MW00651422

WHERE DAWN LINGERS

WHERE DAWN LINGERS

The National Library of Poetry

Melisa S. Mitchell, **Editor**

Where Dawn Lingers

Copyright © 1996 by The National Library of Poetry
as a compilation.

Rights to individual poems reside with the artists themselves.
This collection of poetry contains works submitted to the Publisher by
individual authors who confirm that the work is their original creation. Based
upon the authors' confirmations and to the Publisher's actual knowledge, these
poems were written by the listed poets. The National Library of Poetry does not
guaratee or assume responsibility for verifying the authorship of each work.

All rights reserved under International and Pan-American copyright
conventions. No part of this book may be reproduced, stored in a retrieval
system or transmitted in any form, electronic, mechanical, or by other
means, without written permission of the publisher. Address all inquiries
to Jeffrey Franz, Publisher, P.O. Box 704, Owings Mills, MD 21117.

Library of Congress
Cataloging in Publication Data

ISBN 1-57553-065-1

Manufactured in The United States of America by
Watermark Press
One Poetry Plaza
11419 Cronridge Dr., Suite 10
Owings Mills, MD 21117

Editor's Note

Poem. From the Old French *poeme*, from the Latin *poēma*, from the Greek *póēma*, a derivative of the verb *poeín* meaning *"to make, to create."* The word *poem* literally means *"something created."* *Poet.* From the Greek *poētés*, meaning *"maker."* Thus, the poet is the creator of the world of the poem. He or she has complete control of all of the elements therein; anything can happen. It is through this power which the poet possesses as maker that each poem is rendered completely unique. Each poem, each created piece is the link between the unfettered and abstruse emotions of the poet and his or her conscious mind. Furthermore, once the poem is created and the emotions made more concrete, the words become the link between these emotions and the audience. The individuality of each poem creates a rare connection between poet and reader, and through this connection the reader can experience events and emotions which may never have occurred in his or her life. This is the magic of poetry.

There were many excellent works which were considered for the contest in association with this anthology, each an important tool of expression for its author. Among the most notable of these pieces was H. Izadpanah's "Acacias Unbloomed" (p. 238). The persona speaks of watching a woman performing daily chores, noting her actions with extraordinary detail:

> *I see her clutching my soiled shirts in nervous hands,*
> *And breaking sheets of dripping ice from a frozen stream.*
> *Her blue hands, still vigorous but shaking,*
> *Will wring them snow-white again.*

The woman being described is doing the wash in a stream during the wintertime. The cold water and ice are causing her hands to shake and to turn blue. Nevertheless, she continues to wash the shirts, to "wring them snow-white again." In the following line, "she prays shuddering before purgatorial fires," indicating that she is praying for forgiveness for something she did, or perhaps for something that happened to her for which she holds herself responsible. This repentant praying coupled with her persistence in cleaning the soiled shirts suggests that she is trying to cleanse her soul, which has been soiled and must be made "snow-white again." Also, while she prays, she remembers "a soft April night with the sound / Of a flute and bitter scent of acacias in the air."

Acacias grow predominately in tropical climates. Due to the cold weather, it is probable that the place in which the woman now lives is somewhere quite different from wherever she experienced this "soft April night." Despite the "bitter scent" of the flowers from the acacia tree, she seems to be longing for this time and place. A description of her legs, which have degenerated from age, directly follows. She longs also, then, for a time when she was younger and her legs were "so firm / And lithe as twigs freshly stripped of their green." Her legs are now arthritic and covered with varicose veins: "Tongues of fire lick her bare and varicose legs."

The second stanza begins with the speaker dreaming: "I look through the window of a dream." There is a body swinging from a tree which appears to have been hanged and tortured. Additionally, it has been some time since its death, as it is "bird-pecked and bloodlessly lacerated." This body could be that of the woman from the first stanza, who has been punished for what she has done. In the last section, though, the speaker says that soon:

> I'll shed this rotting and tattered flesh
> And a sweet robin redbreast
> In my rib-cage shall nest,
> Where my restless heart used to sing.

The persona becomes the body "swaying on a bare tree"; the condition of the body represents the treatment of the soul and psyche during life, the emotional "beatings" one endures from day to day; and, finally, through death the persona can "shed this rotting and tattered flesh" and the soul can be freed from all the hardships of life. Because the speaker sees the suffering that the old woman has endured, it becomes certain that there is no way to escape from the pain of life other than through death. It is because of the multi-faceted meanings and the admirable use of complex images that "Acacias Unbloomed" was awarded a Second Prize.

Similarly, Joni Wilson, in her poem "The Awakening" (p. 418), speaks of the trials in life, the discovery of truth and "the way things are," so to speak. Wilson states: "It inevitably comes to this you know." "It" is the realization that "they lied to us," and "this" is the remnants of order in life, the "kicked-over metal marker; / block letters strewn on the ground."

> The dream has exploded madly, and the choice of east or west
> is no longer an option. It happens as the final curtain call
> echoes a distant scream.

The dream is one of an ideal world, where all are safe and protected from harm, where every person has a chance at happiness. "They seduced us with a dream." Throughout life we are told that we can be individuals and can exercise control over our lives and the ability to affect others, to make an impact on society:

> They even used examples, every one of them,
> about those who beat the odds and found immortality
> in the tiny print of thick volume books. They who
> hopped the trains and rode the distance.

The immortals are writers who through their works have achieved a sort of eternal life. They were the ones who adventured and defied society directly, the ones "who hopped the trains and rode the distance" instead of adhering to the established mores of society. They took control over their lives, it seemed, by making unconventional decisions. The speaker is seduced by these models and by the romanticized idea of the life these people led, and believes it possible to have command over her own existence. Unfortunately, when we attempt to defy the establishment, we get thrown by "life's little bucking pony." All we are left with are the "remnants of / visions, intent, and substances not seen." We have the shattered remains of our great life-vision, useless good-intentions, and all the factors which we could not see when immersed in the situation.

The "awakening" occurs when we realize that life is not all good and that we are ultimately powerless and at its mercy. In the end, all that remains is " a kicked-over metal marker; / block letters strewn on the ground." Order and logic have been destroyed, as have any attempt to make sense of life. The metal marker and the block letters evoke an image of a road sign, one of the many attempts by humankind to bring order to its world. The sign, the attempt at control, has been destroyed. What it once said is unimportant, as humans are ultimately powerless; all aspirations of mastering any aspect of life are in vain.

Holly Mayo's "Reptilian Testimony" (p. 160) also deals with the issue of powerlessness on a very personal level. She uses elaborate language and metaphor to create an impressive work of poetry:

> Her words slithered across the page
> In serpentine persuasion
> A smooth hissing of pleasantries
> Veiling intentions to ensnare me

The narrator is reading a letter written by someone who is subtly accusing her of something but who initially tries to hide her intentions behind politeness. The slithering words invoke an image of serpentine script handwriting, seemingly innocuous, but with intentions to "ensnare" her. The letter-writer is likened to a snake, perhaps because of the script, but also because of the sly, soothing way in which she ultimately destroys her victim. Also, the impressive use of sibilance, a difficult technique to use well, creates an overall alliteration which is suggestive of a snake's hissing. The letter is devoid of even a single "angry syllable," and the language is composed of "cool soothing sounds." The letter is innocent but the words are "sure in their destination of my guilt."

The lines of the message begin to hypnotize the persona into being repentant and "invoking a contrite trance," by "rhythmically crooning convictions." The accuser is repeating her belief that the persona is guilty, and essentially talking her into apologizing for something she may not have done. In the fourth stanza, however, the tone of the letter changes from gently accusing to hostile.

> *Relishing the victory she struck*
> *Fangs piercing me she injected her venom*
> *As poisonous invectives oozed*
> *Seeping into my vulnerable wounds*

The writer of the letter has dispensed of all pleasantries, no longer concerned with subtlety and slyness in her accusing or with sparing the persona's feelings. The language changes from "cool soothing sounds" to "poisonous invectives." The writer is enjoying the knowledge that the reader of the letter is certainly feeling the weight of her guilt, and takes advantage of this reaction. Adding insult to injury, so to speak, she lets her poisonous words seep into the persona's "vulnerable wounds." The last stanza merely shows the effects of the scathing letter on its reader. She is a victim of the "cold blooded reptilian testimony."

Holly Mayo's use of complex images conveyed with an economy of language creates a very believable circumstance. Because of her adeptness with written representation, the judges have awarded her the Grand Prize.

Other noteworthy poems in this anthology include Xavier Robertson's "October Cloves" (p. 370), Deborah Laney's untitled piece (p. 604), Frances Boyle's "Resignation" (p. 333), William Norris' "Storm Prayer" (p. 498), and E.C. Moll's "Still Drifting" (p. 390). These are just a few highlights, however, and I wish to congratulate all of the poets featured in this publication. Please carefully peruse each of the poems in this anthology, for you will find a wealth of experience and emotion within.

I would like to thank each of the staff members from the National Library of Poetry, without whom this book would not have been possible. Judges, editors, associate editors, customer service representatives, data entry personnel, graphic artists, office administrators and general services staff have all made invaluable contributions to this effort. I am *grateful* to them for their contributions and support.

Melisa S. Mitchell, Editor

Cover art: Tracy Hetzel

Grand Prize Winner

Holly Mayo / Irvine CA

Second Prize Winners

Frances Boyle / Colorado Springs CO
H. Izadpanah / Simi Valley CA
Deborah Laney / Sanger CA
Jean Lin / Baton Rouge LA
Teresa Manidis / Birdsboro PA

E.C. Moll / Red Hill PA
William Norris / Farmersville TX
Xavier Robertson / Utica MI
Palmer White / Atlanta GA
Joni Wilson / Newport IN

Third Prize Winners

Cathryn Allen / Austin TX
Melanie Beckett / Amarillo TX
Rodger Bolles / Santa Cruz CA
Pamela Bruns / Long Beach CA
Christopher Campbell / Northport NY
Douglas Carey / Aurora CO
Melissa Coleman / Louisville KY
Cynthia Corliss / Bozeman MT
Jayne Cummings / Seagoville TX
Berradette Daly / Edina MN
Fred D'Astoli / Agoura Hills CA
Rebecca Dondlinger / Edina MN
James Flaherty / Annapolis MD
Timothy Flanagan / Missoula MT
Laura Foreman / New York NY
Amber Frederick / Emmett ID
Erica Goodstone / New York NY
John Handy / Huntington VT
C. Haque / Bronx NY
Nereg Hartounian / Fort Lee NJ
Renee Haugerud / Preston MN
LeAnna Herrera / Lakewood CA
E. Manuel Huber / Philadelphia PA
Philip Johnson / Villa Park CA
Susan Julia / Brooklyn NY
Charles Kammer / Wooster OH
Robert Kibler / Salem OH
Pamela Kirtos / Canfield OH
Kerry Kolasa / Phoenix AZ
Joan Krause / Saginaw MI

Susan Landino / Los Angeles CA
Carlton Lear / Grass Valley CA
Phil Lewis / Lakehead CA
Lisa Link / Columbus OH
Susann Maccia / Cambertville NJ
Joe Marchant / Denver CO
Mary Meyer / Anthens GA
Brian G. Miller / Sherman Oaks CA
Shannon Moore / San Gabriel CA
Adam Pagel / Minneapolis MN
Ann Parsons-McNiff / Gloucester MA
Jessica Patulski / Muskego WI
B.T. Windsor Patterson / Memphis TN
Debbie Pento / Somerville MA
James Phillips / Tulsa OK
Anthony Prowell / Tucson AZ
Elizabeth Reed / Queen Creek AZ
Kimberley Riek / Chicago IL
Krzysztof Sacinski / Arlington Heights IL
Nils Sara / Seward AK
Cynthia Sherman / Los Angeles CA
Enriqueta Silva / Santa Ana CA
Anna Skaarland / Onalaska WA
Susan Smith / Redford MI
Adam Stultz / Johnstown PA
Kimberly Terlap-McMahon / Island Lake IL
Katherine Thompson / Humble TX
Antoinette Voget / Aloha OR
Marie Webster-Henderson / Glenwood MD

Congratulations also to all semi-finalists.

Grand Prize Winner

Reptilian Testimony
by Holly Mayo

Her words slithered across the page
In serpentine persuasion
A smooth hissing of pleasantries
Veiling intentions to ensnare me

Not an angry syllable surfaced
As cool soothing sounds slipped
Into lines of utmost innocence
Sure in their destination of my guilt

Questions swayed hypnotically
Invoking a contrite trance
Rhythmically crooning convictions
Spells spun in repititious litany

Relishing the victory she struck
Fangs piercing me she injected her venom
As poisonous invectives oozed
Seeping into my vulnerable wounds

Her victim, I now lie immobilized
Her pages lay crumpled in a heap
Like dried scaly skin discarded
In cold blooded reptilian testimony

The Mirror

Some questions that I ask myself
While wishing on a star:
Does the world show simply what it is,
Or reflect just who we are?

It is possible what I send out
Returns soon manifold?
Does what you give count more or less
Than what you hoard in gold?

Might it be true, when we forgive,
That life begins anew?
Could it be, if your cheek is turned,
They gain less than you do?

Perhaps the life was hold so dear
Comes easiest this way:
Look in the mirror, survey the scene
Make changes there and pray.

Mark Schermeister

Marble Fudge

Life s neither black nor white,
But encompasses grays from
Dark to light.
Since intense problems often arise,
There are solutions we must devise.
Often we tend to deal
In the extreme.
When in reality, the solution
Lies between.

It's like a choice of ice cream.
Think not only of the vanilla,
Or the chocolate dream.
Peruse carefully "the bill of faire",
Make your choice with utmost care.
Seek the compromise, as you judge.
Perhaps you'll select
the MARBLE FUDGE!

Phyllis J. Crockett

"Love - A Treasure Of One's Heart"

One learns to love at birth,
a bonding that's nourished each day.
A feeling that warms the heart,
a sensation so hard to convey.

Love will take many forms,
laughter and tears are just two.
Sometimes it's candy or flowers,
only to mention a few.

But mostly love is a caring,
a yearning deep from within.
To generate this special feeling,
so a new form of love can begin.

For love has no boundaries or limits,
it's shared among the young and the old.
And love both heals and comforts,
its worth is as precious as gold.

So when thinking of gifts that are special,
to be shared right from the start.
Give that something that's held so dearly,
Love - a treasure of one's heart.

Rosemary Sebastian

Shayla Rain

Shayla Rain is
a beautiful girl
Her hair is
full of spiral curls

On her chin is
a little dimple
She looks just like
Shirley Temple

Shayla Rain's eyes are
big, bright and shiny
Her hands are
soft, tender and tiny

Shayla Rain's heart is
full of laughter and love
She is an angel
sent from heaven above

Shayla Rain is
Moma's little girl
She outshines
Every pearl

Teresa Chapman

To All The Veterans

For all the soldiers who've marched on
A braver world has carried on
And for all the ones who know the favor
Freedom has a better flavor
So when you want to speak your mind
You know that you deserve to find
The right that you've been fighting for
Is the dream, that you wish for

So when soldiers fight a country's war
Your home is what they're fighting for
And even though some have to die
The essence is the reason why
While truth and justice make the call
"It's all for one and one for all"
So have no fear then anymore
Soldiers fight for no more war.

Wendy Waldheim

Along For The Ride

Endless dreams and visions of
A celestial angel from above
Reaching out to take my hand
And guiding me upon command
Flying me from here to there
With not a worry or a care
Leading me to sights unseen
Mountain tops and forests green
Far off lands and mammoth seas
When and where it is I please
Taking me to where before
In only dreams I could explore
A symbolic ring of sanity light
Would circle 'round its head so bright
With my angel I could be
A part of what is heavenly
So my dreams and visions seek
An archangel of mystique
With its hand along to guide
I could fly above worldwide

Robert J. Pool

The Forbidden Love

I see your body....
A creamy white liquid passion....
I am engulfed in the beauty
    you possess -
With the innocence that is touched
with a chilled child -
I smell your skin,
Like the dew which kisses a
    morning orchid....
I slowly lay my lips upon you,
I am captured in a whirling rapture
of knowledge that I am the
first traveler to touch the
forbidden love you have kept
locked away -
    I weep,
for with that touch,
    you have disappeared -

Pamela Butler

"Pride Is..."

Pride is to have,
A good happy feeling,
As long as you have that,
You're a terrific being,

It can be something you did,
Or something that's done,
Or it could be,
A wonderful son,

It's all a feeling,
A wonderful one,
So when you have pride,
Just have some fun!!

Ramkumar Nair

33 Years

33 Years to this day,
33 Years seems like a long time away.

One short tender moment did we share,
Feeling to this day it seemed not fair.

That our love was unfulfilled,
Do we yet have feelings still.

Not for a moment can we return,
To a flame that would not burn.

When our hearts have turned so cold,
What shall we do as we grow old.

33 Years to this day,
33 Years seems like a long time away.

Verlon L. Head

Scattered Toys

Most of each and every day
A child is mischief, scattered toys
And "Do I Have To".
But for a few moments
Each and every day
That same child is helping,
Giving, bringing happiness.
Offering you total
Unquestioning love.
And needing your love
In a way only a child could.
Making you forget
All the mischief and scattered toys.

Rita J. Toovey

IF

If is dangerous
A hungry monster
A frosty-eyed politician
Always waiting

Door of uncertainty cracks
Open
If peers inside
Looks all around
Then
Deftly steps in
Straightens his collar
Stands tall
And proceeds to speak
Rambling ruthlessly
Unraveling your faith
With prickly fingers
Savoring your doubt
Like a home-cooked meal

Meg Peters

Uncharted Voyage

From worlds apart they sail a course
A journey of faith to guide their spree
The main so vast sure to be lost
For two so bold to dare the sea

The ships on voyage alone on brine
In darkness move in seek of new light
By chance of nature do come to pass
As dawn ascends to dethrone her night

Waters uncharted oft scary to all
Forever engulf the meek at heart
Treasures that lie on routes unknown
Ne'er to be found by sloops at port.

Ken Patterson

Whisper

Whisper to me
a little voice said.
Whisper to me
bring thoughts to my head.
Make them of
laughter and happiness too.
Show me the
love I should have for you.
Give me the
strength to deal with others.
Show me the way
and I'll call you mother.

Mary Ramirez

Recipe For A Picnic

A beautiful sunny day
A nice quiet spot

A big beautiful shade tree
So it's not so hot

A carton full of chicken
From a fast food place

Potato salad, coleslaw and
A nice and quiet pace

Surround yourself with people
That you love a lot
Relax, enjoy, have a good time
In your peaceful spot!

Renee Granzotto

The Baby

On a snowy night in November
A baby fawn was born and named December,

The wind was gusting high and low
As she walks across the crust and snow,

Her voices so light they did not hear
Even though people were near,

She takes and runs up on a porch
When she see's a glowing torch,

It is warm and cozy all around
As snowflakes fall on the ground,

A act scurry's up by her side
And goes to sleep on her hide.

LeAnn Marie Behrendt

b. d. Poem For g.

you play and sing to me,
a love song
open and gentle
serenading my heart,
my being,
the very essence of my soul.

your tune embraces a melody;
voice so sweet and fine
expressing in such an
endearing way,
all the love you have to give.

and for you, my beloved
not through voice or instrument,
do I have the gift to give;
but I'll serenade you, angel,
with words expressed on paper,

and a love song from my eyes.

robin yost

Friends

Clouds and sky so white and blue
A picture caught my eye.
Something there I just knew
Though it was so high,
A small white dog, his best friend too,
Looking for something to do,
She's looking up at me and you
Let's play some peek-a-boo.
Each hiding in they're cloud of white
Just their faces showing,
Now became a lovely sight —
Each other we were knowing,
A little boy who was a man when
He went away,
His little dog was there and ran
To him so they could play.
Don't feel so bad, I'm not as sad
As I used to be,
I'm almost glad for I can see,
They seem to be so happy.

Mary Gambetta

Dacchau

There is a place near Munich
A place we wouldn't want to go,
Where once all dressed in tunic gray
And stood every day in a row.

These people were not free you see,
Prisoners were what they were.
They had no food like you and me
Nor much to drink, for sure.

The Germans were the guard;
Just staying alive was way too hard.
Of these Jews dressed in tunic gray,
Most are not alive today.

They died in chambers filled with gas.
They were not allowed to wear a mask.
This place which near Munich lay
Is a tragic memorial today...
DACCHAU

Parker Anderson

Strange Changes

ALONE adrift the deep blue sea,
A porpoise tossed a note to me,
Bottled for posterity.

I opened it most carefully
And read the note quite thoroughly,
But all it said was: "RESCUE ME".

I pondered these words, briefly,
When a thought occurred unbiddenly
And I leapt to my feet excitedly:

"AHA!" I yelled, "A kiss will free
This prince porpoise enchantedly;
Then rich he'll make me, gratefully,
And we'll live forever happily!"

WITH dreams in mind I bent a knee
And kissed the fish most eagerly,
Never thinking alternatively.

WHAT happened next is history,
Taught to children repeatedly,
For I became this toad you see.

Sunnia Eastwood

Loves Soldier

Deep within the lovers soul
A raging fire burns
A kiln to forge the soldiers tools
For peace and faith he yearns

Born when first the feelings stirred
The day they met by chance
He toils in the furnace heat
Readying his shield and lance

The couple share a warm embrace
Unaware of the heroes plight
He battles foes of mixed emotions
When the troubled twosome fight

As time goes by and feelings fade
The lovers hardly speak
Their flame is now but embers
Loves knight grows old and weak

The pair now travel separate paths
With no last words to say
The final battle dealt the blow
Loves soldier passed away

Steven E. Donnelly

Tear Drop

I gaze upward into the evening sky
A puddle gathers in my eye

The trumpets of heaven gather
With great anticipation

As my heart is overwhelmed
By Your goodness and Love
With your one and only truth

Made up of Righteousness, Power
And Your Glory

It pierces my heart
Yet comforts my soul

It sparkles and glistens
As it rolls down my cheek
With in it holds the answers that I seek

It pauses at my chin
As I embrace the spirit that is now within

It falls to the floor
Then explodes with thunder
The trumpets sound and Angels sing!

For Lord you are the Alpha and Omega, the
truth

Nigel L. Johnson

Flower Children

They sprang,
A raucous, raging field of bloom;
Colors in the brilliant sun;
Wild.

Attacked and covered
All the cold, hard metal
of Establishment;
And there upon the cruel fortress,
Withered, dried,
Reformed.

And yet, there sometimes leaks
Through crevices in hollow casings
Hints of green, murmurings of the secret
Of their infiltration.

And one day,
The shining coldness
Will be flung by strength of vine,
And blossoms will break forth in glory,
Warming all the heartless world.

Peace, my brothers and sisters.

Karen Shell

A Friend Of God

The clouds are moving down a path,
A scent of wisdom in the air.
Aware of what is going on,
To know that truth is always fair.

The sky is light, my vision clear
Warm tender love of what and where
Words of affection that I hear
My heart will tell me when I'm there.

Calm the wind and make me pure,
For only then can I be sure.
The things I seek cannot be seen,
But in the end he makes me beam.

Laura White

Dreams

A single tear falls from above.
A sign of sadness, strength and love.

A rose shatters from a single touch.
A child cries from withstanding so much.

A dream rises from the dead,
While it's creator is in troubled sleep.

A wish, a hope, a winged beast.
Or, for some, a loved one now deceased.

But the dream may be
a life without misery.
That is the dream that follows me.

Tanya Lea Thompson

Mind Broken Box

I speak to the world in
a small box and pass away
inside, far deep, but no one
hears my words.

Mad they say I am, I
know that I am clear
in mind. There are no
webs that can be fed to me.

A mirror stands in front
of the wall. I find myself
looking through it. I see
the true side of sanity.

Reflecting the moments of
one's life is self-examining.
I say this to find my way to
the true treasure of life.

Death will come, but in
mortal's eyes, life itself
is what eternal youth
can see.

Nikki Pechek

My Kite

Today I flew a kite of happiness,
A tail of smiles, a string of tenderness.
Moments spent, never to reclaim.
For not much, but just the same,
The giving made the gift.

Can you see my kite?
It's high above the smog,
Of selfish minds.
Up where the air is fresh,
And motives clear.

What good is a kite you can not see?
I know it is there, and I can be
  Proud of it.

Richard Carmichael

Desert Storm

As the desert storm approaches
A cactus pine a blows
A rattle snake rattles
and a sun shine arose

Nicole Ann Kelly

Untitled

Is there such a thing
A visit with joys and despair
Oh yes, and a face
that fails to disappear
A face that once was close
and fails to disappear
Patience, a part, goodness too
All are true with much more
Your face that fails to disappear
Looking deep is void
When sight cannot see
Speaking to and wishing for
A face that fails to disappear
A time once more is remote
Yet wishing free for you to own
All can make this face
and deepened thoughts appear again.

Margaret Burik

Imprints On My Heart

Moonlight romance
a warm embrace
a tender look
when face to face
leave imprints on my heart

A loving hug
a kiss, a stare
those special things
that show you care
leave imprints on my heart

Our walks together
a dinner date
the things you do
just for my sake
leave imprints on my heart

The life we live
the love we share
the love we have
beyond compare
leave imprints on my heart

Patricia A. Sowells

"You Want Me To Be Perfect"

You want me to be perfect
A woman who never makes mistakes
You want me to be intelligent
And adapt to all your ways.

You want me to be patient and kind
To be sweet and cordial
To have a mind like your mind
Understanding and loyal

You want me to smile
When you hurt my feelings
Believe me, I don't like to lie
My broken heart is bleeding.

If I am so imperfect for you,
Go, Go up into the blue sky
Seek for an angel of true
And be happy after I die.

Rosa M. Centeno

Remember

Much has been said,
About the right of the people,
To do as they choose,
Both the strong and the feeble.

So often we take for granted,
The sacrifice that was made,
By the men whose lives,
For ours, they did trade.

They had a brave vision,
Of how things should be,
And knew the great cost,
To keep their loved ones free.

They fought for our freedom,
We must never forget,
Because the price that was paid,
Was the blood of a vet.

Terri Exum

Oh As An Eagle

Oh to soar as an eagle
Above the earth and the clouds
An appearance oh so regal
Wings of hope - troubles to enshroud

Oh to see as an eagle
Far ahead - so clear the path about
To keep a constant focus
Each intent - swift to carry out

Oh as an eagle
With expertise and skill exact
Nary a perplexing ordeal
With eagle power we shall distract

Oh as an eagle
To master a situation
Oh as an eagle
To achieve a destination

Margie Ann Filbert

Windy Weather

Clouds roam like buffalo
across a prairie
Huge, cumbersome shapes grazing
on a grassless sea
From blackened lungs, the beasts
are herded west
Thundering across the open
heart of America

Mary Orr

Untitled

Sitting here on my rock
  alone and afraid.
Trying to hold on to hope
  for the life I have made.
It is so hard to smile
  while holding back tears.
But if I dig down deep
  somewhere in my soul.
I will find the strength
  to fill my empty hole.
It might take time
  many hours of pain.
But I realize I have nothing to lose
  and everything to gain.

Michelle Lynn Bragg

I Touched A Star

I touched a star and sparkles fell
  across the sky in showers bright,
and spilled in cascades like the dreams
  you bring my heart each night.

I touched a star and melodies
  arose from out a starlit sea
of tiny silver bells that chimed
  when you would speak to me.

I touched a star. The world stood still
  to bring you here to me once more,
to let us live through endless time
  upon an ageless shore.

I looked into that star and saw,
  reflected magically it seems,
your picture that portrayed for me
  the answers to my dreams.

Now when I sit in pensive mood,
  while thoughts betake themselves afar,
I find that I subconsciously
  reach up to touch a star.

Peppino N. Vlannes

Reach Up

Dance in your little pool
Add light and shadow to the world
Reach up with all your might
While holding to your anchor
Tempt with your color
Reach for your next step
Leap up and grow upon it
Increase your brilliance and color
Leave only ashes behind you
Never to return to the safe pool
Fearing only the wind.

Lawrence Volk

Season's Glory

Fine ladies of the earth
adorned in rich attire
Tall, slender, and stately they inspire
Their limbs they adorn
in the finest hues
gems of rarest beauty for us to muse
A parade of jewels for ever season
variety they say is the reason
Their summer attire shines
in emerald's richness
Arrayed in ruby, garnet, and topaz
autumn shocks us
with winter's wind and snow
comes a chill
but ladies dressed in diamonds
brings a thrill! And at the thaw
how we're in awe as she does gleam
in rare tourmaline
Earth's beautiful wardrobe for all to see
such richness and glory in a tree!

Paula A. Brown

Untitled

Like a sunny sky
After a stormy night
You came into my life
Giving me hope and comfort
Showing me the light

You taught me that love is good
Helped me through all my fears
Forgave me when I hurt you
As only true love could

My heart whispers to me
That you are the love
Who mirrors my heart and soul
Wondering in my heart
If you were sent from somewhere up above

Peggy Sessions

The Gift

I look at the flower
Ah! Most beautiful it is too!
It is then that I think of you.
The Rose- the flower of love,
Love which itself comes from Above.
The more I learn to love with grace...
The more I begin to see God's face.
It is in His Grace...
that this far I have come...
Without the God of Love
I would have none...
It is thru Him that I can see...
the love that you give to me.
Your love eases my burdens...
gives me the strength to live.
The more I learn of love ...
The more I want to give ...
Ah! Rose of love - what so freely was
given to me ...
I can now in loves abundance give back to
thee.

Sandra L. Campbell

"Sea Of Doubt"

Winds drifting
  all about
  surging through
the sea of doubt
  people drowning
  everywhere
sea birds fly around and
  stare
  minds wasting
  valuable
life
Thinking they go through
  pain and strife
no one thinks of beautiful
  things just the terror
  from when the doubt
bell rings people not
  knowing what life is about
so they just drown
  in the sea of doubt

Melissa A. Dettmer

Snow

Snow likes to blow,
all around on the ground,
but it is silent and does not
make a sound,
You can go sledding,
again and again,
Fly through the air,
till you get to the end,
when you are done sledding,
you go home to get warm,
lay down and rest up,
so you can go out
once more.

Rachel Routly

The Highway Man

He walks down the streets all day and
all night,
wishing for a family to hold him tight.

The cars go by with looks of disgrace.

He never looks back because of
his face,

He clutches a case with his tired,
withered hand,

but no one stops for the highway man.

Susan E. Simms

A Place

I've found a place where I can do,
    all the things He wants me to.
A place, where I can see exactly,
    what He wants from me.
A place, where I can pray for all the
    ones, I hold so dear.
Whether they be far away or very
    very near.
A place, where I pray for this whole
    world, here and there.
For all the people in Europe, Asia,
    Africa, everywhere.
I'm so grateful He has given
    me this lovely place.
I'll tell you now it is known
    to us as, His Grace! His Grace!

Lois K. Rathburn

"Alone"

Alone, I shall be.
Alone, I will be free.
Alone, I am leaving all my worries,
Alone, I have no hurries.
Alone, the skies turn gray,
Alone, for that I will pay.
Alone, is a dream wanting to come true,
Alone, I will be blue,
Alone, I will find my way.
Alone, to survive I will eat hay.
Alone, is all I want to be right now.
Alone, but how?

Misty Gillespie

"The Wave Of Life"

The waves flow out and in
    Almost what life is all about
        Changes happening all the time
Everybody noticing something different.
    If a person has their back to a wave,
        How are they to know it's coming?
        It's a surprise, or a shock
Many people experience different new
    Every wave brings something new
        Such as everyday
    Nobody knows what to expect
Except a change of some kind.
    The good thing about waves
    Is that they bring in the new
And take the old back into the ocean,
    Letting go of it's own past.
        But, the past becomes part of the ocean
Which can either be brought back another
day
        Or can be damaged by nature
    In the same sense as memories.

Kimberly M. Herbers

Frustration

Here I am,
    Alone again — as always
At least within myself

In my mind I'm free
    Free from this demented world
Left to watch
    Through all this turmoil
    Through all this love
    Through all this hate
    Through all this violence
Through all this life...
    There is a lack of compassion

But from a small speck in the universe
    A soul cares
    A soul cries
Passionately trying to change everything...
    Everyone
Yelling to the world
    Or, better yet, at the world
But I am not heard

Polly Hutchinson

The Angry Tiger

We lost our way somehow somewhere
Along life's path we cannot share
The things in life, so precious are
Like sands of time off and afar
Perhaps some day a smile will crease
Her crimson lips, a frown will cease
And all that anger that sleeps inside
Will leave her heart before I die.
I do not know the reason being
But there is no life without her freeing
The angry tiger deep inside,
So we can live again with pride
I long to see the girl I knew
She would laugh and smile as I could too
For until that angry tiger rests
Her time is lost and mine is less
Each day becomes beyond repair
And she is left but with despair.

Rosemary Bello

Sins Of Indifference

Do you know someone who lives
alone   you promise to stop
by   but forget to phone

Do you see someone
you really don't like   you
cross the street   take a hike

Do you one an apology wrong
or right   decide the best policy
stay our of sight

Do you pick up TIME only to find
your favorite photographer
has war on his mind

Do you half see hostages chained
to stakes   they're U.N. peace keepers
for heaven's sake

Do you try to skip over
the market place   where people of all
ages were shot in the face

Do you sigh with relief that it wasn't us
turn you thoughts
to a charity affair   wondering what outfit
you'd like to wear

Mimi Eagan

(The life we live also the life!...)

The life we live
Also the life! We may live
May never be in vain
Shame! fear! pain! may never be.
Death may never occurs.

Life! What! Where! When
Days and nights aren't in vain
Words! World! also
human beings.
Darkness and lights isn't
sorry or insane.
Society is never hidden,
Stumbling or murder a close down.

Life and time; the way
we live life is never
occur last or lost

Unborn and born victories
never falls or ends
lifetime victories are
never torn down.

William Yates

Who I Am

I am what I think
and feel and believe.

I am what I love
and hate and fear.

I am what I hide
and wonder and pretend.

I am a being separate
from by body.

I am my soul.

Wanda Killman

Love In My Eyes

It was just like a dream come true
Always being so close to you
There was so much love we had to share
Knowing your love was very rare
But since you walked out of my life
I think about you every night
Knowing this feeling must be right
Oh girl you got control of me
Cause it turns the cold into heat
That it melts my heart to my feet
Can't seem to say the word goodbye
With all this love in my eyes
Wants to shelter you from the rain
And this feeling deep within my heart
We both have shared from the very start
On that day when we first met
We both said our lives were set
From the fire that was in our souls
Giving me love that touched the moon
But now it all grew into gloom

Rocco Pace

Pressing Invitation

Welcome, glorious Friend Divine
Always into this heart of mine
Holy Spirit, please be free
Inspire and work through me.

Higher, ever let me lift my eyes
Onward, with greater purpose rise.
I yearn to be free of resistance
Pressing on with renewed persistence.

I can't fathom the depth you can fill
A hungry heart, empty of self-will.
Continue to stoke this fire in my soul
My deepest desire is you be in control.

Patricia Mester

A Question Of Priorities

This truly is a wondrous age.
Amazing things surround us.
It's the age of modern miracles!
Our progress doth astound us!

Robots do our menial tasks.
Laser beams protect us.
Miracle drugs wreak havoc
On bugs that would infect us!

We see things as they happen
Via man-made satellites;
We read our books and magazines
By nuclear-powered lights!

Before we reach Utopia, though,
Before we think we're there,
I feel that there's a problem
Of which we must take care!

The one thing that they've overlooked
Causes widespread, undue strife!
They just don't make erasers yet
To match the pencil's life!

William Lyle Slagle

Σ Parts > Whole

We're each but a speck
Among all that exists
Our problems monumental
To ourselves we do insist

Back up a few steps
Experience a new view
Welcome the unknown
A trait enjoyed by few

Things in our lives
Cannot remain the same
For life's a dynamic force
In this universal game

On this infinite cosmo canvas
A speck we might only be
But the picture is only brilliant
When the glow of each speck we see

Focus our hearts on love
And we fuel the universal light
Reaffirming that "All" consciousness
That is so naturally right

Memory Anne Rodgers

Untitled

I look into his deep brown eyes
and am lost in a world
of faith and passion.

To be so much alike
and to be so different
all the same fills my deprived soul.

I couldn't ask for
a more generous
compassionate human being.

I long to be near him always
but to be far away
so that I may miss him.

It is unfair that
I am so content
and others may never feel the same.

But I am grateful
for the chance and
will be selfish with my gift.

Kimberly Ward

Dear God

Dear God let me fly away
and be a bird for just one day
To get away from the pain
inside
To free the aching heart I hide

Dear God let her realize
what she puts me thru
Dear God let her realize
that every tear is "true"
Stop the screaming, the
yelling, the pain
and I will never cry again
For all times to be
happy is a wish that can't
come true
For sometimes to be happy
is all I ask of you

Dear God let me fly away
and be a bird for just one day

Sandra M. Coon

Our Sea Of Love

We lived by the sea
And caught the spirit
Of each sparkling wave;
Each foaming crest
Another height to reach
Like our love, so strong
So young, so brave.

The sea subsides—
Becomes a shining smoothness
Of emerald green;
And like our love,
No longer turbulent and wild
But deep, enduring and serene.

Neva Greeson

We As The People

The violence is rising
and death increases.
Family and friends
are left to pick up the pieces.

The stabbing, the shooting, and killing,
will it ever end?
It's creating such unhappiness
at every funeral we attend.

Our government, alone,
can not make it disappear.
We as the people
need to start to care.

We as the people
need to understand
That everyone should
work hand in hand.

Our country has some problems
but all can be mended.
Believe me when I tell you
"The madness should be ended."

Michelle A. Tomchik

Autumn

When the leaves turn brown
and fall to the ground
I know it is Autumn

When we are all wearing sleeves
and there's BIG breeze
I know it is Autumn

When it is cold
and the grass looks gold
I know it is autumn

When the sun is set
and everything gets wet
I know it is Autumn

When frosty comes out
and everybody's about
I know it is Autumn

When the plants turn brown
and then blow around
I know it is autumn

Sara-Jean Marie Mills

Our Crown

Our hearts will leap, when thee we see,
And fill, and flood with ecstasy;
At last to see thee, whom we love
Will be of joy, all else above.

To hear thy accents on our ear,
When faith to sight will disappear,
With sweetness filling every part,
To know from thee, we'll not depart.

To be with thee, and know thy grace,
And look with wonder on thy face,
What peace, what joy, with thee to share,
O, morning star, O love, so fair.

So great thy mercy and thy blood
Which flowed for us, a cleansing flood,
The washing, healing, saving stream,
In thanks and praise will be our theme.

Norma Vinson

A Rose For Mother

I bought a rose
And gave it to you
Not for any special reason
Just because I wanted to.

This rose is to show you
All the love my heart holds
And mother I will love you
Long after I have grown old

If I were a rich girl
You'd have a rose each day
To show you I'm sorry
For the things I do and say

But I'm a poor girl
And have just one rose to give
To show you I'll love you dearest mother
For as long as I shall live

Norma Jean Derryberry

"A Mother's Prayer"

Thank you, God, for this day,
And helping me in every way
I'm sorry for the things not right,
But Lord, Please help me sleep tonight.

Oh God, You're Great and good to me.
I thank You for our family
Please help us love and serve you to,
And help us see that we need you.

My husband is so good to me,
My favorite on our family tree.
He works so hard and helps me too,
We have so many things to do.

We try and do the things we should,
And be to others kind and good.
We love you God, and as we pray
Please help us with another day!

Mrs. Cyril M. Welles

"Little Jake"

He's an English Staffordshire
and he's the cutest thing to see.
His name is "Little Jake"
and he's a champion to be.

His coat is black and brindle,
his body strong and buff.
He likes to strut around
and show off his fancy stuff.

On his paws he has white socks,
and really cute pointy ears.
You think he's sharp at this age . . .
just wait a few more years.

We love you Jake, yes we do,
you're our special little boy.
You make us laugh and smile,
you bring us so much joy.

Lynn Y. Montaño

Bird Of Prey

He glides effortlessly through the sky,
and his wing's seem to touch the clouds.
The search is on.

He sees what is invisible to the human
eye, and he descends all so swiftly his
powerful talon retrieves the prey and
he is gone as quickly as he came.

He is at peace with his surroundings, he
knows no boundaries. The sky is his and
his alone.

His view of the world is to be cherished
for all God's beauty is visible and
opened wide, and at a glance he takes it
all in.

As he sits perched high upon his
mountain nest, one can't help but
wonder if he can comprehend the splendor
his eye's behold.

Tamra Mauck

Untitled

Round Robins Grapple with Air
and I breathe a destiny
of despair

Light green shades of a
post summer day
why delay the winter's edge

Such a tease

Dressed in darkness
giving light smile
breathe

Teach me to sing.

Robert M. Carmenini

Picture In The Water

I am a river,
and I flow,
with strength and grace,
with cunning current.
As sure as intellect
I glide,
Waters calm
for raging thought.
I am a river,
Beauty in my depth,
Wonder in my waves,
Life spilling over
the smoothness of
my surface.
I reflect only myself,
and ripples you make can
not distort that image.
I am a river,
and I flow,
my freshness ever quenching.

A. R. Benish

Autumn Reflections

I've had a great life
And I want all to know
I've enjoyed to the hilt
Don't be sad when I go.

We've had our touch times
But it never seemed bad
Because we faced it together
Made the best of what we had.

I've skated, swam, skied,
And parasailed too.
Sewed, quilted, canned food,
All the usual things folks do.

I know the thrill of sex
The joy of babies too
Had my share of business life
A busy social life too.

Now in the autumn of my years
I ponder what made it so fine
God was always there with me.
With Him life is sublime.

Margaret Toothill

"Joey"

You're in our hearts
And in our souls
Although we're apart
We feel as if we're whole.
   Even though the years have past
We still feel the love today
And know it's enough to last
Because it's in our hearts in every way.
   We still cry a million tears
And hold you so close to our hearts
And even after all these years
We know we'll never part.
   There doesn't seem to be enough love
For such a wonderful little boy
And though you're safe in His
arms above
   We'll always know you brought us
so much joy.

Lori Hall

Country In My Heart

Oh, my name ain't Merle Haggard
And it sure ain't old George Jones
Glen Campbell can rest easy
Cause I'm ready to rest my bones.

I'm just an old dude from the city
Who ate a western tune
Got hooked on country music
And I'm crazy as a loon.

Can't read or write those pretty notes
Tunes just get into my head
Guess I'll keep on writing words
Till the day that I am dead.

If I were to leave a legacy
For those who follow me
Just put your thoughts on paper
For someone to see.

Lord, how I wish that I could write
All those little notes
That would show my love for music
And are heard by western folks

E. George Metzger Jr.

A Dreamer

I dream in elaborate colors
and I've done amazing things.
I have walked across the water
and flown on eagle's wings.
I have listened to an angel
and held a shooting star.
I have captured a rainbow
in a small glass jar.
I have been a waterfall
filled with tropical fish.
I have been a memory
and I have been a wish.
Then I was a rainstorm
inside a crystal ball.
There's a million things to be
and I have been them all.
Some will say I'm crazy
cause that's the way it seems
But truly I have done all these.
I've done them in my dreams.

Sherri-Lynn Bonis

Searching

Searching, searching,
  Always searching.
Searching for something
  You cannot find.
Searching for peace of mind.
Searching for someone
  who understands.
Searching for a friend
  to lend a hand.
Searching for a loving home,
  who never fights and
  keeps its own.
Searching for that great
  friend — Jesus Christ,
  and that's The End.

Rebecca Stewart

Someday

I know your needs,
and I've studied you.
Even when you didn't know,
that I was in the world.

When you look sad,
I want to make you happy.
When you look disgusted,
I want to make things better.

When you look lonely,
I want to know you're not.
When you look like you want to give up.
I want to tell you things will be okay.

When you look worried,
I want to kiss your cares away.
When you look upset,
I want to see you cheerful.
When you smile, you brighten my day.
And I never want your smile to ever go
away.

I always wonder what it would feel like
to be in your arms . . . Someday.

Lisa Fusicci

Untitled

Bless this bed that I lay on
and keep me while I sleep
Place four angels just to watch
One at my head one at my feet
One to guide me through the day
And one to walk along life's way
And this oh! Lord is what I pray
(Amen)

Violet Cozine

Silence

Reach out your silence
And know my nights and days
Are filled with softness
When your eyes lock with mine

My silence screams
That even if two hearts I had
Both would overflow
With what I've begun to feel

Silence is a blanket
Which covers love to keep it warm
  As I wait
  And long to hold you
I clench it tightly under my chin

Lone hours feed me
For weakness melts to nothing
  When I think of you
Then with silence a chilling warmth upon
me
I fall into your eyes
  Through a face of such beauty
And my heart is home

Robert Parkinson Jr.

"He Is Just A Prayer Away"

He shares your every problem
And knows your smallest need
There is never an earnest prayer
To which he gives no heed

He never will forsake you
He knows you've done your best
You can depend on his promise
Trust him to do the rest

Though storms may fear you
He'll guide you through each day
He will cherish and protect you
He's just a prayer away.

Shyna Lailani

He Gave Us The Best

God gave us mother's to dry our tears,
and laugh with us through the years.

For our disobedience, punishment render,
and later show us her love, so tender.

Teaching us to love our neighbor,
to honor God in all our labor.

Should someone slap our cheek, forgive,
turn the other cheek for him.

Nurse the sick, aid the needy,
what err the need, be always ready.

From time to time mistakes she made,
but relied on God to smooth the way.

As these memories fill my mind,
I thank God for being so kind.

For it is He that had the plan
to give to us this love, not man!

We've been so sad since she's been gone,
Yet we have her in memory, we're never
alone.

We praise Go as in peace she rests,
When it come to mother's He gave us the
very best!

Nancy ReFern Jackson

Untitled

  Soft, pale skin; dark, red lips;
and long, black hair. Big, green
eyes; slender, beautiful body, and
a kind loving heart.
  A tender love that lasts for
centuries, and a trust that would
outlive the dawns of time.
  The pain of losing your love
to something so bitter and cold.
So unbecoming of life to do away
with such beauty in a caring
and loving person.
  Love will never be lost or
forgotten.

Patricia Martinez

Open Your Eyes

Open your eyes
and look at me.

I'm a red blooded
American, can't
you see.

I have cells and
skin and bones
like you?

I have a heart
that beats strongly
too.

I walk and talk
and I have
eyes to see

So open up your eyes
and look at me
I have arms and legs
and a back too
I'm a red blooded
American just like you!

Tina Brannon

Personality

Do you have a charming smile
　　and lots of vitality?
It will help you over many a mile
　　and add to your personality.

Do you have charm about you
　　of making many friends?
If they are young, old, happy, or blue,
　　you try not to offend.

Are you always very thankful?
　　Are you merry and witty, too?
Are you sad and wilful
　　when a needy friend is blue?

Be honest, kind, and faithful
　　and always be wise.
Do not be so boastful
　　and never criticize.

Ruth Friese Ressler

I'll at ease

I lie long
and often
I lounge and
lie about

the truth
the real truth
is that I lie

I am lying now

awake
I lie
sleepy
I lie

I get up
and still I'll lie

Natali F. Burr

Night Fright

The night was black as black could be,
And on the lonely streets was me.
I thought I heard an eerie sound,
Scared though I was, I looked around.
I saw a giant at least ten feet
Waving and motioning in the street.
I wanted to run - but instead
My shoes filled up plumb full of lead.
When I got inside the door, I laughed
in hysterical elation.
That weird and ghostly episode was
figments of my imagination.

Ruth Y. Phillips

To Wayne

I have a sister and a brother,
And one other,
He is known as a "half" brother.
The "half" that is not
My brother,
Comes from being begot
From another,
My Step-father.
So I have "half" a brother
And a "full" Mother.
And another,
A "Step" father.
That makes me a "half" sister,
To my "half" brother.
Since he is a "half"
And I am a "half"
And it takes two "halves"
To make a "whole"
That makes one "whole" sister
And brother

Ruth E. Blankenship

Love Lost

The train pulled into the station
And people began getting off.
For a moment I almost forgot
We were saying goodbye to love lost.

You are going away without me
One ticket is in your hand.
We had meant so much to each other
And now it all has to end.

You put your arms around me
And I touch your cheek so soft.
The conductor yells "All aboard"
And we say goodbye to love lost.

Phyllis M. Brundidge

Alchemy

Here where I am is shadow
And the rain
Beats down upon the trees
Dressed in the vestment of spring,
But out in the valley lies
The knife edge
Where the sun has slashed the storm
And turned the leaden drops to gold.

T. O. Thatcher

Mother's Lullaby

Snuggle closer little one
And rest your sleepy head
Sandman's coming nearer dear
You'll soon want your warm bed.
Cuddle closer curly locks
Dream a dream of sweet things.
Never fear for mother rocks
Her child to sleep by singing...
Lullabies of days gone by
Of fairies and of kings
Lullabies of days of yore
Of magic elfin rings
So with these thoughts dear
Dream away, into a slumber deep
And gently I will close the light
And you my little one....sleep

Teresa E. Nugent

I Looked Into My Child's Eyes

I looked into my child's eyes
and saw our road of life.
But mostly my own.
I saw the good and the bad.
I looked into my child's eyes
and realized that child was
trying to be just like me.
I looked into my child's eyes
and realized where ever I went
what ever I did, what ever I said
that child was taking it all in.
I looked into my child's eyes
and realized I made some mistakes
both good and bad.
I looked into my child's eyes
and realized I too was down
a road like this with my parents,
relatives, and their friends

Margaret S. Matyok

A Better Place

We walk down the street,
　　and see the homeless begging;
We go into our homes,
　　and listen to the fighting;
We go to the hospital,
　　and see battered women;
But no one cares,
　　and nothing is done;
Criminals murder,
　　and leave families grieving;
Rapists rape,
　　and leave girls screaming;
But they walk free,
　　only to do it again;
We can help,
　　and make a difference;
Give our love,
　　and care a lot;
If we could all try our hardest,
　　we could make this world a better place to
live.

Nina Paterson

"Little Child"

Dear little child, I hear your cries
And see the tears fill in your eyes
When last I looked, you were asleep
Was it a dream that made you weep?
Little child, please do not fear
You're not alone, I'm always here.
I'll hold you close - so you will know
Dear little child, I love you so.

Holding you now for a little while
Upon your face - I see a smile
A little tremor that came to pass
I realize now, it was just gas.

Nancy B. Waz

Genesis

The birds emerged from the mud
and skittered under a truck
birds made of mud
and streaked
with axle grease

Mud birds

One time we left some cat food out
and from it maggots formed

Cat maggots

Worms with long whiskers
that purred

I was sired from a soup
made of my father and my mother

A gene soup and emerged
half maggot half catbird

I purr when content
and skitter under diesel trucks
I clean out wounds in old tires
and somersault

Long into the night

Laura Foreman

Cancer's Box

She hides her fears in a black box,
And the pain she feels inside,
Can lurk just as a sly fox,
The way that it can hide.

She knows what hangs there is death,
In her room she will sit and cry,
Savoring each and every breath,
She knows she soon will die.

She knows it will not go away,
She just stares down at the floor,
And no matter how hard she will pray,
The cancer lurks hard evermore.
The taste in her mouth lasts forever,
She's in for a painful ride,
The needle goes in just like a lever,
And when it was over, she cried.
She hides her fears in a black box,
And the pain she feels inside,
Can lurk just as a sly fox,
The way that cancer hides.

Sue Kuchli

I'll Wait

For an experience so intimate
    and so precious
I would want that moment
    to be most sacred.....
When I share with the only
    woman I've ever loved
God's wonderful gift of sex.

I have decided to be patient
    refusing to jump the gun
    and thereby deny myself
The beauty, the purity
    and the pleasure of sex
Within God's approved boundaries —
    marriage.

I'll wait.

Terry Lim

Minneapolis '96
The Gift

Washed away by tears
And sunk in blackened pools
Our scarcely beating hearts
Saw we were such fools
To take a gift from God
And keep it to ourselves
As knowledge gleaned from books
And hidden among the shelves
The fruit was not the pleasure
In the cup that we had poured
The love we thought forever
Was endowed to serve the Lord
In fortune there is duty
We sadly couldn't see
That grace abounds in beauty
And charity was the key
To loose the selfish bond
That kept our love between
What was in our minds
And what was in our dreams

Stephen Barclay

I'll Believe

When the babbling brook stops to listen,
And the man in the moon plays host,
When Father Time waits for Mother
And we give up Banquo's ghost,
When the primrose path gets a stop sign
And the murmuring pines speak up,
When the Milky Way turns sour
And the Cheshire Cat has a pup,
When Jack Frost moves to Miami
And Christmas comes in July,
When the Marlboro Man stops smoking
And we eat the pie in the sky;
When the Headless Horseman dons a hat
And somebody finds the Lost Chord,
When folks won't stop to chew the fat,
And we trap the mouse that roared,
And when all these things all come true
That's when I'll believe in you.

Rose Schissell

Untitled

When things get tough
And the road seems far
Believe in yourself,
And who you are.

And when your life.
Isn't going your way
Put yesterday behind,
And think of today.

For when the rain of life
Comes to each one,
Don't give up
For here comes the sun.

For my friend a rainbow will appear
After the storm of life has cleared.

Terry McNulty

What The Future Holds

The grass sprouts green,
And the snow is almost gone,
Across the meadow,
Is a mother and her fawn.

Birds chirp wildly,
Bears awake from their sleep,
The lake begins to thaw,
In the valley deep.

Raccoons and squirrels,
come out to play,
The sun shines bright,
as a rising of a new day.

Fish jump, excitedly,
They have a very good reason,
Spring is here, now indefinitely,
The start of a new season.

Matthew Genuise

School Days

With their shining faces beaming
And the weather turning cool,
Children eagerly are talking
As they wend their way to school.

Now and then they stop to chatter
Or to kick a stone or two,
Spirits high and hearts aflutter
As their chores they plan to do.

Day by day they learn their lessons
As the years so quickly pass,
Bringing new friends to them often
When they reach a higher class.

Soon their school days will be over
And a whole new world awaits
As they choose their avocation
Which will open many gates.

May they always be light-hearted
Helping others on their way,
As they travel down life's pathway
With God's help from day to day.

Sue Myers Dietz

Camille

From heaven on a raindrop she came,
And the world will never be the same!
A tiny star come down to earth,
To lighten our hearts with her mirth.

Stardust twinkles in her eyes,
As she smiles and sweetly sighs.
And the sky shimmers with delight,
At such a soft and lovely sight.

She is precious-she is so dear,
Magic in raindrops now lives here.
Gather the glitter and hold her tight,
Keep danger and darkness out of sight.
        Margaret East

The Hummingbird Dance

I saw a hummingbird today
And then—I saw it fly away.
It took some nectar from the cup
and buzzed around, and yet enough
It took to flight I know not where.

Perhaps it will return to share with me
its beauty, and perchance
I will once again marvel at the
hummingbird dance!
        Suzanne Moss

Untitled

I chant languid need
    And wax pink beneath it

Then lick at winter
    Only to recall an elaborate lie

I froth bitter truth
    And lash light around it

Then slip on jagged fragments
    Remains of a rage worn dream
        Linda Catoe

My Tribute - A Loving Farewell

We both knew the end was near
And there was little to do - or say
But when I looked into your eyes
I knew
That love would find a way
To have you leave - to say goodbye
Was not a simple task
To make the path an easier one
Was all that I could ask
There are many loving memories left
With dreams to still come true
But it will be alright - it really will
Because of my love for you
So please don't cry for me
There is no more to say
I'll go on living knowing deep inside
That love will lead the way
        Violet Wolf

Home

I was there in times of trouble
    and there were quite a few;
And now the pain is double
    and you're wondering what to do.

Can't you see the road you're taking
    is the one you took before.
And the only place it got you
    was knocking on hell's door.

I've been down that circle road
    I still can feel the pain.
It offers no accomplishment,
    On it you'll never gain

Now, I know that I'm not perfect;
    and I'll never claim to be
But, God gave us something special
    the gift of you and me.

I know your head is spinning
    and you're feeling all alone
But, come and let me hold you
    and you'll always be at home.
        Rebecca A. Hohmeier

Dreams Of You

As I sit alone
And think of you,
I dream of the love,
That I once knew.

Everyday of the week,
You're all that's on my mind,
How I loved you with all my heart,
How our love was so divine.

I wish you still loved me,
Because I still love you,
I don't know what happened to our love,
The feeling seemed so true.

A love like that,
I might never find again,
I'll always dream of your love,
Though it's something I know I'll never
win.
        Karen Rodgers

Connection With Nature

My soul searches and stretches
And touches the sky.
My mind floats on clouds
As I ponder and sigh.

As a bird taking wing,
Like the flight of a dove,
I am free from man's rules;
I am feeling God's love.

My soul searches and stretches
And garnishes strength,
As I reach and touch nature -
Yes, my heart is content.
        Linda J. Porter

The Rain

A drop of rain falls from the sky
    and washes all away;
the dirt, the sand, the memories
    of what was yesterday.
The thunder and the lighting,
    the dark and heavy clouds,
all seem to be so angry,
    all seem to have a frown.
Still the rain comes pouring down
    like tears upon my face.
Searching, looking, questing
    for a single happy place.
The rain can wash away the bad,
    can make things new again;
but my tears are pointless
    they always leave the pain.
The rain is always beautiful,
    I love the sound it makes.
So peaceful on my rooftop,
    but never upon my face.
        Melissa Giersberg

Requiem For Victoria Lucas

I dreamt a bright Sarcophagus
And you and I were twins.
Side by side we lay
Though, truly, not the same.

I've imagined your likeness
Dark featured as myself.
Yet, looking at your photograph
I see the girl next door.

No drama to your features
A pure and smiling face
Still, I saw something deeper,
Beyond the light facade.

Your writing paints a picture
Self portrait of the mind.
A poem for a picture
Reveals to me your soul

A secret friend, a secret thought
And you and I are twins.
We share a darker soul
Though you did what I cannot.
        LeAnna Herrera

Shattered Dreams

Another night I cry
Another piece of my heart will die
In the silence of my head I scream
Only to release the tears by streams
Can't hold back anymore
I'm now behind closed doors
Doesn't matter what happens now...
because I'm all alone
Silence - not even the
ringing of the phone
Torture in my head.
As I lay here dying in my bed
Can't stop what's going on in
My heart...or soul
You see he was my life, breath,
My one goal!
But he closed me out and walked away
Did it in the turn of a day
No reason from off his lip
Just opened his hand - I fell I slipped.
        Rita V. Brown

Imagination

I drew a picture,
Appraised it with admiring eyes.
Then I thought I'd like to paint
The green of trees, the blue of skies.
My paint brush I took in hand,
But when I tried to capture
The beauty of nature's scenes
The joy, the rapture
I found an artist was not I;
I sighed but then came laughter.
An inspiration came to me;
I wrote with admiration.
"Ah ha! A poet that's me," thought I.
But alas!
'Twas just imagination.

Mitzie Dawes

Night Butterflies

Sleepless hours
Are all adrift
With
Flitting thoughts
That
Float and flutter —
Like butterflies.
And fireflies.
Some fleeting, floating—
Others drift across the space
Of time.
'Tis well to have chosen
Basic patterns
Of
Looking for the beautiful
And the good.
Enough of shadows and sadness
Are interspersed —
To occupy
Inactive hours.

Marian Smith

The Rope

Dreams and expectations
    are all we ever hope,
Come into our lives
    at the bottom of the rope,
Hand over hand
    we reach for the top.
Just to slip back down
    when undone is the knot.
After all disappointments
    we make ourselves stronger.
Looking up, or not
    the rope gets longer,
So learning to adjust
    we sit back and cope.
Realizing that it's not so bad
    at the bottom of the rope.

Teresa Swift

Untitled

For a horizon to be
Beautiful
It must be admired
For it to be admired
It must be loved
You
Are a
Horizon

Steven Oberdorfer

The Sands Of Time

The sands of time
are at your beck and call
when you understand the hidden meaning
in their individual grains.
It is in trying to grab too much,
that you lose the individual feeling
in each grain.
Learn to count each individual grain;
then, and only then,
will you understand time's true meaning.
Within each second of each minute
is time's true meaning
and the meaning of who you are.

Ron Rathbun

Trees Of Life

The trees in the forest
Are so high
I can hardly see the sky
But some how
I can always hear
The voice of God

He speaks to me
In pastel colors
Spread across the western sky
Like a blanket
Of falling stars

Filled with the sparkle of
Raindrops from the heavens

As each rain drop falls from
Above, it slowly and tenderly
Caresses each leaf and branch
Of the trees
In the forest of life

Nourishing and renewing hope in
Each and every one of us.

Patti Willis Wendt

Forever Friends

Stephie—
Are we forever friends because
we have the same relatives,
love the same people,
or act the same way?

Is it because we share the same name,
have the same hobbies,
or wear the same clothes?

Are we forever friends because
we love the same food,
or like the same music?

Is it because we love our good times
and cherish our moments of seriousness,
or is it because we are sisters
and have a friendship that is more
beautiful than words can describe?

Sister,
We are forever friends because we
share the same happiness... each other.

Thanks for being you! Your friend forever,
Sheryl

Sheryl J. Malpezzi

Prayer Battalion

Standard bearers reach to Heaven
Arms, and essence, all unfurled:
Lifting hearts, like flags, to Glory
Praying — one voice — Shooting Star!

All these soldiers, many ransoms
Paying dearly to be freed;
Ease and comfort, roads not taken:
Offerings on the road to Peace.

Melissa Lynn Taylor

Untitled

Seconds gone as fast
as a lightning bolt.
Minutes going like a
train going by.
Hours gone as fast
as a picnic
Nights gone as fast
as a song.
Days gone as fast
as the night
Weeks gone by like
counting to one hundred from ten.
Months gone like
the wind.
Years gone like
melting snow.

Lorri A. Radford

Seasons

Grief is what makes the arctic cold,
as gradually it does entomb
numbing whatever it shrouds.
When frozen tears mask pain untold,

Spring seems as it if will not come.
Yet given time all things change,
gradually the days grow longer
and a rose appears when winter's gone.

Kimberly Coates

In His Eyes

In his eyes I see tenderness
As he holds me tight
The touch of his skin
Warms my heart

In his eyes I see love
As he whispers in the night
The touch of his skin
Becomes apart of me

In his eyes I see doubt
As he turns away
The touch of his skin
Becomes memory

In his eyes I see no more
As he goes away
The touch of his skin
Haunts me

In his eyes I must believe
As he lives his life
The touch of his skin
Remembers me

Teresa Rasmussen

My Dentist

My dentist is a real nice guy
  As I can plainly see
But as I sit in his fancy chair
  I'm as nervous as can be.
The little tray in front of me
  With all the tools in a line
Makes me wonder what he would do
  If I added a few things of mine.
He tells me in a soothing voice
  What needs to be done to my chopper
Then in a voice that can hardly be heard
  The price he quotes is a whopper.
I know that I can't get along
  Without his dentistry
And the price he asks isn't half as bad
  As my pain and misery.
When the work is complete
  And my pain disappears
I can tell at a glance, with half a chance
  I'll be paid up in two or three years.

Richard E. Mitchell

My Shadow

Who is that person in my shadow?
As I look at it, it looks at me —
During the day it passes and goes.

Who is that person in my shadow?
I watch for it —
It stays when I'm in sorrow.

Who is that person in my shadow?
Does it speak?
How will I know?

Who is that person in my shadow?
It tells me this,
I will come back tomorrow.

Who is that person in my shadow?
It's love I feel —
Like a river it flows and flows.

Who is that person in my shadow?
Will it stay forever?
Oh please God don't let it go —

That person in my shadow.

Natalie D. Sinks

My Winter

The world was all ice and snow
As I took my walk today.
The bitter cold wind stung my soul
And took my breath away.

The distant sun gave no warmth
As if swallowed by the sky.
And all creation seemed to feel
The same despair as I.

How far away spring's green joy!
How bleak icy winter's strife.
Yet silently, secretly there,
A promise waits — new life.

Season of rebirth, come so
To me — God's love felt anew.
Like gentle breezes melting ice.
Like warm seeds bursting through.

Kathy Bowman

Untitled

Oh, what queenly beauty
As if on her throne
Surveying her domain
Darkness prevails in
corners not apparent,
though known
A sound
A whisper
Unseen ghosts
Graceful, feline agility
But unladylike pouncing
Hissing, white drooling
Sharpness extended
bounding in mid-air!
On top of
the movement.
Gotcha, Mouse.

Priscilla Anderson

Untitled

Neither love nor passion be
As lasting as deceit.

Tiffanie L. Fennell

Sweet Celestial Being

You sweet celestial being,
  as old as father time.

Never have you failed me,
  with silver beams divine.

You worked your mighty magic,
  made him my only love.

I know that you are watching
  from somewhere up above.

You must feel very special
  to make a perfect match.

Without those perfect moon beams
  the man I could not catch.

So if you'll shine down on him
  for he's away you see,

And keep him in your moon beams,
  watch over him for me.

Melda Whittle-Blackmar

Left Alone In Your Last Days

  Trapped in a bed with your voice
As the only one heard.
  Trapped in a bed with no window
Near to peer.
  Hooked up to a mechanical heart,
Revengeful from the start,
When you were put in the bed by your
Love ones to decay and depart.
  Minutes move so slowly because
Nothing is as holy, in the bed
Where times is spent imaging if you
Can prevent life from slipping away.
  As thoughts flutter in your eyes,
You know it is time to say you last
Goodbye,
  To the world that left you in a
Bed, where loneliness was your only
Friend.

Scott Wolf

Memories

Memories -
as they slowly fade away
I try to remember
the thoughts of yesterday
as I try to cling to the past
remember everyday
I think of a time
not so far away
when you kissed me tenderly
time just slipped away
as I continued my thoughts
of the old days
I remember you now
you've been with me all the way
so I look to the future
while I keep my memories of yesterday

Tammi Houston

Tracks That'll Never Be Again

The quiet sky so gentle
As time proceeds
The leaves begin to flee.

The trees prepare for
The snow that will cover their twigs.
The sky darkness and proceeds with
The plans for the nocturnal hours.
The rumble of the season
Approaches much faster now.
As the families prepare for the worst,
The white glistening snow flakes
Fall one by one.

The lightness of the new season,
Warms the hearts of the children.
They laugh and play as they
Catch the white snow on their tongues.
Warmth and darkness now settles in the
sky.
The children run to the house
Looking back at the tracks
They'll never see again.

Nick Snyder

Was It Really Silent?

We sing the song called "Silent Night,"
As we sing of Jesus' birth.
But was it really silent,'
When God sent His "Light" to earth?

It shown on lowly shepherds,
It shown on mighty kings,
It shines on you and me today,
As all heaven and nature sings.

The shepherds ran to tell the news,
Of Messiah's heavenly birth.
The heavens rang with angel choirs
Singing, "peace to all on earth."

He is our only hope today
In a world so deep in sin, and
We must tell of His great love,
If the world we hope to win.

So let us shout for joy today,
As did the shepherds long ago,
And fill the world with praise to Him,
So God's Son the world will know.

Roberta Landon

Grandchildren

Oh, what a joy, a grandchild makes,
As you look into that tiny face,
And see yourself as a child,
Especially, the part of you that's wild.

Fingerprints on the glass, or
Spills upon the floor,
No one cares anymore.
Oh, what a few years make you realize,
As you look into those wide eyes.

Grandparenting is best of all,
You can spoil, hug, run and play ball,
Only to return them to Mom and Dad,
Who wonders why, they are so bad!

Sue Ann Scott

Untitled

All that I know
at such a price
I often wish I had not paid.
I used to separate it
another me
and another
and another
and another
different lives
that still are not this one.
But now I don't wish
sometimes it just comes over me
A brief dizzy spell
blinking and stuttering
knowing that it's just me.

S. Kelley Harrell

Learning To Live

I don't believe I can say just why,
at times I want to soar and fly.

To fly above without a worry, where
all is calm, no need to hurry.

To soar with ease from day to day,
to see my life from far away.

To leave my problems far below,
into the sky is where I'll go.

And when I look at the life I have,
it's then I must return.

Back to my life and all my cares,
to learn what I must learn.

Kelly White

Jester

Everyone laughs at the Jester,
at whom does
the Jester himself chuckle?
For the Jester is the
wise one who knows what
makes all laugh.
But there is a fine
line between laughter and tears.
The Jester knows this,
and can play on your fears.

Wendy Lavella

A Bonding Between Us

A bonding between us
Awakening souls
Came with the day
As the sun rose
Pedals unfolding
We were to find
Love in full bloom
We shared it's birth
    You and I

Pausing a moment
Taking in
A breath of fresh air
Brought it to life
Loves was born
    Alive
It showered the night

Natalie Bryan

The Unknown Me

Sometimes I want to run
away from the fear inside, and
travel to a distant place where
I can sit and hide. To walk
along the water, feel the sand
beneath my feet, to sit, to
dream, to wonder, why am I
not free. Inside myself I
often feel like I'm so very
trapped, deep within my heart
and soul, God's gifts lie
untapped. At times I sense
the nature of the me I'm set
to see, and then with fleeting
quickness, I'm left with only me.

Tony Perricone

Black Sunshine

Happiness,
Barely filtering through the darkness.
Light
Trying to overcome the bleakness.
Being strangled by shadows,
Suppressed by an unseen weight.
Black sunshine
Seeping into my soul.

Shera Thompson

Things Of Beauty

Beautiful roses growing in summer
Beautiful leaves falling in autumn
Beautiful life with love all round
Beautiful snow for christmas abound
Snowballs are wanting
Christmas trees have been decorated
Oh what a beautiful sight
The children are excited
What a beautiful time
Beauty beauty all around

Mary Corbin

Guardian Angel

Don't worry my children
Because I'm not around
Weep not for me
And stop feeling down

Life doesn't stop, it must go on
I'm where I need to be
So help the children along

For today is a good day
So you must be strong
I'll be waiting and watching
And I'll help you along

I'm you're guardian angel
And I will always be near
Hold me close to your hearts
And the one's you hold dear

For if faith is the one thing
I have imparted to you
Know that I am happy
And will always look upon you

Susan Grissmeyer

A Cry Of Help

I know you can't see me,
because I'm so new.
It's so dark in here, deep within you.
Wait, I feel something wrong.
What can it be?
Oh No! I think my Mom
wants to get rid of me.
Doesn't she know
God's already given me my soul
And with her help my body will grow.
I'm know I'm small, the size of a spoon
And it would be so easy
to just let me go.
Please don't take my life
just to make yours easier.
I have lots I'll be able to do
And I promise to always love you.
Please let me Grow.
Please let me Live,
Please let me be born!

Patricia Hesselgrave

Farewell Mr. President

The trumpet has summoned a gallant man,
Beloved by all the free,
Like brave men of old, he goes to keep,
His date with destiny.

He gave his life for his country,
Now his soul rests in peace,
But the glow from the fire he kindled,
Will surely never cease.

His brave deeds will long be remembered,
Engraved on history's pages,
With heavy heart, we bade him farewell,
Now he belongs to the ages.

Ruth A. Gilbert

Shadows

I close my eyes, the gateway
Beyond the realm of human sight.
Poised above, a lone wolf howls
Towards the dark side of the moon,
In awe of its celestial shadow.
This is the world of my creation,
The residue of past light.
Here, I'm but a desperate onlooker
In search of the final clue;
An unlocked emotion,
Meaning in harmless play,
Shadows of doubt
In the eye of the storm,
Masking the thoughts of men.
I cower in uncertainty,
And await the dawn of dreams.

Trent Grover

"Mother To Be"

She is near death when she gives
birth to life.
The pain she feels, no one can describe.
Her heart beats faster as her blood
pressure starts to rise.
She yells out a groan and tears
fill her eyes.
Hours seem like days as she begins
To pass out, finally the child is born.
Thru nine months she has suffered
for this day.
She wonders can this blessing from
God! Truly be worth all this pain?
Then the child is laid beside her,
in her arms.
She looks to heaven with a smile
and tears in her eyes and says; "It was"
credit to the Dad for being at her side,
and from him the seed did come.
However the birthright belongs
to the Mom.

Robert V. Criss

Thinking Of You

This morning when I wakened
    and saw the sun above.
I softly said, "Good morning Lord!
    Bless everyone I love!"
Right away I thought of you
    and said a loving prayer;
That he would bless you specially
    and keep you free from care!
I thought of all the happiness
    a day could hold in store;
I wished it all for you, because
    no one deserves it more!
I felt so warm and good inside,
    my heart was all aglow
I know God heard my prayer for you,
    he hears them all you know.
Just to let you know I'm thinking of you!

Larry A. Miller

Into The Rainset

Pale somber faces
blending with damp heavens
cold and clammy
walking slowly
trudging in soggy dark green earth
And the weight would be too much
if necessity didn't persist
like the night consistently pushing
Red eyes and the whites of the lips
quivering like a virgin sky
Smoke to the west
spreading to the east
into the rainset

Matt Shears

The Illumination

Blood on the clouds
blood on the sky,
flowing, spreading
in time with the motion of the earth.
The night is pierced
and bleeding in the East
spilling the colors of its wound
across its paling body,
and drowning the stars
in its liquid light.

I am stone—
a statue
watching the face of God
rise with the glaring brilliance
of the sun
and seeing the echoes
of the first dawn
in the blood-light colors
of the dying night.

Nathan M. McTague

Love Is Like A Rose

Love is like a rose
Both begin with a seed of hope
Quickly growing, strong and deep
Filled with buds, blossoming with hope
Bursting with colors deep
Love is like a rose.

Love is like a rose
Both are full of thorns
Quick to bring tears
Yet the gentle beauty...
Can wash away your fears
Love is like a rose.

Rebecca A. Patterson

Colors

Rainbow colors form
boundaries between
reality and play.
While youth sings songs of joy.
Picking series of red,
orange and pink,
from freshly cut green.
As the yellow shines
onto the earth.
We are all one,
just as the colors.

Sarah Bluman

Freedom

A glass cage
breaks free
Freedom
the rest is
bear to become
who knows
patterns distorted
shields break
emotions nurtured
Forgive combat
Strive for
    Paradise.
    Water runs clear
        can you see
    Food is good to
        eat
    Life
        flows through
    the years

Michelle Morrison

A Moment Of Freedom

The gorillas sleep in the afternoon sun
Breathing deeply after hours of fun
Babies tug at the blades of grass
This day is slipping by all too fast

Something isn't right, the gorillas stir
The peaceful picture becomes a blur
The giant awakes from a restless night
Looking around with a sudden fright

Familiar bars enclose his home
Suddenly he knows he's all alone
No one there to ease his pain
No one there to feel his shame

Gripping bars made of steel
No one knows just how it feels

Slowly he stumbles back to his bed
To find his peace in dreams instead
Where gorillas sleep in the afternoon sun
Breathing deeply after hours of fun

Shannon M. Morrison

Lost Love

I seen him one summer day
Bright eyes color of dark hay
Who he was I did care
But I knew I had to beware.

I asked him his name but was
ignored. I kept pushing and he said
"more" He said that he couldn't be got
right away I knew he had to be sought.

He looked like a lost dove never
Knew He would be my "Lost Love".
As time past we grew together
through beautiful and foggy weather.

He used me and he also lied
And last but not least damage my pride.
I kept my mind above.
Never knew He would be my "Lost Love."

I was hurt deep inside he never could
See how much or why. God please help
me from above never ever knew he
would be my "Lost Love".

Marilyn Townsend

Ascent From Hell

Darkness of the dampened night
bringeth forth thoughts despair
For life's complexities wrong or right
matters much to him who cares.

Somewhere beyond by memory's reach
a plea pathetically heard
'tis not the plea of one beseeched
more the cry of a wounded bird.

Oh! Memory where hidest thoughts of joy
canst thou feel my desperate yearning
Dost thou care my heart destroy
left disposed of satan's burning.

Will not the morning shed this fear
uplift the thoughts depressing
Or wilst they all again appear
torment me everlasting?

Wouldst thou Lord in Heaven dwell
makest me plainly see
And lead me from the depths of Hell
to live in peace with Thee.

William Henry Jones

"Gotta Go"

Cars going - People coming
Busy schedules everywhere
Sorry, not home, the machine replies
Gotta go Harry, see you later
Can't cook now, get it catered
Micros with their speedy meals
Computers - are they for real!
Our brain in recess
While machines take over
Sounds like the age of the 666
Or is Satan up to his old tricks
What ever happened to the good old days
Perhaps we should slow down and renew
Our ways
It wouldn't hurt to give it a try
And see what happens by and by.

Margaret Belleret

A Silent World

My world is silent
But I can see what you do
Your actions speak loud
As I look at you.

My world is not dark
For I see what you say
And watch your expressions
As they pass my way.

I see and hear more
Than you think - it's true
So be wise and careful
What you say and do.

Marilyn Stevenson

Poem

I thought I'd write a poem
But my brain this morning
would only roam!
So, guess what?
No poem!

Marlin K. Brandt

Loss

My throat is tight
But I cannot cry...
No tears will come,
Hard as I may try.

Tears to ease the pain
That won't go away...
From losing a love
I knew would not stay.

I grieve for this loss
And always will....
He gave me the world
With his own special skill.

His moon always smiled,
His stars twinkled bright
And his rain always soft
Be it day or dark night.

I'll always remember
His voice soft and low
That bid me good-bye
Before we scarcely said "Hello.

Sondra Weiss

I Can't Get Over You

I thought I was over you,
   but I guess I was wrong

My feelings for you are still
   there and maybe just as strong

You're someone special and getting over
   you is something hard for me to do

I've overcome many things in life,
   but as much as I try.
   I can't get over you

Ruben Ramirez

Masks

They wore masks of deformity
But I saw something more
A child's heart enveloped
A light behind the door

They wore masks of emptiness
But I felt something cry
A yearning from a desert
A world within a sigh

We wear masks of shadows
And who will see us clear
With a vision that breaks through
All the masks of fear

Robert C. Tomlinson

Depression

My soul is dead,
But I'm alive,
My heart pounds,
My body thrives.
I have no love,
Nor any friends,
I really don't think,
This sorrow could end.

Sarah Whitby

I'll Miss You

Dad I'll surely miss you,
But I'm glad you're not in pain.

The fact that I'll always love you
Will never ever change.

And now you're in a peaceful place
Looking down from above.

So I feel my loss I must face
With all your special love.

Linda Dunn

"In Flight"

   Two birds in flight on a quiet
but mysterious night...one goes through
clouds, the other through rain, both
feeling each other's heartache and pain.
Shall we come together on a new
but different flight or go our own ways
this special night?
   Say the decision is mine and
together we'll be; say the decision
is yours? Would you rather stay free?

Susan Kaiser

Untitled

A drifting soul in search of love
But never know the truth
A glimpse of hate beyond closed doors
Showing all but proof
A deserted sign on nowheres earth
Shines into the sun
The heartache follows every step
And tells me I'm the one

I have a hope but lost a love
And feelings come apart
So all the battles of the trip
Are kept here in my heart

I fear the end but seek the fields
Of which my gardens grow
The hands of ice and heart of steel
Would only like to know

Tricia King

What Is Black

Black is a color,
Black is me.
Black is a thing in which
You can be free.
Black are the people tall
Around you that say, hey!
What's happening, what's going
On, brother man and so on.
Black are the people with a
Desire to fight, for their
freedom, their color and their
legal rights.

Pamela Cook Chavious

My Grandpa

My Grandpa is Love,
But now it's time for
Him to fly on the wings
of a Dove.

The memories will always stay,
until it's time for me
to go away.

Life must go on for me,
and that's just the way it must be.

Future generations will be
taught of his way,
and how he fought in his day.

He will be dearly missed,
while they try to cope
with the bliss.

Dedicated to my Grandpa
Bernard L. Russo, 9-27-95

Michael Anthony Colbert

I Seem To Be

I seem to be a lazy cub...
but really I am a wild tiger.
I seem to be a calm goldfish..
but really I am a wild shark.
I seem to be a day dreaming cow..
but really I am a charging bull.
I seem to be an annoying cactus..
but inside really I am a blooming flower.

Stephen Stica

Sometimes

Sometimes there's thunder
But there is no storm
Sometimes there's a drawing
That has no form
Sometimes there is crying
Without any tears
Sometimes there's a courage
Hiding in fears
Sometimes is sometimes
But is never always
Sometimes there's a mist
On bright sunny days
And sometimes there's hope
When all is in vain
And sometimes there's love
That eases all pain

Karen F. Wynn

Children Of Rwanda

I looked into the eyes of death
Black children's eyes, the laughter gone
Sick bodies and dead bodies lying there
Lying and dying all alone.

To be buried in some nameless grave
Without a marker, without a stone
Like tender lambs, slaughtered too soon
To lie un buried under an African moon
I sobbed as I looked
And I held my breath
For I had looked into the eyes of death.

Margaret I. Hodges

Cover Me

The days go by the years they pass
But this ache it seems to last
The loss I feel can't be denied
I got this pain deep inside

I feel the world closing in
When will it stop when will it end
I need your pleasure from on high
I plead and pray don't pass me by

Please take this ache it's plaguing me
I've got two eyes why can't I see
Oh I need peace with-in my soul
Will this river of sorrow stop it's flow

The loss I feel can't be denied
I've got this pain deep inside
Oh won't you come and cover me
Let this heart begin to see

Stephen L. Raley

Message Of The Butterfly

Human souls and
butterflies; aren't
they a wonder to
behold?

Each, is a beautiful
work by GOD, more
precious than any gold!

We are daily proof,
that GOD had made
a plan for each and all.

Let's strive to help Him
keep those plans, and heed
his beck and call.

Ken D. McCarty

Granny

I remember granny's rocker
By the old wood stove
It sat upon a braided rug
From rags that she had wove

With twinkling eyes and wrinkles
She would smile to me and say
I love you dearly child
Stay sweet in every way

Granny was a kind soul
With love in her heart
I cherished her completely
Hoping wee would never part

And now I have granny's rocker
Before my fireplace
And as I sit down and close my eyes
I can still see her face

As memories fill my mind now
I can feel her warmth around me
I smile to her and say
I love you dearly granny

Sherry Marie Rupp

Circle Of Life

Bloody body bogs
    by the perfume river lie.
Life is so short -
    why'd they have to die?

So that we could live -
    so that we'd go on.
So that we could give,
    and maybe have a son -

Who'd go some day
    to a place like hue',
and give his life too -
    for his squad,
    for me -
    and for you.

Thomas J. Leavy

"Minds Of Men"

Lashed
by the whip of insanity,
Warped
by the rains of hate,
Confused
by the fog of security,
Enraged
by the hand of fate.
Caressed
by the cool autumn breeze,
Relieved
by the fertile, sod,
Enlightened
by the morning sun,
Calmed
by the hand of God.
So Man is born-is reared
Survives
Lives his life — until he dies.

Martin Israel

Music Of Love

The revelation of love
can be musically implicit,

For in my soul there is
an instrument.

I play a beautiful rhythm
from my heart.

There is a harmony to which is
grand when the music doth impart,

And when the music stops,
I know my love is trite.

But should the love I give
cause my heart to sing,

I will know my heart of music
gifts me love which is right.

Linda Wanat

Conquered

Eat my sunshine
Drink my blood
Use me up
Until I am none

Zilla May Martin

Mask

I wear a mask that nobody
can see, no one but you knows
the true me.
   I hide my frown behind a
smile, but it starts to fade after
awhile.
   If anybody just knew, everything
I have gone through.
   They just may understand, that
I to need a helping hand.
   But you handed your hand out to me,
and told me to set myself free.
   Free from all the hurt and pain,
and not to hold myself the blame.
   So I did as you asked, and
I no longer wear that mask.

Sharon Gardner

Passion

   I hate you with a passion and
cannot comprehend I wear it
like a cloak tight around my
soul closer than a friendly, O, what
has happen to me that once I loved you
so that I bathed in your glory
from head to toe only knowing you
and no more. Dreaming of a life we
two could share now. I don't even
care as I run my fingers threw your
hair. I wonder do you know have
I ever let it show you smile says
no. I kiss you on your lips. You say
I taste like wine but. This wine
my love is from a poisonous vine. As
you drift off to sleep I ponder in my
mind. This feeling, this anger, this
passion of mind and do you to feel
as I do thinking the words I
hate you with passionate to.

Katina Collier

Hour Glass

The man in the hour glass
cannot tell time
his thoughts and emotions
have become poisoned
and now blind
The man in the hour glass
is covered in sand
keeping sane thoughts
as best he can
The man in the hour glass
cannot understand
how he grew up so fast,
his world
has turned upside down
and now the sand
has become his past
and soon he
shall be free
from this hour glass...

Rebecca M. Sasena

Time Isn't Enough

Not enough time in life
Can't do everything that you want
Everyone thinks that time is everything
They are nothing
A time to wake-up
A time to be home
Curfews
Due dates
No freedom
Like we are trapped inside a clock
It is our king
It rules our life
We have no control
We have to over throw it's throne
Over power it
We have to free ourselves
The one who knows no time, know
themselves that they are truly free.

Kelly Kooperman

Coral Reef

Could such beauty
capture the mind's deepest rapture
and leave it stunned
to never again behold such wonder
or would such beauty
awaken a resonant chord
to be reinforced again and again
never to be lost
by
its haunting repetition

Theodore James Hovey

Mom's

Mom's are just a special breed
Caring for our every need,
From the day they give us birth,
Through the years they spend on earth,
Always listen to our needs
Helping with their thoughts and deeds
Never asking to be paid
For any sacrifice they've made.
When at last we're fully grown
Tell the world we're on our own.
Thank God for mom's who are still there
Always showings that they care.

Paul E. Johnson

Where Did The Summer Go?

Icicles replace bicycles
And snowballs form from leaves
Wonderland instead of sand
We're amazed that it could be
No more hot sun and summer fun
Just hot cocoa and cold toes
I get a chill inside my spine
Every time it snows
So next year
When the trees turn colors
And the ground is filled with snow
I'll remember then to ask myself
Where did the summer go?

S. E. Risbon

Goodbye

This will be our last goodbye
Cause I won't be around
Its time for me to disappear
You'll find I can't be found

You reminded me how much love hurts
When you opened up my heart
I never wanted to hear those words
I told you from the start

But you had to say it anyway
I tried not to feel the same
I was pretty sure it wouldn't work
Now all I feel is shame

You know you really hurt me
You also hurt yourself
I'll take the pieces of my heart
And return them to the shelf

I'll never forget your beautiful eyes
I'll remember what we had
It's just to bad that I won't smile
Cause all I'll be is sad

Loretta A. LaForce

Angel In Heaven

My heart is in so much pain
cause it's longing to see you again
I sit here as each day goes by
wondering to myself saying why.

Memories of you are in my room
seeing them puts you in bloom
If only I could touch your little face
to feel your loving warm embrace.

Courtney I know where you are
and memories not very far
Someday I will up there with you
to hold and kiss and say I love you.

Angel in heaven give me strength
Angel in heaven give me hope
Angel in heaven give me your hand
Angel in heaven give me you.

Stephanie Rau

Love

The lonely girl sat in the dark
Cautiously she played her part
Careful not to make a start

She regressed and remembered her past
Very lucky that it didn't last
Sadly remembered escaping it fast

Looking for her doll in the ominous room
Sweeping her fingers across the gloom
Realizing that it was gone

Inhuman to isolate her in this spot
He was never found, never caught
Did everything to her as she fought

Now she was cast into this lonely place
Spending time in this deserted space
No one around to calm her crying face

There must be an easy way out
Beyond a shadow of a doubt
It's absurd for Love to be without

Traci Lynn Usrey

Growing Up

Whenever I smell
chalk,
it is a hot summer day
and I am in my basement
playing school with my aunt.
She lets me be the teacher
while she is the student.

But that is not my story.
My story is my aunt
who has grown up too fast
and has left me behind
holding the chalk.

Kari L. Pohlman

Woodland Winter

Rabbits hopping in the snow,
Chipmunks wanting you to know,
That Christmas is almost here.

So ducks, listen
Your pond will glisten,
Winter has put it on ice.

Spider, winter has chosen
To make your web frozen,
I fear some of you may die.

William D. Roussel III

"Morning Dew"

So high in my thoughts,
Choking on stale clouds
of puffy intoxication.
She floats like a butterfly...
in my fields of flowering love.
Just touching my petals, long
enough for a rest
Then she's gone with the,
"morning dew."

Nicholus Jones

The Resurrection

clear
cold
alone
the barbarian's memory
crystallizes in the silence
at the end of time.

He walks the frozen rainbow to Valhalla
crisp glowing colors on the brittle air.

He stands possessed a moment
sword arm raised
to hear the epic songs around him
now distant echoes down forgotten fjords
and cryptic whispers
all around in snowflakes.

Wendy Myhre-Levy

Untitled

Love is colors
Colors of beauty
Light-rays of sunshine
Love is like a rose
Its petals unfold to the light
Blossom to sunshine
Time to grow with rain.
Love is like a rose
That has thorns like pain
If caressed will unfold
Letting out its inner beauty

Susan Regenauer

Nature's Detriment

In the fields I have seen
    colors that screamed
    of the injustice nature has seen
As I walked on it seemed
    it was just a dream
Oh when would I awaken

Then I started to get scared
    and for my death I prepared

Preparations being set
    caused me to forget
    that nature was ever different

It's propaganda that was sent
    that hid what was meant
    to be obviously ecological betterment

If evil runs so thick
    that we can't cut it to the quick
    then we all shall reap the pain
    of nature's detriment.

Keith H. Rigdon

Concept

Though death has
Come and taken me
I am not far away
Ever I am with you
Around you night and day

By night I am the darkness
That envelopes you in sleep
The stars, the moon, the sky
That enfold you in God's keep

By day I am the flowers
New buds upon the trees
The melting snows of winter
The depth of countless seas

Do not grieve for me dear one
I am happy and ever free
Admit to your soul God's wonders
When you would commune with me

Nancy Price

"Happiness From Within"

I don't believe true happiness,
Comes to us from another,
It must begin within ourself,
our heart and soul, no other.
Materials find us empty, for
The meanings we may seek,
Their monetary value, without
Feeling's for the meek.
The places we may wander, will
not seem to satisfy,
Although the plan was well
Thought out, an absence still defy's.
Encounter's find's new meaning
with the making of Good friend's,
with barrier's up, we're closed
to see beginning's not just end's.
And though it seems so hard to
find, our happiness in this place,
I'm sure compassion from beyond,
help's find our niche in space.

Katt McCray

The Puzzle Of Life

Life is like a jigsaw puzzle,
composed of many pieces -
some round -
some square -
some jagged -
The round ones are happy times,
The square ones - solid times,
The jagged ones - troubled times.
I suppose —
looking at the overall picture -
there are equal portions of each -
But, - just when you think you have
    it all together -
It falls apart!

Marian Di Stefano

February 1st, 1995

Twenty-five years of life
converge
to result
in tiny hands and feet,
helpless little-boy cries.
Nine months of growth and change
result in life,
unnamed as yet
mother shocked with sleep and pain,
and Joy.
Twelve hours of agony and fear
give way to bliss,
and as medication wears off
the cuts ache,
but she fights the hurt,
"It was all worth it."
And I fight back tears
for my sister
and her undying strength.

Maria Coley

Legacy

He beholds his wife,
Cradles his son.

Awestruck—

Bequeathed by letter,
Sealed with a prayer.

He remembers—

Love's brilliance aglow;
In his smile her legacy told.

Patti Jo Dieringer

Child Of Sorrow

Child of sorrow - born to loneliness
Dark tomorrows - where's the happiness?
Seeking love in sordid places
She looked for love in strangers' faces.

Eyes were blinded by the snow
She couldn't see which way to go.
Fleeting days - night without end
Downward spiral - hooked again!

Look up, sweet child, the sun is there.
Look around for those who care.
Learn to love the inner you.
God's love within will see you through.

Winter ended - spring began.
Hope had blossomed in her mind;
And as she started life anew;
God said: "I have other plans for you."

Now she's home to perfect peace
No more sorrow, no more grief.
Once she entered heaven's door,
She's child of sorrow nevermore.

Pamela Heydel

Thought of You

Months gone by,
days so fast, but
thoughts of you
always last.
I laugh sometimes
at how I try, to not
think of you... but
I cannot deny, you've
made a dent into my
mind, and try as I
might I cannot find a
way to forget you,
you're just so fine.
I guess you are
worth thinking of.

Peter J. Tirpok

Dream

Close your eyes and go to sleep,
Dream of good things that you eat,
Not of bad things in the night,
But of good things glowing bright,
Seas that sparkle,
Birds that sing,
Just go ahead dream anything.

Trystn Talley

Untitled

It may still rain
deep down the river
where we came from.
dry here,
    There? Unknown.
It may still rain
    when hearts pity the old slave,
    man where is my shrine?
it may still rain
    sad anxiety.
It may still rain
poor soul,
lonely.
It may still rain
deep down the river
where we came from.
hard, touch feeling
    still pouring...

Manzila Nsimba

Recognize

Movie madness
Destruction sadness

What will we face today
Should we go to the far left
Should we make the right our way

Why does the system make you weak
When sometimes bitter
This causes us to weep

Drugs, war, homeless and alcohol
Recognize its a struggle we all fall

One day at a time
This is how we make it
Its not a perfect world
So the poor have to take it

We want solutions
Not racial pollution

We all should recognize
Not disguise

Renita Rachal

Did You Stop Dreaming?

Did you stop dreaming?
Did you know it was time to die?
Did you lose sight of a dream
You held so close to your heart?
Did you let go of a love;
Slip up and fall apart?
Did the rain fall on your face
As you stood in silence and cried?
And no one could tell how deep it was,
'Cause through the pain you lied.
Never showed us a glimpse of the truth;
You chose to hide behind a needle.
Not quite the voice of a generation,
But definitely one meant for an angel.
Did you stop dreaming?
Did you know it was time to die?
Were you ready for this change in your
life?
Now, forever, you'll silently lie.

Kristul Straube

The River Of Love

The river of love flows
Dividing the land
Where it leads, no one knows
Not of mortal man.

The river runs fast
And is very deep and wide
Many rocks and undertows
To keep us from the sides.

At one point in our lives
We all must take a chance
Jump into the river
In search of lost romance.

Many before have failed
Many will fail again;
But if you find that certain love
For you the river ends.

But if that love should tarnish
And you realize it's a fool's gold;
Before you know what happened
The river of love will flow.

Mason Dunkerson

Rolly My Kitten

If he died would you care?
Do you miss him purring in your hair?
In the trees he would climb and was
very hard to find.

Today he's not here, don't fear.
Don't fall apart cause you know
he will always be in your heart.

Tammy Thomas

Inside

I know you see me but are you looking
Do you see inside
Behind fears of refusal
And past my lying eyes

I know you hear me but are you listening
Do you hear inside
Past the words I say
And into the truth I hide

I know you hold me but do you feel
Do you feel inside
Beyond the walls around my heart
And to the love inside

K. ellis

"The Serpent"

Look into my eyes little one,
    Do you see the pain,
        the anger,
            the hunger?
If you look farther you will see.
I look into yours and see fear. You
are distraught. Your flesh is no good
to me if you are not sedate.
Either way you are mine to feast
upon. So now relax. That's better.
With those last words I lavished
over the small child and swallowed
him whole.

Misty Michelle Cook

A Tribute To A Friend

You were always
Doing a good deed,
Helping all that
were in need.
Everyone you met
you called friend
and you were always
Ready to end lend
a helping hand
to all that asked
regardless of how long
or hard the task.
You loved all
or so it seemed
always friendly
never mean
about no one
you ever spoke ill
you were the kind
to live and let live.

Virginia Hunter

Save The Little Children

Save the little children.
Don't let them starve and die
Share your blessings with them
Don't horde those war supplies.

Save the little children
Give all you can to care
Bring an end to suffering
and sadness every where

The great leaders of our world
Pray to God they find a way
To work and strive together
So the world may yet be saved

Save the little children
End the suffering and disease
Don't let atomic weapons
Destroy humanity

Kenny Rickard

The Waterfall

The dark waterfall
Flows swiftly
Through the air
Racing for revenge

Niki Wilson

Dream

Dream me a dream love.
  Dream me free of pain.
Dream me love, so that I won't cry again.
  Dream me pretty, dream me nice.
Dream me free of vice.
  Dream me a love dream.
Fill it full of cheer.
  Dream me forever.
So I won't really be here.

Vicky M. Williams

Alligator Junction

There's a symphony playing
Down in Alligator Junction
Let's go down there together
And listen carefully.

To the croaking of the frogs
And the chirping of the crickets
To alligators snapping jaws
And swishing their tails.

The fish are happily splashing
As they jump out of the water
The mosquitos are humming
As they flit in the air.

The shrill-sounding cicadas
Provide the background music
While birds sweetly sing their song
In pleasant harmony.

There's no audience require
Down in Alligator Junction
The symphony is played for
The simple joy of it.

Millie Hull

Uisge Beatha

Take it all, always
drink deep with greedy mouth
all that is offered
all that another freely gives

take nothing for granted
drop to your knees at the muddy bank
drink until you gasp and choke
sucking at the air, laughing
then try again to drown

we rage at the passing of our time
the passing of our lives, our loves
but there is no stopping
the rushing of the stream

hold nothing back
give all without thought or measure
until the rending current
sweeps back all the gifts

Michael Simonetto

Take A Chance

Rain
Drops
Fall on my head

Soaking
Wet
On my head

Pull me from the cold
Warm my chill
My bones
Stimulate

Take a chance

Laurie Patelunas

Untitled

Lying in a room.
Dull and lifeless.
People all around.

Machines running on full.
Life running on empty.
People crying.

A breath.
Possibly the last.
People, family, friends; praying.

Heartbeat is down.
Life ebbing.
Somebody comes; holds my hand.

Speaks; his name through tears.
He loves me. "Live! Live!"
Shocked; he can't continue without me.

I want him, I'll live.

Yet...
One week passes.
Two weeks pass...
Third week..."pull the plug."

Staci Attwood

Life...

Only players
dwelling in the game
are known to realize
none are the same

Time after time
pieces fall but never decease
the lost fade without contact
others fail to defeat

Without a right or wrong
rules remain but a question
stakes become endless
by choice few seek confession

Residing with the fact
accepting all that you chose
seeking glory is the key
to the door no one knows

Kate Vickers

Untitled

You're the one that makes
each day worth looking for

You make me smile
each time I see you

Your shine that are with-in
your dark brown eyes

And that smile, that never
goes down;

That smile always let me
know that I'm not in a dream,
but within a realistic of life.

How to see your smile and
the shine that keeps me always
happy to be yours
  for today
    the one whom
      will always love
        you.

Mary Connie Perez

Like Oak

My love for you
Each passing day
Grows like oak
And never sways

Its tough, its strong
And full of life,
And helps me make it,
Through this strife

My heart, my love
You have for sure
Is tucked away
And will endure

Till the day has come
When we must part
And leave this world,
You'll keep my heart.

So, my love for you
Each passing day
Grows like oak
And never sways.

Kerry A. Burke

Friendship

"No man is an Island!"
Each person needs someone!
The strong, the weak, verbose and shy,
Should not remain alone.

A problem, when it's shared,
Seems lighter than before!
How can listening ears lift mountains,
Ease pain from troubles stored?

True friendship is not bought
With things you may possess;
It's built on stones of trust and faith,
And exists on nothing less!

Margie P. Hitte

Parting

My sudden sadness is only uncontrollable
   emotion set off by fears
Of days apart that will seem as years.

They say that love can only grow
   stronger with time...
Then why do I feel my heart will weaken
   with sorrow, though I'm fine?

Because I feel I will love you
   an eternity each of those days,
And will between each meeting until
   our last, true parting of ways
      and my love is genuinely eternal.

Shelly Knapp

"Clouded"

Cold, sullen, vacant,
Eyes like a brick wall;
Distant, hidden, shut,
Emotions have been withdrawn;
Pitter, patter, thump,
Heart of stone;
Quiet, blank, sedate,
Soul that feels alone.
The epitome of emptiness.

Sonia Waters

"Lost Of Feeling"

Here I sit, pen in hand.
Emotions tumble, unnamed.
Too tangled up
From years of neglect.
Much easier to ignore
Than to identify.
Time flies by and so do I
Like a leaf twirled by the breeze.
Never a cause - only a result.
Never act - only react.
Blame it on the wind.

Margaret Basford

In A Flash

  In a blink of an eye
Everything is gone
You open up your eyes
To find you're all alone.

Your mind flashes back
To a life you once had
You don't understand what's happened
You think you're going mad.

Your senses go crazy
As you see the sign of death
Your mind flashes back again
To when you took your last breath......

Tonya A. Milton

Untitled

Who knows
Exclusion
Seclusion
Alone
Intrusion
Inclusion
New friends
Collusion
Confusion
Betrayal
Delusion
We use our imagination to find new and
ingenious ways to hurt ourselves
Why?
We think deep and profound thoughts
Why?

Vann Nicholas Daugherty

Alone

One mind and body
expressing one being,
one world,
extends naked fingers
out to touch
other bodies, other beings.

One many pointed star
crossing, cycling,
overlapping
many heads and legs
and arms
with no point quite the same.

Mary Bridget Joy

"A Summer Rose"

As "a summer rose" blossoms,
expelling fragrance
and radiating beauty,
affixing to life as only hers.

Then pedals, fall one
by one, in accord,
wilted tarnished, as
only untold death can bring.

Enlightened eyes, to vision
tomorrows rose bud, comes,
instead of one there's two,
twice the fragrance, twice the beauty.

In life, unity we hold dear,
as "a summer rose"
affixed to life as yours,
a grandeur of beauty.

In accord life and death,
as "a summer rose" to unite,
your tomorrows living, sharing,
twice the fragrance, twice the beauty.

Verda McCafferty

Stars Of Love

Starlike moments in time
explain much
But just how do times
like these arise.

It's when many glorious
stars turn into a bunch
Then it branches out and
almost doubles in size.

Love is practically the
same disposition
Only love gathers upon
time manifested in itself.

Now upon which star
is your love wishing
is your love based on
truth or pelf?

M. Elizabeth Poole

Destiny

   The sun rose early that morning with
eyes of fire and flames glory
   Though I stood there not knowing
my destiny
   I wanted to see the heavens with
my heart and soul
   I wanted to be a bird and fly with
the stars
   To see the people below and heal
there scars
   Through fire and flame, glory and
shame, I am like the sun not knowing
how the day will end.

Nesha Sexton

Life Of Dreams

She reminds me of a story book,
Face that has that snow-white look.

In the world she has created,
Hangs the curtains that are faded,

To intruders who would see,
The truth and life's reality.

The strength she holds in keeping safe
Her fairy tale life for all to take.

To be with her, you'll get entwined,
Her dreams and schemes, all, in her mind.

Stay too long and you'll believe,
The tale of hers, without reprieve.

Is mine the life that's full of dreams,
No, hers is the one, or so it seems.

Robin Laurie

Condensation Point

Watching the dew
fall onto the leaves
outside windows
one cannot help but wonder
why is God crying?
My God is strong
and so they say
who is the stronger
the man who cries?
Or the man who bites his lips?
Strength is required to cry
tears fall down your cheeks
and it all ends up in the same place
we all die
but hanging on makes it worse
and so they say
hold on - suck it up - be a man
and I respond I am a man I just cry
maybe you should try it sometime
just ask God

J. Louis Hathaway

Fall

Leaves are turning yellow,
Falling off the trees,
Landing in the grass,
Floating with the breeze.

Temperatures are dropping,
Squirrels are gathering food,
Woodcutters are chopping
Logs for a fireplace mood.

Pumpkin pies are baking
Smells of turkey fill the air,
Many folks are raking,
Children play without a care.

Its autumn, can you feel it?
Can you sense it everywhere?
Just slow down and then enjoy it
Winter's coming, see it there?

Melissa McKinney

Untitled

I am who I am.
Feeling the wind
As it touches my face
Like a lover's tenderness,
Soft and gentle.

I am what I am.
Feeling the freedom
Watching miles sweep by
Pulsating iron beneath me
Traveling winding roads.

I am why I am.
Feeling the purpose
Knowing no other lover,
Eagles soaring above me
As I ride.

Michele Dewey

1 Left Shoe

Our love is like one left shoe
Feels good but just won't do
Does one wing make a flight?
We need one more to a right
No more stub toe'd of a fright
We needs both soles for the height
Our love is one left shoe
And I don't know what I do
Rough ground is a hop-a-long
But 1/2 of a whole is no song
Our love is one left shoe
And I don't know what I do
We need to pair afore it's thru
Our love is one left shoe
And I don't know what I do

Matt Berry

The Freedom Makes Me Cry

My heart struggles with my mind,
Fighting an endless sorrow.
Maybe it can be cured with time,
So I wait for tomorrow.

The journey is long and restless,
As the battle has no fears.
I cease to own a simple kiss,
To wipe away my tears.

My heart belongs to a jealous soul,
My mind is out to kill.
And you are it's only goal,
So tell me how you feel.

As the battle continues on,
I can't help but wonder why.
The union I had is now gone,
The Freedom Makes Me Cry.

Kendra Roche

The Dances

Wild music
Fills my soul
Spinning around
My thoughts a whirl
Soaring in emerald
Dipping into shadow
My body all golden
Soaring over the world
On the edge of a dream
All numb and cold
The world ceases
And the vision blurs
I am free free free
Open wild and burning

Marion Hawkinson

Witness Cauldron

Double, double, toil and trouble,
Fire burn and cauldron bubble.
Toe nails,
From people in the jails,
Venom of a snake,
Sizzling as it bakes,
Frog legs,
It will make you beg.
Double, double, toil and trouble,
Fire burn and cauldron bubble.

Vanessa Richards

I'm A Red - Blooded American

Don't judge me by the clothes I wear
Don't judge me by my skin and hair
Don't judge me by the way I walk
Don't judge me by the way I talk
Judge me by what's inside.
It's on, I have nothing to hide
I'm a Red Blooded American just like you
I have a heart that beats strongly too
I have bones and muscles that grow
I have a brain now don't you know
So next time when you look at me
Don't judge me by what you see
If you look inside I'll guarantee
There's a lot more to see.

Rasheeda Barnett

To J. L.

It's high noon in my life;
From sunrise 'til now I've
Seen it, done it, been it.
What a busy morning!
I can't believe it's noon.

The rain stopped a little
While ago - the sun's out
And I want to spend the
Rest of my day with you
Laying back, chilling out.

We'll celebrate sunset
Like they do in Key West
Savor it - taste it - not
Just let it slip away.
Sharing is beautiful.

Priscilla Howell

For Tina

Through misty waves of pain you came.
Flesh and blood and bone of me.
How was I to know
How was I to see
How brief your visit was to be

Seasons came and seasons went.
A fair young maiden came to be.
Flesh and blood and bone of me,
How could I ever see
A long life was not yours to be.

In the glare of lights too bright
And the hum of beeping machines,
Through waves of soul wrenching agony
You quietly slipped away.
Flesh and blood and bone of me.

It was my fulfillment to be there when you
came.
It was my deepest despair to be there when
you left,
My daughter my heart you took.
Flesh and blood and bone of me.

Linda S. Dant

Peace

If only to be a
flighted geese
beyond a flagpole
waving peace.
Somewhere heading
to a home
where bombs have ceased
and guns have gone.
Somewhere serene in space
away from gavels, and
laws that take.
Away from senseless, shouted words
away from lands now so
disturbed.
Far above envy's sight.
Somewhere amid God's calming
light.

Wayland W. Williams

Alone

A young man dies
Fog hangs low·
Clouds grow dark
The world cries and why
Must young men die?

Rain drops hang
No sun this morn
No song of bird
No out cry heard, but,
Gray fog creeps - a world weeps.

Alone, we come
Alone, we must go
Weep clouds bugles blow
Birds will sing
Sun will glow

D. Kwasniewski

My Heart

I have no heart no more
For he is now with you
I lost him on the day you left
When you said that we were through

I told my heart what would happened
I warned him all the time
But my heart just wouldn't listen
When I spoke my piece of mind

I told my heart you'd leave us
Never to return
And heart you'll break in pieces
And the hurt will always burn

But he would not believe me
He said this love was true
And he said that he would leave me
For the sake of loving you

So now he's gone forever
That loving heart of mine
To be with you, the one he loves
Until the end of time

Marvin L. Ballow

When You Talk

To me, talk not of poverty
  For I know it's many faces
I bid you, talk of purity
  For I know not it's many places

Speak not to me of foul and evil
  deeds
For many have I seen, and also done
  myself

Speak to me of righteousness so I
  may heed
As you may have done thyself

To me, speak not of sin and fear
  For in it's darkness I have been
Speak of a light, so glorious and
  dear
That I, perchance have seen

Nay, talk not of sorrow and tears
  For it's not that path I choose
Talk of glad things and full cheers
  For it's my world I stand to lose.

Manuel Soto Romo

My Mother

She is a hero to me,
For many reasons I can see,
Even though she's far away,
In my heart she will stay,
I really do miss her so,
But on with my life I must go,
Why we must part is a mystery,
Though later in life I will see,
Someday we'll be together,
From then until forever

Melissa Kohls

This One Child

His heart must be of gold
for one of flesh was not
given. In the blink of an
eye from my womb
God's rocking chair is where
he abides, to be an angel
before he opened his eyes.
How precious he must be
for God to need him
more than me.

Liz Anderson

Earth

The Earth is such a great wonder
For small minds to search and plunder
People care for it with great love
Clouds are white like a dove

Why do people abuse the ocean
You can't fix it with some secret potion
Now they're hurting the land
Why don't they understand

Poor babies just born and already hurt
These days you must always be alert
Young girls are giving birth
More lives to live on Earth

Shelly Marie Cross

"No More Will I Cry"

No more will I cry,
for there are no more tears.
No more will I cry,
for the pain is too great.
No more will I cry,
for death is not the end.
No more will I cry,
for I know you are with me.

Kyle Witt

Love Of A Son

I stayed with you,
for thirty plus years.
You loved me so true,
and calmed my fears.
But, for all I could find,
you gave me advice.
And when I was blind,
I never looked twice.
Through thick and through thin,
you have remained.
My mother, my friend,
just the same.

Robert Rainey

Generations

We will miss you here with us
For your strong, but silent ways.
We knew that you were always there;
No matter how bad our days.

Your understanding of our lives
Joys and sorrows that we shared.
The pride that you had in all of us;
Special deeds that showed you cared.

You taught your children to stand tall
And when down, to rise above.
You gave us courage to be ourselves;
And you always gave us love.

Unselfish ways you gave from the heart,
To stranger, family and friend;
We have taught to our children,
So rest assured, this is not the end

Now your time to leave is here,
As you pass through Heaven's door;
The memories will cause us to smile,
And will make our spirits soar.

Marilynne Burton-Ristau

What I Feel For You

Feelings so strong they
form a bond,
    But miles apart doesn't
mean there gone.
    The distance is so great,
but the Love is so near,
    Hold deep in my heart
with nothing to fear,
    It's hard to describe the
Love I have in side,
    Freely flowing through
me like an on going tide,
    I miss you dearly, I miss
you much, but with your warm letters
    my heart you touch,
So love me as I love you,
    and together we'll make our
dreams come true.

Mike J. Eberhard

Remembering 1945

On the 8th of May, Nineteen
Forty-Five,
We jumped for joy,
We were alive!
We danced in the streets,
We had lots of fun,
We were winning the war,
We had beaten the Hun.
But in the Pacific
Lay a long road ahead.
There, many were captive,
Many were dead.
Japan would fight on
To the end we were told.
Its leaders were stubborn,
Its soldiers were bold.
Then out of the blue
Came a B-29.
The rest is now history
Japan toed the line.

Tony Ralph

Dreams Of A Tomorrow

Dead loved ones,
Friends' betrayal,
Dreams of a tomorrow.

Hopeful wishes,
Unbreakable love,
Dreams of a tomorrow.

Unbearable pain,
Crazed minds,
Dreams of a tomorrow.

Shameful embarrassment,
Unforgotten pride,
Dreams of a tomorrow.

Cold-hearted strangers,
Brutal Nazis,
Dreams of a tomorrow.

Wanted freedom,
Desires to live,
Dreams of a tomorrow.

Kelly Kleinert

"Foolish Heart"

Why do you run away
from my love,
    I think its a match
made from up above.
    You say that you found
someone new,
    When all along the truth I knew.
    You are nothing but a fool,
    You could never stay
with just one girl.
    You are just a childish boy,
    Playing with love as
though it were a toy.
    You say that you only love one,
    But in the end you
will love no one.
    I wish there was a way you knew,
    Exactly how I feel for you.
    But love is just a game to you,
    But as for me it's a gift shared by two.

Marissa G. Conley

Where Did It Go?

A love that was born
From the days of our youth
Full of passion, full of fire
Built on honesty and truth
Together we add the sparks
As the early years go by
We later grasp for answers
Why we no longer want to try
The love has turned to anger
The fire has turned to cold
We've lost our hopeful dream
Of sharing life until were old
Our intentions were sincere
The love we had was pure
But it somehow got away
Where it went we are not sure
It happens in a flash
Like the twinkling of an eye
We are only left to ponder
How to tell our marriage good-bye.

Richard L. Everett Jr.

Until We Meet Again

I pick up the dried rose petals
from the garden our love fed
they symbolized hope and friendship
and now have fallen with the dead.

I hold the petals in my hand
and draw then near my heart
wishing I had said goodbye
now we are too far apart

You are now in a better place
so close but yet so far
but I will be strong for you
you are happy where you are.

I will never forget you
my prayers I will always send
and my love for you will never die
until we meet once again

A new rose in our garden will grow
in its beauty at full bloom
all the pain and sadness will depart
and I will move on without you.

Valerie Carzello

"G.P.O. Tidbits"

"My discharge occurred in forty-five,
From the U.S. Army Band—
After five long years of military life,
It was time to see what's at hand."

"I decided on a career in the P.O.,
I'd enjoy working in Civil Service—
I took the P.O. postal exam,
And passed, boy, was I nervous."

"I was assigned to the Registry section,
Where I hoped to do my best —
Every year I took the Registry exam,
I made a perfect score on every test."

"The happiest day of my life occurred,
July twentieth, in forty-six —
My sweetheart and I tied the knot,
Our love will endure, like bricks."

"I retired from the P.O. in seventy-seven,
After thirty-two years giving my best —
Still married nearly fifty years,
Next year, you will all be my guests."

Marty Rollin

Eternity

Eternity is like a
grain of sand that
sits on the beach.
A bird with one wing
comes and retrieve it,
fly away towards the
sun and fly's back to
retrieve another
Time is forever, forever is time
It awaits for no man
It just passes on.

Renita Weathersby

Forsythia

Enter Pagliacci
Full regalia, colors aloft
Boldly foretelling the story

With youthful exuberance
Haphazardly reaching with confusion
and grace
Defying and teasing the retreating
chill

Echoing the sun's color
Demanding attention
It is the messenger of hope
As spring's curtain goes up

Paul R. Rice

Seasons Of Life!

Summer breezes, winter scenes
Fun with friends, sick all week
Weekend nights, partying right
Playing hard, hurting bad
Trying to cope with the summer sun
Dating some guy I met last month
When the snow begins to fall
How come you never call
When the sun begins to rise
You never heard my cries
For something happened last summer
I'm afraid to tell you now
Because you found someone for you
And I'm beginning something new
Some call it "motherhood"
I call it "being used"
For you no longer have me
But I'll always have a part of you
For as you have guessed, like the seasons
I have changed
I am no longer one, I am "two and a fool!"

Robin DuPont

Wolf

Wolf,
gentle and full of
beauty. Nurturing to
its young and spiteful
to its enemies.
Misunderstood and
ridiculed. Destroyed
through story, song
and fable. Never
spiting man and too
beautiful to be
destroyed. Yet it is.

William C. Dockstader III

Sky Song

Gonna catch me a rainbow,
Gonna catch me a cloud.
Gonna ride on the wind
While singing out loud...

I have colors to sail me
Through pieces of sky,
And when I come down
I'll still be up high...

Yolanda Robinson

Little Brothers

Little brothers always
get on your nerves and
yell out its hers. They
always get you in trouble
and when your mom
has twins you have double.
You take the wrap for
all they do and they
never say thank you. Mom
always says you do something
wrong and then he sings
the I got you in trouble
song. No need to worry, no
need to cry because when
he's hurt he comes to
you with tears in his eye.

Nafeesah Allen

Snowing Poetry

Poetry is as bright as the
glistening light off the snow.

Bouncing off thing to thing,
place to place,
every place it goes.

The writing glistens and
dances and bounces in the light.

For those who look into the light
go blind with fright.

Katie Berk

Prayer

When no one else seems to care
God is always there
Your every problem to share
Just take them to Him
    In prayer.

V. Patricia Smith

Renewal

Whisper a prayer
    ....God listens.

Accelerate a cure
    ....with the next step.

Vanquish the pain
    ....God love you.

Virginia Knight

Purification

White jade with
Gold like a cloud rising
From the river
Translucent
Hovering silent and still.

Behind, within or perhaps beyond
A beam of light made more brilliant
By its slivered form
Pierces
Shatters and scatters.

The now dust-turned gold
Disappears...
Only jade and its whiteness remain.

Marie Annette Kirk

Quiet Passage

A perfect feather,
graced upon crisp, white linens.
Lace curtains frame an open window.
Soft music, gentle strings of harp.
Dancing sunbeams form an aura
of tranquility and purity.

Gentle winds stir and shadows shift.
Day's aura, now an evening glow.
The feather is at peace,
though ravaged by disease.
Weightless, febrile, anorexic,
yet at peace.

The winds gain strength.
Sunbeams transform to moonbeams.
Stirring drapes and increased winds
send the feather on its journey
to the windowsill, atop an angel's wing,
to the world beyond.

Suzanne Creighton

Gargantuan Grandeur

Gargantuan,
Gravity-geared,
Geodesic giant,
Grind!
Rotate and revolve,
Cuddled in a quilt,
Of clouds.
Tranquil,
Tender, tendrils, trail,
Along the hallowed hollows,
Of the vales,
Wending their way,
Over holy hills.
View the cornucopia!
Fountains overflow —
Cast coins into canyons,
Containers, cans, corroded cars,
Mulch with mounds of mud.
Grind on,
Gargantuan grandeur!

Ray Suzan Strauz

The Spark

A small spark starts deep within
growing stronger with time.
Soon the spark is full grown
demolishing everything in it's path.
In time the spark, which was so tiny,
Is out of control.
It burns away, dreams, memories,
and laughs to come....
Until there is nothing left
except regret and sorrow.
Then the spark grows weak,
it's damage has been done.
Finally the spark dies,
but in my mind it lives...
Burning through my thoughts,
and terrorizing my dreams.
When will my suffering ever end?
No one knows except the spark,
and it will never tell.

Marla Carter

Nineteen Years ....And Still

Nineteen years of working
Hard for everything I've got
Nineteen years of working
And still don't have a lot

Nineteen years of learning
At home and in the schools
Nineteen years of learning
And still feel like a fool

Nineteen years of wondering
What in life I want to do
Nineteen years of wondering
And still without a clue

Nineteen years of going
Where to? I don't really know
Nineteen years of going
And still a long long way to go

Robert C. Rollins Jr.

Finally Free

All the anger, old anger
has left me
I can see me at 16
and remember me
without seething

And I can think of it now
your hands, hard hands
and not feel so sad
for so long thinking
I was so bad, too bad

Finally, I'm me again
just me, only me
not smashed down by memories
smothered suffering
finally, I'm free
I'm free

S. Laine Reeves

Pearl

A pearl
has many shapes.

Not only round,
but soft.
Not heavy,
but full of pricelessness.
Warm and delicate to touch

A pearl
has many colors.
Not only white,
but black.
Shining with beauty

A need to feel
with feelings,
to caress and admire.
An object
with no objection
to being loved,
an object of my affection.

Rea Lynn Russell

The Awakening

What seemed to be a millennium away
Has now come to pass.
The time to put childish dreams away,
Putting innocent youth in the past.

Yet there is a child inside,
Struggling to evolve into womanhood.
Ever changing like the tide,
Unspoken things are understood.

A stranger inside keeps beckoning.
The child wants to stay.
What is this strange awakening,
Pushing the child away?

A new person is emerging.
Mysterious and powerful.
Yet like a lost child lying alone,
Feeling afraid and incapable.

The child of youth is forever gone.
In it's place, the child of intuition.
Guiding the new child to face the unknown.
Preparing the old child to accept the
awakening.

Kathleen King

Brooklyn Pale 1996

Lies and betrayal
hatred and torture
weave the pattern of my shining heritage
tenderly passed
parent to child,
and on stage
my pale demon-self dances
in my place
amongst the bones
clean, hard and white.
While in the labyrinth
beneath the dance
I stumble and fall
on limbs long since bruised and broken
unable to speak
my tongue rots in my mouth.

Susan Julia

Without Form

God is a God without form.
He created the universe in all its calm.
God is a God without form,
Yet without him, man can't perform.

God is a God without form,
By his spoken word, the seas are calmed.

God is a God without form,
It is he worship, praise and adorn.

God is a God without form,
he knew us, before we were born.

God is a God without form,
I thank him for all he has done.

Mae L. Moten

Thankful

I saw a lad who had no eyes.
He did not fret nor pine.
I said a prayer in this wise:
"Thank Thee, Lord, for mine."

There was a beggar with one leg
Who did not seem to rue
His loss, and was content to beg.
"Thank, thee, Lord that I have two."

A woman without hands came by.
Her joyous smile appeared to say:
"You can't be happier than I"
I clenched mine tight to pray.

Those of us who are bereft
Of limb or sight; sometimes of mind;
By nature, chance or time are reft.
They are God's most blessed kind.

Stephen Poch

Ito, Lance

Has big pants
He got a lot of money
For sitting around looking funny

Zach Young

Reunion

After fifty years of marriage
he had to go away
Leaving her alone to face
day after lonely day.

Memories were her crutches now,
the only thing she had
Thoughts of how things used to be
always good and never bad.

Time which once had been a friend
became a hated thing;
The bell of life had tolled so sweet
now had an empty ring.

And then a miracle occurred for her
where life had lost it's charms;
She went to sleep in bed one night
and woke up in his arms.

Two people whom we loved so much
have died and gone away;
Together again, happy and waiting
we'll meet again someday.

Linda Hallock Reinsager

Opening My Heart To The Lord

I have opened my heart to the Lord.
He has given me a new song,
I can't begin to tell you
The warmth of feeling belonged
I called on him today and,
He did not let me stray
When I put my hand in his
He carried me the rest of the way.

Linda Shaw

Sixth Grade Psalm II

The Lord is my crossing guard,
He helps me across the street,

He steers me away from cars,
He guides me through life,

He waits for me at the corner each day,
and He knows my name.

I thank him for being there for me.
I will always remember my crossing guard.
6 Gr Sunday School

God's Care

God is everywhere,
He keeps me safely in His care.

He watches o'er me day and night,
I trust in Him and need not fright.

When dawn appears and all is bright,
I thank Him for a restful night.

I rise and ask what is in store,
For this new day He's given more.

Then on I go, and hope that I
Can cheer someone who passes by.

Our God is real and a true friend,
On that we can trust and always depend.
Rachel Spangler

Sorry That He'd Lied

He knew it from the start,
he knew it wasn't wise
keeping all the secrets,
telling all the lies.

How could he stop now,
it's been so many days
so he went and got his ring back,
and they went their separate ways.

Girlfriend went home crying
because she wants him back,
then she took a walk
along the railroad track.

She never saw the headlights,
or heard the whistle call,
or saw the shadow of the smoke stack
standing straight and tall.

Boyfriend went to the hospital,
sorry that he'd lied,
that very night in his arms
his ex-girlfriend died.
Shea Metcalf

Broken

Sadness falling all around,
I can no longer hear the sound,
Of my heart beating.
Sadness in my head,
I feel that I am dead.
My heart is no longer beating.
Is there a way out?
Can I make this madness stop?
Without my heart beating.
My mind has gone insane, and
I no longer feel the pain,
Of my heart beating.
Tanya Ray

Love Too Far

I loved him and
he loved me
I thought it would
last till eternity.

We loved each other
very much and so
when we saw each other
we couldn't let go.

His school started and
things got strange
our love drifted away
and I began to change.

I cried and cried
till I'd fall asleep
and when I'd wake
I'd sit and weep.

We loved each other
very much but
lived too far
and had to let go.
Sandi Lubiewski

My Dog, Willie

My dog, Willie
He loves me silly
With eyes that shine
A coat that's fine
And long, black, curly ears
When I say let's walk
He can almost talk
I've loved him through the years
He barks and yaps
Takes lots of naps
Eats biscuits by the dozen
I love him so
He has to know
I'll protect him to the end
He's one of a kind
A special find
A loyal, faithful friend
Mary Ellen Steinhagen

Some Of The Things My God Made

God made the night;
He made the dawn.
Sunset glow and evening shade.
Pretty flowers son the lawn...
Some of the things my God made.
God made the land;
He made the sea.
Mountains tall, shady glade.
He made them all for all to see...
Some of the things my God made.
Of all the things my God made...
Oh, so sweet his empty...
He read my lonely heart
Then he made my wife for me.
When it rains on our parade,
Her hand in mine, I'm not afraid.
I look at her, I see
One of the things my God made.
Mel Stites

This Is How Deep

"For you", she said.
He tasted the old woman's bread.
"Oh, how I love you", his reply.
When that man died
She cried
So many tears
That parts of her fell with them
Dropped from her eyes in streams
And flowed from her cheeks
As waterfalls.
It seemed forever.

She spoke aloud
To the old man today.
"You know we loved
To last, and last".
And smiled . . .
To a reply.

Dry streams
And waterfalls no more.
Today, the old woman bakes again.
Stacey M. Hallbeck

Untitled

I knew a man once, long ago.
He was a man of God.
A finer man I've never met
As o're life's road I've trod.

He always thought of others.
Why think about himself?
If he had any pain or cares
He put them on the shelf.

His phone rang morning, noon and night.
And he was always there.
To be of help to someone
Was in answer to his prayer.

He was a very quiet man
He did not have to speak.
He talked and walked along with God,
And did His guidance seek.

His friends, and they were many.
To have met him they were glad.
You see they called him Reverend
And me, I called him Dad.
Lila F. Crosby

Trust Me

Put your trust in no man,
  He will always let you down.
But whatever trials you go through,
  I will always be around.
The many things you face,
  are only there to test your faith.
Let me be the strength that guides you
  to that safe and wonderful place.
I am the beginning and the end.
  I have always been your friend
Come, find your rest in me,
  and I will set your spirit free.
Trust me to light your pathways,
  I'll make them narrow and straight.
You'll never have to wonder
  just how long you'll have to wait.
I put you here for a reason,
  let your loving kindness show.
Let me lead and then you follow.
  and you'll know just where to go.
Phyllis D. Raymond

Alexander At Four Years

I couldn't imagine
He would be so sweet
So completely boy
(With a capital "B"!)

His grin makes his
Face and his eyes light up
As he lists for me what
He'll be when grown-up;
A... cowboy, construction man,
Engineer, fireman, and power ranger!

I say "Alex, I believe you can
Do all of those things"
And he firmly replies
"I know I can."

Dear Alex — I'm so glad
You are here!!

Shirley J. Birmingham

Heaven's Stairs

Kevin St. Clair is now on
    Heaven's stairs.
Not so long ago, it seems, His
    life was full of wishes and dreams.
Always smiling and full of love,
    Who knew someday he'd be
    leaving for above.
He'll be with Jesus, when the
    Time is right, the sun and moon
    will be ever so bright.
Stars will shine and sparkle with
    light, and then we'll know
    everything's alright.
He'll soon be where there are
    no cares.
Kevin St. Clair is now on
    Heaven's stairs.

Marion Rosser

Crime Of The Heart

He's robbed her of
Her innocence
He stole her
Youthful exuberance
He has taken her
From who she loves most.

Though he has given her
Heartache
And emotional distress
Things she keeps hidden
About
This crime he did commit,
Will haunt her for life.

Melissa Rich

Summer's Night

I see two stars in summer's night,
hovering lost, in blinding light,
ever so dull in heavens net,
so each remains, as yet unmet.

But fortune moves in strangest ways;
it lengthens nights, it shortens days.
May this night end, and day begin
and bring two lovers back again.

Michelle Simmons

Her

I know I don't see,
Her that much.
I got to say.
That I love her,
Much, so much.

Most people want
To keep us away
I'll seek away
To tell her,
I love her.

I love so much.
I give her my,
Heart what the,
Pure love.

In the above.
In the sky.
With my love,
That is white
As a dove

ILOVEHER

Tori Spade

The Rose Garden Of God!

He walks in beauty and light,
His majesty worn like a cloak,
His face lit with a golden aura,
His feet are shod with gold.

He weeps and tears fall down
Watering the garden beneath.
Each with a face of beauty fine
Each one a child of His.

As He bends-he touches gently
Each lovely flowers face.
Ripping away the weeds of strife,
Of sorrow and of grief.

He tenderly caresses
Each petal worn with brown,
And as He touches it so light . . .
It wears a golden crown!

God loves all His flowers,
Each one an earthly child.
But when they come to be with Him,
    His garden will be gone!

M. Joan Hanson

A Teacher

Listening with my heart
hoping to hear the beat
of ambition or even hope.

Some days spent dozing
certain of only an empty room
crumpled dreams, broken thoughts

Remembering the flash of
promise so brief that it
might have been imagined

Some days spent searching
certain of only this room
so full of life and light
and my imagining.

Which one? Who is to
be my gift - the gift I leave

Patricia Curtis

"Miss You"

Fear can be your prisoner,
Hope can set you free,
Love is something special,
It's only shared by you and me.

Death is something crucial,
You lose someone who is your friend,
You remember when you both used to talk,
He always had his hand to lend.

You wanted him to stay,
But it was his time to go.
It was for a pretty good reason,
He expected you to know.
So, now he's gone forever
you just want to cry
He passed on and went to heaven,
You wish you could say bye.
But now that is impossible
You can't see him anymore
You think about him almost everyday
Because that's what friends are for.

Valerie Lackner

Thanksgiving Day

Times have come to call
Horrendous leaves begin to fall
And all colored leaves turn to snow
November winds begin to blow
Nestling down God's creatures lapse
Settling in they all collapse
Giving into a long Winter's nap
Idle deer standing by a lake
Voices call and off they make
In woods they quietly wait
Now hunters will decide their fate
Graceful Tom's fanning their feathers
Sure looks pretty in this weather

During this time of year
All friends and families gather near
Yes! Thanksgiving time is here

Lynn Valentine

Good Morning Darling

Good morning darling,
How are you?
I missed you a little
The whole night through.

I knew you were near,
Just out of sight.
But in the morning I see you
In the new daylight.

Even if you are not close
To me each night,
I can dream and pretend
That I hold you tight.

Though I know sometimes
The dreams we want
Play hard to get
And gaily taunt.

Us, till finely we
Come out on top
To reap the harvest
Of our ripened crop.

Tom Lynch

Children

Children do not realize
How deep a father's love, or
  How wise.
  They do not fully understand
The joy that's in his
  Guiding hand,
  Yet they hold him above
The childhood things that
  Children love.
  And they grow as children do;
Their love for him keeps
  Growing too.
Until they learn the full extent
Of what a father's love has meant.

Myrtle Renee Terry

Your Touch

Loving you means to feel your touch
how I love you so very much
just to feel your hand in mine
makes my life so divine
your touch means the world to me
wish it could be forever with thee
in your life forever more
holding you is not a bore
but your life is not free to give
if it only were you and me to live
we would go together hand in hand
into a beautiful fantasy land
your hand in mine, my hand in yours
I love you so very much
how I long for your sweet touch
I'll love you always in my heart
and hope our dreams will never part.

Veronica Odell

Such Words

I wish that I could tell you
How much you mean to me.
I wish on every single star
In this enormous galaxy.
I could call you cute and caring,
But that'd be just a start,
On all the different reasons
You captivate my heart.
If I said you're sweet and gentle,
Would those worlds tell it all?
I wish that there were words to say
How deep in love you've made me fall.

Lisa Rivera

Laying In The Sun

Laying in the sun
  I feel its warmth
My cheeks become flushed
  And my mind fills with dreams.

Laying in your arms
  I feel your love
My cheeks become flushed
  And my heart swells with desire.

Laying with you in the sun
  I feel your warmth and I feel love
My cheeks become flushed
  And my life feels complete.

Margaret H. Bark

The Sitter

I barely worry anymore,
I baby sit not as a chore
With these two boy's whom
Are filled with joy and
Cheerful greetings, they
Also bring a happy feeling.

  Then off to school on
the bus one goes. The
one remaining on the
sofa, he snores, until
at twelve thirty he is on
his way, to kindergarten
and a happy day.

  Little angel's in
their sleep and full of
fun upon their feet.

P. Jean Evans

Vigil

My little son you've no idea
  how often I have stood
  beside your crib so late at night
  to see you sleeping good.

You have no clue as to the times
  I woke up to your cough
  or gently raised your blanket up
  when you had kicked it off.

My little boy you couldn't know
  in slumber sound and deep
  the times I crept into your room
  just to watch you sleep.

And all the times I gently touched
  those tiny quiet feet
  to see that you were warm enough
  wrapped up in dreams so sweet.

My little son these things I do
  at night will go unknown
  until the day my little love
  you have one of your own.

Mark Lutz

Rocking

Rock
  I
  N
    G myself to sleep
you came along
Broke my rhythm
Rocking, rock
      I
      N
        G myself to sleep
As far as I can remember
That's how I fell asleep as a baby
Rocking, rock
      I
      N
        G myself to sleep
You prefer stillness
What, does my rocking hinder?
Rocking, rocking before you
ever tagged along

Kristina Rebecca Kula

Reunited

I wish that you could see me.
I always wish for you to be
by my side—watching the distant skies.
I know you could dry my teary lament.
Oh, tell me, can you feel the past?
Our memories shall forever last.
Hold my heart, it is all I have to give.
I wish you could be here—
without you I cannot live.

I can see you, my dear—
I have always been near...
The distant skies are not so distant.
Feel my breath in the wind,
and dry your eyes of the past.
Our future shall be together at last.
Extend and reach for the sky with your life.
Spread your new wings and clutch my
hand—
"Eternally embracing, our souls reunited;
man and wife."

Lee Richard Mather

A Sister's Prayer

Over the years,
I ask,
Of only one thing,
Remember
Me putting Bandaids,
upon your knees,
When you were two,
And three,
The chalks,
the crayons,
all those silly things,
I did,
Just to make you grin,
remember,
us, as friends.

Wendy Keel

Never Alone

Single, but not alone
I can truly say,
Jesus is my friend
He's with me each and every day.

Single, but not alone
I tell Jesus my deepest concerns,
He's my confident and friend
For him my soul yearns.

Single, but not alone
My master comforts me,
When I cry out to him
He hears my plea.

Single, but not alone
Jesus guides my walk,
He has changed my ways
He has changed my talk.

Single, but not alone
Jesus is dear to me,
He brings me joy and happiness
He's the one who set me FREE.

Olympia Williams-White

My Elusive Smile

I tried to find my smile
I can't seem to find it
I don't know where I left it
I can't find my way
Through the coldness
Through the darkness
Through the emptiness
Of my heart
I search my soul
I look for life
Then I see the one and only light
The rays of hope through dark and bright
That helps me discover the elusive smile
I once had
Am I hopelessly in love,
Or am I just hopeless?

Tracy M. Concepcion

Dreams

To weep at such beauty
I couldn't do,
So I laughed and I laughed
At the reds and the blue.

I laughed by myself
That day on the beach
And what life promised
I stood up to reach.

I walked back to their house
To check on her baby.
I'd have my own
Some day-maybe!
I'd have a husband
And children three
And a beautiful home
Built by the sea.

Thus I dreamed dreams
That day by the sea,
And they all came true
They were meant to be.

Mildred E. Roethlisberger

Cycle

Drowning in a sea of despair
I cry out for help
A wave of hopeless prayers
And cries of hatred
Drown out my own
I need a lifeline
A safe, secure place
To help me
With my problems
There is no such place
No way out
One way out
They cry for me
I laugh at them
I'm happier than they'll ever be
I listen to their cries
So much like the ones that drowned out my
own
And I think:
"This is a cycle."

Nanalyn M. Lopez

Curtain Call

Each time the bright lights dim,
I die a little death.
My life is empty—gone—
My lungs clamor for breath.
I turn and see you there,
I know you feel the same.
Not all joy and cheer,
But fear. You smiled, they came
Back to congratulate.
We all smiled, and said, "Thanks,
We're glad you enjoyed it,"
But each time the lights dim,
I die a little death,
And know the time will come
When there is nothing left.

Kate MacKinnon-Rorer

Love From Your Daughter

Mother,
I don't know you,
don't you want to know me?
Was it your age,
Or that your weren't
ready for me?
I love you Mother,
don't you love me?
For 19 years, I've
wondered who you are,
wanting to know you,
hoping to have the chance,
the chance of knowing, and loving you.
I want to know you,
won't you let me?
Love,
Your Daughter.

Lana May Sager

Freedom

50 Stars and 13 stripes
I don't understand why people fight
I'm so glad to be free,
To have the choice of being me.

50 stars and 13 stripes
I don't understand why people gripe
I'm so glad to be free
Or I couldn't sit on my grandpa's knee

50 stars and 13 stripes
I don't understand why people gripe
I'm so glad to be free
Because we have the Statue of Liberty

Shannin Lewandowski

"Old Age"

My hair is getting white and thin,
I have wrinkles under my chin.
My husband said
With a twinkle in his eye,
And a mischievous grin,
"Don't worry baby,
You're still pretty good
For the shape you're in"

Mrs. Sherwin Griswold

Now My Reality

As all little girls do,
I envisioned many dreams.
Still one continued,
The most meaningful one of all!
An only child was I.
Pampered with affection.
My response was immense.
The other love?
Dream of dream, man and woman.
Prince or knight on a white horse.
That was my fancy,
Surrendering to love
Difficult for most
Accepting love
Complicated for some
Confident I could do both
My dream was out there?
Searching for me!
Donning a Ponytail and Beautiful green eyes.
Just as I had dreamed....

Noni Alvarez

Where Are You

I thought I heard your footsteps,
I even felt your presence;
when I looked around to see,
you were not there, just me.
Where are you?

Why did you go away?
You left without a word,
I'm sure we'll meet again someday,
or am I being absurd.
Where are you?

My days are not the same.
It hurts when I mention your name
Lord, lift me out of my hurt, my pain,
Set me upon my feet again.
where are you?

Penny Bagby

To Be A Victim

If I would a victim be,
I first must find a malady.

What deficit disorder lurks
In genes that cause my funny quirks?

I'll pick a name to fit my case,
Let someone state it's commonplace.

Ignore the ones who overcame
Travail beyond the blight I blame.

To be a victim is my right.
There's comfort in a common plight.

Each member of the human race
Can find some weakness to embrace,

But let me choose mine carefully,
For it may be my destiny.

Les Welch

"One Road"

I claim no religion
I follow no human
For I am a daughter of God
I cannot be tempted
For I give no entrance
To the darkness that threatens the heart
I believe no interpretations
Offer no explanations
I stand alone, a part
I have no fear
My path is clear
For I am a daughter of God

Lynn N. Rowland

Cameo Dream

As I walked through the garden,
I followed the stream.
Beneath the bright moon
I started to dream.

The rose petals glistened
A droplet of dew.
Amid the fragrance of flowers
My thoughts were of you.

My dress was of lace
And the neckline adorned
A pink ribbon from which
Your cameo was worn.

Then I heard your voice echo
Through the rustle of trees.
A sad figment drift
Of a warm summers breeze.

Margaret A. Brennan

My Peace

When I close my eyes,
I go to this special place
where dreams do come true

It's so beautiful
Log cabin by the river,
with a stone fireplace

Wildflowers dancing
all around the cedar trees,
greet the morning sun

At night the stars shine
just enough to see the love
you hold in your eyes

With you, I've shared this
Which brings it all together
for a soft good-bye

Over the hillside,
just along the riverbank,
my soul rests in peace

Shelly Steiner

I Want To

I want to blossom like a flower.
I want to feel my inner being.
Stretch and open my petals of my soul
    and find my place in life.
At night I will close up by getting
    my needed rest but most of all
I want to be me.

Rosette Mines

Future's Past

Due to recollections,
I had to cry today.
I had to simply wonder,
How would life've been
    ...if you could have stayed?
Due to recollections,
I turned back, pages of time;
To help me with my memory,
With all those jokes
    ...caused by the mine.
Due to recollections,
I had a hopeful dream;
That you had stayed forever,
To share the ride
    ...down life's cruel stream.
Due to recollections,
I had uncontrolled desires.
For I know, deep in my heart
Your passion was real
    . . . and not for hire.

Rhonda L. Forsthoff

Someone Cares

Winter has gone, spring is here,
I have shed some tears.
Tears of happiness - because,
Spring is here.

Winter has gone - happiness is here,
I have shed some tears.
Tears of happiness - because,
Happiness is here.

Winter has gone - love is here,
I have shed some tears.
Tears of happiness - because,
Love is here.

Winter has gone - someone cares,
I met someone who loves and cares.
I have shed some tears,
Tears of happiness - because,
Someone cares.

Ken Coe

Shadows Of My Memory

I listen to your every thought
I hear your every prayer
And even in my dreams at night
I seem to find you there

You are my inspiration
the courage I possess
When all alone, and in my tears
I walk in loneliness.
You hold my every hope in life
And all the love I own
It's when you are gone from me
That I feel so utterly alone.

If only I could turn these pages back
And make them fall in place
These shadows in my memory
That time has not erased.

Lucille Cook

My Dad

I kissed his head,
I held his hand,
Forever I will love this man.

He guided me from wrong to right,
He held me when I felt a fright,
Forever I will love this man.

His memories will always be,
A piece of life he left to me.

Through good times and through bad,
This man will always be my Dad.

Roxanne Sprague

The Night We Danced

That night we danced
I held you close.
I prayed this night would never end.
I prayed you would not
notice how nervous I was,
just to be near you.
I dared not look into
your eyes, for fear you
would see the passion
for you, burning in my own.

Kyle D. Walker

Untitled

As you walk through life
I hope you keep your eyes open.
I hope your confidence never runs out,
And your dreams never be broken.

As you walk through life,
I hope you remain at a steady pace.
I hope you don't try to compete,
And that you run a fair race.

As you walk through life,
There are definite's and doubts.
There are smiles and tears,
And laughs and shouts.

As you walk through life,
There are challenges to beat.
Whether they be big or small,
I wish you an overwhelming defeat.

As you walk through life
My hand to you, I always will lend.
And I'll thank God everyday,
For bringing me a wonderful best friend!

Nicole Telford

Dreams

In my last dream of your world,
I saw your body's hunger,
And you reached for me.
But I burned you,
And I scarred you.
As I soared into your pain,
The tears shattered my wings
And scorched my sight,
So I can no longer fly,
And my empty eyes
Can no longer dream
Of the world within you.

Tara Wolfe

Comfort

When ever you're sad, or feeling blue
I know a man who will comfort you
His name is Christ the one above
The one whose willing to share his love
Not to many know of his name,
But he loves you just the same
You may not know that you're his child
But look to him once in a while,
And you will see that his love is true,
And he's always there to comfort you
He died on the cross to conquer sin
That one day you would let him in
So open your heart, and you will see
That his love for you is meant to be
The love of Christ is the best of all
For his love for you is all and all

Rebecca A. Sookdeo

Grieving Yesterday

A tear escaped my grieving eye,
I never got to say good-bye.

Years have passed since he died,
and yet the pain remains inside.

Bitter emptiness had hung around,
In the air and on the ground.

A child he was, a leaf in the breeze,
Smiling and laughing with perfect ease.

And when he left my heart went too.
But after time my heart re grew.

I was young when we last met,
face to face without regret.

When we were together then,
We only fought, and fought again.

I wish I could just let him know,
that I would never let him go.

I miss him like I'll miss no other,
For he was my precious, older brother.

Tami Barrows

No Way Out

Sometimes it seems
I no longer have a soul
Things are really scary
I think I've lost control

When I look in the mirror
I get an icy cold stare
It has a silent scream
Telling me I don't care

Life is destroying me
Leaves me in confusion
Someone is there to help me
No, it was just an illusion

I don't want to be here
Please God, take me soon
Maybe while I'm sleeping
Under pale light from the moon

Words can't express the sorrow
For the damage I've done
All I'm asking now
Is forgiveness from everyone

Randy Allison

Your Shadow's Intrusion

Once when you were in my mind
I reached but you weren't there.
I knew that I could never find
Someone so willing to care.
I always dreamed of us together
As we laughed and had some fun.
But then you left me for another
And my life, I felt, was done.
I woke to see the blackened air
And realized that all was illusion,
So I fought to regain slumbers snare
But lost to your shadow's intrusion.
I heard you crying over someone's death
And felt the urge to hold you,
When a chill, as from an ice cold breath,
Through my poor bones blew.
A feeling of helplessness filled my brain;
I panicked as it began to spin,
For the body you had just Laid to rest
Was the body my soul lived in.

Tom Gens

Loneliness

Alone and needing a kind word
I reached out to her as our eyes met
Mine craving acceptance,
And hers answering, "I understand."

No vocalizations,
Yet the subtle smile
Which crinkled in her glance
Said far more than words.

Her entire being seemed
To stretch outwardly
As our psyches met, and each soul
Responded to the other.

Or was it only my emotions
The craving for companionship
That caused my tortured soul
To believe I saw acceptance?

And that which I perceived
As welcomed companionship,
Was kindly but regretful rejection,
And again I was quite alone?

F. Clyde Schofield

His Gift

As I look out from my window,
I see a large from elm tree.
'Tis glorious in the sunlight -
A gift God has sent you and me.

Yesterday we had an ice storm,
And today the sun shine bright,
So the ice on that tree is sparkling
Like millions of stars in the night.

'Tis another of God's great wonders,
And I ponder if you or me
Will ever be as shining in Glory
As the ice on that elm tree.

Nellie McPherson

Smiles

When I see you,
I see a smile.
That brightens your face,
and brings joy to my day.

When I see you,
I see your eyes.
The pain flowing out
in streaks down your face.

When I see you,
I see something
that I wish
I had.

When I see you,
I see just
a little
of me.

Marion L. Smedley

Lonely, I Am

As I go through each day of life,
I see all of my friends and family.
I see all the people that I know,
Who love me and care for me.
Alone, I am not.
Lonely, I am,
For I do not have you,
The one whom I truly love.
The one, to me, who means
More than anyone or anything else,
I wish I could see you,
Touch you, hold you, smell you.
But for now we cannot see each other.
Yeah, I do love you, and
Yeah, I do miss you
And even though I am not alone,
Lonely, I am.

Shane W. Peterson

Seasons

I feel spring in the soughing pine,
I see it in the laughing shore line,
I hear it in the early morn,
When the day is scarcely born.
Ah! But I know it's really spring
When the oriole makes the Gloria ring!

An artist at play at break of day
Wanton nature colored disarray
A sunburst of tint across a lake,
Sunsets trailing a stolen wake,
Legions of birds packing their nests,
Circling for farewell roosts and rests,
Pines that stand staunch and firm,
For the biting entry of winter's term.

Rita O'Cannor

Rain

Gray clouds darken the sky.
I turn my face upwards,
The big wet drops caress my face.
A flash of lightening
And a crash of thunder.
The storm has passed,
The earth is rejuvenated!

Shawna Gray

Stars

I look in the sky
I see some light.

The stars are dancing
I recite.

I laugh to think they
turn round and round.
I cry to think they'll
fall right down.

Mom's a saying they're candles
in the sky. I'm a thinking
if they fly.

My dogs a barking 'cause
he's scared.

Those stars I wonder
what they are.

Ryan Mcleod

Wake Me If I'm Dreaming

I know that you are there
I see you drawing near
Flowing closer in the night
I hear you whisper in my ear
Wake me if I'm dreaming

The sweet words you whisper
Show me how your love does burn
Flaming eternally in the night
My heart, too , begins to turn
Wake me if I'm dreaming

I reach my hand out to you
And feel yours fall into mine
The silent touch grasps my heart
Assuring me everything is fine
Wake me if I'm dreaming

My heart beats in harmony with yours
Knowing that our feelings flow together
Never will the flame burn out
Because our love will last forever
Wake me if I'm dreaming

Susan Thielen

Me

It's fun to be me,
I stroll through my mind,
Remembering the experiences,
That made up my time
I feel my heart race,
When I plan for the days,
That will be my future.
I have so much to live,
And much more to give,
I'm not just a whisper.
Get to know me,
You shall find,
That it's fun to be with me,
Most of the time.

Medrith F. Rogers

Untitled

Red, what does this color mean
I think it describes the innermost
thoughts of everyone and if you gave
each letter a word it would stand for

Romantic Erotic Desires

I would send you a dozen red roses a
day if I could afford to. But right now
all I can afford are the petals.
If you dissect a rose aren't the petals
the most important part anyway?
For the petal has all the color
It is soft and smooth like your skin.
The fragrance is so erotic and inviting
just like your eyes.

To touch it to my lips makes my desire
and passion grow stronger an stronger
in every way. Are you excited? Are you
hot?
Do you feel the passion?
That's red!

Suzie Pustelniak

The Snowfall In June

When I raised from my bed this day,
I thought that everything was okay.
Then I saw that it was still dark,
But my clock is always on the mark.

The clock said it was nine o'clock,
So I was in a great deal of shock.
Nobody was out on the street,
Except for some people who looked beat.

I then saw that it was snowing,
That is when my face started glowing.
My calendar said it was June,
So it could not be snowing so soon.

I heard a laugh across the way,
It might have to do with this weird day.
It was my brother mocking me,
He was the one playing tricks on me.

I went to bed again this day,
I hoped everything would be okay,
When I wake I will remember,
It is now morning and December.

Ryan Morra

My New Hobby

I have a new hobby
I want you to know.
It's cracking the faces
Of the high and the low.

How do I do it?
Just watch me and see.
Here comes someone and
She's looking at me.

Her face is care-worn,
Weary and sad.
Her lips turn down,
My, she looks bad.

But I greet her and smile
And she smiles right back.
There! Did you see how
I made her face crack?

Mildred E. Benton

The Concentration Of A Race

Swish swish
I turn tightly
  Around each gate.
The edges of
  My skis carve
  Precisely into
  The deep snow.
I concentrate
  Only on my form,
  Keeping my hands
  Out in front and
  my skis close together.

The blustering
  Wind picked up,
  But with the finish
  Line in sight
  I couldn't be
  Stopped now.
My heart pumped... I
  Crossed with a swish swish.

Michelle Goheen

You And I

You surrounded me with love,
  I turned away.
You warned me of things to come,
I did not listen.
Now I'm alone.

My loneliness is a reminder
  of how I failed.
If nothing else, I have learned
  and learning is not easy.

As I say goodbye,
  my heart aches.
As I close the door,
  My soul stays behind.
I loved you and always will.

When the bitterness ebbs
  and you feel alone,
Know one thing for certain,
Someone will defend your honor
  against all who speak against you,
. . . That someone is me.

Lawrence James Mellon

I Wish

I wish I had a handsome man
I wish he had an awesome tan
I wish I had a swimming pool
I wish at night I didn't drool
I wish that school was full of fun
I wish I had my homework done
I wish all merchandise was free
I wish I could go on a shopping spree
I wish the mall would never close
I wish I had some Oreos
I wish I had a stretch limo
I wish I was Pinocchio
I wish I was loved by everyone
and now my poem is finally done

Tracy E. Doyon

If The Demon Calls Again

As the night takes over day,
I wake from my sleep,
and call forth the spirits
of the dark underworld.

We dance to the chants
of the human world,
and take their sacrificial child
to be prince when I am gone.

Stars of blood burn dark in the sky
as the prince is named.
I chant the words of Darkness,
and send the spirits to haunt the night.

I wait,
and watch as a girl joins
her lover in my spirit world,
her grieving at an end.

Dawn's bells ring through the air,
and the spirits return to their rest,
awaiting the next night, when they will
again rise
and haunt the dreams of the human world.

Tawnya Clardy

The Forest

Before you were,
I was...
my limbs stretched forth
to catch warmth and life
from a friendly star.

Before you were,
I was...
providing habitat and nourishment
for beings large and small,
a way of life for all and all.

Before you were,
I was...
happy to live with friend and foe
until you came and took my very soul.

Of wooden alters ever reverent to God,
only shorn stumps remain,
bereaved roots clinging to terrestrial earth.
Before you were,
I was...

Louis Lazaro Enriquez

In The Wilderness

In the wilderness,
If you wander there and look,
The sky and ground
Don't make a sound
The trees,
The birds,
The bumble bees,
And me,
In this tiny hide-out tree
In the wilderness.

Kasey Schlienz

Wrong

You thought
I was going to be here forever!
You did
Didn't you?
You thought
I didn't need nurturing, tending to

You thought
You could go — fly — try
Something new
When it caught your eye.

You thought
Because you were everything to me,
I'd look the other way
and just not see.

Well, my darling,
Now you know
All of the above
Is just not so
"Forever"
Is over!

Patricia Young

Dreams In Your Eyes

I will make dreams rise in your eyes
I will unlatch the gates to Paradise.
I will rest upon your sun-gold thighs.

I will make dreams rise as fairy castles
You have but to touch the velvet tassel
Before you will stand your vessel.

I will make dreams as the Phoenix rise
Do not despair as passion dies,
Love returns in beauty as the butterfly.

Pierritz

My Fiddle

As I pluck on my fiddle
I wink and go diddle diddle
I think of Dingus
And that's no Mingus

It's just McGee on a spree
That's a Cowboy on the loose
Not what you call Mother Goose
Only a diddle on my fiddle

And that is another diddle diddle
So I diddle diddle on my fiddle
That's a tush
Behind the Bush

And only a riddle on my fiddle
And another diddle diddle
So I diddle diddle on my fiddle
That's a Bull

With no Pull
You can fall off
You may just cough
And that is another diddle diddle

Michael A. Martin

Eternal Loving

I wish you were still here with me
I wish we were together
I wish it didn't have to end and
banish what we had forever

I wish you could still hold me,
giving me your eternal touch
I wish you could realize that
I love you oh so much

I wish you knew my love for you
will never die or fade away
For my heart will always be yours
loving you everyday

I wish things weren't as they are
I wish I didn't cry
I wish you'd come and tell me
that this is all a lie

But most of all I wish you loved me,
as much as I love you
Because I know my love for you
Will always be: Forever true

Michelle Juanita Ybarra

Left Over

As I sit here all wrapped up.
I wonder if I'm left to rot,
or will you be back to get me.
Oh! Look! The light is on and now
its off again. Always wondering when
the last time you had seen me.
Always wonder if you have forgotten me.
Everyone else you've taken, only I
remain. Maybe no one cares for me.
Here I sit with a bowl of casserole
from last week Friday night.

Michelle Engelhardt

Fade

I wish I could fade into the night.
I would disappear without a trace.
I would run like a free spirit,
Running, fading, dying.
I wish I could fade into the sun.
I would burn into oblivion,
Burning, fading, dying.
A free spirit in oblivion - fading.

Leslie Wilson

Love

To speak of love,
Ignore the pain.
Pretend to be normal,
Not insane.
Heart's been broken
Gotta keep control
Try to hide it,
Burns my soul.

New dawn is breaking
Lighting up my heart.
Hands are shaking,
Brand new start.
Do you love me?
Will you be mine?
You know I love you,
Sweet little valentine.

Karl Nicholson

If I Could Choose My Parents

If I could choose my parents
I'd choose the both of you;
So many hearts you've lifted
By what you say and do.

You're always there to carry
Us through life's road so long;
Lending forth your hand
To all who pass along.

You've always been a friend
To those you got to know;
Proving to be faithful
By the kindness that you show.

You are a true example
Of what love should really be;
You're there for all who need it
With complete humility.

I am so very honored
By having both of you;
I know you're always there for me
And so I am for you.

Lisa M. Lauro

My Learning Experience

In the beginning I was told,
"If at first you don't succeed
Try, try again."

Being young and fresh and bold
I tried - and failed - and in my need
Tried to try again.

Experience as I grew old
Allowed some wisdom to be freed
And I decided then
To just do it!

Rose Mary Bryan

Endless Thoughts

I'm thinking what would happen
If I died today
I'm thinking what would happen
And where would I stay?
I know about heaven
I know about hell
I know what the people, try to tell
I'm thinking what would happen
If I were Christian or Jew
I'm thinking what would happen
If I believed like you
I know about seance
And Oujiboards too
I know about all the bad things
That they are said to do
I'm still thinking what would happen
If I died today

Lynn Haney

Life

Is like a waterfall
it's never very sure at all
we try to live it day by day
but who's to say what
will step in our way...
So to keep our lives worth
LIVING
we just keep right on
GIVING!!!

Ken Horricks

Angel Voices

My Father spoke to me today
In a very special way
Not with words, but just the same.
I walked outside,
I heard the birds.
The snow fell softly on the ground.
I thought what wonders life can hold
If only we would hear the sound
Of angel voices in the wind
Telling us to just slow down and lay our
worries onto Him.

A. Bonita Irvin

Like a Rose

I too will blossom
if watered with love
   like a rose
and will grow thorns
to shelter myself
from pain and fear
of being used for
awhile and just for
   beauty's sake
and discarded when
I no longer bloom.

And like a rose
I will wither away
fall upon the earth
and turn to dust
   unseen
making room for
other roses and
other loves.

Migdalia Rosa

Forever

I live in forever
I'll return, never.

Today is dull and cold.
Forever is wild and bold.

You can not live and do
If tomorrow is closed to you.

Put away your fear,
Look ahead, straight and clear.

The war inside you will cease.
Your world can be filled with peace.

So, I live in forever,
It gives me a lever,

Into the land called tomorrow,
Where I can purge all my sorrow.

Tomorrow never really comes,
But you can hear it in distant drums.

Do not be bound by snow and ice,
The cost in time is too dear a price.

So, I'll live in forever,
And return here, never.

Mary E. Neman

When Mama Comes To See Me

When Mama comes to see me, Nursie
I'm gonna tell her
What you did to me
You'll see, you'll see

I'll tell her how you left me
All alone in the dark
How you quickly patted my back
And told me, "sleep"
You'll see, you'll see

I'll ask Mama why
You held my arms down
And stuck that thing in me
That hurt so much
You'll see, you'll see

I'll tell Mama that I cried for her
And, you came
And held, and kissed me
Rocked me till I slept
You'll see, you'll see
When Mama comes to see me, Nursie.

Wanda Jeremiah

Let Me Write

I'm gonna be a writer one day.
I'm gonna write the book,
I've been down in the gutter so long.
I don't know how up looks.

I'm gonna dot all the I's
And I'm going to cross the T's
And when I get to the very top,
Excuse me if you please.

I'm gonna get up of my rump
And I will strut my stuff.
I'm gonna put my best foot forward.
I've sit down long enough.

Collard greens and black-eyes peas
is something of the past
Cornbread, fatback and fried potatoes
is all we poor folks had.

I'm gonna move out of this dump
Into a house-with my own name.
The knowledge that I have comprehend
Will land me in the hall of fame.

Margaret Lanier

Being Different

I'm different
In a way
That is unique
For being different
Doesn't mean
I can't do things
It means
I have to work
Extra hard
With what I want
To do in life
That makes me happy
And that is to
Work with television

Susan Traxler

To A Dandelion

Bright yellow dandelion on my lawn,
I'm smiling down at you.
I needn't ask who placed you there
or made the sky so blue.

You are the first harbinger of spring
and have been since ages roll,
your tousled golden head
brings sunshine to my soul.

All to soon your life is spent,
and you are old and gray.
Then a gentle breeze will come
and blow you far away.

I too have known the joys of youth
now silver hides the gold;
I don't know where the years have flown
I too have grown gray and old.

But I'll not fret in growing old
I'll just be blithe as thee,
I'll go some day where you have blown
and find you smiling up at me.

Wilhelmina Lukezic

Bye, Bye Winter

Bye, bye winter, bye, bye snow
I'm so sorry, I have to see you go.
We had Christmas.
We had Valentine's Day.
But, bring on the spring,
Hip, Hip Hurray.
Bring on the baseball bats,
Bring on the gloves.
Dethaw the ponds,
Do it for the doves.
Bye, Bye Winter, I hate to see you go.
But, bring on the grassy fields,
Throw away the snow.

Nathaniel Alan Price

Alone

Alone, all alone
I'm suddenly, forever alone!
My tears are now falling
My own voice is calling
Oh God, how can I go on?

There's no one to hear me
The darkness surrounds me
I wail in a voice from the past
A touch on my shoulder
An arm comes around me
My heart finds peace, at last

Though the love of my life is gone
Your presence is with me
In daylight or darkness
I know I'll find strength to go on
To fill my life's promise
Whatever the days bring
I'll work to be happy and strong

Lela F. Dodds

"Baby Girl"

Tiny fingers;
Imprints of reality.

Tender whispers;
Only to fascinate.

A moment of animation;
Proclaiming attachment.

A little reflection;
Delightful and warm.

A vessel of endless love;
Cautious and determined.

A precious spirit from above;
A gift never to be repaid.

A dainty simper;
A portrait of a season.

A silent whimper;
Minutes of affection.

Nightfalls of seven;
A constant snuggle.

A rain drop from heaven;
A priceless treasure!

Michelle Heemeyer-Caldwell

An Endless Road...

Standing
In a seemingly endless road,
He looked fixedly
At the bleak and desolate house
On top of the hill,
Which held
All of his desires.
The rain fell
In dreary sheets
Encompassing him.
All he had sought after
Disappeared
Arm in arm
With her.

Tiffany Diamond

A Great Dream For The World

I wish I was there
In a wonderful place
Where no one knows the word "race"

I wish I was there
In a wonderful place
Where no one knows the word "hate"

I wish I was there
In a wonderful place
Where no one know the word "hurt"

But most of all
I wish I was there
In a wonderful place
Where everyone know the word "peace"

Rachel Vaughn Bloom

In Honored Glory

In honored glory my brothers died,
In battles not meant to be;
These fights they say are for freedom,
But is man yet free?

And if again my brothers go,
To fight across the sea;
Will they come home in a box,
Forever haunting me?

Will we then raise up a wall,
In silent memory;
Or a statue on some hallowed ground,
For their victory?

Those heroes die a lonely death,
Born of tragedy;
Who battle to the very last,
For God and family?

Or for some politician's gain,
Or for some company.
Where peace and love and life are lost,
Our brothers pay the fee.

Sandy Treat

My Strength

The Lord is my strength and refuge,
In him do I safely abide;
He leads me around the pitfalls,
And holds me closely to his side.

He is my rock and my fortress,
No stronger wall could I desire;
His arms enfold me, sin and all,
As he lifts my feet from the mire.

All my ways to him I entrust,
No truer friend could I find;
He's faithful in his promises
They've been proved by the undersigned.

Mary L. Shelton

My Point Of View...

... My point of view
- in life -
where hearts find together
and emotions go lost
people grow ages
in joy and in pain.
Between time and distance
we are so far apart,
that tells my story
in long and in short.
... My point of view
- in life -
where roses are contempt
to be broken, and the thorns,
don't even hurt anymore,
that's how the world seems to be
from my point of view.

Ramona Sehler-Downey

Common Treasure

Oh praise! Most high for voice.
In song of every choice.
For what is good and right
Morning, noon and night.
For messages of old
And history foretold.
Through every race and every tongue
Something of want by everyone.
For greats of old who are now dead
And left us treasures to be read.
Enriches lives and gives us joy
On faces of each girl and boy.
How blessed we are for gifts to keep
That make us cry and oh to weep.
And never, ever fade away
Resounding voices here to stay

Marion Preyer

When Words Fail Us

When the sun rises high
in the blazing noon sky....
When the crops are withered,
and we're ready to die...
When words fail us.

When the tides come washing in,
and they wash away our sin...
When there's nothing left to see,
and no shelter to live in....
When words fail us.

When a stag jumps high,
and is seen against the sky;
When the hunter spies his quarry,
and the proud beast must die...
When words fail us.

There's a language that lies
in the depths of our hearts,
and it's spoken in our souls
through the windows of our eyes...
When words fail us.

I. Khanani

In The Brush Of Voiceless Words

We live in slumber
In the soft pillows
Of one another.
Engulfed
In down quilts.
Entranced
In fluid movements.
In the feverish flow, of the stream,
That draws us on.
The source in the light brush
Of voiceless curved words.
Together we fall
In unspoken agreement,
Intermingled like fluids
In the furious flow
Of our passions.
Flung into the calm
Depths of the other.

L. E. Kamphausen

"Cancer"

Cancer is painful.
  Is taking loved ones away,
Find a cure now; please.

Wanda Reyes

Nature

The sun flowers lay cheerfully
in the valley, the wind whistles
in the air the summer birds
make a perfect pair.
The water runs so freely
Thru the stream the pine
Trees are so tall and green
The sun beams on the grass
making a sparkling glow
This is all Nature's Beauty
to show.

Sarah Riggsby

Vision Of Peace

A vision of peace so calm and bright
In this world, so torn I pray!
Erase the long and dark, dark, night.
Please, won't you show us the way?
To end all wars, near and far
And live once more in peace.
Men only try, then leave their scar,
But you, all the suffering can cease.

Marion Tarle

Untitled

Clouds lazily float
Like piles of driftwood looking
For a resting place.

Lee Pearson

Lord, Make Me A Blessing Today

Lord, make me a blessing today
In word or thought or deed,
To someone who is hurting
And Your Good News they need.

Lord, make me a blessing today,
To all who come in touch.
So that they may know the Savior
And that He loves them very much.

Lord, make me a blessing today,
Give me Your Word to share.
Help me to show a broken heart,
That You're always there to care.

Lord, make me a blessing today,
So that all may see Your Son.
And know that He gave His very all,
To bring life to everyone.

Vicki J. Preston

A Forgotten Child

A baby forgotten
inside of her mother.
A heart beats,
like no other.

Don't tell me this child
is no longer alive.
Please tell me this child
will have a chance to survive.

A miracle from God,
like no other.
A beautiful miracle,
for every father and mother.

Meghan Tippy

One Little Tear Drop

One little tear drop falls
into my aching soul,
one lonely heart beats and cries
as it aches for you my dear.
Tell me, my love why is it
the love I find always flies away.
and my heart lies aching
with pain and
sorrow, this lonely heart
fills my eyes with tear drops,
my lonely spirit will
soon die form a heart that's broken,
your voice I hear echoing through the
darkness, trying to save my dying heart,
but one little tear drops rolls from my
broken heart. A lonely heart dies
without ever knowing
the passion of real love, but this lonely
broken
heart will someday find a love that will
never
depart.

Paulette Cain

A Daydream Into Heaven

As I stop and take a look
into the back of my mind
and into the bottom of my heart
I realize how wonderful it would be
to be able to reach up and pull
Heaven down to me and in that thought
I realize that it is not me who
can reach up and pull Heaven down
but heaven that can reach down
and pull me up yesterday, today,
tomorrow, and forever more. Amen.

Matthew Lee

The Man In The Moon

The man in the moon
is a friend of mine.
He likes to shine on me.
He can be big and bright
or small and dim rite out
of sight.
He looks as if he's
smiling at me.
I would like you to
meet my friend too.
He's the man in the moon.
The man in the moon
Lives way up high,
In the stars and above the sky.

Kimberly D. (Ivey) Smith

Untitled

Why does darkness envelope me?
It's chilling grip is tight,
  unwilling, unforgiving.
I once knew warmth and love,
  the sun did shine,
But now winter is my lover.

Kristi Lamb

A Better Tomorrow

Just a few minutes of your time
is all I want to borrow...
To tell you how to make, tomorrow
a better tomorrow...

Why don't you try once in a while,
To give someone just a friendly
smile...

Forget your worries and troubles,
listen to a friend....
Two heads together are better than
one, you both will feel better in
the end...

Your time, your smile, your will,
to listen, will be appreciated to,
because others have problems
just as you and I do...

I'm sure you would find tomorrow,
not just another day,
If before you go to bed,
you would kneel down and pray...

Lilly Ann Snell

"My World"

The life is this world
is coming to its end
I would love to warn you people
But I want to stay your friend
If I had the money spent
You know it is yours to lend
Snow white wings are promised me
My Lord will surely send

Hate and love, Good and weak
Pray to Angel's the devils weep
Hide the bad, tears roll sad
Hold my soul, fear the bad

Now you hear what I have learned
Parent's, teachers manners earned
Come and see why I am free
The Devil with his horns cannot frighten
me
.....Bow down to love - not hate....

Tim J. Bremser

Free Speech

The neat thing 'bout America
Is freedom to express
Our views on subjects dear to us
Without fear of redress

Expression is our heritage
It's in the Bill of Rights
And it applies to all who speak
It is a point of light

We've had to fight so many wars
To keep this right intact
Much blood has spilled upon this land
To maintain this contract

So when you see that flag of ours
The red, the white and blue
It stands for letting each of us
Express his point of view

Remember when you hear someone
Though you may not agree
It is their right to speak their mind
That's why our country's free

Tom Farrar

The Pressure Is On

The pressure within me
is seeking to escape.
My heart is pounding faster
as I reach an exploding state.
But, powers that obsess me
hold the steam inside.
Making be boil
till there are tears in my eyes,
When the pressure bursts
my mind is in a fiery.
And, once this confusion passed me
I can see things clearly.
Now that the pressure is gone
and there is no turmoil.
My heart can finally start
to beat like normal.

Pater Gennardo

Our Savior

Christ.
    Is the blue in the sky,
    The earth under our feet,
    The sea that keeps us going.
He keeps us.

Christ.
    Is the blood in our veins,
    The beat in our heart,
    The love that keeps us warm.
He keeps us.

Christ.
    Is the music we sing,
    The word we read,
    The little voice we hear.
He keeps us.

Christ the Lord.
    Is the love in our heart,
    The feel in our soul,
    The chance we have.
He keeps us alive, Open and see.

P. J. Smith

A Tear

Every minute I am with you
Is the happiest I have ever been.
The love you hold for me,
Shows through in your eyes
And every embrace.
As I watched you drive away
A tear ran down my face.
I could only wish you were here,
Loving me with your eyes.
And embracing me with your arms.
Every minute I am away from you.
Is the loneliest I have ever been.

Marla Rattenborg

Lavender

How, Lavender loves heat and sun!
Its flowers are sweet to smell.
We dried the blooms and put them
in these little sacks to sell, so
people can on snowy nights
remember summers smells and sights.

Melissa Jean Clontz

Weave On S.T.

Life seen in Black and White
is life limited and trite

Life seen in global shades
is life vibrant and unafraid

Life is a series of colors
that weave themselves into shades
of creations beyond all trades

So weave on with delight
with vision unafraid of the night
for to achieve one's dream
one need only weave the dreath!

Obi Obi-Bandale Jr.

Baggy Pants

Baggy pants, Baggy pants,
is what we would yell,
at the crooked old man,
who walked up and down the hill,
where did he come from,
where did he go,
that is something we would never
know.

Many years have gone by,
what I'll never forget,
is that crooked old man
carrying his worn out sack.

The lines on his face,
that look of despair,
everything about him,
what a great story was there,
but we were only children,
we just couldn't see,
what a crooked old man.
could give you and me.

Maurine Mullikin

Untitled

Loneliness engulfs my being
    Like a world void of God or,
    The love of God.
My spirit yearns, to escape
    Like water from the tap.
Beautiful Pan, save me!
Soothe my soul with tones of life.

Leslie Dutton-Allen

Being Within The Lord

The reflection of you Lord
    is within my soul.

Your holy name shall reign
    within my spirit.

Your grace shall walk
    within my feet.

Your love shall shine
    within mine eyes.

Your gentleness shall touch the
    world within my hands.

Your word shall be heard
    within my mouth.

May the Lord be
    within your souls.

Kathy Buck

"Yes"

When I swing out for a star...
It behooves me just how far
    All the twilight from the vast
On a spell, of me, it casts...

    Now, I swing out for the moon..
And I know that very soon
    The whole universe will agree
It's a joke, it played on me..

Patricia E. McInerney

Again For You

The rain has come
It darkens the road
Makes things stir
    different you know
You wish for some sun
A light to feel
Can't change the rain
But the sun shines
    in my heart for you

Richard Lawrence Neidhardt

Take Time

Take time to think—
It is the source of power.
Take time to play—
It is the secret of perpetual youth.
Take time to read—
It is the fountain of wisdom.
Take time to pray—
It is the greatest power on earth.
Take time to love and be loved—
It is a God-given privilege.
Take time to be friendly—
It is the road to happiness.
Take time to laugh—
It is the music of the soul.
Take time to give—
It is too short a day to be selfish.
Take time to work—
It is the price of success.
Take time to do charity—
It is the key to heaven.

Rose Hladky

The Anointing

My soul cries out for thee
It longs to be heard, to be
near thee
It longs to feels the presence
of God
Oh, my soul does cry out
The spirit awaits, the soul
longs to feel thy presence
The song in my spirit speaks,
Amazing grace
Oh, the anointing fall down into
my spirit, my soul
Continue to cry out
I feel the anointing
God heard my spirit, my soul's
plea,
The anointing fills my soul
The inner cries of my SOUL has
manifested
The Anointing

Katie G. Brannon

Things That Go Bump In The Night

From an evil sound I awoke last night.
It made me suddenly set upright.
Whatever it was made my hair
stand on end.
I'm telling you this because
you're my friend.
In the dark I looked all around,
to see what made this horrible sound.
I slowly reached to turn on the light,
Knowing I would see a terrible sight.
But really it was a great surprise.
Nothing was there before my eyes.
I left the bedroom to search the house.
But all I found was my dog Klouse.
He was lying there by the door,
sound asleep there on the floor.
People have told me of dreams like this.
When everything sane seems to run amiss.
I lay back down and in soft laughter.
I plan only to dream of the sweet hereafter.

Paul Sidebottom

Summer Tide

The sea is quiet,
It no longer roars,
As it lazily carries,
The sand to the shores.

The sky is blue,
The day will be fair.
A promise of warmth,
Can be felt in the air.

The gulls softly wing,
In their silent flight.
They drift and they float,
On the soft summer light.

And out in the distance,
Just off the shoals,
The spout of a whale,
Can be seen as she rolls.

As the waves slowly drift,
To the beach from the sea,
The summer tide brings,
Peace and solace to me.

Susanne F. Salem

Moon Magic

The pale moon teases as
    it peaks from the shadows.
It shimmers-gives off
    gleams of brightness
Then dodges in again!

Breathlessly we wait.
There-in the full glow
    of its light
The beauty dazzles.
A fleecy cloud drifting by
    catches it for a moment.
Then it is ours
A pale orb of celestial beauty!

Velma Owen

A Rest From Reality

Her mind needed a break
It whispered his name
Panther, Panther, Panther
A seductive tease
Feeling like a cool breeze
His eyes of dark chocolate
His laugh, a thrown pebble in a lake
His body movement, flowation ease
A festival of thought
Reminded her of a starry night late
A rest from reality

Pixi

Maria Rose

Maria Rose, Maria Rose
it whispers through my head.
I do not know a Maria Rose
maybe from the park or so
or maybe from class or phone
but I do not know a Maria Rose.
Maybe heard in a book or so
or maybe on a boat or shore.
Do you know a Maria Rose?
But I do not know a Maria Rose.
But the name whispers through my head
    "Maria Rose, Maria Rose."

Rachel Auguste

My Gift

If I had one thing to give you,
it would come from above;
They'd be footprints of an "angel",
for theirs are prints of love;
They're footprints that we never see,
but we know that they are there;
To watch over us and guard us
and keep us in their care;
So until you get your strength back
to face each day anew,
Its comfort to know that angels
watching over you.

Pat Collins

Untitled

It's how,
    it's how I see you.
A burst of colors, that hug me.
Sunshine from your heart, that warms me.
Kisses that adore me!
    Love only me.
It's how,
    it's how many people love you,
and how much love you carry in your
heart for others.
Then everything falls into place.
That's how it works...

Rita Cappiello

Only God Could Create A Star

Only God could create a star
It's light shines both near and far
It brightens our night and lends a glow
For the people of the world below
It gives us something to wish upon
But disappears upon the dawn
To come again the very next night
And fill our world with guiding light
Only God could create a star

Kathy L. Stephan

Much Easier Said Then Done

I'd like to be friends
It's no big deal
    just friends

Much easier said
    then done

To be able to talk
Not just what makes me happy
Not just what makes you happy
    just talk

Much easier said
    then done

To be able to listen
    really hear one another
Not just when the volume is up
    along with your temper
But hear whispers
And to feel thoughts

Much easier said
    then done

Nan Johnson

My Dear Madam Alexander Doll

This precious doll
I've had for years,
Has seen my joys
And all my tears.
She's stood beside me
through thick and thin,
Her dearest face
And sweetest grin.
It doesn't matter
How I feel,
She makes me happy
And makes me heal.
For fifty years
We've been a pair,
Together we can always share
Our love for one another.

Susanna G. Taubenberger

Each Moment In Time

Soar high, soar high
Kiss the clouds as you climb
And laugh 'til the tears
Beg to flow from your eyes.

Drink in the sweet mist
Of the heavens surrounding
And caress and enjoy
Each moment in time.

N. O. Lacey

In Search Of

I've lived my life in search of you,
I've lived through pain and loneliness;
I prayed to God that I would find you,
But He said "It's Not Time".

I never knew what life had in store,
Why he felt I was not ready;
I've made mistakes and broken hearts,
And He sat back and waited.

I gave up hope of finding ONE,
My search for you was over;
Then He stepped in and set me straight,
My time was right, your wasn't.

Three years alone went by so fast,
I kept my faith alive;
But when I met you, you were not alone,
And I felt God had lied.

I prayed one night - "What to I do,
Is he not the one for me?"
God smiled and said "This Love Is Right,
In Time He Too Will See."

Teresa Y. Spell

Walking The Endless Road

On our road to nowhere we
journey very far no transportation,
not boat, nor plane, nor car. We
stumble down this road feeling
all the pain lost loves lost souls
and lost friends never to be
seen again. The road is endless
everyone will go and when the
end does finally come you'll be
sure to know, your eyes will
close, your blood will boil and
you will feel no more. With love
in your heart and Jesus Christ
raise a smile for what's in store

Scott Dickens

The Quiet Moments Of Night

In the quiet moments of night
just before I sleep
Eyes closed against the darkness
My mind begins to soar
with thoughts of you

I feel a pressure against my being
My breath quickens
My body tingles
My heart is full

Have you come?
Have you slipped into my space?

I move — ever so slightly
to enclose you
and you are gone

The pounding of my heart surrenders
to the softness of my tears

I pray for sleep
to bring me peace
in the quiet moments of night

Yvonne Clarke-Forbes

Untitled

Oh happy June bride
Just let me confide
A wee little secret to thee
A bright cheerful smile
Makes life seem worthwhile
And a frown makes happiness flee

If hubby gets cross
When you try to be bass
'Tis useless to argue or pout
And a frown will annoy
Even vex the dear boy
Where a bright sunny smile will win out

A. P. Bundy

Untitled

I was sad I even cried
just to know a good friend died,
but now I feel, I truly know
just how come she had to go.
Because people come and people
go even though you love them so.
  Life is good,
    life is great,
      as long as you
        can put off fate.

Roxanne Wilks Robins

To Gina, From Your Old Dog, Freddy

I lay alone, away from home
Just wondering why, as time passed by
The dim-lit room felt like the womb
Of one who bore me years before.

I wasn't sure how I'd endure
This loneliness, but I could guess
That something grand was near at hand.

And then I knew how you felt, too
When I just heard that glorious word
My name, repeated o'er and o'er
Your hands, your kiss, just as before.

I lay in peace, as questions cease
I feel your love calm all my fears
My life above will hold no tears.

And at the end of my sweet journey
I'll meet my friend, Woofy, who went that way
Before I did, and waits for me
So we can play eternally.

Marian Triolo

Don't Give Up

I almost gave up
Life was so cruel
But you came along
And told me the rule
You said not to forget it
And I never will
For you said —
"You must not give up
for if you do —
The flowers will not bloom
The water won't be blue
'Cause if you give in
the world will too!!!"

Lori A. Ruffe

A Baby's Cry

But what do we
know of a baby's cry

Is it that of hunger
or need of changing or
comfort
    Or does God reveal to
this infant the road it
must take
    The mountains before him
This journey he must
follow the hardships he will face

    Does God give this
infant it's future while
it lay in its crib

    Why infant cry
Do we all know our
Destiny

    In its purest Little Form
Linda Jane Jacqueline Malak Bickford

His Promise

"Read - that you will know Me,
learn - that you will recognize Me
from all others.
Remember - that you will never
forget the gifts I have
given you.
Come to Me when the circle
has been drawn together,
And I will take you home."
Shirley Pullano

Leaves

Strewn along the path they lie,
leaves' faces round and smiling.
Some sad and worried faces.
Others on the fly.
Leaves get stuck in fences.
Some rest lightly on the ground,
ready to flee with frightened senses.
Leaves with stems like bending ears
go which way the wind is blowing.
Some soak in puddles drowning fears.
Leaves cup upward, hoarding raindrops.
Some cup downward shedding tears.
Leaves there are of many shades.
No growth from ideal forms we see.
Took those leaves to grow the tree.
Volney Faw

Mojo Rises

Hearts broken
Left to die
No one is kept
all is left
someone
something
could any one stop
a big drop
of fire
from the sky
your life is left
all are kept
break the mask
it's the biggest task.
Nyki Sebby

Beginnings

My baby started school today
Left his toys and pre-school ways
Onto the bus,
His wave was quick
Camera out, I began to click
And hoped he didn't see the tear
Of sadness for the passing years
Swiftly they've gone, I know
But part of growing is letting go
So love him, school
Hold him near
My precious child
Ease my fear
Bring him knowledge, love and cheer
Challenge him so he will care
About family, friends and peaceful living
Not just getting, but the joy of giving
My baby started school today
I'm going home
My time to play!
Madge K. McCartney

Trapped In By Discipline

Life is full of mystery
Left uncaptured by the mind
Lingering from history
'Til the future depths of time.

Forced in by discipline
Yet desiring for freedom
Knowing it would be sin,
Yet still desiring freedom.

Knowledge with its limits come
Restriction in its action
For discipline brings freedom
And freedom brings satisfaction!
Laura J. Bjork

Love's Eternal Soul

My love for thee is so very strong,
Let the waves crash loudly,
Let the mountains burn above
I could look into your eyes for eternity,
But never be tempted to look away.

As the sands of time pass by,
Uniting our souls forever,
We are each other's futures,
Now and for every day to come.
Sherry Kathleen Boes

Epiphany

Let us take prayer from the school
Let's ignore the golden rule:
Take God's name from coin and bill,
Bend no longer to his will...
But rather hail those other ones
Who seek to lead with gold, or guns
And when we face the impending doom
We'll pray... but oh, America to whom??
Louise Hockman

Whatever Do You Think It's Worth?

Whatever do you think it's worth,
Life on this planet they call earth.
Is it just a place of mirth,
Where all of man has had its birth.

Or maybe it is right to think,
That man and his are on the brink,
To fight and die and finally sink
And when it's over, to become extinct.

Now I ask, above the roar,
Whatever are we living for...
And if we live here just to fall,
Why is anyone born at all...

So here it is another day,
And you have heard what I've to say.
I ask you now about this earth,
Whatever do you think it's worth?
Wayne McGan

Love

Rhyme without reason,
Life without name,
Time without season
Who taught you this game?

Mountain without valley,
River without sea.
Who am I O precious one
That thou shouldn't favor me?

Rainfall without clouds,
Fountain without source,
Questions without the slightest doubt
Great ruler without force.

Life and death thou authoreth,
Darkness and the sun,
Myriads of form thou surely art
Yet thou art truly one.

Love thou art the burning quest.
Love thou art the goal.
Love thou art the place of rest.
Love — thou art my soul.
Kirbie L. Greene

"Daybreak"

Day by day dawn's early
light gleams like fine gold.
    Trees with drops of dew on
their leaves; precious as royal
jewels.

Winds blowing gently as
a whisper.
    Clouds as fluffy as a cotton
puff,
    Birds begin chirping, thanking
earth for all its gifts.

Sun smiling with its warm
rays
    Telling the world it's a wonderful
place!
Lisa Holland

Cacophony

The night never sleeps:
lights burning
sirens screaming
cats screeching
neon blinking
babies crying
people dying

More gray than black.
More pounds than lean.
More blood than wine
spilling in the street.
I feel the heartburn
of my conscience.
I hear the silence
of man..
I weep for those
I cannot touch.

Sandra James Snider

It Somehow Looks Familiar Like . . .

It somehow looks familiar
Like drama on a stage,
But players have no faces
And no one knows their age.

It somehow sounds familiar
To hear the plot unfold,
But muted end within me
Won't allow it to be told.

It somehow feels familiar
As happenings occur.
I'm here and yet I'm also there.
Then all begins to blur.

Oh, yes it is familiar.
The truth I shall explore.
I know I must have been here
Many, many times before.

Sandra Seidl

Hear The Children

They stand in front of me
Like trees after some disaster
With such starkness against the sky.

Their naked limbs reach
Toward me in search
Of relief from the emptiness.

Their silent cries echo
Over me with urgency
To alleviate the pain.

Their misshapen trunks reveal
To me the desperate need
For aid in adversity.

Their waning looks awaken
In me the responsibility
To mitigate this oppression.

Tina Harvey

"Dream"

Come and hear my story,
Listen to my dream,
They are all I have,
And they are all I need,

In my mind I see a home,
With happiness inside,
This is where I live my life,
This place where I reside.

Children roam our hallways,
Their tiny smiles so sweet,
They have their daddy's dimples,
Blue eyes make them complete.

Our love made this happen,
This love that is so true,
I thank the Lord every day,
For sending me a you.

Now you've heard my story,
You know the dreams I keep,
This is where I live
When I am asleep.

Traci Lee Fulco

Who

Who will listen?
Listen to the cries;
Cries of the children
The forgotten!

Forgotten is where
Our children lie.
We try hard to keep
Them small and insignificant.

We don't mean to;
Don't set out to;
think that we aren't.
Wouldn't do that!

Give them a chance!
They have ideas and hopes.
They can talk.
They can think.

They are our future.
They are our hope.
Let them grow.
Let them try. Let them speak!

Wanda King

The Breeze

In the stillness of the hour,
long awaits your gentle whisper
in to which I meditate
on your wings
that see me flying free.

I feel you passing through me,
— My Breath
— My Life
my motivation you are
into achieving such great lengths.

Blow,
Blow and begone,
your wind has cleansed me...

I am now
as fresh
and pure as the breeze.

Scott Douglas Bauer

Untitled

Omniscient question
longing in every crevice
of my being.
Haunting the endless boundaries
of my soul.
Daily encounters ending with
why?
Seemingly mocking me
and my fears.

The days pass
a timeless blur of
faces, stares, taunts
immune to all but one.
The memories penetrate
delivering their paranoia.
Spreading their nihilistic tendencies
leaving me numb and forlorn
knowing he always wins
at his game
still the question lurks.

Shannon Staloch

Reasons

I stood on the edge of yesterday
Looking back upon my years
Remembering the battles I had fought
Diluting my pain with a million tears

Salty tears on the raw edge of sorrow
Seared a path deep in my mind
Sucking the good times like a vacuum
Reality becoming so hard to find

Having so little, yet having so much
Dreams burned on the altars of time
I feel compelled to try to retrieve them
From the ashes of the smoldering shrine

One by one, though badly scarred
I clung to what remained
Five good reasons thrust from my loins
Was the balm that eased my pain

Marie Pitts

A Friend

I was sitting on a hill one day
Lost and all alone
Nothing to hold onto
For bitter seeds I'd sown

When all at once a man appeared
He came as if to say
Take up your cross and follow me
I'll go with you all the way

I leaned on Him and then I knew
My old life was at an end
I took up my cross and followed Him
I knew I'd found a friend

Lillian A. Davis

Vice - Versa

Without death,
love is pointless.

Micah Clayton

Love Is.....

Love is caring
Love is sharing,
Love is hoping that you are loved,
Love is nice,
Sweet as spice
Gotta have it,
That's what love is
Love is, well many things
Love is
Liked
Overrated
Very nice
Extra sweet
That's what love is

Melissa Lynn Stiltner

Love . . .

Love takes time,
Love takes pain,
Love causes anger,
in different ways,
But love also gives warmth,
Love also gives passion,
But most of all,
Love gives us the happiness
we've always imagined.

Mayra Alejandra Salazar

The Hot Air Balloon

Still,
majestic,
floating brightly
against a soft warm
summer sunset sky . . .
pushed on
by the force
of the glowing evening fireball,
golden red . . .
the backdrop
moving,
deceptively,
slowly,
across the graying twilight
and out of view . . .
gone
but to a bright speck of memory
taken in
and turned to words
upon a page . . .

Kathleen Schongar

Dear Chad

With love and goodness in your heart,
Make honesty a big part.
Lots of laughter in your soul,
Is what keeps a wise man in control.
Only you can make it right,
To make your dreams shine so bright.

Sherry Lynn Blaze

Searching

What is this that consumes me, and
    makes me search and search?
To find some peace within my soul, I
    know not where to go.
I laugh, I cry, I hope, I dream, I do
    all that mortals do
But I cannot find my place within
    this world of mine.
In dreams, I live another life I
    hardly recognize
The feelings that I long far, I
    begin to realize.
So Lord, when I awake tomorrow
    please help me find the way
To live my life, and feel my life,
    with all my heart, I pray.

Shirley R. George

This Cowboy

What makes this cowboy so special?
Many have asked this very question
What is it that spurs him onward
To rise to every occasion

He's off his horse into knee-deep mud
In the middle of a driving rain
To round up a calf that has strayed
Yet, this cowpoke will not complain

The ranchero will stay in the field
Even though it's well past sundown
To mend that busted barbed wire fence
Never making a petulant sound

He triumphs over any challenge
This wrangler stands above other men
Having success when others do not
It simply must be from within

What makes this cowboy so special?
It is hard for many to understand
But to him it is quite simple
He places his faith in God, not man

Randall C. Tadlock

Broken Levy

When you see
Me cry,
It is not
That I am sad
But a display
Of emotions
Which I can not
Control.

Rex V. McCoy

Peace

I wish the world was war free
miles and miles of peace
exceptional people
making new friends
talking to everyone
helping the homeless
butterflies, world peace, calm days
small animals

Vanessa Lopenzina

You Lie, You Cheat, You Steal

The way you treat
me is unreal,
    You expect me to sit
around and wait, when I could
be out with another
date,
    I always thought you
where the one,
but now I've deceived were
over and done.
    Sure I'll always love
you,
    But not until you
can love me too.

Samara Anthony

Beauty By The Road

The path of finely ground up dust,
Meandering through the wood.
Inviting treetops formed an arch,
With blue birds on it's hood.

Hibiscus bushes by the way,
With spring wind in their hair,
Beckoned with a whisper soft,
For me to enter there.

And oh, the beauty that I found,
As I wandered where it led.
To the right of bunch of daisies,
And soft grass for my bed.

Then, on the left a babbling brook,
Sings softly in the sun.
So I think I'll lie down for a while,
'Till day is almost done.

Then when the dusk of Springtime comes,
I'll slip to my abode.
And thank the Ever-Living God,
For Beauty by the Road.

Maude Alley

A Christmas Dream

Merry Christmas, Merry Christmas,
Merry Christmas,
    Xmas, Xmas, Xmas,
Spoken and hearing Christmas for us.
    The snow capped are beautiful to see
another place of Christmas for me.
    Someday the Xmas will turn around,
and say it's Merry Christmas I've found.

Linda June Mesaros

Dear My Love

I love you so, so
much you may
never know. Day
or night you'll be
in my eyes sight
maybe not in my
Arms but in my
care and in my
heart forever there.

Stacey Shaw

The Spring Wait

This is a season of waiting,
  Mind's camera reversed and
Backing out old slides of sunshine.

Thoughts of spring warmth
  Carefully, quietly
Are measured in our mind.

In an act of unseeing wisdom,
  Forsythia branches
Picked bare swell, now, in the kitchen.

Ready to burst like our spirit,
  Programmed responses
To an inescapable life vision.

We all know the inner feeling.
  After waiting, wishing
The freedom of sun come singing.

Then let fireplaces smoulder out
  TV silent, books shelved
Beauty and fragrance, it's spring come
winging.

  Sienna Sowatsky

Pass On

  We have but a
moment to stand erect
  and be proud,
But a moment to live
  and enjoy our
humble existence.

  May life always
have in store the very
  best for us and others
For the moment is soon
  swept by and we must
pass on.

  Pass on to where
spring never ends but
  winter still exists,
where we never again
  pass on.

  Lee Liddy

"Eulogy For Myself As Well"

Gone now from this imperfect world,
mother fades into earth
no storms to mourn her,
only the sun shining cold,
oblivious to summer sorrow.

Now, I look the moon in the eye,
with sudden grief of knowledge
that my prayers drift in a dead-star sky.

Buried among breathless dead,
put fairy tales and God beside her,
For I've grown tired from pretending.
to be unconscious at last,
of empty promises, and faith.

In the heartless beauty of a day
mother fades into the earth.
The same end everyday
as we slip from this imperfect world,
Godless on our way.

  Mary Meyer

Silent Words

A child was born and the young
Mother spoke silently.
I love you my darling
With a love that will never die.
When you are happy and when you are
sad
Look behind you and I'll be there.
O silent words never spoken aloud.
Silent words which were never heard.

A mother dies and the young
Woman cries silently.
I love you my darling
With a love that will never die.
When I was happy and when I was sad
I looked behind me and you were there.
O silent words never spoken aloud.
Silent words which were never heard.

  Patsy Dees

Judgement

Since I walked many a
mountain, not knowing
where the moon lay,
I stay under the
helm of disdain, a sane
man of old age with
a sad story under
his right arm,
He fell from grace
the day despair was
brought upon us all,
Not evil, just a hint
of melancholy on his
breath,
Where do I stand
under the eyes of greatness,
where shall I be destined,
As a joke, soak me with
sarcasm
Yes, he is a very old man

  Louis A. Bottino

Night Prayer

Night
Move quickly
Take me
From my tearless tears
Wake me
From my sleepless fears
Heave me
Atop your wavecrests
Beach me
On Dawn's silent shore.

  Sandy Wicker

Weary

The moment is here
my life is Dear.

Each breath I take
is it good or a mistake.

My life is chaotic so therefore
it is idiotic.

I am one with the Universe,
so how can it get worse

  Lee Harry

November

Leaves reign down

  waiting
  mutating
  Leaving long limbs
  Exposed like raw pain.

"The Lord gives and the Lord takes away.
Blessed be the name of the Lord?"

Blessed be
blessed be
  because pain weathers
  well.

As leaves to earth
We return to the genes of our souls

  bare — not barren,
  becoming at last
  who we always were.

  Rita Hemmer Kowats

Keesha

I walked through the woods,
my best friend at my side.
We frolicked in sunbeams;
We drank of the sky.

I sat on a rock
and told her my dreams;
We danced across meadows and
Played near the streams.

We strolled down the lane;
she sniffed every blade.
She's the greatest creation
that God ever made.

We lay down together;
I started to know:
It soon would be time
For my best friend to go.

I walk through the woods,
We're never apart.
We frolic in sunbeams
deep in my heart.

  Lee P. Mahle

"Alone"

The music begins,
my body fades into the wind.
I wait for the voice to return.
My ears are ringing,
  my eyes burn.
I can feel his hands on my hair
his lips on my body,
my breath is lost in the air.
I hear his beating heart,
he's coming near.
My dress comes apart,
is He here?
He's all I Feel
The rain comes again.
Is it Real?
The music ends.
I stare into the mist,
alone
My soul is Kissed.

  Kristen Cheney

Affirmation

I am a Woman, My heart is pure
My body is my own
Sexuality is my crown
Loveability my code
Openness my edge
Willingness my cross
Trust are the pearls I wear
Emeralds my tears
Rubies my fire
Diamonds my humor
Lilies my flower
My feet are bare
Connected and grounded to the earth
Solid, sure and stable
My spirit is untamed
It cannot be caged
It won't endure chains
Now you see me, now you don't
I am a mystery, I am a woman!

Phebe Von Achen

Deathless Death

I feel as if I'm the color black
my death is here as I disappear
Does anyone at all notice
I look at the prints that I've made
    as I've walked along
Mistakes here and there
    More then I wish I'd made
I don't really mind my absence
for I feel less pain
I love the thought of not thinking
for when I think I go insane

Natina Gunter

Writing In Wonderland

With sweaty palms and hopes alive
My dream has come in sight
But I can't reach my fantasy
For nothing comes out right

I try to find my happiness
I try to show I care
As I share all my emotions
I say a silent prayer

But prayer or not, it doesn't work
It always comes out wrong
And every time I feel like this
I write another song.

And in these songs are feelings
Which I cannot express
And these verses are my savior
That pull me from distress

I wish to hold you in my arms
But you don't understand
I'll stay alone and be depressed
Writing in wonderland

Michael Bartleson

October Haiku

The Red Hibiscus
makes me miss my lover's lips.
Ah! Fresh coyote tracks!

Laura Dailey

Palouse Hills Soft With Grain

Palouse hills soft with grain,
My eyes move over fruitful curves,
Hands tingle at the sight,
Though reality is dirt and stubble.

Running across the beauty,
Brings pain through knowledge
of failing strength.
Though hope grows going down
in stumbling strides,
It is exhausted in scrambling
up the opposite.

Coyote's laugh, bounding ahead
to an endless horizon.

Phillip Spencer Gale

The Shaman

i am of the earth and wind
my garden stretches to the sea
i know the sound of winter frost
i know eternity
i know the hawk and fox
as one
i drink the gold of setting sun
it is a part of me
i know the heights
the rock and air
they taught me of the secrets where
the eagle reaches free
my spirit is
the light of day
my spirit is
the depth of night
i vanish
even as i stay
within your chains
of sight.

Nils P. Sara

Mary Elizabeth

I put them on,
My grandmother's earrings.

I never met her;
But I know her
    Through thoughts
    Traditions
    Sayings
Absorbed and repeated by her daughters.

When did she wear these jewels?
    To celebrate?
    To knead bread?
    To greet friends?

I wear them and wonder . . .
Our two lives joined by these baubles

And, perhaps, tied
    By family
    By womanhood
    By common experience

Lynne Mokler Simpson

Dreaming Of You

When you sit and smile at me,
my heart seems to skip a beat.

My day is so true,
walking hand in hand only you,
my night is yet so blue,
cause all I do is wish I could hold you.

I wish you could understand,
that forever you will be my man.

I look forward to dreaming at night,
because in my dreams we never fight,
when you leave it breaks my heart,
it feels like we've miles apart.

Dreaming of you and me,
I see how happy we will be.

While I dream of only you,
I dream of the good things I hope come
true,
I'm so happy we're together,
the way I feel we'll last forever,
I wrote this poem to say,
that in my heart you'll always stay.

Lisa Terwisscha

Oh California

Oh California,
My heart yearns for you,
Beating in memory of your
Spring's grassy green,
And your summer's ocean breeze.

Oh, California,
My heart yearns for you,
Beating in memory of your autumn hues
Reds, oranges, and yellows,
And your winter's cool rain showers.

Oh California,
My heart yearns for you,
Beating in memory of your
Gentle seasons,
And your ever blooming flowers.

Yvonne Croxen-Steffens

My Queen

My queen:
My lovely queen:
    The mother of this earth:
The beauty of life
    That blossom from seed to seed:
My queen:
    My lovely queen:
How I treasure thee
    My lovely queen:
Your smile and strength
That only a queen such as yourself
Possess:
    My queen:
My lovely queen:
    How I treasure thee
My lovely queen:

Larry Neal

Happy Birthday To My Mother

Happy birthday to you
My mother, my friend.
A poem - some flowers,
This love without end.

I write this rhyme
From myself to you,
For giving me life,
For showing me through.

You're always there, mom
The first one I call,
Like fear of the dark,
You're the light in my hall.

You're my inspiration
More that an idol,
Like a working heart,
The beat is vital.

Your being is sweet
As sweet as a truffle
I owe you my world...
Sincerely, "The Fuffle."

Sandra P. Miller

Sweet Sleep

My eyes are getting heavy,
My senses—beginning to feel numb...
My thoughts—now incoherent,
Here comes sleep...I gladly succumb.

Babies resist sleep during the day,
Darkness comes—they cry for light,
Yet I so easily surrender...
To sleep, the quiet shadow of night.

There's so much more I need to do,
But again, I must confess,
I seldom put forth a fight
Against sleep—the sweet nothingness.

Since time flies through the years,
How wonderful if I could send
Sleep away...for only one night,
Just a thought...here I go again.

Sheree Taylor

After I'm Gone

When I die, don't cry for me.
My soul, like a bird, has been set free,
To soar away, in the great beyond.
Our Lord, in Heaven, has called me home.

My life on earth was filled with love,
And I'll look back from Heaven, above.
I'll see you and hear your laughter,
I'll be fine in God's hereafter.

There'll be nights when you're asleep,
Into your dreams, I'll silently creep.
You'll feel my kiss and see me smile.
I'll only stay a little while.

Then in the morning, when I'm gone,
You'll think of me and carry on,
Knowing that I'm always near.
Remember me, but shed no tears.

Laura Moon

My Cologne

Papa used to tell me at times
    Myndi, you're smelling like a doggie
As he went and ran the water
    to scrub me from end to end.

Boy, I hated that warm water
    But he never had it cold;
Then he'd have to find me
    Cause I surely wasn't bold.

But after it was all over with
    I was just as proud as could be;
Then he spoiled it all, cause
    He sprayed me with cologne!

Anyway, I feel much better now
    For I'm fit to be around you, see
And MaMa likes the smell I have
    As the old doggie's gone down the drain.

Whittier E. Clark

More Than One To See

Shape shifters
Name lifters
A wolf a bear or a tree
Who or what is it that I see
When and where should I be
Is it really even me?
The eyes of a fox
Over there on the rocks
The howl of a wolf
Calling to his pack
Planning for their next attack
Nightfall arrives
The lone owl flies
Softly gliding through the skies
Is it truth or is it lies?
It's all behind the eyes.

Robyn Marie Glosson

I Stand Alone

I've never had someone beside me
Never known what love could be
If only one could understand
If only one could really see
I stand alone.

Even when I'm in a crowd
And the world around me seems so loud
I hear no voices see no face
In this world I have no place
I stand alone.

As I listen to the pouring rain
I know that I'm the one to blame
I mean no hurt I mean no pain
The world no longer seems the same
I stand alone.

As the bustling world pass us by
The time will come when all will die
I know I need to find a way
To make the best of everyday
I stand alone.

Katie Miller and Kellie Vignia

Blur Vision

Dark circles and sunken eyes,
never shown to the lighted skies
living a disillusioned high
committed to a chaotic society
doing with no question why
lost in rampant thought
defeated but never fought
walking the halls
a skeletonized shadow of a man
til you fall
subconscious depression
blurs your vision of home
love died with addiction
retarded concept of life
kept you in death
losing your precious happiness
with every shallow breath
a mind so blind.

Scott T. J. Edwards

"Life In My Eyes"

Day always follows night
night always follows day
Some people say "such is life"
I must be different
I don't see things this way
There's color not black and white
You must smell all the smells
You must see all the sights
Just open your heart and mind
You must open your eyes
All the lights are so bright
And only then you will find
That the secrets of life
Are not out of your grasp
They're right in front of your nose
And you'll never again
Let tomorrow go past
And say that's the way life goes

Scott T. Boettcher

I'm Here

    No problem is worth dying for.
No matter how Big or small.
    Life is a wonderful gift.
Live it to the fullest.
    Cry if you have to.
No one is going to laugh.
    Not me.
Not ever.
    If you ever need someone to talk to,
I'm here.
    If you ever need a friend,
I'm here.
    If you ever need someone to talk to,
I'm here.
    I'll always be here for you.
Let it all out.
    Scream, if you have to.
Fight, if you have to.
    I won't say anything.
But remember, I'm here.

Melanie Reese

The Senses Of Love

I feel your gentle caressing touch.
No one has ever pleased me this much.

I see the beauty you hold inside.
Your caring nature you shouldn't hide.

I smell the fragrance of your skin.
Now I know that love can win.

I taste your mouth upon my own.
Trust is something you have shown.

I hear your heart beat with mine.
Who knew that love could be this fine.

You satisfy me in every way.
Here beside you is where I'll stay.

Sue Swanson

Pilar-Star

Pilar, Pilar, Pilar,
No star on the Tower-Marquee,
No notes along no fence,
No ribbons on any trees —
How fitting in a kiddies playground,
You fought and died,
Poor little Crybaby cried her
Last tears for me —

Dios Mio! there goes another
Angel, torn from her Mother's
Arms, so Gabriel sound the trump,
The final alarm, Our Lord is
Coming back, Yes, Just like it's

Told, And there in his Train of
Gold, Oh there in His train of
Gold, Yeah, there in His train
Of gold, Cheri and Pilar-Star —

J. J. B. Sharp

I Stand With Awe

I stand with awe, of much each day,
Of how you always lead my way.

I stand with awe in what you do,
In all the things you guide me through.

I stand with awe, that trials become,
Because of those I try to shun.

I stand with awe, in what I gain,
When sometimes I'm in a lot of pain.

I stand with awe what happiness is there,
When in times I'm in complete despair.

I stand with awe of the joyful news,
Will sometimes come when I cry the blues.

I stand with awe, because I need not cry,
You are always, always nearby.

I stand with awe, when I realize
You make me say words that are wise.

I stand with awe of what I feel
Because I know your love is real.

This I know, my Lord above,
Is all because of your great love.

Phyllis J. Summitt

Everybody Knows Her...

She's not a full-fledged fisherman,
Nor does she sail the salty brine,
And yet she is a wizard
At getting something on her line.

She doesn't sit for hours and hours,
Beside a shady nook,
Just waitin', waitin', waitin',
For a nibble on her hook.

The dear old sun has kissed her,
Till her skin's a gypsy tan,
Which would be the pride and envy
Of any fisherman.

She's at it nearly every day,
And most everybody knows,
It's not fish she's getting on her line,
She's hanging out her clothes.

Marion Reed

Rocket Man

I need a love
   not her or she
You are the one
   the one for me

Yes you are
No, you're not
However, only you will decide

If your answers is "Yes!"
   I'll wear a great big smile:-)
If it's "No," however
   I'll walk an Indian mile

It doesn't really matter
   'cause it's all good, until you think,

"Well, maybe I should of
   But I wonder if he could of
      And then, if he would of"

Shoulda, Woulda, Coulda, but then didn't
   And it's all really just to bad
      'Cause that poor Rocketman just burned
outta fumes
      And hit the Earth a bit to hard

Shaun Reeves

I Will Be Gone From Here, Someday

I can not say
Nor will I say
That I will not die someday,
Yet when I do
Be sincere and true
That you not forget
This was my wish.
Know that I am happy
And have no regrets at all.
For I am in my heavenly home, I'm free
This is where I want to be.
I love you all very much, I always have
That will never change.
Yet even when I'm gone from here
I will love you just the same.

Phyllis M. Johnson

The Perfect

There once was a person.
Not a woman or a man
They had not an eye,
And they had not a hand.

With the mind they saw everything,
And every part.
And they felt everything
With the tenderness of the heart.

They walked eye to mind,
And hand in heart
But never did they sin.
For they were The Perfect.
Only seeing what was inside,
And feeling from within.

Karen Lynne Wolf

A Grandmother's Song

Hands offer pleasure
Not because they grab,
Manipulate or move things,
But because they feel.

Life in the same way
Offers pleasure because it is felt.
Mourn not when it is lost
Or has left.

Rejoice to yourself
Because it was here, at all,
For however fleeting an instant,
Let that be felt.

Life my friend is infinite.
It is the forever's
We build for and around ourselves
That are short lived.

Kynan Alexander Cooke

Feelings

One has many feelings hidden inside
not knowing when to let them out
or knowing when to hide.

You feel like a glass that someone
can look through, and see that your
heart has been broken in two.

Feelings have a lot to do with
the way a person dreams.
you may try to hide your
feelings or so it may seem.

But the more you hide,
the more you show.

Then you find yourself at
realities door.

Knocking knocking, can I come
into your hidden feelings deep within.

Sheri Coutee

A Glorious Moment

Down on my life
Not really, ever knowing
What next to do
With the wild wind blowing.

It was time for a change
Time to ask for "forgiveness"
Forgiveness from my husband
To help me find happiness.

In mid-November of 1995
At the lowest point in my life;
Not knowing how he missed me,
I was allowed to be his wife.

Together, learning each other;
All about our need for love
We are taking "One Day at a Time",
Giving thanks to God above.

Pauline Phillips

Shadow

I am always there with you
    nothing can take my place,
I am as beautiful as you
    but without a face.
I stand by your side
    unseen by the eye,
Only a figure of me
    stands close by.
I am there in the darkness
    when the moonlight shines,
I follow you in the day time
    trailing close behind.
I will never leave you
    by your side I will always be,
In the past, the present, and the future
    it will always be you and me.

Tara C. Henderson

My Friend

Forever you are, my true friend,
Now I see, you're my friend,
    till the end you will be.
Now I know,
    What a true friend is,
No matter what,
    you have been there indeed;
    through good and sad,
    you were there for me,
Thank you Lord Jesus, for
    that special friend,
    for you have given just for me;

Marian Rodriguez

School Days

The house seems much too quiet now.
My ears, attuned to summer months
Of shouting, shrieks and cries,
Cannot endure the silent air,
Nor can my heart, no matter now it tries.

I wander through their sunny room,
So newly neat and orderly, not cluttered
Now with toys, and for a moment
Want again, the satisfying frenzy of
Those happy, playing boys.

Louisa Jean Roediger

Symbols of Faith

Bright warm glow
of Chanukah candles,
Shining star
a top the Christmas tree;
Star of David
twinkles bright,
Delicate angels float
in the red and green night;
These symbols of faith
all around us we see,
The Holiday traditions
of each family;
And though our beliefs
may not be the same,
If we look beyond differences
We'll see what remains,
Is a common hope
and people with prayers,
for peace, love and joy
in this world that we share.

Tammi Wallace

If I Could

If I could mend hearts broken
Of dear ones who I love,
I would build a road of freedom
And a bridge to rise above.

If I could change a tearful past
To bright and sweet memory,
I would fill their thoughts with smiles
And make them strong and free.

I hope for peace and joy for all
Who I hold in my heart,
I wish them all true happiness
And pray we never part.

I mourn their sad and troubled minds
And feel their pain and sorrows,
If I could change just one small thing
I'd hand them bright tomorrows.

If I could have one single wish
It would be clear to me,
My dear ones would be full of hope;
Their pain would be set free.

Rebecca L. Brown

Touches Of Love

A mutual respect
is a touch of love.

Infinite caring
is a touch of love.

Soulful empathy
is a touch of love.

Caressing tenderness
is a touch of love.

Open arms of understanding
is a touch of love.

Heart-felt validation
is a touch of love.

Please endow me with all of your love.

Sherry Reeves

"November"

Sometimes cloaked in the sunshine
Of Indian summer
At times wrapped in the frosty
Coat of winter.
"November" heralds the closing
Of another year.
"November" with its traditions,
Memories and its hopes.
Thanksgiving traditions.
Veterans remembered.
Elections-our hope for
The future.
"November", capricious, volatile.
"November" like its zodiac sign
"The scorpion"
Will flip back and sting you!

Virginia Wilkins Hillery

Alone In Reflection

Alone in a world
    Of mirrors and glass,
    In my own special world;
Alone in reflection.

Through my eyes
    see your eyes.
Through my eyes
    see mine.
Seeing my world
Alone in reflection.

Through glass covered shadows
    and crystallized hands,
A place full of stillness;
Alone in reflection.

Alone in my world
    Full of dark, peace and quiet
It's my own, special world
Alone in reflection.

Valarie A. Holscher

Nobody Deserves That

The lies, lies and more lies.
Nobody deserves that.
Man or woman.
The pain, pain and more pain.
Nobody deserves that.
Man or woman.
Emotionally and physically
    both ways it hurts and
    scars you for life.
Nobody deserves that.
The lies and pain is all the
    same to me.
Once he lies to you;
Once he hurts you;
It'll happen again and again.
Nobody deserves that.

Rana M. Wolfert

Gold Country Winter

Gazing past tamed gardens to the wild woodland beyond
Suddenly transfixed in wonder at the austere beauty
the special "flavor" of Earth in Winter.
A fresh dampness in the nippy air
gnarled dark trunks of ancient Apple and Grape
rust and straw of spent annuals
vivid yellow flashes of falling Willow
ever-greenness of Cedar and Fir
thrusting upward thru Earth's sere browns and greys
flanking Her reddish brown curves
freshly plowed furrows, curiously moving
like a psychedelic landscape
teeming masses of tiny brown birds foraging for a Winter meal
something Van Gogh might have noticed, and painted.

Waves of déjà vu flow at the edges of my awareness
images from other lifetimes
someplace long ago and far away, like Gaul or Vikingland
seeping through the profound quiet into the here and now
with all their familiar Winter flavors
Lost in the eternal "isness" of those moments.

Hope Winthrop

When Noah Smiles

When Noah smiles, I smile.
When Noah smiles, I sigh.
A warmth erupts in my soul.
A glow shines upon my face.
For one moment, nothing else matters.

When Noah smiles, it's bright.
When Noah smiles, blue sky.
I love to see him laugh again
Hear his wordless chirp of glee.
Relaxed, becalmed, laughing free with him.

When Noah smiles, such joy.
When Noah smiles, I cry.
But of contentment not of grief
To wish this way will always be
Knowing each smile builds a memory.

Jeffrey J. Lyons

Me

I've spent my life walking in circles searching for myself,
But what I found was that I always expected others to tell me who I am.
In doing so, I've tried to live up to their expectations only to
find anger, frustration and rejection by not being able to be,
all that was expected of me.
I've now learned to love and embrace myself for the ability of just to be.
I've learned to set my own goals and achieve them at my own pace,
I've learned to enjoy the company of others, but enjoy time to
myself and demand my own space.
The best lesson I've learned that the one that is truly real,
Is that no one can make me happy or feel the way I make me feel.
And the greatest gift that I can give to those that truly care,
Is the me that lives inside myself, the me I choose to share.
I find that I'm like a mirror, I can see myself outside and in,
I know just where I'm going, and I praise the places I've been.
No longer do I walk in circles asking others to define who I'm supposed to be,
I now walk with my head held high because I'm able to define myself for me.

Glendora Holden

A Picture of Me Without the Picture

Making plans and sharing gossip, are popular subjects on my phone.
Between shopping and hanging out with my friends, I never seem to be at home.

Eating shrimp fried rice, strawberries, or stuffed cheese pizza, is
sure to make me happy.
Always keeping money in my pockets, so my hair won't get too nappy.

I like to draw, sing, especially write, and sometimes even dance.
Listening to good music like jazz or R&B, can keep me in a trance.

Often thinking of boys and how to deal with their difficult antics.
Receiving long stem white roses or a big teddy bear, sure would be romantic.

Anticipating getting my license since I finally became sweet sixteen,
going out all weekend and still make it to church on Sunday, now
wouldn't that be keen?

I play golf and sometimes basketball just to keep me busy.
In my free time I think about college plans, which really makes me dizzy.

Computer games and reruns of "My So-Called Life" pass the times as
well. Writing songs of the piano or playing with cute little
puppies, always seems real swell.

I love the Christmas holidays and summer vacation, because then I get
to be free. I travel to Missouri, Kentucky, California and Texas, to
visit my family.

Always laughing, trying to stay cheerful, I have a smile that just won't hide.
A sweet, smart, modest young lady that's me, of these qualities I take great pride.

I'm really cool person you can find out, come talk to me and take off
some loads. I'm always nearby, glad to say "HI!" Come meet me,
I'm Billye Norma Rhodes.

Billye Rhodes

Good-bye My Friend

I once met a man who for a short while gave my life a purpose. We
talked - we laughed - we shared. His gifts to the Universe were many -
The music in his mind traveled through his fingers and the sound came
out of a guitar. His thoughts surfaced on pieces of paper in the
form of the most beautiful and meaningful words - words that inspired
one to believe anything was possible. His eyes, looking through a
camera, found the most vivid sights to share with the world. His
touch was one of gentle meaning of teaching of sharing of comfort.
Poetry flowed from his eyes - the deep blue color of the ocean a
glance into his eyes and the troubles of my world disappeared.
My hands in the hair made of silk became instruments of his.
His concern and giving to others made the world a better place.
His mere presence electrified a room. The words from his lips
comforted a crying baby. Action was his manner not only words.
The time he walked among us was cut too, too short. We are all better
individuals by the time he shared with us. When I feel his being
around me, the tears surface in my eyes a smile comes upon my lips
and I thank God I met him - I thank God that the road he traveled
I crossed. His given name was AARON - and he took my heart.

Carla Jenkins

Time

Time is something we each are given everyday.
The sun rises and sets and all too soon "this day", too, has gone
away.
Time is ours to use as we will, we all have a purpose
that's needs to be fulfilled.
Minutes to hours, hours to days.
Time is slipping by, have I lived my life the right way?
Days to months, months to years.
I wonder how long "My Time" is here?
Time is something we'll never get back, it moves ahead,
leaving only traces of what we did with "Our Time."

Annette Good

Turning

Turning away . . .

Turning upside down . . .

Turning around and around . . .
. . . in circles.

Finally . . . . . . turning inward . . . .

      tapping the vessels of strength
      that lay buried in the sawdust
      of past pilgrimages to this temple.

      Hidden beneath my faith that would
      move mountains . . . . stability.

    Ginger A. Sims

"A Miracle in Bethlehem"

Long ago in the town of Bethlehem
  A baby boy was miraculously born.
He was placed in a lowly manger
  For room in the inn, there was no more.
The angel appeared to the shepherds
  As they watched their flocks that night.
They were told of the Savior's birth
  Then they went and rejoiced at the sight.
God sent Jesus to earth for a purpose
  Jesus, was His God given name.
Because of God's love for us
  Was the reason why He came.
Jesus was more than just a baby
  God's only begotten Son, is He.
For all the sins of you and me
  Was the reason He died on Calvary.
All He wants is our trust and repentance
  Eternal life is the gift we're given.
Along with the peace and assurance
  That our eternal home is forever in Heaven.

    Debra L. Ostenson

Homeless

This is all I've known,
A better life, I'd like to be shown.

When you walk by,
I try not to cry.

I know you have a home,
Here on the streets, I'm all alone.

You have nice shoes on your feet,
I don't even have food to eat.

You are lucky you have someone to care,
I wish you had a family to spare.

They would take me home and show me love,
They would give me clothes, food, and things I've never thought
of.

But I know a life like that is only for people like you,
Living like this, my dreams will never come true.

    Cheryl Welty

"Glimpses"

A candle flickers, in the night
  A bird will soar - in desperate flight
A baby is born, in the world somewhere,
  And a soul passes, does anyone care?

A train can be heard - on a lonely track,
  A plane has landed - a loved one is back,
A mountain steam, rushes to the sea,
  And everything - has a destiny . . .

A country road, will twist and bend,
  A chance meeting - with an old friend,
A Sunday picnic, the smell of food.
  A tender kiss - to set the mood . . .

To dream of places - and never been,
  To want to be, somebody's friend . . .
In this world - all things - must fade away,
  Life and death - just brings another day!

But . . . there is an exception . . . to every rule!
  The strong will see - the weak it will fool,
Yet . . . you'll always see it, in your loved ones eyes,
  It's . . . the gift of love . . . And . . . it never, Never, dies!!!

    Daryl Gaertner

My Child Strong Black Lady

Tough tar baby
A black and strong lady
Made for these times
Must live off a dime
Alright for her to cry in these times
Rough and tough in the ghetto I lust
Always I long to make a bust from this place
  of darkness and fright.

Surviving on a dime I must make a flight,
Away from this place from darkness and fright,
Nothing can keep me here another night,
Dreading the time will never be right,
Evil lurks in every corner out of sight,
Running and screaming trying to change these wrongs to rights,
Strong tar baby, black lady, shines bright.

    Betty Sanders

American Salad Bowl

America is like a salad bowl.
A bowl which fulfilled by harmony of beautiful
colors and delicious taste.
Do not need to stir to mix up, even though
you detest the taste of it. Instead, be more open
minded and take a good look at each of vegetables.
Isn't it looks tasty?
If one of them is missing, it would not look as tasty
and beautiful as it is now.
It has colors of green, yellow, red, white, black
and purple.
Do not need to stir it. Instead, try to taste each
of them carefully.
Soon, it will taste better and looks more beautiful.
This is what American salad bowl
makes special and unique. Hope you like it.
One last thing, do not forget to put
salad dressing. Which dressing?
Choice is yours.

    Hiromu Homma

Time, Pain And Peace

Time is just an hour class. Mom and Dad what for you.
A Boy or Girl. You just become a part the love of their live. With
unconditional love. From day to day every thing you mean so much
with mom and dad love so true. From first step first word and when
you say (I love you) and you grow so fast as time goes by. You
find friend and only this by and by. Then you said I'm grown up now
time to said bye-bye. The light is still on in the window
for you. Mom and dad pray you're safe and ask God to take
care of you. Make many phone calls to them even just
to say hello and remember little one to say (I love you)
Don't let the pain from inside of you. Remember if you
called them and the phone rang and rang. There be no
peace for you. Open your heart and hear me please
when no one answer. You begin too say did I tell them.
I loved them every day. Don't ever there
they won't go away. Sometimes down the road
pain and peace will take fold. You only get one mom and
dad. Thank God for them cause you know they did for you.

Jeanette C. Fildes

The Angel From Above

Angel has come to us
A brilliant light was shown
Not a lot of words was spoken, but it wasn't a hush tone
She the Angel, spoke of love and caring for everyone
Telling us what we should already know but haven't practice all along
When the Angel with her brilliant light
Placed her hand on our shoulders
We could feel the chill of love and life all the way down to our soul
That chill open up long ago feelings that was felt so long ago
They were still there but long ago forgotten
But now resurfaced not buried anymore
For the Angel who came from above
Had shown us what was misplaced long ago
In one quick moment the brilliant light was gone
We can still feel her presence in our soul
For her the Angel left her love and joy of life
As the reminder of what we had misplaced long ago
The Angel will be with us for always
To keep that light shining in our soul
For the love of God, He has sent her to us, the Angel from above . . .

Brenda Colclasure

Pictures Of Grace

The premiere brush of light when morn breaks anew
A brisk, cold winter's day with the sky brilliant blue
The unbridled excitement of a curious child
Summer winds that blow warm, hazy and wild

The marvels of life displayed as a baby just born
Spring flowers that bloom. In the midst of a nation war torn
When fond memories bring a smile and light an old wrinkled face

These are pictures of grace.

A comforting word spoken by a dear close friend
When there's a breath taking view as you round "the next bend"
A festive, crunchy blanket to tread on as trees shed their leaves
The season's first snow as to the branches it cleaves

The sweet thick scent of lilacs as it perfumes the air
The comfortable squeak of an old rocking chair
The hues and textures of sky as daylight abates

These are pictures of grace.

A man who left Heav'n to die on a cruel Roman tree
So that mankind's sins will be nought if we'll only believe
When He takes me Home for eternity, I shall then fully see
That God alone is the truest picture of Grace.

Danita R. Senzel

Scrapbook

My shiny red radio flyer 2000
a bump, ump. Bump, ump
Pony princess and Raggedy Anne griped the wagon sides.
Burrowing picked dandelions and daisies in yarn hair and baby doll
clothing. I kicked up my heels and sat
reading a book in one hand, holding a radio in the other.
My dog, Mandi, dragged me around the neighborhood
Until she yelped!
Parking my flyer on the sidewalk, stuffed animals
march to greet me and my red vehicle.

I lugged the black handle over my shoulder,
sweat from my puny palms withered the paint away.

I sprayed the flyer down with a garden hose.
Rusted paint pieces and flower stems trickled
through cracks of the sidewalk.

Dumb, cheap, red wagon, too old to play.
Pony princess and Raggedy Anne sit in a cardboard coffin
in the basement.
And the radio flyer 2000
dangles on the garage wall.

Diana Myers

Untitled

Driving down an emotional highway, I pass
a car. We play a game. I speed up, he slows down.
Speed up, slow down. One day my brakes and
accelerator will die, but will he keep going?
Will I lose my partner in our game of tag? Will he
stop, or keep going, and find another willing partner?
Will that next partner know what we did? Know
where he's been, where I've been, where my last
partner was, where the partner before his last partner
was? Will he tell her or will he give her the disease that
now rots my body? Or will she be a smart one? Anyone can
be smarter than I was. I was so stupid, so trusting. I didn't
see the lies in his eyes. The word just floated out of his
mouth. He looked so healthy. How could he have been affected?
How can I be affected? Everybody knows that you live forever,
give or take a life or two. So, every morning I wake up, take
a deep breath, and live. Of course no one else knows about
me, I still look healthy. I could go out right now, and have a great
time. But maybe later, I've got a doctor's appointment. Maybe
he'll have some great news. I doubt it, though. Every one says
it can't get any worse, but then again it can't get any better.

Bridget Burke

"Transformation"

I once had a butterfly who still was
a caterpillar. I asked him "why have you
not died yet? Why have you not yet wrapped
yourself in a white coffin and charmed the
world with new born color?"
He did not reply. Only closed his eyes
and went to sleep. A while went by and
I came back to see my caterpillar, but I
could only find a glorious butterfly.
I asked him if he knew where I could find
my friend? He smiled, folded back his
wings, and said "look close at me and you
will find that what you are looking for."
With that I knew what he meant and
watched my butterfly take to the sky.
Leaving behind a little white tomb.

Andrea Baker

Fractured Reflection

Do you see perfection in the contours of your soul?
A clean and radiant conscience, contented and whole
Did he make you unbreakable with his expert hands?
And endow with a goodness I cannot understand
Have you never had a thought that was less than pure?
Or a diseased emotion you found impossible to cure
He did not sculpt me in the pristine essence of you;
You saw in me an ugliness you could not construe
Must I be ashamed of this darkness I show?
Such darkness, you swear, you could never know
Is there only sweetness in the fruit of your being?
Or do you carry bitter seeds you cannot bear me seeing?
Perhaps you hide cracks that you fail to acknowledge;
Then I would be the embodiment of that broken image.

Kalpana Vijayan

Traveling Cockroach

Never had I seen in all my travels far and near,
A cockroach, not in a room, not on the ground, but on my plane, oh dear.
It walked around with confidence and took in the scene without fear.
People didn't seem to matter to it, not a bit.
But when it got too close, I knocked it to the floor with a quick lick.
I didn't dare squash it for I didn't know,
If it were maintaining the air balance and if it went, so would the plane go.
I've never been a lover of roaches;
And felt, as he climbed onto my blanket again, that it was exercising a bit of encroachment.
I had some respect, however, for its choice of a destination.
To travel to Hawaii, maybe receive a lei and a kiss, must have been a cockroach sensation.
I wondered where it would travel the next time?
I needed to know so I could find,
Another time, another destination, another plane, and another air safety sing.

Henrietta A. Smith

Ode To A Friend

Beneath the cotton is velvet
A combination of leather and lace
All her movements are languid yet fluid
Poetry in motion; a softness with grace

She's alone in a crowd, the last soldier standing
In a war she fights every day
With herself and loved ones, always demanding
And the obstacles that stand in her way

Yet someday one will honor her
With the love she truly deserves
It's a friend who relishes all she is
But hasn't quite got the nerve

To let her know there's more to life
Than what she's seen to now
Confusion breeds a sort of wisdom
She won't know why or how

But soon she'll see what she really wants
And how she wants life to be
Through all the anger, the dreams, the tears
She'll know the answer is me.

Joe Pavelka

A Deny That Was Found

A heart of a dream,
a core of a religion,
a diseased beauty,
the cursed voice soothed the wounded and worried frail of sadness.
My brilliant art stunned the love of words.
My sneeze lifted the pollen to brighten
and seize taunted minds.

But like bread to rot,
and life to bury,
A sun must shine
no more.

Anita Kingsbury

A Mother And Daughter

A mother can grow just as her Daughter grows.
A daughter can cry just as her mother cries.
A mother can hurt just as her daughter hurts.
A daughter can love just as her mother loves.
but, the one thing a mother and daughter can't
do is replace one another.
There's a bond that keeps them together like shoes
mended with leather.
They can grow apart or go back to the start.
That's when the mother and daughter should
Reopen their hearts and put the past deep in the dark,
Look toward the future in the big bright star . . .
Mother and daughter you certainly are.

Jill Irene Morin

"In My Heart"

Gentle, soft and strong,
A diamond among the stones.
The light she brought was so bright.
Our paths will always be lit.
Thinking of days to come.
The silence in the air, she was there -
The simple jester of a sisters hand,
Will make me think of her again.
My dreams start when I wake
Sleep my only escape -
Does the pain ever end.
Or become an eternal fate -
Then all the sweet memories come rushing in,
And save me one again.
The gentle touch of her hand, upon my tear stained face.
And to rest my head upon her breast,
A child's safest place
I can't let go -
I won't let go -
She remains here in my heart.

Ilona J. DeSiervi

Untitled

Passionate flames that leap like
a forest fire devouring it's victim
caught in its own intensity, unbridled
heat of the moment, propelled by the
wind of its own invention

Driven, scorching, searing, paying homage
to no earthly power or persuasion,
it is bent on total destruction
not unlike human flesh it must have oxygen,
without which it diminishes with
the swiftness of light
glory so powerful, so suddenly
nothing at all

Agnes Caldwell

Thunderstorm

I see the birds flying high;
A dragon fly flitters close by.
The squirrels play from tree to tree;
A woodpecker hunting for bugs I see.
The wind is blowing oh so cool;
It makes you tingle, like a dip in a pool
I hear the thunder and just can't wait;
For a bolt of lightening, its mate.
It lights the sky to let you know;
The grass will be growing for you to mow.
The clouds are gathering dark as can be;
A thunderstorm comes to wash all clean.
The dust will be gone, the earth anew;
God's love will show, all bright and true.
Catherine Hunt

Phases Of Love

The beginning of Love a thought a word a glance
A feeling of heights and depths unchanced
Love knows no boundaries of time or of space
But leaves its tale upon each face

Love means learning how to risk and to trust
And accepting the truth becomes a must
It means joining of present and past
Of sharing and caring and memories that last

Love is the comfortable part of giving and taking
And the anxious part of forgiving and mistaking
The loss of One's Love means longing and grieving
And hurting and finally learning to Love again . . .
Betty L. Noyes

The Encounter

A bright, luminous light, screeching, high-pitched sounds,
A figure sits in the forest, looking nervously around.
A space craft cuts through the sky, the man becomes paralyzed with fear,
He tries to flee but cannot, as the mysterious ship grows near.
When he finally recovers, he is encircled in a beam of light,
He glances up at the saucer, in this windy, cloudless night.
The noise and lights now cease, the ship proceeds to land,
The man's heart begins to race, he clenches his trembling hands.
An alien steps out, he stares at the man in awe,
Both freeze where they are, both scared at what they saw.
For the alien was covered in a silver space suit, his real body inside,
And the man had a broad, triangular head, his eyes were large and wide
"We come from Earth in peace," the alien said to the man,
But the man only nodded, for this he could not understand.
Another quick flash of light, as a camera photographs the man's face,
The aliens return back to the ship, and in a moment are off in space.
The man was hesitant to leave, but his walk broke into a run,
After his encounter, with the third planet from the sun.
Garrett Dancik

Moving Down Day

a smile
a nonsense belied by your eyes
slipped between thoughts
doubt damned
demanding
why that filthy tile,
must shoot it's chill through your naked feet

the question hangs
under peeling paint
as you unwrap the silver
from yesterday's papers
James Nash

A Fathers Best

No one gave him books to read, just a little advice,
a great task given to him, which would not always seem nice.

Four young lives bestowed on him to mold.
Four young lives in which his hand he would try to hold.

Working hard to provide for them,
seemed to take up most of his life.
At times he would wonder, "When did they all grow up?",
he would ask his wife.

He sometimes might wonder, did I meet all their needs,
was I there to answer questions of these four life seeds.

Did I nourish and advise them the best that I could.
If there was something I could do for them,
you know that I would.

To answer your questions the best that I can.
I first start out by saying that you are only one man.
It may have seemed at times that you might have not been there,
but let me remind you, we all knew that you did care.

You did a job, you were on a quest.
Concerning your youngest seed,
You are my Father and Friend, and you are the best.
James E. Nusl

The White Sea

The white sea descends as a promise to be kept;
a healthy vapor of mine mingles
with it single file.

Parting it with an extended hand proves grueling;
as I tread around wheeled lifeboats in our dock -
Gramma's and mine.

Long minutes bathing in the white sea and I am parched;
I fantasize of its first cousin:
engulfing the pure sparkling moisture.

I, under layer upon layer to keep the sea's nature from me,
welcome exquisite zephyrs that scatter the socializing vapor
and particles.

Once the journey's done, I imagine
splashing in the white sea: floating in its midst,
imitating heavenly bodies
that watch over us along uncertain trails.
Dionne Kinch

Untitled

Offer her love warm and tender
A heart that cares takes the time to remember.

Blow her a kiss from across the room
Call to say, honey, I'll be there soon.
Send a card on that special day
Brush her arm as you walk away.

Hold her hand as you walk
Listen to her words as she talks.
Dry her tears when she cries
Forgive her mistakes and don't ask her why.

Offer her love and she'll surrender
A heart that cares takes the time to remember.
Catherine M. Rise

Camelot's Promise

Somewhere I have never been
A land filled with lovers and dreams
Peace keeps the heart full of laughter
Eyes wide, alive, and free
Believe and bring to life Camelot's Promise.

Somewhere, a hidden treasure
Wind carries a song above the trees
A melody of strength and wisdom
The leaf's quiet kiss upon the sea
The carrier of Camelot's Promise.

Somewhere, caressed by the light of the sun
Blending water to sky
A never ending circle of hope
Heaven's garden blooms on the untrodden earth
The dew's mirrored path to Camelot's Promise.

My world is hazed by immense fog
The green mist of envy and currency
Red flows the anger and blood
You look upon this land but are blind
Somewhere, Camelot's Promise grows dim.

Denise G. Tsoi

Untitled

I see a yellow light open to the night.
A lantern is burning in the coldest of night;
In the coldest of storms,
In the darkest of skies,
In the brisk of winds,
In the darkest of caves,
In the night sky a light shines.

A warm flickering flame.
It is my imagination!
So powerful . . .
So comforting from the sharp winds of the outside world . . .
And from the evil that lurks and simmers
In the hearts of people.

It is a refuge,
A place of comfort that everyone has . . .
That they possess . . .
In their mind.

Amina Sattar

A Promise Kept

Furious winds, booming sounds
A lightning bolt streaks across!
Drops of water, crashing down
Everything becomes drenched.
The clouds move on, place to place,
Gray colors travel with them.
Nothing is spared.
The rainstorm sweeps the sphere.

Soon, just a short while, a hand reaches,
Stretching past the sky, past the clouds,
The calm fingers of God touch the air.
The earth is taken, everything hushed.
Even the birds are silenced.

At last the sound of chirping;
The family watches as the colors shine;
The rainbow has come,
Arched with beauty all over the land.
The promise is kept . . .
Mankind has been given another chance.

Eurie Jennings

Eternal Bloom

He will water His garden;
    a living rainbow shall shelter
    the Sleeper
with its flesh of colors.

Wilted, the Flower - tho' forever adorned by mortal fancy.
    Petals stretched to
        Divinity,
the Blossom so nurtured in His Love and acquired,
    in mind and soul,
        Serenity.
Success, sought and strived, showed strength —
    the Goal was reached,
    the Dream thus lived.

She blossomed for understanding the World, and
    Compassion saved the Bitter Ego.
        Fulfilled was the Life of the Flower;
    Now, shall she retire for the New Seed.

The Bloom has died; but the
    Roots still implant deep in
        the Soil.

Cammy Wang

Live On!

A sudden whisper, a sudden sound,
a loud explosion echoes all around.

The cries and yells of a horrified crowd,
are scaring me as they point to a cloud.

I look to the sky, there is a cloud of red,
a surprise fills me, someone yells the Challenger is dead.

All seven aboard died on their way,
on their way to space, turned to heaven in a day.

And very deep down inside my soul,
I knew that they played a much greater role.

They were not astronauts leaving the earth,
they were heroes going into rebirth.

They are now living in heaven above,
living with God and The Great White Dove.

They are living with God's own Son,
And That is why I say today live on Challenger, live on!

Annemarie DeGenova

Spring's Secret Smile

Spring wears a secret smile of sun and warmth and joy, like
a lovely maid in a trysting place as she dreams of her handsome boy.
For Spring knows that time is short, and summer heat will come,
swelling the dreams of bright new love 'neath the warmth of
Summer sun.

In March, her temper cold as steel, brings weariness and pain,
But April is apology, paid for with tears of rain.
June brings the blue of azure skies, of joy and warmth and sun,
ending the season of Spring again, that seems 'twas just begun.

Spring's hair is worn in leafy green, her blue eyes two limpid pools.
Her dress caressed by blossoms pressed to her throat like gleaming jewels.
Yes, Spring can wear a secret smile as she acts the shy coquette,
for she knows she has us all beguiled—but I'm sure with no regret.

Frank C. Sibley

Life's Journey

As I travel down the road of life, I'd love to have with me,
A map of where I'm going and where I soon will be.
If I knew what lay around each bend, and where each road would lead,
I could plan my trip more carefully and know the things I'd need.

As it is we're all explorers in a strange and foreign land,
Traveling a road that we don't know or understand.
We climb mountains and cross deserts, forge rivers deep and wide,
Always hoping that a valley lay on the other side.

Sometimes a loved one shares the way, sometimes we're all alone,
But there will be a day when we meet everyone we've known.
For some the journey's long and hard, for others short and fast,
We never really know how long the trip will last.

So take your time, enjoy the things you see long the way,
You'll never find tomorrow the joys you passed today.
And when you come upon those crossroads and have to choose a track,
Take time in your selection for there is no turning back.

As you climb those mountains and cross those rivers wide,
And wonder if you'll make it to the other side,
Remember someone's watching and He'll lend a helping hand
To aid you on your journey to that far and distant land.

Elaine Ticchio

The Meadow

Silence.
A meadow green and peaceful.
Whoomp go boots trudging through the grass,
On flowers, through dirt, water, and mud.
BOOM goes the guns.
Crash, swords smash.
Yelling, screaming of dying
Days go on more dying, suffering.
One sides line breaks.
Run! There they go.
Running from death.
Over all gone. Meadow stained red.
Smells of death. All but the dead are gone from this place.
That once was just a peaceful meadow.

Chris Winton

"My Love"

The rose, fresh and tender gives a beauty of it's own
A newborn baby, warm soft, amazes one of it's miracle
The river flows quiet and free, seeking out new depths
So is my love for thee;

The rock of Gibraltar stands firm and sure a sign for all to see
Summer rain showers, unexpected, welcomed eases the sun's dryness
A mother's caring eyes watches and protects her young from harm
So is my love for thee;

A ring, made of gold represents pureness and never ending
The candlelight is a "way giver" showing one's soul the way
A highway, winds up mountains, to valleys, takes you to your goal
So is my love for thee;

The Christ was moved with compassion to the point of tears,
Wanting so much more for those He loved
He lifted his hands and died, sacrificing His life for us
So will my love for thee.

Cynthia M. Morris

"No Place To Cry"

There's a place for pleasure; there's a place for all our toil,
A place for the happy and there's a place for pure joy.
There's a place for success and a place for those who win,
But there's never a place for the heart that's caving in.

No place to cry Lord, no place to cry.
No place to cry Lord, no place to cry.

There's a place for success and a place for those who win,
But there's never a place for the heart that's caving in.

Then I hear a whisper and my spirit tries again.
I hear my Lord calling, "You use my arms to cry in."
"You need a hiding place to renew your soul within."
"There'll always be a place for the heart that's caving in."

Some place to cry Lord, some place to cry.
Some place to cry Lord, some place to cry.

You need a hiding place to renew your soul within.
There'll always be God's love for the heart that's caving in.

Esther M. Thomas

A Heavy Heart

Tears run like rivers from a sinking heart,
A poor raft cannot make it to shore;
Pain seeps in through the cracks in the logs,
And what is all this suffering for?

The world of the mind is a scary place
When dusk leaves and darkness sets in;
To let the light just float away
Is committing a deadly sin.

For the raft rapids are quickly approaching,
There's a bumpy ride ahead,
A pulsating sound can clearly be heard,
And it's yelling, "You're better off dead!"

This raft may not make it through the rapids,
But only fear stands in it's way;
And if fear tips it over, sadly enough,
There will only be hell to pay.

But if a raft of a mind can make it past the fear,
Then the darkness shall meet the dawn;
And the raft floats across the tears to the shore,
And life will carry on.

Jenna Stram

Rectangles

Two rectangles of steel and glass.
A portal with no way through.
On one side, artificial light,
    bleak surroundings,
    and stale air.
On the other side, life springs forth
    with vibrant colors
    and movement.
The air is fresh. The boundaries are limitless;
    but, only a few understand.
People move around, never stopping to gaze
    at the beauty of it all,
    until it is cut off
    and they are on the side where I am.
Only then do they realize how precious it all is.
Two rectangles of steel and glass.

John S. Ford

Faith Of The Flowers

White mums,
A potted plant,
Given to convey a friends concern
At our time of sorrow.
White mums,
Trimmed to the perfection of a hedge,
Strange how a flower could show faith
And stand by to help us face a long tomorrow.
They will not bloom, said critics, inside a room,
But, still potted, they remain and bloom.

The winter lived again, cold, smirking,
Reminding us of the saddest season of our past.
Two autumns came, the search was through
And certainty was known to us at last.

And now within their graves
Sister and sister lie.
With the prolonged agony brought to an end
The white mums die.

Beula Ashment Chesak

The Silver Casket

A silver casket I see for her
A restful death was too much of a lure,
Her curly hair weaved like a basket
as she lay peacefully in her silver casket.

Pale and cold was the skin on her cheek
as they kissed her good-by and began to weep,
She was doing what she thought was best
by giving herself eternal rest.

A shadow began to cross her face
as they shut the top of that silver case,
She would never again see the light of day
from the satiny bed in which she lay.

It was deathly quiet as she was lowered down
there was crying and tears as I looked around,
In that hole she would forever be
sleeping for eternity.

On the quiet country side
is the grave sight where she lies,
Upon her grave I feel the pain
my life will never be the same.

Elizabeth Oermann

After The River (The First Kiss)

I remember a dying July
A slow, timid moment, a soft saddened eye.
Fireworks lingering - twinkling, sprinkling
Melodies eulogy mourning July.
The moon rising slowly, boldly and lowly,
Coldly controlling the black summer sky.
Guiding and guarding the feelings, new, starting;
A spotlight patrolling a night in July.
The air, in connection, was thick, and affection
Was quickly becoming a reason to cry.
Then - we kissed! And the kiss that we kissed
Was a promise,
And Heaven smiled down and poured blessings upon us;
A dowry that all of the love now upon us,
Would forever don us, and never would die.
Love never dying . . .
Forever, lying . . .
There, neath the air of a dying July.

Corey Christensen

Flickering Life

It stands alone quietly in the corner
A spark of amber, then a warm sensation
as if a gust of the warm mid-summer winds
were attempting to carry it away

It twitches, then a long-lasting
groove of it's most colorful light,
At first reaching as high as it could,
almost touching the top,
but then begins to fade
Drowning in it's own body, it flickers,
throwing it's last breaths of life

It silently darkens
A long streaming tail of gray rises up
as if it's spirit has been lifted,
And all was well

Joellyn Stoneberg

Turning The Corner

Voices past and present split the morning sun
A spot on the horizon has been shaken from the clouds
Former shadows compromise the soul

Patterns of destruction
Locus of control
Landing is the battleground
Journey out of bounds

Deception flows through the veins of reality
Amidst the carnage belies the inroads to safety
Pain must be challenged
Embraced
Beaten
But not forgotten

Cries for help reflect the past, present, future
The turning point to success intersects the point of no return
So take care, when
Turning the corner

John P. Moir

Untitled

This is a story sad but true
A story I think should interest you
Of a man who gave his life to free
His home, his people and dear country.
At last while on duty he was caught
By the enemy, the man for whom they had long sought.
He was given that terrible sentence to die,
When the sun's first rays entered the sky
And while the sky was still lit dim
The general appeared and asked him
"Is there any thing you would like to say
Before you leave here today?"
In answer "I regret that I," said he,
"have but one life to give for my country,"
Two minutes later he passed away
To another land forever to stay.
He had answered his call faithfully and true.
Would you have answered, had it called to you?

Barbara Walters Cole

The Smoking Room

In the smoking room somehow dark and light coexist; throwing a strange hue on already strange circumstances. The ever present smoke clouding our heads. All of us attached now detached.

The conversation, a dulled discussion of feelings, ideas, impressions; all rising, curling, intertwining like the smoke. Some things resolved, some disappear through a window left ajar for their escape.

But still, a trace left; a small smudge, a lingering odor. Things said gone, maybe, but not forgotten. Just put away for another day. The small feeling inside, a tiny reminder of those things said in the smoking room.

Jeannine Lagomarsino

Why?

I stared out the window
A tear running down my face
Wondering how I ever got in this place

Nobody listens
Nobody cares
They just don't know that you're standing there

You scream in there ears
You jump place to place
Can't they see the sadness in your face

Why don't they listen
Why don't they care
Why don't they understand and that you are there

I stared out the window
My hands in my face
Wondering how I ever got in this place

Allegra Azzopardi

Man

Formally, with a soft swift brush across me,
A very Careful procedure.
Very concerned about what's in my heart.
He seeps into bed, all open and ready for love.
This Man, so bright, so cool.
His energy to me, faithful. As mine is to him.
He feels so bold and gracious.
My Man asks me questions.
My love appreciates my answers.
My love is an individual.
My love is sensitive.
His hands have the power to heal, but his touch,
unyieldingly powerful.
I am glad I am his love.
I am glad I can trust him, count upon him.
My Man is the best friend I have ever had.
So gentle in manner and precise with his movement.
His mind is brilliance and one I adore.

Brandi Christine

"Illusions"

I think we sometimes build illusions
Against love's hurts and life's confusions;
To give's comfort, make us warm;
Give our hearts shelter from life's storms.
And thus deluded, we send up kites
Of inflated hopes which reality bites.
It's wise to stop and clearly see
That others are who they have to be,
Not whom we need or hope to see.
Learning this, we'll be set free
To make our self-discovery
And deal with life's uncertainty.

Fred Rollins

To Where Shall The Eagle Fly?

The eagle flies to nothing but
a void space, a vast land and not
the colorful world that it used to be
when life embraced this land and sea . . .

To where shall the eagle fly?
When Lords of dynamite destroy
The fingerlings in the ocean wide,
in a bang, schools of fishes die . . .

To where shall he search his food?
When the mighty greed takes the wood,
cut the narras in the forest to sell,
leaves the mountain land no tale to tell . . .

To where shall the eagle rest?
When rain floods the valley's breast,
Shall we need another Noah to save the crops?
or another sun for these land to dry up? . . .

Let hope exist in the next eagle's mind,
stop the greed, give them a chance to find
a life where rainbow colors still remain
the promise of sunshine, the gift to gain?

Eusebio C. Noblefranca

Assurance Of Life . . .

I awaken wiping my moist brow, head turning toward
A whispering light,
Eyes peering through the ashen smoke, debris and
fallen lives lay still;
Dreams of piece now breathe true, faith again reigns
to the fullest;
It's roots weaving beyond illusive hate, flowing
blood comforts the bitter cries;
Petals above in rich beautiful crimson, bellow a
stem erected of strength.
A tranquil tear of serenity falls, smile spanning
across my sanded face;
Thunderous heart of rhythm loudly applause,
I stand proudly corrected and forgiven;
War of men has finally concluded, the almighty
God has truthfully won.

Angel C. Gomez

Just In Case I Haven't Told You

You're a woman full of vigor
A woman full of fire
So strong and so determined
To obtain all that you desire

You're a mother and a father
You're a sister and a friend
And no matter just how much you've done
Your roles, they never end

You're unselfish—always caring
And giving of yourself
Always willing to lend a helping hand
To comfort someone else

You're a healer and a mender
You put your all in things you do
You're a positive influence within my life
And I'll always look up to you

For over the years it's been just you and me
And for one thing I am so glad
And that's that you're my mother
The best that one could ever have

Crystal M. Onorato

The Wall

I see a wall there in front of me; black, tall, insurmountable.
A world lies on the other side, blocked from my view, deaf to my cry.
My vision is gone; my pain only grows.
This wall blocks me from all that I know.

My world is dark; I'm cold and alone, but still I know He's there.
The wall moves in closer, but why can't I move?
All I can do is stand there and watch.
It comes from all angles, from all different sides.

I'm locked in between its darkness. No one knows I'm here.
They see a different side of me.
No one can see the pain because of the wall;
And while they can't reach in, I can't reach out.

Nothing makes me happy; I try so hard.
I keep myself busy, but it won't break down the wall.
While I try to keep on running, the wall only slows me down.
It crushed right through my body, now it's crushing through my
    heart and soul.

Lord, lift me up. I'm calling on you!
I see you there on the other side.
Break down this wall that I've put up.
Take me out of this hell! I want to be with You again.

Angela Michelle Brunson

Catharsis

I had a sunken pallor,
a yellow green sick color.
My loose strings hung moodily.
My hollow sound screamed melancholy.
My chord chaotically twisted to the amp.
I played in familiar cant.
My wail was heard, my cry understood
as it rang throughout the neighborhood;
as it went burning through the night sky;
as it went tearing, and crying, and screeching, and flying.
The full harmony ripped, it sang and roared
and in this sound let out the demon horde.
I cleared up my sickened hollow.
I blasted out sound in reverse swallow.
Now I was empty, and all was well
no more phantoms inside my shell.
At last I was free from heaviness,
clean and clear, I rested in bliss.
Oh happy day when I am free
from that which rules inside of me.

John McMullen

"The Ladybug"

As I sit here wondering
About the many things,
A ladybug flies down
With black spots on his wings.

How very delicate he may seem,
His red and black coat makes him gleam.
He is curious and often goes where he shouldn't,
But nobody said that he couldn't.

Then as he approaches a weird,
But furry looking thing
A fuzzy paw swoops down on him,
But he squeezes out and sets to wing.

Then away he flies into the pale blue sky,
Already setting out to a new place.
Leaving the playful little kitten
With a strange look on its face.

Karalee M. Mulsow

Untitled

There are so many things I could say
    About this man I loved.
He loved me and told me so in every way
    I know our union was blessed from above.

We followed this man to far away places
    And he always made sure we were safe and sound.
His military record he never disgraced
But when needed at home, he was always around.

There is no way I can describe this man.
    To each of you, he was so different.
He was a friend to many in his life span,
    And the time he spent with you he made an event.

I loved him deeply as husband and wife.
    Always my pal, my lover, my friend.
As a father he may not have always been right.
    But his unspoken love he could never pretend.

So I send him to join the family who loves him.
    And know they will welcome him into their arms.
The cup of love they serve him will be filled to the prim.
    And the arms around him will keep him from harm.

Jane E. Knowles

Until I Went To The Mountains

I've been to the city, where it is never truly dark.
Above all those lights,
Only a few stars shine bright
As small, dim sparks.
And I've been to the towns beyond the city streets.
Here the lights are low,
And many stars in the sky glow
Even in summer's heat.
I went to the country where the lights are few and far between.
Here above darkened fields and woods
Hundreds and hundreds of stars could
On any night be seen.
But oh! Until I went to the mountains I never knew
How many, many stars the sky could hold.
In the darkness atop a mountain's height
Countless stars shine where there no other light.
I looked up and saw a millionfold.

Daynell Stankiewicz

A Forgotten Friendship

I crouch in fear, from the shadow above
abusive hands, that contain no love.
The pain still throbbing, in my wounded side
would have been merciful, should I have died.

I look into those angry eyes
that used to be, so kind and wise.
But don't remember, what I did so wrong
to be without food, or water so long.

It really is sad, to live this way
to cringe in fear, till I'm old and gray.
I used to run, and play all day
but no more fun, I'm sad to say.

My heart goes faint, when I think of him
sitting there drinking, with the light's all dim.
I lie awake, on the cold hard floor
hoping for love, from my friend once more.

I sure do miss, the way we were
when the one I love, would brush my fur.
To be a dog is not so bad
unless you live, with a man gone mad.

Edward Pethers

Fire In The Forest

Sometimes I ask myself why should I be
afraid of a fire in the forest.
I guess I'm afraid that I wouldn't be able
to look up and see the beautiful birds flying
across the sky, or to see the squirrels in
the trees, or the lizards that keep the
annoying little flies away, or to see the bees
that nest in the dead branches of a tree.
I guess I'm afraid that I would lose a picnic
spot, or the shade, or taking hikes on the deer
trails, or I guess I would miss running away
from the skunks hoping they don't spray me.

I guess I shouldn't worry.

Kamen Lane

Bleak Outlook

It is so easy to ignore the pain
After a while
It all passes by

To wait for the corpse to fade from plain sight
It will cover over
The weeds will hide it

Out of mind gone from sight do not hear it
Cut off from the world
Severed the life cord

It is so easy to ignore the pain
But you must wonder
Does time heal all wounds?

Daniel R. Robichaud II

Apple

I'm a little white flower with not much power on my own.
After the frost, the bee has the power and along comes the
rain and now's the hour.

A bee with the power, a little rain shower, I'm the flower
of the hour.
The sun's shinning rays and summer's long days, makes me grow
in many ways.

As I move down the road of life, not any work and not much
strife, I travel down the road of life.

As the tree branches blow, with the coming of falls woe.
As I'm in my prime, it becomes the time to grow.

As many changes have come about, I'm an apple and the secret's out.
Now you know what I'm about.

Connie Fehr

The Loss Of A Special Friend

The music of sadness plays in my heart,
all my thoughts strum over the strings

It lingers, taking hold of each moment,
becoming a part of people, places and things

The melody composed in feelings of loss,
the notes emerge with every tear

The music of sadness continues to play,
it's heard each day, every week, all year

Ann Keegan

Shattered Anxieties

Her fears and anxieties pulsate through her temples as her feet pound
against the pavement.
She looks back and glances and her anxieties come back into clear,
painful focus.
The perspiration on her chest drips loose as she pounds harder,
pulsates harder.
She strides past the flag a third time and rushes past the anxious crowd.
They have all surmised that she will be victorious but she has not
come to the same conclusion.
Victory will be hers if she can succeed. She must only stay ahead
a moment longer.
She takes a leaping stride forward and her arms flail forward in an
extemporaneous motion.
The dark silky strands of hair bleed onto her face and back as she
gallops further.
She passes the flag a final time and f-" ᵤₑ earth with a
shattering impulse.
She raises her head and gazes at the light above and prays.
The water pours down her back and face as her legs begin to tighten.
She begins to move and shakily stands. She smiles at the
amicable crowd of people and waves. But her smile and wave
cannot conceal her tired hands, her troubled eyes,
her tortured mind.

Alison Feigles

The Gift

I had a dream last night, and were there,
    aglow with your magic, you descended the stair.

Into the night, thru the door did you stride,
    where fairies and unicorns joined by your side.

With joy, I watched you play your magical games,
    could tell as I listened, you knew all their names.

Then you ran 'cross the meadow, and filled it with laughter,
    when you caught the silvery moon beam you had chased after.

With a twinkle in your eyes, you run to where I stand,
    "my gift" you say, and press something into my hand.

To see what you've given, I slightly lower my head,
    and suddenly I'm awake, sitting up in our bed.

Only a dream I say, but that's not how I feel.
    The sights, sounds, and scents were all so real.

Then I looked in my hand, and my eyes began to smart,
    your "gift" was a moon beam . . . in the shape of a heart.

Barton L. McNabb

Dreams

When I see the seconds hand running behind the dial,
I feel my life shrinking, and the lump I've in my throat getting bigger.
I closed my eyes.
Hot tears are going all over my cheeks.
I'm dreaming of the sea, infinite space. Symbol of liberty.
I'm lost among the warm dunes of the desert and, curiously,
My only desire is to stay here and contemplate this eternal beauty.
The snow, creative of extreme sensations,
Brilliance in the name of her magnificence. Symbol of purity.
I'm looking at the peaceful clouds gliding along the bluish
reflection of the sky,
hanging through the blazing rays of the sunshine. Empire of fire.
I'm swimming among dolphins,
Whom are making me cry even harder by their freedom and grace.
Sliding with these reincarnated creatures through the lightness of the water,
I'm going into ecstasies. Evocation of intelligence and love.
The birds, undulating among the winds,
Are lightly touching the world by their stares. Feeling of well-being.
I opened my eyes.
The luff of wind makes the leaves flying around me,
It's good, but I'm back among reality.

Janis Leblan

My Neighbors Are Eagles!

My neighbors are eagles!!! I see them out there,
  Alive in the trees on our beach.
At first light each morning they rise in the air
  To dance on the wind out of reach.

Oh, to see them soaring, spinning circles in the sky
  Takes my heart exploring all those dreams where I can fly.
I know my friends who dream with me are smiling at the thought
  Of riding wings above the sea pulse pounding, nerves held taut.

Try it! Oh, friend, try it!!! Spread your wings and soar!
Find your dreams and fly it into that sky and more!

Reach out to grab the wind and glide, rising as you go,
  Until your troubles fade and hide midst all the world below.

Oh yes, when flying you forget petty things,
  And all that small worry stops
For you're sharing the air with eagles on wings
  Looking down on mountain-tops.

Life on the wing is joyous and free
  As herons and ravens and seagulls,
And the days of my life are precious to me
  When lived where my neighbors are eagles.

  Ernest B. Meloche

The Subway Train

I felt the strangeness
all around when I first came on board but time
wore it off, faces and voices became familiar, bonding
us together as we shared the blissful,
sometimes downcast, unpredictably bouncy, serpentine
journey in our assigned section of the subway train.
Many times I've mourned and struggled with the miserable
desolate feeling when a member suddenly exited
at an unannounced stop without a word or gesture of farewell,
leaving only priceless
memories
behind.
I rejoiced when a newborn
joined us, even though, it might be for a short time - others
never made it aboard; one day, my tour will terminate
I will come to face what is beyond these doors,
they will open,
I will get off without looking back.
I wonder
if I'll have a chance to say good-bye?

  Helen S. Brodeur

Betrayal

When I think of you, I think of all the pain,
all the hell you put me through, all your little games.
To you it was harmless,
the scars you left upon me are deep.
They run far into the depths of my soul.
How could you hurt me so bad?
Why did I let you tear me up inside, even when I was mad?
Now you ask questions,then you didn't even care.
You blame it all on me, knowing I'm innocent,
and you're in the wrong.
WHAT IS WRONG WITH YOU?
Why don't you understand my pain?
Why do I have to suffer, and you always gain?
Those piercing words burst through my soul.
So hard, so long,
I've got to stop you now.
No more will you hurt me, the pain will eventually disappear.

  Jennifer R. McGuire

Heaven In The End

Sleep, dreams Space and time
All illusions nothing's tangible 'Cause when it's all over
everyone ends up the same Cold and alone sleeping listless
in our graves, and our dreams? . . . Well, I think we dream of
Heaven (Perceptions of the Blissful Kingdom) Huge white
clouds and cherry blossoms for some Or a spacious darkened
room with a desk in the corner to write endless prose Maybe
books stacked so high you could never finish Eternity day
Full of Whitman, Kerouac, or whoever the hell else you
wanted to explore through type And for me? . . . Well maybe a
lovely oak drafting table with limitless paper and unlimited
medium And the books, they would be nice too Create by day
Read by midnight-light And when I tire of both I could see
my friends We'd say what we never could Cry, if need be,
without ridicule A clean genuine existence - Honest Pure

And during our lives nothing came true, all bets were off . . .
and the more we planned, the more we failed.
And during our lives all we saw were angry faces everybody
was angry, they all seemed angry, the whole world was angry
I'm not angry I'm just sad

  Christopher B. Morris

"A Tribute To The Veterans"

Take a moment to remember,
all of the things they did for us.
How they fought the wars,
And risked their lives,
and protected America's golden doors.
Many were wounded in battle,
bodies were scattered askew,
they valiantly fought to save,
their country and you.
Many families torn from reunion,
faces grieving in sorrow,
for fear that their country wouldn't have,
another tomorrow.
The soldiers were masked with depression,
their lives seemingly unclear,
as America was slowly covered,
with sadness and fear.
The disheartened soldiers with many a thought,
The terror of having a friend depart,
for the loneliness was relentless,
and was constantly tearing at their heart
Take a moment to remember.

  Chris Rosen

King Of The Dew

Drought, flood, and rain
  all controlled by the same

We can't touch the clouds in the sky
  but oh how we try

In our frustration we just scream "why!"

I'm glad to know that it's a power we can't have
One making a lake would love a flood
A carpenter would choose the drought
A farmer would make the rain
  and after a while simply close the spout

Each would hate the other
  and eventually the clouds, too

We would sell them for a profit
  make ourselves kings of the dew

So I stand on the ground gazing
  at whatever is in the sky

Spending my time preparing
  I want to be happy wet or dry

  Anna S. Critz

A Just World

Food, clothing, shelter, health care,
All the needs of life are there.
Hungry, naked, cold no more,
There are no sick, there are no poor.

As employment, education, opportunity arise,
Equality for all is no surprise.
Debts are canceled, gaps are sealed,
There is no more fighting in the mountain or the field.

Decisions are made with council and prayer,
Power is shared with everyone there.
A perfect world is not guaranteed,
But it all begins with one little seed.

Common dreams are shared with your brother,
And now you work with, instead of for another.
Society is there to help you be right,
With God by your side through day and through night.

Jennifer L. Willard

Clear Doubts

What will change this feeling
all this hate, which I still breath
It has just disappeared
It is something I still need.

Feel my dreams that follow
emptiness that feels like home
can you hear the be silence
does it have to be alone

I'm drowning in my only fear I'm blinded by the change that's hear
take away my only doubts help me, help me figure out

Still drowning in the sorrow
Wash away these thoughts I taste
I can feel them fading
Taste the pain just melt away.

What will change the future
Everything that I still need
I can't change tomorrow
I still need my misery.

I'm drowning in my only fear I'm frightened of the change that's hear
take away these lonely doubts help me, help me figure it all out.

Adam Martinez

Hope Deferred By A Dream In 1972

Last night in a dream,
An ugly hag hailing from Endor
Pulled a curse from her large wrinkled bag,
Placed it on me, and became my predator.
How does prey cope with a predator?
Like the wild hare I could lie still
Until she passes through this dark wood.
Or I could play the game of the gander
Who flies south and out of winter's ken.
Even her swiftest broomstick
Couldn't reach me then.
No, I'll consult a physician, a magician,
An exorcist or two, to perform
A trick which I cannot do.
Saul had his Samuel,
The Gadarenes their Immanuel.
Can curses be lifted in '72?

Gary M. Johnson

Cake

But what you see is different from what I see.
All you see is the icing on a cake,
I see the cake.

Are you the only one?
I don't know.
Could be.

Does that make me special, you ask?
No, anyone can see the cake.

Is the cake as nice as the icing?
Not always.
Sometimes the cake is better.

Barbara Kutis

Life Changes

For you see my son has come to me lately, ever so lately,
Almost never, but come he did and just in time,
Before life's fall, fortyish winds blew silver in my hair
And dried my skin, my soul and heart.

Gone the life of sure sophistication, the bridge, the golf,
And never missed, like the dates and desires of early youth.
Here now are purpose and dreams. Fulsome and rewarding.
For you see my son has come to me lately, ever so lately.

Betty Farrell

Chances Are . . .

If you always doubt, then you'll never be surprised
always look before you leap, never ever aim too high

Almost always look both ways, always quit while you're ahead
if you never talk to strangers, then you'll never make a friend

Never ever take a chance if you think you might get hurt
you shouldn't play with fire, if you're 'fraid of getting burnt

Never argue with the facts, never speak your mind too loud
always laughing at me 'cause, I've got my head up in the clouds

Never dream something too big, never go too far from home
far too shy to make a friend, too afraid to be alone

Never go out on a limb, always stop and think it through
you shouldn't fall in love, if you're so sure no one loves you

Never ever get your hopes up, too afraid they won't come true
you always say I'm crazy, but I'm just not scared like you

Heather Mackey

Samantha Faith

With the face of an angel
And a body so perfect and whole
We held you for only a moment
And love you with all of our souls

Our hearts ache because of your suffering
And the loss of your innocent life
There's so much we wanted to give you
But most of all, a happy, full life

We know how much love can hurt us
And through life we thought that we knew
But nothing compares to this tragedy
Of our daughter, our angel, our child

From heaven we know that she's watching
And feels the souls she has touched
She will live in our hearts and our memories
But now lives with God in His love

We love you Samantha Faith . . .
  Forever!!

Jamie Martinez

The Beast?

Watch him move silently thru the brush
always on the alert but definitely in a rush

He is the wolf, the scourge of man
kill them all off that is the master plan

The leaves rustling, twigs snapping, a distant human sneeze
each new sound he hears causes him to freeze

Is he on the trail of some poor rabbit or deer
chasing them tirelessly, filling them with fear

There seems to be no prey, or at least none that I can see
but yet he moves in such a state of emergency

As he approaches what appears to be his lair,
he stops once again just to check the air

He enters his home and his spouse is the first sight he sees
laying in a corner on a small pile of leaves

He moves toward his mate sensing something,
first a howl, and a whimper and then there is nothing

But he is not a monster, beast, or cad
because you see, he has just become a dad.

Jeff Holmes

"Forever Love"

Just listening to your soothing voice, it make me tremble
Amazing feeling, I'm afraid to feel
My heart is beginning to love you
Eternally I want to be with you
Same feeling, I'm hoping from you.

Can't you give your love for me?
Once in my lifetime, I yearn for a never ending love
Only you can sustain me with love that I long for
Paradox situation we're in, our love will bring us together for an
Eternal, forever love . . .
Romance that never ends!

Love, we will share now and forever, even in
Another place, another time
Never end your love for me, 'coz
Every beat of my heart, body and soul I wish to be with you forever.

Flora C. Doligon

Hiding The Pain

Troubled times, crying times, loving times,
and hard times

Want to leave but can't, want to run but don't
know how, want to get away but scared

Trying to hide the pain, trying to show the
happiness, and trying to show the kindness

Learning to love, learning to live, and learning to care

Cassie Lavergne

Our Greatest Friend

When you bow your head and fall on your knees
And all you can pray is dear God please
No words will come and all thoughts flee
Remember the Holy Spirit will pray for thee
For when we are weak God is still strong
And when we seem powerless He'll give us a song
For the Spirit that generates the longings within
Will soon give us victory and new heights we will win
We'll sing praise to our Savior the redeemer of men
For Christ is our victory our greatest friend.

Janna Chapman

Walt Beauty

I remember it bound in apple-green
An interwoven mat of a thousand leaves of grass
Pages edged with gold romanticized by age fading
Intimating ageless treasures bound within

I sit among the leaves of grass in the Yard, age-old oaks towering
  above . . .
Ahh, finally the awaited moment
What other souls have they watched over,
Leaves yellowing, ripening with the passage of inevitable Time
The ageless whispers murmur their wise secrets, insights
Windows to the soul

Soaking in the sunshine of his verses
Becoming his essence
Adjusting only to the altered light of Time

Listen carefully, and you will hear their Hollers
Resounding for miles and miles, aeons and aeons,
in saecula saeculorum, ay, forever in Eternity, *in perpetuum*
I sound my barbaric Yawp
I listen for yours

Jean Hai-Fay Lin

No Man's Land

There's a place where the young find their courage,
and a time for their season to start;
a sacred estate where they go to escape
the invisible ties to Dad's heart.

Small hands in doubt that always reached out
for a lap or the bounce of a knee,
must pass through this zone where our hugs were outgrown
and the ache in our hearts had to be.

Time played its part on a somber-faced clock
whose numbers where naked of hands.
Through the night, as we slept, life measured our steps
like so many grains in the sand.

Big button eyes had learned to disguise
all the tears unlicensed to fall
when the little toy train took the teddy bears home
on the loneliest trip of them all.

Time slowly falls outside the walls
of this land undiminished by chart.
But time cannot dim the light from within
where Dad's little boy left his mark.

James O. Kelly

Autumn

Another beautiful autumn is here
And always seems more beautiful than last year
By the ponds groups of cat-tails can be found
And the yellow leaves of the cottonwood carpet the ground
Indian paintbrush and bright red sumac bushes too
And goldenrod nodding in the breeze at you
The ageless ever new cry of geese in flight
In the woods hooty owls calling to each other in the night
The sharp yapping of the coyote can be heard from afar
And somewhere a dog is howling at the moon or a shooting star
I love these scenes and sounds of nature every year
And I'm always glad when autumn is here.

June Carrick

Timmy

I was sitting, enjoying my coffee at dawn
  And attempting to wake myself up for the day —
When the picture that came with our yesterday's mail
  Seemed to capture my eyes in a fanciful way.

It was Timmy, our very young grandson, who posed
  As he sat in his colorful "carry out" chair,
With a smile that would win any heart within reach;
  And then, quickly my thoughts ran away with a flair.

Through his face I could see his intelligent mind
  And the goodness and charm he would share every day.
With his hand at the rein — the lace of his shoe,
  He was telling the world he was well on the way.

    Ann Demprey Burke

"Love Is Like A Flower"

Our love is like a flower that blooms in the spring.
And blossoms into a bouquet of sweetness.
Our hearts beating as one.
Come with me and be my love.
Until the morning comes.

Our love isn't perfect, this we know.
But, with help from God, I know our love will grow.
What a beautiful flower, sent from above.
And this shall be our perfect love.

Love can bring sweetness of pleasures untold.
A lifetime of treasures to one that is bold.
Come, and be my love, until we are old.

    Clara M. Cotton

The Migration

When autumn's icy winds denude the trees,
and chase the summer goslings from the nest.
Then some who hear the calling of the geese,
will feel a kindred stirring in their breast.

Their hearts will yearn for some more friendly clime.
Where gentle breezes heated by the sun,
caress them as they while away the time,
the way their feathered counterparts have done.

But many more who cannot heed the call,
that they have heard so many times before.
Must stay and face the chilling winds of fall,
and in their sense of duty mind the store.

    George Bloczynski

Dreams

As I lay my head down to sleep,
And cover my body with a soft sheet,
What I'll dream I'll never know,
Until I turn on that imaginary T.V. show.

Dreams can be frightening,
Dreams can be nice,
Like being struck by lightning,
Or skating on ice.

There are some dreams that you can't control,
Like the one where you're falling in a hole.
There are some dreams that can be quite sour,
But sometimes they can be under your power.

When you rise and awake,
You come out of a world that was very fake.
Now the show is over which lasted an hour,
Then your mother comes in and says, "Time to take a shower."

    Beth Buckley

Mother

When I was just your little child
And did something to get you riled
You punished me for doing wrong
I knew your anger wouldn't last long.

Because the love you had for me
Was felt full force and so you see
The love's what I remembered best
Even when I left the nest.

I still feel that love so strong
Though years have passed, I sometimes long
To be a child once again
Of seven or eight or nine or ten.

Then I would hold you close once more
And my spirits they would soar
To have another chance or two
To tell you how much I love you.

But I don't have to turn back time
And I don't have to make it rhyme
I'm sure you know that it's still true
The simple fact is I love you.

    Joyce A. Reisman

"God's Might"

As night's dark fingers touch the earth
And dim the setting sun
Our thoughts so often turn to God
And the wonderful things He's done
The twinkling stars, the velvet night.
The brilliant sun, tis God's great might.

It seems our life is oh so brief
As we savor every moment given
For earth is just a stepping stone
Our destiny is Heaven
And God who controls our world from above,
Controls our lives with eternal love.

    Ethel Williams

Soulmates

Lock eyes with me under a full moon,
And draw near enough to gently touch.
Until we can feel each others hearts,
Beating to the very same rhythm.
Our energies have joined as one now,
Dancing around us though we are still.
The loneliness that was there for each,
Has subsided for at least this moment.
Don't yet look away and break the spell . . .
We could be soulmates, but how to tell?
Do we each make the other feel whole?
One heart, one mind, complete and loved.
Sensing each other's thoughts and feelings,
Hopes and dreams, needs and desires.
Bound together by love, now and forever . . .
Soulmates.

    Bradford L. Williams

At Last, At Last I Have Found You!

At last my days are not blue
and everybody knows, it's because of you
at last my nights are true, because of you.

You are like a tornado coming thru
standing, strong and only taking a few
honesty, love, faithfulness and bonding will follow too!

.. when I'm in your arms the skies are so new,
the stars, so bright the moon so full.
It seems the heavens have opened to show me you!

Sleet, snow, or rain my heart hurts
with great pain for the love I hold for you!

Idell Cowan

Fantasies

I know that I'm not on Fantasy Island
and Fantasies don't come true,
but all I want is just one night
To make sweet love to you.
I've waited for you patiently
I'm waiting for you still,
I'll always want you, as long as I live.
I see you every day, and when I
see you, I have so much to say,
but I know it's best for me
To turn and walk away
I know that we shouldn't be together
because we both belong to someone else
but you look so good to me I can't help my self.
I would climb the highest mountain
and swim the deepest sea, if I
had a chance to be with you
it would mean so much to me.
I don't believe in Fantasies, they don't
come true, but in my dreams I'll only love you,

Ethel Sutton

"Nanny's Backyard"

(For Josh and Alex)
I sat out in my backyard one warm September day,
And felt the gentle breezes blow and watched the green ferns sway.

The humming birds drank nectar with their long and slender bills,
While tiny ants were crawling all over big, brown hills.
The butterflies were visiting the flowers all around,
While lizards scampered over rocks and crickets there they found.

I walked back in the house and out the window saw
A little, grey, bushy-tailed squirrel, with something in his paw.
He scampered quickly up a tree and found his cozy nest,
Where he hid his little nut, and stretched out for a rest.

This place is filled with many things from butterflies to bugs,
But what Nanny's backyard really needs is two little boys with hugs!

Ann Suddith Hickson

The Jewel Of Life

The jewel of life can not be bought
and finding it is hard
You have to search for it everyday
to realize it was there all along
For each person this jewel is different
but that doesn't mean they are wrong
It is these differences that helps life continue
and that's the most precious jewel of all

Gina C. Oughton

Thank You

Thank you for all the love you've brought
And for all the understanding I've sought

Thank you for all the warmth—now in my heart
And for the never-ending start

Thank you for your help during those trying times
And for your shoulder during those crying times

Thank you for your company through those lonely nights
And for all your patience during those silly fights

Thank you for all your advice and those long talks
And for taking me on picnics, parties and those long walks

Thank you for all the trouble we've been in together
And all the times we've looked back and laughed at them together

Thank you for missing me whenever I wasn't near
And coming to my side whenever you had fear

Thank you for all the things I've learned from you
And all the experiences that we've learned through

So many thanks I owe to you,
Together, let's open the future and see all that is new.

Barbara Page

My Love For Daniel

The waiting game and so much more time to go. The endless worry
and frustrations of not knowing.

The time has come when you appear and my heart is filled with so
much joy and no more fear.

But the fear comes back when the truth is known and my heart aches
with hurt and the futures unknown.

Time again has passed with the same fear and frustration. Only one
thing has never changed and that is the love I hold for you is
unconditional and everlasting.

Charleen M. Keefe

Obey Today

Scripture pops into my head
And gives me good conscience clues
To guide me in my daily living
And separate don'ts and do's

But I just say dear memory verse
No thank you go away
Your word is sweet, and so complete
But I'll do it my way today

While the sun goes down I'll keep my will
And I'll offer satan my heel
There's time tomorrow to obey
And come to the cross and kneel

And the Lord says . . . no there isn't time
My word is pure don't be so sure about the way you feel
I'm a jealous God you belong to Me
Don't let satan steal

Beverly M. Jensen

Naughty Diabetic

I am a diabetic,
And I'm really quite pathetic,
When cravings for sweet posses my soul.

I am on a diet,
You really ought to try it,
Let's discuss it while we eat this jelly roll.

Carolyn L. McKee

Wishing You Were Here

Sometimes we wake up at night
and go to see if you've come home.
It's still hard to believe
that you are gone.
We find ourselves waiting
for the late night sound of an opening door,
And the sound of your steps
across the kitchen floor.
The thunder rumbled,
and the rain came down last night
Could it have been you in heaven,
still fighting this last fight?
I think if only we could see you again
it would be easier to let you go.
Just to tell you we love you
and be certain that you know.
All of us have been to your grave,
and all of us have cried.
I know it 's been over a week,
but it seems like just last night that you died.

Jim Garrison

Elijah's Poem

I'm looking at my kitchen floor
and how it was empty just months before.
Now it is strewn with blocks and toys
thrown from the walker with smiles and joys.

I'm looking at our extra room.
It was the catch all for boxes and broom.

Now it's cleaned up, painted and dressed
all tiny and pretty for baby's best.

I'm looking at our bedroom now
it is our peaceful, sacred bow'r.

Our love and hope it safely keeps
and in it our babe so peacefully sleeps.

Cynthia L. Travers

A Mother's Arms

I'm frightened because I see you fall
and I am helpless to pick you up.

The shadow sees your innocence, your
insecurities, your desire to be,
your need to belong.

I try to wrap my arms around you, to
protect and guide, but you want
independence, and you push
me away.

I must step back and let you experience.

My love is now a shadow.
A shadow for you to find protection and comfort.

My arms open and close as you need,
Arms that can squeeze you tight,
but arms that refuse to squeeze
you out.

Denise K. Kacir

"Thoughts Of Yesterday"

A cold wind blows, as my heart is filled with pain;
And I find that I have only myself to blame.
A calm breeze on the ocean, a soft cry in my heart;
A feeling of loss, as our souls drift apart.
A soft touch, a quiet whisper, a last glance as you walk away;
A feeling of pain, of wanting to know why you can't stay.
A spark of love, once there now gone;
I'm left to wonder, how will I ever go on.
Feelings of emptiness still linger inside;
Left to wonder, when will this pain subside.
As the sun sets, I shed a last tear;
A final thought of our love, that I will always hold dear.

Jennifer Lyday

God Provides

I know what it's like to be rich
And I know what it's like to be poor.
And I would rather eat a quiche
Then be short a dollar minus four.

God said, "I'll supply all your need."
Do not look to your left or your right.
I only need faith as a seed.
He'll give me what I want without a fight.

I'd receive a check in the mail
When my bills reach the top of the hill.
A bill that's all paid for is God's will.
See? It's all paid for, without fail.

Then someday my ship will appear,
It will come up out of nowhere.
When seen, I'll be waiting for it.
I will pay everyone just a bit.

They're some things that can't be repaid
Like friendships that want to stay that way.
I'll not pay back what has been laid.
I will see them in Heaven someday.

Candi Meinders

As The Years Go By

As the years go by
And I look up at the sky,
Where another of my brother veterans,
Has reported to our commander in the sky.

I ask will it hurt to see our ranks thin out?
Of this I have no doubt.
We, who have been through so much,
Fighting through jungle, mud, snow and such.

As brothers in arms we came together,
Living, at times crying and dying.
We followed orders knowing the cost,
Of lives that would be lost.

And now as I leave the fight,
Where I tried to make things right,
Even tho I trembled with fright.
I fought with all my might.

So my brother veterans,
The time has come to say goodbye,
As the years have now gone by.

Julio Y. Martinez

Looking Out A Window

Looking out a window I see many fond memories.

I see a warm spring day in the garden with my grandmother,
And I see my friend and I jokingly running for cover.

I see my soccer ball lying on the ground,
And I see the swing in which I sit when I want to say,
"Go away frown!"

I see the tree where my cat got caught,
And I see the yard where my brother and I have fought.

Yes, looking out that window I see many memories.

That window isn't tall at all,
In fact, it's not a window at all.

I can open this window just by lying on my bed;
Because this window is in my head.

Amie Glover

As I Pray

Lord I thank you for saving me,
And I thank you for now I see.
My voice shall keep on singing,
And my feet shall keep on dancing.
A holy dance O' Lord! I want to do,
And a love song I want to sing to you.
You are all I can think of O' My God!,
I am saved by your grace and for that I am glad!
My life I give you now to shape,
You are my shelter and there I am safe.
Who am I Lord that you call me by my name?
A wretch such as I who brought you nothing but shame!!!
My Lord Jesus I pray that you'll save all who are lost,
And bless all of those who deed the most.
That the people from all over the world,
Know and say that "You alone are the Lord"!!!
Give them a song like you gave to me,
They are captives Lord Jesus! Please I beg you set them free!!!

Elena Sforza

A Toy's Lament

I'm sad that you no longer care,
And I was too blind to see
That it simply is no longer there
And that it can never be.

I was your robot, your toy, your possession
To satisfy your every whim.
For a while I was your obsession,
Now my future is pretty grim.

I'm broken now, your toy doesn't work,
The controls are jammed and corroded.
There's a leak in my eyes, an annoying quirk,
And my circuits are overloaded.

My buttons won't push and my spring is sprung,
And my string won't pull as it should.
I'm battered from being trampled upon;
You've forgotten I used to be good.

So you've cast me aside to forget me
'Cause I no longer can bring you joy.
Though I've now become your catastrophe,
I once was your favorite toy!

Cassandra Cail

The Mystery Machine

What a wonderful, intricate, mystery machine,
And I'm hiding gleefully deep inside,
Observing the delicate sensory lines,
Sending messages, causing movements alive.

The brain is the master of it all.
It receives stimuli great and small,
Sends orders to body parts below,
So understanding and cognitive action can show.

There I watch the big pump working away,
Sending good blood from head to toe.
Little pipes and bigger pipes carry the flow,
Thumping heartbeat steady, firm and slow.

What a marvelous, complicated machine am I.
Fascinating perfection, no skill need I apply,
Just enjoy the life it gives to me,
Silently grateful for the great mystery.

Emily J. Ham

Mozart Meets Metallica

Genius is said to be 99% perspiration
And inspiration a measly 1%;
This statement is true of all the greats
From Einstein to Mozart to Yeats.

Mozart was a musical master, who despite natural gifts
Labored day and night.
Musicians soon followed his path, along
With their own symphonies, operas and songs.

Beethoven's Fifth never rocked the house
Or brought tears to the eyes;
Yet he will not be forgotten in years to come,
While heavy metal and alternative groups will succumb.

Bach and his peers belong in a league of their own
And though Schubert never finished his symphony;
Modern songs lack the beauty and moods,
But include curses, screams and everything crude.

One day in the future you'll reminisce;
When you're older everything is different.
It takes years and deep thought to comprehend:
What's classic remains, what's forgotten are trends.

Jana L. Gasn

Earth Kiss

A soft light smiles through the trees
And into the quiet of the morning.
I open the windows to let the first
Breath of fall whisper into the room.
The cool air smells clean and sweet.
If I could paint a picture with words
I would say that it feels as though my
Spirit is dancing with the light, and
The wind is making love in the softest
Way to my skin.
Kissed by the earth and given the first
Breath of life, I feel alive again.
The wind will forever kiss my spirit
And my soul will someday return the favor.
This fall morning I promise to feel
And savor
To not take for granted the wind or
The light.
Earth kiss me gently, moon kiss my night.

Faith L. Ketterman

"God's Peace"

Lo, I awoke this beautiful morning
And into the valley I looked below.
Then raising my eyes into the realm of God's heaven
I finally saw the road I must go.

The ray's of God's sun lit the road to the valley
Encompassed by lushness of grass growing green.
As I walked down this road, a pleasure engulfed me
I kept pinching myself, but it was no dream.

There in the valley, God laid out before me
A serenity so peaceful I halted my stride.
This calm and this peace filled my heart to it's fullness
A contentment of heavenly peace lay inside.

As I walked on this road, down in the valley
My thoughts turned to awe as I walked with my God.
How could a creature like me be so lucky?
To trek down this road where no other had trod?

Then God in His goodness knelt in this green lushness
And taking my hand, we prayed there for peace.
I've prayed to our Father, the one great Jehovah
Who heard, and we were into His kingdom released.

James D. Mack

Lost Remembrances

When the pain is too much to bear
And life and love are withering;
When thoughts of hope turn to fear
And your heart is tearing;
Lost remembrances may heal your wounds.

When your faith turns to dust
And you feel that all is dying;
When white innocence turns to black lust
And you are made to keep fighting;
Lost remembrances may help you see light.

When you stand alone in darkness
And no sun or moon is shining;
When nothing remains of beauty and likeness
And all has been forgotten;
Lost remembrances will fill the void.

When you need someone to be close
And stop the crying and the fears;
When you want depression to repose
And content life to overcome the tears;
Lost remembrances will offer love.

Jennifer Christina Cimorelli

First Love

As I sit alone in the still of the night,
  And look out over the sea;
My thoughts go back to the girl I love,
  The one who is waiting for me.

Until we met, I knew nothing of love,
  Except that of family;
When I saw her I couldn't explain,
  The feeling that come over me.
She was fragile and small, like a china doll;
  When she smiled her eyes would dance;
I longed to touch her, to see if she was real,
  But afraid to take the chance.

There are many good feelings God gives to a man,
  As he travels this roadway of life;
But none can compare to that "first love" I felt,
  For the girl who is now my wife.

Donald Gene Stevens

If I Had My Way

If I had my way, I'd be a writer or an artist,
and make things glow in the dark, and
write and draw to my heart's content.
If I had my way, I'd be a cowboy or a farmer
and tend to the cattle and pigs all day long
and go for a ride on my horse named Tony.
And if I could do anything, I'd do it all.
Be a preacher for a day and a dancer the
next. Just imagine all the possibilities I could be.
I'd travel the world and see a rainforest;
go to a jungle in Africa, ride the seven seas
in a ship yelling "Ahoy Mate" and watch for pirates.
I can do it all from where I sit. I can write
and read and dream with all the charisma
and flare of any of my heroes, because I am.

Jim Friedman

Thoughts Of You

dedicated to Bruce

Thoughts of you skip across my mind, serene
and melodious. Like rain falling softly from
cloudy skies; and like angel dust blowing
softly past virgin eyes.
You must know how you touched my life. We
shared smiles, laughter, and deep thoughts,
as though we'd known each other a lifetime.
I think we have . . .
Then you left . . .
You must know how you touched my soul
with electrifying currents, sparking a depth
of passion never to be forgotten.
Then you left . . .
You must know how you touched my heart,
filling it with joy and love. Two
hearts . . . beating as one . . . a friend no other could replace.
Then you left . . .
Hear me cryin' on . . .
I need you to come back to me, if only to say
you missed me too . . .

Beverly A. Stamp

What's Next

I've traveled through this world six decades
  and more
I've watched the rushing river
I've seen the eagle soar
I've trod the burning desert, and crossed
  the grassy plain
I've felt the searing sun, and the coolness
  of the rain
I've gazed in awesome wonder at the moon
  and stars above
I've felt the sting of hatred, and I've seen
  the power of love
I've ridden the rails with soldiers to
  countries far and wide
I've flown the skies with airmen with a
  friend close by my side
What awaits me down the road or just
  around the bend?
If you can tell me sir, I wish you would
  my friend.

Homer H. Pollard

Coffee Hour Blessings

I had my juice this morning in a mug from "Calvary",
And my coffee in a mug ablaze with "Holy Trinity".

My lunchtime chicken soup mug said, "God's Chapel by the Shore",
I had a second helping from "St. Alban's Open Door",
And my yogurt filled with berries
Proclaimed "St. Martha's and St. Mary's".

At four, my tea mug rimmed with birds recalled "St. Francis and St. Clare",
It seems I have a mug for every moment, and to spare.

My dinner stew sustained me in "The Annunciation",
And I drank my after dinner brew from "The Transfiguration".

I look at all the mugs I have to use, ad infinitum,
And I think of many blessings from the churches where I got them.

What would I do without these treasures reaped from all the time I spent,
Making new friends and talking over the Third Sacrament?

Clarice L. Dietrich

The Love That Never Was

So many words never spoken, so many feelings never revealed.
And my heart which was broken,
From our love that never was.

Those words will never be said,
Those feelings will never truly descend,
And my heart will always hold a memory of you inside it,
For the Love that could never be.

When we had the opportunity, the words could not be found.
When the feelings were there, they could not be seen.
And when my heart was whole,
There was no love that could be shown,
For the Love that would never be.

So, please remember,
Those words that were never said, those feelings that remained hidden,
Never now to be revealed.
And remember my heart, which without you
Will never be truly whole again.

Remember these things,
Remember our love,
Our love that never really was.

Ginnie Lin Clarke

Untitled

When things go wrong, and I don't know why;
And my whole world seems to have gone awry;
Instead of stars in my eyes, a sty;
I cry.

When I need a friend and he's not there;
When there's nothing in my closet to wear;
And everything seems so damned unfair;
I swear.

When I've offended in any way;
Or I've caused someone to go astray;
Or inflicted pain for even a day;
I pray.

Esther A. Rannow

Tiny Dancer

No one is as agile on her feet as she,
And only she hears the music to which she dances.
Quiet and serene, joyous and nearly frenzied,
    oblivious to anything or anyone,
    she dances to the breeze,
    dances to the strong wind.
At least once a day, non-stop,
    she dances to get through
    the rest of the day.
In her own small favorite spot
    with no need for an audience,
    she dances.
And come the day when her energy is
    totally spent,
Does she get total credit for
    her ability,
Or the candle that spent itself
    for her?

Joela Leinberger

Undertone

Last night while listening to the gentle rain
    and pondering the squirrels in the woods,
I wondered if they were scurrying
    to find shelter from the same,
Or simply running to play, wondering if they should

The crickets and frogs were in perfect form,
    their harmony uniting
Aided by nature alone
And all the while their voices creating
The sweetness of a perfect song

My thoughts slowly turned to you
    as they often do
With smiling eyes and gentle hands you caressed me
No words were spoken but somehow I knew
That one small moment was all that would be

Then suddenly you turn away, yet again,
    and leave me alone
The conception of our souls was not the same
The thunder rumbled and lightning struck close to home,
And again, softly, I whispered your name

Deborah K. Sherrill

Untitled

If tomorrow I don't wake
    and rise to meet the dawn
if tomorrow you should find
    that all but your memories are gone
reach back to the time and feel my touch
    my tears upon your chest
know that I love you like no other man
    my fears you laid to rest
I want you to know the way I feel
    each day until I die
You are my hero, my shining knight
    you listen when I cry
You're my life, my breath, my song
    and always in my heart
cling to these things if our time should pass
    and never will we part
if I could twist the hands of fate to ideal reality
I'd hold you close within my arms and never set you free

Jennifer S. Hayes

Blessed Deviation

At the ripe old age of twelve I took a pen in hand
And sat me down to write about all of the things I planned
  To do in my lifetime;
Be it short or be it long, my intentions were complete
I was young and full of confidence and did not intend to let
  defeat—interfere
I thought I'd be a writer with fame and fortune my lot
And even illustrate my works and be the heroine of my plot.
  Instead, along came wife time;
I met a man and married him, raised a family of five
Lusty sons and daughters who with care and love did thrive—to me most dear.

One gloomy morning I awoke and felt that I had failed
I had missed my call to fame and such and my life had slowly
  trailed—away to mediocrity;
I surely had no fortune and the world knew not my name
I'd let circumstances interfere, yet I had only myself to blame—my
  pusillanimity!
The thought possessed me day and night—a haunting thing to know
'Til suddenly, like dawn upon the world there stole over me a
  glow-my redemption.
I was wealthy in my own name as the Mother of my brood
My fame with them exalted—their heroine where none could intrude—
my salvation.

Gena E. Morgan

"My Mom Is In Heaven And I'm Glad"

She's got big giant wings of Satin and Gold.
And she's happy and healthy and no longer
old. She told me not to cry, or to be sad! My
mom's in heaven and I'm glad. She kept a
clean house and mended and sewed. She
stayed up past midnight paying bills that were
owed. She polished our shoes and ironed our
clothes and taught us of Jesus so that all of us
knows, that my mom's in heaven and I'm so
very glad. Cause I'll be with her too with our
Savior someday. And there will be no more
suffering and anguish to pay. My mom fought
for her life with all of her might. Right up to
that Glorious day. And now she has wings,
and is an angel who sings:
MY JESUS MY SAVIOR HE'S THE WAY
My mom 's in Heaven and I'm glad. And she's
saving me a place, with our Lords saving
grace. And we'll all be together someday.

Jill Maxwell

Number Three, John Starks

  I've seen Oakley grab a rebound,
and Smith go in for the jam.
  Patrick Ewing from the baseline,
and Harper for an easy "three" to can.
  I've seen Mason dribbling up the
court with his tongue hanging out,
and Anthony playing tough defense
without a doubt.
  Herb Williams playing back-up with
knowledge and wisdom, and that
Hubert Davis can shoot jumpers
with the best of them.
  But number three is the one that I like,
even more so than the Admiral or Mike.
  Like the time you went over Grant
for the jam, number three, John
Starks, you're my man.

Arlen Harris

Grandparents! Grandparents! Grandparents!

They are so nice, like spice,
And so sweet, with neat smiles,
  With the happiness of me.

They're wonderful in every way,
and their joy with me,
will never end.

Christopher Urban

Sisters

Sisters are always around
and sometimes don't make a sound.
Sisters are sometimes a pain
But they just want to help you gain.
Sisters don't mean any harm
But they do have large amounts of charm.
Sisters sometime look the same
And sometimes their hair needs to be tamed.
Sisters get along so well
But some could go to . . . heaven.
There are many sisters in the world that are fine
But none are compared to mine.

Chelsea C. Crisp

Men Who Cry

Men who cry think with their brain
and speak their heart.

Men who cry are not afraid to show
their true feeling.

Men who cry are showing they care, love and
and understand and help without being asked.

Men who cry are human beings.

You ask, do I cry?
I care, I love, I feel pain; yes, I cry!

Billy A. Davis

PISCES

The porpoise, the whale
and the crippled minnow in the mud
  -breaking the sea line, a great swordfish
his dorsal fin stark to the sky
twists and peeks at the sun:
but some have swum
in water poisoned by oil
have sunk with gills glued
  -others stiffened by harpoon
and the fishing nets of entire fleets.
So the man-fish who'd ne'er leave the reef
where gleam the coral colors
should go as the salmon through bear, eagle and eskimo
to leap the torrents to the place of peace.

John Barclay Cowper

Silent Thunder

Where will it stop
All the hurt, lies, the pain
Each one wanting to come out on top
To me there all insane,
One wants freedom, one just wants out
All they do is yell and shout
My mother so sure and aware but
yet wanting to belong
I lay awake at night and wonder
But I know it won't be long.
Won't be long til I hear the silent thunder

Crystal Young

Unity Broken

Times of change have blown past,
And the hate builds with every breath.
Where is the peace?
Who started the hate?
Whom can we trust?

Those whose lives are destroyed by hate,
And those who feel for them,
Raise prayers of peace;
In hopes they'll soon be answered.
Others sit and watch as another life is taken.

Babies aren't born knowing how to hate,
They must be taught.
When are we going to step in and stop this cycle?
Society is producing a generation of more hate than ever,
You can read it on their faces and with every breath they breath.

So, when is this going to stop,
And, with whom?
Where do you stand?
And tell me this . . .
Are your children going to know how to hate?

Christine M. Guzior

A World Where Dreams Come True

Where life's challenges no longer create broken dreams
and the jealousies of those that inspire hateful acts
no longer have strength

Where petit differences feasting on hate and vengeance
are tapered by the flame of just behavior

Where pride in oneself is achieved by concern
love and respect for others

Where good acts and virtue are no longer replaced by
greed lust criticism and hideous crimes

Where rainbows of laughter and daisies of hope have replaced
the storm that brought pain suffering hurt and despair

Where one can live in harmony
in a world where dreams come true

Joann Pelliccia

Space

When the water stands still
and the mystics come ashore
to rob me of my dreams
I am tempted
to abandon my rock
and journey with them straight into the sun
but a voice
inside of my head
says "be a man"
so I tell them that I must be left alone
to live in this barren land
where no vines grow
in hopes of one day breaking free
from the empty space
which surrounds my soul

Chris Adler

Your Smile

Give me your smile so I could see the sun setting
and the new day be able to challenge.
Give me your smile so with it I could hold on
to an anchor of hope, when I am about to give up.

Give me your smile so I could describe with it, the
path I still have to go.
Radiate the spaces of my environment with your
angelic resemblance, laugh and be joyful and always
go around in your musical carousel.

Give me your smile so I could never forget that
in spite all life's miseries one's life could be restore.
Laugh and always laugh that your bright smile
as a spring of water in the midday awaken my feelings.

Laugh and amuse me with it since your laughter
make me invoke desires which are universal.
Give me your smile and let me see the ray of
light that is visible in your gentle sight that like
mirrors reflect your soul without dissimulation.

Give me your smile so I could conjugate the word love
and your smile will always be my banner to struggle for thee.

Hannia E. Beckford Zamora

Sunset

As the sun descends beyond the Hudson
And the Palisades develop a glow,
The curtain rises on nature's spectacular show
Each evening the great scene unfurls
with a mackerel sky and a golden hue,
Certainly never quite the same, but always on cue

The orbit of the sun seems to follow a
pre-determined path
First touching the ridges pausing and blinking
than disappearing in an amber bath

Indeed such a scene
Can God only render
While man stands in awe and marvels at the splendor

John J. Maddocks

The Presence Of God

He is in the wave that washes on the silver sand
and the wind in the tall pine tree.
It's his gentle voice, the touch of his hand
that calms the storm on Life's Sea.

He is in the beautiful song that a mockingbird sings,
it's soft melody in repose.
In the fleeting shadow of an Angel's wings
as it kisses the dew on the rose.

He is in the beautiful rainbow after the rain
fulfilling his promise from above.
In the flutter of a butterfly's wings,
in the cooing voice of a dove.

He is in the sun and rain that makes the flowers bloom,
in the sunrise golden hue.
The butterfly that comes from a rough cocoon,
the whisper of life anew.

He gives us rainbows, butterflies and beautiful flowers
His presence in these we can see.
But his greatest gift was the gift of His Son.
Who died to set men free.

Alethia Bruner

Into The Wind

INTO THE WIND THEY FLEW.
  And then clouds appeared across the great expanse.
INTO THE WIND WE MOVE WITH ANXIOUS HEART,
  while the drums beat, beat, beat from the past.
INTO THE WIND WE RUN,
  knowing that all will be as before, and yet never again.

INTO THE WIND
  turn and feel.
INTO THE WIND
  know and see.
INTO THE WIND
  now we disappear.
INTO THE WIND,
  Into the wind,
   into the wind,
    the wind,
     the wind,
      wind,
       wind,
HOLD ON AND BE.
   Gail Batty-Ryan

Untitled

A promise is a promise only until it is broken
And then it falls in a splatter of tear drops
The tears are dried and leave a bit of salt and a vapor of steam
Rising into the sky. Never to form into a promise again
But, mayhap, they'll fall as rain with a rainbow of hope at the end.
   Evie C. Miller

And Then . . .

The house grew dark, like the still quietness outside
and then it happened.
The lightening shrieked across the sky with arms stretching
in all directions. Nothing moved and nothing was able to move.
Everyone knew, although they could not see, that it was happening.
It was here, right upon them, what was suppose to happen.
It was dark, then it grew light. A thunder was heard and then a
voice. The people listened as though hypnotized.
Words were spoken, commandments were given and the JUDGE took his seat.
The people, the nation, the world stood before him.
And then . . .
   Juliette L. Sharpe

Mistaken Identity

"Thank you for the flowers you sent," she said
And then she pouted and appeared coy.
"Forgive me for the words I spoke last night;
Your flowers have proved that you were right."
I pressed her hand gently, forgave her . . .

But as we strolled down the path
through the garden
I wondered
who had really sent
the flowers.
   Hazel Uhlir-Devine

Forever Love

There was a little girl about three years old,
And there was a lady standing close by.
The lady called to the little girl to come to her.
When the little girl was beside the lady,
The lady picked her up and held her very close to her.
She said to the little girl,
"Mommy loves you very much, and I will always love you."
She told the little girl that she had to go away,
For a long time; but she would see her again some day.
The little girl said, "Mommy, I don't want you to go."
The mother said she didn't want to go, but she had no choice.
She stood her daughter on the floor and knelt before her.
The Mother crossed her arms in front of her
To show her daughter how to hug herself.
Then she said, "when you feel sad or lonely do this and
Know that it is really me holding you."
The little girl grew up without her mother
And when she became an adult she recalled
That day when her Mother showed her
How a mother's love can live forever.
   Forrest Kirby

Along The Narrow Road

Along the narrow road we walk
and think there must soon be a fork
where we decide of left or right,
to reach the point what life provides.
What will we find,
what will we see,
a river, stream, a pond or tree.
A lovely lake, a clear blue sky,
a robin and a butterfly.
Will we walk on or stay awhile
and follow little butterflies
beyond the hills, meadows and streams,
hoping to find the perfect scene.
Life is a road with many stops,
how do we know where is the perfect spot?
   Anna F. Haberzettl

This Town

Out of all the towns
And this is the capital
Its headed by clowns
That's intolerable

I walk around
Take in the sights
In buildings . . . much abound
And in them many fights

Struggle, struggle, struggle little people
Getting in deeper
Thoroughly incapable
Oh, stop . . . its the beeper

So, I row down the Potomac
With a Roman candle
Oblivious to my sneak attack
This they can not handle
   Adam Meredith Dash

Clouds

Have you ever wondered about the rain
And those big dark clouds from which it came?
Well the clouds come from a place you'll never believe,
They come from the water from which we play and retrieve.
Clouds come from lakes, pools, and seas
In a way you can't quite see.
When the sun comes out and it's hot outside
The water begins to rise and hide.
The water turns into a gas and the gas is invisible,
What could be more incredible?
The gas rises into the sky
And forms the clouds way up high.
When the clouds can't hold gas anymore
It starts to rain and pour.
The rain returns to the water from which it began
And the cycle starts all over again.

Dawn Marie Wyatt

"Goodbye For Now, Dear Friend"

I salute the passing of that moment when he stepped into my life
   and time stood still.
In crossing my path he has left his footprints behind.
I hear his footsteps, I see the man, I feel his touch,
   and I remember.

So, the time has come when he must place his hand upon my heart
   and say goodbye.
The magic of his soul that has given me moments of surprising
Happiness, sometimes the mystery of unsettling sadness,
   will have to last a lifetime.

Only in memory will his shadow cover me with his strength,
   and give me comfort,
His fingertips gently stir the spirit within,
His presence dance over my walls and the sound of his voice
   create the first smile of the day.

Judith R. Hinchman

For Me

He was always there to hold me,
and to take my hand, didn't want to
scold me but he had to take a
stand. He walked me in the
darkness, and showing me the light
I would always be ok with daddy by my side.
Hard times I did give him precious moments to.
He looked at me with strong eyes,
and the love came shining through.
Yes there were some bad times, but
those were rare and few.
But I rather have the bad times
then have no time with you.
No one could ever take your place
your hands so soft and strong
you've always been to me that is the
greatest dad of all.
I never thought I'd lose you and now
that you are gone. I have to live from
day to day for you I'll carry on.

Dina Millner

Life Wind

From where do these winds blow?
And to where do they go?
What meaning do they bring?
And what songs do they sing?

Erratic do these contrary winds speed.
Over flats and hills, bearing the seed.
Seeds of our future, good or ill.
Our life's path is at their will.

It is futile to search their direction,
For nothing can give protection,
From that, which to me is apparent . . .
The fickleness of the life wind's current.

Cecil R. Daniel

Northern

The grass was not the same as when it grew there in the past
And trees grown larger through the years some diff'rent shadows cast.
A shaded concrete bench may not have seen the shade before,
Nor Seymour's lentils framing 'round the very self-same door
Through which you passed a thousand times completely unaware
That some day one who loved you so would find your spirit there.

But grass was just as green in summer's days so long ago;
The trees, though smaller, spread their leaves to shelter those below.
You'd daydream there where I am dreaming, seemingly alone,
While I was in your soul though I remained to you unknown.
Unknown to me, but always there, you were yet with me then,
As soft I walk where you had walked and touch your heart again.

Henry Travers

The Stone Crop

Fields of stone await the laborers:

   Some see boulders — heavy, immovable —
      and turn aside.

   Some bring hammers — reducing mass to dust.

   Others chisel forms — and bow their heads.

   While those who lift and carry — build walls
      encircling fields soon fallow —

Ready for the seed.

Jean M. Aloe

My Sons And I

We used to sit upon the stairs, my son and I,
   And watch the clouds roll by.
We saw the birds, we heard the wind,
   We felt the breeze that caressed
Our cheeks as it passed by.
   That Hudson River breeze, we loved so much.

We shared out laughter, talked of our fears.
   Sang songs we loved, as we sat upon the stairs.
As we made our plans, we felt the gentleness
   Of that Hudson River breeze.
A special kind of breeze, that meant so much to us.

   Sometimes at night, when thoughts begin to roam,
I think of those happy times, my sons and I,
   As we sat upon the stairs and felt the gentle touch
Of that special breeze, we called our very own
   In our long ago home.

Hattie C. Scott

Focus On The Future

We must set our goals to reach,
And we must learn, as well as teach.
We must set aside what doesn't matter,
If ever we want to climb life's ladder.
We must decide, make up our mind,
Work for only that and leave the rest behind.
We must focus everyday, we must be strong, and do what we say.
But most of all we must both agree, what we
want from life and where we want to be.
Let's start tonight and together we'll make a list,
Put it in writing and seal it with a kiss . . .

Christine Bright

When I Have Wings

I greet the sun, the wind, in their infinite space
And welcome the freedom we share
The eagle and I are alone in the sky, aware
Of our need for this air-borne flight in the limitless light
From the bindings and boundaries of men
And our spirits unite as we soar at a dizzying height
Until, reluctant, with sadness, I leave mine with him,
To bask in his freedom and indulge in his whim,
To remain unbent to the will of my world, and see thru the
   eyes of the eagle . . .
I'll re-claim it again and again, until, one time,
This spirit of mine will prefer the eyes of the eagle
And I'll be bound to escort him home.

Dorothy F. Smaltz

Skipping Through The Night

We'll skip through horizons declining
   and welcome the rising stars,
   anticipate coming tomorrow,
   discovering who we are.

We'll dance with Saturn and Venus
   and play with the archer and bear,
   fulfilling innermost feelings,
   learning how much we care.

We'll frolic, inquire and banter
   and when the night is done,
   We'll venture through untouched sensations,
   And roast marshmallows on the rising sun.

Diana M. Lane

The Lonely One

His big brown eyes tug at my heart,
   as he stands there in shabby clothes,
His arms stretched out in defiance
   at a world that has wronged him.
Beyond his anger is a loneliness,
   that I have never known.
without a home, a family to love him,
   he stands alone against the world,
crying out the only way he knows how.
   How ironic it is, that many misinterpret
his needs and callously push him aside,
   Leaving him to try and gain a sense of identity.
This little boy, a child cries out
   and I smile and touch his hand.

Karen M. Beavers

Oh, Sweet Panic

Oh, sweet panic,
Anguish of longing,
What phantomless hunger.
Yes, desperately desiring life's share of love.
The twilight moments come and go,
Why do you hesitate?
Life lies in the soul of being,
The beauty of communicating hearts.
Why do you hesitate?

Florence Gaspar Muzi

Life Is Like A Rose

Have you ever looked at a rose
And wondered why God created it
With both pedals and thorns?

Could it be because he knew life
Would hold times both good and bad,
And that the rose would be given
As the universal symbol of love?

If so, he must have know that the good
Times would exceed the bad, for if you look
Closely you will find that the pedals in
All their beauty far out number the thorns
And the pain they carry with them.

If this is so,
May your life be represented by the
Pedals of a rose and all it's
Thorns be pruned away.

David J. Herrle

A Frustrated Mother

I'm real tired
and worried too,
Cause you can't feel my love for you.

I try so hard
to make you see,
But you just don't seem to understand me.

Sometimes when things get really tough,
I feel that I don't love you enough,
But I know that I do,
And you will too,
Maybe someday when I'm gone.

Deborah East Tucker

"Wanting Freedom"

I have experienced all the seasons
and yet you still occupy a fragment of my mind.
It's not that I am lovesick and
am longing for your touch or which we could
rekindle that love we had and such.
I anticipate the day when a thought
of you does not cause my stomach to twist.
For the anxiety and mental anguish you have
caused will not in the least be missed.
The necessary severed relationship with
your family, pains me the most.
So, in honor of you I drink this toast:
To the BETRAYER!
May you never cause such suffering to another.
Why God? I ask why?
Please Dear Lord
spare me from such future pain as this
or my spirit will surely die.
My only plea
is to be free.

Jennifer Chappell

Unrecognized

It's the first day in a new town,
and you don't know anyone around.
As you look around to recognize faces,
you realize you're looking in the wrong places,
and although Tampa seems like a nice place to be,
you'd much rather be in New York City.
As you're looking around for room 123,
everyone else seems to know where to be.
You take a seat and sort of plop down,
and hope that there is a new friend to be found.
Your hands are sweaty, you don't know what to write
and the people behind you are having an insight.
So you start to wonder if anybody else is confused like you,
doesn't know where to go,
doesn't know what to do.
But then you think, that can't be true.
For only my eyes seem slightly glazed,
and only I seem a little dazed,
And there you go, thinking again,
and hoping one day this will all end.

Eugene S. Stumpf

My Dear Sweet Mother

Mother you have been patient with your children
and you have handled us with tender loving care.
Always taking time to kiss us good night and to remind
us to say our bedtime prayers. Always had us looking
good before you sent us on our way. And always making
sure we had a good breakfast before we left for the
day. There to correct us when we were wrong, and punish
us when we were bad. But you always said to us . . . "My
children I still love you" to let us know you weren't
mad. I know I don't often say "I love you mother".
I am so sorry what I say is true! That I sometimes take
advantage of the many good things you do. But I want
to take time to say "thanks mom" for keeping me in your
care. For sharing your everlasting love with me and
keeping me in your prayers. I wouldn't trade you for
anything in the world mom and I know I wouldn't dare
find another. Who could ever take the place of you
"My Dear Sweet Mother."

Cynthia Hunter

Blessings

When the steps you take are all uphill,
And you want the world to just stand still,
And you think that you have had your fill,
That's when a blessing happens.

When your friends turn their faces aside,
And you want to reach for a true, wise guide,
When you fall in troubles heaped so high,
That's when a miracle happens.

When you think that all is care and woe,
And you have nowhere safe to go,
When your heart cries out, and your steps get slow,
That's when a miracle happens.

When you hate to face the light of day,
And the darkness just won't go away,
Then a rainbow suddenly comes your way,
You'll know a blessing happened.

When you feel that everything is gone,
And you turn to God, and you're not alone,
When you find you still can sing a song,
You'll know a blessing happened.

Gladys Clark

My Family

My family is a sandwich.
Andy's the meat in the center which everyone enjoy's so dearly.
Jamie's the special sauce that drips on your shirt and can be
rather annoying, but still tastes delicious.
My Raphie, she's the cook for she's always making sure
everything perfect.
My Mom's the funky tofu because that's just the way she is.
I'm the potato chips that gives that sandwich extra crunch.
And my Dad, he's the bread that keeps it all together.

Emily Machado

Young Love

Two captives set sail in a leaky boat
and wondered where to go.

So many streams streaming, screaming as
waters washed the sandy shore.

"Which port to hail?", they might have asked,
as currents carried them afar.

But neither wondered or cared to know,
so through the channels they drifted.

Gwynn Kelley

Life's Dream

Only I can feel the pain so deep, the confusion that lurks inside.
Another screaming let me out, only to depress the thought.
Let it be known that it is I who control the power not I.
The moments of bliss shadowed only by the dark side of power.

A battle, of futuristic proportions, again wages on in the mind's eye.
Only hope, can be seen from the outside as a faint glimmering light.
Participants from all the same are the only forces taking action
A fight with oneness that only one can hope to win or loose.

Feelings, they say nothing more can be done to stop the flames.
Experience the realness of reality and walk away with a bad taste.
Could it be a falsehood or is true, only the shadow speaks to tell why
All a mistake or just the right way, only a stranger could answer wise

The positive is not the norm in a world full of negative thoughts.
Thoughts so intense that life has to move out of the way of the
tempting. Keep quiet my friend, good things will wait for those who
let their enemy die. Peace shall over come the reality that seems so
real at this point in life's dream.

Daryl A. Briggs

Rivers Of Red

Shot fired . . . run away fast!
Another shot . . . stinging back.
Third shot . . . I'm falling down.
Body's cold on the hard, black ground.
Pavement burning, scratching as I crawl.
Silent are my thoughts . . . quietness is all.
Footsteps coming near . . . closer . . . STOP!
Clicking sound . . . it's over . . . POP!
Body surrounded by rivers of red:
Another day, another one dead.
Sirens approach, he runs away:
Be back to kill another day.
Mother cries as the world sighs;
Rhetorical thought "How many must die?"

Erik Nieman

Friendship

I stood just like an island, Protected by the sea
Appearing on the surface, To be happy and carefree
But somehow you looked deeper, And saw beyond my pride
And knew I was a prisoner, Of my secrets deep inside

Although I was resistive, And put up quite a fight
You never gave up trying, You worked both day and night
You listened to my anger, You wiped away my tears
You helped to heal the wounds, That had deepened through the years

You helped me to climb mountains, That all appeared too steep
Together we crossed rivers, I thought would be too deep
You carried all my burdens, And stayed right by my side
And when I gave up all hope, You just kept up the stride

You taught me how to trust again, And say just what I feel
To sort out all my fears, And know which ones are real
You are always kind and caring, On your strength I can depend
You are so much more than that, You're a very special friend

Gemma Mazzella

Angel Of Aquarius

Run with me
  Aquarian Angel of the night
 Fly with me on the wings
  Of destiny's tomorrow.
 Threw the threshold of time
And beyond the shadows of illusion
    There's no stopping us.
  Meet my Gypsy soul at the edge of darkness.
Dance with me
  Angel of Aquarius
  Crawl with me into the fire
  Of loves sunrise.
  We can define the ancient mysteries
And discover the sacred universe of a dream
  Two spirits danced naked
  Into the drunken wilderness
   Dance enchanted souls
   Into the dying midnight sun
   Spread your wings and fly.

Crystal Stief

The Golden Rule

The opinion of others may not always agree what is truth and what are dreams.

The truth is what has always been taught to free the spirit and the life can continue.

Dreams are told only to be dreams, never to become truth.
If the two paths were ever to cross, insanity is the name given.
But if insanity is the name given, whose to say that it is not the right way.

The opinions of others would cast you aside, with no remorse or concern of well being.
But whose to say that truth and dreams are not but one in the same.

Amy Lynn Morales

Happiness

Happiness is anything that you want it to be
As long as you know that from deep within it is true,
Some motives may not be your own,
Especially when you find, that you're beating upon a stone.

It's that inner being inside
That will give you the drive
To survive within your stride
And find happiness flourishing right at your side.

Dorothy Swygert

Untitled

the feelings which rage up inside
are impossible to deal with constructively
she thinks of everything at once
yet nothing at all
fearsome images race through her mind
urging her to strike out at something
dark emotions beg to be released
her self-control barely contains their force
realizing she has a safe outlet
she allows tears to fall
and soothe her anguished soul
opening her mouth she silently screams
slowly sinking to the cold floor
she hugs herself giving into the sadness
the tears wash away the anger
soon she'll be prepared of face another day
smiling at everyone she meets
no one will ever know her terror
none will ever guess how she hates the nights
the long empty nights she spends alone

Jeweldean Patty

Tides

Along the vast, rocky shores of life
Are many a sharp shell and splinter
And long the course of a lonely man's life
Are no summers or spring times
Just winter
And the old writer who cannot compose
Can only grow haggard and worn
Can you see how a poor man who owns just his clothes
Can only regret he was born?
And then to the blind man
Who sees not a mirror,
Feels only the lines on his face
So, too, for the runner whose
Legs have been crippled
Can no longer finish the race
And so goes the course of our lives
Without failing, our youth dwindles out with the tide
Sculpting and shaping
Our old age thus causing
Misfortune and woe be our bride.

Jennifer D'Andrea

Thoughts

At nine fifty six a.m. on Sunday
are those thoughts, my thoughts, though scattered, able
to be comprehended by God, who is
overloaded at this particular
time in this time zone. As the earth turns, he
has to consider everyone who
kneels before the service. I am not pure
enough to talk with him. I try to say
the learned verses but skipping along,

I wander — so as to make my requests and questions
More specific and more encompassing, — I wonder

If these learned verses were created
to allow a mass clumping of a mass
revival and blessing. There are many
wandering and wondering to allow
for prayers to be specifically
answered. God takes for granted that we will
recite the catch-all phrases so we will
feel steered and saved and free yet to wander
and to wonder about our verses.

Jacki Stevens

Consecrated Ground

A wind howls and a bird cries
As a baby is born and an old man dies
A leaf falls on its journey down
As a tortured sun shines upon consecrated ground
As I look up a crowd stands all in black
Their emotions awaken me from my nap
In unison's their prayers, are bound
And many tears fall upon consecrated ground
Cold tendrils pierce through me now
As peace permeates my body somehow
Someone has placed a blanket upon the mound
It is the snow that has fallen upon consecrated ground
Twilight has turned into the darkness of night
I look to the stars to behold the sight
There is a stillness here that was never to be found
That lingers with the rain that falls upon consecrated ground

Andrew Balasa

Fighting

The chills of conscience numb her severed self,
As her soul reaches out with shining wings
Her flesh stays behind to toil and delve.

Darkness closes the day and loneliness rings;
Piercing waves penetrate the truth in her
And the dreaded dark voice sings.

Fate all her efforts futile renders;
But random motions in her tears,
Her life reforms again as she remembers.

Morning's early waking nears;
In the tiny bundle her hopes dawn
In soft and sonorous mocking jeers.

Sometimes she sees the face of the long-lost man,
When the waxing moon tints mother and child
She feels the naive honesty of emotions swell again.

Memory saves her as her eyes lay mild
Upon the new cheeks wrinkling into a smile;
She is reborn: rescued by Love, renewed by Pride.

Jamina Oomen

"Death Becomes Me"

The feeling of an aneurysm in my heart drifts among me slowly,
as I glare into the window of that big, black car.

Ringing the door bell, my hands tremble.
You can hear the shakiness in every ones voice,
but the world around me is of the silence of standing in front of a
    church alter.

I sit beside the hospital bed, seeing him for the last time.
Feeling his spirit rise up, out of his body, like God himself is
    taking him away.

He knew he was leaving, for he told me himself.
He wants to be with his wife, in Eternal Life.

My heart catches a slight drift, as no one is there for me.
No one loves him, not as much as me.

As I hold his hands and give him a kiss, the tears flow freely from my eyes.
My heart throbs, my eyes stare, my head drops, I'm in shock.

This man was very close to me, my best friend.
My grandpa will be in Heaven waiting for me, when my time comes.

Bobbijo Lea Reich

Night Thoughts IV

Alone in the night, I'm shaking with fright.
As I lay in my bed, I am filled with dread.
My mind has gone numb, my tongues stricken dumb.
I no longer think clearly, I'm missing you dearly.
You left for another, he's one who won't bother
To hold you so tight, in the dark of the night.
Or give love to you, the way that I do.
He may take my place, but you'll still see my face
I am lost and alone, I want to come home.
I do still love you; I don't know what to do.
For I've nowhere to run, in my hand a cold gun
I see you in my sleep; I pull the trigger and leap.

Joseph R. Forzano

The Pilots View Of Man

The earth has much to show to man
As I soar like an eagle into the sky.

I lift my plane to leave the land
To fly from earth's lowly bonds.

There is no other flight to match this joy to glide
As a pilot who steps into the heavens
Who sees the land like God above, the valleys, hills and plains
below.

As God Himself were observing man
As finite and minute on His creation, the world.

The cities, towers, spires and roofs
Barely touch the sky, they shine so brightly in the morning sun
And outline the fields with fences and lanes
To show to man his boundaries of his home.

A pilot looks at earth and sees as only God can see,
Who looks from above on His green creation.

I only wish that all mankind could know the world as from above
And see his fellows with love
Thus his God on earth would surely find
A man who is loving and truly kind.

Conard D. Moore

In A Quiet Moment

How gentle the cool breeze against my cheek,
As I stepped into the darkness, gazing into
The star studded sky, in a quiet moment, I feel
Your spirit beside me, in the deep recesses
Of my mind, and with sadness in my heart,
I treasure the nearness of your lost being.

For a brief time, I believe you too, can feel
The oneness we once shared, and you know the
Unspoken love the years have not erased.
Reflecting on the error of my spent youth,
Bring the tears, as I once again embrace
Your memory, in a quiet moment.

Joyce Howe Landrum

"Sheet Of Love"

Love is the fear of hate,
as is hate the rival of love.
They battle a never ending war,
never to be won or lost.
I ask,
could one triumph over the other,
as fear to bravery,
as life to death,
as light to darkness,
as love to . . . to hate.
Love and hate are never to be found
only to received.
Searching forever you could not find love,
or so hate.
You must earn them,
and receive them.
For once received, it is placed over you
like a sheet never to be removed.
And you will always hold it dear.

Jonathan Pretz

River Of Life

The anger pours from me
As little foamy bubbles frothing and flowing
Down the twisting river bends, full of
Frustration and dancing in dismal distress.
The clouds quickly surround, falling down,
Bringing on the feeling that I'll slowly drown,
In this swift river of life-lulling sound.
Frantically floundering for freedom,
From the foul stress of life.
My organs crying out in pain.
My mind crying out in vain.
Rushing, roaring, rapidly soaring,
The water keeps on pouring in.
Fighting, fighting, the rocks of the river,
Reaching to find my rolling bones
That crunch and crackle
As I struggle against the shackle
Of roaring rapids that fill me with stones.
And I swallow the emptiness full of shattering,
Cold, wet water from the river of life.

Brighton A. Mangini

Of Thee I Sing

Looking up to's not half as crass
    as looking down on
    (to the ignorant bystander)
but much harder to believe in.
This day of ours is just about
face it, we scratch ourselves
when no one's looking
and find something like unto Hyde —
a strange bedfellow we compulsively
second in murky dawn's daily
waterloo against other automatons.
Unless, that is, the truth shall make us
see what really lurks beneath
the ultrabright ivory framed in a
fleshly crescent no man in the moon would own.
Ecce Homo? How dare this ego
remain so alter?
Looking up to's not half the class
of looking down on
but much harder to believe in.

8/12/72

Beverly Harris

Thoughts Of You Shine Through

A body so fine, a mind so divine, lips so soft,
As my thoughts of you, shine through
A day long I wait for you,
A night strong with love so true,
As my thoughts of you, shine through.
A song to sing only to you, of romance of two,
A smell of passion in the air,
Are my only thoughts of you.
Dreams so wild, just like a child
Imagination takes hold, I become bold
To a life long future awaits
As my thoughts of you, shine through.
Today unfolds, memories untold
In the arms of only you,
As the day is done, and the night becomes
All my thoughts of you, shine through.
And carry onto the next day, to be with you.

Amanda Bauer

There Is A River

There is a river, that flows so free,
As on the mossy green bank I seek,
time alone for God and me.
To humble my spirit, I wait to hear and see,
The whispering of his heart,
Listening for the wisdom He will impart.
Take time from my busy day
to find this quite place
Slip away, to renew, and seek
His Holy face.

There is a river, I know, where
peaceful waters flow.

I talk to God and feel so refreshed.
The day then seems brand new,
For the love we share with
our Savior,
He will give it back to you.

Irvina F. Renea Crull

Beyond Redemption

The sands of time fell too swiftly through the glass
    as passion touched my life, but life I let pass.
The moon, the stars might have been my crown,
    but I chose lesser things much closer to the ground.
In my youth, at the crossroads of my life,
    the road I chose was gold and glittered in my sight.
Many years would pass, before my fears I'd meet,
    when that golden road turned to brass beneath my feet.
Then aged, broken and alone, the brass road I trod,
    waiting for death to give me that welcome nod.
Those same grains of sand that fell so swiftly through the glass,
    now betray their master's hand, and time moves slowly past.

Charly McDonald

"The Essence Of Love"

There's serenity in knowing you care
at the waning of love we should beware,
with the enhancement of your total giving
you erase
the head above water, times of living.
Everyday strife is easily dismissed
and life is enriched, with your each and every kiss.

Cordell Anthony Irving

Purity Born Upon The Wind

Upon the wind, purity was born.
As the tears of Angels graced your face,
the down of their wings touched your soul.
Out of the darkness and into the light.
Sweet child of mine,
you were born untouched by humanity,
perfect in your innocence,
purity born upon the wind.
As the first light of God shines in your eyes,
the Angels depart,
but forever shall the tears of Angels
grace your face.
For you truly are purity born upon the wind.

Ellen Scott

As Summer Comes

As the summer trees turn red
As the beaches empty out
As the barbecues cease
We know that summer has ended

As a cold wind blows in
As school starts and it's back to work
As our footsteps crunch on the fallen leaves
We know that autumn has arrived

As the snow lightly comes down
As we sip our hot chocolate
As we build snowmen and play outside
We know that winter has begun

As the trees start to tint green
As we abandon our heavy sweaters
As the snow melts away
We know that spring is here

As the days give away to bright sunshine
As we splash in the ocean
As the aroma of hamburgers fills the air
We know that summer, once again has come.

Dina S. Paulson

"The Keeper Of The Lighthouse"

My lamp lays blind fearing the raging storm,
As the foghorn barrages Mother Natures scorn.
The sea thunders at my weak and feeble walls
And soon she'll fall through and grab me by the balls.

Maggie, although not a generous sacrifice,
Was willing to appease the seas dreadful sight.
Aye, if I were Neptune, I'd throw her back too,
But it's true! It's true! She did and done fell through.

Satan shall indeed knock at my door one day
And this I'll have but once and only once to say:
My wife, she was good from far but far from good,
And those that knew her, understood.

So do not cry this stormy wake of a night
I am alone at last and far from her sight.
I praise the good Lord for bottomless whiskey,
And my dear wife, floating somewhere beneath me.

Christopher Miller

Water That Moves

The trees along the shore deposit their life
As the leaves fall to the water as if severed by a knife
That gentle wet substance creates a mood
And I could watch forever, water that moves

It swirls and ripples as it carries the leaves
It goes around and through, in and out as it weaves
And as it cuts into itself lands and grooves
I could watch forever, water that moves

Oh, the picturesque patterns that the water takes on
As it travels its way to some distant pond
That soft steady sound, oh, how it soothes
I could watch forever, water that moves

It bounces along swiftly to where it will fall
As it jumps and dances having a ball
Then the water again becomes flat and smooth
And I could watch forever, water that moves

To put a hand in the current and feel the cold
To taste that liquid which touches the soul
That life giving fluid has nothing to prove
I could watch forever, water that moves

Edward Allen Bray

Footprints Of Life

Life is like a sparkling timeglass
As the sand trickles slowly through as
the early morning dew.

We grow to learn frightening desire
And our souls burn with everlasting fire.

The precious time we have on this earth
We should learn to grow and share, and
Let others know we really do care.

These moments shall be treasured in
each other's heart — each day will unfold
something new until we part.

Prints are to be left behind of
Laughter — living loving in life,
So let's stop carving with thy knife.
And start building with a blessing strive.

Cheryl Lynn Sprague

Reflections In An Autumn Day

I stood in the crisp November air
    as the sun shown its dying rays
        through feathered layers of pink and purple clouds.

I realized my world is not the world of others.

In my world feelings are intense and not
    the drug deadened numbness of the existing.

My moments of pain
    would be celebrated with death,
        and my moments of pleasure are the birth of a child.

Colors are the flashing brilliance
    of a fourth of July nighttime sky.
My passions meet in a point
    north and south through the stars
        and my heart screams the emotional intercourse of love.

I'm blinded by what others are blinded to.

For my life is kaleidoscope of words
    and a poet writes his soul.

Calvin R. Smith

First Born

Stars hung in the heavens,
As the wind blew quietly cool,
And on that far away eve,
You decided to be here.

Your hair, fine and fair,
Matched the brown of your eyes.
Your plump, pink belly rolled,
Your masculine voice filled the air.

Your father was awed by your appearance,
Your mother elated but weary.
Your grandparents were enraptured, delighted
By you, the first grandson.

For some unknown reason, however,
All our joys were not enough.
After a few weeks of being with us,
You looked for a better place.

It's been a long time now since you left us,
Seasons have turned months to years,
But there's no sadness that we're without you,
Only a joy that you were here.

Evelyn M. Guthrey

Untitled

Aimlessly observing the clouds
As they drift lazily across an azure sky,
My mind fills with respect for our mother nature;
While the beauty of her creation unfolds around me.
With the mottled browns of our earth
And the gay greens of vegetation,
Our nature's loving hands paint the wondrousness
Of Earth's living canvas.
And even the rocks, so dull and dead to most,
Are beautiful;
For they are the splashes of immortality
Our nature has impressed upon our planet.
The birds sing in contrast overhead
To create a harmony that only nature understands,
While the sun crawls slowly towards the horizon
In an effort to bathe our world with warmth and light.
Soon, though, darkness drowns our world in shadows
So that all may appreciate the twinkle of the heavens,
And anticipate the glory
Of another beautiful day . . .

Brandon C. Boyd

Life's Merry-Go-Round

Life, resembles the horses, on a merry-go-round,
As they prance forward, and sway up and down,
While galloping in a circle, as the music,
From the calliope is heard playing, as in a mystic.
Life, duplicates the horses, in all of the details,
As they circle their laps, with long tails,
Following behind, giving off a bigger display,
And, leaving the mind to think, is life this way?
Life, imitates the horses, as they show off
Their strides, in the circling gulf,
Of the merry-go-round, and the eyes of man,
Follow intently, relating to this, and how it began.
Life, resembles, duplicates, and imitates,
The antics of the horses, before they stop, for heaven's sakes!

Eva M. Roy

The Wall

Their shoulders tremble, their eyes fill with tears,
As they relive the horror and the pain.
The agony, the suffering of those years,
Comes flooding over them again.

They come, these men whose faces are etched
With grief and sorrow.
They bow their heads and touch the names
Of those who will never see tomorrow.

Their haunted eyes tell the story, oh so well.
Perhaps they shared a bunker, or even just a meal.
These are their comrades, these are the men who fell
Please, God in your mercy, let this visit help to heal.

Christine Wayland

The Black Coyote

He was loping parallel along the hill
    As though without a care
To me it was a memorable sight
    To see the coyote, black as night
    . . . but I wouldn't tell

Many times I sat and watched
    He too, sat on the trail, as if we talked
About the hills and trees and all
And the coming of the fall.
    He saw me, but he knew
    . . . I wouldn't tell.

The fall and winter have passed
The hunters have come and gone
I turn the curve and strain to see
But nothing shows . . .
    Someone must have seen
    . . . and told

Gen Bancroft

Lost Love

The years that separate us must not be scorned.
As vintage wine enhanced with age, cherish a greater love
And tenderness matured and magnified by time.
I awaken and reach to touch you . . . my hands grope barren
emptiness.
The pain of never touching you or seeing you again are scars
Of long past wounds.
I miss the burning joy of your body encircled by my eager
Arms, of the exciting softness of your nippled breasts. The
vibrant joy of cloaked anticipated lust found in the depths
Of your embrace. Remembered odors of our closest moments,
The perfumes of your intimate body parts engraved in my
Mind must not be erased or nullified . . . all are precious
Dewdrops gleaming brightly in the storehouse of my brain.
When love has dwindled and the joys have ebbed . . . when there
Is no more love to share and icy winds chill our souls . . . we
Have experienced another way to die.
The years that separate us must not be scorned but
Welcomed as a greater love and tenderness, as vintage wine
Enhanced by time. Empty desolation chills my plexus.
Deliberate pounding of my heart reverberates in all my
muscles and arteries. Solemn sorrow, no more to feel the
warmth of your lips, your loving body.

Joseph L. Cittadini

Untitled

I collapsed in the arms of security
Ashamed of myself for my knowledge
Knowledge of the forthcoming
The legend of Mt. Olympus

Visualization of the sacred
Unknown revealed in the nude
As I stare in the face of isolation
Simplicity overcomes me and I break

I enter a world of artificial joy
Through the shattered mirror and chaotic cries
The ghost of virtuosity has possessed me
And left my soul in complete isolation

Resentment of thy kindred
Speaks the mind of the abandoned
In many ways so intense
But yet I still lift my eyes to the illuminated sky

I bear the pains of destruction
And seek forth the knowledge I resent so much
As I uncover the face of monstrosity
Reach for the courage, you're alive . . .

Anna Skaarland

The Cloud

From a Heavenly cloud, two raindrops fell upon a mountain.
At a great distance apart, soon came together and joined a
fountain. It flowed over rocks through valleys, eventually
becoming a stream, that flowed into a much greater river,
that carried one another's dream.

Flowing and building, overcoming obstacles great in size.
River, sea and sky he saw by the reflection in her eyes.
Soon an ocean surrounded on all sides, wave and tide.
Building and consuming . . . neither could run nor hide.

Two raindrops, a fountain, stream, river, and sea . . . who
might have foretold of what these two would eventually be?
Soon the sun and salt had carried them away. Forever, now
above, as a cloud they will stay.

Bryan K. Blakemore

Meeting

Let's meet at the place of trust
At a street of faith
At a time of confidence
The best among darkness when we cannot see each other's faces
Take with you some courage and a smile
Just as I will
And take with you memories
Of what we went through together
We will talk about the past,
Our friendship, and how we have left each other
Maybe you will tell me about your new girlfriend
and I will tell you about my new boyfriend
And maybe . . . maybe we can be friends again

Eva Grzegorczyk

Skin Deep

Snug in my skin,
At ease, I wander freely.
Smug, incognito, I am on the prowl.
Then fate . . . cavalier . . . sneered, and
I met you,
and you threw me off kilter!
I don't know what, where, who . . . how I feel!
Who are you? Where am I?
No man's land! Outer limits! Off limits!
I must touch!
So I can breathe,
so I can see,
so I can be!
Your revulsion to my touch rip away my sensuality!
Torn from myself,
Disconnected from you,
captive, flayed and blind,
I sink into a murky, lonely descent toward oblivion.
For a time, the balance of energy will be reestablished.
Sleep Narcissus, sleep!

Christine Perez

"Waiting"

I wait all day for the phone to ring hoping you will call.
At last! The ring of the phone!
How will I sound?
What will I say?
Be coy and decline, not to seem too anxious or
Shall I be filled with excitement and say, "Yes!"
Quickly! Answer the phone least he hang up!
"Hello," "What?" "Would I like to subscribe to McCalls?"
"No" I say.
So again I wait.

Jean W. Griffen

Dream Lover

You sneak into my head, and steal my thoughts away.
At night when I lay sleeping, my dreams you invade.
Everyday, I am living, you touch my heart.
My soul you've taken, to leave me here shaken.
My life will never be the same, because of you,
True love has came!
Everyday, I ache, to be with you.
To hear your voice, to see your smile,
To touch your hand in mine.
The dreams bring you to me, and me to you.
I long for the day to have your arms around me
The smell of our bodies, the passion, the love.
Dream lover,
Is that what you are?
A vision in the day, a dream into the night.
Our dreams,
Will they ever be together?
Or, will they always be apart.

Jenny Rhea

Pause And Reflect

Life is precious; live each day to the fullest.
Be aware of the sights and sounds that surround you.
In the course of a busy day take time to pause and reflect,
Perhaps at the birth of spring; at a blossom that will soon
Burst forth with new life, after the deep sleep of winter.
Listen to the song of a morning dove as it greets the new day.
Delight yourself with the beauty of virgin snow, as it silently
drifts down, covering the earth.
Accept each day and make it yours to enjoy.
This is the constant wonder of life; the miracle of God's work.

Consuelo H. Otero

Untitled

The wind blown fields danced a ballet
At the feet of the girl
Who performed a sacred pirouette on the rim
Of her ziggurat,
A "castle in the sky,"
A silo on ma and pa's farm.
She was sure she could fly.

Seventy one years past sixteen,
Her mind and soul ascended
Back to her imagination and dreams.
She had climbed down the long welded ladder,
And tugged through his expectations and demands.

She should have taken the leap,
And sailed like a dove
Into the mystery and magic
Of what never had been danced before.

Daniel Koenig

Home

As I stare in wonderment
at the white door of the blackened home,
Horror and misgivings run through my mind.

What lies behind the door, what is my fate and destiny?
Should I turn back or go
and face the most horrible
sight that I may face,
For it is only the doing of one
that frightens me so, that
I never return to the place
for which I call home.

Carolyn Briguglio

Memories Of The Future

There are but several summits in life,
At which you look both forward and back at your years;
As time is ever-swiftly approaching the present,
Beyond the past; in constant measure to the future.

Upon the reflection of this remembered past, we see:
That which brought us revelry, and smiles;
That which brought us sorrow, and tears;
And that which brought us nothing, and pain.

Such remembrances in unison with carefully cultivated reason,
Have summoned us from sable darkness into light.
Some of us will willfully drift wantonly in raging rivers,
While others will wisely travel forward in calmer waters.

Perhaps incited by destiny, or perhaps by choice;
We will choose our river, and our memories;
Whether they are stained by the crimson color of regret,
Or imbued by the brilliant and magnificent glow of fond rapture.

As for the past, and of the hope for a mirthful future;
Never forget the memories, but do not allow them to blind you,
And aspire to swim in the sea of your own dreams,
But choose thoughtfully your own way to happiness.

Jackie P. Hines III

Wonderful World

Today is thee first day of
Autumn.   A diamond fell from the sky,
into a locket for me to wear.
I read time in the clouds,
The sky is bright blue
and today I cried blue the world.
This day is the last day of time
Please understand there are only days left
and it is urgent that I must tell all
the people I love how much I love them.
So the way I am trying means I am trying
to become more of myself
I want to be an individual.
There is peace and joy
and goodness in this world.

Cindy Cudworth

To My Dearest Friend

I don't know what to say now that you've gone away.
No one can fill this empty feeling that you have left behind.
To go in a car accident is no way for a friend to go.
I wish I could have been there to say one last good-bye.
I hope that God is taking care of you just like we
   took care of each other.
I've loved and lost you.
I don't know what to say now that you've gone away.

I MISS YOU

Dana Andresen

Night Time

The presence of night is coming; coming . . .
   Awe struck with beauty; patient but true,
   The air seeks through the pink and blue sky
   Ruffled, rounded, clouds await the darkness,
For the presence of night is approaching; approaching . . .
   Unconventionally sound; radiant but calm
   Trees whistle while their needles stand still
   Swish! Swish! Are the only fortunes of clamor,
For the presence of night is growing; growing . . .
   Profound with excitement; silent but candid
   Flying creatures soaring, snaking amongst the breeze
   Birds; birds, making their presence felt one last time

Winter is coming, summer has past
As I sit trapped in this cycle withering through me;
Galloping by while I watch nothing but peace; nothing but peace

But then, I look up; nothing is seen!
The air; the trees; the clouds, the birds-nothing but another memory . . .

For the presence of night is upon me; has engulfed me;
   For the presence of night is here . . .

Aaron Levine

My Mom

She carried herself like royalty and rightfully so you see
   Because she was the best mom in all the world to me
Never did she fail me, her strength was always there
   And she never tired of giving, much more than her share
She always set high standards, but by example set
   The rules of honest principles and these were always met
She taught me oh so many things to get me thru the day
   She stood by me thru laughter, thru sorrow, grief and pain
She stood by me in every way until her dying day
   Oh Mom, dear Mom I love you, you've taught me well you see
For now I know I'll always have a part of you in me.

Joan Shettle

The Years Roll By

Two smooth hands held tight, one large one small,
Bands of gold encircle shiny and new.
A key in a lock, a switch of a light.
Trembling fingers fumble with satin buttons,
A pile of satin, a flushed red face.
Whispered words of love to calm her fears.
Moonlight walks on sandy beaches, footprints trail behind.
Sleepy little faces searching under the Christmas tree.
Training wheels, puppies and tooth fairies,
A family portrait, some graduation pictures too.

New sleepy little faces searching under the Christmas tree.
The years roll by . . . with a blink of the eye.

A monitor beeps and she comes back to reality.
The shiny gold band now faded with time,
Caresses her finger now wrinkled and brown.
A band of white now encircles his finger,
The strength now gone, in a once strong hand.
He squeezes her hand, one last look, a loving smile.
Whispered words of love . . . a last sigh.
"Good-bye my love." And she cries.

Judy Bechtle

Arm Of Flesh

With the Arm of Flesh we work the ground till our sweat rolls off like beads
And with the Arm of Flesh we prepare the soil for the coming of the seeds
We agonize and fertilize till the crops are tall as trees
And with the Arm of Flesh we reap rewards that fulfill it's very needs
But the Arm of Flesh can't give new life not like the Hand of God
And it's abundant supply can never satisfy like a touch from the
  Finger of God

With the Arm of Flesh we handle life as it comes forth from the womb
And with the Arm of Flesh we nurse the torn and gently dress their wounds
We sterilize and specialize but so much we still assume
For with the Arm of Flesh we take our dead and place them in the tomb
For the Arm of Flesh it can not heal not like the Hand of God
And the grace of the soul can never make you whole like a touch
  from the Finger of God

O the Arm of Flesh is a mighty lord all robed in victory
And the Arm of Flesh is a gallant knight in shining bravery
But with all it's fame and great acclaim it can never set you free
For the Arm of Flesh will pass away like a fleeting memory
For the Arm of Flesh it can not save not like the Hand of God
And it's greatness within won't deliver you from sin like a touch
  from the Finger of God

Glade Hoffman

The Holocaust

During the Holocaust 11 million innocent victims were to die,
Because of Adolf Hitler who was a powerful guy.
Hitler killed the gypsies, handicapped and Jews,
Also the homosexuals, cripples, actors and those who would refuse.
They were tortured, hung, starved, gassed and shot,
And men like Schindler who knew they could be bought.
Some escaped and some survived,
In spite of the horrific demise.
If the Holocaust were to happen today,
I would do everything in my power to keep it away.
Some prisoners were shipped in cargo trains like cattle,
Everyone else did things to help Hitler in the battle.
Anne Frank died in a concentration camp and wrote a diary
which was left behind,
It was left for her friends, family and public to find.

Heather Sanders

Words Unspoken

Words unspoken are a dangerous thing.
Because of the pain and misunderstanding they bring.
Words unspoken get locked deep inside.
Hiding behind my false pride.
My false pride wasn't with me, when I realized.
Words unspoken are no different than lies.

Yes . . . words unspoken can only convey,
the exact opposite . . . of what you really
want to say.

Anthony Kerlegan

Our Immigrant Relatives

How can we thank you? We really wish we could.
Because of your courage our life has been good!

Far away in a Volga village, you heard of a great new land.
With opportunities available to make your life so grand.
A new freedom of religion, to worship without fear,
With services in German, the language to you so dear.

How can we thank you for the heritage you gave?
You left your home and family, our ancestors so brave!

As you started across the ocean, fear must have filled your heart,
But still you were determined to make a brand new start.
America did welcome you when you arrived upon her shore,
You kissed the ground, shed tears, and prayed to stay forever-
more.

How can we thank you? You worked hard to survive.
And kept our German ancestry very much alive.

U.S. citizens you became when you passed the test,
Thanking God who helped you to do your very best.
Life was not always easy, sometimes not as you planned,
But God was still beside you here in this new land.

How can we thank you? The answer's plain, you see,
By worshiping and trusting God, as you did so faithfully!

Joanne Krieger

"The Innocent"

I can't tell you how long this poem will be,
Because you mean everything to me.
There just aren't enough words to explain it.
I know I've messed up and I've done wrong,
that I know it looks like a habit.
But, I'm telling you now, I want to die when you frown.
I know I've hurt you and this I'm not proud.
I want to say I'm sorry but that's not enough.
What to do when you goof up to much?
Please forgive me and don't blame it on the innocent,
If anyone deserves rejection, it's me because I sure did it.
I know everyone will read this, but I don't care,
I messed up before, but this is beyond compare.
I have so much guilt and hurt inside, I feel I can't go on
I love you so much, honey, please don't leave me alone.
I've grown a lot since this happened, yet I feel so old.
I'm sorry, oh so sorry for everything I've done,
I'm doing my best to carry on.
I'll end this with one last thing to say,
I need you so much, all I can do is pray.

Donna Dabo

Dear Friend

I just have to let you know how much I honor your friendship
Before it's too late.
In unionism we walk the halls of friendship, in times of despair
We turn to each other for encouragement, in periods of weakness
We hold on to each other for strength, in times of pain and
Sorrow we give each other comfort, our joys and laughter we share
With each other unconditionally. Our friendship is very special,
I want you to know you mean a lot to me, our friendship is unique,
I want you to know I treasure it dearly. Thank you for being
My friend, thank you for being my confidant, thank you for
Your kindness, your thoughtfulness, your praise. Thank you for
Your patience, your concern, your loyalty, thank you for inviting
Me to walk with you down the road of peace and harmony.
Through you my life has been full and enriched how fortunate
I am. Through you I have learned how to appreciate the little
Things in life. May your soul be greatly blest,
May your wishes and aspirations come true;
And may we be "friends forever."

    Euriel C. Simpson

Greed

Some people buy the land
Before they get to see what
That piece of land may turn out to be.

Some people buy the land
That little tree is growing on
Before they get to see how beautiful it will turn out to be.

Some people see how beautiful that tree turns out to be
And take all of what they see.

But people like me will just watch and admire
That beautiful tree and maybe ask
"May I have one of your leaves, please?"

    Denise Forte

The Mask

They play charades, and masquerade
behind their cloak of many shades

And play their part, rehearsed at dark
in hopes they'll score another mark.

The lion slayers, lie in layers.
The prize unto the master players.

It's all the same, it's called the game
that's played with unrelenting shame.

Their wasted lives that are their wives,
they rendezvous within these dives.

As the night unfolds, stories are told.
Beneath the mask the face is old.

Sublime and sweet, jubilant defeat.
Trade victims at opponents feet.

When the dawn has come, through the wine and rum,
self esteem lies deaf and dumb.

They never learn, and for those who yearn,
next week shall bring another turn.

    Carly Miller

Untitled

My eyes beheld before the dawn,
Beneath the moon upon the lawn,
Beside a tree beneath a sky
Of sticky black, a shadow lie.

It searched beneath my rubber knees,
And nosed its way between the trees
Toward the blacker shadows there.
My feet began to beat the air.

I turned about and ran rough-shod
Across the lawn I once had trod,
'Til looking back, my fate to see
I saw the shadow chasing me.

The fright now gripped me, heart and soul;
I breathed a whimper, slinking, stole
Beneath my dog house, turned to see
And found the shadow part of me.

    Charles L. Martin

Relentless

To be 29 and write your own will . . .
   better days are ahead still.
To do everything they say to do . . .
   and realize it's all up to you.
To carry on with stinging tears . . .
   only to march into deeper fears.
To know you did all you could do . . .
   yet knowing he will always find you.
To pray, and hope, and keep your chin up . . .
   only to know that your time's almost up.

    Deborah E. Mundy

A Time To Live - Always

If life were death, then Heaven and hell are within us.
Birth a departure.
Death a returning.

Would not the unborn child in amniotic flight
View its own leaving with fear, and fight
   to extend its life in the womb.
But time has decreed it go to its doom.
   and it passes the veil protesting and screaming
Never dreaming, its death is but a rebirth,
   and the host that it left awaits on the other side,
   with love.
This then is what? Life or Death?
And what should we fear as the ultimate threat!
   Here, Now, the World of Man.

    John A. D'Agostino

"The Years Of The Locust"

Little by little the cracks were opened.
Bit by bit God's armor left untaken.
Fallen from grace, wandering in disgrace
The years passed by while living a lie.
Lights avoidance the one true concordance.
Life that's worthless: soul without focus
The path of destruction the catechism.
Finally, coming to the Lord looking for more
Desperately searching for God's sweet embrace.
Knocking, Jesus comes and opens the door
Offering up peace and a final release,
Giving the chance for a different romance.
He took the old and cast a new mold.
The lie of life he exchanged for the truth.
Years forsaken dearly bought and paid.
Locust ate life till he took the blight.

    George A. Kessler Jr.

Peace

People are people, what do you see?
Black and white living in harmony.
We need to start loving one another, yes, today.
Start loving each other right away!
Peace on the street, what a wonderful thought
Children are the future, they learn what they've been taught.
All are equal in God's eyes.
This truth is real it's very simplified.
Love is the answer you'll find it in your heart.
Just look in the mirror, that's where to start. Peace.

Antonia Pavone, R.N.

The Blackness We Have

Black is being beautiful, so many people say,
Black is being proud, being proud everyday.
No matter how badly treated, no matter how tough the task,
Being black you are beautiful, being Black you are blessed.
I think of all the hard times my mother used to have,
Being Black is just a part of God's love from the start,
God loves us for the Blackness we have, our coloring he's very proud,
Let our Blackness be known about, we're proud without a doubt.
So no matter how badly treated, no matter how tough the task,
Being Black you are beautiful, being black you are blessed.

Gloria Newbill

The Difficult Dream

Grows with an old man's thirst -
Blinded, by life's endless itchy questions.
Freedom is the wound and the sword of his sadness.
Once asleep, the cut is redder with each, silent dawn-
Slivers of soaring visions and children brawn.

What is the sense of sleep's mission-
An eclectic quest to shrink its distance,
To linger, unmeager, like truth-
To harden its shadow,
To live the forbidden rage,
To break out of its rough or gentle cage?

If only he could become these passing thoughts-
Swimming through the sea of true orion time
Passing fast the flicker of some andromeda night
If only he could be the one to make this flight.

Jeffrey Schwab

Remembering

I remember autumn, green leaves turning to gold
Blistery winters of snow, the mornings very cold.
Thawing spring times, crocus popping up everywhere
Steaming hot summers, beaches and swim wear.

Rolling hills, where wild deer ran
Run off brooks, where suddenly streams began.
Large open fields, pheasants spring to the air.
Chirping and chattering, a squirrel on a branch up there.

I remember schoolyards, playing basketball, one on one.
Choosing teams for boxball, having lots of fun.
Playing stickball on narrow city streets.
Touch football, testing individual heroic feats.

All the school years pass through my head
All the friends, all friends, not black and white instead.
The many fine teachers, very tough, not one bad
Many times they were the best friends we had.

Yes I remember, thanking God that I still do
For it carried me through all these years with you.
It gave me courage, instilled morals from the start
The love of Mom and Dad, a love from their heart.

Herb Meisinger

Having A Wonderful Time Wish You Were Here

In May the Eastward hill
Bloomed cumuli of green
The shades of frogs, seasurf
And meditations.

Winter's blind eye, kindled to proximate star,
Fired sticks on the high ridge
Northward ascending dawn by dawn,
To summer,
  Spilling over
    And down
      To us
        In sunspilled falls
        And eddies through the clouds

There was no hope in it
And no reprieve,
Only remembrance of the Winter ridge
And the sound somewhere of disremembered
Voices.

John Handy

Our Friend

Our friend is like the browns of the earth, grays of the wind,
    blues of the sky and crimson of the sun,

Our friend is the keeper and teller of stories which he humbly
    shares with us from time to time,

Our friend is like the illusive breeze that lazily moves through the summer sky,

Our friend is like a butterfly that moves from flower to flower,
    taking nourishment from one and giving it to another,

Our friend lights up the space that he is in, like a full moon
    glowing in a starry black sky,

Our friend surrounded in peace shares it with everyone that
    knows and loves him.

Our friend who walks with beauty . . . Meketi.

Bobbi Foster

Same And Different

When you look around, you will see a
blur of color and differences.
But in many ways we are the same.
The biggest way we are the same is,
we all have feelings.
Even though we are all different, we all
care about something or someone.
We may be different races, some of us may
be handicapped and even some normal, or so we say.
What is different?
In a dictionary it means "unlike" but
does that mean that we have nothing in
common?
Well that's what it sounds like.
But - even if we are different, we all have
similarities.
Some of us are tall, some of us are short,
some of us are big, some of us are small,
but we are all people.
I think we have no right to criticize each other.

Amy Watson

Mourning

Her eyes sluggishly awaken from their slumber, her
body renewed as it emerges
from its cocoon of sleep, while still
restless and disturbed
as it has been
for now seemingly an eternity. The
birds outside her window
croon ceaselessly in beckoning this
day to come, the
sun with its glaring intensity
discovers her bedroom, filling it
with warmth and light and hope.

She cautiously raises herself up
from her new bed, struggles
to reach her bedside cup of water and
toast the morning.
She is victorious
once more.

Gregory A. Leos

Remarkable Reptiles

Slithering snakes who are
born to swim,
Eating mice and shedding skin.
Crocodiles and alligators
look very much alike,
Though one the crocodilian
has a very watery life.
Sensitive tongues, natural
camouflage and a question of heads or tails,
Eggs and babies, walking on
water and even a lizard with frills.
Clever and deadly, long distance
travelers,
Giants, and old timers basking
together.
Dancing rattlers, double
trouble,
A successful rescue . . . and then a turtle.

Jessica Barkhaus

Slightly Schizo II

What is that green-eyed monster,
brain-chemical snaps-stompster?
He shot my soaring spirit,
swallowed joy and all life's merit.

Drunk from all my sucked-up mirth;
he vomits apathy on today's worth.
Tomorrow I pretend he's not here,
"No, I'm not mad, just serious," I swear.

Needing an experienced soldier on my side,
I take Yeats' book and therein hide.
He holds my hand and strokes my heart,
grins and chuckles when I fart.

I'm the monster's favorite whore,
that's why I'm careful leaving his shore.
K-marts, shops and malls are shallow stuff,
chemicals, monsters and Yeats are deep and tough.

Josephine Holzberlein

To Stella Star

Stunning, stellar Stella Star,
Brash and shy and candy-sweet:
What is it makes us stand and spar,
And laugh and scream when we two meet?

Dive and swim, you won't catch me!
I'll wait for you at the other side,
Then pull you under so you can't get free
Till you kick and punch and thrash my hide.

Or run! run fast, run high, run wild,
You won't see my face, but a sideways glance,
A grin and a chuckle will lead you, child,
And confound with rage your furious prance.

But I was born first, and you know that that matters
But little when we get to life's finish;
And if you've the notion to see me in tatters
Just wait around awhile, you'll see me diminish!

And even as my sun sets over riotous shores,
I'll be in your corner, Stella dear;
I'll be the ropes, the lights, the crowd and the floors:
My days've been better since you've stayed near.

Dan Kelly

The Stallion

Wild as the prairie winds,
breath as hot as fire,
prancing and dancing by the seashore.
That stallion that stallion
what a sight to see.
So free with a swift
natural force and power,
standing alone by a running stream,
birds singing with their sweet high pitched voices,
nibbling at the wild grass and flowers,
drinking the pure fresh water.
That stallion will never be tame.
Black as night, fast as lighting,
but it is alive just as you and I.

Jessica Paul

Wind

Breath of ancient history, alive today,
Breath of forest vastness, washing Earth and Sky,
Breath uncolored of the Pharaoh's memory,
Breath of eagle's loft and crashing oak's regret,
Breath unquenchable, devouring monuments,
Breath of fire and water, carving continents,
Breath of sighs and whispers floating in treetops,
Breath of Time, dimming the warrior's battle-cry,
Breath of all being, beyond death or rebirth,
Breath becoming breath becoming breath again.

Gene Bivins

Excerpt From The Mind

The touch of night comes softly creeping.
Bringing to some, the healing caress of sleeping.
To others, the dark of night rises unbidden.
Numbing their souls, so doubt ridden.
The sounds of night, "All", do fascinate.
For some, a blanket of peaceful harmony.
To others a manifestation of the fears they anticipate.
Tranquility and fear within us dwell.
Within our minds, nights heaven or hell.

Howard R. Buchholz

Lifelong Tears

Whispering winds blew soft, white snow,
Bright young faces were all aglow.
Even the nurse had cried that morn
With tears of joy when he was born.

For his parents, the years flew past.
Knees were skinned as he ran too fast.
Father helping his first bike ride,
Mother wiping the tears he cried.

Eager to work and start his life,
Happiness found him with his wife.
Food to be bought, bills to be met,
The tears cried then were blood and sweat.

Wondering where all his time went,
Wishing his kids better time spent,
Golden years now spent in a bed,
Regretful tears are tears he shed.

Whispering winds blow a cold rain,
Missing his love evokes their pain.
Reliving times things went unsaid,
Tears from their cheeks fall on his head.

   Glenn A. Kirkpatrick

A Means To Our End

   Drugs and guns have left us undone. They have almost
broken our will to even try to carry on. When I was young
I had hopes and dreams for my children, when I would become
a parent. But now that I'm a mom I pray to God for my daughters
and my son. A gun don't care who it will leave in a ditch, on a
highway, in some lonely alley. A gun will claim our innocent
love ones lives. A gun won't fire without a cold hearted you
are I. But if it do some one is sure to suffer or even die,
and that's no lie.

   Drugs have taken over the young and the old. Drugs
will leave our love ones, silent and cold. Drugs will make our
loved ones rape, rob, steal, kill and live in fear.
Drugs fool our children. It is the only way for them to
gain fame and fortune. It have invaded our neighborhoods,
homes and our schools. It takes us as a nation to pray off
all these burdens, tries and tribulations.

   Geraldine Claiborne

The Wraith

The return of a wraith
Brought back memories of faith
From days past now like a dream
Faint twisting trails through
The chaos of time and things
Called not like them seem
Death to the spirit of fear
To raise the shield of faith
Between me and the bandit beggars
Trying to silence the voice of a wraith
They increased against them the odds
As they ground their axe in the name of their God's
To keeps us out of the market place
But we were foxes in the race
Outsmarting the hounds of hell
Stacking the deck
While ringing their funeral knell

   Janet Hyatt

Mississippi Fog

The weariness creeps in the Mississippi fog crawling over hot marsh—
bringing wet. It lurks on the sidelines then slides stealthy over
my body silently invading the borders—quietly consuming all
territory, making it's acquaintance. It glides—slips soundless into
the depths of all ideas—chills the animals living there. The
supreme "God" that ignites-burns the flames serving the "Gods" of the
pith of soul—movement passion is reduced to shimmering coals
sending out the flickering shadows—designs. No constant—seductive—
lulling. The fog seeps deeper, entering the core. Returns—spreads
outward covering ground already claimed. Fingering its way under
molding dreams. Gliding underneath stagnant waters, waking them up.
I reek of weariness. I carry the stench of hot decaying swamp. I am
spent. I ache to surrender, but the animus agitates itself against
the flickering coals—sparks fly. I'm moved against the weary, then
collapse and succumb to the lulling flickering shadows. I want to
rest, to stop, to still. The fog moves easily into opened paths
quelling the effervescence cinders, any desire of movement. I
abdicate—wooed and embraced as this quiet lover draws this blanket
of still over me. Life strikes the fire again sending out ripples
of sound—it echo's its voice into my dulled senses. I cry out!
"do not call me now—let me drift into stilly". Between breath.
Into my eye, my cry finds no resonance. Faintly I hear the distance
call—stirs the still. "Animus, pour fuel into and around this bog,
strike the flint to steel." Ignite, breath on, make fire . . . Cinders
glow, flames flicker, I move, a slow motion shadow against the light.

   Bonnie Cannon

"The Star"

In memory of Pedro Zamora of "The Real World"
"Through the weather beaten window the star is seen,
bringing quiet wisdom and understanding far beyond its years.
A path of light in a time of darkness,
for a star always shines brightest just before it fades."

   Barbara Ocola

For My Mother

For all you've done without my asking
For all you've done as a favor to me
For everything you've put up with from Dad and me
For all you hard work
For all your patience
For all that you are
Thank you, Mom!

   Rosalind S. Grady-O'Toole

Independent

There are no words from the loud,
Raw bands you see on a nightly basis
Stand as a way of living.
Anything can be done, the label is a small
Tattoo to intimidate the norm.
I am me.
Moving from home with nothing
But a runners numbers and an entry form
To social Darwinism, and the confidence
Moving and speaking; giving orders.
Should I shoot up?
Life is filled with dinners,
Decisions your parents made for you.
Eggplant parmesan? Chicken kiev?
A self evolves from decisions with bias a Mamma's boy at first.
Independence runs with Hansel and Gretel into oblivion.
Faster, it gets darker inside the forest of life.
It is never obvious to anyone.
Decisions are yours.
What am I?

   —*Brian G. Miller*

Caught Between A Smile And A Tear

Through all my trials and tribulations,
Brought on by grief, or joy, or fear,
With each success, as I progress.
I'm caught between a smile and a tear.

Life is filled with stumbling blocks:
and paths we don't expect to bend,
When, I can see this, simply as another challenge,
The light of hope is never dimmed.

And as I've journeyed onward,
throughout my each and every year,
At each plateau, of success I've found,
myself caught between a Smile and a Tear!

Elizabeth Ann Moritz

"The Baking Of The B's"

Beryl Brown baked a better batch of
brownies and bread than Betty Boop because
of using Brummel and Brown butter. But Betty's
bigger sister Betsy bets that a non-butter
batter of brownies bakes better
than bread! Beyond that, Beryl Brown
bought a basted turkey dinner from
Boston market, which was a beautiful
sight to the beholder.
(Whew!)

Dave Eschhofen

The Tunnel

He flew through a broad tunnel into a dim, secretive place, sturdily
built into the ground by peace-seeking men with careful attention.
The men were grave and beaming bright against the stale dirt inside,
that obviously was attached permanently onto the structure. A
shadow moved across the room, moved light in at one end and toward the
distant wall-like structure, decorating it up across the gleaming headboard of the wall, and then spiraling over the coffee colored table,
creating a picture on it, as the night does through a lamplight.

The only partially visible piece in the room was a tiny pawn by which
two knights were stationed as though upon a cautious decision.
They were both bronze, and their amours were battling and protecting
as if they had just been attacked after an offensive more across the
board. Father must have sat for several seconds thinking about the
tension and excitement of the game and the fury of the world above the
soil. There was a draft as she closed the iron gate and the collected
people paused inside the room, and the shadow and the breeze and the
two strong knights smiled graciously to the party.

Jennifer M. Duke

My Confused Pain

Her friends say she is all smiles, and laughs,
but deep down there are frowns and confusion!

They say she's smart and fun to be around,
maybe it's just a way to cover up the hurt inside!

They say I know just when someone needs a little
"hi", "how are you" or just a good joke
to laugh about to make them feel better,
maybe that's because I've been there before!

Maybe I have to be all these things,
to cover up what's really hurting inside . . .
my heart!

Brittany Rapp

A Burning

The light of life
burns bright, . . . inside all
living, feeling, breathing, working entities.
It shines in different shades
from lush greens,
to brilliant flights
of purple, oranges, yellows, and reds.
Each being
special in its own right,
beautiful in its own right,
belonging in what is essentially right.
A working whole
with sounds, smells, and majestic sights.
That trudge through days,
that trudge through night, . . . with ironic ease.
That loves and laughs,
that hurts and sobs, . . . with all meaning
and yet seeming to have none.
Life, a light burning
BRIGHT.

Jessica Sarah Rackley

The Empty Desert

The unrelenting sun
    Burns the desert day.
And all the ghosts of ugly past
    Are free to have their way.

And as the killing wind blows
    The empty desert grows.

Time has come and gone and left a legacy.
Hard reminders of it's power, it forced itself on me.

And as it comes and goes
    The empty desert grows.

No path already taken,
    No footprints for a guide.

No rock, no trees, no hint of shade.
    Nowhere for me to hide.

And as my weakness shows
    The empty desert grows.

I don't know where I've been, nor what lies ahead.
Despair has claimed my blackened heart
    Now that hope is dead.

And as the death bell tolls, the empty desert grows.

Al Baxter

God's Autograph

Life isn't a motionless photograph,
    But an opportunity to enjoy the beauty of God's autograph.
His Son, Jesus was made sin and died on the cross,
    But to choose darkness over the Light, then it's a loss.
His signature of suffering erases everyone's sins.
    And by believing in Him, all can overcome; then victory wins.
Since the sacrifice was made
    And the price was paid,
Accept the plan of salvation
    And the Lord will stand as a solid foundation.
Surrender your all to Him who cares
    And generously with you His love He shares.
He promises to forgive and forget all wrongs,
    And replaces old things with new songs.
Read His Word and hide it in your heart,
    For all that receive Him, He will never depart.
As we strive to accomplish our best and grow in grace,
    God will provide peace, rest and spiritual strength to succeed in the race.

Deborah A. Young

Can You See It?

Afros and Dashikis are good for a laugh,
but can you see the aftermath? Can you see it?

Extra padding on the butt, and over emphasized
lips to make fun of some peoples God given gifts,
Can you see it?

Keeping you out of the political game, by questioning
your character and besmirching your name.
Can you see it?

On most commercials you sing and dance. Light and
bright on the others; do you stand a chance!
Can you see it?

You must be name brand from head to toe, play sports,
make records, and a music video. Can you see it?

Fighting for equality, the majority of your time is spent
Go to the Olympics! Be a proud American! Our country
represent? Can you see it?

Many material possessions you own, a diamond ring on
every finger of your hand. So tell me, "Will you ever
attempt to acquire a house and some land?"

    Can you see it?
    Allen L. Melton

From Concentrate

Pinch me if you're real
but don't burst the bubble we lived in
for a handful of days from concentrate
as I protect this lifetime of memories
in the dark cave of my palms
that I can't seem to share with anyone.

Hollow in the reality I've returned to
I look over my shoulder with near-sighted eyes
to see the events of my life have led me to you
and I wonder how I walked away.
A kaleidoscope of answers in sharp focus for even a moment
or a blurred eternity of questions?

Separated from the heat of your touch by several states
I can hear your laughter in a stranger's smile
taste your kiss when the sun hits my face
and reflect on a hope I had buried.
Pinch me if this is real.

    Diana Juhasz

Steven

He was very upset and cold inside,
But he knew I would be by his side.
But this one time I was not there,
It was not because I did not care.
I really don't understand what happened that night,
All I know is it was a big fright.
He took his own life in a blink of an eye,
We still all wonder really why.
He left us a note when he left that day,
We all wondering what it might say.
He told us why he left us that way,
But saying he hoped to see us again one day.
We buried him where he wanted to be,
Asking that someday we return and see.
If only we would have looked deeper inside,
At least we would have known we tried.
Although he is gone and not with us today,
There is a lot of things I wish I could say.
Every night I kneel and pray,
Just hoping, maybe I could see him, just once, someday.

    Cristal Demonbreun

The Thought Of Losing You

The thought of losing you did me no good.
But I did all I knew I could.
Why are we in so much pain?
When in my eyes, there's nothing but rain.

The thought of losing you was, oh but a dreadful sight.
When our love was once like a beautiful starlit night.
Why do we do this to each other?
I wish we could forever be together.

The thought of losing you, kept running wild through my head.
Especially, those three little words you said.
Do those words mean anything to you?
Coming from you, I think they do.

The thought of losing you, I don't want to think about.
When in our hearts, minds, and eyes, we love each other no doubt.
So can we forgive and forget, go back to the start?
Don't ever run from love; always follow your heart.

    Jenny Beary

Wind Of Happiness Brings Release

I don't know your pain
But, I do know hurt just the same

I can feel the depth of your sorrow
I can visualize the discontent of tomorrow

Because of the depth of your despair
You should know that I really care

There is nothing that can be done on my part
Except to be there with you in heart

With each passing day
You should understand how I pray

For the Rainbow of Love
To be sent to you from above

Gaze quietly and be content
Upon the gift of God's tent

For only then will you know
The release of which way the wind of happiness does blow

    Aurore Black

Changes

Summer's nice; so is fall,
But I love Spring the best of all.
Winter's cold and Summer's hot,
And Fall's a blend of all they're not.
Winter's snow north winds will bring,
But they can't bar the surge of Spring.

Listen, child, and you will hear
That life's like seasons of the year.
Summer comes, and Winter goes —
The breath of Spring melts Winter snows.
Nothing happens without reasons,
For life keeps changing like the seasons.

God put us here and with good reason
To face each change like each new season . . .
It's up to us to face each test,
To pray and trust and do our best,
To seek His guidance from above,
And work and play and live and love.

    Cecil Haywood

The End

They say it's the end of the world
but I think it's just the beginning
for we just met
for we just fell in love.
We are like a journey with no end
we are a bud waiting to grow
and together we can make a blossom.
So why do they say it's the end of the world?
When it's really just the Beginning!!!

Angela Yates

Don't Call Me Brother

Many people who are black will gladly call you brother
But if the situation presents itself, some would betray their mother

How in this world can you be my brother
Especially when I am treated no better than any other

If advancement is your game and your goal is the riches
Why are you bothered when I'm lying in the ditches

I'm just one person who is out of your way
And you can progress - if you call it progress - for another day

My main concern is your support, especially when I'm down
Instead of giving me what I need, you prefer giving a frown

So until I'm treated as someone special - not like any other
Don't you dare breathe my name - no less call me brother

Harry H. Martin

Happiness

Happiness is living in peace one day at a time;
But it's hard when we see so much crime.

Our children are living on the streets,
While parents are working for more treats.

What happened to the family and the neighborhood?
Do people run around, and do not what they should?

Happiness is loving yourself and neighbors too;
But instead we see people in a living stew.

Young girls get pregnant without true love;
And our boys fight, and push, and shove.

What happened to the marriage relationship?
Do people think divorce is really hip?

Happiness is for anyone who wants to try.
Don't be afraid to set your goals high!

With hard work you will succeed:
And will for family provide and feed.

If you choose to do what is good and right,
Happiness will then be yours today and into night.

John R. Johnson

Darkness Of A New Day

I believe in love and hate,
But murder is an empty sin.
One should not decide another's fate.
The pain and Darkness they have caused,
Goes beyond one's sanity.
For the victims lives have paused,
Staring a new day of uncertainty.
Showing they have no remorse for feelings,
Stating clearly, how one can act selfishly.
In their minds they've justified these killings.
Reality

Duane Standifer

Untitled

You said that my love would flee with the rising sun
But my love I sweetly protest to thee
I shall love thee until the flesh has been flayed from my bones
Until the last drop of blood has trickled forth from my veins
My heart is thine until my bones wither and crack
Until a plague of rats devour my flesh I shall love thee
My soul belongs to thee until my eyes are gouged out with
scalding hot iron rods
Until day is night and night is day; until the sun kisses the
blessed moon
I shall worship thee until the sands of time cease their descent
Until the moon ceases spinning in her orb around the earth
I exist as thine slave until an angel's tears burn my cheeks
Until the stars cease to burn bright and the moon is consumed in flames
My spirit shall be infatuated with thee until all passion is extinguished
Until the seas form land and the land melts into oceans
My passions shall burn only for thee until life is but a hollow shell
And until a kiss burns and corrupts

Alexander L. Gordon

Nana, My Gift From God

My Nana was a special one,
But now here life on earth is done.
Although it's hard to say goodbye,
Her pains are gone in Heaven on High.
She fought the good fight, she ran the race
And now she's in a much better place.
Her prayers were heard by God above
As she spoke each word in precious love.
She loved to sit and talk awhile,
How I'll miss her voice and sweet, sweet smile.
One glorious day I'll see Nana once more
For one day I too will pass through death's door.
And as those golden streets we trod,
I'll hug my Nana, My Gift From God.

Donald R. Thetford Jr.

Never Forgotten

You were special to me;
     but that was a long time ago.
You touched a part of my heart;
     that will forever belong to you.
You filled many voids;
     where for so long there had been nothing
     but emptiness.
You were at times my sanity;
     when many times the madness was overwhelming.
You brought many smiles;
     to a face filled only with sorrow.
You wiped away each and every tear;
     long before they ran a river.
You wrapped me in comfort;
     to shelter me from the storms.
You told me that although miles may separate us;
     we would never be alone.
You gave to me as no one ever had;
     it was as though our souls existed as one.
You will never be forgotten;
     as memories of you are often in my thoughts.

Brenda L. Wilson-Davis

Do Angels Forgive?

She was nine or ten when he passed away,
but the pain grew stronger each and every day.
    As a little girl she now feared death,
for she had seen him take his final breath.
    Now four years later, and in the eight grade,
the pain still hadn't gone away.
    Yet continued to grow throughout the years,
and continued to bring many more tears.
    Now many questions she has come to ask,
like will she always remember the past?
    And if she can't remember his voice, . . .
is that wrong?
And will she forget more as time goes along?
    Do angels forgive someone forgetful?
And will her grandfather always be near her?
    Brandi L. Baker

True Love

I noticed that there were no stars in the skies
But then I saw them in your eyes.
It's not that I smoother you too much
It's that I know you so well 'cause I love you so much.
It's hard to miss those beautiful angel wings
That in one person lies so many things.
It seemed that there were only seven wonders of the world.
Until not long ago I met the eight.
There is nothing I wouldn't do
Just to be with you.
I will do whatever it takes
And along the way, I will not let your heart break.
Is this true love?
That I might be the one to rescue you.
That as we go through each day
There is only one special way
To show my true love for you.
    Jason Neighbors

A New Life

It was no delight to lose her sight overnight, it was a serious plight
But through her loss of sight, many others saw light.
After knowing her sight was gone, a special new life begun.
Sharing her blindness with others around, who was just sitting on the
ground, with not enough strength to cope and with no hope.
Her blindness gave strength to the weak, as she remains so
humble and meek.
Day after day she was able to seek those who thought blindness
was for keeps.
God bless her with some little sight, to encourage others to fight.
When things go wrong we must not grieve, for God knows why.
He will relieve.
For in One's power we all believe, to teach others to live.
Regardless of the pain she bears, there is always someone ready to share.
The concern for others is beyond compare, this is a lesson for us
all to prepare.
She accepted her disability, with her high mentality and ability,
she continued to share and care for that was her way.
As she awakes every day, she bends her knees to pray,
"Lord help me stay and from God not to stray but teach others the way"
She can walk, she can talk, God has given her her lot.
For that, she will never be forgot. Even when she lay in her plot.
    Emelda Cox

We Choose

In our lives, we do not have guarantees.
But we do have the choice to make commitments.
We choose to live life with each other
For such a time is immeasurable to man.
We choose to rejoice with each other in times of triumph
And grieve in times of sorrow.
We choose to give of ourselves, in any way,
To make life a little better
And the days a little brighter

We choose to love one another unconditionally.
    Beth Ann Davis

God Gave All Beauty

God gave all beauty for us to see.
But we were too blinded, in our own needs.
God made rivers, mountains and trees.
But we were too blinded, too blinded to see,
God made Adam, God made Eve, but
They were too blinded, so they ate from the tree.
Then God sent Jesus, to save you and me,
But we were too blinded, too blinded to see,
God put Jesus, on the cross to die
For our sins, but still we were too blinded, too blind to see.
What will happen when we fall on ours knees?
God is forgiving, he will set us free.
He will say you were blinded, but now you can see.
All that I ask child, is you abide in me.
Come my child, come abide in me,
All is forgiven. I have set you free.
    Carole L. Bohn

Untitled

The grains of sand are slipping through our fingers
But what powers have we to bring them back
None
We just reach down and scoop up another handful
Not stare with a blank expression at out empty hand
So why do we then, dwell so much upon the past
Wishing we could go back and change our mistakes
    Joshua Kawachi

Address Unknown

I thought I saw you just the other day,
but, when I turned to call out your name,
once again, you had gone away.
Once again sad and with tears in my eyes,
I turned back around and looked up at the sky.
I started wondering if I was going crazy,
so, after 16 years, I thought I'd write you a letter
thinking things wouldn't seem so hazy.
In the letter, I asked how you've been,
and what you've been up to
all the while remembering the fun things we used to do.
I then stamped and addressed the envelope,
the best way I could
not knowing if it would get to you,
but hoping and praying it would.
It was returned to me marked simply "ADDRESS UNKNOWN,"
Daddy, I guess getting a letter to you in Heaven,
is harder than I could have known.
    Karen H. Boehm

Paths

Pathways must be taken, and paths we must choose,
But when making decisions, our real goals we can't lose.

Success is a word that we are taught to embrace,
But its meaning to one, to another's hard to place.

Complacency is touted to make our lives stale,
But if you are happy, then can life only pale

These are things to remember when setting your course,
Can you tell dreams from ambitions, and what is their source?

Is that promotion you're taking worth all your free time?
How high up Their ladder will you let yourself climb.

Is it Money or Power that makes your heart rise,
Or is it seeing your wife being Mother in his eyes?

Not all of life's lessons can be learned in a school,
It takes courage and insight to grow Old Man not Old Fool.

Jason Bailey

Children First

You've heard it said, "Put children first."
"But why?", some will reply.
"They're just kids who want to play or sit
around and cry."

But think of this and maybe you'll see clearer
what I see . . .
If we will put our children first,
Think of what they can be.

Just give that child a listening ear,
And listen to what she says.
She may be a psychiatrist with you on her couch,
Feeling a need to confess.

Teach him social studies and history,
and how to learn about his world all around.
He may become President of the United States,
and help world peace to abound.

Our children are our future,
We must lead and guide them as such.
So, that, as they grow and accomplish their goals,
We'll live in a world we want to very much.

Denise Gray

I

I a woman skin flesh and bone
But yet a woman who turned to stone
I a mother but yet no mother
with a heart so cold it's going to smother
I a wife and yet no wife
The day will come to end this life
To love to hate to want to cry
To want so much but not to wait
What's right what's wrong what's good what's bad
They cannot say the chance I had
To try so hard to make things right
And yet to end to quit the fight
Can it be my life is through
To finish the things I have yet to do
Then prey to God who lives above
To take me then and keep my love
So much to love so much to need
Can't someone near come hear my plea
I love them all but who loves me
The love I need where can it be

Barbara Smith

Holding On

It has been a little over a year,
but yet what has happened I still fear.
He took a precious gift away from me,
but no one will ever realize, no one will ever see.
It is so hard for me to ignore that day,
but the memories will never go away.
The pain is still very much there,
but I have to deal with it, I have to bare.
I wish people could understand,
I wish through it all someone would have held my hand.
I just need someone to be a guide,
someone in whom I can confide.
Even though this 'nightmare' will never go away,
it will get better with each day.
So I guess I will hold on and stay strong,
hoping nothing else will go wrong.

Jamie L. Gray

Seasons

Having life torn at the roots like a tree,
by an unforetold hurricane.
You're in a whirlwind of emotions that
were unseen by your serenity of basking
in the sun, turning in a cycle with nature
(Summer, Fall, Winter and Spring).

When you land, your world is upside down.
You can't find the spot where you once knew happiness.
You prop yourself as best you can hoping the
roots can take life again, but nothing happens.

All you feel are your roots dying, trying to
reach the top where there are still green leaves,
but as the days go by, these green leaves change
colors as if for the last time of a quicker season
gone by, till at last there is nothing left but a
rotten tree, which will disintegrate with the soil,
as a body when buried will, to ashes

Connie S.

Untitled

I live in a glass bubble, protected from all evil. I'm surrounded by lace-edged hearts and the reflections of thousands of smiles. Inside my crystal palace is where golden wishes covered in melted dew drops are bountiful. Inside my shimmering snowflake I am confronted by silver unicorns and mystical fairies from all angles.

I am suffocated. I'm drowning in sugary sweetness. So unbeknownst to my disguised enemies. With my icicle dagger of crushed diamonds, I'm slowly digging my way out of my icy cottage.

One day I break through the last sliver and I fall from the heavens. Nothing is left of my dream house. My laced edged hearts are piles of dust, my walls just broken glass, my stars no longer glitter and I am nothing but a fallen angel. Left alone to face the dangers of the dark.

But I am free! At last! And though all odds are against me, hope blossoms within, and through the veils of shadows, you'll see my shining grin.

Christy Chesnet

Only once . . .

Only one time in your life
Can you find your one true love.
The one who will be faithful in all things,
will always love you, and never leave you.
And when you see him,
you both escape into your own world,
where nothing can harm you . . .
And you are safe.

Brandi Bloodworth

It's Happening Again

They say history repeats itself, I know this fact is true;
By looking at past experiences and now it's me and you.
In the beginning it is great, we're as happy as can be;
But then something changes and it's happening to you and me.
I don't know what happens to change the way we feel;
But the happiness is gone and the tears are all too real.
The reason for the change, this I do not know;
For if I knew the answer, I would have fixed it long ago.
Why don't I see it coming, so I could stop it then;
But it seems to just sneak up on me and I get hurt again.
Whatever the hidden purpose, I wish it would refrain;
I can't handle another problem, the crying, or the pain.

Carolyn Hovorka

A Gathering Of Crows

A gathering of crows
By the withering corn stalks
Sit silently, sullenly waiting.
Grasping fingers of shadows
From the tips of bare skeletal tree branches
Menacingly stretch out across the cold river,
And relentlessly creep up the banks strewn with brown, limp leaves.
The sky is a palette
Of gray on gray
Cocooning the landscape
As the crows rise
Screeching like avenging angels.
The retiring sun
Casts a purple twilight
As the gathering of crows
Wheel above the woods
On into the descending Halloween night.

Irma Garbarino

Black Sunrise

To understand my carnal rage one must lie inside my blackened cage
As you sleep is my awake
From this I have no escape
Memories are all I can see
Future visions will never be

Crystal is no longer clear, and there is no longer far and near
Writing that will be never read
Blackness stuck inside my head
Smiles on a gentle face
How quickly memories do erase

How little things can mean when once things saw are not seen
All I have is a spoken word
One day I will see what now is heard

Aaron H. Williamson

Beauty So Deep

How silent the beauty so deep within
calling out in waves of joyous clouds
Spirits raise . . . a shadow oak's distant horizons
ancient memories sound so near
dancing divas breathe in harmonious rhythm
a luminous light sounds forth
the illusions begin to fade
dusk and dawn are one . . . together
LISTEN
the sky breathes LIFE
bell chimed tears are swept into SAND
now silent
beauty so deep
graces My child within

Gloria Federwitz

"How Seasons Change"

I fear the seasons change like no other change in life,
can it be that where there is reality there is no change but phases . . .
the answer exists before me.

In winter, picture a tree that has withered from coldness, so does
my heart and soul.

In spring, the birds sing songs of relief from coldness and dullness,
so does my heart and soul . . . fly, fly, unleash your love.

In summer, the burning unbearable heat releases my soul and heart to
show how much, once released, my love makes me do crazy and wild things . . .

In fall, this season like no other, shows the reality of evolution
of life's subtle changes. My oh my how seasons change . . .

Charis Desirae Cannon

"Wondering"

Have you ever stopped and wondered . . . why the world seems
such a mess?
Can it be the people in it, not giving it their very best?
As you walk along life's highways and there's a stranger standing there.
Who is having trouble getting someplace . . . anywhere.
Do you offer him assistance in a kind and friendly way?
Or do you even bother to glance his way today?
This life is full of highways, some long, some short and such.
There's some that's traveled little and there's some that's traveled much.
But there's none that's oh, so lonely, as the one that's traveled alone.
So do your part in helping - whether it be lots, little or hardly none.
For it might be Jesus calling, asking help, alms or love.
It might be He who's testing - to find the size of your space above.

Helen Smith

The Journey

Can you see up there, how big is that boat
Can you admire, the beauty of it's whiteness
I am overwhelmed, with what I witness
Because instead of fear, it is giving me courage and hope

Sorrow is heard, discreetly, from behind
Even then, I am drawn by the warmth surrounding me
But still, it is hard letting yourself go to sea
When there are so many loved ones on our mind

We will be there, as before, together
As guardian angels, looking on our children affectionately
Such beautiful faces, that our love has created tenderly
Now covered with sadness, but keeping all the memories alive, forever

Why the ignorance of the unknown is so chilling
And it is with anguish, that we speak about this journey
Nevertheless, all mankind with is belief, will be taken, night and day
Turning this painful end, to a new beginning.

Dediated to the Lacombe's Family

Josee Labranche

Peace And Hope

The gangs, the drugs, the murders.
Can't we make them see, that this is
not the way to be?
We don't have to fight.
We don't have to scream.
We can make them see,
that there is a light at the end of
this dark tunnel, and that peace and hope
is what we need.

Christy Thompson

At Days End

At the end of the day when you lay down to rest
Can you honestly say you have given your best

Have you done something good for a neighbor or friend
Or been unfair and mean and would not even bend

Life is too short which you've often seen
So try to be pleasant and not be so mean

Be patient with others and be a good friend
You'll be able to rest better when the day comes to an end

Don't forget to thank God for the things that you have
And remember to thank Him for your mom and dad

Thank Him for friends that you meet on the way
Some that have left us and ones here today

You could never be happy life wouldn't be worth living
If you keep holding a grudge and not be forgiving

For the way that you act from January to December
That will be the way that you'll be remembered.

Bill Adas

A Hand For The Tears (A Villanelle)

Someone's hand through these long lonely years,
Can you see this heart that's torn inside?
It is filled, it's a cup full of tears,

Too many pains, sorrows, aches, and fears,
The heart is broken, the crack is wide,
Someone's hand through these long lonely years,

The heart was screaming, yet no one hears,
It gave up, it just sat there and cried,
It is filled, it's a cup full of tears,

The storm - it settles, the sky - it clears,
Help has come, stemming the hopeless tide,
Someone's hand through these long lonely years,

Out pours the heart to these lis'ning ears,
The river runs free it's not denied,
It is filled, it's a cup full of tears,

Brightness and lightness the heart now wears,
Where went and sadness you tried to hide?,
Someone's hand through these long lonely years,
It is filled, it's a cup full of tears.

Charles W. Hacker Jr.

Contraction

I
can't tell
if the life
we were made to
share is going to be
an easy and happy one, but
what this promise can do for you
is assure you that from this moment until
who knows when, as long as you're in this
world, there will be no one who will
love and care for you as much
as the one who holds you
so close but so far.
I only ask that
you are excited
to see
me.

David Doughton

Invitation

Care to walk with me through time and space;
Care to touch the wind and really feel nature's embrace.

Come along and breathe the mountain air,
       pass through trees stout and bold;
Sit in the world's finest school and learn of wisdom ages old.

Watch the great dark clouds churn and muster about the peaks,
Giving gifts of rain and snow in exchange for the passage they seek.

Come wander and wonder with me,
       leaving society's security without a care;
To witness the grandeur of the good earth —
       come along with me, if you dare.

David C. LaRue

"Emily dreams"

Baby voice, babbling and sighing
dreaming of a warm embrace and rocking arms,
a happy day of dry diapers and no tumbles,
of mashed bananas and no strained peas,
A sample of big brother's chocolate cake
Good even left over on the rug.
For a non-fussy outfit and a second longer than yesterday
Standing without any help.

Cindy Glass

"Cracked Glass Escape"

What would you do if no one was there
Caught is your body trapped without air
Breathe through a bottle with spidery hair
Tranquiled delusions of minds that aren't there

Because another cracked glass escaped
While the reels go round erasing the tape . . .

Your beyond this life without direction
Thoughts of another is one's exception
Your a changing product of it's conception
Behind closing doors of perception

Mirrors reflect another cracked glass escape
As the reels go round erasing the tape . . .

Oceans of sand sounds within the sea
Teachers of zen learn theosophy
As a Pharaoh of fortune invades a country
While a pill burning amber is smoldering free

Smoking cracked glass to escape
While the reels go round erasing the tape . . .

The sun in time space within the moon.
Bottled flies free die only too soon.

Daniel R. Iazeolla

Love You Baby

I wish I could talk to you every second of the day
Cause baby I'm thinking of you anyway
Every time I hear your voice I have no fear
Cause I know you'll always be near
I've only been without you for a little while
But when I see you again I'll surely smile
Across the miles I miss your touch
Cause baby I love you oh so much
You are that light of my life
We share our laughter and tears
We help each other to overcome our fears
I love you baby I really do
I'll always hope our love is true

Kara Banda

Life

Tongues of fear lashing up at me, as I walk to the
cave of the unknown.
I enter the cave full of hesitation, but through sheer
determination, I walk through to the other side.
As I walk to the forest of silence, the noise is
hurting my ears.
And then I know life is a contradiction and time
is the fear kicking at my heels.
Now I am in the forest of silence, as I walk on
the leaves, they do not crunch; they crumble just
as we do at death.
It is like that all throughout the forest.
Life is a raging sea of obstacles that doesn't end till
we crumble at death.

Jessica Merkel Keller

Life's Changes

Change, Change, Change, so few things remain the same -
Change your address, change your name
Change the rules, change the game.
Change of attitude, change of expression,
Change your major, change your direction.
Change the temperature, change the time,
Change of a dollar, change of a dime,
Change the menu, change the page,
Change your mind, change your age.
Change the color, change the size.
Change your clothes, change your exercise.
Change gear, change telephone number
Change job, change the hours you slumber.
Change in weather, change in fashion,
Change the tune, change the passion.
Change the tempo, change the date,
Change old habits, change your mate.
Change the blame, change the reason
Change of winds, change of season.
Change, Change, Change, so few things remain the same.

Eleanore Johnson

"Songs Sung By The Journey"

Songbird flies upon dissolving, white clouds,
Climbing and descending - windward, she sings.
Guided by moonlight when the pale night shrouds,
She flees from Fall's presence, and waits for Spring's.

Flocks of crickets creek and croak to the dawn,
Calling anew the day — with past behind.
Away, like the crickets, day will pass on,
And new crickets croak to a new dawn shined.

The songbird sours through the pale, windward flights
Singing for her songs silenced by the breeze,
With her wings weathered by the endless plights.
Below, whistling winds dance about the trees.
Cricket's croaks are swallowed by midnight's mouth,
While the songbird breaks night's wind to fly south.

Jason Ludwig

The Love I Seek

I have always thought of love as something everyone
could experience.
Love would bring happiness and joy into my life.
The love I seek I've yet to find, searching time and time again.
Love closer than a brother, love more than a friend.
Diligently I've search for love, love without hurt, sorrow or pain.
The bible tells me this love can only be found in your name.
Thank GOD my search is over. Please come into my life.
I LOVE YOU JESUS!

Adolphus Life' Foster

I Am On Ocean

I am on ocean.
Caressing the sandy shores of life,
with light fingers of tides too strong to be denied.

Softly rippling,
touch by the warm breezes.

Majestic waves
thrown upon the tempests of the fates.

Crashing upon the high cliffs,
and eroding them into rocky shores.

And peaceful waters return.

Claire Greyling

A Poet Song

Poetry and leaves burst forth from reaches uncharted —
Come Spring, fresh and green, shining Cezanne green, blue green,
Bright green gifts of Winter's, hiding, bid by the voice of God,
Buds twirling, twisting birth's journey from Adam,
Dogwoods and words flower, coaxing colors before emerald bows,
Plows turn sweet earth loam — froth rows plead for barefoot children,
Shouts and glees push the poet from sleep and words meet paper
Sun sets — moon burns — seeds jump, bump through dew damp-
ened shell of loam,
Rake and smooth — prepare — weed — hoe, chop
Chop, chop, this weed, this word, this seedling,
Stop! Let it flower, — songs must always be sung,
Words must live — life is ever,
Never break the root or hand,
Let the farmer tend the earth and let the poet write.

Anne Cecelia Armistead

Lilies Of The Valley

From under winter's white blanket of cold
Comes a genesis; the young from the old.
A sprig of lush life, sprouts up fresh and new
Witness to the spring, the wind, and the dew.
On splendid wings of jade, it flies through May,
Releasing its flowers one sunny day.
Silently supreme in the valley green
It is by far the purest to be seen.
Soft white bells chime out their magical tune,
Swinging gracefully in the month of June.
The proud rose smells of passion and of love,
But these lilies perfume is far above.
As sweet honey is to the golden bee-
Lilies' sensuous fragrance is to me.
Simply perfect, and mighty as the oak;
Surviving rain, thunder, fire, and smoke.
Their perfumed voices will forever sing,
Of beauty and peace on every heartstring.

Josh A. Getchell

"To Weave A Soul"

Certain threads convey somber, others are livid
But certainly some are gay, some are thick, some thin.
Each motley rug, once woven, or in progression,
is as diverse as the snowflake, yet more vivid.
With hope, the loom is girded by diverse spindles,
which the weaver uses to derive a sharp soul.
For, the more threads, the better the rug, (as a whole).
Threads can't be dismantled, once entwined, nor dwindle
with age. Thralling on the girth of the loom, the rug's
dimension acquires variance with duration.
Fluxing patterns change with each new thread's perception,
and hold tightly together with the weaver's tug.
The weaver's goal is for most threads to be of love.
Love, O' yes love; enough love to complete the rug.

Alexander J. Noser

Being Different

Condemned for wearing braids in their hair
Condemned for being breechcloth heir
Looked down upon because of red skin
And for being of savage kin

They wanted a peaceful way of life
Instead they received pain and strife
Riding ponies, hunting buffalo and living in tepees
Raising children, caring for elders and working with beads
Moving around from place to place
Finding camp grounds became a race

Once their tranquil life was broken
Anything else was but a token
In a white-man designed life
For the Native American brave and wife

    Deborah C. Leichliter

Pow Wow

Red, brown, white, and yellow feathers
   cover your head and back.
Bells tied around your ankles,
   your feet make music as you dance and sing:
    Hey Ya! Hey! Ya!
     Hey Ya! Hey Ya!
Ground shakes below, sky darkens
   rain begins to fall.
Not far from the chanting site, a woman and her children use
   their hands as machinery.
Her children laugh while they make multicolored
   bead necklaces. Each bead put on one by one,
    until the black string can be seen no more.
The sun shines down, reflects onto your big
   brown eyes, as you pound silver metal into jewelry.

Hand made rings, necklaces, and bracelets, with turquoise stones
   ranging in size and shape, cover your table.
Next to you, an old woman is weaving blankets
   and rugs. Hands hard and dry. Wrinkles
    darkened by the sun, cover her face.

    Irene M. Lopez

The Disdained

They lie on cardboard remnants braced against worn brick walls,
Covered with ancient newspapers sheltering from the cold,
Their shopping cart nearby loaded with worthless debris.
Unkempt, uncared for, unwelcome, scorned by the scurrying rabble.

Their faces are gaunt, soiled, their hair an infested tangled nest.
Mouths tremulous, gaping toothless holes, eyes rheumy and vacant.
Parched lips cracked and bloody, mumbling to themselves.
Clothes threadbare and shabby, feet covered with squalid rags.

My embarrassment yields to disgust and revulsion
As dirt-encrusted hands reach into bins of discarded waste
In search of a crust of bread, a shred of cast-off clothing.
Anything to ease the pangs of hunger and cover their naked shame.

But I have become inured to their self-abasement and despair,
Hardened to their misery, unmindful of their pain.
I renounce their humility, repress the horror of their plight.
I reject my feeling of guilt and refuse to acknowledge my impotence.

I pass them by on streetcorners, ignoring their outstretched cup.
I am deaf to their appeals, their blessing echoing in my wake.
I have become oblivious to their misfortune, calloused to their fate.
I barely see them anymore.

    Harvey N. Lippman

Raggedy Ann

Deep in an old trunk beneath all the clothes;
Covered with grime from her head to her toes;
Dressless she was and her head minus hair,
A pitiful sight she was to me there.

Memories suddenly sprang to my mind
Of this Raggedy Ann you left behind;
Like the time you set up the barber shop,
And hair from her head you began to crop.

Your love for this doll was often made plain;
You'd lend her to me if I were in pain.
Rememb'ring this love, it seemed 'most a shame
Not to resurrect this mem'rable dame.

So, into the bath and off to coiffeur;
New clothes she will need her poise to assure.
Cleaned and undaunted by years in the trunk,
She smiles up at you with wonderful spunk.

If she could but find a place on your shelf.
I'm sure that she'd be most proud of herself.
Wherever you go, whatever you do,
The sign on her heart still says, "I love you."

    Ira W. Finger

Inner City Life

Turmoil, strife, guns, and a knife
crack, dope, smoke, and no hope
litter, being alone, bleak, and stoned
dirt, rats, poverty, and stats
garbage, smells, graffiti, and no one tells
pimps, hoarse, police, and abandoned stores
death, gangs, destruction, and loud bangs
young, bold, helpless, and old
no grass, trees, plants, and nothing to see
despair, concern, poverty, and no where to turn
hopeless, welfare, frightened, and no one cares,
wholes in the walls, babies cries, no food, nor future
and all that leaves is major attitude!
you call that life?

    Debbie Powell-Everett

The Valley

The stream flows gently through the valley
creating beauty once again on Earth,
Grass grows ever so quietly through the valley
making a softer landing for a future fall,
Winds whisper through the valley
calming all those restless and waiting,
Trees growing in the forest of the valley
protect the life of us,
The sun sets along the horizon of the valley
and its rays become one with us,
Life is brought to the valley
a child is born,
Growing up in the valley
the children know you watch over them,
Walking through the valley
they are protected by you,
Being put to rest in the valley
we are now one with you, You,
Our Father above,
Have allowed us to love within your valley . . .

    Angela Lincoln

The Promise

Scudding clouds and pelting rain
dance outside my windowpane.
The weather speaks of changing times,
and marks well summer's swift demise.

Mother Nature is busy tidying her house,
sweeping all that lies before her.
Creating naked branches of maples and oaks,
that resemble charcoal smudges on an easel.

The blustery winds makes me feel like pulling
my little house around me,
to protect me from the coming storm!

And yet, life becomes one cyclical change of seasons,
Birth, Childhood, Youth and Old Age;
or Spring, Summer, Winter and Fall.

The Birth of Life in Spring is full of promise.
Childhood and Summer arrive, hopefully full of sunny days.
Too quickly followed by Winter, cold, stiffness and old age.
Finally, Fall appears and all must go back to the earth.

But, we must remember that the Promise of Spring
is Eternal and always follows the Fall.

Claire Ford

A Glimpse Of Eternity

I've been tossed and I've been driven and the waves were
dashing me
against the jagged rocks of oppression and life's anxieties;
I was trying hard to keep my head above the waters of life's angry
and turbulent sea,
I was drowning and I saw a huge mountain hovering over me!

Darkness was all around me, and this mountain was blocking
my view, I cried out for help, and I heard a kind voice whisper
"Don't be afraid because I AM here with you".
He stretched forth his hand and I took it, although the
light was dim,
in the flash of a moment, I recognized his voice
and by faith I followed him!
He moved that mountain, so that I could clearly see
I saw a light so bright and beautiful, yes I saw eternity!

As I stepped out into the sunshine, I had a glimpse of eternity,
I looked up and saw a rainbow looking down on me!
Underneath his wings he lifted me up from the troubled sea
I'm following the rainbow onto the path of righteousness
for I know that if I walk therein I will find true happiness!

Delores N. McKinney

The River And I

To sit by the great Mississippi on a warm summer
day is one of the joys of living. For here (to all who
worship at her shrine) nature casts an hypnotic spell.
In this setting of pristine beauty my thoughts soar to
new dimensions, and I am free of the boundaries of time and space.

The vaulting sky reveals the existence of other
worlds. Towering trees defy the pull of gravity. The
warm summer breeze is the elixir of life, the soft
green grass offers comfort and rest. While the inexorable
power of the river over life and death rides on its crest.

I identify with the river, struggling in its
currents - sometimes submerged - sometimes
my head above water - reaching frantically for
branches of trees to pull myself to high ground.

Henry Botts

God's Promises

God has not promised us lives without pain
Days without troubles-sunshine without rain
Comfort at all times, blues never to show
And always love's treasures wherever we go
All our wants granted as soon as we ask
Our lives full of pleasure whatever the task

But God has promised us strength from above
Help with our burdens-a sign of His love
If we humbly ask for favors we crave
He will grant them and tell us always be brave
To carry our loads until our lives cease
When he'll help us to glory with comfort and peace

So with that Great Promise from Heaven above
Let us endure to the end and thus merit God's Love.

Phrona Furman (Deceased)

Submitted by Her Son Gordon Furman

Autumn Soldiers

The golden rays reached
deep into the woods,

Turning rows and rows of trees
into shining soldiers,
layers and layers of leaves
into glorious flags.

The color of the carpet spread under their feet,
the golden soldiers marched to nature's song.

As the darkness crept into the woods,
the soldiers marched the final march.

In the last flicker of orange light,
the flags waved for the last time.

Silently, the soldiers retreated
into the crisp dark night.

Junko Geddes

Untitled

I'm falling
Deeper and deeper and deeper
Until
Aaah, sweet landing
Resting upon this cozy kidney
Watching the reds and blues
Grasping all that is throbbing and pulsating
I'm engrossed and engulfed by this scene
Gone on a tubular journey - in search of my destiny
Sweet destiny - then agonizing discovery
The blood is too thick, the skull too hard, the bones too brittle
But I'm trapped
The cavity is closing in on me
Banging, pounding on the chest - let me out! Let me out!
I'm not released
Pounding harder on the walls - let me out! Let me out!
I'm imprisoned
Oh, my fate is here
To suffer and struggle here forever
('Less I slip out through the belly-button)

Antonietta Tarnell

I'm Traveling On

I wake up each morning to face a new day.
Depending on Jesus to show me the way.
By faith in my Savior I'm traveling on.
Rejoicing while trav'ling through pathways unknown
I'm trusting in Jesus to always be near.
Because He has promised I've nothing to fear.
Although I may falter or fall by the way.
I know then for certain he hears when I pray.
Some-times I grow weary, the road is so steep.
But I must keep going I will not retreat.
If night overtakes me, I'll still travel on.
With Jesus beside me I'm never alone.

Adele Plunkett

Curtain Of Doom

A thin sheet of doom slowly
    descends upon my body disturbing my thoughts.

Now they turn into the direction of gloom,
    ever so slightly the darkness falls upon me,
        leaving me groping for brighter thoughts.

Reaching back into the depths of my memories,
    I struggle to bring forth something
        glowing with love or sunshine.

It is so hard to tear open the sheet of blackness,
    Its dusty film is spotted with tears as
        I try ever so hard to stretch apart
            this steel curtain of doom.

It's blackness is so domineering and strong
    always trying to get the better of me.
But slowing into my veins, the blood is surging.

It's warmth tingling into my fingers, heart and thoughts,
    Making me rip open this depressing gray curtain.

Behind it glows the sunlight or moonlight
    with beams ever so bright and warm,
        filling my soul with life again.

Donna Castelo

Tempest Wind

The Tempest Wind - cold it is, hot it's not
Destroying all in its path
It can't be stopped

Reckless, Rough, Rolling 'Round
Rare it is, it can't be found

Likened to a Merry-go-round
'Round and 'round it goes
Where it goes no one knows
If it can't be found
How did it get here?
Disappearing as quickly as it appears

Likened to a candle once so bright
it grows dim
Slowly, slowly dies the tempest wind

The beauty of Life is Death
From Death comes forth Life
Surely this is a mysterious life
My love for Life will always last
But only until I breathe
my very, very, last.

Anderson Roache III

Destruction

So much destruction in the land,
destruction here, destruction there,
and no one seems to care,
that we don't even share anymore,
even out time seen so unaware,
sometime it seems like a roller coaster,
that goes round and round,
but never stop anywhere,
even our family never get together anymore,
is it because we don't care,
or is it because we don't have love anymore to share,
but think about the love our father in
heaven gave us,
and you know what he was aware,
and think about how he is always there,
because he's everywhere,
even when trouble comes he is there,
when death comes he is there,
when sickness comes he is there,
his love will always be there.

Hattie L. Moyler

Thy Blackened Soul

Wolves cry, pierce thy heart.
Devils dig deep within.
Fresh blood drips from these blackened lips, my heart beating still.
What wrong have I done to taste such a wine.
Illusion pass beyond reach, wings have broken, will I find my light
    forbidden?
Faith is gone, what is left to believe?
Will you believe my relinquished truth; drink from my heart taste a
    wine unpure.
Touch the edge, death reclaims thy filthy soul.
Devils promise, bargains made, soul's gone evermore.
Wolves cry, pierce thy heart.
Devils dig deep within.
Fresh blood drips from these blacked lips; my heart beating still.
Illusion pass beyond reach, wings have broken, will I find my light
    forbidden?
Dragons circle my wasted caress, stretched upon a moistened earth.
Wars began, actions taken, souls escape reality, driven to the after
world of truth not taken.
Secret shadows awake within, rest before time.
Banish the thought, banish me, drunken savior fill your goblet once more.
Nightmares haunt a dawning shadow. Awake to taste my wine.
Sleep to ear wolves crying.
My soul's gone evermore.

Jamie Quirk

Dew

On the leafless branch
dew visits and lays herself,
her movements so delicate and graceful
like long and slender fingers of a Javanese dancer
immersed in the magic of the gamelan tune.

Then, look at the greetings offered by the breeze
on the leaves that begin to sway.
In a little while longer
the dew will vanish with the drift of the wind
to the ethereal world on the other side
beyond the reach of my spirit.

Anna Maria Siti Kawuryan

Ascent From Disillusion

I find myself living in other worlds, other times
Dimensions beckon to my spirit, to my very soul
This world grays to petty political bickerings
Doing nothing and blaming every other fool

Or descends, spiralling into unimaginative murder
Mayhem and chaos ever on the brink
Of that fine and flimsy madness we call civilization

Where is the magic? Where are the dragons?
Where is the good that battles and wins against evil?
I long for those worlds where even in the shades of gray
We can sort out which side to take in the war

This world crumbles into ambiguity
The strain and burden of day to day life
Enormous in its mediocrity

I fall, seeking shelter in the realms of enchantment
The far future, the ancient past
The parallel worlds that exist just beyond
My fingertips touch

Julia M. Alldredge

The Colorado

The baton of creation
Directing forest and cliff steeply upward
To challenge clouds
Boldly surrenders such architecture to blazing blue
At altitudes attended by stars and eagles,
Where renewable primeval music
In myriad atonal murmurs
Is yielded from sun-dazzled snow,
Whispering past the roots of pine.
Liquescence of melodies ensue, and grow,
Accompanied by eventual cascading power —
Finally to carve colossal landscapes.
Guiding itself toward the sea
This symphony crashes downward
   only to lose its destination,
   dismally transposed where depleting deserts wait
   and lavish cities drain its life —
   the glory is diverted to a muddy finale' —
   the mighty theme unfinished.

Dorothy St. Clair Bradshaw

Suspense

From keep of stolid dark, a lawless knife
Dislodged reclusive shadows from the room,
Pried hapless calm and vexed dry seeds to life;
Faint ends of yesterday, now, coarsely rued.
It stirred the stealth of hope she most esteemed,
So safely furled elsewhere; lulled from harm
Deigned if the eye should crack and wit should spring
Aloof dismay, fraught 'neath her proper charm.
Unschooled when braving dull tears not to wet,
When flesh or paltry shields prove less than fair;
So fierce this throe some early tempest set
On artless youth, it, since, enlisted her there.
'Til I know why bleak folly plagues the sense,
'Side love, I shall e'er linger in suspense.

Frederich Lange

Seed Of Thought

The ability to reason
distinguishes the animal from the man . . .
yet, when looking around, 'tis simple to see
the lack of the same throughout each land.

"Allegiance to the Flag",
they cry, most as taught and trained . . .
All for the right, forget the left
The victors record the game.

Always looking out for, yet never into
the thoughts for "which it stands".
Waving their flags, "Allegiance", they shout
still yet to comprehend.

Circles spinning,
history repeats again.
For all thought springs from a single seed . . .
Love your fellow man.

Christian Ros

My Quest

My quest in life — what should it be?
Do I do what the world demands of me?

Since I was a child, I did what I was told;
Working hard, saving money should be my main goal.

Attending church, a must, to thank God for His blessing;
Instead of love, I learned to fear — oh my was that oppressing.

In spite of it all, I knew that God was loving as He could be;
Who else would send His only son to suffer for you and me?

Mankind has made all the rules and claimed they're from above;
The only thing God wants from us is unselfish, glorious love!

Kindness shared everyday in things we do for others;
Doesn't matter what color we are, after all we're sisters and brothers.

Wouldn't life be wonderful if money was never invented?
Worry and strife to make ends meet — God surely never intended.

Isn't it time to throw away the old and begin to start anew?
If each of us would change just a little, our world would start to change too.

It will begin with me I swear - today my quest will start;
Stop thinking with my head — instead start feeling with my heart!

My life will be so much enriched — not my bank account;
My spirit will grow in leaps and bounds — that's what life's about!!

Josephine Ann Bonomo

The Little Sparrow

Little sparrow has; fought a good battle, and now he's ready to collect his reward, by taking his flight.

The Blues; of anyone which, has one's heart feeling a lost; has their blues painting their skies.

The little sparrow, was just born, and now dies the cruelty of Cancer in the bone marrow, has shot an arrow in the hearts of the little sparrow's parents . . .

They had just gotten little sparrow, and Oh! What pain the thought of little sparrow slipping bye.

The arrow of sorrow, hits little sparrow's parents hearts; in having to tell, little sparrow good-bye, as they part tomorrow.

The pain that little sparrow, has suffered will pass away, and as the days go away; little sparrow's parents are left here to say. "Our Little Sparrow has, taken his flight, and has flown away."

Dorothy Lewis

Accepting

Lies, falsehoods.
Do I really know you?
Give me hope — that was shattered months ago.
Forgive me for not seeing you for who you are through the lies.
The need to lie is overwhelming.
Believe your lies, live your lies, but without me.
I married a falsehood.
I've been cheated. Cheated out of everything, that was sacred to me.
May I find those sacred things again.
Holding close to my own God, forgiving myself, knowing my
Mistakes I have made, lying to myself and others during
This time.
Let me live my life truthfully again, from here.
Let me go
Without a fight, knowing the lies will not cease with you.
Please let us part with what love is left.
Heal yourself, as I have.
God loves you, God loves me,
Please know that.

Eileen Millsop

A "Do Not" Prayer

Dear God:
    Do not always give us the strength
    to speak about ourselves at length,
    But, instead, make us sit and hear
    A lonely person's doubts and fear.
    Do not always give us the sight
    To see the darkness and be in fright
    But, instead, please let us see
    That darkness brings serenity.
    Do not always make us haste
    That we do no have the time to "waste,"
    A precious day with the very old
    And hear the stories they unfold.
    In short - dear God - do please train
    Our hearts to over-rule our brain.

Gina Grazia Squadrito Hoppinthal

The Reflection

When you look in the mirror, what do you see?
Do you say to yourself, only I know me?

When you're laughing and smiling,
Is it sincere?
If you're not really sure,
Take a look in the mirror.

The reflection you see is what you display
To the people you meet
Day after day.

Is kindness and sincerity
Seen in your face,
Or is anger and suspicion
There in its place?

Your expressions can talk
While not saying a word.
People can hear
The face can be heard.

So remember the next time
Your face shows expression, keep in mind
It's a tacit confession.

Dennis Burkman

The Key

You look in a mirror and what do you see?
Do you see a locked door and you're the key?
Or are you trapped deep inside?
Now looking for a place where you can hide.

Only you can't hide from yourself and your thoughts.
And there's no escape routes or big empty pots.
You might try to run away from all your strife,
But you can't run away from your real life.

To lift this burden will take more than a day.
You'll have to go back and right the wrongs you've made.
It won't be easy, it will be very hard.
But when you're done you'll be holding the highest card.

You'll then be the key to unlock that door,
And like an eagle you'll be free to soar.
Now look in the mirror again and tell me
Who do you really want to be?

Cholana Nichols

Happiness Found

Is happiness so difficult to find, where should one begin,
Does it come from those around us, or does it come from within;

Is happiness so important we search our whole lives through,
Looking for someone special or something of great value;

Why can't we look to just ourselves to find the happiness we seek,
Instead of blaming all the others, when it's ourselves who are so weak;

Cast your doubts your fears, be strong in what you do,
Happiness can't be bought or sold, for happiness is just being you;

Open up your heart, let the sunshine light your way,
Let the peace of God within you make your happiness today;

Count your many blessing, be thankful for what they bring,
Be secure in who you are, make life a lovely thing;

For when you know deep inside that you've done the best you can,
You'll find a brand new happiness to share with your fellow man.

Gloria Marshall

Daylight Saving Time

Daylight saving time
doesn't make the day any longer -
Neither does it make it shorter
no weaker or no stronger,

Daylight comes just before sunrise.
And dark just after sunset -
There's still twelve hours in a day or night
and that makes twenty four hours yet,

That's the way it was in biblical times.
twelve hours in a night or day -
and I don't care how you set the clock.
it will always be that way.

There's fourteen hundred and forty minutes
in a day and night -
Divide by two that's seven twenty.
if I have it figured right.

I never was too good in math.
but my horse sense is fine -
But I never could figure where we gain.
With day light saving time!

John Wright

Lay Then Down

Lay then down and leave then at his feet;
Don't let satan weaken your faith, and make you know defeat.
He will take your burden whatever it is, when you leave it to Him.
And your pathways will never be dim.
When you trust it to him, he will make you strong,
And put within your heart a song.
Nothing is impossible, when you entrust it all to Him in everything
And much blessing and refreshment to your soul
He will bring.
You truly will be a conqueror when you entrust
all to Him in all you do,
And let him your strength and faith renew.
The joys and rewards of trusting him are truly
beyond compare,
And a true, total peace He truly will give
when with Him you share.
Lay then down, each and everyone,
And entrust them to Jesus, God's Son.

Hope Rhodes

Untitled

The pictures on the wall
don't tell the stories at all.

The way she really feels
is hidden deep beyond discussions
at family meals.

The exterior facade that she portrays
helps her to disguise her inner rage.

She knows she must fulfill her one true dream,
a dream others always disapprove of it seems.

But it is a challenge for her you see;
and no matter how dangerous,
she must answer to her inner "me".

So she now starts down the inviting road,
not knowing what her future will hold.

Camela Krebs

Steps

A cold wind blows as I leave my car and walk up the steps to my front door.
I listen to the sound of our bracelets as they chime together.

Mine, a silver birthday present from years ago.
Yours, I found today in the glove box behind the ice scraper and
some old Christmas tapes.

The gold plating is fading, but not the name engraved
"Tabatha" (with a tiny heart in front)
is still so clear on this bracelet and in my heart as well . . .

But the judge said steps don't matter. (not stepmothers anyway)

We don't get to have a say. Or a hug. Or a kiss. Or a visit just to
say, "I LOVE YOU"

No; not even to return a little girl's lost birthday present —
A child who called me "Mother" and once gave me a silver bracelet.

Dauphne Rhodes

Flight . . .

Skillfully, the wings of gulls
    draw forth a crimson edge of morning sky
Dispersing the cold veil of night.

Soaring in long slow circles,
    their mournful cries pierce the stillness
    (My heart in perfect resonance . . .)

Beneath their flight . . .
    distinguishable becomes the shoreline,
Where tracings of night waves
    and the pungent brine of seaweed
Expose the clinging oysters on jagged rocks.

Hidden within each calloused shell lays a secret
    of pure cool succulence . . .
    (Awaiting the sweet moisture of your tongue . . .)

Golden now the sun's warmth upon the shore
    transforming the deep primordial sea of night
The myriad stars falling to grains of sand.

Sadly, . . . the rhythm of incoming waves
    echoes the memory of your heart, against my cheek
    (Softly whispering goodbye . . .)

Ginia Pati

Alive In Your Eyes

Looking in your face my heart's captured,
Drawn in by the ghost that was once real,
Tauntingly invisible but seen,
Emotions thought lost I again feel.

I touch the flame of a candle burnt,
Here in her soft glow I want to drown,
While painfully aware that she's lost,
In a mirror never to be found.

Like going through pictures from the past,
By your memories I'm taken back,
In your eyes I see the me I was,
The me before my soul dressed in black.

For the moment I stare in silence,
I can see the smile that hangs brightly,
My eyes glistening and filled with life,
This warm image I embrace tightly.

In this gaze I can almost feel that life,
Though I know in me it can't be revived,
So longingly I journey through your eyes,
To where the me that died remains alive.

Bria Eli

We'll Join In Heaven . . .

As I see you pass from here,
Draws us close, I want to be near.
Embraced from the earthly day,
In heaven shall your spirit lay.
Open arms, Jesus awaits,
As you enter through the Pearly Gates.
Knowing you'll find such wonderful peace,
The love left behind shall never cease.
No more disease, no more pain,
To be with our Lord is a Christians gain.
I look towards Heaven and see you smile,
Someday we'll join, it will be just a short while.

Jennifer C. Grammer

Life's Illusions

Smile at me, from your twisted realities.
Dream with me of fairies
dancing on magic carpets.
Carry me away to your desert islands
thick with blackberry vines.
Sleep with me
on plains of endless grey
where black turns to white
and white to black,
and colors fade to meaningless sepia.
Envelope me in beautiful seas of your
manipulated words.
Caress me,
make
me
forget.

Christina Piluso

"My Dad"

A beep of the horn, a flash of the lights,
he drives all day, he drives all night.
He's known for his belts, his buckles and boots,
no one would guess he owns a blue suit.
He's suppose to be naughty, loud and a drunk.
At home drives a heap, with stash in the trunk!?
The road is a game, his truck is his toy,
he thinks like a man, behaves like a boy.
The highway's his friend, his wife he can trust,
cafe's are no good, and cops are a bust!
Where did this image of truck drivers come?
Not from my dad he isn't the one.
He doesn't like belts, buckles cause sores,
he doesn't wear boots, his foot was broken before.
Rowdy and loud, maybe just once or twice,
but most of the time my dad is quite nice.
At home, yes a car, and maybe a heap.
Of course it's real special, it's real name is "Pete".
The road is a living, cops help give him life,
for you he is giving, RESPECT him alright!

Judy Fenn

Beach Days

The soaring sight of gliding gulls floating in the wind
Dropping down their prey, looking like they have sinned.

The sound of waves sitting still but yet moving
With the sand in your toes it seems so very soothing.

The peaceful singing of a loving loon
As the sun goes down and wakes up the moon.

The crabs dancing into the dark blue night
When the moon is a big round dazzling sight.

The sun comes up in all great shades
And then the ocean bellows for days.

The day is bright and the sand is warm
As the clouds collect in one great form.

As a slight pitter-patter hits the sea
The wind rushes to be free.

The clouds get dark as a dark blue night
Then the lightning makes an enormous light.

The seashells wash upon the seashore
And then the ocean comes up in a big huge roar.

As nature's fight comes to an end
The beaches sand begins to mend.

Danielle Pappalardo

Ocean Wind

Wind blows, ocean roars, sand specks fly,
  Dunes shift, clouds rift, surf roars high,
   Clams burrow, seagulls roar, fishes hide,
     When west wind comes and brings the tide.

Light changes, sun streaks sky, evening comes,
  Shadows lengthen, beaches shorten, day's lost sun,
   Water's grey, moontime's nigh, waves are wide
     When west wind comes and brings the tide.

Bernice M. Gray

A Tribute To Ron Goldman And Nicole Brown Simpson

Ashes to ashes,
Dust to dust,
In the quiet grave you lie,
Only now did you find peace.

Your secrets still untold,
Your mysteries unrevealed,
Shattered fragments of your life,
Were spilled on court floors.

Your tragedies were impressed,
Into the hearts of all Americans,
Whether black or white,
Young or old.

The glowing embers,
Of your lives,
Continue to live on,
Forever in all of us.

Jenni Schopper

Darkness

   His mind races through the clouds as he lays
dying on the cold street soon the darkness devours
him his heart stops beating, his mind goes blank
and as the sun begins to rise his body goes cold and stale.

   I ask myself why do evil things have to happen
to the innocent? Why must the innocent die to please
the guilty, but then why are the guilty pleased with
killing the innocent.

Alisha Sprague

King Of My Soul

Within my soul, a garden behold with wondrous beauty within,
each flower characterizes each picture of life,
each person of past, through all toil and strife,
but deep in the garden of my soul, my heart showers a unique flower
alone, leader of the blossom, amazingly he grows,
showered with my deepest devotion, each petal my love coats,
as the fertile soil caress his body his roots dig deeper into my soul.

Oh! dear prince,
here you shall remain for all seasons to come,
as I shine my love onto you,
showering you with your utmost needs,
as you grow,
yes, as you grow,
a budding knight,
you become my king.

Jodi Ann Cortez

Tribute to a Friend

Phoebe, Dear Phoebe, we all love you so;
Each in our own way. None want you to go.

You know where you've come from, you know what you've done.
You've been a great influence on myself, and everyone.

You've loved your husband, your family, your friends.
That's what he taught you, and this never ends.

The look that you have shows how much you care;
Always thinking of others, and so willing to share.

You know where you're going how good you must feel;
To know he's there with you through all your ordeal.

He cares for all of us deeply, and he loves you so.
This you've come to believe. This surely must know.

The place he's given you, is easy to see;
The contentment of knowing His promises . . . will be.

Your a precious beautiful person, you remind me of another.
The look I see on your face, is like my own loving mother.

Joan Gunther

It

It oozes out, dripping, collecting at my feet on the cold granite
Each puncture forms a stream that flows down my chest
It falls slowly at first, then drops and darts
The drops clutter, chasing one another and the puddle increases
As it grows vastly at my feet, I step back afraid of drowning
Of being pulled by its incredible powers
So dark it seems from a far, but close up I can see its shimmer
The brightness of its nature calls to me
I curiously plunge my finger into its deepest measure
It disappears under the pressure and vanishes from eye sight
Startled I pull it back, only to find that I am unable
It eats my hand, from knuckle to finger to wrist
The puddle increases, growing in strength
It continues up my arm and follows to my shoulder
Gnawing now at my neck, I tense my upper body
Faster now it is gradually engulfing me and I close my eyes
Relaxed, I enjoy its presence as it circles all around me
A warm bath of unknowingness gives me a surprised pleasure
Instead of fighting it we unite and become one
And I sink deep below to the other stage of knowing

Amanda Samet

Be Still Before The Lord

Be still before the Lord, oh my soul; listen
Earnestly, reverently; for he gives comfort,

Strength . . . he is the rock to which I cling in
Times of hardship, suffering and temptation.
In silence and meditation I can find what was
Lost . . . peace for my soul and my burden is
Lightened. How great is the love of the Lord,

Bearing all my sins . . . taking my punishment,
Enduring the torment and pain that was mine,
Freeing me from the bonds of sin and death.
Oh how awesome is my Savior, for he daily
Refreshes my spirit and renews my hope as
Eagerly I go to him in prayer, listening quietly.

Then in those sacred moments of silence, oh
How my soul rejoices, for I feel his presence
Enveloping, enfolding me in such warmth and

Love that I feel my heart will surely burst. Lord
Of all creation, help me to be still and listen, to
Rest in this quietness of spirit and body for my
Delight is in drawing closer to you, knowing you.

Donna J. Clark

The Happy Trio

Three little squirrels sat on a wall
Eating the nuts they stored last fall.
They listened to the birds singing in the trees
And their bushy tails moved with each little breeze.
Their names are Beppy, Boppy and Boo
And they're wondering what they can find to do.
Beppy said "I think we should make up a song
To sing to the people as they walk along.
They jumped to the ground and cleared a place
And each one chose a nice clean space.
With twigs for pens they wrote on the ground
So busy thinking, they didn't make a sound.
Then said Boppy "What word rhymes with love?
Cried Boo "that's the word I'm thinking of!"
They wrote and erased, then one by one
Laid down their pens and looked at the sun
They sprang back on the wall and all agreed
That writing songs was very hard work indeed
It would be much more fun to scamper and play
Than sit on a wall and sing songs all day.

Geraldine Roberts

One Touch

Two hands that brush so casually so innocent for all the world to see.
Electric current from one to the other, it passes and you quickly recover.
The beat of your hearts seems to synchronize-one touch, one
look, just as you fantasized.
More and more by chance you meet, it's surprising how intensely
you feel the heat.
Your eyes and his, they lock in place, and memorize the details of a
special face.
That certain smile when it's only you two, quickly ignites the
passion in you.
It's drawing near - a final confrontation. You know-without
   communication.
Sooner or later you'll end up as lovers, in bed, intertwined beneath the covers.
But maybe it will be for just one night, feelings gone with the
arrival of morning light.
Is what you feel going to last, or will dreams turn to dust, the
craving true love or animal lust?
If the feeling is strong and there's love to be shared, one touch is
is what will take you there.

Candy Burnaine

Nobody But My Soul

When a number of brilliant stars tonight
coloring the sky slightly
hold the tired wings of crying angels tight
I am turning into the fragile drop
slipping off a tilted cold wineglass
like an eagle flying with its wings wide
Through the deep blue sky of mountains
and across the rainbow over the sea
to the further corner of the earth

Now I see the sky burning to the red
The past time rises from the dead
and gets into the present
The shadow of the life
would be never seen at all
And the wind is leafing gently
through a book someone left on a window sill
And my story's tracing back
to the preface from the climax
There is nobody reading it but my soul

Akihiko Higuchi

Angels In The Snow

In those first years of life,
    embraced in the loving arms of childhood,
We basked in the innocence of the moment,
    lying in the green meadow on the hill beside our house.
How we loved to make pictures in those snow-white clouds
    that drifted across the blue canvas above us.

And our greatest concern then,
    was the twilight that came to claim us in the evening.
Remember how we laughed as we chased the fireflies?
    We were certain we could capture the last light of day.

Those were the days that forged the bond between us,
    the brother and the sister who would someday grow up,
And then somehow grow apart, as their own lives
    led them across other meadows more important.

But even now, when the evening shadows beckon to this aging woman
    who once chased behind you on the lawn,
You dance across my thoughts, Brother, and I remember
    how we loved to fall backwards in the first winter snow,
Making the snow angels that our grandmother told us
    would always see us safely through life.

Candace Viers

Little Boys

God made this world with skies of blue,
Enormous hills and mountains, too . . .
Then paused, and said "It needs something more",
Someone to run in the sand and on the shore . . .
To walk along the river and sing and wail . . .
And put some sand in a pail . . .
To make a castle and pretend it's home,
Go into the woods and roam.
To romp and play and jump and laugh,
Forget about taking a bath . . .
To fill his pockets with rocks and frogs . . .
And frolic with the cats and dogs.
Play baseball and other kinds of sports . . .
Pretend to be cowboys and Indians, making forts . . .
God made little boys, to be loved by you and me . . .
For without them, there is no pleasantry.
God was joyful when his job was complete . . .
A little boy makes our world a happy retreat.

Helen L. Moore

"Nancy Sue"

Long lean and worn her hands have seen
enough of life to know
as she stares at them she can see
the years behind her and those beyond
each crease cries for love every knuckle wants to crack
she watches as her hands melt away
there is nothing to be done so she stands to walk away
she stops and stares at her feet
her toes so calloused and worn
remembering where they've been she wonders.

Joyce E. Shipley

A Poem For My Wonderful Grandmother

I'll miss my grandmother so kind and so sweet, she was quite the
entertainer, a piano player was her feat. Her hands would glide
across the keys, so smooth, so precise, a front row seat would
always be nice. Family and friends would ooh and ah as sounds of
sweet music would touch us all and oh yes oh sure, she could even
play the saw. I love you grandma, my dear, my sweet, for now you
are in heaven saving me a front row seat.

Charles Adams Jr.

A Journey To Home!

A Journey to home . . . a path for everyone . . .
Envision your path of many memories . . . of different journeys . . .
A journey of being a child . . .
A journey of being playful . . .
A journey to fight for freedom . . .
A journey searching for peace, faith and forgiveness . . .
A journey of being open-hearted . . . to the world . . .
A journey of giving, sharing, and loving . . .
Through the days and nights of a journey, you will seek comfort,
patience and joy . . .
A journey has many twists and turns . . .
A journey across a bridge . . . searching for the unknown . . .
A journey to sing praise (give thanks) to our Father, our Creator . . .
A journey with trees, flowers and grass to give the breath of life . . .
There are many journeys of choices . . .
A journey is a continuing challenge of endless emotions . . .
A journey is a flowing river with a glimmer of hope . . .
A journey through space and time . . .
The rays of light from the sun, moon, stars in the sky gives us all
energy and vision of our journey to home!

Jodi A. Landry

"Deep In My Heart"

Love is something you don't run across everyday.
Especially, if you love someone in a certain special way.
I loved you since day one, and from one little look,
I knew you were the only one.
I love you dear, and you can bet on it.
It's the kind of love that last over hundreds and
thousands of years.
Until the day I die and past eternity.
You and I will have the ultimate unity!
Listen to my words and you will see,
That your love is everything in the world to me.
And this my love is why I say,
Love is something you don't run across everyday!

Heather Nuhfer

Holiday Blues

The holiday season can be such a low,
    especially if your job has you in tow.
This time of warmth and families aglow,
    is harder than most folks will ever know.
You have to be there because it's your job,
    these special moments, of you they rob.
The joy of the children which you only occasionally see,
    they're all gone and grown, how can this be.
While the rest of the world celebrates this season,
    you must provide for your family and sacrifice for this reason.
There are others in this boat besides myself,
    but at this time it's as though your life's been put on a shelf.

David Ehlert

The Warmth Of Christmas

Christmas is a time of joy. It comes around every year.
Even if you don't get a toy, it fills your heart with joyous cheer.
Even if it's winter time, you feel a warmth in your heart.
Strawberry ice cream topped with lime and a scrumptious turkey part.
Christmas is a time to gather. There's snow in the air.
Give or receive it doesn't matter. It will touch people everywhere.
So, when it's December you must remember that Christmas is a
time to gather.
Give or receive it doesn't matter.

Andrea Joy Martin

The Fishermen's Memorial

A man there is down on the shore
Even when a bitter wind whips;
He's watching and waiting forever more
For "they that go down to the sea in ships".

A silent watchman on the coast -
His heart is cold and his lips
Are grim as they speak with the ghost
Of "they that go down to the sea in ships".

His eyes stare out on the rising tide,
Where a single gull screams and dips;
'Twas a hell where no man could abide
For "they that go down to the sea in ships".

Year after year and wave after wave,
Steady the wheel that he grips,
And sad he thinks of the watery grave
Of "they that go down to the sea in ships".

Far out the horizon he tries to scan,
While fog envelopes his hips;
'Tis not the home for a cowardly man,
But "they that go down to the sea in ships".

Jeanne Marie Bouteiller

"The Memory Keeper"

(A tribute to Alzheimer's Patients)
Events of years past are written in a face;
Happiness, sorrow and all those emotions
That fit so neatly in between.
The eyes have seen it all,
But, not always able to remember.
Yet, it's all been recorded,
In the conscious or subconscious.
There's a vast storehouse of memories;
They've been carefully locked away.
Each day that passes,
Is filled with new material.
The key is always nearby.
Now, it does not fit properly.

There's difficulty unlocking the vault.
There must be another entrance.
But who takes care of the records
When the keeper is gone?

Carole Dombroski

To The One I Love

There is a star that shines in the heavens,
Ever so brightly that it lights the sky,
It glitters in such a magnificent manner,
That it touches every fiber of my being;

And this sparkling star is you . . .

There is a meadow in the darkness of the night,
But, it is illuminated by the brightness of the moon
A moonlit night that brings a warmth to my heart,
This heart of mine that is aglow with thoughts of love,

And this radiant moon is you . . .

There is the sunrise that reflects the early morning dew,
That brings forth the birth and beauty of a new day,
The heavens are reflecting the wonders of the creations;

And the exhilarating sunrise is you . . .

This is all a joy to behold, a thrill to experience,
The stars, the moon and the sunrise from above,
All this just lifts my beating heart, ever so,
And I will never let it go, it is deep in my soul;

And all because of you, wonderful you, Dearly Beloved.

Joseph De Cicco

Back To The Basics

Why are we in such a hurry? We need not make such a fuss.
Every day we see people scurry, hailing a taxi or chasing a bus.
The drive to better ourselves is in all our heads.
We relinquish our dreams and desires and act on our dreads.
Insecurity and fear shape our goals at what cost?
Our whims are thrown out, our spontaneity is lost.
We push and we shove, we put blame on others.
We cast out our friends, our sisters and brothers.
And once in a while, as we take a step back,
we try to remember what it is that we lack.
Why we are not happy when we've come so far.
Should we not be proud of who we now are?
We have it all, so what could we possibly miss?
Could it be laughter, love, and kindness? Could it be this?

Becky Kolvek

Heart

The single element of our being that separates us from everyone
and every living thing that exist.

Our heart is our life line, it can break us or make us and it solely
determines our destination.
Our heart feeds our determination and strengthens our purpose.
Our heart gives way to fantasy and allows dreams to become reality.
A strong and giving heart, can conquer any challenge.

For the characteristics it inherits, gives power to achieve, where others fail.
It's as if everything it touches becomes gold after a matured time.

It shares the same characteristics as gold, a precious and very unique.
Substance pursued by all. (Or many).

It's uniqueness and worth, far out weighs any other substance in the world.
"A heart gives solely to be giving".
"The reward is found only in the eye's of the receiving".

Gina A. Whitacre

Mission District 1990

I see a homeless woman, walking barefoot on broken glass.
Everyone is high.
Crack hotels, dimly lit windows, red lights, flowery ripped drapes,
loud voices from inside, sirens.

I cross the desolate street.

The smells of Mexican food, pungent, stale.
The sound of broken glass and tin cans kicked around streets' corners.

Drunken eyes lost in stoned wonder.

A burning haze rises over the Mexican designs on the tiles at
Mission High School.
The sun shines on everything.
But the darkness of night is never withered by this merciless
golden Californian light.

Lives wasted and lost consume these streets.

In my daily ramblings through the crowded streets I weave a
blanket of dreams.

Alessandra Pasquino

Heaven

H Happy people live up there.
E Every one is under God's care.
A Angels live in glory above.
V Victorious songs they sing with love.
E Eternal joy is felt by all.
N Neighbor loves neighbor, large or small.

Jenna Lee Motyka

Ode To My Man

Everyone knows that life is a struggle
Everyone knows that life isn't fair
Everyone knows that you reap what you sow

   BUT

You are not Everyone . . .
You are a Black man, my Man
You are the drumming heartbeat of Mother Africa that lulls me and
   rocks me to sleep at night
You are the picture of Strength and Courage that I carry with me as
   I too march out into a hostile world
You are the warm, hard voice of Reason that says we can still have
   dreams of better tomorrows
You are the Force compelling the elements to converge to make those
   dreams attainable
You are a safe, warm and welcoming Haven into which I flee when the
   storms of life and the perceived storms of life threaten to engulf me
With you at the helm and me as head yeoman we can conquer any raging
   sea and regain a steady course back to our goal
You and I together sow seeds of happiness through the struggle, wrench
   from life what joy we can and reap all the benefits of mutual
   admiration and Love

Everyone knows that Two is better than One
Everyone knows that the Dream is no greater than the dreamers
Everyone knows that the key to life is Love

   Jeaunice C. Pulliam

Christmas Thoughts

T'was the day before Christmas and all through the office,
Everyone was working, including the bosses.

The thought of a holiday gave everyone and a good reason,
This thing of returning to piles of work unfinished,
Made even the workers just a little bit skittish.

A spirit of good feeling toward all mankind
Is something, which today, is hard to find.

In the hurry and bustle of everyday living
We simply forget that life takes some giving.

Not just our money, our efforts, and time,
But a hearty greeting and a cherry smile,
Makes everything seem really worthwhile.
So here's a glad and happy greeting,
Best wishes to our friends and a pleasant meeting.

As the true meaning of christmas and all its cheer,
Brings together our thoughts of those we hold dear.

May we each, in our own particular way,
Have a very Merry Christmas Holiday.

   Eloise Moore

Beginnings

In the beginning we did not know,
Everything that our hearts would show.
The feelings, emotions, and the desires,
All the things that love requires.
We start out slow, afraid to making mistakes,
When patience and understanding is all it takes.
When love is new and full of wonder,
There's always someone to try to rip it asunder.
But when your love is truly strong,
No matter what happens, your heart still sings it's great song.
So listen carefully lest you forget,
That I'm still yours, you can make a bet.
So until next time, I'll miss you so much,
To miss and feel the love of your touch.

   Frank H. Green

A Place Of Dreams

Twenty-two miles off the main highway
Everyone wondered why so far and how long our stay?

A winding country road with ole John Deere's and Muscatine melons
And fine dining as promised by flashing windowed neons

At last a posted sentry round the bend pointed our way
His bright dress referring to the "Upper Deck" - but we intend to play!

The white farm house at road's end up on the hill
The diamond surrounded by corn fields, bleachers empty and still

Oh but the field . . . lads and lassies with mits and bats everywhere!
In the outfield dream seekers swallowed by the corn only to reappear

From everyone came easy smiles - young, old, the hardy and the lame
Frozen for a short spell in mutual love for the game

Old timers lined up for a turn at the bat
A "Shoeless Joe" offering up pitches with a wink and a doff of his cap

There wasn't a lot of noisy chatter and it was crystal clear
A slap of the glove, a flashing signal, subtleties of a pastime so dear

We left as the sun went low - in the mirror new players to the lawn
Someone had thrown the switch and the dance went on

In the distance we could see more beacons meeting the soft twilight
More dreamers to the field of dreams in Dyersville tonight.

   James J. Everett

Untitled

Through the relevancy of the rock
exists time, representing each line
throughout to make different signs.
As the current takes it makes its life
as the ocean sends ancient artifacts.
The fact is packed with information
which leads to mineral creation
which leads back to creating my sanction
with no complication this is my indication
that the existence of life is not only about
humans, animals and trees but what lies in the seas.
And as I am making myself free on this earth
I am growing and expanding my birth.

   Asher Bell

This Nurse; She Sleeps

Surrounded in quilted softness
eyes at rest but mind still twitching
like a child with the light switch switching
on . . . off . . . on . . . off, she sleeps.

Yet wrestles with time,
time for pills, tablets, capsules
or was that an injection?
Be sterile no infection
She sleeps.

And murmurs a response unclear
to cries of pain or fear
from her charges who see and feel
terrors imaginary and real she sleeps.

But does not rest.
For each day's a test
of her need to nurture
those with no or little future she sleeps.

And in the futility to express
the depth of my feelings for this nurse,
I watch over her as She sleeps.

   Gary S. Collins

Aging With Delight

Little One, challenge the wind!
Eyes bright, gleaming, head high,
Running the Wasatch, anxiety within
To consume the universe passing by.

Your torrid pace abandons all care,
Faster, faster lengthening the gait,
Golden tresses flying taking the dare,
Surging forward the hunger cannot wait.

First leeward, windward, whatever sight,
Ever pursuing in bounding determination,
Show me more, left, next to the right,
New faces, fauna, flora, a constellation.

Mother Earth, teeming, a welcome college,
In wonder and awe see and listen to learn,
Acquiring, understanding, seeking knowledge,
Always back to the oft used road you return.

The tumultuous joy of a discovering embrace,
Is it conceivable to reap even much more,
Are there adventures yet an unknown place,
That will be explored after you reach four?

James F. Iaconis

Untitled

Alas poor Ed, by the love bug has been bitten.
Faith and be sure, it's by Wanda he's been smitten.
Through the years many times it's been written
The prize will go to the quick to propose
While the faint hearted are among those
Who can only pine away and yearn
For the day when love she'll return
To make happy my life's sojourn.
So not only a Kansan but a Toledoan too
Share the company of being smitten by you
While I prayed to hold you again in my arms
And once more be smitten with your charms.
It was lucky Gene from West Bend, who is the winner in the end.

We well remember as a lark, Wanda week-ending at Asbury Park
When unannounced from Okracoke came Ed
And undaunted went to the Stork Club instead.
Tho we sipped champagne on another day
Still that Sunday could've been our Funday
To show off my beauty queen, while the rich and famous and in between
Would be envious of your sailor tall and lean.

Edward A. Breitfelder

Open Your Eyes And See

Open your eyes and see how the world is today
Families and their children can't go out to play

Open your eyes and see how we treat each other
Why can't you treat me as if you were my brother

Open your eyes and see how hateful we can be
Why can't you just open your eyes and see

Open your eyes and see all the guns, the gangs, the violence
Soon the whole world is going to come to a great silence

Open your eyes and see all the people on the street
Their families have hardly enough food to eat

Open your eyes and see how selfish we can be
Why can't you just open your eyes and see
    Open your eyes and see

Brandy Raden

I Hear Rhode Island Singing

I hear Rhode Island singing — it is oceanic playful tunes I hear,
Families in for the summer — over the Jamestown, down from the Cape,
over the George Washington, through the Lincoln Tunnel.
They are crawling, flocking out as if they were bears returning from a
long Winter in hibernation. Their purpose?
To have fun, see relatives, and reminisce.
They can all be seen on the beaches — Narragansett, Matunuck,
Scarborough, Charlestown, Ninigret, Misquamicut the list goes on yet —
They are all searching for the same.
Rejuvenating themselves in the rays of the sun, with the fresh salty
air, coming in from the continual crashing waves,
With aromas of the local summer menu, cold, crisp, refreshing ice
cream cones, warm sauggies, newly made grinders —
All joined with the musical intrigue — carousels, ferris wheels, bumper
cars. The Westerly Chorus sings — every summer,
Similar to the Chickadee, Robin, and Cardinal —
Each returning every year as if being 'on call' for life.

Dorothy L. Mcdermott

Forest Love

Sun weeping through the canopy
Far above the steamy primeval
forest floor . . .

Earthy smells rising, caressing senses
As the musk of a well laid woman . . .

Rich and dark and sensuous and swirling
Drawing into the next performance
Recalling, returning again and again and again . . .

Sounds as moans of a long lost lover
Seeping into tortured souls
Lonely breathing turn to panting
Quiets again to seething breast . . .

Until exhaustion claims the age old battle
No winners . . . only players still . . .

Faye G. Smith

A Peaceful Place

A peaceful place lies far beyond,
Farther than one's eye can see.
It has lush green trees and gleaming waterfalls
There it is very calm, quiet, and peaceful.
This place is deeper than any canyon,
Wider than any ocean waiting to be found.
We must find this wonderful place,
For it lies within the soul.

In this place, oceans are more calm
Than a baby's blanket.
The sun's rays are always shining
With love and prosperity.
The green grass is softer than a feather
And it never turns yellow.

If you want to find this place
Look within your heart and if there is love there
You will live in this peaceful place forever.

Amanda Brooke Hughes

A Kiss

A kiss is freely given from time to time.
For when we get one we, feel so sublime.
It makes ones blood rush through ones veins.
It builds little sparks of fire in us it seems.
Our minds reel rock and sway.
As we receive one in our, plain and simple way.
Our bodies flicker with a small burning fire.
For deep with end we are filled with desire.
A kiss makes us so sublime, for a kiss is freely given
from time to time.

Calvin T. Altman

Violence

Violence, thrives like a fatted calf,
Feeding on harvests of anger and hate.
Feeling no remorse for sorrow that's past,
of victims mourned, buried and waked.

There are no boundaries of age or color,
that hold back its rage, its intent to destroy.
It cares not if you are sister or brother,
a dry sponge in life, it sucks up your joy.

Talons strike deep, digging into the core,
disrupting thoughts like floods through streets.
Sometimes subtle, sometimes it roars,
trampling and wounding everyone that it meets.

There is no cloak to cover its face,
it wanders at will during day and at night.
Thriving on fear that it finds every place,
turning things wrong that should have been right.

It continues its course with boldness, with cunning.
Succeeds in its quest if given free reign.
In order to stop this generational running,
we must birth the seed of love once again.

Chris Stienstra

White Clean Sheets

She lies alone between white, clean sheets
feeling complete and spent within herself.
The sun shone bright then, clouds fleeting across
misty blue skies. Darkness was light's compliment
providing the backdrop for change.

She lies alone between white clean sheets
feeling trapped, confined and twisted, exhausted at breathing.
The sky is heavy, and storms rage. Energy like children is spent.
Time has been a foe pretending to be a comrade. Hours and days
running together like noise from a man made water fall.

She lies alone between white clean sheets
heavy breathing at her side. He used to run with the wind
playing tag with yellow daisies. Commitments, schedules and
white
newsprint breath of time spent chasing chroma skies.

She lies alone between white clean sheets.
Footprints beating a path to her quiet, finding comfort
within the ageless tradition. Innocence understands the fragility
of
warm, pink sunrises.

She lies between white clean sheets seeking the embrace
of rain-soaked evergreens and hopes of red skies at night.
Breathing life, breathing herself as one.

Cynthia Corliss

Moon Thrall

Oh pale golden slice of light.
Feeling the faint twinge I ignore the sight.
The new moon cloudless sailing high
Slowly growing toward the crescent scythe.

Then the half moon and last quarter
And from within the slow stirring begins
It changes now from pale to bright
The stirring is wildly rising. I must soon take flight.

Growing, pulsing, thrumming, singing,
Two days to full moon. Something wild
has come alive within. While trill after
trill ripple through my throbbing veins.

Sol is down, the full orange globe floats,
It's power draws me to the night.
My ears are pointy, feet changing, arms like wings at the sight.
Shedding clothing I rush headlong into the soft pale light.

Over meadow, over field I fly to the place of the dead.
Leaping fence and stones to romp with the moon folk.
With ghosts and werewolves I play, Shouting
Singing to the moon till sun brings the day.

Clayton Ball

Unity Or Defeat

Changes, changes, changes
Fight, fight, fight
Each one holding tight to the reins
Each one thinking he is right

While they are seeking their own will,
Our great nation is standing still
Our dear country was founded on solid rock
Guided by God's hand around the clock

Our wise forefathers worked together,
  prayed together, and built together
this Nation.
Their motto being united we stand,
  divided we fall into another's hands

Wake up, America and see the guiding light
Before it is too late.
For God alone is master of our fate

Berniece Waddell

Autumn Morn

I've roamed these streets since the day you left me. Liquid pain
filled my eyes so I knew not where I stood. This world of concrete
and steel, so hard and cold, unforgiving and rigid. I came here in
search of a poem. A song whose melody takes your Autumn life
and returns it to me as the Spring.

A heart so broken and torn it bleed through my eyes, and passed from

my face to the ground without a sound. This time my love was left on
these streets where no one noticed and no one cared.

The pieces to my heart have been scattered across this filthy ground,
its coldness leaving my soul numb from its touch. The pain still
falls from my eyes. Leaving a trail for the broken hearted.

Tonight the streets are in peaceful silence. Desperately I listen
for the words to sing by themselves, without my breath to lead them
in their cadence. For I know when the words become their own melody,
And the stars renounce the bounds of earth, my heart will stop its
rain from forming, and once again you will be in my arms, where you
belong, and never leave.

But words will never go unspoken, stars will continue their love
affair and never renounce its mistress. So my heart will always rain
down in an Autumn morn, where nothing grows and peace comes
in the form of a dream.

Anthony Ryan Morris

Love

Love is a fickle, cold emotion
filled with pain and aggravation
its painful arms of torment and trial
treat its victims to a fate most vile
want, and need, and loss of hope
how can anybody cope?
its strangle-hold grip is never loosed
just chokingly tightened, like a hangman's noose

Heartache, loss, distress, and fear
overpowering and impossible to bear
the weight and stress of love's cruel bliss
just to long for one sweet kiss
but is it worth this strife and pain
her love, I know, I can not gain
so with heavy heart and longing soul,
I trudge along, and hide it all.

Chris Nicholson

"The Northern Lights"

My love is somewhere up yonder
Filled with sparkling red ornaments when he calls
It bursts the universe
With divided colors untold.

Some days he rides his brilliant sleigh of silver dogs
Over the northern plain in a dash
After that . . . a quiet repose lingers in the air.

Nights I stand under the stars
waiting as I listen to the tales
My heart at times throb
Warmth pouring in like the tide

It is told to me in reality
By those who trodded this land before
That great is the love in a soul
Who look to the sky with peace.

What banner have you?
For me, it's my love for a warrior of the sky
If it need to be, I shall wave it high.

Yes, no greater love is this who waits patiently
Counting the stars as blessings each day.

Dorothy M. Epchook

The Dance of Love

We're writing a story of love, it's true
Filling the lines that were me and you
Heartaches, heartbreaks, we've known so few
Today you spoke of "us"
A new chapter — always something new.

We're creating the future, creating the past
We both want a story in time that will last
In print it will sparkle, a remarkable pair
So noble, so worthy, sharing each care
With glamour and style, dancing to glory,
The quill to our love is a timeless story.

Quanah Parker

Soft Heaven

Listen, I'm telling you, sit softly alone.
Find the voice with the night to guide you.
You could be chosen.
Don't start to panic.
Don't hide from your cosmic encounter.
This is the hour you rule and invite ventures, guest,
Trips to hypnotic wilderness, led out of bondage.

It's where dreams are made,
Where everything is possible,
Participate in creation, hands on experience.
Your mind will work wonders
Enlighten us for a spell.
An open window, a soft new slave.
Escape back into the land scape and laugh.

Then reappear, search for jewels,
Self image propagation.
Images of illumination
Put all your screaming fantasies into seed.
Plant them where I can find them
    and wait for my return.

James H. McBride

Untitled

A bird who was easily tricked
Finds it hard to flee
    the hindsight,
      the memories
        and poor chance
of owning her American Dream

With her green innocence open wide
Too young to comprehend
And his hungry reckless lust
Too mixed up to defend

There's a drunk horse prancing around the bandwagon
and the Peer Pressure Crew wildly cheers
The motherhood you have tripped upon
and from fatherhood he will run

Jay Ellis

Managing Care 4 Patients

Cold, cold hands; warm, wanting and wandering eyes,
Finely trembling fingers with blueing tips,
Rapid, irregular, yet fine pulse
The beating heart that nears its last,
Whose finite beats get another chance by us in the long white coats
Who blaze through the wards like demigods
Deciding who will 'stay' and who won't
Deciding who 'we' can afford to keep
'Managed care' or 'Managing our care 4 us'?

The rhetoric question resounds again in my mind.

Trading old fashioned bedside clinical medicine and morals,
4 plastic, greenbacks and a slick office room with a view,
And not to forget the members only club room marked 'HMO Physicians
Only'.
The discordant clash: Bona fide medicine and bucks for medicine,
One comes out the winner, the other smothered by the tidal wave we surf
But what about the patient
"CODE BLUE, CCU, TWELVE D DELTA"
Did we forget about him for a moment?
NO! 4 without him, we are without a use,
And without us, who would there be to be Managed!

John P. Higgins

A Christmas Star

Twinkle, twinkle little star, oh, how I wonder, what you are?
"Five little points am I; for God so said, `Let it be'."

"My first point is `Wonderful'.
It has the sense of miraculous; anyhow, we get ahead in the
`game' of life."

"My second point is `Counselor'.
One may think of a lawyer; but it means, One who guides through life."

"`A mighty God' is my third point.
The meaning might be the feeling of just `winning', but it is
incomparable with being a `champion'."

"My fourth point is Everlasting Father'.
With God as one's Father; One will be with him eternally."

"My fifth point is `Prince of Peace'.
Within is the sense of prosperity; yet clothed in poverty, He came."

"One may say, `How can it be?' or `What is that to me?'
But after all, I am A CHRISTMAS STAR!"

Edward Terrell

The Beginning

A little white dove;
   Flew overhead.
      As they pledged their love
         The day they wed.

That was long ago and far away
   The love, that little white dove
      The wedding day.
         Still; it repeats to those who love.

The dove still flies.
   The wedding take place.
      No-one denies,
         God's precious grace.

Beginning to ending
   With an eternity pending

George S. Bryant

Colours Of Italy

Piazza San Marco hosts silver gondolas
floating quietly through Venice.

The aroma of fresh Italian dolce' panne'
baked with sweet anise.

Open market places sell salami
hanging by thin ropes.

The heavenly Vatican in Rome
occupied by past and present Popes.

From snow-capped mountains to giant cathedrals
marble statues found shelter.

We traveled by train to Pisa
to climb the Leaning Tower.

Hungry, lonely gypsies
camped out by an abandoned roadside.

Pick the fruit of scattered fig trees
in the darkness of the night.

From a terra cotta tile rooftop
you can see

The beautiful colours of Italy.

Jo A. T. Thiede

"My Reasons For Seasons"

It's fall and the leaves are falling.
Flowers start to frown because they won't be around.
Squirrels and birds are settled in their brown covers.
All summer long they hunted for the best.
Hid everything from the rest.
We know we'll get through till spring is sprung.

Mrs. Glen A. Davis

Angel In My House

I saw an angel in my house; her smile was bright; her dress was flowing.
I wanted to ask her where she was going.
And then it occurred to me; her visit was short, but shed some light.
I was to ponder, use my sight; I was to keep my spirits soaring.
My burdens were really few; I just had more work to do.
Good work that HE has given me; I just had forgotten how to be.
Instead of giving and I knew how; I looked for others to give me a bow.
My journey here is just beginning; and as I gain new energy.
I share my love with my spouse; let my child be a child.
Use my creativity.
Write down my thoughts; make some dolls.
Smile more smiles.
And now after that special day, I slide comfortably into my couch.
I recall how my angel leaped in and out that doorway!
My soul is bound.

Dolores Stephenson

The Shape Of The Soul

The soul, like the river, is wide by its estuary,
flows slowly, spills widely.
Our spirit becomes more beautiful when the time is passing,
brightens up in the fire of the world.

I went behind my God, like my Bible tells me,
I was involved in the beauty and the power of my Lord.
Today, when the years passed, the Voice of God is calling me,
He is, in my heart, like the member of my family.

There are the souls, like the lonely flower,
they tremulous up high in the sun,
they look into Eternity from the Earth . . .

Another, like the flourishing bushes by the house,
are blooming by the love to their children,
and the Angels are counting their flakes.

Josef Siwolowski

Rite Of The Sissor Tails

Hovering in flight, so graceful were they.
Fluttering, hovering, oblivious of time.
Lost in some mystical ritual inherent of time.
Upward, ascending as though gathered in a
whirlwind, they circled and flew.
The colors of their feathers meeting in one vibrant hue.
Whirling rainbow shadows ablaze, against a
curtain of blue morning haze.
Downward, descending tiny enchanting spirits captivated in
their courtship ballet, left my mind to wonder, my thoughts to
inquire, the mystery, the fascination of these small winged creatures.
But before my thoughts could gather to understand, as if to deceive,
upward, upward in flight they disappeared into the golden light.
These conquer's of the wind left no query of their kinship with the heavens,
They offered no invitation into their domain,
But they left behind in the golden dawn the beautiful echo of their
   courtship song.
Young, their ritual as they.
Old as the light they followed.
Thus the rite of the Sissor Tails.

Doris Booth Bryant

Black Butterfly

Fly free God's child. Fly above the clouds.
Fly circles around the stars. Soar above the Heavens.
Black Butterfly you are amongst friends now, so fly high, fly free.
Soar into God's house, your house and if we who are left behind,
if we live right and we are deemed worthy. Save a place for us.
We shall miss you dear sister, our Black Butterfly.

Bobby McFadden

Ode To God

Rise up my soul and take flight,
follow the great golden light.
Go home to the joy and bliss,
something that has long been amiss.
Go back to the everlasting love,
on the wings of the faithful dove.
To catch that loving memory that glimmers in my soul.
To know that unconditional love.
A quest, a journey I have been on,
but eternally yearning for the place I love.
Guide my path, light my heart, let me accomplish my job.
Then home to the God I love.

Carol Radzus

The Lost World

A world lost, another gained,
Foolishness traded among victors unnamed.
Through sweat and blood, tears and pain,
Nothing seems real to the one's that remain.
Is there a plan from up high above?
Some method in chaos, is there no love?
How to find the answers unknown,
is to open one's heart to all that is shown.
An idealistic thought, this vision of love.
Hung from the trees as others above
Swing back and forth from side to side,
All clenched together facing no more time.

Jeff Charbonnet

My Prince

Foot step by foot step I hear him coming the
footsteps echo in my mind. Hurry I think
to myself. In the opposite direction I can
hear more than one human coming.
Hurry please! I need you, I need your love,
hurry I plead to him but what's that?
The group of humans are now running.
He starts running. I see his silhouette in
the light he's here, he's here I think
to my self. The group of humans run
faster. He picks me up and brings me to
his castle. I can hear the group of humans
weeping outside the castle. I weep too but not
out of sadness out of happiness that my
prince has saved me from what I would
have become.

Emily Camp

Thanksgiving

O let us give thanks to the Lord,
For all his blessings and his bountiful care
For life and love, for freedom and joy;
For a harvest of fruits and grain with a little to spare.

O let us give thanks for a bountiful harvest of food;
For the freedom of religion and speech in our beautiful land.
The early Americans decided that all should give thanks;
For all this the national thanksgiving day began.

As we look at the origin of thanksgiving day,
When the pilgrims sat down together to eat;
The first thanksgiving dinner, so we are told;
Five grains of parched corn was the treat.

Our tables are set in splendor and we fill up to the brim,
But there are some who know hunger and want in our land,
O teach us Lord not to be greedy, nor to boast of what we have,
But teach us to share and give a little to the needy if we can,

O, let us give thanks for freedom, and friends, and for all that we
have;
For church and home, and, a place to live, work play and pray;
O, let us give thanks to the Lord above,
On this great a national thanksgiving day.

James T. Davis

"Within The Eyes Of Love"

The Eye sees the beauty it chooses
For beneath the temporal exterior
We are all the same
With needs and desires, goals and dreams
The hope for a better life
From those who came before us
Yet it is the differences between us
That we should learn to cherish
As much as the likenesses
Each difference a gift
Unique within each other
And within each other, the beauty of diversity
Though not always appreciated
And at times not easily understood
However, if opposites truly do attract
And the likenesses keep us together
Then why is there so much in the way of this unity?
For everyone is beautiful, in their own way
For us, we understand, we see the truth
All within the eyes of love.

David A. Richman

"Proud Without Shame"

Lead me into darkness, oh deadly piper
For beneath thy cloak there lurks a viper
With a taunting melody from a sinful flute
Lure me to thy garden, but offer no fruit;

Bare thy sabre fangs, oh wicked parasite
Feed upon sweet dreams, oh phantom in the night
Inject me thy venom to coarse beneath skin
Bittersweet addiction, manipulate within;

Love, most sacred emotion, I gave unto thee
Now lifeless and limp, deformed by disease
Strip thy shroud to reveal the face of true sin
Once again foiled, the viper hath shed her skin;

As a soul in disbelief cheats both Heaven and Hell
I walk the earth alone, a shallow empty shell
But just as the phoenix doth emerge from the flame
I will celebrate revival, proud without shame.
Proud without shame.

John L. Carson Jr.

Ode To A Plebe

Hail noble plebe on Severn's shore, pursue your lofty goal
For drills and tests and shaven heads, enrich your heart and soul.

Let nothing slow your progress, though the road you've chosen's tough
You wouldn't be there bold warrior if you didn't have the "right stuff."

Yes, hit the books and swab the deck. Anchors Aweigh, Ahoy!
Learn to shoot and raise the flag, you're now the Navy's boy.

Where mighty smithies forging men fill rigid vessel's holds
But you will not be cast in stone, you'll overflow their molds.

There's not an ocean deep enough to quench your restless spirit
No prison dorm too dank and dark could quell your sparkling wit.

No nautical vise seafaring prince, rope or chain though crude and rough,
Can crush the gifts I've come to love, of repartee and tender touch.

They're yours to keep, to hold, to share and can't be bartered, stolen, sold
And won't be lost amid the dross, while this fire tries your gold.

So carry on intrepid mariner, ready to hoist your sail
Struggles soon behind you'll find, you've reached your hallowed grail.

Peer now at that distant chalice. The reflections that you see
Are the mirror of your future and your coming victory.

Connie Mastbrook

The Stand

Fear is a well known word
For everything that is going on is just absurd.

Violence is everywhere you look
Anymore people just don't follow the good book.

A gun short ringing out
Another body falling without a word or shout.

No explanation.
No confrontation.

Just a bullet in the head
Another brother is declared dead.

Sorrow fills a mother's heart
For she needs to find a brand new start.

His body is lowered into the ground
Tears of pain fall without a sound.

Too weak to see anymore
His mother walks away with a permanent sore.

Her heart in her own hand
She just wants to know,
"What was his stand."

Elizabeth Smalley

"Trucker's Wife"

The tears are dry;
  for I can cry no longer.

My head is full of words;
  but yet I speak of not one.

Yearning for your love;
  my heart fills with pain.

Words can not explain the loneliness;
  for there are many miles between us.

The twinkle in your eyes . . .
The gentleness of your hands . . .
The warmth from your caress . . .
The tenderness from your kisses . . .
  Keep me anticipated while I wait for your return.

Denise Gayle Shumate

Grandma And Me

My name is Angela and I'm not one two or three
for I go to school now yes indeed. My Grandma is special
she dances, plays and sings songs with me. We make up
our own toons and animal sounds to. So you see I'm
no longer one, two, or three. Sometimes she acts foolish
but I know its just for me, that's my Grandma yes
indeed. We live so so far apart and sometimes
it really breaks my heart.
We talk on the phone when afar, she calls me Honey
and I say, Hello Grandma, she visits in summer
and what a treat, she really is so neat I think!
The two of us read books, and walk, and talk I'm
no longer one, two, or three, almost grown yes indeed
I know my prayers now, and she thinks that's
Just great, I'm almost grown for goodness sake.
If I had one wish it would be that my
Grandma could come to live with me. So you
see I'm no longer one, two, or three and Grandma
and I are best friends yes indeed.

Judith J. Arruda

The Master's Cup

Weep no more for me my beloved
For I'll always be near in your hearts if you looketh
Upon the NAME blessed at birth,
And the one who was crucified here on Earth.
Oh the hours of sorrow are much to bare
But to question His wisdom we do not dare
For the Lord hath given and taketh away
His only Son that glorious day
So that He may join Thee in heaven above
But leave behind to all his love
The spirit that binds us and sets us free
From Satan's power and evil deed
Will soon be coming to lift us up
And forever we'll drink from
The Master's Cup

Janice Sobel

The Eight Wonder

  A wonder of the world, that's me!
For I'm more magnificent than a tree
I have a smile that when turned upside down
quickly becomes a terrible frown.
I've always wondered how he knew
to make the sea such a glorious blue.
But when I consider what he did with me
his earlier creations must have come easily.
How did he know each hand would need a thumb,
each body a brain to keep it from appearing dumb.
He gave me five senses to enjoy his earth
and intelligence to determine my own worth.
So that when I think of all the wonders he created,
it surprises me what he anticipated!!

Betty Carroll

To Life

Where have the years gone by?
Give me answers to questions so I don't die
I won't die because I look before me
All my family are a part of thee
Flashbacks of memories, photos and locks of hair
Bind the threads of life
And the threads weave a cloth
Dedicated to eternal love and overcoming strife
For the hands of time may tick a healthy body away
But the soul lives on forever and a day

Diane Dedrick

There's A Man

There's a man no one talks about
For it would bring too much pain
To reflect on his memory would cause
One to remember how he was slain.

There is a woman no one speaks of
The many things she did while here
Why she is gone is still so unclear.

There's a child no one mentions
The most innocent of all; much time has gone by
How they left, many don't recall.

Then there is those who are left
Trying to live with their loss; trying to find some rest
While also paying the cost.

Society is the biggest victim of all
Choosing what or what not to recall.
Take note to what goes on; help those around you no less;
    and pray for those gone and left,
Knowing that lesson is always best.

Jackie A. Kniep

"The 6th Of November"

There's never a moment that's right in our lives
    for losing a person we love—
It's hard to know why things should happen like this,
    so we turn to our Father above.
He'll lighten the loss and the sadness we're feeling
    with strength only He can impart,
And, just as a Father embraces a child,
    He will shelter us near to His heart.

It was a cold December day, I'll always remember,
    she came home to be with us after being diagnosed
    in November.
She entered the field in the fight for her life,
    she was a daughter, sister, mother and wife.
But as the months passed and her condition worsened,
    we felt we were losing her but have memories to remember;
And so she left us, the family who loved her, as she lie
    in our midst,
And it was dark and cold on the sixth of November,

John Kozlosky

The Raven Part II

I will never forget that haunting December,
for months have past, and now it's September.
That stupid bird I will always remember,
the raven that stayed above my door,
with words that were spoken "Nevermore".

curse this raven, curse him to Hell.
I picked up my shotgun and put in the shells.
I pointed the gun straight at his head,
with hopes that the raven soon would be dead.
BANG! Went the bullet, the bird fell to the floor,
I knew he was not dead because he said, "Nevermore".

Shut up, don't speak, won't you please go away!
With a smile on his beak and a limp to the door,
the last thing he said was "Nevermore".
My eyes turned red from the horror before,
so I fired the gun and shot him once more.

I picked up the bird and stuffed him with cotton,
with a hope that this nightmare soon would be forgotten.
I nailed the bird above my door,
with a gold plaque under it that reads "NEVERMORE".

Carl W. Cassady

Bill

I passed by what you said to me
for my ignorance would not let me face it and see

I'm sorry for the war that you were in
I can't imagine to be shot at and to lose good friends

You were young and taken in without much prepare
I'm sure you were lost and very scared

The things you saw we can't even begin to know
Until you open up and let some of your pain go

It was not your fault that you were there
It was not your fault no-one seemed to care

You may never forget some of what you were in
But, I ask you to let go of some of the Anger
And any guilt you hold deeply within

I will keep praying for you at the wall
for our brothers and sisters and families of us all

Jane K. Watts

Moonlit Dance

My lady, I ask the chance,
for my only wish, one quick dance,
of this I have dreamed for a great many years,
while laughed upon by all of peers,
but I know you are not the same,
you wish not to spread pain and shame,
I must confess, I love you,
and I wish you would love me too,
I would love to hold your hand,
on a moonlight walk in the sand,
watch Artemis moon shine of Poseidon's sea,
it would be only them, you and me,
but, alas, this shall happen to me never,
for you will love him now and forever,
but please, my love, give me the chance,
to hold your hand and have a moonlit dance.

Eric Carlson

A Dose Of Patience

It isn't very easy to keep our patience every day
For our hectic pace of living often makes it go away.
When we become angry, we may say things we don't mean;
Instead of stopping to think, we may create a scene.

If only we could bottle it and save it in a jar,
We could take it with us when out driving in our car.
And when another driver or the traffic made us mad,
We could take a little spoonful and soon we'd feel glad.

When waiting in the grocery store at the checkout line,
A little patience candy would make us feel fine.
While standing at the bus stop or waiting for a plane,
A cool taste of patience would help relieve the strain.

If we were tired or angry and feeling quite upset,
A little drop of patience would help us to forget.
And if we had a headache and were feeling very ill,
A tiny dose of patience would be a welcome pill.

The best we can do is to try to keep our cool.
Don't panic; remain calm; use patience as a tool.
Say a little prayer, "Lord, please give patience to me."
You soon will feel better. That I can guarantee!

Elizabeth S. Gill

Old Mrs. Green

Old Mrs. Green, that's what we would say and somewhat with contempt,
for only young and foolish judge the old that way I think. We would
watch her as she made her way down the dusty gravel road, to Granny's
house, for that's where I stayed with brothers and sisters four.
She always stopped to see if there was some thing she could do, to help
my Grandmother mostly, though I think she liked us too. For scrubbing
clothes on a washboard, was quite a chore back then but work she did,
all day long and never did complain, we thought it was her duty for
there was no monetary gain. She would stand and iron our clothes with
irons heated from a wooden stove, and hardly say a word or two
till it was time to go.

Then she would leave and up the road to her house she would go to do
her own chores then I guess, for no one else would I suppose.
She took me on a trip one time to a town called Neosho, where I went
swimming in a pool then ate all the ice cream I could hold. I can't
remember if I thanked her, for at that time you see, I thought it was
just as much a treat for her as it was for me. How foolish,
thoughtless, false pride, that I had way back then; kept me from
seeing what she was, a true and thoughtful friend. She has long gone
now where good people go when their earthly time must end, and if you
are judged by the deeds you have done how special her's must be, it
would have to be a nice one in the land of golden dreams. If there
is a way from the other side this writing can be seen, I want you to
know how we really feel - we loved you Mrs. Green.

John I. Porter

For Ruth

So let us sing a hymn and breathe a prayer
For Ruth, who now is one with all that's fair
That's Good and perfect, breathing that pure air
Of souls, who shedding outer garments, glow
With pristine GOODNESS. Thus do we below
Perceive and clearer vision. She will know
The answer to life's riddles, reap her prize
For any pain she bore and now full wise,
Will Recognize her GEMS with open eyes
Bestowing on her LOVED ONES - full and free
Pure Love! She'll share this knowledge graciously
unhindered. To her own a part she'll be.

Now to the Heavens — our soft song we send
For Ruth, 'Fair Daughter, Sister, Mother, Friend,

Ellen L. Barnette

Friendship

What's in a friendship one might say?
Friendship is thinking of someone each day.
Of sharing great laughter and good cheer
Letting friends know if needed your near.
Friendship's not something money can buy
Friendship comes from a feeling inside.

Friendship's the greatest gift you can give
You treasure friendship as long as you live.
You have offered your friendship through the years
And many a times have wiped my tears.
Yet I know I've neglected to say
Thanks so much for coming my way.
So through this poem I hope you can see
Just what our friendship means to me.

Ginger Bird

The Puzzle Of Peace

The puzzle of peace is a probable ploy
for the famished spirits who roam,
They seek and they search well outside of themselves
for a place which they can call home.

Look deeply within for the pieces of peace,
They vary so greatly in kind,
A calm will beset you when coming to terms
In the world of infinite mind,

Within is a universe seldom explored
Where you may break trails every day,
The legerdemain of the soul's black and white
Insists it is here you should stay,

The pieces that fit in the puzzle of peace
Are many and varied it's true
The shape of the puzzle will change over time
As your soul growth changes it's hue,

Delight will encompass each day of your life,
More vivid the colors you see,
Beginnings and endings will blend every day,
For the peace of soul makes you free.

Graydon Landahl

Whispers In The Night

Continue on and upward child, let nothing keep you down
For there are more deed to be done
And treasures to be found.
Did drama's stop with shakespeare
Did inventions end with Bell
There is no time for "ifs or buts"
There's no use for, "wells".

Life has its many shadows and obstacles face
There's hatred, fear and prejudice
Throughout this human race.
Yet you must fight, with all your might.
I pray, you do not stop.
Until we meet at Victory Street, and sit down at the top.

For hours I lay is darkness, and urge to carry out
Those pressing words, some unseen one just told me about
When fame and fortune all are mine
Nought shall be mince by right
I owe my entire future to
Those whispers in the night.

Anna Howard

A Message

There is murder, death and hate.
For we analyze, judge and rate.

Time moves on through a blackening hole.
As we are destroying our very soul.

Change, we must change our destructive path.
Or let no man avoid his deadly wrath.

We must find love and unity of heart.
Today is the day we all must start.

So start, don't wait, and set a fast pace.
The race we are running is the human race.

Barbara Fitzsimmons

In The Garden

Everyone needs solace on life's pilgrimage
For we are weary souls traversing paths unknown.
Life at times is a catalyst for fear and rage
So be mindful of the seeds that are sown

We need to cultivate a beautiful garden
It can be spiritual, metaphysical or environmental
The end result will not require a pardon
For real solace could never be detrimental.

Our lives ought to resemble a well nurtured garden
Refilling others from our inward spring
Those who are struggling with a heavy burden
Can pray to God and receive forgiveness for their sins.
Andre L. Procope

Labor Not

Labor not to be rich in goods below,
For who can gain in wisdom of his own?
And seek not that which men on you bestow
Of fortune, fame, and beauty they have sown.
Set not your eyes upon his dainty meat,
For who can trust the veiling of the coat?
Speak not to him who wraps a package sweet
With words of smoothness - feign, and foolish dote.
Instead, lift eyes - trust Him in yon above;
Apply thine heart as he instructs thy way.
Rejoice! Rejoice! He fills thy soul with love;
Imparts his knowledge rich - enough, each day.
Then, hearken now to Him and rest sublime,
Forever in His presence - O joy - 'tis mine.
Evelyn Felkins

Spring

The time has come and it is now
For winter to take it's final bow
The winds that once blew cold from the north
Give sway to allow south winds to come forth
See the trees, they tell the story
Of brown leaves gone to greenish glory
Honey bees, yes, they know the hour
They too enjoy the fragrant flowers
While kites sail high on the winds of March
Picnic and playing fill the park
I love the Spring, I'm glad its here
And I'll be glad again next year
K. Tigert

Spirit On The Wing

Through my eyes as an Eagle I can see far and wide,
From deserts to oceans to the most majestic mountainside,
I can fly at great speeds and as high as I dare,
With grace and beauty and awesome flair.
Proud, strong, magnificent am I,
As I glide through my territory of boundless sky.
With the Great Spirit guiding my every flight,
I deliver your messages both day and night.
You may not see me return but you will know I was around,
Because you will find a single father on the ground.
Connection was made between Mother Earth and Father Sky,
As I wing off silently without even a cry.
My sole, my spirit, is free to explore,
Follow me and be lost no more.
Barbara J. Danskin

Endless Love

From when I first saw you, until this moment today
For you to be mine, I have endlessly prayed

I find a sense of contentment when you are with me
With you I am secure, with you I can be me

Your touch relieves me of my greatest fears
To see you go makes my heart swell with tears

God has so graciously dealt with my desire
For you to be mine, which I so long aspired

I do not deserve your love, nor does a king
No one is worthy of such a beautiful thing

I have found such a treasure
One of God's works of art

Though I can't always be with you
You are here in my heart

Forever you'll be there, forever you'll stay
Nothing of this world can steal you away

We will always be two, together as one
And together our love will outlive the sun.
O'Quinn

The Pearl

It was so long ago when they first met
Friends said, "the perfect pair, a matched set"
Everyday was a joy of love
Heaven blessed from the skies above.

He placed the pearl on a circle of gold
The symbol of never ending love to hold
His eternal devotion was the pearl of life
Frank asked Bertha to be his wife.

They made their plans for a wedding date
Then tragedy struck and an unkind fate
Took his sweetheart before their wedding day
And the pearl of life ring was put away.

For theirs was a love so true and pure
Her passing was difficult to endure
The years have ticked on by the score
As the endless ocean waves pound the shore.

Another generation now has the ring
And the new owner proudly does cling
To the memory of her aunt as a young girl
And beholds the beauty of the pearl.
Betty Yaus

Osiris

Within the womb of the winged scarab all is light
From fire light and the inner dimensions of space
From the mouth of the crocodile from the inner winds of Time
What is immortality to a God, who was dismembered by Seth
Within the wind the sun and the moon

Inner dimensions inner planes the Nile and its mysteries
The Mystery schools are never dead
Upon the wind the smoke of time and space
The winds of Egypt blow upon the Nile
Within the breath of a God all is life

Upon the sun the moon and the eclipse of the Nile
Ancient Mysteries Ancient Thoughts of the Gods
Upon the pyramids the moon over Egypt and Fate in the balance
Within the wind the sun and the moon and all the stars
Within the sun the moon
Antoinette Voget

A Friend

Some people live an entire life
From its inception 'til its end,
And never know what it is to have
A person they know is a friend.

Someone you don't see in your day to day
Activities but when there is trouble,
If they only know what you're going through
They come to your aid on the double.

To give of yourself, to fill someone's need
Is as far as many people will go,
You unselfishly share whatever you have,
And that is why we all love you so.

To just give my thanks with a word, hug or kiss,
Does not somehow convey how I feel,
The appreciation and the love felt for you
Is deep and wide and it's real.

Because your heart is so full of love
Is the reason you do what you do,
I love you so much and I thank God above
To have given us a friend such as you.

Charles Lee Taylor

It's Monday Again

At 5 a.m. the alarm on the clock commences to ring.
From my warm, cozy bed with malice aforethought I spring.
Darn that clock! Kill the thing! Oh no, it can't be Monday again.
I stagger to the bathroom, shower, and dress,
Not with much alacrity I confess.
I make my way to the kitchen, moaning and bitchin',
Feed the dog, feed the cat, and do other stuff like that,
Grab a bite of breakfast then off I go,
With an unenthusiastic hi ho hi ho.
After all, it's Monday you know.
Back to the paper shuffle, back to the grind,
Egad! I must be out of my mind!
Memos to type, letters to file, hurrying, hurrying all the while.
Take these minutes, make this call. How can I do it all.
Schedule a meeting. Am I ever taking a beating!
At last 4:30, I thought it would never come.
Now to face the traffic home. Oh, what fun!
Home again to cook and clean; if I complain I'm just being mean.
At last Monday has come and gone; some days I don't think I can
go on.
There must be more to life than this.

Judith A. Reichard

He Is There

Jesus will be there for me
from now until eternity.
In the night I need not fear
for I can feel that He is near.
I pray for love and serenity
and Jesus whispers, "Let it be."
When I'm in pain the Lord is there
to heal me with His loving care.
He shields me from evil ways
and blesses me with brighter days.
Jesus is in the hearts of all mankind;
as He once said, "Seek and you shall find."
Thank you Lord for all you do.
Your love will help me see things through.
All the days of my life I will declare,
"Keep the faith in Jesus for He is there."

Grace M. Coppa

The Cry Of Homelessness

What is the cry of Homelessness, Is it a cry to be freed
from poverty or stress,
Could it be the cry of mental depression, mental state,
or moral evolution.

The cry of the homeless is heard only sometimes by very
few, they wander in a world of confusion hoping that one
day they can escape that dream world back into a society
which previously existed in which they once knew

So just maybe if they scream and cry a little more
for help out of their present mental state, for society's
politicians to hear and apply support through their
forever forgotten fate,
  Scream! Scream! Scream!

For one day you may be heard, even though society may
not answer, the Lord Jesus Christ makes the final decision
for all, and gives the final word.

Bruce Pettaway Sr.

Daybreak

Travelling down the road it is dark and the road is drying
from the recent rains.
Each lane looks like the back of a shirt drying on a clothes line.
The winds are blowing and the dampness remains in the center
of the lanes.
Soon the roads will be dry.

There are no lights except occasional bright headlights that
appear to be dancing when they hit the tree lined roads.
I drive through lights of green, street after street, and
I don't slow down until I reach the tolls.

"No traffic problems exist in vicinity of ___and___ ."
I try to listen but still I do not hear.
The street names are not important as my direction is clear.
I park my car and go into work and daybreak is still not here.

Helene A. Baker

Inside Of Grandpa's Heart

You've been my little buddy,
From the very start.
We've walked and talked and fished;
And watched the stars; when it was dark.
We have loved to be together,
And been sad, when we've had to part.
But we're never really separate,
Cause you ALWAYS STAY; inside to Grandpa's heart.
Now, you're growing up, changing
From a little girl.
Too soon, you'll be a young lady;
And head out, into the world.
But no matter how big you get,
Or, how important might be your part.
You'll always be, that little girl,
So precious;
Inside, of Grandpa's heart.

Herman Birdsong

My Life Story

October 16, 1961, Gwendolyn and Joseph had a son,
From Trinidad/Tobago, they both came, I was given my dad's name,

A New Jersey kid I grew to be, a little Yank and TNT,
I did well in Catholic School, A's and B's were the rule,

Music and sports were my life, I stayed happy and away from strife,
It was fun at Rutgers University, I worked and graduated in '83,

Now as middle age draws near, I'm still in school for a health career,
I'd like to get married and be a dad one day, so I must work and
   continue to pray,

I'll keep myself focused on being a mentor,
As I work at Hackensack Medical Center,

I went through a lot of ups and downs,
But I'll try to stay happy and erase the frowns,

As I approach the end of 1995, my life feels vibrant and alive,
For my life, I give God the glory, for this my beautiful life story.

Joseph Gittens Jr.

Evening In The Barrens

We milked the blueberries from their stems,
fruited so thick the earth was gemmed with sky,
sky-blue drops that streamed into our buckets
as if the dark-faced being beyond the barrens
had for a moment relented,
metamorphosed into angel.
Late sun poured, burnished,
between the cloud banks.
We tramped the wheel tracks home, unheedful,
with the savor of blueberries heavy in the air,
of what soon would shrivel, rot, betray
in the chill-locked winter
until the next brief wave of blue illusion
broke over the short stiff rusty branches.

Harvena Richter

The Rainbow

Teeny, weeny drops of water high above the air,
Full array of a million million, myriad mire,
Transform'd to colors fresh and pure, deftly shaped with art and will
By the hand divine a painting in the sky, so serene and still.

T'was a rainbow crisp and clear, radiant brightly fraught with cheer,
Freely arched across the sky, over misty mountains steep and high,
Dispelled the dawn of eve around with alluring
   splendor without a sound.
Wispy clouds floated by past a spectrum of wondrous hues unsurpass'd,
Before the glare of the sun like a glowing ember falling in the west,
Behind yonder distant shades of hilly chilly crest.

Didn't you say a splendid rainbow, huge and bold?
Come then, show me, lead me to its pot of gold!
Won't it be a treasure rare and great? What a dream
To dream when it could be had and not seem'd?
Let's tarry not, but take the route to bounteous gold delight.
Alas, it's far beyond the reach of any jet of speed in flight,
Beyond the horizon of men of red, yellow, black or white;
For none will ever reach nigh the cherished site!

Ernest T. Lim

Tragedia De La Rosa (Tragedy Of A Rose)

I remember a rose outside my house.
Full, lush, beautiful,
The scent seducing me every time I stepped outside.
I would feel the velvet petals, take in the sensuous redness
Carefully observe
The bodyguard thorns.
I wanted to pick it, bring it in, give it my love . . . but
No, I hesitate . . . would I disturb it? I saw
Love, Passion, Sex, me making love,
Even a funeral inside that rose.
While I hesitated, the floodgates above opened. I was
Sheltered inside my ice blue room while the sensuous rose
Took its beating.
I decide to make those rose my foster child,
Nourish it . . . I rush outside . . .
It's gone! The flowered brethren drip and shake their
Soggy heads in bereaved tribute. Near
My foot, a lifeless rose petal lay, limp and stuck to the
Ground. I pick it up, seeing my friend, who had gone too
Soon . . . No time for goodbyes . . .

Dinah Tutein

Life's Road

Life's road twists, turns, and spins.
Full of places, people going where.
All seems to be in a hurry, rushing.
Down the roads around the bins.

Children growing up with material things.
Parents time is a desire for money.
Love, family, friendship seems un-important.
Life's Road, is this suppose to be what it brings.

Beauty all around, God's gift to life.
Wonder, excitement, truths ours to behold.
Inside out, comes forth our soul.
Instead of seeing beauty, most see strife.

I wish I could slow down time.
Sprinkle some magic dust in everyone's eyes.
So they could see were all the beauty lies.
Life's Road the greatest journey of all.

Barbara J. Stallard

The Night

Whisper unto the winds my love,
   gently speak my name.

To feel the wind upon your skin,
   and imagine it's from whence I came.

Close your eyes and embrace the night,
   as the sensations surge through your veins.

The peace within as you let me in,
   for I bring you pleasure and not pain.

Only ecstasy for eternity,
   to stand the test of unknown time.

To walk with me endlessly,
   and begin to cherish true delight.

While the stars are in bloom,
   give a kiss to the moon and call this paradise.

For it's serenity, peacefully when,
   you open your arms and welcome the night.

Cynthia Wegman

Cliffs

Funny - the edge always seems so much farther away than it is
someone said jump so I did only I took you with me
and now we're falling how much farther? Funny -
you're always so cool except for the heat that radiates from within
I'm still waiting that one person who supposedly understands
and the ground is still too far away
it's been 16 years though it seems like hundreds and how long have I
been falling and were you always there and I just missed, it
Do you really understand? Or is the velocity screwing up my mind?
The ground isn't that much closer than when I first fell
How long ago was that?
Bloody scenes, hellish nights, silent minds screaming, tempting.
Funny - how one too many makes you believe that somehow falling
might be better than standing is that your hand or my imagination?
Mirror images reflect a past and
glass shatters on the ground that is still so far away.   Funny -
I hope there's someone to catch me cause you're with me or are you
another fleeting memory passing in my supposed flashback
as I keep falling looks like there's no one to catch me. Funny -
the ground is getting so much closer

Cate Wardell

Madness Strikes To Make Suffer

Running into a deep fog.
Further and deeper to see what it feels to be inside.
Turning around after the experience within, and the curiosity
   has been satisfied.

Running back,
On the same way,
As the forward track.

The loss of bearings, as the panic of fear wears in.
Dashing in every way, attempting to escape the pain I feel each day.

Panic on the defense.
No longer will it remain at my expense.
The anger burning bright with rage.
A monster becomes with the command from his sage.
Madness strikes with his powers of evil,
Say goodbye to all gentle and tranquil.
For all must suffer for my pain, that is equal.

Jeff Longo

Do You Know Me? — Memories Of A 50th Year Reunion

From far across the room they came,
Further still across time they came.
Fifty years or more ago came these time travelers.

Seeking those they thought they remembered well,
Who, once long ago, with another face and another body
Knew, liked, even loved them well.

They had talked, walked, and worked with them,
Played, prayed, and strayed with them, and
Shared pleasure, pain, and sorrow with them.

As they greeted each other
They first sought
Only memories of a kinship
That would match their own.

James M. Davidge

Our Loving Mother

When we were little girls, my mother was there. She
gave us love and the courage to give to others and taught us to share.

The laughter that came from her truly was of her heart. I
know now why she always made it possible for us to
always be together instead of apart.

We have to let go now, and know how much she really
was a wonderful mother. But there's a better place and
there are a few others that need her most.

A time when it seemed impossible for her, the Lord came
and gave her peace. She'll always be watching over us
saying that's my girls to everyone she meets.

The smiles and the love she has given us will always be
up in the heavens above.

With this we let you go and carry your spirit where ever we go.

Karen L. Leinhauser

Can't Get Over You

When I look into your eyes, it's like I
get hypnotized.
   It's like I am in a daze or stuck in a
maze when I start to think of you.
   When you come around, I keep my head
down to the ground, because I can't get
over you.
   When I think of you I think of the beach
water's so blue I remember when I was
stuck on you like glue.
   Now I gotta get over you, some way,
some how, I gotta keep my head up instead
of down.
   When people ask me out I don't know
what to say, I just tell them I'll get back
with them another day.
   The reason why I say this is because
I can't get over you, and you didn't
believe me, when I said I love you.

Danielle Williams

On Being Eighty

The fickle hand of fate that placed us here
Gives little guidance thru the passing year.
As we rise or fall in the tour thru life,
We give ever greater sign of exceeding strife.

From the unguided ways and frivolities of youth
We gradually proceed toward the seeking of truth.
To strive to reach higher is life's great goal,
To deny this effort is to concede to death's toll.

The chance that each will make a mark in the world
Or be greeted as conqueror with flags unfurled
And be considered by one and all as a grand hero,
Is the stuff of idle dreams that adds up to zero.

A man's appearance is no real clue to his age,
Looks can change fasts as the turn of a page.
And time is a relative thing they say
Your life is your own and for it you pay.

The rigorous march of time may not be turned back,
We can only march on in the once chosen track.
By all that is holy and thoughts that are weighty,
It gives a feeling of pride to arrive at age eighty.

John H. Rust

"Feeling The Joy And Pain"

The joy of talking and being with you.
  gives me more courage to go on living.
Gladly sharing the jokes, laughter and woe.
  makes me feel life after all is not boring.

The happiness I felt working and playing with you.
  strengthen my confidence and stop my crying.
Lending a helping hand in everything I do . . .
  I found joy in a friend who is so caring.

The stubbing constant pain of losing you . . .
  gives me sleepless nights and eye sore of crying.
To think there's no one to share my deepest woe . . .
  makes me feel the burden of losing is overbearing.

The sadness I felt of wanting to be with you . . .
  drive me nuts and my head go spinning.
Crying, walking, running to and fro . . .
  to ease the deepest pain of losing.

Deliah M. Lim

The Belles

Afternoons we would see them
Gliding down the sidewalk
Straight-backed, careful
Out on their errands and visits.

Miss Carrie and Miss Lillie
With large brimmed hats (always tastefully trimmed)
Cocked just so, and white gloves,
Pressed flowered dresses - all elegance and jasmine.

A neighbor called them "the girls from New Orleans."
I knew nothing of that place but I knew the neighbor must be right.
New Orleans in my imagination, far away and exotic
Just like these women in our midst.

And us, we ran about — rough dungarees and flannel,
Dusty from day of play; Loud, racing, twirling —
A counterpoint to their ephemeral elegance.

Down the sidewalk into their gate they'd come.
Past the dahlias, glowing in bloom,
Up the stairs into their tiny house,
Closing the door behind them and disappearing
like butterflies on the wind.

Ann Eastman

Letting Go of Love

Sometimes in the end I cannot let you
go you meant to much to me. Everything
I ever needed and everything I ever received
came from you. Sometimes I would say
I did not need you at any point in
time. But you were a shining star.
You picked me up when I had no beauty
within myself. You made me happy when
I felt bruised up inside emotionally.
You know your smile was so magnificent
and it was to good to be true. I wonder
if you miss me? I wonder if I can be
strong? I wonder if I can get along
without you by my side?

Brandi Matranga

Meet Me On The Clouds Heave's For Singing

The universe are yet a snowy on God's mantel piece
God believe me into existence, that's why I believe in God
Why is the creation of all answers
"Why?" "because I love you."
Love love's love love, God is love
Only God can love you more than I can
God I love you, thanks for loving me
I love loving
God pray my prayers for me
My whole life's a prayer

Not for the threat of hell
Nor for the promise of heaven
But because it's right

God only remembers the good of you
Find the master in everyone, and you've found God
If you're alive, you're a hero
I'm not afraid to fear
If anybody's lost 'no body's won (one)

James Michael Walker Jr.

You Are So Special

No matter how bad you think things seem,
God made you special in a parent's dream.
No matter your looks, brains, or your size,
God made you special in his eyes.

You are a likeness, from heaven sent,
God made you special, how he only meant.
Your likes or dislikes, quiet or loud,
God made you special, sent down through a cloud.

God gives you challenges, sometimes quite hard,
Many will catch you, way off guard.
When things are so tough and you don't understand,
Call up a friend for a helping hand.

When you feel like giving up,
Call a friend and say cheer me up!
You all are needed each one of you,
Ask for help to get you through.

You're all so special I know it's true,
'Cause God and your parents created you.
Always remember each day when you wake,
You're a very special person God did make!

Judy Bittner

Autumn Colors

Beautiful Autumn of many colors
God must have thought you special and dear;
Mixing together ten thousand colors
Touching each leaf with love and care.

I stand in awe before its beauty
In search of words that could explain;
My heart is full, there's no description
Tho I try and try, and try again.

God's gentle hands have shaped these mountains,
with beauty beyond the mind of man.
He planted these trees on hills and valley,
and far beyond the rivers span.

He planted the dales with beautiful flowers,
To brighten the spring when all things grow.
To bring new life to all his creatures,
After the passing of winters snow.

He made the sun to warm the valleys,
To makes the trees I love grow tall.
So now he will mix ten thousand colors,
and paint again for it is fall.

Dallas Laws

Life That's Given

To take each and new born day
God will make your life
Brighter in every possible way.

The Lord our master is the inspiration
So you must never never fear,
With any unknown situation
But always know life is very very dear.

He always comforts and sustains you
Whenever you feel in despair,
you can be sure he is the one
Who holds your hand and is always there.

Your hope and confidence must be
In your heart when you have distress
Because God will gave you the shining light of happiness.

Though we show our sins as we all have them to be
But our Lord our God will be there,
With his love so you can see.

Stay on the road with his footsteps of love
So you can always see the beautiful
Sunshine always coming from above.

Berné

In The Garden

I was there in the Garden of Eden,
  God's Glory, how it shone round about!
But I doubted the Truth that He told me
  So in kindness He made me go out.

He tenderly gave me a body, wrapped in blankets of time and of space
Picked a home here on Earth where he sent me,
  To grow with the rest of the race.

How I cried as I felt separation from my Father in heaven above,
Then I saw in the eyes of my mother the reflection of His blessed love.

With patience supreme He has waited
  While I battled the problems of life
Self-centered, self-righteous and ungrateful;
  Only He, knew the depth of my strife.

With delight I remembered the garden
  And surrendered myself to His care,
Now my life must express to all others
  The love, peace and beauty found there.

I'll return to my home in the Garden; with desire I await the great day.
Until then may I act as His servant,
  To build Heaven on Earth here, I pray.

Alberta Bair

Pinholes In Heaven

Pinholes in Heaven winking at me
God's little windows from which He can see
Wishing on one, watching if fall
Imagine the fun of creating them all
For all little girls that are born here each day
A little red star He puts on display
And then for the boys that giggle and coo
Out God's window a star shines blue
So every pinhole you see that may flicker and fall
A little lost angels the best gift of all
A soft pair of wings, a halo of gold
Three tiny rings and God's hand to hold.

Christie S. Wells

Across The Potomac

Across the potomac, in the darkness of night lies a
great American by a flickering light.
The thirty fifth president of this great land, struck
down in his prime by an assassin's hand.
On the twenty second of November, nineteen sixty three,
the blackest of Fridays in the land of the free, a city
named Dallas was set as the scene, a nightmare emerged
from a political dream.
The people all waved and cheered as he passed, no one
could know that it was his last. Three shots rang out
amid the cheers, the next thing to follow was sorrow
and tears.
Their at his side as life ebbed away, sat his wife on
whose lap his bleeding head lay. His trip to the
hospital was swift but in vain, a lifeless cold body
was all that remained.
His body was laid in a flag draped coffin, beneath the
capital dome where he walked so often. Our leader had
fallen our respect we paid, to Arlington he was taken,
at rest to be laid.

Eugene Michael O'Hara

Roots That Will Remain

The quickening has begun.
Green Wytches, through the forest run.
The dark embrace lets you merge with this place.
A leaning pine sighs above full moon water,
Whispering of drifting ducks and playful otters.

The fish can see that I am a tree.
Sound and scent, crawl and climb, no longer mine.
I am ancient now, Divine.
A cricket chorus sings of secret things.
The river calls, cool faerie mist falls.

Sand and stone caress, their soft songs bless.
Against a shadowed cheek flutter velvet moth wings.
Wandering go the wild things.
Upon a shadowed brow whisps of Willow fall.
The Earth . . . She remembers us all.

Now recognize little ones once lost.
Witness what ignorance has cost.
I have known this, the beginning of old remembering.
All life is reflected in a single flame.
And wild are the roots that will remain.

Dianne Keast

Love's Nest

I cry crimson tears . . . look up to the
grim grey skies bellowing . . . when will
we live in harmonious days of love
filled days. Children running briskly
with adolescent thoughts of and frolic
Dreamer . . . believer . . . Imaginer. Rainbow
thought of love's nest for mankind . . .
No hatred, jealousy, back biting, violence
the many facets of the demonic evils of
the world. Blood-stain tears of skeletons
singing their praises of joy . . . eternal
love . . . no sorrow . . . no suffering.
Moments of silence . . . angelic guard . . .
comforting thy neighbor thru the love's
nest hunt for peace and eternal life.
Fulfill your spirit . . . embrace your
blessings thru God's unchanging hand.
Living, giving, caring . . . begin the
journey to the tree of everlasting
life thru the tunnel of the love's nest.

Charlotte M. Williams

Teen-Age Years

Oh the frivolity of the teen-age years!
Growing away from family and closer to peers;

Capturing the moments to completely enjoy;
Forgetting the future, thus parents annoy.

Partying till they almost, if not drop,
Then sleeping, sleeping but the phone can stop.

The telephone is an important part.
It connects them with friends for another start.

When does reason and responsibility start?
Please do tell if the answer you can impart.

Charlotte Eaton Powell

Untitled

I was dancing in a meadow
   hand in hand with you.
The sun was over the horizon
   and it was shining on the dew.
My heart was so bright and gay;
It was a beautiful start to any day.
And then, just as I turned to steal a kiss,
My eyes all full of mist

RING . . . Another rude awakening
As the alarm clock does it's thing.
Every morning it's the same,
Yet my heart still bears the sting.

Life goes on and years go by
   so why do I still remember?
All those touching moments
   they haven't turned to cinder.
I'm in love again, and so are you,
   yet memories still remain.
And in their afterglow I smile and I think,
   I hope you feel the same.

Geri Fridriksson

"The Portrait"

The portrait of Papa most precious to me
Hangs not on the wall where you'd think it would be.
Instead, in his bedroom behind closet door,
Not hung from a nail, it is there . . . on the floor.

The canvas upon which his portrait is made:
An old square of rug, where all burdens are laid.
Its frame: a small altar-an old wooden stool
his grandson once made, long ago, while in school.

My grandfather's likeness was not made by paint,
but, by long devotions without one complaint.
The portrait I speak of: Two imprints I see . . .
Result of his years spent upon bended knee.

Carla Christian Helmke

Black Butterfly

I curl into a ball,
   go inside where the dark is full of color,
      go inside where it's warm to the touch but bright to the eye,
         where meanders my long lost black butterfly.
   I dance unseen,
      I chant in unknown languages to solemn stones,
climb to the pinnacle,
      let the wind pass through me like a hot knife through ice,
         let me fall, only to rise again on the wings of pitch and velvet,
      to once again caress the midnight sky with my lone soul.

Joshua R. Evans

My Father's Roses

Silently they fall to the table.
Haphazardly they arrange themselves around the vase.
Large, velvety red petals from the last
roses of the season.
They speak to the man who lovingly
grew and tended them.
He, too, seems to be in his last season.
Once vigorous and proud and even a little vain,
his body, like the roses, has shed
much of its outer shell.
But, like the inner petals that refuse to fall,
continuing to cling to the flowers' centers,
So, too, my Father clings to the core of his being.
The fragrance of the roses fills the room
stirring my senses.
The perseverance of my Father fills my heart
stirring my soul.

Doris E. Italiano

A Mother's Sorrow

Oh dear and beloved son: You went on that trip, full of life and happiness, with many plans and dreams on your mind. But it was a trip from where you would not return. They brought me your broken and cold body, and with my warm, loving hands I longed to give you life. But death was stronger than I, and stronger that my mother's warmth. I kissed your forehead, and touched your hands, but they were so cold, and I felt a pain so deep at not being able to give you a second life, just as I lovingly gave you life the first time.

Oh my son, you don't know how sad I feel when I look at your photographs and see you smiling, full of life, or when I see all your belongings. And I cannot accept having lost you, so I ask God: "Why?" But He doesn't answer me — these are things of destiny, and mysteries of life.

Emilia Blazquez

Gods Gift

Majestic
Hardy
And as tall as can be

Just another of Gods many gifts to me

It's strong
Home to His creatures, those oh so small
So beautiful
So silent

Speechless
Yet graceful
And special to me

Oh what, Oh what, Oh what can it be?

God painted it with nature and called it a TREE

Anita Waller

Bondage

Although he is younger, he is wiser somehow.
He seems to know all the answers to the emotional questions.
We both came from the same place, only he was sent from somewhere.
Life's memories always dwell on him.
I may not act it-but I admire him for his courage, and his quick thinking.
I love, respect, and envy him more than anyone will ever know.
He is my hate, my love, my sorrow, my excitement, my feelings.
He is my writing.
He is my brother.

Amanda Cogburn

With Harp And Lyre

Sing to the Lord with the harp and lyre
Hark to the sound of the angel choir
Worship the child of our heart's desire
Praise to the king who sent tongues of fire!

Cherish the lamb swaddled near the wall
Held by the virgin in manger stall
God's only son, Christ, the Lord of all
Issuing mankind its final call

Pierced by a mocking soldier's stave
Nailed to a cross, sealed in rocky cave
Conquering death, rising from the grave
All for the children He came to save

Sing songs of praise with the harp and lyre
Tell what He did, let your words inspire
Power He gives lest his children tire
Witness for Him as with tongues of fire!

Anne G. Marean

The World's Birthday

Now that Summer's ravage
Has almost passed,
And the school bus comes
In its yellow form with squeaky brakes,
Things seem more what they are.
Like wearing sunglasses in the rain.
The ticking clock knows no pain.

I think of you today.
I thought about you yesterday.
Tomorrow scares me a bit,
Just like a child's first ride on the school bus . . .
That ride we all once took.

But, today is different.
Different as Autumn's breath
Whispers its colors to the Wind.
Reveals secrets to those who listen.
Exciting the restless seekers,
As the World, once again,
Puts on its party dress.

Joni Starr

Love Lost

When love so deep and love so true
    Has ended by a final breath,
The heart of one who stays behind
    Lies broken by the robber; Death.

The tears that fall unceasingly
    As droplets in a summer rain,
Are understood by few who see,
    But cannot know the pain.

Time heals he's told, just trust and pray,
    Your heartache soon will fade away.
And happy memories will soon replace
    The painful yearning for her face.

But alas, such trite remarks
    Give little comfort to the one
Who only knows his grieving heart
    Remains unchanged when day is done.

And yet through all the pain and grief, the promise
    Of a life complete doth stir within the breast,
And gives the shattered soul and relief
    And the broken heart its rest.

Frank Roberts

The Long Grey Cloak Of Winter

The long grey cloak of winter
has fallen all around,

through the dark and endless night
nothing stirs a sound,

and the leaves were once so gold and green
are dead and faded brown,

sailing through the wind blown sky
then rustling on the ground,

till bitter cold brings swirling snow
and blows it all around,

then settles with the howling wind
and shouts aloud with sound,

and the moon comes out to bring the tide
with waves that reach so high,

pounding on the ocean floor
then leaping to the skies,

the long grey cloak of winter is a dark and mournful thing
that lingers on until the spring flares its skirt of green.

Joan Overton Hogue

A Stronger Love

The distance we have grown to understand
Has unnoticeably open windows to a real love,

Like the awaiting hug with open arms
Anxious to give, when he walks in the door,

The softness of a kiss when our lips meet
Turns into a desire of intimate touch,

Leading to the once closed doors
Of the heart, to the sensitivity within,

Has arrived to a better understanding,
And a love stronger than before!

April Zerbe

Cosmic Nook

Dashing high over the hill, rays of sun
    hasten the call
Wholly, completely, all

What joy (and how) to discover here
    in the kitchen, a rather unchoatic
    cosmic nook

Where in awaits the teacup, pen, and
    notebook

Now, if only space time congeals
    into some fanciful wit

Be bewildered? wavering, I sit

Seems there are some thought
    barriers to cross

Then, laughingly, beguilingly, the writer
    comes to yield to the bidden task, no loss

Hustling sounds of the big pine trees
    thrust through the indoor spaces

The world reinvents itself in the
    impetuous movement of the curtain laces

Agnes Anna Barron

Emptiness

This lonely house — it's floors are cold and bare,
haunted by lingering footsteps no longer there.

Its walls are solid, silent and sad. Once family
and friends gathered together, sharing love and
care — their happy voices echo everywhere.

The door is warped - worn - dwindling from neglect;
yet crossing its threshold one feels wonderful
stories waiting to unfold — eager to be told.

Once outside on the overgrown lawn, the large oak
tree glistens with dew — branches swaying,
beckoning me to stay and return the soul to this
house anew. I will. I really will.

Constance Cornwell

Untitled

She was everything to him, some might say she was the perfect woman.
He felt as though he could spend the rest of his life with her, all
of sudden it all changed.
His days were always dark and depressing, because what he had
was now gone.
She was the silver lining in his dark cloud.
She was the ray of sunshine on a rainy day.
She was that warm, cuddly spot on your favorite "blankie".
She was everything to him, and now she is everything to somebody else.
Days, weeks, months, maybe even years after she's gone his heart
won't forget about "the one that got away".
The pain is awful, but he will make it past all of that.
The only hard part is starting over, he has to look for someone new.
But will he find her?
As the saying goes "every cloud has a silver lining" and that
means there's hope.
Now who will be his silver lining?

Jerry Andrews

What He Doesn't Know

When I try to tell him how I feel;
he simply disregards to me what is very real.
The daily conversation about work, money, kids,
and our home; but something is missing, I feel so alone.
He says he is happy and everything is fine;
but in my mind I am just passing time.
I cannot escape, I have nowhere to go;
perhaps if he reads this he will realize
what he doesn't know.

Cynthia Eveland

The Gentle Giant

I will never forget the man himself,
He never achieved any fame or wealth.

With eyes as deep as the dark abyss,
And wrinkled hands as soft as a kiss.

In his outstretched hands I could always hide,
They made me feel warm and safe inside.

He gave all he had without any doubt,
No finer man could I talk about.

The face will forever in my mind remain,
His memory has drenched my heart with pain.

For I miss him so and I always will,
My days with love and kindness fill.

Until the day his face I see,
I will carry on the legacy,
Of the man who set my spirit free.

Allison J. Giger

My Inspiration

My inspiration comes from a little boy.
He gives me hope and a lot of joy.
He makes my world a better place.
Without him, my heart would have an empty space.

Every new day gives me another chance to try,
and every tomorrow gives me the answer why.
A little boy is always the answer I need.
He is always my final push to succeed.

And when times get a little rough,
I stop and think I need to be tough.
There are times, though, when I may stumble and fall,
but there's a little boy who helps me through it all.

The little boy of whom I speak
makes me strong when I am weak.
He's the biggest and best part of me.
He is my child - He inspires me.

Jennifer L. Payne

Father's Day

Our dad was poor in wordily goods,
He had no claim to fame.
No history book or atlas will ever list his name.
But we remember him today and will for years to come;
He labored long and hard to give us
A happy love filled home.

We often see him in ourselves and in our children, too;
A spoken word or action, just as he used to do.
Although a Jack of many trades, his first love was the soil;
And rest was sweet at evening after a day of sweat and toil.
His words were few and far between, but actions, we are told,
Will endure much longer than a speech of purest gold.
We place the roses, which he loved, upon his grave and pray:
"May your spirit live with us, dear Pop, forever and a day".

Helen W. Rank

Alzheimer's Unit

Old hands, Old eyes, Old voices
   Have you been there?
Long halls with rails -
Small rooms with beds -
Pictures of children, grandchildren - Their children
Smells of Pine-Sol, Lysol, age
A sink that drips away time
Pastel peeling walls with huge calendars,
to remind how old today is.
All is temporary and ancient
A holding pen for those once loved - Perhaps still
   Can you watch old used hands reach out
   and not be touched?
Can you see old eyes fill with light and tears and confusion
   and not see?
Can you hear old voices sigh incomprehensible stories
   and not listen to the song?
Time's quilt has unraveled
They have lost their sequence
They are new-borns of now.

Bill Gorman

The Gift

"Thou Mayst," said the Lord.
He handed to humankind his precious gift — freedom of choice.
Thou mayst abide or disavow from birth till death this
miraculous flow of wisdom from the Kingdom way up high.

Thou mayst wear ten commandments as thou cloak, glory crown thy soul.
Trust in the Lord, onward to ascension, there floating clouds befriend
as guides Where angels await rocking the cradle of peace.
Doves will speak and tell
the story, tears nor sorrows fly on misted wings.

Or blind thine eyes, thou mayst, and choose thine own sins.
Find crooked roads blend and bind hearts to stone, leaving wicked
minds alone, ignoring God's word.
Surely, eternity follows choice, beckoning hollow shells
as flaming souls melt. Listen to the promise!
You have chosen chains that bound.

Or thou mayst hear whispers seeping into breath releasing
sweet eternity, beginning of life.
I behold God's precious gift. My freedom to choose right or wrong.
Judgement stands high above watching over earthly journey.
The choice is mine, I'll follow the Lord.
When he calls my name, I think he'll remember.
I made the right choice.

Barbara Kelalis

Jesus Has Been Waiting On Me

I found someone to help me through trials and tribulations
He has been talked about in all generations

When my life would go down and then raise back up
I though it was just something called good luck

But when I said my prayers one night
The Lord touched me with all his might

When I became filled with the Holy Ghost
I then knew my Lord Jesus was so close

Though I have been blind, but now I see
My Lord Jesus has been waiting on me

Yes, my Lord has forgiven me for my sins
And I must say that I have been born again!

I am now filled with the Light
And serving my Lord Jesus with all my might

For prayer is the key and Jesus is the door
If you open it up it is guaranteed you will come back for more

So don't let your life go astray
Chose the Lord and he will lead you the right way.

Carolyn D. Johnson

Christmas

Jesus birthday is Christmas Day,
He was born in a stable on a stack of hay.

We remember him with such joy,
He went to the temple when he was a boy.

He came into the world when we were gone astray,
To show us all how to live the right way.

Jesus lived and died to save us all,
The cross he bore was very tall.

Amy D. Durham

The Church Passed By

Jesus came to earth one day to visit all his churches,
he knew the singing and the shouting would help him in
his searches, he carried his bible down the road until
he heard the sound, the joy and music were so loud it
could have shook the ground, he opened up the door and
was shocked at what he saw, the people so happy and gay
were not his church at all. Jesus dropped his head in
shame and turned to walk away, then he saw a little boy
and ask him where is my church of today? The little boy
replied, you passed it two blocks down the road. So Jesus
started back down that way, but now he carried a heavy load
when he got to the church it was so quite inside, he could
not hide his sorrow, no matter how hard he tried. No singing
shouting, or praying his christians were asleep. He was so
sorrowed and ashamed, he could not help but weep. He
returned to heaven and told God the story with a sigh.
If Jesus came to visit today, would he find us, or just
pass us by?

Gail Mayfield

Chocolate Man

He's short and cute and full of fun, his skin is chocolate brown.
He runs, he jumps, he squeals, he shouts and acts just like a clown.
All kinds of ball he loves to play,
There's often a ball in his hand, baseball, football, basketball and more.
I call him "chocolate man."
"How old are you?"
With a great big grin, he holds three fingers high.
"What a big boy you are!"
Such praise brings a dimple and puts a sparkle in his eye.
"Can you climb on Grandma's lap,"
and I extend a helping hand to chubby legs and chubby arms,
My little chocolate man.
He says, "Dad, let's make water balloons and go outside and play."
With anxious eyes and prancing feet, he'll tolerate no delay.
Balloons are filled, bright yellow and blue with the mischievous
contents for two.
Dad says with a teasing laugh, "One for me and one for you."
"I'm going outside now, Grandma," he says and blows me a kiss with his hand.
I laugh and say, "Have a good time, my little chocolate man."
With laughter and tears he tackles each day trying out everything he can.
Until exhausted and finally asleep. I love you chocolate man.

Genetter Bell

Strength Of A Man

Like a fine silver it is in his eyes.
He searches for it like gold for treasure.
Strong will it make him when he is weak.
When trouble comes like thunder claps in a storm.
It soothes his spirit like a calm autumn breeze.
When it speaks its soft.
But wrong it its voice cuts deep like a knife.
Beautiful will it appear to him when he brings gifts.
Gifts of love through the years will bring it wrought.
In his sight through the years will brings many a comfort and
praise to his heart.
It speaks sweet words in his ears and smells just as sweet as
flowers from a summer meadow.
In the morning with a kiss it rises above him.
Sugary things will it brings him for the days trials.
Before he leaves to face the day it embraces him and with a kiss
he replenishes his puissance.
As he leaves he turns his face as he walks away.
She waves her delicate arms and hands then blows the man the
strength of love.

Byron Auguste Hoesman

126

Jim

Hair like separate shocks of wheat,
He stands, skinny and unkempt,
In a shirt too big, patched and frayed,
Faded beyond guessing its color.
He's come by rail from a rural slum—
For want of a word, he calls it home—
Not yet sixteen, looking younger.

Asked his age, he chokes out the lie:
Just turned eighteen. (In his reply
Are all the hope and hopelessness of his young life.)
Mom died. Dad remarried.
No room for this son at the new wife's table.
He'll say no more, but sets full child-lips in manly line.

No matter. His eyes relate the rest.
Pale blue, they're cold as mountain streams he fished —
And older than his need.

Judith K. Parker

Why?

He looked at you and it filled you with love
He told you that he loved you and that he could never hurt you.
You trusted him and you loved him back.

He slapped you when he found out you were talking to your ex-boyfriend.
He looked at you and it filled you with pain.
He told you that he was sorry and that he would never hit you again.
You trusted him and you loved him back.

He screamed at you and threatened to kill you if he caught you
with another man.
He looked at you and it filled you with fear.
He apologized and said that he loved you too much to kill you.
You trusted and you loved him back.

He slashed your throat when he thought you were cheating on him.
He looked at you and it filled you with hate.
He begged for forgiveness and said that he loved you as you died
in his arms.
You trusted him and you loved him back.

Jonathan Ezarik

Silence

Silence should never be a story.
He who holds a death tool at another,
Who pretends he is greater than this sacrifice,
Will stand seduced at the awful muteness
Of blood spilling poetry left unspoken,
Never realizing that humanity
Has stolen his angel's face.

Tranquility will always follow death or love
Or conflict distorted into righteousness.

The millennia of earth or rock tearing
Itself apart at the novelty of war
Produces only the quietude of the grave
When the bones of enemies sleep together.
And the sight of men playing God
Is greeted with the stony silence
Of a mother recoiling from her infant's touch.

Anita L. Gonzalez

The Mechanical Dog

The mechanical dog was well-behaved,
He was shiny and silver, clean cut and shaved.
He listened to all commands fairly well,
Knew how to read, write, and even spell.
Peculiar even though has he may be,
Was quite a sight for people to see.
He lived in a town for about three years,
Always wagging his tail with pointed ears.
Name changed to Rusty after the accidental day,
When left outside, and the clouds came to stay.
Rain poured over all morning and all night,
Rusted his hinges, a truly horrific sight.
Now Rusty was spotted and brown,
It got his owner kicked out of town.
He's loved by everyone in his city,
Ruined by rain, what a pity!
He's still the same old Rusty that everyone knew,
But how would you feel if it was a mechanical you?

Bill Martlink

Our Great Little Callings

Lord, I hear you calling and my
heart, it jumps with glee.
I do not comprehend why you would
want to choose me.
My spirit runs ahead like a free and happy doe.
Is this what you are thinking Lord?
Is this where I'm to go?
I see the possibilities and I'm ready for the war;
But your voice is getting fainter,
Perhaps I've run too far.
I run back to my loving, all-knowing gracious king.
I'm so happy to be chosen, you're praises I do sing.
Give me just a hint Lord, of what you know I am.
Only you have all the answers, you wrote the master plan.
He looks down at my smiling face and takes me in his arms.
"To tell you all my little one would only bring you harm."
"I'll tell you this sweet dreamer. We will win this holy war!"
"So back to why I called you. Let's scrub this temple floor"

Amy Frahm

Father's Day

My Father is the perfect picture that I see myself to be,
He is always there to guide me and shows me
the obstacles in life that I should see.
He guides me through the hardships,
and he always listens to the bad,
He is always there for me to cry on his shoulder,
And he always makes me laugh when I am sad.
He always works hard at work to give us luxuries at home,
He would give us everything he had,
before he would buy something for his own.
My Father is a great person that should be known throughout history,
But, even though everyone will not know him,
he will always be special to me.

Beth Barry

deeper than all roses

something
in me
knows this
that there's
something
about you
that
ponders and poses
and
the smell
of   your   lips
goes
deeper than all roses
roses and roses and roses and roses

Chris Lee Wingler

Pacific Northwest

Pacific Northwest
Sun Abreast
Ocean
Enchanting and Near
Where
Tides Awake
Evoke and Break
Pacify Console and Endear
Our Emotions
Sweet Emotions
Abreast on this Sphere
To
Rejuvenate and Invigorate
Simply Sifting Clear
Effortlessly and Carelessly
Dancing in the Tide
Cleansing and Purifying
Body Soul and Mind

Daniel Byron Krevitsky

Amputation

I said, "Come by me."

Did you need some convincing?

You just walked away . . .

I am consumed by your smile.

I want to bask in the rays.

Amy Krause

From Far

Never
May the thunder
Of guns, of storms disturb
The solitude which memory brings
On tiptoe to the tiny haven into which
You have been tucked away
For just this
Moment

Dean E. Dowling

Fear

The darkness of fear.
A desert on one's tongue.
Sounds of silence and nothing.
Loneliness engulfs the life.
When living with nothing dear.

Andrea Littig

Upon Awakening

There is an interesting realm,
Somewhere . . .
Just between consciousness,
and the abyss
did I see it? Hear it?
Was it real?
Or simply a construct,
Of the mind.
A phantom of thought,
Gremlin of the synapses?
I enjoy this place.
I visit often
Never awake though.
The rules don't allow it
So come with me!
(we can fly)
Not on the map.
(we'll be free)
The spectral world.
The Power Nap!!!

Joey Martin

Rain

Echoes of time
   A thought — space
Only a drop of water
   In a empty barrel
Oftime:

Connie S. Gasperson

Again

Heavy again
A burden
of conscious
and desire and ambition
disorganized
lack a dazical
The foundation
is impossible
to conceive
if that's how its'
perceived
wow
the revelation
Again
History must be repeated
by those who
don't learn
to change
Again

Eric Willson

Zoot

I see the park through wire mesh fence
a burial ground for my memories
my pain filled heart crying out
thoughts of the dog make me cry out more
sorrows turns to anger
Questions fill my head
Why did his owner move away?
Memories fill my head
hours spent with him
summers days that never ended
tears roll off my cheek
the image blurs
I turn away from the fence
and return home.

Joy Roberts

Demo Rapture

Sea of Galilee.
A chosen place,
to close friends
who looked
upon His face.

Seven miles,
east to west,
when darkness came.
The waters rough.

Half way out,
for His friends,
that was enough.

Then a crossing over.
Yea a shortened trip.
And only by Gods Son,
see John 6:16, to 21.

David W. Domansky

Realization

What is a color to you or me?
A color is something you see,
I don't understand why a person should
Die,
For nothing more than a color seen by
The eye,
To me it's violence nothing more,
To me this seems an everlasting war,
Sometimes each one may cry in their
Sleep,
Feeling the tears as they silently weep,
For why are these tears falling down
These eyes?
It's maybe the sorrow of helpless cries,
We all have to come to the realization
We all live in the same nation
One nation under God with liberty and
Justice for all!!!

Daneen Botero

Party Of 205

The lights go out.
A door is locked.
How can we go home,
with a party still in progress?

How would you like chains,
on your nice picket fence?
A perilous quest at best,
can you tell by the evidence?

The dreams of many,
to be taken by few.
A little chunk of time,
to be paid by a myriad.

The white mercenaries,
to be paid by minimum wage.
Packing a gun of sort,
not a good report.

John Virden

Untitled

When I was but a little girl,
A favorite teacher said to me.
I want you to write a poem,
Write it about a tree.

Many years before, a poem
about a tree I'd read.
So when I wrote, this tree
of mine, was dead.

This tree has only limbs
With no leaves to clear the air.
No shade in which to place a swing,
For children playing there.

No branches into which a bird might fly,
and maybe build a nest. No cooling
shadows, a pup might claim
to take a needed rest.

And yet there's beauty in this tree,
and I saw it oh so plain.
As a small boy sat on a large bare limb,
and wave to a passing train

Jean P. Garcia

"A Day"

A man stands alone in the dark.
A fire burns at night in the park.
A child cries on through the night.
A mother holds her shaking with fright.
A gun shot echoes in the sky.
A man falls dead in the blink of an eye.
And another day just passes by.

Jorge J. Wahner II

When I Care

The way I care is when
a friend is drinking to much
and needs to go home. I
Take them. I care when
a person is on the street
with no food to eat. I
Feed them. I care when a
person is hurting and need
someone to talk to I
care. When I care I care
with my whole heart and the fear
in my heart goes away when I
care.

Angeline Showers

There was a sound . . .
A look
a touch
caressingme—
For a brief instance
I was filled with
joyous love . . .

Then

There was a sound
of shattering hearts
Shards of our souls
hit the ground
Echoing . . .

Then Silence . . .

Charlene Campbell

Untitled

This life of mine—
    A history book
Of valiant deeds
    Left undone,
Of moving words
    Still unsaid,
Of worthy thoughts
    Quite unfinished,
Of emotional battles
    Yet unfought,
With many volumes
    Still to come.

A thousand years
    Shall I wait,
    Till history's end.
    Then shall I write
    The final book,
    Left unread.

Jadz Morrison

Solitary Region

On the cracked hard concrete
A leaf blows by,
Catching an edge on the fractured
Earth.

The mourning dove sits
On a black stiff cable,
Raging with the sun.
Gray silky wings
Thrash the ground below.

My neighbor's dog works the soil,
Forging his single pathway.
An axe lacking a handle
Wishes for one more taste
Of a stately hard wood.

Anthony James Frelo

Jack G.

He battles death every day now.
A losing battle, he knows,
but still—
He sits at the breakfast table
surrounded by people.
Friends, hangers-on, what?
His bandanad head is kept lowered.
He raises it slowly.
Under his bushy eyebrows
wide opened eyes speak volumes.
Questioning?
Angry?
Hurt?
No. A mad bull, she thinks.
A mad and a cornered bull.
He battles death every day now.

Janet B. Donaldson

Market Of Death

I'm searching in a market
A market of death
Where everything is hatred
Yet nevertheless
I know it will lead
To the end of this world
Yet I keep searching
In this market of death

Jenny Edmiston

Memories Of Mario

I have in my heart
a memory of you.
Of your face and your walk
and the things you would do.

I loved you my darling
but now you are gone.
Just drifted away
Like the words of a song.

Now if it wasn't for memories
How lonely I'd be
I'd forget you
Just as you've forgot me.

Janet Iriarte

Hope

Hope is such a small word
A nebulous thing,
Buried in the glitter
And carols we sing.

Hope for our country
It's such a mess.
Hope for all people
With racial unrest.

Hope for the stressed-out
And elderly sick
Where the nursing home
Just can't do the trick.

Hope for the children.
What will be left
As they trod this land
On their earthly quest?

Hope is such a small word,
Not a tangible thing,
But a part of the message
That Christmas brings.

Estelle Wise

Eternal Life

A place of hope and glory
A place so undefined
A place that's universal
This place withholds no time

A place that's everlasting
A place that's mine and yours
A place that judges no one
This place holds open doors

A place that sees no evil
A place that forgives bad
A place that sees no color
This place hinders the sad

A place beyond mortality
A place of godly love
A place I will one day know
Heaven up above

Diana Hayes

What Is This?

A ball is passed,
A point is made,
A player falls,
A ball is stolen,
A game is won,
A team is glad,
A crowd cheers on,
WHAT IS THIS?
BASKETBALL

Elizabeth Bowerman

Untitled

Mind's peace
a rarity of its own
into which this bliss
can't find its way.
A lost direction
is an aimless delight.
If a laugh can be found
treasure the moment
for through the mire
can be found your way;
one must only
desire the peace
within the heart.

Jessica Lee

Untitled

Inside me lives an iron man.
A rigid frame of steel.
He keeps my face towards the sun
Despite the fear I feel.

The man is nothing if not strong
And dominant in will
He drives me on when days are long,
And when the path seems all uphill.

Inside me lives a stubborn child
Who wants the world his way.
He cries in fear, and all the while
His world is dying day and day.

With idle threats the boy cries on
And pleads to save himself.
But he can see his time is gone;
No boyish toys upon the shelf.

the boy, the man, who will control,
The body, mind? The heart, the soul?
If you doubt this struggle lives, and if
you doubt my child dies,
search for strength and search for fear
behind the glare upon my eyes.

Cameron Carr

At The Center

There is a joy in silence . . .
A soft, soothing envelope of peace.

Shutting out the noise of the world,
Assuring all "Prisoners" their release.

A haven removed from the violence,
A harbor in the midst of the storm.

A sanctuary in the heart of the soul,
Where God's love keeps us warm.

Jan E. DeRouin

At Eventide

There comes to me, at end of day,
    A strange sweet longing,
As the twilight tries to linger
    Against the advancing night.

An inner calmness, not born of day,
    Pervades my soul,
As I now behold . . . the glory
    Of the twilight hour.

Within the vale, the village kirk
    Now breaks the silence,
And tolls its requiem
    To the passing day.

Someday, I'll remember,
    I'll remember when . . .
I looked upon this scene,
    As it became a part of me.

Forever . . . to know, there was
    A time . . . a place . . . a sight,
That touched my heart . . .
    At eventide.

Glen A. Lougee

Who Are We

"Who are we?"
A two-sided spirit
Can't you see,

With a mind
And a will to choose
Who we wish to be,

"Who are we?"
A two-sided spirit
Can't you see,

Good or bad
Weak or strong
Being what we wish
For however long,

"Who are we?"
A two-sided spirit
Can't you see,

Now that you know,
"Which will you
Choose to be?"

Carol F. Burnett

Dawn

Upon the darkness of the night
A vision I search not in sight
A clue of my beleaguered plight
A wish I may be blessed with sight
To know to understand my in ward light

With age and time there came a clue
Who was I and what I was to do
To think of me as I of you
With this in hand works I must do

With the breaking of the night
My vision has given me sight
for now I see the light - Dawn

Darrell Raphael

The Pain You Feel

A cloud of gloom
a world of hate.
Who said you
could decide my fate?

A lonely star in the sky . . .
dampened cheeks from crying eyes.

A beaten child
shivers from fright
as he haunts her
day and night.

A single family worlds apart . . .
a slowing beat of a dying heart.

Words of wisdom
never heal
the pain inside
that one feels.

A lost soul wandering about . . .
in a world that shut her out.

Deanna J. Griak

"Love"

What is love, that we forget
    about it?
What are feeling that we forget
    about love?
Love is not something that man
    created, but its something they
destroy with their behavior.
If love dies, does man perish
    God forbid.
For it was this reason he died
    on the cross, because it was
man that he cherish.
If a man hate, he shall have
    his place, but if a man
shall love, his place is Heaven above.

Bermoine Lindsey

I Thought I Knew

All about love I thought I knew
About romance I knew all too
But fate has now shown to me
How much more there is to see
Into my life she walked one day
Now in my heart is where she will stay
Love found me but I didn't see
Now I've seen love pass by me
All about love I thought I knew
But now I know, how little I knew.

James B. Dreslinski

Dreams And Memories

I dream that I walk in sunlight.
Across a spacious lawn
I want to step into that dream
But my walking day are gone.
I shed a tear as I awake.
Then I know what I have to do.
I turn my dreams into memories
When I walked in the sunshine with you.

Evelyn Walker

Untitled

"On the battlefield of war
  after all is clear"
"The only sound that you will
  hear"
"Are the voices of spirits
  as they arise above"
"To say that heaven is all Love"
  "And as these spirits ascend
    With a mighty yell"
"To tell all mankind
  that war is the only hell!"
Donna Crowder

Monument

Come close my love
After it's all said and done
You've been a friend to me
I've been a friend to no one
Yet
It seems to me
That you cut my dreams apart
On the altar of a promise
That was never spoken

My love for you
Is like a whirlwind in my heart
I'm spinning faster
Falling through a wheel that turns

Mark my descent
By an oil slick on the clouds
Let my debris be
Seagulls in the setting sun
Brendon Michael Walker

A Sailors Creed

All alone in the dark of night.
Against the currents, we have to fight.
To the dark blue waters and ocean floors.
The foreign lands that we explore.

Where men hate men and fire guns.
Where missile soar above rising suns.
A soldiers roar, when he has won
A brave mans cry, when he has none.

Defend our country to the end.
A helping hand we will lend.
All the bodies that we send.
To the fights and to the graves.
Their families heart we must mend.

A sailor keeps his line of sight.
Though borders loose or borders tight.
He will always be alone, against the
currents in the dark of night.
Ariel Colon Jr.

Roses

Every day I like to see
All the children walk by me
I love the wind to blow around
But not my peddles on the ground
I like my leaves
So soft and green
I like the lovely morning grace
I love when the sun touches my face
Me the rose has no more to say
Just have a nice and lovely day
Ashley Abbott

Untitled

Gentil touch de mon amour
  al(l) ways
tugs/Pulls; My heart with the
Strength of Rolling
thunder: overwhelms, — loads
my Mind, my Soul, mon Coeur

you i reach, (con) sole — (me)
    hold me, love me
Be me / for all that i Am,
  i AM
  for you: (la vie, not
for gain: jamais) shades
de blanc, mon cher
  Bewilder, amaZe (others
do not compare to MY
love) my life; mon amour.
Christina Stamper

The Aura

The energy, it flows
  all around
My emotions, it's feeling
  it just may overtax me
Love, its power
  will be my deliverer
Hate, its taste
  oh, so bitter sweet
But Jealousy;
  Yes Jealousy
it hurts right to the bone
Can Revenge,
  All revenge
be all right?
  Or wrong?
Human being, be it as it is told
  we are bright and able
and even so, dumb and blind
John Lee Spragley Jr.

My Mind Is Gone

In my state of destitute
All I can do is think of you
In my dreams of waking terror
I think of you in the twilight hour
  My Mind is Gone.
Nothing matters as I rot away
No one here, no one stays
People come and then they leave
There's nothing left to believe
  My Mind is Gone.
Now I sit in my darkened room
Would you like to see my view
Nothing here but silent screams
Nothing here but broken dreams
  My Mind is Gone.
Will you come and taste my pain
Then you'll never thirst again
To see what it's like on my side
Come and take the last ride
  My Mind is Gone.
Denise Cooper

World's And Countries

World's and countries
all in war.
Countries used and
Countries tore.

World's and countries.
With no rules.
Just run by killers,
Slayers, and fools.

World's and countries
In religious confusion.
And weapon's made
By nuclear fusion.

World's and countries
Need to pause.
And see if the fighting
Is for a worthy cause.
Christi Miller

Wonders Of The Butterfly

Butterflies were fluttering
All over the trees.
You could hear
A rustling like a breeze
Fragrance of flowers
Filled the air,
As I strolled beneath
And watched in awe
The sight above me
Unfold.
The trees seemed to move,
In union
As each wing opened
And closed.
The color before my eyes
Was a breath taking view,
So beautiful to see
All this color in motion.

Frances Dare Johnson

nowhere

crates cartons containers
all sizes shapes
line cross zig zag the room
stand at attention
like soldiers
some taped tightly shut
solemnly protect
their precious wares
others mouths agape
bellies wait to be filled
shrill ring of a phone
sorry truck broke down
and here i am
in limbo
  not here
  not there
  just

      nowhere
Barbara Hoffman

Jeffrey

I know that we weren't
All that close,
But I have a feeling that
We would've been.
Why you were given
Such a short time
I will never know.
You were a really
Great guy
And you will always
Be missed
And will always
Hold a special place in my heart.
I would be willing to trade
You places
If it would mean
Bringing you back
Even for a few seconds
I would be willing
To give my life forever.

In Memory of Jeffrey "Jeffco" Acker
April 8, 1977 - February 3, 1995

Gandy Baker

Forever Friends

I don't know how to say
All the things I feel for you.
Thank you is too little, but
'I love you' is difficult too.

To say how much will frighten
To say too little will never do.
For you need to know how much I care,
But not how much I love you.

Your smile in the morning light
Makes my heart and mind brighten,
Your hugs in the afternoon
Let me know how much I'll miss you.

As the night draws closer
My heart sinks with each passing minute
For I know too soon you'll be gone
And I will once more be alone.

Here's to a lifetime of friendship
Of caring and being there for each other.
As our lives change and develop,
May we always be together, somewhere.

Debbie Gadd

The Final Farewell

It seems so hard to say good-bye,
all the time I thought you were true.
Then after I hear all your lies,
I knew I wasn't meant for you.

I must remember that life goes on,
even through all the memories we shared.
I now know my love for you is gone,
but in my heart you are concealed.

Julia Eh'e Grow

To A Calendar

On a single sheet
All those days — weeks - months.
Happy moments - troubled hours.
Plans, schemes - events
Fears, disappointments - pure joy
Memories - associations - anniversaries
Each a little numbered square.
Dear days - weeks - months
Some like granite building blocks
Supporting us a lifetime.
Others - children's blocks
Inconsequential and frivolous
An alphabet of color
Running thru the year.

Delight L. Millspaugh

"Hit And Run"

The speeding auto sped,
along the road that led,
to certain death of red.

Feathers flew on impact,
no wing was left intact.
The hit? It was exact!

Raspberry red ran out;
pouring as though from spout.
But was he dead? No doubt!

Grayish feathers mangled,
long, lanky, legs tangled,
by his blood he strangled.

Life was gone in a blink,
he didn't have time to think;
dappled dove, now extinct.

Joseph Henderson

Salt Air

Oceans moving
Always changing
Always the same

Tides rising
Tides falling
Ending higher than before

Currents swift
Changing fast
Keeping current

Waves silent
Building, louder
Crash

Repeating, echoing
Roll in and
Crash, crash, ash, ssshhh

Takes me out
Leads me back
But means much more

Derek Adam Warner

From The Beginning Of Time

From the beginning of time, we were
Always we have been one with God.
Through the dark veil the soul remembers.

Those souls we know in this time
We will meet again
We know not where or when.

There is no death; no parting.
From the beginning of time, we were
Always we will be one with God.

Florence D. Nordquist

Alone . . .

Another day lost
among the pages
in the book of life.
The book is filled
with many empty pages -
days forever gone,
not worthy of recall.
Wasteful, tragic, true. . .
Not all pages are empty
thank God, a treasured few
are filled with meaning -
these can be read
again, a pleasant trip
down memory lane.
When the book is closed
the memories die -
we know not why.

Dorothy A. Wallace

Melting Innocence

Winter shelters innocence as it falls
amongst the gentle white of snow
But in time both melt away
Bringing only the rain and tears
eroding trenches to form the
bridges forever uncrossed.

Footprints of the past mark trails
of pain
Always unforgotten are the haunting
memories with only time to resolve
their sadness gathered in the journey
But surely as there is night and day
Life too will blindly slip away
As did the time that faded
With melting innocence

Jeremy D. Chrane

Dream Star

I close my eyes
An I see a star
I look into the sky
An their you are

I see your head arms an feet
Then I wonder when we will meet
I keep watching the sky at night
Waiting for the day of your flight

Many light years from now
When you fall down on my turf
We will be together here on earth

James E. Long

The Coyote

Lumbering, limping,
   (an uneven gate)
Whining and whimpering,
   (a terrible fate)
For one who's so agile,
   noble, and cunning,
A life filled with stealing,
   and hiding and running.
Finding a refuge
   to lick at long last,
the burning and searing,
   caused by the blast.
To bleed and to die,
   and not ever know why.
Hated and hunted,
   with no place to hide.
Howling her haunting
   hymn from the old
The long hated coyote
   dies alone in the cold!

Jennae Earnhart

With Mama And Me

It's like we started off on a tree trunk
and a lumberjack cut it down
My smile then got replaced with a frown
With mama and me

Or off on the sand of a beach
and the sea washed it away
and colors transformed to gray
With mama and me

Or off just simply on some paper
and it got erased
And put things in an awkward place
With mama and me

But now we're going to start
where things won't come to grief
a stable place with such relief
is unmistakably the heart

With such a component I will succeed
With mama and me

Right away
Without delay

Ebony Dean

Precious Moments With Me

With a gleam in your eye
   and a smile that was sly,
When you entered my room,
   You soon had me in tune
and had precious moments with me.

Ataka Rhodes Royse

StarStuff

All that is,
And all who are
Were processed in some ancient star.

Now, only clouds
And scattered dust
Are faint reminder of its' past.

Where planet tracked
Around its' globe
Is empty, lifeless, dark and cold.

And memory
Of why it shone
Is locked forever in our bones.

That distant sun, from whence we came,
Will never have a proper name.

And ages hence
When Sol does wane
We shall return to star again.

To Mother Earth
To Father Time,
To journey celestial maritime

Charles L. Davis Jr.

Mom

You are my heart
And always will
So gentle and loving
I love you still
As years go by
Your beauty stays
Your caring heart
And loving ways
I love you Mom with all my heart
You are a beautiful work of art.

Camille Bass

Girls

Through diapers and rashes
   And baby bottle crashes

Through crawling and walking
   And the constant talking

Through rollers and ribbons
   And lipstick and polish

If "she" would be a "he"
   This could be abolished -

There'd be trucks and tanks
   And "walk the plank"

There'd be knives and guns
   And Gooey Yuck
So maybe girls is really luck

Through dates and dinners
   And boyfriend winners

Through rings and all the "I do's"
It makes me glad and yet so sad -

That I only have a few.

Heidi Donat

Behind The Badge

From behind the badge
and beneath the vest,
Lies a heart and soul
Always put to the test

Standing tall and proud
in his uniform of blue,
He speaks with a sincerity
that is found in so few.

He tells of a way
if you want to achieve,
It is in yourself
that you must believe.

Despite all the chaos
in his day of events,
there's still time for an ear
or shoulder to be lent.

So! This poem I've written
is dedicated only to you,
'cause behind that badge
is a friend in Blue.

Janice M. Harmony

Reality's Child

Reality is, reality was
and cannot ever be
the same to any one of you
what it is to me

A child 'til touched
by you and me
A tree remains,
just a tree

Reality's experience shared
becomes the same
for those who cared
when hearts did meet
'neath souls which bared
within that tree,
nay, at its feet

A child is born to you and me
immersed within reality
and lives and breathes
and learns of love
as it was ever meant to be

Howard A. Bristow

Untitled

The dawn has broken
And my eyes see the light.
That which I vowed
Never to look upon again.

Turn back time
So that I may see darkness;
The darkness that holds my heart.

My dreams were so sweet
Now awakened, I see
The sour aging of reality.

Constance Ann Deveres

The Flight

Let the children be thirsty
and come to our spring
let them eat of our fruits
may they soar by our wings.

Take each moment, unpromised
for nurturing song.
By example, we teach
Let us not guide them wrong.

Rather, seek out the course
upon which one should fly
be unto such the wind
that will keep e'er high.

'Til darkness approaches
borrowed wings needing rest
unto these be the branch
upon which one may nest.

For some days later flight
by own wings shall they soar.
as the course e'er taken
is free to explore.

Erika Akeo

'Eagle'

If I was an Eagle,
And could take off in flight,
I'd come and sit on your house,
And protect you day and night.

So nothing would ever come your way,
That wasn't good for you.
I'd keep you always safe from harm,
Till you could be there in my arms.

We'd go everywhere,
We'd see everything.
When you and I are finally one,
Then we've only just begun.

Fern E. Howe

The Computer

Just when my program is running well,
And everything seems to fit,
A glitch comes out of nowhere,
And blows it all to bits.

It just takes one comma out of place,
A period now and then,
The whole thing will refuse to work,
And I have to start again.

Garbage in, garbage out,
No truer words can be said,
I'll never learn computerese,
I think I'll go to bed.

In the morning when I rise,
To set the thing to working,
The lights will all come on again,
And the glitch will still be lurking.

Jane Reinmuth

Lizards Are Lickable

Lizards are lickable
and extickable

And even if you try
you can't make them unstickable.

They stick to logs
and rocks by frogs,

They stick to sticks
covered with ticks.

They even stick
to the ticks on the stick

And to one another
what a trick!

They stack like logs,
they stack like pogs.

You think there's one,
there's twenty-one!

You'd think they'd run,
they stick for fun!

Justin Lepper

Nightmare

Shame
and fear
oh screaming
violent tears
sleep

Dream
escape
and forget
try to forgive
heal

Scars
painful
and haunting
oh the visions
scenes

Life
goes on
to forgive
try to forget
heal

Kara L. Leonard

Insong

Oh, to stand on the summit of a hill
And feel life vibrant around me
In silent joy,
Till I am living, too.

Jane G. Osler

Another Child Gone . . .

I stared into this mother's eyes
And felt the sorrow from tears she cried
The tears of past days gone by
And wondering why her child had to die
The answer she will never know
Why her child would not grow old
She thinks back to a happier time
When this child could always find
Something that would make her smile
And make her tomorrow's all worth while
Now this mother sits with flower in hand
And wonders if her life will end
Because this pain she feels so deep
As she watches her child's eternal sleep
She looks up toward the heavenly sky
And once again I heard her cry
Lord please give my child a loving home
for now I know my child is gone

Jodie D. Robinson

"A View"

To sit upon a rock up high
And gaze out to the sea and sky
To feel the sun warm on my face
To watch the current glide and race
To hear my heart sing deep within
To feel as if I'm cleansed from sin
To know release from daily strain
To let the joys of life take reign
The light blue sky, the deep blue sea
The wonder of it inside me
The distant shores so real though dim
Craggy rocks 'round the waters rim
The peace and quiet that fills the air
With precious moments sweet and rare
All this and more I think of when
I take myself with book and pen
And sit upon a rock up high
And gaze out to the sea and sky

Hannah F. Turner

Winter Wonderland

One day as I sat by the window
And gazed at the view outside,
It was just all so amazing
That I almost sat there and cried.

There were icicles on the wires,
Hung from houses and the trees too,
It looked like "Winter Wonderland,"
Sure made for a beautiful view.

It looked like millions of diamonds,
Sparkling all over the place,
It certainly was God's work
Giving beauty to the human race.

If it wasn't for the accidents
These bad storms cause everyday,
I'd vote for these pretty ice storms
To always come our way.

No artist could paint such a picture,
'Twas just so beautiful to see,
Felt I could gather those diamonds
'Cause they sure looked so real to me.

Evelyn M. Swenor

Let Us Play

Remember that life is a game,
And give your child time to play.
When was the last time
You skipped down the street?
Was it yesterday?

We take our lives too seriously,
Trapped in our own pomposity.
The ever ready antidote
Is to see the humor in it all.

So blow up your big red balloon,
Let it fly high in the sky,
Soar on the wings of fantasy,
And skip down the street tomorrow.

Hap Barhydt

Just You and Me

We're waiting and watching
And guarding the sheep,
the dog and the cat both sit at our feet.

She meows and he barks
And make lots of noise
they lunge and they pounce
And sit in their poise

The ticks and the fleas —
Will sure as you please
All wait for a chance for a ride,
When the day is through
There's me and you
To tend them side by side.

Just me and you
And the day is through
When all the work is done
Do sit in repose as this day goes —
By the setting of the sun.

Evelyn Carrie Meschefske

Issues

The death will happen sooner
And if that might be good
The cops and goons will look at
The violence in the hood
The druggies and loons
Will stop and think a bit
Before they carry on
To take that lasting sip
And if that ain't enough
To hear the children's pleas
To stop the violence
And make the druggies drop
Down to their knees
And then I hope the keys
Will be found at last
To save the children's souls
From the violence of the past.

Julie Dodge, 14

Cats

Cats
Beautiful, majestic
Pouncing, sprinting, purring
Very proud and confident
Cats

Ange Wang

Song of the Heart

I love you more and more each day
And in my heart you'll always stay
Along with all the memories
Of how much you love me.

You are worth more than you know
I hope my love for you I show
And I will wait forever just
To have you by my side.

Someday this world may fall apart
But you will stay here in my heart
Always safe and always loved
Forever you'll be mine.

Jennifer Phillips

Build A Wall

Smile upon a world so grim
and keep your thoughts
buried deep within.
Close the blinds
behind which you hide
and build a wall
so very high.
Share with no one,
and let no one in
live a life
so very dim.

Cherrie Hiles

Memories That Bind

You went away
 and left behind
 the memories of
 the years that bind;
that bind together
 years we shared
 from dreams we planned
 and how we cared.
You may be gone
 but still remain
 deep in my thoughts
 tho' not in vain.
I remember clearly
 what love can do
 the strength, the power,
 miraculously, too.
Your absence leaves
 what you left behind
 the meaning of life
in MEMORIES that BIND.

Cesarina Maria Rossetti

Finding A Perceptive Listener

"Have you ever felt terrified
And paralyzed,
Like you were caught within a trap
And victimized?
Did you feel like you dare not move
Nor even speak
And all your future looked real bleak,
Gloomy and bleak,
Because someone's anger was high,
High to the sky
For no reason?" . . . "Oh my, oh my,
Yes, so have I."

Evamae Luenberger

My Fortress

You are my husband
And my friend;
My life I know
I must depend.
You are my fortress
Strong and high;
I know in you
I can confide.
When sad emotions
Swell within;
Your like a high
And rushing tide
You bring me up
To make me see;
I must face reality.
I love you now
Don't you see,
Until we reach
That golden shore
I'll love you more in our Eternity.

June Ruth

Untitled

The days have passed so quickly,
 And now the time has come.
For the two of us to separate.
 And act as one and one.
When I last looked in your eyes,
 my heart was beating fast.
My body shook all over,
 and I prayed for the moment to last.
As our lips came closer together,
 my heartbeat continued to rise.
The future seemed to vanish,
 the second I shut my eyes.
That moment lasted forever,
 though still not long enough.
When it suddenly seemed clear to me,
 that all you need is love.
As the kiss was ending,
 and our lips were forced to part.
I realized very quickly,
 forever you'll be in my heart.

Erin D. Eltman

In The Beginning

In the beginning, God,
And only empty space,
The only tool, His word
The only means, His grace.

In the beginning, God
Almighty, sovereign Lord
The world came into being
Created by His word.

The mountains and the valleys,
The rivers, lakes and seas
The flora and the fauna
He created all of these.

In His hands, some clay
He formed it into man,
His breath gave light and energy
And human life began.

In the beginning, God!

Jane Godfrey

Voyager Contemplation

I strive to greet each silent star
And pass to galaxies afar,
To climb the attic of the skies,
Discover where creation lies

To view the vaulted vestibule
Established where some Titan tool
That forges astral entities
In celestial identities
Is scattering its sacred sparks
Where eon's history embarks,
And from whose crucible cascade
The spores from which all space is made.

With emblems of this empyreal span
How minuscule a mite is man!
Yet he, with mind attuned, can vision
This panoply of pure precious.

Ione Newby

The Last Song

I have song songs for King and Queens
and people all over the world
I song songs of life and love
and great story were told

I lived my life and sing songs
along the way
To mother and father
and children as they play

Song of happiness and sadness
I did sing
Now my songs will be ended
but my memoir will
linger on
So dear God please
let me sing one more song
for my last will be just for you.

Betty Jean Herron

Oh So Young

I went to the park,
and played on the swing.
I thought for a moment,
I must be the king.

I spotted the monkey bars,
and thought, oh how high.
I climbed to the top,
and let out a sigh.

Off in the distance,
a sandbox for two.
I thought to myself,
could I play with you?

I ran to the slide,
and slid to the ground.
Look at all the fun,
I somehow had found.

Aren't you to old
to climb on that tree?
I said oh no ma'am,
I'm just ninety-three.

Diane F. Hoffman

The Black Heart Inside Of Me

Love is such a strong
and powerful word. It
expresses your emotions
and feelings from deep within
your heart. It seems like
such a harmless, word. You
hear it everyday. Just another
word in our vast vocabulary,
right? Who knew what LOVE
could mean to one person?
Who knew what LOVE could
do to one person? Who knew?
If only, they knew.

Brandi Green

The Blue Spruce Tree

I stand in silence with other Spruces
And preen in the brilliant snow
I stand quietly this way
Day and night as the winds blow.

Then one day in a home I was placed
I knew not what was in store
They dressed me in lovely colored bulbs
With ribbons, lights and more.

So I had been a part in a plan
Of some kind of holiday ploy
To be amid laughter, fun and children
Indulged in something called joy.

Days later I was lonely and sad
Abandoned and garlanded no more
I then wished to stand again in silence
Quietly with the Spruces, wind and snow.

Johnnie F. Kirvin

"Lost"

Insignificantly it began brewing
    and returned to him fast
unconsciously he was cluing
    that he must let go the past
It stirred in his head
    as if some huge recital
but came to him instead
    that he was living in denial
to the mirror he crept
    saw a different race
and it was met
    with his own face

Antonio Royuela

Bitter Words

Poisoned hearts, damaged minds,
and shattered emotions are all
that we have left of the love
we once held dear.

With bitter words of anger, we
wield them at each other, like
the men of old with swords
of steel — striking deep within
each others' hearts
to rip asunder at the thing we
cherished most about each other —
our love.

Brian Clites

A Mother's Moment

I look out in a field of green
And see it's not so bare.
For in the center I see a boy,
Not moving, just standing there.

Hair of blond, eyes of brown,
His skin a golden tan.
Should I see this boy tomorrow
Perhaps he'd be a man.

But this is not tomorrow,
A man I do not see.
In this field I see a boy,
My son who's only three.

My heart goes out to this little one
Who'll one day face the world
For today he sees only love in life
With all its beauty unfurled.

C. Lynette

Distance

It's something you can drive
    and something you can run.
It keeps people in different places.
    It has been said to make the
    heart grow fonder.
But it has also separated many.
    Lovers. Friends. Family.

It keeps enemies apart.
    And can drive a wedge
    through friendships.

It sometimes can be measured,
    and almost always can be felt.

The strong do survive it.

Only time can prove
    just how strong
    we are.

Amy L. Monastero

Veneer

To walk along the cobblestone street
And stagger as it twists my feet
A desolate mile that only one proceeds
Wandering among peeling birch trees

Sky above splintered crimson tangerine
Simmers over the forest green
Birds in their song now relate
Life, death, and impending fate

Tiny claws, rugged bark they leave
Smooth perfection, vandals and thieves
Tearing the silver paper bark
Flutter off and leave their mark

Standing tall with still defense
Accepting quiet helplessness
Sighing through rustling leaves
Falling, gathering around my feet

Sadness, sees the staining flaws
Pillage left by usurping claws
Standing under the shady tree
Remaining flaws it shares with me.

Jim Grube

A Dream

Each night a dreams comes
And takes me away
Sometimes good
Sometimes bad
Even if I try
Some are bad
Though I wish
They we're never bad
Some are
Some times a bad dream
Is not as bad
As it seams.

Dean-Anna Hicks

Faith, Hope And Love

The wind blows swiftly by my face,
and takes me to a far off place.
To a place I once dreamt of,
a place of laughter, a place of love.

Over the hills and mountains tops,
my spirit soars - it never stops.
Hoping, searching for the day,
I'll find this place so far away.

I'll climb the highest hill or slope,
to grasp hold of my only hope.
To find true love and strength of soul;
undoubtedly my greatest goal.

Then suddenly I start to shake;
my tender heart begins to ache.
I hope and pray the day will come,
my soul and love will join as one.

Anthony Benedict Fox

The Scooterville Incident

It was hot that night in Scooterville
And the bikes were rolling late
The doughnut vendors, on the street
Ran out of cyclamate.

The law sprang forth in force, of course
Asked, "What here evil delves?"
The doughnut guys, cried out, "Surprise!
We cycled it ourselves!"

Squimbo

Untitled

Spin the tapestry of life
and wind the ball of hope
For if the world were half mine
Then all I have's a joke
 In this world
 To which I'm hurled
In spinning hangman's ropes

Take a hand to run the race
Four eyes to teach the path
The cobblestones of smoothing words
Lending kindness to wrath
 It's all a hated enterprise
 and none are more the wise
It's all for naught and then some more
When we muffle baby's cries

Christopher J. Reid

Where The Poplar's Roots Are Buried

Now as Summer gives way to fall,
and the leaves descend to nestle
upon the ground, the poplar's looming
branches spread out unhidden.
Deathly and bony, wrapped in weathered
ropes. Black blood draining through
the soil and into the poplars buried
root. Now this tree, the black
man's tree, and a different soul
for each different leaf.
The blood in the seed grows another
tree, that will hold a rope of
it's own.
We, like this tree, keep our ropes
'round our hands, as the blood
enters our root, and we become
no different than the men we have
hung. Though we spread a seed that
will grow a tree that will hold
a rope of it's own.

James Clayton Fiddler

Lands-End: A Simple Question?

Feel the smells of sightly dells,
and the pollen rolls over me.

I see the Why,
of lands spread thighs,

Where went its Virtuosity?

Jeremy Clow

"Transition"

As the cool gentle rains begin to fade
And the sun sleeps for tomorrow's shade
Stars in the twilight sky play
And mother holds child to allay
Those thoughts which produce great fears;
Causing him to let loose his tears.

Chicopee Quidnet

"Jack Frost"

Summer is gone and Winter is here
And this is the time for him to appear
 all clad in ice
 all clad in snow
He'll bring good cheer where
 e'er he'll go.
He'll dance upon your windowpane
And paint it with an icy stain
He'll clothe the houses and trees around
And place his mantle upon the ground.

Grace Wagner

Royalty

My favorite bird sat near my window,
 and wished me a happy day
His song was light and pretty
 his song was bright and gay.
Thank you God for the Cardinal
 he's a reminder of your creativity
Such a lovely painted coat of red,
 it has the look of royalty.

Janet Johnson

Holding On

When the dreams have all gone homeward
 and tomorrow's sun is here
Will I still be holding on
 to dreams I now hold near?
There was a time in yesterday
 when dreams were all around.
But when tonight's dark moon has passed
 can they still be found?
No one knows when dreams are born
 or just when dreams will die.
Some may see the other side
 that teaches them to cry.
For this night I'll just go on
 and pray that love is true.
When the sun comes out today
 I'll tell you I love you.

Judith E. Bailey

The Times We Share(d) Together

We've had our good times
and we've gotten through our bad

We've shared our deepest feelings
that we didn't know we had

We've said things that we
sometimes have regret

But, we always come to our senses
forgive and forget

We've managed to make each other
feel good in all sorts of ways

Which brings me back to those good
and loving days

We've shared a love that no other two
people could share, and because of this
we know our love for each other will
always be there

Crystal D. Lockett

It's All Right To Chase Rainbows

As he faces life's challenges,
And with God's help succeed.
Like after a storm,
He sees the rainbow.

For man to face life's challenges,
And succeed, he grow as a person,
When he gives the glory to God.
Like after a storm, he sees the rainbow.

As the earth welcomes rain,
Man should welcome the challenges.
For as the earth needs rain to grow,
It's God's plan that man needs
Challenges to grow.
Like after a storm, he sees the rainbow.

So as you go through life, accept
life's challenges, and remember
"It's all right to chase rainbows."
Just remember, it's God's grace,
That put them there.

Earl Johnson

Forever Near

And my life begins anew,
  And with me, my mother.
So I yearn to play,
  And there is my mother.
And with such, I learn,
  And with me, my mother.
Of education, I toil,
  And there is my mother.
And with work comes counsel,
  And with me, my mother.
Post counsel I fall, as all,
  And there is my mother.
And when I fall, I learn.
  Thank you mom.
From high and afly to briefly awry,
  You are with me.
  Thank you mother of mine.

John Hamilton

Cosmic Unity

The cumulus clouds
Are all piled up
Like whipped cream
Around the rim
Of the towering sky
A beggar's bowl
Upturned to beneficence
Of rain - wind - sun

The people scurry
In the ratholes
Of their minds
Lunch with Millie
Meet a client
Court at two
Catch the train
Fight the crowds

The indifferent earth
Continues as it has
In millenniums past

Gerrie Kretzmer

The Eyes Of A Child

The eyes, they say
Are the windows of our soul
Revealing our innermost thoughts and
desires,
But none are so bright
Like the eyes of a child,
Shining passion that burns like a fire.

But the years that pass by
It's sad to say
Can begin to take that gleam away
The innocence -- the passion
That mark tender years,
Give way to suspicion
And too many tears.
So if you're looking for joy
And hope that abounds,
It's in the eyes of a child
That these too can be found.

John W. Granger III

"Race"

What does it mean to have a "race,"
Are we in competition?
Who wins a battle fought with hate,
Prejudice or derision?
Is race a color of the skin
Or something else that shows?
Could it be just a difference in
A mouth, an eye, a nose?

To me a "race" is just a word
Which keeps us from our brother;
Something so small it's quite absurd
For us to hate each other.
Perhaps we should forget the term
That causes so much bother,
And try to live our lives as one;
The children of our Father.

Joanne C. Kriston

Artist Of The Fall

A kaleidoscopic artist
arrives at summer's end
to brush the wooded landscapes
with fiery, russet blend.
Color inspired by sunlight
and evenings brisk to cold
turns all the shrubs to crimson
while the trees are etched in gold.
A sky of misty silver,
or sometimes, azure blues,
contrasts with newly-fallen leaves
adorned in brilliant hues.

Of all the famous paintings,
there's no other half so grand,
as a vivid autumn masterpiece
created by God's hand.

Gloria Jones

Blood On The Moon

She saw the love in his eyes,
As he stood nearby;
She felt the warmth of his heart,
As he watched her die.

He knew it might happen,
But not that soon;
And if did happen,
Last night at "Cactus Moon."

The doctor has told her,
"No more drinking,"
But she was having a blast,
And she want thinking.

She took one more drink,
And her heart feel;
Now she is lying in a bed,
Forever to dwell.

Deana Ross

Untitled

Tomorrow is gone
as twilight becomes darkness
our lonely travels.

Douglas S. Milne

The Ballet Shoes

I am a pair of ballet shoes,
As I dance everyone coos.

My age is ten,
I was made by men.

I can't help but bourree,
When the music starts to play.

I do my best points,
As she flexes her joints.

As I changemont across the stage,
I hope to get my name on the
Program page!

Amy K. Swartz

My One True Love

God's untainted offering to me,
As I gaze upon it with unbiased eyes,
Appears as a flawless realm
As the sun slowly setting
Casting a beautiful glow of fire
red, majestic purple, and cerulean blue
Across the soft ripples of a river
Slowly cascading through a fertile glen
Peaceful
Beautiful
Unblemished
Once again I look at it
How is it possible for me to thank God
For His gift to perfection . . . You.

Christy L. Williams

Early Snow

Winter makes a one step gain.
As snow falls gently on the pane;
She softly sifts the icy rain.
Blotting out brown autumn's stain.

And I am watching, safe inside.
As flakes on puffs of northwind glide,
Swirl, and spin until it's tired.
And dropped then in a snowy tide.

Calm penetrates the silent fall,
As snow creates a misty wall,
That spreads enchantment overall.
I watch, spell-bound by it all.

David Abel

Untitled

A moment . . .
As the dawn blushes shyly,
  the sun paints
  a new day,
  over Fuji mountain.
Into a no longer night sky
  I raise my arm,
  casting a shadow
  upon perfection.

Breathing stillness
  I free my soul to glide.
And walking through sorrow
  barefoot
  I shall a life unfold . . .

Giuliana Blackwell

Untitled

Weep for the slain
   as the so-called
peacemaker's cause pain
   and death and wars.

Great iron slave
   to selective peace
through some sadist
   form of genocide.

No war ever really
   ends but just
bleeds into another and
   another and another.

War upon war.
Death by the scare.

Kill. Die. Kill. Die
   for your kings and dictators
and presidents and priests.
   They're all the same
     self-proclaimed Gods.
   Douglas Freeze

Appreciation

The leaves on the tree wave briskly,
as the wind blows,
The grass is forever green, in the
eye that beholds;
The sky, so ever blue, as the clouds
mount into shapes,
The warm glowing sun, beams down
upon my face;
Birds fly with freedom, they land
with much beauty and pride,
Each breath I take, is not a must,
but a gift from the man who died;
These things are truly miracles,
just as everything you see that lives,
The impossible could not be done,
only through the God that gives;
Before my eyes were closed, such
darkness surrounded my soul,
For now, my hand reaches out, to
the one that lovingly paid my toll . . .
   Jenny M. Blake

The End

Time was standing still,
As we danced to the end,
Only you and I were moving.

No one could have known what we felt,
It was the beginning,
The beginning of the end.

We thought that nothing else
mattered,
It was the end,
The end of the dance.
   Cathy Jo Turner

A Little Pumpkin

I'm just a little pumpkin,
as you can plainly see.
Won't you take me home and
make a jack o lantern of me?

Carve two large eyes
and a big round nose.
Give me a toothless grin,
with a candle that glows.

Then I will keep you safe
as I shine so very bright.
I'll scare away the goblins
this spooky halloween night!
   Dorothy Baker

Rites Of Passage #7

I saw Romeo and Juliet
at a train station
in Berlin.

Both glanced towards miracles
as the train pushed away.

Both waited,
and waved good-bye.
   Drew Mullen

The World As I See It

I see the world as a jungle
At times I'm very confused
When I think I've found away out
I just get deeper into the problem
When I think about it, many tears follow
It makes me feel trapped inside,
Trapped inside of a world of loneliness,
fear, sadness, and even anger
for there is no one to turn to
The world as a jungle brings sadness
to my heart
I hope the confusion all ends soon
   Carrie Elliott

Daybreak

The hour was a half yawn
away from rising;
Her restless night
had stolen sleep
And the eyes of streets
were moist with early
rubs;

And she was clean
and ready
Torn in spots; broken
mendings here and
there;

And from the distant
thoroughfare
above the silent grey;
The gold crowned sparrow
flies
Breaking waves of still
   Gloria Goldsmith

"The Roses Of Love"

To Brian Jarboe, Producer
In life on earth there so many
Beautiful things to see
with our eyes -so
Beautiful flowers
Of all the flowers the
roses in all there beauty
And various colors are
so beautiful and bright!
roses come in many kinds, and
types. "Ironically," like
life, and love there are
many kinds of love in life!
   Abel Lee Collins

An American - Rose

Do we cry -
Because roses have thorns
Or do we rejoice -
Because thorns have roses.

Do I cry -
Because my hispanic has European
Or do I rejoice -
Because my European has hispanic
   David Daniel Pickrum

Untitled

Live one's taste for love.
Because there is no other way to live.

Be that one on which you savor.
To glorify, and be glorified.
   Jonathan Milici

Dreams In White

Last night I dreamt of snow fields,
Beds of land neath sheets of white.
Layers look of warm left there by storm,
Glow boldly through the night.

The earth has served it's purpose,
From spring throughout the fall.
Bearing grain, washed soft by rain,
Plain, proud, and tall.

And now desired rest,
Is prescribed by wind and sun.
Lie still and sleep, while watch we keep,
In search of spring to come.

It is hard to imagine,
The potential of the soil.
As it lay the solid clay,
Seems far from greening toil.

So good night for now sweet winter,
Till spring I bid adieu.
Last night I dreamt of snow fields,
And each year my dreams come true.
   Dave Dalton

Night Time Prayer

I just want to thank you, Lord,
Before I go to sleep
For the blessings that were mine today,
For watching over my feet.

Strength and joy
Were your gifts, dear Lord,
And the food
You gave me to eat.

We oft take things for granted, Lord,
It seems easy to do,
But how weak and frail we'd be
Without help that comes from you.

As I sit upon my bed,
Before I take my rest,
Remind me of my blessings, Lord,
Less I should forget.

Janet S. Wheeler

Untitled

A long time ago
Before the whiteman came
We hunted many buffalo
And other wild game
We were very happy it so seems
Though we didn't have life easy
We had many dreams,
Then one day our dreams were shattered
For in our way
Wagon trains clattered
Before we know that was going on
Gunshot begin to ring
And our buffalo were soon gone
We too began to die
For what the whiteman promised
Was just another lie
Now, today they wonder why we fuss
But do they realize
That it will soon be over for us

Jack Jarvey

Being Sick

Being sick is not fun,
being sick is very dumb!
Runny noses,
Snotty tissues,
achy stomach,
throw up puddles!
Throat's sore,
Feet are cold,
Bones achy,
and can't get comfortable!
Yes, being sick
is very dumb,
being sick
is not fun!

Jennifer Galvin

Time

Time has been long since I
cannot see you. I can't
erase to you from my mind.
The love we felt was real.
Way down deep there is pain.
I can't understand. I
feel alone and numb. Deep
inside my lonely, broken heart.

Catherine L. Katona

"Ode To My Mailbox"

Emptiness? Alas, sadness
   beyond belief,
But wait! The shadow
   of my mail today
brings complete relief;
Having trod the long
   paved driveway
to open your cold
   gray door
I ask of you Oh Mailbox,
   "Isn't there anymore?"
Words, precious news
   I await
Bills and Catalogs I anticipate
Thank you dear friend
   Mailbox my heart sings,
God Bless the Postal system for all the joy
it brings!

Carol Clary

Highway

Moon on my shoulder
Black ribbon of highway
And many more miles to go

Ghostly sage, black shadows
Of mountains,
Touched with blue-white snow.

Whisper of wind
Going breathless by.
Passing glance as the night owls fly.

Darkened houses softly sleep.
Twinkling stars their
Vigil keep.

Cloud swept moon
Bids fond farewell,
Gently brushing my sleeve.

As I fade from sight
On a ribbon of dark,
And only a memory leave.

JoAnn H. Ward

I Am Old

I am old—
But age is only passing years
A pause in fleeting times
I still can greet the dawn each day
And find new heights to climb.
I feel the warm sun on my face
The wind blowing in from the sea
While robins sing their cheery notes
High in my tamarack tree.
I sit here on my garden bench
And life has much to hold
I watch my children's children grow
See their cherished dreams unfold.
I am old—
But old is for remembering
A haven from daily strife
Time to turn another page
In the record book of life.

Francesca C. Hines

Take a Tripp With Me

You speak from higher ground
but are no higher being
You see not what I can see
just what I am seeing
You, alone, can do better
but do not have the right
And we, ourselves, can adapt
but always have to fight
So journey along with me
come and see what we can see
Tripp
and fall unto my road
unsew the seeds that have been sewed
again
Thinking back along days' end
long before, a wanting hand
That longing is now for something new
what was many, now are few
Remember when, remember how
all are just but memories now.

Bethany Sweeden

Friends

Friend is such a simple word
   But greats the meaning of
To have a friend is sure to be
   a blessing from above.

You've been my friend for many years,
   You know my deepest thoughts.
You're always there to help me out
   and over look my faults.

In you I share my secrets
   and all my silly fears
And when the time comes that I'm sad,
   you even share my tears.

In worldly things, I come up short,
   I have not much to lend.
But riches are what can't be bought
   When someone calls you, "friend".

Gay Nell Synder

"My Deepest Prayer"

I know I'm not the church goin' one
But I still believe in you Lord,
And I only ask that you listen to me
When you come knockin' at my door.

Please accept me in to heaven
And forgive me for all my sins,
Lead me through those pearly gates
And not into the devils den.

If I should go to heaven Lord
Will I see the ones I miss?
Will I be able to hug a touch them
And maybe give them a kiss?

Will they still Look the same Lord
Will they remember who I am?
Will they greet me at the pearly gates
And reach out and grab my hand?

This is my deepest prayer Lord
That I see those pearly gates,
And be with the ones I Love Lord
Cause I know in heaven they wait.

Kandi J. Bailey

This Too Will Pass

"This too will pass" I use as a slogan
But it's built on faith and on truth
Through thick and through thin
It has worked for me,
Waiting way back to my youth.

Now life is surely no bed of roses,
The Bible tells us it's true
The rainfalleth on the good and the bad
The sunshine sometimes finds us sad
But faith and time see us through

So when I see suffering among my friends
And watch their troubles amass
I hurry to tell them,
Indeed try to sell them on these words:
"God willing, this too will pass"

Alice M. Huber

Love, What Do You Think?

Love opens your eyes
but makes you blind

Love makes your heart race
but brings you to a complete stop

Love brings you new journeys of life
but takes you in the wrong direction

Love brings out your inner beauty
but is it really recognized?

Love gives you a focus on life
but are you truly happy?

Love, is it good or bad?

Love, we need it, we want it
could we ever live without it?

Angela Mueller

Autumn

I love the seasons one and all
 but most of all I love the fall.
A tapestry of red and gold slowly
 beginning to unfold.
A feast for the eye every year
 to let you know that winter's near.
The wheat all tied in neat sheaves,
 and showers of golden leaves.
The pumpkins in the market place
 all waiting for a smiling face.
The crisp cold days and chilly nights,
The apples and cider, all autumn's
 delights.
Now it's known to one and all
Why I truly love the fall.

Joan Mullen

In Time

Sleep sweet moon
For the time of shadows
Is incubate
And the forest lies in watch
Beneath your breast
For the delicate moment
When light and sky become one

Denice Behdad

Untitled

"Get out!" I say.
But please, do stay.
Question everything,
but don't question me.
I'll hear you, I'll see you.
But tomorrow I will be you.
One with you, two with you.
Is that the answer?
The question is the matter.
I'll smell the air, I'll taste the wind.
In the morning, anyhow,
But not to me.
Don't leave me here, alone.
I'll feel you there, I'll sense you near,
When you come back to me.

he who was loved, was also hated;
And betraying as he was devoted.
Stripped and robbed thin,
As he was clothed and provided with
All of nothing.

Carrie Hathaway

"Love"

Love can bring us to the top,
But sometimes it can make us drop.

Love is in our dreams at night,
Never ever filled with fright.

Love can give us gifts of joy,
But shouldn't be used as a toy.

Love is always in the air,
Showing how you really care.

Love is like a red, red rose
Always showing, no one knows!

Brandy Illges

Belonging

Though we may be
but tiny ripples
of relativity
on the ocean
of the absolute,
ultimately, in essence,
we are one.
We do not see the one,
for we are the one seeing.
We are pulses of a universal
space-time probe
seeking to experience
all that is possible.
Our challenge and adventure
is to tune in to the
cosmic frequencies
that will guide us
back to the homing signal of the
Absolute Radiant One.

John P. Huibregtse

Without You

For it's only been months,
 but what seems like years.
Since that last tender moment,
 when I held you so near.

Your eyes, your lips,
 your oh so tender touch.
With each day that passes,
 I miss them so much.

Once our hearts were afire,
 but now I've caused yours to bleed.
If I'm to change and help heal.
 then a chance is what I need.

Now if that flame we once had
 shall never burn again,
Renae, I promise you can count on me,
 "I'll always be your friend".

James M. Smith

Family Ties

Shared emotions
But you love 'em
Mistreat you and misunderstand you
But you love 'Em
Dubbed selfish and unfeeling
But you love 'em
Missed Birthdays
But you love 'Em
Unexpected disappointments
But you love 'Em
Additions
You gotta love 'Em
You can't choose them
So you love 'Em

Donna R. Smith-Tobias

Precious Rose

As I doze
by this precious rose
I dream of love at first sight
A love that just might
Feel the same way
Oh well, maybe someday.

Someday precious rose
I may have one of those
One I can walk with
One I can talk with

In the park
After dark
By a pretty fountain,
For this I would climb a mountain
But this will never happen,
And I will just doze
By this precious rose
And dream of days to come

Juan DeLa Cruz III

Tunnel Vision

Never breaking from one's choosing
    can create extensive mental errors
And can close one's mind to answers
    creating paradigms to bare

Like proof reading one's own writing
    when one overlooks mistakes
Because determination to get it done
    prevents taking proper breaks

Tunnel vision is what some call it
    because they only see the end
"Can't see the forest through the trees"
    getting lost where trails begin

So take a break and seek a change
    pursue some other skill
Return refreshed, with new insight
    for, enhance your task, it will

Dennis Wheeler

Nature Weaves Love

Evergreens and snowy scenes
Carved in the bright moonlight
Chickadees, the winter breeze
The setting was so right!

Crocuses saw their first kiss
True love had just begun
Tulips knew, as their love grew
Those two would be as one.

Sweet lilacs and loving acts
Kept blooming in the spring
Daffodils balk winter chills
Bet he'll give her a ring!

Pansies sigh, true love won't die
For they're in love to stay
Hummingbirds and loving words
She'll be a bride in May.

Parakeets heard words so sweet
As those two pledged their hearts
Roses nod, all's right with God
Until death do them part!

Barbara Wilson

Golden Reflections

Golden reflections upon the sea,
Cast their spell on thee.
Waves bask in the sunlight,
Ponder a moment all is right.

A bird ascends into flight,
Slowly soaring out of sight.
Darkness gathers upon the night.
Life's challenge is a plight.

Old age blessed by another name,
Life's struggles are the same.
We live our life as it should be,
Golden reflections upon the sea.

Anita Douglas

Evanescence

Torn skin, broken bone
Cause no greater pain
Than the distorted silence
of alone.

Ripped apart, hearts bleeding
Emotions run red
Washed with tears of
desolation.

Loneliness dissolves, hearts mend
When the world is healed
By the arrival of my friend.

Dolly Ness

Whether We Know It Or Not

Change, a friend.
Change, a foe.
Use it as an energy flow.
A threat,
fearful thrust.
We must! We must!
It ebbs, it flows.
It comes,
and it
goes.

Alicejean Leigh Dodson

Forward Woman

I will change my Pains to Gain
Change my disharmony to harmony
Change my situation to Creation
Change my dark to light
Change my hurt to love
Hell
I'll change water to wine
Get drunk in my soul
and allow it to soar into the ethers
free
All beginning with the change
in
me!

Greer Sha Fredericks

Innocent Love

The fantasies of days gone by
changed quickly into realities
with one intimate encounter.

But one has to ask oneself
if the fantasies were
indeed more fulfilling.

Perhaps disappointing realizations
have clouded the once
unknown excitements.

The innocent flirtatious moments
that were magically arousing
have faded away to leave an emptiness
of uncertainty.

Uncertainty in the embodiment
of translucent intentions
that have gnawed away
at trusting feelings within.

Oh! To be able to retreat and retrieve
the satisfying flirtatious impulses
of days gone by.

Jacqueline M. Nemec

"Insanity"

Wild eyes aflame,
Chaotic thoughts.
Is there a way to stay sane,
From all that's sought?

Another of those balms,
To keep me calm.
When will this end?
This suffering.

Amuck, is what they say,
Tell me is there another way?
To end this affliction,
On my brain.

I will ameliorate,
Or will I asphyxiate?
A struggle with my soul,
That will never be told.

Carla Curry

The Sounds Of Christmas

Sleigh bells in the frosty air;
Children's laughter everywhere.
Santa's jolly Ho-Ho-Ho,
Carolers singing as they go.

Church choirs singing "Peace on Earth",
Commemorating Jesus' birth.
Sorts of little girls and boys,
As they open up their toys.

Crackle of the yule-log burning,
Welcoming the days returning.
Children's happy sleigh sighs,
As they close their sleepy eyes.
These are the SOUNDS OF CHRISTMAS.

Cheryl Newman

Butterfly

It began in a bundle; a shell of love.
Closed in from the forest,
Yet lit by the sun.

As light shined without,
Growth stirred within,
As the Love creature escaped
To a world filled with sin.

Though its colors so brilliant
And dance so unique,
It graced all the skies,
Luminous hues of peace.

Gretchen L. Peer

Bird Of Love

Bird of love
Don't fall for me
If you fall
I will weep for thee

Bird of love
Spread your wings
Engulf the wind,
the earth, and me.

Dianne Pekie

Silent As Frost Falling

There was no thunder, only
clouds of white petalled dogwood
on the hillside.

Beneath leaning, green willows,
a shy fawn bent to drink.

Kiss crushed the golden pollen
that tumbled from boughs.

Green dawns of summer
shared sun-long laughter
with the butterflies.

Autumn tears are falling,
silent as memory of love,
silent as frost falling
in each moon-rise loneliness.

An icy dagger-time stabs the heart
thrusting laughter into darkness.

The eastern sky reddens —
Red-fire of dogwood on the hillside.

The shy fawn returns to drink
Beneath the leaning yellow willows.

Emma Crobaugh

When Love Dies

When love dies
Clowns cry
Angels fall from the sky
Becoming morning dew
On the earths crust

When love leaves
Flowers die
Unable to bloom
They return to earths bosom
To become fertilizer for hopes next try

When hope dies
Man's spirit stretched to endurance
Asks why?
What did I do?
How will I survive?

Only God can make a love
From a flight of doves above
Our spirits soar, confused and misused
Only man and woman can break it
Was that the plan all along?

Dennis M. Obrien

"Self"

I like searching for, and
collecting rare things, it is
a hobby of mine. Take you
for example you are very,
unique there is only one like
you, you could search the
world over, and find only
one, like you. Very special,
  You don't have to be attractive,
or intelligent.
  Come with me, gaze
into the mirror, ask your
self this simple quiz.
  Am I worthy? If the
answer is truly yes, then
I would like to add you to
my collection. For one that
is worthy is a rareity indeed!

Clydia Estelle Bishop

Self

In your innocence you knew me
Clutched me as a gift from God

Once a blessing
Now a dormant restless inert memory

Locked away so tightly
Squeezing the breath out of my jailer

Searching from release
The path grows more narrow

Loudly growing
Restless Seclusion

No rest in denial
No peace with suppression

The escape comes —

Feeling exalted
I am strengthened with renewal

My victory is pointless
Lest you finally recognize

You know me—I am you
At last, WE ARE

Carole S. Schulz

Juxtaposition Of Seasons

Reality like ocean waves in winter
cold and crashing onto an empty beach
of east or west coast - doesn't matter
  Sand in sand
  time is time
  love is love
Or it isn't. Spring evaporates, a
fragrant memory. Inland lurks the
honest doubt, the ifs and buts
of intimacy, the stops
(as if tide could be halted giving us
time to assimilate, figure it out)

What if reality like ocean waves
in summer pounds on melted feelings
if putting it together is an act
of cause against the tide? Hot
immediate, it's now or not at all

Then, what would you make of it
as leaves fall?

Ann H. Hutton

Razor sharp
Cold as ice
No delay
Now sacrifice
Hard to handle
Kind of small
Say good-bye
For that is all
Memories hurt
It can be done
Be afraid
Try to run
Stop to realize
It can't be saved
It has been done
It is engraved
Feel nothing
It had to end
It was the only thing
It was your friend!

Christine Dobbins

Passage

The tinkling sounds of laughter
  come skipping down the hall.
There seems to be a smile,
  dancing on the wall.

Children's happy voices,
  float gaily on the breeze.
A shout, a squeal, a whisper,
  then silence - what a tease!

Today there's lots of happiness,
  no sadness, pain, or wrath.
They do not know what lies ahead,
  no cares have crossed their path.

All too quickly, time marches on
  and childhood's left behind.
The struggles of daily living
  weigh heavy on their minds.

They yearn to hear the music
  of days once young and slow.
But bridges age and crumble,
  ever onward they must go.

Brenda Kinsey

Upon The Ridge

Mountains high, valleys low,
come with Me we will take it slow.
Walk upon the ridge so careful.
Slowly, peace will over take you.

Many trials will come your way,
remember Me and do not stray.
Walk upon the ridge so careful.
My love is with you always!

The wind blows fiercely and unending
God is with you, there is no pretending.
Walk upon the ridge so careful.
Hope will guide you there is no doubt,
faith is what this is all about.

Debbie Ann Mason

A Joyful Sign

Maintaining a vision
Concured in my head
Awake with a dream, only
dreamt in bed.
There are bouquets of flowers
in the midst of a pond
a canoe dressed with lilies,
a paddle and a fawn.
His ears are erect
his eyes full of cheer
his tail give the signals
that Christmas is near.

Douglas Washington

Untitled

Oceans roaring
Crabs biting
Lights shining from the sky
Birthday drums banging
Children finding shells
People playing volleyball
Boats jumping off waves
Surfers surfing off boards
Friends swimming
Clouds shining

Edward Schlageter

Confrontations

My demons assail me
Confront me
Bedevil me

I've anguished
And languished
And death-wished

Till racing them
Pacing them
Finally facing them

I see them - nearly
Now clearly
And merely

For the simple
Paper tigers
That they are

Jean Lewis

Reflections In A Cymbal

The blue of the uniforms
contrasting with
the green of the football field.
The in time cadence of the drumline
contrasting with
the crude yells of the crowd.
The soft notes of the flutes
contrasting with
the harsh bellows of the tubas.
The warmth of excitement I feel
contrasting with
the cold of the air.
The thrill of victory
contrasting with
the sorrow of defeat.
Life can be like a marching band.
Similar
yet different.
I'm glad to be a part of both.

Anthony Forte

The Western Star

Gary Cooper,
(Crack Shot)
A plain, honest western star
Had importance of
Wearing a hat!

Acting greatest days of motion pictures,
As other actors like
Jimmy Stewart, Henry Fonda
Randolph Scott, Clint Eastwood,
Gregory Peck and John Wayne, etc.

Silver Screen magazines commended
By written articles of
Fisty, fighting, comical movies, etc.
In filmsdoms variety.

Ellen Skogster

This Day

This day is mine,
Created and given
To me by that
Inner force I call God.

Given to me in trust
That I may live it well
Without wasted minute,
Or drifting dream.

Given me to create
Understanding, to
Sweep away cobwebs
Of fantasy.

Given to me to
Let love flow freely
To all needing hearts,
This day is mine.

Francisca McCluggage

Shadows

As the night falls,
creeping over every
little thing that's in
it's path, the shadows
overcome the night.

Over the trees and
across the sea's the
shadows pour out.

The shadows like to
play games with your
eyes so your vision will
be very lost.

But when day rise's,
the shadows do not have
anymore fun with your
eyes and settle's down.

Amber Bowles

Shades Of Grey

Desert frost,
Creeping through the sands,
The moon and the stars
Imprisoned behind invisible bars
Searching and searching for the unknown.
Like life alone
Threw upon a dream
And covered in ashes,
We fall and never remember why?
Fallen colors, and fallen rainbows
seem to fade away.
As the cold desert night creeps upon
the summer day.
But not black or white
But in shades of grey?

Albert Dean Woolridge

Mementos

Sigh for the memories of the past.
Cry for the loves that didn't last.
Wrench your heart with pain and sorrow.
Lie and say "I'll forget them tomorrow".

Although the dreams of yesteryear
Somehow always disappear.
The mementos will remain alive
In the treasure box that I hide.

Cathy Rice

Her Way

I like the way she looks at me;
Dancing emeralds, sly smile
Glowing heat pierces my heart
Igniting fires I've never known.

I like the way she touches me;
So soft caressing and warm.
Her heart where fingertips touch
On the path that leads to my soul.

I like the way she kisses me;
Warm lips inviting sweet taste.
Lifted to heights beyond reach
When tenderness draws close to hand.

Real love this love she offers me;
Childlike flirtatious and hopeful.
Stirs memories long forgotten
In a heart that's hungry for love.

Joe Halfaker

Travelers Of Arcadia

Sweeping white on the wind
dangle upon blue
Touch the currents
above gray and wet
silent and open
high and swift

Point to the edge
Head for home
from where there is end
from where there is beginning
where line upon line
of shadowed reflections
caress the lucid terrain of old

Travelers of Arcadia
Sweeping young pilots
Glide the breath of time
Exalt in rapture
Repose in solitude
for you have arrived
You have arrived.

Carlton Lear

Behind A Locked Door

The grey walls
Dark and gloomy
Surrounded the room
As he sat in the corner
The sun
Shining in through the glass window
Showing hope and fear
Fear.
Fear, of something unknown
Caged in
Like an animal trying to get out.
The wishing of freedom
Of peace
Of tranquility
The wishing of hope
Behind a locked door.

Davina Harounoff

Death's Door

It came quick
dark and night
descended like a heaven's light

The end came quick
though much to fear
under death's lazy leer

The darkness ended
the tunnel began
and the memories ran

From the beginning
to the end
with nothing more to lend

Then the light began
at the tunnel's end
and my spirit began to mend

From here after
I can tell you no more
for I have gone through Death's Door

David Kirlin

Untitled

I seek a wisdom
    deeper down than
        meets the eye
        on printed page.
    I'm of the age
where facts are blurred
    and lie interred
        amidst the ashes of forgotten days.
    Perhaps the haze
of memory
    gives way to yet
        another mode of being —
        a way of seeing
that transcends
    complexities of "Now"
        to touch "Forever."
        Yet never
will I know
    for sure till God —
        and thus, the search!

Anne T. Dillen

Editor's Note

The man that's lost inside his head,
Determines now that he is dead.
And takes some pity, hence to wed,
But finds himself, at once, instead,
And then attempts to annul his dread.
But receives double sad, instead.
And though his bridesmaid he had led,
She is addiction; brings her to bed.
And crying fears, he bravely said,
"The tears I cry are turning red."
And this poor man with sorrow bleed

His youth onto the floor.

Jeffrey M. Schall

Someone's Treasure

Bidding was high as the auctioneer
Displayed a box of intricate design.
"Going-going-gone!" he called
The small velvet box was mine.

Inside, no jewels or money,
Only a photo of a baby girl
A faint smile, two tiny teeth,
Hair in dark brown curls.

A tiny broach adorned the neck
Of her dainty, lace trimmed dress.
She once was someone's pride and joy,
A baby girl, so picturesque.

No name, no date on the photo
A sentimental, untold tale,
Someone's treasure of long ago
I bought at an antique sale.

Bernice Bottoms

Sing A Little Lover's Song

Do Re Do Re sing a little lover's song
Do Re Do Re everyone sing along
Sing it swing it either high or low
Do Re Mi Fa So La Ti

-Do Re Do Re sing a little lover's song
Do Re Do Re everyone sing along
Day time night time any time you go
Do Re Me Fa So La Ti Do

Love is always in the air
Love is always everywhere
In the fall and in the spring
In the lover's heart that sings

Do Re Do Re sing a little lover's song
Do Re Do Re everyone sing along
Sing it swing it in the rain or shine
Sing it swing it for your love and mine

For your love and mine

Fred F. Heitzig

Mother's Day, 1995

Mother, are you listening?
Do you hear me when I speak
Do you know who I am
Can you see how I've grown
Am I making the right decisions
Have I turned out alright
Am I similar to you
Do you remember our life together
Do you still protect me
Do you still love me
Do you remember me?
I'm the one who used to pick
Bouquets of dandelions for you.

Jeanne-Marie Montgomery

Doubt

He is a man of emotion
Does he love me?
I have given him much
Is he deserving of my trust?

Does he love me?
Will he help preserve my identity
Is he deserving of my trust
or will he bend me to ashes?

Will he help me preserve my identity,
a multifaceted mask,
or will he bend me to ashes
lost in the ceremonial web

A multifaceted mask
covers my face and pain
lost in the ceremonial web
I pledge my bond and my freedom

I cover my face and pain
as he turns and walks away.
I pledged my bond and my freedom
but he is a man of emotion.

Jeanne Emerson

Tomorrow's Yesterday

Walk slowly little one.
Don't hasten on your way.
Tomorrow comes so suddenly,
Too soon it's yesterday.

Elizabeth Snow

Draw Them, Lord

Draw them, Lord.
Draw them with your loving power
Draw them through each weary hour.
Draw them, Lord.

Show them, Lord.
Show your plan for their redemption,
Show them your supreme intention.
Show them, Lord.

Heal them, Lord.
From the sin of their condition.
From their pain - you bring remission.
Heal them, Lord.

They have tried it their way
Now the best I can say is
Jesus, please - today,
Draw them, Lord.

Dorothea Talbot Thornton

mmorality

Would it be a gift or a curse?
Eternal life
What could be worse?
An unending journey without relief
Being denied the greatest gift of all
Death and release
This is what fools dream of
For without death
life could not be.

John Nixon

The Passing

As I lay on my bed last night
  Dreaming of what might have been,
I found no peace in the quiet
  Reminding me of him.

I feel the wind on my face
  From the window ajar,
Lying here in his place
  Makes love seem ever so far.

With the morning comes light
  Breaking gently as rain,
All the memories of night
  On the bright window pane.

The empty place on the bed
  Seems as still as the day,
The memories in my head
  Must last the rest of the way.

Then love comes edging in
  As swift as the wind,
Bringing joy to my heart
  And the closeness again.

Billie R. Lee

The Starfish

I walk along the sandy beach.
Dreaming things I think to teach.

The sand is soft in my toes.
The sea is calm,
Why?
Who knows!

I see the starfish laying there.
Washed upon the sandy floor.
Soon the sun will take their lives.
The time to save them I will prize

I throw them in the cool calm sea,
and they turn back to wave at me.
Smiling inside I see,
saving a life means a lot to me.

I go home and tell my story.
No one thinks it is such a glory.
I shrug them off and walk away.
There in my memory it stays hidden,
locked, and tucked away.

Jeanette Newton

Incense

Silent swirling wisps of smoke
drifting steadily skyward
amorously engulfing the upper shelves
throwing horizontal tentacles towards me.

It's sensuous scent is everywhere
mood setting mystery of ancient lands
skeletal tendrils eerily dancing
amongst my exhaling breath.

Carol Mueller

Windows Of The Soul

Eyes bottomless pools.
  Drowning.
Darkness leaps before me.
  Dying.
Flickers of disjointed emotions.
  Fading.
Pain, sorrow, anger.
  Hope.
Loneliness, hopelessness, desolation.
  Peace.
Everything fading away.
  Falling.
Eyes shutting me out.
  Crying.
Returning to reality.
  Confusing.
Looking back into eyes.
  Empty.

Anna Schmidt

Untitled

Bach's Swirls
drunken Girls
pubescent Curls

Crow's feet
Wind   and   sleet
      within the peat,

Why look upon
      or a back suit don;
what — nothing   is beyond?

Young with goal
all on the dole
  a mine   of   coal

Strive   or   stand
        and
the world is manned

Sickles   circles
  . . . evening purples.

Daniel Orlikowski

Thank You Lord

I thank you Lord for:
ears to hear your Word preached,
two eyes to read the same,
a mind your Word can reach,
a mouth to speak your fame,
friends who share their insights,
their prayers to keep me whole,
but most of all, I thank you Lord,
for Christ, who saved my soul!

Dorothy M. Ellar

Untitled

Spire framed by clear green mountains
Equinox etched against summer blue sky,
Resting secure above the valley
Enhanced by such calm and beauty
Not afraid when sheltered here
Infinite peace
Tomorrow will surely come as
Yesterday fades to a memory.

Joann H. Prout

The Tears I've Cried

A love that spans o'er 30 years,
E'en tho we said goodbye.
I've been alone for 28
With just the tears I've cried.

They told me that I'd love again,
And Lord knows how I've tried;
But every time I think of you,
I think of tears I've cried.

I close my eyes and see your face,
And wish I were your bride,
But then reality sinks in,
With all the tears I've cried.

If I could only see you dear,
And have you by my side,
I know that I would soon forget,
The million tears I've cried.

Cathryn Howard Teed

Untitled

I loved her so much
especially her warm soft touch
We were together for so long
we thought nothing could go wrong,
but it did, now she's gone,
cuz of me, we're no longer meant to be
I broke her heart and inside
it tore me apart
I said sorry, but that wasn't enough
and I didn't know what else to do
yet I deserved it, cuz I wasn't true
I thought we'd be together long
enough to say "I do"
but,
When she said good-bye
I couldn't take it and
began to cry
and its all cuz of me
we're no longer meant to be

Gabe Orellano

The Last Call

The air was crisp and cool, as the water
  rippled in.
And repeating sounds of gunfire were
  heard upon the wind.
The pastel shades of evening, were
  dancing on the trees,
And the scorching sun of noon had
  drifted behind the seas.

He had lain there on the beach that
  day, with his face upon the sand
And the closest thing that he could see
  was the rifle in his hand.
He knew that he would never move.
  and on that beach would lay;
Because his greatest general was to
  call on him that day

Nicoletta M. Kowalczyk

Her Beauty

Her beauty speaks without words
enchanting as the night;

A veil of stars she wears in her hair
and the moon the light of her eyes

And a thousand nights the measure
and yet none compares

For all that moves in the heavens,
like stars in galaxy's flight;
and is the mystery of the night
pale in the beauty of her light.

Jean Marie Nast

Alone

Alone walks my soul
Empty of love and calm
Breaking fate
Wondering ties
Secrets of untold
Binding mortality
But my own

No one sees the pain
The dagger through the heart
Aches in silence
Plays the game
Again she plays the part

No lies I speak
Evil I hear or see
My true soul
Only knows
I am keeper of me

Jenny Brooks

Untitled

I think I can see
eternity
when I look into
a deep ocean of
blue
an ocean where
Hurricanes
never cross
and boats never
sail
only the cool
blue water
and the peaceful
sunshine play
in the doldrums
of the water
throughout the day.

James Thomas

Namesake

The same name for,
Four is quite a bore;
We really didn't need more.

Then there were only three
including me.

All too soon there were
just two, and now sadly
only thee, and how I miss
the other three.

Grace Ardean Trossbach-Schleutermann

Precious Lord

Hold my hands precious Lord,
Every day, every hour
In my heart, wash me clean from sin.
Died for me upon that cross,
I do share the Word of God.

My Lord bled his precious blood,
Crucified upon that cross.
Made me free from all my sins.
Innocent, yet he died,
Leaving me, His Word as guide,
Loving me, so I can be saved.
In my heart, he truly lives.
Alleluia, Praise His Name,
Nearer my God to thee.

Irene K. Seto

"Destination"

Train whistles in the distance
eyes focus on the light
coming round the bend
whistles, shrill in the night

The track rumbles
birds scatter from the rails
as the train goes by
puffing smoke leaves a trail

Where are you going, train?
Where have you gone?
From the sunset,
traveling to the dawn?

The steam overflows,
a great mist appears
Train, a burning soul
travels, not knowing where

Christopher Helm

Hypnotized

From the deep darkness I
fall into a trance
hypnotized by your stare
Should I take this chance?
Embraced by your gentleness
intrigued by the wonder
Thinking of you constantly
What spell do you have me under?
I'm speaking of your eyes
and the mystery they hold
the warmth of your stare
Cradles me when I'm cold
the temperature is rising
your eyes are a burning flame.
Since I looked into them
I have not been the same. Fascinated
by the shadows at the same time
consumed with love. I try to
fall asleep, and you're all
I dream of.

Christy Lynn Schrage

The Ocean

Miles and miles of water,
farther than the eye can see.
It's beauty enchants me.
Myths and magic, powder white
sand.
The water cools me off as it
touches my hand.
As I slowly walk down the
beach, the outside world is out of
reach.

Cerelle L. Valerio

One With Nature

Nature makes me
Feel like soaring
Soaring up into the sky
It makes me feel
Like I'm in a forest
With tropical birds above me
All the trees
High, high above me
Wind rushing past me
The clouds look so beautiful
Blended with all the colors of the birds
The trees so magnificent
Just the right amount of leaves
And branches
Here comes the sunset
Such a marvelous scene
The right amount of each beautiful color
Red, orange, yellow, pink, purple, and blue

Jennifer Perez

Inner Pain

It burns behind my eyes now
Feverishly dark it roams
Wreaking havoc everywhere
Ruining my inner home.

Silently I bear the pain
The evil creature brings
For no one can take it from me
No one can share this thing.

I am so very sad now,
Forsaken by my past.
Quietly I move forward
To face what the future asks.

God please don't forget me
In this, my hour of need
For I am so alone now
I ask only for one deed.

Help me find my way Lord
As only you can do
So I may find my way in life
That helps me live it true.

Amy Snyder

147

To A Runt Named Chewing Gum

Can I forget when we first met
Fifteen years ago in El Paso?
A tiny ball of fur, a plaintive purr,
Soft velvet paws, sharp clinging claws
Sticking like chewing gum
To my coat. "Please let me come,"
You cried, "to live with you!"
What else could I do?
Today, a tabby cat full grown,
(How quickly time has flown!)
Curious, playful, petite in size,
You gaze at me with eyes
Full of mystery and love.
I thank the saints above
That there was just enough of stuff
Left for God to make you,
My exquisite chum, Chewing Gum!

Elizabeth Dacanay

A Turbid Odyssey

Throughout the course of history
flowing down a river called time,
many dreams are shattered,
and some are met,
the experiences of love, joy, and pain
are remembered in part, by those
who lived them out.
Like a piece of dust,
caught in the winds of change,
our lives keep drifting on and on
down a path called fate.
But in the course of living,
this river and breeze will meet,
and everything we've done
will start to settle down
and flow in the river of time,
and through its course
most memories are forgotten
of the dreams that we have met.

Craig Howell

Visual Serenity

River of dreams
flowing ever so gently
Knowing the power that you possess
invade my soul

Churning waters splashing
misting my face
Knowing the peace that you possess
invoke my thoughts

Pebbles and sand rinsed
by your touch
Knowing the healing that you possess
enlighten my heart

Dianne St. Peter

small Life

There's a vase sustaining a small Life
Fragile, independent;
It sheds tears of pedals;
Water with not nurture it,
Sunlight will not revive it,
And yet the world around it lives;
It lives to tell the small Life's tale.
Why?
small Life is already telling . . .

Jisun K. Lee

My Gratitude

My gratitude is beyond words
For all thou has done
The gifts of love, peace and joy
perfectly provided by your son.

For the peace of heart for mankind
For work, play, food and sleep
For pain and sorrow to make us strong
That make the heart secure and sweet

My gratitude of praise is unworthy
of your gift so true
But with humble heart I come before
your throne
To thank you for all your earthly
gifts
Also the eternal gifts from above
For my sorrow, pain and unmatchless
love.

Carolyn Voss

"Country Days In Kansas"

My heart still yearns
For country days
For country folk
And country ways

For country roads
And country lanes
To hear the robins
Sweet refrain

For country meadow
Washed with showers
To brighten up
The meadow flowers

For country streams
So bright and clear
Keep rushing on
Year after year

Helen L. Zickefoose

A Heart Of Dreams

The house stays clean
For guests that don't come.
I rush home to cook
Supper for one.
The pillow is cold
When I get there
No one smells
The perfume in my hair.
Life goes on for all who live,
But there's no one receiving
The love I want to give.
Dreams of roses, candy and wine
All, still fade from an earlier time.
A tender kiss from yesterday
Brightened my heart,
But didn't stay.
Night time's here, again, it seems
Setting on a heart of tender dreams.

Cyndy Ryan

To My Beloved

Do not weep over my grave,
For I am not there.

I am the wind that blows free
and gives voice to the leaves
that fall from the trees and
speak of my love for you.

I am the spirit mist that comes
softly with the soft patter of
rain drops that drift across
the meadow and kiss your lips.

I am in everything you say and do,
the breath you take, asleep, awake!
Fret not for I am free.

But shall watch over you
until you are again with me
and we shall be as one
to be apart no more.

Charles White

Second Place

Take away this heart of mine.
For it has worked far too well.
It breaks and breaks and breaks again.
Mesmerized by a woman's spell.

Take away these loving arms,
Longing for a warm embrace.
Strong, warm hands within deep pockets,
Unable to caress a beautiful face.

Take away my azure eyes.
Endless oceans of saline tears.
Despite a sparkle the stars have envied,
Brilliant seclusion endured for years.

For all these traits I possess
Do nothing for me, I confess.
Lonely, tired, weary of this race.
Forever shall I be in second place?

Dan Jones

Wings

If I had wings
for just one day
I would fly far, far away.
I would go to a place
where the sun shines bright,
and the sky is clear.
And there are only two people here.
Me and God.
We would talk,
Work out my problems.
And then as my wings faded away.
I would fly far, far away,
I would come home,
And go to bed.
My mind would be clear,
And I'll have no fear.
But whenever I need him,
God is here.

Erin Jones

Christmas Cheer

Christmas is a time of year
For love and good cheer
Making peace with those we love
And sending greetings far and near.
A time for mistletoe and holly
Church bells and sleigh bells
A time to be jolly.

A time to relive the birth of Christ
And the glory of that day;
O, if only all through the year
This feeling would prevail
The world might be a better place,
With year round Christmas Cheer.

Helen A. Holland

"First Of All"

First of all I'd like to thank you
for loving me at all
you should know if you need anything
I'll be there

Don't you know the starlight shines
to remind us
we needn't touch to feel the warmth of
love we left behind

Though you travel to some distant star
while I stay behind
there's no distance far enough to
keep you from my mind . . .

What was that?
I heard your voice whispering again
it's louder than all the noise in this
crowded room I'm in . . .

You're telling me to just hold on
don't worry about tomorrow
when we finally meet again
we'll laugh away the tears . . .

Gayle Greene Vasulka

I Died For Love

To this place I do not dwell,
   for there was a boy I loved so well
He took my heart right from me,
   and now he wants to set me free
I even know the reason why,
   for there was a girl better than I

My father came home late one night,
   and looked for me left and right
He went up stairs and broke down my
door,
   and found me hanging above the floor
In my pocket this note he read:

   Dig a grave, dig it deep
     marble stone head to feet.
   On my grave, place a dove
     to show the world
     I died for Love.

Amanda O'Brien

The Church

God said, "This Church is my house
For you I built it here.
So you will get to know me,
In love and faith, not fear."
This Church is built on nothing less
Then my own blood and righteousness
Poured out upon a cruel cross,
So your soul will not be lost.
In this holy sacred place
I will meet you face to face.
Put a song within your heart
And a smile upon your face.

Evaline Walker

Chameleon

Chameleon
Forever changing its color
Never showing its true color
Vibrant shades of life
Forever changing

Chameleon
Hiding in the world
Forever melding into the crowd
Never showing its face
Forever melding

Chameleon
Hiding behind its mask
Forever hiding its identity
Never being itself
Forever hiding

Chameleon
Lonely in the world
Never allowing the release of its soul
To any other in its presence
Forever alone.

Eileen Fitzgerald

Day

I see silence sleeping
Found fear falsely fading
I have pain stored down in side my brain
feeling my objectives leaving
feel my tears escaping
deciding my distant decisions
blocking out my involuntary visions
staying still
staring away
from each long lonely day!

Christopher Keith Howell

Randy's Eyes

Seductive and passionate.
Full of love,
Full of sadness,
Full of fire
when he is jealous.

Romantic and sexy
looking right through me,
Randy's sapphire blue eyes.
Dedicated to: Randy Poffo

Heather Estruch

Freedom Stands

In the darkness of the night,
Freedom stands tall and bright,
As the flag is raised up high,
All our brothers turn to heroes,
And we never question why.
Silence is finally over,
we can now speak out,
guaranteed these freedoms,
beyond the shadow of a doubt.
Ambitions and dreams can now turn
to reality, expressing our spirit and
also personality. We can live now,
in prosperity, and no longer in fright,
for even during the darkness,
freedom still stands, TALL AND BRIGHT.

Joan Wilson

The Soft Touch

Soft is the light that comes
From a summer's moon;
Soft like velvet are
The feet of a baby raccoon.

Soft are the petals of a rose
From the garden we may pluck;
Soft is the yellow fluff
That covers a baby duck.

Soft is the summer breeze
The leaves in the trees to stir;
Soft is the pussy willow
Like little balls of fur.

Soft is the pillow on which
I lay my head to sleep;
Soft is the voice of a new born bird
When it utters it's first little "peep!"

Soft are the wings of butterflies
As from flower to flower they dart;
But nothing's any softer than
The softness of Donna's heart!

Jean D. Wisner

Fear

The dark, forbidding shadow crawls,
From around the corners,
And from every inch of us.

Fear is the most feared,
For it can destroy a persons mind,
And can destroy in great numbers.

It is neither seen, smelled, nor touched,
Yet it can attack so quickly,
Many are left stunned.

That is why we avoid it,
Shun it,
Trying to hide it.

But it always finds a way out,
And when its out,
Who knows when or where it will stop.

Allison M. Ruotolo

One People

We say we're different people
From different worlds
We speak of many colors
And the way we talk
We go along separate pathways
thinking of ourselves
We say it doesn't matter
The path our brothers walk
We build this endless distance
To make us seem apart
We dance in our light
When the other people sulk

Why can't we break down the space
That seem to keep us apart
Because in this race
No man is different from the other,
It's all in the face,
The harder you try to look
The harder it is to trace
What the different is, and God Smiled.

Charles Udoutun

Dangerous Dinosaurs

They're wide-eyed creatures
  from lands unknown.
Their long, sharp teeth,
  eat chunks of meat.
They stamp around,
  and crush the ground
  with overgrown feet.
They come in different sizes -
  long and tall
  short and small.
With a gigantic head.
But best of all, they're dead!

Erin Scott

Roller

Skating
fun, challenge
crashing, falling, bruising
skates, helmets, bat, ball
hitting, catching, throwing
fun, cool
baseball

Justin Best

Empty Promises

Empty promises
have been heard before
how quickly forgotten
my ears hear no more.
Rhythm in motion
to view, to adore
fine lines and curves
my eyes see no more.
So satiny smooth
with touch to explore
stirs unknown desires
my hands feel no more.
What now is left
but to close one more door
the trembling heart hushed
love speaks no more.

Brenda L. Phlipot

"Give Me Your Completeness"

Give me tomorrow
Give me today
Give me your shoulder
When I should sway
Give me you love
Give me your strength
Give me your time
At any length
Give me your positive thoughts
When mine are not so
Give me your input
So that I may grow
Understand my grief
When I stand low
Understand my sorrow
Born of long ago
Forgive my Mourning
For I have not the control
Of a childhood taken away from me
So long ago.

Donna V. MacHardy

Country Treasures

Dusty country roads
Give the soul a peace,
A peace unlike any other.
The wheels of the car
Kick the dust up into the air.
It quietly lays in a thin sheet
On all that it descends upon.

You know that you are alive
Fated to return to the land.

How many generations?
How many have passed this way before
you?
Did they pause in wonderment,
Or pass by the treasures of
  old houses,
  plots of land,
  and unkept graveyards.
And if they did,
Was the sun shining on the dusty country
roads?

Jerushia L. Graham

"Windchime Dreams"

In the windchimes of my soul,
glass rainbows catch (those)
lost childhood dreams,
and turn around those youthful schemes.
We seldom ever become what
we would have been,
and faded aspirations are only
hoarse whispers in the wind.
To try again to be
what we could have been,
Perhaps can soften
disappointments of
old men . . .

Cyndy Lowery

Something Bad

When something bad happens to you,
go tell your mom and dad. Tell them
every single thing that made you
mad, even though it makes you
sad. Don't keep it locked up like
a diary. Let it free so you can breathe.
Just forget about the past at least
it went fast. So when something
bad happens to you don't forget
to tell your mom and dad. Remember
to tell them every little single thing
that made you mad.
So don't forget to tell your mom
and dad, when something bad happens
to you like that.

Evelyn Ibarra

Bless This Little One

Bless this little one,
God from above,
Born into this world,
With a family and love.

Bless this little one,
God from above,
He who is weak,
Needs plenty of love.

Bless this little one,
God from above,
As you take him from us,
On a snow white dove.

Bless this little one,
God from above,
Show him the light,
And an abundance of love.

Bless this little one,
God from above,
A sweet little angel,
For all to love.

Debbie Dillon

Failing

Whenever I fall down,
God pick me up with his hands.
Brush the dirt off me,
Stand me upright on the land.
He turn me in the direction
That I'm suppose to go,
Points His finger and say,
"Don't come this way no more!
Remove thy foot from evil,
They know not at what they stumble,
Ponder the path of thy feet,
And let all thy ways be humble."
Whatever I was doing,
I've promised not to do again,
In Jesus name I pray.
  Amen.
    Amen.
      Amen.

Carol Watson

"It Takes Both Fathers To Raise A Son"

You can take him fishing,
God will help him catch a fish.
God can make a shooting star,
You have to teach him how to wish.

You can take him hunting,
God will provide the game.
You can make mistakes in life,
God will take the blame.

God loves you and your son.
He knows us all by name.
You must teach your son of God
So he can teach his son the same.

Mothers are great and loving,
Their best they always do,
But a little boy needs God in his life,
And he needs his father, too.

There will surely come a time in his life
When he'll face choices concerning drugs or a gun.
There's only so much parents can do at that point.
That's why it takes both fathers to raise a son.

Edward J. Good Sr.

God's Gift Of Love

A treasure to be treasured,
God's gift of love to me
A gift so far unmeasured
The gift who has set me free.

A Savior pure and humble,
So great and free from sin.
Why then now should I grumble-
When He has placed such love within?

This Savior is my Jesus
Who died for you and me.
He bore my sins on Calvary-
He took it all instead of me.

Where else is there a Savior?
Where else upon the earth?
Unchangeable and forever pure,
Is Jesus from His birth.

He's gone to live with God above,
And yet He's here with me.
Because He is the gift of love-
God gave to you and me.

Bernadine Carlton

Squish

Tiny hands grip the
gooey cone and
strawberry ice cream drips
onto the pavement
and squishes
between small fingers as they
cling
with all their might
so that next time
unlike the last,
it will not be a cup with a spoon.

Amy Simkins

Water's Victim

Toward the waves, washed over by despair,
grief will overcome in the end

Walking slowly into the water,
blue above and below

Sea lapping at my feet,
aching to swallow me

Licking hungrily around my legs,
tears are streaming down my face

Sapphire swirling about my waist,
glistening like the stars above

Twilight has fallen above my head,
coolness is tickling about my neck

Feeling the sand disappear from under me,
I look up at the sky for the last time.

Erika Duncan

Love And Hate

Love is hate . . .
Hate is love . . .
But when joined together
Can reach ones inner self and
   last forever
The pain is so grave
The pain lasts until you forever long
   a cure
You then remember there is
   no cure
There is only love
Love is hate
Hate is love

Bridgette Gordon

Be Free Loved One

Be totally free,
have lots of fun;
think of me,
when the day is done;
unique and grand,
you are my left hand
loved one.

Bonnie R. Shannon

"The Charmer"

He tells you what you want to hear,
He even shares you of his fears,
He sweeps you off your feet,
He knows how to make you weak.
Always knowing what to say,
To make you feel good in every way.
Always a kind word to share,
Pretending like he cares.
Only in it for the fun
Not realizing what he's done,
Wanting to still be friends,
Always leaves you in the end.

Beverly Robinson

Walking With Jesus

I love to walk with Jesus
He protects me as I go.
He stays close beside me and
defeats my every foe,
   He never will forsake me
He'll always be right here,
   There's no reason for me to
Worry I have nothing to fear.
   He's a good and loving
savior, He cares so much for me,
   He gave his life as calvary for
me, from sin to be set free.
   He sticks closer than mothers
father or friend. He'll always be with
me right to the end.
Some day I'll be in Heavens to
look upon his beautiful face
because he saved me with
his amazing grace.

Eleanor Johnson

The View

Dax
Healthy, good looking,
wild, pet lover.
Son of Fred and Judy.
Cares deeply about Dad,
Mom, and my dog.
Who feels happy.
Who needs skates.
Who gives baby toys to babies.
Who fears a big rock
falling on my head.
Who would like to see
Terminator 2 again.
Student of Flint Hill
Spanogle.

Dax Fredrick Spanogle

Looking In On An Outlook

Gather all the love that you feel
From the world around you;
Spread the love that is real
And put the hatred behind you;
Search beyond the walls,
Which minds build;
Climb until you see the truth;
For it is there that you find yourself,
Mother Earth's youth.

Whether you're a warrior,
Or one who unlocks the gate;
It's your decision to reach,
Your destination to seek;
For over the wall lies your fate.

Freida Baugh

Her First Gold

Nature's first green is gold.
Her hardest hue to hold.
Her early leaf's a flower,
but only so an hour.
Just as leaf subsides to leaf.
So Eden sank to grief.
As dawn gives in to day,
Nothing gold can stay.

Daniel Lee Roumell

Ode To A Sense Of Humor

Many of us have our troubles,
 heartaches and woes,
And it takes a lot of "doing"
 to keep on our toes
For in this, most of us think we
 all one of a kind
But the best antidote is to
 keep this in mind;
Through-out all our complaint and wails
It soon disappear with our fears
 when a sense of humor prevails

Our sorrows suddenly seem smaller
 than those of the other man
By allowing a sense of humor
 to rescue us, as it can
But the most important things
 to remember are the stamina
 faith and courage we show
While throughout this life
 we go.

Dorothi Lemont

"Dawn"

Dawn is a ghost.
Her duties as Hostess of Morning
And Pursuer of Night
Carry her to being as Light.
'Though gray and ill-seeming
Her garments are teeming
With hope
Of a new day,
Not forlorn but bright
When sight
Is here.

John M. Mays

Hidden Self

Monster, monster where are you
Here I am inside of you
Behind your eyes so bright and blue
I sit in darkness, waiting for my cue
Everyday I grow inside
I'm taking control of your mind
I live and breath for your soul
Soon it will be mine forever to hold
I bring your nightmares and your fears
so I can feel all your tears
Your blood is the tea that I drink
Delicious and tasty the more I think
One day soon we will meet
My power and strength you cannot beat
I live inside you and you and you
I live inside everyone that I do.

Jennifer D. Miller

Words

Sometimes when I'm talking,
I am most surprised to hear
The things I am saying;
Where they come from is not clear.

Then, if on whom they fall,
They are wont to leave a bruise,
I feel very sorry
I spoke words I did not choose.

Etta B. Cory

Back Home

One hundred miles or more
Here in another state
In search of work
The hour is getting late

Somewhat in desperation
My mind does roam
Thinking thoughts of others
Especially the folks back home

The television showing commercials
Dad in his easy chair
The family dog asleep
Mom's cleaning up somewhere

Sis is in the bedroom
Playing with her dolls
The cat most curious
Is scratching on the walls

Closing my eyes but a moment
Floating off somewhere
In just a nod or two
I'm back home there.

Betty Ann Estes

Oh Friend!

Hello, dear friend
here we are again.
It has always been us
Who can say why?

I've seen people go
and others just leave.
but when you turn around
here I am alone.

Promise I had not yet shown
yet you loved me still.
Soon we were friends
but always this and nothing more.

I tried to repress the truth
but now I dare not.
Still the best of friends,
But now the love of my life!

Bill Newton

My Granddaughter

I love you Grandma and Grandpa too
Here's a great big kiss for you.
My granddaughter just four years old,
What a wonder to behold.
She always has a twinkle in her eye
And a smile on her face,
Laughter to her is common place.
Why, there she is now, just over there
Fast asleep in her Grandpa's chair.
You know she's the apple of my eye
She's strawberry shortcake
And blueberry pie.
Soft brown hair and big brown eyes
What's next with her?
It will be a surprise.

George Kolar

Lies

Lies are used to,
 hide the truth.
Lies are another,
 form of abuse.

People don't care about,
 who they hurt.
People just keep on,
 dishing out their dirt.

Lies are from people who,
 won't or can't deal with themselves.

Lies are from people who,
 steal from everyone else.

Hey, stop, and take a minute before
 you open your mouth;

For if its gonna be a lie
 tell it to someone that's listening
 like only yourself.

Evelyn Forman

The Ferris Wheel

Round and round about it goes
High and low, and all around.
 People get on,
 The door closes.
And then starts the big circus fun

Three times it goes around
As the people scream of enjoyment.
 People get off,
 The door closes.
And then starts a new ride

Hilary Puzak

That Intimacy Called Friendship

I like to remember
His hair blowing in the breeze
Like his spirit, unrestrained.
Dark eyes that dart and tease,
Then focus with intensity
Above a wide, mustached smile
That takes my breath away.

I stare wide-eyed
At the ease of his acceptance.
Dropping my robe of mistrust,
I bare my tarnished soul,
Unashamed. He sees no flaw.
His words caress my spirit.
Oblivious to time and place,
We soar in ecstasy
On golden wings of friendship.

Charlotte L. Rust

My Dream Of Yesterday

My husband so tall and thin
His retirement just begin
Our plans to have fun and play
Were soon taken away
When he was called to heaven to stay

My daughter soon come to stay
Our plans were to have fun and play
Suddenly she too, was taken away
Now I'm old and gray
I have more children to play
But what happened to yesterday?

Grace Brandon

Real Illusion

When the darkness in the early
hours of the afternoon.

When the thunder sounds further
than the leaded clouds,

When the wind cries further away
in the monotonous sounds of the storm

I remember you.

When the clouds start dropping
their heavy drops,
When the wind sounds threatening
between the neighboring trees;

When the sky and the earth
get together in a tempestuous night

I have you with me.

When the night is close
without a promise of a Moon,

When the loose wind cries
with tempestuous broken gusts

When the steady rain drops
in the needles of the pines

I cry.

Josefa Rivas

My Love For You

My love for you is so strong
I can't even hold on

Why is it like this?
Is it because of yesterday's bliss?

Can you love me, too?
The way I love you

Caroline Cosing

Feelings

Love is like a romance.
How can you feel love?
That's what we all ask.
Love is like butterflies in your stomach.
Or how you feel about someone.
When you finally
feel love you never want
it to go away. But if
love goes away you always
love the one you love. That is
what I think about love.

Jaime Darland

Paralyzed Thoughts

Imprisoned in my own reality
How could this be?
Helpless to save my soul
Drowning in a gigantic bowl.
Afraid of what could have been
Knowing that my life is a sin.
Scared to say nothing, Petrified to talk
Nervous to stand, Paralyzed to walk
I am dying slow, slowly
When my life will end I do not see
Why must I be
Why can't I see
A end to my torment

Chris Kuznia

Seasons

Have you ever sat to ponder,
how our lives are truly blest.
Nature sets it's stage with seasons,
beauty abounds within earth's zest.
Spring renews all birth to the land,
while summer offers flowers so grand.
Autumn spreads its colors in splendor,
while winter's delicate snowflakes
show God's creative hand.

Beverly A. Kaehler

"Children Of My Children"

Just didn't realize
How wonderful it could be
Children of my children . . . loving me.
Didn't realize how special
It would be to watch them grow,
Beautiful God-like beings
Of someone I love and know.
So now their lives surround me
In so many special ways.
I thank the Lord and bless my children
For giving me these wonderful days.

Allen J. Vangelos

Untitled

I am the one you hate
I am the one you despise
I am the one you can't stand
But now I realize . . .

I am that loser
I'm the abuser
I am the one you abhor
I won't stick around anymore

I hear the whispers in the halls
I see the writing on the walls
I feel you kick me in the balls
I am that loser

Why can't you please just tell me why
So long I've been living this lie
I thought my life was apple pie
So much pain I think I could die

I am that loser
I'm the abuser
Sometimes I just want to fly
Sometimes I just want to die . . .

Chatam Miracle

Let Me Go

Please let me go
I can't take this,
  it's hurting me
  it's hurting you
Please let me go
I'm in pain.
  you can see it in my eyes
I can see the pain in yours,
  it's just like mine,
  because you can't help me
I love you, you love me too,
  but let me go
Please, let me go,
  I'm begging you,
  Please, set me free from pain
Let me go.

Elizabeth Z. Guerrie

A Dying Poet's Wish

When I am gone
I ask but this;
On my cold brow
Plant not a kiss.

No love nor lust
Can e'er revive me.
Urn not my dust
If you survive me.

Raise not my bust
Nor bow before it.
Adoration?
I deplore it.

I wish no peer
To eulogize me
But, if you must —
Anthologize me!

Harry Merritt

Past, Present, And Future

I'm worth more than gold
I can never get old
I'm famous
Everyone knows me
My name is on the cover of a
Famous magazine
I can never be owned
I can never be bought
I never give up
And I cannot be fought
I'm passing by
Right before your eyes
You can not see me
But you sure can feel me
We met when you were born
And you've felt me ever since
Oh haven't you?
Just give me some . . .
Time

Bryan A. Zardeneta

When You Were Here

When you were here,
I could hear you wishing,
wishing hard that you could take
all your memories and keep them safe.

And now its me
oh yes its true that has to keep
them safe for you.

When you were here,
I could hear you crying
Crying about the saddest part
that dwelled inside your hollow heart.

When you were here,
I could see you trying,
trying to see from others perspective,
Playing the part of a simple detective
Wondering how could death possibly
be and now your gone and now you see.

And now your gone but there's a part
for you inside God's humble heart
for every death there's a
price to pay I'll see you again one special
day.

Charlestaneca Caprice Coats

Room At The Top

If we had a room at the top
I could lift the shade at night
We'd dance with the wondrous stars
The moon would be our light.

If we had a room at the top
With windows that opened to sun
We'd waste away the day
Wouldn't we have fun!

We'd be closer to snowflakes
Closer to sky
Closer to heaven
You and I

If we had a room at the top
Above the city's roar
We'd hear each other's heart
How could we ask for more . . .

Harriet Sidney

Christmas Tree

I was once proud and very tall
I dared the wind to blow me down
now my many branches lay
useless in the snow
the little birds no longer
perch in my crown
please take care when you
set me in your stand
that you break not,
my leader before the end.
And when you burn me on
the pile, remember me when
I stood so proud and very tall!

Dwight Eich

To Soar

The eagle soars.
I drift
and wait
for his return.
He turns.
Showing me
his playful tricks.
The sun is setting.
I turn
and know
he's taught me
something about pride
in what we do
and
enjoying it
every step of the way.

Becky DeWitt

"Tender Thoughts"

Dearest One:
I heard the birds chirping outside
   my window pane,

and the wind blowing softly in
   the rain.

And deep within my heart
   I thought of you -

by my side always, with all
   my love, too.

Dorothy T. LeViness

Christmas Love

Christmas is coming
I feel it in the air
It's the season to be jolly
For people everywhere.

The houses are decorated
With wreaths and red bows
There's magic at Christmas
And everything glows.

We celebrate Christmas
In a very special way
Because our Lord Jesus
Was born on Christmas day.

May we always be blessed
With peace from above
As we worship the King
Merry Christmas with Love.

Alta Jean Kuhn

The Sky

   At night I look into the sky, and
I feel so wild and free;
   There's so much beauty in the air,
so much for me to see

   Sometimes I wonder if there's
somewhere out there, like another world
above;

   Where all there is happiness,
and a constant show of love.

   As the wind-blown trees sway
into the night; and the leaves land
on my face;

I pray somehow to get away
and find this special place.

   Someday I'll find this
dreamland, but until then,
I'll just wait.

   And give out all the love
I have, cause there's no
more room for hate.

Justin Wahl

The Horn

In the forest this morning
I found a horn.
It was the horn
Of a unicorn.

It was lying there
On the soft, green ground
As if waiting
To be found.

I picked it up
And held it in my hand.
It took me with it
To a foreign land.

A land where nothing evil
Does exist,
Where fairies dance
In the morning mist.

It is the land
To which unicorns
Go with joy
When they have lost their horns.

Ida Carlen

A Day In June

While working in the yard today,
I found ample time
   To worship and pray,
To thank God for
   My family and friends,
And to praise him for Jesus
   With whom love begins,
To intercede for the sick
   And shut-in,
As well as for those
   Still lost in sin,
To thank Him for the beauty
   Of flowers and trees,
The refreshing rains
   And cool summer breeze.

Doris DeVault

Taken

From the time I realized
I had given life to you,
You've been a part of me
Even tho' you never knew;
The day you were born
And I held you in my arms . . .
I vowed to keep you
From the world and all it's harm,
Back so many years ago
Father's seemed to have no rights -
Tho I never signed a paper
You were taken from my life.
Long days and endless years.
Turned into troubled sleepless nights,
I couldn't erase your precious face
From my mind or from my sight . . .
So my search for you began.
Hoping for the very best -
That we would meet again;
And let God take care of the rest.

Jan Knox

My Song

Why do I sing, you ask?
I have no sorrow?
No, but I have learned of life
That grief exalts my song.
Life heals where it has given hurt
And what matter pain,
If tomorrow, I can sing again
And sing more sweetly?

Brenda Patrick

Wonder Why

Oh lady, oh lady why
I have so much sorrow
I could die.
But I know not why.
I look to the sky and
Wish I could fly.
With a shy sigh,
I wonder why.
This isn't a lie,
I just want to be high in the sky,
With the guy, so I wave bye,
Because this is my pie,
And I wonder why,
Oh my, oh my, oh my.

Charles Littlefield

Reality

When I see
I have thought
When I close my eyes
I have vision
When I sleep
I have relief
So real are my burdens
Exceeding belief

James Michael Williams

Innocent Hunger

You loved me once
I have yet forgotten
and
now
you're somewhere else

Not far
yet
journeys from my touch

See me now
caress me with your tempted eyes
for
I'll wait

Devon O. Savaj

Someone Cailed My Name

Someone called my name
I heard it, oh so clear
It was only just a whisper
But, the sound was very dear.
Someone called my name
It came out of the blue,
I heard a very special voice,
I asked, "Lord, was it you?"
Someone called my name
In the dark and quiet of night
It startled me, at first,
It gave me such a fright.
When I asked, "Who called me?"
I heard not another sound
I do not know the reason
But, there was quietness all around.
Then I thought of Jesus,
My fears went right away,
Someone called my name
And it made a special day!

Eloise Harmon

Untitled

Waiting ever waiting
I know I am.
I shine the stars in blackened nights
Nature myself,
I dance the ocean waves
I sing the song of sails.
Crystals I am
Thoughts I purge
Desires I loosen,
Judgements battles not yet won.
Light I am,
I wait
Love and trust sit on the fence
My heart remaining fallow,
Hope I am.

Diane T. Valente

My Sympathy

I'm sorry you've lost your mother
I know she was precious to you.
I understand how you feel,
For I lost my mother too.

I know you loved her very much
But, Jesus loved her best.
There's much consolation in knowing
She is now His heavenly guest.

Of course you'll miss her more and more
As the days go by.
And sometimes you may even
Breakdown and cry.

So go on and mourn
The lost of your mother
Knowing that Jesus
Is closer than a brother.

And soon one day without a doubt
You'll rejoice in remembering
What a mother's love was all about.

Amelia E. White

My Daughter, The Carpenter

My daughter is a carpenter;
I learned that by surprise.
She telephoned excitedly to say,
"Come see my prize!"

Of course, I, as her mother, went
immediately to see.
"What is this gorgeous Super Prize
she has to show to me?"

She had a typing table
unassembled from a box!
And there it was! Now all set up!
complete with drawer and locks!

"Beautiful!" I said to her.
She laughed and said to me,
"I built this table by myself.
I'm proud as I can be!"

The best part was the cash she saved,
all stuffed and in her pocket,
Could buy the folks a Christmas brunch
and for herself, a locket!

Alice E. Nelson

Father's Gift

Eyes blue, cheeks full and rosy,
I like to hold her nice and cozy,
Sweet she is, as her mother,
I love them both, like no other,
When I wake to go to work,
I look at them both,
And let out a smirk,
I know at night, when I come home,
I will have them both, to myself alone.

Clarence J. Harris

"Goodbye"

Why i live i live
i live for her.
Why SHE died,
SHE died for me.
Now SHE's gone,
So i must say . . . "Goodbye."

Jon Zackula

Night Games

These foolish games
I like to play when I am all alone.
    I pretend I am everything I'm not
    and everything that I haven't become.
My tears are frozen inside my eyes.
    My ears are clogged with fright.
I have become everything that I despise.

Upon the window,
dreams take the place of stars
being thrown, hurled through
the night's sky.
Relentless, unfulfilled
they drift away.

Broken and desolate,
the stars take over my eyes,
my mind.
    I am the stars,
with only the wondrous galaxy
    as my boundary.

Amanda Schomas

Future, Past Or Present

I live for the future,
I live in the past,
But in the present,
I will not stay.

The future holds promise,
The past adventure,
But the present,
Is dull and gray.

The robots of the future,
The knights of the past,
The wear and the tear,
Of the everyday.

The future will come,
The past is gone,
And in the present,
I must stay.

Geoffrey Richard

Rapture

I met Love the day I met you
I looked at you and said to God
Is it really him?
To grant me such a wish is joy.

I said thank you Lord
I will take care of him
Until we meet again in Heaven
When I will bring my Love back to you.

Anita Wales

Autumn

Autumn to me is the best season of all
I love to watch red and gold leaves fall
Then Mr. Wind his breath will blow
Big leaves, small leaves, high and low
They scatter north, they scatter east
As if they were going to a feast
I know not where they disappear
Red leaves, gold leaves, here and there.
Then all this must come to an end
When Mr. Winter his big wind will send
All the leaves one by one disappear
Red leaves, gold leaves, here and there.

Dee Laukonis

My Valentine

I love you in the morning,
I love you at night.
You're my little star,
Who's always shining bright.

You're always in my corner,
With love and ever giving.
You're always sharing something,
To make life worth living.

Johanna Fratrick

My Love

I loved you before you knew yourself
I loved you when you were a
Thought sitting on God's shelf
I loved you before time began
I loved you long before you were a man
I loved you before there were stars
I loved you before there was Mars
In a place where love has no friends
I loved you, without sin

Dena Marie Hughes-Ebo

Magnificent Is My Guardian Angel

Angel from above
I marvel at your splendor,
an aura lined with gold
and a heart so tender.

No melodious sound compares
to your ethereal expression of song.
Only in the choirs of Heaven
could such a delicate voice belong.

Gracefully, you ascend
to the heavens far above.
You illuminate my path
with your radiance of love.

Effortless are your motions,
every miracle performed with ease.
You never cease to obey
the Father you wish to please.

Loving messenger of God,
guardian of my soul,
divine in every way,
your presence I behold.

Heather E. Yopp

Untitled

Daddy, where are you?
I miss you so.
Just once I would like
to here from you.
Tell me you're all right,
and ask me that to.
Do you know how I am?
Do you care how I am?
Tell me that you do.
Daddy, oh, Daddy
Where are you?
Daddy, Oh, Daddy,
I love you.

Jessica Gayleen Fisher

Absence

You go away
I miss your face
Time goes by
I long for your smile
Days are lonely
I want you here
Sleepless nights
I miss your touch
Disjointed thoughts
I need your love
You come back
I live again

James E. Earl

Early Frost

That final fragrant bloom
   I never paused to hail
Nods limply from its stem,
   Laid waste by autumn's flail.
I didn't heed the sounds
   Of Nature's vocal seers:
The rose has gone again
   And left me in arrears.

Del Joost

Hope For Rachel Lavinsky

I do not pity her she can't forget.
I pity her she won't forgive.
The wounded heart will never heal
Nor ever truly feel again
Till spirit falls upon it knees
And begs Oh God! forgive them now,
As through my bitter pain I also do.

The tattoo numbering her arm
Will never fade;
But if the heart cleave still to hate,
Hate will slowly kill
And death be then twice magnified.

Love was made
To make the body whole again
That broke and died.
Let it enter - oh sweet dove of peace!
And surely then
It will release the prisoned soul
From death that Life be then
Thrice glorified.

Ernest C. Allison

Untitled

With arms outstretched
I reach towards the sun
And I am drawn upwards through the sky
Until the Earth is but a speck of dust
And, drifting through space and time
I feel great joy as I go ever higher
Into the deep blue vastness
On a peaceful journey home

Holly Mock Kadota

In Terminal Sound?

Poems that rhyme and poems that don't
I really hate them both.
Cause when I find a word that rhymes,
usually the next line won't!

Makes no sense to really bother
to rhyme or not to rhyme
just pour your heart out right on paper
now that is not a crime!

Please let there be no more
"Roses are red
violets are blue,
because violets are really purple!

Why bother spending all your days
with a catchy, matchy phrase
where's the rhyme or reason?
unorthodox, that's what I say,
would be a bit more pleasin'!!!

Deborah McDonald

God's Gift

By the dawn's early light,
I received my first fright.
It was the air that we breathe,
Compelling me to leave.

Up in space, I thought,
Is where I'll go.
I'll find free, clean air
For everyone who's there.

Little did I know
Others were thinking so.
But enough free air was there.
For everyone to share.

Dedicated to my Father,
John Sebastian III, 8/20/25 - 6/21/95

Bernadine Sebastian

A Moment In Time

As I was walking through the wood,
I saw a fallen tree.

It lay there never moving, still,
decayed as it could be.

Around it little saplings grew,
as if they never knew that they, too,
would live and die and lie beneath
the clear, blue sky.

How could it be so near to me and
yet so far away, that death may be
so close at hand, might even be
today.

Donna Baughman

Defined

"Before I wrote
I was a poet
Then I became a laborer
And the pen was still in my hand.
Even pages empty
But for thought
They called to me."

Gregory Broder

The Unforgiving Light

It was on a cool summer night,
I saw a shimmering light in my sight.

I felt the breath of fear appear,
knowing it came from far to near.

I watched it silently come this way,
now knowing if it was safe or okay.

But, I was moved by a long gentle force,
I started to feel a little remorse.

As I drew closer and near,
I realized there was nothing to fear.

But, then the light was gone;
It felt so very long.

I kept looking around,
But, the light was no where to be found.

I was back on my way,
With my mind astray.

Wondering if it would come back to me
fast,
Or just be a vision from my past.

I prayed for the light to come back to me,
But, that was only a hopeless plea.

Candace April Williamson

Sonnet No. One

Should I write like Robert Frost?
I search within my heart
Looking hard for talent lost
Which might incite a start
From where does it come?
To pen such verse
So flowing to some
To others a curse
I wish to know, seeking to aspire
To place my writing
On the muses fire
Hoping there to receive a knighting
Thus it is my poetic fate
To attempt and ponder how to create

Andrew Agnew

To My Son

As I look upon your perfect face,
I see a boy changed to a man.
Those eyes, so dark, so full of hope,
That smile, I keep within my heart.

You stand so tall and strong,
I can't believe your grown.
Where are those years of little boy hugs,
Of games and toys and little boy tears.

I loved you then, as I love you now,
This boy turned into a man.
You fill my heart with pride and joy,
This mother's heart is given to you.

I ask no pay for giving you life,
I prayed for you from God above,
Never could I choose so well,
As God has granted me your love.

Cherish my love and keep it close.
It stays with you for all your life.
I take it with me when I leave this world,
To give it back when we meet again.

Carroll Knapp

Dreaming

I look into his eyes
I see into his soul
To me there is no disguise
To me he is a whole
He never lies to me
He means it when he says
He will always love me
24 hours, 365 days
Love is forever
We will never part
He has changed my life forever
He will never break my heart

Becky Ring

Eyes

When I look in your eyes
I see me
The way I never seen before
Please don't close your eyes
I ask
I don't want to wake up

Agnes Biondi

Zace And Grace

Grace stepped on my toe.
I started to push her to the floor.
Instead, I zoomed rapidly out the door.
Grace ran and grabbed my hand
And stared very sweetly in my face.

Then she gave me a big bear hug.
And we went back inside and sat
On our grandmother's soft shag rug.
She looked at me and said
"I love you Zace."

When I looked at her, my anger flew
Into the thin summer air.
I returned Zace's warm friendly stare
And said, "I love you too, Grace."
We reached and clutched hands.

"My twin," . . . we repeated thrice.
Life is more fun when we're nice.
We acted in a friendly way
Which made us have an extra special day.
Then Grace gave me another big hug.

Florence M. Jones

Whenever I Think Of God

Whenever I think of God,
I think of joy, of peace, of love
I think of joy God gives to me
With late night talk and serenity
I think of peace we all could have
With just believing what he has said
I think of the love within my heart,
Just knowing that God has done his part
Whenever I think of God,
I think of Christ his only son
The son who died for you and me,
The son who set us free
He walked on earth a little while
To make things right for one and all
Whenever I think of God,
I think of Christ the risen one
He came, he preached, he died, then rose
He gave to all the greatest hope
The hope that comes after we're laid to rest

Brenda Means (Walker)

My Feelings

Time and time again,
I try to tell you how I feel.
Yet I can't even tell my friends,
they don't get the big deal.

Every moment I'm with you,
I want you to hold me in your arms.
That's because when I'm with you,
you keep me safe from harm.

There's nothing left to say,
nothing I could tell you.
There's nothing left to say,
except maybe I love you!

I wish I could tell you,
tell you everything I say.
Wishes don't always come true,
but if they did, I'd face a brighter day.

This poem is at it's end
I love you, I love you, I love you!
You'd probably say, 'were just friends',
if only you said, 'I love you'!

Annie Wong

The Clown

Hurt, angry,
I want to cry,
But I dare not try.

People Watching,
Laughing at me,
I perform, I joke,
No one takes me seriously.

Stand up,
Be brave,
Show no anger, fear, or sadness.
Hide it, cover it, pretend gladness.

Soft side,
Serious side,
Aching to be shown.
Not here, not now,
Perhaps when I'm alone.

I am the clown,
From day to day,
Mood up or down,
That's how I must stay.

Chrissy Lee

Untitled

Yesterday has come and gone
I was glad and I was sad
It did not end up with a song
It could not hold to what I had

Yesterday I tried to live
To make a friend, to see the sun
I did not have enough to give
I really failed the distant run

Yesterday will not be back
And now I cry with but regret
My frame of mind is not intact
My inner self with grief beset

Yesterday has come and gone
Today is here and I am glad
Yesterday, happened wrong
Today, old life, I won't be sad

Jean C. Talbert

Rosebushes

From out of my natural orbit,
I was pulled by a rosebush.
Upon my arrival,
I found myself hungry.
So . . .
You fed me apples, berries,
Peaches, cherries, and plums.
Apricots and quinces, fruits
that are equally pleasing
to the palate and tongue.

As your fragrance drew me nearer,
I was overwhelmed by your loveliness.
Rose, tea, and fruit blended so well.
Scarlet of colors, crimson and rare,
Eclipse yellow, fragrant red.

While I was staring, entranced by
Your beauty, I hadn't noticed your thorns.
Ouch!! It's too late,
I've been stuck by more than one.

Rosebushes
Annalisa S. Burch

Like A Flower

I was planted.
I was watered.
I was given a lot of sun.
I grew up tall.
I had a nice color.
I gave off a nice smell.
People from all over came to see me.
I was always center of attention.
I got older.
I got tired.
Like a flower,
I died.

Daria Nikole Butler

"My One And Only"

Without my one and only
I would be so sad and lonely
So I give to her all my dividing love
Because we are like two soaring doves.
We have are ups and downs
But we never keep our frowns
And when I look into her eyes.
I feel safe as the stars in the skies
For my one and only, is my wife
To which I would give for her my life
So with my one and only
I'll never be sad or lonely.

Harry Johnston

Dead Life

What I say no one listen
If I die no one will christen
For some reason I do not exist
For hell I'm bound to enlist
My life and soul will be gone forever
But there my life will last forever

Jodi L. Frank-Johnson

The Seasons (In Haiku)

Spring
Ice melts. Pods explode seeds.
 Robins dine on Spring's larder.
 Faith reaffirmed.

Summer
Garden wars! Blooms vie for sun.
 Marigolds win in
  pungent skirmish.

Autumn
Crisp and brittle, leaves whirl color.
 Long shadows say
  the party's over.

Winter
Snow gentles the earth.
 Come stars - shine ways through
  our drifts - that we may
  find peace.

Jacqueline Kozuch

Happiness

Oh how pleasant it would be
 If all of us were to agree
On just the basic things in life
 So they don't gender war and strife.

We cannot each have our own way
 On everything from day to day;
But each must give and take a bit
 So peace and harmony can sit.

God does not hold His blessings back
 From each of us because we lack
Some small or very great possession
 Or sour or happy disposition.

So friends, as days go marching on
 Let's fill our days with happy song
And think of others without blame
 Then peace and harmony will reign.

Gloria Sharp

Not Mine

I stepped into my dream,
If only for a moment,
I felt the warmth of his hand,
As it rested on my breast.

We laid side by side,
Not looking at each other.
I breathed in slowly,
To catch his body scent.

This is what I've wanted,
When he pressed his lips on mine.
To know what it felt like,
This time it was time.

Now my lips feel haunted,
Will I feel his lips again?
I close my eyes gently,
Trying to pretend.

What do I have to give up?
My purity, my mind,
You see he's with another,
He isn't even mine.

Donna G. King

Wouldn't It Be Nice

Wouldn't it be nice
If people were like trees
Tall and straight and strong
And never do no wrong
They'd plant their roots so deep
And never have to weep
They'd spread their arms out wide
And shield every one inside
Shed their rotted leaves
As pretty as you please
Wouldn't it be nice
If people were like trees

Anna Mae Lockhart

The Message of the Dove

There's a message of peace
If we listen well,
On the wings of a shadowy dove,
For the shadow dove speaks,
Softly sweet, softly low,
"There is no peace without love."

But oftentimes earthmen
May meet and agree
With strangers to live without strife,
So we say to the dove,
"Though we live without love,
Cannot there be peace in our life?"

"To be so divided
By a cold unknown wall
Though strife and all warring may cease,
Is to exist, not to live,
In this measured life span,
For love is the very heart of peace."

Betty N. Owens

Untitled

It's hard to tell
If you really care
About me
At times I think
You really do
Other times I think
You possibly can't
Confused
Yes, that's me
I wish I knew
How you really felt
Just friends
Or maybe a little more
It could be great
You and me
Wishing
Hoping
Wondering
Someday
Maybe

Danielle Green

Autumns

As I look out my window
into the yard ringed with trees,
the leaves ablaze with colors,
falling in the breeze.
Then I become nostalgic,
thinking of autumns past.
All of them beautiful,
but none of them last.

Faye League

I'll Be There

When you need me
I'll be there
I'm the one who cares

When things are good
But sometimes bad

I'll be there so don't
Be sad

When you need me
I'm around

I'm the best friend to
Be found

Just say the words
And it will be heard

I'll be there
I' the one who cares

Brenda P. Stellmacher

Goodnight

Go to bed sleepy head
I'll wake you up in the morning
So we can play in the dew
Sing with the birds and
Watch the sky turn
Orange, pink, purple,then finally blue
We'll play in the flowers
With the wind
Then watch the sky turn
Purple, pink, orange, then black again
Mama will call us in
Go to bed sleepy head
Tomorrow is another day

Courtney Harral

Return To Reality

The stress of life is killing me,
   I'm captive from reality.
The power of money is destroying,
   the values of life worth enjoying.

So I escape to the sea, where
   calming waves welcome me.
Now my senses come alive, I'm
   free again I will survive.

For He has made the oceans roll,
   like soothing rhythm for the soul.
Hear the birds how they sing,
   sweet music to the heart it brings.

Sunset and sunrise displaying
   splendor in the sky.
Many colors all so bright, to the
   precious gift of sight.

This is reality, which God creates
   for all to see.
Come and share this world with me,
   and stress of life will cease to be.

Helen Miles

Winter Tribute

She rests in peace
   in a garden of Christmas wreaths.
The snow falls softly,
The wind blows gently
Across the sweep
   of snow covered evergreen boughs.
A tiny bird chirps the clear,
   sweet notes of a winter song.
She rest with God,
   in peace.

Annamae Murphy

Whomever Made The Earth?

Whomever made the earth?
I'm not so very sure.
The grassy lands,
The colorful bands,
On the planet Jupiter.

Whomever made the rainbow?
I do not really know.
The beautiful colors,
Including all of the others,
A beautiful place to go.

Whomever made the earth?
It seems a little odd.
I know who made it,
The one and greatest,
The only man named God.

Eric Steven Warman

A Mother (Mine)

A mother
Impressions in my
Soul . . . shaped
like Love bonded with
her beauty

Her words are
Strength
Supported on the
Beams of life

Touch of security
the stroke of her
Hand, a gentle
Rain on an
Autumn day

A mother is
Once . . .
but a reflection
Always, in the
Shadow of life

Garret Abeyta

A Sure Sign

I know a sure sign that fall
is here, do you know a sure
sign that fall is here? Well I
do, and I'll tell you if you'll
just only listen. Of course,
it's the leaves. They're always
on time and they will never
be late because the weather
reminds them.

Denise Hansen

David's House

Lonely echoes
In a house without furniture.
Empty rooms
Filled with memories.

Working late
To avoid the inevitable return.
The palpable loneliness
Of an empty heart.

You can run
But the past always sneaks up on you
And taps you on the shoulder.
Reminding you.

Claudia M. Howard

Kindness

My happiest days have all been spent
In doing things for others -
Perhaps a smile, a hand, a hug,
To sisters, friends, and brothers.

The things I do seem small to me,
To little to be counted-
And yet when kindness comes my way,
My soul, it's wings are mounted.

I fly away above the clouds,
My spirit soars forever -
Until it's time to do again,
A kind deed for another.

Joy Komnick

Dream Chasin'

Dreams hold a special place,
   in every man and woman's heart.
It's almost like a race
   where everyone plays a special part.
Dreams flow slowly through our heads
   in school or at night,
As we lay in our beds.
It's a never ending fight
   where only one can be the victor.
In order to catch our dreams,
   we must chase them with an open mind.
It's so hard it may seem,
But it's not you will find
If only you chase them and not
   give up.

Brian Bollinger

Wings of Faith

From the road
   In graceful flight,
Four crows arose
   In morning light.

For this day
   No troubled thought,
What it brings
   Or yesterday brought.

Though they live
   In shroud of black,
For joy of life
   There is no lack.

Arise my soul
   And follow them,
Our Father cares,
   Trust in Him.

Jack Conn

Reflections

Reflections of the past
in memory of who we were,
time stands still long enough
for everything to become a blur.

Remembering how it used to be
knowing how things have changed,
people going separate ways —
lives being rearranged.

Friends losing touch
as we each take separate roads;
learning about life and love
in separate, unique modes.

Jennifer Washwick

Memories

Oh Scottish Lochs and Ben's
In memory of you I am sad
Memories, when I trod upon your soil
Clothed in a tartan plaid

The ship sailed down the River Clyde
While loved ones waved from shore
And out into the open sea
A thousand miles or more

Each passing day in farther from
The ones I hold most dear
And sea and sky were all around
But then land did appear

And as the years have swiftly flown
I often stop and think
Of that far away place I left behind
A remnant of my past.

Agnes McMaster

Gentle Piranhas

Safe but for the mirror
in my hand
steals my identity
only allows one to see
the part of me that needs
improvement
reflectively
collectively
I look to see
the real me
surprisingly,
inside of me
I find
my true identity
is starving . . .

Heather Girouard

Guilt No More

Ghosts
in my mind
Pounding
a closed door
I want
Never opened,
Hounding
me in sleep
Until
I shoot
Straight
up in bed
Screaming
guilt no more.

Jennifer Sheeran

Reptilian Testimony

Her words slithered across the page
In serpentine persuasion
A smooth hissing of pleasantries
Veiling intentions to ensnare me

Not an angry syllable surfaced
As cool soothing sounds slipped
Into lines of utmost innocence
Sure in their destination of my guilt

Questions swayed hypnotically
Invoking a contrite trance
Rhythmically crooning convictions
Spells spun in repetitious litany

Relishing the victory she struck
Fangs piercing me she injected her venom
As poisonous invectives oozed
Seeping into my vulnerable wounds

Her victim, I now lie immobilized
Her pages lay crumpled in a heap
Like dried scaly skin discarded
In cold blooded reptilian testimony

Holly Mayo

In Silence

We will make music
  in silence.
Listening in the stillness
  for the melody
    of our souls
    melting together.

Our love goes deep
  beyond all four walls,
    existing freely
      flowing continually
        in mute
        solitude.

Harmony escapes our minds
  in rhythmic overtures
    with our bodies
    blending together.

And,
  in silence
we make music, forever.

Carol Ann Yasuhara

In No One's Name

I am the virtuoso
in the real of despair
with operatic voice
I sing
soprano, only warmed
bass, only chilled
I am the dredge of society
I am the wind
that sets the birds to fly
I am the arrow
which kills free wings
I am the blackness
you see buried
deep within white
I am the soulless God
who sails the night
Thy kingdom come
Thy will be done
In no one's name
I pray

Amber Frederick

Untitled

The lights burn bright and radiant.
In the distance I see the future;
Not defined or complete, but luminous.
Not knowing what it holds,
I feel the confidence of its presence.

Waiting for me to come to the door
Where it waits in anticipation
Of my awakening into myself.

This map has no roads; only destinations
that are for me to find through
routes I make up along the way.
Some take longer than others;
some have bumps, where others
have deep trenches; and yet I
keep getting to new locales with
familiar strangers appearing along
the way, to guide my soul through
a life that makes no promises, but
allows for the possibility of a magical
contentment that is often mistaken for a
dream.

Daniela Kurland

Whisper In The Night

When the moon hung softly
in the dust sparkles of street light
you held me closer and closer
There was magic in the night.

Silent whispers . . .
are released by the words we say
the romantic night
fades into the break of day.

But the night's not over
for in your eyes I see
the moon has not faded
and our love is a mystery . . .

We whisper in the night
to say our love is true
We'll be together forever
and I will always love you.

Joshua McCown

Apples It Seems

In the mist of September
In the fall with the leaves
Trees burst with red spheres
Apples is seems

The luscious red
The greed of the sea
Falling down like pebbles
Apples it seems

The sweet dripple juice
Make the brightness of the tree
A very desire
For apples it seems

Do not leave it
For the color will fail
Making all brightness not prevail
But in the world
Greatness it be
I long for the taste of
Apples it seems

Christina Calloway

Music For St. Peter

When we meet
In the here - after
And St. Peter
Hears our laughter
He will greet us at his pearly gate
With open wings and cheers.

He will call
His angel chorus
Have them all
Around before us
To adore our heavenly laughter which
Is music to his ears

Genie Grimmett

Sailing

Silently, we set sail
In the light of the moon so
    pale.
A strong wind lasted through
    the night,
But ended with the morning
    light.
We finally reached our
    destination
Through strength, courage,
    and determination.

Andrew Corrigan

Remembering You

As I walk along the seashore
In the setting of the sun
I remember all my blessings
And I count them one by one

All the stars come out to greet me
As I gaze into the sky
And the joy still overwhelms me
When I think of you and I

For my dear I can't forget you
And the wonder of our love
But God needed one more flower
In his garden up above

So just keep a look out for me
As the clouds go drifting by
When once again I'll hold you darling
In that mansion in the sky

Alice E. Jones

Untitled

My love for you,
is so true,
like the ocean blue,
and the star filled nights,
the moon shining so brightly,
I think of you,
only memories I see,
of me and you,
together I wish we could be,
forever I cherish,
those words I heard from you,
it's hard to forget the past,
but I always give others a try,
come with me and I'll show you,
true love can last forever,
till eternity.

Jaime Lynn Boswell

Anna Lodena Noel

At four score and fifteen
in the years of man.
When McKinley was in office,
I was born to this land.

To the tribe, Hunkpapa
the Sioux of Sitting Bull.
With five generations living
to keep our family full.

Lived through the great depression
and saw both of the great wars.
Now a gold star mother
for the bronze star that he bore.

Riding in our horse back
or in a drawn carriage.
Lived at a boarding school
Fort Yates after marriage.

A school teacher, a Riveter
and fifty two years a wife
Closing in on a century
to see three in my life.

Belmer L. Graff Jr.

Breaking The Cycle

Frustration overwhelms my mind
In training these few words to dance
There is hope when I see the light
from the heavenly beams in clouds
casting down with translucent rays

What enigmatic force drives me
from the negative power's clutch
with such a metaphysical
allegiance; I cannot withstand.

Like a child willing to receive
but unable to understand
the unscrupulous life ahead
holding the vast majority
in a shackle of ignorance

Lives interlocking by harsh words
clinging, blaming, judging, telling
Those who use and have discernment
Accomplish impossible dreams!

Janice M. Eaton

Untitled

What is beauty?
Is it really skin deep?
Is it with you always
Even when you sleep?

Does everyone have it?
Can you buy it at a store?
And if it fades away
Can you get some more?

Is it born like a child
Or does it blossom like a rose?
Do you have it all over
Even on you nose?

True beauty as I see it
Is like a shining star
That radiates one's love for God
And which no one can mar.

Betty A. Perry

The Contest

May I comment on your contest
in which you asked the public to write
only 20 lines per poem???
Oh, c'mon! That's just not right!

I've written many things
about people that I've known:
expressing love, or poking fun,
in the form of a poem.

Lengthy stories I love to tell,
spinning yarns of truth and fable:
molding our lives into a backdrop;
putting events out on the table.

In an age of fast-food restaurants,
sound bites, and spray-on hair,
to compact the lives of those I know
in 20 lines, would be unfair!

Enter me, if you wish;
though a winning chance, I doubt.
My poems win the hearts and minds
of those I write about.

Christopher James Cotter

Violin Concert

Warm wisps, strong flurries
Insinuated notions, jaunty romps
Deliberated statements
    pulled over strung gut
    past curved maple, aged and elegant

Gentle person, hung there
    before us in sound
At once master and slave
Executor of beauty
    and exquisite sound

With silken strands of equine hair
    you ply your pain and pleasure
And so they're ours
As calmly you dispatch your songs
    with skill acquired in your years
    of willful toil

Wear now your laurel o'er your sweated
brow
    and move one step closer to the gods
    whom you have pleasured with your gift
    while we, in reverie, attend, applaud.

Barbara Kelley

Untitled

The weaving of a quilt,
is that of life.
And of all Gods creations,
which grovel upon him.
And of all life,
as we know it.

The end will come.
Life will be a memory.
While we're here,
treasure life.
For it may be the last
in the weaving.

Angela Lentini

Prospecting For God

Have you ever prospected for God
Instead of for gold?
If you haven't, you are
Missing fortunes untold.

There's many a treasure
You surely will find,
If the worldly riches
You erase from your mind.

Prospects for God
Let all of us seek,
Spreading the gospel of Jesus,   .
We must not be meek.

All of our material possessions
We must cast aside
And prospect for the "Master"
No matter what may betide.

Share the "word" with your neighbor
As you plod along lives way
And you'll be richly rewarded
On the "Great Judgment Day".

Eugene H. Channell

Untitled

What I feel
Is not what
I think
Poems can open
A window
Slam a door
I can't let
You in
A poem can
Give a clue
You must decipher
What I mean
What you come
Up with
I do not
Care
For all I know
Is that I
Wrote a
Poem

Carolina Vizcarra

Untitled

My decision.
It is done.
Over and over.
Now, like a thorn in my side;
These splinters of life
Always here.
Never fully healing.
How do you move on?
To forget.
To replace.
All that was known is gone.
Life, a series of starting over.
Waiting, wanting to exhale.
On the brink of madness
Is it fair to throw memories away?
Layers of soil.
Something primitive
Something novel
One cannot escape the past.

Amy Hayden Nutt

My Best Friend

My best friend
Is there through thick and thin
All day waiting, patiently alone
Lying by the door for me to come home
When I'm feeling alone and depressed
To pick me up the tries his best
Asking nothing in return
But friendship or new tricks to learn
A dog you say . . . perhaps
He doesn't know while in my lap
Maybe a person he thinks . . . or not
Surely he'll not be forgot
When it's dark in the house
He comes quiet like a mouse
Not to play or to be fed
Just to lie next to my bed
We go through a lot and have some fun
Playing games or lying in the sun
When it's all over and near comes the end
He and I will always be the best of friends.

Jim D. Carver

The Tree Outside My Window

The tree outside my window,
It changes now and then.
From blowing in the summer breeze,
To fighting winters wind.
It waves to me good morning,
And softly rustles in the night,
Welcoming the sleepy birds,
Or sending them to flight.
I gaze upon the towering tree,
And think back to my past.
For with the tree my childhood lies.
It all went by so fast.
But never through these trying times,
Did the tree give in or relent,
Changing through the seasons,
It's beauty, heaven sent.
It's a comfort and memory,
I shall keep within.
The tree outside my window,
Changing now and then.

Alisa McMillen

Love

Love is in the air tonight,
It comes and goes, but we never fight,
We'll never brake-up,
We'll never shut-up,
So leave us alone and we'll get up.

We love each other so very much,
No one can stop us,
only God's touch.

We get up in the morning to go to school,
But we can't do our work,
And we can't follow the rules.

We call each other on the phone,
But when we call no ones home,
So we wait awhile and call back soon,
And there they are waiting in their room.

We talk about this,
We talk about that,
Then we wish that we could be together at
last.

Cynthia White

Contest Or Not - A Real Dilemma

Please don't order me to write!
It comes to me in its own time.
It's not like turning on a light.
It's from my soul, not idle rhyme.

Please don't tell me to compose!
It started when the stress was high.
The verse helped vent my daily woes.
And caused the frequent pain to die.

Please don't urge me for a poem!
For each one is a part of me.
I'd rather share my humble home
Then share my humble poetry.

But if you ask me now to write
As well as I might try and do.
It may not be my brightest light,
My soul will try to rhyme anew.

For writing is its own reward,
And so is love that's true.
To lose a prize I can afford,
But, never to lose you.

Eric W. Barteldt

"A Rose"

I saw a yellow rose today;
It gives me new life!

In the rose I saw
"gentleness" reaching out.
The "soft fragrance"
is a gift from God
It's "beauty" was beyond
man's touch.
The round curves wound
around so perfect!
Each leaf "sang out"
it's beauty!
Even the stem, so green against
the sun; gave off a "glow."
'Tis a shame roses have to die;
for their beauty would fill the skies!

Arnold R. Willis Sr.

I Love My Time With You, O God

I love the time we spend together
It has made my life so much better
My life is now far sweeter than ever
I give you my every endeavor
I love the time we spend together
I love it more and more

I love my time with YOU, O GOD
This is what I say; I love it more
and more each day; because I know
whose I am, and who I am in YOU—
MY GOD, MY FATHER, MY CREATOR

I truly love my time with YOU, O GOD
It has been long over due
I am destined to soar, as I direct my
praise and worship to YOU, MY GOD
YOU are more precious to me than
silver and gold
I truly love my time with YOU!

Delores Mooring-Grimes

River On A Run

I see it fall off a ledge.
It hits the ground with a splish, splash.
Flowing fast.
Bubbling white, over rocks,
Plowing sand.
I see fish making ripples.
Skimming on its bed, pulling
Creatures behind.
It joins with brooks and streams
And more of its own kind.
On a stormy day it would flow too
Fast with waves crashing back and forth.
Ripping up plants, destroying animals
And even its very own bed.
Till it calms down and then slowly
Flows to its destination.

Brian Farber

My Life Is A Rose

I give you this rose today,
It holds my spirit and my life,
If you love me, you will keep it,
If it gets old and dies, don't let
  looks deceive you,
The spirit is still left inside,
If you take a petal, and bury it,
Take care of it as you have taken
  care of me,
It will live again, and you should,
Love it as you have loved me.

Jacki Ramsey

Untitled

Darkness is a thing
It knows you, it feels you
But you can't sense it
Darkness has a mind
It thinks of its needs
It thinks of you
But you think of avoiding it
Darkness is an emotion
It desires, it needs
It needs you, it desires you
But you can't escape it
Darkness has a need
And it needs you, it wants you
It'll hunt you
And it'll haunt you
But if it scares you
It'll get you

Ever McKinney

Race

As important as it may seem,
It really is not.
The obvious difference stands alone.
You suddenly realize,
No two people are the same.

It clearly symbolizes a rich history
Of tradition,
Worthy of your respect.
Others look at you . . .
Then think the same.

Beyond the book's cover,
Your stories are identical.

Christopher Linares

Writing In The Sky

Watching the storm
it makes me think
of writing in the sky
the ultimate pen and ink.

Flash of brilliance
sometimes frightening
the sky's ablaze
with strikes of lightning.

Quietly
as I gaze in wonder
I hear the words
in the sound of thunder.

Words of freedom,
speed and might
subtle hints
written in the light.

The exclamation point in blue
the art of light,
power and might
all at once come shining through.

Andrew S. Pettigrew

The Bird's Message

There was a bird perched in a tree.
It seemed to be there for a year.
Every morning it sang to me,
Songs which only I could hear.

I really couldn't understand,
What it was trying to say.
I only know it did demand,
My attention every day.

Then suddenly it disappeared,
It sang its song no more.
Then I found what I had feared,
A cat with a mouthful of gore.

Now the message seems so clear,
Like the brightness of a light.
"There is tragedy always near,
So live your life just right."

Alton Matheny

Life Related To Geometry

Life is a segment.
  It starts and stops
A choice is an angle.
  You can go 2 ways.
   The right way or
    the wrong way.
A dream is a ray.
  It starts and keeps going.
Family is a line.
  It goes in 2 directions.
   Ancestors.
   Future.
A person is a circle.
  We all are a whole . . .
   360 degrees.
Friends are perpendicular
  We each have different personalities
Death is infinity
  It lasts forever.

Christine E. Schaub

Dandelion

The dandelion is a weed
It starts as a baby seed
It's puffy, fluffy head is yellow
It sways in the breeze
It's very mellow.
I like to pick them
And tickle my feet
Or blow at the dead ones
Full of seeds
And plant it in a hole that I dug
On it comes a little bug
The bug is what I shoo away.
I plant the seed and think
A new dandelion will grow
Someday!

Joan Bosco

No Cure

It over came him,
it took over his body,
he had no control.
Never telling, never
sharing.
Eating away at him.
Thinking life may be a
never ending story,
but the end is coming
the end is near.
Taken over by a deadly
disease.
There's no cure AIDS.

Dana M. Rocheford

Captain Hook

I read a really good book
It was about Captain Hook
He sailed the blue seas
And liked to eat peas
Now he is a famous cook.

Janet Montgomery

The Sky

The sky is blue as blue can be.
It's a heavenly picture to me.
I lay and watch the sky all day.
In hopes that soon the clouds will play.
The clouds form pictures in my mind.
Pictures no one else can find.
These pictures make me feel free
Pictures no one sees but me.

Jake Joslyn

Roses

Roses are seeds,
  Just like we were.
They turn into buds,
  Like we were when once a baby.
Roses bloom and blossom,
  When we turn to adults.
But most special of all,
  Each rose is beautiful,
Like we each are inside.

Candace Brush

Eternal Fire

True love
It's an eternal fire
In a heart that lives inflamed.
It's a violent pulse in the memory
That burns the soul without compassion.
If, in my being, exists only essence.

Fire of immortality
Annihilates the fear
To perish in the far and away.
Untamed fire without rancor
When offended, always forgives.
It never compares.

Resplendent light
Illuminates in the distances
Inextinguishable passion.
Flame of pureness and humbleness
Without demands or exigencies
Fire heating my solitude.

Jorge M. Leyva Rodriguez

Untitled

My world has stopped revolving
It's completely still
It's as though my soul is dying
But my body never will
I try to think of happiness
But then it always dies
You have the only life I need
I see it in your eyes
I thank you very deeply
From the bottom of my heart
You brought light to my empty world
And chased away the dark
I need your help to stop my universe
From crashing all around
The life you hold within you
Keeps me from being down
Although it may mean little
I feel that I must say
The mere thought of being near you
Turns endless night into day.

Jama-el Hakeem Mills

Written Communication

A poem,
its' essence heartfelt
a pouring out of ones' soul.
An expression,
in verse or free form
created from words written down.
Such pleasure,
it brings to the writer
a forum to publicly speak.
And yet,
so very private
as ideas take shape from the ink.
Entertaining,
or thought provoking
or just giving vent to emotion.
A legacy,
to the one who reads
a kindred spirit perhaps.

Jean A. Smith

My Michael

If there is one thing I'm glad for,
It's having part of me that I adore.
Watching the picture of innocence
Change to maturity and common sense.

His smile is refreshing.
His laughter is enlightening.
The sparkle from his blue eyes,
Gets sad when he cries.

At times he has been a drain,
Because he has given me much pain.
I have plenty of love for this one.
After all, he is my ever-loving son.

Gloria J. Flitcraft

Spring Is Here!

Spring is Here, Spring is Here
It's in the Air, Everywhere

The Birds are out
The Kids can Play,
The Streams are Flowing Everyday.

We're Eating Ice Cream
Playing catch,
Teaching our Dogs, how to Fetch.

We're Playing Sports
In our own way,
The Flowers Sprouting Everyday.

The Grass is Growing
The Animals are out,
It's the Best Season, Without a Doubt.

Jaclyn Hubbard

When

Anyone can create
it's just a question of
when.
When will you shed
those tight controls?
When will you peel away
that annoying standard?
When will you melt that
frozen self and
reveal the fantasy within?

Only when you realize
that present styles were
once the dreams of others
who dared,
and you have a mind of your own.

Janet Pelliccio

The Best Side Of Me

When the night is long,
It's like a song,
Carry it in your heart,
Like a fire,
Truly yours,
Never a liar,
Save you from loneliness,
Fill you with happiness,
Make things a little warmer,
And love on in the memory,
Of the best side of me.

H.D. Maye

"Over Avalon"

In your smile, I find happiness,
It's your heart, that's my soul,
Your arms are where,
My dreams unfold.

Time goes by, we've laughed and cried,
Never for long, we've said goodbye,
You teach me, we grow,
You love me, I know.

Over Avalon we flew,
That moment I knew,
The flight we were on,
Would last my life long.

I sometimes feel the need to say,
I think about you everyday,
It's simple, it's true,
In my life, my love was you.

Dana Sher

Untitled

I've always loved you from the start.
I've always loved you with all my heart.
Then we were married,
And my love grew stronger,
And the line of love,
Got a little longer.
With each day passing,
My heart starts racing,
Like a hurricane in spring,
And a summer rain.
Each day with you,
Takes away the pain.

Brandi Hunter

Company Man

I can't wait until I retire
I've been here twenty years plus four
I can't wait until I retire
All I have to do is twenty more

I have to work this job
Because I'm not that brave
And I can keep this job
If I work like a slave

My boss says he cares
And I won't break my back much more
Besides, he pays me well
It's not like I'm a whore

I just moved up the ladder
For stabbing my best friend in the back
My boss says don't worry
My friends work was beginning to slack

I have to keep this job
I don't know what else to do
I'm too much of a coward
And the world is so cruel

Christopher P. Perkins

Untitled

Sunlight falling through the trees
Kisses our skin
As our lips bind our hearts
Closer together

Dana Lis

"My Buddy Ron"

I met old Ron in 49.
Just a skinny little kid, at the time.
A little boy just past six,
Full of mischief and lots of tricks.

I watched him grow and become a man,
No finer guy in this whole land.
We used to sit and talk about his truck,
And how some day he'd run out of luck.

But Ron loved the work he done,
Never boring and lots of fun.
He loved the trucks, big and small.
Kw's Pete's he drove them all.

So guys when your out on the lonely road,
Making time to deliver your load.
Take a look, up towards heaven,
You just might see old Ron, and old 37.

Dwane R. Jones

Untitled

Joe was a little chicken hawk
Just big enough to walk
He had a little limp in his leg
He walked down the road
Talking to the road, and said,
"Some day I'm gonna fly away!"
The toad laughed aloud,
and jumping all about said,
"Son, the way me break out
It was the last day in June.
The frog was singing his same tune,
and walking down the same rocky road
He looked to the sky.
and flying real high
He saw the chicken hawk,
Go sailing by.

Audrey H. Wilson

Untitled

Pine and cypress, deep blue sea,
   land where dreamers dwell.
Heaven lost a little piece,
   and there I found Carmel.

Helen Lewis Brenner

Untitled

Dog
large, smelly
jumping, barking, running
fur, leash, paws, litter
pouncing, hissing, scratching
cute, small
cat

Janet Wagner

September Silence

Silence, penetrates the quiet air
Laughter, actions all dispersed
Trees in gentle rhythmic sway
Missing children hard at play
Blades of grass shall not retreat
from under chasing little feet
Nature's sadness all around
   School, Beginning
      Silent Sound!

Dolores Mary Rose

You Two Were Sleeping . . .

. . . When I tiptoed into your room
   last night.
Soft sounds of breathing
   a dreamers duet.

The moon was waning
   as I gazed at your still small forms
who just an hour before
   were teasing and laughing.

Sister child in somnionastics
   one knee in the air;
hair draped across pillow
   like soft, dark silk.

Brother child's body
   sprawled across bed;
head cradled in pillow
   as I once cradled his infant self.

I watched you two sleeping
   last night
and fell in love again.

Jeannie O. Harsha

Untitled

The angry waves
leaped at the inert shore,
like a hungry lion
prepared to devour
its defenseless prey.

The land, calm and brave,
painfully disengaged itself
from the brutal embrace
after each assault.

The fury of the deluge abated.
Land and sea
achieved a tenuous truce.

The apologetic tide
returned frequently,
gently asking reassurance
for its restless pacing.

Each was aware
of the danger of the other.
Each knew, one day,
mortal combat would be renewed.

Alan Shafrin

Her Young Niece

Death,
like still-wood.
A baby girl.

Sad.

John R. Howley

The Fireplace

Tend the damper of passion
   Lest the wild flame should thrash
Too quickly reducing the fuel
   To a gray pile of ash

Be warmth my friend and glow
   Remain basic in design
For life is but an ember
   In the fireplace of time

John L. Fletcher

Time

If I could stop one moment in time
Let it be you who stand before me
If ever a song could remain in my heart
Your words would be my melody
If I could capture a feeling
It would be your touch
No promises, no lies
Just a dream as such
If when I awaken my moment is released
Walk with me
   Talk with me.
      Touch me.
Forever in time.

Deborah A. Brooks

Let Me Be Somebody

Instead of a nobody.
LET ME BE ME,
and not a color to see.
LET ME BE ONE,
as you are one.
LET MY NAME BE KNOWN,
and not my color be shown.

Carolyn Singleton

Untitled

Come into my sickness
let me enfold you with disease,
kiss you with darkness,
embrace you in dementia.
Die to me
Surrender yourself.
I will use your body
abuse your mind.
You are now a wholly fractioned thought,
a maniacal, manipulative puppet.
Immortality flows through your veins.
Make love to my insanity.

Joanna Babcock

Never Part

Please Lord do me a favor.
Let this memory always be savored.
Don't ever let me forget,
That one heavenly event.
Don't let it slip or fade,
Fade into the shade.
Don't let it leave
Like the trees.
Let it remain.
Remain in my heart.
Then no matter what,
We will never part.

Corey Harris

Together

Let's walk in the rain
Let's run in the sun
Run through the fields
Right through the fun
Kiss in the dark
Make out in the sun
We'll have it all
Together as one

Amanda Lisowski

Old And Waiting To Die

Far into the darkness
lies many of the needy.
They are not helpless
nor are they greedy.

You can't touch them
cause the glass is too thick.
No way to steal their gems
cause the colors flash too quick.

They're old and waiting to die.
Old and waiting to die.
Why do you lie?
You know we're all going to die.

Out of this world
there are no boys, no girls.
Only strange beings
with no meanings.

They're just old and waiting to die.
Old and waiting to die.

Bill M. Whelan

The Unfolding Of Grace

A broken, shame-filled man;
Life bound by worthlessness.
Self love a long-lost dream.
His grace unknown to me.

"Forgiveness offered you";
Agape was the hope.
Full cleansing for my soul.
GRACE WAS HIS master plan.

My tear-filled eyes looked up;
Beheld his offered hand.
New hope a wrestled thought:
CAN GRACE BE MEANT for me?

He saw beyond my past;
The wrongs and pain I'd wrought.
His pardon offered me
"MY GRACE SUFFICIENT BE."

My trembling hand touched his;
Rich peace enveloped me.
Renewal filled my frame
GOD'S GRACE HAS SET ME FREE!

Dan Kohn

Lost Love

You loved me then you
left me

In your dust like
yesterdays sorrow

Now you want me back
but I love you no longer

So here's the love and
the sorrow take it and
leave because I love you
no longer.

Cristin Miller

The First Snowfall

Snowflakes are falling
Lights are coming on
The beauty that surrounds us
Is coming from above.

Little children love it
Adults say, "Oh my back",
Doctors say, "Don't shovel,
You'll have a heart attack."

The differences are many
From childhood to old age
One looks at the beauty
The other at his age.

God sees us just as one
From the beginning to the end
If we live our life completely
He'll be our loving friend.

So don't worry about the snowflakes
Just look ahead to spring
Your spirits will be lifted
As the snowflakes turn to rain.

Brownie Todd

Sunset

The sunset is a show,
Like a bird its plumage bright
Trying to attract a mate,
The sunset outdoes itself.
Everyone has to look,
How can one duplicate!

The bright colors shimmer in the water
Not one but two sunsets do we see.

Yellow, orange, red
Intermingle with purple, grey and blue,
Women of fashion
Can not duplicate, it is true.

The sky is alive with color,
Trying to dazzle
A world in a frazzle,
Oh what a sunset can do!

Evelyn Hunker

Silent Tears

Silent tears
like a laugh, without sound
no distinct tone of expression
an endless path
without a given direction
My past is still with me
like echoes of chimes from blowing winds
my future, I can not see
cause my present in blocked with fears
A wall is building of emotions
if touched, it will shatter and fall
Things are kept within myself
I'm trapped in my own decisions
there is no way of escaping
I stare into endless space
As a tear trickles down my cheek
the tear falls from my face
no sound of its landing
no one hears me crying
Silent tears

Darcy D. Olson

A Whispering Voice

I hear whispering around me,
Like a voice is praying,
I want to get closer,
I need to hear what it's saying.
It's the voice of Jesus,
He wants me to hear.
He said if you believe in me,
Then you have nothing to fear.
I said I have faith,
He said yes you must.
God sent Jesus to help us,
He's the one we can trust.
He said if you believe in me,
With all your heart, mind and soul.
Then I will never never leave you.
Not even when you get old.

Jonathan W. Cormier

"Clouds"

Clouds can form so many patterns
Like chameleons in the sky.
Great big pussy cats, that flatten
Into forms, just drifting by.

Changing clouds like thrifts of cotton
Move, like little herds of sheep
Clouds like smoky great big dragons.
Clouds, like pillow, where I sleep,

Clouds, like sprays of snowy mountains
Glow, like little peaks of fun
Peek-A-Boo, there by tall fountains
Flirting, with the passing sun.

Clouds, can leave you in such wonder,
With its moods, that change in hue,
Change to smoky, angry thunder
Rain, then fade to skies of blue

Clouds, return and take their places
Once again, at varied play
Like a slate that one erases
With new imagery each day.

Domenique Saint John

Falling Leaves

My how they fall, one by one
Like dancing ballerinas
So graceful but some rather "clumsy"
They seem to be in such a hurry.

As tho they know winter is coming
And they must protect the earth
Together they form a blanket
Where they will rest for this year.

It's been a long spring and summer
Now fall brings out their beauty
Of reds and golds and yellows and
Jack Frost will be coming soon.

Their many many shades of green
Have protected us from the sun
Have provided homes for lots of birds
Made covering for animals at play.

Now they must take a rest
Their job is complete and well done
Winter is nigh upon them and so
They fall, one by one.

Daisy M. Cassia

"My Brother"

My brother he is just a boy,
Like dozens you have seen.
But to me he is much greater,
Since he donned that suit of green.
He was just a local shearer,
When the seasons came around.
But now he is away fighting,
With his body close to the ground.
With his gun in correct position,
He is quick on the draw.
His one ambition is to say,
The enemy is no more.
Then homeward bound he will go,
The proudest I have seen.
For that soldier is my brother,
That boy in jungle green.

Emily Florio

Did You Ever Get That Feeling

Did you ever get that feeling
    like nobody's on your side?
That everyone cares only about
    their own personal pride?

Did you ever get that feeling
    when you're all alone?
That you want to go to someone,
    but nobody's home?

Did you ever get that feeling
    on a bleak and dreary day?
A feeling that you think
    will never go away?

Did you ever get that feeling
    that there's no blue in the sky?
Did you ever get that feeling
    that the lakes have all gone dry?

Did you ever get that feeling
    of a young child crying?
Did you ever get that feeling
    that millions are dying?

Did you ever get that feeling
    that the candle will never be lit?
Makes you think of a lot . . . doesn't it?

Janine Bobko

"Outside And Inside"

Some fall quickly
like raindrops splashing
on chipped paint porches
and spilling to walks below.

Some fall instead
like leaves from October trees,
first soaring high, sketching crescents
in the sky — then
dropping to be stepped on playfully.

Some fall coldly
like delicate snowflakes
crossing once, then drifting far apart
forming separate mounds of white.

Falling apart from
you could never happen so easily, for
so many words and feelings won't escape.
The only falling I can accept
happened on that remarkable day
that I fell
in love with you.

Janet Rethaber

To An Unknown God

In quietude our paths crossed
Linking together two strangers
Across a lonely gap of solitude

Two strangers forging an unspoken path
Together walking through doors
Of untried emotions that never opened

Into valleys deeply in bloom
With unknown pleasures
Of risks not taken

Into the hush of canyons
Stilled by the silence
Of our meeting speeding by

To be broken only by the thunder
Of two stars never touching earth
As they collided into a timeless sky

Jewell I. Filion

"Thoughts"

The fish swim upstream
little boy falls down
and loses sight in time
to see another shattered dream

And the sky
turns grey with rain
as an old wise man
grows wiser from the pain

And just the other day
In a town not far from here
two different lives
met at the same path
just in time to disappear.

If I could see the future
things would be more clear
but I can only see the past
and presently I live in fear

Jeremy Richardson

A Cabin In The Woods

In the woods a
little cabin sat with
it's wooden deck.
As winter comes the
snow appears and the
blue birds leave their
trees. As spring turns
the air warm the
blue birds speak of their
return. The smell of
green summer with apples
so crisp with the deer
eating in the hills by the
cabin in the woods.
Fall appears and chills the air,
deer in the runt and harvesting
in the mountain hills
by the little cabin in the woods

Claude Burns

Letting Go

Turn away and don't
look back I love you that
is my fact.
    This fall you have taken
will not be long.
    I still live here in your
heart, even though I'm gone.
    I am sorry for I broke
many hearts.
    When God called I went.
    I did not know your life
was so badly bent.
    Still I move on and I
know you can too.
    So turn away and don't
look back I am not
afraid that is a fact.

Cherron Walker

Geese In Flight

Light of day with geese in flight.
Looking for places to spend the night.
Natures way to give them rest
While flying north at their best.
Eating, drinking to fill a need.
Varmints, sickness are dangers they heed.
Graceful birds always free.
Home soon spring it'll be.

Jimmy Spence

Dad

A mountain, amidst a snow laden field
Looking out across the horizon
Where life becomes surreal
A wise man sits content

He's fought the battles
Cheered and cried
Held strong to his beliefs
And has watched them die

He has crawled through shame
Agonized in defeat
Twisted in the clouds
On the winds of victory

Pure in his heart
And his actions there of
Provider till the end
And giver of love

If I could have one wish ever be mine
I pray these sights be held in his eyes
And these thoughts be his
When we say good-bye.

Chaning L. E. Simnitt

Passion

Tangled in Ebony coils
lost in Piercing blue desire . . .
Infatuation
Feathered by Silken porcelain
caressed by Blushing wine . . .
Obsession
Hovering above rational Sanity
rising above Passé fantasies . . .
Passion

Barbara Ann

Empty

I felt my life was empty.
Love had come to me, yet
Still, there it was, empty.
Life was not inside of me.
Just empty, empty, empty.

A life came to me; empty?
Feelings came alive.
Then, two more lives; empty?
Yes, there was still
That empty, empty, empty.

Was it God that had not come? Empty!
A heart with so much joy and love,
Could still feel empty.
Then when I opened my heart to him,
No more empty, empty, empty.

Donna Cook

Love Is . . .

Love is caring
Love is sharing
Love is daring
Love is learning
Love is yearning
Love is concerning one to another
Love is appealing
Love is feeling
Love is knowing
Love is showing
Love is true, never blue
Love is growing
Love is strength
Love is without length
Love is the time I spend with you
Love is from within
Love is never without
Love is knowing what we're about

David Kastner

Love

Love is something very powerful.
Love is strong enough to knock the
    tallest giant to its knees.
Love is strong enough to make
    any heart grow.
Love is like something that
    never goes
Love is needed everywhere
It's not something that will disappear
Love is something you can wear,
    But best of all love
is something you can share.

Jana Wilkins

Life

To be born, and then grow up,
maturing through the years,
ever drinking from God's cup,
tasting happiness and tears.

To accept, with joy, a smile,
As you cope with death and strife,
To love someone forever
is to take a sip of life.

Colleen Cruikshank

"Dreamer By Your Side"

The Nazarene
made of loneliness
do you really believe he wanted it?
reluctant messiah
lover without love
his message for you is
not
crucifixion not
death this
message is of love.
Love all humankind
but
do not doubt (christ-man)
that you will be
killed for it

Adam Stultz

The Wall Of Tears

Here is built a wall of tears,
Made of sorrow, pain, and fears.
Without a door, lacking gates,
Seals us inside our angers and hates.
It locks us in yet has no key,
Those inside will never be free.
Here is built a wall of tears,
Made of strife and ill-spent years.
Tears for those who marched away,
Tears for those who wouldn't stay.
No army can break down this wall,
Once built up it cannot fall.
Prisoners inside a well-masked rage,
Trapped like rats inside a cage.
Those inside will never leave,
Here they are, here they grieve.
Will the people never learn -
Many go but few return?
Here is built a wall of tears,
Made of many, many fears.

Beth Grimaldi

Piano

The piano, my favorite instrument
makes beautiful music. I know that
my whole life and until I die I
will always love the music a
piano creates As I lay on my bed
I listen to the music from my
radio, and dream of myself sitting in a
beautiful field, all alone, with
a pond nearby, and the sun's
warmth on my back. I then
take a seat at my very
own piano and play many
pieces, old and new, classical
and rock. I finish and
notice a crowd around me
applauding and yelling "encore".
I see roses, being tossed
all around. I've always
dreamt and hope this
will someday be of me playing the piano so
gracefully.

Alysha Nicole Hernandez

Love

When I was a child and asked as one,
"Mama, do you love me best?"
She answered,
"Better than any on the place—"
Youth took no note of being alone
with her there
Older, now, I cherish each similar
moment with child, lover, friend—
The beloved, to whom I confess
"It is you, alone, I love the best—"

Billie Thompson

Suffering

The first day of his birth,
Man uttered the cry of pain:
He suffered.
In fact, there is some suffering
In each domain of life.
But the realm of love
Between man and woman,
Makes much more suffering.
In the sincerity
As in the insincerity;
In the fidelity
As in the infidelity.
And we really suffer
When we love sincerely.
However, we must always love sincerely
And with unselfishness.
For it is better to suffer
For well doing
Than for evil doing.

Daniel Cinevert

Heavy Ladened

My heart sounds an alarm
many can't hear;
That I sometimes can't bear
alone.
It cries of desperation,
exasperation;
many can't feel;
That I sometimes can't bear
alone.
It suffers from
weariness,
The agony of pain,
many can't see;
That I sometimes can't bear,
when I'm alone.

Anita Lee Wyatt

Untitled

The leaves of fall come in
many different colors.
They look like a painting
in a rich family.

The leaves like the summer
but dislike the autumn
for they fall and get stomped on.
They make a loud crunch.

The leaves make a rustling sound
rolling and blowing all around.
That is why these are the leaves
of fall.

Joe Wills

Tear

Teardrops glisten my cheek
Mascara smudged under swollen eyes
Lipstick smeared all over my face
No one to lift me up
Nowhere to go - except straight down
Hanging on a single thread
about to fall into the depths of hell
can't be worse than staying here
Down falls another tear.
What should I do
will no one tell me what is left
nothing - that's it
that's what you don't want me to know
Hell is the only place left for me to go.

Betty J. Rolph

Canadian Rockies

Towering peaks surround them,
Masked by billowing clouds.
The lone whistle of a train echoes

The soft raindrops fall,
The rays of sunlight
Struggle to shine -
The peacefulness of nature
Settles around.

Freedom fills the soul
Overflowing the everyday
Realm of reality.

The rising of the moon,
Soft reflections on the clouds
Dark blue velvet -
Wisps of light miles away,
Its' fullness penetrates.

Canadian Rockies fill my soul.

Joy Brook

Untitled

If I ever must remain,
May my spirit not suffer with me.
May it leave in death's dark shadow,
Then to have to stay with thee.
I must live and ride the wind,
And sail upon the sea;
And if I can't and never will,
May my spirit always remain free.

Jael S. Rodgers

Ocean

Come see my ocean out before
me it goes, out to the edge of the earth
where the bright flaming sun waits
to brighten your day.
Come see my ocean it carries
me out, out into that world of happiness.
Come see my ocean, come into
my ocean feel my waves, feel them
go through you and into your soul.
Then finally guiding you backwards
to where you stood before.
Come see my ocean out before
me it is a beautiful place.
Come see my ocean out before me
it's a life of eternity.

Andrea Giacomotto

Before My Time

Once, this land flourished
miles of trees
Once, this land flourished
free from the screams
Once, this land flourished
blooming of flowers
Once, this land flourished
dying by hours
Once, this land flourished
rivers ran through
Once, this land flourished
the waters not true
Once, this land flourished
I could be proud
This land malnourished
as we break the ground

Erik Wood

To My Wife

After all this time, it is so clear
more than any sweat or tear
In my heart,
Over come with this feeling
Is this thought,
Filled with overwhelming
meaning
It is something that is clear and
true,
Love is something
that I share with you

David John Ventrano

Song Is Music

Song is music
Movement is dance

Time is forever
Love is romance

White is pure
Black is sin

Sadness is open
Joy is within

Pain is gone
Fear is here

Life is now
Death is near.

Amber D. Botts

Life

Pure and sweet
Swift and bleak
Life comes and it is taken
Purity has left me now
I know I am forsaken
I do not know
Where to go
My light still shines
But faintly glows

Josh L. Lively

She Asked For a Poem

"Write me a poem",
My dear wife said
"If you think you can
In that dumb old head."

"Then we'll send it in
"And win us a prize
"And wouldn't that be
"A complete surprise."

"If you win one
"I'll take you out for a treat
"On a fun filled evening
"That can't be beat."

"Then back home we'll go
"For a late night snack
"Then two lovey-dovies
"Will hit the sack."

Al McCreary

Phantasma

Now he has started to invade
my dreams. Dreams bring us together
in nocturnal pleasure where we
kiss and touch without facing
the truth of our differences
In my dreams I have no power
I abandon myself to this naive
young man who's smile and blush
who's timid touch arouses me
When he enters my room in the
light of day we talk of small things
in soft tones. Behind veiled words
we exchange glances and sift
feelings. Then the time comes for
his next class and I am forced to wait
for the next phantasma

Dori Calhoun

"Thoughts"

When I think about my Savior,
My faith begins to grow;
The window of my mind is opened
and I learn much I need to know.

He guides me through each morning,
Reminds me of my prayers
and helps me through each troubled day
To show how much He cares.

An angel tucks me in each night;
My Shepherd holds my hand;
One day I'll see his loving face
and then I'll understand.

I feel His love, His grace, His peace,
But only in a part;
The day will come when I will see
The longing of my heart.

Eve Kuehn Whalen

Winter

Babies bloom.
Mother's love.
Friends play
With father's trust.
Soon snowflakes fall
From the ancient sky
With God watching
From heaven high.

Christian Thompson

Mikie

I just wanted to let you know,
My feelings for you will only grow.
And honey, you will be missed,
Where, ever, you go."

That I, will never, forget, the
Hours at work, since, first we met.
That work is nicer better by
Far, because of the person, I
Know you are!

Now my only thought will be,
I know I miss him but, is
He missing me? I love you!

Gladys Cuttle

Freedom Throw

I threw a rock across the park,
My friend and I were there.
He said the rock would set me free,
Just throw it in the air.
He tossed his first so furiously,
And then he smiled at me.
But when I went to throw my rock,
It didn't go far from me.
I know inside he's hurting still,
I guess he'll heal in time.
My hurt I will just pray it out,
In Christ I'll be just fine.

Joyce M. Hahn

Cookie

Cookie, oh Cookie,
My friend so dear.
I'm so glad
That you are here.

Cookie, oh Cookie,
Every night we walk.
I really wish
That you could talk.

Cookie, oh Cookie,
So proud and true.
I really hope
You like me to.

Cookie, oh Cookie,
Come give me your ball.
Then you can fetch it
From the end of the hall.

Joan M. Brown

My Sister And I

My sister and I are mean.
My sister and I like to play together.
My sister likes grasshoppers.
I do not like grasshoppers.
My sister has blond hair.
I have black hair.
My sister is white.
I am black,
But, I love my sister

Jessica Harrell

Heart And Soul

My heart holds many fears.
My soul holds many worries.
But most of all my life,
it holds my dearest memories.

Cara Newhouse

Mother In Waiting

Dear little baby yet to be,
Nestled so deep inside of me,
Do you know how much I care?
Or are you dreaming unaware
Of how your mother longs for you,
Waiting for your life's debut?
Love unending, without measure
Awaits your birth my blessed treasure.
How I shall marvel at your charms
The day I hold you in my arms!

Edna Moldrem

The Man Above

So many times I've tried, but
never could succeed.
Not knowing I wasn't doing
your deed.
I feel myself falling apart, no
pep in my step no love in my
heart.
But then one day something new
came to me, a voice I never heard
before.
Kept telling me there's an open
door.
Come with me for a walk, and then
we can talk.
Trust in me that's all you need, then
my child you will succeed.
I'll put pep back in your step, fill
your heart with love, but it can
only happen with the man above.

Jameica Richardson

Untitled

A story unfolding
never-ending
Every chapter a piece of the whole
Each piece new
expected or unforeseen
with potential to change to soul
Remember the faces
the lines and words
Memories of places we've met
Minutes become months
Years become a lifetime
A time to cherish without regret
New chapters begin
as others end
The tale continues to unfold
The end forever remains untold

Jennifer Shettler

The Grandmother I Never Knew

I've heard and heard but
never saw who everyone loved before.
  She died young.
Now only memories of how
she lived and all of her
ways of living.
  Now I wonder about my
grandmother, Elizabeth.
  I have a wonderful different
grandmother.
  But I would have loved
to see my real grandmother.
  Though I know I can't
I do know she is there
in a way, always.

Andrea Elizabeth Roussel

Ohio Spring

A line so markèd and discrete
Never shall snow and water meet

But in increments
brought on by the sun

Dripping snow
helps water to run

Ever faster
away from its endless source

Spill out to the ocean
O stream of the North

And with it
Memory, plainly marked

Brought on by the distance
and force of the dark

Memory
and the tales it tells

Returns to the wellspring
to shout down the well

Debora Crosby

My Love

My love is everlasting,
Never yielding,
Forever strong,

And will last throughout the ages,
Until all we know is gone

But it will not fade with my body,
Which holds my soul within.

So I may rise up to the heavens,
Where we will join again.
God made us a promise,
He gave his only son.
So that we could have forever,
And forever be as one.
You see, He brought us together.
He has already joined our hearts.
We will always have forever,
And never be apart.

Jeremy S. Nielsen

"In The Blink Of An Eye"

In the blink of an eye
night turns into day
or day into night;
one soul is saved
as another takes flight.

In the blink of an eye
one year loudly begins
as another softly ends;
lovers become newlyweds
as rocky marriages end.

Halos are given to angels
followed by silken wings;
dreamers start their days with smiles
realities come from dreams.

Memories gain in value
time that just flew by;
life turns to death
in the blink of an eye.

Angie Strickland

Depressed

Life is Great
No it's not
I want to sleep
To take my mind off it all

I hate the sun
too friendly and happy
I like rain
so grim and dull

But I'll get over it
it's just a mood
and anyway . . .
There is nothing else to do

Holly S. Grass

You Can Reach Out

There are many things you can not do
No matter how hard you try.
You can not mend a broken heart
And you can not touch the sky.

You can not force the birds to sing
When they're not in the notion,
Or cause the flowers to bloom in fall
Or fish to leave the ocean.

You can not stop the blowing wind
The water, snow or rain.
You can't erase the abuse of a child
Or take away its pain.

You can not tame the eagle
Or the wild things of the earth.
And you can not stop the labor pains
Of a mother giving birth.

There are some things that you can do
To make this life worth living.
You can reach out and help someone,
And to everyone, be forgiving.

Billy G. Jennings

Friend?

You said you would be my friend
no matter what.

You said you would be there for me
no matter what

You said you would hold my hand while
I was crying no matter what

You said you would hold my hand while
I was laughing no matter what,

I say what happen?
You were not there when I was crying
You were not there when I was laughing
You were not there when I needed you

So what happen?
No matter what

Alveda G. Walker

Eternal

I am lost in the world,
no one cares what I do,
when my heart falls to pieces,
no one cares, I know this is true.

I'm not special to my enemy,
I'm not kept near the coldest,
I'm the flower that freezes,
alone in the forest.

The frost of all hurting hearts,
is that which freezes my petals,
a dagger which plunges my heart,
only to be made with the hardest metals.

Material that has but one name,
is that of which creation wills,
the dagger is made of loneliness,
has been doubted, but is known to kill.

A blaze rips through the forest,
A deathening, consuming inferno,
the dead flower turns to ash,
but it's loneliness remains . . . eternal.

Catherine R. Sox

The Kiss I Never Had

She loved me for a moment,
No one loves me long.
She gave me wings of an eagle;
And my spirit a song.

She loved me for a moment,
But only in my mind;
Her lips I could not conquer,
A day or in a night.

That smile that I cherished,
With an intent of pain;
As of one bright star light,
Or a reed in the rain . . .

After all the laughter,
I lie in the anguish;
Day and night it haunts me.
The kiss I never had!!

Daniel Michael Davis

I'm Getting Old?

I'm getting old
Not in years or mind
Nor in great wisdom's wealth.

I'm getting old
And seem to find
I lack in physical health.

I'm getting old
I need my sleep
Yet, sometimes sleepless toss.

I'm getting old
With aches and pains
And memories I have loss.

I'm getting old
And hate to think
Of tasks I cannot do.

I'm getting old
And have to face;
It's all in one's point of view!

Diana Luna

Time Ain't Money

Time ain't money
not on my clock
'cause I live in poverty
by the stinking dock
sitting and sitting
I talk to myself
damned for quitting
no better than dust on a shelf
hopefully I'll die before forty
the dock is where I roam
this life is very dirty
everyone should have a home
excuse me, 'Can you spare a dime?'
time ain't money
and money ain't time

Everett Starnes

Something Keeps Me Hanging Round

What use to feel like home
now feels like a cell,
What use to feel like heaven
now feel's like hell.

The day's feel like months
and the months feel like
years, sometimes I have
to laugh to hold back
the tears.

When I took in the mirror
I don't like what I see,
I don't like the person
looking back at me.

I'm glad that I'm sober
but I miss being high,
I use to think that I
wanted to die until I
looked death in the eye.

Glenn Rosas

Hope

I am not alone
Now I know
It's still
  hard.
to share though
the hurt is
down
deep
and at
  surface
I keep
I must erase
the pain
so I can live and gain
The flowers from the rain.

Debra Ann Vidas

Thoughts For A Friend

Nights are lost and days have order
Now our thoughts the sole recorder

Of all the things throughout our lives
That helped us live and made us wise

When we reflect on all we are
We find that we are not so far

From parents who have raised us whole
Who touched us to our very soul

Then it comes, they pass away
Our hearts are pierced, our sea is gray

For those who made us, gave us life
Have now moved on to God's great light

David A. Nesbitt

For A Love So Rare, So Warm, So Complete

For the memory of our years
now twenty and five
we have shared it all that
which life could derive
But beyond all our dreams
we held a love so strong and true
Dear, I thank God in my prayers
for giving me you.

Babette Amy DeGrocco

No One Wants To Leave Their Home

This is what I write to people in a
nursing home.
  We wish you the very best in your
new surroundings in life.
I know no one wants to leave their home.
We know that God is with you and
looking down from above and is
watching over you.
You will be provided with your
personal needs also. You won't
have to be alone or eat alone.
We will continue praying for you
everyday. We will pray for you
that you will meet and enjoy the
company of new friends. You
have worked hard and deserve
someone looking out for you now.

Elaine Zimdars

Untitled

Cataract clouds in the eye of the moon
Obscuring these mem'ries of mine —
The taste of hot coppery sunsets
Washed down with a wintery wine.

So brief, like the flight of a mayfly,
Yet sweeter than clover in June,
And fleeting as leaves I see tumbling
By the light of a late autumn moon.

If only these moments precious,
That slip through my fingers like sand,
Could be trapped like an insect in amber,
And held like a gem in my hand.

Donald Nollet

Chain Reaction

A dozen doves were feeding there
Observed by a feline stranger.
Not one of the doves seemed aware
Of the impending danger.
Neither was the cat aware
Two eyes had him in view.
A mongrel dog approaching there
was only passing through.
The dog tore after the cat,
Causing the doves to flee
To a natural habitat
The safety of a nearby tree.
Speaking of the cat
Whatever happened to him?
Just below the doves
Sat the cat safe on a limb!

James W. Faucette

From My Window

From my window I can see the
ocean, the deep blue sea

From my window I can see the snow
on the peeks that glow to be seen

From my window I can see the
grass and trees so, so green

Also from my window I can see my
family waiting for me by the deep
blue sea

Amber Rhodes

Travelin'

Ain't nothing like the bliss
  Of a hug and a kiss,
When my daughter welcomes me home.

She scolds me for staying,
  She's sure I was playing,
And next time she won't let me go.

Someday she'll be gone,
  And I'll be at home,
Wishin' her here with me.

With mem'ries of the times
  She'd laughed and she'd cried,
An old man's last company.

Fred Hudgin

A Second Chance

I sometimes see an image
Of a little girl that plays,
But, I don't know who she is
Which I regret to this day

She holds her little dolly
So gentle and so kind,
Then she calls for mother
Which her mother looks like mine

She dies an early age
Then my vision becomes so blind,
I realize now I have a sister
That I will never find

If today she'd be around
She'd be the middle kid,
I will never get to see her though,
Since she has run off and hid.

I wish I could have met her
But, I will never get to see,
My second older sister
Who will regret that she missed me.

Jamie Shee

Love

LOVE is the greatest
Of all the talents
Found in the hand of man;
It links souls together,
And binds dreams and visions forever.

LOVE is the key
That lifts the latch to the heart of man;
Prompting him to remove
All thoughts which are unkind,
And freely give soul, heart, and mind.

LOVE is a special feeling within,
That can brighten the darkest of souls,
That seem to have reached their end.

LOVE is the spark that reaches in,
As life continues to roll,
And warms the most unrestful soul.

LOVE is from little things in life,
Not from fine mansions or fortunes untold;
But the feeling that intertwines
  two human souls.

Alice Lesh Russ

Dreams

As you grow older you begin to think
Of dreams you have had.
Some have been completed,
While others are in a holding pattern.
You ask, "Will they be fulfilled also?"
Only God knows the answer to that.
How many have been realistic?
I do not know, but dreams have helped
Through life's challenges.
Young dreams are of love
And finding yourself,
Also finding where you belonged
In this busy world.
We build our life on these young dreams.
With God's love and help
We are able to understand
When the dreams have been fulfilled.

JoAnn Young

Understanding Love

The consumption of my mind
of my thoughts
and of my actions
are but my own obstacles

I love you with the very
breadth and depth of the words meaning

It is my preoccupations
with my path that I request
your understanding

"And know" my darling sweet
that you flood my eternal
and forever changing existence

Frank A. Ridgell III

The Healer

Midst the pain and suffering
of needs and deeds for survival
Our thoughts to thee are always free.
A flood to our beings of spirits,
Uplifted unto a soaring plane.
Unborn, unspoken.
A silent tribute in humble
surrender to an unknown wonder.
That is in truth all of that which
we are.
    Thou art, I am, we be.

Francis E. Snyder

"The Untold"

    Once life unfolded a story,
of new, of old. Then the story grew
thin, the story grew cold. When
no one even bothers, to tell the
tale of old, the death of the story
grows nearer. When the story comes
back, it is not new, it is not old.
It is a story of the untold. But
when the untold story, unfolds a
message of modesty and truth, It
comes to behold a child's youth.
So when you hear a story that
needs to unfold.
Tell the tale of old.

Chrystal Dean

Happy Birthday Little Carolyn

On the 16th of December
of Nineteen Sixty Two,
The Lord was making angels,
and He named one Carolyn Sue.

She had hair of flaxen ringlets
and eyes that sparkled bright;
And a magic halo overhead
that lit the skies that night.

She's the last of Daddy's angels
and though we're far apart,
She'll be a timeless angel
in the warmth of Daddy's heart.

John R. Watts

Dreaming . . .

Heads weaving day dreams
of puffy clouds -
Glorious colors intertwine
reflecting onto sparkling waters
while angels hover round about us.

With purity
simplicity
loyalty
and unconditional love
that is timeless,
angels whisper into our being

Frances Noble Smith

Never Tomorrow

And in the shadows
    of shredded visions
    past worlds
        emanate to future decisions

(Life-like) obscured by waterfalls
    in the bleak
    undistinguished
        person vs. being

There hovers a nest

Lost and empty cocoons
    of worldly voids
    and tampered souls
        placid and peaceful
        assume rectified death

Take away the fruit of desire
    lustful humanities:
    inspiration
    hope
        kindled flame
        cradled fire

Fred J. Matteson

These My Dreams Are Yours

I'm a labyrinth of hopes and fears
Of tears of frustration and of anger
But if you can break through this wall
And search amongst it all
You'll find a man there
Who has a heart of love
Who is afraid of getting jaded

I know I have a darker side
A cruel streak
I'm selfish and demanding
But I'm a man with a vision
It just takes a little understanding

And in my hands
The grains of sand
A thousand million moments of emotion
Oh these
Oh these my dreams are yours

Brandon Fincher

April

April - is the fourth Month
    of the year - as
April - is the Month for showers
    that bring May flowers
April - is the Month that Spring
    starts after the long cold
Winter is over - as trees leaf
    out and green grass starts
And Winter wheat starts
    to green up - as
April - is the month that
    Spring starts

Irene Mary Larson

To Dream Of A Better Place

To dream of a better place
Of there's no sorrow
Climb up the highest mountain
With hope for tomorrow

Always have love in your heart
Ride the steady gale
A ship cannot stay on course
When holes are in the sail

Search for knowledge and wisdom
To gain all insight
For ignorance is darkness
The truth is in the light

If there will be no regret's
In all of time and space
The sun will shine on everyone
If we dream of a better place

Eric Nordgren

A Murder

As I walked the cold grey city concrete
Off in the distance a sound so discrete
I wondered and for a moment thought
of mountains and streams
the calling oft.

But what of the present sound?
Here in this place surely can't be found

The callers, the players
the rowdy winged noisy flyers.

As the cold wind whipped around me
in the East the sun fractured the night

Nearer the sound - clear
I could not be mistaken
Above my head the laughter came
The calling of the crows.

Christopher M. Garrick

"Christmas Blessings"

I could be homeless
No place to rest or eat
I could be clothes less
With worn shoes upon my feet
I could be jobless
Without a goal in sight
But think God for his mercy
As well this holy night

John Hartzell

A Lie

Moonlight Sonata
on a fabricated dance floor
a faux pas of love, from you
to me . . .
spinning around call me a fool
for someone . . . anyone . . .
Gullible?

You lead up the spiral staircase
and force me from the stars,
spinning
a pit of nothingness.

Lonely ears hear the spiral voice:
yes, the one without the echo . . .
The bird sings it and hears it
believing.

Adam F. Braun

A Hunting Trip

Once on a hunting trip
On a rock I slipped
And cracked a stick
My lip I bit.

I saw a deer
It showed no fear
Until I moved
Then it moved.

The sun went down
We returned to town.

Jeremy Born

The Beauty Of God

A child at play
On a warm sunny day
Reaching for shadows
All along their way

Dorothy A. Hayes

Possibilities

Possibilities - and my hopes rise
on flights of eagerness and trust,
earnest longings long disclaimed
to fit, or force to fit, no,
retrofit myself to match the
yet unrealized whatever.

Someone that I was meant to be
came by and had a word with me,
am I the one you wish to be, or
maybe just a parody?

Jana Targova

Confusion

Constantly
On going
Non stop
Furious
Unforgettable
Stress
In the
Option of
None but one

Amy Nicole Johansen

Shadow Of Woman

As I rock back and forth
on my metal chair
I wonder the purpose life
cold chills tickle spine
The darkness overcomes me
It seems to be a comfort
I waste my life sitting
in a locked room imagining
I still await day for happiness
or even a hallucination
Is there heaven is there hell
that's in store for me
I'm shaken up confusion
day after day, week after week
month after month, year after year
I scream lethargically
but am ignored by many others
but I mustn't speak
Silence is golden
But talking is silver

Jillian Batman

Reminisce

In the distant heat and haze,
on sunwashed shores of whitened sand
shimmer thoughts of yesterday,
while the sun shines in ignorance,
blithely performing the duties
to which we have become so accustomed,
as waves break on the shore,
and gulls whirl overhead.
The scent of flowers lingers,
of saltwater, of warm air,
the scent of things held
in memory, waiting for
the day they will be retrieved,
pulled back slowly, cautiously,
as if on a string which might,
at any moment, snap in two,
severing the ties not only to
yesterday, but to tomorrow.

Carol Thompson-Taylor

Artist's Farewell

Dedicated to Chester Hayes
What is it like
On the last day of your life?
It's like:
Leaving a fabulous friend,
Who has shown you,
Wonders beyond belief!
Oh, the colors, my friend
Everywhere - the colors!
Days like jewels,
Of which I've had a few.
Jewels! Green, white, and blue,
Born in fire
At the center of the earth.
Life - hospitable friend
You have given so much.
Life! The earth!
And thirty thousand days.

Geraldine P. Trory

Looking For A Home

I saw a little boy
On the T.V. Air
I just wanted to shed
A great big tear.

He looked so alone.
He was looking for a home
with a mom and a dad
For which he has never had.

Someone to care
Too hold him dear
Looking for someone to hold him
that would never let go

He's just patiently waiting
For someone to take him home.
Take me home
Before I am grown
And all alone.

Cindy M. Taylor

"The Morrow"

Aye, 'tis no time to be dour
on the thirteenth hour,
at a melancholy time
of the season;
Spirits fly so high
s does time go by,
with irregularity
and no reason
Colors blend together
birds flock together,
in one mass
To give the skies a brilliant dash!
As the time grows near
we have need to fear,
for the future;
who says to-morrow will come?

Burton L. Strid

Love

A child was crying in the street
One cold and rainy day.
I thought I'd simply rush on by,
But Love got in the way.

A frightened puppy lost and starved,
Came up to me today.
His soft, brown eyes tugged at my heart,
And Love got in the way.

A friend distraught and needing help
Called on the phone to say
She couldn't handle things herself.
So Love got in the way.

I turn to God in times of need.
I bow my head and pray.
I'm glad he's always there for me.
His love gets in my way.

Anne R. Johnson

The End Of The World

One day I was walkin'
One day I was talkin'
And that's the day I saw it
The end of the world as we know it

I could see everything
I could see hate
I could see murder
On that particular date

I tried to run
I tried to hide
But I couldn't get away from
Seeing blood by my side

When the day comes
We can't run
We have to face our fears
Without any tears

We don't need weapons
To harm each other
We need love to
Heal one another
Jessica Jacobsen

Marching On

Fierceness, boldness, courage, drive,
Onward through the world we strive,
Pushing, pulling, pressing on,
Marching, marching, on and on.

Leaving footprints, making names,
Satisfaction, fortune, fame;
Conquer, capture - caution gone,
Marching, marching, on and on.

Running through the soldier's fire,
Trudging through the muck and mire,
Pushing, pulling, pressing on,
Ever gaining, going on.
Amanda Severance

To My Wife

I cannot build an edifice,
    or mansion in the blue?
Unless a firm foundation, I build,
    with love so true!

Whether tis my duty,
    my obligation must be sewn.
To hold close the garment,
    and kiss each fallen stone.

Yet, there is now, and ever will be,
    love, upon the shore.
Blissfully tinted by the waves
    and shells of one or more.

So raise your eyelids, first and then,
    slowly look about;
And you will see me,
    not far, without a doubt!
Daniel J. Evans

A Forest Aflame

Red, russet, and gold
Orange, yellow, some green, too
The colors of a fire so bright
To feel the warmth, can you?

There's even brown, and a bit of black
But, still the air is clean.
A quiet, crispness can be felt,
Ah!, for you the joy to glean.

What a riot of colors!
The forest is aflame with light . . .
Why! Can't you guess?
Autumn is announcing her delight.

An excitement for the eyes
As you please, slowly or fast.
Long after this wondrous day
Special memories will surely last.

While the forest remains aflame
Giving the senses an unexpected lift
Thoughts of thankfulness abound
For appreciation of this yearly gift.
Dorothy A. Mitchell

Sunday Is

Sunday is
Our bare feet side to side
engaged in a playful duet
as our bronze palms clutch
together in a moment of oneness

Sunday Is
A sentimental Coltrane ballad
muffled beneath a thick blanked
of contentment, where lovers
whisper secrets inside a quilted
dream of restful completeness

Sunday Is
A day spent adrift in the bend
of my lovers' applauding arms

And

Under the noon day saffron sun;
a hushed merriment drapes itself
over my bedroom decor, watching
us as we nod on pillows made of
peaceful down.
Cynthia M. Sherman

My Prayer

Bless O' Lord,
    Our boys in far off lands
At home; and on cold, cruel
    bloody strands.
In turmoil, trial, and in fear.
    Let thy comforting voice be heard.
By a heart of faith and a pious ear.

Then endow with unwavering strength,
The wounded warrior struggling
    from death's brink,
Cheat lustful death!
And give him life that he might
    live a righteous way.
If it be thy will Lord,
    this I pray.
Henry Wilson Swift

I Will Never Let You Down

As we plant a seed
our leaves will
begin to grow.

When a leaf of
your branch falls,
I'll make sure
that you won't
feel let down.

Everytime we're
together, another
leaf will grow,
but when we're
not together,
two leaves will die.

By remembering all
the good times
that we've shared
like the sun and rain
our feelings of love
will never change.
Christina Feliciano

Travelers In Eternity

As travelers in eternity
Our thoughts are turning home.
We have become so weary
And lack the strength to roam.

So take my hand, my darling;
Let's slowly move along.
You smile your pretty smile;
I'll sing a happy song.

Sixty years together —
It seems like just a day.
Let's dream about the good times
And brush the bad away.

The sun is slowly sinking
Beneath the sky's great dome,
And we will rest forever
In our eternal home.
James H. Hart

Inside Me

I'm lost inside of me
    Outside you can not see
I'm lost inside of me

I'm not quite what I seem
    I sleep instead of dream
I'm not quite what I mean

I'm lost
    Untrained assault
I've lost my eyes in salt
    No one to name for fault

I'm not one to look like you
    Won't change to fit in to
Your narrow field of view
    I'd be lost inside of you
Christopher Worley

"Ending Feelings"

Lightning across the sky is like the
pain in my head, the thunder roars
again as anger comes to an end.
Feelings of guilt, relief and loneliness
take over and still my heart aches.
Not knowing which way to go, this way,
that way, who cares? I don't need to
know. For now I'm like a bird flying
in the sky, free, free, to fly.
You see, no one can tell me do this,
do that. I'm now able to do my best,
like the bird inside of me, I can build
my own nest.
The thunders stopped but the rain
still pours, like mismatched feelings,
my love still soars.
Don't let anyone get you down, for
now I know, a true friend I've found.
Search your soul and look within,
you hear a sound, you're your own true
friend.

Amanda Bullen

Untitled

Insanity, my inspiration
Pain is to be my cause
Evil surrounds me
I can feel the demons claws
Ripping at my flesh
The pain grow strong
Blood leaving my body
Still I go on
Because my love holds so very strong
These words I can say
I shall fight the evil
And live another day.

Dale W. Foreman

Look Where He's Brought Us From

Everyday the school bus
"Passed right by us"
had to walk for miles
"but was always on time"
look where he's brought us from.

Had to use the bathroom outside
"but was done with pride"
with God right by our side
look where he's brought us from.

"When we went in a store"
"had to use the back door"
Mama and Daddy, "work from sunrise
to sunset"
Just to put food on the table
thank God not anymore
look where he's brought us from

Brenda Shoots

Morbid Thought

Morbid thought
Peaceful night
Someone overwrought

Sharpened knife
Silky throat
End of a life

Alicia Anne Pell

Peckwaddle Special

Chicken huge and Alba Duck
Pecked and waddled
All night long.

Feathers and down!
Thy went to town
To visit for the day.

They clucked and quacked
And ate and ate—-
But suddenly they stopped.

Black clouds rolled in,
Then rain poured down
And shrank them both away!

Dorothy R. Green

Lake Side

Alighting from the car to the ground
Peering through the shoreline trees
My soul cried out
Not in pain or anguish
But with rejoicing!
An aura of calm prevailed
And firmly took hold—-
Peace settled over me
With its web of gossamer thread
Like a protective cocoon.
My soul was enchanted!
Everyday worries, anxieties, fears
Were no more;
Only the rippling water,
The warming sun,
And the nuzzling breeze,
Bringing sublime serenity in its wake.

Karen C. Allen

Penguins In The House

Penguins! PENGUINS! They are a thrill!
Penguins just LOVE cold and chill!

Penguins! PENGUINS! In the south!
Stuffing fishes in their mouth!

Penguins! PENGUINS! In my room!
Nipping penguins I assume!

FIGHTING penguins! Fight themselves!
Fighting penguins on my shelves!

MANY penguins crowd my room!
Many penguins! ZIP and ZOOM!

I've got to get them out of here!
Those thrilling penguins are my fear!

GET OUT YOU PENGUINS! GET! GET! GET!
I WILL NOT HAVE YOU FOR MY PET!

Athena Carr

Away From Home

As I walk down the street without shoes,
people stare at my calloused feet.
I know what they think.
They wonder if my calloused feet
really do stink.
But it really doesn't matter
for when I fart, they scatter.

Joshua Videto

The Waterfall

A conscious impression,
perceiving motion,
I listen to the waterfall.

The colorless liquid,
in a transparent downpour,
a sight of compelling force.

An odorless flow,
a spirit in the mist,
Do I sense a presence?

I experience flavor,
pure of quality,
the tastebuds of time.

To hold in my hands,
slipping through my fingers,
My opposition?

Jacqueline J. Lal-Kissoon

Life's Departure

Family and friends
Please do not grieve for me
As always, death is meant to be.

When the Angel of Death cuddles
me to her gentle breast,
I will rejoice, for I have
grown weary of the pain.

While I would have liked to
see you fulfill life's dreams.
I will be ever watchful from above,
Monitoring with love.

Think of me when you see a butterfly
light on a lovely flower petal;
Or when a leaf floats gently to
the ground.

Be glad for me, because as I have
left my earthly body behind
Oh, how my spirit will soar!

Carol J. Rawlings-Morrow

Come In

Come in - come in
Please join us in our hall

Come in - come in
There's food and drink for all

Come in - come in
The fires burning bright

Come join us in our merriment
and shelter from the night

Within - within
hearts are full of thanks and love

Our blessings are abundant for
they come from him above

Come in - come in - come in

Easter Varso

A Thanksgiving Song

Magnify him with thanksgiving,
Praise the name of God with song
There will be blessings through the day,
Although everything does go wrong.

Let's marvel at the love of God
It reaches the depth of the sea
He sent His Son to redeem those
Who call on Him to be set free.

For that indescribable gift
There is gratitude in the heart
Eternal life with the redeemed
From the Savior we'll not depart!

Thanks be to God for health and strength,
For eyes to see, and ears that hear
Making peace with our Creator
Removes every doubt, and great fear.

From sunrise to sunset we must
Remember to praise the Lord's Name,
With a new song we sing to Him,
Jesus Christ, who's always the same.

Carolyn Marquis

Seeking An Escape

Asian American with slanted eyes
Prejudice and racism fill the air
Wishing I could spurt wings and fly
To a distant shore away from there

As I seek a place to hide
Far beyond their words of spite
So overwhelming that out loud I cry
A painful scream that fills the night

My almond eyes flood with tears
As they mock the fact I'm not the same
Their slurs bring out my greatest fears
What a cruel and wicked game

I try to run, I try to fight
But from the flashbacks, I cannot cope
But in the distance shines a light
A small reminder that there's still hope

Austin Chung

Beyond Dust Dreaming

Galaxies in grandeur springing
Pristine primordial order bringing
Surging searing gleaming streams
Searching floating glistening dreams
Dizzily drifting dancing mazes
Tracing opulent shapely hazes
Ethereal dramas drinking spaces
Beauty bending
Thoughts unending
Triumphs tenderly descending

Chrystalla Mars de Lucca

Expressions

Stirrings of emotions
Recoiling from assaults
To the senses —-
Youthful innocence besieged
Raining torrents
Of naked reality—

Ireland E. Ray

Fall

Leaves
red, yellow, gold
graceful pirouettes
dancing
a pas de deux with the wind
singing
a requiem to the summer
heralding
the coming
snow.

Dawn Marie Larsen

The End

Dusky clouds move in
Pushing blue skies further,
Further from my mind
The end is approaching
Is there time?
Time for that final thought
Time for that final dream
Time for one last regret
Time to move on . . .
Darkness moves in,
Time has gone,
The end.

Dawn Ricci

Quilted Memories

I sit here by my window
quietly contemplating
the twilight of my life
pacing the sunset, facing the onset
of the Golden Years

And your friendship looms before me
like a beacon in the night
your laughter safely guiding me
through the haze to the brighter days
when I was young

But today the sun seems colder
and the fear of growing older
blinds me like a winter storm
and rips apart that inner part
of my soul

So I clutch my dreams around me
like a familiar winter coat
and somehow these thoughts of you
p-i-e-c-e-d together like quilted memories
keep me warm.

Carlos T. Sams

Farewell

My love has departed, to
   return no more,
And today is filled with
   sorrow and past regrets
But no longer future hope nor fears.

The flower that once bloomed has
   withered and died
And cannot blossom for all my tears.

Another chance, another summer,
   another snowfall.
Never more, my love, never more.

Hilda Brown

Frozen Leaves

Persimmon teardrops
rain down dead
amidst fruit drops plops bombs
loud and heavy with frost
first sound of mourning.
The tree shakes
with so much leaving
all at once.
Cries of hurt fear
are strangely absent
or perhaps
five senses aren't enough
to appreciate
the pain
of being caught
in such an obvious cycle
of small livings and dyings
between births.

David Webster

Life In The World

Treat everybody the same
Regardless of creed, color or name
Even though life is nothing more
than a big game.

Everybody in the world is doing
their own thang.

Whether it is right or wrong
No one seems to be ashamed

But down through life
It will most likely make them lame.

Gloria J. Shaw

Thanksgiving

Giving thanks to the one above,
Reminds us of the good that's here,
And all the special ones we love.
The precious things that we hold dear.
It's wonderful to have a day,
To share our blessings with others
Unity in spirit, to pray.
Daddys, Mamas, Sisters, Brothers
Everyone! This is a good day!

Dawn Cahoon Kniff

Flowers

Daisy daisy tiger lily
Roses and clovers and more
Flowers oh flowers
What do I see
I see colors so bright
Colors like
Red and purple, green and orange too
Blue and yellow can you see them too?
Oh flowers I wish I were one of you

Jennifer D. Larrivee

Blue Dolphins

Blue dolphins
sail the sea
under the ocean
and above with the bees.
They cannot breath
on ocean floor, so they
must breath up on the sea.
where the nest.
We must help dolphins survive,
if we don't they will die.

Caressa Welligiton

Not Just Me

Little boats just one inch high
Sailing across a bright blue sky.
I watch them move across the sound
And through the pass to the gulf beyond
Little boats just one inch high.

They're far away from me, you know,
Making their way to the sea below.
I travel with them in memory
Of distant places I long to be
With you- but "not just me."

Effie Douglas Henderson

Untitled

Your words become hot with intensity
saying what your body is feeling
Our breath grows heavier
as your mouth nears mine
My body starts to tremble
with the feel of your touch
Wills become weaker as
our worlds collide around us
Your fiery lips leave a blazing trail
down my neck
Then you say what I need to hear . . .
        "I love you"
And I die in a whirlwind of passion
your words have created in my heart
My life is in your hands
and my soul is in your eyes
My senses are screaming out to hear you,
feel you, have you
"I love you" - "again - "I love you"
Keep breathing them until my mind
believes
what my heart is feeling

Jennine Dwyer

Searching

Many today are searching.
Searching for a way to fill the
emptiness they feel in their lives.
Some are waiting.
Some are filling the void with
the wrongs that they feel
is the answer.
Living in the dark
instead of the light.
Rejoicing in the evil and the
delight of perverseness.
Many are avoiding and ignoring the
voice that is within.
And denying the truth that
Can show them the light.

Jan Phillips

The Elements Of Earth

The northeastern winds,
seem to quiver the leaves,
As swiftly a fawn,
has shiver the trees.
Thus the howling of wind,
like a fast moving train.
Which will not stop,
no matter what's in the way.
For the tempest was strong,
as the earth starts to spin.
Causing destruction of structure,
where ever its been.
For near the heavens,
a disturbances occurs.
As if time has distinguished,
what a man has built.
The elements of earth,
are only of four.
For when there together,
they create a dangerous wind storm.

Catherine C. Mondragon

Survival

Far away in a land
Seen only in books,
There was a war.
People are fighting for freedom,
There is bloodshed and destruction.
People fall on top of each other,
As they tumble to death.
The grass turns red,
From the dark thick blood.
But the sun still shines,
It shines on a single flower.
The only thing left untouched,
And unbroken.
It is alive,
But lonely.

Jennifer Ferris

Man . . .

Self reliant man . . .
Self indulgent man . . .
Intelligent man . . .
Wise man . . . heterosexual man . . .
"Real" man . . . police man . . .
Religious man . . . your own man . . .
Everybody's man . . .
Woman . . .
Strange man . . .
Unusual man . . .
Strong man . . .
Polluted man . . .
Evil man . . . good man . . .
Corrupt man . . .
Dirty man . . . super man?
Educated man . . .
Spoon man . . .
Better man . . .
Nothing man . . .
Human . . .

Brian Bednarek

A Celebration Of Love

Today is a special day
Set aside to celebrate our love,
The love I feel for you,
The love that comes from above.
To express feelings for friends that
Don't get shown every day.

You're my whole life.
You're my lasting dream.
You're always on my mind.
What a blessing that was sent to me.
Together we will shine.

Now is the time that we stand
Together as one.
A new life inside us will shine.
Together we will shine
Throughout eternity.

Joan Stretch Haskin

Nature's Apron Strings

Roses and sunlight
    share elements.

The moon and oceans
    are tied.

Stars and lovers
    exchange a glow.

The trees and I
    trade breaths.

I call out,
    and the hills
    echo my cry.

Barbara Schick

Ode To A Friend

My best friend can no longer see
She sits in silence near to me
Disease has robbed her of her sight
No longer shine her eyes at night
Or look at me with trusting gaze
The world to her became a maze

My friend and I, we used to run
Play ball, go for long walks, have fun
She used to swim and fetch a stick
And bring it back to me so quick
Now all these things we do it seems
When she is sound asleep and dreams

My best friend lost her sight today
I pray it may come back some day
We slowly walk together now
I guide her, try to teach her how to find her
way, to carry on.
My heart aches seeing her empty stare
Confusion, anxiety and despair
My friend don't be afraid
I'll be your eyes, I'll be always there.

Christine Perry

The Passing

The flag at half mast
Signalling someone's demise
The war is over

Andrew LaBerge

Rain

A drop is like a tear
Shed from one's eye
To smile upon a bud
Which blossoms into
A beautiful flower
Droplets, liquified
Shower
For a more purposeful meaning
Breathing a new life
Anna Gilmore

In My Garden Green

Like to lover's tears
(shed in heartfelt joy)
   fall the petals of a rose
in my garden.
My garden
   (lush and green)
   would bloom for you if
you asked for it.
   (A flower)
Knock, and the door opens.
Call, and I will hear.
Cry, and I will answer.
Need, and I'll be near
   (hiding in my garden.)
Forever, in my garden,
   my niche,
     my home,
My Love,
You are welcome.
   (Please, do come.)
Deirdre M. Maisannes

Claire

This is Claire, God
She's starting school today
And I wanted to ask if
You will sort of pave
Her way.

I know it's asking a lot
For, of course, she too must learn
That life is not an easy path
And there may be danger
At any turn.

But she's such a little tyke, God
She hasn't as yet reached six
A frail, a gentle child
She's not ready for life's tricks.

So I thought I would ask
Though I know·you'll do what's best
Would you look after her God
Just a little more than the rest.
Catherine M. Felber

Dust Of Snow

The way a crow
Shook down on me
The dust of snow
From a hemlock tree

Has given my heart
A change of mood
And saved me part
Of a day I had rued
Cheryl Norcutt

The Gift

soft white
shimmering light

settling down
upon your crown

prickly thorns
that you adorn

gentle breeze
tempts the seas

vast shrouds
of parting clouds

ultimate price
of life sacrifice

graceful love
from heaven above

cleansing away
our sins at bay

leading us home
no longer to roam

eternal life
free from strife
Cory Calvin Cannella

Prisms

Prisms of light
Shining through crevices of intuition
Prisms of light
Illuminating my mind
Revealing my vulnerability

I see through rose colored glasses
Covering the thorns of my mind
Marring the misty roses
I reach out for the flowers
My rose colored glasses are shattered
Prisms of light

Light comes in digging out
Those darkened corners of my mind
Rose colored glass falling
Intuition untold yet unmasked
Prisms of light
Illuminating the crevices
Of my broken heart
Donald Brown

No One's Listening

Screams of terror,
shrieks of fright.
Cries for help,
each and every night.
Ignored and put aside,
accused of telling lies.
Adults saving adults,
fearing the truth in his eyes.
Excuses to explain,
lies to deceive.
A child is DEAD,
because we didn't believe.
Dana Fry

Childhood

I closed my eyes
Shutting out
Childhood
Bidding farewell
To life I once knew
Secure shells
Of warmth
Withered away
Sun-warmed existence
Set into a
Horizon of disillusionments
Fading
In the night sky
Of reality
Gone for always
Never returning
Emily Skelton

Mountain Magic

I descended the rugged mountain
   side
After sharing of its treasures
   untold.
"Good bye high Majesty.
Your gifts are more precious
   than gold."

I've followed your rivers,
And gazed at the awesome terrain.
Such peace and contentment,
Will not fade in vain.

The city is calling;
The crowds push their way.
But stored deep in memory
Are the mountains in glorious
   array.
Carol M. Stevens

A Letter To My Dad

Though it's been months now,
since you were taken away.
The memories are still strong,
and I wish you were here today.

I remember all the good times,
with you there was so much to gain.
But now there's so much emptiness,
and ever so much pain.

I can't see or touch you,
so I know that your not here.
But I've still got the past,
in my heart your still near.

I wake up in the night,
crying aloud and calling your name.
Its hard to realize your gone,
and things will never be the same.

If I could see you just once again,
you know what I would do!
Hold you tight and say,
I love you.
Elizabeth Wolf

Promises To Keep

Leaves rustling,
singing me to sleep.
Restless as I am
sorrow I keep.

Staid on memory,
constant in my mind,
the world around me,
leaving me behind.

What's in a word,
a promise gone sour.
Many times wishing,
every minute, every hour.

Uneasy with trust,
not knowing where to turn,
over and over,
when do we learn?

Have faith in the heart,
its mind like a dove.
Forever returning
for something to love.

Alura Charbonnet

Bay Watch

I had a kind of lonely feeling
Sitting there all alone
On the sandy shore,
With nothing to do
But watch the sailboats pass.
And all the while the great golden sun
Was sinking lower in the west,
And the waves played chase
With each other all the way
Up to the sandy shore,
Where their journeys came to an end.

Becky Myers

Dear Daughter

To my little girl, born twenty
    six years ago.

From your Mother, who desperately
    wanted you so.

Birthdays comes, and birthdays
    will go.

The only thing missing, is the
    warmth of your glow.

I look at all the little faces,
    time after time.

Wondering which one, will look
    just like mine.

I hope and I pray, to see you
    once again.

I know in my heart, you also
    wonder when.

I miss you, more than you will
    ever know.

I just wish, I could see you,
    to tell YOU SO.

Donah Tryder-Rogers

Deference

Your style of poetry,
so different from mine;
More eloquent, continuous,
absent of rhyme.
Meter is missing, it
covers too many years;
telling how you coped
with destruction and fears.
Yet it sends us a message
untainted within;
Reveals saving graces
from wherever you've been.
Your poetry is substance,
with facility;
thank you for enhanced,
redeeming reality.

Constance Barrett

Life

Life is a wonderful thing
so don't mess it up
by doing drugs and getting pregnant
doing drugs you could end up dead
if you get pregnant your parents
might kick you out and they
may never talk to you ever again
so watch what you do
cherish your life
or you might end up dead or
homeless.

Jessica Blymire

Inner Strength

A child entrapped,
so eager to speak.
Begging please.

A world so cold,
let her go.
Let her feel
the warmth.

Darkness lifting,
images clear.
I've come . . .
home.

A strong woman,
steps from
the shadows.
A survivor,
set free.

Christine Frizzle

Black Momma

Tough nails but
Soft spots in her
Base of being.
Like a hundred year old tree
Staunch, steady,
Soaking the sun
To warm the base . . .
The roots.

Annette T. Craighead

God Bless The World Today

God bless the world you have made;
So far from thee we have strayed.
'Til we recognize thee
We shall never be free;
For too long we have strayed.

God bless the world today
In a most unique way;
The world you designed,
A part it is mine
You're our only hope for today.

God give us the strength that we need,
Bring us together as one, indeed;
Lord, pour out your blessing
As we are confessing;
The world has grown full of greed.

For the dawn of a brand new day
Let us learn to live and pray.
Lord, cheer each heart
Thy grace to impart;
God bless the world today.

Beatrice Montgomery

Ode To A Toad

Here's to your life,
so green and so true.
Here's to your home,
of water so blue.

Here's to your family,
is that them over there?
Here's to your health,
don't be caught unaware!

Here's to your croak,
heard often at night.
Here's to your silence,
that stars when there's light.

Here's to your friends,
with you they do cheer.
Here's to your hop,
your there now your near.

Here's to your work,
tell me what do you do?
Here's to the toad,
how amazing are you.

Brian W. Jeffrey

How I Love The Ocean!!!

As I wake up with the
soft yellow sun I feel the breeze
of morning and hear the water
slapping the soft sand.
The sea oats move with the soft breeze.

As I stretch my long legs and
pull my blue quilt off I hear the
call of the seagulls.

I step outside on my balcony and
feel a soft mist of salt water,
oh how I love the ocean!!!

Brittany Sims

Jump Start

You laid into me,
rhythmically.
My eyes closed.
My soul released.

My arrhythmic heart
struggled to survive.
Could the years of neglect
be overcome?

The past flickers:
first love, romanticist,
adulterer, summer fling,
clogged my heart with waste.

Until your lips
breathed lifesaving
fire into me.
And I responded.

You laid into me,
rhythmically,
and resuscitated
my love.

Janet Carol Fasig

"A Friend In Jesus"

Where are you running my child
so lost and alone
looking for shelter
from the darkness and cold
where are you running my child
your eyes filled with tears
running from the pain
you no longer can bear
many painful memories
from days long ago
looking to find a way
just to let it all go
How long can you keep running
before the road suddenly ends
don't be afraid my child
to reach out to a friend
your not alone my child
for I am with you by your side
never will I leave you
you have a friend in Jesus Christ

Elizabeth Ann Woodruff

The Bethlehem Star

One dark and lonely night,
So many, many years ago;
In a humble stable
A King was born;
And soon, man came to know,
He was King of all the Kings,
Born of a Virgin Fair.
He was the Son of God,
He, of whom Angels sang,
All man's cares come to bear.

Yes, in the little town
Of Bethlehem, was born,
Jesus, King of all Kings!
A star, who with its light
The Little King adorned,
Led shepherds from fields,
And wise men from afar.
All who came, were led
To this Sacred Place
By the Bethlehem Star.

Joanne I. Casmo

Seat Belts

It's seat belt safety week
  So please buckle-up.
You could save a life
  if you only buckle-up.
Tell your mother,
  your father,
  your siblings too!

It's easy to forget,
  but please don't try to!
Buckle-up for me
  so you won't die.
You'll save your life
  and maybe two.
So please buckle-up
  before you get caught.
There's a price to pay
  if you get stopped!

Buckle-up
It's the law.

Darci L. Bruns

One Nation Under God

I was born into a country.
  So vast, and rich, and free.
Yet taken so for granted
  Maybe it's up to me.

This country stands for freedom
  Fore fathers fought and died,
To worship God in one's own way
  As Christ was crucified.

I pledge allegiance to this land
  I cherish all my dreams,
Of mountain tops and ocean shores
  All races join as teams,

United we can go ahead.
  And keep our goal in sight,
We'll work together all as one
  Our future will be bright.

Tomorrow is another day.
  Great men this land have trod.
Will my footsteps lead the way
  To one nation under God?

Amy Martin

Memories

Memories are all that's left.
Some vague, some clear,
Some strong, some weak.
You left us with these memories,
No warnings you'd be gone.
It's hard to picture your face
Each night as I close my eyes.
The love for you will never die.
You mean too much to me,
To let you go.
I love you too much,
To let you fade away.

Janette Loupe

Lonely

Can I fall knowing
someone will be there to catch me.
Can I make a mistake
knowing someone will still love me.
Can I cry on a shoulder
when I need a friend
I feel so alone.

Brooke McKay

Special Thoughts

I long to put my thought into words,
So you would be sure to see,
How many of them are of you,
And how much you mean to me.

I also wish that I could tell you
About the special way,
That loving you brings such luck
To me each and everyday.

But it's my very deepest feelings
That are hardest to convey,
Because I care and love you,
More than words could ever say.

I can't describe what love is
But I can feel it in your touch,
And honey I need your warmth
And understand oh so very much.

Just knowing you are my happiness
And my reason for living too,
I simply want you to know these "special thoughts"
Are always going to be in "my heart for you."

Deborha McKibban

Ancients

Voices of the Ancients
  Speak softly to me
Of blue sky
  And calm, cool breeze

Eternal whispers
  Of duty and peace
Tall grass rippling
  Alive in the sun

The circle of life
  The sea of hope
Seasons cycle
  Evolving birth

Heart-Reaches-Through-Flame
  Once walked this earth
With infinite stride
  Proud of what was

These thoughts I leave
  Love what you see
When you gaze
  Into the mirror

James A. Bowles

Untitled

Children are precious,
special gifts from above.
Handle with tenderness,
mercy, and love.
As each day goes by
precious memories, you'll find,
will forever be etched
and engraved in your mind.
Take time as a family,
do things together,
cherish the time with
your children forever.
For the time that you spend
and all that you do
are constant reminders
of God's blessing on you.

Diane Blanton

Tryst In Time

I waited
spending my life
in minutes.
She did not come.
I did not mind waiting
spending my life in
minutes.
I walked out
to get a better view
to see if she were coming.
She was not.

All minutes were gone.

As I lay dying
suddenly I knew she
would not come.
She was dead
or had forgotten
They are the same.

James Corbett Tasker

Labels

Look long at the label.
Squint hard at the print.
Insist on a list
Of what is and isn't.
If there's a big build-up,
Is it getting out of hand?
Or is it as familiar
As your favorite brand?
Not what they name it,
But what it does.
Maybe it's famous for what it was.
Clamor of commercials
Is apt to lead astray,
With so many virtues
On tap to display:
Tested and targeted
As the best on the market.
Come, pick it up.
Yes, you can charge it.

Genevieve R. Griffin

Zen Painting

Such is the tree across the street
Standing barren of leaves,
Such wooden arms stretched out
Measuring the breeze.
Under such ease
A child waits to sneeze.

John L. Mazzuca

A Portrait

Looking bravely sternly down
Standing handsome holding roses
Bearing headdress like a crown
To his beloved smiling poses.

Appears facing loving spouse
In life source to his strength
Picture gladly in our house
Portrait hanging full in length.

Father to four children young
Loving husband city's son
Upholds rulers country's wrong
Disciplines own household fun.

While I admire posture here
I will forget never father
Handling to me roses dear
Yet now always giving mother.

Henri Joseph Dolega

Cloud

I saw a cloud the other day, as I
Stepped outside to my car.
    I couldn't see it very well it was
    Far oh so far.

Just by seeing and knowing its glare
was but a helpful hint
That God was sill at work in heaven
And our life was not full spent.

The cloud was oh so beautiful
With cone's of Vanilla White
And mountain's of luscious peaks
That would be a skier's delight.

I took a ride out thru our town
And though all our bless, but
Never in all the clouds, I've seen,
Has given feeling like this.!

James D. Davis Sr.

Writing Complaints

Poem after poem
Story upon story
Piles of essays
Files of reports
Please oh please
I beg
No more for the year
Writing never comes very easy
it is always tough and very cheesy
Teacher bubbling with cheer
Saying one more line dear
I dare say
I should flunk
And be back for more
of this
junk.

Jamie M. Gerkin

An Ode To Dennis

A bond of commitment
Strengthened by time;
Who can explain it
With meter and rhyme?

How can a poet
Describe the foundation
Built with respect
And mutual admiration?

A mere "I love you"
Seems shallow and trite,
As saying the immeasurable
With the finite.

So understand the inadequacy
As I struggle to reveal
As realistic portrayal
Of the love that I feel.

Donna Nelson

Hope

An angel comes each season,
Symbolized by "Hope!"
She speaks to each believer
And helps one learn to cope!

No matter where life takes us,
Or doors that we come to . . .
There stands "Hope," as always,
In each season, guiding thru!

We find that mind and spirit
Unite under one name, for
"Hope" is meant to conquer!
"Hope" is eternal flame!

As "Hope" is always with us,
We know she's burning bright!
And with "Hope" we'll face the future
Guided by eternal light!

This angel is now waiting . . .
"Hope," is always kept alive,
Her flame will burn forever. . . as . . .
Onward, upward, we strive!

Billie F. Netterwald

Lie

She's got all the laughter
    that I'm after
She's got your loving eye
    I'm the lie
She's got all the happy years
    I got the tears
My heart is starting to bleed
    I got the need
To have someone there
    who really cares
Someone to hold me
    let my feelings free
Someone who loves from the heart
    and won't tear mine apart
Someone like you
    I wish we could be true.

Cheryl Miller

Slow Steps

Let's go walking, Grandma.
Take my hand. We'll see
the world and all it's wonders
awaiting you and me.

That stone, that bug, that tree leaf,
we take the time to hold.
With you we note the marvelous things
a strolling walk unfolds.

Who says your eyes are dimming!
Who cares your steps have slowed.
The 'tension that you give me
is worth a pot of gold.

You say I make you happy,
a smile is on your face.
We even share a giggle,
all worldly cares erased.

The walks I take with Grandma,
are enough to make my day.
The times we share together
in memory they will stay.

Germaine Draeger

The Ebony Soul Of Man

Two lovely daughters, so very dear,
   taken from me here.
No one, no God, can explain
   the hurt, the wrath, the disdain.
Two roses yet to bloom
"Man" sealed their doom.

This is not a world for me,
   thee and thine:
This thwarted wonder, this phenomena,
   this savage "man" kind.

Men! Easily overpower and kill
Woman; most gentle, loving:
   Give birth to man
   From man give birth
Only . . . to die by their hand!

Why? For what? We cry! We call!
The devastating finality
   almost surpassed . . .
By the senseless, brutal, stupidity
   of it all.

JoAnne Coleman

Phantom

What is it with the night
that makes us long for light?
Perhaps our failing sight
feeds fears appetite.

What is the mystic power
that causes us to cower?
Our dreams it does devour
that lonely midnight hour.

Why yield to an ill force
that plots a darker course,
and wallow in remorse?
You are the phantom's source.

Jewel Jackson-Shahan

Long Overdue

Veterans standing at attention
Taps blowing so clearly and so loud
A misty rain gently keeps falling
Mingling with tears in eyes of the crowd.

A monument just dedicated
To heroes from the Vietnam War
Prisoners or missing in action
Or gone from this earth for evermore.

Some alive and suffering affliction
Or tormented in mind and in soul
Some, although now healed in the body
But still bearing many losses untold.

Let us who are present this morning
And everyone else across this land
Give thanks to these men and these women
Who for this country, did take a stand.

Let this land of the free acknowledge
Their contributions so bold and so true
And from now on continue to give them
The gratitude that's been long overdue.

Elizabeth M. Jedrzejewski

When

   Pains of the heart
tears within the eyes
   heads throbbing, fists
   clenching, flames burning
screams, wails, cries.

   Time never ending
death's all around
   cancer, aids,
   epidemics
that's what they have found.

   Life so short
none left to waste
   birth, mid-age,
   it's all over.
Don't be so quick to make haste.

   So much to do
no time to spare
   life's a bitch, a bowl
   of cherries, who knows,
who cares?

Amy Lynn Tavares

Dear Mother

Dear mother,
Tell me, just what did you think;
when they handed you a baby girl
dressed in pink?

Did you ever really care?
Do you wish I was there?

Do you ever wish you knew,
what kinds of things I like to do?

Do you know how easily I cry?
Do you know I'm sometimes shy?

But, after all this I can't honestly say,
that I wish you were here today.

I wonder does it hurt you,
to be the woman I met; but never knew?

Karen Clevenger

Nurse Beth

I know the moment it happened
That her smile, unexpected,
Pierced my heart.
Now I lean on her shoulder
As she guides me up the stair
To my shared room.
I know that this is love.
What else could it be?
Each day I hold my breath,
Waiting for her arrival.
When she comes through the door,
The sight of her white dress
Reminds me that love
Has come too late.
My life is almost over,
Hers hardly begun.
I would tell her (if I could speak)
Of this love, this joy.
But it must remain
An old man's secret.

Donald Gregory

"Jesus"

   He's the hands and the feet
that never admits defeat.
He's my hearts brightest song.
   He took a tree and set me free,
when the gift of love was shed.
   He took a thing and made it a ring,
to wear upon my head.
   He took a wrong and made it a song,
to sing for eternity.
   He took an old rag and made it a
flag, to fly for all to see.
   He's the king of Kings, the maker
of all things, the beginning and the
end, and I'm glad he's my special
FRIEND.

Barbara Lamping

At Peace

I'm gone.
Tears may flow.
The house may seem quiet.
Things unfinished may gather dust.
These things I will never know.

But, I remain,
for Love is strong
and Memories bring smiles and laughter
and Hearts will forever hold me.
THIS I know.

Jill M. Basar

Untitled

There are so many things
that we all share
Even the others think we
   don't care
God created us all at one
time or another
Gave some of us a sister
   or brother
So please let us pray
To God up above
To once again unite us
   in love.

Adeline Larsen

"The Wall"

You built a wall around your heart
That no one could break through
You promised yourself
No one would get close to you
Your heart has been broken
And you suffered a lot of pain
You tried to stop them
But your tears fell like rain
They hurt you so much
More than you could take
And you knew
Your heart would soon break
Brick by brick
I tried to break through the wall
I tried my best
To make the wall fall
With each brick I took away you put in two
more
Now I've lost the key to an open door
I eventually gave up there was nothing I
could do
You didn't love me, but I loved you.

Jason Houston

My Faith, The Hand Of My Soul

Thank you Lord for this faith
that you have given me,
with its warm embrace
it keeps me close to thee.

My faith is the hand of my soul
reaching out to contact thee,
seeking neither silver nor gold
nothing my eye can see.

I have no need of these things
as this earthly path I trod,
only the rapture that it brings
when my faith is in touch with God.

Sometimes I lose this touch
when I neglect my prayers,
then the rapture becomes engulfed
and tarnished by worldly cares.

So I ask that you clasp your hand
within the hand of my soul,
and keep it in your command
so my faith may never grow cold.

Irene Couts

A Challenge To Fill

There use to be a mountain
That was so very high
It was thought impossible to climb
But somehow we learn to fly

There's always been a river
That started as a stream
And as long as I can remember
Man always lived for a dream

Now they say there is a heaven
Where love like flowers grow
A place so beautiful in the sun
We all should get to know

Cause like that river and mountain
This too can be real
Cause life ain't nothin'
But a challenge to fill

Arthur Gurlly Jr.

History Repeats

I am so used to your extended absences
that this feels like just another
and I have to wonder "Is this really the
end?"
because it hardly seems real.
With you I could never see clearly
further than my hands could touch
even now I half expect your call
in the middle of the night
knowing I'd take you back
even after seeing your selfish expectations
magnified by a speakerphone in a quiet
room.

Your sharpened words cutting into me
I hardly felt the pain that should have been
there
because we've been loving each other
so long and hard and mean
that I could build you with my fingers
out of dust and your taste has become a
part of my tongue
and our tangled roots continue growing
deeper
to drink from strange waters
and I have come to expect nothing less
from you.

Diana Juhasz

God's Creations

Angels look upon the stars,
that's where God's Heavens lay.

Astronauts look upon the earth,
that's where people stay.

When we go to church
we think of God,
to Him we pray.

When I go outside I think
of a rose so beautiful and pink.

A rose is as enchanting as a new
day's dawn in May, and
soft as a cloud in a certain kind of way.

Often I stop and wonder why rose
petals are the way they are today.

Ah! They are the way they are
because God made them to say
My love shines for all on this very
special day!

Arwen Morningflower McGinnis

Family Ties

Family ties are precious bonds,
That passing time endears
For they begin with memories
Of our childhood years.
Family ties are growing bonds,
Nourished by love and laughter,
And a thousand everyday events
That are cherished ever-after.
Family ties are lasting bonds
That are woven in each heart.
To keep a family close in thought,
Together or apart.

Catherine A. Manson

A Sister's Love

To know you is to love you . . .
That's the way it's always been.
I'm so proud that you're my brother
And also my dear friend.

When we were growing up,
We shared many joys and tears.
You always took good care of me
And chased away my fears.

I was just a "little kid"
And you were my "big brother".
I'd always seem to pester you
In one way or another.

Even though we're grown up now
And living miles apart,
I'll always feel you're near me
And keep you in my heart.

I may not say it often,
But you must know I care.
May God be with you always . . .
For you, this is my prayer.

Jo Coody

Relief

Monotony:
the act of
doing something
over and over
and over again.
My life:
An endless cycle
nothing new
no change, no excitement . . .
Sometimes Death
seems
enticing,
sweet,
(something new)
an escape,
Relief.

Amanda Larger

Autumn

I see the world a million colors
That shadow the candor of natures lovers
Like a butterfly on a flowers wings
Free to fly as the soft air sings
A gentle sonnet of sweet harmony
Humming the tune inside of me

Colors fade at autumns call
And beside the sun so we fall
With our tears falling down, down, down
Desperately seeking the higher ground
That we seek no choice to be
A lonely cry the dying plead

Corey French

Untitled

There's a box in the corner
  of my room.
Like my mind,
  It is dusty and dark.
In the corner of my mind
  there is a box.
Like my room, but there's chains
  and it's locked.
Like a circuit, like the box
  in my room.
It never ends because it never begins.
Like a cycle that never opens.
Like the box that's so dusty;
Like my heart, it's so rusty.
This box, it confused me.
Says my mind "it eludes me"
It's so dusty and dark
And I speak from experience
These locks do not unlock
Says my heart "please excuse me".
    Michael Paul

Retrospect

Looking back on the remote possibility
of once upon a time
Was there "something" between us?
Did I imagine it or was there a gleam
of affection in your eyes?
Could there ever have been a
you and me.... us.... we...?

And if there was a spark, a flare,
an infinitesimal flame,
has it been extinguished
or does it will reside within
waiting to be refueled, rekindled
into a bonfire?
    Patricia Jones

Nostalgia

Some of us have fond memories
Of places once important to us,
But it's not the same anymore.

We can go back to where they were,
But not back to the way they were.
They aren't the same anymore.

There is still some nostalgia,
But we can't relieve the past.
Times aren't the same anymore.

When we try to relieve our memories,
Nostalgia plays a deceptive role.
It's not the same anymore.
    Philip J. Wicke

Intoxicating Ride

Gliding down the highway
  On a steed of pure delight,
The wind runs its fingers
  Through my hair in its flight.
The air caresses my body
  As a lovers fingers do,
With passion rushing through its need.
  It makes a hearty brew!
    Scheri Martin

Sunrise

No grander introduction
Of rank or royalty,
No welcoming more splendid
Ever could there be,
Than that of each new morning,
As the night fades away,
And a glorious sunrise
Ushers in the day.

An artist's inspiration!
It's easy to see why:
It's beauty, overwhelming,
Lights up the eastern sky.
For Kings roll out the carpet,
Blow trumpets loud and clear,
But for the birth of each new day,
A sunrise first appears.
    Ronda C. Colwell

Your Blessing Sis

Your blessing Sis, is like a gift,
of silver and of gold.
And sometimes it is almost more,
Than I have strength to hold.
Sometimes God showers so much joy,
And happiness on me.
That life is like a paradise,
Of perfect ecstasy.
And that is why I do not mind,
The time I've done in jail.
Or any hail or thunderbolt,
That makes my body frail.
I have my disappointments,
And my share of griefs.
But I always do remember, Sis
That there is some relief.
Because when I have said my prayers,
I heard God's soft reply.
And when I lift my eyes I see,
A rainbow in the sky.
    Rocky Johns

The Innocence Of Youth

Speak while I listen,
of the idleness of youth.
For my own sad existence,
is the great living proof.

While we search and we wonder,
as if lost in a haze.
All we know that's for certain
is the passing of days.

Then time seems to be endless,
Na, we will never grow old
Why, to even make mention,
You must be so bold!

But the years slip behind us,
Like the waves neath our sails.
Then at last we give over,
as our first grandchild wails!
    Stan Simpson

Differences

Many times I stand in awe
Of the things that God has done.
The different kinds of people
That we have all become.

Some people are so outgoing
While others draw away,
Some people seem so much alike,
Some different as night and day.

I look around and see the ones
That I have come to know,
And realize some differences
That each of us do show.

A different size, a different shape,
Each person is unique.
Some will talk so endlessly
While others barely speak.

I'm glad God made us different
Because how dull the world would be,
If I were just like you
And you were just like me.
    Marty Mason

The Chair

Rings
  of time,
An eon
  of existence,
Of growth,
  history.
Reaching
  bright leafed,
Knurled limbs
  embracing blue, domed sky,
Then felled,
  cut, planned, honed;
A simple Chair.
Oh, but the sights
  you have seen!
The ultimate high,
  ethereal sky,
And many a bottom!
    Simone Mary Grace

Laughter

Once an integral part
of you and me
Now seldom comes at all
Touching
Once there was never enough
Now distance reigns
Loving
Once so easily shared
Now put aside for others things
I search for you in my dreams
Reach for you in the darkness
My need so deep
For all we once were
The ache inside so real
As I grieve at the loss
Of what we could have been
What we used to be.
    Mary R. Willis

I Wish I Could

Don't get mad at me if I can't hear you
oh how I wish I could
hear the sounds that everyone should
to hear the train whistle blow
I wish it weren't quite so low
To hear the birds sing in the trees
To hear the rustling of the leaves
Blowing in the wind
To hear the raindrops on the roof
To hear the sound of ocean surf
These are the sounds that make me sad
Oh bring back that which I once had
Don't get mad at me if I can't hear you
I wish I could
Hear the sound that everyone should.

Mary Kathleen Pelikan

"Sheila, The Child"

Rescue me, I am a child
Oh save me from this wicked Wild
Save me please, but please don't say
I can't retain my childish ways

My fairy tales forsake me not
They keep me warm
when life is not
They blind me to the painful truth
And desperately maintain my youth.

And dreams, my dreams, I shan't abade
from grim reality my shade
They make me worth what I am not
and give me hope I haven't got.

Stephen B. Johnson

I Wish

I wish the sun would shine
  on a cloudy, rainy day,
I wish the moon and stars
  would never go away.

I wish life could be
  like a cloud in the sky,
I wish life would be
  where you'd never have to cry.

I wish the pain could go
  to a place I've never been,
I wish I understood
  how a heart could ever mend.

I wish now and then
  that I were some bird,
I'd wish for forever flight
  so I would not be heard.

I wish it could be that easy
  with no problems at all,
I wish for only love
  so I'd feel forever tall

Kimberly Hunefeld

Paradoxic Day

Daybreak, boisterous
paroxysm, cloudburst, tmesis
prismatic summit.

Lisa A. Valentine

The Wall

There are many heroes;
On a great wall that stands.
They represent our glory;
And fought in distant lands.
They represent pride in our country;
A country standing tall.
They risked their lives for freedom;
A freedom that belongs to us all.
All they received was their names
Engraved on a wall;
But memories of our great heroes
Will be forever standing tall.

Kelly Smith

I Was A Whisper

I was a whisper
on a purple summer day;
A tear in a river
that just washed away.

A deep black whole
that goes on for eternity:
Nothing to break my fall,
nothing to cushion me.

I was a whisper
in my mysterious crowd;
Never wanted around
like a dark, lonesome cloud.

Never to be heard,
no one to understand;
I was different
like a beach of pure black sand.

Soon I shall go,
a bit of dust on a windy day;
A tear in a river
that just washed away.

Sarah Janis Kay

Wind In The Trees

I love to wander thru the woods
on a sunny, breezy day.
And listen to the wind in the trees
and the words they seem to say.

To let my mind just wander
To another sphere or plane.
To think they might hear my thoughts
or hear me call their name.

Then I hear "Mom, I'm doing fine"
"Daughter, don't worry about me."
"Sister, we hear your thoughts
as we wander thru the trees."

My mind becomes calm and peaceful
My heart does feel at ease.
I know soon I'll walk with them
and listen to the wind in the trees.

Reba Lyon Gulley

Cosmo

Oh, Cosmo is a dapper cat.
On each small foot, a neat white spat.
His suit of gray and vest of white
Are elegantly just right.
A cane to swish up, down and back?
He has his tail—so that's no lack.
Oh, Cosmo is a dapper cat.

But mostly, he forgets all that
  and pounces and chases,
  darts, jumps and races,
  begs food, chews shoe laces,
  climbs screens, scratches on places
  he shouldn't.
In short, all elegance forgotten,
He's just a cat.
We like him like that.

Margaret C. Taylor

"This World We Live In"

We all must have someone
on something to turn to
A bird in his flight finds
a tree
A rose looks to heaven for
sunshine
I too have a need, Mon Ami
I find peace all alone in
A garden
I'm surrounded with love
on a hill
I know that "God's" love
won't desert me
Man-kind has and perhaps
always will

Marta M. Hart

Drowning

We stood there in the dust
On the tomb of the kings,
Staring into the sinking sun
The sky all around it
Coral and blue...

And I,
Lost in your eyes drowning,
Drowning in those deep pools...
Then you smiled
And I broke through the surface
Breathing again...

The sky had grown dark
As the sun fell away
We stood there in wonder
of the flickering stars
All silver and blue...

And I, wondering
How deep those pools had been
Was lost again
In the depths of your eyes...

Kevin m. Kincer

Melancholy

Slow beats my heart,
On this long day,
Slowly a tear,
Goes on it's way.

My thoughts have turn'd,
To loves long lost,
Oh' Father Time,
Dear is the cost!

Tell me how long,
Must this grief last?
How many years,
'Til this has past?

Slow beats my heart,
On this long day,
Slowly a tear,
Wends on it's way.

William H. Ball

I'm A Leaf

I'm a leaf on top of a cottonwood.
On top of a very tall cottonwood.
Reaching out for the blue of the sky.
I feel I'm close to the God's country.

Sunshine in March helped me grow up.
Warm rains in May helped me shape up.
From baby green to adolescent green.
Soon a lot of us all in mature green.

We gave shade for children to play.
In the melodious breeze we sway.
Beautiful and strong and free.
A poet called it a laughing tree.

September song was sentimental.
October gust was detrimental.
One by one our friends went away.
I hanged on though dry and wrinkly.

November chill took away more friends.
Now I'm all alone on top of a cotton wood.
When my time comes to go, Dear God,
Please gently scoop me up in your hand.

M. Josephine Bucol

What Is A Vampire?

What is a vampire?
Once a man.
Changed irreversibly into a creature
Of long-lasting life, or underneath.
A creature with a lust for blood,
Among other things.
A creature with incredible powers.
Powers physical. Powers metaphysical?
A creature that acts on its own,
Or is controlled by something within?
A creature of the night.
One that hides from its worst enemy,
The light of the sun.
A creature that should fear its prey.
A creature whose prey can fight back.
A creature whose prey is men.
A creature that is imagined.
Or a creature that is real?
Who knows?

Nathan Austin Mandehr

Ode To A Handkerchief

A pink handkerchief I can see through.
Once gorgeous and large,
now lifeless,
like the person who gave it to me.
My grandmother.
I was a few years old,
she bought it for me willingly.
Over the years it was played with...
worn...
used....
Now it is nothing but rags,
Under my dresser it lies,
with other possessions...
lost.

Katie Schlesinger

Individuality

In a room full of people,
one remains individual.
In a room full of spirits,
one stands above all.
In a room full of minds,
one determines presence.
In a room full of hearts,
one beats loudest.
In a room full of dreams,
one carries on.

Valerie Baxter

Progeny

They are like the trees,
One short, one tall.
They are like the leaves,
Every changing like the fall.

They are like the branches,
Always reaching towards the sky.
The morning dew their leaves will snatch,
For their hunger that never dies.

They are like the bark,
Growing stronger as the years go by.
And when the evening sky turns dark,
They are the stars up in the sky.

The roots they become,
When the wind blows to and fro.
From the winds gentle hum,
They never bend or begin to bow.

Yes they are like the trees,
Always together never apart.
Love for them will never flee,
For nellek or lark.

Paula L. Holden

Into Silence

Fade from the fear
Open the voices
Beyond anything real
Above all that is pain
and melt it away
Painting visions on memories
Close to forgotten
Smiling deep inside
If only to dream
Toward and until

Kenny Whitfield

Fontanelle

One look is not enough
One touch cannot control the emotions
One whisper soothes the soul
Needs more, wants more
Love overwhelms the body
One smile, one cry
At times impossible
At times wonderful
Holding, fondling
Fontanelle resting in arms
Helplessness brings tears to the eyes
Unexplainable
Unimaginable
Perfect.

Peter Hastings

Changes

Nothing stays the same, it seems,
Only that, that's in your dreams,
First it's one thing, you think it is,
Day to day you try to live,
Changes come with no concern,
Suddenly, it makes a turn,
Try to live from day to day,
Tomorrow is too far away,
The pace too fast, and I'm too slow,
When I start to change,
Then this you'll know,
It's time, dear Lord,
   For me to go!
      Guess I'll never change.

Leona Cliburn

Untitled

The tiny bud, the child's eyes,
open so wide, toward the sky,
reaching outward, all around,
intrigued with life, wonders abound.

The child grows into adult.
Summer brings Spring to a halt.
The wonder seems to disappear.
The days pass by as do the years.

Looking back, Summer's so brief.
Lore and color, now clothe each leaf.
Quiet beauty has settled in.
Wonder sparkles, once again.

Winter's blanket, white and cold,
shimmers across the days of old.
Still childlike eyes, gleam within,
spirit awaiting to begin.

Terri Thomas

Untitled

Stare into the darkness
Peer into the night
Immerse yourself in shadows
Suspend your need for light
There is no hope for lucid dreaming
with life in the obscure
You've ventured into darkness
submerged your mind in fear.....

Michael S. McCracken

Who Am I?

Who am I?
Please tell me
I sit and think, I might be shy
They say, "Who is she?"
I pace day and nigh
Am I just another Sara Lee?
Who am I?
Please tell me
Why don't I know who I am, why?
Who will I be?
Am I as pretty as Dee?
Always to myself I deny
Who am I?
Please tell me.

Maggie Friedl

I'm A Poor Mutt

I'm nothing but a has been,
Or so I have been told.
They make me eat broccoli
And things that look like mold.
I sleep outside in the shed.
At least I'm out of the rain.
A potato sack for my head.
How I want a sugar cane!
My birthday was forgotten,
Got no Halloween treat.
The only thing they gave me
Was some cheese that smelled like feet.
The people who I live with
Don't ever seem to care.
When I'm sad or lonely,
They're never really there!
Like I said in the first line,
I'm nothing but a has been.
But once I did sneak some good food.
I am a dog, that is my sin!

Susan Fore

Full Circle

If I save but one life
or teach one unknowing
than my life is not in vain.

As I reach out to one alone,
or guide one through the pain,
I am jealous of my attention.

For it is I that needs guidance
to learn again to be.
For I am that lonely figure,
I am the one in pain.

So if there is one life
that needs to be saved,
take the risk and reach out;

for that one is mine.

Sharron Unger

In My Garden

I walked in my garden at twilight
reminiscing of our love so true,
when we walked together an promised
each other we will always be true,
as I sat watching the brook rippling
on by with the fragrance of fresh
flowers in the air,
I will wait here my darling till
we can walk in my garden as a pair.

Vina Pusateri

Tomorrow

Always there will be tomorrow,
Or that's what most people say —
When you'll be free of the sorrow
And the pain you feel today.

When the new day has its dawning
And your hopes are riding high,
You will feel that your potential
Is no lower than the sky.

In the glory of a sunrise
Clouds are sure to fade away
As you gaze into the blue skies
Of another perfect day!

Soon you'll feel no trace of sadness,
Strength will quickly smother pain.
Faces 'round you will be smiling
And reflecting cheer again.

So be careful not to worry,
Not to fret and not to grieve,
Joy will surely come tomorrow —
If you truly can believe.

Melvin Gammage

The Penguins

Our noses are frozen,
Our feet are too numb,
We stand in a circle
And feel pretty dumb.

We are birds you see,
But cannot fly.
We swim in the ocean
Instead of the sky.

We're found in Antarctica
Where it is freezing cold,
Our diet is fish
Even when we are old.

We do not do tricks
Like a lion or bear,
I'm sure if we did
No one would care.

Life as a penguin
Is truly unfair,
Most of us wish
We could fly through the air.

Lisa M. Einhorn

"Memories Never Say Goodbye"

There are special moments
Our heart can not erase
There are special times
That have memories to embrace

There are also special people
Whose love they freely share
To light our path, in life's road
A precious gem, so rare

My mother, is one of those people
Who has a special place in my heart.
The sparkle, the twinkle in her eye
Brought joy to me, from the very start

Let me tell you, that I hear
The angels singing on high
They are singing a special song to me
The song is:... "Memories never say
Goodbye"

Marilyn J. Trainor

"Forever Yours"

You took my hand and led me
   Out of the darkened night.
You touched my lips so passionately
   And made it feel so right.
You held me in your arms
   And sheltered me from the rain
You touched my body with your own
   And washed away the pain
Your gentle fingers wiped my eyes
   And washed away my tears
Your gentle voice whispered to me
   And turned away my fears
Each time I look at you I seem
   To want you more and more
And deep inside my heart I know
   I am forever yours.

Sjah Y. Short

Rain

Flowers, trees, bushes, rain
Outdoors, outside, plants, rain
Oceans, lakes, rivers, rain
Mountains, hills, plains, rain
Grass, dirt, sand, rain
Fields, yards, glades, rain
Moon, sun, stars, rain
Galaxy, milkyway, rain
Forest, woods, boonies, rain
Leaves, stems, petals, rain
Storm, lighting, thunder, rain
Woodlanders, foresters, pets, rain
Animals, people, machines, rain
Wings, beaks, talons, rain
Paws, claws, fangs, rain
Tails, feathers, fur, rain
Scales, fins, gills, rain
Hooves, ears, eyes, rain
Water, everywhere is rain.

Tonia Berry

Light

That light
Outside my bedroom window
Shining thru
In subtle tones of white and
Silver gray

Like magic
Turns familiar into fantasy
And night
Becomes a place where
Shadows play

The trees
Which in the daytime seemed
Such friends
Now send grasping fingers down
My wall

And just
About the time I'm most afraid
My mom
Turns on my light and
Ends it all!

Suzanne McGrath

Euonymous

Stagnant I'm not,
overgrown with life,
a kudzu vine
entwined
in too much of itself,
a portrait green.

Not finished or new,
exploring pilgrim, vaguely lost,
I inch across
into uncharted
fertile, fallow ground.

Sprawling or
strangling
or giving birth?
Life and death do coexist
in splendid union
kissed,
by instant need.

Ruth-Anne G. Hammes

UNTITLED/UNSIGNED

I long to be with you

NOW

Even in the never-nor-dare-ever

ALLOW

SOMEHOW

Love does contain

The single pain

We learn

To smile to....

Would that you

Ask me once

Could that I

Say "I do"

YES...YES...YES

NOW you
Owe me two
QUES...
tions.

Mila Vonderheid

Memories Of Love

I never really felt much,
Pain encompassed every day,
These feelings seemed to be such,
That there was no other way.

But a special gift God gave to me,
When I was but a child,
It came to me so easily,
My heart rejoiced and smiled.

For when I smiled the sun came,
And I suddenly felt alive,
My life took on a different frame,
When she finally did arrive.

Her name was "teacher" and also
"friend,"
And she gave with all her heart
Memories I'll cherish-never to end,
For it's love she did impart.

Kathleen M. Anthony

Untitled

Like specters from ages past, we
pass over the railway track.
The iron rails divide the forest
prime evil and the garden of stone.
On the wind the sirens wail to
me, the Pendragon reborn with Merlin
ny my side.
Autumn chill, dragons breath,
purgatory, burning leaves and
crystal care.
The store Angel of my deep desires
touched my face.
His unicorn heart and sylvan
lips capture mine with the heady
wind of medieval zephyr.
Excalibur shatters my gargoyle
of defence as his kisses lay waste
the garden nosferatu.
"Patri Draus, whilst thou be my
king?" the dark Queen of Mysteries cries.

Shelly Isenhoff

Heaven

Into the depth of darkness
Past the shining glimmer of the stars
Lies a place
A place of ease and comfort
All held is of love and pleasure
Peace and kindness
Heart and soul
Not a problem or worry
Just care and sentimental ideas
With no consequences and no fears
And as the dawn breaks
And casts the light upon the stars
Everything beautiful fades away

J. Alexander Evans

Beads

Pretty beads, refreshing, dancing
 pit-a-pat, pit-a-pat on the deck
All-a-wash

Glassy beads varnished, refinished
Sealed radiance
 pit-a-pat, pit-a-pat
All-a-glow

Beads of sweat off a brow
Droplets working free
Beads in rows straight and narrow
Growing secretly

Beads, bonds, and plowshares
Furnaced from the deserts of pioneers
Tarried time come forward
In glass hardware

Marbled beads in an apothecary jar
Kept in the ground safe
Once lost, then found
Pretty beads
All-a-wonder

Marian K. Baker

Life

Like a violin
playing its romantic notes
like a guitar
strumming the songs
from the heart
early in the morning
I listen to the breeze
singing to me
the gentle songs nature brings
birds are singing
trees are swaying
rivers rippling
oceans soothing
do you hear my songs
that my heart is playing
all day long my mind is humming
to the gentle sounds
and the melodies surrounding me
life is but music
waiting to be sung

Martha Arellanes

Seasons

Daffodils and April showers,
Poems of love and fields of flowers,
 It's spring!

Picnics, vacation - a break from school,
Suntans, the seashore, fun's the rule.
 It's summer!

Crunchy leaves and golden skies,
Brisk, crisp air and pumpkin pies.
 It's autumn!

Shorter days with snow and ice,
Roaring fires make it nice.
 It's winter!

Mary Ellen Hess

Diana's Place

How I sit upon my balcony,
pondering thought that meant to me.
Thoughts of hurts, love, and serenity.
That's how I sit upon my balcony.

Looking out upon the ocean,
thinking—Why aren't I'm happy?
Where is the magic potion?

I seek for El Rey "THE KING OF THE
SEA",
for answers that are beyond me.
And then, at once, I get a sense of
serenity.

 I'M HAPPIEST SITTING ON MY
BALCONY!!!

D. M. Cazarez

Crossroads

Spirit has no ethics,
rides dark wisdom,
runs stark wild.
Flares in shadows dancing,
unexpectedly subsides.
Conjures up blind crossings
where serenity and madness
must tenderly collide.
Then delivers sanity,
their quiet only child.

Susan Ritter

The Rain

Another year,
Pooling of tears,
Humid with dreams,
Storms without you.

Sheets of sleet,
Cascade my heart,
Cold and hollow,
The empty safe.

Unforgettable dreams,
Drafty, yet sweet,
Awakes me,
Thinking of you.

Sweet, but so
Brief. Long, it
Has been so long.
Since the last

Time I was awake
And was drenched
By my dreams
Of you.

Lori S. Kaderavek

Home

Apple apple in my eye.
Premium milk,
The wolf has died.
The chair stands watching,
The couch has cried,
The table loathes,
And the bed can fly.
The door so opens,
Passes itself.
The carpet bathes,
And it hugs itself.
The oven reeks,
of a jaded pie.
Apple apple in my eye.

Sean Thibodeau

The Man From Yesterday

Another relationship down the drain,
Puppy love is such a strain.
His, the name I won't forget,
He hasn't learned to like me yet.

Just to be my life-long friend,
While he has someone else to tend.
Why does it have to be this way,
Why can't love come to stay?

Nothing I give is good enough for him,
To him, I seem a light that's too dim.
Faithful, and yes, I stayed by his side,
But near her alone is where he'll abide.

Here I remain by myself,
Tossed like a doll on the highest shelf.
Alone and rejected, here I'll stay,
And I'll dream of the man from yesterday.

Tiffany O'Quinn

Bravo (Company - B)

B - is for the bravery we have
R - is to remind you that we care
A - is for our all and all and all
V - is for the Victory we share
O - is only to remind you we are
    The tough and the bold
When you put it all together it
    Spells bravo
Company - B the whole wide
    World should know
Company - B I thank GOD
    For you so

Linda A. Merkison

Remember

Remember it doesn't always have to
rain before you see a rainbow.
Not every flower is perfect, just like
anything else.
Remember to follow your dreams and
never let them go.
Never forget the sky is the limit,
the sun will light your way as the
stars do, the rain will help your
love and everyone else's to grow and
the rainbow is the sign of happiness
and will someday be your pathway
to heaven.
Always remember I love you and
when I look at the sky I will
see the same thing.

Rennie Lucius

Memories

Fall leaves from the trees
red, yellow, gold and brown
fall leaves upon the ground
from shades of green
in trees so tall
from green to brown
and then to fall
Memories are like the leaves
swaying in gentle breeze
Memories in trees so tall
turn gold, turn brown
and then they fall
Yes they'll fall
there comes a time
Memories of yours
and those of mine

R. D. Sauers

Lost Innocence

Angelic eyes full of innocence
    reflective pools of light
hide from this darkened night
Take thyself captive
    in a sea of mist
Devil's advocate closes in for your soul
    words do not escape
breathless whispers left unknown
    Belong this you do not
Devilish eyes peer through your heart
Flesh and blood, bone to bone
    for you have been torn apart
Unrecognized you have become
    Blink of an eye
Now slowly you wilt and die

Krissy Grant

The Twilight Horseman

Powerful steed beneath his heel,
Riding night with arms of steel.
With the moon's angelic embrace,
And the helm upon his face.
He knows bravery and songs of deed,
In battle he will always lead...
And lo!
He leaves with the dawn,
To reappear with weapons drawn.

Ryan Mitchell

Night

Night comes to soon with its
    rising stars
    rising moon
Darkness engulfing everything
    in its path leaving nothing
    to spare for it don't care about
    A child's fright
    a sleepless night
Its full moon without a
cloud in sight the fear
insinuated with darkness, night,
fear to turn out the light
fear to close your eyes
fear of what's waiting
for you in the night
But, darkness slowly turns
to the early morning light
and the night slowly disappears
Along with all your fears.

Tisha Wesseldine

Reflections

Raindrops falling, gently beating
    rivulets on my window pane.
Life remembered, slowly fleeting
    tears upon my cheek do stain.

Loving always, warm affection
    seeing life unfold anew.
Life departing, souls unleashing
    wilting flowers in the dew.

Loved ones come, departing always
    children grow so soon it seems.
Tightly hold them, while they're with us
    help them mold their future dreams.

Striding slowly, meadows blooming
    footsteps crush the morning grass.
Birds arising, loudly cursing
    secret homes within the ash.

Wind gusts blowing, whistling past me
    sadness finally disappears.
Warming sunlight, rays that blind me
    smiling through remaining years.

Pamela Weil

I Love You

As the sun arises every day
So don't you and I.
We always say good morning
To the one's we love, the most
And every night when we go to
Bed we say good night to the
one we love the most.
    I love you.
    The most

Mary Wilt

Wintertime

Snow, cold, dreary.
Romantic, carriages, fireplaces.
Holidays, families, gatherings.
Food, laughter, singing.
Lights, music, trees.
Snow - big flakes, small flakes,
all shapes and sizes.
Sledding, skiing, skating.
Snuggliness, lovingness, kindness.
Warmth, caring, giving, receiving.
Happiness.   Joy.
Wintertime.

Nicole Karaffa

A Collection Of Haiku

FALSE SPRING

Fat hyacinth bulbs,
Roused by a warm winter sun,
Shiver in the night

PATIENCE

The old orange cat
Stares through the cold, dark window,
Pale eyes holding mine.

CONCERTO

The sweet violins
Pierce my cool and armored heart,
Singing wild and free.

HARVEST MOON

The pale, swollen moon,
Released from its daytime bonds,
Haunts the cold, clear night.

Lois Lannin

Together In The Sand

They laughed and played together,
    running across the sand,
And stopping only briefly,
    catching their breath as they ran.
They had never seen the ocean,
    the power of its waves,
Or the beauty of its beaches,
    felt the coolness of its breeze.
In the sand they built their castle,
    while the tide was at its ebb,
And stood and watched together
    as the water reclaimed its land.
They cried for joy at shells they found,
    watched crabs crawling to the sea,
And widened their eyes in wonder
    at gulls sailing the ocean breeze.
They laughed and played together,
    their first day in the sand,
And tonight they watched the stars come out
    and then fell asleep — my sons.

William Allen Walker

Endometriosis

Jagged pain
Running through my body
Aching everywhere
Moods are up
          and
             down
Swinging everywhere
Never ending pain that controls my body
HELPLESSNESS
No control over emotions
Which brings HATE and DESPAIR
Always there gnawing at my life
Taking my body
PIECE by PIECE
and R-I-P-P-I-N-G apart my soul
NO CURE
Which brings hopelessness
All ALONE in this pain
Which leaves me....

.........HELPLESS.......

Tiffany Marie Shield

Rivers Of God

Rivers of God
Runs through our veins
Filling our hearts
And mountains and plains
Washing our spirit
Free from sin
Cleansing the soil
To plant again
Bringing forth harvest
of spirit and soul
to sift the good
and tally the toll.

Sherri Patton

Love

Love is like the river,
Rushing strongly from side to side,
Love is like the ocean,
When you are watching the coming tide,
Love is like the valley,
Where the lions growl and roar,
And love is like that day,
When you came knocking at my door.

Yes, love is very special,
To everyone indeed,
But, love is even more special,
When it's you loving me.

Kristin Heller

Silent Scream

Crystalline waters,
Sapphire skies.
Pain in tears
Shed from her eyes.

Freedom once gained
Apparently lost...
Will she rise like a phoenix?
Or to the ocean be tossed?

Plundered by Greed,
Corruption, and Crime
Her people were always
Ahead of their time...

Kelly Youngquist

Love Ago

Jacoby of Lion's Head
Rushing wither hands to meet me
Laughter ringing shining starward
Bands of wrinkles shadow headstream.

I could never love another
With young Jacoby's wondrous face
Brightest eyes in purest simple
Forest clothes in handsome flight.

In my dress of oaken flowers
I approach the wood-crest glen
Softly spoken eyes of aqua
Lilith fingers showing ways.

We a pair of blessed creatures
Stowing apples in our breasts
Quiet feet on earthen pathways
Find each other everlast.

Sandra Lee Fulgoney

Collecting Novembers

The falling leaves
sail through mist
glide down past
a wet country that turns

into a road
a truck
a rush
the leaves settle

November's dust
wrapped in plastic
bags thrown in the back of locked
sheds behind the stucco

pages of a photo album
voices in the corner
echo with the faint familiar
still in the yellow
lights of the window frame
when trucks go by

Krzysztof Sacinski

My Firstborn Son

I've given birth to my firstborn son
Saw all his firsts, now he's one
Independent and says "I can do"
Just looked up and now he's two
can ride a 2 wheeler so carefree
my goodness gracious, now he's three
He does cartwheels out the back door
Can it be that, now he's four?
So energetic and alive
Ready for schooling, now he's five
Doing Karate chops and kicks
With a wink of an eye, now he's six
Praying to God up in heaven
My little boy just turned seven
Growing up fast, my boy won't wait
Hold on a minute! Now he's eight
My son is handsome and fine
I wasn't there for birthday nine
Feels like yesterday he was born
my firstborn son that I adore!

Trina M. Stone

Watchful Eyes

Watchful eyes waiting still
Searching for the way to feel.
Confusing thoughts cloud your mind
You're looking for a clearer sign.
A tender touch upon your cheek
You look at him your knees go weak.
The love you feel he'll never know
This hidden love can never show.
As painful as the thought might be
You can't express your love for he.
The feelings of guilt are growing strong
This burning passion for him is wrong.
You long to feel his warm embrace
See the smile upon his face.
In peaceful dreams you hold him tight
Somehow here it all seems right.
You're falling and you're falling fast
For a love that could not last.
My body aches when you're not here but
when you are I feel the fear.
For all the thoughts I can't explain I have
no one but me to blame.

Victoria K. Falconburg

Life

　　You are helpful, you
see people threw, you bring the
sun and moon, you make people
get up in the morning, you make you
wonder about you, you make people see
the truth, you make the world go around,
you are always on time, you make
people sad, you hurt people threw
your disaster, you can make us all
wet, you make people come together,
you are the reason for the news,
you are the reason for green peace,
you make the world riches,
you know everyone who walks on
the grass, you feel the hurt of
the trees as they get cut down,
you are what makes the world
work, you are LIFE

Lisa M. Bishop

Untitled

Look about you as you move around
See the wonders to be found
Wonder, wonder everywhere
See the grass beneath your feet
Calling out "look at me, look at me
I am here, framing flowers and trees
—Almost everything you see"
Feel the wind caress your cheek
As it choreographs the leaves
Watch the fluttering humming bird
Sipping nectar from the flowers
And the eagle soaring high
In the vastness of the sky
Open wide your heart, your mind
And be aware there are wonders,
Wonders everywhere
And all of them are free

Lydia Leona McIlroy

Invisible Hands

Someone from above
Sent you my way.
Someone watches over
Each passing day.

Invisible hands
Guided us together.
Invisible hands
Knew what we would find.

Hands unseeable but felt
Making us stronger.
Showing us love
Is all that matters.

With skillful perception,
These protective hands
Molded two separate lives
Into one heart.

Our love is held
In the comfort
And the warmth of
Invisible hands.

Skip R. Zagorski

Untitled

Faun form he frolics
shattering my solitude
skipping cavorting flippantly
freeing my imagination
to wildest fantasy

Creature of sun fountains
and lightly falling air
a priest of errant air
a priest of errant daffodils
closing in sun drunken
disarray at moon time

If naiads dream
in sleeping trees
it must be of
puckish dancers
such as he

Wild hair
furry ears
nimbly leaping
goat feet

C. L. White

Adversity

In her cruel arms she takes him
She bends him, but doesn't break him,
Although it hurts,
she molds him,
Teaches him patience
While she scolds him,
A friend or foe is what he asks her
I am friend and one day you'll know sir
All the time you're sure you hate me
But given time you will embrace me.
I am friend,
I am adversity

Laura Thompson

Give Us Your Hungry

With matted hair and sandaled feet
She held a sign that read
"Will work for food" - nothing more
Not coin nor clothes were pled.

Searching for reasons in her eyes
That brought her to this plight
I wanted a tale that terrified
To make my gift seem right.

What is this need to justify
Giving from the heart
Auditing her life was I
Ah-smugness from the start!

Where she goes or what she's been
Is not my place to be
Her doors to hope are present
And I handed her a key

With lowered eyes and quickened step
My people pass her by
Once beyond, with guilt now gone
I heard Miss Liberty sigh.

Lori Campanelli

Ocean Mover

The ocean mover moves with Grace
She is a girl with a pretty face
She wear a beautiful skin tight gown
And upon her head lay a beautiful crown
When she pushes the water ashore
Her beautiful fins touch the floor

Sara O. Laing

Black Woman

BLACK WOMAN, strong and versatile.
SHE is a queen to black man.
SHE is a nurturer to black child.
BLACK WOMAN DIVINE!

SHE is a shining star in the sky.

HER mind a taproot,
　　always thirsting for knowledge.
HER heart, pure as gold,
　　filled with love from her soul.

A BLACK WOMAN walks with a stride,
　　full of finesse and pride.

BLACK WOMAN unique,
　　never to be duplicated,
　　can never be underestimated

　BLACK WOMAN!!!

Stephanie L. Kidd

Green Thumb

Each year in the spring
She plants a few seeds
But all that come up
Are a few hardy weeds
So down she went
To the corner store
To buy oodles of flowers
To plant at her door
Now when folks stops by
With praise enthusiastic
She never lets on
That her posies are plastic.

Viola Southin

Mother's Day

My mom is really wonderful
She is good to me.
She helps me with my homework
And is as nice as can be.

Whatever she does,
She does it right.
When I ask her to help
She can because she's bright.

I know she gets mad at me
When I don't clean my room
She goes to then closet
And comes back with the vacuum.

She always nags at me
To play with my little sister
She doesn't understand
She's just my little sister.

My mom she gets real mean
Just like a mother
But that doesn't bother me
Cause I still love her.

Sharron Maria Diggs

Misty

There is a horse named Misty
She is pretty nifty.

I once rode her.
She has pretty white fur.

Her back is covered with dots.
Her name is always full of knots.

She sometimes has a stall.
Barely ever in the Fall.

I don't ride her anymore.
Guess what! She almost broke the door.

Now I ride Katrina.
Who never belonged to Nina.

I rode Misty on an english saddle.
She never fought in a battle.

I ride Katrina Western.
I really have to be stern.

I really miss Misty.
I hope she lives to be fifty.

Well that's all.
I have to go clean her stall.

Sara Johnson

Darkness

Darkness
Silence all around
Light shows
Going through your
Mind
You see
Lions and Lambs
Playing in the meadow
Ravens and doves
Flying formation
God
Then
You open your eyes
Darkness

Richard E. Preheim Sr.

On Trial

What did I do so wrong?
She was sitting there asking for it
Sitting there in that glove of
A mini dress
And carrying on with every male
That surrounded her
Tricking her was easy
She fed on every line
And was hypnotized by my presence
My face showed love
My heart felt hate

No outright screams
Or physical traces

Now the crack of a gavel
Threatens
As I face
Judgement.

Tracy Allyn Warrick

My Little Sister

My little sister is two,
she wrecks everything I do,
from projects to games,

She drives me insane,
that's what little sisters do.
If you try to give,

Her a nap at noon,
if you never seen anger,
you will see it soon.

She eats like a horse,
oh of course that's what little
Sisters do to you.

But she's kind a cute,
when she's not a little brute.
My little sister.

Steele Kott

Untitled

Somewhere out there
She yearns and she calls
Are we separated by oceans?
Or, perhaps only walls?

Having yet to meet me
Will she settle for something less?
As I, myself, have compromised
I humbly must confess

Although the odds are astronomical
That someday our paths will cross
I still dream of her often
As I turn and toss

My heart holds a reservoir
To flow with love for her
For all that I am longing
Her love will be the cure

Will we really ever find each other?
And share our loving fate?
The possibility that we might not
Tears me apart to contemplate

J. Peverly Saunders

Empty

There sits the cradle,
shrouded with a white blanket.
Empty, so empty.

She stands at the door
remembering her lost dreams.
Empty, so empty.

He stands next to her,
but she shows no emotions.
Empty, so empty.

He can remember—
a few drinks, a fight, a fall.
Empty, so empty.

Her heart is broken,
like his feeble promises.
Empty, so empty.

What once was alive,
she will never have again.
So very empty.

Lynn Trall

"The American Rodeo Cowboy"

The American Rodeo Cowboy,
    Silver spurs upon his boots,
Ridin' tall upon his saddle,
    Ragin' bulls within their chutes,
Levis and bright belt buckle,
    Brimmed hat upon his head,
The time it now approaches,
    To meet the bull "Big Red".
Now when that gate bursts open wide,
    And out snorts hell on hoofs,
He's stompin' left, he's stompin' right,
    Must beat his every move.
Eight seconds upon mean killer beef,
    It's hoofs and horns can kill,
But for the Rodeo Cowboy,
    It's the fans, the ride, the thrill.
So when the day is done and gone,
    And luck has seen him through,
It's the American Rodeo Cowboy,
    A friend to me and you!

Ralph B. Lopez

"Simira"

Simira's my Mother
Simira's my sister
Simira's my friend
With a significant other
When she walks down the street
The trees bow their heads
With their leaves rustling in the wind
They wave to her
But she is steady as she
Walks with a destination
The sun swoops down to greet her
She smiles with a light of her own
Here she comes draped in her
African attire, she's a proud
Beautiful black woman setting
The world of fire.

Zita Ann Hymes

Moonset

Two days ago I watched a moonset
Simultaneously with a sunrise
The more brilliant became the sun
The humbler the moon slid away

It did not seem to me
A contestation
Rather it was a lesson
In harmony
And the beauty that results
When we complement
One another
Let's try it early this morning!
You be the sun
I'll be the moon

Mary C. Rowland

Poet In Prison

How long has it been
Since you have seen
  milkweed:
  Down and seed
Blow in the wind?

How oft do you find,
Caught in your mind,
  Day-dream,
  web and gleam,
Etched on your heart,

How oft do you start,
In world apart,
  Stanza
  (Bonanza)
Spread on a page?

How oft does your "cage",
Cleansed of all rage,
  Lightened
  And heightened —
Burst with your love?

Madge Chidlaw

"Music Of The Bow"

The music of the bow
sings to me a melody
standing watch by the spirit

Waves strumming the side
as the water rushes by
winds gently whistling, thru the rail

The porpoise splash, an occasional whale
a night birds cry
the vessel joins in with a creak

The enormity of the sea
orchestrating music for me
playing a sonata, from the bow

Riding up and down, an exhilarating trip
I feel I'm a part of the ship

Looking aft, to the billowing sails
tantalizing, as great dazzling breasts
is it their strength, or shape, that so
enraptures

I wonder, how long have seamen felt
the desire to sing with their ship
accompanied by the music from the bow

R. E. Caldwell

Untitled

Tabula Rasa is the mind
Sitting here like a mime.
Know of nothing that's around
Feet not firmly on the ground.
Life goes on without a care
Left behind, and in the dust.
No love around, just a frame of mind
And everything eventually dies.

Rachel Dougherty

Untitled

There we were
Sitting side by side
In the room.
With nothing to hide
Holding a conversation
With wander in our minds
When we're together
I feel so at ease
He says we are only friends
And I feel that too.
But what's going to happen
If one of us draws to close
Will things remain the same
Or does it really have to change
Because we are suppose to be
  just two friends

Patricia Haines

The Way You Make Me Feel

Like a fragile, beautiful butterfly
Skipping through the air
Playing tag with the gentle breezes
Living it's brief life fully

Like a playful, lively kitten
Racing around the house
Pouncing on everything it sees
So full of adventure and glee

Like a fast moving mountain brook
Tumbling and leaping
With gusto and force
Through its' twisting, turning bed

Like a little child
Reaching out tentatively with
Exploring senses
Ready to laugh and love completely

So many feelings you create in me - so many

Sandra M. Ward Gursky

Untitled

Drip dried dreams
slowly scatter through sheets,
finding their way
to the girl who remains,
but there I lay with my disease
alive to hope.
So saturated this mind of mine
with thoughts of her,
was my heart destined to die?
for I find the sword
twisting and turning,
my essence quick to absorb it.....

Michael Dudley

Listen For Silent Words

Lo, watch the wind blow.
Smell that what it is, subtle.
Feel that which it does, surrounds.
Taste and know that it is
The breath of life.
Listen to whom it calls,
Your name.
And so it is just the same.
He who makes the wind blow
Lo, he has made us too,
Even my love for you.
Watches inside my heart.
Smells that what it is, burning.
Feels that which it does, longs.
Tastes and knows that it is
Salt in the rain.
Listens to whom it calls, your name.

Robin Sunde

Snow

Snow is white
Snow is soft
Snow is slippery
Snow is fluffy
Snow is pretty
Snow comes from the sky
Snow comes in different shapes
Snow comes in different sizes
Snow comes in a lot
Snow comes in a little
Snow comes everywhere

Summer Capasso

Endless Possibilities

  Cocoon-like,
  Snug deep in the fleecy
  Pockets of Time,
  Unknown to the clash and
  Clacking of the World,
  I float;
  I bounce.
  My significance is yet to be.
  I backstroke comfortably,
  Body and soul curled
  In the magic web
  Of Hope.
Unmarked, unpinched, unscathed
  By hand or tongue or pride,
  Purely, chastely waiting,
  For birth.

Saralyn J. Richard

Nature

Nature is a beautiful sight,
So delicate and delightedly bright,
Filled with lovely brilliant colors,
Plants, butterflies, and flowers.
Colors as dark as the midnight sky,
Can hold someone's breath till they die.

Kari Caldwell

The School Bus Driver

We get to work at time each day,
so eager to be on our way.

To take our precious cargo to school
so they can learn the golden rule.

But as we do the job we love,
our strength is given from up above.

One driver has gone astray today.
Now we are all made to pay;
for something that we didn't do!

But that's o.k. we know the truth;
that "were in love with what we do!"

So when you hear upon the news
a school bus driver has been accused.

Please do not abuse the rest,
because we just might be the best!

Sharon L. Atkinson

Whom Will I Leave?

God, who made the universe
  So easy to admire,
Have man a gift called, "free will",
  To choose what he'd desire.
A meteor that's burning out
  Becomes a "wishing star"
Yet God, in His magnificence,
  Caused it from a far.
In learning all about the earth,
  About its people, too..
Man forgets his own creator
  To choose his point of view.
But surely as our very earth
  Revolves around the sun,
Our will must be in time with God's
  So that His will be done.
Let us kneel to our Creator
  For we are His creation
And celebrate the gift of life
  By serving with elation!

Margaret Peterson

"A Tiny Rosebud"

A tiny rosebud can mean so much
So I'm sending you one today
A tiny rosebud means sincerity
From a loving heart to say

Each petal means I'm grateful
For all the things you do
And to let you know in every way
It fills my heart with gratitude

When the petals wither and fall
And they are scattered all about
Each and every one of them
Is the love my heart gives out

A tiny rosebud can mean so much
So I'm sending you one to say
A tiny rosebud means sincerity
From my heart to yours today

As a lovely rose unfolding
Will bring new beauty into view
May all your dreams in the future
Bring new happiness to you

Mary Lovell

Time

So much can be gained,
  so much can be lost.
For time is the prize,
  and time is the cost.

With time there are memories,
  with time we forget,
Some places we've been,
  and people we've met.

And then comes the cut
  of that familiar old line,
"I would have, I could have,
  if I just had the time".

If time could stand still
  or this moment would last,
We'd have no future
  or thoughts from the past.

So remember this
  when you're pondering 'whys',
When you want less it lingers,
  when you need more it flies.

Teresa Nicole Ross

Devil's Mission

All alone I feel
So much, no one can heal.
No one shows they care -
So with this, I try to bare
My heart from pain,
But so far, there's nothing to gain.
The laughing and taunting will not end -
So I will show them what I send.
Death to all, this glorious night -
No matter how hard they try to fight.
Each one will get there prize -
Without being the less wise.
They see it coming, oh yes they do -
The sky is turning an evil blue.
Here I come, to return your deed -
All you should do, to me, is heed.
My anger is burning -
As the hour is turning.
Beware of my spirit, which haunts -
It is you my appetite wants.

Lisa Williams-Raykovich

My Garden

Little flower
so tiny
water and sun
a sweet song
a special place in my heart
see you grow
today my seedling
tomorrow my bloom
Oh! So fast
I see you shine
one little flower
among the rest
I see only you, no more
your the best.
You are my creation
my years of hard work
for that season of bloom
you are worth.
In my heart and my soul
forever, you will never be old.

LuAnn Russo

Similes Of Life

Life is like a lion
  so strong and full of might.

Life is like a distant star
  that sparkles in the night.

Life is like a puzzle
  that's made of many parts.

Life is like a lover
  we love with open hearts.

Life is like a sunny day
  that greets us with a smile.

Life is like a raging storm
  that blows for quite a while.

Life is like a diamond
  so filled with beauty rare.

Life is like a precious gift
  a gift that we all share.

Life is full of smiles.
That fact is very true.
Sit down and think about your life
And what it means to you.

Sheila B. Roark

Answers

I needed you then
So where have you been?
You left me too soon
To understand me, to know me.

So far from me
Did you wish to be?
Broken trust, anger, confusion
These left for me.

Did you care
when you weren't there?
Did you care
when I was scared?

My innocence
  lost
in a sense
  to you.

Daddy...
Is that who you are?
Tell me then,
where have you been?

Kimberly Rae

From The Shadow....

Standing in the cool night air,
  soft white skin and silky hair.
From the shadow she moves with grace,
  she's closer now, I see her face.
Eyes of fire her passion burns,
  day and night for her I yearn.
A scent, a touch, a gentle kiss,
  throughout the day it's her I miss.
The smile, the gaze, the whisper too,
  the her I write about is you!

Michael D. Bender

Lamentations

What a soothing means to cleanse!
Softness, purity, and innocence,
Overshadow the stern and probing
glimpse.
How creatively sculptured,
Just two eyes!

R. D. Griffith

Untitled

We are all like flowers;
Some are flashy or showy
Some are plain but perfect,
Some are naturally pretty
Some are lovely!
Some are classic
Some are short-lived
Some are tall and big

But, what makes us all the same;
Our distinct differences that make us
UNIQUE!

Laura Duffy

Roads

Many roads I've traveled
some happy and some blue
I've many roads to tread,
I hope, before I will be through
From my travels I've obtained
items I hold dear
I hope I will have many more
this time, perhaps, next year
As I walk down these roads
Many thoughts pass through my head
I look forward to each new road
with hope, quite rarely dread
I look up to my Father for
guidance and advice
Many people I meet are courteous
but some, well, just aren't nice
This poem, of life, a metaphor
To which I hope you can relate
No road is the same as the previous
But I find that quite great!

Ralph William Evans II

What Is True Love

What is the meaning of True love,
Some says it's when a man feels
something for a woman, or the
other way around, but what if
a man feels something for
another man, or a woman feeling
something for another woman?
I think true love is an emotion
that anyone can have for anyone else.

Shawn Gregory

Rapture

Beings hurtling through now
Starpoints in all that is
Find a moment of matter
Upon which to train their love -
A choice
Forever altering the song of time.

Rhys Stevenson

Untitled

To someone special and true
Someone as perfect as you.
I want to say
we gone a long way.

But through it all
You've held my hand
and helped me understand
That we were meant to be
together you and me.

Priscilla Villavicencio

"I Love You"

I love you
Something people like to say
not knowing what it really means.
It is a very strong emotion
that can cause a lot of pain
it is used quite often by people
but do they really mean it
saying I love you should be saved
for someone very, very special

Terra Laughton

Sometimes

Sometimes - the load is too heavy
Sometimes - my faith is too small
Sometimes - the pain overwhelms me
Sometimes - I can't even crawl
Sometimes - the days pass so quickly
Sometimes - the nights are too long
Sometimes - God seems on a journey
Sometimes - He gives me a song
Sometimes - the clouds hide the sunshine
Sometimes - the winds blow so strong
Sometimes - in crowds I feel lonely
Sometimes - I like being alone.
　　At all times - I know God is working
　　　to show me His undying care

　　Ever and always - He loves me
　　Not sometimes - but always
　　He's there!

Sylvia Occhipinti

Essence Of My Life

Essence, essence of my life.
Sorrow, sorrow pain and strife.

Beat up, knocked down and kicked again,
Never, could see how I could win.
Shameful, humiliated too.
Hurtful, what am I to do?

When will, will you be satisfied?
Why must, your feelings from me hide?
Why do, you always criticize?
Why aren't, you ever on my side?

Lonely, and isolated too.
Never, a friend that would be true.
Leaving, and never looking back.
Put all, my feelings on a rack.

Hiding, the pain I feel inside.
Detach, from things I can't abide.
Don't want, to see inside myself.
Keep all, my feelings on a shelf.

Essence, essence of my life.
Sorrow, sorrow pain and strife.

Rose Shuff

Shades Of Hue

I see her green eyes, green vision, envy
Space to you allows me to see the truth
Conquering you is a feat of distress
Fate is to hope for something new
Love can be truth or you
Wanting, thinking, being, touching
Having, hoping, fearing, lying, doing
Will be me.

Will Salas

Human Doll

Take a human doll
split its heart into two
put new emotions and perspirations
and glue it back together.

Create a nest of flesh and bones,
and plant the soul as you like it.
Let the stream of blood flow
from its toes to the tiny skull.

As the heart begins to beat,
let the doll swim and roll,
until it is hardened from all sides.
Then pull the curtain away.

Then listen to the doll's song
from cradle to the grave;
and when its last dance is over
pull the curtain over its soul.

Vishnu P. Joshi

She's Gone!

Winter is almost gone,
Spring is very near,
Birds sing their lovely song,
But who is there to hear?
Mother's gone...she's gone!

Spring is already here,
Soon summer it will be,
Flowers break forth in bloom,
But who is there to see?
Mother's gone...she's gone!

Lovely music fills the air,
Life, in spite of sorrow,
Joy, in spite of pain, we share
But mother's gone...she's gone!

What shall I do while she's asleep?
Flowers I'll see, the songs of birds I'll hear,
But I shall weep, oh yes I'll weep
My mother's gone...she's gone!

Zoila E. Flores

Truth Revealed

At times, I tend to feel that I'm,
standing still, merely marking time -
Thou revelations continue to burst,
In the obscure corners of my mind -
I hear the voice of truth from within,
yet choose to listen not.
Knowing I deserve the best of everything,
Yet I merely settle for what I've got.
A knowing within continues to shout; of
a better world, as soon as I,
Stand up! arise-to the truth that I know.
My inner self I'll no longer deny!

Oscar L. Cormia

Good-Bye

Memories remembered, dreams once
dreamt.
Staring at the face I'd never forget.
Blackness I'm blank,
brightness you see.
A world given to you, and taken from me.

Tears of awakening, mind of non-belief.
Look down unto you, reality?
Smile swiped away,
laughter not heard.
Angel laid down,
angel overhead.
Protected and guided,
yet, I'm mislead.

Sunny sky, darkening day,
bottomless pit soon displayed.
Rose of red petals lay on a ground of
death,
becoming their home,
becoming their end.

You are gone,
  Good-bye.
  Rae Melvin

Question On A Springtime Walk

O swollen bud on
stark gray limb
about to burst
in glorious green,
is there hope
that dormant life
locked in my heart
will also surge
and greet the sun?
  Muriel L. Hastings

Blue

Roaring silence..
  stops me with you.
Let's hide
  -behind the shine-
  of blue.

Slippery motionless dolphin,
gliding through the waves,
  turning changing
and
My Hunger it staves.

The shutters hide
  me from them,
But not you from me,
  As you can
  - see!
  Rebecca Binkley

A Bird's Playtime

Flying up there oh so high,
Suddenly seeing the perfect guy,

Flying down really low,
Aiming at his ugly foe,

Finally dropping his big white bomb,
Missing the guy but hitting his mom.
  Thanh Kim Ngo Tran

Untitled

Sunrise catches day's hair
  streaming down mountain sides
birds caress the wind
  while spirit stalks the wood
    stirring in the
  soft breath on my neck
This is a day to spend
  drawing the sun
from its distant lair
This day will lie in my arms
  swallowing fire
and whispering her name
  in white capped waters
    as it meets the shore
  singing down eternity
  Robin McKann

Black Brother, Black Brother

Black brother, black brother
Strong, loving and wise

Black brother, black brother
The apple of someone's eye

Black brother, black brother
continue to stand strong

Black brother, black brother
Even when things go wrong

Black brother, black brother
No one has to die

Black brother, black brother
Just ask yourself, why?

Black brother, black brother
Your time has come

Black brother, black brother
You are the lucky one!

Black brother, black brother
Continue to love

Black brother, black brother
Good things come from Gods love!
  Theresa Solomon

Re-Entry

Hurray for re-entry,
Successful breakthrough scored,
The crew, they glowed with pride and joy,
To see the waves that roared.

Descending in their capsule
They could hardly wait
To splash into the water,
And watch their raft inflate.
  Pamela Dunstan

A Gift

My Mother, she made a man of me.
  Such an enduring responsibility!

My Mother-in-law, she made a wife for me.
  A task requiring great ability!

My Wife, she made a child for me.
  A gift given so miraculously!

A family these women made for me.
  Thank-you God, for allowing it to be!
  Phillip E. Gunnels

Sun Break

Just before the
sun does break,
Within my arms
My lady wakes;

While her contentment
Is mine again,
Another day is
Set to begin;

Comes to us now
Our little girl,
Her eyes a wide as
The world unfurls;

I wonder what
She shall see,
Just how exciting
It all must be.
  Scott W. Alexander

His Love

His love is a precious treasure,
surrounding me,
slowly embracing all that I am.

His love leaves no emptiness,
filling my whole world,
burning with love.

His love is a majestic ray,
illuminating,
a beautiful dream.

His love is sensitive and understanding,
it elevates my spirit,
trembling with happiness.

His love will never be discouraged,
parting will never alter our love,
I love him and he is the beloved.
  Michelle Wernsman

Don't Settle For Less Than Love

A collage of images,
sweet delicacies to behold
and pleasures beyond description,
her countenance my heard remolds.

The wonders of her spirit
combine with those around her,
giving fate a full embrace,
I revel that I found her.

Eyes like facets of a diamond glistening
reflecting rays of light
flowing deep into my heart
making lesser things seem trite.

True love is where peace does dwell
I will not settle for some mask
love comes not without its pain
and compromise its task.
  Mark D. Kale

A Time To Remember

With varying shades of purple and pink,
Sweet morning is born from the night.

I jump from bed with such great joy,
And gaze at this wonderful sight.

God's given beauty to the world,
On this day when Christ was born.

This splendid sight now greets me,
As I gaze at this beautiful morn.

Sweet thoughts of Him come to my mind,
And I think of all He's done.

For saints and sinners He has died,
For each and every one.

I think of how He suffered,
Of the brutal way He died.

Nailed to a cross by hands and feet,
A sinner at each side.

Then I think of how He loves us,
With our sins both great and small.

And somehow He forgives us,
For He loves us one and all.

Lois Thomas

Untitled

Humble yourself to life
Take not more than needed
Give not less than taken
For life can be a cruel master
She will twist and bend you for her own
Selfish pleasures, or,
Simply discard you

Shawnee Purcell

Tears Of Pain/Tears Of Joy

When we're in pain,
    Tears we cry and cry.
Is this the way for faith we gain,
    Or is it when WE try and try?

This pain leads us to fear,
    Our salvation we may lose.
Jesus is there, ever so near,
    If, HIS way we choose.

When, in HIM, our faith we keep,
    In the dark we shall sleep.
In the morning's light,
    Comes our joy; ever so bright.

Linda I. Hertwick

A Tribute To The End Of Our Lives

    The time has come my own dear love
that you are gone from me.
    I'm sure I'll drown in all this
loss into the turbulent sea;
    Our children are no longer small,
but such a comfort dear;
    Tis proud you'd be
to see them try, to take such
good care of me.

Marjorie Elizabeth Lear

"Marooned In Monterey"

3-10-95
The news report this morning came
Telling what happens with too much rain
Vacationers from far and near
Stranded in Paradise without fear.
Not thinking of the time allowed
Were caught unexpectedly in the crowd.
Forgetting schedules work demands.
Enjoying surroundings near at hand.
While all this was taking place
Salinas Valley was losing the race.
Lettuce, broccoli, and celery too
Strawberries, artichokes, and honeydew
All went down the drain
Caused by such torrential rain
Don't be surprised when to market you go,
You'll find prices have skyrocketed,
    wouldn't you know?

Mary Barrett

Ten Little Fingers - Ten Little Toes

Ten little fingers,
Ten little toes;
How could I make something
As wonderful as those?

Little one who needs me,
Who sees my face and smiles;
How could I resist someone
With all your charms and wiles?

When I look upon your face
I must hold back a tear.
How could God have known how much
You'd be wanted here.

I know that God loves us
When I look into your eyes.
All the wrongs quickly forgotten
Through strong paternal ties.

How much God must love us
To give up his own son.
Could I do the same
With you my little one?

Susan Cooke

"Thanksgiving Expressed"

Without the miracle of life,
Thanksgiving would not be,
we thank you for the feast we share,
with friends and family.

We thank you for just being there,
and guiding us each day,
we thank you for the gift of love,
and showing us the way.

It's said that Heaven holds a place,
for all who heed your word,
so, on this day I give my thanks,
for letting me be heard.

Susan Ongirski

"Jesus Is The One"

Jesus is the one,
that all of us should turn to,
and put our everlasting faith,
in him, to see us through.

Jesus is the one,
that carried the cross for us,
he never cried, he never whimpered,
cause in His father, was his trust.

Jesus is the one,
to whom we should pray,
for all of our blessings,
and to show us the way.

Jesus is the one,
that stated I'll be back,
so let us all try,
to get our lives in tact.

Solomon Jones

Untitled

The images I see
    that aren't really there
Are seen through someone else's eyes
    Consumed with despair.

    So
Darling, I may not always
Eat your body and drink your blood.
Spoken too soon with no
Participation in this ceremony;
Aligned with celestial
Icons - never to be touched and
Removed from my space.

Melissa C. Gay

"Love Is Like A Candle"

Love is like a candle,
that burns deep inside,
full of happiness and joy,
that some seem to hide.

The wax on the candle,
it melts each day,
don't take it too fast,
or it will all melt away.

The candle will flicker,
and sometimes go out,
but another will light it,
without a doubt.

So please just remember,
don't get depressed,
your true love will come,
so give it your best.

When you find,
your one true love,
stay with that one,
till the heavens above.

Michael Allen Jr.

The Poem is Yours

If you find beauty in these lines
That doesn't come from me.
It's what your dearest heart defines
In everything you see.

My rhymes are poor at their best
Any beauty that you find
In some little thing that I suggest,
Lies deep inside your mind.

The joy and love, you see is yours,
In the melody I sing.
The magic, the tone, the sweet allures,
It's you, dear one, who bring.

Simple hints are all that I can give,
Your heart brings them alive.
Only you are blest to make them live,
And to make these words survive.

If you see grace and beauty true,
Which brings you sweet delight
All good things in it - come from you,
And it's you, indeed, who write.

Robert Simmons

Autumn Time

Nature is painting every leaf,
That hangs upon the tree.
Strokes of every color,
for all the world to see,
Maybe they are dressing up,
for a party on the ground.
I can hear the children laughing.
Trying to catch them tumbling down.
The picture tells me summer is gone,
And Autumn time is here.
There is beauty as for as eyes can see,
It's my favorite time of year.

Rosa Webster

A Pawn

I stand before you a man
that has aged well beyond his years
and what I lack in experience
I have made up for in tears
an alcoholic by age ten
addicted to anything by age twelve
no need to try to fill me up with fear
I already know I'm going to hell
I am a pawn in the game of life
easily moved from square to square
but just as easy I am captured
never to be known that I was even there

J. J. Campbell

Untitled

Round as a ring.
That has no end
So is my husband's head,
A hummingbird did lite,
and fluttered his wings
'Twas no nectar he found
so on he flew.

Norma A. Callison

"There Is Not A Day"

There is not a day
That I don't wish,
I could take your pain away.

There is not a day,
That I don't think of you,
Close my eyes and pray.

There is not a day,
That I don't wish,
I could help you in some way.

There is not a day,
That I don't wish,
I could take your pain away.

Mattie M. Stewart

One Day At A Time

One day at a time
That's the way it should
Be between you and me
So when your feeling
Down and blue
Turn to me because
I love you.

Richard Harris

Secret Stories

This piece of rock
that I hold,
Has many stories
that are untold,
They are as clear
as day and shining bright,
They show up in the
darkened night,

They are secret stories,
No one knows,
They come and go
like when the wind blows,
They touch the heart,
the soul, and mind,
These are stories
without a bind,
Secret stories for
you and me,
Secret stories that are free.

Lindsey Czech

Scarlet

She had the prettiest red hair,
that I loved to run my hands through.
She was very playful and happy,
there wasn't anything she couldn't do.
She had a very good life,
that only lasted a couple years.
But she will always be in my heart,
that I will hold very close and dear.
I loved her so very much,
even though she just died.
I know she's in a happy place now,
but I never got to say good-bye.
God take good care of her,
and keep her safe.
Because I'll never forget about her,
in my heart for her there will always be a
place.

Melissa Barz

You

'Tis that I ride the winds of love
That I would soar to heights above
And only at a time to be
Shall I my long sought dreams to see

'Tis you that wings my flight so high
Yet beckons me to long for thy
As I shall find these dreams afar
Twill be of thee, my visions are

Could I continue on to live
Not having thee, or love to give
Could I be able, strong and sure
And nourished well, to long endure
Would I without thy hand to hold
Be bold enough to brave the cold
Not having that which I so need
Could I extinguish, the lonely heat
I think sure not, I'd rise above
The emptiness, without thy to love
Then cast me not away from thee
For hold me close, eternally.

Rodney Davis

Spoke Too Soon

Now everybody knows fair well,
That I'm a married man.
I never laugh, I never smile
I don't know how I can.
For when I asked my wife if she
Would come and share her life with me,
She said, "I'm yours forever,
But mama will fret and fuss."
Says I, "My darling, your mama
Can come and live with us."

Now I'm sorry that I spoke.
Now I'm sorry that I spoke.
Tho' they talk to me most every night
It seems they always want to fight.
I can't go out, drink beer, nor smoke.
Now I'm sorry that I spoke.

Ruth F. Mitchell

Loneliness

The feeling
that no one is ever around.
When tears of sorrow
reaches for the ground.
Searching for help and no one is there.
Questions cloud your mind
you wonder who cares.
You feel so empty
this situation of your soul.
You feel left out
with no control.
Your heart is in pieces,
there is no one to share.
Or fill this void, you call
Loneliness.

Nigel N. Douglas

Angel On My Shoulder

There's an angel on my shoulder
That only God can see,
And everywhere I go in life
"Angel" watches over me.

Through life's trials and tribulations,
Deepest sorrow, endless pain,
"Angel's" always there to guide me
Bringing sunshine after rain.

There are clouds on the horizon,
Distant rumblings in the night,
But then an end to darkness
When at dawn appears the light.

Each new day brings so much promise;
With spring new life begins.
Every season brings rich blessings,
Treasured time with special friends.

Yes—there's an angel on my shoulder
And a rainbow up above,
And in life's journey here on earth
I'm surrounded by God's love.

Sue Froseth

Untitled

Take my hand
That says so much
If I had
But one to touch
And by that gesture
I could reach
A compassionate heart
That would then breach
The walls of silence
That round me climb
Keep me prisoner
With thoughts in mind
A life imperfect
But full spent
I need a hand
Mine - not lent

Sarah G. Solomon

Wondered

Inquisitive child clutching
that shell —
stroking it
listening for its message
imagining its creation and
likewise its ultimate fate.

Do you know that you are
our hope for the future
and a key to the Universe?

Patricia E. Arnao

Untitled

Full moon appeared
The hour late
Window open
Gentle breeze caressed.
Alone upon my bed
I had no lover, but God.
Sleeping in His embrace.
Loneliness was gone.
Kiss of sunlight
Waiting to touch my face
In the morning.

Margaret Leeman

Expressions of Grief

Dark, sleepless nights, no stars
that shine. Grief!

When? Does it stop? When will the
pain end?

I miss you, so much, my precious
friend.

Your warmth comforted me.
You were my sun.

I long for the days we were
together as one.

It is cold here.
I feel frozen in time.

I so badly want back, what I
took for granted as mine.

Everyday I look to the sky
I ask the higher power for
the reasons why?

All I can do is hope and pray
that the sun may warm and
Comfort me, on this very cold day.

Mary Tabbi

Answer Me

It seems to me I've come to learn
That strife is part of every day
There may be time to play
But not for me
I can at times feel so sad
I cry inside sometimes it comes outside
There is so much I don't understand
You have to earn faith from hope
But if the end isn't what you planned
What is it all for anyway?
There is nothing I can do
I'm stuck here
Answer me "what is LIFE for?"

Tina Simpson

Teacher, You Just Don't Understand

There is unlimited time I've heard it,
That teacher doesn't understand.
If you only knew my problems, miss!
You would take me by the hand.

If students only knew the late nights,
Away from their families they spare.
To grade, figure and plan to teach.
All because they care.

They do not choose the profession
Necessarily to get rich quick.
They want to make a difference,
In Susie, Bob or Rick!

Student, before you go to class
And give the teacher the blues.
Just remember the one behind the desk,
Is human and may have problems too.

Say a kind word,
And thanks, for all you do.
You will be surprised how it will make them
feel
It will make you feel good too!

Sandy Graham

The Many Years Of Friendship

The years are now behind us
That we'll forever share
They're filled with hope and kindness
That always will be there.

Please take time to realize
How lives are meant to be
And how our friendship through my eyes
Meant so much to me.

Our lives will surely open
And we will truly find,
The answers to our problems, and
Then let our hearts unwind.

Time will truly tell
When things will be the same,
And know that how the friendship fell
Could give no one the blame.

We must look on to better years
And put our pain aside,
Forget all the fights and tears
And let happiness reside.

Nicole Isaacs

A Woman Of God

I AM SHE
   that woman,
that claps,
   and sings,
   and praises,
the Lord.

I AM SHE,
   that believes,
and receives,
   and knows,
   it's mine,
it's yours.

I AM SHE,
   that woman of God,
   a woman who prayed,
   God delivered
God saved.

Shannon DeWitt

Stands Alone

Who would have known
that you where it,
who would have known
that I was the one
the one you would
chose to bare and
be your wife
The one who now
stands alone
we were together
and apart
I am a widow
of your heart
the one who now
stands alone

Lova Miller

There But Not Seen

There is no feel
that's really real

We try to seek
the hidden mystique

All beauty must escape
and not abide the mental rape

Though it knows our longing
sensing our clawing

It just won't be thrust
into a heart without trust

But it leaves a trace
memories won't erase

And the longing remains
and the feeler complains

This knowledge we seek
requires us to be meek

For each of our days
are but time in a haze

If we insist on the part
of a cold old heart

Naji Mourad

The Undying Magic

Grandpa has a banjo
That's so shiny.
The sun hits it
and you could go blind.

The cords look like invisible string
The sound they make
Are like angels singing.

Grandpa be showing me
What cords to hit
But my hands be too little.
He say "You'll" get it
I se believe it too.
His banjo be magic.

His banjo can make anything happen.
Make me a country prince
or a jazz player.

His banjo make everything alright
His banjo seen hard times
but it's still here.
So it be magic his magic banjo.

Shannon Dunbar

"O, Father"

O, Father how I've hurt,
the hurt you'll never know.
Years went by as I felt the pain,
the pain you'll never know.
O, Father so much sorrow and
grief for all you've done,
all the heartache you have caused me
the battle not yet won.
As I grew from a small child,
the heartache you'll never know
but I have to ask myself —
O, Father did you know?

Robbi L. Trevethan

Untitled

For months I've watched
The anguish and pain
Holding on to anything
To keep from going insane

With prayers to God
Who is so wise
I lie here at night
With tears in my eyes

Still without answers
I go through another day
Hoping, begging for someone
To show me the way

But I awoke this morning
From a sleep I never had
Today I go to a funeral
The funeral of my dad

I'm thankful his suffering is over
And wished mine didn't have to begin
I'll take everyday, one at a time
Until I see him again

Mitchel Abshire

My Prayer

Thank you God that I can hear
The bird's singing loud and clear.
Thank you God that I can see
Every living growing tree.
Give me the strength every day
To act with wisdom in every way.
Let me not hurt a living thing
Help me only joy to bring.
Give me each day a loving heart
To those I love let me impart,
A touch of wisdom and of love
Mixed with your blessings from above.
When life becomes more than I can bear
Please give me someone who will care.

Sallie Belle Neary

"Poets And Poems"

I looked into the book received,
    The book "Beyond the Stars."
And never dreamed the poems within,
    From poets near and far.

Page to page I read and read,
    My inspiration grew,
So many poets in this world,
    To which I never knew.

Today I blend with those within,
    A dream I had come true.
How could a mere soul like me,
    Share this book with you.

My hurtful thanks I give to you,
    Who took me in their fold.
This book "Beyond the stars" received,
    Is worth its weight in gold.

For all the years I wrote and wrote,
    I never thought I'd show it.
You took me into the fold,
    And said I am a poet.

Richard L. Parker

"The External Equation"

When I have outrun time and
The cacophony of the flesh,
Will my identify be intact in
The regions of hell or in the
Garden of Paradise?

Will I know another by a touch
Or a cry, a long embrace or a
Wretched sigh?

In the eons of loneliness
Between one borning and the
Next, is there only a
Recognition of our being within
Another's caress?

Marjorie Liebman

Untitled

Memories pass as
the day and night
can't hold on even
to the fond chemical interludes
age clings to pull me in
as I struggle for youth

K. P. Smith

Age Is Upon Me!

The books upon my shelves
The dust that they collect,
Covers never cracked
titles I just can't recollect.

Pictures in a box
The faces that I see,
No labels are upon them
Names all of which escape me.

Numbers on a paper
What on earth could they be for,
Seems I can't remember
I'll put them back upon the door.

Someday I will remember
Until then we'll wait and see,
If any of them will come back
To my old memory.

Karen J. Simpson

Hunger

The rumbling and the growls,
the empty feeling inside,
your body becoming weaker
because nutrition has been denied.
Steady, continuing to wither away
bones covered only by skin,
no muscles, no fat, nothing left around
and starvation is setting in.
Longing for some food
But knowing you'll be without,
and expecting to die before your time
is what starvation is all about
many are exposed
to hunger everyday
But we close our eyes and turn our heads
and continue to look away.
We need to help our neighbors
it's time to take a stand,
Because this problem has a solution
you just lend a helping hand.

Kelley Mask

No Good Byes

This night I see the stars above
The eyes of angels, eyes of love
Placed gently in a mystic sky
The souls of those in love, did die
A breeze brings on a cloak of clouds
A lonely lover sobs aloud
Angels eyes so bright and strong
Cannot endure one's grief so long
It rains the tears those souls do weep
For pain below, their lone mates keep
Until clouds break and drift away
For sunrise and another day
Though time may help to clear the mind
Of one which life did leave behind
Still together always, in the heart
Two love bound souls will never part.

Michael J. Hegarty

Mirror

When I look in the mirror
The figure that I see
It seems so very clear
That figure is me.

I'm not getting any younger
More wrinkles every day
I look for an answer
Of why it's this way.

The tears begin falling
I'm crying out loud
The face that once was shining
Is just another face in a cloud.

Tiffany J. Moore

Untitled

Though the distance was far,
The friendship was strong
I can't stand the heartache now,
But I know I must go on.
I miss everything about you,
The big as much as small.
From friendly chatter,
To painful moments,
It all means so much to me.
Whenever I was lost,
You knew how much to find me.
Now I'm lost in such sadness,
Knowing you are gone,
But I still think of you often,
To keep the memory strong.

Michelle A. Quinn

Sunset

I stayed around to watch and see
The sun so bright go past the mound.
Where we once stood, with hand in hand,
where we had pledge our love so true.

The sun has set with warning none
for days have come and nights have gone.
My love was yours without neglect.
I've loved you always without regret.

The night is black with stars so bright,
And now you've gone, and tears I lack,
For when you left no bye's were said,
and now I stand, where we once stood,
so all alone and oh, so sad!

Tony Ramirez

Miracles Abound

As the morning sun gleams softly from
The horizon in the east
And hugs me with its gentle warmth
And wakes me from my sleep,
I thank the Lord for keeping me
Through another night
And for all the things that come to life
With his morning light.
The birds all sing in harmony,
Oh such lovely tunes.
The flowers will soon fill the air
With sweetness as they bloom.
We sometimes take for granted
All the little things
That God has put here on this earth
And the joy that they bring.
So, when you wake each morning,
Look to God above.
Thank Him for His blessings
And his wondrous love.

Sandye Applegate-Hager

Dying Ember

When I lay still, so very still
the last day of September
God made a spark of life
out of a dying ember
When I tried to eat
use a fork or knife
God turned a dying ember
into a spark of life

When I didn't know for sure
if I'd ever again remember
God made a spark of life
out of a dying ember

I learned to walk, I learned to talk
and be a mother, friend and wife
because God turned a dying ember
into a spark of life

He leads me along the byways
through all the troubles, hardships and strife
because He turned a dying ember
into a spark of life

Marian Moore

This Poem is for You

In a place called Nazareth
The Lord God gave him birth
The Son of God
Sinless and so pure
Come to save a world
Sinful and unsure

They nailed him to a cross one day
He could have cursed them
He could revile them
Spit on the ground
But he said "Father forgive them,"
"For they know not what they do."

This poem is for you
When times were tough
You saw me through
I knew what I had to do
You said "Pray for those who persecute you."
"And turn the other cheek."

Renée Balise

Untitled

A tree does not a Christmas make
The love is there to give or take
We can feed the hungry, visit the sick
Go visit a prison, play St. Nick
We can go to church, and cookies bake,
No, a tree does not a Christmas make.

A baby's born to share the joy
Should we do less for Mary's Boy?
In our hearts and in our home
Christmas is the love we share
With loved ones, strangers, everywhere.
God shared this love that we may be
Happy in Eternity.

Maud Macsurak

Untitled

With our souls wearing thin
the march of man malingers on

Destiny's flame burns ever dim
future melts into the waxing now

Yesterday's tomorrow
still reaching for today

Lost in man's hell
a child hungers for the way

Swallowing sin
spooned from undigested guilt

Life's due debt
gratitude pays without will

Leaving whence we came.

Mark Reeder

For Me

Why try?
The more I try
The more I cry

Why cry?
For me
I cry

A lot I cry
The more I cry
The more you cry

This is killing me
Get ahead, who?
When I take one step,
Back I go, two

This keeps me humble,
 I repeat
In hopes of preventing
 The feeling of defeat

Priscilla J. Anderson

Anticipating Springs

We each seek
the obvious bloom
for its gifts...

Our hope
yet tempered by the weight
of petals lost

Margene Mastin

Rewards

I've invested in a stock not listed on
  the N Y S E
A blue chip stock, with yields
  immeasurable to me.
This investment is called children,
  and dwells within the heart.
And I am called a teacher — from
  that special breed apart.
My investment will increase, and
  multiply and grow
From the myriad seeds I will nurture,
  and the myriad I will sow.
The high returns are countless, coming
  from students and from peers.
Together they help to erase the
  anxieties and the fears.
For my investments I am grateful,
  in my life they are profound.
This dividend of my profession, like
  interest, will multiply and compound.

Lillian Tisherman

A Place I Know

It never quite dries under
the old bridge. At no time
is the sun agile enough to
embrace its cool underbelly.

The dew-filled mists of
morning seem to advance
from, and withdraw to, this
darkened haven of the damp.

Thick clumps of rich green grass
spot the exaggerated median
which separates the puddled
ruts in the forgotten road below.

Gangling weeds droop in
all directions, move little in
the breeze, and shield the moist
topsoil from the determined sun.

Mosquito, snake and spider
frog, toad and turtle all
prosper under the bridge.
People never go there.

Michael Landy

My Shell

Where has my true love gone,
The one I once counted on.
Inside I have become ice cold,
It seems as though I'm growing old,
My pain I keep hidden deep inside,
I can't face the fact that you lied.
You said, you would never leave me,
Then you walked away one free.
When you left you took along my heart,
Alone again I knew not where to start.
So here I stand looking to the past,
Wondering why your love couldn't last.
I can't forget the nights I've cried,
So in this shell I chose to hide.

Vickie L. Beer

The Poets Know

The poets know the feelings rare
The pain that leads the way to care
The ink that lives on paper white
The moon that spills to give him light
The rhythm giving way to rhyme
The poets know the way of time
The poets dream of feelings deep
Of flowing words that wake from sleep
Of crying hearts that grope alone
The poets dream to lead them home
The poets love beyond their ink
Beyond their stars and sunsets pink
Because their words cannot quite quote
The ones who live the words they wrote
The ones who live the Poets dream
The poets rhyme the poets scheme
The ones who cause all words to fail
The heart must now in silence sail
The ones who live each moment new
The poets love someone like you.....

Larry D. Marshall Jr.

Shattered Dreams

The shattered dreams, the broken heart
The promises unkept.
The silken sheets so neatly spread
On the bed where he once slept.

The room is dark, the pictures gone,
But the memories are there.
Like a child alone and all forlorn,
She stops a while to stare.

On the table lay a ring of gold
With little stones of blue,
That ring meant more than words untold
It meant his love was true

Come live with me and be my love
The words so often said
This ring you'll wear, until the day
Both you and I will wed.

But as the years went quickly by
Another at his side would lie
And then those words which he had
spoken
To his first love, were forever broken.

Ruth Wilson-Brooks

Hot Summer Nights

In the dead of the night
The quiet becomes a roar
As the stench of days gone by
And love that never was
Rises
From its sewer pits
Far below
And no one ever notices
Except for the few
Who recognize the familiar scent
For it is one
Which they have felt
Many times before

Hot summer nights
Were made
For lonely cups of coffee
And empty highway lines

William F. Rhoads

Achieve

Over and over
The questions of life,
Need more, want more
Who's willing to give.

To see the pictures
To read the news
The thought of standing up
Stays just a thought.

To be the few
Discourages the action
to turn the other cheek
Is easier than doing the work it takes.

To give, to give
Somehow is never enough
For the people who take
can never fill the emptiness.

Now close your eyes;
Imagine
Now open your eyes;
ACHIEVE.

William K. Dias II

Babies Are . . .

Babies are . . .
The shadow of angels;
The flowers of heaven;
A gift from above;
The light,
Of love.

Lisa Sunahara

"No Better Friend"

The day is warm with sunshine and
the sky is extra blue,
  because in all the world I have no
better friend than you.

Because you always greet me with
a kindly word and smile,
  and in a dozen different ways you
make my life worthwhile.

You comfort me whenever I have
any fears to hide,
  and when my heart is sad I know
that you are at my side.

As well as inspiration for my
every daily deed,
  and all the stars are silver bright,
when the sky is young and new,
  because I know in everything I can
depend on you.

Sylvia LoCicero

Hope

Help me to understand
This chaos inside,

Help me to believe
the hope you put in my heart.

Teach me to face
the ghosts in my soul

Put faith in my mind, heart and soul
to believe in me again.

Lisa Culler

The Softness

The soft sounds of swallowing.
The soft breath of a sleeping child.
The soft warmth of a little body.
The soft curves of a pudgy cheek.
The soft feel of youthful skin.
The soft cry in the night.
The soft flow of falling hair.
The soft gleam of expectant eyes.
The soft laughter of glorious joy.
The soft padder of busy feet.
The soft color of a flushed face.
The soft touch of a miniature hand.
The soft hug of open arms.
The soft kiss of innocent lips.
The soft nestling of a sleepy head.
The soft beating of a trusting heart.
The soft comfort of presence.
The soft pleasure of seeing.
The soft sound of, "I love you."
The soft tug on my heart.

Laura Jones

Listen!

Listen to the happy sounds,
The sounds of the children playing,
Carried on the lilting breeze,
The branches gently swaying.

Listen to the stormy skies,
The gusty winds of teen-age years,
The rosy dreams, the broken hearts,
The silent, painful tears.

Listen to the clouds now clearing,
Pierced by shining rays,
With idealistic dreams to dream,
And lives to touch in many ways.

Listen to the blowing wind,
Strong and sturdy as can be,
Steady hands upon the helm
Steer through the treacherous sea.

Listen to the songs unsung,
Whispering from above,
The torch has now been passed along
In the final act of love.

Richard E. Slaughter

An Alzheimer Day

Today
  The sun
  No clouds
  No breeze
  No sound
It slips
  Away
  No friends
  No news
  No fun
It hurts
  To say
  No use
  No abuse
  No love
It's time
  To end
  And see
  Tomorrow

Marie N. Kuebel

Cynthia, My Love

I stand, alone in a field
The sun going down
A cloud passes by
Tinted red
I think of you
Your hair, a cloud
Blown by the breeze
And I know Love,
Alone in a field

Mike Beevers

Terrible Two's

Hello, world! What do you say!
The terrible two's are on their way.
Just one year is all they last,
I personally plan to have a blast.

Watch out, sister, here I come,
Move over, brother, I'm on the run.
Baby's too little to get in my way,
I think I'll go outside to play.

Dad says Jesus is King of Kings,
That He created beautiful things.
Mud to splash, rocks to throw,
Flowers to eat, delicious you know.

Mom says I'm special, one of a kind,
That step by step, my way I'll find.
Terrible two's? No, not really,
It's just my time to act real silly.

Norma Vano

Tears

The time is now.
The time is near.
Every time is ripe for tears.

Be they joy
or be they sorrow,
none will keep until the morrow.

Todd A. Blandin

Grandpa's Earth

Ecology psychology,
The way we think the earth should be.

We cut down trees and cleared the land,
We built beach houses on the sand.

The birds that soared above our heads,
Became extinct and now are dead.

My grandpa knows the way it was,
And longs for younger years because.

He knows my kids will never see,
The earth the way it used to be.

The sky so blue, the stars so bright,
The buildings didn't block the light.

The wildlife that ran so free,
Are now in zoos for them to see.

Salmon runs in crystal streams,
Are only found in Grandpa's dreams.

We've mastered our technologies,
But lost the forest in the trees.

Mark Roberts

The House

The house stood still.
The wind blew strong.
The people who lived here,
Had now all gone.

The windows they banged.
The chimney, it creaked.
The old shingled roof,
Had now sprung a leak.

It's funny how people
Can roam
And leave this old house,
That once was a home.

Patricia A. Laudette-Held

Raindrops Fall

Silence disturbed
The wind starts to blow
Bright sun
No longer a glow
Calm sea
A wave starts to form
From silent trees
The leaves are now torn
Light of the sun
Now faded to night
Rain starts to fall
Ever so slight
Heavenly tears
Shed from above
Our Father watches
His heart full of love
Raindrops fall
Our Father cries
He watches His world
As it slowly, slowly dies

Kendra J. Shields

"Pledge To Myself"

A new beginning.
The wish upon a star,
Can become real,
If I make of it.

I will try,
Not to lose its light,
By doing all I can.

I am in control,
Of the life,
I plan to live.
Let me flourish in God's blessings,
And become what He,
Wants me to be.

When opportunity knocks,
I will open its door;
Strong, patient, and with good common sense,
I will make it so.

Sandra Rene McDonald

Winterwolf

Winter night;
The wolf walks,
    stalks,
        cries,

Under frozen
Sliver moon.

On grey-white coat
Snowflakes
    falling softly,
Counterpoint
To cold within.

Journey stating,
Never-ending,
Seeking
    solitary
        heart.

Let it go;

Come into the wind.
Come home.

Ron Rogers

Untitled

The sun comes up each morning
Then goes down again each night
Leaving me alone
To face a never ending fight.

And each night it gets harder
To stop the tears that fall.
I keep praying that God will help me,
But I don't think he hears my call.

Each day someone gives up
Says they can't take the pain.
Some how though I'll keep fighting;
I'll soon get through the rain.

I know I'll make it down this road,
For God walks along my side.
Even though it seems he hasn't heard
All the times I've cried.

I realize now He's in my heart
And that He has filled the hole.
The Lord took back from sorrow,
The space that sorrow stole.

Kristen Fieker

A Choice

If allowed to love just one,
Then I choose that there be none

For I would have to blind my eye
Even memories of you deny

My ears could hear no waterfall
Or respond to a sweet child's call

And I would always have to state
My loves before you were mistakes

Since none of that was ever true
I cannot give my love to you

Mary Sue Arias

God's Grace

There are days I feel your pain,
Then I remember...
God's Grace is still the same.

It makes no difference how old we are,
We can look up into the darkness,
And see the beauty of God's stars.

The light of each star...
Is a reflection from the sun, EVEN SO,
God's Grace is for every one.

May you bask in HIS LOVE and GRACE,
Until that time comes, and you,
See Him FACE TO FACE.

Viola Venters

Teenagers

First they're mad,
Then they're glad,
Then they're sad,
Then they're bad.

Next they fight,
Say they're right,
Think they're bright
Stay awake all night.

Always ask why,
Never ever lie,
Sometimes really try,
Oftentimes cry.

Love to win,
Hate to begin,
Pick their skin,
Look like sin.

Always on the go,
Acting like they know,
Putting on a show,
Just trying to grow.

Tom Price

"Jesus You Are Precious"

  Jesus you are more precious,
then words can ever say.
  You took this life of mine,
and turned it into something sweet.
  I had my doubts, but you were there.
You eased my mind, you calmed my fears.
  Jesus you are more precious,
then words can ever say.
  Because this life of mine,
is the best you ever made.

Katherine Harvey

Thy Praise

Oh, Lord
There are not mortal words
That sound as sweet
As songs of elfin birds
Nor any quite as meet
To praise Thee with

We who think ourselves quite blest

Because we are not dumb
And have the sense to think
Are not as blest as some
Who can but sing Thy praise

Thelma M. Jarvis

Horses Graze

Out in the pasture
there are beautiful
horses, standing with
no riders

Horses graze on a
meadow of grass, they
stand in peace, with
the breeze

Breeze of cool air
blowing in their manes,
and little colts
jumping

Jumping and playing,
the colts have a way
of enjoying life, in
the plains.

(Jumping for joy)

Rebecca L. Curtis

Midnight Star

Once in a moonlight night
There bloomed a star in the midnight sky.
It twinkled like a pearl,
Danced like a doll,
Roved about here and there
Pretty Jolly and shy.

But suddenly what happened.
Much before it was dawn
It ceased twinkling,
Stopped roaming,
Disappeared once and for all
Without saying goodbye.

I still pass sleepless nights
Gazing into the sky,
Looking for the midnight star
That touched my heart, my soul,
And then left me in anguish,
Never, never to come back again.

Syed M. Haque

Summer

Here it is
there is goes
Miss it, kiss it
where did it go?
Vivid memories
of times come and gone
how could something
so simple slip, and be gone?
Times that were more than
precious, less than perfect
beautiful places, faces,
words and wisdom
all stain a patch of your brain
growing, feeling, caring, hurting
warm summer nights full of
mystery and romance
but wait! Don't go too deep
school starts next week!

Niki Bordner

Our Hideout

In the corner of the attic
there was a secret place
That had our little rocking chair;
to get it we would race.

It was always hot and humid,
but we didn't give a care.
We called it our secret hideout,
but everyone knew it was there.

Last week I was in the attic
and saw the tiny chair.
It brought to me the memories
that I had gotten there.

I walked into the hideout
to remember the old times.
I could not sit in the rocking chair,
because, in time, I had doubled in size.

I will not forget the attic
even when I get very old.
I will always remember the hideout
and the memories that it holds.

Patrick J. Rogers

Hiding

Deep inside where no one knows,
  There's something locked away.
Even though they don't know I'm
  Fighting everyday!
I'm looking for an answer to this
  Mystery inside,
So I'll know what happened on that
  Day and time.
It's hurting me so bad and true,
  To know that it's actually to
Do with you.
  My hurts for real and I know
I make you feel so awful all the time.
  It's because of me that I can't
Say the feelings on my mind.
  Just hold me tight and pull
Me through, because when I'm ready
  you better be too!

Stefanie Marie Carnevale

Feelings

Feelings are very strong
they come and go
they make you laugh and cry
they make you happy and sad
some you keep all locked up inside
and some you let out to fly
and when you do
you end up hurting someone
so what do you do then
if there going to hurt someone
then do you not let them out
and keep them locked up inside
to hurt your own self

Stephanie Lawson

Rivers Of Time

These are the rivers of time,
They flow quietly over the rocks
of heartbreak and sorrow,
slowly erasing the hurt and
blotting out the pain.
Their small waves lap gently
against the banks of reality, and
over time seem to alter the
memories,
until everything looks different
and strange and very far away.
The rivers of time will flow
forever,
and for eternity they will cry out
in vain to the world,
every droplet will whisper a
message for the earth to
remember...
"Nothing is forever"...

S.A. Fraser

Halloween

If witches come out
They have had a party.
If Halloween is near
Then monsters are here.
If ghosts come out
Then they disappear.
If you see a skeleton
Then your bones will rattle.
If a scarecrow comes to life
Then say, "Good Night".
If monsters get killed
They will have purple blood.
If monks come to the door
They will push you to the floor.
If you see a scary thing
Then don't you scream.
If a goblin comes to scare you
Then scare it back.
If you find a big bat
Then you better scat.

Tabitha Hornby

Black Out

Oh, do I hate black outs
They scare me so
But, do not fear my parents are near
My mind tells me so

I'm under my covers
so warm and safe
But my flashlight I have to see
Until the light comes flying back to me.

CAB-R

The Whale

Calm sea, alone with
thoughts of a life, sorrow
Joy, Love lost, Love new,
Sudden great beautiful
majesty breech's silver
waters, oh glory, oh
creature one with God,
this man wishes to be you,
Nothing to prove.

Robert F. Michalowich

So Far Away

As I sit and ponder
Things, like yesterday
Gone, but so close
And yet so far away.

As I enjoy things of nature
And watch wild animals at play
I think how close
And yet so far away.

As I stand above a loved ones grave
And the winds make the treetops sway
I think how close
And yet so far away....

I look at the sun, moon, rainbows
And clouds of gray
And I think how close
And yet so far away....

We perceive things to be near
Things that are near and go unseen
Makes our thoughts go astray

For they seem so close and yet so far
away...

Kenneth Zeitler

Well Of The Tears Of God

Light, make your attempt
This desert it oozes contempt

Life, it thrives near here
This oasis feeds the hunger

Words, will not fly here
This cocoon envelops the ear

Breath, it eludes you
This space denies all that is due

Senses, distorted
This universe defies order

Silence, surrounds you
This world is studying the new

Death, everpresent
This graveyard buries the unkept

Dark, remains in wait
This paradise arrives too late

Mitchell L. Hearne

Dreamer

Rainbow and straight roads,
This is a dreamers last dream.
Darkness and utter loneliness,
Will no longer be feared.
Green fields and colorful flowers,
Shows natures pride and beauty.
Sunshine on crystal clear water,
Puts glittery sparkles in all eyes.
Sensation of rain in the air,
Smells of purity and freshness.
Communicating, expressing true emotions,
Can lead to better understanding.
A true friend and a joyous smile,
I am the dreamer, dreaming till the end.

Martin Ed Hall

Untitled

Please-make no comment,
this is a "senior citizen" lament.
How? When? Where? Or Why?
In the end we all must die.
What difference whether then or now?
The only difference is the how.

Maybe in the fury of a hurricane?
A wrecked ship on the bounding main?
A downed plane if we decide to fly?
Or a drunken motorist zipping by?

Do I my "Seniors" duty shirk
If I decide to go to work,
and not worry myself to death
about how I will draw my last breath?

Wilma V. McCoy

A Baby

Wait a week, wait two weeks.
This is what the doctors say.
I feel the blood go to my cheeks.
Deeply I breathe, I pray.

Will we gain a life from love,
Or is my body out of line?
Can anyone tell me up above?
May I receive a message, a sign?

Earthly mortals do not know
The complete miracle of birth.
Just as we predict first fallen snow,
Yet are amazed when it falls to earth.

So now we wait a week or two,
A sense of hope, a maybe.
Perhaps the sign was right, was true.
Then the greatest gift—a baby.

Michelle A. Greer

Early Snowfall

What's this nonsense that I see,
This ugly sight offending me?
Frozen crystals drifting down,
Icy carpet on the ground.
Surely it's too soon for snow,
Much too soon for Fall to go.
The flakes collecting on the trees
Must share the branches with the leaves.
And where the earth's white coat is lean,
Clumps of grass show Summer green.
Some migrant birds who linger still
Are scolding the unwanted chill.
Anxious now, without delay,
To get their journey underway.
As I recall my Emily Post,
The early guest offends the host.
And modern manners indicate
It's more in fashion to be late.
So come with ice and snow and slush,
But, darn it Winter, what's the rush?

William D. Mackey

Only Me

What is a man's soul
Though his soul may
Not bleed
To see the end
Of a dying need
I awaken from dark
To a new day of birth
I taste the pain
Of a dying earth
Though I'm strong
They'll never see
The tear of a child
An empty need
As I reach to love
There's only me

Sherry L. Opper

Old Folks

Some spoke that old folks in my town
Thought and even walked quite strangely.
This talk, to me, was empty sound
About unimportant people, mainly.

But when I reached that middle age,
The time most folk reject;
I started feeling those at my stage
Deserved attention and respect.

As years rolled by I learned much more
That living makes us wiser.
Most things we couldn't know before
Now help us turn advisor.

"The last for which the first was made"
Seems sad, like hindsight come to life,
Yet we seem to wane and slowly fade
And most old folks live in strife.

Texora Satterwhite

"Desperation"

Feelings without a name
Thoughts of no origin
    or destination
Fill me so fully
That I feel like
I'm drowning in nothingness -
Engulfed by a void
    and suffocating
Alone and afraid
    in a box I call home
I hang my memories to dry -
But they always seem
    to wilt and die
Filling my room with emotions
And now there's no longer
    room for me
I slip through a hole as
My life drains through a straw
    sucking me dry

Michael Crosby

I Love Your Laugh

I Love Your Laugh
Thrillingly Unique And Distinct
Flashing Of Hope And Relief

The Truth Of Your Eyes
Warm As The Morning Sun
Bright As The New Day's Dawn

The Feel Of Your Touch
Caressing As A Midnight Pillow
Rejuvenating As A Brand New Promise

Summer Evenings Dialogue
Exciting Previews Of Nights Never To Be
And With A Blink Of An Eye, They End

The Press Of Your Lips
A Truth That Cannot Be Repressed
For A Minute Time, That I Cannot Digest

I Love Your Laugh
It Haunts My Memories

Sam "Balamb" Anastas

Nature

The wind is restless as it sways
through the trees,
I am breathless by the sight of the
birds and bees,
Flying around in their habitat,
Never wondering where they're at,
Nature is beautiful and glorious,
Especially in the woods or forests,
Where we are is nothing more,
Than walls of bricks and a wooden door,
When we see nature,
What goes through our minds,
As we stare across the wide, blue skies,
And the beautiful animals of all
different kinds.

Nikole Carroll

Many Winter Memories

The winter season sends a chill
through your bones.
The days grow shorter. The
nights longer.
You stay cuddled up by a
warm, crackling fire.

Families gather for holidays
sharing laughter and love.
Decorating christmas trees
and wrapping presents.
We thank our heaven above.

The children get toys
Adults get paper fans.
The ground is covered in white
let's go make a snowman.

Everyone fills their insides with
turkey and applesauce.
Hurry kids! Get to sleep
Here comes Santa Claus!

Lynn Burton

Anticipation Of A Bride

She lays awake at night
Till she sees the morning light
  This season she did invite
Since she was but a mite
  Anticipation of a bride

  Her eyes a star
Her thoughts a far
  Not a soul can mar
The moment she left her heart ajar
  Anticipation of a bride

  He came in; she made him king
Now her lips will forever sing
  Of the joy their love will bring
For soon the bells shall ring
  Anticipation of a bride

     Lisa Peterson

Sojourn Of Sleep

Fringes of a lucid dream
Time, not a life, insignificant
Springing to being - by shadow light
Open the arms of Morpheus

Her mantle ablaze
Dormant fields awaken
Virginal whites, earthen tones
Isolate the night

Secure in their lust
Her creatures, her liege
Frolic in her presence

Through dance they revel
'Til all breaths escape
Constructed - a realm exists

A pariah to the affair
I can not bear witness
To the grandeur
Of this procession
And the waters which slake
The thirsts of heaven

     D. B. Parsley

Jack Frost

I woke up this morning
To a beautiful sight
The ground was covered
With a blanket of white
The rays of the sun
That shone all around
Revealed millions of diamonds
There on the ground.

The blanket of white
Jack Frost had spread;
During the night
While I slept in my bed.
Millions of diamonds
Were frozen droplets of dew.
Rays from the sun
Also revealing...
Emeralds...rubies
And sapphires of blue.

     Peggy Joyce Whitfield

Just A Dream

Come ride with me
to a place reserved just for us,
  No war,
    No hunger,
      No hate,
        No disbelief.
Where love and peace
are the only feelings
a world of enchantment
and make believe.
Where dreams are reality
and everyone is equal,
  No money,
    No disease,
      No jealousy.
Won't you come ride with me.....

     Tammy Leaverton

The Letter

I wrote a letter
To a young, handsome Marine
An old man did receive it -
As he held the pages and started to read
The spots on those hands began to recede.

His lungs were filled
His hearts beat strong
His eyes were clear
His legs were long —

The bells did ring
We stood and prayed
The sun shone hot
The ocean sprayed

And when the letter was finished
It fell to the floor -
The old man sighed,
A youth no more.

     Marion Codd

I Haven't Found the Words

I haven't found the words
To describe how I feel
This pain; this hurting
It's all too real

I sit all alone
And stare at the light
My love for you
Has stolen my sight

I wish I could tell you
It will be all right
I wish I could hold you
And kiss you goodnight

I've given my heart
Please hold it tight
I know this love
Will turn out right

I hope someday
We will be together
Because my love for you
Will last forever

     Willard Slivinski Jr.

The Gardenias Are Dying

We thought we were meant
To dine on their scent
Forever.

When fair fragrance filled the air
One into the other's eyes we'd stare.
Together.

Far longer than this
We wanted to sit,
Drinking that perfumed wine;

But white fragrant shrouds
Wasted with rust,
Fell to a useless death;

And bequeathed in the earth,
A bitter-sweet taste
Of remembered remorselessness.

So for better or for worse
With no redress:
The lingering smell of loneliness.
Forever.

     Rosemary Paul

Thelma's Sunset

When a family comes together
To do what you always liked doing
When they gather to show
How much you were loved
and to say goodbye
For the very last time
When they laugh and they cry
Although you are not there
And though time has stopped
Just for a while
They can see by the sunset
You are close, so close
And forever near...

     Lyman L. Trescott

Special Prayer

If I could ask my Heavenly Father
To grant one special wish.
I would plead that he would impart
A loving change in human hearts....

Then he could give each dog and cat
A home with loving care.
For everything that walks and flies
Protection everywhere.

Perhaps someday we will all realize
How much our life depends.
On the care and comfort that we give
To all our animal friends.......

They cannot ask for kindness
Or for our mercy plead
Yet cruel is our blindness
Which does not see their need.

World-over, town or city.
God trust us with this task:
To give our love and pity
To those who cannot ask!

     Marilyn Cronin Castle

Untitled

Broken thoughts;
to hurt to say,
to hard to think,
to push away.
Crumbled lies;
fell to the floor,
love is dead,
friendships war.
All was found;
then lost again,
strange encounters,
forgot right then.
Hope had flew;
far away,
and will be found,
some other way.

Melissa Uroff

Playmates

Eagerly I asked His Mother
To let me hold Him for a while;
Just lift him from His manger bed
And play in baby style.

At first she seemed reluctant
As mothers often seem to be,
'Til smilingly St. Joseph said
To give the child to me.

When she laid Him in my arms
So unfounded were all fears;
His baby eyes looked into mine
And mine smiled back through tears.

In silent words He spoke to me,
His little one held captive here;
And as I pressed Him closer still
I heard His message clear:

"Oh if My playmate thou wouldst be
Take up thy cross and follow me!"

Katharine Brenner

A Rose From My Heart

Here is a rose from my heart,
to let you know we will never part,
and as long as we are together,
there will be no stormy weather.

We will walk hand in hand,
along the beach's golden sand.
We will look up at the sky,
and watch the beautiful birds fly by.

You mean so much to me,
and our love will always be.
Through all our heart ache's and pain,
our love will always stay the same.

We are as one now.
Our love we will always vow.
And this rose is from the heart,
to let you know we will never part.

Mary K. Coleman

"The Dawn Of Cycles"

Waves churning
  Tide returning

Stormy sky
  Seagulls cry

Whirling breeze
  Dancing leaves

Rain or snow
  Where to go

Enjoy His plan
  All you can

Sunset to dawn
  Life cycles on

Rex Trowbridge

There are so many of them

So take them all one at a
Time Do you see
how they accumulate over
time They are barnacles

And heavy So

much is made of the blue sky
above but so
little clear of the breathless deep
above which barnacles

have accumulated thickly

Around that shifting swelling
place do you see
it now The boundaries between
Place and place are not things

But the weight carries through

Rick Hutchins

"A Gift"

A gift is such a simple thing
To mean so very much
It tells I'm thinking of you
And long to have your touch.

A gift though small in quantity
In quality may reign supreme
If the thought behind its message
Is sincere and yet serene.

But if the thought is tranquil
And has no meaning being there
Then the gift reigns supreme in quantity
And the quality's no longer there.

So to keep an air about us
So that all we give is good
Let's work to build understanding
And keep our relationship good.

Vincent R. Bujan

Writers Block

Pen is the conduit
to my soul
sitting prosed, prepared
for nothing

The mind races
in this storm of empty thoughts
blinding me

Still, remains the body
time escaping, like a breathe
with eyes searching a blank slate

There is always tomorrow
dreading another day
searching the dark place
four walls in a quite storm
of nothing

Wilfred Torres

Sing My Song

I want someone
to sing them for me
the words I have
inside my head
are yearning
for a lilting voice
a voice so clear
and sweet
the angels
would wake the dead
just to hear the sound
of heaven on earth
and the children
will twitch their ears
to listen
the old folks
will tap their feet
such a sweet beat
a song for all souls
young and old

Sylvia Marie Blanton

Today

I have not the courage
to stand by you today.

For today is
the day of all days.

It will bring grey waves
for a cold dark finish;

Deaden the feelings
which have lived so long.

It will seal with confidence
the heart of close friends.

It will take you away.
Forever. Today.

Stacie Easterwood

The Light

Slowly fading away
Tries to stay a glow
Slips farther away
Soon to disappear
Not a sliver of light
Just darkness

Kris Lynch

Holocaust

From the halls of U.S. Congress
To the Nations everywhere
The sales of guns and talks of wars
Are not pleasant to hear.

But it seems that there is never
Any peace for a mother earth
As she has evolved so many times
From the raptures of those

Who call themselves peace makers
Who want to sedate everyone
With their talks of peace and love
But it's only a game

For the vastness of a Universe
With all it's mysteries
That men have tried to conquer

As the new horizons
That come and go
Like belts of lightening that fill the air
As we pray for new beginnings
With the passing of each day
Kathleen L. Chanay

Are You Experienced?

Grandfather of experience
To those who come alone.
Here to teach the teaching
That our fathers have bestowed.

Ignorance is nature
Please learn to come in peace.
Spanning new ideas
Until the brain has been deceased.

Passing new philosophies
In a subconscious realm.
Dreaming in reality
My thoughts are overwhelm.

Conspicuous analysis
Too many to rehearse.
Feeling mass confusion
My mind is yet to burst.

Seated upon my throne
I wait to plant the seed.
To those I feel are worthy
To pass along the deed.
Miguel Vargas

The Question

Man, the human animal
Toils his life away
Ideals abound, but false do prove
Till the cold, withering grave.

The sunrise, the sun sets
Foretell the onrushing end
That inevitable final curtain
That ore takes all mortal men.

Then we shall know the final truth
The awful summation
Will it be eternal life?
Or soulless, mindless
Disintegration...
Sue Wilson

The Beauty Of Love

I was loved for a moment
too fleeting for my taste

And beautiful, I was
striking in fact
if measured by the fullness of my hip

And feminine, indeed.
Oh, I remember
all perfume, red lace, velvet breast.

A more ardent lover
I had never been.
It is true. I remember.

Oh, to have witnessed my grace
sculpted through the gaze of that man
polished by the rhythm of his speech.

It's hard to imagine this, I know,
I know

Now that my spirit is hollow as bone.
Kendall Lynn Leeper

Photographs

I often wondered why my dad,
took photos of me, asleep in my bed.
Was it because it was a time,
my mouth was closed for a brief time?

But now I gaze at you and see,
what my dad too, must have seen.
The beauty made with God's good grace.
The child and angel in that face.

So peaceful are the moment when,
I look at you and remember him.
And laugh and cry at dear old dad.
Wishing I had a camera at hand.

Traditions die hard it's plain to see,
I see in you, what he saw in me.
Ursula Mitchell

Oakland Hills

The whimsy of the aureate hills
tossing their manes of yellow blooms
under a light and petulant rain

The crows are circling
and the clouds are shredding
at the edge of the sun racing
in advance of this year's dissolute rain

Time and nature mend
the charred ruins of yesteryear
and soon we'll build again
over the tentative stubble
over the newly composed earth
we'll build again
since lightning never strikes
this space but once.
Violet R. Lippett

China Winter

The horizon on this cold winter's eve'
Touches the earth
Like the rim of a china cup.

Pale pink, turquoise, translucent blue,
Lavender light,
A few faint stars showing through...
No clouds to mask my sight.
How still this winter eve'!

I must stand in silence, for my sake;
If I move, this lovely cup will break.
Lillian Volkmer

Black Brother

Oh Black Brother, you have been
tried, falsely accused and even
died. Your hopes have suffered
your dreams denied, but still
you continue to struggle and
even survive.

So fight on black brother, until
freedom comes, fight on black
brother, until victory is won.

Until God grants you rest and says,
"Well Done." Fight on black brother
until tomorrow comes.
Marlena E. Jones

Untitled

Sadness guilted from shame
Truth covered in pain
Bluebells, red roses just signs
Fragrant coverups like pines

Flowers don't correct sickness
Only appease a soul's sickness
Breaking promises of remorse
Beatings are only one source

To stay or to go? Where?
To walk away or to stare?
People help no one! You?
At least to yourself be true!

Hanging on a ledge of hope
Overcoming cruelty's steep slope.
When with hope,
outside the hurtful home
at least then,
consigned to freely roam.
Russell G. W. Hilton

Love

Falling in love is like having a friend,
Two hearts together that forever mend.
With each other throughout the day,
Hoping that together you'll stay.
When alone and far apart,
You feel each others beating heart.
Then when back together again,
Wishing the day would never end.
Love feels so good, Love is divine,
Love is something that just takes time.
Love is in the heart they say,
Love will never fade away.
William Candido

This Too Shall Pass

This too shall pass...
tumbling toddlers,
catching lightning bugs,
picking dandelions.

Friendships,
nervous first dates,
first kiss.

Sleepless nights,
high stacks of bills,
life long mates.

These too shall pass... on
knowledge,
possessions,
memories.

So shall thy spirit,
where is up to you.

Sharon Kay Haggerty

Undying Love

I miss your smile — your dimples, too.
'Twas all so much a part of you.
The mountain hikes on trails we knew —
Each time to me it seemed brand new.

My memories are all that's left
My aching love, my hope, bereft.
You were my life, my all, my love.
I pray that you're with God above.

My heart longs to feel your touch,
See eyes again I loved so much.
Promise that you'll watch for me
At the open gates of Eternity.

Mary E. Beery

The Gift

Beneath the tree of life I spied,
Two gifts, laying side by side.
One wrapped in red and gleaming gold,
The other in brown paper had no bow.

Two strangers came along the road,
One appeared lofty and very bold.
The other was bent under life's load,
Struggling to feed his body and soul.

The high minded man quickly grasped,
The gift tied with the golden sash.
Leaving for the man to slow to react,
The one wrapped with a brown paper sack.

Without delay the man of the world,
Ripped paper away, his trophy to unveil.
He found to his sensual appetite,
Riches of money, desire and delight.

Savoring the worth of the moment in time,
Slowly, the second man revealed his find.
Unexpectedly, angels ascended from within,
Inside, A Babe in a Manger smiled up at him.

Sandra J. Starks

Untitled

On this day
  two hearts soar —
to join two spirits
  But so much more.

Love is given
  a commitment made,
May your feelings
  never fade.

A blessed gift
  this love your share,
With communication
  you'll never despair.

Love surrounds you
  as it must,
Throughout your life —
  Keep the Trust

To one another
  you must hold —
And together
  will grow old.

Vicky Lynn Forester

My Prayer

I pray for the children
Unborn and unloved
That they will be with You
On high, up above.
I pray for the husbands
Both young and old too
That You will instruct them
On what not to do.
I pray for the black folk
That they can believe
The hatred soon over
No more to receive.
I pray then O Lord
For my very own kind
That Thy voice will be heard
That women will write.
I pray these things
In Jesus Christ's name
Remaining Thy servant
Always and forever the same.

L. Prosise

A Message From Grandma

I look at you and see
  Unborn generations.
Then I recall
  When I was small
I thought the world
  Had waited just for me!

But now I see
  There are those yet to come.
Only God knows their destiny
  And yours
Or when they will be here.

But, for now,
  I know the world to be
A better place,
  Since you are here, my dear.

Mary M. Landry

Your Tree

If I were a tree you could sit
under me, and shade yourself
from the summers sun.
Or cut my branches for your
fire-place, to keep you warm
when the winters come.

And in the Fall to look up and
see, all the colors I've painted
for thee.

Then in the Spring to gaze
through my foliage at the blue,
and know that this tree belongs
to you

Oh there are greater trees who's
branches are stronger, and leaves
brighter sparkling with dew,
and I wish I were that too

But don't you see, as hard as
I try; I can only be me
but... your tree

Samuel Viola

Mantis Religiosa

I thought it was a stick
Until it began to move.
I finally realized
It was a praying mantis.

Slowly it moved along
Eating bugs and hay.
I tried to talk to "it."
But no word did it say.

Nature is wonderful!
Colors change with the season.
First it's green, then it is brown.
That's the praying mantis.

It was my pet all summer.
Where does it stay in winter?
Since it did not answer me
I guess I will never know.

Virginia B. Guthrie

An Old Time Christmas

Little brick streets
Up hill and down...
Wooden frame houses the
Churchyard, surround...

The old church bell rang
On Sunday at one....
Knocking us down as
The porch swing, swung...

The town was so small
There was no town hall...
One guy bought a paper,
Passed it round, that's all...

The night before Christmas
We went out to chop wood
For the Franklin stove...
Feeling tingly and good...

As the sparks flew up
The chimney with ease...
Santa came through the
Front door with his keys...

Tobi Kumar

The Cottage On The Hill

There sits a little cottage
Upon a wooded hill
It looks so uninhabited
Yet very lovely still.

Its garden full of flowers
And moss green on its walls
While on its thatched roof
Woodbine and ivy crawls.

There sings among the roses
A love-lorn nightingale
Until the golden moonlight
Goes down the woodland hill.

Oh, why must lovely roses
With seasons fade away?
Soon chilly winds of winter
Will bite away each day.

Yet amid this fading beauty
A maiden merrily sings
Against all odds of winter
And what the future brings.

Teofil Dumitru

To A Teacher

If freely written in chalks of white
Upon the dark your self could write;
A blackened board would there I be,
As contrast to your certainty.

And damned thought could there lie plain
That fortune and future, torn and slain
Held once itself to be a love
In eyes of both a thing approved.

But darkness falls into the light
Obscuring thoughts in chalks of white.
Whilst all becomes, like needs are must.
The message fades in chalks of dust.

And future now in hearts are known,
We create what we have grown.
In all things change and possibility,
To be a part of your certainty.

So as the purpose rends its' way
Playing host to life conceived.
Perceive'd voice to my self will say,
"Once misled but not deceived."

Paul Moore

Innocence's And Fear

Innocence dispersed numbness
  upon the scent of fear.

Deafness encountered innocence
  and fear during the mutation
  of horror.

Horrendous dreams of death glorified
  in an innocence mind.

Illumination beyond this earth
  kept innocence's from insanity.

Illness strikes fear and powerful
  strength weakness.

Innocence wept with pain when
  fear was abandon by love.

Shedding tears made innocence
  understand fear,
  and forgiveness emerged.

Maria Barth

The Gift Of Life

God sent a little angel for
us to watch and hold.
The precious gift of life,
a mystery of old.
We watch you as you sleep
as peaceful as a dove,
A present come to us on earth,
a symbol of God's love.
Such tiny little fingers,
ten perfect little toes,
Two bright and shining eyes,
a turned up little nose.
It is a wonder to us
just how you came to be,
But that is only part of
this awesome mystery.
Each day brings new awareness
reflected in your smile,
of the promise of new life and hope
in a tiny newborn child.

Tracey L. Short

Ode To A Dew

Roses are red
Violets are blue
I love mountain dew
and you too!

Kristina M. Cundiff

Colors

Roses deep red,
virgins in white
black is the best
after midnight
mauve in the morning,
greeting the day
coffee with kisses
roll in the hay
sheets should be satin,
erotic to touch
regal in purple
and reeking with musk
afternoon tea time,
the green of the fern
enveloping shadows
that too quickly turn
from apricot sunset
to quiet repose
enfolding us back
to the dark of the rose.

Patricia J. Porter

Talisman III

Summer strangers; does it matter?
We are far beyond the spring.
Summer's loves lie with its roses
Fragrant for remembering.
Autumn offers for our viewing
Beauty to bemuse the gaze
Long warm afternoons reflecting
Summer in the Indian haze.
What though Winter soon will follow?
Can another season show
Amid all its bud and blossom
Beauty to surpass the snow?

Libby Pinar

Gathering People East To West

I look at my painting
  waiting to be done;
Iraqi boy
  and you,
Christ's feet
  I have given both of you.

So long ago
  I had that dream
  —seems only yesterday
In the city of St. Francis
  rich brown ruffle
  underneath the door.

Artists know
  what feelings show, Christ's feet
  watch where they go
  gathering people,
Butterflies are helpful
  protecting the sun.

I give you Christ's feet
  the Iraqi boy and you.

Theresa R. Donahue

Sea Urchin

As of late daybreak finds me
walking the beach, waiting for the sun
and seagulls to appear.
I sit on the sand
and talk with the driftwood
(once trees that stood tall
now twisted scraps of wood).
They tell sad stories
of the axe-laden forest thieves
who brought their ruin.
I cry tears for them and for me.
I know how it is to drift and drift.
I wonder how many shores
they'd washed up on -
was this to be their last and mine?
I pick up dying starfish,
return them to the sea
search for seashells, comb the sand
hoping to find myself or the memory
of someone who cared.

Tim Currier

Assurance

The look of pain that crossed his face
Was more than I could bear
Because I knew, because of me
He was hanging there

His eyes met mine and there was no blame
Looking back at me
There was only love, compassion, warmth
And so much victory

No words were uttered from his lips
Only silence there
But in his gaze I knew he said
"Child I really care"

I care about those years ahead
I want you close to me
I shed my blood, I give my life
For your eternity.

Patty S. Toller

Untitled

All I ever intended,
    Was to find a way home
      And only when I scribble
        The last word,
          On the last page
            Will I get there.
Keith Khon

Winter's Snow

When the winter wind begins to blow
We all know it will snow

The kind of snow that piles high
Just enough to touch the sky

Making snow forts with the snow
It's a good place to hide and throw

Father's coming out to plow
Brushing snowflakes off the boughs

Mother's making cocoa, it's real hot!
In the house the kids all trot

Wet clothes everywhere
Even on the wooden chairs

Father comes in for a warm drink
Put his wet clothes in the sink!

Everyone's as warm as toast
This is the time we love most!
Mary Robin Corson

If People Were Flowers

If people were flowers
We'd handle with care,
So they would continue
To grow beautiful there.

We'd pull out the weeds
And stir up the dirt,
Trying to be careful
Our flowers aren't hurt.

With Hope we place them
Very gently in a row,
With Faith we watch
How our flowers will grow.

The Love that we give them
WILL return equal measure,
When they grow and blossom
What a beautiful treasure.

People aren't flowers
I'm so happy to say,
If they were I'd know
A very beautiful bouquet.
Mary A. Fulton

It's A Girl

A girl? A boy? Twins? Triplets?
We're here!
Exhausted mom on the bed.
Small baby in a crib.
A girl, or a boy?
It's a girl!
Two big sisters watching.
Kristina Van Dort

Untitled

Gone are the days
When children play
Hide and seek was
A favorite game
Life today is not
the same
Parents, teachers,
preachers
One they trust
Respect an obedience
was a must
Bible sits full of dust
Life today is full of lust
Lily Arreguy

Autumn Makes Me Cry

You say that you love Autumn,
Well, Autumn makes me cry.
The colors are so beautiful,
Its does say good-bye.

Good-bye to summer fun,
Like going to the park.
Or just sitting outside,
Watching silence in the dark.

But, now that it is Autumn,
I put the memories away
Of some mornings in the rain,
Or just watching the kids play.

The sun does set as you drive away,
And silence fills the sky.
You told me you loved Autumn,
Well, Autumn makes me cry.
Penny Malloy Deckert

Progress

Birds
Vanish
From nations
Guided by man's
Greed.
Marilyn Brown

How Is It?

How is it that you've touched me so
What is this magic that you've done
How is it that you've freed my soul
How did my chains all come undone

How is it I did not notice
you charm my guards to sleep
or nonchalantly force your way
deep inside my keep

How is it I did not see you
slipping through my gate
or feel the danger of your presence
until it was too late

I built this cage myself you see
I placed each bar most faithfully
and then I threw away the key
how did you find your way to me

How is it that you've touched me so
What is this magic that I feel
How is it that you've freed my soul
Is this a dream, or is it real?
Tracy Roth

Untitled

Time will always tell
What one's heart can never say
The eyes are always blind
To what is to be faced the next day
The solace of the dark
Becomes the soul's salvation
Creating a cove
For the mind's true aspirations
Fear will always hide
One's true desires
Leaving only dreams
To relinquish or aspire
The sanctuary of the mind
Can never be achieved
For the eyes of life
Shall always be deceived.
Theresa Rivera

Life Is Like A Painted Picture

If we all see in a picture
What the artist tries to convey
We wouldn't be individuals,
Only puppets pulled for play.

Life is a chain of colors
Some bright, some dark, some grey.
The color of our life reflects
How we live from day to day.

The colors on a palette
Are but there for all to use
How we brush them on our canvas
Is entirely up to you!

The scene will change in many ways
As we walk throughout the land
No artist could ever paint the beauty
Like the touch of the Master's hand!

If there was only one painting
For me and for you.
The picture should boldly emphasize
"To thine oneself be true!"
Suzy Thompson

Prepare Me

Prepare me for the time
When days have gone past
When moments have rushed by
And do not carry the same elements
Upon their breath as today.

Open my eyes to be one with my mind
To be able to fly with the eagles
To dance across the tree tops
To a waltz of life
Ever so graceful ever so light.

Release my chains of fear
That bind me tight and show me
Teach me the secrets of yesterdays
Show me the mysteries that keep us
Driving us to tomorrow's tomorrow.

Melt away the walls of ignorance
Bring forth the knowledge of the ages
Tempered with the wisdom of the elders
I am but a babe in this trek called life
Thirsty for the journey of higher insight.
Pat Barnes

Why Don't You Hear Me?

Why don't you hear me?
When I call out to you in the night.
Why don't you hear me?
When I just can't fight.
Why don't you hear me?
When my eyes are filled
  with tears.
Why don't you hear me?
I've been here for too many years
Why don't you hear me?
When I feel hurt day after day
Why don't you hear me?
I really don't want to stay
Why don't you hear me?
Am I crying in deaf ears?
Why don't you hear me?
For you have forsaken me all these years
Why don't you hear me?
I answered your call.
now, I beg of you, answer mine.

Sharon Reppert

Faith

  Why do we cry . . .
when it goes unheard.
  If only in our ears . . .
we listen to the pain.
  And in our hearts . . .
we feel the sadness.

  If not for faith . . .
would we forever be . . .
  Alone to deal with the burden . . .
That God would shoulder . . .
  And carry us . . .
to that peaceful place . . .
  in our hearts, souls, and minds.

Rose Ann Rapp

Our Lord Is Always There

Trouble come in every shape,
When no one seems to care,
Please do not give up,
Our Lord is always there.

We have to count our blessings,
Pray to the one above,
He is the one we look to,
How beautiful his gifts of love.

How great is our dear Savior,
His truth is everywhere,
When we are faced with problems
Our Lord is always there.

Thelma Lee Freeman

Silent Whispers

Silent whispers in my ear
Whispers only I can hear
But Day and Night my thoughts are of you
The air smelling so fresh and sweet
I start to cry and drop to my feet
The whispers tell me of the day
My pains and tears shall go away
I love you and you'll never know
How very much I cherish you so.

Tera Teafatiller

My Dream

Without a dream
Where would I be
Life would be boring
And that's not me
Without a dream
I'd be just little ol' me
Some day I'll be famous
Just wait and see!

Robin Weber

Time Spiral

There are times
  When our anger over powers us.
There are times
  When rage surrounds us.
There are times
  When mental abused belittles us.
There are times
  When physical fatigue reduces us.

Time is there
  When understanding empowers us.
Time is there
  When love surrounds us.
Time is there
  When kind words improve us.
Time is there
  When hope strengthens us.
Time is there
  When our actions unite us.

Lynda J. Bryant

When Things Go Wrong

Sometimes one is discouraged
  When our life seems to go astray,
And we cry out for more courage
  To help us meet the day
Sometimes when pain over-powers
  We find our thoughts amiss.
Then we must close our eyes
  In prayer, seal it with a kiss
Oft times we need greater courage
  When our days go all wrong
One needs our faith and courage then
  To keep us truly strong
Our heavenly father understands
  And he is always there
To give us strength to meet the day
  To show and guide us on our way,
To give us faith to make us strong
  On days when everything goes wrong.

Ruth Beaufait

A Spring To Remember

Spring is the loveliest time of year
  When sun and flowers warn "it's here"
Few people notice the signs, you see
  For their tiny buds upon the trees

The daffodil, the first to appear
  Declares that spring soon is near
While the lazy rose stays in it's bed
  Winter clothes will soon be shed

The tulips flower, like a crown
  Tells us winter will soon be bound
To other regions of the earth
  For spring is a time of joy and mirth.

Sallye Beth Jordan

The Rooster

In the early part of morning
when the sleep is in your eyes,
You can hear the still of daybreak
and anticipate the rise
of the bright and cheerful sunlight,
and the crisp and chilly air.
But the covers they won't come off,
and your slippers aren't there.
You're tempted just to linger
and sleep awhile more,
when you hear the strange enchanted
call of the bird who lives next door.
He calls and calls and calls to you
until you come around.
Oh, to hear the cock-a-doodle
when the dew is on the ground.

Susan Walsh

What Will Be

What will the sky be
When the stars have all fallen
Some empty hole in space
We are sent to explore

What will the sea be
When the fish have all died
Just a landmark of time
We are told to remember

What will the land be
When the trees have all burned
A vast waste land
That will never be admired

What will brotherhood be
When the races are all conquered
A word that was thought about
but not often followed

Rosina Valvo

Murmurings

I have tender moments for you,
  when the world is so unkind;
A gentle hand to stroke a wounded
  heart.
I fancy myself a sentry, steadfast,
  between you and fear.
I see your face, the face of a
  woman hiding a little girl —
Trying to keep her in, to persevere,
  to live a life in disarray —
To hold up one end as the other topples.
Step back a pace and let me help,
  if only with a chosen word;
For if words have power, then surely
  they must give comfort too.
My heart murmurs in the night,
  speaking softly to you,
Words that only I can hear.

D. A. Smallwood

Storm

Clouds building
Wind blowing
Rain whipping
Thunder rolling
Waves crashing
Souls thrashing
Lightning strikes!

Laurel Schamber

You

I smell your pillow,
when you leave.
I see your face
smiling at me.
I hear you whisper,
in my ear,
I really love you
have no fear.
I feel your arms
around me so tight.
I taste your kiss,
when we say good night.
All those words couldn't
tell you what I mean
Forever in my heart
you will always be!

Lisa Tyson

Somebody Cares

Miracles do happen every day
When you turn your eyes to Jesus
Bow your head and pray

When the mountains in your life
Seem to steep to climb
He'll lift you up and free you
In your spirit and in your mind
Miracles do happen every day
When you turn to Him He'll always
Make a way

Miracles do happen every day
When you turn your eyes to Jesus
Bow your head and pray

Mary Eva Taylor

And The Flowers Bloom . . .

And the flowers bloom
   Where angels play
Amongst the treetops
   The mapling maze
. . . And the flowers bloom
   Upon hills autumn grey
land fertile
   Pine box decay
. . . And the flowers bloom 'UNWRITTEN'
   Unspoken graves
TO SEED . . . The Wind
   Asters in sway
To ALL
   A new may
   . . . And the FLOWERS bloom

Kim C. Teachout

Home For The Holiday

Home for the holiday
Where loved ones wait
They watch from the window
Hoping you won't be late.

The door opens inward
Where they wait with open arms
Their greetings and love,
Your heart it sure warms

You get that special feeling
Please keep it all year long
Not only for the holidays
To everyday it should belong.

Margaret Gardner

Good-Bye

How do I start?
Where do I begin?
To close a chapter in this book,
When I'm not ready for it to end.

So much life
So much love all rolled up in one,
How can I say good-bye to my
Bright shiny sun?

I could start with I love you,
And I always will,
And how special you are,
Or how lonely I feel.

I could list all your good points,
But that would take too long.
Or how much I'll miss you
But that will forever go on and on.

So all I can say is wait there for me,
Save me a place where we can be free.

And someday my love, my promise to you,
I'll be there to hold you until forever is
through.

Shawnna S. Prehm

Time

Tick, tock, tick, tock
where is the time going
thinking, dreaming, about days
to come. What do we do?
Is it wasting time in what
we do or what we don't do.
   What shall happen
if you sit back and watch
it go bye. Flying from north to
south and east to west.
   The questions is "Do
you catch it or watch it fly
right in front of you?"
   Tick, tock, tick, tock
where does it go? I know it
flies right in front of me and
I catch it.

Vashti Eleesha Bocker

Our Love

Oh precious one of gentle heart
which beats with love for me.
What would I give, if given chance
to become but one with thee?

If I were king, then kingdom all
would I give to reach that goal.
For nothing less could I ever do
if by doing, our halves grew whole.

For nothing in life is worth as much
as a love so shared by two.
Not wealth, nor things, nor life itself
if I can't spend this life with you.

So when that day, that sacred day
has come, and come it shall.
I pledge to you, oh precious one,
more than words can ever tell.

And if by chance, old we become
and our hair turns white as snow,
this gift of love will still burn bright
so all that see, will know.

Stephen C. Sample

Message Received

Autumn colors! Fountains
Where the mountains
Meet the terrain below.
Yellow, green, and red flow,
Shimmering in the sunlight,
To form for us a sight
As they wend their way
By winding stream and say
Without words that life
Is to live, without strife.
Life is to live with love
From the heart, from above.

Robyn Runyan

West Virginia

Where the sun shines the brightest
Where the shade is cool and still,
And the water slowly trickles down
Between the West Virginia hills.

In the spring the flowers are sweetest
In summer, the grass more green,
In the fall the leaves are brightest
In winter, wonder lands are seen.

Where the snow is piled the deepest
On the hills that are so high,
And it looks like many pyramids
As they soar against the sky.

It is where the birds sing sweetest
And our hearts with rapture thrills,
And our hopes all rise the highest
Back in the West Virginia hills.

Kathleen Caldwell

Trapped

I am like a butterfly
Who sings but cannot fly
I am like a butterfly
Whose sorrow cannot die

I am like a wailing baby
Whose mother left behind
I am like a wailing baby
Whose still has love inside

I am like a wilted flower
Whose petals cry for loveliness
I am like a wilted flower
Who needs the sudden sun rays

And so I am all these things
Still no one seems to see
That there is aching love
Lying there within me.

Melanie Diaz

Tomorrow

The love, the hurt, the pain, and sorrow
Will hopefully end tomorrow
But if it doesn't
I shall wait
alone
filled with the
Love, hurt, pain, and sorrow
Hopeful for tomorrow

Pam Hicks

The Runner

I am a runner, one of a few,
Who's only as good
   as the tread on my shoe.

I am runner, who knows determination
Can only be found
   On the 5th mile marker,
When 6 miles bound.

I am a runner, my spirit is free,
Til the tread is all gone,
   And I damage my knee.

I am a runner, my soul has no ground,
Til the last mile is over,
   And my wind can be found.

I am a runner, and only confined
By the strength in my legs,
   And the depths of my mind.

I am a runner, as I'll be til I die,
Then, my shoes won't need tread,
   For then, I will fly!

    Katherine L. Morgan

Dear Grandpa

Dear Grandpa in heaven above,
Why did God take you from our love?
Why did you make me cry?
Why do I remember you at times?

Did you see Grandma when you died?
She went to you and said Good-bye.
With her hand close to yours,
She was near you, her heart so sore.

My heart broke when I saw her there.
I had to leave, I could not bare.
To see you once before I left,
I glanced, I saw, I shouldn't have.

I went outside to start to cry.
Then I felt you at my side.
It's all right, I heard you say,
You'll be up there with me someday.

When I turned to see your face,
No one was there, just an empty space.
Why didn't you stay with me some more?
But it wasn't you, it was the Lord.

    Kerry A. Dutoit

Menuki

Menuki, beautiful, black, slave-girl
why you crying?
Mama's gone be alright though she's a
dying, but Lord knows she'll be better
off in her new home, which is heaven
above.
Menuki, beautiful, black, slave-girl
why do you look at me like that?
Maybe you'd like to say through your
sad, big, brown eyes instead of with
your mouth that you don't want to walk
this life along, but don't worry, Menuki,
for I'll always be here just for you
my beautiful, Menuki.

    Virginia McIntyre

Love Is Like A Rose

Love is like a rose,
Wild or tame it grows.
Evident but silently,
Developing slow you see.
Be patient - it takes time,
As it makes its gentle climb.
Beauty flourishes as it blooms,
And in the heart it takes up room.
Then suddenly the rose is cut down,
And slowly death is found.
The rose is weak - no longer tall,
One by one the petals fall.
Left behind are stem and thorns,
Apart the rose is torn.
The sadness soon dies,
And broken are the ties.
But look on the bush and you will find,
Many more roses of all sizes and kinds.
So don't give up over just one love,
Remember the rose and climb above.

    Tammy M. Brown

Our Love

A rose healthy and strong
Will live very long
But with a little neglect
Their is a harsh effect

So show some concern
And you will learn
The rose will prosper
Like no other...

But if you choose
To abuse
The rose will wither and die
And eventually become dry

But once the rose goes bad
Remember what you had
And please do not make
This very same mistake

For the rose
In this pose
Is much like a dying dove
or should I say our love...

    Kevin Weaver

Four Seasons

I love the beauty of the seasons:
Winter, spring, summer and fall.
Each one has its glory;
That's why I favor them all.

The drifting snows of winter
Bring joy to my heart.
Blooming flowers in springtime
God's beautiful work of art.

Oh, the joys of summer living,
When we can swim and play.
The cool, cool days in Autumn
I sometime wish would stay.

God gives us these resources
To benefit one and all.
We should thank Him daily,
Work hard, be proud, stand tall.

    Lillian E. Hart

"If"

If I give you my heart
   Will you handle it with care.
Will you say you love me
   and always be there?

If I give you my hands
   will you let them do
Works that show
   my love for you?

If I give you my moments
   and my days
will you keep me happy
   in endless ways?

If I give you my lips
   for you to keep true.
Will you fill them
   with messages from you?

If I give you myself
   will you let me be
yours alone...
    ...eternally?

    Lisa Rodriguez

White Is

White is the fluffy snow falling in the
winter sky
White is the cleanliness we see in our clothes
White is the taste of marshmallows
cooking on an open fire
White is the soft clouds soaring above us
White is the smell that rises above all smells
White is the ice cream rolling down your
throat on a hot summer day
White is the feel of a waterfall's mist
White is the air on a crisp winter morning
White is the joy and smell at Christmas
time when family and friends get together
White is

    Sean Colahan

Clara

Such a special woman
with a heart made of gold
God saw you suffering
He called you home.

In this world you are no longer
but in our hearts you still remain
and the love you gave to all of us
will help us through our pain.

The void you left within our lives
no one can ever fill
even now that time has passed
we feel your presence still.

And though we can no longer touch you
we feel your love so strong
and in our lives you'll always be
the music to our song.

    Melissa Avery

A Rose

A thing of beauty, but for to share
With all who choose to linger there.
No lovely face, no golden hair.
Only leaves of green and flower so rare.

Would I choose to paint with care?
To loosen earth and water fair?
Perhaps a thanks to God up there?
Or to look and smell a scent so rare?

A warm, red delight, we do see there.
A lovely form of silent prayer.
A tender gift of God so fair.
A flower, a plant, indeed so rare!

Louise Kantenwein

Our Love

Walking hand in hand,
With each other in soft sand.
Looking up at the sky,
On you now rely.
Kissing under the lighted stars,
What happens now is ours.
In our hands the future lies,
Side by side without the cries.
The ocean sound brings us together,
On the sand we stay forever.
In our hearts love it true,
I only want to be with you.
On the beach my love I need not show,
You hold me close while the wind blows.
I love you with all of my heart,
Never shall we need to part.
We will never split because of fights,
Making up, is our delight.
With our love will stay together,
This screwed up world, we'll make it better.

Melinda Werner

"Our World"

The world seems to be shrinking,
With every passing year;
There was a time when thinking
Could be done without fear.
Perhaps past wars have taught us,
Along with science too,
And meeting men has brought us
To see life, in review.
We must learn now, to do all
We can, in worldly scope;
To live and learn, and, to all
Give peace, give love and hope.

Violet Touch

In Two

Early in the morning,
without any warning,
nobody knew, only but two,
when all of a sudden,
a big explosion in the morning.
Everyone was worried, all but two,
the two who knew.
And all of the hearts in Oklahoma
were shattered in two.

Zachary James Miller

"This Heart"

This heart has many doorways,
With hallways that are long,
Only few are meant to open,
Some are not too strong,
The hinges are all sagging;
From too much use and wear,
Some are better than others;
Cause no-one ventures there.
The hallways ring with echoes.
Of the doors that have been slammed,
Never to reopen,
The pain too much to bear.
My souls the only one,
To pass through every door,
The halls are dark and shadowed,
The lights are lit no more.
Some things are to be shared,
But not in this heart of mine.
These doors that will stay bolted,
Through the end of time.

Regina Denise Moats

Waves

Flying like a wild bird
With no care in all the sky,
Scurrying like a tiny ant
Quickly passing by.
A wave can carry dreams away
Or lift your heart in gladness,
Then quickly bring you down again
And fill your heart with sadness.
Coming and going,
A never ending flow,
A wave is oh so many things
With a never ending glow.
It lifts you up so very high
And lets you dream of things to be,
But just before you touch your dreams
They're washed away to sea.

Kathi Snead

The 60's

Hippies walking down the street,
with no shoes on their feet.
Oh, the 60's were so neat.

People smoke Mary Janes,
while Jimi Hendrix sings Purple Haze;
and the band behind him plays.

Come with me; we'll take a ride,
and break on through to the other side.
Come on now, you can't hide.

We'll protest the war.
And what's more,
we'll scream until our ears are sore.

We'll go to Woodstock; it's the best.
We'll be a mess,
and slide in the mud with all the rest.

What would we have done,
if the 60's hadn't come;
and we wouldn't have had ten years of fun?

Spring McAllister

Facing The Light

From strength in spirituality,
with quiet dignity,
I face the light.
Challenged by nature,
resilient with man,
I face the light.
Tempered with age,
seeking peace in my soul,
I face the light.
Sharing with others,
to cast a small shadow,
I face the light.

To find new direction
and leave darkness behind...

Quentin C. Rath

Headache

A vulture lives within my head
With quiet patience waiting
Each day he sharpens talent bought,
I feel his beak's almighty bite.
It greets me at my waking.

Some days he gives me respite,
My spirits soar in vain.
I've searched to find his hiding place,
My friends help in the awesome race
Next day he bites again.

Dear God, Please help me find him,
Please help me set him free.
This bird should fly to meet his kind,
To feed on carrion, not on mind,
And stay away from me!

Miriam Schoenhoft

The Sight

When you sit on a moonlit night
With stars a dancing across the skies
And a cool breeze in the air

When your teeth are clinched tight
And the tears fill your eyes
Thinking that nobody dose care

Look up into the night
Let loose those lonely cries
Then ask GOD if you dares

To come hold you tight
Make you forget your sighs
And to you his love he will share

He gives us the sight
To see thru lies
And find them that care

So turn on his light
And open your eyes
Cause GOD do care

Steven Sandusky

Beautiful Day

I woke up early in the morning
with the light just peeping though.
I heard the birds singing in the trees.
And soft wind blew through and
the sun come peeping in the sky.
I said O, what a beautiful sit to see.
And I thank our God I could see
this beautiful day.

Nellie Le Compte

A Solemn Tide

And behold a hush falls over the world
with the ocean of pain
Bringing tidings of chaos
sweeping across the soul

Lest smash our mouths with
the lies of a billion
Fools
One and all

The end of the era of light
which is dark
Cascading, undulating
insatiable pain

The damage done
the agony achieved
With no eyes to look up to
but those who sneer

Bring you shadows do I
to hide behind
Hide away, wretched refuse
within the tide so solemn

Russ Stillman

Nature's Touch

As I sit on the sand
with the waves at hand,
The pinkish glow of dawn
which is gentle as a fawn,
This beauty is such
that it can only be made
with nature's touch.

Katherine Ann Combs

Retirement

My father dear
    Worked thirty years
        Of this there is no doubt

And now at last
    With Christmas past
        Just forty-five days about

Till ma and pa
    Can see it all
        And not of the days keep track

Able at last
    To go slow or fast
        And not have to hurry back

With retirement here
    And freedom so near
        Like two birds on the breeze

I believe in my head
    What my parents said
        We'll do as we damn well please!

Karen A. Oliver

Inside

Let me ride
with you

let me enter
your dream

walk your floors
of dried dust
blowing—
of old hope

walk your stairs
of pain

your windows
of fear

the blowing curtains
of your love

soft breezes
of stories you have heard

your garden
of peace

the oxygen of desire
let me breathe.

Lydia Szkodzinsky

Recovering

How can I function
Without an injunction
How can I live without "don't"
Why do I worry
Future all blurry
Knowing I can't and I won't
I'm easy to stifle
You don't need a rifle
A cluck or raised eyebrow will do it
Except when I'm manic
Or into a panic
In which case I'll tell you to screw it

Virginia Knight

I

I question myself,
    without doubt.
I answer myself,
    without lies.
I believe in myself,
    without arrogance.
I trust in myself,
    without fear.
I know who I am,
    and I am happy.

I laugh at myself,
    without malice.
I look at myself,
    without secrets.
I live with myself,
    without shame.
I love myself,
    without conditions.
I know who I am,
    and I am happy.

Wendy I. Keathley

If I Only Had A Brain

Sometimes I wish my brain would work
without it's faults and little quirks
But I'm afraid if they were gone,
I could not tell if it was on.

Shannon Dunlap

I Mean Nothing To You

You treat me like a rag doll,
Without the emotions to feel.
Loving me for a moment,
Then, not wanting to deal.
Your shoulders are so cold,
Your words are like heat.
Feelings don't mean anything,
Halfway you won't even meet.
At times I feel so cared for,
Others like nothing at all.
Your words are so harsh,
Their power makes me fall,
Tears now fall like rain,
Where happiness used to be,
Nonexistent emotions,
Mean a hell of a lot to me.
Are you just using me,
For reasons I cannot see?
Hurt and fear unraveled,
Are all I seem to be.

Melissa Millinger

Who?

A mindless vagabond I am
Wondering aimlessly
Feeling so alone
Nobody to talk to,
I talk to myself
Longing so for company,
Companionship.

Am I a mindless vagabond?
Complete in the lunacy
Of my own private madness
I ask out loud,
Only to be answered by
My own voice
A mindless vagabond I am.

Sarah Ann Thomas

Listen

Listen, can you hear, can you feel
    Words coming from a ghost.
Are they real or just an illusion
    Just imagined, just a hoax

Listen, do you dare, do you see
    The words are a power
Eternal once spoken, once written
    Do they wither or do they flower.

Listen, darkness is with-out and void
    Words come from with-in and fill
Are they a light or raging fire
    Do they help or do they kill.

Listen carefully, you can hear
    The words have feel and they can kill
Listen gently, carefully, feel it.
    The words are feeling and they can heal.

Mark S. Clements

"No Words"

There are words that tell of beauty
Words to tell what you see
Words that speak of loving
But no words to tell what you mean to me

I can say I love you
That you're dearer that life you see
I can say you're my everything
But no words can say what you mean to me

Words tell of beautiful sunsets
Of waves on a stormy sea
Of beautiful moonlight for sweethearts
But words can't tell what you mean to me

So I'll just say I love you
They're only words I know
So look down deep into my eyes
And the love shining there will show
Mary Ann Motl

When You Were There

The times the world
Would seem most fair
Were all the times
When you were there.
Patricia Wolery

Needed Trees

If peace grew on trees
would you pick it?
If love grew on trees
would you take it?
If laughter grew on trees
would you listen?
If money grew on trees
would you be greedy?
If all this grew on trees
the world would be better
Right? Wrong!
Everyone would take
What they wanted
And leave behind what they needed.
What if one day I came
Running to tell you that
Trees like this exist?
You wouldn't care, you wouldn't believe,
You would just simply turn away.
Sharla Drew

Pretty Boy

Your wandering eyes
Yearn to see it all.
Your wavy hair
Flying with each step you take.
Your beautiful smile
That stretches for miles.
Your fascination
For everything around.
Your dimples
In your cheeks and on your chin.
Your favorite foods
I like a lot.
Your just something special.
To me.
Sophia Coleman

K.I.T

Keep in touch
write me sometime,
anytime!!!
To let me know
that all is well,
any new or exciting news
to share with me
or I with you
words scribbled
upon the pages
the only thing that is
sad...
is sometime
we have to
say...
I gotta go,
take care,
write back soon,
AND
KEEP IN TOUCH - okay?!
Kristen Marie King

Silent Poetry

Poetry is like the silence
wrapped exclusively around you
teasing your imagination
stirring strong feelings
from the farthest reaches of your soul

Stillness and beauty of the earth
seen through silent eyes
as radiant beams of light cascade
opening the doors to your heart

Meaningful words
dance through your mind
blanketing your thoughts
deep within yourself

They take you somewhere else
away from the hurt
away from the pain
into a whole new world
of eloquent silence
Katie Brown

The Beauty Of Autumn

The trees in all their splendor,
Yellow, red, orange and brown,
The blue sky above us,
There's beauty all around.

Pumpkin's corn and squashes,
Still lie basking in the sun,
Waiting to be gathered in,
Before the winter comes.

The beautiful chrysanthemum,
Rustic, purple, yellow and white,
With mixed array of colors,
It's quite a lovely sight.

Sometimes there's Indian summer,
When the sun warms the air,
God sends all this beauty,
For each of us to share.

It's the brilliance of autumn,
With color around us spread,
Soon it will fade in darkness,
Cause winter's just ahead.
Nancy Klinger Heller

Moods Of Aeolus

The wind sings his theme song
Written so long ago

He blows across the meadows
He skips merrily over the lea

The flogs the sailors on the decks
He rides the angry sea

He howls his music in the beating rain
And taunts the driven snow

He hums it softly in the moonlight
When shadows dance on the walls

He croons a baby's lullaby
He murmurs to gulls in flight

He moans in concerts through the trees
And vaults his notes to the sky

He wails his theme over the prairie
He chants in the mountains high

And when at my final rest I lay
Bathed in autumns glow

The wind will whisper his theme song
Written so long ago.
Stelle MacMullen

More Than Fun

Never ending sunshine
Yes, it's all very nice,
For one could easily get used to
This sea of paradise.

Lying in the sunshine
Dipping in the pool,
If anyone dare complain,
They'd surely be called a fool.

Yet there's more to life than this,
Like helping our fellow man,
Because there's so much suffering
That perhaps God didn't plan.

Oh yes we should enjoy
The pleasures of life that are near,
But we never must forget
Why God has put us here.
Nancy Shrader

The Most Precious Gift

Happy Birthday precious Jesus.
Yes, it's that time of year
To celebrate your birthday;
Or, so it would appear.
But, with the hurried frenzy
That takes us everywhere:
Do we stop and take the time
Just to know that you are there?
With the Christmas trees, the presents,
The exchanges friend to friend,
Will we feel Your very presence
Before we see your birthday's end?
As we plan our celebrations,
Will we even do our best
To remember it's Your birthday
And invite you as our guest?
For it was on that day so long ago
That you were sent to be
(Wrapped and tied in God's own love)
The most precious gift the world would see.
Rachael M. Working

"Unknown Future"

My mind is full of questions
Yet no one knows the answers
How will my life turn out?
Every day I ask myself that
Are my friends going to stand by me
Ready to help me in my time of need?
Thinking of this I do always
Besides these there are many more
Every one a little different
Like the one I ask about love
One what will never cease
Now there are yet still more
Gone right into my head
Some however go straight to my heart
Take me into the land of dreams
On a plateau will I stand
Keep me safe there
Until I return
Recoil my fear of my unknown future
Take me back now to the present

Poppy Kay Cecilia Heinze

Priceless Jewel

It doesn't cost us anything
yet we spend it feverishly,
we never know what it may bring
still we don't take it seriously.
Everything depends on it,
nothing, can be without it
way ahead of everything waiting,
for know one
lurking, around the darkest corners
peeking, through the brightest lights
but you can't see it.
Even though it's right in front of
our eyes when we blink,
we miss it
it's more precious than diamonds
worth more than gold,
it's the one jewel,
we, can't put a price-tag on . . .
time.

Preston Maurice Vann

Parent's Love

When you were, a little girl
you always kept, us in a whirl
we never knew, what you might do
like bringing home, a cat or two

On top of your head, a cat would be
and then of course, we'd laugh with glee
you seldom ever, did get hurt
while digging with a spoon, in the dirt

When it came time, for your nap
you would crawl upon, your Mama's lap
regardless of the dirt, in your hair
your Mama would rock, you in the chair

Mama would wash, your little feet
and soon you would, be sound asleep
you'd wake with a smile, never a fuss
you were and are, a joy to us.

Tom Sibley

The Dreamer

I am the dreamer of the universe
You are a fragment of my imagination
Anything less and nothing more,
Just that!

I've scanned you on oceans deep
And swam far to greet you
Only that from me you seep

I've imagined you on the mountains
Yet feared you in the valley
As you appeared to me in the fountains

I am the dreamer of the universe
And you I conjured, wherever I ventured
Anything less and nothing more,
Just that!

R. Elaine Mazyck

Unexpected Storms

Through the unexpected storms of life
You are always there
Though the clouds gather overhead
You never cease to care

As incredible as it is to find
The snow upon the beach
I find it just as awesome
That your throne's within my reach

Help me to remember
To see and understand
As surely as waves break on the shore
My life lies in your hand

May I always be reminded
That your majesty abounds
I find it in your faithfulness
And in nature's sights and sounds

Thank you for the eyes to see
What you have given me
For all the gifts - both great and small
All glory goes to Thee

Peg Antle

Little One

Oh Little one, oh little one,
You glow so tenderly.
And every time I look at you,
What wonder do I see!

A little one who's just begun
To grow so gracefully,
That every time I hear you smile
I know who you will be.

'Cause ever since this small one came,
My heart has been set free.
You've brought me to tears and laughter;
You mean everything to me.

So little one, oh little one,
Upon my bended knee,
I thank the Lord of love above
For sending you to me.

Vickie Young

Betrayed

You touched my hand and heart today,
you listened, wiped my tears away.

You encouraged, comforted my soul,
you became my "hero" . . .
more then you know.

You were my strength,
the wind beneath my wings . . .
little did I know,
how things would change.

We agreed to be friends,
to "keep in touch" . . .
for unknown reasons,
I didn't hear from you much.

I do not understand,
even to this day . . .
why our friendship faded away?

I ask for consolation . . .
my spirit feels betrayed.

My hand and heart was touched today,
as I knelt down and prayed.

Vicki P. Whetzel

Contradictions

I saw you.
You saw me.

   I noticed you.
   You didn't notice me.

      I loved you.
      You accepted it.

         I smiled.
         You smiled.

            I dreamed.
            You dreamed.

               I sang.
               You heard.

            I cried.
            You went away.

         I screamed.
         You strolled.

   I suffered.
      You stopped.

Finally, I forgot you...
Finally, you remember me...

Rosa Maria S. Bugarin

I Love You

Your hair so brown
Your eyes so blue
Every time I look in them
I see deep down in you
Your lips so pink
Your skin so fair
Every time I look at you
I know you'll always
Be there
Every time you blink
Every time you move
I always think I
Will always
Love you.

Lainey Sharp

"I Just Can't Take It Anymore"

Today we had an argument,
You stormed out the door,
You came back, and said you loved
me like all the times before.
How long is it going to last,
Before you walk out again
like a fool I'll take you back,
I just can't never win.
I don't know what happened to
change my sweet use to be
It's like you locked up the door,
I am left without a key.
You took our love for granted
and thru it all away
I tried everything I can to make
you want to stay;
I fought so hard to keep you
there is something I can't ignore,
I still love you to pieces,
I just can't take it anymore.

Ruth M. Wilkins

Let Me Know

When it was dark...
    You were my sunrise.
When it was cold...
    You brought me warmth and comfort.
When I was angry...
    You soothed me until I was calm.
When I was lonely...
    You were there for me.
When I was lost...
    You came looking for me.
When I was confused...
    You helped me understand.
When I was sad....
    You made me smile.
When I was crying...
    You gave me a shoulder to lean on.
When the times were tough...
    You brought strength into me.
When I needed to talk...
    You were a good listener.
When you need anything...
    Let me know.

Michael P. Wielenberg

Contentment

Father God in heaven above
Your arms reach out to me in love
My head is pillowed on your breast
My soul is calm in perfect rest.

The storm is swirling out of sight
The lightening splits a darkened night
The thunder claps; it rumbles near
But I have nothing, nay, to fear.

You hold me close in arms so strong
Your voice sings out in gentle song
I hear the beating of your heart
And know from me you'll never part.

The storms may come, the storms may go
But this one thing I surely know
When held by your Almighty Arms
I am forever safe from harm.

Minda S. Graff

After The Loving

Many days later,
    your aura still surrounds me;
Your smile, your caring,
    pleasing me, teasing me.
Where have you been all my life?
    Were you waiting for the right time?
Is it now...shall we be?

I come to you
    not in naivete, nor you to me,
For we have known love;
    But know this now I am as vulnerable
As I have ever been
    and yours I am alone; shall we be?

Your aura still surrounds me...

Sheila Conary-Thum

Cry, Child, Cry

Cry, child, cry
Your daddy died
    in battle
in vain
in war
Cry, child, cry
    There's nothing more

There's nothing I want to do
'cause you're not here
But there's everything I need to do
but I don't care

Without you
    I have no meaning
no vision
it all just falls
    to darkness
like your eyes

All I have are my cries.

Mark Morris

"Say No To Drugs"

If you do drugs
your dumb
You'll probably be
a bum
So lets be smart
make a good start
So your future will be
bright and fun

Reno Reddis

Thank God

When you awake by mornings light
    Your eyes see a glorious sight,
The sky of blue and meadows of green
    Are the most beautiful things seen.
Now, if you listen close
    Your ears will hear
The sounds that say God is near.

The gentle breeze in the air
    The smell of flowers everywhere:
Songs the Robins sing
    Early morn in spring.
The hoot of a wise old owl
    And the long sound of a coyotes howl.
From the cows moo, to the horses neigh
    We thank God for each new day!

Pat Eilert

Just A Thought Of Adolf

Imagine...
Your name is on the list.
Mine is not.
I am full of joy.
A sigh is heaved from my breast.
I would laugh,
But this is no laughing matter.
I do not look into your eyes.

Imagine...
My name is on the list.
Yours is not.
You are full of joy.
A sigh is heaved from your breast.
You would laugh,
But this is no laughing matter.
You do not look into my eyes.

Paula C. Helm

Whenever...

Whenever I'm down,
your smile keeps me going.
Whenever I feel like crying,
you cry with me.
Whenever I get an attitude,
you never take it personally.
Whenever I feel no one is listening,
you act as if you care.
Whenever I feel a slight chill,
you seem to keep me warm.
Whenever my heart is cold,
you fill it with love and tenderness.
Whenever I feel guilty of doing wrong
you seem to make things right
Whenever you say you love me,
I will say I love you, too.
Thanks for being you.

Rita Renee Johnson

"Longing"

We sit here every evening
You're absorbed in your books.
There's no exchange of loving terms
Nor even wistful looks.

We're almost like strangers,
Never sharing repartee.
You're deep into your reading,
I'm wishing you'd read me.

I'm longing for the revelry
That we two used to share,
Big bear hugs and thrilling strokes
With tender, loving care.

Our trysts and "little moments"
When your fingers pressed me tight.
The sighs, your touch, the kisses,
The passion in the night.

How I long for contact
A pat, a touch, a glance.
Show me that you still care,
Arouse me to romance.

Lorraine Vianelli

Hot Tears

From his pains and his suffering, he is relieved
But he has left me here to grieve.
How long, for how long will I sing a sad song?
How long, for how long will I cry?

I had thought the reservoir of tears had dried
But this morning it overflowed,
Cascading in torrents from my eyes.
How long, for how long will I cry?

Father I know, yes I know he has gone
To dwell in his mansion on high,
But I am bereaved, and I am undone,
Oh, when will I ever cease to cry.

I miss everything about this man
His humor, his caring for his family,
His sincere concern for humanity.
I remember, I get sad, and then, I cry.

This man was my husband of 55 years
This man had been healthy for 53 years
Then he fell very ill and died in two years
And left me bereaving, grieving, and shedding "Hot Tears."

Lynne A. Brown

Portrait

He knows the places where my paint has peeled,
Edges curled and charred by ancient fires,
Where the gilt is gone,
And where once-lovely traceries are worn.

He knows, (how well!) the textures rough and smooth
That time has drawn unseemly and made plain.
And yet, despite the shade I am become,
With caring eyes and gentle hands he finds
Some substance, beauty, truth, design
worth loving.

I, now loved, am loving in return:
Recreated, am uniquely his;
Possessed, am somehow unconfined,
And being his, he is uniquely mine . . .

Stephanie K-F Beery

Hooray For Whom?

Tinsel town was once her name - adorned with glory, myth and fame.
All the dreams one could conceive, she made alive through make believe.
Princes, Kings and Queens we were - films were Magi - gifts of myrrh.
We became the roles portrayed, royally dressed in grand parade.

Regal, opulent movie house places - thrilled our heart and awed our faces.
Romantic mystery - tears and laughter - ending happily ever after.
The wonders swept us off our feet, often glued us to our seat -
Cowboy, comic, song and dance man, actor, actress, autograph book fan.

Hollywood life was oh so amorous - sometimes tainted, always glamorous.
Divorce, romance, all rumors nourished; gossip columns, how they flourished!
Imagination ruled supreme, letting us sustain the dream.
Hollywood was true escape, to look and leer - to stare and gape.

Busby Berkeley: Extravaganza's - magnificent voices: Mario Lanza's.
The Keystone Cops - those bathing beauties - Clara Bow and other cuties.
Valentino - the Sheik of Sheiks, reached beyond artistic peaks.
What was epic was dramatic - we enjoyed it, were ecstatic!

What it was, it is no more - as la-la-land, it's quite a bore.
The heyday's gone - the glamour's famished, all time greats have slowly vanished.
No more life or ecstasy in deadened halls of fantasy.
Modern things are here you see - attribute it to your TV!

Wally Malins

"Midnight Flowers"

Essence of a midnight flower rare; tantalizing fragrance in the air,
lures me down a pathway to the sea, exciting my desires, enchanting me,
inviting me to lie flowering beds of rare, exotic blossoms passioned
red. Intriguing me with esoteric songs that drifted down the path I
walked along. And lucid was the music in the wind that breathed so
warmly on my tingling skin. Intoxicating was the midnight air perfumed
with the fragrant essence rare, and brilliant was the light that shown
on me and midnight flowers growing by the sea. When suddenly, I felt
an eerie chill that shivered me with terrifying thrills, as weird,
fantastic forms in ghostly greys began to weave a strange, foreboding
haze, and grotesque shadows danced like flames of fire and clothed the
night in ebony attire, and waters in the sea began to ebb and spin the
earth into a giant web, that trapped me in an evil, wretched scheme as I
searched for the flowers I had seen, but each path led me to a desert
land of wilted blossoms dying in the sand, and petals strewn around the
flowering beds turned into ashes burning passion red, And essence of a
midnight flower rare evaporated in the grim nightmare, and left me
helpless in the garden tomb of sooted dreams that smoldered in the doom.

Nashel Houldin

"To My Dear Mom And Dad"

It is truly an honor and blessing for me to be standing here with all of
you, to celebrate something that's so rarely seen, twenty years of love,
still shared by two. So many have felt in their own heart of hearts
that you can't find true love anywhere and I'm so proud my parents are
both living proof, love will always exist if you care.

It's hard to find beauty in this world today, since most of us search
with our eyes. But our Mom and Dad did find beauty out there, and
they saw it by sharing their lives. What's kept them together for
twenty years now, they can't touch, can not see, but can feel. It's
amazing this invisible thing we call love, is the most visible power that's real.

I thank God for the mercy he gave to our Mom and his mercy she truly
had earned. He threatened to take her too soon from our lives, before
we'd shown her the love she deserved. It was then that split second,
I opened my eyes and I witnessed how my life would be. Without her,
there'd be no sun left to shine, and no heart left to beat within me.

I thank you dear Daddy, for your loving arms that cradled Mom through
her sick years. Alone it was you, who carried her through her
acceptance of death and it's fears. I wish I'd known better and been
there for you and forever that cross I will bare. Across made of lead,
turned to true love instead. Where that love goes, you know I'll be there.

I've learned not to take things for granted. Each moment can not be
returned. There isn't a person, a place or a thing that he'll lend
us if love isn't learned. So I think we should focus on the here and
now, just like my Dear Mommy and Dad. They would have lasted these
twenty-plus years without appreciating the love so few have.
"I love you both so much!"

Marie Currie

A World Without Music

It would be like a bird without song
A bell without a gong,
Flowers without bees,
Trees without leaves,
Autumn without color
Winter without cover,
Spring without rain,
Summer without showers,
I love music and song
Bells with a gong
A world without music and song would be wrong.

Ollie E. Kenney

To My Second Granddaughter

Precious little Teri Sue, with
your tiny features, dark hair and big
eyes — a little doll — with a chin
that "quivers" when you cry — who
came to us twixt "night" and "night"
to reign supreme o'er the Marx household as Queen!!!
Your sweet little Mother is a joy
to behold — Your Father as proud as
proud can be as he singles you out in
the nursery and says, "That's my gal"
— the adorable little gal in the
crib next to the wall!!!
Doting grandparents all — uncles,
aunts, and cousins by the dozen will
be your pet enigma I'm sure — but
they matter not as they all file by
for Mr. Sandma has sprinkled sleep
dust in your little eyes!!!

Reva Mart

A Tribute To Mary

This cold and windy day we laid to rest
A beautiful lady named Mary Celeste.
God called her to this heavenly throne
And left me here to be all alone.

Mary gave me the strength to go on in this life,
Because she was a loving and caring wife.
A woman devoted to God's holy mother,
Suffered in silence and prayed for some other.

She cared for her family as most mothers do,
But became saddened that she wouldn't be here as they grew.
Her smile lit the room as the little ones came near,
She read them a story which they wanted to hear.

The doctors and nurses enjoyed as she teased,
They knew that she tried their pain to be eased.
As time grew shorter and death close at hand,
She gave them the nod that meant I understand.

Mary kidded and said God wants number sixty-one,
My numbers sixteen so my life here is not done.
I won't know what to do in the presence of God,
So hopefully Mary will give me the nod.

William R. Leimkuhler

Words Of A Ship - Captain's Wife

He sailed away on his boat Nora Lee;
A beautiful ship, she was named after me.

He kissed us goodbye, it was early one morn'
With sweet, tender words, he promised return.

Our children cried out, in the dawn's early light,
But I waited and wept in the darkness of night.

I was left all alone as he went on that day,
Three babes at my side, and one on the way.

The years, they went by, and our children, they grew,
His voyage was long and I knew not where-to.

My sorrow grew deeper, as night after night,
I watched for the "Lee," but never caught sight.

At last, one morning, some news of the "Lee"
She was coming this way, drifting in from the sea.

I met the first - mate as he stepped on the shore;
"My husband?" I asked, but then my heart tore.

The whole crew survived, but I quickly did learn,
It was only the captain who would not return.

Sandra McLean

Ache

As tears roll down my cheeks, I'm caught in the emotion of you.
A better understanding of love has released me to new heights.
My insides ache to share all of that love with you.

In this atmosphere of change, growth has become inevitable.
As we give of ourselves, our hearts become exposed.
Love provides the protective coating we need for survival.
My insides ache to share all of that heart with you.

My faith has been strengthened by the security of following a
Will greater than mine; following has meant giving up me for
Something that is more steadfast and unconditional.
The freedom that grace provides allows my spirit to soar.
My insides ache to share all of that spirit with you.

I search not for all the right answers, but for the right
Questions that challenge every part of me.
Those that challenge my love, my heart, and my spirit keep me on
The path of all that is good which awaits.
The ache does not diminish until all the answers have been
Questioned . . . I invite the challenge of you . . .
My insides ache to share all of that which is me, with you.

Pam Ogilvie

Little Girl Lost

Somewhere in the silence a voice cries out,
A blood curdling scream that arouses me from my sleep,
To suddenly hear the words that have cut
This poor soul's spirit like the double edged sword of Hamlet.
Slowly she glides across the room and gapes at the image,
The pale complexion, blank stare, the invisible lesions.
She sees a picture of a spirited lady with gleaming eyes.
She reaches out to the picture, but it remains
Beyond her grasp, as she again sees a glimpse in the mirror.
Terrified by the figure, she smashes the glass with her fist,
But the glass would not break.
Pounding, beating, harder and harder she lashes at the mirror;
She soundlessly cries out, but it will not shatter.
She glances at the hour glass and sees the eludement of time.
Breathless by this sight, she sobs a bit more.
Staring at the half empty timer she mutters,
"Where has all the time gone?"
As she turns the time machine over, letting the grains fall
Anew, glides towards the door, with the picture of the spirited
Lady, a voice remains for the little girl lost.

Lisa Marie Bossier

Winter Walk

Sparrow in a cherry tree, fluffed up in the cold-
A cat lying below, too bright and orange in the drab
Where sea and sky match — a dismal slab broken only
By the waves breaking with a frothing white.
A rugged up child in the cold wind, flying kites, the tide coming in
And washing up a sandy shore, filling the senses with a muffled roar.

The sun absent for the day, blanketed by clouds
Like a soft mixed grey cotton ball shroud.
Smoke drifts from a smoldering pile of dead leaves on the sidewalk
Under an avenue of trees, color turned into grey, grey and grey.
No parallel here to make with a picture by Monet, just the tint
Of green with eucalyptus and branches bare of deciduous trees
Around a cobbled square with old iron railings rusting in the wet.

But wait! A flash of hue in the winter gloom - reds, pinks,
Masses of flowers in bloom - the brilliant camellia a part
Of winter's botany and the bright yellow under skeletons of trees.
The daffodil, with the jonquil and snow drop lightening the gloom
Make one stop to look at the winter garden that opposes the rule
Of a depressing winter grey, colors of nature's ridicule.

Simon Blair

Silent Heroes

The Vietnam war took men to fight
  A cause many did not endorse.
  Placed in prisons, with no recourse
Let us bring them home—we must unite!

By the side of our Red, White, and Blue
  Soldiers stared at the face of death.
  Piercing screams consumed their last breath,
People back home never had a clue.

Men torn between what was right and wrong
  A country served in countless ways.
  Spoken words will never repay —
Blood shed by weapons weep sad songs.

God grants glory to silent heroes
  Who were scared still they remained strong.
  We as humans did them great wrong,
Honor them all with Heaven's glow.

The Vietnam war brought mankind pain,
  Remember what each soldier lost.
  The time has come to pay the cost —
For peace and unity to be gained . . .

Victoria A. Thompson

Winter Along The Yukon

An eerie silence seems almost contrived.
A clear sign that winter has finally arrived.
The swift Yukon current has visibly ceased.
Creating a land bridge for man and for beast.

Fishwheels and boats have been hauled up on shore.
Signaling an end to fish camp and more.
Hunting and trapping bring fresh stores of meat
Moose meat or Caribou just can't be beat.

Snow machines are fueled and ready to fly.
Over powdery snow, under crystal blue sky.
Wood is stock piled beside log cabin walls
And fluffy down parkas now hang in the halls.

The land of the far north has a wisdom and peace.
To the careful observer who is bundled in fleece.
Its magic transcends the harshness that's real.
And gives the soul time to think and to heal.

Peggy Freeman Purdy

The Good Old Days

Memories linger like a catchy phrase
a kaleidoscope of my yesterdays.
Childhood was carefree - innocence at play
The joy of living, filled every day
Raggedy Ann dolls, and a blue wooden soldier
Ball games and dancing - when we got older.
Savouring first love - tender and sweet
The highs and lows, made the circle complete
at times there was sadness, many times were gay.
Mistakes we learned from, and grew on the way.
Closeness of family, etched deep in my mind
Rewards came from friendships, the treasured kind
I return to the present, with a sigh of regret.
Patches from youth - are hard to forget.
Tomorrow may be better in many ways
But never forgotten - are the good old days.

Rose Batt

What I Remember Best

When I was five or six, my Thursday spent in Lens, France
A coal miner's town sad and black with dust, like Emile
The quiet little man my Grandma had remarried.
Also the big rabbits I fed in their cages,
Only to hang later for a stew.

Those Sunday visits to the cemeteries of Vimy in the North
In winter, when the wind blew hard over the plains
The trances were left intact after the massacre of W.W.I
But later in the day, the friendly diners with the neighbors,
With my baby brother in his pink brand new bassinet.

When I made my first Communion in North Africa.
I was all in white organza and I carried a huge candle.
That day our villa was decorated with olive branches.
My secret desire then was to die and join the Angels,
As the priest in brown robes had promised us, girls.

After being liberated in June 44, I came to America,
On the "Edmond Alexander", a ship full of brave men.
Six years in New York, six more in the South,
Finally California Sunsets - Marriage - one boy, one girl
Today, my heart full of gratitude beats on . . .

Nadine Sauvajot Speck

A Day At The Fair

We wait all year for this time to come.
A day at the fair is number one.
Share this moment with a special loved one.
This happy place, it's lots of fun.

Hold on to your mother
The ride is scary, but she's like no other.
Cotton candy, junk food.
Enjoying ourselves we're always in a good mood.

Playing games, winning teddy bears.
It's good to be with someone who cares.
With your loved ones, family and friends.
As you grow closer, the love never ends.

Having fun on a scary ride.
You won't feel fear with a friend at your side.
The ferris wheel and bumper cars.
We stay til it's dark, to see the stars.

Watching rides close one by one.
Remembering this day of joyous fun.
As we leave, we turn around.
We will not hear another sound.

Krystal A. Reeve

The Way

Nothing quite says what I feel today,
A little bit silly, a little bit gay.
Two parts thoughtful, three parts sad,
A whole lot of lonely and just plain mad.

What I want out of life isn't too clear.
Can it be love or just some cheer?
What about peace and happiness too?
Why in this world do I have to choose?

I'm so mixed-up and in a big hurry,
To find life's niche amidst all this flurry.
Help me my Lord to find the way,
And just be grateful for one more day.

Shirley Drage

We Died Before We Died

Today, to be faced with the grim reality
   A dead mind may proceed the body in actuality
If so then perception is naught
   As everything viable begins with thought

The mind is our cerebral soul
   That steers us along Life's rocky shoal
Our psyche is our very essence
   Breathing individuality into beneficence

We have lived that we might ponder
   Conjecturally with hope and wonder
Having traveled the world so far to date
   To share creativity that's hopefully innate

And now to be death the brutal blow
   That our mind may be the first to go
Oh! Fate thy wicked sting
   Take our body - before our mind - and ring

The Bereaved Bells of Life to deplore
   The theft of an active mind before
A bereft body that's unwilling to surrender
   "We died before we died" - despite loving life so tender!

   Wayne Field

Grandmother

A face in the window of my mind
a face in the window of all time
she spent watching and waiting for a glimmer of life
to pass by that window that she might view
her body ached from all the years in bed unable to walk
her soul cried to touch the earth again
to joyously run or walk or even crawl
her mind alert as ever wishing it would go
her heart moaning with sadness day in and day out
she thinks what good am I alive I wish I were dead
yet when someone comes to visit she smiles and laughs and reminisces
no one knows the thoughts she thinks
thank you grandma for the time to love
the devotion to God and prayers
the strength to forgive
the sadness of our tears unseen
and the courage to dream
I am still a dreamer

   Maureen Keith

Life Unlived, Endless Time, Precious Love . . .

Life is a dream,
a fading moment of nothingness.
It passes by,
gone in the blink of an eye.
Everything vanishes, nothing is real;
time is a harsh overlord.
Love makes that one instant worth living;
infinite in possibility, endless in truth.
Not all are meant to love true,
few are granted such privilege.
For those who seek it, obtain it, cherish it,
everything else is nothing.
Love is everything, the only thing worth holding on to,
without it life would crumble,
all would be lost.
Money, power, status, all have no meaning in the end,
only love crosses the boundary of time unscathed.
Should love embrace your dying heart,
covet it, risk everything for it, for in the end . . .
Love is everything, and everything is love.

   Spencer Schoenewe

Wings Retrieved

A mortal and angel fell in love
a fine union, it was fate.

Into her mortals life she bounded
her own life she did forsake.
She placed her wings on a shelf
covered them carefully with her wedding veil

Years passed, the angel grew weary
wanted to be with her angel friends, who moved with the wind,
danced on the clouds and whirled through the trees
and skimmed the waves on bended knee.

She missed the frolicking, singing, harps and flutes
A decision the angel did make.
She took the wings from the dusty shelf
shook them lightly and put them on with a shrug

Freely followed the angels to move with the wind,
dance on the clouds, whirl through the trees
and skim the waves with bended knee.

With feathery wings she whirled away
departing to a loftier place.

   Lois Nunn Russell

Untitled

Sitting there exactly as you left it, I spot your favorite toy.
A freeze where I am standing remembering my precious little boy
Anger courses through my veins why was it him task
I remember the first time I held you I also remember the last
It is so hard to think about you without tears coming to my eyes
You never even had a chance it is too soon to say goodbye
I have asked myself a million times what I had done wrong
If I had caused this tragedy or if it was meant to happen all along
I am still waiting for the answer, to my question of why
Praying for the strength to be able to say Goodbye!

I have spent my time on earth with much suffering and pain
I have faced more challenges than most people could sustain
I have fought for every accomplishment in actuality, I achieved a lot
Now it is for me to rest I have used all the strength I have got
I know that this is hard to accept but I am in a better place
I am with my father no more suffering or pain I will have to face
Each time you think of me remember that you gave me all you had
You will always remember the good times right along with all the bad
I will be watching you from above so when you need reassurance
look only to the sky.
Know that of the questions asked to end my suffering was why.

   Sherri Wise

Hurt

The web of branches blocks out the sun
a girth of brush keeps in the damp
dirt smeared windows framed in tattered shears
nothing enters the long low house

The house holds secrets - nothing else is allowed
memories and statements of hurt, love and despair
they rot and smell from simmering neglect
nothing leaves the long low house

An innocent key could unlock the fowl
a sincere broom could sweep in the fresh
such simple tools should be easy to find
but no one knows the house is there

   Mark J. Ioli Sr.

Friendship

A friend is a person to share good time and woes.
A good friend will help you with many of those.
A great friend will listen and help dry your nose
A best friend will lift you and tickle your toes.
A friend is a person who will back you in a fight.
A good friend will stop you and say that's enough tonight
A great friend steps in and takes over the fight.
A best friend stands beside you and says this is our fight.
A true friend asks questions that may make you think.
That will lift up your spirit from the dark black as ink.
A true friend is honest and cuts your no slack.
They kick you in the rump or pat you on the back.
A true friend is one who sticks with you like glue.
And laughs at your old jokes as if there brand new.

Ray Thibault

The Message

Low on a blossomed branch I saw
A gray bird fly to sing -
And all the trees stood motionless
In silent worshiping.

Long he stayed and warbled there;
Each note so flute - like clear,
I knew no sound had come before
As sweetly to my ear.

And yet, though high the scale he touched,
A sadness filled the air -
For bending close to earth I heard
A moaning violet there.

The dusk descended cool and soft;
His mission fully done,
The bird faced slowly to the sky
And soared to whence he'd come.

Meribell Boniece

Comic Girl

A breathing, beautiful Venus.

Moxie girl with woman's eyes of an emerald hue,
a halo of dime-store fire
frames her luscious smirk.

With a whirlwind laugh and f***-me stare
she talks s*** and prophecy most convincingly.
With an auburn flip,
and the sway of her hips;
demure seduction in motion.

A lolita-dream
evoked by aching boys lying in feather-soft beds.
Waiting for a delicious touch,

In the wax and wane light of the moon.

Kat Swaro

The Death Of A Rose

There is a rose reaching for the sun
A cloud comes and hides it
The rose wilts and starts to loose it's petals
While hanging it's head the final petal drops
The rose dries up and dies from despair
The cloud moves on and the sun is seen again
But it is too late
The spirit of the rose is now running with the cloud
He has captured it's soul

Lori Jones

Looking For A Heart That Is More Than Just A Muscle

I want a thinking heart . . . a feeling heart
   A heart shaped like a heart
   not a muscle.
A heart with a drumbeat . . . a rainbeat
   Not a deadbeat bankrupt heart.
I want a full heart . . . a passionate heart
   Even a broken heart!
A heart that can move . . . and cry . . . and rage;
Not just move blood from point A to point B and back again
   Pointlessly
I want a light heart . . . a butterfly heart
   a dandelion puff float-on-the-breeze heart
   even a tempest-tossed heart.
I want a blood-red heart . . . a ruby of a heart
   a jewel beyond price king's ransom of a heart.
Not a stone heart
A heavy heart
A hurt heart
A heart that's just a muscle

Kay L. Halbert

An Immigrant's Pledge

This is my land, a beautiful land
A land of my dreams, my opted land
I love you and adore you
America, my gorgeous America
   You are my oasis in all my crisis
   A powerful land of happiness and peace

Here I work and am honored
Here I live and am loved
I pledge my heart and soul
To you my ever dear America

Where I go and whatever I do
You shall be always in my thoughts and prayers
Seeking His Almighty's Heavenly Blessings
For you my beloved America.

Roma

Grandma's Place

Breeze blowing softly against my face, reminds me of a gentle place.
A large white house with pillars four, stained glass windows line the door.
Children laughing, flowers bloom, I see her face across the room.
Steel blue eyes, and pale gray hair, a crooked smile that signals care.
Scents of cookies baking, linger, we lick the bowls and then our fingers.
Family picnic in the yard, Jimmy threw the ball too hard.
Davey tipped the pitcher over, lush green grass mixed in with clover.
Grandma's place always neat, tidy, gracious, mats for feet.
Never tiring, never shrill, even while she's growing ill.
Grandma's place is different now, quiet, empty, sad somehow.
We sift through treasures great and small, Not wanting any or even at all.
   Nothing can take grandma's place,
      her smile, her touch, her sweet round face.
      If only the breeze could turn back time,
         when grandma's place was hers and mine.

Paula Rutan

The Mirror

As I look in the mirror I see in my eye,
A vacant expression where love used to lie.
The emptiness consumes my heart and my soul,
I long for the day when I may be made whole.
The face in the mirror makes me cry when I see,
And I think to myself, there is no way this is me.
The mirror may show my face and my feature,
But it can't show inside this poor broken creature.

Lori Hunter

This Sweet Boy

Born on the first day of June,
a little after noon,
this sweet boy came from heaven too soon.
His eyes and smile could put the sun to shame,
with no one but God to blame,
for this sweet boy came from heaven too soon.
Image of his father,
whose dreams couldn't go farther."
My little superior being said he,
an astronaut or scientist someday you'll be."
This sweet boy with a twinkle in his eye
just laid back with a sigh
"Oh Dad, thought he, get your head out of the cloud,
I will someday make you so proud."
With Gods help and all of our prayers
this will be true for
this sweet boy came from heaven to soon.

Thelma Milanoski

"My Only Love"

I saw you standing in the cool night air
A lonely soul, I began to stare.
You took one glance and caught my eye,
I turned away, I was oh so shy,
You brushed against my shoulder,
I felt shivers through my spine.
I knew deep in my heart,
One day you would be mine
As time went by visions of forever danced through our heads,
"We'll always be together," or so you said.
You came into my life without any warning,
No thoughts of a love, and you left me the same.
Now visions of loneliness is all that remains.
Broken hearts and broken dreams,
Too sad to be true or so it seems.
My love, my only love has gone away,
So much pain I feel from day to day.
Please dear Lord from heaven above,
Please help me live without my only love.

Linda Blood

Oh Lord, Forgive Me

I find in my heart someone I'm ashamed of:
A merciless critic who won't make amends.
All the time knowing you call me your friend;
Oh Lord, forgive me; oh Lord, forgive me.

I find myself judge, am I quite in your spirit
if I think I'm in court to win a case?
If love is bound, the trial's a waste;
Oh, Lord, forgive me, oh Lord, forgive me.

We're not here to judge one another,
and I confess I do.
But Christ has died, let us not lay a charge
to the ones the gives his life to.

I've been speaking your words.
I've been telling your story.
But do I speak to be seen and praised by men?
As if I would to steal your Glory!
Oh Lord, forgive me, oh Lord, forgive me.

Patricia Weber

Just Me

My joys are many, my sorrows are few,
A mother of four children, what's there to do?
From youth you turn into daddies and mothers,
You feel your burdens, you think like no other,
Have you ever been there? That's me brother.

Prayer and faith in our Good Lord above,
Sends you answers, mercy, and grace through His love,
Your troubles and problems, on the alter lay all,
But don't be too anxious for sweet Jesus to call,
Because He hears everyone, no matter how big or small.

Sometimes it takes awhile for answer to prayer
Not that Jesus has the attitude, "I don't care."
Though often through temptations and trials
He wants to know, if under a heavy load we'll smile
And go with Him to that very last mile.

If you feel each day, something you must sell
To some lost soul, "The Story of Jesus", tell.
For out of bondage, it could be someone's bail.
If under your problems, you feel you'll smother
Take Jesus with you, like me brother.

Verna Carter

A Mother's Lose

In the later part of June,
A mother's thoughts were turning.
In the dark sky there was a beautiful moon.
No one knew but, her heart was burning.

If ever there was hurting
She had it all that night.
Life is never certain.
Life is never right.

Life does go on
When, will it not?
When one of us has gone,
You must stay for what you've got.

Though her lose was great
She knew she had to stand strong.
She, through experience saw her family's fate.
And knew they would go one by one.

When a part of you has left you,
And you had to let it go.
You couldn't keep it no matter what.
As the wind, life will flow.

Nanette Laraine Wood

There Is

A gratitude and reverence for boundless love
A need for the quiet peace of a dove

An abundance of wisdom, humility too
A pure heart that dictates what idle hands should do

A seeking mind that is open and free
A beautiful spirit that too few can see

A physical temple in which to dwell
An expectant soul not bound for hell

A steady gait of weary feet
A lofty place of divine retreat

A struggling heart so in need of giving
A generous love that makes life worth living

A dormant spirit that wants to awaken
A need to achieve its ultimate goals long forsaken

A myriad of dreams and visions of success
A mischievous soul evading redress

E. Faye Fleming

The Game Of Life

Life deals the cards at which we play.
A new hand's dealt out day by day.
It's up to us to build our hand.
To lay them down, to make a stand.
So everyday the cards will fall;
Our hand we'll play: Win, lose or draw.
There's days the cards fall just our way.
Content to win, content to play.
There's days of doom right from the start,
But from this game we'll not depart.
No choice is there, whether to play
For chance or fate comes our way.
We all must play this game of life:
A husband, son, a daughter, wife.
No one's exempt to play the game.
Each hand's diverse, not one the same.
For once we're born until we die,
This game of life, we all must try.
Phillip Ewing Clarke Jr.

An End Of Sorrows

From inside comes a light,
a peace that passes all understanding,
From tragedy, a coming together
to remember a friend

Thoughts of peace, not forgotten, still pending,
as a nation mourns, and is torn, and longs
for consolation, and an ear to bend, life goes
back to normal when the mourning period ends

Day after day, it gets easier to let go
of sorrows,
Pressing towards the mark of peace on
time short yet borrowed.

From above one sees a smile, marking the
end of grief, a cloud gently folding by
the wayside, soft tones of blue and golden white,
Ones soul is quieted and can rest all
through out the long days and nights.
Marisha Gutherez

The Golden Thread

I am a mountain;
A peak who overlooks glory.
As creme is to coffee,
I am to you my dear friend.
An unremitting, never undermined confident —
A woman.
Yet, not only or merely "woman;"
I have choices . . .
And, after climbing and sweating over the mountain,
You shall see me,
For I am the river.
I never end and know all,
Yet, I learn so much from the current;
Yes, I am the wind.
A woman.
The goodness of thy sea and thy holder of mankind.
The world's future is contained deep within my soul.
I have choices . . .
I am woman; beauty and wisdom wrapped in such glistening paper.
I am the sun light that shines upon the mountain.
Kerry Kolasa

A Perfect World

A perfect world, a perfect world, what is a perfect world?
A perfect world is a world in which a person can be himself
A world that is drug free, a world that is war free.
In a perfect world, a person can walk down the street
Without being scared of being robbed or killed.

A perfect world, a perfect world, what is a perfect world?
A perfect world is a world that is free of violence,
A world in which parents can send their children outside
Without the fear of them not coming back.

A perfect world, a perfect world, what is a perfect world?
A perfect world is a world where a kid can walk down
The street without the fear of the drug dealers hassling him.

A perfect world, a perfect world, what is a perfect world?
A perfect world is a world with clear blue skies.
A world without pollution, and a world without homelessness.

In a perfect world you can lie down and watch the
Different shapes of clouds. You can also watch your
Problems drift away. A perfect word is a world without racism.
A perfect world, don't we all wish for a perfect world.
Lewis W. Taylor Jr.

Moonlight Mystique

A peaceful presence seems ablaze,
a planet fills the sky so bright
reflected in a rosy path of light
across the lake, like a maze,
for lovers in a dreamlike phase
on which to float across to the other side
in a mystical fashion as betides
those who are unconscious of the days.

Then a soft wind, like a whisper, ruffles,
circles the tiny nocturnals dancing,
stirring the magical path, prancing
across the water, tip-toeing ripples
until all is spent, fading into the mist
behind them, forgotten as they kissed.
Lillian Martinez

The Closet

I spent my naughty times repenting in the closet; it was not a pleasant place.
It was dark, quiet, and scary, and I wondered if I had fallen from grace.
My sin was being a bad boy but I was only six or seven.
Surely I would be forgiven by the One who lives in heaven.
I cried and cried and begged forgiveness until there were no more tears.
My sobs, my sighs, my pleading gave me no relief, because my
wailing had fallen on deafened ears.
I was a scaredy-cat; to that my siblings all agree.
They scratched on the door that Frankenstein would get me and
it was more than I could bear.
They liked what they were doing, it was done with joy and glee.
This all happened five and a half decades ago, and memories do grow dim.
My family loves me, and I forgave them all.
However, never put a child in the closet, the place is mighty grim.
My God did not forsake me for all the wrongs I've done.
I have asked for His forgiveness through His only Begotten Son.
Ruben A. Pro

A Reminder . . .

I watch her as she plays
  a reminder of God's glorious ways;
Perfectly pieced together from head to toe
  in a way only God would know;
Her little button nose and chubby little cheeks
  her ears so soft and sweet;
Her eyes shaped like almonds
  her lips ruby red;
Her smile glistens like diamonds
  her perfect little head;
Her arms and legs are long
  her hands and feet so strong;
Her fingers always having fun
  her little toes on the run;
Her tiny body so precious and dear
  when I see her I know God is near;
I watch her as she sleeps
  a reminder of the promise He keeps;
That we are fearfully and wonderfully made
  bought with the price He paid.
      Kim E. Smith

Untitled

She's waiting,
a ripe peach, dangling heavily,
casting thick shadow.
She tastes of rain, of dirt, and, once, of purity;
now tainted deeply by stagnation and self-control.
She wants to be warm, always
without need of clothes.
She berates him for his blatant ignorance,
and instantly pities him
for she realizes it's hereditary in this case;
a huge fish, top of the food chain, swimming around in his
gene pool.
In trying to save herself she knows she is killing him.
She's waiting,
a ripe peach dangling,
anticipating the final wind what will detach her from
the tree and send her plummeting into reality.
She'll go quickly, quietly
before her fruit
takes root
in another man's soil . . .
      Kerrie Hilyard

Restless

I gaze at a pebble and see a mountain.
A ripple in my bath smashes the shore, eroding.
  Eating boulders and me nibble by nibble.
Fractals infest my dinner plate,
  Revealing uncountable dimensions within my broccoli.
  All ripe for plundering by my patch-eyed pirateous
  intestinal villi.
Cellular automata pulse and wash over my dreams,
  like a technicolor caress of confusion that fails to
  dissipate with morning's light.
Déjà vu has ceased to amuse.
  The movie of my life (starring the three stooges as me)
  stuck in a perpetual loop.
Somewhere over Japan a monarch butterfly beats it's wings
  and a thousand die in a hurricane.
  Or a tornado.
The analogous nature of existence is like a cruel taunt
beckoning and repulsing all at once.
Or maybe it's not.
      Warren Tandoc

Winter's Day

A bbrrrrrrrry day
  a shhiverrry day
a deep down inside cold to the toes day
  a mitteny scarvery
    Big Bulky Boots day

Finger-tingling
  eye watery
a drip at the end of the nose day

  Blue haze smothering the sun
Crunching, squeaking
while walking through the, trudging through the
  drifted
    sifted
      melted
        glazed-white

Outside.

Oh, such a bbbrrrrry day
  a ssssssshhhhhiverrrry day
a stay inside under the warm blankets
  day
      Vernamaree Nelson

Recovering

A kind of smile - not much of one, I know
a smile it was, at least. The wound appears
but superficial, bruises cannot show.
Her ego's scars revealed in brushed-back tears,
in muffled sobs in distant rooms they flow.
I dare not venture there to calm her fears.

Forlorn, but game, she carves uncharted trails
with instinct, hope and love her only guides.
I follow her. Although the jungle's veils
were woven by my folly, I'm the one who slides
behind. I see no out, my courage fails.
Upon her shoulders frail, our future rides.

The victim is the victor: she shall choose
to what extent we two shall win and lose.
      Robert S. Olive

The Wind Of Kaleidoscope

The endless song through my mind,
a sweet, soft melody whispering to the sun, to the moon,
flowing, soothing my soul of the memories;
he brushes aside the tears from these windows of solitude,
wondrously caressing my fears.
Floating down the lane to the soil I have yet to cross,
nudging me to the next scene,
he erases the words spoken so harsh, the deeds so cruel.
Glancing, he leaves the past for I to dredge,
as he carries on and on . . .
circling alongside till he shall touch me once more,
gliding me forward to our new sanctuary.
      September Schmidt

Untitled

I glide through other's lives
a wafting ghost
I am the blackness, the lane peripheral
while real folk
bustle within a more permanent medium
my dark eye beams
catch their forms through passing portals
though they may see me
their unconscious glance
soon fixes upon more concrete distractions
      Kurt Debban

A . . .

A walk through a field, on a warm summer day
A talk on the rocks, by the water filled bay

A long narrow path, to see flowers and trees
A sound in the distance, of birds and of bees

A man and his friend, playing songs by the fire
A love of your own, the need for it dire

A father and son, playing ball as a team
A boy and his tree house, the American Dream

A storm and some thunder, ever so frightening
A pitter-patter of raindrops, or beautiful lightning

A call on the phone, to a cared about loved one
A poem you've written, to no one or someone

A day to live, and breathe on your own
A dream that is shattered, to mourn and condone

Mike Gershman

Coming Of Dawn

"Coming of Dawn" to all creatures will be
A time for celebrating, jubilee.
Every one thoughtfully will show
Many acts of kindness, love bestow.
Gone drugs, drunkenness, cruelty, urge to kill,
Once ravaged bodies, minds, cleansed of ill will.
Greed, problem of the past,
All hatred gone at last.
Nations shall welcome peace.
Hurt feelings find release,
Contentment for all, now here to stay.
The golden, rule to pattern each day.
Prophesies in old testament did come true.
Overwhelmingly proved studying the new.
The lion, lamb, shall rest side by side.
Our risen Savior with us abide.
All people will understanding be.
Coming of Dawn; fulfilled prophesy.

Margaret Story Myers

Christmas

Christmas is a time of joys,
A time for little girls and boys,
A time to remember Christ our Lord;
He was born for us on Christmas day.
He died for our sins the people say,
He loved us so with all his heart,
And we will love him and do our part.
The Bible talks about his life;
He was born to Joseph and his wife.
He was born in a stable, his cradle was a manager.
As he was born on the twenty-fifth among them lay some strangers;
The strangers spread the word of God;
The angels sang their songs of joy;
The wise men brought him gifts of love.
The scene in a stable, the animals, they lay around, they watched
the Lord and lay there sound.
So remember this great scene, for it certainly was not a dream.
So look up at the stars and pray, for today is a very special holiday.

Tiffany Holder

Time . . .

This is a quiet time
A time of waiting
    For new growth to appear
    New life patterns to originate
    New thinking to germinate
This is a time to still urgencies of the mind.
A time to let greater possibilities for
    the rest of my life take root.
To recreate spring time thinking.
Even though this is the fall of my life.
A time to grow in understanding
A time to realize there are no limits
    to my possibilities
A time to cry, be sad, be fearful,
    even lonely.
But a time for a new beginning.

Norma J. Ables

If I Were A Tree

If I were a tree I would plant my trunk in the ground
a tree where there are children around
there I would grow through winds rain and snow
a tree which did rapidly grow

The children would play and story up a scheme
the plan it seems is to build a house upon me
so each new day brought a tool for each hand
so far so good they continued their plan

As they hammered away with lumber and nails
their work was a success their plan did not fail
I was happy as they finished their house upon me
for they had succeeded a lesson to work as a team

Yollanda L. Garretson

A Star Lit Night

Once upon a star lit night,
A trillion stars twinkled bright.
Yet one stood out, a brilliant sight,
An eastern star of glorious light.

Wise men followed its wondrous rays,
In search of a king in a far away place.
The light of that star illumined the way,
To the town of Bethlehem and a tiny babe.

It's mission complete, the star stood still,
The king of kings, it had revealed.
To wise men seeking, their spirits thrilled,
To see the light, God's plan fulfilled.

Teresa M. Jones

Recipe Of Love

Take one girl-add a pinch of moonlight,
Add one boy and a star filled night.
Mix two hearts, add a dash of a dreaming,
Mix two smiles, happily beaming.
Blend several kisses soft and sweet,
Add several hugs for a special treat.
Mix in a shiny golden ring,
Add two hearts with a song to sing.
Simmer under a summer moon,
Blend two voices in a tender tune.
Add a pair of shining eyes,
Mix together with gentle sighs.
Add a dream for two to share
Blend a lifetime to spend and care.
Mix with a glow from the moon above,
For you and me, it's everlasting love!

Lisa Renae Pendergast

A Tattered Mind

The blackness of night has spread
A veil of misery a shadow of dread.
The deed so perverse, the murdering of a soul
life but a curse, the debris of what was whole.

His mind had been shattered,
his bleeding soul in hell,
for his twisted brain had cut him
with each piece as it fell.

Though you'll find no stains of red
and no remains of the dead;
But there is a walking corpse
searching for a grave,
there to find the soul
of which he could not save.

The murder is his suicide
as he finally comes to face,
the killer dwells inside
among the rubble and the waste.

Lisa Bostjancic

For Laura Lee, Aged 4

No time ago, or else a sigh,
(A vision, perhaps, who can recall?)
Before beginning this crab-scuttled pace
Along the mangled angles of space,
(Ah, Infinity sings, but not of the Fall!)
I caught your face, more than love and gently,
(The eyes that smile, the lips that bless,)
And I, turtling-hurtling my ebony stair
Came face to face with, at last, Yes!

Ronald H. Kickasola

Softly Did It Whisper

One day as I was walking
    a warm and gentle breeze began to blow.
So softly did it whisper, scarcely could I hear it.
The name it had spoken, I did not know.

I saw a butterfly fluttering through the air
    and asked what name was in the wind?
With a great and gentle ease the butterfly replied,
    the name you seek my child is Steve.
Although the bug, he brings you will have the bite of a bumble bee,
    you should not fear it.
The strength it will use to hold you
    shall be as vast as the ocean is wide.
The gentleness it shall use to nurture you,
    as tame as that of a Newborn baby.

In surprise I ask, "What bug could bring all this?"
The butterfly, he laughed at me
    and replied simply, "My dear sweet child,
    the bug he brings to you is Love!.

And the butterfly, with that same great ease
Fluttered away as quickly as the breeze had spoken your name.

Pamela S. McParland

The Wind

The wind is like shooting stars, stars that shoot
above and beyond,
as the wind blows on the trees as leaves fall on
the ground.
The wind is a beautiful thing. It makes the
ripples in the water,
and the eye of the hurricane.
THE WIND

Montana C. Elliott

Snowflakes

A gentle stir, the chilly air,
A wind shift, oh so slight.
The clouds sweep in o'er snug-thatched roofs;
The moon slips out of sight.

The wind picks up its tempo,
Cause trees to dance and sway.
Dry leaves sing plaintive melody
Before the break of day.

The first of many flakes drifts down,
A feather in the air;
Downward, rising, then down again,
Free falling without care.

Soon joined by other snowflakes,
God's purity displayed;
The downward spiral more intense,
Silent painter on parade.

Now all is white, and clean, and pure,
Delightful to the eye.
Snowflakes caress each other.
They rest, no longer fly.

Rosanne Gartner

Why Do I Love Thee?

The heart has reasons reason does not know,
A wise man once observed.
Why love I thee Mother Nature?
Merely because you're my mother?

In your emotions you're inconstant,
Unpredictable in your actions.
In thee are wells of affection,
Also a brewery of hate is within thee.
In a moment you adorn your children,
And suddenly you cover them with shame;
Of their garments you strip them.

Alas, the prettiest flowers you reduce to vanity;
You give them the term of the evening gold,
And to my delights the brevity of a dream.
Gloomy days are the dwelling you give me,
And into my lungs you pump your chilly and misty breath.
Yet, like a weaned child I am and will be tranquil;
In expectation I will wait till your fury ends.

Mother Nature, I still love thee.

Lwanga M. Semikenke

Rites Of Passage

You're a maximum woman with a maximum mind,
A woman of the '90's and won't waste no time,
Got a corporate image and sensitive soul,
Out there making choices in either denim or gold,
Won't take a back seat cause now it's your dime!
You're a maximum woman with a maximum mind.

You're standing at the top and you'll have it all,
For too many years you've followed his call,
Now, you're a maximum woman with a maximum mind,
A woman of the '90's and now it's your time,
You can win with the power or win with the pain,
Your searching's not over too much more to be gained.

Your eyes see the light for years you've been blind,
You're a maximum woman with maximum mind,
You can dress it up, dress it down, don't mean a thing,
You've got the stage,
You've found your voice,
You're just starting to sing!

Phil Allocca

Untitled

In the morning, when the mist has cleared from the sky,
A woman rises from a slumber, which she so desired.
Clearing the rest of the night from her weary eyes,
She wipes the petals from her ivory body.
Descending into a pool of clear blue water,
She lets the water run over her flowing brown locks.
She always seems comfortable underneath the water blue.
The water, drowning over her face, makes her feel tranquil.
Not wanting to rise she tries to keep herself under as long as possible.
But just as she realizes she has no more breath to spare, she finds
Herself at the surface once again.
She is the innocence inside of us.
The man is a thing she has never encountered.
Never will she feel the tenderness of a man's lips against her body.
She can never understand her own sexuality.
She is ignorant to all others, but what would this mean to her?
She is in peace within herself, not afraid of anything.
She walks and lives freely in nature.

Sarah Arnold

A Special Woman

A special woman I must say
A woman who graces me with her love each day.

A woman with confidence and tremendous pride
Who gives me strength when I want to hide.

A woman who listens with all her heart
and helps me fulfill the dreams I thought were torn apart.

A woman who wipes away my tears
and hopes that I can conquer all my fears.

A woman who lends a helping hand
and lets me know she is my one best friend.

This woman is the beat of my heart and soul
and the breath of my life which I hold.

This woman I would not trade for the world,
she is no other she's my mother.

Yvonne Elizabeth Leilani Wright

A World Without Sound

What is it like?
A world without sound.
Can we really imagine it,
When we ourselves have always known different sounds?
How would you feel?
Seeing the rain falling from the sky,
But never hearing its soft patter as it falls gently to the ground.
Watching the waves ripple,
But never hearing their rhythmic sound as they lap to the shore.
Feeling the air rushing by you,
Without hearing the wind's whistling sounds.
Seeing the lightning and feelings its vibrations,
But never hearing the loud crash of thunder.
Seeing water fly high in the air from an incredible dive,
But never hearing the tremendous splash.
You may think these sounds are not all that special,
Having heard them all your life.
But what if you were born into a world without sound?

Sharon E. Smith

School Days

I'd like for you to know
About schools of long ago.
If things didn't go well with us,
We surely knew not to fuss.
We didn't go home and tell
Things we didn't like well.
When we were corrected at school,
We knew our parents' rule.
After school days were through,
We had work at home to do.
No time did we have free
With television to see.
I can see that old school days were best
Because now some students can't pass the test.
I'm thankful for the good days we had.
Now some school problems make me sad.
I thank my teachers every one
For the hard work that was done.
May God bless them all
Until their Heavenly call.

Lois Earle

Who Do I Love So Dear?

Someone who loves you in their heart, someone you cherish and care about. Someone who loves you deep in their heart, and has always been there for you from the start. Someone who hold you tight; and makes sure you're save through the night. She makes ure you say your prayers and is always saying "don't let the bed ougs bite." But you never worried as long as she was there. She would work late and was lowly paid; but she made do with what she made. Her feet ached, her neck was sore, but for you she worked more and more. For she took herself to the limit trying to get things you always wanted, when Christmas and birthdays roll around. Though you didn't get what you wanted still you turn to her and thank her, for at least you did get something. Even though she worked so hard, she taught you right from wrong. She always told you to do things right, so you wouldn't have to struggle for the rest of your life. As time passed and people changed, she always seemed to stay the same. She taught me as I grew older, for now I have a college diploma. With the money I shall make, I'll take care of her until she's in her grave. For the love I have for her will never go away. By now you're probably wondering who she is. Well . . . my aunt (my mother) who I love so dear.

Victoria Simmons

Gift Of Love

A man who had nothing but love, was raised on timbers to the sky above.
His body was nailed to a rugged tree, his blood was spilled for you and me.
He took away our sin and shame, this man of compassion, Christ was his name.
They lowered him down from where he lay, and placed him in his grave that day.
The stone they placed on the tomb to stay, had three days later been rolled away.
They searched the tomb but nothing was found, and news was
  spread for miles around.
This man who they mocked and placed thorns on his head, was
  crucified buried and rose from the dead!
He lives. "Hallelujah!" the Savior lives, and his never-ending
  love he still has to give.
Everlasting life is yours to grasp, all that's required is that you ask,
Jesus the Lord into your heart, and let your life take on a new start
It's up to you which road you choose, I know with Christ you cannot lose!

Randall T. Kelle

God's Land

Warriors on horseback, line the cliffs and the wall,
All dressed in their war paint, all sitting so tall,
War paint and bonnets bows and arrows at hand,
They'll fight to the death for this God given land!

Onward they move faster, and one by one they do fall,
Now to sit with the great master at the end of it all!
Pamela J. Young

Celeste

In her masculine femininity, she will rise.
Above in the everlasting eve of dark and light.
Never to see our faces nor hear our cries.
Yet knowing every change of a nation inside.
She takes the lead in all parts of the play.
Without recognition and yet with praise.
Within all that is, since the birth of time.
Gently guiding, possessed . . .
The sea's rise to her strength.
Should she stray from her favorite chosen path . . . just slight.
Would cause great havoc to all under her spell
And thus she continues her star speckled trail of desire
Hiding behind a blanket of sun, in our hours.
She awaits her entrance at his mighty dissension.
Her majesty in her court winking down upon us
Raise your Gaze and know with lips unseen, she is smiling
J. Alkadri

A Critical Element

The basis of all behavior is chemistry.
Add sodium to water, prepare for fireworks.
We had it - we ached for each other's nearness.
To see her, electrifying. To touch her, explosive.
We planned our working hours, the food we ate,
our wakefulness, around each other.
She'd say, "Lets . . .", and I'd say, "go."

I saw through her eyes and she through mine.
Laughter was easy, every sadness shared.
Everyone we knew remarked on how obvious it was
that we were in love.
Our daily paths intertwined without design.
Promises were made, vows exchanged.
"I'll always love you, with all that I am."
We shared eternal bliss within single magical moments.
The joy that was mine remains without equal.
A critical element was exhausted, her fire went out.
I weep as I continue to burn . . .
alone.
H. Ernest Dodd

Mother

Disarming smile, slender arms, and toothpick legs.
All aerobics and coffee.
Uncompromising plans go well with your emotionless fix . . .
Another promotion?
Let's celebrate with diet cupcakes.
"Hold the icing."
Liberation keeps you free
except from me.
But I am different.
I speak when told to suppress my feelings.
I wear my heart on my sleeve
and my ears are pierced with
too much silver.
My dreams collide
with your own;
but although I'm not a shoe-in for society,
I do hope to be just like you.
Marisa Torrieri

"A Soldiers Epitaph"

A cold dead wind, incessant it blows,
Against my face, thru my clothes, cold it is,
As I lay hidden, in the brown grassy field
Lead bullets whistling by me, whizzing near me.

Cutting twigs, splitting branches, killing
Fighting for a cause, fighting to be free.
Wrestle thoughts of fear and death,
Chaining them tightly, to an empty coffin.

A bead of sweat trickled so lightly, down my face
Gently, it flowed, down past my brow.
Hands raw, withered from blasts of cold air
Gripping my rifle, clutched near my trembling side

A crackling, ruffling of leaves in the distance
Gun clutched and raised, ready and searching.
Thoughts of death and life melted as the sunset
Oppressed no more, the other bullet streaks thru my soul.
Roy H. Johnson III

Beloved Enemy

Quietus has laid claim to my body
   All are destined to this fate I'm told
Paradise or hell may now await me
   An empty shell is all this cask will hold
Were I a flower, you would be my vase
   As kerous faces mourn my faded bloom
Fate decreed that we would make assembly
   The sullen mass may now unmask their gloom
Coffin, casket, mummy case, call it what you will
   Heartache's vessel, chariot of pain
Desolation, anguish, and despondency
   Are all the elements that will remain
Unnatural stillness permeates the chapel
   Whispered voices reminisce as one
Hope for immortality is dying
   The reign of the Grim Reaper has begun
To eternity you'll be my transport
   Your cauldron shields my soul throughout this quest
Sarcophagus make easy my departure
   End this journey with eternal rest
Marie Ellen Webster-Henderson

"This Presence"

It was there,
All around her; everywhere.
There was no place she could hide,
For it was also inside.
A presence . . . a destiny,
A fear . . . her eternity.

All at once she relived her past,
And realized she wanted something that would last.
With tears slipping from her face,
She knew the old paths she would not retrace.
She silently thanked God for this new revelation,
For she had just chosen salvation.
Kimalee Jane DeCosta

If It Was Meant To Be

Now it's too late, to prove what you mean to me,
all I remember, is how our love used to be.
I can't handle the torture, of not having you by my side,
I could tell you I'm doing fine, but it would just be a lie.
I keep thinking of you, every night I come home,
I want to talk, but I just can't pick up the phone.
I try to have fun, until loneliness sets in,
you'd think I would've adjusted, these few months it's been.
Once I saw you again, I felt something wonderful deep down inside,
after we had our talk, that something had died.
I want you to hold me tight, and never let go,
I don't see that coming true, since apart we've grown.
You need your time, I can't argue with that,
if it were meant to happen, I'll have you back.

Vicki Davis

Voids

Everybody has a void
All need to fill one, if not many.
For some it may be money.
Others — would be power.
One's full of courage and adventure look
To tempt death and hope to win.
There are some who crave knowledge,
Always a need to learn
Then some — sex, sex and more, crazed by.
Yet for the few, the tender hearted,
Maybe love — love is their dream, their void.
Yes, love is mine.
There is a woman with love for me,
And I hold love for her.
One day, I hope and pray we will
Unite and fill two voids.

Kevin D. Radican

The Masquerade

The risk is too great, the chance too much
All of it lost with one verbal touch.
Years of understanding swept away by the tears
Replaced by the pervading stench of the fears.

It torments me every tick of the day
It chases and follows, yet begs me to stay.
It's too fast, too big, too tall, and too smart
It knows where to find me, it simply looks for my heart.

There's no trail or signs that point to an escape
The only available is the one offered by fate.
My body, my mind, my soul, and my heart
All fight in concert, yet always acting a part.

Judges and juries all frown down on me
I've been numbered and housed, yet given no keys.
Why are others free when I am so trapped
My life already planned out, easily mapped.

I beg for forgiveness, for what I don't know
Carefully, skillfully, I search out my foes.
But I am also gentle with the ones that are dear
Saying what's right, what they want to hear.

Kelly Van Amburg

Union Of Separate Paths

The crisp clear night had removed
all remnants of the twilight.
Abundant stars of all brilliancies populated
the velvet blackness.
Soft ocean fragrant breezes cooled
the sand still warm from the sun's sojourn.
Glowing embers enhanced the tranquility
with occasional popping and crackling.
Portions of fresh bread and fine cheese remained
after whetting yearning appetites.
Champagne fumes mixed with the night air
as they escaped from a near empty bottle.

One form comprising of two confront
the chill with the fire of their affection.
Burning desires finally ignite
after an eternity of smoldering.
Each one's eyes and heart filled
with passion for the other as they nestle.
The paths to this encounter were beset with hardships
but their union will lead to ecstasy.

Tom Brammer

Regret

My eyes that are hazy will never completely see
All the pain you inflicted upon me

A reckless impulse can not control my anger
Confined to a fatal deceit of a well known stranger

The love you gave was so suffocating
your haunting presence is always tormenting

When you were gone, who was left to blame?
Disgrace was abundant, what a shame

When I'm angry, I'll choose to hate
When I love you, its too late

Infecting disease inside my mind
to ever believe that you were mine

Invade the space reserved for death
wishing or hoping? Don't hold your breath.

Go back to where you think you belong
You always said I could survive, I'm so strong

Living a life now full of misery
Content not knowing the reality

Like a debt never paid, I can't move on . . .
Because I wanted for you way too long

Mandie Gibson

Smokie

I wish I could have been their for you on the day you died
All the times that I was sad
You sat there at my side
You'd lay your head upon my lap
While you would rest and take a nap
You opened up the sliding door
And tiptoed in across the floor
Climbed into the bed at night
Who got the blanket became a fight
You sat at peace with your paws crossed
And helped me find things when they were lost
You'd put your nose under the gate
And wait up for me when I was late
You always made me feel so safe when I was all alone
I should have taken you with me
The day that I left home.

Tracy Reimer

An Arctic Wind Blowing

The sky became overcast in a cloak of bluish-gray.
All the universe it seemed changed from night to day.
Late one Fall afternoon an Arctic storm kept drawing nigh
that had played havoc on the lowland plains and over mountains high.
For one brief moment an awesome silence hovered all around,
Then came the invisible howling wind smashing objects to the ground,
stripping trees of autumn leaves sending them rustling through the air,
interlocking now with sparse white flurries floating everywhere.
Little wildlife critters scampering hurriedly for a place to hide
from the icy sting of Mother Nature to a safe haven to abide.
The few white flurries have turned into a wintry scene of snowing,
still escorted by the unseen roaring giant . . . an arctic wind blowing.

LaRue C. Huckabee

Bobby

To me you are a statue, weathered by a storm.
All those tough times you've seen, have given you your form.
    You are so very thoughtful, you'd give anything you could.
This I thought I'd tell you, this I thought I should.
    That I can see it in your eyes,
    Regret of what you've done.
    Times when you stuck it through,
    Are times I would have run.
Now you've something to bring you joy, and brighten up your day.
    And what it is, is very special,
    No one can take her away.
    And I'm so happy for you, you now have a fine life.
You've found someone you deserve, and she will be your wife.
    I want to say that I respect you,
    In every way I can.
Brother, you've turned out to be
    One hell of a special man.

Renee Beliveau

More Love?

The tears of ages I have endured, never extinguish my-heart's fire.
Alone, I cry at night the tortures of desire.
Sleepless nights have taken it's victim.
Out stretched arms fail to touch.
I have given to you so often, my precious best.
Spurn is my reward.
Passion's greed, I feel it true!
My selflessness is high, my love never low.
Will you return to me a lover's admiration?
I want to be there; To love, to hold, to bow, to share.
Why won't you hear the winds from the South and East?
Your heritage red, plays the bagpipes of Amazing Grace,
But your heart feels Clapton's song of a Blue's place.
Am I more to you than mere droplets of compassion?
I want to free us from generations wrath,
Not to beg my hopes to be met.
Barriers to be removed in this house of wonderment.
Will you give me the ultimate sacrifice?
Without it, I will surely feel death.

Paul Waldmiller

Death Of A Friend

ALONE- is the heart that is far from the body.
ALONE- is the devil who haunts the soul.
ALONE- is the eyes of sadness and regret.
ALONE- is my heart without you here.
ALONE- is gone with each tear I shed.
ALONE- my friend you'll never be . . .
        because you are the keeper of my
        heart, who holds the only key.

Wendi L. Palmer

John Henry

You pace the fence with timeless strides of grace.
Along the white slats you are entertained
by dancing patterns of the oak lace.
You own this land that you have been ordained.

You pound the blades of grass with all your might,
as if you want the earth to always know
that racing was your life and your delight.
Sir Henry, aren't you weary from your show?

Now claps are muffled by white linen gloves
and crowds are drunk from sips of gin and mint.
Will sober souls stir up the race they loved
indulging bets on your most graceful sprint?

Fear not, great horse. Your ride won't be in vain.
The fury of your soul forever reigns.

Theresa Short

As It Is Written

Revenge is sweet, 'tis often the truth
An eye for an eye, a tooth for a tooth.
But how much sweeter for the one who is meek,
And learned to turn the other cheek.

Lenore Karp

Faith

Seasons come and seasons go this is nothing you
already didn't know. Although this is a bit different
than a season you endure, life is a challenge
while forever changing my dear.

This isn't Winter, Summer or Fall. Its not even
Spring till you've sprung through it all. One day
at a time is all you can ask or even endure. For
there are no answers to the questions of the past
or present nor of the future the come, for this you
must know and truly fear my love.

So as each new day gently unfolds at down, have
the best yet most positive thoughts as the day
quietly rolls along. Look onward, for there's no looking
back fore like the seasons that have gone and still
the seasons yet too come, so will this surely
come to pass. My dear!

Live, laugh and love is all one really needs
to know. Faith is the basis for all of these
three things, for this you knew my dearest, my love.

Linda Lightner

Don't Fall In Love

Don't ever fall in love my friend, you see it doesn't pay,
Although it causes broken hearts, it happens every day.
    You wonder where he is at night, and wonder if he's true,
One minute you are happy, the next day you're feeling blue.
    Each time you meet him, your heart begins to dance.
Your world revolves around him. Boy! There's nothing like romance.
    And then it starts, you don't know why - you worry day and night,
You see my friend, you're losing him, it never works out right.
    Love is nice, but it hurts so much, and the price you pay is high.
If I were to choose between love and death, I think I'd rather die.
    So, when I say, "Don't fall in love," you'll be hurt before you're through,
You see my friend, I ought to know, I fell in love with you.

Sarah Ahlstrom

The Rainbow

The storm is there.
Always building up,
Always feeding on anger.
The tornado of your essence rips to get out,
The mass of howling wind tears at your soul.
The tidal wave of your emotions
Meets the venomous whirlwind of your rage.
The two collide,
The tidal wave is thrown off balance.
Then, with one flash of lightning
You lash out at the world with all of your fury and hate.
And in a rumble of raging thunder
The peaceful rainbow of your spirit
Overcomes every thought of hate.
Everything is okay -
For when you make up with a friend,
That is the true rainbow's end.

Stephanie E. Batterman

Eternal Life

I've seen the beauty of His eye's
Although I've never seen His face.
And felt the tenderness of His touch,
In all His love and endless Grace.
He walk's with me when day is new,
And light is bright, And air is fresh.
And carries me when dusk does fall,
And star's a sparkle, and flesh be tired.
With Him a promise of endless life,
Of endless love, and endless beauty.
I keep Him here deep down inside
For Eternal Life Be Mine.

Sherrie E. Robinson

"Pirates And Pails"

Walking through the palace looking for the jewels
always finding guards and snares
What shall we do

Appearing everywhere with no where else to go—we are lost now
Where shall we go

Choosing a left or right—a correct exit
so many hidden ways
Which way shall we go

Up Down—Where? I know over there
over there we went discovering a grave of bone

In this spot we saw the left matter—it was quite a bladder
Now it was gone—Where did it go

It disappeared or maybe it never was there—all I know is that I
have been here to long
Why was I wrong

We left and hid in a walled room with black curtains and a handled
broom, so we swept it clean
And said, "What Now"

We slept until noon and went on our way, remembering our day,
in the palace of malice—and never did we return to this spot
For it was time to stop—and clean the garage

Mike Hilton

Soar High, Sweet Dream

Last night,
   Among the twinkling stars above,
A dream I had of a flying dove.
   Soaring high in the space of life.
Every yearning,
   For peace among the nations' strife . . .
A dream I had,
   That peace was near,
Though nations small and large lay in fear;
   Waiting for my dream to clear.
A dream I had,
   That the flight of my dove
Was not a sign of lasting love.
But an end to a troubled way of life.
   A dream it was
Of a universe once filled with ways to cope
And lasting peace among those who hope
   To soothe man's thirst
      For justice as its quest.

Luis Jake Varela

Points Of Light

The endless motion of the tide bestows the breeze
an amorous mist to disperse along the shore.
A train of silver races across the ocean surface
while the silent junction of sea and sky is punctuated,
by three hovering points of light.

There among this beauty, stands my beauty like a grecian
statue overlooking the mediterranean, or a New England
Lighthouse illuminating the night, casting the warmth
that is glowing from her two emerald points of light.

Classic elegance is how she is described, my victorian on a
quiet New Orleans Street or like Davis, Bacall, Haywood and
Grable, the essence of a movie queen. She's my Lucille Ball,
her mischievous smile and lovable humor are captivating.

Enough! She is my friend, my wife, my lover, my life.
We are two stars endlessly traveling the cosmos.
Drawn together, we have met, united, evolved and gone nova,
we are one glorious creation,
we are one shining point of light.

Mario Collazo

"Danny"

An angel came to our house a year ago today
An each time I recall it, I'm very proud to say
Our little boy is perfect, he's our joy and he's our light
And if you'll just but listen, I'm sure you'll say I'm right

His hair is blond, his eyes are blue
His skin as white as snow
And when he smiles his big blue eyes
Just glow and glow and glow
Oh sure there's times when he is bad
But name a boy that isn't
If something's broke or out of place
You'd think it's him it isn't

What would you say to a little boy
With blue eyes big as buckets
How could you chide such a rollicking joy
with a smile as welcome as nuggets
But perfect he is, an perfect he'll be and when he's a man
We'll still be proud as we can be, because he is our Dan

William M. Dixon

My Light Of Life

A half-burned candle breathes it's light, as it flickers in the wind
An erie sense of hope bestills me, emerging from within
The night is black, but never bleak as I go on ahead
Following with barren feet through mist with might I tread

Parts of my path are obscured although obviously well-worn
Despite the lack of footprints, Someone's been here before
Trying to disguise my way, the wind howls to deceive
But upon this earth that I do walk, I am only to believe

Urgency and determination is now my only force
To follow with my gut and gumption, a dim light as my source
I know not of my destination, but only of my goal
To live on and survive and to save my mortal soul

Ultimately I'll reach the end of the destiny I do seek
And when I get there all will know that I am sure not meek
The arms of the trees can wave and the leaves at me may weep
But all I've encountered along my journey is only Mine to keep.

Laura L. Regner

The Shadows Of The Deep

In the darkest corner of the mind
An evil demon creeps.
Crouching, ever waiting, even now anticipating
For consciousness abating,
To slip into your sleep.

While thoughts are spinning into dreams
Into your chamber he will peep.
No time spent in delaying, for no conscience is he weighing,
As he observes your peaceful laying,
In the realm of deep, deep sleep.

He manipulates your mentality
And enters while you sleep
A claim forever staking, your dreams he will be taking,
A nightmare of his making,
The terrors of your sleep.

Your soul begone, replaced by fear
Through any crack his magic seeps.
But Innocence sustaining, as the nightmare moon is waning
You try to stop your dreams from draining
Into the Shadows of the Deep.

Kristine Marie Aman

Unraveling Friend

You were a supposed friend.
An unraveling young woman,
I couldn't mend.
We started off great,
I guess everyone takes a toll from fate.
I chose the brighter side,
You always chose the darker side of life.
I never wanted to analyze,
Something that could end in a fight.
I was always there, you were never near.
I didn't see,
How you placed them over me.
I can't believe how disastrous you turned out to be.
I don't think you even know what you have done to me.
You told me to watch out for conniving monsters,
You failed to mention you, my fellow sister.
Your innocent aim,
Was overturned by your sinister prank.
Now everyone will see how a disastrous friend,
Starts from an unraveling person, like you, which no one will mend!

Rachel Maurer

"Creation Of Beauty"

With an array of many colors
and a beauty of their own, within
this peaceful haven, a garden, she has grown
romantic rambling roses along the brick
pathway, and the sweet fragrance of the lily
as it blooms each and every day
entwined English Ivy surrounds the garden
wall, and with her varied creations, she admires one and all
at times, we speak with an opened heart
as each flower has a language
of beauty and art.

S. K. Hennekam

On Being 96

Hope you are able to eat cake,
And a cake you won't have to bake.
Plenty of best wishes we say,
Please do have a very good day.
You will 96 bows have to take.

Blessings on you we certainly wish,
Incurring 96 years is no swish.
Rural and city life was your dish,
Then on the great lakes you ate fish.
Here in columbus it's october 19,
Day 19 is usually bright and serene.
At the stadium, Purdue will pick OSU clean,
You will not have to witness unexpected scene.

Grandchildren five and great grandchildren ten,
Retailer wool worth may have done the same (back when).
All wish you good health and strength for your years,
Now together we salute you with cheers.
Down in Gallia Country sounds the refrain.
Many wish you well again and again,
And you dear sweet lady can reflect on your fame.

William M. Snyder

Re-union

Lincoln institute - a school of Barracks and children of destitute,
And a haven for children with wide-eyed resolute,

We meet and bring our children so they can see what was before,
And to heart the ideals that are ours forever more.

Our credo says do the best you can and you will be among the best,
Cast out idleness and put negatives to rest

We meet and honor our instructors who guided our endeavors,
We meet to celebrate the success of their labors.

The roads we have traveled were covered with snares and snags
And at times strewn in all directions, like tattered rags.

A salute to all who have survived the times of destitute,
And returned for the remembrance of our home away from home
Lincoln Institute.

Travers S. Vance

A Breeze Of Confusion

A small suburban town lives among a plague of Lost angels
   and a school grows in this sadness.
While the future lies in the hands of the young in masses,
   this school, my school, breeds the individual.

Laughter and criticism mask fear in each; trepidation hides
   beneath trends, cliques, pressure, and idealism.
The masks create a Mardi Gras of clowns; we look for the
   ultimate and dismiss what we cannot afford to lose.

Though I am one to mock these games that conform all,
   I know the masquerade game and play it well.
Born, not from the soil, nor clean air, as those before me;
   My soul consists of city air and the concrete hearted
   ghosts that frequent its breeze.

The future is beyond my control, still this phantom
   conscience flows with good intentions.
This school is a center for my social growth, yet as the
   confusion lingers in this suburban breeze it provides
   hope for further understanding.

   Shannon Lee Moore

That Beautiful Batch

A tale from a gangly scarecrow overlooking a pumpkin patch . . .
And all the wonder he was able to catch . . .
A tale well maybe a mystery . . .
You be the judge now listen and see . . .
Now pumpkins sit there all orange E . . .

As dignified as pumpkins can be . . .
Then harvest time comes . . . the mystery . . .
Why many will have their heads cut off . . .
Or shrivel up in an old barn loft . . .
But they stay beautiful as can be . . . Destined
My . . . such chivalry . . .
Just a scarecrow's view . . .
   of a pumpkin patch . . .
Every year I see that beautiful batch . . .
And every year I think they have no match . . .
Those . . . oranges . . . in the pumpkin patch . . .
God made them to delight you and me . . .
They're an inspiration don't you agree . . .
Perhaps a symbol of destiny . . .

   C. Jeannette Myers

She

There are Angels watching when women feel
And Angels staying, when women kneel
Heroes came from you and me
Who make coffee and serve tea
Women who rock and mend with art
Those who cherish with broken hearts
Who live through war to see men die
Angels who love and then cry-
Mothers and sisters, daughters and kin
Who with their whole being want heaven to begin!
Yes there are Angels watching
When women on earth are praying
And working and loving from birth
Angels are watching as faithful she goes
Angels are writing the name of the rose
While Queens and Saints, Thinkers and Mystics
Of glory and grace pray for a kingdom for humankind
For God to make people a good place -
Who serves and grieves and loves thee!
What a noble piece of work is She.

   Shirley Bauder

"Another Chance"

All my life I tried to look through eyes that weren't my own.
And as I lived by others views, 'twas me who hadn't grown.

I'd never felt that I fit in, so acted and performed.
Others were impressed by me, but for myself I'd mourned.

My talents, skills, my gift for words, saying the "right" thing,
Had me too confused to know I had a broken wing.

Then when I could fly no more, not knowing I never had,
I lost the things I thought were me, and then life made me mad.

Cause after losing all "my things", 'twas me I had to defend.
But I had yet to realize I was merely on the mend.

I'd lost my skills and material goods, not knowing that "things" weren't me.
I never knew that things were things, and still wasn't ready to see.

I found that what I thought had been a gift for the "right" word,
Was actually being "appropriate", saying what "should" be heard.

When all the damage had been done, and all I saw was rust,
It took time and help to see it's me that I can trust.

Dad spoke few words; that's how I see what he was trying to say.
And I cry as I grasp it all: He meant "Baby, go your own way."

It's been two years now since I lost the "things" that made me see,
I had to lose "it" all to see I'm free to just be me.

   Lauren Gail Payne

Acacias Unbloomed

I see her clutching my soiled shirts in nervous hands,
And breaking sheets of dripping ice from a frozen stream.
Her blue hands, still vigorous but shaking,
Will wring them snow-white again.
She prays shuddering before purgatorial fires,
Remembering a soft April night with the sound
Of a flute and bitter scent of acacias in the air.
Tongues of fire lick her bare and varicose legs, once so firm
And lithe as twigs freshly stripped of their green.

Now, with dazed eyes, I look through the window of a dream
And etched against the lucent fires of a summer twilight,
I see a body swaying on a bare tree.
Shredded rags reveal ashen flesh — macerated,
Bird-pecked and bloodlessly lacerated
Where the thorny branches slash and sting.
Soon — I say — I'll shed this rotting and tattered flesh;
And a sweet robin redbreast
In my rib-cage shall nest,
Where my restless heart used to sing.

   H. Izadpanah

Life

Filigree clouds pass over my head
   and cast shadows that dance with the wind.
Brief glances of shade move swiftly along
   but leave not a trace of their pattern.

It's not with carelessness but grace
   that clouds can mask over the sky
And cover intentions for glad or sad days
   or decorate a soul's mirror.

Clouds cover thoughts of a pensive sky
   that longs to bring peace to the earth.
Clouds cover the longings of peace too
   and enhance the angry heart's hate.

Clouded visions of yesterday's deeds
   or clouded thoughts of tomorrow's bright hopes
Will dance to the rhythm of life's storms and breezes
   and leave not a trace of their pattern.

   Pama-Lynn Hartman

Need

I need a gentle rain, to wash away the tears
and chase away the pain, that has followed me for years

I need a summer breeze, to thaw my frozen heart
and blow away the memories that are tearing me apart
I need a stormy sea, to sail these broken dreams
of what will never be, where no one can hear my screams

I need a raging river, just to carry me away
to a place that will deliver, not another lonely day

I need a sandy beach, to walk for endless miles
a place where time will keep, as I collect my thoughts awhile

I need a roaring waterfall, to drown these worried thoughts
and forget the future, past and all, no matter what the costs

I need a shady woods, to pass these lonely hours
and leave behind for good, all my troubles and their flowers

I need my moment in the sun, another friend or two
but when everything is said and done, all I need is you . . .

        William C. Mitchell

Life

Birth is the miracle of life,
   And death is the end of strife.
Life is that which is in between,
   The birth and death of any being.

Once we're born we learn and grow,
   And become someone that no one knows.
Through all my life I've hidden here,
   Trying hard not to show my fear.
Torn apart by emotions hidden,
   For it's been that, that's forbidden.

Life is sad, and not fulfilling,
   But friends are nice and just as thrilling.
Given a chance by all around,
   Sensitivity and love cannot be bound.

When, at the end of life, it comes,
   All will be forgiven and I shall be done.
Homeward I'll go to be with my Lord,
   To live for eternity on Heaven's bright shore.

        Ross C. Edmonds

"Beliefs"

Who walks the rough and lonely roads of old,
And does such deeds both brave and bold.
A simple young colonel is who I mean,
Strong and simple with a dream.
Colonel Shaw was his name,
And a hero he shall remain.
He led black troops and fought the sins
With freedom fighters who had to win.
He freed his horse and walked to death,
Gave his troops his final breath.
Proved black and white were equal all
Gave us all strength to believe
In Gods way we're all conceived
and equal.

        Stef Kirkendall

Diminished Dancer

She dances with an empty space
and glances with a brittle face.

A thin scent of sweat blows through her halls
and sends her across the apartment walls
tripping dizzy very easy,
fading weightless as she falls.

Deeper shadows hang on the walls,
pictures of postures of paper dolls
that danced with an empty space.

She picks up the pace in case
they pity her size, her sinking eyes,
diminished arms, calves and thighs.

Smaller now than she used to be,
just living on diet and herbal tea,
and her face and waist are caving in.

Like the paper dolls are paper thin
she dances with an empty space.

        A. J. Schuermann

And There Passed — A Man

F.D.R. April 12, 1945
I strode the streets of Washington, the night our leader died,
And I couldn't hold the tears, however hard I tried.
Hard boiled am I, an Army man, and punishment can take,
But I loved the MAN, and in my heart, there's terrible ache.

I watch the cars go by - I hear the newsboy's cry
And from the people's lips, I seem to feel their sigh
As a husband feeling seems settling o'er the town, while the flag
On the hill comes half-way down.

Rest in peace, oh strong and kindly man
While we carry on, the very best we can.
You gave your all, till your heart gave out
We'll carry the banner now-we'll finish out this bout.

And when the drums of war have rolled their very last,
A calm and grateful people, searching deep into the past
Will come to know and realize your worth,
And place your name in history, among the greatest men on earth.

        Samuel I. Tafeen

"Love"

Love hurts so much,
And I finally found out why.
When you have real deep feelings,
For that one special guy.
Love breaks your heart when you love him so much,
Your heart starts dying.
You'll finally find out,
When you can't help but crying.
If you try to hide your love,
And just let your heart break.
Then that just makes another day,
For your heart to overtake.
Now I must tell you my friend,
If you love him, let it show.
But if you don't,
Then let him go.
I know these things,
I tell you no lie,
For I have just lost,
The one and only love of mine.

        Sherri Torres

Dawn

One day you finally caught my glance
And I raised hands to skies and kissed a wish
So crisp and cold and new . . . I sucked it in
And closer became a new form of heaven
Fusion.
And the sky was ours, viewed with new eyes
Digital red - the only remnant of reality
And circumstance surfaces
As the pink dissolves black, scraping tips of green hills
(and you hold me and I wonder if you understand)
My night is trickling . . . and the moon turns it's back
I alter my gaze so tears won't flash in your eyes (so compelling . . .)
I wait for you tell me it never was
It never penetrated through your chest to where it belonged
I wait to be told that animals and dreams never existed
And they slide away as eyes squint at the arrival of the ellipses
Where words trail off (fragments . . .) and the pink is sliding into blue
An instantaneous eternity - silhouetting a memory
And I am fixated on you fading.

Melissa Jett

The Woodlands

The beauty of the forest beckoned me into it's realm
And I trespassed upon a nature not my own.
The rustling of the thicket whispered softly of it's calm
and I surrendered to it's pacifying tone.

The warbling of a brook enticed me to it's edge
and I reclined upon a verdant bank of down.
The current of the streamlet ran unhindered on it's way
and I was soothed to sleep by the tranquil sound.

I awoke in the afternoon refreshed by peaceful slumber
and endeavored to depart this wondrous place.
But the splendor of the woodlands gave me a peace I'd never known
and bid me not return to my own race.

Vicki Roblin Lee

Dearest Santa

As a child you were a fantasy my fondest dream come true,
and I waited patiently each year for my cherished visit from you.

One night I thought I saw you out walking through the snow,
I wanted to run and catch you but of course my Dad said no.

When they said there was no Santa I didn't believe it was true,
I wandered and worried all year until again you came through.

Later I learned you are the Spirit of giving the gift of Love and Joy,
and in the end it doesn't matter who actually paid for the toy.

And that value isn't for the issue it's from the heart that we give,
at that special time of year and through-out the lives we live.

Thank you Santa for being there and for all the Joy you bring,
For the light in children's eyes and the meaning in songs they sing.

You teach us Love for one - another it's better to give than receive,
and race and color are forgotten when it comes to those who believe.

Your image has survived the ages and you're Loved by young and old,
thanks to what you give each year your story will forever be told.

Lora E. V. Myers

A Positive Day

The Lord has given me this new day
And I want it be positive in every way
I want to look up, not down
I want to smile, not frown
I want to speak encouraging words
I want to be cheerful like the singing birds
I want to extend a helping hand
I want to be helpful to my fellowman
I want to do some worthwhile thing
I want to help some sad soul sing
I want to help carry another's pack
I want to feel part of his load on my back
I want to feel at this days end
I've helped someone and been his friend
Help me dear Lord to work not faint
Help me keep going when I feel I can't
Help me dear Lord your love to share
So those I touch will know you care
Do help me dear Lord in all I do
To bring Glory, and Honor and Praise to You

Truitt J. Beard

Selfishness

Whenever I come home upset, I've had a bad day
And I'm embarrassed to share
That it's usually something stupid or unimportant
Like a bad grade or maybe just my hair

As I sit there pouting with a frown on my face
Unlike so many less fortunate than me
I realize how easy and carefree my life is
Compared to the hardship that theirs must be

I start thinking to myself, do we have the right
To get mad or throw a fit?
When we have a home and food on our table
Where a box or a crumb might be all they get

In a world of death, abuse, and hunger
So full of sadness and pain
People like you and I get upset over the smallest of things
What's happening to us? Are we going insane?

Molly Bennette Pendergast

All Things Considered

Square numbers in the box flipped toward the hour
And in my car, the spotted windows sealed,
I. Measured pavement respirated foul,
Oppressive heat. The roadside view, concealed.
A yellow bus blocked all that lay ahead.
Immovable and Trapped. The air and I
Are still, beyond the city that I fled,
But passing cars still move quite swiftly by.
I cannot stand to sit behind the wheel
That's driven by another person's hand.
My minds explodes in movement I can feel.
I, saddened, think it hasn't any chance.
  But I can listen to talk radio
  And learn from voices while I wait to go.

Susan Donley

A Whispered Cry

You felt a need to isolate yourself from me
And, in your freedom, cast your lot
With those who honor, hopelessly and needlessly,
A spirit that denies the very soul its full expression.
You made my life an endless night,
A mirror casting for the light,
A wave that lost its place upon a stormy sea.

My bitterness betrays my desperation
And my soul is torn
Between my longing for you and your sacred forms
That keep you at a distance from a dream we shared.
I still relive the joy I knew
In wanting you, in having you;
A spirit born of flesh is no less spirit.

Your touch evokes my whispered cry:
"How could you do this to me?"
Lorraine L. Todd

Poetry

A leaf blown on the breeze passes the soul
and is reflected in the lake-mirrored
consciousness of the prophet's story.

Seemingly the words unspoken,
feelings throughout man and womankind
pulled through the mind to the
hand holding pen.

What is poetry,
if not the disintegrating pages
of a yellowed book
reposing in that musty archive
and sounding a silent beauty
heard on the current of God's wavelength?
Nena Louise Cummings

Feeling

I can stroke its beautiful shapeless outline
And its untouchable thorns start to shine
As they pine.

I can smell its scentless and wonderful gale
And its odorless banes start to sail
As they pale.

I can watch its imageless stunning profile
And its invisible flames start to smile
As they while.

I can hear its amazing and soundless sweet call
And its inaudible cries start to roll
As they fall.

I can savor its insipid but incredible sap
And its tasteless molds start to flap
As they snap.

I can feel it by feeling bits
Of its own its.
Serban Maris-Sida

Untitled

There's all kinds of bones and biscuits and toys,
and no one to scold us for barking our joys.

And though I do miss you and walks by your side,
I'm in puppy dog heaven dear master, inside.
Thomas S. Whitehead

Forever Friends

When we first came together
And joined up as friends,
A flame was kindled between us;
A flame bright and warm.
Others joined with us in friendship,
And, as our circle grew,
So did our flame grow into a blazing fire.
But the time has come:
The circle is beginning to dissipate.
We must break from this circle to join another.
Somewhere - sometime
A new flame will be kindled,
But we don't have to let the old fire die.
It can live on in our memories,
And burn forever in our hearts.
And indeed
Friends can be friends forever.
Tanja Lucas

Untitled

A city awakens with its urban roar where another day is being born,
And just last night, hours before, a man took his life to hollow blackness.

Miles away near a country abode a farmer walked upon a gravel road.
To a stranger he smiled, as the foreigner rode into a forest of smiling faces.

The busy streets come alive in the city where the people thrive
Like ants, seeking food, arrive at the fallen candy of a child.

Back to the west the old man smiles on his porch as he watches
the early sun rise.
His dog flaps an ear as he shoos off a fly
As the man sits whittling with his knife.

Night falls upon the graveyard of streets as a woman walking home
chances to meet a youth who steals her purse and beats her
Until darkness engulfs her eyes.

A knock is heard upon the door of a country home where stands
before it a friendly neighbor who visits for
An evening of laughter and smiles.
Richard D. Johnson

Ireland

Take me back to Knockmany Mountain
And let me retrace my steps up the winding path,
Surrounded by the quiet presence of the forest.
Once more, let me gaze out over those vast, endless fields of Irish green,
Remembering times gone by.
Let me feel again the dampness on my skin,
And let me experience the overwhelming calm of this panoramic dream.
Let me hear the voices of the past chanting their prayers to the heavens,
. . . And let those voices merge with my being; past with present.
Let them speak to my spirit in soothing whispers,
. . . And let me feel their peace deep within my soul.
Loretta Allen Cash

Fire Flies

In the misty dew lit night frequently you can see
    an array of jubilant lights
near the smoky forests edge there is a buzz
    in the distance
sounds of quiet munching
    of fruit and tree bark.
The hub-bub is like an orchestra playing
    sweetly in the dusk.
Ever so often one can catch the most magnificent
    of life's brilliant treasures,
A phosphorescent light
The fire fly.
Mary Gleeson

241

It's A Beautiful Morning

I throw open the window,
    and let the warm breeze fill the room.
The sun is shining,
    and the birds are singing.
The frosty air no longer carries a bitter gloom.

I whistle a sweet song along with the birds,
It's the best song I have ever heard,
    although it has no words.

The sun beats down warm on my face,
The birds begin a new sweet song with a slower pace.

I brush my hair,
    and I gaze into the sky.
The tune is carried everywhere,
    and a young bluebird flies by.
I lean back in my chair,
    and sit adoring.
It truly is a beautiful morning.

Meghan A. O'Meara

Untitled

I wait for the time when people become the wiser,
and life to be served with happiness.
I fan the flame of the innocence, so we can laugh together in unison.
I wait for a stronger, brighter day.

They sleepwalk through empty lives,
sad and scared of something unseen.
Turning on the light of life brings fear to those who wallow in their misery.
With my arms outstretched, I will comfort them.
Come silently now to the tower of time.
I can't see my future, but I see it coming.
Oh that great sight to open my eyes and see clearly.
Now I paint my pictures with my own hands, and celebrate my youth!

Strangers are all ahead . . . empty faces . . .
What are these things to me?
Why are the world's best people locked inside their eyes?
Can I fly with my wings of steel,
soar into the night to capture the sights of the world?
That place where all is alive, yet no one can admit it . . .
I SEE IT AND I EMBRACE THIS LIFE.

Vanessa Long

Your Dreams Can Be Found

Be very quiet, don't make a sound
And listen to where your dreams can be found
Some find their dreams above in the sky
In the midst of the clouds many miles high
Some find their dreams in the mountain tops
Close to the heavens where snow never stops
Some find their dreams in the depths of the sea
Where no one's around and they can feel free
Some look for fortune, some look for fame
They want everyone to remember their name
But to some, dreams can be very hard to find
For they keep their dreams in the back of their mind
So If you want to be happy and you want to be free
I offer advise, if you are like me
Keep your dreams in your heart, never let them get old
The end of each rainbow could be your pot of gold.

Terrie Webster Kubasiak

The Little Things

I walked a thousand miles one time to see what I could see,
And met a thousand souls each day that won't remember me.
The sights I peered, the things I saw are like a pane of glass.
You stare, you look, you see, you touch, but continue on you pass.
Then one day, your head it clears like day, and memories you hold,
The little thing in life you value until you're tired and old.
'Twas not the buildings you did see, or the medals that you won,
Nor people and paper, or any waiter, things you've said and done.
What stands tall, above them all, are the small things you don't notice,
They sky of blue, and tiny socks, too—the times you were a novice.
'Tis the hand of the child, two inches wide, you hold within your heart,
And walking down halls, the sound of dove calls, from which you never part.
I walked back a thousand miles one day to see what I had missed,
And saw a thousand sights each day that my memory hath kissed.
I stared, I looked, I saw, I touched and the memories stayed clear.
The wind that day, the month of May, I all remember dear.
A crack in the pavement, an unfinished basement, this time did make me smile.
The nail on my toe, a red bow, I memorized each mile.
When the day comes, after many suns, when I can walk no longer,
These memories I hold, the things I have told, will only grow much stronger.

Kate Graves

The Fatality

Happy the tree that is barely sensitive
and more the hard rock because it does not feel.

For there is no pain greater than that pain of being alive
with the heavy weight of life's conscience,

To be and know nothing and
    To be without a certain path,
To fear not being is a future of terror and
    The sure fiend is to be dead tomorrow . . .

And suffer though a shadowed existence
    Because what we do not know and what
    we hardly suspect is that our flesh will be tempted by the
    fresh wreaths and a tomb that guards us with its withered limbs
Because we don't know where we're from!

Noemy Alvarez

My Heart

If beauty is fragile, then now you are shattering,
And my heart trembles like rain's pit-pattering.
As I gaze into thine eyes, I stareth at love,
Undisguised and flowing like from the sky above.

Thy grace is a-flowing, a river of wonder,
And my heart trembles like the blasts of thunder.
I would challenge those both high and mighty,
To win your precious heart, my sweet Aphrodite.

As you walketh, my beauty, young hearts do crumble,
And my heart trembles like an earthquake's rumble.
When I watcheth you with loving eyes, my belle,
I would not even notice if all the stars fell.

Oh, my love is as pure as a Cherub's heart,
For which I am grateful that you take part.

Parhaum Toofanian

The Outdoors

When your outside your wild and free,
and there's nothing but, trees and yellow bumble bees.
You can think of a kingdom,
And really be there.
Even though it's just clouds in the air.

Mandi Novak

Journey To My Soul

I've sailed the sea of uncertainty
and nearly capsized
when I got caught up in the storm of reality

I've swam in the ocean of hopelessness
and almost drown
because I was unable to see the land

I've walked on the beach of tears
never touching the water
for fear of being pulled in
when waves of memories
came crashing down on me

Tired and exhausted
I climbed the mountain of pain
where I could see
the stars light up the night
letting it be known to the world
I am ready for this fight
Laurie Erickson

My Grandparent's Door — The Door Not Closed

I see a frosted ship upon the sea
And oh, it's whereabouts did it carry me!
I'd travel far to places of my dreams someday
For inspiration her sails gave to me
I love that ship upon the sea
For it all became more than childhood fantasy

A ship, a door, great inspiration — Yes Siree!
A part of my past no longer to be
The door is not needed
For the "secret" you see,
The frosted ship is always there
To far away places, she still carries me!
Kathleen Anne Cave

The Path

Today I watched him from afar as he caught fireflies in a jar,
and once again my memories fade, back into my childhood days;
back to the times that now are gone, and once again I felt alone.

Where did he go, that little lad that followed close behind his
dad, and made each step along the way another little game to
play? Another game that led him home, and once again I felt alone.

Where are you when I need you so? I searched the paths of long
ago, I tried so hard to find you there along the paths my
memories bear; but now I know the paths are gone, and once
again I felt alone.

Then I heard the noise behind, the sound of steps that were not
mine. Then I knew it was the lad walking close behind his Dad.
The Dad was me, the lad was mine, and as we walk the paths of
time, I knew that I was not alone.
C. W. Gandy Jr.

Death Watch

Eileen fought death today and tonight;
    And, so far, she's won a tough fight!
So now it's tubes and machines and a I.C.U. nurse
    To see if tomorrow she'll be better or worse.

But, if there's a God, and I'm sure that there is,
    He'll show her that her life is his,
And send her home cured for me to love
    Until she goes up to his home above
Ralph G. Sisk

To The Dedication Of An Organ

The fingers touch the instrument
And out upon the waves of time
    the music pours its glorious harmonies
Never to be caught again
Soaring through all years, all time, and all eternity,
Beautiful and poignant, dulcet and serene.
There is no going back within the being
Of the man-made sounding board.
This music has become our inspiration, hope, and joy
Reverberating waves of sound - victorious,
    magnificent and acclaimed,
Piercing through desolation and despair
It brings the gift of hope to those residing there.
It climbs upon the shoulders of the night
And down the cloak of morning's first grayed light,
It rests upon the cheek of ever-blushing day
And sails on sunset's rainbow hue
    to heaven's be splendored way.
Vibrant music, acclaiming God's hope and plan
That love and peace and brotherhood may fill the heart of man.
Lorna M. Martin

Golden Rose

A tiny seed gently settles in the fertile soil of two young hearts
and quickly takes root, pushing expectantly upward
through the uncharted darkness.
Before long the sun bursts forth, shining its blessings-
children, upon the union,
and the seedling grows stronger, their love expands.
Troubles and disagreements-passing storms
that humble and depress, but leave in their wake
refreshing peace and resilient vigor.
Many years have passed, many seasons
of sunshine and rain, times of joy and of sadness-
the seed has changed, yet remains.
For with each knowing glance, tender touch, or kind word
a leaf, a petal, has been added.
And though a few thorns may occasionally be noticed
in this intertwining of personalities,
what is truly breathtaking to any who pass is the beauty,
the wonder of how a tiny seed of love
has endured in two timeless hearts these 50 years,
to stand now with quiet pride as an exquisite, copious rose.
Michael A. Hanslip

Solace

There are moments when you look around
And there's just no one around for you
No one to talk to or complain to
No one to cry to, none to sigh to
There are times when life's got hard and rough
I look around for a soul who cares
There's just no one to pour it out to
I'm left so lonely in my despair

That's when you came around, soothing as ever
Tears rolling down my face, wet your long brown hair
Just the consolation I need, you know it best
'Feel a lot better crying in your arms
Sometimes I've got a pack of friends
When with all the company, I still feel hopeless
The thousands that pass by me in pain
Don't match my solace, . . . in you alone.
Mark C. Okafor

Certain Young Male Soul

In Heaven, God came to this certain young male soul;
And said, Son, you and I . . . we must take a little stroll.
I've heard many prayers coming from my children down below,
So I'm sending you to them; soon it will be your time to go.

I'm sending you to this earth because it is my plan
For you to become a fine physician so you could help your fellow man.
There's a pestilence that's killing men; for it you'll find a cure.
Be faithful, always praying that you'll keep your garments pure.

Many faces that are frowning now will be smiling once again;
And all my people will be thanking Me for sending you; you'll be their friend.
You'll be kind and gentle and to them your love you'll freely give.
Stay worthy, and then soon again, together we will live.

They walked along the golden streets until they came to the Pearly Gates
Then God looked down upon the earth at all the things He did create,
Tears filled His eyes as He exclaimed, "Son, all I see is doom!
You see, you'll never be; for they just took you from your mother's womb!

Marsha Walters

The Rose

Winter storms and frost have come,
  And thirsty earth has welcomed early snows.
The growing season has been stilled
  Except for a lingering rose.
    This rose that yet blooms 'neath my window
      Graces the top of a slender, thorny shoot.
  It's upward thrust to life is precious,
    Which brown, dead leaves cannot refute.
      After the seasonal shedding of nearby trees
      And the harvest of what summer grows,
    Mother Nature has truly blessed my landscape
      With this fragrant red, red rose.

Vivian Jenson

Confidence

I really know I can make it I just have to try
Ask myself the questions what where and why
Believe in my morals which are very true
Give that 100 percent to everything I do
Get what I need and get what I want
Don't hide a problem that I could confront
For me to succeed I must believe in what I write
For I know I can win every battle and not lose a fight

Michael J. Reilly

Peace Be Still

Dream a dream
And take hold of yourself
Dream a dream
And level off your thoughts

Don't let depression hold you hostage
Dream a dream
And escape with your thoughts to a nearby Serene Cottage

Let meditation begin this process
Take a deep breath and enjoy the scenery
Relax and mellow out as you begin to dream your dreams

Pamper and be good to yourself
Much love and care are due to you
Dream a good dream
And make it come true

Sheila Whisenant

Circus Memories

The trucks move slowly down the street
And soon the tents are lined up neat
The animals are led out two by two
The lion, the elephant and the kangaroo

They pace back and forth in their wire cage
As they wait for the show on that giant stage
The man in his tall hat and carrying a cane
Smiles as he walks by, saying something 'bout rain

Here comes someone with balloons on a string
Bright colors flying high, I can hear him sing
He is closer now, I can see his face
All painted up, why it's quite a disgrace

His hair sticks out and he looks so funny
As he smiles at me and calls me honey
His big red nose looks like a cherry
No wonder he makes the children so merry

His feet are so big with curled up toes
And he's squirting water out of a rose
Tomorrow it will all be gone,
But the memory of the circus will linger one.

Verda Gingrich

Untitled

I wish that the words would flow from the deep waters of the spirit
And that my heart would know what my soul is trying to say;
When the music rises in my mind and makes my being stop
To notice, the rhyming that I find in the pattern of my breathing.

The words can't speak of the deep passion that would swell up
Like the oceans, and the waves creep to the shore
Like fingers reach into the cavities of the dreams
That lie unrevealed in the shadows, and the silent screams
That force their way to the top.

Passion drives me with blind eyes into the raging of the storm
And once I can get beyond the lies of my life and what they've told me
I can make the words come again and speak from the wellspring
So that my soul speaks as a friend and my heart dances in the sun.

Linda Mynatt

Autumn

The world is changing colors now,
And so am I.
Laughter and smiles are taking the place,
of the times I used to cry.

I've learned how to solve the problems,
of feeling all alone,
It is you I have to thank for this,
And all the colors you have shown.

I know myself much better now,
more than I ever did before,
I have made so many improvements
and now I have the strength to make even more,

I have met someone so special,
who sees the colors like I do,
and if we can make a life all our own,
then all will seem brand new,

My colors are really changing now,
more than I have ever seen,
and I'm waiting for my leaves to fall,
And my world to change to green.

Roger W. Brown

Bequeathal

The moon rose cold over the desolate beach
And the breakers scourged the shore
The stars above have judged the scene
From now until before.

A woman rose cold in the crying surf
Cold water runs down her flesh
Her supple gown flows one with the foam
O night, her mission bless!

She quickly held her child close
Then lays him in a cradle of sand
A mobile of sea oats and stars
Goes swinging over his hand.

A scream is stifled in her throat
A tear runs down her face
A voice inside her head
Demands she leave this place.

The sea stretched up with grateful arms,
The woman now returns
To castles and towers under the sea.
Impatient, the future burns . . .
(I was inspired to write this poem
after watching sea turtles lay —
and leave — their eggs on the beach.)
        Rebecca Lauren Love

"The Demon's Hand"

As the Earth quakes,
And the demon awakes.
  As his eyes spread to peer,
  Every thing can feel his power, far and near.
He comes from down below,
Amongst where the Lavas flow.
  As the flames rise,
  Without fear in his eyes.
His unbegotten spirit will arise,
Beyond the darkest skies.
  He rises above the ground,
  To spread fear all around.
His mission is for destruction,
His mind filled with corruption.
  He thrust his body forward,
  Never turning to look backward.
Never turning back until he has conquered all,
Making sure all, has heard his fierce call.
  Casting his curse through-out the land,
  Spreading his dementation through the palm of his hand.
        Steffani D. Matney

The Cave

In the blank darkness, all time stands still.
  And the only thing stirring is the breath of God's will.

With a deep pit of paleness and a never ending sky,
  The only sound surrounding, is the water flowing by.

Under soiled earth we stand, in peace we fall.
  But if I should stumble in, . . . who will hear my call?

A simple light breaks the bleakness and shows an onward path.
  A tunnel of darkness with no way out, it's almost like God's wrath.

Blindly following only touch to reach no certain destination,
  I reach the end of the cave, and face the light in fascination.
        Melinda Wells

Treasure In The Message

She controls the humming bees
and the wind's raspy song
She controls the rustling leaves
and every life short or long

And every step she doth take
a pool of light adorn
with every step she doth take
a brand new life is born

And as the waves crash and roar
upon the limp meek sand
a hope will rise, spread wing and soar
the song of peace it will demand

This hope is in the voice of a child sweet and dear
while shouts leave at all no marks
his whisper shall engrave and sear
listening hearts, far and near
        Nili Hirsh

Ibrahim

The birds are still singing
and there are no tears in my eyes
For you were a teacher
of strength, of peace, and of self-respect.
You had a vast understanding
of the world and the people in it.

Your thoughts and ideas were worth more
than any text book could hold,
and the knowledge you shared,
was priceless.

Your conversations were more valuable,
to those who heard you, than anyone
could ever imagine.

Even in your weakest hour,
you forced so many of us
to think very deeply and
question everything

You can trust that the words you spoke
will be carried in the hearts and minds
of all those who listened and by the generations to come.
        Sana Saah

Our Promised Vows

I promised to give you the best of myself
and to ask of you no more than you can give,
I promised to receive and accept you as you are
and give of my life to shore and live.
I promise to respect you as your own person
and to realize that your interest, desires, and needs
are no less important than my own,
I promised never to disrespect you, to honor your
goals and treat you as royalty upon a throne.
People can make up beautiful love poems
or put down the perfect words in a love letter,
your beauty seems to come from within and
shows me true feelings far better.
I've tried to tell you and show you in my
own little way just how much I care,
our own little ways are genuine and real
and for one another true love will always be there.
        Michael Evans

You Were There

You were there the day I was born, counting all my fingers
and toes to make sure they were all there.

You were there the first time I ever had a cold and stayed
up all night to make sure I was just asleep and nothing more.

You were there when I cut my first tooth and made that first
crawl across the floor.

You were there when I said my first word for all the world to hear.

You were there when I fell down and scratched my knees. You picked
me up brushed them off, kissed them and said that will make them well.

You were there the first day of school. I was scared, but you cried all day.
You were there the first time I went away to camp. You cried then, too.

You were there the first time I loved and lost, telling me
it would be alright, you wait and see.

You were there the day I left home, to start a life all my own.
Times has past from then to now, but I'll always love you
because you were there; the most important part of my life.

    Robin Brown

Time

Time and time again I look out my window
And try not to see the end of the rainbow.
Ashes are all that's left and I scatter the remains.
I wonder where to go and just what to do.
I'm all alone now, feeling cold and out on my own.
Time passes by, easing the pain
And slowly I gather in my remains.

But time after time I look behind me
Reaching out for my past
Knowing it's gone forever.
And time hating time.
Time pulling time.
Time needing time.
Time drags me forward yet pulls me back.
I'm torn between
Time past and time now.

So I look out my window.
I search my heart
And try not to see
The rainbow's end of time.

    Laurie S. Tannenbaum

Break Of Dawn

I like to get up at the break of dawn,
and walk out upon the lawn, when all
the grass and flowers are sprinkled with
dew; and to watch the swollen buds open
as the flowers burst through.

I look up at the sky so blue, as
the sun's ray's cast over it a glorious
hue, the sun just peeping over earth's
brim, making everything so beautiful again.

I wonder why anyone could feel so
blue, looking at the earth in all her
sparkling glory, when God made all
these things for you.

    Una F. Owen

Remembrance

He walked among us for a little while;
And we are the better because of it.
He was just a simple but sort of complex man.
His western cowboy brand spoke to us of dreams in a far off land.
Where man was man and work was play, with endless plans to fill.
"Ah, Shucks, Ma'am," he would with smiles in face and voice reply,
If compliments around him came, too numerous to claim.
Yes, his charm and wit we all acclaim,
they were so comfortable for him to wear.
The children, young and getting older,
did respond to that grace and gentle way in him.
There was a kindness and laughter all about him,
tho he spoke of tales of war and other times that were behind him.
He gave, he truly gave his heart and life.
To his country, that with pride and valor, he served so well.
Can we ask more- yet more-yes, we can and will.
For to be his friend is gain, to greater heights,
and courage for what tomorrow holds.

    Mary Anne Lilly

Owed To Hunting Season

I get up in the night
And what do I see?
A caller in the wee small hours;
Oh, it's probably Theron or Lee
After all, it's open season on
The deer that roam our place.
'Grand Central Station' is again upon us,
Dear deer, don't you dare show your face,
For if you do, I'm warning you,
It's deterrent to your health.
The hunters are out there after you
To serve on their table with wealth.
Stay low, my deer friends,
Your meat, how tasty t'would be.
I'd no longer see you in my garden
Keeping the rabbits company.
Oh dear, my dear deer, I know
How distractive you can become,
But it's hunting season now
And they'll have you on the run.

    Mary Ellen Van De Car

"Something"

I look into the nothing
"And what do you see?"
You ask and I respond
"Nothing's looking at me."
Nothing but a cold, morbid whisper
That echoes in my ear
It's the ominous cry of my death and fear
"Who is it that speaks and why is it there?"
You ask too many questions and why do you care?
It's nothing I said
As nothing as dead
Leave me alone so I can die in my bed.
Do you now understand as to what I see?
It's that beautiful ugly looking at me.
So beautiful to look at
so ugly to think
That nothing there is killing me.
"I ask you again, what is it you see?"
The ugliest nothing something could be.

    Sandra R. Melendrez

Do You Love Me?

Do you love me when the cold winds blow
And when the raindrops fall?
I guess only you could know
If you love me with your all.

Do you love me when the bright sun shines
Or when the dark clouds loom?
Would your heart's love equal mine's?
Or is your heart filled with gloom?

Would you love me when all is dark
And when the world is through?
When on the earth you've left your mark.
For I know that I'd love you.

Natalie Sypolt

Reflections

'Tis sad when the leaves begin to fall,
And when the winds of Autumn start to call.
That's when the children throw the pigskin ball;
'Tis sad when the leaves begin to fall.

They're gold and yellow and bronze and red,
But the sad part is they're already dead.
They flitter and flutter on their journey down,
Where they get together to cover the ground.

I reflect on the summer as I start to gaze
At some of the trees that appear to blaze.
With their colors of red and yellow and gold,
As time demands it, they've grown old.

Their replacements will be here before too long,
With the warmth of the sun and the blue bird's song.
Then we may or may not recall,
'Twas sad when the leaves began to fall.

T.V. Riley

The Right One

Some guys will treat you as if you were a jewel,
and will quickly make your eyes fill up like a pool.
They will be as sweet as they can be,
as you soon will see.
They are there for you no matter what,
knowing the right words to say
and will never make you pay,
even if you treated them in the worst way.
But there are some guys out there that are just like the wind.
They can never be caught or held down.
If you open up you mouth to make one sound,
it could be the end
of what has really never been.
So down come the tears.
Stick with the guys who will treat you right,
and will not fly away as quickly as a kite.
Don't let those guys carry you away with the things that they say,
then drop you as quickly as they swept you away!

Nicole Lamoureux

Changes

I stood and watched the changing skies,
And wondered as the patterns passed by,
Is life just as the skies?
Sometimes cloudy, sometimes bright,
Sometimes not the slightest hope in sight.

I sighed!
It's time to move on!
Life I'm sure is just as changeable
As the skies.
But I'll not let it pass me by.

Shirley Rodney

My Footsteps Echo

My footsteps echo in the empty corridor
and yet I hear the clanging of lockers and
milling together of young voices.

The classrooms are deserted except for the
careful passing of notes and bored heads
slumped over open notebooks.

The cafeteria rings with clinging of forks
and loud laughter.
It whispers with the terminal secrets of youth.

The gym is barren save for the smell of sweat
and the screeching of the sudden stops of
sneakers on a wooden floor.

In the red room with the red benches
I feel my sides ache in memory of
endless laughs. My lips smile as I remember those
I laughed with and those I laughed at.

Here I see the faces of those I have already
forgotten. Friends, enemies.
All equally lost in the rush to move on.

Rebecca McDougall

Another Man's Wife

Today you married someone else
And you looked so incredibly happy
All you could think about was him
You had no room for thoughts of me

But as I sat there watching you
Thoughts of us flooded my mind
You made me feel like I was the one
I can't see now how I was so blind

I thought we would be together forever
All I could see were happy times ahead
Every part of me was in love with you
And I dreamed of the day when we would be wed

I love your laugh, your smile, your lips
I love you more than I love life itself
It's for these reasons and so many more
That I could never put my love for you on a shelf

I guess it's just my fate
To love you for the rest of my life
I guess it's just my fate
To always be in love with another man's wife

Randy R. Reed

Untitled

One tear trickled down her face
as he stood by the vacant place.
A white chalk outline flawed the floor
where once sat he, whom she adored.
Harsh words from her ripped him to shreds
and he died with one bullet to his head.
Memories of him haunted her day and night.
She wished she could take it back, and not've had that fight.
She totally blamed herself inside . . .
Now it's a double suicide.
Both dead, now never to be apart
and all to ease their hurting hearts.

Nichole M. Allchin

I Won't Forget

I won't forget how it felt when I opened the door
and you were there. It was hard to control my feelings.
     When we first touched it was like a fire that lead to
a fascinating desire. I could feel your heart pounding as
I lay against you. Your heart was pounding with desire
and love.
     Your arousal started almost as soon as we touched.
I was amazed to have that effect on you so smoothly.
     My body burned with desire as you were removing
your clothes and I can close my eyes and feel your
calmness as you were undressing me. Being as gentle
as if I were a child.
     Every touch and kiss that lead to our love making
was like fire-works going off in the dark on a winter
night.
     I was astonished at your love-making. It was a
spell-bound time for me.
     It seemed like my whole spirit and soul trembled
with desire and I often wonder,
          Will we ever put out the fire?
          Thelma Johnson

Untitled

Yearning for your tenderness
     and your love . . .

Dying for the warmth
     of your caress . . .
Lying close together
     in a endless embrace . . .

Kissing so passionately . . .
     so affectionately . . .

Intense cries of love making,
     and romantic fantasizing
That for fill dreams so . . .
     full of life, inspiration, and compassion

Sacrifices of the heart kindle
     through out our minds and our souls . . .

As time passes hard and long,
     your smile keeps us strong

For the crave of true ROMANTICISM
     lies deeply and completely
          between you and me . . .

That we were meant to be . . . .
          Lisa Crim

Endings

Walking down the dirt-pocked path
Angled into a rushing wind
I shy from drifting, distant shadows
Gaining warmth from sun-ray strength
Gaining strength from sun-ray warmth

A chapter closes, no resolution
No destination, no completion
I trudge toward places I don't know
Swollen joints slow progress
Damp dreams lie limp before me
As the morning dew bubbles on leaves of broken limbs

An era exits abruptly
Dirt shovelled on a vaulted box
Life pulses in wind-whipped daisies
Beginnings end and ends begin
There is no choice
But to trust in an unseen hand
And press against an unforgiving wind
          Linda Mastaglio

Don't Do It When Daddy's Around

Wake up to the noise of the children at play,
Another hot coffee, another long day,
Get ready for school, it's not time to play,
They do it when Daddy's away.

One's on the table talking to Mr. Nobody the ghost,
One's in the kitchen burning the toast,
It's driving me crazy; they're never this way,
They're only like this when Daddy's away.

It must be a plot, or a well planned-out scheme
To drive me to drink, it's working, it seems,
Life is a circus, happy and gay,
They just go crazy when Daddy's away.

They color the woodwork, and paint my hair gray,
I don't understand why women should pay,
It seems that he's gone forty hours a day,
I swear they grow horns when Daddy's away.

Another day passes and I've aged ten years,
The children are sleeping, too tired for tears,
He won't understand, he won't see them that way,
For kids only do it when Daddy's away.
          Peter M. Contonio

Nile

You are with me like the Nile
Appealing to my ancient side
Part of the soot and steam
Of old Europe in my soul

Gathering dust in the desert
Letting it settle upon my brow
Reminds me of the neglect I've felt

Half seen corners create opaque surprises
As I walk through the pyramids
and find you posing
In a triangular world we remain part of
but can no longer construct

Crevices and stone smooth and tight
form a backdrop leaning toward me
Glistening in the night air
Galvanizing a hope in my soul
at once large and mirrored
and yet I stand alone

Distanced by the wonder of you
I fall forward and smell the
fresh clay . . . the earth's blood
thick and sweet
still . . . I wish I could be stone
          Susan Daria Landino

Burnt Popcorn And Chili

One day young Phil was in a hurry
Around the kitchen he did scurry
He set the microwave way too high
Burned the popcorn, black and dry
He was feeling very silly
He mixed the burnt popcorn with some chili
Much to his surprise
A new recipe formed right before his eyes
The popcorn must be burned as black as midnight
To make the recipe taste just right
Burnt popcorn and chili may never go down in the hall of fame
Phil claims that it is delicious just the same
          Winniferd Gilchrest

248

Untitled

The night unravels
as
I whisper words into the curves of your ears
neither of us listening
even the shadows are dirty here
(not velvet like in other lifetimes)
and I think of
how I used to dream of you
lying naked in Antarctica
melting into all the oceans
until
nothing came to exist
but your body floating through the wet world
like silver silence

Neelanjana Banerjee

Untitled

Children playing in the water,
As a young girl you admire your father.
Birds fly away from the cold,
In your arms a newborn you hold.
An old couple walk hand in hand,
Your entire body covered in sand.
The young boy becomes a man,
Set out cross country without a plan.
The sun shines down to warm your face,
You sit on the river bank and watch fish race.
Snowflakes on your tongue you taste,
Where there is love there is no waste.

Tammy McDonald

For Sissy

Re-claim your inner child, they say
As an adult, begin to learn to laugh and play
Become carefree, re-born anew
Tell your thoughts in groups of ten, like you
This is all just well and good
for anyone to say
But, perhaps they did not grow up
in quite the same way
As we did and you know who you are
The adult children left with just a scar
Where their child-like soul once was.

Michelle Fedirko

Another's Opinion

Seasons change, so the sky,
as bright blue day, turns to teary eye.

And colorful leaves that fall to ground,
prepare the way to winter sounds;

of silence, and sleep, and falling snow.
Temperatures so cold, waters cease to flow.

The Earth lay still, with time to mourn,
death waits the day, for spring reborn.

North winds bemoan a lonely song,
days drag on, dark nights so long.

But in a bare branch of higher tree,
calls out a tiny Chickadee.

"Chick-a-dee-dee-dee, chick-a-dee-dee-dee,
Winter is a lovely time for me."

Leanna S. Jagta

These Days

On these lonely days, I dwell in solitude
as I glare into blank, empty walls
battling with the great riddle of life.
I wonder why the days are so short,
why the sun is so dark, and the moon so gloomy.
As I venture into new thoughts, I am terrified,
What are the ominous answers?
Has God forsaken us? Or,
Is it the end of time?
But why? . . . What happened . . .
to the once playful babies,
the cheerful gentlemen and merry ladies.
The old man never tells happy stories anymore,
and grandma just mumbles sorrowful dirges.
Are you scared? Yes I am, . . . Oh! Wait, No! I know . . .
I just want better days full of life, smiles, and laughter.

G. Mutua

Growing And Moving On

As I grow, help me with the things I may not know
As I grow, don't hurt me for it may not show
Give me space but still be concerned for me
For at this moment I'm as fragile as a newly planted tree

For now and tomorrow let me feel my pain
For when it is over it will be my gain
I must deal with my feelings good or bad
I know this must hurt and make you sad

Just remember you have to stay strong
I am trying to learn that I did nothing wrong
These times are tough, but I refuse to quit
I only hope you can stick with it

There are time in our lives when things aren't right
This is when I know I must stand up and fight
Remember this when you go to bed at night
And one day I know I will see the light

We all know the world doesn't stand still
And we all know it never will
And so I know I must move on
It's the only way I'll ever be someone

Lisa M. Holley

The 27th Of October

The smell of medicine lurks through the hall
As I walk down the corridor so quite
You could hear a pin fall.

I catch myself looking out into space
I start thinking of what could happen
My heart begins to race.

I calm myself down, knowing God's on my side
As I drop to my knees and pray
I can't help but cry.

Please God be with him and help him get strong
We need him here, this is where he belongs.
As I end my prayer I get a feeling of peace
As the nurse walks in to end all our grief.

"Mr. Hodges will be fine," she says with a smile
"He's responding real well! You can see him in a while."
A large smile comes on my mamaw's face
As she reaches for me with a warm embrace.

In my mind I say a little prayer
Thank you so much and for all your care.

Melissa Snyder

Aloha Oe

The hills were lonely that night,
As I was lonely.
At the edge of the woods the wind
Whispered sadly through the tall pines
But there, where no one saw, I wept
For the stars that had gone from the sky.
And the wind called, and the trees called
For the lost stars in the sky.

When the stars hid behind the clouds,
The wind called "Come" and led me gently
To the edge of the woods - but when I saw
That the trees were alone in the darkness,
And the moon had drawn the curtain of night,
I became frightened and begged the moon
For one little star to light my way,
And fled back to the hills -
As the wind whispered sadly through the pines.

Louise E. Schmidt

Life's Great Mystery

I want you to know, your story told
As if standing there, was beautiful.
From on high, looking over the edge
I start to cry, it was a story I use to know
Feeling pain and pleasure,
Hearing life's great sound.
It's hard to know you're walking in sin
With your feet never touching the ground.
When giving love no matter what the cost
Would be the need of all of us.
Then we might see, before we leave
Life's true, great mystery.

Todd Van Marter

Love

Is a special feeling.
   As it appears
      you think you behave
         foolishly sometimes.

Luck has maybe come across I.
   Love has nothing to do with luck.

Love is a blessing.
   There are your ups and downs.
Can you think of any time you
   moved forward without going down.
Progress is the turn out.

They say its better to have loved and lost
then to have never loved at all.
Whether this is the case or not
you need to come up with your own scenario.

Patricia Ann Bruno

Keep My Hand In Yours

Lord keep my hand in yours until I reach my journeys end
As the road twists and turns, help me make it 'round the bend

There are times Lord, I'm weak, help me not to lose my grip
If I fall and call you, please help me continue my trip
When the road is easy, I may forget to hang tight
And let some distraction pull me away from your dear sight
In your grace and great love, help me my sinful way to mend
Lord keep my hand in yours until I reach my journeys end.

Opal Braaten

I Am . . .

The rain is my friend.
As it patters down upon me,
It soaks into my body
And penetrates my soul.
The rain is a friend to me,
So that I may be a friend to others.

I witness the stories of many generations.
The roots of families are my cane, my backbone.
I see every marriage, every separation,
Every life and every death.
No one hides from me;
I am everywhere.
My all - seeing eye
Is everywhere.

I teem with life,
But I am not alive.
I am the basis of all life,
But am taken for granted
Like the sun that shines overhead
And the wind that whispers in the trees.

Stefanie Bluemle

The Beauties Of Nature

Have you ever watched a daisy wave
As it says "Hello" to the breeze?
Or listened to birds as they sing or rave
From their perches high in the trees?

Have you noticed a tear that was left on a rose
As the dew disappeared with the dawn?
Or observed a deer standing still in a pose,
Keeping guard for a helpless fawn?

Have you watched the dawn on summer's day
As the sun breaks over a hill?
And felt at a loss for words you would say
To fully describe such a thrill?

The wonders of Earth are great to behold.
Among them we all have trod.
And wherever we see Nature's beauties unfold
We witness the hand of God.

Thomas R. Willwerth

As The Days Go By

As the days go by I wonder if there is peace anywhere I did not look.
As the days go by I wonder if this dirty world ever thought
what it's putting us through.
As the days go by I pray everything will be all right from
the time I rest my head at night until the time I rise in the morning.
As the days go by I look at the news in hope that no one got
hurt or killed by the problems of guns.
As the days go by I look at the stars and it seems they
understand me by sparkling as bright as they can.
As the days go by I ask the Lord to help me and my family
get through another day.
As the days go by the people of the world understand that
the world can't get better if they don't put effort into it.
As the days go by I hope to tell my children to reach for
the stars because God only knows what the next day holds.
As the days go by I fight with my brother but that's my way
of saying "I love you Randy".
As the days go by I thank the Almighty for giving me two
people in my life who teach me my responsibilities and they
help me. I love you Mom and Dad.

LaShonda Wooten

Travelling Home

The wind was whistling through the sails,
As the gallant ship beat through the gales.
The crew aloft, and none below
Across the deck the spray does blow.

The Captain is standing by the helm,
As our gallant ship's in King Neptune's realm.
The clouds still darken the evening sky,
We're setting sails as the wind does die.

The sky is clearing as morning breaks,
The sun is rising, the rigging shakes.
We're heading north by polar star,
But through the day there's lines to tar.

The Cooper's working on the deck,
The water swirls around a wreck.
The seagull sings his solemn tune,
And now we know we'll be home soon.

Michael LaRocca

Casa Solista

I have always spent some part of each year by the sea.
As the moon pulls the tides, it must zap my amphibian brain,
For, no matter the season, I'm compelled on my lemming-like
        trek to the sea:

In thrall to the big picture, "Unlimited Horizons,"
  With silent, stealthy, furtive freighters,
The animated close-up trafficking of work-a-holic birds,
  The changing plots of condescending clouds.

To lie on the drum-white drum-tight sand,
Eased by the roll and rock of the waves,
  A comforting heartbeat, the first panacea.

The shore is my spa:
More than green pastures, it restores my soul.

Robert J. Wetmore

Roller Coaster Of Emotion

The stench of alcohol fills my nostrils
as the squeaking of wheels forgotten fills the air.
strange faces hover above me as I am
being rushed into the O.R. This can't be me. It's too soon.
I am at home in bed. I wake as if in a drugged sleep.
Smiling faces above me look down and say
"Congratulations! It's a boy." All of 1 lb 14 oz. 14
inches lifts me from adolescence to motherhood in 20 minutes.
Euphoria fills my body and soul,
"He is doing well, we can take him off life support at 3:30!"
My wheelchair rolls me to the NICU to see
this 'bundle of joy.' His teddy bear is a giant compared to him.
The tight little grip of his tiny hand on my pinky
bonds us together. We are now INSEPARABLE.
Warning beeps go off in a cacophony like hysterical birds
"I'm sorry, you will have to leave. This is not a good time."
Worry begins to eat me up inside as tears float down my cheeks.
"It's your choice." I decide. 8:35. His last tiny little breath
fades away. He is in my arms. My last tear
falls on his little cheek. My baby. My Kyle.
Dedicated to Kyle Christopher Grimes

Jan. 28, 1995 - Jan. 29, 1995

Teresa Grimes

Beneath The Bridge

In the sun they sat beneath the bridge staring out above the rail.
As they watched each others light brown skin turn to bronze from slightly pale.
One shared a thought, the other a feeling, and both exchanged a bit of humor.
Being oh so careful all the while not to start the slightest rumor.
They walked along the waterfront it seemed with little meaning,
until the moment became more intense, as the sun continued beaming.
Their eyes met once, and met again, and then became a gaze.
As they suddenly found themselves a mist a definite but pleasant haze.
Although, this space was different they enjoyed it all the while and
to capture this special moment they stole a kiss, then a smile.
It felt so good they wished it could last forever, but of course, no way.
Would Father Time allow that to happen as he began the closing of his day.
They captured and sealed the moment, and the feeling will always be there.
As that warm thought was the only thing to help them weather the
now dampened air.
Nightfall has come and with it a chill like that out of a fridge.
But what a wonderful day they shared when they sat in the sun
Beneath the Bridge.

William Curtis Venters

Christmas

This year Christmas has a special meaning - LOVE.
As though angels had delivered sweet music from above.
The peace of mind, I have now, for the first time in my life,
Has removed most memory of the past and the strife.
This Christmas I'm wrapped up in a ribbon of love,
As though angels had gently dropped rose petals from above.
They've sprinkled down, over before saddened eyes.
They've evaporated clouds and restored clear skies.
This year there's magic at Christmas - it's love.
Sent down from the heavens sent down from above.

Rosalie Todd

I Have To Let You Go

I have to let you go now. It is not good for you to remain.
As time has passed, you have caused me grief and filled my heart with pain.
Although I am attached to you, and it's very hard to let go — I must
release this grip I hold because it must be so!

Why? Did you hurt me in this way, was I that bad to you?
I handed you my heart and soul but you returned them too!
I feel I can never love another because they may hurt me again.
Time brings healing to all wounds, I'm just wondering when?

I thought for years God was punishing me — for what, I wasn't sure.
Well since that thought I've often asked how much can I endure?
A broken jar that's all poured out is how I feel; along comes a mop
to wipe me up so no one will notice the spill!

How many nights I lay awake hoping you could see, the unsung
song within my eyes each time you looked at me!

But now the day is dawning and may have already begun; my
music isn't read nor my song sung.
I'm just waking to smell the roses only to find that summer is gone.
I feel so empty inside, so abandoned and alone.

I have to let you go now because they say it is best, for me to let
you take your leave because I need my rest.

Theresa V. Posey

A Moment Of Time With Grief

Shades of dark and trees and gloom
  Attract my thoughts; alone in this room.
Silence shattering noiseless sound,
  Security sent beneath the ground.
A wind with no breeze is blowing
  Cold and Colder . . .
  My soul is snowing.

Patti Davis

Reflection

A mirror reflection of myself,
As true as true can be.
A look into the silver glass,
See through my eyes, to me.
The eyes of pain, the eyes of shame,
In a face for all to see.
The tears, they fall, the tears that scald,
Become a sea beneath my feet.
Shattered looks betray the truth,
Reveal a world to be.
Lips of wine, pale face-divine,
Soul in chains, yet heart so free.
A lingering look, a burning stare,
A moment frozen in time.
I touch my fingers to the glass,
A face, for eternity, mine.

Kelly Mcphee

My Dream Of You

The weather outside is so terribly cold
as we lay by the fire with each other to hold.
I whisper "I love you", your lips start to smile.
We move closer together, you say "I've known for a while."
You come even closer, our lips start to touch.
My heart beats much faster, I've never loved you so much.
Your hands are so gentle as they hold to my face.
You treat me with warmth, with patience and grace.
I open my eyes and they shed a few tears.
You wipe them away and say "there's nothing to fear."
I ask "do you love me?" You say "yes, I do."
I give myself fully and wholly to you.
Suddenly you vanish, I can't see your face.
The room is so dark, I don't feel your embrace.
I don't know what's happening, I then start to scream
Only to find out that it was all just a dream . . .

Michelle Louise Newman

Harvest

We are all daily sewing
As we travel the highway of life:
Our seeds face many vital challenges
In this world of mortal strife

Some of the "seeds" find fertility
And yield "fruits" that bring much joy;
Others may lose their identity
And become irritants that annoy.

We exercise our free agency
In many ways each day,
And the "harvest" we hope to reap
Will reflect the price we are willing to pay.

If we aim for the highest goals,
And want the very best,
We should be supportive citizens
and share with eager zest.

We are constantly being reminded —
All promises we must keep —
Because from the "seeds" we have planted
Will come the "harvest" we shall reap.

Raymond N. Malouf

Butterfly

It floats through the sky
As weightless as a feather
In the warm spring breeze.

The bright array of colors
Which are spread throughout its wings
Brings a certain beauty
To the first day of spring.

It floats through the sky
With not a destination
Just the desire to bring beauty in this world.

It lights easily upon a small branch
Gently waving to the world.
The wonderful bright butterfly
Is such a beauty to behold.

Susan A. Cotter

Whispers In The Dark

Darkness makes a veil across the face of the earth.
As whispers of yesterday slowly gains their birth.
I hear voices from the past, some laughing, some crying,
Or saying a familiar phrase, recollections of old times and my better
days.
I hear my mother's wisdom, speaking truth before I fall.
I can hear my children's laughter but they don't answer my call.

I call out to their mother and I hear her ask "why"?
Why did I leave her alone, and I hear them cry for a simple reason why
My fears have a voice that tells me I've failed.
Reminding me I took my life and confined it to a cell.

The voices in my mind have been recorded in my heart
The voices that I hear are "Whispers in the dark."

Richard Price Jr.

In The Man That I Love

With all my mind, Heart and soul,
At this time I set my life's goal.

To be happy and satisfied,
To be loved and gratified.

To find these things in a man that I love,
And be able to pray, Thank You, To the heavens above.

To find someone to teach to me the things I need to know,
Such as how to trust, Love and to spiritually grow.

If you are the one that God has sent,
Then I shall pray on knees bent.

Because I find these things in the man I love,
I will rejoice and praise my God in the heavens above.

Kimberly Ann Ortiz Parton

Manic Depression

My mind has a climate all of it's own . . .
at times it is drenched and at times dry as stone.
The times when it storms and seems out of control
it feels as if I'm falling down an endless hole.
Yet when the sun replaces the soggy truth
it cultivates pleasure that is sweet as fruit.
When it is dark it soon will be light
I can count on these seasons to always be right
so today it maybe raining, but tomorrow I know
that the sun like a river will silently flow.

Michelle Lynn Miller

Legacy Of Life Passes On

At times they are tears of sorrow
At times they are pearls of joy,
Oh dear life, but I always live for you.

The impermanence is your fortitude
Every moment is fleeting, every object is mortal,
But your legacy passes on . . .
And so do the tears and the pearls,
Oh dear life, I live every moment for you.

Call this love or call this compromise
I live with the mundane, I live for surprise,
How the heart-beats never leave life silent
How the thoughts never leave life lonely,
Oh dear life, I live for your company.

I am mortal, so death will do us part
But I shall live in other's memories
For, the living are mortal, but life continues.

Sohang Chatterjee

The Gift

The gift of satisfaction cannot be received
At your (the gift giver's) expense.
That is not a gift . . .
Only a barter, and exchange of energy
without suitable recompense.

Let us not re-create
'The gift of one Magi'
Where no one wins, yet does lose
Their sense of joy.
Learning only the saddest lesson
of misdirected selflessness.

Give to me what you can.
When you can with safety
and common sense.
Let the gift be a gift . . .
Not another opportunity
for us,
those karmic weights
to adjust.

Mason Clare

Colors In My Day

Brightly shines the sun on these glowing autumn days,
early in the morn the air is peppered with a haze,
shimmering reflections on lakes, leaves and love,
hundreds of colors falling down from above.
The glitter of the sun on the water so bright,
acorns dive in at the end of their flight,
high soft winds murmur silently for a time,
autumn days with thoughts of love keep you on my mind.
Leaving now are the birds of warmth and sun,
gathering together they're preparing for to run,
coats of fur grow thick to prepare for the way,
when clouds and cold windy snow color the day.
And when the ground is covered white with
snow, and the leaves are buried and cannot blow,
you are the one joy, the thoughts that I find,
that brings color to my winter's day mind.

Marc S. Simon

Like A Tree

Here I am like a tree,
At your side is where I want to be,
Close to you is what I need,
Your love was like water to my seed,
You were like a water spout,
A hug I want, my branches are stretched way out,
I was fooled by the sun,
Now it's gone, there is no fun,
As the wind blows through my leaves,
My heart was stolen by some thieves,
Now I know, I am not real,
All my bark doesn't peel,
When I take a good look at me,
All I see is an artificial tree.

Shamel V. Stilwell

A Midnight Rendezvous With Lucifer's Death

Alone I sit on marble glass
awaiting Lucifer's Death
before my eyes I see changing
a tree
from birth to death
the tiny seed of hope budding,
maturing and finally mushrooming
into a fantastical journey
I watch the rainbows fly
butwait—
It begins to wither and die
goodbye, I assumed it was real
but nothing is everything, remember
thoughts flicker;
Angels ascending to heaven
or caterpillars emerging from a cocoon; anew
before my senses

Ever yours
ever mine
forever

Meredith Neal

Baby's Prayer

Oh heavenly father up above help my
baby rise up with love. Help him by pass
all this hate and worry. Help him be strong
and have lots of courage. Make him bright,
shining and true, help him know not to fall
away from you. Let him live long and free
from harms reach, but please dear Lord don't
preach. Keep him strong, willful and bright,
please oh Lord just make him right. Don't
let him fall into the wrong hands of evil. Keep
him safe from upheaval. Protect him when I
cannot and please give him a good life too.
For if you do all this I'll always be in
debt to you. Amen.

Maria L. Sindledecker

Darkness To Light

Each day of dismal dullness
Attempts to take away the ray of hope
So deeply felt, yet almost dimmed
By the challenges of darkness one apprehends;
Suddenly a beam of light appears
Through the recesses of despair
To strengthen life's anticipation and faith
One struggles to forever hold so dear.
For this light and peace of mind
Gratitude is to the Eternal Father of Mankind.

Pansy M. Keatts

Man Without

The slender, stoop shouldered man
barely moving his feet
As he trudged along the lonely road.
How long could he keep this pace?
Must he travel alone and lonely.

Memories elude his mangled mind.
There was a time when he could think,
But now the sometimes thoughts drifted
In and out of a mind that was hazy and weary.

Once he could smile and life had purpose,
Now the ticks of time meant nothing to him.
Gone were the memories and substance
that, like glue, held him together.

In infinite frailty he lingered.
The expression in his aging eyes
was like a draped veil.
He knew he had somewhere to go,
If only he could remember
where and why.

Mabel Welch

You Never Said You're Sorry

Over the years you have had difficulty understanding why I seem to
be so full of hate and resentment for you. Is it your fear and guilt
that keeps you preoccupied with when and how might I take my
revenge upon you?

Things had to be done I'm told to build this great Nation. No matter
how cruel, demoralizing, insensitive or insane; the end definitely
justified the means. But now you look at me with such disdain and I
at you with much anger and confusion. I'm treated no better than an
unwelcome house guest. You tolerate me only at a distance.
You're cordial only to the extent that it shields your true thoughts;
when is my visitor going home? But home is here sharing all the
wonderful jewels that make this country great.

We are like parent and child, you and I. Oh yes, many years have
come and gone while sharing this land, yet we don't know each other.
Maybe you don't realize how deeply you've hurt me, and I like a
child am incapable of explaining how I feel. Oh how I wish we could
cry and embrace. I wish we could plan our future together. But
how can we, both our hearts so heavy?

America you never said you're sorry.

Marvin R. Wallace

"Love"

Without love do we have a meaning?
Because the world is leaning-
Toward race and hate.
If they could see the light of love-
The racial walls would fall.
For some love is just a distant light,
Lost out in the night.
Some wonder when love will find them.
Others go searching in the cold,
Because they long to hold love in their hearts.
But where do they start?
First, follow your heart and soul,
Let your heart surpass your mind,
And you will find the world is open wide.
There are no more racial walls they have all fallen.
There will be no more sorrow,
Because there will always be tomorrow.
Love and peace have conquered all.

Sarah Gansmann

Commands To My Soul

My soul, I am weary. My soul, I am torn. Why must life
be so full of heartaches, setbacks, pressure?

A husband killed in a drug raid. Gin, cocaine, a careless
smoke—a house now ashes in the wind.

Behind Carl's Deli, I see a woman gathering her meals from
trash bins. In the shadows, a boy is shivering. Weak
from hunger, he closes his eyes and fills on the aroma
of fresh baked bread.

My tired soul, I feel myself sinking, choking, dying in
the mist of alcohol, drugs, violence.

A sip, a swallow, a way out! With moments of time, a stranger
will venture my soul to another land.

My weary soul, my torn soul, That's not the way! Like
branches of an oak tree, Be strong! Hold on! Seek my
inner strength. Caress it, draw from it. Stir my emotions,
Dance and run with them.

I'm free! I'm glowing!

Thank you, my soul, For returning my burning! Thank you,
my soul, For new hope!

Katherine Bassett Miller

Visualized Fire

Dancing flames burning my legs,
beauty rises.
Enclosing the blackness with a life I've created.
Helpless thoughts enter my head as I feel the heat.
Crackling, burning so bright, this warmth I can not comprehend.

Specks of orange cling to the walls,
vanishing as fast as they appear.
Pushing you away deeper towards the blackness that clings onto life.
When will you die?
Will I watch you?
Will I be here as your flames slowly vanish away
into the ashes on a rainy day?

Michelle Fratini

Am I Different?

Because I use a wheelchair, am I different?
Because a dog is my eyes, am I different?
Because I talk with my hands, am I different?

In your eyes, I may appear different,
But I'm not, I'm just like you.

Because I can't speak at all, am I different?
Because I don't understand you, am I different?
Because I use a walker, am I different?

On the outside, I look different,
But God made this way.
I have feelings, thoughts,
And opinions just like you.

Look past my flaws,
And you will see someone
Who has a heart and feelings
Just like you.

The answer is: No, I am
Not different.

Nyetta Charboneau

Today Is The Day

Today is the day to be happy and gay,
because on this day I do you will say.
Today is the day your family all gathers,
for on this day no one else matters.

Today is the day when all up above,
hear you pledge of caring and love.
Today is the day we all celebrate,
and we hope your marriage is always great.

Today is the day your Father and I,
Are telling your our little girl good-bye.
Today is the day you begin a new life,
you take a husband he takes a wife.

Lynnette R. Bechtel

Untitled

A colorful blossom unfolds itself
before my wide staring gaze
such simple beauty, amongst the grand
powers of organic wonders. Alone it sits
surrounded by a plethora of greens.
Take this bit of magic into my soul
and appreciate its delicate stance.
Soon it will be no longer, its soft
petals strewn among the currents wind
but it will stay, for I remember

Robert E. Purick

Worldly Colors

Green is the color of the forests,
Before they are destroyed and burned.
Red is the color of angry fire,
As it consumes the fuel not earned.
Many people do not care,
As if they have not yet learned.

Brown is the color of the air,
When air pollution comes to claim its share.
Gray is the color of the ground,
As cement is drilled down with care.
Many people do not cast a tear,
For all the precious life stripped bare.

White is the color of the clouds,
Before the industrial revolution came.
Black is the color of the hearts,
Of those who cause the world to be maimed.
Many people will definitely not act,
Until they realize it's not a game.

Nathan Leung

Fable

Count all the stars in the sky
before you sleep
Let them fill up your eyes
so you see only beautiful things

Imagine each one's a dream
only for you
to relive when needed
to help carry your weight and see you through

Michael Ferrara

An Ode To Autumn Color

For all my sixty years and four I've harked to autumn's call
Beheld the green of summer give way to brilliant fall,
At first just one or two appear, these leaves from green to red,
As if each one had suffered a wound from which it bled.
Then as each day progresses, more different colors show
Until each hill and valley is splashed with vivid glow
And never in my lifetime will I find an artist's brush.
That can capture all the beauty expressed in Autumn's blush.
A bit of sadness touches me whet first they start to fall
My eyes will mist a trifle when wild geese give their call.
But o'er the years I've come to know as Autumn takes it's bow
I'll live this beauty once again just one short year from now.
And tho' I may be miles away when it's time for nature's show
I'll find a way to journey back for Autumn's vibrant glow.

Lawrence Earle

Never To Live Again

I live
beneath the lulling tides of the grand heights of my roof
entrapped in the city, freezing, capitulating ice-box of my home.

Through the burning heat of the endlessly stinging sun's embrace
between the barricades and obstacles you keep giving me,
I slip never to fall again.
Ignited by that stinging, sneering stare
the pessimistic, peculiar, petrified, pitter-patter of my heart
pounding I fall never to fly again.
Endless miles and stories flow and shatter my mind
millions of kisses, caresses, and smiles
beyond them all, I fly never to jump again.
The feeling of your hand in my hair,
your arms wrapped around me so tight.
The light shattering emptiness devastate me when those arms leave me.

Tears cascade and destroy my happiness
I can't come back up without those arms.
I can't lift my head up,
the light beyond is too charismatically blinding.

I jump never to live again.

Melissa Edmond

Hand In Hand

I can taste the salt of the sea, as I sit along shore with sand in
between my feet. I open my eyes as the sun rises to greet me. It's
so refreshing, as I begin to feel the soft drops upon my skin, as our
conversation begins. As they slowly flow together, hand in hand,
I whisper thank-you. As our talk has ended. I can now feel the
bright warmth come shining through, over the sea and also me.
For not long ago my clouds were a dark gray, now have turned a beautiful blue.
He has lifted what I have hidden way deep inside. I know ask,
please walk along side. Come sit next to me along the shore, as we
sketch in the sand and feel the rich warm colors shine over the land.
For I have again the sand in between, but now its so soft I could lay
and sleep. The wonders of life have returned to me. I can smile and
even laugh, for I have this new friend that walks in my path.
I can run along the shore, hand in hand, even in a down pour.
And now as I smell the salt of the sea, a smile appears from within me.
And I will not hesitate when I see the gray, that is when we will meet
along shore and begin our sketching once more. And beautiful blue
will color the sky with love.

Vickie A. Kendall

The Game Of Life

What a different there is
Between what you want,
And what you can have.
Those selfish desires
Can drive you mad!

Sometimes we fail to realize
That those desires of ours
Can sometimes hurt those we love most,
And leave such horrible scars!

I can't explain it - nor do I like it,
But that's the way life is.
I don't understand it - nor do I want to!
The game of life is strictly for a mystery whiz!

Sheila D. Giglia

To My Beloved Husband

We are both fruits of fall,
Blessings from Heaven above.
Hundreds and thousands miles apart,
Bring together two honest loving hearts.
Hardships, hard work, and harmony living,
For golden harvest in life to come.
Love is so sweet like honey flowing in my heart.
My body wrap with your charming smiles,
And my soul rest in your warm arms.
Millions stars shining in the sky,
But you are my only brightest star.
I am proud and honored,
That you are my hero and my sweet heart.
Husband - honey, you full in my little heart.

Lydia J. C. Brown

A Piece Of Mind

As the bright stars shined in the deep, dark night, as the cool wind blew through my hair, as the tiny raindrops fell on my feet, I would sit there on my mountain and wonder.

Not about anything important, just about simple things.

Not really caring about anyone or anything, just off in my own little world, all by myself. I would pretend that being up there, on top of that mountain, I could see everything and everyone . . .
   almost like I ruled the whole world.

Just me and there's nobody above me.

But at last it's time to wake up to reality, I'm not there anymore and I don't rule the world, I'm jut one more person, trying to make it through this rat race called . . . life.

It's like everyone is so busy trying to survive that no one stops to smell the roses. No one that is, but me.

When I feel things are going too fast I stop and I think of my mountain. Where there is me and only me. Not a hundred other people . . . just me.

Call it what you like, escaping, daydreaming, whatever.

But to me, that is my little piece of mind, to get me through those busy times.

Lena M. Shipman

Point-Of-View (Or Of Misunderstanding)

Color of night, of death, of dark,
Blind as the created who exist within its boundaries.
An impenetrable shroud, clouding all thought,
And waiting for improvisation to break its holds.
Color of night, (descriptive no less)
Of pain, of anger, of hatred, - of faith.
Of light, and not of light.
Of confusion, and utter disbelief.
Of indifference to its likeness, and likeness to its indifference.
Of evil, and of that which is good.
For association lies within the minds grasp.
Oh! If only to break this may we be free!
To rip this crown of thorns from our brow! To be free!!
Of hate, of anger, of confusion, of dark.
To see and be seen eternally in the light of day,
And its darkened corners.
To live and to let live. To free and to be free.
To wear black or white or yellow or red. OR PURPLE!!
To know and to be known. To hear and to be heard.
To be understood, without really understanding — at all.

Katharine Adriana Heeringa

Weeping Willow Tree

Oh! Weeping Willow, crying Willow tree why do you look so lonely and blue.
Why do you cry! It makes your leaves bend and then you began to lose a few.
You look so sad and seems to be filled with many lonely tears, yet you stand bravely through rain, storm, tornadoes, and many long years.
As your leaves began to twinkle in the moonlight and birds began to rest on your branches, you hang your head and cry.
Know one understands or can tell me why.
Oh! Weeping Willow crying willow tree what could it be that troubles and hurt you so?
Is it the sun or the icy cold winter's snow?
What is it that makes your heart bleed and wouldn't let you sway straight and free?
Please tell me, Weeping Willow crying Willow tree.

Thelma Bryant

The Sunset

The purple and blue horizon,
Blue-black clouds stretching to the distance.
A golden egg surrounded by a nest of clouds,
Casting a pillar of light
On the shimmering water below.
Shadows stretch,
Strengthened by the setting sun.
Sailboats dock,
Crickets chirp,
And the children of the night awaken.
The sphere, now red as rubies,
Dips below the skyline,
Courageously firing one last wrinkle of scarlet,
As darkness swallows the world.

Ryan J. Bonneville

What Is Blue

Blue is a bird flying.
Blue is a shirt that waves on the clothesline.
Blue is eating an ice cold popsicle
   that melts in your mouth.
Blue is a wave that hits your feet.
Blue is your cold face in the winter time.
Blue is the paint I want in my room.
Blue is the sky that blows a cold breeze.

Raymond Nunn Jr.

Wash Day

He swipes at muddy knees, the faded blue overalls hanging from
   bony shoulders
A grimy, brown mop of hair falls over his beseeching eyes.
A pointing finger.
A firm command, "Empty them!"
He stares at the floor.
Resigned, he shoves a grubby right hand
Deep into the depths of the pocket in his overalls.
Yanking his hand back out,
He clasps a handful of muddy glass marbles and plunks them on
   the washing machine.
They clunk and clatter and roll, spreading fuzzballs of lint.
"All of it!" A voice booms.
Groaning, he reaches into his left pocket and slowly pulls out
A few battered baseball cards,
Seven prize rocks, a worn sling-shot,
A sticky bubble gum wrapper, the stub of a pencil,
Left-over lunch money, several dazed lady bugs,
A squirming green frog.
Oh, the humiliations of wash day!
    Sarah A. Russell

no Boundaries

a deep tangerine sunset
bordering the black belt of the coniferous night
   reminds me to take a closer look
  and
    sure enough
    a walleye (or maybe a northern or bass)
      carves through the surface . . .

it's noisy now
   and delightedly self reminiscent
    with at least two loons in an incessant trill
      dissecting the rigors of the late afternoon
   and the quiet pleasures of on coming dusk
just Living

their soulful wails will come at midnight, and
   in the early morning
when the raconteurs by day give way
   to the cuneiform compassions of the night.
the stars are arriving
I can't see them yet
      but they are there
    Renee L. Haugerud

Untitled

   Pinecones hanging on branches
bough - like dripping candles oh so
low, upside down they glow.
   The flame does get snuffed out,
just give sweet breath to bring this 'bout.
   Snow crystals melt ever so slow,
just rest the mind and puff a blow.
   Snuffed do they show, no more
light does glow. Make a wish so
ever quickly, the eyes do blink and sink.
   Show no darkness told, but do
sell the soul unto heavens above
have the stars shine bright and
with them they'll bring their light.
   Upon that all is said and written,
may the hand come down upon so I
can be found.
   Let the image arise, let the prize
open the gifts of life to live!
    Libbie Hopwood

"Just Thinking Aloud!"

So often I'm asked why I choose to write
'Bout my engulfing thoughts in the midst of night.
I've asked myself too! What can I say?
Perhaps it's because this heart of mine
Is closed in the midst of day!
    Shirley J. Bench

Where Are Our Friends, Dear

Where are "YOUR KIDS", asked a voice from aside?

They're hiding in the cupboards with puppy -
Breaking brown sugar and cinnamon toast,
Boasting of having the wants they have not -
Like big wheels rolling - down make - believe slides,
Virtual fantasies sharing their rides . . .

In go - mobiles racing let's - pretend lanes,
They float o'er crumbs of toast coasting on high,
Helium - filled - wheels to fly without chains -

Laughing their way to grown - up adventures.
With credit card 'maginings they buy - up
Youths dreams on test tracks of middle - age themes:

Til the "NO's" flip their smiles, so - as they "CAN'T"
Tempt to wile mimes, caught 'tween youth and old - age;
Or rinse, from time's mirrors, reality's
Hands what rock cradles and block-in such rules -
Much like a rock chocks their wheels in mid - stream.

We buzz like flies in their ointment of dreams;
Til God's love amends us in memory.
And bends us to play as "GRAND" - children's friends.
    M. L. Farahay

You Make My World So Beautiful

For sharing my world, for warming it with your thoughtfulness and
brightening, it with your happiness and laughter . . .
   "I Love You"

For always listening with patience and somehow understanding
what I can't find words to say . . .

For reaching out so often with a tender look or smile and gentle
touching my heart . . .
   "I Love You"

For being a part of my happiest moments and bring then sun to
My Cloudiest days . . .

For giving so much of yourself and helping me discover so much
about myself . . .
   "I Love You"

For encouraging my Highest Hopes and praising even my smallest
successes . . .

For being the caring person who makes my world so beautiful . . .
   "I Love You"
    Tracy Koens

Purple Napkins

A dandelion at dinner;
Both of us exploring unexplored ashen
    depths for that hidden treasure.
"Penny for your thoughts!"
Networks, loss of sleep,
    Poetry, summer pursuits,
      And, yes, purple napkins.
    Susan Abrams

Newborn

Ten little fingers, ten little toes
Bring such joy that God only knows
Tiny fingers reaching - patting - touching your face
Tiny little toes kicking wildly - invading your space

Hair as soft as the clouds above
Eyes that sparkle and twinkle their love
Rosy little cheeks - a button of a nose
A tiny little mouth that never seems too close

Cooings and gurglings quietly come out
And sounds of little laughter tinkle all about
What a sweet gift from heaven God has sent
How grateful we are for this blessed event.

Rosemary Nugent

What Is Love?

What is love but an endless waterfall
Bringing you to great heights of ecstasy
Only to drop you to the lowest of depths
To sink into abyss.
What is love?

What is love but a lustrous magnolia flower
Blooming to luscious magnificence
Only to spread its magic, then
To close and die.
What is love?

What is love but a walk on a deserted road
When the glow of a streetlight reveals itself
Only to unveil a path
To a dark and winding road.

What is love?

K. C. Peters

"Jesus"

Life of today, A world locked in sin.
Brother against brother, no way we can win.

Colors of man, too clearly defined.
The answers belief, we've left it behind.

Modern society, machinery so cold.
To laugh with a friend, a child to hold.

Beauty is nature, life everywhere.
Help one another, learn how to care.

Look at your neighbor, seeing yourself.
Money's not riches, love is true wealth.

There's a path to be followed, he'll lead the way.
Open your heart, see him clearly today.

Don't you remember, how can you forget.
He gave us his life, he showed no regret.

He came to this world, so many were lost.
He loved us so much, he died on the cross.

Paul C. Devlin

"Vision Of Love"

As I looked into his burning dark
brown eyes, he said hi how are you?
I told him oh I'm okay, when he
looks at me his eyes make me feel
like an M&M melting in his mouth.

He's husky just like a Teddy Bear,
Gentle as a baby, loving as a mother.
The wind blows his hair everywhere
I can't find him anywhere. I've looked
and looked but he's nowhere to be found,
but maybe do you think that he'll ever be found?

He looks and looks but she's nowhere
to be found, yelling, crying, kicking and
screaming he doesn't think she'll come.

His heart aches for true love, the
girl of his dreams with brown eyes
and brown hair she smiles with care.

For one day they'll meet. He'll run to
her side, and now we all know that
true love does abide.

Susan Davis

Reverie

I watched you
    building castles of Sesame Street blocks.
Big Bird smiled with me.
My dreams grew with your castles . . .

    You are a ballerina, gazelle like,
        pirouetting before a breathless throng:
    A concert pianist, lithe fingers racing
        across ivory keys;
    A skater, blades aglint, slipping across
        silver ice:
    You are lawyer, physician, whatever you please . . .

What is it in blocks? Why does my mind drown
    in fantasy?
I have but one life.
Big Bird comes crashing to the terrazzo floor
    pulverizing my fantasies with his orange claw.

Mary Ann Massaro

Remembering The Lost Child

Sometimes the day begins like a wildfire ablaze,
burning through a field of poppies glowing red,
radiating hope for mutts and other lost strays;
so with awe I evacuate my prison bed,
pardoned from solitary pain to race to the park.

Unfolding leaves tremble in the retreating chill,
not able to contain their marvel for the new day
born to mourn yesterday but rejoice today's thrill:
a concert of soprano-giggling girls busy at play,
unnoticed by swarms of tenor rascals on a lark.

Afternoon flames gently lick the soles of my feet
that prance like a puppy after a morning dove.
I marvel like a child over its acrobatic soaring feat,
a ballet for angels seated in clouds above,
their presence as certain and near as the faceless bark.

Late day comes like a brushfire across a field of time,
engulfs me faster than skateboarders down the asphalt
etched with more cracks than grampa's face bent over
a boy only three, soft sunlit cheeks without fault.
My heart quickly turns stormy and swiftly I de-park.

Kenneth Hightower

For Our Daughter

Our lives have changed since we've been together . . .
But -
The love in our hearts will continue to grow forever . . .
And -
Not only for the two of us, but for our extended life . . .
Our daughter -
You -
So -
We will always share what's dear to us, to our daughter,
and nothing will ever compare . . .
Now!
We must teach our daughter everything we know . . .
We will help her in this world of constant change, and with this
constant change watch our daughter grow . . .

Melissa Riddle

Untitled

I could give you the sun, the moon and the stars,
but all you take is the moon.
The sun shines too bright,
and you don't see the stars sparkling in my eyes
when we meet in the night, you take a trip with me to the moon,
we always come back to earth too soon.

You want to give me the flowers, the grass and the trees,
but all I take are flowers.
The grass is much greener on other sides,
the trees are busy guarding your bicycle rides
but flowers are the one gift you give me sometimes,
the sweet fragrance lingers on in our minds
after their beauty has wilted and retired,
and their shelf-life has expired.

I would give you the sky, the wind and the sea,
but all you'd take is the wind.
The sky's clouds are ever-changing, the sea's tide is re-arranging
and to far off places you will drift,
but the wind's breeze blows you to me,
then the motion will carry you off just as swift,
we can only flow with the movement of the wind's lift.

Karen Orbach

"I Have Let Go"

I write my words, to create my rhymes,
But honestly, I'm empty, deep down, inside.

There's nothing left, inside of me,
I gave and gave, and now I see,
That I was foolish, but only myself,
Now I will put my heart, up on the shelf,
To gather dust, to let time pass,
To wait, to grow, to heal,
And to learn to once again feel.

Until then, I'll stay alone,
Feeling glad, because I've grown,
I've learned, adapted, altered too,
And realize that I am new,
I found myself, and happily,
Accept the madness life brought to me,
Though I've been hurt and very sad,
Time for the good, The sad
Belongs to yesterday,
I will let go,
I have let go.

M. R. Velez

My Fantasy

I am in the house of fantasies.
But I can not find mine.
The house is built on the shoulders of the giants.

Maybe my fantasy's lost
Between being and nothingness.
So I'll wed by essence
To the hardest substance
To give birth to a long-expected fantasy.

Maybe it's somewhere
Between matter and anti-matter.
Then I'll glide between the lines,
And pass through the solid walls
Looking for my ethereal fantasy
In a non-ethereal world.

Or maybe it's fallen in a black hole.
So I'll wait for the monster-or God to explode;
And the meteors shower.
Then I'll hold the cup of my hand
Toward heaven-or hell,
Waiting for my fantasy to land.

Suri Dalir

Years Gone By

I went to visit your grave today,
But I did not take the time to pray.
I stood upon the solid ground
The empty space so threatening.
I starred awhile and all I could see
Were the years that had slipped away.
Where has the time gone - what have I done?
Oh father of mine where did I go wrong?
You wanted so much in life for me.
So many dreams so many years.
Where did they go so fast so soon?
Get hold of yourself I did say,
But I could not calm my fears this day.
Is death near or far away?
What is this turmoil inside of me?
I feel so weak, I must go.
I must not let fear take control.
I looked at the tombstone and the heaven's above.
Oh spirit of my father calm my fears
Did I tell you I love you after all these years.

Rosemarie Stuber

Epitaph

I didn't ask to be born into this world;
but I didn't ask to leave it either.

I sought no reward in my life which I felt I hadn't earned;
likewise, if there be a hereafter,
I seek nothing undeserved in it.

I tried to live my life in a manner
which would neither hinder nor harm another;
and if I sometimes failed,
it remains only a reminder that I,
as all men,
was only mortal, and, as such, so imperfect.

I was fortunate in that I was able to love,
that I was able to touch and to be touched,
that I was able to see and to be seen.

And I was fortunate that I was given enough time on this earth to know
and to be able to say, simply, that

I lived.

William J. Luzmoor III

I Dream No More

I used to dream of so many things,
but I dream those dreams no more.

With pad in my lap and pencil in hand
my dreams became real; so bright . . . so grand.

A poem here and there. A few words I once
shared . . . Brought smiles to those who cared.

Muffled words reduced to a murmur. Once colorful
and bold, now empty and cold. My words go on no further.

I used to dream of so many things,
but I dream those dreams no more.

Teresa Anderson

Toy Box World

Toy box world, something like these days,
But in every young childhood, where lives are only for play.
We set up our play things to live like pretend,
Grooming our minds in a "Motional Trend".
Dreaming "I Love You's" is the cure for world peace,
Growing older and realizing you still believe.
Faith for adventures are the games you once played,
And the thirst for life's vigor is now a serious game.
And just like the toy box dolls that did fall,
Mending by imagination brought them back after all.
And as the years go by you still dream and pretend,
Thus you're never quite off of that "Motional Trend"
Going everywhere to find you go nowhere at last,
Because your memories always bring the Toy Box World back.

William Monroe

Farewell

It's so hard to say goodbye to the ones we love;
But it's especially hard to say goodbye to people such as my
grandparents.

People who are kind, generous, and sincere;
Who carry Christmas in their hearts all through the year;

People who always try to pick you up when you fall;
no matter how big the problem is, no matter how small;

People who give their advice of wisdom, when they feel it is in need;
They are like gardeners, nurturing a growing seed;

People who are both comforting and supportive;
With nothing but "love" as their motive;

People who are always giving and expect nothing in return;
continuing to show excessive love and concern;

I choose not to say goodbye to my grandparents, for goodbye seems so final;

Instead, I'll say farewell for now, and wish you nothing but happiness and love;

And may all your days be blessed by our dear heavenly Father from up above.

Sakena Anderson

Choices

There are many choices in life you make,
But one's you are trusted not to take.
Don't be afraid of what will come,
Those who are won't find the path that
leads them home.
Take the path that you know best,
Take the one that you like best.
It's not your parents choice to make,
Which road you pick, what choice you take.
Some choices you make may not seem right,
Those are the one's that can change your life.

Stephanie Minchew

From The Moon And Stars

I counted the stars last night as the night before
But last night there were two less
Today I saw them again, for in her eyes
Were the two missing stars from the skies

I watch the wind move the clouds
I hear it whispering through the trees
But today the wind did not blow or speak
Until I felt her breath cool my blushing cheek

I used to watch the sun burn the horizon
But yesterday's dusk held no color
This morning I saw her eyes full of it's flame
Still the wonder was breathtakingly the same

If you find it hard to understand
Why men become lost in the moon and stars
The answer lies within the deep pools of her beautiful eyes
There you can find every aspect of heaven's glorious skies

J. Treadway III

"He Always Wanted Action"

'He always wanted action,' said the mom about her son.
But nobody listened as the crowd began to run.
They didn't seem to notice; they didn't seem to care.
The sirens in the background meant there was no time to spare.

'He always wanted action', she said about her boy.
'The pellet guns, the slingshots, they were his favorite toys.
My boy fought with his brother, pushed his face into the sand
I always feared what he would so when he became a man.'

'He always wanted action,' she said about her son.
'Well now he's had his action; the damage has been done.
The wounded and the dying are running in the street.
The children all are crying beneath the trampling feet.'

And as the dreaded fire clouds descended from the sky
The mother raise her voice to make one final angry cry.
'He said he wanted action; I knew just what he meant.
Oh how I begged you not to make my son the President!'

Steven S. Smith

Jessica

Jessica is a name
But not just any name,
Its the name of a very special person
A person who means very much to me,
Jessica is the name of a caring person
Who takes time to listen to your problems
And at the same time telling hers,
She is a very loving and caring person
Who is a big part of my life
Without her I wouldn't be myself,
She has helped me with everything
She's been there for me through thick and thin
I don't think I could live without her
She is what makes me whole
She is me and I am her
She's my friend; my best friend
I'm thankful God made such a wonderful person
And I'm thankful to have her as my one
And only, true, best friend!

Stuart Johnson

Life's Final Certain

Life is so confusing
but one thing is for certain
a day will come when fate will
draw life's final curtain

When the curtain is drawn, and all the
audience walks away, you will wonder
how long in their memory will you stay

Will their love for you always last
will you always remain in their present
or will you become part of their past.

I live each day to show you all my love
for there will come a day when I can only
see you from above.
When the day comes that we are forever apart
my love and memory for you will remain in my heart

When the day comes that fate draws your
final curtain and all the audience walks away,
one thing is for certain
For you I will always stay
For you I will always stay.

Martin M. Clasen

Our Forever Friendship

It seemed like this day would never come,
But reality tells us we have only just begun.
This day seemed like an eternity away,
But it came, it's gone, and tomorrow's another day.
It seems so hard to understand,
That our life will take on a whole new plan.
Our hearts seem heavy, but the load will get lighter,
With each and every day, the future becomes brighter!
Our memories will never vanish,
Nor will they ever disappear,
They are thought we will always cherish,
Every day of every year.
We have to move on to our awaiting lives,
So that we may gain new goals and new strives.
For our new friends we will open up and make more space,
But the old friends are priceless and can never be replaced.
Together we have learned and shared so much,
You are a special part of me because my soul you have touched.
Once you move forward you will never regret,
Because there will always be something you can never forget . . .

OURFOREVERFRIENDSHIP

Kimberly Joan Ostwald

Pamela Sue Goes Home

Not many homes are blessed by an Angel
But that's what Pam was from the night of her birth,
There were very few times while we had her
That she gave us naught but laughter and mirth.

She grew with a wisdom rare to age
A truce maker she was 'tween Mother and Dad,
Creating laughter and joy and love was her trait
Very few times was she found to be bad.

Then came the day God was looking for help
His heavenly choir needed help in some phrases,
So he looked down the highway—coming and going
Then picked out our Pammy, with all of her praises.

Our home is still never too quiet
Nor is it gloomy, dark, or sad,
'Cause we have our Pam - maybe not in body
But in soul to keep us ever glad.

Richard E. Bruening

Remembering My Roots

The beauty of a flower is always praised,
But the bud that is displayed quickly fades away.
In our grief we forget the roots anchoring and nourishing our prize.
Without roots, that moment of colored brilliance could not have transpired.

So is it with me. I may bloom at the moment, but only because
I was anchored and nourished by the best roots of all —
My parents, who nourished me with love and support and
anchored me with conviction.

So remember the roots, when you praise the beauty for the colors
of spring last a short while,
But the plant grows on prospering and fruiting, because of the
duty quietly conducted by the roots sublime.

Sandra Owen Alderson

A Helping Hand

I loved my mother and wanted to stay,
but the drugs she did there was no way.

She drank and drove and tried to be brave,
I couldn't bear to watch her dig her own grave.

I tried my best to give her my hand,
she took it as hurt and didn't understand.

She was slowly killing herself and seemed not to care,
I mentioned her name every night in my prayers.

I had to go, I couldn't stand the pain anymore,
I wish she could have realized that life is worth fighting for.

People can't say that God isn't true, he did more for
her that I could do.

He took her hand and turned her around,
he finally put her two feet on the ground.

She still needs to have God's powerful leading,
she still does drugs, but now knows life's meaning.

She's in my thoughts and heart every day,
I love her dearly and I'll help show her the way.

Monica Jo Reynolds

Reminisce

As long as you were all alone, I was really satisfied.
But the moment you found someone else, something deep inside me died.
Out of sight, out of mind, you know that old cliche,
If I could apply it to myself, I'd feel much better today.
That congratulations card I sent, I wish I could redeem it,
Cause when I said best wishes, I really didn't mean it.
Oh I want to see you well and all, and in the best of health.
But if your heart and soul should prosper, I want to share the wealth.
I'll never let you see this poem, I'll put it on the shelf,
And every time I reminisce, "ooooo!" I could just kick myself.

Rosie J. Ingram

Night Fall

Surrounded is my soul,
By struggles that shield my purpose and my goal.
My lips could lie, and say that I am the same,
But my head and heart have long refused that game.
In the dawn of day my heart was light,
But as I question my purpose, it is faded to night.
The thunder claps, and the days role on,
And as the lightning streaks, I fear my desire has come and gone.
This chance past,
The next must be seized and held to last.
I know that I am confused by the questions, and I look for the best,
But my heart seems to be fading, and my dreams will not lay to rest.

Melissa Elliott

Sonnet

The strongest thing on the earth is not made,
By the hands of a man or by machine.
It is not a stone of diamond or jade
And still has remained untouched and unseen.
Under the worst circumstances, it still,
Continues to gather more and more strength,
Acting upon its own instinct and will,
Pushing itself to impossible lengths.
No one can conceivably comprehend
The immeasurable power inside,
But everyone knows that wounds it helps mend
By facing things, not escaping to hide.
  Look closely and listen and you'll hear it,
  The fearless cries of the human spirit.

Kelly M. Robinette

The Geometry Of Monday

The scars of evening fade in the morning sunlight
but the pain does not, she thought as she stood
on the porch and carefully noted Monday's birth.

The dew awaits death as it lies on the petals
of the red roses, she thought and wondered
why people make such a fuss about love and death.

She arched her neck, looking heavenward once more,
but she said no prayer. Clouds dressed in cruel white
marched across the morning to attack the sun.

She thought it would rain. She wanted a storm to come
and refresh her soul. She wanted to ask
the rain what had happened to a life of promise.

It is with a kiss that we most often betray.
Night sighs are weapons, she said to no one
and started to wash his clothes as she always did.

Mike Billington

The Eyes Of An Angel

My eyes were still blurry from the deep sleep
But the shadow that engulfed me was clearly visible
A breath taking mist boiled over and waves of anxiety
Soared through me, as I saw it had a life - filled with emotion
It was there solely for me, to watch, to comfort, to protect
Blackness streaming in behind from a closed window
It hovered just above the lightly stained hardwood floors
The glistening of small ice speckles formed to the shoulders
From the evening snow that had been falling for hours
I knew that if I motioned towards it, its presence would be known
I suspected surely it would disappear; captivated, I did not reach out
Its draping white cloak, feathered wings, and delicate praying hands
Were gentle and warm, like a past friendship never known
It was not until now that I could see the illuminating light
It was not until now that I understood what it was I was looking at
  I was gazing into the eyes of an angel.

Leaha Weaver

Untitled

I don't understand . . . sometimes.
But what I do know no one seems to understand.
Mr. Farmer is so good at it.
I try to listen but I move on.

The mind is so limited (especially mine).
I don't want to be a God.
I just want answers.

I hope it will come to me,
but I'm still going to sit and wait.
And if it doesn't, then I'll just wait to die.

Mark Papellero

Mother Nature's Cry

A Rhino is butchered for its horn
But there is no one there to mourn
Hawks are shot dead for a single feather
Chopping down rain forests is no better
Human beings are said to have the largest brains
Yet we cause Mother Nature all her pains
Recklessly we slaughter animals left and right
Except they have neither the weapons or voices to fight
Since our arrival we have destroyed the Earth
Before our time the planet had infinite worth
Habitats are burnt to the ground for a bigger home
Now many creatures are forced to roam
The blood of these animals is on all our hands
Only to live free without being hunted are their demands
Hunters mostly kill just for fun
But how would you feel if the bear was the one with the gun

Shaun LaRosa

Last Chance

  My eyes are large and golden brown, my hair a fiery red,
But things like this they'll never know, for I'm the last chance they had.
  God gave me to my parents, a gift money can't buy,
Yet they weren't very thankful, because they made me die.
  I never had a chance to live, to hear, smell and see,
They said I was just a tissue that wasn't meant to be.
  The doctors came with instruments, the pain was so intense,
As they pulled me from my mother's womb, I had no defense.
  Now you can plainly see, just because I wasn't big and tall,
They took away my rights of equal justice for all.
  Why doesn't justice protect people like me?
I can't even press murder in the first degree.
  Yes, I was just a tiny person, but I only needed time,
If they would have let me live, I would have been just fine.
  They said I wasn't a person unless I'd actually been born,
But if they knew the sad truth, my death they'd surely mourn.

Karla Griner

Our Lives

LOVE is a powerful word that can mean so much.
But you must learn its values
Before you earn its trust.
LOVE comes from within the heart,
And this is a must.
For without this fact, there is no trust.
LOVE can make you happy . . . and
LOVE can make you sad.
What great power this word has.
LOVE should never leave your heart,
It should be shared with someone from the start.
If you then become apart,
You will know that person was once loved by your heart.
To live your life without love in it, is sad for some,
For they don't know how to give it.
In the end the heart that gave.
Goes on to learn and find its way.
It may then become apart,
But it will find another heart.
For the one who has lost, will learn in time its powerful cost!

Karen Halowich Zieglar

I'm In Love With You Girl, But You're In Love With Him

I'm in love with you girl
But you're in love with him girl
I'm in love with you girl
But you're involved in his world

Sometimes I sit down and I wonder
Your love hits me just like thunder girl
When I look into your eyes it's frightening
For the glare I see it strikes like lightening

I'm in love with you girl
But you're in love with him girl
I'm in love with you girl
But you're involved in his world

I know you love this man dearly
But I love you more girl, really I do
He only wants you when he's ready
But I really want you for my steady

I'm in love with you girl
But you're in love with him girl
I'm in love with you girl
But you're involved in his world
        Ronald Daley

Surprises . . .

When I thought my life was arranged,
By a phone call, life's questions were changed . . .
The windmills keep turning, and I keep on learning . . .
From life I WILL NOT be estranged:

There is no moral to my story,
(Although my hair has grown hoary.)
But the strengths that one gains, when hard fall the rains,
Keep blooming like Morning Glory!
        Virginia Pease Ewersen

Halloween Fright

The man sat on a stalk,
By a woman in white.
He was unable to walk,
But ran into the night.
A child cried in fright,
Unable to see, she had no light.
Because of the awful sight,
A dog let out a frightened bark.
It's plight, no one was there to hold it tight,
There was something out there in the dark.
A youth let out an unheard of scream.
It could just be a great big lark,
Or a knock on the head by a broken beam?
The trees in the forest began to chatter,
Could it possibly be this was just a dream?
But everyone agreed it didn't matter.
Then, there rose an awful clatter.
        Pamela Sue (Potter) Gilbert

Desert Mystery

A calm and peaceful sky for all to see,
Cacti bloom in full array, with quail
and rabbit on their way to a busy, scurrying day.

Then, in a moment, a sky that is dark and
threatening with thunder and lightning,
and the rain begins.

The desert is a beautiful, ever-changing
place.
        Lee Ross

Heartbroken (Again)

That sudden sunken feeling when reality hits home,
By being used, you feel abused and very much alone.
Reflecting on the past "if only" fills your mind,
"If only" with open eyes you had read the warning signs.

The signs were there right from the start,
There is a lot at stake when you play with the heart,
But in your heart you long to believe,
That which you hear will not deceive.

But deceit comes in a great disguise,
Too well rehearsed to realize,
That which is shared tonight with you,
Will be shared too soon with someone new.

Unable to see behind the mask
The illusion is held, no questions asked,
Until a mutual voice remarks to you,
Don't you know whom he is with, when he is not with you?

Astounded by the facts that followed
Like the bitterest pill to hard to swallow
Déjà vu, felt this before
History beating at my door.
        Katherine Mina

An Unveiling

Slowly, as if it were too much to bear
Came dawn with its first fairest rays
And beam upon beam alighted where
The face of my lovely did lay.

Discerning from night her sleeping smile
Well pleased with its gift to the morn
It rested upon, then lingered awhile
Admiring what dimples adorn.

Stealing a glimpse from their evening's shade
Impatient to wait any longer
A mild flutter uncovered the jade
Of beautiful green eyes, as the light grew stronger.

Full morning showed the dawn was spent
Its pleasure now seen in full view
Happier though, it must have went
In love, as I, with you.
        Ken Sarna

Untitled

When I was a cocoon, an old lady
came up to me, while I was searching
for pearls in the sea.

In the blue depths, I saw shadows,
I saw movements, I saw figures.

I stood firmly planted to one spot
and gazed into the horizon. I took
no notice of the fine spray of mist, or
of the blue, blue sky.

I turned and asked her, "Jajja why am I here,
Why am I alone, why can't I see like the
rest of you? Why do I see the fear?"

"My dear," she sad,
"Stop looking too hard with your eyes.
It is only one of the senses, life flows
it never stands still. Life was meant
for people to live and no characteristics
make people alive."
        Sarah Sendi

I'm Not Gone . . . Not Really

When I'm gone, when my arms can no longer reach you, when my eyes
can no longer see you and my legs can no longer walk to you . . .
don't be afraid.

When you look and cannot find me, don't be sad. Remember the good
times. Remember the love that I have for you. Remember that I
tried to do the best I could.

If you need comfort, if you need to have a part of me . . . put your
arms around someone that I loved and there I will be.

I'm not gone . . . not really. I'm alive in your heart and in your
mind. Love does not die, and that's all that is left of me now.
So take it and use it up. It's my gift to you.

Death does not bind you, it sets you free.

So love, my friends, that is the key. It is the only thing you can
leave behind that will last forever.

I'm not gone . . . not really, we will all meet again.

Staci M. O'Connor

A Second Chance

So delicate is a rose and perfume alluring,
can one create a love that is enduring?

So precious is love and always deserving,
it is not that which brings one back to another almost intruding?

To free a love can be deceptive and yet
to continue on with the same words repetitive.
Can we not forgive for is not that what love is?

Yes, forgiving one spirit creates love so delicate
that in time as perfume and roses do fade away.

Will love be forever as sometimes can be even when
surrendering the fear and reawakening the priceless passions
can we not ignite a love that is everlasting?
Yes, love is forever.

Kelly L. Flurschutz

Dear Momma and Poppa,
I'm growing so fast, just look at me!
Can you believe I will be "BIG THREE"!!!

I eat happy meals, and go to bed by myself;
I can push the chair up to reach "stuff" on the shelf!

I tattle on the boys and catch Dad running red lights,
Use Mom's perfume, and wear pantyhose, not tights!

I love Barbie dolls (not baby dolls), draw, bake and cook,
But when Nighttime comes, I love a good book!

My favorite thing to do is swing, swing, swing,
Dress up is fun, with scarves, hats, and rings!

Look at me "BIG THREE!" Can there be anymore?
Careful . . . when you blink . . . I will be four!

All My Love,

Chelsea

Two Hearts

Two Hearts, one young, one not so young,
Came together entwined one night,
And shared an ecstasy unforeseen,
Through the darkness shone love's faint light.

Yet still Two Hearts are estranged and apart,
Ignoring the gift life did bring,
That Two Hearts so different such as ours,
One night did beautifully sing.

Susanne Mary Watson Dell

Endless Love

How much do I love you? Can you count the ways?
Can you count thousand of years, and, endless days?
Do you know the size of Jupiter and Mars?
Have you ever tried to count the stars?

Have you climbed a mountain or sailed the seas?
Or, when in a forest, count the trees?
Can you name the many hundred kings?
Or, the countless birds that nightly sing?

Add all these together and you will know
The breadth of my love that continues to grow.
And, only God knows that when I pray
How much you are deeply loved, today.

Kenneth Andrew Simpson

Love Hurts

When you have thought you were in love,
Come to find out all it is, was a fantasy,
You will always have part of you wanting that someone,
Who you have long to love, but never can have.

Then one day that someone comes along again,
What you have to do is make a big decision
Of not to love or to love that someone again
Because that someone broke your heart in a million pieces.

Sandi Raines

The Dove

A dove that fly's so high with pride
Can't always find a place to hide
A place to be sad, a place to cry.
No one to know the dove, just wanted to die.

It's so hard for the dove, to be graceful and pure.
To flutter about, through the storms, she's to endure,
Her head in the clouds, feathers so white
No one to know, the tears she sheds each night.

The dove flounders aimlessly, trying to keep her ground
She gets frightened of the storms, that are all around.
Winds blowing hard, the tree tops are bent
This is one flight, she'll be glad when ended.

Her wings are still moving, her head held high
A beautiful sight, as she flies by.
The winds cease, a roof top she found
She's tired, and cold, but homeward bound.

The little nest built with labor of love,
Has given strength to this little dove.
She's still tired, cold and alone
But finally, made it home.

Phyllis Rutledge-Oien

Your Spirit's In The Clouds

You left this life a few months ago, because you were so ill,
Can't question why you had to leave, we know it was GOD'S WILL.
When I look up to the big white clouds, floating in the sky,
A peace surrounds me and I hear you say "Honey" it's still you and I".
I know you are watching over us and telling us what to do,
You want to protect us, that Quality, which made YOU - you.
I'll be so glad when the time comes and we can stand hand in hand,
We can see the beauty of our heavenly home and hear the ANGEL BAND.
The way you loved your family and Country, makes us proud,
Until we all can be together, keep your SPIRITS IN THE CLOUDS.

Nida Callaway

Players

Can't try and plan it, being hopelessly romantic
Caring for you was easy to do,
the bold stupid things,
unrealistic shadow of beings
Finding the creation was just recreation to you
Believe everything is simple
Time is only a guide line -
To think, I am just a memory in your mind
Reeling in feeling has to be,
a natural part of your daily routine
Time continues, like a melody of a song,
the players know that it won't be too long
You hold nothing back
Once you've shown how easy life should be,
it's back to reality
You're no angel, changing lives, of your friends
It's still two cents - Goodbye is the end
    Terri Tint

No More Walls

As a small child, I started collecting garbage
Carried it with me, all day, every day
Slept with it, all night, every night
Growing older and stronger, I collected more garbage
Arms so full, piled it on my head
Head so heavy, could carry no more
Started building walls with all my garbage
The more I built, the more I collected
The walls climbed higher
It grew dark, the cold winds hurled
Those beautiful walls caved in around me
I hit bottom, in pain, buried by garbage
Still for a long time, bits of garbage strength
Starting to squirm, bits of garbage tumbling aside
    I can see light again
Maybe, just maybe, if I keep squirming
I can free myself of all this garbage
To stand tall, stretch, run free
No more garbage, no more walls
    Linda Finnegan

Largo

The evening light from picture windows
Cast softly a subtle veil of a misty scarf.

It outlines our bodies as we stand on twilight
The dusk of the part of an evening time.

Kneel down—recline MY DEMON OF LOVE!
Let part, if not all of the shroud entwine us!
The silence is pierced your soft, exhaled breath
meets . . . touches mine as our bodies meet.
I hold to your strength, and take it within me
This moment says: It is right and very much welcome
The moist of your nectar ornates my loins . . .
my being as I absorb this offer in me.
The evening keeps setting through the picture window
becomes a solemn night, OUR SPECIAL NIGHT!
I watch, as the growing moon outlines its light
on our bodies now resting in its soothing caresses
on a fulfilled aftermath.
    Silvia Guardi

Above The Ruins

On through the days we ride
Casting our shadows in the sun
With quickest glance to the past
We see there is nothing we can hide

All the beautiful rolling hills have been replaced
By mountains of concrete and shame
We seem to think that living above the ruins
We have laid our sadness to waste

But, when time comes to look down
We realize that our wins were only lost
And our faith buried in the misery
Of knowledge that to our lies we are bound

There is but one chance at redemption
Call back that soul which has traveled on
Reward the open doors to truth and
Alight from our lofty elevation
    Slash Sihlehallah

"What Am I"

I am small in size, not a large as your little finger. I can cause a two hundred pound man to swing at me in annoyance.

You may try to sneak up on me, to give me a whack, but I am an "illusionist," I will mock you. My feet are fast on the track. You chase me all around, but I am hard to beat.

One moment I am sitting in the lowest gutter, the next one I am sitting high on a shutter.

"Do Not Enter" signs don't hinder me. I go where others dread, even with the dead.

I watch you do things, you, think are secret. I hear your laughter, taste your tears and see your sins.

I discovered I could go with you into Courtrooms, bedrooms bathrooms, and barrooms. Even under covers.

You say, "I am dirty, but I have the dirt on you." Don't worry, I won't tell your secret faults, I am harmless.
    I'll just sit here on the wall.
    Melvina McClain

"On Feminism"

When you're standing, 2 a.m., grocery store isle. Four dollars change and you gotta buy condoms and cigarettes. You remember they told you something . . . you have the capacity to get what you want . . . in your arms, legs, breasts and in your mind and not so much that. They don't always want a piece of that. It doesn't seem worth all that much to you in old alma-mater sweats and your ponytail.
    And why? And work is okay but you could do something else. You've got these legs and arms and breasts and a mind and why? You know how it feels to be lost.
    2 a.m. He should be buying the condoms anyway.
    Yes, I am woman, hear me roar. In some vague nonspecific direction. A billion more like me at 2 a.m. with legs and arms and breasts and four dollars change and why?
    They lied to us . . . and we got lost.
    Melanie F. Beckett

Farewell

People come and people go.
Each acquaintance helps us grow.
If again we should meet,
Perhaps, on a crowded city street.
I hope that you remain the same.
Don't lose yourself in life's game.
By your smile - I'll pick you out.
By your face, see what your life's been about.
    Tony Smith

November

The season hath circled now
Changing the world, creating anew.
'Tis November once again
A year, a year, a year soon passed.
'Twas November when mine eyes first met thine
And how I prayed, I prayed, I prayed to our Lord
That thou shalt not see my stare.
Memorizing thy face and smile
Captured by the life in thine eyes
Intoxicated with the laughter thine humor do giveth me.
Thou is far from me, yet never far.
We shall know one another in time
For is there no such thing as fate?
Then, pray tell thee, why did we meet?
Patience, my beloved, for if thou wish
Myself will know thou and thou will know myself.
Look close, my dear, the seasons hast come full circle.
'Tis November, November once again
And thou remain strong in mine heart.

Patricia Ruth Mayhew

A Soulful Soliloquy

I've climbed mountain slopes reaching for lofty heights,
Chanted with the babbling brook in search of eternal life;
Ethereal peace, where are you?

I've listened to the ocean's roar,
While the sea raged and thunder resounded;
Nature's attempt to upstage my soul.

Empty stares in deep pools of blue,
I've watched these forever,
. . . But, where were you?

I've ridden heaven's majestic skies,
Felt God's forgiving grace,
And witnessed the Solitude of Peace.

Still, blue eyes look but cannot see;
A faint glimmer, a wan smile,
My name you know once in awhile.

I never knew what lay behind that cloud of blue,
Reflections of the soul mirror a deeper hue.

Incarnate spirit, reveal what remains to be;
Rest on me for all eternity.

Muriel A. Carroll

Listen To The Night

Listen to the night. I like to sit and listen to the night.
Cherishing the stillness and quiet, minus all the bright lights.
The sound of the wind busily rustling through the trees, calms my fears and places my nerves at ease. I like to sit and listen to the night; alone in the dark gazing up at the stars in sight. Letting my mind drift and wonder endlessly; forgetting who I'm suppose to be. But, I can't forget the times I've made many mistakes; nor can I figure out how to restore my life to a normal state . "It's not too late", the night says to me; "You're free to be whatever you want to be"! So, I sit and listen to the night, where there is no worry, no stress and no strife. Because I've profited from every mistake I've made, and I realize that my soul has been saved! I like to sit and listen to the night; feeling peaceful, serene and confident that I fought a good fight. All downfalls happen for a reason; because one should never lose eye contact with the Creator of all seasons. But for one brief moment, I looked away; I never will forget that day. God's spirit seemed to scurry from my life; but, once again I've found Him by listening to the night! So, when you have problems, and no where to turn. Take it from me, the hard way I've learned. Open your heart to the spirit above and allow him to teach you to forgive and love. Then you will realize that your days will be bright; if you meditate with God, while you listen to the night!

Rhonda Morrow Little

Burkina Night (From The Sahel Of West Africa)

Darkness has come, two hours past
Chill and pungent with the scent of the surrounding
Cows.
The huge orange disc of the moon
Rises majestically from the smudges of cloud at the
Horizon
Into the glittering sky.

I sit and hear the guttural murmurings
Voices rising and dipping, vague and lulling.
Shrill and insistent mosquitoes dart about me.
The hard rods of the grass mat absorb
My slowly numbing legs.

Fires glow in the distance,
Few and far between.
As the moon floods the sandy millet fields
And the voices drone
My eyes long for sleep.
I rise stiffly and fumble my way into the tent
To sleep.

Susan Smith

Christmas

Christmas joy and Christmas cheer
Christmas comes but once a year.
Christmas is gone after a season
So please don't forget there is but one reason.
And to Him we should give all the glory,
For without Jesus there would be no Christmas story.
There would be no gifts under a tree;
No happy children giggling with glee.
No Christmas lights; no singing of a Christmas song.
No "season's greetings" as you walk quickly along.
No Christmas love in eyes would glow.
No innocent kisses under the mistletoe.
So let's take a moment to give Him praise.
And thank Him for bringing blessings in so many ways.
As you do this, remember the way He came,
With the only luxury being His name.
A better man, there could be none;
No one is as great as Christ the Son.

Stephanie J. Beard

Awakening

The mind . . .
　. . . churning, racing . . .
　　. . . twirling in the currents of the past
　　and tossed on the waves of the
　　undetermined future
　　　. . . planning
　　　. . . regretting
　　　. . . criticizing
　　creating storms that blind the present
　　　. . . the now . . .
From behind the relentless winds
　an old forgotten voice is heard
　bellowing through the storm
　　. . . BE STILL . . .
　　　. . . the clouds part
　　　and wind stops . . .
　there is silence . . .
The crusted eyes open
　. . . this world is seen for
　. . . the first time . . .

Kristan A. Anderson

266

Dream Away Your Fears

Dream, dream, dream away, dream away your fears
  Close your eyes, block your mind, hold in your tears
You see the day, in a way, no other can see
  Now you sigh, then you cried, hold in your fears

The sun gleams, the sea steams, sweet, sweet dreams
  Close your eyes, block your mind, dream away your fears
Seek your mind, for a time for never ending fears
  I see what's mine, your cries not mine, dream away your tears

Cries at night do not fright
  The ending light is near
Fears of dark on a walk ever lasting years
  Wake only once on a hunch you never had to fear!

Dream of light and of flight yours never to fear
  In my mind your dreams I do not find
Your dreaming away your fears!

    Robert C. Watson

The Journey Of The Milkweed Capsules

Tiny capsules, the seeds of milkweeds
Clustered in close embrace in a pod
Warm and peaceful in their slumber
Were suddenly ejected into the air
Upon the explosion of the pod
The infection of the excitement
Appeared as bursting plumes on each capsule
Plumes, feathery soft, fluffy, downy and white
Caught in the updraft of warm air
Up, up they rose high into the sky
Like rising wisp of smoke, so light
They quickly disappeared out of sight
Tiny, teardrop-shaped, plumed capsules
Where are they going on their journey? No one knows
For they follow the whim of the wind that blows
To hover, and touch down at a distant place
Like a capsule returned from outer space

    Yoshiyuki Otoshi

Dear Little One

You came to visit grandma last night,
  clutching your dolly with fist clenched tight.
We lit the lamp in your "special" room,
  and peeked out the window for "our" moon.
Now time to create shadows on the wall —
  scary creatures of great — others small.
We shared make-believe; some wished too.
  Our secret world stood still — for me — for you.
Your green eyes laced with blue and brown
  captured by a face with a golden crown,
soon fell heavy without a fight —
  and as slumber crept in and stole the light,
I felt your breath of life kiss my face —
  like a wispy butterfly in haste,
building precious memories for grandma to hold —
  more priceless treasure than any gold . . .

    Maxine Haddox

Damned

Did you know change is within growth
Did you know death is life
We are all created to God's perfection
Casting shadows among the living
Seeking spirits among the dead
As they put brain washing thoughts to our head
Our countries greed is drugged like speed
All of our hate is built on fate
And for this we will be damned.

    Paul J. Queenan

From Nothing

The moist strands glide gracefully across the clean white paper
Color appears out of the nothingness of spotless surface
The first stroke, a stroke of genius
The formation is already set on it's course
With every swoop of the wet bristles a certain shape
Becomes more and more prevalent
A beautiful face appears from the tears of color
Life is brought from death
Animation brought from inanimation
Expression without words or letters and almost as distinct
as a scream
A visual sound is created a voice from nowhere
As quiet as the fox stalking it's prey
While simultaneously as loud as stampeding elephants

    Michael Bergin

Joy

Joy beyond compare, a life without despair.
Comfort in Jesus' name, not just for those of fame.
A race that knows no hue is best me and you.
God gave us hope divine, so, let's give it back in kind.

O Lord I love you so, it's your way I want to go.
I'll share your love with friends, on that you can depend.
Without your loving hand my life would be so bland.
As long as I can stand, I'll give a helping hand.

Love starts with ones own rapture, a feeling that must be captured.
For a life of peace and tranquility, with God one has the ability.
Please listen and comprehend, God is more than just a friend.
A Savior so divine, he gave his life for mine.

I'll spread his love to men so that they may understand.
A life without despair, I'll show I really care.
I'll tell it to you first. I'll tell it to the universe.
Put God in first place and he'll be your saving grace.

    Patricia Richey Lee

An Autumn Day With Gusto

Steel gray clouds
Cornered patches of baby blue
Leaving dark eerie gray.

Late afternoon sun
Spawned long gray shadows
Spotlighting leaves of reds, oranges, and yellows.

Sporadic winds and misty rain
Touched dying blooms of summer
Spiriting a wake up call to prepare for change.

    Marcine Pensiero

Riding The Dragon

Deep inside my inner self lies an endless maze of well traveled
  corridors that I have wandered through all my life.
Yet no matter how far I go, or what direction I take I always end
  up at the cave.
The cave, so big, so dark, so mysterious, where inside waits the
  dragon within myself.
A fabulous winged and scaly serpent with a crested head, wings
  and enormous lion's claws.
This strong majestical supernatural beast that flies carrying me
  high in the neverending blue skies of my very existence.
Oh, how I long to ride the dragon, to be free of all that haunts my
  every waking hour.

    Nadine Langston

Forever Now

What is forever to you?
Could it be a drop of blood?
A moment over and done
Or perhaps a memory relieved
And feelings recalled.
Or maybe the wind through the empty halls.

The Ocean flowing over the same sand of
centuries ago.
Yes, the same wind and sand, exactly the same
But to me forever is forever
Continuous always.
Like the light of a heart
And a smile from memories
Feelings are recalled Now.
Do you remember how it felt?
But in forever you will
If you do not yet, It will happen someday
After forever is half through,
You will remember what forever is
And how much I miss you!!!

Karen E. Sharrai

"Robert"

The moon, the wind, the rain, the sea,
  could not bring his soul back to be.
He had a smile brighter than the sun,
laughter louder than the pain, and
dreams which were infinite, but could
never come true.

  When the day the sky turned from blue to gray
  and he left the realistic world, we realized in
  our hearts that the memories of him will always
  remain true.

  To say goodbye is hard to do.
One day our sky will turn blue
and we will know in our hearts he is here
even though him we cannot see or hear,
but we can feel his laughter, his joy, his pain.
  So we say goodbye, though he is not gone,
  because he will live in our hearts for our life long.

Kim Hubbard

Please Excuse Me . . .

Please excuse me if I should say . . .
  Could you remind me of the day?
They say Alzheimers has begun its reign.
My fading memory is causing a strain.
For with each passing thought,
  I wonder how much more time can be bought.

Remind me again . . . What is the date?
And did you say I had a mate?
Some days are worse than others, you see,
  I don't know you, but you know me.

Please excuse me but its time to go,
I didn't mean to be a burden, you know.
Time slips away fast for me,
  so now it's time for you to hear my plea.
There comes a place in everyone's life,
  when decisions are made, no matter the strife.

You need to hear me, so hear me clear.
There's no one ever I've loved so dear.
And don't think for one minute we will ever part,
  because I'll never forget you . . . in my heart.

Dedicated to my family, in memory of my father.

Marsha Denise-Turner BeDen

A Thought

When fog creeps slowly in
covering the city with a grey blanket,
hiding murderers, street walkers
and addicts. Offering a cloak of escape
to the vice-ridden city — think of me.

When night falls and the lights
make fabulous a dirty, crowded
city and gaiety overcomes the sorrow of the day — miss me.
When rain floods the city and cleanses
Cain's hands of his brothers blood — love me.

For I am only human, with human
thoughts and human weakness.
But with a love that never falters,
a faith that never fails and a hunger
that can never be satisfied.

So loving you, I must leave.
For staying would destroy you.
Look for me in crowded bars,
in jostling crowds, on a beautiful wind swept beach . . .
Remember me . . .

Lea Jerez

Snow On Memorial Day

The snow came down silently, like a thief in the night,
Covering the trees and the earth with a blanket of white,
Turning everything it touched into a veritable Fairyland:
A vast splendor of ice and snow created by God's majestic Hand.

This snowy scene was magical, to whit:
Snowstorms on Memorial Day just don't fit!
In place of green fields where wild flowers grow
Everything is covered with falling snow.

The snow kept falling down so stark and white,
Covering all in a snowy mantle bright.
That snow fell as though it would never stop,
Covering fields and trees and chimney top.

I stared in awe at this white surprise
Of a summer's day in winter's disguise.
What a wondrous sight for a morn in May;
But, oh, how soon it all melted away!

Marjorie Thompson Sims

Twenty Lines To Broken Desire

Because I am no longer a poet

Night and stars, sequenced lace of indigo blue,
Covers your bare torso against the day's delirium

Because these words are no longer meant for you

The white of your breasts replaces the absent moon
And your breath's soft surging the ocean tide reminds

These were not lies my hands told you

I take these last broken relics of my desire . . .
The pink anemones of your fingertips
The round, wan moon of your hip bone
The shattered crystal of your laughter
The rhythmic siren-call of your heartbeat
Against which my ships love to collide
Our Chopin—chords more caress than sound

Memory is a shattered vial of perfume which spreads
Its pungent scent to all corners of the world
You are everywhere and nowhere at once

And each vision of you forming a recognizable body
Which I name "closer to myself than myself."

Palmer White

268

Memories

Starlit skies on Summer nights, moonlight on the sea.
Crickets chirping merrily, these things are just a memory.

Sunshine warm upon your face, free to go most any place,
Bluebirds singing joyfully, these things are just a memory.

Chainlink fence across the skies, sunlight that hurts your eyes,
From being locked inside so long, never hear the bluebirds song.

You never miss what used to be, until you are no longer free,
Locked inside your two-man cell, what's it like outside,
You can't tell.

Soon my time to leave will be here, then I'll see the things I now
   hold dear,
No more bars to keep up apart, I'll be making a brand new start.

My memories will renewed, and they will include you and
The things I've missed for so long, like the joyful singing of the
Blue birds song.

   Michele Loftis

Forest Fire

There was a time, a time when I was a happy little fellow; I had
crisp, crunchy leaves on my head and birds chirping merrily on my
limbs as the wind kept swinging me back and forth, back and forth

But now, I'm worthless, as worthless as a needle without thread
Laying in a bed of ashes as I look high into the sky, as the wind
swooshes by, and as it carries me away, I dream of the days, the
days when the wind swept me back and forth, back and forth.

Then suddenly the wind stopped blowing and the sun stopped glowing
I was completely surrounded by darkness and the crystal-blue sky
suddenly turned black, I looked back, and what I saw I will never
forget as I will never forget about the times when the wind swept me
back and forth, back and forth.

Faintly in the distance I saw a bursting, bellowing flame speeding
toward me; things will never be the same; I do not like what I see
But it came, just the same, speeding toward me, collapsing my fellow
friends into ashes on the way, I say, I'll never forget this day
Speeding towards me, stretching within the second speeding towards me.

That's all I can tell for now, but how? It cannot be, why me? The
wind rushed by and swept pieces of me back and forth, back and forth

   Marie Funaki

Life On The Sea

   Blue rolling water, far out in the sea, a
crystallized sky so distant and bright, the
horizon stretches on forever, and life seems
endless by day, and by night.
   The work is hard, and you do sweat and strain,
the old lug steams onward, perhaps home again.
   Billowing black smoke leaves a long trail behind,
and the stacks bass bellow is one of a kind.
   The salt in the air and the heat on your back
are all a part of the sea, if to sail the
globe is your destiny, then a man of men you'd
better be.
   Soon the sky will turn crimson, the water
glows back to the sun, as night is hurrying on.
   All duties are done and a full stomach was won
as reward for being a man.
   You sit out and watch the first star appear,
then millions come out, and all look so near.
   A cool sea breeze will keep you alert, then
rest will be needed, for tomorrow's more work.

   Stephen A. Reimann

"X-Angst"

(Again she screams, in frustration, of the conflict with her generation)

It's hard to be new, she says,
cutting through another modern age - edge,
gorging on the metaphoric
subtle illusion of liquid friends and lasting love
lost on the tips of seamless pricks
impaling nature, dreams and visions
of false romantic risks jumped
for the simple sake of
why not?

(And I reply, in quiet tones, for the contrast of, our generation)

It's time to dance, my fairy friend,
trailing along the edge
of water rushing in the distance,
a melody found in the treetops,
laced through with the quiet fall
of yellow and red leaves touching our shoulders briefly,
on the way down to
a pile of dry flames about our feet.

Why not.

   Katie McMenamin

On A Memory

Yesterday the world was gray,
   Dark and cold as a winter grave.
This morning rose to a world so bright,
   Long pine tree shadows on a field of white.
A multitude of hungry birds,
   Drawn by some mystic, arcane signal
To the bits and scraps thrown from the farmer's table
   On a barren spot among the drifts,
which the wind, like a tidy housewife, swept.
When once more the skies are cold and gray,
   I'll warm my soul with the memory of this day.

   Lee Hunter

Untitled

On a purple midnight
crawling through your dreams
I saw you screaming and could hear your
body twisting. Tears fell from glass eyes,
ran down alabaster skin.
   Anger had turned in your heart
you held fear in your hand.
Fists closed tight and eyes wide open.
Your lips kissed by summer
your mind twisted by man
your body beaten by time
I have seen your inner soul
I have touched your fear.

   Katie R. Beggs

Infancy

We are one year old, you and I.
Despite the time we have lived
each in our own nonsensical lives
here in this mutual one
we make our way on uncertain limbs
that we cannot trust to hold us,
speaking unperfected sounds of declaration
as we try to reveal
what we have just begun to know.
Still our child creature is wise.
We can satisfy all yearnings
with that word, spoken softly in the dark.

   Sarah J. Thistle

Untitled

The sounds of night are closing in,
Dark came like plush velvet being kissed by the wind.

The stars appeared swiftly and I knew not from where they came.
The full brilliance of moonlight cascaded about with no wish to be tame.

I felt the dew fall and the thirsty plants opened
their leafy arms to embrace each crystal drop.
Could this dark be need in motion which now has
surfaced to the top?

This breeze I feel is ever close to a caress of eternal love,
From where did it come? Without as much as a mere
whisper from a place far above.

Oh those distant sounds of night I shall reach out
with my heart to keep this love in full sight.

A. Flowers-Martin

Into The Night

The sun is setting, the night is upon us.
Darkness is falling, the stars shine bright.
The city's aglow as the street lights go on.
The killer stalks you, death is near.
He want's you dead, you don't know why.
You hear his footsteps in the night.
You aren't sure how far he'll go.
You draw the curtains and put out the light.
You hear the doorknob squeak and turn.
You freeze to the spot, overcome with fear.
You want him to leave, but know he will not.
The killer's before you, death is here.
He raises the knife and starts to thrust down.
The knife glitters in the dimly lit room.
You feel the pain, you fall to the ground.
There is no escape, you've met your doom.
The sun has set, the night is here.
Darkness has fallen, the stars shine bright.
Police sirens scream as they race down the street,
But the killer escapes, into the night.

Stephanie Smith

The Elven King

The night will be filled, by magic and love.
Enchantment so close, the spirits above.
The silent trees sway, seeking their domain.
Laughter fills our hearts, nothing else remains.
Amid in the far, and off to the right,
The unicorns play, obtaining delight.
The whispering winds, enchant us with song.
Teaching us patience, so we can be strong.
Down through all the trees, and out by the brook.
The Elven King stands, whose come for a look.
Up upon his head, there's a crown of gold.
Gleaming through the night, with jewels of old.
His whistle was loud, as loud as can be.
Up came his servants, nor frightened was he.
The servants were gay, the drink was not stale,
The Elf King stood up, and began his tale.
   "The trolls in the hills, are like not of us.
They tower with power, and make a big fuss.
The battle was fierce, through war and glory.
   Through fountains and mountains, that is my story."

Merlin Pryde Knapton

Morning

It is morning, and the first sun of a new
day is reflecting off the frosty grass.
The birds are saying "good morning" to the world,
and it is peaceful.
It is a new day, a gift from God, for He has
given us another chance,
a chance to make peace,
to make new friends,
to renew old friendships,
and to love one another.
Each new day is a gift from God,
It's too bad that we forget that, for this
may be the last day we have,
and it should not be wasted.

J. W. Duley

A Mothers Prayer

Mother whispers a prayer to God up in heaven,
"Dear God take care of him"
And then softly and tenderly
Holds him close to her heart again.

Walk with him ever dear Jesus
Please guide him along the way,
Though the way may be rough and rocky
Keep your hand in his I pray.

Keep your hand in his dear Jesus
Give him strength to meet each new day.
Impart in him, strength, patience, wisdom
And mercy for those along the way.

May he ever seek your face, dear Jesus
And walk in the light of your love,
When his days on earth are over
May he dwell in heaven above.

Pauline Gard

"Death"

What is death?
Death is pain,
When it hurts so much to know He is dead,

Death is denial,
When you want to believe it isn't true.

Death is sadness,
When you miss HIM and wish He was here.

Death is loss,
When you have lost HIM and you can't have HIM back.

Death is emptiness,
When you have lost a part of you.

   "Death is the end of life."

Stephanie Baldwin

Depression

Depression is a great obsession to doctors with
degrees. They lie, they cheat, they give you
drugs that bring you to your knees. You beg,
you plead, you ask for help. They put you in
a ward. You feel like a knight fighting a war
without your trusty sword.
It's finally over, it is now ended. The
way I got out was extremely splendid. I
don't think I'll tell you because I don't care,
you wouldn't understand unless you'd been there.

Ryan McMurtry

Boundaries

Creating a place with nothing to strive
Death on my mind and fear in my eyes
Holy land is where I tread
Pushed so far, I've no longer lead
Extreme deception is close at hand
Feeling with one and killing demand
Boundaries of love are meant to last
With dreams and skills to make a cast
Believing you're one when no one cares
Extending a vision to where they dare
Sadistic pleasures are where you dine
You want your greed and then to shine
Oppression is belief which takes you there
Your life in your hand is only a stare
While others remain and never know
How to spend a cry and when to bestow
A world is alone while some dance
All is silent, the death of romance

Melissa Embry

Déjà vu

Déjà vu, It's feelings in time
Déjà vu, It's feelings in my mind

I can't look forward because the forwards the past
I can't step out because there is no release
Yet real it all seems

Creations of images present and past
Illusions of scenes front and back
Possessions of knowledge inside and out
Events already seen

Paramnesia, heaven sent
Remembrances, haunting ones thoughts
I can't look forward because the forwards the past
I can't step out because there is no release

Déjà vu, it's feelings in time
Déjà vu, it's feelings in my mind

Melissa Garrett

Amazingly In Control

On and on and on, time goes by, bye bye!
Desperately searching, find myself turning and turning
Just like a puppet with chain on my feet, following my master's dream
Dream! dream! dream!
  Who am I? Master of the beast!!!
  Where am I? In an infrangible site!!!
  Why am I? Make war, war? war?
Dream! dream! dream! our own dream
All you need is your hijacked soul
Leave your feet and BMW behind, can't voyage far enough
Close your eyes, can't envision far enough
Let's meet on the moon, let's meet down in the bottom of the ocean
Let's feel the extension of our soul and meet our forgotten friends
So much power when you know your soul, so easy and in control
But so much trouble for your master!!!
It is only your life, show you want it
It is only your soul, show you can keep it
It is about happiness, show you deserve it

Mori Seyedan

My Son Has Left His Nest

My heart swells as a mile stone of memories fills my heart.
Despite the fact the place is empty, the scent of him fills the room,
And I can still hear him speak, as the tears run down my cheek.

The memories linger on, the first kiss, though wet and sticky.
The first flower, even though the peddles lost their way.
The promise of a house and a brighter tomorrow.

His cloths are now gone in addition to his precious treasures.
The wet and sticky kisses, are for someone new.
The flower with their petals, and I know she'll get the house too!

Precious are my memories for their all that I have now.
While he still promises a brighter tomorrow.
My heart is sad, melancholy and sings the blues.
While its also blissful, joyous, singing a happy go lucky tune.
For his wedding day is tomorrow.

  My son Has left his nest!
  Mary Fitzpatrick

Time's Troubadour

I'll do a "To Do List" tomorrow
Didn't have time today
Empty an' worn, fed-up and frazzled
I'll be a smarter, faster and wiser winner
After a spate of slumber.
In the morning I'll take time to plan
Setting priorities every day — beginning tomorrow.
I must, I should, I shan't, I ought, I will, I won't
Today got sidetracked — fell for what it felt like
Tomorrow, I design my program
Seldomore drift, dream, drown, dally, or doodle
If only I could cultivate Procrustes' Code
All things would fit so neatly.
Tonight before I sleep — I know —
I'll strengthen my inner resources
By reading the "Revelations of Julian of Norwich"
Right now, I'll follow Steve McQueen in "The Great Escape"
Then I'll feel like one of those tenacious conquistadors
I'll net a home run built on will power —
  — beginning tomorrow!
  Norah Rohan

Untitled

What do you need to know of me to see the mood I'm in?
Do you need to see my face, or just the way I stand?
Can you see from where you are if I will laugh or cry?
Or do you have to be so close that you can see my eyes?
Do you even need my name to know that I'm alone?
Or can you rely upon my smile to see I'm going home?

Where do you see upon my face the feelings in my heart?
Is it my eyes, my mouth or brow, where do you get your start?
What do you need to know of me to see the way I feel?
Should I stand still, or move around? How do you know I'm real?
Can you tell I'd like to mourn the passing of the day?
Or celebrate all new things in a brand new way?

Does the way I hold my head tell anything of me?
Like how it feels to be with friends, is this something you see?
Am I happy, am I not? Please look beyond my face.
There are so many secrets that you've overlooked in haste.
I have many hopes and dreams, but what I feel is lost
If you can't find in any way what's hidden in my thoughts.

Rebecca Tewell

What Do You See?

When you look at me what do you see,
do you see my soul, my heart?
Or do you just see me, my skin, my height, my hair?

When you look into my eyes what do you see,
do you see my thoughts, my dreams, what's in my mind?
Or just their color, their size?

When you listen to my words what do you hear,
do you hear my words, their meanings, their purpose in time?
Or do you hear just their tone and words but not their emotion or
intent in my life?

When I dance do you see? I dance for me!

My thoughts are don't just look at what's there,
read their motions and meanings!

Listen to the words of my song! Watch the steps of my path!

See me for who I am not for who I used to be,
and not for my looks see me for who I am.

Don't let others judge you, respect yourself and others will respect
you, like yourself and others will like you.

YOUR OPINION IS THE ONLY ONE THAT COUNTS!
Michelle Zunker

Untitled

Sitting on the
dock with lily pads surrounding me
and the crisp cool water
peeking through the empty spots
flowers emerge from few of the pale green sheets
floating upon a watery darkness
to me these things are so very small
but to smaller forms of life they're long strips of land
leading to no one knows where
the peacefulness is only interrupted if the train of thought is lost . . .
sparkling
like a crystal diamond
the surface adds a pleasant serene feeling
and it feels as if the whole world has stopped time
so that I can enjoy this short moment
Lindsay Boehler

The Time Has Come

It's so hard to believe how fast the days have gone.
Doesn't it seem strange, that now we've got to change,
That now we're moving on?

A new chapter has begun; now the page has turned.
It won't be the same again . . .
It's so hard to understand how long this flame has burned.

And some time far away, will you remember me?
Because I'll remember you and all that we went through,
In all that comes to be.

The time has come to part: now the road divides.
Don't you think it's strange, knowing things must change,
And that we must say goodbye?

Yes, it's so hard to believe how all these years have passed.
But—
How great it is to find that I don't have to leave behind
A friendship that will last.
Sharon Grace Silla Bugante

Baby

When I was younger I was a Baby
Doing Baby things small children like to do
One day Baby was outside
Watching birds fly
Checking out the blue sky
Baby things, you know?
Baby went inside
Saw a BIG man on T.V.
of much importance
Walking a big walk, talking BIG talk
Mama comes in
Saying Baby do that, make sure you do this
like a BIG man should
BABY did,
and afterwards I stuck out my baby chest
I'm going to be a BIG man soon.
Tyrone Parker

Christmas Cheer

When you spread around that Christmas cheer,
don't come too close or too near.
Don't ask me to help you trim the tree,
or I'll cut it down right to your knees.

Don't sing any carols or ring any bells,
Don't try to get me out of this evil spell.
For Christmas means nothing,
means diddley-squat, although some people want
me to appreciate it a lot.

The egg nog, the socks are just some excuse,
to get the family together for goose.
Everybody gets in a rush,
all panicky with fuss, but not I, for I'd rather play in the slush.
Katrina Hofbauer

Raising Grandma

Her hair has turned to silver and gray, she grows more beautiful
each and every day
Her heart is filled with pure truth, even though she is losing her youth
Her days are filled with memories of the past
To cherish them and make them last
Her needs are met each day she lives, to see the glow only a child can give
She needs so much love and care
Because she has so much Love to share
Let us be as close as we can
For the bond of Love is always at hand
Theresa A. Wiedmyer

Flames

Flames of hate rise up around me, consuming, engulfing,
Destroying my very existence,
The flames lick my face and scorch my soul, setting it free,
It falls into the jaws of death, being consumed by the flames of hell,
Slowly it burns, becoming dust,
I ride the wind in a cloud of dust,
Dust that is blown away because no one cares,
Just ashes in the fires of our creator,
I am stoked until the fires burn all my ashes,
Now I am nothing, and still,
No one cares,
Flames of heat rise up around me and,
I am destroyed.
William Bulck

From Top To Bottom

Skiing down a treacherous mountain side,
Don't forget to step and glide.
Always make a lot of "S" shaped turns,
A lesson that must be learned.

Prepare for your descent down the summit,
Down the fall line you will plummet.
Carving out turns like an orange Halloween pumpkin,
Hittin' a patch of ice or somethin'.

Skiing leisurely down to the base lodge,
All the kids trying to dodge.
People wearing powder pants,
Working on their pole plants.

People heading for the base lodge to eat,
All tired and sore, especially their feet.
Aching from head to knee,
Some people are best at Apres ski.

Buddies buzzing in the bars.
Kids not wanting to get in their cars.
Putting the skis in the trunks,
Kids yearning for their own bunks.

   Neil Richardson

Baby Dreams

Sweet dreams little one.
   Don't make a peep.
We'll have some fun
   once you're fast asleep.

Close your eyes and take my hand,
   let's go on a journey to a magical land.

We'll race on unicorns faster than light,
then ride a shooting star to the moon so bright.
We'll visit the castles and dragons of old
and slide down rainbows into pots of gold.
We'll dance with the leprechauns
until the break of dawn . . .
and play with the fairies
until your mommy is here.
   You'll give her a smile full of pure delight.
And she'll think to herself
   "I wonder what my baby dreamed of last night."

   Tracy A. Devlin

The Journey

There are no leaves on my branches
Don't threaten me with autumn

There are no oars in my boat
Don't intimidate me with storms

There are no clouds in my sky
Don't menace me with floods

The flock has abandoned me
Don't frighten me with loneliness

This mountain I must ascend
Don't scare me with its crooked paths

I am on the brink of a broken heart
Don't terrorize me with hate

This journey has been tiring
Don't burden me with the thought of relief

   Milton Christian

It's Just Me

Can you see it's just me
Don't you fear or shed a tear
Evil should not exist, but when it does I get pissed
When it has fully grown it's cruelty is fully shown
Is it just me, or something I can't see
Will this evil ever leave or will it's pain shall I conceive
Give me rest and relief or will I become a thief
Is it a small price to pay just to get away
God please show me that you care, this pain and grief I cannot bare
So nothing's perfect or nothing's pure
Why must I marry just to score
Is it bad or wrong and why shall I have to wait so long
Who shall I be for you to see do you realize it's just me

   Victoria Blackwelder

One Heart's Broken Dreams

As I watch the beautiful moon beams
Down they flow
Even in the silent solitude of sleep
Away my heartache won't go.
Your work, your family, a busy life
Consume every second of your time
To find a small place for the man you love
is merely a crime
Just for a few moments, my angel;
I do beg
"Wait" you say
While my heart cracks like the shell of an egg
For so long we've fought against the force of fate
I'm sorry lover. Cause forever I can't wait.

   J. Alan Dean

The Idea Of The Kiss Is Greater Than The Kiss Itself

Oh, bright Lucinda! whose lunar magnet lips
draw me nightly to mirthy froth,
bare-bosomed I am rightly struck thru the heart.
Turn to me not the face of Narcissus
but be more than lovely Andromeda
and keep away Morpheus long enough that I,
who maintain an ardent hope,
may be Prometheus, Apollo, Dionysus, and myself.
Be splendours and ribalds and Parnassus!
Bring wine and songs and heralds of the night.
Above all loose your veils that I may see
that brightest of stars light the round heavens
When your lips I brand with my fiery wand!

   Leglaion Templeton

Yellow Morning

Down by the great valley, where once the great reptiles met.
Down by the great waters from once I came.
Where mountains rose while souls rested
. . . and where the voice of reality is unheard,
I searched for your beauty, the one I wasted.

They say rain and thunder is the true beauty of your sleep
how bad can it be . . . when your warms and your fate is that of what I see
that of what I taste, that of what I feel?

Oh dusty yellow morning so fogy and so mystic, tell me . . .
tell me, how much beautiful can you be?

   William Roman

Dream

Dream to wish all your wishes true
dream of hope for me and you
dream of tomorrows fresh new day
dream of all the right words to say
dream of old friends from deep in the past
dream that your happiness will always last
dream of new friends you have not met
dreams are too special for us to forget
dream of togetherness of former foes
dream of how fast a child grows
dream of past lovers warm and true
dream of how much they meant to you
dream of unknowns you still have to face
dream of going to that special place
dream of skies clear and blue
but dream to wish all your wishes true

Scott A. Michaud

In Between

Sun set, night falls;
    Dreams and fantasies begin to call.
Peacefully sheltered from all the day;
    Filling my untold desires in every way.
Having no perimeter my dreams silently reside;
    In the night for me to beckon, share or hide.
As hero of the night my fantasies take flight;
    Surrendering my failures to the dark of night.
Soaring in success, a rise of strength;
    In control of the night I become at any length.
Now sun rises, night falls;
    Awaiting soon the day calls.
Few will ever know this depth of my soul;
    As being sole proprietor I have all control.

Lorraine Macias

Dreams

Dreams
Dreams are powerful
They can hold you within their grasp
Until your drug to the depths
Of where they live.
Dreams are unyielding
They dwell within your mind
They encourage you to go on when
Everything around you beckons you to stop.
They can be golden, like the sun
Colorful, like a rainbow
Dark, like a shadows.
They can be a person
A place
A goal
A desire.
Dreams

Shanna Golden

Mope

What does one do, if she is not happy?
Does she sit around the house and mope,
or does she get out to see the world?

She cannot think, life will get better
if her house is her prison.
She meets no one, she does nothing
if she stands like a tree.

How can she sit there and complain,
yet does nothing to change the state of her mind or body.
She must motivate to elevate
or be condemned to that fate.

Lilith Terry

Mother Nature Sews

Each second a beat.
    Each beat,
    Each second closer to waking.

Mother natures heart beats strong.
    Pumping warm, invisible blood through golden veins.
    Prompting her earthly body to awake.

Healthy limbs of Oak and maple reach out,
    Pulling handfuls of green from the blue sky,
    With which she sews a patchwork dress for summer.

Whistling sparrow sweet songs to lighten her labor,
    She buzzes busily through her day,
    Trimming the gown with flowers of red and yellow.

By August she stands dressed in summers glory.
    And then with a slow, bashful, blush to red,
    Begins work on falls fashion.

Robert J. Bloczynski

"God's Wisdom"

God individually selects each soul, before he sends them to this earth.
Each is destined to be of benefit to Him, from the day of their birth.
It is marvelous how God selects each of us, and on earth gives us our day.
And when He is through with us down here, He calls us all away.
If we each as He desires for us, make Him our pattern, while on this earth below.
When this life is over are assured of, a heavenly place to go.
Where we will dwell in peace and tranquility, with Him there above.
Surrounded by friends, neighbors, and family, whom the Lord so dearly loves.
Therefore it behooves each one of us, in this journey here below.
To acknowledge Him and lift up His name, where ever we may go.
For our life to reach it's full potential, before this world we depart.
We must so live before the world they can see, God's love shown from our heart.

H. Fitzgerald Durbin

Turns And Concerns

I am what is known as elderly
each morning I walk for my many health concerns.
During this walk I make many turns.
Some of the people I meet are friendly
others look down to keep from speaking.
This morning while walking and turning,
a very thin voice said "Wait! I
have something to tell you" - and
this is what I heard "I found
this place called 'Peace of Mind' and
I've learned that all I needed
was to treat you the way I wished
to be treated."
So tomorrow we will walk together
for health concerns and make many
pleasant turns.

Maezell Davis Dickerson

What Happens To The Dreams?

What happens to the dreams of those who are gone?
Do they fade away and die, or do they live on?
Are they somewhere in heaven, carved into an eternal stone?
What happens to the dreams of those who are gone?

What happens to the love of a mother for her child?
Is she watching from above, does she see each wistful smile?
Could she be a guardian angel bringing comfort for awhile?
What happens to the love of a mother for her child?

What happens to the rainbows God paints across the skies?
Are they on display forever, under watchful angel eyes?
Will the Master Artist save them for His glorious sunrise?
What happens to the rainbows God paints across the skies?

Mary Moore Ezzell

Jester's Song

Feeling as a fool for falling at the feet of love, I can only laugh,
Each sound filtering through the corridors of my heart, chilling,
The laugh as is cold as a tear, for I must laugh or cry in defeat.
Finding control to separate my heart, I stroll through every corridor.
The laugh, yet echoing, ringing through my head, will it ever cease?
My raiment is as black as the raven's wing, fitting for death itself,
Though no rustle is heard as I find my way to the main hall.
As I enter, I hear a song being performed, I see a jester without a smile.
"Dark and mysterious, cursed and vile, love is a bitter conqueror",
she sings,
"Sweet and beguiling, gentle with . . ." her voice trails off as she
looks my way . . .
Smirks form on our lips, the jester has my face and I hers.
In time with each other, we begin the song . . .
"Dark and mysterious, cursed and vile, love is a bitter conqueror", we sing,
"Sweet and beguiling, gentle with death's hand, it always destroys
though by only one voice, the jester is out of sight."
I've found once again, the part of me that laughs at love,
And I walk back out, holding the jester's hat, singing the jester's song . . .

Roberta M. Smith

A Place Closer Than Home

The sound of trees swaying in the wind
   echo the voice of a child crying out - return
      your memories were left behind.

A beast in the house forces us away. We retreat
   to a secret park where monsters can't follow.
      Our prints erased by the swooping motion
         of protective branches.

A happy boy in a swing, being kissed by the air,
singing softly, in this sanctuary of lost souls.

My heart and eyes are full of emotion
   for an eternal friend - the park
      I rely on her to keep old memories until
         returning to once again hold
As a new born.

Sandra Hawkins

The Answer

The pain is too much to bare
Empty rooms filled with suffocating silence
Noise so loud it hurts
Burns my ears
Terrorizes my mind
Paralyzes my body

I try to climb from the inside-out
Grasping for any thread of Hope
But Hope is liquid and salty
And gravity keeps me from escaping
The force that pulls Hope from me
Also keeps me planted on this ground
Rooted, with no chance of flight

So tonight I sit and wait . . .
For the sun to come and lift that thread to the sky
So that once again
I can try to grasp it
As it falls from a-high.

Wendi Walser

The Artist's Part

Thank God for talent and the will
enabling one to snare the prize
of beauty, where she lies so still,
invisible to common eyes.

She waits but for the artist's touch
to flush her into open flight
where all can see, to know as much
her glory as the artist's sight.

Her figure may be traced with pen or paint;
her wit the poet's phrase will oft' enhance;
her voice be heard in soft symphonic plaint;
her grace be felt in supple movement of the dance.

Yes, thanks for those with talent and the will
to sacrifice to play the artist's part;
that others might be caught up in the thrill
of beauty which transcends the finite mind
   to spark a movement in the human heart.

Yes, thanks for those who care enough
to play the artist's painful heart;
else might He have created all in vain
the wondrous worlds of beauty and of art!

Robert L. Brown

"Visions Of You"

My Darling Love,
Enchanting thoughts drift to and fro,
Mild pain, torrid passion overflow.

This thought of hope, desire, this love,
Transforms the senses,
And speaks aloud.

Of dreaming desires and loving thoughts,
These I have for only you.
Gracious compassion wells inside,
Secretly, and so true.

A feeling of warmth, a purest essence,
Reaches deep in my soul,
For always within my mind,
The sweet visions of you
Shall dance without end, and brighten my time.

Mary Schlaepfer

Even Though . . .

My father is with me day and night,
   even though he is out of sight.
He's in my mind, my soul, my heart,
   even though we are far apart.
He will always be there watching me,
   even though him, I cannot see.
I miss him deeply and love him dear,
   even though he cannot be here.
My memories are many of my dear Dad,
   even though in the last days some were sad.
"Daddy you're so special and always will be,
   even though it was time you had to leave me.
One day we will walk together in the Heaven's above,
   even though I can't go now, I send with you my love.
I'm not ready to be without you in my life,
   even though, I must accept all the pain and strife.
I will say good night for now but will not say goodbye,
   even though, I know in time, we will walk together
again, you and I.

Wendy Greer

The Maestros Touch

The Maestros touch brings the symphonic sounds to Celestial height.
Encompassed by the swelling of the great organ.

The striking of keys increasing to a tempestuous motion.
The piano makes her grand entrance.

With Genius attack, the strings join in long caressing strokes,
Announcing their prolonged absence.

The trumpets blast warn all brass the near arrival of the cymbals.
While the drums roll in frenzied harmony.

Calm, subdued by a diminish, the harp inserts her ethereal tones,
Bringing a peaceableness with her.

The Maestro continues his journey looking for a rest to suddenly appear.
Where all may come together as one.

A thunderous applause resounds the air as bows are taken and
emotions are released.

My footsteps slowly depart, knowing that with the passing of time.
I will return again to the feast to be filled.
Familiar sounds will awaken my memory and the journey continues with the

Maestros Touch.
Vivian Bell

The Sun

The sun burns into my heart like an
engraved letter in the locket I wear
around my neck. For the locket shines like
a single ray of sunlight and fills my heart
with joy. This joy I share with family
and friends for the sun has provided
me with it. They feast upon this joy and
look to it as their provider as I look
to the sun to be mine.
Kimberly Spalliero

Things Remembered

Things remembered of long ago,
even before childhood.
Pictures past, faces, places.
Sitting in the same setting with others.
Though names have changed thoughts remain.
Of picnics under trees that once were saplings.
Sunny, but hazy, lazy days.
Making of new remembrances.
Children of before, now adults.
Adults of before, now mostly gone.
Still even now those that were the youngest,
have the memories that they keep
in their hearts and minds of things remembered.
Sarah Dzikowski

Snow Flakes

In Winter observe the Snow Flakes blowing in the wind.
    Far away they are all the same.
But, at a second glance, a closer look,
    No two are the same;
Different shades of color, size and pattern.

We are so much like the Snow Flake,
With different thoughts, different likes, dislikes, goals,
    Size, shapes and shades of color.

Our lives of scurrying here, scurrying there,
    Sometimes bonding, sometimes not.
In a world of such fast pace,
    Are not we as they?
Just Snow Flakes blowing in the wind.
Sue Carol Filerio

Mommyhood

The bond between Mother and child, the strongest in existence.
Even in a dysfunctional situation, the strong bond still exists.

Little girls practice being mommies, mommies to their dollies.
Practicing for their future, preparing for their destiny.

Girls having babies strengthens the relationship with their own mother.
They are giving their mother the gift of being a grandmother.

They have more in common; both are mommies.
True adulthood as a mommy; otherwise, forever a child.

Do you miss it? Child birth? Being responsible for that small life?
The ultimate in creating together- a special bond with spouse.

The Bible says that unmarried people may better serve the Lord.
Could it be the same with mommyhood?

Maybe women who are not mommies— and men who are not daddies
Can better serve the Lord. Just maybe — perhaps . . .
Penny Gillett Silvius

Goodbye

I could never let him see me cry,
Even though I had been dying inside. The whole time he was near,
I could feel his breath on my skin, I wanted him to kiss and hold me,
But I had just stood there, holding back my tears.
As I got on the northbound train on that wet and rainy day,
I almost wanted him to run to me and tell me to stay.
Yet still I turned to look into his eyes and deep inside
I knew the love I felt for him would burn forever like a fire's ember.
For a moment, I stood then turned slowly away and walked for hours
it seemed until I reached a window seat where he could see me and
I could see him, one last time.
And as I looked it seemed as thought he might cry
But I saw just a hint of a smile, and as I remember, he sort of waved
    goodbye.
As the train started moving, I pressed my hand against the glass,
and I tried to make a mental picture of his face in my mind.
For it seemed the only place I might see him again would be in my dreams.
Yet before I knew it he had slipped from view and tears had begun
to fall from my eyes.
Mary Elizabeth Grove

Money Fever

Most people today, usually get their way.
Even though their in office,
They still take advantage of us.
Just to make us pay,
When things go their way.
The desire for control, won't let us go,
Until they reach their goal.
But we are only told, "Just be bold."
Things are under way, for a change some day,
But that day never comes,
Because their out of funds,
So they continue to say, "Send more money our way!"
Will it ever end, this spending trend,
We're engulfed in, not until the end,
My friend, so they say,"We've got to pay!"
Marvin G. Richens

A Spooky Sort Of Shadow

There's a spooky sort of shadow, and it's on my bedroom wall, and
everytime it growls at me, it makes me want to fall.
It really is so kooky and I know I'm really dumb, to think that this
monster would eat me till I'm gone!
Sara Tuttle

A Better World

The world is so cruel to people at times,
every night on the news you hear about crimes.
The run away kids alone on the street,
are asking for help for their parents that beat.
The parents that hurt and abuse their young,
should be put away, tortured, and hung.
The stabbing and killing that goes on every night,
gangs meeting gangs as they shoot, stab, and fight.
The drive by shootings killing innocent kids,
the poor crying parents screaming look what they did.
The homeless that wonder and sleep in the street,
start over each day struggling to make ends meet.
We seem to ignore them as we pass by,
and think how lucky I am, then I start to cry.
We need to start helping to change all the bad,
we need to be laughing, be happy, be glad.
Please God we need help to take away crime
to make our kids glad to belong in this time.
        Melanie R. Roderick

What's True To Me

Life for me is total confusion
    Everyone says it's just a delusion
    I wake up everyday knowing that nothing has changed
    As the world turns around me I feel deranged
Something is inside of me, I don't know where to go
    No one cares, everyone is screaming no
    I think a lot, I don't know what to say
    I feel like leaving going up to stay.
As I look high above
    I feel nothing but love
    Everyone is strange no one looks the same
I hear everyone calling Mary Jane
I live different lives, no one knows the same
    To me its like a game
    Parents are not blind, they don't know what to do
I have no philosophy of life, I wonder what they go threw
I get scared, I don't want control
    I'm limited I need a goal.
    I need space, do you know me?
    I wish I was set free
        Mary K. Lauria

Frightening Future Felt

The storms of change raging, invading our dreams
Everywhere the power - big technocrat machines
Industrial and economical strains
Enough even to rattle electronic brains.

Surging great power, hear the futures machines
Their angry noise ripping up memories scenes
And not one reminder, no wreckage or rust
Not a sign of a care, no, the past only dust.

The old neighborhood places can never return
Gone the stores and Churches that knew our concerns
Our own small events, our private public lives
Scattered like bees to apartment house hives.

The threatening sounds; commerce, progress and change
It saddens old hearts and it worries old brains.
What philosophy leads us? Who holds the reins?
Is it good for our people? Is it a gain?

The old and the new thing, the bitter, the sweet
In political law storms be threshed out like wheat.
Individuals upright, to themselves true
In verbal struggle win the best of what's new.
        Kenneth Voegtly

Rememberings

The dusky echoes of remembered things
Evoke the joys of half forgotten dreams
Whose fancies flow in misty silver streams
Along the course of dim rememberings
And elevate to heights aspired by kings
The beggars in the mundane world below
Until the past parades in golden glow
A panoply more real than this day brings.
In retrospect, on lies serenity
If not contentment, firmly clinging fast
To recollections of tranquility.
Anticipation of his future hangs
Upon his present memories of the past.
        Robert L. Marsteller

Sweet Justice

Masters of deceit—lying with straight faces and steady
    eyes, concealment, dripping with sugar-coated words.
Words, causing a slow death of all emotions, an urgency
    to scream vengeful thoughts of misplaced trust; and,
Misplaced loyalty in those thought to be friends and loved ones.
A growing, gnawing cancer of hate and revenge—but,
    oh, SWEET JUSTICE!
        Pat G. B. Hall

Your Choice

One drink and that's all it takes, to knock you down flat on your face.
You feel that tingling feeling in your nose, and a numbness down to your toes.
It would seem at times that you just learned to walk, not to mention the word talk.
The flavors, oh so many. Some bitter as they are sweet.
Some weak, some strong. That first drink is sometimes so wrong.
For some it will be the last night to see the moon so bright.
For some it will be the last time to commit such a crime.
For some, they will go to jail in a small crowd cell.
For some, they won't even know what the hell they've done.
It could ruin your life and cause great strife.
One should commit to the limit.
One should know when to say No! Because it could be your time to go.
        Kelly David

Untitled

Do you know this man who is staring at you from the painting?
Face is not so old but reflecting impending demise.
Not because of grey hair or wrinkles it's fading.
Brutal loneliness conquered his forehead, his lips and his eyes.

Do you think he remembers his being somehow related
To the happiest group which created such mess and such mirth?
Friendship, delicate cloud, at winter becomes separated
Into lonely snowflakes, drifting till meeting on earth.

Telephone, sleeping cat, doesn't twitch, doesn't make any sound.
Only son sometimes calls; he is busy and must not pretend.
He is busy, of course, no time for turning around.
He's consumed with his work and his young intellectual friends.

Conversation is gone, short on substance and long on emotion.
Old man squeezing the phone and not trying to open his hand.
Silence flooding the room and surrounding him like an ocean.
Old man staring at you in his slow and quiet descent.
        Yakov Yablonovich

The Chair

In a dimly lit room, you could see the old chair . . .
faded and worn, even then.
For hours we'd sit and she'd talk of her youth,
telling tales of the times she would spend . . .
silly games, dressing up, sharing dreams, finding love,
having daughters to hold on her knee.
I'd nestle real close, smell the clean of her dress,
and know Angels were smiling on me.
Then we were two as we entered the room,
and she'd call to my child "come sit!"
White hair framed her face, now weathered and worn,
still a beautiful, radiant gift.
Now the rooms light, the old drapes have come down,
The chair cannot take the bright sun.
It sits all alone, just a nudge from the wind,
but our memories have only begun.

Linda S. West-Riehn

So You

Though my eyes are now filled with tears
Fading memories of fond moments
time spent gazing, longing, laughing
hanging on your every word.

I knew then that what we had, this so much
so far, so forever, so were the good
dreams of lasting, leaving everything
else behind to dance on stars.

You never told me how you could really be
you threaten to leave at the mere idea of
physical aggression though it never met my mind as you
learn to crush me - and only with a glance you scream.

And so always I crouch in fear waiting
wanting the feeling to pass never to live cautions
expectations of you walking out, picking
up and leaving behind what you so forever had forged
deep in my soul as you dance, finally free to pursue
whatever it was that we both always knew you really
wanted and the screaming baby-so very, so you
will never wish to speak my name again I weep.

Steve Balle-Gifford

"A Poem For My Lady"

As fingers of moonlight bathe you in their glow, I see the rise and
fall of your body, in its slumber. Your hair flows across your
pillow, and yet, all I see is your face, moonlit and beautiful.
I clasp your hand in mine, and feel the rhythmic beating of a heart
as full with love as my own. You alone have taken me from the depths
of loneliness into the pleasures of paradise. You have done all this
and more by just by being yourself . . . a woman.

Robert Wayne Coughlin

Backstairs

Sitting on the back stairs
Family's blown away
Know they won't come back again
Why, I just can't say.

Thinking on the back stairs
The time has come and gone
What was once can't be again
It didn't last too long.

Sitting on the back stairs
Waiting for dawn to bring
Some light and warmth to this bitter cold
It doesn't feel like spring.

Raymond T. Camanelli II

And Your Eyes Shall Open

Falling!
Falling! Falling! Falling!
Catch me before I dream.
Something to come,
But I remember, some of what was done.
Some time tomorrow,
Could come today.
Falling! Falling! Falling, falling far a way.
Falling in a world of mystery.
Could be sometime far a way.
Could be today,
Falling far a way
Catch me before I fall.
Falling far a way,
A dream a way,
A dream today,
Falling in a world of mystery.
Catch me if you can, catch me
Catch me if you can, before I fall far a way.
catch me if you can, catch me.

Mona Lisa Matthews

The Man And The Boy

Singular thoughts expressed without word;
Father and son need not even be heard.
  No sound but the rustle of leaves underfoot
  As a press of the hand
  Silently signals the hoot
  Of an owl as wise as the boy and the man
  Attuned to each other
  Without sanction or ban.

Instilled in these depths of this forest of joy
Is the warmth and affection of the man for the boy.
  The man will grow older;
  The boy will attain
  The strength of his manhood to continue the chain
  Of relating to nature; to handle life's strife
  By the love that was fostered
So early in life.

Seville R. Shack

Sunsets

The sun shone down on me today
Feeling its presence has drawn me away
The distance, its redness - its becoming unclear
I'm losing what once was held so, so dear

My eyes are puffing, I've lost what's inside
The caring, the warmth my sun tries to hide
Yet, once again it came down on me
And then faded from what it used to be.

Misty Harloff

Life

The taste of chewing on an oak twig.
Feeling of being drug through the mud, heart first.
Zipping around in a dream, flying and floating
Whirling, twirling, and flipping.
Talking on the phone with your computer at your
Fingertips accessing all information: World wide web!
Being paid, having worth or just a full belly.
Walking endlessly, with enough time.
Speeding in your car, late; on an empty tank
Contentment: Not wanting something.
I thought I was really here until someone
Tapped me on the shoulder.
Then I realized I had to get back to the present.

Roberta Kuntz

Silence Broken . . . Truth Spoken

As children of abuse, we were forced to ignore our
feelings and to never ever tell.

We were forced to live alone with the pain and shame . . .
truly a living hell!!!

Keeping the silence was all-consuming and hurt us deep . . .
within our souls.

We may have had some short-lived moments of
happiness, but our lives were filled with woes.

We first had to break the silence to ourselves . . . which
was difficult because it had been buried so very deep.

With help, we learned that in order to heal . . . the
secret silences . . . we could no longer keep!!!

Silence kept and silence broken are both acts of
tremendous courage indeed!!

And we have learned that only when silence is broken
and truth spoken . . . can we finally be freed!!!!

Zona L. Hackett

Emotions Create Confused Thought Writing Absorbs Life

I am lost in a page of EMOTIONS —
feelings come out — they won't organized — they
won't connect-form-CREATE — I see them here
down in front of me — I can't I'm CONFUSED —
what can they mean — how can I work it out —
the page is lost — lost in my hopelessness —
the page is me — my outlet of THOUGHT —
it knows not why or how or what to do
it only receives my ink — my WRITING —
does not deceive — does not solve — it ABSORBS —
pain — solve the confusion that is my LIFE.

Keri Davis

Ribbons of Asphalt

Ribbons of asphalt, humming and churning
Fields of golden wheat, glistening and sparkling
Majestic sky of blue hues, with
Angels floating on snowy white dew.

The Lord smiles gently down upon you
Keeping you safe on those asphalt ribbons of life
Sending you peace, faith, hope and love.

Clocks are ticking, there's no time to waste
Be safe and go in peace
Ribbons of asphalt carrying you home
For tomorrow may not be ours to take.

Kerri Demarest

"50" Is

Fifty is old enough to start losing your hair;
Fifty is young enough to still care.
Fifty is old enough to get a job done;
Fifty is young enough to wrestle a son.
Fifty is old enough to cry when you hurt;
Fifty is young enough to flirt.
Fifty is old enough to appreciate life;
Fifty is young enough to please a wife.
Fifty is young enough to keep yourself fit;
Fifty is old enough to want someone else to do it.
Fifty is too young for social security,
Fifty is a case of mistaken maturity.

Lanelle Bearden

Untitled

He smiles as he opens the door for her,
filled with eager anticipation.
He takes her in his arms.
He loves her long neck and curved middle.
She makes him feel bold, courageous and ready for the day.
He has to see her, everyday.
He can't be without her.
She rules his life.
His mouth meets hers.
He waits, eager and excited.
His head begins to spin.
His heart and pulse beat faster.
He's ready to take on the world.
Once again, she's come through for him!
The day now looks brighter,
as the alcoholic has his first drink of the day.

Patti Kassay

Please, Oh, Please, What Is Happening To Me!

Oh me! Oh my! Please, what is wrong with me!
First the elbow, then the foot; well, now it's my knee!
Please, oh, please, what is happening to me?

Once I walked and talked with ease!
Once I did any and everything that I pleased!
But now each day I panic if I sneeze!

Bifocals, false teeth, and a cute double chin!
Thoughts come to me about the days I was thin.
All these wrinkles! Well, you know the mood I'm in!

Long sleeves I must wear for these baggy arms!
Thick hose keep my varicose from more harm!
I do believe this is the time for great alarm!

When I look at this gal with aches and pains from head to toe;
I am thankful the Lord put our eyes up high and not too low!
Cause what I don't see, I really don't need to know!

At the rate this memory is fading, with absolutely no care!
I truly won't know about what is happening here or even there!
But now when we talk about backs, butts, bladder, or hair;
You can see right now, we will have a lot to share!!!!!

Marcia Chris Crabb

Anger For An Unbalanced Oven Rack

A small change.
Five sweet potatoes instead of six.
Two on one side of the roast,
Three on the other.
He took with him the stability of a once solid oven rack.
Yeah, a small change, but God it was weird to see him go.
He threw the closet clothes on the bed and
The hanger heads tangled together
Almost mockingly.
The littlest walked in, smiled at the hangers.
He wanted to shake her, tell her there was nothing to smile about.
But he untangled the hangers in a shaky way
And bounced back a cellophane smile instead.
Closet empty, he left. Just left.
Gone, just before the roof started to leak.
It figures.
Nobody here knows how to fix it.
And then there's the oven rack.
It's such a small change,
But no one's quite sure what to do about that either.

Kelly de la Rocha

Song Of Renewal

The winter winds have soften to the gentle breeze of spring
Flowers sing the song of renewal declaring the world is king
The earth in transformation never fails to amaze me so
This wonderful song of renewal creating joy instead of woe
Once again life splashes it's numerous shades of green
To give back to the maker the praise that it should bring
But caution is the watched word of every thinking man
Protection of our living space should be our primary plan
The song of Renewal will be sung for years on end
Question is will mankind be a forgotten verse by then.

J. M. White

Where Is Myself Now

I am piece of paper in the street,
flying around the stirring winds, going everywhere
the winds want me to go, doing everything
the winds want me to do.
I'm Picasso's art work.
I am a light bulb sitting stable in it's socket,
alone, never knowing when I'm to go out.
I'm a poem, written by someone deaf
and blind. I am a soft pillow on which
one can sleep, weep, cling and get comfort.
I'm a machine fighting you all the time,
sweating, and struggling for a better life.

Yanira Burgos

Save The Light Of Love

People we tried to reach you through new age tunes
Folklore, fantasy stories, forgotten ruins
You turned away blindly, saying it is not true
How could you not see this will happen to you

The lights will cease to exist some doomed day
No sun, moon or stars to guide your dark way
You'll be lost and helpless as fate sets in
And the world will swallow, you and your sin

It was the greed and dreams that kept you going strong
But the shallow needs you sought,will not belong
Victims of circumstance you all seems to state
That won't help you now, you're crossed off the slate

For the simple, true people who did your best
Somehow you will separate from all the rest
You'll find the reward for being kind and right
And may the warmth of God find you that night

The night of endless darkness
Save the light of your love

Kathleen M. Castile

I Never Got a Chance To Say Goodbye

I never got a chance to say good-bye,
For every tear up in the sky.
Life passed on so quick.
After all thoughts that made me cry,
I realized: I never got a chance to say good-bye.

To die so young is so unfair
Isn't it the gift of life that we're suppose to share?
With a quick glance of a glaring eye,
I realized: I never got a chance to say good-bye.

Though the decision was made by a higher order.
The feeling of loss, emptiness is everlasting, forever,

The feeling to be free,
The feeling to fly,
Made me realize: I never got a chance to say good-bye

Michelle Baker

And This Is What I Ask

If I ever needed hope
For a desperation traveling to its end,
If I ever needed the blanket of a friendly word,
Would it be too absurd
To ask one ounce of encouragement
To set me free — and would it be me
To ask you to be there
In the shadow, in the hour,
Of my greatest need?
    It's so easy to be a lover.
    But could you be my friend?
Could you simply be a soul
With no sexuality to contend?
Could you just be that someone to talk too,
When all that was assured
Never finalized, and was never really meant?
    Could you silently be
    The love
    We all let
    Slip away?

William Mayer

Thoughts On Child Abuse

I want to scream
for all the things she could have been
for all the things she could have done
I want to scream
to a world that said it wasn't right to tell
of things that happened in that hell
I want to scream
for all the lost and broken ones
who were never free to be
I want to scream
for a little girl
who never had the chance to dream.

Nancy S. James

My Golden Anniversary Prayer

Thank you Lord, for this our golden anniversary day.
  For all your blessings, love, and mercy you have given us along the way.
Thank you Lord, for each other,
  and that together we became parents of a daughter and then her brother.
Thank you Lord, for our children, other family and friends.
  They are to us a treasure and a comfort, they have always been.
Thank you Lord, for our old house that stands beside the road.
  The yard with the tall oak trees where the purple wisteria grow.
Thank you Lord, for our churches with their preachers from far or near.
  They bring us words of wisdom through prayers and sometime cheer.
Thank each one of you for coming. It has been our pleasure and delight.
  May the good Lord take us all safely home and watch over us through the night.

Mrs. Roscoe Fussell

Giving Thanks

I am thankful for the morning light,
For safety and comfort through the night.
I am thankful for another dawn
And for the strength to carry on.
May I always be thankful for each new day,
Nor fret at the tasks that come my way,
But strive to do them without delay
And when each day its course has run;
Then I am thankful for Evening's rest
With peace of mind, knowing I have done
My very best.

Vi Smith

Angels Blessed

I have seen the Angels—they are blessed!
For each day they have been put to the test.
Caring for our sick and elderly is no easy task,
And helping their families put there mind to rest.

Imagine the fear—to be alone.
Unable to walk, confined to a chair.
Nothing familiar—not even a phone
No familiar faces—anywhere.

Imagine a world—diminished of sight and sound.
The Angels know those unable to cope.
Small wonder these lost souls scream and fight.
Their minds once bright, feeling less then hope.

The daily doses of affection given,
Hugs and kisses quell the fears,
This means the world to those so stricken.
With loving hands the Angels dry the tears.

Shirley T. Eager

The Earth's Poem

Once there were trees, once there was clean air, for you and for me,
     for everyone to share.
Now they are all gone, The Great Chief took them away,
His work is all done - and let us all say:
You should have kept them here, and let them all grow,
So nice and so dear, He told you all so.
You tried to do good, but why you just couldn't, you got too greedy,
     and no way - you wouldn't.
He told you to listen, to keep the Earth clean,
That wise Indian, but it was all just a dream.
He loved the whole earth with all of his heart,
Then we went and killed it - that wasn't too smart.
So when you are walking down a road far away, just try and listen,
     a tree might say:
Listen to me - I've seen it all happen, men cut down the trees,
     and people start clappin',
They build their new homes where my friends used to live,
Now they are floor boards - nothing left to give, so please,
     little one,
When you go to the store, pick up some seeds, then get lots more.
Plant them and feed them, and nurse them to health.
Then plant them in them in the forest, it is much more fulfilling than
     wealth.
There will be new trees, new plants and new shrubs,
More deer fawns and hatchlings, lots more new bear cubs,
The Earth will be better for such a small price, and just think -
     you helped make it so nice.

Scott Caraveo

To Commune

I need to commune with what lies in me
For if I don't forever trapped they will be.
My hopes, my thoughts, memories and dreams.
Stored up unrevealed - forgotten it seems

To commune with me they try desperately
I hush them up - but they want to be free
Dare I sensitive be to their need?
The voices are urging me to listen and heed.

Quiet! communion we can't have today-
For just a little while longer you must stay
Tomorrow, I promise, I'll spend time with you-
For a day of conversation is long over due.

G. Helene Treadway

My Friend

Thank you for being my friend Lord,
for guiding each step of the way.
For helping me over the rough rocky path,
and turning my night into day.
You help me to see that no matter how hard
and steep the pathway may be.
That you are my friend and will always be
here to guide and to comfort me.
No one could be a fraid like you and care
as much as you do,
Nor could they be as kind, gentle and loving,
always faithful and true.
Thank you for being my friend Lord for
giving me courage to face each new day,
And knowing no matter what ever may come
you are my friend all the way.
You said you would always be
with me even unto the end.
Now from my heart I thank you Lord
for being my dearest, most precious friend.

Katherine Crickenberger

Gaslight Square

Sidestreets and Carnivals provide second-hand judgment days
for hard-to-forget dramas and discarded dreams.

Musical hungry-eyed hipsters spin rollicking jazz-like limericks,
were densely familiar if hard-to-forget fantasies,
are revealed in close-knit transcription.

Dippy androgynous dead-wrong cynics frolic indifferent vistas . . .
Hyperbolic poets, lip-synch infectious tales
of pagan worship and hangars on . . .
while down and out deadbeats croon.

Precarious balance precipitates, magnificent disorder . . .
Heelprints of apostrophes self-destruct when lifelike pantomimes
of national heroes, disappear in rain-soaked landscapes . . .

Meanwhile, the True story survives in language ghettos . . .
untouched my minor characters, ignored by critics,
and accepted by several eccentric aborigines . . .

In a tattered coat of fog the tiny narrative continues . . .
in Dreamland, or the muck of awakening, slightly loony leftovers,
come scrambling along rafters, and leaking from seams.

Alive with misconception, berserk and ignoble nightmares, join
hard-won truths unravelling, from the loose folds of our dreams.

Timothy Martin Flanagan

Hero

As I sit here in the darkness of my room, I wait in sorrow
for him to call. As I bawl my tears away I think of my hero
far away. Daddy was his name. No more is his name.
Daddy's are there for you through thick and thin, and always
there with a helping hand.

What would you do if his hand was gone or spending thick and
thin by yourself always went on?

Love is there but not always shown. His back to me and his
hand out for someone else.

I sit here in the darkness of my room. What should I call
him now? Father, Dad, Daddy or just that man who calls
once every two months? I don't know and I don't care, these
things I would ever dare ask, so how will I find out?

As I sit here in the darkness of my room, I wait in sorrow
for him to call.

Tiffany Lave'

Addiction - Addict - Recovery

I may want to belong, but for me it's wrong
For it controls me, and makes me sing the same "old song".
Excuse all the if's, but's, and's, and then's,
And look at where the problem lies in the end.
Oh my, Oh Why did I ever begin?
Was it to hide the pain within?
I see, I do see, how you've controlled me,
But now I've learned the way to be.
Mind over matter is the way I see,
Which means putting the "I" over the "E".
No more lies, trickery, or stealing for thee,
For my God will be with me constantly.
Despite, despite all of my might
I can not walk freely without God's sight!
Looking down the road may seem too long.
But now I'm sick and tired of singing the same "old song"
"It won't be easy", I've learned this too!
"Breaking up is never easy to do", and my apologies must now come through
"On with a new life," I now say, along with "action" towards that way,
and may God help me stay clean and sober, just day by day.

Kevin Echols

This Thanksgiving

I am thankful for each new lease in life,
for me to enjoy the sun, the moon and the stars;
the trees, the rocks, the mountains and the seas,
for these were part of what was given to me.

I am thankful for my family,
the source of my joy and security.
From it's great love and devotion,
a child has grown with compassion.

I am thankful for having the things that others don't,
and for being content with what I have.
For whatever it is that I may lack in life,
does not outweigh the things I got.

I am thankful for my friends, who helped me paddled through
the rough, stormy sea of my life; who had been there with me,
throughout the blustery ride.

Indeed, a lot for me to thank for
but life, itself, deserves it more.

Lourdes S. Dar Santos

For No One Knows

  As the wind blows
For no one knows,
  How precious life is
When all done, the decision is his
  If everyone was smart
Love and joy would fulfill the heart
  For no one knows
Only he, which one stays and which one goes
  He is the one who protects us all
Even when life brings a big downfall
  For no one knows
When that fragile moment could come
  Just remember those loving hands we came from
  For no one knows
When that faithful and surprising time
  Maybe could be yours or maybe even mine
If I could save souls with another line
  Then possibly, they could be ready by that time
  For no one knows

Michelle Smith

A Significant Home

Perceive significances within our universe and set a goal
For reality has milestones of aggravation therefore be bold.
As you awake and arise to a new day always ask for guidance
To achieve unmentionables in the path, on God put reliance.
With self-assurance ignore ungodly unspoken worldly things
As you aim for higher ground where the saints do reign.
Yes, life is hectic and full of strife but we must tarry on
And one day, someday, we can see our Father on the throne.
Since his chosen ones will acquire a home without strife
Set life's aim today to gain the everlasting sweet life
With riches untold and hindrances will not affect a soul.
A precious inheritance deemed for each to have and behold.
In Paradise, Eternity forever where we'll never grow old
And Heaven is to be A SIGNIFICANT HOME, this we are told.

J. C. Flowers

Ode To My Goaltender

If it wasn't for his quick glove hand,
For saves he'd make when down by a man.
Under pressure he wouldn't crack,
When on his side his pads he'd stack.
He'd sacrifice his body to make a save,
And all the fans would do was the wave.
For what he did he got no respect,
Every game he was the cause to the effect.
No one cared to think that way,
But he did his job day after day.
Sure he'd give up some really soft goals,
But when he didn't he covered his holes.
He played the puck from post to post,
And to tell you what he never boast.
If anyone came near his treasured crease,
He'd slash their legs with his wooden piece.
Everyone seemed to love the guy,
No matter where they were they always said hi.
And to tell you the truth he was my best friend,
And my heart was broken when his life did end.

Scott McWilliams

No Fear

There is no need to fear the end of our time,
for somewhere there's a land so supremely divine,
where the sun shines all day and the air is so sweet,
from heavenly flowers in the garden where we will meet.

No we will not fear the end of our time,
when the Lord calls us up we'll be waiting in line.
Through the golden gate to His heavenly throne,
to hear the Lord speak "this is now your new home."

There will be old friends and new, all gathered there,
to hear the angels sing and join the Lord in prayer.
What a gathering it will be
all gathered there, under a persimmon tree.

No we will not fear the end of our time,
When the Lord calls us up we'll be waiting in line.
Through the golden gate to His heavenly throne,
to hear the Lord speak "this is now your new home."

Dedicated to Dorothy Elliott

D. M. Seely

For The Want Of Love

Love's flame has flared and my heart has been seared.
For such a torch, my heart was inappropriately geared.
I've witnessed the agony of sleepiness nights.
I've been frequented by the presence of zero appetite.
Rest for me has become a perpetual dream.
My heart has cried out and my soul has screamed.
Be there for me, o loveable one.
Cause not my heart to beat a millionth scorn.
Thrust out your heart to put out the flame.
Put not my love to a miserable shame.

Rowena J. Long

Thanksgiving Thanks

At Thanksgiving time we're mindful of the harvest close at hand . . .
For the bounty of the goodness God's brought forth from this great land . . .
"Thank you for this food." The prayer goes as we soon are
going to eat . . .
But the nourishment your soul needs can't be met with turkey meat!
Not a wing, nor thigh, nor turkey breast can satisfy the soul . . .
When it's hungry for the Word of God you won't find it in a bowl!
So put down yer fork and knife and leave yer napkin on yer plate . . .
Grab the Good Book and get readin'. . . feed that soul for Heaven's sake!
Well, there's recipes on how to love yer kin both good n' bad . . .
And there's recipes 'bout mustard seeds and some recipes are sad!
But the one, by far my favorite, serves all peoples in this land . . .
It's the recipe for salvation served up free as God's great plan!
So remember this Thanksgivin' there's more to life than just the bird . . .
There's the promise of God the Father and His recipes are in His Word . . .
Gather round with all yer kin folk and thank the good Lord up above . . .
Then start dishin' double portions when your servin' up the love!

Kristy Friesen-Ritchie

Reality

Believe in who you are
for things aren't always what they seem
You can stretch the limits of
imagination, fantasy and many wondrous things
But keep reality as the factor to
balance your mind, your hopes and
your dreams.
Remember to always shut your world
down when it seems to take you beyond
your own self.
Sometimes what is within reach is more
than good enough if you open your eyes,
your heart and your soul.
Reality is what you make of it, it
is always alright to strive for more
But remember to keep your head
on straight and you will know when
there is no more.

Michael Madalo

A Touch Of Light

A touch of light that always glow
From that someone who inspired my soul.
Oh how I love to be like thee,
So carefree, happy and cheerful as can be
But through these eyes I begin to see,
That journey may not be as easy for me
So with that little touch of light
I hope you will be there for my sight.

Lila Hicks

Our Beloved Mother And Dad

The light of love forever burns,
For two so loving and dear.
Golden memories remain here
They blessed us in countless ways.
As on the wings of a peaceful dove.
Dear Lord, our ultimate Father, we pray
You lift them gently to your love
As we meet here the tears abundantly flow
But within us all, the light of their love
Will forever glow.
When it comes our time to go,
Where you see a single rose like no other
There is where you'll see our Mother.
Where there's a garden lush and green
There's where Dad will be seen.

Sharon Pankey

"Jesus Precious Love" (Thank You God!)

Thank you "God" for Jesus precious love
for we know that it came from above.
All these blessings we truly don't deserve;
that's why it's only "you we wish to serve.

Thank you God for touching me with your
Holy Spirit for I know that you will give me
strength to keep it. Thank you for giving
me enough love to share with others with
it we can all dwell on being sisters and brothers.

Thank you for giving us the greatest love on earth.
You thought well enough to give it to us from birth.
Thank you most of all for not being like man,
for if you were; we'd all be a non-existent
worthless plan.

Thank you God, for your precious love. Thank you for a
love that means more to me than anyone can
understand; for I know that a love like yours is not
sinking sand.

Laura J. Cawthorne

Reality

Today begins something wonderful,
for which I have waited all of my life.
Through awkward years of one frustration after another,
acne, flat chest, hating boys, changing, waiting,
watching, hoping, longing, and yes even praying,
that someday my dreams will be realized.
Dreams which bring great joy to me because,
I love someone who truly loves me.

Of course though, you may disagree
and take your loneliness in stride,
not miss that warm sweet feeling I get,
way down deep inside.
The man for whom I have waited all of my life,
has just asked me to be the mother of his children,
but first, he wants me to be his wife.

M. J. Glover

Forgotten Past

Forgotten me
Forgotten my love
I live only for my children now
Looking for guidance from above.

Never time for me
Never time for my love
I only think of my children now
The past is so far away.

Parties, Banquets, Proms
A long time will pass.
My memories of our love
Will be fading fast.

The windows blow open
The storm is raging.
Through the roughness two people walk separately.
I can no longer see clearly.

Somewhere our love has gone.
I no longer remember.
Our children are grown, we did a fine job.
But for our love, it is in the forgotten past.

Rebecca Lynn Kingston

A Serial Warfare

Breastplate of Righteousness
    Forwarding THE CALL FROM HIGH
Mockers of confusion and distortion
    Flocking in curves that repeatedly pry.

Brass of the tinkling cymbals
    Dutifully glitter through deceit
Breaking past the umbilical pride
    In hereditary retreat.

Pinnacle of Love opposing
    Amputating scrutiny
Bearing the smoldering fray
    Of the inexperience mutiny.

Breastplate of Love and Faith
    Pervading a rehearsing enterprise
As to challenge the Alumni
    Of the IMMACULATE ON HIGH.

Terri H. Johnson

Call Him Special

Flipping TV channels at a fast pace
Found a program called "The Pet Place"

Finding good homes for dogs and cats is what they do
Today was a special showing, handicaps needing homes too

A young black lab, blind from birth was shown
I knew he was the one I had to give a home

Told by friends it was a mistake
My freedom and time I would forsake

A year later he's proven me right
Pumpkin is not handicapped for not having sight

Heel, sit, stay he tries very hard to please
In obedience school taking second place with ease

Knowing his way around furniture and down the hall
Playing tag, tug of war and catching a ball

Life to him is what a normal dog should be
Not knowing normal dogs can see

Words like gifted or special I say a lot
Calling Pumpkin handicapped, I think not.

Linda Mayer

Winter Angst

The snow falls softy; the birds seek eagerly for food
Found only now in crannies; peaceful is earth's mood.
A blanket of white now covers all but the leaden sky o'erhead
Mirrors the shades of greyness reflecting my heart that feels dead.
This peace of earth dwells not with me; with frantic thoughts I pray
How can my arms give up this child; hands bury a babe on such a day?

Mary Joyce Norwood Rodgers

Where Were You

The news today
Four more men dead
And who cares anymore
It's always the same thing

There was a little boy
Car drove by, shots rang out
The boy lies in a pool of blood
Who should we hate
Just another story on the 6 o'clock news

One man's tale too long to tell
Is another life cut short by ignorance
And the deadly silence
Sweeps across the land in a shower of hate
What is wrong with the world

Made it through another day
The sun slips behind the trees
Bringing in a darkness
That never really left
And something's gone wrong today . . .

Megan Sawyier

If I Was In Charge Of The World

For if the world was in my hands;
Friendship would be the lifelong band.
There would be more hugs,
instead of illegal drugs.
And the voice of violence . . .
would hush to a silence.
Instead of gunshots ringing through the air,
the sound of voices who really care.
Peace would be all around,
for this would be the perfect sound.
Racism would be banished;
for the thought of hatred would vanish.
For if the world was in my hands . . .
I would make love my main command.

Mandy Eise

Cristin

God picked a sweet little bud
From amongst his garden of love
With much love and tender care
He picked the sweetest of them there
While little angels sang in softest voice
Our father made his grandeur choice

From amongst his garden there
With deepest concern to select the perfect pair
While heavenly music was played on harps of gold
The little angels were silenced and told
From among his garden there
To take this little darling to Judie and Eddie Hair

While little angels sang in softest voice
Our Father made his grandeur choice

Mildred J. Douglas

284

I Care

The very thought of you drifts on by,
from a dark entranced cloud floating high.

Can I grasp a feeling that we too both share,
but ones thinking is deeper, do I dare?

I've shared my life, my personal mind,
to reveal such a tenderness sharing kind,
a moment of joy can only fulfill,
my wish to open the arms that remain still.

My frantic endeavor to be close,
takes over my soul, trusting it most.
Forever before, shall I dare speak a word,
To the one that's nearer but never feared.

Oh, please hear my thoughts, feel my tender care
For a moment in time can I only spare
A feeling of love growing stronger yet tame,
Speaks only the truth, but hides no shame.

This truth I share, and unspeakable thought,
in caring with you, I can only be caught.
Shall I plead, shall I beg, never more can I think
Of caring for you through this unbreakable link.

Kelly Witt

The Aleutians

Torn
from earth's convulsive womb,
Threatening
since time primeval,
Stirring
with volcanic fume,
Straining
with inherited upheaval,
Sharp
from clawing seas to restless skies,
Endless
through the clothy clouds
Glacial stumps of jagged rocks rise,
storm scratched stones beneath sepulchral shrouds:
Joke of God —
for nothing lives
and nothing dies.

Lou Guttman

Pain

Pain clouds your heart, it stops your soul
from living the best that you can.
It's a feeling of hurting deep inside
from all of Life's demands.

It may be an illness of Mental Mind,
or Physical from your being.
Pain stops the vision of greater love
it blinds all that you are seeing.

Pain is an sickness inside and out
that torments you day to day,
It's a suffering from other things
You know that leads the pain astray.

You may feel so hopeless bearing pain
Whatever the cause may be
Learn to trust Forces Of the Universe
and the pain will cease . . . and leave.

JDenise

The Day After

Tomorrow smoke drifts up
From the smoldering carcass
Of a once beautiful home.

The children's rooms,
With armies of wooden soldiers
And herds of stuffed animals,
Have forgotten their proud animation
And stand no more.

The immaculate kitchen that once smelled
Of steaming apple pies and freshly baked bread,
Is now an ugly pile of wreckage,
Which only reeks of a fatal smoke.

A family mourns as they stand together,
Facing this monstrosity,
The rooms, the kitchen, the beautiful yard,
Have all been robbed of their vitality,
But, deep beneath a worthless pile of ash,
A tiny seed drinks from fertile soil,
Fighting to begin a new generation
Of beauty and life.

Rebecca Benson

Plagued By Problems

When problems are holding you back
from what you want to achieve.

When you feel like the pain is just so
much to bear.

When you lose someone who you love so
much.

When anger rises in your eyes at
someone for minor reasons.

When you want to scream out the
things wrong with your life.

When you feel like ending all the pain,
anger, losses and problems.

Then look at all of whom you love
and respect, then think about trying
again.

Melizza Pelrine

Am I?

My heart is like a river,
From which flows forth waves unknown,
My thoughts like the wind,
Racing through the shores of time.

My light is in my eyes,
By which I perceive all things,
And my utterance is my tongue,
From which I speak forth good or evil.

But by what do I know I'm a person?
And through what must I judge my being?
To create an end of perfection,
Through a means that's not short of divine.

Well, I know that God gave me a mind to reason,
To control all my thoughts and emotions,
So if I reject this wondrous gift, and put myself to shame;
I think not, therefore, who am I?

Mercy Alu

God's Love Is Splendid

God is to be treasure, a possession, a shining light and a
fruit that need to be tasted.
The spirit radiance beauty, it's beyond human comprehension.
For the formal things are no more, for He is the laud in my book.
God's love is splendid and I know it.

I pray that my relationship will grow in truth and goodness.
For prayer expresses life into my spirit.
Balance of service and worship is the key to my success.
Agreement gives me the power to withstand difficulty.
God's love is splendid and I know it.

Seeking His kingdom first is better than investing in silver,
gold and rubies - soul no gain.
I'll invest my time in pleasing you, it's the things I value the most.
The more I work for you, the greater the respect I will show.
So my heart will be loyal to my God.
God's love is splendid and I know it.

Thurman P. Jones

The Year Of Discovery

I'm consumed by the chill of solitary
Frustrated by your apathy
In a world taught by tragedy
A cold pain rains down on me

Ripping and tearing into me
Anger bites out at me
Taking away any good, if any left in my soul
All I ever wanted is to find peace

When one day that peace was found
Many unanswered questions arose
Burning through my skin
Challenging me in unthinkable ways

Looking back at these times
I came to an understanding
That such things are meant to be
And others are meant for learning

M. J. Fell

Shadows Of Themselves

The dance floor is full
Full of shadows of themselves
I see a shadow of a cheerleader
of a basketball player and a valedictorian

It was the valedictorian doing the wheelchair dance
He danced round and round in his wheelchair

They are deaf, but hear the music
They are blind, but see each other

He stands at the back of the gym
His dreams are filled with driving and girls
He wears a leather jacket and his tie is undone
He is the cool dud shadow
He is the shadow of my dreams
He is my son

Susan Williams

My Dad

My dad is the kind who is loving and caring.
He is the one who is willing and daring.
He is the type who is adventurous and fun.
My dad is not just anyone.

Melissa Sullivan

Tree Of Seasons

Strong, bare oak tree
Fury, stretching out for all to see
Snowy, blowing frigid day
Soon spring will come and fury will
   no longer be for all to see
Soft breezes blow and new leaves grow
Re-birth of a new time
Oak tree branches shaking with laughter
   as children run around my shadow
It makes the summer shine, so warm and bright
Soon the chill in the air will start to sap
   my trunk
While my leaves will dance with sorrow
   and joy
For soon my strong bare seeds will be at rest
Until another time, I will always live to
   be a Tree of Seasons.

Mary P. Bowers

Kaleidoscope Of My Expectations

My expectations are colorful fulfillment, memories, and
future fantasies. They are a chrome colored circle in
my mind. Whenever I want to bring them out, I let them
slide off my umbrella, and they fall to the floor with
little splashes of dreams.

The rainbow in my mind is hidden behind stained glass
windows, kept there by walls of laughter. I can be a
doll of delicate lace, that lives in a jewelry box with
a mirror that spins in a wondrous motion, a mannequin
in my own personal store window, filled with chocolate
creams and little toy drums, or the soft song that
plays on the phonograph.

My mind is a pinwheel of color, pattern, and shape.
Without this beautiful kaleidoscope, I couldn't have
all the things I'd like to; no dreams, adventures, nor
images and their worlds. My kaleidoscope is just a
small part of my soul. My kaleidoscope is a world all
its own. My kaleidoscope is my imagination!

Lori Peterman Joesting

Untitled

For you I fell from the Grace of God,
Gathered stones,
Wandered barren, cold and alone.
To you I was like pennies to the rich;
You spent me like the hoards of conquered king.
Love to you is a silent language lost,
That deftly falls on deafened ears
I can hear.
Your is of flies, maggots and hens;
I thought me once to be content
With the company of spoil
But no more.
You left me licking for little drops of love;
You left me reaching, stretching - kicking
For little scraps of you.
You toyed and played and tightly let me go
Rightly so.
A maid needs no mess and a dog needs no bone.

Megan Heffernan

Mother

She carried you for nine long months and then she
gave you birth. She thought you the most precious
thing God put upon this earth.
She dried your tears, she shared your smiles, she
gave you faith and hope. When times were darkest in
your life she taught you how to cope.

A caring ear was always there when you needed most to
talk. When no one else was there for you, you could
always count on Mom. A mother's love can be compared
to nothing on this earth. She'll love you just as much
in death as she did at your birth.

She's been called home as all of us eventually will be.
To live in peace with our Heavenly Father for all eternity.
So when you think, think happy thoughts, for that's what
she would want. Dry your tears and carry on and don't ask
why or how. She's grown her wings, she's been set free,
for she's an angel now.

Sandy Cundick

Bosnia

Shrieks, screams, terrified cries,
genocide, people lamed, bodies lie.
Blood splattered over wall and dirt
a child clings in terror to his mother's skirt.
He looks up at her with haunted eyes
his mother falls, her child cries
he calls her name
again, again,
why doesn't she speak, where has she gone
a child alone - an orphaned son.

K. A. Stephens

My Boy At Ten

There lives a boy at my house
Gentle ways, quiet as a mouse
Freckles placed and oh so sweet
His glances show him looking neat.
A bell within his head; it rang
Our door went shut, with quite a bang.
Two lions loose he lit a fuse
Anything you wish to choose
This boy I fathom, things to come
Counted all and here's the sum.
Change not my son, for when your grown
You'll have your Kingdom and I my Throne.

Marcella New

A Winter Walk

I took a walk on a pristine, sunlit, winter day.
Gentle windswept patterns lay in the snow at my feet.
Trees are lightly dusted with feathery wisps of snow.
The slanting sun sends sparkling glints of sunlight amid
crisscrossing blue shadows of trees.
As the walk nears the end, the setting sun glows red
across the frozen icescape of the lake.
Painters, sculptors, photographers,
Images only, they create.
But this is the handiwork of the master artist,
who's canvas is the universe.

Sue Olson

My Christmas Gift

As I sat and I talked on the phone with my friend; I stared at the
gift I still had to send. Although Christmas was only one day away;
at home alone I was to stay. Lonely you wonder, why would I be?
That's how I've spent Christmas ever since I was three. My mother's
run off and my father's in jail; no happy stories do I have to tell.
When all of the sudden, what could this be? My friend asked me to
spend Christmas with her family. My eyes got wide and my heart all
aglow; but what kind of gifts would I have to show? Penniless poor
not a dime to my name; my heart fell back and my face was in shame.
But again my friend raised my spirits with one single reply; she said
that no gifts would I have to buy. By the time the night fell and the
sun show bright; my friend's house was almost in sight. She came out
to greet me and pulled me right in; my best Christmas ever was about
to begin. That year I learned more than you'll ever know; not just
about Jesus or new fallen snow. I learned that love can't be put in a
box; it doesn't come in the form of bicycles or sox. It's not like a
pencil which easily breaks; truth, strength, and trust is what true
love takes. Through all of the hustle of the holiday season; warmth
and trust are some of the reasons. For celebrating with joy and
cheer, and welcoming in the start of the year. My friend has shown me
a brand new love; like sent as a gift from far up above. She's proven
to me that real friends do care; of the reasons for love she's made me
aware. Love comes when someone wants to share feelings with you;
desire and hope can make a love true. So what am I trying to tell
you? It's simple you'll see; that some of the greatest parts of
Christmas are friends and family.

Rachel Murphy

If I Could Give The World A Gift

If I could give the world a gift, I would
give a day of only love with thousands
of snow-white doves flying above.

If I could give the world a gift, I would
give a day of only peace, free from lies
and endless cries.

If I could give the world a gift, I would
give a day of hard work, to shelter the
poor from the cold rain and help ease
their pain.

If I could give the world a gift, I would
give the children a day of play with no
monster standing in their way. I would
give them a day free from guns and
their fear of always having to duck and run.

If I could give the world a gift, I would
give a promise of a bright, brand-new
tomorrow free from pain, anger, and sorrow!

Stacey Almany

Season Of Thanks

Gone are the sweltering days
Given way to the cooler northwestern airs
Gardens no longer need tending
Great harvests are greeted with festivities
Grilled foods are replaced with baked meals
Ginger and Cinnamon scent overtake all other aromas
Grains that once billowed in the winds become part of our feasting
Grand Display of fruitfulness and homecomings
    line our thoughts of thanks

Linda Pliodzinskas

You Are Love To Me

Seeing all that you go through, doing things I used to do
Gives me joy and love and laughter, hate and sorrow, happy rapture
Knowing those mistakes I've made, teaching you the dues I've paid
But words can only be the start of love that reaches lonely hearts
   And you are love to me

Playing games that never end; to be together, being friends
To laugh with you and see you smile or even just to spend awhile
Riding horses, planting flowers just to look at them for hours
Growing up is all a part of love that reaches anxious hearts
   And you are love to me

If I could tie you in a chair and hold you high up in the air
To save you from the growing pains like heartache, boyfriends;
Loves own shame and show paths to learn loves truth . . .
Oh, what I'd give to save your youth
But words can only teach so much, its love that adds the final touch
   And you are love to me

Your life's beginning to take form and though I try to help and warn
You of the dangers that you face; what's done today you can't erase
Tomorrow when you look around to see your past and smile or frown
Remember, Mommy told you so . . . it's love that deals the final blow
   And you are love to me

Virginia Botica

Mother

Crystal light broken
Glass edges sharper
By lunar light reflected
I blue eyes vastness
Turning your head towards me
By silken hair of brown smells swirl
Your by hazel eyes whole and open
Moon, star, planet turn inside out connection.
My love my sacred lover.
Summer breeze with milk cloud scent
Of grass cut leaves burning
Bring home your warm body offering
As doors close and sunlight drops
Never separate our embrace
My love my aching love.
Morning calling with busy screams
Of our children's nest disturbed
By worries of what's to come or how small they are
Your soft embrace assuring quietness
Their love my mother earth of all love.

F. Jeffris Elliott

Just Get Down And Pray

Though you may be sick and ill
God is gonna love you still.
When your feeling down and out
and maybe can't make it through the day
Don't scream and shout, that's the devils way
Instead just get down and pray.
The Lord would never hurt you or make you sad
Remember he is a good God, not bad.
The Lord is by your side all the while
Ne need to say thank you, just give him a smile.
Everything is going to work out okay
All you need to do is just get down and pray.
God loves you and all the people in your life,
Your children, Grandchildren and your wife.
Your well being is in Gods hands
Just like the poem "Footprints in the sands".
So when times seem to get rough
and you think you've had enough
Just remember what I say
All you need to do is "Just get down and pray."

Theresa Wahner

Por Joaquin

The sun of Cortez awaits, splendid creature;
glide on across the *verrraanda*.
Indio, northern, Azteca by height —
flaunt before me your ancient glory.
Obey, conquered race!
A cowl of black feathers glistens so
in the huge yellow eye of the sun.

Speak of yourself, mighty Montezuma;
of a past violently severed.
Dreams of dreamers superimposed,
I am a conquistador deserving of revenge.
Obey, conquered race!
Passions possible remain aloof, distant and
unfathomable as galaxies far flung.

Glide on now, I bid you — *con permiso*;
toward passions less urgent, more familiar.
Dolorous yet resigned to our parting,
dismissal remains my only power over you.
And I say, "Obey, conquered race!"
Above a cowl of black feathers triumphantly waves
the tattered remnants of regret. — *Adios*.

Susann Maccia

A Rose

I awoke one Spring morning so alive, full of freshness.
Glowing, secure in my bed, I was ready for this world.

I knew my beauty and perfect shape were tempting,
virginal; not one could pass without wanting me.

I was sure a battle was evident to remain untouched,
when I felt his stout grip tugging at me.

I fought back daring, clinging to my bed with
all my might. Stabbing at him was my only defense.

I trembled, though relieved. His hands trickled with
blood, as he walked away. I won that time.

I am uneasy this morning, unsure why, till I see him,
coming towards me again, armed more heavily than I.

I know his hunger is my doom, though death won't be sudden.
He cut at me, I fell limp. He carried me away.

I was drenched in liquid to ease the pain. I know
only a few more days until all my beauty fades.

Katrina B. Findley

Untitled

This Billy Graham whom we all know
God gave Him a master plan to help souls
Were all looking for something (of what we don't know)
But just call up Jesus He'll let you know
Just think no appointment to even make
He'll even listen to us without wink
He never say no only at times take it slow
As he's our Master He ought to know
Regardless of how bad, dirt all the way down
He's always reaching out as all good father do
To take our lives mold and heal them to his own
He makes a better person of us in everyone sight
No more worries about the coming years
As we trust more in him the fears disappear
Gee it's great to lie down at night, knowing when I awake all is alright
When my year or numbers is a all up
I'll go to join him in heaven angels and all
Once again I'll thank him for sending a Billy Graham
A man who made me see I have a Great God
As my dearest and best friend.

Shirley Snyder

"Murder's Mime"

He came in time to watch it go, in time it was to see her low,
Go and hold and leave alone a hardened face staring moaned.

Ourselves at ourselves—a wall most hold—if by patience soon
Unwilling thy grinds go cry: Enfold!

Drawing back yielded more too kind, see in the eye how looking pleads,
Longing begs some ordinal deed.

Why should this blow not be brought around, deeper looking longings
Found. In the eye milky glassed the haze of death comes strong
for Mass.

By first blows which opened fat, man's left eared and hearing flat.
No more lost to this imbalance crossed, of upright standing
watching Light,

Falls from a strike again' the night. One so twitched and twitched
Did thrash about, spewed, and sputtered, was spilled in flout.

Distraught, open, broken carriage same thoughts pour from both:
Perish! Chilling, petrified, belly churns, the nauseous living
Learned yet yearns.

The dead one spun and turned and turned now his is resting,
Anon mine shall burn.

Richard Jackson Ussary

A Sparrow Falls

A sparrow fell from the sky
God has seen, he cares, he will cry
Since he cares so deeply for one little sparrow
Think of this love for you in your time of harrow
God want's to pick you up however far you fall
He will always be there to answer your call
God will solve all your worries, don't fret
Trust in him and have no regret
He knows you just as well
As that little sparrow that fell

Linda J. Anderson

Untitled

Jesus is God, beware of the jew.
God is God, is the belief, they chose.
Burning in hell, if Jesus isn't thy Lord,
Is a sentence hitler proclaimed, in the war.
You can be an atheist, some will understand,
But a catholic, protestant or jew, woe unto man.
Every belief on earth, claims they are true,
Lord, God or nothing, leaves only you.
Who's left to ask, "What shall I do?"
When you know peace, and are no longer lost,
You've heard the truth, from a voice very soft.
Your soul can rest, your mind is set free,
When all are equal, you have seen me.

Maurine Fergueson

The Grease Fire

No one understands her cry every night she
goes to sleep and wonders why
people ask her are you okay
she replies tomorrow's another day
she hopes everyday will get better,
but the grease fire is only getting wetter
by the water that keeps on flowing
that grease fire keeps on glowing
no one understands at all
that baking soda is what's needed for a call
the solution to the problem is great
but, there will still be burns
on that pan's bottom plate.

Lacee New

God Sees

For all the struggling ones trying in the night
    God sees.
For all the lonely ones crying in the night
    God hears.
For all the little ones dying in the night
    God cries.
To all those oppressing the struggling ones
    God sees!
To all those tormenting the lonely ones
    God hears!
To all those snuffing out the light of the little ones
    God cries.
For your life will be swallowed by eternal night!
    And God laughs.
For the little ones now play in His garden.

Nancy Mako

Master Piece

Empty and void darkness on the deep,
GOD spoke into existence a world fast asleep.
Gave light to the heaven and earth down below,
Hung the stars out on nothing gave command to glow.

A gentle stroke at the universe the artist worked so at ease,
To fashion and create such a great master piece.
While skillfully working and giving command,
He looked at the blueprint of his great master plan.
Things brought forth after their kind, He spoke and it was so,
Yet still He kept pressing; He had more work to go.
Looking at all His labor, yet still more creating to His plan,
And last but not least, He made a man.
From the dust of the earth in His likeness to be,
He molded and shaped him carefully.
And given dominion over all he could see,
All living creatures, every green herb, every tree.
In six days finally all things were done,
Heaven and earth were finished, and all things under the sun.
On the seventh day all labors did cease;
And finally completed was a great Master Piece.

Linda Sheppard

Buds

Like the petals of a newborn rose
Gradually unfolding into life
One velvety petal at a time, till open to the light.

Blossoming into beautiful completeness
Over time and trials immense
Ever struggling to maintain and grow
Gaining strength that wasn't hence.

Sharing in the sunshine, the warmth of summer days
Thru loves who come and taste the scent
Then wander on their way.

Even tho the rain falls sometimes
Thru the darkest storms of life
Hanging on with all the strength
Manage somehow to survive.

Thru all our life together
Till our winter comes to claim
Even then our lives incarnate, thru lives to come again.

My best and closest bud . . . my friend . . .
My strength thru times distraught
May our friendship flourish and forever grow — never to be forgot.

Linda L. Hightshoe

Pretty Pretty Things

A shop window withered with time, tissue paper sprinkled with snow
Green boughs and holly, twinkling lights, the window comes alive.
Shoppers stop by, a gift for someone dear,
From the pretty pretty things in an old shop window.
The moon rides the ridge making diamonds sparkle on crystal snow.
Somewhere I hear a sleigh bell, could it be Santa's sleigh?
Piled high with pretty pretty things for Christmas Day.
Busy hands doing pretty things, placing a wreath upon the door.
The angel to the top of the tree, someone turns a switch,
The tree is all aglow, casting its light on ribbons and bows,
And the pretty pretty things below.
In the stillness of the night a church bell rings.
The lighted windows on the snow, lights a pathway to the door.
In candlelight the choir sings the pretty carols,
Prayers go out for peace, and the beauty of Christmas awaits us,
With all the pretty pretty things.

   Louise Murdock

Psychedelic Realities

Forests lost to nothing relevant
Green skyscrapers wafting no longer in
The North Pacific wind.
Indians losing more than just their identity
Americans, not native, using catch phrases to
Sugar coat their indecencies.

It's a hungry world we live in,
And nothing quenches our thirst
It's a crazy life to live in,
When we no longer believe in psychedelic realities.

Supernatural's not the in thing
He can't believe in a greater presence
Who can make his life have purpose
It would mean he'd lose his rationality
Are we the next endangered species?
Perhaps we've always been.

It's a lonely life we're living, running
Into everything we're running from
It's a crazy life we're living, never letting
Ourselves believe in psychedelic realities.

   E. A. Deering

My Love

For this Winter's cold is upon me
Ground turned hard and still
Our trees, bare and lifeless
Sky bleak and filled with clouds of gray
The silence of Winter hath fallen upon me
All is asleep, but nay for me
For there is sleep not
This cold pounds at the warmth of my heart
And it will not be still
As soul laden with such deep sorrows
I can only but, long for this Spring
Flowers to awaken in the warmth of your sun
Birds to return to trees filled with new life
And our seeds to plant
My heart longs for the rose in my garden to bloom
So, I hold to the scent of this distant flower
For now,
My love, this Winter's cold is upon me
And I can but, only wait . . .
   for Spring.

   Juliana

Gift To The Bride

There was a young man named Tim,
had a dark-haired beauty betrothed to him,
now, if he gets haughty, or ever treats her naughty
a rolling pin's wrapped here within.

Wooden spoons are here also, all three,
in case any children there be
'cuz one never know if naughtiness flows
from father to child, possibly.

This rhyme's just a tale, you know,
all can see that this groom's not a foe!
We all wish you the best—pray this marriage be blessed
by the Father, the Son, and Holy Ghost.

   Kathleen Finney

Rachel

She walks through the wheat field, an obvious contrast to her dark hair.
Thinking of nothing, yet everything as well.
Careful yet carefree

With book in hand, she sits and reads, and soon sings, and writes,
and dances, and is gay.
When night grows nigh, she travels back home, not the same path
but different,
for tomorrow she will rise again
and walk through that wheat field and read,
and sing,
and write,
and dance,
and be gay.

   Megan M. Kesterson

College Daydream

Costumed are we for order and rule
Hair arranged and buttons tight
Pages we read and lines we write
Quietly, with great rewards in mind.

Hidden is our inherent urge
To throw off bonds and wave our hair
To dance like natives in the night
Clad in loin cloth.

What a joyous sight our tribe would be
I ponder with affection
Laughing, smiling, passions of the flesh!
But no—there's work to be done.

   Michael B. Bratten

"Contrasts"

Buzzards can be beautiful,
Hang-gliding in the sky,
Gracefully floating on currents of air
   as if motionless.
Suddenly rising,
Softly banking,
Lazily idling.

Abandoning flight-sustaining winds,
Like cackling witches round their bubbling brew.
They dive earthward to begin a bloody-orgy,
   a putrid ritual,
Ripping flesh,
Picking bones,
Tearing life.

Oh, Spring skyward,
Soar swiftly,
Circle unceasingly,
Be beautiful again.

   Martha McConnell Oekerman

Always With Me

There once was a girl
Hair coal black; gentle like a pearl.
  She comes off outgoing and wild;
But on the inside she is timid and mild.
  'How do I know,' you must wonder.
My answer is, 'It is to me this girl ponders.'
  It is to me this girl tells her worries;
I am the first to know when her glasses get blurry.
  This girl can laugh all day at school;
Then at home she'll cry enough to fill a pool.
  At her desk she'll reach over for a tissue;
While writing notes saying, "Dear friend, I miss you."
  She is always with me; I have no choice;
When she had no thoughts I use to rejoice.
  But now I cannot live without her;
I guess I'd forgotten what I have to offer.
  You are probably wondering who I am;
I do not have a name like Laura or Sam.
  All at once I am here, watching and sitting on a bell;
For I am that girl's guardian angel.

   Nicki Zevola

I Lived Once . . .

I lived once, where a little boy with rosy cheeks and muddy
  hands reached up to me.
Where there were chickens and cows and horses, and the little
  boy ran free.

I lived once, in a small town where a young boy could walk to
  school.
I told him it was a nice place with streets and stores,
  but he wasn't fooled.

I lived once in the city, where a young man could work and
  get a college degree.
He said he would learn and earn all he could, so he could go
  back to where he once was free.

   Phyllis Sackman

What Am I To Do Without You

Every day I begin my endless search for someone new.
Happiness eludes me, love excludes me, what am I to do without you.
There are too many faces of lost souls.
That seek escape from the pain they hold.
In the vast emptiness that surrounds the lonely heart.
Begins a bond with the pain I feel since we have been apart.
The days get longer, the nights get lonelier, and the pain grows stronger.
I ask myself every day how I could love someone that cause me so
much pain.
I look for answers, I ask the questions but it's just something
no one can explain.
It's been two years since you left and the pain isn't gone yet.
There can be only one answer I love you, so what am I to do without you

   William J. Weeks

Rushing Water

Rushing water through the woods.
Hear the wind, hear the birds, hear the trees.
Rushing water through the woods.
Hear the crystal clear water
roaring down the hill.
Rushing water through the woods.
Hear the world all around you.
Rushing water through the woods.
Thank you God for
sounds in the woods.

   Sara Marie Martinez

Amaranthine Dirges

Lurid conflagration in the acrid aureole of this culpable angel
  has emaciated in the abyss of dereliction,
We belong to a celestial ambiance, skies of incandescent
  carmine which possess no restriction.
Amorphous complexions embowered by calamitous shadows;
  amidst the realms of phantasm life is dormant and ligneous,
Where cravens once hid beneath a desiccated salvation, the eyes
of
  the sardonic grow phlegmatic and igneous.
Credulous alacrity distorted by eradication left you defiant
  with a soul irreparable from the ambient mordacity
Volant convulsion divulged your concealed apprehension, yet
  rigidly relentless you were the lyrics of audacity.
Indissoluble aspersion deafened each menacing fiend, and
  conquered their futile minds, but like all evanescent luminaries
  you too slept in the embers of demise,
Dolorous lamentation deliquesces through duration, yet these
  Amaranthine Dirges shall be sung as immortal cries,
Callow to caliginous triste you are temerarious and eradicate all
  sorrow.
Today, love is only cacophony, Cupid is inaudibly droning for
  he subsists only for a nebulous tomorrow

   Lisa Ann Menzel

The Stranger

The stranger walks along the streets,
Hat pulled low on his brow.
He slinks along, feet over feet,
And looks up every then and now.
The street light glints off of his sunglasses,
Hiding eyes of love and of passion.
He makes his way through the crowd of masses,
Determined not to take action.
His collar is pulled up against the wind,
A futile attempt to fight it.
It's useless for the cold slinks its way in,
Clawing and numbing and biting.
Most of his life is fighting and struggling,
Not hand to hand but wit against wit.
It's all these problems that he's always juggling,
He's tired of biting the bit.
The stranger is struggling with the stranger within,
Set up for a major fall.
You know, I really identify with him,
But then again, don't we all?

   William S. Entrekin

Autumn

The forests beautiful; So green to behold
Have now turned to shades of crimson and gold
Magnificent trees stand majestic and tall
In all of their splendor; For the season is fall

A wonderful day; Gently a breeze blows by
The rustling leaves seem to whisper and sigh
And as if ever so weary of waving around
They silently let go and float to the ground

The little squirrels so frisky and gay
No longer run through the trees at play
So busy storing food for they seem to know
That soon cold wintry winds will blow

And so as the sun slowly sets in the West
With the last lingering rays the trees look their best
Like waves of the sea they shimmer and sway
To a gentle breeze of a bright Autumn Day

   Romano Vergerio

So Much Beauty To See

Have you ever seen the moonlight on the ocean?
Have you ever seen the mist across the moors?
Have you ever seen the gleaming snowcapped mountains?
Or watched huge waves that pound against the shores?
Have you ever seen the Grandeur of the Canyon?
Or seen the splendor of Niagara Falls?
One can only feel an awesome wonder
As the sight of their magnificence enthralls.
Have you ever seen the Islands of Hawaii?
Or the islands of the Caribbean sea?
Have you ever seen the gardens throughout England?
They are all as charming as can be!
Have you ever seen the loveliness of Venice?
(When it was the way it used to be?)
Have you ever seen the sparkling bright blue waters
That form a sapphire setting for Capri?
Have you ever strolled the Boulevards of Paris?
Such delightful sights are there to see!
And have you ever seen Grenada in the twilight?
All these things are beautiful to me.

Madeleine Matthews

Untitled

Darkness is so full of mystery,
Having a past of an evil history,
It seems so still and very soothing,
Yet that is because nothing is moving,
When you hear a creak or even a noise,
It tightens your muscles and lessens your joys,
You begin to think what could that be,
But because of the darkness you cannot see,
You hear it again and now you're aware,
That it's not just the darkness so you take a dare,
You jump off your bed and run across the floor,
As you reach the other side you grab for the door,
As you flick on the lights and look all around,
You realize it's the cat as he lies on the ground,
Now very relieve as you turn off the light,
You are back in the darkness without any sight.

Mike Southwell

Life Is Just Too Short

Breathing, coming into a new day,
Having no control, nothing to say
Being held in your mother's hands,
'Til the time you stroll in the earth's sands.

Talking, having fun with all your friends,
Striving to go straight through all the bends
Do not mind what they say of your wrath,
Never slide over, stay on your path.

Schooling, making something of your life,
Doing it for yourself and a wife
Don't worry about each little shove,
Nothing will wrong you with your found love.

Aging 'til God calls you to his side,
Leaving your love with nothing but pride
Not coming back, with all left to sort
The clock ran out, Life was just too short

Mike La Ham

Wisdom

See with your eyes the depth of the heart.
Hear with your ears the voices of strength.
Feel with your hands the joy of creation.
Taste with your tongue the flavor of differences.
Smell with your nose the scent of hope.
Remember the innocence of being a baby and grasp the
   truth of love.

Linda M. Farha

Our Dad

Our DAD was always there for us, no matter what it was.
He cared and did all that he could, he did it just because.
We fell out many times; You see, he argued, fussed and swore.
But when we needed him to be, he was there just like before.
He loved us and we loved him; we needed never to despair.
No other DAD could take his place, no other could compare.
Through ups and downs he stood his ground, as stubborn as a mule.
But mean and hard as he made out to be, he stretched out every rule.
He worried and cared not just for us, but for all of his loved ones.
He helped not only us, but everyone, who needed something done.
Healthy as a horse, or sick as can be, he never turned away.
He, always, helped everyone he could, until his dying day.
Now he's gone home to pearly gates, he'll suffer pain no more.
I know he will be welcomed into heavens open door.
We love him and we'll miss him, but the LORD, HE Loved him best.
That's why the LORD touched his soul, and took him home to rest.
He's in good hands, he's doing fine, this life he did depart.
But he'll always live amongst us all, because he's in our hearts.

Lillie Lewis

Ernie A Memorial

He drove too fast - the boy at the wheel.
He caused the death of his "friend", the heel.
The driver went free, justice not done.
The law wasn't fair, the guilty won.
Though years have passed, we can't forget
His handsome face before us yet.

So many things he liked to do,
Music, fishing, cooking too.
Still, most of all, like any boy,
He loved his car; his pride and joy.
He fixed and fussed; new wheels he bought.
Had it painted, got rid of the rot.

Beloved by all who knew him well:
Now gone to heaven with Christ to dwell.
He left a legacy of love.
A gift sure given from above.
We miss him so, this lad so fair.
Lord tell him Please, how much we care.

Rose D. Krikorian

"Gentle Ben"

He was a gentle man; unable to hear, yet he heard:
   He couldn't speak, yet his soft 'voice' gave
Credence to improvised decibels, and his eyesight
   Was impoverished, yet he 'saw' things others only
'THOUGHT' they did!

And he was always stroking hair that has long since
   Left him bald; his skin was rough and lined, like
The bark of an Oak still standing strong.

While this description might fit many, it doesn't,
   Really; in reality it was my own image as an old
Man when looking in the mirror, but in dreams of
   Days long past!

Robert H. Wyatt Sr.

The Tundra

While standing on the frozen tundra, I notice a polar bear
He is walking across the tundra which is older than the sands of time
His coat is like a giant, wooly blanket
In the subzero temperatures, it keeps him warm and snug
The whiteness of his coat is equal to a thousand opal rings
Making his coat shine brighter than the crown of a king
A penguin is the next animal I see
He always dresses very elegantly
This allows him a pass to the ball or an opera hall
The glaciers look like frozen skyscrapers
You could also say that they are giant ice cube towers built by a child
When pieces from the glaciers break away, they produce a giant spray
They tumble into the cool, blue water without a bit of grace
A whale shoots out a column of water from her blow hole
Welcoming me during my stay in her frozen Arctic home
The sky overhead looks dark and overcast
If anyone asks, I would forecast more snow
In my igloo, I will stay until the snow goes away
Hopefully, it will now last the whole day

Margaret Barry

Through The Rug

I saw a soul of a man
   He knelt down before me and shook my hand

This apparition of a man was old
   But the words he spoke were true and bold

He spoke of words I have not heard
   About some event that had occurred

In the horizon he faded off
   But before he left, he took me to a loft

In the lost I saw such strange things
   Purple trees with flapping wings

The lost was filled with magic, colors, and stars
   Green people driving in walking cars

I made my way through the throng
   While singing a sunny blissful song

While in daze, I turned back
   Then felt I a great smack

What I had just seen I thought was reality
   But, there was my sister hitting me

I sat and thought had I touched a drug?
   No, I had fallen through the rug.

Tom Targonski

The Griffin

The griffin sniffed the evening air,
He scented an enchantment there.

He wondered what the magic bode,
As the stars across the heavens rode.

He stretched his wings to feel the breeze,
That blew the glamour through the trees.

He splayed his claws to pull it in,
And then . . . he let it go again.

He somehow knew his time was done,
Though it seemed to him it had just begun.

He felt griffin-kind begin to fade,
Into patterns of light and dappled shade.

His sigh of resign was never heard,
As he passed from earth without a word.

Sharon Pasach

My Happy Snowman

I made a happy snowman, when the winter snow had come,
He made my friends and me so happy, we had so much fun.
I made him very big, he stood so straight and tall,
I made him very carefully so he would never fall.

He made feel so jolly around him I would run,
Then one day he disappeared in the morning sun.
I was so sad, I cried a tear, when he went away,
Without my happy snowman, it's hard to run and play.

I dreamed of my snowman so happy and so tall,
He said "don't cry, I'll be back after the leaves fall,
Just watch for a snow flake, and many more will come".
I waited for that storm, so long it made me numb.

I put my mittens on my hands, and boots upon my feet,
I went to work, he needed my help and soon we would meet.
There he will be, my happy friend, with a smile upon his face,
He'll stand so straight and be so tall in that very same place.

He's here again, I'll run and play,
Until that next warm sunny day,
Then on that I won't shed a tear,
I know my happy snowman will be back again next year!

Sharon Munoz

"My Dream"

I dreamed I saw Jesus coming down from
Heaven above.
His face looked so gentle and filled with love.
But he saw that I was frightened and held out his hand to me.
He said "take my hand and follow me and see."
He showed me the fields the flowers and trees
also the lakes and the great big seas
all this I have given you while down here on earth.
But God up in heaven has laid away treasures
for greater than all these earthly things are worth.
Then he slowly faded away from my sight
and I learned to have trust and faith
from the dream I had that night.

Margie Carhill

Help

Help! I think I'm falling.
Help! I don't know what to do.
Help! I'm going down fast.
   I don't know if I can last.
   I've had a bad past.
   What should I do?
   My past has caught up with me.
   I'm going down.
   Faster! Faster!! Faster!!!
Help! I'm going to hit the ground.
Help! I don't want to die this way.

   JESUS SAVE ME!!!

Whosoever shall call on the name of the Lord, shall be saved.

Acts 2:21

Lela Pendergrass

A Mother, A Son, A Divorce

The shadows look down upon us,
Hiding the moon.
Or is it the lampshades upon the lamps,
In this room.
I look in your little eyes, not as glowing as before,
You look into mine too.
I see the pain in those little eyes,
I'm sorry I hurt you.

Richard Maltsbarger

293

The Vestal Virgins

To a cold goddess with a marble face we give unending praise.
Her face is noble, her figure purine.
But beneath her smooth, snow-white surface there beats no heart
warm and human,
No blood traverses her body of stone, no flicker sparks her vacant eyes,
No glint of compassion, no hint of passion

She merely stands before us, her perfect mouth tightly pursed,
her perfect brow slightly drawn
With an expression of ice, with eyes that never blink, not even for an instant.
Then she must have seen me when I looked up from my prayer in
this monastery of stone
And silence. When I quickly sent a glance and my heart towards
the mountains where you are

For this treason, unfaithfulness, I could be killed.
From earliest youth I have been consecrated, condemned to live a perfect life.
For but one of my dreams I could be buried alive in a cave of stone
with only a dim light to guide me, with nothing to sustain me but a
loaf of bread and your love

But my whole life I have been buried alive in my world of stone;
I am sure I should find comfort in such a final resting place.
If, but for a moment, our hands would touch and, for an instant,
our lips would meet, for this I would suffer a thousand more years
of idle prayer or an eternity buried beneath fertile soil

From my living grave I would sing of love and life and joy and you
Sing till my lungs would fill no more, till another goddess, being
moved to pity, would let me fall asleep, cradled in the earth's
loving arms, dreaming of you.

Teresa Manidis

Grandma

Her eyes grow dim as the years grow on.
Her hair has turned from brown to grey.
Knitting needles are now packed away
where once they were as important to everyday
life as a coffee spoon.
She had taken care of me from the time I was born,
now I take care of her.
Life is strange like that.
She has lived a long life full of good times and
bad times alike.
The last dozen years have been especially
hard on her since grandpa passed away.
She feels alone, yet never reaches out to anyone.
Her house was once as alive as a puppy
in springtime, but now reeks of loneliness
and shattered dreams.

Lisa L. Pingatore

Through The White Piano

Maria sits at the white piano.
Her hands fly over the keys
like caged birds, beat their wings
on the bars,
and trapped, they seek freedom in a song.
The melody so wild and sweet; it whispers, shouts,
of a thousand wishes and desires.
Her slender, bird like body rocks with the music,

The rhythm

Pulses in her heart, runs through her blood.
The music is in her soul,
upon it's wings she flies.
Maria sits at the white piano
on cold dark nights,
because freedom is expression,
and the bird within her sings.

Rebecca Dondlinger

My Mother

Because she's there when I need
her most, and I know she'll always care.

My mother's like no other mother,
because she's Her and Only Her!

She's loving, and kind, and beautiful too.
I love you mother because you're YOU.

Keyonna Diane Kidd

Love, Above And Beyond

In time of need and distress she will always be there
Her motherly love is beyond compare
Will anyone else in this world be so dedicated
As she who is often loved and appreciated

I have seen some Mothers begging on the street
Carrying their dear ones and hugging them complete
May be this is instinct that keep together
Because she is the one who bore the pain and stormy weather

Some are unfortunate but some are lucky
To have them with you to love and be plucky
Well! these are plans from the one above
Trying our patience and endurance and love

There are times when in trouble you really need her
But alas she is gone and come back never ever
Some day let us hope we'll meet her on the other side
To bring back good memories and walk far and wide

P. Samaranayake

Daddy

Alas, this day is born a child
Her presence makes my heart beat wild
The love I feel for this new child
Can't be known by thoughts most wild.

Alas, this day is born a child
Who one day soon will call me "Daddy"
I hope she will feel as did this child
When I first called my father "Daddy".

The world is a place of people gone batty
So driven, so urged to act to badly
The world is a place where people live sadly
Because they have no one to call their "Daddy".

A "Daddy" must be a beacon of light
To help his children get through the night
A "Daddy" must be a beacon of light
To teach his children to do what's right.

Alas, this day is born a child
God's love is gentle, meek and mild
A "Daddy" dreams in dreams most wild
That his love, like God's, will be so mild.

Michael P. Masek

Year-End Reflections

Summer's gone with all its flowers
Here to stay are winter hours.
But, do not fret my friend, for you will see
The holidays will bring good cheer and glee.
Snow will cover all the ground
No singing birds are to be found.
Nature has this change of season
For us to meditate and reason.
The gift of love we must give
To nourish us and help us live.

Terry Scatola

Euthanasia

Euthanasia, euthanasia, garishly graceful euthanasia.
Here I am, here I stand; ready, holding heart in hand to greet you
And meet you. Come to me sweet and light, envelope me
From the heights to the depths of my soul surrounding
Me with the whole of your seeing and your being.
Euthanasia, euthanasia, shockingly soothing euthanasia.
Over here, take me now, gently, as you see me bow in submission
To your will. Poised with trust upon the hill of the void, not
Annoyed, I hear your promise. No alarm is in your tone or fingers
Warm as you touch and retouch me.
Euthanasia, euthanasia, cruelly calming euthanasia.
I have sought you far and wide, questing your aid to decide.
Asked your name, traced your fame, then you came - yes, you
came.
Euthanasia, euthanasia, patiently promising euthanasia.
Take me now, here and now, on this warming grassy mound in
morning's
Light, crisp and clean. Magnificent is nature's scene cloaking me
And choking me, but nothing here I do I fear, all is rightly bright
And clear. Take my core with my share of grief, intensely hiding
There, never to sever, forever and ever.
Euthanasia, euthanasia, deadly definite euthanasia.

M. Margaret Clark

Untitled

I grow in a place where I feel safe, it's always silent to the sound
Here I stay praying for the day that I would soon be found
Trying to live on my own would be impossible for me to do
A combination of the sun and rain make all my dreams come true
My purpose in life is to spread my joy, at least that's what is said
I appear in several pretty colors but, my prettiest color would be red
In summer I grow, in winter it snows which causes me to mourn
At this time, I have thorns representing those who have been
scorned
Buried beneath the snow, I cannot grow, in time I will start to wilt
And if I die, my dreams are gone for I personally cannot be rebuilt
It's not dying I'm afraid of, it's the thought of being dead
Hopefully I will go to heaven and tell of the joy that I once spread
For those who haven't figured this out, like me you are left in the cold
But before I close, I'll reveal my name, I'm the one and only
precious Red Rose

Randy Darnell Ramey

Nothing More

I guess you think, I'll go somewhere to cry
hide in shadow, my feelings, hope to die
in sorrow, run to vengeance seek,
forgetting how to turn the other cheek

Not so! Heartless one! You know me not!
Since yesterday, I've changed a lot
Time was to throw caution to the wind,
time lost, never to come again
So few the feelings that we share,
lost awhile ago, somewhere

So walk away, so tall so proud
no sorrow here, a laughing crowd
my love waits! I've yet to meet,
to take my hand, to kiss my cheek
So walk my love, just close the door,
we'll say goodbye,
  and nothing more . . .

Renee Pimental

Ballet Of The Boughs

The street I live on leads to the sea,
High rise condos cut off the view for me.
However, the trees that border
each side of our street.

Have a message for me that is wild and sweet!
As far as the eye can see green boughs are etched
Against a cloudless sky in traceries
a consummate artist sketched;
Below my terrace the gentle palms
with sun-silvered leaves
Bow, pirouette sweeping the ground, coquettishly sky!
Opposite them, the stalwart oaks stand silently by;
Then I recall that many philosophers
Hold that someday Nature will come to gold!
Everything in Nature will come to consciousness . . .
In nature's mysterious progressiveness!

As we, as humans made our way
Upward through millennia
So too does Natures strive to reach Arboreal Nirvana!
Is Nature our partner or rival in the race for survival?

Marguerite M. Moore

Carson

Waking up to my son, his smile a sweet reward.
His brilliant eyes liberating me with their love.

Words that follow a new title, syllables he pronounces
just for me.
A hand in mine directing me towards play, reluctant
breakfast needs to be made.

A face with traces of his meal in quick flight to
catch the day as it unfolds.

The garden draws him with the smell of earth wet
and enticing worms burrowing out of sight.

His fingers knead the dirt as if to form a pie,.
tasting the gritty texture he smiles with delight.

Katie Schilling

Resolution

Passing weeks wearing, at a once fecund mind
His dearest memories . . . fading with the time

He know she is waiting, but does not know why
He knows the look of recognition in your eyes

The comfort of your presence dissipates
quickly, like the heat from a long embrace

The solemn stare of a sole confused
His only son, a stranger he once knew

He wants it to end, but the means has escaped
He wants to remember, but the memories evade

His only past is his present thought
His only past . . . consumed, sitting alone in the austere room
By the audible ticking of the cold clock

Steve Paul Woodard

Painful Separations

Three days since I saw you last.
Heart rotting with black cancer.
Across a wide ravine, unable to touch.
Thirty miles away, across a turbulent sea.
Speaking as easily as to the mighty hawk,
Flying far above me.
I know soon we shall meet.
Patience bridging the wide gulf.
Longing to hold you, to ease the painful separation.

Douglas Ward

Austin

As I crawl from my warm bed the night sky is still filled with heavenly stars. Their beauty and stillness are so tranquil. I say a silent prayer. The eastern sky is rosy pink as the sun chases the stars from the sky. The promise of a new day and all it's challenges is reflected in the brightening colors of the sunrise. I say a silent prayer. The splendor of the sun as it rises through the morning mist behind the hills. I travel a new road through orchards and hillsides that soon will be houses and shopping malls. The still quiet beauty is reflected in the hills. I say a silent prayer. An owl out hunting late swoops silently across the road. A lone hawk sits on a pole watching for his morning breakfast in the fields. I thank God for His wonderful creatures. I marvel at all Gods splendors I have seen already. How warm and comfortable we are and I wonder about how many more splendors our ancestors experienced each day when they lived outside and knew each star in the heaven by name and position and waited to see if the sun would rise or would the world be dark forever. They too must have said a silent prayer. Evening. The western sunset, as beautiful and colorful as His sunrise pinks, golds, silvers, blues and cremes, a display of color. The ocean sparkles and reflects the setting sun and the lights come on as a huge full moon peeks over my shoulder. I say a silent prayer.

Betty Winchester

Untitled

Is it not her lips you long to kiss;
Her arms that draw you in and hold you close?
Is it not her eyes that lure you deep inside
To another realm of being?

Go there now to find her waiting;
Go there now to find yourself —
Free from the chains that bound you,
Free from the walls around you;
Naked in the light of her soul,
You will find your heart.

Amy Leonard

Messenger Of Love

Tonight an angel is with us
Her necklaces is the glow of the stars of yesteryears
Every feather of her wing is a rainbow
She is flying
Her wing feathers are pointing in toward her heart
and stretched out to the outer universe
Tonight she is the messenger of honest and unconditional love
She is getting closer to the sun
The sunlight swallows her feathers one by one
There are no more signs of the rainbows
She melts and becomes a haze
She then turns into a drop
With the rain she lands on a rose pedal
hoping, that some day
a bird will sing the story of love to her
Tonight an angel is with us

Fereidun Shokatfard

Mom

From the time I met her she was so good to me,
her laughter and love were so obvious to see.

She invited me to her home and her cabin as well,
and of those times they were all really swell.

With her, there have been so many firsts for me,
cheddar cheese, Maui, Las Vegas too, you see.

She likes to sit in the sun and also take a nap,
but soon she is up and ready to go when your fingers snap.

She works too hard and cares so much
and has a beautiful quiet touch.

He actions have shown me what family is supposed to be like
and she accepted my children from the time they were little tykes.

When God made her, for us, he completely broke the mold.
because of what she means to me I'm completely sold.

I hope that she knows what her love means to me,
it's hard to put into words, but I hope she can see.

Most people in this life just have a Mom,
I'm luckier, I got to choose mine.

June Alexander

"I Dream Out Loud"

A shot rings out, a mother cries, in her arms, he slowly dies,
Her only son killed by a gangs drive by, tears fall from her eyes.
As her son is lowered into the ground, lightening fills the sky
To live on the mother tries.
But the world can hear her mournful sighs.
The violence is no surprise, but the questions why?
Now I dream out loud
I dream for us to understand, to come together hand in hand,
For peace among woman, and for man,
From country to country, land to land.
Now I dream out loud
For mankind to set a pace, to no longer be disgraced.
To take time to see through their mind opaque lace.
To let love again retrace, to see there is no such thing as race.
Again I dream out loud
For people to pretend they have one mother,
To live together like sisters and brother.
For us not to fear one another,
And to love the color of the other
To everyone I dream out loud.

Jennifer Aleshire

A Void Is A Void

Richard, the class bully has moved to Maine
His seat is vacant and we don't miss the pain
There is a void where he sat and teased

Sergeant Barnes filled her glass jar with delicious cookies
She missed her chocolate treats, eaten by 39 rookies
There is a void in the empty jar

Hurricane Andrew was devastating and horrifically noisy
The winds are not missed, they were damaging and too busy
There is a void in the clear and calm skies

Giant Dinosaurs used to roam the earth
There are no more to bring new ones to birth
There is a void in the animal kingdom

I used to purchase all kinds of pretty made checks
Don't really miss them because of over spending you bet
There is a void on my last check

Christine Bell Wiggins

"Finding Charlie"

We walk patrol all night just looking for Charlie.
He's hiding on us, his tricks are so foxy.

No contact at all.
But you know Charlie, he's watching for us to fall.

As morning dawns a cold mist fills the air.
Chilling us all, no extra clothes to wear.

We take a rest and eat.
No gourmet breakfast here, just cold meat.

As the sun kills the mist it grows hotter.
We pack our gear and move on farther.

Through the jungle bush and diminished mist a hamlet we see.
Silently we hope there are no VC.

The hamlet chief quickly arrives.
As he sees a bunch of tired G.I.'s.

Our leader, a young first Louie takes command too boldly.
As the hamlet chief scared begins to run clumsy and slowly.

Shots ring out from all directions.
Charlie has surfaced with deadly intentions.

A fire fight has started, our casualties are high.
You see, Charlie has found us and proudly he watches us die.

John Lalino

Teardrops Are Forever

Teardrops are forever, in the dreams of every day,
hiding behind the rainbows, till you chance to come their way.
They are really just a friend, of another kind,
for when they come they wash your soul, and help to ease your mind.
Some people who don't understand, like to hide them deep inside,
they don't know to just let them go, tears were not meant to hide.
The best way to show your heart to a friend, is let them see your tears,
it will help create a love for you, that will last through out the years.
So let your tears mingle, like the woman with her man,
it will create a love so strong, that forever it will stand.
Teardrops are forever, in the dreams of every day,
dancing behind the rainbows, till you need them to come your way.
They are really just a friend, of a special kind,
so just share your tears with me, and I'll share you mine.

Elmer J. Neuman

The Wind

Loud yet soft, wind
higher than a bird but always free.
Sometimes calm and docile, sometimes raging fury.
Changing the empty surroundings
into words of beauty or tales of great display.

The wind is I
flowing free, yet locked in.
On the run but unchased,
in quick and unseen movements.
Unseen, the same as I.

Danny McNabb

Alone

I searched for the pot of gold despite the fading rainbow,
I reached out to touch a drop of rain despite the sunshine,
I listened for the sounds of the ocean despite the closed window,
I fumbled in darkness for love and found only emptiness.

Dorothy C. Maruscak

"One And Only"

There'll never be another Dad to give with all his heart,
His family ties were number one, right from the very start.
There'll never be another Dad to reach to those in need,
And give his love unselfishly in every thought and deed.

There'll never be another Dad, so brave and strong and true,
To serve his country loyally, in all that he could do.
There'll never be another Dad with memories held so dear,
Of lazy days and Sundays when we all were near.

There'll never be another Dad who knew just what to say,
To make the hurt a little less and brighten up our day.
There'll never be another Dad with tender eyes of blue,
To look upon a saddened heart and make it shine like new.

There'll never be another Dad with arms to reach the sky,
And smiles to warm a child's heart, or soften a baby's cry.
There'll never be another Dad to hold the key to life,
The magic of his marriage to a sweet and loving wife.

There'll never be another Dad, so sure of that I know,
He's a rainbow in a colored sky or an angel all-a-glow.
There'll never be another Dad whose missed as much as he,
But someday we'll be with him, what a glory that will be!

Cindy L. Call

A Man

There once was a man so lonely and sad
His house was rotted, but that's all he had
He sat all day long in his small wooden chair
Hoping that someday someone will swing by there
The floors creaked as he walked on them
His windows were old, dingy, and grim
He had no plumbing, his pipes were all rust
His furniture was covered with a blanket of dust
Food in the cupboard, so few, so old
His light is a candle of gold
For he had no power, nor even a mind, since love is so blind
Desperate for happiness, or even some care
As the grey gains more on his hair
And that night he sat alone to cry
Then peace came over him, for it was his turn to die

Jennifer S. Combs

Candy

Make me laugh, Oh Sister in Law
  Hold me with your arms so wide
  Give me someplace quiet to hide
Make me laugh, Oh Sister in Law

Give me strength, Oh Candy Dear
  Help me calm your brother's breath
  Help me hold my sobbing son
Give me strength till this day's done.

Help to guide me by and by
  Memories will not fade and die
  You'll still be there if I call
To give me strength to get through it all

A part of you is in us all
  And you'll be there when we get our call
When we travel to the other side
  You will be our Trusted Guide

Live through me, Oh Sister in Law
  Let me hold the Child for you
  Let me calm their fears and sorrows
Live through me, Oh Sister in Law

Dale Caswell

Looking Back

As I look back and ponder on this past year
I remember so much, that I hold dear
So many things I wish I had said
It's too late now, for she is dead
Her frail, soft voice is silent now
To be her best was her ardent vow
Life's battles for her were long and hard
But never once was her spirit marred
She had more than her share of love to give
You knew by her touch, it was unconditional and real
She passed away at Christmas time
This sweet, gentle woman, this mother of mine
The day we buried her was crisp and clear
The sky so blue, you could feel his presence near
I don't remember all the words that were spoken
I was so racked with pain, for my heart was broken
As I looked back, when we were leaving for home
God gave me a sign, she was not alone
I'll always believe that; I know it is so
For the sun on her casket reflected a beautiful rainbow

Judith B. Yow

Abyss

Lost in an ocean of swirling iridescence,
Hopelessly bewildered
I grasp at a crystal shard of water,
But it slips through my fingers
As if it had never been.

Helplessly I flounder in a never-ending sea,
The frenzied currents pull me further away,
Groping, groping for a solid form
On which to rest my defeated body.

Twisting and turning to my immortal destiny,
A beaten path to a black void,
But an atom of my being resists.

And then —

Far above me a shimmering vision appears,
How quickly it flies!
Boldly, gracefully, swoops down, pulls me up
And wings me back to yesterday I remember.

Cheryl Walker

Where Does Love Go?

Where does love go when it just slips away?
How far does it go? How long will it stay?
What made love so beautiful?
What made love so grand?
How can you push love away with a hand?
You can feel it consume you, a warm feeling inside
But where does it go when its trying to hide?
What makes love so special it makes you aglow?
And when it leaves, what makes you know?
Love is a loss you feel deep inside.
Knowing its gone no matter how hard you tried.
When it goes and in its place there's only pain.
How do we forget it? What do we gain?
Love is so different for each time and place
Can you still love many just missing one face?
Loving and caring is it all in vain?
Will it ever be replaced with something other than pain?
All these questions need answers. I need to know.
Will love ever come back or does it just go?

Jean Rosenkrans

In Remembrance . . .
Chuck, On The First Anniversary Of Your Going Home

It was just a year ago this August 26th that I sat in your quiet
   hospital room and prayed that somehow you'd be all right; but in
   the darkness and the gloom,

I heard the Lord calling and you went home to the Heaven of our faith,
   to take your place as a member of the church eternal, with the
   saints to celebrate.

Oh, how I miss your gentle touch, your strong hugs, a mile wide;
   but knowing where you are today helps bring to me some peace inside.

No one can say that life for me will ever be the same.
   I carry you down deep in my heart and on paper bear your name.

I know that with the company of Heaven you truly sing in bellowing
   notes so bright; for your faith in our Lord carried you to Him,
   making everything so right.

As you celebrate one year in the Church Triumphant strong,
   I know that one day we will celebrate together in that great
   triumphant throng.

Until that joyful day shall come, Lord, grant all I need on earth,
   that with you, Chuck, I shall soon say,
PRAISE GOD and JESUS CHRIST, my Savior and my Lord, for the patience
   and strength that have brought me to this day.

Joyce L. Kaestner

Feelings Of The Wind

Cool as Billy Dee walking down the stairs in Lady Sings the Blues.
Hot as my passion some nights.
Brutal as having five instead of six numbers on the lotto
Warm as your lover's lips.
Cold as a day in my life.
Smooth as a con-man's lines.
Damp like not quite dry clothes.
Thick like your tongue after one too many.
Oppressive as life as a slave.
Whistling like men on the corners when seeing a pretty woman.
Calm as when you know that you don't have to go to work.

Donna J. Taylor

Come To Me In My Dreams

Come to me in my dreams, come forth through the endless
   Hours of the night. Where the gates to forever
Await your sight, and where the darkness of tomorrow
   Turns light. Come talk with me in my chambers.
Come walk with me among my gracious flowers. Come
   Drink with me in the Fountain of Youth, and feel
It's lasting powers. Come sit with me in the meadows
   Of everlasting skies. Come run with me and cheer
On the racing horses that fly across the starlit sky.
   Come watch with me and see the world as it seems.
Come to me in my dreams.

Deveney Gallant

A Parent's Dream

Oh, precious child of our, though your birth is yet to be,
How much we long for your beautiful face to see.
For your tender little body to hold in our arms,
We learn to protect you from all worldly harms.
For to see you born, watch you grow, to always love you,
and come to know,
The man or woman you will grow to be,
Is the dream that means everything to your mother and me.

Joseph W. Gurka

My Brother And Friend

In the autumn of time, I've lost a good brother and friend
How can one understand, when the heart's filled with pain
He was more than a friend, in a sense my only friend
Unforgiving at times, but generous and kind
Always lending an ear in time of despair
And, in time I will always remember his concern was sincere
I know that for me he truly cared
So is why the affection we shared in my heart will always be there
Where I walk, I will always feel his presence near
As we did throughout the years
We shared laughter and tears and so many family affairs
My brother and friend, companion till the end,
I'll see you again, I'll see you again . . .
Eugenio Cepeda

Looking Back

How did this happen to us?
How could so much pain come from something
That once gave so much love?
Was it meant to be?
Or were we so lost in life that we didn't see
Our true destiny?
Joyce K. Morales

An Aged's Lament

Oh Time, how did you steal my youth? No trumpets did I hear!
How did you come and take from me the things that I hold dear?

The many dreams I laid aside to care for on the morrow,
were all for naught. Now wise I sit alone and in my sorrow.

I made the journey at your side. You never stopped to rest.
Although you did forsake me not, you put me to the test.

Those numerous tasks I planned so well, were perfect in design.
But they, with all their lofty goals had withered on the vine.

For knowing you were at my side, I thought together we
could plan until I found a better opportunity.

You tarried not, your pace was set and I strode by your side.
New plans were made and goals were set but yet my dreams had died.

How happened this? How did I fail? Had I been led astray?
You did not speak. You knew 'twas wrong to wait another day.

Without a word you journeyed on but well enough you knew
within me lied the means to make my fantasies come true.

Oh how I fret to find that many years I held that key
that opens wide the door of every opportunity.

So I lament and in my dusk it comes so clear to me.
'Tis "action" one must take to warrant opportunity.
August R. Carnevali

Life - From Birth To Death

A drop of life to begin the spirit
I am but a sponge for knowledge
I crawl, walk, and run

My childhood is that of many memories
My adulthood is that of many experiences
My maturity is that of many acceptances

I grow to wisdom, but my body to weariness
I lie my body to rest

My spirit is rekindled
James Edward Carroll

Enigma

I am an enigma.
I am a rock, I bleed.
I am a butterfly
I have been caged. I soar on the breath
of the wind, my feet planted firmly on the ground.
I have the voice of a hundred angels,
and I am mute.
My mind can decipher life's most perplexing entity,
yet I can't remember my way home.
I am lost.
I am all that is familiar and comfortable,
although a strangeness and discontentment
surround me.
I give all that is mine to give, and I keep everything within.
You thought you knew me and all I was about but . . .
I am an enigma.
Denice Warling

My Fantasy

The love in me,
how I wonder if he sees,
I want to embrace his arms,
and sing along the melodies of our song.
Crying 'cause there'll be no tomorrow,
filling my eyes with tears full of sorrow.
Camping brings joy to his heart,
yet for me there's got to be another start.
Our lives are with serious emotions,
giving him my care and devotion.
Campfire, a tent, a sleeping bag,
as a little boy, yes - he always wanted to have.
I dream with him under the heavens starry night,
although I'm not there, together we gaze 'til morning's light.
My racing heart pitter - patters,
can he be with me? Does it matter?
Alone I sit waiting for him to walk through the door,
wanting to be in his arms once more.
This is just fantasy,
the love in me, I really wonder if he sees.
Iris R. Montague

Emily

Emily, Emily our beautiful Emily.
How I wonder what thoughts run through your mind.
If we could only see into your soul what would we find.

When you are away I think of you often and miss you too.
Many nights I've stayed awake praying for you.
I pray that God might heal your tongue that you might talk.
I beseech the Lord on your behalf that you might walk.

Your very presence warms my being.
My heart leaps inside when your smile I'm seeing.
You've taught me to love deeper and deeper somehow.
If someday you are not healed in this chapter.
I know for sure you'll be healed in the ever after.

As we walk together down those streets of gold.
I want you to tell me the deep thoughts that you hold.
As we soak up the light of the Son,
Let us shout with glee as we run.

Emily, Emily our precious Emily.
Sometimes I think of your pain and cry.
Someday those tears will fade away because you'll not only
walk, but fly.
Benita Joy Hardy

A Christmas Prayer

Oh, Most High and Heavenly Father,
How precious, how worthy Thou art.
The love You so have for Your children,
Is the love I now pray for my heart.

The Son You so lovingly gave us,
Shall live on with Your Word so divine.
He's our Guide and the Light in abundance;
He shall reign with His love for all time.

Celebrating and feasting await us,
With remembrance and faith in His birth.
Please remind us, oh Lord, of His Presence,
And our purpose of love on this earth.

May this season abound with His glory;
May His peace and His joy warm your heart.
May His Light and His Presence surround you;
These are wishes to you I impart.

Alicia C. Peña

River

This River it has dried right out,
How quickly it has drained,
Where will all it's beauty go,
Why has it fallen victim to fame,
Now who will wet the thirsty trees,
And quench the peoples thirst,
Why has it drowned beneath the earth,
To rot beneath the dirt,
It's soul has left the rolling waves,
And drifted into time,
How long will it be before this River leaves our minds,
Forget the sparkling blue it had?
Neglect it's heart that roared?
Never look up again and see the Eagle's that have soared,
That River it has tried right out,
It's time has come to fade,
Never will River feel the warm sun,
Or its rays.

Barbara R. Davila

All I Ask of You

At a time in my being, in our antiquity, of our yesterday,
I asked for entirety.

But time surpassed a bond of foreverness and at the same moment,
condoned our finale,
I revolted to meaningless utters of silent weeping.
It is elegance and grace . . . I ask of you to remember me by.
Bury the words of frustration I bolted out,
When all you were after was to be your own person.

I neglected your pleas and distorted to inadequacy.

A kind thought of me, when you say goodnight, Is all I ask of you.

To think my love would have turned relentless.
As days subside to an approaching nightfall, reassuring prayers
are of what I am.

Indecisive worrying. A circle of a past well-maintained, is what I
touched upon.
The wind lit candle . . . as its flames flicker,
Its wax molds to a portrait of your face.

Forget is to forgive, a pointless form of recreation.

It is a reflection of me,
Which is all I ask of you to glance at when you feel you are
Drowning in your own world . . .

Alexandra Ann Wisnowski

Do You Think That You Know Me?

My day consists of unknown, and silence,
I am a child of secrets. Before, and after.
A burden to all who knows me, I know not myself.
Who am I?
I am a woman of many sides. One, mother, one, child.
I belong to no one, and to all.
A side of dark, and then, a side of discovery.
Who am I?
Torn is my heart, to a way that should have been,
and the way it was. A wrestling inside me.
And now I'm in the role of someone else.
Who am I?
A soul who's known me all these years
knows nothing at all, and can never know the pain in me.
She's confused, but someday will understand.
I am life, and pain, a mother, too. And a child of my environment.
Do you think you know me? Your friend, wife, sister, child?
You know me not at all, for I know not myself.
Every day is the same for me, I cry, I ask, I wonder,
Who am I?

Cheryl Palmrose

"Mama"

Hey Mama, could I dance for you, my brother and I?
I am proud to be dancer, my brother and I.
You scrubbed floors, Mama with your bare hands
Until they were blistered to be able to send me to dancing school.
Now, today, I stand here gracefully and dance for you, Mama.
Some day, I'll dance before the Queen and King.
My brother dances as swifts as Alvin Haley.
He dances to the music of waves in the water.
My brother dances as swiftly as a lion in the jungle of Africa.
Oh, Mama, you should listen to the drum beat of Africa.
I feel like a great eagle, gliding in the air on a beautiful, sunshiny day.
Oh, Mama, take my hand.
I'll show you my beautiful Africa Dance.

Gerry Miller

Getty Trip

Dedicated to Professor Ruth E. Trotter

University of La Verne, CA
Notepad and Sunshine on my back
    I am ready
To breathe-in a wealth of history
    hidden in the Getty.

Years of human emotions in Marble and Canvas
    The Wondrous joy, and Agonized Pain . . . .
        Simply Flawless.

Goddess of victory from long ago Italy
    captures the essence of Art and Mythology.

What a trip back to the Past in Malibu
    Thank you, professor Trotter,
        For a modern dose of the Ancient brew.

Celini Lam

A Mind's Game

As darkness falls,
I become prey to the shadows of my imagination.
The blackness gnaws at my sensibility,
Creating demons in the moonlight.
They lurk in the obscure.
With a crescendo of creaks and groans they approach,
Waiting for slumber to overtake me.

Deborah Kilsdonk-Schultz

The Beach

As I stroll along the beach in the early morn,
I anxiously anticipate the coming of dawn.
The bright sunshine of the new day,
The cold wet feeling of the spray.

The sand rising up between my toes.
Helps me to forget all my woes.
As the seagulls fly out to greet the sun,
I get the urge to flee, to run.

To hide my feelings once again,
To let them free I know not when.
I feel like a shell upon the beach,
Stranded and alone wanting to reach.

The heart of someone that can see my beauty,
This is why I tend to be moody.
This is why I look for the dawn,
The rays of beauty of the morn.

To light the way of the darkness ahead,
To release these unwanted feelings of dread.
Alone I stand among surf and sand,
Waiting for someone to take my hand.

James F. Kriston

Love Hurts Within Your Heart

My heart is sinking in despair;
I believe that life isn't fair.
Through tears of sadness and lost hope,
Thinking and trying ways to cope
Wishing and wanting to feel of your touch,
Please understand that I love you so much.
Don't you know that this great pain
Is making me so very insane.
Hoping that the love between us is true,
I'll be waiting eternity just for you.
My life would be nothing without your love,
The love I believe that was sent from above.
Remember this:
When you're not with me, you're always missed.
I won't forget you, no not even
Because I love you, always and forever.

Chandra Huffer

The Whisper Of Pets

Everyone enjoys a pets love.
I can almost tell what my animal thinks, as time goes by.
She is the king of her backyard. at least you let her think she is.
There are little tell tale signs that you learn from each other,
    as time goes by.
My dog is ready to love me even if I am wrong, I always love her
    the same.
As I sit, she might lift her paw or sit on guard between my feet.
Sometimes she has her ball, ready to play, even if I have had a
    bad day.
Her love can always cheer me.
Her whispers of love are always dear to me.

Elaine Ashley

Tomorrow

Tomorrow had come,
I didn't plan it that way;
I was only a child and fast at play.
As a child, I never thought of tomorrow,
I never thought of love and sorrow.
Tomorrow had come in a moment so fast;
It was something, I thought, would never last.

Charles Small

Untitled

I can smell the sweet smell of the winter air
I can feel the snow falling on my hair
I can feel myself slipping into a daze
As I slowly begin to trail life's crazy maze
There's familiar faces on the wall, so many things to see
People floating back and forth tugging on me
The end of my maze is no where to be found
I find myself going round and round
I feel a hand take hold of mine
It's at this moment the end to my maze is what I find
All of a sudden the light is no longer dim
I have found Jesus he is my friend

Ebonee-Dawn Hardmon

As Near As Distance

You can hold me in your heart, even though we're miles apart.
I can feel you next to me in my thoughts and in my dreams. My dreams . . .

In my dreams our bodies dance as one; our spirits intertwine.
I am yours and you are mine. Our love transcends all time.

Ever so far apart, and yet so near, sharing so many new feelings and fears.
The distance is long, but my heart is strong, and I'll dance with you
    through the years.

Thoughts and feelings travel over mountains and seas.
When you feel a pang of hurt or sorrow, your pain emanates to me.

You're not alone, and neither am I. We're together beneath this
    blanket of sky.
So smile, maybe I'll smile too; not knowing why, but that my smile
    came from you.

Hold me in your heart, and I'll dream of you.
Till we meet again and our love becomes a passionate sea of deep blue . . .

Till you no longer have to hold me in your heart, but in your arms.
And I no longer have to reach for you in my dreams, but touch
you with my hand of flesh and blood.

As near as distance, you'll find my love.

Amy Lynn Bigler

Rhyming Rookie

The National Library of Poetry
I can hardly believe it could ever be
That an organization I had never heard of before
Might award me a prize of money or MORE . . .

The chance to be included in the anthology!
A critique of my poem and its artistry!
Or the let down and evidence that I really am
Just a rookie at rhyming and at being a ham

For I love writing poems and the truth of it is
I dream of a paid job in the poetry biz
A slight talent has become an obsession of sorts
As I write about kids, birthdays, vacations and sports

Each work contains many pages to read
Choosing just 20 lines is an impossible deed
And I failed to do so, as this poem is the proof
Guess I'm really a hacker and a poetry goof

While my finest work remains in an album at home
Remember this is a sample and not my very best poem
I am honored and humbled by the possible chance
To be noticed . . . so please give me more than a glance!

Jean Anhalt

Love For An Irishman

Oh Irishman of Loretto Ridge.
I cannot forget our encounter that seemed so long ago.
I see your face in daydream visions,
with eyes so blue that beckon.
I hear your name in dreams of desire,
the whisper of it still upon my lips as I awaken.
How I long for us to meet by chance once again.
For I would tell you of my deep desire to kiss you.
And show you once, if you so let me.
Oh Irishman, dear Irishman.
I wish you were not so very far from me.
Over the valleys and across the ridge.

Candace Corral

The Dawn

As I sat and watched the day quietly turn into night,
I could only feel fright. I heard the old man getting his
submarine ready for the test for the night . . . I knew
that soon I would be deep into darkness of the
cold eerie lake. The old man roared with laughter and
defied God to stop him if he dared. I felt hypnotized
by the stars and pretended not to be scared. From a
distance the old man yelled "you shall feel no fright."
As we went down deeper I could feel the cold black
water wrap around me like a tomb, as we went
deeper into the darkness I felt as though I was
entering into some other space. So quickly I released
my safety belt and felt happy to feel the water slap my face.
As I stood on the bank I watched and wondered if the
old man would be gone without a trace.
His reply as he surfaced was "you see no one can stop me.
I am John Green and this is my submarine."

Karen Ann Niver

Wistful Thinking

If, for just one moment in time, we could connect,
I could see deep into your soul, and no longer wonder.
Who you are, I would know.
But then, the mystery would be gone.

Some stones must be left unturned;
Some questions never have answers.
Just as the sun and moon cannot share the same space,
So we must be, . . . separated and alone.

Jennifer A. Lantz

Grandpa

I miss you so much it hurts deep inside
I couldn't bare my heart to say my last goodbye
All my life your love was pure and right
My heart was broke into many pieces that
    cold, lifeless night.
Can I try to hide the hurt, which furrows
    it's way out?
Keeping quiet, small and lonely, is that
    what it's about?
I try to understand it the emptiness is
    not right
I try to hold back tears and hate, but it's
    a losing fight.
Being here without you the world grows old
    and dead.
Your voice, it floats inside me, exploding
    in my head
Each night I say a prayer to you and empty
    out my tears
How can I let go of you, after loving you all these years?

Courtney N. Ehmann

A Small Town

It was a small town, I knew everyone there but her
I couldn't help but wonder who she was
Her head was held so high
A look of elegance was about her I'd never seen before
How proud of herself she looked to me.

One day a tall stranger came to town
He stood there looking in her direction
As she came near, I couldn't help but wonder
Did he know who she was
He then straightened, a scowl appeared over his face
There could be no doubt, he knew who she was.

Then she saw him
Sparks seemed to fly from her eyes
Her head went high
She smiled then and went on by.

I nudged the tall stranger and said
Do you know who she is?
With a sigh and a shrug, he turned to me and said
She is the one I left behind.

Howard M. Fisher

Is There A Poem In This Text? Or SOS!

I WANT MY MEANING BACK

   In my identity crisis
   I cry for help

   I used to signify
(good old times when subject meant subject)

   Now my soul's gone
I've been scrutinized,
      deconstructed,
      demythified

   When I say it, I don't mean it
   I mean more (when I'm absent)

My creator has been killed
My reader has to rescue me

   I don't mean anything
   I'm no body

   In case of help
Dial 1-800-SOS-SIGN

Denize Araujo

I Did Not Cry

I saw your face, you looked so still.
I did not cry

All around me, people were sobbing, you laid
there with your arms folded across your chest.
I did not cry.

I kissed your cheek. It was cold and soft.
I did not cry.

I held your hand, your icy fingers laced in mine.
I did not cry.

I lay my hand on your heart, to let you know
I'll always stay there. But still,
I did not cry.

I covered my own heart with the palm of your hand
to let you know you will always stay there.

And at that moment a single tear fell from my
eye onto your cheek. And then I had to smile, we
said we wouldn't, but we both cried, when you died.

Alexis Esquibel

To The Landlord

I'm sorry about the mess I caused, and the monumental debt.
I didn't mean to wreck your car, or sell for cash your pet.
I'm sorry that I broke your pipes so now you have no water.
I really couldn't help myself when I left with your daughter.
You were gone one night, and allowed the house to be right in my hands.
Now cracks are in the walls that are held up with car-jack stands.
So you see, I guess I have to move, and this here is my notice.
- Oh yea! I also drained your bank account and bought myself a Lotus
It takes great care and months of plans to turn it out all right
(That's why I snuck out of your place in the middle of the night.)
You'll never see me from now on- I moved out of the country-
But if you ever need a friend, pick up the phone and call me!

Greg Pahanish

Their Victory

A war wages inside my heart.
I do not want to fight in it but, they say I must.

They say that there are battles I yet have to face,
but I have fought, and lost so many.

They want to break into my self-imposed, shell-shocked den
of textureless sound and monotone sensation.

They say I must name the fear that I've comfortably
refused to confront. "I must give it life".

They say I must battle this now breathing enemy that lives
within me, to free "the myself" that is held there; captive.

They send me no troops. No rear or flanking support. I am one
soldier. I have one weapon. One bomb.

I'm not so insane as to ignore the victory-to-death equation. I
know that it will be me who silently, privately coils in exquisite
pain until mounting . . . ever mounting pressure, sparks and ignites the
fuse . . .

The bomb will explode my prison into bits of bloody guts and
shards of entrails.

I will have won their war.

My tormented screams will announce my "freedom".

Jeneen L. Kugel-Yonkosky

"I"

I wish I had a reason for the way I feel . . . . .
I don't.
Keep thinking I'll feel different in the morning . . . .
I won't.
The last thing I want to do is hurt anybody, but . . . . .
I know I will.
I can't cope any longer, I've got to get away from it . . . .
I've had my fill.
I honestly didn't know I was falling in love . . . .
When it became apparent to me, I cried.
I can't explain to anyone the guilt I carry around . . . . .
But the burden of this guilt, is tearing me up inside.
I wish I could say I'm sorry for it even happening . . . . . .
But I would be saying something untrue.
I feel glad in the sense that it's finally in the open
Even though I stand the chance of losing you.

James H. Moy

Lonely And Gone

I don't have to be alone to be lonely
I don't have to be going to be gone
Because I'm always lonely and I'm already gone

Yes I'm lonely and gone
I've gone all alone to the place where it's warm
The place in my head where nobody hurts me

Like M.C. Escher there is no up or down
I just spin my cocoon around me

No one knows the path to my place
Even I find myself lost
The path is new every time
Sometimes it's twisted; others it's straight

When I come out of my place the world hurts me again
but I have to come out

So I'm always lonely

Don't ask me
I'm already gone

Julia West

Tight Rope

This tight rope I'm walking is starting to wear thin,
I don't know where I'm going. Don't know where I've been,
Help me out give me a hand to hold on to,
Make it so I can stand on my own,
This tug-a-war is starting to get old,
Everyone on one side, and you on your own,
What's the point to this game you're playing with me,
my rope is slipping I can feel it starting to break,
will you be there when I fall,
Will you be there when I break.

Jennifer L. McIntyre

Nobody To Turn To

Running through the darkness, counting the stars
I don't know where to go, how about Mars
Feeling bad right now, sleeping in the night
Feel worse in the long run, I'm high as a kite

Where can I go, to whom can I turn
Going to school, I'm willing to learn
Now at the bridge, as every night
Wanting to jump, with all of my might

Seeing my mother, watching her cry
"Don't think about it, I can't have you die"
Collect all my thoughts, bring them together
Ready to do it, ready to do whatever

I'll help you she says, she's talking to me
I'll help you she says, I know you want to be free
Listening to all that, taking it in
Now what I'm doing, is really a sin

Pinching myself, seeing if it's a dream
Waking up, I give out a scream
Hi ma
Morning sun.

Jeremy Elias

My Love For You Hurts

So many things I want to say,
I don't know where to start.
I guess by saying I love you,
from the bottom of my heart.

I love you for the person you are,
not for what you want to be.
Though I do admire your hopes and goals,
but only wish they would include me.

I am feeling a lot of pain inside,
For you are leaving in a few days.
I so badly want to make love with you,
but fear it will strengthen my pain in many different ways.

I just want you to know how I feel,
because when I am in pain, the quieter I grow.
I would do anything to be with you,
but understand you have to go.

Please don't forget me when you're gone.
For I could never forget you.
I want you to know I will miss you so.
And am doing my best not to be blue.

Heather Horton

A Mother's Love

When I lay to sleep at night,
I dream about holding my baby tight.
I can't help but wish she was already here,
so I can love and hold her near.
This pregnancy has brought me love and joy,
and I often do wonder if it's a girl or a boy.
Whichever it is doesn't matter at all,
I'll love it the same from winter to fall.
I can't wait to count her little toes,
and watch her bloom just like a rose.
We'll raise this baby the best we can,
into a strong and healthy woman or man.
But no matter what, she'll always know,
her Mommy and Daddy love her so.
And through all the good times and the bad,
she'll always have her Mom and Dad!

Author and Mother: Jesseca M. Terrado

Father: Francisco Garza III

A Blind Man's Vision

When my darkness for eternity came,
I drew many tears from my useless eyes.
With my arms extended, I groped with shame.
I thought with my vision, so my life dies.
But her sweet scent alone captivates me.
I need not see her face to know she's near.
Like a trained bloodhound, my nose is the key
To knowing the beauty of her, my dear.
Sight is not all that constructs a true man.
To smell, feel, taste and hear you and your sweet
Words. They do for me what no picture can,
Though I don't feign feeling whole and complete.
    So there's no chance that I will cry and hide
    And miss the joys that to me you provide.

Joseph Monteiro

Decision

I reach to open your door, hesitate, reconsider.
I enter and am not surprised to find what is there.
Shattered remnants of the stained glass that is my mind lay scattered
On your carpeted bedroom floor
Reflecting the passion and thought that once was me.
With an understanding that comes only from rabid dog pain
I know what I must do.
I begin to pick up the pieces, perhaps this time a little bit wiser or
A little too late.

Jim Finn

Dreams

Before I go to bed at night
I erase all thoughts of you.
    My dreams are so sweet
    that I am stirred awake
Only to notice that I am by myself.
    Before I go back to sleep
I pray I will forget about you
    but my dreams only persist
    so that I cannot bear,
but when I wake up you're still not there.
    The only thing left to do
is to accept the fact that I still love you.
    My dreams are so sweet
    but they are no longer true.

Dawn Smith

Untitled

I fall at the feet of Jesus
I fall on my face
I fall on my face at the feet of Jesus
My glorious, wonderful Lord.
Sweet, how sweet his touch
Sweet, how sweet his voice, his words
Sweet, how sweet his face shining upon me.
He is holding me, sheltering me,
    drawing me ever closer to himself.
My heart says . . . let me know him, let me see him,
    let me love him,
O Lord, how did I live without you
Life without you was too hard,
    too lonely, too empty.
I am placing myself in your hands . . . Jesus . . .
And trusting you to make me Christ like
    for your glory.

Gloria Mitchell

Around Us

As I walk in the forest nestled around my house,
I feel an awe at the beauty of it all.
The silence which surrounds me and goes deep inside,
Is only broken by a bird or squirrel, to my sheer delight.
The trees remind m of wise ancient Gods standing guard and
protecting me, as I pay homage to their size and power.
The air so sweet with pine and cedar,
I expand my lungs wider, desperately trying to inhale it all.
Walking in nature as God made it,
makes me realize how we should appreciate all the things around us,
and become a part of it.

Denise Massaglia

My Brain's Expanding

My mind seems cluttered, no room remains.
I feel my thoughts, they're blocked by chains.
Chains of homework left undone
Coming to haunt me in my fun.
My Chemistry flows in and out of my mind,
Making no sense each and every time.
With each new problem, my brain expands.
I search for help, but no one understands
These problems which I will never use,
Certainly not if I have to choose
Whether or not they apply to me.
It's useless, Oh why can't they see?
If I hear once more of beta emission,
Or if I have to read of fission,
My mind won't take it, it'll come apart.
A fate I'm certain I've had from the start.
From the very first day I saw the lab,
I knew I'd wish I never had.
But no . . . I'm here, there's no doubt.
My brain's expanding from the inside out.

Joey Hensley

The Day My Father Wept

He was always there to help me when I fell.
  I fell a lot.
His hands were strong. His face, full of love.
His eyes, worried what I'd do next.
  I tested his love, his patience, his trust.
Day after day. Year after year.
He held me close. But not close enough for me.
I demanded more. I was selfish.
  Then one day, that fatal day,
there were bars in between us
  The cold, cold bars of my jail cell
  in between my father and me
And he could no longer hold me.
  He could no longer protect me from my mistakes,
from myself.
  And that was the day,
the cold, dark day
  that my father could do nothing more.
That was the day my father wept.

Betsy Mastel

Cliffs Beyond The Dry Waterfall

As I stand at the summit of serenity
I gaze down and behold every bend, fold, and crease the land
makes
I absorb the tranquil beauty and majestic scenery.
Where do those twisted mountain paths lead?
Perhaps an intricately woven maze
Carved out of the rugged stone,
Placed to engulf one's soul till the end of time . . .
Or possibly to hinder those who have no purpose in life.

Yet those cliffs seem to hold the mysteries of age . . .
Though the surrounding shrubbery may be lush,
These cliffs are parched and call out for water.
The savage cry of a wolf resounds over and over,
But no one can hear, no one can answer . . .
For a brief instant time seems to stand completely still,
And then . . .
    continues.
But the cliffs still call out for water . . .
And are answered only by a mere drop,
  rolling down their acute and jagged curves.

Anna Venizelos

Sweet Surrender

Can you smell the refreshing sweet blossoms,
  I give to you in the springtime.
Can you feel the warm breeze,
  I touch you with in the summertime sun.
Can you count all the colors,
  I give to you that set a fire the autumn horizon.
Can you see in the winter my reflection,
  On the frozen frostbitten pond.
It takes strength for me to make,
  All this beauty for you . . .
It hurts me for you to abuse me like you do,
  So much pain fills my heart.
I am getting weak.
  I wish for your own happiness you will help me,
Alone I stand helpless.
  I can't take very much more,
Please, please help me,
  Signed . . .
Your loving Mother . . .
  Nature.

Barbara Pavilonis

Missing Me

Sometime between two seconds ago and now,
I found I lost me, back from sometime forgotten.
And in my place stands
A woman with secret-darkened eyes,
Who laughs and smiles and touches hands . . .
While in an inner room, another
Crouches in the corner — and cries.

Fides Capati Agapito

Untitled

Being a victim.
I felt so alone, so weak,
I screamed, yet no one heard me.
Why, Why couldn't anyone hear me.
Was it a dream or was it real.
All I felt at first was fear,
As his cold, sharp fangs,
Slowly punctured my fragile skin,
Ever so gently,
As if he cared about me,
And about my well being,
As he lay me down upon my bed,
He kissed my cheek, with his warm, wet lips,
As he left, all that was left from
his final visit, was the blood bound kiss,
Which I left on my cheek.

Alyssa Wright

Four Seconds Lost

Looking deep and deeper into your eyes, looking for your soul, as if,
I could swallow it up, so we could be one.
I imagine myself swimming in the dark, sensuous chocolate that
surrounds me as I look deeper, then deeper.
Finally I am lost, lost in you, or maybe myself.
I try to imagine what you are thinking, but the place I go, in my
mind, to imagine is torn apart into pieces. I frantically try to
put them back together, but unable to do so, I stop.
Then, at that moment, I realize I have escaped your heavenly prison,
even my own chaotic mind.
To you a meaningless glance, to me an eternity.

Jordan DeBlieux

The Angels Called You Home And You Weren't Even Aware

I did not want to go
I had so much more to do
But the angels called to me
And then I knew

I left my children, my friends
And all on this earth
It was like I had no control
Like it was my birth

I had traveled many roads and highways
And taken many wrong turns
But the angels were always with me
And God forgave so I would learn

There was no light at the end of a tunnel
Nor were there golden stairs
There was only a man beckoning to me
And his smile took away all my fears

He had given me the book and I knew without a doubt
I laughed and cried and felt so sad
Until God put his arms around me and said,
"The Angels called you home and you weren't even aware".

Ann D. Howard

Homework, Oh Homework

Homework! Oh, Homework!
I hate you! You stink!
I wish I could wash you away in the sink,
If only a bomb would explode you to bits,
Homework! Oh, Homework!
You're giving me fits.

I'd rather take baths with a man-eating shark,
Or wrestle a lion alone in the dark,
Eat spinach and liver,
Pet ten porcupines,
Than tackle the homework my teacher assigns.

Homework! Oh, Homework!
You're last on my list,
I simply can't see why you even exist,
If you just disappeared it would tickle me pink,
Homework! Oh, Homework!
I hate you! You stink!

Ashley Dianne Brown

Wisdom

I have known great love.
I have been filled with unutterable
   delight at the sight of my lover's face.
I have lain in the embrace of my other
   half and known nothing could be more perfect.
I have shared wild joy, and deep despair,
   and reveled in it all.
I have loved deeply, more deeply than
   was wise
and I have lost that love.
I have known the pain of a spirit torn
   asunder, and felt the sorrow of each grieving heart.
"It is better to have loved and lost . . ."
Cruel lies of a foolish soul.

Amber L. Hollingsworth

Let Me Be A Soldier

God, Oh Mighty God, Please help me with this pain.
I have nothing else to lose. I have my whole life to reclaim.

This is the lowest point of my life, so I'm going to start right here.

Alone, I know I cannot win this war; countless lost battles
have made this quite clear.

Lord, give me help with my addiction. It has changed me so completely.

Now, when I look into the mirror, I don't even see me.

But I know that your are with me in this hour of need.

You have a purpose for me and this struggle is certainly the seed.

I will never give up hope or quit trying. This drug will not win.

I know you would not forsake me, despite all my sin.

I have always been unworthy and you have blessed me many
times before.

Lord, lead me out of temptation so I can be your soldier,
now and forevermore.

Frederick Turner Thomas

"Because I Want More"

I have money, everything the eye can see,
I have or I can buy.

I have a great personality,
one that can light up a room
in need of glowingness.

I have the looks that turn heads
everysecond, everyminute, everyday.

But it isn't enough
Because I want more.

I want love, that tender touch,
everyone talks about, except I.

Is it I have no time, or is it no one takes the time,
to know me.

Does everyone think I'm just plain out spoiled?
Or are they just jealous, I have all the green
they always dreamed about?

But all I ever dreamed about is just being normal,
just being respected, just being loved.

But that's not all I want
"Because I want More"

Jamie Kay Ward

Love My Love

   Since you and I have been together,
I have realized how much you really care for me.
When you show me that you do, it just makes
me care for you even more.
   I love you so much, my life has turned
into you and only you. If you ask me to show you
a love for life, I will show you our love.
   Your love is why I live. I would do any
thing just for you to stay with me forever. I will
love you until I die.
   My love will put a million smiles in your
heart. Love comes from the mind, and when you
have true love, it comes from the heart, and my
true love is you. I love you with all of my heart.

April Bishop

Memoirs Of A Survivor

Murder after murder
I have seen before my eyes
I sleep, thinking it'll all go away,
I dream of the many faces that I once knew
Suddenly there's silence, darkness
But there still lies a faint sound of death . . .
It's not over.

I never want to wake up again.

The scene only bloodier, colder,
Harder to bear.

Hoping it's over, I awake.

But everyday it seems like
He has come back in forms of Drug dealers,
Gangs, children with guns . . .
To finish the brutality he's started,
Fifty years ago.

The man has passed
But his ideas still remain
What will it take to end the killing?

Will it take another six million?

Amardeep Sangram

Vision Of Hell

The terror rages throughout my body,
I hear the sound of a stallion trotting,
Screams and shouts and little kids crying,
And I know that they are there for lying,
I picture in my head of evil creatures laughing,
Or maybe little witches doing witchcrafting,
The flames of hell are always burning,
Sometimes I think of blood wheels turning,
I always pray before I go to sleep,
Or I might wake up in the devils own keep,
And then one night when you are in bed,
You hear me screaming before they cut off my head,
He doesn't care what he does or say,
He knows that God can't punish him anyway,
And he doesn't care if your dead or alive,
Because as long as your in hell you'll never survive.

Karen Nissley

Remember

On a soft quiet night, once in December,
I heard a sound, it made me remember.
It was the sound of a time stood still,
The kind of time when all was real.
It reached as far as my mind could stretch,
Past the present to which past it did catch.
So warm it felt that my eyes grew glazed,
With the thought that had been rattled and raised.
I laughed at first, then I cried,
And with a blink I let out a sigh.
It flashed so quick my body did shake,
And my hands grew still as my heart started to quake.
And then I knew all was ok, for in my mind it would stay.
Nothing is more precious or quite as shimmery,
As the one thing that keeps us all, a good memory.

Jesse Blank

Fright Night

Pumpkins with their wicked smiles
I hesitate on the stair
The dark rectangle opens - what lurks in there

The black cat watches warily
The wind scares leaves down the street
Goblins with their ransom devouring their treats

I'm caught by bony fingers - ropes they bind my feet
The clouds reveal a sickly moon
Branches and vines that's all - at noon

My heart and feet they race with fear
I drown in fog like foam
All the way my mind it screams
Will I ever make it home?

Elizabeth Stevick

"Long Ago And Far Away"

I thought I knew you—
I knew I did.
Somewhere in the long ago and far away we were friends and I loved you.

What happened between then and now has blown everything apart—
I was flying . . .
shattered in a million tiny pieces far too small to ever hope to recover,
much less reassemble; flung into the long ago and far away.
Time is a healer, and our wounds were almost nothing more than old scars.
But now, they have been torn . . .
and they once again hurt as they did then in the long ago and far away.

The silence and calm I possessed to protect myself was taken, stolen,
   now there's nothing left
The one I could turn to for help has been lost somewhere —
somewhere long ago and far away.

Someday—somewhere, things won't be so hard, so cold, so lonely.
But that's not now, that's someday.
And someday is just as distant as long ago and far away.

Annalea Martin

Why Cry?

Why cry people; when I'm going to a nice home.
I know it is hard, because you can't reach me by a phone.
Just come to my funeral and I'll be glad.
Don't just sit there, talk; but don't be sad.
Don't walk pass me getting ready to cry . . . because when I go home
to Jesus, I'll fly, fly, fly.
I'm going somewhere, where the Angels are;
and I know that it's really really far.
Don't walk pass me with all those tears . . . because now you'll
know that I have nothing to fear.
God made His choice and He chose me.
So I'm really really glad . . . and I want you to be.
I'm going somewhere nice where there's lots of peace and quiet;
So all I want to ask is . . .
Why Cry? Why Cry? . . . Why Cry?

Darryl Pride

Sunday Morning Stroll In The Park

I tried to shoot the shadows in between you and I
I lied and asked the angels to wipe the beauty from my eye
I talked to you for hours even though you were not here
I walked out of view between the trees and water on concrete
   hoping that you were here
I sat on a bench and wrenched my mind in need of lasting peace
but she floated past me and that moment ceased
I spat on the beach and clenched my fist
drowning the vision in a blowing mist
The moment ended in waiting for the kiss
wake up and do more than merely exist

Edward Leer

Motherly Love

I know my mother loved me
I know she loved me so
It truly broke her heart to have to let me go
I never once heard her sweet, loving voice
As it seemed I didn't have a choice
She gave me life, love, and care
But as a mother she couldn't be there
She loved me enough to give me up for adoption
At that time in her life it was her only option
She gave me up out of motherly love
She is now one of God's angels above
Sometimes I see her warm gentle face
Smiling down at me from a better place
One day mother we will meet again
I'll forever keep you in my heart until then

Cindi Jones

Gone Forever

As I sit out on my porch at midnight
I look across the trees and there I see a light
I was oh so scared
It was only my loved ones coming to tell me they cared
They do not come around anymore
Now I love them as much as before
If they only knew how much I did care
Everyone would call us the perfect pair
Where as their souls do now rest in peace
My precious memories of them, I can not release
Oh how I wish I could hold them one last time
If only a careless intoxicated driver had not committed
Such a terrible crime
As the love I have in my heart will endeavor
I know they are gone forever

Goldie Ann Thomas

I Love The Days

I love the days when no one is around, but I am not alone.
I love the days when nature fills the air with folk music that turns
     me inside out.
I love the days when I can hear my sandals hitting moss-covered
     soil.
I love the days when there is no tomorrow, but there is no fear.
I love the days when I can fly across the earth and know that
     it is all mine, but all yours at the same time.
I love the days when I am a Muslim, Christian, Jew, and
     Hindu all at once.
I love the days when I know who I am.

I love the days when I can walk through burlap fields and know
     that what I am doing is good for the earth.
I love the days when I realize how foolish everyone else is
     because they are not doing what I am doing.
I love the days when my soul and I walk and hand-in-hand.
I love the days when I love me.

Justin McKinney

A Journey Read

The sun shines softly at day-light
I read a tattered book at night
But only if by candle-light
The hoot of the owl floats astray
As I lie day-dreaming
On my soft huge bail of hay
So as not to be cold I rummage up a cover
But still the huge dark clouds start to hover
And when the sun's to shine again . . .
. . . A new day at dawn I shall begin!

Chezre M. Harris

"My Sun"

There was a boy full of hope and joy
     his eyes were as bright as the stars.
There was a boy who found a new toy
     each day in the things around him.
There was a boy whose sunny smile
     brightened the world surrounding him.
There was a boy so quick to beguile
     that loving him was as easy as breathing.
There was a boy who chased after life
     to find out what it would offer.
There was a boy who met up with strife
     and dealt it a blow with his humor.
There was a boy who lived happily ever after,
     and then there was a man full of laughter.

Verna K. Wagster

A Life Not My Own

In a life not my own,
I must be the soul of discretion.
My nature's wish to be manifested,
shrouded by a veil of scarlet.

It is not a transgressor I wish to be,
only to be as authentic as I was made.
To permit myself and God to fashion me
and be the adjudicators of my deportment.

Yet in the habitat of my existence, critics prowl,
laying in wait to ambush my efforts.
And so in a disguise of normalcy I remain concealed;
Unexposed, unapparent, and unexplored.

Jamie Farris Moore

Child In A Corner

I am sitting in a far corner.
I must not be heard or found.

I hear yelling and fighting.
What did Mommy do wrong?

My body begins to make noises and tremble.
I am scared and I start to cry.

Someone is beating and hitting.
What did Mommy do wrong?

Why must they fight?
Mommy is starting to cry and scream.

Mommy does try and I try too.
What did Mommy do wrong?

Our phone signals for me to come.
I dial and say, "Mommy's being hurt and she's crying."

Don't worry Mommy, I did right.

Debra LaKay Wilhelm

Turned Away

When I was a little girl,
I never thought life would be this way,
It's that one word divorce that drew us away,
There were many choices that needed to be made,
It seems those choices were to be made everyday,
There was little times of laughter, mostly lots of tears,
But many times of tearful fears,
I never knew how much was really cared,
Until the moments were missed that we shared,
It really hurts to be turned away,
By my own father in every way,
And even though we're far apart,
He'll always be in my heart!!

Julie L. Siefker

"Unrequited Love"

I paint you, Love.
I paint your eyes.
I paint you love, in deep disguise.

I paint you love your curly hair.
I paint you, as you're standing these.

I paint you love, as deep as the ocean.
I paint you, with mixed emotion.

I paint you love, as the world is wide.
I paint you, 'till it burns inside.

I paint you have, 'till the end of the earth
I paint you, for what it's worth.

I paint you Love, 'till the end of time.
I paint you, wishing you were mine.

I paint you love - you'll never know.
I paint you 'cause I love you so.

I paint you love but I shall never see
  you, with a paint brush, painting "ME".

    Eleanor Carpa

Thank You My Friends

Out of the sea of consciousness,
I placed my feet upon this earthly ground.
Thank you my friends, for having walked with me.
For your comfort in my time of need,
will be infinitely cherished, as I stand,
at the edge, of the sand in time.

I see the pain, and the tears in your eyes.
Please, let them be of joy, and happiness,
and they will set your soul free.
If only, your eyes could see, all;
all, of the friends, that have come to greet me.

As they take my hand and guide me back,
back into the infinite sea of consciousness,
I would like you to remember one day,
Soon, I will be back, to meet you.
To comfort you, in your time of need,
As you stand, at the edge, of the sand in time.

    Albert E. Pearce

My Coach

I've never played this sport they call volleyball
  I always thought you had to be big and tall,
Giving it a try, I was nervous with fear
  I did not want to get cut and be in tears.
But one person stood alone and proud
  She could easily put on a show for the crowd,
Support and confidence she gave to me
  Otherwise I'd be home, just a "want to a be."
She taught me the game, I now love
  How to be an athlete and rise above,
She's an unsung hero in my book
  How she has us all hooked.

From day one, when we knew nothing at all
  That sweet phrase, "Champions," we hear the call!!!
I'll never forget all she has done
  She has made the sport o so fun.
I hope when I coach I'll do the same
  That is why she should be in the hall of fame.

    Cheryl Stotsenburg

A Supplication To God

As I give my prayers, towards the heavens above;
I pray for God's touch, of serenity and love.

A love that only, our Lord Jesus can give;
And serenity for which, our soul needs to live.

My prayers request all, your wisdom and truth;
To be wise in God's word, to pass on to our youth.

I pray for God's patience, to enter my soul;
With Jesus Christ in my heart, and for him to control.

I pray for all those, who choose not to believe;
May their heart and their soul, be yours to retrieve.

I pray for all those who stand firmly in you;
That they remain strong and courageous and true.

I pray that all those, who speak of your name;
Will do so with love, and not so in vain

I pray all in bondage, will soon be released;
As our Lord Jesus Christ, brings - world peace.

I pray that all actions, in which I fulfill;
To bring forth the glory, of God's mighty will.

I pray in thanksgiving, for all love and care;
And thank you Lord God, for hearing my prayer.

    James Walt Sniegowski

Annunciation Day

When dusk began to fall
I put my plane away on the workbench
brushed the shavings from my tunic
and sat down outside my shop
with a plug of hashish
thinking of my beloved.
I watched the day pass over unsewn fields
and the soil darken beneath.
From a grove beyond the village street
the hot breeze carried a love song.

And before I knew it night had come
out of the woods fragrant with myrrh
gossamer darkness covering crimson cheeks
eyes twinkling brilliantly
through a slit in the veil:
the eyes of my betrothed.

And the day fell into the arms of the night
and the night became one with the day
and it was morning.

    Hallberg Hallmundsson

My Little Angel

Last night in my dream.
I saw a little angel on your knee.
Can't you see, she kinda looks like me.
For I am the boy whose only joy is
Loving you, loving you.
And kissing you the whole night through.
And I am the guy who will always love you
Forever more, forever more.

    Gene C. Dahilig

Grammy Is My Name

A Grammy's love is one to remember
I really don't feel like a Grammy
As I looked into the mirror today

She is always on the go
Her tights and workout clothes on
While her mobile is ringing
    and wondering what plans are for the day
Having her nails painted red
Her roots are gray for you would never know

The housework can wait for another day
Six grandchildren I have

Where is the Grammy I use to know
One with hair of gray
Wears round spectacles and colors of black

She is more modern
She plays with the computer, uses the fax,
Turns the recorder on to see who called

When the backdoor opens and somebody calls Grammy
My heart pounds
I am old enough to be a Grammy.
    Judtih A. Pattison

Lullaby For A Missing Father

Yidele, Yidele. Tatele, Tatele.
I remember you I remember your white hair
Sitting on a chair in the sunlight on a Sunday

Yidele, Yidele. Tatele, Tatele.

On a Sunday you do not work on that day
I climb all over you kiss you and tickle you
I comb your white hair and sing aloud in the air

Yidele, Yidele. Tatele, Tatele.

I wind a scarf around your neck
Your favorite color, white
I pinch your cheeks and pull your ears

Yidele, Yidele. Tatele, Tatele.

I climb on your knees and you embrace me
Sing me a lullaby and I fall asleep
In the warmth of your love

Yidele, Yidele. Tatele, Tatele.

Your arms around me keeping the outside world away
Just you and me. Now I embrace the cold air
And you are not there

Yidele, Yidele. Tatele, Tatele.
    Greta Herensztat

Forever In My Arms

The early morning sun catches my eye,
I think of you,
And start to cry,
Sadness is not the reason though,
Divinity, that's why.
A gentle wind wipes my cheek,
I look around it's you I seek.
I hold an angel,
And I shall protect you from that which harms,
I hold an angel,
Forever in my arms.
    John J. Chaisson

Untitled

They told me: "Write some poetry"
I said: "I don't know how,"
They told me: "There's this contest, see
You'd better write some now!"

    Well, I'm not certain which is worse
    To fight—or try to write some verse,
    But though I'm filled with mucho doubt
    I'll sit down here and write some out.

Walt Whitman never won, they say
No more did Gertie Stein,
Alas! No scribbler in their day
Wrote lovely odes like mine.

    So stand back, Robert—Look out, Wilde!
    No poetaster meek and mild
    Will ever have the title: "Best"
    Now THIS girl's in this verse contest!
        Cassandra Morrison

Shadows

I hear a voice in the distance
I see a figure in the mist
I call out, but no one answers
I can only see a man the shadows

I see this man everywhere I go
In my thoughts, my dreams
No matter what I do he never leaves my side
My guardian angel
This man in the shadows

I once loved this man
But I painfully let him go
With all the lovers, all the friends
No one can take his place
The man in the shadows

To this day, I can see him clearly, without seeing him at all
My heart, still filled with his love
In the end, I'll always love
The man in the shadows
    Anjanett Goehring

In My Soul . . . Alone

I've lost my courage and my desire to be here.
I sit in solitary,
    as he is willingly caring for another.
Seeing him with her should make me happy,
    but understand I've spent my life loving him - embracing him.
He's been neglecting me because of her.
Would he notice me if I were near . . .
For he is so distant: I can't be with him.
He's in another world - a world he aspires.
I've longed for his friendship, I've longed for his love,
    but he doesn't understand that.
He's been ignorant.
    I wonder . . . Does he care? Does he want to care?
Unhappiness is what I'm feeling; Discordant is what I've become.
It's like my soul has left from within me.
There's something inside of him, that brings him to me when we're apart.
We have this eminent bond, that no one else can ever withhold.
Except there's something keeping him from grasping this bond
    and never letting go of it . . .
I don't know whether I'm lonely or alone anymore . . .
    Carol Ann Jorg

Save This World

As I travel along in life,
I see so much toil and strife.
If I were in charge of it all,
I would make a call;
A call to all who could hear.
Please save this world now,
Save it for the children who know not yet how
their future will be when they are twenty-three!

April Collins

My Grandson

Again through his uncharted eyes
I see the pictures in the skies,
and watch the dancing of the trees
in rhythm to a wayward breeze.

How fresh the fragrance of the rose!
How lush the grass on hillock grows!
We watch in awe the steady pace
of spiders spinning webs of lace.

The snails cling fast to garden wall.
He wonders why they do not fall.
The raindrops sing a wavery tune;
he hopes that it is ended soon.

We hear them as with measured beat
they cleanse the world and make it sweet.
His eyes are ever seeking out
the daily miracles about.

Things to me so trite and worn
I find are now through him reborn.
Through him once more the world is new
A smile is real; a tear is true.

Doris Baillargeon

Abandoned Past - Future Found

I reached my hand out to you - you were not there.
I shared my joy with you - you did not smile.
I had experienced sorrow - you did not console.
I tried to share my children with you - you only found fault.
I tried to share my happiness with you - you did not listen.
My sorrow of your abandonment comes to the surface at time and affects
my loved ones - for this I must tell them "I am sorry."
I've made a life of joy in spite of your non-acceptance
my outlooks, my accomplishments and my pleasures have grown in many ways.
I have found there are people who share my joys, console me when in sorrow,
love my children and accept me for myself and add to the fulfillment
   of knowing another person in this lifetime.
Love and kindness are within so many - it is a contagious pleasure
   to share.
You missed so much in not seeing me for me - knowing me - loving me
living in your closed world.
I'm sorry for you - but pray you are truly at peace within yourself.

Connie Schlingmann

Untitled

As I stand on the side of this mountain
I yell into the great open sky
to feel alive to take in all that
God has made to let it resound and to
set myself free from all that holds me to
this earth so I can truly set my inner-self
free to soar with the birds in the clear
clean blue sky.

Camie Golladay

The Best Part Of My Days

Your light shines through the years of time
   I see your face in every day,
Each place I go I call it ours
   No one will ever take your place.

I wonder how life would have been
   While living it from day to day,
If you were here to help me through
   How different would it be.

But thoughts like that can make me sad,
   If I should stumble, if I should fall,
'What its' don't work to fix the days,
It's only going on as is.

You'll always occupy my thoughts
   Each day is full of you and me,
I know you cared while you were here
   Daddy, to me you will always be.

Dottie Peacock

Signs

I see the current, changing
I see my hands, shaking
I see the power of the government
A temper with, capital punishment

I don't need to see the nails
that hold up my hands
Like everyone else, I don't need
to be hanging from a crucifix . . .
I don't want to love the voice
I can't recognize
Like everyone else, I don't need
to be tested all my life . . .
There's sighs crossing over, to my decease . . .
Tear drops crack and fall, I have been released . . .
Sunset cries in the deep blue sky, showing signs to all lives . . .
But that don't take away my linger . . .

Christopher Williams J.

Colors In The Sky

In the evening, in the summer and the spring,
   I sit quietly on my giant redwood swing.
Sunset is my favorite time of the day,
   Oh, how I wish those colors could always stay.
Ahh the pinks, purples and bright shinning golds,
   What a brilliant sight for all to behold.
I watch the birds soaring high into the clouds of white,
   Wishing I had wings to join them in their flight.
I want to search through the clouds and hope to find,
   The faces of loved ones who've left me behind.
But I'm here on the ground, so I search with my eyes,
   Each and every fluffy cloud that passes me by.
I know they're altogether and smiling down on me,
   As they once again pass over on their floating balcony.
Then darkness approaches and takes it all away,
   But keeps the colors safe and bright to use another day.
But even the darkness paints a picture with it's light,
   It brings with it the moon and stars shining bright.
So when I look at the heavens, I know it has to be,
   That the angles have painted a beautiful mural for
all of us to see.

Cheryl Daenzer

It's A Beautiful Morning

I feel the softness, of the breeze on my face.
I smell the fragrance of the flowers in my garden
IT'saBEAUTIFULMORNING.
Sense of smell and feel will be with me today,
as I enjoy the fragrance of the ruby, red, rose
and the bright, purple, aster.
As I work in my garden, I feel the softness and warmth,
of the soil as it sifts thru my fingers.
IT'SaBEAUTIFULMORNING.
The kittens and dogs are with me, and I feel the
softness their fur as they brush against me.
IT'SABEAUTIFULMORNING.

Evelyn R. Roberts

Passing Moments

Sitting here, looking there, not knowing if I care.
I stare outside the window sill, as if to say how dare!
When silent dreams and thoughts of you come creeping in my
head,
I think the only place for me is wrapped inside my bed.

Tell me now about your dreams, are they as bold as mine?
Or do you dream at all my friend, perhaps from time to time?
When night awakes and so do I, and birds sing silent prayer,
That's when I feel alive my friend, and know too that I care.

How could you know of what I feel, or do you really care?
I think you do, when times I hear, my darling please be there.
Should I doubt your gentle touch, your sweet caress, your kiss?
Not something that I want to do, but forced to when your missed.

Could this be love, disguised with hate, why should I even ask?
Perhaps from fears of loneliness, which all stem from my past.
Have I any strength at all to tell you how I feel?
Would you laugh, or understand that I'm not made of steel?

Will my life be full of doubt with everyone I meet?
Someday I hope to find the one, with whom I don't compete.
Are you the one, sweet friend of mine who softly says to me,
That every time we are apart, with you I long to be.

Judith S. Wayne

Carcinoma

I am looking for you "Where are you carcinoma"
I test your blood, but can't find your source.
I look into your bones, and can not find your
   roots.

Give me another drink, OOH. You taste like
Over ripe, Bananas or Pineapple.
Even chalk has a flavor unwanted.

Where are you carcinoma?
I probe and poke, is this a joke?

I can not find you "Where are you carcinoma".
This game you play is no joke, you are for
Real and it is a steal.

You attempt to take me away from
The one I love.
So where are you carcinoma.
Your game is over and I shall win.

Benjamin Harrison

"Life Is Passing Me By"

As I sit here alone, feeling sad and blue,
I think about our life, I don't know what to do.
I know love hurts, when you have to say good-by.
When all our hopes and dreams, must one day die.
For all the bad times we have endured,
There were good time for us, I'm sure.
Even though life is passing me by,
I think about you, and I started to cry.
Tears may fall, tears may drop,
My love for you, will never stop.
Someone help me get over the pain,
There is nothing left, and no one to blame.
As I sit here alone, wondering why,
Life as I know, is passing me by.

Betty J. Edgerton

All Together Praising His Name

As I praise the Lord on this new day,
I think of the hands that formed this clay.
The vibrating sounds of music sweet;
The crossing of threads in stitchings neat;
All together - praising His name.

Sowing the new seed in fresh worked sod;
Tending the young plant, hand work of God.
Dainty the blossoms, of odors sweet,
The fruit soon to come so tasty to eat.
All together - praising His name.

To see lines take place on blocks of wood,
Visit the lonely — talk of their good,
Aroma of food in fresh cooked stage,
Reading of books from masters page.
All together - praising His name.

James Liggett

Us

   Though you are so far away
I think of you all night and day
   The love I feel grows ever stronger
Patience - it won't be much longer
   Soon you'll be where you belong
Right here with me, in my arms
   I miss your kiss, your love, your touch
I miss you baby - so very much
   Without you, life just passes by
Without your love, I know I'd die
   The minutes tick away like years
Because you baby, aren't here
   The nights are dark and oh, so cold
I miss your warmth, your hand to hold
   I cry myself to sleep at night
But - for our love - I see the light
   I find the strength to make it through
Cause you love me and I love you, to love and honor - to have
and hold
Together as we both grow old, together - till the end of time
A love that's ours - just yours and mine.

Julia Chimenti

Where Eagles Dare

The eaglet falls from the safety of his world in fright.
In desperation he spreads his wings and soars in flight.
Even higher than the pinnacle from whence he came,
And discovers his safe domain was only a thatch of twigs
Balanced precariously on a wind blown precipice.

Charles Bullard Sr.

Sunrise

As I lay there on the cold park bench,
I thought of all the wrong places I'd went.
If only I had listened and did,
what my mother had said.
If I had stopped to look at the rising sun,
all of this poverty wouldn't have come.
I would be watching the sun through
the window of a school auditorium.
And then it hit me with an awesome blast,
that what no better way to begin then
right now in this cursed place.
I sat up filled with joy!
as the sun hit my smiling face,
I knew my life had begun!
Here in this awful place,
my new life had begun!
Wealth and riches could surely come
because of the rising sun!

Julie Bergstresser

Harvest

Is it not that we reap the corn planted in our fields?
~ I throw my body into the sugar cane rivers.
And swim deep down; dark rocks speak only solitude ~

We prepare for feasting. The burning sun has turned our fields red
& flaming. Brown baskets with sesame breads, soft butter, and vats of
honey milk on the table stretch. Many a man and woman will sit here.

~ I scrape my children from the Sky.
I saw the moons in your eyes, and reaped my first kiss ~

Is it not that we reap the breath taken from the Winds?

Our feast continues. We look at the purple trees & the sinking of
sun into the Earth. Burning bark and ripe fruits are ready to burst.
We lick the sweet nectar from our shoulders.

~ The Ocean lays its salt on strong green leaves; baking under the
hot sun. Children scatter about the soil clouds ~

We dance; smiling at our precious bodies and faces.
Potential mates appear when the curves of our thighs rumble;
seeking the fire of the eyes. Wild orchids caress
the ears and dust moves through us.
Is it not that we reap; the life we've planted . . . and harvest ourself?

Danielle de Waal

Face The Fact

I don't know where my life is going,
I try to live each day without a frown showing.

But it is hard for me to understand why,
Everyone close to me, has to die.

First it was my boyfriend, and now soon my dad,
I just don't understand why, everything is going bad.

I just wish everything could be normal again,
But I just don't know where I should begin.

I try to live my life day by day,
With a half smile on my face, but nothing to say.

People keep trying to help me out,
And I just brush them away, and give them a doubt.

I am trying my hardest to take care of my mom,
It's just so hard for us to move on.

All my friends keep offering to help me,
Sometimes I wish they would all let me be.

Now I must face the fact,
That they are gone and not coming back.

Amber Love

Who Did What . . .

I want to kill my Television,
I used to love it so much . . .
Everything designed for my own entertainment,
Comin' into my room like an angel's touch . . .
Sometimes I think I've got it terribly wrong,
Common sense say's it's only a rock and roll song . . .
But what I've got surpasses all logic,
I've heard it said and compared to a kind of magic . . .
You can understand this like light from the sun,
And you saw the life force when it raised by one . . .
But the television's artificial sunlight made me watch,
And the spirit on the radio had me turn it up a notch . . .
And it's like a mirror to a stranger,
Someone who can't remember sleeping in a manger . . .
Stars of Power, and a reflection moon,
Comin' back again, see you soon . . .

<jay@pstbbs.com>

Jay Hanning

I Remember

When I was young with chores to be done
I was given a broom.
Now I was small and the broom was tall
And I longed for the day when I would be
As tall as the broom.

What things we would do, the broom and I
We would sweep the cobwebs from the moon
And brush the dark clouds from the sky,
Oh! What things we would do, the broom and I.

Now I am tall and the broom is small
But the world hasn't changed very much at all
I still see cobwebs on the moon
But now I sweep them from my room
And dream of the day when I was small
And the broom was oh-so-tall.

Hedwig Partenfelder

Forgetting

Forgetting
I was once young, a child,
didn't remember where my sweater was
or my new pencil with the blue eraser
or that mommies die, too.

Forgetting
I am pretty even when I cry,
when I feel anger churning me like butter,
frothing, foaming, coating my insides.

Forgetting
I have pain that will always
grind my bones, then turn upon itself
for validation, become the aches that have no answers,
the scars that have no skin, the dies that leave
no cuts to show where I must heal.

Forgetting
I alone can find my ancient stone,
pull its belly from the mud,
wash its surface in my dripping sweat,
and turn it, remembering, to the light of day.

Berta A. Bollinger

Patty's Day

I came to the hospital for surgery today,
I was scared out of my wits, and didn't want to stay,
I cried and got nervous and very upset,
The doctor and nurses said, you can't go home yet.
They wheeled me up to the O.R. Room with
   very much concern.

Now I'm here for a couple of days
But I'll be going home soon,
With all the medicine and drugs in me,
I'll be so glad when they let me be.
With flowers and cards and phone call galore
With visitors knocking at my door,
I'm laying around feeling so lazy
Climbing the walls and going crazy!
Back to work, I'll be glad to go.
But I can't go back until the doctor says so!

   Betty Rice

Untitled

You tore me in two when you ran that day.
I was scared you were hurt or dead.
What were you thinking?
Did you care about any of the people you left behind?
At the time, apparently not.
You put me through hell, but who cares, I'm no one special.
I thought about you day and night for what seemed like forever.
I felt like there were only two people who really cared about me;
They weren't mom and dad or, at the time, my supposedly two best
   friends,
They were God and the devil,
God wanted me to pray to Him to make sure you got back home ok.
The devil . . . the devil wanted me to come and leave everything
   and everyone to come to him,
But by the last words of this poem you'll see what I did . . .
I didn't run from my problems.

   Belinda Gould

Exile

I am an exile.
I was sent away from my home.
Why?
I crave freedom.
I want to choose my own life.
I loved a man,
But they said I could not love him.
I could not love the man they chose for me,
So I spoke out against them,
And they exiled me.
Who is this man I see?
It is my love.
Now we are together,
Two people rebelling against totalitarian rule.
We may live in the jungles.
We may barely survive.
But we are free.
And our children will be free
No one will tell our children how to live.
I may be exiled, but I'm free.

   Brenda Kay Hale

The Charms Of Marifran

As we walked together holding hands
I was so proud of the charms of Marifran
Her pleasant smile and winning ways
To this day they stay and they stay
Time slipped by like a breeze
She left us many happy memories!

When she was a little tot
Of her future we thought and thought a lot
We bought silver charms
To Mark each event
Quite surely, she was heaven sent.

Eight silver charms
hanging on a bracelet covering her arm
There were tiny shoes, a Virgin medal and go-cart
Faith, hope, love - one even says you're smart
And, of course, the head of her class
As a reward to Washington we went the lass.
A wedding license now, she's on her own
And, of course, she's always welcome home.

Eight silver charms hanging on a bracelet wrapped around her arm.

   Joe McFarland

Does She Know I'm Only Eight?

I sit across the sea of desk.
I watch the brown bun nodding.
My chair is cold, black leather.
It chills my bare legs.
Does she know I'm only eight?
She says I should talk to her.
I try to think of things she'll want to hear.
I try so hard.
But I'm only eight.
Now the bun is moving.
She says Mommy is very sick.
Will she be next in the cold chair?
I wonder if I'm sick, like Mommy.
She says Mommy loves me.
I'm so lost in all her words.
Why does Mommy want to hurt herself?
I'm only eight.
But I know the answer.
I can't make Mommy happy anymore.

   Christine Shuey

Hope

Today it's snowing.
I watch the snowflakes drift in blinding storm.
Each like a frozen tear the world adorns.
Does God weep o'er this troubled world of ours
Or grow more angry with the passing hours
To see the strife that greed and ignorance cause?
The sordid, brutal, senseless grief of wars.

Spring is coming.
We search for signs of early blooming flowers,
The heralds which announce fresh April showers.
Hope wells afresh in every human breast
That God relents, and once more were are blessed.
Forgive us Lord for all our worldly sins
And fill our hearts anew as April sings.

   Doris W. Bane

"I Am"

I am a warm and caring kid.
I wonder how the world will survive in the future.
I hear the wind talking to me at night.
I see, sometimes, my old dog that died last year.
I want to have my grandma and grandpa back.
I am a warm and caring kid.

I pretend that my grandparents haven't died.
I feel that my grandma and grandpa are with me.
I touch their hearts and my parents'.
I worry what my life will be like in the future.
I cry when something touches my heart.
I am a warm and caring kid.

I understand no one can live forever.
I say help one another.
I dream about growing up.
I try to do my best and to help others.
I hope the world will be peaceful when I grow up.
I am a warm and caring kid.

Brett Radler

A Different Drum

Marching to the beat of a different drum
I wonder if I'm the only one
The rhythm is sweet, low, and methodical
Listen closely; but, don't tap your feet

Listen carefully; you'll catch the beat

It's the sound of someone pounding away
At the walls of self-pity, self-recrimination, and dismay

The rhythm is sweet, low, and methodical; I say

And I'll keep marching any way
Marching, marching, marching on
I hope I'm not the only one
Marching to the beat of a different drum

Joy L. Linton

"Thoughts"

Oft times I stop and wonder where with God I stand,
I wonder what his purpose was when he placed me on this land.

I wonder what I might have been 2000 years ago
When Jesus walked upon this earth teaching friend and foe.

Would I have been a boatman fishing the galilee
Or, a greedy tax man collecting the Governor's fee.

Perhaps, a lauding statesman running government affairs
Or, a tiller of the soil raising corn, wheat and tares.

Perhaps he meant for me to teach the sinners and the poor
Leading them from darkness into light thru salvation's open door.

As my thoughts wandered on, a still small voice spoke to me
Saying, "Dwell in the present not the past, you are what
   I made you to be,"

Burnell A. Raphael

The Miracle

As I woke up, I felt a cold breeze slide against my face.
I went out and realize that is finally the time.
As I gazed at the glimmering snow hovering over my yard
I felt warm and cozy.
I laid on my back and looked at the sky.
After a while, I started to move my arms and legs.
Then I got up and the imprint looked like an angel
Tall and proud.
When spring came, the snow melted and it got hotter
But it was still there
As summer came I looked outside and
I saw the imprint outlined with dirt.
Then fall came and it started to rain hard.
It got washed out.
I felt sad.
Then it was winter again, it started to snow,
And it was right there
In my face
I must have thought it was a miracle
And it was, because I believed in it.

David Brumaru

Another Night

I wish I were
I wish I might
I wish you were here
For me to hold tonight
Someone sweet and always true
Never depressed, never blue
Always there to help me through
Maybe someday you'll come along
Until you do, I will listen for your song
I hope it's soon, don't take too long
I know it will work, we can't go wrong
Love is sweet, love is strong
But, love is not a phenomenon

Douglas K. Hopson

"Nature Of Death"

Black is my heart. Stone cold is my soul.
Ice is my blood. Death is my name.

In the night I walk among you. Unknowing you walk with me.
Many come with me, but few return. I have learned the power of uncaring.

I am not prejudiced in what I take. I do not care what age, sex, or
race. My kiss is eternal, but chill. It is not for the warming of souls.

Many fall in love with me, loving me for the danger around me.
For the mystery surrounding me, for the chance of eternity.

I walk yet in the path of the dark. My lips are sweet, but my eyes
are cold. My face is calm. My cloths are black. The sword I carry
is on my back.

When I look upon you, I see the time you have wasted and time you
have left. The wolves are my messengers, the crows are my carriers
leading souls for me.

Many try to mimic me, to take the life before its time
or to lengthen into antiquity, but they shall also fall to me.

A lonely job have I, always taking lives.
It is against my nature to save, to love.

Many fear me and many hate me, but they all come to me eventually.
Be it in peace or with a struggle, none can stop my unrelenting pace.

The soft dawn light glows upon the hills, a symbol of rebirth.
Yet I know not of it, for my way lies in the dark depths of death.

Heather Rossmann

I Am

I am different from everyone, because champions stand alone.
I wonder what the future holds for me.
I hear success yelling from the walls of the pool.
I see gold medals and ribbons waving to me.
I want to be an Olympic swimmer.
I am different from everyone, because champions stand alone.

I pretend I am a great white hunter.
I feel like my shirts going around and around in a drier.
I touch the hand of the power who gives me strength in the water.
I worry if I am ready for the end of time.
I cry for the boy I want to be, but I am just a kid.
I am different from everyone, because champions stand alone.

I understand that my mistakes have been my choices.
I say everyone deserves a caramel cashew sundae from Adele's.
I dream of being a champion.
I try to be the best I can, sometimes it just doesn't work.
I hope my hormones kick in so I will get huge.
I am different from everyone, because champions stand alone.

Bram Olson

I Am

I am an old cuddly teddy bear.
I wonder where the child that used to hold me went.
I hear him come near, but ignore me.
I see him walk away without even a hug.
I want to be loved, just once again.
I am an old cuddly teddy bear.

I pretend that the little boy that loved me is still there.
I feel what used to be little fingers,
    now big strong hands throw me across the room.
I touch the cold floor feeling hurt and afraid.
I worry that one day he will leave me forever.
I cry on the days that he does.
I am an old cuddly teddy bear.

I understand that he's growing up.
I say, "please, can't you take me with you."
I dream I'll be in his arms once again.
I try to be there for him.
I hope once again he'll tell me his problems.
I am an old cuddly teddy bear.

Kalynda Pearce

To Daddy

If I could see you one more time,
I would do anything I could.
But my clock never chimes,
And my hands never move.

Let me borrow your clock,
And tell me when to come.
I'll be there as soon as I can,
Even though I'm young.

One more thing,
As Cher would say,
"If I could turn back time,
If I could find a way."

I would give you, Mommy, and Sean everything I could.
You would never have to say a word of thanks,
Because in my mind,
I could hear you tell me that I'm doing good.

Hannah M. Conley

Winter

The majority of winter is bitterly cold.
I would not go out without a jacket, never!
The world looks new and not too old.
You are instilled with awe at the beauty of the frozen river.

The untouched snow that falls looks like one sheet of ice.
In the winter there are many things to do.
Sledding in the winter will certainly suffice.
Everyone is out on a winter day, along with me too.

All the windows seen are covered with frost.
To see this frost is so much fun.
Snowballs are what is usually tossed.
When the sun goes down, we stop, we are done.

As I sit by the fireplace at night and stare at the burning embers,
I think of all the wonderful things that I will surely remember.

Edmond Nunes

I Would If I Could

I would take your pain away.
I would wipe all of your tears away.
I would make you laugh real hard.
I would if I could.
I would trade my life in to make you happy.
I would give you my heart if yours was broken.
I would if I could.
I would take you to paradise to forget about your problems.
I would give you my love if you were in need.
I would listen if you needed to be heard.
I would if I could.
I would speak if you needed advice.
I would run for miles if it would make you happy.
I would if I could make your life the best it could possibly be.
I love you and I would if I could, do anything.

Candice Simpson

He Can't Hear Me Now

All sons want the approval and the encouragement of their dad
I wouldn't know too much about, that's something I never had

He kept to himself in his garage, a place we weren't allowed
Hey dad, come look at what I did, but he can't hear me now

He never saw a game I played, never saw my winning hit
I'd try to tell him afterwards but he never slowed up a bit

Listen Dad, we won the league, don't you want to know how?
He'd keep right on working, he can't hear me now

Years later. I go to visit him, out in the evening chill
To say the words he never said, if he wouldn't I will

As he lay underneath the earth, the words come out somehow
I love you dad, I always did I know you can hear me now.
I know you can hear me now.

Jonathan W. Benke

The Gate

Right before you lay your future
in behind you'll find the past and present,
All your work in all your life
brought together in grief and strife.
Here you are in my dead land,
you sing the song of death and mourning
although you died without a warning.
I wish I could give what was taken from you
instead I give two final choices
good or evil.

James Myles

316

Untitled

If I had wings - the places I would fly to.
If I were a flower - the things I would hear.
If I were a tree - the things I would see.
If I were a lake - the people I would know.
If I were a sunset - the beauty I would have.
If I were a star - the wishes i would grant.
If I were a cloud - the balloons I would see float by.
If I were a balloon - the smiles I would see on children's faces.
If I were a rainbow - the brilliant colors I would have.
If I were a path - the people I would lead.
If I were a cartoon - the laughter I would hear.
If I were the earth - the people I would love and the people
  I would hate!
    Dalet Zepeda

Can You Feel Me?

Sitting staring into beyond, wondering
if there had been a misunderstanding
after my expressions had been exhausted,
not wanting to ask. Fearing awkward,
reactions, so I'll take more time to
define the statement.

When I ask can you feel me? I'm not
speaking in hands on terms, but the
bodily functions of a speedy pace of your
heartbeat, when my name being mentioned
makes you pay closer attention.
The glistening in your eyes as I enter
your presence, how the nerves gather in your stomach feeling
somewhat queazy, but with a relaxed sensation
and at the same time wondering if I'm having
the same side effects. But afraid to question the
curiosity! So I ask once more!
Can you feel me?
    Ellis Sallis

"Change"

No matter, who you are.
If you're big or small,
girl or guy.
People want things to stay the way they are.

Changes can make people happy, mad
or even cry.
All because people want things
to stay the way they are.

But no matter, how hard people try
things change each and every day.
People can do something about some changes
but others . . . there's just now way.
Because things don't always stay the way they are.
    Jacqueline Bourque

The Wind

The wind, it swirls to and fro,
In the sky,
Above the meadow.
Up with the clouds,
Puffy and white.
It swirls through the day,
It swirls through the night.
I have come to the end of my song,
But you can hear the wind song all day long.
    James W. Smithy

Untitled

Sparkling vacant glances
ignite hopeful trances
marching to the pulse of eroding times
In a celebration of decadence
she walks above my waters
above my immaturity sometimes
Whatever song the hand decides to play
sometimes love, some of forever
but never when the curtain falls
Take my hand
in a visible display
Cast me towards heaven
towards this bed of my shame
I lit my candle for her
because she put the fire in all of my stars
I am her life
I am her breath
when clouds cast shadows on a shivering moon
I howl her midnight call
I am her ritual
    Dave Soberg

Heaven

Some day beyond this vale of pain and tears
I'll go home and meet my savior face to face;
I'll spend the endless ages of eternity
Praising Jesus for his matchless grace.

To be there in that land of milk and honey
Where never comes the grief of death or pain
Will satisfy my soul — so long a'searching
And I'll see my friends and loved ones once again.

Yes, heaven is a place of joy and gladness,
Where my savior wipes away all tears,
Oh, how sweet to know I'm going to a city
And evermore be free from all my fears.

So I'm looking and I'm waiting for that day
When Christ himself will come and take me home
What a day of celebration I'll be having
When I make that final trip — no more to roam!
    Frances Noel

Be Mine

Be mine, and my life with you I will share
I'll hold you close and show you I care

Be mine, for you know you're my one desire
The one who sets my heart on fire.

Be mine, for eternity and I'll do the same
Share your life with me, your love, and your name.

Be mine, and always love only me
Together, forever is the way we will be.

Be mine, and I'll be there throughout the years
to share the joy, the laughter, the pain and the tears.

Be mine, and completely I'll give you my heart
Together, forever we'll never part.

Be mine, and I will always be true
Because darling you know I love only you.

  Be Mine!
    Cristion Haywood

For Grandma

Grandma, you'll always be in my heart.
I'll never forget the fun and games we had and played since my life on
earth just began to start.
You will never be forgotten and always loved.
Maybe in your new home you'll be a peaceful dove.
I'll never forget your "shut your mouths", "fiddle sticks", or
"fridgidare" or the way you always showed you cared.
Your life was full and very long,
I guess it's because you knew how to fight and you were strong.
You left us on this twentieth day.
And behind you all of your pain, stress, and worries must stay.
You gave your sons that powerful last good-bye hug.
So powerful, just hearing about it makes me feel your love.
The tears did run because your days are done,
but they dried at the knowledge of your being with the Almighty One.

Candace Brown

"Why Me"?

"Mommy" hello it's me
I'm deep inside of you
Can't you hear me calling
But I got something to say
Why can't you hear me
I'll try not to get in the way

All I wanted
Was you to see I'm real
Can't you hear me breathing
Don't you know what I feel
We should be together instead we're apart.

How can you love a child with a broken heart
Take its life away and just tear the script apart
No words were spoken
Given no thought
From a child of silence
With a broken heart, Why Me?

Chad Wells

"Strong And Sane Sista"

Always being put down because
I'm a woman of the black race.
Called names such as: Skeeza, hefa, trick, etc . . .

But have I lost my mind?

Am poor, can't take care of myself, more less
the two kids bore from me by my ex-lover
who doesn't give any support . . .

But have I given up?

Men who want to know me try to feel on my a**
when I turn to stop them I get knocked out
not knowing where I am the next day . . .

Have I lost my mind?

Go to a club with a few friends, hip hop
music pumping the degradation of black
females. But still sistas dance to the song,
and when someone personally degrades them they
must fight-protest.

Have we given up?
Have we lost our minds?
And the only answer is no, not yet.

Asuefa Y. Ozaka

Untitled

One of these days I am going to write a book
I'm going to paint a picture, I am going to . . .

One of these days . . .
    When?
When I have some free time.
    Why not now?
Too much to do.
    What are you doing?
Well . . . nothing
    So do it now.
I can't.
    Afraid?
Maybe.
    Well, try.
I might fail.
    Then don't.
Don't try?
    Don't fail.

Grace McKinney

As I Can See God

Dedicated to my Papoú
As I can see God behind the white light.
I'm bird I'm bird in flight!
As I can see God's gentlest face.
He smiles down at me, I'm floating in space!
As he starts talking to me with his strong and deep voice.
He tells me not to worry, not to worry but think twice!
As we are talking together in that long, and dark tunnel.
I see him pulling away from me, he's now in a funnel.
As God starts fading away he tells me,
"Go home. I'm here to stay!"
Until next time, but I don't know when he'll call, but he'll call me again.

Despina Damianides

Changeable

I'm changeable and I wonder why
    I'm sometimes happy or I want to cry
I hate those feelings what can I do
    I want to change, be someone new.
I'm reaching for something that is not there
    I want to do something but should I dare
Will I find it or should I care.
    I wish I could it isn't fair
To live this way with nothing in sight
    Or try to do something that isn't right.
Somewhere out there I'll find a place
    Where all my cares will be put in a race
And when that test has come to past
    I would have found myself at last.

Annie Lorraine Morris

"Ready To Go Home"

I have traveled this ole road, and its seemed so long.
I'm tired and I'm weary I'm so ready to go home.

Jesus promised he was coming someday to meet me.
What a glorious day when his face I shall see.

When the gates of Heaven open, and the
host of angels step aside.
And I see God on his throne with his arms open wide.

I can hardly wait for that wonderful day.
When he steps down from his throne and I can hear him say.

You have won the race and he takes me by the hand.
There's no more troubles or trails here in Glory land.

No sadness or sorrow, no pain you will find.
Yes you won the race you are a child of mine.

Now, we know not the hour, or the time of the day
If we are not ready what an awful price we will pay.

We have his word, and I know that its true.
So be ready to go home when God comes for you.

Dura Mae Dumont

Untitled

Don't weep for me because I'm gone,
I'm walking in heaven, with Jesus, Gods son.
The angels were here to welcome me home,
I'm singing, God's praises and around the Great Throne!

I know that you'll miss me and the times that we had,
But you know that I'm home now, so please don't be sad.
Just hold to God's promise that we'll meet again,
And when you get to Heaven, we'll welcome you in.

Jesus is with you and my spirit is too,
With each step you take in all that you do.
So keep pressing on, until you reach home,
And child please remember, that your never alone.

Although we must part now, it won't be for long,
For God will send Jesus, to escort you home.
And what a reunion when we meet again,
We'll sing out his praises all over Heaven!

Debbie Williams

Untitled

A loveless life built up in side me
Immune to guilt and pain
It shatters all within me
In which I can't maintain
Run with me and you will see
What all I can undo
shattered dreams of broken lies
That I can tell to you
Lies that which once haunted me
Don't hurt me anymore
All which was omnipotent came back to you and tore
A friendly face that sees no pain
Smiles and says hello
I smile and wave back to them, it makes me feel so low
I felt you there to stand and stare.
The hated people I know took all the lies and blames
shame shame you silly mortal
I see you once again
All I wanted was you to know on me you can depend.

Erica Van Pelt

"God's Special Gift To Me"

As I arise to start each day
   In a hurried, harried life,
I always thank my God above
   For His special gift - my wife.

It's for sure He knows what's best,
   He proved this with His gift.
A friend who's always there to comfort me
   And give my life a lift.

She does so many little things
   The make my life worthwhile.
Like thanking me for chores I've done,
   And coaxing me to smile.

Should God decide to call my prize
   To Heaven for His own,
Part of me would surely die,
   Yet, I would not be left alone.

My fondest dreams and memories,
   Provided in my life,
Are shared with God's special gift to me,
   My friend, my love - My Wife.

Charles Owings

Are You Aware?

When the sky is gorgeous in its splendid colors,
in Autumns brilliant multi wonders.

Brown, yellow and orange leaves, high
on the trees etched against the changing sky!

They drop in circular motions down
on the now dying, faded green lawn.

Patches of fresh fallen white snow,
that did not stay long, under the trees below.

Squirrels hop around in a skittish dance
to look for food, that was in abundance

In the passed summer, that has vanish
they know to save food, as not to famish.

The rules of Nature had to be obeyed;
for all animals everywhere these were made.

At least, where the season will come and go
and the sun, in the sky goes to and fro,

To cause these Winters, Autumns, Summers and Springs.
Notice, when birds're leaving, spreading their wings!

Be in awe for the Only one, who's in complete control
of this world and the Universe too in its whole.

Johnanna A. Garretson

Insulin

A look into the future can cause fear,
imagining items of concern that could be real.
When 252 becomes a regular reading
on your blood sugar machine.
"Please, someone, do something to help!"
I scream from the bottom of my heart.
Reaching, searching always looking
for a caring soul to hold dear my cry,
and bring about the miracle I need.
At long last, this week my prayers will be answered,
someone has finally heard and answered
"there is light at the end of my tunnel."
Coming from a very thin point of metal
poked with gentleness into my flesh.

Janet Lee Frazier

The Three Stages Of Man: Youth, Middle Age, Old Age

My love lies beside me, her breathing slow and steady,
In dreamless sleep she renews herself, and by morning she'll be ready.
Now I'm satiated, so why won't my poor brain relax?
'Cause if congress finds out how much fun this is, there'll surely be
a TAX.

The clock keeps ticking as we get older,
So we put our desires in gear and try to get bolder. — BUT!

Surging thighs press up against the rounded buttocks,
A hand reaches out and cups a pendulant breast;
The recipient of all this wishes the great big lummox
Would leave her alone so she could get some rest.

Time passes by and our hair turns grey
And we wonder if something could happen today. — BUT!

I watched my wife one morning as she got dressed.
She whipped off her nighty and I'm sure I felt desire,
But while I sat there wondering what to do next,
She stood before me fully attired.

John M. Stiff

Endometriosis: The Demons

It is hard to find a diagnosis for Endometriosis, but when you do your
in for a lifetime of surprises, these cysts that cast upon my female
organs, I call them Demons who have no mercy on women, they come
uninvited - I wish we can have them indicted, these demons bleed and
make me have painful periods, which makes me all too serious, much so
that I do not even smile or laugh anymore, what is the use of joking
around for, nausea, anxiety, dizziness, bloating and headaches, that's
all I can experience, fever and back pain are my domain, itching
burning sensations just like scabs all over my abdomen and back, hey
endometriosis give me some slack, after the party the demons allow me
to relax, though not for long, they come back for action, pain during
intercourse they would not let me have all the satisfaction, abdominal
pain other than menstruating, lower immune system so I can get sick
easily, suffer from sinus, I assume it is allergies, these demons
inside me play with their forks, stabbing my female organs, twisting,
pulling and tightening, it can be very frightening, it is a wonder if
they ever get tired, drugs, surgery, hormone treatments, my emotions
abused I feel like I have been beaten, time to go to another meeting,
if you see me depressed, you know I am in distress, for it is that
time the demons are having fun once again, so, If I want to stay at
home, just leave me alone, give me support and just talk to me, I can
become irritable and be a witch, not all friends stay, most of them go
away, just bear with me, for I need people and not only the demons
inside me.

Debbie Congello

Listen To Me, Take My Advice

Listen to me, my dear girl, take my advice
If your mate is hurting you, then don't think twice
Get out of your home, stay away from him
If you take that abuse, then it is your sin

Look for the signs, they are there
The door knob blacked your eye, to people you'll swear
You are sitting there crying, to old country songs
Cause even though he lives there, he's never at home

You're reading romances stories, every minute of your life
Wishing you were in the book, instead of being his wife
No matter how much for you, his heart will burn
You cannot go back, the lesson would not be learned

It's for the next woman, who comes his way
That you must have courage, and stay away
Now that you are gone, it's a mistake he thinks
Cause even though he has the muscle, you have the strength

Carolina A. Baker

The Sands Of Time

Feeling alone, she sat by a window
in her luxurious home near the ocean view
with seagulls flying high, just below was
the ocean crew. She looked into the blue
ocean with a telescope and saw a rocking
motion which was shining bright. Her curiosity
took her on a boat ride during a high tide
towards the light. Her eyes opened wide as
she came on the side of a large metal
aircraft with carved words on it; "If you're
lonely too, will you be my friend so my
heart can mend to see what life is to be?"
Her eyes filled with tears also she was in
great fear. Her eyes looked side to side
for this being which is to be unseen. A shadow
of a man appeared, her eyes gazed with fear.
He took her hand as they reached land and
spoke of his human form existing when he was
born, but vanished when his hopes and dreams
were torn, they cried by each others side and found
their souls bonded by time and faith.

Christine Matsueda

Do You See

Hunched over little old ladies
In out-of-date clothes
    and earth-bound shoes?

Diamonds shine on wrinkled, crooked fingers
That can no longer manage
    keys or keyholes,
    or jelly jars,
    or vacuum-sealed packages of processed frozen foods.

Their men have left them, for one reason or another.
Any separation is a death,
The end of anything they might have been together.

Please,
    can you help me with this?
Cathryn Allen

"Sugah"

"Sugah," he would always say
In so many different ways.
I knew the sound and what it meant
In the course of all our days.

It was always just one single word,
But it means so many things,
Like the urgency when he needed me,
Or soft as the bubbling springs.

"Sugah, see the sunset"
Meant, "Share this gorgeous sight with me."
"Sugah, we'll be late"
Was for the Sunday matinee.

"Sugah, hmmm, this coconut pie" . . .
"The best one I had made."
When he was ill, his eyes would smile.
"Sugah" would slowly fade.

Though several years have passed on by
Since "Sugah" went away.
"Sugah" was . . . "Sugah" is . . .
"Sugah" will always stay.

Cora S. Blair

. . . And Again, And Again

I cannot say that we have met before
In some forgotten time, some distant place,
Yet sometimes, when I look into your face,
I catch a glimpse as through a closing door;
And sometimes, when you smile or speak my name,
It seems an image long upon my sight,
An echo half-remembered through a night
Of shifting shadows round a candle's flame.
If hope survives the night to greet the morn,
If time stands helpless to erase what's been,
If life's sweet promise out of loving born
Endures through an eternity of pain,
Then what seems lost for now we need not mourn.
Of this I'm very sure: we'll meet again.

Joyce W. Glauser

Tinsel Dreams

How I love to look upon the city lights all glowing in the dark of night

They glitter and gleam and light the dark skies for miles around.

As I gaze upon these wondrous sights, I am amazed at how brilliant man really is.

But, awesome is the brilliance of this wonderland of ours;

With sequins and tinsel all frozen in place;

To remind us of God's majesty and grace.

To be allowed to travel in this winter paradise;

To visualize the marvel of this beautiful ice palace,
And ask never to be awakened from this dream!

Joyce Hixson

Clouds

Hear my cries
in the ever-shifting clouds . . .

Graceful as they are,
they are blown without permission;

always changing form,
never immune to the same wind
at their souls each day.

It tears them apart
leaving them only to feel the chill
of an absence of what shape
they may wish to have maintained . . .

And I wonder how distant I am
from what I once was,
from what I will be,
and if there is a wind I can actually rely on
other than the force within myself.

Jordan Slutsky

Awakened

Tethered to an expectation fueled by false hope,
In the grip of silent rage disguised as longing,
Shackles so insidious they went long undetected,
Only to appear in a relationship masquerading as a promise.

The button of compromise pushed, engaged my being,
The mission was determined light years ago,
My psyche (read secret weapon) set toward destruction.
This would be the last time betrayal found a resting place in denial.

Your life was spared by cosmic indifference and your walled of Innocence.

Alice Lake

Cat Fancier

Do you believe dog owners who say, "I don't mind walking my dog.",
In the heat and humidity of summer, winter's freezing cold?
The hours spent training and grooming them, teaching them to beg for food???

No thank you! Definitely not for cat lovers like me
They are much to independent, to be led around on a leash!

Yet, cats are loyal, loving, intelligent friends and companions
Who adore chasing each other, frolicking, or, just playing around
At times they seem strange, especially, when they run up and down
curtains - of all things! Then, somehow, manage to reach the ceiling beams???
Such funny antics are cause for hilarity, then —, screams!

Felines are proud, dignified (ahem!), and clean
Which makes them all the more appealing; you want to cuddle them —
Hug them, careful! Only, if they allow you to!
Don't ever assume you own them; quite frankly, the reverse is true

Take it from a cat fancier of many years who believes
That these sensitive, beautiful creatures
Should be treated as if they were kings and queens

YOU OWN THEM? HA!, ONLY IN YOUR DREAMS!!!

Elizabeth B. Baldwin

In The Name Of

In the name of POWER I will fight till the last hour.
In the name of COURAGE I will make up for my errors.
In the name of CONFIDENCE I will never be incompetent.
In the name of DISCIPLINE I will be one above dissension
In the name of LOYALTY I will strive for unity
In the name of RESPONSIBILITY I will be for real, for me
In the name of ENCOURAGEMENT I will do what is necessary to avoid disturbance
In the name of POSITIVITY I will be sensitive to those in need.
In the name of POTENTIAL I will prove myself to be essential.
In the name of MATURITY I will let no one be sure of me
In the name of RESPECT I will treat others with it in all aspects
In the name of LOVE I will love through the feeling of being shunned.
In the name of LIFE I will live it to the fullest.

Gerald Cooper

I Was There

There is a place where the sun meets the thunder
    In the night,
And I was there.
Where? You say, is this place so fair?
Go where the desert meets the Rockies
    And the air smells right.
The air is dry beyond belief
    And the mountains rage with fire.
Uncontrollable fire.
One realizes the flames are near,
Death is here, but there's no fear.
For I was there . . .
    When flames hit soil and faith came to bear.
I was there? . . . I was there!
And now I'm not,
    And I don't care.

Dennis Chatham Jr.

Memories

Now you can soar like an eagle
in the skies with no pain
Please watch over me if you're able
and I will only have good things to gain
I saw your sign when you found
your pot of Gold
and I knew then, you weren't left out in the cold.
My love for you will continue to grow, for
you it was always above the chart
I want you to know, you will always hold
a very special place in my heart.
I know I didn't have to say good-bye
'cause in my heart you never left me
To me, you were always and still are a terrific guy
you were everything I always wanted to be.

Julia Ann Marx

Untitled

Mothers have a complicated role. They must teach us to know
our soul.
In their instruction we must learn. To love, share, care, and show
our concern.

Mothers are that by virtue of a father
With whom they create this new introduction
This doubles the things we expect from them,
For now they are the support of the mate
Often someone, by whom, for granted they are taken.

My Mother handled all her responsibilities with joy and grace
Always everyone can see her love exude from her face.
She gave birth to me, happy as if I was perfect;
Mending my body when the experts said it would be correct.
Working hard each day while she gained a higher education,
A living example of life without sedation.

Her mate she made feel as if he was king
In Camelot, as they frolicked in the joy their love did bring,
Waltzing through life like each challenge was a new song.
An occasional "ouch" when something did go wrong - wrongs
happen in
everyone's life. They handled them together to reduce their strife.
Together things were held with a "glue" called Mom.
The one stabilizing force I could always depend on.

Karen Burress

Mistress Truth

Oh mistress truth where do thee hide?
In what dark place do thee abide?

Oh, elusive maiden whom all men seek, but most have never seen,
Do you live your life in logic or in dream?

Most men profess to know you, their vanity strangely fed,
With the past starving their minds,
They feed easily from the dead.

The danger in life would be finding you, this I know,
For the pious and principled would cry out -
"This is not so!", and truth - would have to go.

Convenience long disguised as her, if unmasked,
Might make them think, and proud man, his pitiful thoughts,
And fat ego, rightly shrink.

No, truth, you shall remain the elusive mistress,
Who has slept in each man's bed,
And before the dawn of reason,
Has shamefacedly fled!

Grace A. Davis

Swallowing

The words spoken by her tender lips were truths
in what once was a believing soul. I am only left
to swallow the poisonous jealousy . . . shoving it down . . .
. . . forcing it down my eternal throat that is unable
to produce any sound to protect her. To one that
can not allow himself to believe, all truths are lies
and all lies ar truths.

I can only retrieve to a familiar surrounding where
the voices of past conversations yell over the sound
of the howling wind crashing against the defenseless
windows . . . whispering her soft breath. I can not
bare to lose her nor can I confine her, yet my thoughts
stab . . . stab . . . stab . . . stab my eyes
so that I am unwilling to see the truth, that which
is the light.

Gary Diaz

Revolutions

Revolutions of a thousand earths, behold,
incessant visits upon her weary soul.
Impervious to guests unknown,
however, vulnerable to yours alone.

Unjust to her slumber, as well as her life,
She beckons upon you to be by her side.
The inflamed heart of a feeble mind,
despairs to release two hearts intertwined.

Respond not to impressions of love,
for she knows not what she is speaking of.
Governed by music from the harmony of spheres,
and blinded by the inundation of tears.

Take your flight, but not in its entirety,
A million other nights has it's complexity.
Within one circle of the earth around the sun,
the lady's misery may well come undone.

Jaymie D. Crisostomo

Untitled

Dances at dawn . . .
Innocence, Sincerity
The love of an irrelevant fool
Destiny has no honor
For the valedictorian lies
    peacefully sleeping in the cell
Perception . . .
the question of our soul's mind
Where is common sense?
Lost within the self searching
    for answers to life's questions
On time goes without a minute of satisfaction
We lie, live, see and change
Happiness . . .
Souls undescribable tasks
We yearn.
Someday . . .
Worlds merge
Souls bond, love tangible
Life liveable

Denise Belyea

An Answer to a Prayer

Porcelain heart in a bed of rose petals.
Innocent smile reveals your soul.
Hypnotic eyes mirror forbidden words.
Words are so often empty and filled with unbalanced thought.
Fear, apprehension and insecurity yield unquestionable doubt.
I yearn to break free of chains that confine
To fly free out of the cage that inhibits my soul.
Together, yet alone.
Close, yet far away.
I reach out to you; are you really there?
Sing to me, hold me close and communicate you
   mind and dreams.
Seep into my body and hold my fragile heart close to yours
Feel its pure intensity and commitment.

Deborah L. Torgersen

Woman's Power

A woman has some power,
Inside of her own self.
Some women take that power,
And forget it on the shelf.

Those women go to others,
And think they'll solve it all.
But the others just give them one big push,
And leave for them to solve.

We really don't need others,
To make us better, no way.
Cause the power lives inside of you,
Any and every day.

You must learn to respect yourself,
And you are not so far.
To know that you are number 1,
And respect you, who you are.

Listen to my words my friend,
And bloom like a flower.
Always, always respect your self,
And respect the woman power.

Crystal Dawn Trujillo-Humiston

Untitled

Sensory moments suspend time
Inspiration fans the flame.
Color is so beautiful
Why does it cause such shame.

Compassion heals the wounded heart
Laughter dries all tears.
Pray that we each do our part
To nurture ourselves throughout the years.

Catherine Frinier

Lost

  Lost is the way I feel today.
In search of the means to make it all okay.
  Lost is the way I see myself.
Like my life goes by while I sit on a shelf.
  The days are too long, the nights even longer,
The feelings of emptiness and contempt grow stronger.

  What happened to me? Where did I go?
Why do all my life's answers turn out to be no?
  Have I lost my mind, my conscience, my soul?
I reach and I reach, but never quite to my goal.
  I am lost and searching for answers within,
something to release me from all my years of sin.

Denise E. Ramey-Hood

Touch Of An Angel

When depression has enter into your soul
Instead of friends - there is only darkness
To push you down and smother your spirit
Let the touch of an angel guide your steps
To beyond the darkness, where light awaits
Within your being is stored a spark
Reach deep and trust it to be revealed
Light can pierce the overwhelming dark
Dark has never pierced the light, it is your right
Take the hand of an angel, follow the light.

Forsake all the negative your sure is true
The one remaining truth inside of you
Is that the darkness will not reward you
With a smiling face or a happy heart
Every beginning starts with the first step
Come out of yourself where you've been hiding
When your done with the darkness and pain
The light is waiting to make you whole again
You'll find that the tugging of the angel
Was your own soul - reaching, searching for the light . . .

Colleen Graham

Coming Home

I ran down the path to the wide wooden bridge
  Intending to go to the orchard beyond.
But I stopped at the bridge to look down at the stream
  Just to cherish my joy in this Eden of mine,
While the leaves on the trees asked to dance with the breeze
  And went on with their shadowy dance down below.

Again I went home and the bridge was no more.
  The stream had been dammed and the trees were laid low.
The orchard was paved and a freeway placed there
  With the noise and the din of fast trucks screaming by.
And I said to myself as my heart broke within,
  "Your childhood is gone! You can never come home!"

"Oh no, that's not true", I mused one long night
  As I tossed on my bed lost deep in my thoughts
"You can always return to that dear time and place.
  You can bring back that bridge and the sound of the stream
And the trees with their beautiful dancing green leaves.
  For give thanks—they're gifts from your mind to your soul."

Doris Barnard Bragdon

Mirror Of A Barbie Doll

Just to behold your beauty is like looking
into a mirror of a Barbie doll.

Your reflexing so new . . . so carefree,
I find myself loving you more each passing day, for
a prayer have I to pray, that we will remain,
and stay till the end of time.

Not seeing the mirror of Barbie dolls, is like
a absent voided deep inside that one finds missing
when she is no where to be found.

This Barbie doll has her up's and down's, but then
again don't we all?

Trying to get things together as fast as they come,
for things happens for a reason, as sure as the coming
seasons of winter, spring, summer, and fall.

As time beats on, and the seasons pass, I still
long for the opportunity to find you, . . .
. . . and call you, . . . my Barbie doll.

Delton Culpepper Jr.

A Mere Speck Of Dust

A mere speck of dust, a polished imperfection born
into a world of claims that never hold true.
Speaking of peace but achieving war, putting
trust in men blinded by their pursuit of power and money.
Calming of words between world powers,
religious strife and hatred for sacred soil fill other
lands with bloodshed.
What is to happen to a world that only knows how to hate
those that don't the same beliefs?
Has there not been fair warning of what will be our future?
Holy writings have supplied the answers all along.
Thousands upon thousands of people dying from sickness
and starvation, a simple act of kindness is all some ask for.
While many consider life a precious gift, is it not a greater gift
to love?
Choose your role models well, for the day of the separating
of good and bad is near.

Dimitri Frant

Promise Fulfilled

In faith borne up from out the depths of eons past,
Into dark, dank soil I buried beauty, locked in bulbs of brown.
'Twas in the autumn afterglow of life's fickle fleeting form,
When summer's verdant richness a sweet memory had become,
And wondrous multi-colored splendor rashly reigned o'er the whole
From the tallest mountain peak to the very valleys of my sheltered soul.
Expectantly, the hasty planting now, ere nature's pristine blanketry
Of pathway and portico should reality become, and sleep o'ertake the all.
In one wee fraction of ageless time this rime-rimmed earth-globe stirred,
Rose up from out the torpor of it's quiescent lassitude,
As exultant spring rent wide the strictive bands of frosty bondage there,
And in my garden those lowly little knobs of earth-hued hope
Loosed their frigid fetters and pushed sunward sleek, strong stems
Pregnant with the promise of fragrant floral fantasies of flame,
Such as to put last autumn's portentous promenade to lasting shame.
Then in that mystic moment of rampant beauty-blaze, God touched me,
Conceived awesome wonder in my heart and spoke in kind and gentle vein,
"Lovely this but 'tis only sun scorched shrub half sunk in sandy loam,
When viewed against the gloried garden grandeur that'll welcome you,
When your journey here is o'er and faith will have led you Home!"

Isabel Hintzman

Epic Cafe

Street lights outside leak illumination
Into the desolate air and onto the window
Which frames the reflection of lovers at opposite ends
Who are dragged by the whistle of each other's
Howl scraping reconciliation
Purging more than true feelings warrant

Different angles mix at intersections
The views shattered by a cornered laugh
Its echo explodes across the cafe cave
And rumbles the table legs
Disrupting unconsummated chocolate crumbs on white china
The lone survivors from a chocolaholic's raid

Outside a few cats scurry and scamper
To dark places beneath parked car shelters
Absorbed into black paved silence
Magnetic force swallows my vision up now
As I am pulled to a handsome smile on the velvet couch
Like a fall into a deep canyon
I slip into a sip of darkness

Amber C. LaPointe

Inspired Thought

A strong idea soars as if on wings,
Into the hearts of people who accept
The knowledge that it carries and it brings.
And in the minds of people most adept
At seeing that which seems quite unexplained,
Their minds reach out and grasp the foreign thought
And gently let it grow as kindled flame
Intensifies, and finally flaring hot,
Bursts forth in glory bright and genius that
The people all look up to and admire,
But think that they could never be looked at
As ones who could spontaneously inspire.
But if their souls are active and aware,
The winged thoughts just naturally come there.

Elizabeth Hoffecker

My True Friend

Life, that brief journey through humanity,
Invites me to search for a few true friends,
Leads me to ponder my own sanity.
Looking for one who truly comprehends
Intimate friendship's goal and objective
Aroused memories of the year just ended.
Never doubt you are among the selective
Few who has with no purpose befriended
Rogues and mischievous fellows such as I.
A true friend will tell you when you are wrong,
Never afraid to seek the reason why,
Courage and honesty makes friendship strong.
  I know upon you I can always depend.
  Surely you will always remain my true friend.

John W. Weaver

Dragon Flight

The quiet buzz of dragonflies
Invites the slumber
Just listen to the constant hum
Relax and let the worries of this world pass you by
Lying under the sky
And watching the dragonflies whiz by
Provides the peaceful resting place
To imagine simple meaningful thoughts
Or dream of things to be.

Carolyn Milicia

The Thrill Of Gymnastic

Watching Shannon Miller,
Is a real thriller.
She does a lot of cool tricks,
In doing her gymnastics.
I know that I'm only in level four,
But I do my best and even more.
My favorite event is the beam,
I leap across it like a gleam.
Flipping across the patted floor,
Doing round off back-hand-springs and even more.
Shoot through's and hand-springs off the vault,
Are my worst tricks to be taught.
The hardest of all are the uneven bars,
It takes a lot of strength an I have many scars.
Although watching Shannon Miller,
Is a real thriller,
I know I can do my best,
If I put my mind to the test!

Christina Marie Otey

Ode To A Son

A little son just like my own long awaited boy,
Is every mother's pride and joy.
His best friend, a faithful dog, is waiting close by,
For this lad with so much wander-lust in his eye.
Without a dream, life would be so very drear,
And a boy has many, a few without fear.
He views the world as all his own;
He feels he could tackle the wild kingdom alone.
There is not one malicious thought in mind;
No one has told him, a new world he must find.
He just reaches out to what ever is there,
Hoping to find excitement and fulfillment somewhere.
Hiding mixed emotions from parents, who see right thru;
He bolsters up courage and seeks for everything that's new.
I remember mine with such sentimental thoughts,
And know, without a vision, all reason for living is lost.
So with sweet memories of days and years gone so swiftly by;
I wanted to pass this on to you; my now grown-up little guy!

Eutha Fletcher

We Think The Same Thoughts

Is it my color
Is it my size
 Is it the shape of my beautiful eyes
Is it my hair
Is it my charm
 Is it the way I bend my arm
Face to face — eye to eye — no reason to attack
No way I can fight — when I'm down on my back
 Is it my language
 Is it my slang
Is it my pain you'd like to obtain
 Is it my teeth
 Is it my feet
 Or just my old clothes being so neat
Face to face — eye to eye — no reason to attack
We see the same thing — when our vision is intact
 We share same fears — we cry same tears
 We think the same thoughts

Carol Janette Hickman-Gayden

Scales

A scale some employ to weight WHITEWATER
        Is ill-adapted to rightly equate
Intending to calm, they preach composure
        . . . Assuring, "This isn't a WATERGATE"
In acknowledging such weak assertions
    I'd have to respond, "That's a bit too late"
Since WATERGATE, while strewing destructions,
        Also at first, wasn't a WATERGATE
It amazes me, but I'm not surprised . . .
    This world's corruption is part of its norm
Though truthfulness lives, yet be well advised
        Its counterfeit masquerades to conform
And as it conforms, it shrouds its broad course
    Upon which the blind are led by the blind
But those that have sight aren't fooled of course . . .
    Instead, their straight paths are clearly defined

The scale that is used among those who see
    For judging between the right and the wrong
Does not balance man's expediency . . .
    It measures the weak to outweigh the strong

Bob G. Martinez

Time

What is Time?
Is it only a humanistic ideal
Applied to a natural process?
Or is it something more . . .
The fire in which we burn,
A predator that stalks
Relentlessly, always victorious in
The End.
Oh, men have tried to elude it,
But no matter how wealthy they are,
Or how much power they hold,
Time will always be right behind them, waiting to
Strike.

Ironically,
When death becomes imminent,
No one wishes for that power or wealth
That was so dear to them in days of health.
What they want is exactly what is quenching
The very life from their being:
Time.

Eric Svendsen

Helping Hand

As the bombs explode all over this land,
I wish we all would give a helping hand.
The world is here for us all to share.
We must let each other know we care.
As we see our loved ones lose their lives,
we wonder what we must do to survive.
All the suffering and pain we feel,
Will it never stop this spinning wheel.
The trouble and hardships, the losing of friends.
When will this nightmare ever end.
We walk through the cities, and the streets of the towns.
And glance at the homeless lying on the ground.
We do not help, just walk away.
Even though we could be like them someday.
We hear the cries of hunger, depression and despair.
Yet, we keep on walking as if we do not care.
We don't even have time to help a friend.
When will this nightmare ever end.

Beth Ann Mosher

Who I Am

Do I upset you
Is it the way I walk or the way I talk?
I don't understand, please tell me.
Is it the curve of my hips or the shape of my lips?
If you don't tell me, I'll never understand.
Is it because I don't do what you command?
Or is it because you want to be in demand.
How dare you try to tell me who I am?
I am a proud young female doing the best that I can.
So don't tell me who I am!
It's hard trying to succeed if all these young men keep
trying me.
You don't understand, I don't want to give you commands.
Nor do I want to be in demand.
So don't tell me who I am!
I am not a toy and I'm not to be played with!
So don't tell me who I am!

Jaquaya J. O'Neal

325

For The Love Of Her

Why does he love her.
Is it the way she walks or the way
She loves him, perhaps the happiness she gives him.
What is love.
Love to him is a never ending thing and
dedication to her.
He is a man that has so much love
for her that he can not cheat on her.
He is the man of her dreams, a man everyone wants,
He is a man who will listen to her
when he knows her jokes are dumb
yet he still loves her and she loves him.
This love he gives is never ending love.
This love he gives is never ending love, but can
she hold on to him forever.
His love and faith is in her heart and mind.
He is a man of true love.

Becca Havard

Untitled Love Poem

What would I give to touch your lips just once;
is my life enough?

What would I give to touch your lips just once;
something from the heart perhaps?
A house, mansion, or a castle, and in that palace
I would place a vault filled with all the worlds precious jewels
for only you to behold.

What would I give to touch your lips just once;
something from my soul perhaps?
A garden, the world's most beautiful, and it would grow
beautiful, red roses around the year.

What could I give to touch your lips just once?
Is my life enough, or my soul, my mind,
or the connection that binds?
If only my love were enough.

What may I give?
For it shall be . . .
As You Wish . . .

Delbert L. Collins II

Untitled

The loveliest flower to ever be found
Is the dandelion that in Spring doth abound.
For when it's picked with tender care
By a precious child with long blonde hair
And offered with much pride to me
Its unmatched beauty do I see.
Its worth surpasses the fairest rose
Its value, only my heart knows.
For there is no bouquet that can ever compare
To the gift from the girl with the long blonde hair.

Jill A. Cunningham

All Will Be Revealed

Is it valid to fear the future?
Is the unknown valid?
If we know not what is impending, should we fear?
Shouldn't we rather welcome the future in hopes of
    betterment?
Hark! Trapped in tyranny of emotion, we shall
    succumb to dread!
The very bowels of our souls shall be revealed to
    the scrutiny of, and taunted by, the unknown . . . the
    wilderness beyond . . .

John M. Dannemiller

More Sense Than Syndrome

The worse thing a woman can suffer in America
Is to be trapped by a crazy man.

Why does he beat me? The answer is simple . . .
Because he can. Because he can.

Why do I stay? He'll hurt the children.
He'll kill me. Then, my corpse will take the blame.

Until he kills me, there's been no crime.
When he does, he walks and wins the game:

He reaps the power he so lusted after—
Now, no one else can ever have me.

He's coddled by cops; my children cry.
It's easier to die. So what? I'm just a she.

Jan Kemp

To Walk Without Love

To walk without love
is to walk with a burden of
death on your shoulder. To die without love
can be denied if in our shadows, if we break out
of our eternal shell.
To walk without love, what a great burden
to never hold hands with another
to be alone.

To walk without love, to see others

Enjoying their mid-afternoon picnics
with their loved ones under a shade tree,
to be without love is to know sorrow

To be without love.
But to their I'm not
without love, I have family.
Still I don't have someone to say to
that I love you girl you're the one of my dreams,
but to be without love is a greater tragedy than
death.

Jonathan Pelosi

Don't Know How To Live Long 'Cause You Don't Know How

Sometimes I wonder, but that
isn't the answer "time is running
out the wise old man would
say not know that was
a key concept of what was
happening to me.

But I didn't understand, 'cause
of the magnetic things in the
presence, and in my possession,
that kept me from focusing
on the principle of my
existence as a human being on
but someday before I
go away, I hope that I
find out the proper
answer about living, as long
as I can, and wish I
do know how to live long

Henry Glover

"Farewell My Friend"

Remembering back to when our eyes first randomly would lock;
It appeared opportunity, was pleasantly destined to knock.

Cherished memories of a young pup, growing more graceful by day;
His appearance most elegant, in his own spirited way.

Swiftly gliding across my path, with a fast paced prance;
Beckoning me impulsively, to take a second glance.

Energetic you were, performing with agility and speed;
Rapidly winning my heart, filling an unspoken need.

Frequent journeys we shared, through the changes of season;
Suddenly illness felled you, I'll never know the reason.

Picturing your excited shadow, scratching at the back door;
How I wish I could hug you, lovingly embrace you once more.

Looking back on my memories, of a devoted trusted friend;
My mind still has trouble, comprehending why it had to end.

With a heavy heart carrying sorrow and much grief to bare;
I gently laid my dog to rest, with guarded painstaking care.

Forever his memory, tucked in a comforting spot in my heart;
Shall remain uniquely treasured, we will never be apart . . .

Debra L. Cempellin

Grandma's Grocery Cart

The sparkling teddy bear stood proudly on the shelf
It caught my eye as I walked by as if it shouted out.
It seem to say, here Grandma, I'm waiting just for you,
Buy me for your granddaughter, that sweetie-pie of two.
I took the sparkling teddy bear and placed it in my cart
Continued down another aisle 'til suddenly I stopped.
There I was a fire truck in the tea and coffee aisle,
This is just perfect for my four year old grandchild.
The gaily fire engine in its brightly colored box
Was added to essentials in my so-called grocery cart.
I came across a video tape as I hurried on my way,
That box office smash . . . it just came out today.
Why, this is it, I thought, that much sought after one,
Placed it in the cart for my eldest grandson.
Those clever marketing people who place enticing things
Know who to get to grandmas to make that register ring . . .

Eleanor F. Basinger

This Rhythm Is Not Mine

This rhythm is not mine
it comes from all hearts beating
all valves opening and closing
it comes from the silent movement of fishtails in the ocean
and from the swinging of waves and tides
it comes from the woodpecker
and from the way the ants parade across the ground
it comes from the circling sun
and the swaying leaf that falls every autumn

no this rhythm is not mine
but none of these can claim it either
not even the spinning moon in her waning and waxing
can boast its creation
This rhythm is old and as constant as our sure death
and as sure as the way morning appears
again and again on the horizon

Nothing does not dance to this rhythm
it is heard in every speck of all worlds
even the God's are forced to step in time
it's been around so long it never began

John DeKadt

Truth

What is truth but love spelled backwards

And what is pain but lies multiplied,

A lie is a cancer never stopping until
it devours a relationship.

Is a thought with held a lie?
Only if it causes pain.

How can truth hurt if it frees the spirit.

Does honesty cause pain, or does pain
make us honest?

A lie always catches somewhere, like a
web, it clings and gathers until the weight
finally breaks it and all the ugliness is seen.

If I could but burn it out like a laser.

A germ crushed before the body becomes
malignant will itself.

Only to be reborn in the cleansing
light of truth.

Catherine M. Warzynshi

Desperation

Run! Run!
It doesn't matter where . . .
As long as the wheels keep turning.
Shout it to the trees.
They listen attentively but offer no solutions.
They cannot keep your secret
For it is swept away by the first breeze.
Beware of outstretched arms that care not!

Estelle Rapp

Wild Flower

I left the garden to pick a wild flower
It drew me through its magical power
I tasted its nectar, much like a bee
Soon I had pollen all over me
I returned to the garden, to smell it's bloom
Tasted its nectar and also to groom
The flowers leaves, but I smelled the scent
Of the wild flower to which I had went
It drew me from the garden like a curious child
Out to the field to that flower so wild

Andrew Thomas

"The Meaning Of Life"

What is the meaning of life?;
is it driving a fancy car or is it owning a big house
or is it trying to improve the life of others or
could it be that it is all of these meanings. But still I wonder,
how people can be so ignorant yet so aware. And where do we learn
these things? Are they dictated to us by society or are they
taught to us by our parents. For all I know, is that taking these
ideas in consideration there is no real meaning to life, just
loneliness.

Danielle Gatewood

The Trail

There is a trail I like so much,
it has so much to offer, things to
see and hear and touch.
You can see trees for miles and miles,
and so many flowers and animals that are wild.
You can hear the water of a bubbling brook,
hear the rustling of leaves through the
wind as they shook.
Perhaps you might hear the croaking of
a fog, hear birds singing, or see a deer
jump over a log.
So many plants and flowers and shrubs to see,
so much quietness in all that beauty.
It takes me away from life's stress
a oneness with nature, a place to rest.
No cars or people just nature all around.
I sit on a rock and listen to all
those wonderful sounds,
as I walk this trail each time,
Its splendor and beauty give me peace of mind.

Jane Lavin

Love

Love is always patient and kind,
It is never jealous.

Love is never boastful nor conceited
Never rude nor selfish.

Love never takes offenses, and it is
Never resentful.

Love takes never no pleasure in other
Peoples conscious, it delights in the truth.

But love is always ready to excuse,
To trust, hope and to endure in whatever
Surpasses your way.

Love does not ever come to and end!

Diane Garcia

Beauty

Beauty is neither money nor power
It is not selfish or abrupt
Beauty can not be bought or created
It is not greedy or corrupt

Beauty can not be lost or stolen
It can not be achieved or found
Beauty is not just in your face and body
But it is inside of you and all around

Beauty is in the way you feel
When you awake to a newly christened day
Beauty is the Christmas song your heart sings
When its just the middle of May

Beauty is not lonely
It is filled with joy and love
Beauty is in the way you show friendship
And the way you rise above

Beauty is in the words you speak
For they are nothing to fear
Beauty is the sparkle in your eyes
As they forever shine loud and clear

Brad Goldvarg

World War I

Remember in 1914, the first world war.
It killed, and led many people to being poor.
Many people died;
And many cried.
You can't forget those years.
They hold most of everyone's fears.

The shots rang out;
And soldiers ran about.
The bombs were dropped;
When the war ended, they finally stopped.

Whoever survived got to go home.
while the deceased just stayed and roamed.

Britney Patterson

Untitled

Everything was so silent on the waters edge
it moving, swaying, an unknown mind
I looked afar, seemingly to the ledge
I saw a dance of the ethereal kind
they called to each other
and moved and danced in time
all moving together
a mysterious and unknown mind
I turned to go and then
as a chill rose in the air
I stopped to watch again
but as I searched nothing was there
was it just a trick, an illusion
all that I saw
did I have a vision
was it really there at all

Emily Bryant

I'll Always Love You

I can't forget that first night we met
It only meant - have fun, be gay
Then fate stepped in and took a hand
My heart changed, love was here to stay

Your love for me grew very dear
Through hopes and plans we made together
Our dreams, our longing for much we desired
The nearness of love, and vows we made forever

Times of silence, with the warmth of your love
You held me close - not a word was spoken
I knew you loved me, alone or in a crowd
Our hands clasped tight, these moments were golden

This love grew stronger day by day
This love we knew as yours and mine
I built a home for you, deep in my heart
Our hearts beat together and proved the bind

Now I sit alone with only memories and tears
My heartbeat is heavy - I'm lonesome, I'm blue
My arms are open to welcome you home
Please come back - I love you, I'll always love you

Chuck Hawkins

From A Window

Do you know the joy a window can bring?
It opens a wall, so you can see
The fluttering leaves on a tall green tree
And a blue sky above with white clouds full of glee.
A joyous blue bird is singing his song,
Come with me, come with me, come along, come along!

At his invitation I followed the bird,
Hearing his song that had to be heard.
Bird did not know the joy he would bring,
His only desire was to sing, sing, sing!
Over soft rolling hills we flew with no notion,
Soon we were over the beautiful ocean,
Over that sea with it's long sandy beaches
Embroidered lace edges to it's last reaches.
Soft breezes caressed as we seemed to glide
Over shinning wet sand and the singing tide.

Then, upward we flew through white clouds full of glee,
Back to the window and the tall green tree.

Delight Melaragno

My Uncle Joe

I remember Uncle Joe as being gregarious.
It seemed like everything he said was always hilarious.
He made us feel special, even when we were young.
And he could make us laugh so hard we thought we'd bust a
lung!!

But then came a day there was sadness Upstairs.
Seems like mostly all they heard was weeping and 'gimme'
prayers.
Said St. Peter to the Lord, "Ya know, I heard a rumor.
It's too solemn here in Heaven, we really need some humor."

The Lord thought a moment, then said, "I have the answer.
My blessed servant, Joe, is having trouble with cancer.
I hate to see him suffer, his heart is so dear.
Send a messenger down, and bring him up here."

Joe said, "Lord, this is great, so much better than life.
Please just do one thing, take good care of my wife,
and all my kin and friends. You know, there are quite a few."
The Lord said, "Of course, Joe, in fact, I already do!!"

I can picture God with Joe, relating events of the day.
Joe looks Him in the eye and says, "Ta Hell ya say!!"
All the saints gasp, wondering what will come after.
Then the skies become filled with heavenly laughter.

Janet Littlefield

The Times

People these days are always running to and fro
It seems as if they are in a hurry to go.

Instead of taking time out and saying hello.
They just write a quick check to say they gave to the poor.

What happened to the days when mothers braided their children's hair
Or even when hearing of a murder on TV was so very rare?

Bring back the times when nights were filled with peace
Not all the violence that takes over our streets without cease.

It's time for a new beginning, a new way of life
No more of this hate, envy, and strife.

In order for this to happen, change must begin with you.
With that said, this poem is through.

Jamila Pratt

Dad

Memories of my childhood will never fade.
It seems like only yesterday when they were first made.

Like the time you taught me to ride a bike,
You realized through the years your children weren't alike.

Practicing softball at times seemed like a chore,
But with your encouragement, I enjoyed it even more.

The summer trips to the state fair were always a lot of fun.
We waited anxiously in line, despite the scorching sun.

Your patience was tested when you taught me how to drive.
I'm sure, however, you were thankful that you did survive.

High school and college seemed to fly by over the years.
I remember our good-bye with sadness and many tears.

Now I'm on my own with my new family,
But I want you to know that you still mean a lot to me.

Thank you for being such a great dad with support and abundant love.
Though you may not know it, you're a blessing from above.

Anita Cuellar

Mother's Day, Or The Milkweed Nosegay

Among the sweet-smelling primroses there grew a sour milkweed:
It sustained the most fragile of the primroses.
Never mind that it was shut out of the richest supplies of minerals
    and water
Never mind that the youngest primroses scorned their protector.
The milkweed watched over the flora in her vicinity just the same:
Unbending in a windstorm,
Nourishing herself without special grooming,
Refusing to be plucked during mulch or petal preening time.
No one writes a lyrical "Ode to a Milkweed,"
No one gathers it on a Scottish hillside like
Wild mountain thyme — tethered to make a romantic bouquet.
Only the Creator saw her as the earth mother of mothers,
And cherished the sour milkweed on her special day.
That's the origin of the milkweed nosegay,
Now ever so popular on Mother's Day.

Barbara Hantman

An American Ironworker

What makes a man rise to the challenge of building a skyscraper?
It takes a certain type of man to work high above the street.
He performs his daily job without missing a single beat.
The huge crane hoists the steel beams, one piece at a time.
To watch the connector's work, is smoother than any rhyme.
They climb the steel columns like a squirrel in a tree.
There's an overwhelming feeling of a man being free.
The connectors hang a floor in just a few days.
To look up from the street, its a giant steel maze.
The rest of the men work just as hard, watching every step,
always on guard.
They'll put in the bolts and deck all the floors.
Soon they'll reach the heights where the eagle soars.
The building will rise higher each day,
in just a short time it's there to stay.
We're almost at the top, the last floor is here.
Tomorrow it will go up and the end is near.
This work has killed many good men,
but this job has ended without losing a friend.

Angelo Paolone

Negro

Down life's dreary road
It travel, alone.
No friends, no companions,
no home.
The world sees me pass,
but it knows not who I am,
nor does it inquire,
rather pushes me aside,
to be cared for
by some kind passerby.
For centuries I've had to take a back seat,
except in times of war,
while shedding my blood and dying,
asking, Lord, what for?
Tomorrow, I'll reach the front,
by today's steady pace,
where I will stand with other men
and take my rightful place.

Johnie Carlisle Jr.

Untitled

I bought myself a present today.
It was a stick of Super Dry Right Guard.
It allows me to go outside and play,
and not smell like the rest of the yard.

Maybe if I smell good she'll let me stay,
But she'd still rather have me go.
She'll never look at me the right way.
She'll miss her chance to know.

She'll miss all the times that would have been;
She'll miss our kids with the nobel prize.
She'll miss the sunsets we would have seen,
She'll miss the feeling inside her thighs.

She'll miss everything my loving gives.
She'll experience everything the wrong way.
She'll go on and live the life she lives,
But for her, April showers will pour through May.

And for me, I'll be worse off than her,
Because I'll have known what my life should be.
I'll be a disease, I'll have no cure,
Until her medicine works on me.

Adam F. Pockross

Momma's Gift

I found a dusty old book in my House today,
It was along time ago that I put it away.

I found the old book while chasing a mouse,
Who has apparently decided to share my house.

It was hidden way back in an old book shelf,
I had placed it there my guilty old self.

The old book was worn and yellowed with age,
But I could feel Momma's presence on every page.

Momma carried this book most places she went,
And always to church where her sundays were spent.

I've dusted it off, and I hold it with love,
As I think of my Momma in heaven above.

I leaf through the pages so weathered and bent,
And I thank the good Lord for a gift heaven sent.

This Old Bible gives memory to a Momma so sweet,
And as I follow her through it, I feel strong on my feet.

George A. D. Mann Jr.

The Fortunate One

I still remember me laughing.
It was yesterday, I think.
Oh, no, 'cause yesterday I was still hoping
That I would laugh again someday.
And I don't think it was last year.
Maybe last month, maybe last week.
The memory's so alive, that I can almost hear
My laughter. Then, I guess I do remember well
That I did laugh one day.
I hope the time will mind me not
And will not make my memory fade away.
Oh, God, I am so grateful for letting me laugh once!

Anca Sorin

The Love That Could've Been

At first glance, I couldn't quite see your face
It was your voice that drew me near
The song you sang, hushed the place
My being there, suddenly became clear

We were introduced, and you became my friend
It all seemed to happen so fast
A new romance was about to begin
This was special, and we wanted it to last

As each day passed, the love would grow
Our hearts had connected in such a way
What the future would hold for us, we didn't know
I thought the love of my life, was here to stay

But now my love, we have been torn apart
So much we still had yet to share
Throughout this lifetime, you will remain in my heart
For you, I will always care

So much time has passed, but even now I cry
Remembering how we were back then
I still ask God "Why" When I think of . . .
The Love That Could've Been

Denise Vicker

"We Will Meet Again"

When I die shall we again meet
It will not be on earth, but in a land
that is oh so sweet

When my time has come please don't stand
above me and cry
For our time to meet gets closer as the days go by

My spirit will always be with you
even though I have left
But you will remember me most in the memories
you have kept

Will you look the same as you did the day I passed
Or will you look older, but still your best

No one knows how long it will be
No one knows when this life we will leave

Our day to meet again will be a happy one
Our time of waiting to see each other will be done

In loving memory of my Pa-pa

Amanda McFarland

Peace

Shhh . . . Whisper; look up at the moon.
It will tell you a story. A story of when it was young.
When the earth was at peace.
Look up at the stars shining in all their beauty . . . shining for a
   reason.
Look at the sun, for he is strong, he's been through the battle of
   time. He can relate.
Look at the never-ending sea, stretching before you,
Silent one minute, crashing against the shore the next.
Never-ending beauty, bringing up shells and creatures to the sand.
Look at the trees, they are strong. They stand proud against the wind.
Look at the clouds. They move diligently, silently.
Look at the grass; a sheltering place for those in need of shelter.
Shhh . . . Whisper; look inside yourself, for you are the moon,
You are the stars, you are the sun,
You are the sea, you are the trees,
You are the clouds, you are the grass,
You are beauty, you are serenity,
You are peace.

   Carolyn Elizabeth Anderson

A Vision

The ground is tainted
It's black with hate, fowl and evil
The pieces are falling, down . . . down . . . down . . .
They almost all fit
A time to expect, a time of regret
A time to accept, not wanting to
Fighting this feeling, the stillness of the night
With all its sounds; loneliness, betrayal and sadness
Uncertainty and confusion, cold and mislead
Where it used to be sunny and bright
It is now dark and empty
Memories fading, wanting to forget
Ill from no nurturing, no purpose no answers
No love and no trust, walking a thin line
A real need for sympathy, an ounce of compassion
A smile a hello
Wanting honestly with assurance
Master of deception will soon fall
So will the mountain, for which it
Was never solid and concrete

   Jewelly Kaalberg

A Magnificent Tree

Gracefully swaying back and forth
It's golden color shining bright in the sun's beams
The sun's warmth and glow make it seem peaceful
The long leaves go for miles
The giant tree goes so high up
Its shade is like a cool blanket of darkness
Its like a dream
It becomes so magical your spirit soars
When the golden sun goes down it disappears into the
darkness like turning a light off
What a magnificent tree

   Amber Bartley

Black Man in America

Being a black man in 1995 America is hard
It's hard for injustices we must still face
It's hard for the looks of fear we receive
It's hard for those who still must hate
It's hard for the ones who try to put us in our place
It's hard for the men working so long
It's hard for the women who stood by strong
It's hard for old men who fought for their rights
It's hard for young men tempted by easy living
It's hard for the fear, the grief, and the hate
It's hard for stereotypes, symbols, and falsehoods
It's hard for the neighborhoods plagued by decay
It's hard for the drugs, the booze, the sin
It's hard to keep faith, keep belief, keep strong
It's hard for those who do not wish to do wrong
It's hard to rise up when you're being put down
But most of all, it's hard for the children . . .

   James Barry

Lazy Sunday

On this cold wet wintery day,
It's here on the couch I plan to stay.
Light from the windows, gloomy and gray,
Under a nice warm blanket, I will lay.

Anxiously awaiting the big Sunday game,
For now an old movie, I don't know the name.
All these chores to do; I have no shame.
They'll be here tomorrow, they'll be the same.

A lazy day made just for me,
On this Sunday, I'm worry free.
Places to go, things to see,
There's no where I'd rather be.

   Dale Cravey

My Southern Star

When the dawn came today, the sun roused me.
   It's light was warm, and soothed me.
As I basked in the morning's silence,
   I thought of you.
My mind's eye saw your face, and you smiled.
   A warmth equal to that upon my skin filled my heart.
My mind's ear heard your laughter, and the stillness of
   the day broke into song of joy.
My mind's arms reached out, embraced you, and
   lifted my spirit from its resting.
You lingered in my thoughts as the task of
   my day drew to an end.
The sky reclaimed darkness; the stars harmonized
   their light in the great reservoir of black space.
I looked up to see a brilliant white light
   shining above the horizon.
I thought of you.
The star that I gazed at extended it's light
   from the Southern Sky.

   Diane Van Ornam

Life . . .

Life—it isn't something you know-it has to be learned
It's not a given-it must be earned
We all make mistakes, sometimes we do things wrong
But what doesn't destroy us serves to makes us strong

You must look ahead to where you want to go
Strive for a vision that will make you grow
Don't let the challenges get in your way
Face them straight on-come what may

You can't hide behind a bottle, a drug or pill
Or you'll end up doing things against your will
You must make the choices that are right for you
No one else can tell you what you should do

You have to work for what you desire
You have to pay for what you acquire
It won't be easy-life wasn't meant to be
Nothing worth having comes to you free

But if you need a friend along the way
I'm here for you tomorrow and today
There is only one thing I ask from you
Accept me in your life-my friendship is true

Jamie Kinion

Where Are You Now Father?

When I fell off my tricycle, you comforted me,
"It's OK Sweety, when you fall you have to get back up."
Daddy, where are you now with your comforting words?

When I was afraid to go to kindergarten, you soothed me,
"It's OK sweety to be afraid of something new; everyone is."
Daddy, where are you now with your soothing words?

When I woke up crying, you reassured me.
It's OK sweety, "Bad dreams help you understand your fears."
Daddy, where are you now with your reassuring words?

When I was cut from cheerleader try outs, you consoled me,
"It's OK to fail, it helps you find your strengths."
Daddy, where are you now with your consoling words?

Daddy, You could always make me feel better.
Where are you now?

Erika Nunez

Beginnings

As the sun slowly rises,
  It's rays wafting through the window,
    Taking the chill out of the air,
      It brings with it a sense of freshness,
        and newness; like a newborn babe,
          It brings chances of hope and dreams of the future.

The clock is ticking,
  The creak and groans of a settling house,
    The oil burner clicks on,
      Implied harmonies and melodies,
        A complete symphony to the trained ear,
          One might call it home.

George A. Wilkes III

Gods Glorious Creations

I often wonder about the world
  It's roof the vast blue sky,
Sprinkled with puffy snow white clouds
  that go sailing by.
The rising sun that shines so bright
  announcing the break of day
Twinkling stars, like jeweled kites
  moon beams to light our way.
The stately trees with heads held high.
  Flowers with colors so bright,
The cheerful songs of birds that fly,
  God shaped snow flakes, soft and white
Mountains and valleys, hills and planes
  Oceans and rivers swelled by rains
Lions and tigers, sharks and whales
Floppy eared, wiggly nosed cotton tails
All of these wonders, more precious than gold.
God's majestic creations, for we to behold,
Breath taking beauty, how blest are we
And all of this beauty my Lord comes from thee.

Clotilda Tullio

Love

What is love?
It's the smile that brightens my day.
It's the joy you give me each and every day.
It's the comfort when I'm in pain.
It's the gentle touch of someone's hand.
It's the smile on my children's face.
It's communication so we both can understand.
It's compromising; not who's right or wrong.
It's knowing when to comfort and when to stand by.
It's saying I'm sorry and take the blame.
It's working together to accomplish one goal.
It's giving your heart without losing one's soul.
It's being the one, that I should comfort and hold.

Andrea Harry

Thanksgiving

Oh, how the months do fly by,
It's time again for thanksgiving pie.

The hassle and bustle of a turkey dinner,
Has changed a bit, to keep us thinner.

Old-fashioned gatherings have decreased in number,
While folks are staying home, taking time to slumber.

Years have passed in one direction,
Time has come for profound reflection.

It was to grandparents' house we used to travel,
Just enough time to become unraveled.

We are grateful Lord, for these memories of gold,
And do reach out to all, so they may come to know you,
  in the world-wide fold.

We renew our prayers of thanksgiving this day,
For all your great gifts, in utter dismay.

Please accept our humble prayer of thanks
And always keep us faithful till we
Reach your Heavenly ranks.

Esther Turbak

A Rosebud Unfolds

Conceived in the love of God, a rosebud unfolds
Its velvet soft petals, kissed by the morning sun.
Its inner, fragrant beauty as yet still untold,
'Til the sun's warmth unwraps each petal one, by one.

The tiny dewdrops cling still to its tender lips,
Glistening mirrors of the blue heavens above.
Each drop reflects its vision of the world then slips
Gently over velvet curves to return God's love.

A whispered breeze causes then its leaves to tremble,
Stirred to life by God's beloved breath they awake.
Each rib and vein embraced by His touch resembles
A hand outstretched, all the gifts of God's love to take.

A rosebud has become what God meant it to be.
The delicate heart has opened, its love set free.

Julie M. Althaus

No Face

I no longer have a face
I've become a number
To my family, a disgrace
I can still feel, I know what is real.
I no longer have a face
I'm a number in this place.

I no longer have my privacy it doesn't matter
No one cares, no one sees
I've become a number
Stripped of all dignity
I no longer have a face
I'm just a number in this place.

Someday when I am free
My face will come back to me
My privacy will return
My dignity, I will have earned

I am no longer a number
I no longer see this place for now I am free
I can now see my face.

Barbara Jean Hard

The Other Side

I've seen what I had to see,
I've been where I had to be.
I've talked the talk I had to talk.
I've walked the walk I had to walk.
So rescue me from this stag net world I live,
Give to me so I can give,
Let me cross the bridge I've burnt.
Take away the pain take away the hurt.
I've heard a lot about this place.
A place where time stands still.
A place where no one kills,
Where the sun always shines,
And people are accepted as all kinds,
The odds are even and their in my favor.
The odds are good this will be a life I'll savor,
So take down the sign that say peace sells but who's buying.
I've bought my peace so I guess their lying,
Turn on the light so I can see,
Turn on the light and I'll show you just how this place can be.
Take my hand, lets go far a ride

Derek Daling

Mom

Every since the day you died,
I've never felt the same inside.
My heart is broken,
and my love is unspoken.

I just wish you were still here,
So I could wipe away the tears.
But, I know you're not and I feel so bad,
Because I know the last words I said
made you sad!
I didn't say I love you, or have a great
day, instead I said I hate you and then I
ran away!

Only if I knew it would of been my last
chance to say good-bye to you, I would of
said, please don't go, I Love You!!

Angie Jannicelli

Resignation

Framed in the barn door
John watched a dappled dawn tarry on the horizon
Curling hazy fingers around fields not quite mower ripe.

    Languidly loosing her dreams, Earth Mother sighed,
    Misting the heads of wheat, bearding them with dew
      For the Sun's amusement
    As, newborn,
    He'd toddle down the hills,
    Exploring the valleys, poking transparent fingers
    Into cool green bogs and waiting fields.

John nodded a farewell,
  Knowing that tomorrow,
    The auctioneers finished,
    He'd wake smog smothered
      Distracted by city-sound
      Bereft of this communion,
      Soul shrunk.

Frances Boyle

Hurricane

Dark faced clouds thundering their anger
Join together in a swirling mass over the sea.
Plotting evil destruction, their whispers turn to shrieks
And their hot breath roils the sea into tumult.
Unwitting sea, racing, jumping, trying to escape
Can't you see you're helping as you race to shore?
Helping bring destruction to the land that lies before you.
Little ant people, scurrying hurrying
Worrying that they will lose the battle.
Batten down the hatches, hide behind closed doors.
The dark faced clouds whirl closer, lightning flashing from their eyes
Opening great mouths of razor teeth, ripping, chomping, chewing
Grinding down in fury, spitting out the remnants as they shriek unholy glee
Satiated at long last, they tie and their fury ebbs
As they depart the scene of battle.
Dark faced soldiers, resting, gaining strength,
Knowing they will come again together over the sea.
To plot the course for future battles
Against the mounting encroachment of the lands and seas.

Carolyn Graham

A Dragon Dreams

A dragon dreams, with tail wound round
His four large feet on a bed of down.

He dreams of knights, and princesses fair;
He dreams of gold to fill his lair;

Of jewels and crowns, of swords and battles;
of elves and trolls, of fiddle faddle.

But when he wakes, he looks around;
the elves are gone, the trolls abound.

And with his gold they claim as booty;
their sacks stuffed tight, their faces sooty;

They run, they cry, they flee, they fall.
For he's awake and sees it all.

His anger, but a fleeting thing.
The flame he shoots
Restakes his claim.

He stretches twice, he lays back down.
A dragon dreams, with tail wound round.

Linda Ankeny Watson

Glorious Sunset

Every evening when I see the picture - perfect sunset, I feel like jumping in excitement.

Instead of jumping though, I just stare in awe and breathe a prayer of thanksgiving to our powerful Almighty God.

Lord, I believe you made the beautiful sunset for our enjoyment only. You could have just made the sun go down, dull and boring. But no!

Father, you decided to show us your glory by sending the sun down blazing with colors and full of glory.

How anybody could not notice the fireworks of the evening sky is beyond me.

Thank you, God, for sending us a sunset full of magnificent colors.

Brooke Ashley Thompson

Yesterday's Dream . . . Abused And Battered

Young and innocent, dressed in white
Just became the American virgin wife

Appeared with, I was told, the perfect husband by my side
Nothing ever would I have to hide

Little children were given life
Appeared everything was going right

There is no reason to live he cried
The little children hung to my side

He flung at us with all his might
Often times all through the night

In our escape, we lost some pride
Felt somehow to us life had been denied

At the end of the tunnel, we saw the light
Abused and battered we pray, oh God, may we never fight

Though it was a hell of a ride
Often times we sat and cried

Thankful now to still have the gift of life
When even ours could have ended with a knife.

Doris Helverson

Soliloquy

i walk through a disarray of wet tears and broken glass,
His hands obscure my eyes and don't permit me to pass.
Hard hands and soft bodies collide with my touch,
Smoothly relating that i must not have amounted to much.
The sun has gone down and all is revealed,
As i look around, i find i'm alone in a barren field.

Like thick claws clasping a slender neck,
A fog envelops me, almost choking me to death.
Carefully, like the petals of a rose slowly wilting away,
Those warm hands grasp mine and cause me to sway.
i am utterly speechless, my mind draws a blank,
The only thought i can rear is that it must be a prank.

He studies each finger with inexplicable detail,
Though he labors hard and long, there is no story there to tell.
In a moment, he is gone with the words "Cry no more,"
Yet that, as he well knows, is an uncontrollable force.
As i had expected, and you may have too,
It was all just a dream, as harsh as the morning dew.

I awake with the bright sunshine glaring on my eyes,
This is why, my dear, the morning I have come to despise.

Sameena Azhar

Reminiscence

He walked along the shores of yesteryear,
His toes digging into the moist, damp sand
That stretched for miles and miles from far to near —
A small stretch of the universe's hand.
His eyes bore the gaze of a lover in thought:
A look of seeing something faraway
That never can be recaptured as it ought
To drive the mists from eyes that see not day.
And every step left footprints on the beach,
For yards along sands where foamy waves swelled.
And yearning, extending their arms out to reach
The shore, they returned once more to sea, repelled.
    And he, of wistful heart and dreamy eye
    Pondered not sea but sweet memories gone by.

rani

Angels Hither And Thither

I dispatch angels and bid them to go
Hither and thither to friends that I know;
They carry comfort and hasten to be
Valiant protectors that come silently!
We never can tell just when they'll appear
And help us to claim our victory here.
Jesus, our shepherd, has us in his care
His angels, with us, are just everywhere!

Lydia Neubuck Harper

Still Of The Night

Praising him for his love and glory,
honoring him for his power and might.
Everything will be alright, is what I
hear in the still of the night.

Knowing he is my everything,
knowing he is my guiding light.
Through all that I have endured,
He is there for me in the still of the night.

Overcoming during the battle,
holding out through the fight.
He is always there to hold me,
in the still of the night.

Lisa Sewell

A Place Of Learning

For sixteen years I have been yearning
Hoping for a better place of learning
Some place to learn to read and write
Without being criticized or pushed into a fight
A place where everyone is your friend
A place where the quest for knowledge never ends
A place where everyone can go
To teach each other and not put on a fashion show.
In a place of learning this violence must cease.
In a place of learning there should only be peace.

Micheal Kemper Jr.

Glorious Day

Wasting away day by day
Horrified of the truth
Constantly lying
Who am I fooling
I know I'm dying
Days on end of being alone
I feel as if I've turned to stone
Silent screams in the night as I
    take this painful plight.
Faster-faster slipping away
I finally hear, it's okay we love you dear.
What a Glorious Day

Sandra King

What Life is About

You will find when you walk through our door, an old farm
house with unscrubbed floors, cluttered up cupboards, worn our rugs
toys everywhere and stains on the couch.

You will find when you walk through our door, a bright burning
candle with treats on the bar, spills in the refrigerator, garbage
not taken out, a VCR playing and children walking about.

You will find when you go upstairs, six unmade beds and
stuffed animals everywhere. Dressers so packed that the drawers
don't close, night-light still shining and pajamas on the floor.

You will find when you walk through our door, a mom and dad
who live for this all. A loving little Louie, a cheery Charlie Brown,
a happy Miss Hillary and more babies to come.

And we all know when we walk in our old house,
our love and our happiness is what life is about.
For our greatest asset is our family and our love,
and we thank our Dear Jesus in the Heavens above.

Mary Jane Hengesbach

Sister Lost

She closed her mind, she closed her heart, left us bereft and sad,
How could she turn away from us and make us feel so bad.
She couldn't make us see her away and didn't really try.
Just turned her back and left us crying why?
Does she ever think of us, does she remember how it used to be
When we could laugh about the past and giggle at the now.
Does she remember how does she recall does she ever think of us at all
We often think of her, the funny things she used to do
Her thoughtful ways and kindness too
We think of her and wonder, does she care, does she know
How sad she left the ones who loved her so.
Oh, will we ever meet again to laugh and maybe cry
To forgive and to hug once more before we die.

Leonie F. Nulle

"Guardian Angel"

From moonbeam rays descends my angel
Hovering over the lush grass carpet of the earth
Illuminated with the radiance of the moon and the kindness of his heart

A silk robe drapes decoratively on his body
The bluest shades of the sea are captured in his eyes
Dewy skin glows beneath the rippling cloth
While golden hair frames his sculpted face

His voice is a soft, deep bass
Soothing any forlorn thoughts or painful memories
Rising to the heavens when singing praise to our Creator
Hypnotic and alluring when speaking of love

He holds me in time of sorrow
He dances with me in times of joy
Devotion and unconditional love are his strengths
I am his only flaw

Sunshine and alarms bring sadness
In the morning I am alone
For the daylight dissolves my angel
Till my dreams will I meet with my angel again

Tricia Crowley

Forever Gone

Forever's a lot shorter than we'd like to admit
How can something that's infinite cease to exist
Love should be flourishing when two people care
But turned one sided tempers will flare
The caring and sharing your mutual trust
Eventually turn to hate and disgust
The one that you'd be with forever and more
Becomes something different staying together a chore
Just to love and to be with that person a must
Now you can't even muster the feelings of lust
Nothing left to cherish the flames been put out
Did they find what they're seeking what's love all about
The times that you shared both as friends and as lovers
Getting used to is hard for those times are now for others
But life is too short you can't build up a wall
For the mistrust for one should not consume all
So remember in forever I is we me is us
Become selfish and greedy forever will bust
Forevers are great whenever they last
It takes two for forever, or else they end fast.

Thomas J. Babiasz

Untitled

Bob, years ago when we first met.
I always seemed so upset.
You were going with my friend.
I hoped your relationship would end.
I know that seems so wrong.
But my feelings for you were so strong.
You may not of seen the way I felt about you.
I always hoped one day you could feel it to.
I just wanted someone to care for me.
Maybe someday it would be you for me.
That is now in the past
It's finally you and me at last.
You are sweet in a funny way.
You make me want to live every minute of everyday.
A lot of guys don't treat me good.
But from what I hear you would.
I need someone special in my life.
Don't get me wrong I'm not asking to be your wife.
Now in my life you are a big part.
I love you with all my heart.

Kristel D. Fisher

You'll Never Know

You'll never know how much you've loved until you've loved and lost.
How eagerly you seek the thrill, no matter what the cost.
One sweet moment that you share with someone dear to you
    that you must pay for with heartbreaking dreams that won't come true.
You'll never know the agony of tears that can't be shed -
    of tears that never fill your eyes, but flood your heart instead.
You'll never know the joy that one surrendered moment brings;
how to the ghost of love now dead your heart in torture clings;
how it seems to stop it's beating when, just by chance, you meet
    and you both pass by, not speaking, the pain so bitter yet so sweet.
You won't know endless solitude when dreams of long ago
    parade before your aching heart, the torment that you'll know
when you waken to reality and face the fact that you
    are remembering the happiness that once was shared by two.
You'll learn how very empty a lover's promises can be.
Your heart will know the hopelessness your eyes refuse to see.
You'll never know how to and fro by fate your heart is tossed -
You'll never know how much you've loved, until you've loved and lost.

    Margaret B. Cramer

Keep Your Head Up

Keep your head up and think positive no matter
how hard life can be. Whenever you are down and
you need a friend, you know I am with you every
step of the way. Don't be afraid, keep your head
up and look up to the sky. Look into the sky and
never be discouraged for never let anyone tell you
that you're wrong. Whenever you think of anything think
about tomorrow; even when we do go thru the joy
and sorrow. "We have to be encouraged no matter what
goes on; cause in our hearts we have to believe our
father in heaven, will make everything all right, keep
your head up and never forget to look up to the sky only if you
believe in your self, always keep your head up and know that
when one door closes the Lord will open another. Keep your head up
and know that it is never too late to speak from your heart and don't
be ashamed to let your emotions show how you feel. Keep your
head up and let God guide you along the way. He will never let
you down. god has given each and everyone a blessing and he
will never let your love fade away. May God bless and keep us
safe for we shall never have to be afraid.

    Melissa Andrea Hernandez

Untitled

How long does it take to walk from the bedroom to the kitchen?
How long does it take to walk from the kitchen to the living room?
How long does it take to walk from the bathroom to the balcony?
How long will it take for me to go mad?
What is madness?
Is madness counting the steps between the rooms?
Is madness all around us and you're the only one to notice it?
Is madness a compulsive behaviors that consist of cleaning or cooking?
If that is the case than I am not mad at all. Hallelujah!!!!!!
Mind
Attitude
Determination
Don't allow yourself to be taken under by the undertow.
Undertow is a horrible and unseen happening that takes a lot of us
by surprise.
Be a strong swimmer. More importantly be a strong person.

    Paula Upchurch

Untitled

The weight of the world seems destined to fall
I don't feel that strong no not at all
In his eyes you see heavens blue
Yet in his arms you feel hells pain too
Cry for ever and yell a thousand silent screams
For tonight he just might kill you

    Michelle Ramirez

"Listen Those Who Care"

Close your eyes and imagine
How they must live in the dark
Scrimping and saving every crumb
Hoping for some light or at least a spark
Listen with your heart
To hear the children cry
Feel with your soul
Their pain as they die
Lift them up with
Your spirit and your hope
Instead of watching them fall
Into a world of violence, crime, and dope
Teach them with your heart
As much as they can learn
Let them know through "Him"
There is a better life for which to yearn.

    Margaret Elizabeth Rice Bridgers

Dilemmas

What to do...Where to go
How to start...Who to know
Go to the left....Go to the right
Walk that middle, dark path of night
Nothings for sure, except confusion
Gotta keep movin' to avoid the illusion
Others don't know, and usually don't say
Even if they've found the sun-lighted way
But what works for them, don't work for me
Its so damned hard to get myself free
Free in life's flow and know where to go
Rejoice in the highs... persevere in the lows
And so I now go to find my own place
The mirror has the answer.....it lies in that place

    Keni Lee

Friends

If my dear, you only knew
How very much I think of you,
Would you now and then
Think of me too?
As very often I come around
And always look for you up and down,
Sometime my friend
You are nowhere to be found.
If we do come, by chance, on the same day,
Would you, my dear, always say
"Darling, I'm so very glad
That we both came today."
Since there are days we come and go,
My dear I hope you'll always know
It's so wonderful to be FRIENDS!

    Lucy C. Greer

E Loa Ke Ola - May Life Be Long

Well, this certainly has been another fast year,
However, I have much about which to cheer.

The first four months I studied Hebrew on the west coast,
And the printing of letters I enjoyed the most.

Attending opera on sunday afternoons was a treat,
San Diego in February would be hard to beat.

March found me singing with a Choral group,
Also with Kayso Folk Dancers and City College Troupe.

April I enjoyed the beautiful - Romona Production,
Traveled in May to Israel for a slight reduction.

June I flew to my beautiful - hideaway - Hawaiian home,
Received a wedding announcement, I was eager to roam.

Saw the eclipse and began to smell the flowers,
Visiting good friends and playing golf for hours.

Oct. I flew to Calif. to visit David and girl friend,
Then took a train to Minn, Burkhardt wedding to attend.

Traveled by Bus to Rapid City, South Dakota,
Picked up and taken to a ranch, spiritually lakota.

How great to study and ride horseback in the Fall,
Really enjoyed the Elderhostel group-one and all.

Virginia Doyle

On Racism

Harsh term,
Human reality.

Man has grouped together from the beginning.
Religion, Sex, Language, Nationality
Differences are feared,
Similarity is safety.
Simply,
Color is easier to distinguish.

Fear is human.
Militants reinforce fear,
As do families, teams, and communities.

To stop racism,
Stop fear!
Without interference
Slowly, with time.

Gains have been made.
Set asides slow the process (acceptance),
Time is the Answer!

R. Joseph Pikowski

I Am

I am a spider spinning a web of diamonds
I am a piece of paper waiting to give a paper cut
I am Emmitt Smith waiting for the pass at the 30 yardline
I am the long awaited bell at the end of the day
I am a hat on a small child's head
I am a page in a book with only a few sentences on it
I am a single white rose in an english garden
I am a beautiful monarch butterfly soaring threw the sky
I am a frog on a log waiting for its prey
I am a football being thrown in the blue sky
I am a half of a heart with out the other half yet
I am a speedbump on the road of life for my parents
THIS IS ME HERE, NOW, AND FOREVER!!!

Megan Woods

Dear Family

The tree is trimmed, the dolls are dressed, the stockings have been hung,
The choirs are busy practicing the songs that will be sung.
The gifts selected for each one are being wrapped with care,
And as they're placed beneath the tree, with each I say a prayer.

A prayer that God will bless your life and guide you with His hand,
That you may know His power and strength, as for the Right you stand.
A prayer that you will feel His love through deeds done from the heart
Through gentle words, through kindness shown, with love in every part.

It's Christmas-time and in my heart I feel that special glow,
Put there by God, who in His love, His perfect love did show.
This heav'nly song keeps ringing in my heart throughout each day,
It gives me peace and utmost joy, to know He points the way.

I'm thankful for each one of you, more than you'll ever know,
You're always in my thoughts and prayers, as through each day I go.
I'll carry you within my heart as long as life shall last,
I'll ask for wisdom for each one, for faith to hold you fast.

I want to wish each one of you a blessed Christmas season,
Filled with hope and love and joy, cause Jesus is the reason.
I thank you for the love you show in many different ways,
And thanks for all the memories and the love of by-gone days!

Lois M. Polinder

Finish The Dream

Emotions are a part of human life
I am a human, I feel emotions

Through your eyes are wide open
You can see my true beauty that lies in me

You see as others do, the skin that covers me and you
Whether black, brown or yellow, we are all still human

Sometimes the blind may see quite better than you or me
For they do not judge a person by the color of their skin
Or their nationality or if they are skinny, short, tall or obese.

Martin Luther King said, "I have a dream",
But the world wouldn't have heard if he had screamed.

For as long as we segregate into our own little groups
And let the opinions of the elders affect the youth
There will always be bigots in our schools.

Prejudice isn't right and the battle against it
Won't be won with a fight, we must unite as one
Will the battle ever be won.

Richard Brian Scott

Sitting, Not Knowing

The dull light, in a quiet room, slowly warms the air.
I am sitting, in that room, living.
With an unmade bed to my right, and newspapers on the floor,
    I will fix it later (the newspaper and the bed).
But at this moment, in my chair, I am and will be sitting.

The music is pleasantly loud, and the air it's not yet warm.
I ponder over things, I still don't understand.
I want to be more than something, and it hurts not to succeed.
My accomplishments leave 3 second smiles
    while my pains will remain in me.

I continue to sit, in my chair, in a quiet room.
For reasons, I don't yet know, but I will think of later.
The air is warming, from the light, in that room;
And I will find some guidance.

Regina Chern

Shadow Waltz

When the jagged layers of night electrify the celestial heavens,
I am beckoned to the spirited woods.
The moon's shimmering glow bejewels the ancient ones as their
overhanging limbs steal touches and quick embraces.

Shadows dance along beside me, and I waltz for a moment or two.
I close my eyes to the bedazzling display of nocturnal visions.
Imaginings of a gentle love encompass my dreams.
Have I become a woman found, or a maiden lost?

The shadow waltz teases me with unanswered prayers.
Its charming beguiling lullaby woos me with perfect rhythm.
From the shadow you rise, and love pours from you.
Tenderly you lead through my field of dreams.

Like chattering demons you reveal all my secrets.
You are the warming breath in the wind, caressing my soul.
You are the artist, molding me, and I am but the clay.
I fill my lungs with your scent so intoxicating.

As the night diminishes, from my arms you leap back to the moon.
Your compassion bathes me in peaceful serenity.
I will float wistfully through dreams until our hearts touch
again, and forever dance the shadow waltz.

Valerie Virginia Kinnebrew

"Good-Bye"

What you see, lying before you is my shell, my body.
I am not moving or breathing, my body is dead.
You cry in sadness and yet I wonder why?
I, meaning my spirit or soul is alive and free,
No longer caged or spoon fed by society.

You are in denial. You think I might wake up,
That I'm just sleeping and will come back soon.

I cannot.
I awoke to a new life the moment my heart gave off its last beat.
If you cry now, the weight of your sadness will bind me,
To a world that is no longer mine.
My work is finished here.

"Good-bye" is only good if you mean it.
Please say it peacefully and in truth.
Send me on my next adventure,
Let me go.

"Good-bye".

Michelle Vozenilek

Relying On Instinct

Good-bye morbid world, good-bye lonely heart;
I am off to begin anew, with a very different start.
Many say it can't be done, but I believe in myself;
To be as happy as I wish, without relying on wealth.
Sometimes I roam around, wondering why I'm here;
And once I finally realize, I never have need to fear.
For every time you look, straight into my loving eyes;
The time that once sped on, stands still and merely sighs.

Hello beautiful world, hello caring heart;
I am here with you now, and never wish to part.
I see too that I was right, to have faith in my selection;
For I have finished my journey, with ultimate perfection.
Now I have no need, to roam anymore;
For in you I have found, what I was looking for.
Forever in your arms, is my home in this case;
I found love to be something, wealth can never replace.

Pamela Gullotti

Through Your Eyes Only

You, my friend, deserve to feel the very best.
I am sorry that some people made you feel much less.

If you can forgive them, why does your inner self dwell?
Harboring feelings holds you back and keeps your soul
from being well.

Don't punish yourself for all that has been done.
Bring your selves together, compromise, become one.

The two of you fight to stay alive inside;
One comes out forcing the other to hide.

Only from within yourself can you release all the anger
and pain.
Answers lie not in condemning yourself, but by releasing
emotional chains.

We are all victims of circumstance so let your soul
be free of blame.
David, judge each individually, so you may trust and love again.

Siubhan Dewar

Us

I have tomorrow, the dream of today.
I am the future, I'll find a way.
You are the memories fading one by one.
Today when I saw you, I remembered our past.
We shared something wonderful, but it just didn't last.
I can't stay any longer.
I have to move on, to find tomorrow,
Because yesterday is gone.

Lindsay Lagoe

The Water Of Life

You are the water
I am the life within
Two signs synchronized

Without the water
The life dies
Without the life
The water dries up

Each taking from the other
Giving tenfold in return
Fish breathing water, water feeding from fish

Unspoken harmony, unbidden sustainment

Sandra Marshall

One Of The All

I am the quiet whisper upon the wind.
I am the lingering sweet aroma of a newly blooming flower.
I am the crisp clean air you breath on a brisk Autumn morning.
I am the beautiful brilliant orange of the horizon at dawn,
the magnificent shadow of dusk and the peaceful purple pink
sunset.
I am the fresh clean smell of rain soaked earth after the first
spring shower.
I am a winged dove flying high on a hint of Winter wind.
I am a dolphin or a hump back whale spraying mist as I rise.
I am a soft eyed doe lying in a sheltered meadow.
I am a great white wolf howling in the stillness of night.
I am the sun, the moon, the stars, Mother Earth and Father
sky.
I am one with the universe, one of the many, one of the all...

Laura Hill

I Am Unique

I am unique
I am the one and only person in the world
I am a very special girl
I am special to my family and every friend
and always have an ear or shoulder to lend.
I am special to my mom and dad
to have them I am very glad
I am unique in my own way
And I am happy to be loved everyday

Latisha N. Lowther

Weeping Willow

As the weeping willow weeps her tears,
I ask her why she weeps through the years.
And she says she does not know,
Why oh why she does weep so.
So I say are you sad?
No, she says, nor am I mad.
So I think and think some more.
On why she doesn't smile anymore.
So I think maybe she is tried of being alone.
Or maybe the constance of her leaves being blown.
No she says, it is none of these.
I just ask you, let me weep by myself, if you please,
So I leave this beautiful tree.
And do as she wishes and let her be.
To let her weep her lonely tears,
For the rest of her lonely years,

Rebekah Anne Titus

A Perfect You

We all have souls of a different degree
I am different than he or she
Our bodies too - are not alike
Some are heavy - some are slight
Our skins are varied of a different hue

White - black - red - yellow too
But within this vast array
Is the perfect you trying to say
Love one another and to your own self be true
Then you can realize the perfect you!

Vivian Mullen

He'll Be Right There

When I was just a little girl,
I asked my father this question.
I said, "Daddy, please tell me how to pray.
Just what is it I should really say?"

He answered, "Child, prayer is merely talking to God,
There is no special way to call.
Just relax and know He'll be right there,
And just give Him your all and all."

As I grew through the years I surely found,
Many days I could turn only to Him.
For my earthly father was called home by God
Early in my life, and when.

When I take time to talk with Him daily,
This great, great friend of mine.
Over and over, he brings me through,
The dark storms in my life to bright sunshine.

That's why I stand humbly before all today,
And declare that I know it's true.
He's been right there for me all of this time, and yes,
He'll be right there for you.

Rayette P. Scruggs

What Can I Do...

I'm sitting in a corner, thinking what
I can do. I'm trap in the middle of silence
and pure sadness. I want to live, I want to
love, so tell me what I can do.
I'm looking for the light that will give me
my life back, I want to smile, but I can't.
I'm all alone with nothing to loose, so tell
me what can I do.

I see my shadow, that's my company, does
what I do, it's not enough, I need more.
Someone to love me and someone to love. I need
to feel happiness. I'm all alone, so tell me
what can I do.
I'll look for you my darling one. You're
the one for me, you'll bring my sunshine, I
need your love, so tell me what can I do for
you to return, to cherish our love till the
day we die...

Nellie Aguilar

My Box

As I walk down the street,
I can hear my lonely heart beat.

I see you and run your way.
You notice me too and begin to stray.

A stranger witnesses and comes near,
Only to see one lonely tear.

He comes to comfort because he sees
    my sadness,
And with his words, it turns into gladness.

After a while I'll give him my heart,
And without me realizing, he rips it apart.

Again I withdraw into a private box,
He says he's sorry and undoes the locks.

I don't want him to come in, but he seems so true.
And I know within time I will again be blue.

Michelle Lear

Between The Rain Drops

I can smell the dampness in the air.
I can hear the drops falling.

Regardless of the type of day I still must
Go out the door if things are to get done.

Regardless, the sun always rises and
The sun always sets.

Today when I go through the door
I'll go quietly without complaint.

Enjoy the peace I find in the stillness
As the world takes cover.

Today I'll not feign the sunshine,
But just enjoy the rain.

I'll be not cynical of mother nature for
As perennial is the rain so is the sun.

I will try to take kindly to the day and
Nurture its strength while others try
And shield themselves from its considered misfortune.

Yes, today I'm going walking,
Walking between the rain drops
Where I've discovered the sun shines through...

Laura Anne Lord

The Real Me, That I Can Be

The time has come to be myself.
I can release these feelings off the shelf.
The world for me has become my stage.
To blossom like a flower, to come of age.

When you find the truth, the world you leave.
Because out into he world, people do deceive.
Once upon a time I was very bad.
Stayed in trouble, and made my family sad.

Alcohol and drugs were my life's ambition.
In the school of life, I paid no tuition.
Life for me was one big game.
But now I've changed, and I'll never be the same.

I can now stand tall and spread the news.
That the new me, never sings the blues.
Times have changed for the best you see.
For now I am, the real me that I can be.

Thomas D. Love

Day Dreamer

I look out of the window with a distance in my eyes,
I cannot hear a tone of voice or anyone else's cries.
I don't know quite what I'm thinking of, but I know I like it there,
This place presents a certain peacefulness that no one could impair.
Everyone does it now and then, though some don't do it as much,
They say that they don't have the time or use an excuse as such.
Day Dreamer dream away and don't you blink an eye,
For if you do time will tell of how the children cry.
Day Dreamer fly away, whisk upon a dream,
And hold it close to your heart, for it's not what it may seem.
Day Dreamer remember your dreams and keep them from the start,
For if it is worth dreaming, it's worth keeping in your heart.

Kelli Carter

Deep Black Hole

Sometimes I wish
I could crawl in a little black hole
To get away from the problems I have not yet solved
When I feel
Used or abused, mad or sad
Nervous or shy, embarrassed or unwanted,
Cheated or ugly
I feel sorry for myself
Or things aren't going well
I wanna dig a deep black hole
For myself to crawl in
And get away from it all
When you came along
Nothing else went wrong
I have crawled out of my deep black hole
With no worries
I cherish the land you walk on
The air you breath and the love and care you give to me
Let heavens light shine down upon you
For you have shined a light down on me

Luke Siciliano

And Then At Night

And then at night in blissful sleep, my peace and visions are so deep.
I drift around in wispy haze, remembering times of happier days.
Walking slowly through my mind, I find the peace which is mine.
To stop and visit with the dead and smell the freshness which lies ahead.
I touch and feel the thing I like, for freedom comes to me at night.
If only life would understand, that I am but a mortal being, holding
on instead of fleeing.

Ronald G. Dahlke

Jack's Neighbor

"From just above pine-scented soft-needled ground,
I do my extreme best to look all around.
But growth so much taller than my shrouded self,
Obscures field-of-view, and shouts quietly at me:
'You're not, then, much more than a quaint little elf!'"

"Well, I'm Jack-of-the-Pulpit, taller than a flee,
No matter that, whether flee, pea or bee.
How do I stack next to my looming pine tree?
My neighbor, my mentor, my cover 'bove cover,
who spires toward heaven as the skies one true lover."

"My roots are quite shallow, while his go quite deep,
both buried in brown-ground, quietly asleep.
Once free of my tower, should I stand still by the hour,
in soil so dark, mixed, with nourishing bark.
Roots would I again grow, or like mankind have none?"

"Great pine-tree with needled-branches holding nigh the sky,
when free of my pulpit, shall I remember you that high?
Or, shall I feel challenged or threatened like man,
and cut you down dead with tooth-twirling fan!
Can't do that, you know, for I shan't be that human!"

Schuyler

The Wing Of Kiss

I fly to see your face on the wing of kiss
I do no remember a flower other than you
I never plant a tree in the garden of my heart
Never plant but in the garden of your love
Reminiscent of times in your arms
Having no other dreams better than this
Kissing your lips, drinking from your cup
Becoming ravished and dancing, now in love
You are a garden of rose, you don't come
Have no other flowers but you
O cloud, rain in the spring on every flower garden
Perhaps my thirst will be cured, for I am restless
I will speak of love, wine, your face
For I am lost without the tavern by your quarter, I am
"Parnia's" poem became many curls of your hair
Baskets of my poems I offer you

Parnia Razi

Failings

I don't care what you do.
I don't care what you say.
I'm gonna do it my own way.
I don't care if I get caught.
What I do I did for nought.
I spent some time by myself.
I put our friendship on the shelf.
The cracks and groans come before the words done.
Now I realize there's more than one.
I look back over my shoulder.
Thank God, that chip didn't turn to a boulder.
I'll be taking more time to think.
While I'm trying to fix that sink.
Remembering all the good times we had.
thinking about some things I did.
I gotta let your children know.
That they just gotta show.
The love I never let mom and dad know.
Oldness comes just some quick day.
Too late, we be going too far away.

Larry L. Ball

About Painting

I feel a storm that is in me.
I don't know yet what it might be;
But it has a form that is swirling about...
Soon, sure to come out —
An image I feel forming inside me.
Await. Asleep. About to be.

It has big strokes.
All colors on white paper showing through —
Red, orange, yellow, green, blue.
Half light. Half dark.
Half me. Half you.

Susan A. Leonard

Need

Don't let me die
I don't want to die alone.
You said you would be here
but you're nowhere to be found.
I need the love you once had for me
I need someone's love
or thoughts or feelings.
You don't know what's happening to me
what's going on in my head, heart, and body.
I feel pain, I feel alone, I feel the need of warmth
two arms wrapped around my aching soul
I need... I need...
I need to love myself again.

Naomi Elliott

Desmodus

Strangled by the lengthy shadows you cast within my mind
I feel and reel at the web of confusion traced and faced by me
till all I know is ensnared in concentric lines of contradiction

It matters not to you who slips the knot that binds and finds
the feelings of anomalous love betwixt the silken chords or tours
the state of my confinement with fanciful art

Thou so cunning, you sought to dominate to late to drain
the essence of my love for your refreshment you see I'm free
to wonder no more where you are I am where I am, you are too.

Susan Rison

Jesus How I Love Thee!

As I see you in my mind, nailed to the cross
  I feel so sad, blue, empty and lost;
Been there — there's something I could have done
I feel like if I'd been there's something I could have done
  To help prevent the death of the mighty Father's Son!

I just can't get the picture out of my mind
  How could so many people be so cruel and so unkind,
To treat the mighty Father's Son as if he was the Devil-himself
  To take away His loving kindness and His precious health.

I close my eyes and I see from the crown of thorns the blood
running down his face
  And when he was thirsty the bottle wine I can almost taste;
I want to reach out and touch him and tell him how sorry some of us are
  Even though he seems so close but then again he is so far!

Shelia T. Terry

Winterwind

The cool winds blow across my face.
I feel the breath of winter.
It blows my hair.
It seeps through my clothes.
My breath becomes cool.
I become winter and winter becomes me.
The snow begins to fall.
Ice falls as well.
Spring will be arriving and I will be me again.

Katharine Dessoir Bojanek

Another Broken Heart

  My heart has been broken yet again.
I fell deeply in love with him, but he broke my heart.
I pored out my heart and soul to him.
In return, he dumped me.
It felt like a razor blade cutting open my heart,
from top to bottom.
All the love in my heart, flows out like a ragging river.
I've been hurt by love many times before, but the
hurt is worse when you're really in love with another person.
I guess I'll get over him someday, somehow.

Paige M. McNeill

"Us"

The day I heard the news,
  I felt all the blues.
I used to stand up for you when anyone said anything.
  Except now I know what you bring.
As I realize how much I cared,
  It makes me so scared.
That I could love someone as much as I loved you,
  Except now I really don't care what you do.
You called me a slut,
  I felt as if my heart had been cut.
Pieces fall to the floor,
  But you don't care anymore.
I thought we'd last forever,
  But no way, never.
Why couldn't you say it to my face?
  Why did you put someone else in the chase?
Where you scared of what I would do?
  To me it wasn't anything new.
It may seem to you like I'm done,
  But inside I haven't even begun.

Rebecca Morse

The Immensity Of The Sky

I was lying on the sand looking at the sky.
I felt the gentle breeze softly caressing me.
I heard the waves breaking at the shore's edge.
There I saw the immensity of the sky.

A white little cloud, quietly, swiftly went by;
A cloud, a puff of steam, perhaps only a dream.
It came, I saw it; it passed by, I know it.
Above I saw the immensity of the sky.

A pelican, wings spread, gliding in the blue;
A living creature flying to somewhere there,
Born to fly, gracefully on his own journey.
Around I saw the immensity of the sky.

The rays of the bright and shining sun,
Radiating everywhere to nowhere, to heaven.
I felt a warmth within, like love forever.
The light embraced the immensity of the sky.

Eternity . . . I saw it.

Silvino R. Foglia

Adulthood, Fast Approaching

As the years go by, and my childhood slips away,
I find myself longing for those carefree days.
The days I'd play non-stop and forget to eat,
The day before school let out,
and I had a fun-filled summer to look forward to.
Now, I don't think I could ever forget to eat,
and the ending of the school year means the beginning of a summer job.
Those lazy days gone by have been replaced with deadlines,
stress, tests, jobs, etc...
I find my life is spinning,
and I often fight with my maker over who should take the reigns.
Slow down I say,
when I'm the one stepping on the gas.

Michelle Miracle

City Of Angels

Flying from ten thousand miles away
I found a place called the city of angels
A dangerous place to be..
The smog, the traffic and the smell of death
Hovering in all the unbounded places.

For a little angel like me
I learned to flap my wings
Carefully...
But oh...what a beautiful place to be..
The sun embracing me like the light from heaven
Every day

Through my windshield, I thread
The ever changing highways...constantly listening
To the sublime...the ultimate...
Innuendos of the day,
While collecting my thoughts, I pray
My tasks to be...

Worthy...
Of my wings to fly in the City of Angels,
For a ten thousand day stay.

M. T. Canoy

Flight Of Life

As I spread my wings out
I glance at the ground.
That's along way to fall.
A big price to pay for failure.
Why take the chance?
A wise man once said: So what!
So I too will say: So what!
If I don't live, then I'll die
and I will die if I live.
So, I think that while I breathe
I will fly and have the best of both worlds.
For, If I never do
I'll never feel the breeze on my face before I die.
But, If I do
I'll feel the breeze on my face before I die.
And I will die knowing that I lived.

Mark Simmons

Windows

A smile spreads across my face
I remembered how to look through windows
I watched the sun glow around the clouds
Sometimes our eyes are blinded
It's wonderful to see again that most things are circles
And you need to walk all the way around them
Not sink in the thick water fogging the windows

Rachael Jones

A Time To Pray

I got up early one morning and rushed right into day
I had so much to accomplish that I didn't
take time to pray.
Problems just tumbling about me and heavier came each task
Why doesn't God help me I wondered
He answered you didn't ask.
I wanted to see joy and beauty but the day toiled on gray and
bleak
I wondered why God didn't show me
He said but you didn't seek.
I tried to come into God's presence I used
all my keys at the lock.
God gently and lovingly chided
My child you didn't knock
I woke up early this morning and paused before
entering the day
I had so much to accomplish
that I had to take time to pray.

Vivian Reed

Did You Ever See A Rose Cry

Did you ever see a rose cry
I have and I've wondered why
Crying for rivers that should be so pure
That are covered with sewage and garbage for sure
Crying for butterflies, that used to fly so free
You may look a month and you might find three
Crying for young kids that could have so much
But no, they want to smoke pot and such
Crying for the old people who should be enjoying life
But all they have is pain and strife
Crying for littered mountains and polluted streams
Crying for the blind who only wonder and have dreams
i don't wonder anymore, I know all above is true
I stooped over and wiped the tears and it was dew

Leonard Doyle York

How Well Am I? Well...

There is nothing the matter with me, I'm as healthy as can be.
I have arthritis in both my knees, And when I talk,
  I talk with a wheeze.
My pulse is weak and my blood is thin,
But I'm awfully well for the shape I'm in.

How do I know that you youth is spent?
Well, my "Get up and go" has got up and went.
But I really don't mind when I think with a grin
Of all the grand places my "Get up" has been.

Old age is golden, I've heard it said.
But some times I wonder as I get into bed,
With my ears in a drawer, my teeth in a cup,
My eyes on the night stand until I wake up.

The moral is this as the tale unfolds,
That for me and you, who are getting old,
It's better to say, "I'm fine," with a grin,
Than to let folks know the shape I'm in.

I get up each morning and dust off my wits,
Pick up the papers and read the Obits,
If my name is still missing, I know I'm not dead,
So I get a good breakfast and go back to bed.

Paul A. M. Krow

I Have Become

I have become the woman my parents raised for me to be
I have become the student my teachers taught me to be
I have become the individual the church preached for me to be
I have become the employee my boss expected me to be
I have become the citizen the authorities trusted me to be
I have become the peer my friends challenged me to be
I have become the neighbor my street fashioned me to be
I have become the consumer that society advertised for me to be
I have become the American the media convinced me to be
I have become the person which means the most in life
I have become who I wanted to be-
Me

Stephanie Sue Maruschak

An Adult

I have grown up, I'm an adult,
I have joined the world in an aging cult.
I work, clean, and run all about,
But feel my life shows no results.

I take all my duties, from deep in my heart,
I try to be all, right from the start.
Be it mother, wife, daughter or friend,
I will be there for all till the very end.

I have learned that no matter how hard I try,
There's part, that never grew, way down inside.
It's the little girl, who lives deep within,
Who carries the hurt, and feels she can't win.

She never grew as an adult like me,
She enjoys life treasures, like hugs and trees.
She laughs loudest and feels more than me,
She breaks and cries, but the adults can't see.

Yes, I'm an adult for the world to see,
But when you look, look inside of me.
For the little girl, who just can't get out,
Is a big part of me...me an adult!

Luanne M. Doyle

A Cry In The Dark

Ooh! I'm so cold,
I have nothing to keep me warm.
How I wish I had something warm to hold,
To keep me out of natures harm.

Ooh! I'm starved.
I have had no food to eat.
Could I have some of that turkey you carved?
For I have had no meat.

I know I don't look nice,
And that I don't smell good, but twice,
I had to lay where others stood.

Oh please!
If you can hear me,
Do not mock or tease,
Can anyone hear me?

If I had been like you,
Then it wouldn't be me,
For if I had heard, then I would listen to you,
But, is there anyone listening to me?

Leslie Samuel Orr

My Little Sister

Let me tell you mister
I have the best little sister.
She grew up so very fast.
It's long ago now in the past.
At first she took up a lot of our days,
But when you're young, those are the ways
That little sisters learn to grow.
And I'll tell you something else, you should know,
She grew up very smart.
I say this from the heart.
She has shown me a thing or two,
Made me laugh when I was blue.
She would lend me her last dime,
Almost every single time,
And even when I couldn't pay her back,
She understood and cut me slack.
Yes my little sister means a lot to me,
I want to make that plain to see,
And even though we're far apart,
She sends her love and warms my heart.

Les Ritter

When I Thank About My Life

When I think of all the many trials that life has sent my way,
I have to stop and thank my God for giving me the strength to stay
And fight the many battles that I have to fight and win
And even when I falter, take defeat gracefully with a grin.

I know it's not always easy to deal with life's bitterness and fears,
To face each day with confidence, and to ignore the pains and tears.
I know that often I must cry when hurt and harm do come my way
But I can still stand and thank my God for giving me another day.

I will not always win the race, nor boldly brace each fall;
But I will make every effort to meet life standing straight and tall.
For I know that God's within me and that with His love divine
I will always be the victor, for He's my anchor every time.

LaReine A. Miller

Faith

Yes, I have touched it
I have touched in so many ways, so many times
with love, with shock, with anger
Yes, I have touched it
The pain, this horrible pain
that became a blessing, but still hurts
Yes, I have touched it today, yesterday, forever
I touched the PAIN of trusting completely someone
and being discarded, betrayed persecuted
in his madness.
Yes I have touched it
today in the morning when I looked myself in the mirror and
faced the abandonment
I have to face it and feel loved by myself and my God
"I am your FATHER and I love you"
YOU whispered in the back of my head
sometime last June
So do love me and help me
to touch it, face it, smell it
and continue to be WHOLE

Zulma D. Alvarez

Anonymous

My name is Anonymous,
I hide in the shadows of the night.
Pleading to be noticed,
Hungry for the light.
My life is a secret, wearing its disguise.
No one meets my sadness,
No one hears my cries.
I feel like the forsaken one,
Living all alone.
Crawling to desolate corners,
Fearing the unknown.
But there must be others like me,
Afraid to show themselves.
Hiding their true feelings,
Stashing them on shelves.
We are the chosen ones, running in life's race.
Wanting to be winners, but settling for second place.
Trying to speak up, give us courage, we pray.
Our chance comes and goes.
Well, perhaps another day.

Tina Miller

Answered Prayer

You came to me, like you knew, I'd be the one for you.
I prayed I would meet someone, completely new.
A companion unjudgemental, steadfast and true
who would answer this prayer for love - it could only be you.

Now we've grown so tight so soon
It makes me wonder, can this be real?
God sent me an angel to fulfill my destiny.
Is this just a dream, how could this be true?

A love like ours should be for everyone.
For when we touch I find it hard to breathe.
There's no need to go further, this is heaven you see.
I need you more than air, your love revives me!

This love sent from God shall not go unnoticed
It burns in us forever nurtured by His kindness.
I'll recognize this gift, till life leaves me
and cherish each moment proudly, this I vow to thee.

For you are me and I am you
I love you entirely, always waiting for you.
Now you've come into my life and made me whole.
What are the chance of anyone touching my soul?

Peter D. Rookey

Life: An Inner Exploration . . .

Before I can truly live my life in self-acceptance
I must ask *questions*; I must find *answers*.
In hopes of finding solace within, I turn to my inner-self.
I have many components that make me an individual.
All my personality parts give me a different key
To many doors that must be opened, a light
To shine upon dark corridors... and I walk in cautiously . . .
The poet in me wants to explain "the meaning of life"
Through use of metaphors, similes, and word pictures
The philosopher in me a has theory as to what
My purpose in life truly is . . . my reason for living.
The writer in me busies herself with painting life
As a field of rich, red clover, a salty sea breeze.
The actress in me is relentless in acting out
Her never-ending melodrama, life as a *continuous* play!
The pensive ponderer pounds in me, thinking
My life away, borrowing thundering trouble —
The communicator in me displays and shows
To the *world* what *I*, myself, really *do not* understand —
So I must continue to seek what I yearn to *know*.

Ruthie Boldt

My Love

Ever since that first night I looked into those incredible eyes
I knew you were special
Like a beautiful flower
on a deserted island
Wondrous to behold and yet all alone
And then you came into my life.....slowly.....cautiously.....
and turned my world upside down
I can't even remember what life was like before I met you,
you have become such a big part of me now
You influence the way I think,
the way I act,
the way I feel
and I will be forever grateful
Whenever I think of you I feel a warmth deep within me —
as if my very being is smiling at the thought of us together
You are my companion,
my sweetheart,
my best friend
But most importantly, you are
my love

C. H. Bauer

Alcoholic Mother

The emptiness of the house when I come home from school,
I know she's out drinking...breaking all the family rules.
Daddy's heart can only take so much,
He feels so lonely and out of touch.
Even though I love her, I hope she doesn't come home
Daddy and I would be better off alone.
There has got to be a reason that she feels she has to drink,
I fear the day she doesn't realize that she's gone beyond the brink.
Today I'll find the courage to tell her how much it hurts,
Dear Mommy, I need you all the time, not just between your spurts.
Tonight we sit as a family and Mommy begins to cry,
Daddy and I hug her tight and tell her that we'll try.
Mommy is going to A.A. with our family spirit guiding her through,
When her goal is reached we'll have her back and she'll feel brand new.

Luke Hickerson

A Widow's Ode

Now that I am eighty two,
I live alone and not with you,
I miss the good times that we had,
The good the better the best the bad,
I miss the flowers I use to get,
Every occasion you'd never forget,
Although we're separated by death you see,
I know you're better off and happier than me,
Of course I don't know how long it will be,
When we'll be together just you and me,
But until then I'm perfectly content,
Living the life that I guess was meant.

Patricia Germani

Untitled

My new neighbor:
I hear her singing as she goes about her housekeeping
I admire her lovely voice, and am envious, but can sense she is happy.
She is readying her new home for occupancy by her family.
So busy - a tiny, energetic little thing, she hustles and bustles.
When she gets settled in, I shall call on my new neighbor - Mrs. Wren.

Ramona Maxine Hart

Untitled

I devote my life to my Father in Heaven.
I live to serve Him and his Son.
I try to live what Christ has taught,
But fail when I am naught.
I want to be like my Savior,
To love and hold the gospel true,
To sing Hosannas to His name
And never think of Him in vain.
To have a love that is never unknown
To all the world and all of Rome.
To be His love, His friend, His companion
And all that he does adore.
To be like Him is all I want.
To walk the steps of a simple man from Galilee.

Lori Ellis

Shame

As I sit here alone unhappy once more
I look at the pictures spread all over the floor
with my innocent face and filthy bare feet
and your smiling eyes so loving and sweet
it's hard to believe what once went on
but the haunting memories will linger long
I refuse to speak with you and yet
deep, deep down I feel regret
I say I hate you but then, how can I?
I won't say I love you, for that is a lie
I must forget what we once had
I must forget you were my
Dad....

Tina Burgell Mann

Harmony And Perspective

Gazing from the driveway on this new September night
I looked up among the clouds to find a beam of light
I'd been wondering all day if a full moon was drawing near
Due to craziness at work that all seemed rather queer
As I waited for the cover to crawl off the moon
The shimmering almost sang to me-somewhere it is noon
I turned a quarter circle and a solo star had died
Though I wasn't even born when that star fell from the sky
I listened to the crickets chirping out a requiem
The gravity of the issue was the weight that fell on them
As cloud smoke unveiled quite to my dismay
Half a moon was rendered and half was still at bay
Perspective is a teacher that plays in every key
The more we're in his band the more we learn the harmony
But this search light has me puzzled yet
As to what the beam is going to net
They've been swinging it around the sky
Does their interest lie in the clouds up high
If they're looking for the star that's mine
They will never find it-it already died

Robert Glen McIntyre

In The Morning

As I'm walking to the bus stop in the morning
I see and hear the birds singing,
the trees swaying back and forth,
the cows mooing.
The mountains in the distance
with the pink and purple sky.
The wind blowing the leaves off the trees.
Five minutes later the rumbling of the bus...
The kids yelling and having fun.

Tiffiny Bernabei

The Lamp

Late one night, I was walking alone.
I looked up and saw
a lamp in a window where no one was home.
I stopped where I was in the middle of the road
to squint up through the trees
and feel its soft hold.
The beacon was not bright
But serenity and joy
Radiated from its yellow light.
I don't know how long I stood,
My heart conversing with the flame,
But I felt its quiet friendship
Offered to help my wild game.
The light then flickered once
and left me by myself,
To walk home on that snowy road.
No longer alone.

Kendra M. Laffe

"True Love"

You hear people say
"I love you" but you can't help
Wander if it's true.

Why do we wander
About how people feel.
But when we hear this
We wander if it's real.

We try to believe it but we can't
Because all it is,
Is a Friday night chant.

They say in the
morning they will respect you,
When all they do is take advantage of you.

After a while
They leave you
And now you know what is true.

True love waits
For all who knows
That in only one true person
Can their true love show.

Melissa Dawn Weatherly

All Alike In Some Ways

Darling, I think you're mighty sweet.
I love you, dear, from head to feet,
And I would do most anything
To have you wear my diamond ring.
Should you consent to be my spouse,
I'll make you queen within our house.
I'll be your slave if you require.
I'll serve you to your heart's desire.
Your dishes I will wash and dry.
I'll walk the babies when they cry.
I'll even serve your Sunday dinner.
Your friends will know you've picked a winner.
But there's just one reservation, hun,
Before the parson makes us one.
When there's on tap a football game,
You'll find us men are all the same.
When the referee blows that whistle, pet,
You'll find me glued to a TV set.

Luna E. Newton

"I Am A Fool"

I ask questions for other people.
I make statements for other people.
I give in to people ideals.
I give from my heart part of what
I have and do as much as I can.

I accept someone else wrong doings.
I am blamed for other people mistakes.
I meet people over half the way.
I listen to people problems and trouble hearts.
I allow children to ask me questions.

People use my car without replacing my gas.
People charge me to take me off in my car.
People stand in my face and tell lies on me.
My relatives charges items in my name and
Pay part of the bills, then I pay the other part.

I was not born a fool.
I have not lived as a fool.
I have found myself being everyone fool.
I wonder if I will die as a fool.
I hope I will not die as a fool.

Norma Jean Mitchell

Nana

Nana, I missed you, where were you today?
I opened my eyes and you were away.
I thought we'd play ball and throw it up high
But you were nowhere in my sight.

My little pet, Nana's never very far
I had to go away in my car.
But I'll come back and see you again
We'll play with the ball and watch it spin.

Nana, remember when I stayed all night?
We laid on the floor and you held me tight.
I opened my eyes and you were still there
With me and my blanket and teddy bear.

We'll do it again someday, little friend,
Summer will be coming right around the bend.
We'll water the flowers and play in the park
You can ride your motorcycle until it gets dark.

And then home to Mommy and Daddy you'll go
You'll see Nana again, this you should know.
I'll always be back another day
I will never go far away.

Shirley Duffy

The World Where the Spirits Soar

Shot from the earth like a stone from a sling
I pass the moon as my ears begin to ring
The stars seem extra beautiful tonight
In the spirit I travel at the speed of light
I travel the universe for what seems a year
I pick up speed as the edge draws near
A burst of colors as I enter the other side
My vision clears as I continue my ride
What a wonderful feeling! Mysteries no more
I've entered the world where the spirits soar
It is total peace there is no doubt
There is no heaven or hell to wonder about
It makes me think, is this the end of the line
I need no more for bliss is mine

Ray Combs

The Last Poem

For now,
I put the pen down.
Another day, another hour,
Maybe, next time,
I'll shout a little louder.

For now,
Just remember this
A kiss is just a kiss
Unless you miss.

See, sometimes it's okay to be the class clown,
And turn a frown around.
Or spend a day running across a field in bare feet.
Ain't that neat?

Here I am watching ants play.
Happy to know a part of childhood will always stay.

But for now,
I put the pen down.
Another day, another hour,
Maybe, next time,
I'll shout a little louder.

Thomas Berntsen

Help Me Help You

He wouldn't ask for help, but I could see him struggling to stand
I reached my hand across the chasm
he was afraid to lean over the edge
at last he did
our fingers brushed
but he looked down
downward to infinity plus an inch farther
then looked at my single, tiny hand
and was afraid
He pulled back like a child learning the lesson
of a heated pan on the stove
the ground beneath him lurched violently, yet it was still land
my hand was only a hand
four fingers, one thumb
My grip was strong enough to be his bridge
from violent blows to gentle arms
but my arm wasn't long enough, he had to reach too
he wouldn't risk it
All I could do was watch him struggle to stand
and with two quick strokes of a razor blade, he fell

Louise Cosand

Disappointment And Delight

In a moment of reflection, filled with tears and then dejection,
I recalled someone I love more than I know.
As the years sped there before me and his life was all I could see,
There were memories in vivid kind of show.

Many memories of laughter and love forever after,
And deep devotion filled with sacrifice.
But beneath it flowed a yearning for the unknown facts of learning
What I could do to mold a better life.

Disappointment where we failed him; all of this was so detailed in,
That I wished that we could just begin again.
Then to the surface came the good things; all the great delight a son brings,
And I knew for certain love had won again.

Proud are we of things he shall be, not of ribbon, plaque or trophy,
And we wish him all the good things life can hold.
Hopes and dreams and fun and laughter, and a love forever after;
Then a tiny life that he might help to mold.

Laverne E. Cowles

Tribute To Grandma On 75th Birthday

Sometimes when I'm far away, and it's way past my bedtime,
I remember Summers spent playing in the dirt
Beneath pecan trees in your back yard,
And running real fast to jump over the ditches by the road,
and throwing sticks at the cats that crawled out of every hole
in the neighbor's house.

You would tell me to hush! be still,
when there was a storm; and I would,
because you listened to Grandma, or else be sent out
to fetch a switch to whip your behind.
And Lord help you if you brought back a twig,
because Grandma knew how to pick a switch.

Pecan trees turned into Pecan Pies! Flour into Biscuits!
and how I loved your biscuits.

Sundays we dressed up and went to Church
to learn of something greater than ourselves.
You sang praises with the Choir and I listened.

Sometimes when I'm far away,
and it's way past my bedtime,
I think of you.

Tracy L. Jamerson

Megan

I gazed into the field
 I saw a flower
It's beauty stood out from all the rest
 It was a pale rose with a pretty fragrance
Like you, it is the best

I looked up in the sky
 And saw a shining star
As you brighten my life
 Because of who you are

I walk through the warm waters
 So blue and so clear
I walk by your side
 As your angel, my dear

You are my little princess
 You bring me so much love
So on this birthday, and everyday
 With warmth, you're always thought of

Teresa Macaulay

Rat, Mashed Upon The Road

Yesterday, I think it was . . .
I saw a rat mashed upon our road . . .
Today it was still there.
I examined it carefully
Dispassionately — for its sufferings were over.
However, except for its instantaneous agonizing death
This rat seems to have suffered little, if at all . . .
For it was a Fat Rat
Probably had been eating where
 the neighbors feed the 'coons
So I told the papergirl
That I would probably
Pick it up by its tail
And throw it into the bushes
When I came back from my walk
And I did.

Patricia Lindsay

The Fashion Show

My garden was a fitting stage, and much to my surprise
I saw a special fashion show unfold before my eyes.
The first bird wore a suit of brown tailored plain and narrow,
His shirt was simple white on white modelled by a sparrow.
A blue-jay wore an azure hat with matching satin coat
His breast displayed a muted vest and black tie at his throat.
A cardinal dressed in flaming red posed beside a yellow rose,
He turned a bit so I could see the splendor of his clothes.
A robin came in casual dress; he must have liked that better,
He wore a coat of charcoal gray and a russet sweater.
A hummingbird in stunning green was too dazzling for words,
He lingered not, but stole the show from all the other birds

Rosemary Muntz Yasparro

A Young Man Wise

I sat in the park under the tree
I saw an old man thinking of the sea.
I started to feel pity a little despair
for he was alone with himself and his chair.
He turned and looked me straight in the eyes
so bright and cheerful it had to be a disguise.
Straight into his soul as far as I could see
I felt unaware of what was to be.
His white hair was his dignity
and his wrinkles his pride,
for he wasn't an old man but a young man wise.

Rebecca A. Constans

People

When I look into your eyes,
I see everything that makes me realize
No matter where you've been or where you're from
How you got here or where you begun,
it's just that you're here right now,
That's all I ask not why or how.

You may have different beliefs, we may not agree,
That's what makes you special to me.
Being different is the spice of life.
If we were all the same it just wouldn't be right.
You are the reason I live for today. To be witness
To grand hour of existence in each and everyday.

So to you, the people whom I co-exist,
Thanks for making life the best.

Richard D. Trautman

I Am

I am the spring peepers chirping in unison.
I am the tree blowing in the gentle breeze.
I am the resting squirrel in a tree.
I am the soft blankets of new grass.
I am the pond, soft and calm.
I am the hungry fish chasing a bug.
I am the lone hawk soaring the skies.
I am the deer quick and agile.
I am the morning fog, caressing the damp ground.
I am free.

I stand small and almost insignificant.
I stand in my own world; free of sufferings.
I stand together as a people.
I stand proud.

Ryan Anderson

Autumn Senses

I watch the trees wilt and the days grow shorter,
I see the colors of a rainbow by just walking down the sidewalk,
I feel the lake water colder on my toes,
I see my tan fading day and day and week and week.

I have never heard such aggressive a sound as the dry Autumn leaf
loudly crunched beneath my soft stepped rhythm upon the whirlpool
Autumn ground.

I have never seen such savoring a sight as the flattering Autumn day
of the bitter, shiverful Autumn night.

I have never smelt such as smell as the damp and soggy air of Autumn.
The smell flows in and out of my cold nose as though I have never even smelled it.

I have often dreamed of living an Autumn life, always smelling the
fresh scents, always seeing the graceful leaves slither down to the
rock solid ground and always hearing the geese fly south and the
rakes scratch against the dried grass. I know that I must not take
Autumn for granted for it happens but two months of the year.

Peter Dolan

Looking Forward, Looking Backward

When I look at my grandchildren,
I see the future, I see past.
I see in them people they never knew,
nor loved, since long gone,
they belong to the past, the children to the future.
It all seems to be the same,
time moving swiftly or standing still.
To be a part of it, is all that counts.
Pictures of my Grandchildren in my wallet are not;
I only carry them in my heart.

Thelma R. Lilly

"Childless Mother"

When the children cry and play about,
I see their dirty hands and mouths,
I look and see within my being,
If only I were a mother, how lovely!
  my world would seem.

I weep and sigh all through the day,
As years go by, I hope and pray,
To be a mother, if only, for a day.
Mother, mother, I hear children call,
And running to the door, I stumble and fall,
I then realize, it was not for me,
  but for my neighbor that call.

Richard Lisboa

Living In My Present Mind

As the days go by
I still live a lie
Problems everyday
Wondering why I stay
Only if he knew
I don't know what to do
Thoughts running through my mind
The words I cannot find
Anger building up inside
Stress, I try to put aside
My mind putting him as an authority
But my heart's desire should be my first priority
Blind as he may seem
My words to him are just a dream

Tanya Johnsen

Harmony

In the secluded meadow,
I sit watching the gentle twilight.
The quiet washes over me like a gentle breeze.
Here there is no crowd,
Only solitude and peace, a softness
that is slow like water about to freeze.
The sky shifts in its ever flowing spirits
to form a canopy of streaked flames.
I feel a tightness in, my chest.
The beauty is my souls food.
For each time, each place,
When I am alone, none are the same.
Each time a deeper peace,
Each time a deeper sight.
These times are all mine,
When I renew my inner-self
with a shaft of inner-light.
And now these, moments are only mine.
Alone, an interlude of quiet times.

Kathleen E. Holbein

Emotions

My life has almost come full circle
I should be joyous, eager, ready to meet my Lord.
How do I feel?

My heart is full of hatred, bitterness
I feel depressed, unloved, unwanted; I am in the way.
Heartaches are tearing me apart.
Painful memories whirling through my mind
As leaves blown about by the wind.
I am tormented by the past, no hope for the future
No reason to live, not yet ready to die.
Thoughts imprison my very soul.
My mind is a tangled web of feelings.
My prayers go unanswered, my burdens are heavy.
My faith is shaken, my strength is gone.
I am desperate, reaching out, trying to find my way.
My life is full of darkness, no light to guide me.
The unhappiness inside me is so agonizing
I feel I might crumble at any moment.
I am sad, lonely, frightened, no one to care
What is the answer? Where do I go from here?

Mary W. Tyndell

Is It All A Dream?

   THE ENTIRE EARTH SHAKING, slowly cracking, like glass breaking,
I shout out "It's all just a dream". . .
   DEATH a pitch black shadow slowly creeping up on me, like the
shadow of an evil cloud, but softly, I yell "It's all just a dream". . .

   ALLEYS dark as night, barely any moonlight still I call "Isn't it
a dream?". . .
   BUMS on the streets, a bunch of deadbeats, I say "It's still only
a
dream". . .
   MURDER on T.V., still I wonder could that happen to me?
"No,"
I murmur "It's still just a dream."
   WALKING home at night . . .
   NIGHTMARES full of fright, but I whisper "It's still only a
dream". . .
   MY WHOLE HOME FLOODING, still I go on shuddering,
thinking "It's
still all in my dreams . . . or is it?"

Katie Lally

Stare

In a silent blurry stare
  I sit and ponder into air
    I push finger-hand through hair
    And have no wish, but to stare.

      My soul has put my mind to rest
       In empty sky of a mountain crest
        Empty air — empty space,
          Above the plane of the human race.

        Not today do I want to care.
         Today, I only wish to stare.
         Tomorrow I'll come back to.
           The wanting world I once knew.

J. Steven Evans

Morning Coffee

When I awake early in the A.M.,
I stagger to the coffee pot and finding it empty,
I could commit mayhem, in frantic movements, I prepare the pot
and count each eternal moment until the water gets hot

Waiting and my nerves about to break,
I feel as though I could truly cry
Oh, please coffee, hurry, hurry before I die

When finally I pour my very first cup,
I give toast to the pot and pet my little friendly pup

While dressing, with a gleam in my eye and a smile on my face
Suddenly, the cup slips and falls and goes all over the place
Watching it run across the floor, only these words
I find to say, oh damn, oh hell, Quickly my spirits do arise as
I remember the pot and its heavenly smell
I dash to the kitchen, knowing its either coffee or doom
Stopping only once and that's at the bathroom

Now dressed and with three cups down
I'm ready to face this world and stand my own ground
As I open my door to leave, my coffee so freshly drank,
I turn and salute the pot and to the pot my thanks!

Nancy C. Brayton Hudson

Passion Tide

Yesterday,
I stood over the jaws of the beast
Jaded, green and angry.
White-hot froth, lapping, itching to taste,
Calling—wanting.

Seething, even as the brown, acidic juices whirl below,
Someone woke it, and now it's hungry.
Hissing relentless, it's cowering prey reflected in its eyes.
Strength . . .   A million years old,
Its teeth withered and gray.

Whispering its summons—roaring its anger.
Gleaming, hypnotic eyes . . . pleading.
And, throngs of quarry tread eagerly into its attending lair.
Mesmerized, they wait their turn for the beast's affection.
Each hoping upon hope that they'll be next.

Taking, pilfering, usurping.
First goes the fight, then anger, then will.
Utopian fools give it their souls, and it feeds hungrily.
Gorged and blue, it recedes again.
Waiting. . .

Wally Kim

"An Unsaid Goodbye"

When I see a plane flying high above
I think of the one who everyone loves.
So far away yet so close at heart
As if he never had depart.
When you left a part of me left, too.
I wish I could say this to you.
Not a minute goes by you're not on my mind,
We shouldn't leave the past behind.
Memories of you stay on our hearts and minds,
You were always there when we got in a bind.
You help us in our time of need,
You were always there doing a good deed.
Every time we're together,
I wish that it would last forever.
Morning, day, noon or night
I know that you will be alright.
Helping us out or just having fun
On a rainy day you can bring out the sun.
Always smiling and full of laughter
We will all live happily ever after!

Mary Anne Kopecky

Mother

Suspended in time and space
I thought madness had taken hold
Search and find the truly good and fine
Be quietly diligent in my quest I was told

A reasonable request I mused
Certainly worthy of time and effort
All that could be seen I viewed
With my heart and soul in rich support

A woman tall, not in stature
But in love and kindness
A wife and mother mature
Full of youth and outlook fresh

Sister and friend extraordinaire
With a voice of comfort, a face of hope
Intangible riches she fully shares
Thus all who she touches learn to cope

Should it be your good fortune
In life's travels to meet her
You will learn what I have known
Throughout all time, she is my Mother

Saundra F. Lesesne

Memories

Memories of you run deep in my mind.
I thought we'd be together until the end of time.
I remember walking hand-in-hand by the sands
of the beach, talking till midnight about all
different things. Loving me endlessly seemed to be right.
Why oh-why did we suddenly fight?
The ways of the world seemed to take control.
I lost my emotions and you decided to go.
I begged and I pleaded you quietly whispered
"I'll love you forever, please don't make it harder."
You kissed my left cheek, my tears ran so deep.
You departed your way and I went mine, until
we meet next time I'll remember your face,
and think of the memories that now take your place.

Sarah Gitchel

"Kiss Me Softly"

Kiss me softly, gently with care.
I too have feelings for the love that we share.
Please don't hurt me, don't make me cry.
Things will work out but we both have to try.
I love you truly and I hope that you love me,
but into your heart you won't let me see.
If you do love me show me how kiss me softly
please tell me now.

Scott W. MacKenzie

Decision

I have decided to put my roots down in this town.
I traveled around the world and found out that Stillwater is the place
I want to stay. Through my job I have the opportunity to work with
the public and have the pleasure to get involved in peoples lives.
I have three special people in this town which friendship and love
I always will cherish.
  People make me happy
  People make me sad
  People make me cry
  People make me laugh
  People are the greatest miracle on this earth.

Maggie Luft

The Passing Of Time

Where is the little child
I use to tuck in every night?
Listen as she said her prayers,
And give a hug so tight.

Where is the little child?
With her dolls she use to play.
The sweetness of her little voice.
Brought joy to everyday.

Where is the little child?
Why did she grow so fast
I hoped the clock would just stand still.
But, alas, the time did pass.

Where is the little child?
The little child is grown,
She's now a wife and mother.
With children of her own.

She now has a little child
She gets to tuck in every night.
Listen as she says her prayers.
And give a hug so tight.

Lori Campbell

Untitled

Set me no date when love's lease must expire!
I would not have my tenancy so brief
It could in days be numbered; nor conspire
To dispossess me of my hearthold's fief.
This fair apartment in your breast I'd keep
With you as landlord, mistress; nor desire
A fitter place to take my tranquil sleep
When done with passion we two should retire.
But banish me this lodging! Lose the key!
Then vagrant would my sullen days be spent.
Of nights, no hospice should asylum me
Save star-fixed shelter of the firmament.
Mendicant exile, pensioner to grace,
If not with you, I'll lie no other place.

Kate Skattebol

Ice Mixed With Rain

I am like ice mixed with rain, I feel no love I feel no pain,
I used to say, It began one morning in the month of May
A baby girl was born on a rainy day
Abandoned by her mother, she was beaten and worse
Day after week after week month after month year after year
Beatings and tears

Till one day she said enough is enough!
She ran and she ran till the road ran out, Lost and lonely, full of self doubt
Is this what life is all about? At the end of her rope
She had lost all hope

Then she met Jesus, a ray of light penetrated a cold black
place inside, it shone so bright that it was hot!
He melted away all the ice and pain, and gave her a reason
To live again

The heart that was shattered, broken, and scarred
Is healed and no longer marred
God had blessed her with a family, with kisses and hugs
She is filled with sunshine and love
No longer bond to humility, suffering, and shame
I was like a ice mixed with rain, I felt no love I felt no pain

Katherine D. Rogers

Spotted Pony

I want to ride a spotted pony.
I want to climb upon his back.
I will then straddle without a saddle;
The reins in my hand will be slack.

  And as I gallop o'er the ground
  I'll seek adventure where ere it's found.
  I'll revel in pastoral sounds;
  Stop and bask on a sunny mound.

And if I should ride before sun rise,
I'll see the glorious painted dawn;
And if I have luck, I will see a duck
Or maybe a deer and it's fawn.

My exploration of hill and dale
May lead me to a silent brook
Or maybe ripples will dot stipples
While I write of this in my book.

  The breeze will caress me as I ride along.
  I'll savor the aromas. I'll sing a song.
  I'll solemnly swear this is where I belong.
  Ah! Such serenity. What can go wrong?

Walter H. Kester

Leaving The Fast Track

I want to be a turtle, I'm tired of being a hare.
I want to walk the slow pace and have fun getting there.
I used to run the fast track and though it was a blast.
But now I know I missed life by running much too fast.

  I need to re-examine, of myself I must take stock.
  When can I sit and daydream or have a quiet talk?
  I need to contemplate the things my Mother taught.
  I need to pause and ponder, I need to think deep thought.

The fast track doesn't get one where you really need to be-
To find life's hidden treasures or to know one's destiny.
This hurried pace makes life pass as sudden as a blink.
I want to stop and listen, I must stand still and think.
I need to count my blessings, I need more time for prayer.
I want to be a turtle, I'm tired of being a hare.

Ruby Alberts

Untitled

What's going on! I ask myself
I want you back I said
Please baby, came back to my arms...

I need you more than ever
I need you day and night
I need you all day and all night..

You are my sunshine and life
You are my honey, milk, blood and life
Please baby don't leave this way...

You don't have to love me
Just let me love you like I want
You will see that my love is true at that.

Don't leave me dead
Please, bring me life back
And all you have to do, is came back...

Remember, you don't have to love me
Just let me do you like I want
You well see my love for you..

And you well give up you life for me
Because my love is everything you want...

Rodriguez Heriberto

Visit With Myself

Today I slept with open eyes, into a dream I crept,
I was awake beside the bed, my younger brother slept,
The loneliness showed on his face, he turned his head and smiled,
I saw my self sitting there, as a young child,
I sat with him and held him close, only for a while,
I'm in his place, eyes filled with tears, still I had a smile,
The time had come for me to go, a voice called out, one I know,
I held on tight as if to say, no matter what, I want to stay,
Again he looked with eyes that knew, he let me go and I did too,
Someday I hope to return, but this time I had to learn
To say goodbye to myself from inside and no where else

Malory Flournoy Jr.

Flames

As I lay and stare out of my pale blue eyes
I watch the flame burn up to the sky
Out of control it blazes wild
Like an abandoned wilderness child
Destroying everything in its path
No control over its wrath
So hot to the touch, so cold to the heart
No way to tear it apart
I stare in amazement at its damaging power
No backing out, you can't cower
The flame goes so fast it actually dashes
Then there will be nothing left but ashes
Then the flame slowly dies away
With nothing left to remember but that day.

Katie Updegraff

"Rose Bud"

I am the petal of the rose that you bloomed.
I want to be colorful just like you.
Every tint that you gleam brings out the best in you to the extreme.
Each person looks at you and says how beautiful you are.
They want to take you home and plant you to make more.
Some kind of flower you must be.
It's because you're a wonderful mother.
And a garden is what everybody really sees.

Natalie M. D'Acquisto

My Prayer

While riding in the car one day
I watched the scenery pass my way.
On the radio, a song played there
and in my mind, I formed this prayer.

Dear Lord,

If I were a rock or a grain of sand
with my home along side of the road,
I'd never have to worry about death or disease
or watch myself growing old.

And I wouldn't care if the sun shone all day
or if the wind came along and blew the clouds my way.

Nor would I care if we went to war,
or the ocean no longer rushed up to the shore.

But if I were a rock or a grain of sand,
I'd have never known your love
or the touch of your hand.

Theresa Holloway

From MN to ML

Little ML has the big MS.
I went to get a card, cried, and made a real mess!

Fright, anger, terror, I wanted to scream.
I wanted to wake up and find it all a dream.

Questions - "What can I do? What will you do?"
Millions of questions - "Are they sure? What can they do?"

Just when we thought we'd been through it all,
First Mother, then Daddy, now you, I could just bawl.

He only gives what he thinks we can handle.
But this time he's wrong? Let's light a candle!

A family that's strong, with lots of love,
We know that's what we're all made of!

Our love is yours and you know it
Even when we're afraid to show it.

Mary Lombardi

"No Shelter From The Rain"

It was a cold and rainy day
I went to work my usual way

Exiting the highway - and what did I see
Living in cardboard boxes - a family of three

Mom reassured her child - it won't always be like this
Dad will find a job - and we'll live in a world of bliss

I offered to bring them - to a shelter of their choice
But there are none - replied a little child's voice

Government funds stopped - more important issues were at hand
Trying to solve the homeless problem - was not a big demand

I asked what could I do - in their time of need
Dad shook his head and said - "We appreciate your deed"
But until people speak out - this problem will never go away
The homeless will increase - each and every day

Until we each realize - that this can happen to us
No one's going to do anything - or even raise a fuss

When people speak out - and decide to take a stand
Then we'll have a chance - to stop this problem that's at hand.

Robin Scott

"The Widower"

The time will come when I am weak and weary
I will stare at deaths welcome door
If my life continues to be lonely and teary
Eternal sleep will be a welcome chore
Do not mourn or weep for me
My life was full and a wonderful one
Filled with love, devotion, respect and glee
A beautiful wife, wonderful daughters and a son
My grandchildren too are really great
They bring me love, joy, and fun
When I see them act, it was worth the wait

They do it with style and grace
For forty-six years Dorothy made a heaven here on earth for me
So at my final resting place
It's by Dorothy's side I want to be
For she was and is my only true love
My fear is that I will be down below and Dorothy will be in heaven above
If that happens I will be lost and alone forever.

Robert Levine

I Am A Stream

I am a stream.
  I wonder if the fish like swimming in me.
I hear the birds tweet as they drink from me.
  I see the sun shining above.
I want to know how the flowers like me.

I am a long stream that runs into the river.
  I pretend to be a river sometimes.
I feel the sun on my back.
  I touch the stones as I run by.
I wonder that one day I will dry up.
  I cry with the water thinking about it.

I am an ocean when I leave the river.
  I understand I will dry up one day.
I say I'll never run to the river, but I do.
  I dream of staying a stream and letting
Everyone drink from me.
  I try to stay, but I just keep running by.
I am a stream.

Selena Headley

Untitled

  Looking out the window
I wonder where my grandpa is on
this cold, wet day.
I wonder if he's sitting above, looking
down, watching what his family is doing.
I wonder if he is sitting there
listening to his granddaughter read her
poems to his wife and daughter.
I wonder if he is sitting there
thinking "that's my granddaughter and
I'm proud of her."
I miss my grandpa, but I know he
is always watching over his family
making sure that we are all happy and healthy.

Sandra Best

Knocking At Your Heart

I'm knocking, please let me in
I'm cold in the wind
What are your thought, what are your fear
What bring you laughter, what bring you tear
There isn't any shoulder, there isn't any ears
If no one is near
Knock, knock, knock

Lan Tieu

Me, Myself And I

I am a person who dreams of glory, and longs for humility.
I wonder . . . why are boomerangs loyal enough to always come back?
I hear the songs of the unsung.
I see through the haze of what society calls reality.
I want to be me.
I am a person that dreams of glory, and longs for humility.

I pretend that animals understand what we say, but are just too offended to retort.
I feel like a dog chained by my owner's expectations.
I touch with my mind, nature's spirit.
I worry about people that don't dream of flying.
I cry out to be heard.
I am a person that dreams of glory, and longs for humility.

I understand the language of the silence.
I say, "Darn the torpedoes, full speed ahead."
I dream of the future, ponder the present, and reminisce in the past.
I try to seize the day and the night.
I hope my nightmares are eaten up by the sandman's pitbull
before they get to me.
I am a person that dreams of glory, and longs for humility.

Karl Kruse

If I Were A Leaf

If I were a leaf,
I would dance in the air.
A gust of wind could
Take me anywhere.
If I were a leaf,
I'd fall from a tree.
I'd yell to my buddies "you can't catch me!"
If I were a leaf,
I'd glide far, far away.
And I would land in a soft stack of hay.
If I were a leaf,
People would rake me into a pile.
Kids would jump on me with a joyful smile.
Every winter I'd disappear,
But I'd right back the very next year.

Treis Scotten

I'd Give Anything

I'd give anything to hear her call my name.
I'd give anything for things to be the same.
I'd give anything for one more fight,
and everything for one last kiss goodnight.

I miss her so much I can't even explain,
more and more I feel the pain.

Sometimes I look into the clouds and see her profile,
and then all I can think about is my abandoning her in the
now empty domicile.

I miss her so much I can't even explain,
more and more I feel the pain.

I'd give anything to hear her swear up a storm,
expressing herself as free as a bird.
And I'd give anything for one last wise word.
I'd give anything to hear her forgiveness,
for all of my cruelty and selfishness.

I miss her so much I can't even explain more and more I feel the pain.

I'd give anything for her to be across the hall,
I'm descending in a tragic fall.
Mostly, I'd give anything to hear her whisper; I Love You.

Michelle Lynn Harman

I Didn't Kiss Them Enough

I wish that I could turn the tick-tock's clock around,
I'd like to give the past another sound.
Communicating with my parents was so tough
Because now I know, I didn't kiss them enough.
I'm not one of the guilty throng,
Feeling that I always did wrong.
I was a wonderful daughter,
Doing all for them that I oughta.
I'm not one of the repentant mob.
I stand at their graves; I don't sob.
I know now they were not so gruff -
I only wish I had kissed them enough.

Wilma Askinas

Shine On . . .

Brilliant star up in the sky, I'm suddenly reminded when
I'd talk to you of dreams and wishes, all excited for the future, and then . . .

Where did I go, what did I see, that had me focusing in
on heartache and lost chances, instead of moving on to begin again?

I used to wish to turn back time, to recreate the past;
by doing so, I was convinced, unhappy times could all be missed
and dreams be made to last . . .

Then something awoke inside of me that shouted out to say
"Turning back the hands of time will make you miss TODAY!"

Life is full of mysterious happenings I can't begin to understand;
it's time to begin to dream again, and to be willing to accept a
helping hand . . .

Thank you, my friend, for shining on through the dark and silent night
guiding dreams and possibilities to be pursued in the new days light ...

Lisa R. Szalapski

But, She Loves Him

It could have been day and it could have been night,
  idle conversation is like fuel to a fire that leads to a fight.

There is never any resolution only twisted words like a sense
  less riddle, questions un-answered are empty beginnings
  without any middle.

Just a kind word filled with compassion needs to be spoken,
  her heart he could mend but chooses to leave it broken

Alone in the dark as tears fill her eyes, he falls asleep not
  bothered by her pain as she silently cries

Gone all morning and most of the night leaves them so little
  time, it's others he tends to thoughts of her never enter his mind.

She gets lonely but never feels alone when they are apart,
  her love for him she carries deep inside her heart

Lorraine B. Orosco

My Friend

If ever there were a friend on whom I could depend
If ever there were one to trust, to say it is you, I must

If ever one cared to share the joys and sorrows
To be a friend today and not be gone tomorrow

If ever once could live life more fully one day to another
And throw herself into betterment, not just for herself but for others

Then, my Friend, it is you, for you have been dear to my heart
And never has there been a waver of friendship and love from the start

Your sparkling eyes and your smile are a pleasure to see when you're near
And your cheerful, spontaneous laughter rings long after you've gone from here

May God bless us with years more of friendship and grant that we always may share
The loyalty only a friend knows when someone really does care.

P. E. T.

If Everyone Were Just Like Me

If everyone were just like me, would the Gospel grow?
If everyone were just like me, would the Savior they want to know?
If everyone were just like me, would God's work get done on time?
Or, if everyone were just like me, would they only sit and whine?
If everyone were just like me, would they do their very best?
Or, if everyone were just like me, would they leave it to the rest?

Lord I am so thankful, that it's not just up to me.
I'm thankful that you have made us all, with such variety.
You've given us each a special gift, to serve you with each day.
And we must learn to use these gifts, or You may take them all away.

Lord there are many times, I stumble and I fall,
Because I did not ask you first, to help me give my all.

If everyone were just like me,.... I'm thankful they are not.
But Lord by Your Grace, I know I can be taught.

So Lord this is my earnest plea, I ask You now today,
May I always bend my knees and never forget to pray.
Show me Lord your will for me, guide me each step of the way.
Lord may I spend each and every day and everything I do,
Living in Your sovereign will and serving only you.

Sandra E. Schlessman Yung

Angels

There has always been this thing,
  if I am an angel, how do I fly?
If I was sent by God, why shouldn't I fly?
  These are things that cross my mind.
If you are an angel, why should you die?
  Cause with God, there is no reason
Why.
  If Lyssa is an angel, why can't she
Fly?
  Why don't we just all die?
  Some of the things we cannot answer,
  But God has the power to all our
Answers.

Wendell Stanley

Do I Truly Forgive And Understand

When I see the faults of others am I grateful I'm not there
If I am, I'm false to myself
For what I don't like of you I don't like of me
And I'm afraid to see
I have no understanding of them because I have
No understanding of me
When I see how empty I was and how I hated me
When I gave up on life, I gave up on me
But, when I walk in there shoes and feel and see
Then I truly forgive and understand
I forgave me.

Mary E. Palazzolo

Silent Scream

Deep within my mind I wonder
if I were screaming would anyone hear me
would it matter if I were to scream
no, no one would her my silent scream
my silent scream is not so silent anymore
and would it matter if I weren't here
sharing my silent scream with you

Sarah Wagner

353

Lament

If all my prayers were answered,
If miracles truly happened and
every wish I'd ever wished came true,
    you would live forever.

Loving you was so easy,
I never really thought about it:
As natural as breathing,
    as uplifting as laughter.

Your affection knew no bounds,
Required no conditions,
Never demanded more of me
    than I could give.

(I'd like to think) I gave back your dignity;
Because I could not offer life
I granted peace. But
    I am no consoled.

You see, I am human: selfish
and weak. I made the mistake
of loving you too much;
    and I believed in miracles.

Peggy J. Wallace

My Purpose

I thank you my Jesus that you died for me;
if not for your love where would I be?

As new as the morning is your mercy and love;
which flows from your heart like a sweet morning dove.

Refreshed and forgiven again I'm made new;
like green blades of grass with fresh morning dew.

I thank you Lord Jesus for helping me cope;
for teaching and guiding and giving me hope.

You show me the purpose for which I now live;
anointed for services, anointed to give.

For my purpose in life which you want me to see;
is to share your great love and lead others to thee.

Binding the wounds inflicted by sin;
that only you Jesus can heal from within.

Pointing the way to the Father of life;
who longs to protect us from anguish and strife.

Use me Lord Jesus to the glory of your name,
and I promise to give you all the honor and fame.

Nisel Pardo McDonald

Untitled

Come lay beside me,
If not in body
    then spirit.
And I will write in bed
Because I cannot feel,
But lay in placid folds of memories
    beneath your absent touch.
I'll prepare a face
For the faces I must meet,
Then look for only yours amongst them.
Because the minutes gone from you are endless
I've buried myself inside forgotten hours —
And because it hurts to count the seconds,
My clock has no hands . . .

Sandra Camp

Knowledge Is Heaven Tower: God's Grace An Eternal Power

Give ear, O heavens, and I will speak O earth,
If the beginning of my knowledge would be as that of God!
Who knowing all things, being all wise, all mighty, and eternal.
Creator of all things, Infinite in wisdom and power, in all growth to life.
This is how I would find master ship, in my special endeavors.

I would comb the universe by spirit, then become the tree of life;
that burning bush of wisdom, the same that delivered Christ.

The continuous growth so perfectly, perfected!
Setting the end of darkness strife, and the shadows of death in my life.

Truly there is a place for all things in life, a vine for silver, and a place for gold.
Yet, not one destroying the other one's mold.
The tongue of the just and it's choice words of understanding,
gold being well used when wisdom is the tool.

So, give ear O heavens, and I will speak O earth, pertaining to the
    growth of my new birth.
There is no wisdom nor knowledge or counsel against the Lord.
However, His just weight, is a balancing scale of our every talents,
    of wisdom and knowledge flow,
an acquired understanding that will always continue to grow.
Steams the trees of life; the end to all darkness and strife.

I would hold the vase of wisdom and touch understanding's heart;
I would aspire to be so gracefully smart!

Margaret Zamorano

"Mind Your Own Business"

If there is something suspicious going on,
    Ignore it and move on,
        Mind your own business...
If its really not your concern,
    Then it's not important for you to learn,
        Mind your own business...
If the gossip is flying high,
    Just let it pass on by,
        Mind your own business.
If you hear a little rumor,
    No need to repeat it for the humor,
        Mind your own business...
If what you thought you saw,
    Could hurt anyone at all,
        Mind your own business...
So have some respect for what I say,
    Go about your business, and look the other way
For there may come a day, when your in a mess,
You'll find yourself saying:
    "Mind your own business."

Tammy L. Bortel

With Pen In Hand

With pen in hand, I'll take my stand.
I'll tell the world, of that special girl.
I'll let them know, I love her so.
And when they yell, and give me hell,
I'll stand right there, to prove I care.
From the top of the hill, I'll state my will.
The love we grow, will brightly glow.
To show the way, and never stray.
I'll show them all, and I'll stand tall.
Being gay, it's just my way.
I see no wrong, I feel just as strong.
I bleed, I cry, I love, I die.
With pen in hand, I took my stand.
My Love and I walk hand-in-hand.
Along with God, in His great land.

Terry Aversano

Working Girl, Again!

Look for a job. It's no trouble at all.
I'll look through the paper, then give them a call.
Where have I worked? How long has it been?
I ran things so smoothly, I can do it again.

I quit to have babies, they needed my time.
They kept me at home wiping tears, washing grime.
Do I have experience? Can I handle stress?
Why I have stayed calm when the whole house was a mess!

Can I handle people, or talk on the phone?
I've reasoned with teenagers wanting to leave home.
Perhaps I'm old-fashioned, or a bit out of date,
But I'll always be honest, and I'll never be late.

Please sir, be willing to give me this chance.
I'll be open-minded, I'll learn the new dance.
I'll use a computer, send copies by fax,
Yet still smile at people and never be lax.

I'll work very hard, giving only my best,
Learning quite quickly, surprising the rest.
So, thank you for listening, please hire me today,
And some day in the future, you'll beg me to stay!

Theresa Weisenbeck

My Thoughts Of War

As I sit here I hope and pray
I'll never see the darkness of today.
Our father's lovely created world.
Which men threw away with just a twirl.

He's wasted and thrown away, the beauty of life,
The brightness of day,
He's made life miserable for others as well.
He's torn our country and freedom to hell.

It isn't his country, to waste like that,
To make our nations fight like rats.
It's ours to mend the wrong from right,
To help the honest win this fight.

We've done it once, we'll do it again,
So now is the time for us to begin,
So fight, fight, fight until the end.

Truman Lawfon Russell

My Best Friend

Nur die guten sterben jung = Only the good die young

Well you say your going out, well that's ok.
I'm a li'l sad, I lost my best friend today.
One monday morning, I noticed he was ill,
It happened so quick, it gave me a chill.
I know he's with God and he's gone for good,
But I can still see him now, just as he stood.
He was quite a man, my best friend,
But I'm sure I'll catch up to him in the end.
He was taken to early, but who am I to say.
Yes I'm a li'l sad, I lost my friend today.
He had a green thumb, made everything grow,
It seemed like his vehicles were always in tow.
When on our vacation, we loved to go,
Our second home was Old Mexico.
We plan to scatter his ashes in the sea.
Hope you wish him well - my best friend

Michael A. Covington

Sea Otter, Sea Otter

Sea Otter, Sea Otter what you be?
 I'm a mammal. Can't you see?

Sea Otter, Sea Otter what do you eat?
 Shellfish, Sea Urchins, and Crab Meat.

Sea Otter, Sea Otter how do you swim?
 By moving my large, webbed, back fin.

Sea Otter, Sea Otter why must you dive?
 To find my food to survive.
 Nicole Wells

Hopelessly

Now that you've gone away from me
I'm not sure what I'm going to do
Without you in my life, I can see
That living alone will only be blue
And I'll be yours forever...hopelessly

If I could only make you come back
Then all my dreams would be fulfilled
On the day you left, my heart cracked
And all my hopes and dreams were spilled
But I'll be yours forever...hopelessly

Hopefully, one day you'll come back to me
And I'll be yours forever...hopelessly

Micheal North

Doctor Joan

Would you like to be my teacher?
I'm very fond of you
We could play, and learn together,
Even hunt the caribou.

Thanks for the 'Check', 'My Medico'
Pleasure and business seemed to meld
From West Virginia to Mexico
With lingering thoughts of the hand I held.

When you're clear of obligations,
Let us plan a pleasant spree
Joan, you're my star and I'll be Santa
You can light my Christmas Tree.

Roy Christiansen

A Final Image, Moments After Death

As I stand here in this God forgiven day, I see
images and it reminds me of you.
As I stand here in the cold, I feel a little warmth
and it reminds me of you.
As I stand here in the dark, a distant light whispers
in my ears, a spark appears in my eyes.
And as I stand here all alone in these final moments,
a whisper, a spark, leads me to my final wish and
it becomes an image of you.

Nazih Hannush

Three Stars

Three Stars have appeared -
In conjunction with Light -
Preparing the way for terrestrial flight!
From out of the depth -
Of the stillness of night -
Come A Voice saying -
"All of this will pass away -
My Word will never pass away!"
Did you hear?
What a sight!
Never - No never -
Were stars ever that bright!

Sharline Maria Thomas

Untitled

The world - a forest of men
Implanted in a vast labyrinth
Of reason, faith and discipline,
Seeks roots in this disparaging earth.

Some seeking mounds of knowledge
May choke and over run others,
Only to be lost in their own hedge
Losing sight of kindness to another.

With all emotions and feelings
In their own beauty is bound,
Hatred, buds sprouting
Branches of prejudice all around.

Few project with comprehensive vision
Root hairs with a sense of direction
To develop knowledge with roots of wisdom
Steeped in sympathy and affection.

Vivian E. Mathews, PhD

"Why"

Why can't people understand what's most
important in life?
That loving and caring for each other is what
helps us get through troubles and strife

Why do we say so many cruel things to each other.
While it could be times well spent loving and caring
for our sisters and brothers.

God is the answer in him we should abide
And all the bitterness and hatred in our hearts
we'll be able to set aside.

If we allow him he'll mold us and shape
us and make us brand new!
He'll do it for me and he'll do it for you

He is our master oh Lord
Divine
He can be yours and he'll surely be mine.

Kay Saam

An Indian's Blessing

As I drift in quite solitude, along the river's edge,
In a distance I see a figure, standing on a mountain ledge.
The sun is slowly rising and it's beams dance across the dew,
And I'm momentarily blinded, from his figure's view.
The river is gently lapping against my small canoe,
A rainbow canopy of leaves, show bright against the sky so blue.
The figure stretches forth his arms as if to catch a beam,
And I feel as though I wish not, to wake from such a peaceful dream.
Then all at once as if on que, from the figure along the ledge,
All the sounds begin to awaken along the river's edge.

Michele M. Mijares

Me

Vagabond, vulcan, torpid I am not,
impressions are more than meet the eye,
descriptions of me would fill the page,
for I am many things indeed!

Soul, heart, compassion yes!
smiles, hope but, mostly humble.
Above all there's one word that suits me,
I would say I am mysterious!

Man has spent a lifetime studying
trying to get under the surface of our species,
there is more comprehension,
but, then again there is uniqueness.

There will always be a part misunderstood,
for we all withhold what is most precious.
The precious is our most delicate secrets,
the ones we are afraid to reveal!

Can you guess who I speak of,
the one who I describe with mystery,
with adlibs, verbs, and underlying meanings?
It is none other than simply me!

Mary E. Pollara

Lost Civilization

Transgression leaves us lost and alone,
In a desolate world of darkness.
The shadows swallow our hope,
We are curtained off from the world.
No one hears our cry,
As we stumble through the heartache.
The distance is too great,
There is no hand to hold onto.
We have wandered too far,
And fallen over the edge.
Our minds are clouded over,
We are left with an empty shell of a body,
Riddled with the fever and pain of regression
And as our days are numbered,
And breathing troubled, we see
In transgression,
    Silence is intangible,
        And truth is irreparable.

Sarah K. Kistler

Magnetic Poem

Delirious with the summer sun,
In a garden of honey as sweet as your dreams.
Whispering of juicy peaches and black shadows,
A music so beautiful you ache for its touch.
A moon goddess,
A love,
A bitter cry.
A vision of chocolatey lust,
Beneath a cool blue mist on a lazy day,
The spray of the sea and the smell in your heart.
Scream and no one is there to ask why,
Swim to your symphony, your diamond in the sky.

Rachel Bender

It Isn't Any Wonder

It isn't any wonder that the world is
   in a quandary,
When most of today's women are out protesting,
   instead of home doing the laundry.
They say there isn't much meaning to
   their dreary everyday lives,
Somehow it just isn't enough to be
   mothers, to be wives.
When will they come to realize this role
   that they reject,
Is one that has and always will, command
   the highest respect.
For in their hands they hold the Power
   to mold the future generation,
How sad to think they'd settle for less
   Women's Liberation!

   E. Picariello

No Answer Why

I thought he had everything that money could buy
In all the years, I knew him, I never say him cry
A home, a family, financially secure, but
Thinking back now, I'm not really sure.

Was it unfulfilled wishes or just life's
daily strife, that made him decide to
take his own life.
Did he realize the heartache he
would leave behind?
It was never in his nature to be so
unkind.

Friends and family offer comfort but when
all words are said, nothing changes
the fact that my brother is dead.
I'll go on living, we all have to try
for only God knows the answer
to the question, "why"

   Tommie Joyce Miller

Sunset

Light dashes beyond the horizon
   in an effort not to be drown in the dark,
colors of flame spread across the skies
   as the sun fought hard not to be vanished,
an instant which behold with such spectacle
   that unfolds an end to a nice day,
darkness has taken the domain over light
   as the day-star solemnly bows to the moon,
a death of a moment it may seem
   yet it denotes the birth of another,
though a summary of a period's events
   it also is a preface of tomorrow's concerns,
lost's of things can be said about it
   people look at it with different meanings,
but no matter how one will view it
   still it will be a glorious and magnificent
   sunset.

   Kenneth Fabugais

"Welcome To The Home Of A Pilot"

I pilot here, I pilot there,
In fact I pilot everywhere,
But a pack rat I am not.
I don't go get the things I've got.

But what my loved ones bring to me,
I love to have it where I can see.
So since I'm older, don't move a lot,
There's love around me, in what I've got.
So I pile it where I'm bound to be.
There's love in everything I see.

When I hold a grandchild on my knee,
There's a glow of love on the face I see.
When they see the treasure that they brought
Is right by, where grandma sits a lot.

So don't condemn the piles you see
When you come to visit me.
Just try my style, it's comforting,
With the love you get in piloting.

   Laura Mae Ross

Ageless, Seasonless, Memories And Time

It moved in so quietly, unnoticed.
In its corner of the room so cold.
So we closed up the doors and windows and turned up the heat.
We did not see it, we weren't looking
A new season, but there was always time.

The seasons quickened
Turning today's and tomorrows into memories
Each smile warming all but its corner of the room.
It was in no hurry watching the seasons pass.
And there was always time.

Memories were shared
Empty glass heirlooms given life
Through eyes so many seasons past.
A memory recounted a new one created
We were sharing time

In the clearest of mornings one last memory
No more seasons she'd have
No struggle, a final sweet breath
It held her hand warmly as they left
But we had memories, seasons and time.

   Lisa Holder

In My Dream

You were with another not me
   In my dream
I walked to your car, for my eyes to see
   In my dream
My heart filled with hurt I could not believe
   In my dream
The man that I love so every much could deceive
   In my dream
I told you please just go
   In my dream
But, you tried to explain so
   In my dream
I woke my wanting to scream
Realizing it was only "in my dream"

   Suzette Davidowski

A Dream

It stumbled over rocky shadow

While beneath hair and behind the eyes
In one memory hidden from lies
Lain wonder why darkened pillow of
Life of one who gave through unselfish time

Absent screaming regressing tear
Lay fallen vulnerable of feeling fear to
Which humming tune matched non-careless rhyme
Aside to travel distance to find a game
Yet mind whose truth fallen tear
Said that masked contentment unfair

Letting so ugly hurt pave thick pain
On delicate lips so sweet
Vivid images surround such mind
Every hope may someday find

To awaken and change the scene
Having felt only sorrow shown this kind
Every night — its only a dream for-
Ever

Robert Herz

"In Loving Memory"

I think about my Dad every day
In speech, actions in every way.

My Dad taught me things I'll never forget,
the tools I use daily my own goals to set.
He taught me that Love,
Hard work and Honesty are the Golden Rules,
those three basics are my tools.

My life goes on with ups and downs,
Wondering if I can keep my head above the ground.
Life should get easier as you grown older,
I've found that it has made me bolder.

Given the tools, I mentioned
before, wouldn't you think
that would open many a door?

My father is gone now but
the rules remain that I was taught,
For Love, Hard work and
Honesty are the things too
Many people "Forgot".

Mary Toolan Clarke

Canyon Land Cultures

Beauty abundant surrounds the beholder
in startlingly harmonious hues subdued
by purple shadows. The Anasazi
made homes here so long ago that modern folk
puzzle over their genius is solving mysteries
with surprisingly accurate assumptions.

Our modern philosophers and sociologists
wonder at their evident perspicacity
and the more artistic minded observers
draw the conclusions very similar, but laced
with scientific research they find useful.

We modern visitors to the land of Navajo
and Hopi, often condemn use of peyote
and refuse to accept their way of life
and their insistence upon ancient culture,
but when we want solitude and relief
from daily stress of buzzing doorbell
or ringing telephone, we find surcease
here among the vestiges of Acoma and Mesa Verde.

Veda N. Steadman

Campground In The Sky

Do you have a space for me, to park my R.V.?
    In the big Campground in the sky?
I have made my reservation, for this long awaited vacation
    to my happy destination by and by.
My time "on the highway of life", has many a conflict and
    many a strife.

As, I am placed upon the gurney,
    for my long awaited journey.
I'll travel over the streets of gold to join the loved ones,
    that I have longed to hold.
And I will see the familiar faces of friends of various spaces.

We will share the memories,
    of the roads we have trod.
On the way to our long awaited Campground
    to see the face of God.

Paula Yeamans

Conscience Clock

I kneel and pray all alone
In the center of a garden of stone.
Some don't live life to its fullest and regret it later on,
There is so much missing, but the time is gone.

When you walk down the street and see a dollar in the road.
Most are quick to claim it as their own.
But that same old person on that same old street,
Can't stop to help a homeless on his feet.

These people are quick to take and last forgive,
Fast to fight and slow to forgive.
They don't realize until it's too late,
That they've lived a life full of hate.

A tender soul isn't hard to find.,
They pride themselves on being kind.
They are remembered through years and generations,
Long after their souls enter heaven.

Don't lose your life before its too late
And the keepers of heaven lock their gates.
Live with a sense of pride and a clear and open mind,
And you'll never run out of time.

Katrina D. Flatt

Search

Rowing across the shores of life
    in the darkness as we came
We hardly known as once before
    and die in darkness as the same

Glancing to see the star lit sky
    in the cool cloak of night we sit
Here in we cry, the truth must lie
    we try remember, yet forget

With fleshy birth of life is launched
    a crooked rudder for the soul,
And swerves far from straight, the prison ship
    as o'er the tossing waves it tows

Then frightful storms oft rise at sea
    in ignorance, fear we of the deep
As such, we can not abandon ship
    in weary sickness on we sleep

At length, at length the port is reached
    then with the key of death is wide
The prison doors which bound souls tight
    to purest freedom then we glide.

Rita Hurst

Broken Trust

On that fateful night when you went berserk
in the early hours before I left for work.
Why this happened to me I do not know
but since it did, I know that I must go.
I didn't want to leave but you left no choice.
It's hard being in a relationship when you have no voice.
You say that I'm beautiful, perfect, smart and all that
but when you get angry I'm just a miserable rat.
With you there are times that nothing I do seems to be right,
and I'd like to scream out, "go fly a kite!"
But I don't as you know,
because I don't like to fight.
Maybe this time apart will help you survive,
and I know it will be hard just staying alive.
You can do it, you know, there was a you before us.
And getting the old "you" back will be a definite plus.

M. A. Koman

Deb And Beverly

I look at Deb and Beverly and see the innocence of truth
In the want to be my fried
They see I hurt and know I keep a pain locked within myself
They hear the silence of the tales I can't bare to tell
And they see in my eyes the tears that I won't cry
They hold out their hands and offer to take hold of mine
To walk me where I fear to go, or to sit with me in silence
They offer to help me, to try to work through feelings and
emotions
I dare not to face alone
When I look in their eyes, I see sincerity and truth
And I know that here - the seed of trust can grow
Yet God, I still fear so much
I fear letting them close, so I keep them at a distance I feel I can
                    control
And yet I know no hurt they've ever caused, no harm they've
ever done
And then I have to wonder what it is I've done
How much truth and trust I've built by keeping them away

Laurie St. Louis

Connections

Tiny little people,
In their tiny little world.

Won't even look,
Or seem to care
What happens or where...

Until its on them.

No place to run...
Waited too long, to escape the gun.

Too busy having fun
To help someone.

Can't make the connection that we're all one.
What happens there, affects what's here!

Wake up! Wake up!
Empathy, not apathy is key to our fears.
Make a difference! Don't just sit there and talk...
Do it! My dears.

G. Steven Hilton

A Dance Of Color

Once a year their colors reveal
    Inner beauty creeping uphill.
Dressed for the ball in lovely gowns
    While a whisper brings rustling sounds.
Some will blush, while others will glow
    It is a magnificent show.
Waiting for a chance at the dance
    To descend, to curtsy, to prance.
Drifting, dancing, downward they go
    Blanketing the earth, bowing low.
A dance of color has no end
    With a whisper it shall begin.

Lisa Ann Robertson

After The Bombing

The little white casket is covered with flowers.
Inside lies a child who was too young to die.
People gather around and speak in soft words,
By my grief blocks them out and I ask, "Why?"

He'll never know his first day at school.
He'll never board the big yellow bus.
We'll never see his little face in the window
As the bus rolls by and he waves to us.

I try to be brave as friends are sincere
When they say , "He's an angel now in God's heavenly place."
They don't know that I'm angry with God
For taking my child whom I can't replace.

I'll remember my child's laughter and his trusting face.
I'll always be grateful for my short time with him
These many gifts that he has given to me by his being
Will renew my faith, for there is good and my anger will dim.

Polly Maxsom

Untitled

The God-given color of skin...
instead of diverse, it's treated as sin.
Inbred prejudices and scornful eyes
look down upon pleading cries.
Accomplishments and growth silently ignored
as double standards linger behind closed doors.
Our "one nation under God", a melting pot
for which valiance was fought
side by side for a common cause
yet, it is long past time to pause,
realizing good and bad exist in all of the races,
not solely those donning different faces.
There is pride and ignorance among the white man
who conquered and explored upon entering the land.
The unfair treaties, the trading wars
eventually opened the door
to a passage of division, growing with time
making respect and empathy difficult to find.
Surviving, alone, is a difficult task
without be punished for the color of our mask.

Traci L. Schlenske

Signs of the Times

Milan is a city in constant motion and change.
Those who dwell here live in a time warp of style
from ancient to commercial.

Milan teenagers are only as different as the universal jean wearing
teen;
involved well into their fast pace, do-your-own-thing kind of life.
A crowd of them, advancing from the opposite direction,
saunter past ancient Roman columns and a crucifix,
Christ
with his arms outspread.

A colossal billboard advertises a bra as "soft as skin."
The model in this billboard appears seductive, voluptuous and
topless.
Her crossed arms placed over the product's purpose as if in false
modesty.

The Ticinese neighborhood of Milan, Italy subtly reveals its
layered
character.
A scene from left to right:
a temptress model presenting herself on a billboard,
the holy man himself — Jesus Christ — in his usual stance,
an imposing series of fat, cylindrical Roman columns,
last of all, a group of trendy Milanese teens
who wear those world renown, funky blue jeans.
They stride by this sign of the times.

Soma Pal

Broken Heart

The Broken Heart of a woman to be shared by another
Is but a mysterious thing
That places her in a state of Sorrow
That cannot be healed by the Giving of Love to another

The Broken Heart of a man to be shared by another
Is but a painful thing
That places him in a state of Depression
That cannot be lifted by the Happiness of Loving another

Together the Sorrow and Depression are constant companions
That man and woman dwell in
Only to be forgotten by the Happiness and Loving
That is given freely in the union of Companionship forevermore.

Kimberly Suhr

"Windsong Of The Sea"

The song of the wind, the wind of the sea
 is here, within the heart of my soul;
It blows, it howls, it whispers to me
 Go now - in the sea lies your goal.
Go now, while the dawn is painting the sky,
 Before darkness can hide the way;
When you reach the sea, your heart will know why
 It is here your young soul must stay.

 Wild is the wind of the sea
So free, unkept, uncaptured, untrod
 It bows before no one
 Except for God
It has no heart to feel life's woes
 It has no boundaries to stop where it goes.

Free is the wind of the sea
 So wild, so free
 I wish I could be
The windsong of the sea.

Marylou Hansen

Nasia

Sweet, lovely and all so bright
Is how you are morning to night
A splash of humor and giggles too
And more is what I find in you

Tenasia a Goddess in a special way
Who'll steal your heart without delay
Untouched by the sins of despair
Because mommy will always care

Sorry there couldn't have been two
Cause I could love one million of you
Your bring nothing but joy to me each day
As we cry, laugh and excitedly play

Why you're so important I can't explain
It must be the way you pronounce my name
No matter the reason I'd like to say
You're the best granddaughter in this world today

Tana Brown

Memories Lost

Is it better, or is it worse?
Is it a blessing or a curse?

Long ago before today
someone dear took hers away.

Memories she won't remember,
her nightmare started in December.

Many, many "I love you" 's
created her hell of sexual abuse.

Time has put a lock on her mind —
a sadness now that she must find.

Sadness prevailing, she couldn't have known,
that her happiness might well have grown.

A single bullet through her head —
she fell down on her bloody bed.

Is it better, or is it worse?
Is it a blessing or a curse?

Memories she won't remember,
her nightmare ended in September.

Linda Walberg

In Mother's Care

On a spring morning he was born
Into this world to endear and adorn.
A lad so obedient and so fair
Nestled safe and serene in mother's care.
In the early years, mother made the usual sacrifice
In the later years, was a source of frequent advice.
At various times when his matters went askew
Usually, it was mother who made the rescue.

Like Siamese twins, they often shared a day
However, it was not in the cards for him to stay.
At age thirty, the illness came
And though mother was there to ease the pain
On a summer evening, he succumbed at home
To acquired immune deficiency syndrome.
Neither fright nor doubt was present there
For as in the beginning, he was in mother's care.

D. L. Perry

"To The Moon"

Your brilliance this night is dulled by the clouds,
Is it because of their envy of your beautiful splendor?
Black are these storm clouds that ascend and descend,
Desiring in their efforts to eclipse your brilliance.

Do not worry beautiful moon, because they meddle
Being fleeting they quickly will go
Toward distant places, they will go intertwine
And at little while slowly they will vanish.

Then you, remain radiantly shining
Lovingly lavishly the earth with yours rays
Illuminating cheerful, quiet and vividly...

To men eager to see your brilliant face,
You continue shining gracefully, despite the war
With the such dark clouds envious of your peace.

Martha Ake

Untitled

I don't understand I can't tell what I'm made of
Is it me or you that I'm afraid of
Sitting here the same things being hard
Is it me or is someone else disturbed
All around me stories of confusion
And so I sit in a world of disillusion
But knowing not I only understand why
It seems to me that everybody stands by
Watching me in a world of utter chaos
Understanding I'm not the only one lost
But ever more I'm trying not to hurt you
I wonder if I'm coming to deserve you
And now I see nothing that I'm made of
Nothing here and nothing I'm afraid of
Nothing more to tell you that I know
I'm nothing here that's why I have to go
And so I leave I never get the chance
To feel the pain I'm dying in a trance
A shattered soul with nothing more to bleed
A broken heart lost into the breeze

Toi Saporiti

Weeping Willow

Oh, weeping willow, why do you weep?
Is it that birds do not come to your branches to sleep?
Or is it that children do not play upon you,
Oh weeping willow, I wish I knew.
Is it the water is too far away,
Or is it that squirrels do not come to play?
Weeping willow, what makes you so sad,
I wish so much that you were glad.
Is it the animals who don't use your shade,
Or is it the flowers that you have not made?
Oh weeping wiilow, I wish I knew, what is
really wrong with you.

Malinda Wistrom

The World Needs A Facial When It Comes To Being Racial

Stop the killing, stop the hurt
It shouldn't matter what color is under anyone's shirt
All around the world someone is at the mercy of prejudice pain
Oh God, what we need is a cleansing rain
Love your neighbor as you love thyself
Don't make judgements based on race, religion, or wealth
Tear down hatred walls of the past
Let us rejoice in peace at last

Whitney Bates

A Cynical, Middle-Aged Woman, Greeting-Card Poetry Response to

Rimbaud's "The Drunken Boat"

Falling in love
is like diving headlong
into a bottomless chalice
of rich, dark, sweet, voluptuous
Puerto Rican rum
and drinking it straight in
through the pores of your skin.

Then you wake up with a terrible hangover.

Katherine Claire Thompson

Life

Life what does it mean,
Is it a big ol' dream,
Life what does it mean,
Does it mean to have happiness and glee,
Life what does it mean,
Is it a door that you go into that is locked with a key,
Life what does it mean,
Does it mean you must be a queen,
Life what does it mean,
Does it mean a hill that is steep,
Life what does it mean,
It means a part of you that is hard but... very sweet.

Kristi Root

What Is Love?

What is love?
Is it Venus, Is it Cupid? Is it liquid? Is it solid?
They say love is blind. Others say love is kind.
But what is love?
Love is exciting like evening dances,
Love is sweet like childhood romances.
Do tell me, what love is?
Is it something we say? Like "I do" on wedding day?
Is it songs that we sing; or holiday bell's ring?
Valentine hearts to candy tarts: do tell me what letter it starts?
Is love soft like a kitten's fur?
Is it like courtesy, "yes, ma'am", "yes Sir?"
Love can make us feel free,
But sometimes we must first pay a fee.
No! No! Mister you have got it all wrong:
You are making this poem way too long.
Listen carefully to what I say,
For I will tell you what love is, without delay.
Love is not what we receive,
LOVE IS WHAT WE GIVE.

Nerchi Nermal

The Never Ending

Lonely. Deserted. Secluded.
Is that what you think I am?
No! I am just imaginary to you.
I have no beginning, I have no end,
When I go through oceans and lands, I do not bend.
Crossing continents, people I do meet,
Saliferous sweating, scalding at their feet.
While some enjoy me, satisfied by the sun,
This job is unending, it's never done.
Zero is nothing more than I can be,
Dividing is my specialty.
Such power I do possess,
Deserted. Secluded. Loneliness?

Micki Bodtke

In My Name

What I could have became
is present in my name
What I am is what you see in me
anonymously my name signifies all that I should be
All that I could have been
is my universal name without and within
I could be a constant companion and a life long friend
my name instinctively instructs me
but I cannot always be the person I so desire to be
still my name is always me
through my name came all that you see in me
a broken part of this vast universe
with a name sometimes complicated and diverse
a name that enhances every fiber of being, every part of me
a name specifically designed and created for me
the relationship between me and my name
may cause me ridicule, but cause me no shame
because all that I am is formulated, demonstrated, and orches-
trated by
my name

Marilyn Gipson Smith

Neil

When a simple music staff
Is secure and stable
And prepared to denominate
My full blown
Discouraged epidemic,
This waxed tension within my rib cage
Expands throughout
The entirety of a disguise I call my own.
For the masturbation of
A mirrored field of roses
Only disables the thorns from
Residing on their stems.
(Targeted)...my heart,
The Central Starvation First Aid Kit that
Entitles what use to be,
becomes a criminal
And provides handcuffed hourglasses and memories
To my journal of
Convenient Amnesia.

Melissa Coleman

Natural Wonders

The wonder of a drop of dew, suffused by the sun,
Is the magic of nature to everyone.

If you are lucky, you may see,
A spiderweb, transformed with a million of these,
A myriad of crystals, that you could not do.

But you better look quickly, for a sparrow flies by,
Destroying the crystals that nature provides.

But who is to say, he's not part of the wonder,
Even though he destroyed it and tore it asunder?

To fill your heart with wonders like these,
Is the magic of life, and it is a great sorrow,
Not everyone can treasure nature's wonder.

Teddy Wessels

World's Very Best Dad

The man I will describe,
Is the man Mom chose to stand by her side.
Stand by her side through thick and thin,
Through sorrow after sorrow, again and again.
He left a legacy to each of his kids,
Through the life he led and the things he did.
He taught each of us to be honest and true,
And all the other things he knew.
How to add, subtract, divide, and multiply,
How to reach for the stars and touch the sky.
How to care for others and always lend a hand,
To a sick child or a tired man.

Now he's the one who's tired and needs a place to rest,
He's carried his share of our load and that makes him the best.
We were never too far away for him to come if we needed him,
His helping hands, we could always count on them.
His tears we never saw when we were young,
But we know all of our praises to others he sung.
We know that he loved us though the words were rarely said,
We will love him always, because he is, was and forever will be the
 BEST DAD.

Patricia Rogers Martin

Keep Your Knees To The Ground, Your Chin To The Sky

The best advice I've ever heard
is to live on bent and willing knees
looking up to the heavens, seeking His will
to ask, to receive, to believe.

A full and honorary surrender
exemplifies a commitment and a love
giving all the Praise and Glory
to our Savior in the heavens above.

Praying in the name of Jesus
exalting Him on high
your knees firmly placed upon the ground
your chin humbling up to the sky.

Pulling your hands together
a plea in a prayer embrace
a heart to soul solutions
in the presence of our Lord and Grace.

For His tender mercy we kneel before Him
forgive us our sins, the defects to us unbeknownst
strengthen weakness' and provide spiritual guidance
to follow His will and not that of our own.

Randall E. Woods

Round And Round

  As the world turns, we wonder if what we're doing
is what we're supposed to be doing.
  As the world turns, you just sit there watching TV
just turning the TV channels, not helping this world at all.
  As the world turns, their are very few of us that are
trying to make this world be a better and safer place
to live for our next generations.
  As the world turns, you and I go places and see people
throwing their garbage on the ground (as in food they
don't want.) And they aren't even thinking what consequences
there are for doing that (animals dying from hunger, homeless
people eating out of garbage cans, because they're so hungry.)
  As the world turns, not very many people think about how
this place is going to turn out for all our next generations.

Marcie Fockler

My Heart

My heart is my soft spot,
It also can be really hot.
It hurts when I think everyone don't care,
It makes me want to pull out my hair.
That makes me really depressed,
Which makes me wish I was put to rest.
But when everything gets better,
I always receive a really sweet letter.
My letter tells me thing,
That makes my heart ring.
I always get really happy,
Which makes my heart sappy.
My heart loves everything in this world,
Which makes me fell really good.

Trisha Ellis

The Poet In The Sky

Radiating against the black of night,
it appears like a diamond glittering in the sun.
First star; one wish.
A childhood memory that makes us all a child again.
One who feels no doubt
that our special wish will come true.
A sense of security that grows up with us;
we almost believe we can manipulate our lives
with this one wish.

If that star could pen
all the decades of wishes we bestowed on it,
it's writings would not be fiction,
but a true account of our innermost desires.

Starlight, star bright . . .
We continue to recite our little poem.
We continue to dream our dreams,
and we find solace in the fact
that we were able to share our fantasies . . .
and yet our secrets are safe and secure,
locked away forever.

Sandy Martin

*My friend, Mary Dunnwald, found
a Christmas card in her belongings
that she had forgotten to send me.
The card was years old, but she mailed it to me.
This poem is dedicated to Mary.*

Lost and Found

I've had this card since 1910
It came from olden time
My other soul did purchase it
For a special friend of mine

Now this other soul did pass away
And never mailed the card
So my present soul went searching
And the tracking got quite hard

The secret's in the finding
My soul has been quite true
It led me to your inner heart
And outside.......there was you!

Lynne M. Grenier

The Morning Sun

The dawn is amazing with it's warm and vibrant glow
it comes from the sky, the trees, it makes me fall to my knees.

It is bright yet hazy with oh so many colors
of red and blue and purple it makes you crazy.

It's such a warm feeling beneath this glow
it's the best love we will ever know.

There are many aspects of this amazing sky
many strange feelings you just want to cry.

I look at the dawn and see an amazing thing
even though it's been here for many days now.

We are all living under this hazy sky
even the animals are here to view it with their eyes.

It goes on forever never seeming to end
the wonderful colors such an awesome blend.

This is a mysterious thing which I know little about
will we ever know more if we keep polluting and cutting pieces of it out?

This dawn of which we speak is like a painting
Who is the painter? Is he or she still existing?

The dawn has always been here even before you and me
I have never seen anything better than she.

Nicole Michelle Wachter

He Doesn't Know

I think about him all day long
it feels so right how can it be wrong
I wish I could tell him I love him so
but that day hasn't come and he doesn't know

Just a few feet away yet so very far
I stare out the window watching for his car
in my dreams he comes to me, he loves me so
but those are just dreams because he doesn't know.

What am I to do I wonder to myself
these feelings are deeper than any I've felt
will he see it in my eyes that I love him so
or will I suffer in silence because he doesn't know

This has to end soon it's driving me mad
my eyes are tearful, my heart is sad
if he ever comes to me I'll never let him go
until then it's my secret because he doesn't know.

Patty Griggs

Close

Frustrating
It is all so close to my home . . .
. . . close as the answers to my being here are in my mind
Close . . .
. . . yet strangely beyond reach
I know I am a warrior
Close . . .
. . . yet strangely beyond reach
Frustrating
It is all so close to my home . . .
. . . close as the answers to my being here are in my mind
Close . . .
. . . yet strangely beyond reach
I know I serve the cause of justice
I know I am a warrior
Close . . .
. . . yet strangely beyond reach
And there is part of me which feels that should be enough

Scott Ransopher

Home

As subtle as love feels,
It is an anchor heavier than any and worth its weight in gold.
It creates a peaceful harbor by virtue of its presence
And even the deadliest billows or the most violent winds
Cannot rend the ship in its care from its lifeline.

It requires simple attention,
A polishing here and there
To keep the barnacles from corroding its surface
And weakening its form.

The anchor can be borne up on the ship's deck,
Taken to foreign ports,
And always signifies home when it is again lowered into the depths.
Adventure on the high seas!
Breezy sails,
Troubled waters,
Lonely lapping of the waves against the ship.
All are weathered by the anchor that is love.

Michele L. Krause

Autumn Memories

Autumn holds memories long since forgotten.
It is the time when those memories are reborn
into a care-free day of sunshine and happiness.
Those memories come flooding back, like the sun's ray's
pouring into a dark room when the curtains are drawn.
You remember those pure days, the sun shining on
your back, the leaves crunching between your toes,
and for a moment you could have sworn you were in heaven.
Soon the sun will sink back behind the clouds, and the
leaves on the ground will be replaced by dead grass
and frost, and those memories will be hidden in solitude
and darkness, until they are again uncovered.

Scott Daniel

Pedestal

You tell me that you can't
it is too far to jump
you're afraid, you say
you've never known the world

And I ask, how this can be
why are you trapped away
we should walk a while together
and share the world

And you tell me you wish that you could,
but you see the world clear enough from here
and you see the one who trapped you here
and you tell me,
                    it is me

Tom Pritchard

Web

Silver is the color of this very fine string
It supports the dead and many living things
Clinging tightly with the most powerful grip
By continuous movement you're unlikely to slip
Victims struggle in frantic to get clear
Then flying high the creator appears
Moving slowly on that silky fine string
This eight-legged insect victory begins
The web of power keeps him alive
Without it for certain he wouldn't survive
Silver is the color of this rich fine seam
Blowing in the wind invisibly remaining till the end

Patricia Johnson

Road To Anywhere

There is an old, old house on the road to Anywhere,
It is weathered, and run down, it has seen its' share
Of love, and laughter, and tears, and pain,
It sits through the wind, and sunshine, through snow, or rain.
It has housed so many families, through all of these long years,
And, could tell many volumes of stories, it could sometimes bring you to tears.
Or sometimes bring memories back of special, happy times, for
These kinds of tales, well, they could never be a bore.
If this old house could talk, it would say many things to you,
Of how it loved its' occupants, maybe tell some secrets, too.
It now has a lonely, haunted and empty look outside,
But, inside it is warm with memories that move like the tide
Over oceans of nostalgic moments, big and wide.
You may pass this old house, with its' weathered, rundown look
On the long road to Anywhere, stop and think of how it took
The heartaches, and happiness of many a family,
And, the joys this old house can give to ones like you and me.

Ruth Milstead Myers

Sometimes

Sometimes, when your eyes shine with the fire of love,
it is your soul that reaches thru and touches my heart.
A gentle pressure of reassurance is in your touch,
    and I return the fire to you.
Often when we are close, I close my eyes and I see
the brilliant white blue glow that clothes the stars at night.
Instantly transformed into heavenly bodies we float
    into a time when we alone exist.
Our forms are the bodies of light that began the creation
that has become our world, yours and mine together,
    and we will live forever in it.
Watch, — the eyes of the cat are upon us, and we know that
what we have is as sure and steady as the sun.
    Pray, — let the fire of love burn bright
    and we can light the world we share.

Katrina Joan Merikas

"Impressionism"

Prosaically the farmers say,
"It looks like rain today";
And weathermen show up on the screen
To say, "The skies today are looking mean";
While reflections in the cow pond show
The way the tinted clouds sweep low;
Over the dark and humble earth,
Mingling with the grass and dirt;
As amateur artists sketch their masterpieces,
Unaware of the expirations on their leases;
While tired citizens cast their ballots
For the politicians who'll keep a promise;
As the religious pray for those gone wrong,
Wondering why God takes so long
To make the world right
Or to give the blind better sight;
And the clouds look like something out of a painting by Van Gogh.

Sarah Barber

What Life Is Like To Me

Life is fun
It shines like the morning sun
Life is like a breeze blowing through the trees
Life is like a hill
You can never stay still

Life is like a rainbow
It has a nice glow
All in a neat row
But in the end
Life can be very wonderful
When you find a friend

Kimberly A. Austin

How To Read A Poem

A poem is like a feeling or idea that you start with
It should be treated with respect because of all the
Hard work put in it.

And if you can not read a poem the way the writer
Has wrote it then do the writer justice and do not
Insult it.

Poetry is a universal language that we all can
Understand. It comes from the heart and could help
Us to become better men.

So when you pick up a poem to read, read it as if
You were the writer and maybe someday we all can
Become better writers instead of striving to become
Better fighters.

Trina B. Harrell

Holy Cross - The School We Believe In

Our school is tall and strong,
It was built in a time so long.
Two buildings of red, the school is not dead,
The workers did nothing wrong.

The school was made just right,
With a flagpole painted white.
It was made out of bricks, not out of sticks,
And the boys and girls did not fight.

Education is our plan.
We do the best we can.
The school is great, there's nothing to hate,
To become a woman or man.

The teachers and students are kind,
They all have a willing mind.
They really are caring, they do lots of sharing,
Such a school is hard to find.

We love our school very much,
We learn by thinking, and touch.
The boys, they race all over the place,
While the girls play double dutch.

Grade 3-109

Laura Mae Maxamillian Ann Hesseltine Harris Herring Washington

The day we met was when I knew, I'd be someone special to you.
It was evident in your eyes, and in the way your lips set to smile.
It showed in all the things you did, your love of me you never hid.
In your arms you'd hold me tight, even as I cried during the night.

When daddy died, you gave us your best.
Never putting yourself first; hardly stopping to rest.
Even as part of you lay dying; your eldest, your first born
You smiled through your crying; weathering the storm.

You've taken on a task most could not;
Raising a teenage grandchild, boy that's some lot.
I ask how you rise to the challenge with such ease.
Again you smile and say, "staying on my knees".

Through your strength of character, and love of God and family
You've taught me almost all I know.
How to give love, feed it, and make it grow.
That's only some of the reason why my love for you shall never die.
You're a friend like no other, and why I'm proud you're my mother.
This is why I can truly say,
Laura Mae Maxamillian Ann Hesseltine Harris Herring Washington
I love you forever and always.

Sharlotte Herring Castro

Ink

What is this thing called ink?
It will be a thing of the past,
Replaced by toner and phosphorescent displays.

What is this thing called ink?
A black, fluid substance that can stain the soul,
A dark, volatile liquid that can bring fear to the mind,
Consternation to the enemy,
And desire to those in need of desire.

It can satisfy that desire!

It can inflame a hatred, or it can strengthen a bond.
It is a tool not to be taken lightly,
Not to be handled by the uninitiated,
Not to be violated.

In the wrong hands, it can kill.
In the right hands, it can build nations, chart the heavens,
And control destiny.

It is not the pen that is mightier than the sword;
It is the ink within... and the hands of those who guide it.

V.P. Turner

Imalsan

Once the earth was clearly glowing,
It's beauty priceless, magnificence stirred.
While river streams are sparkling, flowing,
It's future happenings, Eden unknowing.

Then the sound of chaos was heard,
As these figures came to succeed.
The constant chirping of a bird,
Screamed out, loud and angered.

This black plague progressed on with speed,
Destroying innocent faces with ease.
Not knowing that it was greed,
That had started this tiny seed.

The bird reappeared from the trees,
To mourn the loss of his precious friend.
"Stop the slaughter," were the birds pleas,
But the shadow continued to take them to their knees.

The numbers decreased from this bizarre trend,
The bird's last cry, a muffled choke.
"Don't worry, we will soon mend,"
But this plague never came to an end.

Ryan John Williams

The Forgotten Oak Of Old Monterey

There was an old tree which sat on a hill,
it's branches and leaves were very, very still.
A bird alit on a branch up high,
And sang a song to a beautiful sky.

The tree was bent and crooked and old,
If it could talk, many stories would be told.
It's weathered appearance, both strong and quaint,
Many good artists tried to capture in paint.

It once stood strong and mighty, sometimes looking gray,
But some men mistakenly threw it in the bay.
Many people worried that it might be lost,
So all began searching, no matter the cost.

Great numbers of boats covered the sea,
As they sailed further, some seemed small as a pea.
When the old tree was sighted many cheers made a great sound,
The tree was replanted, and near a church it can be found.

Michelle Toth

"Our Ailing Mother"

If you listen, you'll hear something ticking.
It's deep in the heart of the Earth.
    We've been given this planet as a precious gift,
And we do not yet realize it's worth.
    So we cloud up the blue sky above us,
And taint the generous fertility of the soil.
    We ravage and cut down our forests,
And poison our waters with oil.
    It's up to us to correct our mistakes,
And wipe clean the face of our mother,
    Because we must realize that when we take care of
our home,
    We also take care of each other.

Mariah Bowers

A Wounded Friend

A wounded bird is in my care
It's down and out and no one there
So I must take it and heal it so
Give it support so it's confidence will grow
I'll be there for you each and everyday
Sometimes it takes a friend to make it all go away
I look to the sky and what do I see
My friend who is wounded better from recovery
So my friend you fly and oh you fly high
It made me so happy it brought tears to my eye

Sherrie Olivia Spencer

Love Is Like a Wave About To Break

Love is like a wave about to break.
It's formed and it's nurtured.
But it can come crashing down on us like a boat against the rocks.
There are survivors and there are those lost in the dizziness of the currents.
Some are picked up by passing ships disguised as people and some get
tangled in the web they weave of seaweed they call life and are
forever bottled; engulfed. Looking for love, many places.
Empty, hopeful faces. Spaces; people's space.
Bars where people wait to be picked as if a ripe fruit or vegetable
in a market On streets driving, looking, playing.
Toying eyes playing with people's hungry hearts and lonely souls;
    wanting, needing someone to hold.
Talking, laughing, crying.
Times to remember; times to cherish before they can't remember
anymore.
Having arms and longing to reach but they have no control are
slapped by the weapons they use.
People never seem to learn that love is something we don't conquer;
    it conquers us.

Kevin Redmond

Fire Dance

Before my eyes the fire dances;
it's golden flames reducing log to ash
and twig to dust.

The flames dance in lines and circles;
their silent ballet warding off the darkness
and the cold.

The dance comes to an end as the flames take their bows
sinking into the dusty grey ashes
of time.

Shane Vanderbilt

A Lesson From The Birds

Thank you, Lord, for the beautiful trees
It's inspiring to sit quietly under one of these.
While watching the squirrels run up and down
Noting the colorful birds as they fly around.

In the distance, I hear a bird sweetly call
Closer by, another sings out giving its all.
Soon there's several pouring out chimes
All sound so sweetly, yet nothing rhymes.
Each bird does its own thing and yet they relate
Never a note of unhappiness or a tune of hate.

Now all of us are different too, yet made of the same dust
Created by God in whom we should trust.
It would be good to be like the birds and learn to relate
Tuning out all unhappiness and all that's of hate.

La Verle Rhodes Boyd

What Is Christmas?

What is Christmas to me?
It's more than decoration on a tree
It's more than lights, tinsel, and things.
It's the spirit that Christmas brings,
It's more than goodwill toward man
It's a time to reflect on Christmas past, and the memories of family and friends.
It's the church bells that ring on Christmas morn,
It's hearing the carolers sing.
It was a gift that was sent from above, to show the world of Gods true love.
The sacrifices had not yet been made...the price that one day this
    child would pay.
The star shown bright that Christmas night, to lead the way for all that came.
Three wise men brought their gifts, of frankincense, myrrh, and gold
    to worship the child.
The savior was born.
So Christmas is more than presents and nice things.
It was the greatest gift God gave...the greatest sacrifice ever made.
And to think it all started in a manger and some hay,
a child was born on Christmas day.

Trisha Baran

Flying Solo

On the wings of time I must embark on a journey far from home.
It's not a trip I care to take for it carries me out to roam.
It's easier to avoid the stress of learning to fly alone.
I'd rather curl up by the fireplace like a dog with a bone.
To know the origin of this pain will allow me reprieve
from the pressures that daily life I so often receive.
To have some point of reference helps put life into view
with clarity even though at times it seems precious moments are few.
So.....it appears that flying solo is what I truly yearn.
We'll see the contrails as the plane begins it's turn.
Then I may begin to see objectively as I try to learn
not to be afraid of it's wake and know I will not burn.
Place important trust in myself along with the Lord above.
I'll land safely and surely as I am bathed inside with self love.

Lisa Lindstrom

Joy Child

No one can imagine what kind of joy
I've gotten from the birth of my little boy
A precious gift from the Lord above
He easily, receives all of my love
When I see his smiling face each and every day
My heart goes aflutter, what else can I say
With lottery and such that can be done
Thank you, Lord, for my miracle son
Through your gift, Lord, I have won

Susan Chiucarello

Arising

It fires a hue of red, like none I've ever seen.
It's not pleasant or passionate, not painful or spiteful.
It sits above me and holds me in its embrace.
And in that instance, it's the only thing I see.
So grand, as I watch it climb, from where it was once denied.
But how can one deny it, when it comes round again.
I've seen it countless times, and still I don't know.
How it happens, and yet, I do it myself I'm sure.
It will say what it means as it reveals itself, for it is like no other.
And even though it seems the same, I don't know what I'll discover.
It reflects on me in a way only I can see.
But I, I am for all of what it wants me to be.
And as it circles around me, never coming to close.
Others look at it, and wonder how it rose.
I know it comes around, and I know I understand.
But how can it be so grand, when it comes around again.

Good Night
Vincent D. Giacoia III

Altared Embers On Assignment With You

It's okay, God — we can take it!
  It's okay, Lord — lay it on!
It's okay, Daddy — we can take it
  as we travel on with You

What a privilege, Holy Spirit
  to bear a burden just our size
that we might show the world around us
  how to lift each sorrow High

Just as your folk never grieve without hope:
  Daddy, your chosen suffer - but not in vain.
Peering tearfully into our faith microscope:
  We see your contagious joy mixed with our pain!

Jesus, make us worthy
  to do our suffering joyfully
Remind us often this life we're living
  in your Name is not a game

It's for souls who are hurting
  People You have been alerting
Who watch us in each rough place we're Given
  Hoping we'll point 'em to the Grace of Heaven!
    Val Anne Lynch

The Old House

Have you seen the cottage, that sits by the stream
Its old stone walls ever serene
It has a timber frame and a roof of thatch
And it sits at the end of a timber patch
Have you gazed thru the windows of this old home
To see the statues that come from rome
All the furniture looks as though made by hand
And to watch the old hour glass and its dripping sand
Have you looked real close at the home inside
And noticed its all one room and no place to hide
Have you wondered who lives in this house so plain
It has to be a person who has no shame
O, this house, if it could only talk
To tell us who built it and its beautiful walk
Here comes the owner, ever so slow
To chase us away, never to know
    Robert R. Duwe

A Christmas Letter

She said, a Christmas letter is presently due
It's only October, three months more must accrue.
I complain for more time to begin the report
Last year we were late she replies in retort.
It won't hurt to be early, wife says, looking glum
Halloween has not come yet, I plead feeling dumb.
While she's in her element setting the pace
I must follow directions or fall out of grace.
It's a chore for you, yes, at this time of the year
When it's done you will primp in bloated good cheer.
I'll begin if you promise to leave it alone
Poking fun at my family's my humorous tone.
When first draft is finished I really must gloat
She reviews it until I can't see what I wrote.
This is better she says, there's truth in this missal
I have to admit it's as clean as a whistle.
When everyone mentioned must add his remark
My footprints seem hardly a mark in the dark.
When Christmas is over and all is at ease
I'll add an Addendum, and write as I please.

Raymond Martin

Goodbye

Dear Mom,
It's so hard to say all the things that are deeply ingrained in our heart
Cause we thought we'd be able to tell you before we ever would part

But you left us without any warning and the void is so hard to fill
We love you and miss you dear mother and know that we always will

Oh the years they went by far too quickly but the past remains vivid and bright
And we'll bask in the glow of our memories until you're again in our sight

The one thing that will help to sustain us is a feat we attribute to you
It's the love of the rest of our family and a bond that is shared by so few

We thank God for our brothers and sisters and the kinship we all have known
We felt it when we were mere children we embrace it now that we're grown

And we hope we've succeeded in passing this feeling along to our clan
May it flow from generation to generation with the guidance of your gentle hand

So good-bye mom till we meet you in heaven and remember to pass on our love
To our family who departed before you and are now by your side up above
Your loving children.
    Roberta C. Sibley

Don't Give Up "Just Try"

Wait not my child; "It can be done."
Just try! If you don't succeed.
It can be done, by you the only one
With faith and hope indeed.

If the cause is good, it's sure to stand,
No matter what the task may be.
Hold high your head with prosperity
and most of all, honesty.

When the blows come hard and seem to last,
'til patience has reached its end.
Forget the past and hold on fast
for the good will always win.

As long as there's the will power,
you can always make it through
Grit your teeth and raise your chin,
never doubt what you can do.

Wait not my child; "It can be done."
Just try! If you don't succeed.
It can be done, by you the only one
with your faith and hope indeed.
    Muriel D. Bland Roy

"Reach For the Stars And You'll Walk in His Shoes"

I love the world I live in
  Its the only one I'll ever know.
The stars above are shining brightly
  And the moon is glowing too.
As I stand here on firm ground
  Knowing that our future is to be found
In the stars above us and beyond;
  And I'm sure we shall land
  Close to a brilliant star.
And also to that mystery planet called Mars.
  We shall land there as I'm sure,
A comet will hit a planet like ours;
  And meet a demise like that befell our Dinosaurs
We'll be safe on Mars and also I know
  The "man upstairs" will guide us
To that dream
  That will sure come true for "He"
Only knows the "Score."
  When we reach that beautiful
  'shore' called "Mars."

William Weber

The Flag

The Flag is blood spilled on a foreign shore
It's what drives men to fight when they can fight no more
The Flag is a symbol of all that makes us free
Of the rights and privileges given to you and me
The red is our valor, the white our purity
The blue shows to God our reverence and sincerity
Our Flag has been through war upon war
Yet it still holds the freedom our fathers fought for
Most people do not pledge the flag seriously
They forget the sacrifices that made us free
Our Flag stands for all that makes us free
And we should treasure our Flag for eternity
We should not drag it in the dirt
We should not wear it on a shirt
But respect the Flag we love
And thank the Lord above

Mark Hudson

Love

It's what makes the wedding bells ring,
It's what makes the blue bird sing,
It makes the flowers come up in the spring,
It has great power over everything.

It strengthens the weak, and weakens the strong,
It will consume every body before to long.
It's the basis for peace in this twisted world,
It will keep people together, for richer or poorer.

If it's true and for real, even death cannot part,
It's the greatest thing on earth, it comes straight from the heart.
No matter where you're from, or what race you're of,
The greatest gift is the gift of love.

Melissa Marn

The Glow Of Love

The "Glow Of Love" is precious, so enjoy it while you may,
Keep the embers glowing, in the strife of "day to day".
Many problems enter in, but you can face them all,
When you have the "glow of love," problems become quite small.
Just remember, there is nothing that two can't share as "one",
And forget petty animosity before the day is done!
For if you harbor ill-will, the "glow" can be put out.
You have to work together, and that's beyond any doubt!
As you start along the pathway, as a loving man and wife,
May you have "God's Blessing" and a long and happy life!

Phyllis Reese Fuller

Union Chapel

Union chapel — meeting place of lost souls.
It's where they decide if your destined for heaven or hell.

Lifeless bodies empty and cold.
Souls have left to find their final home.
The fine line between life and death has been broken.
Where you'll go is not your choice,
The empty body holds your voice,
Does it matter whether your good or bad?
Will you be happy or will you be sad?

Life is darkness - life in light,
Is your soul black or is it white?

When we die, Union Chapel is where
We'll meet, without shoes upon our feet.

Red Brick Chapel with stained glass
Windows filtering sunlight,
Casting rainbows on bodiless souls.

Who will judge our destination?
Does it matter?

Kelly Rogers

Silken Wings

I spot a delicate angel gently kissing the flowers petals.
It's wings like silk, it's body light as a feather.
A breeze carries this fragile creature from
Mother Nature's breast.
The wind ruffles its detailed wings,
Blending a palette of colors.
The wind dies.
My butterfly sails in the morning air.
It's persian carpet wings embrace the sun.
I watch it loop, its charm seems to release me.
I daydream of drifting toward
The Heavens one day also.

Melissa Ayn Lynch

God's Love

Jesus loves me of this I'm sure
I've felt his preserve with in me stir

I have praised him for the things he's done
So many Blessings and victories won

But after all the love He's shown
Why do I stray and walk on my own?

So many times I fall in sin
And Evil thoughts will enter in.

When I lack in the word and time in prayer
I can easily fall into Satan's snare

I have stood in church and testified
Then lived my life as if I had lied

But when I think that sin has won
I stop to Dwell on God's Dear Son

He paid my debt at Calvary
He gave his life to set me free.

I can have God's fire within my soul
By letting his spirit take control

Lord, keep my focus less on me
that your Holy Child I can be.

Kevin M. Wright

The Final Solution

My life is a sad story at that. Hello, my name is Cory
I've had a tough time dealing with life, and here's my story

My life is a sad story at that. My heart cries night and day
But no one sees my agony, I've got to find another way

My life is a sad story at that. For I wish to die
My tears extinguish the once Present fire in my eye

My life is a sad story at that. I must confront my fears
And I cry out for anyone's help, but they fall upon deaf ears

My life is a sad story at that. And I cry tears of pain
But you can't see them, for I cry in the rain

My life is a sad story at that. My once black eyes are blue
You would understand me if you knew what I'd been through

My life is a sad story at that. Life is what I fear
I cry out to you, but you don't want to hear

My life is sad story at that. And I no longer have to worry
I hope you can understand my actions, I have decided to end my story

My life is a sad story at that. For just the other day I died
I finally found a perfect way out, my final solution . . . suicide

My life was a sad story at that, and here's the end of this story
I could not handle life. I'm sorry, Goodbye, my name was Cory.

Michael Horan

"The Man"

There is this wonderful man I know,
I've known him for quiet a few years.

It's been a struggle to find out who he is,
through lots of laughter and tears.

I've been so blessed, I've looked inside,
and found this wonderful friend.

And with God's help and lots of luck,
I'll have him until the end.

He's taught me so much in all our years,
he's been there through difficult times.

I could never repay what he's given me,
I thank God every day that he's mine.

This big man I speak of is so strong,
he has been just like a rock.

If you ever need someone, he's right there
on the spot.

His strength never waivers, and his
heart is as big as a tree.

I'm so very lucky he's by my side,
and that God gave him to me.

Viola M. Fels

Time Steals

Time steals what we don't wish to lose,
It's not something we can choose,
Life takes away what we need,
And gives us back a seed,
Of which to grow anew,
Something different to do,
But we always take with us a portion of the loss we had,
Even though it's often sad,
Then this seed blossoms into a rose,
For all the world to know, the beauty we hold in our heart,
Is ready to make a new start.

Martha Mary Meyer

Today

Today is the first day of the rest of my life.
I've lived my life in the shadows of others.
I want to give up, on this so called life
that is bringing me down.
Remembering that each day that went by
was not my own.
Forgetting about the old and making my life anew.
Waking up in this brand new world, where I take charge.
Oh how I could fill that tingling sensation.
Deep, deep down to the core of my being.
Don't give me that look, that turned up look you
always despised.
Today is the beginning of my new existence.
Instead; smile with me, and give me the courage.
Come break forth the joy and the laughter.
Which was shielded by the clouds of others problems.
To make this, today, the first day of the rest of my life.

Ruthie Lewis

Old Man, Help Me

Old man, tell me how to get through this life.
I've reached out and found emptiness.
I've walked down an endless road.
I've looked up and been blinded by tears.

Old man, do you have a secret for living?
Or, did you too reach out, walk down lonely roads -
only to be blinded by tears?
Old man, help me.
I've tried to find the goodness in people.
I've sought the goodness in myself.
Other people can't make me happy -
I must find the happiness within myself.
Old man, have you been happy?
Or have you also found sadness?
Have you lived your days, one after the other,
Not looking forward to the next?
Does time just run itself out?
Or is there a meaning to life?
Old man, help me.

Sharlyn Stephens

Without A Word

Around me it falls, but I am immune
I've seen it before, I've seen the second moon
So dark it reigns, throughout the veins
yes, and so hard it rains, it rains down —
Down around me
But just like before, no one has found me
Or was it dyslexic behavior
In such desperate search of a savior?
The thought was cast, don't want to know . . .
But if you come in last, there was a reason to the slow
How could you not know?
It's just not right, but I won't say a word
If you want it badly enough
The truth shall be heard
If not, the deafening silence shall be king
A piercing ring shall bellow to be heard
Without a single cesspool of any sort of word
Without a word, the tyranny was heard
It all became more clear to me, our sun was one to the third
It all drew near to me, WITHOUT A WORD

Kristen Kemp

October Cloves

Scarecrows of lost and stolen envy
Jack-o-lanterns of lustful promise
Is this what is meant by putting feeling into art
Busted in a bourbon state of grossly overrated jealousy
I stood in the hallway smoking cloves
The death of one is naught but a statistic
In the slated graphs and charts of a nation of limited consciousness
Such a bogus way to think
The smell of dead leaves
Falling in October's lost in paradise and forgotten gives me
feelings of regret
I laugh bitterly in that cold thought on a single moment of irony
The cloves making ghosts dance in the strangely wrought breezes
of the eastern winds
Should humankind ever fall
What would be the hammer of our cold and untimely disaster
There are no questions or answers only thoughts
I drop them and walk away fading like a dying ember
Into the cold darkness of a sleepy October night
Lighting a fresh cigarette of cloves

Xavier Alexander Robertson

"A Wonder"

I looked up and saw a big beautiful moon;
Just hanging there in the sky,
As I stared up I do believe I saw a face with a big smile:
Just smiling down on this earth from up there on high,
I just sat there and looked up at that big moon for awhile;
Just hanging up there with a smile that seemed
to stretch from sea to shinning sea;
I know by this, that the Good Lord loves you and me;
Because he gave us this big beautiful wonder up there so proud;
Makes us want to praise the Lord out loud;
We thank him for this proud moon that seems to
say, "I am the one and the only" shinning down
for you, me and, especially for the lonely.

Virginia Brooks McClanahan

Insight

What if there wasn't a way to see
Just how blind some can be
What if a person could tell the truth
And somehow get away with it
What if a lie meant you believed
Or you have an idea that someone else conceived
A thought of something gone
A gesture to right a wrong
Tying a string to remember
Not knowing what you forgot

Nicole K. Hansen

Is It Too Much To Ask?

There are times when I what I want is an ear
Just to listen, to hear, to really hear
Not just what's said — what isn't said too
Listen to the tone of my soul
Its laughter, its tears
Feel with me for awhile — understand
Embrace me with your soul - gently
Sometimes I'm very fragile — handle with care
I need just a little time to sort my thoughts
Comfort me as I go deep into my soul
I want to lean on you just a bit — stand by me
Hold me through the pain and into truth
So peace can come — joy too
Lend me your ear — listen to my soul
Is it too much to ask?

Richard Hough

Untitled

How many nights I've dreamed of leaving this place
Just to be by your side
So many times I've held that pillow
Silently kissing you and cried

I have never known such loneliness
Total isolation with-in my mind
The hurt, the pain, the anxiety
Of worse there is no kind

Soon I will look upon your face
See the beauty within your eyes
Kiss you soft and tenderly
Listening to each of your sighs

I'll hold you in my arms so tight
Being real I want to make sure
I swear I'll never let you go
And be away from you no more

Again my dreams are being answered
My hopes are all coming to be
All my desires in this world
Will be sitting right next to me

Tom Jones

Am I Who I Am?

Am I who I am?
Just when I think I know,
Someone says that's not who I am at all.
I've been called everyone's name this week but my own.
I feel like nothing more than a shadow.
Mom keeps asking me if I want to go home.
"No, not at all!
I'd just prefer to roam."
If I should find myself along the way,
I hope God will look at me and say "that's OK!"
I am who I am.

Sondra L. Kinner

Stormsong

Night has gone wild! The Wind,
keening in unrivaled ferity,
shatters my somnolence;
Tension coils me like a Spring!
I wait in blackness.

Eerie light-play directs my attention
to Shadows dancing on frightened trees.
I hesitate, shivering in expectation,
and can almost taste the cold, acrid Fury
before I am embraced by its Passion.

Teresa Hunter-Degueurce

The Window To My Soul

The window to my soul is clouded with imaginary dust.
It's swept away, but still a cloud remains.

I want to feel and see the world around me,
But I am blinded and my hands are tied.

I try to listen, but there is no sound.
I cry out for help, but there is no one there.

Where do you turn?
What do you do?

Running toward the light, but it grows quite dim.
The dust is collecting, and there is no way to be rid of it.

So the soul is lost behind closed doors and covered windows.

Laura J. Prescott

Nature's Song

The gentle beat of summer rain
Keeps time upon the windowpane
The rhythm and the tempo seem as constant as the day

The silent humming of the breeze
That rustles leaves within the trees
A tuneless tune that sweeps about whatever's in the way

The simple song of grasses green
They rustle as someone unseen
Will play them as a harp with strings or is it just the air

A stream rolls by like voices raised
In tender song as I have gazed
Along this land I now can hear its music everywhere

Wherever one can look around
There's Nature's Song in every sound
Seek with your heart and from the start you'll hear the music play
        K. C. Fahel

Gran's and Grampa's Christmas In Their Golden Years

(Dedicated to our children, grandchildren and great-grands

Who make our years golden!)
Gram and Gramp are havin' Christmas, all the
        kids are comin' home.
They will all arrive tomorrow, but tonight
        we're all alone.
So, we're dancin' on the carpet (neat!)
A-doin' it in our bare feet!
And, wow, it feels so funny
O-o-o-o . . . it tickles, Honey!

Jingle bells and laughter pealing — Christmas
        tree up to the ceiling!
Kids a-throgin' in the driveway — bringin'
        presents through the doorway!
Birthday cake for Him Who sees us
Children in exuberant choir!
Singin' "Happy birthday, Jesus!"
(S'mores now roastin' in the fire.)

Turkey splutterin' in the oven—great-grandchildren
        full of lovin',
Gram's and Grampa's pride's a-showin' by the special
        way they're glowin'!
But Gram's and Grampa's biggest treasure, celebratin'
        Christmas cheer,
Is the deep love without measure, that our family shares
        all year!
        Faythimes

A Child's World

Turtles, guppies, three-wheeled trikes
Kittens, puppies, two-wheeled bikes
Piggy-back rides, building blocks
A plane that glides, a chair that rocks
Words that rhyme, grass that's green
A sun that shines, a sea that's clean
A book to read, a song to hear
A picture to dream, and love to share
A hug, a hand, an I love you
So much to have, so much to do
And not so much to ask, and not so much to give
Yet all it takes to smile, and all we need to live
Whether two or forty or ninety-three
It's all the same for you and me
A child's world and yours and mine
We come back to this in a matter of time.
        Roberta Kern

The Beauty Of Pain . . .

A fearful cry and a piercing coldness, unto this world I came, without knowledge of purpose or destination . . . I endured all of its great hardships and difficulties . . . I endeavored to find meaning in my existence and failure waited for me after each voyage . . . From crawling to falling, I cried many a tears of misery and pain . . . My blood spilled in many dark places; my flesh rotted in many dark corners. My smile broke into many different pieces . . . I was breathing, but I was lifeless. My only friends were Misery, Pain and Condemnation. I knew the existence of joy and happiness but never met them; I searched to find some light but my walk through life's dark tunnel seemed to be endless . . . Time became a catalyst for each experiment and at times, Time even showed me compassion . . . It was in these brief moments of compassion that I met Hope . . . Hope seemed unfamiliar at first, but in my desperation I clung on to it . . . The healing medication of its gentleness nurtured the sight of my heart . . . And with this ability to see, I saw from afar the beauty of love. Its warmth gave me life and acceptance of myself and with this gift I met wisdom, a most powerful friend . . . The beauty of pain; the redemption of anguish; a purposeful birth
        William S. Paik

On This Rose

As he walks down a path in the darkness and thinks of things no one knows, he wonders if he will ever be free of
The thorns that he picked with a rose.
She lies with consciousness drifting away, and struggles to hear any voice reassuring decisions she made in her past and confirming she's made the right choice.

He wanders to places he doesn't recall, not knowing quite how he'll return and not really knowing the people he's with as they change and each takes a turn.
She wanders in darkness, not knowing her way — not knowing what truths lie ahead, and not really knowing what future is hers or down which path she'll be led.

He continues his journey and happens upon another who's equally "lost," he reaches to her so they walk aside by side not yet knowing, this time, there's no cost.
As she walks down the path in the darkness and thinks of things no one knows, she wonders if he will ever believe that
There is no thorn on this rose.
        Nancy A. Lisak

Untitled

What may I ask, takes place in this home,
Laid bare of things, like Queens and Kings,
Tables and chairs, dollies and bears
Spindles and cots, poodles and tots,
What may I ask, does take place
In just such a place?

Memories are there of weddings and such,
Laughter and tears, and silks to touch.

Sadness too, for all to see
And feel the inner pain,
For when we leave
It follows me, throughout eternity,
It calls to me, "Remember me?"

Echoes do remain, "I miss thee."
        Mario C. Zeoli Sr.

Our Future World In Review

Seems so long ago, that our world was all aglow, people
laughed and sang their song's about A future we all hope
to know. Now that all seems to have past, people grumble
growl and grasp. Our SCHOOL'S back then then were for the learning,
no Gun's no Gang's or Knives - were in the planning,
OUR PRAYER'S were SAID each day we were there, us KID's
joined in and made it A pleasant affair. Now, that has
past, and we LIVE IN FEAR - OUR KID'S want make it
thru another year Our NEW'S is filled with grief and
strife, our KID'S know not our kind of LIFE, we were
BLESSED to have lived back then no Drug's no Gang's,
or Enemies. Seems our FUTURE is at last - just a MEMORY
of the past.

Viola B. Jelinek

Green Eyed Witch

She was a wild free spirit long ago
Laughing as she played games.
The green eyed witch soon came to know
A man she would try to tame.

She was mistaken thinking he was a man
So she played by mortal rules
He saw the weakness and devised a plan
Where only she could lose.

He made a chamber that would hold her love
Only he had the key to the lock
You see he too was born in witches cove
And grew up to become a warlock.

He warned her not to play with his heart
That the stakes were just too high
She forced him to play so he played it smart
He took her love and said good-bye.

That green eyed witch is locked inside me
And she laughs at me from within.
When these green eyes shine it's her you see
Unlock the chamber so we can love again.

Pamela J. Scollon

A Dreamer

I'm a dreamer. With echoes of children's
laughter and visions of Florida Sunshine.
I now endure the pristine Alaskan snow.
Life is different here.
Death is the Center of my existence,
Service my torch. At night, alone,
I silently cry — searching, struggling to break these chains of
mediocrity and poverty; to find and grasp opportunity.

It's here in the house, the land, the sun.
An award of freedom for myself, my children, the next generation.
A chance to feed the fire of independence;
To build new dreams, new hopes,
new lives — that is why. And so, I dream on.

Richard C.

Starlight

Let's assume we were under the guiding
Light of the full moon
When our eyes first met?
May I be so bold then, as to
Presume that what I felt
Was something less than sparks from stars
ERUPTING at a glance;
Or better yet, the beginning
Of An Infinite Affair?

Peter Gonzales Valentin

Prayer Of The Flowers

O Lord! Teach me the sermon of the flowers.
Lead me along paths of beauty
To morning-glory and sunflower,
To violet and lily,
To cactus bloom and orange blossom,
That I may profit by their example.
Implant in my soul a seed of faith and hope
To germinate and climb with the morning-glory.
Irradiate my countenance with light
Reflected by the sunflower.
Impart to my spirit the true humility
of the violet.
Instill my mind with thoughts of that purity and nobility
symbolized by the lily.
Make manifest through the cactus bloom
The good in the worst of us,
So my words shall not be bitter,
But pleasant and sweet as the orange blossom.
O Lord! Teach my heart to flower with love.

Stuart F. Knauss

Natural Disaster

There's a choice to make a choice to not make a choice, but no one
leads. The tsunami can fade into waves washing into a whispering
lullaby-lake. Another natural disaster is all she needs.

Cradling the tornado with fire arms of flames he feeds.
Eruption threatens. We cannot sweep away the ashes that we make.
There's a choice to make a choice to not make a choice, but no one leads.

Spinning so fast, every February, she doesn't know if she bleeds.
Tremor kicks in - The floor's life cycle begins to shake.
Another natural disaster is all she needs.

Molten dreams and rocking chairs are contagious and ignorance breeds.
She defiantly spoon feeds all that she cannot take.
There's a choice to make a choice to not make a choice, but no one leads.

Mud slides into an avalanche that sucks its thumb and plants its
seeds. Child-like innocence soothes; naivete burns, stings, bites
like a snake. Another natural disaster is all he needs.

There's a Voice of Love between the faults and in the spaces of
aftershocks that no one heeds.
Death is the day a bundle of joyous hope turned noise keeps them awake.
There's a choice to make a choice to not make a choice, but no one
leads. Another natural disaster is all anyone needs.

Lori Ann Shea

Dreaming Into Reality

Hold on to your dreams for they may become transcended
Life isn't always as it seems
Lives may be torn, yet mended
Focus on quality, and not how much
For those that do become quite out of touch
Reality is forever - Fantasy explores
If you remain conscious there may open many doors
Closed minds oppose
Preparing a lifetime of chaotic chores
One's spirit may be broken
Please endure and take stride
Wisdom breeds not a token
And one should never hide
Freedom is a state of mind
Fly, soar, dream
For bondage may leave you blind
Resort to intuition
Leave nothing left unsigned
Through love there's restitution
Remember to always be kind

Toni Warren

"A Race For Life"

I entered a race, this race for life,
leaving behind all anger, lust,
bitterness and strife.

When I got started I was full of joy
I was ready to win,
I could see myself in the end,
jumping, shouting and praising the Lord.

The prize for winning the race is eternal life,
with the Lord my Savior Jesus Christ.
So, I ran with this in mind. Some that ran with me began to slow
down, but I couldn't, I didn't have the time.

Some ran and fell on the way,
satan tried to tell me this would happen to me some day.
I ran and ran with the finish in sight, every day seem like a fight.
I leaped over holes that were big enough to see,
traps my enemies set out for me,
but at times I stumbled at small cracks
weakness I had not conquered yet.

I'm running a race this race for life and when it's all over,
I'll have a life with my Savior and Lord Jesus Christ.

LaSonya D. Callahan

Ralphie

He moved into my life, a grey whisper on cushioned feet,
leaving shallow prints in the snow.
Pointed ears tipped by silver round the corner, so discreet,
like radar seeking his needs, telling him where to go.
Green-gold eyes peeked warily, saying he'd give much more than he'd take,
tho he'd already stolen my heart.
He lived quietly inside my life, but I'd laugh out loud at his comic ways.
Ralphie, one of a kind, tho one of many "strays."
Some stay a lifetime, for others that's cut short
by the hardness of man, still, softly they depart.
The wound goes deep, like a pawprint cut out of my soul.
How is such pain felt by the loss of such a small thing?
GOD only knows, so he placed him off the road by the creek,
and covered him with Autumn leaves, so I'd find him in the Spring.

Rise Chontos

Ours To Keep

Life is to short to ponder on
life's innocence.

To try to behold
life at it's finest moments of all.

Will only concede
it's uncommitted fragility.

For us all to reconcile it's
relentless domain,

And try to stop the flowing tide
the dam will break,

Drowning us all in the waves that follow,
loosing what was

Our's to keep,
till the dawn of time shall sweep us away,

Like the cluttered leaves that collect at our feet
in the fall of our lives.

Toni DuBrel

Windy Day Yearnings Of A Young Mother, Alone

I would like to be a leaf blowing, or a wave of sand
Lifted, hurled helplessly about, beating upon the land.
It seems the only way to make my mark on this world,
Is to be helplessly blown through it by the wind.

I was briefly romanced by that seductive satyr, Wind;
With his lips he brushed my cheek, caressed my hair,
My neck lay bare, and whispered urgently,
"I will free you, come with me."

I lingered, being tempted so, then solemnly I answered, "No,
My nest I've filled and feathered, go and leave me be,
When these sweet birds have flown, come back for me".

The wanton Wind withdrew and chilled me through with his reply.
"You may never leave here if you wait too long to fly.
You'll grow to love your comfort and forget me by and by."
. . . "But, tell me, am I chained then to this limb until I die?"

The song will be a different tune, swelling from a sigh,
But a bird can sing as sweetly from her nest, as from the sky,
If she has the heart to try, and so will I.

Except, of course, on days when the Wind begins to blow,
And to rock me wildly to the fro.

Sherry Staker

A Dream

Soft as a feather
Light as a cloud
The smell of heather
Never loud

Pure white snow
Firm as the ground
The first rays of light
Never square, always round

Fluffy like cotton
Sweet as a scent
Like the roll of the ocean
And the beauty of a rose

This is a dream, a dream in its self

The words I have written, are a dreams wealth

You can always dream if you have a mind.

So dream a dream and enjoy the sunshine

Sierra Baker

Beauty

Slowly the sun reached into the protected center.
Light gently coaxed beauty from her hiding place.
Slowly, timidly, beauty turned to face
The warm caress of the distant fire.

As the warmth spread through her
she began to open.
Peering through her petals, beauty smiled at the sun
Winking to me with her dewdrop eye.

My soul was captured for a moment
As the drop clung, desperately, for one last second
Just a gleam in light's eye
And then dropped from the petal of the rose.

G. Dean Blackshaw

Time Will Tell

You walked into my life
like a fresh cool evening breeze
and sent chills up my spine
with your loving eyes
and your casual smile
each time I see you
I fall more and more
in love with you
I've never spoke these words out loud to you
for I don't know if your
feelings run as deep as mine
I do feel a special kind
of magic between us
I pray to God every night
that you are the one
who I will spend eternity with
but the Lord works is mysterious ways
and only time will tell
if eternity will be
ours to share together

Kelly S. Kirkman

A Mountain - A Man

A mountain in valley houses a stream
Like a man's lifelong dream
Forever flowing from it's source
Altering and changing it's own course.

The mountain folk of years gone by
Worked long hard days to preserve the eye.
Now museums hold the lore
Of mountains dreams of years before.

Tho slow the change of mountains be
Man spends most time in eternity.
Let man's eye focus not on time
But in mountains glory - today are mine,

Man is like the mountain.
It is valley's sure to come.
  Until the final cry
  Until the day they die.

Martha C. Evans

Season Of Suffering

When our hopes and dreams lie shattered
Like a precious, broken vase
Our mind begins to wonder about God's heavenly ways

Our hearts cry out "Why Lord?
When things were going so great?
How could you let this happen?
Why am I in this state?"

Have faith my child, - God knows what he's doing
But he also knows your pain
He is not trying to hurt you
But is molding you in his way

Remember the suffering servant
We too must walk in his steps
If we are to become like him
Holy and pleasing and blest

So in this season of suffering
In this time of pain
Look to Jesus your comforter
His likeness to be gained.

Patti Gawlak

"Don't Look At Me"

Our time together passes silently,
  like a predator in the dark.
Our eyes seldom meet, and when they do,
  briefly, we fear that something in them
  will break the silence . . .
  that we will see the truth.
Don't look at me.
In the silence,
In the dark,
  no one is wrong.

Laurie J. Knowles

Snow Covered Understanding Of Emotion

The snow blankets the town,
like grandma's soft quilt erases your body from the neck down.
Everything from tree trunks to potholes has been eliminated,
and there is a cry of honesty from the sugar highway,
a black hole pulling her heart into her sparkling eyes.
I wish she could kiss me,
like the snow that hangs underneath my lips cantilever does.
I wish she could hold me,
like the cold wind that wraps me from toe to ear.
So as I walk away humbly,
I completely understand,
just as the coldness invades,
so does the thought of a close companion,
into the part of the heart reserved for human affection.
This town is whole and pure for a few blinks of the eye,
and my heart is sad and lonely because of it.
Tonight I love you,
I love you both.

Michael W. Nolin Jr.

Free To Be Me

I desire the need inside to be free
Like the little girl bouncing on Granddads knee
No chains or restraints holding me back
The freedom of the train speeding down the track

The wind behind me, the first light of day
Really laughing and singing, whenever I may
The freedom to sit quietly next to a stream
To drowse, to sleep, to laze, to dream

To run when I want, to stay when I need
To follow sometimes, then again, just to lead
To do everything, or just nothing at all
To be the child within, or stand ten feet tall

The freedom to choose to give you all my time
Without feeling that I'm committing a crime
To feel the joy of the sun on my face
No matter what time, no matter what place

At night when I look up into the sky
To play with the stars, I would like to try
Twinkling and falling and shining on me
That would be the ultimate, to be free!

Susan Ramsey

Fortaleza

Like the force of a sword's blade
Like the stronghold of a hurricane
Like the fortifying rays of the blazing sun
Like the strength of an eagle's wing
Like a vigorous action of an ocean's wave
Unparallel to what I feel

Maria Clarke

Racism

Words of HATE mindlessly pouring out . . .
like water speeding over the falls to its DEATH
The tables and chairs FIGHT . . .
with more FURY
Than the March winds that blow through the EMPTY trees.
FEAR pushes against the walls.
closing in,
Making the ANGER quickly,
shoot small shots stabbing some.
Different colors EQUALIZE the room,
Each one knowing it's PRE-decided
RANK OF IMPORTANCE,
for themselves and their . . .
IDENTICAL OPPOSITES.
The voice of REASON steps in . . .
and RESISTANCE . . . to ANGER
in the form of LOVE and HOPE are his SHIELD.
Yet HATE is still TRIUMPHANT over ENEMIES . . .
and HOLDS its POWER till its Final Victory . . .

Tanya M. Pereira

Reminders Of Our Love

Sunshine - The Reminder of Intensity
Lingering warmth caresses my skin
Calming strength secures me within
Spiritual bliss kindles the flame
Soothing moments that can go by no name

Moonlight - The Reminder of Serenity
Luminous glow envelops the air
Intimate gestures no two other share
Heady enchantment seizes our hearts
Bonding so strong we're never apart

Stars - The Reminder of Destiny
Wistful hints of morrows to come
Paradise hints of morrows to come
Wishes of Godspeed which shall never pass
Yearnings for eternity to be everlasting

Wind - The Reminder of Reality
. . . clouds appear
Your voice is a whisper only I can hear
To regrasp our life is for what I await
To be with you always, my loving soul mate

Susan J. Sylvia

Listen Listen Listen

Listen to the falling of the leaves
Listen to the rolling of the dust
Listen in this calm noon silence . . .
The birds chirping
How sweet they are
Melodious too.
Listen to the swaying of leaves
They mingle with each other
That's the life of Nature
Listen to the sighs of your heart
Weighed down with worldly worthless nonsense
Monotonous, tedious, fatigued
This wonderful silence breaks them
Wait and live in Nature
That boosts you up
To lead a life of serene supremacy!

Sreelatha Shankar

Our Baby

Someone once said, "Babies, they are all the same."
Little did that person know . . .

For deep in the eyes of that newborn bundle
could be seen
  -his first smile
  -his wobbly first steps
  -his arms open wide, running to greet
   daddy home from work
  -his first day of school
  -and on and on . . .

With loving arms his parents hold him.
Knowing that in those eyes, looking out at them,
are all the riches he will fill their lives with.

So with patience they wait and watch this
precious little baby.

Knowing . . .
  No baby could be the same as this one.

Tamara Lynn Jensen

The Valley of Sin

   The Valley of Sin, it is my home. I
live next to the Church of Desire, I know
the address of Deceit. I walk through the
Meadow of Passion everyday on my way to the
School House of Lies. I am best friends with
the Blackness of Death. The road to my house
in one of Anger. The animals here all live their
lives in Hate and die in Hate. Across from
me lays the Graveyard of Good. The stores
of Sin sell hot food for the Cold hearted, and
cold food for the Hot, passion driven. The
Valley of Sin, it is my home.

Miranda Whitehead

Dandelion

The dandelion sways in the warm summer breeze
Like the Hawaiian hula dance — so exotic — so free.
With the buzzing bumblebees kissing its petals and sipping out its
   nectar so sweet.
It's a honey of a romance — that can't be beat.
The very mellow and yellow sun - the brightly lit star shine - exchanges
Exhilarating glances with the passionate wild flower.
Enriching it with a deepest love and an uncommon power.
The love — to express it, be it to many or one.
The power — to grace with peace and beauty, a land plagued with pollutants . . .
Pollutants in the air we breathe; the water we use to drink and bathe in;
the food we eat; at the times even in the people we meet.
The dandelion is a masterpiece of nature - sent from God to this Mother Earth.
Oh Glory to the golden, buttery blossom - that buds and blooms
with each spring's rebirth.
When the dandelion is growing old and is ready to die
Its dew drops become teardrops falling from the Heaven's sky.
The life it once breathed, now leaves it dry
Floating away in the wind, it softly whispers goodbye.
To me, the dandelion is a gentle glamorous breed to show - just as
The famous flower - the rose.
There is a bounty of flowers in life's bouquet it seems
And to many the dandelion is just a mere weed.
But keep in mind - it's one of a kind
For it's the only flower upon which you can cast a dream.

Lori Colton

375

Majestic Moon

Mighty hooves cantor fast around the ring stride after stride,
Long silky mane whips my face as we zoom around,
A jump approaches, and as we near the animals muscles
Tighten and he lifts off the ground,
With a flying leap we soar over, and land safely on the other side,
I pat his mighty neck, and he tosses his head in pleasure.

Stephanie Howard

Just Us

In ways that you will never know,
Long years together, and we closer grow.
Over time I hope you can really see,
Vast love I have, for you till eternity.

Every time I see your smiling face,
You try to, all my troubles erase.
Only time together that lasts and lasts,
Until we grow old, it's coming fast.

My heart is warmed by your bright smile,
Remembering each and every together mile.
Some times the rough ones seems to win,
Some times we have to take it on the chin.

Just so you know and don't ever forget,
Burdens are shared, even though we fret.
Each time a problem knocks on our door,
Let us pull together, just once more.

Let us lighten our load by pulling as one,
A new day will break, a new ray of sun.
Remember I love you forever and ever,
Down here, even though we have just each other.

L. Darrell Bellard

"The Wall"

Warm eyes that said "I love you" by just the way they looked.
A smile that captured my heart and instantly had me hooked.
A hug that always gave me a strong safe feeling.
A kiss that made me tremble and left my body reeling.
Silly words that made me laugh. Sweet words that made me cry.
Soft hands that caused a quiver and lifted me oh so high.
Caring ears that heard my troubles and listened to my fears.
Strong shoulders that supported me and caught my many tears.
Where is this person who possessed all of the above?
He's standing behind the wall I've built because he betrayed my love.
For a few nights of stolen sex he took my reason for living.
It's very hard to forget and so much harder to be forgiving.

Linda Kay Bernthold

First Day Of School

As I entered the school, I stopped and
looked down the long hallway. I listened to
nothing but air, I felt my stomach tighten
and my blood turn cold.
My hands felt warm and I felt sweat
on my hands and neck. I was scared,
I took a deep breath and walked forward.
I stopped shortly . . . than I turned
around and ran out the door away
from the school toward home.

Kris Walmsley

I Wonder

Little old lay sitting on a bench,
Looked so lonely eating her paper-bag lunch;
No one to talk to, no one to share
Her innermost thoughts,
I wonder what they were?

I felt so sad when I passed her by,
I don't really know why,
But I could have cried.
Maybe it's the "one-ness," so all alone.

I hope there is someone near or afar
Who will write to her or call her on the phone,
This sadness prevails, it haunts me, why?
Perhaps I see myself, too, all alone
With no one to write me or call me on the phone.

Marian Tietz Anderson

Triumphant Is The Battle Cry

Only those who have caused me pain
Lying on the ground the slain,
Lying in a pale surrender,
Death itself they do render
Though silenced are there evil words
And ne'er again, shall I feel their swords
Pale am I, with knife in hand,
Waxy pale, they can't understand.

For every tear, every cry I've heard,
I long to stand, and say a word,
But silent, cold and pale I stay,
For them to see, I hope, I pray.

And as I lie in pale surrender,
To the very death I render,
My words ring out, in silent strength
I tell my life, though short its length

My figure lying there doth speak,
And tells a tale to those not weak
That only those who have caused me pain,
lying on the ground are slain

Lisa Tittle

Untitled

Hey Mr. Lonely Man sitting all alone
looking into space - a world that's all your own.
What is it that you see? Why is it that you stare?
What thoughts possess your mind? What pain do you hide there?

Hey Mr. Lonely Man why do you seem so sad?
Did someone hurt your feelings? Did someone make you mad?

Hey Mr. Lonely Man staring into space, is that a
tear I see? Or is it the sun upon your face?
What pain are you trying to hide? What pain can't
you let go? How fresh is that new scar, or is it from years ago?

Excuse me Mr. Lonely Man, I don't mean to interrupt -
but seeing how upset you are I hope you don't give up.

Goodbye Mr. Lonely man who sits to dream alone, I
hope that you find peace in that world that's all your own.

One more thing Mr Lonely Man, I know you'll never know,
but I to am sitting here starting into this our world.

Patricia Bugarin

A Sister's Love

You left us all one year ago
Love was in your eyes
Don't be afraid you said
God has called me to his side

We miss you so very much
In everything we do

The love you planted while still with us
Has grown in so many ways
We feel you, we see you each and every day

There will always be that empty space
A birthday party
The new babies christening
Your attendance on christmas day

In our hearts we know
If our love could have saved you
You never would have died

God only takes the best they say,
We know this to be true
For one year ago today
From our lives, he took you

Krista I. Clement

"Mermaids And Fairies"

This cold winter day, with the wind blowing, clouds laying
low. "Snow is falling, the sun shined yesterday, but not today.
I set alone feeling blue, as I watch the snow drift slowly by
my window. "My mind goes back to my youthful days when I thought
Mermaids and Fairies were a child's best friend.
I was much too young to see my future back then. "So it was
Fairy tales, I believed in old Santa with his red nose so cold and I
dreamt of Mermaids and Fairies, where magic and wonder encircled my mind.
My trees were as tall as the sky, my flowers smiled as sweet
as honey, the ground was covered with shells from the sea, my
wonder of a bird on my shoulder, and pink eyed lions roamed my
fields, they would cross their legs and help string a bean.
"O" I was a dreamer, but I had fun!
This land I saw it's still there in the minds of a child, with
a quiet breeze blowing over a water pond of fun. "Wrap it tightly
in your mind and tie it with magic and wonder. "One day come back
unwrap the magic, see the wonder, and let the winds blow where they may.

Patricia Cordell

"Austin"

Each tiny move you make
Makes me prouder everyday
All the smiles I receive
Makes every cry a dream away.

When I look into your eyes
I see a Daddy far away
Who will come home to us real soon
But for now we'll take things day by day.

I see a Mommy in the distance
Waiting for your next move
Encouraging you to keep trying
And soon a new challenge will come for you to pursue.

Your smile lights up the day
And your cry helps me know too
That every day that passes by
My love will keep growing for you.

Melissa Turney

Close To You

The way your eyes light up when you smile
Makes my heart go completely wild.
The sound of your voice when you speak
Is like a soft caress.
Your lips are as the dew softly
Touching the petals on a rose.
Your arms are as steel
But when they are around me
My body feels as weak as a
Weeping willow when a breeze is
Whispering through the leaves.
When I am near you I feel the warmth
That radiates from your body.
Your breath on my cheek is as tender
As a butterfly touching a flower.
When I am apart from you my body
Feels incomplete as it unceasingly
Reaches for you.

Polly L. Spainhour

Fall

Fall is not what it seems to be.
Many new dresses are bought by the trees.
Colors so vibrant in the cool autumn shade,
You'd think the dresses are born not made.

Fluttering in the wind the dresses swirl,
Every maiden in the court dances and whirls.
In the breeze of the forest the dances stop.
Queen snow has arrived the temperature drops.

The dancers all shutter as a hush gathers round.
The queen plants her icy roots in the ground.
The dancers fear greatly her frozen wrath,
They drop their dresses on the snowy path.

They stand very still in hopes she will go,
But she will surprise them with a blanket of snow.
Another breeze comes no dancing begins,
All dancing stops until fall comes again.

Mary Elliott Neal

A Light Amongst The Clouds

Through the clouds in the early morning sun
Many tremble for he has truly come

Saddened are those with parched troubled souls
Digging deep under the earth like moles

Trying hard to hide from the coming light
Along with Gabriel's wings of might!

The Holy one had arrived upon earth
The eyes are still, no one is full of mirth

Like the days of Noah building the ark
Save your soul, avoid the beast with the mark

The days have been shortened, and nights are long
Only evil remains, the good have gone!

Linda Simpson

To Mom

Today is for Mom and all the tomorrows
Mom is so dear and we the children should be near
She loves and gives each day, her smile, her happiness and her
very special way
So remember tomorrow what was today and give to Mom in
the very same way
For we have but one Mom and her love is so deep and so
tomorrow all her love we all must keep

Peter J. D'Amico

Seasons

Autumn . . . is a silent Indian artist, her sun painted days are
  masterfully done, in vibrant colors on lush green canvasses.
  Her ice tinged nights glow with enchantment.
  Witches hex and pilgrims blessings echo within her being
  as dreams of a straw filled manger bathed in starlight
  fills her sleep . . . Transition

Winter . . . is a white bearded wanderer, icy breath reaches out,
  freezes air, and slows time. He causes us to cover
  ourselves from the elements, and seek the warmth hidden
  within our souls. He inventories past year promises
  with new year hopes, to equal experience
  gained . . . Reflection

Spring . . . is a pregnant mother whose fetus develops deep within
  the bowels of the earth. Her frozen surface belies the
  warmth of her womb. Until tears from her birth pain refreshes
  the land and life reaches for the light . . . Conception

Summer . . . is the eternal youth inside each of us, it's
  ageless smile encourages us to believe in
  dreams. Extended days laugh at our comedies,
  while silken moonlight hides our indiscretion . . . Imagination

   Larry J. Harper

The Sea Of Life

May your ship set sail for higher ground,
May God's great grace and love abound.

May the waters in your life be calm,
For God shall have you in his palm.

May the sky be blue and the sun shine bright,
May God be with you day and night.

May the pearls on your ocean floor,
Sparkle as they never have before.
For this is what I hope for you and then, even more.

   Tracy Ann Berrett

Blessings

For Mark and Michelle
   Whatever paths you follow,
may these blessings come your way . . .
Cherished friends and loved ones
to brighten everyday.
Work that makes you happy.
Rest that makes you strong.
A sense of humor to see you through
whenever things go wrong.
The strongest faith, the brightest hopes
that heaven can impart.
Serenity and wisdom . . . an understanding heart.
An awareness of life's beauty . . .
An answer to your prayers.
The blessed reassurance that God
understands and cares.

   Lisa K. Sellers

Eternity

I love you, you are my life. I give
myself to you that I might be your wife.
My love for you is honest and I have
asked God that every happiness be
blessed upon us. I am today as I shall
be tomorrow. I am for you, as you are
for me and it shall be this way for all eternity.

   Linda Ann Breitkreuz-Dackiw

Ode To Scotch

Hail! Thou idol of the lonely; hail to thee, Despair's Demise!
May thy golden glow bring only my love's face before my eyes

Sought I love and understanding, gentle touch and spoken word.
Unfulfilled but undemanding prayed my pleading soul be heard.

Found I hope both brief and burning; helpless now I feel it die.
Here I'll wait for its returning, the eternal *Butterfly*.

In thy arms I feel no sorrow; gently eased away is pain.
Yea, e'en though I know the morrow brings it all to life again.

But for now, if thou wilt have me, I would lie in thy embrace.
I have need to thee to salve me, grant to me a hiding place.

Grant me patience for the waiting; give me rest - allay my fears
'Til the time of my awaking to his kiss upon my tears.

Hail! Thou idol of the lonely, hail to thee, Despair's Demise!
May thy golden glow bring only my love's face before my eyes!

   Rosemary Zamiska

Best Friend

Friend is such a strong word which many people don't tend to use.
Maybe some fear to get close while others are just afraid to lose.
But I've found my special friend whom I like to call my best.
She's been with me through thick and thin and has
   totally surpassed the rest.
She never feared to stand by me and take my hand and guide me through.
For that's the kind of friendship we have, the kind of friend I have found in you.
Strong is the word that suits us best.
Many a day have tried to break us, many more troubles coming with the rest.
But we will oversee them, yes I know we will.
For you never let go of my hand, friends we remain still.
I appreciate you being there, your words touch my heart so much.
In my soul, the things you do for me leave their memorable touch.
If you ever need a thing just think of me and ask.
It'll be done no matter what, if its moving a mountain
   or some simple little task.
You were there for me when the whole world had gone out.
You truly are my best friend for you have shown
   me what love and friendship are all about.

   MaryBeth Delevan

Aunt Sally

   When I was little Aunt Sally was always there for
me. She made time for me no matter what.

   Aunt Sally always was my favorite Aunt.

   I heard today that Aunt Sally is in the hospital.
She fell and broke her hip. I really should go see her.

   Aunt Sally always my favorite Aunt.

   I heard today that Aunt Sally has gone to a nursing
home. I should really go see her. But I have such a busy
life, and the football season is starting. I'll do it soon.

   Aunt Sally always was my favorite Aunt.

   I heard today that Aunt Sally has passed away. It
doesn't seem like five years since she broke her hip. I
feel so bad that I never had time to go see her.

   I wonder when they're going to read the will? I'm sure
she'll leave me something.

   You know, Aunt Sally's always been my favorite Aunt.

   Kay Zinn

Clouds

As a child my grandfather taught me to enjoy the beauty around me, to appreciate all the world had to offer.

He showed me the beauty in the puffy white clouds. How much fun it was to try and see the animals and shapes in them. Anything you could imagine was in those clouds.

Well, I've grown up now, and Grampie has been gone a long time. and somehow with hurried pace of life I'd forgotten about the clouds until today.

I arrived at work early, as I sat in my car I noticed some big white puffy things floating by in the sky.

I think I remember now, those are the clouds Grampie showed me so long ago.

Kim E. Bridges

Woman In Black

Never worn much black, don't think God wanted
Me to wrap-up in the color
Of death, sex, and mourning.
Only had one dress, once.
Low cut, tight, and showed, the tops of my breasts.
The Devil made me buy it, enticed me to wear it.
He dropped a veil over my heart,
And waltzed me out in public.
I danced all night long to a wicked tune sung by
A forked-tongued monster.
Lost that dress, black stockings,
And a few other thoughts,
I had placed on an altar, the day before.
Can't get back a sacrifice,
Given in the Devil's honor.
Only wear white now.
Feel drawn to it, as angels to heavenly clouds,
Adorned in white, waiting to enter
God's holy hiding place,
Safe from the Devil's song.

Sarah Joel

Memories . . .

No, I am never alone, for with me travels
memories . . .
Miniatures in my mind of the many people
I've met.
I cannot take credit for my accomplishments,
for without the parts played by past friends . . .
My life would be an empty stage.
And when I die it will not be the
lonely death of one person . . .
But the disintegration of the many pieces of
the people who've touched me.

Sandra Turchiarelli

"Twisted"

The deep complexities of love can look like an enigmatic, illogical maze such that "concrete" details involved become "twisted" in terms of their stock, eyes clouded by jealousy can easily, psychologically cause one's to feel "fazed" while, in reality, the origins of such suspicions should earnestly be defrocked ,the Holy Grail was a "Union of Opposites" that could heal those in such a daze for procreation of "Higher Consciousness" lies with He who guards the flock, Gold is this "symbol," but not of things that send greed or hormones into a craze, for real, "literal" wealth cannot buy happiness, and lust cannot stop the clock but imperishable truth, candor, and admission of weakness can have one amazed, such that it can reverse the deception that can "hit" harder than sticks or rocks, a "wishmate" won't stay for your "body," or your money if your hair is gray but one whose "Heart of Gold" will be with yours inseparably "interlocked!"

Lyndon Lundgren Nash

The Three Colors Of Mourning

There is a ring of black —
men facing inward;
there is a ring of purple —
women facing outward;
five in each circle
And me.
I stand in the center
of the two rings that spin — clockwise — counter-clockwise
I, clothed in white, sit
my face gazing upward,
illuminated by starlight
I gaze at the stars that spin, and the white bear that never sets
while the black-clothed wear a face of rage
while the indigo-clothed wear a visage of joy
I am shielded from the present world — I can see both past and future
I remember
everything
I cry
silver water tears stream down my face

Lena Katz

Autumn Holiday

NIGHT knockers—
Midgets stunted and stooped
Fistfuls of apple and oranges
Weighting their frail but searching forms.
Warted noses
Running noses
Bubblegum chewed by charcoal-blacked teeth.
Witches and goblins
She-boys and he-girls
Trick or treat or soap on your windows
Danse macabre for an autumn night.

Curtain raiser for a life of violence.

Walter E. Brown

Liberation

Who are my friends?
Migrating birds gathering over Tuskegee lake;
The ragged woods, herds of sheep,
The night, the dream, the homeless wind.

Who are my friends?
The uncrowned king Booker T. Washington;
Whose mission was to serve the people,
Stressing the practical and not ignoring the real.

Who are my friends?
The flowing flames of learning in Tuskegee students;
The flames to become productive citizens,
I balance all, bring all to mind.

With a smile of secret triumph,
I wish to go to the university;
To teach Pound and Eliot,
To enrich the knowledge of the epicures.

I am no more in the narrow mesh,
This city enrolls all real;
God's divinity harbours me forever,
My mind is hushed in a wide light.

Rashmi Roy

Worshiping

Worshiping, thought chiseled idols formed from vain imagination,
  Mind created deities justifying self emancipation.
Beguiled by the Goddess of Power, Fame, Wealth and Pleasure,
  Man surrenders his soul, life's highest prized treasure.

From time immemorial, anthropology has found
  All men have worshiped, his hallowed ground.
So worship he will, and worship he must.
    Whatever it is, that he feels he can trust.

For some it is Power, feeling destined to rule,
  Bound by a yoke that is endless and cruel.
For others it's Fame, and the applause of the crowd
  The chance of a lifetime, that ends in a shroud.

Wealth attracts many with it's glittering gold,
  But like quick silver, not easy to hold.
Then there is pleasure, promising life at it's best,
  Only an illusion, vanity's jest.

God is a Spirit, infinite, eternal, and unchangeable in His being,
  So difficult to grasp, let alone worship without seeing.
Lift your eyes to the heavens, ethereal and glowing,
  God's declaration, I am not beyond knowing.
    Paul W. Unruh

Untitled

Images of a distant time flutter like the wings of a butterfly in my
mind. I try desperately to capture the essence of the message
they leave behind.

The images vanish so quickly, they leave me mystified.
They speak to me of days gone by, of a part of me that has long
since died.

If I could just hold still this moment in time.
I know the answers will be mine.

Do I want to know the lessons they hold?
Will the knowledge make me weary, sad and cold?

I know it's time for old wounds to be healed.
The past forgiven, sad memories tightly sealed.

I ask God for strength to look inside.
Please give me reassurance, be my guide.
    Lisa D. McCullough

"September Falls"

Green, glass grass
moist, cold understood
in a way that only you could understand
shiver in the chill
as the mornings dwindle still
in a way only you could not possibly understand
September falls upon your heart
Suffocating and choking, gasping and grasping
only to tear it apart
and then drop it like confetti
in that way you cannot stand
and the leaves too
drop as if confetti but are more so ready
for September as it falls
Prepare for the white and still shiver in the night
as green silently turns orange
before . . . your . . . eyes
again, in the silence cries
a man who tries to cover your eyes
in a way that only you must understand!
    Michael John Rich

Ladders To Fire

Wander by the ocean blue
Moist salt air, sand in my shoe
The sea blue seduction, like ladders to fire
The stairways to sweetness, reach higher and higher

Treading down the boardwalk mile
All the stars fell in a pile
The rigid professor, a master of bleakness
In a picture frame window, is my sultan of weakness

Bury me in deep fantastic
Soothe me with your soft caress
Caught in your realm of comfort
Take me from my consciousness

In the lucid light reflection
Fearful of the words I say
Catch me in a thought correction
Words leave me alone at bay

Feel the flame from up above
One more step and I'm in love

Higher and higher
Ladders to fire
    Kerry L. Cuddy

"Android"

Why does time seem to pass lightning
Moments seem like a fading memory
And sometimes it seems somewhat frightening
That I will remember just to bury
The deep thoughts that dwell so terrifying
Some moments are bad, some quite merry
But in the end I find myself thinking
About all the hopes and dreams I carry
I am in between the past and present
A precise point for which I can exist
And through the course of time I will mature
But the older I get I will resist
I'll eventually grow up in time
'Cause life is just a riddle and a rhyme
    Michael Chen

"America"

America a beautiful land of opportunity full of wonders
Most powerful nation on earth, Neil Armstrong a legendary
  Astronaut first man to walked on the moon President
  John Fitzgerald Kennedy his prediction came true
Everlasting partner of friendship prosperity in economic growth
Role of America a peacemaker all over the world
Industrial country with wonderful inventions a melting
  pot nation of all races of mankind
Christopher Columbus discovered America landing in the
  Bahamas in 1492, Cherokees American Indian people
  original of Tennessee and North Carolina
Abraham Lincoln president, a national hero abolished
  slavery the land of rich in natural resources,
  George Washington father of the great nation, first
  President of the United States of America. United
we stand America a biblical nation, life, liberty,
  peace, happiness, freedom, democracy greatest
  champion of the planet earth.
    Leonides S. Sales

Unity

The breeze whispers and the bamboo sings.
Mother Nature vocalizes and to my soul brings . . .
Wonder, Laughter, the desire for our union.
Warm rays of sunshine become my companion.
I sit beside the river of my mind . . .
Touching my thoughts of rippling water and sand;
Twittering birds, chirping crickets
The scent of newly mowed hay, sunset at the end of the day.
Inhale! Breathe deeply the quiet stillness.
Look around you- enjoy and see Reality.
Can you feel God's mighty touch?
Can you see his gentle Love?
When Life's color hues reach out to smile.
I feel somehow, I can conquer each trial.
As I allow nature's sensuality to enveloped me.
Feeling the tension released with our joining.
Within my soul I know,
God meant it to be like this . . .
Peaceful and Serene.

Mary H. Pusey

Very Special Xmas

'Twas the month before X-mas; I was busy as a
mouse . . . buying a new home for my wonderful spouse.

The home is a beauty, custom-ordered by me . . .
I've kept it a secret for a month, you see.

Some people may observe that this is quite funny . . .
To buy a house as a X-mas gift, for my Honey.

But she's very special, a great Mother and Wife . . .
and deserves the best I can give her, for the rest of her life!

And tho she wasn't with me to pick this home out,
her spirit accompanied me, without a doubt!

And as we continue down the rest of life's road . . .
We'll be together in this fine abode.

Thanks for the blessings from the Lord, above . . .
HONEY . . . THIS HOME IS FROM ME,
WITH ALL MY LOVE!!

L. L. Burns

The Intersection

The concentrated spirit of one so shrill,
Movement of control so defined and strong;
Overshadowed with a sharpness so faint,
Drive far beyond any balance;
I try to adhere.

Sensing other forms that change within myself
We prayerfully move, somehow to meet, and to be each other;
In everything, we are one.
My soul cries for a consistency in life,
Not to be misled by those which loom, larger still.
Our force is represented and contained in my very being,
Which aligns itself within a certain space,
Ever forth to flow and change.
The boundaries of those which are collimated and constantly
Adjusted for the good.
All points so designated beyond
My heart, will move deeper within the compartment
And begin a contemplative effort, which exceeds their tangents.

Richard Alan Kelton

'Tis the 17th spring I have seen now,
my 18th soon to bloom,
I look at the great oak and bow.
I see the birds and hear them croon.
The soft awakening breeze,
and the sun so bright,
shines on the willows and poplar trees.
It appears it shall never become night.
Yet when it does - it is as if another world comes down from
the skies.
It is quiet now and all looks strange
I see the reflection of a thousand stars in your eyes.
Night turns into day, but why make the change?
For when the sun arises and I awake,
the sweetness of your eyes will fade away.
Even though you are simply a dream, my love I will stake
for when night comes again this time you will stay.

Phaedra Mykel Herndon

You

I watch you drift near me, your sleek lines set my heart racing.
  My blood boils with the sense of adventure at becoming one with you.

I want to hear you whisper in the night as you carry me to places I
have never been.
  Through the mist of time together will ride the swells of life.

The thought of being surrounded by you gives my soul wings,
  so that I can fly high above you like the bird on the wind.

Let me steer you through the starry night while I sing songs of
love for you.
  I will touch you with reverence as I guide you safely
  through the darkness.

Together we will face the storms and the calming of seas;
  I will never desert you.
You give me a sense of freedom along with a certain feeling of power.
  You are a part of me so I never alone.

You show me many wonders few men ever see,
  As you carry me through life's stormy seas.

You rock me gently as I sleep
  While you give me shelter from the night.

Together we will drift through time
  Under the warmth of the sun.

You are my debt to man, you are my life, you are my soul.
  YOU ARE - MY BOAT!

Linda Murray

Last Days

There are things that trigger my thoughts
Minor things that are trivial to most
Maybe I am too sensitive towards love
Or maybe I am just imagining my reality
It feels too real not to be tangible
These feelings of despair keep pounding inside
I am awaiting the day it surfaces
My rage will erupt like Krakatoa
And spread my weeps across the land
Never to be heard of again
I sink into a world of self-hate
No real reason for my haunting cries
These tears of loneliness fall from my eyes
Alone in my burial plot
No real love by my side
But when I'm gone how will be remembered
Good bad . . . mediocre
Will I even be remembered at all?

Shawn J. Clark

"Four Chambers"

The sound triumphant in it's quiet, yet
My ears hear nothing.
While nature sings all around
Her mighty rivers flow within me

There I proceed with such tender oblivion
My cherished life endures what peaks and valleys
This great wonder I possess
Is mine. A treasure. A blessing.

Deep within the hour of the setting sun
There will come the great rest
For the time which this wonder has bestowed upon me
Can only bring me to one enduring moment.

How I have tried to share this gift
With each I love so deeply
Before the time for the long long sleep begins
My wet eyes shall see the mirror of you.

I place my hand upon my chest
There feel her power delicately raging
I close my eyes and see
Faith. Life. A gift from God to me.

Peter Dach

What Am I Feeling?

What are my feelings?
   My feelings are deep.
I can't bear to be without the sound
of your voice even if it's the voice
in your telephone machine.
When I feel trapped in my world,
I tune into your world.
When I feel lonely, I just imagine
our togetherness.
When I feel sad, I think about your smile.
Handsome you bring me happiness and that
happiness keeps me together.
The only thing is, that I'm confused about
my feelings.
   What am I feeling?

Khaira S. Polanco

My Friend That I Had

   I could have sworn she was there,
my friend in white,
she floated in the darkness,
all through the night.
But when I'd awake,
she would not be near,
and all I could do was shed a tear.
I could have cried forever,
but something stopped me.
It was the voice in the wind,
that was calling my name.
I ran outside and she was there.
As I waved good-bye,
I closed my eyes tight and blew her a kiss, with all my might.
The pain is still here and forever will be,
for my friend was like a sister to me.
   She's in my heart and that's where she'll stay.
I hope I can last another day.
Now you're up there for good, not bad.
Oh how I wish you were here, my friend that I had.

Toma-Jean Cox

Searching In The Midst

Like a hurting animal in the forest
My heart cries out to you.
I was left hurting and all alone,
Where you have gone, I have no clue.

Searching for your love every night
And walking the streets for days,
Returning home all by myself,
Tears streaming down my face.

I pray before I go to sleep
And ask the Lord, "where has he gone?"
He answers with a gentle voice,
"His tasks on earth have all been done.

The pain was strong and taking over.
He was dying and didn't want you to know.
Because his love for you was never-ending,
And knew one day he had to let go.

Stop your crying, no need to search,
He's home with Me, and you're not alone.
We're watching over you,
From this place called, "Sweet Home."

Minerva Rivera

"A Mother's Day Card"

Seems like we are always **running** around
Looking for your keys or purse that can't be found.
Dashing about the highways of our state,
pursuing jobs or just plain real estate.

We have traveled from California to Canada,
in cars named Pontiac, BMW and Toyota.
Through rain and snow we found our way,
always believing tomorrow would be a sunny day.

You are the one, who started this journey.
I'm happy you have been there to ease the worry.
Navigator, coach and Mom, let me just say.
God bless you, I love you and
Happy Mother's Day!

William R. Gohlke

A Promise Fulfilled

Long, long ago and far, far away
My heart was captured by love that day
It's music was light and free as a bird
The softest sound that I'd ever heard
It took me to places I'd never been
Showing me beauties that I'd never seen
I indulged myself in it's cool overflow
Taking me under that I cared not so
This was fulfillment of a promise to be
Something I prayed and you were the key
You unlocked my heart from loneliness bound
And gave me a joy that couldn't be found
Through many paths I searched and searched
Looking to find a love that was worth
So wrap your heart inside with mine
Thank God, at last together entwined
Two made as one let no one put asunder
Blest be the ties that bind us together

Susan Sandell

If

If you could have stayed here with me,
My life could have been so much simpler.
If you could have won the battle,
So many hearts wouldn't have been broken.
If you could have shared with us,
There wouldn't have been so many unanswered questions.
If you could have only said goodbye,
There wouldn't be so many quiet moments and sad eyes.
If God didn't love you so much,
He would have shared you with me so much longer.
If and if and if
If I could have been more understanding and more patient,
I could have been stronger for you.
If I ever fall in love again,
Will I ever be able to love like I loved you?
If someone falls in love with me,
Will they make me as happy as you did?
If I give my heart away,
I know you'll always be in it
For you were my best friend

Kate Barreca

A Lengthy Blink

In the very moment of a lengthy blink,
my life was threatened, affecting how I think.

To break the routine and habit of life everyday,
I gathered with friends, to just get away.

We drank and danced and shut down the bar,
I headed back home, alone in my car.

Longing down a lonely road going forever on,
with a crash to a wall, my memory was gone.

The total influence of alcoholic drinks,
consequently caused me, to take a lengthy blink.

I look back now and what a price to pay,
to learn that life's pleasures, come a little each day.

Don't drink and drive no matter how you feel,
it only takes one second, and the price you pay is real.

Rebecca L. Cole

Timeless Cry

Help me I say!
My mind is running crazed,
Mixed emotions of love, laughter and death entwined.
My tears, are they of joy or of sadness?
I scream from within, of pain I can't control.
What can I do?
My life is not a whole.
Victimized from all directions, I cry inside.
Questions exhausting me that I cannot answer.
Just leave me alone!
I lost the past, I hate the future.
My heart is not my own.
I just can't handle this!
Please, I don't want to remember, the pain hurts too much.
Leave me alone, please, leave me alone!
All those memories are far from gone.
My heart has been ripped away.
I love you so much!
Help me, help me I say!

Marleen Stracener Lehr

My Man

My man is someone who never does wrong.
My man is someone who sits on a throne.
My man never cheats; he's with me all the time.
He gives me everything I need and I only have to
    give him ten percent of what's mine.
My man supports me in the good things that I do;
    and the bad situations he help pulls me through.
If it wasn't for him my world would crumble.
But I truly thank his father for allowing him
    to help me to become humble.
I know I have done things to make him upset.
But I'm glad he has the heart to let me come to
    him clean and correct.
I really thank him for always being there.
Even from time to time I thought he didn't care.
Oh, his name, it shouldn't be so hard.
He's so perfect, you should have known his name is God!

Melissa Williams

The Art Of Being Enclosed

I was enclosed too many years of the state of the mind
My mind was a captive prisoner and cramped of too many
ignorant selfish states I was to grow up to be. They
told me that my life must be diplomatic, and very
crafty to enhance my future. They just plain out lied.
They also told me that only the small minded people
would fail. So they pushed, pushed, and pushed some
more toward insanity. That led me mad, which led me to
the stage of erratic. It lead me off.

This stage that has a very strong hold on me, threw me
wondering if their is any more pain. My mind is so confused.
Mind the fact that, my head feels the hunger to expel.
Mind the fact that, my head feels ersatz. It . . .
is defective from all the lies, enclosed messages, and
magnetic forces that they have on me.

Yvette Medina

"The Image"

As I sit by my window just staring into space,
My mind wonders off and soon I see a face,
A very familiar image of someone I once knew,
Someone tall and handsome, someone honest and true,
Oh why do I sit and stare into the sky so blue?
Why are my thoughts only of this man I once knew,
Is it just because I miss him; his company, his laughter and all,
I even miss the kisses of this man so tall,
The trees seem to fade as time drifts away,
The sky grows dark, the image begins to fade,
But even though the darkness has stolen the familiar face,
The memories that I have of him can never be erased.

Thelma J. Vahl

A Stolen Moment

I was motionless in our bed.
My lover by my side.
If only in my thoughts and desires
A lover just the same.

As morning turned to noon
We kissed.
Warm breath enveloped my mouth
As those soft lips touched mine for the first time.

I had longed for this.
Times before I had played the scene in my mind.
And as my dream turned into reality
I knew this moment would forever change my life.

Theresa DeLucca

Rain

He, my friend,
  my neighbor, my kinsmen,
stands alone in the darkness,
  rain pours down from black clouds,
lightning deceives his eyes for a moment
  pretending to be the sun . . . he watches me
  with loneliness and grief,
joy is in his mind,
  but the pain remains in his heart . . . he watches me
  through the tears of his very soul,
his tears dripping like the rain that falls,
the light
  has not yet come,
the peace
  is just within my reach . . . he watches me
  trying to say good-bye . . . he watches me
  with fear and frustration,
lightning flashes . . . he watches me . . .
  being lowered into the ground.

    Kelly Cory

Slow Growth

When the earth was young and time was old
my soul was born in a break away mold

God was curious in those early days
casting souls in various ways

Trying one thing then some other
seeking perfection was his druthers

But souls are not stable like they ought to be
casting only begins their Odyssey

Mine is no different in that respect
could even God forecast such a predilect?

When time is old and the earth has gone
will my soul still blossom as God looks on?

In that time, times ten, can God find at last
that spark missing since the day it was cast?

Only if time gets old enough and only if God will wait a while
can my soul ever hope to see God smile

    Tom Morgan

Oh Surreal

My Life, is the harvest, is the Jewel.
My Task, though seemed easy, turned out Gruelling.
the Duality of the psych, I wear like a Coat,
the Reasons mostly buried, engraved in Code.

  (this Immortal breath that animates the bones,
  the Scream of life, entombed in Stone . . .)

my Death, is the long sleep, the Hibernation of the soul.
my Task, though complete, turned out Far from over.
the Moon, mirror magic, the spiral of Tragedy.
the Sun, fiery element, brings it back to Being.

  (the Fire that drives this wheel of strive,
  the Rush of blood that gives me Life . . .)

My Transcendence, is the crown, is my Resurrection.
my Pearls of understanding, being my portion of Life.
Your kings would enslave your souls, if you pledge allegiance to their goals
Your road, is Your will, your Way . . .

    Lodewyk Le Roux

"My Son"

This is for you my beloved son and as you know you were my only one.
My tears are flowing, I am so sad; I can not believe the news I've had
You made me laugh, you made me smile; I thank God I had you for a while.
A tragedy has happened, Death knocked at my door; you will never know,
  I can hardly breath anymore.
Although the Lord chose to take you away, all I can do is pray . . .
and pray . . . and pray.
The pain is so great, my heartbreak you will never know, the hurt . . .
  the sadness here below.
All your friends came by to express their sorrow; I have begged them
  please come see me tomorrow.
I can not imagine that Gary and I must live on, but we must accept God
  chose you to go beyond.
Your room is so empty and all around the house is sad; I can hardly
  bear to look at all the things you had.
All the fun we had, all the laughter we shared, it's so hard to
  believe it's no longer there.
The wonderful memories I will cherish in my heart will have to sustain
  me as I make a new start.
My heart is broken, I feel like I can't go on, but God will be my
  strength through this storm.

    Lana Adkins

"Who Can Describe It"

As I travel down life's highway, and watch the world unfold
Nature tells me a story, that no man has ever told
Could words describe the beauty, of the lily in the field
Or match the simple glory, that a single day will yield

A blade of grass, a cloud above, a meadow lark, a graceful dove
The eagle soaring there on high, magnificent against the sky
The flowing stream, a river great, a roaring sea, or a quite lake
A simple rose, or a giant tree, "Who Can Describe It" you or me

The smallest insect here below, or the beauty of the falling snow
The colors in the sky that show, as against the rain they form a bow
The grandeur of a mountain high, sculptured there against the sky
In fall the colors on a tree, "Who Can Describe It" you or me

The rolling hills, the desert floor, such work of art, yet there is more
A lamb rest in a meadow green, while a lion roars to show he's mean
A mountain wall that rises steep, while in the valley willows weep
Such contrast we so often see, "Who Can Describe It" you or me

Can we accept these works at hand, and realize how lost is man
Knowing that our ways aren't right, seeking now to find the light
Then follow down life's simple path, with Jesus and escape the wrath
And all God's love in nature see, "Who Can Describe It" you or me

    Theodore R. Ormond

"Mates"

We marry our mates, creating our lives
Needing to reach our ventures so wide
To forsake all obstacles in our way
We forget our vows and begin to stray
Goals enter in our daily grind, omitting
our trust, leaving forgiveness behind
striving for wealth, we forget our aim
wanting not, to share the same
wrapped up in self we continue our
plight, no time for love or peace in sight
Beseeching our hearts with sorrow and pain,
enhancing not love, but worth of gain
Seeing not we move so fast, heeding
not the warnings blast
We've climbed too high to see our fate
love is lost and filled with hate
What happened you say to our lives one day,
remembering not, you led the way.

    Linda Mazurek

You Should Be Thankful

So many people take life for granted,
Negatively their minds are planted,
Their faces vacant, they have no glow,
The seasons come and the seasons go,

But see the people who bear the most,
Still on their face, a smile they boast,
To be self seeking, is not their way,
They just thank God, for another day,

Stop and look, at the world around you,
The beauty and love will surely astound you,
Take a good hard look at your past,
and live each day, to be the last . . .

Kathee M. Felty

The Look In My Eyes

Listen to the warnings,
Never change the light of day,
There's no danger in my darkness
And deaths not what they say,
Their are thunderclouds rolling through the skies,
And my darkness is slowly keeping in,
But you can feel electricity in your veins,
I have no fear till I stake my claim,
Surprise, disguise, better run and hide, now you realize,
The Kiss, Abyss, knowing that you can't resist,
The electricity in my veins,
The thrill, the kill,
And you know that it's not over,
With one look in my blue eyes,
I am your ocean of temptation,
With every sweet drop of red wine.

Tina Louise Weinert

Someone

   They never did anything without each other;
never did they part.

   I was always with them one way or another
and seeing them tore at my heart.

   When I was with them I was really alone.
They paid no attention to me.

   Of their friendship I grew jealous
for in my pod, there was only one pea.

   Finally, I gave up on all of my dreams;
I accepted my friendlessness.

   I shut my world and heart to others
in hopes of happiness.

   Yet, for me, this method was much too harsh.
I needed someone to love, to pull my heart from this marsh.

Sorrow overcame me until I found new hope.
   There must be someone who cares about me!
   So my heart caught hold of a rope.
For I knew that someday I would have a friend, too.
   Now that someday is here.
   And that someone is you.

Kristen Schulze

The Inner Owl

It's the owl's owl I wished to touch.
Never thought that was asking too much.
If I could gently stroke the inner owl's wing,
I might be the first to hear an owl sing.

Roy D. Parsons

First Love

I met him during the first week of college.
Never knowing love, I knew there was chemistry involved.
His eyes deep as an ocean, I felt as if I could drown in them.
Deep Russian accent always echoing in my mind, and his smile
brightened my day.
Many years separated us, but age was not a factor.

He opened a door to a whole new world filled with nothing but happiness.
His presence made my heart skip a beat.
A feeling so strong, nothing else mattered.
At night, he was constantly in my dreams.
Never did I imagine would I meet someone so special.

Little did I know about how he felt.
Expecting to hear the same feelings, I was not prepared for his thoughts.
"I have a girlfriend" was something
I never expected to hear.
I was devastated beyond comprehension.

He broke my heart into an infinite number of pieces.
I cried buckets of tears until I could cry no more.
He's history now, and we hardly acknowledge each other.
My world had come crashing down, and I never expect to find that
   happiness ever again.
He was my first love.

Sukanya Desai

No Turning Back

All my life, I always thought I was right,
never listened to any one, a sinner by the night.
So many heartaches and so many pains,
so much to change, so much sorrow and shame.
But then one day by the bed I now sleep,
I picked up my bible, to the Lord I did speak.
Forgive me I've sinned to the Lord I did say,
I'm hurting inside, every morning, night and day.
And right at that moment, I knew He was there,
right by my side, to show me He does care.
The tears came like water pouring from a spout,
it was like He was holding my hand, and erased all doubt.
I couldn't believe, after all I've been through,
the Lord would forgive me, and make me new.
I put all my faith and trust in He,
the Lord is the way; yes, Jesus is the key.
He will guide my path, and with Him I made a pact,
I'll be His serving child, there's no turning back.

Michael Haley

No Snow?

Alaska, November's end, no snow yet?
Nights still dark and cold,
but yet no snow to warm the night air.
The cars on the highways, lights hitting the windshield,
but no snow to cloud the view of what's around the next bend.
No ice to skate on or snow to sled the arched hills.
No snowmen with faces of carrot and coal.
Mountains peeked with snow and mist,
but still no snow on the dry towns below.
Sleighs and sleds still in the garage awaiting brother snow.
Children's cheeks of pink, noses of red awaiting the day their friend
will show his face once more in Alaska.
No snow yet!

Nicole M. Scaletta

No Dream Street

It's a rainy day on the streets of paper houses.
No food, no water, no happiness; just emptiness.
Where there once were dreams and hopes, there is now cold, hard fact.
The streets that only knew love and laughter now only know
hardships and tears.
There is no hope for these people, the sad sorry people who have
forgotten how to dream.
Most just want something a little better, but they just don't
know how to get it.

Tanya Schneider

My Little Girl

Why has my little girl gone no longer to see her smile,
No longer can we take our walks mile after mile,
Why can I no longer see her playing with her friends,
Dressing up in my old clothes in a game that never ends,
Why can I no longer take her to her first day at school,
Running and playing with her friends and forgetting to follow the rules,
Why can I no longer patch the boo-boo on her shin,
Smiling through her tears she was out the door again,
Why can I no longer see her going on her first date,
Did life pass me by and now it is too late,
Why can I no longer feel her in my arms today,
Why can I not - she has gone far far away.

Marjorie Roop

Out Of Love

Out of love? When everyone else is in?
No longer wild, tormented, crazy, full,
full of desire like the world around me?
May I finally belong to myself, own my own
thoughts and feelings, keep the turbulence down?
Order my life and let the inner god triumph?
No more Medean madness, Junonian jealousy?
The eye of the hurricane swirls in other oceans
now; the Furies seek other victims — hand-wringing
rhymers, divided selves, guilty lovers
knotted and churning. Tellers of lies, they read
their St. Augustine "My love is my burden"
and suffer their pain, despising the tranquility
and peace of non-love.
    My temperature currently
is normal, classical; my exertions for the loved
over — no pampering, affirming, irritation.

Out of love? It's just talk.

Mary Wren Small

Resolution

The sky caves in, the stars are wrong.
No lover cares to share her song
Of empty dreams and words of pain,
Of passion dancing down the drain,
Of furtive pleas to just belong.

The rain drips blue and green and red
On the window pane inside her head.
As Elvis moans in the room next door,
A wrapper settles to the floor.
"I'm all that's left," a small voice said.

"I'll take you, if you'll follow me.
My darkness gives you company."
The shades are drawn, the bed is made,
Her lips caress the razor blade
That promises to set her free.

Michael Gabryszewski

No Matter

No matter the kind of life you lead or where you've begun,
No matter the kind of season you've lived in the winter or the sun,
No matter the way your children were raised or even what you think,
No matter the kind of life they've led or the type of world their linked,
No matter the common places you go day after day,
And their yet to be troubles somewhere along the way,
No matter the resources you got just to stay alive
Or the way you went about getting them in this world to survive.
However it is in your life and whatever you have done
Sword, famine, desolation or affliction, no place safe to run,
If your wounded and torn flesh and soul within,
God's loving touch is upon you and you will shine again.

Linda Dever

"I Cannot Cry"

Wish I may, wish I might
No matter what I do I cannot cry
THE TEARS WON'T COME

No matter what, how hard I try
No thing can bring tears to my eyes I simply cannot cry
THE TEARS WON'T COME

I've felt worry, I've felt pain
At times I've hung my head in shame
And still things stay the same
THE TEARS WON'T COME

I've seen suffering, I've seen death
I've seen souls taking their last breath
Others gone, and I'm still left
And though I should've wept . . . THE TEARS WONT' COME

Tears of love, tears of joy
These are just two of the things I do not know
THE TEARS WON'T COME

I've seen it all, still my eyes are dry
My heart is hardened, I wonder why
And still I cannot cry . . . THE TEARS WON'T COME

William J. Glatfelter

Dark Reign

Living in a nowhere
No one anywhere
My world is full of disappointment and disapproval
Where am I? And where?
Who am I? And who?
Where am I to go now?
I'll take the bow that I deserve
And go on my next nowhere
But it's got to be not here, not there and nowhere

R. Whitby Kinney

Love Flow

The music flows through me like the sweet smell of pastry.
My heart longs to feel and caress the music that flows through me.
It's a wild beast of satisfaction,
like a man as he makes love to the music that flows through me.
The boom of the beat gives him rhythm to do his dance.
That junglefied, funkified beat of the music that flows through me.
I sometime wonder who or what is the creator of that wonderful music,
but it doesn't matter as long as the music never stops flowing.
For the music that flows through me is my life and soul, my reason of being.
So when you walk by and hear that junglefied, funkified beat
know that that beat is the beat of my heart that belongs to me
and the music is the love that flows through me.

Nikia Thompson

Train Of Thought

There is a train
No one can see
Many are on board
Including you and me

We are traveling through life
Where some stations are dim.
With one true conductor
If you care to know him

Some will follow an untrained mind
Some will seek but may never find
Many will think they're on the right track
Purchase their ticket and never come back

Only the ticket is not what they bought
Because after all
We are all just a thought.
Ruth M. Jackson

Summer

Summer's here
No one has a care

Going to the pool, sleeping in late
No homework, No having to be at school by eight

The days are filled with sun and fun
each one never seems to be done

Now that all the kids are free
school is only a memory

July 4th brings firecrackers and
barbecues
Screaming kids and people's
patriotism, too

Each day starts to turn from warm to hot
When your fan doesn't work and neither
does the pool, then you know the heat
can't be fought

When the August heat is all around
that's when you know summer's winding down

Then summer starts to go away
Work and school comes back to
everyone's dismay
Lauren Earl

Untitled

What do you do when you have no one to turn to?
No one to tell your troubles to
No one to understand you
No one who cares about you.

Who do you run to when you're down?
Do you flee from your home town
And pray that you'll find comfort
In some stranger who will listen?

What do you do when you're in love
And you know you have to keep it to yourself?
You know that they won't understand
And say that you are just a kid.

What do you do when you long for his lips,
For his touch, for his warmth?
Do you just ask for it
Or do you wait and hope and pray?

What do you do when you know
Your mom won't approve of him,
The one you love?
Do you run away with him . . .
Linda Going

Mother

Spunky and lively and all full of fun,
No one would guess she will be eighty-one.

She's not very big, but all full of pep,
Anyone who crosses her, best watch their step.

A life of hard work is second nature to her,
But she would be the first to tell you, works a sure cure.

Keeping busy and visiting give her good health,
Although in this life she has had little wealth.

On Sundays and Wednesdays to church she does go
It chases the blues that would make her feel low.

She's a lover of nature and flowers and such
With plants in her care, she has just the right touch.

Faithful and steady all of the time,
God bless her and keep her, Mother of mine.

Years have gone by since this poem I penned
The life that was lived has now come to an end.

She's passed from this world to another one fair
Full of peace, love and rest, not one filled with care.

The work she does there will be done with great ease
For Jesus our savior, she lived for to please.
Shirley Merryman

Tom Wingfield

I have thought many times the way I lead my life
No two days are different
Always the same
Ambitions and Dreams call
But I don't go
What makes me stay
Not my dreaded days at the warehouse
Not my endless trips to the movies
Maybe my devotion to the family
Or my love for Dear, Sweet, Laura
I'm growing restless
Longing for my destination, freedom
I must go
From this torturous life I lead
I can have, one memory
Of what I'm about to leave behind
My memory of Laura
Always there
But always silent
Always in my heart
Nicole Love

What Is Life?

What is life? And what does it all mean?
Nobody knows really, or is it just me?

Sometimes life is good, sometimes life is bad.
Everyone's life is dandy, but why is mine so sad?

People come and go, and really do not know,
that I sit home and cry myself to sleep.

Sometimes life is exciting, other times is not.
For me . . . life isn't all that hot.

There's nothing to look forward to, every days the same.
When I get up in the morning, I think I should change my name.

What is life? And what does it all mean?
Nobody knows really, but now I think it's just me.
Sarah McManus

Love

Love is no limpwristed thing
nor hedged about by the things
of hate, greed, envy, jealousy, comparison, fear,
in which in the total inner, outer, negation
of all that worldly raggedness
love then is already there
Vincent Francis

Perfect Friend

A perfect friend would not lie,
Nor would he cheat and steal,
A perfect friend does not judge,
Rather he looks inside you for what is real.

A perfect friend does not laugh,
When you are not your best,
A perfect friend comforts you,
When you're at odds with all the rest.

A perfect friend would not befriend you,
Just because of fame,
Rather he take you as you are,
And love you all the same.

A perfect friend will be true to you,
And love you from the start,
My perfect friend is my dog,
And I love him with all my heart.
Yasmeen Sands

Memories

Time flows along; a constant ticking of the clock.
Not a thought is given to the moment
that will be cherished someday soon.
In no time at all, memories come back
as a flood of emotions.
Do not think of them too much
for fear that the memories will be used up;
yet, in a moment of doubt, there is always a loner
that replaces what was thought to be the last . . .
Memories are the greatest gold of all:
Memories are richer than the moment itself.
Stephanie Skinner

The Stormy Heart

I constantly wonder why this has to happen, how did we grow apart?
Not coming to you with my souls deepest pain is like a knife in my heart?
But you've changed.
I feel the winds of my heart pounding against my soul.
Its piercing cries of sorrow rings in my ears.
My heart is broken by tremors like an earthquake,
My tall trees of love, that took so many years to grow and mature,
   rock like saplings in a hurricane.
I grieve for love lost for branches bare for loves fruit forsaken.
Though rain comes it does not water my trees,
   but pelts the defenseless earth in loves last curse.
The dark clouds hide my sun and offer me no warmth or comfort.
The flowers of hope for which I so tenderly cared, have withered
   and wilted and lie on the ground in deaths agony.
My river of dreams hath dried up and exist no more.
Oh, how I long to dream once more!
Please, vanquish this storm and restore my dreams and my hopes, too.
Let me be with you!!
Melissa Ditty

I Want To Be The Someone

I want to be the someone one needs everyday,
Not just another someone one helps along the way.

I want to be the someone one must talk with before they sleep,
To make the dreams all pleasant ones, that in one's head will creep.

I want to be the someone one will miss when miles apart,
The one who dominates one's thoughts before the day can start.

I want to be the someone that whenever I am seen,
Will stir the feeling of desire to a height it's never been.

I want to be the someone who brings joy into one's life,
That special someone who is cherished, and is wanted as a wife.
Sandra Deifenderfer

Soul Desire

In a dark room I lay
Not my body, just my soul
Put to sleep by humanity and all its cruelties.
Let down time after time,
And shut down day after day.
Sleep beautiful one,
The day I let you out
Is the day I sell you to the devil.
Learn to have patience,
You are not tough enough
To withstand blow after blow.
Inner-beauty,
Put to sleep.
Outer-body,
Wrecked and ruined.
Shimmering red hair on a body
Built out of pain.
And a love that is lost in the silence
Of sleep.
Taylor Day Nevis

A Life Worth Living

Every time I look at you, so many thoughts flood my mind. I think
not only of the past, but also of what is yet to come.

The thought that you have seized victory fills my heart with joy,
and yet, the thought of losing you has me feeling numb.

I think back on the good times, the bad times and all the inbetweens;
all the lessons we have learned and all that we have seen.

I can't help but wonder, just where do we go from here, but it's the
time we've already shared that to me is most dear.

No matter what happens or how things may seem, just
remember God is our Father and it's on Him that we must lean.

No one can ever take from us all that we have shared, God has a
purpose and He'll never give us more than we can bear.

Your life has a purpose and your story must be told to every man,
woman and child, from the young up to the old.

We will tell it in the valley and on top of every hill. Someone
will be changed today, for I know it is God's will.

So don't you worry, don't you fret, take each day as a new one.
No matter what the devil tries, we've already won.

And when you cross over into that timeless zone, just remember
we'll soon be there. One day we'll all be home.
M. Diahann Clapp

A Lost Soul

Who will morn me when I'm gone? Not a single soul, save me.
Not the lonely dove or the tiny finch, or anyone I see,
In a home below the ground, underneath the open sky,
is where I'll come in final rest, the fateful day I die.
Or has faith chosen yet another path, with icy waters round me?

That of the gently lulling ocean, beside the vastly stretching sand,
where, along the windy hill tops, my soul and I walk hand in hand,
flying to the sea, racing toward the sand,
I catch a glimpse of what's to be, and softly do I land.
Sinking beneath a silver wave, drifting below the sea,
sinking to a watery grave, to spend eternity.

And who will morn me when I'm gone, save the ocean and the dawn?
Swallowed up in salty tears, shining down on countless years.
A lost soul taking flight, falling silently into the night.
Finally come to rest beneath the sea,
alone, in darkness, to face eternity.

Leann Sickafoose

My First Kiss

You ask me, if I remembered all about my first kiss?
Now it is really one that no one would really want to miss.
It was in the month of May in 1937
When my friend politely kissed me and I thought I had gone to Heaven!
You see he dated my sister when I was just a tot
And I would wish that it was me, not knowing what was what.
As time went by they parted and each one went their way
But that night at the party I knew it was my lucky day!
We were sitting outside talking and he said, "I must go."
Then he bent over and kissed me and I tingled to my toes.
It all happened so suddenly that no one would ever know.
That one day I would marry him and settle down with four.
Now fifty years have come and gone and I write this essay
Telling all about my first kiss as if it were yesterday.
Now a kiss is a sacred and private thing, done by only two
Whether short or long, sweet or small, it's just the thing to do.
And it will keep on growing right up to the end
If you start out kissing someone who is really your best friend.
Yes, that kiss has lasted fifty years and more
And it is just as sweet and tender as it ever was before.

Vivian Webb

Dad

I had a dad, just yesterday,
Not young, it's true, but well and gay
And full of life and love and vim.
Today, but memories live of him.

He had not set the world on fire.
Great fame was never his desire;
But, oh, his name is much revered
By scores of friends whose heart he cheered.

He had a gentle, patient way
Of hearing each one say his say.
He never argued — just sat still
And let the hot-head rant at will.

But after they had gotten through,
You glanced at him, and then you knew
That not one argument's height
Had altered his clear view of right.

His God came first, his family next,
And "Love thy neighbor" was his text.
His riches he was laying by
In that far land beyond the sky.

Seaborn T. Stone

Primordial

We, the children of hippies past,
Now adults,
Coming from present addicts and empty philosophers,
Scolded by inconsolable vets,
    We ask you to remove your branded "X"
So we can walk away from the cleverly hidden pain of your kindness
With dignity.

Sara Pritchard

A Portrait In Words

Her facial features, once young and vibrant,
Now look as if they have aged at a year to a second.

Her eyes, once showing bright blue life,
Now clouded and streaked with scarlet.

Her lips, once supple and carnation in color,
Now tight and rigid and cracked.

Her skin, once blessed with a youthful look,
Now lifeless with a pale white tint.

Her hair, once the color of polished gold,
Now listless and grizzled and split.

Her body as a whole, once alive with self assurance,
Now torn - but not only by time alone.

Lacey O'Hara

Our Girl

We had a little girl who used to laugh and play
Now she is sad and troubled not happy like she once was every day
Our girl is needed we want to let her know
This love we have she needs to accept let it grow
With hair or none it's all the same to us
These things we need to discuss
We realize the problems that do arise
The ever changing feelings the bodies telling lies
Womanhood is special some reach it way to soon
Being pushed into it can change the morn to noon
Our girl we love you accept the help you need
Our prayer will be with you all the council heed
Our arms and hearts are open wide
Listen to these words come back with healed mind and pride
You are our girl your grandparents needed one
Come back to us like the brightly lighted sun

Lois Lumsden

She

She saw it happen, her brother's death,
Now she was the only one left.
To survive the pain, once seen from afar,
Every time her dad came home from the bar.

She sat in the corner to think things through,
Wondering, what she would do.

She'd seen her brother's beatings,
And knew she could never be that strong,
When thinking about her family,
Always wondering, what went wrong.

She couldn't keep this secret anymore, she thought,
As she ran out the door.

Sarah Lindahl

Gone Forever

I took no time for my mom and dad
Now they are gone I wish I had
I made a mistake of neglecting them too
I was so busy I forgot what to do

If I could start over I'd try hard to find time
We would do things together and not
leave them behind
Now it's too late and I feel so bad
I'd give anything to be with mom and dad

If your mom and dad are still here
Please take this to heart
Do everything you can before they depart
Oh how I wish I had but it's too late now
I ask forgiveness please forgive me some how!!!

Maxine N. Fite

The Two Of Us

They never told me that there was two of us
Number one wants to rule the world
Number one tries to destroy number two
Number two is fighting back
It is only a matter of time until number two wins
She has to
For the sake of her sons
For her old age
To prove she is not lost
And wandering down the road
In darkness.

Lily Elaine Beach

Silence

The say we separated and said goodbye
Numerous tears fell from my eyes.
The soft colors soon turned to a Seemingly gray
With the endless flow of tears,
I looked away.
Knowing this was my last chance to look at you
The best qualities came out,
Through and through.

It's hard to even imagines us apart
With these deep emotions of pain
We hold in our heart.

But just knowing we'll be united
Soon one day
All the pain and anger will slowly
Melt away.
And with that last silent glance,
You said goodbye to me.

Melody Ann Burgess

Sweet And Twenty-Two

O, bachelor mine, where are you going?
O, stay and hear; your hue love's coming,
that can chance both modern and classy:
cry no more, sweet darling
journeys end in lovers meeting,
every wise man's daughter doth know

What is hope? Tis not here after;
present both loyalty and honesty,
what's to come is still unsure
my path winds somewhere
come, kiss me, sweet and twenty-two,
though it be far
youth's a stuff that no one will ever endure

Linda M. Chambers

Still Drifting

There you stand on the decrepit corner of Palisade and Franklin,
October nighttime is crisp, stinging winds swirl trash beneath the traffic light,
Jersey City stooping by the bodaga just like the night before,
The yellow glow of La Faraona Grocery lights the pavement,
Your thin silhouette opaque against the phosphorus night.

Been a long hot summer, there where you stand,
There where you stood tall and waited for them,
While your brothers and sisters floated like flotsam,
Over the swells on the Gulf,
You stood by and wore the flag,
Draped over your car as you cruised by the shops on Central Avenue,
Veiled over your heart, the flag that is libertad,
One star and one dictator,
The home across the sea that you love and had to flee.

No need to flee the undercover car that pulls to the curb on Palisade,
The two plainclothes stepping out will never cease to intervene,
"Loitering is against the law. Haven't I told you this before Sanchez?"
Arms spread and legs apart you stand against the bodaga,
You may stand in this land, but your soul is miles and miles away,
Trapped by fifty stars, barbed wire and Guantanamo Bay.

E.C. Moll

Thank You, Jesus!

My life has been so differ'nt, since I met Him on that road, a change
of course that takes me back to before the days of old. A promise, a
cross, black skies and shaking ground. The veil of darkness lifted,
rent, for mankind to be found. Before the day I knew His peace He was
just a name you see. Empty traditions, for some but not for me.
But on that road He broke my heart, I found He is alive. He is just as
real today as when He rose up in that sky. If you don't know the
Lord, my king, as your friend and saving pow'r, You can have Him as
your own, indeed this very hour, just bow your heart, and ask Him in,
He's faithful, tried, and true. He gave His life on this earth to
live in heaven with you. Your life will be so different, from what
you know today, a change of course that lifts you up, beyond this
worldly way. Courage! And Triumph! Will be your battle cry, as you
walk this ground, let the trumpets sound, sing Glory Hallelujah on
high! So I, thank You Jesus! For opening my eyes, bearing my all
burdens, walking by my side, and I, thank you Jesus! For giving me real
life taking all my sins away, and your healing stripes! I thank you
for the things you've done, and for all you've yet to do, but most of all
I thank you, just for being You.

Scott Chaney

Wedding Vows

Two hearts coming together as one, a lady in the late summer
of being, a man in early autumn, together as one, a oneness
reaching beyond either individual soul.

Two streams converging, of springs flowing distant and
different, sources unique unto themselves, into a river of
life, together strong and enduring. A lifetime awaits,
Michael and Diane as one.

Two lovers, soul mates, and friends, unite in the early
snows of winter, under a covered bridge in the heartland, two hearts as one.

Diane (Michael) I love you from the very depths of my being,
forsaking all others, now and forever more, to be by your side,
one with you always.

Eyes meet, husband and wife smile, the eyes speak of love, a
love immense and deep, like the mountain snows, covering all
that has gone before.

Michael A. Dishnow

The Wind of Life

The trees are singing with the cry
of death.
The grass no more of green is laid
to rest.
The sky of gray humbles to the
thunder and, caresses the tears from heaven.
The wind of life has changed
from a warm fiery heat to the
chill of an early fall.
The birds call to their mate,
for its time to move on.
Winter is on its way and,
summer is gone.
Time stands still for no one.

Susan Amis

Untitled

I, broken lover of this universe,
of far-flung grasslands
of fast moving waters
carrying boats laden with produce
to the sea whose waves proclaim
their power is host to people's needs, rejoice.
Of slower streams lightly burdened
with sunbeams until at eventide
the blazing sun pulls itself
into darkening sky replaced by
moon's reflection in the water,
to end yet another instant
in time's wondrous design.

I, broken lover of this world
appreciate how pink slowly stains the sky
at dawn, awakening bird song to
dew glistening on animal backs.
Now seen less brightly; heard less clearly;
walked upon less swiftly
but remembered no less sweetly.

Mary Agnes Anderson

50th Class Reunion

Walking into the room, memories came to mind
    of friends and incidents of time gone by.
You're a little nervous, because it's been so long.
You're wondering if they'll remember you or are
    the memories gone.
Most of us had not seen one another for 50 years,
Yet sweet loving remembrances came rushing
    back through tears.
Our lives had all gone in different directions,
But on October the 26th we all made connections
With a past, that went back
To friendships, basketball, football and track.
The memories will live on till the day I die
Of our 50th class reunion of New Brunswick High.

Marie Thompson

Tears For Eternity

He waited in his mother's womb,
Not knowing of his coming tomb.
He will never know of joy or pain,
For an unjust reason he will be slain.
Just another grave today,
When they take his life away.
Why does this cruelty exist?
To a defenseless infant who cannot resist.
She made the decision, she thought it best,
a tear is shed as he lays at rest.

Peter Thomas

Echoes Of Love

Each day we hear the echoes
of God's wonderful song
It lingers in the whispering trees
The birds the notes prolong
Though wild flower bloom
or snowflakes fall
We hear the message still
from low in the valley
or high upon the hills
It shines as the sun in the mornings
It's heard when the gentle rain drops fall
Echoes of his love keep on calling
To each and everyone of us all.

Reba Dziekonski

Songs Of The Desert

After a full days meal on the green
Of a leaf upon a tree,
Buzz-bugs sing, playing their music
. . . the buzzing of their wings.
Buzz they would because of the warmth
Of a slow moving sun upon their tails,
The sun hangs heavy, preparing for sunset
Soft breezes carry sounds of buzzing wings.
What a sound!
What a melody of breezes!
Thanks, Arizona . . . for a summer's heat
Mixed with harmonious, magical songs,
It's locust season upon the desert,
Tributes are sung to the Creator,
. . . the God of nature.

Rena A. Fehrer

Beautiful Dancer

Have you ever seen a water mammal travel thru the sea
Or skim along the top to dance just for you and me
I wonder if the water lapping up against the shore
Is what they dance to when they hear more, more, more
The only way we'll find out
The only way to be beautiful dancers
Is to dance beneath this beautiful sea

Melissa A. Larrivee

Granddad's Graces

Today my Granddad is on the highest mount
Of heaven looking down at me.
Reaching out his arms
To hold me tenderly.

Not the reddest rose holds any comparison to his cheeks.
Not the finest silk compares to his hair.
Not the fastest boy can out run him now.
Not a thing in the world can make him bleak.

As giddy as a school boy,
As happy as a groom,
Granddad waits for us all
To see him again soon.

The man he was,
He now still is.
Just more than before,
Because he's with our Lord.

The reunion to come,
Will be soon enough,
But until then,
We'll just send him our love.

Stacey Hummel

How Do I Grieve?

How do I grieve for the loss of the living?
Of hugs not received from those that aren't willing?

How do I grieve for the longing I feel
For kisses not felt . . . for words that won't heal?

How do I grieve for a Daddy that died
Not in the flesh - but deep down inside?

How do I grieve the lost hope of acceptance
When I'm ridiculed, judged, and given Life Sentence?

How do I let go the critical voice
Of blame I don't own — convicted by choice?

When abuse takes it's toll there comes a jade day
When you choose in your soul to just walk away.

Yet, by burning your back a part of you's lost.
You accept what's not there: You realize the cost.

You choose to protect that small child inside
That cries "I'm OK!", "I am strong!", "I have pride!"

Your future looks peaceful, your heart feels forgiving.
But, tell me . . .
    How do I grieve for the loss of the living?
        René Corey

A Wolf's Shangri-La

It's Spring, we romp through medleys
    Of marigolds - I and my wolf
And chase the lop-eared rabbits over
    Rocks and beneath blackberry brambles.

It's Summer, we race through fields
    Of fresh strewn hay - I and my wolf
And cool under tree's green foliage,
    While awaiting evening's chill to come.

It's Fall, we caper through leaves
    Scorched with red - I and my wolf
And chase the chit-chat squirrels,
    And we laugh a laugh on winds forever free.

It's Winter, we bound through shadowed
    Snows - I and my wolf no more - for she's
Gone now - and it was I
    Who sent her away.

It's Spring again and Elsa laughs with a laughter
    Most free - into the beautiful breeze of
    A Wolf's Shangri-La.
        Melissa Philpott

"My Minds Heart"

My mind yearns to understand the actions
of my heart. I listen to the voice of my
heart if only for a moment. The time has
come for the arena of my heart to be filled
with non other than the clues of my mind.
I feel so impoverished with the facts of my
heart as my mind sees them. As I continue
my existence through life's journeys, I often
wonder if there is a purpose behind the
thoughts and actions of my minds heart. You
see the two are interconnected with the desire
to please the palate of life. I cannot fathom
the depth of my minds logic, much less understand
the meaning of my hearts end. When my
heart begins to rule over my mind, I remember
that I often don't adhere to the logic of it all.
For what seems logical to the decision of my mind,
may not always be my hearts embrace.
        Shelly Yocom

I Turn My Heart Toward Home

As an infant, my home was the love and safety
    of my parents arms.
I knew nothing of all the worldly harms.
When I learned to walk, my world magically expanded.
Often, no doubt, on the floor I landed.
I was picked up, encouraged, taught many, many things.
My parents gave me exploratory wings.
All grown up and living on my own at last,
I reap great success with teachings from the past.
It's tough, coping with the worldly harms from which
    I had been protected;
Rare to find true friends in this world I had elected.
In the quiet times, often in the middle of the night,
I cherish favorite memories with all my might.
Drawn by the love and safety in the house where I
    had grown,
I humbly, joyfully, turn my heart toward home.
        Lois Puckett

Cries For Help

We are all a part
of one whole which we call society
we make mockery and tauntings
of our brothers and our sisters
we block out the silent cries of our people

We are afraid of what lurks in the shadow
of the darkness and unknown
we have an image of what is there
but do not know the true suffering
as a people we are lost in a flood

We have built our selves an image
which we hold and will not let go
we are afraid of change
afraid of what it does

The violence and the misery
are tearing us apart
we are afraid to listen
to what the people have to say
we listen without understanding
the meaning of these cries for help
        Sean Powers

Piazza Della Republica

From the core of her soul, burning bright roars forth an avalanche of passion - and succumbs the path to her threatening eye.

Overdue is her new found liberation; each breath conquering yet concealed by its gentle glow.

Alive is the river - a larva of love - dancing her soul to the conforming niche.

She conquered the valleys and tamed the monster, only his clawed hand a semblance lies.

And in her wake a mantlepiece of possessions, still dusted to revere her throne.

"The Piazza della Republica" in honor of her liberation, still steals a fleeting glance from the passer-by.

Of forgotten indoctrinated admiration - a big ornament or prize.

Once moulded with feeling, now to stand idly bye.
        Richard Barenblatt

Specifications For A Painting

Paint me a tree with wide spread boughs
Of sun flecked green;
Make it tall and stately, of willow design,
To look as though a wilful wind
Were riffling through its leaves.
Beneath it, lightly trace
A stream of sun silvered water,
Swift-moving over stone,
So it will seem as though
I catch the breathlessness of its running.
Outline a bird in clear relief,
Sharp against the blazing blue of a summer sky.
I would prefer a meadowlark;
Few are the birds that sing in flight.
Make the surrounding field a paler green
Than is the tree, with small flowers
Beside the stream, of a softer yellow than is the sun.
This would be all. Start with the tree.

Virginia Lindsay Miller

"Open Door"

Pondering over the question
of whether convincing myself will help, nothing seems to work
and no one seems to have an answer,
searching far and wide looking for a clue,
things just repeatedly become worse
as though life is melting between my fingers,
desperately calling out with anguish
hoping that someone will hear that can help,
what is out there for myself if I cannot enjoy life,
not knowing what kind of answer
makes the answer hard to find, although it is plain and simple
staring me right in the face, whispering in my ear
and following my shadow around,
never being able to catch it in time
missing it through the melting fingers, looking into the sky
looking to hopefulness, my tears can't always fall down
maybe one day they will be for happiness,
as for now waiting patiently,
knowing the answer will come someday
the door will stay open.

Taegen Annunziato

In Your Footsteps

In Your Footsteps, the older my sister gets, the more she reminds
me of you, Mom.
I see, through her, you are here, in body and spirit.
Though gone seven years, You are still here.

In Your Footsteps, her figure, her features, and her face reveals
Your tears and smiles.
Her presence alone shows me you'll never be gone;
From earth, Yes.
From us, Never!

In Your Footsteps, we're always here beside You.
Your death was a loss,
But not a good-bye.
We are all a resemblance of you and your love,
Our actions and lives are all in Your Peace.

I know you are resting in God's eternity,
Where one day we will meet
When, in Your Footsteps, God will bring us home . . . for you to
greet.

Kartney Bass

Love

Love is a warm candle burning the petals
off a red, red rose.
Love is a warm, gentle feeling right
down to your toes.
Love is like a wild roller coaster
that is not on wheels,
Love is like when a man kneels.
Love is when a man and a woman
never part,
Love is when they give each other
a piece of their heart.
Love isn't always perfect though,
it's full of agony and pain,
Sometimes love can cause a fight
and make the tears fall like rain,
But in the end, love finds them in
each others arms, begging for forgiveness.
Making them say, "I couldn't live
without you, my life was full of loneliness."
Love will give strength to begin again,
And through love, the sun will shine again.

Shannon Damon

The Hunt

Yesterday, frigid winds howled from the north,
Offering signs of the seasons coming forth.
Under crisp stars of the warrior's belt,
Rising before the sun can be felt.
Ethereal time between night and day,
Mists in the canyons, soon swept away.
Yellowing leaves are blown to the ground,
Peaks in the distance rise without sound.
Assailing their heights in the morning air,
Standing silently for those who would dare.
Seeking the prey in its' own domain,
Impregnable rook where they remain.
Orpheus plays his notes on the wind,
Needing nobody to comprehend,
Muses tickle the senses with delight,
Yielding feelings long held from sight.
Longings stir from the distant past,
Ingrained in us from a primitive cast.
Flesh and spirit becoming whole,
Extolling life from the depths of the soul.

Phil Lewis

Side By Side

Two people alone searching for love,
Often getting caught up in push and shove,
When no one takes time to share,
Sometimes afraid to care

Two people were given a fresh start,
Wanting the loneliness to depart,
Tenderly she took his hand,
Soon he gave her a golden wedding band,

Married life brought some new pain,
Leaving them both under a strain,
Side by side,
They faced each high and low tide.

Sometimes she would feel sad,
He would help her smile and be glad,
Their home became a shelter of love,
One of God's precious gifts from above.

Mary E. Johnson

A Chance For Happiness

Many miles have my calloused feet tread,
often without a pillow to place beneath my head.
Searching for something, someone, someplace,
when out of the darkness appeared your face.
The face of an angel, so warm, so true,
The Lord answered my prayers and lead me to you.
You took away the pain, the sorrow, the doubt,
you replaced it by showing me what love and
caring is all about.
I want to hold you and comfort you and have
you as my own,
and repay you forever for the kindness you've shown.
Given this chance, in time you'll see,
together we'll make it, yes, you and me.
And so my love, I will leave you never,
for our love will be one that will last forever.

Rebecca Oliver Catterton

Family Amendment

To my undeserving family, you mean so much to me. Yes it's true.
Oh, how can I ever have deceived and lied to you.
In my heart I feel so much shame. I know most of the problems thou
I were to blame. Just the thought of living without you - I feel so
alone and it hurts deeply too.
And without you I am nothing, that's true.
It's plain to see, I love my family, after all they're the world to me
I can never expect you to just forgive me. All I can is that I am very
sorry how could I have done this when you are my life.
My beautiful daughter and my lovely wife.
And with a son that is soon to be, how can there be one as foolish as me
people would kill to have what I got, and I ran around with my head up my butt.
I almost couldn't face my sobriety, and wanted to take the life out of me.
But all I could see through my teary eyes, was two little blessings
looking at me. One Celina Monique, the other Andrew Lee.
That is when the light slammed down on me. That I was their guide,
the one they would pride. I want to be there to love and provide.
I promise my wife, my beautiful bride till death do us apart. And
that I'll abide. Love Me.

Phil Russo

Missing You

A teardrop rolls down the side of my face
Oh how I miss your warm embrace
I miss your tender kisses
I need your loving care
Whenever I needed to talk
You were always there.

I'd give anything to have you back
To see you one more time
I wish more than anything in this world
That you could still be mine.

Kelly Wettstein

The Gardener Among His Truths

Sometimes, soil closes like coffin top locked on one still living.
Air and water can't get to grass roots- insects can and do.
It's a matter of too many people walking the grass, over compacting earth.
Today, I earned good wage coring lawn, removing thatch.

For an alert man with sense, there's
always a living and more, where much
can go wrong in what someone else
considers precious.

Stanley A. Fellman

Memories Of Dad

Memories are all I have left of the things of my dad.
Oh, I have a few pictures of him as a lad.

But things that he cherished, I have nothing at all.
Not even a lead rope, a brush, or a stall.

His harness is old, probably only worth a buck,
The old barn boots were worn and covered with muck.

No one would want the worthless of stuff,
But to me, his belongings would not be enough.

You remember my dad, with his hat cocked to the side,
You never saw him it, he had so much pride.

I can see him each day and almost hear him call,
It's time to do chores and do the watering after all.

The horse sale on Fridays are a things of the past,
The time has fled by, oh so terribly fast.

I just can't believe he won't be driving in
with a horse or a team, from wherever he's been.

A banty rooster to most — but if only they knew,
He had a heart of gold, known only to a few.

Our dad was our friend, our buddy, our pal
"Memories" are all we have of him now.

Ruby Huggins

Jesus, His Name Is Wonderful!

Blessed be His wonderful name,
Oh what peace and joy it brings,
He's a wonderful Savior to me,
Because He died on the cross that I might be free.
Hand in hand we walk together
I whisper His name and things get better
I talk to Him as we go on our way,
And when I finish talking I start to pray.
I tell Him Jesus don't ever take your hand from mine,
Because I've tried walking alone so many times
But no peace in myself could I ever find
Always having so much on my mind
Then Jesus stepped in and took control
Oh what joy and blessings to behold
He renewed my life and reshaped the mold
And today I'm walking toward a brand new goal.

Kathleen Baker

Oh Brave Soldier Of The Storm

Oh Brave Soldier of the Storm,
On desert sands our colors you've worn.

Your gun out front, our flag held high,
Ready for battle, ready to die.

Ever close to enemy fire,
To protect our freedom is your desire.

Another missile lights up the night,
Oh God, I pray, is my buddy all right?

Two sets of footprints in the sand,
Someone is there, guiding your hand.

From "The Eye of the Storm", orders are given,
From this land the enemy is driven.

The war has ended, our liberty is won,
Home again, my favorite son.

Home again, where freedom was born,
Oh Brave Soldier of the Storm.

Sarah V. Halbert

Why My Child?

As I watch the pictures of violence
On the television screen in deadly silence,
The mothers and fathers stare in pain.
"Why my child?" Is the question plain.

They dig and search in earnest hope
As the days go by, we try to cope.
That some survived the deadly blast
There is no rest, 'til they find the last.

They watch in tears as another is found
Pulled and laid lifeless on the ground.
A family claims the body of their infant now
Asking "Why my child?" "Who?" "How?"

For those who survived, the vigil is still
In the hands of care and good will.
With love and guidance, they will all grow
With a memory none should ever know.

We may never know the reason, we hear
As a nation stands by and cries in fear.
As they are laid to rest, our comfort is mild.
They are in heaven, now God's child.

   Thomas C. McDonald

No More

As of late, the world is too much with us with its hate.
One against another - a beating heart stopped.
   No More
      to see the sun rise.
   No more
      to hear the trill in a bird's song.
   No more
      to smell the fragrance of flowers in full bloom.
   No more
      to feel the crispness in the air.
   No more
      to gently touch a soft, small hand.
   No more.
   No more.
As of late, the world is too much with us with its hate.
One against another - a beating heart stopped.
   No more!

   Louise S. Kaltenbaugh

Here

Dank and deep the darkness fell,
One Autumn evening long ago.
Leaves were falling, curiosities crawling,
Shades of terror, hues of grey.
Smashed pumpkins lay by the roadside,
Their stems truncated, lifeless limbs.
The moon, inebriated with light,
Illuminates the sky with nuclear ferocity.
The angels of the creeping crops -
Their sullen silence alarms
And confuses me . . .
Suddenly a path,
A well-trodden walkway appears.
There is an ax,
Resting at your feet.
Pick it up -
It only hurts for an eternity . . .

   Nicholl M. Vallee

Two Invincible Peas

Happy as can be, the two peas.
One becomes mad, the one pea,
The other becomes quiet, the other pea.
Ones become sad, the one pea,
The other becomes sorry, sympathetic, the other pea.
One becomes hurt, the one pea,
The other becomes furious, the other pea.
One becomes scared, the one pea,
The other becomes protective, the other pea.
One becomes daring, the one pea,
The other becomes nervous, the other pea.
One becomes frustrated, the one pea,
The other becomes helpful, the other pea.
One becomes happy at last, and the other follows,
Like two peas in a pod, they take on the world together.

   Nicole Marie Gerardi

One Chance

One chance she had that day but now it is gone . . . blown away.
One thing she needed to say but now he is gone . . . blown away.
If only she had used that chance, to say what she needed to say . .
.
If only his heart didn't stop before it had the chance to die . . .
If only she did not live by if only . . .
One thing she needed to do, to make her dreams come true . . .
If only she could let this chance, slip by too . . .
One chance she has today . . . to say what she needs to say.
She took that chance today . . . to say what she needed to say.
Now they are both gone . . . BLOWN AWAY.

   Stephanie Fleetwood

Friends

(Dedicated to Amanda Marie Smith)
Friends are those who care,
One with whom you dreams can be shared.

A friend is one who shares your tears,
One who will always help with the pressures of peers.

When your feeling blue,
Your friends will always stand by you.
Friends won't let you fall,
And they'll always be there for you to call.

Memories of great friends go on and on,
Memories, which from my heart can't be drawn.

Friends will help you again and again,
That's when you know you've got a true friend.

If you're wondering where a friend like this may be,
You can always find that kind of friend in me!!

   Sarah Sikorski

Winter Is Here

Winter is here,
Play and run.
Go sled riding and have some fun.
Drink hot chocolate and have snowball fights,
Go to bed on real cold nights.
The sun comes out,
And winter goes away.
But still I remember those cold white days.

   Stephanie Thacker

Forgotten Soldiers

Names and faces only a blur in time
Only a few remember the men that gave their lives
Many can't forget the era of bloodshed and terror
But what did we give to the heroes that survived
Did we wait for them with open arms and a firm embrace
Or did we turn our backs and close our eyes
Shunned by the society that created them
Never honored, only forgotten like useless rubble
Their great deeds and sacrifices go unmentioned
Society cruel and unforgiving
Was it their choice or just their duty
They followed their orders and gave their commands
They fought for an honored creed and a defenseless nation
They gave their lives and become silent heroes
And forgotten soldiers

Sean M. Lynch

Light Of Its Fire

Dark county road narrows and winds.
Opposing headlights attract, then blind.
A drunken young lad handles the wheel
Controlling the fate of what I imagine is real.
Headlights illuminate the dead end road.
I turn in terror to duck the death blow.
Bones feel crushed, and flesh is sheared.
I stare into death with no emotion. No fear.

Eye's corner scans a sky holding unsteady light.
It mocks in parade at the dead of the night.
Overview of the wreckage sees me battered and bruised.
Soul may abandon my body, or pay the dues.
Shocked awake, the event becomes real.
Still unsure of this scene, it's now anger I feel.
For the burning pains of my hearts desire
Can only be seen in the light of its fire.

Russell C. Allen

Turtled

When senses have a chance to sense, they can explode your head,
or at least your nose, or mouth, or soul.

They usually sneak up and just wham! The next think you know,
that thing that can't really be talked about, just felt
takes over, silently, stealthily (stealthily?), slowly making its way
from toes to head, inclining without taking large steps.

Nevertheless, like the turtle taking a trip to the Bahamas,
it goes whether we like it or not, never buying a ticket and maybe dying first.

Our senses can die first too, turtled in our face someplace deep
within the sense place; sloppy, and open without control of our heart.

Kurt Aschermann

A Special Mom

When a person puts you before themselves
or does for you before anyone else
they are sending you a message of love
so take time to thank the one above
for blessing you with this burst of glow
that brought you in this world you know
A true mom possesses these things.
She observes her child like a diamond ring.
To her you are a sparkle and a pro
that stands out from the world she knows.
You are her everything, pride, and joy;
Mama's little girl or boy.
She tries to understand what you are going through
and takes time out when you are feeling blue.
A special mom has more than physical features
She is one of a kind; a beautiful creature.

Laverna Walker

Respect

Is there a word like "Respect"?
Or has it vanished from this earth?
There is no respect for God.
There is no respect for love.
There is no respect for parents.
Nor is there respect for old people.
Have we gone and lost our respect?
The devil said, "I am the root of all evil.
Respect me,
And you shall vanish from this earth."
Respect is no longer for our kids.
Or ladies nor men.
Must we go on and hate with no respect?
Wake up before it's too late.
Learn to love each other.
Respect thyself.

Wally Fuchs

Traps

The soldiers job is question not,
Orders followed and answers sought.
They fight for lines, drawn on maps,
The lines are hills and jungle traps.
They fight for the strife of the common man,
In the jungles and in the sand.
The soldiers plight is known by few,
Memories and feelings not shared with you.
Loaded up and trained to kill,
To give their lives for one small hill.
Once again the lines on maps,
Borders move as men collapse.
The courage of man, so wild and fierce,
While the armor of man is so easily pierced.

Michael B. Egan II

You Are Near

When I see a sparrow fly,
or the bluest of all skies,
   you are near.
When a star shines bright
on the darkest of all nights,
   you are near.
When I feel alone and need a hug,
I will think of you and feel your love,
   you are near.
When I look into your child's eyes,
I see you look back, but I will not cry.
Because . . . you are near.
When I am sad and you are all I need,
I feel your touch and your arms embrace me.
   and I know that . . .
      you are near.

Vicki Mears

Given Time

Like the berries ripening on the vine,
   our love will grow much sweeter, if given time.
Given time, new branches will form and grow.
   While sharing time, the more we will learn and know.

Like the beauty of flowering buds with nothing to hide,
   I have shown you all I have to offer from deep inside.
With the beauty of a flower, but growth like a weed,
   the good Lord above has planted our love as a seed.

I have learned a lesson that is seldom found,
   love grows only if planted on solid ground.

Tara M. Best

Fear

Have you ever seen a child's silent tears
or witnessed their silent fear?

Afraid of their own shadow
and use to all the domestic battles.

Their constant prayers for a better tomorrow
A life without so much sorrow.

The gun shots going off on the street
The gangs that fight over a certain beat.

No where are they safe no more
Not even behind locked doors.

Prostitution on the streets
Education no easy feat.

Parents laying their kids to rest
All because someone had to prove who was best.

Drive by shootings on the street
No safe place for kids to meet.

When will this all be done?
When we have buried our future one by one.

Tamera Stradt

Endlessly Pressing

Endlessly pressing against the magic's moonlit shore
Or arching our backs against the blistering sky
Bodies in motion cannot pretend
Or else they'd be crushed

Expectations whirl with yellow ribbon above our heads
It's spirit pure and simple
A holy outpouring
Yearning for warm pockets and hair

Its taste is in your mouth
Water glistens in your hair
Purple passion heats the sun
With endless possibilities

Come let's crash the sun
Let us brake the mold and see
But not just with me or the lover you love
But with the vital world we know so little of

Richard Fuerst

A Woman With Multiple Vision

Black cat paws hover. Life lo these twenty-nine years ending . . .
Orphaned herself, no children still.

Reality shattered into dangerous shards, each a distorted mirror of herself.
Single-minded sharpness sliced from nothingness.
The first step outside the glass walking on rising bubbles of air
as Spirit friends floated near spiralling with coming intention:

Melding into golden, rising yellow
   flaming tangerine, soft pink,
   gushing into cool aquamarine,
   sliding into misty, tranquil blue
braided with pulsing red
   plunging into a royal violet glow
   from a seed in the womb

A purse of muted colors moistened in quivers
Heart racing, lungs expanding she drew breath with this life,
   she'd begin the life trip with both child and woman.

Two selves meshed; beaming a new dawn.
A higher vibration a self birth mother could not give.

Kimberley Riek

Our Eyes

I'm going to take a journey, follow me if you'd like,
   our journey's going to take us into a pair of eyes.
Don't worry about whose they are, just see what they see,
   for what they see is important, for both you and me.
These eyes have seen anger, they've also witnessed sorrow,
   these eyes have seen the past, and peered into tomorrow.
These eyes have seen the times change, while some things stay the
   same, these eyes have seen accomplishments, they've also seen great shame.
These eyes have seen friendship, and the cruelty of rejection,
   these eyes have seen the most excited, they've also seen depression.
These eyes have seen the wealthy, and the lives of those so poor,
   these eyes have seen extreme kindness, and evil like none before.
These eyes have seen the morning sun rise, and seen the same sun set,
   these eyes have seen people they know, and those they've never met.
These eyes have seen other eyes, and in them pain and fear,
   these eyes have seen true love and hate, things you cannot hear.
After this Journey one might ask: To whom do these eyes belong?
   Some might answer; mine . . . or yours. Neither would be wrong.

Larry M. Northam

Affairs Of The Heart

A day to remember or one to forget
Our minds count on peace that our hearts won't let
It came without aiming at race, color, or creed
But its force wound up maiming and killing indeed.
An incredible nightmare, this unspeakable act
Our lives have been bombed by this uncommon fact
Children were ripped from our arms and our lives
Without them now, we must somehow survive.

Heroes were born that terrible day
Grasping for signs before breath slipped away.
The carnage unequaled, they never lost hope.
Together they mustered the strength to cope.
The smoke, the rubble, the scene was so grave,
No consideration of self, there were others to save.
But as quickly as this bomb devastated our land
We pulled it together working hand in hand.
From where comes the strength to prevent our fail,
One nation, under God with justice for all.
Oklahoma's "OK," can't be torn apart
When as Americans we take care of affairs of the heart.

Tom Evans

The Evolutionary Challenge

What a view a bystander has this day . . .
Our spot in the bleachers - or is it time we play . . .
To view events, so long practiced - in preparation of flight . . .
For together - we can all win . . .
A remarkable time to see the corner make . . .
The dimensional fit vibrates true . . .
Generations turn anew . . .
So much we have learned . . .
So far we have come . . .
To form the "Man" . . .
Connect body, mind and spirit . . .
To know we have arrived . . .
The gift is ours, the gift is "Us" . . .
Now to spread the word,
   for the thought has been waiting - so very long . . .
You choose for yourself, you choose for us all . . .
Evolutionary time does tick - destiny now by choice . . .
The show's in progress, the show's about to begin . . .
Make us proud . . .

Lynne A. Riedy

Anamnesis

Loquacious mercurial words flow
Out of my heart, setting aglow
Once again the passions buried deep below
My mind's labyrinthine dungeons - so empty, so hollow.

Why now? So many murdered memories later
These almost acidic words like holy ablution water
Resurrect the dead dreams, the forgotten emotions,
The vengeful volatile fears, the almost poetic aspirations.

Could a few words, written in unorthodox honesty start
An unseen revolution designed to tear out my cold heart
And replace it with a chaos of live and obscene emotion;
Tell me, for what other purpose could be this Resurrection?

C. Haque

Mountain View

As I sit on this rocky perch and look
out over the green, lush valley I close my
eyes and listen. I hear the breeze
whispering through the trees telling the
secrets of the past. I also hear the creek
far below running over the rocks and
carrying away the tracks of time. I open
my eyes and see a buzzard flying in
circles looking for some prey. I look up
and can see for miles and miles. I see
the green and reds of the leaves and smell
the fragrant of the flowers wafting up the
cliff. I never want to leave my rocky
perch, but I must go and join the rest
of life. I know that my special place will
always be here for me to come back to
and listen to the new sounds and see the
new sights of Mother Natures symphony of life.

Wesley McClarren

Alone

In the mind the walls enclose.
Outside who knows.
Shy wondering man reaches out and fails.
Rooms empty in silence.
Memories noisy, hard to forget.
Madness creeping upon you.
Boring, sadness, nothing to do.
Absolutely everything you perceive,
There's no mystery, nothing to see.
Bleak, dark, colorless day after day life.
What shall I do? Should I run and hide?
From what, from whom?
I seem to be lost,
But maybe I will find friends elsewhere.
Oh, darkness settling on my escape.
Now I am alone like before.
I've been cheated by myself.
I am worse than before.
Can't return, wish I could,
It wasn't so bad, some understood, but now, alone.

Ken Miller

A New Day

The morning, crisp and blue. The sun rising between the
peaks of two majestic mountains far off in the distance.
Deer prance around on the snow packed plain, like children
playing tag in a playground, and a whimsical breeze blows
into my warm sunlit face. My hair waving about like an
eagle's wings as it soars high into the pure air.
As the sun continues to rise, I can feel the warmth
of the sun melting away all the sorrows of the past because
today is a new day, and this day will be better than the one
before, but only if I make it that way.

Scott Grandfield

Words Interpreting Pictures

Flocks of geese and doves to pray
Over murky waters and bay to bay
River and falls of gushing blue water
Flows under bridges and grows broader

As the geese and dove flies and flies
Tibet's mountain tops reach the skies
Monks and temples and Buddha prayer
Only the enlightened who will dare

Ancient cities from dynasties past
A market place they will amass
Weaving baskets from the lightest wood
Anything they mastered was what they could
Candles lit and basket woven
Beware, your heart be stolen

Sunlight through trees will shine on them
And their day will grow dim and dim
Joyful and bright they may be
Their future is communist destiny
Shadowy mountains and misty skies
Is when their dawn has died

William Temple

A Picnic After Dark

The delight of the night
    overlooking the city life . . .
The dark sky spread
    across a blanket of exquisite delight . . .
An explosion has occurred at dusk.
The sun has disappeared
    slipping down past . . .
      the horizon.
All you may see is . . .
Those brilliant, bright, blinking
    lights,
      On a Saturday Night.
Embrace as you may
    once or twice in your lifetime.
The breathtaking embellishment
    of the night.

Sandra J. Doyle

The Old Porch Light

I am flooded with memories when I drive up that road, grateful my
parents have never sold . . the house where I spent my childhood years
and made lifelong friendships with my peers; I can remember clear back
to rollerskating and receiving my parents advice, when I started
dating . . . It amazes me as the years have went by, how everything looks
such a smaller size, and though now I have a place of my own,
there's no place as warm as my childhood home.

A hundred memories flash by as I drive, in just those few minutes
before I arrive; I can smell dinner that's probably on and see the old
porch light that's turned on when I'm gone . . . I picture mother out
picking her roses, to fill the house with scents, that delighted our
noses; Dad's out there too, working in the yard, that always looked so
perfect, because he worked so hard . . . I'm laying in the grass now,
picking three-leaf clovers and playing ball with my dog Rover.

I can still feel the thrill in my heart, when the first snowfall began
to start, and we would all go out to play throwing snowballs at each
other all the day . . . How big I felt when I learned to ride a bike,
then gave my little sister my red trike; I remember the pictures upon
my walls, that were covered with my favorite teen idols; and from
these thoughts my heart gets full, and I begin to get a bit emotional,
for in the distance I can see, the home that means so much to me . . .
and still the old porch light is on, waiting for me, while I've been gone.

Shelley Liston

A Tribute To Our Ancestors

You are like a rose in winter, that
Pass's away,
With the shocking coldness of the day.
A rose only sleeps until spring's smile,
It may seem long, tis only awhile.
Soon new life blossoms, descendants of you,
Generation after generation, of life brand new
This message is for the souls of their being.
Their past, our present, the unborn not yet seen.

Virginia Middleton Fellie

Peace And Love Should Live On

You ask what's wrong,
Peace and love should live on.
When I cry before I sleep,
It should be your love through which I seep.
You tell me to be strong and bold for it's a good thing.
But all I should want is your back bone on which to lean.
When I cry before I awake it should be your love I want to take.
Why this must go on, oh for so very long.
You ask what's wrong,
Peace and love should live on.
You as now why I cry, then I ask why I lie.
Sin is forbidden, but is it truly ever forgiven.
I cry these tears of horror and I don't know why.
You look at me and do nothing but sigh,
So I try but don't truly know why.

Lisa Rodman

Stage Fright

LIGHTS! CAMERA! SHOCK!
Paralysis hits like an unknown storm.
The lights went down and no voice came up.
What happened? I was fine just seconds before.

A mystical force has captured my courage.
It happens every time, but why?
The bottomless pit in my stomach begins to ache,
And I am now a part of the spinning stage.

People without faces . . . void of any feeling.
Only eyes staring at my incompetence.
Why did I think that I could do it?
A fool like myself should know better.

Reality wakes me and the stage is now my bed.
The lights are stars peering through the window.
The curtain shall rise again tomorrow
Will stage fright reoccur, or will the show be my last dream?

Kym M. Pizzano

"My Mom's An Angel"

She took me in a stranger when I was only four, my
own birth mother couldn't love me anymore. With the face
of an angel, at the time I couldn't see, that this woman I'd
never met was God's wonderful gift to me.

She took me in her arms, as if I were hers true. How little
I knew then, all the good that she would do.
She chastened me when young, and taught me of God's love,
this wonderful little angel sent from heaven above.

Though small in size, she has a giants heart. And when
she held me close, all my fears would part. In time I had my
own, and she held them close you see. And loved them all the
same, just as she'd done for me. So I wish to tell you now,
and this stands for all time. I love you more than ever, this
little angel of mine.

Dedicated to Mabel O Klinge

Richard D. York

To People Blessed With Dark Opportunities

Do not be afraid . . .

For God provides all things.

She gives strength to our spirit,
    peace to our souls,
    and joy to our hearts.

She presents us with grand doorways
to flow through with grace,

And constant opportunities to expand.

We have only to open our minds
    and souls,

To see each challenge as a gift.

Reach out,
embrace the goodness found within
each moment of darkness.

For I know,
    with as much surely as I breathe,

That when the struggle of my days is greatest,
So also is the presence of God.

(And I give thanks.)

Talibah L. Chikwendu

The Definition Of People For An Alien Nation

People pass people and can't say hi,
people hate people and can't say why.

People talk with people and sometimes lie,
people hurt people this cannot be denied.

People love people with and without shame,
people die for people for no apparent gain.

People sleep with people for love or new growth,
people cry for people with little or no hope.

If people ask people what do real people do,
without this definition they may have no clue.

Since I'm a people and you maybe people to,
I would say people with be people this much is true.

Linda Brooks

I'm Surrounded By Beauty Wherever I Go

I turn on the television only to see,
perfect people staring back at me,
their talent and looks make a wonderful show,
I'm surrounded by beauty wherever I go,

I open a magazine and see smiles of models buoyant and keen,
everyone should look like them, I know,
I'm surrounded by beauty wherever I go,

Then I look in the mirror,
a disgrace I see, who is this behold of me?
It is not like the sunshine the media portray,
but more like the rain in the month of May,

Yet if my heart is tough and my will is strong,
beauty is nothing but a song,
it will soon cease as your age will increase,
and the attractive will be left below,
I'm surrounded by beauty
wherever I go.

Shannon Flannigan

Neon Garden

Heavenly arranged sound of two pan flutes harmonizing
perfect sounds, as loud as I have ever heard a sound borne.
And they comforted me, and warmed my soul. These sounds
secured me, and in them I found a total pale blue bliss.
A happiness no mortal could consciously fathom.
   A muse next beckons toward me in white gown and
Perfect sight. This miracle leads me through a downpour,
under angry Gods, for this angel has given me undeserv'd love.

Confused and calm entered the neon garden,
   an Eden at only night for me.
Barefooted, toes make love with crisp, cool puddles resting
   at my feet as I stare simply into my dream.
One cobblestone path, with reflections of twilights passed, guides
   these feathered feet away from my thoughts of a reality
   cautiously abandoned.
Ahead, by eyesight, seems raven with tattoos created by
Music, love, and belief.

   Now surrounded by the sole aspect I have truly known and wanted,
I can not breathe for I am finally happy. A tear cascades from the
virgin's cheek and I smile. The teardrop finds a home in a blue pool
beneath me to live among others with harmony as their shepherd.

   William Morris

A Mothers' Torment

If I could but know your reasons why,
Perhaps I would understand why you needed to die.
Your memory haunts my mind and still
I don't understand, I guess I never will.

An accident, on purpose, I'll never know, and yet,
I wonder, you said—this I will not forget.
The times in your short life, depressed and sad,
Lost, bewildered, believing you were 'bad'.

If only you had waited, perhaps you would have seen
Life wasn't a horrible, terrible thing,
But a chance at living - survival - an everyday thrill,
Something to constantly challenge your will.

It's over - you're gone my son, now you are free,
No more suffering, you can be what you never
thought you could be.

   Sharon Mansukhlal

Thoughts Tonight

Perhaps we will all be o.k. tonight
Perhaps no one will fight tonight
No one will hurt or feel any pain,
We all will hear the leaves again

That's my wish for this night
However you might weigh my might
Autumn reins, leaves all around
Peaceful and true is the still of the ground

No one's crying, but tears of joy
Babes are asleep and dream of a toy
Divine and right are prayers in the wind
It's the mothers that pray, their hearts within

Sometimes I think it is this way
When the ground is still and the leaves all astray
Not a whisper can be heard
Everything's all right and just one word . . .

Comes into my mind, that thought
That feel, it feels all right, it's caught,
That thought, you may not think it's true
But, yes, that very thought is you.

   Keri Crowther

Cheep, Squawk

I clean my house on Mondays, I finally now an rest;
Phone rings, in-laws coming, must pass the white glove test.
I gather up my soap and rags, put Rover out to play;
Let Tweety free, whilst I clean his cage, what a grueling day.
I've dusted, mopped, and made the windows shine;
I hauled out HULK the sweeper, to finish up on time.
There's something I've forgotten, but have no time to dwell;
HULK is raring to go; he does his job real well.
He looks a little suspicious, but most focus on getting done;
When I hear cheep, cheep; QUICK, Call 911.
SQUAWK. Is it too late? Hurry, please,
Tweety bird is missing, I fear he is deceased.
How could I have forgotten my little feathered friend;
I open up the vacuum bag, I fear it is the end.
No. Wait. Tweety staggers out, a little worse for wear;
As HULK grimaces, foiled again, but beware.
Tweety jets quickly, toward his cage's open door;
So the morale of this story is for now and evermore —
Before you start to clean, let Rover out to play;
Put Tweety in his cage, for the entire cleaning day.

   Sharon J. Boan

A Place

Close your eyes and clear your mind, and listen to these words
Picture yourself by the sea and hear the song of the birds.
It's a place where you can walk along, and never have a fear
A place where JESUS will always be, to wipe away our tears.
With beautiful mountains and glorious seas. A place where you'll
always find rest.
A peaceful setting all around. I know it will be God's best.
Try to imagine, if you can. Walking along the shore
Hand in hand, with our God. Together forever more.
The heartfelt talks, I know we'll have. Just between us two
The peace and love and joy we'll feel, I know you want that too.
A place where no-one hurts you. A place where everyone cares
A place where no-one is crying. A place where everyone shares.
No more destruction. No more pain
No more sorrow, no more shame.
A place where no-one will ever hear, all the poor children's cries
Or the sound of breaking hearts, Because there no one will die.
A place of freedom, A place of hope, A place of fellowship dear
A place where there is always joy, Because JESUS is oh so near.
I know we'll be there someday soon, And you know I just can't wait
So come along and get in line, To enter those pearly gates.

   Martha L. Hartley

Serena's Prayer

Dear Heavenly Father,
   Please hear us as we pray, for a
child we love has passed away. Her
innocents untouched by the harshness
of life, her soul now journeys to
your guiding light. Her sweetness
and love has touched our hearts, the
loss of her laughter now tears them apart.

Please Lord hold our hand as we say
our good-by, to this precious one
with smiling blue eyes.

The joy that she gave in her special
way, we cling to it now with each
passing day. So many lives touched
by one child's birth, thank you for
loaning you angel to earth.

   Sharon Pitre

Untitled

Oh dear Lord, God in heaven,
Please watch over my husband Kevin.
Let him know how much I miss him in my arms at night,
And the tears I hold back are a terrible fight.
No stone walls will ever keep me away,
He can always count on his wife Renee.
Together we vowed till death do us part,
Kevin will always be deep in my heart.
Renee will love Kevin till the day she dies,
Between them there are no secrets, no lies.
It seems so sad he's missing so much of his life,
But I promise you this, forever more
I shall be his wife.

Renee Westfall

Bovid Brown Oxen

Like the monotonous circles
of the bovid brown oxen
strapped to a lonely stone mill,
I labor under the oxbow burden
of my indecisive will.
The ponderous silence penetrates,
languid with travail,
with no end in sight
to change the helix trail.
But I continue to endure
amid the voiceless strife,
subdued to the sedimentary thought
of creating illusions to life,
struggling among photographs and tomorrows;
breathing the lethargic melodeon toxin
from the dust of my bovid brown oxen.

Neil T. Butcher

The Question

I search my soul in days and nights
Pondering this world with thoughts of fright
Who am I to question HE
I ruler, creator of a thought so free

I be only a man, no more no less
An atom among many yearning for the best
What is the question of which I speak
If man knows then maybe life be not bleak

Maurice D. Lewis

Silence

Silent screams
pounding in my head,
inner thoughts
rambling through my mind,
and frequent tears
never seeming to help the pain.

The scornful words
laughing at my discomfort,
causing tiny mirrors to roam my cheeks.
The cruel remarks
never-ending but forever
mirror the jagged edges of a cliff.
Never being accepted
like a withered dandelion in a rose garden.

Thoughts of the pain disappearing,
thoughts of the tears never trickling again
then the darkness
slowly washes over me.
no pain, no tears
there I lay with a smile upon my lips.

Sophia Liang

God Of Winds: Porthole To Peace

Soon I'll spread my broken wings, then
pray the God of winds will bring, a
mighty gust to carry me, far away,
across the sea. Amidst its breast,
again I'll soar, away from man, to
hurt no more. When once away from
mankind be, my soul will rest through
eternity. To which man's so-called love
I've seen, never will it I use, to
mend my heart that man doth break,
and overall abuse. So with heavy
heart, oh God of winds, you must
return alone, for I wish not to travel
back to man's world I once called home.
Blow swiftly back now, and whisper not,
my name to anyone, let fate remove all memories,
and bid its will be done. When once you've
reach their world I ask, the porthole be closed to me,
keep man's cruel ways amongst themselves,
and I amongst my peace.

Susan M. Cooper

Ponder

Ponder the clouds, so lovely passing by
Ponder and dream yet, try not to wonder why
Ponder a field, so golden in the sun
Ponder the touch of, the earth that it comes from
Ponder the hills, the mountains in the air
Ponder the colors, and beauty we can share
Ponder the night, the glowing of a star
Ponder a moonbeam, and float from where you are
Ponder a stream, it's crystal liquid love
Ponder the raindrops, that join it from above
Ponder the trees, that dance upon the wind
Ponder the freshness, the loveliness of spring
Ponder the sea, the many gifts it gives
Ponder a desert, the hidden life it lives
Ponder a lake, a mirror of the sky
Ponder a sunset, so pink it makes you high
Ponder a smile, of flowers in the fields
Ponder the good things, in life that nature yields
Ponder a time, when nature has her way
Ponder and join me, in working toward that day

A. Kelly Jones

Teardrops Of The Gods

Billowing white clouds, in the sky above,
Pregnant with tears of life, and love.
Zeus commands Helios, illuminate the sky with sol's ray,
Harsh earth beneath, only water will pay.

Accumulating together, clouds move around the globe,
Watching the world, shrouded in bright rainbow robe.
Glacial summits, streams, rivers to the sea,
Man and woman, will always be.

Forever rising in the air, life's force,
Collecting in the heavens, on it's course.
Through high pressure, low pressure, choosing neither side,
Clouds travel on, paying no attention to the shifting tide.

Stricken earth, parched grass, changing seasons,
Clouds see all, meaningless life with no reasons.
Clouds billowing high, above mankind,
Pregnant with tears, for humanity to find.

On Mount Olympus, Zeus sees his destiny,
Fated to lived in memories, for all eternity.
The Gods and Goddesses, live on man's forever,
Shedding their tears, for the clouds cry never.

Vincent C. Knull

White Dove

I see now all the pain and suffering that held your life that of a
prison cell with no door for escape.
I see now your spirit longing to be free as a dove in flight to warmer climates.
I see now the troubles which lurked behind every corner and
every shadow that surrounded you like a thorny barrier.

I see now what a fool I had been to believe that I could have
prevented your pain, your suffering and your troubles which
surrounded your spirit every minute and every hour of every day.

I see now the pain and suffering I caused my self when I should
have been rejoicing and celebrating for you.
I see now you spirit no longer suffers.
I see now your spirit no longer is troubled.
I see now your spirit is as free as a beautiful white dove in flight
in the heavens above.

J. Kathleen Williams-Brown

"Peace"

The bombastic fury of fireworks in the brain
produces a simple, tired thought that comes into being periodically.
Each generation expects it to happen;
it never does.
Because the strength of life in the mind
is never stronger than the strength of hatred in the soul.
And the only new creations create destruction,
numbing the senses to the miracle of existence.
Is it too late in the day to dodge the inevitable carnage?
The dirge of the planet lies softly on the wind.

Sandra David

'My Toast Speech To My Son, David'

My son, my son, my love flourishes
Proud father with patience,
Nurturing and time has been challenge with
Distance, priorities and time,
but with family determination,
Devotion and support, our relationship
Has conquered and by the results
of one of my greatest accomplishment in life, son.

I will always be in total awe,
to be your best man. Lisa, oh young Lisa, may
You and David with all the
love and support of everyone
present, share the love of life,
for all eternity, peace, all my love and
congratulations
I am very honored to ask
everyone to please
share in a toast to
Mr. and Mrs. David and Lisa Jasso.

Manuel Jasso

Seasonal Relationships

The spring blossoms, though sweet and pure,
quickly fade and leave no trace as
The summer blooms seem straight and sure,
but unwatered fail to keep the pace and
The fall leaves, dazzling colors unfold,
are fickle and fly away like a dove
for only
The winter flower survives the cold,
for those are the petals of true love.

Kenneth Engelbart

Time Out (Jan., 1994)

Grimy snow stands piled along the roads,
Pushed aside by plows and cursing men,
All that's left of that wondrous time,
Some few days ago,
When winter offered to this troubled world,
A measure of tranquility.
When, for just the briefest spell,
"Time out" was called.

Snow fell in softness through the night,
And the old familiar simply disappeared.

A world of purest white,
Nearly one dimensional
But for an obscure glimpse of color
Here and there,
Which gave it just the slightest touch of depth.

No streets,
No birds,
No traffic noise,
Not even wind.
Just the hiss of falling snow.

Stephen W. Cone

Thoughts

Of God's begot but not forgot,
    Quoth the Raven in the tree.

But all souls drain of sin and thought,
    But all except for me.

As I walk through the forest of tarnished silver,
    And walk the trails of life.

All my thoughts are to but one,
    As the sharpness of a knife.

I realize that to what I've done,
    There is not much relief.

And to the sounds of all around,
    I'll steal them like a thief.

If there's sin in what I've done,
    I pray in my belief.

And finally I find some answers to,
    The hurt I wish relief.

But agony still wanders free,
    In the inner links of me.

And all that I can still remember,
    Is what I am to be.

Ken J. Boff

"Arrays Of Wine"

A glorious rainbow forms above,
Radiated as such with our love.
As tidings of love mount our lust,
A deepening of friendship enjoins our trust.

Today sends no storm or strife,
Only the bonds of Holy Matrimony for life.
'Tis you I love til death do us part-
-And you my love, I give my heart.

Wendy L. Sweeney

Snow

Snow
Pretty, sparkly and glittery
Drifting, dripping and melting on the deck
NATURE'S WHIPPED CREAM.

Mark Bomberger

Midhills

Sunrise warms the frozen compressed granite rock
Raven wings beat the rapidly heating air
Shock waves boom from the shifting Kelso dunes
Barrel cactus flowers open to the darting hummingbird
Diamond back lizard flexes muscles on the agate outcrop
Sap drips from the aged broken pinion pine limb
Whirling devil wind lifts debris into the sky
Juniper berry falls to the needle covered ground
Startled jack rabbit bounds off through the mesquite
Cholla needles glisten in the fading evening light
Sunset orange hues reflect off the desert floor
Venus and Mars appear over the volcanic cinder cone
November full moon lights the jet vapor trail
Freight train rumbles across the Cima Dome plain
Yelping coyotes rend the flesh of hapless prey
  Lawrence Turner

Hands Lovingly

His Hands lovingly folded in prayer
  Reach out every second every hour.
Only those who have tried, tested, and proven it true
  Can know of His love and the strength of His power.

Come all ye who are heavy laden
  with the burdens and cares of this land.
Stretch forth thine arms with thanksgiving
  and accept the touch of His almighty hands.

His hands lovingly in prayer sooth the heartaches
  as we cry to Him in distress.
He is always waiting with patience
  To love, to forgive, and to bless.

Those same hands reach out and touch the afflicted
  And they cause the blind to see.
Giving out a message of such great love
  with that message of "Come unto me."
  Priscilla Gordon

What's Going On?

Going on with my life, leaving mistakes behind,
Realizing things between right and wrong.
Other people are starting to see me differently.
What's going on?
Interested in new things.
Never stop learning.
Getting to know different people.

Undecided about almost anything.
Possibly I'm growing up.
  Rachel Julia Norton

Untitled

The frozen bite of the autumn wind
Reminds me of the conflict brewing within
The warmth of my heart is stolen by the frost
Of cold emptiness by love that is lost
Now I am a solitary traveler, I exist alone
My life is set in its course, etched in stone
Never again will my arms embrace
Never again will I caress a face
No longer will the sun shine its light
I travel alone, in the dismal night
  Robert F. Urban Jr.

A Dawning Memory

I will never forget the faces
Of the past and my present today
Some were kind, some were giving and gentle
And yet some had a critical way

For the casing of body adorned so
Gets worn and frizzled and frayed
By age and stress and illness
And it seems we are oddly displayed

To others who grew to know us
And to some who walked our long road
Of a once was or had been mere mortal
In a time when our prime could explode

But now we are reaching an ending
But beginning a newness of dawn
And we hope that our God will be with us
As we learn to sing our new song
  Virginia Nancy Riley

Footsteps

I stood beside my father's bed,
rearranging the pillows beneath his head.
"Father tomorrow again I will come".
"No for tomorrow I will not be here my son".

"You see something at my soul now tugs,
and I feel the warmth of Our Father's love.
There is an echo so quiet and nice,
It is the echo of footsteps from Our Lord, Jesus Christ".

I fell to my knees and I cried:
"My father please don't leave my side,
I have a love so strong for you
and day to day it carries me through".

His weekend hand covered mine,
he said; "My son you'll be fine.
You will see it won't be long
until we meet again in the life beyond".

As I lay asleep that night,
my father's STRONG arms held me tight.
Then I heard the echoing sound,
of the Lord's and my father's footsteps, homeward bound.
  Tracy A. Schotanus

Untitled

One special angel waits at the gate
  Recalling his angel of yore.
Other angels meander and wait
  To learn whom he's waiting for.

Someday, he said you'll open your wings
  to the dearest angel of all;
When she's finished her earthly angel things,
  She will respond to our heavenly call."

"Don't rush her - there are so many needs;
  Things she's determined to do-
Her monday puns, her exceptional deeds,
  The same she will do for you."

The caring angels now knew of his mate
  and of the earthly things she must do -
"Hallelujah," they sang to the man at the gate;
  we'll be honored to wait here with you!"
  Marian S. Harris

Pacific Coast Highway

Asphalt river time machine
Rectangular streaks of white
Like bookmarks
Guiding me through an H. G. Wells inspiration
This recollection road
Stripping away all pretense
Like an old friend who knows you
Too well
A moody, mirrored measuring stick
Of dreams
Illuminating and evaluating
Bittersweet and humbling
Flash card images of a freer time
Froze colored glasses
Imagination unfettered, unfolding, unending
Nurtured in the bosom of your mighty Eucalyptus
Vanishing obstructions
In my blue Western gaze
The possibilities
Remembered

    Keith Steinbaum

Twenty Years Of Dedication

For twenty years you have always been there
Regardless of the burdens you might bear.

With your timely schedules and meetings
You always manage pleasant greetings.

Being devoted to your beautiful daughters and wife,
You always have time for your spiritual life.

Your excellent sermons are so uplifting
Leaving little time for our shifting.

When we lose a loved one, you are always there
Giving comfort and words of prayer.

When we are troubled, and need to talk
You are eager to take our hand, and we walk.

When our graduates have their degrees to share
You are always present, to show how much you care.

When it is time for Fellowship Hour, you don't hesitate
To give the blessing so we can help our plates.

And now after twenty years, with great anticipation
You are here for us . . . to receive your dedication.

Happy 20th Anniversary to you, Pastor McCreary!!!

    Norjean Butler

Matters Dealing Solely With The Heart

The passion seeker's soul will never die,
Regardless of the wounds that make us cry.
Emotions wears the wings on which we fly,
(Even hatred blends the colors of the sky
In a world that's made of every tear and tie.)

Hell begins where love has never been
Love stands outside with pity looking in
Pity, you see, understands the sin,
That fuels the wars the heartless always win.

Pity sees the soul who never felt . . .
The altar where the sinner never knelt . . .
The winning hand the player never dealt . . .
The friendly hand the heartless never held.

Pride can see what pity can't behold,
The heartless bears no scars upon his soul!

For him the sin is never taking part
In matters dealing solely with the heart.

    Michelle L. Cordova

Christmas Day

The Christ Child was born with a loving heart.
  Rejoice in the Lord we will never part.
The innkeeper gave them a place to stay,
  It was in a stable for a night not a day.
Trust in the Lord all the time,
  Let the stars forever shine.
In the manger was were he slept,
  The angels came to him to protect.
The star will shine on Christmas Day,
  When all the little ones come out to play

    Stephanie Rumage

Always Within

In your solitude moments, search deep in my eyes you
remember. Sense the beauty of words I dare not speak,
but tremble to have you understand. How intense.
Transcendent as the grandeur of Niagara Falls in effusive
mute for fear of overflowing into forbidden pleasure . . .

You who are so distant from me, have nevertheless
slipped into my hearts depth where you shall remain
despite the fate I may deplore. You have crumbled
the structure of my being with the helpless majesty of
a king. You have flooded my heart with an eternal
symphony of beauty.

During acceptance of last moments before we part,
I feel exposed and close my eyes, warmly flushing.
And even now, when I think of you, I find reflected
and measured, the mortal reaction you have on my soul.

    Leah R. Ennesser

A Love Sonnet

And when the music begins to move us
Our feet have no choice, and our hearts, no chance.
Because the melody overtakes us;
We are suddenly engaged in the dance.
If by dancing we gather our moments
And if our moments, they gather our soul
'Tis our soul that demands all the moments
That God alone has allowed us to hold.
So when God agrees in his giving
The miracle of a madrigal plays.
When the madrigal sings about living,
For the sake of Creation, Love stays.
Remember if faith our minds do shift.
Love is the Song, and the Song . . . the Gift.

    Lance Rhinehart

Departure

  As I left her, feelings of loneliness and
remorse overtook my soul.

  As the tears streaked down her face, I
knew without a doubt that our love was whole.

  She carried a life in her, that I wanted
to share.

  As I walked toward destiny, the pain
was more than I could ever bear.

  But I know that she is waiting, while I
helplessly roam.

  To put her loving arms around me, and say
once and for all, "Welcome home!"

    Matthew W. Dillon

The Songs We Sing

The full moon draws me ever on -
Resistantly, I wait for dawn . . .
Stillness makes me feel as one
With creatures swimming in the deep . . .

As I sit here, I'm one in time -
The light of night is really mine . . .
As I survey that oceans wide
And feel the pull of ebbing tide . . .

Nonentity; perhaps a common thing
To those who cannot feel - thus cannot sing . . .
Purpose does enhance the things
That spring from endless pools
Caught in the depths of waters high
That match the blue in childhood's eye . . .

The matchless men whose visions are
Caught somewhat on yonder star -
The same men who feel just as I -
That all of this ties in with one
"Nonentity" who made the sun . . .

Lona L. Cook

"He Stalks Our Dreams"

As I lay down my head to sleep, I pray for
rest no sounds not a peep.
In the next room my daughter does lay, in a
peaceful sleep I hope she does stay.
But there's those times you do appear again she
awakes in terror and fear, for the pain you have
caused you fill her with fright, taking pieces of
days invading her nights.
In that memory she see's so clear shows in her
face I to feel her fear.
All I can do is hold her tight and help her
through this awful night.
Again she passes on to sleep she looks so innocent to
pretty and sweet.
As I turn, and walk back to my room my body is
heavy my mind filled with gloom.
Now I lay down wiping tears from my cheeks praying
and hoping she'll find peaceful sleep.

Vicki Saxton

A Child's Imagination

I see the stars,
Resting upon the night's heavy palm,
To shine brightly, then fade away,
Before the sun's fingers touch the horizon.
I dream of being a star.

I hear the birds
Chirping gaily to the beautiful day's arrival,
Brushing the morning dew
With their soft, feathery wings.
I wish I were a bird.

I smell the roses,
Faint in the summer air.
Raindrops trickling down their pointed leaves
Like tiny spectrums dangling on a thread.
I wish I were a rose.

I dream of being any of these,
But I am not.
I am only a helpless human child,
With imagination as
My only weapon against life.

Kristi Leonard

Untitled

Seasons change.
Rhythms rippling across time,
They carry with them our hearts and souls.

Spring, full . . .
Ripe with promise throbbing within.
Gently, incessantly, the rains force life,
   too, love from seeds hardened by
   winter's chill.

Summer's heat
Burns fire inside.
Passion grows, then overtakes,
Relentless and unstoppable.
A life apart.

Then, autumn's relief.
And lust fulfilled, love dies?
Or goes to ground, armor encased.
Oh yes. Nature protects her seeds.

Winter. Time
To reflect, perhaps to yearn.
I can almost hear the rain begin to beat.

Marty Stokes

Just As June Falls On The Death

Just as June falls on the death of May when a loved one leaves,

Your words dropped into my heart like pebbles in a pool,
Rippling around my chest and leaving it melting cool.

All night, through the eternity of night, pain was all I could feel,
Deep in my heart was sorrow overwhelming that seemed would never heal.

How dull my living hours have grown . . .
My wounded heart sinks heavier than stone.

Yet suddenly a wonder came and filled my nightly sleep,
Like a comet in the sky so I could no longer weep.

Wishing a conversation between you and me could rewind,
Instead, you leave this cold world quiet to worship your shine.

But just like beckoning flowers beautifully blown,
I won't have to mourn your beautiful memory alone.

Your task here is done, now its off to the eternal quest,
You bathe my spirit while I anchor yours to rest.

Roger Traynham Jr.

Art

It was Pop-Art I loved in the sixties
Robert Indiana's "LOVE" was among the nifties
This poster I owned, framed and cherished
Sadly in all of our moves it perished
Then abstract art caught my attention
Rosenquist, Rauschenberg well worth a mention
Jackson Pollack's works had a life of their own
Splattering, dripping, no brushes I bemoan
Now it's Claude Monet's incredible works
Acclaimed to this day with beauty that lurks
"Water Lilies" popularity is at it's height
The waters drink in the brilliant light
There's Renoir, vanGogh, and Seurat
Rodin, Matisse, and Picasso I like a lot
Not to mention Rubens and all his plump ladies
His cherubs always most angelic babies
These are the works best loved by me
And millions of others who all agree
They are the Masters among a few others
I'd own one of each if I had my "druthers."

Marge Kriston

Beyond The Clouds

Just yesterday I saw her
Rocking slowly, in her chair
Her bright blue eyes dancing
The silver shining through her hair

Oh, how I wish it were yesterday
There's so much I have to say
To the woman who loved and raised me
I owe a debt I cannot pay

I look toward heaven beyond the clouds
And cry out tearfully
God, please tell her I love and miss her
Please tell her that for me

Don't worry, he said, she knows your heart
And she's standing by my side
Beyond the clouds, in sunlight
Your love for her abides

She asks that you be joyous
Let your praises ring loud
And she'll be patiently waiting
Just beyond the clouds
G. M. Penland

I Saw A Child Today

I saw a child today
Rolling merrily down a grass-covered hill.
I joined his grandmother and
Shared in her delight,
And in so doing—
I, too, became DELIGHTED!

But most of all that hill SANG with joy
For what greater delight
Than the feel and touch of that carefree baby boy!

Yes, children and grass-covered hills belong together.

   Oh, that we all be such children!
   Oh, that we all be that grass-covered hill!

I walked away with a SINGING heart.

Yea, we climb many a hill —
How great is the privilege to be able
to roll down some!

   I shall seek another child tomorrow—
   And another grass-covered hill.

In so doing, maybe I shall find
   MYSELF! HOW ABOUT YOU?!
Rona H. Desser

On Viewing A Tapestry Or The Lions Fantasy

In the forest of the primitive I the lion rule supreme.
Ruby petals of cyclamen reflect in my topaz eyes . . .

The striped zebra lies dead at my feet.
And once sated I am free . . .
To hear the noisy kookaburra laughing in his tree.

"My kingdom is the garnet snake and every winsome bird.
Emerald grass carpet my satin-pad feet.
Turquoise water is a loquacious drink to slake my royal thirst.
My heart is the forest's clock-beating seconds into each hour . . .
And when I roar —
Each creature shudders and runs
To be caught in the cycle of time's changing prism.

I dream of a golden unicorn and the noble Pegasus galloping
Across the milky way . . .
And I with them . . .
In timeless wonder Ad Infinitum . . .
Roberta Rozwaski

Epitaph Of The King Tiger

When the King Tigers roamed the ground you could hear the
   rumblin' for miles around.
Sherman, Grants and T-34s all alike, were no match for this
   beast with its blazin' guns of might.

It struck fear into men like no thing could; it destroyed,
   crippled and maimed all that stood.
For all its valor it could not win, for the Reds were already
   upon the Fatherland.

The Reds crossed the Oder Line and the Allies crossed the Rhine
And not even the Mighty Tiger could prevail against the odds
   that were before them this time around.

They came from the East 150 divisions strong and all we had
   was 30 divisions and that was all.
All was lost, hopelessness reigned, Hitler blundered and
   20 million paid.
Neil W. Reich Jr.

My Runaway Child

Oh! My runaway child, running wild
Running so endlessly into the street
my child running in her bare feet
Her heart beating an uncontrollable beat
Even her mouth getting dry from the Summer heat
Her hair blowing in the wind, wind.
Running, so fast her energy wearing thin.
Sweat pouring down her face and back.
Her fingers constantly slipping from the back-pack
she's running, only God knows "how many miles"
Oh! My run away child, running wild.
In her mind, many thoughts crosses.
"I'm getting away, won't have to cope.
Doing! Whatever I want-even smoking dope.
Run — ning away helps to avoid facing reality.
No! More! Pressure nor pain for me.
Letting a parent suffer - is comforting you see.
But if, I'm found in my secret hiding place -
Pleased, overjoyed, relieved parents, they'll be.
If they worried? I'm pleased! Now I know what they do, when I
leave.

Macie Stall

The Color Of Life

   Violet reminds me of the ocean
rushing through the rugged rocks at
the bottom of a cliff. It signifies
the morning air like the end of a rainbow.

   It makes me smell the spring in
the air as it brings to life the
lonely pussy willow tree.

   The words of wisdom surround
violets as the rivers flow sweetly on
a summers day. I am in a world of violet.

   Violet is the evening sunset. It
smells like the misty rain that
collects on my window. The cool breeze blowing
through my hair is the violet inside of me
waiting to be out in the open.

   In the summer violet feels as bright as the sun.
The innocent children giggle over an adult acting young again.
I feel as if I am in a wheat field reminiscing about my future plans.

   The sandy beaches on a deserted island with a loved one
is the violet life. The color of life is violet.
Lori Barbieri

Deathsong

Sing
　Said the mocking, relentless voice.

I must not
　for passion, prejudice, and true holy love rest in the bowels of song.
　The bitter, merry word gurgle from within one's inner pools.

Laugh
　Said the annoying echoing voice.

I must not
　for if I do it will shatter the silent nothingness, awakening the
　life that has slumbered inert in my restless soul for eternities.

Love
　Said the cold insane voice. I am not capable of love. I cannot
　give myself to true passion to expose my bleeding and wounded heart.

Forget
　Said the painfully true voice.

　She knew her conscious was right. But on that dark uncaring
　night, she took her life. She turned out the lights, for without
　him she could not go on. She finally had sung the
　DEATHSONG
　　Tim Ferro

Another Chance?

Stubborn. Insolent. Vain.
Sassy. Brazen. Disdain.
Disobedient. Lazy — won't even try.
"Why?" I say, "Why?"

　"He's a dear, cute child,
　So innocent and sweet."
　"Get his own way?" "I'll say!
　Yells, cries, screams — stamps his feet."

　"Peace at any price." "Yes,
　He's so little and young
　It's hard to say 'No'.
　He'll grow out of it." So—

　There's work to be done.
　I'm tired. I'm so busy each day.
　"Of course I love you, child,
　Now run along and play!"

You need understanding love;
Compassion instead of hate.
"Will you forgive me, Son?
Please say it's not too late."
　　Pauline Stonesifer Hockensmith

Surfer

One with the intermittent rise and fall,
Savor the softening mist
At edge of wind;
Glad of the arched unending sky
Above it all,
Glad of beginning, and of gentle end;
Lean to stand upright
In the constant shifting,
Welcome the daring balance-seeking stance;
Wing of the creature-crowded life web,
Locked in it's subtle, mystic, spiral dance:
Over the undulating surface,
Over the spreading tensile floor,
Borne on the upward force insurgent,
Riding the dream's full metaphor
Help me to catch the shining wave insouciant
Soul's swift tide will ebb
From body's shore.
　　Ruth R. Rains

Mem'ries

As we go thru life a bit of one's heart
Remains with each love left behind,
Where it calls us back 'tho we're miles apart
As mem'ries dear come to mind.

One by one, playing memory's fool,
We renew each love gain:
Ageless and timeless each dear one remains
The same as 'way back when.

But Old Father Time, who winds us up
Like tops - just to see us run -
Knows live ones fall and real ones break,
And all of us are soon done.

Only in Memory-Land unchanged
Do our loves live on as before,
And their smiles and kisses stay as sweet
While our aching hearts beg for more.

Yet its better by far to dream them away
Than to know the fate of each love.
Let's pray life and dreams someday will be one
Re-united in Heaven above.
　　Walter R. Young

Star (Spangled Banner)

A frozen con bound by the edges of time
Sands of life experience the array of the sea
Toil not as the lilies of the field, of my mind
Please guide the conscience of my essential soul, of my being
Air lifted to an unknown quiescent truth in my
cognizance, it's me I'm disquieted for, it's the world I
hanker to bequeath
Escape while you can o mountain cleave to another earth
Leave while you can o sea your array needs appreciation
in me, in they
I will long for truth in thee, I will adhere to quiescent
truth in thee
It will be there for us to see, and see
　　Rebecca A. Outlaw

There Are No Shortcuts To The Cross!

There are no shortcuts to the Cross!
Please listen to what I say!
There will be mountains in your path,
As you travel along the way!

We must keep our hand in God's hand,
As we travel the road of life.
We must remain filled with good cheer,
Even when experiencing sadness and strife!

Gathering worldly things won't help.
These are traps Satan lays in our way!
We must leave all things behind,
As we live our very last day!

There are no shortcuts to the Cross!
There will be many curves in the road.
Remember, as we travel toward Eternity,
God is helping us carry our load!

No one can earn or buy God's Grace.
It's always there for us. It's free!
We must learn to obey God's Laws,
For the best is yet to be!
　　Leonora A. Wyatt

The Story Of The Eagle And The Frog

A little green frog, sat on a wet log
Just drowsing and blinking its life away
Unaware that up above an eagle was watching
And soon that little green frog, would be its meal that day.

When out of no where a boat appears and speeds by
So into the water and weeds the little frog did get
The eagle got so surprised, it fell into the lake
And got itself all dripping wet.

I think each creature learned a lesson
That what one thinks is sure thing, may not be
That the one who wasn't watching almost got'et'
and the other tho' watching fell into the lake and got wet
For life holds many surprises, you see!

Beulah Pradels

Trisha's Poem

(To my dear sister and her shining reflection Trisha)
    She never put her toys away,
Just left them scattered where they lay.
    I tried to scold her and I'd say,
you make me mad!

    When to bed she had to chase,
the toys she left about the place,
    would remind me of her shining face,
and make me glad.

    Now she's grown up and gathered poise,
I now miss her harum-scarem noise.
    I often look in vain for scattered toys,
and I am sad.

Glenn Lyvers

Smitten by the play of the wind. The foxtails whip
savagely as they hang suspended like primeval monsters;
each pyramiding against the other.

Gray icicles now replace a once verdant green. The
stink of death and decadence are its commonplace partners.

Denuded of its elegance by parasites that wind
and creep endlessly — the stand of might oak
and cypress is humbled.

So, another virgin forest dies — its virginity
in tact. Another victim claimed by the Circe of the swamps.
Spanish Moss

Stan Kroen

Footprints

Footprints embedded upon the paths of life
Leaving a mark to be envisioned by all
Seldom seen by it's maker
Always in view of it's follower
Left upon carpets of green, wet with dew
Upon meadows painted with wildflowers
Upon fluffs of snow blanketing the earth
Upon dried beds of mud and slime
Upon blood-tinged vines of thorns
Upon the ashes of burning memories
Climbing high upon the tops of mighty mountains
Stumbling low into seemingly endless valleys
Footprints which are the echoes of our lives
The legacy we leave for those behind us
Often erased by the sands of time
Sometimes entrapped in the cages of our minds.

Judy Harris

The Picture

A picture sat upon a desk. Look at it
Just what is it a picture of?
Maybe it's the love of my life.
Look at it some more,
Who is it or what is it?
Is it just a girl, is it more than that?
Could it be a piece of your heart,
missing just waiting for you to find it?
Did you pass it up
and let someone else have a piece of heaven?
When you see the picture, what do you think of,
a moonlit night when you held an angel,
a moment in time you wish you had forever.
It could be.
Why did you let it slip away?
Did you realize what you had?
You don't know what you've got 'til it's gone.
Is it gone or will you find it again?
Even if it is, you still have a memory.
What is it, the picture.

Chad Easterling

Katie

Katie lying on pillows.
Katie a princess lying on pillows.
The princess in a fairy land,
sitting on a throne of
feather stuffed pillows
eating chocolates out of a golden box
petting her dog and Asian turtle
each on a throne of its own.
Princess Katie in her gown of silk
and tiara of gems laid in silver

Katie, lying on an old pillow.
Katie, in a torn sheet lying on an old pillow.
A child in make-believe
sitting on many old pillows
eating raisins out of a bag
caressing her stuffed animal dog
and plastic turtle made in China
each wrapped in a pillow case.
Katie in an old cotton sheet
with a saucer on her head.

Emma Sydenham

Sand Castle

For a long while I strolled along the beach
    kicking at discarded shells,
    skipping over flirting waves,
    carefree, but drifting.

Then I happened on the beginnings of a sand castle.
    Stopping, I gazed in wonder,
    imagining it complete
    and it was beautiful.

Kneeling, cautiously I continued another's inception,
    molding its structure,
    smoothing its surroundings,
    timorous, but committed.

Each press on the sand generated joy,
    hope-filled visions,
    warming promises
    until I was nearly bursting.

Suddenly, like a darling intruder, a wave
    splashed across my castle,
    levelling my lofty dreams
    and leaving in its wake . . . emptiness.

Helen M. Lambert

Untitled

She rests upon a hill beneath a twisted old Oak tree
Keeping silent vigil, and each other company
Her image, through the years, for him grows old but never dies
Sitting 'neath the Oak tree he recalls, and softly cries

Her strength allowed concessions to her young and growing son
She knew just when to hold him - and when to let him run
He ran with wild abandon, never knowing where or why
'Til fate, like changing seasons, brought him back again to lie

Within the warm hold of her arms, amid her knowing smile
That always told him, rest assured - and always know that I'll
Be here when storms befall you - be strong and do your best
But if, at times, you cannot bear them all, I'll bear the rest

She nurtured him and gave him all the strength she thought he'd need
To let his hand go free from hers and follow his own lead
She shed a silent tear, and let him pass from boy to man
And God knows that I promised her I'd do the best I can

I've tried and failed and tried again and sometimes I've pulled through
If, for no other reason, than because I somehow knew
That she was smiling down from high above that old Oak tree
And whispering softly in the breeze "you're still apart of me"

Brian A. Provan

Don't Blame The Children

We read in the paper and hear on the air of
killing and stealing and crime everywhere. We sigh as
we notice the trend. This young generation when will it
all end. But can we be sure it's their fault alone, maybe
a part of it is our own. Are we less guilty who place in
their way, too many things that lead them astray.

Too many books not fit to be read; too much
evil in what they hear said. Too many movies of passion
and crime. Too much money to spend, too much idle time.

Too many children encouraged to roam,
by too many parents who won't stay at home.

Kids don't make the movies, they don't write the
books that paint gay pictures of gangsters and crooks.
They don't buy the cars, and they don't peddle the drugs
that addle the brain. That's all done by older folks
greedy for gain.

"DELINQUENT", TEENAGERS oh we
condemn the sins of the nation and we blame it on
them. By the law of the blameless the Savior made
known: "Who is there among us to cast the first stone,"
for in so many cases it's sad but it's true. The title
"DELINQUENT," FITS OLDER FOLKS TOO!

Cindy Kaercher Lee

Death

Oh Gloomy Death!
Knocking on the door,
Piercing the sinews of my heart
Tearing my soul apart
Then, beckoning me slowly . . .
And tantalizing me with visions
And I, honorably acquiesce to your commands
My dancing eyes lit with laughter
At the splendor of your show
Suddenly, you plunge your dagger
I gasp, my heart cold
Relentlessly but contentedly
You claim me as your own.

Cheryl-Ann Butts

Grateful

How grateful it is that I am here,
Knowing that you are ever so near,
To help me face each newborn day,
And keep my feet from going astray.
How grateful for the things I do,
But I couldn't do it without help from you,
You have watched over me through thick and thin,
And hope you can forgive me for every sin,
And when I reach the pearly gate, Saint Peter will say,
"I've been waiting for you for ever so long,
Come on in where you belong."
How grateful I would be if he were talking to me.

Daniel C. Courtney

"Buenos Noches"

Sitting at the desk in my hotel room by the light of a vanilla-shaded lamp descended from a Holiday Inn of the Mid-80's, staring at the marble cover of my composition notebook, I wait for revelations and profound analogies to bleed on to my paper to satisfy my desperate need to occupy time between sleeping, eating and dreaming of owning high-rises, coffee shops and the taco stands that serve up Carne Asada burritos — and heartburn — that keep me up at night charting the stabbing riffs of Tejano brass that pulses through the veins of the Barrio. In constant orchestration they complement and culminate the spirit and essence of its spanish libretto playing out on the cracked sidewalks of West L.A. The sharp gallop of the trumpet is constant on a Saturday night. The bellowing crescendos and belting poetry of the singers flow with a mellow sensuality, but whose foreign bravado are as mysterious to me as are the thoughts of God. Yet some secrets are best-kept. As the provocative lullabies serenade me to sleep I realize it doesn't matter to me what they are saying, it only matters what I am being told.
And they tell me, "good night."

Christopher Campbell

Last Night

Last night I had a dream.
Last night I dreamt about you and me.
You kissed my lips and held me tight.
You made my dreams come true last night.
It seemed so real I didn't want to wake,
but that's the chance I had to take.

You really don't love me anymore.
I've had this kind of dream before.
It brings back memories and a lot of pain,
just knowing we will never be together again.
Last night when I dreamt about you and me,
for me it really was a bad dream.

Julie Ann Spitaleri

Scurrying

It was a chilly, blustery fall day.
Leaves were swiftly rolling down the street
As the tall oaks leaned and swayed.
The leaves danced in agitation
To a music of their own.
The whirlwind was carrying them
To a far away home.
The leaves were in a frenzy
From the gusty gale.
They were a hasty bunch
As they swirled and sailed.
It appeared to be - a marathon race.
As they rustled with one another
Creating a lively pace.

Christina Forbes

In A Cloister

A yellow flower, cradled in my palm,
lay in neither languor nor repose,
its spirit gone.
The drooping head the flower's fragrance held,
And thorns protected still along the stem.

The path on which the flower lay
Led to a garden in a grave.
There the aged tombstone, hoary gray,
Resembled clerics, fathers of the church.
Sterile fathers, whose progeny,
The credos and orisons, resolved for once and all,
That life eternal is possible through death.

I lay my flower, now in deeper sleep,
Brown stigmata on its lower leaves, in the garden
Down to final rest.
The aged fathers murmur benediction.

Fred D'Astoli

"Escape"

"Come" called the wind, "Come over the fields away from the life you lead.
Come skip in the fields of brush and grass. Come run away with me.
A brand new life awaits you, all you have to do is say my name.
I'll come and I'll take you away from your sorrow and your pain.
I'll carry you upon my wings to the place of your dreams.
Where everything you see is not as it seems."
"No" I replied "I cannot escape. I cannot run away with you
For in my life, I've discovered there's so much left to do."
"Come" called the wind with a final plea "Come with me to this place."
But finally, I had decided, my problems I had to face.

Christina Modl

First Hunt

Moss, hanging freely from the trees.
Leaves, falling heavily in the breeze.
Sun, shining bright through the tree tops
All around you, little snaps, crackles and pops.
You take a step or two, then you stop and wait.
What did you hear, your prey's quiet gait?
You give yourself a minute or so.
But, you see nothing, so onward you go.
Green ferns grow freely from the ground.
Mushrooms of all kinds, some pointed, some round.
Birds hop around, there are quite a few.
Pine squirrels in the trees, they bark at you.
A stream is singing, gently down the mountain.
You picture your big buck at its drinking fountain.
As you sit and wait, you wonder why,
All living creatures in this world must die.
Then, as you meditate and silently pray,
You realize, you don't need to wonder, about God's way.

Dalphne Kile

Fragility

How fragile is man's existence on this orb.
Like a candle burning for awhile,
Wax running down in rivulets
The tears of life . . .

Man learning to live
Like a bird learning to fly.
Falling from our mother's arms
The nest of security.

How tender the inner self—the soul,
Breaking forth from a cocoon
Wings drying in the warm sun
Till taking flight
A beautiful monarch.

Claudette Clarke

Magic Season

On high, in many wooden manors,
Leaves rustling, having won their yearly game,
Are capturing the blazing banners
Surrendered by the faded summer's flame.

Above them, birds in their migration,
Concealed in clouds of flannel, low and gray,
Beat whispers of their destination,
The cotton clouds of balmy yesterday.

On porches perch the harvest greeters,
The lighted candles gently glowing dance
Behind a jack-o-lanterns countenance,
To welcome wide-eyed trick-or-treaters.

Through ruby lips slip faintly frosted sighs
While turned-up collars, noses rosy,
The subtle scent of woodsmoke in the skies
Remind of fires and covers cozy.

Still, mother natures golden reverie
Enchants some so; they need no reason
To bask in autumn's bright tranquility,
Ecstatic in this magic season.

Jim Swords

The Miracle Of Tomorrow

Yesterday descended into the valley of time
Leaving lightless night
Trailing a mist o'er the dawn of today
But exists no more.

Yesterday, today was tomorrow
Yet tomorrow is only a dream
Self destructing into the reality
Of still another today.

Would we live today
As we might have yesterday
Receptive to the communion of boundless joys
Cast to the wind in pursuit of a rainbow.

Then each today could well be brighter
Than all yesterdays
Foregoing the urgency of man's flight
To the miracle of tomorrow.

Jayson Filet

Bluebird

. . . I visit Bluebird and say,
"Lend me your wings." I fly away to a better place.
Oh what glory to soar up feeling the wind whisper in my face.

Weeping willow dry your tears; you've known pain for years.
Soldiers drop your arms. There's no need to be alarmed.
Come. Come all of all. Answer the call.
The voyage is long. The path is rough. Still we have love.

The deaf, blind, and crippled notice not their afflictions.
In their minds there are no restrictions.
The haters cease their spiteful doubt.
They finally realize that true beauty illuminates inside-out.

I ask Fish to lend me its fins.
I swim away to a wondrous world.
The journey is unkind, but we shall get it unfurled.
I tell Cheetah to lend me its legs.
I run away to I don't yet know where.
The idea of no one there I will not bear! What if no one cared?

We're close to the end, or so it may seem, only it's a dream!
But whatever our hearts lay we shall be there someday.

I visit Bluebird and say, "Lend me your wings." I fly away . . .

Celia Foster

Let Me . . .

Let me add meaning to your day;
Let me add a smile;
Let me add warmth to take away your pain.

Let me give you a meaning for today;
Let me give you a smile;
Let me give you strength to go on one more day.

One more day to laugh;
One more day to cherish;
One more day to feel the love you give.

One more day to hear;
One more day to see;
One more day to feel the love you give.

Let me give you one more day of laughter;
Let me give you one more day of hugs;
Let me give you one more day of Love.

Let me be your arms when you cannot reach;
Let me be your legs when you cannot go on;
Let me be your pillow when you get tired of today.

Let me help to make your miracles come true;
One day at a time, let me help you go on, One More Day.
Colleen Harmon

A Lover's Wedding Vow

All the riches I sought so long and so hard for
Lie next to me in my bed at night,
Smile on me from across the fire,
Whisper to me in deepest forest,
Gently touch my naked heart.

You've shared with me your greatest wealth;
Your secrets, your fears, your dreams, and hopes.
I can only hope I have given to you,
As often, and as much, of myself.

After today, as we grow old and our eyes dim,
And our days together number in the 10,0000s.
May the smiles we've shared outweigh the adversity.
May our bonded lives shine brighter, and touch many
with the love that brings comfort to the soul.
Knowing the souls who know us will be loved.

I choose to love you and will give myself to you.

Will you marry me?
Amy Luesebrink

Temptation

In the darkness of the night,
lies the beast that empowers us all.
    When you discover him, he will be stunning,
and he will try to lure you to his chambers.
    "Curiosity shall lead ye to seek me out!", he exclaims,
but only a fool would be willing to apply.
    The sensation that travels up your pulsating
vertebrae is like one never experienced before.
    If you listen closely, you can hear him whispering,
calling out your name, taunting you with promises.
    The demented laughter floating from his voice is
enough to make your chest heave with anticipation.
    Some find their expectations were far too great of this beast,
while others are in bewilderment of the intensity in which he rules.
    "Thou hast not been one greater than I, for I see
any manner in which you beg of me to bless you.
    You shall deny the desire to search for me, but that
shall not make my perseverance perish, for I am
everywhere, you cannot and shall not escape me,
for I am temptation."
Brenda R. Harris

Bewildered France

The bewildered France
lies upon enchant and beauty.
On the low country side
lie peaceful villages with the air fresh and clean.
The clear-fresh water is a beauty to be seen.
The Mont-St.-Michel is a large rock
which lies the abbey town.
Off the coastal line, lies the
wonderful sights of dreams and desire.
The sun slanting at the crack of dawn
to come upon the country side.
And the set amid fields are done by paradise.
The Eiffel Tower slanting the moon at night.
As though beyond the stars above.
The moonlight stroke give France a feeling of romance.
The violins whistling for couples to romance the night.
Wind of a sacred breath of love, single bloodshed
rose is thou purity of France.
Thou France the place for romancing.
Like two pure doves crystal dancing.
Anna Kull

Thinking Of My Very Precious Mother

Once a young boy so full of doubt,
Life full of love, not doing without.

A mother so strong, four kids to raise,
Proud and true, giving God all her praise.

Worry and bust-ass all that she could,
Hoping for children to do as they should.

A bond grew between them so strong and so true,
Fending off many, growing close to so few.

All of the good times, the laughter and cheer,
Forgetting the bad times by shedding a tear.

I remember a song ole' Mom used to play,
It's called Scarlet Ribbons, thank God for that day.

Oh, Mom, how I miss you, I'm crying right now,
For wanting to be with you someway, oh, somehow.

But, until that day I'll remember your smile,
I will run like hell to get that last mile.

Laughing and embracing you, tears will be shed,
Following happily where the good Lord has led.

So, with a prayer I end this poem to you,
God, bring us back together to praise at your pew.
Edward C. Glover

Waiting

Waiting, waiting for what?
Life is waiting
Waiting for someone, waiting for something
Remembering as we wait, what has passed
Beautiful thoughts, terrible thoughts
Waiting to be remembered
Planning, planning for what?
A child to be born
The flowers to bloom
Dinner to be served
Life is waiting, remembering, planning enjoying
Memories and dreams
That's what life is made of.
Reminded of memories
Waiting for dreams to come true.
Elaine Freund

411

Motherly Love

Both were born within a year, I bore you both without a fear.
Life jumped from 1st into 4th gear, Destiny's calling now perfectly clear.
Both were born within a year, neck to neck, ear to ear.
My darling sons you are so dear, watching you grow, so glad I'm here.

Watching you grow, and grow, and grow.
For out into the REAL world, you prepare to go.
To stand tall in life, and fill your chosen role.
Proud of who you are, in all that you show.

Stepping aside so you can learn from your own mistakes.
From the lessons you've learned, you'll get the big breaks.
Finding in a while, you've always had what it takes.

The REAL world not pretty, and CAN drive you insane.
The "roadless travelled" reaps higher gain.
"Come on. This way, to the Road Less Travelled Train."

Peace and love, on guard against pain.
Happiness in life, your hearts will sustain.
Very truly your mother, I shall always remain.

Honor yourself, as well as your brother.
Live a long happy life, and expect from no other.
The love and wisdom of your Earth given mother.

Jeanette Trauth

Rose Petals On The Grave

White, pink, and red laying on the death bed.
Life's lived; life's done; Rose petals on the grave.
Used as symbols of love to those going down below or up above.
Grasping life till the ending day; Rose petals on the grave
Sometimes young and sometimes old; laid to rest in
white and gold
Picked instead of flowers; with trembling hands;
Rose petals on the grave.

Emily R. Lynn

Evaluating Life

Life is often extremely complicated
Lifetime accomplishments very overrated
Common sense sufficiently important key
Which perhaps shapes our future and destiny
For many wise choices we shall have to take
Surely, no one wants to make a serious mistake
Education is certainly quite beneficial
Through it someone can become influential
Experience is undoubtedly a wonderful friend
A realistic yardstick of how life has been
Possessing an abundant portion of self esteem
Allows easy access to a worth while goal or dream
Life has a simplistic twist as well
If we will just answer the righteous bell
Be mindful helps this proper operation
Benefiting every citizen of a great nation
Children often indulge in said endeavor
Exhibiting our youth as being clever
Achievements conquered by the straight and narrow
Pierce our universe like a shot from a bow and arrow

Elizabeth Wallace

Now Gone Blues

Today I felt so lowly and blue
Like an aging detective without a clue
Like a love-given gift never once used
Or an old yellow pencil somebody chewed.

Then a friend dropped in with time to lose
And we chatted little matters of no big news
Later laughin' we reacted as to Merlin's brew
Friendship gifted spirits lifted over now gone blues.

Betty Tuley

The Fallen

The enshrouding mist, slowly
Lifted from the field.
Replaced by a blood-red sunlight
Engulfing an even redder scene

Rays of tinted brightness, sparkled
Bouncing off the remnants of steel.
Broken swords, notched axes, shattered shields,
Defeat in its finest, the outcome bitter and real.

Tattered scraps of bloody banners hung,
Marking the site, men made their stand.
Noble warriors strewn, their bodies flung,
Bravely, as they died.

They were slaughtered to the last,
Beaten not by the trolls and orcs that day,
The hidden danger, treason in the ranks
Promises made in greed, by those who did betray.

Christian Angeles

Dreams

Subconscious images no scientist can explain,
Locked up in our brain,
Waiting for the right time to come out
And bear a strong influence on us
For the rest of our human existence,
Or else fade away into oblivion.

Joy Song

Pieces

In my room I shred myself
Like a cabbage cut into pieces
Tears glistens on scattered parts
Prompted by searching for my internal self.

Clearing the table of past dependency
Opening the door to loneliness
An hour ends I pick up the pieces
Sometimes in disorder to face the world.

During the day I look for order
In a place where chaos reigns.
I go home licking my wounds
Holding the child looking for hope.

I long to be held in human arms
To feel warmth to be safe.
I must face each tomorrow
Pursuing the truth of right over wrong.

Jacqueline E. Perley

Untitled

Lying on the bed with hands across the chest,
  like a corpse in the coffin.
Memories flowing through the brain like flour through a sieve.
Recollections of the day, the week, the year, the decade.
  Happiness, joy, grief, fear, jealousy, excitement, resentment.
Plans for the future;
  anxiety, love, hate, commitment.
Yesterday, today, tomorrow.
  Emotions run wild and rampant.
What will happen,
  when will IT happen.
Lying there,
  hands across the chest.

Daniel Schmitmeyer

Enigmatic Cycle

Fulfilled, complete, content,
Like a full moon resting gracefully in a peaceful sky.
I cherish its wholeness;
Illuminated by the full weight of its predictable cycle,
A transitory pulse that captures infinity in a moment.

Such is the enigma of life,
That I predictably wax and wane
Struggle, unfulfilled,
Search for that elusive full moon;
Find it, bask in its glory,
Content, complete;
Helplessly feel it slip away,
Left again to wonder and hope for its return.

Brian A. Binder

The First Snow

The brown leaf scurries across the pavement.
Like a hand with tiny brown fingers,
Each point on the leaf touches the black road surface.
It is the dark beginning of winter.
Today was the first snow.
It drifted down this morning quietly.
It was sentimental and enchantingly beautiful,
Like being in front of an empty church in the country.
The stained glass windows only partially pass the light,
Like the cloudy sky prevents the sunshine.
The light trickles into the church,
Like the snow trickles through the sky.

Janet Shubock

Spring Is Now

The spring of life is full of exuberance,
Like a happy child who knows only now;
No weight of guilt for the past with its turbulence,
Nor tremulous fear of what the future may endow,
No futile doodling daydreams.

Only now.

All may know presence of mind in this present moment,
Feel the joy, spontaneity and enthusiasm
For what they desire and long for accomplishment.
How? Is it not to the task—consecration?
Presence of mind in the present moment?

Only now.

Let us love each of those moments in every way,
Adore and cherish their winged thoughts
And where they will lead who's to say?
But in the fullness of their affluence let us be caught,
And the springtime of life is ours today.

Hermona C. Beardslee

My Thoughts Of Loosing You

The thought of loosing you, cuts through me like a knife.
I want to stay and be with you, for the rest of my life.

I love you more and more, with each minute that passes away.
I'm always thinking about you, each and every day.

To me, loosing you would be like committing the biggest sin.
I don't want anything to go wrong, I like everything the way it has been.

If I ever hurt you, I want you to tell me so.
Just please, I beg you, please don't go!

Brandi Perkins

Like No Other

Have you ever known a person so gentle and kind
Like a precious jewel, so very hard to find.
They always seem to know your need
With words they say, they plant a seed.

They never boast about things they've done
About a trophy they have won.
They take your hand and help you walk.
Their voice so gentle when they talk.

They wear a smile on their face
Their hair woven like fancy lace.
Their eyes are like stars in the night.
When days are dark, they see the light.

When things are going so very wrong,
They hold you tight and make you strong.
Have you ever know a person like no other
I do. She's my mother

Erma Hill

The General

There stood a bear of a man,
Like an Arabian Knight he rose
From the sand.
He was the General.
He was in Command.
He stood by every soldier,
From the front lines to the seaport,
He was the General.
He was their support.
Forty days and forty nights, he and his men
Put up a hell of a fight. He was the General,
A bear of a man, like an Arabian Knight
He rose from the sand, to oppress aggression
Of a small land. He was the General.
He was in command.
Forty days and forty nights he had won.
His job, it was done. He was the General.
The General. The people were happy and free. It was all
For Democracy. He is the General. The General.
A bear of a man. The General.

Aubrey G. Dudley

"Fusion Of The Heart"

As the rising moon seeks out a cloudless sky
Like the dawn anticipates the first ray of sun I await your love
As the bubbles caress the flutes curvaceous form
Like the waves tumbling over the welcoming shore
Your touch both soothes and excites
As the ripened fruit's juice both satisfies and entices
Like ripples from dew drops alter the lakes reflections
We exist at an eternal cross roads
As sleep calls out to the distant dream to awaken it
Like crying conjures up laughter to maintain life's balance
I now know the value of self love
As eternal life sits patiently beyond deaths door
Like faith finding something to finally believe in
I know I will love you forever
As time is allowed to open up each new moment
Like the womb readies itself to introduce a new life
I anticipate tomorrow in your sweet embrace
As the days when sky is shared by both sun and moon
Like the earth where ocean and dry land coexist eternally
We are two meant to live as one.

Austin H. Pilgrim Jr.

Snow

Falling softly,
   like the gentle tears of a woman
She is caressed by the wind,
   gliding in swirling patterns,
to flirt with the earth below.

A silent lover,
   she casts a haunting spell over the land,
staying only for a moment before darting away.

Much like a tangled web,
   she leaves her pattern etched
in the minds of all until, again,
   she returns to fill the world
with her silent love.

Dale Fukura

Vampire Knowledge And Romance

Mad? To seek a taste of your lethal kiss,
Likely to be spoilt by a bloody slash,
A ludicrous folly of heart is this,
With one who should have long since turned to ash.

Your fierce eyes, razor fangs,ever-growing hair,
These weapons gained; your humanity spent,
To recover buried pain from skin so fair,
Your fury onto a harsh world to vent.

Your excessive years have a wise mind built,
Alas! A man slain by despair remains,
Whose rage makes carnage, whose remorse never spilt,
Never to die, forever bearing these pains.

Through you, I know me, and my wish on sight,
To steal away to the black romance of night.

Aglaia Venters

Expounding On Ignorance

Blissful is ignorance for those so inclined
Limited their perspective, unaware they are blind
Groping in darkness, they extemporize and prate
Emoting pretentiously to condemn and denigrate.

Assuredly ignorance is often naive
When the ignorant expound their doctrinal belief
But ignorance confines reason in a cubbyhole
Restricting intelligence and smothering the soul.

I suppose I should make this concession
A kinder word for ignorance is nescience
And an ignoramus is a blockheaded fool
A bombastic egoist with a flare for overrule.

So; naivety as ignorance can be forgiven
But expounding· in ignorance should be forbidden
If I know not of what I glibly write
Tell me gently I am wrong; I'll try to be contrite.

Elaine E. Kelso

Sewn In The Serpent's Belly

My horned headed ghost sways
Lonely and terrified in the realm of it's pain
As it kisses the side of the dawn of Satan's breath
The poisonous bite of the pale gold snake
Slowly killing it's existence of happiness
Perhaps, the antidote lies
Beyond the shadows of its sword
Which is not sharp enough
To slay the dragon of its destiny

Jeffrey Joseph Mlak

The Dealer

If you're looking for something to cut your life short
Listen to me and lets get taught
My rap ain't pure the stash is no delight
I'll run a game on you both day and night
I don't give a damn if you're just as Average Joe
Athlete, Superstar or Eskimo
What I got on the street is deadly stuff
Rat poison, Quinine or Jessup Cutt
Buy from me - lose your soul, chasing bad drugs or fool's gold
Cash money is what I'm about; I'll help you OD, watch Mama shout
Men, women, children - I don't care, as long as the money's there
I'll string you out and watch you sweat
Keep away from me, I'm not finished yet
You'll have plenty of friends because you all get high
Who'll lift the casket the day you die
When it come down to it, I'm a deadly drug store
Only green money unlocks my door
I am the Dealer
A greedy, heartless crack or heroin dealer
Waiting for a fool; don't let the next one be you!

Joseph Turner

White Against White

Seeking answers in our dreams; illusions in a looking glass;
listening through a mystical shell to echoes of our past.
Never hearing melodies; playing pretty harmonies;
opening doors to fantasies; music always sets me free.
Darkness ends each night at dawn; dreams become reality.

Building bridges of our days; standing high upon a hill;
we set our sails against the sky; alone, together, you and I.
Nestled in a crowded harbor we lose sight of who we are.
Sailing, gliding past each other, never drifting off too far.
Under rocking sails of love, never reaching for the stars.

Trusting winds rustle by, easing paths of slippery stones.
A blinking eye; sunshine to rain;
love from an empty soul brings pain.
Seeds dying in April show man intervenes;
like a calendar in pencil, changing hopes, changing dreams.

The pendulum swings away from now, until tomorrow becomes today.
A blanket of fog on a snow-covered love
rolling in with doubts and fears.
White on white.
Love disappears.

Janet E. Davis

"The Working World"

Planes of all sizes roar overhead,
little children still in bed.

Fathers creeping down the stairs
into the early morning air.

The freeways filled with traffic sounds
at home, at work, all around town.

Industry's wheels begin to turn
from pipes the smoke begins to churn.

Trains, trucks, tractors, cars,
screws, wrenches, poles and bars.

These are the tools of the working man
from four in the morning till six p.m.

Christine Aine

Goodbye

I cannot release my gaze from her eyes
Locked within the depths of her soul
I am colored a melancholy shade of blue

The disturbing sound of silence breaks the lock
Delicately I wipe the tears from her porcelain cheeks
She says not a word, her breath fluttering

The misty clouds pass over the moon, casting shadows
A breeze moves them along, rushing them quietly
My whisper of goodbye floats echoing through the clouds

She kisses my cheek, moving towards
My lips, a warm passion builds in my mouth
A muted orange happiness masks the blue

But only for a moment, then I turn to leave
My rain soaked hair clings to hers
Two hands trying not to slip apart

Hurriedly I turn, her angelic figure flitting through my mind
I raise the collar of my trench coat
Trying to keep her from seeing my tears

Grant Outerbridge

Astray

There are people I remember,
long ago,
but have left me astray
I have friends that are coming and going,
who am I to tell them to stay
but I know I'll always remember,
even though you may not like me at all,
    For I wish I've known you better,
maybe then you would of stayed where you were,
but I know you will get better,
cause I know I'm not that great at all,
and if you don't find any better
just give me a call,
and you know I'll be right over.
    Cause I'd never leave you astray.

Jenny McGovern

Fisherman's Heaven

Here I sit in my fisherman's heaven
Long before the hour of seven
I've cast my line far out into the lake
Now I'm hoping for a lunker to partake
Wow, what a strike I just had
Bet they'll be hitting today, am I glad
Golly look at that rod bend in the middle
The tip is quivering like a bow on a fiddle
He's breaking water trying to get away
Lord, please don't accommodate him today
He's about the biggest I ever caught
I'm so nervous I can hardly hold my line taunt
Bet he's going to shake the hook and swim on by
If he does, I'll just die
Lord, should the excitement take me from my favorite sport
I know I'll have to appear in your court
I beg you, sentence me to your fisherman's heaven
I'll always be there long before seven
I promise to bring lots of laughter and cheer
We'll have a ball year after year

Jean D. Corcoran Cathey

People

Queer girl
long hair
burgundy in braids with yellow ribbons
three t-shirts, red, blue, green
Grateful Dead patch on the red
black and white flannel tied around her waist
hanging to ankles
covered by dark green Doc Martin boots
I walk to her
in Gap Khakis and light blue shirt
Eddie Bauer wing tips
we talk
she's got views I don't agree with (she is pro-choice!)
she likes horror flicks and boring books
but I respect her
I would never
dare to look like her

Becky Phillips

The Voice

Is this what you want your life to be the Voice did ask of me
look in the mirror and don't look away
play by the rules the Voice did say
not theirs but your own
you know what's right, you feel it in the bone
hard it may well be but consult yourself and see
rewind the tape and visit your life
the love the hate the grief the strife
the answers to the questions is always known to thee
see the conclusion not the illusion
all that matters when push comes to shove
is that you did it all with love and the Voice spoke no more
but it had touched me deep and to the core
for now I see
rich man poor man beggar man thief
it is how you treat others your sisters and your brothers
don't indulge the selfish libido this is now my credo
be kind be true
for in the end there's only one sin
to look in the mirror and not see clear

Craig O'Rourke

Eternal Search

Throughout the centuries I have traveled the night;
looking for something, someone,
searching for you, my love.
You come to me solely in my dreams;
only for a moment, then you disappear;
And I wake to realize that the night has
dawned for me once more.

In despair I rise and prepare to stalk the night.
Alone in the eternal darkness I begin my haunt.
I remain unseen by all; an immortal ghost,
condemned by fate to rule the night.

The moonlight is my sole guide.
The mist surrounding me; my only comfort.
I continue on, without you my only love.
My fault, I know, for leaving you so long ago.

In the centuries to come I will travel the night;
always seeking, wandering endlessly.
Looking for you, my love,
Forever searching for you.

Joann C. DeSantis

Untold Destiny

Time and time again, as I lie upon the bluff above my home,
   Looking upon the midnight sky of incalculable celestial bodies,
I find myself drifting away from this world and approaching another.
   A world of unlimited space and of undefined boundaries.
    But I am nowhere near . . .

I am there again, as every time before, in pursuit of some place I
      have yet to ascertain,
   A territory of my world I have envisioned but have not seen,
A precinct of my essence guarded by forces beyond my deepest
   perception.
   A portal of unknown location my only entrance.
    But I have found the way . . .

I must find this gate of my existence, or forever be in wonder of
      what lies beyond,
   A heaven? A hell? Perhaps both, I do not know,
But I shall find this arcane continent, I must, for it is my
   inevitable, Untold Destiny.
   An unknown force draws me toward the ambition of truth.
    But I am getting closer . . .

I have reached the epilogue of my journey and finality closes in
   upon me,
   Is this one oasis I desire? The trophy of my mission?
As the weight of the unknown dissolves from my chest, the clarity
   fades slowly away.
   The light of Helios ascends in the east, I am awake upon the bluff.
    But I am there . . .

    Chris Hogue

My Father Was Not There

In a condition of desolation, I reflect on my existence . . . Lonely,
lost, confused, afraid. Caged like a bird with nowhere to fly. I
look to the sky, but only the ceiling is there. Trapped like the lion
caught in the snare. Despaired, I feel as my hands cover my face.
The race of life is finished for me, and I have lost. I can't
progress. So I regress, as I fall into a state of numbness.
   My chin touches my chest, as I bow my head in disgust of what
I have become. Representing many, I am just one. The offspring of a
man, if one so chooses to call, who left his son destitute —before
he was able to crawl. Now I have nowhere to run. The end of the
road of aberration, by way of a gun. My son, he would say I'll always
be there. Whenever you need me. I solemnly swear. But he was not
there when I took my first step, bounced my first ball, or cashed my
first check. In debt, were we because bills were not paid. I felt
so helpless with no father to aid.
   Tears begin to huddle in the corners of my eyes. They fall off my
face as I ask myself why. Why did he leave me with no one to look up
to, no one to guide me, and no one to talk to. How can I respect man
if man did not respect me. He left me as a child, to grow up in the
wild. Alone, I was, in the wilderness of humanity. Profanity was my
guide in a life full of insanity. Love was not given, so love did not
exist. I am the fatherless.

    Efrem Z. Gause

"To My Son"

Look ye my lad, there are children at play
Look to the sun on this beautiful day.
Remember my lad, this day full of bliss.
For many young lives have been mortgaged for this.
Hear ye my lad, across the land
Guitars are strum by peaceful hands.
Think now my lad, of a world at peace
A permanent status not just a lease.
For the price my son was your own dear life
that rid us all of war and strife.
Remember my lad on a distant shore
When a bugler called you to the corps.
I saw you my lad walk away that day
Now look ye my lad, there are children at play

    Cicely Rigdon

Here I Am!

Here I am! Come rescue me from;
Loud dance music,
In a Los Angeles night club.
Uncrowded dance floors and
Flashing stained glass effect lights.

Here I am! come rescue me from;
Metal tables, high wicker chairs,
Couches with cushions and low wooden tables,
Come talk to me and take me away from here.

Here I am! come rescue me from;
An empty bar room late at night
And the beer and soda of designated drivers.

It is hard to hear conversation,
Over the music the D.J. is playing
In a dimly lit, downstairs bar
Filled with cigarette smoke and memories.

Here I am! Come rescue me from;
The loneliness hidden behind a smile
And from shyness hidden behind a
Facade of confidence.

    Anne-Marie Daly

Prelude To A Child

Love exceeds all boundaries and yet
love doesn't exceed the boundary of ourselves
Love is contained within everyone
within themselves-within each other
to love one another
Hate and greed rule this planet we call
Earth
My wish to you
dear child . . . my child . . .
that though you have not entered this
earth,
You never will enter it . . .
never enter the greed
nor the
hate
instead,
enter the planet with
Love.

    Chrissy Shultz

Love

Love at first sight can work, and cannot-
Love is like no one else is real-
Love is a flower,
  It lives,
  It blooms,
  It wilts,
  And never lives again-
Love is a memory of a person that lives in
  Your heart,
  Mind,
  Body,
  and sole forever -
Love takes over your life,
  Once it's there,
  And then it's gone-
Love, after it's over,
  You always want someone to talk to,
  But you told all your friends to leave-

After all this,
  You decide never to love again.

    Crystal Callahan

Love Is

Love is patient, kind, and true.
Love is tender, gentle, and sweet.
Love is cuddly, cute, and soft.
Love is not mean, boastful, or proud.
Love is not fearful, or scared.
Love is not cold, hard, or untrue.
Love is what you make it to be.
You can give love; and it can be given back.
Love can be strong; if you love your fellowman.
Love can be courageous; if you love your enemies.
Love can be shared; if you love your neighbor.
Love can be soft; if you love your children.
Love can be warm; if you love your friends.
Love can be bright and lovely; if you love your loved ones.
Love can be you; loving the whole human race.
Love is not bittersweet, it is sweet.
Love rejoices in truth. Love is hope.
Love believes all things.
Love is the greatest thing you can give.

Ernestine Lister Clendenin

Love

Love, what is love?
Love is the warmth, in your heart,
The purr of a cat,
The commitment of being together,
Love is the time you share thinking of one another,
It is that sweet, warm, and important feeling,
It is the warm sun or a cold day,
And when you love someone you know,
Because the warmth is there and the togetherness is there to share,
It is about being there,
About sharing your life,
Love will make you cry,
It will make you laugh,
But most of all when you love, you can feel pain,
Hurt, heart break, the dreary winter,
The cold rainy nights,
The cold cement floor, cold, damp and lonely,
But love goes both ways,
And you must face them face love.

Amy Carey

In The Arms Of Night

Touch me, touch me night,
love me, love me night,
red wine is sliding through my fingers,
burn me, I wanna die in your arms.

Kiss me, kiss me night,
kiss me with your sharp lips,
with your wet drops - you excited wanderer.
Your wounds are smell of flowers,
throwing tenderly moonshine in my eyes.
Full of love I'm watching your movements;
morning will take all our sparkles away
everything that we can have.
Love me with your trembling nuances!
Nobody can see us transformed into leaves of grass
waiting for a sunrise when we will disappear together.

Kiss me, kiss me night,
through doors of your kingdom I can see myself in your eyes
playing with sparkles you're throwing,
whispering into your heaven's ear;
kiss me, o, kiss me with your magic sounds!

Bojana J. Nikolic

"The View From Above"

How does the world view love?
Love of convenience
No time for fellow man, not in the plan
Schedule existence
Money and power on my brain
No trust, false gains
Houses of gadgets
Microwave dinners, computerized shopping
Internets, faxes, Oh!, no more taxes
Beep, beep, beepers
Idolizing, idealizing, cliquishness
Favorite reigns!

God, so love the world, he gave His only begotten son - remember!
How does the church view love?
We love our anointed and appointed, what about the disap-
pointed, ouch!
We love our elected, what about the rejected, ouch!
We love our selected, what about the neglected, ouch!
Jesus said, love one another, as I have loved you

Brethren, what does love really mean?
Angels fell silent . . . heaven waits

Carolyn Henderson-Shepard

"Love Is, Love Was"

Love is the flower,
Love was the honey bee that made it flower,
Love is the tall oak tree,
Love is t he acorn that made it be,
Love is the maker of the
pearl in the sea, love is the oyster
that made it be,
Love is in the heart of every child,
Love was the mother who gave her love,
Love is the pitter patter of the falling rain,
Love was that sound on my window pane,
Love is the falling of a leaf on an autumn day,
Love was the leaf on a spring day,
Love is, love was polliwogs and frogs.

Fran V. Rumbaugh

Beverly

In Memory of my Beautiful 19 year old Daughter
Beverly Precious Child of Mine

God loaned you to me for such a short time.

But He knew with your sorrow, fears, energy, smile and
loveliness, you would be One of A Kind.

Beverly Precious Child of Mine.

He knew though that this Mother would love you with a love
so intense, that to everything else except your smile and
loveliness it would be blind.

Beverly Precious Child of Mine.

Mother knows too, He needed another Angel to light His
Heavenly Place, where love rules sublime.

Beverly Precious Child of Mine.

Jannie Davis

The City's African-American Bicentennial Salute

A pioneer's silence of love is lonely.
Love's lonely quietness. Love's lonely silence — the yoke.
Inferiority, forbidden and outlawed; 'cause 200 years yearning the
eternal unchanging principles of the Holy Spirit against such servitude.

Civil liberties direct struggle and suchlike calculating.
with the "All American Flag," a beam of stars and stripes
bursting in the East, West, North and South in the city of Middletown.

The American flag symbolizes freedom and justice.
Love's lonely quietness, love's lonely silence.
The sun is bright, shining with light.
Just to foresee the "Big Dipper" as far as Darkest Africa, piercing at night.

And in the night comes forth a full moon,
The "North Star" is beaming in the East, West, North and South.
Be true, treasure a great soul endowed beyond a surpassing power of wisdom.

Love's lonely quietness; love's lonely silence.
Allegiance to heartaches seek to someday heal one's wounds.
Love is Christ and even precise. Love's lonely quietness;
The African-American Pioneer Bicentennial Salute.

by Cheryl Wilson

The Awakening

It inevitably comes to this you know. Red lights flash wildly on
lowered railroad gates as the 40-year-old man sits at the corner pub
sipping his brew. It happened to him, too.

The dream has exploded madly, and the choice of east or west
is no longer an option. It happens as the final curtain call
echoes a distant scream.

They lied to us, you know. With their tied back hair,
pointed ruler and books, they seduced us with a dream.
They even used examples, everyone of them,
about those who beat the odds and found immortality
in the tiny print of thick volume books. They who
hopped trains and rode the distance.

A mirrored heart never lies, but strikes the epiphanic
truth when life's little bucking pony throws us
on our brainwashed asses, leaving mere remnants of

visions, intent, and substances not seen.

Unclouded now, the best that can be said for
cataracted eyes. A kicked over metal marker;
block letters strewn on the ground.

Joni Wilson

"Virtues Of A Friend"

Friendship, responsibility,
Loyalty and honesty.
These are the things I look for in my friends qualities.

Friendship is the first thing I look for in my friends.
She should take time for me,
And help me when I'm down.
She should also be happy to see me.

Responsibility is another quality that is important.
She should stay out of trouble,
And keep promises on the double.

Loyalty,
might even spoil me,
Because she needs to be good to me,
And must be understanding.

She mustn't lie to me . . .
Must use honesty.
Honesty is the best policy.
And these are my virtues of a friend.

Julia Marie Allen

"Gibbs And Me"

Mysteriously, seductively, enticingly
Lying in the dark
Holding each other tight
Looking at the old oak tree
Through the aged, narrow window pane
Gazing at the stars on the horizon
Twinkling and glittering brightly on the sea
Sincerely wondering how this could be
Yesterday you were a stranger
Today you feel very close to me
It surprisingly happened inadvertently
What could possibly endure between you and me
Perchance the night is a unique gift to you and me.

Laura Elizabeth Ashley

Earth's Beauty

As I sit in my silence and view all that is around I am struck by the
magnificence of all earths beauty. I can only express what my two
mere eyes can drink in the lush greens, the golden shimmering tones,
the creeping vines, the unaccountable wild flowers that fill the soul
with their sweet scents the trees intertwine like lost souls that have
been reunited. The sun in all it's glory is warming all who sit below;
all the flowers and the animals down to the smallest insect and someone
like me. I am absorbing all the sun is giving although I know I do not
deserve it's strength. Sweet enchanting melodies I've never heard are
being chirped in my ear. Smells that will never be forgotten and
could never be described are filling my senses. It is snowing golden
flakes as the leaves separate themselves from their mother tree. I
feel as if I am a part of this earth for this one moment mother earth
has opened her arms and I am by her side to be one to feel her
heartbeat and know how insignificant life's worries are. This
moment is why I exist; this is life our breaths are one and I feel all her glory.

Fonda Faulkner

Little Boy's

They climb a tree and scrape their knee,
make mud pies and get little girls to cry.
They play in the dirt mostly get hurt,
tease dogs and walk on logs.
These are what little boys do.
Making lemonade stands and dirtying their hands,
Catching toads making dirt à-la-modes.
Baseball cards to martians on Mars,
steam engine trains to football games.
These are what little boys do.

Christy Fisher

Swim Lesson

I stumbled over my terry cloth towel to
make my way to the apples
my just off the Sportmart rack Speedo suit
hugged my shivering body

Nervously I gazed at my fellow apples we
were ready for our first swim lesson

I plunged deep into crystallic chlorine
waters and
attacked the red and white border ropes
that marked the distance to test us

Sweet rushes of icy coldness flowed
through my hair clogged my ears as
I kicked and maneuvered so swiftly like
a newborn chick released from its shell

I grasped the rough plastic of the ropes and
waltzed out on the concrete platform
a new banana

A step up on the swim lesson fruit chart.

Jill Prosi

Spring

Spring is the season with the sun that
makes you warm.
It is mostly sunny with some rain and
a storm.
The flowers start to sprout and the birds
begin to sing.
Then the butterflies come out their
cocoons and look at it's beautiful wings.
Some people go the pond to look at
the beautiful fish.
But some people like to catch them and
put them on their dish.
I like to hear the bees buzz while the
deer come out to play
Then I smell the fresh air and say, "What
a beautiful day."
So you see the spring is beautiful
and is very fun.
But the thing I like best of spring is
looking at the setting sun.
Emmanuel Adetunji

Visions Of Togetherness (The Million Man March)

As we looked into the crowds, we couldn't help but feel so proud.

We saw our fathers, our grandfathers, our brothers, our sons,
among the many faces, how proud we were of all the races.

We also saw our mothers, grandmothers, sisters, and daughters,
and many friends, the many faces there seem to be no end.

People of all ages came to unite, this was such a wonderful sight.

We came together that day, together we plan to stay.

We are such a blessed race, there is no reason to live in disgrace.

Bring our mothers, fathers, sisters, brothers and children back home,
this is where we all belong.

Together we can bring our families back, all we have to do is stay
on the right track.

The march had a message for all of us, as many arrived by train,
planes, cars and bus.

The march had a message for the U.S., as we all prepare to do our best.

Men, ignore the negativeness, be strong as we are put to the test.

Today is the beginning of the begin, there shall not be no end.
We will unite as a great race, as we prepare to take our place.
We are in a state of revitalization, as we cultivate our civilization.
Claudia Thomas

Smokey

Who will you be today, Smokey? You have so many moods, so
many mysteries, so many faces for the world. Will you be the
steadfast friend today . . . passionate in your loyalty, eager to
take your place of honor in my lap? Will you be sensitive to my
feelings and ready to soothe each hurt with purrs and nudges and
other intimacies, or will you be cool and aloof, indifferent and
independent and determined to go you own way? Or will you be
someone else today?
To the world you are a puzzle, an enigma, a mystery too rich
in dark unknowns ever to be lit. But I have solved the riddle
that is Smokey, for I am much like you.
For you . . . and me, the world is still a place of wonder. We
experience each new day as a new adventure with new sights and
sounds and experiences to be savored. Turning our attention in
different directions, we explore the world around us and the
worlds within us, seeking to know, seeking to understand.
Because we are resolved to see things as they are, from many
different perspectives, we reveal the many perspectives of ourselves.
Christina Deming

Farewell My Friend

Many tears I shed for you my friend,
Many nights I sit trying to comprehend,
Only sad and angry emotions boil within me
Like violent waters rushing to meet the raging sea.

Question after question run through my mind,
I pray to God for the answers to find,
Still not sure what I am told
My heart tries hard, the pain to unfold.

Your beautiful words of wisdom ring in my ears.
Your gracious smile, I capture, will always be here,
I cherish the lessons and guidance you gave, my friend,
Fond memories of you, I will never allow to end.

My dearest friend, the golden gates of heaven there await
For you to march through into God's hand to take,
The guiding light will take you to a peaceful place,
No more worrying about having to win the race.

No more suffering, no more pain to fear
But in my heart you'll always stand clear
Like the glittering stars around the moon I see,
No more obstacles or traps, you are free.
Joan Allum-Oskoui

Birth Of Christ

It was a beautiful Christmas day.
Mary and Joseph were very gay.
There was a miracle that came to past.
Jesus, our Savior, was born at last!

The three wise men came to see
Jesus so beautiful as can be.
They brought myrrh, frankincense and gold;
Brought it only for Jesus to hold.

Jesus and I will never part.
I will give him a place in my heart.
Joseph R. Klima

God's Given Acres

Mountains and valleys, river and stream
meadows of color and pastures of green

The air is filled, with whiffs of grain
nourished in sun-light and bless-ed rain

With an everlasting peace of mind, what more
could I ask for, when this land is mine

I take on my chores, with tractor on fields, it moves
on with ease, without strain on it's wheels

The Lord is my shepherd, for He somehow,
gently takes hold of my hand and my plow

In the midst of day, by the spring running fresh,
I quench my thirst and bathe my flesh

The toil of man is richer by far, when his
friend is the earth and the good of it's worth

When tables are set and the hungry are fed,
with crops of my kingdom and Thy daily bread

I thank the Almighty, who looks down from above
for my wage in return . . .

is the Gift Of His Love
Anna Disimone

You People

YOU people
        mean nothing to me
YOU   are never on my mind
YOU   and your selfish hearts are worthless
YOU   will never know how it feels to be me
YOU   can never see the light shining in my eyes you
YOU   are someone I will never need you
YOU   who watches me fall you
YOU   will want to be by my side you
YOU   can say you understand you
YOU   might think you know what it's like you
YOU   can never see inside my mind you
YOU   will never know my thoughts you
YOU   meaningless and unimportant you someone I will never love
YOU   the horror in a child's dream
YOU people
        mean nothing to me

Christa-Althea Chiarenza

All Things Anew

Flowers stand straight, in first golden light.
Melody replaces, the long silent night.
Deer prancing through the lush green vines.
An owl hoots, through the whispering pines.
I lift my face to the soft cool breeze.
And notice the beauty of the big pine trees.
Everything sparkles with fresh morning dew.
As we start our day with all things anew.

Cinda L. Lynn

Free to Play

As the wind whispers
memories of how it was enter my mind
now I've come to realize
it is time . . .

Time to release the one I treasured most
who has shared all my dreams
the one who was close

The green grass and leaves have long gone
and the beautiful birds
no longer sing their songs

Happiness I have lost in my past
a lonely spell on myself I have cast

It is difficult for me to accept
that you have forgotten what we once had
but in a gloomy way
in these gloomy days, I am glad

For I am no longer there
to stand in your way
now you're in this earthly domain
free to play.

Jo P. Balaoro

Sweet Remembrances

Sweet remembrances of long ago
mutely etched in Winter snow.

Tree tops silhouette skies of blue
an eerie feeling of déjà vu.

I've walked this path with reflections small and
now I notice my shadow is tall.

The years have changed me but the picture remains
Because sweet remembrances never change.

Frances Joyce

"Thinking Of You"

As I sit an listen to the caressing breeze,
Memories of you speak, as the wind in the trees
When we were young, foolish, so in love,
Never thinking your love being in the heaven's above,
Now I am alone, memories of you on my mind,
Old dreams, thoughts, passing with time,
Must I be a prisoner of your love
Shall an answer come from the heaven above
To start my life anew, as thought we first met
When will time release your love when will I forget
May I find someone to love just as before
Happy in love, your memories no more
Sharing a new life, will my heart be free,
Always knowing your love will be part of me.

Francis E. Wells

These Things!

These things come to me . . .
memories, scenes from long ago in my childhood.
    Nothing ever dies, they just go away,
sometimes, they come back; others do not.
And when these things come to me I can't help,
but think of them with a mixture of sadness
and happiness. For those were the happiest for
me; yet the most sad because they can no longer
be; they are forever gone and can only come back
in my mind.
    Other things come to me, things that will happen,
I now talk of the future, not the past.
I see happiness as well as sorrow and pain.
I see death, but I also see new life.
Happiness comes and goes.
The sorrow of death will finally fade to dull ache,
and then nothing but fond memories and
disappointment for what could have been!

Jennifer Anderson

"The Village Of My Past"

Far away . . .
Midst this self-inflicted reverie,
Distant drums thunder through the chasm of time and space
To hear ancestral chimes
Of song
Of dance
Of laughter.

Childhood becomes a yesterday thing,
Today, I spill my guts
To caress the Gods of recent knowledge
Such cosmic transformation . . . part body, part soul
For a moment in this green and alluring pasture.

The drum beats on . . .
A cold, feverish sweat on an aching, convulsing body
Journey begun
Journey ended?
May send a reluctant self
To a speck of earth that history has not noted,
Where dreams were made and feelings flourished
And heart and spirit were everywhere.

Ivan Watson

Graveyard Postcards From Your Bathtub Heart

If I were a billion
  miles away
When you got your long lost
  graveyard postcard
And it broke
  your half-baked
    bathtub heart . . .
Would I still feel
  the awful pain . . .
Still taste the ugly
  salty tears
Go dripping
  down
  Our sad communal drain?

  Chet Mysliwicz

Memory Unsolicited

Bleak mountains - rocky backdrop for narrow winding road.
Model T Ford with parents and small child aboard.
Radiator steaming - then a sudden stop!
The car's on the edge of fifty foot drop!
Crumbling dirt - teetering slide can't be stopped!
It's a backward, agonizing ride!
How long? Who knew? Maybe a lifetime or two
Before the bottom is reached
With father, mother and child wedged in front seat.
Lucky for them, bed rolls and camp gear stashed in the back
Are strewn on the hillside with car wheels detached!
Parents grab child and scramble away
From a chance gas tank explosion should they stay!
Minutes pass by. The danger is over.
There's wonder with gratitude.
Just scratches and bruises that bother!
God spared their lives in Idaho that day
On a Summit called Galena
So remote in time, so far away.

  Bea L. Richardson

Common Place

   With arms open and eyes clear all our hearts come so near. A day a
month, oh so many years. The valleys and hills keep us afar, but
always the winds carry our calls.
   Always hopeful, endlessly gripping factual matter, and in one way
seeing a prosperous path, in another fear keeps the search alive.
   Living this distance stretches our bind-living this distance our
thoughts and ideals run afar.
   A new and alive a quiet peacefulness surrounds boisterous laughs.
The steady drone of a distant waterfall is swept through the falling leaves.
   Alas the winds need not blow so hard, nor shall we struggle with time.
For in a common place time stands still.

  Jeffrey C. Greene

Eternal Love

The flame of a candle reminds me of you, warm, caring, and
loving too.

The wax which is sliding down the side, is my heart which
you melt, when I'm by your side.

The stick is our souls mixed together. Our flame will keep
burning through all the bad weather.

The stand is our feet on which we will grow, together with
love in a constant flow.

Keep the fire burning, the wax steadily flowing. This way
we'll know our love will always be growing.

  Amy Abbott

Romantic Notions

Follow the fragrance of a lady,
most pleasant her air that lingers on.
Sets the mind to romantics wanderings,
like love in Spring-time makes me long.
Stole my senses and sent me reeling,
forever in a moment to dazzling heights.
Created true magic in her passing,
notice her total presence with delight.

In following the fragrance of a lady,
can you hear her melodious songs?
Like wings a - flitter and vivid colors,
her delightful distractions can't be shun.
So, enjoy the pleasure if only for a moment . . .
I'm sure most men would agree
that she's by far nature's gift most surely
and to man her beauty he will always see.

  Faries Williams Jr.

Dark And Light

Even the darkest life has glimpses of gold
Most slink away, while some clasp as need preside.
Rare those whose sunken best feels like, make bold
Reach for where Noble and Sublime reside.
She, untouched vessel welling with pure love
All good, simple truth tempered by strength
And beauty, glowing natures product of
Moon fair, anchored by family and faith.
Sweeping storm as like and unlike collide
In one alone and both together: Yet
Fear and fact of his dark nature decide
Clouds and rain overwhelm sun, leave weeping weather.
Time hath poured by and etched soft Memory torn
Lifted you remote, my last hope foresworn.

  David H. Lerman

Return To Innocence

You were born small and innocent.
Mother rocked you in her arms.
Mother kept you safe and warm.
Keeping you away from all the worlds harm.
She loved to see her babe smile in her loving arms.
A child so sweet.
A child so perfect.
A child for her to be proud.

Her child now grows distant.
Time leaves her mark upon the child's face.
The child turns into man.

The world now holds the man in its arms.
All the harm mother tried keeping from her babe is now holding the man.

The man grows cold.
His tongue spreads lies.
His eyes stop seeing the love he once knew.
His heart seeks lust.
His heart needs power and money.

His heart stops beating . . .

  Denise M. Searight

421

The Battle

With a dull heavy tread, like a storm cloud overhead.
Moves the march threw the wide plain so green.
A field for strife where men will fight, to protect what's rightfully theirs.
The ground which was green, now, is a bloody scene, with death looming overhead.
Though the battle is long and the fight rages on, I stand bravely
    and fight for my cause.
I stand tall and fight, for my own heart's delight.
To vanquish my enemy's breed.
Yet if the battle is true it's inside of you, the true battle lies in
your heart and mind.
So we must fight everyday with true grit and might to withhold the
    pressure so grand.
Choose your side between your heart and mind because the battle
    rages each day.
All skillful in war as I know you are.
Choose a weapon or choose none at all.
Choose logic or heart.
You must choose now for the battle has begun.
As night is in fight and the sun's in site I must leave.
As the cold dawn of death draws near.

Corey Johnson

Three Good-Byes To Mrs. Mermet

The first good-bye:
  Mrs. Mermet died!
  The church's loss.
  She done the work of three. I worked with her.
    So I guess I'll go say good-bye to Mrs. Mermet.

The second good-bye:
  Mrs. Mermet dead! Unreal.
  She was such a loyal usher.
  I did this with her for years. Could she cook.
    I must help with my club's yearly bash.
      I can't go say good-bye to her,
    but I'll send a pie to her home.

The third good-bye:
  Dead? Not Mrs. Mermet. A gash in my life.
  Her church was not mine, but her true-iron smile
  Vitalized our mutual fondness when we met.
  Would we talk.
    Sickness in my family makes a problem,
    but I will go say good-bye to Mrs. Mermet.

Dorothy Randle Clinton

My Wall, My World, My Tears

No one listens, no one hears
My cry for help as I drown in my tears.
As I lay behind my dark blank wall
I think to myself why must I fall.
As you stand so proud and tall
I shatter to the ground behind my broken wall.
My wall of tears, my wall fears
My wall that hides my world no one hears
My world put away like a letter unknown
I am shattered, broken, and torn.
I stand alone by myself, as you walk
by and stare and laugh.
You can not know the pain I hold
that will not let go to of my heart unknown.
Can you be so cold, so cruel that you
won't look inside at the warmth I hide.
The heart you hold, the warmth I
hide, the tears that lay by my side.
The tears that helped me weep
and the tears that let me sleep
The tears that let me forget the laughter that I hear
If I drown in my sorrow, if I
cry to many tears please don't pity me
because of what you hear.

Catherine Swarts

Diamonds By The Sea

Walking through the sands of life,
Much perils have arisen since that first day.
Found to fall at the least of things,
Was I, to be standing in strife.
Yet was I so susceptible and only having plebeian taste,
I finally found life to be:
Life is as finding diamonds,
Diamonds by the sea.
For through year of much reaching sorrow,
I found to be true, It is what others do with it,
The rest to you.
Though lightning, thunder wind, rain,
and His love eternally the same,
'Twas not all taken!
Rejoice with what remain.
Yet was I so susceptible and only having plebeian taste,
I finally found life to be:
Life is as finding diamonds,
Diamonds by the sea.

Curtis R. Wood

Untitled

I miss you.
My arms feel strange,
As though I must embrace you,
As though they feel how an embrace would feel
And yet hang empty.

I miss you so!
I want the step I hear on the stair
To be your step.
I want to expect that you might open the door.
But you won't come.

I know no change will come
Just because I want it.
To want with fiercest strength has never meant
That you could have.

These words I say alone.
You're gone and won't be back.
No anguish, fear, despair, regret; no grief
Will bring you back.

And with you gone
The good of life has all been lived.

Jean Rosenberger

Well Of Wonder

My mind floats adrift in a well full of words.
My mind finds my contemplation quite absurd.
Where is the master of my well full of words?
I wane and wish for those words yet unheard.

My eye peers to the sky and I wonder why.
My eye peers to the perplexity in the sky.
Where is the master of the luring sky?
I peek and ponder and wonder why.

My ears tingle with a wondering pride.
My ears hear and aware I assert and abide.
Where the master speaks to me from inside.
I seem and sigh and try to reason why

My mirror tells a very tainted tale.
My mirror peers to peek just as well.
Where the mirror speaks to tell me to tell.
I found GOD in myself within my well.

Darby

It Hurts

At this moment I feel an emptiness.
My deepest feeling one of such sadnesses.
The shame as one part of me lets the other down.
My memory taking me back, how I felt there by
your side. The rush, it was happiness like I've
never known.
You see, I was with a friend and there she was
I found so many smiles as I held her close, we
danced, she held me and oh how I held her.
With the seasons telling of what could never end.
And now, the shame as one part of me lets the other down.
The fear, for now I have learned and know
nothing is forever.
It hurts.

David Thompson

From The Eyes Of A Patient

I am weak now and uncertain.
My diagnosis cannot be forgotten.
To fill my needs I touch a button.
Sometimes I feel so dependent and in despair.
A feeling that I have regressed to childhood.
I am not in control, my environment is unfamiliar
    and I am so frighten.
I need understanding and patience some
    kindness with caring.
Please understand I have not chosen this illness.
I would like to be able to function as a whole person.
You the nurse are my savior and I depend on you
    to fill my functional needs.
I want you to know I appreciate you and
thank you for your loving care.

(In Memory of John E. Foy Jr.)

Donna Foy Jones, R.N.

Process Of Life

My love flounders in the wild wind, as it blows rapidly across
my face blowing my hair all around.
I sit quietly on the soft, bleached, white sandy beach.
The ocean waves roll onto the shore roughly pushing the sand
and leaving them there.
The little children run quickly to throw the jelly fish back in
the water, saving as many lives as possible, before they drown in
the soft sandy beach to their slowly but silent death.
Just think what a death like that would be like.
Being buried alive with no love, friends, or family.
Dying with no one noticing you're missing, like your never
existed.
Death is such a sad, but wonderful thing.
Dying slowly to that wonderful pleasant place waiting for you
when the process of life is done.

Joy Neely

Traveling Water

As the snow began to melt, streams quickly formed and ran down the
mountain side. Six streams headed for a miniature box canyon where
three hills of the mountains met. Three streams fell over the end
of the canyon and three streams fell over the side. Then they all
flowed together forming rapids that raced down the mountain side.
The rapids then became a brook that hurried on its way to the river
in the valley that would carry the water to the sea.

Alyce M. Nielson

"My Fantasy"

When you first entered the room
My heart pounded and my body zoomed

When I saw the ring on your hand
I said "Damn" — he's a married man

The past six months went by so very fast
Thank goodness — you're a free man at last

I had no idea we would become so close
Our friendship is definitely better than most

You always know what to say
To make me smile and brighten my day

You're always in a pleasant mood
And knows exactly how to soothe

Making love is a very special treat
Especially when I'm with you between the sheets

It didn't take me long to know you are a nice guy
Strong, intelligent, sweet and fly

Thanks for fulfilling my fantasy
It was everything I had imagined — I was quite pleased

We may not know what the future holds
But, I will always remember you deep down in my soul

Deborah Jewell

Awake Without You

As night falls and the moon rises, once again
    my heart professes it's undying love for yours,
    and as a blanket of stars cover the night's sky,
    my day dreams and night dreams become one inspired prayer.
A prayer of reuniting two into one. One body, one spirit, one love.
Destroying the loneliness and giving life to a new soul.
    A soul with two hearts that beat as one.
But alas the moon must stumble into it's deep sleep and
    just as the sun must awake for another day, so does
    my love awake without you . . .

Denise De La Torre

Where Smiles Are Born

I don't know why she makes me smile, but she does
My heart starts to sing just because
she is near.
There's a brightness in her eyes, hers alone,
that penetrates my soul; let it be known
that although we just met, we speak
without words.
Do I hear stallions galloping? Thunder?
Or is it my heart, I wonder,
at the thought of why she makes me smile.
To this end I must know
whether be still or simply go
To a place where smiles are born
and lonesome hearts embrace.
But will she enter this realm with me
of endless possibility?
For though she makes me smile, you see
Does she smile with thoughts of me?

Jay C. Harden

Moving

We've changed we've grown now it's time we've
moved on.
The thoughts, the feelings, and times here
will always be fond.

Erin Kelly

Reflection Upon Pieter Van Aelst's "Massacre Of The Innocents"

How many it has slain!
Mykris—
How it drools the crimson salve of
Many a man-child's bowels.
It heals the land,
Our land.

'They must die!' I have heard
Screamed through dust-fluttered streets now
Strung with small, fleshy bundles that our dogs
Make wishes upon.
Yet some . . .

'Faithless whores!'

Hide their children's wails beneath
Woven wombs
And their fingers pry at our faces
As our daggers weave through their children's pulp in
Ripping maroon rainbows
To beg our dreams to dwell.

   Douglas E. Carey

Under The Willow Tree

Thinking nothing but me, under the willow tree.
My life is half over, feeling scared some,
Wondering how long one must wait,
for all good things to come.
I keep the faith, most of my days,
Try to do good, in my own little ways.
Long ago, I found love,
But the ole mighty, needed him more for above.
Here I am thinking sorrow for me,
Under the willow tree.
Listening to the breeze, that rings the chimes,
dreaming ahead for precious times.
Hoping to find that magic key,
Under the willow tree.
Looking below, the stream still flows,
and with the stars above, sparkling a glow.
My heart still pounds,
praying it will be found.
Keeping my faith, yet thinking,
nothing but me, under the willow tree.

   Jill J. Neal

I Belong To Jesus

I belong to Jesus,
My life is not my own,
He shed His blood on Calvary,
To shield me from my wrongs.

I was lost and destitute my heart filled with despair,
Sorrow was draining all my strength it was all that I could bear.
My burdens had grown heavy from the evils of mankind,
I was reaching out for anything to ease my troubled mind.

But then I found my Jesus and put my life in His hand,
And I haven't had a burden since that He did not understand.
He healed my wounded spirit and guided me on life's way,
Now I belong to Jesus never more to stray.

Jesus I thank you for your blessings and I give my life to you,
'Cause without your tender mercy there is nothing I could do.
My life is not my own and I'm very glad to say,
That I surrender Jesus never more to stray.

Yes, I belong to Jesus,
My life is not my own,
He shed His blood on Calvary,
To shield me from my wrongs.

   Dorothy A. White

I Belong To Jesus

I belong to Jesus,
My life is not my own,
He shed His blood on Calvary,
To shield me from my wrongs.

I was lost and destitute my heart filled with despair,
Sorrow was draining all my strength it was all that I could bear.
My burdens had grown heavy from the evils of mankind,
I was reaching out for anything to ease my troubled mind.

But then I found my Jesus and put my life in His hand,
And I haven't had a burden since that He did not understand.
He healed my wounded spirit and guided me on life's way,
Now I belong to Jesus never more to stray.

Jesus I thank you for your blessings and I give my life to you,
'Cause without your tender mercy there is nothing I could do.
My life is not my own and I'm very glad to say,
That I surrender Jesus never more to stray.

Yes, I belong to Jesus,
My life is not my own,
He shed His blood on Calvary,
To shield me from my wrongs.

   Dorothy A. White

Twisting And Turning

My life keeps on twisting and turning
My mind, my soul and heart are always burning.
I know something great is going to happen only if I pull my
     life together.
I tell myself wisdom is knowing the difference between right and
wrong.
So live your life from day to day, but from drugs please stay away
If you don't your life will end
And you won't be able to know the difference.
So I looked up and saw the sunset.
It was different from any sunset that I had ever seen.
It was truly magnificent with some of the most vibrant and
beautiful
     colors.
Looking at the sunset made me forget all my troubles.
It gave me hope as I stood there and gazed into space.
I wish it would never fade, but as time went by so did the sunset.
Now these images are locked in my mind as if it was a dream.
Now I know what it is so see God's beautiful nature
And to know that our unhappiness can become hope,
While my life keeps on twisting and turning,
I've got to keep the faith, love God and live, hate God and die
Even while my life, still keeps on twisting and turning.

   Eugene A. Parkes

You

The moments we share are precious and few —
my joy, hope and energy renewed.
The warmth in your words ignite a spark,
that removes my soul from the lonely dark.

Bathed in the warmth of your smile,
I'm blessed to linger here awhile.
To find someone so dear,
it matters not if we are near.

A friend I've found in you,
through good and bad I will be true;
One on whom you can depend,
from now until the end.

A treasure I never knew,
I thank you for being, you.

   Daniel Bryant

A Letter From Heaven

Though many years have past and things have changed down there, I
know my mom and daddy love me and that they really care. But don't
worry about me mommy I'm the best that I can be and it sure is nice to
be able to sit on Jesus' knee.

Sis, though you never got to know me, I'm still watching over you,
you're doing good in softball and I'm so very proud of you, you know
if I could be there I'd be your biggest fan. Take care of mom and dad
sis, by doing the best you can.

To grandpa and grandma Stroman, thanks for every little toy, I've
passed them on to others and it gave me such a joy. I saw grandpa
and grandma Gowdy and they were holding hands, it sure is nice
to know they to were part of the masters plan.

It may be years before I see you, but I'll be waiting here with out
stretched arms to hug you, the ones I hold most dear. So I want for
all my loved ones and all my other friends to believe in God's great
promises before their journey ends. So just reach out and touch
God's loving hand and he will draw you near.

I have to end this letter now, so to all of you down there, just put
your trust in Jesus because he really cares.

Iva Grussendorf

A Mother's Prayer

Lord, thank you for the gift of life
  My tiny babe you made;
You lent me for so little time,
  I wish she could have stayed.

I never knew this child you formed,
  Only held her in my palm;
But great is my loss and greater my pain,
  Her memory lingers on.

In sovereign wisdom you took her home,
  From earth she had to go;
Please tell her how I miss her,
  Tell her "Mama loves you so!".

Please wrap her in your loving arms
  And keep with tender care;
Remind her that I'll hold her tight
  Someday when I come there.

But until then I'll carry on
  Encouraged by Thy love.
I now can rest, you've done what's best,
  I'll trust my God above.

Elaine Fram Distad

Infernophobia

I crouch on the burning pavement,
My tough exterior melting as streams spill from my eyes.
Bedeviled, I had fled my netherworld address, but now
I reach into my frayed pocket and tearfully pull out
A loathed quarter that clinks into the rusted payphone.
I can just imagine the hell I'd get for skipping out.
Spray-painted gang symbols clutter concrete walls;
I want out, dammit, I just want out!
My mom's ardent response shocks me.
I thought she wouldn't care, but she's frantic.
Everyone was looking for me, and she's coming right away.
I was only trying to ditch the devil around me,
The rodents, the reek, the rogues, the wretchedness
That permeated my infernal life and neighborhood.
I wanted to prove to the world who I really was—
What I was truly worth; it was my right!
Gangfight gunfire thunders — Aiee!! —
I seize a sting in my gut—blood-bathed—
I lie on the burning pavement—I dim—
I cross the River Styx—and I crave my mommy's embrace.

Eric Krieger

No Healing

I dream of seeing roses bordering
  my unhappy heart,
While withering roses begin to break
  it apart.
They signify the absence of loved ones,
  determined to destroy my only someone.
Togetherness will never mend, the softest
  petals cannot love again.
Once fallen, deterioration begins, another
  available happy heart is still never
  seen to the end.

Joy Michelle Krimmer

What Time Is This?

What time is this?
My younger sister was killed 3 years ago
My father died this spring
My mother valiantly gropes
In this unending ring.

What time is this?
What is the common thread?
Where is the support I need?

Thanksgiving's a week away . . .
. . . I thank you God for each day.
Christmas is rapidly approaching . . .
  "Fear not, for behold I bring you good tidings . . ."

I know the answer is near
I feel the unspoken love around me
I feel the caring and the sharing.
And I need it, right now, right here!

". . . and His name shall be called . . .
And He shall reign forever and ever . . .
Hallelujah!" . . . and we sing.

Joy M. Steele

November

. . . after an Ozark Colorful Autumn
Pine Needles and Gold Dust, falling after fall . . .
Nature's menopausal leaves of brown . . .

Very still, you are, November,
Unnoticed and not raved about at all.

You are the bare tree before the crystal
  teardrops visit winter branches.

You are the strength after ALL is gone.

You are the power in your changing storms of wind and rain
  that must be present for the new to emerge.

You are the Great Pause between the seasons.
You are the Great Menopausal Change.

Carolyn Amrit Knaus, M.S., M.T.

States Of Mind

One state of mind is the state in which, I fulfill
my obligations to myself and others in the outside
world in which we share.

Another is to fulfill my obligations to my soul, and
eliminate the outside world for the time being, and
create the inner world which I share with my shadow.

The two states reflect upon each other, and thus
create the ultimate state.

Donald Larsen

Cheated Oil

The shadow essence of an untrue love
Neatly assorted on the wall
The paper recollections brag of my ignorant slip
In his eyes
And what of those eyes?
In the perilous pursuit of passion
What face did his memory grasp?
Maybe the wary soul of another insecure
Or the filthy character of an angel fallen
Love turned vengeance
In his absent feelings of guilt
Cogitations I own transform to fury
Contemplating the different insides to water and oil
Understanding only I hold the oil,
And he owns the water

Jessica Andrea Hernandez

Moving On

Always running from an unexplained emptiness,
Never stopping for fear of self-examination.
Always hoping to move on and forget the past,
Never realizing how the yesterdays affect the tomorrows.

What is it that is so hard to face?
They say understanding comes with time.
What is it that keeps holding you back?
They say you could make it if only you'd try.

If only you could try to forget the pain,
That aches in your heart as a constant reminder.
If only you could try to forget the love,
That once was felt so powerful and strong.

Jennifer Trapp

"Emotions"

All ye, all ye, all set free!
No longer will you remain imprisoned in me!
Anger . . . the sharp, bitter taste!
Worry . . . the precious time you waste!
Fear . . . the joys you deny me!
Courage . . . I know "you" won't flee!
Denial . . . you blind, stubborn fool!
Confusion . . . the havoc over which you rule!
Sorrow . . . sip the tears, before they overflow!
Defeat . . . I'm someone, you'll never know!
Happiness . . . pledge to me, devotion!
Love . . . you precious, abundant, emotion!
Go, drain, you're drowning me!
My soul is dying, hurry!
All ye, all ye, all set free!

Jill D. Weidman

Remains Of You

Pain, so searing
my body wants only to surrender its being.
A void, so tremendous
no person can ever hope to fill it.
Tears, so abundant
only a storm can compare.
Questions, so many
will forever remain unanswered.
Forgiveness, that came so easily before
eludes me now.
Hate, so prevalent now
consumed all good feelings for you.
These feelings, so new to me,
is all that remains of you.

Heather P. Gill

Realize In Yourself

There comes a time in your life
No matter your age, be it 5, 15, 23, or 37.
It happens: Maybe when you cross the street,
Or get your mail, check out at the store,
Accept a delivery or look up in the library . . .
You find some eyes looking at you
Attached to a face; perhaps the same sex as your own.
The repression rushes over you, feeling
Constricting, heavy, unhappy and unfulfilling
To name but a few. Perhaps the lies and denial
Have finally overcome your personal damn.
Suddenly you realize you desperately hope for those eyes,
Those other eyes . . .
To look at you with affection, concern, understanding
And love; yes love. No different than any heterosexual.
So you realize, in truth to yourself, that you are gay.
Accepting with a freedom of spirit, the love
From another, like yourself, with pride.
Welcome Home.

Heather K. O'Brien

To Die For . . .?

Friends are friends, right?
No! Not this one,
She was special.
When all else fails, follow your heart,
and meet your soul.
That's what she is, my soul.
Nobody could take it away. Never.
For if I lost her, I would perish.
I could never smile or laugh again.
Even God's loving arms could not pull me away,
from the sorrow I felt.
Nor could I resist the temptation of losing the rest of me.
My heart would be empty and lonely.
Only cold air would touch my body,
and only I'd breathe the darkness from the sky.
Never again would sun touch my face,
nor music reach my ears.
Life would be lost.
That's how much she means to me.
So tell me, are friends just friends?

Amy Justen

When You Left Me

When you left me,
No other lover there could be
To take your precious place
For you were always my "Ace."
We said "Hi",
But we never said "Goodbye."
Whenever I cry,
I always ask myself "Why
did you have to go away,
why couldn't you just stay?
We shared so many memories, good times, and fun
we were great together, we were number one.
I think about you all the time.
There's not a day that you're not on my mind.
From the very start,
You always had a place in my heart
I was there by your side
Until the day you died.

Janice A. Ross

Dear Love

I walk alone among the trees
  No sounds there be, but for these . . .
A murmur, a tinkle, of a tiny stream
  Forever on to what must be,
No birds warble to the sun . . .
  No forest creature poised to run.

I walk along among the trees
  In search of why? These things must be . . .
The light grows dim- the shadows fall
  To ease the pain, the grief, to comfort all.

Perhaps its best we never know
  The why or when, the call to go.

I walk along among the trees
  In hope that time the hurt will ease.
Someday I know the trees will part the path will end
  And waiting there, my Doll, you'll stand.

Until then, my Dearest Love, I walk alone —
  In the silence of the trees-
    Eldred A. Pilant

The Real World

This is the Real World.
Not everything goes your way.
You have to live in the now,
And take things as they happen.
You can't plan the future for
It may not happen the way you plan.
Sometimes people say things they don't mean
And you get offended.
In your mind you say what you will do.
It may not happen the way you plan.
When things go your way
Don't get your hopes up too high
But make sure they stay your way.
It may not happen the way you plan.
People come and people go
But there are more people out there
And one is just for you.
It may not happen the way you plan.
For this is THE REAL WORLD . . .
    Daniel Oftring

Soar Like An Eagle, Please

I wanted to keep you with me, safe, free from harm, but you were
not happy, you needed to be free.

I had hopes you would soar like an eagle if I could just open the
door and set you free.

You flew out the door, taking my heart with you.

I see you now, your wings clipped, fluttering about trying so hard
to fly but, never leaving the ground, beating your wings so hard
against the wind needing so desperately to be free, flying high in the sky.

Fly. Fly away. Fly my beautiful bird for I love you, so you must be free.

Go. Go and make me proud for you'll always carry my heart on
your
wings.

Soar like an eagle, please!

Happy and free . . .
    Cindy Dodson

Old Plumbers

Of all the tradesmen that I know, the Plumber is unique
Not only knowledge must he show, but have a strong physique

To be a plumber in yesteryear, required considerable skill
Working with lead was his career and making water run uphill.

He brought the liquid into the sink, in bath tubs it did flow
The outside Jon became extinct, he brought joy to Jane and Joe

The old plumber was a friend to man, the Nation's health he did protect
His unique skills were in demand, as he gained wide-world respect

Progress was made as years went by, new materials supplanted lead
Old plumbers were forced to try the new techniques that lay ahead
The new and modern plastic pipe, he cut it with a saw
He used a solvent of a type that satisfied the law

The laws old plumbers are governed by, are codes and diverse rules
But old plumbers never die — they just cannot use their tools
    Cecil Freeman

Armored Flight

Exit the daylight, enter the night
Now is the time for me to take flight
Encased in armor, with wings extended
Now is the time for this war to be ended

Many have tried and all have failed
But death took their souls as their screams wailed

I am the master of all I perceive
Like a spider I live in the web that I weave
Anger and hatred are all around
Corpses are buried in shallow ground

The picture is an ugly one, the colors grim
But their lives fade, as daylight grows dim

Night is coming, it is my time to fly
Time for the leaders to pay for their crimes

They send out the soldiers, with no sense or reason
Any opposition is considered to be treason

No one can stop them, or so they believe
But one man is coming, to make them bleed

My name is Vengeance, my creed redemption
Payback is coming, there shall be no exceptions
    Edward Kraynak

1:00 A.M.

I light three candles —
  Not to be alone in the darkness.
As the lights near me flickered, look.

The trees stirring outside my window,
A scene that for three nights prior
Stood quiet and still and magical,
All aglow in the strong light of a full moon.

A storm now brewed — in that same spot.
The noise, excitement and fear won't let me sleep.
The trees swaying in the heavy winds,
Graceful but powerful,
Like an elephant's trunk as she dances in the parade.

The leaves that are still on the trees,
Whipping each other around,
Look like faces in an audience
Laughing and bobbing their heads at the "joke."

Doesn't bother me —
  any of it —
I have my three friends.
    Doris Cunningham

Untitled

Youth in peace and kindness giving,
no more will walk among the living.
A soul so free and a body so strong.
Living life as one whose time is still long.
Taken away in an instant from this.
That we will never again have chance for a kiss.
This baby, this boy, this young man of late,
newly touching life, never wondering of his fate.
Life seems so peculiar, full of wonder and time.
Death seems so final to those who remain behind.
Why was he taken from those who loved him so dear?
Never causing in life, but in death too many tears.
My friend was one of the rarest of kinds.
Caring, considerate, thoughtful and mine.

Cheryl Heckbert

April Snow

"Occasional rain", the forecast told.
Not unusual for April,
especially in our town where weather is bold,
and most anything goes,
even late spring snows.

Sure enough, it happened again —
the mercury slipped in the midst of rain.
The flakes were graceful as they fell;
but with sticky wetness they clung
persistently to branches now low-slung.

Next morn we were greeted
by an eerie sight —
in April, Christmas white.
The crocuses were heavily covered,
and the robins wondered - were the worms smothered?

The stark beauty was there for all to behold;
but, alas, there is more to be told.
Out came the shovels, salt and plows,
as again we rose to attack the snows.
How else can we find how our garden grows?

Donald W. Ramsey

Heart Murmurs

"If your father really loved you . . ."
Note well the words you voice.
They can empower and create
or damage, mar, destroy a fragile spirit
in process of becoming.

"If your father really loved you . . ."
Words uttered from the depths of
shattered dreams and broken promises
were not meant to hurt, but to tranquilize
the writhing self-blame of an agonizing child
who died within that day.

"You are profoundly, deeply loved,"
child of mine, children of the world.
Listen to the whispered truth in silence.
You are our only hope of rediscovering
the mystery and awe of abandoned innocence.
You challenge us to heartfully embrace
precious gifts of forgiveness, love,
and fullness of life!

Helen T. Smythe

Alone

Sometimes you feel completely alone;
nothing and no one to call your own.
Every day is like another day in hell,
but when does it end? No one can tell.
Life's just a lonely room with four bare walls;
no walks in the park and no trips to any malls.
You listen to your voice echoing in the night,
remembering when you used to put up a fight.
Now, I'm all alone and I couldn't care less
because this is who I am, at least I guess.
Now, this way, no one can break my heart,
rip it to shreds, or tear it apart.
After a lot of experience love's not worth the trouble
because every time you fall, someone bursts your bubble.
I think I'll remain alone because I know I'll be protected
from that cruel, harsh world outside and the
feelings that are affected.

Christine Deane Garber

And A Branch Scrapes Against The Window Pane

She sits alone in the painful silence
Nothing breaks the screaming quite
Nothing stirs
And a branch scrapes against the window pane

A sad and lonely sound
Like some sad thing wanting in
Or in her mind something wanting out
And as she sits in a room among the blues and greens her thoughts
run in her head like an old possessed movie projector running wild
And a branch scrapes against the window pane

A whimpering, pitiful sound
Like the cry from her heart as she looks at the old and dying thing
A thing wasted and spent
Too late she sighs
And a branch scrapes against the window pane

A desperate and mournful sound
Like the moans from her soul
As she holds out hope for those wasted lives
But a faint and whispering sound stirs her to hold out that hope
And a branch scrapes against the window pane

Amy K. Bailey

Grandchildren

As a mother my children are everything to me,
Nothing in this world more precious could there be.

My life was complete when my children were grown,
And I saw them married and starting lives of their own.

Little did I know that the best part of life was yet to come,
And it all started with Grandchild number one.

He touched my heart in a place it had never been touched before,
It's a wonderful feeling I will cherish and hold onto for evermore.

Grandchildren are your second chance to make your mark,
With love and wisdom and enough hugs and kisses to fill their hearts.

You have the best of both worlds and can make the rules as you go,
Have fun, enjoy, spoil them rotten and never say no.

Grandparenting is the ultimate unlike parenting which is sometimes the worst,
If the process was reversible I would have had my Grandchildren first.

Darla A. Corsette

And So It Is!

Emptiness . . . loneliness . . . buffeted in a void . . .
Nothing to cling to . . . no one . . . devoid . . .
But it will pass, it always does!
It just makes you wonder, what will be, what is, and what was!
The climb is slow from nowhere to somewhere . . .
Each footfall laden with disappointment and despair.
But with each higher movement you can see the stars shine
You know you're coming out from under and behind.
You resume what you believe in and what you know that "is"
You stand back on your feet and get back to "taking care of biz"
And so it is, until the next time you fall . . .
And so it is, 'til you hear the call . . .
And so it is, that you emerge as a whole . . .
From the depths and the shadows of the crevices of your soul.
And so it is!!

Elaine Kalatta

In The Darkness Of The Night

It's a dark, damp, and cold night.
Nothing to eat, no where to sleep in the darkness of the night.
I have no shoes, I have no socks, no sweater not even a coat in stock.
This isn't fair, I say to myself, in the darkness of the night.

My body is cold and chilled to the bone;
I am a homeless man looking for a home.
A homeless man living in the city streets,
A homeless man looking for a place to shield me from the rain,
snow and sleet.

In the darkness of the night, my belly craves something to eat.
Tonight and every night, hunger grips my soul,
But the real story could never be told
When you come face to face with the darkness of the night.

The only warmth I'll feel tonight
Will come from my bottle of wine
Which only cost me a nickel or dime,
For this is the way I spend all of my time.

I beckon to you far and near,
I need you to lend me your ear.
Want to come — for I am near,
A homeless man's plea has been made clear. Help!

Beulah Hemby Roach

The American Choice

In twelve short years the country was economically buried,
Now both sides claim to want to fix it in a hurry.
Thanksgiving may give us a loud, boisterous lizard,
Since a decision to run comes after his eating the gizzard.
The two party system is overloaded with dribble
And we may again have to vote for the lesser evil.

There must be "good men" who might vie for the presidency,
But look at the cost to the person and his or her family.
No one is sure who represents the common man
And that's where most people are who must really give a damn.
The proposed tax break will not help the common working class.
Obviously they feel that the laboring force also spells jack-ass.
Who cares about political party or christian right or left views,
While within the needs of our country we may all loose!

Anthony Torres

I Dream

I can dream clearly
Now that you are gone
I wake up in the morning and
I actually have stories to tell
I see the world in red, green, blue and yellow
Not just black and white
My breath has come back
The air is no longer stifled

I can dream clearly
Now that you are gone
I wake up in the middle of the night
With sweat on my brow
Dreams of lions roaring, butterflies flying
Mockingbirds singing, and women
Lots of women dancing wild and free

I can dream clearly
Now that you are gone
Now that you are gone
Clearly
I dream

Cecelia Harshaw

A Second Chance

"As for man, his days are as grass . . ."
Now we know mortal life shall pass
Each day is a gift to savor and treasure
To reach for the goals that we've missed by measure
To give of ourselves as never before
To right any wrongs from the days of yore
To retrieve our trespasses as we've been forgiven
To prepare while we live for the gates of heaven
Leaving on earth with those whom we love
Fond memories yet to be spoken of

Eleanor E. Brenneman

You Left Me

My love, you meant so much to me.
Now you're gone, your face I no longer see.
I never wanted you to leave, especially to die.
Now I feel so low and I'll always know why.
There is a place in my heart that will never be filled.
Now that you are no longer living and your breath has been stilled.
I am asking God why, and listening for a sound.
Letting me know that later in life I won't feel so down.
We've had some times together, both good and bad.
And now I am all alone and it makes me feel so sad.
When I think of our love and how much we shared.
My pain is lessened knowing how much you cared.
Oh, that you died and left me so.
You know I didn't want you to go.
My love, I wait until the time will be.
When your face, I shall surely see.
Bye my love, my sweet one, for your life has ended.
At least until this gap between us has been mended.

George H. Cebrynski

Sorrowbirds

Singing all night chirping all day in their own special way.
Not songs of joy or songs of happiness.
Songs of the sorrowbirds.
Sorrowbirds cry.
Sorrowbirds try.
They try to be loved.
They try to be cared for.
Still they cry.
Still they try.
Singing alone, chirping alone, still a sorrowbird.

Jenny Shotwell

The Coral Tree

When my Love is shy and hides from me
nowhere in the house to be found
I become window bound
face to a mute and desolate sea
framed by an ever green Coral tree
Come says a voice, look at my skin of bark
smooth and dark
with translucent blue veins showing through
at my slender limbs, crossing, touching
as yours do in a shared hammock, sleeping
Look at these childish legs
issued from my womb of wood
I for ever give birth
nourished by a generous earth
With my head in the ground
my feet stretched to the sky
my arched back ready to leap and fly
I gather shade in my skirt of leaves
Come cool your fever at my side
the two of you often come here to hide

Colette Larra

My Dream

Far, far away I will go,
    O'er the flowing river,
Beyond the high mountains and hills,
    To a place never seen before.

My place where I can be alone.
    My place where I can think, where I can dream.
A place where I can get away,
    Where there is peace, where there is love,
Where there is care.

To the place I've dreamt about all my life.
    A place where I can get on with
My life the way it was meant to be.

I have only one life to live,
    So I might as well live it to
My fullest!

    Far, far away I will go.

Joseph P. McNeill

The Hunted

Frolicking in the gay hills does the deer
O'er the master's meadows cut so clear
Wherein we did linger in the summer's breeze
Flowing through the hilly grasses and trees
Knoweth now the deer its time for it a hunter chaseth
Up and down rocky inclines that the man loseth his breath
Sport it seems to the man seeing the cotton tail
But nay he knows he's sport to what time wilt for him entail
Long through the chase the deer doth pause looking aback
Leaving betwixt the two a ravine which hurrieth his attack
Bracing his musket and aiming for the eyes he sought a prize
Yet in the moment of the shot sprang did the deer
And the force of the gun moved loose the rocks clear
So that down went the man falling with such surprise
That then only knoweth he the hunted, death the more wise.

Douglas Ryan Brown

City Lights

Alone in the night, looking down on the light
    Of a city's evening attire,
I muse in the glow that the lights down below
    Are a thousand flickering fires.

Who lies be each flame, wondering what they became?
    Who tends the fires all night?
It is those who have missed the warmth of a kiss,
    Much more than just oversight?

Of childhood dreams, pounding thoughts, quiet screams.
    Years passed without feeling pain.
Until much older in years, then came the tears
    Of regret for what is inane.

Alone in the night, looking down on the light
    Of a city's evening attire,
I muse in the glow that the lights down below
    Are the flames of a souls desire!

Amy Welch

Dreamin'

Upon careful considerations
    Of a life long dream,
I came upon the conclusion to change to a bird,
    or so it would seem.

I would be able to fly above the earth
    and see things from a different view.
I could swoop down low when things were good
    Or soar up high when things weren't so.

When my wings became tired, I could sit upon a limb and wonder
    About life, which people hold so dear.
Life is the subject on which one could ponder.
    But no matter how much one muses,
    the reason for it never becomes clear.

Whether flying down low, or flying up high,
My dream could end with an arrow and a bow.
    Because living forever is only a lie.

So ending my dream and coming back to reality,
    I have to let my life begin
And come back to mortality,
    Or at least until I can dream again.

David Clark

Grandma

I had a vision the other night
Of a sagely lady dressed in white
Short and thin, yet emitting power
And in her hand she held a flower
A rose it was, she removed a petal
And all my fears began to settle

She spoke in a soft voice, yet loud and clear
And in her eye there formed a tear
"I miss you all," she said to me
She looked so sad, yet she seemed so free
"We miss you, too" I said to her
And I wished things could be the way they were

She ready my thought, "My time was done."
"But while you were here we sure had fun."
"I miss all the good times that we shared."
"And it was good to know that you really cared."
"You all walk not alone, remember this."
She bent over and gave me a warm, loving kiss.

The petal of the rose was struck by her tear
And the vision of Grandma disappeared

Daniel W. Myers

For The Birds

I turned around and a page has been turned
Of all the pages turned chapters have been made,
not written nor captured, but
distorted by my mind.
I remember those I wish;
I change those I do not like;
And I made up those that never happened.
We are seven, or so I wish to think.
Maybe numbers do not even matter.
The memory I have is always of summer.
There are only two to choose from, you see.
We are birds of every kind and of any time.
Each of us are of different species
and from different families.
We get together at sunlight
like free spirit fowls we are.
We gather around nights in search of flickering fire
not of lust, but of another desire.
We are birds of every kind and of any time.
We were birds, or so I always wish to think.

Jolly De Guzman

The Thoughtless Prayers Of A Dreamer

To thee, my Lord, I pray,
of amber leaves, and shallow dreams
and silver clouds of grey

To live by the rules of Death Himself,
to inherit the bulk of the poorest wealth,
to ride the waves of the calmest seas
and hear the buzzing of silent bees.

I see the sheen of green moon beams,
I know what it is, but not what it means.
The sun is colored a blinding black,
it's covered by clouds, but the lining's cracked

Endless beaches, that turn to grass
a hundred snails, rushing fast
hummingbirds, faster than time
tasting the nectar of the peach-colored lime

In this world I will fly,
up the stairway to heaven
never land, and never die
God grand me power, Amen.

Casey Dokoupil

Her Wish

Can you imagine the life that she led
Of bearing ten children then keeping them fed.
Just having ten children itself quite a chore,
But our mom was special, she could have raised more.
Her patience, her caring, and of course there's her love
She was lovely and precious a gift from above.
Our memories may be different though reality the same
For our love and our happiness were just part of her game.
Whatever we needed she'd try to come through
I miss her so much, I'm sure you do too.
God took her too soon, it doesn't seem fair
Nothing left here on earth will ever compare.
I pray that she's happy, that she's feeling no pain
A new life in heaven with much more to gain.
May we all keep our promise to always stay close,
The last thing she asked us, what she wanted most.

Carol Garrison

Serenity

The waning seasons and the sad eclipse
Of beauty, while their lips
Sing sweetly, as of old,
Eternal things in temporal unrolled.
And man, in his brief hour,
Is happy, too: his scope
Little extends beyond his little dower
And, knowing little, hath much room for hope.
But I, alas, alone.
Although immortal am bereft of peace,
In a world not mine own
Enacting fated sorrows and foreknown,
And yet unwilling, that my pain should cease.
I only of the Gods am yoked in love,
Having an earthly brother
Begotten with me from the lions of Jove.
Alta, unwitting mother,
Too late suspected on olympian strove
To be her mate. Else had the fatal law.

George John Guerin

A True Patriot

As I sit alone listening to the sounds
of fireworks, the anthem, and cheering crowds.
I think back to when I was home.
Sitting on the riverside waiting for the show.
The light is in the sky were so colorfully bright.
Able to light up the rocky mountain night.
I wish I were there.
Enjoying the cool, fresh air.
The forth of July parade.
The fireworks of independence day.
The land of the beautiful, the home of the brave.
I'm just a military man.
Fighting for freedom and my homeland.
Wearing the uniform and doin' what I can.
Living away from home.
Ready to be sent to a combat zone.
Feeling proud but feeling alone.
Remember me on independence day.
I'm the one who keeps it that way.

Jason F. Eldredge

America Revisited

America I've given you nothing and you're the s***.
Of Generation Why I can't assume,
But On the Road was not meant to have Cliff Notes.
So why is Kerouac collecting dust on night stands next to
ashtrays and toilet paper?
America keeping paying the lawyers and f***ing the teachers,
keep one profession noble.
Toss out your umbrellas and listen to nature, nothing's that important
Must I be black, gay, or politically correct to be heard, America?
America, Colin's a whore too, the journey led from your pocket into his.
If I must sell-out my past to buy a future to whom do I write the check?
America, please don't make me learn how to use my Commodore 64.
America, my life is passing me by and I didn't even know I had one.
Give me some life, America, don't let it trickle down.
Pocket quotation books in everyone's stocking.
Let's get John 3:16 out of the stadium and back into the church.
America, where is Carlo and what have you done with him?
Ann, I have no resolve, I'm into unchartered waters.
In Media Res — I finally know what it means.

Cam Martin

Forever Enemies

My tears are lost forever in the emptiness and the darkness
of his heart.
My one time love, my forever enemy.
My eyes reveal to him my hopelessness, my surrender.
My reasons for living, they have lost their purpose.
In the wickedness of his eyes I see his laughter.
In the emptiness of his soul I see his satisfaction.
To me, he is everything, my every reason for being.
To him, I am nothing.
Escape his only reason to pretend he loves me, to torture me.
My strength leading to my innocence he thrives on.
Hoping to destroy me he assures me that he loves me.
While, with every word his attempts to lie are known.

Ileane Lopez

The War

I often reminisce about the things I've seen and done,
Of lands afar, and people there, how governments are run.
I think of songs and tales I've heard, of customs quite unique,
Of stormy seas of placid lakes, of undercurrents and reefs.

I remember ships I've seen with bent and rusted steel,
Of knocked-out trains and airplanes, of craters in the field.
How men can maim and kill each other is hard to comprehend
Yet it goes on and on this way, when will it ever end?

Harvey K. Knutson

70th Reunion and Millennial Closure: 1930-2000

The vast winds of shifting galaxies, in the solemn mystery
    of new black holes, find fruition in
An infant's gurgle; human eyes record all things as
    inter-related: clearer, surer, better.

The mystic glow of sure-footed equations lights up
    man's unfailing tie to reality; what else
Have we learned: to eliminate want? to elevate
    breeding? to proclaim generosity without end?
Clearer, surer, better.

Is our boundless joy in God's world ahead of circuses
    and gladiators? The hunger to leave our mark —
Awakened in hallowed halls of remembrance was fanned
    by magical tomes still enshrined in our souls
As the shining prize: clearer, surer, better.

We jump into eternity, with no visible beginning or end,
    savoring the sweetness of an emerging smile.
The global dream, nurtured in Ithacan-lakes and rills,
    at last trickles home eagerly,
Enraptured by the always transforming now:
    clearer, surer, better.

Grace Blakeslee

"You"

There are so very few
of people just like you,

You filled me up with joy inside
with which I could never hide,

There are so many piles
of smiles after smiles,

You cheered me up when I was blue
But how could I think it would be anyone but you,

The presents that you did bear
Were not roses, but it was your care,

I know I'll always remember you
Because who was the one who cared?
Who?

Colleen Connors

Summer Sunset On West River (The Covenant)

Across the rippling surface
of the river's blue-green depths
there steals a ray of sunlight
more molten than the rest.

It widens, ever widens
before my enraptured gaze
and forms a bridge of rainbows,
wrapped in mists of purple haze.

All too soon the colors fading,
ruby red and vivid blue;
but in my mind remaining
though obscured from my view.

And it seems I hear a voice
like a whisper in my ear
that tells me to rejoice,
that my rainbow's always near.

For God has made a promise —
a covenant with man —
and the rainbow is the bridge
to cross to reach the promised land.

Betty R. Kurtz

James In August

On a hot August night, I met you on the corner
of two out of the way streets by your shiny, red car
under the flickering, electric orange light of a street lamp;
it was impossible to be inconspicuous.

On a sunny September afternoon I went to your Victorian house.
The lace curtains blew in the breeze and the unpredictable
Maine coon cat licked my toe, half buried in the thick aqua carpet;
you said I was lovely, in the way the English use the word.

I waited for you one windy October morning at nine o'clock
and the day went by so slowly, sitting on the worn, wooden stoop
wondering and watching shiny, scarlet leaves fall and all around;
at three o'clock I went inside, still certain I would see you.

You never came around and October ended on Halloween,
without one word from you about why, and the faded leaves
had all broken free of their branches and gathered on the porch;
I still remember the wind, the leaves and the waiting.

In November, we met on the street and you apologized for October
and extended your hand as if to make a peace offering
or close a business deal, and I said it was really nice to have met you;
I want to remember you — the way you were in August.

Debbie Pento

Earth Brown

EARTHBROWN
Old as creation, created in me
A devotion to the clay
From which was fashioned
The original mans' first mold
EARTHBROWN
Sun-kissed, skintone, speak
Of the life you spring forth
EARTH grown, all new,
All colorful, treasure for the world to behold
A New sense of worth Good Lord! I've found
For you've blessed me
Made me naturally EARTH BROWN
Not many more blessings can you send
Image of creation, Image of Birth
Image of the Beginning yes Lord!
Is what EARTH'S BROWN skin
is worth

Chuck D. A. Walters

"Advice From The Heart"

Many have spoken of equality
Often enough, from unequal points of view
Please lend me an ear for a second
As one places this into perspective for proper use

When angry, confused, depressed and/or exhausted
"I" is placed in front of any statement spoken or thought
There's no consideration, respect or room for another
To willingly give compassion, understanding . . . basic love from the heart

Without the proper wisdom and knowledge to assist
This heads straight into a cul-de-sac known as destruction
"Love is patient," is the first aspect given about hope
For this assures a clear path of options for construction

"Love never fails," is the last inexhaustible aspect of faith
Because uncertainty has a tendency to get in the way
Doubt causes an unbridled and enormous amount of fear
That blinds the view of the guidance, from within, displayed

When properly used, love is a formidable companion
With an open mind, there rests the ability to perceive
All that is needed to seek a peaceful solution
One full of grace, mercy, forgiveness . . . The essence of which is in need
Jean P. Juniel

The Tin Foil King

Let the secrets unfold from the soul untold
   Oh! Will you let me in?
I'll only sit and watch how you fit in the world in which you live.
I will not pry on even try to squeeze into your dream
Of scattered pieces, white and black
   under shadow of the crossed beam
Oh let me stay and quietly pray to the emptiness above
By candlelight all through the night
   'til on moonbeams flies the dove.
Let me lie for a very long while here beside the fire
To watch the dancing flames that pass
   from this marshmallow pyre
Let me walk and silently talk
   inside your second skin
And from your warmth a fire all my own
   may someday soon begin
And if you go cold and the fire old,
   around my campfire kneel
And reclaim the fire from inside me
   that from you I managed to steal.
Geraldine McDarby

Summer Solstice

Sticky and twisted she flies
on firefly's back tumbling sunshine
and tattered pages tastes of peaches
old quilts all brown and weathered
her grandmother's hands are over her again
swelling and smooth she gapes
at baby blue skies under his heaven
she is safe upon meeting
cool brown ground of the day old
sprinkler's dew she teases the grass
with her malnourished fingers toes in the mud
she stares lemony scents
disperse from her lions as she feels into air
and is feeling more alive breath is coming back
sugary dirt beneath fingernails
and smiling stomach her flesh
opens to itself inside
the dark past is escaping
and sticky and twisted she flies
on firefly's back to herself.
Aubrey Durrence

This, Our Creation

I will go now to visit old, sick men,
   Old warriors young when they for our defence
Went off to far-flung, foreign battlefields
   To brook the foeman's arrogance immense.

Old soldiers never die, they say, but some
   I see in these aseptic wards now pray
That they could die, and bid life glad goodbye,
   From postwar agonies could flee away.

The battlefields were rampant, rabid hells
   Where men went wild, their actions scarcely knew.
Are not these legless days in wheelchairs spent
   A hell for men who like the eagles flew?

Are not they who would minister to them
   All dying, too, in their own destined turn?
A paradox of sorts let none infer.
   Brave armfellows, their hearts for others burn!

Accursed our hoary, now genetic strife
   Since Cain, accursed, his brother Abel slew!
Oh, fated curse, this modern spawn of wars
   That makes us enemies, both me and you!
Everett Francis Briggs

"Read" Or Listen To The Call!

Come one, come all, and listen to the call,
of the written word, the spoken word both far and near.
Come dance with me, through the pages of romance and mystery
Take flight, across the sea to read, is to be alive, inside.
Eleanor M. Hudo

A Special Night

Warm evening walks in the nights
on the cobble stones in the city lights

People dinning on the sidewalks
with flowers and special talks

Dressed so nice with a dab of cologne
I keep quiet from the danger zone

Horses galvanating at a slow pace
with couples staring for a kiss on the face

Taxi drivers so wild and mean
but nothing tears me from being so keen

I walk pass the beeping cars
and gaze at the crowded bars

Holding me by the hand
It's great being equally in demand

Side by Side
with a look in his eye

Hating to say
GOODBYE!
Antoinette Simmons

Carpe Diem

The sun touches down beyond the bay
On the horizon awaits another day
And tomorrow we'll see the sun rise out of the sea
And memories of yesterday are alive in the ocean breeze
Creating a scene with a special touch the moon lights the bay
And tomorrow we'll seize another day.
Edward A. McCann

Untitled

There's a beautiful church, on top of a hill,
on the land of flowers called Florida.
And in this church there is the most
wonderful choir and an organist
that plays like the angels.
The members of this choir work
together in harmony, like no
other choir I have contacted.
They are good and kind in their
daily lives and live just for others
and I hope when I get to the great
beyond that we shall all be
there and sing together.
To the glory of God, forever and ever.

Doris Bueckner

October Fantasy

October fantasy fills the air
On verdant leaves I see changes there
Autumnal mystery, display your song for me
Engendering rhapsodies rich with flair.

Amid its flaming garments fashion's wear
With tossing gestures bright, putting on aires
Vermilion eyes I've seen, peeking through evergreen
A painted wondrous scene beyond compare.

Ribbons of falling leaves, not a care
Among the husks and sheaves, their bounties share
In every arbor glade, red, yellow and orange cascade
A full and lush parade of harvest fare.

In the breezes leaves drift down to bear
A softest ecstasy, nature's affair
As the warmth aspires, to trim enchanting fires
The Indian Summer bids us to admire.

When the daylight fades, it lingers there
October fantasy, a vision rare
Hinting of Halloween, a Jack-o-lantern's dream
All saints a spirits smile, laugh and gleam.

Barbara Baczek

White Kid Gloves

She woke up to a sunkissed day,
One not too hot in the month of May.
She'd traveled far to see her man,
And in the church, she posted her bans.

He'd left her several months before,
To look for land and build a store.
He found a spot in a town called Austin,
But it was far, so from Boston.

There were hills around and lakes galore,
But the Indians and ranches were true folklore.
It was rough country, wild and untame,
But nevertheless, on a train she came.

The church bells chimed, it was time to go,
To the altar and say her vows to her beau.
She opened her trunk and placed on her hands,
The white kid gloves that matched her headband.

They were purchased in Boston to match her dress,
They were silky and smooth, like a soft caress.
She'll keep them forever, but wear them today,
And preserve them for her daughters who'll marry someday.

Deanna J. Dougan

Untitled

One tear rolls down my face not in fear but in grace.
On word falls out of my mouth, why? Why does the world have
     to be so cruel?
I don't know why or if I want to know why. I just want some
answers about life.
Why are we here, is it for love or is it for fear? Are we here to
     listen to the wind blow?
Or is it to learn how to take it slow?
Why are we hear, for laughter or for fears, loving or for tears?
This world is a crazy place, love has been dangled in front of my face.
A blank look at space is my only place too find love and inspiration.
I look up at a black sky and suddenly I don't want to die.
Instead I laid own and cry. And all I can do is wonder why.
Why this world is a crazy place, all I get is a lonely pace.
The pace I set as I walk alone. No one to follow, or a place I can call home.
And all I can do is wonder why.

Aaron W. Kuehn

Becoming

What time is, now!
   Once forever hoping . . . to be,
     just outside our reach.
Always striving to keep up.
   Like water held, slips away . . .
     tomorrow, our fret; we lose today!

What time is, now!
   Our joy contained in things obtained . . .
     to strive for dust the wind has claimed.
Our hearts we break, our focus dim.
   We see not past what we take in . . .
     the loss of becoming, our greatest sin!

Jan Michael Cohen

Heroes

I see no Heroism in dramatic public exploits.
Only those enduring Suffering, are Heroic.
Within this anguished Fellowship,
Are those who have found Pain to be a Lord of Man
More powerful than Death itself.
It is because of Pain we ultimately perish,
For then; the Flame of Spirit wanes.
And Life may only be sustained by other Heroes,
Brave enough to scale the barrier walls of human hopelessness,
Immuring those in Pain,
Within the darkened habitat of Human Agony,
To lead them out into the healing Light of Day.

John F. Zaleski

To Celine and Dave

To the church the people will go,
On this special wedding day we know,
To exchange their vows for all to see,
Will be the most important key,
For Celine and Dave will be married,
Over the threshold Celine will be carried,
On their special day,
For the bride and groom we will pray,
To the altar Celine will carry,
A rose from her bouquet of flowers to the Virgin Mary,
Their parents will be full of joy,
If Celine and Dave have a boy,
If Celine and Dave have a girl not a boy,
Their parents will still be full of joy.

Anthony De Curtis

The Family Unit

It seems the family unit just isn't the same today.
One of the parents are at home, the other has moved away.
The family unit is being ripped apart, for so many reasons.
And it doesn't matter when it is, it has no time, no seasons.
It's happening more and more with each passing day.
One left with false hope, they'll be happy again someday.
It leaves our children feeling lost, unwanted and wondering why?
And when the one whose left behind has no answers, all they do is cry.
For then this creates resentment for the lost one's left behind.
And the parent at home to help them believe that "We will be fine!"
For the family unit isn't scared no more, it's falling apart.
And with it's destruction, it brings and leaves a lot of broken hearts!

Gwen M. Fisher

When We Were Young

Two little sparrows nestled in a tree
One represents you, the other me
Shy of the feeling and loving it too
Knowing together we'd never be blue

It took five years to get us together
But this true feeling will last forever
No one can take us apart
Because this started in our hearts

As time goes on our love grows deeper
And the hills of life are even steeper
Without love, faith and God's grace and love
We would never make it on earth or above.

Elsie W. Peterson

My Way

   I was born on the banks of a hot muddy river. The child of
one stupid, steamy night. Born to room beneath the sun. What
do you think of me, I'm better left alone. I met an old man. He
said he knew the way. And he would like to show me so my life
wouldn't go astray. He told me, "Take my hand child - now little
boy don't be afraid. I'll take your soul and walk on water."
"But old man, you don't understand. The cuts on me, they run
much deeper. Old man, you righteous man, I've been shown the
way a thousand times—not one a keeper." Then he said, "I'll tell
you boy, you planted rotten seeds. And in the land of happiness,
they'll grow us evil trees. Guided minds and eyes that will never
see. Old man, I'll tell you what it is I believe. I gotta look away.
Old man, you gotta believe in what you see. I don't need your
spells or the little games you try to pull on me. Come to think
of it I don't need your religion. I gotta get away. I wish you
would understand. Everybody prays. Let me find my own way!!!!

Dale L. Sullivan

"Nine Roses For A Bloody Lip"

Blind black eyes, bruised brown skin,
One woman cries, man thinks he wins.
Love tolerating rages, powerful blows of hate,
Life inside of cages, trapped by your soul mate.
Commitment requires strong bones, in this painful relationship,
Never wanting to be alone, nine roses for a bloody lip.
Others see the hidden marks, so who's the one in the dark,
Believing each time is the last, only staying to relieve the past.
A life full of constant pressure, find yourself on a stretcher,
Or in a box six feet deep, say your prayers before you sleep.
Cycles never end once they start,
Find love for yourself in your heart,
When he raises a hand, it's time to take a stand,
She's gone and out the door, he's life to live no more.
When reality is a slap in the face, all the answers fall into place,
Under a brutal fist, true love never lies,
Weak man never wins, strong woman sighs,
Tired of bruised brown skin and black eyes.

Dana Zadia Hardy

I Would Be If I'd Only Give In

Only true comfort is found in the uncomfortable
only in the place you don't belong do you most fit in
there is great peace to be found outside of yourself
for in dependence you are found again

I struggle and fight to be the one
I push and pull to fit in
I search for the right formula
I would be if I'd only give in

Yet time and time the same rings true
for through His image I see
there is a way that I should live
I know what I should BE

What Hell I live what misery
to think and not attain
to reason and to understand
yet victory never came

We have been given all the tools
we've been given all the ways
but because we chose to walk alone
we'll fail for all our days
I would BE if I'd only give in

Christa Essinger

Untitled

What is love more like: a rose?
or a ring?
There is only one answer and only you can answer it.
A rose is beautiful but only for so long.
A ring goes round and never ends.
If you say a rose, you feel love can end and will end.
Life has not been fair to you and probably never will be fair to you
feeling this way.
If you choose the ring
then you are at peace,
for love will never end.
Life is and always will be good for you.
A ring is a never ending circle of life.
So answer this question truthfully
for it matters not what you answer, if you lie you are only cheating
yourself.
Love,
peace and harmony

Feliz Regino Tovar

Justification

Did Noah take mosquitoes in the Ark?
Or did they sneak in after it was dark?
It really doesn't matter
But I think it was the latter,
For who would want mosquitoes to embark?

And once they were inside.
They grew and multiplied.
For food was very plentiful and good.
And Kosher they were not,
They ate Ham on the spot,
(And Shem and Japheth too whene'er they could.)

How lovely for mankind
Had he left them all behind,
But frogs and minnows really would protest.
It takes all kinds you see,
In our e-col-o-gy
So I suppose it happened for the best.

Helen P. Voris

Have We A Chance?

Never were we promised time
Or given any proof
That peace would one day come
With attitudes aloof
And morals on the run
In awe, we stand, undone

The easier we make life - the harder it all gets
Can we understand the paradox
We stir our children's heads?
They're shown and taught
By fragmented thoughts

Love is truly obsolete
The word itself is drained
Universal peace and love
Turned into hate and pain

Until there is another plane
In which we all have ceased
Paradise awaits to gain a race of total peace
We've wasted all what we call time
There's no more room to reach

Barbara Samolyk

What Is Love?

What is love? Is love emotions
or is it the way you feel about a person?

What is love? Is love a feeling
and, if it is, how do you know
when you're in love?

What is love? Is love a curse
that God put upon man and woman?

What is love? Is love a
thought or is love when you long
or desire someone's touch?

Is love blind like they say
or can you see what will come your way?

Is love heartache and pain
or is love happiness, flying freely like a dove?

I will never understand
why we fall in love!!!

Junemarie Davis

Facade For Section VIII

Dare I ease the reins that hold my furies fast?
Or lift the latch that locks my vengeful thoughts?
Or drop the rod that bars my cruel retorts?
Or cut the cord that ties my selfish wants?
Or snag the sash that wraps my fancied wrongs?
Or loosen bonds that bind my broken dreams?
Or crimp the shade that hides my private tears?
No!
Never!
Unless to live in shrieking chaos,
I dare not crack my lean facade.

Florence Whitty Schneider

Musing

If I had eagle's wings
    or the eyes of the wise old owl
I would eschew human things
    and inhabit the world of the fowl.

If I could penetrate the forests
    where unknown mysteries live
I would drink deep of the wonders
    these beautiful creatures give.

I would frolic with the deer and the rabbits
    and run with the gentle fawn
I would wait with them thru the darkness
    and watch for the rising sun

I would lift mine eyes to the heavens
    and give thanks to the God of us all
for the magic gift of the animals -
    these creatures great and small.

Elaine S. Freeman

Searching

She is a lonely hunter and what she's looking for
Or what she needs to make her whole, she's not even sure.
She was such a pretty girl with laughter on her face
Now the years have drug her down, there's sorrow in its place.
Sorrow for the things she's missed, the life she threw aside
Her son, a home, just daily living, but most of all her pride.
The only time she speaks of love is when she's flying high
Makes promises that she cannot keep, more often she won't even try.
She skirts the world of danger with her drugs and alcohol
I worry for her two little boys, when for months she doesn't call.
Then she calls me in the night to cry it breaks my heart in two
I tell her you must help yourself there's nothing I can do.
I would help her if I could I'd give her peace within
I'd bring her back from that dark place she's long been living in.
I'm so afraid there'll come a call or someone at my door
To say she's gone before she finds what she's been searching for.

Judith M. Sperling

Resolution

This is the hour for which I've searched. The hour of naked wisdom
purged from jealousy and insecurities; earned by deeds or
darkness of mind.
Guilt that most wear as a badge of honor, treachery that
makes the eyes go blind, and fear of losing what was never mine.
Release me, oh spirit of monster green. Plant my feet in wheaten
pastures, blown by breeze and new kiss of dreams.
My life anew, my mind replenished; begin the new,
the old now finished.

Bess Radosta

Understanding

I understand that thread must go through an eye of a needle in
order for the needle to complete it's function
I understand that looking both ways before crossing into traffic,
insures my safety
I understand that the sun comes up no matter what, even if the
day doesn't shine, isn't bright
I understand and do not question that there is God and He has a
Divine purpose for us, He is all before and after it began
I understand as I breath air, swallow water, digest food and walk
the surface of this earth, I am not the only one
I understand that two and two is four, forever more
True love between a man and a woman, I don't understand
But, I understand that I will accept it
Understanding

Mrs. Donna

Donna M. Crowley

A Living Nightmare

I stand in a line with death camp awaited, some will be executed,
others cremated. Little children stand beside me with a look of
confusion, I wish this was a dream, just an illusion, as I to my
right, my family to the left, I knew that we would all soon meet death
How could this happen? We did nothing foolish, was it because
we were different? Or us being Jewish as I stand here with my
thoughts beginning to rise, I wish we could just sit and talk, or
compromise. As my fingers were gripping upon my thigh, I only heard
my conscious say, we all will die. I fell to my knees and there I
prayed, I prayed for my freedom and of school days. As I knelt on my
knees I felt so demised, shaking on my knees, a tear in my eye. A
soldier came up to me and grabbed my arm I wish someone could
help me, or ring an alarm I was thrown into a fiery pit of hell. I was
about to meet death, who now, I know so well. Over six million
lives were lost. All over a living nightmare called the Holocaust.

Brennon James McKay

Your Parents Must Have Been An Architect!

Young lady, you are so fine your
parents, must have been a brick layer or an architect,
Because the sleek design of your body
with everything in places is perfect.
Those smooth curves, and those well rounded hips,
Meet and blue prints or specifications
and dimension, straight up to the lips.
Because you, young lady are designed, straight
and perfect to scale for me,
Nothing but perfection is all that I, see.
The design of your body, and legs are so
smooth as you walk,
Has got me so flabbergasted as, I, watch you talk.
Your eyes and your facial expression well set in place,
Perfectly was done your hair, so beautiful
with no time to waste.
I, wonder what scale was used to measure
your personality,
After all you are so fine; having all
of you, is to much for my reality.

Danny C. Coutee

The Dark People

Some people call them "Bums."
Others . . . "homeless."
And even . . . "The unfortunate."
But . . .
I like to call them - "The Dark People."
They have secrets.
They have dreams.
The night is over . . . looking for a place to stay
Nowhere to go
What to see
What to feel
Afraid to turn their backs
Waiting
Waiting again and again.
Closen eyes
Tighten bodies
"The Dark People."
It doesn't fit the pieces.
So dark - and . . .

Dylan Strazar

The Mirror Of A Dream

As the clouds dance in the space
Our children play in the streets.

The shades on the walls are the upcoming events of our young generation.
The life of this monster of a million heads, seems to be
convolved in the Milky Way.

The souls come and go like a sailboat in the middle of a sea storm,
or the souls come and go like the ecstatic light of an static candle.
What is happening in this world that I don't know?

Is this a dream? Or a reality?

I am secure with the unknown.
When I march abreast with my Redeemer.
Let me listen to the sounds of quiet.

Let me sleep, I am tired.

Cesar Quinones

Our Memories

As we reach out our hand
Our family we do grasp,
While we think of our memories,
Of the years in the past.
Tears fill our eyes, because it's all gone.
You're starting a new life, you have to move on.
As the days pass us by,
Although it hurts inside
We'll try not to cry.
We think of your life, and your first years
Now you've reached the end
You are going away.
How do we say we'll miss you,
How do we say goodbye to the one who means so much?
Will there be time?
We'll always have our memories
Of your life from day one.
Don't think of death as an ending,
Think a new life has begun.

Jennifer Cassidy

The Growth Of Love Like A Flower

He came in my life one late August day,
our love was planted forever to stay.
Our love soon blossomed with time and care,
It continued to grow, charming and rare.

Through times of drought when our love was not fed,
However the pain or how our hearts bled,
It was all worth it for what laid ahead.

More time and some sun soon healed our sore spots.
Our love grew stronger, our stomachs in knots.
We knew what we had, and wanted it back,
We tried really hard and got right on track.

My smile shines more than ever these days,
I see what we have, forever, always!

Karen Cheverie

Life

I see life as a cluttered closet because some things you just wear
out but you still keep them just like an old memory you may not want
to but you remember it for the rest of your life and it doesn't mean
you don't like the memory it's just it doesn't fit into your life.
Just like your favorite pair of jeans that don't fit you anymore.
Even though you keep all the old memories, you just keep piling the
new things on top. Your old memories just seem to fade away but they
are still there and everything you do just reminds you of another
old memory. So the next time you clean our your closet maybe you'll
think twice about throwing away those old jeans or that favorite
sweatshirt that doesn't fit you anymore and that's what I think about life.

Jennifer Winkler

I Cry Alone

I cry alone, once again you are gone
Out in the oceans, away from home.
I think of you often, memories vague and to few;
Wishing you were here, I cry alone.
You are my hero, my pride for you is true;
Defending our country, as many others do.
I cry alone, many a night
Alone in our bed, where you once held me tight.
Soon you'll return, love and joy fill my heart
And never again do I want us to part.
With your arms outstretched, I run swiftly to them
And look at your face, I know that I'm dreaming;
In the corner of your eye, a sign of a tear
I wipe it away and then it seems clear . . .
I have never, cried alone.

Jennifer Boynton Blessing

A Desert Poem

As the morning mist lifts,
Over tranquilizing mountain cliffs.
Gigantic robotic figures stand straight in a line,
Their out-stretched arms not making a whine.
For miles and miles they traveled,
In a forgotten land unravelled.
Swift, twirling, whirling sand,
Casting a painted desert program.
Air filled with fragrances of sweet perfume,
Somewhat of cactus flowers in bloom.
Bursting of colors forming shades within a cell,
The sun's penetrating heat upon my shell.
Decaying mesquite huddling close to the ground,
No life form that which could be found.
Stars of the heavens now forming a maze,
Upon a land that once herds of cattle grazed.
Oh! No more shall I seek at the shadow of night,
But be sure I'll be back when it becomes daylight.

Harold R. Harrison

Silent Feelings

The feelings I have inside are so very emotional.
Pain, nervousness, and hurt reckon my soul on this day.
The pain of a loss on the court is a pain I wish not to feel.

Nervous, the first time this year
I don't know what to expect or what to feel inside.
I am hurting internally, but I refuse to tell anyone.
I have to be strong willed to keep my feelings aside.

The eye of the tiger with the intensity of a winner
Is what it will have to take to win it all.
I must be the almighty today,
Refuse to let loose the feelings I have inside.

Jason Nevitt

The Beauty Of Night

Black velvet blankets the sky
Overflowing with sparkling diamond stars
The giant pearl moon dances on crystal water
That whispers and caresses the shore

Tranquility overcomes me
As I am lost
Captivated by the beauty of night

Crickets serenade on their violins
As owls sing with the night orchestra
A gentle wind sings his song through the trees
And carries the fragrant scent of flowers in his arms

Tranquility overcomes me
As I am lost
Captivated by the beauty of night

Jennifer Compton

Pity The Poor Poets

Pity the poor poets, we feel our lives so intensely that pins and
papers are all that keep our souls within our skin.

Pity the poor painters who can't sleep until their heart and hands
will let them rest.

We . . . who are half crazed to express what we feel to anyone who
will take the time to look . . . hear . . . to try to understand.

And most of all, . . .
Pity the poor souls who never allow themselves to be insane enough
to have sleepless nights and emotional days in search of
expression.

We all have so much to say. We all have so much to share. We
all have so many needs to fulfill.

And for me . . . the intensity keeps me alive. The nights I can not
sleep . . . they put another part of me at rest.

For me . . . mixing color is clarity; abstract thoughts on paper are
my only way to view reality.

So, pity the poor poet only for the days she refuses to feel. Pity
the poor painter only when his feel of light, size, shapes and colors
are not at hand . . .

And pity all others for the lovely insanity their lives have sadly
missed.

Barbara Ramsey-Duke

God Knew It

Before we ever said hello, and before our
paths met.
He knew that we would fall in love, before
our wedding day was set.
He knew that we would say "I do," and that
we'd be together.
God knew our hearts would sing a song, and
he's known it forever.
God knew our hearts would sing a song, and
he's known it forever.

Before you ever kissed my lips, and before we
made love,
God knew that we would conceive a soul,
be blessed by him above.

God knew the troubles we would go through and
knew they would not last.
God knows just what our futures hold, just as
he knows our past.

Denise L. Huckaby

Can We Talk?

Anorexiame. meAnorexia. We share the same heart. Till death do us part.
Big getting BIGGER, SMALL getting smaller. O powerful Voice, so smart.
Speak for me, hear me. i hear You. i don't see You, but They do.
Conceal and protect me. Fight for me, notice, nurture and love me too.

Anorexiame, You're winning, i'm crying again, again too tired to fight.
Continue to kill me. If You go i go. If i go You go. Tonight.
You are my feelings if i have any. i don't, do You?
We're loved, for money, in the hospitals we go home to.

Anorexiame, HELP. Leave me alone. You consume our blood and spirit.
i cry, they drown us with feeding tubes and act like they don't hear it.
We're starving for life, living for death. Dizzy and nauseous, I panic.
Pain, shaking, choking on you, I can't sleep through you. You're manic.

Anorexiame, we're getting colder as the scale screams louder, so loud.
Louder like the fainting crashes. Was that us? Are You proud?
Ambulance on the way again? Too late, here they come.
Parents don't visit. They're daughter is "sick". Will you send someone?

Anorexiame, They say they know and care. Do you have love to share?
Does anyone care? Does anyone have anything to share but fright?
If i do you do. If you do i do, but my heart is empty tonight . . .
As They turn out the hospital light . . .

Jacqueline R. DeMarco

A Valentine's Poem

Red and white flowers
Pink candy hearts
Banquets and dances
Cards and a song
A day of love and laughter
Do you have someone with these to share?
Sweethearts, lovers, and friends
All brought together by the three simple words
  "I Love You"
Cupid plays match maker
And makes a new, an everlasting love,
A friendship or two
All of these things put together on one day
Just to help us remember
What it is like to love
And to be loved
On Valentine's Day

Angie Figgins

God Bless My Daddy Who Flies In The Sky

God bless my daddy who flies in the sky
Please guide him and love him don't let him die
First it was grandpa called off to war
To cover invasions and end war of wars

Peace was declared and grandpa came home
But soon uncle Robert to Korea was flown
He fought long and valiant but never came home

Then there was daddy to Vietnam called
Decorated with medals, but in the dark of the night
Death came and called him
In his very last flight

Now I am grown, to the Gulf I was called
Little Kuwait was being destroyed

I hear my little son now praying
God bless my daddy who flies in the sky
Please guide, and love him, and don't let him die
And to all the Presidents, Kings, and Emirs.

Please do something to stop
A small child's fears

Dottie Egan

Untitled

Abruptly silence involved the moment, the time and place . . .
Places and experiences are coming to me; I'm disordered, I'm anxious.
If don't see you, if I see you as well, I'm in love; suddenly moment of silence . . .
A moment of recall . . ." The laws what we have to do? right?
Wrong? . . .
All writhed? All consent . . . I'm stumble in sin and reprehended . .

Is not lawful? Seem dishonest. What is happen to me? What is
happen to you? . . .
And you know everything which way? You way? My way? . . .
We discuss; we changed; we altered; and meaning while what is
happen with you? . . .
I can't speak out; I'm have to be shame and I was born way out . .

And outside I have to grow it . . . no body understand when I speak out
  knowing when
I'm tell Three, I'm tell land, I'm tell sea nd love . . . but they said
  I spoke to much . . .
I'm have been born outside that's why! I speak only with you when
  I said so . . .
Three isn't table? Land isn't seed? Sea isn't fish? And love isn't
  a son? That's why . . .
I speak only with you; you know about ancients and horizons;
that's why you think . . .
And understand . . . you know and they said! . . . I'm speak to much . . .
Only when I talk to you . . .

Ernesto Cervantes

Virtuoso

Sunday October blue Steinway centerstage
poetlength tresses breeze Celtwide shoulders
anchoring tender sentiment surging power.

Magical millisecond seated violinists
loping coatsleeves meet pianistic
rectangles freeze framed haloed.

Lull ends eyes nod Mozart K503
luxurious sonorous seamless
clean clear direct honest.

Cloudsoft hands of steel ripple
changing key mood time zero gravity
tension heightens emotion peaks interest.

Into the listening soul rainbow
hued bubble notes siphon dazzling
beauty elation serenity serendipity.

Facile fingers bravura inspire ovation
enchanted listeners echo note tone touch
sans scales fourteen hour practice days.

Harriett Buckingham-Clark

Untitled

I'm in a
prison Dry skeletons
of trees click together
in the carrion breeze
it was cold I had not noticed amid
its grandeur the gardens dead cold and
buried underneath frozen ground that hears
no sound except that of blackbirds. Ravens if
you will so soft the call It beckons like light
to the blind like cold to heat yes it is sour to
sweet. The dancer leaps to twirl the beauty
you cannot reach streams of satin fluid dressed
in pink to music cloaked in black
velvet like the night illumined in feeble flickering
candlelight - waving like marsh grass in the wind
It scatters the tosspots full of gin far away and
around the bend.

Joey Suzannah Stampley

I Gotta Get A Job

A long time ago I sold
portrait album programs door-to-door
for a man that had a drinking problem.
   Every day, after we finished,
he would buy alcohol with our
earnings and we would "Socialize."
   Unfortunately, this made for poor economics.
Finally, I said, "this can't go on." So I wrote him this poem.

   "Well, T.C., I guess you know,
I decided today, I gotta go.
   You've been swell and
all the others are great,
   But it's time that me and
my babies ate.
   The cupboards are bare,
The bills are due.
   And pretty soon they'll
probably sue.
   So to avoid that suing mob,
I gotta quit work and find a job."

   Jeanette E. Cook

America

Pray for America, land of the free,
Pray that America will bend her knee.
To our God and creator - before its too late,
And judgment falls to seal her fate.
Why, oh why can't the people see!
The destruction of morals and family.

Where is the justice for those who have died?
Who have paid the price with honor and pride.
Pray that America the land that we love,
Will repent of its sin to our God above.
Our God will heal this land if we pray,
America! America! Please do it today.

I weep for America in the day and the night,
I will not give up without a fight!
America! America! What else can I say,
Humble yourselves, let God show you the way
To redeem your land, so it remains free,
With your flag flown high for the world to see.

   Irma Elizabeth Mendonca

In The Beginning

A chronicle of unwritten pages, no past, perfectly centered in this
precise moment. What a sorrowful cry. Necessity or impulse? A
saga yet to be told.

Wordless directives, "Hold me, please, for I am misplaced in this
oneness, my senses violated by glaring and clamor! My tender
skin smarts from cold.

Oh, to float again in your kind, tepid waters, abate a fresh my
surrendered soul. Still my racing heart, press me tighter to your
warm tender breast."

Jerky movements, unrestrained. "Engulf my flailing limbs. Grant my
lips the solace of your bosom. Yield me the rhythmic comfort from
within your chest.

Surround me with your substance, for I am so small and you are all I
know, the purr of your voice, your emotions my own. Your minds
eye my sole sight.

Just yesterday we were one, naught but muffled sound to disturb my
slumber. Cruelly compelled by your compressions from my haven,
I tremble with fright.

Cradled in your arms, weak from exertion, my breathing deepens."
The silence is broken . . . you whisper, "Quiet, my darling, all will be right."

   Elizabeth Reed

Pegasus Sky

The sun is rising up and up
Pretty colors in the sky
Pegasuses wake up too
And then they start to fly.

What a fun variety!
Green, pink and blue
Colorful wings spreading far
Soaring just for you.

They fly and float all day
From sun up to sun down
It's dark now, the pegasus Night Queen comes out
With her beautiful starry crown.

Again the sun comes up and up
Again the pegasuses fly
Again, the colors way up high
Way up in the sky.

   Amanda McCaustland

'Dad'

'Dad' — it was an entreaty, a query, an accusation,
Printed on an envelope taped to his office door.
In jaggedly round letters,
A divisive 'A' between two clenched 'D's.
The contents a mere reflection of betrayal.

One and one seldom make two in a world replete with threes.
The office was no longer his,
But a vortex still flowered from behind that locked door.

A vortex, funneling to his suit's lapel,
That all its life only whirled one way,
Can bring all to its center yet swirl it all away.

What's a wife, a daughter to think when a man,
From his conference never returns home,
And his colleague's skirt seldom touches her knees.

Douse the envelope on a fiery door.
The hate, the hurt, the whore,
All fixed on a man one must strive to hate,
Condense to blood, rivulets towards the floor
When seeing him, stalled at his former door,
Reading his soul in three letters: 'Dad.'

   Brian Anthony Bell

Life's Awakenings

Thump Thump Thump rhythmic beats time to sleep. Awakening
pushing and playing in what seems to me impeccable
surroundings. Now feeling enclosed in these once familiar walls
anticipating of times to come my heart pounds for the new world.
Reaching my new destination I've found it beautiful and bright.
Forced to cry and the pain of hunger hits hard. Joyfully I play
pulling my feet to my mouth sucking on hard earned efforts.
I can stand! And have so much I need to say, but how?
I'm walking, now talking. It seems somehow I'm becoming a
part of this new world I was so curious about.
Trees, bees, cars, airplanes, school, work, parents, spouse,
to live, to live for, to die, to die for, survival.
I've grown and these feet I used to suck on have now
carried me threw the world I once was so excitedly anticipating.
Now death to this world is reality, the walls will be closed and a
true impeccable life awaits in an everlasting world outside.
Time is ever changing. You grow, learn, and are awakened
to the experience of life.

   Dawn Hall

440

Christmas Time

Sparkling diamonds is the snow,
Pure and white as ermine.
Soft and lovely, all aglow.
Speaks to us, as does a Sermon.

Christmas carols in the air,
Proclaim the birth of our Savior Dear.
Children's hearts are filled with glee.
As they view with wonder, the lovely tree.

There always is such fun in giving,
That is part of the joy of living.
But God's gift was best, He gave His Son,
Who is pure and Holy, the Omnipotent One.
Helen Martha Baldwin

Courage

COURAGE is the color of the
purple heart the war veteran
received, reminding him of the
war at which he almost lost his life.

COURAGE smells like the gunpowder
from the bullet that pierced his spine.

COURAGE sounds like rumbling cheers
proclaiming, "THE VICTORY IS OURS"!

The taste of COURAGE is one that is
bittersweet. Bitter because so many lost
their lives; sweet because the battle is
over.

COURAGE looks like the tattered, bloodstained
fatigues our soldiers adorned.

Their COURAGE makes me feel proud that
I AM AN AMERICAN!
Jesica Pennigar

In The Army Now

It's up at 4:30 in the morning.
Push ups and running with the sunrise.
"Drop and give me twenty,"
"Or I will kick your wimpy behinds."

Obstacle courses are so rough,
Being gassed just wasn't enough.
Down on the ground with mud in your face,
You will never forget that time nor place.

Firearms going off over your head,
One mistake and "BOOM" you would be dead.
Think about your plans hard and long,
You must be willing and be strong.

In the army now, yes, that is what said.
When I think WOW!!!
I can not wait to get into bed.

So now you know how to defend your country,
You are ready to fight.
Finally made it soldier,
It's graduation night.
Angela M. Peters

A Frightening Ride

The departure of a deeply loved one
Puts your emotions on an emotional
roller coaster that at
times seems to be careening out of control
with no ability to slow down
and stop.

The highs are made possible by
the fond recollections of the past
experiences and events.

It permits us to laugh and smile,
making the present a little bearable.

But the lows are a frightening,
agonizing plunge into depths of
sadness and remorse unknown and
unthinkable until now.

It takes its hold on you and penetrates
the deep recesses of your body and soul.

You see no end, you feel as if you will
suffocate, and that the ache and pain will never subside.

Your only consolation is your shared loved and memories.
Donna M. Landers

The Poet

It's so easy to be a poet
Putting words down on a page
Just write of love and loneliness
Of caring, compassion and rage

You write about God in his heaven
While you live down here in hell
You pen of your errors on the road of life
And your sins, to God, that you'll tell

Tell about the beauty of nature
And draw the readers right in
Make them see what you're seeing
To help their journey begin

Have them listen to the noise of the city
Let them run through fields of wheat
Take them to the top of the mountain
Where the flower fragrance is sweet

It's so easy to be a poet
Just jot down words on a line
Anyone can do it
Just express what's there in your mind.
Bill Drasher

The Butterfly

I once saw a butterfly as
pretty as can be. Red, yellow, and green
are the colors that it wave to me.
I often look up in the sky
hoping that I'll see it again, but it
never return maybe it already have a
friend.
But if that friend should ever
let you down, please feel free to fly
back in my town. I will always be around.
I will remember you even
thou we are apart. I just wanted
you to know that you will always be
in my heart.
Juanita S. Griffith

Nietzsche's Dream

Black impending night, dark shadows race by. Light passes with a quick glimpse. The clatter of the streets quiet. An unsteady stream of noise rises from the caverns, honks and screams. Automobiles limp through the streets. The rusted heaps beep and lay at the side of the road. Cracked cobblestone ways lead to toppled granite structures where the people live and only the wind blows change. Change of color, change of time, change of rhyme: change, change, change. Blow up the moon. I say moon the moon! The dark shadows turn to black. Colors are polarized. The world is flat. One dimensional planes I fly twisted, torn through the ages like the maniacal eye of plastic satan. Watching. Hunger is its source man's diseased soul its course. Heavily laden bearing spirit like a phantom flung from me raging hate for my tempter. Oh my suffering and tormented gods. In a fit of paranoia raving the insanities of the world. Falling into the abyss I burst the eye. The stench of dead Indians, Jews, Blacks and revolutionaries. I looked upon the souls and saw the fossilized bones of man's eternity and I laughed.

Arthur Mellos

Goodbye Daddy

So this is what it's like now
Quiet, the kind of quiet that makes you nervous
Nervous that I might trip
And fall into the space that was your life

Your things, all gone now, like the nicotine stains on the curtain
Only your presence remains; longing to break the silence

You died yesterday
I know how hard you tried to be my Daddy
How hard I tried to be your little baby girl
To live the life you had forgotten
Left alone in the sunset of your reality

I tried to memorize you
Swimming, laughing . . . laughing
The way you lived your life changed how I live mine
Turning dreams into memories, all bitterness wrong out

You left us on the diving board
Not knowing who'll jump or who'll run
Or who will do a perfect swan dive
And risk imperfection by being happy . . . without you.

Charlotte V. Blair

Un Named Friend

Walked gently into my heart so sweetly,
Quietly disappeared, leaving love with out promise.

His influence still lingers near
It brings me love and cheer.
When I need strength to go on
Our friendship holds a steady bond,
It's like sun shine that appears
From some one very dear.

Through out the years that come and go
I'll always honor that young pro,
How he gave so much to me
And set my passions free,
Of all my love-he'll never know
How he melted me like snow.

inspired me forever, made life a new endeavor
To write love songs every season
Why he came and went away
Took my heart, with him, that day
Left me forever - loving him -

Jean Freeman

Friendship

F amiliar are the memories,
R eluctant to be alone.
I ntensified of a new beginning,
E motions and feelings have grown.
N eedless to mention,
D esire brings about love.
S hared amongst two incredible people,
H appiness fitting like a glove.
I ntimate enhancement destined to be shared,
P articularly because I've always cared.

Joyce Eileen Thomas

Clouds

Clouds boiling with creative vision.
Rains driven with perfect precision.
Pixies in puddles multiply.
Raindrops fall, flow swiftly by,
My window view, kaleidoscope,
Jewels and gems in liquid smoke,
Shattered diamonds, splashed with tears,
Flooding memories of my years.
Ghostly winds, hug colorful trees,
Caressing limbs of shimmering leaves.
Sunlight peers with great surprise,
Through racing clouds, that dip and dive.
Still! Listen! Hear the quiet;
Musical sound of natures rhythm brings sheer delight.
Spring, Summer, Fall and Winter;
With each passing next is better.

Alda Crance

The Beach In Summer

Heat shimmered off the asphalt
Rays of the heavy August air
Suspended in motion
Like sleeping puppets on a string
Hot: The shrill aria of a boiling pot of water

My feet hopping on the summer warmed sand
Find relief in the waves
The water salty; pungent
Beckoning me to the shore

Carefully my wet feet
Beat footprints in the sand
Back to a terry towel
To bask, nearly nude
There I lie, bathing in the warmth

Lotion melts on me
I broil in the sun
Littered with oil of coconut
Shiny and fragrant

I lie back, and let the sun
massage my wintered bones.

Julienne Lambre

Rainbows

A rainbow is a gift from God,
Red represents the blood Jesus shed for us.
Orange is the nectar from God's flowers.
Yellow is the light that glows from heaven.
Green is the new birth we see on earth.
Blue is the forever in the sky.
Violet is God's royal color,
A gift I wish to give you, as he gave to me.

Christina Wetherall

Now There's You

Once, when I played crazy, silly little games, there wasn't much to really care for or about. So I played hard and worried about merely me; never caring about when and if the sun would shine that next day.

But that next day you were there, smiling a lot, dancing a little, and just being nice. From then until now, it doesn't matter much about the weather outside, for inside all my days are sunny and my nights are warm; even when I'm away, just from memory.

If we walk in the park through the rain, or have a picnic on an island with a name most people don't remember, or just lie together in the dark listening - to each other and the quiet - not moving or thinking - just being there. It's times such as these that I remember best.

There are also times that I don't like so well either. Like leaving your side in the chill of early morning, while you are lying there all warm and still full of sleep. And you turn softly, just the way I love, sometimes waking, when I kiss you as I leave.

Now, when I see the sun set over the horizon at the end of a day and darkness takes its place in the sky, I know that for me, at least, the sun will come up again when I'm home with you, and once again, there is someone to care for and worry about besides myself. Now there's you!

John H. Fort

Fallen Branch

Gazing up to see its siblings flourish,
recalling days not long ago since past
It once anchored life abound
Now it wonders how long its own life will last.

Leaves once sprouted from its bark
It outfitted a shelter for the meek and the mild
Though its green counterparts acquiesced to the seasons
It defied elements, providing a canopy to the wild.

This time, it could not brave a strong autumn wind
Perhaps it was slighted, ignored or neglected
It was not critical to the tree's survival
Its mother turned her back leaving it unprotected

How could the body let it snap away so carelessly?
It used to be as significant as any other limb
Cast aside like a stillborn or an orphan.
I guess the old mother will surely survive without him

A limb once vital to its source
A presence of power in nature's state of grace
Once a balance beam for creatures to traverse
Now, soon to be kindling in someone's fireplace.

Christopher Delfino

Summer, Late August

Watching the grass grow on a hot summer day,
reclining in the shade,
not troublesome responsibilities,
no homework to plague my tired mind,
empty time to twiddle my thumbs,
but in the secret depths of my mind,
I almost wish to go to school,
and see my friends,
terribly ashamed by this weakness,
I can only wait until fall,
and see a reflection of my apologetic glance,
all is forgiven and suddenly we remember

Complaining is an art.
(a confession)

Caitlin Reynolds

Friends

Share my laugh, share my tear.
Recognize the truths that you see in yourself, in another.
The common darkness which were once held,
are now revealed with sincerity, trust, and fear.

We see dawn from our own mountain peaks,
and we marvel at the sight time and time again . . . yet
We never see the sun on our own faces.
Look to a friend and understand.

Find solace with your own feeling of warmth and light,
but find comfort in the closeness of a friend.

Gian A. Cossa

Hold A Hand

I want to look into your eyes
reflected the green of grass, the blue of skies
rich in beliefs from one's own origins
leads us in circles, to where it begins

The eagle flies high and low
seeing the chaos reflected below
the gangs and the wars, the drugs and hate
leaving him to wonder, what will be his fate

Eyes are slanted, skin is darker
hair too long, language a marker
peace is a word that is laughed at
fear has made many pull in the welcome mat

Look at yourself, deep into your heart
With one leading to others, it's a start
humanity at work, all making a stand
just be human, and hold a hand

Elizabeth Marie Pursley

The Art of Friendship

As I close my eyes, I see pictures of us
Reflections of our everlasting friendship
Such original portraits!

Created
With the brushes
Held in the hands of my heart and soul

Painted
With understanding demeanor, encouraging conversations,
And unconditional love

Accented
With spontaneous fun, warm-hearted laughter,
And inspirational words

Preserved
With open honesty, sensitive spirits,
And empathetic hearts

Revealing
An incessant beauty
That enhances with each passing year

I shall treasure our friendship always

Beth Brown

Sounds

Tic toc goes the clock hanging on the wall.
Ring, ring goes the phone;
maybe there's nobody home.
Swish, swash goes the wash, the clothes are almost done.
Don't know which one to tend to first,
for all the sounds are one!

Christine Manns

"Silently Dreaming"

Sitting here in silence, I dream about tomorrow
Remembering the pain of yesterday, I live today in sorrow
And I can not help but wonder why, my life is so unfair
I feel as though I'm being trapped, inside a world full of despair.
There is very little I can do, and barely much that I can say
My world is free of hope and strength,
    and happiness has never passed my way.
My heart, it feels so empty, and confusion fills my mind
My life is dark and dismal and loneliness is all that I can find
As I snap back into reality I see a portrait of a girl,
She is lonely and depressed and she hates her little world
As I recur my dream, I realized that I failed to see
That the lonely girl inside the lonely world is me.

Jamie McGorty

The Tide That Binds

The ebb tide of intolerance
Reveals stark shorelines of the bay,
Bares the boulders of suspicion
Stymies thought that would lead the way.

Unseen, the force of gravity
Causes tide to obey and flow,
So changes in the hearts of men
The cause, an unseen force we know.

Flood tide then begins unnoticed
Midst great angst, despair, faith and hope,
Gaining power with every hour
Inundates hate upon the slope.

Dauntless high tide measures all men
And binds all kinds within the bay,
Man knows he cannot stop the tide
Nor upward soaring mind can stay.

Donald Haynes

Morning To Remember Me, My Bike And God

I wake to see the morning dew
Said good morning to the Lord
Grabbed an orange from my tree
Climbed my bike to ride along the ocean path
And feel the mist upon my face
The seagulls fly above my head
The sun soon comes to greet me in splendor all its own
After hours of sheer joy and much content
Returning home, now accepting
    the chores I face with vigor and not discontent
For I have once again experienced
    the beginning of a truly beautiful day

Dolores M. Fuller

Daydreams

Letting the song of the daydreams of love left behind
Rhyme out the sound of her name echoing to your mind
Feeling the depth of an ocean of tears that seem blind
Slip past the dangerous tides that lie in the darkness
Of your heart, if you can't
Love me please hate me, though the difference is blurred
By the same words that speak out of something
Whose meaning's not clear
Except in the warmth of the sun where the rain never falls
To wash out the traces of my feverish desires
If you love me don't hate me
Pretend to be nothing but westbound strangers rolling by
In the hillside of sorrow where love and ambitions collide
You can dance the sweetest of jukebox songs but who can deny
The drug scenery you harbor as life you would not change
If the way you despise me is the way that you wish
To let go the scent of the daydreams of romance behind.

Christian Hohmann

The Bear

I am glad I am a bear,
Ruff and tough and wander everywhere,
Climb trees and eat sweet honey,
Bask on rocks when days are sunny.

Fish in streams when pleases me,
Hope this life will always be,
Fun and frolic, fresh and free,
That's the way it pleases me.

But a bears life is not all fun,
We must beware of the hunters gun,
Of nets and traps of the such,
That would mean our life with a cruel touch.

But I would never ever change,
My free life on the open range,
For the life of a human man,
For GOD has made me what I am.

Heather R. Scala

My Sonni Delight

Silken black hair in points round a face
Rose petal cheeks swirled ribbons and lace
Eyes black as coal peeking out from her crib
Drooling on much of a fancy laced bib
Holding on tightly with two little hands
In ruffled pink bloomers determined to stand
Eyeing their form she lazily lingers
On one tiny hand and delicate fingers
Each look intent upon what she has found
Pursing her lips not making a sound
As I peer from my book our eyes briefly meet
Just look who is standing on both of her feet
Scooping her up my need to enfold
A pudgy pink cherub to kiss and to hold
Silken black hair as it brushes my cheek
Humming a song I rock her to sleep
May God bless this heavenly bundle of joy
Brightest of angels so sweet and so coy
Blinking her eyes and turning her head
Smiling she poops and wets half the bed

Alessandra Matteo

Loneliness

As I wonder through this house at night alone, many thoughts run through my head, many strange and unusual noises pierce my ears. Things that my eyes imagine makes me wonder if I'm really seeing things, are they real, is another thought that flies by many of times. The loneliness creeps up from behind, it doesn't scare me because it had me once I walked in the door. Day after day, the same routine surrounds me over and over, again and again, is there no stopping this. Music helps, but that loneliness just seems to hover above me till the music stops. Every day at the same time it strikes me in the same way that gets me to the point of no return. Checked the phone, its not unplugged, but on the other hand dead. Cars pass, but none to stop. Soon sleep follows, about the only way that I reach total happiness is when I'm dreaming, there's no one to hurt my feelings. Loneliness is forgotten, no pain, only peace, happiness, and serenity. Now I go to my dream world quite often. Makes me wonder if eternal sleep with forever dreams would be the best answer to my soundness. Surely, I would be missed by those who know me, for those who didn't normal life continues. Now I shall lay down for one more dream night. Good night!

Erik Jay Batalia

A Thought

Slowly, a churning thought forms,
running, bleeding.
It jumps upon a star and flies out of reach.
The world,
A fingertip's touch away,
I can only grasp, sense a presence,
Nearer, nearer, it draws me into it,
a hole.
I see only blackness,
I have been swallowed,
No longer in touch with myself,
I am scattered,
Shattered glass on wooden floors.
Pick up these pieces,
Start again.

Annika Nagy

Do You . . .

Do you love me more with the tears
running from my eyes, and the look of
confusion on my face.
Do you like to see me upset sorry I
was alive, and wishing the days that
were coming would never arrive.
Do you love to see me afraid, frightened
of what you might say or do, and upset
because I can never make you smile.
Do you like to be with me, because
you barely talk to me and you won't
even look at me.
Do you love me, do you like me,
or do you just not want me to be
around you?

Holly Ripberger

Beauté de Dieu

The rose with its upturned face,
Released its perfume with sweet grace,
Leaves shiny and dark green,
Adorned this stately queen.

At her feet, her subject
Bowed her head of violet.
Queen and subject perfume and beauty different,
Yet found equal in God's environment.

Georgette Moraud

For David

He interrupted us
Rudely.
Not stopping to ask you
"May I come in?"
(As if we would have answered 'yes')
But barging in unannounced
As is his custom.
I think I hear you laugh at him,
For he can never conquer you.
You still survive,
An heir to mansions in our Father's house.
We remain for now - a slight pause
Between us.
For who can separate us
From the love of Christ?
Not tribulation or distress,
Nor principalities nor powers.
And certainly not death.

Dorette Saunders

A Fall Evening

The sun has left
the air is crisp
and leaves spin in long graceful dance
beneath the autumn moon.

Darkened landscape dashes past your car
in quiet streaks of light.
And the scent of smoke
from chimney tops
float about the night.
Under trees of old
that whisper tales
as the wind blows upon them,
Cold hands are warmed
by someone near
two hearts alone
are one.

Anthony Matero

The Mother Of Many

With snowy wings unfurl
The angel spoke to Sister Merle.

I have come for you today
We must soon be on our way.

The days of toiling now are past.
The day desired has come at last.

No more nights of worry and fear
For the child or loved ones dear.

You have been a mother to all
So many names I can't recall.

Caring and loving each and everyone,
Always praying their souls be won.

There was washing and ironing to do
With mending and lots of cooking to.

She never grumbled or seem to mind,
Always spoke in a tone that was kind.

Thanks, dear Mother, for the memories of you.
You were always so faithful and true.

Someday when the Lord and Master shall call
I want to see again the mother to us all.

Clinton E. Riddle

It Is The Dove

It is the dove that Noah sent out of
the ark. It is the dove that God sent
upon his Son. It is the dove, it is the
dove. It is dove that brought
happiness. It is the dove
that brought peace. It is the dove that
Noah sent out into the air. It is the
dove that God rested upon Jesus'
shoulder. It is
the dove, it is the dove, it is the dove.

Jerry D. F. Duke

Your Lightning Eyes

Your lightning eyes
your fiery lips
and the magic of your touch
magnetize me to you
so you and so I
should create
new us.

Phil Parker

"Green"

Green is a fragrant forest,
the aroma of damp, fertile soil,
and thick, lush vegetation,
that mankind has yet to spoil.

Green is the rustling of leaves,
stirred by a balmy breeze
that perfumes the air
with the woodland scent of trees.

Green is a chorus of birds singing,
or perhaps a solo by a song thrush,
and the scurrying of tiny creatures,
hidden by dense underbrush.

Green is a solitary walk,
far from the noise of "civilization",
time to be alone with one's thoughts,
and to marvel at God's creation.

Green . . . is serene

Cynthia L. Cooke

I Wish, Wish, Wish

I could put in words
    The Beauty of
A woman with Child
    The Strength of
A woman with Child
    The Power of
A woman with Child
    The Glow of
A woman with Child
    The Peace of
A woman with Child
    The Love of
A woman with Child
    The Giving of
A woman with Child
    The Something about
A woman with Child
I Wish, Wish, Wish

I had the words

George Stewart

Wild And Free

Today is a new day for me.
The birds are singing,
The sun smiling,
And I let myself, body and mind, go free.

The wind blows wild,
My hair whips free,
I smile to myself
While thinking of my past,
And what my future can be.

The sun sets
As I sit on my front porch steps.
While sipping a cup of tea,
I think about the past and future
Letting my mind wander free.

I run a hand through my hair
As I stare at the sea,
Memories run through my mind
Letting me go free.

Amy Levins

In November

The mockingbird softly sings,
The church bell gravely tolls,
With it solemnity brings,
And the hearse slowly rolls.

The priest reads a quiet psalm,
The rain gently falls,
All is enveloped in calm,
And the whip-poor-will calls.

The coffin is lowered down,
The grievers move away,
Move away to town,
And yet, one will stay.

She will always remember,
True love died in November.

Elizabeth Marie Warburton

Rain

Here comes the showers
The cleansing rain
Oh, what power
It washes away the pain

I love to feel
The drops on my face
It seems to fill
All the empty space

Fall faster
Than you ever have before
So heavenly master
Let the rain pour

For all the pain
Ever inflicted
Through the rain
Can be lifted

Washed away
To be never seen again
Hear what I say
Let it rain my friend

Carl Davenport

The Daisy

"I'm just a common flower"
the daisy sighed to the breeze.
"I wish that I were more than
a stool for the tired bees."

"I'd like to be tall and stately
with petals of brilliant red
and leaves that are long and slender.
But I must be this instead.

God gently touched the daisy
it turned a flaming hue.
Its stem grew higher and higher.
At last the dream had come true.

But too soon the foolish daisy
missed the hum of the friendly bees.
It longed to be hidden in the grasses
that swayed with majestic ease.

"Dear God" it cried, "Forgive me
I've found that I am wrong.
I'd rather be a daisy
a common flower, unsung."

Ellamay Stufflet

Dear Sister

You were given to me,
the day I was born
You're the one special person,
that I can count on.
You have picked me up,
when I have fallen.
Dried the tears from my eyes.
And even took the time to tuck me in,
when I was afraid of the dark.
You're my best friend.
And you're someone who holds a
special place in my heart.
You are a gift that I will cherish,
as the years go on.
I love you, for you are my sister!

Dariel VanDett

My Treasure Chest

Underneath
The deep dark sea,
Beyond the dull sounding,
Purple waves,
Hidden is the keeper,
Of all diamonds.
They belong to me,
The most precious jewels.
Locked up in my chest:
Intangible, invisible.
The key is useless.
Blind are the eyes,
And deaf are the ears;
They all drown.
Yet, there is one,
Who'll unlock his way
To the most valuable:
My treasure chest.

Jenifer Kim

God's Neverending Beauty

I see every fall
The early morning frost
And it reminds us all
Of the summer we've just lost
The geese soaring
South they go
Our first warning
Of the coming snow
But as the leaves fall to the ground
Slowly without a sound
I come to realize
That it's never too late
To see the beauty before my eyes
That only God can create

April Cooley

Dewdrops

Sun glistens on a cool morning day,
The leaves blows so far, far away.
The children running to play outside,
The animals run to hide.
The dewdrops flow off a leave,
It looks like beads.
The dewdrops go up in the sky,
And the children wave goodbye.

Charley Eloff

Death

End
The End
Is death the only true end
Or is end only saying good-bye
End is leaving behind
Something you love
Looking back yet not seeing
Bleary eyed you can not tell
End is sorrow
Yet also a beginning
All things must end
Things start in order for them to end
End is what we may never know
All good things come to an end
Just like this book

David Bluestone

Thoughts

When you try to understand,
   the mind grows
When you do the best you can,
   the heart glows
And when you take a strangers hand,
And give him all the love you can,
   The soul knows.

Bernadine L. Betz

Shattered Dreams (Icarus)

To fly
The eternal dream
To soar endlessly
Towards the sun
To ride the wind
Over the sparkling water
To laugh with the sheer joy of
Flight

To fall
Spiraling towards the gaping
Maw of the sea
Cast out of heaven
Seared by the great heat of the sun
To tumble forever through the cold ocean
To stare at the wings that let you down
And wonder
Why?

Carley Schacter

Leprechaun's Treasure

The leprechaun sits upon his gold;
The fairies dance their ring.
The banshee its woeful wail does hold;
A tiny voice of peace softly sings.

One hundred million sons of Erin wait
With breath held taut,
As five hundred years of hate
Melts slowly in the mist where
   brave celts fought.

For thousands of years a people stand,
One nation to create.
And though it was twice close at hand,
'Twas not to be their fate.

Yet, now perhaps, has come the time,
Mighty champions to a final rest;
And bid the rainbow brightly shine
On the gold in the Leprechaun's chest.

Denny Jennings

Ode To A New Day

Out of the night
the first glow of color
are fading out in thin lines
heralding the sunrise
nature's master painter
warmly tinting the sky
overlain with dark cloud shapes
to add perspective . . .

Then as in a travel poster
airbrushed rays in
dramatic symmetry
fan across the horizon
pleasuring the eye
uplifting the heart
giving us joy to be alive
to greet another day.

Jack Spiro

Static

Remember
The first time you saw
The whiteblue crackle under your covers?
And how you felt
Like a God
When you realized
You had created it
Rubbingandrubbingandrubbing
Do you know how you
Lost that talent
That pride
That control
And let others be yours Gods
Making you cracklepop . . . spark
Only for their enjoyment.
Learn to be again
and bring back that spark
That is
Your life.

Abby Rosenbaum

The Garden

The sun shone through the trees.
The flowers nurtured in its rays.
All was peaceful in the garden.

The birds tweeting so high.
The deer running in the distance.
All was peaceful in the garden.

Then came the fire,
Like a blanket thrown from the heavens;
It covered the garden in destruction.

The embers left behind
Did not discourage the life.
All was again peaceful in the garden.

The grass sprouted,
And the deer returned.
All is now peaceful in the garden.

Life has returned;
Nature survives.
All will always be peaceful in the garden.

Justin Zak

Reopening Defined

to start again
The formation of opinion.
Oh, to think.
Estimation of my person causes
hypocritical speech; it
grows and spawns from ignorance.
Shield your soul my brothers,
from this state of being
destitute of knowledge.
One might be hiding
behind self hypnotic imagery.
Mental pictures of disdain arrogance
To the time and degree or
until, one realizes
we are not worthy to judge another
Be lovelorn, sisters also,
with heart and mind open.
We are of the same race,
the human race.

Carl Edward Davis

Gloria

You move with style,
    The grace of a cat.
You can have any man
    With moves like that.

You have a beautiful personality,
    With a heart of gold.
With a lady like you,
    I would love to grow old.

Hair of a crimson sunset,
    With the eyes of an emerald sea.
A complexion so sweet and clean . . .
    It takes the breath from me.

You're sleek, lean, and oh so sexy.
    You move with style so fine.
By the Lord in heaven
    I want you to be mine.

Fred Ardain Jr.

Betrayal

A wounded spirit, I am complete.
The hurt you caused
It burned so deep.
My happiness was delusional
My life you tossed
You never understood about
Total loss.

Imagine a lark that
Never flies again, remember
The heart that won't try
To mend.

Jodie Carmen Brown

War Game

War, a game, is of two foes.
The box is filled with tears and woes.
The cards are marked each with a fight,
The dealer gives each man a fright.

Each throws the dice to pick their fate,
While the devil smiles on Heaven's gate,
For evil men, to plan their schemes,
Their wars turn into hellish screams.

Chris Akers

Dedicated To Lincoln County

In a pleading soul a heart is expired
The inner darkness within
Has come crashing again
With no strength to try to rebuild
In desperate despair the sun is black
Under such hallow shadows
In the faint mist of ones shade
A green leaf is ones friend for the day
A new life has begun
One not so true
Fake within the abyss of ones mind
With an undignified altercation
Melancholy becomes one
And the inner soul has no where to go
The bridges have crashed and burned
Trying to excel by hurting you
And still only the fact to be true
In a pleading soul the heart is expired.

Ginger Mitchell

Seasons Time

The wind is blowing, blowing.
The leaves are falling, falling.
Can you hear Autumn is here
and Winter is very near.

The rain will soon begin to pour.
Fountains dry begin to flow.
With the rain and with the ice,
rivers and lakes begin to rise.

The trees are beginning to undress.
In the winter they take a rest.
Until Spring comes back in Lovers' Lane,
then they will dress up once again.

Leaves are blowing here and there.
Trees are shaking cold and bare.
Beds of leaves are everywhere.
Nature has just put them there.

When Spring will bloom in Lovers' Lane,
then lovers will walk through it again.
Songs of love will be in the air,
from Lovers' Lane where lovers refrain.

Antoinette Spitaleri

Freed

It was like being a bird,
    the life she lived.

Locked up in a cage,
    not allowed to fly free.

Grabbed by the wings,
    shown off like a prize.

Finally,
The time came for it to end,
    all of it.

It's not always right,
    but she's free now.

Ashley Knight

The Death Of Love

I know that you shall always be,
The life, the breath inside of me.

The sun, the stars, the moon above,
Hang lifeless there, without your love.

No flowers, or mourners by my side,
Though something in my life has died.

You act like life is just the same,
Totally oblivious to my pain.

With loves death, my feelings chilled,
A tender love, you cruelly killed.

I'll play the part, use all my will,
Till the beating of my heart grows still.

Edith Petty

Labor Of Love

Busy and happy
 The Mom of the house
Dusting and cleaning
 And cooking for spouse
Humming and mending
 And kissing each bruise
The pathways they shouldn't
 The young always choose
The fences they climb
 They've heard all the can't
Then without thinking
 A tear in their pants
Shoes worn thin
 By hopscotch scuffle
A dainty miss with a drooping ruffle
But Mom wends her way
 Gets everything done
At the end of the day her battle is won
She must have great help from the Lord up above
To be sure she did it he blessed her with love.

Anne Porter Boucher

Star Fantasy

Little children of
the moon.
Swaying to the midnight tune.
When our nighttime job is done,
We stars take time to have some fun.
Having tea with Mr. Sun,
Looking down at everyone.
Thinking, "Boy, those kids look strange.
The points on them are not arranged.
Their arms and legs are much too close.
They look like us, though, for the most."
I said this to all my peers:
I have good news that will
bring cheers.
I've watched them close
from up this far,
And everyone's superstar.
We both look different, yes that's true.
But what makes you good is inside of you.

Jillian Vieira

Dwelling

In my heart lies the Sun,
the Moon, the Stars and Everyone!
God, The Universe, and all that be
lie within this heart of me.
For I am all Joy, and I am The King.
When I Love I Am Everything!

Yet, should I hate become I small
and back again to earth I fall.

Joseph A. Pagnanella

Untitled

Stay with me God. The night is dark.
The night is cold: My little spark.
Of courage dies. The night is long;
Be with me God, and make me strong.

Eugene Lowman

The Looking Glass

I see the mirror before me,
The one that was my mother's.
A long silvered glass joined with pine
Made from boxes ripped asunder.

Upon graduation, Mom gifted it to me
With words both wise and true.
This mirror will be your friend or foe
Because it will be a reflection of you.

It will be your friend if you're
Honest; your foe if you are not.
Through the years the looking glass
Was my foe, more often than not.

So daughter, I give this mirror to you
And to these words please listen.
Be honest with yourself and others
And your reflection will glisten.

Elizabeth Meyer

"Time Is Absolute"

Outside my door the wind does blow,
the rain is pouring down,
the night has come and spread its cloak
across this tiny town.

Outside my door the children die,
by other children slain.
For want of just a pair of shoes
they lie dead in the rain.

Outside my door a raging beast
grows stronger every day
The hatred of another's skin
holds many in its sway

Outside my door this storm rolls on
much stronger than would suit
Yet each of us will meet the end
For time is absolute

Outside my door the answer lies
If only we could see
If we could learn to live as one
what beauty there could be.

Don Sylvester

Fall Is Coming

The leaves fly by,
the sky goes dark.
There's nothing but,
naked trees in the night.
We had fun in the Winter, Spring,
and Summer and now it is finally Fall.
There will be kids,
trick or treating on Halloween.
A turkey roasting on Thanksgiving.
We're so happy to say . . .
Fall is coming!

Elisha Ann Gonsalves

The Firestorm

Beyond the horizon
the sky rages with fire
smoke fills the air
and obscures my view
the roar of destruction
threatens
the scent of loss
overpowering
people defending their homes
now ashes
neighbor helping neighbor
families separated
searching
loved ones embrace
debris smoldering
remind of the storm that passed

Jullianne Blommer

Puddles And Souls

Cloudy day, cloudy day.
The rain that washed
Our souls away.
The tears that make up
These puddles . . .
Where we see our reflections
Mock the confessions
Of all those who join us
In the puddle of souls.

Jeremy Adam Lind

Stop The Hate

You're not the right size
You're not the right shape
You don't have the right style
You're not the right race

Sometimes they say
You have the wrong friends
Oh when will these words
All come to an end

Do they feel that bad
That they have to put you down
Why does it give them joy
Whenever you frown

Don't they know on the inside
We're all the same color
And everyone looks
Just like each other

We all have a heart
That no one can take
So why can't we stop
All of this hate

Sharon Cross

America

America, the beautiful
the snowy mountain tops,
the green grass lands,
the rolling hills,
the sandy, rocky desert,
the snow covered ice land,
and the big open oceans.

The Soaring eagles,
the prairie dogs,
the white, haired, horned goats,
the sidewinding rattle snakes,
the snow land Huskies,
and the ocean traveling whales,

America
We are the proud,
we are the few patriot people,
and we are proud to call our
selves americans!

Daryll Yarger

My Blessings

My ears are tuned to listen for
The sound of tiny feet,
Or whimper in the dark to tell
Me of a restless sleep.
My hands are shaped just right
To soothe a childish bump
Or ease an aching head.
No matter if they're rough,
Or if I have not read
The latest books, or seen
The plays they recommend
I'm much too busy with the work
You gave me to attend.
As I strive to finish all the tasks
That seem to have no end,
Help me to still remember, Lord
How blessed I really am.

Gertrude B. Wilson

Nothing Is The Same

When I was young,
The stars were just night lights,
The sun could say, "good night",
The moon was my friend.

When I was young,
The world had just two sides,
My life was a free ride,
My fun had no end.

Now that I've grown up
The world is a cruel place,
My life is a car chase.
Nothing is the same.

Now that I've grown up,
The stars are so far away,
The moon never stops to play.
Nothing is the same.

Nothing is the same
Now that I've grown up.
Nothing is the same
Now that it's all mixed up.

Jeremy M. Young

The Barrier

White walls all around me
The stones are outside
Grim faces I don't see

White flowers all too soon
Turn black with withering sun
only to die.

Why should I want to escape
When quiet abounds in peace
not in dreams.

The withering flowers will cry
The stones may beat in wraith
maybe not.

The one that stands alone
Will soon search and seek
What is not to be found.

How can I know
With no voice to hear tell me,
Not to go.
You answer.

Heather Albee

Seasons Of Our Lives

Drowning in the plight of the season!
the sun rises today awfully in the west
the hopes of the setting is east laden!
I wallow in the agony of my expectation,
alas' the time of reckoning,
the residue of the shifting season.
Drowning in the plight of the season!
the moon steals a light from darkness
turning the darkness of the night into
an autumn afternoon,
alas' summer eclipsed in indian fashion!
Drowning in the plight of the season
the rainy foggy days, turns the night
into a dreamy drenched trenchcoat night
Drowning in the plight of the season
the leaves shed greeny shine for
dry sun baked saharan dust
alas' old man winter arriving on
a slow turning coal powered train
oh drowning in the plight of the season!

Daley J. Obi-Bandale

Moments We Share

The things we say
The things we do
In some little way
Show we care about you

Even though we have a voice
Many times we have said yes
But when there is no choice
We pray the Lord will bless

Our thoughts are with you
Your well being we care
It will always be true
Your sorrow we share

Jerry L. Shelton

Unseen Things

Why do we take for granted
The things we do not see?
Those things that bless our life,
Yet pushed aside impatiently.
Like stars up in the noon day sky
That will not be seen till night,
Unable to outshine the sun,
They still magnify its light.
Or the heart, that works like bellows,
To pump life through everyone,
The thought behind a simple gift,
Or a prayer for a son.
The wind that plays within the leaves,
The love in a parent's hand,
The blossoming of a single flower,
Or the dew upon the land.
Not upon our daily works,
Or whatever we do best,
But whether or not we're thankful,
That is what He'll test.

Charles Brian Jacoby

Lady Snow

Oh, queen of winter, Lady Snow,
The time has come that you should go,
We urge you to be on your way,
And linger not another day.

You look lovely in pearl white dress,
But we deplore your iciness,
And wish you gone, please melt away,
So Spring can move in we pray.

We long to hear the sweet birds sing,
To feel again the breath of spring,
Retire now and do not wait
To end your cold reign . . . abdicate!

Gwyndolyn Smith

Ending To Beginning

Oh dawn's early light
The time of refreshing has come
Red tired eyes to bright
A few stretches here and there
Flexing the legs to withstand the day
Shoulders relaxed to balance the gait
Stretching the mind,
Setting the attitude
A BRIGHT CHERRY SMILE
Silently thinking . . . "KISS"
The one my heart loves
That portion of my journey that keeps me
Going, going, going . . .
A beautiful sight for sore eyes
HELLO,
GOOD MORNING!

Dolores Bugg

Rain

Hear
The rain.
Drip, drop
Is it the rain
Is it my heart!
Pitter, patter
On the roof.
Outside my window
It is dark.
Rain, rain
Go away

Betty Scheider

Light Of My Life

The littlest fingers
The tiniest toes
The beautiful eyes
The cute button nose
You mean so very much
Your precious smile
Your sweet little touch
I brought you into this world
but you've given me so much more
You've taught me how to love again
You've taught me that even before
You can heal the pain
You need to try to care again
Thank you my darling son
I love you so much, you are the one
Truly the light of my life

Heather Erin Kane

Tender Moments

The twinkle in your eyes,
The touch that's in your hand.
Let's me know you love me,
And I'm your special man.

Tender moment's we spend,
With every breath we take.
Two heart's that beat as one,
Can only mend, not break.

Precious than the diamonds,
That shine upon your hand.
Stronger than the gold,
That's in our wedding bands.

Our love is our bond,
That only comes from above.
Purer than the olive branch,
That was carried by the dove.

Tender moments that are lost,
When ever we're apart.
Always remember never forget,
Your always in my heart.

Gary W. Willey

Warrior's Song

The weather scorching hot
the track a battle ground,
the rider just a warrior
few survivors found.

They train for this a lifetime
at least that's how it seems,
taught since birth to win
fulfilling all their dreams.

Each corner a test of skill
each lap a test of strength,
hot, tired, full of doubt
can I go the final length?

Only one can win
the warrior cries out loud,
there is no second best
to lose is not allowed.

In the final moments
when push comes to shove
the warrior who perseveres
will be the one to rise above.

Dawn Ferguson

Passion's Fever

Passion's fever courses through,
The veins without the poison's few.
It's timeless rhythm twangs my mind
To see what pleasures it may find.

I try to hold on painfully
Through tortures I'm not meant to see.
But, passion flows so easily,
Like liquid on my soul.

It finds my heart, it skips a beat,
Then slowly trickles toward my feet.
Making bold what once was meek.
Can you see it in my eyes?

Time, it passes steadily
While passion holds its eager beat.
It makes all other thoughts retreat
Relentless to my cry.

Jill Dehner

Eternal Nap

Understand now the patience
The waiting, the grievance of death
When the ones we love are taken
And upon their last whispery breath
They mumble about something they've seen
That they want us to know all about
But what whispery breath is so soft
That nothing but hisses come out
We strain our ears to hear the sound
As our lovers die in our lap
But the voice is silenced fatefully
When they slip into eternal nap.

Jenn Herbstreit

The Sun

I love the sunshine.
The way it feels on my face
makes me want to smile.

April Tolison

The Sounds Of Nature

How silent, how silent,
The world appears to be
The whispered sound of river flow,
Among the strong, tall trees.

Look about so you can see,
The beauty all around.
Quiet now and you will hear,
Natures lovely sounds.

The songs of birds fill the air,
Their beauty to behold.
While within the roaring wind,
Are tales never told.

Karen Lowry

Without Your Love

Without your love there is no home.
The world is around me, yet I am alone.
We never said our last farewell.
We never said our last good-bye.
You were gone before I knew it.
For only thy Lord knows why.
You won't be back for I know that's true.
But someday my love, I will come to you.

J. Kevin

Her Scent

He buried his face in her robe, but
the years had passed and so had
her scent. Passed from her robe but
not his mind.

He drifted into a peaceful
sleep, his chest raised as his
body with his permission drew
its last breath. His chest lowered
and her name whispered across
his lips one last time.

Her name was heard on the
other side and the angels
ascended to summon her,
and on their wings they
brought her forth to greet him.

He opened his eyes to her smile,
her scent glowed all around her.
She reached and gently took
his hand, and with them the
angels ascended again.

Deloris Miller

Untitled

God is awesome who can know
thee is he that all knowing
spirit or is it just me

I know it as love not just
something coming from above
I look for it as a white dove
or a hand in white glove
I don't know it but I know me
I walk each day and night ever
closer to thee

Elizabeth Jenkins

Night Duty In the Children's Ward

At dusk my lambs are folded in
Their little stalls; the daytime din
Is hushed, and I, their shepherd, keep
A lonely virgil while they sleep.

No enemy must enter here,
No labored breath escape my ear,
No changing pulse, no fever heat,
No heart that falters in its beat.

The morning light must find all well,
My charts a peaceful night must tell
My ailing lambs must stronger be
Healed by the night's serenity.

Then shall I seek my own warm rest
With thanks to him who shepherds best-
Who finding us all erring sheep,
Yet never fails his watch to keep.

And if perchance I once might save
A sickly lamb from dangers grave-
I'd feel like him who all alone
Sought the lost lamb and brought it home.

Alice Surdam

Hate

If hate is a fire
    then give me a pool
If hate is a trick
    then let me out fool
If hate is a story
    then I'll close the book
If hate is a vision
    I just won't look
If hate is music
    then I'll break the beat
If hate is food
    then I just won't eat
If hate is a broken heart
    then I just won't love
If hate is a bird
    then I don't like the dove
If hate is a brother.
    then I'll let him be
If hate is a person
    then don't let it be me
      Beth-Anne M.

To Be Free

    Inside of me,
there must be a place
of forgiveness, sadness has
filled my heart, send this
burden away, I pray to the
Gods of Wisdom. I want
to be free, like the wind.
Excepting the things I
face. And knowing they are
meant to be. I want to win
the challenge, then I'll truly
be free.
    As I journey
blindly down this road, in
desperate search. Have
you compelled me to
write this. I summon
you to peace!
      Bridget Eddy

Future

Here there is sadness.
There, there is doubt.
Up in uncertain.
Out is alone.

Here there is known.
There, there is hope.
Up is unwanted.
Out is unknown.

Here there is hate.
There, there is like.
Up is related.
Out is cruel.

Where should one go?
What should one do?
There is only one thing.
That is hope!
      Cheyenne Walker

Silent Night

The world is silent
There's a crash
A deep sorrow
A friend
That has no tomorrow.
      Faith Ann Payne

Mistakes Can Kill A Heart And A Soul

I'm all by myself
There's no one around
My hopes all desert me
As darkness surrounds

Will it swallow me now
Or will it wait another day
For my hopes to return
Only to again take them away

It surrounds me with doubt
And chases away my dreams
When I close my eyes at night
I can hear Hellish screams

Screams from my past
Causing grief and despair
Is it just me
Or is there no air

As my last breath is taken
My vision starts to blur
Just think all this happened
Because of what I did to her
      Josh Duran

The Dance Is Over

The great hall has emptied,
There's nothing but wax on the floor,
The lights have all turned to black,
A padlock embraces the door,
The dance is over,

The moonlight has awakened
Shadows on the windows and wall,
The bandstand seems so lonely now,
The only thing left in the hall,
The dance is over.

The silence stays unbroken,
There is not a note to be heard,
The musicians won't come back now,
For goodnight was their last word,
The dance is over.
      John N. Barry

The Lonely Sailor

Sail on constant wanderer,
the seafaring vagrant you are,
to the secluded isles,
to the desolate stars,

a staid and ghoulish shadow,
drifting by moonlit tide,
monotonous salty sprays,
horizons spread so wide,

outcast a rocking vessel,
stifled to and fro,
a singled handed oarsman,
has not a place to go.
      Bonnie L. Smith

Bitter

Bitter thoughts are in my mind,
They are in my heart as well.
Those bitter thoughts I cant control,
Will they take me straight to hell?

Spiteful gestures and angry words
Have driven my friends away.
The answer is in the Bible, you say?
It is not — don't be absurd!

God is not mean; He is not cruel.
He wouldn't doom me to this chair.
I'll end my life. It's over anyhow.
Nothing left but dark despair.
Oh God! Don't you even care?

Lord, what did you say?
A small price to pay?
To no longer feel uneasy, no longer feel
tossed.
My sins are forgiven,
By Christ, on the cross.
      Debra Bennett

Best Friends

Best friends don't fight
They brighten the light,
And stand by one another
Like a sister or brother,
You can trust them til the end
If they're really a true best friend,
They'll wipe away your tears
And help overcome your fears,
If they're really a true best friend!
      Julie Shadowens

Friendship

Friends are very special,
They don't laugh or call you names.
And when you really need them,
They're there to hear your pains.

Friends are people who you can talk to,
Even about the important stuff.
They won't tell you secrets,
Even when they've had enough.

True friends won't cheat you,
Or stab you in the back.
True friends won't hurt you,
Or you can hurt them back.

Friends will always love you,
No matter what you do.
Friends will always be there,
All through the hard times too!

True friends will stay together.
No matter what comes between you.
Friends can last forever,
The choice is up to you!
      Elizabeth Trosell

"Two Hearts"

Two young hearts fall in love.
They soon marry.
Promising to love each other
Till death do them part.
This was not puppy love
It was very real.
So real it has lasted over fifty years.
Two middle age hearts struggling
But still together.
Two old but young at heart, hearts.
Alone, like they started out.
But still together.
Till death do them part.

Beatrice E. Dimas

An Angels Whisper

Angels whisper softly
They'll whisper in your ear
They sit upon your shoulder
And they'll wipe away your tears

No need to feel so lonely
He's right there by your side
Yes he's your guardian angel
And he'll always be your guide

One more note of reassurance
He's especially for you
You'll always have an angel
No matter what you do

So listen very carefully
To the whisper in your ear
Never again feel lonely
Your angel is always near

Elizabeth Vega

Time Tomb

I walk among the graves of friends
thinking of what I've done
I set the bomb that killed them all
each and everyone.
A homeless vagabond I've become
since that fateful day
when I pushed that little button
that blew them all away.
I think of the bomb which is myself
and ponder that which I've done.
I've taken their lives, snuffed them out
what is it I've become?
I look into mine own eyes and see
purest hatred staring back at me.
I avert my eyes and trudge along
thinking of just how far I've gone.

Adam Lowery

Ellen Pompper

I think and pray in
this fine land
about homeless
who needs our hand
some of us, are high
and above. To even spare
an once of love.
Lets all work together
because they are on the
Street living in all kind of weather

Doris Denby

Life, To Death, To God

I see a great light,
this is not right.

For where I stand,
it is dark and bland.

This should not be,
but yet the light I see.

An angel by my bed,
looked at me and said.

I now take your soul,
so now God shall hold.

Jason Micheal Nelson

Untitled

I wonder what life is all about
This life with all its tears.
I try to plan what I'm about
But all that comes are fears.

They say that I am warm and nice
so very easy to be near.
But, dear God in heaven, don't they know
I'm, filled with my own tears.

I'd like some comfort to come my way
and ease this heavy heart.
He left me one cold night,
was here then gone from sight.

The night before he was laid to rest,
a shimmering gold light appeared.
It wrapped itself around me,
so comforting and warm.
He came and said goodbye to me,
my love I thought was gone.

In that night I knew what life was all about
He gave me strength to live and face this
life with all its fears.

Francine Ladinsky

This Old House

This old house is loosing its shingles,
This old house is loosing its doors,
This old house is loosing its windows,
Including its all wood floors.

This old house has a lot of history,
This old house has a lot of charm,
This old house has a lot of character,
Including its all around farm.

This old house saw a lot of wind,
This old house saw a lot of pain,
This old house saw a lot of sunshine,
Including a lot of good rain.

This old house saw a lot of mosquitos,
This old house saw a lot of flies,
This old house saw a lot of bees,
Including its good old pies.

This old house it is still standing,
This old house was built in seven,
This old house saw five little children,
Including all hoping to go to heaven.

Eldon D. Johnson

Safety Net

Safety is the byword
This we must respect
It is best for all
Who wish to grow tall
In order not to fall
It seems a shame
Because we must
Take the blame
Looking ahead
Gives us a chance
To provide at a glance
This which we need
To prance.
New ways are here
If we would only adhere
The choice is ours
Which can be very far
With a little help
There is less of a yelp

Edward T. Philpitt

Prayer For Inky

O, Great Master,
Thou art all knowing,
Caring, Loving and Kind.
Thou knowest all Thy
Creatures Great and Small.

Accept into thy Kingdom
This Creature of Yours,
You know he has suffered greatly,
Let him, O, Master
Roam to his hearts content.

Great Master, I know cats
Have no soul, but somehow there
are special ones that wait for
Their friends, and somehow
Inky is one of them.

Great Master,
Your understanding is Great,
Please accept into Thy
Kingdom this Creature of Yours
Amen.

Bonita D. Whitmire

As I Dream

As I dream, I think of you . . .
Though it seems, moments are few.
Love, there is always mine,
Cut above, till the end of time.
As I dream, I think of you.

As I dream, I think of you . . .
That one beam, kept is as two.
This message deep in my heart,
Lifts the essence of thoughts apart.
As I dream, I think of you.

Sometimes our life's have stayed.
Love sublime, raptures delayed.
Unlike the rest, we have power.
I longed for you by the hour.
As I dream, I think of you.

Passions surreal can't compare,
To what I feel, and how I care.
Every second that is ours,
Is the light that opens flowers.
As I dream, I think of you . . .

Heather A. Whitlock

Memories of a Day of Love

'Tis true we should have waited
Though kindled by our love so strong,
Let us reflect upon our memories
And treasure them, my love.

I sat upon thy lap, with arms
Embraced around thee.
What happiness, my love.
Gentle kisses upon thy cheeks I placed.

The sounds of music playing,
With laughter in the air,
And simple chores seemed such a pleasure
When shared with one whom I adore.

Oh how gentle was the night,
With full moon glowing oh so bright,
And angels watching from above,
And a chance to share in love, my love.

So keep these treasures with you, my
darling,
And carry them with you always.
If when we meet again, my love,
You know I love you always.

Gail Carson

Married Lady

My thoughts return to her again
though logic tells me better.
My heart cries out to her in vain
and yet I can't forget her.

She needs me now - she needs me not
and vacillates between her aims.
She dearly wants to (but cannot)
give in to our hearts' claims.

Steadfast she stands upon her pride
and will not break her honor,
and though her heart cannot decide,
the cloak of courage is upon her.

For which of thee, "ladies fair",
would dare to take her place?
Could YOU refuse to loose your hair
and gaze into your lover's face?

But all things come in proper season,
in their rightful place and time,
and in that hope there lies the reason
and the purpose for this rhyme.

Bernard Kerrick

Virginia

A special lady is Virginnie
Though some may say she's windy.
She's thoughtful and sweet,
and wouldn't be complete
without her good friend, Franci.
She's a teacher, a healer,
A counselor and friend.
She believes in what they call karma,
That's cause and effect.
But, she wouldn't dream to harm ya.
For she knows she would pay in the end.
She means a lot
To those who've got
An ache or a pain in the shoulder.
For to me, you see,
She'll always be
My mentor, my friend, Virginnie.

Gail Condon

Faraway Comfort

I often feel you close
Though you're far away
I even hear your voice
In the songs that the wind plays
The words of love flow softly
Gently through the breeze
Bringing a message of comfort
The messengers are the trees
The love you have for me
I will forever hold inside
Never showing to anyone
The tears that I have cried
They aren't tears of sorrow
Or of a deep and burdensome care
They are tears of joy and remembrance
From the times that we have shared
I know we can't go back
For time isn't so kind
But, you truly are the best friend
One could ever find

Catherine M. Richmond

The Fly

It flies;
through air of hate
and lies,
racism kills,
it will die
labeled and chastised,
though still,
it flies,
a pest through eyes
but no one knows,
what's inside,
analyzed and despised
it flies,
until swatted
so
it dies.

David Berman

As The River Goes By

As I sit on the bank, thoughts ran
through my mind.
Feeling how I once felt, I could
break down and cry.
I turn to the water to see who
I found, it's me and my life now.
I see through the face of this
beautiful child and look deep
inside to find, she's not really wild.
While she sits on the bank all
her old feelings start to die,
and all this happens as the
river goes by.

Christine Lynn Williams

Valentine's Day

A day that's put aside,
to say how much we love.

A day in winter's chill,
clouds menacing above.

A day to pierce the gray,
with the brilliance of the sun.

A day to say how glad I am,
that you're the only one.

Jack Troyanovich

Thinking Of You

"Thoughts of you drifted ever so softly
thru my mind,

Listening to classical music from
where I recline,

Light waves in the harbor dance a design,
    The phone rang and it was
you on the line,

The prose you read me, was
simply divine,

For you, my dear, are a romantic,
To me your call was a sign,

I am thinking of you, all
Of the time.

Edward L. Davis

Forsythia To My Heart

You are forsythia
To my heart.
Like springtime
you slip along
its musty hallways
scattering sunshine
to seed and bloom
forever there.

Betsy V. Jacobson

Untitled

The wounding of a mine
Time have past
Day have gone
Many have die
Baby's have born
None to tall
None to small
But life go on
Sun come up
Moon go down
The things I know
But when my breath will go
And my body dust to dust
The wounding of a mine

Barbara Voline Delaney

Lovers' Time

When Lovers make Love,
time stands still.
Minutes may Seem Forever,
When Hearts beat Together.

In Lovers' Time,
Months go in quick Course.
Time to Love on Earth is too Short,
There is no time to Court.

Minutes are too Long to hold a Breath,
Days are too Long to Run.
Months are gone when Their eyes Blink,
Years are Here tomorrow.

Years are Minutes,
In Lovers' Time.
When Lovers make Love,
Time stands Still.

James M. Breeden

Smile!

A smile without the "S,"
'Tis a mile under the Sun.
The best, I must confess,
To be cherished by everyone.

Denotes the distance it will shine,
Which is really very fine.
An' remembered forever more,
Like the welcome on the door.

Demands a like return,
Of all that does receive.
A spontaneous concern,
That gives Us a reprieve.

And like as not,
The feeling we got,
Draws us back for more.
Of that smile, for sure.

This is to say,
That You brighten the day.
So don't change, pretty one,
And here's hoping, you have fun.

Joseph C. Woods

"Heavens Just A Prayer Away"

Come pray with me,
To a far away land,
Where departed love,
Walks hand in hand.

A place that's home,
For the holy man,
And the sins of life,
Have all been banned.

No more hurt,
And no one cries,
No more death,
And no goodbyes.

Eternal life,
For those who pray,
And all the children,
Can laugh and play.

Oh, dear Lord,
Please hear my plea,
And reserve a place there,
For my family.

Jimmy G. Simmons

Foolish Heart

Physical attraction, lust leads
To passion.

Reality escapes, heartfelt
Desires await.

Our feelings we share.
You say, you don't care.
Those are the words,
I most feared I'd hear.
My eyes have suddenly
begun to well up
full of tears.

Oh, mind of mine,
(not worth a dime).
True love is endless,
But it takes time to find.

Debbie Kirchgessner

Untitled

I have enough inside
    To be strong for you.
When you're looking for
    Light in this great darkness
Let me be your candle.
    To lead you to the dawn.
Come to me when your needs
    Make you empty within
I will fill you with me,
    I will make you whole again.
I will slip in and out of
    Your life,
Like the tides.
    I will not drag you under
Only hold your aloft
    To be warmed by the sun.
Come to me
    With your needs
I need only give to you
    To be fulfilled.

Christine Moores

The Idiot Am I

The idiot am I,
to be stupid is essential.
I feel the fool,
I am.
What could I have been thinking?
What was on my mind?
Foolish thoughts.
To think I was ahead,
I'm not.
It places me to the rear,
The place where I began.
Hard work. Determination.
All shot down
Like a bird of prey.
Dear God, help me
My life is turning backwards upon itself.
I can do nothing to save myself.
Can you?
For I am the idiot,
I am.

Estonia Narey Stampley

The World Today And The World Tomorrow

The world today is about
to come to and end.
We kill we rod and do all
kinds of sin.
The world tomorrow how could
it be if we do bad things you
know you and me.
To make a brighter tomorrow, we
must do right to day.
Before tomorrow is faded a way.

Erwin C. Phillips

Jesus I'm Seeking!

Jesus, sweet Jesus, I'm seeking thee.
Though oft in this life I fail in thee,
In the next life, I shall surely be!

Joseph E. McMillan

Generations

His arms open wide
To embrace and I,
Pulling my askew
Hat to rights,
Hold his thin body close
Looking at this miniature
Version of my first born
My heart swells
With love as the
Magical word erupts
From his lips "Nana"

Bettye Hodge Culbreth

Pollution

There is always a solution
To every kind of pollution!
You have to keep the world clean
So that everything can be seen,
But please don't be mean
And please start to clean!
The world use to be clean
But some people aren't keen.
It has to be the way it should of been!
So, make a resolution
To stop pollution!

K-Ming Lee & Kent-Fuh Lee

To Granny

We are as two stray sheep trying
to find our way, only I am young
and you are old.

You lived your life on earth and
finally found your way with the
dear Lord above.

Now I must live my life until
someday I shall meet you in the
great beyond.

We loved each other dearly until
the time came that I couldn't reach
you. You were ill and I couldn't
help you, but you know I will never
forget you.

They say on that final judgement day
we shall not know one another, but
I am sure when I see you I shall
know you were someone special.

Carolyn Duncan

"Illusion Of A Smile"

Who brings dancing shadows,
To frighten my night?
'Tis only the moon,
Bearing his light.
Who watches my steps,
And smiles in the dark?
'Tis the moon once again,
Showing his mark.
Who dances with stars,
'Til dawn is reborn?
'Tis joyous moon,
Who sleeps come morn'.
Who reminds me in darkness,
Light's at the end?
'Tis the man in the moon,
With a smile: Faithful friend.

Andrea Furguiele

Laughter

I like to hear the sound of gentle rain;
To hear the singing of a bird.
But the laughter of a little child
Is the sweetest sound I've ever heard.

A sunny day- a waterfall-
Oh, what could bring such joy!
It would have to be the laughter
Of a little girl or boy.

Laughter is a little smile
That bubbles into sound.
Wherever you hear that laughter, sweet,
You know a child will there be found.

Gloria H. Koplin

You

GOD had just blended a color tint
   To paint a rainbow and a dawn,
But paused a moment for a bud to burst
   Lo, He looked and His paint was gone!

Jesse M. Beck

Buried Treasure

A never ending probing quest
To points unknown within my chest
Must be buried treasure there
Surely valuable and rare
Surgeons open me, they dig within
Quite often much to my chagrin
All who see me thus incited
I myself not that delighted
They'll have to seek another pastime
I've been prospected for the last time

Bob Strauss

My Wonderful Gift

GOD gave me a wonderful Gift
To share all the days of my life
In sickness and health together
We struggled to keep things just wright

We vowed on the day of our wedding
To love each other for life
To bear all our troubles and sorrow
It was not all sugar and spices

And now on this day may I tell you
We kept the promise we made
We cared for each other in sickness
We shared all our aches and our pain

And now this day is upon us
To tell each other again
I love you now more than ever
Dear GOD, please keep it the same

Caleb Hess

Always

I sail on a sea of dreams,
trying to escape reality.
I travel through time
To many different places,
As many different people.
But where ever I go,
And who ever I am
You are there with me . . .
   Always.

Darren Lee Malloy

A Gift

"Yes my child God looks down,
To the circus he gave a clown.
Blessed them with the gift of love
The kind that comes from above."

Clowns dry the tears
Of a crying child
To a troubled world
They bring a smile.

"Yes my child God looks down,
To the circus he gave a clown.
He took a man painted his face
In the center ring he found his place."

In his lapel
He put a rose
dressed him in some
old baggy clothes.

"Yes my child God looks down
It was God's idea
To make a clown."

Gary Schwebs

The Man I Never Knew

To the man I never knew
To the heart I never reached
May the wind carry your voice,
and the country house echo
with your forgotten laughter.
To the man who was always old
To the man whose cane swung about my head.
May the land which holds your body
know the treasure it has engulfed,
and the body by your side sleep
peacefully
knowing your love for her.
To this man your father and my
grandfather
I say rest in tranquility.
Forever

Jeff Vining

I To

I sit alone and watch
To you I'm just a freak
I pray you give me help
To buy something to eat

I sit and dream of simple things
To you they're just a joke
I cry when you will laugh at me
To slowly loose my hope

I sit and stare at humble coats
To dream of being warm
I pray that God forgives your heart
To you I've done the wrong

I sit and wish and dream your life
To you this breeds a grudge
I see you are your brother's friend
To me an unfair judge

I sit and ask of humble things
To you not worth pursuing
I think at times an Erie thought
To you I am not human

Jorge Luis Segarra

The Angry Sea

I awake
To the pounding roar of surf.
The birds wheeled silently,
Voices muted,
Searching for food.
Even the leaves
Ceased their rustle,
In the damp cloud
Of salty mist.
Breaker after breaker
Curled and hurled
The foaming water
To the sand,
Daring any and all the enter,
Tomorrow is another day.

Beverly J. Liarakos

Blow Ye The Trumpet

We are called to be a trumpet,
To sound forth the message of God,
To call the saints to attention,
To walk where Jesus had trod.

To confront the forces of evil,
Take over the strongholds he rules,
To put him under subjection,
And free the ones he has fooled.

Our mission is laid out clearly,
We must obey the word that we know,
To hail the return of our savior,
So pick up your trumpet and blow!!

Irene Phillips

Untitled

Lavender days and drab moons,
To the neurotic world you waken.
Thrown from the womb into the race,
Your innocence has been taken.
Stabbing knives twist in your back
From colleagues seeking promotion.
Your morals thrown out the door,
For the game calls not for devotion.
So by hard knocks you drudge along
Underneath your white starched collar;
Through hardened eyes you see no blonde,
Only deceit of the mighty dollar.

Godfrey Finch

A Place We Used To Go To

I remember a place we
used to go to when
we were happy sad or
needed someone to talk
to you helped me with
my problems we talked
about life, friends, family
or just to listen to
the birds. No one knew
except me and you now
our place is gone and
so are you. I just
wanted to say I love
you and I miss you
very much.

Jessica Hershkowitz

Ties

We go together like left and right,
Together forever, day and night.

We were on our final trip,
Soles together, tongue and tip.
We were on our greatest climb,
And all of the sudden, you fell behind.

I watched you fall, down and down.
I never thought you'd hit the ground.
Then I saw the dust cloud rise,
But would not reach to wipe my eyes,
For I was fixed with stubborn ties.

Now you're gone, they don't need me.
I've ended up where you can't be.
The deep dark box I've been before,
Sitting on an empty floor.

I hope in near fate,
I will have another mate.
One with also weeping eyes,
Another fixed with stubborn ties.

Jayne Lynn Roberts

To The Newly Weds

As you walk down the aisle
Together holding hands
As you repeat the marriage vows
And place the wedding bands

You will be starting a journey
Down the road of life
No longer alone, but together
As husband and wife

Two very special persons
With hearts so full of love
I'm sure they have been blessed
By heaven above

May you always be as happy
As you are on this day
May God bless and keep you
In His own special way.

Barbara Mallett

My Daughter

I have a daughter who is one,
Together we have all sorts of fun.
When she smiles I feel a glow,
Sometimes I wish she would not grow.
When she sleeps she has no fears,
Because her daddy is all ears.
When I'm gone I know I'm missed,
Because I'm rewarded with a kiss.
When she gets hurt and starts to cry,
I just feel like I could die.
I thank the Lord for this swell gift,
Because it gives me such a lift.
When its time to say, "good night"
She doesn't want me out of sight.

Joseph A. Waschensky

Vows

Take hold of my hand.
Together, you and I
will share the joys of this life.
As we grow stronger,
together, as one
we will see the
wonders of the Earth and Stars:
Flowing water,
Magical breezes
Restless Ocean tides,
Flowing meadows,
Glowing sunsets,
Trees soaring to the sky,
Dancing flames,
Floating snow,
The birth of our children.
**Our life together will sing
the joys of the universe**.

Greg Thomas

On Wings Of Eternity

Your life like a bright, precious gift
Touched me fingertip to fingertip
With emotions fragile as a flower petal
Substance sturdy as a lustrous metal
Bringing with it forgotten hope
Man was not lost in murder and dope

With a laugh to lighten the distraught
A smile to warm those with cold hearts
You sprouted like Jack's beanstalk
Reached for the sky like a fearless hawk
Proud of our men in aviation blue
Silver wings was what you wanted too

Always striving for life's utmost
This pilot flew to our divine host
When spirit and mind were cloaked
  with flesh
You were still apart from all the rest
A regal peacock in Air force blue
Longer do I wish you had cooed

Janice Marie Forbriger

The Lord's Touch

The finger of the Lord points high
toward an eternally blackened sky.
"Let there be light!" The Lord does say,
and the sun arose to make the day.
The earth and all within, it's said,
was made by GOD as He was led.
Man and woman He also made
and gave to them a garden pure,
theirs for as long as they obeyed.

A certain tree in the center stood
with fruit of wondrous power. "If
they did eat," the serpent said,
"all knowledge it will shower."
As they did eat there came the shame
and guilt that wrong will bring.
The finger of GOD pointed to the man
and He took away everything.

The moral of this story is as clear as glass.
Listen to the Lord, my friend,
and not that snake in the grass.

Francis B. Frappier

Seasons Of Time

The mountain peaks reach
Toward heaven
As the snow falls gently
On the pine trees
Warmth and contentment
Flow through me
As I watch the scenery
From my cabin door.

The cool breeze whips
Against my face
As I'm watching
The birds in flight.
The sun shines
Brightly in
The sky above
As I feel God's
Love
Embrace
My heart.

Brenda Grosdov

Christmas

Lights
Trees, ribbons
Music, talking, family
Stars, angles, cookies, marshmallows
December

Laughter
Wassail, kisses
Warm blankets, smells, popcorn
Songs, spices, gingerbread, bells
Starlight

Candy
Egg nog
Life savers, nuts
Pumpkin pie, hot tea
Chocolate

Santa Clause
Merry, bright
Helpful, giving, loving
Fulfillment, disappointment, happiness, joy
Christmas

Esther Gausepohl

Your Mine

Something inside
tries to arrive
making its way to your world

The feelings are out
the damage is done
wondering deep in your mind

Another year older
what have you learned
only that time seems to fly

Summer is here
your not so near
wondering deep if your mine.

C.R. Fuentes

Winter Imprint

Large fluffy snowflakes
Tumbling everywhere
Laughing, twirling
Full of life and glee

Clinging collectively
Swiftly assembling
Breathtaking fairyland
Awesome to perceive
'Til the sun gently nudges
With glowing reality

Eleanor Taylor Anthony

Elegy On The Doppler Effect

At last we understood why leaves
turn red in fall;
saw it was not just botanical
but that they are in Doppler's red-shift,
moving away from us
in time, so rapidly
by that phenomenon of physics
which explains why,
by the time we
reach the tree
to gather autumn foliage,
the leaves are gone,
it is December
and we have changed
irreparably.

Cie Christian

Wasted Youth

Iridescent orbs of amber light
twisted and turned
whilst politic unfurled
and mounted wenches cried aloud,
sigh of pain and orgasmic death,
filtered browns and blacks, out, cast
minions of hatred, bought,
and sold, cattle lead to slaughter.
Innocent lives not unlike our own
pawned for petty cash accounts
spent and wasted, a nation
of youth, lost to fuel the fires,
ignited two thousand years ago.
By another, youth, wasted,
truth turned round
spinning lights, the club
closes, another night of
dead dreams and screamed
comforts left behind.

Chris Wiener

Love Poem

Troubled by the world's deceit
Unable to write verse
A shattered spirit dying
The soul sought its retreat.

Gentle darkness waited
Where pain went unexposed
Engulfed in sensual desires
An inner peace arose.

Strong arms held fast the weakened one
And helped the moment last
Renewed the faith, restored the hope
A better day would dawn.

Jean R. Sweigart

I Did Not Ask For This

To lose something is tragic
Unless the pain is ephemeral
To redeem it is victorious
Unless the joy is temporary
To love someone is ineffable
Unless it is at random
To want someone is passionate
Unless it is dangerous
To hate something is perverse
Unless it is relentless
To give yourself is genuine
Unless it is a one-way street
These emotions together are confusing
Unless there are explanations
But I did not ask for this.

Karen Brennan

Untitled

Hold my heart and squeeze it tight,
Until it weeps no more.
Please place it in a better man
Who knows what hearts are for.
To love, to care, to burdens share
And many a secret store,
But not to place upon the threshold,
Only to slam the door.

Eva Ivans Scott

The Poor

   When poverty and strife weigh
upon one's life.
   Where trouble and sorrow lead to a
narrow path.
   Hero's they become, with unswaying
character.
   With God and Christ they walk hand
in hand.
   Giants of freedom so ever free
comes a precious gift, of abundance and
quality of life.

Cecil R. Blackwell

Say No More

Came up from the South, lilting
voice tripping all over those vowels.
Met her in the hard-edged street.
Oh, she was soft, lovely and it was
summer with all those long, hot days.

Dropped by, talked up a storm
of pictures - so like home, she said,
since she was from the islands.
Oh, she was happy - can't-wait-to-
see-him dizzy, and it was
evening: all those cooling breezes.

Asked her to step with him,
everyone else is doing it!
I'm not everyone, she cried, hearing
the summer songs in his voice,
knowing she was butterfly to his bee.
Oh, she was quiet and a little sad.

Left so soon, down to the South,
Yielding her to all those cold, frosty nights.
Mamma, did I do right? Mamma, did I do right?

Joy R. Scott

Naked November

Tiny tit-mouse atop small maple,
upon which still cling
few gold leaves.

Fire bushes maintain their fire
and black squirrels
have puffy tails.

Still nakedness is all around.
Thanksgiving passing
and Christmas coming.

Silver bark and bright red berries,
hope of blossoms
to follow in spring.

Giant russet oaks
won't yet pose nude, holding fast to
shriveled finery.

Frisky gray squirrel
leaps, lurching along slender
branches of leaning spruce.

Tiny scarlet, gold trees protected by
taller naked ones, show off.

C. Warren-Gayda

Believing

At night I lay my tired head
Upon the pillow in my bed,
And ask the Lord to give me rest
So in the Morn I'll do my best.

I ask the Lord to keep me safe
And let no harm come to this place,
I thank you Lord for all you do
For now I know your Word is true.

Diane M. Anderson

"Heidi's Dawn"

I saw your back
Walking out my door.
I got up and ran behind you.
I wanted to catch up
To you one last time.
I couldn't.
I know you knew
Why I was there.
You couldn't turn.
And I didn't run fast
Enough to ever explain
Why I love you.

Barbara Rosch

Untitled

In this world of pain and sorrow,
We often ask why
Why must the young and the
Innocent have to die?
God, in his wisdom, tells us it
Is not for us to know.
But we, being mortal, fear
The day we must go.
In the end, in spite of the
Pain in our heart,
God will decide when it is
Time for us to depart.

Dorothy M. Olson

457

A Mountain Stream

I came upon a mountain stream,
Was born up high in melting snow,
As souls that start somewhere unseen,
The spark of life to them bestow.

The mountain's womb from whence it came,
Gave forth this child of water clear,
The babble of this bubbling brook,
Like coo of baby did I hear.

With downhill flow it grew in rage,
In swirling curls like silvery hair,
On rust brown rocks advanced its age,
Descending from its mountain lair.

Through forests green it rambled down,
Toward graveyards dug in oceans deep,
On polished stones it sang its song,
Its promised journey's end to keep.

I thought about this stream I found,
So destined to merge into sea,
And my own soul, so earthward bound,
To blend into eternity.

John H. Wright

Early 1930

The butcher shop
    was clean and white
Sawdust covered its floor
Fresh parsley separated
    rows of meats
And bells hung on the door

Behind the counter
    weenies hung
And sides of beef did too
There was a different
    smell in there
I wanted to say "phew"

The butchers wore white aprons
Tied twice about their waist
And if I was especially nice
A weenie I could taste

So it was fun to visit there
And see Uncle John and Dad
The weenies that they gave to me
Were the best I've ever had.

Juanita Leese

"Walls"

Sitting alone.
Watching the walls,
Twiddling my thumbs,
Nothing at all.

The walls whisper.
Staring perpetually,
Invading my mind,
A tangled perplexity.

Utter "psycho"
Thoughts in locality,
Touching vibrations
Outside of reality.

The walls love me.
Giving all,
To have some friends,
To be a wall.

Jeremy Bolden

The Love In Your Heart

The love in your heart
Wasn't put there to stay
The love in your heart
Can be given away

The love in your heart
Can be called "Priceless."
The love in your heart
Can never be "Heartless."

The love in your heart
Can be broken
The love in your heart
Although, will never be soaken

The love in your heart
Can be confused
But make sure the love in your heart
Will never be used

The love in your heart
Will choose that special someone
And the love in your heart
Will bind your hearts together as one

Cresyl A. Nevado

Look

Look at dots
Watch them form pictures.

Look at lightwaves
Watch them form colors.

Look at nothing
Watch it becomes real.

Jacqui Hughes

Trying To Shine

Did you ever see a shining star
way up in the sky?
You try and try to reach it
but it's just to high.

It seems that no matter
what you try to do
there is always someone there
trying to step on you.

You've tried your best
to get to the top
then two-thirds your trip
it all has to stop.

It seems to me
it's just not fair
to lose the battle
before you've ever been there.

Dawn K. Bapst

Working for Jesus

When we think of others,
we bring joy to ourselves.
Let us bring happiness to many.
This wonderful christmas season.

Do some work for Jesus
Help the poor and needy,
tell them of Jesus
He will be their friend.

Donna Sisson

My Brother

There is no other like this one!
We are best friends, but
Sometimes show we're not.
We will stay this way forever, I hope,
For without him, life would not go on.

I have found the greatest
Friendship in this life,
That no one can take away!

We will be separated soon,
(Our graduation day)
And I want him to know
I will never forget him
And the special way he makes me feel
When we're together.

And I hope he knows
I love him,
Specially,
Because he's
My brother.

Eli David Mazet

Our Lives

In the springtime of our lives,
We enjoyed our youthful fun,
But even then, my darling
I knew you were the one.

Now in the summer of our lives
We work and play and love;
To give the best to our children
That God gave from above.

In the fall of our lives
Our children grown and gone,
It will be like springtime
As when it first was known.

Now in the winter of our lives,
We can review the years.
And hold each other more closely,
Then say, "it was good and shed no
tears."

James Brown

True Love

Through the experience of heartache
We often learn to see
The other side of the coin of life;
That which is meant to he.
Through our physical senses
Our vision is often blurred
The message true line has for us
Is often never heard
Yet God knows how to reach as
And reach us he surely will
When we take time to listen
When we are calm and still.
Death is not he end of life
As often we've beau taught
Its just another dimension
Into higher realms of thought
God's love is the only answer,
His love is the glue, you see,
That keeps us one in spirit and truth
Through all eternity.

Evelyn S. Huber

Come Play With Me

Do you remember when
we played in the fields of green;
our minds recreating us each day
as cowboys or movie stars,
or heroes to save the world?

The fields have turned to gray
and no more we play.
Our minds burden us each day
with headlines and deadlines;
our lives all a swirl.

Won't you come and play
together with me
again in those fields of green.
Perhaps you'll discover
you've really become
some of what
you dreamed of back then.

Jeff Jaekley

Father

I will never forget the first time
we saw each other
You looked at me like you could not
believe I was real
I must have looked at you with
confusion, misunderstanding
I was expecting someone
a little taller, a little bolder
Some one more like a God than a dad
Some one to put on a pedestal
rather than put a smile on for
Now I see you are my dad, only mine
I should be proud
I am

Chanda Rothstein

Poem

Destroy your Fennel Stock, my friend.
We fear the Atom's blight.
It's "defence" is fraudulence,
Atropos guessing might.

Dare not ignite it on the Sun
Lest Zeus, his wrath unfurled,
Pronounce a ten-fold punishment
And, lastly, fuse the world!

Alma Marie Ravgiala

Trees In April Snowstorm

Bowed by the weight of driven snow,
    we stand and etch the sky,
We bend, our heads in mute appeal,
    for help, lest we should die.
O Great Lord Sun, we do beseech
    you melt this heavy weight,
With muted tongues we cry to you
    before it is too late.
O Brother Wind, that you may come
    and shake us 'til we're free,
Of weighted burden, and of lace,
    that we may live to see
The promises of springtime
    which we answered weeks ago
With swelling buds and faintest green,
    and rising sap aflow.

Fredericka Borges

My Cup Of Coffee

Let's have a cup of coffee, before
we start our day.
Before we have our coffee let's
take time to pray.
Let's thank our Lord and Savior
for everything we have
cause without him things surely
would be bad.
Now take a sip of coffee,
see how good it taste.
Because we took a little time
to put everything in place.
We thank Him for the lovely day
and everyone's good health.
Why on earth do people think
they need a lot of wealth?
All we need is lots of love and
learning how to pray.
Then our cup of coffee will
taste better every day.

Betty L. Cain

My Mother, My Friend

Mother,
We weren't always friends;
We've had our differences.
But we've learned to accept each other;
For who we are and what we believe.
We still don't agree on everything,
But we do believe in each other.

Mother,
You've always been there;
Through the years;
Through the miles;
And in my heart.

I hope that someday,
I am able to give to my children
What you have given me . . .

A handclasp, warm and strong,
Filled with everything you've been.
Your ever thoughtful ways,
Loving me whatever I did.
My mother, my friend . . . I LOVE YOU!

Christine Malcom

Puppies

With sharp little teeth,
Wear some shoes on your feet.
Running around to pee,
Guess who gets to clean me.
All those toys to chew,
Hope he don't get my shoes.
Clumsy on their paws.
Give them plenty to gnaw.
Maybe push around a ball,
it don't matter how small.
Always running around,
Never knowing where they are bound.
Needs his own little bed,
No, he can't sleep with Fred.
Once you give them a name,
Life will never be the same.
Don't look at it as a chore,
You'll never be bored,
Lifetime of memories are in store.

Carol Mahan

Fly

Come fly with me
We'll fly across the emerald seas
We'll fly to the top of the trees
Come fly with me

Fly with me, our bodies entangled
The gleam in your eye
The sweat of our bodies
Now, before we say good-bye

Fly with me
Where nothing can hold us
Where nothing can touch us
We will fly above all reality

Come fly with me
I will fly to the darkest of your hell
I will hold you, I will comfort you
Only to return to soar, and never shall we
tell

Come fly with me, far above all
We shall share and that we may see
But, my friend, I pray thee . . .
Never, take my wings from me

Dona Jourdan-Gantner

Don't Forget to Smile

We're not on Earth forever
We're here only for a while
So make the best of it while you can
And don't forget to smile

For if you go through life
Not showing how you feel
You'll end up having enemies
Who say you don't act real

But you have to be yourself
Not someone else you know
You can learn from your mistakes
For they will help you grow

So, don't hide how you feel
Let the world know
That you are definitely real
And you can really grow

Cindie Novosel

Take Two Hugs

If only hugs
were medicine . . .
No prescription
no cost
no traveling . . .

We would all
be doctors.
All we need
are two arms
and a body
to hold.

Just think
how easy
it would be
to cure someone . . .
a hug
filled with
a dose
of love.

Janet Hill Cushing

Untitled

I cannot help but wonder,
What a child
   would think of thunder,
If he were alone
   upon the sand
With no one
   to hold his hand.
No one to smile and say,
Now the rains will come today,
  to wash the faces
of the flowers
and make new places
   in the sand
for you to play upon.
When the rains
have come and gone . . .
Have come and gone . . .

Irma Provorse Jones

Wondering

  I wonder what went wrong?
What could have been done,
to make it better for everyone.
  I wonder if they cried at night or
did they pray and hope for everyone?
  I wonder what went through
their heads, as they laid there
in their beds? Did they toss and
turn, scream and cry or just
lay there to die?
  I wonder if they didn't care
and just gave up on hope and God?
Or if anyone could have
stopped it? And if not now come?

Jillian Quinlin

Untitled

  In the eyes of a child
What did he pick up? You ask
of a little boy in a blue shirt,
golden blond hair and sky blue eyes
Then I said "I think it was attention.
as me closer looked—we saw
it was crumbs that had fallen
  to the floor
from attention given
  to someone else

Evon Cohernour

An Ode To Mom

We laugh when we want to cry
  When grief is in the air.
A loved one dies and leaves us.
  Can that be really fair?
Dear Mom has gone to Heaven,
  That's the only place she'd be.
Tied no more to life's confines
  Her spirit is floating free.

Those she has left behind her,
  With whom she shared her love,
Will feel her presence always
  As she smiles down from above.
And now, dear Mom, we're sure
  We know wherever you are
We'll always feel you near us
  You cannot be very far.

Harland Hausske

Untitled

My sister had an abortion
WHAT! I didn't even know . . .
she had sex

She cried later
she still cries

So do I

Mom, what did mom say—
The usual, go pray
you know . . .
confession

God, saves us all
"Trust Jesus" painted in blue
all the way to Asheville North Carolina
on the bridge posts

Whatever
Try again 1-900-GOD-HELPS

I would never do that.

Barbara Jo Quamme

"Ariana"

Beauty, elegance, grace.
What I experience when
in her presence.

Warmth, serenity, peace.
What I experience with
each embrace.

Never before, nor since,
have I had the pleasure
to encounter such experiences
with any other.

Within my heart shall
always remain,
never ending love for Ariana,
until its last beat of life.

Francesco Furguiele

Thought

Do you see in me
What I see in you?
If I'd ask to hold your hand
Walking on slippery ground
Would you?
I'm not the same as you
My skin is fair my eyes are blue
My beliefs wander far from years
Would you let me fall?
Thinking I'd do the same?
Would you take the chance
To stop and ask
Do you see in me
What I see in you?

Elizabeth Sharp

War, Peace

What is hate?
What is greed?
What is evil?
What is war!

What is love?
What is caring?
What is sharing?
What is peace!

Joan Reego Gully

The Dove

I want someone who'll remain true.
What is it that entrances me?
My thoughts always come back to you;
The one I loved, that turned to flee.
I gave you everything I had
Which came out as my own, true love.
You took that and just left me sad;
A beautiful, broken-winged dove.
But never shall you have a fear,
For crushed love one day will regrow.
Not that you ever cared, my dear,
But my good friends all tell me so.
As heart-broken as I have been,
Someday I will love once again.

Joshua Kronman

"Sometimes I Wonder"

If I were to go
what would you do
how much would you know
would you have a clue

Who would you go with
if there was never me
where would you be
who would you see

Why should I go with her
when I'd rather be with you
why do anything for another
If I'd rather die for you

If love is forever
why does it always go away
and if we're so clever
why can't we get it everyday

What if I couldn't be here
would you be lost
would you be happy because your in the clear
or would you try and keep me at all cost.

Isaac Chavez

Unending Love

In the autumn of your life,
When all seems cold and drear,
Do not despair my dear,
My love for you will never end.

In the autumn of your life,
Come to me my dear,
Come and do not fear,
I long for your caress.

In the autumn of your life,
Reach out and take my hand,
That I may bring you to my breast,
That yearns for your embrace.

Charlotte Lujan

Epitaph

Will they remember me
when I die go to my
grave and cry?
Will they?
A question to ask
but please don't laugh!
For when your time comes
will they go to your grave
and cry? Remember you when you die?
Laugh yes laugh . . .

Bridie Christos

The First Star

Try to describe a summer's night,
When all the world's asleep.
When every child big and small
Are all tucked in and dreaming.
When you take your cover off your bed,
And quietly tiptoed down the stairs.
You open the door, you're just in time,
To see the first star in the sky.
What a joy to see,
What a moment to remember.
You lay on your cover on the porch,
And wish upon that lovely star.
What did I wish for?
You cannot know,
Or it won't come true.
It's time for me to go inside,
I need my rest, so I can see,
The first star tomorrow night,
And wish my wish again,
And maybe, just maybe it would come true.

Aziza Zuwena Hull

A Mother's Tears

A Mother's tears are never dried.
When her children are happy,
And prospering well.
Tears of happiness, she will shed.

When her children are grown
and out on their own.
Tears of sadness, at being
left all alone.

And when the Father calls her home,
To join him at the Royal Throne.
Rise up my child and dry your eyes.
For now is your children's time to cry.

Ann Lamberth

Grammie

Words of wisdom
When hope is gone
Unconditional love
Even when I'm wrong
Letters sent
So many mile
Just to say
"I thought of you and smiled."
I wonder what you'd say
If you saw me now
I can't always see you
But I know that you're around

Jamie Mitchell

It's A Grey World

I was raised in black and white,
Where things were wrong,
or they were right.
As I got older, I began to see,
things are a little bit different to me.
You say one thing and mean another,
even trying to trick your brother.
It's all sort of fake to me.
Can't we say what we see?
Use your own judgment because
it's a grey world

John Imboden

Visions

I have visions, graphic visions;
when I close my eyes.
They haunt me, intrigue me.
They are with me always.
Morbid visions, demented dreams.
I avoid them and seek them.
I am afraid to know.
Yet, long to ask.
What do they say to me?
What are the hidden truths?
That part of me I fear.
The demons speak, caress my mind,
embrace my fears.
The chasms widen; they deepen;
and still they overflow,
with dark illusions.

Am I the demon or the demons lover?

Karen A. Craig-Thomas

My Sons

Don't cry for me
When I die
for my spirit will soar
and dwell in the sky
to look down upon you
and see how you are
I will be close
I won't be far
You will feel my love
Till the end of time
To see you happy
I will rest sublime
Don't cry for me
When I die
Just look up and smile
and know I'm near-by

Belia H. Linares

The Best Friend

Roses are red, Violets are blue,
When I rest in bed, I think of you,
Life is made with sugar and spice
to me you are very nice.

Your hair is yellow, like the sand
We are happy holding hand to hand,
One day you will grow to take the stand
to join hands with the man of the land.

You are pretty and young,
but will grow to be healthy and strong,
Your mind will wonder as the years pass,
Just remember Mom knows right from wrong.

You can learn to explore,
Just remember Mom is always at the door,
When life seems rough,
She will help make you tough.

When you get turned around, just keep
both feet on the ground.
There is one through your whole life,
A friend in need will always be a friend in deed.

Calvin L. Robinson

True Love

Priceless is love
when it is true
To take it for granted
is the worst thing to do

Cherish the love
every day and night
Because love only grows
if you treat it right

Hold it forever
close to your heart
Then troubles will fade
and happiness will start

Love is the ultimate
no feeling is above
The supreme sensation
they call true love

Bob Pyan

Our Mothers

We were carried near the heart
when just an embryo,
and very near our mother's heart,
we stay wherever we may go.
A mother hurts the most
if to her we are unkind;
and she hurts the most
if we are hurt in body, spirit or mind.
She always thinks the best of us
and believes that we will do
our very best, and will succeed
in carrying our tasks through.
She will reason with us
whenever we do fail
to live up to the standard
she taught us to entail.
So, let us tell her everything
as we know she always cares
and she will do her best to help
and she'll ask God's help in prayers.

Gladys White Stewart

The Prophets Song

Why have I tried to combat life,
when my faith is so weak and my
limbs to numb and subtle to touch
the fresh dew on the meadow leaves?

My hope has bowed to a sorrowful
path, then my feet slow to follow
drags on. Now my heart feels a limbo,
I crumble unto the dirt of the land
from whose warmth the seeds
of life sprouted, greeting spring.

The earth and the atmospheric
universe being two entities
and betwixt is life and love,
where nothing else abounds but
the power of God.

Benedict James

Life

LIFE can travel in circles,
When our destiny remains unknown.
People and places become part of,
life's big fast pace.
You must master life,
leaving yesterdays pain,
in it's place in life's race.
Catch a rainbow and reach for a star.
Put them in your pocket and you,
will go far.
Never let life pass you by.
YOU can make it don't fake it,
life just try.

James E. Nichols

Tranquility

At that hesitation in time,
When the day stops being
And the night has not yet become.
In a moment's breath
As blue melts to red,
And purple and azure abound,
When peacefulness reigns,
With silence as her sister,
And beauty is in every vision,
Tranquility is in the heart of every man.

Douglas Smalley

The Lone Pine Tree

The pine tree cried
when the wind shook her limbs.
It swayed and bent her bough.

But the wind showed her no sympathy.
As she roared and blew
She had only one intent.
To take her madness out,
on any object in her view.

The beauty of the pine
Lay crushed and mangled
All because the anger of the wind.

No more whispers,
No more sighs,
All because the anger of the wind.

Eva Wilkerson

Angel

On my aching shoulder
Where no one else can see
Sits a little angel
Who watches over me.

She doesn't ask me questions
She doesn't tell me why
She just pats me gently
When I begin to cry.

Protection is her middle name
Its me she cares about
Not for fortune, wealth, or fame
I know this without a doubt.

I love my little angel
It's clear she loves me back
For, yet has there to come a day
When she's led me off my track.

Anna Tomaskovic-Devey

How?

How can I cry?
When there's no tears,
left to fall.

How can I try?
When there's no strength,
Left at all.

How could you say you loved?
When there was nothing,
Inside.

How did I notice?
The unnoticeable,
When I tried.

How come I didn't fall?
When I was standing on air.
How come life isn't fair?

How could I know?
Something that wasn't true.

How come I thought,
You loved me too?

Eva Marie Spagnolini

"Riches"

You ask too much of me
When you ask nothing.
What shall I do
With all these riches?
I push and strain
Trying to crowd them back in a box.
The lid won't close.

Carol S. Heiser

Empty

My heart is empty
when your not here

Somehow I know
that you are near

I know we look at the same
sun, moon, and stars
but I can't accept that you are so far

I want you with me forever and ever,
but somehow I know you'll
never come ever.

My heart races when you are here,
my heart fills full when you are near

I never want you to leave
but I know you have to depart
so when you come home
I will be waiting with open arms.

Crystal Markuson

White Is

White is light
White is bright
White is the color of some kites

White is a big June moon
White is the color of sand dunes

But beware, I've heard that the KKK's
favorite color is white

But, I like white

Justen Ward

My Mind

Ok! Where is it?
Where did it go?
I've looked everywhere,
I want you to know.

I've gone here and there,
Gone round and round.
Looked everywhere,
Upstairs and down.

I really do miss it,
Can't go on this way.
Please somebody help!
Please find it today.

They ask, what it is
I really must find?
You're sure you can't tell?
Why, I've lost my mind.

Gladys Stewart

The Snow Day

There once was a day
Where the snow got in the way.
It made everyone get stuck
Because of all the muck.

There wasn't a bird in flight
Only snow was in sight.
The children played in the snow
While others built their snowmen to show.

Snowballs were flying
While inside bacon was frying.
The snow was getting higher
That meant trouble for the limo driver.

I hope it snows more
Because without it, it's a bore.
With snow, school will be out
And everyone will be about.

Before I go out to play
I must say:
You should go out and play
And have a nice day.

Gabriel Facini

To Snow-White

You were only a cat
White, and crippled at that
You couldn't catch birds
And you lived off the fat
  Of my love.

Yet on a dark winter night
Sensing my fright
You dragged your leg
To meet me on the trail;
  A loving guide.

When the tide of life
Forced a move from our beach
We couldn't explain
And no one would fain
  Have our cat.

You were only a cat
And crippled at that
But no one could be
More loved by me
  Or mourned.

Janice W. Krenmayr

462

Success

Some folks think that money,
where we live and how we dress
and the kind of car we drive
is the proof of our success.

But I submit a different view
and while all this may be good
I tend to think that true success
is seldom understood.

To lift someone whose fallen
and help them on their way,
to visit someone lonely
and brighten up their day.

To be a friend to others,
to help someone in need,
to guide someone to heaven
is true success indeed.

For no matter what you've done
you'll never make the grade
if all you've left behind
is the money that you've made.

Aubrey Ellis

Untitled

There once was a cat named Samson
Who always got into a fight.
He never yet won;
But his time will soon come,
For Samson will be the new champion.

Jack Delouya

Purpose

In life there is a purpose
Which is very hard to know
One that is rarely found
One that says the meaning
Of your life, here on earth
One that people fear, not knowing why
Afraid of this, and afraid of that
Because they have no purpose
If they'd look up, they'd find it
Unwilling to try to reach it
A life without a purpose
Is a trail without a path
It goes nowhere.

Bruce D. McDonald

"A Daddy"

A daddy is a special person
Who listens to each word,
That is uttered ever so softly
From a child who wants to be heard.
He's a kind-hearted person
Who will wipe away the tears.
He'll heal the wounded heart,
And will soothe the little fears.
A daddy has a special job
To discipline with respect.
And teach the proper way of life
So that values will be met.
It's not always an easy job
That daddy's usually obtain.
But when that child smiles his way
There is everything to gain
A daddy can't be just anyone
Its a gift from above.
A blessing wrapped up in
The daddy's special love.

Cassandra Olson

Jimmie

Now Jimmie is a little boy
  Who means a lot to me
He's full of tricks, and full of fun
  As happy as can be
Jim never seems to stop and rest
  He's always on the go
We ask him, aren't you tired Jim boy?
  He smiles and don't you know
He takes of like he's jet propelled
  His stick horse bucks in style
His six guns bang, as on he goes
  He rides mile after mile
Today he is a cowboy
  Tomorrow a soldier true
Next day he'll be a pilot brave
  Spinning ore the ocean blue
His imagination it is great
  Beside him others haven't any
But no matter who he thinks he is
  He's our precious little Jimmie.

Amy M. Sylling

Friend

A friend is someone you can trust,
Who never treats you like dust.
A friend helps you with your work,
but sometimes can be a real jerk,
You see through the jerk in them,
And then you find a real friend,
When a friend dies its really sad,
it makes you feel really bad.
Then you meet a new friend,
Who always helps you to the end,
You never forget your old friend,
because their the nicest ever friend!

Christine James

The Hidden Rain Forests

I am a lonesome ladylove
  Whom loves to romance
The world of charm
  And relish
The world of hidden peace
  The green sensuous mist
Of the forests
  Of hidden innocence
The mystic water
  Encircles the dancing
Of the hidden
  Heavenly drama of nature.

Daina M. Snyder

Marshmallow - My Cat

I have a cat,
who's fur is white,
he curls up on my bed at night,
his eyes are blue,
my room is green,
at times he makes me want to scream,
he purrs so soft, mussing up my hair,
sometimes even jumping into the air,
he wildly runs around the room,
then my mother comes in with a broom,
she takes him out,
which makes me pout,
and then I feel I want to shout,
no more will he be soft and sweet,
laying there beneath my feet.

Jennifer E. Hollins

When Friendship Dies

How did it happen, friend?
Why are we now apart?
We who once were one.
When did the break-up start?
No harsh words were said,
No bitterness expressed,
Yet a tender, loving friendship
Was quietly laid to rest.
We soothed each others pain,
And as the years went by
We laughed and cried together.
Was it all a lie?
Can friendship be so fragile
It cannot bear the truth?
Then let it rest in peace, my friend,
A figment of our vanished youth.

Corinne Bernstein

Mothers

There are certain women
Who can hardly be described,
But I can put them in these words:
Sweet, gentle, and kind.

They give their children many things
That can never have a price.
Mothers give their children love,
Whether they've been bad or nice.

Jessie Hughes

"Burning Flame"

I didn't understand the reason . . .
why did you leave?

I ask your friend . . . if you forgot me,
He said "He never did

He just has to leave
to the border, they had to fight."

After a while . . . He showed me
the way and the place
to find where your body rests.

Leaving the lace behind
of the wedding dreams unrealized,
you won the fight and paid the price!!!

In a heroic way to cover the stain
from your people which you feel love
but again, there is a burning flame
to make me feel that you are alive.

I couldn't stop the tears of my eyes
and laid the Hero to Honor our Pride!!

Gloria Isoronis

America

Violence is everywhere
Why does no one care?
The President
He is hesitant
A three year old was shot!
For being on the wrong block
Can we please make this all stop!
Disarm America
So no more harm is done
Bring Peace to everyone . . .

Joanne Sachs

I Wonder

Sometimes I wonder
Why God loves us so
and takes good care of us
no matter where we go

He knows our thoughts
He knows our mind
He knows our hearts
He's the best friend one can find

I want to be just like him
Oh how wonderful that would be
I often think of how he suffered
out there on the wooden tree

Although it was called a cross
They made it from a tree
that is where he suffered so
He died there for you and me

Emma J. Baxley

Thoughts

Have you ever wondered
Why the good Lord made you wait
Because you were not ready
To enter the golden gate
He put you on this earth
To love learn and play
But you must remember this
We didn't come here to stay

Ann Mills Filmore

Stars

Sometimes I wonder about stars
Why they shine, who we say they are
Why we revere things so high
That dwell in distant space and time

What is it that we think they give
What is it that we think we missed
A dream once held so close and tight
That washed away in an aging tide

But ask is not the star the one
Who's light traveled far from home
To reap the awe within our eyes
But then burned out alone and died

So when we ponder with heavy heart
About our dreams about the stars
Ask only this of your mind and soul
Is there a love to call my own?

And if you know that there is
Then gaze upon the stars again
And think about what he missed
Way back when his light still lived

Franklin Fellenbaum

The Clock

Tick . . . tock . . . tick . . . tock
Would someone please, break that
clock. Ticking . . . ticking all day long
Tick . . . tocking that stupid song.
Every second, minute, hour, day
Someone please take it away.
Finally, finally it stopped I've
finished my rhyme. Excuse me
though "Do you have the time?"

Emily Taylor

Will This Fighting Ever End?

Laying alone and wondering
Will this fighting ever end?

Crying
Heartache
Trying to understand
Will this fighting ever end?

Different views
Different beliefs
Trying to ignore
Will this fighting ever end?

Yelling
Screaming
Listening
Blaming
Will this fighting ever end?

Understanding
Realizing
Blaming no one
Will this fighting ever end?

Jaci Craver

Autumn

Cool, rich, peaceful
Winter it does greet,
The requirement for satisfaction,
It does smoothly meet.

A nicely painted canvas,
Yellow, orange, red,
The leaves then gently fall,
And make a leafy bed.

The autumn wind blows softly,
Through the colored trees,
Insects start to hide away,
Including wasps and bees.

Autumn is a time,
To breathe in cool, crisp air,
To roam among the fallen leaves,
Without a single care.

Autumn is filled with so much goodness,
And so much more,
So pleasant, so great, simply wonderful,
One season of the four.

Hila Katz

Saddle Horse

You remind me of a Saddle Horse
with its long legs;
on its way to the Horse Show
So proud.

When you walk
every muscle in your body
has a rhythm like a fine horse
on its natural gaits.
So slow to move and so erect.

And when you're proud
your natural trot shows
your gallops,
when you're not touching the ground.

I wish I were a skilled rider
to exert control.
To be the complete master
of your mount.

Winnie Lisojo

"Wishing"

A memorial to my mother
Wishing I could have you here
Wishing I could have you here
  Still lovingly stroking your hair

Wishing I could hold you tight
  far away from the lonely night

Wishing I could love you
  and feel your love for me

Wishing I could hear you say
  your love will always be

Wishing you could see my heart
  the way it looks at you

Wishing we could still do
  the things we use to do

Wishing I had told you
  How much you mean to me

Wishing this was just a dream
  and I could have you here
  the way it use to be.

Donna Marie Howard

Mother Is Waiting

As a lad I'd stay out late,
With a friend or on a date.
Going places I dared not go,
Forbidden for my mother, said so.

As I'd turn the key at night
Trying my best to be so quiet,
There in silent prayer
Mother was waiting for me there.

With a voice calm and low
'Hon, you were out too late, you know!
How the guilt would flood my soul,
For adding pain to this heart of gold.

I know she prayed and sought the Lord,
That I would soon be back in the fold.
I heard her cry and call out my name,
And ask Jesus to remove all sin and shame.

Mother is gone now, she's on heaven's
shore.
There to be with Jesus for evermore.
I too will be crossing, but not alone,
For mother is still waiting, for me to
  come home.

Karen Durhan

Study Of Love

Muscles of the human vines ache
With ecstatic disbelief for him
And the urge to tangle for both.
Giggles come from playful eyes
And the arms for her only
Snare their passion again.
Winding endless whispers together,
Tighter the bond of hearts and limbs.
A mind at peace, souls on fire.
One more squeeze makes them real,
Entwined lives growing around each other,
Spinning with a need to hold fast,
To thrive in the technicolor bed
Beneath the pomp of a home-made heaven
And the circumstance of a night alone.

Anthony Simeone

My Assurance

Sometimes I am overwhelmed
    with God's love for me
I see it in the morning sky,
    and feel it in the breeze.
I see it in my garden, as I
    pick tomatoes from the vine.
For though, I've tended the plants
    the fruit is a gift divine.
And, here, the lovely flowers
    such beauty to behold.
Surely, there within the petals
    is God's love for me retold.
The building of the mighty clouds
    where awesome, thunder rolls;
And fearsome lightning zips and
    cracks - it shakes my very soul.
This too, is in God's scheme of things,
    for cool rain must soak the earth.
My faith and strength is greater
    still, with the green plants rebirth.

Eva V. Clark

First Love

I love poems to sit and ponder
With mind to think and wonder
Verses course my mind to give
Paper life
My thoughts to live

Carter E. Fairbanks

I Have Twin Boys

Sean of dark hair and eyes
With skin soft white as Irish down
And a smile lit from a keltic lamp

And Charles fair and slim
His eyes cold blue as the northern sky
A Viking's heir from a time far gone
When raiders, fjord born
Drove south in dragon ships
To flog and flame dear Ireland's shore

Then be spun into the Gaelic woof
Through the generation's labyrinth
An eon from the pillage plume
A Norseman and a Celt

Brothers from the same womb.

James E. Flaherty

G.I. Joe

Why were you so discontented
With your plastic toy soldiers
That you had to become one yourself?
This is not a game now.
You're standing on a fault line
Waiting for an earth quake.
Someday they'll ship you off
To Bosnia or another foreign place.
I can picture the scene -
Daddy, with his worried look,
Giving you advice on how to survive.
Mommy crying, wondering why
Her baby boy wants to "be a man".
Inside my head I'm screaming -
    My little G.I. Joe
    My big brother
    Don't go away.

Alicia K. Gadecki

I Saw A Man

I saw a man
With soles on his feet
His heart in a back pack,
He lives on the street.

Walking slowly
Nowhere to go
Do I know him?
I don't know

Children playing
Running and free . . .
"Will they grow up
To be like me?"

Swinging high
Sliding low
Young ones, listen,
Watch him go.

. . . I saw a man
He lives on the street
The holes in his soul now,
Go deep . . . very deep . . .

Christi Vila

Have You Ever Met A Person

Have you ever met a person
    with whom it's hard to say "Good-bye"
    who whenever you first see them
    puts a twinkle in your eye

Have you ever met a person
    who you knew right from the start
    had a certain magnetism
    that began to tug your heart

Have you ever met a person
    that put smiles on your face
    where just a minute earlier
    there were frowns upon that place

Have you ever met a person
    whether destiny or fate
    when you felt that darned attraction
    made you think "I've met my mate"

Have you ever met a person
    that you thought you'd like to date
    then just sat back on your laurels
    'till you realized it's too late

James E. Vale

"This Road"

I cannot walk this road alone
Without a star to light my way
A happy thought to speed my time
A song to drive my fears away
I cannot climb this hill alone
Without a hand to lead me on
A trail to guide my blinded steps
A sturdy staff to lean upon
I cannot live this life alone
Without a hope to lift my soul
Without the fellowship of friends
And love I need to make me whole

Audrey Gibbs

Through Children's Eyes

Have you ever seen the
World through childrens' eyes?
Each day to them is a
Precious new surprise
Their loving hearts embrace
New things with hope and love
They trust in all the powers
From above
Oh! don't you wish that
Once more we could be
as innocent as those
at two and three!

Cloudia Emplroy

Lady In Red

Lady in red, will you cause
World war III so soon,
or, will you pause
and follow some cue?!

The cue to life,
instead of death -
will you give us a chance,
or will it be death's dance?!

O, Lady in red, will you cause
World War III quite quickly?!
Or, will you hesitate and soon see
the difference between you and me?!

O, Lady in red, will you please see
the cue to life, instead of death?!
will you give us a chance,
or will it be a story of death's dance?!

Florence Ann Kelly Stults

Wrinkled Ribbons

Tossed wrapping paper
wrinkled ribbons
crushed boxes
gifts strewn about
how quickly we lose
Our delighted surprise
of presents we received
from people in disguise
The merriment is lost
our feelings of content
as we look about the room
for more of what was sent.

Jacqueline Ciaburri

It's California's Fault

It was a casual quake
Yet quite a noise did make.
Maybe only intuition
But it was an intermission
In his nap upon my bed.
He turned to me and said,
"Mee-oww" then stared in space.
I looked into his face.
We heard and felt the rock
The roll, more rock, then aftershock.
We prayed together, cat and I.
'Twas over. Then he asked "Why?"
"Another seismic record," I said.
"No harm done; go back to bed."

Jean Philipp

Dreaming

The darkness scares me
yet calls me
I'm sent hurling into
it unwillingly
Words and thoughts
flying by me
Nearly hitting me
yet no sound is made
My head spinning
my body still
I feel left out and all
alone
Blinding colors flashing by me
Time and motion
standing still
I'm scared yet
not afraid at the same time
I lift my chin up and wake up
Sweating and screaming
I realize I have been dreaming

Beth Zimmerman

Your Voice

I really don't have anything else to say.
Yet, I don't want to stop talking.
I can't hear enough of your voice.
The tone.
The sound.
The rhythm.
It touches my heart.
It moves my soul.
It becomes a part of me.

Almeda-Princess King

Remembrance

I saw you in a crowded room,
Your smile lit up the night.
Amazed was I to see such grace
Of the gentleman I write.

All gathered at the starlit ball,
An elegant affair;
In honor of the Faerie queen,
Where we met upon the stair.

Moonlit walk on sultry night,
The mighty river near.
My heart near bursting with each kiss,
And at my eye a tear . . .

The night belonged to us alone,
And we belonged to night.
The moon looked down upon us,
Wept tears of silvery light.

Fate brought us there together,
A Princess and a Prince;
But now she cruelly takes away
The one I truly miss.

Christina Loumeau

Watching Me

Thine eyes upon me
wrapped within
embraced, protected
so gentle, so pure
thy keeps me always
no one knows secretly but me
my guardian angel
I love thee

Gary L. Billington

Past

I remember you when you were lonely,
You sat in the dim twilight,
And not a sound could be heard
Except the soft splash of your tears.

Your thin shoulders trembled,
As you shivered,
From the cold
And your loneliness too.

I wish I could have helped you
I could have told you,
That at least I cared
For the little girl that once was me.

Jan Osmussen

You, The Butterfly

Fluttering like the butterfly
you're born to be free
soaring beneath the endless sky
for all the world to see

embracing each fragile flower
as you touch its jealous lawn
reveling in your power
as proudly as the swan

rejoicing from the freedom
you know is your commission
fearing not what might come
you welcome each transition

knowing when you choose
to love only me
transforming, I'll not refuse
to become happy and free.

Charlotte Underwood

Memories

The first time you rode your bike,
Your first friend you really liked.
All the good times, all the bad,
Al the happy, all the sad.
Your last birthday.
The time you spent at the bay.
The time your mom found a job.
or the time you met Bob.
Memories are pictures in the mind,
If you look, you will find.

Christopher L. Meyer

Untitled

You are like a fresh rose.
Your fragrance stays with me
wherever I go.

The sweetness of you touch
Overwhelms me.

The beauty of the image you
leave in my mind . . . everywhere
I go, the thought of you leaves
me smiling, as if I had seen the
most beautiful creation on this earth;

I hear and it is you . . .

Joann McWilliams

My God In Heaven

When I am alone, I dream of you.
You are so sweet, so loving, so caring.
I don't know what I'd do without you.
You teach me of sharing.

I know you are still living.
I confess my sins.
You are so forgiving.
Will I let you in? Of course I will.

I love you so much.
You make me feel good.
You are such a good father to me.
You are here to give me food.

I love you, oh dear God.
You are here for me.
You are my loving father.
I want to sit in your lap when I get to
Heaven.

Jenni Gilman

Forever

Darling
    Your love is like the touch of spring,
    With dreams of tomorrow,
    A joy to bring
    Your touch is so tender
    To help to remember
    Today tomorrow and forever,

Alberta M. Mitchell

Compliments On The Complements

Hey, God . . .
You made a wise choice
Selecting green
Well - for trees and shrubs, I mean —
Good color! Cool and clean!
As artist to master
I avidly aver,
with your choice of color
I heartily concur.
My plaudits!
For when audits on hue
Be submitted,
For shrubbery—
May only green be permitted!
Ah! . . . but, then again . . .
Had I been fed
—onRED,
I might now vent my spleen
At the sight of Grrreen!

David Glaser

Me

I'm me;
    You're you;
You're me;
    I'm you.

I, you, he, she, these, those, them,
    We all contain ME in vast theorem.

Stripped of color, race and creed,
    The shells in which we abide,
Why don't we love each other?
    We're all the same inside.

Jane Barnes Moore

A Queer Day

A day might be dreary, macabre, grey
Yet seldom as queer as this
Tho' not as strange as yesterday,
It certainly ranks high on the list
See, yesterday I lost my job
And wrecked my car in a ravine
A shepherd devoured my persian pedigree
And I choked on a pinto bean
Some days however, are rather plum
Unlike today and the one before
Tho' three days ago I broke a tooth
And slammed my foot in a door
That day, that day was just a fluke
A wrinkle in the fabric of life
As long as tomorrow eludes today
I'll avoid its rigor and strife
I suppose today hasn't been so bad
But certainly one I won't miss
Cause a day might be dreary, macabre, grey
Yet seldom as queer as this

Antonio Womack

New Year's Eve Without You

"Should auld acquaintance be forgot . . ."
You were always there for me —
                now you're not.
You were my strength, my anchorage.
To every challenge you said "I will" —
                now you won't.

You were everything a person should be.
Sympathetic to the point of empathy,
You made every pain bearable,
Every dream possible even probable —
                now you don't.

You kept every promise,
Fulfilled every vow — until now.
"Till death do us part"
You were there for me —
                now you're not.

June Davis

Some Helpful Hints

There are times when you say things
you don't really mean There are times
when you see things that are different
then they seem be careful and don't be
to quick to misjudge and if you're in
a fight, make up its not good to hold
grudge try not to be in a bad mood and
look at the bright side meet new
people, don't be shy, some out of the
corner where you hide be nice to
others and when you catch someone's
eye smile don't be in a rush all the
time stop and talk to someone for
awhile instead of keeping your
feelings inside tell others how you
feel send flowers to sad ones or sick
ones to help their hearts heal these
are just like complete just to make
sure the good things in life you don't
delete

Jennifer Schuldt

Untitled

Parting is now necessary,
saying good-bye with much sorrow.
Here I sit looking back at yesterday,
but concentrating more on tomorrow.
Looking back-remembering all the times,
trying to sum it all up in a few short verses and rhymes.
We can both proudly say;
we've been through good times and bad,
always staying together,
despite the fights we've had.
Now I must look onward,
setting my standards high,
and thinking once again,
how fast it all went by.
But now is the time
to put the past behind,
and go on with the rest of our lives.

Katrina Allaire

To Cindy

Searching within, nothing I found to free my soul, so strongly bound.
Searching within, nothing could ease the pain of my captivity.
Seeking without, in my despair, someone with whom my love to share.
Seeking without, like Noah's dove, a wond'ring soul, inspired by love.
Alone, afraid, wintry the day, with cold remorse the fare to pay.
Alone, afraid, I found no rest; I sought to end the futile quest.
My hands outstretched, I cried in vain for balm to soothe the constant pain.
My hands outstretched, I did resign my soul to Fate, life's dark design.
Just then you came, out of the dark, with eyes aglow, you calmed my heart.
Just then you came, from whence I know. 'Twas God above did you bestow.
Your eyes, so bright, new life displayed, with love so true, new love repaid.
Your eyes, so bright, made clear to me, my soul at last would be set free.
Your touch, so warm, it fired my soul to rise from death, achieve its goal.
Your touch, so soft, instilled new peace; my heart's long quest
with you did cease.
My life, my love, hear thou my plea, song of my heart, eternally.
My life, my love, my fate to know, upon this bloom my love bestow.
Accept this rose, the love it bears; a kiss return, your love to share
Accept this rose; it asks of you, from heart to heart, "One life from two?"

Warner G. Eiben

A Debt

Winds are howling deep in despair
Secrets locked in a glass cage, watched with care.
You wear a mask, hiding fear
Turning a back, not shedding a tear.
In the shadows you stay hiding
For your time you are biding.
Minutes, hours, days pass by
No one hears your lonely cry.
Shouts and cries to heaven above
Somewhere you lost all your love.
Never to see those great sights again
For now you are paying for all your sin.

Sheila Anderson

Memories

Walking through shadows, looking for light
    seeking the warmth of love, in the dawning night.
Fire without heat, joy with despair
    lingering images of life and all that was shared
Searching . . . searching for embodiment of that which should be
    but only touching shadows; twilight, with eyes that cannot see.

Linda Taylor

Strangers To Lovers

The first time I was aware of you
seemed so long ago

Strangers we were did you also feel
this wasn't so

Now you know me and I know you
all along it was love now we know its true.

Lydia Malutin

A Special Prayer

Oh father, as I pray this little prayer,
Send your guardian angel to watch over me.
Listen to my words that come,
As I pray softly from my heart.
Hear Oh Lord my cry for help,
As I call out your name.
For to start the day without you,
Would be a big mistake.
Come, watch over my steps,
As you lead me along the way.
Teach me to be more like Jesus, I pray.
Look into my heart and humble me if you may,
Just come and live in me, I pray.
Oh, thank you Lord for taking the time,
Just to listen to my heart.
And for sending your angels to guide me,
Along the way.

Velma Carpenter

Imagine

Morning sun coming over the horizon,
sending out all colors,
from mauve, lavenders and blues, all golden in light.
Salty tang of sea spray, hearing the foghorn in the distance,
seagulls crying, seals barking, and the waves hitting the shore.
Sand squishing up between your toes, sand crabs scuttling away,
Warm sun that sends sparkles like diamonds over the blue-green water.

Smell of the warmth on a horse,
Earthly smell, sweat, smell of hay, drying up grass,
hear the galloping of the horses hooves as they gallop over the ground.
Feel the vibration.
The smell of sunshine, warmth, life.

IMAGINE

Mary Hoots

Her Soft Unspoken Speech

"Past powers, passing softly into death,
shadows first, brisk breath will follow,
grounded life soon to be hollow.
Chilling souls hiding till black cats hour
and old men again gain their power.
Crystals flying, stone stars truth revealed in lies.
And all the kings men change their mark of arms,
while secrets pass through the minds of men . . .
and women watch the skies.
The creature below does know,
and the fruits of today take away what May.
Burrowing deep into the night till death is the day . . .
and night knows no other way.
Every whisper of the flame, praise.
Fire yesterday deemed deadly,
God's forgotten, worshippers feel Satan's warm breath,
and the water of the fire soothes your satanic soul.
Holding the delicate sun days' soul,
it whimpers, powerless to natures way.
Behold the twelfth hour and my power," winter whispers to me.

Robert R. Lung

When I Open The Door

Eleven secret skies that all lead to your door.
Seven days I wait before I'm coming back for more.

All my life I wonder how it is you make me smile?
And I wish you would come back because I haven't smiled in a while.

I want to row my boat through your sky,
But I lost the oars in the mouth of a dove.
And I just can't let one more day go by,
Without expressing my desperate love.

My blind eyes don't see your lies.
And my deaf ears don't hear the tears.
And my mute voice refuses the choice,
Of revealing to you all of my fears.

So I take my myself and my little row boat
Into your sky but I have to float,
For the dove has died who swallowed the oars;
Yet I know I'll find peace when I open your door.

Megan McGrory

Yearnings

The music plays on
shadows dancing upon the walls
As though they too are searching
for someone to keep them company

To occupy their time
'till the light shifts
And they disappear
imprisoned once again in some useless form.

Longing to escape
to have a soul of their own
No longer depending on the light
that taunts them with only a brief taste of freedom.

Tony M. Peppers

The Room

All lights are off, a darkened room.
Shadows like the trees of a dark forest.
The monstrous laugh of the stuffed animal.
All within the room
The room inside myself.

The window is a separate entity;
It is the scene of my life,
The life I have not yet lived.
Out there is the sound of beauty
That waits for me to touch it.

I can not.
The room holds me tightly
Against its chest, only to allow
Me to view this phantasm of reality.
I quietly scream to break free.

Occasionally the light of human touch
Enters my room and I see the ugliness
Of what's inside. Frightened, I turn to
The window. The picture is gone and
The room is the prison of my soul.

Melinda Feyes

Winter Song

Quiet
shattered when, suddenly, the wind blows from the east. Out of the gorge it comes, to whip through city and town, proclaiming mastery of all in its path.

Frantic
the naked branches of the trees outside my window rattle like bones rising from a moldering grave.

Quixotic
closing my eyes, flying to a far off, golden beach. The sun ever shining, a gentle whispering among palm fronds.

Bemused
finding no seasons to change the world day-by-day. No more to witness the birth of Spring, the growth of Summer, and the small death of Winter. To stay is unthinkable.

Grateful
to be home, snuggled in my warm bed, gladly listening to Winter's song. Knowing it, too, is only whistling in the dark.

Linda France

The Plane That Said Goodbye

The songbird sleeps outside my window
She could sing the song of beauty and life
I heard the plane speak inside my head.

I could always confide in the songbird
She could bring no wrong, until she said so long
The songbird sleeps outside my window.

The hood I hide under, became attached after the songbird stopped singing
I listen for the song, I realize the songbird didn't belong
I heard the plane speak inside my head.

The pain will never subside from not hearing the songbird
I hear the ring of the bell but realize the songbird bid farewell
The songbird sleeps outside my window

The plane's words ride to my ear like the breeze on a breezy day
The words I've always feared, but faced, there still here
I heard the plane speak inside my head.

I do not know where the songbird resides
There are many birds, not like the songbird, this bird left on a plane
The songbird sleeps outside my window
I heard the plane speak inside my head.

Scott Maxwell

A Day With Lovebucket

My love bucket just went home.
She spent the day with me.
That's my granddaughter you know,
Sweet little child, and she's only three.
We went to the mall and then to the park.
By the time we returned home,
It was almost dark.
We played horsey and I was down on one knee,
As I stood up, she climbed on my shoulder,
By then I was a tree.
The day was so wonderful.
It really was a treat.
Now as I rub on my liniment and soak my aching feet,
I can still hear her say
SEE YOU GRANDMA, SEE YOU NEXT WEEK…

Marsha A. Reynolds

Blind Man

He cannot see what they feel
She does not know what is real

She feels his heart and hears his mind
She loves his soul but must be blind

He does not know what makes them tick
Adores them all but still seems tricked

How can he live with all this strife
He would someday wish for a wife

She cannot seem to get past the glitter
Which makes him feel extremely bitter

He knows the game as well as any
But can't seem to find the elusive golden penny

She gnaws away at his soul
But feels great relief when he consoles

Tom Dick and Harry one and all
Make him feel unjustly small

She seeks out all the rest
But in reality overlooks the best

Man is blind or maybe not
Perhaps just positioned in her blind spot

Stephen G. Hauk

I Could Talk To Mom

When I was just a little girl.
She dressed me so I'd look my best.
She used the brush and my hair would curl.
I'd pull on her skirt. She would laugh and say "You little pest".
Oh, what a happy time! Because I could talk to MOM.

She cried, as I started to school. I was so eager to learn.
I would read, spell and write. In a paper bag I carried my lunch.
Hanging clothes, washing dishes, I liked to take my turn.
As I walked home, under my feet the gravel would crunch.
I hurried to get home. Because I could talk to MOM.

We shopped, went to yard sales and laughed when we talked.
Enjoyed the rain, snow, flowers and the bright sunshine.
Thought of our family living far away, as we walked.
Remembered vacations and could hear the sound of tires whine.
Those were the best of days! Because I could talk to MOM.

Seems I can still see her cross the yard to my back door.
Then I remember and heartache takes my breath away.
Where did spring and summer go? I can't remember any more.
The brightest sunny days all seem so gray.
I pray, Jesus send me an angel. Because then I could talk to MOM.

Margaret Polly Shepherd

The Girl In The Back

The girl in the back is quiet and thinks deeply to herself
She never says much and never smiles
They stare and laugh as she walks in
She sits down quickly as usual
Sometimes I'll look back and see bruises on her face
Her frown seems almost painted on
And once I thought I saw a tear run down her cheek
I turned back around and wondered,
If I was turned inside out, is that who I would be?

Whitney Ray

Mother's Day

You think she knows it all and that she can do no wrong.
She holds you and protects you; to help you sleep she sings a song.
Everything is wonderful when her hand is holding yours.
You believe she can do magic as she opens up life's doors.
The sun rises and it sets, the moon shines only for you.
She makes all of this happen and you know there's nothing she can't do.

But, sadly, as you grow older you realize she doesn't know it all.
Everything is suspect; you want to run now, not crawl.
You treat her like an alien, you always look at her in doubt.
When she tries to impart her wisdom, you just run to your room and pout.
Though we're all individuals, in this our lives share the same course.
She'll try her best to teach us, but she can talk until she's hoarse.

We can't wait to go our way just to show her that we're right,
But it's only as we mature that we can value her insight.
She's our mom and we love her; no one can ever take her place.
Though we're now adults ourselves, we still need her to feel safe.
So because we may not show it as often as we should,
This is one time when we'll say it: "Hey Mom, you raised me up real good!"

Kathryn R. Mattern

North Alabama

The House is old, worn, ready to die she is also
for she was born when the house was new.
All of her children are dead
and she is forgotten by her grand-children
save stray checks written in haste and goodwill.
Her only companions reside on a cracked wall,
next to Jesus on his cross
all in broken frames and on yellowed paper
faded memories
tacked on walls
they will have to do.

Lani Merritt

"A Good Woman"

Her qualities are beyond the price of silver and gold.
She is rich in her heart and her strength is in the favor
of God and mankind.
Regardless of her life's vocation, she travels a narrow road.
Her supply never ceases because her heart is generous to the
needy and by this principles, God keeps and endless supply of
food and shelter for her family.

Her husband, children and love ones will praise her.
Love is her strength, it rings from her voice and is her shield
of protection and wisdom is her cloak.

Her time is never idle, she is wise and fervent in all her business affairs.
She bridles her tongue from evil words and dwells safely by her neighbor.

She is not insecure, her security is in the Lord and he hides
her in troubled times.

A good woman always receives her just reward from the Lord
for he considers her cause.
The eyes of the Lord and his angles are ever on that good woman.

Linda Sue Blassingame

Linnea

I wonder what she is thinking about, standing there so quiet.
She looks over at me and runs into my lap. I embrace her little body
and comfort her from her fears of the big world.
She sits quietly and closes her big blue eyes, now in slumber.
Her limp body, heavy in my arms, drifts into dreamland.
She chuckles, and I wonder what she is dreaming.
It must be a happy dream.

Shawn Clark

Harmony

(For my daughter, Harmony)
Harmony much like Wisdom, is inclined to seek her own.
She is the consummation of Camaraderie and Atone

Harmony is arrayed, in flowing robes of white
Holding hands with Unity, she takes us to the light

The beacon of Brotherhood, the escort of our Peace
The Hope of humanity, a harvest of increase

Harmony's words are woven; silky soft and honey sweet
As she pauses to petition, beckons daily in the street;

"Come to me for Comfort, I'm a haven from the storm"
"My heart is full of Love, my embrace, safe and warm"

"My feet are ambassadors, the epitome of Kind"
"I see with sharp awareness, and clarity of mind"

"My aim is Fellowship, my path is ever straight"
"I lead to Tranquility, a calm and soothing state"

Resonant are her chords, a sweeping soft caress
Her core is made of Strength and true Togetherness

Harmony is like two rivers, teaming into one
Both Beauty and Enlightenment, warmer than the sun

You may know her Good spirit, if you so desire
Gladly will she greet you and take you ever higher.

Pam Jennings Spencer

One Day

The little boy helps an old lady across the street.
She leaves him with a "Thank You."
The child smiles with delight.

The traffic light turns green.
A car speeds by and someone hollers "Nigger!"
The boy's face saddens in an instant.

"I watch this all through a cafe window as I sip
   on my espresso."
My imagination goes full throttle . . .
In a cave, the little boy finds a magic lamp.
He rubs the lamp and out I come, his genie.

"I am your genie and I grant you a wish."
Will he wish for every toy ever made?
Will he wish for all the ice cream and candy he desires?
Will he wish for all the money in the world to be his?
Will be wish for a world without school and homework?

The boy remembers the old lady saying thank you.
And he screams, "I wish the world was blind!!!"
   "Back in the cafe window, no desire to finish my espresso.
   Too disgusted with reality."

Vanessa Yanez

Love Has Left

It is too late she is gone,
   she will never come back, she does not belong.
I feel a grudge,
   but she will not budge.
I say, 'come back to me, come back to me I say,'
   she just looks the other way.
It is too late she is gone,
   she will never come back, she does not belong.
I remember the days we used to play,
   just like it was yesterday.
She has gone, gone far away.
   I don't think she's coming back,
because she took the kitchen sink.

Nick Tchokoev

My Shadow

My shadow never talks to me, and once I asked her why,
She simply shrugged her shoulders in a black shadowy reply.
She goes wherever I go, her loyalty seems not end,
She is my lifelong buddy, my ever faithful friend.
She is about my height, and has an equal length of hair,
She plays the games I play, and even wears the clothes I wear!

When I'm feeling lonely, I just go out in the sun,
and Shadow stands with me, and we play and jump and run.
But if the day is cloudy, a stormy sort of grey,
My shadow doesn't come to me, she goes somewhere away.
But I am never sad, for inside I know what's true,
Shadow will come back for me with the blazing sun and sky of blue.

Rebecca Beyer

"A Housewife's Reality"

4 AM Insomniac
She stares at the ceiling,
her pillow,
his back that rises to follow each slow breath.
Awake,
she creates her own dreams.
A wealthy mistress,
she baits each lover with another's jealousies
in time to steal a diamond or a mink.
They think it is love still handcuffed to the bed.
Instead maybe
She'll be a rising business tycoon
soon to redefine the ways of open market trade,
paid to travel the world and drink champagne.
She paints the next Mona Lisa,
decreases the deficit, determines a cure for cancer,
lives in Japan, hikes the Alps, flies over Spain,
lies in his bed at 4:15 AM
and he has begun to snore.

Rebecca Wyngaard Wright

Another Love

My husband found another love,
She takes up all his dreams.
He eats and sleeps and breathes her thoughts,
I should be jealous - so it seems.

Late at night, with the TV on
His eyes twinkle and lips do smile.
And so his mind does travel
For her, he'd drive a hundred miles.

There's no rage, or anger spoke
For I knew her from the start.
And for each night that he's with her,
I know he's handled each and every part.

Every man has dreams and hopes,
A good wife, a job, a home.
But when your man loves racing
You'll spend many a night alone.

You watch him cuddle and baby her,
That race car sure looks sharp.
But when the checkered flag is dropped,
They both have won my heart.

Sandra L. Oxford

She Stays

She stays, knowing the price she and the children will pay.
She waits. She tries to convince herself he really means what he says
She wants a father for her children but what kind of father will he be
She is choosing to have a dysfunctional family.
She knows what it's like to wake up in the middle of a fight.
She knows how the children will feel when they fear for their lives.
She plans to live with the violence the rest of her life,
And the children will be with her, right by her side.
They will live the kind of life she has always known.
The children will grow up without the security of home.
They will hate their father for abusing them,
And they will blame their mother for letting it happen.
So the cycle is set into motion again.
Will the violence, the pain, and the fear ever end?

Susan Pendley Kier

Exposition Of Fall

Feel the crisp sweet air as fall ushers in. Look at the trees
shedding their colorful leaves. In yellow, brown, red and green
they're the starring cast of this scene. From tree branches
they dance into the air to softly land and cover earth with care.

Oh, Mrs. Spider spinning your web with care, that beautiful silk
array upon which hold captive the sun's rays. Lying motionless
in wait, vigilant in guarding your egg - perhaps resting til
disturbed by long awaited prey.

And Mr. Grasshopper, the browning of your haven will soon render
it dormant. Still careless and free have you not yet learned from Mr. Ant.

Mr. and Mrs. Squirrel dash across the lawn, up into the trees like
acrobats, limb to limb with ease. Frantic in search they find that
nutty prize, that under a tree they choose to hide.

I stand in ovation and awe, spellbound by this exposition of fall.

Robert Ramsey

Is Death Our Friend?

Is death as wonderful as some people say?
Should it only happen to the old and gray?
Do people deserve to die?
If no, then why?
Is it because we need to make room for more?
Or is it like a kid with a toy, the old one becomes a bore?
Is death a cycle we repeat over and over again?
In the end do we pay for our many sins?
Are we just put in coffins and left to rot?
Some people may think not.
Is there Heaven and is there hell?
This is a story I do not know well.
These are all questions we ask about our end.
But the question I ask most is, is death our friend?

Tara Briley

Rain

My mind goes back to another time and hour
Sitting on the porch during a rain shower
How pretty the green of the trees - all shades
You could almost see the grass grow
shooting forth new blades
And as the rain began to cease
out came the birds for a new treat.
A gentle breeze began to blow
Favorite flowers are starting to grow
Raindrops glistening under a peeping sun
Gives a sense of peace and joy to everyone.

Lurline A. Vaughn

Alone

An overwhelming sense of rage has taken over me.
Should retaliation be the end of my means?
Gazing into a hallow darkness for an answer, the heart draws back.
One more time, the criminal steps in.
Experiencing only shallowness, depression possesses every breath.

Closer towards the end of my mortality, the weakness is even
stronger than ever before.
The anticipation becomes much too excruciating.
I grow weak . . .
My fervent mind awaits more agony to come.
The strenuous dissension amidst myself, overtakes me.
The pores of my being, bleeding with fright.
Feeling trapped within my conscience, I try to escape my wickedness.

Searching deep into the depth of my soul, I wonder why I couldn't
   escape and leave it all behind me?

Why did I give in once again? But . . . nothing!
Retaliation steps in.

Now all the depression, anxiety, and pain relapses.
The war within my being . . . terminated.
   ALONE!

   Lynn Goff

Reality

A cold night the wind wrestled my emotion the stars
show me my devotion. I'm still alive, but what is living?
The bees came from their hive, flowers, pollen are they giving?
I feel you near, but you are so far, the sky is clear and the poor
musician strums his guitar. You are so overwhelmed, how the hell
did it get this way? Most peoples reaction to the world today
Too little too late, if you fall in love it is fate. Why can't we
all be equal? This is a universe for people. Why so much
destruction? I have a glare upon my face, but do not make an
assumption. Darkness and light what do you do when your fear in
it all, isn't right? Lets go away and set ourselves free, this world
is giving, no way to be happy. I'm going, going gone, but really
I'm still here, well, that's just my luck, I found one quarter so
I put it in the starving musicians cup.

   Stacy Ann Ashman

Untitled

Tell me which road to take, so that I won't make any mistakes.
Show me which way to go so that in the future I'll know.
Stop putting me down and laughing at me because I was not put
here to amuse you.
So look at me and be proud because I determine what happens to you.
I am your future.
If you put me down and leave me here; never to make anything
of myself and let me go down all the wrong roads; what kind of
leader will I become?
Don't think more of my future as what will happen to me, instead
think of it as what will happen to you and the world.
So do not let anybody tell you that you can not make a
difference; because you can.
You can even change the world.
I am a glimpse of what the future holds.

   Yolanda Redmon

Child In Me

I often wonder how the child in me will come out
Slumber's fragile veil reveals heaven's open door
Twilight cover calls for freedom of dawn
Dancing of clouds and coloring of rain
Seeking and finding
In mysteries and miracles
Simplicity inside

   Ken Habib

Waiting For Cadeau

As the old man crouched down,
Silently mumbling words I'll never know.
His face contorted as his mind filled with
Thoughts of years ago.
"Curse this man and his thoughtlessness!
When will he ever show?
Time spent and wasted sitting here,
Always waiting for Cadeau."

His frail hand extended to touch the stone,
Tracing the name carved decades ago.
The ground beneath him housed the shell
Of the one for whom he filled with woe.
The blade was long and sharp in his hand.
Thus, it only took one blow.
He fell to rest clutching the earth,
Still waiting for Cadeau.

   Stacey Atkins

The Silent Vigil

Like barren trees in a burnt forest,
Silently they stand for an hour.
On the placards in passing by
You can reads the reasons why
Like stark sentinels they silently stand,
Waiting for peace throughout the land.
Barren silence——barren people.

God, in His wisdom gave Nature a new birth,
that His handiwork should continue upon His earth.
As the years pass by
There's a new surge of life
Once more, we can see
The budding and branching of barren trees.

So, be it with us today,
The sentinels of despair have had their sway.
Their season now is ending,
A new birth is beginning
Once again, we will see
Green, growing, living things on the barren trees.

   Sally Ferrell Cook

Fountain Of Gold

Fountain of gold
Silver waters
Crystal waterfalls of love

Reaching all across the earth
Sapphire pools of majesty
The madonna stands by the side
Watching with serene promise
Maiden of magic

Proud circle
The fountain isn't anywhere, but everywhere
Part of everyone
Once in a long wait, a child is born of the Love
That the fountains house
The Gods and Goddesses
Messenger of God
Sent for life
The true angels
A legacy of love . . .

   Michelle Hazen

Your Special Days

Several years have come to pass
  Since God gave me a special task.
A baby girl upon my breast he lay,
  That was your Birth Day.

As I held you in my arms,
  I promised to love you and keep you from harm.
One day you were small, sitting on my knee,
  The next, a beautiful woman stood before me.
With pride I watched you walk away,
  That was your Graduation Day.

Now my little girl is grown,
  This day you make a home of your own.
Dressed in white, you walk down the aisle,
  and through my tears, I give you that special smile,
Then close my eyes, a prayer of thanks I say,
  For this is your Wedding Day.

    Terri Cramer

Autumn Equinox

Duets of leaves plummet,
singing in epiphany and threnody,
songs coalesce one tessitura.
I envision her,
last of her tribe, residual gold.
We leap headlong
into warm harvest winds.
The earthen breath swirls us,
captivated by this
windswept dance.
Twirling, rustling pirouette through
naked treetops, reveling in our own nakedness.
I reach out, caress her honeyed skin.
Kissing feather soft,
wedding bed, silk waters synchronous
with a gentle caress.
Euphoric warmth ebbs slowly away,
residual ochre fades,
forest whispers to kindred souls.

    Robert Kibler

"My Love For You"

My heart is full of gratitude as I watch the morning dew,
singing songs of Godly praise, my mind still envisions you;

Knowing there is a great distance which separates our touch,
Longing to gently caress and hold you, oh! I miss you so much;

Determined to do my best, and enjoy freedom once again,
Saddened by the truth that our love is going through such pain;

Will you once again stand by me, as we strive to better our life,
Even delighting my soul and commit to me, a vow to be my wife;

Take time, don't rush to answer, for I want you honest and true,
But for this moment be silent, and satisfy my heart, as I share
my love for you.

    Zell Bradley III

Rose Of Love

The rose dies in its full color of red.
Slowly one by one the petals fall,
Hardening as they reach the ground.
The fragrance of its existence fills the air,
Slowly diminishing with each passing hour.
A mangled mess of pollen and stem,
Shivering for the love of its petals have fallen
To dust.

    Mandy K. Mach

His Littlest Inheritance

Cotton red quilts and pastel blues
sit amidst a snow white crib.
Teddy's and tigers and bells satin shoes
Wait in wonder for a dream come true.

God grows the dreams within our hearts . . .
a button nose lad with sugar brown skin . . .
a dimple with charm and soft dark curls . . .
and boyish delights with Heaven's twinkle in his eyes.

Joy in the morning and songs in the night,
our dearest request are dreams come true . . .
God gives to us his littlest inheritance . . .
a mother's joy and a father's pride.

    Mary L. Archer

The Rescue

A man alone in devastation
Sitting there in a railway station
Meets up with a lady he doesn't know
Opens up to her, his heart he shows.

His thoughts had been of other places,
Of other times and other faces.
She clears his thoughts and changes his mind
With her heart and voice that are so kind.

Then she takes him home to meet her kids,
Wonderful children with whom she lives.
He opens his heart to this family
Life and a future he can now see.

The kids ask questions to blow his mind
Answers unknown of a different kind.
Will you stay awhile and talk to us?
We have faith in you and lots of trust.

The bond is there, a natural thing.
A life of goodness to him they bring.
Another time or another night
He'd have been on the train, out of sight.

    R. J. Lessard

"For All Of God's Children"

Step forward, Earthchild being, with your chin raised toward the skies.
So alive with life's breath, drink in the wondrous beauty, behold
the miracle of one's eyes,

Boundless Creations of the Lord, We are allowed to explore,
Our thirst for knowledge of his gifts, neverending, our quest for more,

Perfection was created, in glorious days, numbering seven,
Bequested upon all beings, from our beloved Lord in Heaven,

His creations with no number, such perfection in their casting,
All hues of the Rainbow, their existence, all being equal, now,
And for everlasting,

Step forward all God's children, seeking hand embracing hand,
Live as brother and sister, we're so blessed to share, on our
Father's Land,

Be never blinded by treacherous light and pigmented shade of cover,
Hold love in your heart, for all friend and foe,
Then, forever in God's house, You will hover.

    Ronald Selkowitz

The Steps Of Wisdom

Walk not to the beat of yesterday's drum;
Skip joyfully along with today's surrounding fun.

Climb up wisdom's ladder.
Don't be a fool to miss the steps
And watch your life shatter.

Promises from unknownledgeable lips do
Portray the future of one's destination.

But the Word of God can and will
Always be a wise man's revelation.
Michele Linda Gill

Silence

When there's no one left, and everyone is gone
Slowly slowly drifting away, no one notices as she walks astray
If just they knew the pain she's been through

Raindrops on her skin, her hair blowing in the wind
Standing there alone she hungers, for the sweet sound of thunder
And are her eyes deceiving, as a cloud awakens, with every streak of lightning

When everyone wants to control you, and you feel your
   body empty, of every ounce of energy
When we've gone from bad to worse, and wonder if suicide hurts
When the blood is not enough, and the pain is too much

What can we do
Where can we go
How do we know

This knife she holds piercing her skin, drawing blood from within.
A vibrant smile turns a shade of gray, and her soul, fades away
Tiffany Mercado

Wedding Bliss

I want to go where you go, taste what you taste, without haste . . .
Smell what you smell, feel what you feel, see what
you see, just you and me . . .
I want your love, I give you mine, inside and
outside, as we stand side by side . . .
I want to ride the wings of life with you.
I want the ups and downs, the good and the bad,
I want to be there when you are sad . . .
I accept no challenge, experience no new adventure,
wish for nothing, dream not, nor cope,
without our rings of hope . . .
I want the bitter and the sweet, otherwise I fear defeat . . .
You are my teacher my lover, my friend,
You are my heartache, the one who keeps me awake,
you are my soulmate . . .
Today is the day, of hope, of love, of my future,
the start of a new life, for you will become my wife.
R. T. Miles

Within Our Mist

Two little trees blowing in the meadow
smiling, swaying, oh so mellow

The sun was bright with the moon coming in that night
for Christ has shown his love so bright

Within his mist of unknown ways
we find peace in all our days

For it is upon the rock that we stand
reaching back for another's hand
Loretta Balbi

Help!

The rain forest's demise, the spotted owl's plight,
smog and pollution light up the night.
The rivers are tainted, the fish die in schools,
who is the captain of this "ship of fools?"
Save the whale and the dolphin; they are our friends.
The list of endangered seems never to end.
The Earth and its dilemmas are put on the shelf,
when faced with the problem of maintaining self,
there's still planes to catch and still bills to pay,
so the system perpetuates day after day.
It's time to revamp, we must act as one,
or there'll be only one species under this sun.
We must pull together and rewrite the text,
'cause after the animals, guess who goes next!
Sylvester Gillner

The Year Of The Snow And Ice

Oh! This year of 1994,
Snow and Ice, we want no more.
In sub-zero weather it's mighty cold,
I stay inside, but I'm told.

I brew the coffee and make the stew,
And keep the fires burning, but this isn't new.
Things like this, I've done most of my life,
Growing up in the country, a mother and a wife.

Oh! This weather in our Golden age,
I'm compelled to stay inside at this stage.
But the memories of a long time ago,
When we used to sled ride in the snow.

The year of 1994 will be hard to forget,
Schools all closed, but the children didn't fret.
Built a fire, and rode down the hill.
I watched from the window, couldn't stand the chill.

The ice on the trees is a beautiful sight,
The snow on the ground is a blanket of white.
But staying inside is not my cup of tea,
Oh Lord, give us warmer weather, is my plea.
Rosie Peer

Promise

The brave little flower stood in the courtyard.
Snow had fallen and the wind was bitterly cold.
The other flowers about him had all withered and died.
Would he be next to fall - he wondered?

His leaves were drooping and brown, yet he stood tall with
blossom still red.

Each day might be his last - yet still he remains. An example of
   dignity, tenacity, and strength.

Soon he knows the deep snows will come. Has he served a
purpose is there a reason for his being here? He hopes so.

Finally, God says "Brave little flower its now time to sleep and wait
to be wakened again." A time to go on perhaps for many suns and moons.

"Sleep little friend you gave joy and beauty to all with out
consideration."

"Come to your rest it is well earned. Yes little friend you have
   given your all."

"I love you, wait for a new day to burst into blossom again."

It's truly not death, only a resting time.
Noreen Rood

Hidden

A wrinkled withered hand pulled down the shade
so afraid the light and life would sear his skin - burn his soul
How many countless times this gesture done
until the time that daylight ceases.
The risk of a smile, perhaps a tear
too much to bear. Too much may shatter his crystalline cocoon
Fingers tapping at his door
tip-toed eyes peeking for one glimpse of the man that was.
A time when his skin was taught and strength supported him
Where did the years go

Lynne F. Hazard

Vessel

The silver vessel awaits its charges
so many, so varied.

Once entered, they wait, they gaze.
Some converse, some relax.
And then in a blink of the eye, it's over.

They have traversed river and mountain,
and flown higher than the clouds.
They have almost touched the hand.

Robert A. Siebel

Bye To Fort Ben

It's time to say goodbye,
so hold your head up high,
although your tears may fly,
our esteem to you rate high.
You've stood the storm bravely,
you've seen them come and go,
all sizes, ranks and nationalities,
during war and peace time.
You've been the cure for all ails,
you've been the answer in the dark,
you've been like a chicken over her brood,
you've trained and you trained well.
Like every good thing must come to a end,
your closing is now at hand,
you'll go gracious down in history,
named the greatest instillation.
Three cheers for Fort Benjamin Harrison!
from the military and civilians everywhere,
but especially from the great city,
of Indianapolis, In. Three Cheers!

Rosa M. Howard

My Teacup Of Roses

Please join me - won't you
so I can share my teacup of Roses.
I'll share my hopes, dreams, fears and loves.
Please join me
for my teacup of Roses.
My soul is waiting for you,
while my body lies in despair.
I've waited so long to share everything
with someone like you.
Now that I've found you
won't you join me,
so I can give you, my teacup of Roses?
Why won't you come, I can see you
drifting into the midnight fog.
Are you afraid, are you ashamed?
No worries, you have nothing to fear.
I love you - no matter what
so won't you join me, and share
your teacup of Roses.

Tiffany Clay

The Desert

"Write a poem!" somebody said.
So, I took myself outside thinking to pen some epic thing,
A vociferous and lofty rendering forming in my cluttered head.
But fickle words confounded me so that I looked around
Where jagged mountains kept their stoney peace,
An ancient sky spread himself in blue and purple fleece,
And falcons keened up high
A lonely, moving sound.
At some point I forgot my quest of words and fell into the tides of mind.
My arrogant pen settled to its page bereft,
While the swollen sun swept down behind the peaks to rest,
And left me to ponder night's endless diamond mine.
How feeble glanced the written line when aimed upon such grace.
The solitude is old as God, and deep, and sovereign
And ten thousand syllables could not its visage paint again.
So leave the pen to other things,
The desert is a thinking place.

Morgaus

November Night

How could I have been
So mad at you,
Little brown dog,
For waking me at 2:30 a.m.
On that November night?
You clawed my back and
Insisted it was time for a
Backyard hike.

I was sure your only plan was to
Lift your leg beside the cottonwood tree.

Suddenly, your ears shot up.
Together, our eyes widened.
What was that amazing burst of
Light and color in the sky?
We learned the next day
It was not an exploding sparkler.
It had been seen thousands of miles away,
A magnificent meteor streaking across the horizon.
Thank you, my best friend, for such a sight.
I should have trusted you.

Lindsay Cooper Calhoun

Locked Up Inside

So many people, so many things,
so many feelings that are locked
up with me. But should I keep
them locked up as I do? I guess
I should face my problems and
talk about them to someone,
to those who I love and to those who love me.
I just don't know how. No one can
understand, and I know this for sure.
For I'm not just the average kid!
I want to talk, but no one will
listen because they're full of their
sorry excuses. All my feelings
locked up. Not because of puberty.
Not school and not boys. I'm not
sure why, nor how to explain it
but it's a very depressing thing
to have them locked up inside of me.

Katie A. Halling

Thank You Mom

So many words unspoken
So many opportunities we let slipped
  Not that I am grown
And have a life and family of my own
  As I face the motherhood
Dealing with sickness and sleepless night
  I wonder if you to
Sat up throughout many a night
  Calming night frights
Or fighting fevers that still lingers
  The many hugs and I love you
As you stood and wave goodbyes
  The reprimands and many praises
The guidance that lead me through
  Yet did I thank you
For all that you have done and for the love
And care that you have shown
  And if I hadn't said it before
Thank you mom from my heart
  Thank you so much for being you.

Lamai T. Edge

Little Miracles

This morning I didn't get up late,
So my mind was in a fairly calm state.
My shower was hot, not cold, which I hate,
And my towel was in reach with the help of my mate.

It was not raining when I went to the car,
There was no accident, I didn't drive far.
I found a parking space without a spar,
The construction was gone, therefore no tar.

Once at work there was lots to do,
I began wondering if it wasn't a zoo.
I got my work done right on cue,
And then came a stack that was all brand new.

Out to the car, once again on the run,
I'm thinking of dinner, I'm under the gun.
I want something different, I want something fun,
But when I got home the dinner was done!

So each day as I go plodding along,
And thinking of things that could have gone wrong,
I say a prayer and sing a song,
God's little miracles keep me strong.

Teresa Olson

A Mother's Love

A Mother's love
So pure and as white as a dove
You can search to try and find
The love she radiates that can blind
But I'll tell you this you'll never find
Her unique love that's so kind
Her love is made up of understanding
She's going to admonish you
That you'll sometimes think is commanding
But it's only her deepest concern
To tell you your mistakes in order to learn
So don't get mad and let your anger run wild
Because she'll get so mad, and that's only putting it mild
And if you ever stray, then decide to come back home
Her loving arms will accept and enfold
And right then and there, you shall know
What a beautiful thing a mother's love's to behold.

Shondell A. D'Ornellas

Untitled

Like a sea gull in flight
Soaring through the clouds
But never feeling the feathers of another bird
It's a lonely atmosphere clouds don't speak
And the rain only makes noises
I fly by myself and feel like I'm falling and falling
But never reaching the coming ground
In my descent I have found
Someone to share space with
and I hope that our plumage
Will vibrate with excitement
as we soar towards infinite happiness.

Lucien Hébert

Mirrors Of The Soul (inspiration)

Mirrors of the soul, flashing by like in a dream.
Softly she speaks to me.
Somewhere I reach for her but,
Like a stream of light, an eel, that
slips thru the silent deep,
She's gone, until then I,
Stop searching and she is there again.
Softly she comes when I do not seek her.
Softly she speaks when I am not listening.
If my fingers can only see when my eyes are closed, she comes . . .
The greater reality is illusion.
Illusion is now and I cannot see her.
Reality is a cloud in the dark and the sun is hiding.
Mirrors of the soul that cannot speak.

Ricardo J. Garcia

Colored Emotions

Love is an ocean that reaches far and wide.
  Some take it in and others run and hide.
Peace is a valley vast and low.
  The seeds of kindness we need to sow.
The world is such a beautiful place.
  Why do we have to be race against race?
Black, yellow, red, white
  Have we lost our sense of sight?
The seeds of hate are planted in our mind.
  Have we left our hearts behind?
If only we could blend in the love
And remove the hate
Take away the races
And of peace partake.

Sarah Adams

Stirring Up Leaves

One crisp fall morning I discovered something,
  something I love to do!
Stirring up leaves around every bend, doesn't
  matter that there were only a few.
Was the thrill in going faster or in making a mess?
Was I adding to confusion or creating any stress?
For a brief moment in time I took charge.
My part so small in a world so large.
The thrill of that moment is over now, a simple
  joy was found.
I so look forward to stirring up leaves, next time
  I'm around!!

Susan D. Benson

Take Me Back

The feelings I have were something new,
Something I've never felt before meeting you.

So special, so happy, so warm and secure,
I thought you'd always be there for sure.

But now you're gone, there's only one thing to do,
and that's figure out a way to get back together with you.

A love like ours doesn't grow on trees,
Take me back Gina, I'm begging you please.

My days have been long, and my nights are lonely,
Please come back, and be my one and only.

Timothy J. Wingell

"A Map To My Heart"

A map to my heart is what you need;
Something that guides you to knowing me.

Because of my past and the way I've been scarred,
Past relationships in which I've been marred;

I keep up my guard and watch constantly,
So that no one can get in too easily.

I give you this map to my tender heart,
So guard it and never let me fall apart.

I know that you will keep it close,
And care for it above all else.

If ever you were to lose your grip,
That map to my heart would surely rip;

Then never in my future days,
Would anyone know the unpaved way,
To the center of my being,
Where my heart doth stay.

Rebecca E. Trease

A Message Within

I woke up this morning, I found something new;
Something wonderful, for me and for you.
Something worth waiting for, each minute of our lives;
Something worth waiting for, it's like a beautiful rainbow you feel inside.
What is the past to you my friend, what is the future without today;
A new life, a new day, a new life, a new way.
So live like it was your last, forget the future, forget the past;
Life is like a song, you sing it and then it's gone.
Your wishing now you had lived for today, helping man learn in a better way;
What can I do, what can I say, but live for today.
So find a path, find a way, find the will and go today;
Who can say if it's wrong or right, just go today for it's almost night.
Tomorrow may never come, just live for now for the day is young;
Living is so hard to do, but the day is here so do what you must do
Live not for me or anyone, live for yourself, it's you who has to prove
You've done your best when the day is done;
You've helped yourself you've helped everyone

Sharon Corley

Together

I sit here thinking of all the things we've said.
sometimes I wish that we were lying down in bed.
I wonder if we'll make it last, the times we'll share together.
I wonder if we'll make it last, always and forever.
i think about you all the time and sometimes even more.
I hope you know deep in your heart, you're the one that I adore.
i hope this once, we'll stay together a long, long time.
to make it last, put in the past, now I will blow your mind.
I see you in the darkness, I see you in the light.
I will rest for now and to my love, I will say goodnight.
ALWAYS AND FOREVER, WE TWO LOVERS ARE TO-
GETHER!

Leslie Schneider

Untitled

Tangled web of bodies like vines,
Sorted souls with hearts entwined.

Blossoming flower that bloomed within,
Hiding with beauty its bitter sting.

Time like molasses sweet and slow,
Love now lost ask, where did it go?

Promises, promises forgotten or ignored
Affection denied to one once adored.

Soft caresses of days gone by,
Now burn flesh and blood boils dry.

There was a time with nothing too small or great,
Could be told now but seems it too late.

Friendly indifference searing the brain,
Hate would be easier, yielding less pain.

Strangers coming closer to the end of the line,
Biting of lips keep words from revealing signs.

Little girl, little boy where did you go?
Did it hurt little one when your heart was torn so?

Thinking it would last, oh how wrong you could be,
Darling, you and I no longer make we.

Maggie Edwards

It's Hard To Say . . .

Sitting on the bank of Mom and Dad's lake,
sounds of crickets, locusts and cranes I hear.
Cars on the highway go hissing by, although
I cannot see them.

It's hard to say . . . this used to be Mom and Dad's.

Monarch butterflies gently flutter south to Mexico,
fish splashing in the water down below.
The tapping of a woodpecker and the whizzing of a hummingbird,

It's hard to say . . .

A large white bird standing just off the shore,
I look up to the never-ending big blue sky,
Monarch butterflies flutter by a few hundred more.

A child at some time has stacked rocks ever so neatly,
one on top of another, wishing,
Possibly trying to escape boredom while his gramps was fishing.

I pondered a thought to myself while gazing at the
neatly stacked rocks;

DREAMING DREAMS WILL COME TRUE.

It's hard to say . . .

Norman B. Ingram

As I Lay Silent

As I lay silent another day is gone
Still all has come to none
Happiness must be illusionary

Daily I go to places
Never visited by me
Yet all faces remind me of where I've been

My still heart strains wanting to run
While I remain afraid to call your name
Knowing an answer will not come

The time we had together is gone
You cannot come back
I can only grow old

R. Fred Kobres

A Moment Of Truth

Watching the surf, hands clasped, about each knee . . .
Spellbound, by rolling waves, sounding reveille . . .
Suddenly, to dawn on me . . . from here, I came to be . . .
The sky illumes, and all, is crystal-clear to see!

The splendor, enlivens, a lethargic jeu-d'esprit;
Awareness, heightens, to the utmost degree;
Words, nor any artistry, depict its facsimile . . .
From the mundane . . . a very willing absentee.

The earth turns, and the heavens, are aglow . . .
A oneness, untouched and pure, as the driven snow;
The essence, of its being, to intimately know . . .
All, is not for naught . . . a manifesto . . . apropos.

Me, myself, and I . . . yes, yes . . . all three . . .
I was the wind . . . a blade of grass . . . and, free!
Cradled in the arms, of the obliging sea . . .
I was everything to everyone, but, true to thee.
        Patrice Tsakálou Hartford

Without Flowers The Weeds

A legion of sunbeams
spilling inexhaustible silence-like decay,
and snatching immutable claim,
surrender the nebulous virgin: the icon of rape

bloodletting grip, and
scorching rightness, and
splattering perished flowers
like Beelzebub's filth

earth dirt, powder dry, frozen in heat, and mute
dullard hybrids relenting nonexistent virginity too late

betrayed by pungent passion, and
innocence, and
promise, and
desire, and
without water, and
without flowers,
the weeds
        M. Theresa Holloway

Billy's Angel

Billy's Angel came to take him by the hand as God set his soul and
spirit free, on a cold November's day.

We shed tears of joy and of sadness and some mourn in silence,
forever missing your worldly presents.

No longer in pain or discomfort, you are at peace finally,
with God surrounded by your angels you look down upon us smiling.

As we put your weary body into its eternal resting place we feel
you, overflowing our hearts and minds with your saintly spirit.

Today we mourn your death but tomorrow we celebrate your life,
each time we speak your name we pay tribute to your being . . .
We honor your memory each and every day of our living.

There may be one less star in the sky, but there is one more Angel in heaven . . .
Now that we must say good-bye, take good care. Though we will meet
again, at the golden gates of heaven.
        Valerie A. Edwards

Structured Phrases Of Chaos

A clamor beckoning forth, enticing like a siren's cry
splendid noises resounding, reverberating in exuberance
a conglomeration of tones thriving in erratic, joyous blaring
evoking dreams, nurturing fantasies
a bewildering rhythmic celebration
conjuring kaleidoscopic apparitions.

A vision infused, a perfect dissonance
thunderous chords crashing in reckless abandon
faint themes of thought blurring
wild, incredible shards of opulent fantasy mingling
with threads of a bleak and dismal reality
rainbows of sound resonating in vigorous expression.

A turbulent explosion of a myriad crowded, lucid notes
a confrontation of forceful vibrations
trickling through every resistance
a tumultuous procession, exultant and triumphant
an expanse without periphery
its madness encompassing all
knowing no bounds, imposing none.
        Szymon Letowski

Dangerous Game

It's dangerous yes the game we play, my heart's at
stake I fear. Despite my flirting ways, you'll
find I long to hold you near.
I see much more than a handsome face, much
more than your deep dark eyes. I see much more
than the ready smile on the mouth that tells me lies.
I see the you that stays in mind, a thought that
makes me smile. I wish to make this game be
real but I wonder all the while. I wonder how
you'd take all this, have you guessed, or would
it be a surprise? I wonder how it would
feel to look and find love there in your
eyes. Our playful words come all the time
but I beg of you look beyond.
    See the meaning behind the actions and
then my dear respond.
        Lillian M. Garcia

Things I Miss About You

The things I miss are listed below,
starting with that look the day it snowed;
Maybe just your beautiful face,
maybe just your long embrace;
Maybe just that little peck,
maybe just your delicate neck;
Maybe just your perfect smile,
maybe I can hold you awhile;
Maybe just your luscious lips,
maybe just your wiggling hips;
Maybe it's your bright blue eyes,
maybe the way you tell your lies;
Maybe it's the way you ignore me,
maybe that's what makes me adore thee;
Maybe it's your precious digits,
maybe that's what makes me fidget;
Maybe it's the way you hold the pool cue,
maybe it's why I love you;
Maybe just your loving kiss,
maybe that's what I really miss.
        Robert Trimble

The Queen Of Hearts

Down to one last bet, I'd gambled nearly all;
Still me fate wasn't set, I'd force them one last call.
I asked the dealer for the queen of hearts, for in the shuffle she lay hid;
And as he dealt me all my cards, I regretted what I'd bid.

Each player stared at me, wondering what could be my plan;
For none of them could see the lady of diamonds in my hand.
She could be the card on which I'd base my every play,
But she was not the queen of hearts, so I could not let her stay.

And instead I threw her back, insisting on a change;
Against me the deck now stacked and this was not a game.
But I got my second hand, the queen of hearts was all I needed,
For she was the only chance that my dreams would be completed.

One face in so many, the chances were so slim,
And as each card turned up empty I knew I couldn't win.
Still no pain showed on my face as all my dreams went cold,
I threw the lady of diamonds away and then life forced me to fold.

Shane Weldon

Hold On To The Night

Cold blooded killers, all around
Still we kill our people, cause they walk our town
What kind of world, are we livin' in
When we're rapin' life, for the price of sin

Infected people, they spread it all around
Indirectly killin' those, who used to walk our town
So Cocaine dealin' junkies, can corrupt our kids
Then they'll grow up just like dad, in his big time world of sin

Everywhere I look there's people dyin', still I don't see no one cryin'
Workin' hard for a day's pay, that theory went out yesterday
So you're spendin' all your dirty money, that you're stealin' from
your old man's honey
Don't worry I won't tell, if you're tossin' Lincoln in the wishing well

People, people, what's goin' on
If I close my eyes, then my son is gone
People, people, oh Lord help us now
We've gotta save our world, but we don't know how

Until then, hold on to the night
And everything will be all right

J Franze

Hobbling Silhouettes

My fathers sat cross-legged on pine infested hills
Stockinged feet, hairless beards, sabers in their belts

My mothers moved between steaming pots and boiling cauldrons
Silhouettes in wooden slippers outlined on rice-paper walls

My fathers spoke on the hills in a tongue I have forgotten
Watched the silhouettes hobbling behind rice-paper walls

My mothers served silently, not allowed to speak
With bowed heads, humble eyes, fed men cross-legged and resolute

My fathers ate under blanket covers of pine infested hills
Outside rice-paper walled homes, ignoring bowed heads

My mothers saddled horses, readied gold-plated armor
Cut their thick, black hair in a mortal mandate of grief

My fathers spoke of war, of duty, of honor as they ate
Last meal before the journey to prophetic pagoda fortresses

My mothers bashfully wept, wailed to calm epileptic limbs
Stood stoic as the procession streamed past, inches from their feet

My fathers rode far from subdued pine infested hills
To war, to duty, to bring honor to their names

And my mothers remained in the forest in black kimonos, shorn hair
Behind rice-paper walls, among boiling cauldrons, hobbling in prayer.

Tarisa Matsumoto

Evolution

The first men who had lived a night
Stood among an ocean of dancing grass.
They searched the sky, bathed in moonlight,
For an explanation of life and death.

Men grew in number as did their problems.
Ignorance and hate blinded them.
Love and respect became shadows of the past.
Death seemed the only quick way out.

Now we gather here once again,
Standing among an ocean of dancing grass.
The moon mocks us with a cruel grin,
For, life was a game, death the reality.

Kristen Myers

Knight-Officer

He rides from street to street
Stopping evil wherever it maybe
And practicing the code of chivalry
He is a valiant fighter in the field
He is an expert of the weapon he wields
He serves his leader so honorable and true
No matter what he battles or who
He's a man with courage of a lion
And he has no real fear of dyin'
He treats his women courteous and right
And carouses with them all through the night
He loves his job this much I know
This man will never be food for a crow
And so I tell you he's a good man
Wherever and whenever he does what he can

Matthew Lapinskas

Thank You

Thank you for all my hands can hold
strawberries sweet water cold the sand so warm on
my feet cookies and candies so good to eat

Thank you for all my eyes can see a sunset gold
like a bumble bee my bunny so soft sitting next to me
while I read a book with my family
Thank you for all my ears can hear the ocean
waves so loud and clear my friends laughing so
happily while my bunny plays with me

Michelle Kent

"My Beloved Husband"

You are my green pastures, my fresh cool
  stream of water . . .
My sunlight, my star that shines in the night,
And you are my light
You are the silent sound of strength
  that comes to me when I am weary.
And the song in my heart when the day is long
And you are the new light that begins at dawn
Our marriage has sealed all that is within
All the things that cry out to be fulfilled
  with longing
Now come to the mountaintop with a
  great sense of belonging . . .
  And you are my lamp

Rosemary Talbert

Shattered Minds

Shattered minds of a useless child,
such a tragic thing. The child confused
and disorientated about it's being.
Psychotic and autistic are the ways of
this child.
    Aggressive and at times suicidal.
Their minds are filled with fear, hate,
and love. With killing, suffering, and
gentleness. Not knowing the reasons why.
They are filled with destruction, neglect,
and joy. Trials, abuse, and giving. All
it knows is frustration, hallucinations,
and complications.
    Shattered minds so desperately
trying to find meaning in this life.
Tell me, what is it that's happened
to my fellow mankind.

    Tamie Nicholls

Man's New World Order

A new world order, vast in scope, what will life be!
Such feelings of hope, will our freedom really be free?
A constitution which guarantees rights from above;
To be based on a creator, who rules by His Love.
Now a world has rights to be decided by the majority;
Just imagine your rights, when you are in the minority!

When man will not restrain himself or his deadly tongue,
He will soon be constrained by another or maybe hung.
Who or what will keep this big world order at peace;
When people are killing each other, rely on thought police?
This new world order will be ruled by fear;
So just remember, the time is now drawing near.

They want to take our weapons from us to start;
But man's killing weapons are hidden in his heart.
To love your neighbor as yourself, do you believe;
Now a world at peace, can we all now perceive?

Such nice and soothing words for most to hear;
That this new world order is soon to appear.
The strong delusion now masks the truth, how odd!
That a man can have peace without being at peace with God.

    Karen Richards

Subtlety, Then Chloe Cried

Through an opiatic obliquity of destiny
Sufferable by means of perpetual finesse
Passes to sweet sorrow an elegant
Rosy hue
Corrupt
And fallen from grace -
Grieved
Yet beautiful.
Pale
Exoteric affections
Each one an inexpressible entity all its own
Left to congregate in the midst of several azure hypochondriacs
One
And the other three sheets in the wind
Taken from side of the house to another.
The sadness of all causes one to weep
And She fills Their wine glasses with tears
Toasting what They'll forever desire
But never possess.

    Scott Staton

Miracle World

It started one day long ago
Sunny, stormy I don't know
The birth of the world
a miracle of all miracles
Images of animals, humans, plants, dirt
and insects all in sight
Good and bad no one knew the difference
No one still does but one person
Reasons for everything but questions
still unanswered
Learning to live in this world is a
commitment itself
To devote the best of yourself is all
that is expected
A small request asked of each and everyone of us
But to find out the meaning of life
and death or to find out the good and bad in ourselves is a
difficult task. Because no one knows of themselves
until they know of their creator
Which usually you will only find in death.
By then it is too late . . .

    Robin L. Tremblay

Sunrise

Open the shades.
Sunrise is the victory of light over darkness.
Sunrise is a tall glass of orange juice when you awaken.

Open the shades.
Sunrise is a ball of fire burning
Its way to the top of the horizon.
Sunrise is nature's wake-up call.

Open the shades.
Sunrise is a message to the moon that it may rest.
Sunrise is a blinding ball of light
Finding its way out of the darkness.

Open the shades.
Sunrise is here.
Star's rest.
Moon's rest.

All earth's creatures roaming about
Sun watching every move.
Its powerful light shining through
Even the smallest cracks.

    Rebecca Allswang

Untitled

Marionettes dance and on the wall,
  Swaying shadows never fall;
Their limbs are free, no strings at all,
Send shadows swaying ten feet tall.
Within this house with not one room,
  Candles flicker in the gloom;
The wind runs by and gulps them down,
And steals a smile from a clown.

The kitchen's full of knives and meat,
  Stairways lie on plates to eat;
You'll still be hungry, still be thin,
But there's the clown's forgotten grin.
So marionettes leap and climb the stairs,
  and gravity's glue drips from their cares;
For as the clock crows, "time to go!"
The wind will weep to end the show.

    Paul Kanter

Shadow-Dancers

Shadow-dancers move along my wall,
Sweeping circles in the darkness.
All but the one, who,
    never moves, never joins,
Remains in the corner, just watching.
Hours pass . . . The silent music stops and starts.
Partners change again and again.
All but the one, who,
    cannot dance, cannot laugh,
Sits in the corner, knees to chest.
Dawn comes . . . The orchestra plays a final tune.
Patrons dance the last dance,
Fraying away to oblivion.
To wait again for the night.
All but the one, who,
    left behind, left alone,
Rises from the corner and goes into the day.
A shadow among shadow-dancers.

Jeffrey Mitchell Beaty

Shannon's Lullaby

Sleep little baby, angel of mine.
Sweet dreams of flowers be in your mind.
All of God's angels watch over you.
They will keep you safe, and your Mother will too!
Close your little eyes and rest 'til you shall rise.
Soon it will be morning.

Sleep little baby, sleep all night long.
Dream of the music playing your song.
Sweet dreams of sunshine, shining on you.
It shall bring you love, and your dreams will come true.
Close your little eyes and rest 'til you shall rise.
Soon it will morning.

Sleep little sweetheart; rest little girl,
Dream of sweet kisses that shine like a pearl
You are my angel, so precious, so new.
GOD shall keep you safe, and your Father will too.
Close your little eyes and rest 'till you shall rise.
Soon it will be morning.

Liv Elise Leftwich

Mine Is The Hand That Wrote, Remembers

  Our extension of heart felt love
symbolically does when hearts intertwine adopth
flow into our word, wisdom divine. Upon my heart is
a glow, laughter, joy in my songs. Do you sense it when
our eyes meet with the sweetness of honey, the soft
fleshy flower peddle, the lightening bolt of energy,
magic given in feeling, thought, all is alive that even
gave a cherished hope, dream, breath and little kisses,
our sensual self, giving, receiving moving in sunlight,
starlight together as one song with voice, melody?
Then if yes, we have a beginning.

J. A. Buck

Bus Driver

Oh driver, what stress is on your mind,
Take them home, leave them behind.
You've been across miles with dozens of them,
Roaring and fighting again and again.
The last is delivered, your nerves are now worn,
Go home, get rest, prepare for the morn.
Oh school bus driver, how do you give in,
To the roaring and fighting again and again?

Rita Smith

Father Figure

I know I have a child. That's why I got a job to raise and
take care of my child properly.

I know I have a child. That's why I stay in school so I can
answer my child's questions.

I know I have a child. That's why I practice at my skills and
talents to give and get more for my child.

I know I have a child. That's why I think before I act so my
child won't be abused or ignored.

I know I have a child. That's why I remember all the things I did
when I was young so I can understand what my child is going through.

I know I have a child. That's why I act like my child; watching
cartoons, playing with games and toys, so my child can trust me
and not think of me as a stranger.

I know I have a child. That's why I pray to stay with the mother
of my child, cause without loving her, I wouldn't have a child
to love of my own.

I know I have a child. That's why I'm not ashamed of being called
a dad. So, what's your excuse . . . Pops?

Yancy Evans

Show Me The Way

Take my hand and help me through this life Lord.
Take my sorrow and give me joy Lord.
Take my hard and give a little easy Lord.
Give me change, oh dear Lord, give me courage.
Take my hate and give me love Lord.
Take my doubts and give me hope Lord.
Take my hand dear Lord and show me the way.

Teresa Daugherty

Time To Listen

If you take the time to listen and cast your cares a-side,
Take the time to listen and in the Lord confide;
If you take the time to listen to the wonders all a-round,
Take the time to listen, miraculous faith a-bound;
The seasons come and go each year —with it's joys and
with it's tears -
If you only take the time to listen,
God will answer all your prayers.

If you take the time to listen, Gods message will be clear,
Take the time to listen and troubles will dis-appear;
If you take the time to listen, hear music bells that toll,
Take the time to listen, feel the beauty in your soul.
The seasons come and go each year —with it's joys and
With it's tears, -
If you only take the time to listen,
God will answer all your prayers.
God will keep you in His care.

Miriam Hildreth

Rocky Road

Don't take my heart down the rocky road,
Tell me now straight and bold.
Don't take my love down the rocky road,
It's too precious to only hold.

Take me now to a brighter place,
That will fill our hearts with love and grace.
To a place you know where beauty grows,
And the air is warmed with a tender glow.

My love is strong, and worth more than gold,
But it can't handle the rocky road.

Michael Stevens

For Sale

Come one, Come all! Step right up,
Take your number, and join the line
Fragments of a madman's mind
Insanity tastes so sweet to the lips of the lucid
How can you turn this offer down?
My wares, carefully concealed-but nonetheless wondrous
A show of pain the likes of which you have never dreamt
The price, though heavy, should not be unexpected
For a show of this destructive quality
and there have been many before to foot the bill
Come, come now. 'Tis an immortal collection!
Worthy of the name: Treasure
Passion and rage, laughter and tears, pride and shame
The Bard could not craft a more perfect division
Images and actions so insanely beautiful
You will not ask for more, I guarantee.
Ah, excellent! You interest is piqued, I see
First a warning, my dear sweet soul
The twisted mindscape you shall enter is beyond
Comprehension, so take nothing with you, for nothing returns

Scott Finnell

A Dad

Any man can be a father, but it
Takes a special kind of man to be a dad
A dad is a gift from God that is
There to help a child grow, and understand
A dad is a man who is there when your asleep,
And when you awake
A dad is a man who can console you when you've
Had a bad dream
A dad is a man who can love
A dad is a man who can feel
A dad is a man who can understand
A dad is a man who can teach
A dad is there no matter what the circumstances,
he is a man who will be there right to the end
A dad in a child's eyes is a king among men

Rick Collins

Untitled

As a child, I knew my father as he was,
Tall and stately,
Perhaps taller and more stately than he was.

I knew him in anger and sometimes caring,
Perhaps angrier than he was,
And more caring than I knew.

I knew him when he was alive
And myself only after he was dead.

I knew him only as I could know him.
And I loved him,
Oh that he could have known me!
We might have spoken.

Virgil Catalano

My Christmas Prayer

My Christmas prayer is for world peace
That all strife and pestilence shall cease
That mankind may kneel in gratitude
And not be bowed down by servitude
That the Christmas spirit shall dominate the earth
And bring back love, happiness and mirth
That each nation shall exist for its peoples good,
That which will create the spirit of brotherhood

Marjorie B. Rogers

The Tapper Or The Dove

Years ago came a tap,
Tap Tap upon a hearts door.
Daylight eagerly came
nights were a maze of unspeakable thoughts
and haunting happenings.
Shut the door, to tappings did she
Entered deeper into unknown travels
and lost portions of herself that resemble pieces of life
that lay scattered, broken and torn along the highways
and backroads of life.

Entered into her, a soaring dove
that perched upon her heart, with desire to
rest inside her being.

Whom be the wiser?
The tapper or the dove?

Both have dabbled in depth that is even too deep for her
and still none possess the key, to open wide up her heart.
For the lock is rusted and corroded in pain
and the key was thrown into a sea of fire,
by someone she loved for many many lives.

Nita Bullard

The Drowning Pit

You need to floss your brain of all that's my fault
tastes like going insane, with a little more salt
you need to see the sky with a more infant view
but it looks like I had an overdose of you
and as you laugh it echoes my walls
it echoes like the crash that destroyed it all
you were nothing but a rerun, I was a block to fill the void
Something easily outdone, something silently destroyed
such a fragrant of a timeline, blending in just the same
we've far since passed the finish line, only this is not a game
we took it like a child's toy and molded it to be
such a picture of dramatic joy that only we could see
you mixed it well and served it up and spoon-fed with your ladle
and now my mind is so corrupt, my bed is now a cradle
it's so beyond comparison, my heart so badly charred
now I'm lost in obsession and from sanity I'm barred
I'll never see the light of day or a sympathetic eye
I could be safe if I could pray, I'd rather sink and die

Lisa Wilhelm

"God And Jesus Loves You"

Miracles so happen if you just believe . . .
    That God and Jesus loves you, yes indeed.

Be faithful, truly faithful, that's the key . . .
    That God and Jesus loves you, yes indeed.

My pastor says, trust in the Lord and only the Lord . . .
    Give God the praise, he must never be ignored.
        Yes, God and Jesus loves you, yes indeed.

Be helpful and kind to your fellow man . . .
    Some don't know him, but we can make them understand.
        That God and Jesus loves them, yes indeed.

That be it big or small, just follow God's commandment . . .
Just do as God demands . . .
Be a true Christian and tell all about God's will . . .
    That God and Jesus loves us, oh what a thrill!
Be a true Christian and it will surely come back to you . . .
    How God Jesus loves, me and you . . . yes indeed.

Susan Woods Patterson

Thanksgiving

Our heavenly father:
Thanksgiving is a day we celebrate
For gifts and blessing which we partake.

We thank you Lord for life and breath
You sustain our being until our death.

We take for granted the air we breathe
And all your love which you do bequeath.

The sun, the moon and seasons too
Are all your miracles that we can view.

We give you honor this thanksgiving day
Ask your blessings on this food - giving you
    Thanks in every way.

We thank you father for the fellowship too . . .
For this family gathering as we bow before you.

We pray this all through Christ our Lord
Thanks for these blessings - so generously outpoured.

Lum Huffman

The Name Game

Parents, beware when you give your child his name;
That as he grows up, he won't wear it in shame.
Don't give him a name that will make him feel old;
Or that will cause him to cringe whenever it's told.

Parents, pick a name that he will always hold dear;
Not one that will cause him to fear,
Though it be shouted from the top of a mountain;
Or whispered in his ear by his beloved at a fountain.

Parents, choose a name that's light-hearted and fun;
Select it with care and let it be one,
That he will tell friend or foe with pride;
And not one that he should try to hide.

The parent that chooses a name out of spite;
Will burden his child for all of his life.

Mildred Hollifield

Untitled

Sometimes it's the simple things
that bring on the sweetest emotions,
the sunrise, the sunset — but it's often more complex.
Sometimes it's people;
"Come here and give me a hug.
You're truly special and you will always be."
But more often our emotions are magical,
overcoming us like a fog, dazing and confusing,
yet we rest secure in their mystery.

I was lying in your arms after dark
resting assured in the brilliant starlight
when the beautiful night released its emotions.
As tears began to fall from my eyes
the stars began to fall from the sky, their glory epitomized
by the golden streaks that painted the black canvas of the night.

Like a bird too soon released from its nest,
your are released unto the world, and you must not be afraid to fly.
Sing a song for home, for hugs, and for shooting stars.
Sing a song for movies, for cool rain, and for the cityscape at night.
Sing a song for sweet emotions, just as I sing when I think of you.

Kenneth W. Farrell

Not About Comic Book Heroes

Heroes are not the fantastic figures
That comic books bred and TV shows raised.
Heroes are those whose ordinary natures
Yield everyday deeds that oft go unpraised.
Such folk e'er emerge, be it day or night
There's no limit to their contributions.
A well-employed conscience is the birthright
That's made heroes throughout generations.
Heroes act based on what they believe in
That is a choice to which all can lay claim.
It's also something they share in common
With renowned heroes of comic book fame.
Comic book heroes do a real service
They show what can be, for those with purpose.

Richard D. Halpern

A Knight's Passion

Little things between us, words that have never been told.
Touches that gave me a rush, kisses so soft, yet bold.
Honesty and understanding, caring, the ultimate desire.
Still, you seem so demanding, when you speak, you turn me to fire.
I'll fight any dragon to love you, guide a unicorn to stand at your side.
For you, the Black Knight I would duel, this love will not be denied.
The sun, arouses your radiance. The stars, arise in your eyes.
The wind, leads the flowers in dance, musical rain in reply. A
beast will leave his beauty, hoping for him your love would stray.
A beauty will escape from her beast, to serve you, no dismay.
Fairies sing you lullabies to the glow of fireflies. The birds,
present you with feathers. For quills, when thou writes me letters.
One I received today, here is what you say. Thou my young
protector, thou mustn't shed blood for thee, my dear sweet knight,
you are my injector, alone you hold my key. I plead with thou, in
grave mercy of thy chastity and heart. Return at once, for Sir
Knight, alas a fortnight, I heard the lark. He spoke to me of the
Raven, he searches for you in vain. Again he returns toward me,
the Craden! Through me, he shall serve you pain. Deliver your
love unto thy kingdom. God speed, I await my prince. At this
message, I called upon all who serve thee. My horse ride with the
wind through the night. The Raven will not have his sin. The
guide of my star light. Alas! I used the key, thy chastity, so true.
Truly, you have loved me, I cast this key out to sea, Nero to
protect, our love has earned respect.

Michelle Renee Sandoval

Four Years And Twenty-Four Months From Heaven

I am a part of an institution
that is forcing me to grow,
thinner and thinner
in my own thoughts and dreams.

And I stir with unrest
in the 3x5 room they have issued to me.
Staring at the stars from my window
and praying for divine inspiration.

It will take a miracle to create
another creative theme
to push my pen towards the greatness
that they are demanding of me.

So I think back tot he days
before everything mattered,
and wonder what exactly it is
that I am working towards.

I am a part of an institution
that is robbing me in my prime.
And I am called to invisible battle fields
to defend these precious times.

Kristin Stoltenberg

I Never Thought

I never thought happiness was within my reach
that is until I met you

I never thought my heart would feel content
and then you came along

I never thought I could express a need for love
and have that desire be fulfilled

I never thought I would be able to feel so much compassion
towards anyone as I do towards you

I never thought I would be able to understand the magnetic force
which unites two human beings as one
then you came along

You touched my soul with your smile
my heart with your gentle touch

You made me realize that happiness is within my reach
that I can endure any difficulty that I may encounter

You made me realize that I too am worthy
and worthy of being loved

I never thought I would understand the true meaning of love
that is until I met you.

Kim Traskell

Death

Death is merely the end of life.
That isn't so bad, because life is just
a mixture of turmoil and confusion.
We have hopes and dreams, but most
are simply illusions.
The search for happiness goes on and on,
until we find ourselves bitter and alone.
The struggle for success takes over our minds,
Always trying to get ahead, but ending up behind.
You work so hard, all your friends admire,
but the days have grown long, and your body is too tired.
Everyday people put you to the test.
You pass, you must, but now it's time to rest.
When you're gone people say, you're dead or deceased,
but I prefer the term resting in peace.

Michael S. Taylor

Needful Things

I need to have the love we had
That lasted a year, then suddenly went bad.

I need to have the comfort
    In which you gave to me;
        The warmth, security, and friendship
            In which I thought would never flee.

I need to know you are there
    As a friend and as a lover
        To solve my inner most secrets
            The ones you have uncovered

I need to know you care
    That you'll never let me go;
        For we once began as a seed
            And suddenly, we started to grow.

I need to be in your arms
    Tell met it's all right;
        Help me through my pains
            Guide me to the light.

I need to know what happened
    One day I'll soon uncover;
        I need you as a friend, but strictly as a lover.

Sandra M. Evangelista

Memories

Why do I hold these memories
That lie deep within my heart,
And seem to wrench my very
Being from its fragile moorings?
Why is it that the loss of special persons,
Those for whom I felt a particular bonding
Can create a gaping void,
And disrupt my mind's harmony?
Who can fathom that indescribable trait
That links soul to soul in the scheme of life,
And leaves one in a quandary?

Patricia Sullivan, CDP

"Nothing's Done Right"

Yesterdays gone and tomorrow hasn't yet come.
That means I only have today.
Another day to struggle through.
A day when I never get everything done and never
get nothing done right.
But somehow, its just not in my plight.
I'm glad when night comes an I can shut out a day,
But sleep doesn't come because my body hurts and creeks,
It just seems to weather an weather away.
Then I start another day
A day when nothings done right.

Lou Ella Stevens

The Angona Family Reunion

You may not remember, or perhaps you don't know -
That on each Christmas Eve, to Grandma's we'd go.
Our very special reason to travel that way -
Was to wish our sweet Grandma "Happy Birthday."

We'd all gather together in her very small place,
So we could enjoy the dear smile on her face,
As she opened her gifts we all brought along
Honoring our precious lady with love and a song.

Then came the day when our Grandma went away,
And her daughter Louise kept us honoring her day.
We still came together in the very same place
To talk and to laugh and 'pizza feed' our face.

We all chattered and ate without even a care
Aunts Louise, Millie and Minnie had put food there.
They planned and cooked and washed all the dishes,
While we merely said a few Christmas wishes.

Now we have a plan that we hope you'll all okey.
To each year honor our Aunts (and Uncles) on THEIR day.
We'll do all the work and they will just eat and sit
And laugh and enjoy all their memories a bit.

Marion Marino Christner

Remembering Mother

Now it seems so long ago
That she sat at her desk all aglow
Writing poetry was her desire
To bring attention to all the beauty on fire
The trees and flowers colors floating everywhere
Children's voices a joyous thing in the air
Just too awesome to compare
With excitement she couldn't stop
Writing around the clock
Beauty that's everywhere
She just wanted to share.
Thank you Mother as I cherish your awards
You left behind
Memories of another time

M. Lorraine McAlhaney

Moment Of Moments

Though, our time seems to be short
That short of time is the best time
I have ever experienced
If ever I had to look for a moment
These moments we've shared
Would be it.
In all my years of living
These moments with you are the very best
Though, without you: It will be different
But, still I'll be living
If only moments could last forever
These moments would never end
'Cause these moments I've dreamed of

Nicole Bartley Tibere

Gloom In May

It was a day like every day,
That started off in the month of May.
There was a sadness in the class that day,
And I could sense this gloom in May

I now sank into a deep thought,
That the night before had brought.
All my friends were in my sight,
Except the one who made it right.

He's been my friend to this date.
I never imagined seeing his own fate.
I could never understand why,
Life could take such a great, great guy.

I found myself sitting in the local parish,
With all the memories of the past to cherish,
And as I sat among all this grief,
I wondered why he was his own thief.

Perry J Frank

Troubles

Don't let your troubles be so deep,
That they effect your mind and alter sleep.
When your nerves seem so frayed,
All your bills seem to be unpaid.
Life will bring about some change,
All your troubles will be rearranged.
When you seem down and out,
Think good thoughts, and clear your doubts.

When troubles seem to come your way,
Find a solution without delay,
If you think in terms of good and bad,
Think of happy things and not the sad.
Everyone has their troubles to bare,
No one said life is totally fair.
If you want to wallow in sorrow,
Your deepest trouble will be tomorrow.

Rick L. Ferguson

"The Little Girl Cries"

A little girl cries many tears,
Tears filled with years of pain and sorrow,

Pain and sorrow of a dream never known,
Dreaming someday, someone, would take her away,
Faraway, allowing her wings to fly,
Flying high with happiness and never ending love,

Until one day the dream became reality,
The reality that pain and sorrow must end,
The someone being "THE LITTLE GIRL THAT CRIED SO MANY TEARS".

Robin Rae Baxter Fann

If I Met The Savior

For at times I have. When he filled my kitchen with great love
that was enough to melt the marrow of my bones. A feeling so
intense as to overcome any conflict. A warm peaceful sublime
feeling of oneness that overcomes any pain.
When in my own private room and excommunicated on my knees in
prayer. A knowledge that comes to me of his most perfect love.
That even rebaptism is attainable.
As I walk, talk or work, with one of his little ones in perfect
harmony. I can feel the truthfulness of someone else's
testimony. In truth all over the world, our Father's Son Quietly
expresses his love if we but knock, Elohim answers.
I would be so unworthy to meet my Eldest Brother today for my
heart is not entirely without guile. But as I travel this road
of mortality I can strive to be more like him and learn of his
love for us all. My example can improve every day and in this
obedience, I can show forth great works, to glorify Him in whom
it is almost impossible to explain.

M. A. Campbell

Sunrise Insanity

Sometimes Moms get so busy
that we forget to say
hey, you're only 9 or 10
and some days it's O.K.
to wake up late or be a kid
and sometimes miss the bus,
or want a morning snuggle
and not a great big fuss.
Us Mommies are not always right
and our moods aren't always great,
but we love you guys so very much
that our hearts would surely break
if we did one thing wrong or made you cry
when all you wanted was a hug,
or yelled at you too loud because
you're moving like a slug.
So my child, here's to say
and believe me, this is true,
the love I feel inside my heart
is all because of YOU!

Pamela L. Winkle

The Aftermath

What is that we cry for so pitifully?
That which is lost from heart and mind
We remember and reflect so mournfully
Grieving silently, we reach for an earlier time

A lost emotion with no chance to revive
We are settled into a cyclical bloc
Cries come forth too passive to come alive
We clutch at the wounds, the bleeding does not stop

All around us virile ecstasy abounds
The throaty laugh of rising passion floats
Couples exchanging admiration without a sound
Caressing clutches sustain fire that the open cloaks

Alas, where do we go? To whom can we plead?
For a reincarnation, a rebirth in consequences of years
An old flame to flicker, lusty smiles again to read
To feel heartbreak, abatement, simple jealous fears

What face in that crowd will smile that smile?
From which hand will come the caress?
Can we guess the colors of the one who stays our trials?
Will we react, commit, or stand and guess?

Kelso G. Sims

The Harvest

Thoughts of the after-math
That which 'twas lost.

The trials; the encounters; the counters;
the mind filled drain; its rain of cost.

'Twere slithering movements; a fore, without
discipline, without askance; but rather it
'twas . . . as you please till' your wants 'twere no more.

To and faith perhaps? Back words then for word?!
Hmm . . . or was it two and fourth, with one
to aft? Or simply the seemingly constant dervish
swirl of a parading circle sway?
But then, who could remember? To say,

That three is was to one, as four is was to none.
Or that the wonderer of the thinly veiled
inquisitional clause had long since tipped
it's consenting cast of reasoning,

Ronnie Godley

The Rhyme And Rhythm Of Love

Have you ever wished that a day would last forever
That you could touch time and hold it still
That moments would turn into eternity,
lost in the depths of each others eyes
That the warm laughter of shared confidences would hold and not wash
away with the tides of mundane daily living
Touching, wanting, urgently needing
Have you ever wished that a day would last forever?

Wanda J. Portee

"The Choice"

Butterflies are free
that's not how it used to be
butterflies come and go as they please
they float with graceful ease.

Days before they had to make up their minds
a world lay outside for them to find
a cocoon is a safe place to hide
would it be alright to stay inside?

To become a butterfly, they had to leave what they knew
only then could they float with the wind that blew
as a result of their choice, they're free
it's the same with you and me.

C. Dorman

Night

The evening is growing dim,
The blue turning black
All the day animals scurry around,
The night creatures have come to take their ground.
The moon rises, a white glow
The wind blows rustling leaves,
As the starless sky peeps out from the trees.
There's a strange essence in the air,
Something no one can seem to identify,
So they just let it be.
A cloud covers the moon,
Total darkness.
Beautiful.
Nights like these are tempting,
My soul yearns for them.
The darkness helps me flee from all possible light,
The blood and heat is all I feel,
The want, the need
Makes my black heart bleed.

Suzanne McEwen

A Time After

There's a time after loving
That's quiet and warm
Yet the tick of a clock
Sounds like thunder in a storm

When she holds you and warms you
And gives you a smile
And says with her eyes
That your safe for awhile

You hear everything and nothing at all
There's nothing too big or nothing to small
Peace and contentment are all that you know
Your heart's full of happiness and really a-glo

Time goes by with incredible speed
You think you got there and its time to leave
Deep in your heart your full of joy
She's made you feel like a little boy

Your supposed to be strong and macho and tall
But she's really the mistress in charge of it all
She's given herself and all I can say
Is "thank you God for this beautiful day"

Richard G. Williams

Two Soul's In One

You and me against the sea,
That's the way it was supposed to be.

We were raised like twins from the very start,
One soul, one heart.

What will I do without you now,
Show me the way, show me how.

Give me your strength so I can see,
Now I will carry on for thee!

Tina Ann Isbell

An Empty Room

In a shaded, pale-blue room, where the cold bright day seeps through
the blinds, sat a sorry, stainless soul, in the quiet corner of this
room, whispering gently a poem of love, in the strong atmosphere of
gloom, "Pity pierced my pounding heart", softly echoed across
the room. I was a shadow in my own disbelief!
As I felt the person's grief . . .

In this silent, boring place, isolated from the clear blue sky,
Lives a longing, lusty love, in the quiet corner of this place,
Peacefully reading a poem of love, a sad sound echoed across the
room, "It will never heal; this deep scar in my heart",
And the future seemed so full of doom.
I was, a reflection of all this grief!
I thought with disbelief . . .

In a pale-blue, shaded room, where the bright cold day seeps through
the blinds, stood a seriously, suffering soul, in the quiet corner
of this room, hissing burning words, from a sad poem of love.
In the foul air of dejection, "You'll never understand: never win
my heart!" echoed the words of rejection.
While I reflected, all day, in disbelief . . .
I sat there in grief . . .

Ronald Antonio

Untitled

Why are you who, and where are you why,
The it is that it was, without the humming cry,
A seeming of pretend, folding in the mass,
The stopping, slowing of the fast,
Hopscotch, butterscotch, sticky fingers too,
So why is there a where, and how is there a you!

Todd N. Rombach

What Is Life

Life is full of surprises,
   that's what life is all about.
You have to be strong and over,
   come trails life bring day to day.
Life is not all about sadness,
   it's about flowers, the sun and the wind.
The wind rushes through your hair and it
   makes you feel warm and cozy.
Life is about such beautiful wonders.
Scientific all about technology and
   what tomorrow brings.
But I talk about natures sweet scent,
   and what wonders what life brings
   for me and my son Austin today and
   tomorrow . . .
    Theresa Baker

Time Stands Still

Time passes and time stands still.

You were the bellows that flames my ambition,
The anvil that shaped my being.

Time passes and time stands still.

You were me and I was you.
Silence held clarity, words understanding.

Time passes and time stands still.

Then you weren't mine,
Whose you were I'm unsure.
Uncertainty replaced understanding.

Time passes and time stands still.

People find people.
People loose people.
Time passes and time stands still.

Then I saw you.
Radiant! Memories!
Then you were gone.

Time passes and time stands still.

Now, we are here in our corners of the world.
And time stands still.
    Sharon Goforth

The Ballad Of The Track

A train ride through the countryside, a wondrous thing to me,
The beauty of a land I'd never ventured out to see,
But times like these are not so fair when you leave dreams behind,
And forgo your own priorities for peace you'll never find.

The tracks converged ahead of us, a beacon of the heart.
They pointed to my destiny, an ending, yet a start
As well, for I am lost among the masses of the land,
Support so far away from me, no one to hold my hand.

My camera's lens is blurred now as the trees move by too fast,
A flash of green and brown that's like a memory, sure to pass.
I wish the train would pause and let me taste the frosty air,
But once I set foot on this path, the train no longer cared.

The rumble warns me not to sleep or I might miss a scene:
A glade, a lake, a mountainside, so calm, and so pristine.
Perhaps a desert's fiery lair, tornado's deadly breath,
The harshness of the wastelands where the lonely hunters tread.

The thunder of the engine roars, defiant in its speed,
Forgetting all its passengers, dismissing all their needs,
Cognizant only of its goal, of its own destiny,
Like life the train rolls down the track, ignorant of me.
    Robert Hope

Whine

Out in the world of a thousand skies
The birds fly and the trees whine.
The mountains climb up tot he heavens,
And the rivers flow into the sea.
All around the sun is shining, and time is ticking
And the children are crying.
The force is great as the weak are crushed
And the days never end until all are lost.

Out in the world the masses cry.
From the immense heart breaks of the lovely lullabies
Why can't they all just live instead of dying
And why can't they all stay instead of leaving
And in the end win with loving

All around the masses cry
As the clock ticks and the birds still fly.
In the end they all will leave
As the children cry
And none will live, and, all will die.
    timothy r. jones

Sonnet

The dark does presage the coming of fright;
The arctic wind sends forth a biting chill;
The land, barren, seeks shelter from the fight.
No breast to comfort me, My heart is still.

Glass, shattered, breaks in a thousand pieces;
The metal can is crushed and made flat;
The rock crumbles, loosing shape; it ceases.
Freezing cold does bite my head with no hat.

Without your love how blank the trees become;
The land dries up and with no tears sobs from thirst;
A blazing sun beats down without a hum.
My heart broken - cries - needing to be nursed.

Only your warmth can radiate through earth,
   waken the spring blooms and bring them to birth.
    Linda R. Ruddy

I See

It saves lives, you see . . .
   The bright blur of beams, the silent screams,
   The bending metal, my instant instincts,

   but I don't look,
   So I am saved.

It makes us aware, you see . . .
   His precise pinstripe three-piece, the hanging war decor,
   His speech, my acceptance,
   And his large wart!

   But I don't laugh,
   So I am hired.

It gives us an edge, you see . . .
   The ball, the clicking clock, my poor percentage,
   The fanatical fans, the open man or the open shot?

   But I don't shoot
   So I am hero.

It should be our sixth sense, you see . . .
   Its never to blame or at fault, it never does wrong.
   Peripheral Vision,

   Do you see, do you see.
    Matthew C. Muyres

The Flight of the Unjust

Mountain of life, are so big and wide,
The cares of our freedom we all take in stride.
America, America, where are we now?
Jesus Christ is real, let him show you how.
The hurt, the bittermen, and unforgiveness, the unjust,
people, help people, love and trust.
Families come together, talk and pray,
This is God's country, let's do it today.

Lila Taylor

Oma Grandmother

"Go down to the basement and get me some beans.
The cellar is dark, but there's a string hanging down . . .
Just turn on the light, and you'll see."

And I see . . .
Jewels in glass jars . . .
Ruby beets, topaz corn, emerald green . . . the beans.

It was fun when we canned them together that fall.
"French-cut!" you explained, as we
Shred them in shifts, and
I got to add . . . the salt.

"Go down to the basement," old bones bid you go.
"Yes, death is dark, but there's a light there for you.
Just call on Christ's name and you'll see."

And you see . . .
Light like jasper,
A crystal, golden glass street . . . Heaven.

Lapis leavings and grievings, together, alone,
In hospital silence, we
Said sad good-byes; and
I got to taste . . . the salt.

Marion Langlo

Heaven—He's Home

The wind furiously howled and whirled. He walked against it!
The clouds were dark and gloomy, they hid the sun. He walked
    frightened!
The weather was cold and damp. He walked shivering!
The days seemed long; the journey endless. He walked fatigued!
The trees, grass and flowers were brown and dry. He walked
    unseeing!
There were cries, there were screams. He walked saddened!
Suddenly, the wind is a soft and gentle breeze. He feels it
    softly on his face!
The sun is shining brightly. He feels the warmth on his body!
The weather is warm, quite pleasant really. He feels content!
The days seem far too short. He feels no fatigue!
The trees, grass and flowers are all so very lovely. He sees the
    beauty around him!
The Angels rejoice, they dance, they sing. He has arrived!

Marie Rie Andrews

Come Go With Me

Come go with me, and you will see.
The dance of a heart, dancing wild and free.
Come go with me, dare to be free,
Where the site of the sunset, sets your heart free.
Come go with me,
We'll find that special tree, that green grass, birds flying free,
Come go with me,
Hear the dancing of my heart, not stopping or thinking that we will
    ever be apart.
Come go with me, set your heart free.

B. Johnson

Simper Fi! (Always Faithful)

A journey through his mind tells the tales of war.
The conflicts, the battles, recon and more.

See the bloody pictures, do not close your eyes.
See the bloody pictures, only truth, no lies.
Simper Fi!
Memories suppressed, intentionally forgotten.
Smells of death, burning flesh, spoiled and rotten.

Nightmares were plenty, day out and night through.
Tormented, tortured . . . what could he do?

Simper Fi!
Twelve gauge in hand, he set out walking.
He sat on the hill, alone, with God he was talking.

With his toe on the trigger and the barrel in his mouth,
According to religious law, This marine was headed south.

Simper Fi!

"Do not pull the trigger," came the reply.
"For I Am with you and I Am . . ."
Simper Fi!

Suzanne West

Daddies

Some people say that the moms do all the work.
The cooking, cleaning and changing of diapers
with a smell that lingers and lurks.
But Dads do their jobs too. From helping with
the diaper changing to keeping baby busy while
moms have things to do.
Daddies help in many ways. They let mommies
relax by taking the babies out to play.
When babies are sleeping sometimes moms want to cry.
But Daddies are always there with a shoulder nearby.
Just like Mommies, Daddies are always there,
they give a family that special love and care.
Daddies work hard everyday. Thus makes the
Mommies life's easier in so many ways.
There are times when Daddies feel unwanted,
yet the days they feel proud they do nothing
but flaunt it. Mommies and babies have something to share
its to tell you we love you and will always be there.

Kristina Sharp

For The Spirit

Off the clothesline, came the least frozen long johns, to go under
the cover that held the flour, before the bread was baked.
Over the head, a gift from the sheep, dyed to nature's hues
Back to the bread, it took just one hour to bake but its warmth
    lasted a lifetime.

Nudged into the bitter night, the wears of this collection of
oddities, felt a push forward, again and again and again.
Not understanding, yet with uncharacteristic surrender,
    looked up at the stars and a response was
    awakened in the diamond not yet polished.

Slowly allowing the heart that was pierced to
    recover enough - to see - for one precious
    moment, the Aurora Borealis.
To return to the hearth, ever so gently, with a
    heart full of love, remembering the bread that
took one hour to bake and provided a lifetime of warmth.

Laura B. Young

"The Night Life"

A darkness comforts me as I awake,
the days long slumber as night I take.
The feast of evening I renew,
the massacre of feeling feels of you.
Now of time I never will know,
of light untouched moonlight grows.
My only vision cannot see
the sounds unheard, unheard by me
what of life I die?
My only smiles that I cry.
Of precious love felt no feeling
that darkness pushed the light to kneeling.
Most pain that feel so sweet,
screams in anguish are my laughters beat.
Now no feeling felt or spent
the night is going, gone, and went.
I return to my day time dead
now my coffin is my bed
till darkness bids me once again
I remain asleep, without pain.

C. T. Stroup

The Unknown

Inky blackness fills the room.
The deadly calm of silence echoes through the night.
A soft whisper of movement . . .
Blazing yellow eyes illuminate a darkened corner.
Slowly . . . slowly . . .
Radiating closer and closer . . .
Blocking any chance of escape.

A heart paralyzed with fear as one lies helplessly . . .
waiting and wondering . . .
Sweat beads upon the skin . . .
Breathing escalates . . .
Peaceful night sounds, now haunting wails.

ITPOUNCES!

The fog of fear evaporates in the face of this unknown terror.
A powder puff of fur lands upon your body.
It's silky softness caresses skin . . .
Revealing it's true identity.

Toby Lynn Perry

The Dreams I Had For You

The crib we bought sits empty there, my arms feel empty too.
The dreams I had for you must die, they never will come true.

I dreamed I rocked you in the night, and stroked your tiny form.
You fell asleep upon my breast, you felt so safe and warm.

I dreamed I combed your little curls and fixed them with a bow.
The tender care I longed to give, now you will never know.

I dreamed I took you to the park and pushed you in the swing.
The pleasure I felt there with you, made me want to sing.

I dreamed I saw you go to school, you were so big, so brave.
Your eyes twinkled with mischief — I hoped you would behave!

I dreamed I saw you as a bride — all dressed in snowy lace.
The love you felt for your young man was shining from your face.

So many hopes, so many dreams, I held within my heart,
Will never, ever come to pass — on earth we'll be apart.

But some sweet day I'll come to you. I'll know you, little one —
And all my tears will pass away as quickly as they've come.

Kay Dunivan

Stand Tall-Young Man

Look into the mirror and what to do you see? Are you pleased
with the eyes that look back?
Would you do what you've done all over again, or start new with
a clean, shiny track?
Would you like to start over and make some amends, to the people
    you hurt in your stride?
Or stay just the way that you see yourself in the mirror full of false pride.
You don't care what you say and you have no respect, do you
really know what that means?
All the people that love you, your family and friends, mean
nothing to you, so it seems.
Did somebody hurt you that makes you so sad and everything
way out of reach?
Forgiveness is needed, should that be the case so you may have
    peace with yourself.
Grow up and stand tall and give of yourself, kind words and respect to us all.
Dreams are fulfilled with a purpose in life and you need to get on the ball.

Shirley Hague

Through A Child's Eyes

To watch a child play, there is no greater joy
The face of a child so innocent and full of wander
Curious and not afraid to ask
Loving with no reservation.

A child is not only willing but, anxious to help
When a favor of them is asked
They do not ponder what return they will receive,
For a smile and a thank you is all they desire.

The love of a child knows no bounds
It matters not of wealth or the lack there of
It cares not of the color of your skin
For it is true love with no restrictions

To lose the innocence of childhood comes with great sadness
For never again will we know the utter freedom
To love and care for others with no limits set
How great life, if we could but see it through the eyes of a child.

Kathy Drake

Sonnet Nocturne

Benignly rolled the full moon through the night,
The fields cast back its soft, cool amber glow;
We sat beneath its phosphorescent light,
And watched the spectral clouds a-scudding go;
In ages past, this moon, with gentle guile,
Cast calm enchantment over lovers true;
And as we sat beneath its gentle smile,
Its ancient magic we explored anew;
And as we sat, we "heard" with hearts in tune,
Two silent melodies fill skies above;
The nocturne fantasy of "Clair De Lune,"
The ancient song of boy and girl in love;
And all the stars that sparkled in the sky
Could not match the sparkle in your eye.

Klahr Loudenslagel

Three Tulips Rose

I am giving you three roses, mon amour
The first is for the intolerable days you pass away from me.
The second represent my name.
The third symbolize my love for you.
I've chosen the color rose
B'cause you belong to someone else.
The color red would represent my life, my heart, my soul
Hopefully, one day
I will be able to offer you the red tulips.

Margarette Rose Peck

The Void Of Conscience

Mother Nature where have you gone?
The flowers and trees are few and none.
I asked who has raped you and left you bare?
Just look around they are everywhere.
Why isn't it a crime, I solemnly cried,
Surely you have rights they should be tried!
Technology is killing you, we should be helping,
Instead we are busy chopping and building.
End the madness, start planting and saving,
We are here for so short a time, we should do more than taking.
So please in your life give nature some space,
Sooner than later, it will affect your place!

Melody Lynn Kelly

Untitled

Forever makes it so tiring.
The forces are already drained, the lights are dim.
What to do, what to forget,
What to pass by without a glance,
For to lose your place would harm the rhythm
Of the motionless treading.
Forever exposes the sins,
But keeps the trembling at a minimum
If the shaking never stops there's nothing to fight.
No need to bulldoze through the screaming valley of quivers.
Forever turns bland with the dismissal of hour upon hour,
Until a stack so high is built up right beside the table that
The roof is no longer visible
And all time's fruity flavor
Has floated out the imaginary window.
No escaping forever, that's for sure.
It stays locked up in the closet
And remains uncultured, exhausted,
Unable to breathe,
Unable to die.

Sally Reynolds

Wolf

   As the shadows pass by in the night, I am there.
The ghost, the chameleon changing with it's life,
in the shadows of the night, with the wind, I belong.
I am the moon surrounded by the stars in the darkness
alone I thrive and grow, watching with pain.
Hear the beat of my heart like the roll of thunder in the night,
the rushing of my blood flowing like a wild river,
as I run through life alone, wild as the North wind.
From the abyss into nothingness I run,
no beginning, no end, just me and the wind together.
I am a creature of the night, I am the wolf,
I run and howl my cry of frustration to a deaf world.
I am the lone protector, the warrior,
fighting to his last breath a war with no end.
Forever alone, forever fighting, a world with no heart.
Look into my eyes and my heart and see me.
I am Wolf, hear my cry!

Rodney A. Guenther

Schizophrenic

   Escape from the dying light and
the place of extreme horror deep inside
your mind. Look upon hope for the pain
and the voices to stop. Wanting to
destroy the throbbing, the terror, and the
screams. Cursed with fierce nightmares
and the lonely souls that cry out to me.

T. J. Clanton

Come And Dine

The table is of silver,
The goblets are of Gold.
The wealth of this great feast,
Truly, the people do not know.

For the food is of the Father,
And the Drink is of His Blood.
As the best was saved for last,
The BEST, is yet to come.

For if the people understood,
And with their eyes they truly see.
They could hear their precious savior say,
"Come, and Dine with me!"

With outstretched hands He was pierced,
With outstretched hands He says "come".
Do not miss this great love affair.
That is meant for everyone.

So the Father says "Come,"
Please, come and dine with me.
The invitation has been given,
To live ETERNALLY!

Pamela L. Higdon

For Megan, "When Fall Nips The Air . . ."

You are the fall . . . September; and the auburn sky of an Autumn night.
        The harvest moon of Indian Summer.
You are golden brown, fiery orange, forest green and crimson.
You are long bike rides and winding roads . . .
        a mid-day retreat: red wine, soft brie and warm French bread;
        sweet strawberries dipped in dark chocolate.
You are the fall . . . October; and the brilliant blue sky of a sun-filled afternoon.
        The crisp, cool air of All Hallow's Eve.
You are bare trees, gray skies, burning leaves, bonfires and folk songs.
You are sweaters and long johns, hiking boots and mountain sides;
        hooded jackets and covered bridges.
You are a cup of hot apple cider with a cinnamon stick, a paperback novel
        and the gentle crackling of a fire glowing in the distance.
You are the fall . . . November. Thanksgiving. My Thanksgiving.
You are turkey and stuffing. Sweet potatoes and cranberries.
        Pumpkin pie with whipped cream.
You are a down-comforter and an easy chair; napping in front a bay window,
        overlooking the ocean.
You are home and family: warm, welcoming, nostalgic . . . sentimental.
You are soft and gentle . . . Cozy. Comforting.
Firm and strong . . . Trusting. Believing.
You are the Indian spirit of this Pilgrim's soul.
And I have fallen . . .
                Higher than the stars.

Kaz Michael Rossetto

Wedding Day Prayer

My friend, my friend, I call you my friend
The journey now begins, and I pray will never end
I wish you love, prayers of joy and happiness
I wish the Lord your marriage to bless;
The journey is long and not always straight
The burdens will come and will have great weight
But remember one thing as your journey goes on
The love you have will keep you strong;
There are no answers to questions unknown
But you will surely get through them with the love you have shown
Compromise and sacrifice will not always come first
But as your journey grows long they will quench your thirst;
My friend, my friend, I call you my friend
Today as your journey begins true
My love and prayers I send
Knowing that GOD has blessed you.

Timothy J. Splane

You Are The One!

Today, Mother dear, you touch
  the hearts of thousands;
As you have touched my own
  heart for so long.
You are the one!

The things you have done— your love, your touch.
The devotion and the care—just for me.
  I love you still.

The silent years pass quickly.
  the tears flow,
Tho' not here, you are the one!

I love you;

The one who gave me a new life—
  I, once broken, crying undone—
Again felt the compassion of a Mother's heart.

You are still the one.

I must continue on;
Knowing that God almighty has indeed touched me . . .
By giving someone like you to me.

You are the one!

   Richard L. Merila

Zazenron

A puddle of water upon the ground.
The heavens reflected.
When the stars of the puddle
Are brighter than the stars seen through the eye,
That is when
Zazenron.

Be silent.
Look down
Until
Nothing outside is felt.
That is how
Zazenron.

Solitude
Without the body.
One hand sound
No sound.
Hear everything. Feel nothing
That is
Zazenron.

   Param Sher

Lines Of Fire

From Doboj to Tuzla
the lines of fire are seen.
But a stillness has taken place,
stirring one's soul.

Occasionally missiles are flying in the air,
and gunfire spatters,
just to recognize that the
"peace" bells have not rung
through the once used to be
Yugoslavia.

Is this the beginning of the end,
or only a false realization of a dream.
As the separate nations of Serbs and Muslims
bring down their bloody swords,
will they see the destruction they have caused?
But since peace is not certain,
the image of the graceful dove
is crying to the heavens
to be heard by all.

   Marian Fevre

Conflict

I feel the anger growing when I see wrong.
The injustice and prejudice that surrounds me
is almost like a blanket of darkness.
There is a sense of doubt; do I belong?

A brother hates a brother, but doesn't know why.
It seems the reasons are not important, are they a lie?
Do they shatter the hopes of the weak and the strong?
Yes, there is a sense of doubt; do I really belong?

Past memories too fade away,
for they didn't survive in the world of today.
A family united, a town that cared;
where are they now, have they all disappeared?

The darkness is heavy but shrinks with the light.
The light is a candle that is made to shine bright.
Who holds the candle that makes the world right?
What have I done to belong in this fight?

Have I hidden in silence, not exposing the wrong;
have I left it to others who really belong?
Is my conscious now clear, knowing I'm in the right?
Have I chosen to die, instead of to fight?

   Thomas Dolan

At Times

At times, I've wished I could not see
the insincerity we all receive.

At times, I've wished I could not hear
the stupidities that people hold dear.

At times, I've begged my soul to respect
the imperfections that everyone accepts.

But, if Time allowed my wishes to come true
and provided humanity in a different view

I may just miss the forest for the trees
and fail to see the beauty life conceives.

   Yvonne C. Julien

Healing?

Rodney King has made his exit, O.J. is center stage;
The jury brought its verdict, yet his debt has not been paid;

His legal team was brilliant; they mastered all the tools;
But now there is an outcry to change the justice rules.
The race card is the problem; it has raised it's ugly head;
Make no mistake about it, that card was never dead.

With hatred in the open, we are no longer friends;
We've chosen sides and take great pride;
In the colors of our skins.

We're guided by opinions; both truth and lies we've read;
In spite of this, let's not forget two human beings are dead.

Is he innocent or guilty? Let's not pretend to know;
But the fear and anger in our hearts must quickly cease its flow.

Our faces brown, black, red and white were sent from up above;
To help us learn to live as one in tolerance and love.

Healing is not easy, but it takes just one to start;
One person with a vision and compassion in his heart.

Let's put aside our difference; this is my fervent plea;
I'll first reach our my hand to you, if you'll reach out to me.

   Ruth M. Smoot

All To Gather A Fall

Bare limbs . . . the fall . . . cold . . .
the leaves . . . brittle . . . tumbling . . .
the wind, heavy but empty . . . the wind
and the wind . . . the dusk, fading light . . .
the cold and the wind down from the mountains . . .
outside . . . inside . . . otherwise . . . together.

We, you and I . . . of the hospital . . . at the window —
see the sky . . . the mountains . . . the town . . .
the water, a canal . . . upon it a pale glisten,
alongside it a path to a bridge . . . again the path . . .
a gate . . . a courtyard . . . a gate . . . a courtyard,
dull and blank but shadow filled.

From the window through the pane
appear the streets in dim light . . . then
the shops . . . the snow — thin but heavy . . .
the wind . . . the limbs . . . the cold . . .
the pale dark . . . down from the sky . . .
a fall . . . a star . . . a streak . . . a flash!

Randy John Steele

The Day My Sun Stopped Shining

It was a beautiful day; an Indian summer day.
The leaves were almost gone from the trees.
I awoke with the dawn and looked out from where I lay
There was not so much movement as even a breeze.

The beautiful day was not long to last
For before it was over, something would happen
And a wonderful life would have passed.
Something I could not even imagine.

The tears would soon come like a torrential flood
And with it bring a broken heart.
For what happened that day would
Forever be with me and forever tear me apart.

I tried to remember everything good,
I tried to imagine his face
The last time I saw him, where he stood,
Until he was taken in grace.

They say you never know how you could feel so sad,
They say every cloud has a silver lining,
But on that beautiful Indian summer day I lost my dad
And it was the day my sun stopped shining.

Vicki S. Flynn

Standing On A Line

The dark side beckons to hear my call
The light side says "Walk slow you won't fall."
One side says "Jump, jump as high as you can"
The other says "Go back, go back where you began."

"That's it little girl jump off of your line
With all of your strength don't waste any time."
"Keep walking the line don't skip any steps
If you skip you'll fall to numerous deaths."

On the light side I see . . . I see nothing no one's there
I'm left all alone on this line in the air.
On the dark there's relief from troubles and strife
And the voice I hear says "Jump and give me your life."

Someone grab my hand or I'll never see day
Slipping farther and farther "Please help me" I pray.
No one's heard my plea or answered my call
So I've slipped out of touch and I've started to fall.

The light side has lost, did I chose the right side?
I chose the dark side which was suicide.

Shalee Smith

Thankfulness

We should be thankful for all that He's done
The life that He gave us through His son

He gave us love,
He gave us peace,
He gave us refuge that we sometimes seek

He created the land, and the animals within it
He gave us the power with arms to receive it

He gave us the day to grow healthy and strong
He gave us the night to sleep with His song

He gave us the stars, to let us know He's watching
He gave us the sun to see what He's done
He gave us the moon, to guide us the way
And we should be thankful for another day.

Tara J. Owens

Dreams

Dreams, awakening imagination
The land of adventure
The land of magic
Grasping on to dying hope
Sleep, the break from reality
Dreams, the eternal questions

Nightmares, terror uncovered
Black mystery
Confrontation with fear
The cold winter
Yet with the hope and confidence in waking
That Spring will soon come

Peter Hazen

The Wizard

Look into my wizard's eyes
the little statue said
The hopes and dreams reflected there
Are things to come ahead
Your daytime fantasies were once so grand
So full of life and childish flare
Now your dreams seem out of reach
Sifted through reality like tiny pebbles of sand
Using your tears to wash them bare
These reflections you see
can be your reality
So dry your eyes precious one
the past is something done and gone
Your future, yet yours to create
can be anything you wish to make

Kathleen Renshaw

The Last Scene

In the night my sleeping dreams, took me to people I once new.
The dream haunted me, for one I once loved.
As I awoke the feeling for quickness remained in my being.
I must go.
And go I did, yet not finding the hurt one I once loved.
For the hurt was for me.
The last scene was to see the one she now loves.
Come from the place I once new as warm and comforting.
I talk to she in that place of warmth, but found it cold.
No longer a place for me to be.
Now the fear haunting my mind, is I must tell the one I hold Dear,
of My Flight in the Night. The haunting Flight in the night.

Robert C. Wall

492

To A Special Friend

I'll remember always the first time we met
The look in your eyes I'll never forget.
We could talk about anything, anything at all
So, make sure your listening when I give a call.

The smile on your face just made my day
And you always knew when you could get your own way.
The tears we cried; the times we shared.
We knew in our hearts we both always cared.

I'll always be there for you
You'll always be there for me, too.
Whether your in my dreams or on my mind,
My love for you, you'll always find.

Real friends are very hard to find
And I know you didn't mean to leave me behind.
So, not a tear will I shed or weep
But your love and laughter I will always keep.

And even though I can't see you each and every day,
You'll always be close, never far away.
Please save me a place in those big clouds of blue
And remember forever, "I'll always love you."
Kathleen L. Reardon-Galluzzo

Crimson Sea

The horizon is pink with shades of blue,
the majestic waves roll through and through

The ships are sailing back to shore,
while the fish all rest on the ocean floor

A flock of swans float to their nesting grounds;
the seagulls' beckonings are the sea's sweet sounds

The crabs close their claws and crawl through the sands,
while the seaweed drifts by in long green strands

A turtle reaches the surface for a breath of air;
it spot its prey with a killer stare

Diving down for its last repast of the day,
its tail disappears as they sky turns grey

The queen of diurnal action has abdicated
from the day's picture frame,
and the stars and moon have declared their reign

So good night my sweet crimson sea,
with your marshes and gentle creatures,
may you forever be free!
Marguerite Corvini

Expectant Heart

I listen for the ring to come,
The meaning always clear,
Expectant, mindful of each hum
Yet fearful lest the taunting jeer
Bring disappointment to this waiting ear.

How can the anxious heart break free,
To find the joy and peace it seeks,
When all around for it to see,
Are longings, sorrows, valleys, peaks,
That somehow echoes, but never speaks.

O aching heart, O heavy heart,
Console me with your prayer,
Restore the loving, trusting part,
That only words of love can bear,
When seeking to the heart repair.
Muriel W. Franklin

The Fall

As I stand here to recall
the memories of my last fall.

As the visions come to me all so well
that it just brings my eyes to swell.

As I stood there in his arm
I knew and felt no harm.

But of all the feelings I feel
I knew these were for real.

As we stood there not knowing what to say
while the light slowly faded away.

It all came down to when he and I
had to say goodbye.

Then he just looked at me and sighed
while I stood there and cried.

He promised he would write and call
but that didn't stop my heart from the fall.
Nichole J. Winckler

A Creation Of Two

The creator of life was looking down on the earth. When in the midst of the madness, what did he see? Two people who wanted to be three.

So with one wink of an eye and a wave of a hand, a baby it shall be within this very plan.

Now with patience and time, it will all come to be; one complete baby for the whole world to see.

To cradle in your arms and sit on your knee, love, guide and teach this precious gift of life - whatever it may be.

An eternity of love from down in your heart, that comes to you from the very start.

A life was passed down from the heavens above and given to you just out of love.

Take care of this gift it is an impression of two; listen to your heart, it will help guide you through.

There is hard work and pain, but with so much to gain, take them in time and things will be fine.

The life brought forth always endure, right by their side, til time is no more.
Noreen Przislidcki

Starry Eyed Dream

Jenny,
The mirror of eyes that speak to me.
The blossom of the morning glory
reaching out with glistening dew
to the sun that wraps your precious face.

Jenny,
All that I want to hold close and dear.
The laughing smile, the soft tendrils,
golden as the dust of a fairy
in your starry eyed dreams.

Jenny,
The wonder of your every turn.
The pirouette that unfolds your secrets
envelopes those who find you embracing
every new treasure.
Linda Admire

Gutting The Feline Shrine

This being your sweet sirens . . .
  The misty distant woods fall off the earth
and reveal the two-sided bridge in odd transparency

And if soulfully innate while the proceedings
  occur, the impetus of vain and motion-
    thought, may begin.
And at the cosmic epicenter, on the sheets of the bed,
  near your headboard is the black of the cat.
Now to puncture the cat, with a dull spear
  as used by Antiphos, causes a swirling devout eclipse.

No presence of sanguine fluid nor throe,
  the cat is fine
But you dive and caress yourself through the wound.
It is dark, as opaque as the feline, yet a vision pierced into
  the jelly is swallowing.

The ecstasy of your anatomical downfall should
  not be frightening, it is like rapture,
    it is love and godly confusion.

The light is just enough for sight, for the
  oracle of blood within the cat.
        Philip Johnson

Untitled

Standing Alone in the open field
The moonlight beaming down
A calm wind sifting through my hair
Crickets chirp simultaneously
As the earth becomes still
The stars fill the dark sky
Watching over me
Far away I hear the sonance of the ocean
The faint sound of waves flow upon the shore
The coldness penetrates my bones
As chills spread over my body
A thin fog begins to fill the air
I suddenly feel heavy
And fall gently into the meadow
Sleep assimilates my every strength
Isolated in my own silence
And dreams begin to harmonize my inner self
Soundly sleeping while the
Night watches over me,
In Peace
        Stacy L. Klein

When Night Meets Day

Darkness envelops the cold of night,
The seconds tick by, time takes flight.
Never before have I seen the sun.
In solitude, I wait for dawn;
Timidly I shake, I know not why;
What is it like to feel the rays of faith?

  My sun aflame with hope;
No sadness, shame or pain to disgrace the soul

Begone creatures of sunless doom!
I glance to the gleam of the enchanting moon.
Nothing shall stop me from my destined path.
To the east I travel those murky depths.
Can the peace I've sought, be far at hand?
Wonder and fear surround my head;
Could it be an angel of mercy calling for me?
My heart a beat with emotion I've never felt.
And to this I owe my angel of light,
The pain is gone a crack in the night.
For once in my life I'm finally free.
When the dark meets the light finally free.
        Kevin Doherty

The Mother I Knew . . .

Lying, helpless, in her hospital bed,
The mother I knew, now looked strange to me.
As I realized with impending dread,
How capricious our fragile life can be.

This once beautiful child, now grown so old
Unable to utter a single word,
Who had given to life, in sons, four fold
The tale of her life, my questions now lured.

Careless errors had caused me to blunder;
Only now, with her life's slipping away
Am I int'rested enough to wonder,
Who she is, and was. What she had to say.

I tried to remember stories she told,
Of her childhood, and life, so long ago
But the tales, whose value would now be gold,
Were lost on a child, to busy to know!

Determined, she struggles for life's last breath;
Fore'er the teacher, my lesson I see
An angel transforms her being with death,
The loss of her life, was only by me . . .
        S. Gordon Fletcher

Deep Yogurt

  From the Region of Preparation,
    the Observing System,
        tainted by consciousness
and entropy,
seeks
    uncertain statistical probabilities,
      gazing through the Realm of Measurement
        at an eternal Creation,
Transformation.
    and Annihilation,
    To discover
        that elementary
particles
      do not exist, except as
abstracted wave functions
  in a tangle of correlations
ceding self-actualized probabilities
        of infinite possibilities.
        Rodger N. Bolles

Love's Tribute

How I do love, thee.

  Let me remember the ways;
The softness of your touch,
  The emotion of your delightful smell,
The exciting sound of your voice,
  The pleasing and tearful sight of thee.

What greater tribute could I give,
  Besides flowers and love;
Than a contribution in your honor
  To help fight Cardiovascular disease.

The number one killer, your life did steal.
  This enemy among us is very real.

How I do love, thee.

  My written words, the world will read.
My contribution, heart research speed.
  My memory of thee will always be.
        Patsy Lee Montana

Dad

Where are you when I need you the most
   the one I need to talk with
   when I'm so alone
The one I need to tell me I'll be ok
   that you'll be there for me
To make me smile and laugh
   or just feel good when I'm sad
Just to see you, to feel safe, warmed and loved
   though we've been apart I can say this
You are here, next to me, so close
   never feeling alone or scared
Because you never did leave my favorite place
   I have kept for you
That's next to my heart Dad, I love you
   and you'll always be, the one I need.

     Nancy Popp

An Important Person In My Life

You're an important person in my life
The one who always makes things right
The one I can always count on
The one whose shoulder I always seem to cry on
You've never turned your back on me
Or let people know what I didn't want them to see
Through bad times you've always been there
And if I needed a friend
You always had a minute to spare
Sometimes I forget to show you how much you mean to me
Or just how important your friendship is to me
You definitely are an important person in my life
And you always make things right

     Sanches McCoy

"Enclosed You'll Find Your Memories"

Enclosed you'll find your memories,
The ones you left behind.
You see I can't keep them anymore they
Only make me cry.

They come from out of nowhere,
And keep me up at night.
Sometimes their even worse I feel as if I'll die . . .

Once they were so happy,
They way we used to be.
But now their only sad.
Like your leaving has left me.

You see I think they miss the ones that I gave to you.
So if their all together maybe then they won't be so blue.

Some of them are not so cruel,
So these I keep with me.
Like the way you made me laugh,
And the love you gave to me.

So these memories I will keep forever and a day.
To constantly remind me,
You once loved me in a very special way.

     Sharon S. Overton

Lady Of The Mist

She frolics along the shadowed path
The sounds of the mist, her muffled laugh
The notes of her song, so sweet, so clear
By listening you will sense she is near
Lady of the mist may appear in reality or dream
So beautiful, yet faint, she will seem
She roams about wherever she pleases
The spirit of her never ceases

     Kristen Gadel

Mirror, Mirror

In this old fancy mirror I see
The only vision known as me
If I could only see right through
There would lie a tiny image of you
Which my mind's eye could not ignore
Along with the passionate, loving heart you tore
And my tears that dwell deep inside
Now exposed without one left to hide
A body so consumed with pain
As I search for answers inside my brain
This dear old glass could not tell a lie
So mirror, mirror, who am I?

     Lisa Arnone

Soul

What is a soul?
The part of you that dwells inside,
And secrets of the past does hide.
And when we sleep does it leave,
To soar the earth above the trees,
And straight to heaven on its knees.
To visit God who lives above,
To ask for guidance, faith and love.
When morning breaks and it returns,
It brings these blessings, so we can learn,
To fill our heart with love and trust,
So it can dwell inside of us.

     Lucy DiLustro

Shadows Of War

A stranger and young lad of ten, suddenly came face to face,
The sky, laden with bolts of lightning-like bullets, as on a battlefield,
cast shadows, as the sad boy whispered into the wind, standing in his place.

With childish tears embracing his lowered cheek,
A quiver slowly crossing his lips, he turned to speak,
I prayed Mama would say, "You are my moon, my stars that shine."
But she wasn't there.

I yearned for Mama to hold me, cuddle me close like a Teddy Bear,
But she wasn't there.
I wanted my Mama to kiss my cheek, tenderly caress my tousled hair,
But she wasn't there.
I asked Mama to tell me all would be safe,
We could have dreams to share, while holding faith,
But she wasn't there.

The young lad turned, pausing momentarily,
Gazing intently into the eyes of this stranger,
A look cast forth a love, deep within an aching heart.
He spoke his last words, while turning, slowly walking away,
"I really loved my Mama and Papa,
But they are no longer there."

     Marki Roberts

Spring

Watch all the snow slowly melt
The sun shining while being felt
Birds singing as they start building their nest
As the newborn begin their flying test
See the children playing in the park
Enjoying with friends until it is dark
Lovers spend sunsets on the beach
That a caring hand is never out of reach
Trees are producing new leaves
Flowers blossoming within the warm breeze
Green grass is again growing
As the rivers are briskly flowing
Spring is now in the air
Everyone breathing it everywhere

     Terence J. Scholz

Blue Warmth

A desert flower dying in the sun.
The stem barely supporting it.
Dead Sea eyes.
Soiled petals on a field of gray.
A decaying blossom waiting to be nurtured.
Embracing the American flag with
Christ crucified secured between her breasts.
She walks her barren wasteland.
Blinding sun, visions, patches of blue, memories.
Innocents playing among the dead.
A fence of thorns, the smell of gas, bleached bones.
She blesses everything blue in her path.
Blue is peace, sky, loving, warmth.
Blue is the lady in whose arms she hides.
A desert flower blooming in a cobalt sun.

Thomas W. Sypek

Sweet Breath Of Wind

Sing to me, sweet breath of wind,
  The song of life in your clear breast.
Sultry, humid, dispassionate and yet,
  Fluent in a languid touch.
A warm finger you run down my chest
  Stirring me, coaxing me to listen.
Stringed and tattered clouds you push
  Across the sky, silhouettes of
  Memories, cherished, past.
The rake and clap of leaves overhead,
  The whistle - whine of the pines;
  Feed me your stories in deep
  Mouthfuls of soul food
Not words, rather, pressures and swirls,
  Invisible eddies, a simple song.
A dance in the language of nature,
  The sound of time.

Sing to me sweet breath of wind.

Paul VerBurg

Deadly Changes

The sun hits the dew drops on the doorway to heaven,
The songs of the birds are those of God's angels.
The babbling brook running down the hills,
Is the existence of life.
Listen. They are trying to tell us something.
The poisoned rain splashes through the doorway.
The rumbling of the chain saws are those of the Devil's disciples.
The laying of cement, cutting off the existence of life,
Overcome it.
For it is trying to overcome you.
As I lay here, looking at the master's work,
I see it slipping away.
This beauty was made for us,
And now we are bent on destroying it,
Why? And for what?
These changes are deadly.
Slipping from His hands, and falling into the Devil's desires is this world.
So reach up and support his weakening hands
For if not, that masterful work will be lost.

Mathew J. Knowles

Walking In The Light

As the clouds moved slowly across the sky
The sun burst forth and sun light caught my eye
I knew that this was going to be a splendid day
So I kneeled and said my prayers and went on my way
Nothing or no one could make me feel uptight
Because all of this day . . . I walked in the light

R. Kearney

The Journey

An old man sits alone beside the river
The springtime sun falls warm upon his face
He shuts his eyes as he thinks about this journey
And he travels back to another time and place.

When as a youth beside this very river
He enjoyed the long and lazy summer pace
Those magic days and nights stretcher on forever
He did not realize how fast they'd race.

Then like a dream he sees her there before him
The only one to ever hold his heart.
He sees her walking down the aisle to join Him
And make their vows that they will never part

The years too quickly pass before him
He can't believe how fast the kids have grown
Yesterday they were playing there beside him
Now they are gone with children of their own

William B. Wilson

Constellation Parody

Discounted and disinherited
the stars of this land do not speak
as if unwanted
    their silence echoes with the rain

The light of their festivals
    burns with the shouting tar
        only on a showboat
            on its way to a lost orbit

Their music is an elegy
    lamented by a deaf carmen
        behind the globeless scenes

But there are nights
    one may find a ticket
        sold only by the midnight gypsies
            who sing the song of the lost stars.

Those are the nights I have not yet found
but if you happen to be there
kiss a star for me
as you dance

Nareg Hartounian

"Junior High School"

School is driving me crazy.
The teachers say I'm lazy.
They say I talk too much and put things off.
And I fake the flu, the sniffles, and the cough
Maybe I am guilty of them all.
But thank God for study hall.

God of the heavens, send down the rains.
The school food is giving me stomach pains.
I need a storm, flood, or fire.
I'd fake illness, but they'd call me a liar.
Just five more years that's all I can take.
Iraq, blow up the school for heaven's sake.

I need a miracle, (a missile, even better).
The principal can't stop me, I won't let her.
The inservice days they don't last long
I need a hundred of 'em, yeah right, that's wrong.
Just can't wait till glorious summer.
36 more weeks, Oh man what a bummer.

Trip DelCampo

"Winter"

'Tis a cold and wintry day,
the sun will not come out to play.

A ghostly, ghastly, eerie sound,
as winds blow ever, all around.

So sad, green grass, has turned to brown.
No leaves are left, falling to the ground.

Songbirds now, no longer sing,
of merriment and a happy thing.

What is left now, for one and all?
Snowmen, snow-angels and of course, snow-balls!

Sheri Maison

Submarine Service "The Silent Keepers Of The Sea"

We are the feared and notorious serpents below
the surface of endless seas

We're called "The Silent Death", according to some people's pleas

Boundless destinies and time seem as though an eternity,
cherished memories in our hearts we keep

We are "The Silent Warriors" of the deep

Ascending from the depths we seek our tormentor

They shall be thrashed and casted below without a single lamenter

We seek our prey upon perilous waters, far and through the deep

The wicked will be silenced, sending their souls for the Lord to keep

Ronald K. Scott

Untitled

The dream team, they're happy and this circus is finally over
The suspect he came out smelling like roses and clover
The media made money on two people that died,
The black people rejoiced, while the victim's families cried.

Two people were murdered by someone with a knife
One an innocent bystander, and O.J. Simpson's wife,
Nine million dollars and nine months of a trial,
The evidence was there, but the jury was in denial.

Two whites, one hispanic, and 9 jurors who were black,
Three hours for the verdict, not guilty, and that's that.
To me, this did not seem fair
Was it because the victim had blonde hair?

Black people of America and yes the white people too,
If we don't join together then our America is through,
We must join together and put our priorities on the line
And criminals of all color must pay for their crime.

O.J. Simpson walked away with a smile on his face,
But only the Lord knows if he fell from his grace,
And when his days are over, his final juror will tell
whether it's the kingdom of heaven, or the fires of hell.

Tom Collins

"As You Are"

True love and friendship excepts you as you are, and if
the time comes you need them they're never to far.
Most people wants to change you to what they think you
should be, which is like trying to calm the tide
of the raging sea.
I'm someone who can take you for just who you are, with
eyes that shine like jewels and a smile that can
send me to the stars.
I hope you understands my love for you is true, for I'm
one who won't try to change you for the person I
love is you.

Steve Moore

"Life's True Colors"

Life is not always simple
The things that it demands
To choose one way or the other
    Each thought balanced in our hands
Indeed "Life" like they say is not just Black nor White
How much easier it would be without so many colors to choose
before our sight
Some will say they have strength, while others seem not to fight
But remember people inside or just like the colors that we see
Not just black nor white
If we try and we know we are doing our best.
Then what right gives others to judge and expect us to meet there
every expectation not less.
So when God calls and they put me down to rest
Lest not they judge me hard unless they have passed
All the colors that life gives them also to test

Susan Killen Foster

Fear

The endless time that is always near.
The undying loneliness that you fear.
For what is fear but the unknown?
That fills each man, even full grown.
Tis not the existence, though numbered by years
But the knowledge acquire, that conquers fears,
That gives man face to realize,
Truth is fear that never dies.

Mary A. Brogdon

Christmas Spirit

I dream for the Holidays when I was young
The time spent together, the songs we sung.
Christmas cards opened, then taped to the wall.
The mistletoe secretly hung in the hall.
Our boxed tree was lit, the ornaments up,
Chocolate milk or eggnog filled ones cup.
Snow flakes twinkled as they fell to the ground
It was a magical feeling you felt deep down.
Rosy-cheeked visitors knocked at the door,
Gifts were exchanged and covered the floor
We laughed, we ate, we felt such love.
This special time was sent from above.
God made us a family, what a precious gift.
When I remember those times my spirits
always lift.

Sharon L. Hernandez

Spring Day

I walk through the park
the sun shines and glistens on the lake . . .
I look ahead and notice the grass swaying
and the motion of the small white waves on the water,
the two seem to dance simultaneously in the wind.

I look up to see birds overhead catching the air,
gliding so effortlessly in bright blue sky.
I hear the song of the birds,
as they sing sweetly among the trees.

I glimpse popping pastels of hyacinth
in perfect planted rows around the park.

I feel the gentle breeze
as it touches my cheek and blows my hair,
my heart smiles.

Kathryn Mets

Rose Petal Touch

Rose petal smooth,
The touch that dusts my bones,
And sweeps my chest from the inside
And pours a waterfall through my mind.

Touch is a welcome thing,
The cleansing with hope,
The softness of silk,
The acceptance of self.

Fingertips on lips,
The feathery back of a hand,
Painting patterns of caring on tingling bare skin.

Lightly calloused heel,
Gently pointed toes,
Sliding familiar along friendly firm bone.

Silent, serious, laughing, smiling, safe and secure.
Lost in open longing of surprise love big eyes.

First love, new love, last love, love of chance meeting,
When eyes catch and spirits collide.

Touch across a room; across the miles; across time.

And touch together; together; together . . . together.

Michael Millay Mann

Buffaloes, Faces, And Places

I took my kids out West,
The trip stands out as the best.
Twenty-three states we saw,
As I look back in awe,
We're luckier than a lot of the rest.

For myself all that it takes
Are mountains, valleys, and lakes.
Sunsets and trees,
Clear skies and breeze,
And deep canyons the river makes.

On mountains there are faces,
In the middle of nowhere, there are places,
Some towns have grown
Into cities, I bemoan,
While others are nothing but traces.

We hear a thunderous sound,
A dust cloud appears on the ground,
I find it amazing
Watching buffalo grazing,
Their slaughter brought the Indian nation down.

Steve Talbott

Untitled

Human beings rarely achieve
the warmth found in angels,
and sometimes words sound better than never
at midnight
in the rain.
As your heart lies open before me
like a broken lock,
I reach for you,
but I don't need to,
because you were inside me long before I knew it.
And I know it's over
once you've begun the search for underwear;
God gave us freedom tonight, but that doesn't matter, because
all the times I told you I'd never leave mean nothing when you
choose to walk away.

Nathan Karpowich

A Storm Prayer

Whipped white peaks of foam spat into the deep blue curls
The undulating blanket that shrouded the turmoil below
reluctantly parted as we sailed into her ominous arms
The breakers crashed and whisked
as they broke over the bow sending rolls of foam and
wisps of stinging salted spray
It filled our nostrils with the sour scent of
Sargasso sea
We cursed the wind and hidden moon that commanded
the tidal hell
The sheets ripped our hands bloody as we scurried to stay the
sails
Rising the bow spirit blessed the decks of dancing demons
And we swore as we rose
a storm prayer
Falling it mocked us as we fell, our knees split
genuflecting on the pitch caulked altars of oak
awash with sea, baptized with blood,
blessed by the souls of those taken by the sea

William F. Norris

"Life"

Love and hate are all the same
The vanity of life makes it all a game
Like a person who pursues fame
Like a mistake where no one is to be blame

When love starts to fade
It makes it feel like being cut by a blade
Wishing sadness and happiness can be trade
Wishing your heart can never again be invade

Like a widow, full of sorrow
Like a lover, waiting to be hit by Cupid's arrow
Like a dreamer, having dreams that are so narrow
Like a child, an innocence that you can never borrow

When you realize what it mean
Life is nothing but a dream
We are under an obligation to be controlled by Fate
By living through our life which he create.

Karin Chau

"Green Confidence"

Daylight alter's black to green,
the way unfold's an ideal being.
Look inside a structure so intrinsically complete.
Let us smell the Lilac's.

Blue, the sky, sometime's lost.
White fairies shade, both slave and boss.
Galaxy past galaxy, the distance grow's feral.
Whisper sweet lotus petal.

A hesitant Moon, hop's from horizon to horizon.
Shadow and light chatter's with the sun.
Here heat temper's glass wishes into silk silver.
Aspen shelter's the wild air.

Earthen tower's, rise and fall,
through eon's, the art, a woven shawl.
Dream's flip, shiver, quiver, and flood the head of a pin.
How quiet the green confidence.

Shiloh Leo Augustine

The Willow

Whistling and wandering among the sweeping breeze,
The willow so tall blows with such ease

It's passing centuries of watching mankind
It's wisdom and endurance can match no mind

Its long history of infinite time stands,
As it gracefully hovers over the land

The limbs so thick and strong,
from trunk to branch so long.

Standing in awe embracing the heavens
Bowing gracefully gently touching the earth

Let our trees stand forever,
So that we may all enjoy earth's sweet endeavor.

Susan Lord Roeder

Praise From All Nature

Nature praises God in a symphony of sound,
The wind sighing through the pines,
The sweet call of the whippoorwill,
The splash of a trout in the summertime.

Nature praises God with its gigantic canvas;
The desert, painted in delicate hues,
Or, the dazzling white of the sunlight
On the fresh fallen snow; or the springtime dews.

Earth offers back to God the fragrance
Of the pungent smell of fresh mint,
Or the heavy sweetness of the magnolia,
And the delicate touch of the rose-scent.

Man, also, offers praise to God
For his uncountable mercies and love,
And for having been made in His image,
That he might reflect God's glory from above.

Margaret Coates Ball

A Moment In Love . . .

She dreams in a realm of eternal joy,
The troubles of her heart have fallen into the past,
Her vibrant silent smile in the stillness of the night,
Shall live forever in the memory of her lover . . .

Lorenzo Cervantez

In The End

Coldness sweeps throughout the room
the wind whistles a saturnine lonely tune.
a chill creeps through the must
indignation left behind by a dead man's cuss.
Hit and run, hit and stun the end has just begun.
Malignant and obscure clouds line the hills
Shadows hidden as one man kills.
Hit and cry, hit and die
the end will slowly creep by.
Chills and shivers throughout the bones
hearts, colder than stones.
Bad dreams in a midnight slum
huddled together as the end slowly comes.
Red as blood is the color of man's eyes
Blood surging down as all the people cry.
A global holocaust is reality once more
We won't see the end of this civil war.
Dawn is only black
the night is always the worst attack.
Desolated while awaiting the end.

Pamela N. Kirtos

Autumn

When leaves change from green to russet and brown
The winds start to blow and bring them down
Down to the ground to be trodden upon
But stand still for a moment, see them swirl and prance
like a Ballerina during her dance
They move in the wind with ease and with grace
A lovers soft touch on a loved ones face
The Autumn sun makes them gleam like gold
Take time to look it's a sight to behold
Please don't be sad that summer has gone
Because the beauty of Autumn goes on and on.

Lily Pike

Out My Back Window

The squirrel scrambled down as
The woodpecker whittled away on his tree
The cardinal cared less as
The bluejay bothered to glance at all the commotion
The raccoon rummaged but not until
The possum pilfered all there was
The dog deliberately scared
The cat curiously peering from under the bush
Nighttime sounds wrenched me from my sleep
Daytime antics mesmerized my thoughtless mind
The show goes on in the yard and
The animals play and laugh at me
So I laugh at me too while wondering why
Animals have so much to do and so much fun in doing.

Thomas L. Tinker

Love Of A Friend

Love of a friend is something we don't understand.
The world is forever in large demand.

But do we really fulfill our heart;
with the right understanding? Or drift apart?

When everyday life keeps the mind from knowing,
then the heart goes on by; like the leaves that are blowing.

Some how we always feel the fear,
of a friend in need to shed a tear.

It's not always how we wished it would feel.
But the love of a friend is a friendship that's real.

Susan S. Hurst

Black World

I'm so confused.
The world seems to be spinning around
Will it ever stop, will it ever slow down?
Ideas are beginning to form in my head
Sometimes I think I'd be better off dead
The pressures keep building, they keep getting stronger
I don't think I can handle this much longer
The ones that I love don't ever love back
I feel as though I'm going to crack
People say things can only get better with time
They don't understand that these problems are forever mine
I want to go somewhere far away
Somewhere, where no one will ever play
Where smiles will fade, the world will turn black
And I pray to God I never come back

Regina Helene Sharron

Moon

The moon, our friend
the yolk of our egg.
only moon can create a
slithering, silver, scarlet snake, snakewalking
throughout the woodlands.
The moon
the yolk of our egg.
Walk up to the cliff
overlooking the turquoise sea
and the densely packed seaweed.
Look up! At the half shattered moon,
and find the beauty within.
The sun, the moon, the land, and the ocean
the four significant changelings for our egg.
The moon has the image of silver,
the image of darkness,
the image of light,
the image of experience,
and the image of the beginning.
Moon, the creator of life.

Maureen Martinez

Seasons Come

Spring comes flowers come,
their beauty all around,
their colors so bright when you look on the ground.
The suns gentle light,
brings you great delight.

Summer comes children come,
from all around they play.
With their trucks and their cars,
with their dolls and their games,
they put on a play.

Fall comes wind comes,
blowing the leaves,
from their branches so far.
Making it cold for a day,
winter is next.

Winter comes cold comes,
no flowers no children,
they are all warm inside,
waiting for spring,
waiting for summer.

Melissa Bland

The Truth

There are many truths in this world
There are many more falses in the world
There are many things that are beautiful
There are many things that lack beauty
There are many honest people
There are many dishonest people
Sometimes its hard to decide that which is good
And sometimes its easy
But this I know for certain
When I wake up in the morning, it is me
When I look in the mirror, I see me
When I speak, it is me I hear
And I know that no matter how people see me
Whether it be
Ugly or fat
Beautiful or thin
Intelligent or silly
Honest or shallow
Or all combined
I will still be me no matter what and that makes me happy

Summer Wednesday Hatcher

Ode To The Million Man March

When God created Adam and Eve,
Their color was never revealed, I believe.
But with love in God's heart and creation His plan,
He breathed life into Adam, the very first man.

Then knowing this man would be lonely alone,
He put Adam to sleep and took out his rib bone.
Out of this God made woman to stand by his side,
And the two, in God's love, were meant to abide.

So what happened next, is known by all,
How Satan, thru tempting them, cause man to fall.
His desires became evil and not what God taught,
They hated their brothers and constantly fought.

And up to this day, I have yet to find,
Why the color of skin can taint a man's mind!
If it be dark or light, I just simply can't see,
Why you can't be you and I can't be me!

We were never meant to fit in one mold,
We were meant to be God's lovely "pot of gold".
And treasures we are, just open your eyes,
And stop listening to Satan's deplorable lies.

K. Kristin Hampton

"A Better Place"

Man meets woman and they soon fall in love,
Their friendship is blessed by the man up above.

They make their plans - they soon are married,
With every little detail carefully carried.

Their love grows stronger with each passing day,
They ask God's blessing as they kneel and pray.

A child is born because of their love,
As God smiles upon them from up above.

A sweet little baby so tiny and small,
With his parents love - he will have it all.

Learning how to love, be happy, mild, and meek,
To avoid bad things - only the good to seek.

As the years go by and the child grows,
He wants to be just like his parents - he knows.

He follows their example right to the "T",
To be the very best he possibly can be.

The world of today would be better to the end,
If we had more families like this to send

Out in the world with their love to share,
 Showing everyone - they really do care.

Sandra E. Spindler

Great Expectations

   People laugh at what they don't understand.
There aren't enough hours in the day.
   Other's expectations weigh my shoulders down.
Tell me how to feel, what to do, what to say.
   Friends were lost and things left unfinished,
I'd sell my soul for things to be set right.
   In my wasted time, every second is used.
Conscience was lost, help me on judgment night.
   Have I sinned or is it all in my head?
My goals were forgotten, my hopes destroyed.
   I try but can't keep holding on.
By everyone else's needs and hopes, I am employed.
   While standing on the ledge, I pray once more.
A cold brisk wind blows on my skin.
   Everything becomes black and freedom is gained
Expectations have caused my greatest sin.

Vincent Pickett

The Mystery Of Life

As days go by and years unfold
there are many special memories we all hold.
We think of good and bad days we've had
that's the past and am I sure glad.
We all have experiences that we must go through,
grown from each and started a new.
That's what makes me, me and you, you.
Each day begins a brand new dream, with hopes,
desires, and craziness too.
Whatever it takes is what we must do.
Times are tough and many things may go wrong,
that's life and life will go on.
Plant a couple of seeds
watch them grow
it's up to life you never know.
What will be, will be,
I guess we all just have to wait and see.

Lisa Dawn

The End

He gazed out the window at the world below.
Then he sighed and turned away
From the same familiar day.
He dared for a moment to let the emotions flow
DarknessDespairSolitudeFutility

The moment passed quickly and he left his room.
He came out from his small cage
For he had to earn his wage.
As he walked down the sidewalk he returned to his gloom
RemorseSorrowEmptinessMelancholy

His seat on the bus he found vacant again.
It seemed that it always was
And he knew he was the cause.
He pondered in silence all the things that could have been
FailureRegretDejectionDysphoria

On that trip he opted to exit the scene.
He rode past his normal stop
Next to his employer's shop.
In this, at least, he would succeed, none would intervene
CalmnessResolveAcceptanceFinality

Ross Johnston

Alas' My Love Has Come Along

I was introduced to my love oh so long ago,
Then I wasn't ready for commitment; I just told him no.

As time went on, life became extremely hard to bare,
Even though I was unworthy my love just stayed right there.

I became a fish out of water trying to put up a fight,
So I decided to call my love and we talked late one night.

I thought he would be angry and simply push me away.
But he really surprised me, with what he had to say.

Now I'm not bound by the simple things you see,
Because he has promised to take real good care of me.

He will never lie or lead me in the wrong direction,
I no longer fear the unknown he's also good protection.

Alas' my love has come to prepare me for my part,
'Cause none will sup with him but the pure in heart.

By now I'm sure you have already figured it out,
That Jesus is my love, the one I spoke about.

Selenda Rena Webb

Heaven's Dove

The dove flew into the wilderness,
then nature burst into bloom.
The higher it flew,
the more the wilderness grew.
Water began to gush forth,
and bubbling springs quenched thirsty ground.
Creatures were making a new sound.

The dove brought strength to feeble hands
And helped weary legs to firmly stand.
The lame leaped like deer
and brought many joyous tears.

The dove will be here to take us,
to the way of Holiness.
Only the redeemed will dwell there.
Everlasting joy will crown righteous heads.
Gladness and joy overtakes the once dead,
but now living wilderness.

Lindsay Hall

The Lord's Supper

I asked my Lord to join me in a quiet evenings sup';
Then wondered how lowly I could fill the Master's cup.

A gentle knock I heard and ran to open the door;
With trembling hands and humbled heart I ushered Him 'cross
the floor.

I placed upon His platter faith, obedience and love;
And hoped my meager offerings would please Him, from above.

His gentle smile and loving gaze filled my very soul;
I knew the food I'd been searching for could be found in no bowl!

I leapt with joy to serve Him, all fear and worry gone;
The Lord gave me the strength to mightily press on.

Although 'twas I who asked the Lord to join with me in sup';
'Twas Him, Holy Host of Hosts, who gently filled my cup.

Susan C. Smith

Marilyn

As far as my eyes can see
There is no ne in the world for you but me
Just as long as the grass is green and the sky is blue
There is no one is this world for me but you
And you are my flower

A flower is but one of God's simple things
But oh! How much love and joy a flower can bring
I see a flower as a symbol of love
More precious than a diamond, softer than a dove

As there are many different kinds of flowers
There are many different kinds of loves
But the love I have for you will never change
No games played, no attached strings
Just simple true love, and what is love?

Love is you, love is a rose
Love can be fragile or unbelieving strong
Love is without faults, no hidden motives
Love is the give and take of oneself, a union of souls
Not two halves to make a whole, but two wholes joined together
Love is simply unconditional

Lony L. Williams

Friendship Forest

Friendship forest is a lovely place to be,
  there is so much to do and see.
We could go there when we're sad,
  and talk to each other so we don't get mad.

We sit and tell each other secrets there,
  that's how we become a better friendship pair.
We share our feelings in this beautiful place
  and when we're there, there is always a smile
  on our face.

This place reminds us that we'll be friends forever more.
It also reminds as of peace, not war.
This is a place where we share special things.
We feel so free that we're flying as if with wings.

It can be a place to feel sad and cry too,
  and to say "I'll never forget you."

This is a place that we have made-
  our memories will never fade.
Friendship forest is for friends like us to share
  and let each other know, that we'll always be there.
We will always visit this place together
  and be best friends forever!!

  Krista Stango

Precious Memories

Tucked away on the plains of Northwestern Kansas, is a farm,
There once dwelled a couple who never did anyone harm.
They were usually cheerful and rarely sad,
These two beautiful people were our Mom and Dad.

A larger family then ours was rare,
But Mom being an only child, didn't dare.
Our farm was peaceful, and the only violence that was for real,
Was when a coyote would snatch a hen for yet another meal.

Even though I was child number eight,
They took special time with each one, and never forgot the date.
Mom and Dad taught us caring and sharing, and they taught us love,
They also taught us of the good Lord above.

Dad had wisdom and he had courage, but we could feel his pain,
When once again the crop was destroyed by hail and rain.
Mom in her creative and efficient way,
Could have changed the saying, "Rome wasn't built in a day."

We think of them often and though we are miles apart,
We gather in Kansas each year to keep their memories in our heart.
Thanks to Mom and Dad for teaching us right, and we shout it loud,
For this you would be very proud.

  Ritha Linenberger

House Of Love

The house of love I grew up in was very small
There was love through each and every wall.

My mother would take a seat
to watch us, as we would eat.
After we were finished, what we left,
she would fix a plate and eat herself.

She cut wood in the winter so we could have heat
She struggled hard to keep shoes on our feet.
When she went to work, my sister would cook
It tasted okay, but oh how it looked.
Hot dogs were almost every meal
That's why I won't eat them still.

That house is still full of love,
From a sweet mother that I was (Mother is gone,
given to from the Lord above. To live with God above.

  Raydell Annie Hargrave

About Grandmothers

Grandma has lived some seventy-odd years
There's been plenty of laughter and
  plenty of tears.
It's been a good life for this wife and mother
She'd never exchange it for another!

Now, twilight years are taking their toll
Memories are fading, she's forgetful and droll,
Can't find her hat, or remember a name,
But loving and enjoying life all the same!

Proud of the family, watching them grow
Praying for them and loving them so!
God has been good, I thank Him each day
For all of the blessings He's sent on my way!
God Bless you all!

  Marjorie R. Devin

Drowning In Blood

I'm drowning in a river of blood, no one will help me.
They are poking fun at me.
My waist is covered in blood.
Yet my friends aren't coming to help me, which means I have no friends.
They're probably laughing too.
Now the blood is up to my neck.
I'm screaming for help; no one comes.
Not even my family, that means I don't have a family who cares for me.
My head is almost under, someone reaches his hand and helps me out.
I have a friend, someone who cares for me.
Now everyone is making fun of him too.
So he pushes me back in.
I still have no one who cares for me.
I have nothing, no one, I'm alone.
The only thing left for me to do is die.
And as the river gets higher and higher . . . I do

  Rena Fisher

A Tribute To All Fire Fighters

They were in the air and on the ground.
They fought the fires all around.
We are grateful for the men in
Yellow, Brown and Blue.
Who fought the fight just for you.
Some homes were saved, many lost.
The men kept working at all cost.
Thank you who came from far and near.
You will all be remembered,
Never fear
When devastation seems most great.
Your work is never finished yet.
You're always ready to perform first rate.

  Odessa A. Brewer

"Loving Memories"

Too many words were left unspoken,
They may never be heard;
Too many dreams fell to pieces around us,
Not making a sound or saying a word.
Too much love that was not shown,
Leaves me sad down deep;
Never too many feelings expressed,
Those I will remember and keep.

  Laura Lynn Gernhardt

Grandfather's Eyes

She has your eyes, you know.
They haunt; the eyes harbor knowledge of some long ago
Daydream, elusive by day but visible in the night's wake.

These eyes Know without knowing.
They Speak without speaking and
Smile without smiling.

These eyes chart the waters and set the course;
Like the sailor in the unpredictable sea, the eyes
Embrace God's Compass while the stars nod above.

She has your eyes, I know you know.
They sparkle and dance even when there's no one there
To spark the spark or to play the music.

These eyes seek Justice for the just and Mercy for the merciful.
They seek shelter from the jealous and
Affirm those in need.

If eyes are the window to the soul,
Her soul and your soul Know each other well . . .

I am glad she has your eyes, my father.
These eyes of hers, so strong and kind,
Are truth that God's Love is Everlasting.

Patricia Devan Barrett

My Dreams

Wealth, power, nor prestige enter my mind.
They hold no sway yet still I am in a bind.
For a dream of someone who makes my heart skip
Occupies me.

I dream dreams of a simple action.
Holding her hand on the beach is one caption.
Simple dreams yet each one with hopes and hints of
Reality.

Her head rests on my shoulder, asleep,
One dream of many which I intend to keep.
I search for someone who can make my heart skip, oh
Where can she be.

Holding her and feeling her embrace.
Is a dream that I truly hope she will face.
Each of these dreams can set me free,
But there is a lock and only she has the key.

Nicholas O'Sullivan

"The Monologue Of The Unknown Soldier"

"They call us heroes.
They say we went above and beyond the call of duty . . .
I say we did our duty.
We are called patriotic zealots, but we are only Americans.
Call us whatever you like,
but we are, what we are.
We know our strength, our patriotism . . .
We know our weakness, our mortality . . .
The front lines, our life story:
the hope, the glory, the peace
the rancor, the sufferance, the war.
We saw the young blood and the old fear.
We are that blood, we are that fear,
We are that sweat, we are those tears.
We march to lift this flag high.
We march to see our anthem prevail.
Through wind, sleet, and storm we march . . .
'till stained red with the last drop of American blood.
Don't cry for us, don't mock us, don't glorify us . . .
We fight for you, we bleed for you, we die for you!"

Reshma Patil

Mother's Hands

Mother's hands held mine as I learned to walk,
They put on my dress, and pulled up a sock.

Her hands, so gentle, would brush my hair,
Then swing me giggling high in the air.

Hands so gentle, yet so firm,
Showed me I had much to learn.

For thirty-five, those hands taught school,
First and foremost, The Golden Rule.

For sixty years I've known those hands,
Which often sheltered me from life's demands.

I now hold those hands to help her stand,
To help her walk, each step now planned.

Mother's hands, once strong, now grown weak,
Still give comfort which I often seek.

Mother's hands, now frail with age,
Tremble as they turn her Bible's page.

Someday I'll have Mother's hands no more,
They will be in God's hand at Heaven's door.

But whether here on earth or from up above,
I know I'll always feel my mothers love.

Wanda B. Gardner

Pencil

Let it be fall or spring
There is no greater thing
Than a colorful pencil
It's the best utensil

Yellows, Blues and even Green
Your pencil will always be seen
The colors are amazing
Things conveyed are surprising

Oh, the things your hand will write
When a pencil is in sight
A pencil is inspiration
A pencil is sheer creation

When ink runs out, a pencil will come to your aide
Even though mistakes are usually made
A handy pencil can erase with ease
I'll always say, "Pass the pencil, please."

Tiffany A. Reed

Teddy Bears

In my room which is quite neat,
There is a doll upon a seat.

A few books are set upon a shelf,
But the place I like best myself

Is a place upon my bed
Where there sit teddy bears in suits of red,

Or blue or green or plaid;
Some look happy and others sad.

Some of them gaze as if in dreams of yesterday,
Others look up at you as if they want to play.

And if you say it I'll agree that it's true,
I like teddy bears, be they old or be they new.

Rebecca Robbins

Wishes

"I wish I didn't love you so," I
Said when I was young, filled
With desire to know your heart,
To hear your dreams, to weave
A silken thread around the two
Of us to make us one. But you would not.

"I wish I didn't love you anymore," I
Said when years had passed, my
Hunger unassuaged, my thirst unslaked.
Neglected dreams for naught,
My soul remained my own, unclaimed
By you. Unrecognized. Unsought.

We were still two alone. Not one.
All then was gone; the silken thread forgot,
The hunger dulled, the thirst ignored the
Soul asleep to ache no longer for
What might have been, remembering, I cried
"I wish I loved you now as I did then!"

> *Janell M. Lindsey*

"Goldfire"

Coiled around a glistening sea,
Sailing above worlds that be.
Seemingly granted by all of man,
Forcing it to till the land.
Filled by citrine rays of light,
Shattered by the darkened night.
That which the floods wash clean,
Until no light shall be seen.
But none will realize this beauty forgot,
Exclusive for me, the humble should it be not.

> *April Ridgeway*

Memories Of A Ragged Blanket

Safe feeling in a shell's curved shape
same security as cotton's sweet embrace.

Smooth as silk, soft as fur.
Cotton's tug,
dragged away to exit into a new domain.

Open spaces freeze the cotton swathed soul,
to fear people's wool wrapped smiles.

Its smell,
sweet and sour.
Catching the drips of mouthed speech.

Sting the eyes,
once alabaster-white.
In an age of new dawned terror,
transformed to gray.

Wispy rags still exist,
small threads unstitched of a great tapestry.

To part with does not secure,
but furthers the gap,
from feathered skin of baby quilt.

> *Benjamin Lowy*

A Last Note

I know you're just joking; it's not time for goodbye.
say you're kidding, or even tell me a lie!
I just got to know who you are in your heart, and
now you're gone, I find I'm grateful in part!
Grateful for the times of your life that we shared,
and thank you for letting me show you I cared.
Grateful for all the lives that you've touched,
and know we will miss you and we love you so much.

> *Elizabeth Turner*

High Land

Must, woven with Chinese spices and Jasmine incense
saturate the air

Sunlight exposes dense dust

The haggard floor squeaks
Chipped walls hum with secrets of past

The sofas are covered with his and hers coverlets
One striped, one pink floral

Yellowing greeting cards, dingy shot glasses and proud
Buddha statues congest the China cabinet

Priceless photographs cover every antique corner
Lamp shades remain encompassed by shredding plastic

Sheer gauze fabric flows gently
as the wind whistles through a narrow crack

A quiet, calm stillness rushes by
The hazy blue tint of the television flickers

Darkness has arrived . . .

> *Casey A. Sang*

This Thing Called Love

What is this thing that people call "love"
    saying it's the best of everything far and above?

Why do they make it such a big deal
    because sometimes I wonder, "Is it for real?"

There must be something that I have missed
    because people say it's more than this.

It's an unconditional feeling of no doubt
    that they'll be there for you even when you pout.

For better or worse, in sickness and in health
    for rich or poor, love will be your wealth.

It has already come to rescue me
    not from a handsome prince, but my family.

It controls my heart and my mind
    letting me know it's "one of a kind".

I have found the thing called "love"
    and it's the best of everything far and above.

> *Kara Heinrich*

And I Alone Survived

The sun shone on the city that day
    sending perfect rays of light that shimmered
        in the pools of water.
Laughter filled the air
    and people played together
        to stay away from what they feared the most.
With a push of a button and the pull of a lever,
    atoms zimmered through the sky
        sending fresh disaster to every machine built town,
            and every shimmery grown farm.
Gray, black smoke filled the poisonous air
    and people fumbled to the ground.
Now a different laughter came around,
    the laughter of wars and their victor's.
Or is there a winner or a loser?
    No, just the dumb and the dumber.
Echoes of dying cries fackled by and by
    and soon everyone on this earth had died.
The clouds faded away and the smoke left the ground
    that was now in jig-saw-meal, and I alone survived.

> *Denise L. Haegele*

September Song

A melancholia fills my heart as summer
  says "goodbye";
A misty haze surrounds the sun as it drops
  from the sky.

The twilight clouds drift slowly; they are
  every form and type
Like herculean puffs of smoke, blown from
  an old man's pipe.

The showy, bright begonias are falling to
  their beds.
The tall and stately roses seem to bow their
  heads.

The year is stretching to its end.
  The days are dwindling, too.
Can it be I'm feeling sad for
  I've reached "those precious few"?

    Frances Favre-Larkin

Sky And Sea

Sky-blue
Sea-blue
Somber sun
The sky is orange
The sea is orange
Lightning, thunder, wind
  Sky turns grey
  Sea turns dull
Waves whip the rocks
Once, twice, three times . . .
The sky dresses in distinguish midnight black
The sea exposes her deep, dark beauty
Moon and stars dance their reflection
  on the ocean-mirror.
A day in the life of a natural union.
Does the sky depart because the sea holds life?
Does the sea fume because the sky is above?
World's apart - a vastness of nothing between them
Yet, on the horizon, they meet as two lovers
  lips on an eternal kiss.

    Azalia Garcia

Finding Joy

Joy—the most sought after prize—
  seems to be in a great demise.

How do I find it—where shall I search?
  I start looking everywhere; but
  certainly not in a church!

Friends—let me start here!
  Some disappointed me—brought many a tear.

Money—the more you have, the more you want! For a year
  It bought many things—but JOY is not here.

Work—is fulfilling they say—work hard, get ahead,
  But look at all the JOY I missed instead!

Fame—ah, this is important—people will notice—
  With JOY I'll burn!
  Alas, Joy still eludes me at every turn!

Church—I have returned and learned,
  That the BIBLE shows how JOY is found.
  Turn to Philippians 2, to see JOY abound:

Study it, practice what you read,
  And JOY will be yours, more than you need!

    Connie H. Place

Pale Man's Light

Anger, came he, with sled and dog.
Searching for bright powder, the pale one's gold.
  Come he, with ravaged face, hate edged,
to kill the animals, to rape the land.
So, brother nature, he fights.   Tooth and claw,
cold and fear he uses to drive the pale evil away.
  The river was our savior. He opened his ice,
took the pale one and dogs.
  Now, the pale one chases his dogs across the sky,
and spills the bright light down the dark.
  A warning, other pale ones, here in the cold lands
brother nature is strong, brother nature will win.
  Your greed and hate stand no chance.

    David G. Toews

"Secrets Of The Dead"

Fields and fields of grass rolling, to the sunset so it seems,
secrets kept, locked and buried, what is this they wish to speak.
Stories held, told in novels, their pasts are books of private dreams.
Experiences only felt from them, just from being down that road,
chronicled on slates of stone, but their thoughts . . . remain unknown,
in the boneyard their to stay, buried, covered, locked away,
sleeping, in their somber states, their loss of victory dealt with
death, overcome by fear of darkness, washed away by tears that wept.
Your agony is over now, rejoice yourself a private victory,
celebrate in state of rest, your battle fought has ended fallen,
to the blackness you have landed, stranded under earth itself,
your presence their will fade away, to what is left but floating
dreams never heard and never spoken.

    Gregory Basey

Get Out Of "Your" World

Look deep into someone's eyes.
See past your reflection.
You can see their world,
Instead of your own.

You can be a part of what you aren't supposed to be a part of.
You can see what you aren't supposed to see.

All you have to do is get past yourself.
Yes it's a tough hurdle.
But I tell you the world is full of hate.
It needs to be stopped.

How you ask.
I will tell you.
Look past yourself and look into me.
If we all did this,
We could all be in the same world.

    Ashley Moskovich

"Then And Now"

She skips and she runs.
She plays and she swims.
She rides her bike as fast as she can.
She smiles and giggles most all of the time
except when she falls, then she cries.
She falls a lot, but when she's not, she smiles
and giggles the rest of the time.
And now when she runs from one job to the next,
she has no time to fall, but she smiles and
knows God will get her through it all.

    Dionne R. Helmer

Untitled

I watched the sun
  set
for a moment it lingered
gracing me with its beauty
then it was gone
swift as a wave breaking upon a shore

Left in its wake
a delicate weave of clouds
held a trace of color

Then it too was gone
into the night

The sky became indigo satin
on the horizon bare branches reached high
their silhouettes delicate as lace

They brought to mind roots of a plant, or the dendrites in my brain,
or the trail of comet as it streaks against a moonless sky

The weave of the universe
is both minuscule and airy
invisible as the wind, yet colorful as the setting sun

  Jody Love

Visions Of Sunrise

When the sun begins to rise
  shades of red, purple, and blue.
I see God's paint brush in the skies,
  He created them for me and you.
Every morning I wait to see,
  a sunrise all anew.
What He has in store for me,
  and the things that I must do.
And when I've done my daily task,
  and laid myself down to sleep,
when I say my evening prayers, for peace I ask,
  in His hands I know He'll keep
My soul from harm and evil too,
  to wake me with the morning light
to see the beauty once again
  what a truly wondrous sight.
So for tomorrow, I will dream
  to see God's paint brush in the skies
Than I'll thank God for another day,
  and for the visions of sunrise.

  Irving J. Bolyard

Tinseltown Of Love

Las Vegas, Heart on fire
Shadow in the mountains
The night's ablaze
With your sweet lips
Opened wide, Inviting arms
Embracing one and all, Come, come
Come inside my tent of joy
Feel my presence
In the groin of your earth
Long for my release,
As your prison bars strangle your senses
Starving you even as your body
Fills with lights and colors
The sounds of lions roaring
Hyenas laughing, as the devil struts his stuff
Melting honey across your chest
Heaving up and down, In and out
In sync and rhythm, With the falling dice
And clanking coins, Money - disappearing
Into the endless night turned day.

  Erica Goodstone

Shadows

Shadows, how they lurk around in my mind
Shadows, which I can never leave behind
Shadows, how they flirt around with no bind
Shadows which I can never leave behind.

Shadows that splash on a mind grown numb
Shadows that flee past a voice become mum
Shadows that sail across eyes moist with tears
Shadows that pierce a heart with lonely fears.

Shadows that clutched never to let go
Now stand as lonely silhouettes, both alone
Shadows that kissed with a prayer on the lips
Now touch only when the heart takes fake flips

Shadows that ran miles together; up and down winding ways
Now tread alone to find their separate days
Shadows that captured all of the other in a steady gaze
Now cry sacred for just a look at the others face

Shadows - they aren't pictures with pretty memories.
Shadows - they are fog. They tell fake stories.

  Anandita Oberoi

Safiya

A mother's prayers travels everywhere
Sharing and caring for a child's despair
A mother's prayers deceives naked eyes
Replacing wisdom to spiritual eyes
So that a child's complexities in life
Are not stricken by malice and strife
A mother's prayers continues
To add to, subtract from, daily menus
Ingredients that boldly bears
A mother's concern as she shares
Prior life experience to present conditions
Shedding enlightenment based on dreams, premonitions

A mother's prayers are steady and continues
Gradually adding to daily menus

Courage to go on, faith to grow strong
Constant jealousies and hate, instant knowledge to debate
Understanding from the soul, currently borrowed and resold
Contents yielding to pretense, lending power to the sixth sense
Love as a healing force, preparing for the advanced course
Denouncing worldwide hate, a mother's prayers are tested, by fate

  Ee-B K. Harris

Sunset

The great fiery goddess is almost through with her journey.
She approaches the horizon, gathering with loving arms the
warmth and happiness.
Blue becomes gloomier, purple engulfing.
Her orange cape is trailing behind her, and her yellow hair streaking
across the sky of twilight.
Remnants of a passing thunderstorm catch her remaining rays, shooting
  them off as pink darkening to turquoise then deepening to blue.
Her enormous sullen suitor pursues relentlessly, spreading his
gloomy blackness through the world.
But she is always ahead of him, bidding his darkness away,
Preventing his dismal control from overtaking the earth.
She sends her servants to give him gifts of diamonds, hoping to
calm his horrendous desire.
But he sneers and heaves the gift in all directions, scattering the
  twinkling beauties into random pictures.
He continues to chase, but she is too swift.
She leaves him, taking the lingering light and beautiful colors with her.
He is left alone, in a sea of blackness dotted with his rejected gift.

  Jill Conradi

Sisters

My sister is a funny girl
She even has a funny curl,
Crooked toes and turned up nose
And giggles loud where 'ere she goes.

She thinks that I am just a jerk
A brother with a funny quirk.
She laughs out loud and acts so proud
And tries so hard to draw a crowd.

One day my sister ran away
It was a bright and sunny day.
She slipped and fell right in a well
You should have heard her scream and yell.

I got a rope and pulled her out
She then began to dance about.
It is a sin to never win,
I wish that I had left her in.

Fern Klopp Bucknum

"Millions Cry With Her"

She cries tears of pain, and tears of anger from the heart.
She feels she is alone when she cries, but she is not. There
are millions of girls, women, who cry the same tears she cries
every day, every hour, every minute. Tears of hate and anger,
tears of sorrow, for they are helpless! They are trapped! No
one to turn to. No where to go! Trapped by who? Trapped by
their husbands, their fathers, their brothers, and lovers.
Trapped by men!! Women who have children, and can support
themselves I envy; for I cannot! I am trapped, and so is my son.

She cries aloud in a towel; so it muffles the echoes
of her cries. She only wants God to hear her, for she feels
he is the only one that will help her.

Dawn Adele Disharoon

Mom

She has seen tough times, times most couldn't survive . . .
She has seen rough times, rougher than I will ever see I'm sure . . .
She has shed many a tear, suffered many a fear . . .
She has felt pain and sorrow, yet makes it through each tomorrow . . .
She has been the beginning of life, then has suffered it's ending . . .
She has loved more than one can love, yet each day she loves a little more . . .

She has been the lamb in life, yet she is as strong as the lion . . .
She has been torn and trampled by life, yet she always gets up and goes on.
She has been the victim of hate, yet she teaches love . . .
She has had the resources to have anything she wanted in life,
    yet she sacrificed it all . . .
She gives of herself on a daily basis, yet she asks and gets little in return . . .
You ask me if such a person exists? . . .
I tell you in a definite tone "YES and I am proud to call her MOM" . . .
And not only for what she gives, but for "who" and "what" she
"is" and for what she has made of me.

Carrie B. Davis

A Child A Gift From God

O LORD, don't ever let me forget that he is heaven sent.
So pleasant and so pure, so loving so dear,
It is hard for us to part from him whenever we are so near.
No one can ever take their place, their smile is so rare,
    the happiness that lingers there.
The joy that they have given us can never be replaced,
    especially when you see that look upon their little face.
OH! Thank you LORD for giving me your child
for a little while, because I know I have to guide
him to you with a smile.
I love this child so dearly LORD. I know that he is mine.
I know I will have to give him back whenever it is time.

Constance M. Weese-Joliet

Untitled

You can smell her, taste her, feel her
she is always within your grasp, in your Blood
The reason you were born.
Never have you loved more purely, more completely
She is your love, your hope, your life,
Addiction.
She opens up to you each morning and you come Alive.
Passion burning in your eyes-She's in your every Thought.
She is Your Private goddess, daily You study her doctrine
You look to Her for Salvation.
Beware
Many have loved her and Lost,
She has no Heart, no soul.
She delights in toying with your Mind
turning away if you falter.
She has caused you doubt, fear, despair but never
Defeat.
For you know her too well, have learned to read her mind,
Have Faith! In You she has met her Match.
Soon She will surrender to You her most prized possession, but
she will Never set you-Free.

Elke Edwards

Margaret

I can see her warm friendly smile,
She is beautiful of spirit and heart, and I love her dearly.

How I wish I could embrace her
Oh, If only I could be with her,
If only I could put my arms around her,
I know I would be safe.

She kept me from harm, all my life.

She fed, sheltered and clothed me.

She went without, so that I might have.

She loves me, I love her - but - but,
Did I ever tell her so?

I love her more than anyone can love another.

I wish that she were here so I could tell her so.
I want to be near her, to run up to her; to embrace her and kiss her.

She gave me so much,
She gave me live.

She is my mother.

Dolores McMahon

Mother's Day

There is nothing like a Mother
    she is the most
precious thing on earth.
Her role begins as Mother blessed
    by births.
Honor, respect, love and obey her
    not only on "Mother's Day."
But all year through, bringing her
    joys, and laughter
and not for one moment making her feel blue.
As the years keep rolling by and by
    and they sure do fly.
Mother starts aging, graying hair,
    wrinkled skin has gone through thick and thin.
So keep on loving her and don't shame
    her into sin.
Don't take here for granted when she
    is around because
another one cannot be found.
Love and cherish her all year round.

Etta Taikeff

Heal A Sick Friend O Precious Lord

I have a friend who is sick, Dear Lord
She needs Your help today
She's having a lot of pain, O Lord
Won't you help them go away

Won't you help my friend, O Precious Lord
And help her get very strong
Let her know that Your with her, Lord
No matter what goes wrong

You'll make it right I know You will
For I have spoken to You before
You're the one who can still
Give her strength to store

She'll carry your word in her heart
No matter where she may go
She'll show you that she is a part
Of everything that You know

I wish to thank you, O Precious Lord
For listening to my plea
I know she'll thank you too, O Lord
For helping her be free

Joseph L. Minnella

The Elephant

My favorite of all is the elephant.
She never talks back, not even a grunt.
She walks softly thru the dry, hot sand
To eat and drink in some far-off land.

She watches over her little one too
'Cause she wouldn't like to live at the zoo.
She may look sad but believe me, she's not
'Cause she's on her way to a favorite spot.

She walks miles and miles o'er the hot, dry sand
To find her food in some far-off land.
Then on to a place where it's not quite so hot
To cool herself down on a nice shady plot.

P.S.
She's funny, she's docile
And really darned cute
But make no mistake
She may give a boot!

Dagmar P. Collova

Reflecting Soul

She returned and the house it seemed the same.
She pressed her face to the window and remembered all the pain.
The life inside was gone, but the ghosts paraded on.

Her tears began to flow and washed the window clean.
She could see her image clear a face she did not know.
Passages of time were silently revealed, and no halting.
of the clock could stall as the lines of time told all.

She could not change the past, and the present
was still unclear, and moving even hear the future
her greatest fear.

The memories of the past hung decaying
on the walls and ghosts paraded greedily
up and down the empty halls.

Her secrets were told and given for all to know
Her shame would be her fame into eternities last glow.
And the ghosts marched past with her demented and dying soul.

Donna Krumm

Death By The Night

Her face, worn with dirt, sand, and the tears which cause her pain.
She sleeps helplessly alone, her thoughts, dreams, visions shattered.
Her love, for what of it remains, diminished within the sands of time,
She lies still, in a midnight corner,
the only light she has, are the reflections of the moon off the brown
shaded tears melting every pore of her face. The only warmth which
she feels, is the blood of her scabs and the wounds which pour within her heart,
She is silent, homeless, yet screams inside in the cold dry air of the
night. Her life is a scrambled puzzle, already assembled,
For she is alone, without a care in the world,
Can she be found?
Her eyes, exhausted; her mouth, glistens
her hands, they tremble; her heart, it bleeds,
her blood, it mourns; her touch, is light, her voice, cracked,
She lay asleep, trying to dream; her soul and hope is dead, trying to live.

Jason Vasquez

Web Of Guilt

She's a black widow spider
She spins her tale, it works so well
Now they're in her web, thoughts are
Not their own for she's sucked them out.

She's a spinner, she'll have you for dinner
She'll have you before you even know
You've been had
She really believes she's the queen bee
She takes no responsibility.

The hour glass upon her vest runs quickly through
If you associate
But take heart, the other side of her will
Destroy herself for she even eats her mate
She's a black widow - tantalizer . . .
Arachne.

Diana Dolhancyk

Lament Of Thirst

Where is the rain that yet hides from the earth?
She swells the clouds that scamper 'cross the skies;
She flaunts herself before the longing eyes
Of parched Terra, languishing for re-birth.
Where is the moisture that would bring sweet mirth
To the scorched meadow, where she, withered lies?
She taunts the sod, as to each cloud she ties
Herself, unmindful of the earth's sad dearth.
Come to the earth! Hear the weary lament!
The hills, the valleys, each seek your caress
To quench the thirst of the billowing sands.
She hears earth's mourning, longs to repent
And yield herself to restore earth's sweetness.
Then fall her tears, subduing thirst's demands.

Betty Golden

No Smoking

I watch as she lights up yet another cigarette
She's shivering and shaking in the cold and wet
Since they've posted those No Smoking signs inside
So on her coffee break she must go outside.

Why can't she put this demon out of her life?
Some day she'll probably go under the knife.
She'll lose a lung, what misery that will be
And her beautiful hair from chemotherapy.

I watch as she lights up another nicotine stick.
Her racking cough tells me that she's already sick.
Oh, Lord Above, let her know this one thing.
She'll be much better off with no smoking.

June Serviss

Mother And Child

A mother bare a child with joy, pain and tear's in her eye's.
She teaches her child to be kind for giving and wise.
Mother gives her child her best never stopping once to rest.
Hoping that when her child become
A man that he will be the very best that he can.
But sometime the child will stray away.
Then mother will get on her knees and pray.
Dear God what have I done wrong.
To make my child go astray from his teaching at home.
Please give me an answer to my prayer.
And deliver me from my despair.
Then as if out of no where come's the answer to her prayer
I know dear mother that you have tried.
So wipe those tear's away from your eyes.
"For I'm omega thy God, and for me there is nothing to hard."
So give this child to me and I will tame him like I calm the sea.
So mother rise's from her knees after getting an answer to her plea.
Mother is no longer hurt or sad.
Because she know's good thing's will come to pass.
She know that God know she was done her best.
So she put the child back into God's hand's to do the rest.

Ever LeBlanc

Untitled

Too much has happened in my life . . . a new relation, an ex-wife, a
single parent, the mom and dad, - one minute happy, the next is sad.
I'm all of these - don't you see? I'm on the brink of insanity.
I feel lost and I'm confused - my head is spinning, I've blown a fuse.
It's too much for me to bare - a padded room - I'm almost there.
Feelings dancing in my brain - I can't get off this speeding train.
I stand at the door and think I'll jump - my heart begins to really
pump - the blood goes rushing through my veins - Let me off - no more
pain! My existence flashes by - tears swell up in my eyes - beads
of sweat upon my brow - I know I'll make it but I don't know how.
Numbness engulfs my heart and soul - I've got to get it in control
Just please don't leave me as a friend, I need you now don't let it
end. I won't always be this way . . . the time will come when I can say . . .
I'm all right I've made it through and part of that's because of you.
So thanks for your time and gentle embrace.
Thanks for wiping the tears from my face.
Thanks for listening and showing you care.
Thanks my friend for being there . . .

Donna Borup

The Flowers She Did Not See

My mother has passed away today
She was laid out beautiful to see,
In silk, she wore and flowers galore
Oh yes, flowers she did not see.

Her flowers were beautiful to behold;
They numbered thirty baskets or more,
I wouldn't have dared to have taken a one
Would have been a sin for sure.

But oh, when you think of the one who morns
For just a flowers or two
For sick persons being in beds of pain.
Or the artist, for painting a few.

I ask, what do you think of covering a grave
With beautiful flowers galore;
Only to die in a day or two
When so many persons are wanting them more
Dedicated to my mother who was an artist

Florence O. Leppin

My Lady

I came into her room silently.
She was sitting all alone
Staring out the window.
I took her hand in mine and kissed her cheek;
A smile and a glint of recognition in her eyes.
I was not sure she knew me.
"I'm Ned . . . your husband," I said.
"You used to call me Daddy."
Her feeble voice, hardly audible,
Spoke words I couldn't hear or understand.
Poor little dear, so thin and weak!

So this is what it's like to die, I thought.
Her little hand, so small and warm
Is losing its warmth as life ebbs . . .
Slowly, silently . . . her hand grows cold
And I say goodbye, but not before I told
Her we'd meet again in happier times
In a place with no pain or suffering.

Edward R. Sargent

For A Friend

Go ahead and cry, for even big boys
    shed tears of sorrow.
Let the tears flow freely now, cause soon
    they'll vanish into yearning memories.
Don't be mad or hold a grudge while
    you toil through the items left behind.
Hold onto memories good and bad;
    knowing she's in the best care available.
Her suffering was short lived and
    now as she looks down, with a smile, you'll hear.

Chuck, it's cold, dress warm . . .
Chuck, it's raining take your umbrella . . .
Chuck, could you stop and get . . .
Chuck . . .
    Chuck . . .
        Chuck . . . I love you!

Bonnie Sue Moore

The Rose Still Blooms

A rose grew where all could see,
Sheltered beside a garden wall.
And as the days passed swiftly by,
It spread its branches, straight and tall.

One day, a beam of light shone through
A crevice that had opened wide
The rose bent gently toward its warmth
Then passed beyond to the other side.

Now, you who deeply feel its loss,
Be comforted the rose blooms there,
Its beauty even greater now,
Nurtured by God's own loving care.

Memories grow
More precious still
When loved ones have to part.
And remain forever blooming
In the gardens of the heart.

Chris Rohde

His Love For Her

They both loved each other.
She was his life,
He was her life.
They both made a mistake,
They talked about it one night.
She said it was over,
But he won't take no for an answer.
He want's to fight for their relationship,
He tried to get her to understand.
She didn't listen she stared right through his tears,
He tries to talk to her but she just won't listen.
He wrote her a note and said he was sorry and that he loved her,
He is miserable without her.
He cries at night for her,
He says he's not going to give up on his love for her.

Jessica Newhouse

Magnolia Miracle

Striving tall and determined,
Short lived your beauty.
Such is life.
Blooms in rebirth, like a Baptism,
Fall to the ground to rot yet no less magnificent
In the sickly sweet decay.
Magnolia memory out of my childhood . . .
The tree so gigantic
Next to my skinny freckled form.
I reached up, small arms outstretched, pleading,
Wanting it to bend down
With it's majestic branches
And lift me up to heaven.
I believed it could happen
With all my innocent might.
A wind blew through the leaves
Disturbing the ancient sleep
And dozens of blossoms fell around me,
Angel soft petals at my feet.
It was enough.

Candace Valenti

A Father's Last Flight

A man can be many things.
Shy, lonely, courageous, or just fly their wings.
Until one day, reality begins
and you're remembering all your sins.
When you are young and full of dreams,
nothing matters, as thought it seems.
Now we're getting older and kind of frail,
everything happens, we can't even read the mail.
We lose our teeth, we lose our hair.
We stumble as we walk, it hardly seems fair.
Some of us are unable to walk,
a tube in our stomach and sometimes can't talk.
Our heart goes bad, our blood pressure's high.
Our only relief, is just a sigh.
We lose our leg and finally two.
What in the world, are we going to do?
From hospital beds to nursing homes, we travel.
"Oh, what a web we have to unravel!"
We pray to God, the angels to send,
So life can end, "Goodnight, My Friends."

Jean Hood

Dancing Joe

Down in the mine, it was dreary and dark
Sixteen horses were his charge.
Up from the mine at the end of the day
A few hours left for pleasures and play.
Home, for a bath, a hot meal, and then
Out for a walk in the park.
Five days this ritual earned him his chance
To pay for his pleasure - a weekend to dance.
No hunting or fishing for him, like his brother
He helped with the chores, made bread for his mother.
From gardens he tended in Spring and in Summer,
Jellies and preserves, mother made like no other.
Bread and his gardens were his staff for life
With muscles and strength to bear burdens and strife.
The dancing a pleasure - never a feat
Made life for Joe completely complete.

Frieda Pantuso Farinelli

When You Feel Everything

When I smell the alcohol,
Sleeping on her breath,
And I see the way she stumbles,
This woman, standing before me,
She becomes a monster in my closet.
There is so much pain inside me.
I want to curl up and sleep until it ends.
But it is so early.
And I can't cry because she can't see what's wrong.
When night finally stumbles in,
I want to kiss her,
To say good night,
But she pushes me away.
And I can't feel anything anymore.

Dorothy Neagle

She chews on the straw and rattles the ice cubes,
slurps watery remains of her coke
Glances around at the tables beside her,
and slowly lights up a smoke.
She sees the tall man walking in through the door,
She knows that he sees her, too,
She tries to look sexy, and gives him a wink,
but her face has begun to turn blue.
An ice cube has lodged itself in her throat,
She tries to breathe but cannot,
As she falls to the floor, she knows very well
Her chances with him have been shot.
"How disgraceful," she thought, "he's watching me die,"
As her fingertips started to tingle,
And what did she think as her soul slipped away?
"I wonder if he was single . . . ?"

Jessica Higgins

Treasure Of A Lifetime

So many troubled words I say,
so many frowns along the way,
so much time till another day,
to say I'm sorry, if I may.
So many laughs we've shared,
so many wars we've declared,
something held us together,
and now I realized that our friendship was so dear.
To cherish,
and to care . . .

Di Wang

Lunch Room Food

Lunch room food
Smelly belly stale stinky
bread, it smells like some kid is dead.

A littered floor that blocks
the door. Bursting chomping chocking and more.
Please let me out the door.

Line cutters, head butters
and hair, netted helpers

Greasy smelly sticky
food no one wants to eat that dude.

Dingy dirty stinky
table please don't make me sit I'm not able.

From dirty faces to unclean places.

No one is happy and no one is said but whatever
you do don't make the cook mad

The food is already very
bad from the start from mystery meat
to stinky feet this is not the place
where I want to eat

Brandi Ciullo

Who Is Me?

   Once a child was born filled with
smiles and love to give, only to be taken away by love.

   Enter a part to deal with the pain and suffering, scared and
afraid to die.

   To help she splits again to cope
with the horrible truths, keeping facts.
Strong and alone enters another to
ease the pain with laughter and play.

   One to perform the acts that is
called for her to do "Out of love".
Three to deal with everyday things,
and others to help to forget.

   But who is me I ask? Havoc runs
wild, life a mess, when will it end? Is it
you or is it me, could it just be I? Is it
we that is you and me or only just I?

   The child within knows she saw it all.
"The children are the ones who is
really me and time is the answer to who is me?"

Cynthia Lynn Price

This Empty Feeling

Here alone in the night, only light I see.
Smoky shaft of moonlight creeping over me.
Lord, it's unreal,
How empty a bed can feel.

Roll back my mind to those wild times;
The smell of weed, the taste of wine,
And your hot body
Throbbing against mine.

I can still see the fire in your eyes,
Can still hear your moaning and sighs
My body aches.
My soul cries.

No I guess you couldn't call it love.
But there ain't a better word I can think of.
And no words can describe
This empty feeling inside.

Alan Tetrteault

Marjorie-Elyn

Love can't be bought and paid for . . . or alas, it turns to sand . . .
So, as you curl into a ball . . . please try to understand . . .
I shall work hard at hardening . . . this broken heart of mine . . .
But you . . . will you remember . . . Do you promise you'll be fine?
Yes, you were my one reason to come home when day was through . . .
Your soft Meow at our front door . . . made certain that I knew . . .
How much you loved your Mommie . . . And how happy we both were . . .
In the silent chambers of my heart . . . I hear your tender purr . . .
I do not know who bought you . . . And I hope I never know . . .
For with her sordid money . . . she snuffed out a priceless glow . . .
That once lived here . . . within these walls . . . A love so pure and free . . .
An epic love . . . A chapter closed . . . my Marjorie-Elyn and me . . .

Catherine Patrick-Newman

Angel

Oh to see an angel bathed in the light,
so beautiful a woman, tis hard on the eyes . . .
With hair so golden and pure,
serenity is in the air . . .
To watch her graceful flight,
as she passes thru a meadow, flying home to God . . .
If only I could see —
To be able to touch . . .
I wonder could that ever be?
You are my angel - Identical in every way . . .
your beauty surpasses those of any other woman . . .

   May the wings of love
   Bring you back to me.
   May God bless my soul
   For I have found my true mate.

Joseph Forlenza

The Soils Of Home

I haven't touched the soils of home for a century . . .
so it seems.
Blind I am to it.
Wanting I am of it.

I haven't touched the soils of home in my thoughts for one minute . . .
or rather one second, so it seems . . .
The feel of it, earthy and sticky.
The smell of it, damp and rich.
Against my skin, it's rough and welcome.

I have never left and soils of home, for it is where my spirit dwells.
And this I know:
In the corners of my mind it stretches, bends and comforts.
A hearth of woeful pleasures, it ignites my dreams.
Stoking in me the fire of home, that I never abandoned.
The soils of home lodged within me.

Illya L. Azaroff

The Holocaust

Down through the ages,
So say the Sages,
Jews were deprived of all their wages.
Then, in Hitler's Germany,
That was done to the extreme,
It was a nightmare and not a dream.
Mother was taken from father and son.
Gas chambers were for every one.
For cruelty, Hitler had no rival.
But God's children learned the power of survival.
Faith and goodness will prevail.
The power of prayer will never fail.
We'll be brave and we will pray,
Now that we're in the U.S.A.

Inge Levy

Our Journey

There is always so little time to share and spare
　So let's do the country, so we can see
　How wonderful this life can be.
Let's stop here and there - enjoy it all as best we can.

We will cruise the spaces wide, then decide to stop or ride.
　To do a visit here and there, and rest a night or two.

For all too soon good things come to an end
　With so little time to spend.

We will look back to where we have been
　And to what we have seen in the joyous time of
　Togetherness that will be missed.

There in the sunshine and through fields of flowing grain
　We'll look forward to the Autumn's rain.

And then look up to the soaring birds in flight,
　To the heavenly skies and stars at night.
It is there where each of us will meet again.

　　Blanche A. Cook

To My Wonderful Parents

I thank our Heavenly Father, for parents like mine,
So loving, respectable, sweet and kind,
They carried me to church when I was small,
And taught me about Jesus, who died for us all,
The scars on my shoulder meant many a sleepless night,
While you both rocked me and held me so very tight,
You are the best parents a child ever had,
I love you Mom, I love you Dad,
My childhood days were such happy ones,
There was so much love and lots of fun,
Your getting older now, and up in the years,
And to see one of you sick, brings to my eyes tears,
Just trust in the Lord and walk in the light,
And all your tomorrows will be happy and bright,
Although there may be some pain and some strife,
But just living for Jesus means eternal life,
I thank you for the rules that you had,
I did not understand then, but now I'm glad,
I can't do for you both as much as I'd like to,
But just wanted to tell you, how much I love both of you.

　　Barbara Walker

My Dear Child

Blowing breezes through the trees,
so much distance between you and me.
Flowers blooming in the sun,
spring is here, your life is done.
Grass is growing with the rain,
be near me now, feel my pain.
Children's laughter, lives of new hope.
Alone in my sorrows, trying to cope.
Skies are threatening, a storm they warn.
My love so simple, so different than norm.
Thunder booms and lightening shatters.
You're dead in heaven with all that matters.
Skies are clearing, a new day has sprung.
Your life I treasured, your praises I've sung.
Blowing breezes through the trees,
each whispering wind carrying you further from me.

　　Kara Lynne Bandy

Untitled

Eyes that sparkle and shine in the night.
So soft and cuddly, when I squeeze him tight.
His eyes are brown, and so are his ears.
Knowing he's there take away my fears.
Each time I squeeze him tight, he knows I care.
Who is he? . . . my big brown teddy bear!

　　Diane Sturdivant

Ella

I knew her not but feel I do,
So much of her she left in you.
Ella's son, that's who you are,
Though she died in birth and left a scar.
What greater gift could a mother give,
Than her own life that a child might live?
Her absence felt with great despair,
Diminished not her love and care.
For she's been with you all these years,
She's seen your joys, she's felt your tears.
The watch goes on with love and pride,
Such odds against you! All defied!
The love, the joy, that's always there,
She left with you for me to share.
In Ella's debt I'll always be,
So much of you she's given me.
She's far away and yet so near,
"I love you Mom" she's there to hear.
Yes, you and I, we have each other,
And also share your loving Mother.

　　Dianne Flack

Smile

Twenty-nine years from one years old.
So much time passed, with nothing to show.
Living for the day, and too wild to care
What will happen in my senior years.

Thirty whole years from one years old.
Noticed the loneliness of elders alone.
Yearning for a partner to share my life.
Someone to stand beside me, everything
would be all-right.

Thirty-one years from one year old.
Found that someone I was searching for.
Sharing ideas, hopes and dreams; with
the one that was meant for me.

Thirty-two years from one years old.
Now we are blessed with what we have sewn.
Finding true happiness, that we wished would come;
We both just smile at our son who is one.

　　Jim Bailey

Oyster Bay Wedding Day

Oyster bay enclaves a perfect day for a wedding
Soft green dampness from the park glistens anew
While salty ocean breezes wash ashore with the drift
Approaching midday an island not alone knew the panoramic view.

Darkly tinted windows of the silver limousine in stealth
Matching blue skies shimmering hue with the haze of the waves melt.
Whose white caps stretch to the top of the cliff
Leaving behind the reception party and getaway trip.

Newly laid wedding vows in their holy sweet anoint
Humbly remain amidst the one-way drive to look-out point.

Rows of stones follow the path across on foot
Aside a mysterious minstrel wallowing unrequited love
Slipped discs, gray wood structures, dainty debutante gloves
Tranquility transgressing the waters now raging the cove.

Unknowingly swept away with the drone of a helicopter in air
An abducted misfortune unseen only in the depths of despair
The sun set lows behind a long-forsaken stream
Leading to an ocean under veil as if lost in a dream.

　　Jena A. Summer

Eagles

His powerful wings lifted in thankful praise, the endangered eagle
soars upward to heaven through life's endless, offering blue sky;
lowered in submission, he glides downward towards the earth's gifts,
skipping lightly over green tree tops.

Reaching gently for his mate, she joins in flight under a watchful
and protective eye, their feathers ruffled, enduring the gusty winds.

Showing no weariness, they dance gracefully among the white, cotton
candy clouds and warm rays of the sun; their powerful claws meet
the challenge of survival; a balance of work and play is achieved.

Illuminated against dark mystery, they shed the tears of the night.
Peaceful in their surroundings, sharing the cave's secrets, they
lay safely cradled in the arms of the towering mountains whose
intimidating shadows are thrown carelessly.

Screams of love, uncertainty, fear and security float through the
air with whispered comfort and goodnights echoing softly.

Janie Carol Muennink-Fagan

Untitled

A mixed girl living in a truly mixed-up world.
Society defining race, lifestyles and our
pursuit of pleasure.
Life is now not our own.
All politics, renters of property,
never the owners, dreamers instead
of achievers. We've learned to settle for things
never pushing issues. We never use to walk away from
battles worth fighting for, losing our passion
and desires, we use to have as
red-blooded Americans. We once were so
proud and dignified. Now it's a race war,
a world of hell bent people, either out for
themselves or too preoccupied to care.
God Bless America!

Catherine Anderson

Untitled

In our hearts, there are many rooms.
Some contain loves and some contain glooms.

As we walk down the hall and remember our past,
We lock many doors and loose the keys with a cast.
This room is bitterness, that one is hate,
The one over there is parents and that one's called fate.

Though life's experiences both good and bad,
We look at the closed rooms that we once had.

And with every room we've locked up tight,
Satan takes his lasting bite.

You see God gives each heart a special design;
For our hearts are like mansions, luxurious and divine.

Is it fun to live in a house and be trapped in the den?
So why don't we reopen doors and learn to live again!

Blake Altman

Friendship Is . . .

Someone who always listens
Someone who's personality glistens
Someone who always cares
Someone who always shares
Someone who's smiles are like the suns rays
Someone who's unique in so many ways
Someone who's full of love
Someone who reminds you of a pure white dove

Detta Milnar

It Must Have Been Love

We've been together for 31 years.
Some have been happy some full of tears
We have four beautiful children who are dear to our hearts.
Who help keep us together instead of apart.
Now that we're older and look back on our past.
And see our mistakes oh how did it last.
it must have been love a true love so strong.
That has kept us together for so long.
If we are blessed to grow old together
Our mistakes from the past will make it much better.
Cause you can't see then when your so young.
You always call it I'm just having fun.
If 31 more years dear we still have to live.
Instead of just taking we bath have to give
And our Golden years can be joy untold.
Now that we've realized we're both growing old,
If I showed lose you it would be a great loss,
but don't push your luck dear cause I'm still the boss.

Audrey Sutphin

The Gull

Passive, submissive, watch the gull ride,
    Some men's traits personified.
Never to beat a high wind in the head,
    Blown off course, an acceptance instead.

Floating through life at ease in the breeze,
    Where do they go, when the lakes freeze.
Regal in beauty and simplicity,
    Quest the skies, soaring and free.

Take what is offered, a scavenger's lot,
    Caw coarse and mean, when a meal is lost.
Many people are like gulls, you see,
    Scooping up what's offered when boast they are free.

Gerald E. Doubet

A Song Before Dawn

A cardinal was singing today, before the total dawn;
Some might say he's misinformed;
But perhaps it's that his faith is strong;
And feels he can face the complete unknown.

Frieda Wyatt

Together Forever

Love's been described in many ways some good and others bad.
Some say its a gamble that you take that often leaves you sad.

Others say it's like a journey, a road we all walk down.
This time will your dream come true or will your smiles just
Turn to frowns?

The path I chose led straight to you, a choice that I'm quiet
Certain,
Was aided by the unseen hand that knew my heart was searching.

Now we walk together, hand in hand down life's road,
Prayful about tomorrow, unsure what the future holds.

Will our road be one that's rough, full of turn and curves ahead?
Or simply wind its way through trouble, as a needle pulling
Thread.

Whatever lies ahead, all the blows that life can give,

I'll have the sweet assurance, that I walk with my best friend.

Gregg Miles

513

Untitled

This is not the same as it was awhile ago
Some think that it is just a game to be played
All I can say is go day by day
You must not listen to others always pay attention to your heart

We have all seen people come and go
Loved ones walk in and out the door
So take some advice take a chance with your life
Remember that you don't always have to say good-bye

Know that nothing remains the same and we are all to blame
So think before you sink
This is what was given to us
Time is more than just a clock or a watch
It is a gift that GOD has given to the both of us

As you turn around or walk down that long road
You will know that you will never walk alone

For time is the friend that will be
until the very end
Charlotte Johnston

Lord, Help Us Win The War

Oh Lord, help us win this war. Oh, be with us till we die.
Someday, make us free from them all take us back to the ones
We love so true and call our own.
Make it so beautiful there that we will never more roam.

Oh Lord, give us strength to fight back to win this war.
When the war is over, we will thank the Lord for the glory and power
He gave us to carry on.

Glory to the Lord, glory to the Lord. Glory to the Lord that gave
Us peace to go back home.
Glory to the Lord that gave us power to win this war. We thank the
Lord in heaven that gave us peace so we could go back home — never
More to roam.

Allen F. Herren

Letting Go

When we first got together. I thought I found
someone . . . I thought I found a friend whom I
could poor my heart to . . . and that you would
look at me with unprejudiced eyes . . .
But, I was naive enough to think that you
actually liked me, I don't know if you felt
obligated to me not to hurt my feelings . . . If
you thought you were doing a good deed, doing
me a favor, you made a massive mistake.
Damn you, you hurt me, I cry at night, I
never did before, I know it sounds stupid
because we never had anything; did we . . .? I
should've known not to smile to show myself
or emotions . . .
Fairy tales don't come true do they . . . I
dropped my shield, and let you peak inside of
my magical land of dreams, I'm sorry that
I burdened you, and I'm sorry I let you
fall into my soul . . .
Jennifer R. Sentz

Again . . .

The watching eyes of a thousand
    souls, the sadness seems to open new holes.
I feel myself falling as the words
    resound, the only way to go is down.
The blackness rolls over me in waves,
    it's my sea my wind my night that saves.
Brandy Wagner

Friend

A friend is a companion, pal, or mate,
someone to understand, realize and appreciate.
A friend will listen to what you have to say
whose continuous love is like a golden ray.

When you are in pain and fear,
they care enough to linger near.
A true friend will not leave you alone
though it tears their heart to hear your moan.

And when you are happy and full of glee,
a friend will be with you. He will not flee.
And when you have finally achieved fame,
a friend will be happy you fulfilled your aim.

A friend will be with you night or day,
if not in body, in spirit anyway.
Your happiness is important but also your fear,
That's when the word friend is especially dear.
June Wiley

Time Bomb

Tick tock tick tock
someone's come to adjust my clock
five more minutes till the big bang

my head so dead
five more minutes till I'm put to bed
seems as though my luck ran out before it even came

I'm a time bomb
I'm an explosion waiting to happen
I'm a time bomb

tock tick tock tick
being here is makin' me sick
feeling every second, the pounding in my brain

it's all me, all you
my friends, my family, and the media too
pressure pressure pressure till you go insane

I'm a time bomb
I'm an explosion waiting to happen
I'm a time bomb
Jessy Napper

"Forever More"

I witnessed something that was very sad
Something that would not make you glad
I stood in the corner of the room
Although standing by the door
Was someone I will love forever more
I stood there with flashes running through my head
The horror, the pain, the dread
I stood there feeling all alone.
Frightened and not knowing what would happen next
As a tear ran down my cheek I knew what would happen next
The scares, the screams, the pain, proved how sad it was
After the boom, the tears, I immediately fell to the floor
I grabbed his hand and his last words were, I'll love you forever more
As we walked down the hill in our dark and black clothes
The words of forever more ran through my head
There was a lonely chanting sound
As his casket was buried beneath the ground.
Alicyndra Valencia

Voices Of Love

The voice in your eyes, your human touch,
somewhere I've never seen.
When I first met you, I didn't see,
how bitter, how cold, how angry I could be.
I couldn't look at you and see, that softness, of love in your
eyes, yet still hold all that armor up.
The warmth in your eyes, melted threw that cold steel,
your gentle voice, opened my heart,
layer by layer, till a seed appeared,
the precious child, very dear.
The sparkle of love, in your eyes,
the sunshine, that helped it grow.
In morning light, I found the rose,
the meaning of, light and life.
Reclaiming my faith, leaving my fires of hell,
no longer, fearing my nights.
That voice in your eyes, opened the flowers of life,
those petals, never to close.
Your human touch, reached threw my darkness,
gently holding the petals, as the roses touched.

Debra Mulholland Strom

Pleasant Dreams

Sleep succumbs my quivering eyelids taking me off somewhere.
Somewhere where dark prevails over light.
And light is dark and dark is light.
Darkness thick, people sick, bitter hatred, words come quick.
A world where it seems to be with no sensitivity.
Children's screams, bad dreams, apprehensibility.
Be still my shaking body! Be still my trembling hands!
My tears are hailing, dark demons wailing.
Will someone break these bands?
But no one's there, not one brave soul.
No one to shake me, not one to wake me. It's up to me to free myself.
Then wake my body, fight the dark.
Then sweat my body, sweat away the pain.
I awake in complete solitude. I cry away my freakish attitude.
Stay out damn pain, don't dare stay.
For now tis morning, a brand new day.
Push out the darkness. Let the day light in.
Does this darkness ever end?
I'm falling, I'm falling through complete nothing, then . . . light.
'Twas it a dream or am I dead?

Anjella Bailey

Ode To The Mourning Dove

Sweet bird of peace and love.
  Song bird thou never were,
But I think that I shall never hear
  A sweeter sound than thy soft cooing.
Like rare pearls of sound so soothing.
  That drift across the sea of space,
Between my home and thy nesting place.

  Thy voice is poured out just at dawn
And floats over the grassy lawn,
  As if to break the silence of the night
And announce the very first light
  Of a brand new lovely day,
In a hauntingly beautiful way.

  There seems to be some primal bond
That makes me feel so fond,
  Of thee sweet bird of peace and love;
Please dear God let no one hurt or destroy
  These precious, priceless doves.
Who give to everyone so much earthly joy.

Billie Perry Prpich

Cherish

The music of spring time is in the air.
Songs of love birds sing this dawn.
Your beauty is that of a rose.
Soft as the petals strong as the stems.
There is a pot of gold at the rainbows end.
But, for me you are the treasure I seek.
We will grow as one with every kiss.
Prosperity is in the future for us.

James R. Downing II

A Winter Wonderland

The snow flutters down softly and it will
  soon accumulate on the ground.
It covers all the hovels, trash, and
  debris that is scattered all around

To look at it when the sun comes out, is
  looking at a winter wonderland.
The snow has covered everything; making it
  all beautiful and seemingly grand.

The snow sparkles like diamonds; the
  rivers and creeks are all iced over.
The trees and the shrubs also sparkle and
  glimmer with all that cover.

The children ice-skating on the ponds and
  lakes, pretending to be champs.
Their dreams may come true, of the Olympic
  gold medal, they have their chance.

You stop and stare in awe and marvel at
  all the beauty that is near.
It's hard to comprehend how God brings
  this miracle each and every year.

Ada Stein

The View From An Isuzu

Lovely Nova Scotia, so beautiful to see,
Soon became another exercise in stupidity.
We went four wheel driving, Jim, me, and the dogs,
having lots of fun 'til we got stuck out in the bogs.
A nice man named Alan, who came from around there,
tried his best to get us out. It's nice that strangers care.
His uncle's front-end loader could not pull out the truck,
so I just sat there with the dogs, waiting; we were stuck!
An hour passed by quickly, there was nothing I could do.
I composed this little poem and enjoyed the view.
I hoped we be out shortly; I was tired, I was cold
(though I could see the humor in it, if the truth be told.)
Four men came; they looked, they talked and then they walked away.
Oh how I wished that they could get us out of there that day.
Mr. Reid had a wench truck with 500 feet of chain
and as luck would have it, we got out before the rain.
Thank God for trucks with wenches, they really saved the day.
And it was even covered by my Triple A!
We learned our lesson very well and can clearly say
that once we found the MARKED TRAIL WE NEVER MORE DID STRAY.

Angela Kathleen Meister

Constraints

How are we to break the bonds of constraints upon our
souls? By appealing to man to define God as ultimately just
and fare, beseeching man's soul, not degrading his "superior
nature," but up-lifting it by acknowledging that women's
superior nature can only elevate man to his peak, which is
his maximum potential. By raising woman to equal status
amassing woman to their full potential of equality,
dissuading man with values of life and justice equally
linking man and woman.

Elizabeth Lowry

Planting Seed

Plant a see and watch it grow,
Sow a seed and watch it show.
Appears to me that I must find;
a treasure of the seed.
Plant the seed in firm soil;
Feed the seed by listening for the sound,
of God's voice all around.

Hidden treasure made real to me,
soon will produce a fruitful tree.
How can this be that a tiny seed,
could release in me,
a faith in God that will forever be.
Which brings me back to that seed in my heart;
that with the sound of God's voice,
will be an eternal force!
Dimi Waters

Speak True

Speak true to the world around you
Speak true from the heart beating inside of you
Speak true from the soul that guides you
Speak true to the community reaching out to you
Speak true about your loved one beside you
Freeing the soul is everyone's continued goal
Becoming one to make the mind and body whole
Don't be ashamed or afraid of how other's will view you
Thank's for the honesty that has been so revealing
Be proud of your achievements throughout this process
We're no different from the rest
We'll strive to be our best
We truly know the meaning of pride, respect, and dignity
This is a reminder to embrace life
There are endless possibilities
Continue to speak the language that represents meaning
in every moment of our lives.
Donna E. King

I Remember

I was young the day you went away, but I still remember the special days.
I remember your thinning red hair, and watching T.V. with you in your chair.
There is one memory I wish I could shake, I keep hoping I'm
    dreaming and soon I'll awake.
I remember all too well the day you died, Oh Lord, how long I did cry.
It hurts so deep, and it's hurt for so long, before I knew it
    my best friend was gone.
I miss you and I'll always love you dearly, it's all a part of life I
    know to clearly.
I guess what I'm trying to say, I love and miss you Dad, more and
    more everyday.
Debra Billen

Black

Jet black ink from a pen of mystery
Spills out onto a tapestry of the unknown.
Sparkling, white paint chips
Are like diamonds aloft this ebony universe.
Secretly, large drops revolve
Around a master of their origin.
The inhaling of nothingness
Makes for a baffled mind.
So much undiscovered . . . too much discovered.
The raging secrecy of the dark outer space
Is much too fascinating to spoil with knowledge.
When gazing into the damp night,
Think not what you know,
Only what you don't.
Kamela S. Gladich

Faerie Dream . . .

Slip into the darkened night and stand within the rain,
    Spread your arms and close your eyes: break out from the grain.

Dance with me below the moon where flitting shadow's shorn
    lie with me below the stars and await the misty morn.

Run among the lonely trees without a single sound . . .
    When angels cry and heaven breaks upon what we have found.

Let the earth recede from your feet, and the sky slip to your hands
    Where freedom calls in every voice the echoes from the lands.

Fly upon a singing breeze and ride upon the waves
    Feel their power as they call to the dark, forbidding caves.

Immerse beneath the clinging depths or sprint across the sand,
    Freedom's King and Queen shall wear crowns of seashell strand.

Mistress of the moon is she, and Master of the light:
    Crowned; they dance in silv'ry paths above the realm of night.

Sit the thrown to slip away, while faeries wave and weep,
    To return to chains of window panes and awake from fitful sleep.

But not alone do you lie, there plays the night's full tune . . .
    And across the skies and horizon lies the sister: awaiting moon.
Alicia Milan

The Magic Of Love

The magic of love strikes again and again
Spreading warmth and happiness throughout the land
It gives you hope and courage and takes away all fear
It brings you closer to the ones you hold so dear
You feel the magic of its touch as love begins to flow
You hear laughter and music as love begins to grow
Love will rescue you from a sea of hurt and pain
It will put joy in your heart that you can't even explain
Love makes you feel wonderful, excited and even sad
It feels so good but yet love can hurt so bad
It will take you from the valley to the top of the highest mountain
It will over rule your senses like an ever flowing fountain
Love know no boundaries, it will not nor cannot be contained
No one can measure nor number, the couples that love has
sustained
Color has no bearing on the path that love takes
Its not governed by our demands or even our foolish mistakes
Love won't stop because the one you love don't care anymore
It will compel you to keep loving just as you've done before
No, the magic of love will never leave you nor grow old
Even if the flame in ones heart go out, the magic won't turn cold
James M. Pegues

The Goddess

Her eyes are those of a jaguar
stalking its prey
waiting for the moment when it will pounce
devouring your soul
taking it all
leaving an abyss

Her hair is finely woven into her head
it is perfection at its finest
the long locks are whispering serpents
hissing for you to come forward
so that they might bring about your hearts demise

Her seductive body entangle's your whole mind
in the web of a black widow
where it spins round you
binding every thought to this goddess
Frost Smith

East Coast Seduction

Alone, barefoot
standing at the edge
late night tide washing over my feet.
Undertow pulling
relentless;
gently luring me out
into her wild, untamed splendor.
Spellbound;
blind to her merciless fury
her fragrant elixir seduces me.
Warm, sultry breezes caress
my sun kissed body.
Mesmerized;
I watch the full moon rise
taking his rightful place among the stars.
Dazzling brilliance dances across
the ocean
in all her magnificent glory;
such a formidable beauty
humbles me.

Colette Barnhouse

Cardinals

I remember the Cardinals so red and bright
Standing out like a traffic light
Against a blanket of gray and brown
Brightening the winters in my Iowa hometown.

They'd always be at the backyard feeder
Leading the group with their cherry song
Dressing the trees with the essence of Christmas
Soft red feathers and furry down.

I'll always remember the cardinals
Etched in my mind like the morning frost
Warmed by the memories of childhood
So pleasant they will ne'er be lost.

Betty J. Townsend

The Sun And The Moon

The beautiful sun lights up the sky,
The birds are happy and float through the sky.
The grasshoppers jump through the nice green grass,
And have a contest to see who wins.

The yellow moon comes out to play,
The stars come out and dance in the sky.
The sky turns black as a bicycle tire rolling down the highway.
One, two, three, four, go black sky go.
Five, six, seven, Eight, the black sky disappears.

Amber Churnick

Humanity's End

With my bloody cheek on the dirt I lie,
staring longingly at the sky.
Blood mixes with oil as it drips down my face,
and it's their fault.
They built better weapons to fit their selfish desires.
And now, we must burn in the fires of hate and distrust.

A light gust blows across this wasteland,
which was once a beautiful grassland.
The sun sets slowly, giving way to night.
The day ends, but the war rages on.

The immortal dove has died.

Candice Carter

The Sky

Here I lay
staring up into the clouds; so many shapes a dog chasing a ball
there's a lady with a purse, she's walking alone on the street,
waiting for a bus I look up for a longer time . . . soon a fish develops I
see him dancing as a fisherman catches him The sky is so peaceful . . .
I see a circus clown juggling three tennis balls wearing a big red
Nose and suit
There's a big fat elephant jumping through a hoop; I watch him as
He slowly fades

The sky is so peaceful . . .

But then I take my eyes away from the sky and focus on the world
Around me . . . the dog is being chased by men who desire his death the
woman with the pursue is standing by a man who want's to kill
Her for her $$ The bus she was waiting for blows black smelly air that makes
me Sneeze . . . There's a struggling fish trying to free itself from a
plastic pop Ring by a pond . . . The vandalized circus tent covered in
spray paint and bad words holds An elephant in chains being
beaten to do a trick . . .
He gives a loud cry-and just gets beaten harder . . .

Sad and depressed, I slowly turn back to the sky . . .
The sky is so peaceful . . .

Helee Hillman

"Stormy Days"

The sea is like love's torment.
Storms begin with an angry shout.
Followed by the waves arguing with the shore,
Pulling towards each other, then backing away.
Neither force giving, just scattering remains on the sand.
When it's over, quiet calm descends in the night.
And the debris that was thrown out, scattered,
Is taken back to the bottom and forgotten.

Ilene R. Bush

America's Forgotten Minority "Native Americans"

Once you were a proud people;
Straight and tall.
Until "White eyes" came and took it all.

Willing to live side by side,
Giving and sharing, their way of life

Big Foot, Black Kettle, Sitting Bull,
Chiefs of their tribes, wanted peace but instead they died.

Red Cloud said that day,
"I was abused and slandered for my way."

Uprooted from our homes,
To be sent west and left there to die
Pushed and prodded along the way
Cold and starving, thousands died along the way.

Carolyn Brady

Summer Is Gone

The sun is red and sad
Summer is gone I am glad!
The air is cool and sweet.
The grass is brown from the heat.

Everything is different in the fall,
The children's voices, in play no longer call.
The trees are red, orange and brown
In the morning there is frost on the grown.

The crisp cold smell of winter is near.
New songs from the birds I hear.
The days grow short and the nights long
Yes, winter is on it's way with a new song

June Fields

A Step Into the Future

A step into the future, a glimpse into the past.
Standing here together wanting this moment to last.
With thoughts of our childhood memories
Fresh in our minds, frightened to take the
first big step and leave our friends behind.
As our future brightens our pasts fade.
We say goodbye to the best friends.
We have waited for this moment for so long,
It is now time for us to sing our theme song.
We have finally reached our goal that we sat so high.
It is finally our turn to take the leap and fly.
Now the world sits in the palm of our hands
We all now need to take our big stand.
Our hearts sadden as the time grows near.
We hold each others hands as our eyes fill with tears
We hug each other and start to cry.
We all now realize it's time to say good-bye.
Our memories will live forever more
Best of Luck, Class 2/96 Mountaineer Challenge Academy

Brandi Speaks

For My Mother

The original mother
strong - willed
sweet
gentle and caring
The woman sprung from the soil of the land
Made in God's image
The original mother
Black, African - which are one and the same
A woman of spiritual and physical strength
She tilled the land
and built our house
but still had time to hear
our sorrows, our woes and comfort us
her tears watered us
as we were fresh, young shoots
and we grew because of her
The original mother
and yet she wasn't superwoman
she was alive, is alive and as a matter of fact . . .
THERE SHE IS!

Akasemi Newsome

Lonesome Phase

Feeling so heartbroken.
Stuck in one place.
Recreating a world,
That has never took place.
Tried to stand proud,
And not below.
Holding in your breath,
So your feelings won't show.
Let it all out, and let it out with a shout.
Don't mind the others,
Let them fall under.
Around some place,
You'll win the race.
Your main concerns,
Will or should be to learn.
The more you worry will turn into stress,
At those standards you'll never become the best.
So remember to say "I shall stand tall always"
Don't make your day fall in to a Lonesome Phase,
Or you'll be lonely for days in all kind of ways.

Chantel Haney

God's Helper

Sitting in the living room floor I begin to see sadness,
suddenly all around me. No one came instantly to my side to explain
I was just a child.
People came to my house; many at once.
I've never had this much company.

All the children were sent to play with me.
They, like me were cheerful and happy,
unlike the adults who are sad, quiet, and grimm.
Among all the company I never noticed my father was not home.
Maybe he was working late again.

Now all of the people are leaving; the children
must go also. But the memories linger, of a happy day of
playing and many flowers which had arrived from somewhere.
Beautiful, Beautiful flowers!

My mother is still sad. She softly combs my hair.
I ask "Where is Daddy?" Mother replies, "He is not
coming home anymore. He is working with God."
What a beautiful day!

Dawn Catron

The Wind

I sit in the field,
swallowed by the long green grass and the smiling daisies.
I think,
I reflect,
I ponder,
I regret.
In the distance I see
the long green grass start to sway gently to and fro,
like the waves of the ocean.
It's coming,
I rejoice in its arrival.
The wind!
Gently it touches my face,
Oh, how I love the wind!
Take me with you, I beg,
But the wind only whispers in my ear,
You cannot come with me; for you know not where I go.
And then the wind is gone and I am again alone.
But I will wait for the wind to return.
Oh, how I love the wind!

Elizabeth Julia Baker

Feelings

When I am happy I'm a Cheetah,
　swift and clever
I'm a Christmas tree, fun and joyous
When I am happy I'm bright orange,
　clear and sunny
I'm a clover, lucky and rare
When I am happy I'm the number 1,000,000
　high and important
I'm copper, vulnerable and flexible
When I am happy I'm water, fast and together
When I am unhappy I'm a Kangaroo
　clumsy and awkward
I'm a thistle, sharp and prickly
When I am unhappy I'm dark brown
　mixed and confused
I'm a circle, pointless an spinning
When I am unhappy I'm a negative 25
　unimportant and insignificant
I'm granite, closed minded and hard
When I am unhappy I'm ash energyless and flat

Brad Beltz

Untitled

She looked around the room,
taking in each new face.
And thought of all she'd left behind,
when she'd come to this new place.

Leaving all her friends behind
had been really hard to do.
She'd cried for hours when she found out
her dad's job would force them to move.

At school the first day, she felt lonely,
and she thought making friends would be tough.
She sat all alone in the lunchroom,
and sat by herself on the bus.

The next day at school was different.
Some kids asked her to come play ball.
As their friendships grew she realized,
moving wasn't so bad after all.

Jessica Miller

The Golden Thread

Julia McDaniel, the quiltmaking queen
Taught me to quilt the perfect seam
I went to visit one day out of school
This day, I was learning to use a new tool
She gave me a needle and snow white thread
Before I was finished, I was sure I'd be dead
Don't take your thread and pull it to tight
It will forever be an ugly sight
The patterns for quilts are really the same
If you notice, they all have beautiful names
Each quilt is designed with more pieces and color
That is how we all will remember each other
It was time to go with a tear in my eye
She hugged me, gave me a thimble and whispered bye bye
This quilt is for you and quilted with love
The idea behind it came from above
The ideal she gave me has never died
When I finish a quilt it is always with pride
I love you Julia for the lesson in art
Your soul and my soul will never part

Betty W. Kenner

As The Door Closes . . .

As the door closes I bury my feminine side.
Tears are as close as my best friend, but appearing
with no place to hide.
They fall into the palms of my hand.
The appearance of my eyes are like a glass window
as someone stares aimlessly inside.

My heart is broken with no key to spare, the pathway
to my heart is damned and no one seems to care.
He has departed and left me alone, my head is buried,
my voice, monotone.
I will always love him more than he'll ever know,
I wish he never left, never decided to go.
As the door closes . . .

Catina L. Sinches

The Leaves

Look at the leaves on the tippy tops of the trees. They
sway so gently down to the warm surface of earth. The
bugs have their fun in the leaves, too. They play games in
the leaves, avoiding the silky cobwebs hanging in the
sunlight. How pretty it is when the leaves change colors
to bright green, yellow and red, leaves. All waiting their
turn to become part of a heap for you to leap in and play
for hours and hours. Just feeling the leaves crumble up in
your hand makes you shiver. Then you dance in them. It
feels like you'll want to be in the beautiful sunlight playing
in the leaves for the rest of your life.

Esme Cullen

Black Angel

Halos shines above thine head,
tears flow forming a river bed.
Hair so soft and skin so smooth,
mountains and worlds your looks do move.

When you smile the sun does shine,
making me proud that you are mine.
Your gentle whisper is a very light breeze,
heard as a song through the flowers and trees.

The glint in your eyes, the gleam in your heart,
they light the skies and make the clouds depart.
Worlds revolve and meteors soar,
but the key to life is locked in your door.

There are so many attributes that you do hold,
A culmination of all?
A PURE BLACK SOUL!

David Darden Jimmy

Success For Sale!

Success is not what you get or create.
Success is what you learn and
become along the way.
It is a process, not a tangible thing or place.
If success was a tangible thing, we
could go to the store and buy a case.
If success was a place, we could go to
the travel agent, purchase a ticket and celebrate.
Life would be easier if
success was a thing or place,
But what meaning or lessons would
the journey have, if success was as easy
as buying a piece of cake?

Dean Kacher

Jimmy

Jimmy had a sly sense of humor. Hell, half the time you couldn't
   tell if he was serious or not.
Jimmy was always squared away. His gear was in perfect shape as
   was his rifle.
Jimmy knew why he was here. He would tell us over and over so
we wouldn't forget.
Jimmy brought all the joy that was his with him. He shared that with us.
Jimmy told us of his family. He even passed around cookies his mom had sent.
Jimmy helped us on patrol with our heavy loads. He always
carried more than his own weight.
Jimmy, with a hole in his head, was carried by his friends. Jimmy
   was going home to his family where he belonged.

Bill Di Roma

Into Me

Look into my eyes
tell me
can you see my faith, hope
can you see me
my soul
look into my eyes
do they hide the pain
touch my brown skin, feel the strength
look upon my face
look at me and see my people
see through my eyes the never ending struggle for freedom
look at my scars and feel the pain endured
years of hard work and hard times
look at me
I am alive
full of my past, hungry for my future
look into my eyes
tell me what do you see
do you see my soul
can you feel me?

Callie Jean Johnson

Untitled

I follow the dents in these prison walls,
Tempt, me Lord not from the outside calls
I'm seeing you now, but feeling you more
Yet I can't seem to enter your heavenly door,
Help me dear Lord, save my sinful soul
For I'm ready to exit my sinful hole,
I'm lost in your beauty, as I reach for the skies
Please wake me before I drown in my cries,
When the evil one comes to me in the dark
"SHUT UP" I say for here you no longer mark,
He's chasing me, chasing me, he's in my head
Get away evil one, to me you are dead.
Fly down to your hell get out of my cell,
I no longer want you, it's you I rebuke
I want my life to change for the heavenly Duke.

Andrea Marie Thompson

Untitled

Ten little fingers
Ten little toes
Mighty like the petals of a rose
God in his mercy has made it so
Earth, with a wee bit of heaven here below.

Helen Rielley

Sonnet For My Daughter Upon Having Her Daughter

When it comes to having babies there is nothing any greater
Than the longing of a mother knowing she can hold her baby later.
All the months and months of waiting, then the days go slipping by —
Into hours and then minutes, then she hears her baby cry!
Seems like only yesterday when I held you close to me.
And now, my dear, you'll understand what mother love can be!
Enjoy every minute, dear, of your baby's first few years,
For when they are gone, they are gone, nevermore to reappear.
First she'll walk then she'll talk then off to school she'll go,
And you'll sit back and wonder, dear, was it really that long ago?
Yes, there'll be tears and laughter, and there'll be heartaches, too,
But teach her well, and love her, dear, for she's God's gift to you!

Freida E. Farrell

The Greatest Gift

What greater gift can one give today,
Than to say I love you, In every way.
I love you for each simple thing you do.
And I love you also, for merely being you.

Sometimes my love is hidden; I might not say,
What I want to express, with each passing day.
But there are no secrets here, everything is real
I want you to know, how genuinely I feel.

There's nothing more precious than my gift of love
For that's the greatest present, I give myself of.
Love has endless value; there's really no price
It cannot be duplicated, nor be given twice.

So of all the presents, that I might give to you,
Please always hold this one; special and true.
For I love you more than I could ever say.
And I would like that to be,
   Your Greatest Gift Today.

David Clark Wallace

Thank You

Dedicated to Hazel McDowell
Thank you for the things you've done
Thank you for the things I've got
You've given me so much strength
I really appreciate it a lot
You've helped me when I was happy
You've helped me when I was sad
You never gave up on me
And you never got mad
You gave me a piece of mind
When I thought that there was no such thing
I want to stand up and sing
I asked the Lord to bless me
And I wondered what he'd do
He put his hands together and for
Me he created you

Gail Matthews

I Am Blessed

Today, I count my blessings in many ways;
Thanking God for a beautiful day.
I look around and what do I see;
All the beauty that will always be.

I count my blessings one day at a time;
For there are some who do not even have a dime.
There have been some hardships throughout the years;
But I'm thankful for the ones I love so dear.

I am thankful for many things in life;
My greatest blessing goes to my wife.
I am thankful for the food we eat;
For the clothes on my back and shoes on my feet.

Sometimes we forget to thank the ones we love;
Especially our Father in Heaven above.
We are blessed to live in a land which is free;
To share our love for the world to see.

As our families get together on Thanksgiving Day,
We will be blessed in every way.
Today our blessing go to the ones we love;
But the greatest blessings come from Heaven above.

David Adams

We Remember

It was down in Dallas Texas in November 63
That an Assassins bullet struck John F. Kennedy
He was the nations president, the 35th in line
He had a wife and children John and Caroline
Oh! How the nation mourned him how the people cried
When the news flashed o'er the air our president had died.
He was working on the civil bill and was happy as you could see
Trying to straighten the country and set the negro free
But now his voice is silent his hands are cold and still
His body lies a resting in Arlington on a hill.
That was John F. Kennedy we'll not forget his name.
Even tho' he sleeps beneath the burning flame.
He will always be remembered his name in history
A great and courageous man was John F. Kennedy.

Agnes Hull

Season's Wonder

What wonderful time for the year
That brings us such glorious cheer
To all whom know what happiness is about
The feelings so great you'll want to shout
No more sadness or tears of sorrow
Only the bright hope to see tomorrow
As we dance and sing our melodies
And we pick and trim our trees
So that everyone around us will know
That soon we will see the snow
As that leave nothing us to ponder
Only the joys of the season's wonder

Jennifer D. Denson

Renewal

An interlude —at last I rest from toils
That fill each day. The rest is pure and calm.
A respite from trivial cares which spoil
The beauty all around. I feel the balm
Of relaxation cleanse my wounds in realms
None others dare to touch. So soft, so light,
It heals me through its tranquil veil. A psalm
Of praise to God for sending me by night
This blessed sustenance to wage the fight
The endless days bring forth. At times
My need is not so great; hence, less my plight.
Then once again the dawn breaks forth. The chimes
The new day tolls. So face each one as it
Appears. At dusk a new-born flame is lit.

Jack M. Stokes

"America's Babies"

Sometimes I think, how lucky I am,
That it didn't happen you me.
But why did it happen to them?
Our little children; America's babies.
America's babies were taken away,
On that sunny April day,
Why were they taken?
Lord give us a way,
To understand why America's babies were taken away.
I can't forget the images in my mind,
Of those babies, with me all the time.
America's babies were taken away,
From Moma's arms swiftly away.
Never again to hear those words whispered softly,
Never to hear again "I love you Mommy!"
Never again to hear "I love you Daddy!"
Sometimes I think that I am lucky,
But why did it happen to them?

Annette Leann Read

Silent Eulogy

My season ended with the later light
    That glanced the mountain ring about the plain
And my last gleanings occupied the sight
    Where part of me would evermore remain

For under heaven everything betides
    My time had come to die, to recommence
To seek the sheltered creviced mountainside
    To rest. To weigh. To gauge my recompense

For plain and pain and Hemet heat and wear
    Were plowed and planted in the bones of me
And honest labor matched with honest care
    Was only just a silent eulogy

And with our death we leave the sullen land
    We take the cryptic channel to accord
Obeisance to the *ultimate* command —
    The passageways of death are of the Lord

And what of me? And whither do I go?
    And does this channel open to a see
Of mighty granite round where sometime snow
    Engenders bright Yosemite?

Freeman D. Blake

Fresh Flowers

O' how beautiful it is to see
That grand ol' tree,
Standing tall aside the riverbank.

O' listen as the wind
sings sweet lullabies through the leaves,
Hear melodies of the river
trickling o'er the reeves.

So, my dear, when this body is mine no more,
Plant me there
By that grand old oak tree.

And please my love, one last request,
Now don't forget,
Lay fresh flowers,
For my head.

Brenda J. Greer

Does My Father Know My Love?

I pray to heaven above
    that my father knows my love.
He died a long time ago.
    How? I just don't know.
You see, I didn't know my father.
    He never wrote nor called, maybe I wasn't worth the bother.
But nevertheless, I think he loved me.
    My mother says I look and act like my dad,
you know, the one I never had.
Sometimes when I think of him, I just want to cry.
    The thought of not knowing him makes me want to die.
Late at night, now and then, I wish I could fly.
    I would fly to heaven and tell my father good-bye.
I pray to heaven above
    that my father knows my love.

Brandi Ann Hudson

My Dad

He's sitting there, there in the front yard. Just cleanin' potatoes in
that old chair he sits in. Got a big garden this year, lost of cukes
and tomatoes, watermelons and strawberries. Lots to do to keep him
busy in between going fishing. Has that damn arthritis so bad since he
was twenty six couldn't work a regular job, the one he did at home was
harder. Nancy, that's my mom, worked a job at the Twin Cities Arsenal,
lost of traveling everyday, took an hour and half just to get to work.
Dad took care of us six kids, cooked, cleaned, went to school meeting
when one of us acted up and took us for rides at night to calm us down,
we loved it, even if we still fought each other till 11:00 P.M. He was
always there, grumpy sometimes cause of his bones aching but always
there. Knew when we were gonna get in trouble even before we did,
used to bust us every time, he knew us so well. Everybody liked him tho,
he used to get drunk and act crazy, fun crazy, singin', dancin', puttin'
on old goofy hats. Some say I'm just like him. He told my friend
one time, "someday, someday, she's gonna really be somebody,
she's gonna makes something out of her life." He never told me
that, but made me happy inside that he said it. Cause if I'm like
him and he's somebody, then I know I'll be somebody. He's not
dead. He's with me everyday.
My dad.

Cynthia E. White

The Angona Family Reunion

You may not remember, or perhaps you don't know -
That on each Christmas Eve, to Grandma's we'd go.
Our very special reason to travel that way -
Was to wish our sweet Grandma "Happy Birthday."

We'd all gather together in her very small place,
So we could enjoy the dear smile on her face,
As she opened her gifts we all brought along
Honoring our precious lady with love and a song.

Then came the day when our Grandma went away,
And her daughter Louise kept us honoring her day.
We still came together in the very same place
To talk and to laugh and 'pizza feed' our face.

We all chattered and ate without even a care
Aunts Louise, Millie and Minnie had put food there.
They planned and cooked and washed all the dishes,
While we merely said a few Christmas wishes.

Now we have a plan that we hope you'll all okey.
To each year honor our Aunts (and Uncles) on THEIR day.
We'll do all the work and they will just eat and sit
And laugh and enjoy all their memories a bit.

Harry R. Christner

My Dream, A Horse Called Blue Dancer

The horse that could have been
The best that she could be.
One of my favorite dreams
That wasn't meant to be.

She was foaled one early April day
And that's when I learned, it was a she
She had to legs and the spirit to match
With those combined, she would be the catch.

Fast and sleek as she could be
She had her flaws and I could see
Proper training and some luck
This blue dancer could turn a black

Time was short
As it turned out to be
For one beautiful animal
No one would get to see.

Jeff Langemo

Too Much Of A Good Thing

Hey Jim, havin' a great time at the bar?
That's good. How many glasses of beer is that one?
Eight? Wow! It's getting late, Jim, I'll take you home.

What do you mean you can go home by yourself?
No, I'm not trying to get you angry, Jim,
But I think you drank too much.

No I'm not trying to tell you what to do, Jim.
Fine Jim, I'll just follow you home.
Yes, only to make sure you get home safely.

Hey, where are you going, Jim? Your house is this way.
That's right, Jim. Good you remember.
Very good, Jim, maybe you didn't drink as much.

That's the wrong way Jim. The cars are
coming towards you! Jim, turn around!
Think Jim! Think!

Look at what you've done, Jim. The girl is being
buried with her teddy bear and here you still sleep
and sleep and sleep . . .

Jessica Jocson

The Accident

As she walks down the dusty dirt road she remembers only one thing,
the accident. The shadows and the bushes taunt her and reminds her of
only one thing, the accident. The brightness of the headlights blinds
her and reminds her of only one thing, the accident. She suddenly found
herself driving the car and was reminded of only one thing, the
accident. The burnt bones and the ashes from her friend sit silently
beside her and reminds her of only one thing, the accident. Now she
awakens from the accident to find herself in a cold white room, just
like the accident. An old man walks in, in a starched white gown.
His shaking hand waves towards her in a threatening manner.
Cautiously his shaking hand laid a single piece of paper upon her desk
She stared at the paper, and noticed two big black blotches across the
top. She looked a little closer and saw two words that made her
want to scream.

Those exact words were DEATH CERTIFICATE!! Now she felt terrified.
She didn't know what was going on. She felt anxiety of not knowing
why she was dead. The screams from her mind suddenly awoke her.
She had fallen asleep in her car, in the parking lot of the mall.

Jessica Goss

Ghostship Of Stars

As it approaches at night,
The air goes still,
Evil souls look for thrills.

Demons come flying down,
From port side under,
And all you hear is cracking thunder.

Looking for cover,
With nowhere to hide,
Blackened souls found at the turn of the tide.

Trapped and belonging to the ghostship of stars,
Your spirit now travels,
And wanders afar.

Now searching the world,
So barren and cold,
For evil children and desolate souls.

And once they are found,
You move in for the kill,
Because it gives *your* soul an evil thrill.

Clayton Hall

522

My Rainbow

The rainbow has always intrigued me.
The beautiful colors, so perfectly blended.
The rainbow, a promise of good things to come . . .
But my rainbow, is long overdue.

I've seen a thousand rainbows
Shining brightly, yet subtly, in the sky.
A rainbow of dreams to catch,
unanswered in the question of why?

The full rainbow I see,
makes me want to walk the sky.
Walk to look for the gold waiting there for me . . .
But my rainbow, is long overdue.

Somewhere over the rainbow
colors glisten and gleam.
Someone gently nudges me,
dream, go ahead and dream.

Reach for the stars,
grasp the magic wand.
Blend the colors of your life . . .
create your own rainbow in the sky.

Deborah J. King

Celestial Seasoning

If only mankind could see
The beautiful gifts, the creator
Has given me
To share and bless and reaffirm
That the whole of creation is really one
Earth is heaven for those who see
For heaven resides in the mind of the body
When we realize that heaven and earth are one in the same
The evolution to heaven will no longer be a game
Man is mind, and if you "will" agree
Together we will seek love and harmony
This is my calling - it is a command
That I spread love throughout this desolate land
Love and divine reason are the keys
If not for others it is for me.

Dael Spencer

Joy And Pain Embrace

My back is in pain, the bed is too lumpy
The bed is too lumpy, it causes back pain.

Come eat, come eat, the red bird ticks
The red bird ticks, it's time to eat.

Coffee smells good, I don't drink it
I don't drink coffee, but it sure smells good.

He takes my hand, as the hours proceed
As the hours proceed, we are holding hands.

A phone call to come, will tell of new life
New life will be announced, by the phone call to come.

Children are playing, oh what is that tune?
Oh what is that tune, the children hum as they play?

Ring ring, ring ring, she has taken her place on earth
She has taken her place on earth, before the ring ring, ring ring.

We rejoice and cry aloud, praise him, praise him
We praise him, and rejoice and cry aloud.

The bed is so lumpy, Tylenol is needed
Tylenol is needed, for the pain in my back.

Death doesn't come, it's only sleep
It's only sleep, death is delayed.

Dee Stanley

Bird of Life

Passing through the summer breeze,
The bird of life glides,
How hard this must be,
But, with so much talent he makes it look easy.

The bird's silky feathers sparkle in the sun,
As rain drizzles on him.

The rainbow on the distant horizon,
Dazzles us all as we stare,
We're mesmerized by both.

The Bird of Life heals us all,
We recuperate as he flies by,
He makes us live long in prosperity,
With him as our soul,
We can never die.

He makes us prosper in our minds,
This is only an illusion, though,
But, if we believe it'll be there,
The Bird of Life told me not to reveal him,
But you'll know when you see him.

Bryan Walker

Changing Times

On a cool spring day
The birds sing their praise.
Life sprouting all around
No more cold, snowy days.

As the sun shines hotter
All the young are getting strong.
They are forced to try their wings at flight
For there is where they belong.

The leaves are turning colors,
It won't be long before they fall.
Playtime in the sky is halted
For the south is soon to call.

The ground puts on its blanket.
An icy whisper fills the air.
It's time for us to leave now,
To find a warmer place somewhere.

Janice E. Ditty

Becoming

Within the dualities of nature in time
The body of a girl matures
She alone carries the secret of life
Alone she must carry the weight
She alone must bleed
Will the world accommodate
Will she ever be the same

Alone she must watch for the rain
Listen for the thundering laughter
Tears of childhood
She looks for the cycles of the waterfall
To discover the grim craziness of being

Along her path she learns about herself
She watches icicles melt
Into crisp clean
Resonating water drops of new life

Gabriela Mendoza

Seems Like Yesterday

The battlefields are empty
the cannon no longer roar,
But for me and many others
we can't forget what we heard and saw,
In our nations capital
their names adorn a wall,
But for other combat vets like me,
their my brothers one and all
A name can be a gentle smile
a bright young life no more
What greatness could we all have attained,
without that old man's war?

Fred T. Reisenauer

Tomorrow

She inherits consolation through her mothers caress
The child anticipates, glances at the ground;
her hair shines, it's summer now

In attempt to aid her understanding; her mother yields,
brushing away weeds and sand; tries not to reveal
the pain as she releases the flowers from her hand

The child's recall is but a whispered urgency of Daddy
cause when he departed she was only three, only three

Your Daddy; she says, we'll accompany him again
and the child asks - When? And Then
replies - "Tomorrow would be okay with me" . . .

*Medals that once adorned his chest
are left but with traces, in a hearts remembrance.*

Daisy M. Brown

little bird

quail with fear, little bird;
the danger is near.
stop with your licentious ways, little bird,
you are nothing but a whore here.
have you no probity, little bird?
lying is perjury, dear:
if you are honest with yourself, little bird,
you will have nothing to fear.
gaunt like a snivelling child, little bird:
why does weeping make you so thin, dear?
augur the future, little bird:
prophesy me an omen, a seer.
what's your prediction, little bird?
do you prefer there, or here —
to hang from the gibbet, little bird —
'cause when you traffic with witches
you must die, dear.

Jennifer Lynn Noz

The Quiet Of The Morning

The rays of the sun are so bright.
The dawn it begins the crack of daylight.

See how the trees they nestle there.
The fresh morning air, there is none to compare.

The birds fly in the sky up above,
The quiet of the morning, the wonders of the dove.

The sounds of the dawning are quiet and dear,
The beauty of daybreak on a morning that is clear.

These are things that cannot be replaced,
And often are hard to try and retrace.

Remember forever the peace that it brought,
The quiet serene time that you sought.

Devona F. Cotham

Nostalgia

We wandered by three years ago,
   the day of the reunion;
Where I was born one day in June;
   I'm glad we went.

They burned it down two years ago,
   the day of the reunion;
The house where I was born;
   I'm glad I wasn't there.

"All mown and smooth", is what they said,
   this year at the reunion;
"You'd never know 'twas there".
   I didn't go to see.

"Oh, who was she?" is what they'll say,
   some day at the reunion;
"All's mown and smooth, you'd never know",
   Because I won't be there.

Charlene M. Bennett

My Fall

The wind whispers in my ear
the dead time is coming again
feel it coming
down in the banes of the earth
ice growing
the trees are dying to my eyes
the green goes its way
to oblivion and I am alone
shut away in my warm little cave of plastic and glass
waiting for the white
shivering in anticipation
of spring
or from the wind that sneaks by
my eyes break when it's cold
brown grey white
's far as you can see
bring me back life
give out the visible greentime
life.

Jeremy Marr

Her Sea Life

Birth brought her to this place.
The distant sound of gentle waves, comforts.
The foghorn's mournful cries, at times, disturb.
Thus, began her sea life.

She languishes in transparent blue, solitary pools.
Brown, big-eyed crabs skitter among slippery stones, hiding.
She feels, afraid, from the black, brutal, majestic surf.
Strong, scrapping gulls hurriedly dip to feast on death.

She's a child, an otter, floating with splayed, seaweed-hair.
She's unconfined, yet unable to traverse the enormous distance, alone.
At times, she's a strong, sleek seal, surfing the charging breakers.
She's on the edge, the unknown within her reach.

This giant is moody, alive and mysterious.
He represents new color, pattern and feeling, each day.
He's lovingly embracing, seductive and warm.
He's, at times, all ill-content, cantankerous old man.

There are sweet summer mornings, with contentment and peace.
There are cold winter afternoons, with raging and turmoil.
She's drawn to this life of inconsistency and will stay.
It's familiar.

Ann Parsons-McNiff

"Past And Present"

Together we sailed the Nile,
The Egyptian night sang it song of love,
I was your champion, Your knight in armor bright
You were my Beloved
I have known you by a thousand names,
A thousand faces,
Different, yet still the same
I have been lost in your eyes since the dawn of time
We have kissed, I remember the taste of your lips,
May I try is it still the same.
We have touched, I feel it as I hold your hand
Is it time again for our love to unite,
Hold my hand old friend,
Let us explain our comfort, our easy,
This love that has grown over time

Anthony Prowell

A Love-Song For America

America the beautiful, I do believe you are
    The envy of the whole wide world, of countries near and far!

Your grace and generosity is felt around the globe;
    Instead of animosity, you spread good-will and hope!

To lands in turmoil and despair, you send your rescue mission-
    With dangers luring far and near and hateful opposition!

Your men and women bravely fought on strange and foreign soil,
    Where death had been their grim reward for months-or years-or toil!

America, I'm here to day: I'm proud for what you stand;
    Oh what a grand, exciting day, when you became my land!

I'll love the country I was born until my dying day;
    But my allegiance now I've sworn to the beautiful U.S.A.!

My attitude of gratitude may not be what it should;
    Yet may my actions show my love toward brother-and sisterhood!

God bless this land from shore to shore, from sea to shining sea!
    Bless it's kind people evermore through all eternity!

Hildegard Weber

The Fallen Few

We will miss them,
The fallen few.
The ones that lost their lives
on that tragic night.

The world is a smaller, darker place
for losing a few small, but bright lights.
And heaven is larger and burns brighter now,
for earth's loss is heaven's gain.
Nothing can crush the immortal strain
with which God weaves our souls.

Weep not, for the fallen few
For their home is now of greater hue.
Honor them instead, with your hearts and in your heads;
By remembering what they did and what they said
Love their loves, be caring and kind.
Weep not for the fallen few,
Weep for those they left behind.

David Allen Cole

A Tribute To My Mother

There was a day some years ago
The father above said it's time to go

Your going to earth to be with some friends
They'll be waiting there to let you in

One will be called mother, and one will be dad
No matter what happens, don't you be sad

The one you'll call mother will always be there
The one you call mother she'll always care

I'm giving you that one cause she'll understand
And she'll be there to hold your hand

There'll be days when you have to cry
But on those days she'll be close by

The one called mother will have a look of gleam,
That's because she has a dream

A dream that you will one day be
The gift her Lord meant you to be

And because God my father has given me you
I know you care about me in everything you do

So mother I know you love me so
Cause the Lord our God already let me know.

Joyce A. Wakefield

Melting Away

We had just finished dinner and a glass of chablis.
The fireplace roared with flames all aglow.
The champagne is chilled, the music is chosen.
As we settle next to the couch and talk about our dreams.
As you look into my eyes I feel as though I'm melting.
Like a candle in a flame, I'm just melting away.
The evenings perfect, the mood is set.
Our love is in the open,
Our feelings to share.
Tell me your problems and I'll show you that I care.
If you ever need a friend,
Just call me and I'll be there.
As you look into my eyes I feel as though I'm melting.
Like a candle in a flame, I'm just melting away.

Joseph S. Siano

Unconditional Love . . .

The first time we met
the first smiles we shared
the warm and helping hands
Right from the start
we knew in our hearts we had found
someone who cared and would understand
Through all the years
we'll share laughter and tears
Never a reason to pretend
in the rush of the day
always a way to think of the one who cares
So before you we'll stand
while exchanging our hands
and together we'll grow with the love
we both know will last throughout the years.
Unconditional love.

Juliana Bliuvas

Misdeeds

For the devious and mischievous things we do and say.
The games of treachery we foolishly play.
There's a penalty to pay, due the devil, some may rave.
That remorseless, reckless attitude, devil may care
On our carefully selected, unsuspecting subjects
Sadly and helplessly unaware of what's in store
When we think we've gone unnoticed, here this! next time you're
Having down times at your door, and you're asking why me?
Feeling hurt, unfulfilled, unloved and unappreciated, think
back for just a moment to the misdeeds you initiated! And know
that, we can only reap what we sow, when we betray a trust,
hurt others so unjustly (beware! when we began to lust,
<Body wasting precious time and efforts on things
that are clearly not ours to have.
    Those little lies, so disguised, falsified alibis
that only leads to consequences of our own demise.
    They will come to haunt us someday
If you think this is just some silly superstition
"Prepare! For your conviction.

Ernest T. Lambert

You Are Divine

When smile shines on all your face, like the sun shines on every place
the glow glows on everything alike. Let us say you are sublime
and you are divine.

The silky scarf around your nestly neck flirts with every sight you
set Intrigues every heart and intoxicates every soul with a newly wine
Let us say you are sublime and you are divine.

When every fluid flows through your glassy veins, all clouds are
filled with rain and showers ceaselessly, equally on every tree and
twine. Let us say you are sublime and you are divine.

When every daydream goes through your eyes, it devils your whole being
with hidden delight climbs and clings like a grape vine. Let us say
you are sublime and you are divine.

When your fondling fountain of love makes everybody feel like a dove,
everybody becomes untied no distinction and nothing to define.
Let us say you are sublime and you are divine.

When your invasive intimacy runs all over, luck seems larking like a
leaf of clover, everybody unfolds like a blossoming flower and every
touch turns wild. Let us say you are sublime and you are divine.

When your blazing buzzing beauty sings a song of eternity, and in
its full ecstasy lifts me loftily to your shrine.
Let us say you are sublime and you are divine.

Bhajan S. Badwal

Carrie

Granddaughter, you're twelve.
The golden halo that crowned you at birth,
Told me you were special, can lead the herd.

"I'll be a doctor", you said,
The leap of my heart left me out of breath,
With your father still in my womb.
University studies, took me in that route.
Men interfered, my struggles crushed,
My dreams are fulfilled now my love.

You said, "I'll come visit my parents, if there is still a home".
Why that attitude, what do you know?
Many, many years before your birth,
I saw you frolicking at the beach, your hair belonged to the wind,
Something horrible had happened, your father had grieved,
Somewhere from space his voice thundered "Mom wait for me"

You see darling, we're in sync.
Please tell me what you think.

Ara Santos

Autumn

The sky deep blue above,
The grass bright green below,
The trees sway slightly in the breeze,
The sunshine's warmth touches you like a gentle glove.

The leaves of green have begun to turn,
Bright orange, red and yellow,
Groups of deer graze calmly in the meadow.

Although, the sun is bright and strong,
It is not hot, only slightly warm,
Our clothes and shoes we must change,
You're known by one of two names.

You float in after summer like the evening tide,
You waltz in like a lady, with "Old Man Winter" at your side.

Nature's burst of color seems to be a welcome call,
Your arrival ends our summer fun,
However, there is apple picking in the fall!

Deborah Lang

I Love The Way

I love the way he makes me feel like living
The happiness in his smile—and his spirit of giving
I love the way he touches me and holds me when I'm blue
Because he's all man and he's oh so true
I love the way I see him as a part of me
That part of my life which is exciting and free
I love the way he takes the time to make all kinds of plans
And when I feel let down, he listens to me and he understands
I love the way he has that special sparkle in his eyes
When it comes to loving him—it comes as no surprise
I love the way I can trust him without having a second thought
That he may someday leave me; lonely and caught
I love the way he tells me things that he doesn't want anyone else
to hear only because we love each other and I want him to be near
I love the way he holds my hand firmly and strong
While we stroll down by the ocean as we walk quietly along
But when he is away from me for a long, long while
I love the way his memory lingers on, in my heart and in my smile

Karen I. Drolette

A Game Of Chess

Wind, earth's messenger in the game of chess,
The heavens make their first move, calling in Lightning to terrorize the earth,
Sun is overtaken by brutal combatants on horseback,
Many horses riding in, kicking dust up wherever they go, coloring
the clouds with many a drab shade of dust,
The people witnessing this on the earth below cower at this horrible sight,
There is no defense that the sun is capable of, for it is too feeble at present,
But, Mother Earth has one for the animals,
Their little world is covered by what seems to be a glass bubble,
Undisturbed by the flashes, of nature's strobe light.
The many knights become angered at Mother Earth for her wise
trick and begin thrusting spears of light at the closest thing,
Thus forcing it to become a victim of the storms toll, the battle rages on,
Sun and Darkness fight to win the sky.
Lightning hears many sirens, and realizes what he has done,
Begging the earth for mercy in the only way he knows how,
He cannot talk for he doesn't know the meaning, only rumbles,
Fire eats through the mother's protective coating and has outsmarted her,
Swallowing up her precious babies,
Sun has gained enough strength to take over the sky once more,
"Checkmate!" she says.
And regains her throne in the sky ready to play many more a game of chess.

Karen E. Mulvey

An Awakening

I turn on the news and what do I hear,
The horror of assassination.
More terror, as hatred runs rampant
In the world, throughout every nation.

My heart it weeps from deep within
For those that are left behind,
To suffer and mourn from such tragedies,
These attempts to destroy mankind.

Our fears begin to rise from inside,
As we dread what the next day will bring.
Have our hopes and dreams for peace on this earth,
Been brushed away by an angel's wing?

Is the rain that falls from the heavens,
His tears of betrayal from us?
That we, his most precious creation,
Have forgotten his love and his trust.

Only time will tell but with faith in our hearts,
That our prayers for peace, he will hear.
Maybe then, his arms will embrace the world
And his love will take away all our fear.

Anita J. French

Sunshine On The Bay

It was a cool and quiet summer morning
The house was such a gloomy place to be
I drove away to seek the golden sunlight
That warms and cheers me there beside the sea.

Each time I go there's something new to charm me
The birds, the boats, the children at their play
The tide, the sand, the ducks, the far horizon
This time it was the sunshine on the bay.

The sun shone on the bay with such a brilliance
The bay reflected every shining ray
In shimmering, glittering, rippling, sparkling water
That had a cheerful message to convey.

It made a path across the shining water
A path shaped like a big broad letter V
Starting on the far distant horizon
And pointing all its brightness toward me.

As I looked out on all that gleaming brightness
So dazzling that I had to shade my eyes
My thoughts proceeded upwards to the Master
Of this great realm of earth and sea and skies.

For He had brought the beauty of the morning.
And He had cheered my heart when it was low.
And I was thankful for the sunshine
That warmed my heart and soul and body so.

Iva P. Owings

Pondering Love

Unexplainable — the word that comes to mind; pondering
the love of friendship, within this group we find.
Unsure what to call it; unfound without a source.
Too often taken for granted — this love of inside force.
My God, He makes reality, this closeness we all share.
Lack of love for from present — replaced with love so rare.
From time to time it gets me, just how close we are
One group with Christ the center; His love is far from far.
The need to reach to others outside our comfort zone
Them longing in their hearts to know what we've been shown.
I thank my Lord and Savior
  For treasures like you all.
You laugh when I laughing,
  You catch me when I fall.

Joel Denning, age 16

Mother Earth

Mother Earth she whispers . . . a soft song of lament
the humans she's supported, multiply, dishonor . . . torment.
Her intricate weave of balance . . . growth promoting growth,
life erupting from that which has passed, life death . . . both.

Green blade of her sword, through cement cracks
gentle reminders of her power . . . laid forth in our tracks.
Her human children take and take, no longer do they give.
Forests of her hair ripped out, how much longer can she live?

Her energy fields retarded, by sub-atomic blasts
so few can hear her sing . . . only the "lowest" human casts.
Her blood it flows in rivers, diverted by man's hand
who pump in their contaminates, her fish children die . . . on land.

We grow and grow and multiply like green on molding bread,
but unlike mold we don't produce, the key . . . lies in your head.
We all were born with innate love of Sun and Wind and Earth
It's time we stopped to honor her and thank her for our birth.
The Crow Woman

  Bonnie L. White

The Day After Christmas Blues

T'was the day after Christmas when all through the house,
  the kids were so noisy, and so was my spouse.

The toys were all strewn - this way and that;
  A doll house and train, a baseball and bat.

It looked as if Santa grew tired of his trip;
  So when he reached our house he emptied his grip.

And under the tree the gift-wrapping lay torn;
  ribbon all wrinkled, and boxes all worn.

The poor tree itself was so brown it looked rusty;
  The tinsel was wilted, the ornaments dusty.

The big Christmas dinner, a 'connoisseurs' treat;
  now nothing but leftovers that will last for a week.

And stacked in the sink, piled high to the sky,
  are dishes, and dishes, and dishes - oh, my!

My head how it's aching, my spirits are numb;
  The day after Christmas had finally come.

As I surveyed the mess I exclaimed with a tear:
  "Thank God Christmas comes but one day a year!"

  Elcy L. O'Neill

"Leaving Me Wanting"

I gripped your hand as I laid restlessly next to you
The love that we had made left me wanting for more
I danced with you in my dreams for I found it too difficult to sleep
We danced together in our nakedness with only a flickering
candle illuminating the room
Our shadows became entangled dancing upon the wall
Passion grew once again wildly and through our shadows we made love
I cannot bare to see you leave come morning, come dawn, though the
hours in road upon me against my desire to have this dream live on
And just as our silhouettes fade becoming meshed into the glow of
light that now beams radiantly through my window, you have now gone
Leaving me wanting . . .
Leaving me wanting . . .

  Alyana Vincente Alvarez

527

Love

Love is a word that is used in many ways.
The love we had was bright and warm as the sun's rays.
We were so close when we were together.
It was so sweet and getting much better.
One day the love started slipping apart.
Oh, it really hurt and nearly broke my heart.
Why does love have to be so hard on me
Please let someone tell me so I can finally see.
I have written this poem especially for you
Please come back to me, I love you yes I do.

Allen Ellis

Morning

The morning light appeared over the horizon
the mist came up to meet it.
Creatures of the day sing their songs
happy to be here to greet it.
Men, women and children open their eyes
to a brand new day.
They hustle about to get on their way
adventures and undescribable experiences lie ahead
it's time for all God's children to leave their bed.
To see, smell and taste God's creations
makes one grateful to be living in this nation.
This is the land of the free . . .
Yet some are not so free
If we love and walk together
one day we all can be . . .
Be what! People living together in harmony.

James Henry

Trophy Night

Wind surging in a black spruce forest;
the moon hanging, half - sliced and still, in a paled sky.

The eagle hurtling from a creek - bed;
golden splendor, harbinger of great things to come.

On the ocean sand, the young boy runs
into fading shades of red; a silhouette,
bonded with the earth, focused in space.

A dim auditorium; a table waits,
white - draped, laden with gold and colors of glory.

Above the revolving planet, one star
speeding into the nocturnal universe, illuminates.

Dawn Gallt

For You

Add up your blessings as they hatch;
The next may be a poorer batch.
Yesterday has left its flavor,
Today is here for you to savor.
Feelings may come and feelings go;
Many, like seeds, we tend to sow.
Their fruits are sweet, their fruits are sour;
Sweeter ones provide a dower.
Today is here for resolution;
Throw out the fruits grown in pollution.
Thus do you gain your self-esteem,
And know that dreams is only dream,
And then go on to cast your role,
To make decisions, set a goal.
With each achieved, another set,
Here fulfillment, there a regret.
Wisdom comes when you manage both,
Lessons they teach will nurture growth.
So, on to knowledge that "I am me,"
With hand so firm on destiny.

James Edward Jeffries

My Dad

You are my Dad and will always be,
The most favorite man in the world to me.

We do not speak of love out loud,
But in our hearts we are very proud.

I know that I have been a pain,
But when it was over it was my gain.

Now that I have moved away,
It seems I love you more each day.

I miss our chats when I would stop in,
Your words of wisdom come from deep within.

You're more intelligent than most can see,
And that's why you mean the world to me.

Please feel my love from across the miles,
And it will leave us with lots of smiles.

Enjoy your Father's Day as I know you will do,
And remember that I am thinking of you.

Judy Podlesnik

Untitled

"There," I murmur, "it's perfect."
The note falls to the table as I pick up the Beretta.
My fingers close around the cold steel.
Over the barrel, over the safety,
Over the trigger my fingers go.

It feels like a weight in my hand
Like the one upon my heart.
How did things get so complicated
that it had to come to this?

The clock reads ten, I must hurry
They'll be home soon.

I slowly raise it to my head.
Mom, Dad, it's not your fault.
It's no one's fault but my own
I just couldn't handle it.

A single tear escapes,
My finger hovers about the trigger

The gun's at my heed now
I take one last look about my room and smile.
The weight's been lifted.

Christina Patton

Aura

Still I see it in your eyes
the pain of a thousand bitter tears
numbed by your thousand lies
is it the fear that you fear most
or is it the realization of what has slipped
through your fingers and bares all too much?

Still I wonder yet what has become of two
even though tears soon fall stale
I believe deep down they help you to get through
although many times we had lied to ourselves and failed.
We always really knew
there's something and always will be to conceal
because the pain is too great no matter what we do.

Like the day has never ended
you're still on my mind
lie to act like we never pretended
and hold it in for all time
I bite my tongue to hold all in; to mend,
but all I have to show for it is my crime
I never meant to love you, but it happened just the same.

Dan Huesman

You're The One

You're the one that makes me laugh,
The one that makes me cry,
You're the one that makes me happy,
And only I know why!

You're the one who understands me,
The one who's always there,
You're the one I want with me,
Here, there and everywhere!

Never before have I dreamed like I do,
I love the thought of sharing my life with you,
I pray each night that we'll never be apart,
But near or far you'll always be in my heart!

We've had our problems, but only a few,
Together we've made it, just me and you.
The love in my heart grows deeper each day,
For you in a very special way!

Like a burning candle, my future looks bright,
With you by my side, each and every night.
Through the clouds and rain or the glow of the sun,
Just want you to know, you'll always be the one!

Jayne Anderson

"A Vision"

I sit here by your graveside, surrounded by the dark.
The only sounds I hear is the singing of a lark
and the lonesome whispering wind, with it's eerie whining sound
as it blows the leaves down upon the cold damp ground

As I sit, I have a "vision", a picture in my mind
a picture of a past, we shared for so long a time
I see your smiling face and your eyes are all aglow
as you tell me that you need me and that you love me so

As we go down life's road, we walk together hand in hand
to our future, to forever, 'till we reach the promise land
we've loved, we've laughed, we've multiplied the earth
for life continues with our children that we've given birth

We've started a family tree with outstretched arms and roots of love
and our God has smiled down upon us with his angels from above

I look around and I realize, it was only a "vision" of so long ago
I see your tombstone, I touch a rose, I hope you know I love you so
It's not goodbye, it's only a beginning of some happy future time
I'll never forget you, your love, your memories are in my mind

I stand, I look around and see a hint of morning sun shinning
I go, but not without a promise that someday I'll see you again

Brenda Griffin

Another Reality

I am the one you see in the darkness,
the picture in black and white.
Where emotions lie buried behind closed eyes
and truth departs with the light.

I am the echoes from the words never said,
forever sounding within your mind.
Where all is not as it would seem
and conscious thought is disentwined.

I am the memory never quite recalled
or the fantasy lover without a face.
I am never there when you reach for me
through fragmented time and space.

Where reality is but your perception,
there are no ghosts and yet you scream.
I am the author of incoherent whispers,
when darkness comes, I am the dream.

David E. Hartley

Those Little Words

Those little words I wouldn't speak those days when we first met;
the passion and the touch we shared, the ache not pain, not yet.
Taking more and giving less through days and nights we shared
while exploring and caressing you, denying that I cared.
And hidden far beneath the mask of cultivated rage
a restless feeling lurked inside a dank and musky cage.
Naive and trusting once before this feeling had roamed free
burned in my soul a heightened sense of all that was beauty
perceiving clearly, so I thought, but there and then betrayed
made prisoner of that beaten soul and herein locked away.
"Life without parole, sentence forthwith carried out"
with no investigation what the crime was all about
no thought to pain inflicted on that day some visitor
released in all its fury by this starving prisoner
a visitor who taught and cared and loved, who held the key
embodied in unquestioned love that you have shown for me.
Those little words I wouldn't say those days when we first met
have meaning that I never knew could free me of the debt
Those little words, "I love you," so simply written down
have freed the feeling evermore, I understand them now.

Dave Ison

Untitled

A page of life turns,
The past memories merge,
A birth, A childhood,
A bride, A groom,
Becoming a mother, having a daughter,
Becoming a father, having a son,
Building Memories,
These eighty some years,
Living life and loving God,
Standing by their family, all sixty years,
Always being there,
when asked by family and friends,
Love in life, Love in death,
And now together forever.
God has blessed us all!

Carol J. Beckler

"In Memory Of My Aunt"

For the love of God, remove this knife from my heart.
The piercing pain of yesterday's memories and today's loss
Are too much to bear,
I loved her with a depth of feeling that was always there.

She held me when I was small and I knew not where to turn,
Her arms of comfort were never closed to me.
The two of them were there for me to talk with, be with,
And their pride in me gave me confidence and hope.

How smothering is this pain of loss!
I don't know if I can bear to lose another who is so dear;
I shall miss her strength, her smile, her love,
Yet I know she has gone to join him
Who was her life and with whom, she will smile again.

Arlene Brandon

The First Winter Snowfall

The afternoon passed slowly as I watched the world go round,
The sky was darkening as snow fell on the ground.
The November day felt cold and as I saw the flakes fall past,
My mood enlightened and my heart was racing fast.
The trees outside standing tall and still
Held out their branches at their own free will.
A layer of whiteness covered the path
And as I walked I was filled with a solitude wrath.
The crispness held out all through the night
And when I woke up my world was white.

Emma Hill

"Scorpion Princess"

Having the dazzling diamond eyes, of an angel
The real compassion of a saint.
True poise of stature, of a model.
Radiating beauty, dimmed by no other.
A glistening smile, linked directly to the looking glass of the soul.
The absolute elegance of a queen.
 An inner warmth, that could capture the coldest of men.
The aura of sensuality, surrounds her being.
Her presence alone, an honor to any true man.
My spirit has awaken.
She holds, eternal prisoner, my heart.
The meaning of life, a secret no more.
Her voice is a dream,
Of a life come true.
Destiny does exist.
Truly, the only real lady I've ever loved!

Joe Nite

The Struggle . . .

The man made concrete jungle:
The relentless power of mother nature:
Each side trying emphatically to cast out the other:
Man builds . . . nature tears down,
only to repeat the cycle until one emerges victorious:

Man in his infinite wisdom
wishes to dominate the elements,
only to be crushed by the ominous
vitality and perseverance of natures wrath:
Never will the two converge to an harmonic existence:

At least . . . not in my lifetime.

David A. Cronin

The Love Poem

A nose fell in love with a rose.
The rose fell in love with a hose.
The hose fell in love with some toes.
And those toes fell in love with their owner's bows.

Haley Dona Saunders

Seaside Reflections

I stood on the sun bleached sand and watched
The sea gulls perched out on the rocks
And my ears were filled with a roaring sound
That swelled and then subsided.
Above me the blue sky stretched wide;
Shielding my eyes I searched its every side,
Expecting there to sight,
The author of that sound in flight;
The roaring "Jet" that eluded me.
Then from the horizon, as far as I could see
I saw the ocean rolling, rolling in on me.
Instantly I knew the sound;
The sound of waves that break on ground.
Lord, let your voice like the ocean waves
Swelling and breaking on the shore,
Swell in my heart and roar in my ears,
To crash down my very resistance
Till I can hear your voice and know your will
In the ebb and flow of my existence.

Dorothy Coppola

Creation

Burning through the gray bleakness of the clouds
The shroud is broken
By a sun as new as the first day of creation.
A revelation that embraced us
Suspending us in golden webs delicate, yet tenacious
Transporting us across strands of time and place
You to a space on a bench by a river
I, to a quivering sun, on a forested mountain.
We are spun, separately, together until our very boundaries
    begin to blur
And I am not sure where I begin and you end.

We cling together in fearful love
Above the chaos that swirls below
Afraid to breath, to disturb the moment.
Lying in the Garden before the Fall
Knowing all the while the gates will someday close behind us.
But in that eternal instant the world was, for us,
    created and recreated.
Since that moment we have seen our lives
    through different and each other's eyes.

Charles L. Kammer

A Simple Expression

I basically oppose in all routine,
The simplification that most people are willing to conceive.

Is it not what we instill into each other?
Whether for today, or even tomorrow?

Words of love and thoughts comprise,
The most precious meanings of our lives.

For if we are these people of whom I speak,
Being all that different and all unique,

We will approach this promise, a promise to end,
All fears and frustrations my beloved friend.

A definition I bring and clearly state,
Within this love, I'll learn to appreciate,

This word alone, I truly must,
In order to give you all of my trust.

David T. George

Sonnet Of Silence

In the yellow sunshine the silhouette's were leafy and green
The sky was sapphire - Ceylon to Kanchanaburi blue
And even the sweet fragrance of the spring flowers
Have been etched into the deepest portion of my soul
But far more indelibly was the peaceful silence
Which only your soft voice could break
This peace was more than the eye defined
And love was more enduring than we dreamed it to be
This solitary place is intertwined with memories
I have come back here many times my dear
But it was never, not even once, the same
Today the silence is no longer comforting
You are gone. The sky is no longer blue
There is no fragrance in the meadows or the woods
My favorite familiar place is wrestled from me
For you, my most dearly loved, are forever gone
And with you go the colors and the sunshine and the songs
Here in this peaceful silence does Love inscribe
A cenotaph . . . . . mute . . . . . eloquent . . . . . and everlasting

Jane Ratcliffe

You'll Never Know

You'll never know what I have known, the times of terror I was shown.
The sleepless nights, the endless grief; my mind would scream, but no relief.
I trembled, shook, I begged, I cried; the countless times I'd wished I'd died.
How many hours did they yell and fight? Too many times all through the night.
Yet, then, thank God, the sun would rise and sleep would come to tear filled eyes.
The morn' of peace meant naught to me, for I knew my mother I would see.
To see her bruised, and swollen face, to know her feelings of disgrace.
I dreamed of being her shining knight, to ease her pain, to hold her tight.
But I turned away from her instead; and deep within my soul I fled.
Till there was not much left of me; a creature, without dignity.
To take a mind so young and pure, to leave it hopeless, insecure.
No greater crime, no greater sin, than to seal a soul so deep within.
Then God looked down and saw in me, a light, a life, I could not see.
An angel came and reached within, and brought my soul to earth again.
She filled my soul with hope, with life; and now she is my loving wife.
No, you'll never know what I have known, and you'll never see
what I was shown.
I thank each day the Lord above, for you, my wife, my life, my love . . .

Douglas R. Reeder

The Token

Her eyes are sparkling,
  The smile on her face is dazzling,
    What has happened to this child of mine?

His eyes are gleaming,
  His face shows nervous anticipation,
    What is it that is yet to come?

She cuddles into my arms,
  Head on my shoulder she asks,
    "Mom, do you want to see what he gave me?"

Expecting yet another
  Small token of his love for her,
    I replied, "Sure, what is it?"

Then I saw it.
  The sparkle of the diamond matched her eyes,
    The gleam of gold matched his.

Small? Only in size.
  The token had great meaning —
    A lifetime of love.

Cathy D. Wheeler

Lament

I hope for joy, but soon I'll wear
  the somber robe of sorrow
Today . . . I smile but tears and heartaches
  will I have tomorrow,
I hope for all that's sweet.
For life like purest gold to glitter,
But I am disappointed
For the fruits I reap are bitter.
When I wish for lilies white
Then only roses bloom,
And when I wish for peace
I hear the troubled trump of doom.
When I wish for starry nights
No star shines in the sky,
I see dark clouds only and hear
  the night winds sigh,
Sometimes I wish for fragrant flowers,
But stagnant rills abound,
And now I need you more than all,
You cannot, dear, be found.

Dorothy E. Mittoo Walker

Animal Champions

Every animal including human is a champion.
The snail for its slowness
The cheetah and peregrine falcon
for their speed
The sperm whale for swimming in
such great depths
The giant squid for its stinging
tentacles
The African elephant
for its great size
Chipmunks and squirrels are nut
collectors
Chameleons are
masters of camouflage
But people have the only thinking mind.

Andrew K. Luzincourt

Goodbye My Sweet Beauty

Goodbye my sweet beauty.
The snow blows cold from the west.
Never forget I love you best.
Your departure burns a hole,
In my very soul.
Always, shall I remember our hopes and dreams.
Even as my face fills with salty streams.
I will remember the softness of your sultry black hair.
The finer moments we had to share.
The depth of your brown eyes.
With other memories my tear dries.
The love in your smile.
Has taken my mind further than a thousand long miles.

Until our next moment I say,
In quiet slumber may you lay.
It is the sandman's duty.
Goodbye my sweet beauty.

Joshua Kelley

Country Love

The sound of the wind, blowing through the pine trees
The songs of the birds, and the humming of bees
The warmth of the sun, and a crystal blue sky
The shriek of an eagle, as he slowly soars by
The chatter of squirrels, at work and at play
My soul starts to wonder, if it's here it should stay
Colors on a lake, while the sun's going down
I can find no such pleasure, in city or town
The cry of a wolf, when the moon is on high
Or the hoot of an owl, as he patiently stands by
You sitting with me, by the warmth of a fire
Is just one of the things, that stirs my desire
The cooing you make, sounds just like a dove
All of these things tell me, I must be in love

Donald L. Schoonover

Early Morning Dew

The wind curls and blows,
swirling and glows.
Such like a tornado the leaves dance in air,
with twist and twirls,
floats with all care.
But yet it is often the sun doesn't shine,
raining and pouring while ordered in line.
Even though the tides are low,
eventually the wind will blow.

Always, like the stars in the sky,
the crickets chirp, and hop on by.
Bumps and Bruises, as all kids go through,
the breeze takes a turn into the early morning dew.

Kanoli Mitchell

To My Husband

Heaven laid low as the clouds settled across the mountains.
The soul knew what it had seen and ached at being made to leave.
I thought of you.
You didn't know it, and neither did I really,
But I saw your face playing hide and seek in the trees by moonlight.
I felt your arms shelter me from the wind,
And I kissed you through the misting rain.
I gazed into your eyes through the stars,
And held you close in the grass.
I sensed our children roaming the hills and climbing rocks.
Leaves crumpled beneath my feet,
And I heard your voice calling softly to me.
I tried to answer.
I hoped you heard
And somehow knew
A heart had sung to you.

Alicia Westhoff

War's Regret

The sound was hollow as it hit my ears,
the sound of the scream of my friend.
He was beside me one minute,
and then he was gone.
And I wondered, why did he have to go?
I remember the reason for the war,
Or what I thought it was,
Men pushing back and forth.
Now as I stand beside my friend's grave,
I still wonder, what was it all about?
Why did I have to loose a friend,
Just because men can't get along together?
I hope you never have to feel the pain I did
that day, as many often do.
The hollow pain of a loss, men will regret someday.

Heather Franklin

A Fall Walk

As I walk thru a fall wood of color,
The wind hails the oncoming snow.
The crackle of leaves underfoot brings to mind,
A warm fire where the coals have been nudged.

Erma Hixenbaugh

Untitled

Above the trees, among the stars
The spirits surround me guiding me along
Finding my way to the island in the sky
They flap their wings and sing their songs
"Hold our hands it won't be long"
Their pureness blinds me, I struggle and cry
"When will we get to this island in the sky?"
Silence remains and we travel farther
Not long before us I could see
A glimmer of light break through the darkness
Tranquility began to wash over me
A scent of heather filled the air
Along a path of mist and light
We walked gently through the clouds
A cascade of snow begins to fall
The angels laughed and began to rise
Leaving a spell of serenity and hope
Alone in my world of castles and dreams

Janice S. Groben

The Golden Years

I have climbed the mountain of life
The summit is here
Perhaps another mile or so to go
Now I know, now I know
Why the miles up seemed so slow
But here it is and back I look
Much to remember, I could write a book
But original it would not be
There is no such thing, life originality
The golden years are not golden at all
Truth be told I don't want to answer the call
I will refuse, I will say no
Tho' futile it has to be so
No choice do I have to complete the miles
I will kick and scream with tears and no smiles
So you near the plateau, keep on fighting, postpone the call
The Golden Years are not golden
But better than nothing at all.

Irene Chadwick

Twilight

Day is done.
The Sun moves on to brighten
Many a distant land.
Yet in its passing it bequeaths an exquisite realm
Of unique and transitory beauty.

I stand transfixed in awe.

Waist high meadow grass surrounding me
Is gradually transformed into a blanket of fawn
In the deepening dusk.

Mere silhouettes,
The majestic thread tipped forest giants,
Stand ever watchful, jutting towards the sky.
Each reach up as if to shake the hands
Of the shimmering Stars that poke their way
Through the clear azure ceiling high above.

A brilliant crimson fissure in the dark ragged cloud bank,
Hugging the distant horizon, heralds the ensuing darkness.
Twilight is here,
With night in all its splendor,
Tagging close behind.

Alan Corson

A Whisper Good-Bye

I awoke this morning to the sound of thunder
The sun was no where in sight
I turned to put my arms around you but found that you had gone
You left in the night somewhere between the dark and the light
And like the startling clap of thunder
So bold and so strong
I face the day with you gone
Like the silence of the calm before the storm
I sit and I wonder what was wrong
You said you loved me, this I believed
I took for granted you wouldn't leave
And with a gentle sway of the trees and
   the howl of the wind
I hear your soft voice whisper Good-Bye
Now standing alone, I seek shelter from the rain

Dawn M. Krohberger

532

Untitled

As I lay sleeping, I beheld a smile upon my pillow.
　　The sweetest and most innocent, more pure
than water from heaven.
A smile shining through the chaos of a hellish storm.
So rare it tears my heart to think that,
　　that smile could ever frown.
I look on in wonderment at the fragile
　　lips upturned, to reveal a heart so good
I see through your masquerade, the fog of my dream.
　　Through the cold stone that tries to hide the
　　fire and smile within.
Only I can see the flame, and only I can feel its warmth.
A smile within stronger than a heart beat,
　　more precious than gold.
If I could awake to have a smile upon my pillow.

Catherine Long

Understand?

　　It's so hard for me to understand
The things we do to each other in this land.
　　For life is short and full of doubts
We need not fight or be on the outs
　　As friends are few and far between
Honesty and love are hardly seen.
　　You find a friend then learn to trust
Yet once your gone; blows away like dust
　　I often wonder what our world is coming too.
Will it end up being me against you?
　　It's so hard for me to understand
The things we do to each other in this land.
　　If everyone would watch and learn
from day to day.
Then just maybe the world wouldn't be this way.
　　Now that's why; it's so hard for me to understand
The things we do to each other in this land.

Cynthis Kia Hill

Of Tidbits 'N Tornadoes

Like splinters from a gold nugget
The tidbits of life floated down on me
They came in shiny clusters and I dreamed
Of goals, of riches, of fame.

Radiance dimmed when the tornadoes hit
Grief ripped and tore and shattered
But ambrosia from gold dust moments remained
And the tornadoes calmed.

My nuggets laughed and grew and I learned
Tornadoes will come but cannot crush
And the nectar of time will soothe the tornado
And the gems of life's morsels shall endure.

Doris Smalling

A Gift

The weeping willow stands so large within the creeks divide.
The water rippled and ran on and I no longer sighed,
for days gone by and promise made that wished the creek a river.
I like it just as it is made, a gift from natures giver.
I like the way it moves along as if it knew the way,
to find another place to roam and dance on come what may.
The weeping willow seems to big for me to reason how,
it came to grow within the banks where it is captive now.
Still she could lift her branches up, if she were so created.
Instead she blocks the sun, oft' times, and shade for glare is traded.
So while the creek runs on it's way, winding here and there . . .
The willow tree stands large and bold it's happenstance to share.

Betty I. Held

Loves Sweet Wonder

The sky is blue,
The trees are bare.
The moon is bright,
The stars are there.
Oh, life is beautiful,
Life is grand,
As we go walking,
Hand in hand.
Hand in hand with life and death,
Hand in hand with loves sweet breath.
Hand in hand 'tween heaven and hell
Where heaven prevails with the sound of a bell.
Life when thought of as with heaven above,
Is truly filled with beauty and love.
So, if you must think and you must ponder,
Think of life and loves sweet wonder.

Gail Gobar

O.J.

The circus is done for the vain and obtuse.
The trial is finished for Orenthall Juice.
So Marcia and Johnny, Varadder and Fuhrman,
Kato and Resnick and various vermin
Can gather around in an electric bunch
And call Mezalunas to send over lunch.
And during this lunch the rhetoric would flow
And this is the way it would probably go
"the glove didn't fit" the defense would shout.
"We knew all along there was reasonable doubt."
"But the mountain of facts" prosecutors will say
"Is proof of his guilt - you can trust DNA."
Then Judge Ito rises to tell a short tale
and all you can hear is a dog's plaintive wail
"It's time to be truthful - no need to be cautious
It's time to reveal that the 'N' word is - Nauseous."

David McCarter

Him

I saw him standing there,
The twilight colors bouncing off his eyes.
His hair glowing.
His persistence and charm pulling me toward
　　him faster and faster.
He didn't talk he just stared,
Awaiting my presence.
He stood on the dock with anticipation.
He finally spoke and said,
"The Twilight does something strange to everyone."
Then he disappeared into the silhouette of the fog.

Carrie Santonastaso

Stormy Weather

Clouds close around the far reaches of the sky.
Then the drizzle begins and the winds start to fly.

Rain hits the ground with a terrible sting
While I look around for the almighty Weather King.

To begin my mortal plea to ask that it be stopped.
I wait just to see if my plea is dropped.

After it stops you begin to feel
The bone chilling cold of the stormy ordeal.

The next day when you wake you see with your eyes
That the sun has baked the rain completely dry

Just remember the sun comes out
For whomever doesn't like STORMY WEATHER.

John D. Monroe Jr.

Ffarwel 'Nhad

On that late spring morning,
The white sands of the shoreline
Contrasted sharply with the figure of his body.

The dried salt from the sea was glistening
Through the curls of his once raven, now graying hair.

It was clear that he had finally heard the
"Celtic Angels"
He so often sang about
During my childhood.

A man out of his time, and, some said,
Out of his mind, whose body was gently released
On the beaches of the old world
By his loving soul.

He once said
He believed in the unicorn and I believe He truly did.

Not because I also did as a little girl,
But he could see and hear more than most could
And he taught me to believe in the unseen
And unheard, to listen to my own heart,
Sing my own song, and to dream.

James Phillips

The Parents

In a silence without song
the wind blew the last feathers of summer
from the trees.

The red of autumn lay against the horizon
like a Christmas blankets, the sleeting mist
chilling their bones.

They are young and hold the infant like a gift
thus they held him as day follows days,
month follows months, year follows years,
and autumn returns
with the yearnings of those first autumns
for a shelter against the sleet, the mist,
and the darkening sky of winter.

And so they grew decrepit, derivative
of wounds which only April's promise gives.

Betty Ann Roberts

Brentwood

I hear Brentwood singing . . .

Cars driving all away,
The wind blowing beyond the trees,
Birds singing songs to nature's flowers,
People talking about many different things.

Leaves falling from trees onto the ground,
Trains going to a far away place,
The children enjoying their day,

I hear Brentwood singing . . .

Jasmine A. Rubio

Nature

Trees, large trees, very large trees,
They have an erie effect on people,
To watch the branches blow in the breeze
Or stand firm and still as a steeple.

Is Nature laughing at the human creature,
When looking down from the towering tree?
Or is Nature too proud a teacher
To even care what happens to you or me?

John Briedis

In Your Eyes

I gaze into your eyes
The windows of your soul
Hoping for the answers
The feelings left untold

With your eyes you touch my heart
Can you see the love inside
Do you see me when we're apart
My thoughts I'm unable to hide

In your eyes I can see the fear
Trying to disguise, to not let me near
Look into my mind, you'll see I'm sincere
Your heart I'll protect, your eyes free from tears

With your eyes, look into mine
Inside you will find a home
As thoughts and feelings entwine
Take my heart, no need to roam.

Don Nichols

Where Has Spring Gone?

The autumn leaves have long since fallen and have blown to and fro;
The winds have ceased and all leaves gathered to give way to the snow;
The tiny flakes have turned to ice and set our creeks aglow;
The drifts have melted like subtle rain with quiet, gentle flow.

And now with Ides of March upon us, blowing up a storm,
The lion roars and whips and lashes far beyond the norm;
The winds subside and hush the breeze as the lamb begins to form;
The clouds disperse and clear the way for rays of sun to warm.

The crocus peeps above the earth as if to test its ground;
The other flowers get a nod and quickly gather 'round;
The robin chirps and feathered friends cheerily join in sound;
The babbling brook reveals that the joys of spring abound.

But swiftly with a sudden stroke all is torn asunder;
Howling winds and stormy rains gnash and clash like thunder;
Mother nature dries her tears, as if to hide her blunder;
The calming scene returns once more, brimming with awe and wonder.

What happened to the months of spring, are they forever lost?
What games does nature play with us? Should May endure a frost?
We must return the rains to April when leaves have splashed and tossed!
Give back the winds again to March, no matter what the cost!

Gladys R. Fisher

Lost Need

For years, the key's been missing
The words locked deep inside;
Like a rusty box of memories
Where shadows seem to hide.
Time passed by slowly, and the prose got eased aside.

The years spent with children,
Till the need to write just died.
There was no ache or mourning,
Just a casual good-bye;

For life was good and full of love,
Never wondering why . . .?

Then a man stepped through my doorway,
And the memories flooded back;
The cobwebs have been lifted,
Life's order has a crack . . .

Doubt held the pen, sure of one thing,
The "Lost" feeling only creating can bring!
The door is now open, but where will it lead?
It matters not,

I now have that need . . .

Darlene C. Bozymowski

Untitled

The sun was setting on my life
The world was darkening all around me
My hopes and dreams had vanished
As the night had come to drown me

A snag in time had caused this curse
Had thrown my existence to the wind
My days were numbered, my countenance weak
My bread of life was sliced so thin

The three sisters who guide my fate
decided to give me another chance
Cloth spun the thread so fine
Lachesis provided an extra inch
While Atropos cut with a sparing hand

My life I owe to the Greek Moirae
who spin the thread and guard the wheel
Those who number the days and count the breaths
that measure the minute and shorten the year

Dawn Shields

Two Cats Sleep

Two cats sleep, cuddled next to each other.
Their arms intertwine, one's head resting on the other's shoulder,
It's body nestled against the other's body,
His tail elongated, relaxed and away.
Their chests rise gently and fall again, sometimes in syncopation.

A passing roar and they awake, squint, and settle down again.

As two cats sleep, a world goes on around them.
It is a troubled world, a world full of pain.
Yet, it does not affect them.
They love one another, and they are brothers.
Nothing can disturb their rest or their intimacy.

While sirens blare and alarms ring,
People around may scream and shout.
Dogs may bark and children play,
And two cats sleep.

Craig Sloane

We The God

Falling stars of granite penetrate the glass surface of the pond.
Then water jumps from the dark sea below.
Suspended in the fluid of the air.
Obsidian droplets shine the moons glow.
Waves begin rolling with the sinking of the granite star.
Then the rippled texture populates with falling sheets of rain.
Birth lies under the cold wind where trails splash into life.

A ripple for each drop,
in a pond with one life.

Swimming by the wake,
wake weaved by rain.

Building white crests
moving with the pain.

Over the mountain wave,
Before the ripples.

The star hath fell,
in stark creation.
From that star. I am born.

After one lap, swimming with you.
waves will crash, where faded death spills into the spirit water.

Jon Vanderbeek

Highway 164

Leather laden outlaws tame horses made of steel
their gallop is a rumble that makes a highway dance,
the spirit soar
American made, true blue soldiers of the open road, a modern cowboy
roping the last dregs of freedom
proudly atop their steed, the rushing wind beckons,
calls each of them by name
they answer
digging in spurs made of silver buckle, clinging wildly to manes of
fashioned fringe
bodies fall in unison with a rhythm as sacred as a heartbeat
this rhythm fills the senses
the sweet tingle echoed in aching limbs is recycled
through fingertips that control the reigns of a legend
a ribboned highway is their fodder, sweeter than any honey
desire drips as sweat from furrowed brows
and the horses push forward never daring to stop for water

Jessica Patulski

Life On This Earth; While Facing Death

We live life on this earth, and we try our best.
Then we come to a time when we appear to be put to a test.

It's difficult at times to understand and to cope,
but we put our faith in God for our strength and our hope.

He's there to help us, he's there to understand,
and we give him our love and ask for his hand.

We live life on this earth, shared with family and friends.
The good times, the bad, and our sorrows he mends.

We strive to believe, though there are times that we fail.
His belief in us all shall eternally prevail.

Keep close in our hearts our maker and his power.
Forever he is with us, in both happiness and sorrow.

Believe in his miracles, and the strength he has given you.
Your life will be blessed with God,
family and true friends to surround you.

Carolyn Casterton

The World As It Was In The Beginning

When the world began
There was nothing but matter and energy
Change came and went "unconsciously"
And nature made itself known only
With its gravitational attraction and repulsion
But later on our awareness of this reaction became consciousness
And when the first primordial cells appeared
And arranged themselves into a logical pattern
A unique and simple type of 'nervous tissue'
Took over and with it the attributes of perception grew.

Such was the 'Spirit' of man, then
Such as the understanding of man's development, now

There is a quotation whose author I do not remember
That say "a man is a creature
Who comprehends things he can not see
And believes in things that he cannot comprehend."

Such was the spirit that made-up the world, then
Such is the infinite wisdom we associate with God, now

Angelo R. Duca

Dead And Gone

When you see me shed more than a single tear.
Then you know that I am much more than just sincere.
Our love was so strong, when we were together.
You promised me that it would last forever.
After awhile my love just wasn't enough.
And you left me behind like unwanted stuff.
Now, when I see that she treats you bad.
For you, it makes me feel even more sad.
Now you know that you made a mistake.
And to come back and break my heart again, I just can't take!
You'll never forget me, I know you won't, you wouldn't dare.
Because now you know that I am the only one that will ever really care.
But you played your cards in this little game.
And nothing will ever be the same.
Now that it's over and life goes on.
The love between us is forever dead and gone.

Jennifer L. Oviatt

The Wait

Sometimes life can seem so unfair to us;
There are times when everything just goes wrong.
When we smile it aches, so instead we cuss.
And the radio plays depressing songs.
Ever notice how fun times zip by fast?
"Time stops for no one", so the saying goes,
But when depressed time eternally lasts;
Problems big and trivial always show.
Questions of existence enter the mind:
When will I end or have I just begun?
Many questions with no answers to find.
Hoping . . . behind the clouds there is a sun.
Should I go now, or leave the deed to Fate?
In no hurry for the unknown . . . I'll wait.

Alex Tai

The Hunt Of The Hunter

He stole silently in the night to reach a spot before the light.
With purpose he would wait for that he had pursued of late.

Slowly, then with a rush, light filled the canyon of brush.
In earnest his search began to find his treasured "gain!"

Did he see movement there? Or was it wind "playing" his hair?
It had fallen out his cap . . . but he wasn't sure it was just that.

Out flared antlers, wide and high, reaching toward a clear sky!
Points too numerous to count . . . it didn't matter, he won out!

That is what he figured, until he tried to pull the trigger!

Something inside awoke; something, never heard, spoke:

"Don't hang him on a wall, let live until his final fall!
Just the 'sight' is 'trophy' enough to last one's life!"

He lowered his rifle down, and realized what he found . . .
A wondrous, precious "luck" to witness this magnificent buck!

Dennis Ross

Untitled

An age is called dark but the sun shines
There is no lack of dreams to pursue
Nor lack of ideas to explore
And yet the age is dark
There is no cover over the sun or moon or stars
There is nothing to impede their imaginations
And I tell you now that an age is called dark
Not because the light refuses to shine
But because the people refuse to see it

Karen D. Heeringa

My Silly Heart

My heart is pounding, my eyes are moist
there is something there . . . I feel so lost . . .

I am losing something, no . . . somebody:
the curly girl who loves her daddy

She smiles a little but not too much
her time has come and I need to touch
that little hand that waves bye-bye
it grips my heart and makes me cry

Why do I feel sad?
Why am I mad?

I see it now, I must be a fool
It is my daughter, on her first day of school.

Fabio Lombardo

Rebirth

Beneath the shadow of a tree
There lies a rose,
Made from the delicate whisper of a goddess.

The pink dream shines beneath the moon.
It's sweet breath permeates the air,
The luscious fragrance lightly dances through the forest.

A single petal falls in the rain,
The smooth drops caress the perfect creation.
Spring is born.

Amanda Adomaitis

"Eye Love You"

At the moment our eyes first met
There was no denying the effect,

Of an instant surge of love
That ran through our bodies interwove,

Just caress my body with your eyes
Be gentle and take your sweet time,

We can make this eye affair last
Till the end of time and back past.

Way past the days we were each conceived
Until the day we can no longer breathe,

Now gently tell me with your lips
Is this the beginning of a true love trip

Or is this some fantasy made up in my head
because I am too naive to understand,

The meaning of eye love you.

Esther L. Bowman

"I'll Live On"

Life has changed, yet so have I,
    There's no longer a reason that I shall cry.
Feeling are different my mind is sane,
    I no longer have all of that strain.
Everything bad has turned to good,
So now I'll know if I shouldn't or should.
    Saying no will be an easier word,
Because all my ignorance has been cured.
Those feeling I've felt of anger and pain,
    are no longer feelings I'll need to tame.
Now it's joy and happiness inside,
    I'm no longer along, just for the ride.
That part of me is finally gone,
    Now my heart and soul will forever, live on.

Jennifer Doolen

The World As It Was In The Beginning

When the world began
There was nothing but matter and energy
Change came and went "unconsciously"
And nature made itself known only
With its gravitational attraction and repulsion
But later on our awareness of this reaction became consciousness
And when the first primordial cells appeared
And arranged themselves into a logical pattern
A unique and simple type of 'nervous tissue'
Took over and with it the attributes of perception grew.

Such was the 'Spirit' of man, then
Such as the understanding of man's development, now

There is a quotation whose author I do not remember
That say "a man is a creature
Who comprehends things he can not see
And believes in things that he cannot comprehend."

Such was the spirit that made-up the world, then
Such is the infinite wisdom we associate with God, now

Angelo R. Duca

Another Birthday

Once immortal, beyond time's ken
There was only growing,
desperate anticipation to grasp a first
To know its secrets, and the next

But then we knew, experience unfurled
Remnants of pleasures and defeats
a menagerie of misguided expectation
Creatures of the past engorged
on future visions once so pure

Sort of a drifting now,
past frozen echoes of those paralyzing cries
Hearing instead our children's laugh,
inspired by their innocent wondering eyes

David Schwartz

Freedom

There is a place I see, that doesn't let you be.
There you cry with sadness,
And there you're never free.
There nice words aren't spoken,
Some dreams may be born.
The hope they bear are broken,
I guess they'll never learn.
They're taking me away,
Away from were I play.
Where no one will ever find me,
There I shall sadly stay.
There is a man who binds us, he binds us to our tears.
He always stands behind us,
And now we live in fear.
There is a day of Freedom,
A day we couldn't see.
Our spirits had been broken,
But now we are set free.
I've started my life anew,
Though dwarfed by the memory.

Heidi Lynn Michel

The Cycle Of Life

In the cycle of life there's good and there's bad,
There's pain and sorrow, happy and glad.
In the cycle of life there are ups, there are downs.
The world today smiles, tomorrow it frowns.
In the cycle of life, there's fun and there's laughter.
There's tears and grief and memories thereafter.
In the cycle of life there are feelings, so many,
There's anger, there's joy, there's despair and there's love,
There's faith and disappointment in God up above.
In the cycle of life each day is a year,
Each hour a moment, so precious so dear.
Every second to be lived to its fullest.
Every day to have meaning and goals.
Life has been given true purpose in the sharing of special souls.
In the cycle of life there's pain and there's sorrow
But there's always the hope for a brighter tomorrow.

Carone B. Berman

Hang In There

Hang in there, God is with you, believe it so,
They find you guilty of something you didn't do,
You are blessed for He permitted this to happen to you,
This is your Gethsemane, but will go through.

Hang in there, even though it seems like the end to you,
For people you thought you can trust betrayed you,
And like Judas, they kissed you for a few silver coins,
But remember, you are not alone, we are here for you.

Hang in there, the moment of truth will come,
You are not what they think you are and you know it so,
Despair not, be of good courage and strengthen your heart,
For God in His mercy will free you and crown you with life.

Eden Agamata-Daproza

Bars Of Laughter

I lay behind these bars of pain.
They keep me from the sun and rain.

I sit and stare through these bars of time.
What they want, is my peace of mind.

These bars of steel laugh at me,
as I count the days.   1   2   3

Barbed wire fence, chainlink cage,
confine the lunatics, the thieves, the raged.

The day will come when I'll be free.
These bars of pain are not for me.

Daniel F. White

"In His Eyes"

In his eyes, I see, the special joy and pride I bring.
These are the very precious years, that will always be held near!!!
Kindergarten started so hard - he just didn't want to be apart!!!
In his eyes, I see, the happiness I bring, when another day at
school ends, and by my side he'll again!!
In his eyes, I see, how much joy reading a book can be . . .
Or to count to 100 . . . or even 3!!!
In his eyes, I see, the happiness it brings, when he can write "mom"
and show me how it's done!!!
In his eyes, I see, the special love he has for me . . .
Looking up to me just-so and wanting to go most everywhere I go!!
In his eyes, I see, he's so sincere when he says "He loves me" . . .
In my eyes, I see, he's everything a mother would want him to be!!!

Diana Moore

Friends

I call them Friends
These women who share the bits and pieces
  of their lives every second Tuesday.
The crazy things we do and say
Politics and candlesticks,
Football to lottery picks.
AARP meetings to vegetable dips,
Wedding bells and Reno trips.
The local news to buckle shoes,
The etiquette of don'ts and do's.
Recalling the crazy things we've done
The Good Ol' Days since fifty-one.
Make-shift hats,
Hobo meals.
Broomstick dancing,
Laughter peals.
We share both the good and bad
I dearly treasure the times we've had.
I call you "Friends"

Dorlene Bressan

Just Another Day

It's just another day,
They are all the same way.
Mornings are so bright,
The day ends with a dark night.
Each day looks like the one before,
The streets are crowded, the traffic roars.
Then comes night for stars to keep,
Also comes that peaceful poet, sleep.
The days go and come, they've all been seen,
Every day is the same routine.
The cold wind blows by,
There's nowhere to run, nowhere to hide.
Alone, by myself, it's peaceful now,
It seems another world somehow.
But the real world still awaits out there,
The pressure, noise and worries are too much to bear.
One must fight for himself if he wants to succeed.
That's the code of life that all should heed.

Jim Humay

Legacy

Where have all the children gone?
  They are in my heart but I cannot touch them.
  They are in my soul but I cannot know them.
  Shall we have a Holy Day to remember them?
  Where have all the children gone?

  In my prayers and at Confession I ask for forgiveness
  For the horrible legacy I began
  I am responsible and I know
Where all the children have gone.

  They said that since I was a woman and it was my body
    that I could choose
  But, they were wrong, and I know
Where all the children have gone.

  You are a part of me—who I am and what I believe
  And I hope others realize before it is too late
Where all the children have gone.

  No, I am not an activist, I do not march nor stand
    at the clinic door.
  I am only a simple woman with pen and paper to tell you
Where all the children have gone.

Carolyn Smith

Footprints

Footprints on the wooden dock
They are mine
When that last morning
I wanted to photograph the sunrise
You woke me early with my cup of brew
The sky was dark
There was a heavy dew
I strolled out on the dock
And over the water I gazed
The sun started peeking over the trees
The sky became a blaze
With colors of every hue
That special morning I spent with you
Now like those footprints that are there no more
You've gone from me - HE closed that door
But the love in my heart will never die
You showed me the way, now I must try
To live as you would want me to
Loving and laughing as you would do

Carol Jean Hogen

Villan Valley

You look out your window and see there mark.
they do there business in the dark.
in this town you live in fear
all day long this is what you hear . . .

BANG! BOOM! there goes another life
it's with a gun or a knife.
as you walk down the valley there's nothing but war
Dealer's on the corner, the poor at your door.

if you want to be a hero
it makes no difference
shot to the floor
there nothing but "Hard core"

Day by Day, Night by Night
Power is held if you can fight
Hang with your gang, Hang with your chief
life in the valley it takes a thief.

Frank Marazita

For Seamus Heaney

He forges his poems on the anvil of his soul
They emerge emitting sparks
Patina perfect
Searing my self deeply with his words
Raking to redness the ashes of yearning
for the soft voice, the sympathetic air
of 'the black North'

My life a patchwork quilt,
His a seamless garment woven with strong thread
For a time we smelled the same 'baps' and bluebells
Knew the sweet kernel of the cracked hazel nut
Were kin to the same valleys, hills and fern
cosseted by mists and grayness of cloud
Shared the same syllabus of sounds
Rhymed the rhymes
Derry, Antrim, Down, Armagh, Tyrone, Fermanagh
Our paths never crossed
Yet we have met
For him I need no glossary of terms.

Bernadette N. Daly

Do You Believe

Do you believe in miracles?
They happen everyday, a baby's born, a flower blooms
Your sins are washed away.

Yes washed away by His shed blood
From a man so kind and true.
He knew from the start He would die
For sinners like me and you.

That wonderful man called Jesus
Knew his own destiny, He would teach the true word of God
Then He'd die on Calvary.

He'd love in return, forgive us all
Even the ones who betrayed,
Then carry that cross willingly
While on lookers ranted and raved.

Forgive them Father He said that day, they know not what they do.
Oh, Jesus, Jesus wonderful Lord, the torture you went through.

Without you I'm lost in this world, but with you I'm found - Amen
This dear precious man called Jesus, my hero, my Lord and best friend.

Frances Ripley

Parents

Parents are there when you need them most
They hold you very tight and close

Parents will be there for you
when your down or feeling blue

They bring you the brightest of days
with there kind and loving ways

They do many things to show they care
They hug, they kiss, they love, they share

When they punish you, you've done wrong
They won't be mad for very long

Parents want the very best for you
You often wonder what to do

Just listen to them with all your heart
for they were there for you right from the start.

Dinny'vie Branco

"Reminiscence"

Sometimes when I feel sad and blue
There's something Lord I'd like to do
I'd like to climb up on your lap
And maybe take a little nap - so very tired I am
I feel the need of your embrace.
When I was little may be three
I'd climb up on my fathers knee
He'd stroke my head and hold me tight
And every thing would be all right
I know that you're my father too
And that is what I'd like to do
Just sit upon your knee Dear Lord
And taste the love that you afford.
And even tho' I'm grown up now
Their are times it seems to me somehow
If I could sit upon your knee
And feel you very close to me
Then all the hurts would go away,
And once again I'd run and play
The little girl of yesterday.

Dorothy N. Long

Untitled

Friends are worthwhile, good as gold.
They keep a secret if they've been told.
Now I know this, and it's been said,
friends will feed ya if you need fed.
You would have a bed in their house
anytime you stopped.
They'd never turn their backs on you
even if your points had dropped.
They'll mount you on a horse even if you're tough.
They don't ask nothing back. "Thanks" is enough.

A friend would stand up for ya in any situation.
It doesn't matter if you're up
against the whole damn nation.

There's many crossroads
down there on those old rodeo trails.
We always seem to get back together —
Hell, it never fails.

But someday we'll split up,
never see each other again.
But we'll say to ourselves on that lonesome day,
"Man, he sure was a friend."

Now it's been said, and I know it's true,
I've got good friends —
but the best one's YOU.
To Tygh Campbell

Jay Dean Hall

Shoes Blues

They tread on my soul, use my toe for their goal;
They kick me aside like a heel.
I receive many a scuff from lads who act tough.
They don't give a darn how I feel.

They pull on my tongue, gouge at my eyes;
They tie knots in my tattered laces.
They put me through mud, water and ice
And a thousand dirty places.

In the corner I'm cast 'till it's morning at last
When I get the boot from a house cleaning mother.
I get the brush-off sometimes but never those shines
And for church — they put on another.

It's no easy feat for me to stay sweet
When dirty socks I'm forced to devour.
Everyone knows I'd smell like a rose
If those dirty old toes would just shower.

I've come to conclude, although it be rude,
My mission isn't meant for the feet
Of those who abuse a nice pair of shoes.
I should swiftly be placed on their seat!!

George Vanness

Old Man

See that old man standing there?
They say he's been everywhere.
His clothes are wrinkled and he looks thin,
Wonder where he's really been.
He stands so tall among the crowd,
You can see that he's mighty proud.
Look, there's tears in his eyes,
As he salutes our flag going by.
They say he served in World War II,
Korea and Vietnam too.
See the stripes upon his sleeve,
And the cap he's wearing is D.A.V.

Henry G. Stivers

Leaves Of Lace

Leaves of lace start life shiny and green
They live life's path
And give benefits not readily seen,
Leaves harbor natures creatures
And nurture their bodies,
They soften all natures features
But, in the "Fall"
Their riotous colors signal natures "Ball"!
Then they fall upon the ground
A place for all to rejoice
And life's fullness will be found,
Then they start to decay
To feed the roots of all,
So let us rejoice today
And look upon this leaf
As it's life fades away,
Behold! Look upon it's face
  Miracle of miracles
It has turned to lace

James Edward Arnold

Mothers

Why are mothers always right?
They seem to know if you slept all night.
They tell you "manners are never out of style",
But just keep going then stop a while.

Your brother teases you round the clock,
He calls you names he makes you hot.
Mothers are right whether you like it or not,
They just can't help but tell you a lot.

Angela Fabbri

Why Mommy?

Why do stars twinkle in the sky? Why, mommy, why?
They shine so bright throughout the night, I have to ask the reason!
  WHY?

Do plants sleep or just me?
I'll stay awake; I'll hide I'll look. I need to see all I can see
My mind, my thoughts: could write a book!

Why does a ship float?
But wait. When do we call it a boat?
I sink when I stand in the water.
Why then can fishes swim much faster?

WHY? MOMMY, WHY?
What's that? Why so high?
What makes that rainbow in the sky?
LOOK! different shapes of clouds fly by!
WHY, MOMMY, WHY?
My mind, my thoughts, go
WHY? WHY? WHY?!!

Jacquelyn V. Harris

Facts Of Life

People speak, but do they really listen?
They walk, but can they really stand?
People look, but do they really see?
Oh how hopeless sometimes life can be
Why do people do the things they do?
I don't know do you?
People move, but do they really live?
They write, but do they know if it's wrong?
People help, but do they really want to?
Maybe it's ignorance or just plain blindness?
Or maybe it's afraid of dying or living?
Why do people do the things they do,
Why do I?
I know, do you?

Amy Stuart

The Butte Hands

There never will be miners like they used to have in Butte;
They'd break it by the acre and get it in the chute.

Those days in Butte have come and gone, those miners left the camp;
Off to other holes to work, and some still on the tramp.

Some landed in New Mexico, much softer ground to break;
But soon sacked up their diggers, when they had themselves a stake.

Other found Jeffrey City was the place to try their luck;
The mines were paying plenty for this special kind of muck.

But that sandstone was unstable, and it took a heavy toll;
The tramps took off in search of another distant hole.

A lot of good Butte miners lit in the Coeur d'Alènes;
It must have been the hardrock was still flowing in their veins.

Where it's deeper and it's hotter, they seemed to congregate;
Take that Sunshine fire, where some good hands met their fate.

Though a lot of them are gone now, into other fields it seems;
They still hear the roaring of that jackleg in their dreams.

No matter where one tramps to in search of virgin ground;
He'll find a few ol' Butte hands are likely still around.

Verne E. Boston

Classics

Some things you would not change even if you could,
Things that can't be improved upon, try as one should.
Things appealing to our senses and sensibility:
A look. A perfect moment. A melody. Humility.

Some things take us beyond standards right up to the stars,
Soaring above the level best to Jupiter and Mars.
These things we call classics, cherished for the gifts they bring:
To our homes a quiet magnificence; to our hearts a song to sing!

They often come to us from a time when our vision was clearer,
Able to see through to truths, able to bring them nearer.
How we could live! How much we could achieve
If virtue were the thread of the lives we choose to weave.

Classics are not always lofty or unattainable,
For we have just to reach out to make them gainable.
Though we cannot always add quantity to our daily lives,
Classics can add wondrously to the quality our living derives.

J. Griffin Day

Homeward Bound

I sit here alone in the middle of the night
Thinking of my journey and the ten hour flight
The job I am doing takes me far from my home
I'll be away from my loved ones, feeling very alone

For years I loved traveling and going away
But now all I wonder is how long I will stay
I long for my wife and my sweet little girl
My most precious belongings, my own flawless pearls

My beautiful young daughter is now nearly two
When she came into my life, my world was renewed
With each day together our bonds grow much stronger
And my desire for traveling is with me no longer

The lady I fell in love with nearly ten years ago
Always dealt with my traveling and rarely said no
But as partners in life we have grown to be strong
And I long to be near her at home where I belong

Though I often wonder how long each trip will be
Its just the end of my journey that I long to see
Coming home to my family always brightens my life
Just to hold and embrace them, my daughter and wife

Larry A. Carnes

My Friend, My Love

He touched my heart in ways I've never known
This friend of mine, who's now my own.
Our love as children was always foretold,
We invited the notion of being alone.

Our love has grown to heights unknown,
Surpassing the merger of hearts entwined.
With mountains to climb and rivers to cross,
We shouted with happiness for a love not loss.

The seduction of his kiss; enticed my inner soul.
The fire he ignites will never go cold.
With every passing moment, our plans of growing old,
will always be the path on which we stroll.

The magic of his words relinquish all my fears,
Being together now, struggling through the years.
In a world of uncertainty, where no one else cares,
This friend of mine, wipes away my tears.

Now we sit together and reminisce the past,
This love of mine is home at last.
To whatever may, from day to day
This love of mine, is forever my own.

Orna Husbands

Home

This was our home, the first we ever owned:
This is a house, where I now live alone.

This was our living room, where we sat and talked:
This is a lonely room, where I sit and remember.

This was our dining room, where we ate our meals:
This is a table and an empty chair.

This was our kitchen, where you loved to cook:
This is just another room and a dinner of leftovers.

This was the closet, where your belongings are stored:
This is a place I cannot enter right now.

This was the window, where you waved goodbye to me every morning:
This is a closed curtain that hides my tears.

This was our bedroom, where we held each other every night:
This is a place to sleep, while I hug your pillow.

This was to be the rest of our life together:
This is my life without you.

Nancy Lee Markell

Peace - We All Aspire

"Saying peace, peace, when there is no peace"
- this is the verse from the Isaiah.

It's a terrible truth of the world that,
we see the wages of peacemaking are death!

World history reminds us again and again,
that to achieve peace is a torturous quest;
yet it doesn't despair from our realism.
We all aspire peace day and night,
like others in the beget of war of human civilization.

Imagine, the dream "the world would be one",
dwells in me and you, why then we are at the cross-roads?
Why then there is so much suffering and bloodshed?
Why hunger, disease and homeless life exists on earth,
Why not we bury our rages and stop the war machines?

Let's shape our intolerances into an unequivocal for peace,
to enlighten more life in harmony - not death.
Don't let the peacemakers as mirror images of death,
believe in 'thou shalt not kill'.

Muhammad Ali Bukhari

Look To Tomorrow

In this world of trouble and sorrow,
This lifetime that passes so fast:
Think of the joys of tomorrow
Forget the cares of the past.
Remember yesterdays for lessons and learning,
Remember the loves and the laughs,
Keep all the joy, your ambitions and yearning
Each shining memory of good things that are past.
But look to tomorrow for a future,
That is bright and shining and blessed
Make each tomorrow a new beginning
To make memories of a perfect past.

Ruth B. Jones

Children

   Babies are joy and fun. They can be hard work till day is done.
This little life is part of you it grew and nurtured inside of you.
Now this child that God has given is in your hands to teach and
love. It won't be easy, yet you will find the comfort of happiness
you see on their face. Remember this child is of God and nothing
else could take its place. So as you may feel worn or frazzled at
times. Think of the long run of what joy you will share when this
child's first word is mom.

Dedicated to My Sister Angela Renee Sandwith

and all the other children we have lost too soon

Shannon M. Sandwith

My Thanksgiving Holiday

Early in the morning I awoke, I could not sleep due to anxiety.
This morning was the big morning I've been dreading.
The morning I got my wisdom teeth removed (all four).
But the Uncomfortableness I had from six hours
With gauze in my mouth. I could not drink nor eat.
My parents told me "Well, the worst part is over."
My stitches are to be removed next week-until then, no gum, no popcorn.
Tomorrow is Thanksgiving day, all I can eat is mashed potatoes
and soup broth.
This makes me appreciate my past Thanksgivings, the food, and my family.
I definitely will not take for granted but take advantage of my future
Thanksgivings. I am very relieved that this day is over and done.

Rita Edwards

I Am My Mother's Flower

I had only one flower blossom in my great garden of delight.
This one flower gave off many colors that shown so bright.
As the flower blossomed day after night.
I never let my innocent flower out of my sight.
Years went by as I watched my flower grow.
She became more and more vibrant, and was now perfect for show.
Now it was time to place my flower in someone else's care.
I hope they love and cherish her, with all their time to spare.

There goes my precious flower, leaving me with tears.
I will always remember the time we spent, fighting our greatest fears.
Farewell my sweet flower until we meet again.
I'm sure God would have us together, later
toward the end.

Kyna J. Voss

Rebel Angel

As she sleeps in silent slumber,
this rare specimen to the feminine gender.
With golden hair against fair
skin, she glows from within.

Ever whining, ever complaining ever so sure.
The Rebel Angel is recharging
once more . . .
So tomorrow she can tempt us,
astound us . . . Amaze us.
Delight us . . .

And . . . as the silence that
we are wanted all day is neigh,
something is missing and its the
giggle of this child.
Now we look forward for tomorrow,
for greater encounters.
We'd never give it up cause
there'd never be a brighter tomorrow

Lillian Kelly

A Memory

Remember this I ask myself,
This wallet size picture, just a little beat
up and ragged around the edges.
It still shows clearly though, my wife, my life, my love.
Her golden hair and round blue eyes, like
crystallized rubies from the center of the earth.
They are like deep pits that if stared into
long enough, one will get lost in them.
Before I knew it, I was.
I still get that feeling when I awake and find her beside me.
Her moist lips are shown here brightly in red.
The bursts of emotions I felt when we first
kissed, are still there, like a mirror image
that won't go away.
The secret innermost thoughts we shared,
our wants and desires, our passions
we both found comfort in each other's arms.
The warmth and love, it's all there!

Vance E. Rawson Jr.

Untitled

Where does it come from
  this yearning to be free?
  Free to explore all avenues open to me.
  Free to be all that I can be.
  To soar like an eagle-all the world to see.
  Free of the stench of poverty
  Free to be me. To cry or laugh joyously.
  Free of the fear caused by thee.
  Free to live happily as can be.
Where does it come from-this yearning to be free?

Mary Andrews

On The Inside

A cloudy blue suitcase filled with things of old,
Things said and done and many untold.

Hapless memories tucked under those that brought contentment
The kind of ecstasies engrossed in shameful resentment

This suitcase worn for many many years,
Is languid with sweat and dried tears.

It's dingied corner oblivious to a piercing sight
While broken latches tell of it's struggles and fights

A few more roads to travel this suitcase has
Dismissing bitter memories of a stored past

Nita B. Wood

Friends

Do you remember as I do,
Those days when you knew me and I knew you.
We were great friends, we were together,
We thought our bond would last forever.
Together we felt so very strong,
We thought we could conquer the world,
and right all wrong.
Until one day we were torn apart,
Our bond was broken heart to heart.
We thought of each other day and night,
And through the early morning light.
Our thoughts got less as time went on,
'Til our thoughts of each other were
completely gone.
Except for vague memories, that lingered behind,
In the labyrinths and corridors of our jumbled minds.
We found these vague memories and realized what we'd done,
We had become two when we once were one.
We forgave and forgot and were friends again,
And were where we were when this whole thing began.

Stefanie Allison

A Lucky Mother

As the mother of two boys, don't pity me
Though doll, curls frill and bows are not to be

I soon found out the many varied joys
That come to lucky mothers who have boys.

My interests now have changed, yes quite a bit
And paper dolls have been replaced by airplane kits

And trading cards, and bats and cars and balls
And bikes and bugs and rocks and nasty falls.

Admitted my life is not the same
I've even learned to watch a baseball game . . .

And just this year I had a "heady" taste of fame
The team chose me for scoring every game.

And now and then your glimpse the man they will become
And proud I am to be the mother of two sons!

Martha Fairman

Speaking Of Birthdays

When I was quite young, lanky and lean
Though that I'd never, never reach 16.

In the 20's I felt so wise and vague
And did not mind who knew my correct age.

Came the 30's I started to hedge a bit, asked which
Birthday, I'd throw a real conniption fit.

In the 40's I wept at finding a first grey hair,
That's when "age" became my own personal despair.

In the 50's there were tell-tale lines in my face,
Yet I fibbed about my age with passable grace.

In the 60's I shed frustrated tears,
Yet still refused to admit my number of years.

Now in the 70's "time" has put a permanent tag,
So I no longer prevaricate, I shamelessly brag.

Should the 80's dawn, the cork vaguely remote.
I'd gleefully announce my age from any old house top.

The 90's? That event seems vaguely remote.
But the way Tempest Fugits, I may catch the boat!

The 100's? Hundreds?? Oh, Ye Gods and little fishes,
Would there remain any friends to extend birthday wishes?

Tressie Storer

If Only My Mind Could Shout

Candles flickering in my mind casting shadows about.
Thoughts of us if only my mind could shout.

Walking hand in hand on the horizons of my mind.
My love, my love shadows dancing in time.

Like a lit candle placed in the window of my mind.
Interwoven shadows dancing in time.
Hand in hand, shadows interwoven, walking on the horizons of
my mind.
Lit candles casting shadows about.
If only my mind could shout.

Kenneth Lee Burk

A Gift Of Gold

He made a difference in our lives,
Through all his simple ways.
He never took-he always gave,
His love would fill our days.

His words of wisdom helped us grow,
His faith made us believe.
Now, guide us Lord, we'll miss him so
Help us not to grieve.
You've freed his pain, he now walks with you;
His victory has been won.
Give us his strength and loving touch;
His spirit will live on.

For in our hearts he'll always be,
His love, his smile, his touch.
You gave to us a gift of gold.
Now, dear Lord, with our thanks
We give him back for you to hold
His life was a gift of gold.

Margaret Holinsworth

Love's Gone Away

Ours was a love you said would last throughout the years
Through all the pain, heartache and tears
Then one day you turned to me and said you couldn't hold on
I looked upon your solemn face and wondered what I did wrong
They say that time can heal all wounds and love it never dies
Perhaps that's just a myth, a bunch of pretty lies.
All the love I feel for you is now trapped within my heart
I want so much to give it, it seems to tear my soul apart
Your love's gone away.

Tracie R. Lane

Jelal

Minutes were
those sexy moments
I laid waiting for you,
in bed
lying there . . .
with my eyes closed
religiously separating the sound of your footsteps,
from my pounding heartbeat
I wanted you
as I envisioned grey rain
and a faded green couch
that we could lie upon
naked
dissolving into each other,
gazing at tangerine sunsets
and smoke-blue skies
deciding . . .
what to make for dinner.

Kelly Watson

This Way Before I Shall Not Pass This Way Again

It seems I've been this way before,
  Through eons of both time and space.
The road looks now the same as then;
  Each turn, each stretch fulfills the race.

"This way before", the spirit cries
  As heart-ache yearns for some lost friend;
Who passed too soon from grasp and fell
  To clouded realms with bounds no end.

And if by more than chance it seems,
  My stumbling moved a stone there found;
To smooth the way of those behind,
  Allowed to reach the higher ground.
Now looking back to my slowed pace,
  My shout go win the race my friend!
And though I've been this way before,
  I shall not pass this way again.

And though this way familiar be,
  Through dream or vision in time or when?
But this I know each day I see,
  I shall not pass this way again.

Lysle R. English

To A Bride

Come, let's sail together across the life's stream
Through its many smiles and passing brief sobs
Along its many sunlit paths and some unlit ways.
Pause not to think if we here lost some skirmish
Or there won a life's little battle. The life flows
Unceasingly on, let's take it all as it unfolds, its
Smiles 'n sobs, darkness and light, all, all of it.

Let's take to it, it is yours, mine, our life now.
Never shall we turn back, on, on, onwards along
The happy highway, up above all darkened lanes.
The world? An empty snare, let it just pass us by.

A common life-breath binds us, O friend mine,
Look, the many-mirrored prism of fleeting time
Holds life in ransom. Let's not tarry, our new life
Beckons. This beatific, loving, our common life.
It was yours, was mine, till yesterday. 'Tis now
Ours, my mate, let's sail together on the jocund
Paths of life's unending dream, just you and me.

Rajendra Prasad Harkara

For The Sake Of Science . . .

Twenty years of edification.
Through minor pitfalls and hallowed halls.
Pupating in a bone-encased cocoon.
Developing grand mal, fighting the banal.

Myriad pathways by chance predetermined
lead to science, not a job but a lifestyle.
Or an excuse for grievous inhumanity — experimentation.
Principles of interspecies coexistence defiled.

Wading through the mental pain.
Elbow deep in blood and brains.

Searching for truth, the pursuit of knowledge.
Primate in a cage, shaking bars, eating stool.
Craniotomy, dural transection, cortical intrusion.
Smoke smells of blood and flesh, my cautery the tool.

Forcing perfusate through the venous circulation.
Watching the dead eyes stare clouded, eyelids twitch.
Asking again what I wanted years ago from life.
Am I happy in this — my chosen niche?

Have my travels been in vain?
Through them, what has the world gained?

Timothy M. Woods

The Wind Woman

The Wind Woman whistles through the trees,
Through the thistles, over the seas.
She has the waves at her command,
She screams through caves, flies over the land.
Birds glide on her currents, leaves tremble and shake
With an air of innocence, the whole earth does quake.
The cool breezes blow at her every will,
Gusts of wind are of her skill.
The glassy lake ripples with her silent kiss,
Stillness she cripples with her whispery hiss.
She is invisible yet invincible, kind yet cruel,
She is angry yet lovable, cheating yet true.

Sara Romano

All Things New

Summer time with its gentle breezes whispering
    through the trees,
Beauty of the flowers and the work of the
    Honey Bees.
Autumn Comes with its beauty, then falls to
    the ground.
The winter Snow descends and covers it like a
    blanket never again to be found.
Spring nears and Mother Nature sings her new
    song.
She arrives with new life, refreshed with the
    beauty that cuts like a knife
It reminds me that God will one day make
    all things new.
A new home especially prepared for me and you.

Michael Hood

The Taste Of Winter

    I whiz by nipping at your aged ears and I tear
through your eyes leaving them raw and sore.
    Tender to the touch, I rip off your shelter and
leave your skin bare. My frost lingers in your bitter
tears.
    A drifting scent of betrayal floats among your
bodies. I catch drift of your pain and use it against your
will to live. But, still you push against my gust of cold
snow.
    Out of all my chances of snatching your lives, I
take pity on your nomad souls.

Stephanie Jacobson

Future Fate

Two lonely hearts from different pasts
Thrown astray from love not meant to last
Wonder in search of a love that's true
Looking for something entirely new
What these hearts don't know or realize
Is that in one another is where their fate lies
One day soon these hearts will meet
And one of two will knock the other off their feet
It will begin with one catching the others eye
Then emotions will build as days go by
They'll have several conversations, heart to heart
No one knows exactly when the loving will start
But those, two hearts once in search and alone
Will realize that together true love is shown
These hearts will confess their love and fears
They'll promise to stay together throughout the years
They will become as one, faithful and true
And together they'll share a love lasting their whole lives through.

Tonya S. Cox

Midnight Snow

Fresh, falling, midnight snow blankets my blue yard
tickles the faces of people who go, whoever they are

What a sight to see on this solemn Christmas Eve
consoles me, though not a single word does it speak

Such mystery dwells in the air on the night before
remembering how my heart felt when I was but four

I venture out to greet crystals that dance in my eyes
staring up, I imagine sailing the quiet ebony sky

Flying away to a place of peace, another realm
where hatred, loneliness, and fear are seldom felt

Closing my eyes, head tilted to sky, without a coat
such a warmth comes - as if God touched my soul

Fresh, falling, midnight snow blankets my blue yard
tickles my face, takes me to a place of total disregard

Michael Franks

A Separate Time

As you leave my arms to go again,
Time stops; as if in a dream
I am mesmerized by your eyes
White light pierces my soul
I watch you back float away as you go
Now, a separate time.

The smell of you still fresh on my lips
permeates my mind.
Thoughts and scents flow in and out with each breath.
I am entranced in a half-space.
My separate time is not mine.

The sound of the sea breaks my endless reverie of you and time
You . . . and the sea,
Always come back to me
To cleanse and irrigate the hazy dried paths beneath the jungle
A separate time . . . but you are mine.

Morna McGann

Life's Recipe

Yesterday was filled with beauty,
Tinged about with homely duty:
    Flowers to gather,
      Friends to greet;
    Hope to scatter,
      And love to meet.
So full of joy was yesterday,
I wished for a part of it today.

Today, again, was beauty-filled,
Care and hopefulness o'erspilled:
    A child to hold,
      Reassure the while;
    Take away the hurt,
      Give smile for smile.
Immersed in child's world of books and toys,
I find happiness lies in little joys.

Naomi Shook

Magic Fingers

Magic finger weave a spell from the womb to the grave.
Tiny fingers reaching out, for its mothers love they crave.
Magic fingers of little children as he plays in a sandbox or tub.
Building highways, floating ships, then in bed,
   his tired eyes he will rub.

These same fingers on a teen-age child,
   will be writing homework for school.
They will be used, we pray, to help a friend,
   in pursuit of the golden rule.

Who knows the magic young adults can make
   with busy hands and fingers strong.
With the help of God, those hands can be used,
   to justify some wrong.

With a pen or brush there is no limit,
   to what those same fingers can create.
Beautiful poems, pictures or songs, hidden beauty they can relate.

Builders architects, musicians laborers,
   all depend on the magic of hands.
We pray that only good they have done,
   when God calls them to that mysterious land.

    Louis M. Hatch

We Live Forever

As people move on
To a different life without us.
They still live forever
Within our hearts and souls.

People we care so much for are always there
Within our hearts and souls, Forever, never to die.
Someday, sometime everyone will move on
Regardless of age or how full their life once was.

Always remember they are there
Within our hearts, memories, and souls.
Forever and always to be remembered
By friends, family, and everyone else.

Our lives move on, but the past is still there
To always be remembered, for the good, not the bad.
You can not replace anything that is lost
You can only cherish what you had once long ago.

    Marcy Thrall

Child Of This World

Shouldn't we all begin with the same destiny? Loved, cherished, born
to be free?
   How, when where then does it all go wrong? Why is it I don't know
   where I belong?

I am a child of this world—from which country matters not
   Bosnia, Somalia, America each one needing to be taught
   that without me there is no future and this planet's the only one
   we've got.
Abandoned and abused, never to have a voice in matters that concern me;
   Never to have a choice to love and be loved unconditionally
   because I know no emotion, no reason to rejoice.
Unattached with no conscience, no feeling of self-worth; I'm part of
generation lost and
   Oh, by the way, when I give birth
   what can I hope to pass on to a brand new child of this earth?

Abandoned and abused like yesterday's news
   But through it all hope springs eternal
Won't you recycle me, too, from this never-ending inferno?

    Lynette Perkins

Hate

Hate is a hardening of the soul so much that it is difficult
To break. Vengeance, revenge, and spirits of the like contrary
To love, constitute hate. Hate is mother forsaking child,
Sister against brother black against white. Hate is an
Evil attribute that should be purged from one's heart like
The impurities of flour before its final stage. Hate comes
In unexpectedly as its victims struggle for their independence,
Only to break free when the damage has already been done.
Hate leaves traces as those on its track are slowly carried
Away.
A 19-year old young man is late coming home as his worried
Mother anxiously awaits his return. Thinking the worst,
She frantically begins making phone calls searching for
Hope at the other end of the line. Meanwhile, the young man,
Innocently walking to his destination, is struck by several
bullets. He goes down, limb by limb, as the unexpected pellets
Shatter his young body. An 82 Datsun escapes the crime scene
Leaving behind its screeches of horror.
His lifeless body lay cold, motionless, undisturbed.

    Suzette Jones

Fifty Years Ago

We travel back in memory some fifty years ago,
To carefree days at Cedar Lake when years of time were slow.

Our world was small, but we stood tall on this secluded hill,
Expecting that our hopes and dreams someday we would fulfill.

A quiet village boasted some, renowned for all its charm.
An old shoe shop, a country store, and nothing to alarm.

A quaint hotel two stories high, and everyone could find
A double decker outhouse there just twenty feet behind.

And if you're walking up the hill you cross a railroad track,
And hear old "90" puff its way, smoke rising from the stack.

There's much we could recall just now of study, work, and play,
Of Sabbath walks and vesper hours at dear old CLA.

What joy there is remembering the sound of that old bell.
If it could speak and halls could talk what stories they would tell!

So here are just a few tidbits we've gleaned from out the past,
And hope you will enjoy them all as long as time shall last.

    Larry Pumford

A Walk With Nature

Come walk with me in early morn
to catch the rising of the sun
We'll see the dewdrops on the leaves
and hear the babbling water run
through shiny rocks of misty grey
and as we walk along the way
We'll smell the fragrance of the flowers
that bloom in early morning hours.

Come walk with me when day has gone
in the hush of an evening breeze
We'll walk through fields so lush and green
or through the gently rustling leaves
that cover the path where we always go
to reach the top of the hill and see the sun sink low
To view the earth where only we can see
our world in its glowing majesty
Then we'll return to our home
for which we have been blest
As all nature puts her bounty
to sleep and rest.

    Robbie Miller

The Chipmunk's Adventure

"To see the world beyond" it said,
"To discover the out of the ordinary
To run as fast as a rabbit would
spread wings and fly like a canary."

It was then that an idea popped into his head,
That chipmunk would run away
he would get that life of adventure,
And with that he was off and away.

He made for the meadow, to the buttercup patch
to discover discoveries there,
And it was a great discovery that chipmunk found
When he entered a grey wolf's lair!

The chipmunk ran like lightning,
As fast as a rabbit would,
He ran as fast as he was able,
Back again, back to the wood.

The chipmunk was welcomed with opened arms
Then told to sit down and rest,
and never was that chipmunk off again,
for he realized home is best.

E. Lea Reynolds

Legacy

I leave you light and lofty laughter,
to drown the solemn sobbing sounds.
But I give you not, the gift of grieving
when I escape these earthly bounds.

I leave you peaceful, patient, ponderings,
to prod you through your pensive lows.
And lift your thoughts toward happy endings,
made to quell impending woes.

I leave you soft and sunny mornings,
with the wealth of warming winds.
And evenings laced with brilliant sunset,
where imagination never ends.

I leave you love to soothe your longings,
with strength to chase your future dreams.
And will to you . . . a gift of courage,
should you learn what failure means.

These things I leave in loving legacy;
Yours to cherish or ignore.
Or, just to pass to someone special
. . . should you not need them anymore.

William Doyle Still

Earth

You lay on the earth
to feel its hum
your cheek pressed against the ground
closing your eyes
you feel the pain of the earth

Cries for help ring out
trees crying out as they fall
the oceans weep
rain becomes acid and dies at its touch
animals run including you

You are a part of the earth
the pain is part of you
can't you feel it
is your heart so cold that nothing touches it
or does only pain excite it

Laura Hwang

Oh! How Sweet Thy Love Can Be

To see thy love shine through thy eyes,
To Feel thy warmth of thy love,
To heal thy broken hearts of pain.
Oh! How sweet thy love can be.

To share thy love with me,
To care with love for thee,
To say I love thee oh! so fine!
Oh! How sweet thy love can be.

I shall look for love all time,
  and I shall find the love so kind.
I shall ask for love for me
  and I shall get that love I need.

For when I die my broken heart shall mend.
And I shall find my one and true love.
  Up in heaven he will be!
My sorrows will end; and pain will spread
  throughout your life til the every end.
And oh! How sweet thy love could have been for me.

Rosario Guerrero

Olympic Commandment

Ask the spirit of your best,
To fulfill your will's request.

The exhaustion of body to conquer,
And not let it faint when the fight occur.

The Olympic oath to understand well,
Feel in full its might and spell.

Fly around the world using the imagination's wings,
When youth and beauty from your body still springs.

Of human victory the taste to feel,
With so much bravery and earthly good will.

To listen to the national anthem sounds,
As to divine-service on sport's ground.

Raise your eyes to the Master-Creator of all alive,
And let belief and training for miracles strive.

Roman Wroclawski

Angel On The Moon

It's never to early it's never too soon
to get a good look at the angel on the moon
she is up there watching over us working
with fate making sure things turn out okay
Her silhouette is thin while she stands tall
helping people throughout life no matter how
big or small.
Her presence helps people when we lest expect it.
A miracle or granting a good wish
even if it means not burning dinner
or chipping an expensive plate or dish
Her existence is omnipresent teaching
us all to do what we can to help each
other even after a fall
To get back up to exhibit kindness
To remember and pass along all of the good.
The angel on the moon is a lot closer than I know
She exists and is always here for me.
I can't tell you her name the only clue
I will give to you is that she is my sister.

Sheri O'Brien

Addicting

You feel trapped inside. You can't get out. You have no where to go,
to get away from the feeling. You have to have it. It haunts you
until you have it again. What am I suppose to do without it. You
forgot how to be yourself. Were you really actually your own person
before. You don't know. You can't live like this. How do I get
help. How do I cure this sickness. No one understands. Its a
compulsion. A need. And that need is so overwhelming. I can't get
past it. I have to have just one more. Just one more and I'll be okay
then. Really I will be okay. I get depressed and that's when the
feeling comes to me. Why can't it just leave me alone. I know I
don't need it but I want it. Its a want and an urge. It's like a
high and if you don't get it eventually you die with out it and whose
to blame? Your own self! Your dead now was it really all that good.
While it lasted it was good. Do you feel satisfied now? Not really
so you get that feeling again. That want. And you spin around
on that merry-go-round one more round.

Stacie Marie Hertel

Untitled

What is friendship, you may well ask.
To give you an answer is not a great task.
It is a feeling beyond compare
Knowing that someone always is there
To lend a hand when you're feeling down
Or to give you a smile to replace a frown.
It's a pat on the back, a hug and a kiss;
Or a long letter to a dear one much missed.
It's all of these things and so much more.
It is the result of opening peace's door.
It can never be bought and cannot be sold;
It makes the old feel young and no one feel old.
It's a wonderful gift from God up above.
Indeed my dear friend, it is just love.

Matthew McMaster

The Fortress

Our Fortress was a house near the river's edge,
To God in prayer was our daily pledge.
When storm clouds hovered overhead,
We didn't fret, nor worry, or even dread.
Our Fortress was protected by God's love and care,
He gives us blessed assurance that He would
always be there.

Raymond Cyprien Jr.

In The Year Nineteen Forty-Five

It's mighty nice to be alive
To greet the New Year Forty-Five.
We hope the battles to be fought
Will bring the peace, so long we've sought.

The boys for whom we've prayed and yearned
In Forty-five could be returned.
If most return alive and well,
Then forty-five will just be swell.

Pray forty-five will bring the sun
We've looked for since old forty-one.
Pray clouds will lift and spirits rise
Great triumphs will light up the skies.

Now aren't you glad you were alive
To greet that New Year, Forty-Five?

William V. Rush

The Glens Of Antrim

Oh, to be a sheep in the rugged Glen,
To have the freedom of the road and highest hill,
To greet again each new day in this unawakened world
And wonder at its beauty till time stands still.

To hear the rush of water cascading o'er a cliff,
Falling ever downwards as it wears away the stone
And buries itself deeper in the hills of this land
Where even in the largest crowd, one can be alone.

Alone with the fierce, proud beauty of the Glen,
As the sunlight gleams upon its tear-stained face
Or the mist drops like a mantle, unfurled gently,
To cover in a pall of grey this wild and lovely place.

To meander through the valleys, and see the rivers
Whose waters, weary after their first joyous fall,
Slow to a gentle trickle through meadows lush and green
And flow into a shimmering lake past trees all standing tall.

To drink in this divine beauty every day that dawns
And marvel at the stature, fierceness, tranquility and peace,
Of towering peaks and gentle valleys and waters running free,
And fresh winds which carry the scent of grass and ruffle my
white fleece.

Maggi Tiernan

"A Mother's Love"

To hear a child cry before the sun,
To hear that's not fair as the day goes on,
To hear I don't want to every time you turn,
To hear I'm hungry till the day is done,
To hear a child cry when punishment is done,
As you turn away the tears must come;
To hear I hate you that brings back tears
The heartbreak of love, that shears and shears.

To hear the laughter and see and smile,
When things go right - what blessing my child.
We're always proud, we always love,
Our guidance is needed with God's help from above.
To help and assist all through your life,
If ever a need the words are nice
We love and we care - we're doctors too,
And all we need is a mom "I LOVE YOU!"

Through all the tears and pain and love
"This my child, is a mother's love.!"

Linda Peace

A Beautiful Dream

I had a dream, a beautiful dream, I went
  To Heaven one night.
Jesus was there, and he was so fair, and
  Angels all robed in white.

He called my name, "Zane", and I felt no shame,
  As I looked at His wonderful face.
He said "Won't you come in, I Am Your Friend,
  And this is a beautiful place".

The streets were of gold, there were glories
  Untold, I really wanted to stay,
But it was only a dream, a beautiful dream,
  So I'm still in this world today.

But one of these days, He will call me away,
  My life on earth will be through;
And my beautiful dream, no longer a dream,
  But one that has come true!

Zane Olsen

The Gift

On the table is a gift
To heavy for anyone to lift.
What is in it no one knows
It is just sealed with a big bright bow.

Don't look, don't peek
For we all want to seek.
What is in this big wrapped box
It could be filled with a dozen rocks.

Is it for mom or is it for dad
If it isn't for you don't get mad.
We all wait in curiosity
Just sitting here waiting to see.

Now it is being opened
Careful so what is inside will not be broken.
All it is, is a little note
That Grandma has sent and it wrote,
  "To my family who I love,
   Hope you have happiness
     sent from above."
        Tammy J. Hill

The Helping Hand

  Some people helping, lending a hand
To help the ones around us in need.
  Churches pray, people help
still they need a helping hand.

  "Dear Heavenly Father" the homeless say
Trying their best to keep warm and safe.

  Rich give to charity once a year
Thinking it will help; clearing their mind.

  The rest of the year, we look down on them thinking in disgust.

  Homeless beg, their children hungry
We only think of ourselves and walk away.

  The government says they help, but never do
What are the homeless suppose to do?

  Dear "Heavenly Father", one child prays
"Give everybody homes and make everyone happy."

  As she grows up in a church family
Helping the world is all she thinks.

  Getting her friends to donate clothes
Spending her time trying to help.

  A friendly smile a poor lady gives is all she wants in return.

  This little girl - making a difference the helping hand.
        Kelley Hall

Thank You For Not Putting A Band-Aid On My Open Wound

Lord, I know people mean well when they see someone hurting,
they try to help you to think of the good and the positive;
like trying to put a band-aid on your wound to help it heal.
I know my child that an internal wound needs to have a place
to ooze, just as you need to let your pain out.
I will not put a band-aid on it, for I do not want it to fester;
I am always there with you, to listen to your pain. I know
my child at times it is very discomforting.
Lord, I want my loved one to be remembered and it hurts as time
goes by people forget or maybe just don't want to remember.
I know my child, you need to remember in those times that your
loved one is written in the Book Of Life always to be remembered.
Lord, I don't want people to think of me as a Band-Aid help
us all to let the pain ooze out for it will not fester up.
        Cleda Davis

My Friend!

I have a Friend, you all know his name
To know his name, and to know him is not the same
I have a friend who's gentle and kind,
Loving and compassionate, forgiving and sweet
    God - Man - Savior Divine!

I have a friend, Jesus is his holy name
Ruler of the world, Lord of all lords, king of all kings
I have a friend on whom I can depend,
His power is great, his love is real, towards all mankind.

I have a friend who walked this earth a long time ago
To tell of God's Kingdom, but some say it wasn't so.
I have a friend who died on the cross to make men free,
Free of all sins, sorrow and iniquity.

I have a friend, who's coming back again,
Taking his loved ones to heaven, the born - Again christian
Forever with him to reign!
I have a friend, who's coming for me, too!
But I am now ready, how about you?

Jesus is the greatest friend I have, but he is
your friend too!
        Loraine Camden

"Giving Of Christmas"

  Christmas to me is, the joy of giving.
To know in my heart, that Christ is
still living.
  The love and smile, upon a child's face,
the sweet sound of music,
when they learn to say grace.
  A child in a manger, tiny and small,
born into the world, to save us all.
  He lived on this earth, for thirty-three
years.
  his death was so painful, we're still
shedding tears.
  So this Christmas, when gifts
we give, also give witness that Jesus still lives.
        Sandra K. Foster

My Legacy

Once in a lifetime, we're put to the test
To make our mark —to do our best.

A year of my life I've given to you.
(Never again would I put myself through
The nerve racking boredom, night after night-
Endless counting to be sure I was right.)

It got bigger, and heavy, as months went by.
The deadline got closer - how times does fly!
It was mighty tempting here and there
To put it down - say - "Why should I care?"

With this tablecloth finished as I promised to do,
I've only this thought to pass on to you.
"As sure as the Lord's in His heaven above -
WITH EVERY CHAIN STITCH COMES A BUNDLE OF LOVE".
        Rose Mewbourne

Where Does The Sun Go At Night

Where does the sun go at night?
To me, it just seems to float out of sight.
We see the sun rise in the early morn,
But where does it go when it starts to storm?
If it goes on the water does it get wet?
Is that where it goes every time it sets?
If it lands on the ground, does it roll around.
Like a giant ball, never making a sound.
Who knows the answer? Maybe it's you.
When the sun leaves me, does it come to you?

Keri Sank

Laughter In The Lane

Summer sunshine beckons the children
  to meander the lane to the woods.
Ripe blackberries along the fence line
  furnish dessert—the sweetest of foods.

Reaching the deep green shade of the trees,
  undergrowth of ferns, mosses, lichen;
Birds overhead, butterflies and bees,
  rich treasures all, their day to brighten.

Swiftly pass the hours to head for home;
  they help with evening chores made easy
With their dreams of other days to come,
  laughing and playing, being lazy.

Marian E. Madden

My Dream

For many moons I must declare
To own a business way my fare
Dreaming hard and trying to wait
The day came and the time was right
Looking to my only life
Simply stated my little wife
We embarked upon a plan you see
To eliminate hypocrisy
Providing just the amenities
At the crossroads we did stake our claim
High above we installed our name
Hoping for riches and fame to come from our claim
And to surround our name
Years later from that day
While working hard with no time to play
We ask our selves should we really stay
We decided to close our shop this day
And take the time to simply say
Thanks for the memories

Robert L. Whitsitt

One Man

When one man tries to understand another,
  to see his needs and understand his views;
when one man strives to see each man his brother,
  to find his hidden strengths, to know his truths;

When one man looks beyond established creeds
  and color, knowing these are only part
on which the valued worth of mankind feeds,
  and reaches out to touch the human heart;

Though faltering, a single footstep taken,
  the world trembles, and an avarice, blind,
retreats, old hates and dogmas shaken,
  and brother-love advances for mankind.

Paul K. McAfee

Compassionate People

Thank God that some people have compassion
To risk their own life to save,
To me, these people are every-day heroes in my mind and fashion!
Best of all, to these people, it isn't even grave!

Not to think and react.
Is special, and some people have this intact!

With the way our lives go,
With our fast-paced life and where we are bound,
We lose this concept, you know!
These every-day heroes perform without a sound!

No credit do these people expect!
But to dwell the subject with these people with you they would reject!

These people are unselfish,
I wonder what they do wish!

For these people, I have so much adoration!
I believe that they take life in moderation!

Paula Patterson-Stevenson

Obsession

  When the moon comes over the mountain, and the sun shines from sea to sea, my love shall always follow thee, soulmates we'll always be. It does not matter where you go, what land that you might be. I'll always, always follow you. You can't get rid of me. I know I said I'd give you up, so free of me you'll be. I tried. I did, I really tried, but you'll never get rid of me. You are a passion to my soul. A constant agony!
  It goes too far, the depths too deep, just like the dark blue sea. And so, my love because I lied, judgmental do not be. My love for you is always there, you can depend on me. I think of you only on two occasions, day and night you see. And when I see you with another, it really tears my heart. It breaks me up, it's tears me down, obsession from the start. I know that you could help me, if you really wanted to. I know that you could set me free, my soul belongs to you.
  And when you pass me on the street, you never give a glance. Is that the way you really feel? That I don't have a chance! One day when you are lonely and no ones in your life, remember this, my love you'll miss, can't stand this strife, I'll end my life, I loved you from the start!

Phyllis Mallory

Door Of Life

There is a void that stands before, like a mirror, I should try
To see myself from deep within and look me right straight in the eye.

But through this void I have to travel to meet the other side of day
And confront all that is before me to safely make my way.

The void won't change in shape or size unless I make it so
And I the only key that unlocks doors of pain and woe.

But, too, the keys are double edged, not only pain there be,
But also tears of happiness and joys of revery.

The choice is mine, but early, this decision I must take,
For yet my growth, intelligence, my wisdom I must make.

And who shall I call to lead me in my ignorance sublime,
For certain someone learned, someone wiser, in their prime.

I fear the lessons taken will enrich my confidence,
With hopes the debts of living will lead my dreams to their presence.

Robert E. Lafond

The Children Of The Future

The children of the future have no self respect, they don't know how to show what they have not experienced. They have no one at home to show them what it means. We teach them work is more important than tending to their needs.

The children of the future are being raised by strangers. While parents strive to reach their goals, they deny their children anger. If you asked them how they felt then you would clearly hear, they cry for you, no one else will do, they'd rather you were there.

The children of the future are left to fend for themselves, competing with other children for the attention of one adult, and still we go on ignoring them, these special gifts of life. No toys you bring or material things, will guarantee they'll grow up right.

The children of the future will come to haunt us all, for one day soon they will all grow up, and then become adults. What have we taught them, that selfishness is best, that you have to do what is best for you, not that children should come first.

The children of the future deserve more than that. To be loved and cared for by their parents is not a lot to ask. So show them your priorities are to them and not to you, and teach them that respecting others is the righteous thing to do.

Susan Olson

Oh, Ye Of Little Faith

Oh ye of little faith, what more must I do,
To show you my love and faithfulness, too?

I've held your hand, I've walked by your side,
There all the time for you to abide.

I've entered your heart, I've heard your deep cries,
And I've seen the pain explode from your eyes.

I've wiped all the tears and begun again,
Calmed all your fears, of where you had been.

You still struggle daily from this world's strife,
But I'm here to tell you, I've changed your life.

So pick up the pieces, the good and the bad,
Rejoice in the Lord, and be exceedingly glad!

I love you, my child, I won't close my eyes,
You're headed straight toward the glorious skies!

My home up in heaven that's filled with such love,
Jubilant singing and peace from above.

Praise my name always, for I'll never go,
Away from the path, to you I did show.

Paula M. Holland

Dreams Are My Reality

Dreams are my reality
To some they are fleeting glimpses
   in the night.
To some they are their fantasies delight.
   Others run and hide
too scared to face the other side.
   But to me these are my realities,
to tell of what is to happen for me.
   The fleeting moment shared
by someone new.
   The passions shared by two.
   Or the signs that are all so clear,
to tell of a loss of someone dear.
These are all a Dream, a Dreamer can Dream
Are you the Dreamer? Or the Dreamed?

Robin Avey

A Moral Compass

I long to be a compass —
To stand up straight,
To point the way,
To contemplate the difference
Between magnetic North and true.

Staunch companion,
Hip-pocket explorer,
Lifetime Mariner,
Nightly Voyager.

Sea coasts and pyramids await my love,
And laughing children dance upon her sandy shore.

Verdant carpets,
Jungles underfoot,
Striving for the mountain vista,
Steadfast in high seas.

Thomas V. Silvia

Life's Journey

A baby is helpless, but still has the will
To start in the valley and climb the great hill.
When first tiny feet trace the unsteady way,
They grow stronger and stronger as passes each day.
Then shiny new lesson books, happy school days,
There are many false steps makes them pause in the ways,
Many a time comes a stumble and fall,
Many a time there's no progress at all.
School days are past, there's a turning point now,
But still many turnings to get to the brow . . .
Triumphs, defeats, are all stones in the way,
Feet sometimes falter and cause great delay.
Many grow weary and stop on the road,
Others just rest, then they take up their load.
Eagerly climbing, so close to the brow
Over the brook, it's not much further now,
Over the stile, up the steep path, until
Triumphant and breathless — the top of the hill.

Vilma Holland Fields

Ruth Gould (Argie) Indritz

January 1
To Tahma a Mother, and to me a Wife,
My Sweetheart forever throughout life,
With infinite understanding, patience and love,
A sparkle of cheer from Heaven above,
Each day for us you so unfold,
Thrills of happiness, limits untold,
For ours is a love nothing can sever,
You are my Beloved, now and forever.

February 22
Glad you make us, happiest,
You for us the very best,
February twenty-second, forty-five,
Our Love is growing, fully alive,
My heart speaks, and you have heard:
"Oh Happy Day, this Fifty-Third".

March 22
Each month with you is happiness,
My love for you grows never less, always increasing and richer too,
Today is my Fifty-Fourth month with you.

Phineas Indritz

Mom

There is no day long enough to express my love for you
To thank you for your constant support in everything I do

To tell you how important it is to have you by my side
No matter how much you have had to swallow pride

For always showing me your kind and smiling face
When other mothers frowned in horror and disgrace

To tell you I know this has not always been so easily done
Considering I've not been the portrait of the perfect son

For giving me the freedom to be just me
No matter if I'm not what you had dreamt I would be

For showing me how to stand on my own two feet
And for being there to carry me in the mist of defeat

For giving the strength to believe in myself
No matter what cards I may have been dealt

For showing me how to hold my head high
And for grounding me when I thought I could fly

And for all of these things they set aside a day
To express the words we fail to say along the way

So Mother I'd simply like to say
I LOVE YOU AND HAPPY MOTHER'S DAY

Timothy McAfee

On A Bus In Warsaw, June 1994

It was afternoon; I was coming from the Old Town
To where my brother lived, when we first met.
Outside, cold early summer in the city,
But with sun that bore a promise of warmth.
There was hardly room when you got on
At a stop near the University;
I was pinned to the window, near the door.

We were apart but I could see your eyes;
It was enough to know
That you were there; that I was there;
That the touch of two lives can be fleeting:
The pale glow of dawn disappearing in a blink,
A few notes of music from a faraway radio,
A breath of meadows caught on a city street,
You seen across a crowded bus,
Leaving my mind with the imprint of your eyes.

Magdalena Carpenter

Intruder

Who's to blame for my shame
To whom do I complain?
My youth and innocence shattered
By a branch of my family tree

Broken spirit pleads to God
Please help me through this ordeal
It's past midnight; it's been hours now
But this intrusion still continues

Explain to me, somebody please!
Why won't the pain go away?
It's been fifteen years now, I'm physically healed
Still I wrestle with my sanity

A teenager, someday my child will be
How do I explain about 'Daddy'?
I'll kneel and pray to my God above
That I find the right words to say

Sometimes at night I lay and cry
Vivid memories still linger
Residual anger buried deep inside
Tell me, should I repay the 'intruder'?

Mark E. Moseley

What Is A Friend?

A friend is someone who just stands by,
To wipe your tears if you should cry.
Perhaps there's not much she can do,
Just to know she's near to comfort you.

Sometimes love cannot smooth the road,
Nor can friendship lift the load.
Just to know that she is there,
Then you know she really cares.

A friend will stand by through thick and thin,
She'll help in lifting up your chin.
Her sympathy through all will still endure,
Knowing her handclasp is always yours.

It helps sometime to see you through,
Even though there's not much she can do.
So I'll repeat again to say,
To have a friend to just stand by,
Makes me breathe a sigh.

Mary H. Tucker

My President

You are my President, young and vigorous,
To you we looked up with pride and trust,
To us you gave inspiration,
The young of this generation.

For you my President, my first vote I did cast,
And for you my Dear President, it has come to be my last.

Your ideals were positive,
Your principles were real,
Under you all people could live for yours,
My Dear President was indeed a wonderful new deal.

Into the South you did go.
No visible fear did you show,
Then this day in November, a shot rang out,
That long the world will remember.

There you did slump, silent and still,
Goodbye my Dear President,
To remember you I will.

William Murray

The Message

Suspended in time,
tormented by time,
rushing,
hoping,
that someday we'll find,
that ray of hope,
that glitter of joy,
something to bring us back to the calmness of the mind,
to the days when parents had nothing but time,
to discipline the children,
who were obedient and kind,
teaching them a purpose,
just being a guide,
teaching them values,
hoping that someday they'll find,
that hard work and dedication,
will be rewarded in time.

Marsha Morton

These Gifts

Without the gift of sight I fear to say, life would be seen through touch, not to see the sparkling stars or sunset at the end of day, life would not consist of very much . . .

Without the gift to hear, the first cry of baby could not be heard, oh, it would be so hard to bear, never to hear the sound of bird . . .

Without the gift of speech, beautiful words I could not say, only God would know my painful silence, as I prayed to him each day . . .

If I were to lose these gifts, for a moment say, alone in the darkness not to speak, hear or see . . . falling down on my knees I would pray, thanking God for these gifts that were given to me . . .

Patricia Larsen

The Beach

We sat on a splintered bench
Touching hips and hands
Looking at the water's horizon
As the temperature cooled.

Tensions eased out of me
I sighed and leaned on you
You pictured the house - our house
Designed especially for me
With a spectacular view
Huge master bedroom and fireplace
Jacuzzi-style bathtub
Kitchen with counters and cupboards galore.

We took off our shoes
And walked in the cool sand
Dipped our toes in the waves
Quietly smiling, holding hands.

Kathryn Lincoln

The Undaunted Spirit

As each God given day sprints hurriedly along,
Touching lives in anguish and those with a song,
We praise our Father in his heavenly place,
For His divine assurance, His love and grace.

Though men may be critical and quick to betray,
The strength He provides is sufficient for the day.
Our brothers, so often, carelessly say,
Things that are hurtful, in a negative way.

We must love each other, as Jesus commands,
And strive continually with helping hands.
The indwelling spirit in a Christian's heart,
Is the ingredient that sets them apart.

God empowers and equips us for living,
A life that is productive and tempered with giving.
So, let us be resolute and certain to heed,
Our God is available for our every need.

May we resolve to be ever alert,
To know God cares for us as we hurt.
Listen to these words . . . be sure you hear it,
Our God is the source of the undaunted spirit.

Wayne Farmer

The Key To Peace

The Key to peace we all should fleece
Try to the north west south and the east
The Key to peace can be easily obtained
By respecting each person regardless of brain
The Key to peace should be tried at least once
Or tried and tried again
If tried at least once
And you feel nothings been gained
The Key to peace at least you did fleece.

Thomas W. Dilsworth

Turn The World!

Wake up and see what's going down,
Toy soldiers running all around,
Fighting to see who owns the town!
Is it your fault?
No, Is it mine?
No, who's could it be?
Turn the world!!!
The world is burning, the clock is ticking
And we can't replace the sand.
Turn the world!!!
We have a battle but the weapons are
Not of steel turn the world!!!
Our fierce opponent
Is the anger that
We feel! Turn the world!!!
God looks on!
Turn the world! We've got to trust
now, turn the world!
We've got to learn to pray!
Turn the world the time is now

Mariee Christine Shaffer

Bridges Of Trust

A couples love is only as strong as they make it
Trust is a bridge that can only be built by their bricks of love.
An extra lover should not be able to destroy their love or burn these bridges.
For happiness lurks in the brightest plunders of life.
A loved ones face awaits in the heart and soul of the receiver.
For one day when you reach that light, your lovers face and your children's care will be all that matters in a series of love, pain and bridges.
A message; for all those who cross our bridges of trust, if their heart is not worthy and their love is not strong, then you will fall through - for I am not asking for smiles, gifts or advice - just that you understand the bond I'm looking for.
If you give me your hand as you pass over my bridge, I promise our bridge will never fall through because our bridge is built with understanding and without that, the bridge we build between us will crumble like sand . . .

Mina King

Left Or Right?

So many times
Tumbling across unruly bricks
Molly Dee wondered which way to be

Serving her Molly life came with
Tangled rough edges, yet
Much satisfaction she has achieved

Seems to be
The kind of path a
Mother wants a child to see

Sneaking over to Dee, hard
Thoughts of rebelling loud parties
Mushed its way all through to her brain

Searching for an answer
Though little came
Molly Dee wanted to know what way to lead

Seeking to find herself out
Tethering minds with ideas
My what a headache Dee has achieved

Maybe Molly is what she was has wanted to see.
Which way could it be?

Linzi Wolford

Fall

The trees sway under the breezy gray sky
Tumbling bushes trip people as the wind blows at night
The moon is always yellow as the storm reaches the night
You feel the cool breeze as it hits your face
The sun grows dim

Some flowers blossom in the fall
The tree loses its leaves
The colors of red and yellow, orange and brown fall
Crunchy and easy to rip apart

It always rains in the fall
The sun's light is dimmed
Yet the son that is in me is always bright
  Vaughn O. Nixon Jr-Johnson

"I Dwell In Time"

My past is largely reverie, my future mostly riddle, although I can turn my watch backward or forward at will, time appears to move on with majestic indifference to my convenience and comfort; it moves in one direction only, from yesterday and toward tomorrow through today. It cannot be reversed or even arrested in its course. I am it seems being pushed out to the moving edge of time. I am made to live in the demanding present when I would prefer to linger in the past or leap headlong into the future, we wander in the times that are not ours, and it is time that brings us up short, the one thing we can never do is to get away from time, but I am not frozen in time; instead I am carried along in it current, now slow, then rapid and who can say where it is taking me. I am constantly being remade by time, it is always bringing me up to date and making me out of date, I am carried in one direction only; time heals griefs and quarrels, for we change and are no longer the same persons. Neither the offender nor the offended are anymore the same, therefore; if I am what I am because of time, may not time be what it is because of me, but I am able to make every minute count only by virtue of the fact that time is carrying me forward in spite of myself, because I dwell in time.
  Phillip R. Billups

Christmas Sunday Waltz

Grandpa waltzed across the floor with Grandma Sunday.
'twas the sweetest sight that you could ever see.
The old phonograph played songs that they had cherished.
As they glided round our gifted Christmas tree.

Grandma's pies and cakes were baking in the oven,
But the ice cream would be made of pure white snow.
There was popcorn strung around the fireplace mantle,
Candles glowing as they did so long ago.

'twas blackjack oak and pine logs in the fireplace.
We sat back when flames were cozy and high,
Small crackling sounds chimed in with those old waltzes.
Grandma's eyes just gleamed when they slowly glided by.

Roasted peanuts and the chestnuts were all ready,
As we gathered round the table Christmas day,
We gave thanks to the good lord up above us,
But Grandpa had just one more thing to say.

Let's dance the waltz of old Kentucky - the Tulsa traveler too.
We'll play the waltz of the wind this Christmas day.
Let's play waltz across all Texas, as we hold each others hands.
No other songs could make us feel this way.
  Roy Pierce

Twenty Lines

They wanted a poem
Twenty lines long
A poem they said
And not a song.

So I racked my brain
And I thought thus and so,
But nothing would fit,
No nothing would go.

My poems are bad
My rhyming is worse
I can't think of enough lines
To write a short verse.

I sat and I wrote
And I sat and I thought
But though the words floated and flitted about
They couldn't, they wouldn't, they didn't come out.

So here's to the poet
Who can write and can rhyme
And can do it all
In just twenty lines!
  Rosalind Backus

"The Dance Of Love"

When eyes do meet and two hands touch
Two hearts together to beat and needing much
In a measure of time, so subtle, so sublime
So begins their dance of love.

As the music begins to play
They are but swirled away
To a fantasy world rarely spoken of
Deep in tune to a dance of love.

A smile, a kiss, unrequited bliss
Two lovers drawn together by one soul
To know, to feel, reaching for the heavens is their goal
So goes on this forever dance of love.

If day should break, the music to end
May we never awake, lest for the memory of that friend
Someone we but loved, met, touched
While caught up in a dance of love.
  Teresa Guinn-Garcia

Memories

Sometimes I hear him call my name,
turning to search for his face in vain.
'times I wish to see his smile,
realizing again the distance of a mile.
I dream of things he'd like to hear,
knowing he'd be there with a patient ear.
A lonely porch swing on a cold winter night,
helps me remember his arms wrapped tight.
Small sighing whispers high in the trees
brings to mind times on our knees.
Motion pictures or songs of low brass
help me recall his enchanting laugh.
We created precious memories made to last,
thanks to God our future's been cast.
We shall meet again soon,
perhaps even tomorrow at noon.
No longer will I have to recall,
for at that time, I will have it all.
  Kimberly Renfro

Irony (Good Fruits)

And then I saw in front of me,
Two rows of trees: one brown, one green.
I carefully inspected each little thing;
The green row was dead, the brown — like Spring!

The green row had nothing that could be of worth,
Only thorns and thistles were rooted in dirt.
But the row that was brown gave good things to eat;
Like apples and grapes; fruits that are sweet!

And it came to me, as I woke from this dream,
That words may not always mean as they seem.
So I hear the words and examine their roots,
Then take heed to those that are bearing good fruits!

Susan Heitz

My Brew

An apple core, a liver or two,
Two snake eyes all boiled up in a stew.
Lizard lips, sirloin tips —
crumbled up into little bits.
A gorilla's heart, an elephants tongue,
A cheetah's hide,
A quarter, a nickel, a dime.
Bat's brains, sheep's wool,
A wallabies disgusting lips,
Ought to do the trick.
Insect wings and all sorts of dead things,
A parrots beak and a rabbits nose,
And yet a part of a rose.
Add some honey and ear wax too,
Then mix it till its a slap of glue.
Then say these magic words to my brew:
　　"Boil and Bubble,
　　Keep me out of trouble."

Sarah Smith

In Memorium Joseph Kleinman
Died February 7, 1977

A golden heart stopped beating,
Two willing hands lay still;
The one who did so much for us
Is resting at God's will.

We miss you Dad and it won't stop,
You left a mark no one can top;
On earth you toiled, in heaven you rest,
Treasure him Lord, he was the best.

Words are few, thoughts are deep,
Memories of him are ours to keep;
Peacefully sleeping, free from all pain
Good-night Dad, till we meet again.

Remember this day as one of prayer,
Because in our hearts he is always there;
Our departed Dad is not alone,
As we unveil to-day his memorial stone.

Maurice Kleinman

You

　　As I opened my eyes, I gazed up into the heavens. I watched the stars as they danced across the sky.

　　They winked at me, and I at them. I reached out to embrace them and the universe then embraced me.

　　Slowly, I drifted into the melody. And I danced with the stars to the sweet song of life.

　　As I opened my eyes, I gazed up and saw you.

Sandra J. Beaston

Freedom?

Why are we trapped in these cages?
unable to live our own lives
society overrides our emotions
we don't even know what we feel
our tastes are according to theirs
we live to please everyone else
we buy what they want us to buy
we cry when they say we can cry
we wear what they want us to wear
they are also cutting our hair
our thoughts aren't even our own
we have nothing left to claim
but we can't give them the blame
It is by our choice that we live in a cage

Paul T. Bray

Freedom

Freedom is a wonderful gift.
When black people were slaves many suffered.
Many had lost their friends and families, food and clothing.
But now there's FREEDOM!
Freedom to do what you please.
Thanks to the states that worked together we are one country.
A symbol for this is "The Statue of Liberty".
Freedom is what makes our country so proud.
Freedom is a wonderful gift.

Megan Busken

The Circle

There was a circle, that did endure,
　　Unbroken, for a long, long time,
Three boys, three girls . . . our mother's children
　　Happy, healthy . . . fruit of the vine.

The years passed on, the circle stayed.
　　I guess we thought we'd be alive
From now on. Now we know, that that can't be;
　　One brother's gone, and now there's five.

We really know now, we're not immortal!
　　Let us endeavor, let us strive,
To make the most of every day;
　　To love each other, while we're still five.

Our brother's left us, he is gone!
　　But still I think, he remains a part
Of our circle, 'cause he still lives,
　　In each and every, wounded heart!

Purnel L. Collicott

Lost

Gifted with a brilliant mind,
Undaunted imagination, euphoric splendor,
The earth, the sky, the sea, magnificent;
Infinite entities of profound proportion,
Visions, sounds, feelings, beyond the horizon;
Now, destruction surrounds me,
A catastrophic plight, darkness, pain;
A dumb animal, speechless, mindless,
Crawling, scratching, groping, lost;
Abort thyself into thy cave, a windowless cave,
Minutes, days, weeks, months, years,
Time prophetic time;
Skeletal, faceless, consumed, devoured,
Thy cave filled with snow, I cannot breath;
Oh God, please God, take back time,
I will be born again.

Mary Harter

Listen!!!!

Listen to my words and hear my sorrows.
Understand my fears and be there for me tomorrow.
Don't take me for granted and forget I'm there,
use me as resource but don't forget to share. Recycle my
feelings and give support in return.

Listen to my mistakes and from them yea shall learn.
I don't claim to be perfect, because I know
I'm not, work hard in life and always strive for the top.
Wipe away my tears when I cry and I'll trust you to never lie.

Be there for me in thy time of need. Be supportive and
encouraging if I don't succeed. Lend yourself to me and
just be my friend and you can count on me to be there until the end.

LaQuanda R. George

Poor Beast

Poor Beast what a dangerous life you lead
Unknown creatures of day and night
Slipping in and out of view
The marvelous invertebrate that keeps us at bay in the vast blue
Poor Beast
How weary you must be, left and right peril lurks
But worst of all in the heights above where you
are as blind as we are to the new moon
Poor Beast
What a wretched name you deem
How wrathful can my kind be
Monster, Reaper, Gray and White death
I cry when your blood flows over the deck
Poor Beast
You who understand your role perfectly
Hunter, scavenger, eater of the sick, weak and dead
How you watch from another realm
the plaques that kill and decimate entire flocks and pods of animals
So tell me, creature, who is the real beast? You, shark,
Hunter of the sea? No, No. The real beast are we.

Peter F. Yurkiw

From The Silence Where I Hid

From the silence where I hid
Unspoken sin of what I did.
I say a prayer that you would hear
And wash away my guilty tear.

Will the moon eclipse the sun?
Will the rainbow turn and run?
You are the beacon by which I walk.
I travel its path; its shadow talk.

Roads we have traveled are rural and ruff
The baggage we carry is empty with stuff.
The humblest of dreams with the hardest solution
Are the joys of life at their conclusion.

I witnessed a birth that's oh so dear
Conceived in heaven I have no fear.
It developed so fast it has no guilt
And when it's scared I'll be its quilt.

So I look to the stars and say my prayer
Of wishes and hopes, a gift so rare.
Give me a life time for this be true
He brought us together; what more can I do?

Kenneth H. Kerr

A Year Ago

How can I explain the loss that I feel,
until you are there it isn't quite real.
You see, I have had friends who lost someone dear.
I couldn't understand the hurt or the pain,
until one morning in November it called out my name.
I didn't believe, I couldn't understand,
I just kissed my mother, I just held her hand,
now it is over, my hurt will never end,
for she is and always will be my Mother, my Soul and my Best Friend.
No one can change how I feel, or say in time it will heal.
For time can't stop the pain in my heart or the longing in my
soul because we are apart.
A year ago, I never knew, what hurt was like until I lost you.
Don't get me wrong, I have hurt,
but nothing hurt or cut so deep as losing you and your love so sweet!

A. Caroline Thompson

Pre-Departure To Exile

Reluctant Departure
No time to stay, too soon to go,
Unwanted leaving - to go alone.

Deadline imposed, foreign country calls
what next to do? I don't know

Crossroads branch, each separate apart
Confusion rises, slight Depression despairs.

Decision time rears its ugly head.
Disappear! Go now! Why can't I ignore you?
Decision time, you're the bane of my life
causing loneliness, distress and despair.

Tracy Doherty

Dedication To A Departed Friend

She fashioned kites so they would fly
    up and away, into the sky
Their spirits flew
    so high and free
Like birds, they soared
    for the world to see
And now her spirit has joined those kites, once
    flown so high
        to bless the beauty of the sky.

Lisa Ackroyd

When? Where How?

Heartbreak, sorrow and pain of a love forgotten
    Upon the sands of yesterday.
At what certain day, minute and hour, did all my
    Tomorrows become yesterdays.
When did the smile upon my face turn to sorrow?
    When did the laughter die in my throat?
When did my heart break, as though shattered
    Like glass upon the floor, and
Become a twisting, searing, throbbing pain?
    When did the joy of rising to greet each shining day
Become a damp, dreary storm ridden sea.
    Where did the expectations and dreams of the future
Become the sad and vanished memories of the past.
    How did the delight of each new idea entering my mind
Become only a detached and passing thought.
    When did my dreams that soared into space
Attempting to reach perfection, die on a lonely
    barren wasteland of knowledge.
The answer is simple and quaint, for last night with love departing,
I now walk the lonely dim lite of night.

Rosemary Tortora

Hot Force

Just as steam will rise to reach sublime,
Vapor floating, piercing smog and grime
Mighty wisdom sleeping, lulled by time.

Thin the pipe connecting minds to cosmic scope,
Stretching wide whenever mortals risk or cope.
Slice your comfort, blind to fatigue, dare to hope.

Water, blocks of ice, each shapes a view that's still or dead
Wishing, tricking, musing, wondering what's ahead.
Worlds of thought, ideas trapped in bed.

Now, defrost all cubes, clean out all slime.
Boil creative juices, help them climb.
Energize your droplets, soar to reach your prime.

Mary G. Dimon

Betrayal

He ran up beside her strolling feet. She looked at him, his
wagging tail, so sweet, she thought he was so complete.

His friendly wet tongue soothed her tired salty skin.

She relaxed, thinking he's so cute. He proudly walked beside her
as if playing the flute.

The light blue powder puff sky suddenly looked as thou metal was in it's eye.

She screeched in pain. As a brittle Autumn leaf, she crumbled as
if slain. Her little friends wet soothing tongue turned into fangs.

Blood slowly flowed from sidewalk to street, could she have been
wrong to think of him as sweet?

She fears she's about to sleep as she looked up at the monster, to weep.

She envisions a strong white horse with wings. A back strong to
take the siege. Fly her away to a pastel world where there is no
black or red, she pleads.

WHERE the butterfly doesn't become a vulture we - know
WHERE lush blades of grass doesn't become nails up the a**
WHERE snow capped mountain peaks doesn't become alligators
and freaks

Nancy Messman

Untitled

The fast pace of a new world envelops her like a thick fog.
Vibrant palettes from which Mother Nature so delicately painted
Fade to flat, blurry shades of gray.
The robust colors of the fall leaves
Are no longer seen through her once sparkling eyes.
Instead, she shuffles listlessly through routine,
Deadlines and commitments echoing loudly in her empty soul.
Loss of life is reflected in her now dull eyes and face
Making evident the distance between herself and the surrounding world.
She awakes each morning only to pay yet another day
To watch the black and white movie which has become her life . . .
When one day, she is startled by a splash of color flickering across the screen.
The image of a wise old man who had taught her the beauty of
living life appeared.
Deep blue eyes focused on her from afar, radiating a powerful sense of life.
She questioned her sanity when after only a few seconds, the image
began to fade.
Yet on that eve, she watched as the darkness filled the sky in a
familiar shade of blue;
And a light snow began to float to the ground, blanketing her with a
sense of peace.
She drank in the strength of the beauty she had neglected for some time,
Remembering the wisdom of the old man with the deep blue eyes,
And once again, became one with nature, and truly living life.

Leigh Shelton

Discovered

Beneath the surface, frozen in time, a treasure awaits the light.
 Virgin soil cast aside, the crevice deepens, no end in sight.
Layers uncovered, closer you come, but alone I lay stripped of self worth.
 A fragmented sculpture, it's pieces scattered-without you I am worth
not a spade of earth.

The scorching sun, a sweltering heat.
 METAL MEETS BONE as light penetrates deep.
 I am discovered-no longer hidden in solidarity.
 Resurrected by your touch, made whole by your Archeology.

With a desert in my mouth a dry wind cries.
My barren soul glances up, an oasis fills my eyes-there you are between
 Heaven and horizon.
Stone temple prayers not to God, but to you above.
A hand raises toward my messiah fingering the rays of your divine
 light-stretching, unwavering, reaching for the icons of our love.

Midnight stars guide our way through misty skies of azure blue.
Sounds of thunder chase their light as my primal bones assemble for you.
Swollen clouds darken skies as seaward winds direct their form.
Lightning strikes weathered land my crumbling bones-lost in
temporal storm.

Alone again, my heart is still, darkness fills my world of stone.
And as I sink back into earth, in silence, I await the meeting of
metal and bone.
Of air, there is none-in sand I am covered-solitude again has come
in blackness I am smothered.
And in frozen time, I am as I was, BONES TO BE DISCOVERED.

Timothy Del Vescovo

The Waiting

He sits in a wheelchair by the window
Waiting for something to happen;
He doesn't know nor care what that might be.
Sounds of voices roll through his head:
He hears a call drawing near,
A call which will take him away
Away where he can live free of fear.
He waits and waits, knowing the time will come
The day his pain will end,
The day his soul will be free,
Free from all the torture he has been through,
Free from all the sorrow he has seen.
As the light draws near his heart begins to throb;
The heat of its rays seems to be holding him.
He feels as if help is on its way.
He cries out to the light, "Hear I am, take me!!"
That is it no more pain.
He mustn't wait another day.

Wayne Bailey

In A Rush

Waiting for the moment to come, but silence continues on.
Waiting for the pen to write, willing to, but the mind doesn't
hear the heart speak-if the two could only have a relationship
together so far away.

Rendezvous-thoughts, muscles flex, lungs take in air, heart
pounds, eyes blink, stares, move pen move, write, but what shall I?

And the subject and inspiration come and the pen follows,
following, like a wild river. Release, anxiety, pleasure, the
heart and the mind are one spirit together-making love again.

Roy David Mora Jr.

Ode To Animal Farm

In the beginning one dictator
Was promptly doomed to be exiled later.
A revolt of the public would start a democracy,
But temptations of power would become a prophecy.

One good leader is then driven out.
The banning of dictators is soon much a doubt.
And all who see the lies and deceptions
Just brush them off as misconceptions.

A little is taken, then exceedingly more
The workers were always urged to ignore
The crucial importance of their needs and rights,
Which had eventually changed over the nights.

The labor increases, the food declines
For all except the clever swine
The ones at the top are drunk with greed,
By taking too much when there are many to feed.

What seemed to be best, is now the worst,
Another dictator learns ways of the first.
If all of them rise to such a degree,
What really is the meaning of free?

Tara Driscoll

Mr. Cherry Tree

Oh Mr. Cherry Tree what has been done - my innocence
     was stolen from under the sun
Your branches, they shelter me,
     what shame I feel for such a little Girl.
The thoughts, they haunt me still.
My friend, Mr. Cherry Tree, you were all that I had - safe I could
     feel from the touch of her hand.
No one ever thought, never really knew that the best friend
     I had was you.
Together we'd sit, while I would just cry,
"LEAVE ME ALONE I JUST WANT TO DIE."
Mr. Cherry Tree it was always you who took away my pain,
     when she had nothing more to gain.
Hands all over me most all of the time.
Memories I hold of you so close to my heart, my pain could not end
When we were apart.
Now that I'm grown I'm no longer alone.
Mr. Cherry Tree I remember you who comforted me.
Until the end-My friend.

Megan Christine Gwaltney

My Damn Love Affair

Sittin' on the side of the mountain
watchin' the sun come up
Cops on the one side, death on the other.
Looks like the jig is up,
looks like it's time, I've lost my mind, I've lost my will.
This is everybody's story,
a close friend, a compadre
we called up faith and courage in a bottle every day.
Drunk one more time, drunk all the time,
I'm out of time, my damn love affair.
The stuff that makes me crazy, my friend
my lover, I think of no other.
My marriage made in hell, screamin' for my father,
mother, brother and friend, no body hears my
screams this time, I'm down in hell again.
Looks like it's time, I've lost my mind,
I've lost my will, I guess my time is over.
My life just stumbled by, looks like it's over, and
I know the reason why.
Drunk one more time, drunk all the time, I'm out of time.

Scott B. Robertson

But I Was Afraid

Hopscotch, kick ball, dodge ball
watching all the elders of my school -
being young had its disadvantages.
Apart from the playground's tools, odd shapes surround me.
Heights of bars, children of climbers,
but I was afraid.
I was not a climber—staring at their fun
 upside down, swinging like monkeys—
I wanted to have fun
I climbed this jungle gym of life in fear of falling
Leaning against its arch I looked out unto the game.
The whistle blew,
but I was afraid.
I was starched against the bars; tears flowed down my cheek.
My eyes would not leave sight of a small pebble on the ground.
Trying to dissolve my fear, my eyes approached a dandelion;
beauty in the eyes of a child.
I reached for a flower and fell.
The hurt could not overpower the relief,
But I was not afraid.

Kyra Semler

The Deaf Child

A sweet little child sitting all alone
Watching out the window; what is shown.
Looking up in the bright blue sky
To see the little doves passing by.

He sees a butterfly on the lovely flower
Alas he watches it for an hour.
And then a jet plane flies o'er the mound,
But he doesn't even hear a sound.

He wants to go out and play
With the hearing children all day;
Has lonely feelings for he cannot hear,
He cannot help himself for fear.

He sits by himself -all alone-
On a chair thinking on his own.
He thinks he will live in the world apart,
For he cannot share his heart.

Marla E. Gunning

The Wolf

He walks silently through the forest, pausing every now and then.
Watching, ready to dash away into the thickets.
Alone in himself, majestic, powerful.
The mere sight of him inspires awe.
His long journey comes to its end, he slowly ascends the hill.
A pause, he sits.
Surveying his domain,
From the mountains, through the river, out into the fields,
Even the dark forest.
His black eyes fix on a spot in the distance,
Huge skyscrapers, towering smokestacks, a dense smog cover.
They are an end to his world, a threat to his life.
He looks into the forest, a shield from the city.
His face is sad, it looks like he might cry.
Instead . . . a SHOUT!
He raises his head to the moon,
The big, white, everlasting moon.
The one unchanging thing in his life, the life of a grey wolf . . .

Meaghan Boyle

Ready For Christmas

Are you ready for Christmas?
We ask each casual passer by,
Knowing full well their answer
As they pill high their arms with bundles
While shaking their heads and uttering a heavy sigh!

The Bethlehem Inn Keeper
Was not ready - list to his cry!
Little did he know
Of the child, in his stable to be born.

The shepherds that starry night on the hill side of Judea,
Were not ready to hear the Angelic voices loud and clear,
"Unto you is born this night a Savior, Christ, The King,"
So go with haste to see, this precious one, so dear.

Not ready for Christmas?
We bow our heads with a heavy sigh.
"Lord prepare our hearts and lives for Christmas,
By answering the worlds cries!"

Mary Evelyn McChesney

Imaginary Hunt

Empowerment; the right to bear arms
We began as hunters and hunters we remain
One with nature or against it
Carnal knowledge, primal, raw, and honest
Flush it out, blow away something that moves
Shells in the gun, pump one in the chamber
Safety's off . . . practice shots . . . kaboom!
Wouldn't want to hear that in the dark!
I prefer not to come back stuffed and mounted
So I lay in wait, stalking my prey
Shifting my eyes from side to side
I lock onto it, look, linger, and shoot!
To experience this whole thing . . .
    The hunt . . .
    The kill . . .
It was the dying I couldn't take.

Robin Dbouk

Untitled

Nature is beauty
we can see with our eyes
like the dew of a rose
glistening in the morning mist
as in hearing soft wings as an eagle
soars through the bright blue sky
lifting higher, unaware of our stare
like dancing snow as it feathers the earth
on branches of trees, powdered, fluffy, light as air,
the waves of the ocean as they kiss the shore,
endless motion, and bubbles that drag the sand back to the sea,
Why do we pollute? All the beauty we see is gently balanced
one day it could be gone, and our children may never see,
all of the art is nature that has been our great mystery

Michelle E. Taylor

Angels

Angels flying in the sky,
    Watching over you and I.
Sent down here from up above,
    To take care of the ones they love.
Watching over us through the day,
    While we work or while we play.
So when you're feeling sad and blue,
    Because your loved one is no longer with you.
Smile and thank the Lord above,
    For sending back the one you love.
As an angel from above,
    To guide you with everlasting love.

Kathleen Gaumer

Bed Time Bath (Childhood Memory I)

I remember my bedtime bath. The sound of gushing
water. I remember the feeling of when my body
first felt the warm . . . almost hot water. The
sensation penetrated my skin from my toes to my
skull. The goose-bumps on the top of my head felt
like I was wearing a wig. I remember the bright
ceiling light that reflected on the rippled bath water.
It danced and jumped as if it had been choreographed;
Sometimes it put my weary eyes into a trance . . .

At times, the bath tub was a playground for my
sister and I. We would stay in for hours. Our small
finger tips and toes would be wrinkled and the water
would turn cool and gray. I remember the ice cream
sodas made from suds and the foamy bee-hive hair-dos.

After, the fuzzy towel would wrap around my entire body
and wet hair trickled down my back. The sensation
penetrated my skin from my toes to my skull.

Today, the convenience of the shower has replaced frequent
baths, but when I do bathe, and my toes first touch the water,
the memories of my childhood surface like ivory soap.

Lauren Beath

The Ocean

As I sit in the sand, watching the
waves fighting to get to the end, as if
racing. I wonder when will this pain
end? When will I ever be free from
this heartache? As the tears roll down
my face, the waves come close enough
to catch the tears as they fall from my
chin, as if telling me they understand.
That's when I realize that the only true
friend I'll ever have, the only friend
that will always understand, and the
only friend that'll always be there for me,
is the ocean.

Mandi Phillips

The Door

We open the door, and yet the door was already open.
We are afraid of what's on the other side so we do not enter.
Our lives and beliefs, are closing this door so we do not enter.
One person enters, he comes back with what he saw, he tells the
others of it, he says our minds can control any and everything we
can imagine here and more, they deny it, for it's against the
bible and all other beliefs. This person tells amazing stories about
how the earth, is cleaner than it is, just as clean as it was before
human's and the industrial revolution, how the tree's are more
abundant than they were millions of years ago. When one person made
a difference. Life was peaceful. Were there was self consciences
and no wars between continents. One government of the world,
space being explored, science that doesn't destroy the universe,
synthetics, no guns, no gangs, no hatred, no corruption, and stronger
sense of human kind. The people ask well how do you know about
this you were only in there for 2 seconds? The person says that
"beyond the door, is what ever you want the future to be, it's life
in it's full entirety, it's us and our planet, in whatever way we want
it, but be careful, once you enter you cannot come back, you can only
search for the new door. and maybe then you will chose wisely, I
made my mind. Now how about you?

Kit Jones

"Sand Castles"

We see but shadows as we swiftly move,
We catch a glimpse of faceless forms.
There is no time to stop and see the beauty of a tree.

When night unfolds to see the brilliance of the stars
To be filled with awe just to gaze at the vastness of the universe.
To dare release our imagination and travel far beyond the stars.

We do not stop, we hurry on with only thoughts about
    tomorrow when today has just begun.
How can we see a lonely soul whose only need is a human touch.

A word of comfort to one who now is feeling pain.
We have created the world we live in, it now demands
    so much from us.
Upon the earth we build our castles, in time, as if
    made of sand they will become.
The only treasures that are eternal have been
    conceived through an act of kindness.
In the book of life forever they remain.

Mary E. Wright

"Haley's First Pageant"

Today was Haley's first beautiful baby pageant,
We got her all dressed up and away we went.
We arrived so late at the high school gym,
People were still lined up waiting to get in.
She was so beautiful in her little red dress,
The best looking baby there, I would guess.
Her tiny red shoes matched so very well,
"that's my granddaughter," I wanted to yell!
Then my daughter took her upon the stage,
To compete with nine others near her age.
Haley became second runner up, and best dressed,
I knew then, my granddaughter was blessed.
She won a trophy, medallion, and a blue ribbon,
We were so happy for what she'd been given.
Now she just turned four months old today,
We all love her much more than we can say.
But we must all tell her again and again,
That real beauty also comes from within.

Linda Greathouse

To A Homeless Friend

Where are you now? My friend!
We have had "so long time no see!"
The severe winter has sorrowfully come again,
Have you achieved a suitable place to be?

I can not forget the night of that specific winter,
My home stair was serving you for company;
The woolen blanket and quilt were rejected,
Seeing the dancing snow, I heard: "No, I am not Chilly, not chilly . . ."

And after the Spring drove away the Winter,
We met again at the University of Tennessee;
Facing the beautiful campus and vigorous people,
You announced: "I have ever also earned a B.S. degree!"

Asking the Spring wind, I would like to know,
How can I cultivate a "long life lucky tree?"
If something could be changed to the unfortunate,
I would rather become a working bee!

Fortunately you still engaged in hungry self-study,
I saw you often in the College library;
Don't forget, Guy: Once you are laughing heartily,
Please come to this city again and be sure to see me!

Meyer G. Xie

A Tribute To Mother

Mother, what memories the name evokes.
We hear again the loving words she spoke;
See again the pride in her eyes
When we brought home some special prize.
She taught us values to withstand life's tests
And always expected us to do our best.
But when we failed as we so often do,
She was always there to see us through.
Remember the feel of her hand on our head
When we were sad or sick in bed?
Smell the aromas from her kitchen wafting;
Was ever food so wonderful tasting?
Remember her voice and the stories she read,
The fun, the laughter, and the things she said.
Feel again her soft lips on our cheek
When her love and comfort we did seek.
As long as mother was close and strong
We were children in a world without wrong.
Ah, to feel that blissful joy once more,
Never were we so loved and adored.

Laurabell Urick

Think?

Have you ever sat and wondered 'bout this world in which we live?
Have you ever not received, the volunteered to give?
Have you ever wondered why the people we call cool?
Are often times heartless and other times cruel.
I don't want to be that stone faced punk, not forever or a while.
I rather be that bright eyed boy who could always make you smile.
I know you've been hurt, but by God just who ain't
Be tough and strong to wash clean of that blue paint.
And when I think or some of the time
songs bounce threw my head but the words won't rhyme.
I'll let you judge me by my failures ma'am.
They've hurt, yes, but made me who I am.
Maybe if people took time to look in a losers eyes.
One would see the smiling world sitting in disguise.

Kenny Winkler

Windfall

Toward Morning, in rain
We make love.
            The mud is shining.
In the bed of your limbs
I am the unborn calf
That stretches in its mother's belly.

I watch the grass whipping
            at your legs
My tongue going limp for speech;
I want to run
Like the hunter who follows the hoarse
            cry of the nighthawk,
Its shot body
Hanging mid-air.

I want to be that bird
To plummet and twitch with it
            downhill.
The light dries me as I move,
The smell of death on the flies
            that fill my face.

Pamela D. Bruns

Why Me?

Sometimes we may ask "Why me"
We need to listen to ourselves speak

Days of pain, moments of despair
Why is this happening? Do I really care?

And then I take a moment and think about life
About how God saved me, and how I really have no strife

Look at the thorns on a vine so ripe
Out of it comes a rose, vivid and bright

Merely grip your fingers around life's thorns
And you'll be able to smell the fragrance of the rose

I know life is hard and He will see us through
We need merely ask for his Help and He will do

Sometimes I ask myself "Why me" "What's next?"
And the answer comes so tenderly, "Because I loved you best."

Pat Roberts

Lock-Less Monster

Foliage flocking forth from my head-
weathered and dry.
Seemingly smooth,
but brittle to the touch.
Naked from ornaments and fragrance.

Prickly needles stomp on my face—as the wind thrashes through my
delicate skin.
The frown suites me.

But . . . so comforting is home.
I watch as the crimson tresses fill the inner cave . . . and fill me.
I gnaw at my nails
    yearning with a rigid grip for luscious locks of my own.
Drowning in kaleidoscope potions,
bathing in natures repulsive mirrored image . . .
actively haunted by another's plush meadow.
Bushels of Buttercups,
forests of Cherrywoods,
miles of Chocolate streams, and
rapid Silver Chains . . . linked all around me!
I sigh in relief, for there is a cold steel on my bed . . .

Kimberly A. Terlap-McMahon

"I'm A Sinner Too"

You ask me how I can live with a sinner like You?
Well, Darling, I'm a sinner too.
"Jesus" forgives me, because I ask him to.
"He" will forgive us no matter what we do.
All you have to do is ask and "He" will forgive you anything.
Just be sincere and believe and you'll always feel "Him" near.
So, if you're shy and can't ask out loud,
That's no problem, for "He" hears each whispered prayer.
"He's" with us not matter where we go or what we do.
"He's" always there for us, because
"He" knows we're sinners too.
All I ask when on my knees at night,
"Please be with me, and help me do the things I know are right."
It feels so good, just knowing that "He's" near,
And I know "He" hears my every prayer.
My sins shall not become the master over me.
For "Jesus" died to set me free, that day on Calvary.
So, "Lord", please help me to remember who I am,
And not be passing judgment on my fellow man,
This I'm asking You cause, "Lord" I'm a sinner too.

Rosalie McKim

What Are Dads For?

What are Dads for?
Well lets see,
A good joke or two
for a slap on the knee.
They make you smile,
sometimes frown.
We have Dads,
to make the world go round.

Dads are for reading a book
if you think it's too long.
For always caring
whether you're right or wrong.
They're always there when you need them,
they're right on call.
They are there to catch you whenever you fall.

Dads make you laugh, they're never sad.
They're one of a kind the one and only Dad.
This question's quite simple, it's easy for me,
because my Dad's just the way
I want him to be.

Laura Bartelson

Retired

Ever want to do just what you wanted to do?
Well you can, you know when you're sixty-two.
Worked all those years, reared kids and such,
Never had time for yourself, you give so much.
Now when you get a call from a friend for lunch
Sure, you can go and see the old bunch.
Your hubby announces take a caribbean cruise,
Three whole days and nights to do as you choose.
Were back and its square dancing for us.
Sure we can go, a Friday night must!
If its a rainy dull day, you stay in bed,
Get up about noon only to be fed.
You just wonder when all this bliss will end,
Well, only our Lord knows, so until them.
I'll go on doing just what I want to do,
Cause you see I'm, retired and I'm past sixty-two.

Nellie W. Land

Winter Wind Song

Let the winter winds blow wild
We're snug and warm inside - my child

Let Jack Frost paint patterns on the pane
And snow flakes softly line the lane

Let the skies darken and threaten
By our warm fire we are sittin'

Let the trees look bare and bleak
We have happy things of which to speak

Let the song birds fly way
We know that they're not gone to stay

Let the flowers all disappear
And the winter winds whistle in my ear

Let the cold rain come down
On the brown and mushy ground

This won't make me sad and bitter
For I know spring's no quitter

She will be back before long
And will sing her own sweet song

And she will come with emerald lace
And will our waiting hearts embrace

Moline Hogg

Together

We shared all the beauty of love.
We painted our world with innocence
and a silent understanding of peace.
We were more than one, and it was perfect.
We were each other and lost without one another.
Our hands could dance in fire, and our eyes could
speak in darkness.
We were happiness and laughter entwined.
We were togetherness and hope that thrived.
Your heart could read my soul, and my eyes could
speak your thoughts.
We were a part of what we could not know.
You taught me strength, and I taught you sensitivity.
And we taught the world what love was.
We made desirable memories and history.
We made each other more than before.
What we were is what I long to be.
We were the passion and fire that made love grow;
we were the centers of each others desires.
We were together.

Trista Phillips

Who Was That Man?

K.A.S.

He carried the weight of the world on his shoulders, we listened to
what he had to say —
Found peace in his company, yet deserted him when he needed those who
claimed that his word was the way —
When we wanted a miracle we sought him out, friends, followers, to heal
their ailments and frustrations —
When he took care of their needs his name travelled, and spread to
people of many nations —
How sorry they were then by their lack of faith, it was over and we
cried much too late —
What did we do but crucify this gentle man? Who is now the keeper of
many a man's fate —
When he was alone in depression and sorrow, he slept without a friend —
He knew they would persecute him so, causing his inevitable end —
Now we want him back, hoping till this day that he'll return and save —
Some fear his coming back but he's already here, fully resurrected from the grave —
For those who follow his pattern, you can see what he went through —
When your number is called and you're asked to come forth, let's see
what he has to say to you —

Raymond Lee

Perkins The Butler

And I wonder . . . If I am Perkins — (and I am) —
What kind of a Perkins am I?
How am I emblematic of a doormat?
Am I walked upon to be the very dirt beneath people's feet?
Is it my lot to collect the detritus, the scum, the icky crud from the
bottoms of their shoes?
Perhaps my soul's essence, like yon doormat, is trod upon:
Heartlessly, filthily.
Or, rather, am I the noble structure that protects, buffers, insulates?
Am I the much needed barrier that separates the cold, cruel ground
From the warmth, the fragrant sweat, of the interior of a well-
fitting, non-bunion-aggravating shoe?
I examine the doormat: Yea, 'tis a fine doormat,
With sturdy wood slats, resolutely parallel.
And I . . . and I like that doormat, remain staunch—
Sympathetically yielding, ever fixed.

A doormat is a fender on the car of life,
And Perkins is shined and ready for the strife.

Mary S. Thistle

Black Would Be Better

Grey, everyday — what I see.
What I feel is the pain; sadness, in a way
So I lay in my soul:
    vacant and betrayed; dismayed,
    alone and afraid.
to wake everyday, to my lone world of grey
strengthens my stay —
    but leaves me in pain.
Anguish, my friend,
with me 'till the end — the end of my stay:
    my everyday grey.
But, this is my deal —
all that you can see — is only part of what
    pain I feel . . .

Rachel K. Blackwell

A Thoughtful Tear

When you feel lonely and sad, I appear. You attempt to suppress the
wet, salty sadness of my existence. You find it is futile to resist
my inevitable freedom.

Sometimes I arrive alone, most times with plenty of company.
When a person sees me coming, they lower their eyes and turn away,
for they feel shame for having caused my visit. Or they attempt to
comfort you and dismiss me, but I will not be denied.

I am not hurtful or vengeful, simply necessary.
When the time comes, and it will, that you sense my arrival
remember, that you are only human and I am only a tear.

Vanessa Saldana

"Winter Scene"

Ice blue space
    veiled with sheerest pink,
    weighted with gold
        dissolved in the west;
Skeletons of black lace
    rising behind rows of city blocks
        pointing fingers into pastel skies
Some are fan-shaped, as sea plumes;
Some are round, like tumbleweed
    caught on the rooftops;
Some have sturdier design, rough and gnarled.
Was lace ever more lovely
    than behind rows of city blocks
        pointing fingers into pastel skies?

Winnie Hellams

Nothing To Give

One might often wonder, in this crazy world we live.
What do I possess? What have I to give?
I haven't any money. I have no extra time.
I haven't even talent to write a simple rhyme.

I haven't any extra food. I have no extra space.
I have no fine linen, no satin and no lace.
I have no gas to give a ride, so one won't need to walk.
I have no dime to telephone, nor have I time to talk.

I have nothing of value, so please don't bother me.
Go ask the neighbor, they'll help you out, you'll see.
Please just go, leave me alone. I have lots of work to do.
If Jesus was knocking at your door, would you offer nothing to?

Renea Blegen Witte

561

The Open Door

No one can predict
   what life has in store
So please don't close that open door

Through that door are the secrets of my heart
That only you have taken a part

That door was open for you to come through
You didn't balk, nor did you walk
You came running with, the swiftness of a deer
Wanting to see, if I was sincere
   sincere I was, sincere I'll be
   If you keep, your faith in me

That door was open for you to come through
Now that you've entered you are the center

The center of my problems they will be worked out
The center of my dreams I hope will come true
The center of my future without you there is no

No one can predict what life has in store
So please don't close that open door

Loral Anderson

Untitled

Now is another day.
What will it bring?
Will there be sun or will there be clouds?
Busy people off to work or play.
Day in day out sticking to the grind.
Man has to give time out for the finer things.
RUSH-RUSH-RUSH
Come back down and take note.

The butterfly searching for the flower to rest upon.
The bird arriving to the nest with nature's earth worm for her little
   one's waiting.
The dew on the grass, nature's own watering system.
The blueness of the sky, the whiteness of the clouds.
The sun ray caught between the window pane.
The grasshopper hopping like he was out to win the gold.

These are just a few of the examples of what some people may
never take note.
It is these little things that can make the world a more fulfilling and restful place.

TODAY IS THE DAY THE LORD HAS MADE!

Rest and enjoy.
Try to see some of the fine things and see what rest and peace it will bring.

Linda Shupe

I Knew . . .

I knew how clear it began
   when a moment was true,
   when someone quoted "I love you",
   when secrets could share,
   when faces were there.

I knew how clear it began
   when one reached out a hand,
   when one could understand,
   when promises turned promised,
   when encouragement was never missed.

I knew how clear it began
   when company took misery's destination,
   when honesty was an impression,
   when side by side existed,
   when emotions never twisted.

I knew how clear it began
   But now it ended.

Tamara Pippins

Cats, Bunnies And Boys

On a bright sunny day he was busy at play
When a snow white bunny hopped his way.
The chase was on and the cat joined in
As around and around the yard they ran.

They bounced as they ran into the field
He sometimes fell when snags did not yield.
But up, and off again with a smile.
Tireless, it seemed he might run a mile.

Even an electric fence proved to be
A small challenge to the child as he
Climbed right through it and into the wood,
Running as fast as a three-year-old could.

Willing the bunny not think him a foe
The boy was given a carrot to show;
They eyed one another, the offer was shunned.
The rabbit hopped off and the boy turned to run.

His face shining brightly, the carrot in hand,
Off through the fields the three of them ran.
The bunny, the kitty, the three-year-old boy,
What fun they were having, sharing such joy!

Ruby B. Britt

On This Day Of Valentines

On this day of valentines when red hearts do abound,
When cupids arrows fly with love and candy can be found,
These verses come to you my love to ask you to be mine,
That I might please and treasure you, to fulfill Gods just design,
For surely we were meant to be, together for our life,
To grow each day for to become, an eternal man and wife.
Our unity of heart and soul are sweets upon my lips
To taste each day in joyful bliss, between the many trips,
Gods angels make to us each day, to fill our cups with love,
That we might sip each newborn day, our blessings from above.

Terry A. Gidish

Only You Will Know

Where do you go? Where do you sleep?
When darkness falls upon the street?

Does anyone know? Does anyone care?
Do you want me here? Are you scared?

I talk to you, you ignore me.
Do you here me? What do you see?

You always have a smile, always a happy face.
Are you in denial, or finally found a peaceful place?

Are you hurting? Do you feel pain?
Is your body crying out in vein?

Never ending, you keep going on and on.
I always wonder, will you see the dawn?

Your way of life, a present hell.
Wish I could join you, hiding in your shell.

Where did you go? I can only guess,
Maybe heaven, a place of rest.

Sitting there, you never surrendered.
When I look back, I'll remember.

In the end, your world will close.
Resting finally? Only you will know.

Tammy Haldeman

562

The Empty Nest

A surprising gladness stirred my heart,
When God blessed us just a few years apart.
With two beautiful stars that shined so bright,
Childbirth was a joy and such a great sight

Our sons were so little and so very light,
We planted the seeds of life and the fruits are a delight.
Years passed by and with our love we helped them to grow,
They left home and flew away such a long time ago.

Like birds they opened their wings,
They left the nest to find a mate and see what life brings.
They don't need us anymore,
But their love continues just as before.

And so today we are alone,
With lot's of memories of our own.
Their unseen presence here to stay,
In our hearts every day.

Mirra Flack

Now From Then

Why is it that the sunset relies upon emotion for its splendor?
When I felt strongly about life, red never felt hotter
Nor burned so brightly in the fire of the evening.

But now that I feel little of life,
The fire of the night glows barely bright enough to remark upon;
Now, joy in the presence of life has passed to a new level,
A level where notice is taken, briefly,
Before trudging to the next experience;
Now, words no longer flow-they merely trickle in a disjointed fashion,
No idea clings together as a whole.
Instead, seams pull apart and the river is left to fall uncaught
Like a bottle of ink spilling across a field of white,
Creating nothing worth savoring, leaving nothing in its wake . . .
I miss my red.

Michelle Diane Sebastian Oatley

Tricks

I was reading a book
when I saw a big fat hook

When I got up to see what it was
I saw it was just a ball of fuzz

I went back to reading my book again
when I saw my dad named Ken

He tried to fool me once more
but I saw him put it on the floor

So I got up off the chairs
and I went and hid on the couch by the stairs

When he looked down the stairs and said "Oh Gee"
I jumped out and said "I knew you were the one that scared me!"

Mallory Elizabeth Nelson

Tranquil Peace

This world we're in is so strange today,
We often, always want to get away.
When I'm in my quiet time away from the world,
I go to places far away where there is Tranquil Peace;

Total tranquility like the island sunset,
Total peace when I see your face,
Your warm embrace,
Like a an ocean breeze sweeping me up into the clouds,
Drifting along, I just hold on to my tranquil peace
Never letting go!

Southwell Lecointe

Up From Sleep: (August 13, 1995)

A Major And Minor Personal . . .

In the cradle of the universe
   when I was young
I listened to the symphonies
   of the trees
Debussy's 'sea' off-shore
Mozartian scores
Butterflying like restless angels
In chords of ecstasy transforming clouds and . . .

The cosmos enfolded me
Expanding the selflessness of the self;
And I grew wise awaiting
The be-loved known and unknown
Drawing me on . . .
Beyond the disparities
Conducting time and space.

E. Manuel Huber

"Well Water"

Get me to the ocean
where my spirit will run free.
Take me to the water, in it there is truth and
love of thee.
On land I'm suffocated.
At the Ocean I'm free.
Leagues and Legends are where I want to be;
too much dirt here, that really bothers me.
Neptune wait for me!
I'm on my way . . .
Goodbye my wave is here to rescue me.

Theresa Chalmers Jones

Winter Into Spring

In the end of Winter,
When ice has unfroze,
An ever slight breeze arose.
All the creatures stared in fascination,
At the gleaming anticipation, of Spring.
The flowers started to bloom,
As the robin admires his plume.
Hopping nearby in the green grass,
Lurked a rabbit's kit, a charming young lass.
There are so many babies around,
There's one everywhere on the ground.
There are raccoons and antelope,
And fifteen chipmunks to cope.
All the animals have something to share,
Everyone,
From a bear to a hare.

Kathleen Kelly

Moonstruck

Oh moon, how beautiful are you. You, that lights the sky.
When I'm feeling blue and look to you . . . I must ask, why?

Why are you, oh moon? What are you to me? When I look at you
I'm soon to see, your not alone and I'm not too.

Your beauty tonight is quiet, and we are but a speck
In the sky of the night. Mysteriously, you beckon my view,
Through the night and before the dew.

To look beyond the light of you implies divinity
While overwhelming me with serenity.

So alone and yet together. So much to learn and so little time.
Teach me oh moon so I will know, do I think afar or keep it nigh.
Oh moon, is that what you are to me?

Vance Stevens

Untitled

We saw the tear that formed in your eyes
When it was time to say goodbye
It glistened under the artificial light
You wouldn't allow it it's natural flight.

In our eyes too, were so many tears
We've been together for so many years.
But now the time has come for us to part
We take so much, but leave a piece of our heart.

A relationship such as we have had
When parting, can be only sad
We've been special to each other in so many ways
We've been there for one another, nights and days.

Now a new life we must start
Which means we will be apart
But no one can take away the memories so many
Memories of laughter and joy, there are plenty.

So while we start a life a new
And often times think of you
Grateful for all the years we had together
The wonderful memories that will last forever.

Sondra Eisenpress

Muses And Meditation Upon Reaching

The 50th Rung On The Ladder Of Life

Methinks it be not super nifty
When one turns the magic fifty.
Forsooth it seems both bod' and mind
Hath nature ravaged most unkind.

Unbeknownst, time took it's toll,
And now, though willing heart and soul,
I call to my feet,"I'm in a running mood!"
They answer back, "Forget it, dude!
The only thing we want to feel
Is a padded footstool under the heel."

Durst I know, I anguish and weep
That now I choose an afternoon's sleep
Instead of football, baseball, or track,
And incentive to work . . . I totally lack!

"To be or not to be!" The question rages.
The answers ballyhooed through the ages.
But as for me, my response is thrifty . . .
Don't ask me, bud, I just turned fifty!

Robert L. Downing

Near The End Of Fall

Near the end of fall, is the best time of all,
When the squirrels go and gather their food,
Cheeks turn a bright red, hood covers the head,
And the cold air puts a change in one's mood.

The leaves turn gold-brown, and gently fall down,
The ground is carpeted in nature's own way,
A chill in the air, wind gusts here and there,
Which sweeps all our humanly troubles away.

People stroll through the park, even after it's dark,
Peacefully enjoying the air and the scenes,
But let us be wise, now do they realize,
Just how much the pleasant fall really means?

So next time you're mad, perhaps even sad,
Because summer is ending and fall must arrive,
Think of the cool air, and the peace everywhere,
An atmosphere that fall has long kept alive.

Wendy Burdick

His Only Son, Her Only Son

"He was my only son!" she cried,
When she was told that he had died.
"Oh! Lord, bring him back to me,
I cannot live, this cannot be!"

But in her heart, she heard God say,
"My Only Son died too, one day.
He hung there upon that tree,
And others buried Him for Me.

Then, at sunrise three days thence,
I raised Him from the grave where he had been,
He is not dead, He lives today,
And your son, too, knew the way."

And then God's message came to her clear,
Though her son would no longer be near,
He'd be at home God had prepared,
Because God loved him, and He cared.

And her heart was flooded with tears,
God reassured her He would be near,
That He's preparing a place to be given
To all who believe to live with them in heaven.

Mary Zinn

"Love Shadows"

At the end of the day
When the moon shows its face,
And the light peeks in through my shade,

I close my eyes,
Thinking only of you
And the plans that we recently made

I vision your face
I feel your touch
I smell the sweet scent of your hair;

You whisper my name,
I answer out loud
Loving the feeling of knowing you care

I whisper your name
Caressing you in my mind
Holding you close in my soul, in my heart

I was born for you,
You were born for me;
I pray every night that we will never part.

Lelia Maxine Smith

The Blue Hour

There is a special time at twilight
When the sun begins to loose its power
And slips behind the hills once more
Then there appears THE BRIGHT BLUE HOUR
But first the sky in mauves and grey
Paints pictures to complete the day.
A ROYAL BLUE—this in-between-time
When the world is BLUE for just the mean-time
Trees silhouette, their colors fade
Becoming BLUE instead of jade
Then as each twinkling star comes forth
To give the sky its dazzling power
The blackness of the night appears
To swallow up THE BRIGHT BLUE HOUR

Ruth Chimiklis

When The Tears Won't Come

What do you do when the tears won't come?
When there's no one to call and nowhere to run.
What do you do when you just want to scream?
But your voice just won't come and this is no dream.
What do you do when your soul's torn apart?
When you can't face the end but can't bear to start.
What do you do in the dark looming silence?
When you just want to sit but to do so is mindless.
Where do you turn when you're on your last leg?
Help's so hard to find and it's not right to beg.
How do you find a friend who'll be true?
If there's only the mirror reflecting pale you.
Curl up in ball and hope it will pass.
Good memories so few and the bad ones they last.
What do you do when there's a bump in the night?
Too frightened to move but needing the light.
I wish I could tell you the answers to these
Ponderous questions indeed which haunt me.
And so I'll just sit here quietly all alone
For it's all I can do when the tears just won't come.

Ken M. Carlisle

Broken Wings

Enemies, or are they considered friends
When they hurt you, coming through the wind.
As you inhale the hurt comes in
Through the tiny membraned skin.

Thinking can you lean again
Forgiving them saying lets re-begin.
Then you feel like a power of one
They hurt you again, you're a power of none.

Spreading salt on a wounded cut
Shocking, sizzling, burning cut.
Do they look back or even try
Watching you sit and start to cry.
Tear drop rolling down your skin
When you're the innocent, with broken wings.

Gazing beyond the soft blue sky
Where the devils play, and the angels cry.
Waiting for another friend
Who's come to play or break a wing.

Kaushika Sengupta

The Art Of Quilting

The art of quilting was almost lost.
  When they were no longer needed for warmth.
Then came along THE COUNTRY LOOK.
  And with it came back the hand made quilt.

They bring back memories of my childhood days,
  For it was under the quilt we always played.
I watched my mother cut scrap after scrap,
  And sitting by the fire she sewed them into a wrap.

Once she had it large enough into the frames it went.
  Stretched over a lining and batting ready to quilt.
Day after day in her spare time she would sew.
  Weaving in and out and to and fro.

The nettle on her thimble would make a little click,
  As she pushed it through and pulled it back.
Then flinging her hand in a half-moon.
  She would start the stitching all over again.

When it was finished on the bed it would go.
  Her masterpiece of patterns and colors aglow.
And now that her artful design was completed.
  Its around to-day to be cherished and repeated.

Mary A. Simmons

Fifty Short Years

It was a cool summer evening in late thirty nine
When we both danced together for the very first time
Just teenagers then but the magic was there
That it would last for a lifetime we just weren't aware

Now our schooling was finished but a war had begun
And our lives were on hold until it was won
A wedding soon joined us but a delay in our life
When the Army did send him to join in the strife

For two years in the Pacific he served America well
A sad, worrisome time which the letters did tell
But he finally came back to his loved ones at last
And true love and devotion made up for the past

We were always grateful for the next fifty years
With so much love and happiness and very few tears
Two wonderful daughters and one granddaughter in addition
Before our husband and father was called up to heaven

Our memories are volume of this wonderful man
Who was loved by so many and missed by everyone
And a greater love story has never been told
Of a lifetime of caring, so great to behold!

Marilyn B. Arnold

Untitled

I long for today to mirror yesterday
When we laughed all our cares away.

Taking long walks, she held my hand
I honored her beauty and hoped to be so grand.

Lying beside her watching TV all day
How I wish today was the same way.

Until we find a way to reverse this disease
Walks through my memories will have to ease.

Playing kick ball in the yard, drinking punch
My tiny hands helped her cook lunch.

Her memories dance through my mind
I hope everyone's are so kind.

Her long walks are now guided by the Lord
For he is the shepherd, we the sheep.

Dedicated to those touched by Alzheimer's.

Kelly Ann Rainwater

Take Me, Or Leave Me

Take me, or leave me. But don't expect me to believe you anymore.
When you came home late at night, you have no reason to make things up
For your clothes have an essence of another home.

Take me, or leave me. If I am not awake please let me dream on.
Don't kiss me on my forehead. You know I heard you getting in.
And besides, your kisses taste like such a guilt.

You admire me because I look up at the sky. And because you don't see me cry.
And you feel smaller and smaller everyday that goes by. And you
avoid me every time I look into your eyes.

Take me, or leave me. I don't spy on you nor I take away your liberty
But if you decide to leave me. If you are going to abandon me.
Do it before I can see the morning sun clearly.

You admire me because I look up at the sky. And because you don't see me cry.
And you feel smaller and smaller every day that goes by. And
you avoid me every time I look into your eyes.

Take me, or leave me. And if you return, bring the truth along.
Straighten up the look in your eyes. Bring with you my arch rival.
If he is better than me then I would be able to cry.

Nelson Aguirre

The Crescent Rose

Why Acknowledge the Thorns,
When you can Admire and Cherish the Crescent Rose"

Your voice is a whisper of sunshine's morning dew,
As it caresses each and every scope of its being,
The warmth it transcends in expression,
Is the touch of an effervescent warm mountain spring,

Your eyes enchant the brilliance of the farthest shooting star,
On a night destitute of light,
The anger, the joy, the sadness, the solace are all etched
into the windows of your soul,
For in those windows I see elegance, warmth of character and
captivating reflection of inner beauty,

Your touch is that of a fleeting winter's night fire,
Resting the chill to a comforts end,
Your hands of soft and tender comprise,
Bring forth Heaven's alluring splendor,

As the sun sets in the west and delicately fades into a glimmer,
My eyes can only reflect the luster of it's essence,
And my heart can only cherish the thoughts and warm remembrances,
Of the lady who has and always will be the ardent fervor in my soul.

J. Mark Sheffield

When You Find God, You Discover . . .

When you find God, you find love
When you find God, you find hope
When you find God, you find faith
When you find God, you find peace
When you find God, you find happiness.

When you find God, you find life
When you find God, you find health
When you find God, you find strength
When you find God, you find security
When you find God, you find prosperity.

When you find God, you find truth
When you find God, you find righteousness
When you find God, you find knowledge
When you find God, you find wisdom
When you find God, you find victory.

When you find God, you find yourself
You will realize that He was not lost, but you were
He is the key that unlocks your heart
and fills you with the fruits of His Spirit.
You will discover that every good thing is found in Him.

Lisa Renee Crummy

Anytime, Anyplace

How often do I think of our love
Whenever I'm doing a task.
Are you wondering if I'm thinking of you
All you ever have to do is ask.

You are always on my mind
If near my side or in another town.
Do not fear, I won't do you wrong
Why look for love when it's already found.

Anytime you wonder am I true
Just put my love to the test.
I'll prove anyplace where my love
for you stands,
Why settle for second, when you already
have the best.

The best things come to those of us
Who come clean in the truth of light.
So put away your fears and see
That true love is hard to fight!

C. Michael Evans

"Are You Sleeping?"

Tell me are you sleeping
When you walk the streets by day?
Or is your mind wandering,
At some foreign bay?
Tell me are you sleeping
When the world goes hungry - (the same)?
For as each seconds tick by,
Another child dies again.

Tell me are you sleeping,
When sadness is in their face?
For we all see it - (I know);
Or does your mind just travel to, "another happy place?"
Tell me why do you pretend to sleep,
When we all can feel the pain?
Tell me why do you wander away,
When you awake - to return again?

Tell me are you sleeping,
When we're all to blame
Even though you do nothing,
You're hurting each other - (the same).

Wendy N. Joseph

My Greatest Joy

(Megan's Magic)

Sometimes, I look into your face and see yesterday.
   When you were little,
     round and comfortable in my arms;
   If I close my eyes and reach back
     I can hold you once again
     and smell your sweetness.

Sometimes, I look into your face and see tomorrow.
   All the hopes and dreams,
     all that the future holds;
   Knowing that all you wish for
     and all that I wish for you,
     may not be the same.

Sometimes, I look into your face and see today.
   Happiness radiating from you,
     delighted with the magic of what I know
     to be just another ordinary day;
   This is the most beautiful you.
     You lift my spirits and fill my heart,
     for you are truly my greatest joy.

Rose Beardsley Kukla

"Empty Nest"

How easy to remember the feelings that I had,
When you were very little and my heart was full and glad.
How easy to forget the moments that we shared,
When you proved to me in a billion ways
How much you really cared.
From the moment you were born-I knew my heart was torn,
Between giving you the best, and loving you to death.
Through the years I've tried to keep you
Under my wing,
One hand holding, protecting, stifling.
The other hand trying
to loosen my grasp,
Hoping you would fly - but never too fast!
Although it seems that you have left me
A light year to soon,
I recall that you were always
A child of the moon.
And now that your wings have soared through the night,
I hope that they are not broken in perilous flight!

Tomasina DeCrescenzo

Good Times Gone

Oh, How I remember good times gone,
When youngsters ran and played
till the lightning bugs came on.

Hide-n-go-seek was a favorite thing to do,
While listening for "wipe your feet
and wash your hands too."

Dinner was on the table and all us
kids were seated, with little heads
bowed for our prayers to be completed.

Our food would be eaten as fast as
arms could bend, so we could have a
game of tag before we'd all go in.

We'd settle down with family as day
came to an end, a bubble bath, a
bedtime prayer, so we could start again.

Oh, how I remember good times gone.

Virginia L. D. Elkins

Together At Last

Beyond the realm of understanding, two friends emerge; renewed;
from whence the familiarity arose to remind them,
They had, in another life, given and shared their love one to another.
Unpretentious, knowledgeable, satisfied; that they had loved-mind,
    body and soul.
As majestic as the mountains which rose high in the North, reaching
to the heavens in awe of revelation; these two now stand firmly together,
    peering into the unknown.
Exiting emotions rocked the bodies of the two friends.
Two lovers, two as one-stand as the doorway of tomorrow-hopes and
expectations imbedded in their minds. Two hearts reopened, renewed
    and rejoiced,
Only the gifts freely given one to the other would suffice; quieten
their bonding love; reaching to the depths of their hearts to bring
all the emotions together of love-warmth; brought to the surface
to be shared and enjoyed. HAND IN HAND THRU ETERNITY.

Tula W. King

Seasons Of My Life

I walked along the lane with you
Where buttercups and violets grew.
You asked me then to be your wife,
It was the springtime of my life.

We kissed beneath the apple tree,
How dear, how sweet a kiss can be.
Our hearts were young and filled with love,
A gracious gift from God above.

First, wedding bells, then World War Two
And off to serve as soldiers do.
Long I waited my love's return
With aching heart and great concern.

The years sped by, all golden days;
Three children grew and went their ways.
With four grandchildren we held dear,
Love grew stronger each passing year.

Then angels came, took you away.
Come back my love, come back I pray.
You left a sad and grieving wife,
It is the winter of my life.

Marjorie N. Farison

State Of The Mind

I long for that special place to visit.
Where I can explore the possibilities that life has in it.
It is far away from the hurt, pain, crime, and taxation.
It is my solace, my place to find ultimate relaxation.

I'm young once again and my spirit is full of dreams so real.
All the disappointment and frustrations I no longer feel.
My body worn and tired is no longer old.
My imagination thinks of beauty and ideas that are left untold.
Do I dare share this place I've found?
Give it away - I can't not my limitless bounds.

So as each day of life passes me by - I dare not worry or even cry.
Just long for my special place to visit.
Where I am free to experience the things that life has in it.

This place I speak of has no war, no hate, and no despair.
In this place I have no one single care.
To go there will not cost me one thin dime.
For my special place is created in my mind.
Here the state of the world does not matter nor does time.
All that matters here is the state of the mind.

Melissa Y. Sawyer

Survival

At six corners, in the city,
where Irving Park, Cicero and Milwaukee collide,
life in the street, at the store front, is difficult.
But around back, in the alley,
there is not even the glow of neon to soften reality.

Around back, delivery trucks and alley pirates
cruise through trash and life's leftovers.
A woman's underwear, soiled, torn, discarded in the walkway.
Graffiti - filled walls (pigs suck) (Lords rule).
McDonald's papers and wine bottles, cans and coat hangers.
vomit and discarded love letters are the reality.

But over there, next to the building,
growing out of a crack and holding on to life tenaciously is a thistle.
Dark green, symmetrical, full of seeds and thorns,
with one small flower.
And you know just to look at it
that it is there to stay as long as it wants.

God, do I love the survivors of life.
Just imagine. The thistle had a flower.

Mark Milligan

"Thoughts Of Peace"

Out here in the woods,
    where it is so peaceful and so calm.
Not like the city,
    where violence and conflicts are all around.

I try so hard to forget the problems of everyday life,
    but can't seem to shake them from my mind.

I wish of PEACE and KINDNESS,
    I wish for problems to get solved,
But I know my wishes won't come true.

If people would only join hands,
    and cooperate to solve all conflicts and come together,
Shake hands and forgive each other for the mistakes made,
    then this world would be in harmony,
And only then would we
    begin to LIVE . . .

Tiffany Gregory

Ellis Island

Ellis Island - now an historical place,
where people from Europe had to face
a new life that to them seemed strange.
As time went by, their life started to change.

The rooms were simple - practically bare
hardly enough room for everyone there.
In the sleeping quarters they slept on the floor.
Each day people came - more, and more.

Immigrants ate at a long wooden table crowded end to end,
tasting new food, perhaps making a friend;
when allowed to leave the Island, traveling to all parts of
  the nation.
Just think - you and I were born from that generation.

After all the stories that I've been told,
I'm glad I visited Ellis Island when it was old.

Peggy Raduziner

On Castle Rock Road

On Castle Rock Road 'neath a natural fortress outcrop of stone
Where rare peregrine falcons and red-tailed hawks soar
A clever native California couple has created its timeless clone:
A secure home in harmony with this honeyed land of legend and lore

A tercentenary coastal oak shades the gateless entrée
Near a clear creek where it makes an ox bow bend
The linen-colored dwelling set on a foundation of an earlier day
Invested with love and meticulous care, seemingly meant to mend

They've brought the outdoors inside with lustrous, glass-catching light
The huge hearth erected from native stone from the cooling creek
The warmth of wood adorning every chamber, in the living room to great height
The use of spruce and pine whose aroma your nostrils avidly seek

May God bless this sanctuary and the souls who dwell therein
Here the human and the divine combine; here there's no separation of sin.

Norman R. Nelsen

Wolves

Beneath the blanket of night,
where the screech owl flies,
two four footed silhouettes silently pass,
a top the white covered hills.
They mark their territory so wide,
Telling all intruders to beware.
They are a pair for life,
watching and waiting for the seasons to change.
Hunting and eating, sleeping and playing,
while howling to one another as they sing
to the moon.
Within the shadows of night,
As the owl watches from above,
They silently walk among the shadows,
passing and waiting, and biding their time . . .

Kathy Parrish

Trust

Trust is a thing of Brick and Mortar
which when stood up high and tall,
is there to protect, guard, preserve and shelter
not to worry, it shan't fall.
For when you lean against it
it will hold sturdy and strong
and if the foundation is firm
the bond will hold forever
on and on and on and on.

Mike Vanier

Nature's Ways

For every ocean there's a shore
Where the waters make their rest
To embrace the land we adore
And that the earth bore to be placed in this nest.
The seagull, inseparable to the sea
Which he seems to decorate as he flies
Singing his freedom as he cries,
Enhances beauty for all who may see
His white form in the skies.
There are moments of restless wonder
When threatening anger lies
Making the earth tremble with the roar of thunder.
Challengingly, nature shows her claws in this war
That goes on forevermore,
And which awakens the sea to match the fury of the skies.
The coming of a wave brings another wave
It's the cycle of the earth portrayed.
Everything disappears and goes to it's grave
While new things appear again to be laid
In the place of those things fade.

Martha Guida

A Place

There's a place you can go, where your heart meets your soul
Where your spirit connects and your body feels whole.

Where your mind is enlightened and dawn brings a new light,
And you begin to see life with revitalized sight.

There's a place you can go, and its not very far,
You must look deep within and find who you are.

And you begin to discover the strength you possess,
And you proceed with the courage to accept nothing less.

And with the strength of a mountain, you can risk without fear,
Because a voice deep within you, rings out loud and clear.

There's a place you can go, where your spirit is free,
And you know you can reach all you dreamed you could be.

And you're thankful for life and the questions it brings,
And you soar to new heights on its magical wings.

And you'll feel you're at peace, because your pain starts to leave,
And you move from a knowing, not from what you believe.

There's a place you can go where you're treading new grounds,
But you press forth with great ease, because life knows no
bounds.

You can go to this place when you're in need of a lift,
And when you arrive, you'll receive a great gift.

Karen Winston

"To A Bird I Heard"

May your song never be silent
wherever you may fly
Even to the highest places
where angels can reply.

It is your song of praise
to the loving creator of your world.
It echoes in my heart long after being heard.

I can't own you, little bird, because
you are wild and free
But I grasp the delight of your
gift and express my gratitude.

Ruth Chapman

Endless

The day unfolds in a shroud of darkness,
while the embers of yesterday wither and die.
The soft glow of the sun fills the sky.

Shards of light split my vision here
on the edge of day and night.
Suddenly time is of the essence and
clarity a goal to achieve.
So much to do before the sun leaves.

Once more on the edges of day and night,
where the sun sets and the stars rise.

Once more on the edge as a cloak of
darkness surrounds me in my endless cycle of life.

Michael Todd

The Evening Stroll

The evening stars drew a pattern in the sky
while the sun was setting very near by and
over yonder, in a small lake, a fish jumped
and chomped on the bait,
to naive to understand its fate.
The smile shone on the young boy's face
who took the fun of reeling it in,
and he looked around before he set the fish down
to be sure that he wouldn't lose this precious gift.
Walking home, he paused in the field
looking at the birds flying high in the sky
and then realizing the time, he hurried along in search of his pa.
Oh how proud would he be
when he saw the gift that his boy went to catch
in the little lake just beyond the trees.
Since supper was caught and the preparation done
the boy and his pa took a stroll to the place
where the fish was caught,
and with open expressions and lots of feeling
the boy began to share his exciting story!

Lindsey Veek

Autumn

Silver plane flying west ward without sound.
White jet stream stretches in the blue sky
Like drawing silk yarn from cocoon.

Last flowers in my garden
Frozen fuzzy bee clinging on the bright yellow
Chrysanthemum petals

Far away over the ocean
Aged mother passed away without saying good by

Tell me little bird on the skinny persimmon tree
Every thing going to be all right.

Shizue Tucker

Pretend

The clock ticks slowly, but time races by
While struggling for survival, we try, try, try
To make some sense of a life we hate
While powerful forces watch and meditate.
"What shall we do to them today?" They ask.
While poking and tormenting as a child with an ant.
These are only people, with hearts and souls and fears.
Who live to entertain us for an allotted length of years.
Looking forward gratefully to a time when it will end
This game, this farce, this life, this pretend!

Shirley Evans Scrip

Heroine Or Heroin

It's so hard to tell, isn't it?
Which one is good and which one is evil.
Look at them together and see both blessing and vice.
So which one takes you over the edge of the world,
And will the other save your life or help end it?
Take one to make you feel passionate and free.
The other, take it to put you on a higher cloud.
Lust and scream, turn away from the honor that you
Once hold so high and become like your enemies.
Steal and kill if you think you must, but there's never enough
That you can cherish today, never will you be satisfied by tomorrow.
Or maybe you wish you could be one of them and inject yourself
Into someone else's life, bringing outside every secret
And every inhibition to be burned on a block of red ice.
Maybe you wish you could rain down from the sky to rescue
Lovers from their hanging and give them solace in your embrace.
Whatever you choose, sign it in the sand and mark it with your
Deepest kiss or a few drops of your richest blood.

It's so hard to tell, isn't it?
Which is the Heroine and which is the heroin . . .

Morgan S. Purdom

My Answer, "My Love"

I've heard from your Angel, and she wants me to say,
While she has been lost, she has now found her way,
And the love that lay dormant from out of the past,
Now stirs in her heart with a love that will last.

She's waiting and longing to take your hand,
To share in your dreams, as no one else can,
A friend, a lover, a partner that's true,
To bring joy to your heart in all that you do.

She will walk by your side every step of the way,
To love you by night and also by day,
And all of the things that bring worry and doubt
Will fade in the distance as they are worked out.

Your angel, "My Love," has one final word.
The message is clear, the intent is not blurred.
Your love and devotion and intriguing ways
Will be reward enough for all of her days.

My answer, "My Love," is plain to see
For life without you could never be,
And the love that was kindled a long time ago
Is a love that clearly will never let go.

Martha Wrotenbery

Come, Walk With Me

Come, walk with me, my friend,
While the autumn sun defies the first fall chill.
We will wander 'cross the field to yonder slope,
Where the trees stand tall, arrayed in splendor still.

Come, talk with me, my friend.
We will speak again of precious hours, well spent,
Where the tiny woodland flowers delight the eye
As they raise their faces to the firmament.

Come, rest with me, my friend.
Yon wooded place is certain to beguile.
We'll forget the weary burdens of the world
And know peace unsurpassed for just a while.

I reach out my hand, my friend;
Take it, take it if you will,
And ere this lovely autumntide is o'er,
Let us walk to yonder woodland hill.

Marian Elizabeth Spear

The Blacksmith

He unknowing holds the key
Who has no use for it
By measures trapped by reason is he
Never daring to step in full
The hot breath of the bellows
Never daring entirely to retreat

Then mettle upon white metal meets
The hammer swings full in hand
The assault upon reason repeats
At the anvil, a scarred and blackened stand,
He forges an untempered chain complete
By twilight, returning home a beaten man
Held captive by the heart's conceit
Yet in hope triumphant in reason's defeat!

Mark A. MacLaughlin

The Wonder

My child, to-day you said to me
Who is GOD? What is GOD?
And I said, I do not know,
I only know that GOD IS, and
the WONDER is that GOD loves me.
You see the sky with your eyes so blue?
GOD is of the sky,
And GOD is of you.
GOD is in the sky. GOD is in you.
GOD is in all, for GOD Is.
You see a tree and a leaf from a tree?
There's not one leaf that is exactly like
Another leaf. This is true.
Just so there is nobody exactly like you.
As you grow you'll learn so much —
But you will always be you.
You will always be a part of GOD
Because GOD is in you
The WONDER is that GOD loves you.

D. E. Harris

Untitled

To my Dad: Who is really rad
Who is smart and knows what he has,
He has a wife and children he loves
They have a bond and are really close
This family a tie and everyone should know.

To my Dad: The great working man
He always seems to have a plan
When things go wrong in hid day
He does not pick up and run away
Even though he would rather play.

To my Dad: Who has two mischievous cats
They run all over the place looking for trouble
And sometimes they get more than one, but a double.

My Mom will yell to get them off the T.V.
But where! Would they run but to daddy's knee.

To my Dad: Who is always trying to get a laugh
For that person on their behalf
He does not want to see gloom and doom,
He would rather get after you with a broom.
We love you our special dad through and through.

Vickie D. Masengale

"A Man Called Jesus"

There was a man from Galilee . . .
Who it's said, walked on the sea.
Miracles it's written he made come true . . .
To help all the people, like me and you.
But when all was done and said . . .
He was hung on a cross, until he was dead.
When three days went by and by . . .
The people found out he didn't die.
He tried so very hard to please us . . .
The man that died, was named Jesus.
He said, "I'll be back someday you'll see . . .
And all of you, had better be ready for me".
So make a choice, be it heaven or hell . . .
For he's making a place for us to dwell.
There's a beautiful end to this sad story . . .
We will be living with him . . . in all his glory

Viola Dudley

No One Special

I am no one special, I never sat with kings
Who make the grand decisions concerning the world and things.

I am no one special, I never sat with Lords
Who call to many servant with fear in all their words.

I am but a husband, who with one more presides,
Combining our suggestions til both of us decides.

I am but a father, with children, just a few,
Teaching them with patience, then watching how they do.

I am no one special, but I try to be a friend
To all who feel they need one, and all that God would send.

I am no one special, I'm simply, only me.
A husband, father, friend, is all I want to be.

Richard A. Hickman

Men

I wonder who has told this lie,
    Who said we as men could not cry.
Little did we know we all have pain and fears,
    Just some are better at holding back tears.
Many pillows are filled with stains,
    Of men's tears, sorrows, and pains.
Some cry in public, some run and hide,
    Others are careful because of there pride.
Some learn to live and take it in stride,
    And others that can not end up in suicide.
So here is a question to all man,
    Can we cry I say we can.

Travis Williams

Little Nephew

I have a puppy who's a Pomeranian,
Who seems to be a little doggie vegetarian

He eats the grass when I take him outside to do
You-know-what
But he doesn't even go, so I scold him, sometimes spank him
On-the-butt

Dino is a good boy when it's time to take a shower,
He comes out of the bathroom smelling, but not looking like a flower

Blow-drying his white fur is an exhausting, tiring task,
Wisps of fur somehow fly into my mouth; I guess next time
I'll just have to wear a mask!

At night, when he's lying on his mat, I go in the garage to say
"Good-night little nephew, your mommy Angela will visit tomorrow
So you can tell her everything we did today."

Maritza Nino

Insight

I am not one who broke new land,
Who toiled in mire or reaped the fields.
No battles were won under my command,
I never defeated uprising evil.

My appearance was of no significance,
I was never envied for my beauty.
I did not perform great feats of courage,
Or completed any assigned duty.

I could not stop unrighteous prejudice,
Or thread honesty into others' hearts.
Profound words of wisdom I seemed to miss,
From depression I could not part.

As time went by and my life lengthened,
I realized with great mirth,
I am a being, a person, a soul,
For some reason I remain on this earth.

So I secured my beliefs, became content with myself,
And found that the goals I had not attained,
Were just minor setbacks in a long journey,
And I had the rest of my life to gain.

Laura Longe

Revolution

There was once a grade school student
   Who was not the least bit prudent
When it came to punctuation marks in place,
   So the marks and their relation organized retaliation
That the world of books might tumble in disgrace.

Now the dash got oh so huffy,
   And the period frightful stuffy
And the comma never would march in her place,
   Colon's sweet cooperation turned to gross vituperation
And the question marks just vanished into space.

Printed chaos swept the nation,
   Volumes danced with wild gyration
Punctuation marks made bold to flip their tittles,
   Great tomes fell in rages, tore out half their pages,
Scholars proud productions turned to riddles.

Now the moral of this story (tho it seems a wee bit borey)
   Is that sentences in books have feelings too
So don't ignore your English teachers
   And offend these little creatures
OR NEXT TIME THEY'LL VENT THEIR SPLEEN ON YOU!

Ralph Blocksma

Till We Have Faces

Till we have faces, we'll never know,
who we are, how to grow.
To find this face is no small task.
Is it worth the venture we must ask?
The alternative is rather dim,
Yes, we decide to go out on that limb.
Like Psyche in the underworld
tried and tested, Fates power toward her unfurled.
Forsaken by all,
Alone in the desert, no one to call.
Yet love did answer her distress.
For life, nature desires success.
She found her face, no small task.
Refused to wear the faceless mask.
She found her rightful place,
for now she has a face.

Kathy DeBlassie

Vows Of The Heart

Everyone dreams that one day they'll find someone whose love makes the whole world shine.

Someone to care for and love as an equal. Someone to share their hopes and dreams with. To wake each day and know you are near me, to touch and to hold you and love you so dearly.

You are the one who makes my life shine, you have my heart like the sands run through time. To know that forever our hearts will be one, to love and to honor, our new lives begun.

On this day forward we will have and hold, in sickness and health for better and worse. To you I pledge my eternal love and pray that forever our dreams unfold. Your love will make my whole world shine. To my husband I give my life, my love and my time.

Kathleen L. Curington

boy

this is a poem for boy,
whose broken chest,
symbolizes his broken heart.

i didn't break his heart,
but i feel a responsibility,
for not being strong enough,
to stop the heart breakers.

i can only tell him,
"be strong and trust in only yourself,
for soon enough, my friend,
your fate will lie in your hands."

"but please, boy, I beg of you this,
(for all I feel for you is love),
love those who love you, for without their love,
you are . . . nothing."

kiffin steurer

Something To Think About

You're so very accommodating. Your vision is so wide!
Why are my choices just a Viking princess
Or a Georgian mail-order bride?

Why not an Egyptian goddess? Or even a Roman slave?
Would you croak to discover that I was earth mother
In the days of men in the cave?

Can't you discern my spirit? My mind you say you admire.
You counted the water, the earth and the wind;
Don't overlook the fire!

You have great imagination, and you're so keen on fantasy.
I'm glad that you care, but are you aware
You might diminish our rhapsody

If you insist on confining bliss to only the scripts that you write?
I know you're well-read, but could your passions be fed
By a lady who wants to delight

You with more than just two parts to play?
Would you be willing? Could you find it thrilling?
Is it a thought you might weigh?

Nancy Helen Maberry

The Girl

Once there was a girl
Who was sucking on a candy cane.
While she was in a hurricane.
I think she was a feather brain and on Novocain.
One day, she was walking on Memory Lane.
And disappeared down the drain.

Paul Weir

"Passing Of A Precious Friend My Mother"

Why did you leave me all alone
Why did God not let me know he was taken you home?
Every thing changes, now your gone.
Making me wonder how to carry on.
Over and over you gave to me,
I chance that you knew what you meant to me.
Like our dream, does this emptiness have to an end?
While loosing a love one, I'm loosing a friend.
Mother what I would give just to hear your laugh.
However I know, it would be like waiting for life from a photograph
Oh! to have known you all those years,
All happy, sad, and hard times, all harvest my tears.
Everything matters when your young.
Everything shatters when one has gone, everything falters in the end.
While loosing a loved one, I'm loosing a friend.
So many feelings rushing in,
it's to late to think of what could of been.
Who really knows the reason? What was meant to be.
While loosing a loved one, I'll loose a part of me.
My mother, my loving precious, and best friend till the end!

Robert Bentley

Where Did You Go Dad . . .

Are you really gone?
Why did you leave so soon and unexpected?
I hope you know we really miss you
you just left my world so blue
If you could stay were would you be?
It was so sad to see you leave
did you know I people tried to save you?
I wish I could have seen you before you left.
But, now you're gone, but I'll
see you when I get there.
Will you still be there?

Nicole Carr

Why?

Why do we have violence?
Why do we have hate?
Why can't people figure out how to cooperate?
We were all made equal.
We are all the same.
Why do prejudice people blow out the flame?
Sometimes I wonder what this world's about.
Sometimes I just want to scream and shout.

Toni Bain

Or, So It Seems

Why? I often wondered . . .
Why life is so unfair
When things go wrong.

  Or, so it seems . . .

Why? I wonder
Why some have so much
And I have so little?

  Or, so it seems . . .

And then, I wonder . . . this "some" that have so much . . .
Do they have a child looking at them with love?
Two little arms hugging them . . .
And a little voice saying . . .

  "I love you, Grandma."

I don't wonder anymore . . .
I feel sad, for those who have so much . . .
  Or, so it seemed.

Ruth K. Cole

Wings

Growing up as a teen, youngest of six siblings
wild and carefree, flying and singing
marriage arrange at seventeen.
The naif caged with tied wings
left home and country for new beginning.
Strange country, strange language, stranger man's wife
what was this all about? She knew no meaning.
No mother, no maid, no cook, nor chauffeur,
cooking, cleaning, scrubbing toilets,
watching soaps, eating chips, drinking coke with teary eyes
surviving day by day.
  Time passed . . .
She found opportunities and wealth of this land's blessings
she could no longer turn away from the miracles around.
The stranger before, now loving and caring
the country once foreign, now a familiar home
two wonderful boys now twenty three and fifteen.
The knot loosened, and untied were her wings.
Her mate and her young ones, along with the three.
she is once again quite happily flying.

Sheela Patil

The Sunflower

A Sunflower seed when planted in May
will grow up to be BIGGER than me someday.

The pedals of yellow and center of brown
have a great look and can bring UP a frown;
that makes you feel happy and won't let you down!

The rays of sun and drops of rain
give life to the seed that I call by name . . .
THE SUNFLOWER

Lindsay Ann Wozniak

Mom's Loving Prayer

A mother's love for her son
will never dull or fade away.
She may yell at you for being bad,
or out of plain frustration.
And you may feel picked on
or not even loved anymore.
  Fear not my son.
For in anger or in play
my love for you is constant.
I pray God looks over you
and lives through you.
I pray the angels kiss your cheek
and it pierces and holds your heart.
I pray that you will understand, as you grow,
the never ending love
that the Lord and mothers
have for our children.
And that love will strengthen you
to do anything you choose to do.

Mary Ann Lopes

Love

Love is what keeps memories alive. Love is what keeps the
world alive. Love is what's found in each others eyes. Love
is the reason that one survives. Love can make and love can
break, because love is a feeling not a mistake. Without love life
would be a frown as if the heavens above have come tumbling
down to cast us into sorrow, because we didn't understand that
love is the reason we are all still around.

Reba J. Pace

Commitment

Waves pound unrelenting against the shore
Wind ruffles my hair as I stand in awe.
Insignificant in this boundless might
Your hand slips into mine, squeezing it tight.

Beneath this sky I pledge my life to you.
With you in my life, mine begins anew.
Enfolding you in my arms our lips touch
We breathe for the other, eyes say as much.

The sun's glare now low on the horizon
Casts shadows of our past far behind us.
We turn from the past and into the sun
Love, life and togetherness have begun.

    Lynne Westhead

Wondering

Many times, I've walked this lonely road
Wishing for someone, to help, share this heavy load
Wondering of what, oh what, could have been
If only you had talked, I was your friend!

Sharing our hopes, our dreams and our fears
together, we wiped away our tears.
Who do I go to, now that you're gone?
What did I do that was so terribly wrong?

Never again will there be another like you!
That's why I sit here feeling so blue.
Wondering of what, oh what, could have been
If only you had talked, I'd still have a friend?

    Lois Hutson

To Grieve The Loss

To grieve the loss of an unborn child
With a pain that settles in the pit of your soul.
To ask why, but get no answers
Tears at the inside of your being.
The sovereign God that gives life
Is merciful to his children, but again I ask why.
The child, yet unaware even to its sex
Struggled to be formed, yet failed.
Its life, in the hands of God,
Was prohibited form being brought into this world.
The child I imagined I'd hold,
Now is in the arms of his maker.
A part of the mother that dies with the child
Creates an abyss of emotion.
To bare that anguish and the memory forever
Is too great a punishment for the sin.
The anger she holds-to blame-to blame someone, anyone,
To lessen the pain.
How do I break through to comfort a heart made of steel,
A heart made of stone, that blames God?

    Rachel Puchalski

Loss

As I stood at the window looking at clear mountains
With clouds tumbling by and a strong wind humming in the oaks,
I studied again the magnolia tree I'd transplanted earlier.
The structure is there, the grace of line,
Even tiny buds remain giving a promise of new beauty;
But it will not flower again;
And I think how like my husband is to it.
He looks quite well, stands quite straight sometimes,
And, like the tiny buds, his eyes still light occasionally
With humor, understanding, and thought,
Bearing witness to an intelligence, to a mind
That, like the magnolia, has been damaged too much to bloom again.

    Mary Cavena

Untitled

When we travel thru the mystery of life
With all the pressures, worries and strife
Stop and listen, what do you see
All the wonders, God gave you and me

Trees with their long limbs and leaves
Among them a spider, how wondrous it weaves
Birds and bees, flitting from flower to flower
Dew on the grass, a nice summer shower

Mountains, oceans, prairies and seas
Imagine the wonder, we have all for free
Animals, insects, snow and the sleet
Everything we need, here at our feet.

Will we learn to give and not to take
Learn to love and not to hate
What does it takes to open our eyes
Restore this world to paradise

God gave all this and asks for love.
To him and the father in the heavens above
This will all be here, when we are no more
Since we're killing ourselves with all our wars

    Mary Boone

Spiritual Seasons

I want forever springtime in my heart.
    With blooms of faith there bursting forth in view.
Yet colors fade and petals wilt and drop
    And then they're gone just like the morning dew.

Let's keep them, Lord, their beauty to behold,
    To show the world Your love alive in me.
I struggle with these blooms, yet still they go.
    From time to time my heart is "faith-bloom" free.

I pause to wonder — then I hear Your voice:
    "I know your struggle all too well, my child.
Just let all seasons come into your heart,
    For constant springtime's really much too mild."

"The summer sun will burn your "faith-blooms" pure.
    The autumn frost brings death to selfish pride.
The winter chill starts longings for the fire
    To light those faith buds growing deep inside.

At last I see the beauty of His plan:
    Each changing season's needed in my heart.
My faith's not gone when flowers bloom and drop
    With His transforming love, that's just a start.

    Lucy H. Wilson

Always And Forever

Always and forever, here is where I stand,
With my Savior Jesus, I will walk hand in hand.
Down the bumpy road of life,
When there is joy or when there is strife.
He never ever leaves my side,
And it is his word, I will abide.
Always and forever, I shall stand upon the rock,
With my Savior Jesus, I will always walk.
Someday I will meet him, my Father's only son,
When he calls me home, you know that I will run.
To be with my one and only, in heaven above.
My spirit will explode, and fly like a dove.
Always and forever, this is where I'll always be,
With my Savior Jesus, who gave eternal life to me.

    Valerie J. Lower

Dreams

Dreams are made in the mind
with continual nurturing and silent living.
Dreams are not forgotten and live 'til born
because of faith held in the heart.
Dreams come together when the time is ripe
with laboring of the hands.

The book of the Lord is right
"for everything there is a season."
With patience, nurturing, expectant faith,
and alertness to timing of the season,
the dream is born and even more fulfilling
than ever before realized possible because of
the added ingredient of time.

This Yosemite, is only the assent to the height
of the first and lowest dream,
only three to ten thousand feet in elevation.
Dreams yet to come will ascend
thousands of feet in elevation higher
above the soft white clouds.

Norma Jean Miller

Mysterious Is Woman

Each woman I've met reads just like a book —
With every page set, another new look!
Each time I pursue, I get, more or less,
Additional clues she's yet to confess.
She's simply a ruse befitting a guess.

She's mystery and lies all wrapped in suspense,
With soft hair and eyes, and pink lips intense.
Romantic at heart, she's found the right touch
To tempt at the start, concealing so much.
Directing her part, she acts it as such.

A tigress too wild who lands on her feet,
An innocent child who squirms in her seat,
A princess beguiled, enchantress complete,
One moment, the rain, the next, she's the wind.
So what's there to gain when all is pretend?

Waltzing a shadow, she's light on her feet.
Focused and narrow, she's never been beat,
For each man who tries gets lost to their fates —
A labyrinth disguise with millions of gates.
A beautiful prize in satin awaits . . .

William C. Bradford

Life Corridors

Little orphan girl from the clay hills of Georgia
With fire red pigtails hanging to the waist
Marches off to the cotton field with a smile
Not tall enough to be seen beneath the stalks
Look at me, I am weak, I am strong.

Little orphan girl in those brown slipper shoes
Could cut as much wood as any boy far or near
But come spring the feet would itch from frostbite
Had to bake them over red hot coals until brown
Look at me, I am weak, I am strong.

Little orphan girl growing up so tall and skinny
No time for nose bleeds had to work those fields
Picking peaches in Fort Valley and Roberta too
Just had to knock out a hundred buckets a day
Look at me, I am weak, I am strong.

Little orphan girl now the class valedictorian
No more fields to work college is the way to go
But no sooner graduated did sickness strike
Two long years in the hospital there to stay
Look at me, I was weak, I am stronger.

Rose Constance Howell

That Little Tow Head Boy (A Tribute To My Grandson, Gregg)

Years ago, I knew this tow head lad . . . unlike his mom or his dad
With hair, as white as white could be: A heart, filled with glee
He'd run . . . rushing to hug me at my knee
Yelling, "Nan, Nan" with all his might . . . oh, what a precious sight

At three, he'd climb upon my knee, saying "Nan, please read to me"
We read those books . . . until he . . . committed them to memory
Then we'd reversed roles . . . and he'd read them to me
Sometimes, it was a strain, but we read those books again and again

It wasn't a set rule, but sometimes, I'd pick him up from school
He couldn't wait to tell . . . the happenings in his day
And later, as we parted, he would always say . . .
"Bye Nan . . . I love you" . . . I'd reply, "Sweetpea, I love you, too"

Now, he's grown into a fine young man . . . discovering new land
He doesn't needs my help . . . he can do it by himself
Yes, it's just like God planned it to be
He's no longer . . . that little boy, who spent time with me

Yes, after twelve, that lad was gone . . . memories to linger on
He was the apple of her eye: He didn't say goodbye
And . . . every now and then . . . She yearns for time . . . again
With . . . THAT LITTLE TOW HEAD BOY . . . She knew back then.

Neal Clark Pierce

Voices

I wonder how long this room's been my home,
With it's white padded walls soft and squishy like foam.
It wasn't long after they gave me this coat,
Not too long after I ripped out that guy's throat.
The police, I was sure, held me under suspicion,
But I just told them the truth — the voices gave me permission.
Off to the doctors the pigs whisked me away,
Now I sit in this room all alone everybody
I don't get much company, no visitors come by,
And I huddle in this corner and I can't help but cry.
If it weren't for the voices how lonely I'd be!
But those voices they come and they whisper to me.
They tell me dark secrets that I cannot share.
And such games we play! But they never play fair.
That makes us argue and then I wish they were dead,
Just to make them shut up, I bang the wall with my head.
Yet they won't get out they just talk in my ears,
Telling me stories that fill me with fears.
That's when I scream and I yell and I shout,
Still the voices just chuckle and say they'll never come out.

Peter Baugh

What Should I Say?

A child is born without guilt or shame,
With little hopes and nobody to blame.
I did all I could to raise him with hope,
Keep him sheltered from crime, violent and dope.
A mother I am filled with love,
Keeping him in touch with the father above.
Will I succeed? Or will I fail?
My son may get trapped and end up in jail.
A doctor, a lawyer, a preacher I am not,
Just raising a child on what I was taught.
Being a single mother is not what I had planned,
But when times got hard his father ran.
He didn't look back ever again,
Knowing his son's life has just began.
When my son ask, will I see dad one day,
I will look at my son, as a mother what should I say?

Sandra Culbreth

The Thoughts Of A "Notions" Box

Not long ago, I was sitting on a shelf,
With lots of others that looked like myself.
We were all pure white, and plain as could be,
I really wondered, "What would happen to me?"

But one day a lady came by and saw the whole stack.
She looked us all over, but chose me from the pack.
She took me home and examined me;
And told her husband, "I know what this can be!"

So she took out her brushes, beads and paint,
I got so excited, I thought I would faint.
Soon I was painted, and dressed up with beads,
Then I knew I was being prepared for someone's needs.

So, here I am - all dressed up and ready to use,
For whatever needs you may want to choose.
But, however you want to use me in your home,
"Handle me with care" - for I'm made of styrofoam.

In your home then, I trust, I will be a place
For your needles and thread, buttons or lace.
So as you use me from time to time
Think of how I developed, as told in this rhyme.

    Loralie L. Barth

Colorblind

The world is an interesting place
With people of various creed and race.
To some the world is made up of colors
But despite this known fact, we are still sisters and brothers.
The colors are Brown, Yellow, Red, Black, and White.
Though we may be different, we still shouldn't fight.
Like ever so often, when the Black and the White
Fight one another because one's dark and one's light.
Or what about colors against one another,
If you're not hitting my sister, you're killing my brother.
There's Black against Black, or Red against Red;
That's the worst way to find another person is dead.
Haven't you heard of the march of Dr. King?
He marched for the freedom of every human being.
You learned not to fight and hate one another,
but to love and call everyone sister and brother.
Don't judge anyone by the skin on their face
Instead, look at their knowledge and grace.
If we look at the world through COLORBLIND eyes,
It will make it a better place, and we all will survive.

    Maisha K. Perkins

Quiet Spaces, Quiet Places

It's in the quiet spaces that I live,
With my heart out in my hands for all the world to see
Showing my feelings with the pride of a new father.

It's in the quiet places that I live,
Where the slightest noise can shake the foundations of reality
Showing my surprise, I jump with a start.

It's in the quiet spaces that I live,
Needing never to be lonely and trapped in the body of isolation
Showing my dread when anyone tries to invade.

It's in the quiet places that I live,
Where solace shows up when one of my friends offers a hug
Showing my joy and love, I open my arms.

It's in the quiet spaces and quiet places that I live,
That I have found my God.

    Paul Robert Hoffman Jr.

... Of Time

On a continuing mark of thought, I dare to share and dream.
With precision of movement, I'll tiptoe across your mind, so it may seem.
Words that rhythmically touch first the heart and then the soul . . .
Simple and easily remembered lyrics we work up to gain control.
Together like a piano whose notes are on the same line . . .
A tune set in motion to reveal the precious quality of time.
To share with someone, and make memories that can enhance . . .
A unique way to express, I hope to always have a chance.
What better way to let the truth settle then at the end of a rhyme . .
.
Enter the heart of you, I know I have all of time.

    Sandra Gary

To Be Myself

To be myself, to be only me
With no leaning on, no dependency
On any other being or material need
Is the true meaning of my own identity

We go through life, so many stages
In ourselves, our minds trapped in cages
Of molds defined by the rest of the world
"Do this, not that, it's the way" - we are told

To escape from the norms brought down through the years
To be something I dream of even through the tears
That sting my eyes on a day of memories
I struggle to turn my dreams into realities

My name to carry its own weight in this world
My achievements - my own, not borrowed
To be a person I can respect
My flaws and faults to be able to accept

For I wish to make my world so full
That never a moment is empty or dull
I want to succeed and be joyful and free
I want to be proud to say - this is me.

    Sadhna Disha Chawla

My Mountain

I have a pretty mountain - all my own
With lots of trees and bushes that are very overgrown;
In winter she's a pretty sight
With snowtipped trees and a sunray's delight;
The spring makes her blossom
With a pretty purple - red;
In summer she's as full as full can be,
Her greenness makes her come to life
And light up like a happy face;
Now autumn is different from the rest,
Her leaves and colors are the best;
But no matter what season it may be,
She's just as delightful as a cup of tea.

    Karoline R. Wyatt

Christmas Time

Christmas decorations are so cherry to see
with the beautiful colors to please you and me.
What a fun time the yule season bring,
the hustling and bustling, and the Christmas bells ring.
The little children filled with surprise, and delight
there's a spirit of giving, and warmth which is so right.
Families and friends gather to share this wonderful season
its too bad that Christmas should be the only time for this reason
as we look at all our blessings from above
it would be wonderful for all mankind to show more love.

    Virginia Blakley

"Reminisce"

Oh . . . to be a child once more,
  with spirits free and wild to soar . . .

Sounds of laughter always found,
  seldom tears or tiny frowns . . .

The joy of dancing in the gentle rain,
  mother's kiss which cured all pains!

Cute little leprechauns with pots of gold . . .
  oh yes . . . fairy towns where no ones old!

All those "Keep-out" signs on club house doors!
  Everything so new, fun to explore . . .

Tender talks on grandpa's knee . . .
  Many moments playing make believe!

Can't forget the special place no one knew!
  nor, the closest friend who was always true!

The eagerness at Christmas time . . .
  Valentines, saying "You are mine!"

Needless to say, time passes by . . .
  To reminisce is such a natural high!

My memories and I shall never part . . .
  Though I'll age, I'll stay always, young at heart!
    Patricia Felshaw Anderson

Weep Not, Sweet Knight

I once was loved by a knight of old
With strength of a lion, and a heart as gold.
He raised my head, brushed the hair from my brow
And bade me stay by his side.
But as we walked, I faltered and fell,
I couldn't keep up with his stride.
A patient man, he lifted me up
And cradled me in his arm.
He held me close, enveloping me,
Keeping me safe from harm.
Again, I teetered and fell to the ground.
The thrill of the fall did make my heart pound
As it had never done before
I craved, I yearned for more.
When I looked up, saw the fear in his eye
My heart felt a crack as he started to cry.
At that moment, his love was so true,
Deep in his soul did it burn.
I had to let go and tell him that . . . no,
Your love I could never return.
    Linda P. Ramsden

Christmas 1994

Christmas comes but once a year
With the joys we hold so dear
Laughing children smiling faces
Best wishes from so many places
Good fellowship surrounds us
Harmony that never ends
Neighbor helping neighbor, friends remember friends
Then we help the needy, aid the sick and old
With more loving kindness than any heart can hold
Bells so clear, lights so pretty,
Spread joy and peace through-out the city
Christmas comes—just once a year
What a pity.
    Phyllis Sumrall

Winds Of Fate

The wind blows cold and raw
with the sharpness of a razor's edge.
And yet I feel no wind; I sense
the breathing of the dead.

It whines . . . the mournful cry
of those who watch and wait
and count my numbered days
with patient sighs; and I am late.

I ache and soon must loose my grip;
stop, cursed wind! I linger, for I know
that as the road behind lies dim and distant,
one lies ahead more infinitely so.

I have reached the threshold of tomorrow.
Winds of fate surround and chill my bones.
With longing do I cling to mortal loved ones;
yet plaintive is the cry that calls me home.
    Kay Meyer

Whiskey Hammock

I feel the sting in my gums followed
with the tincture of whiskey as my
lips plait for the warmth.
The hammock ropes strain as the
wooden bar beneath my head creaks
with fruition to hold my body once again.
The wind gingerly rocks me. I ponder,
wish. Is this what life was like
inside my mother?
Heavenly Bliss
I sail back and forth, floating in suspension,
above my mothers hips in the placenta
where I slept. Despite knowing I cannot,
I wish to go back. I pour myself
another libation, bury myself in the braided
ropes and acknowledge my God for having
made the trip this far.
    B. T. Windsor Patterson

"When Death Come Knocking"

When death come sneaking in like a puff of smoke in the night
without warning you won't have time to take a flight.

Death is cruel, it shows no respect of person it will snatch
you whether black, white or green with its bold assertion.

Death is like a thief in the night, it sneaks upon you when you are
least expected whether you be sitting, supine or erected.

When death come knocking at your door don't be so anxious to
welcome it by lying on the floor.
Nor let it take your sight without putting up a fight.

Death is an eminent enemy destined to take your life;
even if you live right, it will not prevent this strife. Death may
be long or it may be slow, but who knows which way they will go.
Oh death I know I can't run and I can't hide;
but please give me a little more time before you take me
on the other side.

If I had known you were coming, I would have been prepared
dressed in my favorite attire, like a bride, awaiting on the stairs.
I would have had my life in order dressed, starched and clean.
Most of all, would have prepared my friends and love ones for this
ungodly scene.
    Nola Grace Holder

Battle Of Mang Yang Pass

They came by the hundreds in the early morning light,
with their guns blazing fire as we joined in the fight.
Slowly we retreated, we couldn't hold our ground,
troopers started dying, in one's and two's went down.
Our ammo was depleted, our bayonets bloody red,
when the Phantom jets came screaming low, firing rockets overhead.
The deadly fight was over, death had stalked the hill,
the smoking guns were silent, the clouds hung dark and still
I was lying in the jungle grass, with the patter of the rain,
drumming upon my poncho, easing away the pain.
My men had died beside me, their blood had drenched the hill,
as I lay wounded, and wondered, at the quiet and the still.
Over-run that morning, my Platoon had fought it's last,
and lie buried with it's Battle Streamers
   on bloody Mang Yang Pass
     Robert Forrest Stauffacher

Wounded

Benightedness abound
With thy virgin woman's candor
Awaiting lusts savage moment to open pleasures wound
Spreading her lushness amidst a darkened room

For love's cadaver must purge his impetus seed
Thus disenchanting thy lady's love
His river a ruse of deliberate need

Then darkness conceives a demented mood
Of one tainted woman's candor
Alone once again with fears of old
Left to the rising moon
No comfort in her twisted limbs
She closes sorrows wound

For the reflection that is mirrored
One not of sorrows stain
Nor a loneliness remained
Yet to descry, a grander lie!
Of a dignified intellect abused.
     Mary Jacqueline Mayer

All Things Reconsidered

Thirty years from now when you're married with two children,
Will you (still) remember who made you a man first?

Or when you're lying in bed twenty years from now engaged,
Will you dream of her under the spring light?

And ten years from now when you're climbing
up a ladder fixing a roof,
Will you stop and remember how she was once
too scared to look up beyond herself?

Five years from now when you're unpacking,
moving into your own apartment,
Will you search non-stop,
until you find her phone number,
that you once knew by heart?
     Marissa Sabatino

Earth

She is smooth like a sanded wooden sphere,
Yet ridged like garbage heaps full of rubbish.
She is beautiful like a tropical island in spring,
Yet ugly like a face beaten from gangs.
She supports us like a mother to a baby,
Yet we abuse her like everything else we own.
She is the ground we walk on and the skies we dream about,
She is our earth and nobody else's.
But, what is next?
     Mike C. Fields

A Poet

A poet is a writer who can tell a story true
With words in rhyme that should appeal to me and you
A poet is a magician who can make trouble disappear
It's done by private reading or a recitation that you hear.

A poet is an actor that plays a distinguished part
In telling you things that bring solace to your heart
A poet is an artist painting pictures with words of choice
Instilling scenes within your mind by reading, or by another's voice

A poet is a philosopher teaching lessons far and wide
Permitting spread of goodness that he dare not hide
A poet is a songwriter, another adds the music on
They collaborate . . . because lyrics are important to a song.

A poet is a teacher who teaches a variety of things
Reaching many people, not excluding queens and kings.
A poet is so many things, all of them are good.
If you're not into poetry, I surely wish you would!
     Mildred Marsh Ruton

The Edges Of Life . . .

The edges of life curve inward, outward, upward and downward;
Within and among one another creating an ecstasy of
landscape that moves one's soul.
It may be high, large, and strong or low, small and elegant;
But, it consumes and allows one to finally see our purpose.

Tiny purple wild violets; bright, sparse dandelions;
awakening buds on trees; vast, stoney, mountainous ranges;
rocks among and within deep and shallow waters;
green grasses mixed with tall and short stalks and twigs;
movements of the wind that transfer and pollinate.

It all ignites into a sound, a smell, a feeling, a taste
that allows us to retreat to our base
The ecstasy of life lies within our senses.
We must realize the power of the natural world and submerge
ourselves deep within so we may curve with the edges of life.
     Stacy Sayles

Your Words Of Silence

As I lay here quietly,
without sleep.
I listen to the words roll off your tongue,
so quiet, I can barely make out.
Time is at hand.
God, if you were only that easily figured out.
Confusing, twisted words,
of silence.
Your thoughts wander around the room.
I can not catch them,
as I learn to hate them.
I miss you.
     Sarah Kausel

Thump Thump

I sometimes wonder at this thing in my chest,
Wonder what day it will begin it's rest.
So much pain it has received,
How much it beats to fulfill it's need.

Strong it must be to withstand this abuse,
How long shall it last with this much use?
Sometimes warmed up by bringing others closer,
Sometimes shut down when those days are over.

Who's to say when it may take it's rest.
I just hope it completes its quest,

This thing beating in my chest.
     Richard Slawinski

Words

Words, what greater armament
Words define the man
Words defile the man
Words inspire, console, vilify, praise
But what good are words if words
are merely words
Let words be the precursor of deeds
be the prime mover of progress
be the driving force that propels humanity
to realize its sublime destiny
Let words inspire creativity
Let words move us to world unity
Let words awaken man from the nightmare
of prejudices and hate
Awake forevermore into the morning light
of love and brotherhood
Let words empower man to achieve his ultimate
goal, the knowledge and love of God
I need words

Norford Thompson

Sad Sad I Pity You

   Sad sad I pity you what in the
world is wrong with you? You seem to find
fault with everything I do so who said you
were perfect any way? You sure left
authority go to you head I wonder if the
shoe was in the other foot live it
would be or doesn't it matter as
long as you get what you wanted someday
when your conscience makes you up
and let's you think of the wrong you
done you might be glad for a little fun
their it will be too late and all
the heartaches you caused your
will want friends and there will be none
And you won't have no fun.
Sad sad I pity you, you had to
climb the ladder and didn't care who you
hurt or how, now the laugh is on you, sad sad
I pity you

Sandra B. Lengel

Vanity Fair

Whoever thought that the love we'd share.
Would be found in our work place called "VANITY FAIR".

A place we thought would always be,
the perfect job for you and me.

A job that kept us satisfied,
but for some unexplainable reason, our spirit died.

Friendship were found because of "VANITY FAIR".
Togetherness is something that we all share.

We took pride in our workplace, that's what we did,
But someone threw a rock and then they hid.

Some of us had only 2 years, but some had thirty-four,
so many people will be without a job when they close the door.

But we must be thankful always for our health and strength,
because I know a man with a plan and He's gonna pay the rent.

Our hearts cried out in sorrow because our jobs will be lost,
This has affected so many, but look who will pay the cost.

So dry your eyes, lift your head up high,
because someone is patiently standing by.

Give God the praise, there is no other
if He blesses us with one job, He'll bless us with another.

Vernice Ward

Testament

If I had a chance to exchange my past,
   would I transform you to my lover,
      or leave you as my friend.
We share the same core heat,
   molten lava in the disguise of blood.
At times my infatuation cools and becomes whetted,
   piercing the love I have for you,
      only an eruption from within,
         launches our passion into a sky of orange flames.
Unsatiable,
   I give in to any second guessing,
      taking all I can handle.
My actions are sinister,
   always avaricious in my lust for you,
      I demand all from you,
         eyes, lips, voice, hands, smell, graze.
Since my first journey deep into your heart,
   I knew I must possess you in every way imaginable,
Forever.

R. E. Augustin

Mother, The Jewel Of Your Heart

The Jewel of your life has slipped away
Would that I could take away your pain and carry it myself this day

The beauty of her soul shines in your minds eye
Making it really not necessary to say goodbye

A lifetime of memories glimmer in a special corner of your heart
So you will never, ever have to part

As you live your life day after day, the things she taught you,
the love you shared
Are all a part of the child you were, the man you are, the man who cared

Know always through your sorrow and strife
She is ever with you, you cannot lose your Mother, the beautiful jewel
who was with you the very first day of your life

Marlene A. Crossett

There's No Child Like A Grandchild

There's no child like a grandchild to keep you on your toes
You brush their hair and dry their tears and you wipe a runny nose
You laugh when they are happy and cry when they are sad
You help them through their highs and lows and at times this can be bad
But you love them more each day and this loving will never fade away.

You know that they're not perfect but then, who is? Pray tell
A perfect child can be quite dull and you know this very well
They drive you up a wall at times and send you down again
Remember, they're just children, they're not grown-up girls and men
So you love them more each day, and this loving will never fade away

And now that they are older, and we are older, too
We see them only now and then since they have so much to do
We try to grin and bear it, and never rave or shout
We take each let-down as it comes; that's what life is all about
Still we love them more each day; and this loving will never fade away

When GOD created children, HE had a plan, indeed!
To fill this world with love and hope from a tiny, precious seed
But when HE sent grandchildren, we knew right at a glance
Our prayers were truly answered; now we have a second chance
How we love them more each day; and this loving will never fade away

Paul C. D'Andrea

Thoughts Of A Flower

As a seed, I have begun
Wrapped in a blanket of velvet brown
A heart that beats in silent sound
Roots taking cover underground
Pushing forward, a will to grow
Eyes to see a whole new world
Changing seasons, pass away the old
The gleam of spring I now behold
In hands of leaves, sapphire green
swaying in blessings brought by the wind
I thank creation for my family it brings
nurtured by the sun a loving mother
life giving air that is my father
caressed by the rain like a gentle lover
these essential elements to produce my flower
crowning my head upon the hour
To stand before you in all my glory
a beautiful thought to a perfect story.

Melissa Alvarez

"Last Chance"

Please do not think me bold as you read these words I have
written for you, for me, for us. There is a compelling
drive, force, passion guiding my hand, urging these words.

We have loved, you and I, across time and space. Loved
fiercely. But by our unknown ways, not agreed upon and
righteous pride, we deprived each other of the fulfillment
of that love we once knew.

Again paths cross, fleeting feelings of what once was grow
in our souls. Will we take the opportunity that lay before
us to fulfill what once was?

Waters will be tested to see if old ways still prevail.
Will our growth since our departure overcome old ways, old thoughts?

I say soul mate, we cannot afford to regard our paths
crossing lightly or look upon them as mere chance — for we
may never get this chance again.

Louise M. Celeste

To My Mother: On Saying Goodbye

The time is here, almost four
years are putting you into the ground.
It is time I walk to where you lie;
to put my fears aside and my
hands on your face.
Were your eyes and mouth sewn shut
so you wouldn't be able to tell me you
were only sleeping?
You see, I couldn't let you leave me.
Not after fourteen years.
What would it bring me?
What would I get when you got the
solitude you always needed?
A desperation to fill the space in my life
you left barren?
I can't even remember what you
looked like the last time I saw you.
How can I say goodbye, when I don't recall
to whom it is I am saying goodbye?

Kristy Leigh Howell

Game

27 years on this ball of f——n dirt,
Years of drugs and changes, years of pain and hurt.
Years of confusion, years full of rage.
Years spent in hatred, years spent in a cage.

The days go by, like ripples in a pond
See the smiley faces, listen to the con.
The reason I exist is not yet known.
I must learn soon, else my mind gets blown.

But my mind, its still clear, my heart it still beats
I will stay in the game, I'll run with the fleet.
I'll jump the hurdles, I'll climb the high wall.
Till the game is over, till I take that last fall.

And so ends these rhymes, and so ends these reasons.
Will some lived dog make this my last season?
But one final thought, quickens my pace.
The sun must one day shine, even on my face!

Richard J. Moniz

Who Are You

I am a child of God; who earn respect by giving it.
Yes, I am a child of God; who know of a journey by crawling.
Patience, knowledge, understanding, and care supplements inner strength.
Daily prayer and faith guides me through the dark unknown.
For being without Jesus Christ, life has no purpose.
Daily praises to God is a way of thanksgiving.
We are all God's children for life, but some will not accept him.
Yet, he continue to love and bless us according to his will.
Thank - you Jesus Christ for coming as our savior.
Keeping the faith, trusting in his will, and depending on his protection;
Gives me the pleasure of claiming, "I am a child of God."

Marilyn Tolbert

Words On A Page

I saw you first
yes I did
there in the harsh light of another place
at first only words on a page
then something — some thing
caught me - yes!
Caught my eye
and spirit too!
Set me wondering and curious
to set a motion free
Flying to your universe . . . I let it be
and there in the light of yet another place
you caught it
and started a game with me
ummmmmyes
I saw you . . .

Marlo Kimmel

Untitled

Dale, I had to write this poem for you,
Yes it is simple and the words are true,
My prayer was answered on the 16th of November,
On the evening that we met at Riverbend.

Now three months have passed and I must truly say,
You've been the light in my life each and everyday.
Please hold me tight and never let us part,
For it would surely tear apart my heart.

Who knows what the future has in store for us,
I guess we'll just have to wait and see,
I cherish the time we spend together,
And I hope our love will last eternally.

Mary M. Grimes

Hand In Hand

Love . . . is the priceless gift you bring to each other on this day,
yet it is freely given from God.

Today is a treasure to behold,
full of memories to carry you forward in the days yet seen;
let love forever be your blanket of warmth
amid fears of what tomorrow may bring.

Turn to one another for the oasis you will need
in the desert this world can so easily be;
the future is gained by living today,
full of beauty waiting for you to see.

When each day reaches an end, and night
awaits your dreams in the darkness that covers the land,
you will be at each others side always
hand in hand.

Roger D. Anyon

Respect

It is lost on accusations and found in empty promises
Yet it never really exists
In worlds it is made from empty bottles, shattered as easily as dreams
Fallen from a crisp page, slit into three
Empty plea's try to mend
Shards still remain
Listen to the broken unrealistic rumors
As they fall upon ears of the unknowing
Not even knowing they have lost it
Something they can't comprehend, forget it all
F*** you for even realizing
Die for not caring about anyone other than yourself
Everything is a contradiction, nothing in right
And only few know this
But they are also wrong
No trust in your life, no respect in the mind of the lost
We are the lost
Our mind is our shepherd
There is nothing we shall want
Except respect from others

Leah Clark

Country Home

An old house upon a hill sits empty now.
Yet memories linger still and always will.

Fond memories of children swinging
merrily upon the trees,
and rolling down the hillside.

Memories of tiny chickadee's resting
gently on fingertips,
neither fearful nor afraid.

Peaceful, calm, quiet summer nights
all natures voces symphonic to the ear.

Winter stillness and blanket of white
etching footprints upon its quilt.

Cheerful, bubbling voices chattering away
inside the walls
Amid the crackling fireplace.

All these things are memories now.
Happy and joyful thoughts
to calm our hearts.

Mary Anne Trask

"Frozen Ballerina"

A dancer twirls on a base of ice,
Yet she is frozen in time and space;
A turn of my hand causes snow,
To fall on her glass cage, only on her,
Yet she still smiles and dances;
How odd, that life's treasures are so small;
Bombs exploding,
Buildings imploding,
Lives lost and ruined,
And no one cares;
All for old debts,
And no one regrets,
How horrid it is that life's pain covers all;
Lucky dancer in her frozen world,
She sees her own reflection in her cage,
And snowflakes, not of water or cold;
She smiles while the world cries,
And before she sees its horrors,
She dies;
Lucky dancer in her frozen world.

Lisa Gibby

Blackbird

Perched proud,
yet unseen;
With feathers sheened
to capture a hidden rainbow;
She carefully distributes her weight
so not to lose her balance.
An endangered species she is
who is rarely seen.

With wings folded like those of a butterfly,
she observes the world
from two sides;
from two extremes.
Her song can soften ones soul,
but hardens her heart.

Oh - can she fly away?
Are those wings able to break its fold,
sweep the air,
and fly her to eternity?

Lora R. Tucker

"I Do"

This is the moment we have waited for;
You are the woman that I love and adore.
I will be yours now for all of my life;
This is the moment I make you my wife.

Darling I know that if you only knew
The love inside that I hold here for you,
A beautiful rose you would have every day
That blooms in my heart, and always will stay.

The dew on the petals is the tears I have cried
When I missed you so much that I just could have died!
So water me, sweetheart, with your love every day;
For I live, just to give, to you this bouquet.

This is the moment "two shall be as one;"
Our life together, today is begun.
Those sacred vows I will make now with you;
This is the moment we both say, "I do!"

Randal E. Kalbfleisch

The Ply

The river runs red from the blood of the dead.
You can hear Mother Earth cry,
"Behave every rule of every creature,
From the great whale to the fly.
Everything's beautiful, no matter its features."
O' listen to her ply!

Cherish each day,
From morning to night,
Care for fellow man,
And strive to do right!

Remember what she says,
For her words are the guidelines of love.
And no matter what happens,
Praise the Lord above!

Victoria L. Burwell

Winter Nesting

In winter when the trees are free of leaves
You clearly see the bird's nests
Planted in the branches.

Count fourteen nests in that one tree,
And none in others: How can that be?

It really would embarrass me to be a tree
Without a bird's nest
Planted in my branches.

Margaret Hofferbert

Eight Graders Beware

   If you're an eight grader
You have a lot of work to do
We have to take essay tests
We have to do reports
   If you're an eight grader
You have a lot of work to do
We have to take a ninth grade proficiency test
If we don't pass we have to take it again and again
   If you're an eight grader
You have a lot of work to do
We are expected to learn three languages and pick one for high
school
This is what happens if you're an eight grader.

Kim Bailey

My Pretty Lady

My lady, my lady, you once said you loved me, now you have left me.
You have gone far away. Though I still love you my pretty
lady, and as I awake at day break to find you not beside me,
once again I still have faith that I will find my pretty lady
and bring her home safely. And then we will be together as
one, so that we may love again. For today, tomorrow, and
forever and ever till the end of time. We will share the new
world that we have found. A fresh world where there is peace,
love, friendship, and caring. With our new life that we have
found, we must give thanks to our maker, the maker of peace,
love, friendship, and caring just for my pretty lady.

Kevin Campisano

All Of Me

You came into my life some years ago
You have help me learn
You have helped me grow
To you, I have given my whole heart
from my life I wish you will never depart
You were sent to me from God up above
all I ever wanted was your precious love
we have been through some ups and downs
You look so sad when you are wearing a frown
Upon your face I want a smile to be
I will try my best you just wait and see

Lincoln E. Ashe

Halloween Fun

Halloween is so scary,
You have to watch out for the monster's so hairy.
Little kids scream with fright in the night,
The parents have to turn on the light.
You're out collecting candy,
Getting twice as much for being so handy.
You are out having all the fun,
While your sister is singing with a nun.
When it's time to go home,
You feel so sad,
But your sadness turns to gladness.
You get to eat your candy!
Wait! Your parents have to check it first.

Melissa Ann Farrell

A Child's Cry

You hear the sound of a child's cry
You hear the scream
You sense the darkness, you know it's a dream
You toss, you turn
You try to awake
You feel so helpless as you hear the cry
The cry of fear
You're finally awake, it feels so real
The sound of the child seems so near
As you open your eyes and things become clear
You realize it's not your dream, but your child's nightmare
You find your way to the side of his bed
You find him scared, victim of the night
You reach out your arms and hold him tight
Sheltering him from the fear of night
He closes his eyes, once again asleep
Your dream is gone, his nightmare complete

Tamara K. Hyde

Poor Man's Shoes

Put yourself in a poor man's shoes.
Would you know which path to choose?
With no possession except you and the ragged cloths you wear.
Would you know who to fear?
Walking the streets with only food on your mind.
Would you then know why life is so unkind.
Wondering if the Lord has ever heard your cries.
Would you wonder or doubt if you already lived your life's highs?
Looking back at your past.
Would you question, why it went so fast?
Hoping for a brighter future.
Would you know what's life's measure in nature.
Do you understand what goes on in the mind of a poor man.
If so, would you lend out a helping hand?
To lift some of the weight off those hard times blues.
Would you know then, what really happens, in the poor man's shoes.

Steven M. Golubski

Colors Of Youth

Something is different about this mirror
You look right at it but it's not clear
Seems to have changed much over the years
Something missing disappeared

Did you ever have something
You didn't notice till it was gone
Like a dream you've forgotten
Or the lyrics to a favorite song

Remember feeling happy and carefree
Memories stay with you
But in this mirror
You do not see

Search your soul and mind
Something special left behind
So hard to acknowledge
Between the lines

Something is different about this mirror
You look right at it but it's not clear
The frame had color once
But it disappeared

Monte James

Daughters

Each daughter is special, one of a kind
You love them and cherish them all of the time.
You laugh when they're happy, you cry when they're sad
Your love doesn't lessen even when they are bad.
You watch them grow up through their young tender years
Like most other parents with the usual fears.
You want them to have all the good things in life,
Hoping their life will not be full of strife.
They grow into adults and go their own way.
You know they must go. You know they can't stay.
So you smile hiding tears and wish them well on their way
Yes daughters are special all of the time, but
none as unique and special as the daughter of mine

Mary Alice Evans

You Are Very Special To Me

You are very special to me
you make me feel so free
this love that I feel
It just seems so real
there's not one day that goes by
I don't sit with my head and cry
thanking the Lord from above
for what he's given me
I never knew, I could feel like this
But when you are not there, there's a mist
No more two but now we're one
Finally, I can sing this happy song
You are very special, how can I count the ways
You are very special, whether night or day
You are very special just you alone
Now I know that you're the one
For there is no other man for me
True happiness is what I feel, so this must be real
Thank you Lord, from which all blessings come from
For I know, without a doubt, He's the one

Loletia Morris

Good Friends

Good friends are hard to find
You need to have someone to talk too
Someone who you can confide in
Someone who is there to listen to you,
Even when things don't seem to be going right
Someone you can laugh with and cry with
She can even make you smile, when you
   think the world is so unfair
You start as friends who are far apart
   and then become good friends who can
   confided in each other
Then you become sister-in-laws
Then something happens: Children come
   into the picture and you seem to
   drift away from each other and
   don't share in the special times anymore
Why? I guess, we just grow up and family is number one now
But, my feelings in our friendship have not changed
You are still someone very special, who I can confided in
You are my special good friend

Ruth Langiewicz

Trust Me

Lord
   You said You would never leave me
   But at times I thought You had
   When in fact You never left at all
   I forgot the things You said
   When in my mind Your hard to find
   Your really always there. I just forget
   Your promises, and all the things You said.
   You said to really know Me,
   I have to read Your word.
   You'll show Yourself, and prove to me,
   Your greater than the world.
   No matter what comes against me
   I never should forget
   I'll stand, I'll rest upon Your Word
   And having no regret.
   You'll lift me up when times are tough
   Your truth will always stand
   Like You said within Your Word
   Don't put your trust in man

William Robdau

Ode To Life

I may not be able to see you directly
You take shelter in all
Granting power, intelligence, kindness
Even though the stars you remain
Bestowing upon all what you see in their hearts
Causing fortune and happiness through your eternal years
Living everywhere from the depths of the ocean
To the vast jungles all adore you
Many times you're taken for granted
But soon will remember how lucky we are
That you are with us choose to guide us
You never seek misfortune
Always keeping a balance
Never opting to desert your home
Holding on when you're pried from the soul within
Strongfasted you clench and survive, you can enhance our world
Inhabiting all new people, influencing them to help all
You make us understand that not just one person matters
It's the day to day contact, the joy of being with everyone know
Without you, where would we be?

Michael Nagle

James

When I was young and still quite small
    You tarried upon a step to smile
You looked at me through eyes of soul
    You left this plane, it was like a knoll

The years that passed were sad and drear
    I did not know that you were near
Sometimes I turned to you in prayer
    And darling you were always there.

Now you are with me day or night
    To help and guide me in the right
You are my brother and now, we see
    The way God intended it should be.
        Norma Malooly

The Light

The way was there but you were the light.
You taught me to use my sinew and might,
That I was intelligent, capable, strong,
Able to reason and think all along
(But you were always before me—the light.)

Analyzing, interpreting, with the passage of time
You drew from your life to make sense out of mine.
There were times of congruence when things looked the same
But times that were different and seemed near insane,
Unknown, but you were the light.

You tell me my children are now on their own
Yet by your example, continually shown,
You've been there to listen, not selfish get
Not thinking of you at all, and yet
You just kept providing the light.

Try not to chide me for stepping behind
I'm walking along in a much later time
In steps that you made when you trod the same ground
Seeking my way for the wisdom you found.
(We're passing a torch to keep making the light.)
        Linda Stoner Yates

Untitled

Playfully you kissed all my bare skin
You teasingly ceased and started again
You seemed to grow rougher and stronger with me
But I pressed into your force so fearlessly
When I finally stepped out of your overwhelming embrace
All the wet tears had been died from my face
And I knew you must have spoke to the wind today
For it had caressed me in your sweet knowing way
Although I had not even been present with you
I felt your love all around me as the wind strongly blew
        Tisha Humbyrd

"Waiting To Exhale"

Some times you'll pass some times
you'll fail but "there comes a point
when you will exhale" there's bad times
and there's good you could if you
would exhale. Exhale the violence
into the peace then you will see
how good it could be to exhale the
late into the great Exhale the mugging
into the hugging exhale the fright
into the light exhale the fight
into life exhale exhale, exhale some time.
You'll pass sometimes you'll fail but
"there comes a point when you will exhale."
        Tyneka Crain

Thank You

In your love for me
You went to calvary
You did it so I might believe
And in exchange, eternal life I would receive
Upon the cross you did die
Mary knelt there and you watched her cry
Inside your heart did break
For all humanity that will forsake
The heavy burden you bore that day
For all our sins so we won't have to pay
Out of your love you gave so freely
So we could live with you eternally
Thank you for your love
Thank you for your grace
Thank you for your sweet embrace
        Sarah Tesarik

"Our Mom"

Thank you Mom for being there when we needed you most . . .
You were proud of your family and proud to boast . . .
You taught us not only to achieve, but to believe . . .
And finally, you taught us your very important theme
To aspire to great things in life and to never give up your dream . .
        Tim Herrick

Do You Know Him?

At times a feeling of loneliness overcomes you.
You wonder if there's anyone out there that knows you're alive,
    that loves you. It's as though no one cares . . .

The crowd screamed words of hatred as the man passed by.
His head bled from the thick thorns that pierced his brow.
Sores from beatings burst upon his aching back.
The heavy wood he carried pressed him to the ground.
His knees gave way, his weary body fell.
Two heavy set soldiers unmercifully yanked him to his feet.
The dusty road led them to Golgotha, the place of a scull.
The guards threw him to the ground and drove nails through his
    feet and hands.
His body convulsed with pain as they lifted up the cross.
As the ninth hour passed, he died.

At times a feeling of loneliness overcomes you.
You wonder if there's anyone out there that knows you're alive,
    that loves you. It's as though no one cares . . .

I know a man who cares.
He loved you enough to die for you.
His name is Jesus, do you know him?
        Valeri Sewell

Untitled

You walk in beauty,
Your eyes on fire,
Your lips caress thy sweet desire.
I watch you from afar,
My presence not known.
My eyes stare at you as if they're stone.
Your beauty surpassed the brightest star,
The world see's your beauty even from afar.
The fire in your eyes, the softness of your lips,
I would drink your love, but only in sips.
Your love is my life, your love is my all,
But without your love,
I am nothing
    At
        All.
        Rick Riddlebarger

Just Another Dream

Last night I had a dream and you were there,
you would look at me but never stare
in my dream we were back together
in my dream we would last forever
when we walked down the halls we held hands
when we talked on the phone we talked about future plans
when I knew I had you I was glad
because you never did anything to make me sad
you were my kind of guy
and I never felt the need to be shy
you would kiss my lips lightly
and hold me tightly
I waited forever for this
it's a feeling I will always miss
then I woke up at last
and realized the dream wasn't of the
future but from the past.

Misty Tolliver

Untitled

Daddy don't leave me. It's too scary out here. I don't know if you'll believe me. I know I've come too far to return there. I want with you to stay. I know if I continue to leave, I'll never again come your way. I'm weary of the day I'll retreat. Sometimes I feel life's too complicated to complete. It's a routine rarely ending. A long, long road barely bending. Daddy don't leave me. Life's long passage keeps me at night awake. All I want is to be comfortable, not so much as to fall down and break. Daddy please don't leave me. There's something missing out here. At home I knew with no question you were always there to make a suggestion. So many times I wanted to come home where I know I'm not alone. And all of your advice, although I fought it, I knew it was right. You never even though it as I told my friends everything you told me and they always bought it. Sometimes in a big crowd, with my friends, we laugh, but they're not really around. They think they know me and my ideas, but to really know me well is to know my fears.

Lisa Kelly

It's Cleaning Time!

You're the first of us to become a "Levine",
You'll need these supplies to help you clean.

By now we all realize it's not just a fling,
this relationship is the real, marriage-thing.

By giving you a precious ring,
You'll be expected to do the domestic thing.

Well, exactly what is that you ask?
It's more than just a simple task.

Do you know what's involved as you marry Mark?
It may mean house cleaning until dark.

First, it means picking up socks off the floor,
And doing the dishes, oh what a chore.

As you work your way through all the clutter,
Just smile and laugh and try not to mutter.

As "stuff" seems to sprout and you can't find the floor,
Remember, he's your husband, the man you adore.

Use these things to make your cleaning a breeze,
Refer to the hints from our friend Heloise.

With all our love from across the states and sea,
From Lori and Melanie, the "Levine's-to-be".

Melanie Fidel and Lori Williams

'Spawn'

You say you want freedom or just some escape
your actions betray you, you've blocked the gate
you say you want happiness for all to see
your actions betray you, you took it from me
You say at peace you want man to be
your actions betray you, you spit on me
you say there's no need for there to be greed
your actions betray you, you steal the seed
Oh yes the seed, the seed of love will
Cure the greed from below and above
and that seed of love can't you see
will release the peace for you and me
Happiness comes just wait you'll see
Happiness comes for all to be
The freedom you wanted so much to find
Now can't you see it's in your mind

J. W. Briggs

In Memory Of A Love

We once lied together with a tender and warm embrace.

Now as we are torn apart by life and death, I cry for your eternal silence.

I only long for your face, your voice in all its most passionate tone.

As it was when we last dreamt together.

Thinking upon your last right, and the horror beyond, I regret and will always hold great remorse.

Because for all my eternity, I will sit alone, although my pain is not for me; yet for your soul, all alone in such a world unknown.

I once dreamt of us being together, once more, forever. Now I dream of nothing. My heart is gone, my soul diminished.

I will never be complete because our love affair will never finish.

Tiffani Knode

Mourning The Death Of Potential

Once again, destiny hands me wilted roses.
Your heart — impossible to find
Are you afraid to love, or to be loved
Or is it just the commitment you fear?
I never wanted to own you.
I wanted to only to be near
To know you
And longed painfully for you to know me too.
A quest for validation
Rapid growth of need
I find myself the fool and the martyr once more.
I know your demons well,
But cared only for the you who you keep hidden so deep.
You awakened hope.
You were a breath of life to a dying heart;
A momentary distraction from the chaos that's my mind;
A glimpse of potential for a love, for once, kind.
Now, it's goodbye, but I could never claim regret.
It was nice not being myself for awhile.
You were a solace that I will never forget.

Kayla Cooley

Judgment Day

The wind will blow and you will see it as
Your just reward
The quench your heated soul

For you worked so aggressively to get your desire
Retribution for your anger
Is what you need to fuel your fire

Proud of your power and your evil fangs
Gloating as you watch others
Feel your inflicted pain

But this time you have read the wind wrong
What you hear and feel
Is the retribution song

Cause and effect are your creation
You are now the new owner
Of your own damnation

But the world was designed for the good of mankind
And evil ways of people like you
Are etched in time

Someday, your etchings will be shown in the halls of hell
by your agent named Satan curator of your waterless well

Steven R. Busch

Adrienne

I remember . . . when
Your little head on my breast
Your silken hair on my shoulder
And tiny hands trembling,
You were sobbing in a whisper
The first grief of your young and tender life.

Because you had dropped your doll
So fair and so beautiful
Her arms delicate were broken
And her legs fine and dainty
Were severed and crumbled . . .

You matured and blossomed and I became grey haired.
Forgotten was your childish grief
For the doll so precious . . .
I remember, remember . . .
Your sobs still echo in my soul
And your pearly tear drops
Are still dripping in my heart . . .

William Hovnan

From Me To You (To Vonnie Fink)

From the moment I met you, your smile and laugh are unforgettable
Your presence is one of ease and comfort and joy
And your scent is soft and irresistible
Now always in your eye is the spark of a little boy

For too short of a time was he with you and Lloyd and Mike
I know of many ways to take a life but not one of how to give
For if I did, I would certainly recreate your tyke
So that more than just his memory could live

But in this world and life
There are choices that we just don't have
So things we'd rather not have happen very often do
And just when it seems impossible to smile and to laugh
That spark in your eye brings loving memories to you

Reminds us of the time that he was here
Photographs and memories help to fan the spark
To always keep his spirit near
Everlasting Mark

D. L. Shaffer

My Greatest Friend

You've been mighty good and a super good friend;
You've been the kind of spouse one keeps to the end.
A home you made complete and one you've kept well;
A marriage built on love with a story we can tell.
Two fine boys you gave that we can share.
I love the way you taught them and your gentle care.
Lonely days I know you often spend alone;
Times when I'm at work or maybe I'm just gone.
I remember the first time I saw you and the smile on your face;
It sent my soul reeling and made my heart race.
From pony tails to curls and from flats to heels;
No matter how you look, you still give my heart it's thrills.
I heard what you said and I see how you've grown;
I see what you've done for our boys and the many seeds you've sewn.
If the Lord passed out wings, you'd have the biggest set around;
Because a better wife, Mother or friend could never be found.
You're the one I want to be with even to the end,
You're the best of all and you are MY GREATEST FRIEND.

Wayne Grant

Wanted Love

A tear rolls down and, the next thing I know
you're by my side.

I need only see a glimpse of you, and many dreams
fill my night.

Let me go with you, and will watch the sunrise
together.

You hear that it's a wave hitting the beach, I
think it's trying to keep up with fast beating heart.

Shimmering nights and mystic powers glow in your eyes!
Magic is done.

I dream of being with you and climbing the highest of
mountains, laughing and having fun together.

Will ever be held in your arms and kissed? Knowing that
you love me through and through and for who I am.

Maybe I'm a fool for dreaming about this but, I always
wanted someone like you.

I real! Are you!

Rachel Chamberland

Promises Broken

Your promise of life was no more than a dream.
Your promise of love was less than it seemed.
I've learned from mistakes that you won't be true.
I've learned from disaster that I don't love you.
Promises made;
Promises broken.
It's all the same in your twisted head.
To being with you I'd rather be dead.
Promises broken like a heart made of glass.
You tell me nothing but lies, you have no class.
Broken
Broken
Like a mirror looking back.
Broken
Broken
Like two hearts as they crash.

Sarah Honaker

Sweet Scent From Heaven

Wine is sweets so are your lips
your smile your walk your body
sweet smell's good as
your taste good as honey
sugar, warm as the sun
so are you at anytime
lying beside you makes my life good as new
watching you grow to me
closer than wine every day
more than year is
more than time could ever imaging
flower's scent from heaven
makes me smile
for a long life time
a love that will never die
one in a million

Phyllis A. Felton

Dear Lord

Dear Lord, please keep us in your favor, for in
your vineyards, we do labor.

Searching for the lost that we can find, giving
them hope and peace of mind.

Dear Lord, help us to be the Christians you
want us to be, by following your commandments,
and giving praises to thee.

Help us to see others, through your eyes, to be
able to see even Satan, in his disguise.

Saving your people, from all life's harms, telling
us you are waiting, with outstretched arms.

Mary Frances Smith

Talkings Of An Elder Man

Young man, he said, Do you know who you are?
Young man, he said, Do you know what your future holds?
Young man, he said, Do you know the true meaning of life?
The young man replied, no sir, I don't, I don't
    have to worry about who I am, or about my future,
    or the true meaning of life, I just live.
Young man, be proud of who are and have respect for others.
Spend your days and nights wisely for they can be your last ones.
    FOR ONE DAY YOU MAY BE IN MY PLACE

Kathy Steelman

How Do You Say Good-Bye?

How do you say good-bye to someone
You've loved for so long
What happens when he suddenly packs up and leaves
What do you do while your heart is breaking
Do you just stand on the side
While he says good-bye
Flowing like a dangerous river
The tears you can't stop them
The pain just won't go away
Just wanna melt away in his arms
You don't want to leave his final embrace
His goodbye hurt you so bad
But you just can't be mad
Staring at his big brown eyes
He doesn't want to leave
It wasn't his choice
He had to go
So how do you say goodbye?

Patti Vitali

It's A Matter Of Life And Death

It's a Matter of Life
Your womb is filled with child.
Your day of birth is drawing near.
It's a matter of time; your baby will be here.

Soon in enters a Tunnel of Birth.
The Lord be with you; a child is born.
It is totally dependent on you.
Without you there is nothing it can do.

It goes through the learning process
And one day it becomes an adult.
Then there are children and grandchildren too.
They are still dependent on you.

It's a Matter of Death —
One day the body isn't the same any more.
You are dependent on others.
Now your time has come.

Soon you enter a Tunnel to Heaven.
The Lord be with you.
Your heart is field with gladness.
It's a Matter of Life and Death.

Lillian Salanitro

Love Pure And True

It doesn't matter what I say,
You're still going to leave me.
I thought about you all day,
Maybe if I told you, you might believe me.

That I love you more than life,
You mean everything to me.
It cuts like a knife,
Why can't you see?

Even though it hurts,
I can still go on.
The pain is beyond words,
You've got me all wrong.

Keep this thought in mind,
Where ever you go, whatever you do:
No matter what happens,
I still love you.

Nathan Gaddis

The Love In My Heart

You've touched my heart
You've touched my soul
You're more precious than gold

You're light
You're fire
You fill my every desire

I give thanks to you everyday
Through my joy and my pain.
As you're love is the blood pulsating
Through my veins

When I look at you I see me
For I know my flesh is only temporary
So I walk with you by my side and keep my head held up high.

B. M. Saavedra

"Friendships Are Golden"

Real friends are loyal, honest and true;
They will stand ever hour of need by you.

They will celebrate days when you are fine,
Have patience and understanding, otherwise.

Friendships are developed among people who are strengthen;
They are faithful, noble and lends an ear to listen.

If you have a problem they are always there;
Watching, waiting because they honestly care.

Their act of kindness is like an everlasting light,
It never goes out or vanish in the night.

Their purpose and meaning of strength can be,
a lasting relationship with longevity.

Thank God for you, good friends of mine;
I pray our friendship will last a long time.

Gloria Michelle Jones

Ode To A Friend

When you think of me,
Think of sparkling lights
High above the trees,
And stars that shine so bright, they light up the darkest night.

Think of a cozy, warm fire,
And hot cocoa steaming in a cup.
Think of friends lounging around in casual attire
Talking about today, yesterday, and what might be coming up.

Think of friendship tried and true,
A house full of cheerful sounds.
Think of someone to support you in all you do,
With a love that knows no bounds.

When you think of friendship think of me.
Just as when I think of friendship I think of you,
And the friendship you've given me so freely.
When you think of me, I hope you see a friend forever true-blue.

To make a friend is easy enough to do.
It's keeping one that is an art.
True friendship is directed by what you say and do,
And comes from deep within the heart.

Cynthia A. Canfield

Josh

I walked in the church, that day in December
This day I knew I would always remember
I walked down the aisle and took a seat,
And I looked at the people I did not want to greet.
I did not want to cry for my best friends sake,
But how could I stop the painful heartache
I looked at the podium at his remains
I tried not to cry but could not stop the pain
The sermon began, I looked at his hat,
Suddenly, then, did I want him back
I glanced at his picture and there my eyes stayed,
And then, I thought, I'd see them one day
For now I'll live with his memory,
And see his face when I look out to sea.
But the pain I know won't go away,
The pain I have is here to stay.

Dana Harris

A Nation Torn

I had a dream and it was red, white and blue.
This is my story that I'll write to you.
Traveling on a bus that was going nowhere.
I opened my eyes up and oh what a glare.
The precious color red had been badly torn.
Tears falling from the heavens for He does mourn.
Yesterdays fears we never did belong.
Governments failing, so where did we go wrong?
The freedom we gained, never no more.
The wealthy get rich and the needy get poor.
We're still at war even to this day.
We're not fighting for land, but for our way.
Children are dying from drugs and violence on our streets
Not enough policemen to walk their beats.
Crime is invading our society, causing much pain.
Our country 'tis failing, are we going insane?
The elites are neutral, never equal or fair.
Playing mind games, keeping us in despair.
The right to vote, is it only a game?
This nation may never be the same.

Debbie A. Bailey

Ode Of The Lion (Tribute To A Lost Friend)

The lion lives though his body lies cold
Though his head has been severed the majesty remains
Though his thoughts are now barren on the fields of his home
The lion lives on for his spirit stalks the plains
For his dreams are now shared by the remnants of his pack
As they move on along to the challenge of tomorrow
Everyone has seen his strength
And there is hope within the sorrow
The courage of a leader like the fiber in his loin
Was long known and now bares for anyone to see
Even still is surges forth in a flow so seldom known
With the blessings of the angels like a voice of destiny
The power in his mind and the crispness of his thought
Link together in a line making progress from the past
For long beyond the overgrowth on so many battled grounds
The lessons will be clear the purpose will last
Even portraits of his body as the wind sifts through his mane
As he moved amongst the bushes show a graceful work of art
There's extension of his thought
As it had right from life's first start
For then too the message echoed into the full sheen of golden fur.

Gerald D. Pallay

Underwear

No one would ever write a poem about underwear,
Though it is part of us everyday.
No one ever writes poems about underwear,
It's a word people just don't like to say.

Though it is said they come as a pair,
It is really only one small piece.
Made of so many different kinds of materials,
Like cotton, silk, satin, or fleece!

Now there always have been brand name clothes,
But I really think it is new for drawers.
From "Bloomies", to "Fruit of the Loom",
Even "Christmas Dior."

Why poems aren't written about underwear,
Will always be on my mind.
But what if they did not exist,
What would cover our behinds?

Dandi Wright

587

Life Complete

Dark, . . . Lonely, . . . Empty;
Though life tries to befriend me.
Blind, . . . Deaf, . . . Mute;
Yet music I hear, falling leaves I see, and words
coming from my mouth refute.

From where does this empty void come?
With what can I fill it to make a full sum?
Emotions fled, have left me empty, 'til time finds
me and to my aid comes.
To replace and replenish what living has done.

My eyes are dim with age and sorrow,
Tomorrow may bring sight and life and color.
The fullness of life in death may be found-
When the spirit of life leaves the vessel in the ground.

Then the words my mouth may speak:
With understanding and empathy without critique,
May breath life and happiness without a sword,
That enters the heart 'til it beats no more.

Julia S. Malmgren

Innocence Reposes

'Twas but a rose, do not cry,
though the petals fall to earth, they do not die.

As tears fall, we shed our grief.
As innocence pales, to our relief

So do our fears and bated breath -
no longer fearing dreadful "death".

So do not cry, 'twas but a rose,
that drifted down in soft repose.

De Davis

Sisters

Sisters before friends, that's what we are;
thought we were friends thus far.
But the pain that I feel in my heart and my soul,
come not from any friend that I know.
I wish that I had known your feelings from the start,
I would feel easier in my heart.
Alas, do not feel sad for me.
For what is not there, we cannot make be.
We can be sisters before friends;
that suits you and me.

Judy James

Back In Time

When I think back to a simpler time
Thoughts of Amelia Virginia cross my mind
I recall many things . . . but the people most of all
Janet, Petey, Gene, Sandy . . . God I had a ball!

The gang would drive to the Rock Shop looking for guys
Of all that we met, David and Cary caught our eye
Trips to the Tastee Freeze in the heat of the day
"Creedence" hits were the tunes our radio would play
Weekend dances in town and bluegrass festivals at night
Drinking and dancing and sometimes a fight

Occasionally we'd take trips to rippling beaches of sand
Tubs of 'purple passion' at Virginia Beach and Bugs Island
Friends for life and memories that are clear
Souvenirs that will be with me through all my years
But the best thing about that very special time I have to say
Is living and sharing it all with my twin sister Rae . . .

Jo Kizer

The Light Of Hope

Another early morning, still dark and cold,
thoughts to myself, growing old.
Wondering why each day I stay?
When I asked the Lord to take me away.

My face shows the heartache-
My eyes tell it all-
The confusion I feel, as each new day falls.

Give me a reason Lord, give me one today,
before I take my life away.

I sit and wait for a sign from you . . .

The sun is starting to rise, the air filled with morning dew,
the sparkle of the tree tops, so clear, so blue.
How could it be, I never noticed this beauty before?
Could this be what I have waited for . . .

Today I see the light, in a whole new way.
You came through for me Lord-
You answered my prayer today.

Jacqueline Joos

Three Bodies On The Road

Three bodies on the road.
Three bodies in disarray.
Expendable sacrifices.
It was meant to be a family, one of joy and love.
The heart was ripped from it and it never could survive.

Do you get to be happy?
Do you get to go on with life?
Is there no consequence when you disregard a life?

I see you without feelings.
Remorse is not there.
Vacant of emotion.
Drowning in denial.
That you could be responsible for three bodies on the road.

So still faced.
Not able to face the past
Kicking under the bed.
Throwing down the stairs.
Screaming in the night,
That you really did not care about three
bodies on the road.

Bernadette Francino

Rosemary Dreams And Ripe Tomatoes

A gentle summer, poetic in nature, with soft air that drifts
through my life dreams.

A time for the joy of living poetry and the gentle sadness of loves lost.
All combined in my summer of rosemary dreams.

The aroma of each freshly clipped prickly branch from the
backyard rosemary plant releases into the warm air.

I lay the branches in a woven basket creating a cushioned bed
for the ever ripening tomatoes.

There they reside on a glass patio table, shaded by a blue
umbrella. Outside the back door, near the mimosa tree.

I bring the rosemary and tomatoes inside to cook together,
leaves of rosemary and rich red ripe tomatoes simmering
together, a visual and aromatic delight

The pungency of tomato reminds me of the loss of loved ones

The healing of rosemary encourages my soul
The poetry of my life brings peace to my summer dreams.

Bette Morgan

Take Heed

Take heed, ye of magic thoughts,
thy passions will defeat thee.
You will trod and trample hearts of those
you love, in your quest,
the poison of your lustfulness.
Desire leads to dismay.
Your heart will never rest.
Take heed, the search is never ending,
when passions fill your soul.
Never free from desire.
Beware of lusty thinking,
adventuresome at heart.
Contentment not within your reach,
you will die ever searching.
Take heed, romantics of the mind,
settle, happy, for those who love you.

Brenda Mallette

A Wakening

I wish I were a cloud, for up in thy sky,
The sun would always be shining,
not a tear in my eye.
All the drugs, poverty, and loneliness
would be banished from this earth,
The world would be filled with happiness
love, and mirth.
There would be eternal Utopia from sea to sea,
Everyone would be equal, him, you and me.
So if I were a cloud I would
see only beauty and love,
To spread throughout this world.
On the wings of a dove.

Edna Streat

Encounter, Judgment Day

The future holds a powerful treasure. Through
time, nature with its mysterious ways,
gives our daily lives. We'll never be able to
conquer the knowledge for the answers we seek.
The treasures that await us, according
to our subconscious mind, that nourishes our
hearts with every day living, justifies the
characteristics our souls search for; our
deeds, good or evil, mankind can only point
to what is written in front of him. In today's
modern living, we are blind. Only by prayer,
we acknowledge, for guidance, through the dark age
we encountered. Mankind has encountered the age
beyond his worst nightmare, he never imagine.
Through time, what knowledge he seeks is
limited by nature. The knowledge we seek may
yet discover what barrier lies
between mankind and the unseen spirits, we are
about to encounter.

Cecil Dean Tenney

Live

Don't lock me in a cage like a wild beast.
Throw me in the jungle with the wild beasts.
Let me run free until my legs collapse.
Let me scream in ecstasy until my lungs burst.
Watch me conquer the prey.
Watch me devour him whole.
Lust after the spirit that fills me,
For it shall never be released.
Help me rise with the sun.
Help me rise with the moon.
There is no time for sleep.
Let me live,
For I refuse to die.

Denice Kurelko

"Dreams"

Ride on, white horse,
Through the eve's dim shadows
Of spirits of forgotten dreams,
Whispering softly in the night.

Ride on, white horse,
Though the moon be clouded by
The hurt of the dying day,
Hasten boldly toward the dawn.

Ride on, white horse,
Through the forest glades that taunt you with the morning's light,
Race toward that for which
So long, so hard you've strove.

Ride on, white horse,
For dawn is breaking through the murky mist,
Reaching out its warmth to clothe you
From the night's relentless cold.

Ride swiftly, white horse,
For with the morning sun all else will vanish,
As does the sparkling dew in noon's clear sky.
And you alone stand with me.

Julieann Ulin

One More Day

Through seasons of joy, and seasons that were sad;
Through times that were good, and times that were bad;
We have memories so dear, memories of love.
For that one more day, we thank God above.
One more day to share, one more day to care;
Thank you God for that day.
Through seasons of bliss, and seasons of sorrow;
Through times full of cheer, and times full of woe;
We have memories to keep, memories of love.
For that one more day, we thank God above.
Through seasons of laughter, and seasons depressed;
Through the times of wealth, and the times of distress;
We have memories to come, memories of love.
For that one more day, we thank God above.
One more day to share, one more day to care;
Thank you God for that day.

Jack D. Kallal

Miracle Roots

Sick, weakened, and battered plants,
Thrown out by their users to die,
Often sink their remaining substance
Deep beneath the soil where they fell,
And begin anew - in beauty and strength.

Not thinking life could return,
The users stare in utter shock
At these once fragmented specimens,
Which were tossed among tall briars,
And stunned by bruises from hard rock and clay.

No skilled workmen tilled the grounds,
Neither love nor nurture they gave,
But the same - different plants still stand
With signs of who they were but aren't,
With sparks not yet consumed by gross neglect.

Raped, beaten, and tormented,
These scarred but dazzling beauties live
With foliage too brilliant to believe,
Born from some unmovable roots,
Sustained by one unseen - who knows their toils.

Bertie Jeffress Powell

Fire Across The River

Herbal tea and
tiny beads keep me
company now that
December's sorcery has
taken leave abandoning
the light polluted night sky
(tree branches clutch at
its nothingness)

Hungry fire gifted
apparition crosses the river demonstrating
the implausible
cold clad in my tissue paper cloak of
aspirations wrap it tighter around
me and watch in exquisite torment

Cabochon streetlights
orderly tangerine gems
illuminate schemes scenes
played out in my Foucault pendulum heart
planning my own resurrection
designing a bridge
            Joan M. Krause

To Change The World

I'd like to change the world
To a kinder understanding place
Where prejudice and hate are no more
And goodness glows in every face.

A fertile earth where justice thrives
And weeds of deceit cannot grow
Where warm light exposes dark secrets
And rivers spread truth as they flow

But could I really change the world
History laughs at such audacious conceit
Would I only be jousting at windmills
Traveling the path to inevitable defeat

NO! Doubt not the righteous road
Prepared with courage, stamina and charity
It's length is that of a lifetime
With each step, fulfillment and clarity

The world can change with changes in me
As pebbles spread ripples across the sea
And God in my soul is then set free
To touch all of the worlds humanity
            Jim Gantz

Silver Haired Love

Come my darling, slowly follow me
To a place where we carved our initials on a tree.
We ran up the hill that day
We were so young, happy and gay.
Now we have to stop and take a rest.
My darling, wait until I unbutton my vest.
Dearest, take my hand.
I'll help you. I understand.
Love like ours is beyond compare.
It will never, ever need repair.
We have been through all kinds of weather.
Through all those storms we have been together.
Darling, look there is the trees!
Let me clean off you specs so you can see.
Our initials are still there
Though the tree looks old now and so bare.
Love like ours is oh so rare.
Togetherness, consideration, thoughtfulness has been our motto
    for you and me
And now the faith we have helped us make it, my Darling, to the tree.
            Emily Kingston

To My Friend, Ray Yvoskis

His genealogy began in the old country; Lithuania by name
To a young maid and man who born there
But met in Chicago - still in their teens
Isn't life a game!?

A game to be played to the hilt
If honesty, decency and Godliness prevail,
So it was with Ray's parents
The same sun, moon and stars to go by,
As they set sail.

Lithuania, their birth place.
America, their new home and life.
Do we not who were born here
See the courage of their strife?

But my dedication is to their only son,
Who is my very, very best friend
He has all the good virtues one would wish for,
My praise for his goodness, without end!

So here's my respect to those of another land,
Be it North, South, East or West.
They've come to America, to make the better, the best!
            Becky Kinser

The Path

Walking beneath pines, to a small brook, then crossing
To an open path amongst maple, elm and oak with wild
ferns along the way;

While listening to birds; Robins, Sparrow and Bluejay.

The sounded like a chorus;

The sun was filtering through branches, to warm a living forest.

Time seems to stand still, with the way you feel,
in the glory of natures bath;

While your walking along the path.
            Carol Barker-Bettencourt

A Wee Little Girl And A Mother's Tears

I hope that I would never see, the time of year that's come
To be, for a wee little girl that belongs to me.
A time when we have grown apart, with all the pains that
Life has brought.

The time is here now—we must part, for she must make her on
true marks. As life goes on and times goes by,
twill ease the pain we felt that night. A mother's love for
a wee little girl, that's grown a woman almost over night.

Even though it hurts to see this day, the parting of this
child and me. The time has come—she must be free,
to complete the cycle of life you see. Then one day she will
come to see, it wasn't so selfish, this love in me.

'Tis only the love a mother feels, for a wee little girl she
Loves so dear. So let this night be not of fear,
But give to all—great meanings here,
Of a week little girl and a mother's tears
            Alice F. Hoppes

Gift Of True Love

True love is:
To do everything you can for the one you love,
To do what ever you can to make one you love happy,
To love the one you love even if they do not love you,
To do everything you can and ask nothing in return.
I give you the gift of true love.
            Eddie L. Dixon

Hide And Seek

I have raced along behind myself all my life, like a shadow.
To be what I used to be, and more.
And while I've never quite captured myself,
To realize my dreams,
My fears have dominated my existence.

There are those needs I cannot express
To you or anyone.
For no one can be so close to share,
As my shadow, which follows me in my quest,
And is my only friend and lover.
It knows nothing - not even me.

So who is it? And who am I?
Is it my shadow who knows me not, or me,
Who without a friend or lover, knows not myself?

But soon someone will come who can know all.
And then my greatest fears will be realized.
For true knowledge of self and shadow may be unveiled,
In full and glorious disarray!

Behold! For it is me, myself, alone!
Or is it the shadow I perceive?

John F. Vivian

Earth's Plea

The world awaits the transformation of the earth
to become whole again and complete within itself.

We the people must show respect for this magnificent
haven in space by caring for the very foundation
upon which we stand.

The soil must be enriched again — the vegetation
brought forth to display it's beauty, or to give
forth it's wealth of produce.

There must be concern for the exchange of air and
water, keeping both as God intended.

What we don't handle - nature will and we will
suffer the consequences.

Billie J. Scott

Worthy Of Possession

If I were an artist I would do my best
To capture this butterfly, just lying here
Just taking in what's free.
I wonder if he can see me smiling
At him with envy.

There's something about these waterfalls
That calls to me to return each Spring.
Word has it that a man died
Going down these waters; maybe that's the reason
I had to run them for myself.

I sit here thinking about the water
The sunshine and the smiles.
I often wonder if it's the natural beauty
Or the memories that beckons my return each year.

I even wonder if he knows I'm here
Because he doesn't appear to care.
I'm just thankful he is willing
To share this place with me.
A wise old man once told me, the only things
Worthy of possession are your memories.

Bud Rowell

A Boy, Eleven And A Girl, Thirteen

We watched them hurrying down the lane,
To catch the school bus and with hearts aflame,
With pride in them we let them go,
From out of our sight, 'round the bend in the road.

She, just thirteen, carried books on topics
From science and math through Home Economics.
He had no books, but wore his Dodger's cap,
And carried his glove and his baseball bat.

And a card from Jackie Robinson saying,
"Good luck in all your baseball playing,
And be a good boy." What pride, what joy,
That card brought to an eleven year old boy.

The years have gone by, how they have flown,
Each one choosing a career of their own.
She teaches music and he, Sign and Art,
Both subjects straight from the heart.

Now, with their homes, and families, too,
It's starting the cycle all over anew.
And we still feel that pride as they come and go,
From out of our sight, 'round the bend in the road.

Doris B. Adams

I'm "My Mothers Little Boy"

Today I sit beside the Seine.
to Chine, I don't go back again.
Where to go? What to do?
My heart is sad, so full of Rue.
I will talk to God and say,
All men must be free one day.
Suddenly I feel a hand in mine,
It's a little boy not hardly nine.
Mister he says, How do you do?
I felt going from my heart all the rue.
I ask pray tell me what's your name?
suddenly he throws out his shoulder his chest the same,
I'm "my mothers little boy."
There I see her all dressed in lace,
   a lovely smile on her sweet face.
She is speaking to me,
   would you care for a nice hot cup of tea?
As we three trudge along the lane.
   to a small cottage by the seine.
Time has come and gone since then.
   Hearts can love and hearts can mend,
The Chinese men have come I see,
   asking questions again of me.
15 years in a prison was not enough.
   always doubting always bluff,
You solved The Pierre Fermat we see,
   I say have you had your nice hot cup of tea?
Oh! Feng Sheng with us you toy!
   Why not? I'm "My Mother's Little Boy"

Feng Sheng Shi

Today

Wondering about the evitable
Thinking on yesterdays bygones
Reaching for what is now before me,
Life is not a beach; lest not all the time
It's not all its cracked up to be
But life is good
It needs to be cherished
It is God's unique and great creation

Reach for what is before you
Grab it! Hold tight! Don't let go!
For yesterday is gone . . .
And now you have Today.

Deborah D. Pauldo

Peaceful Release

There is no more peaceful place than these stretch of sands
To ease your heart and soul of your many plans;

To stifle out the weary days
Of torment and tangled maze;

The water off shore are calm at last
To let the boats up their mast;

To sail off into the haze
Just to relax and enjoy the lazy day;

To get away from stressful times
And hear the waves splashing like musical chimes;

They give you such inner peace
And let you have true release;

From stressful days and weary nights
And now you soul feels like a flying kite;
To fly so high above the stress
And now my soul I'll feel at rest
To give my Lord and world my very best:

No greater place to get release
Than a beautiful, sandy, stretch of beach:

Bonnie Walters

"Hours In A Day"

There are so many hours in a day
To explain what is in your heart,
and, don't know how to say
One must care, and, carry the
burden that's within the heart
There is love within these hours, and, days.
Yet how does one in your
heart explain, is so much in dismay
You search, I say, within in your heart
Then you will know where to
end, and, where to start
Life is given along each path
to take whether it be to
the left or right
Then it's up to you to seek
what is wrong and what is right.

Dorothy L. Guidi

Emotions

When you left me I didn't know what
to feel, me loving and being with you
forever, it all felt so real.
I couldn't believe anything that was
said, there were all of these, "end of the world"
emotions that wouldn't escape from my head.
I wanted to call you and talk to
you so bad, it seemed like you were all I had.
You should've seen the tears in my eyes,
I thought about what you said
and they were all lies.
I suddenly realize how it feels to
be without you, and to be honest there's
no one else I'd rather be close to.
I cried for nothing 'cause now you're
all mine, please let's get it right this time.

Ginger Lucero

Love

Joseph and Mary were on their way
To find an inn in which to stay —

There was not a one to be found;
So, it was in a manger
that the Child was renowned.

A Holy Child, Who would give His life
To a world full of hate
and war-torn strife!

He gave His life that man might live
In brotherly love, and have a peace
within.

"Love one another as I have loved you", said He;
"And, the whole wide world will be
wonderfully free!"

Ann Berta Ludwick

Alphabet

The ALPHABET has twenty-six letters. To learn at an early age.
To form letters to use. We learn to form words.
Put them together to talk to each other.
Did you ever take three letters at a time add together,
then add that number.
You get 351, just 14 days short of a year.
As there are 365 days in a year. Leap year is 366 days.
By doing this you learn to add. Not every one would agree
in this method. I enjoyed doing this.
ALPHA (ETIC) plus NUMERICAL-ALPHANUMBER ICALLY.

Charlotte M. Ryan

"Sunrise"

My dog, Biscuit, by name, and I walked up a meandering path
To get up the mountain before sunrise. With a flashlight in
Hand, it shone the path ahead. When my dog, the lab, and I
Reached the top of the mountain, I sat against a tree. Out
of my pocket, I took out my black New Testament. I sang and
Read Psalms 28 by flashlight and dim light of day. But the
Sun had not risen yet. Slowly the light of day did come,
But the sun had not awaken yet. I watched the clouds for
Any sign of sun while my dog was lying with her paws crossed.
From a lone cloud, I saw a speck of light. The cloud shoots
Forth with a beam of light. Then above the cloud stood the
Orange sun.

Donald James Pitts

Windows Of Time

Time is only a vapor . . .
To live again, the way it was . . .
A happier time . . . so long ago . . .
Memory mourns the death of time
Taunting the soul, torturing the mind.
On it goes, the hands move 'round,
The sands of time, memory bound.
Moment by moment is lived, as time moves on . . .
Vanishing like vapor . . . where does it go?
Captured by memory . . . the happy and sad.
Created by destiny, more a woman or man?
Time has no mercy, each chooses his lot,
With mind as property, but the soul is not.
Our time is spent for Heaven or Hell and
We make it our own to live as well.
Moment by moment is lived, as time moves on . . .
Vanishing like vapor . . . oh where does it go?
On it goes, the hands move 'round . . .
The sands of time . . . Memory Bound.

Char Albritton

Backbite

Isn't it enjoyable to talk behind a back?
to know someone's not listening, never cut them any slack?
despite our better judgement, all of us join in,
at one time or another we all commit this common sin

Be sure and check the stairway, be sure and check the hall
then go ahead and give them a personality overhaul

Backbite
it feels so good to get it out, despite
your own inner secret doubt it's right
still you gotta scream and shout
about the ones that make you crazy, the ones that drive you nuts,
because you know you're a decent person and they're knotting up your guts

We can all be honest when our victim's not around
it's easier to talk 'cause they're not there to hear a sound
somehow it's rewarding to get it off our chest all of us feel better
because we know we've griped our best

Isn't it amazing the problems that we solve?
So go ahead and give them a personality overhaul

Backbite . . .
   Gurukarta K. Khalsa

Death

It comes out of nowhere
To lead you into the unknown.
Should it really be something we should fear:
Heaven or hell,
Light or dark,
Good or evil.
It happens to everyone
Not just the unlucky.
Bringing tears to loved ones,
And an eternity for victims.
We don't get to chose where to go.
The dark, fiery bottom of hell,
Or the light, fluffy raise of heaven.
Is it frightening to think about it?
The days go by faster and faster,
Bringing you close to it.
Does it excite you
Bringing you out of misery or pain?
It will always be a part of life,
But should it really be something we should fear?
   Gina Lauren Dadetto

"Music's Peace"

What has gone wrong I do not know;
To leave the room I do not dare.
I know not why my spirits are low;
I begin to feel I just don't care.

Placing the violin under my chin,
I feel the familiar strings.
Playing makes the grief less than it's been,
And reminds me of the peace music brings.

Melody swells around the room;
My problems begin to seem small.
I no longer feel the pain of doom,
Listening for the music's sweet call.

   Whenever living gets too rough,
   The music's peace is always enough.
   Andrea Ury

Snow

The white flakes fall from the darkened sky
   To light upon the ground so sly!
A picture of so much peace and rest
   To build upon this land's crest.

The wind and moist in coldness of the air
   Dampens the naked wind so bare
Fallen vapor upon this our harden ground
   Make no noise, not even a sound.

The sun's rays will melt its shortly stay
   Taking its natural color away
Leaving the earth in a very slushy mess
   Knowing the soil, will hold in its breast.
   John T. Woods

The Meanest Man

The meanest man God ever blew breath into is sitting next to me,
His words are cold,
His body smells like mold,
And his hands appear to be coming closer to me.
His eyes spell death,
His nose says to kill,
And he appears to be stronger than me.
His fingers look like knots,
His hair looks like snot,
And his overall appearance is scaring me.
I can not stay much longer,
For I will have to leave,
The meanest man ever has just politely said "Hi" to me.
   Carolyn Day

Goodbye Father

Goodbye father you are no longer in my life.
To me you are dead though to the world you
are still alive.

I wish it was not this way but it seems you
have forgotten me so I will say
I have forgotten you.

I have a new father who my mother says
loves me as much as she does though
at times I really doubt it.

It is time for me to say goodbye but I know I
will always hope that someday I just might
be saying, "Hello father."
   Amanda Smith

Shadow Dancers

Shadow dancers in the night,
   to watch you move is sheer delight.
Across the screen you twirl and dance,
   an intriguing story of true romance.
In the night, I watch you sway,
   you don't dance when it's day.
Alone in my room you catch my eyes,
   A lovers dance, it makes me sigh.
My bedroom window sets the stage,
   for the shadow dancers of unknown age.
Shadow dancers In the daylight hide,
   in the willow tree that stands outside.
It's branches low, and motionless,
   the night breeze knows their sweet caress.
My dancers tell of secrets they keep,
   the dance is over, as I drift into sleep.
   Bonnie Master

The Step Father

When I was a child my mother dated you.
To my family, you were to good to be true.
Everyone cooed over you, and said what
  a wonderful thing you were.
I however was not as sure.
I could not understand or see
What exactly was wrong with just me?
And what on earth did they mean by saying
  you were "it"?
And just where exactly was I to fit?
I stomped my foot, and made my case
That there simply was not a place
Reserved for you to stay
Not now or any day.
But my protests were to no avail
That August you honeymooned in vail
Yes I remember way back then
When you were nothing close to next of kin.

Oh how that I have grown maybe sooner if I'd known
What a wonderful bother is this thing called a stepfather.

Ebony Black

Books

Books give inspiration
to poems just like these.
To read a book,
is like expanding your mind,
But you will find.
Dinosaurs, pirates, and hidden treasures,
Are just some of the things behind the cover of a book.

Ashley Hackney

Nostalgia

You've come back to unwalk the trodden path
To reconstruct the destroyed lives,
To justify mistakes in wrath . . .

The road you left is full with weeds of pain
And thorns of suffering forever cried in vain.

You've sought your way to a redemption
Framed by a sea-side lavished invitation
Back dropped violins, the setting sun;
The lights are dim, the sea at rest.
My pain you cannot mask, as if it were Octoberfest!

"Mistakes, I know I have committed,
But can't you find you've been at fault?
Have you not erred, are you pristine?
Is there no sin **you** wish to clean?"

"Ah! Yes, **my** sin — you have forgotten . . .
For which I'll never be forgiven
Nor in this world or the hereafter . . .
The child! You dared demand of me to let him go,
And I, so weak and ignorant, allowed his tender breath to
  breathe no more."

Emily Sarasty

Sara's Turkey Dinner

Sara Cynthia Sylvia Skinner made a great big
  turkey dinner.

The turkey was taller than the clouds,
  and waiting to eat it, people gathered in crowds.

There was a lot of shovin' and shovin'
  'till Sara finally got that bird in the oven.

Then everyone sat down and began to enjoy the eats,
  for who can resist Sara's Thanksgiving Day treats!

Alan Steinberg

I Am Gone

I look down
To see my lifeless corpse
Lying limp and unmoving.
I am gone,
But I am here.
My spirit is no longer dwelling in my body,
My spirit is free from its cage.
Now the cage that once held my spirit
Lies lonely and forgotten
In a deep dark grave.
I am gone,
But I am here.
My spirit is free!

Carrie Thomas

The Veil

I weave a veil with threads of light
to shield my darkening soul

Memories rip then fray the veil
I toil so hard to sew

How much time must pass
till my veil stays woven smooth

Forever covering a heart
broken by deceit and lies

Notice only the veil when you look at me
Don't peer through the tears

The veil is for the world to see
Not the empty blackness inside of me

Where love once was and I was whole
The illusion of my veil will be what shows

Becky Lurz

Christmas Is The Season

Christmas is the season of the year;
To show our love and spread good cheer.
It is the season to give gifts and toys;
to fathers and mothers and girls and boys.
Christmas is a very, very merry season,
But let us not forget the real reason
Of the little Lord Jesus, who lay in a manger.
Let's hope for another year of happiness, and pray
for no danger.
So let us put on our most memories smiles
And send love and cheer over the miles

Estelle Brewer

The Immigrants

They came to America the same as I,
To start a new life and no-one can deny
That life has been good, in this land of opportunity.
But deep in their hearts as it is so in mine.
Are memories that shine far brighter than the sun
They want to return to the land of their birth,
To continue their lives in that one place on earth, . . . England.
But fate intervened and changed their plans
And took that decision right out of their hands
He went first, one warm sunny day
And then she knew she would have to stay
To be close to him and all they had shared
With the help of friends and family who cared.
Two years went by and the pain lingered on
Because they had always existed as one.
And then one day in early spring,
When young buds were blooming,
And birds had to sing, she went home, to him.

Freda Thomas

One Night

One night I wished upon a star.
To take me somewhere very far.
Where there are oceans, valleys and plenty of trees.
I'll except a ride over the seas.
Where the beauty runs deep and the climate is still.
I can say for once, I don't need this pill
the true beauty of this place has made me well.
How long I can stay, only time will tell.
I thank you God for always being there
Because without you life cannot compare.
I know I'm with you, where I should be.
Floating over the oceans and the sea
The peace of this place has made me see
With you is where I want to be
If one night you wish upon a star
Make sure that wish is what you are.

Deborah Lewis

Memories

Memories, they are so colorful, they seem like yesterday,
To talk about and reminisce, of things we used to say.
When you think of days of old, do you speak of tales untold,
When you were young and bold, don't turn cold.
And it's frightening, I'm sure, the future that you will face,
It will come or it will not, according to your pace.

I made a vow to a friend of mine,
To let him down would be the ultimate crime,
To your friend too, you should feel the same,
I promise you brother, there is no pain,
Though our last words have passed in time,
Not a day goes by doesn't cross my mind.
So what if things just aren't the same,
I'm telling you brother, there is no pain,
I swear to you people, it's not the same.

Herb Nelson

Prejudice

From the burning crosses of the Ku Klux Klan,
To the riots on the streets of Los Angeles,
Prejudice has ruined the lives of innocent people.
From the tear filled eyes of a young child
Who has experienced judgement based on the color of their skin,
To the trembling hands of a teenager
Who has seen someone they knew killed during a gang brawl,
Prejudice ruins the lives of innocent people.
Until we can stop closing our minds to knew things,
And open our hearts to God and each other,
Prejudice will continue to ruin the lives of innocent people.
If we are not careful,
The next innocent person could be someone we know and love.

Beth Rackliffe

Victory Living

God is looking for a fellow He can positively trust;
To uphold His highest standard, this condition is a MUST.
That he overcome temptation when it rears it's ugly head;
"There is power over evil, if you use it", Jesus said.

God is looking for a fellow who will hold His banner high;
Who will use the power given and win others 'ere he die.
Souls are longing for their freedom. Who will help to set them free?
Jesus needs an overcomer — could it be that He wants me?

God is looking for a fellow who is faithful, loyal, true!
So that others, when they're looking will see Jesus ruling you!
Then their hearts will be made hungry and their sins will be forgiven;
All because you were the fellow, Jesus chose for VICTORY LIVING!

Elma M. Wine

Unquestionable Beauty

How do we measure beauty;
To what do we give it claim?
Is it a glorious morning sunrise, or
   is it sunset's resplendent diminishing flame?

If we stood amidst a myriad of flowers
   with colors so gaily profuse,
Would we have the courage to choose the fairest all the flowers,
And the rest that distinction refuse?

Or if we discovered an enchanted forest
   where beauty and peace are supreme,
Would we make this our home forever,
And let the rest of the world unseen?

And when we speak of a beautiful friendship,
Are we truly able to judge and perceive
The quality of that beautiful friendship,
Or do we measure by what we give instead of receive?

Beauty is an intangible moment
Created by God in time's rapid flight,
But the beauty of Jesus is permanent and forever,
God's Son, Our Lord, Our Christ!

Alexander J. Kosikowski

"A Road To Travel"

   My journey is just beginning
To where I wonder . . .
   To where . . .
There is a sweet sadness inside of me
For I know not where the Lord will send me.
My will and desire are so strong,
It's the will of — Sister-Mother . . .
Brother-Father . . .
So many things need to be done
Young sister . . .
Young brother . . .
Have faith not despair
Believe in your journey
Believe in yourself
For no one can ROB, STEAL, BEAT, nor INSULT your
journey away from you.
The journey you take are filled with dreams and hope.
But mostly unknown-wondrous
   POSSIBILITIES . . .

Janie Brown

Tribute To My Mother

When I was just a little girl you were always there,
To wipe my tears, to calm my fears and let me know you cared.
You scolded me when I was bad, gave praise when I was good,
And listened to my problems, I was sure you understood.
I know it wasn't easy, I could really be a pain,
But you never turned away, no matter how much I complained.
You prayed with me and told me, "Always listen to the Lord.
Pray and do your best, to line up with God's word".
You gave such good advice with patience, care and love.
You're the kind of mother that was sent from God above.
When I became a woman and my new life was to start,
I packed up all my teachings and put them in my heart.
As the years went by and I had children of my own.
All my fears came back, it seemed they too had grown.
I tried to remember all the things you said to me.
Oh if I could only be, the kind of mom you were for me.
In motherhood I've learned a lot, of giving and of taking,
Of joy and sorrow as it comes, and tender hearts breaking.
I gave them the support, that you always gave to me.
And hope that someday my child, will look that way at me.

Donna Clements

"Today"

Tomorrow is an easy word to say
Tomorrow is an excuse for yesterday
Tomorrow is what we always say,
But, what's the matter today?
Feelings of doubt overcome me,
and my self esteem fades away,
I lay alone, at night just thinking,
why can't I just fade away?
The mental anguish I must be feeling
when people turn away and leave
The disappointment that I face
Makes me wanna forget how to breath
And tomorrow I say, I'll do it then
I'll forget what they said, and start over again,
I'll get on with my life, I'll take that step
But tomorrow comes, and I forget.
So now, is the day, I'm changing my life
Cause tomorrow may never come they say,
So I'm looking in the Mirror, and facing myself
I'm starting over, and I'm starting today

Gwendolyn Weinert

What In The World?

What has happened in this old world,
Too many crimes, so much abuse,
Some people just say, "What's the use."

Have we forsaken the Golden Rules?
Traded them in for electronic tools?

Are we so fooled by the movie screen
that life slips by us as if unseen?

They tell us . . .
"What's black is white" "What's true is false,"
this new thinking sets an evil course,

There are no rules, no boundaries anymore,
Is this what we want . . . to create empty fools?

Has something been taken from our midst,
something our forefathers had on their lips,
Have we neglected to ask Him above,
to help us with His redeeming love?

This is a challenge, to take back what's good,
it means great courage and much fortitude,

It's a "clarion call" to you and to me,
it rings loud and clear . . . it means . . . our destiny

Gloria Peterson Miller

Waterman's Soul

Winter, and the island is cold
trapped by wind and ice's hold.
On sits the waterman, hardy of heart
leaving things to nature and her natural smarts.
Never a cross complaint will you hear him utter
for he knows that all things are as they are for bad or better.
A leathered face and cracked hands are the symbols he wears
of virtues earned by way of the Good Book on which he swears.
His creator is never far in time prayer.
The sun, the ice, the wind, the water, are His ears to the sayer.
In a time when secrets are revealed in technology,
the waterman smiles at the predestined irony.
For he knows that all things are shrouded for reason,
not to be revealed until the right season.
So, on the cold island he sits, warmed by the mystery,
forever content to admire its symmetry.

John James Good Jr.

The Web Of Sex Games And Sexual Internet

Tangled like a web
Trapped in the World Wide Web
The two had an illicit affair
In a provocative, yet sensual manner
Via internet,
They have met
She worked her fingers every night
Typing in the speed of light
She found the only limit is her imagination
For this electronic liaison
As her modem and his modem connect
And nobody can object
He e-mailed her and she e-mailed him back
She did not care if he was using a PC or Mac
Information flowed out,
Like water out of a waterspout
Finally, they reached ecstasy
But there was nothing to see,
Except for this cold place
We call "cyberspace."

Andes R. Martinez

"The Woman In The Moon"

A face of beauty haunted by loneliness
Traveling through the darkness without a destiny
She wears a hopeful expression, yet it is
Riddled with sadness
Of course, she is truly good, for God's
Angels lend her their haloes from time to time
Her personality shoots out in beams, only
To be taken for granted by those it shines upon
A challenger, who is as big as the sun, rushes
Her to leave, so he may take her place
He diminishes her light, and spirit, and
Once again she is isolated in her loneliness . . .
Oh! How she longs for man to touch
Her soil again, and to praise her, not
Himself, for his grand performance.

Amy Lee Lester

Troubled

Troubled is having wondering thoughts of despair,
Troubled is having feelings of heart break everywhere.

Troubled is a life with uncertain happiness, a future dark and bleak,
Troubled is when you toss and turn for hours unable to fall asleep.

Troubled is having no one to talk to with whom to share your fears,
Troubled is having swollen eyes and cloudy vision from shedding so many tears.

Troubled is watching a life waste spinning recklessly out of control,
Troubled is knowing that things would become clearer if you but had someone to hold.

Troubled is living a double life; One with such misery,
One that you hope to see, but you know it can never be.

Troubled is your child asking you "Mama why?"
You just turn and contemplate an answer to reply.

Troubled am I right now, for I can't seem to figure out my life,
It truly saddens me to think of all the pain and strife.

My source of relief through all of my pain comes from knowing that you
Lord are with me again and again. In you, I find peace through all
of my troubles.
With you, I know I can win. On you, I can always depend.

Annette T. Watters

Listening To The Wind

On this dreary winter evening,
Tree boughs are drooping low.
Cold wind weaves and whistles, careening,
And through dry leaves doth blow.

The moon darts into the clouds and out;
A cast of shadows play.
Sounds high-pitched then low whisper about,
And gloom seems here to stay.

Gnarled tree trunks assume nightmarish shape:
Creatures listening to the wind,
Shrubs lifting bare arms pleading their fate,
Self-gestures to defend.

Crescent light scuttles across the sky
As earthly demons bow.
Day brings calm the mighty wind doth sigh,
But night the might to howl.

Dorothy D. Kemp

The Master Speaks

I give you two eyes to see with.
Two ears to hear with.
But before I speak
You will know the answer you seek.
For the eyes have revealed
What the voice cannot hide.
The truth is what you seek.
To cover up, to deny, to defend is deceit,
To deceive another is to deceive one's self.

Jan Simpson

The Best

Friendship is like a rose that never dies,
Trust is like a mirror that never lies.
Honesty is like a fish that won't pretend to be a shark,
Modesty is like a peacock, insisting it's just a lark.
Loyalty is like a shadows sticking by your side,
Determination is a shoelace—trying hard to be tied.

Understanding is a mother, who knows just what you feel.
Politeness is a clownfish, yielding to an eel.
Joy is like life, appreciated by all,
Common sense is like a parachute, saving you from your fall.

Which of these virtues could I name as best?
They all rank first place, when put to the test.
Since you can't simply say, "All of the above,"
You create a "compound-virtue" and call it Love.

Carina A. Gervacio

Pondering

I was setting and pondering once upon a time
Trying to set a spell and trying to get a rhyme
The flies were a buzzing all around me
Making it hard for a feller to see
What are flies and who made the pests?
Can't be God cause he make's the best
Then who could have wanted plague like these
But guess they are better than them old fleas
Was it Noah, Ol' Noah and the ark?
Or did those pesky critters sneak in after dark
Well it don't make no never mind I say
They will be with us until doomsday
I will do my part tho, til I say goodbye
Sitting here a pondering and swatting those flies.

Gaye V. Selover

Think About This

We would surely live in dread, if all colors of the rainbow suddenly turn red.
How boring it would be, if only one idea transpired between you and me.
If crossword puzzles were our only conversation and finding the missing letter our only inspiration.
Doesn't it make you want to rejoice to know that you are unique and you can make a choice.
That your mind isn't small; that differences are tall.
To know that you are not of the minority, those who wear blinders choosing what they want to see; avoiding you, avoiding me.
We are the flowers, we are the rainbows, we are the colors of the earth.
Because we're different, but yet the same, not picky or prodding or laying the blame.
This is a fact we all must face, these cultural diversities make up the human race.

Anita M. Thompson

November Cosmos

There is a tender land where
tumbleweed and sage sweeten
thinning air, where fisher forages
for winter fare—
a skiff of snow whitens
weathered bone, scarring earth
where a lone squirrel runs,
and here the brown bear
finds a way old as stone.
The coyote prickly and wild with practice
barks forlorn
and moon ignites his eyes,
flanks feeding lean
on the sustenance of stars.
Though owl looms near
the cloudless burn of night,
he does not return the call.

Henrietta Meuller

The Journey

A taste in the mouth of fear, yet sweet.
Tuned into the body; to each heartbeat.
First silence, then pleasure as more inward you turn.
To your mind you journey. The place you will learn.

Tread softly friend and to yourself be kind.
Remember it's magic, it's the path of your mind.
What you see there covers so many years.
It encompasses your knowledge, your loves, your fears.

Don't shudder at the bitterness you've often known.
It was a part of you, and like autumn leaves blown.
Don't gloat at the loves that have filled your heart.
Like life itself, loves quickly depart.

Continue your journey slowly as paths unwind.
Tread soft and gentle through the facets of your mind.
Face to face with who you are. No need for fear.
You are so deep within yourself. No danger here.

Diane M. Fry

Untitled

When I saw you standing in the bright sun your shadow cast a spell upon my soul. I was in love.
Never before had we meet yet you were so perfect for me.
The rays of sun reaching deep into my soul pulling out my most intimate feelings.
I was hoping, praying that you would be the one to share them with me.
I shut my eyes to dwell upon your features, but when I opened them you were gone.
I looked again but there was nothing, you were just a dream.

Crystal L. Rowe

Things Mom's Miss

Refereeing fights,
Turning on night lights,
    and making sure
You're snuggled in safe and tight.

Bedtime stories and midnight snacks.
Sounds as a broken glass cracks.
Watching wads of bubble gum smack.

Dirty tennis shoes, balls and bats,
puppy dogs, hamsters and cats.
Toddlers requiring early bedtime and naps.
Teaching kindergartners how to tie and snap.

Parties at school and after school greeting.
Talking to teachers at a P.T.A. meeting.
Excitement of ball scores and winning.
Homework, report cards, spelling and reading.

Washing your clothes and shopping for toys.
Your friends, radios, and all the noise.
At the end of my poem I must confess,
I miss my three boys.

Betty Starnes-Fox

The Window

When I looked out the window what did I see?
Two little golden puppies staring at me.

When I looked out the window what did I see?
The snow falling onto the sturdy trees.

When I looked out the window what did I see?
A wild duck that would not flee.

When I looked out the window what did I see?
A beat-up shed. Could that be their humble bed?

When I looked out the window what did I see?
A red ribbon of silk that pleaded to me.

When I opened the door what did I see?
Two little golden puppies running straight at me.

When I looked down at them what did I see?
Two little golden puppies just for me!

Jennifer Fazen

The Mariachi Man

In the late of the evening
Under a sky of colored stars
The Mariachi Man told me
When I first saw you walk in the room my eyes were drawn to you

The tumbling sounds of party voices
made soft by bitter liquor
drifted in and out among
the trembling strains of the guitar music
like water through stones in a lively brook

He said to me — *You are the most beautiful woman here*

At 19, in my party dress
under a magnolia tree in the cool darkness
of only a late Summer's evening
an ice cold drink in a plastic cup
made my cheeks warm

Or perhaps it was the touch of his gentle calloused hand
as it slipped softly from mine
as a breeze through long hair
or the dew from grass as the sun rises
We parted.

Erin Mahan

Untitled

My friend and I used to ride bikes
under sunny skies. I used to play games
with him and all the other guys.

My friend used to come over all the
time for lunch. One day I gave my friend
a punch.

My friend and I used to play soccer, and
I'd cheat, but he wouldn't care because I
always got beat.

My friend and I used to fly our kites,
and we used to stay outside late on hot summer
nights.

My friend and I can't do any of that
anymore, because we live far from each
other's back door.

I know no matter how far we grow apart
we will stay friends forever, and no one will
come between us. Because we are attached
within the heart.

Chelsea Morgan

"A Sister's Love"

I never knew how great a love could be
Until I came close to losing you
We were more than sisters, the best of friends,
We had no secrets
We beamed with laughter
We had a special kind of love that only few
possess, God gave us his all!
We bonded together from the beginning
There's always that special smile when we
greet each other
I pray I never lose sight of how wonderful
And blessed I am, to have a sister like you.
I almost lost your love but God gave me
the courage and the faith to forgive!
I love her so, my sister, my friend!

Catherine Blevins

The Graceful Goose

Ere the grey dawn broke through
up from the reedy waters they flew,
so graceful in their formation
honking and quacking to their destination,
of fields of golden grain and corn
shortly after they were shorn.
Soaring along in their vees
they'd alight once past the trees,
for a hearty breakfast of golden grain
where they dined again and again.
But today this was not to be,
for hidden below they did not see
the eager hunters lying in wait
for the hungry geese to take the bait.
Slowly they began descending
unaware their lives would be ending
bang-bang-bang and the lead did fly.
So many fliers fell from the sky
the graceful goose lay in a heap
cleared from the air in one foul sweep.

John Scott

Boulder Hike At Joshua Tree, California

Grandpa climbed like a mountain goat. He charged
Up the steep, rugged, stone trail without a
Detour, misstep or rest for unsteady,
Untried grandsons who grumbled far behind.

"Are we men or mice!" He roared them on with
Sips of water and irascible advice.
"To the top!" bellowed Granddad, with robust
Energy they stretched to match steadfastly

They were five and six and followed gamely
Up, up sand-slick rocks and loaf-brown boulders
Until, the summit!
Below them, unfurled, a
Dizzy checkered world,
Their victory, and

Grandpa napping in
The shade of a tree.
Jeannie Van Orden

Like A Bird With One Wing

As I sit patiently in the forbidden corner
  Upon a wooden floor covered with fear
The anxiety that fills the chilled air
  I only imagine what is creeping near

I grip a tight hold to many dreams
  For when dreams vanish to die
Life grows smaller like a bird with one wing
  Striving to take off to fly

My book I hold lies in my palms
  My eyes are grey as around the room I glance
I dream I hear an empty person's voice
  Unknowing the identity of emotional dance

As I long to stand I look out to see a silhouette
  For I am trapped and painfully cannot move
Like the bird with one wing I have no feet
  And my many dreams dance alone so smooth

I must lie down to block the pain. I ask the darkness to hide me
  Or the moon's glare outside to turn to dark so true
The wooden floor creaking - it's my many dreams creeping near
  Light and dark and in between is the same to you.
Angela M. Rohling

Healed

During the night of day
Under the darkness of the sun
I listen to cries for help
Pleas for pity
Lamentations of sorrow

My heart goes out to them
Touch, heal
Heal, touch

To feed them with the milk of His Spirit
To heal them with the touch of His Spirit

His Spirit, my spirit
We are one

We are healed
Diane M. Petrucci

Stolen Dream And Dead Roses

Dreams of the future dance into the night.
Upon rose petals, words etched forever.
Bathing in the warmth of love's light.
Roses with stems, no mortal can sever.

Musing unwritten songs not yet sung.
Far fetched fantasies slowly becoming reality.
Never imagining not being young.
Creating another dream, someday to be.

Grasping clouds and drifting about.
Sliding down rainbows to their end.
Loving without reservation or doubt.
Journeying down roads without a bend.

Suddenly a shadow darkens the way.
Dreams become murky and begin to disappear.
The rose petals begin to wither away.
The end of the path, it's oh so near.

Dreams are stolen and tossed upon an empty sea.
The silence is deafening as the casket closes.
Tears longing for what will never be.
A path now littered with dead roses.
Gary H. Long

Your Family

Family . . . your family, that was important to you. For mom and us kids, there was nothing that you wouldn't do. I know that having five kids wasn't easy, but we thank god for a dad who wasn't easily intimidated, or queasy. Never once did you leave us because times got rough. That act alone, taught us that we can make it when things get tough. If you had to, you would have sold your shoes, even the shirt off your back, if it meant taking up some of the monetary slack. Maybe we didn't have a lot of money, but the love from you and Mom was like pure gold and honey. Most of the time you were quiet, you had a heart of gold, your deep love for us untold. You showed us your love in your ways and actions; Bit by bit, fraction by fraction. You taught us to always stick together, no matter what the circumstance, no matter what the weather. From you and Mom, many things we did learn — the most important was to be kind, honest and firm. And even though life isn't always fair, when times are difficult and hard, the Good Lord and Family will be there. Dad, as I write this, I realize that you are leaving us to go back to heaven from whence you came. This is the hardest thing I've had to do. Preparing for the day that we lose you. I try to keep the thought in my head that we'll all see you again!! Standing at the gates of Heaven with a big grin. Family . . . your family, we were very important to you.

Debi Culpepper-Peters

"Paradise Treasure"

I thank you for your friendship so kind and true,
Valued so highly like a treasured jewel.
The warmth of your smile has a golden touch,
I adore your gentleness oh so very much.
You like to give the very best you can,
Unique characteristics in such a handsome man.
You fill my head with ideas of elegant charm,
And you protect me safely from all hurt or harm.
You are such a challenge in all you do,
And you are so mysterious but wonderful too.
Much more may I say just to brighten the day,
Keep being yourself in that special loving way.
So darling, may you keep being loved and richly blessed,
For you are the Lord's child and one of the very best.
Connie Lynn Stafford

Our Neighborhood

Scattered shots shatter our peace yet again
wailing of children and siren fill our air once more
our fragrance is smoke and powder
we paddle through our blood

It was Tisane today
she was two, a victim of a stray arrow
from the quivers of a boiling heart
It was no lotto odd, it could have been Dan, Grad or Lashonda

Our undeclared war rages on
high on intensity and fury
low on purpose and reason
power is our currency here.

Ernest Izedonmwen

A Dream Of The Past

She is Quiet, she is lonely.
Waking to the new day brings her no Joy.
Every morning she dresses slowly.
Taking great care in her choice of garb.
Feeling lost in a world of all her own.
Insecurity and sadness living in her heart.
Walking as if drugged, she spots her chair.
Placing it in front of the roaring fire.
She sits herself down, and waits.
For what, she is uncertain.
Maybe a spark, maybe a vision.
But to herself, she knows she is lying.
A best friend a lover.
Someone to give all her love and affection to.
This is what she needs, has to do.
But all of a sudden feelings of guilt overwhelm her.
For she can never forget his face.
She remembers happier days, when they would walk hand in hand
And once again she realizes no one could ever take his place.
So forever in time she will sit by the fire. Remembering his smiling face.

Jody Krieger

Autumnal Rhapsody

White cloud puffs scamper 'mid blue skies.
wand-like, branches scatter brightly-colored leaf clusters,
leaf after leaf tripping lightly to its own melody.
black-birds whirl in playful swirls,
in flight on crisp wind-gusts.
summer's heat is dim'd.
snow clouds crest a far-off ridge,
ever inching, eager to shower their dazzling crystals
And silently embrace this autumnal rhapsody.

John P. McCarthy

For My Son . . .

In the Spring, a baby boy, so precious and small
Was born with a destiny to grow strong and tall,
To be wise and loving and a joy from the start -
With a zest for life pulsing in his heart.
This baby was truly a dream come true!
Such a long awaited gift in blue.

The years have flown by like birds on a wing,
But joys and memories each one did bring.
Oh, how many times did I want to stop Father Time?
Just to savor a day, an hour, or minutes sublime!

My baby grew up too fast to suit me,
But what a wonderful young man he's grown to be!
I count not his years by twenty and four -
His understanding and maturity indicate more.
Talented, patient, positive, happy and fun,
He's been a treasure rare - a one-of-a-kind son!

Helen Mackey

Kristopher

Tell me the secret of how you were made
Was it six months of sun shine?
Three months of shade?

How did God make those sweet little hands?
To think that he did this without rubber bands!
No zippers, no buttons to push in or pull out
He made you so beautiful and that's without doubt.

Oh Kristopher, Kristopher, you are a real dream
And grandma just wonders where God put the seams.

Joan H. Sexton

"My Mother's Smile"

The most beautiful smile in all the world
Was mine alone to see
It was the smile on Mother's face
And was given so lovingly.
Her tears of love shone proudly thru
The depths of her soul brown eyes
And the silent message of her heart and soul,
Shown thru the tired and weary lines.
The cares of life fade fast away
As the time of life runs out
And to all of us who take time to see
The love and the peace her soul imparts
will always keep
"The most beautiful smile in all the world"
Close and deep within our hearts

Helen Cole

Just One Step At A Time

The Grandma of the five year old child
Was mostly confined to her bedroom and her
Walker now.

But every morning, she would rouse herself
To coach and encourage her five year old
Granddaughter to the school bus out front.

Telling the five year old — who always seemed
To have a whiff of Colgate toothpaste about her —
To hold the railing steady.   Then proceed:

"Just one step at a time, child . . . "
"Just one step at a time . . . "
"Just one step at a time . . . "

Then after waving her goodbye, would shut the
Squeaky screen door and return to her bedroom,
With the help of her walker:

Just one step at a time . . .
Just one step at a time . . .
Just one step at a time . . .

David R. Lewis

"Love's Illusion"

She's gone, yet I see her face . . .
Was she here? There is no trace . . .
The mood, the theme, this wretched, rented bungalow . . .
I think we kissed, her freshness fair . . .
I think we loved . . . explosions there . . .
I think that she's in love with me . . .
Yet, could it be, that
My desire for her exceeds reality . . .
She's not here now, was she ever . . .
Could this also be . . .
life's game on me . . .?

James E. Wilson III

Stop Look And Listen

Did you ever stop and look up at the tree?
Watch the leaves swaying in the wind
See the water cascading over steep rocky mountains
Why don't you take time to stop for a minute?
Look at the colors of flowers and shapes aren't they beautiful?
The colors can never be reproduced
Were always in a hurry
How about the beautiful colorful, and varieties of butterflies?
Now we're getting somewhere I hope
Have you ever watched a bird feeding it's young?
An American flag waving in the breeze,
to tell us we're still free
We take everything for granted
Suppose we saw a tree with no leaves
Not a sound of birds singing
How bleak everything would be
Take a walk through the woods slowly
Enjoy the miracles of nature, tend a wounded animal
Thank your lucky stars
We still have a place we call home
Alice Vendetto

The Woods

As I walked alone through the winter-killed woods;
Watching the red, yellow, and brown leaves
Falling gently into the clear, still water;
Seeing the squirrels running over the fallen
Tree to the other side of the stream;
I think — how peaceful and quiet it is,
How lucky people are, the miracle of life;
To hear the serenity of this place;
To see the beauty and splendor of just one piece of earth.
Bertie Shirley

Solitude

I built my prison and tightened the circle until my
waterfall became just drops. Secure, maybe too secure,
for now I can't break my very own bars I surround myself with.
Someone calls me, but I can't answer,
And yet the call grows louder with each new day.
Is there hope? Perhaps when the bars turn to rust.
Bradley Coyote Martens

Lady Of The Horses

She's free flowing like the sea,
waves of grass bringing life to the meadows.
She runs with her head held high,
her spirit of love is inside of me.
A whisper of the wind, a solemn sigh,
Lady of the horses, lady of the horses.

A flower of the sun,
a rebel in the night.
A wild spirit she runs,
her beauty's in my sight.
Her love is in my heart and soul,
Like a child, like a flower she grows,
Lady of the horses, lady of the horses.

A galaxy of the stars,
the rivers and the streams,
Songs of musical dreams.
Day break of a new morn',
a fireplace that's always warm.
Lady of the horses, lady of the horses.
Herbert L. Burd

Mollie

When she first came to my home Lord knows,
we didn't get along but as time went by our love grew
strong. And I guess what I'm trying to say is just that
   Mollie I'll never forget you Mollie I'll
always love you Mollie I'll never forget you and I know
you're in a better place now.
   Then that night it happened Mollie was out on the
streets again gambling with the devil not food or money
but her soul was on the line. And then it happened like
a flash of lightning she never knew what to expect she just froze
in fear and couldn't move, and I guess what I'm trying to
say is just that.

   Yes I know you're in a better place. And now for a question
that comes from the heart. Oh Hollie, oh Hollie will you please
take care of Mollie!
Jason Cannon

Just Who I Am

And to me they say "Who do you think you are?"
   "We don't understand you"

Who I am, A Strong Black Woman
A Goddess of Survival
A legend of envy for my Strength

Who I am, A Strong Black Women
A God fearing Woman
A Woman of Pride and Great demeanor

Who I am, A Strong Black Woman
Whom a many of my Caucasian brothers and sisters have
   refused to accept, because of my undying Strength
A Strong Black Woman, whom so many have envied my
   desire and will to Survive the Stream of hurdles that are
   Placed before me

Who I am, A Strong Black Woman
A Strong Black Woman that breathes Hope

Just Who I am,
A Strong Black Woman
Who is the Child of the King
and for this they don't understand
Brenda A. Fleming

Little One And Me

Though he was little and not of me.
We had a bond that little one and me.
He had a smile that melts the heart of one like me.
And though he's gone the little one from me.
I'll bet he melts the hearts of many he sees.
I know there's a place we will meet the little one and me.
For the Bible says there is a place for us to go the little one and me.
If only all could believe they could see the little
one and someday me.
David L. Funkhouser

Nature's Timepiece

The sentinels of the cornfield march stark and tall
   Weary, having given up their precious bounties
To the lusty, steaming hordes of Summer.

   Autumn's gusting winds stir up whispers
Among the battered, staggering columns
   And drive the vibrant plumage from retiring trees.

Ever shortening days create pause for reflection
   As all around the denizens of Nature
Prepare for Winter's peaceful slumber
   And blissfully await the promise of Spring.
Ann Robbins

"Awaken Beloved Mine"

We have watched many suns rise in the sky.
We have walked many moons, you and I.
Yet you lie very still while asleep, with the enemy's
knife buried deep. The blood from your breast still flows.
Now your hands have become very cold.
   "Awaken Beloved Mine"
The enemy is to close behind,
Heart of my heart, I do not wish us to part.
Soul of my soul, it was written we grow old.
Spirit of my spirit, life will be meaningless
without you in it.
   "Awaken Beloved Mine"
Before we run out of time.
Hear me my woman, obey my command.
Return to me Morning Star, to our sacred land.

For I, Black Eagle, promise not to walk these dry
lands alone.
Awaken beloved, we must journey home.
Either life together, or as one spirit asleep.
   "Awaken Beloved Mine"
or my promise I'll keep.
    Eva Tsoukalas

"Clifton"

Rain fell heavy, hard, and fast
  We knew the walls would never last.
With warning we let people know
  Away from their homes they must go.
Many stood watching, they couldn't believe,
  As the river its normal channel did leave.
Forced from their homes by the raging flood
  They ran from the water, debris, and mud.
The water took its destructive toll
  O'er the homes and business it did roll.
Twice we could only watch and pray
  While the river's force o'er our town lay.
When finally the water did recede
  Many were homeless and lost in need.
Faced with loss and showing their grief
  All looked to any who could give relief.
Though many possessions and homes were lost
  Not one human life did that river cost.
    Cheryl E. Warren Williams

It's Just Wrong

It's just wrong . . . I don't get to see you
we made the choice . . . but can I hear your voice
why are they blocking me . . . I don't have to see
but I'd like to hear . . . that would be nice
frustrations coming near . . . is it worth the price
probably depending . . . on emotions not sending
from me to you . . . I can't get through
feelings stuck here
It's just wrong
It's just wrong

It's not right . . . do you get to see me
it was our idea . . . but now what do you hear
are they asking why . . . straining eyes can't cry
blocking ears can't hear . . . so I'm at a loss
I'm all alone here . . . the distance lines are crossed
desired communication . . . discussing something's my mission
impossible apparently . . . you can't stare at me
or even glance at me
It's just wrong
It's just wrong
    Joshua Tiner

Remember

Remember those days,
We played in our yard . . .
Admired the moon,
Even though it was noon . . .
We did lots of things,
Went many places . . .
Sang silly songs,
And made funny faces . . .

Remember our walks,
Or rides, to the park.
We would stay all day until it was dark . . .
Sometimes a swim,
And you with that GRIN . . .
Wasn't it fun, chasing the sun . . .
Ending up home,
In time to meet Daddy . . .

Soon it was bedtime,
I'd tuck you in tight . . .
Read you a story,
And kiss you Good Night . . . Remember . . .
    Diane A. Emmett

Grampy

As I know you
Wearily
You get out of your magical sleep
You put on your usual smile
Happy to breathe the morning air
Your freckled smile grows and grows
As I know you
You put on the socks that are as white fluffy as the clouds
Smiling with delight
Humming a special old tune
As you make your delicious morning coffee
As I know you
You sit down in a chair
You sip your coffee and you are overjoyed
You have as much freedom as a butterfly
And feel as marvelous as a peacock
After you take your final sip
You go out the blushing red door
Knowing the excitement will come again tomorrow
As I know you Grampy
    John Hoysgaard

To Rebuild An Old Man's Dream

He was ninety-five years old and could still drive his car.
We rented a house that was in his front yard.

"Your husband does repairs?" He asked me one day.
"My beach cabin needs some work and I'm willing to pay!"

We drove him to the ocean as he told us of his plan
To have his friends come once again to his house built on the sand.

My husband worked both day and night, though the cabin leaned;
While a skeptic neighbor watched and ridiculed, jealous, it seemed.

"The first high tide will knock it down," the neighbor prophesied.
Unknown to us, this neighbor was ill, and soon would die.

The cabin work was finished and the smile on the old man's face
Was worth the toil and labor, no skeptic could erase.

The neighbor died, the winter tide came rolling from the sea.
The cabin fell and water washed away the memories.

We never saw the old man again, we had to move away.
We've heard that he still drives his car and mows the lawn each day.

Some say that he was foolish to invest in such a scheme,
But I answer, who can judge the price to rebuild an old man's dream?
    Carol Aiken

Untitled

If I could be king and hold the world in my hand
We'd walk arm in arm throughout my land.
By lakes an by streams to mountains so tall
and down by the sea where the seagulls call
Call out a song about love wild and free
as intense as the waves as they wash up a key
The key to my heart which can only be turned
by the eyes of my lover and their fire that burns
As bright as the stars in the heavens above
as pure as the heart of a lone white dove
whose feather as soft as my dear angels lips
as smooth as her curves, as sleek as her lips
my mind wanders back to nights spent alone
walking the beach where the pale moonlight shone
On a friends borrowed car and a blanket of green
A more perfect love has never been seen.

Brian W. McCall

Rural American Homemaker

Why do I grocery shop the way that I do?
Well, mother, I'm becoming more like you
As you were in the home in which I grew.
You never made a trip to the store
For a loaf of bread and little more.
Ten miles was too far away
To waste a trip "uptown" on a busy day.

So you made do, as I do now
With a weekly shopping trip, list in hand,
And I, with stores nearby,
Shop as if I still lived in that long ago home
Of happiness, laughter, and plentiful meals,
Where nothing seemed to run out
And meals were the gathering place to talk things out
In the home in which I grew.

You, Mother, gracious hostess, accomplished cook,
Nurtured all of us with the skills you knew.
Now I, who inherited your favorite cookbook
Prepare meals planned with love and served with pride,
Remembering the lessons of my long ago caring guide.

Joan Grantham Behmer

"Your Only Friend"

You loved drugs because they made you high.
Well, seeing you that way made me cry.
You took drugs in the morning, noon and night.
You never knew your left from your right.
You forgot all about me, but I was there.
I was the only one who really did care.
When you ran away, I searched for you.
When I could not find you, I felt so blue.
Your mother called me after she got the news.
You overdosed on drugs and booze.
I warned you constantly until the end.
But you never listened to your only friend.

Cynthia Arias

Patience

Give your worries to the Lord,
  whatever they might be.
He changes heartache into joy;
  just wait on Him and see.
He works things out as He see fit,
  so hear what He has to say.
Let His will be done in your life,
  and trust Him every day.
Have faith the Lord will take control,
  no matter how troubled you may be.
Those problems that seem to weigh you down,
  Christ took to Calvary!!!

John L. Wright

Teenage Run-Away

I lifted high Leanna and she held fast to me
We were on a sinking island
Above a rising sea

Cold the icy waters
But her body was so warm
If morning had come early
We'd have weathered that harsh storm
Of if I had been taller
Or stronger with my height
We could have lasted through 'till morning
And withstood that terrible night

The wave that finally took her
Didn't wet my hair at all
But she left with faith I'd held her
As high as I was tall

Edward L. Putman

Michele

You came into my life some five years ago.
We weren't best friends, we didn't know.
We grew up side-by-side.
I looked up to you, you didn't mind.
Will we spend the next few years as best friend?
We don't know it all depends.
When the diagnosis came in, we cried together.
We couldn't believe it, why can't we live forever?
When will you be taken away from me?
We don't know, we must wait and see.
I know whenever the time is here,
I will miss you and shed many tears.
Please don't leave so soon, when you do,
I will think of you and look towards the moon.

Amelia Lynn Simpson

Life: A Game Of Chance

We struggle, we work, our lives to enhance
  We win some, we lose some in this game of chance

When your body is aching from your head to your toes
  And you think of your horse that lost by a nose

"Poor me, poor me," you declare with a sigh
  "Life's not worth a penny, I should lay down and die"

You're still alive, whether nasty or nice
  And fortunes are won by a toss of the dice

The winners get up when they fall on their face
  It's the losers who cry that life's a disgrace

So when troubles befall you, take them in stride
  Forge straight ahead and don't step aside

Your past is behind you and leave it that way
  Looking back is taboo, tomorrow's your day

Face problems head on and you'll never fall
  Like a good hand in poker, the winner takes all

Climb up the ladder and reach for the stars
  Soar past the moon and head straight for Mars

Success and contentment go hand in glove
  And be especially kind to the people you love

June C. Dean

The Best Of Friends

I have a slew of sisters, we are the best of friends
We laugh together, we cry together and tell a joke or two
For we are the very best of friends and that's what sisters do

We know when one is happy, we know when one is blue
We are always there for one another, and that's what sisters do

We've shared together through times of loss and celebrated too
For we are the very best of friends and that's what sisters do

We can tell when one is hurting and even feel the pain
We can tell when one has prospered and even shared the gain
We can even fuss and argue and give our separate views
For we are the very best of friends and that's what sisters do

Bonnie Dues

Bright Light, Dark Light

Bright light, Dark light all throughout the world,
We're not the same? Don't make me hurl.
Bright light, Dark light in your own town,
Some people hate those who are brown.
Bright light, Dark light in your own house,
Parents are racists, but we're a mouse.
Bright light, Dark light why do you fight,
Let's group together to make one light.
One light, One light oh how you I love,
All are together, sent from Heaven up above.
One light, One light oh how you shine so bright,
Peacefully, peacefully through both day and night.
One light, One light isn't this better,
We can always stick together, Sister-to-Sister,
and Brother-to-Brother!

David Musacchio

A Child's Playground

Mama bridled, saddled and cinched the pony, for her three little
girls were off to play dollies down by the big muddy creek.
With Mama back to her chores, Judy hoisted little Denise into the
saddle, for she had to hold all the dollies, blankets and pots and
pans that rattle.

The minutes passed, but not very long, wide-eyed and shaking,
back came the pony with not a stitch on.
Here came Mama down the hill, past the water tank, across the creek
and in the mud she sank. As she rounded the bend the sight she saw
made her hair stand straight on end. Kathy, red-faced and yellow
curls flying, was mad as a wet hen, for the pony had run her over;
Judy frantically running first one way then another, wringing her
hands and crying big tears, then laughing hysterically for Denise was
astride the saddle in top of the big old buffalo berry bush clutching
all the dollies, blankets and pots and pans that rattle.

Mama dusted off Kathy, dried Judy's tears then gathered Denise who
was still astride the saddle in the big old buffalo berry bush
clutching all the dollies, blankets and pots and pans that rattle.

Next time we will check that darn old cinch so the pony won't lose his
saddle, Kathy won't get over and Denise won't be astride the saddle
in the big old buffalo berry bush, clutching all the dollies, blankets
and pots and pans that rattle.

Judy Jaramillo

Untitled

The Rose mist says to the dark shadow
what shall you do? The light shall make you dark.
The dark shadow replies . . . I can not help the way I look but
inside me
I'm as bright as the sun . . .

Autumn Amabisca

Untitled

Five years later we
were on the corner (by a vendor)
the street was Haight St.
caught up in the glitz of a single,
wrap-over earring we were
all turning our eyes clockwise, into
its silver. Instantly, my own sky lowered
and I glimpsed us in Clovis, CA, again, and history.

We had been absolutely ourselves; substitutes in lip
glosses, never going very far from who we were.
That one night in bathing suits, shiny as bottles
of wine coolers, chilled, sweating August in warm
moonlight. Draping towels out of the jacuzzi, fat as
we felt we all were, we had secretly been beautiful, so
soft-handed, dripping out with private thoughts
under the pressure of each hot blush and
so innocent.

Deborah Laney

Untitled

Love,
　　When asked to define it, I am speechless.
　　When asked to observe it, I am blind.
　　When asked to perceive it, I am ignorant.
　　When asked to show it, I am shy.
　　When asked to forget it, I can't.
　　When asked to embrace it, I try.

Jeffrey Lefleur

To My New Love

The many moments I have spent with thee
Were so joyful I've forgotten sadness.
I thank the Lord for sending you to me
For now I feel nothing but happiness.
You can be compared to a maiden fair
Because to me you are just as charming.
I love the touch of your beautiful hair
And your passionate kiss does my lips sting.
You are to me more than amicable
For you have treated me so very well.
Even your faults, to me, are beautiful
For love has blinded me and I can't tell.
My new love, I wish I was with you now
Because to love you always is my vow.

Jonathan B. Doyle

"Our Days Of Wine And Roses"

We found each other again! Isn't that wonderful.
What a pleasant surprise, we find ourselves attracted still.
When we talk it's a delight to my vivid imagination.
Your voice is always so sexy and so full of affection.
When we touch, it's a delight to my body from head to toe.
Your kisses are so sweet and passionate I never want to let you go.
Someday soon you and I will be alone in some secluded place.
We'll steal away, without leaving a trace
finally alone, we'll listen to romantic
music, eat strawberries, and sip wine.
At least for a little while, you'll be all mine
I'll kiss you all over, as we explore each other totally.
Then we'll make sweet passionate love
until it's time to return to reality.
In these "our days of wine and roses" we'll enjoy our precious
time together.
Wouldn't it be nice if they lasted forever.

Anna Addino

604

Forsaken

What is it that brings that tear to your eye?
What is it that makes you cry?
Is it the fact you are all alone
With no where to call your home?

This feeling you have in your heart
You just cannot explain;
The only thing you feel
Is loneliness and pain.
Your attempts to love and be loved
All seem to be in vain.

No one there to tell you not to fight,
No one there to tell you its all right.
Your head filled with . . . anger, torment, and fear.
Is that what brings your only tear?

You cry out for help
But there is no one to hear.
All you see is darkness,
All you know is fear.
As your vision becomes blurred
You cry . . . your lonely tear.

Julie Snyder

The Meaning Of Life

Do you ever wonder,
What is the meaning of life?
Why are we here?
I think the meaning is just not clear.
Think about it . . .
. . . We are born.
. . . We grow up and go to school.
. . . We graduate and go to work.
. . . We make money.
. . . We get married and start a family.
. . . The cycle begins again.
What is the meaning of this? Of life?
There are more hardships and sad times than there are happy ones.
Why do we subject ourselves to these?
The answer should be a breeze.
I just do not know what it is.
Do you? Does anyone?
Maybe this life is a part of a bigger one.
The master plan. Only one person knows for sure.
And He's not telling.

Joanne Bischofsberger

Where Is, What Is The Word?

Where is the WORD?
What is the WORD?
That can help me during my turmoil of the mind
Out of that whirlpool of concern, worry and trouble
About our world today
About our precious children and theirs
About the aging, wrinkling, withering body
  Is there a WORD?
  Is there a COMFORT?
  Is there a HOPE?
We went to the sunset
My friend and I
There IT was - another great marvel of life
Hanging low in all its radiance over the sea
They sky becoming changed into wondrous purples, pinks, and blues
That the vision makes me breathless with its beauty
And slowly, slowly the descent of the big ball of fire
Until that special moment of departure. The SUN SET!
I've found it! The WORD! The SUN! The SON! GOD.

Beth Stevenson

World Of Bliss

What would we be if we were clean?
What of our thoughts our desires?
Would there still be evil power?
Would there still be evil?

Would our hearts be cleansed from inequity?
Would our lustful throbs be pure of their prurient ways?
Would our bodies be of art instead of depictions of elicit bedded
  cravings?

If our souls spoke, would we hear holy words?
If our dreams were clear, could we then understand the meanings?
Will there be pain?
Will there be broken pieces?

What then would growth become?
Will we become weak in our sinless habitat?
Will we breed bad from good?
Will this world ever have the face of peace—of hope?
What will happen in the end?

Christine R. Miller

Tale Of Three: A Child, A Girl, And A Woman

There was once a woman and a little girl. The woman knew what she had to do to make her dreams come true, and the little girl kept wishing too because she knew not what to do. The woman wondered around for years and years trying to find herself and begin to live. Ah! but the little girl kept telling her, "You are not you today, you are me." But the woman still fought for her identity. Although she thought the little girl was right because sometimes she would visit her at night. Once she came to visit the woman and this is what she said, "No one loves you, get that through your head. You would be better off dead!" "You see this is not really me, just a body in a shell," said the woman, "You're looking, can you not tell?" "Oh!" said the little girl. I could not tell. You look as though you are well. I would have never been able to tell. Except you be me and I be thee. Where is the other of us that makes us three?" "Ah!" said the woman, "she will be here soon. I saw her this afternoon. She was smiling and feeling very much alive." "Oh," said the little girl, "I'm going away for awhile." "Good," said the woman, "I will miss you." "Oh no," said the little girl, "I will always be with you."

Jeanette Jackson Jones

Untitled

Pale moon, glooming in a lavish sky
What sort of future lies in thy
Vision; Art thou an evil eye
Of the Universe, seeing all bad and good
Or a mirror reflecting any inner mood?

Not weak - not wild, you shine your light
Illuminating coldest darkest night
Giving to man a second sight
Of past mistakes, of future good:
Man that was, or man that should -

Be pure. Fearless and of nature firm,
Knowing, but always eager to learn,
Willing to work, wanting to earn
His place in time, his future reward:
To be God's vessel, not broken shard

Oh! That not lunacy, but lunar sight
Is the force with which you flood the night
With thought for man to make him bright
Beaming with joy - having fortitude
To stay the course, as he rightly should.

Herbert A. Spies

All Alone

Sitting here looking and wondering
  what tomorrow may bring
It may bring sunshine or it may bring rain.
  It's not by our choice
But the choice of the master
  who holds the future in the palm of his hands.
  How sweet to know it belongs to him.
He's the man in the middle
  he can put it together like a riddle
He's an on time God
  He hold the ransom for the soul
Whatever the situation is
  he's a shelter in time of storm
A friend at a lonely time
  a company keeper in a midnight hour
A burden bearer just keep the faith
  look up, look around but don't
Look back and don't look down just
  remember he's walking beside you
And you're never walking alone.

    Doris Turner

Two Gods

Can you imagine
what two gods are capable of
worshipping each other
in compromised darkness
in ten cent city silence
on a mattress that owns no bed
can you dream it?
Oranges and butterflies on beams of eye socket light
electric throbs bouncing
in exposed copper threads
shades forced to dance along the crackled ghost walls
figures raised their fingertips to create beauty in the softness of their hands
see the eyelid flutter or muscle contract
this is it
this is the world
one room universe
just off the thoroughfare
this is the canvas
still liquid and dripping

    Adam Pagel

Valley Of Death

As I walk to the valley of the shadow of death
What will I feel?
  I will feel awe, I will sense knowledge.
  As I lay by the valley of the shadow of death
What will I feel?
  I will feel pain, I will feel anger.
  As I stand by the valley of the shadow of death
What will I feel?
  I sense sadness, I will feel fear.
  As I stand by the valley of the shadow of death
What will I feel? I sense sadness, I will feel fear.
  As I step in the valley of the shadow of death
What will I feel?
  I will sense darkness, I will sense plight.
  As I walk through the valley of the shadow of death
What will I feel?
  I will sense fear, I will know death.
  As I leave the valley of the shadow of death
What will I feel?
  I will feel knowledge, I will sense awe.

    Barbara Payton

To Kill A Cop

If you kill a cop
What will you gain?
A stain in the hand.

A mark which will
Cause additional pains,
and maybe more stains.

God miracle was wrought
on a book made of stone
Number six says,
"Thou shalt not kill".

We are all crying, "Love"!
We are all crying, "Peace"!
There is little Love and almost no Peace.

For we can see many battles
of hatred, jealousy, and prejudice prevail.
Up to this time they have completely derailed.
Do something to help and
live to have fewer regrets for
everyone suffers when you
You think of death.

    Jean E. Bradley

Psalm Of David

I am a man; my destiny is in my hands.
Whatever I shall have or be
Whatever I have been,
Is, was, and will be my own doing.

I could blame my failures on luck.
I could lay the fault at my neighbor's doorstep.
I could say that my wife or family influenced me.

I could thank God for my successes.
I could curse the Devil for my failures
But to do or say any of these
Is to brand myself a liar.

God has made me what I am,
And God granted our forefathers the foresight
To crystallize the American dream,
And thus blessed me with American freedom.
Beyond this His responsibility ends.

Mine is the task, chosen by intent
Or drifted into by default
To be or not to be
The man that God gave me the chance to be.

    David B. Russell

A Worried Lover

The worry of a lover,
When he never showed.

Her heart beating faster,
As time grew old.

Torture of waiting in a big dark house,
I'm a bed so big and alone.

Not knowing where her lover is,
Still sitting by the phone.

The hours go by will this ever end,
Will the story ever be told.

Finally he's home,
The story will now unfold.

Her happy heart skips a beat for him,
Then she runs to the door.

He said, "I'm sorry baby, please forgive me,
I will do this no more."

    David Perez

When Daddy Goes To War

Where is Daddy going Mom?
What's he leaving for?
Where does Daddy have to go, when Daddy goes to war?

You say he's gone to war Mom,
With other army men.
Will he be home for supper, so we can play again?

It's been a long, long time now,
Since I helped Daddy pack.
My birthday's almost here Mom,
Will he be coming back?

Daddy seldom writes us Mom,
And when he does you cry.
At night we say a prayer for him,
But you've never told me why.

You say he's fighting for us, and he'll be back again.
I wish he'd hurry and win his war,
Come home and tuck me in . . .

They sent a crate of Daddy's clothes,
All packed in bits of foam, and in another wooden box,
They sent my Daddy home.

Dana Dulohery

The Soldiers Game

We the damned pray for the day;
When all these memories pass away.
We who played the soldiers game!

Memories of a gallant and gentle man;
His children, his love, and his shedding of a tear,
For all their lives they lived in fear!

We came as freedom for this man, his children,
His love, and his land.
We who played the soldiers game!

With stars and stripes we came from the heartland,
Sea, and sky; to save them from their sworn enemy;
The V.C., then we became their enemy!

With leaps and bounds we pillaged; and burned;
We killed the fathers and the sons;
We who made him take a stand, for his freedom and his land.

Now after 10,000 days of tears and fear;
Destruction, pain, and death;
We their salvation, left them crying in the jungle rains.
No better now than when we came!
We who played the soldiers game!!!

Chester W. Carter Jr.

Life Is Strange

I sat thinking in a chair on my terrace one bright Sunday,
when all at once I saw a rabbit, a charming little rabbit he was.
He jumped about on the lawn, busy and bright like the dawn;
His tail was like a painting brush, his eyes were pink and full of
trust; Oh, what a joyful scene it was.

But all of a sudden there was a change, the clouds covered the sky with rage;
Thunder and lightening struck the fence, frightening Mr. Rabbit all at once.
I went inside and stood by the window,
And saw the alarmed Mr. Rabbit run for his burrow.
It rained heavily all day long and through the night,
And poor Mr. Rabbit I suppose was in a fright.

Early next morning it was bright and sunny,
looking through the window I felt a bit funny,
Mr. Rabbit's burrow was filled with water,
raindrops from the trees falling pitter-patter.

Alas! How cruel nature was, to the sinless Mr. Rabbit that he was.
But of one thing I was sure
That gentle Mr. Rabbit's soul was Pure.

Gangashree Somayajula

Sun Shine

The Lord is my sunshine
When I am down. I know he'll make a way
Whenever I pray. I know he'll answer someday
When I have to cry. I know he'll dry my eyes
When I fall, I know he'll pick me up

He's shining in my life everyday
When I stray, I know he'll help me find my way
When I have a question, I know he has the answer
When I am thirsty, he is my drink
When I am hungry, he is my food
When I am lonely, he is my friend
When I am sad, he is my joy
The Lord is my sunshine
When I am troubled, he is my peace of mind
He is my source of inspiration
Every day, all the time, he is my only sunshine

Joann Jordan

"Lost In Time"

I'm lost in the memory of a cherished time.
When all my children were entirely mine.

I see them smiling and awfully sweet.
Clothes that matched and terribly neat.

Hair was short and kind of cute;
Tan and playful, loving to boot.

Now these children are semi-grown;
Facing the world that they have blown.

Into the scene of the weed called grass . . .
Eyes are staring as if they were glass.

Minds are foggy, bodies are thin;
Where is the answer for me to win?

God grant me the patience not to breakdown;
For my heart is aching, I'm terribly letdown.

Genevieve O'Boyle

Sharing (The Burden Bearer)

On my way home late one night, I was walking a lonely road,
when I came upon a man who asked, "Will you help me carry my load?"
With his shoulders slumped, his back curved down, he had sweat upon his brow,
his breath was short and labored; would he make it? I didn't know how.

He looked at me with saddened eyes as he managed to force a smile,
but the weariness of his soul shone through, he couldn't make it another mile.
Could I afford to lend a hand to him since my load was heavy too?
And who would help me carry mine? Who would see me through?

I decided after a little thought what I had no choice but say,
"I'll share your heavy load, dear sir," and then we were on our way.
We had rocky roads and rain storms and wind to travel through.
His way was the hardest I'd ever seen, but somehow we both made do.

When we finally made it to his destined place, the sunshine came out again.
The wind stopped, the rain ceased, as I was walking with a friend.
When I returned to where I had left my load placed neatly under a tree,
to my surprise nothing was there! Who had taken my burdens from me?

Jan Patterson

Morning Time

Early in the morning I find a quiet time
When I can think, ponder, and even write a rhyme
I listen to the birds their songs to sing
And love to hear their music upon my ears to ring
They are so free without a care
As they flitter about in a pair.
The air is so refreshing, cool, and still
Early morning is a time to ponder God's will
And to enjoy the wonders of the land
It is a good time to seek the guidance of His hand.
I do enjoy the quiet and peace that I find
In the early morning stillness I can refresh my mind
And prepare myself for the trials of the day
That I know will surely come my way.
I watch the sun as it begins to rise
And I enjoy this time of mine as I surmise
All the beauty spread out before me.
It is a wondrous gift and it is all free.
Early morning is a wondrous time to see.

George William Ray Jr.

"Still"

You may wonder, what had been of me, since the belligerent instant,
when I decide to leave, with the old and timorous birds that migrates
to the sun? If my passion has died, as most promises of love?
Still confounding my ill lack of faith, with the grief and the tears
that covered my face, and with those many questions, you'll concluded,
and thus think, I'd forgotten your kiss and unique mien of being.
That it's not really worth, to recall all those chapters of love,
which together, we'd lived. Today, as before, I'm still the same . . .
a lost sheep, a little bit older . . . not yet free of sins.
As I abandoned myself to the falling rain, I felt the absence of your
kiss, but the light drizzle gave me a richness, that your touch and
your kiss, never did. Between sand and seashells, I'd become a
faithful lover my own way, and indulge the legacy of a smile, a
briskly breeze left behind one day.
Here I depend upon oneself . . . no fear, no haste. Something to notice?
My smile, I believe it's changed.
Throughout winter, near the sea, I'd found a friend and some bread to
eat. I got my guitar and a daughter . . . have no need for deceive.
Although much happiness and joy, I still think of your love.

Avilio Milton Espinoza

Directions Home

I never understood it,
when I heard somebody say.
I need to go and find myself, it seems I've lost my way.

So they change all their surroundings,
find a crowd that's fun and fast.
But is that really searching,
or just running from the past.

I can only speculate, what thoughts go through their mind.
What they think their looking for,
and what they hope to find.

As for you my bright companion,
I know where the answer lies.
Its not on a far off island, with big clouds and bluer skies.

It's in the faces of your children,
and the people that you've touched.
Those of us that know you, and care for you so much.

Now keep these words of wisdom,
forever in your mind.
So when you get that urge to search,
you know just what you'll find.

Chris Young

My Love

My parents don't believe me,
When I say that, I'm in love.
They say, "How crazy can she be?"
But believe it or not, I'm in love.

My best friend thinks I'm silly,
Because she knows that, I'm in love.
She's just jealous, she's stuck with Willie,
But I'm not silly, I'm in love.

Why is it everyone has something to say,
About Ed and me, because I'm in love?
Some make jokes, "Maybe you'll be married in May!"
Say what you have to say, but I'm in love.

I love Ed with all my heart,
Mom must believe me, I'm in love.
When we're together I wish we wouldn't part,
Though we must, my heart still says, I'm in love.

Why must he live so far away?
Maybe its a test to see if truly, I'm in love.
I think of him each and every day,
No matter how far away he is, I'm in love.

Erin Patton

When I Think Of Nana

When I think of Nana, I see a big kettle of "fresh" popcorn.
When I think of Nana, I smell a batch of cookies being born.

When I think of Nana, I see friends and family from far and near,
Coming to Eva's "bed and breakfast"; it was open 'round the year.

O what a treat it was to stay at Portland's 8 Fisher Street.
With such fine food and company, a fancy hotel could not compete.

Such meals as shepherd's pie, baked beans, or walnut roast,
Our Nana loved her kitchen, of that we all can boast.

When I think of Nana, I think of Christmas drawing near.
Now where did she put that present, will she remember, Oh my, Oh dear!

Be it Christmas or Thanksgiving, her children always came.
But now 8 Fisher Street is quiet; it won't ever be the same.

When I think of Nana, I see a woman who loved her God.
And though she often went alone, her Christian pathway she did trod.

Playing the organ and piano was her Christian duty call,
And every week she gave her Lord, her hands, her heart, her all.

When I think of Nana, I see a resurrection morning.
I see the smiling face of Christ, as her crown He is adorning.

When I think of Nana, I see a woman that's been true.
When I think of Nana and heaven, I want to meet her there, don't YOU?

Bradley R. Tanguay

Child

On those days all I wish has gone away.
When I was a painter: my crayons spilled
melting together in the sun, painting everyone out.
When I was a baker: my pies smashed by bullies
returning to dirt, no longer edible.
When I was a student: my pink bubbles bursted
with papers bloodied, drenched in ink.
When I was a camper: my marshmallows caught fire
watched by shadows and bug bites on my arm.
When I was a fair go-er: the gum wrappers were empty
under the broken ferris wheel after I'd won no prize.
When I was a customer: my ice cream splattered
filming the pavement and the truck had just left.
Dirty fingernails with tears in-between:
this is sadness.

Briana M. Smith

Mother And Son

When I cried, you the loving remedy applied.
When I was afraid, you always close to me stayed.

When I was lost, you reached me no matter the cost.
When I suffered in pain, your prayers did me sustain.

In trials of teenage years only you calmed my fears.
My temptations took flight, sighting your great bastions height.

My confused life needs, you cleared with the holy beads.
The love of Christ in my heart, you gave it the start.

My birth, growth, destiny, you wrought from God on knee.
Tears, prayers, sacrifice, offered to God did suffice.

As mother of a priest, you overcame the beast.
And your vocation you performed with devotion.

My vocation from God you brought forth with a nod.
My dear Dad I did miss, you filled me with a kiss.

Higher still was your call as God asked from you all.
Son to mission He took and yourself you forsook.

In your twilight year, Jesus Christ was ever near.
Your son He sent to your side, in love to abide.

Your vocation fulfilled, He a just prize instilled.
With Spirit tender, took you in last surrender.

Howard Picard

A Gift From Heaven

Heaven used to be far away
    When John and I were young and gay.
We laughed and played
    and pledged our love.
While God was smiling from above.
    Then He sent a baby boy
To bless our home and bring us joy.
    He brightened the sunshine,
    He brought the flowers
    He enlivened our laughter,
        and enlightened the hours.
Heaven came a little nearer
    Our love with baby was now much dearer.
We dressed him up as cute as could be
    And took him walking for others to see.
We were so grateful and full of pride,
    Then God called and our little boy died.
Now Heaven is no longer far away
    We shall see it and our boy someday.

Alpha Lee Silvers-Day

Excuses

A state of depression that sees only the end
When reflecting and recalling evoke the begin.
And wondering when?
When circumstances turn—turn and do bend,
Until Evil encumbers and twist crisis within.
When Devils come out from caves and their den,
And, turn joyous occasions—strictly to sin.

One wonders if "circumstances" can ever win
When "excuses for bad" become the defend?
Sad innocence Souls just have to rend.

And weak ones are sought—"weak" only gives in.

God, when will your people just know how to share?
And, when will the excuses be not ours to bear?
Perhaps when the Evil just learns how to care!
Perhaps then all circumstances will turn into fair!

Cynthia L. Bartz

Forever And Always

Our friendship was not yet perfected,
When suddenly everything changed.
I thought we'd be best friends forever,
We still might.
I'll love you forever and always . . .
That's what the letter said.
I read it over and over, interpreting every word,
Looking, checking, making sure nothing was over looked,
I refused to believe that those words were meant for me.
I'll love you forever and always . . .
I wasn't ready to slow dance. I was still hung up in
Looking good, being popular. I wasn't ready to have a boyfriend.
Now I'm ready,
You're perfect in every way,
I'll love you forever and always . . .
He has big strong hands, but he's always gentle.
Not a macho jerk, not a snob, but someone to respect.
But now he's being taken away from me,
He can't stop, it's not his fault, he's moving.
I'll love you forever and always . . .

Connie Summers

Broken Records Of The Heart

Fast forward me back to fifty-eight
When that neon box played . . .
Single forty-fives, all the King's greats
Maltshop memories don't fade away

When did we run out of words to say
My old heart's starting to play . . .
    All shook up . . . everyday
    Memories of the mind are . . .
    Broken records of the heart . . .

At lover's point in that red Belair
While Memphis music touched the air
It was love me tender under neon stars
Later on, burning love that went too far . . .

When did the fire burn out too late
My ole heart's starting to play . . .
    Don't be cruel . . . every day
    Memories of the mind are . . .
        Broken records of the heart . . .

Joni Marie Trojacek

Tea at Three

Not every day, but most days
When the clock strikes three
Laundering, ironing, cooking, and cleaning stop,
The old water kettle is filled to the top;
Stove burner set for near full heat.

Anticipation sets in of what the day offers in treats,
Cheese and cracker were perfect for yesterday,
Baked apple with cinnamon for today,
Sunday we'll have the last two slices of cake . . .
A special gift from a dear old saint.

This is our time to share our minds wonderings.
We exchange philosophers of life, religion, weather,
Growing plants, old dogs, and other things.
There is joy in our hearts to have lived so long,
What determines such things we wonder aloud.

The conclusion is so clear, what took so long to see,
It's the tea of course, it's the tea.
The clock strikes four, tea time is over,
We agree to arrange our tomorrow
To be together again for our tear.

Dorothy McClelland

The Gift of Love

When death gets this close,
When the reality, the finality grips you so tightly,
When infinite time becomes finite, you can find more in each moment,
One day at a time is enough to deal with enough to enjoy.
I can't help thinking a lot, I can't turn it off . . .
How will it be — not to be?
I'll miss the music, but there is a peace in the silence.
I'll no longer open my eyes to see the sun, the trees my beloved earth
But the love I leave, and the earth, will remain.
I will not think, or feel, or sense,
But there is healing in leaving the ills of the body behind.
Has my life been just a chance set of circumstances,
Or is this divine passage to a new adventure just beginning?
Yet, if it is God's will that my life continue, may I help in the
healing, cherish each day to live and love to the fullest.
I pray that I never forget the changes I've made.
The power drawn from this adversity,
The appreciation of the fragile gift of life,
The miraculous powers we have within us,
The ability to enjoy the present, friends, family, the earth —
   The gift of love.
   David E. Transue

Peggy Ann Burnett 1954 - 1993

Some nights I just live in memories
When the solitude is all I own
I try reliving all of our love
Now that I'm all alone

I ask myself when times are tough
How would she help me thru this
And I have all those beautiful memories
Of all of the things I miss

Sometimes I draw on her courage
Other times it might be her strength
But mostly I dwell on her love for me
That she always gave at great length

God, I wish our time could have been longer
I wanted all of our dreams to come true
But now at night when I go to bed
I just whisper, "Peg I still love you"

   Glen D. Burnett Jr.

Comfort

There comes a time for both young and old,
When their life's story shall unfold.
May your grandfather's story live among his offsprings.
Take it! Learn from it! Unto it cling.
As head of his family he shall be missed,
But God tells of a far better place than this;
One where love and tranquility brighten the way.
Eternal life is the gift he claims today!
So don't you all mourn too much;
Your grandfather is satisfied as such.
One day the bell will toll for you.
Will you be ready when your soul is due?
This man was ready, God's own seed.
He knew what awaited a man who believed.
Learn well what your grandfather knew, my friends
Death is where life ultimately begins!
So be happy for him! Don't shed one tear!
Unless you're shedding it for those left here.

   Candace M. Moorer

Trust

Trust is asking of the Lord in a prayer;
when we believe with all of our heart,
we know that trust is there.

Trust is like tranquility;
to live each moment as our last,
without worrying about tomorrow,
or the todays gone past.

Trust is being fearless while walking through the night,
like a feeling of security when living by the light.

Trust is giving authority to those who stand to lead,
bringing Peace, Hope and Courage to those who are in need.

Trust is knowing that our Lord and Savior is near,
it's a feeling of protection
and brings comfort to those who fear.

Trust is an unquestionable belief;
it does not lie.
It's our assurance of victory before we die.

Trust is an act of Faith;
by Faith we cannot doubt.
Being able to say, "I love you", that's what trust is all about.

   Amy L. Peck

"Contemplation Of You"

For Alison
When I walk away from here,
(When) Will I see you again?
If you're really here, will you be here again?

Have you come as an angel?
Like a dream in the night?
Will you be my savior?
Will you be my light?

But I'm all alone in my despairing season,
Loving you would give a reason,
For my heart to keep on beating,
And keep my dampened soul from leaving.

When we go our separate ways,
Will you look back at me?
You'll see a man that's been changed,
You'll see a man whose soul is free.

But if I walk away from here,
Then will I see you again?
And if I come in search of you,
Will we ever meet again?

Last night I dreamt I held you in my arms . . . and nothing hurt.
   Aaron Leis

"Skyler"

Where have you gone my baby,
Where have you gone tonight,
Alive in the womb, yet only a soul lies in the tomb
too precious for - even your mother's sight.
A ghost in my arms, an eternal flame in my heart,
I can hold you and love you even though we're world's apart.
Not fit for each other,
yet never replaceable with another,
Skyler, never forget you'll always have a mother.
Who loves you and cares for you and will never deny,
along with your soul my heart did die.
   April Bonaroti

The White Mountain

I've been to the top of the white mountain
where cold beauty tickles blindness in weary eyes.
Where shadows fall far below and the radiant sun
highlights even the oxygen that flirts with my dry lips.

I've been there, where the subalpine fir fears to hang her evergreen
skirts, where mountain ivy has failed to climb.
I've been to the top of the white mountain and I must say;
I prefer the lowness of the valley,
for in the shadows of the lodgepole and the cotton wood
foxtail grass cradles fireweed,
and the roots of nature struggle for reciprocity in morality.
It is here in the darkness, the beauty of the timid
and the shy brush lips with those of the superior,
and crystal water flows
like love from a child's heart.

I've returned to the valley floor,
and all I have to say;
I've been to the top of the white mountain.

Dale Woolwine

"Broken Night"

Was there a time
where death was not a crime
and life became what you choose it

Through the nights of midnight rage
and to a performance of a blank stage
hope is gone from the heart of good
death is among as well stood

From this ruble some lucky will arise
to start a new generation of different domain
to fall even further into the sea
to you my friend I say be free

Fungus cloud of napalm death
history remains as we stow it
minds of time have solved the rhyme
and the world won't end as we know it

Friends of future passion fly
up the golden stairs will climb
wings of silver heart of gold
to this world already sold

Chris Gardner

Grandpa

I have been through so much, fearing one man's powerful touch.
Where ever I went he was also there, following me everywhere.

He was always in my thoughts, reminded of what he has taught.
Given values that are unsurpassed,
  instilled knowledge that will forever last.

Off to the mountains to fish in the lake, or to barbecue a steak.
Trying out a brand-new sled, his blood in me will be forever bred.

Playing catch at the park, running lakes in the dark.
Working on our art, thinking nothing would tear us apart.

Is what I did good enough, always being ever so tough.
Being his first grandson he expected a lot of me,
to live and to do things the way he thought they should be.

Finding his weak spot, told him I'm leaving, I'd miss him a lot.
told to do things the way he thought they should be.

Years have now gone by, I'm standing here wondering why.
taught me to fight my fears, distanced for his hardest years.

I can't give to him what he gave to me, but it's here for my family.
My only goal is that he live through myself,
for Grandpa's life shall not be put on the shelf.

Curtis Haines

The Yesterday Drums

There is a place
(Where I come from, where I dream of, where I'm going to)
Where regret never crawls in the shadow of the wind
Where a backwards thought is a backward step
And there is no road behind
There is a place
(Where the sun only rises, where I dream of, where I'm going to)
Where the eyes wash the clothes of the soul and the mind
Where tomorrow comes before it's here
And the yesterday drums have yet to sound

Dawn Ann Mudie

Tale Of An Immigrant

For many nights my dreams were of the country
where I had spent my early youth, and my heart ached
when silently I woke and could not stop the tears that
flowed from my sadness,

Why did I not see the beautiful hills, the lovely towns,
the winding roads along the river, the fields of corn that stretch
for a mile, the red painted house and barns of the farm?
My eyes were dimmed with tears, my heart longed for the home I left.

It was so strange to see no people walking by, or some who would pass,
and smile and say "hello".
Only car after car rushed down the street, tin cans with no faces,
my heart felt pain and lonely - and I cried inside.

Some years have gone but still the faint pain lingers on,
it was almost grown quiet now.
And more people come to start anew in this blessed land. I understand
them now, those who do not want to change and cling on to the past.

But this is a different country with people who do care, and join
to build this nation to have peace for all.
I love this land, it has grown dear to me,
it is my country now - it is my home.

Hermine Corpaci

Star Track

Stars be our light, for the night is long,
Where one goes right, six may turn to wrong,
Yet one sparking ray o'er all the clouds
May clear the way, and guide a crowd.

God's Saints have long since passed,
Across the hills and streams; steep ways like glass,
Their glow at night like candles shed
Their beams, and light us on our way ahead.

They are our rampant pillar-fires,
The prospect of God's City's shining spires,
Those sword-like gleams still keep us free from sin,
And just as surely, they will lead us in.

Andy Marshall

Reborn

In the middle of my desert, there is an Oasis where I go,
when bombarded by the everlasting spray of hostile, arid sand.
Upon my knees I creep, always keeping my head high,
never conceding to the devastation that surrounds me.
Reaching the Oasis, I lift my eyes to God in thanks, once again
I have reached the comfort of the cool revitalizing waters,
and rest in the shade from the heat that would engulf my soul.
Refreshed, again I start my journey into the vast parched future,
counting my blessings and awaiting the day when my thirst will be
quenched for eternity.
The day I am reborn into the heavens with my Lord.

Betty Bronske

Mystery Of A Dream

Where tall century elms oversee the fields,
Where summer-clover its deep garnet yields -
There honey-bees toil through sunny hours,
And thistles grace their amethyst flowers.

Where the bobolinks chime notes all day long,
Where vermilion twilight lulls a quail's song -
There a pair albino deer came to graze,
While sunset surrendered to evening's haze.

In misty gown I reached out to impart,
These guests who inspired my hand and heart -
T'was I in quandary to choose only one,
Or for the future-winters shelter none?

All too soon my two deer were out of sight,
As I awoke this sequel of a night -
May now forever live on what might seem,
But an enchanted mystery of a dream.

Helen Jo Brew

Cul-de-Sac

The cul-de-sac where I grew up was a dead end street.
Where the bread man's horse would take a p*** . . .
Each day . . .
From June 'til May.
As poplar tree branches sway.
Now, I, an old man, relieve . . . that way.

While eating grapes from the neighbor's vine, and
Watching the neighbor's wife's bath time . . .
A Peter Gowland magazine . . .
Freshly sliced peaches on
Vanilla ice cream.

Charles Prostak

Symphony Of An Unknown Century

The man lights a secluded country town,
where the crickets perform a spring symphony.
Calling.
A little girl's destiny.

Louder than the cotton fields
or a drunk, violent husband.
Higher than the stills
in the Carolina backwoods.

Journeys through decades,
with nightmares longer than years.
Empires fall, and was wage on,
children cry as their families die.

And she stands tall and proud
"Tomorrow" is a better place it be.
Granting a peaceful century ahead
by a battered century behind.

And street lamps light a crowded city block,
where the crickets perform amid winter silence.
Recounting.
An old woman's story.

Alex Hunsucker

Ties Which Bind The Heart

When does an acquaintance become a friend?
Who whispers in my heart that you're God send?
What are the ties which bind the heart
To make a friend a forever part?
How does one touch the core of my being,
While others see, but without really seeing?
A real friend is much more precious than the purest gold,
And the beauty of that rare gem is awesome to behold.

Brenda McKee

Untitled

I belong to the misty isle
where the wind and rain bring me alive.
I belong to the northern shore
where the grey Atlantic swell.
Pounds against the cliff
where rocky tor, looks out on sweeping moor.

I belong to the sound,
of the seabirds in restless flight in
the land of the lingering midnight light,
I belong to the land where stonehenge sits.
Where ancient history and countryside mix.

I belong to the land so deep in soul
I belong to the hedgerows
dripping with rain
I belong to the Celtic
and Druids flow.

Joe Marchant

Surf

Tide pulls the waves ashore,
  Where they pause, recede,
  And rush again to meet,
Clashing with, and mingling with, the ones before.

Footprints fade, softly,
  Smoothed by ghostly unseen watr'y hands.
  Children playing where the water disappears,
The wet sands giving up their glow,
  Make prints again;
Where do footprints and water go?
  — Prints and water go?

When the sunset colors spread,
  and darkness slowly overwhelms the red,
Wait! The nightfall only covers shore,
  And tide returns to sea to rest,
  —rest;

And sunrise tints returning surf,
  And sky, once more.

Albert C. Reed

My Church

My church is a learning institution,
where we take our problems to get the solutions.

My church has a man who preaches to save life,
he is saved, sanctified and married to one wife.

My church teaches me what is right,
because there is no place to hide from God sight.

My church is where I found love,
the love that I am talking about comes from above.

My church is not a supermarket nor a bingo hall,
our church has a God who is waiting for your call.

My church is here for you and me,
a place where every sinner should be.

My church is located in a big city,
where drugs, crime and killing is very high
and the ones behind it has no pity.

My church is where I got set free,
every day I pray and thank thee.
For my church

Doris Moon

A Prophet's Prayer

If only I had prayed enough, "God heal my family."
Whether I love them or not, they are just what I see.

So dear God, heal my broken heart, please teach me to forgive
My loving but controlling father, the way a good child should.

My mother is obedient, always pleasing as she goes
Seldom with any thoughts of self, handling the highs and lows.

A compassionate spouse came as answered prayer
Be careful what I pray for, you answer anywhere.

If only I had listened to my children's quiet cries
The silence was so painful, but I ignored them, then lied.

Forgot to mention my sister, Jesus, I wonder why?
She was seldom in my thoughts, I couldn't even cry.

Thank you for my struggles, I have an aunt in mind
She's brassy, too supportive, busy-bodied, but kind.

Oh Lord, you know my family much better than I do.
Yes, this was how I saw them, until you brought me through.

Now I'm a teachable being with an expectant heart
Because you made things new again, I praised you and did my part.

You ordained me a prophet, here I am, send me
To witness to the church, victorious and free. Amen.

Doris Haynes-Jamison

"Is It Not So?"

Do you not think that a tree
Which has lost it's leaves in the fall
And in now barren,

Is not better off than the barren tree
Which has never had leaves at all?

Do you not then believe that it is better
To have loved if but briefly,
Than never to have loved at all?

To feel a warm touch but for a moment
And then it is gone-
Is much better than never to have ever
Felt one.

To have felt the pain of lost love,
Is better than to never know love.

Is it not so?

Darline E. Lofton

"So Happy"

So happy I've gotten over you
which I never thought I would.
So happy that I just see you as a
friend and nothing more. And those
feelings the ones I had for you are gone
now and I know they will never
return for now I know better.
Maybe it wasn't love that I thought
I had for you because now I'm
moving on without you.
So happy that I met someone else,
someone I know who will care about me
more than you ever did or showed.
Someone I got to know more than I knew you
and someone I will have feelings for, feelings that
will be known to be true.
But for now I'm so happy that
we are only friends.

Blanca Garcia

ALWAYS

I promise-dear sweet mother,
while I am searching
your advice I will be following,

ALWAYS.

Meanwhile-I will be patiently waiting,
religiously praying,
until to God's altar I'll be coming.
my parent's blessing
dressed in white I will be honoring,

ALWAYS.

Praying-wishing—
my dreams I will be reaching,
to be his faithful wife- most deserving.
And finally, 'thanks to God' I will be giving,

ALWAYS.

Before "God" to love Him forever I will be vowing,
because another man like Him,
I never will be finding!

Celia Jasso Munoz

The Mirror

Roses are red and violets are blue.
While looking in the mirror my resemblance came true.
A sweet little smile from those glorious days,
A body pretty small, in all the right ways.
Beautiful hands and fingers so dear, we're so much a like,
I was frightened by the mirror!
For all of your years and mine of sixteen, we've been
Through a lot and however have changed.
For the good I hope and for many years to come,
The mirror tells a story about the life of a mom.
A mom of kindness and spirit of care,
You have seen me through many years.
Now starting to grow up, I've started thinking sincere
Thinking of my wedding day, dressed in white,
You'll be up front holding his hand tight
Sitting there thinking of those glorious days from
Standing up straight, to bad days . . . the mirror
Tells a story of glory and pain.
Live one day to the next and be proud to say,
"My daughters grown up and moved away".

Ashley Paxton

Untitled

The rain just keeps falling,
while our hearts are softly calling.
We love you Dad and Grandpa too,
but if you leave us now,
what will we do?

And he responds,
in that strong loving voice.

"This is not good-bye, nor close to the end.
Our love is to strong, to never meet again.
No more tears we cry, the pain is gone.
The birds sing once, that is my song.
To let you know, I'm truly fine.
Loving you, protecting you, always by your side."

So keep him in your memory,
as that strong and loving man.
Who not only was a friend to you,
but a grandpa and a dad.

Amie Anderson

Apathy

Sitting at my desk, today
while xerox machines purred computers beeped
and clocks tick away the lost minutes of freedom
I glanced out my window at the sun

A being of immense power and love
Playfully sharing its' energy with the universe
So that we may thrive!

It envisions laughter and beauty
Adventure and fun

It magically creates growth vibrant and glory

How disappointed would our mentor be
if it knew we spent our days in cold, drab rooms
jammed with formica desks
and covered with wall papered murals
   of a world we rarely experience

But . . . the clock is ticking my phone is ringing
   God knows why my computer is beeping
   and the xerox machine is jammed

I am sorry my sun we are lost
and no amount of fluorescent light will see us home.

Carolyn McCue

Renewal

The trees speak to me
whispering and sighing with their leaves
weaving a gentle golden spell on soft, summer afternoons.
The wind adds her voice, each whisper a breathless entreaty
to come, come wander with me.

It is a time for dreams
to be carried along, light as thistledown
rising, falling, drifting from hill to hill
then caught, in a slow eddy of time and motion
coming to rest only upon renewal of heart and soul
my eyes open slowly, as a child on her first day.

Cindy R. Lane

From The Crow's Nest

Gray and moving, rhythmically swelling and falling,
White crests, folding and rolling, disappearing—
Flowing and peaking, subsiding only to form again,
Wind-whipped, sky kissed, and dappled by the rain.

Overhead, clusters of moisture waft over the blue
Gradually touching, enlarging, shifting, pulsating,
Forming and re-forming, scurrying, compressing—
Only to fall as mist and rain, then siphoned aloft to re-do.

One lone gull skirting the waves, pits its strength
Against the tempest-tossed sea.   What great faith
Is borne in such as he to brave the uncharted expanses
Of sky and sea, days from land, and others of kind?

One lone person surrounded by throbbing souls—
Who knows the longing, restless spirit abiding within?
What infinite Faith guides him through life
On planned or unplanned paths, who knows not where?

Steady the ship goes westward, pressed by the currents
Crossing and recrossing from this wind and that,
Variable, ever-changing; up and down with the swells,
But forward she goes — bound for Home.

Alice Robinson Freeman

"Marion"

There is a lady on Quebec Street
Who all should have the pleasure to meet.
She has a habit of walking an extra mile
To lift someone up and make them smile.
She sews, cleans and cooks tasty treats,
And when she hugs you, she smells so sweet.
Take it from me as an old survivor,
She is the best dam taxi driver!
So if you ever need any of these things,
Just pick up the phone and give her a ring.

Janice Ann Burns

A Special Someone

I know a special someone
who can break my defensive wall,
and, when all is said and done,
accept me, faults and all.

A person who can help ease my sorrow
while pointing to the joy of a new day.
Someone that shows things can look different tomorrow
and put problems in perspective today.

There are times, I admit, when the toil of life
seems likely to overwhelm, I fear.
This is when help is needed to deal with the strife
and maybe a shoulder for the occasional tear.

A special person can help create new bonds to share
that grow with the passage of time, ever stronger.
These shared ties can help when apart, so that with care
each one's list of shared memories grow larger and longer.

I am at a loss for the words that can express
my emotions in the end.
Human expressions are but simple fare,
to describe that special one, a true friend.

Dale G. Nygard

Mom Will

I'm so little, all I can do is cry
Who will care for me; Mom will

I'm now walking around, I could get hurt,
Who will protect me; Mom will

I had my first fight today, my right eye now shines,
Who will take my pain away; Mom will

I went on my first date tonight, I need to talk,
Who will listen; Mom will

I now can drive, I wrecked the car.
Who will love me still; Mom will

I will graduate tonight, I hope I've done everything right,
Who will be proud of me; Mom will

I was married today, I have started a new life,
Who will be happy for me and my new wife; Mom will

I now have a baby on the way, soon to be a father,
Who will calm all my fears; Mom will

There was a funeral today, my mother passed away
Who will mend my broken heart; Mom's memory will

Connie Chiasson

Friends

Friends are those who really care
Who help you out and really share
They don't talk behind your back
Or give you too much flack
Friends are with you in good times and bad
And when you're unhappy they make you feel glad
Friends will never pretend
They will be with you to the end
When you win something they are glad
True friends don't fight
You might get mad sometimes
But always make up
When you get in fights with others
They always take up for you
That's what friends are for

Christina Johns

Untitled

Who brought me into this world, and helped me through the years?
Who taught me how to speak; and shed the caring tears?

Who kissed me good night, and prayed, God keep my son?
Who babied me when I cried; and played with me, what fun!

Who stayed with me those frightful nights, when I wanted to hide?
Who scolded me and spanked me when they knew that I had lied?

Who taught me God's word, and said, "Son be a good man?"
Who sent me to school and said, "Son learn all you can?"

Who said, "Son, take my car; and here is money for your date?"
Who punished me those times, when I came home late"

Who said, "Son, we'll always love you, even when you have been bad?"
"WHO?" I know and God knows; IT'S MY MOM AND DAD,
   that's who.

Jimmy W. Frye

Grandmother

Here sleepeth a noble lady
Whose body in marble doth lie,
But whose heart and soul shall never die.

In heaven her spirit awaits
And passes through the pearly gates.
Never again to tread below the sky,
She hath become an angel on high.

And so her soul shall always be free
An angel in paradise for eternity,
Forever in my heart as she watches over me.

Dana M. Spicer

Untitled

The earth is warm and my body is cold
Whose breath was once words that stood pillars of gold
I settle alone with my anguish abreast
As I live, below the rest
Down streams her light from Luna above
Please, scorn me thoroughly for I am in love
Birth of the night splashes the crimson mist
The chase goes on, infidelity, abyss
We meet alone and the stars all cheer
I missed you then, I wished you here
Erotic compassion leaves us no words
Symbolic reaction, as free as the birds
Seize the moment! Melts my soul
The end is near, loneliness the tow
I love you dear Luna, you give me life
Bludgeons the day, a razor, a knife

Damon L. Buckley

Eye Of The Storm

I see across the room a once familiar face
   whose eyes look back at me in wonderment.
Do I know you? The shining gray eyes ask silently.
   Have we met, have we talked somewhere before?
The room is filled with other faces, other eyes
   searching, some finding, as I edge around the
human clusters hearing words not for my ears.
   I pause for just a moment to fix upon the beacon,
the guiding light within your shining eyes that now
   propels me to the circle of earth beneath your feet,
The air is warm around me, generated by me, focused
   on you who seem so far away, so serenely calm.
The room grows larger, more crowded with clumps of
   flesh blocking my path like icebergs.
I am a ship on a calming sea gliding now quietly
   into the eye of the storm,
      Into the shining gray eyes of the storm

Betty Rutter

Why?

Why Anthony Ellis? A youth to lose his life so young.
Why Anthony Ellis? His life of 15 years had just begun.
Why Anthony Ellis? Now the tears are flowing down his friends'
   and loved ones' faces.
Why Anthony Ellis? He had things to do and to go many places.
I asked myself the same question when my brother died so young.
Why my brother? His life had just begun.
Why was my brother taken with life's plans left undone?
Why these two? Why did they have to die?
It's a question unanswered. I'm still asking why.

Aaron Waters

King's Way Christian Academy, Corning, NY

Why?

Why can't I do anything to help you?
   Why can't I take the pain away?
Why can't I do something to stop it?
   Why can't I, why can't I, why can't I?
Why can't I hold you and say it'll be okay?
   Why can't I take you and the both of us run away?
Why can't I just do something that can help you out?
   Why is the pain so very real?
Why is the love so easy to feel?
   Why is the distance so evident?
Why are the tears so prominent?
   Why does everything seem to go wrong?
Why have you had to go through this for so long?
   Why must you suffer?
Why do things seem to get rougher?
   Why can't things just go right?
Why do people have to fight?
   Why the punches?
Why the screams?
   Why does this have to happen?

Delaine Elizabeth Creighton

"This Old House"

The old house has come alive again
   Windows no longer have that vacant stare
Frivolity dances in the frilly curtains
   Happiness is afloat in the Springtime air!

This old house where memories linger
   No longer creaks in disrepair,
It's door knobs clasped by warm fingers
   Friendship beckons in the lights patterned glare.

Almeta Cochran

Why?

Why is life so difficult at times?
Why can't it be so much easier?
All of the things that take you by surprise.
All of the things that lie ahead.

Sometimes you just feel like quitting.
Sometimes you just ask yourself why?
But life works in mysterious ways
And there will come a time in life, where
You find someone to share it with.
All of its ups and downs.
So when times are their worst, it doesn't really matter
Cause you have someone to share it with.
It's all put into perspective.
It seems alright.
You have each other, you'll make it through together.

Jacob D. Heinle

Gettysburg

Gettysburg, Oh Gettysburg,
Why did this ever have to be?
Brother pitted against brother in his human sea.
Musket fire, cannonades, searing summer heat;
Bleeding wounds, flashing blades, by chance enemies meet.
Picketts charge. Never died, finer, more gallant men.
Screaming blue and grey waves never yield nor bend.
Bugle calls, muffled drums, scurrying feet
Calling for an advance or quick retreat.
Moaning men suffering through the long hot night.
Spanglers Spring and cool water after a lull in the fight.
Big Roundtop, how you did conceal murderous fire from a distant hill
Little Roundtop, you too, sent your salvos of steel
Raining upon men, to maim and to kill.
A burning, blazing wheat field, an echoing shot . . .
Another foe killed.
A three day fight, thousands slain:
Departing souls flee the insane.
Gettysburg, Oh Gettysburg, Let us all pause . . .
They were all right. Each died for his cause.

Joseph F. Hammond

Our Little Man

Need we ask why?
Why does the sun rise and set?
Why does God take those so young, yet He may make another man suffer?
I feel we need not ask why, but to remember our little man for
  being so brave,
and just being our little man.
So for you Ray and Sharon Croteau,
Look at one another during those hard moments, hold one another,
but just remember what this little man has left you!
What he has left us and his friends.
I can remember the visits with Ray, Sharon and family.
Little Ray being so eager to learn,
whatever there was to learn around the next corner.
So brave to take a chance, yet so adult to learn from a mistake.
So for you Ray, Sharon and Heather,
you need not forget your little man, nor to ponder on yesterday, or
  tomorrow's.
But just remember Little Ray, for being Little Ray.
Along with all the wonderful memories he has given you.
The memories he has given myself,
my family and all the people who entered his life.

Eric Scott

Where From Here

To P.L. from J.J.
Where do we go from here?
Why in my heart is fear?
I don't question why, I just wait with a sigh,
Wondering where do we go from here?

You're next to me I see,
This is where I want to be.
Watching and waiting, anticipating,
Where do we go from here?

The days are shorter, the nights longer,
Especially when you're alone.
I call you up, but you're not at home,
Oh, where do we go from here?

Sometimes I'm blue, but I'll wait for you,
To you I want to be true.
I understand your only a man,
Tell me, where do we go from here?

When we make love it's like heaven above,
But you say we're not in love.
You say you care and that I am so dear,
But baby, where do we go from here?

Jamie Jones

Don't Let My Presence Worry You

If my path is full of stones, which hurt my soles;
Why, shouldn't I smell the roses? . . .

Let me live my life, quietly, just like a whisper,
I am not seeking to find fortune, but to enjoy, what I have . . .
What life wants to give me; ¡Some rain! ¡Some smiles!
¡Some softness and tenderness!, ¡Some pain, tears or a cry! . . .

It does not matter, what life gives me. It is, what it is,
The wheel is always turning . . . sometimes; a bumpy road,
Sometimes; like clouds and snow . . .

The same second, becomes; present and past, and it was future;
¡Nothing to hold! . . . perishable flesh, changing the matter
And the soul; always changing with the experience.

So; let me just pass by do not try to "grasp me," that certainly;
"I am not, what I was", not even my matter . . .
¡Judgement! is out of time, let me continue,
Don't let my presence worry you; I am, only passing by.

An instant in the space, an instant in the time
"End and beginning" "nothing and everything";
¡Our encounter!; is only circumstantial.

Enriqueta Silva

Time

I think of all the times we shared
why wasn't I prepared?
One day I'm with him on the door mat
the next day I'm gone, just like that
now he's with someone new
and I think of him with that same old view.
Time is supposed to heal all pain
even if you're waiting in vain?
I loved him so much
I really miss his touch.
I wish I would bring back those times
every time the clock chimes.

Amber Kirchenschlager

Why We'll Never Know

Death becomes us.
Why? We'll never know.
Does it just appear?
For heaven's sake that's what I fear.
Tis nothing to be scared, just be prepared.
For when it does,
Shall be forever more.

Shall it wilt my family?
Will they always be torn?
We'll never know.

For thy will never see.
For thou should never be seen,
Just heard.

Thou shall be the bird of dreams, hope, and fears.
But please no tears.
After the end why are people so sad or maybe mad?
Why? We'll never know.

Heather Bushway

Finding A Better Way

I sometimes wonder how we came about,
why were we put here in the first place?
There has got to be a reason without a doubt,
who else is out there in the outer space?

They say there is a God, in which I believe
for some this reality is hard to conceive
did you ever wonder what happens to our souls
after we pass away?
Jesus died for our sins and there he lay.

Risen from hell after three long days
To heaven he rose, next to his father he prays
We are the people who have to make a change
For the lives that are hard, we have to re-arrange
To bring in the new lives with peace and harmony
Ridding others of wonder and allowing them to see
That there is always a better way in life, you just have to search
For some a new beginning can even start at a church
Others can work hard by changing the bad to good
Where there's a will there's a way, do you think you could?

Beryl Blydenburgh

One Lost Night

Time after time I think of that night
why you? Why me? I was filled
with such fright

What was so wrong with you to do
such a thing?
Though it was real, it feels like a bad dream

three years later I still feel betrayed
Will I ever forget one day?

As I try to cope with the harshness of life
what is it exactly that causes this strife?

I will do my best to try to forget
but as my actions show I haven't yet

I can't begin to imagine your feelings of guilt
and I still can't believe the friendship we've built

I am getting help to get over my fright
but I will never forget what happened
that night.

Jamie Lynn Schoof

Father

Fond memories of years gone past
    Will fill our heartfelt need.
We're thankful, dad, for loving times
    And nurturing us as seed.

Through you and mom we've learned to live
    A life of truth and care.
To give, to love, to praise the Lord
    And with others always share.

And like a seed we all have grown
    With roots so very deep.
And memories of our lives on earth
    We shall forever keep.

You'll never be forgotten by family
    or by friend.
And this, a new beginning . . .
    Is really not the end.

For heaven's gates will open
    And God will surely let you in
And when our lives too, are over I know we'll meet again.

Dad, you will always be loved.

Ann M. Harris

Searching Soul

Longing of the soul in search for everlasting love.
Will the soul ever be reunited with the one whose memory is so
deeply etched within the cells?
Will love which surpasses time and space be found?

Is this search worthless . . . Like a dried piece of fruit no longer
containing sweet nectar?
The face of disillusionment is before me . . . What to do?
Like a child without a mother, longing, loneliness, pain.

The unknown is not feared
Never knowing the soul's love is feared.
Will yet again many lifetimes go by without reuniting?
Is this the human experience I committed too?

Confusion and chaos are masked riders by my side
Their darkness like the raging of my soul.
The soul is tired, the search has been long and energy is waning.
When will the search end?

Like a hungry pitiless dog seaking food, the soul will never end its search.
Soul, oh yea wise soul, let the love you know be felt and followed
While the questioning ego fades into a gentle slumber.

Christina Ann Compton

Untitled

As I sit here listening to the news. I think
will there ever be world peace?
    It's the time of the year!
What's the world coming to!
    Bosnia in trouble US military troops being sent
on the double.
    Homeless people starving here.
Americans not able to get an education anywhere.
Japanese girl raped by an American will there
be war again between the U.S. and Japan.
Depression recession people desire to leave.
High taxes low taxes where do we go.
Lesbian rights minority and whites gotta get a
woman in that congressional house made of purity and white.
Rage resentment violence and high temperaments at least
soup kitchens there.
This is the time 1995
    Happy Thanksgiving and Happy New Year.

Filomena Polce

Sweet Cherub

The sky opens with amazing light
Wind becomes still for the beautiful sight
An innocence so pure is softly lifted
Heaven grows to become even more gifted.
With a harmony of love the air sings
While the sweet cherub spreads her free wings
And shares a wisdom of love all eternal
The universe forever blessed a lovely angel.

Corie Rae Simmons

Untitled

A whispered wish, a soft-edged saber,
     winks like a star in the dark of night
Cool and comforting, it pierces the storm filled with loneliness,
     doubt and fright
Breeze that blows strong and true, carries hope on wings of
     doves and sparrows
Over the slumbering rooftops and woods, whether the path
     widens or narrows
The moonbeams cast a frosty luminance atop the scintillant,
     undulant stream
Mountains hover in rocky armor, clothed in dewy mist,
     reminiscent of a dream

Can anyone ever be truly alone, when all see the same sun
     awaken and gleam
Warm radiance washes upon both the earth and the sea; distances
     are much briefer than they first seem
My white-horsed knight - tangible or celestial, carved in the
     clouds far above
Heart that waits and eyes that plead, search for what is hardly
     found but most in need - love
For once and for all, tomorrow incessant, a continuous breath
     of the purest air
Eternity without love would be unendurable; a year ever precious
     if that he were there.

Courtney Patton

Dad I Hear Your Voice, Guide Me Through Life

Although you are now at rest, God has made me feel no fears. I will
wipe away my tears; for your voice I will always hear. My heart feels
you will always be so close and near, even though you are not visibly
beside me; I know you will always be there to guide me. My heart and
soul knows you are in the heaven above, God has made me feel this way,
I will never lose your eternal love; which will still be with me
each and every day. Your loving power of love of life, you have
given, no evil destroyer, can take or cease. You have suffered so
much, God has given you now a peaceful rest, the Lord God, witnessed
my fears, multitude of tears, he has made me feel it is for the best.
Why? I know I must keep on living, although I do not feel at ease;
my love I must keep on giving; for there is many I must still please.
Dad with the Lord God, and mom you have given me life; now I, must
respond bring my feelings and love to a brand new height. This
mountain of feelings I must climb, although you will not be there
for the rest of this flight, you will no longer be visibly beside me,
loving memories will assist me and give me strength through out life.
Will I ever feel at ease? I know I can't give into my weakness, hurt
pain and sorrow, I know I must be peaceful, yet be able to fight for
what is right day and night, what you have taught me, will guide
me through life. The Lord God has given me another day, and
through my worries, I must pray to look forward to tomorrow, because
I have been given a gift of love, that I have borrowed. I must have
strength and love for others, the reason for living, life should be
caring and giving. True love is shared, dad, my true American
soldier, I will love, and fight for what is right. Dad I hear your
voice! The message sent from the angels of God, love has been given
for yesterdays, today, even more love will be sent for each and every
tomorrow. Your loving spirit throughout life, will always guide me.

Charlene E. Nichiniello

"Good Friends"

I thought you really liked me but I guess that it's not true
wish you could have been mine, but you would never do
for your not in for commitment and maybe I'm to blame
I might have pushed you to hard and that really is a shame
I could make you happy, or at least I would have tried
but now my heart is broken and all I do is cry
maybe in the future you'll find a real true love
She'll make you really happy and your heart will rise above
sorry it can't work out for a couple such as we
really truly sorry you and I could never be
It would have made me happy but now I can't be sad
cause we'll always be good friends and for that I'm truly glad.

Candida Knight

Fulfillment But A Dream

I dreamed away the moments
wishing through life's picture book.
Imagining that in my grasp
were all the things on which I looked.

As the vision of hoped for possessions
numbed my mind and caused me to drowse,
I allowed myself to be satisfied
with only the feelings my dreams would arouse.

Too soon the time lapsed into hours,
then days, and gradually years.
My life was fleeting fast away,
as my dreams dissolved to tears.

Why had I not pursued these things
and worked to gain their truth?
Instead I settled for paper dreams
and wished away my youth.

Jeanne Robertson

Alone

Have you ever been feeling all alone
Wishing you had a family and some place to call home
Feeling helpless and infantile
Feeling like sitting in a corner crying for a while
Wishing to go places you've never been
Wishing to have a special, yet trusting friend
Have you ever been so depressed
Life burdening you with too much stress
Have you ever felt so strong about someone
They say they love you then treat you like scum
Always fussing and fighting
Simply can't contend with the back biting
Crushed fingers, toes and heart
Everything that ever meant anything seems to fall apart.
Everything is failing, yes, even my health.
Haven't you guessed by now, I'm talking about myself
After reading all of the above
Can't you see, I just want to be loved
Instead, I'm all on my own
No! It's not easy being alone!

Colita L. Dempsey

Reveries

The heart of the bird has faded away.
With broken wing it valiantly drops.
Silken silver wasted and stray
lived for a time when time would be not.
Shadowy dreams cover the sun
postponing a tryst
empowering what enemies have done.
Stirred from sleep, thoughts stab into view.
Did the bird ever fly?
Was the false ever true?

Alice F. Smith

Invitation Time

I'm gonna be there at the marriage of the Lamb
With a crown of righteousness next to the great I Am
All the believers from all ages will be there
And afterwards, a feast of all feasts beyond compare
The banquet table is neigh set
There's still time for you to get your invitation yet
It's something I can't give you but its something I pray you get
You must be born a-new
Die to self
Christ resurrected in you
The spirit of the Lord is crying out to all who will hear
He's saying keep on praying, the time is very very near
We the privileged, whose names are written in the Book of Life
We the church, will be the wife
We'll be waiting patiently for Jesus, the groom
Just think of the size of the banquet table and all the glory of
    that room
There's still time for you to get your invitation yet
You must be born a-new
Die to self Christ resurrected in you

Fred K. Ortega

Cope

How am I expected to cope
With a man addicted to dope?
He's in love with the White Lady.
She comes before his woman, his home, his babies.
He'll deny he is addicted until he needs it.
He would say he is sick and needs to feed it.
So how am I going to cope
With a man addicted to dope?
He will sell anything of value that he can find.
Instead of going forward, he pulls me far behind.
He'll lie to his mother to get money if he can.
Then he will take it to the drug man.
His money is gone in a matter of hours.
The WHITE LADY has him completely in her power.
He'll need his dope then more to follow.
I only pray he'll live to see tomorrow.
"I try to deal with it because I love him," I'd say
But once he gets started, he pushes me away.
This is a small example of what one would see
If their loved one becomes a junkie.

Christine Boyd

The First Snow

I wish I were a small child
With a mouth and nose so very red
I wish I had a child's mind
So I could dream of fairies
And winter wonderlands of long ago.

I wish I could see beautiful stars
In the heaven's above
I wish I could be super human
And wish on many stars and be a part of all the universes
And winter wonderlands of long ago.

I wish I would only have to wish for tiny snow flakes
And they'd appear before my eyes
For the first snow that falls upon the ground
Is the most beautiful, and I could dream of yesterday's
And winter wonderlands of long ago.

Donna L. La Rocca

Love

Morbid and melancholy
With a touch of infinite sadness
From dawn to dusk, twilight and starlight
Fate falls into madness.
It's come to take love away from you
Maybe your heart and a little soul, too.
Beyond a dead silence there are no dreams
Beyond no dreams there are still feelings.
Feelings of hate and suicide
Take these, too, and go die inside.
Just like me you'll rot away
From life and death just the same.
So turn off my sun
Let me rot inside
Take away my happiness
And let me die.
Love is truly suicide.

Jordan Davidson

Island Girl

You came from a land of different race,
    with all the beauty of an island in your face.
The difference in you was golden and pure
    it was all I could stand and my heart endure
For the time was now and it had to be you
    to make my life and dreams come true
Time has come and gone since then
    here we are still - Rooster and Hen.
You are my sunshine, that's why I crow
    proudly I walk wherever I go.
I'll be here til the end of time
    even after we've past our prime
My past, present, and future is loving you
    that's all I'll ever know and really ever do!

G.L. Nicholas

Ode To Luann

I think of you in heaven above
with angels on wing and snow white doves.

You fought, long, hard, and true
but something better awaits for you.

A place; free of hurt and pain,
soft as dew and fresh falling rain.

The special one who laughs and cries,
with awe and hope in those brown eyes.

Remember, Luann, that we all love
and will meet you later up above.

In a place of clouds in the life ever after
along side the watchful master.

Cheryl Stedman

Summertime

Remember those summers of yesteryear
With fresh lemonade and frosty root beer-
Running barefoot in the grass
Wishing somehow the days would last.
Skipping rocks on the pond,
Ice cream socials on the church lawn.
The old porch swing and the evening breeze -
And sitting back doing just as you please!
Oh yes, those summers of yesteryear
With fresh lemonade and frosty root beer.

Deborah Randolph

Terror

Just as shadows of onyx black clouds
with blinding streaks of silver lining illuminate the sky,
It slowly creeps up, sending shivers down the spine with a
frost-bitten chill stunning the body . . .
Terror is setting in.
Weakness endlessly spreads throughout the limp body
as the power of its stare shuts you down . . .
terror is taking over.
Everyone seemed to vanish as you are singled out by the predator.
You become its prey . . .
Terror is pouncing.
Trying to visualize the predator out of the corner of your eye
without showing fear, you swing around,
only to find a helpless old woman . . .
Terror fades away.

Danny Kliber

Silence

Oh oh oh, oh oh yeah. Mmmmhmmm.
With each new autumn leaf, that falls to the ground.
I remember when you, first came around.
You brought me more than I could ever ask for,
What did I do, for this grand reward.

Then came the day,
You went away, I wanted so much for you to stay.
Still in a way, you'll always be near,
Somewhere deep inside, within each falling tear . . .

Silence,
So much louder, so much more in tense.
Silence,
What did I do, to cry, all this tears . . .
But the day came . . .

Oh oh oh, yea . . .
Silence . . . hey yea.
Silence, yea yea . . .

Deborah C. Wilmoth

Dream Leaves

The trees are colored their gorgeous hues,
With elfish brushes and paint pots.
Skies have lost their summer blues,
But cooler days, just hit the spot.

Kids tramping in leaves as they go by,
Dying to dive into those piled so high.
But for me, they better not try,
Unless the rake, they'd like to ply.

Smoky sensations to my nose,
Of days of burning in the street.
Firemen on call with their hose,
When Mr. Wind comes to fan the heat.

Smoke, amid colors of fall,
Lulls minds to wander in dreams.
Indians, campfires, or hear that wolves call,
Seems to be happening beyond that stream.

But alas it's the kids lusty whoops,
As they tumble amongst the leaves,
While I, doze on the ole back stoop,
And fairyland pictures, in my head, weave.

Charlotte N. Foltz

Big Hairy Monster

There's a big hairy monster under my bed.
With eyes that glow a burning red.
With teeth so long and hairy arms.
To reach up. To grab you and pull you down.

It moans and groans all night long. And it growls
for you to come down.
It tells you, "Come under for just a visit."
But you're not dumb, you will be gobbled up in a minute.

It will stay in the shadows all through the night and
hides when you turn on the light. It will grab your
leg if you stick it out and quickly pull you under
with all its stout.

The only thing that saves you from its reach, is that
blanket that you keep, and that night light glowing
so bright with its strong and guiding light.

And when the blanket and night light are gone.
And when you grow up big and strong.
You can stomp on him . . .
and stomp on him . . .
Until he is gone.

John T. Callaghan

The Path

A quiet path leads through the forest,
    with fallen leaves to line the way.
It wanders far into the distance,
    but where it goes I cannot say.

The wind blows gently through the branches,
    beneath the boughs the light is green,
And somewhere in the wood's dark shadows,
    all our futures wait to be seen.

Mine lies somewhere through the unknown wood,
    far beyond, at my journey's end.
Not knowing what grand adventures wait,
    I smile and start for the first bend

The path is such a wondrous thing,
    full of magic and mystery,
And somewhere under the trees there is
    a chance to find my destiny.

Joe Schlachta

The Good Bye

Say good bye with the wave of a hand,
With gut wrenching waves of emotion.
One must leave while one stays behind
To live with the solitary consequences of good bye.
Moving in and out of lives, the human flux comes a wild river.
Blowing straight through and racing on like a roaring good bye.
Friends make friends and cling desperately to the bond,
The deep yet allusive potential for future good byes.
Good byes that can weaken your knees
And make you fall to the ground weeping.
But you can't do that, it's not socially acceptable.
Hide the gut wrenching emotions away, somewhere deep inside.
Bury them in the murky mud until the next opportunistic good bye,
This time covered in sludge and brutally more intense.
Now you can't help but fall to the floor crying.
And someone comes along and picks you up,
And tries to ease your suffering.
But all you can see is the potential for another good bye
So you say it before it has a chance to be said:
Good bye with the wave of a hand.

Brian H. Kern

When Atlantis Rose Again

When Atlantis rose again, she was there to meet me on the new shore
With her sun-medallion and her golden bracelets
She was no longer a Queen; she wasn't Priestess anymore
Now she seemed to be in charge of all the spaceships

She said centuries had passed since when walked in Inca times
And that since the thermal blast, she sat beneath her wind-chimes
Wondering when I'd next appear — perfecting harmonies and rhymes
And now we're here . . .

When Atlantis rose again, I was transported to the new shore
I just suddenly appeared there without warning
I had no recollection what my job had been before
Until they led me to the dome — we worked 'til morning

She said "We won't be here long, we're almost ready to get started
When the solar winds are strong, we'll take the course you charted
There's a world where things went wrong; an entire race almost aborted
Through hate and fear" . . .

When Atlantis rose again, I had no memories of living there before
It took awhile for all the scenes to start returning
When our work down here was done, we launched for yet another shore
To Orion's gleaming belt we'd soon be turning . . . we's soon be turning

Ira Huddleston

Untitled

A baby crying in an '88 Chevy
with its trunk open and handcreme inside
but be careful, the sauce is on the side
because the streetlamps went out
and the paperboy broke his leg
driving a semi to the opera house
in the hopes of reading the whole Nancy Drew series
before the rain falls in Guatemala
Papou glues a puzzle to cardboard
and lovingly dusts the stereo
that sank in a shipwreck, oh, maybe 500 years ago
long before the Titanic
sailed to Libya
with its cargo of lamps and stagebills
but the baby didn't get a dream last night
so he lets a single tear fall
and it drops,
and plops,
and overflows the Nile

Theo

Destiny Of Time

Children are born
With no expectations or fears.
The world is an endless playground
To ride and enjoy.
They make mistakes
And fall off a ride,
But children you see continue to try.
Each new ride is an opportunity
To find and learn something new.
Life is a sandbox filled with an infinite variety of pebbles
Each with it's own shape and color.
Tossed and scattered all over the ground,
Just as children grow up
And travel their own road in life.
They are our future.
Children will etch the roads and pave the path ahead.
But what happens if all the rides break down,
And the laughter of children fade out?

Jennifer Shaw

Castles

To be lost in a world of loners,
 with no frills or fancies.
To be forgotten and invisible,
 yet very much there and aware.
Running in endless and hopeless circles
 around fallen castles built by my imagination.
It all becomes a ruin,
 a shamble, broken and dead.
To the world it was nothing,
 but to me it meant everything.
Neither brick nor steel
 makes the fortress any stronger,
for it is love that bonds
 and builds the human kind,
not material objects.

Heather Grandmont

Old Rain

The old rain falls softly, tiredly
 With feeble wet fingers,
It soaks the huddled gray houses
 And leaves a scent of ancient mold that lingers.
Weary, weary is the old rain.
 Weary of the ghosts it carries -
Ghosts that move feebly in the phantom breeze,
 Old, faded, drooping wisps from a hags head.
The old rain deadens all sound but its own
 As it falls, weeping from the weight of memories -
Memories it cannot tell, timeless old memories
 Some of Heaven, others from Hell . . . over and over and over.

Edie Burt

Empty Eyes

The reflection of the inner heart,
with precious moments stored deep inside,
flooded with memories of days gone by,
scared with bitterness of lost love,
overcome with the grief of shattered dreams,
once strong, vibrant and full of life,
now just a hollow shell;
pain has become its pleasure,
and pleasure has become its pain,
longing for a love so true,
yearning for passion made so complete,
finding a dream come true,
only losing more than it ever had.

Brian S. Campbell

Vision

We are the invisible leaders,
With pride we guard what was ours.
Alone we search for the answers,
Rarely are we recognized, seldom are we understood.

It is alone we fight these battles,
Against the demons of our myths.
It seems the world never listens,
Could it be they truly cannot hear?

Yet all the time soon passes,
Our future, quickly a memory.
It is alone we fight so often,
Which makes me stop and ponder . . .

. . . To the unknown man,
Across from his very own brother.
"Does it not make much more sense,
For all of us to work together."

Kara Lynn Shenk

Edges

Nippy quick sharp a bite gritty, like a carbon blades end, gleaming
with red heat fire smooth moves and sudden stop, pop like a
firecracker with spastic ability the smooth calming massage of a
chiropractor and the sudden adjustment to come, resounding
noises from the experience, flying on a plane, ears reacting to
altitude pop, pop, pop, must hear fear fright up, on into the
night, shake run scream ignore, snore awake moving like the
shivering volcano, tenacity elasticity stretching beyond, snapping
return, feelings emotions love cuddle hurting yearning, like the
broken heart wanted gratification, simple calm solitude a smile,
sunrise glowing warmer to the depths of our souls, holes socks
tattered patches empathy homeless, lost mentality,
rescue thee, like the child in the night fears the dark, shadows
creatures on the wall, frightening stifling teardrops fall.

Jayne Cummings

A Family Reunion

They all come together
With their perky smiles and traveling voices.
Their eyes filled with glittering magic
As they discuss the year gone pass.

Generations young and old
Recounting tales of family departed.
Holding hands to praise The Almighty
Rejoicing in the circle of family.

Young free spirited children
Romping through the tall, green grass.
Hearts overwhelmed with gleeful innocence
Undaunted by the smoldering summer heat.

They all come together
Young in mind and mature with wisdom.
To delight in the feast before them
Uniting in one splendid gathering
Proving that there is no power
Stronger then . . . family.

Audrey Murphy-Davis

Untitled

Screaming silence can't protrude my lips
With these hidden thoughts covered by blankets of fear.
The beholder of my eye is unsure of my intentions.
When the time comes will I face the beauty standing before me
Or will I crumble in the ruins of my fear?
Is it the "one" that is in my presence or is it just a curse?
You tell me. But for now I'm smiling.

Eric Bruno

Doors

Doors shut and close,
Words misunderstood.
It's all inevitable, I suppose,
But not quite fair to those anew to the game.

Rules are made and broken,
Slightly bent, pushed aside.
No advice does anyone send,
Leaving some alone and full of shame.

What is love? Questioned, undefined
In every language known to Man.
Too bad key points aren't underlined,
So that the vicious heart, I will learn to tame.

Circles running all through time,
Get up, fall down, look to the side.
Is it your turn, is it mine?
Doors shut and closed, it's all the same.

Carol Trent

A Daughter's Prayer

send him an angel
with wings to shroud him in comfort when all seems but lost . . .
send him an angel
with hands that touch ever so gently to soothe his pain . . .
send him an angel
with breath like a swift wind to sweep his mind and carry away all
    negativity, leaving only sweet memories of days gone by . . .
send him an angel
an angel bearing gifts from the heavens — the gift of knowing
that he know in his heart that his mother sees him, feels him, and
    loves him — let him see her smile and feel her by his side . . .
the gift of fire
the fire of life burns bright in me — take some, i have plenty to
    spare — may it burn bright in him and give him strength . . .
the gift of protection
when a dark hour is upon him and the battle too fierce, shield him
    from all that is harmful and carry him in your arms to safety . . .
the gift of love
let him know that even though his daughter is far away, that her heart
reaches out to him and that she loves him very much; she needs him to
be there for her — she may be an adult now, but she will always be
his little girl . . .

fawn m. smith

"Once Young"

Young and unconcerned, a time we have all known
without the cares and worries and leisure to freely loan
Our days were long and joyful, the nights were much the same
for when the time to lay thee down, sleep soft and gently came
Young and unconcerned, those good and precious years
when serenity was found in mother
after hardship brought forth tears

Suddenly times change, the youth and folly flee
the cares and worries slowly mount
no time can we call free
our days now seem endless
the nights fly by on wing
we lay thee down in endless thought and accomplish no one thing

At the crack of dawn, when sleep descends
and pulls down tired eyes
a deep and curt lived slumber ends
once again it's time to rise
No longer young and unconcerned, those long loved years have flown
gone too, the maternal hand of comfort
we must now stand alone

Edward J. Carpenter

"Never Part"

The sun above could never set and leave the day behind
without the warm and loving thoughts of you upon my mind.

I sit and stare off into space to the world I am but blind
you may not know it now but eventually you'll find.

This feeling that I have for you etched deep inside my heart
tells me only this, that we should never part.

I've never felt like this before so strong and true and sure
this wonderful sensation, for this I do adore.

Adore as much as I do you, the girl whose on my mind
so confident yet shy and sweet, so gentle warm and kind.

These things I say come swift and clear flowing from my heart
I can only hope and pray that we will never part.

So take these words in which I speak and know that they are true
for words alone cannot express the love I have for you.

The power and the passion of the love in which we share
there will never be another, nothing will compare.

John Callahan

Our Special Place

My days seem so lonely now
Without your smiling face
I often think of those special times
And of our special place
Where we'd talk about our future together
And all our plans were made
But instead of growing in the sunlight
Our dreams fade away in the shade
I wish I could take all those special moments
And hold them in my hand
And turn them around so our dreams could be
The way that we had planned
But I guess it's like wishing upon a falling star
Whose ending we never quite see
For if I had my way in this crazy world
You'd be spending your life with me
So remember boy I love you
And this I tell you true
No matter what may happen in my lifetime
My heart will forever belong to you.

Judy Ramsey

A New Life

Here I sit, all alone at lunch
Wondering why, why did I leave, why am I here
I had so many friends just last year
Why do I sit alone and bored
Why, why am I sitting here
Like a newborn first exposed to light
Learning of the new world all around
Testing, watching, listening . . . observing
Studying the faces of the many
They, the many, all groups of friends
And here I sit, I was just like them
Talking and laughing among my friends
But now I sit alone . . .
That is the consequence of an adoption to roam
A new period of isolation and coldness
A small display of boldness
Yes, then the friends are made
But until that time here I am
Me and the many others like me
I see them and they see me, sitting alone at lunch . . .

Ian Patrick Riutta

His Father's Son

Nothing could give me joy like watching you explore this wide world, searching for answers to questions so few men dare to ask, and being able to say, "He has his Father's eyes."
And nothing could give me joy like knowing you heed my words, search out my advice, and consider my wisdom, and be able to tell the world, "He has his Father's ears."
And nothing, could bring joy like watching you take a position, and make a stand from which you will not be moved or swayed, and being able to say," He has his Father's feet."
And nothing could bring joy like watching, you reach out to life, trying to touch it and make a difference, and being able to say, "He has his Father's hands."
And nothing could give me joy like seeing you quick to laughter, eager with kindness, and slow to anger, and being able to say, "He has his Father's smile."
But all of these would never bring me such joy as seeing others touch you, provoking you to question, and to take a stand, and eagerly reach out to touch them back, trying to make a difference, and being able to proclaim, "He has his Father's heart."

Christina N. Bonesteel

"Careless At 48"

I wondered once, what would I be, and how, in life, I'd fare.
Would I be successful, and have nice clothes to wear.
I was young then, and could not know how many things could change,
And cause all my priorities to all be rearranged.

As years go by, if we survive we find as we mature.
That most things that we fret about, we easily can cure.
Like! Why do we take up a cause, and make a big to-do,
Only to find our best friend see's the other point of view.

With each birth day I live through,
One thing I could suggest,
Is if you start obsessing,
You should learn to "care less."

Clark Wayne Lynch

My Shadow Of Death

If and when, why and how
would such a huge emptiness control my being.
Yet without regard it holds me, never leaving me,
it guides me, yet never showing me, it covers me,
yet never warms me, it defies me, yet it never knows me,
My Shadow of Death.
For oft I wonder of light not shown, and oft I ponder of warmth not felt,
Oft I find myself needing it more.
But how could this be, the dark of my life,
the misery of my day, the pain of my unknown, yet the joy of my faith,
My Shadow of Death.
Alas the glimmer unknown shines through,
the beginning untold and the end so close,
now, my death be told of virtue unlived,
my joy be felt of light unseen,
my desire be held, by those so new, yet old.
If and when, why and how,
my emptiness be filled, and my being seen,
by the light that gives my shadow its death,
My Shadow of Death.

Anthony Albert Rainge

Untitled

Legs long as night and smooth as
woven silk I'm sure
lustrous hair-alive itself
eyes deeper than a butterfly's
and a smile to born the imagination
address as flowing and wondrous as a waterfall
peace resides in her I'm sure

When our passions connect
fires will erupt in the wilderness,
and the mountains will hear of our legend.
Long anticipations shall be realized
dreams finally within the grasp,
enjoyed-together My love, as one

Distant storms shall hear the passion for our world
The heavens shall arise to a beauty only dreamed
Fantasy will become reality's lover
In this world, we shall live.

Brandon Manning

Television

Television is our gateway to the world.
Without it we would be blind
to what is going on around us.
Television informs, entertains, and teaches.
Without it we would be bored out of our minds.
Television is an important tool to humans.
It is the door to the unknown.

Donald Neil Cothran Jr.

March 15, 1995

I remember it vaguely, not very clear; Kind of like it happened last year.
I was crossing the street doing just fine; Then my friend's and my
  life were on the line.
I saw some light and next thing I knew; I was flipping and turning
  with nothing to do.
I heard a big boom, like the Fourth of July; Then me and my jeep
  were flying in the sky.
When I was flipping, after I heard the crash; I was jolted and shaken,
  and hit my head on the dash.
After it stopped, and everything lay still; I felt my head, as the
  blood started to spill.
I got of my car and fell to the ground; I could not find my friend, I
  looked all around.
I was dazed and confused, and had no clue at all; Felt like I was
  crushed by a 10-ton ball.
I finally found my friend, but he looked dead; He was all mangled up
  and bleeding from he head.
My head was torn up, I broke my hand, Felt like I might leave this
  promise land.
Then I can see people, and can faintly hear them yell; I think this
  round is over, God, please ring the bell.
Now I'm bundled up, on a big stable board; I really need some help
  now; please Lord.
Next I'm lying cold, on a strange, bloody bed; Amazing enough, I can
  feel staples in my head.
Now I'm waking up, in a very abnormal room, At least I'm alive and
  didn't meet my doom.
I feel like hell, and don't remember the night I had, But I'm living
  right now, and I'm really glad.
So thank you Lord for saving my life; So I can up to have kids and a wife.

Cameron W. Jones

Without Him

I'm cold.
yearning for the feel of warmth.
yearning for the feel of his hands, of his arms, wrapped tight around
dying to hear his voice, wanting to see his face.
can I make it one more day without love, without him?

I'm lonely.
aching for the feel of love,
yearning for the feel of want,
hoping for the feel of him.
dying to touch his hair, wanting to kiss his lips.
how long do I have left to go without love, without him?

I'm sad.
wanting to see his calves,
aching to feel his back,
yearning to see his chest.
dying to see him smile, hoping to hold his hand.
when will it be over, my without love, without him?

The crow and the raven are making me sad.
They don't have to yearn, or to ache, to want, to hope, or to die.
I'm the one left barely alive and hoping for love, hoping for him.

Amber Keller

That's Life

Sometimes life is mashed potatoes,
you have to live with all the lumps!
Life is sometimes a road of potholes,
you drive on it despite the bumps.
And through the lumps and bumps of life,
you seem to persevere.
For life is just a broken car,
the transmission's gone, but you always steer.

Joseph Di Edwardo

Yesterday

Yesterday meant having no cares no woes.
Yesterday meant dressing in satin and bows.
Yesterday meant laughing and crying a lot.
Yesterday meant having that one special
  friend you sought.
Yesterday meant caring and sharing and giving.
Yesterday meant having a dream for fulfilling.
Yesterday meant saying I'm sorry to someone you love.
Yesterday meant asking for forgiveness from above.
Our yesterdays are gone, but our memories will live on.
From daylight in morn till setting sun.

Brenda K. Holdren

The End Is Near

Your love is sweet, the end is near, but you have nothing to fear
  you've been good, you've treated me right, but I hate to tell you
  I'm leaving tonight.
I hope your not hurt, I don't want you to be.
I know I love you and you love me, But the love I feel is not like
  a lover it's more like the one I feel for my brother.
I'm sorry this relationship has to end, but I don't feel like a lover
  just a very good friend.

Courtney Holub

"She"

You whisper softly how much you love me,
yet I know differently,
you love her! That woman, she!
And you'll love her for all infinity.

She! That devil that stole you,
I shall throw her in the depths of hell,
and with her you shall go too,
and I will laugh when I hear you both yell.

And yet, I won't, I can't
for I love you still, with all my soul,
no matter how much I rave and rant,
only you can fill my gaping hole.

I thought we'd be together forever,
I thought you'd love only me,
yet kiss you again I'll never,
for you don't love me, you love she!

Only you can mend my broken heart
you, the phantom of my dreams
my heart you tore apart
yet you'll never hear my screams.

Jennifer Linarez

Melancholy Thoughts

Family and friends leave us when they answer God's call,
Yet in our memory thoughts of them are ever on recall.
Their likeness may become somewhat fuzzy,
But from time to time life jolts our bonnet's bee.
Maybe a recipe recalls Mom's special apple pie,
A favorite hymn brings to mind Auntie's voice so high;
The old sports car on the highway is Uncle Joe,
Or a young lady's smile is definitely your old gal "Zoe."

That's not the way to do it, is Dad at your elbow;
A teacher's special nudge puts you on the way to go;
And a well-kept lawn is a former favorite friend.
The list of special signs of departed ones has no end -
Brings a tear, a smile, an arm around one's shoulder,
A special nod of understanding, a whisper on the breeze -
  "I love you."
Family and friends leave us when they answer God's call,
Yet in our memory thoughts of them are ever on recall.

Grace C. Allison

Always Alaska Blue

Blazing red sun up in the sky
Yet no heat to scorch the ground
There must be a million birds
Oh, how lovely it does sound.

The trees are alive and green
Everything is so very bright
Even the common darkness of a sunset
Is kept at bay by the sunlight.

Gleaming snowy white mountain tops
So much beauty I can not see,
But I'd pass it all by
Just to hold you next to me.

With a thousand colors it does hold
And a hundred stories you've yet told
There's still 5000 miles between me and you
I guess that's why I always picture, Alaska blue.

> *Curtis Winsmann*

Midnight Blue

It was good this life you shared with me,
Yet so short in flight like the flower to the bee.
A moment not wasted those long summer days,
The night bird comes swooping its unwatchful prey.

I draw close to the river, and momentarily glance,
The white swans reflection performs lonely dance.
The trunk of the willow thus leans towards me,
Beckoning me closer for tears none has he.

All is in quiet, now sullen dark,
The clouds have left the sky, but my eyes trace no mark.
Our back bears its burden so now willow sleep,
Shall never again tears from your eyes seep.

In shadows of darkness all midnight blue,
This vision before me none other than you.
Leave not me now, in this hour of my need,
Lest my soul leave my body as flower turns to seed.

The birds of the river give sullen chase,
While the swan thus looks on with such picturesque face.
Resentful the night as dusk turns to dawn,
Piercing my heart like the rose doth the thorn.

> *Angela Ryan-Allen*

"A Sorrowed Prayer"

I can feel your presence near me,
Yet your presence I cannot touch,
Your love was real, and now you've gone,
And I still need you oh so much,
The times we shared, the laughter you brought,
Leave cheerful thoughts locked in my mind,
A beautiful spirit, a kindred soul,
Taken so long before his time,
You meant so much to everyone,
If only you were still here,
For us to see, your smiling face,
And for one last moment to hold you near,
These things I wish, I know are unreal,
And I know I'll have to wait,
To see you again, to behold your smile,
At Heaven's Pearly Gates,
Until that time, I'll have to try.
To let your memory go free,
I hope you know your a part of me,
In my heart you'll always be.

> *Elizabeth Adams*

Ocean Of Love

If our love is like an ocean that never ends.
You are my sailing ship with all of its beauty and its grandness.
Your voice is soft and gentle and as sweet as the music of the sea.
Your smile is like the sunshine and the warmth of the sun.
Your touch is like the warm mist that comes off the waves.
Your hair is like the flag that blows in the breeze with all of its
    colors and glory.
Your eyes are as beautiful as the sea, and as deep as the ocean.
Being with you is like sailing in paradise.

> *German Deacon*

My Valentine You Are

To me you are the kewpie doll at the county fair
    You are the cutest cuddly teddy bear
You are the jolly clown that makes all children laugh
    You are the one that, by far, is the better half

You are the dancer that is so light a foot
    You are the summer's babbling brook
You are the stars that shine at night
    You are ever my heart's delight

You are the merry-go round with its shining rings
    You are the blue bird that love songs sings
You are the statue cast in a perfect mold
    In my heart you are an angel to behold

You are the moon, the sun, the gentle rain
    You are the object of a singer's lingering love refrain
You are the arms of the tree that give the summer shade
    You are the miracle that God for me has made

You are the volcano erupting with fire
    You are the one that fills my every moment with desire
You are the Valentine of every day of my life
    God bless you, my honey, my adorable wife.

> *Anthony La Mantia*

Honor Father

A Song, Written to the Tune of "How Great Thou Art."
Our Father dear, you know we truly love you,
    You are the greatest man on earth we know.
Our Jesus sees and knows the teaching you do
    That fills our hearts, and make them overflow.

Chorus:
Then let's give praise to father on this day;
    We honor you, we honor you!
Then let's give praise to father on this day;
    We honor you, we honor you!

When hardships come and problems are arising
    And everything begin to fall apart;
You comfort us with love and faith abiding,
    We hear your voice-you say, "Just trust in God."

And then at last, when all your days are over,
    When you shall go to join the heavenly band,
We should be strong - no doubts arising ever
    For the good words you've said will always stand.

> *Carrie L. Braswell*

O Precious Star Of Bethlehem

O precious star of Bethlehem, we love you dearly so,
you are the true and only Lamb who died to make us whole.
We hear the angels sweetly sing a message true and sweet,
a wondrous story to behold, of one whom all should meet.

O precious star of Bethlehem, our King Emmanuel,
who dwells above eternally and loves us very well.
The tidings angels bring and tell are precious to the soul,
let all rejoice in harmony in days of young and old.

O precious star of Bethlehem, the King who reigns on high,
we see the morning star that shines up in the heavenly sky.
It was you, who in manger lay, so innocent and pure,
came down to earth once as a man, all burdens to endure.

Ira Mikell

Rainbows And Promises

Jesus you're special in so many ways
You bring peace and joy, in the things you've made
You make the sunshine, you make the rain
You cause my heart to want to sing.

You make a rainbow, with promises it brings
When the sun is shinning, at the same time it rains
Though the sky may turn gray, when the storm clouds arise
I will never fear, cause I'm kept from harm
By being sheltered in your comforting arms.

Reach out and touch me, dear Lord make me whole
Keep me safe, and in your strong hold
Make me always aware, of the wonders you've done
For you are the creator, redeemer and son.

When I look to the heaven, and see the moon and stars
It makes me realize what a creator you are
How can anyone say that they don't believe
All they have to do, is open their eyes, they can't help but see.

Joan Pleasant

The Dying Breed

This is my land you've taken from me.
You came, you killed, and you burned our trees,
So damned in humane, you took our lives,
Though we persisted, to fight in strife!

You took my people into reservations,
Where there they wasted in great starvations,
Life of an animal you led us through
With promises of hope, that were untrue!

So take my land, as you have done,
For life's much better up beyond!
My father awaits with happy sounds,
In place called heaven, our hunting grounds.

An Indian's not a matter of blood, it's
  a way of life,
A way of living, with guns, and with knives.
So why should I frown, why should I cry,
Today's a good day as any, to die.

Del Aguilar

Monday night football

Monday night football brings Monday night blues,
You cannot win gals and he dare not lose,
You have to watch it although you don't choose,
Monday night football brings Monday night blues.

As even embraces the setting of sun,
Hovers and echoes the days work is done,
Impatience prevailing he drives like a jet,
It's Monday night football and he knows the bet.

Awaiting with kisses she opens the door,
He runs for the TV and sprawls on the floor,
Ignoring his supper, his team in defeat,
His anguishing billow heard trailing the street.

His eyes set like marbles immovable stare,
She walks all around Him, is he really there?
Adorned in perfection, perfume and a prance,
His vision escaping, he's fully in trance.

She comforts the children with blankets in bed,
Emotions exploding inside of her head,
In need of condolence, the shoulder is His,
Her tears frame her smile, she knows right where he is!

Arlene Broyles

Just For Me?

You took what was mine, only I deserved it.
You didn't even ask if it was okay with me.
"It" had been my companion for as long as I could remember.

You wore my trophy. I didn't have a chance to try it on.
You didn't complain about its fit.
I probably would have rebelled in bitterness and pain.

You won my race and said you did it all for me.
When I complained about my trials you are always "one up" on me.
You have already been there.

I am your servant. All I am and have are yours.
You promised me a wonderful retirement with heavenly benefits.
I'm looking forward to the payoff.

You took my SIN.
You wore my CROWN of THORNS.
You gave me VICTORY.
You are my MASTER.

Irma Sue Murtha

Untitled

How many times can I say I'm sorry before
you don't forgive me?
Why do I have to be so cruel and hateful so
I hurt you, the one I love?
Does it make me feel powerful? No
I feel terrible after I say those harsh words,
but then it's too late.
The damage is done.
So why? I don't know.
Maybe one day I'll have the answers that I
wish I had now.
But until then,
I know I've said it many times, but I hope
you can find it in your heart
forgive me one more time.

Jeanette Beck

Memories Of The Heart

You and I have shared so much
You have comforted me with just a touch
Times haven't always been gentle
But they always seem to settle

I will always cherish the memories
And retell your stories
Chances are we'll grow apart
But you'll always be within my heart

When times grow old
I'll have your memories to keep from growing cold
Soon we'll be together again
It's just a matter of when

    Catina Mell

Going Home - A Few Words Of Encouragement

It is a moving experience.
You heart tells you it is
Time for a change.
So many little details to consider.
So many special people
To tell your plans to.
It involves a whole lot of throwing away,
Passing over and wrapping up to do.
It means going back to and forth
Between where you are
And where you are going.
It asks that you say good-bye
To family and friends
It opens up and lot of dusty memories.
It always hurts to close the door
And turn over the key.
But once you settle in upon
Your new hone
You will want to stay forever.
Have a happy home coming!

    Carol A. Melucci

Damaris, My Love

Thoughts fly endlessly through my mind:
You helped me regain my pride;
You healed my deepest wound;
Your eyes glow with the tranquility that calms the world's woes.
And with your caress, I know any man would love to share his soul.
The outer glow that thrives on your presence
Provides me with the life so I can live another day.
You make me feel so good inside.
My love goes well beyond your body —
It is your heart, your tenderness and compassion that drives
  me out of my mind.

So, when you look at me and show me that you care,
I will give you my heart, my soul, my life; these we can share.
So snuggle into my arms and stay for an eternity;
I will never make you leave.
Our souls shall unite in a bond none can separate
And you will know that no other can give me love; only you
  can medicate.

From sunrise to sunset our love will only grow stronger,
And as we dance together, we will live a life-long "meringue";
And I shall live for you, . . . die for you, . . . and I will take care of you
Because with all my heart, I love you.

    Jeremy Hicks

Of The Passion

So much has been written of the passion
You inspire,
The very image of your face can kindle
My desire,
Caught as though in time the lacy remnants
Of the past,
Steal through my dreams as if the boldness of your
Spell was cast,
Coming when I'm weakest like a moth drawn
To the flame,
Blossoming to die again though neither is
To blame,
Not strong enough to bend the rain swept branches
Of the heart,
Were blown with raging fury of the passion at
The start,
The moon in all its glory turned a blazing shade
Of red,
Glowing on the ashes of the fire that
Died instead,
Trying to rekindle one small ember of
Its soul,
Remembrance of the passion neither part could
Ever hold.

    Jean A. Brinkley

New Awakening

Once there was a lady so very fat,
You looked at her wondering how did she turn out like that.
Never knowing how inside she felt,
How her heart was lonely and about to melt.

With food was warmth and pleasure met,
Serving as substitute for love she didn't get.
Upon realizing food is used for our survival,
In her heart and mind started a new revival.

Soon the pounds slowly began to disappear,
Giving her the inspiration in overcoming her fears.
Now a new personality has emerged,
With all her negatives being submerged.

Now you can look at her and ask,
Will this new person last?
Now from food having been set free,
She has achieved all she wishes to be.

Now she is filled with confidence and self-esteem.
Placed within her eyes that special gleam.
Thankful for this awakening even at her age,
Only wishing she had discovered this at an earlier stage.

    Deanna Peal

"Heaven Sent"

Once in every lifetime - heaven overflows
you meet that "special" someone
and your life begins to glow

You are the stars that shine at night
the light that makes my day
you are the twinkle in my eye
you take my breath away

Your eyes, your walk, your tender ways,
your smile charms my soul
my days are filled with thoughts of you
you are beauty to behold

Are you a special angel sent from God above?
Or are you an ordinary person
and I just fell in love

    June Cooper

Always Forever Alone

As I here alone I wonder how can you throw our love away.
You say that you love me but your actions say you don't
I can't take this pain of loving you.
Don't say you love me, when you love another woman.
Please don't lie!
You don't need to hide from or buy me.
All I want is a relationship filled with monogamy.
I have a very small problem sharing you with another woman.
That's not your problem it's mine and I apologize
I can't change the way I feel. I'm a human being with a rainbow
of emotions. I never ask for anything but a little of your
honest time, guess that was asking for too much
you are still at her house for lunch.

Andra L. Lutchey

"Hope"

You helped me find love, you showed the way;
You stole my heart, one sunny spring day.

Now your gone, no one to blame;
When the crying is done, it'll still be a shame.

I lost the love, that I thought would stay;
The talking had stopped, nothing left to say.

Now it begins, the hurt and the pain;
Words were said, for personal gain.

I now live my life, from day to day;
With hope in my heart, I'll continue to pray.

If you return, there's one thing I'll give;
All of my love, if we both can forgive.

It was fate and God's will, that brought us to be;
It's never to late, for you and for me.

Gary D. Bogan

'Tree Lights Reflection'

Christmas Eve, in silence and all is complete
You take time to sit and let past memories repeat.
When without money we were never poor
The Lord, was somehow closer to the door.

Christmas season is a time to be joyous and gay
Christmas morning everyone takes the time to pray
Remembering to celebrate, as it truly is the Lord's day
Then for another year it is all put away.

If only the world could keep it in their heart
All year long after the festivities do depart,
But too soon the meaning comes and goes
With everyone drifting back into their own woes.

Very soon then even the spirit is out of sight
With the Christmas tree that was trimmed just right
Now ornaments are packed in the trunk for another year
And with them goes the Spirit of Christmas, no longer sincere.

Dorothy I. Brown

Your Touch

Oh why do you mean so much to me?
Your very voice sets me free.
The touch of your hand sends shivers down my spine,
And when you touch my cheek I feel divine.
If only we could be alone,
And I could show my affection too.
Maybe we could share a kiss or two,
And then snuggle up to keep warm.
But if we never are alone and are not able to do these things,
Then know that when we're together my soul yearns for your touch.
Your very presence makes my heart race with joy,
And if it wasn't for you,
I would never know what it feels like to be in love.

Francesca Fasso

Another Time

Softly you leave me, gently I go. Only to meet another time, I know.
You touched my life, as you always will, and knowing you'd leave me
   I loved you still.
Two people searching for someone to care brought feelings of
   tenderness only we could share.
Expressing our thoughts, each to the other, our desires and needs
   were soon discovered.

Time and again our knowledge grew as each day dawned a new
   experience with you.
In the quiet moment of stillness we lay, you touching me, no
   words to say.
We knew the happiness which had been revealed would be kept
   close in our minds; ever still.
Memories were made from being together and will linger in our
   hearts forever.
Now, softly you leave me, gently I go. But only to meet another time,
   I know.

Barbee L. Booth

The Wolf

We behold your form in the moon's bright light,
Your calls shall pierce the still of night
And all who hear are set in flight . . .

We know you do hide in the dark of night,
But where do you vanish in morn's early light?

Your heart is wild, and ever so free,
But all of your secrets, pray tell unto me!

What great sadness do you know?
What sorrows of heart do come and go?

Once you were many, but now you are few,
They slaughtered the old and young ones too.

You yearn for the babies you sired in spring,
And lost all the joy, as puppies they'd bring.

In great sorrow we search the land through,
And found that there's only a handful of you.

Your numbers have dwindled over the years,
You've spent your whole life just shedding tears
And all because of Man's ignorant fears . . .

Frank W. Percival Jr.

To Lori On Her 21st Birthday

Lori, now you're twenty-one.
Your adult years long since begun,
But parenting is never done
'Twas sometimes heartache, mostly fun.

Your college days are almost o'er
What does the future hold in store?
Knowledge opens wide the door
But to succeed, there's so much more.

We hope you'll use what you have learned
And useless bridges you'll have burned;
That you will leave no stone unturned,
Armed with degrees that you'll have earned.

And if I had a crystal ball,
I'd ease each blow, make light each fall.
I'd point out every dead-end wall.
Each disappointment I'd recall.

Wherever leads your path in life,
We hope it will be free from strife;
That you'll be sweetheart, mom and wife
And march to your own drum and fife.

Anne Leftoff

A Perfect Mother

Through the years of almost sixteen
You've seen my emotions sway from sweet to mean.
You've seem my hormones go wild,
As I grew to teenager from a child.
Through the years,
You've seen most of my smiles and tears.
You've seen me hyper and depressed,
You've even seen me when my hair was a mess.
Through the years, you've helped me do what is right,
You gave me your power and light.
To help me through the darkest nights,
And even more so when I was filled with frights.
Through years of loving me, when no one else would,
You told me, to make it through this life, I could!
When I was hateful, you gave me love not hate,
And for that, Mom, to me you will always be a saint.
You've taught me how to have a good life,
And how to be a great wife.
So, as I bring into this world a child and another,
I pray to be like you, a perfect mother.

Jennifer Oreshack

"Beauty White"

The moist cold air is still
your body vibrates with a quiet chill.
Tree branches are barren
green grass in shivering sleep
The sun cloaks behind a shining
white corona deep.
Sounds of airships echo near
while anticipation of beauty white is here.
Swirling crystals fall to the ground
and stick then blow around.
One to three, four to six, seven to twelve
is bellowed loud
People scurry to get with the
snow crowd.
Enjoy beauty white, it come every year,
it melts then vanishes as does a love tear.
All that remains is peaceful memory so dear.

John P. Kroetz

Your Guardian Angel

Hush little baby don't say a word
Your every dream will always be heard

For this small little bundle created from love
Is why I was sent here from heaven above

To comfort and protect you from unknown things
Just close your eyes as I spread my wings

I'm here to catch you whenever you fall
To dust you off and make you stand tall.

You've got to be brave and trust in me
That this is the way God wants it to be

He has a special purpose for everyone
Just as He did His only son

I'll always be here to watch you grow
You're more special to Him than you'll ever know

So climb on my wing and I'll take you far
As you close your eyes and wish upon a star

Cindy Loftin

Far Away

You were the best of love I ever had.
Your eyes could look beneath my quiet soul
and waken charm, and playfully and glad
my heart would join with yours and open whole.
We had our own sweet world, and secret names
within our soul-fused wild imaginings.
You knew my deepest thoughts, my favorite games,
so much like yours, but from such different dreams.
Our outer worlds were years and miles apart,
begun before our faces met the stars.
Our histories encroached upon our hearts,
and present lives gave in to ancient wars.
    Now you are far far away, but deep inside
    our distant souls, love's spirits still abide.

Jeanie Roberts

My Grandpa

You gave us all a gift of love, for many treasured years.
Your grace, your strength, your love of God,
    calmed my youthful fears.
A pillar of wisdom, an example to see,
You walked this earth in faith.
You loved your Lord and family,
You are what make men great.
You built your life on faith in God, for all the world to see.
And from the grip of human flesh, your spirit and soul are free.
As days go by, you'll be with us, the memories will always be.
The barn, the garden, the rocking chairs, just sitting on your knee.
So when I think of mighty men, you are the greatest of these.
The measure of a man is found in you,
I'm thankful, I had eyes to see.
I love you, Grandpa, and you loved me and you caused me to be blessed.
Your call has come, I'll let you go,
I love you and enjoy your rest.

Jonathan W. Lankford

Is This A Journey?

You wonder why I get chill bumps when you touch my skin.
You wonder why the days seem long until we see each other again.

You worry when I get quiet and stop talking for a while.
You wonder where my thoughts are behind my evil little smile.

You think you know me and my ways you think you understand.
You are surprised with covered eyes I recognize the touch of your hand.

Often on Saturday night on the dance floor I get totally swept away.
I get lost in the comfort of your arms, what else can I say?

Sometimes our eyes, our hearts, our feelings speak alone but out loud,
So much that they are read by any surrounding crowd.

Where are we going? Are we just having a good time and fun?
Or is this a journey — that has only just begun?

Audrey Diane Goff

I Love You Just The Same

You're not flashy, but quite plain
    You're not rich, but I love you just the same.
You're not very smart, but you're not dumb
    You may not be a great dresser, but you're not a bum.
Although you act conceited, you're modest at heart
    Everyday in my life, you have a big part.
Sometimes you act shy, others you're bold
    You're really confusing, so I'm told.
I'm describing you with such love and care
    So as not to sound judgmental, unkind, or unfair.
It may sound as though I want you to change — but don't,
    Because I love you just the same.

Cheryl K. Luke

Missing You

If I could turn back the hands of time,
You'd still be here, you'd still be mine;

Two years have passed and home you're not,
My life has changed, but my love has not;

I take each day as best I can,
Though I wish you were here, once again;

I miss you more deeply than words can say,
And desire your embrace in every way;

It's a nightmare for sure and still so unreal,
But in time they say, my hurt will heal;

I hope that's right, I hope that's true,
Because life without you, has sure been blue!

In Memory of David Williamson, 7/10/93

Joyce Ann Markarian Williamson

Hope

When the dark wings of depression beat the air around me,
Your love is the rescuing force.

When I find myself crawling through the darkness
of discouragement and disenchantment,
Your love is the guiding light that shows me my way.

When my heart is sinking in a sea of sorrow,
It is your love that lifts me to dry ground.

When I am lost and cannot find my way,
Your love is the compass that shows true direction.

When my days seem meaningless,
It is your love that gives me purpose.

When I feel I cannot go one step further,
Your love pulls me onward.

Hope . . . it is your love that keeps me sane.
You are in my blood,
It is you I breathe.
My life is meaningless without your love.

Forever I am yours, with love.

John Hendricks

Julie

When I awake in the morn I search for you
Your picture stares as if only to see me
Your lovely face shines because I am in your eyes
I kiss you and my day has begun
The sun shines and you are there
So bright so cheerful
When someone laughs it is you
Your pixie humor a delight
Another speaks and it is you
So open so honest
I hear music and think of you
A rhythm of memories
When I feel something soft I sense your touch
Your tender body next to mine
You are deep within me Julie
When I am with you my heart is full
At night my eyes close and you are beside me
In the dark of my loneliness
You are the light of my life
I love you so

James J. Deegan

In My Heart

Your smiling face
Your warm embrace
And the gentleness of your touch.
These are the things I miss so much.

Our love spanned many years
It outlasted the sorrows and the fears.
Our love was the strongest of any kind
A deeper, more lasting love you could not find.

Then one day you were taken away
Never again to pass this way.
You walked the earth so tall and proud
Now your home is beyond the clouds.

Now you live in that mansion in the sky
Where someday I'll join you by and by.
In my heart I'll carry our love so sweet
Until again someday we meet.

Beverly Myers

"Perfection"

Your Spirit empowers me,
Your wisdom makes blind eyes to see.
Your love can crumble hearts of stone,
Your presence keeps us from being alone.
Your kindness measures beyond compare,
Your love is proof of how much you care.
You stand alone in Your purity,
You're the prime example of what a Christian should be.
You were beaten and stabbed, and You paid the price,
Your death for us was the ultimate sacrifice.
You did the Lord's will and not your own.
Through Your life on Earth, humility was shown.
Your commands are righteous and without exception,
Trusting you will keep us from giving in to deception.
Perfection must be the most wonderful of all things,
And for this very reason, we crown You the King of all Kings.

Brian Palmer

Four Little Words

The romantic instrumental music of Johannes Brahms is soothing when you're sitting all alone. But being a bachelor he would not have understood what is music to my ears. Ludwig Van Beethoven suffered isolation because of deafness. At twenty-eight he could only communicate by writing. He too, would not have understood.

That which is music to my ears is not composed, requires no long hours of work, no particular talents; it's spontaneous, comes from the heart!! When I'm sitting alone, I'm never lonely. My memories sustain me. My daughters who live at a distance call me twice a week. Before the phone conversation is ended, I hear "I love you, Ma." This is "MUSIC TO MY EARS.!"

Ruth Ryan Nalls
10/6/23 to 6/20/94

The Child Within

Her tired heart holds on to the magic of hope,
With helpless longing she feels she can not cope.

A silenced child is lost in time's pain,
Paralyzed by fear because love never came.

She waits, and waits, for someone to hug
her loneliness away,
But hushed cries of abandonment, lead her astray.

Faint echoes of past wants ache her pained heart,
For feelings were denied from the very start.

Rage lies dormant and can't forgive,
But, the child within forever lives!

Cynthia Marie Harbaugh

630

You Are Love

You dance through my life,
  enchanted, I watch you
Sleeping sweetly, your face
  so beautiful, so peaceful.

You have brought me more
  joy than my heart could
   hold.
This, the reason it
  overflows with happiness
   at even the thought
   of you.

An extension of life,
  an extension of love,
You are the dancer, the dreamer,
  the child I once was -
You are my daughter
  and you are love.

    Bonnie M. Reeder

"Move Mountain Move"

Miss America we love you so.
You've opened more doors than you know.
Through faith you've conquered over trivial strife
That the word handicapped places on one's life.

Heather Whitestone, you are a great inspiration
To those who live in constant exasperation.
You've set an example for the world to see
That you can be what you want to be.

Deaf, inaudible speech, or totally blind,
One leg, no hands, don't alter your mind.
Take what you have, work vigorously to the bone
Is, no doubt, your philosophy, Miss Whitestone.

Your triumph has taught us to believe in dreams
Regardless to how difficult it seems.
You taught us about conditions causing dismay;
But say, "Move Mountain Move, get out of my way."

To one who radiates beauty, hope, and love,
The wondrous blessings from Heaven above;
Our prayer is for your continued success
And that the years ahead will be your best.

    Alva Menifee

"Motivation's Lover"

Oh, where have you gone my Motivation?
You've left my soul and flown to worlds distant from here.
Gone with other run-away motivations,
You dance around a bon-fire to be beat of strength and excitement.
Flying through the outstretched arms of the flames,
You go off into the night sky.

Oh, motivation, return to me.
You hear my cries of plea, but, just forsake me.

I see your fire as it burns through the night sky.
Over the world, through the heavens, beyond galaxies,
into the city and looking over the desolate souls
in need of a motivation.
I chase for you, my motivation, but you escape me.
Only to fall, in passion, in the arms of another.
My Motivation, I've lost you forever.

My Motivation, as I walk through the park mourning your abandon,
I feel your presence, I sense your grace, I look behind to see you
smiling through another's face.

    Francoise I. Baramdyka

So Much More

You are so much more, than just my mom
  you are my best friend
The way we joke, laugh, and play
  is very special to me
When I'm with you, you bring out the person
  I sometime hold trapped inside me
You give me the strength, and courage
  to be the outgoing person I like to be
The way we talk, share our feelings, and are
  there for one another, is so rare
But for us, it is just the way we are
  Words can't express how special you are to me
I can only pray when I have children
  they will feel for me, what I feel for you
You are so much more, than just my mom
  you are the kind of person I like to be

    Dena M. Lewis

"My Only Love"

I only want to be with you
you're the only one for me and now
I can't imagine what life
would be like without this opportunity
I waited so long for the one that would be
just right for me It was all I could do
to live the life I knew and then I
became so very lucky when I found you
You made me understand what I never
knew before when I thought you had given
all that you had each day you give me
more and more Now it's my turn to do
all the things you would simply have me do
and I will start by simply saying the words
I love you and I'll always understand
just what they mean because for me they
are only meant for you . . .

    Earl Stanley Cook

They Say

Love they say comes your way at its chosen time,
And Love they say sometimes control the mind.
Love they say can make you sad,
And Love they say can bring you up when you are mad.
Love they say can be true,
And Love they say can make you blue.
Love they say can make you think why,
And Love they say can make you cry.
Love they say can stick like glue,
And Love they say can cure the flu.
Love they say is a wonderful thing,
And Love they say can sooth the brain.
Love they say can come from the heart,
And Love they say can fall apart.
Love they say can shine like the sun,
And Love they say can be so much fun.
Love they say is better in the Spring,
And Love they say is the best when you hear wedding bells ring.
Love they say is not about race or color, but how we feel about one another.
If this is true as they say, I think love has finally come my way.

    Melissa Gonzalez

Growing Pains

I'm full of thoughts I must express
in one way or another
to let you know how glad I am
that God made me your mother.

So often I am guilty
of scolding when you're bad
and I forget, as mothers do,
to show you when I'm glad.

I hope that you remember
through your long and grown-up years
that caring means a frown sometimes
and love will oft bring tears.

When you stand your ground so firmly
and your independence shows
deep down inside I feel the ache
that only a mother knows.

And though the years gone by are few
since first I heard your cry
I must accept the fact that soon
I'll let you say goodbye.

Linda Jorgensen

Two Of A Kind

Piercing eyes of truth that cannot be looked upon.
Pain, fear, honesty,
Dirty hands, matted hair,
Please don't touch that designer suit.
Everyone rushing by.
Hey buddy, can you spare that dime?
Did you hear something?
What a shame, what a waste.
Screaming emptiness nips away their souls.
Out of my way, get a job.
They hurried home once, had jobs too.
They used to have friends and family.
They even had shoes.
Quick, look away, you mustn't care.
Besides, don't you know that will never be you?

Tanya L. Ishmael Hunter

A Father On Mother's Day

Despite getting older and grayer
Mothers still keep taking care —
Of all the sons and daughters
with fathers they do share —
Yes fathers love and treasure and
by their kids are always thrilled —
But seldom sees a father do for kids
what a mother always will —
From diapering to burping to putting on their clothes —
To kissing all their boo-boos to wiping their runny nose —

But a mother's love doesn't stop
though kids reach 40 plus years of age —
You still find mom a-mother-in
she is just on a different page —

Most fathers try to see that their kids are well provided for —
By going one step further than
just keeping the wolf away from the door —

But the greatest achievement as a father
I shall ever reach in life —
Is that I gave my sons a perfect mother the day I picked my wife —

Robert Bowen

I Will Always Love You

Mother you are someone who I will always love.
Through thick and thin, from begining to end.
I followed your steps, and learned as you taught,
And admired the things that we shared, and the joy that you bought.
Today I think of the memories we have shared, and
Thank God I had and have a mother and father who cared.
I love you so very much It's coming straight from my
Heart, since the day I was conceived the love begins from the start.
You are the sister that I never had. You are my sunshine
When things get dull or go bad, and I am to you the same
Thing in return, you educated me well so there's not much I have to
Learn.
I will always love you remember that even if your on the
Edge, because my love to you is something that I pledge.

Antheia P. Thomas

If I Could Only Dream of You

If I could only dream of you
tonight as I lay asleep
My thoughts of you, have failed to decrease
My love fore you, so real and true
Maybe life is worth living
My whole life thru
And as each day passes on
I'm thinking of you more and more
Although I feel you've made it to
your heavenly home

If I could only dream of you
I would whistper these sweet words to you anew
My precious love I still love you
stronger than any love I've ever known

If I could only dream of you
For every dream, I dreamed of you
I would wish upon a star
Please God, let me be where ever you are

Shirley A. Jackson

Glory and Praise

There are so many things I want to say
To thank you, glorify you, and give and praise
You heard my cry, and saved my soul
You gave me the peace that made me whole
I thank you, Lord, for what you did for me
You died on the cross, to set me free
The pain you endured on that day
Your precious blood shed to wipe our sins away
But death could not keep a hold on you
You rose again like you said you would do
I was lost in a world all alone
Living a life that meant nothing at all
Glory to God for your mercy and grace
For one day, very soon, I will see your face
I will stand before you and fall to my knees
For with my savior I will finally be
Praise be to the mighty creator of all
To my father up in heaven
Who makes the demons stumble and fall.

Angela Sandoval

One Lonely Night

I saw a man - seated!
From a-far;
A blind, felt true karma:
Green: Health;
I was drawn, hypnotized,
To Him.
His eyes, through my
Blindness were singing,
Allegro: "Der Frühling"
I came closer, unafraid,
And saw the soul of,
This stranger,
One like mine,
And his name was John.

Eddy Marie Tierney

Come Inside My Reign

Come inside, imagine me
Come inside my beauties
Close your eyes, come inside
Come inside my heart
Come inside my reign
Come inside, have a cup of passion
Come inside my love
Come inside my mansion, in the heavens,
Lay across my pillow clouds . . . come inside
Touch my spirit deep within my soul . . . come inside,
Swirl in the wind around and 'round we float . . .
Come inside horizons of dimensions unknown . . .
Come inside, experience ooh!
Just a taste . . . come inside, anticipate . . .
Come inside my infinitive treasures.
Provocative, incredible, sensational . . .
Pure, divine pleasures . . .
Come inside my reign . . .

Yvette Armstrong

Fantasy

Our dreams are what we choose to see an inspiration made,
Life challenges dreams that are envied and forgotten, some played.

Learning to accept why change comes in so many different ways,
Understanding along as you grow stronger over the days.

Having to face change is a fact that makes a world so insane,
No answers for the tears from a place of endless pain.

A place with such greed where innocent wars we've had,
Living in fear from sins of others that's so bad.

Wish for the future, pray for better than this painful past,
It's not what happens in life, our reactions are what last.

So many different ways to take — how do you know what to change?
Curious emotions from unfamiliar decisions, complicated and so strange.

Discovering those easily confused, left only to pretend,
Pretending that you understand will have you alone in the end.

Those unaware of those others, we pray to never know.
All misunderstood having so much hatred in a world continuing to grow.

Only greed causes such an ungrateful behavior, desperately satisfied,
Innocent lives left begging to survive as the existence of pain denied.

A life of no pain is just a dream to escape reality,
We play the game "Life" — only to try to become a fantasy.

Amanda M. Gamar

Lost Love

Her eyes watched for an
approving glance, a loving look, or
a touch per chance.
    The only adults she had ever
known, did not even notice that
she had grown.
    Her lonely appeals for attention
to date, in their declining years
would turn to hate.
    The bottle would attack the
family tree, instead of two,
    "The bottle killed three."

Archie Wertz

I Do Not Understand

I do not understand
    why so many are without homes
    Why we can't make new jobs, yet lay off so many
    or why we think a quarter can stop poverty all
    together
But most of all I don't understand
    Why people think it can't happen to them
    yet it happens to so many
    Or why people think there so generous
    Yet they push them away
    As if a piece of trash
What I do understand is Helping
    That is not a handout
    but a helping hand
    Or helping those many by providing food
    and shelter

T. Neil Sroka

Moonlit Mirrors On A Sandy Night

As I look in moonlit mirrors
on a sandy night,
I sit listening to the radio
trying so hard to fight
the tears that come when
I remember him.

He used to sit here with me,
holding me and singing off key.
I remember the time this song
was played — he chose me
Out of all of the other girls
at the party.

But now he's gone forever
because of his choice.
No one will ever have another
chance to hear his voice.

Why did he do it?
Didn't he know how much I cared?
I'd give anything to have him back
Looking at moonlit mirrors on a sandy night.

Christi Flores

Passage

Girl
Coiffed and costume-jeweled
One hundred hours of teen-age practice prepared your face tonight
One thousand fantasies led you gently to this moment:
His shadow, cast across your rigid brow,
Softens the glare of girlish hope,
Moves slowly down to mark you
Woman.

Felix Laumann

Meeting With Michael

Hey, how ya been?
I'm here
Did you think you'd never see me again?

It's been the longest time
But you've been in my mind
I missed you
For the rest of my life

You still look the same
As when you were twenty three
I've aged since then
Did you know it was me?

I've been waiting
For this time all my life
For you and I to be together again
I hope I've lived it right
To do you justice my friend
Matthew S. Aquiline

Untitled

The sun rose on a chilly June morning.
Nervousness swelled in my stomach as
tears filled my eyes.
For I knew I wouldn't see my family for 13 weeks.
My recruiters footstep echoed up the stairs and I
knew it was time to go.
Giving my family a last kiss I turned out the door and
did not look back.
The fear I felt was like a child afraid of the monsters
under the bed and in the closet.
Driving to Boston took longer than it ever did before.
Listening to the radio and idle talk with my recruiter
was all that kept me from drifting into a blissful sleep.
It felt as if I was in a dreamland where everything seemed
out of focus but yet it was all clear.
If it was a dream I wished I could have awakened from
it, but it wasn't and I was later glad for it because I earned
the title of a United States Marine.
Matthew C. Forsee

I love you,

I need you,
I want you,
I can't live without you,
So why,
Why can't I have you,
Why?
Kristina Blankenship

Snow Covered Night

It's a night like any other winter night, or is it?
It seems somehow different,
It seems almost magical as I look across the snow covered fields,
They sparkle as if they were covered with diamonds.

Lots and lots of diamonds illuminated by the full moon.
Looking up into the evening sky through the steam from my own breath.
Even though its so cold, I choose not to move for, the sight is so
   breath taking
So far away are the stars but yet this night they seem so close.

Yes there is something different about this night.
Everything seems so peaceful,
Perhaps I'm taking a new look at old things,
If this be the results I'll take it.

I'm very happy with what I'm seeing
It's a new verse to an old song
A new print to an old painting
Yes for this snow covered night is truly a night to remember.
Gregg Neff

This Is Mine

I'm writing again
It's a habit of mine
I don't know what I'll write
But what I write will be mine

One of the few things
I can easily claim to
No mountains to climb
This is just mine.

Other than this, what is mine?
Gifts from friends are just fine
I didn't create them, so I cannot claim them
But this I write is mine

It comes from my mind, my heart, and my soul
Nobody else can claim this
People think they can say "This is mine, That is mine!"
But they're wrong, This belongs to me.

Voices like mine seldom are heard
But writing fills up the void
Sometimes it's too hard to speak
But it's not too hard to write my word.
Vanessa Larae Valentine

Christmas 1994

Christmas comes but once a year
With the joys we hold so dear
Laughing children smiling faces
Best wishes from so many places
Good fellowship surrounds us
Harmony that never ends
Neighbor helping neighbor, friends remember friends
Then we help the needy, aid the sick and old
With more loving kindness than any heart can hold
Bells so clear, lights so pretty,
Spread joy and peace through-out the city
Christmas comes—just once a year
What a pity.
Phyllis Sumrall

In A Heartbeat

In a heartbeat the world is not the same as it was before,
In a heartbeat you can love someone that one heartbeat more.
In a heartbeat you can look at your child with new found love,
In a heartbeat someone you love can pass to the angels above.

In a heartbeat you can regret something that you've said,
In a heartbeat a memory can fade, lost inside your head.
In a heartbeat a new life can be conceived,
In a heartbeat a lie on ones lips chooses to deceive.

In a heartbeat the sky can change from blue to black,
In a heartbeat a lost love can find their way back.
In a heartbeat you may recall a dream that you've had,
In a heartbeat you can go from happy to sad.

In a heartbeat you may question your place here on earth,
In a heartbeat you can discover your own self worth.
In a heartbeat your troubles can seem too big to bear,
In a heartbeat you can feel you are under God's care.

In a heartbeat you offer your friend a kind shoulder,
In a heartbeat you can feel just a little bit older.
In a heartbeat we will take a chance because of someone's special smile
In a heartbeat we know that it's all been worthwhile.
Carol M. Vacca

To Have A Child

To have a child.
That I may never know.
To experience the love,
And watch them grow.
With a sweet smile,
And eyes that sparkle and glow.
With a gentle touch,
And a heart as pure as gold.
To have a child.
To watch them sleep as angels do.
Watch them play and be
Mischievous to.
To hear their laughter,
Throughout the day.
To hold them tight,
When things don't go their way.
To have a child.
God's gift from heaven above.
So cherish their life and
Give them unconditional love.

Elizabeth Berrios

Springtime's Holiday

When spring danced astray
with tomorrow's love anew,
and left its yesterday
all the grass was wet with dew.
Then winter came forevermore,
blithe, frosty snow to stay,
and it resolved to never bore
of springtime's holiday!

Friedell A. Strieman

"From My Window"

The beauty of the desert is
Wondrous to behold
It captures imagination and adds
Beauty to one's soul.
The mountains in the distance
Stand in proud array.
They uplift one's spirit and
Add strength to every day.
A roadrunner scoots by, honking
Along the way.
A huge falcon sits on the
Fence top, calmly waiting prey.
While little birds surround
Him, unimpressed by his majesty,
Two wild rabbits scurry across
Unmindful of their destiny!
Even the blowing, blinding sands
Have a beauty of their own
And promise, with faith and
Hope, all will be serene, once more.

Nancy B. Ott

Heaven

Beautiful, joyful,
singing, amen, alleluia,
praising, innocent, arguing, painful
fighting, fearful, burning,
devil, evil
Hell

Shane Baltzell

The Grains Of Water

I hear the ocean waves
And think of all the days
That I've been in the water
Watching, swim by, the others.

All I have's my soul
I have a name no more
All I remember's the day
The day I became the wave.

The second I fell off
I realized that this boat
Could no longer keep
Any body afloat.

It crashed into my head
The ocean's now my bed
The floor is now my home
I will forever, be alone.

Kristen Ryder

Untitled

Lost is our sense of knowing,
All our security is gone.
Ignorance has filled us up,
And left us empty.

We were the ones in the loop,
The ones that people ran to for answers.
Now we wander lost amongst the found people we once helped,
With no one to turn to but each other.

We look upon each other with angst, disdain, wonder,
Of where our lives have taken us,
And look inside ourselves with hope, curiosity, fear,
Of where our lives are headed.

The uncertainty of life drives us,
From one extreme to another,
To push and succeed and do,
Or to the depths of a personal hell.

Maybe this is growing up,
Maybe this will teach us how,
How to handle the happiness and the strife
Of all life's wonderfully horrific possibilities.

Ryan Wafer

Trip To The J.F.K. Library

Muggy days, rainy days, problem days all forgotten
her smile forgot them
her presence made me forget
on the way to the place with the big American Flag
overwhelming stars, the stripes
hanging from the silk formation
the vibrant red, like the blood from the day it represented
from the man it represented
the white, like angels in the sky waiting to catch him
and the blue, like spotlights shining on victory.
To the place where modern screens showed clips from
not so modern times,
captions taking you back to a time where venetian blinds were
$1.79 and nylon hoses were 99 cents
to a place, a site that is overlooking the bay, the city
so beautiful
the view so beautiful, the place so beautiful
and the one I was with, making my problems go away,
sleeping on my shoulder
even more beautiful.

George Bitsakis

Gifts I Did Not Know

The Lord gave me gifts I did not know,
He gave me children to play with in the snow
The Lord gave me life to chance
He gave me a husband with romance
The Lord gave me two parents to love,
He gave me two that fit like a glove,
When I feel alone and in the dark,
The Lord lights the little spark,
What is perfect, and without a flaw,
What do you believe, if not what you saw,
You were created to be with mistakes,
You are within yourselves great!

Cheryl Lynn Wayne

A Mother's Quest

From dawn, to duck she works to see;
The need be met.

No matter what the cost, she pays;
He sacrifice, foundations laid.

Mother, teacher, wife indeed;
Strives to help all those who plead.

Her children cry and set the tone;
Each challenge set for her alone.

No question where her strength has gone;
A press, a strive to carry on.

Her Lord; she reached out in awe;
Of all His glorious works performed.

Though such a frail and fragile being;
"It must be God", her soul is singing.

Her husband looks and calls her blessed;
He knows she strives to do her best.

Her spirit rises to the cause of rest;
Sweet rest upon the breast
Of the mighty one.

She's overcome; new life begun.

Helene R. Wilson

Eternity

Today my soul was one with Eternity!
An awesome trip it was for me.
I left the world on wings, set free
From worries, doubts, anxieties!

My soul soared through the sunlit sky
And claimed a cloud that drifted by.
From this celestial perch I glanced about,
So filled with joy I tried to shout!

Unfettered now, my soul can go
To Mars and back in a day or so
Stand unafraid on the highest peak
Or dive through stormy seas to seek

The perfect pearl withheld from me.
I tried so hard to pierce the mystery.
I shan't complain, for life's meant to be
A struggle on the road to eternity.

Believe me please, part of me I didn't take
Those dear the me I did not forsake.
For Love's not confine to the world we see,
For love's an integral part of Eternity!

Louise H. Hurd

Memories

There is a joy in memories
That time cannot erase.

Close your eyes, turn the pages
one by one.

An echo from the past;
A forgotten face,
Lines from a song and
Days without end.

Walking, talking, dancing, playing;
Mornings of soft fragrance.

Warm breezes, always spring;
Laughter and tears and gentle rain.

My fathers face, forever still.
Close the book; weeping, remembering.

Sharon Ann Barton

Cat

Sitting tall and majestic
Watching the shadows
   From the wall.

Scratching an old tree
   Sharpening the claws
   For the mice.

Stretching full length
To tone the muscles
   Even the tail.

Purring on the pillow
Expecting the call
   For the meal.

Curled by the hearth
Absorbing the warmth
   From the fire.

On guard by the door
Waiting patiently
   For the man.

Rosemary M. Miller

Swiss Mix

Chocolate and champagne
don't mix
Distant dreams
Spill upon
Distant shores
Spilled ideas
are stolen from the sand
and are invested
in a native's yard
Rain dropped
but didn't dilute
the dreamers
fulfillment
was short
but sweet
too bad
chocolate and champagne
don't mix

Michael Milewski

BIOGRAPHIES OF POETS

ABEL, DAVID MARK
[b.] November 22, 1979, Joliet, IL; [p.] Mr. Michael L. and Monica L. Abel; [ed.] High School Sophomore; [occ.] Student, Data Entry, House and Pet sitter; [memb.] AACA, Junior Statesmen of America, Swim Team, Palm Springs Desert Museum, Living Desert Nature Preserve; [hon.] 2nd Date Festival-Ceramics 1st Daughters of the American Revolution Essay contest (2), Presidential Academic Fitness Award; [pers.] I write what I see in my mind, what I feel in my heart, and what I know in my soul.; [a.] Rancho Mirage, CA

ABSHIRE, MITCHEL
[b.] March 6, 1955, Pikeville, KY; [p.] Eugene and Anna Lou Abshire; [oth. writ.] Collection of poems but never attempted to have published before; [pers.] Nothing is more profound than life itself.; [a.] Knoxville, TN

ACEVEDO, TANIA FRANCISCA
[b.] October 4, 1963, Cuba; [p.] Edith and Roberto Leon; [ch.] Shereen and Adriana; [oth. writ.] Writing poems has been my emotional outlet since age nine. My personal collection consists of over 800 unpublished poems.; [pers.] I've had a lifetime love affair with my pen and my book. My love is my word which needs to be set free. My lovemaking is interesting. Read me!!! (My influence has been "life".); [a.] Pensacola, FL

ACHERMANN, KURT
[b.] December 10, 1958, Ossining, NY; [p.] Ernest and Vivian; [m.] Laura, July 25, 1976; [ch.] Jennifer, Kurt, Kristin; [ed.] BS - Springfield College, Springfield Mass.; [occ.] Senior Vice President Boys and Girls Clubs of America; [oth. writ.] Two books - "Coaching Kids to Play Baseball and Softball" - "Coaching Kids to Play Soccer," Simon and Scluster.; [pers.] The words of my poetry reflect a life, hopefully cultured in others, and dedicated, always to the children of the world.; [a.] Duluth, GA

ADETUNJI, EMMANUEL
[b.] January 18, 1984, Baltimore, MD; [p.] Isaac Ogunsala, Julie Adetunji; [ed.] Evangel Christian Academy, St. Ignatius Layola Academy; [occ.] A Student; [hon.] Best P.E. Student, Perfect Attendance through 93-94, 1995-1996 Honor Roll Student through 92-93, 94-95, Best Scripture Memorizer, Best Basket Ball Player 94-95; [pers.] Sometimes when I write poetry it helps me to express my feelings so I could feel better about myself.; [a.] Baltimore, MD

ADKINS, LANA E.
[b.] December 19, 1949, Arbuckle, WV; [p.] Warren J. Sullivan (Deceased), Eleanor P. Sullivan; [m.] Gary Ray Adkins, October 1, 1981; [ch.] Russell Alan Hughes (Deceased); [ed.] Buffalo High School, Buffalo, WV; [occ.]

Lead Customer Service Rep. for APRIA Health Care, Inc.; [memb.] First Baptist Church of Eleanor; [oth. writ.] Personal poems written for my husband - friends and family. "Thank You" poem written and published in local newspapers.; [pers.] I write mostly when I am very upset - the poetry relieves stress and just seems to flow out. FYI — the poem I sent in was one I wrote about my son - my only son - he was killed in a tragic vehicle accident. In all the emotional upset I just kept having all the thoughts that were in the poem in the mist of all my heart break on a day I don't remember a lot of what went on I managed to get a piece of paper and write down my poem, I guess the straight came from the Lord, the poem was read at his funeral. My father had died unexpectedly on May 17th and buried May 20th, my son was killed May 27th and buried May 30th. I have found a lot of peace in poetry writing and I have also made other people happy with it, when I write them poems. I am thrilled you chose to print my poem.; [a.] Eleanor, WV

ADMIRE, LINDA
[b.] May 17, 1962, Fort Myers, FL; [p.] Hopson Gordon, Gladys Gordon; [m.] Burton Randall Admire Jr., February 15, 1980; [ch.] James Ryan; [ed.] Ft. Myers High, Edison Community College; [occ.] Customer Service Rep. Furon, Cape Coral, FL; [pers.] The poem was part of an inspirational time in my life that sparked a desire to search for my birth mother. I met her August 19, 1993; [a.] Cape Coral, FL

AGAPITO, FIDES
[b.] October 8, 1965, Manila, Philippines; [p.] Feliciano Capati, Greta Capati; [m.] Dr. Arnold V. Agapito, February 29, 1992; [ch.] Michael Alfred, David Joshua; [ed.] University of the Philippines; [occ.] Full-time Wife and Mother (and enjoying it!); [oth. writ.] As former Public Relations Counsel to several companies back in the Philippines, my writings are mostly corporate publications such as newsletters, brochures, annual report, etc.; [pers.] I've kept a journal since I was about 7. When the heart speaks, there is almost always a gem in it. That is the story behind this poem, and others that I write.; [a.] Chicago, IL

AGUILAR, DEL
[b.] December 24, 1950, Mathis, TX; [p.] Frank and Dolores Aguilar; [m.] Porfie Nunez-Aguilar, September 3, 1994; [ed.] High School graduate; [occ.] Rancher; [oth. writ.] Boston Kid, Note in the Wall (Time Travel), Life After Death, The Bible, God Spoke To Me, Collection of poems, (unpublished) also forecasting weather through insects, wild life and livestock.; [pers.] Live life day by day, but lit it to the fullest — love yourself, respect yourself and live for yourself and you will bring joy and happiness to others just

by the expression within yourself.; [a.] Ben Bolt, TX

AKE, MARTHA
[pen.] Anhelo de la Paz, Pease's Craving; [b.] July 28, 1946, Campeche, Mexico; [p.] Andrea Ake; [m.] November 20, 1962; [ch.] Israel, Fco. Alejandro, Andrea Panti Ake; [ed.] Elementary P. Vasto. High Vocational MM. NL. College Universidad de Montemorelos N.L. Mex. I obtained Master in Spanish language and literature.; [occ.] Now, I'm learning English still; [memb.] Seventh-Day Adventist Church. Now, I'm Associate Director of Sabbath School Program, in my local Church.; [hon.] I got a Cum-Laude when I finished my career, also a first place on lever school, other first place on level University.; [oth. writ.] "Dame Senor", "Give Me Lord" published in a known in all country of Mexico. Enfoque de Nuestro Tiempo"; [pers.] I strive to show the God's goodness and all his creation in my writing, I have been influenced by Amdo Nervo and early romantic poets.; [a.] Canoga Park, CA

ALBERTS, RUBY W.
[pen.] Ruby W. Alberts; [b.] October 24, 1928, Wichita, KS; [p.] Max and Mary Wilson; [m.] Bernard J. Alberts, August 6, 1955; [ch.] Joel, Jon, Joni, Paul; [ed.] H. Sch. Sedgwick, Minnesota Univ. and Walden Univ. Ph.D - Speech - Language Pathology; [occ.] Speech-Lang. Pathologist - Rehab Hospital, Clinic and Private Practice.; [memb.] Eastminster Presby T. Church, Wichita Rotary Intern. D.A.R. Board of Starkey Developmental Center, Bd Nat. Down Syndrome Congress, Bd - Lifeline - Wichita Member of Am. Speech and Hearing Assoc., Music Theater Wichita; [hon.] Delta Delta Delta Sorority, National Chairman for Down Syndrome Congress Convention Wichita - 1986; [oth. writ.] One article published in a Catholic Church magazine regarding our boy with Dawn Syndrome and family acceptance. (Have many stories written about our trends but have not published - Have lots of Poetry - none publ.); [pers.] I write poetry for spiritual inspiration and Luminous poetry, and I write for God's glory.; [a.] Wichita, KS

ALDERSON, SANDRA OWEN
[b.] October 7, 1965, Seguin, TX; [p.] Ervin Owen Jr., Wallie Ann Owen; [m.] John Alderson, April 28, 1984; [ch.] John Erick Alderson; [ed.] Seguin High School, Southwest Texas State University; [occ.] Counselor, Gary Job Corps, San Marcos, Texas; [hon.] Who's Who Among Students from American Colleges and Universities, Alpha Chi, Golden Key, Alpha Kappa Delta, Liberal Arts Award for Academic Excellence, Honors Program, Graduate Suma Cum Laude, Dean's List, Students Speaker for Commencement Ceremony; [oth. writ.] Poems and stories for personal enjoyment,

Commencement Speech, Thesis - Fear of Crime; [pers.] "Remembering My Roots" was written with love for my parents - to express my appreciation for their love and support. I presented them with the poem on my college graduation day.; [a.] Lockhart, TX

ALESHIRE, JENNIFER MARY
[pen.] Pokey; [b.] September 25, 1980, Cleveland, OH; [p.] Cynthia and James Aleshire; [ed.] Student at Hunter Huss High School; [hon.] Was accepted into the North Carolina's Governor's School of Art.; [oth. writ.] Many other poems that have never been published.; [pers.] All of my poetry was influenced by my friends and family. Special thanks to Christy Ridyard, Lorraine Gear, my mother, Missy and my Gran, for their support.; [a.] Gastonia, NC

ALLAIRE, KATRINA
[b.] December 31, 1978, Rahway, NJ; [p.] Gina Allaire, Kevin Allaire Sr.; [ed.] Bishop George Ahr High School; [occ.] Student; [pers.] Poetry is the best way to express yourself and your emotions; [a.] Iselin, NJ

ALLBEE, HARLAN
[pers.] Footsteps was written about Harlan Allbee, my great uncle. It is the story of his conversation with his son Roger on the day he died. Roger said he'd see his father tomorrow and his father said no because I won't be here. He died that night. Years later years my friend's four year old son, Jordan begun to ask his mother if when you die did you hear Jesus' footsteps coming to get you. Footsteps was written soon thereafter. Harlan Allbee was one of the greatest men I've ever known. He found the good in everyone he met. He lived his whole life in Brookline, Vermont. He loved the land, the people and his family. What more legacy could you leave behind. I will always remember him and hopefully his memory will be passed down through generations of our family.

ALLEN, ANGELA RYAN
[b.] January 1, 1948, London, England; [p.] Daniel Michael Ryan, Daphne Marie Brand; [m.] Thomas Melvin Allen, April 17, 1976; [ed.] Bishop Challoner H.S. London, England Tonybee School of Drama, London, England, Univ. of the Philippines, Philippines, St. Louis College, San Fernando, Philippines; [memb.] The Nat. Museum of Women in the Arts, The American Assoc. of Museums; [oth. writ.] A collection of Essays and Poems.; [pers.] Realism coupled with sensitivity is the basis of my writing.; [a.] Lorton, VA

ALLEN, RUSSELL C.
[b.] August 11, 1959, Mountain Lakes, NJ; [p.] Edward W. Allen Jr. and Gwendolyn Latour Rosler; [m.] Elizabeth Lynch Allen, July 3,

1994; [ed.] William Paterson College, Wayne, NJ, County College of Morris, Randolph, NJ, US Naval Engineering School, Chicago, IL, Admiral Faragut Academy, Pine Lakes, NJ, Mountain Lakes High School, Mountain Lakes, NJ; [occ.] Manager of Sales and Marketing Roflan Associates, Inc., Andover, MA; [memb.] American Society of Naval Engineers (ASNE), Society of Naval Architects and Mechanical Engineers (SNAME); [oth. writ.] Several poems published in the college magazine "The Promethium". I have not attempted to be published professionally.; [pers.] My works primarily focus on segments of the American struggle of why we do what we do, our conflicts, the consequences, and who we are.; [a.] East Bridgewater, MA

ALLISON, PAMELA R.
[b.] September 23, 1958, Johnstown, PA; [p.] Charles and Dora Lorditch; [ch.] Daughter - Ashley Allison; [ed.] High school Graduate; [occ.] Self employed; [memb.] Oakland United Meth. Church Choir, Hospice Volunteer; [pers.] I write about the feelings inside me and express them in my poems.; [a.] Johnstown, PA

ALLISON, STEFANIE KAY
[b.] February 22, 1983, San Angelo; [p.] Diane Kay Osborn and James Edward Allison; [ed.] I am presently attending Shirley Hall Middle School in Weatherford, TX.; [memb.] I am currently in Student Council and Drama Club.; [hon.] In U.I.L. I competed in the Oral Reading and placed 1st both times in the preliminaries and 3rd and 4th in the finals. In science I place 1st both times. I have also received awards in various sports events. I am also an honor student.; [oth. writ.] In the past I have written many works of poetry but most recently I have written Word Power, Step by Step and Grand mother.; [pers.] I realize that my dreams are high for my age, but I also realize that nothing can stop me from reaching for the stars. I would also like to add I am greatly inspired by my Great Grandfather who is a published author.; [a.] Weatherford, TX

ALMANY, STACEY MAE
[b.] July 1, 1983, Kingsport, TN; [p.] Shelly and Michael Almany; [ed.] Student at Gray Elementary In Gray, TN; [memb.] Washington-Sullivan Softball Association, Johnson City Swim Association; [hon.] Literary and Poetry, Competition 2nd place, Gray, Elementary; [pers.] I wrote my poem to try and make people see thru a child's eyes how violent and uncaring the world has become. I want to thank my mom for teaching and helping me to put my feelings into words.; [a.] Gray, TN

ALOE, JEAN MEYER
[pen.] Jean Meyer Aloe; [p.] Jean Taylor and Richard Meyer; [m.] Edward Aloe; [ch.] Jennifer

and Elizabeth; [ed.] Sweet Briar College - A.B., Northwestern University - M.S.; [memb.] Phi Beta Kappa, (AAUW) - American Association of University Women; [hon.] Phi Beta Kappa (Sweet Briar College), A.B. Degree Cum Laude (Sweet Briar College), N.I.H. Pre-Doctoral Fellowship (National Institute of Health) at Northwestern University; [oth. writ.] Poetry published in the Christian Science Monitor; [a.] Greenwich, CT

ALPERT, DONNA RAE
[pen.] Donald Alpert, Kram Niawt Dawn; [b.] November 29, 1959, NY; [p.] Roland and Frances Alpert; [ed.] Great Neck North High School, B.S., S.U.N.Y. at Albany, A.S. Electronics Control Data California; [occ.] Cruise Specialist, U.S. Merchant Officer; [hon.] U.S. Coast Guard Auxiliary 11th Dist Flotilla 16-01 Past Officer Certificate Award Honorable discharge U.S. Air Force; [oth. writ.] Several short stories, essays/; [pers.] You're here make the best of it!!?!!

ALTMAN, BLAKE
[b.] Wichita Falls, TX; [p.] William K. and Doris Altman; [ed.] Wichita Falls High, plan to attend Texas A&M University in the Fall '96.; [occ.] Student; [memb.] First Baptist Church, National Eagle Scout Assoc., National Honor Society (H.S.) Quill and Scroll Society (H.S.); [hon.] U.S.A.A. Academic All-America, Nat'l. English Merit Award, U.S. Nat'l Academic Football Award, Elizabeth Award, Elizabeth Gration Leadership Award, Hugh O'Brien Youth Foundation Ambassador, Eagle Scout.; [oth. writ.] No other published work.; [pers.] It is my desire to deny myself for the work and Glory of the Lord Jesus Christ.; [a.] Wichita Falls, TX

ALTMAN, CALVIN T.
[b.] December 25, 1926, Jacksonville, FL; [p.] Mr. and Mrs. Beulah Iliziptha Altman; [m.] Divorced, 1952; [ch.] Three; [ed.] High School; [occ.] Retired; [memb.] Church of Christ, V.F.V.U. Post 1170; [hon.] 7 Medals from WWII Occupation China, Philippines good conduct victory Medal Honorably discharge bottom Asiatic Pacific Japan Occupation; [pers.] I have over 1,500 poems that are my own poems, written by me alone.

ALU, MERCY
[pen.] Worth, Titi, Aishetu; [b.] February 11, 1977, Owerri, Imo State, Nigeria; [p.] Matthew and Bernadette Alu; [ed.] Ikenegbu Layout Primary School, Bishop Lasbrey Girls Sec - School Irete, Egbu Girls Sec - School, ie Imo State, Nigeria, Urbana High School, IL, Parkland College, IL student, English Pre Law, Indiana University of Penn.; [memb.] Children's Broadcasting and Newspaper Poem Publication, Imo Broadcasting Corporation, Nigeria (5th grade), President Press Club, Debating Society, Class President, Egbu Girls Sec - Sch and B.L.

G.S.S. Irete, Nigeria; [hon.] Parkland College, Champion, IL, Academic Salute Scholarship, Gamma Theta Sorority Academic Essay Scholarship, Urbana Concert Choir Award, 1st place, Urbana Choir Award, National Honor Society, Miss Teen Illinois (1994, Academics, Leadership, Poise, Congeniality, Personality Awards.; [oth. writ.] A Star, Addiction, Sister Song, Despair, also mostly song writing and singing.; [pers.] All my talents are from within. I believe that: Where there is life, there is hope. What I don't have today, as long as I live, I will obtain it tomorrow. I also strive to portray hope to all in my music and poetry.; [a.] Indiana, PA

ALVAREZ, ZULMA DRUMMOND
[b.] July 5, 1941, Varginha, Brazil; [p.] Zilah and Joao Drummond; [ch.] Joao and Vanessa; [ed.] Marconi High, Brazil, Catholic University - BA Brazil, Adelphi University - NY M.A. Stony Brook School of Social Welfare - NY MSW; [occ.] Social Worker - Alcohol Counselor; [memb.] National Association of Social Workers; [hon.] High School Valedictorian MA and MSW - Magna Cum Laude; [oth. writ.] Fist publication.; [pers.] I believe in non attachment to beliefs and ideologies opening myself to others way of thinking.; [a.] Oyster Bay, NY

AMBROSE, JOHN
[b.] September 30, 1964, Watertown, WI; [p.] Aletta Gray and Clarence Ambrose (Deceased); [ed.] University of Wisconsin - Madison; [occ.] Accountant, Law Engineering and Environmental Services, Inc, Kennesaw, Georgia; [pers.] This poem was written about an 8-year-old boy whom I knew while I was a university student. I wrote it for an assignment in a creative writing course.; [a.] Marietta, GA

ANDERSEN, KRISTIN
[pen.] Kristin Andersen; [b.] January 27, 1948, Altadena, CA; [p.] Donna and U. S. Andersen; [ed.] 1 yr. College Member of "Actors Studio"; [occ.] Singer, Actress, Writer; [memb.] Ascap. SAG. Equity, International Society of Poets; [hon.] International poet of Merit, 1995, Editors Choice Award, 1995 Emmy Nomination 1984; [oth. writ.] "Pieces of Time" Compilation of Poetry's (1970-1978) "Auntie K. Fables" Six Books for Children (1984-1992) Songwriter, Warner Brothers Music (1970-1974). 1994 Poem "Moving Day" Published in Sea of Treasures for 1995 - National Library of Poetry.; [a.] Valley Village, CA

ANDERSON, DAVID CHARLES
[b.] January 18, 1975; [m.] Medora Whitney, June 30, 1994; [ch.] One on the way; [ed.] Graduated from Norwich Free Academy, 1993; [pers.] This one is for my father-in-law, Charles Whitney Barners, who has been mere of an encouragement to me than he'll ever know.; [a.] Young America, MN

ANDERSON, JAYNE M.
[b.] March 25, 1963, Piqua, OH; [p.] Gerald and Rosemary Trissell, Emmett Anderson; [ed.] Piqua High School, Eastern Michigan University; [occ.] Occupational Therapist, Miami Valley Hospital; [oth. writ.] Written several other poems this one is the first one to be published.; [pers.] My poems are of personal quality which reflect some of the more memorable experiences in my life, whether joyful or tragic.; [a.] Piqua, OH

ANDERSON, KRISTAN
[pen.] Kristan Anderson; [b.] February 28, 1958, Columbus, OH; [p.] Carol and Denton Adams; [m.] Jim Anderson, October 25, 1980; [ch.] Ben, Jon, Sarah, Mark, Susan; [ed.] Ohio State University, BA in Nursing; [occ.] Stay at home Mom and help manage Key Connections; [memb.] Evergreen Chorale; [oth. writ.] The poem "The Masquerade" published through Mile High Poetry Society.; [pers.] I use my writing as a tool to bridge the inner and outer world into harmony.; [a.] Evergreen, CO

ANDERSON, PARKER
[b.] November 20, 1981, Fort Ord, CA; [p.] Cheryl Rice Anderson; [ed.] Bamberg Elem., Bamberg Germany, McNair Elem., Fort Bragg, NC, Hurst Hill Elem., Hurst, TX, Hurst Junior High School, Hurst, TX; [occ.] Student; [memb.] National Eagle Scout Association, Academy of Model Aeronautics, Smithsonian Air and Space, Boy Scouts of America, Order of the Arrow, BSA; [hon.] Eagle Scout (1994) with 4 Palms, Boy Scouts of America Heroism Medal, Oder of the Arrow, BSA, Sports Challenge USA All-Star Soccer Team, Honor Student, 13th Annual U.S. Eastern Free Flight Championships, First Place, P-30 event, Veterans of Foreign Wars Patriotic Citizen Award, Young Writers Contest and First Place, One Act Play, Boy Scouts of America Religious Award; [oth. writ.] One Act PLay - Young Writers Contest, Cumberland County, North Carolina; [a.] Hurst, TX

ANDERSON, RYAN
[b.] May 16, 1983, Stoughton, MA; [p.] Suzanne and Ronald Gonsalves; [occ.] Student go for a machine shop; [memb.] Civil Air Patrol; [hon.] Plymouth Youth Football award Basketball Medal a certificate of promotion from Federal Furnace School; [oth. writ.] Short stories and a few other poems.; [pers.] I believe there should be peace and kindness towards everyone.; [a.] Plymouth, MA

ANDRESEN, DANA
[b.] March 8, 1977, Ida Grove, IA; [p.] James and Judith Andresen; [ed.] Battle Creek - Ida Grove High grad of '95, attending Des Moines Area Community College; [occ.] Lifeguard at the YMCA of Ankeny; [oth. writ.] Walls published

in a break in the clouds - The National Library of Poetry; [pers.] This was wrote in memory of Cathy Lynn Freese a great friend of mine who was killed in a car accident on November 11, 1995; [a.] Ida Grove, IA

ANDREWS, JERRY
[pen.] Drew; [b.] March 5, 1975, Long Beach, NJ; [ed.] Athens Drive High School, Raleigh NC/ Attending Three Rivers Community College; [occ.] Yeoman in the U.S. Navy, [oth. writ.] Have yet to be published, but they soon will be (I hope) school newspaper-once; [pers.] I have only been writing poetry for a short time and I never thought I was any good so when the chance for me to measure how good or bad I was came I took it.; [a.] Groton, CT

ANDREWS, MARY
[b.] June 1, 1952, Anniston, MO; [p.] Issac and Willie Mae Martin; [m.] Deceased; [ch.] Charles Jr. Barbara, Adam, Brian, Kelly; [ed.] Bloomington School of Practical Nursing, Lincoln College; [occ.] Nurse; [memb.] American Cancer Society, Phi Theta Kappa, Dean's List; [pers.] I strive to touch the souls of others through inspirational writings.; [a.] Bloomington, IL

ANTHONY, SAMARA RAE
[b.] December 31, 1972, Fort Hood, TX; [p.] Robert and Esther Anthony; [ch.] Katia, Brittney, Cody and Devin; [ed.] Minuteman Vo-tech Lexington, MA; [occ.] Film developer and waitress; [pers.] My Poems are written on the basis of how I feel, with great support from my parents and kids, everything I do is in memory of my son Devin Alan, and those who have touched my heart.; [a.] Elko, NV

ANTLE, PEG
[b.] October 31, 1948, Columbus, OH; [p.] Lee Caryer, Betty Caryer; [ch.] Jeffrey, Christopher; [ed.] Bexley High School, Bowling Green State University, University of Dayton - Masters Degree; [occ.] 6th Grade Language Arts Teacher; [memb.] Trinity United Methodist Church; [pers.] My poems are inspired by God to offer love and hope to His children. May you sense His presence in each one.; [a.] Columbus, OH

ANTONELLI, ALYSSA
[pen.] Christy Chesnet; [b.] October 26, 1982, New Jersey; [p.] Basil Antonelli, Donna Antonelli; [ed.] Our Lady of Victoria Regional School, South Brandywine Middle School; [hon.] 1st place in a talent contest, state honor SAT's; [oth. writ.] A collection of is other poems all under the "Heading" (each poem is personally titled), burney into the mind.; [pers.] "Live your life only for yourself and reaching for the stars shining in the ocean.; [a.] Coatesville, PA

ARAUJO, DENIZE
[b.] Brazil; [ed.] BA in Music (piano), BA in Portuguese (Language and Lit.), BA in English (Language and Lit.), MA in English (Lit. and Cinema); [occ.] Ph.D. Student in Comparative Lit. at UCR, Coordinator of Portuguese/English Graduate Studies at Tuiuti, Curitiba, PR, Brazil; [memb.] MLA, Rocky Mountain Review; [hon.] Scholarship recipient - Italy TA award UCR; [oth. writ.] Articles, book and film reviews; [pers.] If fiction didn't exist, the world would be unbearable. After all, what is life if not a collection of fictional moments?; [a.] Riverside, CA

ARELLANES, MARTHA
[b.] April 10, 1951, Los Angeles, CA; [p.] Amelia and Catarino Arellanes; [m.] Divorced; [ch.] Larry Daza and Evonne Daza; [occ.] Cosmetologist; [oth. writ.] I'm now working on a series of children books and hope to get them published.; [pers.] I want to influence my children that "sky is the limit" on achieving anything that you want in life.; [a.] Montrose, CA

ARMISTEAD, ANNE C.
[b.] August 20, 1940, Hackensack, NJ; [p.] Eleanor R. Chaney Falkiewicz and Conrad L. Falkiewicz; [m.] Samuel E. Armistead Jr., April 28, 1961; [ch.] Elizabeth A. Armistead and Eleonor A. Batson; [ed.] Tenafly High School, attended University of Hawaii, Christopher Newport College, Auburn University of Montgomery; [occ.] Artist/Desktop Publisher; [oth. writ.] Wrote for and edited Wives Club Newspapers - Poems published in "Filibuster" AUM magazine; [pers.] The "nature" of humanity is my inspiration and the "humanity" of nature.; [a.] Montgomery, AL

ARNAO, PATRICIA WELCH
[b.] June 2, 1941, Wilmington, DE; [p.] William Welch, Thelma Welch; [ed.] North Miami High, Florida State University; [occ.] Teacher at McGinn Elem. - Scotch Plains, NJ; [memb.] Terrill Road Baptist Church, NJ Seminole Club, FSU Alumnae Assoc.; [hon.] Finalist in "Miss Hospitality" for Miss Universe Pageant, Grant recipient from Scotch Plains - Fanwood Ed. Enrich. Foundation, Dean's List - FSU; [oth. writ.] Poems published in N. Dade Christian Church's newsletter; [pers.] My poetry stems from the emotional and spiritual experiences God has allowed me to have.; [a.] Clark, NJ

ATKINSON, SHARON L.
[b.] March 26, 1950, Malden; [m.] Warren Atkinson, November 27, 1971; [ch.] John, Sheree, Michael and Cristine; [ed.] Malden High School; [occ.] School Bus Driver

AUGUSTE, RACHEL
[b.] June 21, 1984, New York; [p.] Dugravier Auguste; [m.] Marie M. Gisele Auguste,

December 2, 1978; [ch.] Three; [ed.] High School; [occ.] Taylor; [hon.] In school I won Miss P.E.; [oth. writ.] I write stories but I keep them to myself.; [a.] Malden, MA

AUGUSTINE, SHILOH LEO
[b.] October 12, 1952, Denver, CO; [p.] George Leonard, Lorene Ann; [ed.] High School Diploma, New Ramparr Schools (Trade), and just plain living (unheeded); [occ.] Grinder of Springs at Newcomb Springs, CO; [oth. writ.] Editorial Response letter, some more poems that I sent to Vantage; [pers.] As according to Jesus those who win in this reality will lose in the final, so when somebody calls me a loser, I will wear that badge as the prince of fools. The judgment is not finished.; [a.] Thornton, CO

AUSTIN, CHRISTINE BOYD
[b.] September 13, 1966, Baltimore; [p.] Dorothy Brown, Thearchie McCain; [m.] Andre Austin, August 10, 1995; [ch.] Tomicka Boyd, Andre and Tiffany Austin; [ed.] John Eager Howard Elementary, Frederick Douglas High, Sojourner Douglas College; [occ.] Teacher Assistant, Ashland Headstart Nursery Inc.; [memb.] Lafayette Courts Dual Management Team, Vice president, Parents Against Lead, Waters A.M.E. Church; [oth. writ.] I've written several poems. One other poem "Lead" won an award in another contest a few years ago.; [pers.] My poem reflect the different problems in our society. I only which I could comfort someone and soothe their emotional pain.; [a.] Baltimore, MD

AUSTIN, KIMBERLY ANN
[b.] December 22, 1967, Saint Albans, VT; [p.] Shelvajean R. Austin, Sidney E. Austin; [ed.] Bachelor of Science Degree, Elementary Education from Johnson State College, Associate Degree Liberal Studies-Community College of VT; [occ.] Freelance Writer; [memb.] Ladies Auxilary, VFW Post 758, Friends of the St. Albans Free Library; [hon.] Cum Laude Honor College Graduation - Johnson State College, Class Author and Writer High School Awards, as well as History Award in grade school - award for volunteer hours at Apple Tree Learning Ctr. - 1986; [oth. writ.] Three articles published in the BFA Mercury in High School that appeared in the local newspaper in 1984-1985.; [pers.] In life I find it important to please yourself and strive for your dreams, the dreams will come true only if reach out and grab them, do what you feel is right for you, not for others because that is that they want you to do. Most importantly by ourself.; [a.] Saint Albans, VT

AZHAR, SAMEENA VASEEM
[pen.] Sameena Azhar; [b.] January 18, 1980, Bronx, NY; [p.] Mohammed Sadruddin, Azmath Qureshi; [ed.] Carden School of La Habra, Fairmont Academy/Sunny Hills High; [occ.]

Student, High School Junior, aspiring to pursue career in Philosophy/Biology; [memb.] Key Club Service Committee, co-founder of Muslim Student Union, Model United Nations delegate, American Cancer Society volunteer; [hon.] National Honor Society, Rotary Club Award Honoree, freshman class secretary, Academic recognition in literature and biology; [oth. writ.] Poems for various writing contests, short stories published in yearbook and portfolios for the Sunny Hills Writer's Guild; [pers.] "Time to eat all your words. Swallow your pride. Open your eyes. You must unlearn what you've learned. Trying isn't enough. Do or don't. Size matters not." — Tears for Fears; [a.] Fullerton, CA

BABCOCK, JOANNA
[b.] April 11, 1975, Absecon, NJ; [p.] Linda and Jonathan Babcock; [ed.] Holy Spirit High School, Rutgers University; [occ.] Student; [memb.] US Rowing Association; [hon.] Undine Scholarship; [oth. writ.] Several poems and some short stories, mostly written for friends and family members.; [pers.] I like to delve into the darker side of existence and especially enjoy writing fantasy. For me, writing is a good escape from the monotony of daily life.; [a.] Absecon, NJ

BABIASZ, THOMAS J.
[b.] October 5, 1963, Philadelphia, PA; [p.] Theordore and Lillian Babiasz; [m.] Cara Babiasz, February 15, 1986; [ch.] Theodore and Carrie; [ed.] Father Judge High School Graduate; [occ.] Correctional Officer; [oth. writ.] Poem "Behind These Walls" published in "Treasured Poems of America" in fall of 1996.; [pers.] Writing poetry for approximately a year now, I enjoy the opportunity to express other views or viewpoints on sometimes otherwise simple subjects. I have also begun working on other lengthier projects and hope to bring good, positive messages in my works.; [a.] Philadelphia, PA

BACZEK, BARBARA
[b.] May 12, 1947, Hartford, CO; [p.] Tadeusz and Sophie Baczek; [m.] Divorced; [ch.] R. Theodore and P. Gareth Wallace; [ed.] UCLA and Southeastern Mass University; [hon.] Graduated Magna Cum Laude; [oth. writ.] 1968 songs for an album dedicated to Transcendental Meditation and other meditations.; [pers.] This poem is also a song and was written commuting through rural sections of Massachusetts where the autumns are magnificent.; [a.] New Bedford, MA

BAILEY, JUDITH E.
[b.] August 7, 1956, Wichita, KS; [m.] Merle W. Bailey, May 15, 1992; [occ.] Legal Secretary; [memb.] U.S. Coast Guard Auxiliary, KS Arborist Association; [a.] Wichita, KS

BAILEY, WENDY
[pen.] Wendy Craig Bailey; [b.] October 24,

1969, Gallipolis, OH; [p.] Wendell Craig and Ruby Craig; [m.] Scott Lee Bailey, May 22, 1995; [ed.] Buffalo High School - Buffalo, WV, Putnam Co. Vocational Technical Center - Eleanor, WV; [occ.] Keypuncher - Stone and Thomas Distribution, Nitro, WV; [oth. writ.] Poem printed in 1987 Buffalo High School yearbook; [pers.] Cherish your memories and always tell your feelings before it's too late. A poem is the best way to be unique.; [a.] Buffalo, WV

BAKER, CAROLINA A.

[b.] June 1, 1961, Ports Mouth, VA; [p.] John J. and Eleanor C. Ashburn; [m.] Darryl Wayne Baker, April 16, 1994; [ch.] Roger, Melissa and Christopher; [occ.] Flag Fixer at Unifi Spun Yarns, Eden, NC; [oth. writ.] My poem "Our Little Flower" was published in "Walk Through Paradise".; [pers.] I wrote this poem for other women who have gone through hard times. There is a way out. You just have to work very hard for it. I made it, you can too. This is also for my sisters Lou-Ann Joyce and Rosemary Kennedy. Who helped me through my hard times. And for my friend, Linda Holley.; [a.] Madison, NC

BAKER, DOROTHY G.

[b.] December 30, 1938, Blairsville, PA; [p.] Merle and Sarah Allison; [m.] James Arthur Baker, November 23, 1957; [ch.] Brenda, Diana, Judith, Linda, grandchildren: Amanda, Bethany, Rachel, Joshua, Jeremy, Cory, [ed.] Blairsville High School - 1956; [occ.] Self Employed; [memb.] First United Methodist Church, Founding Member of "All Volunteer Blairsville Food Program"; [pers.] Past volunteer of the American Heart Association, American Cancer Association, Latrobe Area Hospital, Secretary/Worker of Blairsville Food Program. I enjoy self expression through prose and poetry.; [a.] Blairsville, PA

BAKER, ELIZABETH

[b.] July 25, 1966, Jacksonville, FL; [p.] John and Sylvia Luscan; [ch.] Emily Jessica Baker; [ed.] Saranna High, Florida Community College at Jacksonville.; [occ.] Paralegal; [hon.] Dean's List; [pers.] Giving up is easy, but going on is worthy.; [a.] Jacksonville, FL

BAKER, HELENE ARLENE SCHIMEK

[b.] April 30, 1945, Chicago, IL; [p.] Arnold Schimek, Helen Schimek (D. December 12, 1995); [m.] George James Baker, October 25, 1980; [ch.] Stepsons: Bob, George, Don, Steve; [ed.] BA - Northeastern Illinois Univ., Richards Vocational HS - Chicago, IL (Honor Roll), Holy Trinity Croation Elementary School, Logistics Military School, Ft Lee, VA; [occ.] Oil and Gas Revenue Acct/Auditor; [memb.] CFE-Nat'l Assoc. of Certified Fraud Examiners, Reserve Officer Association, The Warrant Officer Association, U.S. Army Reserves, USAF-Aux,

Marauder and Homewood Civil, Air Patrol Units (Liaison); [hon.] Liaison Officer - C.A.P. USAF-AUX, CW4, USAR (IMA) Ft. SamHouseton, TX, CFE-Nat'l Assoc. of CEFs, FY94 WEL Graduate, U.S. Army Commendation Medal, TQM Award, Certificates of Appreciation: USAF-AUX-C.A.P., and City of Chicago Cert., Patent Pending Basketball Conference Runnerup-USArmy Germany (BadCannstatt). Performance Awds; [oth. writ.] A welfare package plan introduced to the 103rd and 104th Congress Prompt payment policy and procedural paper adopted by US D.O.D. Contracting. Indices suggestion to Contracting Regulations - adopted.; [pers.] As we strive for tomorrow let us not forget today. Strive to be a leader and accumulate wealth in health and success and never suppress the unfortunate. Remember your "Heavenly Father" can easily fall kings as he has made kings. Always help others.; [a.] Humble, TX

BALL, LARRY L.

[b.] May 22, 1942, Shelby, MI; [m.] Mary Ann, December 15, 1973; [ch.] Joshua Christopher; [ed.] P.R. Degree Grand Valley State, RN Degree Colo. Southern Grad., Work Western Mich. Univ., Nat'l Inst. of Children's Lit Inc.; [occ.] Self Employed; [memb.] Randolph Sheppard-Vendors of America, Merchants Div., Nat' Fed of the Blind, American Counsel for the Blind; [hon.] None that mean anything; [pers.] I am a spirit waiting to be released to traverse the universe.

BALLOW, MARVIN, L.

[b.] December 27, 1958, Selma, CA; [p.] Buford Ballow, Mildred Ballow; [m.] Susan Diane Bailey, September 22, 1979; [ch.] Angela Marie; [ed.] Gresham High; [occ.] Laborer, Artist; [pers.] I wrote this poem about my first and only true love, Susan, who is no longer with me, but who gave me a dream come true, when she gave me my daughter, Angela Marie, who like Susan and my mother, is beautiful in every way.; [a.] Salem, OR

BARCLAY, STEPHEN G.

[b.] November 8, 1957, Hutchinson, KS; [p.] James T., Joan R. Barclay; [ed.] H.S. Highlands High School, National Hgts. Pennsylvania; [occ.] Service Technician; [memb.] New Song Community Church; [oth. writ.] One Lost Sheep, Given By God, Streets Of Gold, A Daily Walk; [pers.] My singular purpose is to encourage people to seek Truth, Hope and Salvation found only in our Lord Jesus Christ.; [a.] Bridgeville, PA

BARHYDT, HAMILTON

[pen.] Hap Barhydt; [b.] November 4, 1928, New Haven, CT; [p.] Steele Kissam Barhydt and Katherine Hamilton Barhydt; [m.] Elizabeth Bleile Barhydt, October 10, 1978; [ch.] Anne

Barhydt Krall, Katherine Barhydt Dickie; [ed.] Hotch Kiss School, BS Yale University, Physics Ph.D Cornell University, Engineering Physics; [occ.] Retired (formerly applied research guided missiles and infrared sensors); [memb.] Current: Sierra Club, Association of Humanistic Psychology, Touch for Health Association; [hon.] Sigma Xi, Dean's List; [oth. writ.] Voyage of a Lifetime (poetry book) Word Impressions (poetry brochure) many technical articles and books.; [pers.] Trained as a physicist, I have learned to look beyond the obvious for the subtle connections between man and his universe. My poetry reflects this continuing quest.; [a.] Groveland, CA

BARRETT, MARY ANN

[pen.] Mary Barrett; [b.] February 7, 1906, Le Mars, IA; [p.] Catherine Breen Flynn, George Washington McAuliff; [m.] Richard Barrett, November 20, 1929; [ch.] Catherine, Richard; [ed.] High School -Porterville Union, Herald's Business College, S.F., University of California, Berkeley Extension Orange Coast College, Costa Mesa California; [occ.] Retired (U.C. Berkeley Campus 1971; [memb.] Woman's Civic League - Newport Beach, Ca, Oasis Center - Corona Del Mar, CA.

BARRON, AGNES ANNA

[b.] Los Angeles, CA; [ch.] Craig Barron; [ed.] B.A. Psychology, Univ. of California, Berkeley 1972; [a.] Berkeley CA

BARRY III, JAMES S.

[b.] March 12, 1975, Saint Lois, MO; [p.] J. Sherman and Janice Barry; [ed.] Council Rock High School Bloomsburg University; [occ.] Undergraduate student; [memb.] Bloom Players Provost's Lecture Series Executive Committee; [hon.] Pennsylvania Arts Alliance Award for Excellence in Theatre, 1992-93; [oth. writ.] Published in campus newspaper, The Voice Author of several screenplays, and stage plays.; [pers.] The solution to racism, and in fact to all conflict, is only to be found in the individual.; [a.] Washington Crossing, PA

BARTELSON, LAURA

[b.] July 6, 1981, Fortuna, CA; [p.] Bradley and Lori Bartelson; [ed.] Graduated 8th grade at Scotia Elementary School and at present a Freshman at Fortuna High School, Fortuna, CA; [hon.] Fortuna Rotary Club Academic Scholarship - Presidents Award for Academic Achievement - 8th gr. Valedictorian - No. CA CHP 1st pl. Bicycle Helmet Awareness Poster and Slogan Contest - Crescent City Jaycees all tourney cheerleading scholarship - UCA All Star Cheerleader; [oth. writ.] 1st and 2nd place awards on poems entered in County Fairs. Other writings published in the H.S.U. Young Writers Conference Anthology Book; [a.] Scotia, CA

BARTZ, CYNTHIA
[m.] Robert Bartz; [ch.] Pam Bartz; [hon.] Pianist - contest; [oth. writ.] Forthcoming is my non fiction book, "The Expert and The Poet". I have written many poems and all are illustrated by Robert and Pam Bartz.; [pers.] My greatest honor has been living in this magical, mystical, marvelous place called earth. My written endeavors are to pick up the roles that each of us play in life's patterns, rhythm and rhyme and to pass the message on!; [a.] Shenandoah, TX

BASS, KARTNEY K.
[pen.] Kartney K. Bass; [b.] August 20, 1981, Sacramento, CA; [p.] Mr. and Mrs. Henry Bass; [ed.] Spring View Middle School, I am currently in the 8th grade.; [occ.] I am a student.; [oth. writ.] I have been published in a children's Anthology of poetry book called Anthology of Poetry by young Americans in the 1995 Edition.; [pers.] Although I am only 14, in all of these years I have accomplished what I have been striving for and am most proud of being a published poet twice now.; [a.] Rocklin, CA

BATALIA, ERIK JAY
[pen.] The Dreamer; [b.] March 7, 1977; [p.] Chuck and Jo Ellen Batalia; [ed.] Graduated at Frontenac High School in 1995; [occ.] Screen printer at National Mills; [hon.] I got a honorable mention in a Art fair for an acrylic printing; [oth. writ.] Currently working on a book for possible publication and more poems; [pers.] I would like to thank Patty at work which helped me realize this talent. And also thanks to all of those whos been in my life.; [a.] Pittsburg, KS

BATES, WHITNEY E.
[b.] January 31, 1980, Borger, TX; [p.] Mr. and Mrs. Alan Bates; [ed.] Tenth grade student at Borger High School; [occ.] Student; [memb.] Wesley United Methodist Church; [hon.] Who's Who Among American High School Students, National Leadership and Service Awards Winner; [pers.] We must not live to exist, but live to make a difference.; [a.] Borger, TX

BATT, ROSE
[pen.] Rose Batt; [b.] February 7, 1923, Buffalo, NY; [p.] Caneo and Sarah Diagostino; [m.] Richard Batt, September 10, 1955; [ch.] Karen McCrea, Grandchildren - Erin and Michael McCrea Jr.; [ed.] Grammar School and East High School Diploma from Writing Course - Institute of Children's Literature; [occ.] Homemaker; [memb.] Member of Public Broadcasting Association; [hon.] Honorable Mention in Poetry Contest, poem published in Walk through Paradise, Poem published in Our Kenmore Community Newspaper; [oth. writ.] Other poems and stories for children and several articles.; [pers.] I find that writing poetry - is my outlet for being able to express my feelings freely - when I am not otherwise able to do so. It is a form of therapy for me.; [a.] Kenmore, NY

BATTERSON, DORIS
[b.] June 1, 1915, Grundy County, IA; [p.] Emil and Dagmar Aegard; [m.] Deceased - 1963, December 2, 1933; [ch.] "W. J.", "Jerry" and Anne; [ed.] Indian Hills, Community College, OTTUMWA, IA; [occ.] I.P.N. Nurse; [memb.] Of Emuel Luthern Church, Kimballton Iowa and of Iowa Poetry Ass.; [oth. writ.] I am a paraplegia being unable to do anything physical, I find that writing poetry helps to be leave the trapped my own body released the tension and stress.; [pers.] I am an 80 yrs. old widow with 3 children, one foster daughter and adopted daughter and a adopted son I was born June 1, 1915, Grundy County, IA.; [a.] Elk Horn, IA

BAUDER, SHIRLEY J.
[b.] April 25, 1940, Saint Louis; [p.] Jean DiLorenzo, Oscar Ballowe; [m.] Mark A. Bauder, August 5, 1981; [ch.] Three; [ed.] Assoc. Degree, San Bernadino Com. College, CA (including 3 yrs. UMSL); [occ.] Homemaker; [oth. writ.] Unpublished Journal, Garden column for subdivision.; [pers.] "The mind's opinions are a reality."; [a.] Bellevue, NE

BAUGH, ACTER
[b.] June 12, 1979, Hanover, MA; [occ.] Cashier at Wendy's; [oth. writ.] Alive Again, Burned, Delirium (in the works), Don't Fall in Love, Grief, Grin and Bear It; [pers.] I would like to dedicate this poem to James O'Harr. You've been a tremendous influenced to me personally and have inspired me to broaden my horizons and expand my mind, to be unrelenting in my pursuits, as you are. In my humble again you've surpassed were Atkinson and for, albeit as fire.; [a.] Macabody, MA

BAUGH, FREIDA
[pen.] Dimidot; [b.] November 28, 1954, Dallas, TX; [p.] James Baugh, Alta Baugh; [ch.] Amber Shay Whiteside; [ed.] Terrell High, TVCC; [occ.] Newspaper Composer/Writer; [oth. writ.] Several articles published in a local newspaper, The Terrell Tribune.; [pers.] I strive to write about that which many people can relate. I have been greatly influenced by the wisdom of my family and my Cherokee Heritage.; [a.] Terrell, TX

BAXLEY, EMMA
[b.] February 18, 1924, Talladega, AL; [p.] Deceased; [m.] Deceased, April, 1951; [ch.] Six girls; [ed.] 12th grade graduate; [occ.] Retired; [memb.] New Jerusalem Baptist Church Mother Board Stien Hospice, Advisor of Sandusky High School Gospel Choir, Mothers for Christ Jail Ministry; [pers.] I strive everyday to show God's love to others. That influenced me to start writing.; [a.] Sandusky, OH

BAXTER, CHARLES
[b.] May 17, 1984, Tyler, TX; [p.] Ann Baxter; [ed.] So for I've made it to the 6th grade and hope to start middle school next year.; [occ.] Student; [a.] Phoenix, AZ

BEARD, TRUITT J.
[pen.] Truitt J. Beard; [b.] July 23, 1920, Catawba County, NC; [p.] John H. and Susie Williams Beard; [m.] Dorothy (Dot) Bumgarner Beard, June 3, 1962 (second); [ed.] Attended Catawba County Schools Maiden, NC; [occ.] Retired Plant Mgr. now doing part time Consultant work; [memb.] First Baptist Church Maiden (Deacon), Choir Member Etc. - Advisory Board, Salvation Army - Advisory Board Branch Bank and Trust Co. BB and T, Board of Directors Catawba County Council on Aging; [hon.] Deacon for more that 40 years-former Mayor Maiden 6 yrs. - N.C. League of Savings Inst. - Distinguished Service Award 25 years Citizens Bank, American Red Cross 8 gal. blood donor and United Fund Liaison to American Red Cross Board of Directors, 1985 Man of the Year by Woodman of the World, featured in January '95 Hickory daily record article, served as Associate Chaplain Catawba Mem. Hospital Hickory, NC also served as Red Cross Volunteer at Catawba Mem. Hosp.; [oth. writ.] Weekly feature writer for Church news letter First Baptist Church Maiden, NC (Previous) Numerous unpublished works of poetry.; [pers.] "I'd rather wear out than to rust out" (unknown) "Whatsoever ye would that men should to do you do ye even so to them" (Matthew 7:12) Author of influence John Ruskin, Man I greatly respect Dr. Billy Graham, my favorite scriptures St. John 3:16, Micah 6:8, Psalm 1, and Psalm 23; [a.] Maiden, NC

BEAVERS, KAREN M.
[ed.] B.S. Behavioral Sciences Un. Md Un. College currently in the Masters Program in Pastoral Counseling at Loyola College; [occ.] Owner of Gifts and More Inc.; [memb.] Volunteer Domestic Violence Center Howard Cty., American Psychological Association, NAFE, American Biographical Institute, Research Association (Deputy Governor), American Assoc. of University Women; [hon.] Psi Chi National Honor Society in Psychology, Honorable Mention in the Bowie State Poetry Contest 1984; [oth. writ.] Works featured in New Voices of American Poetry 1978 and 1981 also in a vision, a verse by poetry press, works featured in Words of Wonder and Best of Feelings anthologies by Anderie Press also "Feelings" magazine Anderie Press "Night Music" lit. mag. Un. Md. Un. College.; [pers.] The Peace Prayer by St. Francis of Assissi inspires me. "Lord, make me an instrument of Your peace". I try to reflect that in my work.; [a.] Laurel, MD

BEDNAREK, BRIAN
[b.] December 1, 1979, Trenton, NJ; [p.] Charles and Mary Jane Bednarek; [m.] September 26, 1970; [ch.] Brian and Michael; [ed.] Hamilton High West; [occ.] Student; [oth. writ.] Several poems unpublished and awaiting to be published.; [pers.] When viewing a situation, look at all angels, and make all of them fifer out of you and your beliefs.; [a.] Trenton, NJ

BEHRENDT, LEANN M.
[b.] March 30, 1982; [p.] Charles and Betty Behrendt; [ed.] Student of West Perry Middle School; [occ.] Student; [a.] New Bloomfield, PA

BELL, VIVIAN M.
[b.] December 25, 1926, Tampa, FL; [p.] Douglas and Margueritte Pursley; [m.] Gene T. Bell, January 9, 1950; [ch.] Vann Allen Beverstock; [ed.] Elementary School, Houston, Texas, Rollins College, Winter Park, Florida.; [occ.] Teacher and Conductor of Choral and Congregational Music for the Church of Jesus Christ of L.D.S, Music Chairman and Vocal Coach. Organist for the Orlando, Florida, Temple of the Church of Jesus Christ of L.D.S 1995; [memb.] Member of the Bach Festival Society of Rollins College, Winter, Park, Florida 1964-1980, Member of the Florida Symphony Opera Gala. 1964-1980, Winter Park, Florida Concert Orchestra Violinist and Vocalist. 1964-1970; [hon.] Bi-Centennial Award for 50 consecutive years of Church Music Service in Florida.; [oth. writ.] (1.) A Psalm, (2.) The Holy Temple; [pers.] Quality music and poetry in addition to the Holy Scriptures, I feel are the iron rod of divine direction through life's sojourn.; [a.] Orlando, FL

BENDER, MICHAEL D.
[b.] August 22, 1960, Baltimore; [p.] George E. and Jean C. Bender; [m.] Tina Bender; [ch.] Michael Scott, Jordan Alexander; [ed.] Loyola College in MD. MS Engineering, Johns Hopkins University BS; [occ.] Engineer; [pers.] I'm happy when with tender heart I'm standing close to you, for you possess the magic charms to make my dreams come true. Love you! Love me!

BENNETT, DEBRA ELAINE
[b.] September 23, 1950, WV; [p.] Mr. and Mrs. Kenneth Scaggs; [m.] Calvin W. Bennett, May 17, 1970; [ch.] One daughter Amber Leigh; [ed.] 15 years; [occ.] Registered Nurse for 20 years now retired; [memb.] ANA, NAACOG, WVNA, NMSS; [hon.] Have served on Advisory Boards for Nursing Programs and Consultant to various OB/Gym Facilities. I have taught Childbirth classes and wrote objectives for the Class; [oth. writ.] "Bitten" is first in a trilogy in an attempt to renew hope in those who are at a desperate point as I have been there.; [pers.] I believe we are governed by a

higher power who has predestined us to lead and follow the pathways we do.

BERMAN, CARONE B.
[b.] January 5, 1942, Everett, MA; [p.] Frances Blank, Barnett Blank; [m.] Stan Berman, August 19, 1962; [ch.] Sherri, Ira, Julie, Carlos, Bob, Lisa, grandchildren Amanda, Harrison; [ed.] Boston Univ., Boston, MA, Hebrew College, Brookline, MA; [occ.] Sales; [pers.] I dedicate my poem to my brother, Melvin Blank, and my sister in law, Phyllis Berman, who taught all of us who knew them the meaning of love, warmth and compassion.; [a.] Framingham, MA

BERNING, MARILYN
[pen.] Marilyn Bublitz Berning; [b.] July 27, 1938, Winona, MN; [p.] Donald and Helen Bublitz; [m.] William E. Berning, September 13, 1958; [ch.] Jeffrey and Jason (Peggy, now deceased); [ed.] Spring Valley, MN. High School also some additional classes; [occ.] Small Business owner and Homemaker; [memb.] Int. Society of Poets; [oth. writ.] Various assorted; [pers.] A poem is usually to say what your soul says to you today. I draw on my good home life, I grew up in when young for my view points on life to write about. My faith is my foundation.; [a.] Stewartville, MN

BERRY, JAMES M.
[pen.] Matt Berry; [b.] August 13, 1960; [ch.] James, Christine; [occ.] In between due to injury, Songwriter, Poet; [oth. writ.] I have numerous songs, poems ready to be put to use.; [pers.] I wish to write poems, songs to be simple on complex, complex on simple thoughts, to break down to see, to explore what's seen - felt - to stimulate thoughts - turn words into personal mini-mind movies.; [a.] Buford, GA

BERRY, TONIA K.
[b.] February 11, 1983, Watseka, IL; [p.] Alayne K. Berry; [ed.] Porta Jr./Sr. High School Petersburg, IL; [occ.] Student; [memb.] YMCA Karate (Goju) West Side Christian Church; [hon.] Porta Jr. High honor roll; [oth. writ.] (Poems) Eyes, A Pine's Love, The Warrior Redwall, Fire and Warriors, Kindness Proves All, Night Sight; [pers.] Don't take for granted that to us has been granted. I have lived my life for thirteen yeas now, and plan on living the rest. I have been influenced by my family, friends, animals, plants and greek myths.; [a.] Springfield, IL

BEST, JUSTIN
[b.] October 24, 1983, Jonesboro, AR; [p.] James and Penny Best; [ed.] Student at Sixth Grade Academic Center; [occ.] Student; [memb.] Ducks Unlimited; [hon.] Honor Roll; [oth. writ.] Tornado Talk Newspaper publication.; [pers.] I hope to help people more to understand another point, of view on mankind.; [a.] Jonesboro, AR

BEST, TARA T.
[b.] September 12, 1970, Ashdown, AR; [p.] Bobby and La Vonne Thompson; [m.] Michael David Best, October 26, 1991; [ch.] Owen Michael; [ed.] Dermott High, University of Arkansas at Monticello (UAM), and Institute of Children's Literature.; [occ.] Full time wife and mother; [memb.] Baptist Student Union, Missionary Baptist Student Fellowship.; [hon.] Honorable mention in the World of Poetry's "It's a Great Life" National Poetry Contest - 1987; [oth. writ.] Several pomes published in local newspapers.; [pers.] I write from my heart. God is the source of all my gifts, talents, and blessings.; [a.] Buna, TX

BILLINGTON, GARY L.
[b.] August 26, 1952, Amsterdam, NY; [p.] William and Beverly Billington; [ed.] Wilbur H. Lynch High School Europa School of Hairdressing and Cosmetology; [occ.] Hairstylist; [hon.] I am an award winning hairstylist with certificates of achievements and diplomas in various fields of hairdressing past present and advance.; [oth. writ.] A poem in the rainbow's end, title: Spirit.; [pers.] Dedication: To Beverly Billington and William Billington (Mom and Dad) special thanks, for always being there and many thanks to all who has touch my life, I feel poetry can be fun its a way to share our inner feelings with one another and it can bring knowledge and happiness to so many I believe poetry can have a great reflection on our lives for the better it's a way we can educate our minds and hearts with good I read poetry to give myself inner comfort and peace of mind. It's very relaxing and I highly recommend everyone to read and write poetry if not for fun than for the challenge of it.; [a.] Schenectady, NY

BILOTTO, PAMELA
[b.] April 30, 1950, Danbury, CT; [p.] Kenneth and Gladys Dimon; [m.] Anthony Bilotto, September 5, 1970; [ch.] Damien, Darren, Vanessa; [ed.] Shelton High School, Conn Business Inst.; [occ.] Executive Secretary Philips Medical Systems - Shelton, CT; [memb.] Make A Wish Foundation, National Arbor Day Foundation; [oth. writ.] To date my poems are of a private collection shared with family and friends. None of which I have taken the initiative to publish.; [pers.] I am inspired by special people and situations in my life. My poems reflect God's love and my desire to share personal life situations and encourage others.; [a.] Shelton, CT

BISCHOFSBERGER, JOANNE
[b.] July 24, 1968, Bronx, NY; [p.] Anthony and Diana Verde; [m.] Larry Bischofsberger Jr., March 4, 1995; [ed.] Carmel High School - Graduated 1986, Westchester Community College - graduated in 1988 with degree in

performing Arts, Dutchess Community College - graduated in 1994 with degree in Business; [occ.] Human Services Working with Developmentally Disabled Adults; [memb.] The Dian Fossey Gorilla Fund, National Audubon Society, National Honor Society (High School); [hon.] Won several Citations throughout regular School And College. Won Honorable Mentions for poem "Mother Nature," about 3 or 4 years ago (1990 I think); [oth. writ.] Mostly poems "Mother Nature" is the only one that has been published outside of this one. Now I am attempting to write a book - which I hope to have published.; [pers.] I strive to be the best I can be at whatever I do. I can be at whatever I do. My writings come from my philosophical way of looking at life. My influence and encouragement comes from my husband. Thank you, Larry.; [a.] Pawling, NY

BISHOP, STELLA
[pen.] Clydia Estelle Bishop; [b.] September 18, 1949, Ramer, TN; [p.] William Thorne, Ester Thorne; [m.] Divorced, June 28, 1969; [ch.] Larry James II; [ed.] Green County Tech. High, Arkansas State University; [occ.] Competitive Sweepstakes Contender; [memb.] Life-study Fellowship, The Nature Conservancy, National Wild Flower Research Center, Supporter of America's Hospitalized Veterans, National Committee to Preserve, Social Security and Medicare; [hon.] National Humane Education Society, National Children's Cancer Society, National Park Trust, Royal Award Certificate, Principality of Hutt River Province; [oth. writ.] Personal writings, of self and love ones!; [pers.] Poem is dedicated to the supreme being of all worthy creations; [a.] Paragould, AR

BIVINS, GENE
[pen.] Ben Vinegis; [b.] October 11, 1946, Pasadena, CA; [ed.] A.A. Los Angeles City College; [memb.] Gay Men's Chorus of Los Angeles; [oth. writ.] Poems in KPFK Folio, Program notes for Gay Men's Chorus of Los Angeles, Articles for the Advocate.; [pers.] All of my writing is concerned, at least in part, with the written and spoken beauty of our ancient language.; [a.] Los Angeles, CA

BLACK, AURORE
[b.] February 23, 1945, Brockton, MA; [p.] Emile Chartier, Aurore Chartier; [m.] Walter J. Black, October 8, 1977; [ch.] Daniel Buck, Dawna Vassalotti; [ed.] Mansfield High, Mansfield, MA. Class of 1963; [occ.] Self-employed Day Care Provider; [oth. writ.] Several un-published poems.; [pers.] All my poems reflect my personal feelings and emotions or, how I interpret be feelings and emotions of other's.; [a.] Norton, MA

BLACKWELL, GIULIANA
[pen.] Blackwell Giuliana; [b.] August 23, 1969, Siena, Italy; [p.] Francesco Sica and M. Adelaide Sica; [m.] Robert E. Blackwell, April 29, 1989; [ed.] ITI C Gambacorti Pisa - W.S.I. Languages School Pisa Italy; [occ.] Teacher Pre-school; [memb.] Red Cross Volunteer; [hon.] Foreign Teacher of the Month - from Alpha Languages Inst. while working in Japan; [oth. writ.] Other poems one children curriculum books used by school as learning program material.; [pers.] When words are written from the heart they are read with the heart.; [a.] Pensacola, FL

BLACKWELL, RACHEL K.
[b.] August 10, 1969, Brantford, Ontario, Canada; [p.] Janet A. Ross, Lurty H. Ross; [ed.] Northern Virginia Community College, Business Administration, Full Sail Center for the recording arts, Orlando, FL; [occ.] Manager of Dispatch, Merit Concrete of Virginia and General Assistant, Cue Recording Studio; [memb.] Audio Engineering Society, Humane Society of the United States; [oth. writ.] Personal Poetry, Anthologies, various lyrics and songs (unpublished); [pers.] You can only leave your mark if you live life your own way!; [a.] Alexandria, VA

BLAIR, STEPHEN SIMON
[pen.] Simon Blair; [b.] November 2, 1960, Bulaklava, South Australia; [m.] Jillian; [ed.] Birdwood High School, Flinders University, Deakin University, South Australian Schools; [occ.] Nurse Manager; [oth. writ.] 100 plus other poems unpublished.; [pers.] I use poetry to draw pictures of God's nature, and pictures of the struggle of man, or pictures of life. Poetry for me is the paint and canvas of the artist expressed as words on paper.; [a.] Stonyfell Adelaide, South Australia

BLANDROY, MURIEL D.
[b.] April 26, 1934, Texarkana, TX; [ch.] Seven girls and three boys; [ed.] Macedonia High, Community Education Business, Adult Learning Center; [occ.] People Creeter-Wal-Mart; [memb.] Union Hill Baptist Church, Senior Choir; [hon.] Senior Class of "51" Salutatorian; [pers.] I feel like my poems can make a difference in someone's life.; [a.] Texarkana, TX

BLASSINGAME, LINDA S.
[pen.] L. S. Washington; [b.] October 26, 1949, Saint Louis, MO; [p.] Shirley Ann Washington McCoy; [ch.] Woodrow S. Blassingame; [ed.] Three years of College General Education Degree State East St. Louis Illinois Community College 1980 Graduate of District 189 School of Practical Nursing East St. Louis Illinois 1982; [occ.] Retired Nurse Home Tutor for Academics grades six-adult; [memb.] St. Augustine Catholic Church St. Louis MO. Knights of Peter, Claver Ladies auxiliary court #339 Hold Office of

Lecturer for 1996; [oth. writ.] (1) No Easy Way To Heaven, (2) A New You, (3) Better Things Of Life, (5) Love Is Not Love, (6) Good By Son; [pers.] "Writing is a joy, a whole new world of creativity projected from the mind of the writer to activate the minds of the readers."

BLESSING, JENNIFER BOYNTON
[b.] September 16, 1972, Portland, ME; [p.] James Boynton Jr., Nancy White; [m.] Troy R. Blessing, August 9, 1991; [ch.] Chelssie Ann Blessing; [ed.] Deering High, South Portland High, attending Florida Community College at Jacksonville; [occ.] Student, wife, mother; [pers.] Everyone has an inspiration. I want to thank my husband for being mine and so much more.; [a.] Atlantic Beach, FL

BLEVINS, CATHERINE
[b.] January 5, 1937, Pierce, WV; [p.] Guy and Mary Polce; [m.] Edward Blevins, July 13, 1963; [ed.] High School Real Estate School; [occ.] Retired. Former Occupation - Office Manager - Gianato Pontiac - Buick Inc. - 30 yrs. Real Estate Salesman - 4 yrs.; [memb.] Fraternal Order of Police, Women's Bowling Association, St. Peter's Catholic Church; [hon.] Served as Sheriff of McDowell County, W. Va. for unexpired term in 1984. Was on County Executive Committee from 1982 to 1986. First and only Lady Sheriff of this County.; [pers.] I have always loved reading poetry. It relaxes my mind!; [a.] Welch, WV

BLIUVAS, JULIANA
[b.] July 6, 1964, Brooklyn, NY; [p.] Severinas and Patricia Bliuvas; [m.] Gregory J. Morrow; [ch.] Kevin Scott, Matthew Steven, Jacobsean; [ed.] Fort Hamilton High; [occ.] Self employed; [memb.] Humane Society, American Heart Association, Donation Comm. for Little League, Parents Club; [oth. writ.] A Mother's Tears, When You Wish Upon A Star, You Are Our Baby Now, What Is Love, The Bond of Marriage; [pers.] My writings are inspired by events as well as people surrounding my life. The message I hope to convey is life and everything in it are precious and you should not have to seek only further than your own backyard.; [a.] Healdsburg, CA

BLUESTONE, DAVID S.
[pen.] David Bluestone; [b.] December 1, 1981, Philadelphia; [p.] Eric and Marissa Bluestone; [m.] March 7, 1980; [ch.] Governor Mifflin, Middle School, Shillington, PA; [memb.] BBYO, USY, GMIS, Jazz Band; [hon.] Memorial Speech, Citizenship Award, Honor Roll, Several poems published, County Band; [pers.] Writing is a way of expressing my feelings.; [a.] Shillington, PA

BLUMBERG, PH.D. J. ANNETTE
[pen.] Anne Blum; [b.] April 12, 1943, Oxnard,

CA; [p.] Sybil and Arthur Buck; [m.] Ex -
Arthur David Blumberg MBA, March 6, 1966;
[ch.] Aaron Matthew and Kenneth Eugene; [ed.]
Ventura College, FAS, (U of B), Kree Institute,
Anthony Business Professions, Simi Valley
Adult Vocations, FED TAX-NCI, ICS, LaSalle
(Golden State Schools, Probe's Investigations
and others); [occ.] Care Provider Security
Officer, Corporate Officer; [memb.] Past: Art
Club of Oxnard, NCJW, NOW (and others),
current: Ventura Chapter BPW (Women's)
IWIG (and others) ie. Universal Life Church,
(Blumberg Associates, Inc.) (Youth Associations
for Years for Sons); [hon.] Affiliations with
persons of note in California, New Jersey, CT,
NY and travels in the USA, Europe: is a type of
honor, Collectors of my work is a type of
award; [oth. writ.] Non published works, for
children sketches for privately published
magazines, skiing, ponds mainly donations for
fund raisers summit Art Center, NJ (Portraits,
Landscapes, still life, sculpture, jewelry, pottery
stainglass hangings).; [pers.] Gratitude for
inspiring praise of creative instructors deserves
thought, each day. To find oneself observed in
perceptions of visionaries as product of mind
shared through education and print from media
other communication concerts.; [a.] Ventura, CA

BOBKO, JANINE
[b.] July 3, 1981, Chicago, IL; [p.] Michael and
Luann Bobko; [ed.] Graduated from St. Juliana
Grade School 1995, currently in Resurrection High
School; [occ.] Student; [memb.] Dance Student 10
yrs., Perform in many dance and variety shows,
plays and musicals. Active in St. Juliana Parish
Church as Sunday School Teacher, Church Lector,
and Handbell Choir.; [a.] Chicago, IL

BOCKER, VASHTI ELEESHA
[pen.] Catherine Bui, Marilyn Cancino, Carmen
Smith, Noemi Vega; [b.] December 31, 1982,
Brooklyn, NY; [p.] Celmira S. Smith, Arturo E.
Bocker, [ed.] School in Immaculate Heart of Mary.;
[occ.] Student; [hon.] Student of the month awards
(more than 2 times). Honor roll first and second.;
[pers.] I wouldn't have done my poem if it wasn't
for my mother or my teacher Mr. Amelotte. I
encouraged people to believe in themselves.;
[a.] Irvine, CA

BOHN, CAROLE L.
[pen.] Carole L. Bohn; [b.] August 29, 1939,
Decatur, IL; [p.] Don and Doris Virden; [m.]
Divorced; [ch.] Cheryl and Mark, grandchildren:
Amy, Amber, Brian, Mark Jr., Tyler, [ed.] Decatur
High, Decature, Ill Nova College - Woodbridge, VA;
[occ.] Salesperson; [hon.] Sales awards; [oth. writ.] I
have many poems and songs. This is my first
published.; [pers.] To lead the lost to the saving
grace of Jesus Christ by salvation. All people need
the Lord. In honor of my Mom Doris Virden.;
[a.] Virginia Beach, VA

BOLDT, RUTH ELIZABETH
[pen.] Renaissance Ruthie; [b.] July 31, 1978,
Birmingham, AL; [p.] Arthur and Sylvia Boldt;
[ed.] 1996 Graduate - Hopkinsville High School
plans to attend Hopkinsville Community
College for first two years and two years at
Western Kentucky, University in Bowling
Green, KY; [occ.] Legal Secretary (part-time)
Wendell H. Rorie, Law Office; [memb.] St. John
United Methodist Church, National Honor
Society, Beta Club, Speech Team (6 Years),
Future Business Leaders of America, Foreign
Language Club, Yearbook Production Team
(1994-95); [hon.] Hopkinsville High School,
Honor Roll - Kentucky New Era (local
newspaper) Carrier of the year, 1991 - 9
Consecutive years of perfect attendance in
school - Speech Team Rookie of the Year (High
School) 1993, FBLA Member of the Month,
November, 1995; [pers.] I write to create a sense
of beauty and comfort in a world of tarnishment
and pain. When I write, I begin by raising the
window only to walk out of the door in the end.
My writings are my letters to the people in this
world.; [a.] Hopkinsville, KY

BONAROTI, APRIL
[b.] March 23, 1978, Pittsburgh, PA; [p.]
Donald and Linda Bonaroti; [ed.] Plum Senior
High School, Penn. State New Kensington; [occ.]
Student; [memb.] St. John The Baptist Church;
[hon.] Award in Elementary tutoring and many
"Excellent Work" awards, High School Honor
Roll; [oth. writ.] Always have kept my poetry
and writings to myself.; [pers.] A person's
imagination is a gift that should never be put to
waste.; [a.] New Kensington, PA

BONNEVILLE, RYAN
[b.] December 21, 1982, Saint Petersburg, FL;
[p.] Randall and Linda Bonneville, James and
Gail Michelini; [ed.] Currently attending White
Lake Middle School, White Lake, MI; [occ.] 7th
grade student; [memb.] Student Council; [hon.] 4th
Honor Roll, Science Olympiad; [a.] White Lake, MI

BORTEL, TAMMY L.
[b.] October 22, 1969, Fremont, OH; [p.]
Marcia and Rich Rahrig; [m.] Tom A. Bortel,
October 22, 1994; [ch.] Joshua Michael, Alexis
Shay-Lyn and Brandon Thomas; [ed.] Fremont
Ross Senior High School; [occ.] Union factory
worker, Mascotech Forming Technologies;
[memb.] Grace Lutheran Church, The U.A.W.
and the W.I.B.C.; [pers.] How do you know
you cannot do something, when you haven't
even tried to do it? No matter what you do or
where you go in life, never forget where you
came from after all it is the roots from which
you grow.; [a.] Old Fort, OH

BOSTON, VERNE
[pen.] H.W. Shortfellow; [b.] July 2, 1936,

Datman, AZ; [m.] Beverly, March 1985; [ch.]
Ten; [ed.] 12th Grade; [occ.] Disabled Hard-
Rock Miner, Fed. Mine Inspector; [oth. writ.]
Numerous poems; [pers.] Enjoy writing poetry
for others.; [a.] Mabton, WA

BOSWELL, JAIME
[b.] September 27, 1977, Cheverly, MD; [p.]
Ronnie and Claire Boswell; [m.] (Fiance) Gary
Broome II, June, 1997; [ed.] Calvert High
School, ICS - Cobol Programming; [occ.] Dollar
King - Cashier and Stock; [pers.] The poetry I
write reflects my feelings. Most of my friends
enjoy it also. I was influenced by a famous
poet, Edgar Allen Poe, for his unique ability in
poetry. Poetry will be around forever.;
[a.] Prince Frederick, MD

BOTTINO, LOUIS A.
[b.] March 28, 1978, Camden, NJ; [p.] Joseph
F. and Mary L. Bottino; [ed.] Atlantic City High
School, Atlantic City, NJ; [occ.] Student;
[memb.] Producers and Song Writers Guild,
Ventnor, NJ; [oth. writ.] Original songs written
for the band, Midnight Sun.; [a.] Ventnor, NJ

BOTTS, AMBER DAWN
[b.] July 2, 1978, Juneau, AK; [p.] Tom and Jan
Botts; [ed.] Hoonah Public High School; [occ.]
Student at Hoonah Public High School; [hon.]
Various School Awards - Geography, Biological
Sciences, Adv. English, etc...; [oth. writ.] Many
other poems that live written for a poem book
I'm putting together and poems that have been
published in our school newspaper.; [pers.] I
express my thoughts and feelings through my
poetry. Most are about love and pain and just
life in general. I hope people can see who I am
when they read my poetry.; [a.] Hoonah, AK

BOUCHER, ELIZABETH ANNE PORTER
[pen.] Anne Porter Boucher; [b.] February 24,
Fall River, MA; [ch.] Three Daughters; [hon.]
International Woman of the Year, National
Woman of the Year, A Wall Full of Plaques,
Thank God for my Talent; [oth. writ.] I have my
life story. But someday I'll have it published,
and if you can give me some names. God Bless
You.; [pers.] Anne Porter Boucher is living in
Blackstone, MA. Comments... Thank you for
all you've done for me. I appreciate having my
poem in a most illustrious Form of Beauty.;
[a.] Blackstone, MA

BOULD, ANNE MARIE SAULNIER
[b.] February 12, 1964, Kittery, ME; [p.] James
Saulnier, Jennifer King-Karsikas; [ch.] Brandon
Montgomery, Clifford Fred III, Justin Alexander
Bould; [ed.] Bishop Manogue, Phillips Jr.
College; [occ.] Mom, Manager, Entrepreneur;
[memb.] Mother's of Multiples, National
Association for Female Executives; [hon.]
Presidents List, Honor Roll Artistic Award,

Business Academic Award, Service Award.; [oth. writ.] Several poems but this is the first I have sent in for publication.; [pers.] My poems are inspired by the people who surround me and the feelings they create in my heart and soul.; [a.] Raleigh, NC

BOUTEILLER, JEANNE MARIE
[b.] May 29, 1931, Great Barrington, MA; [p.] Armand and Isaline Bouteiller; [ed.] Searles High, June, 1949, Great Barrington, MA, Syracuse University Bachelor of Fine Arts, Painting and Illustration May, 1953; [occ.] Retired; [memb.] Was in past a member of MENSA; [pers.] The fishermen's memorial is in Gloucester, MA the last line of each verse is from Psalm 107:25 in the Bible and is on the memorial.; [a.] Syracuse, NY

BOWERMAN, ELIZABETH
[pen.] Liz, Lizzie, Aliz and Lizzy; [b.] July 9, 1983, Madrass, OR; [p.] Jon and Candy Bowerman; [ed.] Fossil Elementary School Grades 1-7; [occ.] Student at Fossil elementary school.; [memb.] American Quarter Horse Association, American Paint Horse Association and Northwest and Oregon, Cutting Horses Association; [hon.] Horse Competitions, Dog Competitions; [oth. writ.] "Love", "Dare Essay", and Historical Biography on grandfather Bill Bowerman.; [a.] Fossil, OR

BOWERS, MARIAH D.
[b.] September 20, 1978, Augsburg, Germany; [p.] CSM William H. Bowers II and Mrs. Judith M. Bowers; [ed.] Buena High School; [memb.] S.A.D.D. Club, Vice President of German Club, Key Club, National Art Honors Society (all are school sponsored); [hon.] Cochise Cowboy Poetry Contest, 1st place, Artwork Exhibited in Mona Puzzi Art Gallery, 1st place in '94 School Poetry Contest (for a poem in German.); [oth. writ.] Poem entitled "Through A Child's Eyes" published in '93 Sierra Vista Middle School yearbook.; [pers.] I believe we're all in this together... our human brothers and sisters, our animal brothers and sisters, and the planet upon which we live. We all have to work together to make it work.; [a.] Sierra Vista, AZ

BOWLES, JAMES
[b.] November 24, 1960, Northridge, CA; [p.] Hugh G. Bowles, Hyla J. Bowles; [m.] Mary Bowles, April 25, 1992; [ch.] Kenneth Albert; [ed.] Clear Lake High Southern Oregon State College; [occ.] Author; [oth. writ.] Moving Beyond Walls: "La Fille De Joie". Poem was written for publication in "Moving Beyond Walls" a Southern Oregon State College Publication.; [pers.] Give a man a chance and you give man a chance.; [a.] Eagle Point, OR

BOYLES, BARBARA GENEVIEVE
[pen.] Genevieve O'Boyle; [b.] May 26, 1943, Bridgeport, CT; [p.] Robert Harley and Ida Mae Barnes; [m.] Charles Eckerd Boyles, December 14, 1959; [ch.] Dennis William, Charles Edward and Deborah Mae; [ed.] Mount Vernon High School Cypress Community College, Long Beach State College and NOVA; [occ.] Computer Equipment Analyst; [memb.] Girl Scouts of America, Heart Association of VA; [oth. writ.] Several poems and children's songs (unpublished.); [pers.] The Lord will provide for these that keep the faith, which is reflected in all that I do. I am a romanticist.; [a.] Burke, VA

BOZYMOWSKI, DARLENE C.
[b.] January 21, 1952, Detroit; [p.] Irene and Zoltan Papp; [m.] Edward G. Bozymowski, March 16, 1979; [ch.] Desiree, Nichole and Juliann; [occ.] R.N. Wyandotte Hospital for 20 years.; [memb.] Christ the Good Shepherd. Catholic Church; [pers.] The written word is not only my outlet, but my legacy and thus the choicest of relics. Influenced by Hemmingway and frost.; [a.] Lincoln Park, MI

BRAATEN, OPAL B.
[b.] July 24, 1919, Fonddulac, WI; [p.] Rinhart and Eva Holts; [m.] Edwin K. Braaten, May 9, 1942; [ch.] Bob, Cheri, Bonnie Sue, Candy, Edwin Jr.; [ed.] Almond High School, Stevens Point Central State, WI, several courses in Writing at Appleton Technical College; [occ.] Former Teacher and Hospital Employee, Writer - Retired; [memb.] Zion Luthern Church Appleton, Salvation Army (Vol) Appleton, Medical Center Aux.; [hon.] Award for Teaching Sunday School for 17 Years; [oth. writ.] Children's stories one published. Poems and stories for children in local church publication and newspapers.; [pers.] To bring out the best in people in the life they live and the choices they make. God is very important in my life.; [a.] Appleton, WI

BRADY, CAROLYN S.
[b.] February 23, 1940, Elizabethton, TX; [p.] Dan E. Mosley, Sarah Elizabeth Guinn; [m.] Robert Lee Brady, March 11, 1959; [ch.] Donna, Robin, Laura, John, Karen, Maureen adopted April and Jessica who are my grandchildren too; [ed.] High School, graduated from Happy Valley High School, in Johnson City, Tenn., in 1958; [occ.] Homemaker; [memb.] American Indian Relief Council to whom I make donations; [pers.] I would like to dedicate this poem to the Native Americans. They were my inspiration and also to my late Grandfather who was part Cherokee Indian.; [a.] Hyattsville, MD

BRANNON, KATIE G.
[pen.] Kate; [b.] April 8, 1955, Donalsonville, GA; [p.] Elizabeth Groomes and Clifton Groomes; [m.] Divorced; [ch.] Yasmin Brannon

- 18, Felicia - 14, Jamopn - 7; [ed.] Seminole Co. Elementary and High School BS Early childhood Fort Valley State, MS early childhood, Albany State College, Library Science Florida State; [occ.] Teacher; [hon.] Woman of the Year, [oth. writ.] My Grandmother Is An Angel, Too Close Too Soon

BRANNON, TINA
[b.] November 7, 1982, Garden Co Hospital; [p.] Teresa and Jackie B.; [ch.] Tina Brannon; [ed.] Pickens Co Middle School. All my life in Pickens Schools.; [oth. writ.] I like to write poems and short stories. I like to write to express my self.; [pers.] When I write I can never think of enough words to express my true self. There are not enough words in this world.; [a.] Jasper, GA

BRATTEN, MICHAEL B.
[b.] December 5, 1966, Bartlesville, OK; [p.] Stephen L. and Carol Hill Bratten; [ed.] Glen Burnie Sr. High School, Glen Burnie, MD, Anne Arundel Community College - Arnold, MD, Del Mar College - Corpus-Corpus Christ, TX; [occ.] College student, Journalism major; [hon.] Award for creative merit in the 1984 congressional art competition.; [oth. writ.] Art work and articles published in various books and magazines.; [pers.] I speak for the thousands of talented and anonymous artists in this society whose daily energy is spent increasing the profits of the wealthy. I am influenced by the realists of the 19th century.; [a.] Corpus Christi, TX

BREEDEN, JAMES M.
[pen.] Jimmy Breeden; [b.] December 14, 1946, Baltimore, MD; [p.] James A. and Earlyn R. Breeden; [ch.] Michele Lynn Breeden, Julie Marie Breeden; [ed.] BA Education, University of Maryland Baltimore County Campus; [occ.] Retired Police Officer, President - 5% Realty Co. Ltd.; [memb.] Fraternal Order of Police, National Association of Realtors, Airborne Society, Society of the 173rd Airborne Brigade; [oth. writ.] Love's Wall, La Mere, Bed of Nails, Nance's Beauty, The Cool Pool, Just Never Tell Me Your Feeling Or The Lady Wore Track Shoes; [pers.] From "The Killing Fields of South Vietnam" comes the message that Love is the most powerful force on earth. My favorite poem is Dante's Inferno from the Divine Comedy. We need romance in our lives everyday.; [a.] Linthicum, MD

BREITFELDER, EDWARD A.
[b.] January 20, 1922, Toledo, OH; [m.] Alice, 1990; [ch.] Stephen, Edward C. Joseph; [ed.] Grad. Toledo CCHS '40; [occ.] Retired Tool Designer (Dana Corp.); [memb.] Life Member American Legion, Life Member VFW, Life Member Society of Mfg. Eng.; [oth. writ.] Alas Poor Ed,... is an excerpt from essay What Did You Do During The War, Papa? Written for

Grandkids written May 1992 (Happy ending to poem, still friends.); [pers.] Though my attempts at poetry are a disaster I keep trying to shed the label of poetaster. I enjoy words. Amuse friends with simple rhymes, all the times enjoying life to its fullest day by day.

BRENNAN, KAREN
[pen.] Boo, Ren, Pretty; [b.] March 13, 1973, Forest Hills, Queens, NY; [p.] Carol Bakich and Robert Brennan; [ed.] Kellenberg-Memorial High School, Uniondale, New York; [occ.] Receptionist, Clerk Ambulance Company; [oth. writ.] I have written many other poems as early as 1987.; [pers.] The greatest thing about poetry is its ability to go beyond our basic "understanding" of the language we use in our everyday lives. Poetry, to me, is the mirror of the soul.; [a.] Valley Stream, NY

BRENNAN, MARGARET A.
[b.] May 18, 1947, Brooklyn, NY; [p.] Mary (Sullivan) and Frank Harucki; [m.] Richard D. Brennan Sr., August 14, 1993; [ch.] Kenneth, James, Richard Jr. and Kimberly; [ed.] High School Grad plus various business school courses; [occ.] Accounting Clerk; [memb.] NRA, Bay Area Poets Coalition, International Society of Poets, America On Line, The National Authors Registry, North American Fishing Club; [hon.] Awards include: Golden Poet, Silver Poet, several Honorable Mentions, Certificate of Poetic Achievement, Certificate of Publication, one first place poem, one second place poem and several published poems.; [oth. writ.] The Whisper of the Wind, Roses for My Mother, My Son, The Gift, My First Born, The Garden of Stone, The Wedding, Rose Coloured Glasses, For the Sake of Sanity, Eternal Love, Hearts, The Big Sister, Passion.; [pers.] I enjoy watching people. I can always find something to write about. Sometimes I just let go and dream. I usually write what I see, whether it is something happening to me, or someone else. Poetry is life.; [a.] North Babylon, NY

BRENNER, HELEN LEWIS
[pen.] Mortimer Mouse; [b.] December 10, 1910, Omaha, NE; [p.] Samuel Arion and Jessie Lewis; [m.] James Clarence Thornton, May 9, 1952, Benedict Brenner (Deceased), July 29, 1966; [ch.] Four Stepchildren; [ed.] Dundee Elementary School, Central High School in Omaha, NE, 5 years of Oil Painting Lessons; [occ.] Retired; [memb.] Founder's Church of Religious Science, Smithsonian Institution, AARPI, Auto Club of So. Cal.; [hon.] Honorable Mention for Poster Front Page of Omaha World Herald on date of birth December 10, 1910, photo at opening of Panama Camalire, State Children"; [oth. writ.] "A Dialogue" Conversation between America and Statue of Liberty on her 100th birthday, "The Church Mouse" and "the Word" for 13 years. "It's Just a Building" The headquarters' building for the church of Religious Science have to be torn down to make way for a modern one. I worked in it for 53 years. I wrote the above article for our last meeting there.; [pers.] "Climb Every Mountain"; [a.] Inglewood, CA

BREW, HELEN JO
[pers.] I dedicate my poem to the former Dorothy Blenker, who was my eight grade teacher at the Dodge School, in the town of McMillan, Wisconsin, U.S.A.; [a.] Stratford, WI

BREWSTER, RANDALL
[pen.] R. Brewster, R.; [b.] May 20, 1970, London, England; [p.] Athelston Brewster, Glenda Alleyne; [m.] Rosa Pimienta - Brewster, July 31, 1995; [ed.] St. Augustines, Union City, NJ, St. Benedict's Prep, Newark; [occ.] Customer Service, New York Times; [memb.] U.S.; [hon.] I received Nat'l Music Society Award for Piano; [oth. writ.] I've written some short stories, songs for producers (mostly just friends), and other poetry.; [pers.] I try to invoke feelings and emotions in who ever reads my writings, so that we can ponder things often taken for granted. Langston Hughes was, and still is, a large influence.; [a.] Teaneck, NJ

BRIDGERS, MARGARET ELIZABETH RICE
[pen.] Meg; [b.] June 9, 1973, Florida; [p.] Tina Morris and Jenvey Rice; [m.] David Michael Bridgers, March 26, 1994; [ed.] High School, home town - Beaufort; [occ.] Desk Clerk; [memb.] Beaufort Support Group for Nervous Disorders, Illnesses, giving Love and support through the understanding of people who suffer any mental illnesses.; [hon.] Certificate of Appreciation for work through the group.; [oth. writ.] Poetry wrote to put in the News Letters from the Support Group monthly, to encourage and bring HOPE to those who suffer.; [pers.] I have just always put into Poetry what I feel an see around me in everyday life. I express my feelings and Hope this way. I believe Poetry is an excellent way to Reach Out and Touch another person's Heart, to bring Peace, Love, Hope and Encouragement.

BRIONES, ROLLY
[b.] November 16, 1957, Philippines; [m.] Helen Nolaso Briones, January 12, 1980; [ch.] Lisa Marie, Azeneth, Mark Anthony; [ed.] Mountain View High, Foothill College; [memb.] Filipino Organization; [oth. writ.] Writing poem, published in publisher.; [pers.] I been writing a sad poet and romantic poet and planning to write a history of world and my life. And story book.; [a.] Sunnyvale, CA

BRITT, RUBY B.
[b.] April 21, 1941, Mitchell County; [p.] Lester Brown and Louise Brown; [m.] John W. Britt, June 12, 1959; [ch.] Donna Faircloth, Debbie McInvale, Dale Shiver and Danny Britt; [ed.] Darton College and Albany State College, Mitchell County High School; [occ.] Postmaster, Baconton, GA; [memb.] Alpha Beta Gamma, Baconton Baptist Church, National Assoc. of Postmasters, U.S.; [hon.] High School Honor grad. recommended by Darton College for Biographical inclusion in the Third Edition of Two Thousand Notable Women released in late 1991.; [oth. writ.] Poems and articles in local newspapers.; [pers.] I delight in the company of children, especially my grandchildren. I believe in the inherent goodness in all people and in the application of the "Golden Rule".; [a.] Baconton, GA

BRITTS, DOROTHEA, M.
[b.] February 8, 1934, Missouri; [p.] Robert and Mildred Oliver, [m.] Thomas Britts - Deceased; [ed.] 11 1/2 yrs. Hermann MO; [occ.] Retired Nurse; [memb.] VFW aux.; [pers.] Country girl. Mother of six with four living. Blessed with a talent in art and poetry.; [a.] Fulton, MO

BRODEUR, HELEN S.
[b.] May 20, 1940, Alburquerque; [p.] Mr. and Mrs. Jose Patricio Sanchez; [m.] Alphonse Maurice Brodeur Sr., February 19, 1966; [ch.] Alphonse Maurice Jr., Maria Elena; [ed.] Sacred Heart Academy, Sacred Heart College, University of New Mexico (BS, MA - Elem. Ed.); [hon.] Nominated Distinguished Teacher Award 1984, Certificate of Appreciation 1989, Selected and included in the first edition of Who's Who Among America's Teachers, 1990.; [pers.] Words are a powerful tool. Therefore, may the words I choose serve to educate, inspire, strengthen, console, entertain, humor, and/or help in any way, those who read them.; [a.] Albuquerque, NM

BROOK, JOY L.
[pen.] Joy Brook; [b.] July 19, 1958, Cameroun, West Africa; [p.] R. N. Lillian Brook, Rev. Ronald Brook; [ed.] The American School of Kinshasa Eastern College; [occ.] Accountant; [oth. writ.] I have been writing poetry since High School, and also play the piano and guitar by ear.; [pers.] My poems are the reflection of life experiences, and the beauty and respect of nature. I treasure the uniqueness of each person that I meet, and accept them for who they are. I have been blessed with an intercultural background and a wonderful loving family.; [a.] Lindenwold, NJ

BROOKS, DEBORAH
[b.] November 8, 1947, Phila, PA; [p.] Mildred and Rozell Pough; [m.] Cedric Brooks, July 8, 1967; [ch.] Jacqueline R. Brooks; [ed.] William Penn H.S.; [occ.] School Secretary School Dist. of Phila.; [pers.] Nature and all of its beauty is my inspiration for writing poetry; [a.] Blue Bell, PA

BROOKS, LINDA
[p.] Mr. and Mrs. Jesse Kingsberry; [m.] Willie Brooks Jr.; [ch.] Winter Kingsberry, Romelo Kingsberry, Pamela Elder, [pers.] I strive to be the best, at whatever it may be. That I am doing. I have been greatly influenced by my loving husband Willie Brooks Jr.; [a.] Atlanta, GA

BROWN, BETH
[b.] November 18, 1965, Cleveland; [p.] Catherine Catullo; [m.] Mark Brown, February 27, 1993; [ed.] Bowling Green State University; [occ.] Elementary Educator; [memb.] Ohio Council of Elementary School Science, Ohio Student Education Association, Volunteers on Progress, Association of Childhood Education International; [hon.] Excellence in Education Award, Apple Award, Special Service Music Award, Dean's List; [pers.] My written words express the feelings in my heart - openly, honestly, and genuinely.; [a.] Mentor, OH

BROWN, DOUGLAS RYAN
[b.] March 24, 1972, NC; [p.] Thomas and Beverly Brown; [m.] Rachael Grace Brown, January 14, 1995; [ed.] Franklin College, IN, B.A. History; [memb.] Lambda Chi Alpha Fraternity; [hon.] Phi Alpha Theta History Honorary, Phi Sigma Tau Philosophy Honorary, Dean's Scholarship, Gold Quill Academic Honorary; [a.] Indianapolis, IN

BROWN, JAMES C.
[pen.] J.C.F. Brown; [b.] July 24, 1970, Denver, CO; [p.] Joseph and Canstance Brown; [ed.] Ivy Tech State College, Indianapolis, Indiana.; [occ.] Assistant manager for Damino's Pizza, Indianapolis.; [memb.] Indiana Patriots; [hon.] Phi Theta Kappa honor society.; [pers.] Duty to God, nation and race.; [a.] Indianapolis, IN

BROWN, JEANA
[pen.] Stormy Smith; [b.] December 10, 1963, Dallas, TX; [p.] Jerry and Anita Farmer, [m.] Divorced; [ch.] Jennifer and Ian Brown; [ed.] 30 Hours Phlebotomy at Tyler Junior College and Trinity Valley Community College; [occ.] Disabled; [oth. writ.] The final passage, a day of love, etc.; [pers.] Struggling with kidney disease has been a hard road, but I have learned that we can always find a piece of heaven in our children's eyes.

BROWN, LYDIA JC.
[b.] October 16, 1967, FuZhou, China; [p.] James S. Chen and Florence Z. Chen; [m.] Robert G. Brown, October 16, 1993; [ch.] Sabrina JC Brown; [ed.] Southeast High School, Oklahoma State University, Oklahoma Baptist University, University of Central Oklahoma - B.S. in Accounting; [occ.] Accounts Clerk, Oklahoma Department of Vo-Tech; [memb.] Mu Alpha Theta Club, National Honor Society, Delta Mu Delta, American Vocational Associa-

tion, Oklahoma Vocational Association, First Southern Baptist Church; [hon.] Who's Who Among American High School, 1st, 3rd and 5th place in Oklahoma Public School Math Contest, Salutatorian of Class 1988, various Scholarships from Universities and Community, President's and Dean's Honor Roll, All City Art Exhibition (1985-86), Honor Scholar Academic Achievement Award from Oklahoma State University Alumni Association (1986-87), Outstanding Award 4.0 GPA from Southeast High School (1985-88), Salutatorian of Class of 1988 - Southeast High School, Principal's Certificate - Highest Honor (1987-88); [pers.] Whenever amazing grace resounds in my ears, it tugs my heart strings, and my eyes are moist with tears... as a lupus patient since age of 15, and immigrant from China to this country with my family in 1985, life has never been easy to me everyday is a new challenge. But, by God's grace, nothing is impossible! Even in the darkest night, they are still stars twinkling from heaven above, and the dawn light is closer every minute, every second. Have faith in God and never give up because to greet your joyful smiles. Hold in your arms of this world with great love!; [a.] Oklahoma, OK

BROWN, LYNNELLE A.
[pen.] Lynne Reece-Brown; [b.] August 9, 1915, Jamaica, West Indies; [p.] John Canute and Margaret Reece; [m.] Karl St. E. Brown (Deceased, September 2, 1995), June 29, 1940; [ch.] Eight adults; [ed.] High School grad. Kingston Jr. in service training in the ministry of housing, Kgn. Ja. diploma in Extension Work-Housing Officer, University of the W.I.; [occ.] Retired - oil painting and poetry writing - (hobbies); [memb.] Christian and Missionary Alliance Church, Hudson Guild Snr. Citizens Centre, Manhtn. Hazel Brooks, Citizen's Centre Bklyn. C&MA Church Snr., Adults and Singles Adult Groups; [hon.] High commendations on my paintings at annual art exhibitions at the Hudson Guild Theatre of Arts in Manhattan - 26th Sts. N.B. neither awards nor prizes are given in these art exhibitions.; [oth. writ.] Many other poems like 'Our Years Together', "Hidden Beauties", Family If Is, etc., and poems in Jamaican Dialect - "Patois".; [pers.] In 1985 at age 70, I started oil painting and excelled in it in 1989 I started poetry writing which I have continued after retiring at age 77. Working writing and painting have kept at least and independent and that was my main objective - retiring so late. I love people and fortunately my jobs always job me involved with seeing to peoples needs. In the Jamaica Civil Service as Housing Officer, Social Work was involved and here in the U.S. I wondered with the elderly. I also did a spot of teaching children in my early days.; [a.] Brooklyn, NY

BROWN, MARIE
[b.] December 29, 1983, Indianapolis, IN; [p.] Joseph Brown, Constance Brown; [ed.] 6th grade, Indianapolis Public School #59; [occ.] Student; [hon.] City Spelling Bee Finalist; [pers.] My favorite poets are Whitman and Poe.; [a.] Indianapolis, IN

BROWN, NAOMI
[m.] Deceased; [ed.] I studied play writing at Bowling Green State University, Bowling Green Ohio; [occ.] My occupation is in social work. I work part time and attend The University of Toledo, working on my BA in theatre. I am active in the Performing Arts Center at the University of Toledo, I am a poet, playwright, actress; [memb.] I am a member of North Coast Theatre Company in Toledo Ohio; [oth. writ.] I write short stories.; [a.] Toledo, OH

BROWN, TAMMY M.
[b.] February 1, 1971, Barberton, OH; [p.] Jerrilyn L. Brown and Edward T. Brown; [ed.] Green High School/Portage Lakes Career Center, Kent State University -B.A.; [occ.] U.S. Postal Service Employee Data Conversion Operator - Akron, Ohio; [memb.] PETA-People for the Ethical Treatment of Animals, American Wildlife Federation - Assoc. member, The Humane Society of the United States; [hon.] Dean's List, Psy Chi Member; [oth. writ.] Many-however all remain unpublished at this time; [pers.] My writing reflects scenarios found in everyday lifestyles. I try to show how bleak situations can become beautiful when shown in a different context - generally a metaphoric one.; [a.] Green, OH

BROWN, WALTER E.
[b.] October 17, 1930, Norwich, CT; [p.] Walter Brown, Margaret Sweeney-Brown; [m.] M. Lillian Arseneault, October 22, 1960; [ch.] Wynn Erin, Wayne Evin; [ed.] High School: Norwich Free Academy, College: University of Connecticut; [occ.] Construction Marketing Director, [a.] Charlestown, RI

BRUNSON, ANGELA MICHELLE
[b.] December 5, 1979, Goldsboro, NC; [p.] Cecil H. and Jean Brunson; [ed.] Sophomore at Germantown High; [occ.] Student; [memb.] Central Church, Key Club, Junior Classical League, Thespians, Christ Living in Christian Kids, Mock Trial; [hon.] Who's Who Among American High School Students, All American Scholar, United States Achievement Academy, Tenn. Miss National Teen-Ager Pageant (top ten and Community Service Award), National Foreign Language Award, All-American Scholar, Top Ten in class of 650; [pers.] I write straight from the heart. All of my works reflect my own feelings.; [a.] Germantown, TN

BRYAN, ROSE MARY
[b.] Piedmont, SD; [p.] William S. Andrews, Mary S. Andrews; [m.] Frederick T. Bryan; [ch.] Danielle Wickham Maria, Frederick Terrence Bryan Jr., Christopher John Bryan, Kelly Rosemary Bryan; [memb.] Westsail Owners Association, Family of Bruce Society in America; [pers.] Other interests include: Sailing, Calligraphy, recording for the blind and dyslexic; [a.] Concord, MA

BRYANT, LYNDA JEAN
[pen.] Lynda Jean; [b.] October 13, 1941, Washington, DC; [p.] Virginia Mae Lamm Darden Zierdt and Jesse Robert Darden, Sr.; [ed.] Suitland Sr. High School, MD, Eckerd College, FL (BA 1984), and Capitol College, VA (MS 1996); [occ.] Program Manager - Computers, Communications, Controls, and Audio/Visual; [memb.] Washington Farm United Methodist Church, Information Systems Audit and Control (International) Association, and small writing groups; [hon.] Federal Systems Integration and Management Center performance awards, Scholarships, Speaker at the Federal Data Center Directors Interagency Conference ('90) and others business, educational, and church groups; [oth. writ.] Several technical articles published in Federal Computer Week and various personal poems for friends, families, and fellow travelers.; [pers.] I strive to reflect faith, hope, and understanding in all my writings both for fun and business. Communication with each other (worldwide) and God is critical. Thanks to my friends and family for the encouragement to learn, write, and persevere towards my dream; [a.] Alexandria, VA

BUCHHOLZ, HOWARD ROBERT
[b.] April 7, Kearny, NJ; [p.] Thomas and Jeanette; [m.] Beckie, Barbara, Suzanne and Linda; [ch.] Greg, Diane, Kevin, Bruce, Patricia; [ed.] BS, Seton Hall University Master of Life, School of Hard Knocks Apprentice of Arts, Theatrical Co's, MA. NH, NJ and VA; [occ.] NOMAD; [hon.] Elected to the Union County (NJ) BA for Meritorious Service, Elected 1st VP Fairlawn, VA, Lions; [oth. writ.] Uncle Howard's game.; [pers.] Each day to see a smile, or hear laughter or applause for something I have done for others.; [a.] Sand Springs, OK

BUCKLEY, DAMON L.
[b.] June 15, 1966, Lynwood, CA; [p.] Hershel and Sharon Buckley; [ed.] Downey High, Cerritos College, California State University Fullerton, Kliment Ohridsky University-Sofia, Bulgaria; [occ.] Bank Teller; [pers.] I dedicate this poem to those friends that encouraged me to write.; [a.] Downey, CA

BUCOL, MIZUHO JOSEPHINE
[b.] September 17, 1916, San Diego, CA; [ed.] M.A. in English; [occ.] Director, Escondido Canter Laubach Literary Council, San Diego County, Inc.; [memb.] California Tanka Kai; [oth. writ.] Tanka (31 syllable Japanese poems); [pers.] Oh, how beautiful! What is? That is. Where? Don't you see?; [a.] Escondido, CA

BUECKNER, DORIS
[pen.] Doris Bueckner; [b.] March 6, 1917, New Jersey; [p.] Mr. and Mrs. Rauch; [ch.] Two; [ed.] Grammar School, High School; [occ.] Retired; [memb.] Church - Jensen Beach Community, Volunteer in Hospital; [hon.] 16 yrs. as volunteer Martin Memorial Hospital - Stuart, FL; [a.] Port Saint Lucie, FL

BUJAN, VINCENT R.
[b.] January 23, 1937, Jersey City, NJ; [p.] Joseph Bujan, Mercedes Bujan; [ed.] Towanda, PA High School, BA Elon College, NC, Post Grad. Marketing, City, Univ. New York; [occ.] Semi-retired, Advertising; [hon.] Regional and National Advertising Awards; [oth. writ.] Articles published in local newspapers; [pers.] I wrote the poem "A Gift" to Peggy Emerson during the summer of 1966, Nothing stirs the words or emotions like being in love.; [a.] Marietta, GA

BURCH, ANNA ANNALISA SUEFAWN
[b.] April 28, 1968, Los Angeles, CA; [p.] Thomas and Arbutus Burch; [ed.] Beverly Hills High School, Beverly Hills, CA, Graduated, June, 1987; [occ.] Fitness Instructor/Child Care Assistant East Los Angeles YMCA, East Los Angeles, CA; [memb.] Harmony Matters Collective; [hon.] Various certificate programs completed for: National Aerobics Certification, Strength Training Certification, CPR and Standard First Aid Certification, International Dealers School, Curriculum: Computer Training; [oth. writ.] A Poet In Stages at 1992, Selections in Words That Matter (Most), New Poems From The Women's Poetry Project at 1995, at least 100 other unpublished works.; [pers.] I nurture the talents that God has given me to serve mankind with.; [a.] Los Angeles, CA

BURDICK, WENDY LEE
[b.] October 26, 1982, Haleyville, AL; [p.] Bob and Sherry Burdick; [ed.] Presently attends 7th grade Addison High School; [hon.] Musical and Academic Awards, Winston County Spelling Bee Winner 2 years in a row.; [oth. writ.] I have written several other poems.; [a.] Addison, AL

BURGESS, MELODY
[b.] July 26, 1979, Bunnell, FL; [p.] John and Elaine Burgess, Grandparents: Edward and Mary McSweeney and Henery and Lucy Burgess; [ed.] Still in 3rd year of highschool;

[occ.] Student; [memb.] Flagler County Sheriff's Posse, Fashion Marketing, ST Elizabeth Ann Seton's CYO, Flagler Palm Coast High School R.O.T.C., Taekwondo Karate-Brown Belt Level; [hon.] Award of Excellence in the News-Journal Design-An-Ad/write An Editorial contest. My poems was also published in the National Poetry Contest; [oth. writ.] Other poems published in school newspaper.; [pers.] I believe happiness is derived by following your heart, utilizing your God given gifts to their maximum potential.; [a.] Bunnell, FL

BURKE, KERRY A.
[pen.] Kirby Burke; [b.] December 17, 1956, Gary, IN; [p.] Joseph and Geraldine Burke; [m.] Brenda K. Burke, September 5, 1990; [ch.] Renee Ellen, Angela, Kerry Jr., Mike Medrano, Nick Medrano; [ed.] Crown Point High; [occ.] Warehouse Supervisor, Pro. Driver - Midwest Siding Supply, Lowell, IN; [memb.] Cedar Lake Civil Defense; [oth. writ.] Home for Lunch, my three o'clock girl, "the love within me," remembering, faith, "my dearest darling.";
[pers.] I try very hard to live by the golden rule, at times, I find it very hard to express myself through conversation, this is what motivates my writing.; [a.] Cedar Lake, IN

BURT, EDIE
[b.] August 18, 1923, Cleveland, OH; [p.] Chet and Irene Conklin; [m.] Joe Burt; [ch.] Debbie and Doug; [ed.] White Plains High, New York American River College, Carmichael CA; [occ.] Retired travel agent; [memb.] Good Shepherd Lutheran Church; [oth. writ.] Remembering Mary Fee Finnegan, The Last Cat, Little Margaret Under The Tree...other short stories and collection of poems.; [pers.] Many writers can write whenever they choose...I envy that, but I write when my vatic voice speaks to me.; [a.] Sacramento, CA

BURTON, LYNN
[b.] January 3, 1973, South Carolina; [p.] Rose and Arnold Pelletier; [m.] James Shannon Burton, December 3, 1994; [ch.] Tanner - 2 years old; [ed.] Cooper High School graduate; [occ.] Homemaker; [oth. writ.] The is my first published writing and I am proud of my accomplishment.; [pers.] My writing is very personal and my moon will definitely show through in the reading. I hope to put a smile on someone's face and laughter in their hearts.; [a.] Dallas, TX

CALDWELL, KATHLEEN
[pen.] Colleen Moore; [b.] December 5, 1915, Paradise, WV; [p.] S. D. and Letha McCormick; [m.] Ernest M. Caldwell, January 9, 1934; [ch.] 3 Girls and 2 Boys; [ed.] Diploma from 8th Grade Tilmon School; [occ.] Homemaker; [oth. writ.] I have wrote between 100 and 200 poems including 2 hymns, one titled, My Saviour and

Me.; [pers.] I was born, raised on a little farm in the rolling hills of W. VA. saved at age 14. Most of my poems were inspired by my love for Jesus whom I will see one day. I have lived my poem, West Virginia.; [a.] Hurricane, WV

CALLAHAN, JOHN
[pen.] Jay Cee; [b.] June 7, 1963, Webster, MA; [p.] Adopted - William and Faye Callahan; [ed.] Technical H.S., Design and Graphics, Santa Monica College, Business and Psychology, Undergraduate Studies - Desktop Publishing and Macintosh; [occ.] Director of Print Services Toyota Motor Sales, L.A.; [oth. writ.] Compilation of poems, greeting cards.; [pers.] "Values are the key to a joyous life. We must choose wisely and live honorably, for then there would be no strife.; [a.] Hermosa Beach, CA

CANNON, BONNIE
[b.] October 28, 1937, Fredonia, TX; [p.] Frankie Greer, Della Byrd; [m.] William Cannon (deceased 1972, age 39), September 14, 1952; [ch.] Bonnie Gail, Diana Lynne, Karen Kathleen; [ed.] A.V. College - Cal Poly Ponoma; [occ.] Recently retired - Director 19 Health Resort - Now pursuing dream of writer-poet; [hon.] College honor - Alpha Gamma Phi Sigma, Dean's List, Academic Scholarship award; [oth. writ.] Many poems essays life story - short novelette none submitted for publishing yet, except 2 poems to you.; [pers.] Pain is the wrapping paper of life - inside the box of life is the gift. What I do with these defines me.; [a.] Venice, CA

CANNON, JASON L.
[pen.] "Wolfe" Cannon; [b.] July 13, 1983, Seattle, WA; [p.] Jennie Cannon; [ed.] 6th Grade; [occ.] Student; [hon.] Visual and Performing Arts; [oth. writ.] I love you and face your fears (not published or entered in any contest).; [pers.] Age does not matter when you put your mind to something.; [a.] Fort Jones, CA

CAPASSO, SUMMER
[b.] January 22, 1986, Lancaster, CA; [p.] Louis and Karen Capasso; [ed.] Now attending Linda Verde School, Lancaster 4th grade. Also student at Viking White Sewing Center Lancaster - 2nd year, Gate program 4th grade; [memb.] Quartz Hill Junior Grange; [hon.] Student of Month: K-2nd, 3rd and 4th grades, Best of show for sewing at Antelope Valley Fair 1995, perfect attendance 4th grade, 1st place in sewing at Grange State Convention 1995 CA; [pers.] Right now I'm wanting to become a teacher and I want to run in the Olympics.; [a.] Lancaster, CA

CARAVEO, SCOTT
[b.] May 13, 1982, Turlock, CA; [p.] Bryan and Genny Caraveo; [ed.] 8th Grade student at Rio Seco. I will graduate this June, then attend Santana High School.; [occ.] Student; [pers.] I

enjoy playing soccer. I would like to play on. The U.S. National Team someday.; [a.] Santee, CA

CARLISLE JR., JOHNIE
[b.] May 16, 1934, Meridian, MS; [p.] Johnie Carlisle, Sr. and Alma M. Carlisle; [m.] Eunice M. Carlisle, May 20, 1955; [ch.] Cynthia, Kenneth, Craig; [ed.] Bethel Seminary M. Div (D. Min 1997); [occ.] Pastor, Bethel A.M.E. Church, Oxnard, CA; [memb.] Alpha Phi Alpha Fraternity Numerous civic and social organizations including N.A.A.C.P.; [hon.] Outstanding Black Citizen 1989, Vta County, Clergy Award 1990, 5th Episcopal Dist, WMS, Citizen of the Year, 1992/93 Delta Sigma Theta Sorority, Vta County Chapter, and 1996 Summit Award, Ventura County (Vta) Jack and Jill of America, Inc.; [pers.] I believe in the dignity and worth of every individual.; [a.] Oxnard, CA

CARNES, LARRY A.
[b.] October 27, 1958, Bay Village, OH; [p.] Robert L., Phyllis A. Tucker; [m.] Michelle J. Carnes, December 10, 1987; [ch.] Britainy Leanne; [ed.] Xenia High (Ohio), All Honors Courses and Premed; [occ.] Plant Manager Alway Inc. (Airline Ground Support); [hon.] 1972 California American Legion State Essay Award Top Ten, National Honor Society 2 yrs; [oth. writ.] Many but all now published; [pers.] 2nd eldest child of 8 low middle class all writings heavily influenced by past and present family ties. My poems are an effort to present one8 persons outlook at real life events.; [a.] Winter Haven, FL

CARNEVALE, STEFANIE MARIE
[b.] January 29, 1981, Derby, CT; [p.] Donna Giusto, Alber Anderson; [ed.] Emmet Oibien RUTS; [pers.] In life we all have a song to sing and it comes from our surroundings.; [a.] Ansonia, CT

CARNEVALI, AUGUST R.
[b.] June 15, 1931, Archbald, PA; [p.] Primo and Vienna Carnevali; [m.] Marion; [ch.] Gina Marie; [ed.] Scranton Univ., Fairleigh Dickinson Univ.; [occ.] Machine Designer, Semi-retired; [oth. writ.] Articles for Spectrum Magazine "7-Oaks" - a 348 line poem - a story of love of family that endures beyond death.; [pers.] Wasted talent is a sin against God!!; [a.] Somerville, NJ

CARPENTER, EDWARD J.
[pen.] Eddie or E. J.; [b.] September 12, 1940, Washington, DC; [p.] Marvin and Helen Carpenter (Deceased); [m.] Sandra Helen Carpenter, December 6, 1963; [ch.] David and Mark Carpenter; [ed.] Cardoza H.S. Graduate, Washington, D.C.; [occ.] Home Decorating Contractor, [memb.] NAACP; [hon.] Honorable Service, U.S.A.F. 1959 to 1962; [oth. writ.] "My Mark" and other poems; [pers.] I only have a minute, only 60 seconds in it. Forced upon me, I did not choose it, but I will suffer if I loose it, I only have a minute, but eternity is in it!

CARPENTER, MAGDALENA MARIA-ANNA
[b.] March 31, 1977, Warsaw, Poland; [p.] John Carpenter and Bogdana Chetkowska Carpenter; [ed.] Greenhills School, Williams College; [occ.] Student, Williams College; [oth. writ.] Poems published in Offerings, articles for campus newspaper, The Williams Record; [pers.] I think poetry comes from the very heart of life itself, which can be found in the most minute events. I have been very influenced by Czeslaw Milosz, Bruno Schulz, and Albert Camus.; [a.] Ann Arbor, MI

CARPENTER, VELMA
[b.] July 14, 1965, Newark; [p.] Roger and Carolyn Long; [m.] Divorced; [ch.] Daniel and Angel Carpenter; [ed.] Licking Heights School and Licking Country joint Vocational School; [occ.] Hair Stylists; [oth. writ.] Poems in the Columbus Dispatch about my brother; [pers.] The words that I write are a reflection of God's love and mercy that he will pour out upon his children.; [a.] Pataskala, OH

CARRIGAN, MICHELE LINDA GILL
[pen.] Carrigan; [b.] October 21, 1965, Carson City, NV; [p.] La Vonne Riley, Michael Gill; [m.] Robert Carrigan, February 17, 1986; [ch.] Laura Loraine Carrigan, Robert Lee Carrigan, Jeremy James Carrigan, Weston Kyle Carrigan, Weston Kyle Carrigan; [ed.] Odessa High, Midway College of Med Dent Careers; [occ.] Home maker, raising my 4 Children; [memb.] First United Methodist Church; [hon.] Volunteer of the last 6 weeks of 95, for my son Weston's first grade class; [oth. writ.] Several poems written, just never submitted. This is my first submitted poem.; [pers.] This is dedicated to all the people with a God given talent, that might be afraid to take that first step. Go ahead take it. It will give you the joy of knowing you did try. Who knows where you will walk tomorrow Glory be to God.; [a.] Wolfe City, TX

CARTER, CANDICE
[b.] January 23, 1981, Baton Rouge, LA; [p.] Mike and Donnie Carter; [ed.] Chesnee High School; [occ.] Student; [memb.] Chesnee High School Band, Chesnee United Methodist Church, American Red Cross Volunteer; [hon.] South Carolina Lt. Governor Essay Award; [pers.] The dove has been known as the dove of peace for decades. Now, in today's world, we are so overthrown by gangs, violence and was, that the dove has almost lost its meaning. I try to touch people, and inspire chance for the better. A single act of kindness, is the beginning of peace.; [a.] Chesnee, SC

CARTER JR., CHESTER WILLIAM
[pen.] Chet, C. W., Mickey, Mick. Cater; [b.] Grassvalley, CA; [p.] Chester Wm. Carter, Viola E. Carter; [m.] Dorothy; [ch.] William Carter, Angela Carter; [ed.] High School-Reno High,

NRI-School of Writing, Washington DC, Retired Executive Chef., Certified in Videography; [occ.] Retired-looking to be pub. as a Poet, Novelist, and Freelance Writer; [hon.] NRI-School of Writing, Achievement Awards with High Honors; [oth. writ.] Several poems, Novel Three Quarters Finished, Mystery Novel, Several Short Stories, Show time Mag., Reno For Radio K-Bul Dave Collin, Second Place-Nothing Pub. Yet!..; [pers.] Only a fool would dismiss, life's trials, love and mysteries. And a fool I am not! With this in mind: I fulfill my life's dreams just a "whisper in the wind", becoming, one with "God! Nature! And Mankind:" Living life, as a Romantic! Loving Poetry!; [a.] Reno, Nevada

CASMO, JOANNE
[b.] July 24, 1941, Columbus, OH; [p.] John J. Murphy and Jeannette; [m.] Ross Casmo, February 2, 1961; [ed.] Grandview Heights H.S., Franklin University (BS degree) Nova University (MS) Business Administration; [occ.] Software Specialist AT&T; [memb.] Norris Lake Presbyterian Church (Elder of Church); [pers.] Writing poetry has always been my way of expressing those inner fellings I otherwise have difficulty in verbally expressing.; [a.] Lithonia, GA

CASTILE, KATHLEEN M.
[b.] May 16, 1957, Chicago, IL; [p.] William A. and Kathleen M. Castile; [ed.] Forestview High; [occ.] Restaurant Service 20 plus years; [oth. writ.] 600 unpublished poems collection, 48,000 pages personal journal, lyrics for several songs.; [pers.] I have written privately since 1975, and am now willing to share my artistry in hopes of touching people's lives.; [a.] Cape Coral, FL

CATOE, LINDA
[pen.] Linda M. Catoe; [b.] June 19, 1955, Winston Salem, NC; [p.] Edith Wilson, M. E. Catoe; [ed.] UNC - Greensboro, NC School of the Arts, JoAnn Baron/DW Brown Studio; [occ.] Actress; [memb.] AFTRA; [oth. writ.] While you're up... Poems from the fridge; [pers.] To thing own self be true, follow your instincts.; [a.] Santa Monica, CA

CATTERTON, REBECCA OLIVER
[b.] May 106, 1966, Pascagoula, MS; [p.] Gresham and Mary Oliver; [m.] Douglas Catterton, June 22, 1991; [ch.] Jonathan, Samuel, Rachel; [occ.] Homemaker; [oth. writ.] Acknowledged on local television station as a child.; [pers.] I believe everyone deserves a chance for happiness. Some spread their entire lives searching for love, peace and happiness yet never finding it. I was blessed to have found all three in my husband and children.; [a.] Clyo, GA

CAVE, KATHLEEN ANNE
[pen.] Kathleen Anne Gallagher; [b.] August 17, 1943, Seattle, WA; [p.] James Gallagher, Norma

Cronin; [ch.] Norie Anne Bauer, [ed.] B.A. Ed., M.A. Ed., M.A., L.M.H.T.; [occ.] Retired Educator, Licensed Mental Health Therapist, - Playing Out Career Monopoly"; [memb.] N.R.T.A.; [hon.] Phi Beta Kappa Research Grant, "Jane Walters" Actress and M.C. Award; [oth. writ.] Articles, essays published in local newspapers, professional publications.; [pers.] "Life is a treasure, dive to discover it's bounties". K.C.; [a.] Irving, TX

CAWLEY, WILLIAM D.
[b.] July 6, 1934, Cleveland, OH; [p.] Deceased; [m.] Divorced; [ch.] Susan Marie; [ed.] B.A. Sociology, Chapman College 1973; [occ.] Retired; [memb.] Former: Junior Cham. of Comm. Lions, Optimist Club; [hon.] Honorable Mention Poetry Contest Lompoc CA; [oth. writ.] "Diamonds in the Wine," "Memories," "Vignettes of the Sea," "The World is Cold Enough," "Spring Valley."; [pers.] Very interested in world peace and a containment of violence world wide.; [a.] Winchester, KY

CAWTHORNE, LAURA J.
[pen.] Peanut; [b.] October 16, 1947, Opelousas, LA; [p.] Clinton Martin Sr, Celisa Jones Martin; [m.] Eddie Marion Cawthorne, January 28, 1977; [ch.] Herschel Maurice Martin; [ed.] J.S. Clark High, Hargest Vocational College, Moses Lake Washington Job Corp Center, [occ.] Teacher's Assistant at Welch Middle School (OH Dept Exceptional Ed); [memb.] Children International (sponsor); [oth. writ.] Several unpublished poems and writings but yet my original work inspired of God; [pers.] "Only what you do for Christ will Last", "He's worthy to be praised," I'm not Ashamed of the Gospel of God that's why I'd rather fight to be his child than to switch to the prince of darkness; [a.] Houston, TX

CEBRYNSKI, GEORGE H.
[pen.] Hoslar; [b.] October 31, 1948, Pineville, LA; [p.] Michael M. and Lois A. Cebrynski; [m.] Martha S. Cebrynski, May 10, 1980; [ed.] Associate Degree in Nursing; [occ.] Registered Nurse; [memb.] United Pentecostal, Church International; [pers.] Find out God's purpose for you in life and seek after that purpose.; [a.] Pineville, LA

CEMPELLIN, DEBRA L.
[pen.] Debra L. Cempellin; [b.] February 23, 1957, Peabody, MA; [p.] Carol Peabody Durland, Richard K. Durland; [m.] Peter O. Cempellin, February 10, 1979; [ch.] Kimberly, Joseph, Jenna; [ed.] Beverly High Beverly Mass.; [occ.] Owner of Deb's Daycare Middleton MA, Free Lance Writer of Poems, Sh. Stories; [memb.] Local Greyhound Rescue Shelters; [oth. writ.] Articles published by local newspapers, local greyhound adoption agencies,

several short stories.; [pers.] To be able to express feelings in words and have an affect on others is a true gift from God, any future writings will be dedicated in loving memory of my grandmother "Florence H. Durland." Her never yielding faith in me still gently nudges me forward....; [a.] Middleton, MA

CENTENO, ROSA M.
[b.] El Salvador, CA; [p.] George Hurtarte and Rosa Maria Hurtarte; [ch.] George W. Centeno, Martha D. Kelley, Richard D. Centeno, Rosalie A. Centeno; [ed.] Elementary and Secondary School Saint Ines Catholic School. El Salvador. Maria Auxiliadora School. El Salvador. Exec. Secretary.; [occ.] Counsellor (Bilingue) Own Buss.; [memb.] Notary Public Association A.A.R.P.; [oth. writ.] I have composed other poems in English and Spanish Languages, including religious poems.; [pers.] I love poetry. It is my passion. Writing is like an incentive to keep me going...it is a good feeling to express in writing what I feel inside of me.; [a.] Downey, CA

CEPEDA, EUGENIO
[pen.] Gene; [b.] March 15, 1949, Saint Croix, VI; [p.] Gregoria and Candido; [m.] Miriam, November 16, 1974; [ch.] Nichole, Dominique, Gina; [ed.] Franklin K. Lane H.S.; [hon.] Medallic Art Award; [pers.] Through my poetry, I try to inspire feelings of the mind and soul, the connection between one's personal feelings toward each other, and that of nature, this poem is in memory to my brother in law.; [a.] Brooklyn, NY

CERVANTEZ JR., LORENZO
[b.] October 4, 1957, Los Angeles, CA; [p.] Christian and Lorenzo Sr.; [m.] Elizabeth Cervantez; [ch.] Destinee, Lorissa, Lorenzo III; [ed.] Graduate - University of Arkansas at Fayetteville, Graduate - Walnut High School, Walnut, CA; [occ.] A law enforcement officer, Los Angeles, CA; [oth. writ.] I have written several poems and have not sough to publish them.; [pers.] Human emotions mirror life experiences. This is what I try to capture in my writings.; [a.] Long Beach, CA

CHADWICK, IRENE
[pen.] Irene Chadwick; [b.] March 1, 1918, New York City, NY; [m.] Divorced; [ch.] 1 - Frank Weisman, married to Joyce, grandson Zachary 16 yrs. old; [ed.] B.A. Degree, Ucha - Extension Courses in PR Advertising, Pers Mgnt., applied Psych.; [occ.] Retired; [memb.] Formerly a Rehab., Counselor - Member in Affiliated Organizations, Speakers Bureau, Business and Prof. Womens Group, Long Beach, C.C.; [hon.] Public Speaker in 'Careers at Any Age', many accolades re same, honoree degrees; [oth. writ.] Published columnist, 1 year plus Pomona Calif., many articles, book - Dear John (1964), Desilou Studio Interest, hobbies:

Painting and Writing.; [pers.] Great interest in all phases in the arts, writing, literature, theatre, etc. As a senior now I participate in volunteer programs.; [a.] Los Angeles, CA

CHANCELLOR, CHARLES E.
[pen.] Dream Painter, The Old Cowboy; [b.] November 5, 1946, Wichita, KS; [p.] William and Stella Chancellor, [m.] Katherine S. Chancellor (Deceased), July 25, 1965; [ch.] Tony, Terry, Shenelle; [ed.] High School, Bible College, Business School; [memb.] Cowboys for Christ, The Christian Fellowship of Horsemen; [oth. writ.] The Cowboy, The Cowboys Mid Night Dream, Rainbows, Angel Flight, The Beautiful Rose, many more.

CHANEY, SCOTT
[b.] March 2, 1956, Fort Wayne, IN; [p.] Glen and Helen Chaney; [ch.] Shannon Joy, Samantha Jo; [ed.] Rudyard High, Kinross, MI, Midwest Horseshoeing, Macomb IL; [occ.] Blacksmith; [memb.] First Assembly of God, New Castle, IN; [hon.] Distinguished Service, USAF; [pers.] Let the words of my mouth and the meditation of my heart be acceptable in thy sight, O Lord, my rock and my redeemer.; [a.] Sulphur Springs, IN

CHAPMAN, TERESA
[b.] May 5, 1969, Bartow, FL; [p.] Sam Granthan, Ruth Grantham; [m.] Ray Chapman, February 15, 1986; [ch.] Shayla Chapman; [ed.] Holmes County High; [occ.] Housewife; [oth. writ.] Written poems for family members on holidays and special occasions.; [pers.] I write poem because it's something I enjoy. Poetry enriches the mind and warms the heart.; [a.] Caryville, FL

CHARBONEAU, NYETTA
[b.] May 10, 1966, Vermont; [ch.] DJ, Josh, Justin; [ed.] Currently going to school for story writing and publishing.; [hon.] "The Elderly" won Editor's Top Choice Award - 1994; [oth. writ.] Several other poems, and tributes, am currently working on a childrens book. Some of my other poems have been published in newspapers in Colo. and N.H.; [pers.] Am I different? Is Dedicated to: My brother... Bobby, my niece... Danielle, my nephew... Micheal, all who are handicapped.

CHAU, KARIN
[b.] June 10, 1979, Taiwan, Republic of China; [p.] Chong Hwa Chau, Tung Lang Chau; [ed.] Francis Lewis High School; [occ.] Student; [memb.] Kawanis, Key Club International; [hon.] Achievement in Conflict Resolution Program, UFT Service Award; [oth. writ.] Few writings in Chinese and English that are published but are dedicated to my friends and family.; [pers.] Do the best you can on everything, no matter what the results are, failure or success. As long as you have tried and done your best, that is what matters.; [a.] Flushing, NY

CHENEY, KRISTEN
[b.] March 11, 1978, Bay Shore, NY; [p.] Gail S. Cheney, Ralph L. Cheney; [oth. writ.] My own unpublished collection of poems.; [pers.] We need to heal the world through expression and understanding, in order to understand and express, we must remember to feel.; [a.] Deer Park, NY

CHERN, REGINA
[b.] May 5, 1981; [p.] Chii-yuh Chern and Po Ying Chern; [occ.] Freshman at Monte Vista High School; [pers.] To mom and dad, I love you with all my heart. A lot of whom I am comes from music and my sisters, Stella and Eugenia. Thank you.; [a.] Danville, CA

CHESAK, BEULA ASHMENT
[b.] Freedom, WY; [p.] Arlynn Ashment, Vella Kronhofman; [m.] Jim W. Chesak; [ch.] Four; [memb.] Was president and Editor of Eda - How Poetry and Writers Group; [oth. writ.] Humorous poetry collection "Dogs, Cats and me" sponsored by Humane Society. Poetry in local newspaper and annual writer's group publication ("Eda How Gems") poems in Hardback "Guild Anthology" and "Author/poet" magazine; [pers.] I'm obsessed with poetry. I walk with frost/cry with Millay, laugh with Parker and Cheer Angelou. I credit my poetic versatility to my fascination with poetry in its many forms and styles.; [a.] Idaho Falls, ID

CHIMIKLIS, RUTH
[b.] May 24, 1932, Chelmsford, MA; [p.] Remi E. Lassonde, Harriet Cornwall; [m.] John Chimiklis, February 19, 1959; [ch.] Ronald Theodore, Cynthia; [ed.] Westford Academy grad. Westford, Mass.; [occ.] Volunteer Ministry; [pers.] I have a great appreciation for the magnificent works of creation which surround us and enjoy writing about them in my poems; [a.] Uniondale, NY

CHIUCARELLO, SUSAN
[pen.] Sue; [b.] August 15, 1959, Waterbury, CT; [p.] Mario and Georgie Cantamessa; [m.] Albert Chiucarello, April 4, 1992; [ch.] A. J. (age 2 1/2); [ed.] College Graduate - Associate's Degree Executive, Secretarial Science; [occ.] Mom and homemaker; [pers.] The three things that children need most in life are lots of hugs, lots of kisses and a total surrounding of love. Every thing else is unimportant.; [a.] Waterbury, CT

CHRISTIAN, MILTON
[b.] October 18, 1976; [ed.] Graduated in June 1995 from Union Hill High School, Union City, NJ.; [occ.] Student; [memb.] National Honor Society, MV Alpha Theta, Art Club, Math Club; [hon.] High honors, award for highest average in Algebra II in 1994; [oth. writ.] 'Tomorrow', 'Sacrifice', 'The Twig', 'Life', 'Often', 'Enigma', 'Sentiments', 'Low', 'A

sinner's fate', 'But I do', 'Perfection', 'The Cure', all poems; [pers.] My heartiest thanks to Mrs. Makar for all she has done (Math Dept. Union Hill High School) To Jesus for guiding me through this journey. What would I do without you? I have been greatly inspired by the music of Phil Collins. "The success of ones future lies in the beauty of his dreams"; [a.] Union City, NJ

CHRISTNER, MARION MARINO STANLEY
[b.] November 17, 1924, Los Angeles, CA; [p.] Josephine and Joseph Marino; [m.] Harry K. Christner, April 27, 1965; [ch.] Richard Stanley, Tomas Christner; [ed.] Hoover High School; [occ.] Retired Typesetter; [memb.] Rebekahs Emblem Club (Elks Lodge); [hon.] High School Scholarship Society; [a.] Tujunga, CA

CIULLO, BRANDI
[b.] August 11, 1982, Chicago, IL; [p.] Doreen Mitchell; [ed.] 8th Grade; [occ.] 8th Grade; [memb.] Library; [hon.] Basketball Award, Honor Roll Award, Soccer Trophy and Award.; [pers.] I strive to finish High School and go to Notre Dame College.; [a.] Port Richey, FL

CLAIBORNE, GERALDINE
[pen.] Jerry Dean; [b.] August 1, 1960, New, Orleans, LA; [p.] John Smith, Georgia Smith; [m.] Hubert Claiborne, May 18, 1979; [ch.] Jana Shantell, Herbert; [ed.] William Winans High; [occ.] Wife and the proud mother of two daughters and one son.; [memb.] Vaugha chapel church, Kingford Baptist Church 2nd a member of shilo, Baptist Church. Where I am an usher and the secretary for the ushers.; [hon.] Vol. services rendered for A.J.F.C. W.H.C. from 1986-87 The Wward was from the Head Start Center for Volunteer Work.; [pers.] I just wish, we as a nation can come together as one with no color lines and love one another as we love our selves. The way God intended and help ones who have went astray.; [a.] Woodville, MS

CLAPP, DIAHANN
[b.] July 30, 1963, Seville, Spain; [p.] Charles and Millie Clapp; [ed.] Dudley Senior High G'boro NC (1981); [occ.] Relief Manager for Motel 6 Greensboro, NC; [oth. writ.] Several articles published in local newspaper, Greensboro Daily News, G'boro, NC; [pers.] This poem is dedicated to and was written for my brother, Michael Clapp who we lost to Aids on April 28, 1995. Through this poem, I hope those afflicted will find the strength to go on.; [a.] Greensboro, NC

CLARDY, TAWNYA
[b.] December 5, 1980, Salt Lake City, UT; [p.] Jean and Tom Clardy; [ed.] Currently in High School, Alhambra High, Phoenix, AZ; [hon.] Won first place in school, district and State poetry contests in Arizona; [oth. writ.]

Currently writing Lullaby and Stonesong, a fantasy novel.; [a.] Glendale, AZ

CLARK, DONNA J.

[b.] October 1, 1940, East Saint Louis, IL; [p.] Robert and Marie Williams; [m.] Randall D. Clark, 1960; [ch.] Susan Marie, Stephen Randall, Angela Marie; [ed.] DeKalb High School; [occ.] Secretary/Bookkeeper; [memb.] Basically church organizations and extensively involved in the Emmaus Community which is non-denominational and works to bring all people together, regardless of church affiliation; [oth. writ.] A Sunrise To Remember, The Walk To Emmaus, The Christmas Story, And They Will Call Him Immanuel, Our God Is An Awesome God, Walking With Christ, Living With The Bears, Your Confirmation, Whom Shall I Send, And Jesus Walked With Them, Wrapped In His Love; [pers.] What I write comes from my heart and the relationship I have with the Lord. Through this unusual style of writing, I try to reach out to others hopefully to comfort, encourage, lift their spirits.; [a.] North Vernon, IN

CLARK, EVA V.

[b.] October 9, 1920, Vale, SD, [p.] Kate and Luther Hill; [m.] Robert W. Clark, May 26, 1942; [ch.] Cheryl, Judy and Robyn; [ed.] College B.E. Degree; [occ.] Housewife - Teacher Retired; [memb.] United Church of Christ, Black Hills Art Association; [oth. writ.] Several poems published in Isabel Dakotan Newspaper; [pers.] I am moved by everyday, ordinary things. I call them small miracles that can shape our thinking and help me cope with the problems I face.; [a.] Spearfish, SD

CLARKE JR., PHILLIP

[b.] November 14, 1956, Warrington, FL; [p.] Phillip and Liz Clarke; [m.] Janith C. Bosarge, July 19, 1982; [ch.] Stacey Lee, Tammy Marie, Oliver Barton; [ed.] Alba High School, Bayou La Batre, AL; [occ.] File Clerk, First Chemical Corp., Pascagoula, MS; [hon.] Chorus Award, Alba High School; [oth. writ.] The Haunted Head of Cedar Point Reef, Night of the Banshee, Samhain, Angel of Darkness/Angel of Light, Hide and Seek, The Captain, Moments Dreams and Memories; [pers.] Anything is possible but it's up to you to be responsible to yourself as well as others.; [a.] Bayou La Batre, AL

CLARY, CAROL

[b.] October 13, 1945, New Orleans, LA; [p.] John and Ann Hoffman; [m.] Benton J. Clary, October 24, 1964; [ch.] Michelle and Jill; [ed.] Associates of Arts Degree; [occ.] Homemaker; [memb.] Girl Scouts, Library Volunteer, Park Women's Association, Church Guild; [hon.] Dean's List, Beta Sigma Phi, Who's Who in Jr. Colleges, Who's Who In American Colleges; [a.] Van Buren, MO

CLASEN, MARTIN M.

[pen.] Marty Clasen; [b.] August 27, 1963, Wichita, KS; [p.] Mathias and Mary Ann Clasen; [m.] Elvia Clasen, October 14, 1995; [ed.] Madison High School United States Navy; [occ.] Frito Lay Salesman; [hon.] Naval Awards Letter of Commendation from a two Star Admiral. Sailor of the Month (April 1986) Good Conduct Medal.

CLEMENTS, MARK

[pen.] God's Fool/Tool; [b.] April 23, 1957, Bedford, VA; [p.] Julius Clements and Anne Edwards; [ch.] Delila Ann, Sheila Marie, Crystal Lea; [ed.] 8th Grade; [oth. writ.] Words from the grave, 1988 more than numbers 1991.; [pers.] I am a student of life. Life is constance change, a never ending cycle. We are only a moment and very small slice of the whole. The whole is timeless and endless. Yet, this moment can ripple, so use it well.; [a.] Chesapeake, VA

CLENDENIN, ERNESTINE LISTER

[b.] March 10, 1955, Rockport, TX; [p.] Verland Lister and Lucile Lister; [m.] David Clendenin, November 13, 1993; [ed.] Cholla High School, Pima College, Anderson University; [occ.] Homemaker; [memb.] Somerville Church of God; [oth. writ.] Poem published in Arcadia Poetry Anthology. Writings for church organization.; [pers.] I hope that my God-given talent of poetry writing may be an inspiration in someone's life.; [a.] Somerville, TX

CLONTZ, MELISSA

[b.] December 15, 1985, GA; [p.] Heidi and John Clontz; [ed.] I am attending 4th Grade at New Ga. Elm. I am 10 years old; [memb.] I am a Peer-Mediator at School; [hon.] I have been an Honor Roll Student since 1st Grade; [oth. writ.] I have written several other poems, and short stories.; [pers.] I have been inspired to write by my second grade Teacher, Ms. Lewis, Fair Oaks Elem. School, Marietta GA.; [a.] Dallas, GA

COATS, CHARLESTANECA CAPRICE

[b.] Taneca C. Coats; [p.] May 6, 1983, Birmingham, AL; [m.] Charles and Chasta Coats; [ed.] Woodbrook Junior High Evergreen Elementary; [memb.] Girl Scouts USA, Deliverance Baptist Church; [oth. writ.] Current poem published in the Deliverance Baptist Church News Letter; [pers.] Certain events that happen in my life, gives me the inspiration to write poems.; [a.] Fort Lewis, WA

COGBURN, AMANDA

[b.] 1980, OKC; [p.] Mack and Sherry Cogburn; [occ.] Student; [memb.] First Presbyterian Church; [hon.] Who's Who of American High School Students, "Student of Today" Award; [pers.] Live for what counts.; [a.] Edmond, OK

COHERNOUR, EVON

[pen.] Beadc or Eadc; [b.] Clio, WV; [p.] Raymond and Gladys Armstead; [ch.] Roy Jr. and James Droddy, Jeanie Addington; [ed.] 1) Herbert Hoover High School 1975, 2) Kanawha Co Board of Ed. School of Practical Nursing 1964; [occ.] Nurse; [memb.] 1) Clendenin Advent Christian Church Member, 2) Rebekah Creed (March 1996), 3) American Association of retired persons; [hon.] The greatest honor I ever feel is when my children call me "Mother" other honors or awards I have never received.; [oth. writ.] Short stories nonpublished, 1) On the Beach - non published, 2) Healing Hands - non published, 3) What Christmas Means to Me - non published, 4) Many poems - non published; [pers.] I try to show deep feelings I have in my heart and sometimes reflect what God means to my life, I love life and I love reading books and poetry; [a.] Clendenin, WV

COLAHAN, SEAN

[b.] May 19, 1982, Danbury, CT; [p.] Gail and Grey Colahan; [occ.] Student; [memb.] Boy Scouts, Band, Chorus, Church Youth Group, Science Olympiad, and Student Council; [pers.] Having a positive outlook will get you far in life.; [a.] Reading, PA

COLE, REBECCA L.

[b.] August 19, 1969, Little Rock, AR; [p.] Robert and Lena Keenzel; [m.] Anthony R. Cole, November 13, 1987; [ch.] Houston Ray, Nicholas Ryan; [occ.] Homemaker, Child care provider; [oth. writ.] Several poems written, but never viewed.; [pers.] I enjoy writing poems, reflecting personal views of lifes experiences.; [a.] Fort Carson, CO

COLEMAN, BETTY JOANNE

[pen.] B. JoAnne Coleman; [b.] November 8, 1937, Portland, OR; [p.] Alfred M. Harris, Frances Harris; [m.] Deceased; [ch.] Angelina Marie and Michelle Suzanne; [ed.] Reedsport U.H.S., Reedsport, OR, Santa Rosa Jr. College, Santa Rosa, CA; [occ.] Oil Painter/Retired (30 years) W/Amer. Express T.R.S. Inc.; [pers.] Written in loving memory of my daughters, Angie and Michelle and with deepest love for my grandsons, Nicholas and Joshua.; [a.] Santa Rosa, GA

COLEMAN, CHRISTINE

[pen.] Praline, McFly; [b.] July 15, 1972, Toledo, OH; [p.] Pariss and Linda Coleman; [ed.] St. Ursula Academy, Toledo, OH, University of Dayton, Dayton, OH; [occ.] Sophomore Health Teacher Bowsher High School, Toledo, OH; [oth. writ.] Found in personal journals and the Black Perspective newspaper - University of Dayton, Dayton, OH; [pers.] This poem is dedicated to my grandfather, Claud Recker, who passed away June 18, 1995. To my parents, who have always encouraged and supported me, as well as giving me the opportunity to explore and live life to the fullest. To my brother, Mike, for pushing me to be the best. To all of my friends in Dayton and Toledo - Ha Ha - I've got published poetry and this is just the beginning.; [a.] Toledo, OH

COLEMAN, MARY KATE
[pen.] Mary Kate Coleman; [b.] March 15, 1941, Ashville, NC; [p.] Mr. and Mrs. Johnny Grice; [m.] Deceased; [ch.] Three; [ed.] 12th grade, Went Cosmetologist School for 13 months.; [occ.] Retired Hairdresser; [memb.] Member of the Church of God in Bristolva; [oth. writ.] I write poems and I have one out now, which I had music put to it and it is beautiful. It is about the little Smith Boys, their mother Putthemin The Lake in SC the name of the song is Mommy God now holds Our hands, it is on the radios in NC, SC town.

COLEMAN, MELISSA
[b.] February 15, 1977, Louisville, KY; [p.] Charlotte and Lee Coleman; [ed.] Doss High, University of Lou.; [occ.] John Conti Coffee Cafe; [memb.] Kentucky Fairness Campaign, Humane Society (KY), PLTA; [hon.] Who's Who Among American High School Students, 3rd Place in National Library of Poetry Contest (Winner '95); [oth. writ.] Poem published in a sea of treasures, other poems and stories in local magazines.; [pers.] Find motivation within yourself, and inspiration from the struggling societies to create a whole new world of words.; [a.] Louisville, KY

COLETTE, LARRA
[pers.] French born and educated, author of poems in French, English and Spanish with own translations, influenced by French, Indian, Chinese Poets.

COLON, LUIS F.
[b.] March 12, 1967, N.Y.C.; [p.] Aracelis, Luis Colon; [m.] Divorced; [ed.] Seward Park High; [occ.] Resident of Hawk-Eye Management, Inc.; [hon.] Certificate of Merit for Peer-tutoring Program, The Governor's 1986 Youth Drug Prevention Campaign, Visual Essay Contest Award, Scholarship Winner Friend, Friend of Seward Inc.; [pers.] Everything you do today dictates the rest of your life so be true to thyself.; [a.] New York, NY

COLTON, LORI
[b.] July 9, 1967, Washington, PA; [p.] Paul and Janet Colton; [ed.] Canon McMillan High School; [occ.] Disabled right now due to Schizophrenia and Leukemia (ALL); [oth. writ.] Personal poetry, song lyrics - "Who Needs a Job?", poetic story - "My Visit With Santa." Poems - "Patriotic" and "God - my guiding star." Working on first screen play - "Be Kind to animals Week."; [pers.] Elvis Presley is

biggest influenced and inspiration - his song - "If I can dream " - symbolizes my philosophy of life - Best song ever. Goal - is to be a successful, "Super screen writer"!; [a.] Cuddy, PA

COLWELL, RONDA
[b.] November 27, 1955, New Castle, IN; [p.] Earl Vincent, Lou Vincent; [m.] Denny Colwell, June 15, 1974; [ch.] Travis LaVere, Darin Vincent, Nathan Todd; [ed.] New Castle Chrysler High Graduate; [occ.] Homemaker; [memb.] International Society of Poets; [hon.] Member of National Honor Society in High School.; [oth. writ.] Personal Collection of over 100 poems.; [a.] Columbus, IN

COMPTON, CHRISTINA ANN
[b.] October 24, 1959, Boise City, OK; [p.] Ralph Stanford Compton and Mary Ann Walters; [ed.] St. Gregory's College, Oklahoma State University; [occ.] Wholistic Health and Consulting; [pers.] I am committed to assisting others in recognizing and embracing their own self-worth and greatness. May the power of love and truth be felt by those who read my works.; [a.] Phoenix, AZ

CONCEPCION, TRACY
[b.] September 6, 1981, Smithtown, NY; [p.] Alberto Concepcion, Milagros Concepcion; [ed.] Freshman at Mount Sinal High School, Long Island, NY; [memb.] National Junior Honor Society; [hon.] High Honor Roll, National Junior Honor Society, Athletic Awards, Painting of the Moral, New York State School of Music Association; [oth. writ.] Several articles published in school newspaper.; [pers.] Never give up your dreams. Hope for the best in the future.; [a.] Mount Ginal, NY

CONDON, GAIL
[b.] December 4, 1942, Sacramento, CA; [p.] William and Hazel Johnson; [m.] Divorced; [ch.] Julie De La Torre, Kellie Condon; [ed.] Highlands High, Barclay College; [occ.] Customer Service Representative, State of California; [oth. writ.] Several poems on family members and friends since 1987; [pers.] One of seven children born into an artistic family. I am the scribe of the family and this is my first published poem. I try to write with humor but also strive to touch the heart of the person I am writing of.; [a.] Roseville, CA

CONLEY, MARISSA GAIL
[b.] October 8, 1981, San Diego, CA; [p.] Willis and Sharron E. Conley; [ed.] Currently a high school freshman at Monte Vista High School in Spring Valley, California; [occ.] Student; [oth. writ.] Poetry, Short stories; [pers.] My writing is a reflection of my emotions and thoughts I write of the top of my head, hoping it will be a success.; [a.] Spring Valley, CA

COOK, EARL STANLEY
[b.] November 26, 1954, McKeesport, PA; [p.] Robert C. Cook Jr., Arona M. Cook; [m.] Single parent; [ch.] Earl Jr., Chanel; [ed.] Seaside/Alisal High, Univ. of Nevada Reno Scholar Athlete; [occ.] Psych. Counselor, CPC Belmont, CA, Creator of Cook Greeting Cards; [pers.] In my poetry the quest is to use precision with every word that is chosen to present a captivating personal moment in time so the reader is compelled to read on and personally identify with the deepest he or she may be experiencing in that very special love relationship, and to do it in a way that never compromises class, style and eloquence.; [a.] Union City, CA

COOK, JEANETTE ELIZABETH
[b.] December 25, 1950, Columbia, SC; [p.] Guy Miller, Mary Mundy, Johnsie; [m.] Richard Ashford Cook, October 31, 1988; [ch.] Shane Griffin Church, Mary Amy Helen Aldrige, Daniel Allen Knight Lewis; [ed.] Columbia High, Midlands, Tech., University of South Carolina; [occ.] Physically, challenged Wife, Mother and Grandmother; [hon.] Only those bestowed on me by my family; [oth. writ.] None published; [pers.] My mind seems to be the most useful thing I have to share, which I do everyday with my loving husband, my dear children and daughter-in-law, Bonnie and my darling granddaughters, Ashley, Elizabeth and Hope Christian; [a.] Lexington, SC

CORNELL, PEGGY
[pen.] PC; [b.] June 26, 1932, Jersey City, NJ; [p.] Michael and Annie Fahy; [m.] Bud Cornell, July 15, 1954; [ch.] Six; [occ.] Housewife, Grandmother and Volunteer; [oth. writ.] Weekly Community Column in local newspaper "The Beacon" L.I., N.Y.; [pers.] I lost my son in 1988, and I was through my faith in God, my church, my family and friends, that I survived the grief and the loneliness. I saw my grief and sadness in the eyes of others and promised to ease their pain whenever I could. Thank you.

CORSON, MARY
[pen.] Robin Corson; [b.] February 28, 1954, Dumont, NJ; [p.] Roselyn M. Corson, LE Corson Sr.; [occ.] Factory Worker (Vacuum Cleaners); [oth. writ.] Poems about 200 short stories (Fat Little Kitty).; [pers.] I write poems for entertainment of others and myself!; [a.] Jersey Shore, PA

CORVINI, MARGUERITE
[b.] November 4, 1979, Smithtown, NY; [p.] Robert Henry Corvini, Joann Corvini; [ed.] Presently a Junior at Smithtown High School; [memb.] Smithtown H.S. Leadership Club, Smithtown H.S. Key Club; [hon.] Who's Who in American H.S. Students 1994, All County Field Hockey Player 1995, All State French Horn Participant 1995, US Field Hockey

National Tournament Player 1994; [pers.] I have always been influenced by the beauty of nature.

COTHAM, DEVONA FEEZOR
[b.] July 6, 1945, Memphis, TN; [p.] Cooper and Mary Feezor; [m.] Jerry W. Cotham, November 9, 1963; [ch.] Tonyi Huff, Lori Christian, Brady Cotham; [ed.] Kingsburg High 12th Grade, Vocational Plaza Beauty College; [occ.] Admission/Emergency Room, Counselor; [oth. writ.] I have written several poems and a few short stories, but I have never attempted to have anything published until this poem.; [pers.] All of my poems and short stories have been inspired by my family, friends and my own personal experiences and dreams.; [a.] Memphis, TN

COTTON, CLARA M.
[b.] December 8, 1938, Duncan, MS; [p.] Clarence and Montella Conigan; [m.] Zack Cotton, December 25, 1980; [ch.] Seven; [ed.] High School Central High; [occ.] Retired Ward Clerk, Memorial Hospital, South Bend, IN; [memb.] New Jerusalem M.B. Church, WIBC Bowling League of Indiana, Senior Choir Secretary, Sunday School Teacher - adult class, USA Health SPA; [oth. writ.] I have never published anything. My writing have been for personal gratification.; [pers.] I try to relate in my writings "Love" that inner feeling, that flows from heart to heart.; [a.] South Bend, IN

COURTIER, ELAINE PARKER
[pen.] Quana Parker; [b.] September 1, 1945, Nottingham, England; [p.] H. M. and Louisa Parker; [ch.] Mark Weissman; [ed.] B.A. University of Colorado, Harvard University; [occ.] Writer; [memb.] Various writing workshops and clubs. Also novel workshop; [oth. writ.] At least 1,000 poems novel and novel in progress; [a.] Dana Point, CA

COWAN, IDELL
[b.] April 7, 1955, Cleveland, OH; [p.] Katherine and Curtis Cowan; [ch.] Mynette Brooks, Deleon Barbee; [ed.] H.S. Grad., 1 1/2 Year Theater Make-up, 2 Years Ion's and Emzymes Studies, Cosmetic Chemistry Studies 1 1/2 of Cosmetology. Hair Color Educator; [occ.] Hairstylist; [memb.] State Board of Cosmetology; [hon.] Certificates in Product Education, Business Management Hair Care Studies; [pers.] This poem was written from my heart for Mr. Michael Coleman 1995/1996.; [a.] Cleveland, OH

COWLES, LAVERNE E.
[b.] August 12, 1928, Johnstown, PA; [p.] Ralph and Della Keiper; [m.] Eugene J. Cowles, June 21, 1958; [ch.] James, Jeffrey, Jonathan; [ed.] Johnstown Central High; [occ.] Secretary (retired); [memb.] Bedford United Methodist Church, American Red Cross; [pers.] This poem

was written for my son James on his 18th birthday.; [a.] Bedford, PA

COWPER, JOHN BARCLAY
[b.] March 17, 1954, Salisbury (Harrce), Rhodesia (Zimbabwe); [p.] Barclay Cowper, Maree Cowper; [m.] Kristin, January 21, 1995; [ed.] Bachelor of Accounting (Honours) Chartered Accountant. Prior to that an infantry soldier.; [occ.] Excel Telecommunications, Inc., Independent Representative; [memb.] Strallers Cricket Club; [oth. writ.] Poetry (Published The Soft Thud of the Beat); [pers.] Love and service keep us dry.; [a.] Grosse Pointe Farms, MI

COX, LISA M.
[b.] February 4, 1969, Vineland, NJ; [p.] Emma Evinger, Hector Negron; [m.] Divorced; [ch.] Kayla (6), Christopher (5); [ed.] High School Grad., US Navy; [occ.] Cashier and Homemaker; [memb.] World Vision - sponsor for needy children, Trinity Assembly of God; [hon.] Honor's List - Christian Academy, nominated for most likely to succeed in H.S. Top 10% in Naval Training School; [oth. writ.] Several poems written for my own pleasure and of my family.; [pers.] My writing comes from deep within my heart. I've been writing since I was a young teenager. This is the first time I ever let any beyond friends and family review any of my writing.; [a.] Westchester, PA

CRABB, MARCIA CHRIS
[b.] November 12, 1936, New York City, NY; [p.] Garland and Anita Wright; [m.] Charles Lloyd Crabb, January 22; [ch.] Charles Kelly, Andrew K, Cayce L.; [ed.] Sam Houston State, Huntsville TE 1957 - B.S. Degree Elementary Ed.; [occ.] Houston I.S.D. Retired Elementary Teacher; [memb.] Alpha Delta Kappa ADK Association of Childhood Education, International ACEI.

CRAIGHEAD, ANNETTE T.
[b.] January 15, 1932, Chicago, IL; [p.] Samuel and Clarice Martin; [m.] Divorced; [ch.] Christine Wyche/Cathleen Craighead; [ed.] B.A. and B.S.S. - University of Chicago, M.S. - Columbia University Psychiatric Social Work; [occ.] Manager - Bell Atlantic's Career Services; [memb.] Alpha Kappa Alpha Sorority. American Counseling Association, Council of Action for Minority Professionals; [hon.] General Electric Foundation Fellowship for Study in Vocational Counseling. YMWCA Black Achiever from Bell Atlantic 1992; [oth. writ.] Published articles in Internal Newsletters, on topics of Diversity or Career Development; [a.] Old Bridge, NJ

CRAMER, MARGARET B.
[b.] January 22, 1920, Toledo, OH; [p.] Gil and Mildred Brackett (Deceased); [m.] James R. Cramer (Deceased January 4, 1976), December

11, 1941; [ch.] Cyndrea Lee and James Rance; [ed.] Central High School, Lima, O; [occ.] Retired - Secretary for 41 Years; [hon.] My Greatest 'Award' has been the smile, and occasionally the tear, from the person for whom I wrote the particular poem in honor of his or her birthday, father's day, mother's day, etc.; [oth. writ.] Poems for parents, husbands and children's birthdays and special occasions - song lyrics with local musician.; [pers.] 'You'll never know,' was written in 1940 after one of many breakups during my 7 year relationship with Jim (who finally became my husband of 35 years) - he never saw this poem but I have read it to myself many times since his death, and it still applies.; [a.] Lima, OH

CREIGHTON, DELAINE
[pen.] D. Elizabeth Creighton; [b.] February 7, 1978, Wheeling, WV; [p.] Deborah Creighton, Jay Creighton; [ed.] Senior at Bridgeport High School; [occ.] Student; [oth. writ.] Several poems written, one published in local newspaper.; [pers.] Hold on to your dreams. Your day will come.; [a.] Lansing, OH

CREIGHTON, SUZANNE M.
[b.] July 10, 1950, Boston, MS; [p.] James and Alice Shrelds; [m.] James L. Creighton, September 4, 1982; [ch.] Jeremy Shrelds Davidson, Jeffrey Cameron Davidson; [ed.] Fontbonne Academy, Faulkner Hospital School of Nursing; [occ.] Registered Nurse, Certified Clinical Hypnotherapist, Certified Chemical Addictions Counselor; [memb.] American Board of Hypnotherapy, American Counseling Association, P-Flag of Ventura County; [oth. writ.] Large collection of unpublished poetry. General articles published in Local Newspaper.; [pers.] There is a raging disease upon whose battle ground many souls have departed. The war is A.I.D.S. The destruction, devastating. The world must never forget its impact. My poems strive to perpetuate the memories of those who have fallen. As a nurse, I have held these brave soldiers in their final hours. As a poet, my words keep their hearts above.; [a.] Oxnard, CA

CRICKENBERGER, KATHERINE A.
[m.] Herbert P. Crickenberger; [ch.] Constance, Cynthia, Brenda, Dianne, Rick; [oth. writ.] Many poems unpublished.; [pers.] I would like my poems to be an inspiration to others, to lift them up to loftier heights.; [a.] Forest, VA

CRIM, LISA REA KATHLEEN
[b.] August 18, 1975, Okarche, OK; [p.] Carol Sue, Earl Wayne Crim; [ed.] In my 2nd Semester in College, striving for my as/degree in Fire Tech.; [occ.] Mark Twain St. Joseph's Hospital, Billing Dept.; [oth. writ.] Personal dictionary you can say, of my own feelings. One I like most of all is called "Dear Friend"; [pers.]

Know your soul, know the world achieve your soul, achieve the world... also - God gives us tears to shed the pain, a heart to hold the love, and strength to get us through; [a.] Altaville, CA

CRISS, ROBERT V.
[pen.] "Night Hawk"; [b.] May 31, 1961, Cleveland, OH; [p.] Doy R. and Deoma Criss; [m.] Brenda K. Criss, July 4, 1982; [ch.] Robert Vernon and Lacy Marie; [ed.] High School, Transportation Training in D.D.C Haz-mat (Heavy Equipment); [occ.] Operations (Sitton Motor Lines); [memb.] National Riflemens Assoc. O.O.I.D.A. (Owner Operator's In Dependent Driver Assoc.) National Safety Council; [hon.] Three National Safety Awards, D.D.C. and Haz-mat awards.; [oth. writ.] "Lover's Dream" (A William Shakespear Sonnett form) song: "Only in my Mind", "If you don't know me", "Rodeo Dreams" "A lady like you", "The Memory of you" "Before Her Brown Eyes Turn Blue"; [pers.] None of my poems or songs have been published, but! No one has see them before now. Thanks to Mr. Howard Ely, that has changed. I always wanted to publish my songs, never thought about my poems; [a.] Carterville, MO

CROCKETT, PHYLLIS J.
[b.] November 13, 1926, Sebastopol, CA; [p.] Russell and Esther Jones; [m.] July 23, 1950; [ch.] Carey Wayne, Carole and Alan Lloyd; [ed.] M.S. Wellesley College 1949, Pupil Personnel - 1962 San Jose State College, San Jose, Ca, also BA from San Jose State 1947; [occ.] Retired Teacher, Coach and Senior Counselor, Carmel H.S., Carmel, CA - 33 yrs. in Education; [memb.] Misc. Scholastic, American Red Cross; [hon.] 1964 - "Good Egg," Carmel Valley Citizen of Yr. Award, Clara Barton Award, Amer. Red Cross 1987, Commodore Longfellow Award "International Order of the Golden Whale" December 1991 (Red Cross, 50 Year Volunteer Award, American Red Cross, June 94, still active as ARC Volunteer at local and State levels - Consultant Health Services; [oth. writ.] None published to date except in Monterey Peninsula College, CA "Women's Students" booklets. Last Christmas I made by hand books of my writing for my 3 children. 54 poems were included and it was called "Dolphin Sounds".; [pers.] I have a great deal of love and care for people, animals and nature. I tend to write on inspirational levels related to love, friendship and understanding life. I also write on current and family issues. Approach is positive and when possible there is humor. We grow best when we laugh at ourselves.; [a.] Carmel Valley, CA

CRONIN, DAVID ARLEN
[b.] May 19, 1962, Owensboro, KY; [p.] Nancy and Blaine Townsend; [m.] Elizabeth Victoria Cronin, June 17, 1993; [ch.] David Blaine

Cronin; [ed.] Governor Livingston Regional High School, Avalon Vo-Tech. College; [occ.] Self Employed; [hon.] Dean's List, Creative Writers Award 1992; [oth. writ.] Editor of College Paper, "Step Beyond"; [pers.] my wife and I hold our future to our son, David. May he strive to make his work for a better tomorrow in this world. Peace to all, past, present and future.; [a.] Hobbs, NM

CROSBY, DEBORA
[b.] June 21, 1961, Fremont, OH; [p.] Nathan and Sharon Crosby; [ed.] Hillcrest High, Presbyterian College; [occ.] Seafood Shop Mgr., Bi-Lo Inc., Greenville, SC; [hon.] Alpha Psi Omega, Dramatic Fraternity, [a.] Fountain Inn, SC

CROSBY, LILA F.
[b.] September 5, 1936, Bertha, MN; [p.] Rev. and Mrs. Lyle Foreman; [m.] Russell G. Crosby, September 2, 1955; [ch.] Curtis, Charles, Crystal, Cynthia and Carey; [ed.] High School and one year of Bible College; [occ.] Owner of Always Uniformly Yours; [memb.] I am involved in Church related activities - Women's Group - Sunday School Teacher Music; [oth. writ.] Several advertisements for my store - writings for holidays and for special people in my life.; [pers.] Most of my writings have been God given inspiration.; [a.] Moline, IL

CROSS, SHELLY MARIE
[b.] March 28, 1981, Concord, NH; [p.] Paulette Lopez, Paul Cross; [ed.] Elementary at Conan and School (Concord) and attending Jr. High at Rundlett Jr. High School; [occ.] 9th Grade student; [pers.] I would like to thank my mom for making me send in my poem also all of my friends in Concord, NH for supporting my poetry and respecting it. Thank you God! Peace.; [a.] Concord, NH

CROSSETT, MARLENE A.
[b.] May 21, 1934, Renville, MN; [p.] Marie and Ben Pingel; [ch.] Kathy McCarthy, Debbie Kamin, Jim L. Richardson, Ron Richardson, Nick Crossett; [ed.] Knapp College of Business; [occ.] Communications - Banking Housewife, currently retired; [memb.] Toastmasters Speech Giving, Volunteer work for Seattle Crisis Clinic; [hon.] Golden Poet Award for poem "Can You" 1991 also Honorable Mention for same poem; [oth. writ.] Poem published 1992, in book entitled "Selected Work Of Our Worlds Best Poets," called "The Miracle of love, Yours, Mine and His," several articles published in local newspapers in Plymouth, Michigan and Seattle, Washington.; [pers.] The poem "The jewel of your life has slipped away" was written for my doctor and good friend William Ross and his family - when his mother passed away this past year - poetry written entirely on my emotional feelings, when hurt and sadness immobilize as life rocks's me to and fro.; [a.] Plymouth, MI

CROWELL, MILLARD DAVID
[pen.] Millard D. Crowell; [b.] October 3, 1909, Lakefield, MI; [p.] Mallard D. Senior and Rosa Alice Crowell; [m.] Minnie Estella Hildorf Crowell, July 14, 1934; [ch.] Sharon Annette and Vincent Dwight; [ed.] B.S. in M.E. and B.S. in E.E.; [occ.] Retired; [memb.] Boy Scouts of America, Kiwanis International; [hon.] General Motors for Inventions of "Air Operated Broken Drill Doctor"; [oth. writ.] Poem "Lassie 'O' the Dale," and a poem honoring President Theodore Roosevelt, "Help Make Us Like Roosevelt"; [a.] North Fort Myers, FL

CROWLEY, CHARLOTTE ALBRITTON
[pen.] Char Albritton; [b.] November 17, 1947, Wauchula, FL; [p.] Kylen Albritton, Helen Simmons; [m.] Dennis, August 6, 1994; [ch.] Scott, Mary Jane, J.T.; [ed.] Plant City Senior High Plant City, Florida, Kissimmee Police Academy Kissimmee, Florida; [occ.] Exceptional Student Ed. Teachers Assit. - Poinciana High Kissimmee, Florida; [memb.] Victory Baptist Church, Intercession, Florida; [oth. writ.] "Diamonds in the Night", (Poetry), "Hudiniis Reprieve". Also original quotes and more poetry short stories.; [pers.] I elect to use my God given talents to help others. My poem "Time is a Vapor" was inspired by James 4:14 (KJV) Holy Bible. My writings reflect my life experiences.; [a.] Haines City, FL

CROWLEY, DONNA M.
[pen.] Mrs. Donna; [b.] November 24, 1954, Chyenne, WY; [p.] Leonard and Dorothy Robinson; [m.] Divorced; [ch.] Asia Crowley and Thea Crowley; [ed.] Soldan High School Forest Park Community College; [occ.] Secretary UAW GM Center for Human Resources; [oth. writ.] I have over two hundred copy righted poems; [pers.] Everything and everyone has a word about it or them that can be expanded upon.; [a.] Saint Louis, MO

CROWTHER, KERI LYN
[b.] June 26, 1979, Sacramento, CA; [p.] Gary and Kathy Crowther; [ed.] Currently in High School; [oth. writ.] When I was in the 3rd grade a poem of mine was published in True Wonders, California Poets In the Schools. Man, was I excited!?!; [pers.] Times of a teenager are exciting, depressing, and awkward. I hope years from now I can remember some of those times through my writing.; [a.] Rancho Cordova, CA

CRULL, IRVIN A RENEA
[pen.] Reneta; [b.] September 13, 1927, Kansas City, MO; [p.] Irving C. Seeley, Rachel Hooper; [m.] Guy E. Crull, November 2, 1968; [ch.] Walter; [ed.] 2 years college, Business School, Special training from State of Illinois, have done much traveling and learning.; [occ.] Retired secretary; [memb.] V.F.W. Aux Lifetime Mem.,

Am. Legion Aux, Past President, Disabled Veterans Aux Lifetime, and Eastern Stars of Chillicothe, (Martha Washington Lodge, V.F.W. Girls State Life).; [oth. writ.] "Whispering Silence", Story of the Dogwood Tree", "Somebody's Knocking", "My Witness", "Angels" have had poems in local newspaper.; [pers.] I do believe all things can be done thru prayer and faith. And everything in life that happens, rather good or bad is for a reason. We all have our own Angel.; [a.] Chillicothe, IL

CRUMMY, LISA RENEE
[pen.] Lisa R. Driver-Crummy; [b.] January 10, 1966, Jasper, AL; [p.] Mr. Howard and Pearlie Driver; [m.] Reuben Q. Crummy, June 25, 1994; [ed.] B.S. in Health Education Minor in Sociology, University of Alabama at Birmingham; [occ.] NC Dept. of Revenue Raleigh, NC Former Teacher; [memb.] Wake Chapel Baptist Church, American Red Cross, Highlite Modeling, Scranton, PA; [hon.] High School Marching Band in Cordova, AL, Certificate of Achievement of a Bible Study Course, and received outstanding recognition; [oth. writ.] Wrote a love poem in College and received outstanding recognition; [pers.] I am inspired to express the goodness of the Lord and encourage others through my writing.; [a.] Raleigh, NC

CUELLAR, ANITA
[b.] September 22, 1969, Sweetwater, TX; [p.] Gregory and Emma Munoz; [m.] John Cuellar, October 13, 1990; [ch.] Anissa Cuellar and Julia Cuellar; [ed.] Sweetwater High School Art Institute of Dallas; [occ.] Cover Artist, Taylor Publishing Company, Dallas, TX.; [memb.] National Honor Society Mexican American Club Future Homemakers of America; [hon.] Wreathlaying participant-Tomb of the unknown soldier, Washington, D.C., Who's Who Award, U.I.L. Scholar Award, Academic Excellence, Award Honor graduate (ranked 10th in class) United States Award in Art, Honorable Mention Regional Scholastic Art Awards Exhibition Winner - Sears -Roebuck Anniversary Art Contest Congressional Scholar Nominee - National Young Leaders Conference Post graduate program, Washington, D.C.; [oth. writ.] Several poems written for family, and friends, as unique and personal gifts.; [pers.] I strive to acknowledge the Lord in most of my poems. It is through Him that I am able to touch other people's lives with my talent in poetry and art.; [a.] Irving, TX

CULBRETH, BETTYE HODGE
[b.] July 3, 1933, Jefferson City, TN; [p.] Lillie and Carter Hodge, September 28, 1958; [ch.] Walter Jr., Lori, Mark, Cheryl; [ed.] M. ed - Trenton State College, B.S. Duque SNE Univ/ Knoxville College; [occ.] Teacher of Lang Arts Trenton Bd. of Ed, Trenton, NS; [memb.]

N.J.E.A., TEA, International Reading Association, (local and county) chosen as Citizen Ambassor to China - 1995, Rec Mellow Grant, 1990; [hon.] Top Ladies of Distinction, Twigs Inc., Friends of Library, Adult Book Club-Founder and Member of 25 years old reading group. Inducted in Kappa Delta Pi 1989; [oth. writ.] "The Guest" published in Clover International Poetry Competition - 1975, published several articles in local newspaper, The Trenton Times.; [pers.] We should never stop growing intellectually. We must strive to discover our talents and utilize then to the utmost.; [a.] Trenton, NJ

CULLEN, ESME
[pen.] Esme Cullen; [b.] May 28, 1986, Connecticut; [p.] Mark Cullen, Michele Barry; [ed.] Academy Elementary School; [occ.] Student 4th grade; [hon.] Pat Wilson Writing Award 3rd grade; [oth. writ.] Poetry Anthology; [pers.] I feel poetry is fun to do any time or place if you're in the right mood and I hope to became a poet when I grow up.; [a.] Madison, CT

CUMMINGS, NENA LOUISE
[pen.] Neena Louise Cummings; [b.] April 3, 1951, Santa Monica, CA; [p.] Lois Lynn Jones, Edward V. Cummings; [ed.] Beverly Hills High School (Class of 1969); [memb.] Granada Park United Methodist Church, Orangutan Foundation International, The Cousteau Society, Inc.; [pers.] It has been my experience to live with a debilitating illness for the past 16 years. I desire to write well as a means of participating in the world of the arts. The challenge is to try to touch others with compassion. Respect nature, seek grace, inherit dignity. A favorite poet: William Butler Yeats; [a.] Los Angeles, CA

CUNDICK, SANDRA
[b.] February 12, 1947, Seattle, WA; [p.] Doreen McCain and Richard Maxwell; [m.] Richard Cundick, March 25, 1988; [ch.] Kelli Contos and Robert Shearan; [ed.] Some College - Numerous Computer Classes; [occ.] Data Administrator - Nevada Bell Telephone Co. - 30 years; [memb.] I have done quite a lot of Work with Abused Women and Children; [oth. writ.] I have written poetry for myself for several years. This is the first piece I've ever submitted. I hope to write a book next year when I retire. It has been a dream of mine for some time.; [pers.] This poem ("Mother") is very special to me as I wrote it for my husbands children when their mother passed away last fall.; [a.] Reno, NV

CURRY, MRS. CARLA
[b.] October 14, 1969, Meridian, MS; [p.] Mr. and Mrs. G. T. Crudup; [m.] Hugh Curry, June 23, 1990; [ch.] Reed and Megan; [ed.] Currently attending Wood College in Mathison, Ms. majoring in English. Future: Attend M.S.U. and

receive a Master's and Doctorate degree in English.; [occ.] Student; [memb.] Petrified Poet Society, Pres. Wood Players, Phi Theta Kappa, Dean's List, International Club, school newspaper, and The Budget Committee.; [hon.] High school - Finalist in state public speaking competition. Play "Wait Until Dark" I had the role of a police woman, under study for Susy and I was Assistant Director.; [oth. writ.] I had a poem published in the school paper. I've written many poems and my school is publishing a literary book with my poems. I am currently writing a short story and have begun a novel.; [pers.] Our self-image evolves from how we perceive others to believe us to be. A kind word or encouragement to another can greatly influence how they perceive themselves and what they accomplish.; [a.] Maben, MS

CURTIS, PATRICIA
[b.] Lynn, MA; [p.] Albert J. Cocozella, Mary Cocozella; [m.] Clayton L. Curtis; [ch.] Daughter - Julianne; [ed.] Simmons College Boston University B.S., Lesley College M. Ed.; [occ.] Teacher of English as a second language Northeast Metro Tech H.S. Wakefield, MA.; [memb.] MTA, NEA (Mass. Teachers Assoc., National Educational Assoc.); [oth. writ.] Previously unpublished; [pers.] I write for my own pleasure and encourage my students to find their own voices when they write. The music of softly scratching pencils in an otherwise still classroom is a favorite sound.; [a.] Saugus, MA

CURTIS, REBECCA L.
[pen.] Becky Curtis, Becky Edin; [b.] November 20, 1950, Bellingham, WA; [p.] Jim and Kathy Jordan; [m.] Jim A. Curtis, April 22, 1994; [ch.] Heath B. Edin; [ed.] Mt. Baker High School, Bellingham Technical School; [occ.] Homemaker; [hon.] Accomplishment of Merit, Creative Arts and Science Enterprises for Poem "Children Play"; [oth. writ.] Mud puddles, wonders of life, an angel from heaven, white caps on a river, poetry twinkle of light, two hearts as one, songs.; [pers.] Poetry is written in many forms. some in beauty and others in many different expressions. I enjoy writing poetry, it gives me a feeling of expressing my inner being, and I feel a nice happiness when one is complete.; [a.] Bellingham, WA

CUSHING, JANET C.
[pen.] Janet Hill Cushing; [b.] November 11, 1957, Boston, MA; [p.] George and Natalie Hill; [m.] Martin F. Cushing, November 11, 1983; [ch.] Patrick (6), Jennifer (4); [ed.] Winthrop High, MA, Endicott College, MA; [occ.] Mother and Writer; [oth. writ.] In the process of working on obtaining a publisher for a manuscript, on various poems, written over many years.; [pers.] I believe everyone has the need to set his/her emotions free. That is why we have poetry.; [a.] East Lyme, CT

CYPRIEN JR., RAYMOND
[b.] September 2, 1933, Port Arthur, TX; [p.] Raymond Cyprien Sr., Hazel Cyprien (Deceased); [m.] Melvia Faye Cyprien, August 9, 1957; [ch.] Charles Dwayne, Chris Douglas, Cass Jay; [ed.] B.S. degree from Lamar University, Beaumont, Texas, Texas Southern University, Houston, Texas, Wiley College Marshall, Texas; [occ.] Retired Elementary School Teacher; [memb.] Associate Minister Mt. Sinai Missionary Baptist Church, Volunteer Worker for Adult Day Care Center AARP; [hon.] Ordained Deacon Licensed Minister, Honorable Discharge US Army, (Korean Veteran), Teacher retirement plaque (33 years of service P.H.I.S.D.); [pers.] It is my desire to share in my writings God's love for mankind. I enjoy the writings of Robert Frost, Emily Dickinson, Paul Laurence Dunbar, James Weldon Johnson, and Edgar Allan Poe; [a.] Port Arthur, TX

D'AGOSTINO, JOHN A.
[pen.] Vanya; [b.] September 3, 1929, Flushing, NY; [p.] John and Catherine; [m.] Anne, September 3, 1950; [ch.] John, Catherine, Chris, James; [ed.] Newtown H.S., C.C.N.Y.; [occ.] Retired; [memb.] Telephone Pioneers, 2nd Chance Band (Piano); [oth. writ.] Several poems published in H.S. Periodicals, unpublished songs; [pers.] Nothing in life is singly faceted. Our perception of what is, is based upon information, background maturity and judgement. As we increase our asset base, any of these variables, we get closer to what is and each other.; [a.] Flushing, NY

D'ANDREA, PAUL C.
[b.] September 29, 1905, New York City; [p.] Beatrice and Donald D'Andrea; [m.] Camela D'Andrea, January 6, 1935; [ch.] One son and two daughter; [ed.] Graduate of DeWitt Clinton High School and Business Course; [occ.] Retired since 1971; [memb.] Music Group in Highland Beach; [hon.] I-appeared on CBS Television in 1952, and placed 2nd with one of my songs, 2-appeared on February 19, 1953 as winner of Brotherhood Week Song Contest, sponsored by the Nassau and Suffolk B'nai B'rith. Song was titled "Judge A Human" and prizes were a one-week stay at the Miami Hotel President Madison for my wife and me, all expenses paid, and publication of song by Charles Hansen.; [oth. writ.] I was a winner 2nd prize in a Tommy Dorsey contest years before the other awards. I also made several appearances in Talent Shows on cruise ships. The song was one which I wrote, words and music, titled: "There's No Child Like A Grandchild." This is the poem which I submitted as an entry in the above contest.; [a.] Highland Beach, FL

DAHLKE, RONALD G.
[b.] August 15, 1944, Watertown, WI; [p.]

Russell and Mannett Dahlke; [m.] Marion, December 7, 1968; [ch.] Jamie Sara Jesse; [ed.] 12 year High School Grad; [occ.] Lithography; [pers.] I write about my thoughts and dreams mostly when I am feeling blue and by myself. It is like I step back in time and all the smells sounds, voices and things of the past return to me. The words come so fast like fleeting visions of many thing from the past; [a.] Waterloo, WI

DALEY, RONALD
[b.] July 8, 1944, P.G. County; [p.] Ileana and Hampton Daley; [m.] Lorraine Daley, January 15, 1966; [ch.] Charlotte, Antoinette, Ronald Jr., James; [ed.] High School Graduate Fairmount Heights High School year 1963; [occ.] Business Owner J&R Auto Electric Co.; [oth. writ.] 1) She left me in misery, 2) ("Watch out" the world's going up in smoke), 3) The love I thought I knew so well, 4) Len Bias Md's Super Stan, 5) I'm in Love with You, since I first layed Eyed on You."; [pers.] My outlook on life is to raise your kids the proper way, with both parents. Also to discipline them for we can develop them in to excellent men and women.; [a.] Lanham, MD

DALTON, DAVE
[b.] December 3, 1962, New Richmond, WI; [p.] John and Carolynn Dalton; [ed.] St. Mary's University Masters Program, University of WI - Eau Claire Education, St. Croix Central High School; [occ.] Educational and Assessment Manager; [memb.] NEA, Phi Mu Alpha, Class Acts Performer and Writer; [hon.] 1987 Teacher of the Year, 1995 Haldorf's Award, St. Mary's Dean's List; [oth. writ.] Lament 08of Tom; [pers.] It is my hope to paint a picture with my words for readers to see an experience through my eyes.

DALY, BERNADETTE N.
[pen.] Bernadette N. Daly; [b.] June 18, 1944, Strabane Co., Tyrone, Northern Ireland; [m.] Michael J. Daly, June 1990; [ch.] Claran, Sean, Naoise, Criostoir; [ed.] BA Fine Arts, Belfast College of Art and design.; [occ.] Teacher of Art St. Raphael's School, Crystal Minnesota.; [oth. writ.] Unpublished (short stories) journal, book reviews for quarterly journal for Lutheran Libraries and other unpublished poems.; [pers.] I enjoy painting with words. Poetry for me is the challenge of saying the maximum with the minimum of words this is what I aim for when I write; [a.] Minneapolis, MN

DAVIDGE SR., JAMES M.
[b.] November 4, 1926, Saginaw, MI; [p.] Walter, Janet (Jarvie); [m.] Marilyn Joan (Heine), August 17, 1957; [ch.] Susan Kathleen Carpenter, James M. Jr.; [ed.] Moose Heart High School, Aurora University, Northern IL., Univ., University of Il, Champaign - Urbana Campus; [occ.] Retired; [memb.] Moose Heart

Alumni Assn., V. of IL, Alumni Assn., V.F.W. Post No 9284, South Church Community Baptist; [oth. writ.] A number of poems in praise of fellow retiring agents, nurses at Hines VA Hosp. and Moose heart and the Loyal Order of Moose and my wife.; [pers.] I believe in telling those who do good things in this world I appreciate what they are doing or have done. I feel better after I have done so especially when the time is just right for words of encouragement.; [a.] Elk Grove Village, IL

DAVIDSON, JORDAN
[b.] October 10, 1981, Miami, FL; [p.] Joy and Robert Davidson; [ed.] South Miami Elementary, South Miami Middle; [occ.] Student, Poet; [memb.] 1st United Methodist Youth Group, Police Explorers; [hon.] President South Miami Middle Band, President of Youth Group; [oth. writ.] Tons of other poems.; [pers.] "Make a wish see on through it, hold right on and don't let go."

DAVIS, AUDREY MURPHY
[pen.] Audrey G. Davis, Audrey Murphy; [b.] November 1, 1961, Baltimore, MD; [p.] Bobby L. Murphy, Catherine Murphy; [m.] Michael E. Davis, June 4, 1992; [ch.] Christopher, Mikal, Jelani; [ed.] AAFCENT American High School Holland, Europe Morgan State University Baltimore, Maryland; [occ.] Correctional Officer; [memb.] NAACP; [oth. writ.] A poem published in "Sparkles in the Sand" called The Birth. Currently working on several children's books.; [pers.] Sometimes one does not discover his passion until later in life. It is never too late to be successful at something you love. Whatever your passion may be season, cultivate it and watch yourself grow.; [a.] Baltimore, MD

DAVIS, BRENDA L. WILSON
[pen.] Brenda Wilson; [b.] April 22, 1962, Alamance, CO; [p.] Lawrence and Mary Wilson; [m.] Mark Davis, April 12, 1994; [ch.] Tiffiny Dawne Lawson; [ed.] Cummings Sr. High, Alamance Community College; [occ.] Alamance-Caswell Area Mental Health, Developmental Disabilities and Substance Abuse Authority/also CNA/PA/NA; [memb.] Professional Advisory Comm./Volunteers Advisory Comm./ and ADM-DCE Comm. for M.H. (VTA); [hon.] Governors Award for Vol. Work in Local Community, Dean's List and also President's List ACC; [oth. writ.] Poetry and short stories.; [pers.] "There is good to be found in all situations, we just have to look a little more closely some than others.; [a.] Burlington, NC

DAVIS, CARL EDWARD
[pen.] Carl Edward Davis; [b.] April 12, 1960, Sandusky, OH; [p.] Ronald G. and Wanda J. Hall; [ch.] Sharlene M., Roy E. Brandon E. Davis; [ed.] Dundee Community High School and Monroe County Community College; [occ.]

(Self-employed) Partner in: Two Ol' Dogs D.J. Service and Writers Garrets, and A Freelance, Artist; [oth. writ.] Children Book: "Bee Helpful" unpublished volumes I and II called "Poetry and Thoughts" by Two Ol' Dogs (From the desktops of the writers Garret) each volume contains 100 poems and songs.; [pers.] Every human on earth is worthy and have their own keys to happiness, and the powers of the will to bring dreams to life. If they choose!; [a.] Deerfield, MI

DAVIS, CARRIE
[pen.] Bea Davis; [b.] March 1, 1964, Sacramento, CA; [p.] Bennie and Ruth Bennefield; [m.] Harvey E. Davis, November 7, 1987; [ed.] Elk Grove High School; [memb.] Supporter of Cystic Fibrosis Foundation, American Heart Association, California Police Activities League, Villagers Neighborhood Association.; [pers.] I began writing in my early teens. My work reflects the hardships in life and the human will to overcome them. I want to give a personal thanks to my Mother. She is the person who taught me how to overcome.; [a.] Sacramento, CA

DAVIS, CLEDA
[b.] May 31, 1959, San Diego, CA; [p.] Harold Andrews, Wilma Andrews; [ch.] Jeromiah Paul, Raelynn Candace, Kyle Burgoyne, Gabriel Nathaniel; [ed.] El Cajon High, Cuyamaca College; [occ.] Assistant Director, Teacher Calvary Chapel Pre School, El Cajon, CA; [memb.] El Cajon Missionary Alliance, El Cajon National Little League; [oth. writ.] I have kept a journal off and on since the age of twelve years, to some day pass along to my children and their children's children.; [pers.] Writing is a way to express yourself and look back on yourself.; [a.] El Cajon, CA

DAVIS, DE E.
[b.] September 17, 1948, Red Bay, AL; [p.] Helon and Earl Myrick; [m.] Divorced; [ch.] Tara, Zachary; [ed.] B.S. Speech Communications, University Central Ark., Minor degree in Journalism.; [occ.] Computer Operator, Office Mgr., Writer, [memb.] First United Meth. Church, Conway, AR., Beta Sigma Phi Int'l., Dean's List, Theatre, Guild, Former Forensics Club; [hon.] University Central Ark. Debate Champ 1994 Fall Semester; [oth. writ.] Have written many more poems, music and lyrics, short stories and have book 3/4 finished.; [pers.] I hope to touch someone's heart make them feel the emotions of the heart, from sadness to ecstasy. I think this is what a writer should do. I have always loved the great romantic poets and French poets.; [a.] Conway, AR

DAVIS, EDWARD L.
[pen.] Edward; [b.] January 13, 1928, Columbus, OH; [p.] Walter T., and Hallie Davis; [m.] Margaret Awoyera; [ed.] Columbia College of Radio and Speech, 1 year Chicago, Illinois; [occ.]

Security Officer, Baltimore, MD, Circuit Court Clerk, Cook County, Chicago, Illinois (Ret'd), Professional Security Officer; [hon.] International Assoc. of Hospital Security Officers. I am honored to receive the recognition from your highly regarded origination.; [oth. writ.] Possess small collection of light poems, all done on a amateur basis. And kept in a personal file.; [pers.] My commitment to poetry and prose is strictly personal achievement. Influenced by high school public speaking instructor, Ms. Jeanette Triplett Jones, Chicago, Illinois. Attended Dusable H.S., Columbia College Chicago, Ill.; [a.] Randallstown, MD

DAVIS, GRACE A.
[b.] March 31, 1932, Philadelphia, PA; [p.] Frances and Grace Lindsay; [m.] Bobbie V. Davis, May 14, 1949; [ch.] Three; [ed.] High School (College Course Business Administration 4 yrs. - by mail), all "A"'s.; [occ.] Lyricist - Songwriter All Genre's - Philosophical - Love - Country - Gospel - Pets - Contemp.; [memb.] Song Writers Guild of America; [hon.] 1990 "Who's Who" U.S. Business Executives of Year, was President of "Hemada Inc.", Chamber of Commerce Award, State Assembly Award; [oth. writ.] 370 copyrighted songs - registered - 1994-1995, author of "The Real Ringmaster", book published by New Leaf Press, Motion Picture Video - "Rock A Bye Terror", I wrote lyrics for "Ghost of my Heart".; [pers.] As a child - I.Q. 168, read most of the classics by age 12. Wrote poetry (Traded Commodities), age 44 wrote book - also produced and directed 13 videos, went P.T.L on satellite TV, President Hemada Corp. Furniture Store.; [a.] Millville, NJ

DAVIS, JANET ELLEN
[b.] November 4, 1945, Binghamton, NY; [p.] Paul J. David, Ruth W. Davis; [ch.] Nicholas Coviello, Carlyn Coviello, Lance Coviello; [occ.] Owner/Teacher, Janet Davis Piano Studio; [hon.] Best play, State of New Jersey, Little Theater Tournament, 1980, - "Bye, Bye Amy."; [oth. writ.] "Bye Bye Amy" one - act play - performed off - Broadway, 1991, produced by Interborough Repertory Theater, a non-profit theater company; [a.] Belle Mead, NJ

DAVIS JR., CHARLES LYNN
[b.] December 5, 1957, San Francisco, CA; [p.] Charles L. and Atha E. Davis; [m.] Marcy R. Davis (nee Perry), July 5, 1986; [ed.] Santa Rose Jr. College, American River College, Petalluma Senior High School; [occ.] Medical Technician at Physicians Clinical Laboratory; [memb.] American Institute Physics, Society for Physics Students, Planetary Society; [oth. writ.] Dozens of Couplets, irregular odes and free verse all unpublished currently writing a screenplay on The Life and Science of Albert Einstein.; [pers.]

Art and science are two aspects of the same creative germ. To paraphrase keats 'Art is science, science is art'. I attempt to marry the two in my poetry.; [a.] Antelope, CA

DAVIS, LILLIAN A.
[b.] November 29, 1941, Cincinnati, OH; [p.] Fred and Thelma Pennekamp; [m.] Denny B. Davis, December 10, 1960; [ch.] Victoria Lynn Vanvelzel, Gregory Scott Davis, Brian Allen Davis, Brett Anthony Davis, (grandchildren) Leah Malanie Vanvelzel, Bradley Alexander David; [ed.] Western Hills High School Cincinnati, Ohio; [a.] Lithia Springs, GA

DAVIS SR., JAMES DEVELLO
[pen.] J. Davis Sr.; [b.] December 7, 1937, Rutherford Co, TN; [p.] Fratos and Corrine Davis; [m.] Jane N. Davis, September 17, 1963; [ch.] James Jr.; [ed.] 1 year College oop's Central Office Egu Spect. G.T.A. Spect., I.T.E. Spect.; [occ.] Electrical Sup.; [memb.] Consumer Reports Safety Advisor member.; [hon.] 7 silver awards from world of Poetry, 3 gold award's and 2 honorable mention for years 88, 89, 90. Presented by Eddie Lou Cole and John Cambell; [oth. writ.] Gross 1989, Take your turn 1988, Cloud 1988, Dreaming my life 1990; [pers.] I love life it's so unique but don't have time for thing's I seek.; [a.] Murfrees, TN

DAVIS, SUSAN HELEN
[b.] June 4, 1979, Fayetteville, NC; [p.] Ralph Davis, Ana Davis; [ed.] Sophomore at Mankato, West High School; [occ.] Student; [a.] North Mankato, MN

DAVIS, VICKI
[b.] November 4, 1973, Paterson, NJ; [ed.] Lakeland Regional High School, Katharine Gibbs Business School; [occ.] Administrator, The Carroll Superchanging Company; [pers.] Never give up on your dreams.; [a.] Haskell, NJ

DBOUK, ROBIN
[b.] Indiana; [ch.] Four wonderful souls to enjoy.; [memb.] Church of Christ; [oth. writ.] "A Promise Broken", "Gay Writes", "Remorse of the Unborn", "Betrayal Never Forgiven", "The Devil's Advocate, rules of the Game" "Acceptance", "In Jesus Name, I Ask You Now", A new author of writing yet to be published on the morals of mankind.; [pers.] As I hold no claim to any experience in writing, the credit must be gives of Him for He is my author. The purpose of these writings are such that we may return to the laws of God. Not withstanding my own sins, if I can use these poems to help the pain of a single person, then my life was not in vain after all.; [a.] Bartlett, TN

DE BLASSIE, KATHY
[b.] June 6, 1958, Los Angeles, CA; [m.] Paul A.

De Blassie III; [ch.] Paul III, Katherine, Maria, Victoria; [ed.] Attended University of New Mexico, Alb. and Colorado State University, Ft. Collins, Co.; [occ.] Homemaker, Potter, Painter; [memb.] International Society of Poets; [oth. writ.] Numerous poems, songs, childrens stories; [pers.] Veriditas, literally meaning greening power, or which gives life. It is my hope that my writing would reflect the triumph of the human spirit in all situations.; [a.] Albuquerque, NM

DE KADT, JOHN
[b.] May 15, 1963, Greenwich, CT; [p.] Norma Nelson and Pieter P. De Kadt; [ed.] Greenwich High, Earlham College, American College of Traditional Chinese Medicine; [occ.] Student of Chinese Medicine and percussionist; [pers.] I love writing about mountains trees or anything wild and about waking up, not from the sleep that nourishes us but from the sleep that slowly numbs us.; [a.] San Francisco, CA

DEACON JR., GERMAN G.
[pen.] German Deacon; [b.] July 22, 1958, Waukegan, IL; [p.] German and Donna Deacon Sr.; [ch.] Christina Maria, Christopher Michael; [ed.] Sheridan High School Denver Inst.; [occ.] Medical Assembler; [hon.] Lots awards from jobs; [oth. writ.] Lots of poems not yet published; [pers.] I try to show people the beauty of this world that is beyond the eye sight and to see thing with there heart.; [a.] Sheridan, CO

DEAN, EBONY
[b.] December 3, 1979, Wichita, KS; [p.] Arnold Dean Sr., Jessie Dean; [ed.] Wichita South High, Mount Rainier High; [pers.] I would like to dedicate my poem to my mother, Jessie Dean, and I would like to thank my freshman year English teacher, Matt Mitchell, who greatly inspired me to show my poetry.; [a.] Desmoines, WA

DEAN, JOSEPH ALAN
[b.] June 20, 1976; [pers.] I enjoy blue skies, hiking, and good conversation my favorite color is purple. I write poetry to express strong emotions I cna't release in normal conversation. When the inspiration hits me, at 3 am, in the showers, or in the middle of a sentence, I just have to write it down. The words flow like water, and like electricity the emotion flows threw them. One heart's broken Dream's erupted when an eight relationship with my fiance fell apart last yr. We had drifted very far apart but I still held her as we cried after she read it. Then she got up and walked out of my life. I never thought any one would like my work. This contest has really lifted my spirits. Maybe one day I'll find someone to help me write brighter poems. If anyone has any advice or comments on my poem please write me at; [a.] Louisburg, NC

DEAN, JUNE C.
[pen.] June C. Dean; [b.] July 6, 1932, Chicago, IL; [p.] Alice and James McMahon; [m.] Donald A. Dean, November 24, 1963; [ch.] Scott, Michael, Steve Symons; [ed.] Lake View High, Truman College; [occ.] Retired - Travelling in RV - no phone; [memb.] National Wildlife Soc. Former Member of Chicago's, Art Institute and Field Museum.; [oth. writ.] Currently working on a children's story in poetry. Have written short stories - none published; [pers.] I have been influenced by the writings of Albert Payson Terhune, Louis Carroll and Dr. Seuss, Anne Rice is also favorite author.; [a.] Newport, OR

DEDRICK, DIANE
[b.] September 23, 1953, Hudson, NY; [p.] Irving and Frances Broomer, (Deceased); [m.] Jerry Dedrick, May 26, 1990; [ed.] Utica College of Syracuse University; [occ.] Senior Occupational Therapist for Broome Developmental Center Binghamton, N.Y. occupational Therapy Consultant for twin home care, Binghamton, N.Y.; [memb.] American Occupational Therapy Association, New York State License; [hon.] Bachelor of Science Cum Laude; [pers.] I wish to thank my loving husband, Jerry Dedrick, for encouraging me to express my poetic thoughts and honor my parents deceased forever - Irving and Frances Broomer.; [a.] Binghamton, NY

DEES, PATSY
[b.] July 18, 1945, Fredericktown, MO; [p.] Antone Dees, Maxine Dees; [ch.] Jennifer Diaz; [ed.] King High School Tampa, Florida; [occ.] Judicial Assistant; [pers.] Writing poetry is an excellent way to express thoughts and feelings.; [a.] Tampa, FL

DEHNER, JILL
[b.] February 2, 1978, Cincinnati, OH; [p.] Margaret Powers and Ralph Dehner; [ed.] I am currently a senior in highschool at the school for Creative and Performing Arts. My major there are commercial art and vocal music.; [oth. writ.] I've written many poems in my spare time, but this is my first published work. I write about what I feel strongest about. I've learned that without feeling even the most noble tasks will die.; [pers.] To pour one's heart out may result in massly confused emotion, but to embrace one feeling and paint a picture for the world can be a very beautiful thing.; [a.] Cincinnati, OH

DEIBLER, MATTHEW E.
[b.] October 30, 1976, Dallas, TX; [p.] Thomas Deibler, Kathy Deibler; [ed.] Apple Valley Christian School, Houghton College; [occ.] Student; [memb.] National Honor Society (high school), Apple Valley First Baptist Church; [hon.] Dean's List, Valedictorian (AVCS); [pers.] I have had many discussions with my family, which grately helped shape my

perspective in writing. I seek to proclaim the love and salvation of my God through my writing.; [a.] Houghton, NY

DEL VESCORO, TIMOTHY A.
[b.] August 31, 1966, New Jersey; [p.] Tim and Joyce; [ed.] Catholic University; [occ.] Architect; [pers.] Timothy Del Vescoro Practices Architecture in the Washington, DC, Metropolitan Area. His art embodies the similarities and contrasts between anthropomorphic forms and architectural elements. Influences are commonly drawn from his extensive domestic and international travels.; [a.] Bethesda, MD

DELA CRUZ, JUAN
[b.] August 6, 1978, Riverside, CA; [p.] Juan and Sylvia Dela Cruz; [ed.] Currently attending High School; [memb.] I was in a college preparation program called A.V.I.D. for two semesters last year, [hon.] This is the first honor I have received and it is truly an honor; [oth. writ.] Behind these bars, Grandma, cold winter day, she doesn't love me, I love you, shadows, Dear Mr. Santa Clause. Precious Rose and a couple more poems in my High Schools literary magazine.; [pers.] I would like to thank my parents and family for being there through all the hard times. My language arts teacher Mrs. Osko for believing in my poems and last but not least the selection committee for selecting this poem as a semi-finalist and everyone at the National Library of Poetry.; [a.] Corona, CA

DELANEY, BARBARA V.
[pen.] Barbara DeLaney; [b.] May 9, 1951, Louisville, KY; [p.] John and Ella Sensley Sr.; [ch.] Brandon and Camille DeLaney; [ed.] Braxton Buss. College Smith Dale Massey Buss College; [occ.] I own my little cleaning company, [oth. writ.] No, I write because it's a way to talk to my soul. I would love for you to read some of my other poems; [pers.] With my pen I find joy happiest love that no man can give.; [a.] Richmond, VA

DELFINO, CHRISTOPHER
[b.] December 4, 1966, Tarrytown; [p.] Michael Delfino, Mary Delfino; [ed.] Undergraduate: Fordham University Graduate: M.B.A. from Fordham, University graduate school of Business; [a.] Rye, NY

DEMAREST, KERRI
[pen.] Kerri Demarest; [b.] October 25, 1941, Wellington, KS; [p.] R. E. Branson and Harriett Branson; [m.] Hal Demarest, June 16, 1978; [ch.] Robin, Tanya, Rob and 8 grandchildren; [ed.] Wellington Sr. High, Emporia St Tchrs. College, Numerous Personal Mgmt and Executive Asst. Seminars; [occ.] Lease Renewal Asst., Chico, CA (Wittmeier Ford); [hon.] Most Professional Secretary - 1979-80, Blood Drive Laision (1985-90) Secondary Mktg., Great

American Bank, Care Committee Member, Great American Bank (1988-90); [pers.] I encourage and inspire my children and grandchildren to be the best they can be and to love each other and their friends.; [a.] Chico, CA

DENBY, DORIS J.
[b.] June 20, 1935, Yorktown, NJ; [p.] Martha Robinson and John Draper; [m.] David Denby, May 25, 1995; [ch.] Five; [ed.] 10th grade; [occ.] Retired Glass Worker

DESAI, GIRISH D.
[b.] November 28, 1930, India; [p.] Dhrubhai and Ratanben Desai; [m.] Mrudula Desai, March 1, 1960; [ch.] Alexis Desai; [ed.] Bachelor of Science, Physics and Math; [occ.] Engineer; [oth. writ.] Poems in Gujarati language (India); [pers.] To be a slave is weakness but to make on a slave is a crime.; [a.] Webster, TX

DESANTIS, JOANN C.
[b.] May 28, 1961, Somerville, NJ; [p.] Victor Eads, Shirley Broschart; [ed.] Bound Brook High School, Fairleigh Dickinson University; [occ.] Accounting Manager, Somerset, NJ; [pers.] Push yourself beyond your limit at all times, the possibilities are truly infinite.; [a.] Middlesex, NJ

DESSER, RONA H.
[p.] Sadie Finkelstein, Jacob Finkelstein; [m.] Irwin H. Desser, December 22, 1963; [ed.] Forest Park High School - Attended Catonsville, Community College; [occ.] Manager - Law Office; [hon.] Appointed by governor to the Citizen's Advisory Board of the Springfield State Hospital Ctr. at Sykesville MD, Elected President of the First Community Support Group of the Springfield State Hosp. Ctr., received several award of Merit for Conducting and Directing a poetry Therapy Clinic at a Baltimore County Community Mental Health Ctr. and Honored by the County Executive therefore.; [oth. writ.] Collection of poetry written by me since childhood—unpublished except for few poems published in newsletter of community support grp. —Shc.; [pers.] I feel that we must truly get in touch with our own feelings before we can hope to connect, in a positive, effective and fulfilling way, to other people and our surroundings. I have been greatly influenced by Philosophers and poets such as Kahlil Gibran.; [a.] Baltimore, MD

DEVAULT, DORIS
[b.] June 10, 1917, Ook Grove; [p.] Robert M. DeVault Sr. and Bess Moulton DeVault; [ed.] Watauga Academy (Baptist high school, Butler, TN), Carson-Newman College (2 yrs), Meredith College, B.A. WMU Training School, M.R.E.; [occ.] Retired in 1982, having been winner youth leader in Alabama and Arkansas (10 yrs), Woman's Missionary Union, SBC, B'ham, AL

for 27 years; [memb.] Dawson memorial Baptist Church: Watouga Associating of Genealogists Upper E, Tenn!; [hon.] Sophomore in high school medal for essay on "music", senior year best-all-round student medal, Valedictorian of class-wrote and delivered talk, "Floating for Rowing?" In college society "Calliopeans", was Miss Freshman and Miss Sophomore; [oth. writ.] Ten years articles for WMU Missionary Magazine - The Window and Royal Service, also Southern Baptist Encyclopedias, Family Genealogy in Washington Co. and Sullivan Co. Histories of East Tenn.; [pers.] Since becoming a christmas at age ten, my desire has been to follow and serve Christ. My home provide guidance and encouragement. We were not rich financially, but wealthy in terms of love, books, music, and biblical teaching.; [a.] Birmingham, AL

DEVINE, HAZEL B.
[pen.] Hazel Uhlir Devine; [b.] October 16, 1926, Verdigro, NE; [p.] Josephine and Richard Uhlir; [m.] Frank S. Devine, June 2, 1949; [ed.] San Diego State College (BA ed) University of NE (MA Ed.Ad. plus Library Administration plus reading) teacher, ed. Admin. Library admin. (ed.); [occ.] Retired - Homemaker, Volunteerism; [memb.] Nebraska Writer's Guild (Official Writers Organization of NE), Adams Co. Historical Society, NE Historical Society, Nebraska State Historical Society, P. Pres. Retired Teachers Hastings, AARP, AAUW, Rep. Party, Friends of Library, etc. was published in Verdigre Centennial Book, published letters to editors, 1996 Reminisce (2 articles, 2 series of humor) pending; [oth. writ.] Presently writing Poetry Book beginning in publishing poetry, wrote several articles 1983 (Book: Kids, Taxpayers and Schools Uhlir Family History, Short stories misc. writings for local Writer's Club sponsor writing class (April); [pers.] I attempt to write about those things that are quite universal and stress the positive everyday occurrences about ordinary persons and what might happen to them concerning their emotions and occupations.; [a.] Hastings, NE

DEWAR, SUIBHAN MELISSA
[b.] August 26, 1964, Johannesburgh, South Africa; [p.] Ronald and Delma Dewar, [ed.] Cal Poly San Luis Obispo, CA, B.S. in Business Administration; [occ.] Associate Benefit Coordinator, [oth. writ.] Trees, View of Life From a Harp Seal, Eternal Peace; [pers.] Believe in yourself and all that you do! The drive inside makes dreams come true... Suibhan Dewar; [a.] Concord, CA

DEWITT, BECKY
[b.] August 3, 1958, Melrose, MA; [m.] David; [ch.] Kirsten and Kendra; [ed.] University of New Hampshire; [occ.] Communications Manager; [memb.] Church of Christ; [pers.] I hope my writing could add to touch of joy and

comfort to someone's life as well as glorify God.; [a.] Danvers, MA

DIAZ, GARY F.
[b.] February 3, 1997, Ecuador; [p.] Franklyn and Elvia Diaz; [ed.] Clinton Elementary School, Mather H.S, University of Illinois Urbana-Champaign; [occ.] Student; [memb.] "Good Guys" Club-Vise President; [hon.] National Honors Society; [pers.] In a time of Koas music is the only real escape.; [a.] Chicago, IL

DICKENS, SCOTT
[b.] September 26, 1970, Atlanta, GA; [p.] Charles and Joanne Dickens; [ed.] Wolfson High School; [occ.] Parts Manager at Copy Tronics; [oth. writ.] A book not titled that was never finished because of his death; [pers.] The value of life can not be taught but only lived; [a.] Lakeland, FL

DIEDWARDO, JOSEPH
[b.] December 11, 1983, Allentown, PA; [p.] Dr. Amedeo and Mary Ann DiEdwardo; [ed.] 1 year local Catholic School, has been home-schooled for past 4 years, is in 7th grade, Honor Student; [occ.] Student; [memb.] United States Figure Skating Assoc. (USFSA), U.S. Chess Federation, Two Homeschool Clubs, (S.E.L.A.H, and L.C.H.E.); [hon.] Two Gold Ice Skating Medals, Consecutive (3 years) winner of local poetry contest, won PA State Federal Junior Duck Stamp Contest 2 yrs., National Story League; [oth. writ.] "Hair", "The Reproachful Roach", "Nonsense", "Homework for Breakfast" (poems); [pers.] "When I write poetry, it is usually about something that occupies a great position in my life."; [a.] Bethlehem, PA

DIMON, MARY G.
[pen.] Emdee; [b.] May 13, 1929, Manitowoc, WI; [p.] Monona Reynolds and Earl Gilling; [m.] Richard Dimon, June 14, 1952; [ch.] Four daughters, one son; [ed.] B.S. Northwestern University M.Ed U. of Calif. at Los Angeles, Ph.D. Claremont Graduate School; [occ.] Retired Education Faculty for Calif. State University System.; [memb.] American Association of University Women, Zetu Phi Eta, Pi Lomda Phi College Volunteers, Retired CSU Faculty Assoc.; [hon.] Published three articles in Western College Reading and Learning year book (blind judging). Recently published in Martha Maxwell Anthology (1994); [oth. writ.] Four unpublished children's books, recently written. Presentations at thru National Conferences on College Learning. Dissertation topic was concerned with high risks College students and their curriculum.; [pers.] Main interest is the continued reflecting of young people from all cultures so they may see their future before they ease it.

DISHAROON, DAWN ADELE
[b.] August 21, 1959, Philadelphia, PA; [p.] DeAlton P. Disharoon, Norma M. Disharoon; [ch.] Myles Christian; [ed.] Woodrow Wilson High School, Bucks County Community College, Barbizon School of Modelling; [occ.] Bood Binder, Delaware Valley Blindery, West Trenton, NJ; [memb.] LPRA, Levittwon, PA; [pers.] "Life's Goals" "Have faith in your dreams, wish upon that star. All things are possible, near and far!"; [a.] Levittown, PA

DISIMONE, ANNA
[b.] February 2, 1920, Detroit, MI; [p.] Philip Marracco, Maria Marracco; [m.] Ignazio Disimone, February 7, 1942; [ch.] Lillian M. Wall, Mary Ellen Pane; [ed.] Sainte Catherine, High School; [occ.] Retired Homemaker; [memb.] Member of "Our Lady Of Grace" Church; [oth. writ.] Writing poems and songs are my favorites hobby, Lyrics for "Now and then", sung by Johnny Desmond. Poem "My Kite and I" published.; [pers.] My writing have always been of good faith.; [a.] Encino, CA

DISTAD, ELAINE SANDRA FRAM
[b.] April 28, 1961, Moncton, New Brunswick, Canada; [p.] Alvin Fram, Enid J. Fram; [m.] Gregory E. Distad, August 11, 1984; [ch.] Tyler Jordan, Charity-Lynne, Adam Joel; [ed.] Emmanuel Baptist Christian School Bob Jones University; [occ.] Home School Teacher; [pers.] "Whether therefore ye eat or drink, or whatsoever ye do, do all to the glory of God." I Corinthians 10:31; [a.] Cincinnatus, NY

DITTY, JANICE E.
[b.] April 28, 1963, Lewisburg, PA; [p.] Harold and Kathryn Savidge; [m.] Steven E. Ditty, September 11, 1987; [ch.] Kyle Steven and Bryan Elwood; [ed.] Milton Area School, Thompson Institute - NEC, Harrisbury, PA; [hon.] Dean's List, Magna Cum Laude; [pers.] My writings are usually inspired by personal moments and nature's beauty. I try to reach out to the feelings of others and to touch them in some special way.; [a.] Lewisburg, PA

DOCKSTADER III, WILLIAM C.
[b.] June 19, 1980, Ithaca, NY; [p.] William and Mae Dockstader Sr.; [ed.] Sophomore in Cascadilla Private School; [memb.] ACE Access to College Education.; [oth. writ.] Enjoy writing short stories and poetry. Have had 2 published in school magazines.; [pers.] Inspirations: William Shakespeare, Emily Dickonson, Robert Frost, Edgar Allen Poe; [a.] Ithaca, NY

DODD, H. ERNEST
[pen.] Ernest Gray Feather; [b.] November 20, 1950, Anaconda, MT; [p.] Harry C. and Rita Ruth; [m.] Divorced; [ch.] Donald Dean Dodd; [ed.] AA, ACS, DD, ASN, RN; [occ.] Sub-

Acute Care RN; [memb.] Planetary Society, Vietnam Veterans of America, VFW; [hon.] Dean's List, Cum Laude, Mattegon Nursing Scholarship; [oth. writ.] Pending; [pers.] The things I have written come to me move-less in a completed state. I can take credit only for putting pen to paper.; [a.] New York, NY

DODGE, JULIE DIANE
[b.] December 9, 1981, Colorado Springs; [p.] Sue and Allan Dodge; [ed.] I'm in the eight grade; [memb.] Pride Soccer Club; [hon.] 2nd Science Olympiad Award for most aggressive player on my soccer; [pers.] "I am there for, we all are"; [a.] Colorado Springs, CO

DODSON, ALICEJEAN LEIGH
[pen.] Alicejean Leigh; [b.] May 13, 1941, Staten Island, NY; [p.] Beatrice Beinert Leigh and W. I. Leigh; [ed.] Gustavus Adolphus College, University Puget Sound, University of Washington; [occ.] Director of Nursing; [oth. writ.] "Whether We Know It Or Not" is a first poem.; [a.] Springfield, VA

DOKOUPIL, CASEY
[pen.] Dokey; [b.] February 15, 1980, Williamport, PA; [p.] Kathryn A. and James R.; [ed.] Liverpool High School, Sophomore 1995-96; [occ.] Student; [memb.] School Newspaper - News and LHS, Edu., Tech. crew, Burnet Park Zoo Explorer Post, Aids Task Force, American Heart Association.; [hon.] National Junior Honor Society; [oth. writ.] Articles, letters, poems, and stories (and babblings useful to no one but me), all lost in my room somewhere.; [pers.] I dedicate this poem to anthony, wherever he is. To L.N. - the sun isn't always black. R.C., K.R., L.B., M.O., K.K., M.C., C.S., M.D., J.H. - word are just words unless they're spoken with heart.; [a.] Liverpool, NY

DOLAN, PETER
[b.] May 3, 1982, Salem, MA; [p.] Marcia Dolan and Robert Dolan; [ed.] Ipswich Middle School; [occ.] Student; [memb.] Beverly Youth Hockey; [hon.] I was selected to be in the Northeast Junior District Chorus; [pers.] In my writing I hope that people realize how precious our environment is and that they will appreciate it more in everyday life.; [a.] Ipswich, MA

DOUGAN, DEANNA
[b.] September 10, 1956, Illinois; [m.] Jeff Dougan; [ch.] Jennifer, Mark, Erin, Luke, Ashley; [ed.] University of Wyoming; [memb.] North Phoenix Baptist Church; [oth. writ.] Western Poetry; [a.] Phoenix, AZ

DOUGHTON, DAVID
[b.] January 11, 1971, Chicago, IL; [p.] Frank Doughton, Carol Doughton; [ed.] San Bernardino High School, Riverside Community College;

[occ.] Retail Manager; [oth. writ.] Several poems in college magazines and the anthology Songs on the Wind; [pers.] If I wasn't writing poetry, I'd be doing nothing at all.; [a.] Riverside, CA

DOWLING, DEAN E.
[b.] February 17, 1942, Daytona Beach, FL; [p.] Edward M., Josephine F. Dowling; [m.] Brenda G. Dowling, August 15, 1976; [ch.] Keith R., Brian E. Dowling, Jo Anne Russo, Julie Rudowski; [ed.] Columbia Univ., PhD, English, 1972, Columbia Univ., PhD, English, 1970, USMA, West Point, NY, BS, 1963; [occ.] Lockheed Martin Corp. also - Adjungant Professor, Park College; [memb.] Philosophy/ English; [a.] Alexandria, VA

DOWNING, ROBERT
[b.] May, 5, 1943, Baytown, TX; [m.] Shirley, August 18, 1961; [ch.] Robert III, Kimberly; [ed.] Lee College, Indiana University, University of Houston B.A. Economics and Russian. Postgraduate, Univ. of St. Thomas - Education; [occ.] Teacher, Turner Elementary, Pasadena, Texas; [oth. writ.] Several volumes of unpublished memoirs, articles for local published memoirs, articles for local publications and for "The Rocky Mountain District News" and "Harvest time," publications of the United Pentecostal Church, International; [pers.] The richest man in the world is he who sleeps with a clear conscience.; [a.] Baytown, TX

DRAEGER, GERMAINE
[b.] June 14, 1919, Marion, WI; [m.] Widowed 21 years; [ch.] One son Leslie, three grandchildren, Jessie, Jenny, Casey; [ed.] Univ. Wis. Stevens Point, Univ. Wis. Oshkosh, Univ. Northern Ill (Bach. Science and 30 cr.); [occ.] Retired Math Teacher, Extensive Volunteering; [memb.] Waupaca Co. Retired-Past Pres. Award, Educators Assoc., Wis Education Assoc., St. John's Evang. Luth Church, Member Building Task Force of local congregation; [hon.] Teacher of the Year Award, Excellence In Teaching Award, Certificate of Recognition from Nat'l. Republican Congressional Comm., Grant from Nat'l. Science Foundation, Honored for most years of service on Church Council.; [oth. writ.] Nothing published. Did many poems, a few lyrics, wrote entire programs for various organizational celebrations.; [a.] Marion, WI

DRAGE, SHIRLEY
[b.] January 22, 1950, Wausau, WI; [p.] Maynard and Alice Wiemann; [m.] Dick Drage, February 16, 1974; [ed.] University of Wis. - Marathon Campus Wausav Senior H.S.; [occ.] Commercial, Lines Insurance Technician Dallas, TX; [pers.] Composing a poem is an emotional release for me. Sometimes it's on a personal level or other times it's to commemorate a specific event or a struggle to establish a

memorial befitting someone you've lost. I like to include poignant phrases or hints of a certain time or place to convey the feelings being directed to the subject of a particular composition. It's meant to strike a chord of memory or emotion.; [a.] Lewisville, TX

DUCA, ANGELS R.
[pen.] Angels R. Duca; [b.] March 26, 1912, New York City; [p.] Salvatore and Katie Duca; [m.] Edith Duca, January 1941; [ch.] One daughter; [ed.] B.S. City College New York City 1937; [occ.] Retired, Art as a hobby and poetry; [memb.] National Library of Poetry 1994, Sparrowgrass Poetry Forum, Great Poems of the Western World Vol. II 1990 - (No longer in existence); [hon.] Editor's Choice Award 1994, National Library of Poetry, Editor - Cynthia Stevens, Editor - Caroline Sullivan Managing Editor - Howard Ely; [oth. writ.] "Faith" page 235 #1, "Dew drops in the grass" p. 46 #2, "Mind and Matter" p. 85 #3; [pers.] I write poetry in Praise of God. The prime concern is rhythm and the words should be placed in the proper and balanced frame work of a suitable 'idea'. In a beautiful poem rhythm, word and idea move and intermingle to form a beautiful blind we call poetry.; [a.] Hasbrouck Heights, NJ

DUKE, JENNIFER M.
[b.] February 15, 1971, La Miranda, CA; [p.] Jim and Diane Duke; [ed.] University of California Santa Barbara, B.A. English, with honors, California Western School of Law-top eight percent of my class.; [occ.] Law student studying to become criminal prosecutor. Legal intern with San Diego District Attorney; [hon.] Dean's honors at UC Santa Barbara and California Western School Law, Miley M. Manuel state Pro Bono Award, Imelda Rosenthal Foundation of the State Bar Scholarship.; [pers.] All that we are stems from all that we dream.; [a.] San Diego, CA

DUNBAR, SHANNON
[pen.] Shannon Dunbar; [b.] December 23, 1978, Fort Campbell, KY; [p.] Shirley and Frank Dunbar; [ed.] Indian River High School; [occ.] Student; [memb.] Sigma Phi Omega, Pals for Poems, Drama Club, Second Calvary Baptist; [oth. writ.] A child's life apart.; [pers.] God helped me when no one else would. If you have faith he will help you too.; [a.] Chesapeake, VA

DUNCAN, ERIKA MARISSA
[b.] November 12, 1980, Bryn Mawr, PA; [p.] Michael W. H. and Peg Duncan; [ed.] Agnes Irwin School, Freshman High School; [occ.] Student; [memb.] Glee Club, Drama Workshop; [hon.] High honors at Agnes Irwin. Multiple English, French, Latin Awards at Agnes Irwin. Latin Poem Award given by Philadelphia Classical Society.; [oth. writ.] Several poems published in Agnes Irwin literary magazines.; [pers.] I do not always experience the things or events in my poems, but everything comes either directly from my heart or my mind's imagination.; [a.] Malvern, PA

DUNLAP, RICHARD W.
[b.] April 29, 1947, Granite City, IL; [p.] Charles L. Dunlap Jr. and Georgia L. (Thomason) Kittrell; [m.] Sandra K. (Hansell) Dunlap, February 26, 1970; [ch.] Mrs. Stephanie J. (Dunlap) Walker, Sean Michael Walker; [ed.] 12th (GED) Madison Sr. High, Madison, IL., Computer training-federal Govt; [occ.] Retired (disable) GS-5 Lead Mailclerk Arpercen St. Louis, MO; [memb.] Veterans of Foreign Wars; [hon.] Several awards from former job, Vietnam war awards, desert storm (Gulf War) award; [oth. writ.] 3 Poems recorded to music, another pub. in "Great poems of the western world, another pub. in "The Gallant Grahams of Tennessee, 205 poems written to date.; [pers.] My poems have in some ways helped me to deal with my depressions and post trumatic stress due to Vietnam; [a.] Camp Pendleton, CA

DUNSTAN, PAMELA C.
[pen.] Pamela C. Dunne; [b.] February 14, 1924, London, Unite Kingdom; [p.] Monty and Maud Broadbridge; [m.] Les W. Dunstan, July 23, 1944; [ch.] Eleven; [ed.] St. Mary's Convent - High School music Major thru High School, Music Major thru High School and beyond L.R.A.M. Instructors and Exams; [occ.] Part-Time Accompanist at Reputable Dance School; [memb.] D.B.E. (Daughters of The British Empire); [hon.] Dance Accomp. at A.S.U. for 12 yrs. L.R.A.M. Exams Grade 5 - Distinction Festivals 1st, 2nd Awards, Arizona State University; [oth. writ.] "The New President," "The New President," "What's In A Name"; [pers.] The Music In Language, The Language in Music. Beauty in accents and brogues are heard in the rolling R-r-r's of a Scottish accent, with the ebb and flow of the lilting Irish brogue, the "blooming loverly" Cockney accent, also the Boston, Louisiana and warm Southern accents to name a few. Now for expediency and efficiency Slang has taken over our expressive wording. O.K.? O.K.! O.K!! Musically, now.; [a.] Mesa, AZ

DURAN, JOSHUA A.
[b.] November 19, 1977; [ed.] Graduate of SELF High School; [pers.] With all the pain in this world, I'm glad to know that all my pain has resulted stronger me.; [a.] Irvine, CA

DURBIN, H. FITZGERALD
[pen.] H. Fitzgerald; [b.] February 18, 1915, Todd, OK; [p.] W. R. Durbin and B. L. Romines; [m.] Nolda J. Walker, August 15, 1933; [ch.] Barbara, Herb, Joe, Bertha, Paula, Dan, Don; [ed.] 8 yrs pub 4 yrs Bible; [occ.]

Retired minister; [memb.] General council Ass. of God, Ok. District Council Ass of God International Society of Poets, The Rutherford Institute; [hon.] Gold Pin Award for fifty years of ministry; [oth. writ.] Poems published by local paper, quill Books, Iliad Press, Cader Publishing Ltd. MWM Dexter, Inc., Sparrowgrass Poetry Forum; [pers.] It is my desire that my life and my writings will always reflect the existence of a kind and loving God.; [a.] Wyandotte, OK

DURRENCE, AUBREY B.
[pen.] Aubrey Durrence; [b.] June 5, 1980, New Haven, CT; [p.] Christine E. Burke, John M Durrence; [ed.] Manual High School; [occ.] Student, Photographer's Assistant; [memb.] Lacrosse Foundation, National Fish and Wildlife Federation, National Geographic Society; [oth. writ.] Several unpublished works; [pers.] Thanks Mom; [a.] Denver, CO

DUWE, ROBERT R.
[b.] October 21, 1937, Cleveland, OH; [p.] Oho and Ann Duwe; [m.] Sandra Ann (Walkley) Duwe, April 28, 1962; [ch.] Robert R., Jr., and E'Lise M.; [ed.] Graduated from Lincoln High (1958) and Graduated from Cuyahoga Community College about (1971) with an AS Degree; [occ.] President of Sales with high performance Asphalt; [memb.] I am a member of the Berea Congregation of Jehovah Witness; [hon.] I've had five of my poems publish in the National Library of Poetry; [oth. writ.] I have other writings that haven't been published as of yet.; [pers.] Every Man, Woman and Child. No matter what race or station in life, has many things to contribute to this world. From their writings to their different forms of art and inventions. But most of all is there Faith, Love and Obedience in their God, Jehovah.; [a.] Brook Park, OH

EARL, JAMES E.
[pen.] James Edwards; [b.] October 29, 1932, Nashville, TN; [p.] Odie Earl, Annie Earl; [m.] Joyce Earl, October 8, 1954; [ch.] Peggy Liles, Janice Earl; [ed.] University of Tennessee at Chattanooga; [occ.] Retired Engineer; [memb.] UT Alumni Assoc, American Legion, The Bible League, The Braille Institute, The American Red Cross; [hon.] College: Various Scholastic Honor, Engineer: Commendations from Air Force and NASA; [oth. writ.] "Days of Youth", an Autobiography. Several poems for various occasions.; [pers.] Writing poems is a beautiful and honest way to express my feelings about life and this world we live in.; [a.] Yucaipa, CA

EASTWOOD, SUNNIA
[pers.] Many thanks to my friend Susan Stauter for introducing me to W.H. Auden and Joseph Brodsky, all of whom have awed, influenced, and inspired me. My accomplishments are

dedicated to my dad, John Connel Joseph Eastwood.; [a.] San Francisco, CA

EBO, DENA M. HUGHES
[b.] November 4, 1964, Pittsburgh, PA; [p.] Sally Hughes, Eddie Wright; [m.] Joseph Ebo, January 2, 1988; [ch.] Jamilahalake, Adomjamil; [ed.] Westinghouse High School, Community College of Allegheny County, Western School of Business and Health; [occ.] Pharmacy Technician; [oth. writ.] Hundreds of Poems with a urban/love slant.; [pers.] Every life, makes someone happy, one day.; [a.] Decatur, GA

ECHOLS, MAGILL
[occ.] Psychologist; [pers.] Emerson and George Russell agreed that all poetry is first written in the heavens, and is my philosophy.; [a.] San Diego, CA

EDDY, TARA
[b.] December 14, 1978, Rome, NY; [p.] Sherry Eddy, Carl Eddy; [ed.] Lake Delta Elementary School, Rome Free Academy (Still in School, 10th grade); [hon.] An award for best artist in school when I graduated from sixth grade.; [oth. writ.] A few of my poems were put in the Rome observer last year.; [pers.] I like to write about things that happen in everyday life and sometimes my personal feelings.; [a.] Rome, NY

EDGE, LAMAI T.
[pen.] L. T. Miles; [b.] May 5, 1962, Thailand; [p.] Alden M. Smiley, Sr., Lek Smiley; [m.] William Wesley Edge, August 20, 1983; [ch.] William Alden and Mattie Thippawan; [ed.] Bolton High Delta Business College; [occ.] 100% Mom!; [pers.] I enjoy writing my own greeting cards. I believe that if you let your feelings guide you then it's coming from the soul.; [a.] Keithville, LA

EDMONDS, RENITA PATRICE
[b.] April 2, 1961, Phoenix City, AL; [p.] Alveta Edmonds and Robert Williams; [ed.] Pershing High School, Central State University, Faith Bible College, Holy Ghost Full Gospel School of the Prophets; [occ.] Special Education teacher at Webber Middle School in Detroit MI; [memb.] Holy Ghost Full Gospel Baptist Church, United Bowlers For Christ; Sigma Gamma Rho Sorority Inc., Delta Omega Chapter; [hon.] National Dean's List Ministers IN, Training 2 year graduate; [oth. writ.] Destiny's Secret, A Call to Prayer; [pers.] What a man thinkest, so is he. I have been greatly influenced by my dear mother Alveta Edmonds, my godmother Darlene Kennedy and my spiritual mother and Pastor Bishop Corletta Harris Vaughn.; [a.] Detroit MI.

EDMONDS, ROSS C.
[b.] April 20, 1974, Abingdon, VA; [p.] Charles W. and Christine Edmonds; [ed.] Abingdon High School, Virginia Polytechnic Institute and State

University; [occ.] Computer Technician; [hon.] Who's Who Among American High School Students, Presidential Seal of Excellence, Governor's Seal, National Honor's Society Seal; [oth. writ.] Several unpublished poems and short stories.; [pers.] "Greater love has no one than this, than to lay dow one's life for his friends." - John 15:13; [a.] Blacksburg, VA

EDWARDS, DAVID S.
[p.] H. Nate and Nyoka K. Edwards; [m.] Frances R. Edwards; [ch.] Amber Nyoka and Seirra Jade Edwards; [ed.] Wabash High School graduate; [occ.] Electrician; [pers.] I would like to thank my children for the strength to keep going when all is against me. This poem is dedicated to my inspiration, my wife, Frances.

EDWARDS, RITA ANNE
[b.] August 26, 1978, Fort Lauderdale, FL; [ed.] Nursing School, Florida Atlantic University Boca Raton, FL; [occ.] Student; [memb.] Spanish Honor Society

EDWARDS, SCOTT THOMAS J.
[b.] November 27, 1978, Anaheim, CA; [p.] Larry B. Edwards, Debby M. Sobin-Edwards; [ed.] High School Graduate; [hon.] Soccer Mid-City Championship, S. Orange Co. Soccer AYSO - Library Arts Finalist; [oth. writ.] Several poems and short stories, including love madness in publication.; [a.] Buena Park, CA

EILERT, PATRICIA K.
[b.] November 10, 1953, Columbia, MO; [p.] Kenneth and Bernice Sparks; [m.] David P. Eilert, May 27, 1978; [ch.] Tina Kay, Shawnda Lee; [ed.] High School and 21 hrs. college; [occ.] Self Employed, Sugar Shack, Branson, MO; [memb.] National Write Your Congressman, Our Lady of the Lake Catholic Church, VFW Auxiliary; [oth. writ.] Several poems and essays published in local papers over the years.; [pers.] I keep a positive outlook on life and look for God as my strength. The love of my husband, David, and family greatly inspire me.; [a.] Branson, MO

ELDREDGE, JASON FORREST
[b.] January 30, 1976, Idaho Fall, ID; [p.] Steven Eldredge, Tammie Harris; [ed.] Skyline High School, U.S. Army Training As Microwave Radio Systems Operator Maintainer; [occ.] Tactical Satellite Systems Maintainer; [memb.] U.S. Army Signal Corps, 58th Maintenance Company of Fort Bragg, NC; [hon.] Parachutist Badge, Expert in Rifle Marksmanship; [oth. Writ.] Poems, song lyrics, short stories, none published; [pers.] Solitude in a great influence in my writings, along with my love of nature, sports, and music.; [a.] Idaho Falls, ID

ELI, BRIAL
[b.] December 8, 1976; [a.] Pittsburgh, PA

ELLIOTT, NAOMI
[pen.] Naomi Elliott; [b.] January 8, 1971, San Diego, CA; [p.] Dameda Grissom and Malcolm Elliott; [ed.] Graduated from Mt. Miguel High School in 1993, attended Cuyamaca College; [memb.] Artists for a hate-free America, San Diego Rock Band Haplo; [hon.] Received a savings bond award for a poem in the 7th grade; [oth. writ.] Short poem published in 1995-1996 Cuyamaca Reader.; [a.] Lemon Grove, CA

ELLIS, KIMBERLY J.
[b.] January 24, 1969, Miami, FL; [ed.] North Carolina State University; [occ.] Marketing; [pers.] Words in poetry are a reflection of the soul.; [a.] Fairfax, VA

EMMETT, DIANE A.
[b.] March 11, 1960, San Diego, CA; [p.] Joyce E. Jones; [m.] Kevin M. Emmett, June 29, 1985; [ch.] Jami Redford and Kevin M. Emmett Jr.; [occ.] Barber, Hairstylist; [hon.] This publication is an awards in its self... thank you.; [pers.] For my son Kevin M. Emmett Jr., I think of you everyday and can only hope you know how very much I love you and miss you. Mommy.; [a.] West Hills, CA

ENGELHARDT, MICHELLE
[b.] April 6, 1975, Neenah, WI; [p.] Margaret and Terry Engelhardt; [ed.] Appleton West High School; [occ.] Employee of Anchor Foods; [memb.] Precious Moments, International Wolf Center; [pers.] My High School creative writing teacher, Gerald Saindon Strongly suggested that I send this poem to a poetry contest.; [a.] Appleton, WI

ENRIQUEZ, LOUIS L.
[pen.] Lazaro Enriquez; [b.] January 11, 1940, Los Angeles, CA; [p.] Rupert and Caroline Enriquez; [m.] Mary Enriquez, June 20, 1970; [ch.] Paul - 1; [ed.] 5 years of college, but for the most part I am self - educated; [occ.] California Insurance Department; [pers.] To find the spiritual beauty of our physical existence and reflect it in the writings so that the reader may comprehend reader may comprehend our relationship to all life forms.; [a.] Walnut, CA

ESPINOZA, AVILIO M. VALENZUELA
[pen.] Milton Espinoza; [b.] February 22, 1956, Cuba; [p.] Pedro Espinoza and Nieves Valenzuela; [ch.] Heaven Leigh, Shayna Monique; [ed.] 1973-1977 University of Havana, Havana, Cuba; [occ.] "Press Set-Ups"; [oth. writ.] Various poems, which I'll expect to publish on near future.; [pers.] If there's a place, a humble small place that with open arms will accepts you, just as you are..., don't ever say no, you might be denying paradise.; [a.] Winamac, IN

ESTANDIFER, DUANE
[pen.] Reality; [b.] February 6, 1978, Gallup,

NM; [p.] Wanda Ewynn; [ed.] High School - Florence Christian School, Florence, CO; [occ.] Student; [oth. writ.] Book called Misunderstood, not published as of yet.; [a.] Penrose, CO

ESTES, BETTY ANN
[pen.] Babe; [b.] October 25, 1943, Boston, MA; [p.] James and Katherine Boan; [m.] Divorced; [ch.] Randall Scott Estes; [ed.] MA. NC S.C. and VA; [occ.] Self Employed (working with the aged).; [memb.] President of the Rebekah Assemblies of S.C. Secretary of York Lodge #17 The American Heart Assoc. (Project for 1995-1996)) The Nat'l Authors Registry The National Arbor Day Foundation. The Long Fellow; [hon.] "Honorable Mention" - Awards The President's Awards for Literary Excellence 1995 - The Iliad Press for "He Makes His Presence Known"; [oth. writ.] I have written many articles for the EC writer Pineville, NC - in The Early 90's. I am Representative from SC for the International Odd Fellow and Rebekah Located in Linden CA. Published and Editor for The York Odd Fellow and Rebekah, York, South Carolina.; [pers.] With pen in hand my mood swings to the tune, Mother nature sings.; [a.] Rock Hill, SC

ESTRUCH, HEATHER
[pen.] Randya, Macho Teen; [b.] September 2, 1975, Downey, CA; [p.] John and Cherryl Estruch; [ed.] Victor Valley College; [memb.] Monte Olive, Presbyterian Church; [hon.] Phi Theta Kappa, Dean's List, Honor Roll, 26 Girl Scout Badges, Who's Who Among American High School Students; [oth. writ.] I have no other writings published. I have several unpublished poems and short stories.; [pers.] I have been a fan of Randy Poffo also known as "Randy" Macho Man "Savage" for 10 years straight. He inspires all of my work. I only have 3 poems that aren't about him.; [a.] California

EVANS II, RALPH WILLIAM
[b.] May 6, 1981, Roanoke, VA; [p.] Kaye and Larry Harless; [oth. writ.] Unpublished Short Stories including: Love By Chance on Thorny Vine Lane, All Evil Ends Sometimes, Of Love and Forgiveness, Samuel in the midst of the Shadow and numerous poems.; [pers.] I do not look to express one emotion in my poetry, but to explore and express all the emotions I feel.; [a.] Salem, VA

EVANS, KRISTIE KAI
[b.] March 12, 1964, Cincinnati, OH; [p.] Robert and Katie Smith; [m.] Sylvester Evans, July 14, 1986; [ch.] Byron, Marquis and Briana; [ed.] University of Cincinnati, Cincinnati, Ohio; [occ.] Member Services Representative - Mid Atlantic Medical Services Inc.; [pers.] When I write I try to reflect the feelings that come from within. Most of the poems that I have written have been love poems.; [a.] Landover, MD

EVANS, MARTHA CELESTIA
[pen.] Martha Evans; [b.] November 8, 1947, Canton, OH; [p.] Celestia Martha Williams; [ch.] Jeffrey D., Marsha, Mary Anna Jonathan; [ed.] B.S., Kent State OH, M.Ed Wright State OH Mental Health Concentration; [occ.] Free Lance Writing; [memb.] A.A. V.W. 11 Years Teaching Washington C.H. 3 years High School Counseling Wash. C.H., OH 5 years Academic Advisor Wright State University; [hon.] Glenwood H.S. - Canton Ohio - 3 yrs. Cheerleader, Jr. Class Secretary - Home coming attendant, Sr. Class Secretary - Senior Attendant Council. Five year service award from wright State University.; [oth. writ.] "Teenagers and Alcohol" - Scholary Paper, Med. Series of newspaper articles "Community Psychology" published in Washington. C.H. newspaper. (Focused on Parents Helping Teens); [pers.] I believe every individual is a unique human being created by God. My poems bind nature and humans to a belief that there is a higher power, which is a part of nature.; [a.] Canton, OH

EVANS, MARY ALICE
[pen.] Rusty Phalen; [b.] August 6, 1939, Columbus, OH; [p.] Edward Baclawski and Alice Phalen; [m.] Jack Eugene Evans, April 8, 1971; [ch.] Kyran, Linda and Christine; [ed.] Holy Family High-Columbus, Ohio Holy Name High-Cleveland, OH; [occ.] Quality control Technician Tridelta Industries; [oth. writ.] I have written several poems, but this is my first attempt of having one published.; [pers.] I write about what I feel is important in life. I try to write from the heart with sensitivity.; [a.] Andover, OH

EVANS, YANCY LAVAR
[b.] October 7, 1977, Saint Louis; [p.] Zenobia A. Jackson, Cloyd X. Evans; [ed.] I'm in my last year at McCluer High and North Tech High; [occ.] Best Buy: Video Salesman, St. Louis Bread Company; [memb.] Track, Jazz Band; [hon.] Who's Who Award; [oth. writ.] Same poem was in my last year high school Marquee; [pers.] I really didn't even expect to get a reply. The only reason why I sent the poem is because I have this mad prayer to get into the music business as a lyricist. I guess I had to start somewhere. And no, I don't have a child.; [a.] Ferguson, MO

EWERSEN, VIRGINIA PEASE
[b.] June 7, 1922, Van Wert County, OH; [p.] Elza and Pearlie Pease (Deceased); [m.] Herbert Ewersen (Deceased), October 18 ,1942; [ch.] Dale and Carol Ewersen, Hoaqlin-Jackson Centralized Schools; [ed.] BS in Education, Bowling Green University (OH), Graduate Studies University of Toledo, The Ohio State University; [occ.] Retired Reading Coordinator - Teacher, Port Clinton OH City Schools; [memb.] Kappa Delta Pi, International Reading Association Sandusky (OH) Choral Society,

Humane Society of the United States, The Nature Conservancy National Trust for Historical Preservation; [hon.] Literacy Award, International Reading Association (Vocational and Conference), Who's Who in American Education and Who's Who in America, Child Development Professionals; [oth. writ.] "From Hyperactive to Happy - Active in Limited Spaces" published 1979 (re Help for Learning Disabled Children), several articles re Learning and published in local newspaper, Chapter 1 Handbook; [pers.] In all my life's endeavors, I strive for excellence, with a cheerful heart!; [a.] Port Clinton, OH

EZZELL, MARY MOORE
[b.] June 26, 1945, Sampson County, NC; [p.] James R. and Elizabeth B. Moore; [m.] Divorced; [ch.] Jessica Brown Ezzell; [ed.] East Carolina University, Batchelor of Music, 1967; [occ.] Elementary School Teacher, Southport Elementary, Southport, NC; [memb.] NEA, NCAE, Southport Baptist Church; [oth. writ.] No previously published writings.; [pers.] Writing poetry and songs allows creative expression of inspiration from my personal life experiences.; [a.] Southport, NC

FAIRBANKS, CANTIER E.
[pen.] Cartier E. Fairbanks; [b.] November 24, 1950, Grand Forks, ND; [p.] William and Helen Fairbanks; [ed.] The study of Psychology at North Dakota State University and the University of Minnesota; [occ.] Non Commissioned Officer in the U.S. Army Stationed in Virginia; [oth. writ.] Several; [pers.] Expressing yourself with poetry enables you to convey your thought as well as your emotion.; [a.] Newport News, VA

FARRELL, FREIDA E.
[b.] June 13, 1925, Pittsburgh, PA; [p.] G.E. Eugene Wilson and Mary Alexander; [m.] John B. Farrell Jr. (deceased); [ch.] John A., Dennis P., Jacquelyn Y., Michael D., Beverly E.; [memb.] St. Bernadine of Siena Catholic Church, LIteracy Council PG Co., AARP #939, VFW #5471, Zeta AMICAE of PG CO., Suitland Citizens Ass'n Inc. (Arthritis Foundation, Support Group Leaders), World S.H.A.R.E. Program Site Coordinator; [oth. writ.] The autograph and love.; [pers.] Quoting Sam Walter Foss "let me live in a house by the side of the road and be a friend to man." His words have been my life's goal!; [a.] Suitland, MD

FEARON, CAMESIA
[b.] February 11, 1980; [p.] Diana Ingram; [ed.] Shortwood Elementary, St. Hugh's High and Teaneck High; [occ.] Student at Teaneck High School; [memb.] Debate Club, Drama Club and FHA; [hon.] Writing Essay Competition; [oth. writ.] Several poems published in school newspaper and personal writings.; [pers.] I

strive to reflect the reality of todays world in my poems. I also use poems as a way of changing society view on certain matters.; [a.] Teaneck, NJ

FEDERWITZ, GLORIA
[pen.] Gloria; [b.] January 26, 1950, Marshfield, WI; [p.] Willy Federwitz, Jeri Federwitz (deceased); [ed.] V.W. of Wis Marshfield, Milworkee, and Madison; [occ.] Creative Consultant, Inspirit and Writer; [memb.] Board Member Marshfield Zoological Society, Institute of Noetic Sciences, International Women's Writers Guild, Treasure at Trust International Mfld, MACCI, Assoc. of Humanist Psy.; [hon.] Marshfield Area Visitors and Promotion Volunteer of the Year 1995 - World Congress of Women Chiropractors distinguished Women of the Year 1995; [oth. writ.] A journey of sacred spirals, lessons in abundant aliveness mandala moon (a greetings card) world congress of women chiropractors (1995) - (1996) calendar.; [pers.] When love and healing work together expect a masterpiece. Let me as a teacher of healing wholeness work with you using creative communication and artistic abundance to reveal your own inspirational presence.; [a.] Marshfield, WI

FELICIANO, CHRISTINA
[b.] June 24, 1980, Puerto Rico; [p.] Marta Malave; [occ.] High School Student from Central Park East H.J., CPESS; [hon.] Junior H.S. - First Place Art Project, Third Place in Science Fair, Art Award and Second Place in the Social Studies Fair. Central Dark East H.S. - Nineth Grade - Math and Science Awards, Writing Award and Communities Service Award; [oth. writ.] Short stories, annotuited biographies, poems for school, autobiography, history essays, time line of my pasts.; [a.] New York, NY

FELKINS, EVELYN
[b.] April 22, 1930, Ralston, OK; [p.] Frank and Annis Felkins; [ed.] Elizabeth Union High, Elizabeth, CO., Biola University, La Mirada, CA; [occ.] Retired Elementary Teacher; [oth. writ.] Several poems.; [a.] Hesperia, CA

FELL, M. J.
[b.] March 30, 1982, Marlton, NJ; [p.] Thomas and Maryanne Fell; [ed.] 8th grade student at Neeta's Jr. High School to Graduate June 1996; [occ.] Student; [memb.] Bridge, Church Youth Group, Lakers Basketball, Lakers Lacross, Medford Lakes Camp; [hon.] Mile Swim at Camp - 1993, 1994 Archery Tournament - 1993, Soccer Championship - 1992, Softball Championship 1991, Top Swimmer - 1993, 1995, Basketball Tournament - 1993, 1994, Honor Roll, MVP Tennis - 1993, Triatheton - 1992-995, Bronze Shied - 1996, Best Female Athlete - 1994, 1995.; [pers.] Mentality. It's good for your soul. Thanks to Ms. Strath and

Ms. Kool. Special thanks to Shawn who believed in me when no one else did.; [a.] Medford Lakes, NJ

FELLIE, VIRGINIA MIDDLETON
[pen.] Ginny May; [b.] January 1, 1946, Burlington, WI; [p.] Lawrence Harvey and Edna Mae (North) Middleton; [m.] Fiancee: Richard C. Van, pending; [ch.] Richard Lawrence, Florence Lorraine, Tammy Marie and Katrina Paulina Anne; [occ.] Retired and doing family research on my four natural grandparents; [hon.] Winner of Valentine's Day Happy Ad Contest, poem called "Hey You!" Herald Times Reporter Manitowoe, WI; [oth. writ.] "Saluting All Veterans of Wars", in The Herald Times Reporter, Manitowoc, WI. During the Persian Gulf Uprising. "To keep this Nation Free, published in the Treasured Poems of America, winter edition 1992, Sparrowgrass Poetry Form.; [pers.] Waiting is an opening to a universe of feelings of oneself that can be shared by others in their time of need. Doing family research has inspired the poem "Like A Rose of Winter".; [a.] Apache Junction, AZ

FELS, VIOLA M.
[pen.] Mazie; [b.] July 5, 1942, Georgia; [p.] Frances Duffey; [m.] Raymond J. Fels, February 7, 1959; [ch.] (Four daughters) Lorena M., Dorothy M., Verna M., Karen M.; [ed.] High School Equev; [occ.] Housewife would like to write for greeting cards; [memb.] Immaculate conception church; [hon.] The honor of being rays wife. The reward is my 4 daughters and 11 grandchildren.; [oth. writ.] "Memories," "Friend," "My Kitchen Table," "Spring," "Just for When," "Time," "Feet," "Life's Journey," "Forgiveness," "My Rosary," "Accepted," "When I Die."; [pers.] Love, respect, and kindness, for all we know and love. Will bring favor and reward, from God up above. Handle all hearts with the love, that you do your own. Anyone with no heart, their body has no home.; [a.] O'Fallon, MO

FELTON, PHYLLIS ANN
[pen.] Phyllis Ann Felton; [b.] April 21, 1965, Elizabeth City, NC; [p.] Hattie Elizabeth Revell, Wesley Felton Jr.; [m.] Boyfriend Micheal Tolliver Jr. plan to get married soon; [ed.] Graduated Hempstead High School, 1) Hempstead New York High School Diploma, 2) Trade School Airline Training, Thompson Career Prep 59 Main St. Port Washington, NY received a diploma in October 1983; [occ.] Produce Manager of a Salad Bar Worker of Supermarket Grand Union, in West Hempstead, New York; [memb.] None membership's yet at the present time; [hon.] I received a Gold Platinum Award at Coehmann's Department Store in Hewlett New York, 11557 in 1984 for Best Dressed and Best Worker of the Year, in Fashion and Design; [oth. writ.] Other writing's

I dove at School Plays when I was Eight and Nine years old in 1976 and 1978, years in the Fulton St. School, Hempstead, New York.; [pers.] I have been writing poems for years as a little girl and decided to send it in this year to the National Library of Poetry in Maryland.; [a.] Hempstead, NY

FELTY, KATHEE M.
[pen.] Kathee M. Felty; [b.] December 20, 1950, Chelsea, MA; [p.] Arthur J. and Margaret M. Gleason; [ch.] Christopher, Melissa, Amanda; [ed.] Wheeler High School, North Stonington, CT; [occ.] Owner of Heath Tanning Salon, Secretary, Poetry, Notary State of PA; [memb.] National Society of Poetry, International Society of Poetry; [hon.] Editors Choice Award 1995 International Poet of Merit Award 1995; [oth. writ.] "Melissa," "Taylor," "Grandmother," "Time," "Again," published in various books of the National Library of Poetry several poems published in The "Reading Eagle Times Newspaper"; [pers.] Love is the beginning and the end, the very essence of mankind. The secret of happiness. Strive to be the best you can be.; [a.] Wernersville, PA

FENN, JUDY
[pen.] Moreno; [b.] April 15, 1951, Salt Lake City, UT; [p.] Clint and Elaine Robins; [m.] Scott L. Fenn, August 8, 1990; [ch.] Anthony, Aaron, Kari, Alex-Elaine; [ed.] Nogales High School, West Covina Calif.; [occ.] Lease Sales; [memb.] N.V.L.A. (National Vehicle Leasing Association); [pers.] After 17 yrs. of being a single parent and raising my 1st 3 children alone. I've realized women should have children after the age of 40 so we are mellow enough to enjoy them!; [a.] Rowland Heights, CA

FENNELL, TIFFANIE
[b.] October 5, 1972, Philadelphia, PA; [p.] Evelyn F. Smalls and Johnie L. Fennell; [ed.] Episcopal Academy, University of Pennsylvania; [occ.] Computer Consultant; [pers.] I'm a 23 year old woman trapped in the body of a 12 year old with the mentality of a 40 year old bitter divorcee.; [a.] Wayne, PA

FERBEZAR, JANE A.
[b.] January 5, 1963, MO; [p.] Frank M. and Helen M. Ferbezar; [ed.] JC Harmon H.S. and Hollywood Scriptwriting; [occ.] Full Time Writer; [hon.] Journalism Award in H.S.; [oth. writ.] Published poem.; [pers.] Having a family that supports me, and having the needed inspiration to write from Steve P. the two things that everyone needs to make it in this world.; [a.] Kansas City, KS

FERGUESON, MAURINE
[b.] February 9, 1938, Park City, UT; [p.] Oren J. and Marie Noakes Anderson; [m.] Ernest R. Fergueson, December 9, 1967; [ch.] David W.,

Linda M., Connie N., Robert C., Judith L., Norma J.; [ed.] High School, 11th Grade; [occ.] Owner Manager Mobile Homes, M.J.N. Inc.; [memb.] ISP Distinguished Member Utah N. Apartment Assoc., Layton Area Chamber, Hill A.F.B. Military Affairs Committee; [hon.] Achievement Award, Layton Chamber, 5 Editors Choice Award, NLP Lifetime Member ISP, Inducted as an ISP Poet of Merit; [oth. writ.] NUAA Magazine "My Attitude" book Noble House parenting in the nineties and control your life. 8 poems in the NLP, including best poets of 1996. Poetry for domestic violence, missing children, victims rights. Neighborhood watch news letter "zero crime."; [pers.] God is answering most of the questions I've been asking him about life, and given me a wonderful gift. The power of the pen. He is the true author, human's are the subject.; [a.] Layton, UT

FIDDLER, JAMES CLAYTON
[b.] April 17, 1976, Bartlesville, OK; [p.] Robert and Nancy Fiddler; [ed.] Caney Valley High School; [memb.] Ramona Friends Church; [pers.] There is no dignity in conformity.; [a.] Ramona, OK

FIELDS, VILMA HOLLAND
[b.] May 17, 1929, London, England; [p.] Harold and Helen Holland; [m.] William Fentress Fields, November 15, 1951; [ch.] Graham, Fentress (twins - Fentress died at 26 years age) Kay; [ed.] London Central School Received equivalent of Junior College at age 15.; [occ.] Part-time Secretary; [memb.] Order of the Daughters of The King; [oth. writ.] Various poems Ten Dramas for performance in churches. One palm Sunday Passion Play. Six Christmas songs telling the Christmas story.; [pers.] Most of my poems were written in London during World War II. The dramas and music were written later after coming to this country. I also continued to write poems, but not as frequently as I did when younger. My writings are meant to encourage hope for better things to come to comfort and inspire.; [a.] Savannah, GA

FIGGINS, ANGELA KAY
[b.] August 3, 1967, Cincinnati, OH; [p.] Donald and Sharon Figgins; [ed.] Western Brown Sr. High, Southern State Community College; [occ.] Receptionist, Biggs Hyper Market; [memb.] All Ohio State Youth Choir Alumni; [oth. writ.] Poem, The Candle published in book Listen With Your Heart.; [pers.] To me writing is a gift God has gien to a chosen few and I feel very blest to have been given just a little of this talent to express the gift.; [a.] Amelia, OH

FILERIO, SUE CAROL
[b.] December 11, 1942, Chicago, IL; [p.] Arvel Daugherty, Margret E. Smith, step-father: Arthur Miller; [m.] Arthur E. Thomas, February 3, 1961, Victorino Filerio, April 14, 1984; [ch.]

Arvella-William, Roy-Arvel E. Thomas, step-daughter: Reene Thomas; [ed.] Libby Grade School (kindergarten), Cooksville Grade School, St. Mary's Grade School, Holy Trinity High School; [occ.] Small business owner of Sue Carol Filerio Household Prod.; [memb.] Our Lady of Lourdes Church, NRA/AARP; [hon.] Raised my children without racial pred., and are drug free. This is the biggest honor I know.; [oth. writ.] None published; [pers.] Wake up greeting the day. Think about the trials of the day. Help what I can, and what I can't put aside without worry, as it may be for someone else to deal with.; [a.] Chicago, IL

FINNELL, SCOTT
[b.] October 26, 1977; [p.] Sharon Finnell, Ted Finnell; [ed.] North Mecklenburg High; [occ.] Student; [memb.] National Honor Society, Academy of Finance; [hon.] National Young Leaders Conference, N.C. Governor's Council or Education; [oth. writ.] Assorted unpublished poems, short stories, and a feature-length film.; [pers.] I write to release certain emotions that build up within me. My favorite writers include Keroval, Poe Ayn Rand, and Shakespeare.; [a.] Huntersville, NC

FISHER, KRISTEL DAWN
[b.] January 31, 1981; [p.] Cindy Fisher and Chuck Lottes; [ed.] Washington Township High School, Pitman Middle School; [hon.] United States Achievement Academy 1993 National Awards; [pers.] "Life is what you make of it," "Live life to its fullest," "Have all the fun you can while you are here."; [a.] Blackwood, NJ

FLACK, DIANNE
[b.] January 15, 1955, Hialeah, FL; [p.] Donald Head, Barbara Head; [m.] Gary Flack, March 29, 1991; [ch.] Dale Eugene; [ed.] Bozeman High, Miles Community College, Eastern Montana College, Rocky Mountain College; [occ.] Advocate for Senior Citizens, Home-maker; [hon.] Dean's List, RMC; [pers.] People and relationships are central to my writing. "Ella" was written in tribute to my husband's mother, Ella Kracke, who died giving birth to him in 1943.; [a.] Laurel, MT

FLACK, PAULINA M.
[b.] July 4, 1926, Philadelphia, PA; [p.] John and Alice Mason; [m.] Claude H. Flack, August 28, 1954; [ch.] Claude H. Flack Jr., Patrick T. Flack and Paula F. Upchurch; [ed.] Graduated 1994 From West Philadelphia H.S., graduate January 1950, Cheyney State Teachers College; [occ.] Retired Teacher, Philadelphia School System; [memb.] Belong to the Drama Club on Cheyney Campus, stared in "Nine Girl", also belong to Youth Temperance Club; [hon.] I recited "Fifty Years" by James Weldon Johnson at a dedication ceremony for the colored

Soldiers Monument in Philadelphia's Fairmount Park; [pers.] I felt that a written voice was needed, so America would know that affirmative action is a very important bill. I was greatly influenced by James Weldon Johnson and Paul L. Dunbar, who wrote about this social problem many years ago.; [a.] Philadelphia, PA

FLAHERTY, JAMES E.
[pen.] James Flaherty; [b.] July 4, 1925, Boston, MA; [p.] James and Mary Flaherty; [m.] Elinor M. Flaherty Nee Flynn, November 17, 1951; [ch.] Charles, Jean, Anne, Jamie; [ed.] Boston University 1952 Journalism, Certificate in Computer Programming from IBM; [occ.] Retired Computer Technical Writer and Sales Executive; [memb.] Veteran Foreign Wars, Caterpillar Club, Society of Technical Writers and Publishers; [hon.] Aside from a few medals from WW II, none; [oth. writ.] A host of books and writings on Electronic Equipment, Manuals on re-entry vehicle and Rocket support equipment and hardware and software manuals on computers.; [pers.] All my life I have been avid reader, and I believe reading is one of the great pleasures in life.; [a.] Annapolis, MD

FLANAGAN, TIMOTHY MARTIN
[b.] September 21, 1951, Saint Louis, MO; [p.] Lois Jean Wilson, James Martin Flanagan; [ed.] B.A. English at Northern Arizona University, also studied at Antioch University, University of Missouri and Cal Poly Pomona; [occ.] Writer, Teacher; [memb.] Amnesty International, ACLU, Hair Salon Student Community; [hon.] Graduated Cum Laude, Dean's List, Member Phi Kappa Phi, Golden Key National Honor Society, have completed CRLA Master Tutor Certificate; [oth. writ.] Published in Surrey Poems News, Montana Kaimin, Missoualian, Missoula Independent, The Lumberwalk, The Daily Sun; [pers.] I write poetry, short stories, essays and guest columns on a variety of subjects.; [a.] Missoula, MT

FLANNIGAN, SHANNON MARIE
[b.] April 16, 1983, Edina, MN; [p.] John and Vicki Flannigan; [ed.] I currently attend St. Odilia School where I am involved in Sports, Drama and Literature; [occ.] Student; [hon.] I have received local awards for writing and have been recognized for my athletic ability.; [oth. writ.] I have written a series of poems that are not yet published.; [pers.] I have been inspired by my teachers David Fink and Jack Kreitzer, also my best friends Anne Murnane Dybsky and Molly Costanzo.; [a.] North Oaks, MN

FLETCHER, JOHN L.
[b.] January 27, 1932, Raton, NM; [p.] Lynn H. and Mable L. Fletcher; [m.] Judith A. Fletcher, August 4, 1965; [ch.] John, Danelle, Collett, Michelle, Beth and Kathy; [ed.] 12

yrs.; [memb.] A.M.A. and I.M.M.A.; [oth. writ.] Numerous poems

FLOURNOY JR., MALORY

[b.] January 6, 1954, Saint Louis, MO; [p.] Malory Flournoy Sr., Lelia Mae Harris; [ch.] Joy Janelle and Janine Michelle; [ed.] Hoover High (S.D. CA), Univ. Maryland, Central Texas College (Japan); [occ.] Asst. Store Manager; [pers.] I find enjoyment to be able to inspire pleasant feelings and thoughts through the aura of my poetry.

FLOWERS, J. C.

[pen.] Bouquet Kid; [b.] November 16, 1948, Broken Bow, OK; [p.] Edward Lloyd Flowers (deceased), Tilda S. Goodman-Flowers); [m.] X-Ethel Jane Sanders, September 4, 1969; [ch.] Kevin Lane, Lloyd Dale (deceased), Jason Charles, Melissa Dawn, Jeffrey Gregory; [ed.] Holly Creek Elementary - First through Eighth, Idabel Gray High - Ninth through Twelfth; [occ.] Supervisor at Pilgrim's Pride Poultry Processing plant in Dequeen, AR; [memb.] Eddie Lou Cole's World of Poetry - Honorable Mention in 1991 three times, Honorable Mention in 1990 two times, Honorable Mention in 1989, 1985, 1984 one time, Golden Poet Award in 1989; [oth. writ.] Several poe published in a books by Eddie Lou Cole, National Library of Poetry still has others yet to be published.; [pers.] Without God nothing would exist. He is the Creator and Father of all things. No need to question his works. Many people believe things done or said is from self alone. This is not so. I believe, God's purpose or reason for happenings is to teach all. Ideas an thoughts with knowledge and wisdom comes from the Almighty God. Any burden or hindrance (all obstacles in life) can be overcome for God is there when no one is. I thank God for life above all things and know without him I would not be on earth. No offence friend but it is something to think about while living on earth.; [a.] Broken Bow, OK

FLOWERS, JESSE

[pen.] The Maximus; [b.] April 11, 1964, Salem, NJ; [p.] Jesse and Leona Flowers; [m.] Kim Flowers, May 1993; [ch.] Lara Ashley; [ed.] Penns Grove High, Rowan College; [occ.] Forklift driver, somewhere in New Jersey; [memb.] No membership affiliations of any kind; [hon.] Captain, Penns Grove High Rutgers Bowl Team, Scholars Program, National Merit Scholarship Semi-Finalist; [pers.] I think of my poems as epigrammatic and sometimes tend to be alliterative because I think that even though rhyme isn't necessary, the juxtaposition of similar words is still a compelling feature of poetry.; [a.] Alloway, NJ

FLURSCHUTZ, KELLY L.

[b.] October 17, 1968, Atlanta, GA; [p.] Mr. George and Mrs. Ruth Flurschutz; [ed.] Guesleyan College 2 years Macon, GA, Georgia State University Final 3 Years, Stone Mountain High; [occ.] Art Teacher at Woodridge Elementary; [memb.] In Dekalb Co., National Art Education Association, Member of Decatur First United Methodist Church in Decatur; [hon.] President National Art Honor Society at Stone MTN High School, Second Place Greeting Card Design at Stone Mountain Park. Honorable Mention on Portrait Exhibited at Wesleyan College; [a.] Stone Mountain, GA

FLYNN, VICKI

[pen.] Vicki Anderson-Flynn; [b.] October 13, 1947, Saint Louis, MO; [p.] Charlie Ray and Virginia Lee; [m.] Harold Flynn, January 8, 1966; [ch.] Sheree Leanne, Jody Stephen, Jason Harold; [ed.] Festus Senior High, American School of Cosmetology, Jefferson College; [occ.] Free lance Interior Decorator; [pers.] I think that life itself is worth writing about. I have always seen the beauty of words that come to me when I see my husbands and eldest son's drawings and when my youngest son sings or plays the piano.; [a.] Imperial, MO

FOGLIA, SILVINO

[b.] September 6, 1935, Naples, Italy; [p.] Domenic Foglia, Bianca Foglia; [m.] Gail Foglia, April 18, 1964; [ch.] Jennifer Foglia; [ed.] B.S. Physics, Mechanical Engineer, Graduate work in Physics; [occ.] President, Sport Oceanic Technologies Corp.; [oth. writ.] Many poems and articles.; [pers.] To live from the spirit within, for it is only in the spirit that we can become truly aware of our Creator's presence and His infinite love for us. To forgive and to love unconditionally. To be honest and a person of integrity, to help others in all what I do. To give to the world the many and many inventions I made thanks to the limitless, incredible mind and imagination that God has given me.; [a.] Jupiter, FL

FRANKLIN, HEATHER

[pen.] Echo Marie; [b.] July 30, 1978, Knoxville, TN; [p.] Thomas Franklin Sr., Evelyn Franklin; [memb.] Civil Air Patrol, USAF Auxiliary. I also do a number of other things that aren't really memberships; [hon.] Several rank increasements in Civil Air Patrol; [oth. writ.] A few other poems, short and long stories.; [pers.] The poem, war's regret was written for and in honor of my grandfather Emmett L. Waller.; [a.] Youngstown, OH

FRASER, STACEY

[pen.] S. A. Fraser; [b.] October 8, 1981, Concord, MA; [p.] Paul Fraser Jr. and Charlene Fraser; [ed.] W. Diamond Junior High School (current School); [occ.] Student; [memb.] First Baptist Church, Lexington MA, International Order of the Rainbow for Girls, Lexington Assembly #37; [oth. writ.] School - and church - published poems.; [pers.] Thanks to my family, my school homies, my church friends, my rainbow and demolay crew, and my father in heaven.; [a.] Lexington, MA

FREEMAN, ELAINE S.

[b.] January 26, 1020, Burlette, AR; [p.] Percy Stanfield, Dovie Cole Standard; [m.] Elwood A. Freeman, March 23, 1962; [ch.] Woody Freeman, Brooks Freeman, Dee Freeman, Lynda Freeman; [ed.] Luxora High School, Memphis School of Commerce; [occ.] Housewife, (Retired Officer of family-owned competition); [memb.] First Christian Church, Jonesboro, Arkansas Christian Women's Fellowship, several Bridge Clubs; [oth. writ.] None submitted for publication. Other poems written: An Ode to a birthday celebration, Night Reckoning, That Man and His Dog, Housewife's Dilemma, How Can We Cherish the Children.; [pers.] I seem to think in rhyme. My poems almost write themselves. Often I get out of bed and write them down so I won't forget them. It's a wonderful world out there. Let's not mess it up!!; [a.] Jonesboro, AR

FRENCH, ANITA J.

[pen.] Anita J. French; [b.] November 23, 1942, York, ME; [p.] Barbara Greene and Richard Wiggin; [m.] Terry M. French, July 5, 1963; [ch.] Eric McArthur, Brian Scott and Teri Lee; [ed.] York High School; [occ.] National Arbor Day Foundation; [oth. writ.] "Let it be angels" (National Library of Poetry - walk through paradise) two unpublished poems, "Me" and "twas the good old days." Am currently working on others.; [pers.] I am very concerned with what is going on in the world today, not only with the destruction of the lands but of its people as well. I am optimistic though, that the day will come, when we all realize, it is never too late to bring it all to an end.; [a.] Canasteta, NY

FRENCH, COREY

[b.] December 2, 1975; [occ.] Musician; [pers.] I love to reflect on the twisted, changing seasons of our emotions.

FRIDRIKSSON, GERI K.

[b.] January 31, 1954, Nampa, ID; [m.] Gudmundur Fridriksson, December 28, 1991; [ch.] Skyler Odinn Fridriksson born February 1, 1993; [ed.] Boise High, Boise State University, Brian Utting School of Massage; [occ.] Homemaker; [oth. writ.] Poems; [a.] Anacortes, WA

FRIESEN, KRISTY LEIGH

[b.] September 3, 1959, Grougeville, ID; [p.] Dave and Dee Friesen; [m.] Steve Ritchie; [ch.] David Friesen, Dan Friesen, Zach Ritchie; [occ.] Domestic Engineer; [oth. writ.] My Christmas Gift, Rejoice, Save Me From Falling, A

Valentine Poem, My Son, Kiss For Kristy, I'm Just A Little Doggie; [pers.] I'm an adopted child raised by very loving parents who have provided me with a wealth of, "life's tools" enabling me to enjoy life to its fullest.. these same tools are now helping me with my birth family which has surfaced by coincidence.; [a.] Boise, ID

FUCHS, WALTER
[pen.] Wally; [b.] March 15, 1919, Chicago; [p.] Deceased; [m.] Marie M. Fuchs, February 8, 1947; [ch.] Four Daughters; [ed.] Four yrs. High School various Schools in the W.S. Army, Sign painting Self taught Oil Painting; [occ.] Retired Sign Painter, [memb.] American Legion Post Courde also V.F.W., Pres, Men's Club, Bolingbrook Senior Citizen of Bolingbrook; [hon.] High score in Bowling, 3rd Highest Center of Il. in .F.W. American Air Award Gold Medal in golf, Lightweight changes in Golden glove; [oth. writ.] Love to write poetry letters and retired to painting oil landscape portraits. In praise and love to be a leader.; [pers.] Right now I'm 77 and brave, I have a very sick wife, must stay with her. I can't afford to spend much money. So please understand my situation.

FULCO, TRACI L.
[b.] June 26, 1974; [p.] Wayne and Sonia Marsh; [m.] George W. Fulco, January 7, 1994; [ch.] Crystal Fulco and Hunter Fulco; [ed.] Scurry - Rosser High School Graduate; [occ.] Housewife; [oth. writ.] I have been writing since I was around 12 years I have many poems. This is my second publication.; [pers.] The death of a friend inspired me to write my first poem and I have written ever since.; [a.] Scurry, TX

FULGONEY, SANDRA LEE
[pen.] Samantha Alexander; [b.] March 24, 1947, Danville, PA; [p.] Ruth and Sidney Steinberger; [m.] John F. Fulgoney, March 21, 1981; [ch.] Nicholas and Rebecca; [ed.] B.A., Penn State University 1972; [occ.] Homemaker raising two young teens, owner of "Fanny Robin Artisan's Gallery; [oth. writ.] Published two poems in "Era", journal, University of Pennsylvania, 1979.; [pers.] With my poetry, I hope to emotionally grasp a moment in dream - like time and then paint pictures with sounds and word combinations.; [a.] Pittsburgh, PA

FULLER, DOLORES M.
[b.] August 1, 1931, Omaha, NB; [p.] Edward J. Stehno Sr., Anna J. Stehno; [m.] Theodore J. Fuller, October 1, 1955; [ch.] Deborah Ann; [pers.] Life is a gift from God. May it always be cherished, lived well, enjoyed and shared with others. Thank you given first to God my creator, my parents, family and friends.; [a.] Los Angeles, CA

FUNKHOUSER JR., DAVID L.
[b.] August 30, 1954, Pennsylvania; [m.] Debra

Gail, July 25, 1975; [ch.] Victoria (22), David (19), Daniel (9), Jonathan (7); [ed.] Graduated from Bladensburg High School, Bladensburg MD; [occ.] Disabled Due to Back Injury; [pers.] If you live for the Lord and give him your best heaven awaits you when you take your last breath.; [a.] Pulaski, VA

FURGUIELE, ANDREA
[b.] May 1, 1976, New York; [p.] Anthony and Cecilia Furguiele; [occ.] Student of Florida Atlantic University; [hon.] First Place Winner of Poetry Contest in High School. Received Second Place Trophy for Palm Beach County; [pers.] In Charge of poetry karaoke.; [a.] Boca Raton, FL

FURGUIELE, FRANCIS
[pen.] Francesco Furguiele; [b.] January 18, 1958, Covina, CA; [p.] Joseph Furguiele and Patricia L. Bissonnette; [occ.] Installation and Repair Technician with GTE Customer Networks Long Beach, CA; [pers.] I would like to dedicate this publication of my first poem to Ariana Kalina, for whom the poem was written, and to my mother, Patricia Louise Bissonnette. I am also interested, and studying about the famous Italian Poet Francesco Petrarch.; [a.] Long Beach, CA

GADD, DEBBIE
[pen.] Anna Carey; [b.] October 16, 1965, Devon, England; [p.] Gill and Charles Knape; [m.] Nicholas Gadd, August 27, 1988; [ed.] BSC. (hons) Animal Science, London; [occ.] Student, Pre Veterinary Science; [memb.] Golden Key National Honor Society; [hon.] Presidential Scholar, Dean's List, University of Georgia; [pers.] Fulfill your dreams by stretching to reach the stars, and never ever give up hope.; [a.] Athens, GA

GALLAGHER, LINDA BARBARA
[pen.] Beautiful Stranger; [b.] December 30, 1965, West Palm Beach, FL; [p.] Roe Schefezuk and William A. Wilson III; [m.] Divorced; [ch.] William (19), Barbara (15), Edward (12), Lisa (10); [ed.] 11th Year High School and Beauty School; [occ.] Unemployed Homemaker, Single Parent; [oth. writ.] The Christmas That Last A Lifetime, Scranton Times and Church Bulletin, Trinity Lutheran, A Parents Prayer Church Bulletin, Grace Lutheran Church Hop Bottom, Prayer For Healing, Alone One and AA.; [pers.] I hope I see Gods grace return to this world. I'm a survivor of domestic abuse and violence my writing is inspired by my love for God and his gifts of peace. I hope to write christian books in the future.; [a.] Nicholson, PA

GANDY JR., CHOYCE W.
[b.] December 7, 1948, Jasper, TX; [p.] Choyce W. Gandy Sr. and Eva Gandy; [ch.] Stephen Gandy, Kandy Burrows, Tammy Pelt; [ed.] High School, Buna High School, Buna Texas, College Lamar University, Beaumont Texas

Masters Criminal Justice (Law Enforcement) I.C.S. Engineering; [occ.] Police Officer; [oth. writ.] Book "The Fourteenth Summer" being received by the TEXAS Wide Writers, Byliners of Corpus Christi book of poetry not published but finished called "Passing The Torch" weekly news paper columns.; [pers.] My writing is inspired by God and it is my prayer that everything I write will be to His glory and Honor.; [a.] Vidor, TX

GARCIA, BLANCA
[pen.] September 10, 1980; [p.] Al and Bertha Murillo; [occ.] Student (Sophomore) at Cathedral City High School; [hon.] May 1988 Student of the Month of Yerington Elementary School, May 1992 at Nellie Coffman Middle School; [pers.] My inspiration is about love, sadness and romance. "To some people saying I love you is easy but then again to some people it's hard to accept it"; [a.] Cathedral City, CA

GARCIA, DIANE INEZ
[b.] December 20, 1976, Downey, CA; [p.] George and Inez Garcia; [ed.] La Serna High Fullerton College; [occ.] Mortgage Company Loan Processor; [memb.] American Heart Association, American Rifle Association, Blackbelt Club; [oth. writ.] Several poems, poems exposed in public newspapers unknown.; [pers.] I strife on reflecting my writing by the way I feel and the environment I'm in. I feel the best thing the future is that it only comes one day at a time.; [a.] La Mirada, CA

GARCIA, SANTOS FRAUSTO
[pen.] Santos F. Garcia; [b.] March 21, 1944, Stamford, TX; [p.] Francisco M. and Josefa F. Garcia; [m.] Graciela Lumbreras Garcia, April 12, 1969; [ch.] One girl, two boys, one grand-daughter; [ed.] H.S. G.E.D. Two Associates, Data processing/Programming; [occ.] Computer Operator, [memb.] Knights of Columbus; [oth. writ.] Other unpublished poems at home; [pers.] To write a poem, one must be inspired. To be inspired, there must be reality. Mine was a beautiful lady, named Laurel Ann Carnine. Thank you Laurel; [a.] Silverton, OR

GARCIA, TERESA GUINN
[pen.] Irish; [b.] May 31, 1948, Shreveport, LA; [p.] Gwen/Troy Uzzell and late William Ed Guinn; [m.] Frank Garcia; [ed.] Texas City High, University of Texas, TWU, Galveston College; [occ.] Nurse/Med. Transcription - UTMB Family Healthcare Cntr. - TX City, TX; [memb.] TNA, AAMT, TAMT, GHAC, various "Forever Knight" Clubs, and President of "Fans of Forever Knight" - Texas, Sec. - "Beauty and the Southeast Texas Beast" Fan Club; [hon.] Various Military/Medical Awards; [oth. writ.] Complete books/poetry collections: 1) "Forever Immortal - Forever Love," 2) On

Wing and Stranger Things," 3) "Under the Looking Glass and into the Stars," 4) Lyrics for Musical Score; [pers.] I write to carry on a family legacy, to honor those subjects about whom I write, and to let mankind know that we all have hidden talents that make us the artful individuals we are. I owe thanks to Zoe, Geraint, and Nigel for mine.; [a.] LaMargue, TX

GATCHELL JR., JOHN
[pen.] John Hamilton; [b.] September 24, 1952, Kansas City, MO; [p.] John H. and Betty J.; [ed.] John Marshall High School south Okc Jr. College, on state grant; [occ.] The Arts; [memb.] The Smithsonian, National Trust for Historic Preservation, National Air and Space Museum, The International Society of Poets, Save the Children; [hon.] 1994 and 1995 "Editor's Choice Awards" from the National Library of Poetry; [oth. writ.] My works of poetry have been published by the National Library of Poetry, several times, as well as the Sparrowgrass Poetry Forum.; [pers.] My writings outline the book of life, today so happy, so wonderful, and tomorrow so ugly, so blue. Balance. My favorite authors are easy ones to categorize, renaissance.; [a.] Oklahoma City, OK

GAYDEN, CAROL JANETTE HICKMAN
[pen.] Net, Net-Net, Brave, Nem, Coach, Red; [b.] June 16, 1958, Bishopville, SC; [p.] Rebecca Lesane - James Hickmon; [m.] Tony Gayden, June 26, 1993; [ch.] Lapetria and Shunlekee Pendleton, Steven Brown Jr., Amanda Scott, Donald Williamson Jr., Kyndall Johnston, and Johnathan Candice Smith; [ed.] Alcorn State University - Lorman MS - BS., Troy State Univ., William Paterson College, Kean College, Jersey City State College; [occ.] Educator - Eastside High School of Paterson, New Jersey; [memb.] Faith Chapel Reform Church, Delta Sigma Theta Sorority, Inc., National Education Association, New Jersey Education Association, Passaic County Coaches Association; [hon.] Woman of the Year - Counselor of the Summer - College Dean's List - Track and Field Coach, Grandparents - Florine and Marion Scott and Rebecca and August Hickmon

GENNARDO, PETER
[pen.] "Chaz"; [b.] May 29, 1963, Brooklyn NY; [p.] Maria L. and Francis K. Gennardo; [ch.] Godfather of Joseph Carmine Barra (Godson and Nephew); [ed.] Bachelor of Arts in Psychology Adelphi University School of Arts and Sciences, May 1986; [occ.] Habilitation Specialist Practitioner and MaryHaven Center of Hope, Riverhead, NY; [memb.] Chapter Advisor -Kappa Theta/TKE Honorary Membership - Tau Kappa Epsilon M.C.S.A. Basketball coach, Junior Division Champions 1991-1993; [hon.] Sportsmanship Award, 1977, Suffolk Lutheran Basketball Champions, 1980, Aggie Spirit

Award, 1983, Most Active Senior Award - Adelphi U., 1986, Student Life Award - Adelphi U., 1986, Leadership Recognition Award - Adelphi U., 1986, Outstanding Service - Adelphi U., 1988, Hoop It Up Championship, 1990; [oth. writ.] "The Pressure Is On", published in the Delphian Newspaper and Adelphi U., 1988, "Without Your Love", published in the Rambler Newspaper and S.U.N.Y. and Farmingdale, NY, 1982; [pers.] "I started writing poetry in 1975. At that time I did it for fun. Later, writing poetry became the most effective way for me to express my inner feelings from my heart. Now, it is passion filled throughout my mind and body. Through my heart and soul. Through my thoughts and dreams.; [a.] Centereach, NY

GENTRY, CHRISTY L. WILLIAMS
[b.] March 4, 1970, Arlington, TX; [p.] Mr. and Mrs. Robert B. Williams; [m.] Benjie Gentry, June 8, 1996; [ed.] High School - Cleburne H.S. - Cleb., TX College - McMurry University, Abilene, TX; [occ.] English Teacher, Coach - Mineola, TX Mineola Middle School; [memb.] Texas State Teachers Association; [oth. writ.] Several poems and writings in college publication.; [pers.] I try to instill my innermost feelings and ideas and beliefs in my work. I believe the most appreciated poets do.; [a.] Brentwood, TN

GIACOIA III, VINCENT D.
[pen.] Van Giacoia; [b.] November 5, 1970, Southampton, NY; [p.] Vincent and Dorothy Giacoia; [ed.] BS in Architectural Technology from New York, Institute of Technology; [occ.] Caretaker; [memb.] Omega Delta Phi Fraternity; [hon.] 3rd prize in east Hampton Airport Student Design Contest; [pers.] Light once shined, but the bulb blew out, so I found a new one, and it shined too, then it blew out.; [a.] Hampton Bays, NY

GIBBS, AUDREY R.
[b.] December 7, 1927, Vermont; [p.] Eva and Roger Keenan; [m.] Warren T. Gibbs, December 27, 1945; [ch.] Three Girls and One Boy; [ed.] Grade School, Chareston, VT; [occ.] Homemaker; [memb.] Greater Plymouth Association for Retarded Citizens of Plymouth, MA; [hon.] Mother of the Year May 6, 1993, as I have a C.P. son I have taken care of for 37 years at home; [pers.] My handicap son has influenced my writing a great deal. I have learned patience and how to accept his handicap.; [a.] Plymouth, MA

GIBBY, LISA M.
[b.] August 30, 1980, Texas City, TX; [p.] Michael and Karin Gibby; [ed.] Current Student at Texas City High School, Texas City, TX; [occ.] Texas City High School Student; [memb.] Texas City Band Organization; [hon.] Consistent Honour Rolls, VIL Honours, Principal's Scholar Award, Rotary Club Awards,

Superintendent's Award; [oth. writ.] Numerous poems and prose pieces.; [pers.] I believe that I have been influenced most by the Macalb writings of Poe, Ayn Rand and Oscar Wilde. My favorite poems, however, are by Rudyard Kipling.; [a.] Texas City, TX

GIDISH, TERRY ALLEN
[b.] May 4, 1952, Washington, DC; [p.] John and Marjorie Gidish; [m.] Laura Ann Gidish; [ch.] Michael and Diana; [occ.] Mechanical Foreman; [memb.] Church of Jesus Christ of Latter Day Saints; [pers.] My poems reflect the deepest feelings in my heart. Love and God top the list and so most of my poetry ends up revolving around these two subjects; [a.] Fort Washington, MD

GIFFORD, STEVE BALLE
[b.] February 10, 1973, Marion, IN; [p.] Thomas Gifford, Linda Gifford; [m.] Mary Balle-Gifford, February 18, 1995; [ch.] Dorian Kai; [ed.] Marion High School, Ball State University, Indiana University; [occ.] Student, Graphics Editor, Indiana Daily Student; [oth. writ.] Published in a local poetry magazine. More poetry available on the World Wide Web at http://copper.ucs.indiana.edu/sgifford.; [pers.] A student of Yusef Komunyakaa. I owe a great debt to him, as well as Lawrence Ferlinghetti for all their writings, and for that matter anyone who has ever taken pen in hand to bear their soul.; [a.] Bloomington, IN

GIGLIA, SHEILA D.
[b.] June 11, 1962, Batesville, AR; [p.] Quincy and Shirley Floyd; [m.] Wayne Giglia, April 19, 1986; [ch.] Jerry Andrew and Alyssa Michelle; [ed.] Jacksonville High, Jacksonville, AR; [occ.] Property - Office Manager, Alpharetta, GA; [memb.] Cross of Life Lutheran Church, Roswell, GA; [hon.] High School Honor grad, Jr. High Speech Awards Musical Achievements (Jr. and High School); [oth. writ.] "Loneliness", "The Horizon"; [a.] Alpharetta, GA

GILBERT, PAMELA SUE
[b.] June 24, 1956, Fort Campbell, KY; [p.] Jurrien J. Potter, Gwen Terrell; [m.] Alvin Gilbert, January 18, 1991; [ch.] Christie Fugate, Granddaughter Courtney Wright; [ed.] GED/ Lees College, Morehead State University after Morehead, hopefully Law School; [occ.] Right now, I'm getting my B.A. Degree at Morehead State University, KY; [memb.] Non-traditional Eagles Society, Societas Pro Legibus, Breakthrough Ministries, Phi Theta Kappa; [hon.] Dean's List, Division of Humanities Award, Who's Who Among Students in American Junior Colleges, Recognition Award for Student Government Association, Recognition Award for Phi Theta Kappa; [oth. writ.] Wrote some short stories and poems which are in musings: The Lees College Journal of Arts and Letters;

[pers.] I want to give special thanks to Maude Cornett, and M. Kay Miller for their help and encouragement.; [a.] Booneville, KY

GILL, HEATHER P.
[b.] January 23, 1960, Barbados; [p.] Stanley Gill and Anita Stevenson; [ch.] Christopher Gill; [ed.] Modern High School, Barbados West Indies, Montgomery College, Rockville, Maryland; [occ.] Library Assistant; [oth. writ.] I have written several poems - some published by National Library of Poetry, I am currently writing a book.; [pers.] My poetry usually reflects the serious side of everyday life. Sometimes I reflect on the many faces of love.; [a.] Silver Spring, MD

GITCHEL, SARAH
[b.] May 28, 1981, Butterworth Hos.; [p.] Nancy Gitchel; [ed.] Freshman at Kenowa Hills High School; [oth. writ.] I write children's stories none which have been published but open for offers.; [pers.] I'm in the process of writing my own book all which will include my original poems.; [a.] Grand Rapids, MI

GITTENS JR., JOSEPH
[pen.] Joseph Gittens Jr.; [b.] October 16, 1961, Newark, NJ; [p.] Gwendolyn and Joseph Sr.; [ed.] Essex Catholic High School (East Orange, NJ), Rutgers University (New Jersey), Elizabeth General Hospital School of Nursing (presently); [occ.] Nursing student, employee at Hackensack University Medical Center (Hackensack, NJ); [memb.] I am a member of Trinity United Methodist Church in Newark, NJ; [hon.] Dean's List, Spring 1982, Rutgers University, Football Team - Essex Catholic High School, Football Team - Rutgers University, presently a High School Football Official, Soccer Team - Essex Catholic High, Chess Club - Essex Catholic High; [oth. writ.] Letters to the Editor published in Jet Magazine, Ebony Magazine, Newark Star Ledger Newspaper, Rutgers University School Paper, Irvington Herald Newspaper; [pers.] I've always loved music, sports, chess, and writing. Those disciplines are expressions of creativity I enjoy. I will probably work as a health care worker for the rests of my working life (in one capacity or another).; [a.] Newark, NJ

GLOVER, AMIE
[b.] Plano, TX; [p.] Joe and Lynn Glover; [ed.] Home School; [oth. writ.] Several pieces published in local newsletters.; [pers.] Don't worry be happy!; [a.] Dallas, TX

GOBAR, GAIL TAMARA
[b.] November 4, 1940, Bronx, NY; [m.] Seymour Gobar, November 10, 1962; [ch.] Bonnie Deborah, Tammy Dana; [ed.] RN, N.Y. Med. Coll. and Flower and Fifth Ave. Hosp., 1961, EdD; [occ.] Registered Nurse; [hon.] Rhyme U., Buffalo, 1985; [a.] Lakewood, NJ

GOBAR, GAIL T.
[b.] November 4, 1940, Bronx, NY; [p.] Anne and Jack Ossin (Deceased); [m.] Seymour Gobar, November 10, 1962; [ch.] Bonnie (30), Tammy (27); [ed.] Graduate Roosevelt H.S., Yonkers, NY, graduate N.Y. Medical College and Flower Fifth Ave. Hospital, NY, Registered Nurse, Ed (Hon) Rhyme University, Buffalo, NY; [occ.] R.N., Writer; [memb.] Lakewood Republican Club, Ocean County Board of Elections, Board of Directors Congregation Dove 'V' Schmuel, FFAH Nurses Alumni Assoc.; [hon.] Listed in 'Who's Who of American Women and Who's Who in American Nursing, Ocean County Girl Scouts Hidden Heroine Award - 1976, N.J. Assistance To Handicapped Award 1984, Rotary Speakers Award, 1985; [oth. writ.] Newspaper Columnist, Ocean County, N.J. - 1978-81, a number of writings printed in local newspapers over the years.; [pers.] I inherited a knack for writing from my father, who never had an opportunity to develop his talent. I dedicate all my writings to him - with love. Am currently writing a book on my version of 'motherhood.'; [a.] Lakewood, NJ

GODBEY, TINA
[b.] June 27, 1970, Saint Louis, MO; [p.] Charles E. and Sally Godbey; [ed.] Pacific High School; [memb.] The Fraternal Order of Eagles, Ladies Auxiliary; [oth. writ.] A variety of poems and free-style writings ranging from romance to fantasy, I hope to share in the future.; [pers.] To live through the words of poetry sets no limits between fantasy and reality. The imagination is only but one burning ember of a dream.; [a.] Pacific, MO

GODFREY, CRAIG
[pen.] Godfrey Finch; [b.] October 5, 1965; [p.] Jan and Todd Godfrey; [occ.] Officer, Veranda Construction; [pers.] In writing poetry or other works, I am influenced by everyday life: The challenges and how we overcome them....the joys and how we embrace them.; [a.] Houston, TX

GOFF, AUDREY DIANE
3[b.] June 4, 1949, Springfield, TN; [p.] Aubrey and Dollie Moon; [ch.] Brian Goff and Angela Cabarcas; [ed.] Springfield High, Baptist Hospital School of Nursing, Belmont College; [occ.] Information Systems Analyst for State of TN - Dept of Transportation; [memb.] Springfield Baptist Church; [oth. writ.] Poem for Church Bulletin; [pers.] I want my writings to remind others of laughter, loving or living with kindness, thoughtfulness or giving. May it inspire you to live life to its very fullest. The work of Helen Steiner Rice has been a great influence to me.; [a.] Springfield, TN

GOHLKE, WILLIAM R.
[b.] November 30, 1945, Long Beach, CA; [p.] Ole and Stephanne Gohlke; [ed.] Masters in Business Administration - Woodbury University, Bachelor of Arts - Calif., State University Northridge, Associate of Arts - Glendale Community College; [occ.] Real Estate Investor and Developer; [memb.] Brown and Root Gold Club and Sandpiper Mens Golf Club; [hon.] Wall Street Journal Award - Woodbury University, Outstanding Graduate - Glendale Community College, Dean's List - Glendale Community College; [oth. writ.] Author of brown and root golf club newsletter "in the cart"; [pers.] This poem is dedicated to my mother, Stephanne, and reflects about our travels and life.; [a.] Burbank, CA

GRABRYSZEWSKI, MIKE
[b.] November 22, 1948, Chicago; [p.] Barbara and Stanley Gabryszewski; [m.] Bonnie, August 29, 1970; [ch.] Mike and Carrie; [ed.] BA Psychology and Education, Northeastern Illinois University, MA Administration, Roosevelt University; [occ.] Teacher - Thomas Middle School - LA and Social Studies.; [memb.] Greenpeace, Amnesty International.; [oth. writ.] Poems, short stories and a novel in the works.; [pers.] Nothing is simple. What is inside us is complex and webbed. I have been influenced by Leonard Cohen and Kurt Vonnegont, men of conscience and vision.; [a.] Mandelein, IL

GRAFF, MINDA S.
[pen.] Selmer; [b.] July 7, 1916, Berkeley, CA; [p.] Bjarne H. and Lillian E. Graff; [ed.] University High in Oakland, CA, U.C.L.A., U.C. Berkeley, UCSF, B.S. in Nursing, "Biola" (Bible Institute of L.A.), Teaching Credential from U.C.; [occ.] Formerly school nurse, teacher, in Kenya and California, Retired-currently; [memb.] Valley Community Church in Napa, American Legion, Alumni Assoc. UC Nursing School, Wycliffe Assoc., CEF, NCF-IVCF; [hon.] Honorable discharge from Navy Nurse Corps WW2, Winner of contest for lyrics for Veteran's hymns, Home Member of Year Award Veterans Home CA 1991; [oth. writ.] Several poems published in "Observatim Post" - Vet. Home bimonthly publication.; [pers.] I like to write poems that reflect my struggles, solutions, and beliefs. I like to write for encouragement to others.; [a.] Yountville, CA

GRAHAM, JERUSHIA L.
[b.] March 16, 1978, Fort Jackson, SC; [p.] Jerry and Miriam Graham; [ed.] Albritton Jr. High, Jonesboro High; [occ.] Full time High School Student to be attending College in the fall of 96; [memb.] Beta Club, 1995-96 Olympic Dream Team, etc.; [hon.] NCTE Award of Achievement in writing, Georgia Governor's Honor Program Participant, Good Citizen Award - Daughters of the American Revolution (DAR), etc.; [pers.] I communicate through the medium of visual art as well as through my

writing. Regardless of how my personal experiences are communicated, I strive to create works that excite and encourage the emotions of a large variety of people.; [a.] Jonesboro, GA

GRAMMER, JENNIFER C.
[b.] November 17, 1980; [p.] Bill and Renee Grammer; [ed.] I'm in the 9th Grade in High School; [occ.] Student; [hon.] First Place Honor and Award for Poetry in a Reflections Contest in 1993. Title: "Imagine That I Was An Angel."; [oth. writ.] "I Dreamed That I Was In Heaven" was published in an October issue of Vital Christianity.; [pers.] With my many illnesses I hope to inspire others through my Poetry not to give up. I would also like other teenagers who have chronic illnesses to know they're not alone. I want to thank God, my family, friends, and special Doctors for helping me through my trials and for being there for me.; [a.] Independence, MS

GRANT, NORMAN WAYNE
[b.] January 15, 1945, Hope, AR; [p.] Norman E. and Ora F. Grant; [m.] Mary Susan "Rowe" Grant, August 7, 1964; [ch.] Terry Wayne, Kerry Lynn; [ed.] Hope High, Red River VoTech Pearl River Jr. College; [occ.] Evangelist, Barber Hair Stylist; [memb.] Assemblies of the Lord Jesus Christ, Phi Beta Lambda (Past President) Boy Scout board for Troop 77 Insoma Council, Chaplain Pearl River Co. MS Law Enforcement Agency and past Pres. of so Ms. Hair Assoc.; [hon.] Dean's List, Honor Grad., Who's Who in Amer. Colleges and University's; [oth. writ.] Several poems and songs (not published), articles for Weekly Church Bulettin.; [pers.] I strive to promote love, joy, beauty and happiness for all mankind and to be proud of America. I've written since age 11 and influenced by poets and above all my father and mother.; [a.] Covington, LA

GRASS, HOLLY SHEREE
[b.] July 25, 1976, Paintsville, KY; [p.] Jerry Grass, Melanie Grass; [ed.] Johnson Central High, Morehead State University; [occ.] College Student; [hon.] Second HM for a contest held by the Kentucky State Poetry Society in 1989; [pers.] Don't give up, because people say you can't do something. If you believe in yourself you can anything.; [a.] Sitka, KY

GRAY, BERNICE M.
[pen.] Bernice May Cunningham Gray, Bernice Gray; [b.] December 22, 1921, American Fork, UT; [p.] Aurelia and Clarence Cunningham; [m.] Orville L. Gray, October 27, 1942; [ch.] Michael Ian, Merrill Ivan, Gordon David; [ed.] Fresno High School 1940, Fresno, CA. Porterville Junior College 1942, Porterville, CA San Francisco State College 1956 San Francisco, CA; [occ.] (Retired) Temple Service Mission for Church of Jesus Christ of Latterday Saints;

[memb.] Life membership in the California Teacher's Association; [hon.] From Church of Jesus Christ of Latterday Saints for recognition for missions served and classes in organ playing and teacher training class. Also Calif. State Scholarship Federation CSF when in Fresno High School.; [oth. writ.] My own personal home made book of "Mom's Poetry" for my children and grand children. Hope to compile my prose, and music. Have written family histories and transcripts of two pioneer Journals; [pers.] I look for the good and beautiful in all things, and in people I meet each poem is an expression of an experience. I avoid criticism of others, and hope my faults may be over-looked.; [a.] Los Angeles, CA

GREEN, KIRBIE
[pen.] 'Oko'; [b.] April 23, 1941, Oklahoma City, OK; [p.] Leroy and Lucille Greene; [m.] Donna R. Stiggers/Greene, April 9, 1965; [ch.] Kirbi, Kellie, Kenii; [ed.] Douglas Sr. High, Central State University, Edmond Okla., (B.A. Degree in Philosophy), Life's School of Hardnox; [occ.] Military Adviser, U.S. Gov't. - 35 years; [memb.] The 'Human' Race, The Oklahoma City Society of the Drum, Loveholies Anonymous (all above are un-chartered and our meetings are un-announced).; [oth. writ.] I have numerous other poems and essays. None have been published to date.; [pers.] This poem is dedicated my dear friends, Mr. and Mrs. Al (R.P.D.) and Ella P. Smith, without whose inspiration, I might have remained all others I sing my song, 'Love is all, all is love.'; [a.] Oklahoma, OK

GREENE, JEFFREY C.
[b.] May 31, 1968, Pittsburgh, PA; [p.] Charles Greene, Rosemary Greene; [m.] Toni Greene, April 10, 1994; [ch.] Quentin Green; [ed.] Shaler Area High, U.S.A.F., Mt. San Jacinto College; [occ.] Flight Engineer, Aircraft Mechanic; [memb.] American Motorcycle Association; [pers.] Each of us may reach deep within ourselves pulling from the depths thoughts and ideas forever lasting.; [a.] San Jacinto, CA

GREER, BRENDA
[b.] March 24, 1952, Houston, TX; [p.] Robert and Alberta Greer, [m.] Divorced; [ch.] Four; [ed.] H.S., Houston Baptist Univ., now studying at San Jacinto College, Houston Community College; [occ.] Licensed Vocational Nurse; [memb.] Eastern Star - Sara Chapter - Queen of the South; [hon.] Member of the National Honor Society in High School, received Jones Scholarship.; [pers.] The gift of life is precious, we must care for others, appreciate our blessings from God, and share our blessings with others.; [a.] Houston, TX

GREER, LUCY C.
[b.] January 20, 1915, Nashville, TN; [p.] Joseph A. Sr. and Beatrice (Williams) Greer;

[ed.] 12th Grade Graduate of Central High School - Nashville TN; [occ.] Retired (from State of Tenn.); [memb.] Hillcrest United Methodist Church Nashville, TN; [hon.] Turner Grammar School - Nashville Tenn., Valedictorian - 8th Grade, Sigma Beta Phi - Honor Society, Central High School - Nashville, TN; [oth. writ.] "Hands of a friend."; [pers.] I am a great great granddaughter of William and Sarah C. Nolen for which the town of Nolensville and the Nolensville Road were named.; [a.] Nashville, TN

GREER, MICHELLE ANN
[b.] Long Beach, CA; [m.] Nat; [ch.] A two year old daughter, Hannah; [ed.] She attended Woodrow Wilson High, where she was named one of the top ten writters. She currently attends Long Beach City College; [hon.] She also received the Bank of America Achievement Award in Drama. where she receive the Jerry And Jeta Jabos Scholarship Award For Scholastic Achievement. She also received Best Actress at the Fine Arts Ceremeony Chachet Awards; [oth. writ.] She loves the creative process of writing and acting. She strives for poetry that is fresh and new, yet embracing traditional themes. She hopes to shed light on the simple things in life, such as love, nature, and family. She believes that such themes are uplifting and give hope.; [a.] Los Alamitos, CA

GREGORY, DONALD
[b.] June 22, 1925, Santa Monica, CA; [p.] Ethel G. and James H. Gregory; [ed.] BA - Univ. of Southern California, MA - Columbia Univ.; [occ.] Retired; [a.] New Haven, CT

GREGORY, TIFFANY LYNN
[pen.] December Sherwood; [b.] December 19, 1980, Ashland, KY; [p.] Angela Elizabeth Gregory; [ed.] Ironton High; [occ.] High School Student; [oth. writ.] Several poems published in local newspapers, anthology of poetry for Young Americans.; [pers.] In my writing I try to direct my solicitude to problems that are prominent to today's polymorphic society. I personally feel I execute these endeavors.; [a.] Ironton, OH

GRENIER, LYNNE MARIE
[b.] March 18, 1945, Rochester, MN; [p.] Marion G. and Monte W. Bingham; [m.] Ronald Raymond Grenier, March 19, 1970; [ch.] Aaron R. and Ranae L. Grenier; [occ.] Insurance - Antiques; [oth. writ.] "Young American Sings" poem published in Anthology Iowa and Mn High School Poetry. Poem published in newspaper Collectors Journal-Iowa 1995. My poem "Antiquity" framed and hangs in Antique Manor Shop in Stewartville, Mn.; [pers.] My life's adventures, friendships, antiques and travels have inspired me to write poetry. I share it with the people in my life. I am influenced by emotion, humor and truth in our everyday lives.; [a.] Stewartville, MN

GRIFFITH, JUANITA S.
[pen.] Wanie; [b.] May 11, 1971, Saint Croix; [p.] Eileen L. Sealey and Everett Griffith; [m.] (Fiancee) Melford Selkridge; [ch.] Dean, Dwayne, David, Denny, and Tamara; [ed.] High School, Class of 1989 Central High; [occ.] Housewife and a Housekeeper; [memb.] Caribbean Health and Racquet Club; [hon.] McDonald, V.I. Half Marathon St. Croix November 27, 1988 1 point 3 miles. Walker 2.50.44; [oth. writ.] Run Freely, The Butter Fly, Wind So High, I'm free. All of the following poems was published in local newspaper, articles for the Sunday and Monday post.; [pers.] As a mother of five and a hard worker. I do hope to maybe influenced someone and saying to that person (be your best in what ever you do and don't give up try and try again).; [a.] C'sted, Saint Croix

GRISWOLD, MAY
[pen.] May Griswold; [b.] May 1905, Wilson, KS; [p.] Elizabeth Frantz - A. Langerman; [m.] Sherwin Griswold, February 28, 1927; [ch.] Dr. Dale - MD, Dr Don Pharmacology, Dr. Mary Ann Hankin, Education.; [ed.] 1 year Teacher's College, Hays, KS.; [occ.] Home maker; [memb.] 1st Presbyterian, Church P.E.O. Sisterhood, Sorosis Study Club "one of woman of year" (1962); [hon.] Golden, poet "One of women of year"; [oth. writ.] Golden poet, award, "poem" bouquet for my sister"; [pers.] I stay to make anything I write to the helpful to family and friends; [a.] Newton, KS

GROVE, JODY M.
[b.] September 19, 1944, Brooklyn; [p.] Alex and Rose D'Alessandro; [m.] Divorced; [ch.] Only one daughter; [ed.] Went to Elementary School, Junior H.S., High School (Franklin K. Lane, H.S. Jamaica, Queens) Graduated High School, General Diploma went to Libbs Beauty School; [occ.] Hope to be working as a Beautician soon; [oth. writ.] I like to write, mostly for my friends, have written several poems for farewell gatherings and special occasions.; [pers.] When writing poetry or any writing, stride to be honest and always make it understandable.; [a.] Brooklyn, NY

GROVER, TRENT
[b.] December 1, 1978, Wichita, KS; [p.] Joan Bixler, Arlan Grover, David Bixler; [ed.] Seaholm High School, Minnetonka High School; [occ.] Student (Minnetonka High School); [memb.] National Honor Society, Minnetonka High School Varsity Track Team; [hon.] Student Recognition Award, An Honor Role, MSAA/SMA Boys 9th grade 300m Intermediate Hurdles Conference Champion; [oth. writ.] Assorted poems, short stories, and children's books (all, as of yet, unpublished); [pers.] Obviously, my writing is heavily influenced by Edgar Allan Poe, along with my own life experiences. Always remember, as I do, that theres always light to balance with dark.; [a.] Excelsior, MN

GROW, JULIA EHE
[b.] January 23, 1984, Abington Hospital; [p.] Mrs. Jeanne Grow, Mr. Robert Grow (Deceased); [ed.] Log College Middle School 7th Grade; [occ.] Student; [pers.] I love animals and when I am older I'm planning to dedicate my life to them. They are the only species that doesn't speak to show emotions. Good-bye seems forever, farewell is like the end. In my heart are the memories of the loved ones we've lost.; [a.] Warminster, PA

GUARDI, SILVIA RUTH
[b.] December 8, 1932, Riga, Latvia; [p.] Janis (a Doctor and Professor in Medicine) and Natalia Sulcs (Opera Singer in Rija National Opera House); [m.] Frank Guardi, April 28, 1959; [ch.] John, Alfredo, Nano, Jennifer.; [ed.] Gramman School, High School, a 1957 graduate from University of North Dakota, Grand Forks, North Dakota. B.A. in Music, English, and Literature; [occ.] Foster Grandparent at St. Vincent de Paul Daycare Center; [memb.] Sigma Alpha Iota (SAI), Music Fraternits; [hon.] I was awarded for writing and composing a song in praise of my honorary fraternity S.A.I.; [oth. writ.] I wish to have several of my poems published (50 or more) in a book, which I would name "Crystal Tears". However - I need someone to help me with it.; [pers.] Each of us carry emotions. They are within us and manifest themselves by coming forth as crystal tears. These tears reflect the emotions of joy, love, sorrow, hate, anger, and much much more; [a.] Chicago, IL

GUERIN, GEORGE JOHN
[b.] November 15, 1922, San Juan, PR; [ch.] Gina, Mercedes, Jon, Noelle, (elder son) George; [ed.] Boy's High School - Graduated, City College Two Years, Journalism, University: Fairleigh Dickinson University, New Jersey, Business Adm., United States Army Special Training Centers, WWII; [hon.] Bronze Star Medal, Three Clusters, Italy France, Germany, Campaign Battles-Anzio-Bulge, Siegfried Line, Editor's Choice Award for Poem, "The World Will Say," "What Mystic." Published in the book in Congress, by the I.S.P. 1995 Editor's Choice Award and 1994 above. Other poems published in a tapestry of thoughts also a poem being published in a muse to follow.; [pers.] You see it's a complicated story, my wife departed six years today, later my elder son in 1989. Want to feel, and I want to know everything. Even if it means to hold on to the worse kind of pain. I strive to reflect the goodness of mankind in writing.; [a.] Petaluma, CA

HADDOX, MAXINE
[b.] 1934, Marshallville, OH; [p.] Sylvia and Glenn Krites; [m.] Donald L. Haddox; [ch.] Jesse and Shan, (Grandchildren) Shawna, Ryan and Marina; [occ.] Painter -- oils Aka Name (Jesshan); [hon.] Editor's Choice Award (2)

1995; [oth. writ.] Article for RY Magazine, poems published (The Garden of Life) 1995, (A Delicate Balance) 1995 by The Nat'l Library of Poetry; [pers.] Poetry is the "silent" song within the heart.; [a.] Fairborn, OH

HAGER, SAUNDRA J.
[pen.] Sandye Applegate-Hager; [b.] February 19, 1953, Hamilton, OH; [p.] Jennings Applegate - Loraine A. Cates; [m.] Leonard Hager, May 9, 1986; [ed.] Madison High School, Richmond, KY; [occ.] Homemaker, Writer; [hon.] Certificate of Merit, Who's Who in Poetry, Golden Poet Award and Silver Poet Award from World of Poetry; [oth. writ.] Pledge of love - published in "Greatest Poems of the Western World." Many others not published; [pers.] Most of my writing has been inspired by the love of family, life and God. "Miracle Abound" was written for and dedicated to a wonderful friend who has touched my life immensely, Jan Rollins.; [a.] Richmond, KY

HALL, SARA KEMP
[b.] August 5, 1922, Cartersville, GA; [p.] David and Grace McDaniel; [m.] Harold Hall (Deceased), October 12, 1946, Hubert Kemp, January 6, 1984; [ch.] Karen Hall, Duane Hall; [ed.] Acworth High, Southern College of Business, Marietta, Ga.; [occ.] Retired; [memb.] Fair Oaks United Methodist Church Pres., Jubileers Senior Citizens Organization, Administrative Council, Senior Net, Charter Member of Women in Military Service.; [oth. writ.] Editorials and Feed Back Articles published in local newspaper. Editorial published in Smyrna Senior paper.; [a.] Marietta, GA

HANDY JR., JOHN L.
[pen.] John L. Handy Jr.; [b.] August 14, 1920, Akron, OH; [p.] John and Virginia Handy; [m.] Jane Fraser Martin, November 24, 1946; [ch.] Amy, Myra, Jane, Nell and Caroline; [ed.] Milton Academy, Harvard College, Columbia University (M.A. English) Brown University, Phd. Residency; [occ.] Retired from Teaching and College Administration; [memb.] 10th Mt. Division Alumni Association; [pers.] I believe very much in the ambiguities of our time, of the existentialists and the french symbolist poets each of whom challenge us, out of the darkness and light in the world, to create.; [a.] Huntington, VT

HANEY, LYNN
[pen.] Lynn Haney; [b.] December 1, 1981, San Jose; [p.] Donna and Steve Haney; [ed.] Payne Elementary and Rogers Middle School; [occ.] Truck Washer, Writer, and Student; [memb.] Peer Helper; [hon.] Honor roll (3.5) average in grade school. Being a semi-finalist in The National Library of Poetry.; [oth. writ.] I write anything that comes to mind. Short stories, events in my life poetry.; [pers.] I would like to

say special thank to Eli. With out him, I wouldn't have started poetry. I would also like to thank my friends for giving me ideas. I write the truth in my poems and what comes to my wonderful mind.; [a.] San Jose, CA

HANNAN, RHODA-KATIE
[pen.] Rhoda-Katie Hannan; [b.] August 28, 1926, New York City; [p.] Blanche Fidler, Wm. Hannan; [ch.] Sharon, James, Scott, Glenn; [occ.] Retired Secretary; [memb.] Unitarian/Universalist Fellowship of Huntington, N.Y.; [hon.] Award for hymn "The Sound of Peace" This hymn has been performed by both Unitarian and episcopal choirs.; [oth. writ.] Blue Mountain Arts greeting cards, Cruising World, Poet magazine, Reminisce magazine, Column (weekly) for Smithtown News Unitarian World and Beacon newsletter - letters to News day and Suffolk Times and song and hymns. 5 Blue Mountain Arts anthologies - 1 poem "The Silent Heart" in the "We Speak for Peace" anthology "The Sound of Peace" words were published in a United Nations pamphlet peace is my favorite topic; [pers.]; [a.] Kings Park, NY

HANNUSH, NAZIH
[pen.] Nezo; [b.] January 27, 1960, Beirot, Lebanon; [p.] Ibrahim and Janet Hannush; [m.] Prisgla Hannush, July 2, 1992; [ch.] Julian Andreas Hannush; [ed.] Rice Aviation, Airframe, Powerplant Mechanic, University of Houston, Major Psychology; [occ.] Bartender at the Fourseasons Hotel (Newport Beach); [oth. writ.] (Unpublished poems) A Silent Wisper from a Rose Garden, The Crying River, Poverty, Thieves of the Morning Sun, Confusion in War, There Was a Moment Like This, Rivers that Became Hard Deserts of Life, A Tear for a Year.; [pers.] My writings are a reflection of imagination and past experiences from a far away culture brought into this American Culture and I hope that they are simply enjoyed by the reader.; [a.] Newport Beach, CA

HANSEN, BARBARA
[pen.] Barbara Ann; [b.] December 28, 1979, Lanstohl, West Germany; [p.] David and Carol Hansen; [ed.] Currently attending The Catholic High School of Baltimore; [occ.] Sophomore at the Catholic High School of Baltimore; [hon.] Academic scholarship The Catholic High School 4 years, Forensics Scholarship the Catholic High School of Baltimore - 4 years, McCafferty Honors Program The Catholic High School of Baltimore, Archdiocese of Baltimore High School Honors Band; [pers.] When you discover your uniqueness, make it known to the world.; [a.] Baltimore, MD

HANSEN, MARYLOU
[pen.] Sammie Labiak; [b.] February 14, 1948, Providence, RI; [p.] Bill (Deceased) and Mary Labiak; [ch.] Ray; [ed.] Hilltop High (San Diego,

CA) and some Jr. College at Pima College in Tucson, AZ; [occ.] Secretary at AMARC ("The Boneyard"), Davis-Monthan AFB, AZ; [pers.] `Wind Song of the Sea' was actually 2 poems I wrote in the early 60's - not until I saw your contest ad did I combine them and finally consent to publish (my teachers thought I had stolen someone else's work because I didn't let them publish the poems then.) God's handiwork is what owes and inspires me.; [a.] Tucson, AZ

HANSEN, NICOLE
[b.] December 20, 1978, Arcadia, CA; [p.] Jim Leslie, Dayle Leslie; [ed.] Junior at Fountain Valley High School, Fountain Valley, Calif. I graduate in 1997.; [hon.] I'm on my high school's varsity track team.; [oth. writ.] I have several other poems I've written over the years. This is the first one that's been published.; [pers.] I'm really excited about having one of my poems published. I think it is a really great honor.; [a.] Fountain Valley, CA

HARD, BARBARA JEAN
[b.] August 10, 1949, Seattle, WA; [p.] Geneva and Roy Maxwell; [ch.] Cheryl, Kelly, Carrie Ann; [ed.] St. Vincent Central High, College of Hampton Rds. Newport News, Virginia; [occ.] Motel Manager, Shell Point Resort, Inc.; [memb.] New Life Christian Fellowship, Church; [oth. writ.] Several non-published poems, and short stories, I've written for my own enjoyment and for my family.; [pers.] I believe you and I can change the world by doing the will of our father in heaven, which is loving one another unconditionally. Also forgetting what is behind and straining for what is ahead.; [a.] Crawfordville, FL

HARDY, BENITA JOY
[b.] December 29, 1959, Hannibal; [p.] Calvin and Eleanor Burnett; [m.] Steven Hardy, June 28, 1980; [ch.] Tiffany Christine, Breanne Marie, Matthew Steven; [ed.] Graduated Mark Twain High School in Center, attended - Central Christian College - 1 yr; [occ.] Children's day care and photographer; [oth. writ.] Raining in My Heart - poems published by N.L.O.P. in 1992. Won several local radio essay contest. Had a short article printed in Woman's World Magazine; [pers.] This poem is in honor of Emily Dawn Wisdom. She is one of the most precious little girls I've ever known. If anyone wishes to spend an eternity in heaven with us, look up John 14:6 in the Bible. It will tell you how to join us.; [a.] New London, MO

HARGRAVE, RAYDELLANNIE
[b.] September 6, 1939, Mount Airy, NC; [p.] Annie Hargrave, Curtis Hargrave; [ed.] J.J. Jones High - Johnson C. Smith University; [occ.] Teacher (Pre-school); [memb.] Missionary Society - Peace Missionary Bapt. Church NAACP; [pers.] I have been writing poetry

since childhood, although I have never had anything published. I was amazed at my mother's strength and devotion to her family and others. This inspired me to share my insight through poetry.; [a.] Columbus, OH

HARMAN, MICHELLE LYNN
[b.] May 12, 1978, Ocala, FL; [p.] Karen and Jack Harman; [ed.] Currently attending Col. Zadok Magruder High School (12th grade); [occ.] Customer Service and Summit Sales and Marketing; [oth. writ.] Numerous poems none of which have been published yet!; [pers.] This poem I'd give anything was written in memory of my loving Grandmother.; [a.] Olney, MD

HARMON, COLLEEN
[b.] January 2, 1954, Caribou, ME; [p.] Harrison, Curtis, Erma Curtis; [m.] Arthur Harmon, August 29, 1992; [ch.] Sherrie Harmon, David Harmon; [ed.] LPN - NMTC - 1973, Business Mang't - 1990, Accounting 1991, Business Adm. - Husson College 1995; [occ.] Instructional Tutor; [memb.] EMA - Volunteer member (Emergency Mgt. Agency); [hon.] 1995 - North Star Year Book Recipient, 1995 - NMTC - Course Development and Instruction on Math Anxiety; [oth. writ.] Poem in "Misty of Enchantment"; [pers.] By making others happy you increase your own happiness; [a.] Caribou, ME

HARMON, ELOISE
[pen.] Eloise Harmon; [b.] October 19, 1928, Cordele, GA; [p.] James Richmond Spears, Louise Spears; [m.] David W. Harmon, September 8, 1977; [ch.] Marvin Tarrant, Mary Ann Chesser, Andrew Jackson Hi, Jacksonville, FL; [occ.] Admitting Dept. Mullins, Hospital/Mullins SC; [memb.] Veterans Foreign Wars, Post (Past President 3 years), Member: Grace Baptist Church, Nichols, SC; 9[pers.] I feel that I have been and I strive to express my experiences in such a way that others may enjoy them. I have been influenced by wonderful people, in my life, that really cared.; [a.] Mullins, SC

HARMONY, JANICE M.
[pen.] Jan Harmony; [b.] April 21, 1953, Allentown, PA; [p.] Martha and Al Harmony; [ch.] Brandon Matthew; [ed.] Louis E Dieruff High School; [occ.] Pt. Times on Emmaus Fire and Police Depts. Full time shipping/receiving; [hon.] Editor's Choice Award from Nat'l Library of Poetry; [oth. writ.] I published in local paper, poems sent to Nascar drivers with response; [pers.] During a time when police officers/departments are shown in newspapers/tv as being corrupt, Emmaus Police Dept., Emmaus, PA. has Ofc. Scott Gross. For believing in me and my abilities and encouraging them, for listening and being trustworthy and an advisor; [a.] Emmaus, PA

HARRIS, ANN M.
[b.] February 17, 1957, Quakertown, PA; [p.] Ann M. Crouse, Rollin P. Kichline; [m.] Timothy Wayne Harris, September 4, 1982; [ch.] Joshua Wayne Harris; [ed.] Saucon Valley High/Hellertown, PA; [occ.] Sales/Export Company; [memb.] Colonial Squares Square Dance Club, Chapman Quarry Methodist Church; [oth. writ.] Personal poems, newspaper letters.; [pers.] That there be world peace for this particular poem I was inspired by my childhood. This poem is in honor of my beloved father and also for my mother.

HARRIS, CHEZRE
[b.] March 3, 1983, Fort Stewart, GA; [p.] Violet and Albert Harris; [ed.] Dover Middle School a 7th grader; [memb.] Power of the pen-an advanced writing club; [hon.] Honor Student; [pers.] It takes mores muscles to frown than to smile so smile!; [a.] Dover, OH

HARRIS, EE-B K.
[pen.] Pendeza, Deeliah Rusalen, Katie; [b.] November 9, 1948, Scooba, MS; [p.] Katie Bee and Bobby Harris Sr.; [m.] Louis James Bailey, March 22, 1974; [ch.] Hariri Rose and Ayanna Chenzira Bailey; [ed.] Anna Strong High - Marianna Arkansas Pasedena City College - Pasadena California University of Pine Bluff - Pine Bluff Arkansas Montclair State College - Montclair New Jersey Atlanta University - Atlanta Georgia; [occ.] Teacher/Counselor/Actress; [memb.] Mt. Zion Baptist Church College Fund, Jamaica - Arts - Association, Saidi Arts Inc., National Arts Endowment, Montclair State Alumni; [hon.] Lionette Club, Witty Poets of America, Ovuad City, De Butantante Society.., Mico Blanco All Star Dance Award, Brimah's Ethnic Dance Award; [oth. writ.] One hundred and nine unpublished sons, thirteen children stories - two books - entitled - key corner road, Venetian Blinds, 5 one act plays. Written, directed, produced by EE-B K. Harris.; [pers.] My eyes are oblivious to the odd odors of denominational preface, my love light shines through Hobnailed situations, sowing words of wisdom, to children with less grain, attempting to enhance The Innate Quality of Light given to each brain by Birth Right, Denied by Human During "The Human Flight"; [a.] Tucson, AZ

HARRIS, MARIAN S.
[b.] May 22, 1913, Norwood, PA; [p.] Lewis Smith and Jennie Vaughan Smith; [m.] Tommie Harris, July 8, 1939; [ed.] Harrisonburg Teachers College 1935 (now James Madison U.); [memb.] Episcopal Church Stratford Book Club, N.C. DAR; [hon.] President Junior Class 1933, President Senior Class 1935. Director of District III, N.C. DAR; [pers.] My husband died 1990. The picture of the angels and the boy at the gate, was the whole story for the thoughts

of the poem. My philosophy: I know I'll see him in Heaven and be with him.; [a.] Charlotte, NC

HARRISON, BENJAMIN L.
[pen.] Benjy; [b.] December 31, 1936, Forth Worth, TX; [p.] Mr. and Mrs. Willian F. Harrison; [m.] Nina Kate, July 28, 1967; [ch.] Craig (Adopted), Elizabeth Nichols (Foster); [ed.] Weatherford High School, Weatherford, TX, Weatherford Jr. College, Lee College Baytown, TX; [occ.] Industrial Instrument/Electrical Technician; [memb.] American Red Cross, First Aide CPR Instruct, American Nondestructive Testing Assc. Meta-4 Poetry Reading Club.; [hon.] Girl Scout Family of Year 1993, Distinguished Boy Scout Leader, [oth. writ.] Read poem Barnes Noble Bookstop, local library, several local coffee shops, Univ. of St. Thomas; [pers.] I attempt to write about life events and demonstrate to the youth of today that poetry is an important part of personal living and enjoyment as a release from common stress.; [a.] Houston, TX

HASTINGS, MURIEL
[b.] August 13, 1926, Madison, CT; [p.] Edward Lent, Doris Lent; [m.] Edward Hale Hastings, June 16, 1947; [ch.] Carol Holliger, Paul Hastings, Patricia O'Neill; [ed.] New Haren State Teacher's College; [occ.] Retired Teacher; [memb.] United Churches of Olympia, WA; [hon.] Beatitudes Center DOAR Volunteer Service Award, 1983, Phoeniz, AZ; [oth. writ.] Article on Bach: A.D. Magazine, 1980, Poem re hummingbirds: AZ White Mountains Magazine, 1994.; [pers.] Being an interior person, I use my poetry to express my feelings and yearnings.; [a.] Tumwater, WA

HASTINGS, PETER
[pen.] Peter Hastings; [b.] April 22, 1980, Minneapolis, MN; [p.] Donald and Susan Hastings; [ed.] At Robinsdale Armstrong High School (present time); [hon.] Several dozen academic awards, several musical awards (nothing big); [oth. writ.] I'm working on several short stories at the time; [pers.] We see possibilities in others, but we should be dreaming of the possibilities within ourselves.; [a.] Crystal, MN

HATCH, LOUIS MICHAEL
[b.] June 27, 1918, Brockton, MA; [p.] Michael David, Agnes Hage Hatch; [m.] 1) Helen Hazam Hatch, November '42, 2) Katherine Rose Hate, August 23, 1985; [ch.] Louise Helen Shea - Ronald George Hatch; [ed.] Graduate Brockton High Class '37 - 64 in Class World Poet Laurente of Class at 50th Reunion 1988; [occ.] Retired Teams 57 years now Chaplain of RI Retrives-Local 251; [memb.] Chaplain Retired Teamster - Poet in Res. RI Past Card Club - Poet in Residence Bellingham Mass. Health Care Center, Past Pres. 4 Years Blackstone, Valley

Writers Guild-Sc. NE now Chaplain; [hon.] Voted Poet Lawrente Class '37 at 50th reunion 1988. (651 in class) I write for my church. I open monthly meetings of retirees with a prayer and original poem.; [oth. writ.] I write many prayers for a church, I also a write for all occasions wedding. Memoriams eati/Gentlemen of the highways. Dray in travelogue" - Inauguration, Poem for 4 presidents (have autographs) practical peace. Give him a chance.; [pers.] I am of Libonese syriva and admired the old custom of men at gatherings telling life stories in sing - song fashion - my meet philosophical statement is aspiration through inspiration with horizons unlimited.; [a.] Pawtucket, RI

HAUSSKE, HARLAND A.
[b.] June 29, 1920, Chicago, IL; [p.] Albert and Clara Hausske; [m.] Luella I. Hausske, June 13, 1943; [ch.] James and Douglas; [ed.] Home by mom and dad and Calvert Course. North China American School (NCAS) 7th thru 2rd Yenching University (1938-39) Whitmon College, 1939-40, Univ. of Wash. 1940-42, BA in History and 1946-48; [occ.] Retired from UFCUW; [memb.] B.S.A since 1947, BAUCC (Congregational Church), Renton Senior Center WA "Writing for fun" class; [hon.] B.S.A. Silver Beaver, BSA and Union Meany Youth Award; [oth. writ.] "I Remember When" I, II, III, IV for family and friends and ("Family Memories I); [pers.] My writing has been done over a period of almost 7 years for "Writing for fun" class. My enjoyment has been in writing anything and everything for fun as it comes to mind. An Ode to Mom was written in the hospital after Mom's death and my other writings have been bossed on their immediately.; [a.] Seattle, WA

HAWKINS, SANDRA
[pen.] Louise Jay; [b.] November 18, 1950, Le Grande, OR; [p.] Betty Pistorius, William Pistorius; [ch.] William K., Jennifer T.; [ed.] Kearns High School, Salt Lake Community College (Still attending); [occ.] Directory Assistance for US West Communications; [memb.] Telephone Pioneers of America, Communications Workers of America, PTA; [hon.] This is the 1st "Honorary Publishing", Summit club, Public Safety Award from West Jordan City; [oth. writ.] I have written many stories and poems. This is my 1st publication.; [pers.] I would like to put forth a message that many wonderful things exist which cannot be seen. I enjoy romantic poetry.; [a.] West Jordan, UT

HELD, BETTY IRENE
[pen.] Betty I. Held; [b.] June 21, 1939, Hammond, IN; [p.] Minnie and Delbert Gootee; [m.] Richard Held (Deseased), December 27, 1958; [ch.] Richard Jr., Bambi, Don, John, Dianne; [ed.] Lincoln Elementary Hammond IN, Irving Jr. High 8th and 9th Hammond IN,

Hammond Technical Vocational High School Hammond IN; [occ.] Retired Homemaker; [memb.] Holy and Ghost Church Knoxville, TN; [hon.] 1993 Poem Dilemma Won Honorable Mention Award in the Hoosier Horizon Writing Contest; [oth. writ.] A precious rendering my life story 1950-1996 poems: Dilemma, Danny? He is Risen, The New England Kennedy's, Varnished Vacuum.; [pers.] I am a believer in encouragement. A strong believer in human dignity. I like the lifting of human expression in writing. And it's accessibility.; [a.] Knoxville, TN

HELD, PATRICIA LAUDETTE
[pen.] Patricia A. Brought; [b.] December 19, 1951, Lawton, OK; [p.] Roy and Lois Laudette; [m.] Sanford F. Held, May 16, 1978; [ch.] Ray Gene, Brett D., Brad D.; [ed.] Lawton High School, graduate Jewish - Christian Institute of Dallas, Texas; [occ.] Teaches Religion, Missionary; [oth. writ.] Programs for churches religions articles; [pers.] I learn from everyone that I meet.

HELLAMS, WINNIE
[b.] September 19, 1923, Piedmont, SC; [p.] Brooks and Vivia Holtzclaw; [m.] John Hellams Jr. July 1, 1950; [ch.] Vivia Jeanne and Richard Hellams; [ed.] B.A. degree, Limestone College, S.C. Double major: Music, French, Post graduate piano study; [occ.] Private Piano Teacher; [memb.] National and Local Music Teacher's Association; [hon.] National Honorary English and French Literary Sororities, College: Chi Delta Phi, Beta Pi Theta; [oth. writ.] Perhaps a dozen unpublished poems; [pers.] My love of poetry stems from immense love of music, awe of nature and the universe, and sensitivity to the collective mind of man.; [a.] Atlanta, GA

HELMKE, CARLA CHRISTIAN
[b.] June 20, 1957, Charleston, WV; [p.] William and Shelva Christian; [m.] Louis E. Helmke, May 8, 1987; [ed.] B.S. in Fine Arts from Pembroke State University, Pembroke, N.C. Scotland High School; [occ.] Desktop publisher (Multi-Business and Bookkeeping); [memb.] Church of the Nazarene, Family Life Church Board; [hon.] Nat'l Honor Society; [oth. writ.] "For Your Glory I Lift This Praise" - a collection of psalms and declaration of praise.; [pers.] The joy of the Lord is my strength - that is the ultimate influence on my work.; [a.] Sterling, VA

HELVERSON, DORIS
[b.] July 16, 1941, Walnut, AR; [p.] Alva and Lora Weston; [m.] Don Helverson, July 3, 1987; [ch.] Three children and three stepchildren; [ed.] Interior Designer, Modeling Business - (Owned and Operated Fashion Shop; [occ.] Consumer in Kansas City, MO, Consultant for Western Auto; [memb.] Cousin to Thomas Fall deceased, Author of Books for Young Readers, Supportive

of Local Charities; [hon.] Trophy's for Submitted Poetry to Women's Club; [oth. writ.] Currently writing a novel, writing poetry, newspaper articles.; [pers.] My writings reflect real life situations that I hope people will learn from.; [a.] Blue Springs, MO

HENDERSON, TARA C.
[b.] May 20, 1971, Dayton, OH; [p.] Crystal Henderson; [ed.] Paul L. Dunbar High School, Grambling State University; [occ.] Reserve Teacher, Dayton, Ohio; [memb.] Buckeye Trails Girl Scouts, Ohio Players Society; [hon.] Kappa Delta Pi, Sigma Tau Delta; [pers.] I strive to reflect the emotions of those unspoken and not heard. My greatest influence has been the world around me.; [a.] Dayton, OH

HENRY, JAMES E.
[b.] April 25, 1939, Manhattan; [p.] James and Mabel Henry (Hughes); [m.] Beatrice Mills-Henry, August 20, 1994; [ch.] Pamela, Stephanie, (stepchildren) Amira, Matthew, Anthony; [ed.] College - Lehman Nursing School - Central School, for practical Nurses; [occ.] Practical Nurse promenade Nursing home; [hon.] Dean's list - Lehman College - Golden Key Honor Society; [oth. writ.] I have written other poems but have not and anything published I've been trying to find a way to bring my writing to the public's eye.; [pers.] Most of my poetry is about women. My new wife has been an inspiration for much of my recent poetry. I like to write about the goodness of people; [a.] New York, NY

HENRY, JEAN DOOLITTLE
[b.] November 19, 1934, San Francisco, CA; [p.] Jean McLaughlin Doolittle, Jefferson Jennings Doolittle; [m.] Charles V. Henry, June 21, 1958; [ch.] Rebecca Henry, Amy McLaughlin Henry, Jean Carvill Henry, Charles Henry; [ed.] 1956 - B.S. Pre-Med, Pre-Nursing, University of California at Berkeley, 1955 - Politics, Philosophy and Economics, Summer School, Oxford University, 1956 - Certificate in Physical Therapy, University of California at San Francisco, 1958 - Masters in Elementary Education, Harvard University, 1974-75 - Special Education and Psychology Courses, Millersville University, 1975 - English as a Second Language Course, Temple University, 1976-1995 Adult Education and Computer Workshops; [occ.] Coordinator, ESL classes and Homeless class, Lebanon Co. Housing and Redevelopment Authority, Instructor Harrisburg Community College, Co-editor of "Bridges", an ESL newsletter distributed in PA; [memb.] County Housing, PAACE (PA Adult and Continuing Education Association) Board member, Legislative Chairman Head Start, Policy Committee, Lebanon County League of Women Voters, founding member, Secretary, Treasurer, Land-Use Chairman, President of the Board of

Directors, Philhaven Hospital, Member Board of Directors, Lebanon County Chamber of Commerce, Legislative Committee, United Cerebral Palsy of Lebanon County, Secretary and Board Member, Lebanon County Visiting Nurse Association, Secretary, Vice-President, President, Board of Directors; [hon.] Delta Kappa Gamma, Educational Honors Society, Massachusetts, Elementary Education, Pennsylvania, Elementary Education; [oth. writ.] Hmong and Pennsylvania German Textiles: Needlework Traditions in Lancaster County, Folk Art, Magazine of the Museum of American Folk Art, Summer 1905, pp. 40-46.; [pers.] A poem flew in the window and what was I to do I ran into the living room and left the chores for you.; [a.] Lebanon, PA

HERBERT, CESARINA MARIA
[pen.] Cesarina Maria Rossetti; [b.] August 23, 1911, Casto, Italy; [p.] Julio Rossetti, Angela Frassa Rossetti; [m.] Divorced; [ch.] Mariae Tumelty, Rossett Herbert, Claren Herbert; [ed.] Burlingame High, Interstate College of Personology, Delores Premiere School of Cosmetology; [occ.] Owner and manager of own properties.; [memb.] Girl Scouts leader, Boy Scouts den mother, American Red Cross, Swimming Instructor, Earthquake Safety Program; [oth. writ.] Poems - published in... At Water's Edge, 1995, Best Poems of 1996, Spirit of the Age 1996, Muse to Follow 1996; [pers.] In my writing, my goal is to express and project, the basic reality of all life, as life is presented to me.; [a.] Hillsborough, CA

HERENSZTAT, GRETA
[b.] July 7, 1933, Paris, France; [ch.] Claudine-Judith, Hannah-Charlotte; [ed.] High School Equivalency Diploma, BA from CUNY Graduate Center, MLS from CUNY Graduate Center; [occ.] Operations Manager, Saks 5th Avenue, NYC; [hon.] Dean's List, Kappa Delti Pi, Pi Delta Phi, Graduated Magna Cum Laude; [oth. writ.] Several stories published in local newspaper and magazines, poems in the process of publishing; [pers.] I am a Holocaust survivor and just started to write about the unending grief of having lost my family at the hand of the Nazis. We have to remember what happened in order for mankind to become human.; [a.] New York, NY

HERLIHY, LISA J.
[b.] October 21, 1961, Stoughton, MS; [p.] Jean Berggren, the late Harold Berggren; [ed.] South Eastern Regional High School, Massasoit Community College, Program Choices; [occ.] Shaws, Packer; [hon.] A personal honor to be recognized by The National Library of Poetry, my award, to have my poem published; [oth. writ.] Articles written for the Brockton Enterprise and Patriot Ledger, [pers.] My poems are a way to express what I see in day to day life,

the beauty of nature and the calming way of nature, this is what inspire me.; [a.] Stoughton, MS

HERNANDEZ, ALYSHA NICOLE
[b.] August 9, 1984, San Antonio, TX; [p.] Joe and Sylvia Hernandez; [ed.] St. Paul's Cath. School in San Antonio, 1st Grade - moved to Harlingen, TX and attended at St. Anthony Cath. School, the last few months of 1st grade to 6th Grade. I will be graduating from St. Anthony 6th grade June 1996. I will be attending another school for 7th and 8th grade; [occ.] Student; [hon.] St. Anthony Cath. School "A" Honor Roll, Student Council President, School Choir, National Guild of Piano Teachers, Catholic Interscholastic League, CIL, 3rd Place Oral Reading, C&R School of Fine Arts; [pers.] The feelings I get when I am writing are overflowing. I love classical music especially when played on the piano, my favorite instrument. I am inspired by poets like Edgar Allan Poe, Children's Poets and many, many, more.; [a.] Harlingen, TX

HERNDON, PHAEDRA MYKEL
[b.] February 27, 1972, La Grange, IL; [p.] Gail, Richard Korpi; [m.] J. Douglas Herndon III, October 25, 1993; [ch.] Jareth Michael; [ed.] Robinson High, USMC, Nova College; [occ.] Nanny; [hon.] Short story contest in 1988; [oth. writ.] Several poems and stories as yet unpublished.; [pers.] The best thing you can do for society is to raise your children to be strong, capable, and tolerant people who believe in themselves, and everyone else.; [a.] Manassas, VA

HERP, ROBERT L.
[b.] September 21, 1959, Euclid, OH; [ed.] Lakeland Comm. College Cleveland State Univ.; [occ.] Toolmaker/Medic; [memb.] Phi Theta Kappa/Alph PSI RO; [oth. writ.] Who will carry me; [pers.] Deep emotions when written are better understood.; [a.] Willoughby, OH

HERRICK, TIMOTHY
[b.] June 17, 1947, Hamilton, OH; [p.] Howard Herrick, Jackie Herrick; [ch.] Lukas Howard Herrick; [ed.] Mansfield Senior High Ashland University The Ohio State University; [occ.] Defense Logistics Technician Columbus, Ohio/ D.O.D.; [memb.] American Heart Association American Legion, First Methodist Church; [hon.] Presidents Nat. Medal of Patriotism, Kappa Sigma Scholarship Committee Ashland Univ., Deans List; [oth. writ.] Several poems in local newspapers, articles for the stars and stripes newspaper; [pers.] It's not always the greatest things that make the biggest show, rather it's the little things that people do that makes this old world go...; [a.] Columbus, OH

HERRON, BETTY JEAN
[pen.] Lee Herron and Kevin Herron; [b.]

October 25, 1927, Los Angeles, CA; [p.] Julia and Harry Lankford; [m.] Lee Herron, December 1, 1950; [ch.] Lee Grant Herron, (grandson) Kevin Herron; [ed.] Jr. Collage Jefferson High School, La Trade Ja Collage Costomology Instructor for Clairol Hair; [occ.] Home maker; [memb.] New Revelation Baptist Church. Metropolitan Baptist Metropolitan Church.; [oth. writ.] Yes not publish.; [pers.] I feel poetry is a way of expressing one deeper feeling and dreams and the love of God.; [a.] Pasadena, CA

HERTEL, STACIE M.
[pen.] Ivy Rose; [b.] June 2, 1977, Painesville, OH; [p.] Wayne and Diane Hertel; [occ.] Secretary/Student; [memb.] Willoughby Hills Friends Church; [oth. writ.] Articles in News Herald; [pers.] Stories, places, and people inspire me and my feelings to create that unforgettable poem, that reveals my heart and soul.; [a.] Mentor, OH

HESS, CALEB G.
[b.] April 19, 1922, Quakaka; [p.] Jacob and Anna Hess; [m.] Vida, December 21, 1946; [ch.] Sharran Susan; [ed.] Self made Machinist and Supervisor; [occ.] Retired; [memb.] National Rifle Assoc. North American Hunting Club, Little Schuylkill Conservation Club; [oth. writ.] Many poems but no books hope to finish my book. My life by Caleb G. Hess

HICKS, GOLDIE MAY
[b.] July 7, 1963, Welch, WV; [p.] Jesse and Daisy Hicks; [ch.] Raven Maureen and Jean Marie; [ed.] Parkside High School; [occ.] Mother and writer; [oth. writ.] Not published yet: Raven, Young Dreams, My World, My Soul, Troll Family, Troll Baby, Rocket Shooter, On My Quest, Don't Shade My Love, I'm Here, We're Not Friends, and more.; [pers.] I want to be a writer of poems, books, and movies. I want my children to be proud of me. I can't seem to do anything else right, except for writing.; [a.] Willards, MD

HIGUCHI, AKIHIKO
[pen.] A.B. Jackson; [b.] February 15, 1968, Japan; [p.] Riichi Higuchi, Yone Higuchi; [ed.] Musashi Univ. in Tokyo, Japan; [occ.] Travel Guide, a self-employed Company, Road and Sky in New York City; [pers.] I saw a lot on the road behind me, and will see a lot more in the sky before me. I'm now standing on a place, where the road and the sky are laced.; [a.] Astoria, NY

HILDRETH, MIRIAM CHRISTINE
[b.] June 26, Pharisburg, OH; [p.] Ivan and Elsie Parrott Miller; [ed.] Magnetic Springs High Grad. Gemological Institute Los Angeles; [occ.] Retail Jewelry and Antiques; [memb.] President and Charter member, Business and profissional Women. UMW and special Music United Methodist Church. Senior 4-H advisor OSU

Extension; [hon.] 1992 Proclamation by Union County Commissioner presented to The Musical Team Miriam Hildreth and Clayton Shanks for Patriotic Songs We'll Never Ration Liberty, Forward Together, Yeah! Ohio, Bring Us Together Again. Music and Lyrics used in Concert, Chancel Choir, Follies and Starlighters Orchestra, O.S.U. 4-H Advisor banquet. 4H-Endowment-Dean's List.; [oth. writ.] Have Copy-R or Pub. records and albums - Music and Words Titles "The Lawrence Welk Polka," "Gift of Love," Little Blue River," "Laurence Welk Waltz," "Christmas Is Love," "I'm A Farmers Daughter," "Jesus My Savior," "Deep Love," "Because You Are Mine All Mine," "Hear The Savior's Voice on High," and many more not copy-R. "Our Golden Years" was composed in honor of Miriam's Parents fifty years of marriage.; [pers.] Respect for fellow man, Admiration for Home State, and Love for the U.S.A. Love and Faith in God is a tremendous help and guide.; [a.] Marysville, OH

HILL, MONTE J.
[pen.] Monte James; [b.] July 26, 1958, Kalamazoo, MI; [p.] Jimmie and Alice Hill; [ch.] Melissa M. Hill; [oth. writ.] Several songs that have been copywritten. A Portfolio of six albums that include 70 songs.; [pers.] To my beautiful daughters Melissa, I love you; [a.] Riverview, MI

HILL, TAMMY
[b.] March 10, 1981, Chaptico, MD; [p.] Zack Hill, Barbara Hill; [ed.] Attending Chaptican High School, I am in the 9th grade.; [memb.] I belong to the Junior Varsity Volleyball and Basketball team.

HINTZMAN, ISABEL
[b.] August 17, 1918, Caddie Woodlawn House, Dunn Co, WI; [p.] Arnold Flick, Ermina Flick; [m.] LaVerne Hintzman, May 31, 1941; [ch.] Dixie Lee, Lonnie LaVerne, Lynn Elliott; [ed.] Menominie High, Mpls. Business College; [occ.] Former Secretary, Retired Personal Banking Officer, currently housewife with many hobbies.; [memb.] Peace Luther Church and PLC Prayer Chain; [oth. writ.] Countless Letters to the Editor of Newspapers: Programs, poetry, prose for various organizational meetings: Personal poetry for birthdays, etc. of friends and family, and in 1994 my first published book titled "Just Like Peas In A Pod."; [pers.] My love affair with words my strong belief in the Divine Trinity are reflected in my writings. Also, my writings stem from a rather awesome moment experienced when I was about seven years old.; [a.] Menomonie, WI

HIRSH, NILI ISABEL
[pen.] Nili Hirsh; [b.] March 20, 1983, Tarzana, CA; [p.] Dan and Mary Hirsh; [ed.] I'm in the 7th Grade; [occ.] Student; [pers.] I enjoy writing

poems, english riding, basketball and reading books. I'd like to thank my parents for their constant encouragement in all I do.; [a.] Santa Monica, CA

HOFFERBERT, MARGARET
[pen.] Marge of the Woods; [b.] February 3, 1916, Marion, IN; [p.] Glenn and Hazel Stover; [m.] Ernest Hofferbert, May 30, 1936; [ch.] Rick, Claudette, Jim, Dave; [ed.] Marion HS, many creative writing course; [occ.] Retired; [memb.] United Methodist Church, Church Women United, La Grange Women's Club; [hon.] Valiant Woman - CWU, Discipline, UMC, over 40 Awards - 6th District Federation of Women's Club.; [oth. writ.] Many poems, essay, skits, short stories, one unfinished novel. Have given programs to clubs, Chorus, etc. reading of my writings; [pers.] I love to play around with words, and some times make them do, with satisfaction deep inside, what I want them to.; [a.] Brookfield, IL

HOFFMAN, BARBARA
[b.] July 11, 1937, Brooklyn, NY; [ed.] Erasmus Hall H.S., State University of Ny and Farmingdale, Adelphi University; [occ.] Freelance proofreader and copy editor; [oth. writ.] Poetry published in several literary publications, newsletters, local newspapers; [pers.] My strongest works of poetry and prose speak out in particular, to issues of women, and homeless and those unable to speak for themselves. Also, I love the beauty in nature: The sights, sounds, aromas of it all!; [a.] Merrick, NY

HOFFMAN, GLADE
[pen.] Edward J. Pullins Jr.; [b.] August 25, 1946, Passaic, NJ; [p.] Edward, Joan Pullins; [m.] Carol, September 13, 1972; [ch.] Sarah, Jennifer, David and Josh; [ed.] Santa Rosa Junior College; [occ.] Songwriter, Promoter, General Contractor; [oth. writ.] Songs published in "Songs of Creation" song book, seven songs recorded by Jim Linzey; [pers.] It is my goal to use my gift for the Glory of God and to show those who read my work the way to Him and Reflections of His love; [a.] Lucerne, CA

HOFFMAN JR., PAUL ROBERT
[b.] May 27, 1965, Takoma Park, MD; [p.] Paul Hoffman, Sally Hoffman; [ed.] Oxon Hill Senior High, Phoenix College; [occ.] Program Assistant, Arizona Aids Foundation; [memb.] Phi Theta Kappa, International Honor Society; [hon.] Governor's Award for Excellence on Arizona Child Support Enforcement Conversion Project; [oth. writ.] Ode to 'it' (not yet published); [pers.] I have learned as a human being that I need to believe and have faith in a power greater than myself and share the gifts I was given by that power.; [a.] Phoenix, AZ

HOGG, MARTHA MOLINE
[b.] October 27, 1931, Dickson, TN; [p.] Hattie Trotter Phillips, Seamon Trotter; [m.] Cecil B. Hogg (Deceased), July 1, 1950; [ch.] James, Gary and Perry Hogg; [ed.] Graduated Shawnee High School; [occ.] Homemaker; [hon.] Easter poem won second place in high school easter poetry contest when the stone was rolled away.; [oth. writ.] Water windows in a tapestry of thoughts.; [pers.] My love of nature is reflected in many of my poems.; [a.] Louisville, KY

HOGUE, CHRIS
[b.] February 28, 1981, Columbus, OH; [p.] Bill Hogue, Ellen Hogue; [ed.] Freshman at Westerville North High School (currently); [occ.] Student; [memb.] United States Youth Soccer Assoc., Central College Presbyterian Church, Westerville North Student Council, Class President.; [hon.] Dale Seymour "Escher-Like" Art contest winner, Stewart Scholar Winner, Soccer Jr. Design Contest Winner, State Soccer Team Captain; [oth. writ.] Published in "Anthology of poems by Young Americans"; [pers.] "If a penny saved is a penny earned, then the government ain't earned nothing!"; [a.] Westerville, OH

HOGUE, JOAN CLAIRE
[pen.] Joan Overton Hogue; [b.] June 27, 1944, Lakewood, NJ; [p.] Carl Overton, Glennie Overton; [m.] Montez Allen Hogue, August 20, 1967; [ch.] Sean Steven, Brent Allen, Ryan Carl; [ed.] High School Diploma; [occ.] Assistant to the Director of the Addiction Program for the City and City of Denver. (Denver C.A.R.E.S.); [memb.] Member of the Parkfield Congregation Of Jehovah's Witnesses; [pers.] Turn negative things into positives. As a very small girl, my mother often put me and my siblings to bed at 6:00 pm as we sometimes has no dinner and the house was very cold. As a small child the nights seemed endless, hence The Long Grey Cloak of Winter. I always tell people no matter how bad your situation is things can and do change.; [a.] Denver, CO

HOHMANN, CHRISTIAN
[b.] April 2, 1958, Chile, South America; [ed.] Bachelor in Architecture, Professional Musician/ Songwriter, Researcher of Mystic Theology; [oth. writ.] Articles in "Noreste", a monthly fictional newspaper sold in corner stands, "Of Trascendental Geometry and the Organic Theology of Time" (book/unpublished) "La Casa y el Arquetipo Centrado" (unpublished); [pers.] I view Art as an emotional liberation from the artificial complexities of life as we know it, but not as it really is in the full beauty of a trascendental Eden, maybe a way of reconnecting our true self to the elemental Origins that haunt us with their meaningful simplicity.; [a.] Houston, TX

HOLDEN, PAULA
[pen.] Paula Holden; [b.] March 22, 1964, San Diego, CA; [p.] Hubert and Charlotte Brogdon; [m.] Karl Holden Sr., August 7, 1982; [ch.] Karl Edward, Kellen Kenneth; [ed.] Great Falls, High School; [occ.] Substitute Educational Assistant; [a.] Cheyenne, WY

HOLDER, TIFFANY
[b.] April 15, 1981, Asheville, NC; [p.] Rustin and Cynthia Holder; [ed.] Freshman Milton High School; [occ.] Student; [memb.] John's Creek Baptist Church Missions Committee; [hon.] 8th grade all around award peace movement 1994 Marithe Francois Girbaud; [a.] Atlanta, GA

HOLLAND, LISA
[pen.] Lee Hughes; [b.] December 26, 1967, Columbus, OH; [p.] Willie and Rayleen Holland; [ch.] Julia Nicole, Christina Renee; [ed.] Hamilton High School, DSSC, Devry Institute Technology; [occ.] Self-employed; [memb.] American Cancer Society, Member - World Vision Sponsor 2 1/2 years; [oth. writ.] Many poems that I hope will soon be published; [pers.] In my writing the wondrous joys of the world comes alive, from trees to star, birds to child. I have been inspired greatly by the numerous poets of early century.; [a.] Columbus, OH

HOLLEY, LISA
[b.] August 5, 1969, Atlanta, GA; [p.] Jim Holley and Beverly Holley; [ed.] Pebblebrook High and Georgia State University; [occ.] Student of Medical Assisting; [pers.] I believe that anyone can be someone regardless of what their past may hold, through all the struggles, hurt and pain, they will be stronger, I thank all who helped me become the person I am through their excellent guidance and support.; [a.] Atlanta, GA

HOLLINS, JENNIFER
[b.] March 28, 1962, Long Island, NY; [p.] Cynthia Duryea and Robert Tait; [m.] James Hollins, May 18, 1985; [ed.] Lowest Valley H.S., Plainedge H.S., Taylor Business Institute; [occ.] Was travel agent 13 years, now retired - Homemaker; [memb.] National Wildlife Federation, National Park Trust, Int'l Fund Animal Welfare, Humane Society of USA, Audobon Armchair Activist; [hon.] H.S. Art Dept. Award, High Honors Senior Year, 2nd Place Plainedge Library Art Show; [oth. writ.] Many, but never bothered to publish any. (This poem I wrote when I was 10 years old).; [pers.] Become involved in a charity. Even if you're an "armchair activist" like myself. Writing letters to those in paper does help. Let your voice be heard!; [a.] Bedford, NY

HOOD, JEAN H.
[pen.] Jean H. Hood; [b.] September 27. 1929, Packard, KY; [p.] Roxie Williams Hamby and

Lloyd Hamby; [m.] James T. Hood (Deceased December 19, 1995), August 12, 1954; [ch.] Five, three boys and two girls; [ed.] High School and Special Credits; [occ.] Retired (Henry Ford Hospital); [memb.] AARP; [hon.] Best Waitress of the Year - Knoxville, TN in 1954, Best Supervisor 1972 HFH Detroit, MI, Excellence Awards 1984 HFH Detroit, MI; [oth. writ.] Grandmothers Like Me; [pers.] This poem was written for my daughter about my husband. He was not one to go to Church. All these things happened to him and much more. Grandmothers Like Me was written for 2 of my grandchildren.; [a.] Lincoln Park, MI

HOOD, MICHAEL LEE
[b.] May 10, 1958, Bardstown, KY; [p.] Eules M. Hood, Willana A. Cox; [m.] Betty Jean Hood, December 31, 1993; [ch.] Stephanie and Allison Hood; [ed.] Nelson Co. Sr. High, Nelson Co Vocational School, Continuing Education for Work with the Physically and Mentally Challenged; [occ.] Supervisor Frankfort Habilitation Inc.; [memb.] Golden Pathway Fellowship, Alton Baptist, Chaplin Christian; [hon.] For Working with Children and Teens, Sunday School Teacher, Vacation Bible School, received and honor from Chaplin Christian Church for 13 years without Missing a Sunday; [oth. writ.] A special thought (my first), my greatest treasure, waiting, searching, children, the cross, these are a few in my first book entitled special thoughts.; [pers.] Most of my poems reflect from situations I see in everyday life, which was inspired by the death of a Sunday School Teacher and friend who never gave up on me. (Robert Johnson) in which the first poem I wrote.; [a.] Lawrenceburg, KY

HOOTS, MARY ANNA
[b.] March 22, 1963, Escalon, CA; [p.] Edward S. and Mary C. Machado; [m.] Jeffrey Hoots, May 24, 1991; [ch.] Robert, Amberleigh, Jessica; [ed.] Santa Cruz High Calif, Killdeer Public, N. Dakota; [occ.] Supervisor, Operator at Killdeer Mt. Manu.; [memb.] Little Missouri Jayceees, Kill Deer Saddle Club; [pers.] I've always loved, poetry, books, plays, anything that involves imagination and thought. Through my writing, I would like to transpose sight, smells and life, excitement; [a.] Killdeer, ND

HOPE, ROBERT
[b.] April 19, 1969, Los Angeles, CA; [p.] Ronald and Juanita Hope; [ed.] Keene High School, New Hampshire College; [occ.] Retail Manager, Chartwell Pharmacy, Boston, MA also Bassist, Boston Area Recording Artists "Bee Charmers"; [hon.] National Honor Society, Who's Who of American High School Students, Winner, Edlee Songwriting Contest, Dec. 1995; [oth. writ.] A book of poetry and song lyrics titled Descent A Look Inside, searching

for a publisher and/or agency.; [pers.] I trust my instincts: I write what I feel and what I know, otherwise, it wouldn't be real.; [a.] Billerica, MA

HOPPES, ALICE F.
[pen.] Alice F. Hoppes; [b.] May 20, 1939, Tucumcari, NM; [p.] Harold Kent and Bessie Mae Kent; [m.] Willard Hoppes, August 24, 1969; [ch.] LaDonna, Gamble, Diedra Faulkner, Linda Hoppes, and Toia Morgan; [ed.] Tucumcari High School, one year at Eastern New Mexico Univ.; [occ.] NIA Foundation, President Albuquerque, NM; [memb.] National Association for the Advancement of Colored people, National Association for Female Executives, National Council of Negro Women; [hon.] The World Who Who's of Women Liberty Bell Award Law day USA Kappa Alpha PSI Community Service Award, African American Studies Person of the year, YWCA Woman on the move, Governor's Award Outstanding NM Woman, Who Who's Among Black Americans; [oth. writ.] Articles for Black History Month Albuquerque Journal Series of Articles on the Trip to Nicaragua during election in 1989.; [pers.] I write poetry to express how I feel on certain issues and during crises in my life.; [a.] Albuquerque, NM

HOPWOOD, LIBBIE
[pen.] Libettes; [b.] February 3, 1953, Minneapolis, MN; [p.] Britton A. Goetze Jr., Martha M. Goetze.; [ch.] Chester, Isabella, Arthur; [ed.] Alice Smith Elem. Hopkins, Widsten Elem. - Wayzata Jr. and Sr. High Vofm. (of Minnesota); [occ.] Pappagallo of Minn. Inc. - V.P. Retail - 25 yrs.; [memb.] Kappa Kappa Gamma Chichaper of U. - of MN. 4-M, Girl Scout - Choir Jr. High and St. Davids, Deca Club, Tonka Teens.; [hon.] State finals in D.E. 4-M, County finals, A&B honor roll, MS. Freeway News, Galleria Board of Directors, Pres.; [oth. writ.] French Journals 4 yrs. 30 yrs. of writings - advertising lay-outs and comp. summarizing and criticizing.; [pers.] "Life is based on experience, in both body and soul, one way to achieve this is through writing and living life to the utmost in ones honesty to "ones-self"; [a.] Minnetonka, MN

HOWARD, VIVIAN WILKERSON
[pen.] Rose Creek; [b.] February 3, 1929, Uree, NC; [p.] Lillie Mae Wilkerson, William Roland Hamilton; [m.] Raymond Howard, January 27, 1955; [ch.] Raymond Michael, John Douglas and Nathan Reuben; [ed.] New Hope High School (1948), Good Samaritan Hospital (1951), Knoxville College, Knoxville TN (1962), BS Degree in Social Studies; [occ.] Registered Nurse on Alcohol and Drugs Unit at UT Medical Center, Knoxville TN; [memb.] Life Member of Disabled American Veterans, Tabernacle Baptist Church in Knoxville TN, S.R. Lee Missionary Circle; [hon.] Served two years in Army Nurses

Corp during Korean War from 1952 to 1954, First Lt. I have been a R.N. since 1952. Have licence to practice nursing in North Carolina and Tennessee.; [oth. writ.] A Matter of Choice, Tornado on Cedar Lane; [pers.] Love God above all others. Love all sisters and brothers. Continue to work all my live. Decrease trouble and strife.; [a.] Knoxville TN.

HOWLEY, JOHN R.
[pen.] J. R. Howley; [b.] January 1, 1949, Providence, RI; [p.] Raymond L., Eileen E.; [occ.] Director/Designer in the Animation Arts; [pers.] Poetry is like capturing life in the tip of a fountain pen and re-writing it your way.; [a.] Santa Monica, CA

HUBBARD, JACLYN M.
[pen.] Jackie; [b.] April 26, 1985, Salem, MS; [p.] Karen and Michael; [ed.] Cove Elementary grade 5, Mrs. McGurn; [memb.] Under 12 Soccer A.T.V. Skiing Program, Flute Lessons; [oth. writ.] Winters coming, Watch out, Halloween's here, Fall, Parents, Colors, Brothers and Oreo (my dog); [pers.] I enjoy writing about things I have seen heard about or done - I try hard to write good poems. I enjoy soccer, skiing, riding my bike and playing with Oreo, my dog.; [a.] Beverly, MA

HUDDLESTON, IRA
[b.] December 3, 1952, Waco, TX; [p.] David and Agnes Huddleston; [m.] Noel Huddleston, November 17, 1989; [ch.] William, David; [ed.] Baylor University; [occ.] Computer Technical Support Analyst; [hon.] Air Force Commendation Medal (1985); [oth. writ.] Computer Software User Manuals; [pers.] I have been influenced by Walt Whitman, Arthur Rimbaud, and Bob Dylan. Robert Bly's own poems, as well as his translation's of Spanish poets and analysis of other poets has been a big influence.; [a.] Garland, TX

HUGHES, AMANDA BROOKE
[b.] August 11, 1983, Monroe, GA; [p.] Steve and Sheila Hughes; [occ.] Student (Cousins Middle School); [hon.] Honors - Beta Club, Gifted Art Program, and Chorus Awards - Science, Reading, D.A.R.E. essay award, honor roll, and student of the Month also Young Georgia Author's Award; [pers.] I really enjoy writing. When I write I escape to another world that is filled with happiness. I try to express the way I wish the world could be.; [a.] Covington, GA

HUGHES, JACQUELINE E.
[pen.] Jacqur Hughes; [b.] February 10, 1968, Baltimore, MD; [p.] Reta T. Hughes, Hugh P. Hughes Jr.; [ed.] BA in Psychology with minor in Business from College of Notre Dame of MD currently working on main counselling Psychology at Bowie State.; [occ.] Counselor at

Potomac Job Corps Center Staff Sergeant Marine Corps Reserve.; [memb.] American Psychological Association, Sierra Club, World Wildlife Federation, National Parks and Conservation Assoc. The Wilderness Society.; [hon.] Who's Who Among American High School students. Meritorious Mass, National Defense Metal 4.0 GPA; [oth. writ.] Several poems published in H.S. Literary magazine. "Ellipsis" 1984.; [pers.] Everyone must be a little crazy, because if you were totally sane, you would see the world as it actually is... and go crazy!; [a.] Catonsville, MD

HUGHES, JESSIE LYNNE
[b.] October 19, 1984, Belleville, KS; [p.] Bill and Jolene Hughes; [ed.] Homeschooling (5th grade); [memb.] Black Belt Club (Karate); [hon.] Super Kids of Summer 1995, (library volunteer), Various Karate Tournament Trophies, danced in "The Nutcracker" December 1995; [a.] Duncan, OK

HUMISTON, CRYSTAL TRUJILLO
[b.] May 29, 1984, Durango; [p.] Caren Trujillo and Mike Humiston; [ed.] 6th Grade Bayfield Middle School, Bayfield Colorado; [occ.] Student; [hon.] Honor roll Bayfield Mid. School, First place in talent contest, Second place in Reflections (grade 6-8); [oth. writ.] "Silence", "Grandma's Garden", "Lacy", "William Dawse", "My Great day", "New Soap", "My Class", "Wonder", "Weird Santa", "Environmental Rap Poem", "Funny", "Dandelion"; [pers.] "I want to inspired children everywhere" "You can achieve anything you seek."; [a.] Bayfield, CO

HUMPHREY, CLAUDIA
[b.] February 3, 1939, Duluth, MN; [p.] George and Geneva Bennison; [m.] Kinsey H. Humphrey, March 8, 1958; [ch.] Steven and Wendy Humphrey; [ed.] 2 yrs. College; [occ.] Homemaker; [memb.] Friends of East County Arts Inc. - Foothills United Methodist Church; [hon.] Citizens of year 1967 La Mesa Woman's Club Jrs.; [oth. writ.] Nothing published - many poems I've written for years as they come to me; [pers.] I believe in the basic good in all people - try to I've by the golden rule and am truly blessed to live in America where I'm able to write freely of that which I choose; [a.] El Cajon, CA

HUNKER, EVELYN
[b.] Pittsburgh, PA; [m.] Walter; [ch.] Susan L. and Jeffrey A.; [ed.] B.A. University of Alabama at Birmingham, many art workshops and classes; [occ.] Artist; [memb.] 8 Art organizations including Birmingham Museum of Art, the water color society of Alabama and The National Museum of Women in the Arts; [hon.] Paintings accepted in National and Regional shows.; [oth. writ.] Other unpublished poems that correlate with original paintings; [pers.]

Poetry and painting are both an expression of the inner sol. Poetry brings out the beauty of words, the music of the mind and the harmony of lines and phrases. Paintings are visual, but the beauty, the harmony and composition are there.; [a.] Birmingham, AL

HUNTER, PATRICIA A.
[pen.] Patricia Hunter; [b.] September 10, 1941; [p.] Frank and Mary Kurrell; [m.] William F. Hunter, August 10, 1957; [ch.] Cynthia Louise, Tammi Marie, William Frederick Jr., Lynn Allen, Cheri Michelle, Patricia Ann [pers.] To enrich the mind and heart reach out with a hand shake to commend. Don't point a finger to condemn; [a.] Sunbury, PA

HUNTER, VIRGINIA
[pen.] Ginny; [b.] January 6, 1953, Union County; [p.] James W. Hunter and Fannie M. Hunter, [ch.] Mar, Windy and Melody Boyd; [ed.] Carlisle Santuc Elementary, Sims High and York College; [occ.] Mental Retardation Specialist Supervisor, [oth. writ.] Now that you're gone. Memories of a friend a wind called you.; [pers.] I would like to dedicate this poem to my friend Nancy Chambers and my sister Bessie Crosby. It is because of their encourage-ment that I write.; [a.] Whitmire, SC

HUTCHINS, RICK
[pen.] Bic; [b.] May 1, 1961, Boston; [p.] Winnie and Rick; [m.] TBA; [ed.] The back roads of New England, the streets of big cities, the mountain, the desert, the library, the small hours of the morning, also, Emerson College; [occ.] Midwife Juggler at Boston City Hospital; [memb.] Cousteau Society, Save the Children, Planetary Society, Southern Poverty Law Center, Smithsonian, Spacecause, et cetera..; [pers.] All of life is the sun of the arts and sciences, science is what we know and art how we perceive it. To know true peace, one must understand that each informs the other.; [a.] Quincy, MA

HYATT, JANET
[b.] February 16, 1935, Iowa; [p.] John Hyatt and Mary Hyatt; [ed.] Independent Study: Verse of Long Fellow Shakespeare, Melody/ Rhyme of Burl Ives, Jimmie Dale Gilmore; [hon.] Angel Trimmer Merit Award, ShenanDoah Iowa 1995 for "Flowers for the Living an Inspirational Poetic Song about little motherless sister Ann and Baby Rose and their father, [oth. writ.] A volume of unsubmitted songs and poems.; [pers.] To encourage more consideration of human rights. I find Gerry Spence's soft spoken common sense words to be inspirational.; [a.] Plattsmouth, NE

ILLGES, BRANDY
[b.] March 26, 1983, Noblesville, IN; [p.] Paul Illges and Dorothy Illges; [ed.] 7th grade at

Sheridan Middle School; [occ.] School; [memb.] Band, Quiz Bowl, Champs, Pep Band for Sheridan Basketball.; [hon.] Presidential Academic Fitness award, 2 trophies for all star pacesetter in 2 years in a row.; [pers.] Although this is my first published poem I hope it won't be my last one.; [a.] Sheridan, IN

INGRAM, NORMAN
[pen.] Norm (Brent Johnstone); [b.] August 22, 1963, Kansas City; [p.] Raymond and Nellie Ingram; [m.] Toma Jo Ingram, June 8, 1990; [ch.] Ashley, Tonya; [ed.] Jenks High School 1981, Tulsa Junior College 1990 Climate Control Institute 1995; [occ.] HUACR Tech.; [memb.] Beaver Street Baptist Church Jenks, Oklahoma; [oth. writ.] Several other writings not yet published, just waiting for someone to get their hands on.; [pers.] "The past is a killer, so beware."; [a.] Jenks, OK

INGRAM, ROSIE J,
[pen.] Buckner Marrimon; [b.] September 11, 1938, Greenwood, MS; [p.] Calvin and Ruth Moore; [m.] Otis Ingram, January 23, 1988; [ch.] Ernest, Rolind, Darwin, Jacquelyn Buckner; [ed.] Paris II Cosmetology School, Sumner High School, Institute of Medical Studies, St. Louis, Mo. - Long Bch, CA; [occ.] Cosmetology, Instructor/Part Time; [memb.] Christian Tabernacle Church of God in Christ; [oth. writ.] Excuses - Excuses The Item - Holiness or Hell The Lord and His Complaining Child. - Big "I" Go, and Sin No More; [pers.] I once wrote a book titled "Innermost. I tore it up but later I realized that life's experiences has inspired me to write poems of my innermost feelings. I'd like to share them. God inspired.; [a.] Gladstone, MO

IOLI SR., MARK J.
[b.] January 14, 1949, Pittsburgh, PA; [ch.] Mark Jr., Jason, Bret; [ed.] B.S. Education California University of PA; [pers.] My writing tends to flow from emotion and/or experience; [a.] Pittsburgh, PA

IRBY, LAURETTA A.
[pen.] Kit Irby; [b.] January 6, 1917, Lucas, KS; [p.] Daisy and Abe Sawyer; [m.] Bud Irby, November 27, 1978; [ed.] American Business College Whichita; [occ.] Retired Nurse; [memb.] Cheney U.M. Church; [hon.] Mayor Cheney Kansas sculpture ceramics painting Voluntary Mission Projects; [oth. writ.] Essays poetry.; [pers.] Reach out to everyone with Gods love as King David, Paul, and Jesus did.; [a.] Whichita, KS

ISON, DAVE
[b.] January 22, 1959, Cincinnati, OH; [p.] Don and Cleo Ison; [m.] Julie Ison, June 9, 1984; [ch.] Jared, Mark, Grant, Amy; [ed.] B.S. 1980, The Ohio State University J.D. 1983, Capital University Law School; [occ.] Lawyer, [a.] Powell, OH

ITALIANO, DORIS E.
[b.] July 31, 1937, Ridley Park, PA; [p.] Samuel T. Dowey, Doris G. Dowey; [m.] Thomas J. Italiano, June 15, 1974; [ed.] Chester High School, Neumann College (Non-credit); [occ.] Retired five years, employed 35 years for PECO Energy as an executive secretary; [memb.] Wallingford Presbyterian Church (Editor of Church Newsletter), National Trust Historic Preservation (Associate Member); [oth. writ.] Article in Fall 1992 edition of Inspired (a qtrly, preservation publication), articles in the following newspapers: Delaware County Daily Times, The United Methodist Reporter; [pers.] I try to greet each day with a fresh eye and maintain an optimistic outlook. My goal is to reflect these attitudes in my writing.; [a.] Upland, PA

JACKSON, VI LYNNE
[b.] Dallas, GA; [p.] Hollice and Maggie-Rachel McGarity; [ch.] Kiara and Julian Jackson; [ed.] Savannah State College Major: Secretarial Science; [occ.] (Norfolk Southern Corp.) Accounting Adjustment Specialist; [oth. writ.] (These are songs I have written) "Come And Dance With Me - A Good Friend Will", "Forever", "Not An Elusive Dream"; [pers.] Practice good mental health, believe in the positive, use your imagination for good thoughts.; [a.] Lithonia, GA

JACOBY, CHARLES BRIAN
[b.] September 23, 1976, Brenham, TX; [p.] Charles and Andrea Jacoby; [ed.] Navasota High School, University of Mary Hardin - Baylor; [occ.] Student - Freshman at the University of Mary Hardin Baylor; [memb.] First Baptist Church, National Eagle Scout Association Youth Council; [hon.] Eagle Scout, Honor Graduate, All-Star Cast; [a.] Navasota, TX

JAMES, BENEDICT
[pen.] Benzi James; [b.] December 18, 1963, Saint Vincent, WI; [p.] Martin James, Dorothy James; [ed.] St Vincent Grammar School; [occ.] Travel Agent/Photographer; [oth. writ.] After poems and songs in English and French on various themes; [pers.] My work is dedicated to the youths everywhere. That they'll grow up with love and respect and show reverence for their elders and the ancient. Fathers who came before them.; [a.] Brooklyn, NY

JARVEY, JACK E.
[b.] June 14, 1954, Great Falls, MT; [p.] Daniel and Lillian Jarvey; [ed.] H.S. Graduate and 2 yrs. College Education; [occ.] I was employed by the I.R.S., for 1 yrs. but had to take a disability due to epilepsy.; [memb.] Epilepsy Foundation; [hon.] Received various awards and letters of recognition while employed by the Internal Revenue Service (I.R.S.) including 2 Peoples Choice Awards from My Peers and Performance

Award based on My Position as a Tax Auditor.; [oth. writ.] I wrote 2 other poems during the same period of time that this poem was written. All 3 were used by a friend who also wrote some of her won poems as a project for English while in High School, and she received an A for the project.; [pers.] I was not diagnosed with epilepsy until 1994 which was a result of an Auto Accident. (Not my fault) prior to that time I was physically fit and very active in sports and the great outdoors. I'm a firm believer in family values, traditions, and cultures and heritages.; [a.] Missoula, MT

JEFFRIES, JAMES EDWARD
[b.] August 13, 1912, Atlantic City, NJ; [p.] Byron Woods and Helen Binckley Jeffries; [m.] D and W; [ch.] Elizabeth B. Klein; [ed.] BS in Ed Brooklyn College OCS Fort Benning, Military Intelligence Training Center; [occ.] Retired Writer, Editor; [memb.] American Medical Writer's Assn.; [hon.] Army Good Conduct Medal, Army Bronze Star Medal, AMSR Campaign Medal, European, Arkandale East Campaign MEdal, 2 Bronze Stars, AMG R JRL of Nursing - Book of year, Ohio House of Reps - Outstanding public service, Syntaxis Homes for youth awards, Jefferson, OH, solution for public service.; [oth. writ.] First poem 1978 Life Is Bitter, Mad Man, Monologue, Child Memories, My Dearest Lizzie and Ben, Haikus, Birthday Remembrance, Reflections on Father's Day.; [pers.] Life is bitter, life is sweet. Having another fitter, It's hard to beat. Love your neighbor if you want to love yourself. A cogent, assertive, considerate rebel gest along.; [a.] Harvey Cedarsboro, NJ

JELINEK, VIOLA B.
[pen.] Vi; [b.] December 6, 1920, Smithville, TN; [p.] B. L. and Novella Atnip (Deceased); [m.] Divorced, February 26, 1954; [ch.] Doug; [ed.] High School Night College Courses; [occ.] Retired. Gen. Services, State of Tenn.; [memb.] AARP, Baptist Church, Nafe, for female Executives; [pers.] Strive to reflect positive imagination with reality.; [a.] Madison, TN

JENSEN, BEVERLY M.
[b.] December 14, 1951, Baltimore, MD; [p.] John Beever, Rose Beever; [m.] Paul K. Jensen, October 1, 1983; [ch.] Maura Leigh Jensen; [memb.] Gunpowder Baptist Church; [pers.] I believe Spiritual Warfare is a real thing. For peace on earthly pilgrimage and eternal life we must all come through Jesus.; [a.] Millers, MD

JENSEN, TAMARA L.
[pen.] Tami; [b.] December 10, 1961, Grantsburg, WI; [m.] Mitchell Jensen; [ch.] Katherine Ann, Bethany Joy, Chelsea Renee, Rosalie May; [ed.] Mariner High School St. Olaf College B.S. in Nursing; [pers.] Life here is

fragile and fleeting - how wonderful it is to reflect in its tender and meaningful moments.; [a.] White Bear Lake, MN

JEREMIAM, WANDA
[b.] Trinidad, West Indies; [p.] Phyllis and Augustus Douglas; [m.] Ricky Jeremiah; [ch.] Fana and Safiya; [ed.] Educated in Trinidad, West Indies. Presently, attending St. Joseph's College, Brooklyn for Degree in Health Administration; [occ.] Registered Nurse; [memb.] American Nurses Association; [pers.] Each human being is responsible for his/her life. Some people want to forset the spiritual law of life. I want to remind them through my writing, what you sow, you reap whether good or bad; [a.] Rosedale, Queens, NY

JIMENEZ, KATHY
[pen.] Tutty; [b.] November 6, 1974, Brooklyn, NY; [p.] Carlos Jimenez and Migdalia Roldan; [m.] Carlos J. River, January 11, 1995; [ed.] Francisco Mendoza High School and Interamerican University of Arecibo, Puerto Rico; [occ.] Secretary and a Salesperson-decorating; [memb.] CSI Collegiate Secretary International, National Library of Poetry, Dean's List, International Society of Poetry, Future Leagues of the American Commercial; [hon.] Third place in the Interamerican University of Aguadilla for best poems and short story. Second place in the High School in the Regional of the Commercial School of Arecibo for bookkeeping etc.; [oth. writ.] Several poems published in newspaper and magazine. I wrote poems in English and Spanish. And I also have a short story and a novel.; [pers.] I've always tried to express the love I feel in my heart in my poems. I believe that if we are to survive as a race, love will be the answer. I dedicate all of my writings to my family, my wife Marilyn and my children Nigel and Nikita for their inspiration.; [a.] Isabela, PR

JOESTING, LORI PETERMAN
[pen.] Susan Snell; [b.] August 12, 1963, Baltimore, MD; [p.] Robert Peterman and Valerie Crook; [m.] John F. Joesting Jr., February 14, 1982; [ch.] Hannah and Olivia Joesting; [ed.] Bel Air High School; [occ.] Administrative Assistant; [memb.] Church of God of Cleveland, Tennessee - National Right-To-Life Committee; [oth. writ.] Several poems published in local newspapers; [pers.] I believe writing to be a God-given talent and an ingraining of one's own soul.; [a.] Churchville, MD

JOHNS, CHRISTINA R.
[pen.] Renee; [b.] September 2, 1986, Munster, IN; [p.] Loren and Renota Johns; [ed.] Mizpah Junior Academy School; [occ.] Student; [memb.] Brunswick Height Church, Mizpatt Choir; [hon.] Honor Roll Student and actress in Little

Company Angels Aware; [oth. writ.] Liars, Kiss Me, Stand in for the Lord; [pers.] My poems reflect my short years on this planet and what I see, and how people act and why we need the Lord so much. I have been influenced by my mother a poet Renota; [a.] Gary, IN

JOHNS, ROCKY
[b.] December 25, 1963, Phoenix, AZ; [p.] Lynn Houston, William Junior Johns; [ch.] Kimberly Lynn and Rocky Johns Jr.; [occ.] Floor Mechanic; [hon.] Gospel Music Award; [pers.] I write poetry to express my inner-most feeling and emotions; [a.] Mabelvale, AR

JOHNSON, GARY M.
[b.] November 26, 1938, El monte, CA; [p.] Mills and Nell Johnson; [ed.] Pryor High School Mississippi State University (Ph.D. in Psychology), University of Tulsa (M.A. in Psychology); [occ.] Psychologist, Tulsa Public Schools, Tulsa, OK; [memb.] Oklahoma School Psychological Association; [hon.] Psi Chi National Honor Society, Dean's Honor Roll; [oth. writ.] M.A. Thesis And Ph.D. Dissertation In Psychology; [pers.] My writing expresses the irony, paradox, and absurdity in the human condition. My favorite writers are T.S. Eliot, Samuel Beckett, John Keats, Fyodor Dostoevsky, and Herman Hesse.; [a.] Tulsa, OK

JOHNSON, JOHN R.
[b.] March 7, 1931, Wisconsin; [p.] Dewey and Eleanor Johnson; [m.] Jackie Kinsella Johnson, August 29, 1993; [ch.] John, Jackie; [ed.] B.S. in Education, Taylor Univ., M.S. in Teaching, Portland State Portland, Oregon; [occ.] Juvenile Court School Teacher Los Angeles County; [memb.] LA Co. Education Association California Teachers Association, National Education Association, Air Force Association; [hon.] 1969, Teacher-Of-The-Year-California Association of Christian Schools High School Year Book Dedication (1970); [oth. writ.] "The Israeli Educational System" published in Thrust, an educational magazine especially for school administrators. (February, 1986); [pers.] Treat others the way you want to be treated.; [a.] Apple Valley, CA

JOHNSON, MARY BETH
[pen.] Cecila Alexander Briar-Rose, CR "Cab-r"; [b.] November 21, 1982; [oth. writ.] "Am I A Crime", "Hopeless Romantic", "Mystery of The Diamond", short story; [pers.] To live life as a game and to seize the day.

JOHNSON, NIGEL L.
[pen.] Noshoj Legin; [b.] May 10, 1959, Oakland, CA; [p.] Cleve and Betty Johnson; [m.] Sharon D. Johnson, July 7, 1995; [ch.] Vaughn, Ryan, Cameron, Trevor; [ed.] Diablo Valley College 1978-77, Monte Vista High

School Graduated 1981; [occ.] Executive Management Castle Management and O.C.C.A.; [memb.] Lighthouse Christian Ctr.; [hon.] Inducted by the International Society of Poets as International Poet of Merit 1995; [oth. writ.] Warriors of God - National Library of Poetry - the best poem of 1996, between the raindrops, east of the sunrise.; [pers.] I am but am instrument in the hand of God.

JOHNSON, PAUL EDWARD
[pen.] Irving Matt Godenuff; [b.] July 30, 1921, Northfield, CT; [p.] Philip and Doroty Johnson; [m.] Nina Johnson, November 19, 1961; [ch.] Lucy Alexander; [ed.] G.E.D., High School, U.S. Army WW II; [oth. writ.] Misc. verse not pub.; [pers.] Dedicated to two great moms my mother Dorothy my mom Dec. and my wife Nina.; [a.] Copake, NY

JOHNSON, PHYLLIS MARIE
[b.] March 10, 1951, Springfield, OH; [p.] Late Ben F. and Mariamne (Hixson) Johnson; [m.] Divorced; [ch.] 2 Rebekah and Mariamne; [ed.] 1969 Graduate Springfield North High School and 1970 grad of Springfield joint vocational school of Practical Nursing; [occ.] Retired LPN after 21 years of service.; [memb.] St. John's Business and Professional Women, The Mary Martha's of St. John's Lutheran Church, and The Springfield Area Emmaus Community; [oth. writ.] This is my first; [pers.] I am a person that does not fear death. I wrote this poem to give comfort and assurance to my oldest daughter about the finality of death; [a.] Springfield, OH

JOHNSON, RACHEL A.
[pen.] Rena Fehren; [ed.] B.A University of Utah; [hon.] In 1965 I was awarded a Bachelor of Science Degree in Music Education (Ogden, Utah).; [oth. writ.] Of poetry (As yet also unpublished), "Wintertime", and "Reflec-tions", and "Harvest". One other, presently in preparation for print, is "Blue Skies".; [pers.] In the springtime of 1995, I began writing my first poems. Writing poetry is an experience of writing I cherish very highly.; [a.] Tucson, AZ

JOHNSON, STEPHEN JEROME
[pen.] S.J.J.; [b.] October 14, 1918, Stephen, MN; [m.] Alma Elizabeth, July 20, 1944; [ch.] Four daughters and four sons.; [ed.] Schooling 8 years, worldly 77 years.; [occ.] Retired, hobbiest; [memb.] VFW the 96th historical society; [hon.] Strictly military.; [oth. writ.] None published, but have written articles on many subjects. In poetry I prefer poetry for special occasions. Such as weddings, artifacts and birthdays. I humbly admit I am humorist, and philosopher.; [pers.] Wise men contemplate facts, but Speak the truth, with confidence.; [a.] Apache Junction, AZ

JOHNSON, VAUGHN O. NIXON
[pen.] Nov; [b.] December 17, 1983, San

Francisco, CA; [p.] Vaughn O. Nixon Sr. Nigel and Sharon Johnson; [ed.] Oak Grove Middle School; [occ.] Student; [memb.] Light House Christian Ctr. - Royal Rangers; [hon.] Honor Roll Kindergarten through 4th and 6th; [pers.] When I wrote this poem I was not myself at all. God just took over.; [a.] Concord, CA

JOHNSTON III, HARRY E.
[b.] August 10,1968, Virginia; [m.] Tara Juba Johnston, September 10,1994; [ed.] Wyoming Area, Johnson Tech; [occ.] Techneglas Inc; [memb.] Army National Guard; [pers.] This poem was written for my wife, it was a little taken of my love for her. She is truly my "One and Only".; [a.] Wilkes Barre, PA

JOHNSTON, ROSS
[b.] July 15, 1968, Little Rock, AR; [ed.] B.S. Mathematics, Rose - Hulman Institute of Technology, M.S., Mathematics, New Mexico State University; [occ.] Investment Advisor; [memb.] The Planetary Society, ASPCA; [oth. writ.] Several short stories and poems published in campus publications, currently working on a novel.; [pers.] Next time I'm going to submit a dirty limerick!; [a.] Little Rock, AK

JONES, DONNA FOY
[ch.] David, Dawn, Dannielle, Darcele; [ed.] Degree in Science Professional Registered Nurse - University of the State of New York; [occ.] Pharmaceutical Sales; [memb.] ANA, NUS Hospital Society of Pharmacist, Poet Society; [hon.] Editor's Choice Award regarding "I Wish I Were A Tree"; [oth. writ.] "I Wish I Were A Tree" publication "A Delicate Balance" 1995 several pieces of poetry; [pers.] "The poem from the "Eyes of a Patient" was written as I worked as a critical care nurse. I envisioned the difficulty the patient endured. This poem is in honor of all nurses in memory of my father John E. Foy Jr. who died of Cancer at the young age of 36 years old. I am where I am because of his appreciation of nurses.; [a.] Clifton Park, NY

JONES, ERIN
[b.] September 1982, Wilkes-Barre; [p.] Julie Jones and Paul McCrea; [pers.] I write my poems by what inspires me in my life.

JONES, FLORENCE M.
[pen.] Florencia, Prudence; [b.] April 11, 1939, West Columbia, TX; [p.] Isaiah and Lu Ethel McNeil; [m.] Waldo D. Jones, May 29, 1965; [ch.] Roderick, Wanda and Erna; [ed.] Prairie View A. And M. University B.S. (cum laude) 1961 Prairie View A. and M. MEA 1968 Rice Univ., Univ. of Houston, St. Thomas Univ.; [occ.] Piano Instructor, writer, speaker, story teller; [memb.] Life Member, Texas retired Teachers Association, Texas Storytelling Assoc. Distinguished Life Member International Society

of Poets, Member: Oak Meadows Church Of God, National Woman of Achievement and Society of Children's Book writers and Illustrator; [hon.] Outstanding Achievement in Education Letters of Recognition: President Bill Clinton, Governors Ann Richards and George Bush, Congresswoman Shelia Jackson Lee and numerous others, Gold cup (Highest Music Award) National Lib. of Poetry Editor Choice, Diamond Key, National Women of Achievement, Who's Who In Art Educ.; [oth. writ.] (1) Science Modules for Houston, Ind. Sch. District (1985), (2) Gifted And Talented Program For Peterson El. School (3) Poems, National Lib. of Poetry Anthologies And Sparrougrass Poetry Forever, (4) Science Pop-Up book, presently writing children's Book; [pers.] Life is more pleasant when we have a forgiving positive attitude. A positive attitude is a powerful asset which can enable us to accomplish fears others merely dream about, faith in God and self-confidence are also needed.; [a.] Houston, TX

JONES, JEANETTE JACKSON
[b.] September 17, 1946, Opelika, AL; [p.] Palmer and Lucy Jackson Sr.; [m.] Freddie Leon Jones Sr., April 3, 1965; [ch.] Three sons; [occ.] Writer, Poet; [memb.] International Society of Poets; [hon.] International Society of Poets (Distinguished member) Poet of Year Award 1989; [oth. writ.] At Water's Edge, Best Poems Of Western World, A Tapestry Of Thoughts, Best poems of 1995, Poem on tape, Sunday Morning By River

JONES, KIT
[b.] May 2, 1978, Winfield, IL; [p.] Debbie and Larry Jones; [ed.] Still in High School Dundee Crown High, Currently 11 grade.; [occ.] Store roomy at Toys "R" Us; [memb.] Biker, with the Dundee Cardinal Bicycle Club.; [hon.] 5th grade presidential Academic Fitness Award.; [oth. writ.] Many untitled works and one short story which is untitled, but the story is a chronicle of an ideal society based on the path of the past into the future.; [pers.] My work is based on life and humans, and the path we take into the future.; [a.] Carpentersville, IL

JONES, NICHOLUS
[b.] June 6, 1976, Chester, PA; [p.] Charlotte Campbell, Curtis Jones; [ed.] High School Graduate of Chi-Chester High School.; [oth. writ.] Christmas Story printed in local paper second place.; [pers.] My poems are a reflextion of my inner feelings, of life, love and a twist on the beyond of a everyday world and the happenings around me.; [a.] Chester, PA

JONES, WILLIAM H.
[pen.] William Henry Jones, Bill Jones, W.H. Jones; [b.] April 1, 1924, Black Diamond, WA; [p.] Helenor Jones and Father Deceased; [m.] Barbara A. Jones, May 17, 1960; [ch.] Denise

Lynn William and Robert Jeffrey Jones; [ed.] B.A. San Diego State Naval School of Hospital Administration; [occ.] Captain, U.S. Navy (Ret); [memb.] (1) Federal Health Care Executives Institute Alumni Assn., (2) Fleet Reserver Assn., (3) Distinguished Member - International Society of Poets; [hon.] Legion of Merit (Navy) Numerous Service Medals and awards, Graduated with honors 5 military schools, Advanced from Apprentice Seaman to Captain during Naval Career; [oth. writ.] "A Tapestry of Thoughts" (1) The National Library Of Poetry, "Beyond the Stars", "Best Poems of 1996", "Spirit of the Age", "A Muse of Follow" (2) Sparrowgrass Poetry Forum, Inc. "Treasured Poems of 1995", "Poetic Voices of America", "Treasured Poems of America" (3) Oriville Register, Oroville, CA "The Infamous Still in Orovillie"; [pers.] I believe in personal achievement, inspiring others to fulfill their dreams, at peace with self and others, all with a sense of humor, dedication and perspective.; [a.] Lake San Marcos, CA

JORDAN, JOANN
[pen.] J. J. or Joe Joe; [b.] August 8, 1941, Greeleyville, SC; [p.] Ervin Davis and Martha L. Davis; [m.] Lindburgh Jordan, August 12, 1967; [ch.] Carolyn Lorraine and Kenneth; [ed.] Williamsburgh City Training, O.I.C. and Crown Business School; [occ.] Home Health Att. and Child Care Provider and Avon Rep.; [memb.] Berean Miss Baptist Church Youth Min. Volentair; [oth. writ.] This is first poem to be published Several others ready and waiting to be discovered or excepted and approved; [pers.] I try to express the beauty of different experiences in life through the love of God, nature and man, to express hope love, joy, peace of mind and smiles; [a.] Brooklyn, NY

JOSEPH, WENDY N.
[pen.] Wendine; [b.] November 18, 1972, Grenada, WI; [p.] Kent G. Joseph, Brenda A. Joseph; [ed.] St. Mary's Junior, St. Joseph's convent (High School), Grenada National College, St. Francis College - Brooklyn NY; [occ.] Psychology student, at St. Francis College, NY; [hon.] Dean's List; [oth. writ.] Several poems, and one short story, published in "The Montague" (A School Magazine), one poem "I Have Much More" published in "All My Tomorrows" (volume IV "Quill Books") and many more unpublished short stories and poems.; [pers.] Creativity comes from inside, but inspiration comes from the people, things, and experiences I encounter everyday. I put my feelings, and that of others - in all my writings; [a.] Brooklyn, NY

JUGAL, RAYMOND YSAAC
[b.] August 12, 1974, Baguio, Philippines; [p.] Rustico D. Jugal Sr., Lolita Y. Jugal; [ed.] Saint

Louis University High School, Saint Louis University College; [pers.] Poetry can be described as a way of thanking and appreciating the good things God has done for us and for the good things that are to come.; [a.] Baguio, Philippines

JULIEN, YVONNE C.
[b.] June 9, 1964, New York City, NY; [p.] Angel Luis Cajigas and Sixta Raman (Foster Mother); [m.] Trevon C. Julien, June 12, 1987; [ch.] Jay Everett Julien, Cheyenne MacKenzie Julien; [occ.] Desktop publisher, The United Way of Tri-State; [oth. writ.] "A Master of None", "Unaware of its Fate...a Tree remains faithful until the end." (Both unpublished); [pers.] I live by and honor respect, faith, courage, integrity and compassion, and try to live life without any regrets.; [a.] Bronx, NY

JUNIEL, JEANPIERRE
[b.] August 18, 1968, New Orleans, LA; [p.] Mr. and Mrs. Albert L. Juniel Jr.; [ed.] Marion Abramson Senior High 12B Combat Engineer (Active Army) 68X Electronics and Armament (Army Reserve); [occ.] Security Officer; [oth. writ.] "The Pointed Finger" (Unpub.), "Seize Life at the Moment" (Unpub.), "The Attraction of a Tear" (Unpub.); [pers.] To my mother and father for instilling the basics, my brothers and sisters for challenging my doubts and to my friends for increasing my strength. "Thank you God for the aforementioned blessings."; [a.] Houston, TX

KACHER, DEAN
[b.] April 21, 1962, Detroit, MI; [p.] Donald and Mary Kacher; [m.] Eun-Ok, September 18, 1989; [ed.] Electronics Engineering; [occ.] Personal Coach and Business Consultant; [memb.] President - Dallas Entrepreneurs Society, V.P. Word Entrepreneurs Society Member, International Society of Poet Consultants; [oth. writ.] Presently writing book titled "No more secrets" notes from a seminar junkie!; [pers.] There are no secrets in life except the secrets we keep from ourselves.; [a.] Dallas, TX

KADOTA, HOLLY DANA MOCK
[b.] December 1, 1957, Riverside, CA; [p.] Theodore and Louise Mock; [m.] David R. Kadota, June 12, 1982; [ch.] Keli Louise, Jillian Leanne; [ed.] University of California, Santa Barbara; [memb.] Alpha Lambda Delta Scholastic Society; [hon.] Bacherlor's Degree with Honors, V.C.S.B.; [pers.] Dedicated to the memory of my mother, Louise Lundine Mock; [a.] Rancho Palos Verdes, CA

KAESTNER, JOYCE LAURIE
[b.] November 8, 1943, Milwaukee, WI; [p.] Laurence and Ruth Farber; [m.] The late Charles A. Kaestner, January 23, 1965; [ed.] Grad. 1961 Wauwatosa High School, Grad. 1963 Spencerian Bus. College; [occ.] Management Assistant, Sr.;

[memb.] Mt. Calvary Lutheran Church Council, South Wisconsin District Lutheran Women's Missionary League - Recording Secretary; [hon.] 1961 National Honor Society 1963 - Outstanding Female Graduate, 1991 Certificate of Leadership Award; [pers.] It is my faith in my Lord and Savior, Jesus Christ, that has sustained and uplifted me throughout the ordeal that prompted this poem from the heart, for it was my thoughts reacting to the Lord's words within me. Praise God, from whom all blessings come. For I know I will see my beloved husband, Chuck, again in Heaven.; [a.] Wauwatosa, WI

KALE, MARK D.
[b.] February 6, 1950, Brooklyn, NY; [ch.] Shana Ann and Jacob Alexander Kale; [ed.] University of California, Los Angeles B.A., Bacteriology; [occ.] Real Estate Consultant, Radivs Retail Advisors; [memb.] International Council of Shopping Centers, Association of Corporate Real Estate Executives; [oth. writ.] Unpublished poetry, including free verse I mostly employ heroic couplets. My poetic side revealed itself about 2 years ago and now I cannot stop! I write mostly of relationships.; [pers.] Be sensitive. Connect with people in a meaningful way. Enjoy what life has to offer. There is no more that what you see so live at the edge.; [a.] Tustin, CA

KALTENBAUGH, LOUISE
[b.] September 24, 1941, Pittsburgh, PA; [p.] Ernest and Louise Sauerland; [m.] Glenn M. Kaltenbaugh, August 6, 1960; [ch.] Robert, Ronald and Donna (three); [ed.] B.A. Liberal Arts - English Literature, M.A. Liberal Arts - English Literature, Ph.D. - Educational Admin., Higher Educ.; [occ.] Director, Teacher Center for Urban Education; [memb.] ASCD, Phi Delta Kappa; [hon.] Recognized by Gov. Edwards as Outstanding Educator; [oth. writ.] The Influence of Prices and Price Subsidies on Persistence by African-American Students: An Analysis of the National Postsecondary Student Aid, a chapter in a book titled Changing Times, Changing Schools, The Comer Project for School Development; [pers.] I believe that as members of a global society we must embrace each other with understanding and caring and we must respect individuality.; [a.] Belle Chasse, LA

KAMMER, CHARLES L.
[b.] December 18, 1946, Pittsburgh, PA; [occ.] College Teacher, The College of Wooster

KANTER, PAUL
[b.] July 20, 1977; [p.] Monnie and Susan Kanter; [occ.] Student at the School of the Art Institute of Chicago; [pers.] One day I'll be dead. What madness and kindness can I give to the world before then?; [a.] Chicago, IL

KATZ, MADELINE
[pen.] Marilyn Di Gatti; [b.] June 12, 1966, Bronx, NY; [p.] Sol Katz, Sylvia Katz; [ed.] Harry Truman High School, Mannes College Of Music - Undergraduate Degree in Vocal Music, Long Island University, Presently Attending for Graduate Degree in Special Education - with Bilingual Extension.; [occ.] Teacher for the Board of Education; [memb.] The United Federation of Teachers, and I.A.P.P.W. - Teacher's Association of Personnel Workers; [hon.] Spanish Medal of Honor, Plaque from the Spanish American Club for fluency in the language and College Level Achievement in Spanish literature, Music Medal of Honor for Achievement in Vocal Music.; [oth. writ.] Has written poetry in other languages as well: Spanish, French, Italian, and German. Music composes have written music to some of my poems.; [pers.] Much of my writing has been greatly inspired by my musical training. Other works which I have continued to formulate are directly related to the people I have had the opportunity to meet, and have played many positive roles in my life.; [a.] Bronx, NY

KAWURYAN, ANNA MARIA SITI
[b.] Jakarta, Indonesia; [p.] Johannes Soemadiman, Henrika Maria Wadjiah; [m.] Keith Owen Fuglie, December 19, 1990; [ed.] 1) Santa Ursula High School, Jakarta, Indonesia, 2) University of Indonesia, Jakarta, Indonesia, 3) University of Minnesota, Minneapolis, Minnesota, USA; [memb.] 1) Ikatan Sarjana Ekonomi Indonesia, 2) Golden Retriever Rescue, Education and Training, Inc.; [hon.] 1) First in class for each semester, 10th, 11th and 12th grades, Santa Ursula High School, Jakarta, Indonesia, 2) Graduated Cumlaude, Santa Ursula High School, Jakarta, Indonesia, 3) Award for Classical Guitar, The Music School of Indonesia, Jakarta, Indonesia; [a.] Falls Church, VA

KAY, SARAH
[b.] August 11, 1981, San Francisco, CA; [p.] Larry Kay and Eileen Kay; [ed.] I am presently a Student at Notre Dame High; [hon.] I received an academic scholarship to Notre Dame High and have received First Honors every semester.; [pers.] I try my best to write from my heart. Each poem is a mirror of my soul.; [a.] Belmont, CA

KEAST, DIANNE MARIE
[b.] May 10, 1965, Crow Agency, MT; [p.] Thomas J. Keast and Mary Lou Keast; [ch.] Kevin A. Wheeler; [ed.] St. Ignatius High School, Life experiences; [occ.] Habilitation Aide, Personal Home Health Aide; [memb.] Reformed Congregation of the Goddess, Missoula Pagan Alliance, Missoula L.A.R.P. Group (Live Action Roll Playing); [oth. writ.] Magda (Short Story), The Illumination of a Vampire, Old Lovers and New Ghosts (Short Story), She Has

Always Been (Poem), Darkness (Poem), Coveted by Darkness (Short Story), The Electric Rure Oracle (in progress); [pers.] I believe that the profound mysteries of our universe are reflected all around us. The trick... is in deciphering them. (Personal Note) I never think of being published when I write. I write because I am a story teller.; [a.] Missoula, MT

KEATTS, PANSY M.
[b.] October 12, 1913, Indian Mound, TN; [p.] Dr. C. K. Keatts M.D. (Deceased), Mrs. Lillian S. Keatts; [ed.] Colleges (teacher), College (business); [occ.] Retired Federal Employee, Retired Teacher; [pers.] Expressions of different feelings regarding the beautiful and meaningful things in my life that may enhance the lives of others!; [a.] Indian Mound, TN

KELALIS, BARBARA ANNALISA
[b.] San Antonio, TX; [m.] Panayotis P. Kelalis, April 8, 1970; [ch.] Steven Michael Fletcher; [occ.] Interior Designer; [oth. writ.] Books of poetry and newspapers.; [pers.] My poetry is to express my love for God and humanity. If I touch one heart through my writing, than I will have accomplished my goal.; [a.] Ponte Vedra Beach, FL

KELLER, AMBER
[b.] April 6, 1980, Tacoma, WA; [p.] Joe and Annette Keller; [ed.] Skyline Elem., Truman Middle School, Wilson High School; [occ.] High School Student; [memb.] Wilson High School Diving Team, Pacific Northwest Diving Team; [hon.] Numerous awards for diving, gymnastics and Girl Scouts, five years on Honor Roll, plus other School related Awards; [oth. writ.] Many others written, none other published.; [pers.] I write about the deep emotions I feel or experience. It helps to lift them.; [a.] Tacoma, WA

KELLER, JESSICA MERKEL
[b.] April 12, 1982, Plainfield, NJ; [p.] Walter J. Keller and Claudia Merkel-Keller; [ed.] Currently enrolled in Far Hills Country Day School (grade 8), Far Hills, NJ; [occ.] Student; [memb.] Member of the Glen Ridge Swim Team in Bridgewater, NJ Member of the Far Hills Country Day School Lacrosse and Field Hockey Teams; [hon.] Am editor of Far Hills Country Day School Yearbook, The Sentina. Have won numerous swimming medals, ribbons and awards. Have won numerous riding medals, ribbons and awards. Am listed in the United States Achievement Academy National Honor Roll; [oth. writ.] Have written other poems and Haiku.; [pers.] Everyone experiences life but few live it. Living is happiness.; [a.] Bridgewater, NJ

KELLY, DAN
[pers.] True love and real friendship are nature's finest treasures. My poem in this anthology is about my darling friend, whose sobriquet is "Stella

Star." Stella is a beautiful, talented, audacious, very competitive, dazzling young redhead. She lives with her family in Orlando, Florida.

KELTON, RICHARD ALAN
[b.] March 24, 1950, St. Albans, NY; [p.] Charles Joseph K., Marie Ellen Froland; [m.] Angela Dance Carrington (Divorced), June 15, 1975; [ch.] Tara Lane and Alan Ross K.; [ed.] Frank W. Cox High School Chowan College, Associate of Sci, Virginia Wesleyan College, Chemistry, class 1973 ICS (International Correspondence-Schools) (Law Enforcement Science); [occ.] Chemist II, (On long term disability) - Tenneco/Newport News Shipbuilding; [hon.] Phi Theta Kappa Fraternity by the Iota Delta Chapter 15th of Sept. 1969 also A.S. Cum Laude, Chowan C. Chemistry Degree, Cum Laude - Virginia Wesleyan College; [oth. writ.] None pub. assorted prose and poetry; [pers.] Exploit not the breath of timeless thought to power...; [a.] Newport News, VA

KEMPER JR., MICHEAL
[b.] September 30, 1976, Port Arthur, TX; [p.] Micheal and Etta Kemper, [memb.] Port Arthur Camera Club, Christian Faith Baptist Church; [oth. writ.] The meaning of "If" Unstoppable Violence, Mist of Madness, "Dead End"; [pers.] Michael was a very lonely young man. He was killed by police at age 17 while visiting a friend's house.; [a.] Port Arthur, TX

KERLEGAN JR., ANTHONY
[b.] March 3, 1962, San Francisco, CA; [p.] Anthony Kerlegan Sr., Mimey Kerlegan; [m.] Christine A. Kerlegan, December 17, 1988; [ch.] Sean Anthony Kerlegan; [ed.] Oceana High School, Pacifica, CA; [occ.] Truck driver, [a.] Hayward, CA

KERN, BRIAN H.
[b.] September 10, 1956, Potsdam, NY; [p.] Lewis A. Kern, Sr. (Deceased) and Donna J. Kern, Vorce; [m.] Donna S. Kern, June 9, 1990; [ed.] A. A. S. Agronomy - Canton ATC, Canton, NY; [occ.] Supervisor of Defense Subsistence Office/Defense Personnel Support Center; [memb.] American Massage Therapy Association; [hon.] Silver Award for excellence in government achievement; [oth. writ.] None published; [pers.] The pleasure I derive from writing poetry comes from the influence of my father who also wrote many good poems before his untimely death. I am proud to be his legacy.; [a.] Hoover, AL

KERR, ROBERT MICHAEL
[b.] November 4, 1954, Washington, DC; [p.] William A. Kerr, Thersia B. Kerr; [m.] Signa Joy Kerr, June 13, 1995; [ed.] Master Degree from San Diego State University in Public Administration, 1978, Master Degree from Faith Lutheran Seminary in theology, 1982, State of

Washington and Alaska Teaching Instructors License in Cosmetology, 1985, Languages Hebrew I, Greek I, II III and German I, II, Machintosh and I.B.M Computers, going to the College of the Desert because of my Brain Injury, 1995; [occ.] Disabled; [memb.] Piranha Swim Club in Palm Springs; [hon.] Nanka Judo Federation, 2nd Degree Brown Belt, then Black Belt in Japan, 1972 High School Academic/Athletic Excellence Award, Recommended approved by Senator Alan Craston for the United States Air Force Academy, Football Scholarships throughout the U.S.A, Victory Valley Junior College Most Valuable Football Player Award, San Diego State University Football Defensive Linebacker/Walk on N.C.A.A. Light Heavyweight Colligate Boxing Championships, Silver Medalist 1977, Professional Boxing, 1979; [pers.] I suffered a stroke when my first wife died in my arms after fighting cancer (1992) griefing over her death. My stroke came in 1993. Then, 9 months later after recovering from my stroke. I was struck by a car (March 1994) while crossing the main street by the "Blue Coyote" restaurant. I was struck by the car going 55 m.p.h. M.D Gregory G. West "Trama Adult Reconstruction" rebuilt my broken left elbow with steel plates. M.D. Sheer rebuilt my entire face from the inside out. I now have a steel jaw, steel eye sockets, a steel top cap. Also, another M.D. rebuilt my right leg from the knee cap down when my bone disappeared on the cars impact. My face hit the wild shield damaging my face, frontal brain lobes and lower brain stem. The Palm Springs police never caught the driver. It is listed as a unsolved hit and run. Then on April 4, 1995, I drowned at the College of the Desert pool. I attempted to break the school record of holding my breath under water when crossing the pools length twice. Take one day a time (24 hours). Live in the present! The past is dead, no one really knows the future except God the creator of all life.

KETTERMAN, FAITH LYNN
[b.] October 27, 1971, Akron, OH; [p.] Charles and Judy Ketterman; [ch.] Jessica and Jacob; [occ.] Line Builder; [pers.] I dedicate this poem to my children Jessica and Jacob - my inspiration comes from the happiness they bring me each any every day of my life.; [a.] Candler, NC

KEYSER, LINDA
[b.] March 9, 1946, Mount Pleasant, PA; [p.] Floyd and Jane Fitzsimmons; [m.] Charles Keyser, May 28, 1966; [ch.] Mark and Jenny; [ed.] Mayetta High, Kansas Children's Institute of Literature (Writing Course); [occ.] Teachers Assistant for Lincoln Intermediate #12; [memb.] Church; [hon.] Pioneer Girls 14 Years Service Pin, Volunteer Work for our Local Church; [oth. writ.] Letter to the editor of a local newspaper.; [pers.] In life you should think so what when

bad or good things happen to you. You shouldn't think what if. I praise the Lord jesus for my God given talent.; [a.] Shippensburg, PA

KHALSA, GURUKARTA KAUR
[b.] March 21, 1958, Houston, TX; [p.] Lee C. Russell Jr., Gloria G. Russell; [m.] Hari Singh Khalsa, June 9, 1979; [ch.] Kartapurkh Singh; [ed.] University of Houston and Glendale College, California; [occ.] Ordained Minister, Sikh Dharma, Houston, TX; [memb.] International Kundalini Yoga Teachers Association; [hon.] 6th Annual Billboard Song Contest, Certificates of Merit - 2 songs; [oth. writ.] Several poems published in various books and magazines.; [pers.] Humor is a wonderful thing. It allows us to see ourselves with laughter.; [a.] Houston, TX

KIBLER, ROBERT L.
[b.] November 7, 1974, Port Charlotte, FL; [p.] Larry D. Kibler, Patricia A. Plummer and Ronald L. Plummer, [ed.] Salem High School, currently Kent State University; [occ.] Freelance Artist, Student at Kent State University; [memb.] KSU Salem Art Club; [hon.] Dean's List, "Reconcilliation Now" USA/Vietnam Art Contest; [pers.] In my poetry, I seek to convey and share the imagery of my artwork, my spiritual beliefs, and capture the voice of nature. I enjoy many poets but find the romantic stylings of yeats influences me greater than others.; [a.] Salem, OH

KILE, DALPHNE M.
[pen.] Dolly; [b.] May 27, 1952, Burley, ID; [p.] Mildred Bennett and Luther Bennett; [m.] May 26, 1975; [ch.] Three; [ed.] Some College - Gen Ed.; [oth. writ.] None published; [pers.] I have written several short stories and poems. I hope to write an autobiography.

KINCH, DIONNE
[pen.] D. L. Kinch; [b.] July 23, 1970, Lincoln, NE; [p.] Patricia and Leonald Kinch; [ed.] Eastern SHS, Univ of Nebraska at Omaha at present; [hon.] Dean's List, Alpha Lambda Delta; [oth. writ.] Articles in the ' Afro-American Weekly' newspaper and 'every Wednesday' magazine.; [pers.] I hope to expose my cultural richness to everyone who reads my work.; [a.] Omaha, NE

KING, KATHLEEN
[pen.] Kat; [b.] September 17, 1953, Houston, TX; [p.] Herbert and Gloria Ehlert; [m.] O. Aubrey, June 8, 1979; [ch.] Shawn Michael; [ed.] Reagan High School, Houston TX; [occ.] Bookkeeper; [memb.] St. John the Baptist Catholic Ch. RCIA Facilitator; [a.] Edmond, OK

KING, MINA
[b.] September 18, 1981, Wichita, KS; [p.] Doug and Anita King; [ed.] Belle Plaine Elementary

and Belle Plaine Middle School; [occ.] Student; [hon.] Won Science Olympiad in 1991, been on Honor Roll for 4 years; [pers.] The views expressed in my poetry all come from my heart. They are my personal views about a problem. I myself have faced or someone close to me. I was influenced by my dad's great poetic skills and my mom's great courage.; [a.] Belle Plaine, KS

KING, SANDRA L.
[b.] July 20, 1964, Woodruff, SC; [p.] James King, Patricia King; [ed.] Woodruff High School; [occ.] Lawn Maintenance; [oth. writ.] My poetry has never been published.; [a.] Naples, FL

KING, TULA W.
[b.] April 2, 1940, Alturas, FL; [p.] Dallice and Florence Wasden; [m.] Widow; [ch.] Renee Brown, James Redlinger, Daryl Redlinger; [ed.] Bartow Summerlin High, American Medical Records Correspondence Course, Institute of Children's Literature; [occ.] Production Coordinator - ADA Consulting Firm; [memb.] AHIMA; [pers.] To search within, sharing in writing, enabling others to soar to destinations beyond the current consciousness.; [a.] Deland, FL

KIRCHENSCHLAGER, AMBER
[pen.] Ambo; [b.] February 17, 1982, Akron, CO; [p.] Dan and Kindi Kirchenschlager; [ed.] Currently in 8th Grade at Yuma Middle School, Yuma, CO; [occ.] Student; [memb.] Jr. America Club, 4-H, Tribal Sounds (an audition choir), Farmers M&M Co-Op, YMS Student Council, Colorado Jr. Rodeo Assn.; [hon.] 4.0 Club, Jr. Beef Champion Showman and Jr. Round Robin Champion, Several Barrel Racing Champion-ships, Honor Swing Choir, Honors Science, Honors Math, Honors English, Ambassador to Australia for the USA through People to People Ambassador Program in 1996; [oth. writ.] Ghosts (published - will be in 1996).; [a.] Yuma, CO

KIRK, MARIE A.
[b.] January 23, 1934, Salt Lake City, UT; [p.] Joseph L. and Anna Broadbent; [m.] Andrew B. Kirk, January 4, 1959; [ed.] East High, Henager School of Business, Art and Music Studies at McCune School and Art Barn - all in S.L.C. Utah; [occ.] Retired Graphic Artist; [memb.] St. Cornelius Catholic Church; [hon.] Honorable Mention Fine Arts Utah State Fair 1995, Commendation Pacific Telephone CEO for Design and Production of Annual Report for Junior Achievement of Bay Area - 1980; [oth. writ.] Several books of poetry - all unpublished; [pers.] The incidents and observations of daily life touched by the finger of God or permeated by the beauty of nature prompt my poetical inspiration. The numerous poems I have written over the major span of my lifetime are my dairy.; [a.] Richmond, CA

KIRKENDALL, STEFANIE ANN
[b.] December 27, 1983, Saint Louis, MO; [p.] John and Patricia Maher; [ch.] Pets: 2 dogs (Beethoven, Doc), 1 wolf (Nikki), 2 birds (Icarus, Bernie), 2 hamsters (Mozart, Pixie), 3 rabbits (Oscar, Bugs, Lady); [occ.] Student at All Saints Catholic School in St. Peters, Mo.; [memb.] World Wild Life, Green Peace, Goal Keeper - Queen Bee Soccer Team (w/135-31-16 Record), All Saints Speech Team, Basket-ball and Softball or All Saints; [hon.] Honor Roll, 1992 Missouri State Tae Kwon Do Champion, 2nd Place at Lake St. Louis Stables Horse Show, 33 Soccer Awards, 18 Karate Awards, 5 Basketball Awards, 1 Softball Award, 1 Horse Show Award; [pers.] I hope to work for green peace as an adult, and am currently pursuing horse riding lessons in hopes of owning my own horse.; [a.] Saint Peters, MO

KLIMA, JOSEPH R.
[b.] November 18, 1937, Brownsville, PA; [p.] Mary and Joseph Klima; [ch.] Colleen Ann, Joseph Louis, Cynthia Marie; [pers.] I dedicate this poem to my grandchildren, Valerie, Michael, Julie Purtell, Monica Joseph, Stephanie Klima, Paul Krotine.; [a.] Euclid, OH

KNAPP, SHELLY D.
[b.] October 11, 1968, Fort Worth, TX; [p.] Ron Rankey, Winnie Rankey; [m.] Lewis G. Knapp, November 20, 1993; [memb.] Officer's Christian Fellowship; [hon.] Marine Corps Honor Graduate Plt. 4019, National Defense and Good Conduct Medal; [pers.] I strive to keep God first in whatever I do. I wrote this poem to my husband Lewis when we were engaged and he was away at college.; [a.] Fort Worth, TX

KNAUS, CAROLYN AMRIT
[ed.] B.S. in English Education, M.S. in Organizational Behavior, holding certifications as a Parent Effectiveness Trainer, as Revaluation Counselling Instructor a Licensed Massage Therapist and a flower Essence Practitioner; [occ.] Wellness Professional; [memb.] Profes-sional Member of National Wellness Associa-tion, Physiology and Biofeedback and Member of the Flower Essence Society of America; [pers.] I am an aspiring poet who is a lover of nature and the changes of the seasons. I live surrounded by the Ozark Forest which is a continual inspiration to me. I am interested in imaging reality in the arts in the contest of the feminine experience. I am gifted to live in a small Ozark Village of artists, bed and breakfast owners, tree lovers mountain bluffs, victorian cottage, caves historical hotels and healing springs. From the woods and these ambiences, I draw much inspiration.; [a.] Eureka Springs, AR

KNAUSS, STUART F.
[b.] July 26, 1907, Pughkeepsie, NY; [m.]

Suzanne C. Knauss, June 24, 1943; [ed.] Cornell U 1927 Class; [occ.] Retired LA City employee; [memb.] World War II, served 4 years retired as Capt.; [oth. writ.] "Hokku and Hokum", a collection of haiku, "Desert Gulch", a poetic opera.; [a.] Los Angeles, CA

KNIGHT, CANDIDA MONTALVO
[b.] April 27, 1968, East Meadow, NY; [p.] Thomas D. Montalvo, Anne H. Zellner, [m.] David E. Knight, August 2, 1990; [ch.] Chrisha Anne, Brianna Joyce, David James; [ed.] McArthur High School; [occ.] Housewife; [pers.] This is my first poem to be seen by anyone else. I've always been afraid that no one would like what I wrote so I always wrote them just for myself.; [a.] Milton, FL

KNIGHT, VIRGINIA
[pen.] Ginny; [b.] December 10, 1931, Cleve-land, OH; [p.] Vick and Janice Knight; [ed.] Hollywood High, LASC, UCLA; [occ.] Interior Designer and Instructor, UCLA Extension; [memb.] ASID (American Society of Interior Designers) U.S.C. Architectural Guild, UCLAX Guidance Committee; [hon.] Barons Who's Who in the West, Who's Who Interior Design, Certified Interior Designer, Honorable Mention Crayola Contest; [pers.] Humor, that is laughing at myself, is a life saver. A.A. Milne and the wizard of oz continue to influence my life.; [a.] Los Angeles, CA

KNOLL, VINCENT C.
[b.] September 20, 1952, Portland, OR; [p.] Edward and Alice Knoll; [ch.] Richard; [occ.] Security Professional; [pers.] Words are what makes language possible, to create is God's gift to man, let no one take his creativity from Him.; [a.] Port Land, OR

KOBRES, R. FRED
[b.] June 25, 1939, Atlanta, GA; [p.] Ted and Kate; [ch.] Mike and Steve; [pers.] The poet is always catching up, but at least he runs the race. And, being first is not his Goal anyway.; [a.] Tampa, FL

KOHN, DAN
[b.] April 27, 1950, Antigo, WI; [p.] Robert and Delores Kohn; [m.] Gloria; [ch.] Joshua, Leah; [ed.] MA - Psychology/Counseling and Guidance, Un. of Northern Colorado, Greelye, Colo.; [occ.] Christian Counselor, Marriage and Family Health Services, Eau Claire, WI; [memb.] American Association of Christian Counselors, Life Member, Optimist Int'l, Toastmasters Int'l, Toastmaster Int'l, Promise Keppers, Lutheran Church - Missouri Synod; [hon.] Public Speaking Awards; [oth. writ.] 1 Professional Article - "Professional Counselor" Magazine, Poetry and other writings in local publications; [pers.] "I am an instrument of Jesus Christ gifted to share and serve." My poetry is inspired through Him."; [a.] Eau Clave, WI

KOREY, BERNADETTE

[pen.] Bunny; [b.] July 20, 1964, Pittsburgh, PA; [p.] John and Helen Stadler; [m.] Frank M. Korey, May 4, 1991; [ch.] 8 children; [occ.] Mother of: Scott, Lita, Kira, Anne, Francis, Andrea, Timothy and Joel; [oth. writ.] Loves to write lyrics for church and to make poems into songs.; [pers.] There will be peace, even if only in the heart!; [a.] Pittsburgh, PA

KORNBLUTH, WILLIAM
[b.] January 8, 1922, Europe; [m.] September 18, 1949; [ch.] Renee, Phil; [ed.] One year at Munich University; [occ.] Retired Farmer; [memb.] Numerous; [hon.] I have quiet a number of plaques - mostly for lecturing; [oth. writ.] Autobiography: Sentenced to remember. Lehigh U. Press, publishers. Also countless poems and essays. Co-editor of quarterly magazine newsletter at Brookdale College; [pers.] I write for the love of writing. I have been doing so since the age of nine.; [a.] Jackson, NJ

KOTTY, STEELE M.
[b.] November 3, 1982, Northampton, MA; [p.] Charles Kotty, Dianne Stankowski; [ed.] 7th Grade Student Whitebrook Middle School Easthampton MA; [occ.] Student; [memb.] Boy Scouts of America; [hon.] Human Relations Award, Honor Roll Student; [a.] Easthampton, MA

KOWATS, RITA HEMMER
[b.] September 13, 1944, Saint Louis, MO; [p.] Marguerite Hemmer Kowats, George Kowats; [ed.] BA in English and German, MA Theology from the Graduate Theological Union, Berkeley, CA; [occ.] Theology Instructor, Bellarmine Preparatory School, Tacoma, WA; [oth. writ.] Other poems, "Jonah" and "Trilogy" deal with themes of nonviolent resistance to nuclear weapons and in just structures; [pers.] I love poetry because it helps me to get back to the "genes of my soul." My poems are therapy for me and often minister to others.; [a.] Tacoma, WA

KRAUSE, AMY
[b.] August 22, 1977; [p.] Daniel and Charlene Krause; [ed.] I graduated from Lockport High School in Lockport, IL. I am currently enrolled at Morounne Valley Community College studying to be an elementary school teacher.; [hon.] I won a poetry contest in 1994 for school. I was also published in our school's literary magazine called Visions.; [oth. writ.] I have written several other poems and short stories that I have entitled The Joseph Chronicles.; [pers.] My greatest influences were Anne Sexton and Sylvia Plath. I hope to one day walk in their paths. I find that writing is a constant source of comfort in my life because sometimes paper is the only thing that will listen to you!; [a.] Orland Park, IL

KRAUSE, DELTA
[pen.] Delta McLaughlin; [b.] May 12, 1939,

Springtown, TX; [m.] Stanley Krause, April 25, 1995; [ed.] North Side High School; [occ.] Dispatcher - Tri-County Electric Coop; [memb.] International Society of Poets; [oth. writ.] Had poems published in Christian newspapers and magazines, have poems in anthologies.; [pers.] I've had many miracles from the Lord. I love to write about how great he is and the mighty wonders he can do.; [a.] Azle, TX

KRAYNAK, EDWARD
[b.] August 17, 1971, Youngstown, OH; [p.] Judith Grove, Edward Kraynak; [ed.] Howland High, Gordon D., James Career Center; [occ.] Sales Person, Spencer Gifts Inc., Roadie - Rock Band Psycho Cafe; [oth. writ.] Many others poems that are yet unpublished and lyrics for several songs.; [pers.] My goal is to show through my poetry, that there are two sides to everything. In this case the side of the leaders and that of the soldiers. My influence for this particular poem was the band "Megadeth".; [a.] Warren, OH

KRIEGER, JOANNE
[b.] November 12, 1935, Portland, OR; [p.] John Green and Frieda Eisal; [m.] Willis Krieger, February 28, 1958; [ch.] Curtis John, Craig Willis, Camilla Joanne; [ed.] Jefferson High School - Portland, OR; [occ.] Homemaker; [memb.] Evangelical Congregational Church, AHSGR (American Historical Society of Germans from Russia); [hon.] Honor Society of Jefferson High School - Music Awards at Jefferson High School; [pers.] I write poems to celebrate and remember special events in the life of my family. It all began 37 years ago when I couldn't find a suitable card to give my husband on our 1st wedding anniversary!

KRISTON, JAMES F.
[b.] May 29, 1958, Rutherford, NJ; [ed.] Graduated Rutherford High School 1977, Pima Community College, Tuscon, AZ; [occ.] Bartender - High Volume-Club W.P.B., Fl.; [memb.] Blue Boar Tavern; [oth. writ.] Numerous (as yet) unpublished poems.; [pers.] My inspiration comes from meditation which is a learning experience for me, and I hope, in written word, it moves others.; [a.] West Palm Beach, FL

KROHBERGER, DAWN MARIE
[b.] July 26, 1969, Kew Gardens, NY; [p.] Fred and Virginia Krohberger; [m.] Divorced; [ch.] Thomas Andrew Collora; [ed.] West Babylon High School, Briarcliffe College - Associates Degree/Legal Assistant; [occ.] Insurance Representative; [memb.] American Diabetes Association Walk to her Fest Committee; [hon.] Briarcliffe, Dean's List; [pers.] I believe in individuality, I feel that each of us are unique beings. Love and respect toward each other can only establish a harmonious co-existence.; [a.] West Babylon, NY

KRONSKE, BETTY
[b.] Tampa, FL; [ed.] High School and some college credits Dale Carnegie Course; [occ.] Worked as a columnist for several newspapers in NY and Tampa area.; [memb.] On the Board of Adult Ed. program, Ambassador for the Chamber of Commerce-Was president of the Tri County Art Guild in LOL, member of the Lut-LOL. Woman's Guild, member of the Lut-LOL. Dance Group; [hon.] For poems, writing songs sculpture, singing, dancing entertainment, making prize winning costumes chosen best Columnist a the Laker News Paper in LOL.; [oth. writ.] Many poems and songs. Newspaper columns. Poems published in newspaper and read on radio. Wrote them song for the "Late Bloomers" dance group.; [pers.] I always accentuate the positive eliminate the negative.; [a.] FL

KUBICA, FRANCES
[b.] October 10, 1949, Bridgeport, CT; [ed.] M.A., Creative Writing, Brown University; [occ.] Writer/Researcher/Composer; [memb.] Dramatists Guild, BMI; [oth. writ.] Ties, a short one-act play, several concern works for solo piano.; [a.] Los Angeles, CA

KUKLA, ROSE BEARDSLEY
[pen.] Rose Kukla; [b.] May 24, 1952, Bridgeport, CT; [p.] Esther C. and Roger G. Beardsley; [m.] Michael W. Kukla, October 7, 1978; [ch.] Megan 1 daughter; [ed.] B.S. Physical Educ. - Univ. of Southern Calif., M.S. - Southern Illinois University - Carbondale; [occ.] Registrar, California Polytechnic University - Pomona; [memb.] Board of Directors, San Fernando Valley Girl Scout Council, various Professional Organizations; [a.] Sunland, CA

KULL, ANNA
[b.] January 12, 1985, Russia; [p.] Tamara Nazaroval, Givi Kull; [ed.] Elementary School 196 Queens; [pers.] In most of my writings I use the goodness of nature. My thoughts play a big role in my writing. My favorite writing of a poet is (Paul Revere's Ride by Henry Wadsworth Longfellow).; [a.] New York, NY

KURLAND, DANIELA
[b.] October 7, 1969, Brooklyn, NY; [p.] Ted Kurland, Liliana Kurland; [ed.] Notre Dame High School, The American Academy of Dramatic Arts; [pers.] My writing has always been for personal growth. My own life experiences are the basis for the words that I put down on paper. They are reflective of how I react to what goes on around me.; [a.] Los Angeles, CA

KUZNIA, CHRISTOPHER PATRICK
[b.] January 28, 1977, Edina, MN; [p.] Clarence and Pauline Kuznia; [ed.] High School - Thomas Jefferson attending Academy of Accountancy; [occ.] Student - Construction Worker; [memb.]

Jefferson Hockey Booster Club, Boy Scouts of America; [hon.] Academic Scholarship to Academy of Accountancy; [oth. writ.] Frightened Whispers Broken Dreams; [pers.] Be true to yourself, don't expect too much and always be happy.; [a.] Bloomington, MN

LA MANTIA, ANTHONY
[m.] Emily; [ch.] Jack, Dr. Joseph, Theresa, Anthony, Armanda; [occ.] World War II Veteran, Army 2 1/2 yrs. European Theatre of Operations. Retired after 41 yrs. of Service as Foreman from a most ethical and employee oriented Pharmaceutical Corporation - Pfizer Inc.; [oth. writ.] This is my first publication so it proves that at any age miracles do happen.; [pers.] My wife and I have tried to instill family values to our children, to be honest, fair and open minded in dealing with everyone. In this, we believe we have succeeded.

LABRANCHE, JOSEE
[b.] April 19, 1968, Montreal, Canada; [p.] Serge Laroche and Louise Benoit; [m.] Jocelyn Labranche, February 22, 1991; [ch.] Katia an Genevieve; [ed.] Pere-Marquette High School; [occ.] Mother full time; [oth. writ.] Personal poems about friendship, relationship, love, families, sickness and death.; [pers.] I would like to say my gratitude to all the people that I love and cherish. You are my greatest inspiration.; [a.] Panama City, FL

LAILANI, SMYNA
[b.] May 27, 1976, India; [p.] Mr. and Mrs. Lailani; [ed.] High School Graduate; [occ.] Job at Taco Bell; [memb.] Health occupations students of America. Columbia House, and American Heart Association (C.P.R.); [hon.] Certificate of Appreciation of Participation in the Junior Volunteer Program and Certificate of Students of Health Occupation of America.; [pers.] Thanks to Allah for being there, my parents, my family, my sister Aneta. my cousin Dimple. Thank you all very much. I love you.; [a.] Woodbridge, NJ

LAL-KISSOON, JACQUELINE J.
[b.] June 16, 1959, London, England; [p.] Cecil Lal-Kissoon; [ed.] Furtherwick Park Comprehensive School and Basildon College of Further Education, England; [occ.] Business Owner of Administration Company; [hon.] Everyday I am honored and awarded by health, happiness and peace of mind.; [oth. writ.] Stories published in Pathways Magazine. Writer of Children's Short Stories.; [pers.] Poetry is an art, as life is an art. Art is an expression of goodness and beauty, and it is life that is my greatest inspiration.; [a.] Dunedin, FL

LALINO, JOHN
[b.] June 2, 1947, Bronx, NY; [p.] Carmine and Antoinette Lalino; [m.] Mary Lalino, October 28, 1972; [ch.] Donna and Janet Lalino; [ed.]

High School graduate, Janes Monroe High School; [occ.] Disabled Viet-Nam Veteran; [hon.] Good conduct medal, Viet-nam Service Award, Army Commendation Medal, purple heart with clusters, Bronze Star with "V" device for valor. South Viet-nam medal of honor; [oth. writ.] All poems are about Viet-nam they are true, "Why", "Shortly", "When Night Falls," "If This Applies To You", "Trick Or Treat", "Deros", "The Village People", "One Day Short" and The Changeling; [pers.] My writings are about the Viet-nam conflict. I would like to have all of my poems published. Since they are all true I would like the general public to know how it felt to live with death 24 hours a day seven days a week and the long lasting suffering a veteran endured forever.; [a.] Hershey, PA

LAMBERT, ERNEST T.
[b.] November 25, 1942, Gainesville, VA; [p.] Deceased; [m.] Separated; [ed.] Completed Vocational School and Bldg. Engineering School; [occ.] Maint. Engineer; [oth. writ.] Titles (What I See In You), (Time Is Of The Essence), (What Can I Tell The Children?), (Am I different?), (The Road to Happiness), (My Most Important Affair); [pers.] I draw on my experiences and surroundings. I seem to seek some redeeming value out of any situation.

LANCASTER, LENORE LONG
[pen.] Lenore Long Lancaster; [b.] April 29, 1939, Cumberland, MD; [p.] Maurice and Edna Long; [m.] Jerry J. Lancaster; [ch.] Kim, Mark, Karen, Lisa, Su; [ed.] Pittsburgh Art Institute, Allegany Community College; [occ.] Freelance Illustrator and Author; [memb.] Grace U. Methodist Church, Allegany Arts Council-Bd. of Dir., Allegany Area Art Alliance-Bd. of Dir., Colored Pencil Society of America; [hon.] Various ribbons for Art, Sparrowgrass Poetry Forum 1995, World of Poetry - Merit Certificate 1990, National Library of Poetry 1995; [oth. writ.] Author and illustrator for childrens book to be published 3/96 entitled Window Well Stories, illustrator for Appalachian Story Tellers Series by author Mark Van Tyne; [pers.] If you have to explain it the message was lost.; [a.] Cumberland, MD

LANDINO, SUSAN DARIA
[b.] January 13, 1960, New Haven, CT; [p.] Maryellen and Joseph Landino; [ed.] Branford High School Manhattanville College, Centre for Medieval and Renaissance Studies, Keble College, Oxford; [memb.] Lord Byron Society; [a.] Los Angeles, CA

LANDRY, MARY M.
[b.] July 7, 1920, Rutland, VT; [p.] Michael and Margaret McDonough; [m.] Deceased, March 8, 1945; [ed.] Local Schools Mt. St. Joseph Academy - Rutland, BS - Trinity College - Burlington, VT, MA - Castleton College -

Castleton, VT; [occ.] Retired Teacher Green Mtn. Now: Foster Grandparent - tutoring and Asst. in Library; [memb.] Formerly Delta Kapa Gamma, Catholic Daughters of the Americas, Variety of Teachers Assoc., Formerly: Business and Professional Women's Club.; [hon.] National Authors Registry, President's Award for Literary Excellence (1994); [oth. writ.] Poems - published (2) Local and State Newspapers (1); [pers.] Poetry can be an instrument for giving wings to the mind.; [a.] Rutland, VT

LANE, KAMEN J.
[b.] October 2, 1984, Utah; [p.] Juliet and Kent Inasy; [oth. writ.] A Leaf, Earth-Quake, and A Tree.; [pers.] My hobby is to play basketball and write poetry. I also enjoy school.; [a.] Burbank, CA

LANG, DEBORAH
[b.] April 19, Newark, NJ; [p.] William C. Lang, Marion Lang; [ch.] Nikol Y. Hines, (grandson) Shawn L. Hines; [ed.] Educated in Newark School System, completed Computer Programming in Basic I 1982; [occ.] Staff Assistant, Customer Service, New York Ins. Co.; [oth. writ.] Nothing published as yet, but I have several poems and short stories I am trying to get published. While in Junior High I was editor of African American Newsletter.; [pers.] I think that reading is the key to discovering a world of knowledge and beauty. If what I write can bring enjoyment or comfort to only one person I feel that I have made a contribution to mankind.; [a.] Mount Pocono, PA

LANNIN, LOIS A.
[b.] September 19, 1941, Annapolis, MD; [p.] Adele Stockett and John Stockett; [m.] Bill Lannin, April 5, 1961; [ed.] Annapolis Senior High School, Anne Arundel Community College, Northwestern Michigan College; [occ.] Retired/Student; [pers.] I am in the process of beginning a second career in Social Work.; [a.] Williamsburg, MI

LARGER, AMANDA
[b.] June 3, 1977, Columbus, OH; [p.] George and Sandra Larger; [ed.] Grove City High School, Ohio State University; [occ.] Freshman at OSU; [hon.] Graduated with honors diploma; [oth. writ.] Personal, unpublished poems; [a.] Grove City, OH

LARKIN, FRANCES FAVRE
[b.] May 18, 1918, Gulfport, MS; [m.] William J. Larkin, November 11, 1994 (a second marriage after the death of first husband of 53 years.); [ch.] Tommye Dale Favre; [ed.] Local grammar and high school, Ms. Univ. for Women - 4 yrs, BS degree in Business and Language, various courses in Coast Community Education throughout many years.; [occ.] Twenty years with Federal Govt in various departments, seventeen years as legal Secretary. Followed by part-time employment in other areas.; [memb.] At 77 years, too numerous to list. Currently,

Volunteer Guild at Gulf Coast Medical Center, Gulf Coast Jazz Society, Community Concert Assn., Life member, Local Legal Secy. Assn.; [oth. writ.] "Drop of the Hat" occasional verse for birthdays, anniversaries, special occasions on request, one small book of verse, "Push, Pull, Mr. Christy", done as a Christmas gift for members of my family and close friends, many skits and songs for various groups.; [pers.] As I age and have reached what some call "the twilight years", enjoying love, the second time around, it seems so much easier to voice and place on paper in inner-most thoughts on paper to share with others. No longer do I hesitate for fear of criticism for my heart does pump to see my words published.; [a.] Gulfport, MS

LAROCCA, DONNA L.
[b.] January 9, 1930, Muncie IN; [p.] Lloyd and Alma Huber, [m.] Anthony R. LaRocca, June 6, 1964; [ch.] Robert; [ed.] M.A. in Education, B.S. in Bus. Ed., Dist. Ed. Endorsement (Just a few credit to receive doctoral); [occ.] Retired; [memb.] Eastern Star #464, past member of ABWA, Honor Society (Delta) (grad.) Moose Lodge - Anderson; [hon.] Grage Mering Award H.S. 3rd in class on grades for 12 yrs. Secretary for Eastern start A.B.W.A. and honored many times; [oth. writ.] Halloween, Winter, Storms, Xmas, Homecoming, Organizations, My Precious Son, Dedicated my Husband, "My Husband," and many more.; [pers.] "All things get better in life's struggles hang in there!"; [a.] Muncie, IN

LAVELLA, WENDY
[b.] April 12, 1972, Dearborn, MI; [p.] Karen and Leroy Lavella; [ed.] BBA Marketing from Easter Michigan University, [a.] Melvindale, MI

LEBLAN, JANIS
[pen.] Janis Leblan; [b.] November 23, 1977, Prades, France; [occ.] Student; [pers.] The purpose of we writing isn't only for my work to be published or recognize, but also for me to express what I can't pronounce out loud. In that way of thinking, I would say that my "masters" are Baudelaire, Rimbaud and Verlaine.; [a.] Middlesex, NJ

LEBLANC, EVER
[b.] April 1, 1948, El Campo, TX; [p.] Matilda Grays; [ch.] Brinnith L. Grays, Shoneth N. LeBlanc; [ed.] E.A. Greer High; [occ.] Batendriss and Waitress, El Campo Country Club - Elks Lodge; [hon.] As far as Honors and Awards I have never received any because I have always thought that I wasn't good enough. But now I truly feel that God bless each individual with his special gift; [oth. writ.] I am writing a book and have three other poems I'm hoping to publish.; [pers.] I have always loved poetry and I always will. In school I would check out library book on poetry. After high school I tried writing poetry. The desire of poetry never left me.; [a.] El Campo, TX

LECOINTE, SOUTHWELL
[b.] April 18, 1963, Grand Bay, Dominica, Carribean; [p.] Helen Lecointe; [ed.] M.A. - Physical Chemistry and Physics B.S. - Chemistry and Mathematics Fisk and Vanderbilt University

LEE, BILLIE
[b.] May 24, 1932, Dandridge, TN; [p.] Mr. and Mrs. S.H. Rimmer; [m.] Curtis B. Lee, August 19, 1952; [ch.] Darrell Lee, Krista Oliver; [ed.] High School Maury High School, Dandridge, Tennessee, B.S. Degree. U. of Montevallo, Alabama, M.S. Degree A and M University, Alabama; [occ.] Retired Teacher Home Economics; [memb.] Home Economics National Honor Society Member.; [hon.] Graduated with highest honors.; [oth. writ.] None published.; [pers.] I write for personal satisfaction. Writing is a means of releasing my feelings to others.; [a.] Addison, AL

LEE, CHRISTINA S.
[b.] February 12, 1983, Morristown, IN; [p.] Franklin H. and Donna D. Lee; [ed.] Witt Elementary School, Lincoln Heights Middle School; [memb.] Beta Club, Honor Roll Attends Faith Baptist Church in Jefferson City, Tennessee; [hon.] Other poems have received either a 1st place honor or have been published. She has written alot of poems. She has also recently submitted a short book to the TRA Literacy Council contest.; [oth. writ.] I thank God for my gift of writing.; [pers.] Morristown, TN

LEE, K-MING
[b.] November 7, 1987, West Covina, CA; [p.] Johnson and Lorraine Lee; [ed.] Mesa Elementary School; [occ.] Student; [hon.] Principal Award; [pers.] Interested in music and hey play recorder, keyboard, saxophone and guitars. Swimming and Tennis; [a.] West Covina, CA

LEE, PATRICIA
[b.] June 7, 1943, Anderson; [p.] Janie and R. B. Richey; [m.] Sidney Lee, September 13, 1959; [ch.] Bea, Sid, Jr. "Buddy," Vaughan; [ed.] Dixie High School, DueWest, S.C., Draughon's Business College, Greenville, SC; [occ.] My husband and I are owners of "Lee's Barbecue and Catering Service"; [memb.] First Baptist Church, Laurens, SC, Laurens, SC Chamber of Commerce, Greenwood, SC Chamber of Commerce; [a.] Waterloo, SC

LEEPER, KENDALL LYNN
[b.] April 22, 1962, Salinas, CA; [p.] Robert O. Leeper and Darlene M. Leeper; [ed.] Parkrose High School Graduate, Portland, Oregon; [oth. writ.] "Where Dawn Lingers" will serve as the first publication of my writing.; [pers.] My work reflects the working out of emotional struggle, and the expression of life lessons. Maya Angelou is a great inspiration to me.; [a.] Los Angeles, CA

LEER, EDWARD
[b.] March 9, 1974; [p.] James Leer, Donna Leer; [ed.] Roger Bacon High School, University of Cincinnati; [oth. writ.] Two poems and a short story were published in a local literary collection.; [pers.] I write as a type of therapy and to educate myself and others. Art and music influence my writing. I fight for the dying dream and stand against the running stream. The pen is mightier than the sword. T.F.O.; [a.] Cincinnati, OH

LEFTWICH, LIVELISE
[pen.] Liv Elise; [b.] March 2, 1925, Norway; [p.] Marie and Oystein Nordsjo; [m.] Richard F. Leftwich, March 1, 1958; [ch.] Three daughters (37, 34, 31 Yrs.); [ed.] High School, Business Training, Home Ec. (Norway), Voice Training - Music, (Classical), (Voice, Norway, London and Rome and New York.); [occ.] Homemaker, Writer, [memb.] Pound Ridge Community Church, Pound Ridge Garden Club, Norwegian Seamans Church of New York.; [hon.] Performing solo, (singing) for the late King Olav of Norway! Several awards for Flower arrangements!; [oth. writ.] Diploma from Institute of Children's Literature, in writing Children's Books. Publishing Myown Newsletter for Distribution Business. Poems published in Local Newspapers.; [a.] Pound Ridge, NY

LEIMKUHLER, WILLIAM RAYMOND
[b.] January 29, 1930, Baltimore; [p.] August C. and Anna M. Leimkuhler (youngest of 11 children); [m.] 1st Helen Mae Adamecz, Nov. 26, 1953 to Dec. 22, 1983, 2nd Mary C. Raley, May 10, 1986 to February 4, 1995; [ch.] Steven A. Leimkuhler, Cynthia A. Lucas, Lisa M. Roeder, Diana M. Viennas, stepson Steven A. Raley; [ed.] 8 yrs. grade school, 4 yrs. Calvert Hall College was graduated 1948; [occ.] (Retired) Electrical 40 yrs., Baltimore Gas and Electric Co.; [memb.] Arbutus Community Assoc., Loyal Order of Moose, American Legion (Dewey Laman), Served Honorably U.S.M.C. 1951-53, St. Agnes Church Choir; [pers.] "A tribute to Mary" was my very first poem. I wrote it on the night of her burial after all of my family and friends left my house. Mary is a special lady and my best friend, very inspiring.; [a.] Baltimore, MD

LEINHAUSER, KAREN L.
[b.] July 20, 1967, Grand Forks, ND; [p.] Connie Allard Leinhauser, Herman Leinhauser; [ed.] Central High, Houston Community College; [hon.] Multiple sporting awards including the varsity letter in track and volleyball, and special recognition for outstanding athlete in track and basketball.; [pers.] I dedicate my poetry to my late mother Connie Allard. A writer herself, she has been my inspiration.; [a.] Houston, TX

LEOPIN, MARK PHILIP
[pen.] Moshe; [b.] April 25, 1952, Port

Jefferson, NY; [p.] Matthew and Marie Leopin; [ch.] Adam, Andrew, Matthew, Eric and Lance; [ed.] Bachelors Degree in Accounting, Governmental Accounting Degree from U.S. Air Force Technical School.; [occ.] Accountant and Tax Consultant.; [memb.] Member of Promise Keepers, an organization nationwide of Men of Integrity. Dedicated to building relationship with God, family and other men who believe in God.; [hon.] Editor's Choice Award from National Library of Poetry, Ron poem published in Anthology "A Far Off Place".; [oth. writ.] Produced album of songs, "Praise be the Lord the God of Israel", which is currently being played on radio and television. Wrote over 200 worship and praise songs over last seven years.; [pers.] Having a personal relationship with God is the greatest accomplishment that a person can attain. Surrendering one's life to the Leadership of God, the Creator, will bring true freedom and real happiness. Jesus is Life.; [a.] Birmingham, AL

LEPPER, JUSTIN
[b.] July 14, 1987, Indianapolis, IN; [p.] Deborah and Patrick Lepper; [hon.] Awards from this poem (1) Third place poetry award from Los Angeles County Fair, (2) City of Claremont Certificate of Recognition, (3) Principals Award for Creative Writing; [oth. writ.] Angelic Animals, The Boys Who Met A Baby Dinosaur, co-author The Wild West Oakmont School, Special Education Publishing House; [pers.] I want to thank my family and Olivia Simpson Ellis, in Special Education, for believing in me when no one else did.; [a.] Pomona, CA

LETTKO, BEVERLY
[pen.] Beverly Grogan; [b.] March 13, 1936, Berlin, NY; [p.] Claude Plank and Violet Betts Plank; [m.] William Lettko, January 6, 1973; [ch.] Rebecca, Michael, Bridget, Christina; [ed.] Berlin Central High, Hudson Valley Community College; [occ.] Legal Secretary, now Retired; [memb.] First Baptist Church, Associate Realtor, Rensselaer County Board of Realtors; [hon.] Business Award; [oth. writ.] "Attic Of My Soul," a compilation of poems, Lyrics for (3) songs: "But He's Not You." "Speak Softly," "In My Heart," Children story: "Billy's Dream"; [pers.] I try to reflect in my writing, an appreciation for the Beauty of Nature around us, and love of family.; [a.] Berlin, NY

LEVINE, MELANIE J. FIDEL
[b.] September 26, 1966, Newark, NJ; [p.] Helena And Irv Fidel; [m.] Tom Levine, June 9, 1996; [ed.] Bachelor of Arts, Theater; [occ.] Administrative Assistant, Tri-Countries Easter Seal Society Ventura, CA; [a.] Ventura, CA

LEVINESS, DOROTHY TERESA
[b.] May 14, 1928, Brooklyn; [p.] Richard and Ellen Fitzgerald; [m.] Frank George Leviness,

September 20, 1947; [ch.] James, Dorothy, Francis, Richard; [ed.] Elementary High School P.S. 203 "Girls Commercial"; [occ.] Housewife; [memb.] St. William The Abbot Church; [pers.] You can't enjoy the fruits of marriage 'til the tree is ripe.; [a.] Massapequa, NY

LEVY, MS. INGE
[b.] February 1, 1938, Vallendar, Germany; [p.] Phillip and Thea Levy; [occ.] George Washington High School, City College of New York, Bachelor of Arts Degree - Concentration in English Literature. Master of Science in Education; [memb.] Retired Elementary School Teacher - was a teacher for over 30 years. for New York City Board of Education; [hon.] Jewish Teacher Association, United Federation of Teachers.; [a.] New York, NY

LEVY, WENDY MYHRE
[b.] January 28, 1950, Kingston, NY; [p.] Ralph Myhre and Lovella Roehr, [m.] Peter Levy, June 15, 1980; [ch.] Jacob Bartholomew, [ed.] BA Reed College, MA (Technical Theatre), LIU C.W. Post; [occ.] Graphic and Theatrical Design; [memb.] Board of Directors: Rockville Centre Guild for the Arts, Production Design: Island Harvest

LEWIS, DAVID R.
[b.] January 14, 1939, NYC; [p.] Paul and Estelle Lewis; [ed.] A.S. Adult Ed. New School; [hon.] Social Studies School Service; [oth. writ.] Matte Robinson's Pearly Confections Clapbook (poems) Cailling Out (childrens poetry); [pers.] 'Not excuses' Models and Heroes W.E.B. Dubois James Baldwin R.H. Tawney; [a.] New York, NY

LEWIS, DEBORAH
[b.] Alexandria, VA; [p.] Romaine Lewis; [ch.] Kimberly, Gary, Tracy, Casey Lewis; [ed.] Parker Gray High School, Alex., VA; [pers.] To my children Gary, Tracy, Casey and Kimberly Lewis and James Edwards. My sister Crystal Lewis and nephews Eric Lewis and Eation Lewis.

LEWIS, MAURICE DWAYNE
[pen.] Maurice D. Lewis; [b.] December 10, 1970, Saint Louis, MO; [p.] Dorothy McClendon, Kirk McClendon; [ed.] B.S. Computer Information System Central State University, Naval Science Cleveland Junior Naval Academy; [occ.] Systems Engineer; [memb.] Toast Masters, International Iota Phi Theta Fraternity, Inc.; [hon.] (4) Deans List (1) Military Order of World Wars-Award of Merit (1) American Legion-Military Excellence; [pers.] My writing reflect the inner being that I am.; [a.] Flint, MI

LILLY, THELMA R.
[b.] May 26, 1926, Auburntown, TN; [p.] John and Helen Robinson; [m.] Widowed (2 times); [ch.] Lowell, Linda, Donna and Diane; [ed.] High School, Auburn Town High, some Business

Courses, College courses; [occ.] Retired - Civil Services 31 years; [memb.] None at the present time have worked with local league and Association in the pass. Cancer Association and etc.; [pers.] My true saying and belief are after God, family and friends. The greatest gifts to humanity, are literature, music and the arts; [a.] Shalimar, FL

LINARES, CHRISTOPHER
[b.] February 22, 1982, Miami, FL; [p.] Anne P. Linares, Victor Reeve; [ed.] Middle School; [occ.] Student; [memb.] MDA, and the Broward Esperanto Club, Florida Esperanto League; [hon.] Proclamation of City of Lauderhill for wining essay, and other misc. awards.; [oth. writ.] First; [pers.] Always strive for what you know you can achieve.; [a.] Plantation, FL

LINDSAY, PATRICIA MARIE
[b.] March 2, 1946, Ashland, OR; [p.] Roland and Mariece Lindsay; [ed.] B.A. in German, OSU, 1973; [hon.] First and second place in Artist's Paint-Out Competitions; [oth. writ.] The Eric Velvetbelly Stories, Frizeline was a Princess, My Pigeon Friends - all unpublished books, illustrated by the author.; [pers.] My life has been marked by a closeness to animals and Nature. It seems I was always outdoors, enthralled by the forms of trees, the blue shadows on the stormy mountains. Admired poets include Poe, Donne, Lanier, Frost, Burns and Bertolt Brecht.; [a.] Medford, OR

LINDSEY, BERMOINE
[b.] December 27, 1968, San Antonio, TX; [p.] Keal Lindsey; [ch.] Bermoine Lindsey Jr. Destiny Lindsey; [ed.] Willow Ridge High Barclay Career College; [occ.] Security Officer; [oth. writ.] A movie about real street Deal Life, Crying World Love Your Race Love.; [pers.] Born with Sickel Cell and I love to write Love to write a book about my life.; [a.] Houston, TX

LINDSTROM, LISA MICHELE
[b.] August 8, 1961, Minneapolis, MI; [p.] Ward and Carol Engebrit; [m.] Jeffrey Rollin Lindstrom, July 25, 1992; [ed.] Hopkins MN - Lindbergh Senior H.S., U of Minnesota 1 year; [occ.] Poet and Housewife, Publisher; [memb.] Distinguished Member - International Society of Poets; [hon.] Editor's Choice Award - 1995; [oth. writ.] Several Anthologies and I just published my own first book of poetry entitled "Adequate Justice - Beginning Healing Through Poetry". And I'm busy writing the second.; [pers.] Words can describe feelings better when written. I have now discovered my passion for Impressionistic Art.; [a.] Yorba Linda, CA

LINENBERGER, RITHA
[pen.] Ritha Linenberger; [b.] March 25, 1929, Hays, KS; [p.] Peter and Rosa Pfeifer, [m.] Ken Linenberger, June 10, 1948; [ch.] Four; [ed.]

Some College; [occ.] Retired; [memb.] Church Organizations; [oth. writ.] Fifty Anniversary Poem Family Christmas Poem.; [a.] Las Vegas, NV

LINK, LISA D.
[pen.] Kat Swaro; [b.] December 5, 1971, Columbus, OH; [p.] Russ and Sierra Link; [ed.] Bachelor of Philosophy, Miami of Ohio; [occ.] Nat'l Accounts Manager - FilmKraft, Inc.; [memb.] Sierra Club Member, work with Women's Groups, Locally - as well as other environment groups.; [hon.] Barbara Nicholson Award at Miami for my Senior Thesis in Women's Studies, Dean's List; [oth. writ.] None published; [pers.] Human's endure passion and pain and love in an endless cycle - I just take notes.; [a.] Columbus, OH

LISOJO, A. WINNIE
[b.] September 24, 1956, Puerto Rico; [ch.] David Jr., Daisy, Alvin; [ed.] B.A. In Psychology, Lehman College, NY; [occ.] Family Counselor, Teacher; [pers.] My deepest thanks to the man who was the sole inspiration of this Creative writing, Mr. Luis A. Carrasquillo; [a.] Bronx, NY

LISTON, SHELLEY
[b.] August 27, 1961, Saint George, UT; [p.] Clyde Evans, Beth Evans; [m.] Kalyn D. Liston, April 18, 1980; [ch.] Skyler, Sarah, Nellie, Nicholas; [ed.] Basic High School (Henderson, Nevada), Utah State University (Logan, Utah); [occ.] Housewife, Daycare Provider; [memb.] Member of the Church of Jesus Christ of Latter Day Saints; [pers.] Pleasant memories and the simple things in life bring joy. Much growth can come when we view life with a positive attitude and fill it with uplifting surroundings. I try to offer these through my poems.; [a.] Liberty, UT

LITTLE, RHONDA MORROW
[b.] January 8, 1951, Birmingham, AL; [p.] James O. Morrow Sr. and Edna Phillips Morrow; [m.] Sylvester Little Sr., December 15, 1974; [ch.] Sylvester Jr. and Jamie Olivia; [ed.] New Castle High, Miles College B.S. Degree; [occ.] Data Conversion Operator U.S. Postal Service; [hon.] B.S. Degree, Office Administration; [oth. writ.] Numerous poetry and Lyric pieces - presently unpublished.; [pers.] My desire is to profile in print my concerns for mankind and my hanger for peace. Hopefully my words might reach someone in need of consultation. My mission is to share with others how to first find peace within themselves, thereby, rebuilding their own self-esteem and self-confidence (As I have thus far) enabling them to help someone else.; [a.] Birmingham, AL

LITTLEFIELD, CHARLES WALTER
[pen.] Chaz; [b.] July 8, 1970, Mineola, TX; [p.] Robert and Katherine Littlefield; [m.] Kelly A. Bissaillon, September 21, 1993; [ch.]

Samantha Renae, Kristen Marie, Amanda Paige; [ed.] Agua Fria Union High School, Phx. Job Corp-Painting, Scottsdale Culinary Arts Ariz.; [occ.] Chef-Ann's Townsman Miami, Okla.; [memb.] International Chess Association, A.C.A. of America, M.D.A. Inc. National Arbor Foundation; [oth. writ.] This is my very first writing of any sort, it will not be my last by any means.; [pers.] I would love to thank our Lord for all his blessings in life, and my beautiful family for their love and support through all the trials of life on earth God bless you!; [a.] Miami, OK

LITTMANN, KATHY
[b.] February 16, 1980, Charlotte, NC; [p.] Laszlo and Anna Littmann; [ed.] Providence Senior High School; [occ.] Sophomore in High School; [memb.] Honor Society, National Beta Club, Literary Magazine, Orchestra, French Club; [pers.] Writing is a way to express emotions once you're drained away your tears, beat all the feathers out of your pillow.; [a.] Charlotte, NC

LIVELY, JOSH
[b.] July 12, 1978; [p.] Wendell and Vicki Lively; [ed.] Currently attending my junior year of high school; [occ.] Learning and studying the great beauty of poetry; [hon.] Silver honor roll and Beta club; [pers.] Live peacefully with your fellow man and write beautiful poems to please them.; [a.] Evanston, WY

LOCKHART, ANNA MAE
[b.] October 20, 1928, Pittsburgh, PA; [p.] John K. and Emma A. Sayers; [m.] Herbert L. Champion, May 5, 1990; [ch.] Joseph and Darlene; [ed.] South Hills High Iron City College; [occ.] Office Manager Rod and Rod, Inc. Utility Const.; [oth. writ.] Short story Poem in school.; [pers.] Ran 3 companies at age 28 long before womens lib Rec. plaque for twenty yrs. of excellent service from co. Be nice to others and they will be nice to you.; [a.] Jacksonville, FL

LOFTIN, CINDY THOMPSON
[b.] November 18, 1957, Charlotte, NC; [m.] David Loftin; [ch.] Jessica, step daughter-Brandi; [ed.] West Mecklenburg High, Elon College; [occ.] Self employed; [memb.] Secretary of (FSA) Future Secretary's Assoc., Notary Public; [hon.] Number one on girls tennis team; [oth. writ.] published article in local newspaper about my daughter weighing two pounds at birth.; [pers.] My poetry is a gift which I call Poetic Specialty, because of the ability to take a situation, weather it be mine or someone else's and put those feelings into poetry.; [a.] Charlotte, NC

LOFTON, DARLINE ESTELL
[pen.] The Black Rose; [b.] November 25, 1951, Los Angeles, CA; [p.] Jay P. Lowe Sr., Dora Lowe; [m.] Ernest Lofton, June 27, 1968; [ch.] Ernest Deon Lofton, Eugene DeJuane Lofton;

[ed.] Duarte High, many college courses, Duarte California; [occ.] Customer Service Specialist-Bank of America; [oth. writ.] Several poems published in school paper; [pers.] A smile and poetry transcends all barriers!; [a.] Chino, CA

LOMBARDO, FABIO
[b.] December 26, 1961, Venice, Italy; [p.] Giampietro Lombardo, Marisa Lombardo; [m.] Catharine Bemiss McGuire, May 20, 1990; [ch.] Alessandra, Daniela; [occ.] Senior Buyer, Beretta U.S.A. Corp.; [memb.] American Heart Association, Scleroderma Foundation; [oth. writ.] Silly, simple poems; [pers.] The pick of my inspiration is given to me by the girls who gave me life: My mother, my wife and my two daughters: I love you.; [a.] King George, VA

LOPENZINA, VANESSA
[b.] May 20, 1984, Hackensack, NJ; [p.] Len Lopenzina and Chris Lopenzina; [ed.] St. Paul's School, Princeton, New Jersey; [occ.] student, St. Paul's school; [memb.] S.P.S. school choir; [hon.] honor roll; [oth. writ.] Other poems published in Anthology of poetry by Young Americans and Creative Communications Inc.; [pers.] I believe that the world should be war free, and the peaceful, just like my poem state, I have been influenced by my parents, and many great leaders, such as Dr. Martin Luther King Jr.; [a.] Jamesburg, NJ

LOPEZ, IRENE M.
[b.] March 30, 1972, Chicago, IL; [p.] Andrew and Julia Weber; [m.] Juan Lopez, August 26, 1995; [ed.] University of IL at Chicago; [pers.] I strive to give vivid descriptions and insights of people, places and things in my writing. I have been greatly influenced by a variety of poets, however the two that have inspired me the most are W. H. Auden and Diane Glancy. My biggest inspiration was Professor Mills, my poetry writing instructor. If it wasn't for him, I would have never known that I had the talent to write poetry.; [a.] Chicago, IL

LORD, LAURA ANNE
[pen.] Laura Lord; [b.] October 3, 1965, Silver Springs, MD; [p.] Jeanette F. Lord, James R. Lord Sr.; [pers.] God has given many of us special gifts and talents and by using and sharing these gifts and positive way we show our gratitude to him.; [a.] Warren, NJ

LOUGEE, GLEN A.
[b.] March 23, 1922, Laconia, NH; [ed.] B.S. University of N.H., M.A. Boston University; [occ.] Retired Media Services Director; [hon.] Purple Heart; [oth. writ.] Destiny of Silence, To Remember, A Poet's Touch (unpublished).; [pers.] I write not for myself, but to focus others through poetry on the beauties in life and basic philosophical truths and values.; [a.] Marblehead, MA

LOVE, THOMAS DUANE
[b.] July 19, 1955, Flint, MI; [p.] Donald and Lillie Hogan; [m.] Glenda (Lady), February 7, 1987; [ch.] Cass, Danielle, Alexis; [memb.] One of Jehovah's witnesses; [pers.] I'd like to thank my mother Lillie, for teaching me about Jehovah God.; [a.] Flint, MI

LUCIUS, RENNIE
[pen.] Rennie Lyn Lucius; [b.] February 17, 1977, Waukegan, IL; [p.] Nancy Lucius and Charles Lucius; [ed.] Wauconda High School; [occ.] Dietary Aide and Nany; [memb.] Wauconda Federated Church; [hon.] Technology Campus - V.I.C.A. Awards, Child Care Certificate and Scholarship from Wauconda High.; [oth. writ.] Other Personal Poems.; [pers.] I am inspired by the people around me and I write what I feel my heart. Never forget who you are and if you ever feel lost look around, Nature will help you to remember the things you forgot.; [a.] Wauconda, IL

LUDWICK, ANN BERTA COLEMAN
[pen.] Ann Berta Coleman-Ludwick; [b.] January 14, 1917, Somerset, NY; [p.] C. Stanley and Marjorie Coleman; [m.] Robert J. Ludwick, July 18, 1942; [ch.] R. David, Jeffrey and Scott; [ed.] Barker High School, Barker N.Y., University of Buffalo - B.E.D. (Bachelor of Educ. Degree), Canisius College - Bflo, NY, Counseling; [occ.] Retired H.S. Teacher and Counselor; [memb.] Assembly of God Church; [hon.] Barker H.S. Honor Society, U.B. Top 25% of Students (1935-1939); [pers.] The Goal of Wisdom is Love!; [a.] Punta Gorda, FL

LUDWIG, JASON
[b.] May 14, 1976, Cincinnati, OH; [p.] Charles Ludwig, Diane Westrich; [ed.] Milford High School, University of Cincinnati; [hon.] U.C. Dean's List; [oth. writ.] Poem, "Atlantic Night", published in anthology, Crossings, Essay, "Home Run!", published in the University of Cincinnati E.E.C. reader. Anticipating many other poems to be published.; [pers.] There is a reason for every event in life. Regardless of the simplicity in a single moment of time, it will always offer to us some profound emotion that is inevitably, and eternally, instilled within our memories. I find the Shakespearean Sonnet an interesting and challenging technique to work with.; [a.] Cincinnati, OH

LUENBERGER, EVA MAE
[b.] June 16, 1924, Cadillac, MI; [p.] Carl Fockler, Eva Ward; [ch.] Three daughters; [occ.] Retired Secretary and Piano Teacher; [pers.] I am nothing until my intelligence and talent are combined with genuine Christian love.; [a.] Curran, MI

LUJAN, CHARLOTTE
[b.] December 21, 1936, Santa Fe, NM; [p.] Delfino Lujan, Frances R. Lujan; [ed.] B.A. English/Speech, M.A. Christian Spirituality, Certified Hospital Chaplain, Certified Poetry Therapist; [occ.] Hospital Chaplain/Mental Health and Oncology; [memb.] The National Association of Catholic Chaplains, The National Association for Poetry Therapy; [hon.] Chaplain of the Year 1993, Lubbock, Texas; [oth. writ.] Articles for Vision, NACC Publication, Articles for Grapevine, St. Mary Hospital Publication; [pers.] As I seek union with God and all His Creation I am inspired to write of life, love, beauty, strength, oneness...; [a.] Lubbock, TX

LUKE, CHERYL K.
[b.] December 11, 1974, Cleveland, OH; [occ.] Insurance Claim Administrator; [oth. writ.] A book of several poems yet unpublished; [pers.] Poetry for me is an exercise of wit and word play; [a.] Cleveland, OH

LUNA, DIANA R.
[b.] November 13, 1937, Gorham, ME; [p.] Henry and Marian Wilder; [m.] Tom Luna, January 2, 1975; [ch.] Dreama, Dila, Steven; [ed.] University Southern Maine - Gorham Central Washington State College; [occ.] Elementary School Teacher; [memb.] Delta Kappa Gamma, ATPE (Association of Texas Professional Educators), Region Officer; [hon.] D.A.R. Recipient; [pers.] There really is nothing like a good book!

LUNG, ROBERT R.
[b.] October 28, 1970, Saint Louis, MO; [p.] Dr. Robert Lung and Mrs. Rita Lung; [ed.] Parkway West High, Regis University, Union Dayton School of Law; [occ.] Law Student; [memb.] Phi Delta Phi; [hon.] Alpha Sigma Nu, Dean List; [oth. writ.] Published in Regis University literacy magazine.; [pers.] In faith and love, cherishing the memory of my grandmother I so dedicate this poem to Granny Franny.; [a.] Chesterfield, MO

LUTCHEY, ANDRA LEIGH
[b.] September 28, 1968; [p.] Harold E. and Lillian L. Lutchey; [ch.] Taren N. Lutchey, D'Andre M.J. Lutchey and Samia N. Garner; [ed.] Thomas A. Devilbiss High School Graduate, Current Student at University of Toledo; [occ.] Home maker and floral designer (Hobby); [memb.] St. Martain De Porres Catholic Church; [oth. writ.] Andra's Alphabet In a Journal called "Honestly" Spring 1995. Published by the writer's workshop at owens community college P.O. Box 10,000 Toledo, OH 46699-1947; [pers.] Crossroads have on unique way of greeting individuals, it's up to the Individual to decide which road is the right one to take advantage of. Not all Teen-age mothers end in disaster.; [a.] Toledo, OH

LUZMOSOZ III, WILLIAM
[b.] April 14, 1944, Webster City, IA; [m.] Single; [ed.] University Of Wyoming; [occ.] President, Communications Corp. of the Americas, Inc (COMCOA), Radio Stations; [pers.] Had I not shared any of the hundreds of things I've written with a friend who submitted this would have not been published.; [a.] Rock Springs, WY

LYNCH, MELISSA AYN
[b.] October 10, 1976, Chicago, IL; [p.] Hollis Lynch; [ed.] I am now a Sophomore at Teikyo Marycrest University in Davenport, Iowa; [occ.] Student; [hon.] First place in fiction for a writing contest at my university; [oth. writ.] Several poems and stories. I have had three or four published in campus and local magazines; [pers.] My poetry reflects the beauty and goodness of nature.; [a.] Deerfield, IL

LYNN, EMILY
[b.] October 10, 1981, Birmingham, AL; [p.] Lee Anne Lynn, Charles Lynn; [ed.] Montevallo Elementary, I am currently in 8th grade at Montevallo Middle; [occ.] Student; [memb.] National Junior Honor Society; [pers.] God has blessed me with a talent to write. I am doing my best to use it for God's purpose.; [a.] Birmingham, AL

M'LAHERTY, VERDA
[pen.] URM; [b.] March 29, 1938, Hudson, OH; [p.] Clint and Ruth M'Elrath; [m.] Divorced; [ch.] David and Jessie M'Laherty; [ed.] 12th grade; [occ.] Disabled; [memb.] North Park Baptist Church; [pers.] To exhume loquacity of emotions so my personage communicates with God and nature the poem becomes the proof of document.; [a.] Warren, OH

MABERRY, NANCY HELEN
[b.] September 21, 1949, Midland, TX; [p.] R. J. Maberry, Floy Maberry; [ch.] Michelle, Tiffany and Joseph McMillan; [ed.] Midland High School, Odessa College, the University of Texas at Austin B.A. - Sociology, 1972; [occ.] Schmidt Electric Co., Inc., Austin, TX; [memb.] Unity Church of Austin; [hon.] Phi Theta Kappa; [pers.] An open and loving heart and a sense of humor open many doors.; [a.] Austin, TX

MACH, MANDY
[b.] April 26, 1975, McHenry; [p.] Gail Mach; [ed.] Johnsburgh High School, McHenry County College; [pers.] We are thrown into this world without a script, no knowledge of what our future holds. But we dare guide ourselves to the path we believe to be true. Though they may turn to thistles and thrones our beings become stronger.; [a.] McHenry, IL

MACHARDY, DONNA V.
[pen.] D. V. MacHardy; [m.] Patrick MacHardy, October 8, 1994; [ed.] High School, Army Reserves currently attending Quincy Jr.

College as a part time student; [occ.] Certified Home Health Aide; [pers.] Thank you to my herses: My husband, Patrick MacHardy, my best friend Patti Timmons, my late father Leon Currier, my late mother in-law Cathy MacHardy. I love you. Thank You for believing in me.; [a.] Plymouth, MA

MACK, JAMES D.
[b.] September 25, 1919, Robinson, PA; [p.] Vincent Mack, Elloda Mack; [m.] Alice Mack, May 19, 1970; [ch.] William J. Mulvihill; [ed.] High School, Air Force Flight School; [occ.] Retired-Pennsylvania Electric Company; [memb.] Life member VFW and 80th Ftr, Sqdn., 5th Air Force Association, Reserve Officers Association, Air Force Assoc., AOPA, Pilots International Assoc., 32 Degree Mason.; [hon.] DFC, DSM Air Medal Bronze Star, Purple Heart, Asiatic-Pacific Theatre Medal with Five Battle Stars.; [oth. writ.] Several Poems written during service days.; [pers.] As I grow older, my aim is to write more serious poetry and to have same published so that others can share my love of poetry.; [a.] New Florence, PA

MACKEY, WILLIAM D.
[b.] February 17, 1923, Newark, NJ; [p.] Henry and Louise Mackey; [ed.] Nutley High School, Nutley, NJ; [occ.] Retired Purchasing Agent; [oth. writ.] A few poems have been published in newspapers and magazines.; [pers.] A sporadic non-professional writer, I usually stick to short humorous verse.; [a.] Warwick, NY

MADDOCKS, JOHN J.
[b.] August 19, 1924, New York City; [p.] Deceased Mary and John; [m.] Irene, July 25, 1964; [ch.] Son - Peter Driscoll; [ed.] Bachelor Civil Engineering Manhattan College; [occ.] Retired; [memb.] Marine Trades Assoc. of New York; [oth. writ.] (Over 50 poems) Riverdale Press, Metropolitan Golf; [a.] Riverdale, NY

MAHLE, LEE P.
[b.] May 8, 1955, Oakland, CA; [p.] Lawrence and Loretta Mahle; [ed.] Undergraduate Studies, Ohlone College, Mission San Jose, CA, Undergraduate and Graduate Studies, San Jose State University, San Jose, CA; [occ.] Educator and Philan Thropist; [hon.] Various College and University Awards and Degrees with Honors and distinction.; [oth. writ.] Various poems, short stories, and essays; [pers.] I have benefitted greatly from the support, encouragement, and patience of my parents and of the muse to whom I owe so much, J. Atwell Scruggs III.; [a.] White Mountains Region, NH

MAKO, NANCY
[b.] July 22, 1958, Verplank, NY; [p.] Blaise and Margaret Mako; [pers.] Experiencing the personal love of God and seeing so much

suffering while being able to do so little about it have been the strongest motivating factors in my life. Returning God's love by helping others is what I want to do. If I can somehow help people through my writing, so much the better.; [a.] Vails Gate, NY

MALCOLM, CHRISTINE L.
[b.] December 24, 1968, Bryn Mawr, PA; [p.] Ronald and Peggy Ann White; [m.] Vincent Malcom, October 31, 1992; [ch.] Vincent, Jr., Anthony Michael; [ed.] Henderson High School, Central Pennsylvania Bus School, Institute of Children's Literature; [occ.] Housewife and Mother; [memb.] Order of the Eastern Star - West Chester, PA, Tall Cedars of Lebanon Ladies Auxiliary of W. Chester, PA; [pers.] I wish to thank my husband, Vince, for his support in my many endeavors, especially writing; [a.] Elverson, PA

MALINS, WALTER J.
[pen.] Wally Malins; [b.] May 18, 1928, Chicago, IL; [p.] Joseph and Mary Malins; [m.] Rita Perfetto Malins, November 2, 1963; [ed.] Kelly High School De Paul University; [occ.] Retired; [memb.] Pi Gamma MU National Honor Society; [hon.] Dean's List - Pi Gamma Mu Honor Inductee for exceptional scholastic achievements in fine arts.; [oth. writ.] Several poems published with corporation publications the book of pet names (Dell Publishing) specialty poems to honor people's achievements; [pers.] To me, poetry stimulates thinking ability to idealize in just a few words the whole essence of life and what it takes into account.; [a.] Chicago, IL

MALLOY, DARREN L.
[b.] April 11, 1965, Springfield, OH; [p.] Lawrence S. and Sharon Malloy; [m.] Ruth Meza Malloy, Pending; [ch.] Expecting first; [occ.] Carpenter; [oth. writ.] Several poems and stories published in various creative writing publications, also a great number of unpublished writings and poems; [pers.] My greatest influences are the great philosophers such as Aristotle and Plato and the mysteries of the universe.; [a.] Springfield, OH

MALMGREN, JULIA S.
[b.] July 7, 1950, Fairmont, WV; [p.] John and Genevieve Suttan; [m.] Erick Malmgren, 1974; [ch.] Five; [ed.] 2 years and W.V.U. then Nursing School for 3 years; [occ.] R.N. - disabled with multiple Sclerosis after work in ER, MICU, ICU, and the last 9 years in as officer in Del. Nat. Guards, a Geriatric of facility, MICU, ICU, and the last 9 years in L.DC (Labor and Delivery) and as cetificare childbirth educator; [pers.] I write at times when I feel to express the true heart of my spirit that none of us always express, in our daily living.; [a.] Wilmington, DE

MANIDIS, TERESA
[b.] April 22, 1973, Reading, PA; [p.] Salvatore and Maria Messineo; [m.] John Bacus Manidis, August 6, 1994; [ch.] John Anthony Manidis; [ed.] Reading Central Catholic High School, Bachelor of Arts from Allentown College of Saint Francis de Sales; [occ.] Writer; [memb.] Delta Epsilon Sigma, Delta Delta Chapter (National Catholic College Honor Society), American Red Cross LaLeche League International; [hon.] Ross Baker Memorial Writing Achievement Award, Diane Danacarte Murtha award for Art, elected to "Who's Who Among students in American Universities and Colleges", Dean's list; [oth. writ.] Poems published in the "Literary Review", article published in "American Builder" Magazine; [pers.] There are those who write for fortune, For money, power, fame. There are those who write so people will ne'er forget their name. But my words are a part of myself, The world 'round, and the sky above. I write for I cannot keep silent. I write because I love.; [a.] Birdsboro, PA

MANN, MICHAEL M.
[b.] October 2, 1948, Moscow, ID; [p.] Paul and Elsie Mann; [ed.] BSEE - Bachelor of Science in Electrical Engineering, University of Idaho; [occ.] Self employed, President Innova Development Corporation; [oth. writ.] Various Corporate Business Plans, The Quiet Claws - poem and short story, various poems and personal journals; [pers.] Set monuments along the pathway of life. The path never ends. And only the memory of the monuments remains.; [a.] Boise, ID

MANN, TINA J. BURGELL
[b.] March 4, 1960, Colorado; [p.] Darvin and Geraldine Burgell; [m.] Robert J. Mann, October 16, 1982; [ch.] James, Jurchee, Jonathon; [occ.] Secretary Treasurer, Gray Oil Co. Inc.; [memb.] Fort Lupton Chamber of Commerce; [pers.] This poem reflects the deepest feelings of an eleven year old girl after being molested by the man she called Dad!; [a.] Fort Lupton, CO

MARCOULIDES, MICHELLE
[b.] March 13, 1970, West Covina, CA; [p.] Mare and Sandra Marcoulides; [occ.] Sales; [a.] Yorba Linda, CA

MARIS-SIDA, SERBAN
[b.] September 13, 1969, Timisoara, Romania; [ed.] University of Timisoara, Romania; [pers.] The perfect poetry is the one that makes every mind and soul think that they understand it completely.; [a.] Oakdale, PA

MARKELL, NANCY LEE
[b.] Chicago, IL; [p.] Warren E. and Nancy L. Bunker; [m.] Joel M. Markell, July 10, 1972; [ed.] North Western University Chicago, IL; [occ.] Office Manager, Sunset Magazine; [oth.

writ.] "When love was all that mattered," Colo, SPGS. Gazette Telegraph, "A Love Story" Colo. SPGS. Beacon.; [pers.] A former advertising copywriter and editor, since the death of my husband in writing 1995, I have started writing again, I am currently working on a book of poetry dealing with the loss of a loved one to alzheimer's and related incurable diseases.; [a.] Colorado Spring, CO

MARTENS, BRAD COYOTE
[pen.] Coyote; [b.] January 27, 1956, Maumee, OH; [p.] Bob and Eva Martens; [ed.] Grade Ten; [oth. writ.] Have had other poems published before; [pers.] I write about the life and world around me I was inspired by Bob Dylan Arlo Guthrie and my older brother Bob Jr Martens; [a.] Maumee, OH

MARTIN, ALICE FLOWERS
[b.] September 24, Monticello, MS; [p.] George and Maggie Flowers; [ch.] Deborah, Carla and Shari; [ed.] Columbia High School Weber University (Attended); [occ.] Retired Asst. Division Chief Ogden Internal Revenue Service; [hon.] (2) Directors EEO Award (10) Performance Awards, Woman Of The Year Sojourner Truth Award, Denver Regional Woman Of The Year Award; [oth. writ.] TJ The Tangerine Puppy (short story) Zesty and Mrs. Em (Short Story) The Black Wind (Poem) Outside My Window (Poem); [a.] Ogden, UT

MARTIN, ANNALEA
[b.] June 14, 1976, Lodi, CA; [p.] Allen and Joanne Martin; [ed.] Rio Vista High School, Currently Attending Brigham Young University; [occ.] Secretary/Student; [hon.] Bank of America Certificate for excellence in English, Quill and scroll for Journalism; [pers.] I wrote what I feel, Think and see, trying to somehow bridge the gap that so often grows between members of the human race by sharing one experience at a time, believing that others may have had the same feelings, or take joy from what I have printed in their heart with words.; [a.] Provo, UR

MARTIN, CAM
[pen.] Cam Martin; [b.] June 22, 1973, CT; [p.] Dave and Sally Martin; [ed.] Vanderbilt University Fairfield Prep.; [occ.] Observer; [memb.] Phi Kappa Sigma Fraternity; [hon.] Loudest Kid in the eight grade; [oth. writ.] Several poems and short stories such as the poem, "Judas," "as Nada 91 my written," "Kohuutek," and short stories "When things change everywhere," "Blind Man On Acid," "Alright," and "Thank You Johnny Gilbert."; [pers.] "Why does every one keep getting off the blue bus?" "Thanks for the ride Doc."; [a.] Stratford, CT

MARTIN, PATRICIA ROGERS
[b.] March 13, 1962, Hayt, MO; [p.] James E.

and Opal B. Rogers; [ed.] Dell Public Schools, Dell, Arkansas; [occ.] Retail management Mac's Incorporated D'lo, Mississippi; [oth. writ.] Several unpublished writings.; [pers.] I have always believed the heart carries the truth and is the center of everyone's personality and existence, I let my heart do my writing.; [a.] Flowood, MS

MARTIN, STEVE
[pen.] Christ; [b.] March 24, 1963, Indpls, IN; [p.] Frank and Nancy Martin; [m.] Maren Hecker, December 24, 1995; [ed.] High School Graduate 1 year college, 4 yrs USN; [occ.] Federal Express; [memb.] Future farmers of America; [hon.] Honorably discharged vet. involved in the 1986 bombing of Lybia on board the carrier USS America CU66; [oth. writ.] Several poems published in the federal express night side paper. Copy writers held on songs from mothers day to Vietnam as well as christian poems of songs.; [pers.] I strive to life kin the abstract from a different point of view hoping the reader will look beyond and with for their meaning to my work.; [a.] Indianapolis, IN

MARTINEZ, BOB G.
[pen.] Bob G. Martinez; [b.] June 7, 1949, Las Vegas, NM; [p.] Mary Jane Martinez; [m.] Annette E. Martinez, February 10, 1973; [ch.] Lita Renee Martinez (19); [ed.] Graduated with honors in 1968 from North High School in Denver, Colorado; [occ.] Security Department; [memb.] Distinguished Member of The National Library of Poetry; [hon.] Awarded the "Best Little Can for a Mexican" Distinction from Annette and was honored to receive the "Smartest Dad" trophy from Lita; [oth. writ.] Own compilation of poems, "Sidetracks" and a single unbroken poem of 302 pages detailing interesting events experienced throughout my first 44 years.; [pers.] Oh what peacefulness when God paints the sky!... on canvas of clouds, His aura gestures. These far away scenes when touched with the eye draw us to His stillness where dawn lingers.; [a.] Denver, CO

MARTINEZ, JULIO Y.
[pen.] Julio Y. Martinez; [b.] December 20, 1924, Riverside, CA; [m.] Florence C. Martinez, April 8, 1946; [ch.] Julio Jr. and Peter P.; [ed.] Grad. San Bernardino Valley College, San Bernardino Ca. Earned teaching Cred. at Ucla Teaching Credential State of Calif. The sun Newspaper San Bernardino, CA. The Military Press Newspaper, Colton, Sacramento, CA.; [occ.] Instructor, Youth Authority, (Ret.); [memb.] I am a life member of the veterans of 9 foreign wars of the United States and life mem. American Legion I have served in numerous positions of leadership for U.S. Veteran organizations.; [hon.] I consider it an honor to have been recognized by the United States Congress, as an American who loves his

country.; [oth. writ.] I have written numerous articles on U.S. Veterans issues, for the Redlands Daily facts newspaper, Redlands, CA. The California Veteran Newspaper on Sept. 7, 1995, My poem "What America Means To Me" was entered into the congressional record.; [pers.] Many years ago on the Montana Indian Reservation, I met an ageless american Indian, who told me when you write from the heart, people will listen to you. I strive to adhere to this philosophy.; [a.] Washington, DC

MARUSCHAK, STEPHANIE SUE
[pen.] Antonia Sue; [b.] May 13, 1972, Youngstown, OH; [ed.] Boardman High School ('90), Mahoning County Joint Vocational School, Canfield, Ohio; [memb.] 3 World Wildlife Federation (WWF), 4 American Heart Association, 1. The American Society for the Prevention of Cruelty to Animals (ASPCA), 2. The Humane Society of The United State (HSUS); [hon.] Honor Award from Boardman High School for G.P.A. Sponsored by Boardman Civic Association; [oth. writ.] Won honorable mention in essay contest. Wrote an article that was published in my 8th grace school newspaper. "I Have Become" is my first major publication.; [pers.] I acquire my ideas from my own feelings at the time I write. My inspiration comes through Mariah Carey's music, as well as my personal thoughts. I plan to someday move to New York.; [a.] Boardman, OH

MARX, JULIA A.
[pen.] Jules; [b.] February 25, 1970, Scenectady, NY; [p.] Nicholas and Patricia Marx; [ch.] Victoria, Sissy and Kathrin; [ed.] High School Graduate, no college; [occ.] Food Establishment; [pers.] This poem Memories was inspired by my Grandpa, Harry Merriman who was the light of my life.; [a.] Schenectady, NY

MASON, DEBBIE
[pen.] Debbie Ann; [b.] September 11, 1954, Honolulu, HI; [p.] Edward and Peggy Coggeshall; [m.] Glenn Ray Mason, August 5, 1970; [ch.] Jeffrey Glenn and Jeremiah Craig; [ed.] W.W. Samuell H.S. Tarrant County Jr. College; [occ.] Admin. Asst, Tyler Bank and Trust; [memb.] First Baptist Church, Overton, Volunteer for various Civic Organizations; [oth. writ.] Quarter view Newsletter (Bank Customer Newsletter).; [pers.] My passion for romance and my family runs very deep. That passion sometime, is revealed to me in a God - given gift of writing poetry.; [a.] Overton, TX

MASTEN, PATRICIA G.
[pen.] Harriet Sidney; [b.] March 18, 1943, Worcester, MA; [p.] William Lillian Carriere; [m.] Benjamin B. Masten, August 6, 1981; [ch.] Lauren Ducharme, Karen Baker; [oth. writ.] I'm working on my collection entitled: Simply...

Poems, earlier poems printed in periodicals and newspapers - Worcester poetess; [pers.] A poem is any thought you feel someone else may be able to relate to; [a.] Worcester, MA

MATHER, LEE R.
[pen.] L. R. Mather; [b.] December 14, 1976, Reading, England; [p.] Kenneth and Christine Mather; [ed.] Carmel High School, now attending Bradley University; [occ.] Full Time Student; [pers.] Who is to say what is and what is not? Those who attempt, are they so beautifully wonderful that they, at will, may create our boundaries? Allow your soul to tick off possibilities, allow your heart to unlock your mind. Only then will your spirit be justified; [a.] Carmel, IN

MATLOFF, ABRAHAM J.
[b.] February 9, 1914, New Haven, CT; [p.] Louis Matloff and Eva Matloff; [m.] Selma Martha Matloff, January 24, 1937; [ch.] Harvey E. Matloff, Adrienne G. Matloff and Lynne A. Maser; [ed.] New Haven Hillhouse High School of Pharmacy; [occ.] Registered Pharmacy; [memb.] Connected Pharmacy Assoc. Temple Emanuel New Haven Worth Jewish Congress Channel Opera of Connecticut; [hon.] College Dean List Alpha Zeta Omega; [oth. writ.] College Class Poem (1934) other poems, and letters published in newspapers.; [pers.] Poetry is the perfect language and when blended with music it becomes a deep touching ballad I am also into classical music, especially opera, expressing emotions of heart and soul.; [a.] New Haven, CT

MATSUEDA, CHRISTINE
[b.] December 25, 1969, Honolulu, HI; [p.] Jack Matsueda and Lorraine Matsueda; [ed.] Kaimuki High School Kapiolani Community College; [occ.] Student; [hon.] Award of merit certificate (World of Poetry); [oth. writ.] "These Years."; [pers.] My personal experiences have inspired and driven me to write I hope my works will someday inspire, others.; [a.] Honolulu, HI

MATTHEW, MONA LISA J.
[b.] August 19, 1956, Goldston; [p.] Johnnie V. and Lois Jones; [m.] Charles Matthews, December 23, 1980; [ch.] Two; [ed.] 2 years College; [occ.] Work in Textile; [memb.] Of The Church; [hon.] Graduated with honors at Central Carolina Tec. College in Associate in Applied Science; [oth. writ.] "No" only poems.; [pers.] My writing is basically about men and women trying to live right, if you don't the ditch you will fall. I am influenced by the world as a whole. "people."; [a.] Cartage, NC

MATYOK, MARGARET S.
[b.] May 9, 1937, Toledo, OH; [p.] Julius and Margaret Fodor; [m.] Lewis P. Matyok, June 29, 1959; [ch.] Pamela Sue and Lewis P. Jr.; [ed.] Waite High School Food Service Coarse in

Sanitation, Nutrition and Management; [occ.] Server at Parkvue Retirement Center; [memb.] St. Stephen United Church of Christ, Chefs Ass; [hon.] Nellie Arthur, family, husband, friends, poets, poetess, the Bible, God who gave me talent and Jesus my friend; [oth. writ.] God made our tears, The window of life, and my first published in the Beyond the Stars, God painter First.; [pers.] My grandchildren are the light of my life. As God gave the me the gift to write, as others have share their with me. My writing have given me the strength to go on no matter what events came into my life.; [a.] Sandusky, OH

MAURER, RACHEL
[b.] April 6, 1980, Michigan; [p.] Roger and Kathleen Maurer; [ed.] St. Anne Elementary School and Bishop Foley High School. (Sophomore year in high school); [memb.] Macomb Family Services; [hon.] Calender Artistry Award and participation in Macomb Performing arts, received supervisor in piano; [oth. writ.] Several poems in school newspaper.; [pers.] "You can look at models, or you can be one."; [a.] Sterling Heights, MI

MAXWELL, MICHAEL
[pen.] Devon O. Savaj; [b.] March 17, 1974, Queens, NY; [p.] John Maxwell and Joann Savage; [ed.] Previously attending Nassau Community College; [occ.] Telemarketing; [pers.] I believe that everyone has the talent to become a poet, for this type of creativity comes from the heart and soul - It's pure. My dream is to become a novelist and screenwriter. Look out.; [a.] Queens Village, NY

MAYER, MARY JACQUELINE
[b.] January, 1964, Houston, TX; [p.] Mary Linbeck Chisolm and Paul E. Mayer; [ch.] Joshua Von Rous; [ed.] Incarnate word Academy Houston Texas, Redwood High School - Marin County, American River College - Carmichael, CA; [occ.] Hair Stylist; [oth. writ.] I have many unpublished writings.; [pers.] "As I bare my own soul throughout my writings, striking the chords of raw emotion, touching the depths of another soul, only then shall I view myself a true poet."; [a.] Northern, CA

MAYFIELD JR., VADERBILT
[pen.] Junior; [b.] January 16, 1925, Ecru, MS; [p.] Mr. Vanderbilt Mayfield Sr. and Ruth; [m.] Mrs. Ella Judon Mayfield (Deceased); [ch.] 13 Children; [ed.] Promoted to the 10 grade; [occ.] Retired but still work; [oth. writ.] I have lots of poems never been published before.

MAYHEW, PATRICIA RUTH
[b.] May 31, 1970, Alamogordo, NM; [p.] Sandra Abarr and Hank Mayhew Jr.; [ed.] John Foster Dulles High School; [occ.] Circulation Manager at Missouri City Branch Library/ Missouri City, TX; [memb.] Juvenile Diabetes

Foundation, Houston Livestock Show and Rodeo Lifetime Member, National Parks and Conservation Assoc., World Wildlife Fund, Officially protect and sponsor, Sirius, "A humpback whale thru the International Wildlife Coalition," "Kamots, a gray wolf thru the Wolf Education and Research Center," "Kouza, a Siberian tiger thru the Siberian Tiger Project."; [oth. writ.] Poems published in local newspapers.; [pers.] Life is love, our world and our children. The human race must stand united for these three for life to continue. Imagine... the power we each carry. Imagine... what we can do.; [a.] Missouri City, TX

MCAFEE, TIMOTHY S.
[pen.] Timothy S. McAfee; [b.] November 27, 1964, Gary, IN; [p.] Steve D. McAfee, Patricia A. Byer; [ed.] Hobart Sr. High, Hobart, IN Miami-Dade Dr. College, 4.0 GPA, Highest Honors; [occ.] Branch Manager, International Freight Forwarder; [memb.] Miami's Forwarders Association Licensed Real Estate Agent, Broward Countries Realtors Association; [hon.] Science Award, various other achievement awards; [oth. writ.] Hobart Gozette; [pers.] I believe that we are all truly created equal, some have bigger burdens, some are less fortunate, and some are just different, but that we must try and learn to accept or at least be tolerant of others and let them be themselves; [a.] Pembroke Pines, FL

MCCARTNEY, MADGE K.
[b.] March 2, 1949, Pittsburgh, PA; [m.] Thomas C. McCartney, December 31, 1978; [ch.] Tom, Brian, Matthew; [ed.] Scott H.S. N. Braddock, PA, Clarion University, University of Pittsburgh; [occ.] Speech/Language Pathologist, Wilson Elem. Imperial, PA; [pers.] This poem was written for worried parents whose first child is entering school - to let them know that school is a safe, loving, caring place; [a.] Weirton, WV

MCCHESNEY, MARY EVELYN
[pen.] "M.E."; [b.] June 24, 1910, Stuarts Draft, VA; [p.] John and Mamie McChesney; [ed.] Fishersville High School, Home Studies; [occ.] Retired Post Master - 35 years Service, 1940-1975; [memb.] Because of age and unable to get out much - Belong to Fishersvine Area Senior Citizens and served as Director from 1975 to 1985; [hon.] Essay "Lincoln", Lincoln Medal given by Ill. Watch Co., Medal given by UDC on Essay, "Va. As She Leathe South In War And Peace", have written six Historic Church Pagents - These I've my copy write on; [oth. Writ.] "For and Old Ladies Pass Time"!; [pers.] "The mind is a great gift - tho, illness and age may come - do something (like writing) to keep it active."; [a.] Fishersville, VA

MCCLUGGAGE, FRANCISCA
[pen.] Francisca; [b.] March 21, 1914, Oregon;

[p.] Unknown; [m.] Deceased - Robert E., March 13, 1959; [ed.] St. Marys High School, Business, College - various development courses; [occ.] Retired; [memb.] Unity West Church; [hon.] Honor Student in High School; [oth. writ.] Independent - Journal, Sausalito, CA Marin Poets Corner; [pers.] My poems are written in the early morning, an inner feeling to help others an extended "helping hand" an understanding.; [a.] Santa Monica, CA

MCCRAW, ARLEAN FORD
[b.] October 6, 1941, Little Rock, AR; [p.] Mr. and Mrs. James F. McCraw, [m.] Jesse E. Ford, February 1993; [ch.] I have 3 my husband has 5; [ed.] BS - Biology, minor in Chemistry, I have Certificate in Bio, Chemistry, Gen. Sci. and Sp. Ed K-12, 1. I have attended (BS) UAPB - Pine Bluff, AR, 2. Attend Bridgewater St. Univ., Tufts Univ., Boston Univ, UALR (cert. insp. Ed., UCA grad. courses in Adm.); [occ.] Teacher; [memb.] NAACP, Shiloh SDA Church, Bi-racial Com. for NLR, AR Sch. District, contributor to AETN-AR; [hon.] 1991 Cuniff Outstanding Teacher Award, Teacher of the Week (at my school), Recruit and Judge the NLR, AR Annual Youth Speech Contest, Ask to help wright the NLR Sch. District Student Handle, Attended Youth Leadership Workshop, TOT (Teacher of Tomorrow) Club Sponsor (N.L.R. High Sch. East); [oth. writ.] I have written 20-40 poems. I made a soft back poem bk. for my children - 1991 "Tried and True"; [pers.] I am always inspired by God when I write, when you reach out to help others (especially youth - you're helping tom old the future for our country and world).; [a.] AR

MCDERMOTT, DOROTHY L.
[pen.] Abby; [b.] April 10, 1978, Seattle, WA; [p.] M. F. McDermott; [ed.] Barrington Christian Academy, Barrington High (R.I.) Covenant Christian, Clover Park High; [occ.] Student; [pers.] Raised in R.I., spent five years in the Westerly Chorus Westerly R.I. attending Sheldan Jackson College in September 1996 - interest in Marine biology; [a.] Tacoma, WA

MCELROY, ERNEST MURPHY
[b.] August 4, 1950, Harrison, AK; [p.] Murphy and Willodean McElroy; [m.] Brenda Moody; [ed.] B.S. University of Art; [occ.] Real Estate; [oth. writ.] 100 personal poems; [pers.] If life is not chosen death will be had.; [a.] Brawson, MO

MCFARLAND, AMANDA
[pen.] Suzy; [b.] September 15, 1978, Cincinnati, OH; [p.] Harold and Nancy McFarland; [ed.] Princeton High School, Scarlet Oaks Vocational School; [occ.] Medical I assistant, Urological Surgeons, Montgomery, Oh; [memb.] National Vocational Technical Honor Society, Vocational Industrial Clubs of America (VICA);

[hon.] Honor society for junior year, honor roll for junior - senior year, State participation award for classroom medical skills; [oth. writ.] Many more poems (not published).; [pers.] I believe poetry is written from the heart. When I wrote this poem the words just came right to me the afternoon my grandmother passed away.; [a.] Cincinnati, OH

MCGAN, WAYNE EVIN
[b.] December 24, 1959, Cleveland, OH; [p.] Janet and Bryant; [m.] Debra McGan, May 2, 1982; [ch.] Josie Bird and Cortex; [ed.] Gwynn High, Cyahoga Community College, P.S.I. Institute of Computer Tech.; [occ.] Production Control Coordinator at Weyerhaeuser Co.; [memb.] I'm a member of a Country Club, Browns Backers; [oth. writ.] None other than poems to my wife and my self.; [pers.] Does it matter about good times, bad times and in between times...; [a.] Cleveland, OH

MCGANN, MORNA
[pen.] Morna McGann; [b.] August 5, 1954, Brooklyn, NY; [p.] Nancy Liddy-Wolfe; [ch.] Kirsten Morna and Inga Lee; [ed.] Cardinal Gibbons High School, Broward Community College, Florida Atlantic University; [occ.] Marketing and Public Relations Consultant, worked in house as publicist and marketing, Director for several companies.; [oth. writ.] Published articles - in Washington post, NY Daily News, fortune mag -nytimes - consumer digest as news and world report- wrote and designed ads - in - vogue - harpers bazaar - town and country - elle womens wear daily.; [pers.] In this age of technological advancement it is important that poetry and the arts in general - (The Real Crafts of mankinds development) not be forgotten.!; [a.] Jupiter, FL

MCGORTY, JAMIE A.
[p.] Debby McGorty and Patrick Russo; [ed.] Roosevelt Grammer School, Secaucus Middle School, and Secaucus High School; [memb.] ICCYG, Key Club, Foreign Language Club, Math Club and School Chorus; [hon.] Foreign Language poetry recitation award, freshman volleyball and varsity cheer leading; [oth. writ.] Several poems published in school newspaper and magazines; [pers.] Strive for your dreams - anything is possible!; [a.] Secaucus, NJ

MCGRATH, MAURA CATHERINE
[b.] January 18, 1983; [p.] Greg and Patti McGrath; [ed.] Currently I am in the Seventh Grade at St. Jerane School; [pers.] I have always enjoyed writing and encourage all poets to keep up the good work. I would like to thank my parents and friends for all of their support.; [a.] Cleveland, OH

MCINTYRE, ROBERT G.
[b.] October 10, 1975, Fairfax, VA; [p.] John S. McIntrye, Sheryl C. McIntrye; [ed.] James

Madison High School Graduate - 1993, (Currently attending College at NOVA Comm. College); [occ.] Salesman at Home Depot; [memb.] Vienna Presbyterian Church, Church Choir; [hon.] Who's Who Among American High School Students 1990-1991, 1993 District Chorus; [oth. writ.] I love songwriting and will settle for writing poetry if the subject is not willing to be in a song. I also love singing, recording, and playing guitar, [pers.] Much time and effort has been spent looking for that which cannot be seen, and the heart that appreciates the intangible is more precious than gold.; [a.] Vienna, VA

MCINTYRE, VIRGINIA A.
[b.] October 16, 1966, Magnolia, AR; [p.] Mr. and Mrs. Bobby Joe McIntyre; [ch.] Kashawa K. Mitchell; [ed.] Magnolia High School Southern Arkansas University Milwaukee Area Technical College; [memb.] Omega Pearl which is an incorporation of Omega Psi Phi Fraternity The Shade Tree Creative Arts Department; [oth. writ.] I've had several poems published in the Magnolia Arkansas local newspaper titled The Banner News; [a.] Milwaukee, WI

MCKAY, BRENNON
[b.] November 24, 1981, Youngstown, OH; [p.] Kevin, Tammy McKay, [ed.] Currently attending East Palestine Middle School; [memb.] Member of Grace Lutheran Church; [a.] East Palestine, OH

MCKENZIE, ATLAS
[b.] October 11, 1981, Warner Robins, GA; [p.] Linda McKenzie and Alvin McKenzie; [occ.] In School; [memb.] Student Council; [hon.] Trophy for Outstanding Student Award in 1994, Plague for Outstanding Student Award in 1995; [oth. writ.] Several poems published in local newspapers. I have written many poems which all try to tell a story. My poems insist of serious events and love.; [pers.] Inb my poems I'm trying to give America a wake up call. It's about time we face the fact about what's going on in America today. We're tearing our own selves apart by hatred and violence. I'm only a kid but I'll do whatever it takes to change the ways of this country, even if it means spending the rest of my life doing so.; [a.] Warner Robins, GA

MCMAHORI, KIMBERLY A. TERLAP
[b.] June 17, 1970, Waukegan, IL; [p.] Roberta Pantel and Marty Terlap; [m.] Timothy J. McMahori, June 24, 1995; [ed.] Prospect High, William Harper College; [occ.] Administrative Assistant; [pers.] I write poems for myself. If others enjoy reading them, that's all the better.; [a.] Island Lake, IL

MCMANUS, DENNIS
[b.] October 18, 1972, W. Slip, NY; [p.] Candice and Dennis McManus; [ed.] Brentwood Sonderling High School, New York Institute of

Technology; [occ.] Museum Guide; [memb.] National Lacrosse Association; [hon.] Most valuable player varsity lacrosse 1988, 89, 90. Captain N.Y.I.T. Lacrosse team, Charlie Hustle Award 1993, Outstanding player 1994; [oth. writ.] All American U.S. Intercollegiate Lacrosse Assoc. Midfield 1994.; [a.] Brentwood, NY

MCMURTRY, RYAN
[b.] July 23, 1978, North Platte, NE; [p.] John and Janet McMurtry; [ed.] Student at Okaloosa Walton Community College; [occ.] Student; [memb.] Singer, Songwriter for local band; [hon.] Numerous Downhill Skiing Awards; [oth. writ.] Poem entitled, "This thing called my Soul," published by The National Library of Poetry in their Anthology, Beneath the Harvest Moon; [pers.] My writings typically reflect my own views and feelings on various issues. I have been greatly influenced by my own experiences and hardships in overcoming dyslexia and depression.; [a.] Niceville, FL

MCNEILL, JOSEPH P.
[pen.] Skedge Jr; [b.] October 26, 1984, Cheverly, MD; [p.] Brian McNeill, Colleen McNeill; [ed.] Our Lady of Mercy School, Winston-Salem, NC St. Bernard's School, Riverdale, MD; [occ.] Student, Our Lady of Mercy School, Winston-Salem, NC; [memb.] JV Basketball, LL Baseball Young Astronauts Club, School Band, Saxophone; [hon.] 6th grade - 3rd place, Spelling Bee, 1st place Science Fair; [oth. writ.] Ramblings O' Mine, McNeill Publishing; [pers.] I was inspired by my great-grandfather (a.k.a. Skedge) to write after reading his poems. I like to write about anything that comes into my mind and also things and places in nature.; [a.] Winston-Salem, NC

MCPARLAND, PAMELA S.
[b.] July 13, 1963, Ellwood City, PA; [p.] Harry D. Kuhrt Sr., Patricia B. King; [m.] Steven H. McParland, January 19, 1988; [ch.] Chassidie Anne, Alaina Marie; [ed.] Slippery Rock High, Butler Community College; [occ.] An aspiring writer, Artist; [oth. writ.] Numerous poems and novelettes, short stories, investigative exposes; [pers.] My writings are a manifestation of the beauty, and the darkness to which I see in the world.; [a.] Butler, PA

MCTAGUE, NATHAN M.
[b.] August 17, 1973, Fairfax, VA; [p.] Michael J. McTague, Nancy L. Dent; [ed.] Sidney Lanier High School, Auburn University; [occ.] Montana Conservation Corps Member, Poet; [hon.] Spotlight on Student Achievement (Montgomery Area High schools), Alabama Penman; [pers.] The purpose of my work is to point out the beauty of life, whenever and however it presents itself to me. There is beauty everywhere, in everything, we have but to see it.; [a.] Bozeman, MT

MCWILLIAMS, JOANN
[b.] December 5, 1963, Dallas, TX; [p.] Chuck and Eileen Blount; [ch.] 1 Boy; [ed.] High School and Paralegal School Completed; [occ.] Executive Assistant; [memb.] Member of The Professional Career Development Association For Paralegal; [hon.] Diploma from high school and Paralegal School of Education; [pers.] This poem I submitted for the contest is very sentimental and his a lot of history and meaning behind it.; [a.] Dallas, TX

MCWILLIAMS, ZAC
[b.] August 15, 1978, Dumas, TX; [p.] Lanis and Paul McWilliams; [ed.] Junior at Lumberton High School; [memb.] Vice President of Coastal Plains Area Youth Ministry Council; [hon.] Served on National Committee of Order of the arrow and I am Eagle Scout; [oth. writ.] I have had little exposure. I have had one poem published in a local newspaper and other various poems published in my church's news letter; [pers.] I merely allow my hand to capture my pain I hope into words. I draw off of tragedy a love for my promised wife.; [a.] Lumberton, TX

MEADE, KISHELLE MARIE
[b.] November 1, 1976, Allegan; [p.] Gary Meade and Connie Housworth; [ed.] Graduated from Allegan High School 1995.; [occ.] Server at Orlo's, a Small Restaurant in Allegan Michigan; [oth. writ.] Oklahoma City bombing poem I wrote for school, was published in our school literary magazine.; [pers.] I've enjoyed writing since I can remember. Friends and family have inspired me, I want everyone to know, it is possible to write if its from the heart.; [a.] Allegan, MI

MEARS, VICKI
[b.] November 8, 1964, Zanesville, OH; [p.] Fred Pride, Norma Jean Pride; [m.] John Mears, December 28, 1981; [ch.] Jessica, John, Heather, Justin; [ed.] Muskingum Area Joint Vocational School; [occ.] Home maker; [oth. writ.] Various poems written for family members and friends; [pers.] This poem is dedicated in the memory of Donald Wayne Shaffer Jr. whose life was taken from him January 9, 1995. May his sweet and gentle voice live on inside of all of us.; [a.] Zanesville, OH

MEISINGER, HERBERT J.
[pen.] Herb Meisinger; [b.] March 7, 1979, Union City, NJ; [p.] Peter J. and Florence L. Meisinger (Deceased); [m.] Marjorie W. Meisinger, August 19, 1949; [ch.] Peter, Marjorie, Lucinda, Donald, Debra and Herb (Deceased); [ed.] Union Hill High; [occ.] Retired; [memb.] American Legion; [oth. writ.] Dreamer's Love - Lyrics writer in 1950 Recorded Hollywood Tunesmiths 1950.; [pers.] To be a good enough poet published for my children and grandchildren to be proud to have known.; [a.] Palm Bay, FL

MELTON, ALLEN L.
[pen.] Allen L.; [b.] Tucson, AZ; [ed.] David Starr Jordan High School of Long Beach; [occ.] Plant Worker at Robert F. Kennedy Elementary School, Part time musician (Saxophone); [hon.] Several service awards; [oth. writ.] "Always Look Beyond The Obvious"; [pers.] My inspiration to get serious about my poetry came after reading the anthology "The Black Poets", edited by Dupley Randall. It was then I realized that someone else may be feeling just like you at a certain plane in time. Adversity can bring about strength. So I've endeavored to redirect negativity into a positive format. My faith in Jesus Christ, love from family and friends and my wife's confidence in me, gives me the extra push I need to prevail.; [a.] Anaheim, CA

MELUCCI, CAROL N.
[pen.] Carol A. Melucci; [b.] November 21, 1945, San Bernadino, CA; [p.] Alfred and Elizabeth (Hosey) Melucci; [ed.] Providence College, Bristol Community College, O. L. Peace Spiritual Life Center; [occ.] Health Services - Caretaker of Retarded Persons; [memb.] Associate Member of the Sisters of Mercy, Providence, R.I., Mass. Am. Heart Assoc: Lifesavers, Inc.; [oth. writ.] First poem published in Grammar School Newspaper. High School poem entered in anthology book in High School Contest, Wrote lyrics to song sung in my parish church this post year.; [pers.] My words reflect my desire to touch reality and also to give glory to God. I am deeply inspired by other people. I write about their lives.; [a.] Providence, RI

MENDONCA, IRMA ELIZABETH
[b.] July 20, 1931, Manitoba, Canada; [p.] Gus and Christina Lepholtz; [ch.] Jennifer Christine Shadbolt; [ed.] Glendale Community College; [occ.] Recently Retired - Trust and Compliance Banking Officer; [oth. writ.] I have written many poems through the years. "America" is the first one I have ever submitted and I feel honored to have it published. "America" was borne out of the depths of my soul and my love for this wonderful country. May the hearts of Americans be stirred to serve their country with more zeal and true patriotism. God Bless America! Where freedom reigns with Liberty and Justice for "All"; [pers.] My writings are true reflections of my personal desire to encourage others to stand up for what is right! To never give up! And to show genuine love to all mankind.; [a.] North Hollywood, CA

MENIFEE, ALVA LA FRANCES
[pen.] Alva Menifee; [b.] February 4, 1947, Auburn, AL; [p.] Willie Arthur and Hester Harper Menifee; [m.] Divorced; [ch.] George Raephael Young and Gregory Renardo Young; [ed.] B.S. Degree Alabama State Univ. Montg. Al. Further studies - Tuskegee University

Tuskegee, Alabama. Univ. of Michigan Lansing Michigan 1973; [occ.] Elementary School Teacher, Souvenir Retailer T-Shirts Cards, tributes; [memb.] Hatchinson Missionary Baptist Church Board of Christian Education and Mamie G. Lewis Matrons. National Ed. Assoc. NEA, Alabama, Ed, Assoc., AEA Autanga County Assoc. ACEH. National Assoc. for Female Executive NAFE. Brantwood children home; [hon.] My poem "I Feel Like Me" is displayed in the Tuskegee Municipal building. I been cited with mentions of honors in various newspapers and books; [oth. writ.] Several poems printed in Montgomery Advertiser - Journal, Montgomery - Tuskegee Times, Westside News, Tuskegee Tribune and The Prattville Progress. And The Prattville Progress. Book "Dream Awakening."; [pers.] I strive to inspire, reflect the human experience, and the beauty of nature in my writing. I have a deep respect for the dignity and worth of all mankind.; [a.] Montgomery, AL

MERILA, RICHARD L.
[b.] May 15, 1947, Washburn, WI; [p.] Toivo and Geneva Merila; [m.] Kristin Linberg Merila, October 8, 1993; [ed.] Washburn High School, Ashland County Teacher College, Eau Claire State University Night Classes; [occ.] Retired; [memb.] Disabled American Veterans, American Legion; [hon.] Salutatorian Award, Latin Award, Social Service Awards, Nominated by ISP as Poet of the Year (1995); [oth. writ.] To My Nightingale, Don't Ever Let Go, Alone; [pers.] I believe in the great personal worth and dignity of each person. Salvation is the beginning of life.; [a.] Ashland, WI

MERRITT, BETH-ANN
[b.] February 14, 1983, Fort Pierce, FL; [p.] Robert and Jo-Anne Merritt; [ed.] 7th grade at forest grove Middle School 12 yrs. old.; [memb.] Crime watch at forest grove; [a.] Fort Pierce, FL

MERSHAWN, ANGELA DIANE
[b.] February 28, 1953, Rome, GA; [p.] James E. and Jacqueline I. Norwood; [m.] Jon S. Mershawn, November 3, 1989; [ch.] Christine Litchfield, Shannon Brown and Myria Ervin; [ed.] Presently attending Navarro College, Corsicana Texas; [occ.] Attending College for Business cerficate; [pers.] I write from the heart and soul. Disease is not discriminating and threatens the future of our world. We must remember there is always hope for mankind.; [a.] Corsicana, TX

MESTER, PATRICIA LEE
[pen.] Patricia Grace; [b.] May 19, 1950, Saint Louis, MO; [p.] Lee and Grace Jones; [m.] Dale Charles Mester, October 28, 1968; [ch.] Rick, Michael and Christopher Mester; [ed.] Christian and Layperson Seminars on hurting people

especially relationships.; [occ.] 8 years part-time lay counselling for premarital classes or marriage counsellings at our church in life Christian Center, Saint Louis, MO; [oth. writ.] Unpublished poems and exhortations to encourage hurting people.; [pers.] Having been through many personal tragedies, I long to comfort during relational breaches, sickness and deaths of loved ones.; [a.] Saint Louis County, MO

METCALF, SHEA MARIE
[b.] June 22, 1981, New Haven, CT; [p.] William and Cheryl Metcalf; [ed.] I am a Freshman in High School at South Haven, Kansas; [pers.] I started writing poetry as a creative outlet to life's trials and tribulations.; [a.] South Haven, KS

MEYER, MARY ELLEN
[b.] June 28, 1978, Athens, GA; [ed.] Clarke Central High School (Graduation expected June 7 1996) enrolled at Georgia State University for the 1996 fall term; [hon.] "Notorious under-achiever" award; [oth. writ.] Just a lot of poetry I've never published.; [pers.] Everything's probable, nothing is possible.; [a.] Athens, GA

MICHALOWICH, ROBERT F.
[b.] June 8, 1946, Johnstown, PA; [p.] Robert and Sara Michalowich; [ed.] University of Viet Nam Life; [occ.] Owner, Kawasaki Motorcycle Dealer Ensenada Mexico; [oth. writ.] Other scribblings of a totality incurable romantic mind; [pers.] I have destroyed I have created I gave love, I lost love, I have love, I live I have nothing to prove; [a.] Ensenada Mexico, Baja CFA

MIJARES, MICHELE MARIE
[b.] April 7, 1961, Michigan; [p.] Winlaw and Marie Bramley; [m.] Omar E. Mijares, June 20, 1981; [ch.] Shayla, Natasha, Omar Jr.; [ed.] South Dade High School Graduated 1979; [occ.] Mother, wife; [pers.] I would like to thank my husband, children, parents, my sister Maureen, and my friend Pam for believing in me.; [a.] Virginia Beach, VA

MIKELL, IRA
[b.] March 21, 1976, Gainesville, FL; [p.] Clifton and Zelda Mikell; [ed.] Trenton High School Florida College; [occ.] Student; [memb.] Sowers Club, Omega Chi, Concert and Pep Band; [hon.] All State Band, Who's Who Among American High School Students; [oth. writ.] Poem published in River Breezes 1994-95 also a poem published in famous poems of Today 1994-95, also, 12 poems published in River Breezes 1995-96.; [a.] Bell, FL

MILANOSKI, THELMA
[b.] August 2, 1937, Catawba Co., NC; [p.] Harold and Rene Barringer, [ch.] Helene, Kimberly and John Jr.; [ed.] Rochester High School - Centralia, WA, Everett C. College -

Everett, WA; [pers.] I have been greatly influenced by the love of my children in all that I do.; [a.] Edmonds, WA

MILES, HELEN
[b.] December 17, Pittsburgh, PA; [ch.] Ron, Dave, Kevin, Susan, Tina; [ed.] St. Mary's High, Allegheny Community College, Duquesne University, Connelly Vocational School of Nursing; [occ.] Staff Nurse, Naples Community Hospital, Oncology Unit; [memb.] International Society of Poets, The Conservancy, National Resource Defense Council, ASPCA, WWF, Sierra Club Legal Defense, National Audubon Soc. American Heart Assoc., DAV Commander Club; [hon.] Clinical Excellence Award, Certificate of Appreciation - Project Helps Hotline, Certificate of Appreciation - National Humane Ed. Soc., DAV-Bronze Leader, Poet of Merit Award, Editor's Choice Award, Special Recognition Award in Oncology Patient Care; [oth. writ.] Have had other poems published; [pers.] It is a pleasure to share my poems with others. My greatest influence my children.; [a.] Naples, FL

MILICI, JONATHAN
[pen.] Jon Milici, JM; [b.] October 27, 1968, New York; [p.] John Milici, Nora Johnson; [ed.] Bard College - New York; [occ.] Artist; [pers.] To God, for who I am always thankful.; [a.] Cambridge, MA

MILLER, BRIAN G.
[b.] July 26, 1974; [pers.] Brian G. Miller is a young dropout, from Virginia Commonwealth University whose hobbies include making fun of the world around him, drinking beer by himself, and masturbating.

MILLER, CHERYL ANN
[pen.] Cheryl Ann McElroy, Miller, [b.] February 22, 1966, Newark, NJ; [p.] Malcolm and Margaret McElroy; [m.] Michael R. Miller Sr., April 4, 1987; [ch.] Danielle, Michael Jr., Donald; [ed.] Colonia Sr. High School; [occ.] Early, Education Specialist; [oth. writ.] I am proud to say that this is the first time I offend my work for publication. Although I have been writing since my early teens.; [pers.] I would like to thank Marian and all those who have encourage me threw the years. My writing has and continues to pull me threw a lot of hard times it has always been there for me.; [a.] Mebane, NC

MILLER, GLORIA M.
[pen.] Gloria Miller; [b.] April 6, 1941, Ardmore, OK; [p.] T. Wade Peterson and Helen Peterson; [m.] Robert Miller, November 11, 1979; [ch.] Cynthia, Mark, Craig and Bridgette; [ed.] St. Mary's High, Blackwood Business, West Valley College (CA), Western College of Natural Health (CA); [occ.] Secretary/Home-maker; [memb.] Bethal Christian Church; [hon.]

Finalist in the non-alcoholic drink competition (Sponsored by Triple AAA), Honorable mention poetry contest awards, (World of Poetry), semi-finalist - open National Library of Poetry contest.; [oth. writ.] Articles for the Hertz Data Chatter, Song Lyricist, Several songs performed Fro an AG Church, write short stories, (3) poems published. Dozens of open letters to magazines and newspapers published.; [pers.] It is my desire to convey a message from my heart, that reflects God's influence on my life. I have been writing poems and songs since I was a young girl for my own pleasure.; [a.] Gilroy, CA

MILLER, JENNIFER D.
[b.] May 1, 1974, Oneida, NY; [p.] John B. Miller and Dianne M. Miller; [ed.] Associates Degree in Medical Laboratory Technology from Alfred State College; [occ.] Office Assistant at Walters Chevrolet and Sales, Inc. and Cashier at Camden Super Duper; [a.] Camden, NY

MILLER, KATHERINE BASSETT
[b.] April 14, 1958, Bentonia, MS; [p.] Eddie and Estell Bassett; [m.] John R. Miller, June 7, 1980; [ch.] J. R. and Bryan; [ed.] Bentonia High, Bentonia, MS, Hinds Jr. College, Jackson, MS, Jackson State Univ., Jackson, MS, The Art Institute, Dallas, TX; [occ.] Freelance Photographer, Mark-Up Clerk, U.S. Postal Service, Dallas, TX; [memb.] Sims Chapel Missionary Baptist Church/Senior Mission, Garland, TX; [hon.] Received Distinguished Recognition of Achievement Award in the Fifty-Third Annual Kodak International, Newspaper Snapshot Awards, 1988.; [a.] Garland, TX

MILLER, KATIE AND VIGNA, KELLIE
[b.] Kellie - July 3, 1980, Redmonds, WA, Katie-May 5, 1981, Tacoma, WA; [p.] John and Rose Miller/Stan and Shirley Vigna; [ed.] Freshman in High School, Kellie - Auburn Riverside HS, Katie - Fife HS; [hon.] Honor students maintaining a 4.0 G.P.A. various published, writings/poetry in students newspapers and magazines; [pers.] The greatest thing about writing is that there is no limit to your imagination and expressing yourself. We use poetry to reveal our emotions and creativeness. If it hadn't been for the inspiration of our favorite teacher, Mr. Nelson, we may have never discovered our love of poetry. Thanks Mr. Nelson.; [a.] Auburn, WA

MILLER, KEN
[b.] July 30, 1949, Morgantown, WV; [p.] Bill Miller (Deceased), Louise Wright; [m.] Sheryl L. Miller, February 12, 1972; [ch.] Kristin L. Miller; [ed.] DuVal High, Prince George's Community College, The American University; [occ.] Grocery Store Checker, Safeway, Dunkirk, MD; [oth. writ.] A number of unpublished poems.; [pers.] My poems can be

pretty intense. However, by writing them I've gotten something out of my system, which seems to be a positive release. I hope anyone who reads something I have written will find the work helpful or cathartic. To have someone relate to what I am saying would be truly rewarding.; [a.] Owings, MD

MILLER, LAREINE A.
[b.] February 25, 1947, Washington DC; [p.] Rev. LaReintz A. and Mrs. Mary B. Johnson, Sr.; [ch.] Lillian M. Bonds, Yvette S. and Andréa L. Miller; [ed.] Eastern High School (DC), DC Teachers College, The Washington School for Secretaries; [occ.] Legal Assistant, Mary Kay Consultant; [memb.] St. Paul Baptist Church, Shiloh Baptist Church (Alexandria, VA), National Council of Negro Women, NAACP, National Association of Female Executives; [oth. writ.] "A Shepherd's Talk With His Lord and God," "My Child, Yes, You Do Matter," "The Private Man," "To My Mother, Whom I Cherish," and numerous poems written for family, friends and special occasions; [pers.] Don't hesitate to use God's gifts; if you do, you'll lose your blessings. God's wisdom flows through me as I pray and express concern for others.; [a.] Capitol Heights, MD.

MILLER, TINA
[b.] November 30, 1978, Wayne, MI; [p.] Norm and Janet Miller; [ed.] East Detroit High School Student, 11th grade; [occ.] Student; [hon.] MEAP Awards for English and Reading; [pers.] I enjoy expressing my feeling in my writings.; [a.] Warrer, MI

MILSOP, ASHLEY
[b.] October 20, 1980, Springfield, MA; [p.] Roger and Ruth Milsop; [ed.] Billings Senior High School; [pers.] Look to this day, for it is life. For yesterday is already a dream, and tomorrow is only a vision. But today, well lived, makes every yesterday a dream of happiness and every tomorrow a vision of hope. Sanskrit Proverb; [a.] Billings, MT

MIRES, ROSETTE
[b.] April 1, 1929, Brooklyn, NY; [p.] Esther, Samuel; [ed.] Erasmus Hall, Brooklyn College Adult Courses; [occ.] Cost Service Mines Press, Inc.; [memb.] Artist League of Brooklyn; [hon.] World of Poetry, Honorable Mention, The National Library of Poetry Editors Choice, Artist League of Brooklyn, Honorable Mention.; [oth. writ.] Poetic Eloquence, Feelings Magazine, Poetry Harbor; [pers.] I want to feel, touch and sense my soul! I want to be me!; [a.] Brooklyn, NY

MIRET, KELLY SMITH
[pen.] Kelly Miret; [b.] April 18, 1959, Mass; [p.] Patricia and William Miret; [ch.] Karen Ann; [ed.] Assoc. Science Massasoit Community

College; [occ.] Radiological Technologist; [memb.] M.S.R.T., A.R.R.T.; [hon.] Scholarship Recipient; [oth. writ.] Several poems, short stories; [pers.] Looking at life through rose colored glasses can have great advantage, as long as you get them down on paper. To feel and share is a wonderful contribution to all.; [a.] Stoughton, MA

MISCHEL
[b.] June 1967, Chico, CA; [ed.] Art Center College of Design; [pers.] One must never silence what is inside, laugh, cry, write, create. Be true to one's self.; [a.] Los Angeles, CA

MITCHELL, ALBERTA M.
[b.] May 28, 1924, Linden, NJ; [p.] Owen David Davis and Talitha Buckman Davis; [m.] John E. Mitchell Deceased, July 2, 1957; [ed.] High Linden School, Newark School of fine and Industrial Arts; [occ.] Retired from 37 years working at Newark Public Library; [memb.] With children first baptist church Linden, N.J.; [pers.] Worked with children for Newark Public Library for 37 years. Attended Newark School of Fine and Industrial Arts. Born in Linden N.J. Love in the answer.; [a.] Roselle, NJ

MITCHELL, NORMA
[b.] August 28, 1942, Saint Augustine, FL; [p.] Jeffie and Willie Mae Mitchell; [ed.] Richard J. Murray High Florida Memorial College; [occ.] Retired Disabled Pre-Kindergarden Teacher; [memb.] Rogers Memorial United Methodist Church; [a.] Brandenton, FL

MITCHELL, RICHARD E.
[pen.] Dick Mitchell (Golden Oldie); [b.] April 6, 1913, Salt Lake City, UT; [p.] Erral Mitchell, Gertrude Robinson; [m.] Deon Smoot, December 23, 1945; [ch.] Richard L. Sandra, Debra; [ed.] High School Grad., 1 yr. Post Grad., University of Hard Knocks and Experience, Travel 50 States - Europe, Athens, Austria, England, So. Africa, etc.; [occ.] Retired; [oth. writ.] "Think It Over" (24 Lines), "You're Never Too Old To Learn" (16 Lines), "Our Anniversary" (16 Lines), "To My Brother In The Hospital (8 Lines), "My Operation" (28 Lines), "My Excuse" (8 Lines); [pers.] I write on: Inspiration, situation, occasion, humor, true happy feelings strive to make people happy and hope what I write is entertaining.; [a.] Redondo Beach, CA

MITCHELL, RUTH F.
[pen.] Ruth F. Mitchell; [b.] December 12, 1923, Payson, UT; [p.] Ella M. Lott, Charles J. Christiansen; [m.] Alfred T. Mitchell, November 6, 1950; [ch.] Brent T. Mitchell; [ed.] High School; [occ.] Retired; [a.] West Bountiful, UT

MITTOO, WALKER DOROTHY ELAINE
[b.] Jamaica, West Indies; [p.] Joseph and Leila Mittoo; [m.] Kenneth Walker, December 17,

1955; [ch.] Jackie Patricia, Michelle, Karen, Richard, Carolyn and Sandra; [ed.] Registered Nurse, - a graduate of the University College Hospital of the West Indies; [hon.] Won a Scholarship to St. Simons College, Jamaica West Indies; [oth. writ.] "The Magical Foundation of Love," a book of poems dedicated to my son Jackie Mittoo who has left behind him so much of his musical talent.; [pers.] The thoughts are the most beautiful part of one, they reflect the true beauty that - lies deep within my soul, a special beauty that you will find in each poem that I send to you.

MOIR, JOHN P.
[b.] March 22, 1960, Sudbury, MA; [ed.] M.A. degree candidate, Counseling Psychology, Antioch New England Graduate School, Keene, NH. B.A. degree, Social Services, Westfield State College (Westfield, MA); [occ.] Outreach worker, student; [memb.] Former member of the Board of Directors to Attention Deficit Information Network; [hon.] Founder/Leader, New England based A.D.D. support groups; [pers.] Seek to show in my writings, the processes by which the human spirit overcomes adversity. Sources of inspiration: Timothy Allan Moir, Dr. Maya Angelou; [a.] Peterborough, NH

MONDRAGON, CATHERINE CANDELARIA
[pen.] Catherine C. Valdez; [b.] January 25, 1955, Pueblo, CO; [p.] Rupert Joe Valdez and Rose Gloria Valdez; [m.] Mike G. Mondragon, February 14, 1987; [ch.] Rupert Leo and Nicholas Augustine; [ed.] Central High School 1972, University of Southern Colorado; [occ.] Domestic Engineer; [hon.] The World of Poetry, Silver Poet award 1986, 1972 contestant Miss Colorado Teenager pageant, 1995 Eidtor's Choice Award (ALIKE), 1995 Honorable Mention Front Range Chapter for (Carousel); [oth. writ.] Published in the Anthology, Alike—Beyond the Stars An Angel Walks—the best poems of 1996 Mother Earth—Beneath the Harvest Moon the Elements of Earth—Where Dawn Lingers; [pers.] In order to succeed in today's generation, one must know what they want out of life. For life itself has so much to offer.; [a.] Pueblo, CO

MONROE, WM. F.
[pen.] Morgan Morgan Monroe; [b.] May 3, 1965, Pontiac, MI; [p.] Mary A. Brookshear and Glenn A.; [m.] Amy C. Monroe, October 29, 1983; [ch.] Eric William and Melesa C.; [ed.] Self teaching, currently Enrolled In APL Program Clarkston, MI; [occ.] Industrial Building Maint.; [memb.] President, "Motional Trendz Artistic Promotions; [hon.] Have worked with many artistic local talents. Published twice in poets Anthologies. Have made points in donations to several charities and hospitals; [oth. writ.] `At water's Edge' "Storms from now her" "motional trendz" darker than black manuscripts of "Here They Eat "Their Own.";" [pers.] No man shall rise above another, but being held on his brother's shoulder. All men will be judged by the brother's he help up. Naught the one's trampled under.; [a.] Pontiac, MI

MONTGOMERY, BEATRICE
[pen.] Beatrice Opp; [b.] December 2, 1926, Champaign, IL; [p.] Walter Opp, Lucy Opp (Deceased); [m.] Deceased; [ch.] Walter, Warren, Ethelda, Aletha; [ed.] South Market School, Liberty School, McKinley High School, Walsh College; [occ.] Retired Head Start Teacher from Martin Luther Lutheran Church; [memb.] Shiloh Baptist Church, Church Clerk; [oth. writ.] Other poetry, one song "It Must Be The Love Of God"; [pers.] I have been writing since age 14 and had booklet published in 1947 "Gems of Thought". Have not been successful in getting another published. Love writing religious materials.; [a.] Canton, OH

MONTGOMERY, JANET
[b.] January 23, 1983, La Plata, MD; [p.] Benedict and Judith Montgomery; [ed.] John Hanson Middle School; [occ.] Student; [memb.] Charles County Junior Olympic Volleyball Team, Johns Hopkin's Center for Talented Youth.; [hon.] Straight A's in school, Student of the Month for Leadership, Principal's List, and President's Award for Academic Achievement.; [pers.] I strive to be the best I can be. Reading and writing to me enhance the mind.; [a.] Benedict, MD

MOON, DORIS
[b.] January 1, 1956, Henning, TN; [p.] Annie Currie and Thomas Currie; [m.] Max E. Moon, November 29, 1992; [ch.] Jimmeca Currie and Jacqueline Currie; [ed.] James Madison High School, National Education Center; [occ.] Certified Home Health Aide; [memb.] God's Greater Holy Temple, Full Gospel Church, Pastor Bishop B.D. Jackson and Evangelist Helen R. Jackson.; [a.] Dallas, TX

MOONIE, WANDA FAIR
[b.] June 24, 1960, Gastonia, NC; [p.] Fannie and Donald Boyce; [m.] Johnny Ray Moonie, September 27, 1985; [ch.] Marcus, Anthony, Xavier, O'Darius; [ed.] Adams Elementary Gordon Jr. High Cardozo Sr. High, All in Washington DC; [occ.] House wife, and mother of four boys; [hon.] The only Honors and Awards I have received in my life is the joy and happiness I see on my children face each day and the love we feel for each other; [oth. writ.] I write poems and songs but none have been published; [pers.] I only write what I feel in my heart and what I think the world and it's populations should be May God bless us all; [a.] Gastonia, NC

MOORE, CONARD D.
[pen.] Connie Dea Moore; [b.] July 8, 1928, Okmulgee, OK; [p.] Conard Milton Moore; [m.] Kitzia Poniatowska, December 20, 1975; [ch.] Connie D. Moore; [ed.] Medical Doctor, Ophthalmologist; [occ.] Ophthalmologist/Chief of Surgery, International College of Surgeons; [memb.] American College of Surgeons, International College of Surgeons, American Academy of Ophthalmology; [hon.] Chief of Staff, Medical Center Hospital; [oth. writ.] Scientific papers; [pers.] Wish to be included in the biographical section of the National Library of Poetry, Houston, Texas; [a.] Houston, TX

MOORE, DIANA L.
[pen.] Deede; [b.] January 23, 1967, Los Angeles, CA; [p.] Tom Wright, Lynn Hansen; [m.] Larson E. Moore Jr., December 27, 1985; [ch.] Larson and Jeri; [occ.] Dept. of Corrections Medical Record Tech. I; [oth. writ.] None published before now.; [pers.] I enjoy writing poems about my children, they are so very precious to me. Once, I wrote a poem "To Forgive" to my brother during a crisis between us - that poem has brought us close again.; [a.] Charleston, WV

MOORE, ELOISE
[b.] January 15, 1915, Aduston, TX; [m.] Deceased, October 26, 1933; [ch.] Two; [ed.] High School - 2 years College Nurses Training (3 years); [occ.] Retired-Nurse; [oth. writ.] Various articles, notices for small neighborhood newspaper.

MOORE, HELEN L.
[b.] May 21, 1933, Indianapolis, IN; [p.] Crave Botkin, Bernice Botkin; [m.] Willie Moore Jr., February 10, 1958; [ch.] 6 sons, 2 daughters; [ed.] Graduate Broadripple High School, Indpls, IN, Business Correspondence School, 1 year Business Courses (Community College); [occ.] Income Tax Preparer, Notary Public; [oth. writ.] Wrote a genealogy book on my husbands family; [pers.] I try to establish the wonders of nature and God's creations. I enjoy poetry. Put my thoughts into verse I've wrote poems Limericks, and satirical verses. I enjoy all of God's creations, and beautiful sights in the world. I wrote a genealogy book; [a.] Seaman, OH

MOORE, MARGUERITE MANELLA
[b.] January 4, 1917, Pittsburgh, PA; [p.] Francisco and Marietta Manella; [m.] Thomas Claude Moore (Deceased), September 15, 1942; [ch.] Thomas F. Moore, Manella M. Moore; [ed.] B.A. Carlow College, PGH, PA, M.A. Univ. Of Miami, Florida M.S. Univ. Of Miami Florida; [occ.] Retired Dade County Public Schools I thought English to twenty yrs. college-bound; [memb.] Graduate School U. Of Miami Carlow College Alumni Ass'n. Soroptomist Club-Coral Gables Coral Gables

Country Club Respect Life Ass'n. Miami, Florida; [hon.] Community Service Award Carlow College-1980, For Outstanding Community Services Exec. Dir. Coral Gables Youth Center and Coral Gables Sr. Citizen Club Plaques in both Blds. as founder; [oth. writ.] Very little. A weekly column in local Coral Gables Paper While Exec. Director Of The Coral Gables Youth Center An article in Recreation Magazine years ago on teenagers; [pers.] I was one of eight children of parents whose dictum was "You are your brothers keeper" so we grew up rooted in the concept of community service which we exemplify to this day.; [a.] Coral Gables, FL

MOORE, MARIAN
[b.] November 20, 1935, Millerstown, PA; [p.] Howard Henninger, Florence Asper; [m.] Richard W. Moore, July 17, 1954; [ch.] Karen, Linda, Roland, Richard, Nichole, Vivian; [ed.] 12th grade; [occ.] Housewife; [oth. writ.] 300 poems, Biography, Mini-Profiles, Christmas Story, Book of Drawings, despising daily happenings; [pers.] Started writing 91 after 4 strokes, writing for therapy 300 poems, autobiography poems about daily happenings cleared my head and soothed me and made me stronger.; [a.] Lake George, CO

MOORE, SHANNON
[b.] May 5, 1978; [occ.] Student; [pers.] Through all the corruption mankind has to show us, I believe in the intrinsic passion that makes change possible for each of us.; [a.] Arcadia, CA

MOORE, STEVE
[b.] May 25, 1958, Columbus, OH; [p.] David and Ludie Moore; [m.] Divorced; [ch.] Cheyenne, Jimmy, Crystal, Amber; [ed.] High School, 4 year trade school; [occ.] Commercial Construction; [oth. writ.] I am in the process of publishing a book (I Love You) and writing my second both are books of love; [pers.] I have great respect for woman kind, to me they're special (or at least most of them). I try to reflect that in what I write. I have my mother to think for that.; [a.] Houston, MI

MOORER, CANDACE M.
[b.] April 9, 1963, Birmingham, AL; [p.] Jesse and Oyweda Moorer; [ch.] Jessica Jerald (12) and Ivana Mbullah (3); [ed.] BS - Biology. I'm currently working on a dual degree - Masters in Business Administration; [occ.] Special Chemistry Supervisor, [memb.] American Society of Clinical Pathologist, Delta Sigma Theta Sorority.

MORALES, AMY LYNN
[pen.] Amy Lynn; [b.] July 8, 1968, Pasadena, CA; [p.] Carl and Pamela Morales; [ed.] California Stat University Northridge, BS in Physical Therapy; [occ.] Student and Exercise Therapist; [memb.] Job's Daughters, Bethel 179,

Temple City CA, Temple City High School Newspaper 3 1/2 years key club, Student against driving drunk; [hon.] Quill and scroll 2 years, TCHS National Honor Society 3 1/2 yrs, TCHS; [pers.] I believe that a persons true soul can be revealed through poetry. A word is just a word, but when combined with other words, a powerful statement is made which can influence society.; [a.] Temple City, CA

MORAUD, GEORGETTE
[b.] Saint Junien, France; [p.] Marcel and May Moraud; [m.] Gene Murphy; [ch.] Maureen, Kathleen, Eugene Jr., Georgette and John; [ed.] Primary, Secondary - France, Under grad and grad. USA; [occ.] Retired Mod. Lang. Prof; [memb.] AATF, AAUP, MLA; [hon.] Elected to: Societe' Des Professeurs En Ame'rique, Ecoles Des Hautes E'tudes, Se'Jours Internationaux Linguistiques et Cultures, PI Delta Phi, Nat. French Honor Society, Phi Sigma Cota Nat. Romance Language Honor Society, Received 5 awards for Excellence in Teaching from, AATF; [a.] Geneva, NY

MORELAND, TERESA JOY
[pen.] Terese; [b.] April 13, 1964, Council Bluffs, IA; [p.] Fred Fezelte, Amy Finkebone; [m.] Leonard Joseph Moreland, July 10, 1981; [ch.] Joseph Daisy, Wendy Moreland; [ed.] 9th Grade, G.E.D., 3 yrs., College at Vermillion for A.S. Degree 92-95; [occ.] Housewife; [memb.] Moose Heart for Children; [hon.] Dean's List at Vermillion; [oth. writ.] I have kept a journal of thought since I was 12 yrs. old. Have had several poems published in school and city newspaper and read at weddings. Also like to write short stories and essays. Hope to publish my collection of poems.; [pers.] Since I was very young people have called a dreamer. I only know that when I looked at the sky full of stars. I became captured by curiosity and consumed with wonders. Wonder never cease, answers are sometimes never seen, still we all dream for world peace.; [a.] Ely, MN

MORENO, TRINA B.
[pen.] Trina B. Harrell; [b.] April 12, 1964, Houston, TX; [p.] Louise E. and Willie Harrell; [m.] Mark S. Moreno, September 1, 1990; [ch.] Jonathan and Kaleb Moreno; [ed.] M. B. Smiley High Texas Tech University; [occ.] Customer Service; [pers.] I have always love reading and writing poetry. I thank the Lord Jesus for giving me the talent and the ability to do so and I treasure this gift.; [a.] Ontario, CA

MORESCO, AMANDA
[b.] April 6, 1975, New York City; [p.] Bobby and Barbara Moresco; [ed.] St. Vincent Ferrer H.S., New York, N.Y. San Francisco State University, S.F. C.A.; [oth. writ.] Many poems and prose: all unpublished, currently working

on a full length play.; [pers.] Every line of every poem written is the beauty of someone's soul transcribed onto paper, words meant to touch a person who can understand and relate to that beauty. I hope that my words have touched you in some way or unearthed something in your souls as they did for me when I wrote them. For then, they will have served their purpose as poets; [a.] North Hollywood, CA

MORGAN, KATHERINE L.
[b.] Franklin, VA; [p.] Robert L. Carr (Deceased), Mary Alice Stewart; [m.] Stephen G. Morgan Jr.; [ch.] Stephen Lee and Justin Gray; [occ.] Registered Nurse; [a.] Warner Robins, GA

MORGAN, RANDAL J.
[pen.] Ladnar S. Nagrom; [b.] November 25, 1966, Milwaukee, WI; [p.] Arthur and Clovious, Morgan; [ed.] Madison Area Tech. College; [occ.] Education Assistant; [hon.] U.S.A.F. Vet., Dean's List; [oth. writ.] "The Man Behind the Door" (unpublished); [pers.] Ha Ha Ha, laugh while you are still able, Ha Ha.; [a.] Madison, WI

MORIN, JILL IRENE
[pen.] Greeney; [b.] July 14, 1967, San Bernardino; [p.] Theodore G. Robinson and Colleen J. Paris; [ch.] Christopher Michael Campbell II and Jenna Melissia Morin; [ed.] Belvedere Ele, Del Vallejo Jr. High, Sierra High-Completed with High School Diploma; [occ.] Domestic Engineer; [memb.] First United Presbyterian Church; [hon.] Singing Awards for best improved choral student, James Sharte Scholarship; [oth. writ.] Numerous poems and songs but I have never submitted for publishing.; [pers.] To Jenna and Christopher I love you; [a.] San Bernardino, CA

MORRIS, ANNIE LORRAINE
[pen.] Lorraine Tyler; [b.] August 27, 1948, Richmond, VA; [p.] John and Catherine Tyler; [m.] William H. Morris, October 11, 1980; [ch.] Katrina M. Morris; [ed.] Maggie Walker High School, Cortez Peters Business College, Northern Virginia Community College, Institute of Children's Literature; [occ.] Disability Retirement as a Secretary, Freelance Writer; [memb.] Organization of Professional Employees with the Department of Agriculture (OPEDA); [hon.] Superior Award 1988, Departmental Awards 1988, 1987, Certificates of Merit 1988, 87, and 1980. Group Award 1988; [oth. writ.] Short stories for children and teenagers. I have several other poems of which were accepted by Advantage Press Publishers.; [pers.] I love to put my feelings on paper so that others might enjoy what I feel.; [a.] Temple Hills, MD

MORRIS, ANTHONY
[pen.] Ryan Anthony; [b.] January 24, 1969, El Paso, TX; [p.] Fred and Barbara Morris; [ed.]

BS of Criminal Justice Southwest Texas State University; [occ.] Insurance Broker Normal Brockerage Agency, Inc.; [memb.] Phi Alpha Delta Pre Law Frat. Visiting Nurses Assoc. Volunteer Church Member Hyde Park Baptist; [hon.] 1983 Who's Who of National Football Awards 1986 - All District Football; [oth. writ.] Several other poems published Locally and many others locked up in hiding.; [pers.] In writing a poem, I wish only to convey the emotions that I feel and hope somehow someone else will experience the same from just the readings.; [a.] El Paso, TX

MORRIS, LOLETIA
[b.] April 2, 1957, Beckley, WV; [p.] Chaunkey Bayle and Robert Bayle; [ed.] Woodrow Wilson High School West Virginia State College; [occ.] I have a ministry of helping others; [hon.] I've been honored to sing at Church Wedding, and talent shows.; [pers.] The poems was originally wrote for a wedding song to be sung by me. I was inspired by a beautiful grandmother Florida Pennel who has entered to eternal rest, and most importantly inspired by my Heavenly Father.; [a.] Loletia, MO

MORRISON, JADWIGA M.
[pen.] Jad'z Morrison; [b.] October 9, 1948, Essex, England; [p.] Helena and Tadeusz Szelazek; [m.] Douglas Morrison, February 1, 1971; [ch.] Douglas and Elisa Morrison; [ed.] Pulaski High School, Central Conn. State Univ., B.A. Degree in English; [occ.] English Tutor to Foreign 10 School System, and Business Consultant; [memb.] New Britain Museum of American Arts, Inc. (Former Bookkeeper); [oth. writ.] I have written songs, poems, and stories merely for the enjoyment of my friends and family. However, by putting this poem into print I've opened myself up to another path in life... previously untried.; [a.] Burlington, CT

MORRISON, MICHELLE
[b.] April 24, 1968; [oth. writ.] I have been writing since I was 6. I have books full of poetry and short stories.; [pers.] I want my writing to guide people to acknowledge their truest feelings and not be afraid to express them.; [a.] CA

MORSE, REBECCA M.
[pen.] Becky; [b.] December 25, 1981, Tabernacle, NJ; [p.] Michael and Ruth Morse; [hon.] Certificate of Achievement in Art; [pers.] Someone once said to me "If you truly love someone with all of your heart your feelings will never change for them." That is what inspired my poem.; [a.] Tabernacle, NJ

MOSELEY, MARK E.
[pen.] Raggamuffin Scribe; [b.] October 25, 1965, Linden, Guyana; [p.] Keith E. Moseley and Lorna L. Tyndell; [m.] Litonia V. Moseley,

June 16, 1995; [ch.] Lorna D. Moseley; [ed.] Polytechnic University and Naval Advanced Technical Schools; [occ.] Gas Turbine Systems Tech. and U.S. Navy Instructor; [oth. writ.] Several other poems, and a novel (in progress currently), short stories.; [pers.] Within the basement of our psyche lies the answer to all our questioning. We seldom visit this location, this mankind continues to wallow in gross despair; [a.] Waukegan, IL

MOSHER, BETH ANN
[b.] November 28, 1970, Saginaw, MI; [p.] Albert Webb Beem, Dianne Sue Beem; [m.] Timothy Jon Mosher, August 25, 1990; [ed.] Meridian High School - Sanford, MI; [occ.] Machinist - U.S. Graphite Saginaw, MI; [pers.] I feel the love of your family is the greatest asset a person can have.; [a.] Sanford, MI

MOTEN, MAE L.
[b.] February 7, 1947, San Marcos, TX; [p.] Joseph Kelley and Teatrice Kelley; [m.] Lawrence Moten, January 20, 1968; [ch.] Sheldon Terrance, Zandria Vedette and Lawrence Jr.; [ed.] Roy Miller High; [occ.] Housewife; [memb.] National Church of God; [oth. writ.] Several poems not published at present.; [pers.] Life is challenging - we take one day at a time realizing that we are not human beings but spiritual beings on a human journey-fulfilling our destiny... Making a difference in someone's life.; [a.] Fort Washington, MD

MOURAD, NAJI
[b.] May 5, 1966, Providence, RI; [p.] Dr. and Mrs. Nabeeh Mourad; [m.] Dina Mourad, July 1, 1992; [ed.] Virginia Polytechnic Institute; [occ.] Systems Engineer

MOY JR., JAMES H.
[b.] January 24, 1949, Camden, NJ; [p.] James Moy Sr. and Florence Moy; [m.] Caroline F. Moy, October 26, 1968; [ch.] James H. Moy III and Melissa M. Moy; [ed.] Woodrow Wilson High, N.J. Correctional Academy, N.J. State Police Academy, Police related college credits from seton hall; [occ.] Police Sergeant, Lower twp Police Dept. Cape May County N.J.; [memb.] P.B.A. Local 59, Cape Masonic Lodge; [oth. writ.] Several poems written but not published as of yet, also several songs written and compiled.; [pers.] I find that by my writing poems and songs compositions it allows me the opportunity to share my thoughts and views to others in the form of verse. It also creates a form of relaxation from the arduous career of a Law Enforcement officer.; [a.] Cape May, NJ

MOYLER, HATTIE L.
[pen.] Hattie L. Moyler; [b.] August 22, 1937, Martain Co, NC; [p.] Columbia Brown, Lindora Brown; [m.] Junius S. Moyler, July 11, 1980;

[ch.] Carolyn Brown, Judson Wright; [ed.] Oak City High School eleven grade; [occ.] Private duty nurse assist; [oth. writ.] This is my first time.

MUELLER, HENRIETTA
[pen.] Henrietta Mueller; [b.] Pittsburgh, PA; [p.] William S. and Helen K. Waters; [m.] Werner A. Mueller; [ch.] Christopher Mueller and Richard Mueller; [ed.] Northwestern University Evanston-Ill., School of Chicago Art Institute University of Wyoming Laramie WYO. B.F.A. (Chicago) M.A. - M.E.D. Univ. WYO; [occ.] Artist - Poet, Oil-water color teacher (Retired) painting Print making (Gravure); [memb.] Columbine Poets (State of Colorado) Alpa Chi Omega - (National) Delta Phi Delta (Art) National Honorary PSL GHI (Psychology) Presbyterian Church; [hon.] Who's Who Of American Art, Who's Who of American Women Who's who of the West Works in Collection, University of Wyoming State Library - Cheyenne, Wyo, Chicago Art Institute (S.A.I.C.) Permanent Alum. Collection; [oth. writ.] Published owen wister review (Univ. of Wyoming) Laramie, WY Boulder, (Colorado) Camera Newspaper Anderie Poetry Press - Easton PA. June 1996.; [pers.] Special application of color and light in creation of form influenced by constructivist (Mondrian Bolotowsky) and 20th C. Concepts, Helen Franken Thaler.; [a.] Boulder, CO

MUENNINK-FAGAN, JANIE
[b.] February 20, 1954, Fort Bening, GA; [p.] Lenwood S. and Betty H. Muennink; [ed.] BBA from Stephen F. Austin State University Nacogdoches, Texas, Richardson High School, Richardson, TX; [occ.] Legal Administrator for Ross, Clapp, Korn and Montgomery, L.L.P.; [memb.] National Geographic Society, Messiah Lutheran Church - member as well as Youth Counselor; [hon.] Graduated from High School with Honors; [oth. writ.] None published or submitted; [a.] Addison, TX

MULL, CHERILYNETTE
[pen.] C. Lynette; [b.] May 23, 1957, Auburn, CA; [p.] Norman and Lynette Owley; [ch.] Darryl Robert and Aaron Allen; [ed.] Has been helpful.; [occ.] Inner Growth and Healing; [memb.] Human Race; [oth. writ.] Personal and unpublished until it's time.; [pers.] Than you to grandma, who steeped me in books and sparked my desire to write. Mom, Dad. Laura, Vernice, Mindy, Shirley Mae and Archie for teaching me that patience is the larger part of love. Kitty for inspiration and understanding. I love you all.; [a.] Auburn, WA

MULLEN, JOAN M.
[pen.] Joan Mullen; [b.] January 19, 1929, Wilkes-Barre, PA; [p.] James and Irene Coughlin; [m.] John E. Mullen, April 21, 1951;

[ch.] Maureen, John and Mark; [ed.] Attended Coughlin High School, Wilkes Barre, Penna., graduated LaFayette H.S. in Bflo., graduate - Sisters of Charity School of Nursing - Bflo. NY 1950; [occ.] RN on Staff - St. Francis Nursing Home, Williamsburg, NY; [memb.] Former Board Member Epilepsy Association of Western, New York; [oth. writ.] Eighteen other poems written - in soft covers that were printed for my children by a dear friend - all unpublished.; [pers.] All of my poems are drawn from life - children, growing older, loss of parents - pets and every day experiences.; [a.] Buffalo, NY

MULLIKIN, MAURINE
[b.] July 8, 1946, Jackson, MI; [occ.] Teacher Assistant, East Jackson Middle School; [pers.] I try to leave a message of how we can learn from others.; [a.] Jackson, MI

MULSOW, KARALEE MAY
[b.] August 6, 1982, Emporia, KS; [p.] Dale and Deborah Mulsow, [ed.] Neosho Rapids Elementary and Neosho Rapids Junior High; [hon.] Principal's and High Honor Roll; [pers.] I'm in 8th grade and beside poetry, I enjoy drawing, sports, and taking care of my animals.; [a.] Neosho Rapids, KS

MURPHY, ANNAMAE
[pen.] Suzanne Wilk, July 25, 1935, Shamokin, PA; [p.] Anna C. Murphy and John P. Murphy; [ed.] Kenmore West High, Buffalo State College of NY, University of Wisconsin, Geneseo State College of NY; [occ.] Retired Teacher, Charles A. Lindbergh Elementary School; [memb.] N.Y.S.U.T. Retired Teachers, Buffalo State College Alumni Assoc., Kenmore Retired Educators Assoc., AFT, Alpha Delta Kappa; [hon.] Canisius College Mentor Award, Kenmore - Town of Tonawanda School District, Distinguished Service Award, Lindbergh Elementary School of Excellence Writing Team Award.; [oth. writ.] Poems for High School and College Anthologies, Lindbergh School publications, children's stories and poems, enjoy writing in personal journals.; [pers.] I believe children have a natural ability for writing and poetry, if it is nurtured. I encouraged my students to read wonderful literature and express themselves in writing stories and poetry.; [a.] Amherst, NY

MUSSER, ANN
[b.] October 31, 1943, Tacoma, WA; [m.] James Thomas Musser, July 8, 1995; [ch.] Christie Chantelle, Ronnie Roy, Lori Len; [ed.] Victoria High School, Wharton Jr. College; [occ.] Home maker; [pers.] I draw upon my inner soul, from pain and love and dreams untold, to form the rhymes, to guide my pen, for all to see my heart within.; [a.] Danbury, TX

MYERS, DANIEL W
[b.] September 5, 1966, Buffalo, NY; [ch.] Michael, Ryan, Earl Myers; [occ.] Press Operator Bison Bag Co. Inc. Kenmore, NY for last 10 years; [a.] Cheektowaga, NY

MYERS, DIANA MICHELLE
[b.] May 28, 1975, Buffalo Grove, IL; [p.] Mark and Janet Myers; [ed.] I'm a full-time student at Illinois State University. I will graduate in 1997 with a Junior High/Middle School Degree; [hon.] I have been published in a magazine from Michigan (Berkley, MI), called U.X. Press.; [oth. writ.] For a novice writer I feel this accomplishment will enhance my growth in my passion for poetry writing.; [a.] Buffalo Grove, IL

MYERS, JEANNETTE C.
[b.] March 2, 1936, Springfield, IL; [p.] Guy and Carmen (Waremburg) Myers; [ed.] Springfield High School - Class of 1954; [occ.] Executive Secretary Electric and Gas Industry; [memb.] Southern Baptist Convention; [hon.] Old fashioned memories (Primitive Painting) 3 Blue Ribbons Ties That Bind (Electric Industry - The Art of EHV - Primitive Painting) Exhibited Layton School of Art - Milwaukee WI - 2-Yr Tour of U.S; [oth. writ.] BOO -Beauty of ORANGE -ES.; [pers.] Well... It would be my... Wishing to see the ..whole... world... kissing.; [a.] Springfield, IL

MYERS, RUTH E.
[pen.] Ruth Milstead Myers; [b.] February 8, 1927, Decatur, IL; [p.] Dewey, Mavis Milstead; [m.] Earl W. Myers, November 13, 1944; [ch.] Patricia Lynne - Earl W. Jr.; [ed.] Decatur High - Argentina High; [occ.] Homemaker; [memb.] Eastern Star Organization Chicora United Brethren Church Cancer Society Allegan County; [hon.] Church - School Awards; [oth. writ.] Church paper - school nothing published yet personal writings.; [pers.] Through teen and adult years, I have loved writing poems and short stories, and have an active imagination, which inspires my writing, also my family has been very helpful and supportive and I love to share my feelings and writings with others.; [a.] Mount Zion, IL

MYLES, JAMES M.
[b.] November 23, 1983, Huntington, NY; [p.] Sean Myles and Margo Myles; [ed.] Presently in 6th grade at East Northport Middle School, East Northport, NY; [occ.] Student; [hon.] Johns Hopkins statewide verbal award, 1995, President education award, 1995; [pers.] I want to become a television writer and create science fiction shows like chris Carter (X-Files, Space-Above and Beyond).; [a.] East Northport, NY

NAGY, ANNIKA
[b.] August 24, 1983, Los Angeles, CA; [p.] Al

Nagy and Kathy Nagy; [ed.] Currently a 7th Grader at St. Margaret's Episcopal School in San Juan Capistrano, California; [memb.] Southern California Blues Soccer Club; [hon.] Qualifier in University of California, Irvine Academic Talent Search and the Johns Hopkins University Center for Talented Youth; [oth. writ.] Several poems and a few short stories.; [a.] San Juan Capistrano, CA

NASH, LYNDON LUNDGREN
[pen.] Thunder Tiger; [b.] February 3, 1969; [ed.] B.A. in Philosophy, from the University of California at Berkeley, M.A., in Psychology from Marist College; [occ.] Pursuing Doctoral Degree in Psychology; [memb.] American On Line, Macintosh Users Group, Save the Siberian Tiger Project; [hon.] Scholarly Achievement in Psychohistory, 1995; [oth. writ.] Psychobiography entitled "'Iron' Michael Tyson's `Superiority Complex'"; [a.] Poughkeepsie, NY

NEAL, JILL J.
[b.] December 3, 1957; [m.] Scott D. Neal, December 31, 1992; [pers.] My poetry within me, is in memory of my grandmother, Florence V. Kerr. My goal is to have this poem be made into a country song-muse.

NELSEN, NORMAN R.
[oth. writ.] Critters Who Aren't Quitters in "Spirit of the Age"

NELSON, JASON MICHAEL
[b.] February 10, 1977, Arlington, WA; [pers.] Attended schools in Olympia, concrete and Yelm Wash. G.E.D. wanted to live in the country, become an art teacher, and publish a book of his poems. Unlike my other poem Jason had written he wrote "To life, to death, to God," three months prayer to his death due to an auto accident April 17, 1995.

NELSON, VERNA MAREE
[pen.] Maree Nelson; [b.] April 9, 1939, Brownton, MN; [p.] Erwin and Mildred Peik; [m.] William J. Nelson, August 25, 1962; [ch.] Leah Maree and Sarah Beth; [ed.] B.A. Bemidji State University; [occ.] Receptionist Southdale YMCA Edina, MN; [oth. writ.] Children's stories, memoirs, various poems for friends, devotionals. Hopefully some will be published in the future.; [pers.] My writing enjoyment comes from telling about experiences, places and people I know. Sharing my faith in God and myself is the primary purpose for writing.; [a.] Richfield, MN

NETTERWALD, BILLIE F.
[b.] June 17, 1932, Marcellus, MI; [p.] Ruth Eleanor Cornish Forbes and Howard Forbes; [m.] C. Edward Smith, 1951, Frederick G. Netterwald Sr., 1981; [ch.] Karen Elaine Smith

Johnson, Mark Edward Smith; [ed.] B.S. and M.A. - Western Michigan University Kalamazoo, Mi, Michigan Music Teachers Association, Private Teachers Emeritus Teaching Certification (Lifetime); [occ.] Private Piano Teacher; [memb.] Kalamazoo Oratorio Society, Music Teachers National Association 1961 - Michigan Music Teachers Association 1961 - Kalamazoo Area Music Teachers Association, National Guild of Piano Teachers, Active Teacher - International Composition Test, National Chairman 1993-1994-1995 and Judge, currently Judge, National Federation of Music Clubs, Suzuki Association of Americas - Active Teacher; [hon.] 1951 Western State High School Salutatorian, Hall of Fame of National Guild of Piano Teachers Lifetime Honor (NGPT), Teachers Honor Roll Annually - Composition National Guild of Piano Teachers 1985 - Had Student High School Composition Winner National Guild of Piano Teachers 1993 Puja Bhargava also same Michael Park in year 1993 and many winners 1983 to present as well as in Composition Tests thru Music Teachers National and Michigan Music Teachers Associations; [oth. writ.] Desiring more music/book copyright 1989, Piano Guild Notes - Magazine and Official Publication of National Guild of Piano Teachers, 3 Articles July/Aug 1995: The Art of Making Music, July/Aug 1983: Teaching Composition/Notes from our readers, May/June 1983: A Tribute to Hazel Ghazarian Skaggs, Music Writings Special Professional Superior and Honorable Mention 1989 Oh Papa! Come Dance With Me!, 1989 Twins! A Fughetta, 1990 A Rose Rondeau, 1991 Suite Seasons, 1993 How Do I Love Thee?; [pers.] The most important people in my life are family and students! My daughters "4" girls have been an inspiration and special blessing! My students enjoy and inspire creativity! A zest for living comes from the young and future generations!; [a.] Kalamazoo, MI

NEW, LACEE LYNN
[pen.] Lacee Lynn; [b.] December 2, 1981, Pasadena, TX; [p.] Rebecca Amison, Gary New; [ed.] I'm still finishing school, I'm in the 8th grade at Katy School District. I plan to finish and go to college.; [occ.] I wish to become a lawyer and a writer.; [hon.] Math, Science, History Awards. Presidental Academic Fitness Award; [oth. writ.] Yes, but none have been published this was my first step.; [pers.] I'm 14 and I will live in Katy, Texas. My feelings are what inspire me to write poetry. I think that my best work is done when my feelings are hurt.; [a.] Katy, TX

NEWBILL, GLORIA JEAN
[pen.] Lady "G", Glo; [b.] April 11, 1944, Saint Louis, MO; [p.] Baby Ruth Hayden, F. D. Myles; [m.] October 13, 1966; [ch.] Yoaka,

Ra'Tiya, Andre, Donito, De'Angelo, Quito, Ivano, Codez; [ed.] Christopher Columbus High School; [occ.] Receptionist Fashion Designer; [memb.] First Baptist Church, Gospel Choir - Mass Choir, Nurses' Guild - Orthodox Missionary Auxiliary; [hon.] Honor Student - 1962, Outstanding Woman's Award - 1976, Miss Design and Originality 1977 - Modeling Trophies 1978-1985; [oth. writ.] Poems, short plays - songs; [pers.] Never think of yourself as a loser - positive thinking always make you a winner.; [a.] Macon, GA

NEWTON, LUNA E.
[b.] February 5, 1908, Goodhope, MO; [p.] Daniel and Hattie Newton; [m.] Helen, April 15, 1939; [ch.] Carol (Mintz) and Judy (Donham); [ed.] Ava High School, S.W. Missouri State University; [occ.] Retired; [memb.] Past President of Tri-State Writer's Club, Founder of "Sermons in Rhyme Ministry"; [hon.] High School Valedictorian, Poet Laureate of the Ozarks in 1937, Missouri State Winner of Senior Citizens Slogan Contest; [oth. writ.] Several poems published in newspapers and periodicals, 2 books, "Voices from the Hills" and "Don't Count on Tomorrow"; [pers.] All of my poems have been inspired, most of my poetry was written after God saved my soul at the age of 63.; [a.] Brownstown, IN

NEWTON, WILLIAM CLARK
[b.] April 15, 1979, Belvidere, IL; [p.] Stephen Newton, Joanne Newton; [ed.] Currently enrolled in Auburn High School (Junior); [memb.] The Club with no name Club; [hon.] Honor Roll, A.C.E. (Auburnites Choose Excellence); [pers.] In my poetry, I attempt to fuse opposing emotions together along with my thoughts. I have been influenced by Emily Dickenson, Kurt Cobain and Billy Corgan.; [a.] Rockford, IL

NICHOLS, DON
[b.] August 9, 1958, Ashland, KY; [p.] Donald E. and Susan Nichols; [ch.] Eric David, Benjamin Christopher; [ed.] Boyd County High; [occ.] General Manager, Parks Welding, Inc.; [memb.] Poetry Ocala; [pers.] Poetry speaks louder than words...; [a.] Ocala, FL

NIELSEN, JEREMY S.
[b.] August 4, 1973, Memphis, TN; [p.] Scott and Linda Nielsen; [m.] (Soon to be) Nicole E. Brendt, May 25, 1996; [ed.] R. L. Turner High School, Brookhaven Community College; [occ.] Carpenter; [memb.] Prince of Dence Lutheran Church; [oth. writ.] Many poems written solely for the love of my life.; [pers.] Do not take life so seriously, it's not permanent.; [a.] Farmers Branch, TX

NIVER, KARENA.
[pen.] Pegasus; [b.] October 29, 1952, West Virginia; [p.] John Green II, Jo Ann Muncie;

[ch.] Shannon Jo Cummings; [ed.] Grad - Killian High, Charron William's College, Paramedical Division; [occ.] Dental Assistant; [memb.] Florida Dental Association, International Society of Poet's, American Heart Association; [hon.] Editor's Choice Award 1995; [oth. writ.] "The Life Guard Stand"; [pers.] My father who invented the first Scuba Submarine inspired me to write this poem - the depth of the voyage enlightened my subconscious.; [a.] Miami, FL

NOEL, FRANCES
[b.] September 28, 1928, Detroit, MI; [p.] James and Hazel Denington; [m.] Frank W. Noel, September 8, 1945; [ch.] Jan Wallis, Tim Noel, Linda Jared, Randy Noel; [ed.] Lincoln High School, Clear Creek Baptist College; [occ.] Ministers Wife, Retired; [memb.] Hurst Bourne Baptist Church, Honorable Order of Kentucky Colonols; [oth. writ.] I have written many other poems, but have not had any of them published.; [pers.] One of my greatest joys in life is writing poetry. As I write, I am fully aware that my talent comes from God, and I hope my poem will be a blessing to others.; [a.] Louisville, KY

NORDQUIST, FLORENCE D.
[b.] August 12, 1921, Taylorsport, KY; [p.] Edna and Lawrence Donathan; [ed.] Taylor High, Studio School of Fashion Art; [occ.] Free - lace writer, Costume and accessories Designer, Genealogist.; [memb.] Daughters of the American Revolution, Kentucky Genealogical Society, Friends of Edgewater Library, Tomoka Gem and Mineral Society.; [oth. writ.] Several historical and antiques articles published in local newspapers, Editor and publisher of Halifax Historical Herald, Publisher of Florida News and Events section of America Collector magazine.; [a.] Edgewater, FL

NORRIS, WILLIAM F.
[b.] August 2, 1946, Bronx, NY; [p.] Walter Theodore, Victoria; [m.] Virginia (Gigi) Norris, January 28, 1989; [ch.] William James; [ed.] Westchester CC, NY; [occ.] Regional Operation Manager - Electronic Contracting; [oth. writ.] A novel in process "Belvue."; [pers.] My attraction to the sea is a reincarnate reunion with my second love. My first, of course, is the inspiration for my words, my wife Virginia.; [a.] Farmville, TX

NUNEZ, ERIKA
[b.] October 25, 1976, San Jose; [p.] Sergio and Leticia; [ed.] High School Silver Creek Elementary School, Holly Oak; [occ.] Student; [hon.] G.I. Forum Scholarship Foundation National Hispanic Scholarship Honor Roll Recognition Award from SC - Latino Student Union; [pers.] I write from the heart. My inspiration comes within the depth of my very soul. To understand me is to understand my work, my art.; [a.] San Jose, CA

O'KELLEY, JENNIFER C.
[b.] July 15, 1972, Saint Paul, MN; [p.] Janice
O'Kelley, Dr. Richard A. McCorkle; [ed.]
Currently a senior at UPENN working toward a BA
in Psychology.; [occ.] Student - UPENN; [hon.] Psi
Chi, Dean's List; [pers.] This poem is in remembrance of my grandfather who will always have a
special place in my heart.; [a.] Philadelphia, PA

OATLEY, MICHELLE DIANE SEBASTIAN
[b.] May 2, 1967, New York, USA; [p.] John
Pennington Snyder, Judith Ernst Snyder, [m.]
John Phillip Sebastian Oatley, May 2, 1992;
[ch.] Michael Pennington Sebastian Oatley; [ed.]
Mount Vernon College and Benjamin Franklin
University of Accounting; [occ.] Patent Law
Secretary; [a.] Washington, DC

OCCHIPINTI, SYLVIA G.
[b.] August 9, 1937, Elizabeth, NJ; [p.] Trygve
and Gudren Tonnessen; [m.] Rev. James
Occhipinti, May 31, 1958; [ch.] Mark James,
Joy Ellen Ferrara; [ed.] Keyport High, Valley
Forge Christian College, Valley Forge, PA,
Institute of Children's Literature, Redding Ridge,
Conn.; [occ.] Licensed Minster - 30 years,
Minister with the Assemblies of God, Ordained
in 1993. Co-pastor with husband in this church-
25 years.; [memb.] N.J. District Assemblies of
God, General Council Assemblies of God,
Institute of Children's Lit- advanced course.
Taught writer's class at local library. Certificate
from Institute of Children's Lit. Continuous
education in Christian Ed. teacher in Sunday
School, Women's Ministries Superintendent of
Christian Ed. in local church, preacher/teacher to
various groups outside the church as well as to
the local congregation.; [oth. writ.] Several
poems published in CHristian publications, local
newspapers, denominational periodicals.
Numerous plays, skits for children and youth in
the local congregation. Lyrics to songs, etc.;
[pers.] I endeavor to write from personal
experience of God's continual faithfulness and
comfort. I have found my most creative times to
be in my darkest hours and deepest trials. The
lessons learned at these times are priceless
treasures.; [a.] Cedar Run West Creek, NJ

OCOLA, BARBARA
[b.] January 17, 1967, Madison, WI; [p.] Wilma
and Eugene Brookmiller; [m.] Leonidas Ocola,
November 8, 1991; [ch.] Alejandro 3 1/2, Paloma
Luz 1 1/2; [ed.] Two years at VW Madison, go
badgers; [occ.] Homemaker; [pers.] This poem is
dedicated to Pedro Zamora of the Real World III
(MTV) I was moved to write this poem after
Pedro's death. I realized how much he has
taught me and millions of other not just about
AIDS but also about life.; [a.] Madison, WI

ODELL, VERONICA
[b.] June 13, 1940, Saint Petersburgh, FL; [p.]

Freida and Alfred Braun; [m.] Stephan F. Odell,
December 12; [ch.] Ronald Cynthia Fred, Pete
and Freida Howard; [ed.] High School Graduate
took personal computer course; [occ.] Home
maker and care giver for family member; [memb.]
Sing in Church Choir Exercise Class; [pers.]
Enjoy poetry writing about personal feelings and
love poems; [a.] Saint Petersburg, FL

OERMANN, ELIZABETH
[pen.] January 29, 1978, Harvey, IL; [b.] Bruce
and Connie Oermann; [ed.] Lutheran High
School North Graduate June 96, College:
Macomb County Community College; [a.]
Clinton Township, MI

OKAFOR, MARK C.
[pen.] Mark Okafor; [b.] April 23, 1976,
Boston, MA; [p.] Edwin Okafor, Chloma B.
Okafor; [ed.] University of Nigeria High School,
Northeastern University, Boston; [occ.] Pharm.
Student, Pharmacy Technician, Boston City
Hospital; [hon.] Several Awards in High School,
Secondary School Principal's List; [oth. writ.]
Several songs and poems, unpublished as of the
time of this publication (same songs recorded on
demos).; [pers.] I enjoy writing artwork and
believe lots of people worldwide will be reached
through my work. God given talents can be used
almost limitlessly.; [a.] Boston, MA

OLIVER, KAREN A.
[b.] December 16, 1949, Vancouver, WA; [p.]
Gordon and Ruth Whitsitt; [m.] Ronald C.
Oliver, June 30, 1973; [ch.] Jason Ronald,
Jennifer Ruth; [ed.] Evergreen High School;
[occ.] Secretary; [memb.] Goodwill Rebekah
Lodge #163; [a.] White Salmon, WA

OLSON, BRAM OWEN
[b.] June 24, 1981, Hutchinson, MN; [p.]
Bradley and Leann Olson; [ed.] Presently
Student (8th Grade) at Hutchinson Middle
School, Hutchinson, MN; [occ.] Student;
[memb.] Watertown Area Swim Klub (WASK),
8th Grade Band; [hon.] Numerous U.S.S. Swimming
Honors and Awards, "A" Honor Roll Student,
Student of the Quarter Award; [oth. writ.] Personal
and journal writings.; [pers.] Never get tired of doing
good for others. In everything you do, do your very
best.; [a.] Hutchinson, MN

OLSON, CASSANDRA L.
[b.] February 8, 1965, Cocoa Beach, FL; [p.]
Glenn Grant, Carlene Grant-Williams; [m.] John
H. Olson, April 17, 1993; [ch.] Hannah Jean,
Sarah Anne; [ed.] Thomas Stone High School,
various College Classes; [occ.] Lic. Daycare
Provider, Artist and Hand-crafter; [oth. writ.]
Several other unpublished, poems, short-stories,
and children's stories.; [pers.] "I can do all
things through Christ Who Strengthens me."
Philippians 4:13; [a.] La Plata, MD

OLSON, SUSAN E.
[b.] March 26, 1960, Minneapolis, MN; [p.]
Gordon and Jean Olson; [ed.] Manhato West
High Manhato Area Vocational Technical
Institute; [occ.] Billing Clerk; [oth. writ.] This is
my 1st published work. Though I do have other
poems I have written.; [pers.] I believe my ability
with words is a gift from God. I hope to use my
gift to honor God.; [a.] Minneapolis, MN

OLSON, TERESA L.
[b.] August 24, 1960, Fort Worth, TX; [p.]
Douglas and Nancy Carey; [m.] Bernard J.
Olson, February 14, 1981; [ch.] Benjamin and
Andrew; [occ.] Administrative Assistant, Valley
Medical Center, Renton, WA; [oth. writ.] Short
Stories, Articles, Humor nothing published.;
[pers.] I'm an average Christian woman with too
much to do, and not enough time to do it. I love
to write, but since I'm my own worst critic, no
one ever gets to read it.; [a.] Renton, WA

ONGIRSKI, SUSAN
[pen.] Jessica Wheeler; [b.] December 8, 1959,
Nazareth Hospital, PA; [p.] Mary and Ted
Ongirski; [ch.] Niece Sarah - is important in my
life; [ed.] Completed 8 years - Grade School,
went onto High School through 11th Grade,
received my G.E.D. to complete High School,
attended college for 3 years (Temple Univer-
sity); [occ.] I am physically disabled and
permanently confined to a wheelchair; [memb.]
International Society of Poetry - World Wildlife
Fund - National Wheelchair Athletic Assn. -
W.X.T.Y 92.5 Country Music, Country Club;
[hon.] Volunteer Award for over 1,200 hrs. Gold
and Silver Medals for Wheelchair Track and
Field - Disabled Bowler's Trophy - 1995
Editor's Choice Award for Poetry - Golden
Poetry Awards for 1985-1987 also several
Honorable Mentions - "Best Female Athlete
Award" for 1990; [oth. writ.] Many other
poems I have written since age 12, published in
local papers - newsletters - anthology called
"Mists of Enchantment" - personal cards
written for family and friends and anthology
called "Where Dawn Lingers."; [pers.] The
three greatest gifts that are sent from above, is
talent - our parents - and children to love, God
gave us talent to express and appease, with
parents to guide us through life's rampant seas,
and children who mean more than errors
unplanned, they are hope for the future, a legacy
of man!; [a.] Philadelphia, PA

OOMEN, JANINA
[b.] June 2, 1978, Klagenfurt, Austria; [p.] Kees
Oomen, Lea Oomen; [ed.] Surabaya International School, American International School of
Mallorca, Yale University; [occ.] College
Student; [hon.] National Honor Society; [pers.] I
would like to thank two very special teachers:

Pamela Dehner and Alexis Mulvihill, for adding a love of literature to my scientific interests. My deepest gratitude and love go to my parents: The greatest teachers of all.; [a.] New Haven, CT

OSHER, REGINA LYNN
[pen.] Gina Osher; [b.] February 11, 1951, Topeka, KS; [ed.] El Cerrito High School, El Cerrito, CA., University of Oregon, Eugene, Oregon; [occ.] Employment Counselor Alameda County Social Services Agency Oakland, CA; [oth. writ.] I have authored approximately 70 poems to date. I have written three children's story's: The Legend of Greenhorn, The Barefoot Boy and Sky and Cloud Together. "Journal of a Californian" about my experiences, observations, thoughts and responses in regard to the 1989 Bay Area Earthquake.; [pers.] I believe people should be connected by the down-to-earth aspects of life and I revere mother earth. I try to reflect this in my poetry. I try to create poetry that will promote pace on earth and peace of mind and which is timeless and enjoyable to all.; [a.] Alameda, CA

OSMUSSEN, JAN
[b.] August 13, 1948, Elvins, MO; [p.] Lloyd and Omilee Stricklin; [m.] Pete Osmussen, May 27, 1967; [ch.] Peter, Paul, Dina; [ed.] B.A. Western International University Honors; [occ.] Buyer Planner, [oth. writ.] Just starting; [a.] Glendale, AZ

OUTERBRIDGE, GRANT HAZARD
[b.] May 11, 1980, Denver, CO; [p.] Cheryl Outerbridge, J.R. Outerbridge; [ed.] Foothills Academy (Sophomore yr. at present); [oth. writ.] Book in progress; [pers.] Thanks to Thomas A. West for all his wisdom, mentorship, friendship, and sense of humor.; [a.] Denver, CO

OUTLAW, REBECCA A.
[b.] April 12, 1965, Erie, PA; [m.] Johnny C. Outlaw, April 26, 1986; [ch.] Danielle, Joshua, Jennifer, Alexandra; [occ.] Pentecostal Evangelist; [memb.] Apostolic Church of Jesus Christ (for 10 years) and The True Churches of the Apostolic Faith Inc. (for 10 years); [oth. writ.] Chapbook Titled "There's A Bird Singing Outside My Window," not yet published.; [pers.] The beauty of poetry is in the eyes, ears, nose, and hands of the beholder. In order to appreciate poetry you have to love it with every part of your being.; [a.] Erie, PA

OWENS, BETTY
[b.] November 6, 1921, Circleville, KS; [p.] Marvin and Bessie Biggs; [m.] Robert Owens, August 30, 1942; [ch.] Sharon Cunningham, Aleta Turley; [ed.] High School, One Year College, Completed Local Art Course, Numerous Workshops, and Northlight Art School, Cincinatti, Certificate of Achievement; [occ.] Artist, Housewife, Former Secretary, Retired;

[memb.] Tablerock Art Guild, Springfield Art Museum Assn., Hill Country Herb Club, Kimberling Christian Church, Ellie's Aerobics, Dean's Yoga Class, Friends of the Kimberling City Library Assn.; [hon.] Former International Quartet Medalist, Arrangement Awards, Current Judged Art Show Awards in Missouri and Arkansas, Past President of Tablerock Art Guild, Numerous purchase awards in Art Shows; [oth. writ.] Meditations for Church, Poems for Greeting Cards, etc. Submitted 2 for publication, first when I was seven and the second more recently, Ozark Mountaineer, both published. I have now been asked to submit poetry for the Branson Daily News, wrote Art Guild News for 3 years for 3 newspapers.; [pers.] Painting, music and writing are so closely related that each seems but a separate avenue of expression from the same package. The creative mind must busy itself putting things together, words on paper to make poetry or prose, notes and lyrics to make music or pigment on canvas or paper to make a painting. Each provides a pathway of expression of that which lies just beneath the surface of the soul and would otherwise lie unreleased for a lifetime. The need to create grows more pressing with the passing years.; [a.] Reeds Spring, MO

OWINGS, CHARLEY R.
[b.] December 11, 1932, Greenwood, SC; [p.] William D. and Mary Elizabeth Owings; [m.] Frances T. Owings, November 26, 1955; [ch.] Russell T., Charles Barry; [ed.] Greenwood High, Lander University; [occ.] Engineer, Textiles; [oth. writ.] "The Pastor's Wife", "Ode To The Smoker" and other short poems for friends and neighbors, none submitted for publication.; [pers.] I gain a great deal of satisfaction writing poems pertaining to special events, neighbors and friends.; [a.] Lumberton, NC

OXFORD, SANDRA L.
[b.] March 3, 1953, Fort Churchill, Manitoba, Canada; [p.] Omer and Irene Shell; [m.] David L. Oxford, August 8, 1985; [ch.] Shawn VanWinkle, Matthew VanWinkle; [ed.] AAS Degree Crowder Junior College, Neosho, Missouri; [occ.] Recruiter, US Naval Reserve 18 Years with US Navy I work under the name Sandra L. VanWinkle; [hon.] Four - Navy Achievement Medals, One - Navy Commendation Medal, One - Army Commendation Medal, All Military Personal Awards; [pers.] I truly enjoy writing where the reader smiles, and laughs, and feels great by the end.; [a.] Broken Arrow, OK

OZAKA, ASUEFA YVONNE
[b.] July 6, 1978, Wilmington, NC; [p.] Fred F. Ozaka, Elsie M. Ozaka; [ed.] Senior attending New Hanover High School.; [memb.] Future Business Leaders of America. First teen to serve on the Vestry at St. Mark's Episcopal Church.

Serve as Acolyte for the same above church and also a member of the Episcopal Young Churchmen of St. Mark's.; [hon.] First runner up in 1994 Omicron Psi Zeta Chapter, Zeta Phi Beta Sorority, Inc. Pageant.; [oth. writ.] I have several unpublished poems.; [pers.] I try to bring about the joys and sorrows felt in the everyday Black woman.; [a.] Wilmington, NC

PADILLA, LATOYA
[b.] July 15, 1984, Albuquerque, NM; [p.] Freddy L. Padilla, Yvonne Y. Padilla; [ed.] 6th Grade; [hon.] Writing awards in Elementary (Adobe Acres), Albuquerque, New Mexico. Academic Awards, and honor roll in elementary and currently in Harrison mid-school.; [oth. writ.] Do You Believe Series, The Tree Library, The Year Five Thousand and The Hidden Microscope (Essays); [pers.] I was 10 years old when I wrote "Who Am I?" I am 11 years old now.; [a.] Albuquerque, NM

PAGNANELLA, JOSEPH A.
[b.] November 19, 1947, Bronx, NY; [p.] Dominic and Frances Pagnanella; [ch.] Daughter - Nicole and Son - Joseph; [ed.] High School Diploma, Advanced Computer Technician; [occ.] Astrologer, Poet, Mystic; [memb.] American Federation of Astrologers; [hon.] Profession Practicing Astrology Service located in the New York area.; [oth. writ.] Several poems and astrological literature; [pers.] "You get out of life what you put into it!"; [a.] Bronx, NY

PAIGE, DENNIS
[pen.] Swiftdeer; [b.] April 2, 1948, Chicago, IL; [p.] Henry and Lucille Paige; [m.] Mary Ellen Knight-Paige, August 4, 1995; [ch.] Joseph, Kristen, Kelly, Allison; [ed.] B.S. in Education-Northern Illinois University - History, Sociology M.A.T. Northern University - Social Studies M.S. - Lesley College - Environmental Education; [occ.] Naturalist, Newspaper Columnist, Environmental Educator; [memb.] Northern University Alumni, Green Peace, Earth Island Institute National Audubon Society Expedition Institute; [hon.] Conservation Award For Environmental Weekly Column (Daily Herald Newspaper) from Northern Look County Water and Soil Conservation District, awarded Benjamin Field Grant 3 years in a row by the National Audubon Society Expedition Institute for taking an exceptional active role in my community for the environmental.; [oth. writ.] I have written over 120 columns for a major newspaper in Chicago (Daily Herald) called "Green Light: Living With Nature," I try to write about local, regional, state and national issues concerning an interest in nature and caring for the environmental in an active way.; [pers.] Every one as a personal journey in life. Mine is to explore an ethically "green" ecologically wise path that searches for deeper connections with nature through simple joys and enchantment.; [a.] Schaumburg, IL

PAIK, WILLIAM S.
[b.] August 20, 1965, Seoul; [p.] Young Ho and Kum Sung Paik; [ch.] Alexis Sae Yeon (one name); [ed.] Univ. of IL at Chicago, The School of the Art Institute of Chicago, U.C.L.A., Lane Tech High School; [occ.] Writer, Author, Business Consultant; [oth. writ.] Modern English (Six Series Eng. Education Book), Basic English (Three series Eng. Ed. book), Campus English (English Conversation book (5 books) for foreign students), various TOEIC books; [pers.] Such words that I write are the voices within me and of me the joys and cries of everyone's life...; [a.] Chicago, IL

PAL, SOMA
[b.] October 6, 1976; [p.] S. K. Pal and Brinda Pal; [ed.] 1 yr. Broad Run High School, 3 yrs. Dulaney Senior High; [occ.] Full time college student; [oth. writ.] Poems, Sequel Magazine '94 and '95, Unbound Magazine '95; [pers.] My greatest tormenter today is myself left over from yesterday.; [A.] Fairfax, VA

PANKEY, SHARON RAE
[pen.] Sunshine; [b.] March 13, 1944, Bend, OR; [p.] John S. Cripe, Violet L. Cripe; [m.] Larry F. Pankey, April 18, 1964; [ch.] Devini Layng and Devin Pankey; [ed.] Graduated Redmond High School 1962; [occ.] Part-time office work-Erickson's Sentry Market Redmond, Oregon 97756; [hon.] Won Poetry contest-local radio-station Valentines Day 1995 "Hearts For All"; [oth. writ.] "Heroes Not Hatred" published local paper Thanks Giving - 1994; [pers.] I would like to be a hero, if only with pen and paper. I always wanted to write poetry the tragic murder of my parents. Started my writing. April 30, 1984; [a.] Redmond, OR

PAPELLERO, MARK PHILLIP
[b.] October 19, 1978, Philippines; [p.] Isidora Adlawan; [ed.] William C. Overfelt H.S.; [occ.] Sales at Cinnabon in Eastridge Mall, San Jose and Student; [oth. writ.] "The Lives of Workers" second place poem for Cesar Chavez writing contest, in the congressional record (May 2, 1995).; [a.] San Jose, CA

PARDO-MCDONALD, NISEL
[b.] July 28, 1951, New York City; [p.] Jose and Esther Pardo; [m.] William Byron McDonald, July 30, 1995; [ch.] Esther Orona; [ed.] Graduated from Damascus Bible Institute; [occ.] Administrative Secretary; [memb.] Vineyard Christian Fellowship of Crestline; [pers.] The inspiration for this poem came as I meditated of the goodness of how through accepting his son Jesus Christ I was saved 22 yrs. ago. I now live with a purpose and you can too. is God Real!.; [a.] Crestline, CA

FARKER, CAROLYN
[pen.] Kala Ji; [b.] August 4, 1940, Morrisville, VT; [ch.] Jual Curtis, granddaughter Nierika Sotya Kimimeiya - graddaughter, [oth. writ.] Forthcoming work short stories, poems and illustrations by author "The Babaji Tree"; [pers.] Compassion is the bedrock of all art.; [a.] Laconia, NH

PARKER, PHIL A.
[b.] August 31, 1973, Iceland; [p.] Richard Parker, [ed.] Montreat College, Elon College, University of NC at Greensboro; [occ.] Student, President - Parker Publishing Co.; [memb.] Alpha Psi Omega - drama; [hon.] Poet of the year nominee - International Society of Poetry 1995; [oth. writ.] Poems published by Logos Literary Magazine - Montreat NC, National Library of Poetry Spackler in the Sand 1995. Sparrowgrass Poetry Forum, Inc. WV.; [pers.] Romanticism is a lost art which is desperately needed in today's chaos.; [a.] Burlington, NC

PARRISH, KATHY
[pen.] Kathleen Lyman Parrish; [b.] February 23, 1960; [m.] Dana W. Parrish, September 26, 1987; [ch.] Andrew, Kris; [ed.] 3 years College Biblical Studies and Business Major; [occ.] Security Guard; [memb.] Sharon Special Police; [oth. writ.] Ecoo's Sharon Advocate, my heart speak to thee, Golgotha and Changes (1985) American poetry Anthology, Remembrance; [a.] Sharon, MA

PARSONS, ROY D.
[pen.] Roy D. Parsons; [b.] June 12, 1926, London, England; [m.] Allyn W. Parsons, September 1954; [ed.] Menlo College San Jose State College Univ. of Calif. at Berkeley Univ. of Calif at Los Angeles; [occ.] Artist and Sale of Artifacts (Ethnic); [oth. writ.] Never submitted anything before; [pers.] Still thinking about it. Honest thoughts forming; [a.] Beverly Hills, CA

PARTON, KIMBERLY ANN
[b.] April 1, 1969, Granite City, IL; [p.] Christina M. Ortiz; [m.] Patrick G. Parton, August 19, 1987; [ch.] Jasmine Paige Parton; [ed.] Business School M and M Word Processing Institute Houston, Texas Graduated Nov. 11, 1993; [occ.] Executive Secretary for Keppel Marine Agencies, Inc.; [a.] Houston, TX

PATERSON, NINA
[b.] September 6, 1981, Wilmington, NC, New Hanover Memorial Hospital; [p.] Mark and Cyndi Paterson; [ed.] So far, Blair Elementary School, Noble Middle School, and I am currently a freshman in Laney High; [memb.] I am a member of the Laney key Club, Earth Club, and Spanish club. I am a member at Grace Baptist Church; [hon.] I have several trophies for reading, small diplomas for A's in several

classes, and my kindergarten diploma. I also received a letter from George Bush for A's for kindergarten - 5th grade; [pers.] I believe that if you have a dream and believe in your dream, it can come true.; [a.] Wilmington, NC

PATIL, RESHMA
[b.] July 21, 1978, Atlanta, GA; [p.] Chander Patil, Poonam Patil; [ed.] Burlington High School; [occ.] Senior of BHS; [memb.] Collab Literary Magazine, Student Government, Math League, Tutoring Program, NEMM; [hon.] VFW Script Writing Award, Brown Book Award for Language, Featured in The Lowell Sun; [oth. writ.] Published in "Collab", The School Literary Magazine; [pers.] Poetry is the highest expression of one's individuality, it defines who we are and who we aspire to be.; [a.] Burlington, MA

PATTERSON, B. T. WINDSOR
[pen.] B. T. "Windsor" Patterson; [b.] December 21, 1969, Cheyanne, WY; [p.] Pat and Wiley Patterson; [ed.] Some College, Life of Extensive Travel; [occ.] Ramp Agent/Dangerous Goods Agent, Student, Publishers Reader; [hon.] I am honored to have the loyalty of true friends and therefore my award is my eternal service to you.; [oth. writ.] Thousands of poems, in my room of waiting Walt, Mr. Whitman, its time to wake up and mingle with the people.; [pers.] Poetry is the clarity we need for the paradoxes we face, daily; [a.] Memphis, TN

PATTY, JEWELDEAN
[b.] July 21, 1968, Dallas, TX; [p.] Jewell and Larry Kline; [m.] Daniel Ray Patty, July 7, 1987; [ch.] James Daniel and Sandrah Leigh; [ed.] Van High; [occ.] Homemaker; [pers.] To maintain a happy home, I use my writing to express negative emotions that might otherwise reflect badly on my children.; [a.] Tyler, TX

PAULSON, DINA SUZANNE
[ed.] Eight grade student at Fairfield Woods Middle School. I work very hard in school and receive straight A's.; [memb.] A member of the Connecticut Audubon Society. Whenever I havd the chance (usually Sunday's) I volunteer) at the Audubon and take care of the animals. The CAS takes in injured animals and regular animals for the enjoyment of others and also so younger people (such as myelf) can have the experience of working with them. I really enjoy working there, as I am fond of animals.; [oth. writ.] My Literature has never been published. My first publications is "As Summers Comes" in Where Dawn Lingers is my first publication.

PAVELKA, JOSEPH M.
[b.] March 25, 1956, Cleveland, OH; [p.] Joseph and Thea Pavelka; [m.] Paula, November 8, 1986; [ch.] Rob and Jessica; [ed.] Independence (Ohio) High School, Cuyahoga Community

College, University of Notre Dame, Cleveland State University; [occ.] Wireman - System controls, Cleveland, Ohio; [memb.] Cleveland State Alumni Association; [pers.] I try to get people to see and understand all the good that exists in our lives. Not just the negatives we see on the news. Words are indeed a tool, and anyone can use them, but when and how you use them is what makes a difference.

PAVILONIS, BARBARA
[b.] October 19, 1966, Newton, NJ; [p.] Walter S. Pavilonis, Dolores Pavilonis; [m.] Single; [pers.] I wrote the poem "Sweet Surrender" because I love the outdoors and to bed part of nature. It is something that can be over looked or taken for granted easily. It bothers me to see the serenity and freedom of nature taken away because of the ignorance of people. See trash among natures, reminds of how ugly world can be.; [a.] Hackettstown, NJ

PAYNE, FAITH ANN
[b.] July 3, 1966, Bellefontaine, OH; [p.] Ronald and Phoebe Cotterman; [m.] Myron Payne, January 6, 1986; [ch.] Miranda, Ora, Peggy-Sue; [ed.] 1984 Graduate of Indian Lake High; [occ.] Nurses Aid; [pers.] I enjoy the outside - football (Pittsburgh Steelers) and always try had at what I do.; [a.] Bellefontaine, OH

PAYNE, JENNIFER L.
[b.] November 22, 1968, Bristol, CT; [p.] Alvin Payne, Beverly Payne; [ch.] Justin; [ed.] Wolcott High, Tunxis Community College; [occ.] Office Administration; [pers.] I have written many poems from my experience in single motherhood, and I one day hope to publish a book of my poems. I have been greatly inspired to my child to pursue my dream of writing.; [a.] Bristol, CT

PAYNE, MARY ANN
[b.] September 16, San Jose; [p.] Ron and Jean Lopes; [m.] Jim; [ch.] 2; [ed.] Alameda High, Diablo Valley College; [occ.] Secretary; [memb.] Full Gospel Church - Concord, CA; [pers.] Say what is in your heart; [a.] Concord, CA

PAYTON, BARBARA
[pen.] Delores Chavez, Ariel, Gypsy; [b.] December 25, 1962, Portales, NM; [p.] Joseph and Eudean Meyers; [ch.] Joshua Meyers; [ed.] Graduate May 1996 with an Associate of Science from North Central Texas College Working Toward a Bachelor of Social work degree; [occ.] Student, Crossing Guard, Prof's Assistant; [memb.] Phi Theta Kappa, North Central Texas College Young Democrats; [hon.] Error Presidents List -X 2, Dean list, City of Gainesville Special Recognition Award of 1994, Editor's Choice Award for Outstanding Achievement in Poetry; [oth. writ.] Many, [a.] Gainesville, TX

PEACE, LINDA
[pen.] Linda Peace; [b.] May 12, 1955, Bradenton, FL; [p.] L. H. (Bud) Peace-Florence M. Palmer; [m.] Fiance' Sam D. Buck; [ch.] Christopher, Crystal, Ricky, Tina and four grandchildren; [ed.] Southeast High School; [occ.] Receptionist Royal Patio Mfg.; [pers.] I write what my heart tells me at the time. I would at this time like to thank my brother David and his lovely wife Patty, also a dear friend Cookie, and of course Sam, for their encouragement along with their love and support.; [a.] Bradenton, FL

PEACOK, DOTTIE
[b.] December 16, 1947, Marietta GA; [p.] John L and Dorothy Peacock; [ed.] H.S. currently enrolled part time at ARC Sacramento California to receive a Asso. degree in Liberal Arts; [occ.] Controller at family owned Linen Supply Business; [oth. writ.] Short stories and essays mostly for school projects.; [pers.] I try to live each day as it comes - writing helps me deal with losses in my life and keeps my Dad and others close.

PEARCE, ALBERT E.
[b.] September 30, 1957, Kingman, KS; [p.] Albert and Christine Pearce; [m.] Cecile S. Pearce, March 25, 1985; [ch.] Albert Christopher, Catherine Marie; [ed.] University of La Verne, La Verne, CA, Professional School of Psychological Studies, San Diego, CA, MA Psychology Hypnosis Motivation Institute, Hypnotherapy; [occ.] Certified Clinical Hypnotherapist; [memb.] American Hypnosis Association; [hon.] BS Psychology Cum Laude Departmental Honors Psychology; [oth. writ.] Several articles for the Local Newspaper: Library of the University of La Verne: "So you want to teach": Handbook on Elementary Classroom behavior: and about one hundred unpublished poems.; [pers.] I have always strived to write from the very depths of my soul. Much of my inspiration has come from reading the works of Edgar Allan Poe.; [a.] Pratt, KS

PEARSON, P. A. LEE
[b.] June 23, 1939, Phoenix, AZ; [p.] Margaret and David Hamburger,; [m.] Divorced, 1979; [ch.] Dennie Pearson; [ed.] Grad. North Phoenix High School "With Distinction" 1957, Yacht Design Institute 20 hrs college; [occ.] Store Manager, Goodwill Industries of New Mexico; [memb.] Society of Naval Architects and Marine Engineers, Society of Small Craft Designers; [hon.] International Directory of Distinguished Leadership 1989, Dove Personalities of the World 1988, 2000 Notable American Women 1989, World's Who's Who of Women 1989, Who's Who in America 1988, Who's Who in Finance and Industry 1989; [oth. writ.] Published "Untitled" 1968 Band, professional articles in magazines, novel "A Pennies Worth

of Dreams"; [pers.] We all have a responsibility to help made the world a better place. Through our everyday actions, I choose to look for small miracles in everyone.; [a.] Albuquerque, NM

PECK, AMY L.
[b.] June 14, 1968, South Bend; [p.] Thomas H. and Jill M. Richards; [m.] Bradley S. Peck, December 17, 1994; [ed.] John Adams High, Michiana College; [occ.] Accountant; [hon.] United States Achievement Academy, 1986 National Arts Award; [pers.] My poem is dedicated to my supportive family.; [a.] Mishawaka, IN

PECK, MARGARETTE ROSE
[b.] June 19, 1953, Port-Av-Prince, Haiti; [p.] Othor Edward, Carmen Afflack Edovard; [m.] Jean Claude Peck, March 22, 1975; [ch.] Marilyn, Marjorie, Matthew, Gabrielle, Sandrine; [ed.] Brooklyn College, Universite de Coupe et de Haute Couture de Paris; [occ.] Designer; [oth. writ.] Written several poems for friends and family; [pers.] I sincerely, thank my daughters and doctor Ronald Beauvais for inspiring, supporting whatever path I've chosen in life. And my mother for guiding me in the right direction.; [a.] Brooklyn, NY

PEGUES, JAMES MICHAEL
[pen.] Robin Michaels; [b.] June 7, 1953, Chesterfield, SC; [p.] Robert Pegues and Mary Helen Pegues; [ed.] Chesterfield Senior H.S.; [occ.] Tractor Trailer Driver; [memb.] Streeter Grove Church

PELL, ALICIA
[b.] November 21, 1972, Los Angeles, CA; [p.] Linda Pell, Donald Pell; [ed.] Currently enrolled in Junior College; [occ.] 411 Operator; [memb.] AA/0A - 7 Day at a time.; [hon.] Honor society; [pers.] Thank you mom. Thank you Dad. Thank you Marcey. Without your love and support I am nothing, with it I can conquer anything. I love you. This is just the beginning.; [a.] Sherman Oaks, CA

PELLICCIA, JOANN
[pen.] Heather Moreland; [b.] January 25, 1945, New York, NY; [p.] Santo and Connie Pelliccia; [ch.] Ronald Jr. and Jacqueline Annechiarico; [ed.] High School grad.; [occ.] Office Assistant - Public Safety Headquarters - Police; [memb.] National Trust for Historic Preservation; [hon.] Various Certificates Relating to professionalism in the office and public contact.; [oth. writ.] Various inspirational and poems of encouragement, and essays on varied topics.; [pers.] "Happiness is intertwined with one's outlook on life. Go through life with a positive attitude and high self- esteem. Then all with go well.";[a.] Coral Springs, FL

PELLICCIO, JANET
[b.] April 14, 1955, New Jersey; [ed.] Alfred

University B.A., Pratt Institute; [occ.] Financial Software Consultant and Trainer; [memb.] The National Academy of Popular Music (songwriter), Marble Collegiate Church; [hon.] Wrote and Recorded pop single called "Crystal" on Select Record; [oth. writ.] Monthly columnist for Financial Planning on Wall Street Magazine, Numerous song lyrics for demonstration purpose.; [pers.] I am a dancer/choreographer. I began writing to complement my non-verbal message and utilize the music video platform.; [a.] New York, NY

PERCIVAL JR., FRANK W.
[b.] May 6, 1934, Fredericksburg, TX; [p.] Frank and Gladys Percival; [m.] Jean Percival, September 5, 1955; [ch.] Linda Christine, Frankie Carol, Sherry L, Karen, Sandy; [ed.] Kern County High School; [occ.] Commercial Artist Owner (Wakefield Outdoor Advertising); [memb.] Bakersfield Art Association; [hon.] Many civic awards, 20 first place awards (Professional) oil paintings and watercolor pictures.; [oth. writ.] 'A Celebration of Life' A collection of reflections by Frank W. Percival Jr. has not been published, my own collection of poems!; [pers.] I consider my poems as reflections on life, in hopes of touching someone life, in some way in a positive way.; [a.] Bakersfield, CA

PEREIRA, TANAYA M.
[b.] May 19, 1979, Brackton, MA; [p.] George Pereira, Joyce Pereira; [ed.] Attleboro High School; [occ.] Student; [memb.] Marching Band, Concert Band, Chorus, Percussion Ensemble, Chaminade Opera Group, Norton Singers, Math Team; [hon.] French Honor Society, Spanish Honor Society; [pers.] To differentiate between what you want and what you need ask yourself what you'd want if you didn't have anything else; [a.] Attleboro, MA

PEREZ, CHRISTINE JOLLY
[pen.] Christine Perez; [b.] September 1947, France; [p.] Henriette Guedon, Paul Jolly; [ch.] Alain and Bruno; [ed.] 2 year college self taught philosopher and writer; [occ.] Retail sale; [oth. writ.] Short, witty French and English stories followed by Philosophical comments... and the other way around also! (Unpublished); [pers.] Inspiration comes in spur and goes incognito!; [a.] Los Angeles, CA

PEREZ, MARIO
[b.] August 13, 1926, Miami, AZ; [p.] Mr. and Mrs. Lee Perez; [m.] Gwen M. Perez, December 15, 1954; [ch.] Lisa Ramona Mark Phillip and John; [ed.] Bachelor of Business Administration Masters in International Relations; [occ.] Marketing Director Parkview Community Hospitals; [memb.] Past President of: Riverside County Philarmonic, American Cancer Society,

Arlington Chamber of Commerce, Riverside Hispanic Chamber of Commerce; [hon.] Too many to list; [oth. writ.] None - This poem "An Ode to Retirement" was my first attempt at writing poetry and reflects my 26 years in the profession of Arms and Retirement.; [pers.] I'm a veteran of three wars: WW II with the U.S. Navy in the Pacific Korea and Vietnam with the U.S. Air Force. In November of 1972 I retired as a Lt. Colonel from the U.S. Air Force thus I will be buried with full military honors and protocol my poem refers to the last valley and taps.; [a.] Moreno Valley, CA

PERKINS, MAISHA KIANA
[b.] April 16, 1979, Bellflower, CA; [p.] Charles Perkins, Barbara Perkins; [ed.] Crenshaw High School, Class of 1996 I plan to attend Howard University in the Fall.; [occ.] Student; [memb.] Young Black Scholars, Crenshaw (Chapter) YBS Club (President), Youth Task Force (Vice-President), Reed College Take Charge Program, California State College Northridge Program, C.C. Church Youth Activity Committee.; [hon.] Proficiency in English Oratorical Contest-1st place, Society of Women engineers Essay Contest-3rd Place, Optimist Club Oratorical Contest-1st Runner up.; [a.] Los Angeles, CA

PERRICONE JR., ANTHONY J.
[b.] March 20, 1965, Mount Vernon, NY; [p.] Lorraine, Anthony Perricone; [ed.] Carmel High School; [oth. writ.] Poem published in church newsletter; [pers.] I believe everyone has a God given talent. Some find their's early, others have to search. Don't give up on yourself! Be encouraged, its there!; [a.] New Rochelle, NY

PERRY, TOBY LYNN
[b.] April 22, 1969, Manchester, NH; [p.] Brent Joseph Perry, Linda May Bose Perry; [ed.] 1988 - Goffstown High School - Valedictorian; [occ.] Reimbursement Specialist, State of Tennessee, Dept. Environment and Conservation, Division of Underground Storage Tanks.; [pers.] My family history and personal experiences have contributed to a discovery of an individual's inner strength. It is this discovery, along with honesty, hard work, and love of animals that has had the greatest impact on my artistic endeavors.; [a.] Nashville, TN

PETERS, DEBRA CULPEPPER
[pen.] Pepper and Toshiba; [b.] July 28, 1958, Los Angeles, CA; [p.] Delton and Mary Culpepper Sr.; [m.] Walter Peters, July 21, 1988; [ch.] Tomas Spain, Alonzo and Aaron; [ed.] Morningside High School, Webster Career College and El Camino Junior College; [occ.] Domestic Engineer/Housewife; [hon.] M.H.S., Principal's Honor Roll; [pers.] I truly believe in families. My family is very special and important to me. I wrote this poem as a tribute

to my dad, who passed away on November 5, 1995. He and my mom instilled a sense of family in me that will remain always. Here's a photo of dad and us kids.; [a.] Los Angeles, CA

PETERS, KATIE COLEMAN
[pen.] K. C. Peters; [b.] July 10, 1950, Chicago, IL; [p.] Colethia Crawford, Richard Crawford, Ulysses Coleman; [ch.] Kenny and Kevin Peters; [ed.] B.A. Northern IL University M.P.A. Calif State University, Stanislaus currently pursuing doctorate at the university of the Pacific; [occ.] Teacher, Garfield Elementary, Stockton, CA; [memb.] Delta Sigma Theta Sorority Jack and Jill of America California Teachers Association N.A.A.C.P.; [hon.] Pullman Scholar 1982 Outstanding Young Woman of America; [oth. writ.] Published article on "School Uniforms" in thrust for educational leadership, published by Association of California school administrators; [pers.] I have been composing poetry since I was eight years old. My poetry is self expression and the reflection of my moods and feelings.; [a.] Stockton, CA

PETERSON, ELSIE W.
[b.] May 9, 1929, Mathews, VA; [p.] Mr. and Mrs. Roger Williams; [m.] Melvin Peterson (Deceased), June 17, 1956; [ch.] 2 boys, 2 girls; [ed.] Graduate of Thomas Hunter (1947).; [occ.] Retired Baby Sitter and Housewife.; [memb.] Member of Wayland Baptist Church, Mathews VA; [pers.] I have always loved to write poems, I wrote many as a child. This is the first time I have entered a contest.; [a.] Mathews, VA

PETERSON, LISA MARIE
[b.] September 20, 1978, Plattsburgh, NY; [p.] M. W. Peterson, Elizabeth Peterson; [ed.] I graduated from high school in 1995. I plan to begin college in the fall of 1996.; [occ.] Layaway Department at K-Mart Stores, Merritt Island, Florida; [pers.] The person who inspired me the most in my literary ambitions is Lucy Maud Montgomery. I hope to write as well as she did, one day.; [a.] Merritt Island, FL

PHILIPP, JEAN
[pen.] Jean Philipp; [b.] Tempe, AZ; [p.] Howe Clary, Lulu Clary; [m.] Gerhard Philipp, 1951; [ch.] Clary Philipp, Gerhard Philipp; [ed.] Tempe High, ASU Tempe AZ, Yeoman, Training, Wave US Navy; [occ.] Church Organist, Santa Cruz, CA; [oth. writ.] Many "Letters to the Editor" in Santa Cruz Sentinel newspaper. Limericks published in students. Poetry collection in Santa Cruz.; [pers.] Courses in "Creative Writing" have taught me to capture everyday overheard conversations worthy of keeping in my daily journal, to be used in future writings. It's a new world, interesting, exciting, heretofore unexplored.; [a.] Santa Cruz, CA

PHILLIPS, E. IRENE
[b.] October 8, 1920, Montrose, WV; [p.]
Walter and Bertha Price; [m.] Percival Q.
Phillips, February 24, 1939; [ch.] Barbara Gail
(Phillips) Hughes; [occ.] Housewife; [memb.]
Front St. Presbyterian Church - Women Aglow;
[oth. writ.] Many poems; [pers.] I seek to show
the love and concern of God through Jesus
Christ.; [a.] Fairfield, OK

PHILLIPS, JAMES W.
[b.] October 27, 1950, Tulsa, OK; [p.] James W.
and Syrene C. Phillips; [m.] Martha (separated
July '95); [ch.] L. Kaitlin Phillips (Kaitie); [ed.]
Northeastern State University, University of
Oklahoma and University of Tulsa, Graduate
Colleges, also the Oxford Summer School of
Religious Studies; [occ.] Hospital/Managed
Healthcare, Pharmaceutical Consultant; [memb.]
I am completing my Novitiate in the Third
Order, Society of St. Francis in the Anglican
Communion. Also a member of the Institute of
Noetic Sciences, The New York Academy of
Sciences, Life Membership in the Oklahoma
Wildlife Federation.; [oth. writ.] "Foundations
of the Celtic Church", "Ecumenical Evolution in
the Holy Catholic Church", Contributor to,
"The Chalice and Tongs", publication of St.
Dunstan's Church, and editorial contributions to
The Anglican Journal. Also, the "Rosamund
Papers", a journal of the Living Literature
Center of Northeastern State University.; [pers.]
"Too long a sacrifice can make a stone of the
heart", W.B. Yeats; [a.] Tulsa, OK

PHILLIPS, JAN
[pen.] Jan Phillips; [b.] December 24, 1971,
Birmingham, AL; [p.] Melvin and Phillips; [ed.]
Bachelor of Science in Business Administration;
[occ.] New Business Development-Southern
Commercial Waterproofing; [memb.] National
Business Merit Award Winner-1993, Southland
Conference Champions-Softball-1995, A former
Member of Alpha Kappa Psi-national Business
Fraternity; [pers.] The thing I like about poetry
is its versatility, but also give many interpreta-
tions and deep meanings to its readers.

PHILLIPS, MANDI
[b.] September 29, 1976, Mississippi; [p.]
Kathy and Gordon Phillips

PHILLIPS, PAULINE
[b.] November 10, 1943, Mound Valley, KS;
[p.] Paul and Dorothy Babb; [m.] James H.
Phillips, December 6, 1993; [ch.] Dow Ray
(Tony) Hawkins; [ed.] LCCHS, Altamont, KS,
University of Florida, Gainesville, FL; [occ.]
Breakfast and Dinner cook at Townsman
Restaurant Parsons, KS; [hon.] Dietary Manager
Certificate, Special Manager Course; [pers.]
Having something publicity has always been a
goal of mine and I finally made it.; [a.] Parsons, KS

PHILLIPS, ROSHELL
[b.] January 6, 1957, Houston, TX; [p.] Rochon
and Hazel Phillips; [ed.] E. L. Furr Jr. and Sr.
High; [oth. writ.] I have written over 120 various
types of poems (religious, love, and friendship).;
[pers.] Each and every poem in my collection is
written from the heart. I feel all of my religious
poems (about 60 or 70) are written with God's
help. I try to make each poem have some type
of message in it.; [a.] Houston, TX

PHILLIPS, SARAH
[pen.] Ginny Phillips; [b.] October 8, 1935,
Louisa, KY; [p.] Raymond and Belle Cyrus;
[m.] Donald R. Phillips, March 20, 1954; [ch.]
D. Bruce, D. Brian; [ed.] Columbus St. Comm.
Call; [occ.] Real Estate Appraisals and Sales;
[memb.] National Board of Realtors, National
Republican Party, National League of Cities;
[hon.] Citizen of the Year Whitehall, Parade
Marshall 4th of July, Republican National
Committee Delegate, in 1988, Republican
National Committee Alternate in 1992.; [oth.
writ.] Misc. poems; [pers.] Both gladness and
sadness cause me to express my feelings in
verse.; [a.] Columbus, OH

PHILPITT, EDWARD T.
[b.] November 15, 1926, Washington, DC; [p.]
Richard and Isabel Philpitt; [ed.] Graduate from
Benjamin Franklin Univ, Wash, D.C.; [occ.] Part
Time Poet and song writer.; [memb.] Int'l
Society of Poets; [hon.] Int'l society of Poets
Poet of Merit 1995 Selected eight times for
"Sound of Poetry" by Nat'l Library in 1995.;
[pers.] When a rat is trapped, it's looking for
away to escape. You will never be happy
thinking about the negatives in life. The best
comfort of life is good health. It's through
individual thoughts that we can entertain the
stardom within.; [a.] Washington, DC

PICARD, HOWARD
[b.] January 17, 1924, Brooklyn, NY; [p.]
Arthur J. Picard, Katherine Yonkers Picard; [ed.]
Newtown High, Elmhurst, NY, B.Ch.E. -
Brooklyn Polytechnic Institute Ole Miss. Univ.,
Oxford Miss. - ASTP Our Lady of Angels
Seminary, Niagara Falls, NY; [occ.] Catholic
Priest - C.I.C.M. - Religious Missionary,
Congregation of the Immaculate Heart of Mary;
[memb.] Alpha Chi Rho - Fraternity (Retired
Contract Chaplin and Ft. Myers, VA. various
Veterans Groups - Heritage Foundation,
Smithsonian Institute; [hon.] Various Army
Medals, Service 3 1/2 yrs. 1943 - 1946 Army
Sgt.; [pers.] Catholic Religious Missionary (40
yrs.) spreading the word of God to all people for
peace, love, human dignity, harmony, freedom
and salvation and everlasting life in the Glory of
God.; [a.] Arlington, VA

PICKRUM, DAVID DANIEL
[pen.] Pick; [b.] April 14, 1956, Warrensburg,
MO; [p.] David Pickrum, Barbara Pickrum; [ed.]
Graduate of Oak Forest IL High School 1974;
[occ.] Electrolytic Plating Process Tech.;
[memb.] United States Marine Corp "74" to
Infinity and beyond.; [hon.] 1991 Malcolm
Baldrige Quality Award, Team Member 1993
Industry Week Magazine Best Plant Marlow
Industries.; [pers.] I am an American. I do not
hyphenate myself, if I did I would be a British,
Polish, Spanish and American-American. To
hyphenate I could pick and choose at my whim.
I was taught that anyone could come to America
and become an American, not a hyphenated
American.; [a.] Garland, TX

PIKE, LILY
[b.] May 5, 1942, Scotland, United Kingdom;
[p.] Robert and Isabella Burleigh; [m.] Michael J.
Pike, December 17, 1960; [ch.] Graham Scott,
Ashley Marie; [ed.] St. Roberts Primary,
Holyrood Sem Sec Glasgow, Scotland, United
Kingdom; [occ.] Bookkeeper; [oth. writ.] Several
poems and short stories in local anthology in
Scotland articles in various newspapers, at
present I am writing a series of children's
stories.; [pers.] I enjoy writing both short stories
and poetry and hope that people find a little
enjoyment by reading my work.; [a.] Norfolk, VA

PINGATORE, LISA LEE
[b.] November 9, 1972, Hibbing, MN; [p.]
Frank and Carolyn Pingatore; [ed.] BA in
English Writing from Concordia College in
Moorhead, Minnesota; [oth. writ.] Several items
published in college yearbooks.; [a.] Missoula, MT

PIPPINS, TAMARA
[b.] June 24, 1977, New York; [p.] Patricia
Pippins; [ch.] Shane; [ed.] Graduate of Andrew
Jackson HS, recently Majoring in fashion
Merchandising at Laboratory Institute of
Merchandising in NYC as a freshmen; [occ.]
Freshmen student of Laboratory Institute of
Merchandising; [a.] Queens, NY

PISCIOTTA, EDWARD A.
[pen.] Dan Iazeolla; [b.] August 21, 1961, Los
Angeles, CA; [p.] Sally and DeWayne Pisciotta;
[m.] Ronna Pisciotta, 1985; [ch.] Rocky and
Tessa; [ed.] St. Mary's College; [occ.] Roofer
and Artist; [oth. writ.] Essays - poems, drawing
for Logo's in Advertising; [a.] Big Bear Lake, CA

PLUNKETT, ADELE
[b.] October 1, 1903, Roanoke, AL; [p.] Henry
Veal and Luola Veal; [m.] Joseph S. Plunkett,
May 4, 1924; [ch.] J. Melvin, William A.
Vernon W; [ed.] Bear Creek, High; [occ.]
Retired; [memb.] Christian Coalition Riverdale,
First Baptist Church; [oth. writ.] As a hobby, I
have written some short stories about what life

was like on the farm around the turn of the country. But have never submitted them for publication.; [pers.] I feel that if I can write anything that will help some discouraged person to see that life is still worth living. I have not wasted my time.; [a.] Riverdale, GA

POCH, STEPHEN
[b.] June 17, 1909, Homestead, PA; [p.] S. George and Mary (Banyas) P.; [m.] Elizabeth Alberta Mrasko, February 1, 1941 (Deceased, September, 1994); [ch.] Pamela Elizabeth; [ed.] Geneva Coll., Beaver Falls, PA, 1930-31, BS in Metall. Enging., U Pitts., 1939, postgrad., 1942-44, 46-47.; [occ.] Retired Registered Profl. Engr., NJ, PA, Conn Metall observer Carnegie-Ill. Steel Corp., Homestead, 1936-39, devel. Engr. Irvin (PA.) Works, U.S. Steel, 1942, Rsch. Engr. Acid Open Hearth Rsch,. U. Pitts., 1942-44. 46-47. Supt. Metall. observer Driver Harris Co., Harrison, NJ 1947-58, V.P., dir R and D Molecu Wire Corp., Farmingdale, NJ, 1958-69. Asst Prof. NYC Tech. Coll., Brooklyn, 1969-74, Metall. Cons. in pvt. practice 1974, fine wire cons. C.O. Jeliff Co., Southport, Conn., 1972-75, Marcal Paper Mills, Inc. Elmwood Park, NJ, 1979-80. Co-author monographs, patentennin field. Judge of elections Republican Party. Homestead, 1935-39,; BD. dirs. Whitaker Depression Coll., Munhall, PA, 1934-35. [memb.] Lt. (S.G.) USN, 1944-46, PTO. Mem. AIME (SR.) IEEE (SR., Life), NSPE, ASTM (Chmn. com. B-4, 1953-54), Metal Sci. Club, Am. Soc. Fro Metals.; [pers.] I like to write about subjects which are not usually considered by other poets. a.] Mollusk, VA

POCKROSS, ADAM
[b.] May 30, 1974, Chicago, IL; [p.] Keith and Mimi; [ed.] BA from Syracuse University, major: Broadcast Journalism, minor: English; [oth. writ.] Many poems, songs, and short stories. None published.; [a.] Denver, CO

POLCE, FILOMENA
[pen.] Phyllis; [b.] November 7, 1966, NJ; [p.] Maria and Salvatore, Diprospero Polce; [ed.] Forest Hills High grad 1984 Major English, Queens Borough Community College, Major Business, Minor Politics Speech; [memb.] Mental Health Cert. Friends of the Library.; [hon.] Mental Health Anat and Physiology Political Speech; [oth. writ.] None published yet my own and personal I derived a lot from Shakespeare and other romantic writes philosophers and political leaders.; [pers.] Live your life to the fullest for it os short and sweet when bitterness comes along take it in stride and write for it's be over come love your friends and enemies for there will always be hope of peace.; [a.] New York, NY

POLLARD, HOMER H.
[b.] June 6, 1928, Newport News, VA; [p.] Roy

and Kathleen Pollard; [m.] Oleta Martin, December 27, 1947; [ch.] Cassandra; [ed.] Bachelor's Degree - Sociology, Univ. of Nebra at Omaha, NE; [occ.] Retired from U.S. Air Force; [hon.] Numerous military decorations and awards; [oth. writ.] Numerous poems - none ever submitted for publication; [pers.] I just write about what I have experienced, and how I feel about different things. My family and nature are my favorite subjects.; [a.] Papillion, NE

PONTICELLO, MAUDE JAMES
[pen.] "Maude"; [b.] August 8, 1915, England; [p.] Charles F. Hart, Mary F. Hart; [m.] Harold J. James, February 14, 1942, Salvador Ponticello, December 7, 1968; [ch.] James, Walter, Edward, Lawrence, Mary; [ed.] Catheral High - N.Y.C., 2 years Hunter College NY, 1 year Ass'sium - N.Y.C. NY; [occ.] Retired Postal Empl., Hicksville, NY; [memb.] S.F.O. (Franciscan Orde) 40 yrs, Outreach - Mother Seton's - Palm Coast, 5 years -Eucharist Minister, 8 years - FL - 5 years N.Y.; [oth. writ.] Poems published - Moment of Time - 1994, poems published Fraciscan News Letter, Catholic Digest, St. Anthony's Magazine; [pers.] On life's journey I try to strive to reach and to know and help my fellow travellers on their journey to God.; [a.] Balm Coast, FL

POSEY, THERESA V.
[b.] June 14, 1953, Washington, DC; [p.] John and Rachel Middleton; [ch.] Marquita, James Jr., Kevin; [ed.] Cardozo High, University of MD-UC; [occ.] Executive Administrative Aide University of Maryland at College Park; [pers.] I am currently working on my auto-biography.; [a.] Greenbelt, MD

POWELL, BERTIE JEFFRESS
[b.] Pittsburgh, PA; [p.] Conway and Bertie Jeffress; [m.] Grady W. Powell; [ch.] Sandra, Dorthula, Grady Jr., Herbert; [ed.] A.B., Virginia Union Univ., M.Ed., University of Pgh., Ph.D, University of Pgh.; [occ.] Professor Emeritus, Virginia State University; [memb.] Gillfield Baptist Church, Tri-City University Women, Ministers Wives Alliance, Phi Delta Kappa, NAACP, Women's Committee of Petersburg Symphony Orchestra; [hon.] Educator of the Year (1994), by Delta Sorority, Various Retirement Awards; [oth. writ.] Encounter, Teaching poetry writing to High School and College Students, Students Can Write (editor) articles (a few professional articles); [pers.] Much can be gained at any level of achievement when individuals realize how important other people are in attaining their goals and in helping them experience happiness in the process.; [a.] Petersburg, VA

PRADELS, BEULAH A.
[b.] May 17, 1921, Steadman, OK; [p.] Bert and Effie Cupps; [m.] George E. Pradels, September

18, 1942; [ch.] Three; [ed.] High School; [occ.] Wife, Mother and Grandmother great Grand-mother.; [memb.] I belong to a church. I attend regularly. Calvary Assembly of God Church San Pablo Calif.; [oth. writ.] I have written many songs and poems I have almost two dozen books of songs and poems. I am writing my familys life story I have 3 books written and another started; [pers.] That we do all we can, while we can, the best all we can also life is to short to bother with the trivial things; [a.] San Pablo, CA

PREHM, SHAWNNA S.
[b.] April 1, 1972, Milton, FL; [p.] Gloria J. Hix and John R. Prehm; [ed.] BA in Liberal Studies; [pers.] This poem is in loving memory of Frank I. Wheeler III March 12, 1969-May 28, 1995. With all my love - infinity...; [a.] Des Moines, WA

PREYER, MARION
[b.] January 3, 1949, Seattle, WA; [p.] James and Lula Mathews; [m.] J. C. Preyer, June 5, 1976; [ch.] Monique D. Preyer, Lisa M. Preyer, Jamese E. Preyer; [ed.] Garfield High School, Griffin and Murphy Business College Lutheran Bible Institute of Seattle; [occ.] Housewife, and mother; [hon.] From 1971-1976 I had the honor to travel internationally with a Gospel-Singing and Communications Group and experience many cultures; [oth. writ.] Many but none published; [pers.] I write from personal experiences and hope to be an inspiration to all who read my work; [a.] Seattle, WA

PRICE JR., RICHARD
[b.] December 9, 1963, Maryland; [p.] Linda Lloyd, Richard Price Sr; [m.] Divorced; [ch.] Jeremiah, Travis, Tyshia, Donte; [ed.] Northern High School, Watternson College SD CA Boiler Technician School; [occ.] Laborer; [memb.] Disabled Veterans; [hon.] Scholastic Achieve-ment Award; [oth. writ.] To prove my love, other printed in school newspaper.; [pers.] I want my kids to always know anything is possible if you never give up!; [a.] Baltimore, MD

PRICE, NANCY BENNETT
[pen.] Nancy Bennett Price; [b.] October 19, 1917, Philadelphia, PA; [p.] William A. Bennett, Josephine Bennett; [ch.] Linda Thayer Price, Ann Price Montgomery; [ed.] Frankforth High School; [occ.] Retired; [hon.] Blue Ribbon for Water Color Sonoma City Fair - 1995; [oth. writ.] Seven years producer, writer and broadcaster on radio.; [pers.] As we look ahead time is interminable as we look back time is infinitesimal.; [a.] Santa Rosa, CA

PRICE, NATHANIEL ALAN
[pen.] Nate Price; [b.] October 6, 1984, Matteson, IL; [p.] Timothy A. Price, Penny D. Price; [ed.] 5th Grade; [occ.] Student (5th Grade); [oth. writ.] Various other poems; [pers.]

Influenced by my 4th Grade teacher, Mrs. Jill Robbins; [a.] Ogden, IL

PRIDE, DARRYL LESHAUN
[pen.] Shaun; [b.] May 18, 1983, Chicago; [p.] Barbara Jones; [ed.] 7th grader at Hefferan Elementary School in Chicago; [occ.] Student; [hon.] Certificate of Recognition for outstanding accomplishment in the Urban Engineering Program. Computer Achievement Certificate; [oth. writ.] Write various songs and poems for different family events.; [pers.] I like writing things that will make people happy. I am influenced by positive things that happens in my everyday life.; [a.] Chicago, IL

PRITCHARD, THOMAS HEDIN
[pen.] Tom Pritchard; [b.] October 7, 1976, Baltimore, MD; [p.] James T. and Kristina H. Pritchard; [ed.] St. Pauls School, Baltimore, MD Falls Rd.; [occ.] Student University of Maryland College Park (Scholars Program); [memb.] Assistant Scoutmaster Troop 306 Catonsville, Presbyterian Church; [a.] Baltimore, MD

PRO, RUBEN A.
[b.] July 26, 1930, Port Arthur, TX; [p.] Fernando Pro Sr. and Incarnacion Gomez; [m.] Marjorie E. Pro, April 23, 1955; [ch.] Andrea M. Pro, Lydia M. Birks, Tracey A. Walsh, Christopher Pro; [ed.] Associate Degree: Criminal Justice, Clovis Community College; [occ.] United States Air Force Retired. 32 years service 1948-1980. Retired Rank Chief Master Sergeant Served Vietnam - 1967-1968; [hon.] Bronz Star, Meritorious Service Medal Air Force Commendation, Good Conduct, Two Battle Stars; [pers.] Learn from the past. Change the present. Prepare for the future. Practice the "Golden Rule and Obey the Ten Commandment to one's ability.; [a.] Clovis, NM

PROUT, JOANN H.
[b.] December 20, 1943, Manchester, VT; [p.] Kenneth and Lois G. Hill; [m.] Thomas P. Prout Jr., November 26, 1988; [ch.] Julia A. MacDonald, Brian Scott T. Oakley; [ed.] Burr and Burton Seminary Catawba College, Salisbury, NC; [occ.] Retired, but taught for 30 years; [memb.] 1st Congregational Church, 1st Congregational Church Choir and Women's Fellowship, Friends of Hildena, Southern VT Artcenter, Ekwanok Country Club; [oth. writ.] Many unpublished poems used as gifts is done in calligraphy and framed. This poem was written for my husband.; [pers.] In my writings, I try to capture the beauty around me and show the amazing wealth of God's creation; [a.] Manchester, VT

PRYSZCZEPKO, PAWEL
[pen.] Pawel P.; [b.] April 23, 1977, Bialystok-Poland; [occ.] Senior in West Babylon High School; [pers.] I love writing poetry in two languages-Polish and English.; [a.] West Babylon, NY

PUMFORD, LAWRENCE JUNIOR
[pen.] Larry Pumford; [b.] January 22, 1927, Saginaw, MI; [p.] George and Lorna Pumford; [m.] Florence (Lewis) Pumford, July 27, 1947; [ch.] Bonnie Lynn Reilly, Dennis Lee; [ed.] High School — Cedar Lake Academy (now Great Lakes Academy), Cedar Lake, MI College - Emmanuel Missionary College (Now Andrews University), Berrien Springs, MI (Post Graduate - same Univ); [occ.] Retired Teacher, Pastor, Youth Director, [memb.] Ministerial Associations, Pathfinder and Camping Associations, Youth Organizations, and life-time member of the Seventh-day Adventist Church.; [hon.] Leadership award — "I Dare You" Foundation Junior and Senior High School Class President. "Master Guide" award Achievement and Temperance Awards; [oth. writ.] About 36 Poems (to list a few) "Old Glory" "Beaver Island Memories" "A Moonlight Cruise With You" "Thanksgiving Reflections" "Life's Journey" Stories — "Haunted House" "Grandfather's Farm" "The Old Log Bridge"; [pers.] In writing poetry my objective is to bring joy and hope as happy memories are recalled and like experiences shared. I prefer to write in such a way that makes for easy and delightful reading, introducing a bit of humor along the way.

PURCELLA, SUSAN M.
[b.] March 11, 1949, Globe, AZ; [p.] Robert and Betty Smyers; [m.] Wayne Purcella, January 6, 1968; [ch.] William Purcella and Elisha Grabe; [ed.] Rose Mar Beauty College; [occ.] Office Nurse's Aid

PURDOM, MORGAN S.
[b.] February 29, 1976, Orange, CA; [p.] David and Patricia Purdom; [ed.] El Modena High; [occ.] Assembly Office Worker, Smooth-bor Plastics, Laguna Hills, CA; [memb.] National Parks Conservation, The Access Fund, Off Broadway West Theatre Arts, America Online (Jedinit 007); [hon.] Honor Thespian, Vanguard Award '94; [pers.] I give my poetry to the way of imaginary setting and visual story telling. Inspirations include E.A. Poe, Stephen King, Nikos Kazantzakis, Jack Ketronac, and the Lord Jesus Christ.; [a.] Orange, CA

PUTMAN, EDWARD L.
[b.] February 21, 1936, Pierre, SD; [p.] Selma Kittelson Putman, Carl Putman; [m.] Patricia McLoughlin Putman, August 7, 1958; [ch.] Hans, Brendan, Daniel, Leanna, Shannon, Mary Angel; [ed.] BS Math, Univ. of Connecticut; [occ.] Computer Programmer; [memb.] Pi Mu Epsilon; [oth. writ.] Porky Thnort - An illustrated child's poem; [pers.] Most of my poems are of the great plains. Not only Geographic Center of The United States, but the great plain within us at least within myself and within all people that I have gotten to know.; [a.] Rockville, CT

PYAN, BOB
[b.] October 14, 1920; [p.] Louise and Burnell; [m.] June 22, 1957; [pers.] I think, there is far too many people, that don't realize the value of unconditional love. They should appreciate it more, before its gone. Poems are a wonderful way to express your emotions.; [a.] Merrill, WI

RAINS, RUTH R.
[b.] October 20, 1927, Champaign, IL; [p.] Ray O. and Anna Day Ringland; [m.] Deceased, April 4, 1948; [ch.] John Ray Rains, 1951; [ed.] Ph.D. University of Illinois, '63; [occ.] Retired; [memb.] First Presbyterian Church Consortium of College and University Media Centers. Former member, several professional societies and honoraries. University of Illinois Alumni Assn.; [hon.] Pi Delta Phi (French), Kappa Delta Pi (Education), Phi Delta Kappa (Leadership In Education), Who's Who of American Women, 5th ed. 1968, Special Service Award, Consortium of University Film Centers, 1981 also University of Illinois, 1987; [oth. writ.] "Les Sept. Psaumes Allegories" of Christine de Pisan, a critical edition, Washington, CUA Press, 1965, Journal and magazine articles. Author/editor Lens and Speaker magazine, service publication of the University of Illinois Film Center, 1971-1980; [pers.] I would like to use any language ability I have to reveal and to preserve and to increase the beauty of life.; [a.] Urbana, IL

RAMEY, RANDY D.
[b.] February 7, 1969, Dickson, TN; [p.] Donnell and Jackie Ramey; [m.] Single; [ed.] Dickson Sr. High; [occ.] Weld Tech., A. G. Simpson Dickson, TN; [memb.] NAACP; [pers.] I write to bring about a smile to those that I encounter as I journey here on earth. May everyone find the happiness they so desire. Expect nothing except only what is given and joy will always come to you.; [a.] Charlotte, TN

RAMIREZ, MARY L.
[b.] January 22, 1980, Toppenish, WA; [p.] Verla and Onesimo Ramirez; [ed.] Student

RAMSEY, DONALD W.
[b.] September 17, 1926, Lakeland, FL; [p.] Arthur E. and Sadie Ramsey; [m.] Suzanne M. Ramsey, December 26, 1964; [ch.] Laura Lynn, Robert Bruce, Christine Ellen; [ed.] B.S. in Mechanical Engineering Massachusetts Institute of Technology, 1949; [occ.] Retired, was Senior Compliance Engineer, Rochester Products Div. of General Motors Corp., and Supervisor, Town of Chili, New York; [memb.] Downtown United Presbyterian Church, Veterans of Foreign Wars, American Society of Mechanical Engineers,

Theta Chi Fraternity; [oth. writ.] Several poems, unpublished, working on autobiography.; [pers.] Have moved from work-related technical writing to poetry, as a means of expressing the passing scene and interpreting life.; [a.] Rochester, NY

RAMSEY, ROBERT C.
[b.] September 1, 1957, Cleveland, TN; [p.] Robert and Hazel Ramsey Sr.; [m.] Loretta Ramsey; [ch.] Ebony Ramsey; [ed.] Cleveland High School, Cleveland State Community College, University of Southern Colorado: Bachelors Degree Business Administration; [occ.] Law Enforcement, Supervisor; [hon.] Semi Finalist 1995 North American Open Poetry Contest, Military: Honor Graduate, Distinguished Graduate, Leadership School, School of Business, Dean's List.; [oth. writ.] Personal collections; [pers.] The inspired writer touches the soul of humanity.; [a.] Lithonia, GA

RANDOLPH, DEBORAH
[b.] June 9, 1948, Dayton, OH; [p.] Harvey Kindell, Louis Kindell, Jobe; [m.] Larry Randolph, October 18, 1985; [ch.] Robert, Lisa, Heidi; [ed.] Fairmont East High School class of 1966 Kettering, Ohio; [occ.] Resident Care Tech. Lincoln Park Manor, Kettering Ohio; [oth. writ.] I have started my own personal collection of my poetry, I had one poem published in our local paper inspired by the tragic murder of a four year old girl also read on national TV. Another poem is being used at Local funeral homes.; [a.] Dayton, OH

RATCLIFFE, JANE
[pen.] Janie Wiles, Jane Sargent; [b.] April 4, 1932, Sheboygan, WI; [p.] Dr. George B. and Ione Gibson Wiles; [m.] 1st Lloyd Sargent, 2nd Roy Ratcliffe; [ch.] Tobi Stoll, Scott, Jaime and Shawn Sargent, Talli Hill, Joyce Shirley; [occ.] Surgical Assistant and B and B Inn Keeper; [oth. writ.] Misc. articles in magazines and newspapers, some historical research and genealogical material published.; [pers.] I love my grandchildren: Stephen, Brandon, Cassandra, Jenna and Ryan Sargent - with them I can go-Kart all day and be a kid again.

RATH, QUENTIN C.
[b.] December 21, 1950, Faribault, MN; [p.] Floyd Rath, Acqunetta Rath; [m.] Julie Rath, June 28, 1975; [ch.] Daniel, Nicole; [ed.] Medford High School, St. Thomas University, Mankato State University; [occ.] State Probation/Parole Agent; [memb.] Olivia Kiwanis Club; [hon.] My Wife and Two Children; [oth. writ.] I write poetry pediodically for friends and relatives, none published.; [pers.] Living in a small town on the Minnesota prairie affords one an opportunity to think and reflect.; [a.] Renville, MN

RATHBUN, RON
[b.] November 21, 1956, Thief River Falls, MN; [p.] Ray and Betty Rathbun; [m.] Lavana Rathbun, August 29, 1987; [ed.] Vista High School, Vista, CA. Chapel of Awareness Spiritual Church, Encinitas, CA., became an ordained minister; [occ.] Meditation teacher and writer; [hon.] Finalist in the 1994 san diego book awards, self help category for first book "The way is within: A spiritual journey."; [oth. writ.] "The way is within: A spiritual journey" currently working on second book.; [pers.] "When people learn to work out the problems from within themselves, we will solve the problems in the world."; [a.] Oceanside, CA

RAUDENBUSH, JENNIFER
[b.] May 13, 1973, Ypsilanti, MI; [p.] Michael and Judy Guidebeck; [m.] Jason W. Raudenbush, August 8, 1992; [ch.] Heather Ray; [ed.] Ada Elementary Vero Beach Senior High School; [occ.] Mother of one, honored wife; [pers.] I try to make writing an outlet for day to day forthcoming and antics. My family is an inspiration to me. With all that they do I'll never run out of material.; [a.] Vero Beach, FL

RAVGIALA, ALMA MARIE
[pen.] Amber; [b.] December 13, 1922, Bath, ME; [p.] Deborah Currant and Arthur Grindle; [m.] Herbert W. Barlow, Sr., (Deceased), William Ravgiala, October 23, 1943; [ch.] Herbert Barlow Jr., Suzanne Ravgiala; [ed.] High School; [occ.] Housewife; [oth. writ.] Too many! Mostly serious social issues. Poems, essays RE: Justice, Tyranny, War, Peace, Bigotry, Racism, Nationalism, Essential Self, Timeless-priceless Self, Behavioral Modification, Prisons Criminal Law, Economics, Drugs, etc.; [pers.] The manipulation of mankind - a study humanity divided from itself and all other life forms by tyranny in its misc. patterns of subtlety. Atom bomb written in early 1940's.; [a.] Hagerstown, MD

RAWLINGS, CAROL J. MORROW
[b.] February 12, 1942, London, KY; [p.] John Brock Rawlings and Othadell C. Rawlings; [m.] Divorced; [ch.] Tracie Ann, David Kelly and Scott Allen; [ed.] Western Hills High, Campbell Business College, Psychology Courses at University of Cincinnati; [memb.] Friendship Baptist Church; [hon.] Outstanding Performance Awards from Veterans Administration for work in helping disable veterans re-enter the job market; [oth. writ.] Have written several other poems, short stories and written and illustrated a children's book. This is first submission of any work also working on a fact-based fiction on growing up in Appalachia in early 1900's.; [pers.] Have always been literally and artistically natured since elementary school days.; [a.] Cincinnati, OH

RAY JR., GEORGE WILLIAM
[b.] May 6, 1939, Durham, NC; [p.] George W. and Leslie N. Ray; [ch.] George Franklin Ray; [ed.] AB Degree East Carolina University Southern Durham High School; [occ.] Retail Merchant; [oth. writ.] "Poems of life and nature" published in 1994 volume II is currently being compiled. Three songs and many unpublished poems.; [pers.] I try to encourage joy, happiness and love for one's fellow members of mankind.; [a.] Wake Forest, NC

RAYMOND, PHYLLIS DENISE
[b.] December 13, 1963, Statesboro, GA; [p.] Roy and Mary Washington; [ch.] Donavan Jaurez Raymond; [pers.] I truly believe that God has a promise for each of us and that we should always in every situation look to him for guidance.; [a.] Statesboro, GA

RAZI, PARNIA
[pen.] P. R.; [b.] July 26, 1936, Iran; [p.] Deceased; [m.] Divorced, 1960; [ch.] Three; [ed.] University of Iran; [occ.] Writing for publishing; [memb.] Air in the Radio Station; [hon.] I have received seven diploma for my designs in Women Apparel in World competition in Austria, Germany and Switzerland and Oil Painting; [oth. writ.] My book "The Wind and Wisdom of an Iranian Woman I try to publish English also; [pers.] Used positive mind and body techniques to heal suffrage; [a.] Laguna Hills, CA

READ, ANNETTE LEANN
[pen.] Leann Read; [b.] December 13, 1978, Silsbee, TX; [p.] William and Linda Read; [ed.] Vidor High School (Junior); [occ.] Student, Sales Associate, after thoughts; [memb.] National Honor Society, French Club, Advanced Choir, and Vicor High School Brigadettes; [hon.] French I Honors Award, Seventh alternate Region V Choir, Perfect attendance, Federal Express Orange Bowl (dancer); [pers.] I write from the heart. It is my way of expressing how I feel at a certain time. I am greatly inspired by daily life.; [a.] Vidor, TX

REDDIS, MENO
[b.] August 1, 1988, San Jose, CA; [p.] Paul and Kathy Reddis; [ed.] Webster Elementary School 1st grade; [occ.] Elementary School; [hon.] Poem 1st place school contest; [pers.] Reno is a very compassionate loving and giving individual with a very creative and inquisitive mind.; [a.] Madera, CA

REDMOND, KEVIN MICHAEL
[b.] June 19, 1965, Fullerton, CA; [p.] Walter Jordan Redmond, Dee Ann Redmond; [occ.] Actor; [pers.] I thank my family for their unconditional support. I thank Brian for being the best of everything. Remember what a very wise man said, "Your playing small doesn't serve the world." Peace.; [a.] Gendale, CA

REDMOND, RITA
[b.] September 3, 1960, Germany; [m.] Michael,

June 9, 1995; [ch.] Alexander, Jacqueline, Cameron; [occ.] Domestic Engineer; [oth. writ.] Written hundreds of poems since early teenager; [pers.] There's no escape from destiny; [a.] The Woodlands, TX

REED, ANNE ELIZABETH

[pen.] Elizabeth Reed; [b.] December 26, 1950, Modesto CA; [p.] John and Marilyn Gant-Johnson; [m.] Robert Bertram; [ch.] Eric (26), Lisa (25), Amy (20); [ed.] Westwood High School, Mesa AZ; Arizona State University, Tempe AZ; School of Hard Knocks, USA; [occ.] Housewife, horse breeder, poet, author, accountant, healer; [hon.] Dean's List; [oth. writ.] Extensive unpublished; [pers.] My poetry is the untarnished link between the woman I am today and her colorful, but troubled, past. My poetry traverses decades in perfect clarity, it is my healing heart unveiled for all to share.; [a.] Queen Creek AZ.

REED, LUCIA LANG THI

[b.] December 7, 1952, Vietnam; [m.] Divorced; [ch.] Four Children; [ed.] Midlands Technical College, Association of Business Degree; [oth. writ.] Sparrowgrass Poetry Forum, Inc.; [pers.] I feel in love with poetry since I was a little girl. The worlds of poetry that I can share feelings, including love, happiness, humor, anger, hurt, fear and loss. When I write poetry I find many answers that lies within me, and help me to cope with many problems that I has been throughout.; [a.] Gaston, SC

REED, TIFFANY A.

[b.] November 13, 1980, Salth Lake City, UT; [p.] Miles and Wendy Reed; [ed.] 1-6 Terra Linda Elementary 7th grade Joel P. Jensen Middle 8-9th Elk Ridge Middle School, Salt Lake City, Utah; [occ.] Honor Student; [memb.] National Junior Honor Society, 4-H, Young Women's Church group, Citizenship Club, Editor of Elk Ridge School Newspaper.; [hon.] Student of the Month, 100% Attendance Award, National Junior Honor Society, Citizenship Award; [oth. writ.] Death of the Two Worst Teachers, The Wicked Office, Katrina Mouse Learns a Christmas Lesson, The Witch and The Alphabet, Alyssa's Love; [pers.] My favorite author is James Herriot, and I hope to follow in his footsteps. I too want to be a veterinary surgeon. I hope my future works will be as funny, touching, and heart warming.; [a.] West Jordan, UT

REEVE, KRYSTAL

[b.] January 26, 1981, Miami, FL; [p.] Anne P. Linares; [ed.] 9th grade South Plantation High School; [occ.] Student; [memb.] M.D.A., F.E.L., E.L.N.A., Broward Esperanto Club; [hon.] Art; [oth. writ.] First; [pers.] I strive to do my best in everything I do and to put all my effort into it.; [a.] Fort Lauderdale, FL

REICH, BOBBI JO LEA

[b.] March 19, 1980, Mercy Hospital Mason City, IA; [p.] Jacqueline and Keith Reich; [ed.] Elementary at Harding Elementary, Middle School at John Adams Middle School Mason City High School, Sophomore at Mason city High School; [memb.] Bethlehem Lutheran Church; [hon.] Honor Roll 1st and 2nd place trophies for gymnastics; [oth. writ.] I write poetry to keep in a note book for when I get older to have as a keep sake of my childhood. I also write stories; [pers.] This poem is written about my grandfather (Harvey Reich) who meant a lot to me but died when I was only 4 years old; [a.] Mason City, IA

REICH JR., NEIL W.

[b.] December 13, 1968, Waco, TX; [p.] Neil Reich Sr., Mary Jo Reich; [ed.] Waco High; [occ.] Part time radio/tech for rock band "Blind Wolfe"; [oth. writ.] Vultures of the Eastern Storm, The Valiant Struggle, and Operation Barbarossa (all unpublished); [pers.] I try to reflect the terrible cost and suffering the German soldiers went through and to tell of the great fighting spirit and determination that kept them fighting the war was long lost.; [a.] Waco, TX

REILEY, JOHN E.

[b.] July 13, 1927, Hinton, WV; [p.] Earle and Gladys Reiley Deceased; [m.] Divorced; [ch.] Patricia Anne Reiley; [ed.] Peterstown, High School, W. Va., Virginia Polytechnic Institute; [occ.] Electronic Servicing, Teach Electronics; [memb.] Roanoke Valley Writers Assoc., Calvary Tab. Church; [hon.] World Poetry Contest in Los Angles, California 2 years ago my poem, a different one, was highly recognized.; [oth. writ.] Published book called "Video Productions", in my library of VA. Three espionage books, two manuscripts and the the third in script. One unsolved mystery, "Death on the Memphis Princess" and a book called "Special Moments" with 18 poems and 12 short stories.; [pers.] In poetry, I want people to identify with the character, and feel the emotion mystery and espionage, the suspense and curiosity to hold their interest. Longfellow, Byron, Shelly, Sir Walter Scott Influence me. I want my life and writings to be an inspiration, my memory a benediction.; [a.] Roanoke, VA

REILLY, MICHAEL J.

[pen.] Michael J. Reilly or Mike Reilly; [b.] October 17, 1970, Sheboygan, WI; [p.] Lawrence and (the late Patronella) Reilly; [ed.] Plymouth High School, Moraine Park Technical College, Associate Degree in Restaurant and Hotel Cookery; [occ.] Culinary production Cook; [pers.] I have always believe in one's own individualism which I try to show in my writings. Before one can make others happy, one must be happy oneself.; [a.] Fond du Lac, WI

REISENAUER, FRED T.

[b.] May 25, 1947, Brooklyn, NY; [p.] Frederick (Deceased), Peggy; [m.] Divorced; [ch.] Christopher; [ed.] High School graduate Academic Diploma. Many forums meetings etc. courses pertaining to the many positions I have had in the Auto Industry including owning a repair shop; [occ.] Auto Parts Jobber Counterman; [memb.] American Legion, Disabled American Veterans, Smithsonian Society WNET, Public T.V. New York; [hon.] Military Service, Bronze Star, Army Commendation Medals, Combat Infantry man Badge, Good Conduct 2 overseas Bars, Vietnamese Cross of Gallantry, Left Service with rating of Sgt. E5; [oth. writ.] Contributed to an article in the June 1971 Auto Magazine "Speed Supercar" Volume 19 number 4 my name was printed with the article. Years of poems and short stories, for my son, future stepdaughter's fiance most of my high school teachers hoped I would become one.; [pers.] Having survived a war, a divorce and Cancer (agent orange related). I have learned to still maintain my mom's sense of humor. And enjoy a talent of expressing myself in words that appears now to appeal even to your editors. Complete strangers to me.; [a.] Franklin Square, NY

REYNOLDS, MARSHA ANNETTE STRICKLAND

[pen.] Marsha Annette Strickland-Reynolds; [b.] May 3, 1943, Akron, Ohio; [p.] Thelma and Alonzo Strickland; [m.] Raymond Reynolds, January 1, 1962; [ch.] Maria Reynolds-Brooks and Renee Reynolds; [ed.] South High, Akron, Ohio, Essex County College, Newark, NJ; [oth. writ.] A variety of poems and short stories.; [pers.] Being a parent is a glorious blessing. Being a grandparent makes that same blessing shine brighter that the sun... Thank you God for such a beautiful light.; [a.] Studio City, CA

REYNOLDS, MONICA JO

[pen.] Doodle; [b.] February 2, 1979, Bedford Medical Center; [p.] Jerry K. and Ricky J. Reynolds; [ed.] I am a Junior in High School, at Medora In.; [memb.] Beta Club, Vice-President of my business class; [hon.] I'm in Beta Club, Business and Office course, I got 4th place at competition for my Business Course, at Bedford North Lawrence, I'm on the high a honor roll making a GPA of 3.7.; [oth. writ.] Secret Tears, Glad You're Here, Only Eight; [pers.] I want to thank my mom, aunt Teresa, grandma, dad, Tommy-boyfriend, Charlotte, Jason, Red, my family, Karen and everyone else who influenced me. Also my grandpa's.; [a.] Campbellsburg, IN

RHEA, JENNY

[b.] December 24, 1967, Indianapolis; [p.] Jon, Shirley Barkman; [m.] James Rhea, February 18, 1989; [ch.] Lacy, Dusty; [ed.] Eminence High School, Eminence Indiana; [occ.] Homemaker;

[pers.] Writing frees the heart and puts your soul at peace.; [a.] Monrovia, IN

RHOADS, WILLIAM F.
[pen.] William F. Rhoads, Mr. Mojoris; [b.] June 19, 1955, Niles, MI; [p.] William W. Rhoads, Donna Rhoads; [m] Dodie A., April 18, 1980; [ch.] Erin, Erika, Eileen, Adam (Grandson); [ed.] Brandywine High School Thomas Edison State College; [occ.] It's better left unsaid; [memb.] Life; [hon.] A lot of old jock stuff; [oth. writ.] Life songs (write me, I'll send you a copy); [pers.] In the end, it doesn't matter who or what you are. We are all reduced to being the same. Greatly influenced by the POET!! James Morrison (not to be confused with the rockstar Jim Morrison); [a.] Alloway, NJ

RHODES, DOLLY MAY
[pen.] Dolly M. Rhodes; [b.] March 30, 1961, Fort Lauderdale, FL; [p.] Lee and Jud Rhodes; [ch.] Jennifer, Eric, and Danielle; [a.] West Palm Beach, FL

RICE, CATHY
[pen.] Cat and Cathy Bond; [b.] January 16, 1950, Great Galls, MT; [p.] Joe and Eunice Burckhard; [m.] George William Rice, July 11, 1992; [ch.] Kandi, Jodi, Sharon, Sandra, Tom; [ed.] C.M. Russel High, College of Great Falls, Computer Schooling; [occ.] Administrative Assistant for American Building Company and Owner - Rocky Mountain Bookkeeping, owner - Miss Kittys Cattery (Persian Cats); [memb.] RLDS Church, Single File Volleyball, RMB Volleyball, Menza; [hon.] National Honor Society, Who's Who of American Women; [oth. writ.] A few unpublished poems, and award wining essays published in state organizational newsletters.; [pers.] I am very active in my church, serving as stewardship commissioner and youth minister.; [a.] Helena, MT

RICE, PAUL R.
[b.] July 28, 1943, Huntington, WV; [p.] Tom and Libby Rice; [m.] Jane Bird Rice, January 12, 1963; [ch.] Allyson Rice-Taylor and Andrew Rice; [ed.] Marshall Univ. - BS, WVU - JD, Yale Univ. - LLM; [occ.] Law Professor - Washington College of Law-Amer. Univ. - DC; [memb.] ABA; [oth. writ.] Many articles comments on evidence and teaching materials. Author: Attorney - Client Priv. - US, Attorney - Client Priv. - States, Evidence - Common Law and Fed'l Rules of Evid., and Managing Complex Litigation with Hazard and Brazil; [pers.] Be a good witness then be grateful.

RICH, MICHAEL JOHN
[b.] March 21, 1978; [p.] Art and Yvonne Rich; [ed.] Moriah Central School, Will Attend Green Mountain College; [oth. writ.] Many other poems compiled into unpublished books.; [pers.] Know when to stop, know when to keep going, know when to not know, when there's no need in knowing.; [a.] Port Henry, NY

RICHARDS, VANESSA L.
[b.] January 9, 1984, Melbourne, FL; [p.] David Richards, Deidre Richards; [ed.] Columbia Elem. Discovery Middle School; [occ.] Student; [a.] Christmas, FL

RICHENS, MARVIN GENE
[pen.] Goose; [b.] August 29, 1947, Vernal, UT; [p.] Melvin E. and Lois Jean Richens; [m.] Ramona Lisa Richens, February 27, 1992; [ch.] Micah Lee Richens; [ed.] Uintah High School, Ashley Valley Junior High, Naples Elementary, Technical Training Welding; [occ.] Rough Neck 25 yrs., Social Security Disability; [memb.] Life Time Member of The Disabled American Veterans; [hon.] Army Accommodation Metal Viet-Nam; [oth. writ.] I have wrote about 50 poems, which I enjoy reading and think the world would to!; [pers.] I had to have a personal experience in all of the poems I've written, would like everyone to hear them.; [a.] Vernal, UT

RICKARD, KENNETH
[pen.] Kenny; [b.] June 21, 1922, Schoharie, NY; [p.] Edith and Ray Richard; [m.] Virginia M. Rickard, September 5, 1942; [ch.] Patricia and Deborah Lane; [ed.] High School graduated for Schoharie Central School June 1941 as class Treasurer; [occ.] Retired, write-songs and poetry.; [memb.] AARP, BMI; [hon.] Four outstanding work as president of local chapter AARP Copyright Office for song I wrote Sweet Baby Jesus, certificate for song in Kentucky Fried Chicken contest signed by Brenda Lee; [oth. writ.] Wrote a song called Stop Your Smoking. In 87 great come out for American Cancer Society played it all over us. We were put on TV news. Have 7 songs under contracts. No money yet.; [pers.] Write 6 kinds of music, love country and gospel music. Home poems and songs make the world a better place to live and give God more love hope to stop drugs alcohol in kids.; [a.] Cobleskill, NY

RIDDLE, MELISSA J.
[pen.] Angel; [b.] May 29, 1970, Long Beach, CA; [p.] Irving J. Klein, Maureen L. Klein; [m.] Ben R. Riddle, February 11, 1989; [ch.] Breanna Meghan; [ed.] John F. Kennedy High School in La Palma, CA; [occ.] Medical Receptionist; [oth. writ.] Personal writings, never published.; [pers.] I live my life for myself and family. My poems are my deepest feelings. I dedicate this poem for Breanna, my first born.; [a.] Cypress, CA

RIDDLEBARGER, RICK
[b.] December 8, 1977, Logan, OH; [p.] Cindy Riddlebarger, Rick Riddlebarger; [ed.] Logan High School; [occ.] Student at Logan High School in Logan, OH; [oth. writ.] Poetry and artwork published in the Logan High School literary magazine "Off the Record"; [pers.] I have been influenced by the writers from the beat generation and the feelings in my heart.; [a.] Nelsonville, OH

RIDGEWAY, APRIL
[pen.] Ivy; [b.] March 8, 1980, Macon, GA; [p.] Alice and Tom Ridgeway; [ed.] Tinsley Elementary School, Miller Middle School, Central High School, Tattnall Square Academy; [pers.] You may toss away rags, which I will pick up as riches.; [a.] Macon, CA

RIEDY, LYNNE ADELE
[pen.] Lar; [b.] March 24, 1957, Lansing, MI; [p.] Marianne and Victor Zucco; [m.] Mark R. Riedy, September 6, 1980; [ch.] Brad R. Riedy and Brian V. Riedy; [ed.] Bachelor of Science degree from college of Nursing at Michigan State University in 1979; [occ.] "At-home-Mom", Community Volunteer, Free-lance Poet; [memb.] International Society of Poets and Noetic Sciences, Current licence in Michigan as a Registered Nurse, Certified Nurse American National Red Cross; [hon.] Chairperson - Antrim County Child Abuse and Neglect Council, Representative - Antrim County Coordinating Council, Representative - Parent Educator Advisory Committee, Representative - Project: Share; [oth. writ.] Anthology - "Beyond the Stars", Anthology - "The Best Poems of 1996", Anthology - "Tapestry of Thoughts", Anthology - "Where Dawn Lingers" Tapes - "The Sound of Poetry" and "Impressions" from ISP.; [pers.] My love of writing poetry spans over twenty-five years. Recently I have enjoyed sharing my poems publicly. I look forward to the next twenty-five years!; [a.] Bellaire, MI

RIEGER, JASON GERARD
[b.] December 2, 1979, New York; [p.] Robert and Gail Rieger; [ed.] Presently a sophomore in High School; [occ.] Student; [pers.] Poetry is my escape. It heals, touches, and soothes. I want to thank my family for encouraging me always, especially my father, my biggest fan. I love you all.; [a.] Coram, NY

RIGDON, KEITH H.
[b.] January 31, 1971, Portsmouth, VA; [p.] John D. Sr., Elva M. Rigdon; [ed.] High School Texas Senior High; [occ.] Restaurant and Net Work Marketing; [oth. writ.] Several unpublished poems on wide array of subjects. Currently working on short stories.; [pers.] I strive to show the pain nature feels due to the in active consumers buying habits. With consumers passive corporations run amuck; [a.] Texarkana, TX

RILEY, VIRGINIA NANCY
[pen.] Vinny Riley, Robert Riley-Dedicated; [b.]

April 23, 1946, New York; [p.] Raymond and Josephine Schuhriemen; [m.] Robert Joseph Riley, December 5, 1966; [ch.] Sandra Riley, Cynthia Riley; [ed.] Bryant High School Bible Education Studies - Studies in Psychology for Children - Prevention of Abuse; [occ.] Self help, Care of Health Systemic Lupus Erythematosus (SLE) advanced; [memb.] Member of Lupus Foundation of America; [hon.] Teaching Volunteer, Children with learning Disabilities, 3 honor Awards for achievements in teaching, Children are to be protected they are precious to us and God; [oth. writ.] The Last Word of Carole, A Look In The Mirror, Enduring Our Problems, A Helping Hand (Ronnie), Little Boy there's No Pleasing Anyone, I Miss Barbara Joan, For All Our Futures, Lord Of My Heart Freedom, Two Angers, Sandra Cynthia Richie; [pers.] This poems that I wrote, a dawning memory was inspired by those in my life Barbara Joan, Carole, Louis, Darlene, Bob, Rob Nancy, grandma Grace, Mom my father Raymond Schuhriemen, my husband Bob my children Sandra Cynthia, Arthur Pasqua; [a.] Jackson Heights, NY

RIPBERGER, HOLLY
[b.] February 3, 1973, Indianapolis, IN; [p.] Keith and JoAnn Ripberger; [m.] Glenn Parmer, March 11, 1991; [ch.] Abigail, Ashley, Adam Parmer; [ed.] Thomas Carr Howe High School; [occ.] Homemaker; [oth. writ.] Had other poems published in books, this will soon be one of many; [pers.] I've wrote poetry for years, but never having the confidence in myself to enter contests. I just want to say thank you mom for helping me you said I have a special gift now I know you where right; [a.] Indianapolis, IN

RISBON, SHANNON ELIZABETH
[pen.] S. E. Risbon; [b.] June 23, 1970, West Chester, PA; [ed.] Berklee College of Music Immaculata College; [occ.] Singer/Songwriter, [pers.] Words and music are precious gifts to our world - may you always posses them, may they always possess you.; [a.] Honey Brook, PA

RIVAS, JOSEFA
[b.] 1921, Spain; [p.] Maria Crespo, Rawiro Rivas; [ed.] Mastery eu Filosophy from University of Santiago de Courfrostels, Spain, Master eu French, Rice University, Houston, PhD eu Literature, University of Valencia, Spain; [hon.] Due high honor in the University of Santiago de Cowfrostelo, the other in the University of Valencie, Spain; [oth. writ.] "El Escrito y su Sendo", Sol y Sourbra" poemas, "Penumbrae" poems, a study of Raviou Sender's works; [pers.] She was a happy person, but very sensitive. Her failures, were her own, did not shore them with any body. I suffered with her. Her sisters Dors.; [a.] Fort Belvoir

RIVERA, MINERVA
[pen.] Minnie; [b.] July 11, 1951, Puerto Rico; [p.] Pedro and Trinidad Garcia; [m.] Eliodoro Rivera, October 30, 1971; [ch.] Rafael, Orlando and Margarita Rivera; [ed.] High School graduate, attended College M.A.T.C.; [occ.] Housewife; [oth. writ.] Writing my own poems, one of which was published in the newspaper.; [pers.] Through my writing of poetry, I can express my feelings without shouting them. I'm sure other readers of my poetry will feel the same.; [a.] Milwaukee, WI

ROACHE III, ANDERSON
[b.] July 9, 1970, Tacoma, WA; [p.] Anderson Roache II; [ed.] Junior in College with hopes of entering Law School; [occ.] Student; [pers.] My poetry has been inspired by the glorious Quran which has opened these once closed eyes and healed the seemingly unhealable heart.; [a.] Tucson, AZ

ROARK, SHEILA B.
[b.] New York City, NY; [p.] Mary and Harry Galvin; [m.] V. Gail Roark, February 10, 1988; [ch.] Meri Galvin, Teri Tramuto, Cyndee Risko; [ed.] Graduated from Notre Dame Academy - NYC - 1964; [occ.] Devoting my time to writing; [memb.] ISP, Poets Guild, National Poets Assocation, WIBC, Board Member of IWBA; [hon.] 1995 - Editors Choice from National Library of Poetry, Award of Merit from Creative Arts and Sciences, Honorable Mention - Iliad Press; [oth. writ.] "Jucumcari Literary Review", Covenant House Texas Newsletter, "Oatmeal and Poetry Magazine" and my poems have been accepted for publication in 29 anthologies.; [pers.] I write for the pure love of it. Along with that love, I enjoy sharing my thoughts and opinions with others and hope they in turn enjoy reading what I have composed.; [a.] Euless, TX

ROBBINS, REBECCA L.
[b.] October 7, 1981, Kerrville, TX; [p.] Donald and Leanna Robbins; [ed.] In middle school; [hon.] 3rd Place in the "Poetry Society of Kerrville", Student Contest 1992 title "The Waterfall"; [pers.] The less you say, the more people listen to you. I am grateful to my parents and teachers for their encouragement.; [a.] Kerrville, TX

ROBDAV, WILLIAM
[b.] July 23, 1948, N.Y.C., NY; [p.] Corrine and Albert Robdav; [m.] Deceased; [ch.] Tara; [occ.] Businessman; [pers.] If my poem Trust Me is able to bring only one person to the Lord Jesus Christ then I will have accomplished a great deal by writing it. I give all the Glory and Honor to the Lord. I know more people should give God more credit for what they can do, rather than to take the credit.; [a.] Island Park, NY

ROBERTS, EVELYN R.
[pen.] Sarah Doyle Roberts; [b.] July 30, 1922, Cincinnati, OH; [p.] William and Ruth Doyle; [m.] Russell Roberts, March, 1943; [ed.] High School; [occ.] Retired had been self employed.; [memb.] American Herb Society Garden club of America St. John Church; [pers.] With all the horrors in the world there is still a lot of good, and beauty, if we look for it.; [a.] Kenton, OH

ROBERTS, JEANIE
[b.] May 27, 1962, Austin, TX; [p.] Royston and Phyllis Roberts; [ed.] B.A. in music, Oberlin College, M.A. in anthropology, University of Texas at Austin; [occ.] Volunteer Coordinator, Austin Children's Museum; [memb.] Association for Volunteer Administration, University Presbyterian Church Chancel Choir and Chamber Singers; [hon.] Phi Kappa Phi; [oth. writ.] Lucky Science, a children's non-fiction book co-written with Royston M. Roberts (John Wiley and Sons, Inc.), poems published in my High School yearbook.; [pers.] In my poetry, I try to reflect Universal human emotions that I have experienced in my own life - love, hate, fear, joy, anxiety, and peace. I enjoy putting a modern twist on traditional farms, such as haiku and Renaissance forms.; [a.] Austin, TX

ROBERTS, MARKI
[pen.] Marki Roberts; [b.] June 5, 1924, Cincinnati, OH; [p.] Lowell Robertson, Ruth Robertson; [ch.] Anthony Daniel, Jerome James, Julie Anne DeNuccio; [ed.] Columbus Girl's School, Columbus, OH, Medical and Dental Secretarial School, San Bernardino, CA; [occ.] Private Duty Nurse, Writer, Artist; [memb.] 2nd degree Reiki Healing, 4th Degree Mayan Order 5 years Chapel of Awareness, Encinitas, CA; [oth. writ.] If The Shoe Fits, Merlin Pub. Inc, (Prose and Poetry) completed Non-fiction On My Merry-Go-Round, to be published. Somebody gave me a penny, (Prose and Poetry), in the works. An article titled, Schauder.; [pers.] My creative ability is all geared toward helping humanity, as a thank you to God for my gift.; [a.] Oceanside, CA

ROBERTS, PATRICIA S.
[b.] March 19, 1951, Washington, DC; [p.] Willis and Octavia Kinsey; [m.] William R., December 23, 1995; [ed.] Some College, and a lot of life.; [occ.] Personnel Mgmt. Specialist U.S. Dept. of State; [hon.] Five Certificates of Merit on five published works, from World of Poetry, Golden Poet Award 1991, Outstanding Achievement in Poetry 1993; [oth. writ.] Several poems published in World of Poetry Anthologies; [pers.] I give my Lord all the credit for my writings. I hope to have my own book published some day.; [a.] Prince Frederick, MD

ROBERTSON, JUNIKKA
[pen.] Nikka Ronee; [b.] October 25, 1974,

Eden, NC; [p.] James Jr., and Devern Robertson; [ed.] 1 yr. College at Danville Community College, Laurel Park High; [occ.] Presently in Basic Training in the Army at S.C. (Fort Jackson); [oth. writ.] Silly thing called love, if that could be, A Dreamer's Love, and others mostly written to and for friends.; [pers.] There is something unique and special in everyone and everything, and if you use more than the natural eye, you shall see.; [a.] Axton, VA

ROBERTSON, LISA ANN
[b.] January 10, 1970, Cornersville, TN; [p.] Harold and Joyce Rowland; [m.] Steven Edward Robertson, June 19, 1993; [ed.] Cornersville High School UT Martin, BS Early Childhood Education Certification: K-8; [occ.] Educational Tutor; [memb.] National Teacher Education Association; [hon.] Dean's List, National Dean's List; [pers.] To see with your heart and write what you see is an eye-opening experience; [a.] Cornersville, TN

ROBINSON, CALVIN L.
[b.] September 14, 1955, Margaretville, NY; [p.] Marion L. Robinson, Freda M. Robinson; [ed.] Grand Gorge Central School U.S. Navy; [occ.] Equestrian Farmer, Gardiner, New York; [memb.] New York Sheriffs Association; [hon.] Two good conduct awards, Honorable discharge from the U.S. Navy; [pers.] I try to put reality in words for others to understand or comprehend.; [a.] Gardiner, NY

ROCHE, KENDRA
[pen.] K. J. Roche; [b.] July 16, 1979; [p.] Vickie Roche, Ken Roche; [ed.] Gates County High School 11th Grade; [occ.] Student - Junior at Gates County High School; [memb.] Future Business Leaders of America; [hon.] Honor roll; [pers.] I hope others can relate or understand my feelings and expressions; [a.] Eure, NC

RODGERS, MARY JOYCE NORWOOD
[b.] December 16, 1924, Davidson, OK; [p.] Joseph Guy and Pearl Franklin Norwood; [m.] Joseph Lee Rodgers Jr., April 9, 1948; [ch.] Joseph Lee III, Mary Ellen Bumdren, Robert Norwood, Lawrence Richard; [ed.] Davidson High School, Oklahoma College for Women, BA in Journalism at Univ. of Oklahoma, Masters of Social Work, Univ. of Oklahoma; [occ.] Home maker, Social Worker, Child Study Center, The University Hospitals, Okla. City Oklahoma Leader, Parenting Skills Training Groups; [memb.] McFarlin United Methodist Church, Univ. of OK Women's Association, Valley View Garden Club, National Asso. of Social Workers, PRO-Oklahoma Active Parenting Certified Leader, Former PTA Pres.; [hon.] Social Work National Certification and State of Oklahoma Licensors, Norman Leaders Plus; [oth. writ.] The Christian Home, The Upper Room, The Norman Transcript, Editor of Child

Study Center, United Methodist Woman, University Women's Association, Wesley Foundation, Catholic Social Ministries, McFarlin Church Newsletters and Brochures; [pers.] Families are my primary personal and professional interest, and most of my writing is directed toward concerns of parenting and family issues, within the framework of my commitment to the Christian Faith; [a.] Norman, OK

RODRIGUEZ, JORGE LEYVA
[b.] November 20, 1967, Mexicali, B.C.N.; [p.] Jorge Leyva, Mario Leyva; [m.] Laura Leyva-Sanchez, June 4, 1994; [ch.] Alexa; [ed.] C.B.T.I.S., Mexicali, planing to go in to Law School; [occ.] Business owner, in San Diego CA; [oth. writ.] Others poems, never published before; [pers.] When I write poems, my intentions are to confirm my deep feelings of love, admiration and respect for my wife. She and our daughter are my inspiration and motive to improve myself and be a man of good will. This is my synonym of love respect for my fellow man.; [a.] San Diego, CA

ROEDER, SUSAN LORD
[pen.] Susan Alexandra Lord; [b.] New York City; [m.] Kevin R. Roeder, December 4, 1994; [ed.] CPI Business Institute - Diploma Connecticut Chiropractic Assistant - Diploma Reiki Certified Practitioner - Usui Shiki Ryoho School, Certified Reiki Master, Universal Life Church - Ordained Minister P.H.D.; [occ.] Ministerial Counseling and Reiki Teacher and Practitioner, [memb.] Connecticut Chiropractic Asst. since 1985, Usui Shiki Ryoho School, Master of Reiti. Reverend of Universal Life Church, P.H.D.; [oth. writ.] Poems - Wedding prayer, Cosmic Gold, Beneath the Stars, Cupids Arrow, The Only Path there is.; [pers.] I am dedicated through my work to assist mankind in recognizing and understanding their oneness with God and that we are all part of this divine truth.; [a.] Norwalk, CT

ROGERS, KATHERINE D.
[pen.] Kit Rogers; [b.] May 15, 1958; [m.] Major Kent Rogers, February 14, 1984; [ch.] Kristen Marie, Aaron Dana, Richard; [ed.] Cerrittios College, East L.A. College North Light Fine Arts School, Longridge Writers Group, The Institute of Children's Literature; [occ.] Mother and wife; [memb.] Home Mission Chapel; [oth. writ.] None published I have written short stories for my children.; [pers.] If I can touch other's heart with my words then will I have accomplished my goals as a writer.; [a.] Tipp City, OH

ROGERS, LESLIE ERIN
[b.] December 7, 1962, Texas City, TX; [p.] Marion and Doris Wilhelm; [m.] Dennis H. C. Rogers, August 21, 1992; [ch.] D. H. Christopher Rogers; [ed.] Mesa High School, Apollo Medical College; [occ.] Wife, Mother, Home

maker; [oth. writ.] Not yet published; [pers.] I believe in honesty and sincerity and everything I write comes from the heart.; [a.] Mesa, AZ

ROGERS, PATRICK J.
[b.] June 29, 1981, Tulsa, OK; [p.] Johnnie and Marilyn Rogers; [occ.] Student, 8th grader, first Colony Middle School Sugarland, TX; [memb.] National Junior Honor Society; [hon.] Sugarland Exchange Club Outstanding Student, Fellowship of Christian Athletes; [a.] Sugarland, TX

ROHAN, NORAH
[b.] March 22, 1943, Annascaul, Kerry, Ireland; [ed.] B.A. Liberal Arts Siena College, Loudonville, New York, M. Sc. in Ed., College of St. Rose, Albany New York, Post Graduate Cert. in Education, University of London, England; [occ.] Special needs teacher of St. Anthony School, Winsted, Connecticut; [memb.] Member of the Roman Catholic Congregation "Franciscan Missionaries of the Divine Motherhood", whose Motherhouse is in Godalming, Surrey England. The Order is dedicated to attempting to live the values of the Holy Gospel.; [hon.] Delta Epsilon Sigma, (College of Saint Rose, Albany, New York); [pers.] I dabble with words mainly for fun!

ROHDE, CHRISTINA LYNN
[b.] March 26, 1973, Scottsdale, AR; [p.] Karen Rohde; [ch.] Tyler James Scott Runkle; [pers.] Poetry was a way for me to deal with my grief. This poem and others I have authored are dedicated to my brother Albert Keith Rohde who died in December, 1987.; [a.] Scottsdale, AZ

ROHLING, ANGELA MARIE
[b.] September 15, 1980, Grand Rapids, MN; [p.] Tom C. and Sandy J. Rohling; [ed.] K-6 St. Joseph's School 7-9 Grand Rapids Middle School; [occ.] Student grade 9; [memb.] Enrolled in the Children's Institute of Literature in Connecticut, and Art Gallery Association; [hon.] Poem published in Anthology of Poetry by Young Americans, and poem published in Poetic Voices of America; [pers.] I want to say thanks to Nancy Whitelaw and my 8th grade English teacher Becky Loomis for their inspiration to me. Thanks for the support from my family and friends. My creative writing I tend to base it on nature outside in.; [a.] Grand Rapids, MN

ROLLINS, FRED MICHAEL
[p.] Danny Irizarry, Anita Irizarry; [ch.] Alicia Ostrander, Lavonna Daniels; [ed.] Hartnell College; [occ.] Federal Employee; [memb.] U.S. Army (Ret.) American Legion, Noncommissioned Officers Assn.; [a.] Paso Robles, CA

ROMAN, WILLIAM
[b.] March 7, 1969, Cuba; [ed.] Bachelor of Architecture; [hon.] Pratt Circle Award for

Student Achievement; [pers.] But man is a part of nature... a war against nature is a war against himself.; [a.] North Bergen, NJ

ROOD, NOREEN
[pen.] Dawn Neilsen; [b.] April 1, 1932, Muskegon, MI; [p.] Howard and Etta Rood; [ed.] High School Left School at 16 returned in 1987 and gained my diploma May 1988. Classes in sewing art writing and communication; [occ.] Retired CBX Operator of Mercy Hospital; [oth. writ.] Other poetry and short stories but not published, except one in the adult education school paper.; [pers.] I owe my love of reading to both my parents, especially my mothers love of poetry. If I can learn from my mistakes, have a firm faith, recognize and appreciate the goodness of life, I can truly say "I am a child of God."; [a.] Muskegon, MI

ROSA, MIGDALIA
[b.] June 10, 1953, New York City, NY; [p.] Manuel and Felicita Rosa; [ed.] St. Simon Stock H.S., Herbert H. Lehman College Master of Science in Education; [occ.] Kindergarten Teacher at John Peter Zenger School, Bx Ny; [a.] Hartsdale, NY

ROSE, BARBARA LUE
[b.] August 27, 1944, Bluefield, WV; [p.] Tom and Mamie Boyles (Deceased); [m.] Gerald Rose, October 26, 1963; [ch.] R. G. Rose, Priscilla Rose and Collette Hall; [ed.] Bluefield High, High School Graduate; [occ.] Housewife and dispatcher for Husband's business; [memb.] Church - Tabernacle, Baptist Church; [pers.] I enjoy taking sometime silly - such as a comment and putting it into a poem or story. I had tried to get someone else to enter your contest. When I did, my family laughed at well, well, well.; [a.] Kingsport, TN

ROSENBERG, PHILIP
[b.] March 20, Poland, Europe; [p.] Samuel and Anna; [ed.] High School Graduate Innumerable college courses-non credit over the years, several on writing, oil painting social/Psychol/Anthro/ and others; [occ.] Retired Occ. Painting Contractor; [memb.] None important! A loner-love of the woods camping-hiking-love of words a compulsive writer; [hon.] Ms. Toni Taylor, staff editor of McCalls and Look magazine, teacher at the New School for social research, "You do have talent (emphasis hers) not only for poetry, but forputting a poetic quality in prose, also for expression" Teacher and free lance writer, Ms. Sylvia Horwitz, most outstanding student and best critic in class; [oth. writ.] A prolific writer (never published) but with no effort towards publish' G; [pers.] Faced early in personal analysis with the crushing inability to verbalize in group, suffering the taunts of others, he resorted in the desperation to writing, inadvertently and unexpectedly tapping a latent resource lain dormant for years.

"Lost Love" is a one of several poems born within the laboratory of the psychoanalytic process. The new magic of discovery opened wide the smoldering volcano of repression and from it burst new hope and optimism and with it ego gratification and self esteem.; [a.] New York City, NY

ROSS, DENNIS
[b.] July 20, 1958, Culver City, CA; [m.] Sharon Ross, December 13, 1980; [ch.] Christopher, David and Elizabeth; [occ.] Minister; [pers.] My love for God and His creation kindled my love of poetry. My great-grandfather, Frank McCullock Sr., who wrote a book of poems mostly about living in Feruly, NV, also greatly inspired me to try and write my own poems.; [a.] Santa Barbara, CA

ROSSER, MARION B.
[b.] August 14, 1950, Alexandria, VA; [p.] C. James and Estelle Bartlett; [m.] Robert B. Rosser, January 17, 1976; [ch.] Melissa and Kevin St. Clair, Dustin Rosser; [ed.] Lord Botetourt High School, F.T.S. Course - Rec Certificate.; [occ.] Cashier, [memb.] F.O.P., P.B.A.; [oth. writ.] For the Ride - November 1989 Nashville Songwriters Suc. - Rec. Song Writers Certificate.; [pers.] I enjoy writing my personal feelings down, and have done this since my early 20's.; [a.] Gibsonton, FL

ROSSMANN, HEATHER
[b.] August 30, 1977, Ypsilanti, MI; [p.] Ronald and April Rossmann; [ed.] Woodhaven High School, attending Michigan State University as a freshman; [memb.] Faith United Methodist Church; [hon.] Detroit Association Phi Beta Kappa Certificate of Recognition, Old Kent Bank Scholarship, Language Arts Department Medal, 7th in a Class of 259 Students; [oth. writ.] Two third place poems and one other in high school literary magazine "Musings".; [pers.] In a world of many problems it's great to sit down and forget it for awhile, by writing poetry. Thanks to Jaime because she understands my writings.; [a.] Flat Rock, MI

ROUSSEL, ANDREA E.
[b.] September 7, 1984, Fall River, NC; [p.] Nancy Roussel and Ken Roussel; [ed.] Little Red School House (P.S.) Chace St. School (K-5), Somerset Junior High School (6); [occ.] Student; [memb.] Somerset Dance, (Assistant Teacher), Melody Shop, Student Council, Band, Chorus, D.A.R.E; [hon.] Presidential Physical Fitness Award, Honors Dance, Jump Rope, Perfect Attendance; [oth. writ.] Teachers of Chace, 5 Grade A Special Monday 5 grade, If I Could Fly 1 grade; [pers.] My grandmother, Elizabeth Ann Gendreau (Tlynn) inspired me to write this poem; [a.] Somerset, MA

ROWBERRY, MICHELLE
[pen.] Little Lady, Goober, Yogart, Shelle the

Jelle Belle; [b.] August 19, 1980, San Bernadino, CA; [p.] Priscilla Wager, Bob Fritzinger, Don Rowberry, [ed.] Right now I'm attending San Juan High School; [hon.] I've gotten Awards from cheerleading and from school for being a good listener. I also work with handicapped kids!; [pers.] I started writing poems about four years ago. My poems are usually about what's ever on my mind. The poem "more than ever" was dedicated to my boy friend Ryan Jones.; [a.] Citrus Heights, CA

ROWE, CRYSTAL LEE
[b.] October 12, 1978, Bath, ME; [p.] Brian Rowe, Judy Rowe; [ed.] Morse High; [oth. writ.] No others published but I love writing in my extra time.; [pers.] I thank my friends for getting me to send in my poem.; [a.] Woolwich, ME

ROWLAND, LYNN NEDA
[b.] April 11, 1952, Pittsburgh, PA; [p.] Eileen Rowland, Ted Rowland; [ed.] CUNY (City University of New York); [occ.] Entertainment Business Manager; [hon.] Dean's List; [oth. writ.] Various poems published in local and university newspapers.; [pers.] For those who choose the path less traveled, I try to serve as guide, unless they were sent to guide me.; [a.] Los Angeles, CA

ROY, MARGARET
[b.] September 15, 1912, Hinckley, OH; [p.] Deceased; [m.] Deceased; [ch.] James West, Sharon Karohl; [ed.] High School Business School, Nursing School; [occ.] Visiting Nurse; [pers.] Never give up your dreams.; [a.] Seven Hills, OH

ROY, RASHMI
[b.] September 12, 1967, Gaya, Bihar, India; [p.] Mr. Surendra K. Sinha, Mrs Shanti Sinha; [m.] Mr. Sanjeev R. Roy, June 17, 1986; [ch.] One, Miss Shipra Roy; [ed.] Sri N.S. Inter College, U.P. India Gaya College, Bihar, India Magadh University, Bihar, India; [hon.] National Merit Scholarship won many awards and prizes in debates and essay competitions. Elected 'Secretary of English Association' Gaya College, Bihar, India; [oth. writ.] Written Papers on the Poetry of D. H. Lawrence, Pantheism in Wordsworth's poetry, short stories of James Joyce, 'Hail to Tuskegee' - poem; [pers.] Poetry weaves deep into my consciousness. The romanic poets and Eliot and Yeats made a deep impression on me. I try to portray the wisdom and spirit of mankind in my writings.; [a.] Tuskegee, AL

ROYSE, MS. ATAKA RHODES
[pen.] Ataka Rhodes Royse; [b.] February 17, 1925, Florence, AL; [p.] Wm. Henry and Myrtle South Rhodes; [m.] Ralph Royse, June 6, 1987; [ch.] Mark Adam and Paul Aaron; [ed.] High School, Nursing Variety of Special Training Courses; [occ.] Housewife, Pastors wife,

Mission Pres. S.S. Teacher; [memb.] Independent Fellowship; [hon.] Hospital Corp. of America Humanitarian Award, Distinguished Service Award, Nazarenen, Distinguished Member, International Society of Poets, Spotlighted, Newspapers, T.V. Radio.; [oth. writ.] Poem, Golden Ann. School Book, National Library of Poetry (several) special tributes, dedication, award services, songs, other.; [pers.] I strive to beauty hope and praise in my writings. My mother was my early mentor and I learned to love and deliver with oral perfection from her later a greek professor, was my mentor. I am indebted to the poets who have gone before me.; [a.] Tulsa, OK

ROYUELA, ANTONIO
[b.] February 25, 1972, Lancaster, CA; [p.] Antonio and Beatrice Royuela; [ed.] Palmdale High School, Antelope Valley College; [occ.] Electrician for MDM Electric and Actor, Hollywood, CA; [memb.] Screen Actors Guild; [hon.] AVC Dean's List; [oth. writ.] Poetry and Riddles published in college newspaper.; [pers.] I strongly believe that writing poetry is an excellent form of therapy for one's mind in expressing hidden fears, anger and love. Edgar Allan Poe's fearless writing has given me no boundaries in my own writing style.; [a.] Palmdale, CA

RUBIO, JASMINE A.
[b.] January 8, 1986, New York; [p.] Luis and Irma Rubio; [ed.] I am in 5th grade at Northeast Elementary School in Brentwood, New York. Went to Ballet since I was 3 and also piano classes. Best subject is Art; [occ.] Student; [memb.] Brentwood Library; [oth. writ.] Other Poems and articles for school; [pers.] I love nature - enjoy reading poems, listen to music and believe people should be happy.; [a.] Brentwood, NY

RUMAGE, STEPHANIE
[b.] January 27, 1987, Upper Heyford, England; [p.] Jeff and Michelle Rumage; [ed.] Holtville Elementary, Gifted and Talented Program Holtville, Alabama; [hon.] An honor roll; [a.] Deatsville, AL

RUNYAN, ROBYN
[pen.] Robyn Runyan; [b.] February 27, 1915, Corina, CA; [ch.] Michael Gracen Runyan Ph.D.; [ed.] Advanced degrees in Education, English and Humanities; [occ.] Retired teacher; [memb.] California Retired Teachers Association, Writers Club of Leisure World, Laguna Hills, CA; [oth. writ.] Travel articles in local newspapers, Novel to be published in 1996, You Can Come Back by Brownell-Carroll, Newport Beach, CA.; [pers.] The ultimate note is upbeat, although man's is humanity to man is confronted.; [a.] Laguna Hills, CA

RUPP, SHERRY MARIE
[b.] November 3, 1949, Cherokee, IA; [p.]

Garland Duvall, Pauline Duvall; [m.] Dennis Rupp, December 4, 1976; [ch.] Gary Paul; [ed.] Washington High School; [occ.] Housewife; [memb.] International Society of Poets; [hon.] 1995 Editors Choice Award by The National Library of Poetry; [oth. writ.] I have several other poems; [pers.] I like to write poems that I have experienced or that other people can relate to.; [a.] Quimby, IA

RUSS, ALICE LESH
[pen.] Alice Lesh Russ; [b.] August 26, 1922, Cassatt, SC; [p.] Amos and Vergie Watkins; [m.] Woodrow Russ, February 27, 1994; [ch.] Winfred, Thiry, Gary Lesh; [ed.] College Graduate Spartanburg Jr. College University of S.C.; [occ.] Retired 1984 Elementary School Teacher Taught 36 years Bolivia Elem. School; [memb.] Former Town Bd Member former member of Beta Beta Chapter of Alpha Delta Kappa Bolivia Lions Club Order of Eastern Star (N.C.) Bethel Methodist Church, Retired Teachers Organization; [oth. writ.] Personal poems, poems written and used for different occasions; [pers.] Write as a hobby used this poem on back of my wedding program in 1994 1st marriage to Winfred E. Lesh 1946, 2nd Marriage to Woodrow Russ 1994; [a.] Bolivia, NC

RUSSELL, DAVID B.
[pen.] Dave Russell; [b.] April 6, 1913, Erie, PA; [p.] Ned Russell, Nellie Bates; [m.] Marjorie Blodgett, March 13, 1941; [ch.] David Jr., Patricia, Peggie; [ed.] Springfield V.T. High, Springfield College, Syracuse V.; [occ.] Retired Personnel Mgr. Erstwhile Farmer, Machinist, Engineer; [memb.] Green Mt. Club, Sierra Club, Audebon Society, Comg. Church, Woodstock Dog Club, Past Pres., current director, Parker Hill Assn.; [hon.] Gold and Silver Medals, Collegiate Boxing and Wrestling; [oth. writ.] Some 200+ poems publisher in various newspaper trade paper, presently historic - nostalgic vignettes in times of Shrewsbury; [pers.] Have always tried to put in writing - mostly verse - my feelings regarding human relationship with working, life, and each other.; [a.] Springfield, VT

RUSSELL, REA
[b.] March 17, 1964, Middlebury, VT; [p.] Louise Russell, Rod Russell; [ed.] Peoples Academy, Community College of Vermont; [pers.] This poem was written as a tribute to a beloved pet I lost years ago. My writing reflects on the unconditional love and simplicity of how pets enrich our lives, and my deepest respect for the happiness they have given me, now and always.; [a.] Montpelier, VT

RUSSELL, SARAH A.
[b.] February 8, 1982, Dallas, TX; [p.] Gary and Catherine T. Russell; [ed.] Currently an 8th

grade student at Austin Academy for Excellence, Garland, Texas; [occ.] Aspiring Pianist and Writer in the making; [memb.] Austin Academy Pentathlon Team, Student Affiliate of Texas Federation of Music Clubs, Staff of Austin Academy Literary Magazine, The Fountain Pen, Lady Eagles Athletics; [hon.] Honor Roll Student; [oth. writ.] Published in Cricket Magazine; [pers.] Thanks to dad for all the late-night typing, to Mr. Maher for the exuberant encouragement, and to grandma for her love and support.; [a.] Garland, TX

RUSSO, LUANN
[b.] March 8, 1962, Brooklyn, NY; [p.] Carmela DeLora and Carmelo DeLora; [m.] Vincent J. Russo, December 22, 1985; [ch.] Michael and Dakota Russo; [ed.] Saint Nicholas Elementary School, Christ the King R.H.S.; [occ.] Homemaker; [pers.] My writings come deep from within my heart. A place where my family lives. A place where love, hurt, sorrow and joy. Take a chair. A place only my pen can take you to.; [a.] Deer Park, NY

RUTAN, PAULA
[pen.] Paula Rutan; [b.] November 21, 1954, Waterloo, IA; [p.] Paul Ellsberry, Mary Steinhoff; [m.] Richard Rutan, January 15, 1984; [ch.] Jason Parr, Kimberlie Parr, Joshua Parr, Amanda Parr and Aaron Rutan; [ed.] Thomas Jefferson H.S. Council Bluffs, IA, Metropolitan State College of Denver; [occ.] Educator; [memb.] Sigma Tau Delta, NEA, CEA; [hon.] Working on a novel; [oth. writ.] I have always loved to write and take pride in my works. I know my writing abilities were nurtured by my high school English Teacher Carolyn Goad as well as my Creative Writing professor Amber Dahlin. Thank you both.; [pers.] Denver, CO

RUTLEDGE, PHYLLIS OIEN
[b.] August 30, 1938, Lansing, MI; [p.] Nick Ellison, Pearl Ellison; [m.] Joe; [ch.] Laurie Kay Larson, James Kenneth Rutledge, Robin Sue Wolfe; [ed.] Okemos H.S. Business School Comp.; [occ.] Community Services; [memb.] VFW Aux Eagles Aux - volunteer services for the aged; [oth. writ.] Newsletters Local Org.; [pers.] Always Striving to reflect the feeling and dreams of mankind, and personal thoughts.

RUTON, MILDRED
[pen.] Mildred Marsh Ruton; [b.] November 2, 1906, Bridgeport, OH; [p.] Joseph Clarence and Pearl Marsh; [m.] Eddie Ruton (Deceased), October 15, 1947; [ch.] William Beckford (Deceased), and Larry Oliver; [ed.] Wheeling High School Graduated 1925 and later by travel in show business and many office positions managing own c/w Park and experienced; [occ.] Retired, Poetry Writing; [memb.] Distinguished Member of ISP, NLP, Order of Eastern Star,

Silver Club, Library of Poetry Associate, Charter Member of Country Music Assn., AARP, locally and national, The Travel Club; [hon.] Have 4 Editor's Choice awards, International Poet of Merit Award at ISP conv. I was a semi-finalist in ISP Conv. 1995, I won a Talent Award for comedy from The Licking County Aging Program it was for improving the quality of life of the aging (by doing my amateur comedy as a volunteer for some of their functions) had poems pub. in Sr. Cit. Publications poems published in NLP Books; [oth. writ.] The Gift of Sight, The Human Liberty Bell, A Good Son, The Invisible, World Peace, Scenes in the Clouds, I like Your Style and "A Poet" (to be published soon) and "So Loved" NLP Books these poems are in as follows: A Muse to Follow, Reflections of Light, Beyond the Stars, At Waters Edge, Best Poems, Mists of Enchantment, Where Dawn Lingers, Spirit of the Age; [pers.] Live life to the fullest, but make it a good life without picking up bad seeds along the way that would only grow weeds instead of flowers.; [a.] Newark, OH

RUTTER, BETTY A.
[b.] January 16, 1932, Tonopah, NV; [p.] George and Kathryn Johnson; [m.] Tom Rutter, February 14, 1995; [ch.] Three by former marriage.; [ed.] Have never stopped formal education - for the sake of learning - not for degrees.; [occ.] Retired from Real Estate; [oth. writ.] Completed metaphysical work of fiction. Have started book number two.; [pers.] Each of us must accept responsibility for our own actions - thereby we have the power to do anything!; [a.] Kingman, AZ

SAAM, JANICE KAY
[pen.] Kay Saam; [b.] March 17, 1942, Seneca, CO; [p.] Charles Wollam, Bertha Whicker; [m.] Donald Frederick Saam (Deceased), January 25, 1964; [ch.] Jeffrey Lee Saam, Daniel Eugene Saam, Michelle Renee Getzinger (Saam) Kristina Joan Saam; [ed.] Bettsville High School graduate; [occ.] Bowling Green, OH., Greenwood Coinlaundry; [memb.] Girton Church of God, National Audybon Soc. Eastern Paralyzed Veterans Assoc. (Church, Rising Sun, OH.); [pers.] My mother has always been an inspiration to me. She gave me all I needed in life, especially love. I strive to be an inspiration to others, be it comfort, religion, etc.; [a.] Helena, OH

SAAVEDRA, BARBARA M.
[pen.] BMS Hope-Joy; [b.] May 2, 1960, Brooklyn; [p.] Jose and Angela; [ed.] New Rochelle High School, Boston University, Westchester Community, Iona College; [occ.] Nurse; [pers.] Live in peace today for the glory of tomorrow.; [a.] Loechmont, NY

SABATINO, MARISSA J.
[pen.] Sea Hag; [b.] August 6, 1976, New Jersey; [p.] Michele and John Sabatino; [ed.] Voorhee High School full sail; [occ.] Student; [memb.] Dead Poets Society Voorhees High School; [hon.] Won 400 dollar for poems; [oth. writ.] 6 Chap books at Voorhees High School under pen name Sea Hag. Images - School Magazine.; [pers.] I write to keep my sanity. And when it comes to writing about myself, I'm as open as a widow is on a Hot Summer's day.; [a.] Glen Gordner, NJ

SABESSAR, EMMA
[b.] Albany, GA; [p.] Mary Martin; [m.] Joel Sabessar; [ch.] Joyce, Linda, Lisa, Cheray, Ferrisha, Tina, Sophia, Chad; [ed.] SCS Business Technical Institute Nassu Community College; [occ.] Freelance Writer; [hon.] Certificate SCS Business published in sparrow grass book of poetry, Editor's Choice Award The National Library of Poetry; [oth. writ.] Children's Books for Calton Press due to be release; [pers.] Believe in yourself. Keep the faith, you will come out alright The sun shine every days cloud come and cover it and yet the sun shines right on, have faith. In your dream; [a.] Springfield, NY

SAINT JOHN, DOMINIQUE
[p.] Lena Louis; [m.] Deceased; [ch.] Two; [occ.] Talent Agent; [memb.] As Cop; [hon.] I am enclosing a write up from what you can exhort what you want from it. It talks about some things I was recognized for; [oth. writ.] Dakata Staton sings "I'm Tired of That" that I wrote. Its on a "Muse" album also I wrote lyrics for a song called "Wende."; [pers.] On an Arista album by Ran Blake - also published poetry in the destal magazine I've written tons of songs.

SAINT PETER, DIANNE
[b.] January 25, 1958, Kankakee, IL; [p.] Delmar and Evelyn Provost; [m.] Kevin Saint Peter, April 23, 1977; [ch.] Jeanna, Kelly, Nathan and Nicholas; [ed.] Momence High School, Momence, Illinois; [occ.] Secretary for Roofing Complete, Inc.; [oth. writ.] Currently writing a novel, striving for completion in Spring 1996.; [pers.] It has been my desire for as long as I remember to have a career in writing. My ultimate goal is to know that my writing has been enjoyed by others.; [a.] Grant Park, IL

SALES, LEONIDES S.
[pen.] Leo; [b.] April 22, 1936, Bacarra, Ilocos Norte, Philippines; [p.] Gregorio Albano Sales, Maria S. Sales; [m.] Divorce, March 3, 1955; [ch.] Victor Sales, Glenda Sales, Anthony Sales, Ferdinand Sales, Geraldine Shemoe, Christopher Sales, Lilibeth Sales, Ronald Raegan Sales; [ed.] High School - Kabangkalan Academy Negros Occidental Philippines, Northwestern College, Laoag City, Philippines, Bachelor of Science in Commerce, University of the East, Manila, Philippines, Aircraft Armament Repair Course, U.S. Army Ordinance Center and School,

Aberdeen Proving Ground Maryland 21005 U.S.A., Special Intelligence Operational Course, Philippines; [occ.] Philippine Air Force Armed Forces of the Philippines, Lieutenant Retired, 23 years of service. Former Security Aide of President Ferdinand Edralin Marcos of the Philippines; [memb.] American Association of Retired Persons, May 1986, Filipino American Community of Los Angeles Inc, 1989, United Bacarreneous of Hawaii Inc. 1992, BNCHS Club of Hawaii 1992, Kiss AM Fun Club Hawaii 1992, Filipino Californians Senior Citizens Society Inc. 1993, International Circle Inc. 1993 to date. International Society of Poets - Distinguished member; [hon.] The Philippine Republic Presidential Unit Citation Badge, Commendation, Official Appreciation, Anti-Dissidence Campaign Ribbon; [oth. writ.] Several articles published "The Youth Grinder" Baccara Provincial High School Newspaper.; [pers.] To try is to succeed. Be brave in the cause of right be coward in the cause of wrong. In order to be a leader you must learn to follow. Beyond the clouds the sun still shining. Smile and the world is yours.; [a.] San Francisco, CA

SALLIS, ELLIS L.
[b.] May 19, 1967, Pascagoula, MS; [p.] Mr. and Mrs. Price Sallis; [m.] Felicia Sallis, April 29, 1996; [ch.] Steven and Elisia, Christina; [ed.] High school, 1 yr college; [occ.] Forklift Oper. I.T.O. Exports; [memb.] Christian Love, Church Of God; [hon.] 2nd Degree Brown Belt. Tae Kwon Do; [oth. writ.] Two Books unpublished; [pers.] Things in life can be so confusing at times usually. But the art of patience and conservation will always bring forth understanding.; [a.] Pascagoula, MS

SAMARANAYAKE, PEARLY
[b.] September 3, 1919, Sri-Lanka; [p.] Marshall V. Rosalind Perera; [m.] Ben Samaranayake, March 12, 1949; [ch.] Tony Samaranayake and Antonette Yayasinha; [ed.] Senior High; [memb.] Distinguished Member in International Society of Poets; [hon.] Editor's Choice Award for Outstanding Achievement in Poetry (1995); [oth. writ.] My Plea, Sunset and Sunrise; [pers.] "My Plea" - Love and Harmony among all nations, "Sunset and Sunrise" - We must learn to take life in any possible way, "Love Above and Beyond" - A mother's endless love and care; [a.] Canoga, CA

SAMPLE, STEPHEN
[pen.] Sva'pe Smetle; [b.] December 10, 1944, FL; [p.] Jay and Frances Sample; [m.] Shelly B. Sample, October 13, 1995; [ch.] April and Scott, Joshua and Amber; [ed.] 12 yrs; [occ.] Carpenter; [hon.] Pres - Cluitans, Civitans of the Year, A.R.C. Pres., E.Y.C. Leader, Pres. Men's Club, Meritorious Mast - 5th Hosp. Co., Marine Corps., Best Supporting Actor; [oth. writ.] Many poems of different types. Have been

writing since age 10.; [pers.] If only I could capture the beauty of a single sunset in my poems, I would then feel content.; [a.] Stuart, FL

SANCHEZ, CONNIE
[pen.] Connie S.; [b.] December 12, 1949, Puerto Rico; [p.] Matilde Rivera, Anthony Perez; [m.] Separated - Divorced in process; [ch.] 4 and 3 grandchildren; [ed.] 2 years at Brooklyn College; [occ.] Human being; [oth. writ.] A publication of an article I'm in. "Penthouse" September 1981 Girls In Gangs, "Sayings" "What color body should the perfect mind above"; [pers.] Book on my life Bibliography, "The Girls In The Gang", "The Girls in The Gang" by Anne Campbell Library publication published in U.S.A.

SANDWITH, SHANNON M.
[b.] August 21, 1971, Bellingham, WA; [occ.] Administration Assist. at a Real Estate Office; [pers.] I want to dedicate this poem to my sister Angela Renee Sandwith and all the children who are not with us now.; [a.] Friday Harbor, WA

SANGRAM, AMARDEEP
[pen.] Amar, Deep; [b.] May 18, 1980, Chicago, IL; [p.] Aruna Sangram; [ed.] Currently Attending Niles North High School (2nd year); [memb.] Member of "International Society of Poets"; [hon.] 2nd place "Young Author's Short Story Contest", "Distinguished" Member of the "International Society of Poets" 1994-1995; [oth. writ.] Poem published in "Journey of the Mind", by the National Library of Poetry, Poetry published in local newspaper; [pers.] Poetry is written by one, read by many, and understood by all.; [a.] Stokie, IL

SAPSER, FRAN M.
[pen.] Fari Smitt; [b.] April 8, Wilkes-Barre; [p.] Mr. and Mrs. Mary and Miko K.; [m.] Divorced; [ch.] Tom; [ed.] 10 years of College which included 3 years of University work in W-B, General Hospital - 3 years Business and 4 yrs. at Marywood and Prott Institute NY; [occ.] After doing nursing for 30 years - am now a Business Mgr. and Landlord; [memb.] Nurses Registry, Automobile Clubs, Photography Clubs, Heart Associations, Animal Lover, Dance Club; [hon.] Latin Award for being best in PA Test, Poetry Awards, Acting Awards for stage and considered the best land-lord in Wilkes-Barre; [oth. writ.] Short stories and a possible novel, a lot of poems and articles.; [pers.] I Always say: "Books are my Life", "Strive to be the best", being an only child with 2 sick parents I read continuously.; [a.] Wilkes-Barre, PA

SARA, NILS P.
[b.] November 19, 1947, Bethel, AK; [p.] Clement Nils Sara and Martha Sara; [m.] Rose Sara, 1982; [ch.] Rebecca; [ed.] High School Graduate and some College; [occ.] Fisherman and carpenter, [oth. writ.] Other poems published in Alaska; [pers.] I try to reflect my heritage of Scandinavian reinder herder and Alaskan Eskimo in my writing.; [a.] Bethel, AK

SARASTY, EMILY
[pen.] Melysa; [b.] Columbia, South America; [p.] Domingo Sarasty, Isabel Morera-Sarasty; [ch.] Claudia and Patrick Rossi; [ed.] Columbia, Mexico, USA; [occ.] Federal Interpreter/Translator, [oth. writ.] Unpublished collection of Poetic dialogues and other poems in Spanish.; [pers.] I hope that someday my poetry will please young an old like, touching the heart, shaking the senses and moving the spirit. "Poetry is the divine music of the soul."; [a.] Lakewood, CA

SARGENT, EDWARD R.
[b.] February 5, 1911, Wolfeboro, NY; [p.] Herbert E. and Marion R. Sargent; [m.] Virginia, July 12, 1980; [ch.] David, Peter and Elizabeth (Azcarate); [ed.] Brewster Academy - Wolfeboro, NY, Harvard College 1934 B.S.; [occ.] Retired - Aerospace Apollo; [memb.] Amateur Radio N3DCS, Fed. Comm. Commission; [hon.] Harvard Club of N.H.; [oth. writ.] Misc. poems not published. Did several french translations.; [pers.] I believe in the essential Lordmen of mankind but we often go astray when we don't follow the teaching and our Creator.; [a.] Washington, DC

SATTERWHITE, TEXORA PIERCE FRAZIER
[b.] March 8, 1910, Blooming Grove, TX; [p.] J. W. and Martha Pierce; [m.] Herbert Frazier, died October 25, 1950 then married T. L. Satterwhite March 9, 1952; [ch.] 3 girls now all well married; [ed.] B. BA degree from T.C.U. in Ft. Worth, Texas in 1931; [occ.] I taught Commercial Subjects in Moran High School Texas - then last 5 years in Baytown, Texas retired in 1960; [memb.] AAUW - League of memory waters - book review club - Baytown Woman's Club and (Churchwomen United) Baytown Area Church Memory I have taught Sunday Schools Classes for 50 years and am an Elder in my church (Baytown First Christian Church); [hon.] In college I was a member of Science Society Queen of BBA Department in 1929, 1931 Senior Class Favorite I was president of Ladies Club in our Country Club in 1981; [oth. writ.] My Story "An I'll Wind" was published in Hollands Magazine, some of my rhymes made the college paper; [pers.] At my age of 85+ I grieve over the seemingly look of respect people have for God and each other. Teachers and low officials are even in danger. The poetry we studied and reserved was full of the appreciation of life and beauty.; [a.] Baytown, TX

SAUERS, R. D.
[b.] March 26, 1945, Port, OR; [p.] Mr. and Mrs. E. E. Sauers; [ed.] North Bend High

SAWYIER, MEGAN
[b.] July 14, 1977, San Mateo, CA; [ed.] Elk Grove High School; [occ.] Gymnastics Coach; [pers.] If you see something in your life you don't like - change it.; [a.] Sacramento, CA

SCARBOROUGH, BERNADETT ELLEN
[b.] August 2, 1967, Sallisaw, OK; [p.] Chester and Elizabeth Scarborough; [ed.] Vian High School; [occ.] Nurses Aid; [memb.] Vian Church of God in Christ; [oth. writ.] Poem published in our local newspaper, a recent publishing by Ilian Press; [pers.] I write to express my feelings and views of others as well as myself instead of talking to others I prefer talking to my pen and paper therefore it can not answer me back. Maya Angelou has influenced me a lot.; [a.] Vian, OK

SCATOLA, TERRY
[b.] May 5, 1922, Wappingers Fall, NY; [p.] Carlo and Francesca Rosignoli; [m.] Anthony, October 19, 1947; [ch.] Martin Scatola, Blase Scatola, Frances Buist, Teri Dumont, Charles Scatola; [ed.] High School (Julia Richman - NY) Stenotype Institute of NY; [occ.] Retired (Formerly Data Control Specialist) Mt. Pleasant Square Dance Club; [memb.] Pelham Promenaders Square Dance Club, Commerce Senior Center, Coyne Park Senior Center, St. Joseph Players, Annunciation Players, I.C. Players (Community Theatre), AARP - Eastchester Chapter, [hon.] Westchester County Senior Hall of Fame, 1995 - Special Recognition Award, Mayor City of Yonkers Community Svc. Award, Certificate - Special Congressional Recognition, NY State Senate Achievement Award, Proclamation - Westchester County Bd. Legislature Distinguished Service Award and Westchester County Clerk, Westchester County Certificate of Appreciation; [pers.] I believe in remaining active especially after retirement. Volunteering in helping people in nursing homes and senior centers is a very rewarding experience for me.; [a.] Yonkers, NY

SCHERMEISTER, MARK
[b.] August 28, 1956, Chicago, IL; [p.] Paul Schermeister, Lisa Schermeister, [m.] Janet Schermeister, September 6, 1980; [pers.] I am expressing a positive view of the world. With faith in Jesus, life is an opportunity to serve God. My poetry is a way to convey a spiritual, optimistic way to think and live.; [a.] Fort Lauderdale, FL

SCHICK, BARBARA
[b.] August 25, Bakersfield, CA; [p.] Adolph and Flora Schwartz; [m.] Doyle Schick (Deceased); [ch.] Christy, Donna, Leila, Shem, Brian Nobi; [ed.] Health Science B.S., CA. State San Bernardino, CA. Post graduate Cal. State U. Long Beach, CA; [occ.] Record analyst, Loma Linda U. Medical Center; [memb.] Armed

Forces, Writers Guild; [hon.] Dean's list, Local Poetry Competition; [oth. writ.] Poems for newsletters in California; [pers.] You can't find happiness you cause it.

SCHLESINGER, KATIE
[pen.] Jo; [b.] June 24, 1983, Glendora, CA; [p.] Hank and Bonnie Schlesinger; [ed.] Lyndon Baynes Johnson Middle School; [hon.] 1st place in Spelling Bee, twice; [oth. writ.] Several unpublished poems.; [a.] Albuquerque, NM

SCHLEUTERMANN, GRACE ARDEAN
[b.] June 23, Washington, DC; [p.] Grace and Dennis Trossbach; [m.] Divorced; [ch.] Michael Jr.; [ed.] Anacostia High and Maryland University; [occ.] Adm. Asst.; [memb.] German Shepherd Club of America; [hon.] I have received many awards through the years both in private industry and govt. as well as AKC affiliates; [pers.] I had a wonderful childhood and happy life. My parents were truly a child's dream and I wanted to somehow let others know my mom's name (Grace) and how she live up to it.; [a.] Camp Springs, MD

SCHLIENZ, KASEY LEIGH
[b.] February 7, 1986, Wiesbaden, West Germany; [p.] Don and Karen Schlienz; [ed.] 4th grade at Parkside Elementary School in Manassas, VA, a participant in the Signet (gifted) Program and attends Bennett School one day a week. Attended school in Pennsylvania and Rhode Island.; [occ.] To be an Entomologist; [memb.] Junior Girl Scouts of America; [hon.] Honor Roll student; [pers.] "I love art and poetry and write about almost anything, usually about how I feel."; [a.] Manassas, VA

SCHLINGMANN, CONNIE
[b.] 1942, Saint Louis, MO; [m.] Robert W. Schlingmann, August 1963; [ch.] Robert II, Michael, David, Mary and Christopher; [ed.] St. Alphonsus (Rock) High School; [oth. writ.] First publication of a poem.; [pers.] I find that in my writing it is a true extension of feelings felt and it in turn gives a view point of this world in a perspective that is quite unique to me.; [a.] Hillsboro, MO

SCHOLZ, TERENCE J.
[pen.] T-Bird; [b.] November 26, 1964, Green Bay, WS; [p.] Don and Rozita Huebner; [ed.] Currently enrolled at Moraine Park Technical College in Ford Du Lac, Wisconsin; [pers.] Writing poetry is like therapy to me. I hope people in the world can benefit from my poetry as much as I have.; [a.] Brillion, WI

SCHOONOVER, DONALD L.
[b.] September 1, 1962, Martinez, CA; [p.] Edward L. and Susan R. Schoonover; [m.] Maria Teresa M. Schoonover, October 15, 1990; [ch.] Edward J. Schoonover; [ed.] High School; [occ.]

Detachment 1, 615th Air Mobility Operations Group, Kelly AFB TX (US Air Force); [hon.] Air Force Commendation Medal, Air Force Achievement Medal, Air Force Good Conduct Medal, Armed Forces Expeditionary Medal, and Air Force Overseas Long Tour Ribbon; [pers.] To understand true freedom, the glorious outdoors, and poetry you must not only gaze upon it with your eyes, but you must be able to feel and touch it with your heart. But, most importantly, you must defend them with your entire being.; [a.] San Antonio, TX

SCHREMP, FAITH M.
[pen.] Faythimes; [b.] May 15, 1921, Pickerel, WI; [p.] Vic and Bess Iames; [m.] Lester "Butch" Schremp, September 19, 1942; [ch.] Four, 3 girls and 1 boy, 11 grandchildren, 3 greats, 2 coming; [ed.] Some College and Scales of Life Experience; [occ.] Writer; [memb.] International Women's Writing Guild, National Writers Club, Wis. Regional Writers and Antegs Writers Club member at large (past pres.); [hon.] Golden Poet from 985 to 1992 annually, Distinguished Member, Int Soc. Poets 1995, Danae Lifetime membership Award 1950 by Int. Clover Poetry Assn Wash. DC, Marquis Who's Who In Entertainment 1992/93, Who's Who in Am. Women 1993-94; [oth. writ.] Novel "The Last Switcherer," novel "Smalltown Wife and Mom" 1992 cookbook "Granis Good Grub" 1992, Poetry, "Mom are we there yet?" 1994, numerous short stories and poems in papers and magazines; [pers.] "Life is short - enjoy," (Let me leave some footprints in the sands of my Life).

SCHUFF, ROSE L.
[b.] August 15, 1950, Harrisburg, PA; [p.] Sara Dockens, John R, Dockens; [m.] Gary C. Schuff, January 12, 1980; [ed.] William Penn High; [occ.] Correspondence Clerk United Concordia, Camp Hill, PA; [memb.] Harrisburg Art Association; [hon.] National Honor Society; [oth. writ.] Have had several poems published in office newspaper. Have written total of 29 poems, and will strive to have them published. Also have written a short story, am working on my autobiography which deals primarily with how I triumphed over being an abused child.; [pers.] The poetry I write is a reflection of my personal struggle to free myself from the chains imposed upon me by an abusive mother. It is an acknowledgement of long suppressed feelings, of injustice done, of deep seated anger. It is the unfolding account of finding who I really am, of learning to nurture, of letting go of the pain.; [a.] Harrisburg, PA

SCHULZ, CAROLE SUE SIVEL
[b.] November 28, 1944, Philadelphia, PA; [p.] Joseph and Mil Sivel; [m.] George R. Schulz, July 11, 1965; [ch.] Ron G. Schulz; [oth. Writ.] Silent Conversation, Donnie, My Legacy, Mrs. Sabatose, I Do, The Farmers Wife, Grandpop

Engelke, My Diary, Regret Me Not; [pers.] Poetry is my freedom to take leave of what I am and in experience whatever circumstance or emotion my imagination inspires until the last word is written.; [a.] Franklinville, NJ

SCHWEBS, GARY NYE
[b.] September 21, 1941, Los Angeles, CA; [m.] Kathleen C. Schwebs, November 12, 1994; [ch.] Kari Lee, Kimberly Nye; [ed.] Buena Park High; [occ.] Salesman/Co-owner of K.C. Sales (Artist); [oth. writ.] Poems A Broomstick Horse Named Clyde, Homeless Man Band, Clowns Lull-A-By, Clown's Laughter; [a.] Bellflower, CA

SCOTT, BILLIE J.
[b.] December 27, 1928, Cromwell, OK; [p.] W. R. and Ninahree Scott; [ed.] High School; [occ.] Reflexologist; [memb.] All Reflexology Assocs. Worldwide - Unity Church of the Desert - Las Vegas Chamber of Commerce; [oth. writ.] Yes - but a few in print - Reflexology Newsletters; [pers.] I have concern for the world in aspect.; [a.] Las Vegas, NV

SCOTT, ELLEN
[pen.] White Raven; [b.] May 12, 1974, Heidelburg, Germany; [p.] Robert Scott and Barbara Scott; [ed.] Seoul American High; [occ.] Marketer Plymouth, MN; [oth. writ.] So far I am unpublished, yet I am striving to have my work put in print.; [pers.] The death of splence is found in the birth of purity.; [a.] Maplegrove, MN

SCOTT, ERIC
[b.] November 12, 1960, Worcester, MA; [p.] Edward and Miriam Scott; [m.] Venessa (we are divorced), September 24, 1984; [ch.] Ericka and Renee Scott; [ed.] 1978 High School Graduate; [occ.] Meat Cutter/Produce Clerk; [memb.] First Congregational Church of Hancock in Hancock NH, Monadnock Full Gospel Church in Ringe, NH, Fire Fighter for the Hancock Fire Dept.

SCOTT, JOY R.
[b.] December 2, 1937, Jamaica; [p.] Flo and Waldemar Thompson; [m.] Dennis Scott (Deceased), October 4, 1969; [ch.] John-David and Danielle; [ed.] University of the West Indies, Sorbonne, Albertus Magnus College, New Haven; [occ.] United Nations Staff Member; [pers.] I have always been captivated by the power of language.; [a.] New Haven, CT

SCOTT, RICHARD BRIAN
[pen.] R.B. Scott; [b.] August 24, 1969, Rome, GA; [p.] Maria McIntyre, Richard Scott; [m.] Linda Ann, April 6, 1996; [ch.] Samantha (Stepdaughter); [ed.] High School Diploma at Cartersville High School, Server in US Navy 3 yr was on call for Desert Storm; [occ.] Arrow Ind., 5db Title Machine Operator; [memb.] Tabernacle Baptist Church, Bushido Karate Associa-

tion; [oth. writ.] Out of the Dark, Rainbow True Beauty, The Answer, The Next Day Girls, Fast Pace, Finish the Dream, Friends which was published but as an unknown author.; [pers.] I enjoy writing for recreational purposes, it also help me express my internate feelings which confuse me. I like to write poetry because it touches people's hearts.; [a.] Cartersville, GA

SCOTT, RONALD K.
[b.] August 11, 1946, Vallejo, CA; [p.] Leslie L. Scott II, Dorothy N. Scott; [ed.] Bella Vista H.S. American River College; [occ.] Civil Service at McClellan AFB, CA; [pers.] Since I was a teenager my mother inspired me to write poems and short stories; [a.] Sacramento, CA

SCOTT, SUE ANN
[pen.] Sue Ann Scott; [b.] January 20, 1948, Portsmouth, OH; [p.] Fern C. Wheeler; [m.] Divorced; [ch.] Eddie E., Jeanne Ann; [ed.] B.S.N. Ohio University - 1982, Wheelersburgh High School; [occ.] Disabled Retired R.N.; [memb.] Arthritis Foundation, Deer Park, U.M. Church; [hon.] Published in First Edition "Who's Who in Nursing"; [pers.] I strive to enjoy life to the fullest, enjoying each new adventure day by day.; [a.] Deer Park, TX

SCOTTEN, TREIS
[b.] November 8, 1983, Fort Scott, KS; [p.] C.D. and JoAnn Scotten; [ed.] Currently in 6th grade Nevada Middle School, Nevada MO; [occ.] Student; [memb.] Lone Star 4H, D.A.R.E., Rinehart Christian Church, Nevada Youth Basketball League. Nevada Little League Baseball.; [hon.] 6th grade "A" Honor Roll Elks "Hoop Shoot" Winner

SCRIP, SHIRLEY E.
[b.] December 28, 1933, Donora, PA; [p.] Alden and Jean Evans; [ch.] Lori, Jeff, Tim, Val, Kathy; [ed.] Donora Senior High, St. Francis Hospital School of Nursing, Pittsburgh, PA; [occ.] R.N., Utilization Review Co-Ordinator, Brownsville General Hospital, Brownsville, PA; [oth. writ.] First published work; [pers.] I have tried to personify the reality of life.; [a.] Grindstone, PA

SCROGGINS, MARY M.
[b.] July 17, 1949, Norfolk, VA; [p.] Floyd and Edith Clark; [m.] Larry R. Scroggins Sr., August 23, 1975; [ch.] Larry R. Scroggins Jr.; [ed.] Booker T. Washington High (Norfolk, VA), Norfolk State University, Baltimore City Community College; [occ.] Fingerprint Specialist, Department of Public Safety; [memb.] Maryland Classified Employee Association

SEBASTIAN, BERNADINE
[b.] December 25, 1952, Navasota, TX; [p.] John and Barbara Sebastian; [ch.] Martin J. Sebastian (15); [occ.] Clerk, Harris Co., Sheriff's Dept.

SELKOWITZ, RONALD
[pen.] R. R. Royce; [b.] June 2, 1936, Brooklyn, NY; [p.] Enrica and Emanuel Selkowitz; [m.] Joan Aileen Selkowitz, December 10, 1989; [ch.] Robin Gail Hernandez, Tammy June Selkowitz; [ed.] Ft. Lauderdale College - Fla., Abraham Lincoln H.S. - Brooklyn N.Y., Dental Tech. School - US nary, State of Fla. R.E. School; [occ.] US Postal Service Clerk Cocoa - Florida; [memb.] America Postal Workers Union; [hon.] Presidents List Ft. Lauderdale College-Miami-Fla.; [pers.] Should I succeed in bringing even a miniscule form of enjoyment and possible enlightenment to a single being reading my writings of personal endeavor, then would I feel complete exaltation and satisfaction in such accomplishment.; [a.] Cape Canaveral, FL

SELOVER, GAYE V.
[b.] February 21, 1934, Miami, OK; [p.] Jim Padgett, Faye S. Landers; [m.] Marion V. Selover Jr., February 14, 1973; [ch.] David Reed, Michelle Hall, Michonne Pieksma; [ed.] Payette High School; [occ.] Teach Stained Glass/Art, Homemaker; [memb.] T.V.A.A. (Art) Glass Crafters; [pers.] To put God first. The rest will follow.; [a.] Payette, ID

SENTZ, JENNIFER R.
[b.] May 6, 1974, York, PA; [p.] David and Karen Sentz; [ed.] Business School, Legal and Management Program; [occ.] Office Support - Quality Control Dept.; [memb.] Greenpeace, Classical Music Lovers Exchange; [hon.] Perfect Attendance Award, Dean's List, SADD; [oth. writ.] Several poems written in creative writing course. Articles for school newspaper.; [pers.] I strive to be the best, and to express emotions through writing. I have been influenced by my grandparents.; [a.] Dover, PA

SEWELL, VALERILYNN
[pen.] Miss Priss; [b.] December 7, 1978, Camden, AR; [p.] Mr. and Mrs. Lonnie C. Sewell; [ed.] Junior at Woodbridge High School; [occ.] Student; [memb.] FCA (Fellowship of Christian Athetes); [hon.] Academic Letter at W.S.H.S. for 94-95 school year. Fine Arts Festival short story metal 94-95.; [oth. writ.] Through The Lion's Den, The Snow-Cap Mountain Ambassadors, The Great Pumpkin Chase, various other poems and short stories; [pers.] I like to share the writings and the talent God has given me.; [a.] Woodbridge, VA

SEYEDAN, MORI
[b.] February 17, 1958, Nahavand; [pers.] I believe, we all want to do good as people, but oftentimes with a little struggle we crumble. I would like to attribute the good things I do and the good thoughts that save me, to my beloved father who has inspired me for life.; [a.] Ventura, CA

SFORZA, ELENA
[pen.] Elena Sforza; [b.] December 15, 1965, Italy; [p.] Nick and Rose Busciacco; [m.] Peter Sforza, April 24, 1993; [ch.] Mario D. Caldararo; [ed.] All schools 1 to 18 attended in Italy; [occ.] Cashier at a Rite Aid Pharmacy-Store; [memb.] Hope of the World Ministry of Beth Israel Messianie Center; [oth. writ.] Just finished working on a booklet "Reasons to Believe that Jesus is the Messiah" which I'm planning to be out sometime in summer.; [pers.] Believing in God brings hope and love to our hurting lives. And if that is what it takes to make us better people. Why not follow his teachings and yield to him.; [a.] Cliffside Park, NJ

SHAFFER, DEBRA L.
[pen.] D. L. Shaffer; [b.] December 23, 1956, Somerset, PA; [p.] Dolores Deaner, Charles Deaner; [m.] Ronald L. "Buntch" Shaffer, July 21, 1994; [ed.] North Star High School, BA - University of Pittsburg at Johnstown, MA - Bowling Green State University; [occ.] Therapy Manager - Gateway Rehabilitation Center, Aliquippa, PA; [a.] Hooversville, PA

SHANKAR, SREELATHA
[b.] January 23, 1969, Pondicherry, IN; [p.] V.K. Shankar, Prena Shankar; [m.] Parasu Nagendran, July 16, 1995; [ch.] Expecting my first child; [ed.] M.A. (English Literature) B. Ed. (Bachelor of Education) DCE (Diploma in Creative Writing in English); [oth. writ.] Poems published in magazines in India; [pers.] Be good, do good, good will come to you; [a.] Richmond, VA

SHARP, GLORIA ESTHER
[b.] October 15, 1930, Battle Creek, MI; [p.] Earl and Edna Babcock; [m.] Edward Sharp, April 13, 1951; [ch.] Lois, Paul, Joseph, Rebecca and Angel; [ed.] High School and some business school; [occ.] Homemaker; [memb.] No club memberships. I enjoy the woman's group in our church. The Seventh Day Adventist Church from Norfolk, Nebr.; [oth. writ.] Some poems published in local newspapers and magazines.; [pers.] As people read my poetry I want them to get a glimpse of our maker and provider of all.; [a.] Beemer, NE

SHARP, KRISTINA
[pen.] Kristina Sharp, Anonymous, Kristina David; [b.] September 20, 1973, Oregon; [p.] William and Peggy David; [m.] Matthew A. Sharp, August 28, 1993; [ch.] Devon Anthony Sharp Joshua Allan Sharp; [ed.] Eric Birch High School; [occ.] Sub. Bus Driver and Mirit Mart Clerk; [pers.] I try to be my own individual and reflect that upon my children. I believe my husband has been my greatest inspiration. The greatest rewards are being a parent.; [a.] Vancouver, WA

SHAW, GLORIA J.
[b.] June 30, 1953, Cumberland County; [p.] Mrs. Minnie D. Shaw; [ch.] Harold Shaw; [occ.] Dining Faculty Attendant; [hon.] Connely Awards in year of 1988, 1994, 1995; [a.] Fayetteville, NC

SHEARS, MATT
[b.] October 16, 1975, Alliance, OH; [p.] Terry Shears, Patricia Shears; [ed.] Boardman High School, currently enrolled at Miami University of Ohio; [occ.] Student; [pers.] I am an alien. I come from the planet Ummagumma. I was born in the back seat of a spaceship, and was left to die on the third ring of Saturn. That is where Chubacca found me.; [a.] Youngstown, OH

SHEE, JAMIE
[b.] December 18, 1978, Rochester, PA; [p.] Larry and Marilyn Shee; [ed.] High School Student, graduate in 1997; [hon.] 1993-94 PTA 3rd Place Bearer Co. 1994-1995 Veterans of Foreign Wars Voice of Democracy "My Vision for America" 1994 PTA 5th Place Pennsylvania District II; [pers.] My writing is not only what I deal with, my personal life, I try to get into other views. I try to open my thoughts and feel how they feel. That is why I have so many poems about different views of life.; [a.] New Brighton, PA

SHELLNUTT, CANDACE VALENTI
[pen.] Valenti; [b.] September 19, 1971, Tucker, GA; [p.] J. C. Murphey and Pat Abbott; [m.] Christopher Shellnutt, September 20, 1991; [ch.] Alex Valenti and C. Justin Smith; [ed.] Newton County High, Georgia Military College (Dean's List), Mercer University (physics major); [occ.] Graphic Artist, Georgia Correctional Industries; [memb.] Future Business Leaders of America, S.C.A., G.C.I. Quality Control Team; [oth. writ.] Several poems published in quarterly papers, "Baby Parts" published in Milledville's Allied Arts, and self published poetry "Picking Appels from a Cherry Tree", a book funded by Arts Clearinghouse.; [pers.] Reaching from the darkness, pen in hard, I grasp for freedom, which is found only in my words. As for truth...my children are the only truth that matters.; [a.] Atlanta, GA

SHELTON, LEIGH
[pen.] Ashleigh Merritt; [b.] October 4, 1967, Frankfurt, Germany; [p.] Charlotte and Richard Shelton; [ed.] BA in Elementary Education, MA in Gifted Education, Maryville University, St. Louis, MO; [occ.] I teach academically gifted and talented fifth graders at the Center for Creative Learning: Rockwood School District, St. Louis, MO; [memb.] Phi Delta Kappa, Alpha Omicron Pi; [hon.] Rose Award Recipient, 1995, 4-time recipient John M., Kastner Board of Education Award, Gifted Education Presenter at the national level; [oth. writ.] A poem, This Lime, won honorable mention in the Wednesday Club of St. Louis creative writing contest. I had a professional article on discrimination of the gifted published in a national journal: Gifted Education Press Quarterly.; [pers.] I write from my heart, drawing on experiences and issues which move me. The poem I wrote for When Dawn Lingers was inspired by the recent death of my grandfather, Charles Haynes. He taught me to live life to its fullest, never losing sight of what is most important: Family, friends and the beauty of nature. He was a wise man with a heart of gold.; [a.] Wildwood, MO

SHELTON, MARY L.
[b.] February 23, 1920, Heber Springs, AR; [p.] John H. and Eva E. Ladd (Both Deceased); [m.] R. Wayne Shelton (Deceased), April 19, 1941; [ch.] James Wayne; [ed.] Flint Creek Elementary, Gentry, AR; [occ.] Retired Homemaker; [memb.] Seventh-day Adventist Church, I.S.P.; [hon.] International Society of Poets; [oth. writ.] Anthologies and Church magazines.; [pers.] I only ask that the reader receive a blessing from the words God has given me to write.; [a.] Phoenix, AZ

SHEPPARD, LINDA DIANE
[b.] March 14, 1950, La Grange, GA; [p.] Douglas Lync, Vener Hill Lynch; [m.] Henry Wayne Sheppard Sr., February 2 1966; [ch.] Henry Jr., Donna Lynn, Mary Diane; [ed.] Handley High, Chauncey Sparks College for Nursing; [memb.] Reynolds Holiness Church; [oth. writ.] Several songs, and the poem Masterpiece published in the Southern Tradition Newsletter.; [pers.] As though the Creator were looking into a sea of glass, and His image reflecting upon the universe, upon man, and nature, let his reflections be in my writing to those who read.; [a.] Chatom, AL

SHER, PARAM
[b.] January 22, 1977, New Delhi, India; [p.] Amarjit Sher, Joginder Sher; [ed.] North Central High School, currently enrolled at Butler University, College of Pharmacy; [hon.] Who's Who Among American High School Students, National Honors Society, Second place in local short story contest; [oth. writ.] Various short stories for contests, a religious biographical essays; [pers.] It is not the fortunate person who arises from humble roots. It is the fortunate person who embraces humbleness, and remembers roots.; [a.] Indianapolis, IN

SHIELDS, DAWN
[pen.] Beth Longworth or Lady Beth Longworth; [b.] April 23, 1979, Phoenix City, AL; [p.] Rhonda Jones and Dwayne Shields; [ed.] Russell County High School; [occ.] High School Student; [memb.] Scholar's Bowl Debate Team; [pers.] I am a romantic and tend to bottle up harsh emotions. I use poetry as my outlet, but I hope it lifts others spirits.; [a.] Seale, AL

SHIRLEY, BERTIE
[b.] August 28, 1948, Canton, OH; [p.] Clifford Stage and Evelyn Rolston; [m.] Robert R. Shirley, October 6, 1972; [occ.] Senior Relationship Associate, Society National Bank, Canton, OH; [pers.] Find the balance from within, happiness makes everyday special.; [a.] Canton, OH

SHORT, SJAH
[pen.] Micah Lee; [b.] September 7, 1977, Oklahoma City, OK; [p.] Debra K. Short; [ed.] Fayetteville, Christian High School; [occ.] Tele-Marketer at Tri-State Publications; [memb.] World Wildlife Federation (WWF); [hon.] High School Home-Coming Queen, Vice-President of my class; [pers.] I try to write poems about my life, writing is a way for me to open up my heart and let my feelings out.; [a.] Fayetteville, AR

SHUPE, LINDA
[b.] July 24, 1947, Saint Paul, MN; [p.] Earl and Phyillis Van Tassell'; [m.] Jerry Shupe (Deceased August 5, 1989), January 13, 1988; [ed.] H.S., some college, Nursing Program and Human Service Tech., unable to complete Nursing because of illness.; [occ.] Nursing Asst., (Disabled at this time); [memb.] Holy Rosary Church; [hon.] Volunteer Award for putting in hours beyond what was requested a Children's Hosp., Award from Police Chief for helping with lookout group in HiRise Safty Programme.; [oth. writ.] None published - few poems - starting short story; [pers.] I see the love of God. The poem I wrote was after I was very ill and my heart had stopped twice. I have always loved and known God was with me but this makes you realize all the little things He has made for us.; [a.] Minneapolis, MN

SIBLEY, FRANK C.
[b.] February 7, 1919, Seattle, WA; [p.] Deceased; [m.] Beryl C. Sibley, October 13, 1942; [ch.] Three, and 8 granchildren; [ed.] High School; [occ.] Retired; [oth. writ.] None published, none submitted; [pers.] It might be of interest to know that we were at church summer camp. Our minister who is a published poet gave us the title "Spring wears a secret smile" and ten minutes to write a poem. This was mine. I have written 3 or 4 others but have done nothing with them.

SIDEBOTTOM, PAUL E.
[pen.] Bud Sidebottom; [b.] September 4, 1919, Ayoca, IA; [p.] Aaron and Ida Sidebottom; [m.] Maxine (McKenzie) Sidebottom, September 19, 1939; [ch.] Loretta and Nick; [ed.] Shelby Consolidated, Marne Elementary; [occ.] Retired; [oth. writ.] Several poems and other articles in local paper.; [pers.] I write for past time and for pleasure as well as amusement. Learn to listen, sometimes opportunity knocks softly.; [a.] Deming, NM

SIEBEL, ROBERT
[b.] February 21, 1946, Philadelphia, PA; [p.] Robert Siebel, Dorothy Siebel; [m.] Ellen Siebel, May 23, 1984; [ch.] Erich, Amanda and Nicholas; [ed.] Hammond H.S. Alexandria, VA Eastern KY Univ. W. VA State College; [occ.] Visual Artist; [memb.] Pres- WVA Int'l Film Festival, Fund for the Arts Development Board Allied Artists (Juried Member), Arts Advocacy, W. VA Artists and Craftsmens Guild, Ascension Church - Arts and Furnishings Committee; [hon.] Strathmore's Who's Who 1995-96; [pers.] The strength's of my life are family, love and the arts.; [a.] Hurricane, WV

SILVERMAN, ROBERT E.
[b.] March 1, 1924, Providence, RI; [p.] Samuel and Natalie Silverman; [m.] Margaret Takacs, December 23, 1949; [ch.] Jill, Pamela; [ed.] Brown University, B.A., Indiana University, Ph.D. (Psychology); [occ.] Retired: Professor Emeritus, New York University; [memb.] American Psychology Ass'n., Phi Beta Kappa, Sigma X; [oth. writ.] Several articles dealing with Psychological Research, Psychology (textbook), How to Write a Program (Text); [pers.] As a late comer to the vistas of Poetry, I am delighted by my newly discovered power of expression. For me, poetry brings life to the world that is beyond words.; [a.] Naples, FL

SILVIN, THOMAS V.
[pen.] Subliminal Kid; [b.] February 7, 1950, Newport, RI; [p.] Joseph V. and Mary E. Silvin; [m.] Divorced; [ch.] Grace Emerald Silvia; [ed.] B.A. Michigan State University, J.D. Detroit College of Law, 1992; [occ.] Attorney; [memb.] State Bar of Michigan, ABA American Indian Law Section, Arts Communication Entertainment and Law Section, Delivery of Legal Services Section, American Immigration Lawyers Association; [hon.] Honorable Mention - Best Brief Jessup International Law Competition 1991, Voice of Democracy 1968, Connecticut Interscholastic Writing Competition Honorable Mention Poetry and Essay CCIC State Champion Cross County Team 1968 Boston Marathon 2:37, 1975; [oth. writ.] Sports Metaphors in Judicial Opinions, copy right Protection in China: Elvisin, Elvis Out, Technology and International Law of Nuclear Weapons. Numerous poems, songs, short stories and plays.; [pers.] I have recently achieved some little notoriety after been detained by the Michigan Court of Appeals for Citing to the Dylan Thomas Poem: "Do not Go Gentle Into That Good Night"; [a.] Ann Arbor, MI

SIMENTAL, NICOLE M.
[b.] January 16, 1969; [p.] Randall, Maureen Head; [m.] Raymond, May 2, 1987; [ch.] Daniel, Nicole, Amanda, Brandon, Randall; [ed.] Mother McAuley and Hubbard High School,

Sauk Valley Community College; [pers.] The "Rose" is dedicate to my dear grandmother "Rose Rossi" January 15, 1910, - September 28, 1995, she was and will always be my inspiration, she was a beautiful, loving person, who touched the lives of everyone she knew. She made God, her family and love the most important things in her life.

SIMEONE, ANTHONY CHARLES
[pen.] Charles Drance; [b.] October 20, 1975, New Jersey; [ed.] English Major at Rutgers, the State University of New Jersey; [occ.] Full-time Dreamer (or student); [hon.] I was blessed with life and creative soul. Those are awards and honors enough.; [pers.] I seek to return balance to the world, to make it a place safe for artists again. We need to embrace the mystery and myth around us, and the artist is our only hope to tell us how.; [a.] Mount Ephraim, NJ

SIMKINS, AMY L.
[b.] January 17, 1971, Hillside, IL; [p.] Marvin Stolarz, Carol Stolarz; [m.] Clyde Simkins, June 26, 1993; [ed.] Claremont High, University of California Riverside; [occ.] International Trade; [hon.] Dean's List; [a.] Ontario, CA

SIMMONS, ANTOINETTE
[b.] April 14, 1966, New York; [p.] Mr. Louis and Vera Fassari; [m.] Mr. Rick Simmons, October 14, 1990; [ed.] Brooklyn Avenue School (Elementary) Valley Stream South High School Briarcliffe; [occ.] Opthalmic Dispenser; [pers.] I like to dedicate my poem to a very dear friend who is no longer with us Ms. Joanne White March 14, 1965 to June 23, 1992 Friends Forever with love.

SIMMONS, JIMMY
[b.] November 11, 1956, Booneville, MS; [p.] James Simmons, Shirley Simmons; [m.] Paula Simmons, March 13, 1987; [ch.] Laura Brown, Jackie Simmons; [ed.] G.E.D., Mt. Vernon Baptist College; [hon.] Honorary Plaques awarded for inspiration and kindness to others.; [oth. writ.] In memory of Jacky Simmons, Daniel Hicks, and all other departed loved ones all over the world.; [pers.] When my words touch the hearts of others, my goal in life is fulfilled.; [a.] New Site, MS

SIMMONS, MARY A.
[pen.] Mary A. Simmons; [b.] January 31, 1929, Madison, GA; [p.] Edward and Irene (Duke) Morris; [m.] Johnnie E. Simmons, July 1949; [ch.] One - deceased; [ed.] High School; [occ.] Retired; [memb.] Flowery Branch First Baptist Church GA., Hall County, GA Home Makers Club, Quilters Club. Hall County, GA Public Library; [hon.] First Place Quilt in Hall County. Georgia Senior Homemaker of the Year 1984-1985, Best Citizenship Chairperson 1984-1987.

(Best Speech Writer) Berry Alumni Association (Active Member); [oth. writ.] Poems, speeches, short stories, play based on Bible written for 7-12 grade V.B.S. students and directed and performed at Churches. Skits for Clown Ministry.; [pers.] I enjoy writing for children. I have not submitted any thing to be published although I would love to have my work put into a book for use in Churches.; [a.] Alford, FL

SIMMONS, ROBERT J.
[b.] August 24, 1925, Chicago, IL; [p.] William and Marie Simmons, (Deceased); [m.] Geraldine M. (Deceased), May 20, 1950; [ch.] Robert, Mary, Cathleen, Stephen, Christopher, Daniel; [ed.] Associate of Science but worked 21 years in engineering because of extensive Naval Electronics Training; [occ.] Retired; [memb.] Fleet reserve, Naval Institute, retired senior volunteer police patrol, Int'l Society of poets.; [hon.] Associate of Science with honors 3.96 GPA; [oth. writ.] Various poems published by NLP.; [pers.] Spent 45 years in Naval service (24 years active duty), (21 yrs civilian) love the sea and writing about it. Influenced by 19th century English and American poets. Favorite Robert W. Service; [a.] San Diego, CA

SIMON, MARC S.
[b.] February 2, 1955, Appleton, WI; [p.] Marcel and La Verne Simon; [ed.] 1 Year College - Sciences; [occ.] Entertainer - Singer - Owner Oldest Full time Karaoke Show in the United States; [memb.] Reiki I Practitioner, [hon.] Member National Honor Society, Outstanding Citizen of the Year, Oedensburg, WI 1993; [oth. writ.] "Colors in my Day" is my first submission anywhere and is part of a collection of poems, I would possibly like to publish myself in the future.; [pers.] Love in life initiates my inspiration and enables me to tap into my higher creative self. Most of my poetry has been a gift to me and also my gift to a very special woman.; [a.] Waupaca, WI

SIMPSON, EURIELL C.
[b.] November 12, 1945, Jamaica, West Indies; [memb.] National Writers Union 1993; [oth. writ.] Walk With Me (poem), published at Boston University 1992, Keep Going (poem) published 1992, A Note of Thanks (poem) published 1993.

SIMPSON, JAN
[b.] August 16, 1937, Cayuga, ND; [p.] Casper and Marie Detling; [m.] Ronald Simpson (Deceased 1958-1992); [ch.] Bruce Alan (Dec'd), Lorie Marie; [ed.] St. John's McNamara School of Nursing, Rapid City, SD; [occ.] Reg. Nurse; [oth. writ.] Just beginning; [pers.] My life has been a mountain, a process of growth thru which I have learned wisdom. As I strive to conquer the Mt. I must stop at the

summit for now, For it is at the foothills I have learned to be humble and share with others the gift of life. If I can enlighten someone's life for a moment, I have truly lived.; [a.] Hill City, SD

SIMPSON, KENNETH ANDREW
[pen.] "Angel"; [b.] July 2, 1916, Saint Louis, MO; [p.] Andrew and Veronica Simpson; [m.] Antoinette Peca Simpson, September 2, 1943; [ch.] Christine Yvonne Simpson, Michael Andrew Simpson; [ed.] Degree in Psychology; [occ.] Retired; [memb.] Kiwanis - Methodist Church; [hon.] Charter Member of Top Value Trading Stamp Company, Presidents Club - years 1967 and 1968, In Top Ten (of 200+ salesman) for two years.; [oth. writ.] Dedicated to "Victoria" 65 unpublished poems and 60 life experience essays from childhood to present.; [pers.] Life experience and mood writings have filled lonely hours. Short essays are true accounts and have not been offered for publication. My entire life passes as I reread these homey pieces.; [a.] Bloomington, IN

SIMPSON, LINDA MARIE
[pen.] Marie Lynn; [b.] April 20, 1956, Tacoma; [p.] Jim and Rose Becktold; [ch.] Christine Joyce Marie Simpson; [ed.] Lincoln High, Clover Park Vocational College; [occ.] Assembly Work; [oth. writ.] Several poems, fantasy and science fiction, short stories - children's picture book stories, one currently seeking publication.; [pers.] Always believe in yourself - never quit trying to achieve your goals.; [a.] Tacoma, WA

SIMS, KELSO GAMMILL
[b.] August 7, 1957, Greenwood, MS; [p.] Kelso F. and Mamie G. Sims; [m.] Katrina Sims, 1st November 7, 1980, present April 30, 1994; [ch.] 1st Stephanie and Blair; [ed.] Greenwood High School, Miss. State University; [occ.] Mgr./Engineering and Quality Assurance; [memb.] Society of Mfg. Engineers; [oth. writ.] 4 songs and 13 other poems (none published); [pers.] I write from strong feeling and experience. Even my fiction is based on strong hope and desire. Hopelessly bound by internal inspiration.; [a.] Boyle, MS

SINKS, NATALIE
[pen.] Natalie Sinks; [b.] August 31, 1979, Bakersfield, CA; [p.] Rick and Cathy Hood; [ed.] Student - a Junior in High School; [memb.] Cheerleader; [hon.] Honor Roll; [pers.] I was greatly influenced by my 5th grade teacher.; [a.] Bakersfield, CA

SISK, RALPH
[pen.] Short Fellow; [b.] October 13, 1917, Chicago Heights, IL; [p.] Ira C. Sisk, Lottie B.; [m.] Eileen, August 9, 1938; [ch.] Ralph Dale (Deceased) Penny Eileen; [ed.] High School and 1 yr. College taught close tolerence quality

control in Learning in Industry; [occ.] Retired; [memb.] Good Sam, First Baptist Church; [hon.] 1. Several driving awards (18 wheelers), 2. Several Commendations when I was a Juvenile Officer in Cook Co. ILL., 3. Made President's Club when I worked for John Hancock Ins. Co.; [oth. writ.] Have only sent one poem for publication. Have many on hand; [pers.] Most of my writings was inspired by my wonderful wife, Eileen.; [a.] Watseka, IL

SLAUF II, STEVEN JOHN
[b.] February 7, 1959, Iornton, MO; [p.] Harold and Norma Slauf; [m.] Divorced; [ch.] Crystal Lee. Slauf, Joshua A. Buelna; [occ.] Writer, Author, Model; [memb.] Country Creations Nashville Tenn, Advantage Press Inc., New York, NY, USA Fitness; [hon.] Advantage Press Writer's Award, Country Creations Song Award, Nashville Tenn.; [oth. writ.] Have wrote words for songs for singers, bands etc.; [pers.] I try to bring out the best meanings in words with feelings behind them. Influenced by Walt Whitman's in the early 1970's.; [a.] Fort Wayne, IN

SLAWINSKI, RICHARD
[pen.] Richard Andrew; [b.] July 8, 1973, Indiana; [p.] James and Linda; [ed.] Various Institutions - none more or less important then the next.; [occ.] Student of life.; [memb.] USLA, United States Lifeguarding Association, American Red Cross, United States Master Swimming.; [hon.] Every time I have pulled a swimmer, or non-swimmer as it may seem, from what may be conceived have saved a life is more an honor then one could with to love.; [oth. writ.] Forthcoming.; [pers.] It is fairly simple to learn something that has already been taught, but it is rather difficult to teach something that is not yet known.; [a.] Scotch Plains, NJ

SLOANE, CRAIG A.
[b.] October 15, 1970, Manhasset, NY; [m.] Donna Garon Sloane, January 6, 1996; [ed.] University of the State of New York, Regents College Degrees. Benjamin N. Cardozo School of Law; [occ.] Law Student; [memb.] American Bar Association; [hon.] H. Bert and Ruth Mark Scholarship; [a.] Tuckahoe, NY

SLUTSKY, JORDAN
[b.] August 13, 1980, Bronx, NY; [memb.] Ice Skating Institute of America, High School Related Membership, Varsity Tennis, Drama Club, Newspaper Staff (Creative Writing Editor), Class Secretary; [hon.] High Honor Roll; [oth. writ.] Many other poems, high school newspaper articles, and several short stories.; [pers.] My poetry represents honesty, maturity can only develop from truth.; [a.] Ellenville, NY

SMALLING, DORIS
[b.] December 21, 1920, Lake Andes, SD; [p.]

Willis and Viola Cleeton; [m.] Duel Smalling, March 4, 1950; [ch.] Roger, Janet, Marcia; [ed.] Eugene High School, OR, Master's Degree in English and Education, Los Angeles; [occ.] Writer, Retired School Teacher; [memb.] Eastmont Baptist Church, VFW Auxiliary, Phi Beta Kappa Alumnae, Wenatchee Christian Writers Fellowship, Portals Poetry Club, Wenatchee Christian Women's Club; [hon.] Phi Beta Kappa, Cum Laude, Outstanding Teachers of America, Valley Forge Freedom Foundation Teacher's Award, Valley Forge Poetry Award; [oth. writ.] Editor for Church Newsletters, National Collegiate Poetry Review, Broken Streets Poetry, Sunflowers Seeds, Dramas for Schools, Newspaper articles.; [pers.] I like to express my love of God and country. I've been influenced very strongly by early American poets.; [a.] East Wenatchee, WA

SMITH, ALICE
[b.] December 15, 1940, Waterman, IL; [p.] Arthur and Agatha Hampton; [m.] Charles W. Smith, June 23, 1962; [ch.] Roderick, Steven, Anita, Bradley, Alexander; [ed.] Waterman High School BS in Ed. Northern IL University; [occ.] Home maker; [memb.] St. Mary Church, Liturgy Commission Assistant Director St. Mary's Choirs; [pers.] My writing began in the form of journalist. I can express a depth of feeling that might otherwise take volumes to say. My poetry becomes an instrument of instruction from the Divine when I use journalist as a meditative process.; [a.] Malta, IL

SMITH, BONNIE LYNN
[b.] August 18, 1958, Chicago, IL:; [p.] Raymond F. and Karen M. Smith; [ed.] Carl Schurz H.S.; [occ.] Semi-Pro Fisherman, and former Banking Sales Rep.; [memb.] American Fishing Assoc., N.O.W., Nat. Dem. Committee, Illinois Spina Bifida Assoc.; [hon.] Illinois Big Fish Award-1994; [oth. writ.] Poems published in local newspaper and high school poetry annual.; [pers.] Having been born with the birth defect spina-bifida and also an amputee, my life has been painful and challenging. Poetry has been an outlet and escape for my dreams and imagination. I am passionate for nature, animals and music and individualism is my personal doctrine.; [a.] Chicago, IL

SMITH, CALVIN
[b.] June 16, 1950, Paintsville, KY; [p.] Charles and Delphia Smith; [ch.] Erin Michelle, Richard Scott; [ed.] As New York regents 1981, currently studying mental health and mental retardation with a goal of creative therapy, Columbus State, CC; [occ.] Student, Columbus State Community College; [memb.] American Legion, Hilliard, OH; [hon.] Dean's List Columbus State; [oth. writ.] Several poems in newspapers, Columbus State, Community

College Spring Street; [pers.] U.S. Army Club Retired. Don't fear the changes life thrust upon you, sometimes they are guided from beyond our sight.; [a.] Upper Arlington, OH

SMITH, DAWN
[b.] December 1, 1965; [p.] Earl and Elizabeth Willitts; [m.] William John Smith, October 22, 1988; [ed.] Graduated from Pemberton Twp. currently attending Burlington County College.; [occ.] Recently transferred from Sales Coordinator to Accounting; [memb.] Board of Directors for Chi Iota a chapter of Phi Theta Kappa; [hon.] Phi Theta Kappa, Dean's List.; [oth. writ.] Childrens short stories and other poems.

SMITH, FAWN M.
[pen.] Fawn; [b.] July 21, 1964, Barre, VT; [p.] Douglas and Cheri Lachue; [m.] Mark D. Smith; [ch.] Timothy Lee; [pers.] We are strong...we are fragile....we are human; [a.] Cumming, GA

SMITH, FRANCES NOBLE
[b.] March 21, 1936, Manhattan; [p.] Camillah and Francis O. Noble; [m.] Dubois T. Smith, October 26, 1968; [ch.] Dubois T. Smith II, Dorothy Miller Smith II; [ed.] Viewpoint School, Hunter College; [occ.] Lay Ministe and Homemaker and Happily Married.; [pers.] I write from my heart and whatever comes becomes. I love children, the out of doors, my family, hearts and angels.; [a.] Bridgehampton, NY

SMITH, JOYCE
[pen.] Joyce Smith Thomas; [b.] April 28, 1934, Canton, TX; [p.] Alonzo and Bethfeenia Smith; [m.] William James Thomas, June 8, 1954; [ch.] Five; [ed.] 12th Grade, Grass Root Organizing Positive Paranting, A servey of the Bible; [occ.] Writing and Prayer Intercessor; [memb.] MAACP, Woman's Voters Leauge, Interracial Council, Creative Women of Positive Motivation, Chairperson and Repersentive of L.A. Housing Authority.; [hon.] Servey of the Bible, Poetic Society Diamon Homer Award, Community Volunteer Worker of Year. The Dove Award Outstanding Parent of Utah Elementary School Volunteers Award; [oth. writ.] Poems: I Am Some Body, 2) Walk With Me My Child, 3) The Black Woman, 4) Wake Up Black America, 5) Gods Glory, Book: Lizzie Jumped the Broom.; [pers.] My greatest satisfaction from my writing go forth to bring some pleasure as well as joy and happiness in reading my writings.; [a.] Los Angeles, CA

SMITH, MICHELLE B.
[pen.] Shalee' Smith; [b.] October 13, 1967, San Diego, CA; [p.] Ethel May Findlay, Rick Van Horn; [m.] Kirk Douglas Smith, June 27, 1993; [ed.] Clairemont High School; [memb.] Order of Eastern Star LaJolla #479, Past Honored Queen, Job's Daughters Pacific Beach #141, Independent Order

of Foresters, Past Miss Hospitality IOF; [hon.] High School Poetry Book, Grand Bethel Poetry Contest, California; [pers.] Open your heart and love thy neighbor. Show compassion be caring and kind. Shun greed and conceit. See the world through the eyes of love.; [a.] San Juan Capistrano, CA

SMITH, ROBERTA
[pen.] Destiny Fate Santangelo; [b.] January 17, 1978, Missoula, MT; [p.] Donna and David Groskopf; [m.] Torben Bender, May 1, 1994 (going together); [ed.] Anderson Elementary, Hobbs Elementary, McKormick Junior High, North Middle School, Everett High, Lake Stevens High (to be), Everett Community College; [occ.] Student; [memb.] Honor Choir '93 and '94, Wyoming Childrens Choir '90; [hon.] Numerous Musical Festivals Contests, from 8th grade to now, winning and rating well; [oth. writ.] Numerous poems, my (some) Favorites being Hells Hands, influence of Nightfall, Jester's Song, Dyer's Eve, Suicide's Dominion...; [pers.] "Light may linger in the skies, but night will return and conquer..." My writing strongly reflects the events of my life, I hope, someday, that whomever reads any of it feels comforted. They're not the only one...; [a.] Everett, WA

SMITH, SANDRA L.
[b.] February 6, 1940, Union, MS; [p.] Eleanor and William Buckwalter; [m.] Divorced; [ch.] Kevin S. Smith and Melinda L. Stinson; [ed.] University High School (Los Angeles) B.A. Elementary Education - U. of Colorado M.S. S.W. Social work U. of Tennessee; [occ.] Social Worker, [memb.] Natl. Assoc. of Social Workers; [hon.] Phi Kappa Phi; [oth. writ.] Poems published in other anthologies through the Natl. Library of Poetry, and letters to the editor of The Commercial Appeal and Modern Maturity.; [pers.] My poetry is a way of reflecting my observations on many aspects of life, as well as expressing my feelings about these aspects. It s my hope that my poems may strike a chord within the reader and plant a seed for thought.; [a.] Germantown, TN

SMITH, SHARON E.
[b.] August 20, 1973, Macon, GA; [p.] Dwight and Frances Smith; [ed.] Southwest High School, Georgia College - Bachelor of Science degree in Biology; [occ.] Veterinary Technician; [memb.] Phi Kappa Phi, Gamma Beta Phi, Tri-Beta Biological Honor Society; [hon.] Cum Laude honor graduate, National Dean's List; [oth. writ.] Several poems published in school literary magazine.; [pers.] When you meet someone who doesn't have a smile, give them one of yours.; [a.] Musella, GA

SMITH, SUSAN C.
[pen.] Sue Smith; [b.] October 21, 1962, Pueblo, CO; [p.] John L. and Sharon E. Goodbar; [m.]

Rodney D. Smith, June 18, 1983; [ch.] Jeromy Ivan and Ethan Cole; [ed.] East High School, Abundant Life Bible Institute; [occ.] Administrative Assistant, Kurt Manufacturing, Pueblo, CO; [oth. writ.] Numerous poems, skits and short stories. "Reflections of Love", a book collection of inspirational poetry.; [pers.] May my words heal instead of hurt, comfort instead of complain. May they be said in wisdom and love instead of anger and vanity for they are a reflection of my soul. May it always speak, and seek, truth.; [a.] Pueblo, CO

SMITH, TONY A.
[b.] Frankston, TX; [ed.] BBA - Major in Marketing; [memb.] Kiwanis Club, Fourth Degree Knights of Columbus; [hon.] Who's Who World wide 1993, Honor Graduate U.S. Army Air Defense School; [pers.] Never under estimate the human spirit.; [a.] Palestine, TX

SMOOT, RUTH
[occ.] Management Consultant; [oth. writ.] Unpublished writer who only recently began writing poetry. My dream is to launch a new career as a fiction writer upon retirement from my current profession in the near future.; [a.] Norcross, GA

SNEAD, KATHI B.
[b.] May 13, 1956, Muskegon, MI; [p.] Dorothy A. Czinder; [m.] David Snead, June 24, 1978; [ch.] David Franklin Jr., Kimberly Michelle; [ed.] Osbourn High School, Northern Virginia Community College; [occ.] Freelance Writer, Family Self-Sufficiency Coordinator, Manassas, VA; [memb.] Manassas Presbyterian Church; [oth. writ.] Feature stories in local newspapers, children's stories and other poetry.; [pers.] My poetry and story telling has evolved because of the family members who told me their stories, taught me to love books and continue to remind me to never stop dreaming, my mother, my uncle Jim, my sister, my husband and my children.; [a.] Manassas, VA

SNELL, LILLY ANN
[pen.] Annie Bee; [b.] January 30, 1942, Auburntown, TN; [p.] Ross Leach, Reba Rogers; [m.] June 9, 1959; [ch.] Jeffrey Ross Underhill, Jennifer Dover, [ed.] Auburn High School; [occ.] Homemaker; [hon.] Poems, published in local newspaper. "Vietnam Prayer", published in paper during the war - kept my phone ringing.; [pers.] Encouragement from my mother, an avid lover of poetry and reading was my greatest influence to continue writing.; [a.] Murfreesboro, TN

SNYDER, BILL
[pen.] The Sage of Hootin-Holler; [b.] August 30, 1914, Pittsburgh, PA; [p.] Sylvester and Musetta Snyder; [m.] Roberta Shaver Snyder, March 30, 1946; [ch.] Carolyn and William, Jr.;

[ed.] Ligonier (PA) High, Indiana V., Purdue, (Occ.) Electrical/Nuclear Engr. Navy Dept., Westing House; [occ.] Retired; [memb.] "Silver Spring Lawn Mowers", Baptist Church, Gideons; [hon.] Completed engineering on "Couldn't Be Done" designs. Leader in delivery "On Schedule" of nuclear plant equipments.; [oth. writ.] Two Patents: Ship Speed Ind. Eqpt.; [pers.] Never got over being voted "Most Witty" by my High School class. (Six grade) Won III, Logan, Matt, Lydia (Snyder) plus Michael, Jessica (Engram).; [a.] Silver Spring, MD

SONG, JOY
[pen.] Dana Lee; [m.] Peter Nelson; [ed.] Mt. St. Mary Academy, Cornell University; [occ.] Computer Instructor, Rental Agent; [hon.] French Honor Society, Jacob Albright Scholar; [oth. writ.] Short Fiction, Essays, and poetry published in literary magazines, poem in Mists of Enchantment, currently working on novels and short fiction, along with my own book of poetry.; [a.] Ithaca, NY

SOOKDEO, REBECCA A.
[b.] March 24, 1963, Martinsville, VA; [p.] Charlie Gravely, Lenora Gravely; [m.] Narish Sookdeo, August 12, 1992; [ch.] Indira Sookdeo; [ed.] Laurel Park High School; [hon.] Pace Setter Achievement Award; [pers.] This poem was layed upon my heart to write, and after you've read it, and need comfort, remember this poem.; [a.] Virginia Beach, VA

SOPER, MIMI
[b.] September 8, 1942, Washington, IN; [p.] Phyllis and Joe Wade; [m.] Henry Soper, April 8, 1989; [ch.] Seven; [ed.] High School; [occ.] Admn. Assistant; [oth. writ.] Local Newspaper; [pers.] I'm inspired by my family especially my husband, Hank. He get's a big kick out of seeing me published. And I must not forget Evelyn Heine, my teacher, who said write something everyday and I do!; [a.] Crystal Lake, IL

SOUTHIN, VIOLA
[b.] June 27, Guelph, Ont.; [m.] Leslie; [ch.] Two sons David and John, two grandchildren Cheryl and Marty; [pers.] We only stay in Florida for five or six months. We'll be back in Canada April 4. Plays bridge euchre and cribbage. Son John is a retired Prof from McGill Univ. in Montreal. We'll be married 60 yrs. June 29, 1966.; [a.] Fort Pierce, FL

SPAGNOLINI, EVA MARIE
[b.] December 17, 1978, Colorado Springs, CO; [p.] Judy K. Spagnolini, Leo R. Spagnolini; [ed.] Fountain Fort Carson High, I'm in my junior year and plan to attend college, to work in a field with children pref. social work.; [memb.] I am currently a member of the Writing Club. Next year I will run for president.; [hon.] I'm always a honor roll student. Presidential Academic Achievement

Award in '91.; [oth. writ.] I was published in the 1992-93 Anthology of Poetry by Young Americans. I'll also have 4 poems published in the Writing Club Book this year.; [pers.] All of my poetry comes from my heart and most is inspired by my true love Michael Ball!; [a.] Fountain, CO

SPANOGLE, DAX FREDERICK
[b.] June 21, 1983, Arlington, VA; [p.] Fred and Judy; [ed.] The Flint Hill School (K-7); [occ.] Student; [memb.] Music (Saxophone and Piano) Flint Hill School Basketball Team's Starting 5 Drama; [hon.] Dean's List, 2nd Degree Black Belt, HWARDO Honor Student; [a.] Oakton, VA

SPEAR, MARIAN E.
[b.] February 14, 1921, Erie, PA; [p.] Roy Spear, Arminta Spear; [ed.] Strong Vincent High School; [occ.] Retired; [memb.] Christ United Methodist Church; [oth. writ.] Poems for church publications, several sacred music compositions (words and music).; [pers.] A brilliant person once referred to my poetry as "Honest". I was flattered.; [a.] Erie, PA

SPECK, NADINE SAUVAJOT
[b.] August 18, 1928, New York, NY; [p.] George and Flore Sauvajot; [m.] Roger A. Speck, March 2, 1957; [ch.] George and Claudine; [ed.] BA in Education; [occ.] Part-time Teacher in Adult Education; [memb.] Alliance Francaise, French Cottage, Club De La Petanque, CCAE (School Organization); [hon.] Teacher of the Year (for Calif. State), Charter Member of The US Normandy Committee; [oth. writ.] Diaries, Short Stories, Essays, Journal D'Exode (in French and English), (War Journal) on The Allied Invasion (1944); [pers.] I derive great joy from writing, both in French and in English. I wish to leave my memories as my humble legacy to my children.; [a.] San Diego, CA

SPELL, TERESA Y.
[pen.] TYS; [b.] November 11, 1957, Durham, NC; [p.] L. P. Spell, Mary V. Spell; [ed.] Southern High, Durham Technical Community College, Shaw University; [occ.] Estimator/In-House Sales Representative, Universal Printing, Durham, NC

SPENCE, JIMMY
[b.] August 15, 1946, Waco, TX; [p.] Quinea Spence, Lois Spence; [m.] Esther Spence, July 31, 1985; [ch.] Four children - four stepchildren, 1 foster child; [ed.] High School graduate, 2 yrs. University High Waco, TX., 1 yr. Richfield High Waco, TX.; [occ.] Work for cabinet shop in Tulsa, Oklahoma; [memb.] Tulsa Moose Lodge #862 for 5 yrs.; [oth. writ.] None published One printed in local Moose Lodge bulletin.; [pers.] Have been writing for 25 yrs. but all were lost or forgotten until about 11 yrs. ago when my wife inspired me to start writing again. This will be my first published poem.; [a.] Tulsa, OK

SPENCER, SHERRIE
[pen.] Olivia; [b.] October 21, 1972, Bronx, NY; [p.] Gordon Jones, Linda Spencer; [ed.] Public School 21, Ollinville Junior High, Evander Child's High School, Monroe College; [hon.] Citizenship Awards (3); [pers.] Thank you. I will continue to write from my heart.; [a.] Bronx, NY

SPINDLER, SANDRA E.
[b.] March 30, 1942, Detroit, MI; [p.] Shirley and Henry Deochoa; [m.] Stephen A. Spindler, June 9, 1984; [ch.] 4 Children, 3 Grandchildren; [ed.] Waterford Township High School, Class of 1960; [occ.] Police Civilian Aid; [oth. writ.] I have several poems I have written but this is the first time I decided to publish one; [pers.] I love to write about the beautiful things of life or of those especially close to me.; [a.] Pontiac, MI

SPIRO, JACK
[b.] March 1, 1920, Queens, NY; [p.] Dora, George; [m.] Divorced, 1946; [ch.] Jan Louis - Gail Lynne; [ed.] John Adams H.S., Pratt Institute, N.Y., NYU (Advertising Program), Dale Carnegie Course, NY; [occ.] Semi-Retired, Adv. Consultant; [memb.] Delray Art League; [hon.] Cornell Museum, Lake Worth Coop Gallery, Delray City Hall Gallery; [oth. writ.] The boosters, (Novel in Development), newspaper editorials.; [pers.] Am involved in fine art (Oils) as well as creative writing, continuous local exhibitions.; [a.] Boca Raton, FL

SPITALERI, ANTOINETTE M.
[b.] Italy; [ch.] Two children; [occ.] Retired; [memb.] Past member of Northern California Songwriters Assoc.; [hon.] Honorable Mention in past contest; [oth. writ.] Numerous poems and songs over the years; [pers.] I have been a poet and songwriter for many years. I have a great respect for life, love, and nature which have greatly influenced my work. I am also a family person and enjoy spending time with my children and grandchildren.; [a.] San Jose, CA

SPITALERI, JULIE ANN
[pen.] Jules; [b.] October 29, 1968, Santa Clara, CA; [p.] Fred Spitaleri, Yvonne McDonald; [ed.] Santa Teresa High School San Jose, CA (Class of 1987). Silver State Beauty College-Sparks, Nevada Licencsed Manicurist; [occ.] Receptionist Santa Clara, CA; [memb.] Nature Conservancy and The Humaine Society; [hon.] Many awards in dance competitions.; [oth. writ.] Currently writing my first novel. (Historical Time Travel Romance) I have also wrote many other unpublished poems.; [pers.] I am supported and inspired by my caring family and loyal boyfriend. "May we all find our hidden talents from God and use them wisely and honorably for him."; [a.] Fremont, CA

SPIVEY, DEBORAH ANN MCVEIGH TINDAL

[b.] November 19, 1955, Montclair, NJ; [p.] Thomas and Elizabeth McVeigh Sr.; [m.] James Darwin Spivey Jr., November 19, 1988; [ch.] Todd, Tanya and Tavis Tindal; [ed.] Roxburgh High, Succasunna, NJ, Wilfred Academy, Succasunna NJ, County College of Morris, Randolph, NJ; [oth. writ.] 1 Book of Poems "A Thought About Aids - A Collection of Poems"; [pers.] Voices of many can make change if only voices of many come together as one.

SPLANE, TIMOTHY J.

[b.] January 20, 1961, Wilmington, DE; [p.] Dr. and Mrs. Francis X. Splane; [m.] Claudine V. Splane, May 2, 1992; [ch.] Casey Alexavier Splane; [ed.] High School Diploma, 2 yrs of High Education; [pers.] Poetry is a reflexion of oneself towards others and the world as a whole.; [a.] Lakewood, CO

SPRAGLEY JR., JOHN LEE

[b.] March 6, 1969, Manhattan; [p.] Mary M. and John Lee Spragley Sr; [ed.] Grover Cleveland High School Medgar Evers College; [occ.] I.R.S. employee Army Veteran; [memb.] Member of the Alpha and Omega Society of the African Christian Teachers Played saxophone for Heritage Symphony Orchestra; [hon.] Army Achievement Medal; [pers.] I write what I feel; [a.] Brooklyn, NY

SROKA, T. NEIL

[b.] April 14, 1984; [p.] Tim Sroka and Susan Kenski-Sroka; [ed.] Pritchett Elementary School, Tripp Middle School, Meridian Middle School; [occ.] Student at Meridian Middle School; [memb.] Boy Scouts of America, Troop 79; [hon.] God and Country award, Tenderfoot in Boyscouts; [oth.] Ode to Life; [pers.] I feel poetry reflects people's inner-self. I dedicate all my work to my family and my 6th grade English teacher Mrs. Borg.; [a.] Buffalo Grove, IL

STABLER, HELEN

[b.] July 21, 1920, Fort Wayne, IN; [p.] Chris and Emma Doenges; [m.] Deceased, June 6, 1941; [ch.] Carole Tscmannen, Barbara Morse, Bob Stabler; [ed.] I had grade school and high school; [occ.] Homemaker, live alone; [memb.] Eagles, Trinity Lutheran Church; [hon.] I live here at North Highlands Hi Rise, and, one of my poems is in the Newsletter each month, I used to have poems in the Eagles Newsletters, Airie 3512; [oth. writ.] 1. The Man with the Red Torch, 2. The Rapture, 3. September Moods, 4. Special Gift, 5. Mama's Journey Home, 6. Beloved Sister, 7. Kathy, six of many. I'm 75 years old. Wrote my first at 16.; [pers.] One of my "Thou Little Angels" has gone back to Heaven. My son passed away 2 yrs. ago in June. We miss him so, but he's gone to a better place.; [a.] Fort Wayne, IN

STAFFORD, CONNIE LYNN

[pen.] Chawn Laurentaylor; [b.] May 15, 1957, Larned, KS; [p.] Anne Marie Zimmerman; [ch.] Ty Rollin Keith; [ed.] Nickerson High - Nickerson, KS., Friends University - Wichita, KS., Bryan Institute - Arlington, TX.; [occ.] Mgr./Medicaı Tech at Irving Healthcare System - Irving, Tx.; [memb.] Classic Car/Truck Club Stampede Dancing Club; [hon.] 1) Honorable Mention of "Those Ole Days", National Library of Poetry. 2) Behind the Scenes Employee at Irving Healthcare System - Irving, Tx.; [oth. writ.] Church Newsletters, Creative Writing in High School, written 2 books, non published as a hobby.; [pers.] Honor and glory to God for all talents and wisdom he has bestowed unto me. Love and appreciation to my family and friend - Irma Shampain, for their support and believing in me.; [a.] Irving, TX

STALLARD, BARBARA J.

[pen.] Barbara J. Stallard; [b.] November 12, 1952, Ohio Country; [p.] Frances and Herman Ray Fulton; [ed.] High School, 2 years Computer Science, Dec. 1996, will have 4 year degree in Psychology, will go on for my Master's Degree; [occ.] Computer Operator; [memb.] Comp. Volunteer; [oth. writ.] Poems that I've written that aren't published.; [pers.] To always believe, dream and feel. To become a great clinical psychologist. To know that true inner beauty lies within my soul.; [a.] Louisville, KY

STAMPLEY, ESTONIA NAREY

[b.] September 29, 1976, Murray, UT; [p.] Luvonia Stampley; [ed.] Campbell High School, University of Georgia (still attending); [occ.] Student at University of Georgia; [memb.] American Museum of Natural History; [oth. writ.] In the process of writing two novels and two screenplays.; [pers.] Whether it's in art where I can see it or in writing where I can feel it, I always try to create life.; [a.] Marietta, GA

STANDFIELD, NADINE

[b.] February 3, 1931, Minneapolis, MN; [p.] Alice and Archie Austin; [ch.] Kathleen, Craig, Duane, Randy, Kevin, Donette; [ed.] South High Institute of Childrens Literature Long Ridge Writers Group; [occ.] Retired; [memb.] Abiding Savior Lutheran Church Childrens Ministries, International Society of Poets, Blaine American Legion Post 566; [hon.] Honored by God awarded a loving family; [oth. writ.] Several poems in anthologies from National Library of Poetry poem in the church vine branch several short stories and articles (as yet unpublished); [pers.] Always keep God near, for with God by your side you can accomplish many great things.

STANG, WENDA

[b.] January 5, 1943, New Orleans, LA; [p.] George St. Peter and Bobbye Nelson St. Peter;

[ed.] Upper Columbia Academy, Walla Walla College, La Sierra College Year Abroad at Collongessous-Saleve, France, School of Veterinary Medicine, Washington State University, University of Denver; [hon.] High School Graduating Class Vice President, Salutatorian, and School Paper Editor, Degree in French with Very High Honors; [pers.] "Tomorrow, at dawn..." is dedicated to my good friend, Dr. Geoffrey B. Heron, who encouraged me in my decision to translate French Poetry after the death of my beloved dog, Buffy. Buffy was my inspiration for this poem, the first of many now completed.; [a.] Denver, CO

STANLEY, WENDELL

[b.] December 2, 1981, Houston, TX; [p.] Dede House and Leroy Stanley; [ed.] Currently in 8th grade; [occ.] Student - part time tug boat work; [hon.] Several school awards in writing; [pers.] Enjoy animals, have 3 dogs 5 cats. Enjoy future farmers of America. (FFA); [a.] Houston, TX

STANTON JR., SCOTT M.

[b.] May 23, 1979, Washington DC; [p.] Diana B. and Wilfred F. Hoyer, [ed.] Currently studying 3rd year at Westview High School; [occ.] Student; [memb.] Charter member of the Red-Lib Procreation, A Creative Arts Club; [oth. writ.] Two original collections of unpublished material.; [pers.] We should all ponder our grim moralities with an erotic imagination. I believe doing so is an essential step in blameless schooling.; [a.] Beaverton, OR

STEELE, RANDY JOHN

[pen.] Round Stick, Favorite; [b.] June 18, 1953, Zion; [p.] Jay and Bev; [m.] Linda; [ch.] 4, two boys, two girls; [ed.] Westminster College, Utah State - graduate of Bryman Business College and have BA English, University of Utah; [occ.] Free lance writer and movie extra. A steel worker, construction laborer, rough-Framer, a father, a husband, bicycle racer, runner, a clerk; [memb.] The human race, LDS Church; [hon.] None other than being alive - that's all; [oth. writ.] School Newspaper, American Express publications; [pers.] Create poetic pieces of prosaic experience. Put together phrases of pedestrian lore that speaks an uncommon truth to each other. Place an image, a written art-print, on the cognitive walls in the reader's living room mind. Access the imagination through poetic bites. Restore daydreaming to its throne.

STEELMAN, KATHRYN

[b.] September 4, 1957, Albuquerque, NM; [p.] Deanna Seibors; [m.] Michael Steelman, May 8, 1988; [ch.] Tommy Steelman; [ed.] Sunbright High School, Tennessee Tech University; [occ.] Nursing Assistant; [memb.] Calvary Baptist Church; [hon.] Essay Contest at Life Care Center of Morgan County, TN; [pers.] I love working with the elderly people, they are our backbone of this country. I try to put in writing of a poem of how the elderly would talk to the world.; [a.] Wartburg, TN

STEINER, SHELLY
[pen.] Shel E. Holliday; [b.] January 21, 1957, Aberdeen, WA; [p.] Denny and Kay Rowley; [ch.] Chad Michael, Cody Ashton; [ed.] Puyallup High; [occ.] Domestic Engineer!; [memb.] Milton Writer's Club; [pers.] I give my heart and soul to my poetry, because I believe in order to reach the very soul of a person, you must first touch their heart with the giving of your own.; [a.] Auburn, WA

STEPHENS, KHADEIJAH
[pen.] Anne Stephens; [b.] September 7, 1940, Bristol, England; [memb.] Co-Founder of the Mosque of the Internet; [oth. writ.] Islamic verses for children on the mosque web site.; [pers.] I am excited that CNN has linked to the mosque and it is discovery channel's choice in Islam. It has received over 100,000 hits.; [a.] Tesuque, NM

STEPHENS, SHARLYN K.
[b.] December 18, 1944, South Gate, CA; [p.] Sheldon and Zena Shrier; [m.] Timothy, January 9, 1965; [ch.] Tim, David, Jamilyn; [ed.] LPN 1978 - Shapiro School of Nursing, Det., MI, RN 1985 Monroe Community College, Monroe, MI; [occ.] Registered Nurse, Main Pre-op Oakwood Hospital, Dearborn, MI; [memb.] Three grandchildren (Matthew, Ashley, Kaitlyn); [pers.] Old man was written about 1980 to my father (Sheldom Pete Shrier) who has since passed away (1985) without ever reading my poem. I dedicate this poem, with love, to my Dad.; [a.] Southgate, MI

STEVENS, DEANNA
[b.] November 6, 1944, Lawrencevile, IL; [p.] Otis and Verdona Greenlee; [m.] Tom Stevens, January 4, 1964; [ch.] Tony Keith, Barry Gene; [occ.] Teach Future Woman Christian Workshop; [memb.] River of Life Church; [oth. writ.] Over 100 poems covering topics from "Todays Life" to the "Politically Right"; [pers.] I am not a poet. These poems are strictly from the Holy Spirit to God's people before Jesus' return.; [a.] Smyrna, TN

STEVENS JR., MICHAEL C.
[b.] September 10, 198, Bloomsburg, PA; [p.] Bonnie S. Stevens, Michael C. Stevens Sr.; [ed.] Attend Waverly Jr-Sr High School, Waverly, NY; [memb.] Waverly School Band, Waverly School Chorus, Waverly Summer Theatre, All County Chorus for Noga County, NY; [hon.] President Award, Spelling Award, Good Citizenship Award; [pers.] I have the emotional goal for people to be influenced by my writings,

and may they relate my poems to the everyday decisions that come and go.; [a.] Waverly, NY

STEVENS, SHAWNA M.
[b.] May 19, 1977, Big Spring, TX; [p.] Douglas and Dorothy Stevens; [ed.] High School Diploma; [occ.] Student, Baylor University, Waco, TX; [memb.] Fencing Club, Herman Sons and Mt. Olive Lutheran Church; [hon.] Certificate of Recognition from the 1993 Olympic Committee for Volunteer Work; [oth. writ.] Two poems published in "The High School Poetry Magazine"; [a.] San Antonio, TX

STEVENSON, PAULA PATTERSON
[pen.] Diane L. B.; [b.] January 25, 1951, Gowanda, NY; [p.] Robert and Sally Patterson; [m.] Terry Robert Stevenson, July 31, 1971; [ch.] Jodi Diane, Tammara Dawn, Tara Denise; [ed.] Troy Area Schools, Troy, Pennsylvania East Forest School, Marienville, Pennsylvania graduated May 29, 1969, Duff's Business Institute, Pittsburgh, PA, graduated April 1971; [occ.] Clerk Typist for a Job Training Consortium/Part-time Waitress; [memb.] First Presbyterian Church, Marienville, PA, MACA (Marienville Area Civic Assoc.), Marienville, PA; [hon.] Salutatorian Class of 1969, East Forest School, Marienville, PA; [oth. writ.] Poem published by: EPS Publishing in the book "Reflections of Life" poem published by: National Library of Poetry in the book "Tomorrow's Dream"; [pers.] Depending on the mood that I am in, all my poems are written from my feelings. Also writing poetry is self-healing for me.; [a.] Marienville, PA

STEVRER, KIFFIN
[b.] January 19, 1978; [p.] David and Judy; [ed.] I am a High School Senior.; [a.] Scott Depot, WV

STEWART, GEORGE J.
[b.] March 6, 1933, Staten Island, NY; [p.] Dr. Geo and Marion Stewart; [m.] Divorced, 1956-86; [ch.] Five Children/Eight Grandchildren; [ed.] AA Bus Norfolk Junior College, Norfolk, Ne., additional course work, Wayne-State Ne., except College Fl.; [occ.] Self employed writer; [oth. writ.] I have written three books which have been recently published. The first, There is the Egg—There is The Seed—Then Life gets Complicated. The second, —We Three. The third, The Circle—Less than one hundred pages to a new look at Life.; [pers.] I have visited many countries and observed several kinds of societies around the world as a tourist, while in the military, and as a two time Peace Corps volunteer. My writing is intended to bring home the different perspectives I learned from those experiences.

STEWART, REBECCA
[b.] April 7, 1964, Greenville MS; [p.] Mr. L.R. Stewart and Barbara Stewart; [ed.] Associate

Degree in Data Processing; [occ.] Self-employed; [memb.] National Spinal Cord Injury Hotline; [oth. writ.] poem published in another poetry book; [pers.] I am a quadraplegic and don't accept no for an answer.; [a.] Gilmer TX.

STIDHAM, RICHARD C.
[b.] January 23, 1959, Upland, CA; [p.] Robert and Patricia Stidham; [m.] Kim Laney; [ch.] One; [ed.] G.E.D. 1 year of College; [occ.] Noble Home Asst. Manager; [memb.] Moose Lodge, Elks Lodge Sons of American Legend; [hon.] Awarded several times in aircraft work, for Zeroins ship under budget and quality work.; [oth. writ.] Just poems and songs I've wrote for my family members.; [pers.] My poem was my inner feeling of myself and my spiritual feelings of what God and I share, that none at the rest of world sees. But perhaps can relate to my visions. With an open mind.; [a.] Lancaster, CA

STIENSTRA, CHRIS
[b.] March 1949, Whitinsville, MA; [p.] Cecilia (Cis); [ch.] Kim, Kelly, Derek; [ed.] Bachelors Degree Industrial Management Technology; [occ.] Sales/Service Manager, Gockel America; [oth. writ.] Published in last years issue of "Tomorrow Never Knows," also published in "Cimera," "Words of Wisdom" and "The Advocate."; [pers.] I write from a love of expression and a desire to make poetry words for everyone to read and enjoy.; [a.] East Douglas, MA

STIFF, JOHN M.
[pen.] "Old Med"; [b.] November 23, 1914, Bristol, England; [p.] Charles John, Winfred Dorothea; [m.] Florence Louise Adams, October 10, 1942; [ch.] Cramer, Brenda, David, Roy; [ed.] Arlington High, Lowell Tech. Adv. Machin Design, Bus. Ind. Management, MIT - Public Speaking, Harvard - Ind. Electronics - (Night); [occ.] Retired; [memb.] Computer Volunteer in Public and Parochial Schools in CT and FL - Member 60 voice Choir of Unit. Methodist Church; [hon.] Awards for work design and build - in space program; [oth. writ.] Have many poems copyrighted but have not submitted to others.; [pers.] I write what I see and I paint and accurate picture with words.; [a.] Osprey, FL

STILL, WILLIAM DOYLE
[b.] August 25, 1936, Dickson, TN; [m.] Wanda Bishop Still, January 18, 1964; [ed.] Dickson High School, Anchorage Community College, University of Tennessee (Undergraduate studies); [occ.] Retired Marketing Mgr.; [oth. writ.] Unpublished poems and short stories.

STILLMAN, RUSS
[pen.] Russell Ryan Stillman; [b.] June 10, 1973, Bloomington, MN; [p.] Julie Ann Stillman and Paul Barnes; [ed.] Graduate 1991 Kennedy Senior High School; [occ.] Food Service

Employee, full time; [oth. writ.] Currently the author of 30 or so unpublished poems, and writing two novels.; [pers.] Poems should not bear names, only the words should tell the tales of the soul.; [a.] Bloomington, MN

STITES, MEL
[pen.] Mel Stites; [b.] March 27, 1914, Hanna, OK; [p.] William and Lou Stites; [m.] Vivian McDonald Stites, April 10, 1940; [ch.] Donald Dean Stites; [ed.] High School Diploma; [occ.] Retired Merchant. Too busy building a business to do anything else. Discontinued all writing for more than thirty years.; [hon.] God has honored me with a lovely family, my wife (Vivian), (The subject of the lyric you have chosen to print), my son (Don), his wife (Sally), grand-daughters (Angie and Cindy), their husbands (Jeff and Charles, great granddaughters (Chloe and Cailin), great grandsons (Josh and Collin); [oth. writ.] Poetry in three anthologies, one song in the Columbia record label, one song re-corded (1995), an Interview depicking life in Oklahoma around state hood time is in the Library Of Congress Archives in Washington, DC. Oh, yes my lyric extolling our big beautiful lake i.e. "Blackjack Shade Is In The Book Lake Eufaula Reflection.; [pers.] Patience..In All Things..Pace One's See. Make the right moves at the right time. Appreciate your blessings, accept all the tears.; [a.] Eufaula, OK

STOKER, SHERRY BOEDEKER
[pen.] Sherry Stoker; [b.] August 18, 1940, Brigham, UT; [p.] Bill Boedeker, Ruby Boedeker Wilson; [m.] Lowell R. Stoker, July 2, 1990; [ch.] Chris Hernandez-26, Jan Davis-35, Laurie Roberts-35; [ed.] B.S. Degree-Weber State University Composite Major Theatre Arts and Communications, English Minor, Secondary Teaching Certificate; [occ.] Teacher for U.S. Bur. of Reclamation, Weber Basin Job Corps Center (High School) Ogden, Utah; [memb.] Daughters of the Utah Pioneers, Western Two Steppers, Utah Education Association, A devotee of the Unity Church, S.L.C., Utah, Member of L.O.S. Church; [hon.] Best Actress award in the State of Utah, 1958 - H.S. State Competition. Best Actress, Weber State College - 2 years, Two awards for outstanding service to Weber Basin Job Corps Center for Christmas plays and winning the National Job Corps Essay contest - 1st place-2 years, 2nd-1 year, my students have either won at nationals or at region all but one year of the seven years the contest has been held - the contest is run by Joint action in community services out of Denver, CO. The students placing 1st place in the nation get #1,000.00 and a trip to Washington, DC, accompanied by me. We've gone twice.; [oth. writ.] I write songs that I like to sing and would like to publish - especially in the Western Venue. I've written 2 or 3 Christmas plays to perform at our center.;

[pers.] God is within each one of us - and that's what unites us. Wherever I am, God is, and all is well. Thank you, God.; [a.] Hooper, UT

STOKES, JACK M.
[b.] July 28, 1933, Des Moines, IA; [p.] Joe E. Stokes and Mildred M. Stokes; [ed.] East Des Moines High School; [occ.] Retired Mortgage Banker; [memb.] U.S. Navy (1952-1965)

STOLTENBERG, KRISTIN L.
[b.] March 12, 1976, Pittsburgh; [p.] Carl and Loretta Stoltenberg; [ed.] Franklin Regional High School (gr. 1994) Indiana University of Pennsylvania (currently enrolled); [occ.] Student; [hon.] Bell Atlantic Technology Grant Program Participant, IUP Honors Convocation Participant; [pers.] A blank piece of paper invites my dreams daily, and it is this invitation that sets my soul free.; [a.] Murrysville, PA

STONE, TRINA MARIE
[pen.] Trina Marie; [b.] September 27, 1964, Columbus, OH; [m.] William Timothy Stone, November 23, 1991; [ch.] Eric Peter, Ryan James, Adam Timothy; [ed.] Fairbanks High School, National Business Academy, Columbus Business University; [occ.] Domestic Engineer (Housewife); [memb.] Plain City Presbyterian Church; [oth. writ.] One poem published in the 1989 American Rottweiler Magazine in 1989.; [pers.] I write poems about my life experiences. Usually my poems are very deep and full of meaning. I was mostly influenced by my Grandma Hodge's poetry.; [a.] Hilliard, OH

STRAUZ, RAY SUZAN
[pen.] Ray Suzan Strauz; [b.] Sweden; [p.] Herman and Golda Weissberger; [m.] October 17, 1949; [ch.] Rachel M. Catlin, Daniel I. Strauss; [ed.] Hunter College, Dean's List, Lehman College, Art Student's League, Extensive Religious Courses; [occ.] Landlord, Realty, Investor; [memb.] UNAUSA, Election Committee; [hon.] Good Citizenship Medal Awarded by Daughters of the American Revolution; [oth. writ.] Spelling textbooks using a unique new system based on my experience in teaching and tutoring; [pers.] I believe humanity's mission is ecology. Law and order are required in order to achieve this.; [a.] Los Angeles, CA

STREAT, EDNA
[b.] December 20, 1954; [p.] Edna and Joseph Hurt; [m.] Donald Streat, October 20, 1973; [ch.] Jennifer Streat, Tina Streat-Graham, Dawn Streat; [ed.] Associates degree (Blackhawk College in Criminal Justice); [memb.] Life Member V.F.W. Bettendorf and Iowa Ladies Auxilary; [hon.] Certified Nurses Aide Degree, Associates Degree; [oth. writ.] Reflections, Molotto, Self Destruction, Dee, Mesmerize, Daughter, G.I. Brother, My Flag; [pers.] My

family and friends have always encouraged me to keep doing something I love... Writing, it makes me feel alive something I can always leave behind.; [a.] Davenport, IA

STRID, BURTON L.
[b.] June 14, 1955, CT; [ed.] W.S.T.C., W.C.S.U.; [occ.] S-Metal/Welder/Mechanic; [hon.] 1st Honors - Trade Occup., Quality Achievement Award, '73; [oth. writ.] Publication of a work by nationwide publishers, "The National Library of Poetry"; [pers.] "A constant demonstration of persistence can only lead to success."; [a.] VA

STROUP, CHRISTOPHER
[b.] November 7, 1970, Lynchburg, VA; [p.] Thomas and Delores Stroup; [ed.] Scottsboro High, Current Student, Hillsborough Community College, Tampa, FL; [memb.] Dawns Early Flight, Feast of Evening, Sacred Dance Society; [oth. writ.] Yet to be published, soon to be seen.; [pers.] Poetry was meant to be lived, not just written and read. Search out true beauty not yet covered by life's distractions, the search is life. Live the poetry.; [a.] Tampa, FL

STULTS, FLORENCE ANN KELLY
[pen.] W. R. Allen; [b.] May 24, 1948, Columbia, SC; [p.] George and Florence B. Kelly; [m.] Robert David Stults, September 30, 1993; [ed.] B.A. Music, Bernard College, 1970, H.B. Studios, Active Studies, NYC, NY 1978-81, 1982 Master's Degree Work in Drama, at University of Houston; [occ.] Writing, housewife, playwright; [memb.] American Mensa Ltd. since 1987 Maryvale Medical Center Auxiliary, since 1991 Wilderness Society member National Parks and Conservation member; [hon.] 1966 Pelham High School, Valedictorian, 1966 American Legion Award for Citizenship, Bausch and Lamb Science Award, National Merit Scholarship Commendation DAR American History Award, Regents Scholarship Women NY State, Philharmonic Symphony if Westchester Award, all 1966; [oth. writ.] Plays "Living Together" in sinning again, A Poet's Love, in progress now A Long Death; [pers.] In base my writing on thought and scientific observation, since I in fact did study some medicine and psychology, I take an impartial look at life, whether sometimes "off the deep end" or not...; [a.] Phoenix, AZ

STUMPF, EUGENE STEPHEN
[b.] September 14, 1980, Manhattan, NY; [p.] Maria Arnone, Stephen Stumpf; [ed.] Plant High School; [occ.] Student; [memb.] Florida Aquarium Volunteer, Ecology Club, PADI, Scuba Diving, Private Pilot; [hon.] National Honor Society, Key Scholar Award; [pers.] Try to see other's point of view.; [a.] Tampa, FL

SULLIVAN JR., DALE
[b.] October 27, 1980, Ashland, KY; [p.] Dale Sullivan, Lorie Sullivan; [ed.] Crabble Elem., Verity Middle School (currently) Ashland, KY; [occ.] Student; [a.] Ashland, KY

SUMMERS, CONNIE M.
[b.] April 28, 1984, VA; [p.] Terrie and Mike Stinski; [ed.] 6th Grade; [occ.] Student; [pers.] I enjoy a wide variety of authors and activities. I have not really picked a style or who has influenced me the most, other than my parents, as I am still learning at 11 years old.; [a.] Bonduel, WI

SUMMITT, PHYLLIS J.
[pen.] P. J. Summitt; [b.] August 18, 1931, Berwick, PA; [p.] Thomas and Sarah Trapane; [m.] Ed Hawks (1954-1983), Marion Ray Summit (1985-1989), 1st 1954, 2nd 1985, Mrs. died 1989; [ch.] Barbara Parsons, Patricia Causey, Bonnie Brannon, Judith Williams; [ed.] Went to the complete 9th grade and quit because of health, 25 yrs. later got my GED, took a 9 mo. course in Key Punch, is 3 mo. studied income tax 30 yrs.; [occ.] Retired - was head bookkeeper and 30 yrs. as Tax Consultant; [memb.] Smith Grove United Meth Church, Smith Grove, KY; [hon.] Won Miss WWRC at the Woodrow Wilson Rehab. Center in Fishersville, VA, 1984; [oth. writ.] I have a few other poems but have never submitted them before.; [pers.] I have had polio for 62 yrs., I kept up my home, my husband, and 4 children, and 2 business for 25 yrs., was divorced after 29 yrs., some reeducation and remarried in 1985. My husband was killed in an accident. On my own since, but post polio syndrome is taking over.; [a.] Bowling Green, KY

SUTPHIN, AUDREY G.
[b.] February 5, 1934, Basin, WV; [p.] Jesse and Callie Poe (Deseased); [m.] Donald Sutphin, October 5, 1964; [ch.] Dale, James and John Sutphin (Callie Sutphin) Fresch; [ed.] 3 grade; [occ.] House wife; [oth. writ.] A song I wrote to my Mom. Some years ago called dear Mom. I didn't have it published. Two songs I had published in the 60 is but I lost the copy and several other poems.; [pers.] Most of my poems are about family. The seasons. One that was published in a local newspaper in Mullens, WV. Title a sign of Spring. Back in the 50s. My favorite is one where we use to slay ride in a Shoule as kids.; [a.] Mio, MI

SWANSON, SUE
[b.] March 2, 1959, Superior, WI; [p.] Whitey Olsen, Jane Olsen; [m.] Kevin Swanson; [ch.] Mike Guryne, Eric, grandchild - Paige; [pers.] I write to use the paper as a sounding board, to use the pen as a spiritual release, to really feel me and to touch others.; [a.] Superior, WI

SWORDS, JIM
[b.] March 19, 1968, Florence, OR; [p.] James L. Swords, Sandra L. Vick; [ed.] Pendleton High, U.S. Navy Service Schools; [occ.] Data Systems Technician, Sterling Software, Ft. Monroe, VA; [pers.] Mother Nature and human nature have a lot to say and I try to record a little of the much they tell us.; [a.] Hampton, VA

SWYGERT, DOROTHY
[b.] May 1st; [m.] Deceased, August 23, 1969; [ch.] Sons - Omar and Samori Swygert; [ed.] Tuskegee University, New York University, New York Theological Seminary; [occ.] Counseling; [memb.] Phi Delta Kappa Sorority, Tuskegee Univ. Alumni, Prison Fellowship Teacher of Social Studies, H. S. Guidance Counselor, 1995 Associate Minister Ebenezer Baptist Church. Concord Baptist Gen. Supt. until 1993.; [hon.] Community Service; [oth. writ.] The Montgomery Bus Boycott (Martial King's Rise To Fame); [pers.] Put on the spectacles of life and see the beauty of the universe for all of God's inhabitants. In all my years as an educator, I have never seen one child who could not learn. Rebuild Community!; [a.] Queens, NY

SYLVESTER, DON
[b.] January 26, 1965, Fayetteville, NC; [p.] Ardwin T. Sylvelster, Jr. (Deceased), Sharon Sylvester; [ed.] Andover High School Anne Arundel Community College; [occ.] Carpenter; [pers.] Having seen, in my life, both the beauty and hideousness of this land and its people, I choose to adopt a sinister appearance. In my experience, people do not bother to hide their true prejudices from a sheep in wolf's clothing.; [a.] Oklahoma, FL

SYLVIA, SUSAN J.
[b.] December 8, 1969, New Bedford, MA; [p.] Sandra and Richard Sylvia; [ed.] New Bedford High School, various enrichment courses; [oth. writ.] Numerous poems and songs.; [pers.] Interested also in: Singing, photography. Influenced by: God, family, friends, love and the sun.; [a.] New Bedford, MA

SYPEK, THOMAS
[pen.] Thomas Sypek; [p.] March 24, 1938, Boston; [m.] Anna and Thomas; [ed.] South Boston High; [occ.] Supermarket Produce; [memb.] Playwrigths Platform. Stage Source Outloud Theater Boys and Girls Club; [oth. writ.] Strangers a one act play hysteria - an aids play don't look back - play around a hundred poems.; [pers.] See God in people around you. Don't look on the surface of things. Love people for what they are.; [a.] Boston, MA

TABBI, MARY
[pen.] Tatum Surface; [b.] June 2, 1964, Boston; [m.] Joseph Tabbi Jr., October 27, 1985; [ch.] Kaitlyn, Sarah, Michael; [ed.] Personal studies and Courses in Special Education.; [oth. writ.] Many others writings to be published in the near future.; [pers.] I strive to reflect understanding of human emotions. I have been greatly influenced by my personal life experiences, as well as other fellow human beings.; [a.] Hamilton, MA

TAFEEN, SAMUEL
[b.] February 13, 1909, Pittsburgh, PA; [p.] Abraham and Ida Tafeen; [m.] Arlene Bricker; [ch.] Debra Welker, Anthony Tafeen; [ed.] Wallingford High, Bentley Accounting School; [occ.] Retailer in apparel; [pers.] Influenced by two poems in 8th grade, "Trees" by Joyce Kilmer, and "Opportunity" by John Sells. These poems have remained with me until this day.; [a.] Tampa, FL

TALBERT, JEAN C.
[b.] May 17, 1934, Sebago, ME; [p.] Guy M. and Lillian C, Crawford; [m.] James E. Talbert, December 14, 1953; [ch.] Timothy, Thomas, Tammy, Teresa; [ed.] Potter Academy U.S. Navy; [occ.] Para-Professional, Boston ESE School, Deland Florida; [memb.] Orange City United Methodist Church, Laies Auxiliary of the Veterans of Foreign Wars, DeBary, Florida; [pers.] My poems are my personal inner thoughts. When I read them I call recall with either joy, sadness or laughter, the reason I wrote each one.; [a.] Debary, FL

TALLEY, TRYSTN N.
[b.] November 20, 1982; [p.] Ted and Babbette Talley; [occ.] Student; [hon.] Miss Port Aransas, Texas Competition 1st place; [pers.] I find pleasure in writing poetry.; [a.] Port Aransas, TX

TARGONSKI, TOM
[b.] October 6, 1979, Boston; [p.] Debra and Thomas Targonski; [ed.] Masconomet Regional HS; [occ.] Student; [pers.] I try to do my best in all that I do in athletics, school work and my writings.; [a.] Topsfield, MA

TAYLOR, CAROL
[pen.] Carol Thompson-Taylor; [b.] January 10, 1968, Jackson, MI; [p.] Nat and Sarah Thompson; [m.] Robert Taylor, December 28, 1989; [ed.] Lumen Christi High School, B.A. University of Michigan; [occ.] Income Tax Preparer; [hon.] Graduate Cum Laude L.C.H.S. and U. of M.; [oth. writ.] Fiction "Vision of Darkness" in process of publication.; [a.] Jackson, MI

TAYLOR, DONNA J.
[pen.] D. J. Taylor, 6[b.] June 4, 1953, Pittsburgh; [p.] Lorraine and Newgene Elston; [ed.] College Graduate - Assoc. Degree Business Admin.; [occ.] Dietary Clerk; [memb.] National Honor Society; [hon.] National Honor Society; [oth. writ.] Several poems as yet unpublished;

[pers.] I write what I feel and about what has happened around me in my life.; [a.] Pittsburgh, PA

TAYLOR, KYNDALL S.
[b.] May 27, 1971, Flint, Hurley Hospital; [p.] Fred and Patricia Taylor; [ed.] Flint Northern, Baker College and Eastern Michigan University; [occ.] Student; [pers.] Poetry has become a way for me to express my feelings. Whether I am happy, sad, up or down, this is one of the ways and heavenly Father has helped me to sooth my soul.; [a.] Flint, MI

TAYLOR, LEWIS W.
[b.] January 8, 1978, Monrovia, Liberia; [p.] Jackie Wilson; [ed.] Essex County Vocational, Technical High School; [memb.] V.I.C.A., T.I.G.S., T.N.T.F.T. (Teens Networking Today For Tomorrow); [hon.] "Who's who among American High School Students" Edward J. Bloustein Distinguished Scholar; [pers.] "Don't count the days... make the days count."; [a.] Newark, NJ

TAYLOR, MELISSA
[b.] May 31, 1951, Long Branch, NJ; [p.] William Forbes Taylor Jr. and Rosemarie Grace Milici; [ch.] Christina Bahrs; [ed.] BA, Momnouth University, West Long Branch, NJ; [occ.] English Teacher, Shore Regional High School, West Long Branch, NJ; [memb.] National Council of Teachers of English; [hon.] Dean's List; [oth. writ.] Poems published in local newspapers, writer for Manual of Idiomatic American English, writer of Marketing Manuals.; [pers.] My poems are lyrical, reflecting intense, dramatic human situations. Many of my poems are spiritual poems, featuring individuals at varied points on the path to God.; [a.] Oceanport, NJ

TAYLOR, MICHELLE E.
[b.] May 18, 1960, Ferndale, MI; [p.] Don Graham and Sharon Bozzer; [ed.] Central Michigan University, BA Interior Design, and Psychology; [occ.] Graduate student in Professional counseling program.; [hon.] Who's Who Among American High School Students, Photograph published in Photographers Forem 1989 Outstanding Graduating Senior in Interior Design Department, 1989; [oth. writ.] Poetry published during school years in Detroit Free Press, 1968.; [pers.] Inner expression, that form words, leaving a small mark on the world human race, poetry in place for God to bless, and history to face.; [a.] Gaylord, MI

TAYLOR, V. EARLENE
[pen.] Ireland E. Ray; [b.] March 8, 1942, Elk City, OK; [pers.] I wish to stir the emotions of those who read my poems toward those purposes which will only be for the good of all - Ireland E. Ray, Pew; [a.] Sacramento, CA

TAYLOUR, NEVIS
[pen.] Tommy; [b.] August 2, 1977, Pacific Grove, CA; [p.] Sandra Coley, James Nevis; [ed.] Aptos High School, Santa Rosa Junior College; [occ.] Student; [oth. writ.] The Bottle of Emotion, The Burning; [pers.] Poetry is like no other, the words come straight from the heart and reaches out, for others to know.; [a.] Santa Rosa, CA

TEAFATILLER, TERA GAYLE
[b.] January 4, 1984, Dequeen, AR; [p.] Ralph and Gail Bilbay and Bruce Teafatiller; [ed.] 6th grade and I'm in Basketball, Math, Science, Computers, Reading, Social Studies, Spelling and Language; [memb.] Church - The Abuntant of Life; [hon.] All A's, Award for almost all my subject, and citizenship, and perfect attendants; [pers.] I'd like to be a doctor when I grow up. I like my life a lot. I like my new step dad a lot, his name is Ralph Bilbay Sr.; [a.] Bochito, OK

TELFORD, NICOLE
[b.] August 12, 1974, Scranton; [p.] Joe and Bladie; [ed.] High School Graduate; [occ.] Manager of Local McDonalds; [pers.] If you most lie about it, you shouldn't be doing it in the first place.

TEMPLE, WILLIAM
[b.] September 3, 1971, Portsmouth, VA; [p.] William Temple Sr., Janet Temple; [ed.] Chamberlain High, Waycross College; [occ.] Valdosta State University (VSU) Student, Education Major; [memb.] Sons of the Desert, Humane Farming Association, Common Cause; [hon.] Dean's List; [pers.] I study Anglo-Saxon history and Germanic Mythology. I hope for Tibetan independence, animal rights, and the survival of wildlife.; [a.] Waycross, GA

TERRY, MYRTLE RENEE
[pen.] Renee Terry; [b.] December 21, 1910, Alabama; [p.] Elizabeth, Theophilus Singleton; [m.] Addison Dennis Terry Jr., July 17, 1930; [ch.] Leon Dennis, Bonnie Jean; [ed.] High School; [occ.] Enjoying life.; [memb.] Baptist Church, Choir Member, Montgomery Art Guild, "SACS" - Arts and Crafts, Bank-New Outlook Club; [hon.] 1st place in Art show, most popular vote in others.; [oth. writ.] I have a number of songs I wrote years ago, only one published. I gave it up. I like art better. Have been professional for 30 years.; [pers.] I have never tried poetry thanks for accepting it for "Where Dawn Lingers".; [a.] Montgomery, AL

TERWISSCHA, LISA
[b.] January 19, 1980, Seattle, WA; [p.] Marilyn and Larry Terwisscha; [ed.] Kamiak High School, Mukilteo, WA; [hon.] Basketball and Soccer Trophy; [pers.] My poem Dreaming of You is dedicated to my boyfriend Jon Sayer, [a.] Everett, WA

THETFORD JR., DONALD R.
[b.] May 5, 1972, Memphis, TN; [p.] Donald and Nancy Thetford; [m.] Allison Lynn Thetford, June 1, 1996; [ed.] B.A. from The University of Memphis; [a.] Bartlett, TN

THIBODEAU, SEAN
[p.] April 28, 1976, Colorado; [m.] James and Lynn Thibodeau; [ed.] Conval High School readings of Jack Kerouak, Allen Ginsberg, and William Burroughs; [occ.] Warehouse; [oth. writ.] "A Collection of Sorts", poems and other writings. "The 'Shepherd' we've Dubbed Him", audio cassette/CD, comp. with John Martz: Guitar; [pers.] It's time to rise, and use what we have, to do the most truly difficult thing imaginable. Think. Through thought, all answers can be found, not by listening to the thoughts of others. The answers lie within each and every creature. THINK.; [a.] Peterborough, NH

THIELEN, SUSAN M.
[b.] January 3, 1977, Elgin, IL; [p.] Leonard and Phyllis Thielen; [ed.] Mission Viejo High School, University of Colorado at Boulder; [occ.] Student studying to become a Physical Therapist; [memb.] Alpha Omicron Pi; [hon.] Who's Who Among American High School Students, Honor roll, Presidential Math award, Top 25 students; [pers.] Far out in the sunshine are your fondest dreams. Reach for them, follow them, but always stay in touch with reality.; [a.] Boulder, CO

THISTLE, MARY
[b.] August 25, 1948, Saint Louis, MO; [p.] Henry T. Schlapp, Warrene Hobbs Schlapp; [m.] J. Jeffrey Thistle, September 23, 1973; [ch.] Joseph Henry, Ellen Warren; [ed.] Univ. of Colorado Florida Atlantic Univ. B.A., M.A., School of Haddknox, The Streets, L. V.; [occ.] Personal Secretary and Advisor; [memb.] Library Board ACL, Sousalarm Club, Procrastinators Club (tomorrow), My family Herman RACE, Fcis, FBI, FSMTA, TZCY ZZRK, Presidential Secret Service; [hon.] Blue Ribbon in Holiday Cump Horse Show, Best Mom Award; [oth. writ.] Grocery List, Names in Backs of Shirts, Signature on Checks, Notes in class (7th Grade) Letters to parents, friends and Children, 1,733,000,000 phone messages, Names on lunch bags, 14 gym excuses.; [pers.] I feel, that in my life time, I would like to count to do, find out what is at the end of the universe, and decide on a color for the kitchen walls. I always see the glass as half-full.; [a.] Delray Beach, FL

THOMAS, ANDREW A.
[b.] September 19, 1950, Deadwood, SD; [p.] Andrew Thomas and Mildred Thomas; [ch.] Angela, Denae, Aric and Devin; [ed.] B.S. in Ed. Black Hills State Univ; [occ.] Chartered Financial Consultant; [memb.] Kappa Delta Pi, American Society of CLU, Natl. Assoc. of Life Underwriters, MDRT; [pers.] Touch each

person you meet with a smile and understanding, it's the least expensive, but most valued gift you can give.; [a.] Las Vegas, NV

THOMAS, CLAUDIA M.
[b.] Meridian, MS; [p.] William Slater, Lillian Slater (Both Deceased); [m.] Divorced; [ch.] W. James Thomas, Lillian Thomas, Daryl Thomas, Diana Powe Thomas, Bruce Thomas, Adrianna Thomas; [ed.] East High School Hammel Actual Business College; [occ.] Secretary Babcock and Wilcox; [oth. writ.] Congratulations for high school graduate. A wedding, birthday wishes and The Trial; [pers.] I strive to express my personal thoughts from within my heart in my writings. I greatly admire Maya Angelou.; [a.] Akron, OH

THOMAS, FREDERICK T.
[pen.] Frederick Turner, [b.] June 16, 1958, Brooklyn, NY; [p.] Columbus and Ineko Thomas; [m.] Cheryl K. Thomas, May 24, 1986; [ch.] Janae E. Thomas, Andrew F. Thomas; [ed.] MA - Central Michigan University, [oth. writ.] Rock Bottom - Crack Cocaine; [pers.] Common sense isn't that common; [a.] Tampa, FL

THOMAS, GOLDIE ANN
[b.] June 17, 1967, Bristol, TN; [p.] Phyllis Johnson, John Dollar and Nancy Thomas, Gene Thomas; [m.] Tony D. Thomas, September 10, 1988; [ch.] Michael Anthony, Ashley Nicole; [ed.] Central High Draughons Jr. College; [occ.] Laboratory PBT (ASCP) Bristol Reg. Med. Center, Bristol, TN; [pers.] I dedicate my writings in memory of Cheryl Hicks and her son Brian Hicks and my Little brother John C. Dollar Jr. I want my poems to be a great influence to my Little nephews and nieces: Courtney Hughes, Cristy Hicks - ACE 14 Courtney Vance - Roger Gibson Jr. - Matthew Thomas and my little brother Charles R. Dollar.; [a.] Bristol, TN

THOMAS, LOIS
[pen.] Lois E. Laine; [b.] January 4, 1949, Belvidere, IL; [p.] Lee Rubeck, Frances Rubeck; [ch.] Nicole Francine Thomas; [ed.] Carl Hayden High School, Paradise Valley Comm. College; [oth. writ.] An assortment of inspirational poetry and prose; [pers.] My mission is to put a smile on everyone's face.; [a.] Phoenix, AZ

THOMPSON, CAROLINE
[b.] March 2, 1964, Brush, CO; [p.] Ed Smithey, Charlett Smithey; [m.] Stephen Thompson, September 15, 1991; [ch.] Douglas Scott, CharliAn Marie, Dale Maverick; [ed.] Rangely High School, CNCC College, 1st year, [pers.] In memory of my loving mother and best friend!; [a.] Rangely, CO

THOMPSON, CHRISTY ANN
[b.] March 23, 1982, San Angelo, TX; [p.] Leslie, Teresa Gray and Dennis, Kay Thompson; [ed.] Wall High School (current); [occ.]

Student; [memb.] Wall High School Band (I have played the claranet for 4 years.); [hon.] UIL, Gifted and talented, and student of the month.; [oth. writ.] Poems and short stories (none published).; [pers.] Over the years I have been in 23 schools in 8 years, and I'm only 13! I was inspired to write this poem because of what I have experienced in the past. I would like to thank my Mom, great-grandmother, and my cousin, Jason, for teaching me even the darkest cloud has a silver lining.; [a.] San Angelo, TX

THOMPSON, KEVIN P.
[pen.] Kevin P. Thompson; [b.] March 5, 1968, Greenville, TX; [p.] Ray, Dena Thompson; [ed.] Terrell Police Academy, Skyline High School Dallas, TX, Fred F. Florence Middle School; [occ.] Tractor-Trailer Driver, [memb.] Trinity Life Baptist Church, Disciples of Christ; [oth. writ.] Many other poems all centered around morals and/or Christian values with aspirations of publishing three other poems about trucking in trucker magazines; [pers.] My poems are all based on good moral values and the everyday situations that face each of us. Mostly influenced by the works of present-day philosophers who put today's problems in a more glorious light.; [a.] Dallas, TX

THOMPSON, NORFORD
[b.] June 28, 1955, Jamaica; [ed.] Master of Engineering, Howard University 1988; [occ.] Electrical Engineer, [memb.] Bahai Faith; [hon.] Tau Beta Pi (National Engineering Honor Society); [oth. writ.] Several soon to be published poems and songs, write special occasion poems and verses upon request. One publication in Vibes International Magazine.; [pers.] I believe in the oneness of mankind and I strive to promote and realize unity in its diversity.; [a.] Hyattsville, MD

THOMPSON, SUZY
[b.] March 12, La Sara, TX; [p.] Jim Huntley, Lela Huntley; [ch.] Kim Thompson, Mark Thompson; [ed.] Associate Degree Arts and Science; [memb.] Bering Dr. Church of Christ; [hon.] National Honor Society; [oth. writ.] Individuals request poems for special occasions; [pers.] In my writing, I try to reflect on truth and beauty from a realistic point of view.; [a.] Houston, TX

TICKLE, DELOIS J.
[pen.] Grannie; [b.] December 14, 1948, Saint Louis, MO; [p.] Dorothy Sample and William Miller; [m.] Ex Mr. James Tickle, February 14, 1965; [ch.] Monique Tickle, Robert Tickle, a Bryant Tickle, and Doris Flowers; [occ.] Homemaker and a mother of 4 children, 2 girl and 2 boys and 15 grandchildren; [pers.] I have been greatly influenced by my children and my grand children over the years. As well as my ex-husband.; [a.] East Saint Louis, IL

TINER, JOSHUA
[b.] May 8, 1972, Somerset Co., NJ; [p.] Gordon Anton, Sheila Susan; [ed.] Bridgewater - Rariten High School East, The Pennsylvania State University. B.S. Civil Engineering.; [memb.] Sigma Phi Epsilon Fraternity; [pers.] Depend on Him with all your heart... though trust is rather rare...; [a.] Bridgewater, NJ

TISHERMAN, LILLIAN
[b.] April 23, 1921, Pittsburgh, PA; [p.] Ida Barris and Samuel Barris; [m.] Zola Tisherman, January 21, 1942; [ch.] David Roy Tisherman, Phyllis Jean Foreman - Barie Ellen Edwards; [ed.] Taylor Allderdice High School, University of Pittsburgh; [occ.] Kindergarten Teacher, Hyde Park Elementary School South Central Los Angeles; [memb.] Phi Sigma Sorority Honorary Mentor Teacher; [pers.] Success in ones endeavors is attainable even at age 74 — I am currently and have been in the same classroom for 18 years so ——— "Believe In Yourself".

TITTLE, ELIZABETH
[pen.] Lisa Tittle; [b.] May 8, 1983, Calexico, CA; [p.] Ken and Diana Tittle; [pers.] I would love to give someone hope, provide peace for someone, if only for a moment, or open someone's eyes to what lies within, and heal an emotional wound.; [a.] Calexico, CA

TOLLER, PATTY S.
[pen.] Patty S. Toller; [b.] August 28, 1941, Vanceburg, KY; [p.] Myrtle Liles, Elmo Flinders; [m.] Lowell Dean Toller; [ch.] Lowell Toller Jr., Cindy Toller; [ed.] Lewis County High School; [memb.] Vanceburg Christian Baptist Church; [oth. writ.] Several poems published in Local Newspaper.; [pers.] We don't have to polish ourselves up to look really good before we come to the Lord. Just come as we are and accept His love, forgiveness, and the gift of eternal life.; [a.] Vanceburg, KY

TOOFANIAN, PARHAUM
[pen.] L. Dulac; [b.] September 14, 1972, Columbus, OH; [p.] Dr. Farshid Toofanian, Dr. Souri Toofanian; [ed.] Freshman at Capistrano Valley High School; [memb.] National Honor Society, California Scholarship Federation, Future Scientists and Engineers of America, Academy of Technology Math and Science; [hon.] 1st place in History Day, Regional, Honorable Mention, State, 3rd place in Odyssey of the Mind; [oth. writ.] Short stories and other similar poems.; [pers.] I would greatly hope to become a known pet, one of the few Romantic poets of the upcoming 21st Century.; [a.] San Juan Capistrano, CA

TOOVEY, RITA J.
[pen.] Rita Toovey; [b.] September 3, 1949, Omaha, NE; [p.] Rosetta J. Best; [m.] Bruce L.

Toovey; [ch.] (Daughter) Kimberly J. Toovey; [pers.] My writings are influenced by everyday thoughts and emotions that we all have. I just happen to put mine on paper.; [a.] Seward, NE

TORRES JR., WILFRED
[b.] September 24, 1960, Dade, FL; [p.] Wilfred and Maria Torres; [m.] Sandra Torres, September 30, 1995; [ch.] Dewitt Clinton High, Borough Manhattan Community College; [ed.] Banker, Chase Manhattan Bank; [oth. writ.] Novel titled "Happy Endings" and other poems awaiting for publication.; [pers.] My poetry expresses personal experience which most folk can relate to, I also delve in writing short stories of horror to generate response as my poetry does.; [a.] Forest Hills, NY

TORRES, SHERRI
[b.] September 4, 1979, Las Vegas, NV; [p.] Victor and Merlie Torres; [ed.] I am attending the Las Vegas academy of International Studies, performing and Visual Arts.; [occ.] Student of the 11th Grade with a 3.75 GPA.; [memb.] Philippine Chamber of Commerce, Philippine Bisayan Society, and Mountain View Assembly of God; [hon.] Miss Teen Asian Universal '94, I received a crown and trophy for 2nd runner-up, Miss Petite Model Search '94, I received 1st place for diamond in the rough. Bike Roded '87, I received 1st place. Gymnastics Competition '8, I received a bronze medal, principal's award.; [pers.] I have always had an interest in writing and hope to attend college to major in English and minor in educational psychology. All of which I will pursue a career as an English teacher of Creative Writing or Guidance Counselor.; [a.] Las Vegas, NV

TOUCH, VIOLET
[b.] Archbald, PA; [p.] James and Marie Badlat; [m.] A. Alfred Touch; [ch.] Lorranne Genevieve, Alan James, Michael Thaddeus, grandchildren - Victoria Courtney, Whitney, Christopher, Matthew, Melissa, Michelle; [ed.] Art Major, Music Minor, Drake Univ., Des Moines, Iowa, Piano Teacher, Waterloo, Iowa, Piano Teacher Waterloo, Iowa; [occ.] V.P. 2nd Sec., Andiphone Company, Inc.; [memb.] Women's Symphony Guild - Founder and Offices, Theatre Guild - First Nighters Founder, First President, International Council For Exceptional Children - Charter Member and Offices, Girl Scouts of America - 35 year pin, National Thanks Badge, Council Member, Leader and Offices, Rees Carillon Society - Lifetime Board Member, Developer, The Carillon Belles Founder and Offices, Easter Seals - 25 year Board Member, Scholarship Committee Chair, Pledge Center Coordinator, Island Bay Yacht Club - Inland "E" Sailor, Trophy Winner, Rotary Ann, Rotary International, National Council of Catholic Women, Illinois State Museum Society,

Municipal Opera - Asst. to General Manager, Springfield Art Association - Artist, Member, Woman's Club - Philanthropic Work, Golf, Bowling, Eagle Forum - Member and Offices; [hon.] Golden Poet Awards, 1987, 1988, 1989, 1990, 1991, Who's Who in Poetry, 1988, 1991, 1993, World of Poetry, many prizes and Honorable Mentions, Poetry Published in: Great American Poetry Anthology, The Golden Treasury of Great Poems, World Treasury of Great Poems, Great Poems of the Western World, New American Poetry Anthology, World Treasury of Golden Poems, When Dawn Lingers, Our World's Favorite Gold and Silver Poems, Our World's Most Treasured Poems, World of Poetry Anthology, Poetry for Friends and Organizations; [oth. writ.] "Most of my poetry is written to be sung to music I compose".; [pers.] "Nothing has happened tomorrow, nothing can happen yesterday, all you have is today, God will see you through."; [a.] Springfield, IL

TOWNSEND, MARILYN Y.
[b.] May 22, 1970, Union City, KY; [p.] Mary Helen Pirtle and Dennis Townsend; [ch.] Tynette Townsend; [ed.] Graduate of Southern High School Class of "88"; [occ.] Lock box processor at Bank One.; [pers.] I just would like to say that I hope that you enjoy my poem because it was a true experience that I will never forget. Thank you and may God bless you.; [a.] Louisville, KY

TRAINOR, MARILYN J.
[b.] July 24, 1938, Watertown, NY; [p.] Valence and Mary Quenneville; [ch.] Debora, Tamara, Kelly, Valence; [ed.] Voorheesville High School, State University Brockport New York, St. John Fisher College, License in insurance, Securities, and Real Estate; [occ.] Sales Rothman Furniture Ofallon, IL; [memb.] National Assoc. Female Executives Secretary for Dandy Dancers Square, Dance Club Belleville, IL Christian Worship Center, Caseyville, IL.; [hon.] Kezk—nominated and Recipient - "Business Person of the Week" - sold over 1 million in insurance — sold over 1.7 million in New Construction Numerous Achievement Awards; [oth. writ.] "In The Midst of It All", "Power In Prayer", "On The Wings of Angels", "Please Help Me God", "A Blessing From Above", "Our Reflection", "Memories Never Say Goodbye", "You Can Make A Difference", "Parents", "Precious Gifts", "The Personal Touch"; [pers.] My poems reflect and project the inner strength from God... my poems are also to encourage, to motivate and to bless others - with a positive attitude - "I know I am a survivor"; [a.] Ofallon, IL

TRANSUE, DAVID E.
[b.] March 28, 1953, Bucks; [p.] Earl and Lola Transue; [m.] Beverly Transue, June 7, 1986;

[ch.] Mandi M. Transue, Chad D. Transue; [ed.] Council Rock High School, Bucks County Community College; [occ.] Transue Contracting; [memb.] Langhome United Methodist Church; [oth. writ.] Several poems published in local newspapers.; [pers.] To all my friends and loved ones. Thank you all from the depths of my heart, for the prayers, the caring, and most of all, for the love you have shown me throughout my long and tiring struggle with this Satan called Cancer. I love you all as brothers and sisters in our Lord and Savior, but without the love and patience and selfless giving of my family, the role of my wife, Bev, and caring family, the children I love so much, and most of all by the pure Grace of God, I never would have been strong enough to love and smile my way through this trial. I know now that I am being called, I also know where I am going through the pure grace of love of God has shown mankind through the sacrifice He made for us.; [a.] Plumsteadville, PA

TRAUTH, JEANETTE
[b.] December 22, 1957, Norton, VA; [p.] Helen and Kyle Jones; [m.] Dennis, February 14, 1987; [ch.] Walt Eric Massengill and Adam Wayne Massengill; [ed.] Appalachia High and Chaffey Adult School; [occ.] Co. Owner Electrical Contractor in Specialized fields; [memb.] Disabled American Veterans, Veterans Commanders Club, Northshore Animal Shelter; [hon.] Honor Roll High school and Grade School; [oth. writ.] Voice of The Angel, Renaissance of Love, The Prayer That I Pray; [pers.] Children are people too. If we, the adults, do not teach them right from wrong, how will they know. Every adult has a responsibility to children. Children who are unhappy, grow up to be unhappy adults.; [a.] Torrance, CA

TRAXLER, SUSAN
[b.] August 2, 1968, Los Angeles; [p.] Beverly Traxler; [occ.] 1360 N Sandburg Chicago, IL; [hon.] Knowing that you like my poem and selected me in the semi-finalist is the greatest honor you have given me.; [oth. writ.] Poetry and short stories; [pers.] I'm interested in writing poetry, and getting into the acting business. Thank you for selecting me in the semi-finalist and this poem comes from my heart.; [a.] Chicago, IL

TREADWAY, HELENE G.
[p.] George and Sadie Lester, (Deceased); [m.] James C. Treadway; [ch.] Bonita Lester Phillips; [memb.] 1st Baptist Church (Erwin) AARP - PTO - ISP; [oth. writ.] Children's poems and stories. (Used at school and church) - I have hundreds of poems of all subjects - unpublished, some poems published by The National Library of Poetry.; [pers.] My poems address the greatest influences in my life. My love for God

family - country - friends. It is my way of expressing my appreciation for each of the above. I cannot ever remember not loving poetry. It has always been a vital part of my being.; [a.] Erwin, NC

TRESCOTT, LYMAN L.
[b.] March 6, 1921, Kankakee, IL; [p.] Edward and Johanna Trescott; [m.] Dorothy L. Trescott, October 21, 1944; [ch.] Robert, Steven, Jean, Daniel and Gloria; [ed.] Two yr. college, Woodrow Wilson College, Chicago, IL; [occ.] Retired; [oth. writ.] Evolution, happenstance by L.L. Trescott; [pers.] Your body may get old, your mind need not.; [a.] West Palm Beach, FL

TROWER, NOLA BETH
[pen.] Father Allahu Akbar; [b.] October 19, 1969, Jersey City; [p.] Garland Wilson, Nola Cavill; [m.] Tyrone Joshua, June 13, 1994; [ch.] Nola Garlanda Brielle, Immanuel Jesus; [occ.] Wife to wonderful husband, presently mother of 2.; [memb.] Nation of Islam; [hon.] "The Honorable Elijah Muhammad is Our Holy Messenger for Allah!", "The Honorable Minister Louis Farrakhan is our Warner!"; [oth. writ.] "All Praises due to Father, Allah for the Million Man March!, "All Praises Due to Father Allah for Coming in the Person of Master Fard Muhammad!" "It takes 24 hours to Digest ONE meal!"; [pers.] Oh my Father, Allah! Thank you for your mercy and blessings! In Shallah, please bless me with resuming custody of my daughter, Nola, and please bless us with a son named Jihad. Allah!; [a.] Long Branch, NJ

TROYANOVICH, JOHN M.
[pen.] Jack Trojanowicz; [b.] August 22, 1936, Bay City, MI; [p.] Czeslaw and Lorettal; [m.] Ilse, December 31, 1984; [ch.] John, Steven, Mark, Rita, Josef; [ed.] B.A. Cum Laude U. of Michigan, M.A. University of Illinois, Ph.D. in German Literature, Michigan State University; [occ.] Manufacturing, Consultant; [memb.] Society of Manufacturing Engineers, American-Polish Cultural Center, Kosciuszko Foundation; [hon.] Woodrow Wilson Fellow, 1960 to 1961, Germanistic Society of America foreign scholarship, 1964, American Association of Teachers of German research grant, 1973; [oth. writ.] Passion for Manufacturing, Society of Manufacturing Engineers, Dearborn, Mich., 1993. The Messenger from Dad. A short story. Bereavement, Vol. 3, No. 2, Feb, 1989, etc.; [pers.] "Mike was among the latter. He still had many miles to go. But he had to see the forests, before they slept in snow." From: To Mike from his grandson, an epic poem by Jack Troyanovich; [a.] Clarkson, MI

TSOUKALAS, EVA
[b.] July 22, 1951, Nashua, NH; [p.] Bessie Velonis; [occ.] Financial Consultant, Domestic

U.S.A./International; [oth. writ.] Recently completed a trilogy of three Romantic Fiction Novels. Storyline is based upon an interracial union between a white settler and a commanche warrior. Setting is mid 1800's in the American West. I eventually wish to submit them for evaluation with a prestigious publishing firm, aspiring to become a successful author and poet.; [pers.] I wish to convey a sense of enjoyment to the public, which will enable my creative nature to expand, both for public acknowledgement and personal satisfaction.

TUCKER, LORA R.
[b.] May 8, 1960, Brooklyn, NY; [p.] Lemuel and Kathleen Tucker; [ed.] Syracuse University, Pratt Institute; [occ.] Interior Designer, Senior Office Designer/Federal Reserve Bank of NY; [memb.] Harlem Writers Guild, New York, NY, Langston Hughes Writers Guild, Sag Harbor, NY; [oth. writ.] Several readings throughout the New York, Metropolitan Area, poems published in community newspapers.; [pers.] Poetry is a window that I open so to get a breath of fresh air.; [a.] New York, NY

TUCKER, MARY H.
[b.] August 4, 1914, Sioux City, IA; [p.] Mr. and Mrs. John H. Tucker (both deceased); [m.] Deceased; [ed.] East High School, graduated 1933; [occ.] Retired Veteran; [memb.] American Legion from 1945-1957.; [hon.] American Legion - Ninth District Commander, Historian. Honorable Mention - Poem - My Little Friend, awarded from World of Poetry, Sacramento, Calif., Sept. 21, 1990. Was in U.S. Coast Guard (Spars) 8 1/2, from February 1944, Sept. 1945; [oth. writ.] Honorable Mention from world of poetry for poem "My Little Friend" September 21, 1990.; [pers.] I write poems as therapy and pleasure. I do needle work and work crossword puzzles. have my own home, which I take care of.; [a.] Sioux City, IA

TUCKER, SHIZUE
[b.] February 13, 1927, Japan; [p.] Koichi Ito, Sata Ito; [m.] James Baker Tucker, April 6, 1954; [ch.] Jerry C. Tucker, Mary J. Terry, George M. Tucker; [occ.] Retired; [a.] Doolittle, MO

TULLIO, CLOTILDA
[p.] Carmella DeLisio; [m.] Anthony Tullio, April 26, 1943; [ch.] Anthony Jr., Thomas, five grandchildren, and two great-grandsons; [a.] Port Richey FL.

TURBAK, ESTHER
[b.] May 8, 1927, Farming, MN; [p.] Rose and Henry Schadeg; [m.] Walter J. Turbak (Deceased, 1984), November 16, 1972; [ed.] Albany H.S. - Nursing School - Registered Nurse - Breckemridge, MN (Diploma) BS Degree - St. Francis College - Joilet, IL. 3/4 Completion of

Masters Program in Health Services Admn.; [occ.] Professional Health (Home) care Registered Nurse - Home Health Care; [memb.] Nurses Asso. — Amer. Cancer So. - Alumni Asso. Semi Retired - Several Senior Citizens groups St. Mathias Cath. Church Choir.; [hon.] 1957 "Nursing Kindness Award." I love classical and Semi Classical Music - Play the Key board for pass time entertainment and enjoy putting music to my poems.; [oth. writ.] Just the last two years., I did a writing and picture book of Individual family members titled "This is your life" so far have completed eight of them and working on two more. These writings include Original Poems - unwally pertaining to the individual.; [pers.] Being a Senior Citizen, I now have more time to reflect on the beauties of the earth that God has put these for us. I believe in the positive aspects of life - "The good - The True and the beautiful.; [a.] Milwaukee, WI

TURNER, ELIZABETH J.
[pen.] Elizabeth J. Turner, Liz Bratten; [b.] July 29, 1956, Spokane, WA; [p.] Patrick Hall Bratten, Druse Ann Guy Bratten; [m.] Thomas Raymond Turner, February 20, 1981; [ch.] Thomas Sean Turner, Kristine Ranee Grigory; [ed.] Las Vegas High School, special Training in Geriatrics; [occ.] Homemaker, now have been Nursing Assistant and Veterinarian's Assistant; [memb.] International Society of Poets, of Smithsonian Institution; [hon.] Outstanding Achievement for my work with Alzheimer's Patients and in Geriatrics. Editor's Choice Award for outstanding achievement in Poetry 1995, N.L. Poetry Nominee Poet of the year 1995, through International Society of Poets.; [oth. writ.] Three other published Poems: N.L. Poetry The Running Man, In A Walk Through Paradise 12/95 What's In A Child, In Spirit of the Age 1/96 Paul Henery, in Where Dawn Lingers Summer in '96 publication now., and lots of other poetry not published. (YET)!; [pers.] This poem is dedicated in memory of Paul Henery Garrett my brother-in-law for 28 years. He was also my friend.; [a.] Las Vegas, NV

TURNER JR., JOSEPH C.
[b.] November 4, 1948, Baltimore, MD; [p.] Joseph C. Turner Sr. and Alma R. Turner; [m.] Yvette Larkin Turner, August 19, 1995; [ch.] Diana R. Turner and Erin Johnson; [ed.] BS Degree - Afro American Studies, 1977 Towson state University, AA Degree - Human Services, 1975, Community College of Baltimore; [occ.] Family worker for Pressley Ridge Schools, part-time Advocate for Martin Pollack project working with Foster Care Youth; [memb.] NAACP; [hon.] Phi Theta Kappa, State of Maryland Certificate of Service Neighborhood Reinvestment Certificate of Service "The Family Place" Outstanding Service Certificate,

South East Community Organization Service Award, Banner Neighborhood Service Award, Turn Table Community Association Improvement Outstanding Service Award; [oth. writ.] 1) Because I Live in a High Rise Doesn't Mean I Have No Pride (Public Housing), 2) Rats Ain't Hip Rat's Are Jive, 3) Sister Twister, 4) Springtime is Our Time; [pers.] I live by faith not by sight. Therefore I am not blinded by life's false realities. I constantly seek knowledge and the opportunity to reach one and teach some in the name of my heavenly Father. Peace!; [a.] Baltimore, MD

TURNER, VINCENT PATRICK
[pen.] Patrick Vincent; [b.] July 3, 1968, Oakland, CA; [p.] Donald E. Sims, Carolyn M. Sims; [m.] Donna L. Turner, January 14, 1995; [ch.] (Step) Melissan Louise, Timothy Robert, Adam Curtis, Randey Wade, David Wayne; [ed.] Independence High, San Jose, Can Cypress College, Cypress, CA; [occ.] Customer Support Technician, Dell Computer Corp, Austin, TX; [oth. writ.] "Cyber Nation", A Feature Leyath Screen Play, several Cable PSA's, several as yet unpublished poems and story ideas.; [pers.] Never lose sight of your dreams, or your nightmares could prevail!; [a.] Austin, TX

TYSON, LISA
[pen.] Love Struckin'; [b.] December 31, 1968, Clairmont, FL; [p.] Lois and Jimmy Long; [m.] Fiancee (Alan Howell), May 25, 1996; [ch.] Danielle and Steven Tyson; [ed.] GED - Paris Vo-tec Paris Tenn., Computer and typing - Flagler/Palm Coast High Flagler Beach, Fl; [occ.] Secretary, for Palm Plumbing and Solar Inc; [oth. writ.] Several poems - but never published; [pers.] True-deep feelings from my heart makes the best poems. I have been greatly influenced by my children Danielle and Steven, also my fiance Alan and our new baby arriving September 30, 1996; [a.] Flagler Beach, FL

UNDERWOOD, CHARLOTTE
[b.] March 1, 1959, Cheverly, MD; [p.] Jeraldine Leverett; [ch.] Trisha, Bryan, Timeka, Bryan, Darnell Underwood; [ed.] Fairmont Heights High, Central High Prince George's Community College; [occ.] Administrative Assistant, Neighborhood Reinvestment, Washington, DC; [memb.] Psi Beta, Uplift Baptist Church; [oth. writ.] "Moon Swings and Spiritual Visions" - a collection of poems 1989, unpublished.; [pers.] "Continue to pursue your dreams - no matter how long it takes - persistence and determination makes the realization of dreams that much sweeter.; [a.] Landover, MD

UNGER, SHARRON
[b.] September 23, 1957, Summit Hill, PA; [p.] John and Pauline Peters; [m.] Richard; [ch.] Eric and Kelly; [occ.] Registered Nurse in Labor and Delivery in VA; [pers.] I would like to help

people experience the pain and the resolutions of growing up in an abusive and alcoholic home.; [a.] Warrenton, VA

URBAN, CHRISTOPHER ANDREW
[b.] June 18, 1986, Boston, MA; [p.] Andy and Barbara Urban; [ed.] Hillside Academy, Garland, Texas; [occ.] Student; [memb.] 1) Weblos Cub Scout Pack 1988 - Garland, TX. 2) St. Michael's Church, 3) Hillside Singers; [hon.] UIL (University Interscholastic League) Maps, Graphs and Charts, Reflections - Best of Show in Acrylic Paint; [pers.] I wrote this poem to increase the awareness of the importance of grandparents.; [a.] Garland, TX

URBAN JR., ROBERT
[b.] September 15, 1972, Kingston; [p.] Robert and Carol Urban; [ed.] Wyoming Valley West High School, Bloomsburg University; [occ.] Pennsylvania State Police Cadet; [hon.] Dean's List; [oth. writ.] First publication.; [pers.] Poetry is an intense and constructive channel for the bevy of emotions that rage throughout our lives. I try to harness this energy. [a.] Swoyersville, Pa

URENOS, ELEANOR MORRITT
[b.] Eleanor Bredesen; [p.] Darlington, WI; [m.] W. Dale and Dorothy P. Morritt; [ch.] John A. Urenos, April 21, 1973; [ed.] Darlington High, B.S. Univ. Wis.; [occ.] Retired Author/editor; [hon.] Grad. with honors U. Wis., 1st pl. 1995 Chgo. Natl. Agri-Marketing Assoc. and 1995 Merit Award, Chgo. Soc. for Techn Communications for annu. rep. Building Consumer Demand through Research; [oth. writ.] 23 publications in nutrition, consumer edu., food science, poem, Chicago People in Walk Through Paradise, 1995 anthology, Natl. Libr. Poetry, 2 poems in nutrition publications, articles in several consumers and professional periodicals; [pers.] Poetry is a source of creative exploration and re-creation for me; [a.] Chicago, IL

USREY, TRACI LYNN
[pen.] Alyssa Lynn; [b.] February 15, 1979, Pontiac General; [p.] Mary Ann and James Bane; [ed.] Pontiac Central High School.; [occ.] Cashier at the waterford K-mart; [memb.] Stage Players (theatre group at my school) for 1 year, Silver Lake Church of the Nazerene youth group, the Talented and gifted group at Central.; [hon.] The LM Cricket Award on Cross-Country for dedication. Being published in your book is the greatest honor I have ever received.; [oth. writ.] I have not published anything yet, but some of my best poems include: Love, Mistreated, Wind; [pers.] I try to explore all of the realities of love in my poems. I'm greatly inspired to continue writing because of this accomplishment.; [a.] Pontiac, MI

USSARY, RICHARD JACKSON
[b.] November 1, 1969, Myrtle Beach, SC; [p.] Mary Lou Dixon, Charles Dixon (stepfather), Stealen Ussary; [m.] Colette Anna Ussary, March 19, 1994; [ed.] I am currently in my second year at Sterling College, Sterling, K.S. My major is English, my minor is Art (pursuing law school); [occ.] I am putting myself through college working for Dillon Stores; [memb.] Westbrook Baptist Church; [hon.] My salvation through Jesus Christ; [oth. writ.] (Nothing that's been published), Popcorn Junction, Vikings Voyage, Little Brother, The Firemen, Mom Thomson, Unknowing Soldier, The Woodsman's Family, other various works that are untitled.; [pers.] My wishes are to produce literature that allows gumpses into the cathartic nature of events as they happen to the person's person. If people can read about trying times, hopefully they will gain some insight into why they did or did not. Make the best choice.; [a.] Hutchinson, KS

VALE, JAMES E.
[b.] September 15, 1953, San Antonio; [p.] Samuel E. Vale, Yolanda G. Vale; [ch.] Jacqueline Erica, Jennifer Eve, James E. II, Jeremy Edward; [ed.] Oliver Wendel Holmes H.S., San Antonio Community College; [pers.] But for the encouragement of family and friends, I might have never tried.; [a.] San Antonio, TX

VALENTIN, PETER GONZALEZ
[b.] March 4, 1943, Puerto Rico; [m.] Felicia Valentin; [ed.] Bronx Comm. Col. Lehman, Col.; [occ.] Self Employed; [memb.] Bronx Poets Alliance; [hon.] Mobil oil poetry award for excellence.; [oth. writ.] 3 acts play, 2 trilogys dealing with the metaphysical tragedy of love unfound.; [pers.] I strive to redeem the spirit from the bonds of human suffering.; [a.] Bronx, NY

VALENTINE, LYNN MARIE
[b.] February 11, 1956, Rochester, MI; [p.] George A. Stein, Norma A. Stein; [m.] Russell Valentine, July 17, 1976; [ch.] Shan Valentine (18), April Valentine (10); [ed.] Graduated from Atlanta High School, Atlanta, MI; [occ.] I'm a Quality Control Person at Fairview Tubular Products Fairview, MI; [oth. writ.] I've written a few poems that have been published in the local newspaper, Poem Titles "Halloween Night," "Christmas Day," "Valentines Day," "One Christmas Eve Night"; [pers.] I began writing poems to bring laughter and to uplift peoples spirits. I strive to bring out the goodness of people and the world we live in. I hope to be able to publish a book in poetry. I was greatly influenced by holidays and children.; [a.] Atlanta, MI

VALENTINE, VANESSA LARAE
[b.] May 11, 1982, Washington PA; [p.] Eric

Gerard Valentine, Jody Rae Valentine; [ed.] Lone Pine Elementary School, Trinity Middle School; [occ.] Student; [hon.] Free music lesson scholarship, regional spelling bee, honor roll; [oth. writ.] extensive number of unpublished poems; [pers.] I write what my feelings are. I write what I want to say when I don't know how to say it, or can't say it out loud.; [a.] Washington PA.

VALERIO, CERELLE
[b.] May 28, 1984, Geneva, OH; [p.] Mike and Dori Valerio; [ed.] Headlands Elementary 6th Grade; [occ.] Student; [memb.] President of STudent Council, Computer Club, Safety Patrol, Conflict Management, Technology Club; [hon.] Honor Student - every semester - 5 yrs. straight; [pers.] It doesn't take alot to write a great story or poem, all you need is peace of mind and a little inspiration!; [a.] Mentor, OH

VALLEE, NICHOLL M.
[b.] October 31, 1975, Cherry Hill, NJ; [p.] Joseph and Shirley Vallee; [ed.] Bishop Eustace Prep, Villanova University; [occ.] Communications major at Villanova University, Villanova, PA; [memb.] Ambassadors Club, News Anchor at college radio station, reporter for college newspaper.; [hon.] President's Service Award; [oth. writ.] Poems published in high school and college literary magazines.; [pers.] I attempt to reflect and eccentricities of life in my writings. I have been greatly influenced by the Beat writers, especially Jack Kerouac.; [a.] Woodbury, NJ

VAN CLOW, JEREMY
[pen.] Nixel; [b.] October 21, 1969, Thief River Falls, MN; [p.] Janice Clow, Arnie Clow; [ed.] Lancaster High, Moorhead State University; [occ.] Security Officer - Asp Inc. of Moorhead; [pers.] Life holds many things of interest. All one has to do is look hard enough to find them, and then accept them.; [a.] Fargo, ND

VAN DE CAR, MARY ELLEN
[pen.] Mary Ellen Van De Car, Mary Ellen - Wright Van De Car and M.E.V.D.C.; [b.] May 23, 1926, Ellsworth, MI; [p.] Frank and Cassie Wright,; [m.] Charles Van De Car, July 4, 1945; [ch.] Charles Jr., Donna, Wm., Bob, Carl, Cora and Ann; [ed.] 8th grade (formal); [occ.] Retired; [memb.] United Methodist Church; [hon.] Of my Church "Century Woman of the Year," of many Friends; [oth. writ.] Too numerous to mention, none published except locally.; [pers.] I want my poetry rhyme, nothing obscene. More on the spiritual side, days of yore and greeting card type.; [a.] Charlevoix, MI

VAN ORNAM, DIANE
[b.] November 30, 1960, Greenville, SC; [p.] Jackie Mouchett, Marilyn Gilreath; [m.] Timothy J. Van Ornam, January 7, 1980; [ch.] Jordan, Graham, Aaron, Peter, Madeleine,

Joseph and Augustine; [ed.] G.E.D.; [occ.] Mother, Homemaker, Artist Crafts; [oth. writ.] Children's Stories and poems, spiritual writings, personal memoirs.; [pers.] As my spiritual being experiences human life, I am provided with a variety of challenges that inspire my writings.; [a.] Bennington, NE

VANCE, TRAVERS S.
[b.] October 17, 1932, Indianapolis, IN; [p.] Kenneth Vance, Alice Vance; [m.] January, 1956; [ch.] Ardeana, Cedric, Charles; [ed.] Lincoln Institute "All The World Academy"; [memb.] St. Mary's Lodge #14 Fort Wayne, IN; [hon.] Graced by God with Health and Sound mind. (Though some people may dispute the latter (Smile); [oth. writ.] Poem for local newspaper-letter to Editor, Etc.; [pers.] Writing Poetry can be so beautiful that it elicits teams like red wine from a tilted stein. Only God grants such a gift.; [a.] Lawrenceburg, KY

VANDERBILT, SHANE
[b.] October 25, 1983, PA; [p.] Thomas D. Vanderbilt, Jay R. Vanderbilt; [occ.] Student; [a.] Dublin, NH

VAUGHN, LURLINE DRISKILL ALEXANDER
[pen.] Lurline A. Vaughn; [b.] January 26, 1922, Heflin, LA; [p.] Charlie Cade Driskill and Maude Toms Driskill; [m.] 1) James Ralph Alexander, April 5, 1946, 2) Oscar A. Vaughn, October 2, 1965; [ch.] Charlis Annette Alexander; [ed.] Heflin High School, Normal State College (Now Northwestern State College) other Short Courses in Typing and Shorthand, Louisiana Real Estate Course; [occ.] Retired - Taking Art and other Participation in Church and some Volunteer Work; [memb.] Calvary Baptist Church, Shreve Port Art Club, Beta Sigma Phi (Past Member); [hon.] American Legion Medal Award in High School Graduation, also Valedictorian of Graduation Class, I have won several prizes and places in Shreveport Art Club Exhibits; [oth. writ.] Many unpublished poems, poem in the Year Book of the Shreveport Art Club, acknowledged short stories and themes in High School and College; [pers.] I express my feelings and write them down immediately, the words don't come back again. I love God, people, places and things and the events that happen to them when, where and why - their response to different situations.; [a.] Shreveport, LA

VEGA, ELIZABETH
[b.] August 15, 1961, McAllen, TX; [p.] Mike and Mary Vega; [ch.] Alfred, Frank, Samantha, Steven; [ed.] Covina High School Gr. in 1979, Samuel Alarcon and Dr. Nicholson introduced me to the Lord in heaven; [oth. writ.] Several poems hoping to be published about life and hope for the after.; [pers.] Angels whisper poem was written for

my friend "Delia" of Glendora, CA who has Multiple Sclerosis and has the hope and desire to go on and for "Jessica" who I believe is an angel.

VENINCASA, JOSEPH S.
[b.] January 9, 1984, Worcester, MA; [p.] Barbara and Steven Venincasa; [ed.] Currently 6th grade at Oxford Academy of Northboro, MA; [hon.] Academic Honors, Headmasters List, Most Improved Soccer Player, Musical Talent, Piano and Voice with many leads in Musicals; [oth. writ.] Currently writing a book and medieval fiction.; [pers.] Some things are not meant to be found.; [a.] Westboro, MA

VENTERS, WILLIAM C.
[pen.] William Cortnii; [b.] May 31, 1955, Los Angeles, CA; [p.] Theopris, Erma Owens; [m.] Corliss M. Venters, November 28, 1982; [ch.] Cortnii, William II, Quebec; [occ.] Salon Owner, Hair Designer Poet, Song Writer, [a.] Fremont, CA

VIANELLI, LORRAINE
[pen.] Elvie; [b.] November 30, 1918, Chicago, IL; [m.] Carlo E. Vianelli, November 1940; [ch.] One Daughter Sara; [ed.] Hamilton High Sch., Art Institute of L.A. Choinard's Charette School of Design; [occ.] Retired Teacher; [memb.] San Gabriel Valley Federated Women's Club, Riohondo Symphony Assn. Pio Pico Women's Club, Children's Home Society, [hon.] Several poems printed in newspapers, Federated Women's Club Award for all around Poems; [a.] Whittier, CA

VIDAS, DEBRA ANN
[pen.] Gidgett; [b.] October 22, 1956, Portsmouth, VA; [m.] John William Vidas, February 1, 1975; [ch.] Clark 11-27-75, Derrick 11-13-82; [ed.] Raleigh Egypty, H.S. Memphis, TN, George Stone Vo-Tech, Cosm. California Miramar College, Business Navy-Military Kid and Wife; [occ.] Hair Salon Owner, Stylist of "Hair Keepers"; [oth. writ.] Songs and other poems not yet submitted. Christmas memories - Charlotte Newspapers 1995.; [pers.] If you have faith as small as a mustard seed nothing will be impossible for you. Matthew 17:20.; [a.] Charlotte, NC

VILLAMOR, PHILIP
[b.] October 21, 1970, Fresno, CA; [p.] Gary and Shirley Villamor; [m.] Marisa; [ed.] B.A of Political Science from U.C.S.B., ('93), Teaching Credential (June '96); [pers.] Hopefully my writings reflect the relative nature of truth, of goodness and everything one night point to as having "quality".; [a.] San Marcos, CA

VILLAVICENCIO, PRISCILLA
[b.] October 6, 1982, Chicago, IL; [p.] Carmita, Patrick Villavicencio; [ed.] Grammer School - Saint Ferdinand; [occ.] Going to school; [pers.] Poetry comes from the heart, not the mind.; [a.] Chicago, IL

VIVIAN, JOHN
[b.] September 11, 1933, Kansas City, MO; [m.] Cari Vivian, March 1982; [ch.] Six Daughters, Fifteen Grandchildren; [ed.] B.S. - University of San Francisco; [occ.] Retired - Former Insurance Executive for Major Insurance Org.; [pers.] My attempt is to write about inner feelings that all of us struggle with from time to time.; [a.] Santa Rosa, CA

VLANNES, PEPPINO N.
[b.] November 9, 1919, Shreveport, LA; [p.] Nickolas Vlannes, Henrietta Vlannes; [m.] Katherine Batzis Vlannes, June 25, 1949, (deceased January 25, 1994); [ch.] Nickolas and Katherine; [ed.] Saint John's High School, Shreveport, Louisiana Centenary College, Shreveport, Louisiana, B.S. Chemistry Xavier University, Cincinnati, Ohio, M.S. Chemistry, Georgetown University, Washington, D.C., Post Graduate Studies; [occ.] Retired; [memb.] International Society of Poets (ISP), Southern Poetry Association (SPA), Poetry Society of Virginia (PSV), Poets Anonymous, The Retired Officers Association, Reserve Officers Association and AHEPA Poetry only: Southwestern; [hon.] Intercollegiate Poetry Meet 1946 and 1948, Southern Poetry Association, Blue Ribbon Awards 1990, 1991, 1992, 1994 and 1996, Poet's Choice Award 1993, Who's Who In Poetry 1994, National Library of Poetry, Editor's Choice Award, 1995, and International Society of Poets International Poet of Merit Award 1995, many other recognitions approbations, Honors and Awards at the National and International Levels, pepping also is an Inventor; [oth. writ.] Poetry only: National Poetry Association, Anthology of College Poetry 1946, 1948, Vlannes Associates Inc., Anthology - of life, and love, and other things 1989 Southern Poetry Association, Ten Different Anthologies 1990-1995, National Library of Poetry, Two Anthologies 1994, 1995, Poets Anonymous, Anthology - Anonymous no more 1995; [pers.] Peppino writes poetry for the love of poetry and the challenges that poetry brings. It is a way to touch the hearts, thoughts and imaginations of all those who love poetry. After all, isn't everyone born a poet?; [a.] Fairfax, VA

VOEGTLY, KENNETH W.
[b.] Alexander Theophilus; [p.] January 21, 1926, Crewe, VA; [m.] Roger F. and Flossie May Voegtly; [ch.] Alice Bissette Voegtly, 1964; [ed.] Maury High School of Norfolk, VA, Technical Training; [occ.] Retired - I was Jacks at all trades - master; [oth. writ.] I have about 60 titles - some verse and some prose.; [pers.] Keep faith in goodness love yourself live and let live.; [a.] Smithfield, NC

VOLK, LAWRENCE
[b.] October 16, 1954, Newport, RI Len and Leona Volk; [ch.] B.S., M.E.D., E.D.S. - University of Virginia; [occ.] Teacher/Professor; [memb.] AFT, ADCIS; [hon.] Who's Who In American Higher Schools; [oth. writ.] Several poems published, including "Liv And Luv" "Lioness", and "Something Lost"; [pers.] Thank you to all the people and places that have inspired the words I've written; [a.] Carolina Beach, NC

WAFER, RYAN JOSEPH
[b.] April 24, 1976, Long Island NY; [p.] George Wafer, Patricia Wafer, [ed.] Student at North Carolina State University, Half Hollow Hills High School East; [occ.] Student, Screen Printing; [memb.] Sigma Phi Epsilon Fraternity; [pers.] My writings are greatly inspired by the Beats, and I believe that life is all about experiences.; [a.] Dix Hills NY.

WAGNER, GRACE MARIE
[b.] February 8, 1928, Brooklyn, NY; [p.] Edmund F. and Graced R. Lamb; [m.] Joseph M. Wagner, November 4, 1970; [ch.] Joseph, Grace Fetta, Edward Pohren, Regina Chadarick, Christopher Pohren, Teresa Pohren, Stephen Pohren, Madeleine Sharp, Eugene Pohren, Stephanie Schoenleber, Rebecca Harsh, Jeremy Wagner, we have 26 grandchildren; [ed.] Adelphi University, Art Major, Public School Art Teacher; [occ.] Homemaker, we are a remarried family: my nine, his two, our one.; [memb.] Delta Zeta National Sorority, former Volunteer Red-Cross Driver; [hon.] Maine Health Care Volunteer of the Year of 1982; [oth. writ.] I have had one poem appear in the Pro-Life Action League publication: "Ransem Babe", Jan. '86. I have written several other poems that I hope to see published some day.; [pers.] I feel all my inspiration is from God and that I am His instrument.; [a.] Liberty, ME

WAGNER JR., JAMES A.
[b.] July 24, 1973, New Prague, MN; [p.] James A. Wagner Sr., Barbara A. Mahowald; [m.] Stephanie Westerlund-Wagner, 1997; [ch.] Red River High School, University of North Dakota; [a.] Kansas City, MO

WAHL, JUSTIN JOSEPH
[pen.] Just and Little Wally; [b.] November 1, 1974, Fall River, MA; [p.] Gerald and Judith Wahl; [m.] (fiance) Janet LaChapelle, June 8, 1996; [ch.] Jordan Joseph Wahl; [ed.] High School Grad. Riverton RI; [occ.] Industrial Worker; [memb.] Holy Ghost Church, Body Builders Gym; [hon.] For Writings Herald News - all Scholastic Award 91-92, RI Baseball at Team 1992, RI Baseball MVP 1992, Soccer Classic 1st Place 1991, East Bay Basketball 2nd Place 89-90; [oth. writ.] Dreams; [pers.] Justin was a beautiful person and left an expression on everyone he met. He was loved by so many and will always be missed. He left part of him with us, his son Jordan. Justin died 12-11-95. We know he's in his dreamland with God love always, mom and dad - Jerry-Jason-Janet-Jordan and Wendy Zan.; [a.] Tiverton, RI

WALKER, BARBARA
[b.] May 27, 1935, NC; [p.] Millicent and Frances Swaim; [m.] William Walker Jr., June 4, 1955; [ch.] Dianne Bodenheimer and Tonya Robbins; [occ.] Retired from R.J. Reynolds Tob. Co.; [pers.] I love to write poetry. But all I have written are true to life events of loved ones and friends. Plus I love to write about Jesus and God's Holy Word.; [a.] Winston Salem, NC

WALKER, CHERRON
[b.] February 27, 1979, Toppenish, WA; [p.] Adrienne and Kenneth Walker; [ed.] 10th Grade Toppenish High School; [occ.] Student; [memb.] Weight Powerlifting Club, Washington State Trappers Association; [hon.] 1995 2nd Place Trophy at Washington State Powerlifting Meet; [oth. writ.] As Dark As Night, My Cousin, Lost Memories, I Understand, All That Matters.; [pers.] My feelings pour into words on paper. Whatever feeling I have, sad, angry, or happy, I write down in poems.; [a.] Toppenish, WA

WALKER, CHEYENNE
[b.] December 1, 1952, CA; [m.] Timothy Webb; [ch.] Ross; [memb.] San Diego Zoological Society and Interior Racing Assoc. of Alaska; [pers.] I want to write books for children and horror stories. My main writing goal is to write a children's book that will be made into a Disney movie.; [a.] Delta Junction, AK

WALLACE, DOROTHY A.
[b.] September 11, 1942, Wright County, MO; [p.] Stephen Foster Dudley, Lois Breman Dudley; [ch.] Michael Huckaby, David Wallace; [ed.] Mansfield High School, Mansfield, MO, Drury College and Southwest Missouri State University, Springfield, MO; [occ.] Director of Special Services, Mansfield Schools, Mansfield, MO; [memb.] Council of Administrators of Special Education, Missouri State Teachers Association, International Society of Poets, American Sales Association; [oth. writ.] Several poems published, articles for local newspapers, family histories for county history books.; [a.] Seymour, MO

WALLACE, ELIZABETH GRACE
[pen.] Elizabeth Wallace; [b.] August 6, 1948, Pittsburg, PA; [p.] Nathienal James and Betty Jane Parker; [m.] Richard A. Wallace Sr., July 16, 1971; [ch.] Richard Jr., Adrinne, Monica, Amber; [ed.] I went to Belmar, Bennett, and Baxter Elementary Schools. I attended Westinghouse High and graduated in June of 1966; [occ.] My current occupation is Supervisory Lunch Aide at Belmar Elementary School;

[memb.] I am presently an adult advisor with the Awesome Authors, an after school children's writing club. I held the position for three years now.; [hon.] My association with Awesome Authors as an advisor is a rewarding experience in itself. In 1986 Governor of Pennsylvania Dick Thornburgh honored me as part of the Parent Partner Recognition Program. I also received a certificate of appreciation in the school volunteer program. In 1995 I was a presentor for Chapter I program explaining to parents about Awesome Authors; [oth. writ.] I don't have any other poem published at present. I would like to one day get a morally positive book of poems published to encourage our children to reach for the best in them. I believe to be a rule model and encouragement to the young is important.; [pers.] I have written this poem as a message of hope to all the youth of the world regardless of economic background. Look at me, an individual coming from modest means. I wanted to write poetry and have it published. Please pursue your dreams and goals always.; [a.] Pittsburgh, PA

WALLER, ANITA
[b.] April 23, 1951, Fort Wayne, IN; [p.] Scott R. Waller, [ch.] Kristina, John, Beth, Erin; [pers.] I am inspired by all of our children, encouraged greatly by my wonderful husband and enlivened by Gods many creations.; [a.] Mukwonago, WI

WANG, CAMELLIA
[pen.] Cammy; [b.] March 23, 1970, Los Angeles, CA; [p.] Armand and Margaret Wang; [ed.] UCLA, Loyola Law School, Los Angeles; [occ.] Lawyer; [memb.] California State Bar; [hon.] Phi Beta Kappa, Chancellors Service Award, Magna Cum Laude (UCLA), Dean's List, Am Jur in Trial Advocacy (Loyola Law School); [oth. writ.] Several 1st place essays in writing contests, some feature articles published in local and college newspapers.; [pers.] Although I wrote this poem back in 8th grade, it still brings much meaning to my life and, hopefully, to others. Blessed am I by the Lord for my family and friends.; [a.] La Palma, CA

WANG, DI
[pen.] May Lan; [b.] October 19, 1982, P.R. China; [p.] Tom and Yimei Wang Allen; [ed.] 7th grade student; [pers.] Dedicated to my dearest mother, my step-father, my grand-parents in China, my friends, and my family who supported me.; [a.] Tulsa, OK

WARBURTON, ELIZABETH
[b.] July 26, 1980, Kalamazoo, MI; [p.] Robert Warburton, Suzzann Tokarz Warburton; [ed.] St. Mary's Grade School, Ring Lardner Jr. High School, Mishawaka - Marian High School; [occ.] High School Student; [memb.] Marian High Golf, Track and Football (mgr.) Teams, Marian

German Club; [hon.] Three time Varsity Letter Winner, English, Biology and World History Honors; [pers.] Life's short, live long.; [a.] Niles, MI

WARD, JUSTEN
[pen.] "Mike"; [b.] December 6, 1983, Oakland; [p.] Roscoe and Dawna Ward; [ed.] Attending Kensington Elementary School - 6th Grade; [occ.] Student; [oth. writ.] Include but not limited to: My Thoughts, Neat Pete, Walter The Tree; [pers.] There are a lot of books written, but poems can touch the heart and cause a person to feel good about themselves - I hope my poems causes inspiration to many.; [a.] Richmond, CA

WARLING, DENISE MARIE
[b.] July 21, 1955, Minneapolis, MN; [p.] Walter Schendel, Mary Schendel; [m.] Micheal L. Warling, October 21, 1978; [ch.] Donald J., Corey V., Lucas N.; [ed.] Lakewood Community College; [occ.] Receptionist; [memb.] St. Michael's Lutheran Church; [hon.] Dean's List - Lakewood Community College; [oth. writ.] Several other poems dedicated to dear friends and family; [pers.] I appreciate the diversity in all people, it's because of our differences we can be awakened to the beauty of life. I personally like to plant a send of hope in everyone I meet.

WASHINGTON, TYRONE DALE
[b.] July 13, 1958, San Bernardino, CA; [p.] Margaret and Arthur Daniels; [m.] Christina Robin; [ch.] Andrea Faith and Starr; [ed.] San Gorgonio High School; [a.] Palm Springs, CA

WATSON, AMY ELIZABETH
[b.] April 10, 1983, Cincinnati, OH; [p.] Alan and Patricia Watson; [ed.] Brantner Elem. now I'm in GlenEste Middle School; [memb.] Glen Este Middle School, Art Club; [hon.] Honorable Mention in Duck Stamp Contest Sponsored by U.S. Department of Interior, Student of the Year 93, 94; [oth. writ.] School Student Newspaper; [pers.] Write about what you know and use your feelings. Speak from your heart and mind.; [a.] Cincinnati, OH

WATSON, IVAN
[b.] March 31, 1943, Guyana; [p.] Rev. James and Elsa Watson; [m.] Phyllida Cleopatra Watson, January 8, 1972; [ed.] MBA (Howard University); [occ.] Analyst/Acountant; [oth. writ.] "To Gain A Land" a collection of poems published in 1970.; [a.] Cheverly, MD

WATTERS, ANNETTE T.
[b.] March 7, 1958, Marengo County; [p.] Mrs. Margaret Brock; [m.] Louis Watters Jr. January 6, 1986; [ch.] Three; [ed.] Registered Nurse; [occ.] Patient Care Coordinator, [a.] Demopolis, AL

WATTS, JOHN WARREN
[b.] October 17, 1925, Bakersfield, CA; [p.] John Frank and Lily A. Watts; [m.] Lois, August

28, 1949; [ch.] Paul, Jennifer, Susan Louise (Decease) and Kathleen; [ed.] BS UCLA and Numerous post graduate courses, most recently short story writing at Univ of Calif. at Irving (USI); [occ.] Retired Real Estate Developer (Diagnosed Parkinson's 1/88) BA the late United States; [memb.] St Andrews Presbyterian Church, Newport Beach, CA, Parkinson's Disease Research National Foundation, UCLA Alumni Assoc., (Past Pres.) Retired from Santa Ana North Rotary Club (Past Reg.) Paul Harris Felloco resigned after 18 years service Watan Medical Board; [hon.] (Oldest Hospital group in Orange Co Calif. member (Past Association) Citizens Direction Finding Committee - Orange Co., past chairman Boy Scouts of America Inner-City Explovers Scouts, Santa Ana; [oth. writ.] Brisbane III, Kangaroo Rat Adventures, Palm Desert (A short story), Med Fly Meandarings (poem), Inequity, The Late, Great United States; [pers.] My poems I hope express a deep concern for long time loyal employees or major U.S. Companies being turned out for short term financial benefits. Accountants and economist seem to be the controlling philosophy.; [a.] Newport Beach, CA

WAYE, DOROTHY
[pen.] "Dee Waye"; [b.] December 19, 1934, Crawfordsville, IN; [p.] Curtis and Faye Quigg; [m.] Michael Waye, June 25, 1992; [ch.] Jeffrey Waye and Carla Janae, Amy and Andrea; [ed.] New Market High School - Indiana; [occ.] Housewife and PT Help with Husband in Own Remodeling Business; [oth. writ.] Poems published in hometown newspaper in Indiana. Have never entered a contest before.; [pers.] I have always enjoyed poetry and have written many poems for my own personal enjoyment as well as my families, but never believed that I had any "real" special talent.; [a.] Carlsbad, CA

WAYNE, JUDITH S.
[b.] October 1, 1954, New York; [m.] David L. Wayne, May 16, 1987; [ch.] Eric Justin Wayne; [ed.] Univ. of Southern California; [memb.] Alpha Epsilon Phi Sorority

WEAVER, ANTHONY M.
[pen.] Tony Weaver; [b.] December 8, 1981, Aspen, CO; [p.] Mary and Joe Weaver; [ed.] 8th Grade Basalt Elementary, Basalt Colorado; [occ.] Student; [memb.] Basalt Lions Club Baseball Team, Basalt Middle School Football Team Aspen Skiing Club - (Full Scholarship) Honor Student every quarter since 5th Grade; [hon.] League Brain Bowl (Winning First Place Team) Basalt Brain Bowl Team 1994. Associated Artists "Participant of Unity Moral Project" Honor Student; [pers.] God, I'm just a Kid.; [a.] Basalt, CO

WEAVER, BETTY
[pen.] Betty Starnes-Fox; [b.] August 24, 1943,

Granite Falls, NC; [ch.] Jonathan, Timothy, and Joseph; [occ.] Dental Assistant; [oth. writ.] Short Stories, Children's Stories, Autobiography; [pers.] I write for pleasure, communication and therapy. I enjoy sharing thoughts and feelings.; [a.] Granite Falls, NC

WEBB, SELENDA RENA
[b.] June 25, 1969, Saint Louis, MO; [p.] Luther and Linda Webb, James and Yvonne Slidham; [ed.] Graduate of Vashon High School, Saint Louis, Missouri and MSA School in San Diego, California; [occ.] Operations Manager, Fast Food Restaurant; [memb.] Member of Senior Usher Board and the Mission Society at the Mount Pleasant Missionary Baptist Church, Saint Louis, Missouri; [hon.] While in the United States Navy Aboard the USS Prairie I received a Navy "E" Ribbon, National Defense Service Medal and a Sea Service Deployment Ribbon; [oth. writ.] Poem published in the mount pleasant news gram.; [pers.] I was encouraged to start writing by Mrs. L.C. Shaw, later I was inspired by the Holy Spirit to reveal the true reason I had been blessed with this talent so all praise's are to my heavenly father for blessing me with the beautiful gift. Praises be to God Almighty.; [a.] Saint Louis, MO

WEBER, WILLIAM
[pen.] William Weber, [b.] November 13, 1911, Yugoslavia; [p.] Frank and Anna Weber, [m.] Mildred Weber (deceased 1992), September 15, 1952; [ed.] Two Years Roosevelt High School and McKinley High School, St. Louis MO, Four Years Evening School - German, MO, as a child I went to Catholic School - Bookkeeping, Shorthand, Tying, Lino-type Operation, Searching - Medicine Army, Mustily self-educated, most of Personages that influenced; [occ.] U.S. Government - Retired; [memb.] My life - Goethe Carl Sandburg M. Dickinson, Haveluck Ellis, the Famous Sexologist, Charles Chaplin, Charles Lindberg, President Kennedy Pre. Roosevelt, NY Carl Sagan; [hon.] June Scubee Rogers, the astronaut raindow, Albert Eistein, Hawkins, English Scientist - Mr. Hugh Downs, Amateur Astronomer - I love astronomy and a great teacher is the a man upstairs and lastly, not last but mostly influential Mr. Orson Welles - and as I love fiction in cryform - I love forever "Benhur"; [oth. writ.] I have one letter sent poem form to reader digest which I never won - the poem in shot said - I went to see man land on the moon before I go up to my God and behold it came true not later but very soon - and I'm still here but I'll never see more fly in space and that will also come true and live on another planet safe from, comets and asteroids - the world of tomorrow will be by my belief, and he will finally work with God at his side or should I say fly - as his side the nature of man we'd finally evolve!; [pers.] To "Quate" Carl Segan we came from the stars and finally we will go back and live with the stars which will be our final adventure!

WEBSTER, DEBORAH MARIA ROBINSON
[pen.] De Webster; [b.] Mount Clemens, MI; [p.] Theodore and Annie Mae Robinson; [m.] Divorced; [ch.] Aaron Demot and Anthony Lee Webster; [occ.] Bookkeeping Clerk, Banking; [memb.] The Arts Council of Montgomery Alabama; [hon.] As a young girl my accomplishments and awards was in music, playing the clarinet. As a mature woman I express myself through Art. In 1991 I won 1st place in Art Contest called "Oh My Own Time" with a portrait called porcha. Again in 1992 winning third place and best of show in the "On My Own Time" art contest. In 1993 my Art work was on display at the Armory Learning Center too, at the Alabama Democratic Conference in 1994; [pers.] I believe your best works comes from your experiences in life. Good or bad the emotions from these experiences when shared with others, brings peace, joy, sadness oneness and understanding; [a.] Montgomery, AL

WEBSTER, SAVANNAH
[b.] March 13, 1983, Saint Louis, MO; [p.] Jon and Ruth Webster; [ed.] Wilkinson, Dewey International Studies, Chaney Accelerated School and A.B. Green Middle School; [pers.] I want to say thanks to all of my English and reading teachers. They are the ones who taught me how to write such wonderful work. Also a thanks to my mom who encouraged me to do this.; [a.] Saint Louis, MO

WEISS, SONDRA
[b.] November 30, 1936, Jamestown, NY; [p.] Theodore and Virginia Peacock Skinner; [ch.] John Mollard (New York City) and Elizabeth Otander (Atlanta, GA); [ed.] Hood College, Long Island University, Pratt Institute; [occ.] Retired Librarian; [hon.] Long Island University, Optimates Honor Society, Sigma Tau Delta National English Honor Society, Albert A. Berman Memorial Senior Honorary Award for Short Story "The Mystic Mirrors"; [oth. writ.] Short story and poetry published in 25th Anniversary issue of Spectrum, long island university's literary publication of the university honors program, musical scores and lyrics.; [pers.] The memory of an intimate word... spoken or unspoken, written or sung... will bring a smile to warm the heart forever.; [a.] Maitland, FL

WELLINGTON, CARESSA RAE
[pen.] Coco; [b.] April 14, 1986, Mineola, NY; [p.] Winston and Linda Wellington; [ed.] Linden S.D.A. School 4th Grade; [occ.] Student; [hon.] Special Award in Spanish Reports; [pers.] "It doesn't matter what color you are on the outside but it matters what is on the inside no matter what anyone says keep on trying your best."; [a.] Springfield Gardens, NY

WELLS, CHRISTIE
[pen.] Memory; [b.] December 21, 1972, Texarkana, AR; [p.] Roy S. Wells and R. Karen Foster; [ed.] Genoa Central High School and Heritage Nursing Center; [occ.] C.N.A. - for the Community Health Center; [memb.] Shiloh Baptist Church; [pers.] My greatest inspirations have always been my family, friends, and life itself! Dreams can come true as long as you never stop believing in them.; [a.] Texarkana, AR

WERNSMAN, MICHELLE DAWN
[b.] January 2, 1980, Haxtun, CO; [p.] Jerry and Cindy Wernsman; [ed.] Attended K-10 at Fleming Frenchman RE-3 School, Currently Sophomore at Fleming High; [occ.] Student; [memb.] FBLA, FCCLA, F-Club, Academic Letter Club, CYO, Knowledge Bowl, and Quiz Bowl; [hon.] 1st Place at Fleming Science Fair- 1995 and 1996. Scholarship Award, Who's Who Among American High School Students, Math/Science Academic Award, Honor Roll 1993-96, Academic Letter, Athletic Letter, 8th Grade Continuation Speaker, [oth. writ.] From the heart - poem, Laura - short story, articles for Colorado FBLA today.; [pers.] "The best writings come from your heart," his love was inspired by a close friend, Benjamin Wyrsch.; [a.] Fleming, CO

WESTHEAD, LYNNE
[b.] June 22, 1955, Manchester, England; [p.] Bob Hodgkinson, Joyce Jodgkinson; [m.] Divorced; [ed.] University of Manchester, England, University of Leeds, England; [occ.] English Teacher, Vintage H.S. NADA, CA; [pers.] My poetry reflects a personal philosophy on aspects of life and love - two precious gifts given to us all but which we often take for granted or abuse.; [a.] Fairfield, CA

WHALEN, EVE K.
[pen.] "Vera Joyce" (Long ago); [b.] May 15, 1913, Hartford, CT; [p.] Edward and Marie Kuehn; [m.] Frank D. Whalen, October 1, 1940; [ch.] Dick and Curtis Whalen; [ed.] William. H. Hall High School Seminars Geo. Washington U and U. of Chicago as Dir. Public Relations and Vols. Alexandria Hospital; [occ.] Housewife; [memb.] Alexandria Hosp. Foundation, Honorary Member Jr. Assoc. Hosp. and Health Vol. Directors, Prince of Peace Lutheran Church, many others when I was a navy wife and worked in hospital.; [hon.] Teenage Vol. Program Rec'd National Award by American Hosp. Assoc. JAHA. Honorary Member VA Assoc. Hosp. and Health Dirs. of Vol. I organized the First State Organization and was elected first Pres.; [oth. writ.] Alexandria Hosp. Patient Handbook placed second in VA Hosp. Asso. - many other poems, some printed in Church newsletter.; [pers.] I am an x-navy wife, was at Pearl Harbor when Jabs attached. Started

a book on my experiences there. I have made 2 and moves in 22 years of Navy life. Was on Guam when the last two Japs pick me visit at night when my husband was away.; [a.] Annandale, VA

WHEELER, JANET S.
[pen.] (Former) Janet Lee Saunders; [b.] November 10, 1946, Tidewater, VA; [p.] Jasper and Mary Saunders; [m.] Earl B. Wheeler, August 10, 1990; [oth. writ.] "Howling Winds Stir", poems "The Journey", Autobiography, 1989. "Through Eyes of Love", Poems, 1990. Articles, poems for "Riverside Nurse", 1990-1995.; [pers.] It's an honor to be a part of this great volume. Inspiration is a gift. Words of grace are better than noble deeds.; [a.] Warsaw, VA

WHISENANT, SHEILA
[b.] January 5, 1963, New York, NY; [p.] George McCray, Annie McCray; [m.] Jay Wesley Whisenant Sr., December 1, 1983; [ch.] Twins - Jay Wesley Jr., Janae Latecha; [ed.] Jane Addams V.H.S., Villa Maria College 1 Year, Private Industry Council Training Center; [occ.] Home Business; [memb.] Coney Island Grace Tabernacle, Auxiliary Police; [hon.] Peace Officers Award, the Citizen Service Award; [pers.] Self love conquers a multitude of inadequate feelings. Self acceptance brings on a full life of joy and understanding.; [a.] Brooklyn, NY

WHITE, BONNIE
[pen.] The Crow Woman; [b.] April 2, 1962, Baltimore, MD; [p.] Wm. M. Collins and Florence L. Canapp; [m.] Wm. C. White, January 23, 1991; [ch.] Fawn and Erik; [ed.] H.S. Dropout - GED, (5 units) 1 Course College Alg. Compl., slowly wkg. on Degree; [occ.] Clerk Receptionist Psychiatry, Kaiser Permonente; [memb.] Church of Jesus Christ of Latter Day Saints, American Red Cross Disaster Team Volunteer, U.S.W.A. Loc 7600, Member of Celtikee Nation (Half breed Cherokee Nation Rejects); [hon.] Poem "Reaching" Honors Award Timinium Fairgrounds - MD State Fair 1978 - Pen and Ink Art Award MD, State fair 1977 - Honorable Mention for "Holocaust", "The Camppost", Florida State Fair 1974; [oth. writ.] Currently compiling poetry book for publication "Within-Without" looking for a publisher.; [pers.] I attempt to re-connect humanity to its elemental roots. Ours is a shared energy and we as a species are committing Matricide to the planet which gives us life. I hope to spark humanity's spiritual awareness.; [a.] Ontario, CA

WHITE, CYNTHIA E.
[b.] February 14, 1950, MN; [p.] Donald and Nancy Miller; [ch.] Tara White and Anthony Branch; [ed.] B.A. Metro State University, St. Paul, Minn.; [occ.] Self Sufficiency Program

Manager; [pers.] The most important way to personal peace is self expression, if you're not afraid to share who you are you have nothing to be ashamed of or to be guilty for and you can grow reaching for your full potential.; [a.] Minneapolis, MN

WHITE, DOROTHY A.
[b.] May 16, 1954, Knoxville, TN; [p.] Oscar and Dorothy White; [ed.] Bachelor of Arts in Sociology - University of Tennessee at Knoxville Master of Arts in Theology, Oral Roberts University in Tulsa, OK; [occ.] Program Analyst (Trainee), Associate Minister First Mount Zion Baptist Church, Dumfries, VA; [hon.] Ordained Minister Via First Mount Zion Baptist Church, Dumfries, VA; [pers.] Through the love and support of my family, the Lord has bless me with a love for writing. The words in the poem "I Belong to Jesus" were once an attempt to capture the living witness of a friend. Now the words are my own experiences.

WHITE, JIM
[b.] July 27, 1942; [m.] Cathy B. Moffet, December 3, 1966; [ch.] Theresa, Tara

WHITE, KELLY
[b.] October 23, 1970, Norwich, CT; [p.] John White and Barbara Barnt House; [ch.] One daughter Rosalinda Marguez; [ed.] Elementary School, Queen Palmer Colorado Sps. Co., High School: Coronado High Colo. Spg. Co.; [pers.] "Never judge a book by its cover."

WHITE, LAURA A.
[a.] Royal Oak, MI

WHITFIELD, PEGGY J.
[b.] May 30, 1942, Casa Grand, AZ; [p.] Cleve and Susie Erwin; [m.] Kenneth A. Whitfield, December 21, 1957; [ch.] Dennis Eugene, Darryl Dwayne, Valerie Annette, David Anthony; [ed.] Arizona, California, and Texas (11th grade) married 15 1/2 half way thru 11th grade; [occ.] Homemaker 38 years; [memb.] First Assembly of God Church, Howe, TX; [oth. writ.] Seven poems published in "Today's Great Poems". I've written 71 poems, 8 Gospel Songs, 1 song written especially for The Whitewright Nursing Home Residents. Where we minister in song and poems every Tuesday morning.; [pers.] Most of my poems are inspired by actual events in my life. How it was in the Cottonfields, school days, wash day with no plumbing, grandchildren storms sickness, travel, family, funtime and etc. Most in story form - to many lines for publishing in most contest.; [a.] Howe, TX

WHITMIRE, BONITA D.
[pen.] Pulaski D. Ethridge; [b.] August 8, 1959, Baltimore, MD; [p.] John and Eva Lee Whitmire; [ed.] Southside High School 1976,

Greenville Technical College 1979, University of South Carolina 1987; [occ.] Marketing Research; [memb.] Member Chancel Choir of Edwards Road Baptist Ch., Pleasantburg Lions Club, Zone Chairman Zone 6 1995-96 (Lions); [hon.] Melvin Jones Fellowship 1992 - Highest Award that can be received by Lions; [oth. writ.] Two poems reed river review 1 poem Palmetto Lion, 1 poem Glimpses of Grove, 1 poem SAM Newsletter, East of the Sunrise, Best Poems of 1996, A Muse to Follow.; [pers.] My writing reflects the core of my being. Often, when I write, what I write pours out of me, as if I have no control over it.; [a.] Greenville, SC

WIELENBERG, MICHAEL P.
[pen.] Wheelie; [b.] March 17, 1965, Saint Paul, MN; [p.] Alvin and Jackie Wielenberg; [ch.] Stephanie Gail Wielenberg; [ed.] Kellogg High School, St. Paul Technical College; [occ.] Service Technician; [memb.] Incarnation Lutheran Church, Great River Valley System; [hon.] Honor Student St. Paul Technical College, Chisy's Outstanding Student Award; [pers.] I enjoy writing inspirational poetry. I enjoy the solitude and peace of the outdoors. Romance and inspiration are the type of writings I have achieved in.; [a.] Saint Paul, MN

WIENER, CHRISTOPHER M.
[pen.] Sebastian Quine; [b.] February 10, 1970, Raf Lakenheath, United Kingdom; [p.] Dale Wiener, Trauti Wiener; [ed.] MALS in Progress University of NC Charotte, BA History and Religious Studies UNCC, AA Brevard College; [occ.] Support Engineer with Microsoth Corp.; [memb.] Microsoft Certified Professional Product Specialist; [hon.] Phi Theta Kappa, Phi Beta Kappa, Eagle Scout, 2 Army Commendation Medals, 3 Army Achievement Medals, National Defense Medal; [oth. writ.] Extensive world wide wed publishing, published in two literary magazines during high school and college.; [pers.] Poets have a mission to revitalize the revolutionary spirit of change.; [a.] Charlotte, NC

WIGGINS, CHRISTINE BELL
[b.] June 6, 1954, Norfolk, VA; [p.] Thurman Bell, Frances O. Bell; [ch.] Bernice Renee, Marlina Derisa, Adrienne Denise; [ed.] Tidewater Community College; [occ.] Recreation Assistant BEverly Manor of Portsmouth; [memb.] Mount Carmel Baptist Church of Norfolk, VA. Ruffner Middle School TPA, Booker T. Washington High PTA; [hon.] Achievements in Therapeutic Recreation; [oth. writ.] Several unpublished poems and stories.; [pers.] There will always be good and evil in the present world but with a mixture of love and forgiveness, and good can greatly outweigh the evil.; [a.] Norfolk, VA

WILHELM, LISA
[pen.] Lisa Wilhelm; [b.] January 5, 1981, Pensacola, FL; [p.] Robert and Barbara Wilhelm; [ed.] Currently attending Leonardtown High School; [occ.] Student; [oth. writ.] I have 4 books full of poetry, but none are published anywhere.; [pers.] I think the reader should decide what they want a poem to mean, so it means something different for each person.; [a.] California, MD

WILKERSON, EVA E.
[b.] February 12, 1914, Republic, MO; [p.] M.M. and F.E. Turner; [m.] Samp Wilkerson, August 4, 1929; [ch.] Two Boys and Five Girls (seven) who are a blessing to me; [occ.] Being happy in my old age; [hon.] For several poems; [oth. writ.] Short stories for my little friends.; [pers.] My mother and brother planted the lone pine tree when it was only 304 inches tall so to them I owe this poem.

WILLEY, GARY W.
[b.] January 2, 1958, Detroit, MI; [m.] Lisa Willey, May 8, 1995; [memb.] Top Records Song Writers Association, BMI; [hon.] Outstanding Lyric Writer; [oth. writ.] Several song's published by Country Gateway Publishing.; [a.] Garner, NC

WILLIAMS, CHERYL WARREN
[pen.] Chery Warren, Liz Warren; [b.] February 9, 1946, Bisbee, AZ; [p.] Edgar Charles and Mary Evangeline Warren; [m.] Fiance - Jerry Pigg; [ch.] Charles Thomas, Robert Michael, Robbie Michelle, Kathy Markaleen; [ed.] Bisbee High, Cochise Junior College, University of Arizona, Northern Arizona University; [occ.] Inventory Clerk for COE Manufacturing; [memb.] Ariz. Education Assoc., National Educ. Assoc., Oregon Bow Hunter, National Field Archery Assoc.; [oth. writ.] Stories and poems (non-published) written while teaching for Arizona schools.; [pers.] I taught 15 years - 3rd grade Ariz. If I can make one person feel better with something I have written - then I have attained success.; [a.] Hillsboro, OR

WILLIAMS, DANIELLE ALEXIS
[b.] July 29, 1982, Queens, NY; [p.] Isabelle Williams, Carl Williams; [ed.] P.S. 150 Queens, I.S. 125 Queens, New York; [occ.] Student; [hon.] Martin Luther King Humanitarian Award (1994); [oth. writ.] Several poems and short stories published in school newspaper.; [pers.] Write it, read it, love it, a book called "Life.";
[a.] Long Island City, NY

WILLIAMS, MELISSA CARLETTE
[b.] April 1, 1971, Sunflower County, Indianola, MS; [p.] M.C. and Dorothy Williams; [ch.] Marveale and Marchristian Williams; [ed.] Received diploma at Gentry High of Indianola,

MS, Received B.A. Degree in Sociology in Itta Benay, MS; [occ.] Wal-Mart Discount Store, Inc. as Cashier/Sales Representative; [pers.] My writing comes from daily experiences and the knowledge that God has instilled in me.

WILLIAMS, RICHARD G.
[pen.] Rick; [b.] June 15, 1941, Fort Monroe, VA; [p.] Bill and Marie Williams; [ch.] Glenn and Amy Williams; [ed.] Rancocas Valley Regional H.S., Mt. Holly, New Jersey; [occ.] Retired - U.S. Army (1980), Retired Construction/Security, Stricked M.S. 1988; [memb.] American Legion; [oth. writ.] Special lady, exciting eyes, it comes as a dream, transparent, dreams, what if, that time after loving. I've mentioned before.; [pers.] Everything I've ever written has come from personal experience. I want to thank 3 of the most beautiful women/people/ teachers in the world. I only wish I'd learned my lessons sooner. Thank you, Linda, Toby and a special lady named Nick.; [a.] Phoenix, AZ

WILLIAMS, TONY LEE
[pen.] C. W. Williams; [b.] May 20, 1958, Georgia; [p.] Major and Cassie Williams; [m.] Marilyn Cunningham; [ch.] Nikita and Nigel; [occ.] U.S. Air Force; [oth. writ.] Feelings, a lover's prayer.; [pers.] I've always tried to express the love I feel in my heart in my poems. I believe that if we are to survive as a race, love will be the answer. I dedicate all of my writing to my family, my wife Marilyn and children Nigel and Nikita.; [a.] Wichita Falls, TX

WILLIAMSON, CANDACE A.
[pen.] Candy Williamson; [b.] November 2, 1981, Lexington, KY; [p.] David Y. Williamson, Ginger Williamson; [memb.] National Junior Beta Club, President of the 4-H Club, Percussionist of the Bath County High Marching Wildcasts Band, Pep Band; [hon.] All District Band, Academic Award, Citizenship Award, Pat-on-the-Back Award; [pers.] I try to show my work as a reflection of awakenings for all people to see and understand.; [a.] Owingsville, KY

WILLIAMSON, JOYCE ANN MARKARIAN
[b.] April 6, 1957, Chicago, IL; [p.] Jerry and Deloris Markarian; [m.] David Wayne Williamson, July 20, 1985; [ch.] Kelly Ann and Nick Anthony; [ed.] Diploma Graduate of: Mennonite School of Nursing, Paxton High School; [occ.] Homemaker; [memb.] American Lutheran Church, American Heart Assoc., WELCA, Mennonite Nurse's Assoc.; [oth. writ.] "War Buddies" published in 1987 american anthology of midwestern poetry plus numerous poems published in my local newspaper - the Paxton Record; [pers.] This poem "Missing You" is dedicated to the memory of my husband David Wayne Williamson who was suddenly taken from us due to a heart attack. He was only 36!; [a.] Paxton, IL

WILLIS, MARY RUSSELL
[pen.] Mary Willis; [b.] September 22, 1949, Manhatten, KS; [p.] Dr. L. Jack Russell Jr., Mary B. Buckley; [m.] Mark A. Willis, October 18, 1994; [ch.] James, Matthew, Meagen, Brittany, Mark Jr.; [ed.] Ygnacio Valley High, Monterey Peninsula Jr. College; [pers.] My writings reflect self realization and self awareness. I really began to write in 1984 while trying to deal with my fathers death.; [a.] Saint George, GA

WILLIS SR., ARNOLD R.
[b.] September 13, 1936, Santa Fe, FL; [p.] Wilma and D C Willis; [m.] Janice; [ch.] Five; [ed.] High School Graduate, Alachua, FL, plus life's daily training ground; [occ.] Supermarket Produce Assistant; [memb.] NRA, Southern Baptist many others; [hon.] Publix Supermarket gave me an award for writing about their supermarket in poem form.; [oth. writ.] Victory, Justice, Peace, A Rose, God's Nature, "Fall", "My Love", "The Old Bay"; [pers.] I never was much of a speaker, so I write to express my inner feeling and the wondrous beauty of our world God has made that seem to pass by so many. My writings express my lack of outward expressions; [a.] Alachua, FL

WILSON, AUDREY HOOPER
[p.] Emmett and Eva Hooper; [m.] Bryant Wilson, December 24, 1949; [ch.] Son; [ed.] In 1945 finished school at Central High School at Ashland City Tennessee; [occ.] Retired

WILSON, MS. CHERYL
[pen.] Cheryl Wilson; [b.] September 25, 1958, Dayton, OH; [p.] Samuel Wilson Sr., Hazel Wilson (deceased); [m.] Henry Heard Cofield Jr., July 27, 1985; [ed.] Middletown Senior High School '76, Miami University, Oxford, Ohio '87, Associates in Arts Degree and a NRI non-fiction writer.; [occ.] Housewife; [memb.] Ohio Association of Historical Societies and Museums (OAHSM), Butler County Historical Society, the Middletown Historical Society (MHS) as curator, local historian, tour guide and membership committee and the National Association of the Advancement of Colored People (NAACP).; [hon.] Received NRI Achievement with high honors, received the National Library of Poetry Editor's Choice Award for outstanding achievement in poetry among the best 3% of entries judged in the anthology "At Water's Edge."; [oth. writ.] "Loves' Lonely Silence", "Treasure Chest," and "Love Is" are parts of the three poems that make up the poem "The City's African-American Bicentennial Salute" to be published in the anthology "Where Dawn Lingers" in honor of Middletown's African-American Heritage.; [pers.] I enjoy writing poetry, researching, family genealogy and photography.

The philosophical statement "Love's lonely quietness. Love's lonely silence" means the non-violence movement that means instituted by Martin Luther King, Jr., "The Yoke" means the chains that slaves wore on their hands and feet, the words "Inferiority" means slavery, "Civil Liberties" the Magna Carta and Bill of Rights. The words "Darkest Africa" means lapses of time, "Allegiance" to the flag, "Heartaches" is servitude and the phrase "Seek to someday heal one's wounds" is a reflection of an apology to blacks for the struggle and suffering of their ancestors and descendants. Words like "sun", "moon," "stars," and "night" relates to the same description of such words in America or wherever you are living, one can image seeing the same 'sun,' 'moon,' 'stars' and darkness. The "North Star" is associated with Harriet Tubmen following the 'North Star' to free the slaves.; [a.] Middletown, OH

WILSON, JONI
[b.] August 12, 1956, Biloxi; [p.] Terry and Nancy Floyd; [ch.] Amber - The light of my life; [ed.] Ohio University - Dean's List; [occ.] Free Lance Writer; [memb.] Historical Society; [oth. writ.] Short Fiction, News Writing, Technical Writing; [pers.] While most of my fictional writings are written from a realistic point of view, poetry allows me to express inner struggles that lie within the heart and mind.; [a.] Newport, IN

WILSON, LESLIE
[b.] February 21, 1978, Cleveland, MS; [p.] Simone and Wesley Wilson; [ed.] Montgomery County High; [occ.] Student; [memb.] Beta Club, Who's Who Among American High School Students, United States Achievement Academy; [hon.] Many Achievement Awards; [oth. writ.] Many others poems written to pass time and convey feelings.; [pers.] The poems I write reflect my feelings and the problems I encounter. They are my way of expression when I cannot share my feelings with others.; [a.] Kelmichael, MS

WILSON, LUCY H.
[b.] September 14, 1951, Burlington, NC; [p.] Robert Hill, Virginia Hill; [m.] Steven P. Wilson, June 17, 1972; [ch.] Robert Paul, Steven Mark; [ed.] Southern High School, Graham, NC Old Dominion University Norfolk, VA (1973), Southeastern Baptist Theological Seminary, Wake Forest, NC (1980); [occ.] Church Secretary for Good News Baptist Church, Roanoke Rapids, NC; [memb.] Good News Baptist Church; [oth. writ.] A pome published in the local newspaper, a poem published in A Collection of Religious Poems by the National Society of Published Poets, poems used in church newsletters.; [pers.] I seek to share my faith and everyday experiences with others

through my writing so they may be encouraged in their daily lives.; [a.] Roanoke Rapids, NC

WILSON, NIKI
[b.] February 24, 1985; [p.] Connie Howell, Dan Wilson; [ed.] Sunset Elementary 3rd Grade - Mrs. Runyan's class my class is cool; [occ.] I go to School M-F, chores to earn money; [memb.] YMCA; [hon.] High Flyers for Accomplishments in Certain Areas from my School, Coloring Contest; [pers.] I care about the environment and I am concerned about its future. I love animals, especially my cat Madi. It makes me hurt inside when I see someone else sad. Mommy says this makes me compassionate.; [a.] West Linn, OR

WINKLE, PAMELA L.
[pen.] Pam Parten; [b.] February 17, 1962, Kissimmee, FL; [p.] Frank and Louise Parten; [m.] Thomas Winkle, August 8, 1980; [ch.] Megan Nichole, Thomas Logan; [ed.] Kathleen High School, Institute of Children's Literature; [occ.] Office Manager of an Architectural Firm; [memb.] First Baptist Church; [hon.] School Volunteer Appreciation Award, Graduating Class Honors Award; [oth. writ.] Several poems and short stories.; [pers.] My goal is for everyone reading my work to feel a remembrance of a similar event in their own life and to reflect our lives as we live them in todays times.; [a.] Lakeland, FL

WINNING, PAUL
[b.] December 28, 1959, Stoughton, MA; [p.] Paul, Pat Winning; [oth. writ.] When I meet someone who is in need, or meets a need, I've been writing something precious to give to them to show them how they are.; [pers.] My poems are expressed to reveal things in myself that are private. I also must write about life and its most beautiful qualities.; [a.] Halifax, MA

WINSTON, KAREN
[b.] August 16, 1961, Washington, DC; [p.] Richard and Barbara Winston; [ed.] Michigan State University, Bedford College London; [occ.] Advertising Manager; [memb.] Lupus Foundation of America, National Association for the Advancement of colored People (NAACP), Urban League; [hon.] Local Poetry Contests, all - State Track Low Hurdles; [oth. writ.] Short stories, songs, children's books.; [pers.] I enjoy writing about personal experiences that move me or touch my heart, and sharing those experiences with others through poetry.; [a.] Boston, MA

WINTERS, SIR JASON
[b.] September 13, 1930, United Kingdom; [m.] Paterna Winters; [ch.] Nine; [occ.] Herbalist and Health Book Writer; [hon.] Laureatte Belgium, Netherlands and South Africa, Knight of Malta, President of Cia Man; [oth. writ.] Books: Killing

Cancer, In Search of the Perfect Cleanse, Breakthrough, Sir Jason Winters Story (four in one)

WINTHROP, HOPE
[b.] May 22, 1936, Mobile, AL; [p.] Hope and Frank Sneeringer; [m.] Divorced; [ed.] Huntingdon College, Spring Hill College; [occ.] Reiki, massage, writer; [memb.] Member of the Board (Secretary) New Frontiers of the Gold Country; [oth. writ.] The Desert pub. in The Motley literary pub. of Spring Hill College. '50s Interviews in The Elysium Journal. Yucatan Experience in Elysium Journal '70s.; [pers.] I believe in the goodness of the great God and Goddess and in the workings of Love in the Universe. Blessed Be!; [a.] Grass Valley, CA

WINTON, CHRIS E.
[b.] December 25, 1981, Oakland, CA; [p.] James Winton, Mary E. Winton; [ed.] 9th grader —first year in High School Creek H.S. Clear Creek Public; [occ.] Student; [a.] Nassau Bay, TX

WIRTH, CANDICE M.
[b.] October 20, 1973, Queens; [p.] Alice and Donald Wirth; [ed.] Expected B.A. in English and Studio Art and a Minor in Secondary Education, 1997; [occ.] Queens College English Club - Vice President; [oth. writ.] Several poems in the Queens College literary magazine, Pandemonium. Several poems were published in the Queens College Quad.; [a.] Maspeth, NY

WISE, ESTELLE DEMARS
[b.] January 25, 1917, Staples, MN; [p.] Harry Hollister, Kathryn Hollister; [m.] Harold DeMars, October 29, 1938, Everett Wise, July 6, 1968; [ch.] Eight; [ed.] BS El Ed - Mankato U, Mankato, MN 1966, St. Benedict's College 1936-37 Staples High School; [occ.] Retired Teacher; [oth. writ.] Children's stories, none published. (I have not seriously pursued publication.); [pers.] After Harold's untimely death, my outlook on life became, "I will take one day at a time, for that I can life, I know."; [a.] Fifty Lakes, MN

WISNOWSKI, ALEXANDRA
[b.] September 1, 1976, Montclair, NJ; [p.] Donald and Patricia Wisnowski; [ed.] Passaic Valley High School, New York University; [occ.] Student; [hon.] Dean's List, Member of the New Jersey School of the Arts for the gifted in creative writing.; [oth. writ.] Collection of poetry and short stories; [pers.] My writings are derived from the sad experiences in my life. I feel these are the most emotional times and when reading my work, I like my reader to feel it and relate to it.; [a.] Little Falls, NJ

WITT, KYLE LYNN
[pen.] Kyle Lynn Witt; [b.] August 28, 1981, Colorado; [p.] Jerry S. Witt, Robyn Hitchin;

[ed.] 9th grade, Goshen High School; [occ.] Student; [memb.] Teen Inst. (Teens against drugs); [hon.] National Honor Society, 2 yrs. honored by United States Achievement Academy, All Star Award (Softball), God, Flag, Country. Runner Up in 8th grade Spaulding Middle School Goshen, Ohio, Cheerleader; [oth. writ.] Frightful Nights I-IV, "Kendra", "Grandpa", "What You Don't See", "Holidays", and "By the Fire", and "Why?"; [pers.] Take life one step at a time. It's priceless. In loving memory of Charles Messmore.; [a.] Goshen, OH

WOLFE, TARA
[b.] January 13, 1979, Lawrence; [p.] Judi and Richard Wolfe; [ed.] Lawrence High School; [occ.] Dietary Aide at Brandon Woods Retirement Home; [hon.] Presidential Academic Award, Lawrence High School Honor Roll for Two Years; [oth. writ.] Poem published in Lawrence Journal World Newspaper; [pers.] For me, influence comes from all my surroundings, but I would have to say I value what life has given me in terms of educational value most. I give thanks to all who have taught.; [a.] Lawrence, KS

WOMACK, ANTONIO R.
[pen.] A.R. Womack; [b.] October 3, 1963, Annapolis, MD; [p.] Dr. Jean Creek, Rev. Charles Creek; [ed.] Associates: Bus. Admin., Bach: Philosophy, Univ. MD Balto. Co. (UMBC); [occ.] Entrepreneur; [memb.] Phi Beta Sigma Frat., Black Professional Men, Co-Founder of Project Fresh Start (Mentoring), Governor's Citation Recipient; [oth. writ.] Abortion, Rights and Obligations, Life and the Un-Lived, Pigeon Hold, Circular Theory, and more.; [pers.] I am, therefore I think. I try to make people think when they read my poetry. Most of my poems have a meaning beyond what's apparent on the surface.; [a.] Baltimore, MD

WONG, LILLIAN THERESA KELLY
[pen.] Marie K.; [b.] August 2, 1959, Kgn, Jamaica; [p.] Detors Smith and Lester Wong; [m.] Everton Kelly Wong, May 11, 1991; [ch.] Three; [ed.] Educated in Jamaica Chetolah Park Rumary, Kingston High School; [occ.] Nurses Aid, Riverdale Bronx; [oth. writ.] Several unpublished poems.; [pers.] There is so much to life to be appreciated and writing poem always seem to capture my thoughts and views. There is so much of ones self, that one can learn, if one only take time to know one's self better one would be surprised of the wealth of knowledge retained.; [a.] Brooklyn, NY

WOOD, CURTIS R.
[pen.] Chris Crowe; [b.] May 5, 1978, Jacksonville, FL; [p.] Winston R. and Blenda A. Wood; [ed.] Morningstar Christian Acc; [occ.] Part-time front-service Publix Associate; [oth. writ.] Many Christian songs and choruses and other poems; [pers.] "But God hath chosen the foolish things of the world to confound the wise, and God hath chosen the weak things of the world to confound the mighty" -I Corinthians 1:27; [a.] Jacksonville, FL

WOOD, NANETTE LARAINE
[b.] January 29, 1975, Peoria, IL; [p.] Mr. and Mrs. Oneal Wood; [ed.] Graduated from Graves County High School, I also am going to be starting college in the Fall; [oth. writ.] I am currently writing a novel.; [a.] Hickory, KY

WOODS, JOHN T.
[pen.] John Terry Woods; [b.] August 20, 1950, Roanoke, VA; [ed.] Livingstone College, Salisbury, NC, B.A. History; [occ.] Local Veteran Employment Representative of Roanoke, VA; [memb.] Prince Hall Mason, Livingstone College Alumni, Member of Personnel in Employment Security, State of VA, Coach A.A.U. Basketball.; [hon.] I have had in the past poems publish in the newspapers, and other books.; [oth. writ.] "Country Living Is The Best For Me", "A Tear", "A Light", Dreams of You, Do Good to Others, When "The Fox Guards The Hen House".; [pers.] As for myself I strive to write about love, history and the goodness of mankind. I have been greatly influenced with the many loves in my life.; [a.] Roanoke Rocky Mount, VA

WOOLWINE, DALE J.
[pen.] The Hidden Boy, D.C.; [b.] October 12, 1977, Jackson, WY; [p.] Willard Woolwine, Connie Woolwine; [ed.] High School Senior, Jackson Hole High School; [occ.] Student; [memb.] Founder of "The Free Style Romantics" a Group of hopeless Romantic High School Friends, who Camp, Fish, and Hold Poetry Readings along the River; [hon.] Young Author's District Finalist, National Honors Society; [oth. writ.] "Everything in Between," a personal collection of my own writing.; [pers.] I've been greatly influenced by the outdoors and the natural environment in which I live. These influences and the ever changing lessons of my life are reflected in my writing. I love the 50's, baseball, old cars, and am an avid fan of the little rascals.; [a.] Jackson, WY

WORKING, RACHAEL M.
[b.] June 27, 1934, Marion, IN; [p.] Charles T. and Julian N. Wilson; [m.] Von L. Working, October 28, 1968; [ch.] Kyle A. and Allison Rene; [ed.] Marion High School, Marion College 1 yr, [occ.] Housewife; [memb.] Nelson St. Wesleyan Ch; [oth. writ.] I have had poems published in the local newspaper, written many personal birthday etc. verses for own use and have written four Christmas verses which we have used to send. I also have written poems for other people to give to others just from information they give me. Also I did not receive a list of prizes as stated in your letter to me.; [pers.] I believe God has given me a talent to use to encourage and uplift others. I became aware of this talent in the seventh grade from a teacher who loved James Whitcomb Riley; [a.] Marion, IN

WRIGHT, DOROTHY
[b.] December 10, 1925, Lima, OH; [p.] Ted and Bertha Hollingsworth; [m.] Ted L. Wright (Deceased), April 18, 1949; [ch.] Kip, Tim, Teresa, Lorrie, Jack; [ed.] Lima South High (1943), Lima Memorial Hospital School of Nursing (1947), Worked as R.N. for 45 years.; [occ.] Retired; [memb.] American Nurses Assoc., Michigan Nurses Assoc.; [oth. writ.] None published as yet poetry, essays, children's stories; [pers.] This poem was written to inspire compassion in Nursing Assistants and co-workers when I worked at a Nursing Home in 1993 and 1994; [a.] Celina, OH

WRIGHT, JOHN L.
[b.] May 8, 1964, Youngstown, OH; [ed.] Liberty High, Youngstown State University; [occ.] Science Teacher, Lakeview High School, Cortland, Ohio; [pers.] Always remember to be led by your dreams, not pushed by your problems!; [a.] Warren, OH

WRIGHT, KEVIN
[b.] September 9, 1962, Three Rivers Hospital; [p.] Charles and Margaret Wright; [m.] Becky Wright, June 30, 1984; [ch.] Ruth Ann Wright; [ed.] High School - Christian College, A.A. Degree at Christian Center Collage South Bend Ind; [occ.] Boxer of Copper tubing at Elkhart Products, Elkart Ind; [memb.] Diamond Cove Missionary Church in Cassopolis MI; [oth. writ.] I write other poems for church specials; [a.] Cassopolis, MI

WROCLAWSKI, ROMAN
[b.] July 13, 1955, Poland; [p.] Fadwiga Lapinska, Dominik Wroclawski; [m.] Halina-Folanta; [ch.] Michalina - 15 yrs, Roman - 9 yrs.; [ed.] Academy of Physical Education in Warsaw 1981, Glass Work Technical School Piotrko'w - Poland; [occ.] Voluntary Coach of US Olympic Wrestling Team; [memb.] US Wrestling Federation, Sunkist; [hon.] World Champion in Greco-Roman Style Wrestling in 1982, Olympian in Seoul in 1988.; [oth. writ.] 350 poems on different subjects but mainly reflecting the power of human soul. Three Cooks, one biographical.; [pers.] "Life is brutal, usually ends with death and coffin does not have pockets"; [a.] Phoenix, AZ

WYATT, ANITA LEE
[b.] July 25, 1972, Davenport, IA; [p.] Jurline

and Donald Bryant; [m.] Royal T. Wyatt, June 20, 1995; [pers.] Poetry is life on paper.; [a.] Silver Spring, MD

WYATT, DAWN MARIE
[b.] February 7. 1975, Norfolk, VA; [p.] Mr. and Mrs. R. Michael; [ed.] High School Diploma from Cradock High School, Tidewater Community College; [occ.] Student; [memb.] Church of the Holy Angels, Religious Education Program for the Diocese of Richmond; [hon.] Five Awards in Regional Science Fairs during High School; [oth. writ.] Several poems for personal pleasure.; [a.] Portsmouth, VA

WYATT, KAROLINE
[b.] October 23, 1982, Grand Forks, ND; [p.] Rev. Joseph K. and Yvonne Wyatt; [ed.] 8th Grade at Growing Grace Christian Home School, been home-schooling 6 years. Kindergarten, 1st Grade was at Mercer Christian Academy; [oth. writ.] This is my first publication. Being a semi-finalist also.; [pers.] Saved, born again Christian. I am a member at Cornerstone Baptist Church. I enjoy writing poems but never sent one in 'til this time. Also I like to write animal stories.; [a.] Thorpe, WV

WYATT, LEONORA A.
[b.] June 14, 1926, Spring Lake, NJ; [p.] Kellogg and Bertha Ashton; [m.] Divorced; [ch.] Wendy, Michael, Wayne and Linda; [ed.] H.S. B.S. in Education Licensed Practical Nurse; [occ.] Retired; [memb.] United Methodist Church, Administrative Council; [hon.] Golden Poet Award, 1988, 1989, 1990, 1991; [oth. writ.] Published poetry books, "Life, Love and Me," "The Best is yet to be."; [pers.] I am striving to spread God's good news to all through my poetry.; [a.] Trenton, NJ

WYNNE, ALICE L.
[b.] January 23, 1928, Brooklyn, NY; [p.] Joseph Zittel, Bertha Zittel; [m.] Donald M. Wynne (Deceased), December 8, 1951; [ch.] Mary, Donald, Jr., Deborah, James, Ann, Theresa, Michael, Patrick, Thomas; [ed.] McAuley High, Suf. Co. Com. College AA Humanities Extra courses-review typing and steno Courses in word processing etc. I also took a Writer's Digest correspondence course "Writing To Sell Fiction" in 1991; [occ.] Retired last position - clerk typist in Patchogue-Medford Library, Patchogue, NY; [memb.] No particular memberships at present time. However, I register twice a year for a class (actually a group of writers who critique each other's writings, with the help of a moderator) Traproot, LI's Community of Older Writers; [oth. writ.] Essay published in LILITH (1981) college magazine. Couple of poems published in local newsletter, BULL GAzette (1985). Wrote weekly staff newsletter TP NEWS (1989-90)

short story published in MY LEGACY, which is an offshoot of FELICITY, a literacy magazine in Penna. (1990) I have completed a novel, a mystery which I am hoping to have published in the near future. A memoir piece was published in Taproot Journal in spring 1995 will have a pome published in National Library of Poetry edition "Carvings in Stone.; [pers.] A writer uses her pen as an artist uses a brush. With the magic of words she creates a picture and presents it to the world. This picture, she hopes will arouse an emotion, whether it be joy or sorrow, laughter or tears. Then, and only then, can she be called "Author."; [a.] Medford, NY

YABLONOVICH, YAKOV
[b.] May 16, Odessa, Ukraine; [p.] Mark Yablonovich, Gitel Yablonovich; [m.] Lidia Yablonovich, February 10, 1969; [ch.] Mark Yablonovich; [ed.] Odessa Institute of Construction; [occ.] Structural Designer; [oth. writ.] Poems and prose published in Ukraine and USA.; [a.] Los Angeles, CA

YASUHARA, CAROL
[b.] March 17, 1951, East Cleveland, OH; [p.] William and Betty Herrin; [ch.] Bryan Chad and Kelli Diane; [ed.] Shawnee Mission South High School, AA - Johnson County Community College, BSE - Emporia State University, MLA - Baker University; [occ.] Foreign Language Teacher - Westridge Middle School - Overland Park, KS; [memb.] National Education Association, Kansas Foreign Language Association, American Association of Teachers of Spanish and Portuguese, Phi Delta Kappa; [hon.] Dean's List, Sigma Delta Pi; [oth. writ.] I just recently had a poem published in the anthology: A Voyage To Remember, this poem was also featured in "The Sound of Poetry."; [pers.] I write short stories as well as poems. I write in both Spanish and English.; [a.] Overland Park, KS

YATES, ANGELA
[pen.] Ang; [b.] January 4, 1981, Cottage Grove, OR; [p.] Debbie and John Yates; [ed.] High School - 9th Grade; [occ.] School; [memb.] Columbia House, Music and Video; [oth. writ.] Poems and stories; [a.] Cottage Grove, OR

YATES, LINDA STONER
[pen.] Linda Yates; [b.] July 20, 1938, Saint Louis, MO; [p.] June Alberta Crowder and Robert Anthony Jerrue (Deceased); [m.] Alan Porter Yates, July 22, 1983; [ch.] Cathryn, Chris, Heather, Sean; [ed.] B.S. (1973), M.Ed. (1975) Auburn, University, Auburn, AL; [occ.] Owner, Telecommunications Company-Power Communications; [memb.] Phi Delta Kappa, AAUW, Christian Women's Club, Toastmasters; [hon.] Secretary of the Year, 1974 National Secretaries Ass'n.), Outstanding Careerist of 1975 (Bus. and Prof. Women), Who's Who in

American Women, 1993, Who's Who World-wide, 1994-1995, Distinguished Member, International Society of Poets, 1995; [oth. writ.] "Appearances", The Auburn Circle and The Chattahorchee Review, "The Donor" published by University of Virginia, "A Serious Illness" in Mists of Enchantment, "This Is Reality" pub. by All Saint Episcopal Church in the Parish Letter.; [pers.] Poetry enables us to share our thoughts our feelings about life's experiences and important issues with others who might benefit from such sharing.; [a.] Tripp Island, SC

YATES, WILLIAM
[pen.] Greasy Pig; [b.] September 30, 1945, Wake Country; [ed.] I have 14 years of Education. I have gin High School Diploma, also two year of Business School also two year of Voc. School; [occ.] Plumber Common Labor, Hospital Worker, also Salesman; [memb.] I am Lifetime Member of Senior Citizen also Lifetime Member of International Society of Poetry; [hon.] I have receive honors and award from Track and Fields. Also quality in road races also three Editor's Choice Award from The National Library of Poetry 1994 yr., 1995 yr., 1996 yr.,; [pers.] As writer I am writing for victories that's never ends, understanding of mankind, also human as greater victories of the know also, know which yet the ends never occurs.; [a.] Raleigh, NC

YOPP, HEATHER ELAINE
[b.] November 23, 1970, Kingstown, RI; [p.] Stacy Warden Jr., Elaine Warden; [m.] Glen Patrick Yopp, June 18, 1994; [ed.] Topeka West High School, University of Kansas, Manatee C. College, Florida State University; [memb.] Westminster Presbyterian Church, HSUS, ASPCA; [hon.] Phi Beta Kappa, Golden Key National Honor Society, National Collegiate Scholar, Dean's List, Selby Scholarships, Geology Scholarships.; [oth. writ.] Many other poems printed in church newsletters, wedding poems featured in marriage ceremonies, children's literature.; [pers.] Through my writing, I endeavor to highlight God's role in our lives and to touch the hearts of many. Writing that has encouraged people to feel, has served a great purpose.; [a.] Fort Myers, FL

YORK, RICHARD DEAN
[b.] January 6, 1957, Beech Grove, IN; [p.] William H. and Mabel O. Klinge; [m.] Lori Ann York, April 11, 1986; [ch.] Ricky Dean II, Nathaniel Everett, Tiffany Pauline; [ed.] Lutheran Memorial Elem., Emmerich Manual High Indianapolis, IN; [occ.] Inventor (Bodyguard Child Auto Safety Device); [memb.] Glendale Baptist Church, Bowling Green, KY; [hon.] I was honored God gave me Mr. and Mrs. Klinge for my mother and father. United States Patent on my invention called "Body Guard" a child auto safety device; [pers.] Problems that

arise show our true character do not fret on them but use that energy to find the positive reason God gave us the problem.; [a.] Alvaton, KY

YOUNG, CHRIS C.
[b.] September 16, 1959, Grand Rapids, MI; [p.] Byron Young, Richard and Kathleen Gruenbauer; [ch.] Kathrine M. Young; [ed.] Caledonia High School; [occ.] Production Sup.; [oth. writ.] I am currently compiling a collection of poems titled "The Life and Rhymes of a Middle Class Poet"; [pers.] My writings are not bias toward politics, religion or race. They come from experiences that I've had and stories I've heard from the people that I've encountered in my life.; [a.] Grand Rapids, MI

YOUNG, DEBORAH A.
[b.] January 7, 1957, Havre De Grace, MD; [p.] John E. Young Jr. (Deceased), Betty J. Young; [ed.] Bel Air Senior High School, Harford Community College; [occ.] Computer Assistant at Aberdeen Proving Ground, Md; [memb.] Emmorton Baptist Church; [hon.] Dean List at HCC, March of Dimes Walk-A-Thon; [pers.] "The rewards of being grounded in God are better than being short-circuited by the currents of life."; [a.] Darlington, MD

YOUNG, JEREMY M.
[pen.] The Stranger; [b.] November 10, 1975, Lebanon, PA; [p.] Stanley and Susan Young; [ed.] Mountain View Christian School, Harrisburg Area Community College, planning to attend Maranatha Baptist Bible College starting Jan. '97; [occ.] General Contractor; [memb.] Phi Theta Kappa Honors Society, National Dean's List '95, Who's Who Among Students '95 in American Junior Colleges, Faith Baptist Church of Lebanon, PA; [hon.] National Dean's List - '95, Who's Who among Students in American Junior Colleges, Academic Fitness Award; [oth. writ.] Several poems published in my High School's Students paper, also had some published in The Phoenix a student newspaper at Harrisburg Area Community College and Thoughts Beyond Insanity IV, V and VI also from H.A.C.C.; [pers.] "In the end, the poem is not a thing we see, it is, rather, a light by which we may see - and what we see is life." Robert Penn Warren, being the greatest fan of Edgar Allan Poe, my poetry revolves around the themes of love and life.; [a.] Lebanon, PA

YOUNGQUIST, KELLY
[b.] June 5, 1965, Columbia, SC; [p.] Julian Hegler, Kathy Hegler; [m.] Robert Youngquist, July 25, 1987; [ed.] B.S. Marketing Management, University of North Carolina, Greensboro, NC (UNC-G), Brookville H.S., Lynchburg, VA; [occ.] Self Employed - Animation Computer Graphics, Copywriting; [oth. writ.] Mostly unpublished poems, raps, scripts for skits and a

couple of children's books still in progress.; [pers.] I love to read as it inspires us to write.; [a.] Winston-Salem, NC

ZAMORA, HANNIA E. BECKFORD
[b.] August 27, 1946, San Jose, Costa Rica; [p.] George Beckford, Clara Zamora; [ch.] Jonathan Schreiber; [ed.] Elementary School, San Jose, CR High School, San Jose, Costa Rica, Touro College NY B.A. Psychology Fordham University MS Adult Ed and Human Resource Dev.; [occ.] Case Social Worker, St. Joseph Services for Children and fam.; [hon.] Dean's List; [oth. writ.] Several poems published in Spanish in a local magazine in Costa Rica; [pers.] I believe my poetry is the result of daily contemplation. My thoughts having been purified sprout as a Chant or a cry from my soul.; [a.] Bronx, NY

ZARDENETA, BRYAN A.
[b.] September 25, 1970, San Pedro Hospital, CA; [ed.] Northgate High, El Camino College; [occ.] Sales Rep., Home Depot, Marina Del Rey; [hon.] Honorable Discharge, United States Marine Corps.; [oth. writ.] None submitted for publishing; [pers.] I find that the poems I have written were used for the sale purpose of communicating to the people I care for how important they are in my life. Maybe someday I shall venture out and write poems everyone can appreciate and enjoy.; [a.] San Pedro, CA

ZEOLI SR., MARIO C.
[b.] October 28, 1922, Weymouth, MA; [p.] Clementine and John Zeoli; [m.] Ruth E. (Anderson) Zeoli, April 27, 1957; [ch.] Charlene, Gwenn, Mario Jr., Nancy and Steven; [ed.] Weymouth High School, Mass., Orange Coast College, Costa Mesa CA, New England School of Art-Boston; [occ.] Retired, Part-time, Maint. Man - hobby Artist; [pers.] I am a first generation Italian American, born and educated in Weymoth Mass. Served U.S. Navy C.B's WW II - So. Pacific Campaign. Poetry writing and painting is my therapy and relaxation.; [a.] Buellton, CA

ZEVOLA, NICKI
[b.] November 19, 1984, Seoul, South Korea; [p.] Robert and Judy Zevola; [ed.] I am a straight a student in the fifth grade. I am also in the gifted program. And I am ten years old. (When poem was written); [oth. writ.] This is my first poem ever to be published. I am very excited! I love to write books and I want to be an author when I grown up.; [pers.] My poem is dedicated to my grandmother, Vi Giovanelli (who is no longer here), but I hope she is my guardian angel. And to my mom and dad, my role models.; [a.] Pittsburgh, PA

ZIEGLAR, KAREN HALOWICH
[b.] September 24, 1949, Waynesburg, PA; [p.]

Steve Halowich, Ann Halowich; [ch.] Kevin Ayers, Brian Ayers; [ed.] Albert Gallatin High, I.C.M. of Pittsburgh, PA; [occ.] Technical Support Specialist, Monongalia General Hosp., Morgantown, WV; [pers.] My writings are greatly influenced by my heart, thru all the travels of my experiences and realities that I have walked, down the road of life.; [a.] Maidsville, WV

ZIMDARS, ELAINE BEIMBORN
[b.] July 22, 1939, West Bend, WI; [p.] Adolph and Gladys Nee Michelis Beimborn; [m.] Harry O. Zimdars, September 2, 1961; [ch.] John and Paul; [ed.] Graduated from West Bend High School in 1957; [occ.] Homemaker and babysitter for our Granddaughter Stephanie; [memb.] St. John's Lutheran Church Newburg - Wisconsin, Women's International Bowling Congress West Bend Women's Bowling Assn., Morning Glories League; [hon.] 1994-2nd Place Weilands Wed A.M. Morning Glories Woody's Flooring, 1995 had a 234 game with seven strikes in a row. I received a watch a key chain and a pin; [pers.] Appreciate and show love to your parents, brother or sister because life is too short. My parents and two brothers are deceased. Don't forget to visit people in nursing homes also send cards.; [a.] Newburg, WI

ZIMMERMAN, BETH E.
[b.] February 25, 1981, Sellersville, PA; [p.] Myron and Faith Zimmerman; [ed.] Attending Quakertown Community Senior High School; [memb.] National Junior Honor Society; [hon.] Distinguished Honor roll; [oth. writ.] Articles for the Panther Paws school newspaper.; [pers.] "Commit to the Lord whatever you do, and your plans will succeed." Proverbs 16:3.; [a.] Quakertown, PA

INDEX
OF POETS

A

Abbott, Amy 421
Abbott, Ashley 131
Abel, David 138
Abeyta, Garret 159
Ables, Norma J. 230
Abrams, Susan 257
Abshire, Mitchel 201
Ackroyd, Lisa 555
Adams, David 520
Adams, Doris B. 591
Adams, Elizabeth 625
Adams Jr., Charles 106
Adams, Sarah 476
Adas, Bill 96
Addino, Anna 604
Adetunji, Emmanuel 419
Adkins, Lana 384
Adler, Chris 73
Admire, Linda 493
Adomaitis, Amanda 536
Agamata-Daproza, Eden 537
Agapito, Fides Capati 305
Agnew, Andrew 157
Aguilar, Del 626
Aguilar, Nellie 339
Aguirre, Nelson 565
Ahlstrom, Sarah 235
Aiken, Carol 602
Aine, Christine 414
Ake, Martha 361
Akeo, Erika 134
Akers, Chris 447
Albee, Heather 449
Alberts, Ruby 350
Albritton, Char 592
Alderson, Sandra Owen 261
Aleshire, Jennifer 296
Alexander, June 296
Alexander, Scott W. 197
Alkadri, J. 233
Allaire, Katrina 467
Allchin, Nichole M. 247
Alldredge, Julia M. 101
Allen, Cathryn 320
Allen Jr., Michael 198
Allen, Julia Marie 418
Allen, Karen C. 176
Allen, Nafeesah 28
Allen, Russell C. 396
Alley, Maude 46
Allison, Ernest C. 156
Allison, Grace C. 624
Allison, Randy 35
Allison, Stefanie 542
Allocca, Phil 231
Allswang, Rebecca 480
Allum-Oskoui, Joan 419
Almany, Stacey 287
Aloe, Jean M. 75
Althaus, Julie M. 333
Altman, Blake 513
Altman, Calvin T. 110
Alu, Mercy 285
Alvarez, Alyana Vincente 527
Alvarez, Melissa 579
Alvarez, Noemy 242
Alvarez, Noni 33
Alvarez, Zulma D. 343
Amabisca, Autumn 604
Aman, Kristine Marie 237
Amis, Susan 391
Amrit Knaus, Carolyn, M.S., M.T. 425
Anastas, Sam "Balamb" 207
Anderson, Amie 613

Anderson, Carolyn Elizabeth 331
Anderson, Catherine 513
Anderson, Diane M. 457
Anderson, Jayne 529
Anderson, Jennifer 420
Anderson, Kristan A. 266
Anderson, Linda J. 289
Anderson, Liz 26
Anderson, Loral 562
Anderson, Mary Agnes 391
Anderson, Parker 4
Anderson, Patricia Felshaw 576
Anderson, Priscilla 15
Anderson, Priscilla J. 202
Anderson, Ryan 347
Anderson, Sakena 260
Anderson, Sheila 467
Anderson, Teresa 260
Andresen, Dana 84
Andrews, Jerry 125
Andrews, Marie Rie 488
Andrews, Mary 542
Angeles, Christian 412
Anhalt, Jean 301
Annunziato, Taegen 393
Anthony, Kathleen M. 189
Anthony, Samara 46
Antle, Peg 220
Antonio, Ronald 486
Anyon, Roger D. 580
Applegate-Hager, Sandye 202
Aquiline, Matthew S. 634
Araujo, Denize 302
Archer, Mary L. 473
Ardain Jr., Fred 447
Arellanes, Martha 189
Arias, Cynthia 603
Arias, Mary Sue 205
Armistead, Anne Cecelia 97
Armstrong, Yvette 632
Arnao, Patricia E. 200
Arnold, James Edward 540
Arnold, Marilyn B. 565
Arnold, Sarah 232
Arnone, Lisa 495
Arreguy, Lily 213
Arruda, Judith J. 114
Aschermann, Kurt 396
Ashe, Lincoln E. 581
Ashley, Elaine 301
Ashley, Laura Elizabeth 418
Ashman, Stacy Ann 472
Askinas, Wilma 353
Atkins, Stacey 472
Atkinson, Sharon L. 195
Attwood, Staci 23
Auguste, Rachel 42
Augustin, R. E. 578
Augustine, Shiloh Leo 498
Austin, Kimberly A. 364
Aversano, Terry 354
Avery, Melissa 216
Avey, Robin 550
Azaroff, Illya L. 511
Azhar, Sameena 334
Azzopardi, Allegra 60

B

Babcock, Joanna 165
Babiasz, Thomas J. 335
Backus, Rosalind 553
Baczek, Barbara 434
Badwal, Bhajan S. 526
Bagby, Penny 33
Bailey, Amy K. 428

Bailey, Anjella 515
Bailey, Debbie A. 587
Bailey, Jason 94
Bailey, Jim 512
Bailey, Judith E. 137
Bailey, Kandi J. 140
Bailey, Kim 581
Bailey, Wayne 556
Baillargeon, Doris 311
Bain, Toni 572
Bair, Alberta 122
Baker, Andrea 54
Baker, Brandi L. 93
Baker, Carolina A. 320
Baker, Dorothy 139
Baker, Elizabeth Julia 518
Baker, Gandy 132
Baker, Helene A. 118
Baker, Kathleen 394
Baker, Marian K. 189
Baker, Michelle 280
Baker, Sierra 373
Baker, Theresa 487
Balaoro, Jo P. 420
Balasa, Andrew 79
Balbi, Loretta 474
Baldwin, Elizabeth B. 321
Baldwin, Helen Martha 441
Baldwin, Stephanie 270
Balise, Renee 202
Ball, Clayton 110
Ball, Larry L. 340
Ball, William H. 187
Balle-Gifford, Steve 278
Ballow, Marvin L. 26
Baltzell, Shane 635
Bancroft, Gen 82
Banda, Kara 96
Bandy, Kara Lynne 512
Bane, Doris W. 314
Banerjee, Neelanjana 249
Bapst, Dawn K. 458
Baramdyka, Francoise I. 631
Baran, Trisha 366
Barber, Sarah 364
Barbieri, Lori 406
Barclay, Stephen 12
Barenblatt, Richard 392
Barhydt, Hap 135
Bark, Margaret H. 32
Barker-Bettencourt, Carol 590
Barkhaus, Jessica 88
Barnes Moore, Jane 466
Barnes, Pat 213
Barnett, Rasheeda 25
Barnette, Ellen L. 116
Barnhouse, Colette 517
Barreca, Kate 383
Barrett, Constance 180
Barrett, Mary 198
Barrett, Patricia Devan 503
Barron, Agnes Anna 124
Barrows, Tami 35
Barry, Beth 127
Barry, James 331
Barry, John N. 451
Barry, Margaret 293
Barteldt, Eric W. 162
Bartelson, Laura 560
Barth, Loralie L. 575
Barth, Maria 212
Bartleson, Michael 48
Bartley, Amber 331
Barton, Sharon Ann 636
Bartz, Cynthia L. 609
Barz, Melissa 199

Basar, Jill M. 183
Basey, Gregory 505
Basford, Margaret 24
Basinger, Eleanor F. 327
Bass, Camille 133
Bass, Kartney 393
Batalia, Erik Jay 444
Bates, Whitney 361
Batman, Jillian 174
Batt, Rose 224
Batterman, Stephanie E. 236
Batty-Ryan, Gail 74
Bauder, Shirley 238
Bauer, Amanda 80
Bauer, C. H. 344
Bauer, Scott Douglas 45
Baugh, Freida 151
Baugh, Peter 574
Baughman, Donna 156
Baxley, Emma J. 464
Baxter, Al 90
Baxter, Valerie 187
Beach, Lily Elaine 390
Beard, Stephanie J. 266
Beard, Truitt J. 240
Bearden, Lanelle 279
Beardslee, Hermona C. 413
Beary, Jenny 91
Beaston, Sandra J. 554
Beath, Lauren 558
Beaty, Jeffrey Mitchell 481
Beaufait, Ruth 214
Beavers, Karen M. 76
Bechtel, Lynnette R. 255
Bechtle, Judy 85
Beck, Jeanette 626
Beck, Jesse M. 455
Beckett, Melanie F. 265
Beckler, Carol J. 529
BeDen, Marsha
    Denise-Turner 268
Bednarek, Brian 178
Beer, Vickie L. 203
Beery, Mary E. 211
Beery, Stephanie K-F 222
Beevers, Mike 204
Beggs, Katie R. 269
Behdad, Denice 141
Behmer, Joan Grantham 603
Behrendt, LeAnn Marie 4
Beliveau, Renee 235
Bell, Asher 108
Bell, Brian Anthony 440
Bell, Genetter 126
Bell, Vivian 276
Bellard, L. Darrell 376
Belleret, Margaret 18
Bello, Rosemary 7
Beltz, Brad 518
Belyea, Denise 322
Bench, Shirley J. 257
Bender, Michael D. 195
Bender, Rachel 356
Benish, A. R. 9
Benke, Jonathan W. 316
Bennett, Charlene M. 524
Bennett, Debra 451
Benson, Rebecca 285
Benson, Susan D. 476
Bentley, Robert 572
Benton, Mildred E. 36
Bergin, Michael 267
Bergstresser, Julie 313
Berk, Katie 28
Berman, Carone B. 537
Berman, David 453

Bernabei, Tiffiny 345
Berné 122
Bernstein, Corinne 463
Bernthold, Linda Kay 376
Berntsen, Thomas 346
Berrett, Tracy Ann 378
Berrios, Elizabeth 635
Berry, Matt 25
Berry, Tonia 188
Best, Justin 150
Best, Sandra 352
Best, Tara M. 396
Betz, Bernadine L. 446
Beyer, Rebecca 471
Bigler, Amy Lynn 301
Billen, Debra 516
Billington, Gary L. 466
Billington, Mike 262
Billups, Phillip R. 553
Binder, Brian A. 413
Binkley, Rebecca 197
Biondi, Agnes 157
Bird, Ginger 116
Birdsong, Herman 118
Birmingham, Shirley J. 31
Bischofsberger, Joanne 605
Bishop, April 306
Bishop, Clydia Estelle 143
Bishop, Lisa M. 192
Bitsakis, George 635
Bittner, Judy 121
Bivins, Gene 88
Bjork, Laura J. 44
Black, Aurore 91
Black, Ebony 594
Blackshaw, G. Dean 373
Blackwelder, Victoria 273
Blackwell, Cecil R. 457
Blackwell, Giuliana 138
Blackwell, Rachel K. 561
Blair, Charlotte V. 442
Blair, Cora S. 320
Blair, Simon 223
Blake, Freeman D. 521
Blake, Jenny M. 139
Blakemore, Bryan K. 83
Blakeslee, Grace 432
Blakley, Virginia 575
Bland, Melissa 500
Bland Roy, Muriel D. 367
Blandin, Todd A. 204
Blank, Jesse 307
Blankenship, Kristina 634
Blankenship, Ruth E. 11
Blanton, Diane 182
Blanton, Sylvia Marie 209
Blassingame, Linda Sue 470
Blaze, Sherry Lynn 46
Blazquez, Emilia 123
Blessing, Jennifer Boynton 438
Blevins, Catherine 598
Bliuvas, Juliana 525
Blocksma, Ralph 571
Bloczynski, George 66
Bloczynski, Robert J. 274
Blommer, Jullianne 448
Blood, Linda 227
Bloodworth, Brandi 94
Bluemle, Stefanie 250
Bluestone, David 446
Bluman, Sarah 17
Blydenburgh, Beryl 617
Blymire, Jessica 180
Boan, Sharon J. 400
Bobko, Janine 167
Bocker, Vashti Eleesha 215

Bodtke, Micki 361
Boehler, Lindsay 272
Boehm, Karen H. 93
Boes, Sherry Kathleen 44
Boettcher, Scott T. 49
Boff, Ken J. 402
Bogan, Gary D. 628
Bohn, Carole L. 93
Bojanek, Katherine
   Dessoir 341
Bolden, Jeremy 458
Boldt, Ruthie 344
Bolles, Rodger N. 494
Bollinger, Berta A. 313
Bollinger, Brian 159
Bolyard, Irving J. 506
Bomberger, Mark 402
Bonaroti, April 610
Bonesteel, Christina N. 623
Boniece, Meribell 226
Bonis, Sherri-Lynn 10
Bonneville, Ryan J. 256
Bonomo, Josephine Ann 101
Boone, Mary 573
Booth, Barbee L. 628
Bordner, Niki 205
Borges, Fredericka 459
Born, Jeremy 174
Bortel, Tammy L. 354
Borup, Donna 509
Bosco, Joan 163
Bossier, Lisa Marie 223
Bostjancic, Lisa 231
Boston, Verne E. 540
Boswell, Jaime Lynn 161
Botero, Daneen 128
Botica, Virginia 288
Bottino, Louis A. 47
Bottoms, Bernice 145
Botts, Amber D. 169
Botts, Henry 99
Bourque, Jacqueline 317
Bouteiller, Jeanne Marie 107
Bowen, Robert 632
Bowerman, Elizabeth 130
Bowers, Mariah 366
Bowers, Mary P. 286
Bowles, Amber 144
Bowles, James A. 181
Bowman, Esther L. 536
Bowman, Kathy 15
Boyd, Brandon C. 82
Boyd, Christine 619
Boyd, La Verle Rhodes 366
Boyle, Frances 333
Boyle, Meaghan 557
Bozymowski, Darlene C. 534
Braaten, Opal 250
Bradford, William C. 574
Bradley III, Zell 473
Bradley, Jean E. 606
Bradshaw, Dorothy St. Clair 101
Brady, Carolyn 517
Bragdon, Doris Barnard 323
Bragg, Michelle Lynn 6
Brammer, Tom 234
Branco, Dinny'vie 539
Brandon, Arlene 529
Brandon, Grace 152
Brandt, Marlin K. 18
Brannon, Katie G. 42
Brannon, Tina 11
Braswell, Carrie L. 625
Bratten, Michael B. 290
Braun, Adam F. 174
Bray, Edward Allen 81

Bray, Paul T. 554
Brayton Hudson,
   Nancy C. 349
Breeden, James M. 453
Breitfelder, Edward A. 109
Breitkreuz-Dackiw, Linda Ann 378
Bremser, Tim J. 41
Brennan, Karen 457
Brennan, Margaret A. 34
Brenneman, Eleanor E. 429
Brenner, Helen Lewis 165
Brenner, Katharine 209
Bressan, Dorlene 538
Brew, Helen Jo 612
Brewer, Estelle 594
Brewer, Odessa A. 502
Bridgers, Margaret Elizabeth
   Rice 336
Bridges, Kim E. 379
Briedis, John 534
Briggs, Daryl A. 77
Briggs, Everett Francis 433
Briggs, J. W. 584
Bright, Christine 76
Briguglio, Carolyn 84
Briley, Tara 471
Brinkley, Jean A. 627
Bristow, Howard A. 133
Britt, Ruby B. 562
Broder, Gregory 156
Brodeur, Helen S. 63
Brogdon, Mary A. 497
Bronske, Betty 611
Brook, Joy 169
Brooks, Deborah A. 165
Brooks, Jenny 147
Brooks, Linda 399
Brown, Ashley Dianne 306
Brown, Beth 443
Brown, Candace 318
Brown, Daisy M. 524
Brown, Donald 179
Brown, Dorothy I. 628
Brown, Douglas Ryan 430
Brown, Hilda 177
Brown, James 458
Brown, Janie 595
Brown, Joan M. 170
Brown, Jodie Carmen 447
Brown, Katie 219
Brown, Lydia J. C. 256
Brown, Lynne A. 222
Brown, Marilyn 213
Brown, Paula A. 6
Brown, Rita V. 13
Brown, Rebecca L. 51
Brown, Robert L. 275
Brown, Robin 246
Brown, Roger W. 244
Brown, Tammy M. 216
Brown, Tana 360
Brown, Walter E. 379
Broyles, Arlene 626
Bruening, Richard E. 261
Brumaru, David 315
Brundidge, Phyllis M. 11
Bruner, Alethia 73
Bruno, Eric 622
Bruno, Patricia Ann 250
Bruns, Darci L. 181
Bruns, Pamela D. 559
Brunson, Angela Michelle 61
Brush, Candace 163
Bryan, Natalie 16
Bryan, Rose Mary 38
Bryant, Daniel 424

Bryant, Doris Booth 112
Bryant, Emily 328
Bryant, George S. 112
Bryant, Lynda J. 214
Bryant, Thelma 256
Buchholz, Howard R. 88
Buck, J. A. 481
Buck, Kathy 41
Buckingham-Clark, Harriett 439
Buckley, Beth 66
Buckley, Damon L. 615
Bucknum, Fern Klopp 507
Bucol, M. Josephine 187
Bueckner, Doris 434
Bugarin, Patricia 376
Bugarin, Rosa Maria S. 220
Bugg, Dolores 449
Bujan, Vincent R. 209
Bukhari, Muhammad Ali 541
Bulck, William 272
Bullard, Nita 482
Bullard Sr., Charles 312
Bullen, Amanda 176
Bundy, A. P. 43
Burch, Annalisa S. 158
Burd, Herbert L. 601
Burdick, Wendy 564
Burgess, Melody Ann 390
Burgos, Yanira 280
Burik, Margaret 5
Burk, Kenneth Lee 543
Burke, Ann Demprey 66
Burke, Bridget 54
Burke, Kerry A. 24
Burkman, Dennis 102
Burnaine, Candy 105
Burnett, Carol F. 130
Burnett Jr., Glen D. 610
Burns, Claude 167
Burns, Janice Ann 614
Burns, L. L. 381
Burr, Natali F. 11
Burress, Karen 322
Burt, Edie 621
Burton, Lynn 207
Burton-Ristau, Marilynne 27
Burwell, Victoria L. 581
Busch, Steven R. 585
Bush, Ilene R. 517
Bushway, Heather 617
Busken, Megan 554
Butcher, Neil T. 401
Butler, Daria Nikole 158
Butler, Norjean 404
Butler, Pamela 3
Butts, Cheryl-Ann 409

C

C., Richard 372
CAB-R 206
Cail, Cassandra 69
Cain, Betty L. 459
Cain, Paulette 40
Caldwell, Agnes 55
Caldwell, Kari 194
Caldwell, Kathleen 215
Caldwell, R. E. 194
Calhoun, Dori 169
Call, Cindy L. 297
Callaghan, John T. 620
Callahan, Crystal 416
Callahan, LaSonya D. 373
Callaway, Nida 264
Callison, Norma A. 199
Calloway, Christina 160

Camanelli II,
    Raymond T. 278
Camden, Loraine 548
Camp, Emily 113
Camp, Sandra 354
Campanelli, Lori 192
Campbell, Brian S. 621
Campbell, Charlene 129
Campbell, Christopher 409
Campbell, J. J. 199
Campbell, Lori 350
Campbell, M. A. 485
Campbell, Sandra L. 6
Campisano, Kevin 581
Candido, William 210
Canfield, Cynthia A. 587
Cannella, Cory Calvin 179
Cannon, Bonnie 89
Cannon, Charis Desirae 95
Cannon, Jason 601
Canoy, M. T. 342
Capasso, Summer 194
Cappiello, Rita 42
Caraveo, Scott 281
Carey, Amy 417
Carey, Douglas E. 424
Carhill, Margie 293
Carlen, Ida 154
Carlisle Jr., Johnie 330
Carlisle, Ken M. 565
Carlson, Eric 115
Carlton, Bernadine 151
Carmenini, Robert M. 9
Carmichael, Richard 5
Carnes, Larry A. 540
Carnevale, Stefanie Marie 206
Carnevali, August R. 299
Carpa, Eleanor 309
Carpenter, Edward J. 622
Carpenter, Magdalena 551
Carpenter, Velma 468
Carr, Athena 176
Carr, Cameron 130
Carr, Nicole 572
Carrick, June 65
Carroll, Betty 114
Carroll, James Edward 299
Carroll, Muriel A. 266
Carroll, Nikole 207
Carson, Gail 453
Carson Jr., John L. 113
Carter, Candice 517
Carter Jr., Chester W. 607
Carter, Kelli 340
Carter, Marla 28
Carter, Verna 227
Carver, Jim D. 162
Carzello, Valerie 27
Cash, Loretta Allen 241
Casmo, Joanne I. 181
Cassady, Carl W. 115
Cassia, Daisy M. 166
Cassidy, Jennifer 437
Castelo, Donna 100
Casterton, Carolyn 535
Castile, Kathleen M. 280
Castle, Marilyn Cronin 208
Castro, Sharlotte
    Herring 365
Caswell, Dale 297
Catalano, Virgil 482
Catoe, Linda 13
Catron, Dawn 518
Catterton, Rebecca Oliver 394
Cave, Kathleen Anne 243
Cavena, Mary 573

Cawthorne, Laura J. 283
Cazarez, D. M. 189
Cebrynski, George H. 429
Cee, Jay 622
Celeste, Louise M. 579
Cempellin, Debra L. 327
Centeno, Rosa M. 5
Cepeda, Eugenio 299
Cervantes, Ernesto 439
Cervantez, Lorenzo 499
Chadwick, Irene 532
Chaisson, John J. 310
Chamberland, Rachel 585
Chambers, Linda M. 390
Chanay, Kathleen L. 210
Chaney, Scott 390
Channell, Eugene H. 162
Chapman, Janna 65
Chapman, Ruth 568
Chapman, Teresa 3
Chappell, Jennifer 76
Charboneau, Nyetta 254
Charbonnet, Alura 180
Charbonnet, Jeff 113
Chatham Jr., Dennis 321
Chatterjee, Sohang 253
Chau, Karin 498
Chavez, Isaac 460
Chawla, Sadhna Disha 575
Chelsea 264
Chen, Michael 380
Cheney, Kristen 47
Chern, Regina 337
Chesak, Beula Ashment 59
Chesnet, Christy 94
Cheverie, Karen 437
Chiarenza, Christa-Althea 420
Chiasson, Connie 614
Chidlaw, Madge 194
Chikwendu, Talibah L. 399
Chimenti, Julia 312
Chimiklis, Ruth 564
Chiucarello, Susan 366
Chontos, Rise 373
Chrane, Jeremy D. 132
Chris, Marcia Crabb 279
Christensen, Corey 59
Christian, Cie 457
Christian, Milton 273
Christiansen, Roy 355
Christine, Brandi 60
Christner, Harry R. 522
Christner, Marion Marino 484
Christos, Bridie 460
Chung, Austin 177
Churnick, Amber 517
Ciaburri, Jacqueline 465
Cimorelli, Jennifer Christina 70
Cinevert, Daniel 168
Cittadini, Joseph L. 82
Ciullo, Brandi 511
Claiborne, Geraldine 89
Clanton, T. J. 490
Clapp, M. Diahann 388
Clardy, Tawnya 37
Clare, Mason 253
Clark, David 430
Clark, Donna J. 105
Clark, Eva V. 465
Clark, Gladys 77
Clark, Leah 580
Clark, M. Margaret 295
Clark, Mary Toolan 358
Clark, Shawn 470
Clark, Shawn J. 381
Clark, Whittier E. 49

Clarke, Claudette 410
Clarke, Ginnie Lin 71
Clarke Jr., Phillip Ewing 228
Clarke, Maria 374
Clarke-Forbes, Yvonne 43
Clary, Carol 140
Clasen, Martin M. 261
Clay, Tiffany 475
Clayton, Micah 45
Clement, Krista I. 377
Clements, Donna 595
Clements, Mark S. 218
Clendenin, Ernestine Lister 417
Clevenger, Karen 183
Cliburn, Leona 187
Clites, Brian 136
Clontz, Melissa Jean 41
Clow, Jeremy 137
Coates Ball, Margaret 499
Coates, Kimberly 14
Coats, Charlestaneca Caprice 153
Cochran, Almeta 615
Codd, Marion 208
Coe, Ken 34
Cogburn, Amanda 123
Cohen, Jan Michael 434
Cohernour, Evon 460
Colahan, Sean 216
Colbert, Michael Anthony 19
Colclasure, Brenda 54
Cole, David Allen 525
Cole, Helen 600
Cole, Rebecca L. 383
Cole, Ruth K. 572
Coleman, JoAnne 183
Coleman, Mary K. 209
Coleman, Melissa 362
Coleman, Sophia 219
Coley, Maria 21
Collazo, Mario 236
Collicott, Purnel L. 554
Collier, Katina 20
Collins, Abel Lee 139
Collins, April 311
Collins, Gary S. 108
Collins II, Delbert L. 326
Collins, Pat 42
Collins, Rick 482
Collins, Tom 497
Collova, Dagmar P. 508
Colon Jr., Ariel 131
Colton, Lori 375
Colwell, Ronda C. 185
Combs, Jennifer S. 297
Combs, Katherine Ann 218
Combs, Ray 346
Compton, Christina Ann 617
Compton, Jennifer 438
Conary-Thum, Sheila 221
Concepcion, Tracy M. 33
Condon, Gail 453
Cone, Stephen W. 402
Congello, Debbie 320
Conley, Hannah M. 316
Conley, Marissa G. 27
Conn, Jack 159
Connors, Colleen 432
Conradi, Jill 506
Constans, Rebecca A. 347
Contonio, Peter M. 248
Coody, Jo 184
Cook, Blanche A. 512
Cook Chavious, Pamela 18
Cook, Donna 168
Cook, Earl Stanley 631
Cook, Jeanette E. 440

Cook, Lona L. 405
Cook, Lucille 34
Cook, Misty Michelle 22
Cooke, Cynthia L. 445
Cooke, Kynan
    Alexander 50
Cooke, Susan 198
Cooley, April 446
Cooley, Kayla 584
Coon, Sandra M. 8
Cooper Calhoun, Lindsay 475
Cooper, Denise 131
Cooper, Gerald 321
Cooper, June 627
Cooper, Susan M. 401
Coppa, Grace M. 118
Coppola, Dorothy 530
Corbin, Mary 16
Corcoran Cathey, Jean D. 415
Cordell, Patricia 377
Cordova, Michelle L. 404
Corey, René 392
Corley, Sharon 477
Corliss, Cynthia 110
Cormia, Oscar L. 196
Cormier, Jonathan W. 166
Cornwell, Constance 125
Corpaci, Hermine 611
Corral, Candace 302
Corrigan, Andrew 161
Corsette, Darla A. 428
Corson, Alan 532
Corson, Mary Robin 213
Cortez, Jodi Ann 104
Corvini, Marguerite 493
Cory, Etta B. 152
Cory, Kelly 384
Cosand, Louise 346
Cosing, Caroline 153
Cossa, Gian A. 443
Cotham, Devona F. 524
Cothran Jr., Donald Neil 623
Cotter, Christopher James 161
Cotter, Susan A. 252
Cotton, Clara M. 66
Coughlin, Robert
    Wayne 278
Courtney, Daniel C. 409
Coutee, Danny C. 437
Coutee, Sheri 50
Couts, Irene 184
Covington, Michael A. 355
Cowan, Idell 67
Cowles, Laverne E. 346
Cowper, John Barclay 72
Cox, Emelda 93
Cox, Toma-Jean 382
Cox, Tonya S. 544
Cozine, Violet 10
Craig-Thomas, Karen A. 461
Craighead, Annette T. 180
Crain, Tyneka 583
Cramer, Margaret B. 336
Cramer, Terri 473
Crance, Alda 442
Craver, Jaci 464
Cravey, Dale 331
Creighton, Delaine Elizabeth 615
Creighton, Suzanne 28
Crickenberger, Katherine 281
Crim, Lisa 248
Crisostomo, Jaymie D. 322
Crisp, Chelsea C. 72
Criss, Robert V. 17
Critz, Anna S. 63
Crobaugh, Emma 143

Crockett, Phyllis 3
Cronin, David A. 530
Crosby, Debora 170
Crosby, Lila F. 30
Crosby, Michael 207
Cross, Sharon 448
Cross, Shelly Marie 26
Crossett, Marlene A. 578
Crowder, Donna 131
Crowley, Donna M. 436
Crowley, Tricia 335
Crowther, Keri 400
Croxen-Steffens, Yvonne 48
Cruikshank, Colleen 168
Crull, Irvina F. Renea 80
Crummy, Lisa Renee 566
Cuddy, Kerry L. 380
Cudworth, Cindy 84
Cuellar, Anita 329
Culbreth, Sandra 574
Cullen, Esme 519
Culler, Lisa 203
Culpepper Jr., Delton 323
Culpepper-Peters, Debi 599
Cummings, Jayne 622
Cummings, Nena Louise 241
Cundick, Sandy 287
Cundiff, Kristina M. 212
Cunningham, Doris 427
Cunningham, Jill A. 326
Curington, Kathleen L. 571
Currie, Marie 222
Currier, Tim 212
Curry, Carla 142
Curtis, Patricia 31
Curtis, Rebecca L. 205
Cuttle, Gladys 170
Cyprien Jr., Raymond 547
Czech, Lindsey 199

D

Dabo, Donna 85
Dacanay, Elizabeth 148
Dach, Peter 382
D'Acquisto, Natalie M. 351
Dadetto, Gina Lauren 593
Daenzer, Cheryl 311
D'Agostino, John A. 86
Dahilig, Gene C. 309
Dahlke, Ronald G. 340
Dailey, Laura 48
Daley, Ronald 263
Daling, Derek 333
Dalir, Suri 259
Dalton, Dave 139
Daly, Anne-Marie 416
Daly, Bernadette N. 538
Damianides, Despina 318
D'Amico, Peter J. 377
Damon, Shannon 393
Dancik, Garrett 56
D'Andrea, Jennifer 78
D'Andrea, Paul C. 578
Daniel, Cecil R. 75
Daniel, Scott 364
Dannemiller, John M. 326
Danskin, Barbara J. 117
Dant, Linda S. 26
Darby 422
Darden, David Jimmy 519
Darland, Jaime 153
Dar Santos, Lourdes S. 282
Dash, Adam Meredith 74
D'Astoli, Fred 410
Daugherty, Teresa 481

Daugherty, Vann Nicholas 24
Davenport, Carl 446
David, Kelly 277
David, Sandra 402
Davidge, James M. 120
Davidowski, Suzette 357
Davidson, Jordan 619
Davila, Barbara R. 300
Davis, Beth Ann 93
Davis, Billy A. 72
Davis, Carl Edward 447
Davis, Carrie B. 507
Davis, Cleda 548
Davis, Daniel Michael 171
Davis, De 588
Davis, Edward L. 453
Davis, Grace A. 322
Davis, James T. 113
Davis, Janet E. 414
Davis, Jannie 417
Davis Jr., Charles L. 133
Davis, June 467
Davis, Junemarie 436
Davis, Keri 279
Davis, Lillian A. 45
Davis, Mrs. Glen A. 112
Davis, Patti 251
Davis, Rodney 199
Davis Sr., James D. 182
Davis, Susan 258
Davis, Vicki 234
Dawes, Mitzie 14
Dawn, Lisa 501
Day, Carolyn 593
Day, J. Griffin 540
Dbouk, Robin 558
Dean, J. Alan 273
De Cicco, Joseph 107
De Curtis, Anthony 434
Deering, E.A. 290
De Guzman, Jolly 431
de la Rocha, Kelly 279
De La Torre, Denise 423
de Lucca, Chrystalla Mars 177
de Waal, Danielle 313
Deacon, German 625
Dean, Chrystal 173
Dean, Ebony 133
Dean, June C. 603
Debban, Kurt 229
DeBlassie, Kathy 571
DeBlieux, Jordan 305
Deckert, Penny Malloy 213
DeCosta, Kimalee Jane 233
DeCrescenzo, Tomasina 566
Dedrick, Diane 114
Deegan, James J. 630
Dees, Patsy 47
DeGenova, Annemarie 57
DeGrocco, Babette Amy 172
Dehner, Jill 450
Deifenderfer, Sandra 388
DeKadt, John 327
Del Vescovo, Timothy 556
DeLa Cruz III, Juan 141
Delaney, Barbara Voline 453
DelCampo, Trip 496
Delevan, MaryBeth 378
Delfino, Christopher 443
Delouya, Jack 463
DeLucca, Theresa 383
DeMarco, Jacqueline R. 439
Demarest, Kerri 279
Deming, Christina 419
Demonbreun, Cristal 91
Dempsey, Colita L. 618

Denby, Doris 452
Denning, Joel, age 16 527
Denson, Jennifer D. 521
DeRouin, Jan E. 130
Derryberry, Norma Jean 9
Desai, Sukanya 385
DeSantis, Joann C. 415
DeSiervi, Ilona J. 55
Desser, Rona H. 406
Dettmer, Melissa A. 6
DeVault, Doris 154
Dever, Linda 386
Deveres, Constance Ann 133
Devin, Marjorie R. 502
Devlin, Paul C. 258
Devlin, Tracy A. 273
Dewar, Siubhan 338
Dewey, Michele 25
DeWitt, Becky 154
DeWitt, Shannon 200
Di Edwardo, Joseph 624
Di Roma, Bill 519
Di Stefano, Marian 21
Diamond, Tiffany 39
Dias II, William K. 203
Diaz, Gary 322
Diaz, Melanie 215
Dickens, Scott 43
Dickerson, Maezell Davis 274
Dieringer, Patti Jo 22
Dietrich, Clarice L. 71
Dietz, Sue Myers 12
Diggs, Sharron Maria 193
Dillen, Anne T. 145
Dillon, Debbie 150
Dillon, Matthew W. 404
Dilsworth, Thomas W. 552
DiLustro, Lucy 495
Dimas, Beatrice E. 452
Dimon, Mary G. 556
Disharoon, Dawn Adele 507
Dishnow, Michael A. 390
Disimone, Anna 419
Distad, Elaine Fram 425
Ditty, Janice E. 523
Ditty, Melissa 388
Dixon, Eddie L. 590
Dixon, William M. 236
Dobbins, Christine 143
Dockstader III, William C. 28
Dodd, H. Ernest 233
Dodds, Lela F. 39
Dodge, Julie, 14 135
Dodson, Alicejean Leigh 142
Dodson, Cindy 427
Doherty, Kevin 494
Doherty, Tracy 555
Dokoupil, Casey 431
Dolan, Peter 348
Dolan, Thomas 491
Dolega, Henri Joseph 182
Dolhancyk, Diana 508
Doligon, Flora C. 65
Domansky, David W. 128
Dombroski, Carole 107
Donahue, Theresa R. 212
Donaldson, Janet B. 129
Donat, Heidi 133
Dondlinger, Rebecca 294
Donley, Susan 240
Donnelly, Steven E. 4
Doolen, Jennifer 536
Dorman, C. 486
D'Ornellas, Shondell A. 476
Doubet, Gerald E. 513

Dougan, Deanna J. 434
Dougherty, Rachel 194
Doughton, David 96
Douglas, Anita 142
Douglas, Mildred J. 284
Douglas, Nigel N. 199
Dowling, Dean E. 128
Downing II, James R. 515
Downing, Robert L. 564
Doyle, Jonathan B. 604
Doyle, Luanne M. 343
Doyle, Sandra J. 398
Doyle, Virginia 337
Doyon, Tracy E. 36
Draeger, Germaine 183
Drage, Shirley 224
Drake, Kathy 489
Drasher, Bill 441
Dreslinski, James B. 130
Drew, Sharla 219
Driscoll, Tara 557
Drolette, Karen I. 526
DuBrel, Toni 373
Duca, Angelo R. 535
Dudley, Aubrey G. 413
Dudley, Michael 194
Dudley, Viola 570
Dues, Bonnie 604
Duffy, Laura 196
Duffy, Shirley 346
Duke, Jennifer M. 90
Duke, Jerry D. F. 445
Dulohery, Dana 607
Duley, J. W. 270
Dumitru, Teofil 212
Dumont, Dura Mae 319
Dunbar, Shannon 201
Duncan, Carolyn 454
Duncan, Erika 151
Dunivan, Kay 489
Dunkerson, Mason 22
Dunlap, Shannon 218
Dunn, Linda 18
Dunstan, Pamela 197
DuPont, Robin 28
Duran, Josh 451
Durban, H. Fitzgerald 274
Durham, Amy D. 126
Durhan, Karen 464
Durrence, Aubrey 433
Dutoit, Kerry A. 216
Dutton-Allen, Leslie 41
Duwe, Robert R. 367
Dwyer, Jennine 178
Dziekonski, Reba 391
Dzikowski, Sarah 276

E

Eagan, Mimi 7
Eager, Shirley T. 281
Earl, James E. 156
Earl, Lauren 387
Earle, Lawrence 255
Earle, Lois 232
Earnhart, Jennae 133
East, Margaret 13
Easterling, Chad 408
Easterwood, Stacie 209
Eastman, Ann 121
Eastwood, Sunnia 4
Eaton, Janice M. 161
Eberhard, Mike J. 27
Echols, Kevin 282
Eddy, Bridget 451
Edge, Lamai T. 476

Edgerton, Betty J.   312
Edmiston, Jenny   129
Edmond, Melissa   255
Edmonds, Ross C.   239
Edwards, Elke   507
Edwards, Maggie   477
Edwards, Rita   541
Edwards, Scott T. J.   49
Edwards, Valerie A.   478
Egan, Dottie   439
Egan II, Michael B.   396
Ehlert, David   106
Ehmann, Courtney N.   302
Eiben, Warner G.   467
Eich, Dwight   154
Eilert, Pat   221
Einhorn, Lisa M.   188
Eise, Mandy   284
Eisenpress, Sondra   564
Eldredge, Jason F.   431
Eli, Bria   103
Elias, Jeremy   303
Elkins, Virginia L. D.   567
Ellard, Dorothy M.   146
Elliott, Carrie   139
Elliott, F. Jeffris   288
Elliott, Melissa   261
Elliott, Montana C.   231
Elliott, Naomi   341
Elliott Neal, Mary   377
Ellis, Allen   528
Ellis, Aubrey   463
Ellis, Jay   111
ellis, K.   22
Ellis, Lori   345
Ellis, Trisha   363
Eloff, Charley   446
Eltman, Erin D.   135
Embry, Melissa   271
Emerson, Jeanne   145
Emmett, Diane A.   602
Emplroy, Cloudia   465
Engelbart, Kenneth   402
Engelhardt, Michelle   37
English, Lysle R.   543
Ennesser, Leah R.   404
Enriquez, Louis Lazaro   37
Entrekin, William S.   291
Epchook, Dorothy M.   111
Erickson, Laurie   243
Eschhofen, Dave   90
Espinoza, Avilio Milton   608
Esquibel, Alexis   302
Essinger, Christa   435
Estes, Betty Ann   152
Estruch, Heather   149
Evangelista, Sandra M.   484
Evans, C. Michael   566
Evans, Daniel J.   175
Evans II, Ralph William   196
Evans, J. Alexander   189
Evans, J. Steven   349
Evans, Joshua R.   123
Evans, Martha C.   374
Evans, Mary Alice   582
Evans, Michael   245
Evans, P. Jean   32
Evans, Tom   397
Evans, Yancy   481
Eveland, Cynthia   125
Everett, James J.   108
Everett Jr., Richard L.   27
Ewersen, Virginia Pease   263
Exum, Terri   6
Ezarik, Jonathan   127
Ezzell, Mary Moore   274

F

Fabbri, Angela   540
Fabugais, Kenneth   357
Facini, Gabriel   462
Fahel, K. C.   371
Fairbanks, Carter E.   465
Fairman, Martha   542
Falconburg, Victoria K.   192
Fann, Robin Rae Baxter   485
Farahay, M. L.   257
Farber, Brian   163
Farha, Linda M.   292
Farison, Marjorie N.   567
Farmer, Wayne   552
Farrar, Tom   41
Farrell, Betty   64
Farrell, Freida E.   520
Farrell, Kenneth W.   483
Farrell, Melissa Ann   581
Fasig, Janet Carol   181
Fasso, Francesca   628
Faucette, James W.   172
Faulkner, Fonda   418
Favre-Larkin, Frances   505
Faw, Volney   44
Faythimes   371
Fazen, Jennifer   598
Federwitz, Gloria   95
Fedirko, Michelle   249
Fehr, Connie   62
Fehrer, Rena A.   391
Feigles, Alison   62
Felber, Catherine M.   179
Feliciano, Christina   175
Felkins, Evelyn   117
Fell, M. J.   286
Fellenbaum, Franklin   464
Fellman, Stanley A.   394
Fels, Viola M.   369
Felton, Phyllis A.   586
Felty, Kathee M.   385
Fenn, Judy   104
Fennell, Tiffanie L.   15
Fergueson, Maurine   289
Ferguson, Dawn   450
Ferguson, Rick L.   485
Ferrara, Michael   255
Ferrell Cook, Sally   472
Ferris, Jennifer   178
Ferro, Tim   407
Fevre, Marian   491
Feyes, Melinda   468
Fiddler, James Clayton   137
Fidel, Melanie   584
Fieker, Kristen   205
Field, Wayne   225
Fields, June   517
Fields, Mike C.   577
Fields, Vilma Holland   550
Figgins, Angie   439
Filbert, Margie Ann   6
Fildes, Jeanette C.   54
Filerio, Sue Carol   276
Filet, Jayson   410
Filion, Jewell I.   167
Filmore, Ann Mills   464
Finch, Godfrey   455
Fincher, Brandon   173
Findley, Katrina B.   288
Finger, Ira W.   98
Finn, Jim   304
Finnegan, Linda   265
Finnell, Scott   482
Finney, Kathleen   290
Fisher, Christy   418

Fisher, Gladys R.   534
Fisher, Gwen M.   435
Fisher, Howard M.   302
Fisher, Jessica Gayleen   156
Fisher, Kristel D.   335
Fisher, Rena   502
Fite, Maxine N.   390
Fitzgerald, Eileen   149
Fitzpatrick, Mary   271
Fitzsimmons, Barbara   116
Flack, Dianne   512
Flack, Mirra   563
Flaherty, James E.   465
Flanagan, Timothy
    Martin   281
Flannigan, Shannon   399
Flatt, Katrina D.   358
Fleetwood, Stephanie   395
Fleming, Brenda A.   601
Fleming, E. Faye   227
Fletcher, Eutha   325
Fletcher, John L.   165
Fletcher, S. Gordon   494
Flitcraft, Gloria J.   164
Flores, Christi   633
Flores, Zoila E.   196
Florio, Emily   167
Flournoy Jr., Malory   351
Flowers, J. C.   282
Flowers-Martin, A.   270
Flurschutz, Kelly L.   264
Flynn, Vicki S.   492
Fockler, Marcie   362
Foglia, Silvino R.   341
Foltz, Charlotte N.   620
Forbes, Christina   409
Forbriger, Janice Marie   456
Ford, Claire   99
Ford, John S.   58
Fore, Susan   188
Foreman, Dale W.   176
Foreman, Laura   12
Forester, Vicky Lynn   211
Forlenza, Joseph   511
Forman, Evelyn   152
Forsee, Matthew C.   634
Forsthoff, Rhonda L.   34
Fort, John H.   443
Forte, Anthony   144
Forte, Denise   86
Forzano, Joseph R.   79
Foster, Adolphus Life'   97
Foster, Bobbi   87
Foster, Celia   410
Foster, Sandra K.   548
Fox, Anthony Benedict   137
Foy Jones, Donna, R.N.   423
Frahm, Amy   127
France, Linda   469
Francino, Bernadette   588
Francis, Vincent   388
Frank, Perry J   485
Frank-Johnson, Jodi L.   158
Franklin, Heather   532
Franklin, Muriel W.   493
Franks, Michael   544
Frant, Dimitri   324
Franze, J   479
Frappier, Francis B.   456
Fraser, S.A.   206
Fratini, Michelle   254
Fratrick, Johanna   156
Frazier, Janet Lee   319
Frederick, Amber   160
Fredericks, Greer Sha   142
Freeman, Cecil   427

Freeman, Elaine S.   436
Freeman, Jean   442
Freeman Purdy, Peggy   224
Freeman, Thelma Lee   214
Freeze, Douglas   139
Frelo, Anthony James   129
French, Anita J.   527
French, Corey   184
Freund, Elaine   411
Fridriksson, Geri   123
Friedl, Maggie   188
Friedman, Jim   70
Friesen-Ritchie, Kristy   283
Frinier, Catherine   323
Frizzle, Christine   180
Froseth, Sue   200
Fry, Dana   179
Fry, Diane M.   597
Frye, Jimmy W.   615
Fuchs, Wally   396
Fuentes, C.R.   456
Fuerst, Richard   397
Fukura, Dale   414
Fulco, Traci Lee   45
Fulgoney, Sandra Lee   191
Fuller, Dolores M.   444
Fuller, Phyllis Reese   368
Fulton, Mary A.   213
Funaki, Marie   269
Funkhouser, David L.   601
Furguiele, Andrea   454
Furguiele, Francesco   460
Furman, Phrona   99
Fusicci, Lisa   10

G

Gabryszewski, Michael   386
Gadd, Debbie   132
Gaddis, Nathan   586
Gadecki, Alicia K.   465
Gadel, Kristen   495
Gaertner, Daryl   53
Gale, Phillip Spencer   48
Gallant, Deveney   298
Gallt, Dawn   528
Galvin, Jennifer   140
Gamar, Amanda M.   633
Gambetta, Mary   4
Gammage, Melvin   188
Gandy Jr., C. W.   243
Gansmann, Sarah   254
Gantz, Jim   590
Garbarino, Irma   95
Garber, Christine Deane   428
Garcia, Azalia   505
Garcia, Blanca   613
Garcia, Diane   328
Garcia, Jean P.   129
Garcia, Lillian M.   478
Garcia, Ricardo J.   476
Gard, Pauline   270
Gardner, Chris   611
Gardner, Margaret   215
Gardner, Sharon   20
Gardner, Wanda B.   503
Garretson, Johnanna A.   319
Garretson, Yollanda L.   230
Garrett, Melissa   271
Garrick, Christopher M.   173
Garrison, Carol   431
Garrison, Jim   68
Gartner, Rosanne   231
Gary, Sandra   575
Gasn, Jana L.   69
Gasperson, Connie S.   128

Gatewood, Danielle   327
Gaumer, Kathleen   558
Gause, Efrem Z.   416
Gausepohl, Esther   456
Gawlak, Patti   374
Gay, Melissa C.   198
Geddes, Junko   99
Gennardo, Pater   41
Gens, Tom   35
Genuise, Matthew   12
George, David T.   530
George, LaQuanda R.   555
George, Shirley R.   46
Gerardi, Nicole Marie   395
Gerkin, Jamie M.   182
Germani, Patricia   344
Gernhardt, Laura Lynn   502
Gershman, Mike   230
Gervacio, Carina A.   597
Getchell, Josh A.   97
Giacoia III, Vincent D.   367
Giacomotto, Andrea   169
Gibbs, Audrey   465
Gibby, Lisa   580
Gibson, Mandie   234
Gidish, Terry A.   562
Giersberg, Melissa   13
Giger, Allison J.   125
Giglia, Sheila D.   256
Gilbert, Pamela Sue (Potter)   263
Gilbert, Ruth A.   16
Gilchrest, Winniferd   248
Gill, Elizabeth S.   115
Gill, Heather P.   426
Gill, Michele Linda   474
Gillespie, Misty   7
Gillner, Sylvester   474
Gilman, Jenni   466
Gilmore, Anna   179
Gingrich, Verda   244
Girouard, Heather   160
Gitchel, Sarah   349
Gittens Jr., Joseph   119
Gladich, Kamela S.   516
Glaser, David   466
Glass, Cindy   96
Glatfelter, William J.   386
Glauser, Joyce W.   321
Gleeson, Mary   241
Glosson, Robyn Marie   49
Glover, Amie   69
Glover, Edward C.   411
Glover, Henry   326
Glover, M. J.   283
Gobar, Gail   533
Godfrey, Jane   135
Godley, Ronnie   486
Goehring, Anjanett   310
Goff, Audrey Diane   629
Goff, Lynn   472
Goforth, Sharon   487
Goheen, Michelle   36
Gohlke, William R.   382
Going, Linda   387
Golden, Betty   508
Golden, Shanna   274
Goldsmith, Gloria   139
Goldvarg, Brad   328
Golladay, Camie   311
Golubski, Steven M.   581
Gomez, Angel C.   60
Gonsalves, Elisha Ann   448
Gonzales Valentin, Peter   372
Gonzalez, Anita L.   127
Gonzalez, Melissa   631
Good, Annette   52

Good Jr., John James   596
Good Sr., Edward J.   151
Goodstone, Erica   506
Gordon, Alexander L.   92
Gordon, Bridgette   151
Gordon, Priscilla   403
Gorman, Bill   125
Goss, Jessica   522
Gould, Belinda   314
Grace, Simone Mary   185
Grade 3-109   365
Graff Jr., Belmer L.   161
Graff, Minda S.   221
Graham, Carolyn   333
Graham, Colleen   323
Graham, Jerushia L.   150
Graham, Sandy   200
Grammer, Jennifer C.   103
Grandfield, Scott   398
Grandmont, Heather   621
Granger III, John W.   138
Grant, Krissy   190
Grant, Wayne   585
Granzotto, Renee   4
Grass, Holly S.   171
Graves, Kate   242
Gray, Bernice M.   104
Gray, Denise   94
Gray, Jamie L.   94
Gray, Shawna   35
Greathouse, Linda   559
Green, Brandi   136
Green, Danielle   158
Green, Dorothy R.   176
Green, Frank H.   108
Greene, Jeffrey C.   421
Greene, Kirbie L.   44
Greene Vasulka, Gayle   149
Greer, Brenda J.   521
Greer, Lucy C.   336
Greer, Michelle A.   207
Greer, Wendy   275
Greeson, Neva   8
Gregory, Donald   183
Gregory, Shawn   196
Gregory, Tiffany   567
Grenier, Lynne M.   363
Greyling, Claire   97
Griak, Deanna J.   130
Griffen, Jean W.   83
Griffin, Brenda   529
Griffin, Genevieve R.   182
Griffith, Juanita S.   441
Griffith, R. D.   196
Griggs, Patty   363
Grimaldi, Beth   168
Grimes, Mary M.   579
Grimes, Teresa   251
Grimmett, Genie   161
Griner, Karla   262
Grissmeyer, Susan   16
Griswold, Mrs. Sherwin   33
Groben, Janice S.   532
Grosdov, Brenda   456
Grove, Mary Elizabeth   276
Grover, Trent   17
Grow, Julia Eh'e   132
Grube, Jim   136
Grussendorf, Iva   425
Grzegorczyk, Eva   83
Guardi, Silvia   265
Guenther, Rodney A.   490
Guerin, George John   431
Guerrero, Rosario   546
Guerrie, Elizabeth Z.   153
Guida, Martha   568

Guidi, Dorothy L.   592
Guinn-Garcia, Teresa   553
Gulley, Reba Lyon   186
Gullotti, Pamela   338
Gully, Joan Reego   460
Gunnels, Phillip E.   197
Gunning, Marla E.   557
Gunter, Natina   48
Gunther, Joan   105
Gurka, Joseph W.   298
Gurlly Jr., Arthur   184
Gutherez, Marisha   228
Guthrey, Evelyn M.   82
Guthrie, Virginia B.   211
Guttman, Lou   285
Guzior, Christine M.   73
Gwaltney, Megan Christine   557

H

Haberzettl, Anna F.   74
Habib, Ken   472
Hacker Jr., Charles W.   96
Hackett, Zona L.   279
Hackney, Ashley   594
Haddox, Maxine   267
Haegele, Denise L.   504
Haggerty, Sharon Kay   211
Hague, Shirley   489
Hahn, Joyce M.   170
Haines, Curtis   611
Haines, Patricia   194
Halbert, Kay L.   226
Halbert, Sarah V.   394
Haldeman, Tammy   562
Hale, Brenda Kay   314
Haley, Michael   385
Halfaker, Joe   144
Hall, Clayton   522
Hall, Dawn   440
Hall, Jay Dean   539
Hall, Kelley   548
Hall, Lindsay   501
Hall, Lori   9
Hall, Martin Ed   206
Hall, Pat G. B.   277
Hallbeck, Stacey M.   30
Halling, Katie A.   475
Hallmundsson, Hallberg   309
Hallock Reinsager, Linda   29
Halowich Zieglar, Karen   262
Halpern, Richard D.   483
Ham, Emily J.   69
Hamilton, John   138
Hammes, Ruth-Anne G.   189
Hammond, Joseph F.   616
Hampton, K. Kristin   500
Handy, John   87
Haney, Chantel   518
Haney, Lynn   38
Hanning, Jay   313
Hannush, Nazih   355
Hansen, Denise   159
Hansen, Marylou   360
Hansen, Nicole K.   370
Hanslip, Michael A.   243
Hanson, M. Joan   31
Hantman, Barbara   329
Haque, C.   398
Haque, Syed M.   205
Harbaugh, Cynthia Marie   630
Hard, Barbara Jean   333
Harden, Jay C.   423
Hardmon, Ebonee-Dawn   301
Hardy, Benita Joy   299
Hardy, Dana Zadia   435
Hargrave, Raydell Annie   502

Harkara, Rajendra Prasad   543
Harloff, Misty   278
Harman, Michelle
     Lynn   352
Harmon, Colleen   411
Harmon, Eloise   155
Harmony, Janice M.   133
Harounoff, Davina   144
Harper, Larry J.   378
Harral, Courtney   159
Harrell, Jessica   170
Harrell, S. Kelley   16
Harrell, Trina B.   365
Harris, Ann M.   617
Harris, Arlen   72
Harris, Beverly   80
Harris, Brenda R.   411
Harris, Chezre M.   308
Harris, Clarence J.   155
Harris, Corey   165
Harris, D. E.   570
Harris, Dana   587
Harris, Ee-B K.   506
Harris, Jacquelyn V.   540
Harris, Judy   408
Harris, Marian S.   403
Harris, Richard   199
Harrison, Benjamin   312
Harrison, Harold R.   438
Harry, Andrea   332
Harry, Lee   47
Harsha, Jeannie O.   165
Harshaw, Cecelia   429
Hart, James H.   175
Hart, Lillian E.   216
Hart, Marta M.   186
Hart, Ramona Maxine   344
Harter, Mary   554
Hartley, David E.   529
Hartley, Martha L.   400
Hartman, Pama-Lynn   238
Hartounian, Nareg   496
Hartzell, John   173
Harvey, Katherine   205
Harvey, Tina   45
Hastings, Muriel L.   197
Hastings, Peter   187
Hatch, Louis M.   545
Hatcher, Summer Wednesday   500
Hathaway, Carrie   141
Hathaway, J. Louis   25
Haugerud, Renee L.   257
Hauk, Stephen G.   469
Hausske, Harland   460
Havard, Becca   326
Hawkins, Chuck   328
Hawkins, Sandra   275
Hawkinson, Marion   25
Hayes, Diana   129
Hayes, Dorothy A.   174
Hayes, Jennifer S.   71
Haynes, Donald   444
Haynes-Jamison, Doris   613
Haywood, Cecil   91
Haywood, Cristion   317
Hazard, Lynne F.   475
Hazen, Michelle   472
Hazen, Peter   492
Head, Verlon L.   3
Headley, Selena   352
Hearne, Mitchell L.   206
Hebert, Lucien   476
Heckbert, Cheryl   428
Heemeyer-Caldwell, Michelle   39
Heeringa, Karen D.   536
Heeringa, Katharine Adriana   256

Heffernan, Megan 286
Hegarty, Michael J. 202
Heinle, Jacob D. 616
Heinrich, Kara 504
Heinze, Poppy Kay Cecilia 220
Heiser, Carol S. 462
Heitz, Susan 554
Heitzig, Fred F. 145
Held, Betty I. 533
Hellams, Winnie 561
Heller, Kristin 191
Heller, Nancy Klinger 219
Helm, Christopher 147
Helm, Paula C. 221
Helmer, Dionne R. 505
Helmke, Carla Christian 123
Helverson, Doris 334
Hemmer Kowats, Rita 47
Henderson, Effie Douglas 178
Henderson, Joseph 132
Henderson, Tara C. 51
Henderson-Shepard, Carolyn 417
Hendricks, John 630
Hengesbach, Mary
    Jane 335
Hennekam, S. K. 237
Henry, James 528
Hensley, Joey 305
Herbers, Kimberly M. 7
Herbstreit, Jenn 450
Herensztat, Greta 310
Heriberto, Rodriguez 351
Hernandez, Alysha Nicole 168
Hernandez, Jessica Andrea 426
Hernandez, Melissa
    Andrea 336
Hernandez, Sharon L. 497
Herndon, Phaedra Mykel 381
Herren, Allen F. 514
Herrera, LeAnna 13
Herrick, Tim 583
Herring Castro,
    Sharlotte 365
Herrle, David J. 76
Herron, Betty Jean 136
Hershkowitz, Jessica 455
Hertel, Stacie Marie 547
Hertwick, Linda I. 198
Herz, Robert 358
Hess, Caleb 455
Hess, Mary Ellen 189
Hesselgrave, Patricia 16
Heydel, Pamela 22
Hickerson, Luke 344
Hickman, Richard A. 570
Hickman-Gayden, Carol Janette 325
Hicks, Dean-Anna 137
Hicks, Jeremy 627
Hicks, Lila 283
Hicks, Pam 215
Higdon, Pamela L. 490
Higgins, Jessica 510
Higgins, John P. 111
Hightower, Kenneth 258
Hightshoe, Linda L. 289
Higuchi, Akihiko 105
Hildreth, Miriam 481
Hiles, Cherrie 135
Hill Cushing, Janet 459
Hill, Cynthis Kia 533
Hill, Emma 529
Hill, Erma 413
Hill, Laura 338
Hill, Tammy J. 548
Hillman, Helee 517
Hilton, G. Steven 359

Hilton, Mike 236
Hilton, Russell G. W. 210
Hilyard, Kerrie 229
Hinchman, Judith R. 75
Hines, Francesca C. 140
Hines III, Jackie P. 84
Hintzman, Isabel 324
Hirsh, Nili 245
Hitte, Margie P. 24
Hixenbaugh, Erma 532
Hixson, Joyce 321
Hladky, Rose 42
Hockman, Louise 44
Hodge Culbreth, Bettye 454
Hodges, Margaret I. 19
Hoesman, Byron Auguste 126
Hofbauer, Katrina 272
Hoffecker, Elizabeth 324
Hofferbert, Margaret 581
Hoffman, Barbara 131
Hoffman, Diane F. 136
Hoffman, Glade 85
Hoffman Jr., Paul Robert 575
Hogen, Carol Jean 538
Hogg, Moline 560
Hogue, Chris 416
Hogue, Joan Overton 124
Hohmann, Christian 444
Hohmeier, Rebecca A. 13
Holbein, Kathleen E. 348
Holden, Glendora 52
Holden, Paula L. 187
Holder, Lisa 357
Holder, Nola Grace 576
Holder, Tiffany 230
Holdren, Brenda K. 624
Holinsworth, Margaret 543
Holland, Helen A. 149
Holland, Lisa 44
Holland, Paula M. 550
Holley, Lisa M. 249
Hollifield, Mildred 483
Hollingsworth, Amber L. 306
Hollins, Jennifer E. 463
Holloway, M. Theresa 478
Holloway, Theresa 351
Holmes, Jeff 65
Holscher, Valarie A. 51
Holub, Courtney 624
Holzberlein, Josephine 88
Homma, Hiromu 53
Honaker, Sarah 585
Hood, Jean 510
Hood, Michael 544
Hoots, Mary 468
Hope, Robert 487
Hoppes, Alice F. 590
Hoppinthal,
    Gina Grazia Squadrito 102
Hopson, Douglas K. 315
Hopwood, Libbie 257
Horan, Michael 369
Hornby, Tabitha 206
Horricks, Ken 38
Horton, Heather 304
Hough, Richard 370
Houldin, Nashel 222
Houston, Jason 184
Houston, Tammi 15
Hovey, Theodore James 20
Hovnan, William 585
Hovorka, Carolyn 95
Howard, Ann D. 306
Howard, Anna 116
Howard, Claudia M. 159
Howard, Donna Marie 464

Howard, Rosa M. 475
Howard, Stephanie 376
Howard Teed, Cathryn 146
Howe, Fern E. 134
Howell, Christopher Keith 149
Howell, Craig 148
Howell, Kristy Leigh 579
Howell, Priscilla 25
Howell, Rose Constance 574
Howley, John R. 165
Hoysgaard, John 602
Hubbard, Jaclyn 164
Hubbard, Kim 268
Huber, Alice M. 141
Huber, E. Manuel 563
Huber, Evelyn S. 458
Huckabee, LaRue C. 235
Huckaby, Denise L. 438
Huddleston, Ira 621
Hudgin, Fred 172
Hudo, Eleanor M. 433
Hudson, Brandi Ann 521
Hudson, Mark 368
Huesman, Dan 528
Huffer, Chandra 301
Huffman, Lum 483
Huggins, Ruby 394
Hughes, Amanda Brooke 109
Hughes, Jacqui 458
Hughes, Jessie 463
Hughes-Ebo, Dena Marie 156
Huibregtse, John P. 141
Hull, Agnes 521
Hull, Aziza Zuwena 461
Hull, Millie 23
Humay, Jim 538
Humbyrd, Tisha 583
Hummel, Stacey 391
Hunefeld, Kimberly 186
Hunker, Evelyn 166
Hunsucker, Alex 612
Hunt, Catherine 56
Hunter, Brandi 164
Hunter, Cynthia 77
Hunter, Lee 269
Hunter, Lori 226
Hunter, Virginia 23
Hunter-Degueurce, Teresa 370
Hurd, Louise H. 636
Hurst, Rita 358
Hurst, Susan S. 499
Husbands, Orna 541
Hutchins, Rick 209
Hutchinson, Polly 7
Hutson, Lois 573
Hutton, Ann H. 143
Hwang, Laura 546
Hyatt, Janet 89
Hyde, Tamara K. 581
Hymes, Zita Ann 193

I

Iaconis, James F. 109
Iazeolla, Daniel R. 96
Ibarra, Evelyn 150
Illges, Brandy 141
Imboden, John 461
Indritz, Phineas 550
Ingram, Norman B. 477
Ingram, Rosie J. 261
Ioli Sr., Mark J. 225
Iriarte, Janet 129
Irvin, A. Bonita 38
Irving, Cordell Anthony 80
Isaacs, Nicole 200

Isbell, Tina Ann 486
Isenhoff, Shelly 189
Ishmael Hunter, Tanya L. 632
Ison, Dave 529
Isoronis, Gloria 463
Israel, Martin 19
Italiano, Doris E. 123
Izadpanah, H. 238
Izedonmwen, Ernest 600

J

Jackson Jones, Jeanette 605
Jackson, Nancy ReFern 10
Jackson, Ruth M. 387
Jackson, Shirley A. 632
Jackson-Shahan, Jewel 183
Jacobsen, Jessica 175
Jacobson, Betsy V. 453
Jacobson, Stephanie 544
Jacoby, Charles Brian 449
Jaekley, Jeff 459
Jagta, Leanna S. 249
Jamerson, Tracy L. 347
James, Benedict 461
James, Christine 463
James, Judy 588
James, Monte 582
James, Nancy S. 280
James Snider, Sandra 45
Jannicelli, Angie 333
Jaramillo, Judy 604
Jarvey, Jack 140
Jarvis, Thelma M. 205
Jasso, Manuel 402
JDenise 285
Jedrzejewski, Elizabeth M. 183
Jeffrey, Brian W. 180
Jeffries, James Edward 528
Jelinek, Viola B. 372
Jenkins, Carla 52
Jenkins, Elizabeth 450
Jennings, Billy G. 171
Jennings, Denny 446
Jennings, Eurie 57
Jensen, Beverly M. 67
Jensen, Tamara Lynn 375
Jenson, Vivian 244
Jeremiah, Wanda 38
Jerez, Lea 268
Jett, Melissa 240
Jewell, Deborah 423
Jocson, Jessica 522
Joel, Sarah 379
Joesting, Lori
    Peterman 286
Johansen, Amy Nicole 174
Johns, Christina 615
Johns, Rocky 185
Johnsen, Tanya 348
Johnson, Anne R. 174
Johnson, B. 488
Johnson, Callie Jean 520
Johnson, Carolyn D. 126
Johnson, Corey 422
Johnson, Earl 137
Johnson, Eldon D. 452
Johnson, Eleanor 151
Johnson, Eleanore 97
Johnson, Frances Dare 131
Johnson, Gary M. 64
Johnson III, Roy H. 233
Johnson, Janet 137
Johnson, John R. 92
Johnson, Mary E. 393
Johnson, Nan 43

Johnson, Nigel L.   5
Johnson, Patricia   364
Johnson, Paul E.   20
Johnson, Philip   494
Johnson, Phyllis M.   50
Johnson, Richard D.   241
Johnson, Rita Renee   221
Johnson, Sara   193
Johnson, Stephen B.   186
Johnson, Stuart   260
Johnson, Terri H.   284
Johnson, Thelma   248
Johnston, Charlotte   514
Johnston, Harry   158
Johnston, Ross   501
Jones, A. Kelly   401
Jones, Alice E.   161
Jones, Cameron W.   624
Jones, Cindi   308
Jones, Dan   148
Jones, Dwane R.   165
Jones, Erin   148
Jones, Florence M.   157
Jones, Gloria   138
Jones, Gloria Michelle   587
Jones, Irma Provorse   460
Jones, Jamie   616
Jones, Kit   558
Jones, Laura   204
Jones, Lori   226
Jones, Marlena E.   210
Jones, Nicholus   21
Jones, Patricia   185
Jones, Rachael   342
Jones, Ruth B.   541
Jones, Solomon   198
Jones, Suzette   545
Jones, Teresa M.   230
Jones, Theresa Chalmers   563
Jones, Thurman P.   286
jones, timothy r.   487
Jones, Tom   370
Jones, William Henry   18
Joos, Jacqueline   588
Joost, Del   156
Jordan, Joann   607
Jordan, Sallye Beth   214
Jorg, Carol Ann   310
Jorgensen, Linda   632
Joseph, Wendy N.   566
Joshi, Vishnu P.   196
Joslyn, Jake   163
Jourdan-Gantner, Dona   459
Joy, Mary Bridget   24
Joyce, Frances   420
Joyce, Mary Norwood Rodgers   284
Juhasz, Diana   91, 184
Julia, Susan   29
Juliana   290
Julien, Yvonne C.   491
Juniel, Jean P.   433
Justen, Amy   426

K

Kaalberg, Jewelly   331
Kacher, Dean   519
Kacir, Denise K.   68
Kaderavek, Lori S.   190
Kadota, Holly Mock   156
Kaehler, Beverly A.   153
Kaestner, Joyce L.   298
Kaiser, Susan   18
Kalatta, Elaine   429
Kalbfleisch, Randal E.   580
Kale, Mark D.   197

Kallal, Jack D.   589
Kaltenbaugh, Louise S.   395
Kammer, Charles L.   530
Kamphausen, L. E.   40
Kane, Heather Erin   450
Kantenwein, Louise   217
Kanter, Paul   480
Karaffa, Nicole   191
Karp, Lenore   235
Karpowich, Nathan   498
Kassay, Patti   279
Kastner, David   168
Katona, Catherine L.   140
Katz, Hila   464
Katz, Lena   379
Kausel, Sarah   577
Kawachi, Joshua   93
Kawuryan, Anna Maria Siti   100
Kay, Sarah Janis   186
Kearney, R.   496
Keast, Dianne   122
Keathley, Wendy I.   218
Keatts, Pansy M.   253
Keefe, Charleen M.   67
Keegan, Ann   62
Keel, Wendy   32
Keith, Maureen   225
Kelalis, Barbara   126
Keller, Amber   624
Keller, Jessica Merkel   97
Keller, Randall T.   232
Kelley, Barbara   161
Kelley, Gwynn   77
Kelley, Joshua   531
Kelly, Dan   88
Kelly, Erin   423
Kelly, James O.   65
Kelly, Kathleen   563
Kelly, Lillian   542
Kelly, Lisa   584
Kelly, Melody Lynn   490
Kelly, Nicole Ann   5
Kelso, Elaine E.   414
Kelton, Richard Alan   381
Kemp, Dorothy D.   597
Kemp, Jan   326
Kemp, Kristen   369
Kemper Jr., Micheal   335
Kendall, Vickie A.   255
Kenner, Betty W.   519
Kenney, Ollie E.   222
Kent, Michelle   479
Kerlegan, Anthony   85
Kern, Brian H.   620
Kern, Roberta   371
Kerr, Kenneth H.   555
Kerrick, Bernard   453
Kessler Jr., George A.   86
Kester, Walter H.   350
Kesterson, Megan M.   290
Ketterman, Faith L.   69
Kevin, J.   450
Khalsa, Gurukarta K.   593
Khanani, I.   40
Khon, Keith   213
Kibler, Robert   473
Kickasola, Ronald H.   231
Kidd, Keyonna Diane   294
Kidd, Stephanie L.   192
Kile, Dalphne   410
Killen Foster, Susan   497
Killman, Wanda   7
Kilsdonk-Schultz, Deborah   300
Kim, Jenifer   446
Kim, Wally   349
Kimmel, Marlo   579

Kincer, Kevin m.   186
Kinch, Dionne   56
King, Almeda-Princess   466
King, Deborah J.   523
King, Donna E.   516
King, Donna G.   158
King, Kathleen   29
King, Kristen Marie   219
King, Mina   552
King, Sandra   335
King, Tricia   18
King, Tula W.   567
King, Wanda   45
Kingsbury, Anita   55
Kingston, Emily   590
Kingston, Rebecca
   Lynn   284
Kinion, Jamie   332
Kinnebrew, Valerie
   Virginia   338
Kinner, Sondra L.   370
Kinney, R. Whitby   386
Kinser, Becky   590
Kinsey, Brenda   143
Kirby, Forrest   74
Kirchenschlager, Amber   616
Kirchgessner, Debbie   454
Kirk, Marie Annette   28
Kirkendall, Stef   239
Kirkman, Kelly S.   374
Kirkpatrick, Glen A.   89
Kirlin, David   145
Kirtos, Pamela N.   499
Kirvin, Johnnie F.   136
Kistler, Sarah K.   356
Kizer, Jo   588
Klein, Stacy L.   494
Kleinert, Kelly   27
Kleinman, Maurice   554
Kliber, Danny   620
Klima, Joseph R.   419
Knapton, Merlin Pryde   270
Knapp, Carroll   157
Knapp, Shelly   24
Knauss, Stuart F.   372
Kniep, Jackie A.   115
Kniff, Dawn Cahoon   177
Knight, Ashley   447
Knight, Candida   618
Knight, Virginia   28, 218
Knode, Tiffani   584
Knowles, Jane E.   61
Knowles, Laurie J.   374
Knowles, Mathew J.   496
Knox, Jan   154
Knull, Vincent C.   401
Knutson, Harvey K.   432
Kobres, R. Fred   477
Koenig, Daniel   84
Koens, Tracy   257
Kohls, Melissa   26
Kohn, Dan   166
Kolar, George   152
Kolasa, Kerry   228
Kolvek, Becky   107
Koman, M. A.   359
Komnick, Joy   159
Kooperman, Kelly   20
Kopecky, Mary Anne   349
Koplin, Gloria H.   455
Kosikowski, Alexander J.   595
Kott, Steele   193
Kozlosky, John   115
Kozuch, Jacqueline   158
Krause, Amy   128
Krause, Joan M.   590

Krause, Michele L.   364
Kraynak, Edward   427
Krebs, Camela   103
Krenmayr, Janice W.   462
Kretzmer, Gerrie   138
Krevitsky, Daniel Byron   128
Krieger, Eric   425
Krieger, Joanne   85
Krieger, Jody   600
Krikorian, Rose D.   292
Krimmer, Joy Michelle   425
Kriston, James F.   301
Kriston, Joanne C.   138
Kriston, Marge   405
Kroen, Stan   408
Kroetz, John P.   629
Krohberger, Dawn M.   532
Kronman, Joshua   460
Krow, Paul A. M.   342
Krumm, Donna   508
Kruse, Karl   352
Kubasiak, Terrie Webster   242
Kuchli, Sue   12
Kuebel, Marie N.   204
Kuehn, Aaron W.   434
Kugel-Yonkosky, Jeneen L.   303
Kuhn, Alta Jean   154
Kukla, Rose Beardsley   566
Kula, Kristina Rebecca   32
Kull, Anna   411
Kumar, Tobi   211
Kuntz, Roberta   278
Kurelko, Denice   589
Kurland, Daniela   160
Kurtz, Betty R.   432
Kutis, Barbara   64
Kuznia, Chris   153
Kwasniewski, D.   26

L

La Mantia, Anthony   625
La Rocca, Donna L.   619
LaBerge, Andrew   178
Labranche, Josee   95
Lacey, N. O.   43
Lackner, Valerie   31
Ladinsky, Francine   452
Laffe, Kendra M.   345
Lafond, Robert E.   549
LaForce, Loretta A.   20
Lagoe, Lindsay   338
Lagomarsino, Jeannine   60
La Ham, Mike   292
Lailani, Shyna   10
Laing, Sara O.   192
Lake, Alice   321
Lal-Kissoon, Jacqueline J.   176
Lalino, John   297
Lally, Katie   348
Lam, Celini   300
Lamb, Kristi   40
Lambert, Ernest T.   526
Lambert, Helen M.   408
Lamberth, Ann   461
Lambre, Julienne   442
Lamoureux, Nicole   247
Lamping, Barbara   183
Land, Nellie W.   560
Landahl, Graydon   116
Landers, Donna M.   441
Landino, Susan Daria   248
Landon, Roberta   15
Landrum, Joyce Howe   79
Landry, Jodi A.   106
Landry, Mary M.   211

Landy, Michael 203
Lane, Cindy R. 614
Lane, Diana M. 76
Lane, Kamen 62
Lane, Tracie R. 543
Laney, Deborah 604
Lang, Deborah 526
Lange, Frederich 101
Langemo, Jeff 522
Langiewicz, Ruth 582
Langlo, Marion 488
Langston, Nadine 267
Lanier, Margaret 38
Lankford, Jonathan W. 629
Lannin, Lois 191
Lantz, Jennifer A. 302
Lapinskas, Matthew 479
LaPointe, Amber C. 324
Larger, Amanda 184
LaRocca, Michael 251
LaRosa, Shaun 262
Larra, Colette 430
Larrivee, Jennifer D. 177
Larrivee, Melissa A. 391
Larsen, Adeline 183
Larsen, Dawn Marie 177
Larsen, Donald 425
Larsen, Patricia 552
Larson, Irene Mary 173
LaRue, David C. 96
Laudette-Held, Patricia A. 204
Laughton, Terra 196
Laukonis, Dee 155
Laumann, Felix 633
Lauria, Mary K. 277
Laurie, Robin 25
Lauro, Lisa M. 38
Lave', Tiffany 281
Lavella, Wendy 16
Lavergne, Cassie 65
Lavin, Jane 328
Laws, Dallas 121
Lawson, Stephanie 206
Le Compte, Nellie 218
Le Roux, Lodewyk 384
League, Faye 158
Lear, Carlton 144
Lear, Marjorie Elizabeth 198
Lear, Michelle 339
Leaverton, Tammy 208
Leavy, Thomas J. 19
Leblan, Janis 62
LeBlanc, Ever 509
Lecointe, Southwell 563
Lee, Billie R. 146
Lee, Chrissy 157
Lee, Cindy Kaercher 409
Lee, Jessica 130
Lee, Jisun K. 148
Lee, K-Ming 454
Lee, Keni 336
Lee, Kent-Fuh 454
Lee, Matthew 40
Lee, Patricia Ritchey 267
Lee, Raymond 561
Lee, Vicki Roblin 240
Leeman, Margaret 200
Leeper, Kendall Lynn 210
Leer, Edward 307
Leese, Juanita 458
Lefleur, Jeffrey 604
Leftoff, Anne 628
Leftwich, Liv Elise 481
Leichliter, Deborah C. 98
Leimkuhler, William R. 223
Leinberger, Joela 71

Leinhauser, Karen L. 120
Leis, Aaron 610
Lemont, Dorothi 152
Lengel, Sandra B. 578
Lentini, Angela 161
Leonard, Amy 296
Leonard, Kara L. 134
Leonard, Kristi 405
Leonard, Susan A. 341
Leos, Gregory A. 88
Lepper, Justin 134
Leppin, Florence O. 509
Lerman, David H. 421
Lesesne, Saundra F. 349
Lessard, R. J. 473
Lester, Amy Lee 596
Letowski, Szymon 478
Leung, Nathan 255
Levine, Aaron 84
Levine, Robert 352
LeViness, Dorothy T. 154
Levins, Amy 445
Levy, Inge 511
Lewandowski, Shannin 33
Lewis, David R. 600
Lewis, Deborah 595
Lewis, Dorothy 101
Lewis, Jean 144
Lewis, Lillie 292
Lewis, Maurice D. 401
Lewis, Phil 393
Lewis, Ruthie 369
Liang, Sophia 401
Liarakos, Beverly J. 455
Liddy, Lee 47
Liebman, Marjorie 201
Liggett, James 312
Lightner, Linda 235
Lilly, Mary Anne 246
Lilly, Thelma R. 348
Lim, Deliah M. 121
Lim, Ernest T. 119
Lim, Terry 12
Lin, Jean Hai-Fay 65
Linares, Belia H. 461
Linares, Christopher 163
Linarez, Jennifer 624
Lincoln, Angela 98
Lincoln, Kathryn 552
Lind, Jeremy Adam 448
Lindahl, Sarah 389
Lindsay, Patricia 347
Lindsey, Bermoine 130
Lindsey, Janell M. 504
Lindstrom, Lisa 366
Linenberger, Ritha 502
Linton, Joy L. 315
Lippett, Violet R. 210
Lippman, Harvey N. 98
Lis, Dana 164
Lisak, Nancy A. 371
Lisboa, Richard 348
Lisojo, Winnie 464
Lisowski, Amanda 165
Liston, Shelley 398
Littig, Andrea 128
Little, Rhonda Morrow 266
Littlefield, Charles 154
Littlefield, Janet 329
Lively, Josh L. 169
LoCicero, Sylvia 203
Lockett, Crystal D. 137
Lockhart, Anna Mae 158
Loftin, Cindy 629
Loftis, Michele 269
Lofton, Darline E. 613

Lombardi, Mary 351
Lombardo, Fabio 536
Long, Catherine 533
Long, Dorothy N. 539
Long, Gary H. 599
Long, James E. 132
Long, Rowena J. 283
Long, Vanessa 242
Longe, Laura 571
Longo, Jeff 120
Lopenzina, Vanessa 46
Lopes, Mary Ann 572
Lopez, Ileane 432
Lopez, Irene M. 98
Lopez, Nanalyn M. 33
Lopez, Ralph B. 193
Lord, Laura Anne 339
Loudenslagel, Klahr 489
Lougee, Glen A. 130
Loumeau, Christina 466
Loupe, Janette 181
Love, Amber 313
Love, Jody 506
Love, Nicole 387
Love, Rebecca Lauren 245
Love, Thomas D. 340
Lovell, Mary 195
Lower, Valerie J. 573
Lowery, Adam 452
Lowery, Cyndy 150
Lowman, Eugene 448
Lowry, Elizabeth 515
Lowry, Karen 450
Lowther, Latisha N. 339
Lowy, Benjamin 504
Lubiewski, Sandi 30
Lucas, Tanja 241
Lucero, Ginger 592
Lucius, Rennie 190
Ludwick, Ann Berta 592
Ludwig, Jason 97
Luenberger, Evamae 135
Luesebrink, Amy 411
Luft, Maggie 350
Lujan, Charlotte 460
Luke, Cheryl K. 629
Lukezic, Wilhelmina 39
Lumsden, Lois 389
Luna, Diana 171
Lung, Robert R. 468
Lurz, Becky 594
Lutchey, Andra L. 628
Lutz, Mark 32
Luzincourt, Andrew K. 531
Luzmoor III, William J. 259
Lyday, Jennifer 68
Lynch, Clark Wayne 623
Lynch, Kris 209
Lynch, Melissa Ayn 368
Lynch, Sean M. 396
Lynch, Tom 31
Lynch, Val Anne 367
Lynette, C. 136
Lynn, Cinda L. 420
Lynn, Emily R. 412
Lyons, Jeffrey J. 52
Lyvers, Glenn 408

M

M., Beth-Anne
Maberry, Nancy Helen 571
Macaulay, Teresa 347
Maccia, Susann 288
Mach, Mandy K. 473
Machado, Emily 77
MacHardy, Donna V. 150

Macias, Lorraine 274
Mack, James D. 70
MacKenzie, Scott W. 350
Mackey, Heather 64
Mackey, Helen 600
Mackey, William D. 207
MacKinnon-Rorer, Kate 33
MacLaughlin, Mark A. 570
MacMullen, Stelle 219
Macsurak, Maud 202
Madalo, Michael 283
Madden, Marian E. 549
Maddocks, John J. 73
Mahan, Carol 459
Mahan, Erin 598
Mahle, Lee P. 47
Maisannes, Deirdre M. 179
Maison, Sheri 497
Mako, Nancy 289
Malak Bickford,
    Linda Jane Jacqueline 44
Malcom, Christine 459
Malins, Wally 222
Mallett, Barbara 456
Mallette, Brenda 589
Mallory, Phyllis 549
Malloy, Darren Lee 455
Malmgren, Julia S. 588
Malooly, Norma 583
Malouf, Raymond N. 252
Malpezzi, Sheryl J. 14
Maltsbarger, Richard 293
Malutin, Lydia 468
Mandehr, Nathan Austin 187
Mangini, Brighton A. 80
Manidis, Teresa 294
Mann Jr., George A. D. 330
Mann, Tina Burgell 345
Manning, Brandon 623
Manns, Christine 443
Manson, Catherine A. 184
Mansukhlal, Sharon 400
Marazita, Frank 538
Marchant, Joe 612
Marean, Anne G. 124
Maris-Sida, Serban 241
Markell, Nancy Lee 541
Markuson, Crystal 462
Marn, Melissa 368
Marquis, Carolyn 177
Marr, Jeremy 524
Marshall, Andy 611
Marshall, Gloria 102
Marshall Jr., Larry D. 203
Marshall, Sandra 338
Marsteller, Robert L. 277
Mart, Reva 223
Martens, Bradley Coyote 601
Martin, Amy 181
Martin, Andrea Joy 106
Martin, Annalea 307
Martin, Cam 431
Martin, Charles L. 86
Martin, Harry H. 92
Martin, Joey 128
Martin, Lorna M. 243
Martin, Michael A. 37
Martin, Patricia Martin 362
Martin, Raymond 367
Martin, Sandy 363
Martin, Scheri 185
Martin, Zilla May 19
Martinez, Adam 64
Martinez, Andes R. 596
Martinez, Bob G. 325
Martinez, Jamie 64

Martinez, Julio Y.   68
Martinez, Lillian   228
Martinez, Maureen   500
Martinez, Patricia   10
Martinez, Sara Marie   291
Martlink, Bill   127
Maruschak, Dorothy C.   297
Maruschak, Stephanie
   Sue   343
Marx, Julia Ann   322
Masengale, Vickie D.   570
Masek, Michael P.   294
Mask, Kelley   201
Mason, Debbie Ann   143
Mason, Marty   185
Massaglia, Denise   304
Massaro, Mary Ann   258
Mastaglio, Linda   248
Mastbrook, Connie   114
Mastel, Betsy   305
Master, Bonnie   593
Mastin, Margene   202
Matero, Anthony   445
Matheny, Alton   163
Mather, Lee Richard   32
Mathews, PhD,
   Vivian E.   356
Matney, Steffani D.   245
Matranga, Brandi   121
Matsueda, Christine   320
Matsumoto, Tarisa   479
Matteo, Alessandra   444
Mattern, Kathryn R.   470
Matteson, Fred J.   173
Matthews, Gail   520
Matthews, Madeleine   292
Matthews, Mona Lisa   278
Matyok, Margaret S.   11
Mauck, Tamra   9
Maurer, Rachel   237
Maxsom, Polly   359
Maxwell, Jill   72
Maxwell, Scott   469
Maye, H.D.   164
Mayer, Linda   284
Mayer, Mary Jacqueline   577
Mayer, William   280
Mayfield, Gail   126
Mayhew, Patricia Ruth   266
Mayo, Holly   160
Mays, John M.   152
Mazet, Eli David   458
Mazurek, Linda   384
Mazyck, R. Elaine   220
Mazzella, Gemma   78
Mazzuca, John L.   182
Menzel, Lisa Ann   359
McAfee, Paul K.   549
McAfee, Timothy   551
McAlhaney, M. Lorraine   484
McAllister, Spring   217
McBride, James H.   111
McCafferty, Verda   24
McCall, Brian W.   603
McCann, Edward A.   433
McCarter, David   533
McCarthy, John P.   600
McCartney, Madge K.   44
McCarty, Ken D.   19
McCaustland, Amanda   440
McChesney, Mary Evelyn   558
McClain, Melvina   265
McClanahan, Virginia
   Brooks   370
McClarren, Wesley   398
McClelland, Dorothy   609

McCluggage, Francisca   144
McCown, Joshua   160
McCoy, Rex V.   46
McCoy, Sanches   495
McCoy, Wilma V.   207
McCracken, Michael S.   187
McCray, Katt   21
McCreary, Al   169
McCue, Carolyn   614
McCullough, Lisa D.   380
McDarby, Geraldine   433
Mcdermott, Dorothy L.   109
McDonald, Bruce D.   463
McDonald, Charly   80
McDonald, Deborah   156
McDonald, Nisel Pardo   354
McDonald, Sandra Rene   204
McDonald, Tammy   249
McDonald, Thomas C.   395
McDougall, Rebecca   247
McEwen, Suzanne   486
McFadden, Bobby   113
McFarland, Amanda   330
McFarland, Joe   314
McGan, Wayne   44
McGann, Morna   544
McGinnis, Arwen Morningflower   184
McGorty, Jamie   444
McGovern, Jenny   415
McGrath, Suzanne   188
McGrory, Megan   468
McGuire, Jennifer R.   63
McIlroy, Lydia Leona   192
McInerney, Patricia E.   42
McIntyre, Jennifer L.   303
McIntyre, Robert Glen   345
McIntyre, Virginia   216
McKann, Robin   197
McKay, Brennon James   437
McKay, Brooke   181
McKee, Brenda   612
McKee, Carolyn L.   67
McKibban, Deborha   181
McKim, Rosalie   560
McKinney, Delores N.   99
McKinney, Ever   163
McKinney, Grace   318
McKinney, Justin   308
McKinney, Melissa   25
McLean, Sandra   223
Mcleod, Ryan   36
McMahon, Dolores   507
McManus, Sarah   387
McMaster, Agnes   160
McMaster, Matthew   547
McMenamin, Katie   269
McMillan, Joseph E.   454
McMillen, Alisa   162
McMullen, John   61
McMurtry, Ryan   270
McNabb, Barton L.   62
McNabb, Danny   297
McNeill, Joseph P.   430
McNeill, Paige M.   341
McNulty, Terry   12
McParland, Pamela S.   231
Mcphee, Kelly   252
McPherson, Nellie   35
McTague, Nathan M.   17
McWilliams, Joann   466
McWilliams, Scott   282
Means (Walker), Brenda   157
Mears, Vicki   396
Medina, Yvette   383
Meinders, Candi   68
Meisinger, Herb   87

Meister, Angela Kathleen   515
Melaragno, Delight   329
Melendrez, Sandra R.   246
Mell, Catina   627
Mellon, Lawrence James   36
Mellos, Arthur   442
Meloche, Ernest B.   63
Melton, Allen L.   91
Melucci, Carol A.   627
Melvin, Rae   197
Mendonca, Irma Elizabeth   440
Mendoza, Gabriela   523
Menifee, Alva   631
Mercado, Tiffany   474
Merikas, Katrina Joan   364
Merila, Richard L.   491
Merkison, Linda A.   190
Merritt, Harry   153
Merritt, Lani   470
Merryman, Shirley   387
Mesaros, Linda June   46
Meschefske, Evelyn Carrie   135
Messman, Nancy   556
Mester, Patricia   8
Metcalf, Shea   30
Mets, Kathryn   497
Metzger Jr., E. George   10
Meuller, Henrietta   597
Mewbourne, Rose   548
Meyer, Christopher L.   466
Meyer, Elizabeth   448
Meyer, Kay   576
Meyer, Martha Mary   369
Meyer, Mary   47
Michalowich, Robert F.   206
Michaud, Scott A.   274
Michel, Heidi Lynn   537
Middleton Fellie, Virginia   399
Mijares, Michele M.   356
Mikell, Ira   626
Milan, Alicia   516
Milanoski, Thelma   227
Miles, Gregg   513
Miles, Helen   159
Miles, R. T.   474
Milewski, Michael   636
Milici, Jonathan   139
Milicia, Carolyn   324
Millay Mann, Michael   498
Miller, Brian G.   89
Miller, Carly   86
Miller, Cheryl   182
Miller, Christi   131
Miller, Christine R.   605
Miller, Christopher   81
Miller, Cristin   166
Miller, Deloris   450
Miller, Evie C.   74
Miller, Gerry   300
Miller, Gloria Peterson   596
Miller, Jennifer D.   152
Miller, Jessica   519
Miller, Katherine Bassett   254
Miller, Katie   49
Miller, Ken   398
Miller, LaReine A.   343
Miller, Larry A.   17
Miller, Lova   200
Miller, Michelle Lynn   252
Miller, Norma Jean   574
Miller, Robbie   545
Miller, Rosemary M.   636
Miller, Sandra P.   49
Miller, Tina   344
Miller, Tommie Joyce   357
Miller, Virginia Lindsay   393

Miller, Zachary James   217
Milligan, Mark   567
Millinger, Melissa   218
Millner, Dina   75
Mills, Jama-el Hakeem   164
Mills, Sara-Jean Marie   8
Millsop, Eileen   102
Millspaugh, Delight L.   132
Milnar, Detta   513
Milne, Douglas S.   138
Milstead, Ruth Myers   364
Milton, Tonya A.   24
Mina, Katherine   263
Minchew, Stephanie   260
Mines, Rosette   34
Minnella, Joseph L.   508
Miracle, Chatam   153
Miracle, Michelle   342
Mitchell, Alberta M.   466
Mitchell, Dorothy A.   175
Mitchell, Ginger   447
Mitchell, Gloria   304
Mitchell, Jamie   461
Mitchell, Kanoli   531
Mitchell, Norma Jean   346
Mitchell, Richard E.   15
Mitchell, Ruth F.   199
Mitchell, Ryan   190
Mitchell, Ursula   210
Mitchell, William C.   239
Mittoo Walker, Dorothy E.   531
Mlak, Jeffrey Joseph   414
Moats, Regina Denise   217
Modl, Christina   410
Moir, John P.   59
Mokler Simpson, Lynne   48
Moldrem, Edna   170
Moll, E.C.   390
Monastero, Amy L.   136
Mondragon, Catherine C.   178
Moniz, Richard J.   579
Monroe Jr., John D.   533
Monroe, William   260
Montague, Iris R.   299
Montana, Patsy Lee   494
Montano, Lynn Y.   9
Monteiro, Joseph   304
Montgomery, Beatrice   180
Montgomery, Janet   163
Montgomery, Jeanne-Marie   145
Moon, Doris   612
Moon, Laura   49
Moore, Bonnie Sue   509
Moore, Conard D.   79
Moore, Diana   537
Moore, Eloise   108
Moore, Helen L.   106
Moore, Jamie Farris   308
Moore, Marguerite M.   295
Moore, Marian   202
Moore, Paul   212
Moore, Shannon Lee   238
Moore, Steve   497
Moore, Tiffany J.   202
Moorer, Candace M.   610
Moores, Christine   454
Mooring-Grimes, Delores   162
Mora Jr., Roy David   556
Morales, Amy Lynn   78
Morales, Joyce K.   299
Moraud, Georgette   445
Morgan, Bette   588
Morgan, Chelsea   598
Morgan, Gena E.   72
Morgan, Katherine L.   216
Morgan, Tom   384

Morgaus 475
Morin, Jill Irene 55
Moritz, Elizabeth Ann 90
Morra, Ryan 36
Morris, Annie Lorraine 318
Morris, Anthony Ryan 110
Morris, Christopher B. 63
Morris, Cynthia M. 58
Morris, Loletia 582
Morris, Mark 221
Morris, William 400
Morrison, Cassandra 310
Morrison, Jadz 129
Morrison, Michelle 17
Morrison, Shannon M. 17
Morse, Rebecca 341
Morton, Marsha 551
Moseley, Mark E. 551
Mosher, Beth Ann 325
Moskovich, Ashley 505
Moss, Suzanne 13
Moten, Mae L. 29
Motl, Mary Ann 219
Motyka, Jenna Lee 107
Mourad, Naji 201
Moy, James H. 303
Moyler, Hattie L. 100
Mudie, Dawn Ann 611
Mueller, Angela 141
Mueller, Carol 146
Muennink-Fagan, Janie Carol 513
Mulholland Strom, Debra 515
Mullen, Drew 139
Mullen, Joan 141
Mullen, Vivian 339
Mullikin, Maurine 41
Mulsow, Karalee M. 61
Mulvey, Karen E. 526
Mundy, Deborah E. 86
Munoz, Celia Jasso 613
Munoz, Sharon 293
Murdock, Louise 290
Murphy, Annamae 159
Murphy, Rachel 287
Murphy-Davis, Audrey 622
Murray, Linda 381
Murray, William 551
Murtha, Irma Sue 626
Musacchio, David 604
Mutua, G. 249
Muyres, Matthew C. 487
Muzi, Florence Gaspar 76
Myers, Becky 180
Myers, Beverly 630
Myers, C. Jeannette 238
Myers, Daniel W. 430
Myers, Diana 54
Myers, Kristen 479
Myers, Lora E. V. 240
Myers, Margaret Story 230
Myhre-Levy, Wendy 21
Myles, James 316
Mynatt, Linda 244
Mysliwicz, Chet 421

N

Nagle, Michael 582
Nagy, Annika 445
Nair, Ramkumar 3
Nalls, Ruth Ryan 630
Napper, Jessy 514
Nash, James 56
Nash, Lyndon Lundgren 379
Nast, Jean Marie 147
Neagle, Dorothy 510

Neal, Jill J. 424
Neal, Larry 48
Neal, Meredith 253
Neary, Sallie Belle 201
Neely, Joy 423
Neff, Gregg 634
Neidhardt, Richard Lawrence 42
Neighbors, Jason 93
Nelsen, Norman R. 568
Nelson, Alice E. 155
Nelson, Donna 182
Nelson, Herb 595
Nelson, Jason Micheal 452
Nelson, Mallory Elizabeth 563
Nelson, Vernamaree 229
Neman, Mary E. 38
Nemec, Jacqueline M. 142
Nermal, Nerchi 361
Nesbitt, David A. 172
Ness, Dolly 142
Netterwald, Billie F. 182
Neubuck, Lydia Harper 334
Neuman, Elmer J. 297
Nevado, Cresyl A. 458
Nevis, Taylor Day 388
Nevitt, Jason 438
New, Lacee 289
New, Marcella 287
Newbill, Gloria 87
Newby, Ione 136
Newhouse, Cara 170
Newhouse, Jessica 510
Newman, Cheryl 142
Newman, Luna E. 345
Newman, Michelle Louise 252
Newsome, Akasemi 518
Newton, Bill 152
Newton, Jeanette 146
Nichiniello, Charlene E. 618
Nicholas, G.L. 619
Nicholls, Tamie 480
Nichols, Cholana 102
Nichols, Don 534
Nichols, James E. 462
Nicholson, Chris 111
Nicholson, Karl 37
Nielsen, Jeremy S. 170
Nielson, Alyce M. 423
Nieman, Erik 77
Nikolic, Bojana J. 417
Nino, Maritza 570
Nissley, Karen 307
Nite, Joe 530
Niver, Karen Ann 302
Nixon, John 145
Nixon Jr-Johnson, Vaughn O. 553
Noblefranca, Eusebio C. 60
Noel, Frances 317
Nolin Jr., Michael W. 374
Nollet, Donald 172
Norcutt, Cheryl 179
Nordgren, Eric 173
Nordquist, Florence D. 132
Norris, William F. 498
North, Micheal 355
Northam, Larry M. 397
Norton, Rachel Julia 403
Norwood Rogers, Mary
    Joyce 284
Noser, Alexander J. 97
Novak, Mandi 242
Novosel, Cindie 459
Noyes, Betty L. 56
Noz, Jennifer Lynn 524
Nsimba, Manzila 22
Nugent, Rosemary 258

Nugent, Teresa E. 11
Nuhfer, Heather 106
Nulle, Leonie F. 335
Nunes, Edmond 316
Nunez, Erika 332
Nunn Jr., Raymond 256
Nusl, James E. 56
Nutt, Amy Hayden 162
Nygard, Dale G. 614

O

Oatley, Michelle Diane Sebastian 563
Oberdorfer, Steven 14
Oberoi, Anandita 506
Obi-Bandale, Daley J. 449
Obi-Bandale Jr., Obi 41
O'Boyle, Genevieve 607
O'Brien, Amanda 149
Obrien, Dennis M. 143
O'Brien, Heather K. 426
O'Brien, Sheri 546
O'Cannor, Rita 35
Occhipinti, Sylvia 196
Ocola, Barbara 89
O'Connor, Staci M. 264
Odell, Veronica 32
Oekerman, Martha
    McConnell 290
Oermann, Elizabeth 59
Oftring, Daniel 427
Ogilvie, Pam 223
O'Hara, Eugene Michael 122
O'Hara, Lacey 389
Okafor, Mark C. 243
Olive, Robert S. 229
Oliver, Karen A. 218
Olivia, Sherrie Spencer 366
Olsen, Zane 547
Olson, Bram 316
Olson, Cassandra 463
Olson, Darcy D. 166
Olson, Dorothy M. 457
Olson, Sue 287
Olson, Susan 550
Olson, Teresa 476
O'Meara, Meghan A. 242
O'Neal, Jaquaya J. 325
O'Neill, Elcy L. 527
Ongirski, Susan 198
Onorato, Crystal M. 60
Oomen, Jamina 79
Opper, Sherry L. 207
O'Quinn 117
O'Quinn, Tiffany 190
Orbach, Karen 259
Orellano, Gabe 146
Oreshack, Jennifer 629
Orlikowski, Daniel 146
Ormond, Theodore R. 384
Orosco, Lorraine B. 353
O'Rourke, Craig 415
Orr, Leslie Samuel 343
Orr, Mary 6
Ortega, Fred K. 619
Ortiz Parton, Kimberly Ann 252
Osler, Jane G. 134
Osmussen, Jan 466
Ostenson, Debra L. 53
Ostwald, Kimberly Joan 261
O'Sullivan, Nicholas 503
Otero, Consuelo H. 83
Otey, Christina Marie 324
Otoshi, Yoshiyuki 267
Ott, Nancy B. 635
Oughton, Gina C. 67

Outerbridge, Grant 415
Outlaw, Rebecca A. 407
Overton, Sharon S. 495
Oviatt, Jennifer L. 536
Owen, Una F. 246
Owen, Velma 42
Owens, Betty N. 158
Owens, Tara J. 492
Owings, Charles 319
Owings, Iva P. 527
Oxford, Sandra L. 471
Ozaka, Asuefa Y. 318

P

Pace, Reba J. 572
Pace, Rocco 8
Page, Barbara 67
Pagel, Adam 606
Pagnanella, Joseph A. 448
Pahanish, Greg 303
Paik, William S. 371
Pal, Soma 360
Palazzolo, Mary E. 353
Pallay, Gerald D. 587
Palmer, Brian 630
Palmer, Wendi L. 235
Palmrose, Cheryl 300
Pankey, Sharon 283
Pantuso Farinelli, Frieda 510
Paolone, Angelo 329
Papellero, Mark 262
Pappalardo, Danielle 104
Parker, Judith K. 127
Parker, Phil 445
Parker, Quanah 111
Parker, Richard L. 201
Parker, Tyrone 272
Parkes, Eugene A. 424
Parkinson Jr., Robert 10
Parrish, Kathy 568
Parsley, D. B. 208
Parsons, Roy D. 385
Parsons-McNiff, Ann 524
Partenfelder, Hedwig 313
Pasach, Sharon 293
Pasquino, Alessandra 107
Patelunas, Laurie 23
Paterson, Nina 11
Pati, Ginia 103
Patil, Reshma 503
Patil, Sheela 572
Patrick, Brenda 154
Patrick-Newman, Catherine 511
Patterson, B. T. Windsor 576
Patterson, Britney 328
Patterson, Jan 607
Patterson, Ken 4
Patterson, Rebecca A. 17
Patterson-Stevenson, Paula 549
Pattison, Judith A. 310
Patton, Christina 528
Patton, Courtney 618
Patton, Erin 608
Patton, Sherri 191
Patty, Jeweldean 78
Patulski, Jessica 535
Paul, Jessica 88
Paul, Michael 185
Paul, Rosemary 208
Pauldo, Deborah D. 591
Paulson, Dina S. 81
Pavelka, Joe 55
Pavilonis, Barbara 305
Pavone, Antonia, R.N. 87
Paxton, Ashley 613

Payne, Faith Ann 451
Payne, Jennifer L. 125
Payne, Lauren Gail 238
Payton, Barbara 606
Peace, Linda 547
Peacock, Dottie 311
Peal, Deanna 627
Pearce, Albert E. 309
Pearce, Kalynda 316
Pearson, Lee 40
Pechek, Nikki 5
Peck, Amy L. 610
Peck, Margarette Rose 489
Peer, Gretchen L. 142
Peer, Rosie 474
Pegues, James M. 516
Pekie, Dianne 142
Pelikan, Mary Kathleen 186
Pell, Alicia Anne 176
Pelliccia, Joann 73
Pelliccio, Janet 164
Pelosi, Jonathan 326
Pelrine, Melizza 285
Pena, Alicia C. 300
Pendergast, Lisa Renae 230
Pendergast, Molly Bennette 240
Pendergrass, Lela 293
Pendley Kier, Susan 471
Penland, G. M. 406
Pennigar, Jesica 441
Pensiero, Marcine 267
Pento, Debbie 432
Peppers, Tony M. 468
Percival Jr., Frank W. 628
Pereira, Tanya M. 375
Perez, Christine 83
Perez, David 606
Perez, Jennifer 147
Perez, Mary Connie 23
Perkins, Brandi 413
Perkins, Christopher P. 164
Perkins, Lynette 545
Perkins, Maisha K. 575
Perley, Jacqueline E. 412
Perricone, Tony 16
Perry, Betty A. 161
Perry, Christine 178
Perry, D. L. 360
Perry, Toby Lynn 489
P.E.T. 353
Peters, Angela M. 441
Peters, K. C. 258
Peters, Meg 4
Peterson, Elsie W. 435
Peterson, Lisa 208
Peterson, Margaret 195
Peterson, Shane W. 35
Pethers, Edward 61
Petrucci, Diane M. 599
Pettaway Sr., Bruce 118
Pettigrew, Andrew S. 163
Petty, Edith 448
Philipp, Jean 465
Phillips, Becky 415
Phillips, Erwin C. 454
Phillips, Irene 455
Phillips, James 534
Phillips, Jan 178
Phillips, Jennifer 135
Phillips, Mandi 558
Phillips, Pauline 51
Phillips, Ruth Y. 11
Phillips, Trista 561
Philpitt, Edward T. 452
Philpott, Melissa 392
Phlipot, Brenda L. 150

Picard, Howard 609
Picariello, E. 357
Pickett, Vincent 500
Pickrum, David Daniel 139
Pierce, Neal Clark 574
Pierce, Roy 553
Pierritz 37
Pike, Lily 499
Pilant, Eldred A. 427
Pilgrim Jr., Austin H. 413
Piluso, Christina 104
Pimental, Renee 295
Pinar, Libby 212
Pingatore, Lisa L. 294
Pippins, Tamara 562
Pitre, Sharon 400
Pitts, Donald James 592
Pitts, Marie 45
Pixi 42
Pizzano, Kym M. 399
Place, Connie H. 505
Pleasant, Joan 626
Pliodzinskas, Linda 287
Plunkett, Adele 100
Poch, Stephen 29
Pockross, Adam F. 330
Podlesnik, Judy 528
Pohlman, Kari L. 21
Polanco, Khaira S. 382
Polce, Filomena 617
Polinder, Lois M. 337
Pollara, Mary E. 356
Pollard, Homer H. 70
Pool, Robert J. 3
Poole, M. Elizabeth 24
Popp, Nancy 495
Portee, Wanda J. 486
Porter Boucher, Anne 448
Porter, John I. 116
Porter, Linda J. 13
Porter, Patricia J. 212
Posey, Theresa V. 251
Powell, Bertie Jeffress 589
Powell, Charlotte Eaton 123
Powell-Everett, Debbie 98
Powers, Sean 392
Pradels, Beulah 408
Pratt, Jamila 329
Preheim Sr., Richard E. 193
Prehm, Shawnna S. 215
Prescott, Laura J. 370
Preston, Vicki J. 40
Pretz, Jonathan 80
Preyer, Marion 40
Price, Cynthia Lynn 511
Price Jr., Richard 252
Price, Nancy 21
Price, Nathaniel Alan 39
Price, Tom 205
Pride, Darryl 307
Pritchard, Sara 389
Pritchard, Tom 364
Pro, Ruben A. 228
Procope, Andre L. 117
Prosi, Jill 418
Prosise, L. 211
Prostak, Charles 612
Prout, Joann H. 146
Provan, Brian A. 409
Prowell, Anthony 525
Prpich, Billie Perry 515
Przislidcki, Noreen 493
Puchalski, Rachel 573
Puckett, Lois 392
Pullano, Shirley 44
Pulliam, Jeaunice C. 108

Pumford, Larry 545
Purcell, Shawnee 198
Purdom, Morgan S. 569
Purick, Robert E. 255
Pursley, Elizabeth Marie 443
Pusateri, Vina 188
Pusey, Mary H. 381
Pustelniak, Suzie 36
Putman, Edward L. 603
Puzak, Hilary 152
Pyan, Bob 461

Q

Quamme, Barbara Jo 460
Queenan, Paul J. 267
Quidnet, Chicopee 137
Quinlin, Jillian 460
Quinn, Michelle A. 202
Quinones, Cesar 437
Quirk, Jamie 100

R

Rachal, Renita 22
Rackley, Jessica Sarah 90
Rackliffe, Beth 595
Raden, Brandy 109
Radford, Lorri A. 14
Radican, Kevin D. 234
Radler, Brett 315
Radosta, Bess 436
Raduziner, Peggy 568
Radzus, Carol 113
Rae, Kimberly 195
Raines, Sandi 264
Rainey, Robert 26
Rainge, Anthony Albert 623
Rains, Ruth R. 407
Rainwater, Kelly Ann 565
Raley, Stephen L. 19
Ralph, Tony 27
Ramey-Hood, Denise E. 323
Ramey, Randy Darnell 295
Ramirez, Mary 4
Ramirez, Michelle 336
Ramirez, Ruben 18
Ramirez, Tony 202
Ramsden, Linda P. 576
Ramsey, Donald W. 428
Ramsey, Jacki 163
Ramsey, Judy 623
Ramsey, Robert 471
Ramsey, Susan 374
Ramsey-Duke, Barbara 438
Randle Clinton, Dorothy 422
Randolph, Deborah 619
rani 334
Rank, Helen W. 125
Rannow, Esther A. 71
Ransopher, Scott 363
Raphael, Burnell A. 315
Raphael, Darrell 130
Rapp, Brittany 90
Rapp, Estelle 327
Rapp, Rose Ann 214
Rasmussen, Teresa 14
Ratcliffe, Jane 530
Rath, Quentin C. 217
Rathbun, Ron 14
Rathburn, Lois K. 7
Rattenborg, Marla 41
Rau, Stephanie 20
Ravgiala, Alma Marie 459
Rawlings-Morrow, Carol J. 176
Rawson Jr., Vance E. 542
Ray, Ireland E. 177

Ray Jr., George William 608
Ray, Tanya 30
Ray, Whitney 469
Raymond, Phyllis D. 30
Razi, Parnia 340
Read, Annette Leann 521
Reardon-Galluzzo, Kathleen L. 493
Reddis, Reno 221
Redmon, Yolanda 472
Redmond, Kevin 366
Reed, Albert C. 612
Reed, Elizabeth 440
Reed, Marion 50
Reed, Randy R. 247
Reed, Tiffany A. 503
Reed, Vivian 342
Reeder, Bonnie M. 631
Reeder, Douglas R. 531
Reeder, Mark 202
Reese, Melanie 49
Reeve, Krystal A. 224
Reeves, S. Laine 29
Reeves, Shaun 50
Reeves, Sherry 51
Regenauer, Susan 21
Regner, Laura L. 237
Reich, Bobbijo Lea 79
Reich Jr., Neil W. 406
Reichard, Judith A. 118
Reid, Christopher J. 137
Reilly, Michael J. 244
Reimann, Stephen A. 269
Reimer, Tracy 234
Reinmuth, Jane 134
Reisenauer, Fred T. 524
Reisman, Joyce A. 66
Renfro, Kimberly 553
Renshaw, Kathleen 492
Reppert, Sharon 214
Ressler, Ruth Friese 11
Rethaber, Janet 167
Reyes, Wanda 40
Reynolds, Caitlin 443
Reynolds, E. Lea 546
Reynolds, Marsha A. 469
Reynolds, Monica Jo 261
Reynolds, Sally 490
Rhea, Jenny 83
Rhinehart, Lance 404
Rhoads, William F. 203
Rhodes, Amber 172
Rhodes, Billye 52
Rhodes, Dauphne 103
Rhodes, Hope 103
Ricci, Dawn 177
Rice, Betty 314
Rice, Cathy 144
Rice, Paul R. 28
Rich, Melissa 31
Rich, Michael John 380
Richard, Geoffrey 155
Richard, Saralyn J. 194
Richards, Karen 480
Richards, Vanessa 25
Richardson, Bea L. 421
Richardson, Jameica 170
Richardson, Jeremy 167
Richardson, Neil 273
Richens, Marvin G. 276
Richman, David A. 113
Richmond, Catherine M. 453
Richter, Harvena 119
Rickard, Kenny 23
Riddle, Clinton E. 445
Riddle, Melissa 259
Riddlebarger, Rick 583

Ridgell III, Frank A. 173
Ridgeway, April 504
Riedy, Lynne A. 397
Riek, Kimberley 397
Rielley, Helen 520
Rigdon, Cicely 416
Rigdon, Keith H. 21
Riggsby, Sarah 40
Riley, T.V. 247
Riley, Virginia Nancy 403
Ring, Becky 157
Ripberger, Holly 445
Ripley, Frances 539
Risbon, S. E. 20
Rise, Catherine M. 56
Rison, Susan 341
Ritter, Les 343
Ritter, Susan 189
Riutta, Ian Patrick 623
Rivas, Josefa 153
Rivera, Lisa 32
Rivera, Minerva 382
Rivera, Theresa 213
Roach, Beulah Hemby 429
Roache III, Anderson 100
Roark, Sheila B. 195
Robbins, Ann 601
Robbins, Rebecca 503
Robdau, William 582
Roberts, Betty Ann 534
Roberts, Evelyn R. 312
Roberts, Frank 124
Roberts, Geraldine 105
Roberts, Jayne Lynn 456
Roberts, Jeanie 629
Roberts, Joy 128
Roberts, Mark 204
Roberts, Marki 495
Roberts, Pat 560
Robertson, Jeanne 618
Robertson, Lisa Ann 359
Robertson, Scott B. 557
Robertson, Xavier
   Alexander 370
Robichaud II, Daniel R. 62
Robinette, Kelly M. 262
Robinson, Beverly 151
Robinson, Calvin L. 461
Robinson Freeman, Alice 614
Robinson, Jodie D. 134
Robinson, Sherrie E. 236
Robinson, Yolanda 28
Roche, Kendra 25
Rocheford, Dana M. 163
Roderick, Melanie R. 277
Rodgers, Jael S. 169
Rodgers, Karen 13
Rodgers, Memory Anne 8
Rodman, Lisa 399
Rodney, Shirley 247
Rodriguez, Jorge M. Leyva 164
Rodriguez, Lisa 216
Rodriguez, Marian 51
Roeder, Susan Lord 499
Roediger, Louisa Jean 51
Roethlisberger, Mildred E. 33
Rogers, Katherine D. 350
Rogers, Kelly 368
Rogers, Marjorie B. 482
Rogers, Medrith F. 36
Rogers, Patrick J. 206
Rogers, Ron 205
Rohan, Norah 271
Rohde, Chris 509
Rohling, Angela M. 599
Rollin, Marty 27

Rollins, Fred 60
Rollins Jr., Robert C. 29
Rolph, Betty J. 169
Roma 226
Roman, William 273
Romano, Sara 544
Rombach, Todd N. 486
Romo, Manuel Soto 26
Rood, Noreen 474
Rookey, Peter D. 344
Roop, Marjorie 386
Root, Kristi 361
Ros, Christian 101
Rosa, Migdalia 38
Rosas, Glenn 171
Rosch, Barbara 457
Roscoe, Mrs. Fussell 280
Rose, Dolores Mary 165
Rosenbaum, Abby 447
Rosenberger, Jean 422
Rosen, Chris 63
Rosenkrans, Jean 298
Ross, Deana 138
Ross, Dennis 536
Ross, Janice A. 426
Ross, Laura Mae 357
Ross, Lee 263
Ross, Teresa Nicole 195
Rosser, Marion 31
Rossetti, Cesarina Maria 135
Rossetto, Kaz Michael 490
Rossmann, Heather 315
Roth, Tracy 213
Rothstein, Chanda 459
Roumell, Daniel Lee 151
Roussel, Andrea Elizabeth 170
Roussel III, William D. 21
Routly, Rachel 7
Rowe, Crystal L. 597
Rowell, Bud 591
Rowland, Lynn N. 34
Rowland, Mary C. 194
Roy, Eva M. 82
Roy, Rashmi 379
Royse, Ataka Rhodes 133
Royuela, Antonio 136
Rozwaski, Roberta 406
Rubio, Jasmine A. 534
Ruddy, Linda R. 487
Ruffe, Lori A. 43
Rumage, Stephanie 404
Rumbaugh, Fran V. 417
Runyan, Robyn 215
Ruotolo, Allison M. 149
Rupp, Sherry Marie 19
Rush, William V. 547
Russ, Alice Lesh 172
Russell, David B. 606
Russell, Lois Nunn 225
Russell, Rea Lynn 29
Russell, Sarah A. 257
Russell, Truman
   Lawfon 355
Russo, LuAnn 195
Russo, Phil 394
Rust, Charlotte L. 152
Rust, John H. 120
Rutan, Paula 226
Ruth, June 135
Rutledge-Oien, Phyllis 264
Ruton, Mildred Marsh 577
Rutter, Betty 615
Ryan, Charlotte M. 592
Ryan, Cyndy 148
Ryan-Allen, Angela 625
Ryder, Kristen 635

S

S., Connie 94
Saah, Sana 245
Saam, Kay 356
Saavedra, B. M. 586
Sabatino, Marissa 577
Sachs, Joanne 463
Sacinski, Krzysztof 191
Sackman, Phyllis 291
Sager, Lana May 33
Saint John, Domenique 166
Salanitro, Lillian 586
Salas, Will 196
Salazar, Mayra Alejandra 46
Saldana, Vanessa 561
Salem, Susanne F. 42
Sales, Leonides S. 380
Sallis, Ellis 317
Samaranayake, P. 294
Samet, Amanda 105
Samolyk, Barbara 436
Sample, Stephen C. 215
Sams, Carlos T. 177
Sandell, Susan 382
Sanders, Betty 53
Sanders, Heather 85
Sandoval, Angela 632
Sandoval, Michelle Renee 483
Sands, Yasmeen 388
Sandusky, Steven 217
Sandwith, Shannon M. 541
Sang, Casey A. 504
Sangram, Amardeep 307
Sank, Keri 549
Santonastaso, Carrie 533
Santos, Ara 526
Saporiti, Toi 361
Sara, Nils P. 48
Sarasty, Emily 594
Sargent, Edward R. 509
Sarna, Ken 263
Sasena, Rebecca M. 20
Sattar, Amina 57
Satterwhite, Texora 207
Sauers, R. D. 190
Saunders, Dorette 445
Saunders, Haley Dona 530
Saunders, J. Peverly 193
Savaj, Devon O. 155
Sawyer, Melissa Y. 567
Sawyier, Megan 284
Saxton, Vicki 405
Sayles, Stacy 577
Scala, Heather R. 444
Scaletta, Nicole M. 385
Scatola, Terry 294
Schacter, Carley 446
Schall, Jeffrey M. 145
Schamber, Laurel 214
Schaub, Christine E. 163
Scheider, Betty 449
Schermeister, Mark 3
Schick, Barbara 178
Schilling, Katie 295
Schissell, Rose 12
Schlachta, Joe 620
Schlaepfer, Mary 275
Schlageter, Edward 143
Schlenske, Traci L. 359
Schlesinger, Katie 187
Schlessman Yung,
   Sandra E. 353
Schlienz, Kasey 37
Schlingmann, Connie 311
Schmidt, Anna 146

Schmidt, Louise E. 250
Schmidt, September 229
Schmitmeyer, Daniel 412
Schneider, Florence Whitty 436
Schneider, Leslie 477
Schneider, Tanya 386
Schoenewe, Spencer 225
Schoenhoft, Miriam 217
Schofield, F. Clyde 35
Scholz, Terence J. 495
Schomas, Amanda 155
Schongar, Kathleen 46
Schoof, Jamie Lynn 617
Schoonover, Donald L. 531
Schopper, Jenni 104
Schotanus, Tracy A. 403
Schrage, Christy Lynn 147
Schuermann, A. J. 239
Schuldt, Jennifer 467
Schulz, Carole S. 143
Schulze, Kristen 385
Schuyler 340
Schwab, Jeffrey 87
Schwartz, David 537
Schwebs, Gary 455
Scollon, Pamela J. 372
Scott, Billie J. 591
Scott, Ellen 81
Scott, Eric 616
Scott, Erin 150
Scott, Eva Ivans 457
Scott, Hattie C. 75
Scott, John 598
Scott, Joy R. 457
Scott, Richard Brian 337
Scott, Robin 351
Scott, Ronald K. 497
Scott, Sue Ann 16
Scotten, Treis 352
Scrip, Shirley Evans 569
Scruggs, Rayette P. 339
Searight, Denise M. 421
Sebastian, Bernadine 156
Sebastian, Rosemary 3
Sebby, Nyki 44
Seely, D. M. 282
Segarra, Jorge Luis 455
Sehler-Downey, Ramona 39
Seidl, Sandra 45
Selkowitz, Ronald 473
Sellers, Lisa K. 378
Selover, Gaye V. 597
Semikenke, Lwanga M. 231
Semler, Kyra 557
Sendi, Sarah 263
Sengupta, Kaushika 565
Sentz, Jennifer R. 514
Senzel, Danita R. 54
Serviss, June 508
Sessions, Peggy 6
Seto, Irene K. 147
Severance, Amanda 175
Sewell, Lisa 334
Sewell, Valeri 583
Sexton, Joan H. 600
Sexton, Nesha 24
Seyedan, Mori 271
Sforza, Elena 69
Shack, Seville R. 278
Shadowens, Julie 451
Shaffer, D. L. 585
Shaffer, Mariee Christine 552
Shafrin, Alan 165
Shankar, Sreelatha 375
Shannon, Bonnie R. 151
Sharp, Elizabeth 460

Sharp, Gloria 158
Sharp, J. J. B. 50
Sharp, Kristina 488
Sharp, Lainey 220
Sharpe, Juliette L. 74
Sharrai, Karen E. 268
Sharron, Regina Helene 499
Shaw, Gloria J. 177
Shaw, Jennifer 621
Shaw, Linda 29
Shaw, Stacey 46
Shea, Lori Ann 372
Shears, Matt 17
Shee, Jamie 172
Sheeran, Jennifer 160
Sheffield, J. Mark 566
Shell, Karen 5
Shelton, Jerry L. 449
Shelton, Leigh 556
Shelton, Mary L. 39
Shenk, Kara Lynn 621
Shepherd, Margaret Polly 469
Sheppard, Linda 289
Sher, Dana 164
Sher, Param 491
Sherman, Cynthia M. 175
Sherrill, Deborah K. 71
Shettle, Joan 84
Shettler, Jennifer 170
Shi, Feng Sheng 591
Shield, Tiffany Marie 191
Shields, Dawn 535
Shields, Kendra J. 204
Shipley, Joyce E. 106
Shipman, Lena M. 256
Shirley, Bertie 601
Shokatfard, Fereidun 296
Shook, Naomi 544
Shoots, Brenda 176
Short, Sjah Y. 188
Short, Theresa 235
Short, Tracey L. 212
Shotwell, Jenny 429
Showers, Angeline 129
Shrader, Nancy 219
Shubock, Janet 413
Shuey, Christine 314
Shuff, Rose 196
Shultz, Chrissy 416
Shumate, Denise Gayle 114
Shupe, Linda 562
Siano, Joseph S. 525
Sibley, Frank C. 57
Sibley, Roberta C. 367
Sibley, Tom 220
Siciliano, Luke 340
Sickafoose, Leann 389
Sidebottom, Paul 42
Sidney, Harriet 154
Siebel, Robert A. 475
Siefker, Julie L. 308
Sihlehallah, Slash 265
Sikorski, Sarah 395
Silla Bugante, Sharon
    Grace 272
Silva, Enriqueta 616
Silvers-Day, Alpha Lee 609
Silvia, Thomas V. 550
Silvius, Penny Gillett 276
Simeone, Anthony 464
Simkins, Amy 151
Simmons, Antoinette 433
Simmons, Corie Rae 618
Simmons, Jimmy G. 454
Simmons, Mark 342
Simmons, Mary A. 565

Simmons, Michelle 31
Simmons, Robert 199
Simmons, Victoria 232
Simms, Susan E. 7
Simnitt, Chaning L. E. 167
Simon, Marc S. 253
Simonetto, Michael 23
Simpson, Amelia Lynn 603
Simpson, Candice 316
Simpson, Euriel C. 86
Simpson, Jan 597
Simpson, Karen J. 201
Simpson, Kenneth
    Andrew 264
Simpson, Linda 377
Simpson, Stan 185
Simpson, Tina 200
Sims, Brittany 180
Sims, Ginger A. 53
Sims, Kelso G. 485
Sims, Marjorie
    Thompson 268
Sinches, Catina L. 519
Sindledecker, Maria L. 253
Singleton, Carolyn 165
Sinks, Natalie D. 15
Sisk, Ralph G. 243
Sisson, Donna 458
Siwolowski, Josef 112
Sixth Grade Sunday School 30
Skaarland, Anna 83
Skattebol, Kate 350
Skelton, Emily 179
Skinner, Stephanie 388
Skogster, Ellen 144
Slagle, William Lyle 8
Slaughter, Richard E. 204
Slawinski, Richard 577
Slivinski Jr., Willard 208
Sloane, Craig 535
Slutsky, Jordan 321
Small, Charles 301
Small, Mary Wren 386
Smalley, Douglas 462
Smalley, Elizabeth 114
Smalling, Doris 533
Smallwood, D. A. 214
Smaltz, Dorothy F. 76
Smedley, Marion L. 35
Smith, Alice F. 618
Smith, Amanda 593
Smith, Barbara 94
Smith, Bonnie L. 451
Smith, Briana M. 608
Smith, Calvin R. 81
Smith, Carolyn 538
Smith, Dawn 304
smith, fawn m. 622
Smith, Faye G. 109
Smith, Frances Noble 173
Smith, Frost 516
Smith, Gwyndolyn 449
Smith, Helen 95
Smith, Henrietta A. 55
Smith, James M. 141
Smith, Jean A. 164
Smith, K. P. 201
Smith, Kelly 186
Smith, Kim E. 229
Smith, Kimberly D. (Ivey) 40
Smith, Lelia Maxine 564
Smith, Marian 14
Smith, Marilyn Gipson 362
Smith, Mary Frances 586
Smith, Michelle 282
Smith, P. J. 41

Smith, Rita 481
Smith, Roberta M. 275
Smith, Sarah 554
Smith, Shalee 492
Smith, Sharon E. 232
Smith, Stephanie 270
Smith, Steven S. 260
Smith, Susan 266
Smith, Susan C. 501
Smith, Tony 265
Smith, V. Patricia 28
Smith, Vi 280
Smith-Tobias, Donna R. 141
Smithy, James W. 317
Smoot, Ruth M. 491
Smythe, Helen T. 428
Snead, Kathi 217
Snell, Lilly Ann 41
Sniegowski, James Walt 309
Snow, Elizabeth 145
Snyder, Amy 147
Snyder, Daina M. 463
Snyder, Francis E. 173
Snyder, Julie 605
Snyder, Melissa 249
Snyder, Nick 15
Snyder, Shirley 288
Snyder, William M. 237
Sobel, Janice 114
Soberg, Dave 317
Solomon, Sarah G. 200
Solomon, Theresa 197
Somayajula, Gangashree 607
Song, Joy 412
Sookdeo, Rebecca A. 35
Sorin, Anca 330
Southin, Viola 192
Southwell, Mike 292
Sowatsky, Sienna 47
Sowells, Patricia A. 5
Sox, Catherine R. 171
Spade, Tori 31
Spagnolini, Eva Marie 462
Spainhour, Polly L. 377
Spalliero, Kimberly 276
Spangler, Rachel 30
Spanogle, Dax Fredrick 151
Speaks, Brandi 518
Spear, Marian Elizabeth 569
Speck, Nadine Sauvajot 224
Spell, Teresa Y. 43
Spence, Jimmy 167
Spencer, Dael 523
Spencer, Pam Jennings 470
Sperling, Judith M. 436
Spicer, Dana M. 615
Spies, Herbert A. 605
Spindler, Sandra E. 500
Spiro, Jack 447
Spitaleri, Antoinette 447
Spitaleri, Julie Ann 409
Splane, Timothy J. 490
Spragley Jr., John Lee 131
Sprague, Alisha 104
Sprague, Cheryl Lynn 81
Sprague, Roxanne 34
Squimbo 137
Sroka, T. Neil 633
St. Louis, Laurie 359
St. Peter, Dianne 148
Stafford, Connie Lynn 599
Staker, Sherry 373
Stall, Macie 406
Stallard, Barbara J. 119
Staloch, Shannon 45
Stamp, Beverly A. 70

Stamper, Christina 131
Stampley, Estonia Narey 454
Stampley, Joey Suzannah 439
Standifer, Duane 92
Stango, Krista 502
Stankiewicz, Daynell 61
Stanley, Dee 523
Stanley, Wendell 353
Starks, Sandra J. 211
Starnes, Everett 171
Starnes-Fox, Betty 598
Starr, Joni 124
Staton, Scott 480
Stauffacher, Robert Forrest 577
Steadman, Veda N. 358
Stedman, Cheryl 619
Steele, Joy M. 425
Steele, Randy John 492
Steelman, Kathy 586
Stein, Ada 515
Steinbaum, Keith 404
Steinberg, Alan 594
Steiner, Shelly 34
Steinhagen, Mary Ellen 30
Stellmacher, Brenda P. 159
Stephan, Kathy L. 43
Stephens, K. A. 287
Stephens, Sharlyn 369
Stephenson, Dolores 112
steurer, kiffin 571
Stevens, Carol M. 179
Stevens, Donald Gene 70
Stevens, Jacki 78
Stevens, Lou Ella 484
Stevens, Michael 481
Stevens, Vance 563
Stevenson, Beth 605
Stevenson, Marilyn 18
Stevenson, Rhys 196
Stevick, Elizabeth 307
Stewart, George 445
Stewart, Gladys 462
Stewart, Mattie M. 199
Stewart, Rebecca 10
Stica, Stephen 19
Stief, Crystal 78
Stienstra, Chris 110
Stiff, John M. 320
Still, William Doyle 546
Stillman, Russ 218
Stiltner, Melissa Lynn 46
Stilwell, Shamel V. 253
Stites, Mel 30
Stivers, Henry G. 539
Stokes, Jack M. 521
Stokes, Marty 405
Stoltenberg, Kristin 483
Stone, Seaborn T. 389
Stone, Trina M. 191
Stoneberg, Joellyn 59
Stoner Yates, Linda 583
Stonesifer Hockensmith, Pauline 407
Storer, Tressie 542
Stotsenburg, Cheryl 309
Stracener Lehr, Marleen 383
Stradt, Tamera 397
Stram, Jenna 58
Straube, Kristul 22
Strauss, Bob 455
Strauz, Ray Suzan 28
Strazar, Dylan 437
Streat, Edna 589
Stretch Haskin, Joan 178
Strickland, Angie 171
Strid, Burton L. 174
Strieman, Friedell A. 635

Stroup, C. T.   489
Stuart, Amy   540
Stuber, Rosemarie   259
Stufflet, Ellamay   446
Stults, Florence Ann Kelly   465
Stultz, Adam   168
Stumpf, Eugene S.   77
Sturdivant, Diane   512
Suddith Hickson, Ann   67
Suhr, Kimberly   360
Sullivan, Dale L.   435
Sullivan, Melissa   286
Sullivan, Patricia, CDP   484
Summer, Jena A.   512
Summers, Connie   609
Summitt, Phyllis J.   50
Sumrall, Phyllis   576, 634
Sunahara, Lisa   203
Sunde, Robin   194
Surdam, Alice   450
Sutphin, Audrey   513
Sutton, Ethel   67
Svendsen, Eric   325
Swanson, Sue   50
Swaro, Kat   226
Swarts, Catherine   422
Swartz, Amy K.   138
Sweeden, Bethany   140
Sweeney, Wendy L.   402
Sweigart, Jean R.   457
Swenor, Evelyn M.   134
Swift, Henry Wilson   175
Swift, Teresa   14
Swords, Jim   410
Swygert, Dorothy   78
Sydenham, Emma   408
Sylling, Amy M.   463
Sylvester, Don   448
Sylvia, Susan J.   375
Synder, Gay Nell   140
Sypek, Thomas W.   496
Sypolt, Natalie   247
Szalapski, Lisa R.   353
Szkodzinsky, Lydia   218

T

Tabbi, Mary   200
Tadlock, Randall C.   46
Tafeen, Samuel I.   239
Tai, Alex   536
Taikeff, Etta   507
Talbert, Jean C.   157
Talbert, Rosemary   479
Talbott, Steve   498
Talley, Trystn   22
Tandoc, Warren   229
Tanguay, Bradley R.   608
Tannenbaum, Laurie S.   246
Targonski, Tom   293
Targova, Jana   174
Tarle, Marion   40
Tarnell, Antonietta   99
Tasker, James Corbett   182
Taubenberger, Susanna G.   43
Tavares, Amy Lynn   183
Taylor Anthony, Eleanor   457
Taylor, Charles Lee   118
Taylor, Cindy M.   174
Taylor, Donna J.   298
Taylor, Emily   464
Taylor Jr., Lewis W.   228
Taylor, Lila   488
Taylor, Linda   467
Taylor, Margaret C.   186
Taylor, Mary Eva   215
Taylor, Melissa Lynn   14

Taylor, Michael S.   484
Taylor, Michelle E.   558
Taylor, Sheree   49
Tchokoev, Nick   470
Teachout, Kim C.   215
Teafatiller, Tera   214
Telford, Nicole   34
Temple, William   398
Templeton, Leglaion   273
Tenney, Cecil Dean   589
Terlap-McMahon, Kimberly A.   560
Terrado, Jesseca M.   304
Terrell, Edward   112
Terry, Lilith   274
Terry, Myrtle Renee   32
Terry, Shelia T.   341
Terwisscha, Lisa   48
Tesarik, Sarah   583
Tetrteault, Alan   511
Tewell, Rebecca   271
Thacker, Stephanie   395
Thatcher, T. O.   11
Theo   621
Thetford Jr., Donald R.   92
Thibault, Ray   226
Thibodeau, Sean   190
Thiede, Jo A. T.   112
Thielen, Susan   36
Thistle, Mary S.   561
Thistle, Sarah J.   269
Thomas, Andrew   327
Thomas, Antheia P.   632
Thomas, Carrie   594
Thomas, Claudia   419
Thomas, Esther M.   58
Thomas, Freda   594
Thomas, Frederick Turner   306
Thomas, Goldie Ann   308
Thomas, Greg   456
Thomas, James   147
Thomas, Joyce Eileen   442
Thomas, Lois   198
Thomas, Peter   391
Thomas, Sarah Ann   218
Thomas, Sharline Maria   356
Thomas, Tammy   22
Thomas, Terri   187
Thompson, A. Caroline   555
Thompson, Andrea Marie   520
Thompson, Anita M.   597
Thompson, Billie   168
Thompson, Brooke Ashley   334
Thompson, Christian   169
Thompson, Christy   95
Thompson, David   423
Thompson, Katherine
   Claire   361
Thompson, Laura   192
Thompson, Marie   391
Thompson, Nikia   386
Thompson, Norford   578
Thompson, Shera   16
Thompson, Suzy   213
Thompson, Tanya Lea   5
Thompson, Victoria A.   224
Thompson-Taylor, Carol   174
Thornton, Dorothea Talbot   145
Thrall, Marcy   545
Tibere, Nicole Bartley   485
Ticchio, Elaine   58
Tiernan, Maggi   547
Tierney, Eddy Marie   632
Tietz Anderson, Marian   376
Tieu, Lan   352
Tigert, K.   117
Tiner, Joshua   602

Tinker, Thomas L.   499
Tint, Terri   265
Tippy, Meghan   40
Tirpok, Peter J.   22
Tisherman, Lillian   203
Tittle, Lisa   376
Titus, Rebekah Anne   339
Todd, Brownie   166
Todd, Lorraine L.   241
Todd, Michael   569
Todd, Rosalie   251
Toews, David G.   505
Tolbert, Marilyn   579
Tolison, April   450
Toller, Patty S.   212
Tolliver, Misty   584
Tomaskovic-Devey, Anna   462
Tomchik, Michelle A.   8
Tomlinson, Robert C.   18
Toofanian, Parhaum   242
Toothill, Margaret   9
Toovey, Rita J.   3
Torgersen, Deborah L.   323
Torres, Anthony   429
Torres, Sherri   239
Torres, Wilfred   209
Torrieri, Marisa   233
Tortora, Rosemary   555
Toth, Michelle   365
Touch, Violet   217
Tovar, Feliz Regino   435
Townsend, Betty J.   517
Townsend, Marilyn   17
Trainor, Marilyn J.   188
Trall, Lynn   193
Tran, Thanh Kim Ngo   197
Transue, David E.   610
Trapp, Jennifer   426
Trask, Mary Anne   580
Traskell, Kim   484
Trauth, Jeanette   412
Trautman, Richard D.   347
Travers, Cynthia L.   68
Travers, Henry   75
Traxler, Susan   38
Traynham Jr., Roger   405
Treadway, G. Helene   281
Treadway III, J.   260
Trease, Rebecca E.   477
Treat, Sandy   39
Tremblay, Robin L.   480
Trent, Carol   622
Trescott, Lyman L.   208
Trevethan, Robbi L.   201
Trimble, Robert   478
Triolo, Marian   43
Trojacek, Joni Marie   609
Trory, Geraldine P.   174
Trosell, Elizabeth   451
Trossbach-Schleutermann,
   Grace Ardean   147
Trowbridge, Rex   209
Troyanovich, Jack   453
Trujillo-Humiston, Crystal Dawn   323
Tryder-Rogers, Donah   180
Tsakalou Hartford, Patrice   478
Tsoi, Denise G.   57
Tsoukalas, Eva   602
Tucker, Deborah East   76
Tucker, Lora R.   580
Tucker, Mary H.   551
Tucker, Shizue   569
Tuley, Betty   412
Tullio, Clotilda   332
Turbak, Esther   332
Turchiarelli, Sandra   379

Turner, Cathy Jo   139
Turner, Doris   606
Turner, Elizabeth   504
Turner, Hannah F.   134
Turner, Joseph   414
Turner, Lawrence   403
Turner, V.P.   365
Turney, Melissa   377
Tutein, Dinah   119
Tuttle, Sara   276
Tyndell, Mary W.   348
Tyson, Lisa   215

U

Udoutun, Charles   150
Uhlir-Devine, Hazel   74
Ulin, Julieann   589
Underwood, Charlotte   466
Unger, Sharron   188
Unruh, Paul W.   380
Upchurch, Paula   336
Updegraff, Katie   351
Urban, Christopher   72
Urban Jr., Robert F.   403
Urick, Laurabell   559
Uroff, Melissa   209
Ury, Andrea   593
Usrey, Traci Lynn   20
Ussary, Richard
   Jackson   289

V

Vacca, Carol M.   634
Vahl, Thelma J.   383
Vale, James E.   465
Valencia, Alicyndra   514
Valente, Diane T.   155
Valenti, Candace   510
Valentine, Lisa A.   186
Valentine, Lynn   31
Valentine, Vanessa Larae   634
Valerio, Cerelle L.   147
Vallee, Nicholl M.   395
Valvo, Rosina   214
Van Amburg, Kelly   234
Van De Car, Mary Ellen   246
Van Dort, Kristina   213
Van Marter, Todd   250
Van Orden, Jeannie   599
Van Ornam, Diane   331
Van Pelt, Erica   319
Vance, Travers S.   237
Vanderbeek, Jon   535
Vanderbilt, Shane   366
VanDett, Dariel   446
Vangelos, Allen J.   153
Vanier, Mike   568
Vann, Preston Maurice   220
Vanness, George   539
Vano, Norma   204
Varela, Luis Jake   236
Vargas, Miguel   210
Varso, Easter   176
Vasquez, Jason   508
Vaughn Bloom, Rachel   39
Vaughn, Lurline A.   471
Veek, Lindsey   569
Vega, Elizabeth   452
Velez, M. R.   259
Vendetto, Alice   601
Venizelos, Anna   305
Venters, Aglaia   414
Venters, Viola   205
Venters, William Curtis   251
Ventrano, David John   169

VerBurg, Paul 496
Vergerio, Romano 291
Vianelli, Lorraine 221
Vicker, Denise 330
Vickers, Kate 23
Vidas, Debra Ann 172
Videto, Joshua 176
Vieira, Jillian 448
Viers, Candace 106
Vignia, Kellie 49
Vijayan, Kalpana 55
Vila, Christi 465
Villavicencio, Priscilla 196
Vining, Jeff 455
Vinson, Norma 9
Viola, Samuel 211
Virden, John 128
Vitali, Patti 586
Vivian, John F. 591
Vizcarra, Carolina 162
Vlannes, Peppino N. 6
Voegtly, Kenneth 277
Voget, Antoinette 117
Volk, Lawrence 6
Volkmer, Lillian 210
Von Achen, Phebe 48
Vonderheid, Mila 189
Voris, Helen P. 435
Voss, Carolyn 148
Voss, Kyna J. 541
Vozenilek, Michelle 338

W

Wachter, Nicole
   Michelle 363
Waddell, Berniece 110
Wafer, Ryan 635
Wagner, Brandy 514
Wagner, Grace 137
Wagner, Janet 165
Wagner, Sarah 353
Wagster, Verna K. 308
Wahl, Justin 154
Wahner II, Jorge J. 129
Wahner, Theresa 288
Wakefield, Joyce A. 525
Walberg, Linda 360
Waldheim, Wendy 3
Waldmiller, Paul 235
Wales, Anita 155
Walker, Alveda G. 171
Walker, Barbara 512
Walker, Brendon Michael 131
Walker, Bryan 523
Walker, Cherron 167
Walker, Cheryl 298
Walker, Cheyenne 451
Walker, Evaline 149
Walker, Evelyn 130
Walker Jr., James Michael 121
Walker, Kyle D. 34
Walker, Laverna 396
Walker, William Allen 191
Wall, Robert C. 492
Wallace, David Clark 520
Wallace, Dorothy A. 132
Wallace, Elizabeth 412
Wallace, Marvin R. 254
Wallace, Peggy J. 354
Wallace, Tammi 51
Waller, Anita 123
Walmsley, Kris 376
Walser, Wendi 275
Walsh, Susan 214
Walters, Bonnie 592

Walters, Chuck D. A. 432
Walters Cole, Barbara 59
Walters, Marsha 244
Wanat, Linda 19
Wang, Ange 135
Wang, Cammy 57
Wang, Di 510
Warburton, Elizabeth Marie 446
Ward, Douglas 296
Ward Gursky, Sandra M. 194
Ward, Jamie Kay 306
Ward, JoAnn H. 140
Ward, Justen 462
Ward, Kimberly 8
Ward, Vernice 578
Wardell, Cate 120
Warling, Denice 299
Warman, Eric Steven 159
Warner, Derek Adam 132
Warren, Toni 372
Warren Williams, Cheryl E. 602
Warren-Gayda, C. 457
Warrick, Tracy Allyn 193
Warzynshi, Catherine M. 327
Waschensky, Joseph A. 456
Washington, Douglas 143
Washwick, Jennifer 160
Waters, Aaron 615
Waters, Dimi 516
Waters, Sonia 24
Watson, Amy 87
Watson, Carol 150
Watson Dell, Susanne
   Mary 264
Watson, Ivan 420
Watson, Kelly 543
Watson, Linda
   Ankeny 334
Watson, Robert C. 267
Watters, Annette T. 596
Watts, Jane K. 115
Watts, John R. 173
Wayland, Christine 82
Wayne, Cheryl Lynn 636
Wayne, Judith S. 312
Waz, Nancy B. 12
Weatherly, Melissa
   Dawn 345
Weathersby, Renita 27
Weaver, John W. 324
Weaver, Kevin 216
Weaver, Leaha 262
Webb, Selenda Rena 501
Webb, Vivian 389
Weber, Hildegard 525
Weber, Patricia 227
Weber, Robin 214
Weber, William 368
Webster, David 177
Webster, Rosa 199
Webster-Henderson, Marie Ellen 233
Weeks, William J. 291
Weese-Joliet, Constance M. 507
Wegman, Cynthia 119
Weidman, Jill D. 426
Weil, Pamela 190
Weinert, Gwendolyn 596
Weinert, Tina Louise 385
Weir, Paul 571
Weisenbeck, Theresa 355
Weiss, Sondra 18
Welch, Amy 430
Welch, Les 33
Welch, Mabel 254
Weldon, Shane 479
Welles, Mrs. Cyril M. 9

Welligiton, Caressa 178
Wells, Chad 318
Wells, Christie S. 122
Wells, Francis E. 420
Wells, Melinda 245
Wells, Nicole 355
Welty, Cheryl 53
Wendt, Patti Willis 14
Werner, Melinda 217
Wernsman, Michelle 197
Wertz, Archie 633
Wesseldine, Tisha 190
Wessels, Teddy 362
West, Julia 303
West-Riehn, Linda S. 278
West, Suzanne 488
Westfall, Renee 401
Westhead, Lynne 573
Westhoff, Alicia 532
Wetherall, Christina 442
Wetmore, Robert J. 251
Wettstein, Kelly 394
Whalen, Eve Kuehn 169
Wheeler, Cathy D. 531
Wheeler, Dennis 142
Wheeler, Janet S. 140
Whelan, Bill M. 166
Whetzel, Vicki P. 220
Whisenant, Sheila 244
Whitacre, Gina A. 107
Whitby, Sarah 18
White, Amelia E. 155
White, Bonnie L. 527
White, C. L. 192
White, Charles 148
White, Cynthia 162
White, Cynthia E. 522
White, Daniel F. 537
White, Dorothy A. 424
White, J. M. 280
White, Kelly 16
White, Laura 5
White, Palmer 268
White Stewart, Gladys 461
Whitehead, Miranda 375
Whitehead, Thomas S. 241
Whitfield, Kenny 187
Whitfield, Peggy Joyce 208
Whitlock, Heather A. 452
Whitmire, Bonita D. 452
Whitsitt, Robert L. 549
Whittle-Blackmar, Melda 15
Wicke, Philip J. 185
Wicker, Sandy 47
Wiedmyer,
   Theresa A. 272
Wielenberg, Michael P. 221
Wiener, Chris 457
Wiggins, Christine Bell 296
Wiley, June 514
Wilhelm, Debra LaKay 308
Wilhelm, Lisa 482
Wilkerson, Eva 462
Wilkes III, George A. 332
Wilkins, Jana 168
Wilkins, Ruth M. 221
Wilkins Hillery, Virginia 51
Wilks Robins, Roxanne 43
Willard, Jennifer L. 64
Willey, Gary W. 450
Williams, Bradford L. 66
Williams, Charlotte M. 122
Williams, Christine Lynn 453
Williams, Christy L. 138
Williams, Danielle 120
Williams, Debbie 319

Williams, Ethel 66
Williams J., Christopher 311
Williams, James Michael 155
Williams Jr., Faries 421
Williams, Lony L. 501
Williams, Lori 584
Williams, Melissa 383
Williams, Richard G. 486
Williams, Ryan John 365
Williams, Susan 286
Williams, Travis 570
Williams, Vicky M. 23
Williams, Wayland W. 26
Williams-Brown, J. Kathleen 402
Williams-Raykovich, Lisa 195
Williams-White, Olympia 32
Williamson, Aaron H. 95
Williamson, Candace April 157
Williamson,
   Joyce Ann Markarian 630
Willis, Mary R. 185
Willis Sr., Arnold R. 162
Wills, Joe 168
Willson, Eric 128
Willwerth, Thomas R. 250
Wilmoth, Deborah C. 620
Wilson, Audrey H. 165
Wilson, Barbara 142
Wilson, Cheryl 418
Wilson, Gertrude B. 449
Wilson, Helene 636
Wilson III, James E. 600
Wilson, Joan 149
Wilson, Joni 418
Wilson, Leslie 37
Wilson, Lucy H. 573
Wilson, Niki 23
Wilson, Sue 210
Wilson, William B. 496
Wilson-Brooks, Ruth 203
Wilson-Davis, Brenda L. 92
Wilt, Mary 190
Winchester, Betty 296
Winckler, Nichole J. 493
Wine, Elma M. 595
Wingell, Timothy J. 477
Wingler, Chris Lee 128
Winkle, Pamela L. 485
Winkler, Jennifer 438
Winkler, Kenny 559
Winsmann, Curtis 625
Winston, Karen 568
Winthrop, Hope 52
Winton, Chris 58
Wise, Estelle 129
Wise, Sherri 225
Wisner, Jean D. 149
Wisnowski, Alexandra Ann 300
Wistrom, Malinda 361
Witt, Kelly 285
Witt, Kyle 26
Witte, Renea Blegen 561
Wolery, Patricia 219
Wolf, Elizabeth 179
Wolf, Karen Lynne 284
Wolf, Scott 15
Wolf, Violet 13
Wolfe, Tara 34
Wolfert, Rana M. 51
Wolford, Linzi 552
Womack, Antonio 467
Wong, Annie 157
Wood, Curtis R. 422
Wood, Erik 169
Wood, Nanette Laraine 227
Wood, Nita B. 542

Woodard, Steve Paul   295
Woodruff, Elizabeth Ann   181
Woods, John T.   593
Woods, Joseph C.   454
Woods, Megan   337
Woods, Randall E.   362
Woods, Timothy M.   543
Woods Patterson, Susan   482
Woolridge, Albert Dean   144
Woolwine, Dale   611
Wooten, LaShonda   250
Working, Rachael M.   219
Worley, Christopher   175
Wozniak, Lindsay Ann   572
Wright, Alyssa   305
Wright, Dandi   587
Wright, John   102
Wright, John H.   458
Wright, John L.   603
Wright, Kevin M.   368
Wright, Mary E.   559
Wright, Yvonne Elizabeth Leilani   232
Wroclawski, Roman   546
Wrotenbery, Martha   569
Wyatt, Anita Lee   168
Wyatt, Dawn Marie   75
Wyatt, Frieda   513
Wyatt, Karoline R.   575
Wyatt, Leonora A.   407
Wyatt Sr., Robert H.   292
Wyngaard Wright, Rebecca   471
Wynn, Karen F.   19

X

Xie, Meyer G.   559

Y

Yablonovich, Yakov   277
Yanez, Vanessa   470
Yarger, Daryll   449
Yasparro, Rosemary
    Muntz   347
Yasuhara, Carol Ann   160
Yates, Angela   92
Yates, William   7
Yaus, Betty   117
Ybarra, Michelle Juanita   37
Yeamans, Paula   358
Yocom, Shelly   392
Yopp, Heather E.   156
York, Leonard Doyle   342
York, Richard D.   399
yost, robin   4
Young, Chris   608
Young, Crystal   72
Young, Deborah A.   90
Young, Jeremy M.   449
Young, JoAnn   172
Young, Laura B.   488
Young, Pamela J.   233
Young, Patricia   37
Young, Vickie   220
Young, Walter R.   407
Young, Zach   29
Youngquist, Kelly   191
Yow, Judith B.   298
Yurkiw, Peter F.   555

Z

Zackula, Jon   155
Zagorski, Skip R.   192
Zak, Justin   447
Zaleski, John F.   434
Zamiska, Rosemary   378
Zamora, Hannia E. Beckford   73
Zamorano, Margaret   354
Zardeneta, Bryan A.   153
Zeitler, Kenneth   206
Zeoli Sr., Mario C.   371
Zepeda, Dalet   317
Zerbe, April   124
Zevola, Nicki   291
Zickefoose, Helen L.   148
Zimdars, Elaine   172
Zimmerman, Beth   466
Zinn, Kay   378
Zinn, Mary   564
Zunker, Michelle   272